A HISTORY OF GERMANY
1715–1815

A
HISTORY OF GERMANY
1715-1815

BY

C. T. ATKINSON

FELLOW AND MODERN HISTORY LECTURER OF EXETER COLLEGE, OXFORD
FORMERLY DEMY OF MAGDALEN COLLEGE, OXFORD

WITH 35 MAPS AND PLANS

BARNES & NOBLE, Inc.
New York
METHUEN & CO. Ltd
London

First Published in 1908

Reprinted, 1969
by
Barnes & Noble, Inc., New York
and
Methuen & Co. Ltd, London

Barnes & Noble SBN 389 01068 5
Methuen SBN 416 15670 3

PREFACE

THIS work is the outcome of an effort to produce within moderate compass some account of the affairs of Germany between the Peace of Utrecht and the final overthrow of Napoleon. In view of the dimensions to which the volume has attained I can hardly claim to have been successful in the task of compression, but I am more conscious of shortcomings in omitting things which ought to have been included than of having dwelt at excessive length on those aspects of German history with which I have endeavoured to deal. It may indeed be urged that the character of the subject must bear some share of the responsibility for the length to which the book has run. Germany between 1715 and 1815 was not a nation with a well-defined national life and history, but was merely a chaotic collection of states with conflicting aims and ideals, constantly engaged in struggles with one another; there can be no history of Germany as a whole, because, as this book endeavours to show, there was hardly anything that could be called "German"; particularism and localism were infinitely stronger than any unifying or centralising tendencies. But one has not merely to follow the fortunes of the principal portions of this infinitely subdivided "geographical expression," the struggles of these various members are so completely merged in the international history of Europe as a whole that the affairs of Germany only become intelligible, if at all, when narrated as part of the history of all Europe. It is no exaggeration to say that

Russia, Turkey, Great Britain and above all France play more prominent parts in German history in these years than do some German states of quite respectable size. Thus one cannot neglect battles fought outside Germany by the troops of German states; Marengo and Arcis sur Aube are quite as much part of German history as are Leuthen and Wagram, while the otherwise abortive victories of Prince Charles Edward in " the '45 " helped to transfer Silesia from the Hapsburg to the Hohenzollern and thus profoundly affected the course of German affairs for over half a century. Thus, then, when one attempts to narrate the history of Germany from the death of Louis XIV to the overthrow of that other great enemy of Germany, Napoleon, one finds one's self committed to relating the course of European affairs so far as they took place in or immediately affected Germany, a very much more lengthy process than that of narrating the development of one country only. But it must also be remembered that while these affairs for the most part took the shape of wars or rumours of wars, military matters must be treated at some length if they are to be in the least intelligible. Indeed I am afraid that in the effort to compress my accounts of campaigns and battles I have failed not only to be succinct but even to be reasonably clear and, still worse, that I have made statements which need more expansion and justification than they have been given, and have pronounced verdicts without a sufficient setting forth of the grounds on which I have formed my conclusions.

In deliberately choosing the military aspect of German affairs as the feature on which to lay most emphasis, I am aware that I have hardly touched upon the intellectual and literary life of the period. However, I have omitted this side advisedly, feeling convinced that it was in the main a thing apart, which affected the life of the country as a whole but little and certainly had hardly any effect on the politics of Germany. The " Potsdam Grenadiers " are more typical of eighteenth-century Germany than are Goethe and his fellows. It was only quite at the end of the period, in the days of the War of Liberation, that German literature can be really called "German," that it ceased to be merely cosmopolitan and became national. Considerations of space must be my apology for the inadequate treatment of the social state of the country ; when there is so much to be included something must be left out, and in preferring to dwell on the military history of the period I have taken the aspect of the subject which appeals to me most and with which I feel least incompetent to deal.

The appended lists of authorities do not of course make any pretensions to be exhaustive bibliographies : the first gives the names of the principal books from which I have taken my information, the second of some books to which I would refer any one who wants more information on particular points than is here given. Other references will be found from time to time throughout the book to other works which I have consulted less frequently or on special points. Some books (indicated by an asterisk) which appear in both lists have been published since the manuscript of the book was first completed, now some time ago, for unforeseen difficulties have caused considerable delay in the appearance of the book. I have thus not been able to utilise several volumes which might have been very helpful. Before leaving the subject of authorities I should like to make special acknowledgment of my indebtedness to two works, Dr. Ward's *England and Hanover* and Mr. Fisher's *Napoleonic Statesmanship : Germany*, the first of which I have found exceptionally useful when dealing with the attitude, not as a rule very rightly represented, of England towards Germany in the first half of the period, while Mr. Fisher's book I found peculiarly illuminating on a subject on which the German authorities I had utilised were copious rather than clear.

Further, I must plead guilty to what I believe to be generally looked upon as the perpetuation of a vulgar error, my adherence to the incorrect form " Hapsburg " in preference to " Habsburg," and my preference for such forms as Cologne, Mayence and Ratisbon. Strictly speaking they are no doubt incorrect, but I prefer to use the forms to which I am accustomed.

Finally, I should have liked to have included a good many more maps and plans, but of such things only a limited number can be inserted, and when the requisite things are to be found in the Clarendon Press *Atlas* and in M. Schrader's *Atlas de Geographie Historique* it would be merely superfluous to have given such maps as " the Development of Prussia " ; I have therefore preferred to increase the number of plans of battles.

OXFORD, *June* 1908

CONTENTS

CHAPTER I

GERMANY IN 1715—THE EMPIRE AND ITS INSTITUTIONS

PAGES

The Peace of Utrecht as a "landmark" in German history—Effects of the Reformation and Thirty Years' War on Germany — Charles V and Protestantism—The Peace of Westphalia and the constitution—Writings of Chemnitz, Pufendorf and Leibnitz—The Emperor and his authority—The Imperial Army—The "Roman Month"—The revenue—The Circles—The Imperial Chamber—The Aulic Council—The Diet and its Colleges: of Electors, of Princes, of Free Cities—Absence of unity and national life in Germany—The Princes and Louis XIV—The Princes and the Hapsburgs— Reasons for the survival of the Empire   1-30

CHAPTER II

THE GERMAN STATES IN 1715

"Austria" and the Hapsburgs—The ex-Spanish possessions—Hungary—Lack of unity — The Ecclesiastical Electors: Mayence, Treves, Cologne— Saxony and the Albertine Wettins—Brandenburg and the Hohenzollern— The Wittelsbachs in Bavaria and the Palatinate—The Guelphs and the Hanoverian Electorate—The Ecclesiastical Princes—Würtemberg: *Das gute alte Recht*—Baden—Hesse-Cassel—Hesse-Darmstadt—The Wittelsbach branches—The Franconian Hohenzollern—The Ernestine Saxons— Mecklenburg—Schleswig-Holstein and its connection with Denmark— Oldenburg—Sweden's German territories—Alsace : its anomalous position —Lorraine—Minor Princes—The Imperial Knights—Condition of Germany, social and economic—Effects of the Thirty Years' War   .   . 31-63

CHAPTER III

THE END OF THE NORTHERN WAR

The Coalition against Charles XII—Intervention of Frederick William I— Russo-Prussian Alliance—Intervention of England and Hanover—Losses of Sweden — Anglo - Russian quarrel over Mecklenburg — Death of Charles XII—Peaces of Stockholm (1719) and Nystad (1721)—Situation in the Baltic   64-71

CHAPTER IV

PASSAROWITZ, SICILY AND THE PRAGMATIC SANCTION

PAGES

Turkish attack on Venetian possessions—Austria assists Venice—Eugene's victories at Peterwardein and Belgrade—Spain's attempts to upset the Utrecht settlement in Italy—The Quadruple Alliance—Peaces of Passarowitz (1718), of London (1720)—Policy of Charles VI—The Austrian succession question—The "Pragmatic Sanction"—Its effect on foreign affairs—Ripperda's schemes—The League of Vienna—The Ostend East India Company—Congress of Soissons—Second Treaty of Vienna (1731)—The Powers and the Pragmatic Sanction . . . 72–83

CHAPTER V

PRUSSIA UNDER FREDERICK WILLIAM I

Religion as a factor in politics—The persecution of the Salzburgers—Frederick William I and his work for Prussia—Economies and revenue reform— Constitutional situation—Judicial and social reforms—The Prussian Army : its increase and improvement—Frederick William's foreign policy— Jülich and Berg 84–96

CHAPTER VI

THE LAST WARS OF CHARLES VI

The Polish Succession—France and Spain attack Austria—Walpole's neutrality : its unwisdom—Campaigns of 1734 and 1735—Preliminaries of Vienna —Lorraine ceded to France—Marriage of Maria Theresa to Francis Stephen of Lorraine—Death of Eugene—Charles VI joins Russia against the Turks—Disastrous campaigns—The Peace of Belgrade— Death of Charles VI. 97–104

CHAPTER VII

MARIA THERESA AND HER ENEMIES

Condition of Austria in 1740—Constitution, army, finances—The Conference and its members—Possible claimants : Saxony, Bavaria—Attitude of "the Powers"—Frederick II of Prussia : his action at Herstal—The Hohenzollern "claim" on Silesia—Frederick's action discussed—Silesia invaded—Maria Theresa's attitude—Campaign and battle of Mollwitz—Its great political results—Fleury and Belleisle—The Treaty of Nymphenburg—Other claims raised—England's advice to Maria Theresa—Policy of France discussed 105–123

CHAPTER VIII

THE AUSTRIAN SUCCESSION WAR—TO THE TREATY OF WORMS

Franco-Bavarian invasion of Austria—Vienna in peril—The Elector's change of plan—Convention of Klein Schellendorf—Loss of Prague—Khevenhüller invades Bavaria : his success—Charles Albert elected Emperor—Frederick II again takes the field—Unsuccessful invasion of Moravia—Battle of

CONTENTS

PAGES

Chotusitz—Peace of Berlin—French besieged in Prague—Belleisle's escape —Death of Fleury—Campaign of 1743 : French driven from Bavaria— Fall of Walpole—England and the " Pragmatic Army "—The march to the Main—Dettingen—Carteret and the "Project of Hanau "—Affairs in Italy—Campo Santo—Austro-Sardinian relations—The Treaty of Worms— Maria Theresa's policy discussed—The Treaty of Fontainebleau . 124-145

CHAPTER IX

THE AUSTRIAN SUCCESSION WAR—TO THE PEACE OF AIX-LA-CHAPELLE

Threatened invasion of England—Saxe overruns West Flanders—Austrian invasion of Alsace, checked by Frederick's intervention—The Union of Frankfort and its objects—Campaign of 1744 in Bavaria and Bohemia— D'Argenson—Death of Charles VII—Bavaria retires from the war—French plans of campaign— Fontenoy—The Jacobite insurrection—Election of Francis Stephen as Emperor—Austrian invasion of Silesia : checked at Hohenfriedberg—Frederick in Bohemia—Battle of Sohr—Convention of Hanover—Joint action of Austria and Saxony : Gross Hennersdorf and Kesselsdorf—Treaty of Dresden—Frederick's success—Affairs of Italy : d'Argenson and Charles Emmanuel—Campaigns in the Netherlands : of 1746, 1747—Negotiations for peace—Peace of Aix-la-Chapelle—State of Europe after the Peace—A mere truce 146-171

CHAPTER X

MARIA THERESA'S REFORMS AND THE DIPLOMATIC REVOLUTION

The Conference after the war—Maria Theresa's new ministers : Kaunitz, Haugwitz, Chotek—Increased centralisation and efficiency—Army reform —Administrative reform—Financial and judicial reform—The outlying dominions : Italy, the Netherlands—Maria Theresa and Hungary—Foreign policy—Austria and her allies—Kaunitz proposes a change of front—Rela- tions with France—Treaty of Aranjuez—Anglo-French conflict—England vulnerable in Hanover—George II's preparations for defence—Attitude of Frederick II : his fears of an attack—Convention of Westminster—Effect of this on France—Negotiations with Austria—First Treaty of Versailles— Its importance and effects 172-193

CHAPTER XI

THE SEVEN YEARS' WAR : CAMPAIGNS OF 1756 AND 1757

Frederick's use of the peace—His expectation of attack—The invasion of Saxony—Saxons stand at Pirna—Battle of Lobositz—Fall of Pirna— Negotiations during the winter of 1756-1757—Sweden, Russia and the Empire support France and Austria—Campaign of 1757 : Frederick invades Bohemia—Battle and siege of Prague—Daun's victory at Kolin—Prussians evacuate Bohemia—Operations of Russians—Affairs in Western Germany : Richelieu's advance—Hastenbeck and Closter Seven—Soubise and the Imperial Army—Frederick moves to Erfurt—Austrians invade Silesia and defeat Bevern at Breslau—Frederick's victory at Rossbach and return to Silesia—Battle of Leuthen—Situation at end of 1757 . . 194-227

CHAPTER XII

THE SEVEN YEARS' WAR (*continued*) : 1758 AND 1759

PAGES

Preparations on both sides—England subsidises Prussia—Ferdinand of Brunswick given command in West Germany—England's part in the war—Convention of Closter Seven denounced—Ferdinand's opening operations : French driven behind the Rhine—Frederick recovers Schweidnitz and invades Moravia—Siege of Olmütz—Loudoun captures a great convoy—Siege raised—Prussian retreat into Bohemia—Russian advance calls off Frederick to the Oder—Daun's wasted opportunity—Battle of Zorndorf—Frederick returns to Saxony—Battle of Hochkirch—Frederick's recovery—Ferdinand's operations : Crefeld—British troops sent to help him—Fall of Bernis : Choiseul succeeds him—Schemes for campaign of 1759—Frederick adopts the defensive—The Russian advance—Battle of Paltzig—Loudoun joins Russians—Battle of Kunersdorf—Daun misses his chance of decisive success—Prince Henry's operations—Maxen—Situation at close of 1759— Ferdinand's campaign : Bergen and Minden   .   .   .   228-272

CHAPTER XIII

THE SEVEN YEARS' WAR (*concluded*)

Battle of Landshut—Frederick assails Dresden—Loudoun takes Glatz—Frederick moves into Silesia—Battle of Liegnitz—Operations of Russians— Raid on Berlin—Battle of Torgau—Ferdinand in 1760 : Warburg—Hesse lost—Plans for 1761—Frederick at Bunzelwitz—Loudoun storms Schweidnitz—Fall of Colberg—Western Germany in 1761 : Ferdinand's victory of Vellinghausen—Negotiations for peace—Intervention of Spain—Fall of Pitt—Death of Elizabeth of Russia—Peter III assists Frederick—Sweden retires from the war—Campaign of 1762—Frederick recovers Schweidnitz —Ferdinand's successes—Peace Negotiations—Treaty of Hubertsburg— Frederick's part in the war—France and England—Attitude of Germany to the struggle   273-293

CHAPTER XIV

AUSTRIA AND PRUSSIA AFTER THE WAR.   THE PARTITION OF POLAND

Condition of Prussia in 1763—Remedial measures—Administrative reforms— Frederick's system of government—Condition of the Prussian army— Maria Theresa's work of reconstruction—The Council of State—Death of Francis Stephen—Joseph II—Ministerial changes—Joseph and the Empire —Affairs of Poland—The succession question (1763)—Internal troubles— Russo-Turkish war—Danger of war spreading—Partition suggested and adopted — Responsibility and justification — Austria's acquisition of Bukovina—Peace of Kainardji   294-309

CHAPTER XV

THE FOREIGN POLICY OF JOSEPH II

Joseph now predominant in Austria—The Bavarian succession question— Joseph's claims and proposals—Opposition of Charles of Zweibrücken

CONTENTS

PAGES

backed by Prussia—The Bavarian Succession War—Peace of Tetschen—
Russia's influence—Death of Maria Theresa—Joseph supports Cather-
ine II's Eastern policy—The Netherlands and the closing of the Scheldt—
Joseph thwarted by Vergennes—The Bavarian exchange project—Fred-
erick II and the *Fürstenbund*—Death of Frederick II—Joseph involved in
Catherine II's war against Turkey—Prussian intervention in Holland—The
Triple Alliance of 1788—Eastern complications—Death of Joseph . 310-327

CHAPTER XVI

MARIA THERESA AND JOSEPH II—DOMESTIC AFFAIRS

Joseph as a reformer—The Church—Relations with the Papacy—The fall of the
Jesuits—Education—Toleration—The Agrarian question—Opposition of
the nobility—Ministerial changes—Finances and commerce—Joseph and
the Netherlands—Localist and clerical opposition excited by his reforms—
Outbreak of Belgian insurrection—The Belgian Republic—Joseph and
Hungary—Opposition to agrarian reforms—Prospect of Prussian intervention—Reasons for Joseph's failure 328-346

CHAPTER XVII

LEOPOLD II AND THE EASTERN QUESTION

Accession of Leopold II—His experience in Tuscany—His policy—Intrigues of
Prussia—Treaty of Reichenbach—Conciliation of Hungary—The Belgian
Republic suppressed—Condition of Austria under Leopold—Peace of
Sistova with Turkey—Better relations between Austria and Prussia . 347-355

CHAPTER XVIII

GERMANY AND THE FRENCH REVOLUTION

Reasons for intervention of European powers in France—The *emigrés* and
Alsace—Condition of Germany, political and intellectual—Little national
feeling—Attitude to France—The *Illuminati* and the Revolution—
Western Germany the only district ready to receive the propaganda—
Effect of Revolution on German unity—The German states in 1792 :
Bavaria and the Palatinate ; Saxony ; Hanover and Brunswick-Wolfen-
büttel ; Hesse-Cassel, Hesse-Darmstadt, Mecklenburg ; Oldenburg and
Holstein ; Baden, Würtemberg ; minor states ; the ecclesiastical territories ;
the Free Cities 356-374

CHAPTER XIX

THE FIRST COALITION

Leopold II and intervention—The Declaration of Pillnitz—French hostility to
Austria—Sudden death of Leopold—War declared—French invade
Belgium—Brunswick's invasion of France : Valmy—Belgium and Western
Germany overrun—Republicanism on the Rhine—Affairs of Poland : the
Second Partition—Campaign of 1793 : the Allies' opportunity ; it is
missed—Wattignies—Hoche and Pichégru on the Rhine—Prussia's failure

PAGES

to co-operate—Campaign of 1794: Allies driven out of Belgium and
behind the Rhine—French conquer Holland—Collapse of the Coalition—
Prussia's policy—The Peace of Basel : can it be justified? .   .   . 375-395

CHAPTER XX

FROM BASEL TO CAMPO FORMIO

Prussia and Poland : the Third Partition—The Empire and its defence—
Campaign of 1795 : Clerfayt's successes—Campaign of 1796 : Bonaparte
in Italy : Archduke Charles against Jourdan and Moreau in South
Germany—Attitude of minor states—Treaty of Pffaffenhofen—Repulse of
Jourdan and Moreau—Bonaparte's victories and advance into Austria—
Preliminaries of Leoben—" Fructidor "—Treaty of Campo Formio—
Austria's acquisitions and losses—Her internal condition : Francis II :
Thugut and his policy—State of Prussia under Frederick William II
and III—Her misguided policy   396-417

CHAPTER XXI

RASTATT AND THE SECOND COALITION

Meeting of Congress of Rastatt—Territorial " compensation " and secularisation
—Treatment of Germany by the Directory—Franco-Austrian relations—
French aggressions in Italy—Formation of the Second Coalition—Prussia's
continued neutrality—Attitude of Bavaria—Outbreak of war—Operations
in Switzerland and South Germany—Archduke Charles victorious at
Stockach—Events in Italy—Dispersion of the Congress : the French
envoys murdered—First battle of Zurich—Thugut's plan of campaign—
Suvorov's successes in Italy : Cassano, the Trebbia, Novi—Suvorov
diverted to Switzerland—Fatal blunder of moving Archduke Charles to
Rhine—Masséna's victory at Zürich—Suvorov's retreat—Anglo-Russian
expedition to North Holland—Discord in the Coalition   .   . 418-439

CHAPTER XXII

MARENGO, HOHENLINDEN AND LUNÉVILLE

Bonaparte's plans for 1800 — Passage of the St. Bernhard—Marengo—
Moreau and Kray : Austrians driven back—Armistice and negotiations
—Fall of Thugut—Operations resumed—Battle of Hohenlinden—Austria
forced to conclude Peace of Lunéville—Its terms—The " Left Bank " lost
to Germany 440-454

CHAPTER XXIII

THE RESETTLEMENT OF 1803

Napoleon and Germany—Arrangements for the redistribution—The Armed
Neutrality of 1800 — Prussia occupies Hanover—The " Recess " of
Feb. 25th, 1803 : its terms—Heredity as the principle by which secularisa-
tion can be justified—Ecclesiastical states and Free Cities suppressed—

PAGES

Results of the redistribution—Gains and losses of individual states—The question of the Westphalian bishoprics—The Recess practically the end of the Holy Roman Empire—Attitude of country to the changes—Effect of the German Revolution 455-466

CHAPTER XXIV

THE CAUSES OF THE THIRD COALITION

The Imperial Knights after 1803—Bavaria's attack on them—Maximilian Joseph and Montgelas—Napoleon and Great Britain—French occupation of Hanover—Abduction of the Duc d'Enghien—Napoleon assumes Imperial title—His tour on the Rhine—Prussia and France : Frederick William III's hesitation—Preliminaries of the Third Coalition : Austria accedes to it 467-480

CHAPTER XXV

ULM AND AUSTERLITZ

The Austrian army in 1805—Mack and his plan of campaign—South-Western states join Napoleon — The march to the Danube — Mack's retreat intercepted—Capitulation of Ulm—French advance continued : Vienna occupied — Prussia decides to join Allies — Convention of Potsdam— Haugwitz's mission—Allies defeated at Austerlitz—Treaties of Schönbrunn and Pressburg—Austria's losses—Napoleon's treatment of Austria . 481-495

CHAPTER XXVI

THE CONFEDERATON OF THE RHINE AND THE OVERTHROW OF PRUSSIA

Projects for reconstruction—" Mediatisation "—The Confederation of the Rhine founded—Its members—Many minor states suppressed—Francis II takes title of Emperor of Austria—Attitude of Prussia—Napoleon and Hanover —Condition of Prussian administration, society and army—Breach between Napoleon and Prussia—Execution of Palm—Campaign of 1806 : Prussians defeated at Jena and Auerstadt — Collapse of Prussian resistance — Ministerial changes : Haugwitz retires 496-512

CHAPTER XXVII

FRIEDLAND, TILSIT AND ERFURT

Winter campaign of 1806-1807 : Pultusk and Eylau—Austria's inaction— England's wasted opportunity—Battle of Friedland—Peace of Tilsit— Humiliation of Prussia : its harsh treatment—Territorial changes in Germany : the Kingdom of Westphalia ; the Grand Duchy of Berg ; the coast-lands—Outbreak of Peninsular War—Napoleon's relations with Russia — The Prussian indemnity — Congress at Erfurt : its delusive character 513-524

CHAPTER XXVIII

AUSTRIA'S EFFORT TO OVERTHROW NAPOLEON

PAGES

Napoleon's policy towards Germany — Austria's preparations : Stadion and Archduke Charles—The best chance missed (autumn 1808)—Outbreak of hostilities—The Eckmühl campaign—The Archduke at fault—Abortive risings in North Germany : Schill's, Brunswick's — Napoleon takes Vienna—Operations in Italy and Tyrol—Napoleon defeated at Aspern— The advantage not improved—Battles of Raab and Wagram—Position after Wagram—The Walcheren expedition—Prussia remains inactive— Treaty of Schönbrunn : heavy losses of Austria—Tyrolese abandoned— Fall of Stadion : Metternich's change of policy   .   .   .   525-546

CHAPTER XXIX

GERMANY AT NAPOLEON'S MERCY

Attitude of Germany to Napoleon : altered by the Continental System. Bavaria under Maximilian Joseph—Baden—Frederick I of Würtemberg—Saxony and the Grand Duchy of Warsaw—Hesse-Darmstadt and Würzburg— Dalberg's Grand Duchy of Frankfort—Berg and the Continental System— Jerome's Kingdom of Westphalia—Napoleon's exactions and annexations— Prussia since Tilsit—Her revival—Stein's reforms : the Municipal Reform Edict ; the Emancipating Edict—Hardenberg continues the work—Von Humboldt and educational reform—Military reorganisation : Scharnhorst and short service—Napoleon's changed relations with Russia and Austria : his marriage to Marie Louise—Causes of breach with Russia—Prussia and Austria support him in 1812—German contingents in the Grand Army —Rise of a national feeling : Fichte, Kleist and the Universities .   547-570

CHAPTER XXX

THE WAR OF LIBERATION : TILL THE ARMISTICE

Situation after Napoleon's repulse from Russia—Yorck and the Convention of Tauroggen—Frederick William's dilemma—His decision—The Treaty of Kalisch—Napoleon's efforts to create a new army—Attitude of German contingents — Prussia takes arms — Attitude of Austria : Metternich's waiting policy—Bavaria and Saxony—Operations begin—Eugene driven back to the Saale—Napoleon's advance—Battle of Lützen—Operations in North Germany—Battle of Bautzen—Allies retire towards Bohemia— Austria's intervention—Armistice of Poischwitz—Napoleon's reasons— Metternich's policy—Convention of Reichenbach—Sweden joins the Allies —Preparations for resuming hostilities—The Allies' strategy—Vittoria— The armistice expires   571-594

CHAPTER XXXI

THE WAR OF LIBERATION (continued)—TO THE BATTLE OF KULM

Napoleon's Grand Army of 1813—German contingents—The Allied forces— Schwarzenberg as commander-in-chief—Napoleon's situation and strategy —Napoleon advances against Blücher, but is recalled to save Dresden from

PAGES

the Allies' main body—Oudinot beaten at Gross Beeren—Macdonald's
disaster at the Katzbach—Allies attack Dresden: Napoleon returns in
time—His victory—Vandamme intercepting Allied retreat is overwhelmed
at Kulm—Situation at end of August   595–614

CHAPTER XXXII

THE WAR OF LIBERATION (*continued*)—LEIPZIG AND HANAU

Ney defeated at Dennewitz—Napoleon's operations during September—Treaty
of Töplitz—Consequent defection of Bavaria—Wallmoden's operations:
battle of the Göhrde—Decisive movement begun—Blücher passes the Elbe
—Napoleon falls back from Dresden—Schwarzenberg advances on Leipzig
—Concentration at Leipzig—Battles of October 16th and 18th—Napoleon
compelled to retreat—Evacuation of Leipzig—Collapse of Confederation
of the Rhine — Napoleon deserted by South Germany — Allies pursue—
Napoleon's retreat—Battle of Hanau   615–633

CHAPTER XXXIII

1814 AND THE TREATY OF PARIS

Napoleon's resolve to continue the war: he rejects the "Proposals of
Frankfort"—Allies' plans and preparations for 1814—Napoleon's skilful
campaign: battles of La Rothière, Champaubert, Montmirail and Montereau
—Bülow called up—Battles of Craonne and Laon—Battle of Arcis sur
Aube—Treaty of Chaumont—The Allies press on to Paris: its capitulation
—Abdication of Napoleon—The Treaty of Paris—Changed attitudes of
the Allied leaders   634–643

CHAPTER XXXIV

THE CONGRESS OF VIENNA

Proposals for reconstruction—Stein's idea — Metternich's intentions — The
preliminaries of the Congress—Its meeting—The principal negotiators—
Question of reconstruction: the Twelve Articles—The Germanic Confederation agreed to — Its members and constitution — Metternich
champions localism—The question of territorial redistribution—Saxony—
Talleyrand's intervention—Russia and Prussia baulked—Solution of the
Saxon question: its ultimate result—Prussia's acquisitions—Other readjustments—Austria finds compensation outside Germany—The settlement
reviewed   644–659

CHAPTER XXXV

THE HUNDRED DAYS

Napoleon's return—The Treaty of Chaumont renewed—Enthusiasm in Prussia
—Forces available—The Allies' plans—Napoleon's strategy—The Allied
armies: Saxon contingent mutinies—Events of June 15th: Ziethen's
containing screen; Ney and Bernhard of Saxe-Weimar—June 16th, Battle
of Ligny—Defeat of Prussians—Battle of Quatre Bras—June 17th, Wellington's retreat—Grouchy detached to pursue Prussians—Gneisenau retires on

b

PAGES

Wavre—June 18th, Grouchy's movements—Blücher moves to Waterloo : his late arrival there, its causes and effects—Battle of Waterloo : part played by the German contingents—Principal phases of the battle—The Prussian share — Total overthrow of Napoleon — June 19th, battle of Wavre : Grouchy's retreat—Subsequent operations—Restoration of peace : Prussia baulked of vengeance—Second Treaty of Paris : its terms, as a landmark in German history—Situation of Germany : a compromise, not a settlement 660–702

GENEALOGICAL TABLES—

    I. The Hapsburgs 703
    II. The House of Brunswick 704
   III. The House of Hohenzollern 705
   IV. The House of Wettin 706
    V. The House of Wittelsbach 707

INDEX 709–732

MAPS AND PLANS

Mollwitz, Chotusitz and Sohr 170
Prague, Kolin, Rossbach, Breslau and Leuthen 228
Zorndorf and Hochkirch 246
Minden, Kunersdorf and Torgau 280
Marengo and Hohenlinden 452
Austerlitz and Jena 508
The Danube Valley 532
Aspern and Wagram 544
Germany in 1811 570
Lützen and Bautzen 586
Dresden 612
Katzbach and Dennewitz 616
Movements between Dresden and Leipzig 622
Leipzig 630
Saxony, Silesia and Bohemia 632
South-Western States in 1815 }
Kingdom of Hanover 1801–1815 } 658
Ligny and Prussian gains in 1815 680
Theatre of Waterloo campaign 696
Germany in 1715 . . . . . . *at end of volume*

AUTHORITIES

A

ARNETH, VON. Prinz Eugen, vol. iii.
,, Maria Theresa.
,, Maria Theresa und Joseph II.
BROGLIE, DUC DE.
Frédéric II et Marie Therèse.
Frédéric II et Louis XV.
Marie Therèse Imperatrice.
Maurice de Saxe et le Marquis d'Argenson.
La Paix d'Aix la Chapelle.
L'Alliance Autrichienne.
CATHCART. War in Germany, 1812–1813.
CHUQUET, A. Les Guerres de la Révolution.
Dropmore Papers. (Historical Manuscripts Commission : MSS. of J. B. Fortescue, Esq., 4 vols. and 1 vol.*)
DROYSSEN. Friedrich der Grosse (Part V. of his Geschichte der Preussischen Politik).
ERDMANNSDORFFER. Deutsche Geschichte, 1648–1740, vol. ii.
FISHER, H. A. L. Napoleonic Statesmanship : Germany.
Geschichte der Befreiungskriege, 1813–1815, especially
VON HOLLEBEN, Geschichte des Frühjahrsfeldzuges, 1813.
FRIEDRICH, Geschichte des Herbstfeldzuges, 1813 (vols. i. and ii., also vol. iii.*).
HAUSSER, LUDWIG. Deutsche Geschichte vom Tode Friedrichs des Grossen bis zur Gründung des Deutschen Bundes.
HERMANN, ALFRED. Marengo.
HOUSSAYE, H. 1815 : Waterloo.
HÜFFER, HERMANN. Der Krieg vom 1799 und die Zweite Koalition (referred to as Hüffer, i. and ii.).
,, Quellen zur Geschichte der Kriege, 1799–1800 (referred to as Hüffer).
Instructions aux Ambassadeurs de France. Autriche (edited by A. Sorel).
Bavière, Deux Ponts et Palatinate (edited by A. Sorel).
ONCKEN. Zeitalter Friedrichs des Grossen.
PFLUGK-HARTTUNG, J. VON. Vorgeschichte der Schlacht der Belle-Alliance.
PUTTER. The Political Constitution of the Germanic Empire.
RANKE, L. VON. Preussische Geschichte.
ROUSSET, C. La Grande Armée de 1813.
Royal Historical Society. The Third Coalition Against France (edited by J. Holland Rose).
Buckinghamshire Papers, vol. ii.

SCHWERTFEGER, B.   Geschichte der Königlich Deutschen Legion, 1803–1816.*
SEELEY, SIR J. R.   Life and Times of Stein.
SIBORNE, W.   Waterloo Letters.
          ,,   The Waterloo Campaign.
TURNER.   The Germanic Constitution.
USSEL, VICOMTE JEAN DE.   Études sur l'année 1813.   La Defection de la Prusse.
WADDINGTON.   Louis XV et le Renversement des Alliances.
          ,,   La Guerre de Sept Ans. (vols. i.–iii. going up to 1759 ; vol. iv.*).
WARD, A. W.   England and Hanover.
Wellington's Dispatches, vol. xii.   Supplementary Dispatches, vol. x.
WOLF.   Osterreich unter Maria Theresa, Joseph II and Leopold II.
YORCK VON WARTENBURG, COUNT.   Napoleon as a General (English translation).
ZWEIDINECK SÜDENHORST.   Deutsche Geschichte in Zeitraum der Gründung des
                    Preussischen Königtum (referred to as Z. S.), vol. ii.
          ,,   Deutsche Geschichte von der Auflosung des alten bis
                    zur Errichtung des neuen Kaiserreiches, 1806–
                    1871, vol. i. (referred to as D. G. 1806–1871).

B

ARMSTRONG, E.   Elizabeth Farnese.
BEAMISH, MAJOR.   History of the King's German Legion.
BRACKENBURY, COLONEL C. B.   Frederick the Great (Military Biographies).
BRIGHT, DR. J. FRANCK.   Maria Theresa.
          ,,   Joseph II.
BRYCE, RT. HON. J.   The Holy Roman Empire.
Cambridge Modern History.   Vol. viii. The Revolution.
          ,,   Vol. ix. Napoleon.*
CHESNEY, COLONEL C. C.   Waterloo Lectures.
CLAPHAM, J. H.   The Causes of the War of 1792 (Cambridge Historical
    Essays, xi.).
COQUELLE.   England and Napoleon (translated).
FORTESCUE, HON. J. W.   A History of the British Army (vol. ii. for Ferdinand of
    Brunswick ; vol. iv. for 1793–1794).
GEORGE, H. B.   Napoleon's Invasion of Russia.
LORAINE-PETRE, F.   Napoleon's Conquest of Prussia.
          ,,   Napoleon's Campaign in Poland, 1806–1807.
MALLESON, COLONEL G.   Loudoun (Military Biographies).
REDDAWAY, W. F.   Frederick the Great (Heroes of the Nations).
ROSE, J. HOLLAND.   Life of Napoleon I.
          ,,   Napoleonic Studies.
SOREL, A.   La Question de l'Orient.
          ,,   L'Europe et la Revolution Française.
TUTTLE.   History of Prussia to 1740.
          ,,   Frederick the Great.

A HISTORY OF GERMANY
1715—1815

CHAPTER I

GERMANY IN 1715—THE EMPIRE AND ITS INSTITUTIONS

THE practice of dividing history into more or less conventional "periods" is always somewhat arbitrary and unsatisfactory, and at first sight there hardly seems much justification for treating the year 1715 as an important turning-point in the history of Germany. If one is seeking for an end, for a point at which some long struggle has been decided, some doubtful question settled, one would select 1648 rather than 1715, the Peace of Westphalia rather than those of Utrecht, Rastatt and Baden. If, on the other hand, a starting-point is sought, the unloosing of some hitherto unsuspected force, the appearance of a new set of actors, the opening of some great question, 1740 and the attack of Frederick II of Prussia on Silesia would seem to possess a far stronger claim. But the conditions which existed in 1740 and the forces which were then let loose did not spring into being in a moment; they were the fruit of years of development, and to appreciate them one must go back at any rate to the Peace of Utrecht. Similarly, great as were the changes summed up at the Peace of Westphalia, when one looks at it as a landmark in the history of the Holy Roman Empire and of that German Kingdom which, to its own undoing, was associated with the heritage of Charlemagne, it may be argued with some plausibility that the true failure of the Hapsburgs to make real their position as titular heads of Germany came with the premature death of Joseph I (1711). Germany from 1648 to 1815 was little more than a geographical expression, its history, such as

I

it is, is a history of disunion and disintegration; but between 1648 and 1715 it does possess a small degree of unity, and that is given it by the persistent attempts of France to profit by the weakness and divisions of her Eastern neighbour, and by the efforts of the Hapsburgs to unite the German Kingdom in opposition to the aggressions of Mazarin and Louis XIV. The Spanish Succession War, fought out largely on German soil and by German troops, had a very important bearing on the fortunes of Germany, and at one time it seemed that one result of it might be a great increase in the Imperial authority and prestige, and as if the practical independence of the territorial princes, established at the Peace of Westphalia, might be substantially reduced.   But this was not to be, and as far as the constitutional condition of Germany was concerned, the Treaties of Utrecht, Rastatt and Baden, instead of undoing the work of 1648, confirmed it, and left the German Kingdom an empty form, a name with no real substance behind it.

Thus the condition in which the year 1715 found Germany differed in degree rather than in kind from that in which the Thirty Years' War had left her in 1648.   The great movement of the Reformation had been fatal to the Holy Roman Empire: it had swept away the last relics of its pretensions to universal dominion by emphasising the national character of most of the states of Western Europe, and by introducing between them differences in religion which were of more than merely religious importance.   The Thirty Years' War had done a like office for the German Kingdom: it had completed the ruin of the Emperor's authority over the lands which were still nominally subject to him.   The forms of the old constitution, the Imperial title, the nominal existence of the Empire were to endure for another one hundred and fifty-eight years, but the settlement of 1648 amounted in all save the name to the substitution of a loosely-knit confederacy for the potential national state which had till then existed in the shape of the Empire.   Not that the settlement of 1648 was the sole cause of this change, even the long and terrible war to which it put an end could not by itself have effected so great an alteration had it not been the last in a long chain of causes whose work was now recognised and admitted.   At the Peace of Westphalia the Hapsburgs acknowledged principles which struck at the roots of the authority of the Emperor, they accepted because they had failed to prevent the results of the disintegrating tendencies which had been at work for so long. The practical independence of the Princes of the Empire was no new thing, but it now received formal recognition; the principle *cujus regio, ejus religio*, now reaffirmed, had been the basis of the Peace of Augsburg. It was all the more strongly re-established because, in the meantime, the Hapsburgs had led the crusade of the Counter-Reformation, and were now forced to leave in Protestant hands many secularised bishoprics as the token of the failure of their great endeavour.

Even before the Reformation the authority of the Emperor over the German Kingdom had been weak and uncertain, though Maximilian I had done much to assert it and had attempted more, while the possibility of converting the German feudal monarchy into a strong national sovereignty like those of England and France was still present. The process of disintegration had, it is true, gone much further in Germany than elsewhere, and localism was stronger and the central institutions were weaker than in France and England. What the Reformation did was that it introduced into Germany a new principle which served to complicate the contest between the spasmodic attempts of the Emperors at a centralising policy, and the disintegrating tendencies of which the Princes were the champions. The already existing aspirations to local independence received the powerful reinforcement of the new spirit of resistance which the revolt from Rome engendered. Seeing how strong the traditions of close relations between the Pope and the Emperor were, and how intimately the idea of the Empire was bound up with the idea of the Universal Church, it was only natural that resistance to the spiritual authority of the Pope should encourage resistance to the temporal authority of the Emperor. Moreover, when Germany was being divided into two antagonistic camps, the Catholic and the Protestant, it was impossible from the nature of the quarrel that the Emperor should be neutral. He could not be the impartial head of the whole nation, he must take one side or the other. It was with a crisis of the most momentous importance for Germany that Charles V was confronted in 1519 when he was required to make up his mind between Rome and Luther. Had he declared for Protestantism, and placed himself at the head of a national movement against the

Papacy, it is possible that the sixteenth century might have seen Germany really united. If the Emperor could have obtained control of the vast territories of the Church, he would have acquired the revenues and resources so badly needed to make the forms of the central government an efficient reality. But such a course must have brought him into collision, not only with all those who clung to the old faith and the old connection, but also with those Princes who adopted Protestantism, partly because they found in it a principle by which to defend their resistance to the Imperial authority; they would not have been so enthusiastic in their support of Protestantism had the Emperor been of that persuasion. Prelates and lay Princes alike would have struggled hard to hinder so great an increase in the Imperial resources and so great a change in the relative positions of the Emperor and his subjects, as that which would have been involved in his annexation of the ecclesiastical territories. As things actually went, the Emperor's continued adhesion to Roman Catholicism gave the Protestant champions of local independence a permanent bond of union in their religion. At the same time, even the Princes of the Emperor's own religion could not but be favourably disposed—as Princes —towards resistance to the Imperial authority and efforts to limit the Emperor's powers.

The Peace of Augsburg (1555) was of the nature of a truce rather than a settlement. The evenly-balanced contending forces agreed to a compromise which actually secured to Germany over sixty years of religious peace of a kind, but it was absolutely lacking in the elements of finality. The omission of any regulations for the position of the Calvinists, the failure to enforce any accepted rule as to new secularisations, were bound, sooner or later, to lead to a new conflict: it is only remarkable that the outbreak was so long delayed. Meanwhile the acknowledgment of the principle *cujus regio, ejus religio* was a fatal blow to the Imperial authority and the first great breach in the outward unity of the Empire.

The circumstances under which the great struggle between the rival creeds finally broke out were such as to make it even more impossible for the Emperor to adopt a neutral attitude. The local troubles in Bohemia which culminated in the famous "Defenestratio" of 1618 were only the match that fired the train, since for some time the Calvinists of Germany had been contemplating a war in defence of their religion. By adopting the Bohemian cause the Elector Palatine and his supporters brought themselves into a double collision with Ferdinand of Austria. By breaking the peace of the Empire they set at naught his authority as Emperor; but he was also King of Bohemia, and by assisting his revolted subjects the Calvinists assailed him as territorial ruler and as head of the Hapsburg house. Thus the Emperor could not interfere disinterestedly: he could not suppress the Calvinist disturbers of the peace without using the Imperial authority, such as it was, on behalf of his own dynastic territorial interests. Not merely was impartiality impossible, he was the leader of one of the contending parties. Much in the same way, by accepting the Bohemian Crown the Elector Palatine made it impossible for himself and his party to disassociate their defence of oppressed co-religionists from their own selfish interests and ambitions. Thus on the one side the cause of order and of unity became identified with intolerance and oppression, on the other anarchy and violence seemed to be the natural corollary to religious freedom. In this dilemma there were but two alternative possibilities. Either the Emperor would succeed in suppressing Protestantism both as a religious and as a political factor, and would thereby vindicate his authority, or by his failure in this attempt he would leave Germany divided between two hostile factions, one of which must always look upon the decadence of the Imperial constitution as the surest safeguard of its own existence.

In 1648 the Peace of Westphalia announced to the world that after thirty years of a most terrible and devastating war both combatants had failed, and had been obliged to assent to a compromise. That the Hapsburgs had failed, was proclaimed by their assenting to such a Peace. To their failure many causes had contributed; their want of material resources, Ferdinand II's incapacity and lack of statesmanship, the lukewarmness of those Catholic Princes whose political aims would not have been served by the complete success of the Catholic cause if championed by the Emperor, but more especially the intervention of foreign powers who had good reasons of their own for dreading the establishment

of Hapsburg supremacy over Germany. Yet such a result
had at one time seemed probable, for Frederick's headlong
folly had given the Emperor a chance a statesman would
not have missed. But Ferdinand had misused his victory
at Prague: he had endeavoured to do to Frederick what
Frederick had failed to do to him, he had then driven the
Lutherans into taking up arms by his efforts to reverse the
compromise on which the territorial distribution of Germany
rested: he had parted with Wallenstein at the bidding of
the Catholic League when that general seemed to have
Protestant Germany at his mercy. Had the Emperor believed
in the honesty of Wallenstein, or in the wisdom and justice
of the toleration advocated by that mysterious adventurer,
sufficiently to stand by him, it is possible that his confidence
might have been rewarded by success; but Wallenstein's
record was not one to inspire confidence, and toleration was
a policy not only in advance of the age but quite opposed
to the traditions of the Empire and of the Hapsburg dynasty.
Thus though the Peace left Bohemia and its dependencies
in the Emperor's keeping, it left the Empire hopelessly and
irretrievably disunited. As the next seventy years were to
show, not even common dangers of the most formidable
kind could weld Germany together effectively. The acknowledgment of the rights of the heretic minority in the Empire
was in absolute conflict with the theory of Church and State
on which the Empire was based; the concessions which the
Princes had extorted reduced the Emperor's authority over
them to a mere form, and made the name of Kingdom a
complete anachronism when applied to Germany. But
signally as the Hapsburgs had failed, their opponents could
hardly claim to have been much more successful. The
Imperial supremacy which Frederick v and the Calvinist
Union had sought to destroy still existed, even if it was a
mere shadow of what Ferdinand had hoped to make it.
The Protestants, Calvinists and Lutherans alike, had succeeded in freeing themselves from the jurisdiction of the
Pope, in wringing from the Catholic majority in the Diet a
recognition of their right to freedom of worship in their own
lands, and in defending their possession of those ecclesiastical
territories which the Edict of Restitution had endeavoured to
wrest from them. But they had not managed to obtain

the rich and coveted abbeys and bishoprics of the South: indeed, on the whole they had lost ground. Bohemia and its dependencies had passed from them, and the skilful propagandism of the Jesuits was rapidly extirpating Protestantism from its former strongholds there. The adoption of January 1st, 1624, as the date by which the possession of disputed territories was to be determined on the whole favoured the Catholics, to whom it left a majority of the bishoprics. Moreover, the religious freedom thus won by the sword—and in no small measure by the swords of the Swede and the Frenchman—could only be retained by the sword. It was indissolubly connected with local independence and Imperial impotence; in other words, the disunion of Germany was its only guarantee. Identified as the Hapsburgs were with Rome, with intolerance, with the forcible promulgation of Catholicism, German Protestantism could not but look upon the Imperial institutions as hostile to its rights and could hardly do otherwise than seek to prevent anything which promised to restore their vitality. Loyalty to the Empire seemed to the majority of German Protestants incompatible with the safety of their religion.

The collapse of the old constitution not unnaturally occupied the minds of the pamphleteers and publicists of the day, and many were the schemes for reconstruction and reform put forward in the second half of the seventeenth century. Among the most important and interesting of these is the *Dissertatio de ratione status in Imperio nostro Romano Germanico*, written by Philip Boguslaw Chemnitz, a Pomeranian jurist of some repute, and published under the pseudonym of Hippolytus à Lapide. The treatise sets out an ideal which was never realised, and was based on a theory which was neither sound historically nor accurate as a statement of the existing facts, the assumption that neither the Emperor nor the Electors, but the whole Diet was the sovereign body. This may be accounted for by the fact that Chemnitz was actuated throughout by an intense hostility to the Hapsburgs. When he looks at them the sight of the sack of Magdeburg rises before his eyes, and the Edict of Restitution is for him the type of their acts and aims.

Chemnitz was not the first writer to find salvation for Germany in the decrease of the Imperial authority and in the increase of the powers of the Princes, but he may be taken as the best example of those who hold that view. He regarded the Emperor as the representative of an aristocratic republic, the sovereignty of which resided rather in the assembled Estates than in the Emperor. To him the Emperor was little more than the nominal head, the minister of the Estates, not their superior. Thus it is by the Diet, not by the Emperor, that the decision as to peace or war must be taken, to the *Kammergericht*[1] rather than to the *Reichshofrath*[2] that the final jurisdiction belongs. Throughout Chemnitz assails the Hapsburgs in unsparing terms; their pretensions are the principal danger to Germany, their power must be diminished, their Imperial authority curtailed and restricted in every possible way. "*Delenda est Austria*" is his panacea for the ills of Germany and the burden of every page of his pamphlet.

Rather different was the account given by Pufendorf, who, writing under the name of Severin de Monzambano, a fictitious Italian traveller who had made the tour of Germany, compared the Holy Roman Empire to the league of the Greeks against Troy, and pronounced it neither monarchy, aristocracy, nor democracy, but an anomalous blend of all three, "a half-way house between a kingdom and a confederation," which the Emperor was striving to make more like a kingdom, the Princes to make more of a confederation. The Princes, he pointed out, though nominally in vassalage to the Emperor from whom they held their fiefs, enjoyed a practical independence, having all sovereign rights in their own territories. Indeed one thing only prevented Germany from being as absolutely disunited as Italy: the possessions of the Austrian Hapsburgs formed a connected state which alone gave Germany some approach to unity by being able and willing to maintain the forms and institutions of the Empire.

Pufendorf's treatise provoked a reply from no less eminent a man than the philosopher Leibnitz, who in his *Contra Severinum de Monzambano* dealt mainly with the need for unity against the enemies of Germany. He dwelt on the defencelessness of the Empire, the utter absence of military organisation, the need for a standing army and of proper provision for its support. But he had also to point out how

---

[1] The Imperial Chamber of Justice; cf. p. 14.
[2] The Imperial High Court, the so-called "Aulic Council"; cf. p. 15.

slight were the chances that any permanent organisation would be established.   To some Princes the present situation offered a good prospect of profiting by the troubles of their neighbours, others for religious reasons entertained suspicions of the use that might be made of a standing army, others again feared that it might be employed by the greater powers to suppress their petty neighbours, and thus Leibnitz's appeal to the Princes of the Empire to cultivate better relations with the Emperor fell on deaf ears.

The substantial accuracy of Pufendorf's description of the state of Germany will be realised when one examines more closely the Imperial constitution and the component portions of this anomalous mixture of a confederation and a kingdom. The Imperial office, nominally elective, had practically become hereditary in the Austrian branch of the Hapsburg family, which had provided the Holy Roman Empire and the German Kingdom with an uninterrupted series of rulers ever since the election of Albert II in 1438.   But the elective element had not entirely disappeared: indeed, it might have been better for the Empire if it had.   Its survival merely served to further the decadence of the Imperial institutions, for, from Charles V onward, each new " Emperor Elect " had had to purchase the suffrages of the Electors by means of " Election Capitulations " which circumscribed and curtailed yet further the meagre powers and rights still attached to his office.[1]   Such influence and authority as the Emperor possessed was his on account of his hereditary possessions, not in virtue of his Imperial office.

Yet on paper his rights as Emperor were still considerable. In addition to the so-called *Comitial rechte*, those rights which he exercised on behalf of and by the authority of the Diet, he had certain " Reserved Rights " with which the Diet had nothing to do.   He could veto measures submitted by the Diet, he could make promotions in rank, confer fiefs, titles of nobility and University degrees.   Further, he represented Germany in all dealings with foreign powers, and it was from him that the Princes had to obtain the coveted privileges, *de non appellando* and *de non evocando*, which removed their law-courts from the superintendence of the Imperial tribunals and made their territories judicially independent.   A certain amount of rather indefinite influence and prestige still, after all

[1] For those of Charles V, cf. Turner, p. 120.

deductions, attached to the Imperial office, and it need hardly be mentioned that the Emperor possessed in his hereditary dominions all the ordinary sovereign rights which the Princes enjoyed in their territories. Indeed, it was the great extent of the rights and powers of which the Princes had become possessed rather than any lack of powers theoretically his which made the Emperor so powerless and his office so anomalous.

The process by which this had come about has been admirably described by Sir John Seeley[1] as "the paralysis of the central government and, consequent upon that, the assumption by local authorities of powers properly Imperial." "A number of municipal corporations," he writes, "which in England would have only had the power of levying rates for local purposes and of appointing local officers with very insignificant powers, had in Germany become practically independent republics. Magnates who in England would have wielded a certain administrative and judicial power as members of Quarter Sessions, had risen in Germany to the rank of sovereigns." With all the Princes of the Empire practically independent in their domestic affairs and almost as completely their own masters in their dealings with foreign powers, not much scope was left for the intervention of the Emperor or of any of the machinery of the Empire. Only in regulating matters which concerned two or more German states was the Emperor likely to be called upon to act, and his intervention was rather that of the president of a federation of independent states than of the King of even a feudal monarchy. What he lacked was the force needed to compel obedience and secure the execution of his orders. The extent of his impotence may best be judged from the condition of the Imperial revenues and from the composition and organisation of the Army of the Empire.

To say outright that the Empire possessed neither revenues nor an army would strictly speaking be inaccurate, but it would be a great deal nearer to the real truth than to affirm that either of these effectively existed. Since 1521 there had been a unit of assessment, the so-called "Roman Month," which represented the amount voted by the Diet in that year for an expedition to Rome which Charles V was contemplating. The sum then voted, 120,000 florins, was calculated to provide

[1] *Life and Times of Stein*, i. 12.

4,000 horsemen at a rate of ten florins a month and 20,000 foot-soldiers at four florins.   Since 1521 fractions or multiples of this rate had been voted from time to time, for the convenience of utilising an existing assessment was enormous. Hard as it was to obtain payment of contributions even when the due proportions were assigned to those liable to pay, as was the case when the Imperial Roll of 1521 was utilised, the difficulty of collection and the friction arising out of it would have been multiplied many times had a fresh assessment been necessary whenever a vote was passed.   But even this was far from giving the Empire a standing army or even the machinery for raising one; it merely settled the proportions, and each new call for troops involved a fresh settlement by the Diet, which required almost as much diplomacy and negotiation as an international agreement for joint action. It was never certain whether the Diet would vote for sending men or money; though whichever form the contributions might take the Roman Month gave the proportion in which the individual states were liable.   It was, of course, to the advantage of the Emperor that the contribution should be in money, but the contributors preferred to send men : it gave them the appearance of allies rather than of tributaries, and, moreover, enabled them to exercise more control over the war : a contingent could always be recalled, it was less easy to recover a money contribution once it had entered the Imperial coffers.[1]   Nor was it certain whether the vote of the majority bound the minority, or whether only those who had voted in favour of a tax were liable to pay it.

Thus though many of its members possessed armies of considerable strength and efficiency, as a military power the Empire was an almost negligible quantity.   More than one attempt at reform was made in the second half of the seventeenth century.   In May 1681 the Diet issued a decree fixing the total force to be provided by the Circles at 12,000 horse and 28,000 foot, each Circle being given the choice between providing its own men or paying another " armed estate " (*Armirte Stände*) to supply its allotted contingent. But though a new unit of assessment was thus substituted for

---

[1] It is easy to see that this uncertainty very much increased the inefficiency of the defensive arrangements of the Empire : a noteworthy example was the delay over the despatch of troops to assist the Austrians in the Turkish War of 1663–1664.

the Roman Month not even now was a permanent force kept
on foot, and in the War of the League of Augsburg there
was continual friction between the "armed members" who
provided troops and the "assigned" who contributed to their
support.   So inefficient was the protection afforded to the
"assigned" states by the Army of the Empire that the
Franconian and Swabian Circles finally resolved to reorganise
their own resources, and by raising troops of their own to
avoid being "assigned" any longer.   With this object a
scheme was drawn up by Margrave Louis of Baden-Baden,
the colleague of Marlborough and Eugene in the Blenheim
campaign, which was finally adopted (Jan. 1697) at a meeting
held at Frankfort.   These two Circles, with the Bavarian,
Westphalian and the two Rhenish, formed the Association of
Frankfort, undertaking to provide 40,000 men between them,
and to draw up definite regulations for their equipment and
organisation.   This scheme would probably have provided a
more efficient *Reichsarmee* than had hitherto existed, but the
prompt conclusion of peace prevented it from being put into
practice, and thus, never getting the chance of being tested
in a campaign and put into working order, it remained a mere
paper scheme.   At the outbreak of the Spanish Succession
War it was necessary to make entirely new arrangements, and
that struggle found little improvement in the Army of the
Empire.   It was lacking in discipline, in homogeneity, in
organisation, in equipment, in almost everything that goes to
make an army efficient.   The states which, like Hesse-Cassel
and Brandenburg, possessed really efficient forces preferred to
hire out their troops to fight the battles of the Maritime
Powers rather than employ them in the less lucrative task of
defending the "lazy and sleepy Empire,"[1] which was thus
overrun again and again by French armies who levied in
requisitions and in unofficial plunderings sums far larger than
would have sufficed to provide troops enough to keep Villars
at bay.   Nowhere, indeed, was the disunion of Germany so
evident as in its defensive arrangements, and the last
appearances of the *Reichsarmee* during the Seven Years' War
were a fitting finale to its career.

Not the least potent reason for the inefficiency of the
defensive arrangements of the Empire was its poverty.   Nearly

---

[1] *Portland Papers*, iv. 441 ; Hist. MSS. Commission.

all the lucrative sources of income had passed from the Emperor to the local rulers. The Imperial Chamber of Justice was supported by a special tax, first voted in 1500 and known as the Chamber Terms (*Kammerzieler*); a certain amount of revenue was derived through the exercise of the Emperor's " Reserved Rights " and the Imperial Cities paid a small tribute amounting to about 12,000 gulden;[1] but these sums were quite insufficient to defray the maintenance of the Imperial institutions, and the want of an Imperial revenue was one of the reasons why the Hapsburgs remained so long in unchallenged possession of the costly dignity they alone could afford to support.

Where there was hardly any Imperial income it is not surprising that there was no common Imperial treasury, still less any administrative machinery. Police was left to the Circles, an organisation the germs of which are to be found in the fifteenth century, but which had only been extended all over the Empire in 1512 by the Diet of Cologne;[2] but this attempt to provide for the execution of the judgments of the Imperial Chamber had never enjoyed more than a very partial success, and by the beginning of the eighteenth century the institution had fallen into abeyance in many parts of the country. In three of the Circles only, the Franconian, the Swabian, and the Westphalian, was the organisation sufficiently effective to demand serious consideration. This was because in these Circles there was no single Prince powerful enough to become predominant, as was, for example, the Elector of Bavaria in the Bavarian Circle; on the contrary, they included a very large number of Imperial Knights and of minor Princes, all so evenly balanced that the Princes chosen from time to time as Directors of the Circle had no chance of making themselves predominant. An even less effective piece of administrative machinery was the Imperial Deputation, created in 1555 to assist the Circles in the discharge of their duties. It was in effect a standing committee of the Diet, comprising the Electors and representatives of the other two Estates and

---

[1] In 1677 an edict fixed the gulden at 60 kreuzer, the thaler being 96: the equivalents in English money may be roughly estimated at half a crown and four shillings.

[2] Even then Bohemia and the lands of the Teutonic Order had been excluded from its operation.

of the Emperor-King, but it was no better able to make its authority effective than was the Diet. After the Peace of Westphalia efforts were made to reconstruct it; it was proposed by the Protestants that the Deputation should be drawn equally from the two religions; but as a majority of the Electors were Roman Catholics, this could only be done by permitting one Protestant to vote twice or by not counting one Catholic vote, both solutions being equally unacceptable. In the end nothing was done to increase the efficiency of the *Reichsdeputation*, and it was never of much influence or importance.

The judicial institutions of the Empire retained rather more vitality; but even they were in a moribund condition and had been hard hit by the anarchy and disorganisation produced by the Thirty Years' War. The most important of them, the Imperial Chamber (*Kammergericht*), had been established towards the end of the fifteenth century as a permanent court of justice in place of the feudal courts (*Hofgerichte*) which the Emperors had till then been wont to summon at irregular intervals whenever enough judicial business had accumulated. These had proved quite inadequate to meet the requirements of the Empire: indeed, the establishment of a permanent court of justice had been one of the measures most urgently advocated by the active reforming party of the day, led by the then Elector of Mayence, Berthold of Henneberg.[1]   Maximilian I had given this court a permanent establishment of a President (*Kammerrichter*) and sixteen Assessors (*Urteiler*), and some additions had been subsequently made to its staff. It was a court of original jurisdiction for those holding immediately of the Emperor-King, of appellate jurisdiction from the courts of those members of the Empire who did not possess the liberally granted privilege *de non appellando*.[2]   During the Thirty Years' War the Imperial Chamber had almost fallen into abeyance, but at the Peace of Westphalia and at the Diet of Ratisbon (1653) attempts were made to reform and reconstruct it. The number of Assessors was raised to fifty, and it was

---

[1] Cf. Turner, pp. 72, 104 ff. ; also *C.M.H.* i. 304 and 317.

[2] This privilege, granted to the Electors by one of the clauses of the Golden Bull, and since then extended to most of the chief Princes, prohibited appeals from the territorial courts to the Imperial Courts ; the corresponding privilege *de non evocando* forbade the Imperial Courts to call up cases from territorial courts.

provided that twenty-four of them together with two of the four Vice-Presidents should be Lutherans, and also that in all cases in which one of the parties was a Protestant and the other a Roman Catholic the Assessors chosen to decide the case should be equally divided between the two religions. Moreover, a commission was promised to expedite the procedure and improve the efficiency of the Chamber. But these reforms produced no real improvement. The revenues of the Chamber were quite insufficient for its expenses and it proved impossible to keep up the full staff. The decay of the Circles involved inefficiency in the execution of the decisions of the Chamber, since it was on the Circles that this depended.[1] And it is characteristic of the traditions of the Imperial constitution that the reforming commission, which was to have begun its labours in 1654, never really got to work till 1767. That under such circumstances efforts to wipe off arrears, to accelerate business, and to check factious appeals and undue litigation proved quite fruitless, will be readily understood. A disputed decision was practically adjourned *sine die* and the mass of arrears grew rather than diminished.

Soon after the establishment of the Imperial Chamber, Maximilian proceeded to set up (1492) a rival organisation which was far more closely identified with the Emperor than was the Imperial Chamber, whose members were jointly appointed by the Diet and by the Emperor. Originally this *Reichshofrath* or so-called "Aulic Council"[2] was intended to deal with all business from the Empire or ˙ the King's hereditary principalities; to it were also to be referred all cases in which he had to adjudicate as King. It was to be something more than a mere law court, it was also to exercise administrative functions in the hereditary possessions of the Hapsburgs. These objects, however, were not realised, and the Council had to be reconstructed in 1518, when it was put on a regular footing, with a President, Vice-President and sixteen Councillors. Its members were appointed by the Emperor, and with his death their commissions were to lapse. It was at this time also that the administration of the Austrian dominions, hitherto entrusted to it, ceased to form part of its functions.[3] In 1559 further changes occurred, Ferdinand I

[1] Cf. Turner, p. 114.   [2] Cf. *C.M.H.* i. 313.
[3] Pütter, *Germanic Constitution* (Eng. trans.), i. 358.

confining its sphere to Imperial business, and giving it jurisdiction as a high court of the Empire. But it was not till the Peace of Westphalia that it received formal recognition as such from the Diet, which then for the first time took cognisance of it, regulating its procedure and applying to it the principle of equality between religions, which was the rule with the Imperial Chamber. At the Diet of 1653 another attempt was made to reform it; but the Emperor, resenting the interference of the Diet and anxious to retain control over the Council, resisted the proposed changes and issued an Imperial edict (without allowing the Diet to intervene) introducing certain reforms. On the whole, it was more efficient as a court of justice than was the Imperial Chamber, its decisions being reached more certainly and rapidly. To a certain extent the spheres of the two courts coincided and collisions were not infrequent; but whereas the Imperial Chamber may be said to have dealt rather with cases between Princes or between subjects of different Princes, the Aulic Council's province included matters relating to fiefs of the Empire and cases in which the Emperor was personally concerned. At the same time its position was somewhat complicated by its political aspect. It had originally been an administrative rather than a judicial body and it had never wholly lost this character. Indeed, as the Empire possessed neither a Privy Council nor a War Office, the Aulic Council may be said to have to a certain extent supplied their place.[1]

There was also another but even less important Imperial Court, the *Hofgericht*, which had its seat at Rottweil on the Neckar. It represented the old royal courts of a period prior to the erection of the Imperial Chamber and the Aulic Council, and had been revived and re-established by Maximilian I in 1496, and again by Maximilian II in 1572. Still it had always been disliked by the Diet, and the reforms of 1572 notwithstanding, its position was most insecure, so that one of the questions which the negotiators of the Peace of Westphalia had left over for the next Diet was that of its abolition. It is perhaps unnecessary to add that the Diet came to no decision, and the Court protracted a useless and inconspicuous existence until the year 1802.[2]

Of all the institutions of Germany, however, the Diet

[1] Cf. *Z.S.* i. 26.   [2] Cf. Turner, p. 136.

(*Reichstag*) was the most important   Its origin may be traced back to the general councils annually summoned by Charles the Great. During the Middle Ages it had occupied a position approximately corresponding to the *Etats Généraux* of France and to the feudal forerunners of the English Parliament. A purely feudal body, in which tenants in chief alone might appear, it had undergone modifications parallel with the change in the position of the great feudal nobles. As the Dukes of Bavaria and the Counts Palatine of the Rhine had developed into petty sovereigns, as their estates had become in all but name European states of the third and fourth rank, so the Diet also had changed. It had really become a congress; those who attended it were, as a rule, mere representatives of the great feudatories who in former days had been wont to appear in person. From a body which was practically an international conference measures tending to the efficient government of Germany were not to be expected. Particularist ideals were bound to prevail over any feeble tendencies towards unity, the interests of Germany were sure to be sacrificed to local aims and objects, any proposal to strengthen the central institutions and to set the constitutional machinery in effective order could not but excite the opposition of vested interests, and was certain to be judged not on its merits but from the particularist point of view. Yet even so, it was in the Diet that the nearest approach to German unity was to be found. The Netherlands, the Helvetic Confederation, Burgundy and other countries once part of the Empire had been lost to it, but not even the strongest and most separatist of the minor powers of Germany had obtained or even sought exemption from membership of the Diet. No privileges corresponding to the right *de non appellando* marred the completeness of its sphere of influence. Indeed, though the link it provided may have been more negative than positive, as long as it existed there could be no formal dissolution of the Empire. It made no attempt to arrest the process of disintegration, it never considered or contemplated a constitutional reconstruction, but the fact of its existence did to some extent check disintegration and maintain the semblance of German unity.

Since the fifteenth century the Diet had been organised in three Chambers, the College of Electors; the College of the Princes, Counts and Barons; and the College of the Imperial

Free Cities.   Of these that of the Electors was the most important, since to it fell the duty of electing a new Emperor when the Imperial throne became vacant.   The privileges of the Electors were extensive: they not only enjoyed the rights *de non evocando* and *de non appellando*, but they received royal dues (*regalia*) from mines, tolls, coinage and the dues payable by their own territories and were to all intents and purposes independent sovereigns.   The Golden Bull, which amongst other things had greatly exalted their status by declaring conspiracy against their lives to be high treason, had fixed their number at seven and defined the great court offices held by them.   The three ecclesiastical Electors of Mayence, Cologne and Treves were respectively Arch Chancellors of Germany, Italy and Burgundy: among the lay Electors the King of Bohemia was Arch Butler, the Count Palatine of the Rhine was Arch Steward, the Duke of Saxony Arch Marshal, and the Margrave of Brandenburg Arch Chamberlain.   Further, the Bull had attached the electoral votes to the electoral territories, which it declared to be inalienable and indivisible, while it made primogeniture the rule of succession to the lay Electorates. It was because of this declaration that the validity of Ferdinand II's action in depriving Frederick V of the Palatinate of his vote and transferring it with his territories to Maximilian of Bavaria was so hotly disputed, the partisans of the dispossessed family maintaining that the Emperor had exceeded his rights.   They did not deny the Emperor's right to depose Frederick, but argued that as Frederick's offence had been personal, so his deposition was a purely personal matter and could not affect the right of his descendants to the Electorate.   At the Peace of Westphalia the question was solved by a compromise, which altered the constitution as laid down in the Bull in several important respects.   An eighth voter was added to the Electoral College; but while Charles Lewis, the eldest son of Frederick V, regained the Electoral dignity for his branch of the Wittelsbachs, he did not recover the office of Arch Steward, which his ancestors had held, but had to be content with the newly created office of Arch Treasurer and the Bavarian vote was recognised as the fifth, so that the compromise was decidedly in favour of Bavaria.[1] This solution left the balance of religions in the Electoral

[1] Cf. Erdmannsdörffer, i. 56.

College inclined to the Catholic side, which with Bavaria and the three ecclesiastical Electors had a clear majority over Saxony, Brandenburg and the Palatinate, even when the Bohemian vote, which had fallen into abeyance, is not reckoned to their credit.

Between the Peace of Westphalia and the end of the seventeenth century the balance was to some extent redressed by the creation of a new Electorate for the house of Guelph, (1692) when Ernest Augustus of Hanover obtained the coveted dignity for himself and his heirs ;[1] but any advantage the Protestants might have hoped to gain from this was lost through the conversion of Frederick Augustus of Saxony to Catholicism (1696) in order to improve his chances of obtaining the Crown of Poland, for which he was then a candidate, and by the accession of a Catholic branch of the Wittelsbachs to the Palatinate.[2] But by this time religious differences were beginning to lose some of their political importance, as may be gathered from the fact that, despite his conversion, the Elector of Saxony remained the recognised head of the *Corpus Evangelicorum*, in other words, the nominal leader of German Protestantism.

The connection which the success of the candidature of Frederick Augustus established between Saxony and Poland is also of interest as illustrating the increasing power and importance of the Electors. Saxony was not the only lay Electorate whose fortunes became closely linked with those of a non-German territory. The accession of George Lewis of Hanover to the throne of Great Britain (1714) started a connection which was destined to exercise a very important influence over the affairs of Germany during the next century, and the conclusion of the celebrated "Treaty of the Crown" (1701),[3] which recognised Frederick of Brandenburg as Frederick I, King *in* Prussia, may be said to mark the point at which the Hohenzollern became of European rather than of merely German importance. So, too, the close connection between Bavaria and France, the result of the policy followed by Maximilian Emanuel in the Spanish

---

[1] Cf. p. 45.
[2] In 1685 the Simmern line became extinct with the death of Charles, son of Charles Lewis, who was succeeded by Philip William of Neuburg. Cf. p. 44.
[3] Cf. p. 42.

Succession War, enabled yet another Elector to play the part of an almost independent sovereign with a policy of his own, and submitting to hardly any control from the nominal ruler of the country.

The College of Princes had in 1648 some seventy-six members with "individual votes" (*Virilstimmen*), forty-three of them laymen and thirty-three ecclesiastics, besides four bodies of voters who delivered a "collective vote" (*Curiatstimme*). Of these last there had only been three before 1640, one being given by the numerous prelates who were below princely rank, the other two by the Counts and Barons, divided for voting purposes into two so-called "benches," the Swabian and the Wetterabian. From this last body a new "bench" had been formed in 1640, under the title of the "Franconian Counts," while in 1653 the collective votes had been increased to five by the grant of a second vote to the Prelates. At the Diet of 1653–1654 a proposal had been put forward by the Counts that a fourth College should be erected for them and the Prelates; but the scheme found little support and nothing more was heard of it. The *Curiatstimme* ranked as equivalent to an individual vote, so that it would be fair to regard the voting strength of the College of Princes as about eighty in 1648, while by 1715 it had risen to over ninety. This increase was caused by the occasional exercise by the Emperor of his right to raise to the princely rank Counts and other nobles not hitherto in possession of a *Virilstimme*. This right, which gave the Emperor the power of rewarding his supporters and at the same time increasing his influence in the College of Princes, had been in dispute until the Diet of 1653–1654, at which it had been definitely recognised, with the limitation that those thus raised to the rank must possess as a qualification territories held immediately of the Emperor, a condition imposed to prevent the swamping of the College by lavish creations. At the same time there were never as many individual holders of *Virilstimmen* as there were *Virilstimmen*, for many Princes had come into possession of more than one qualifying piece of territory. Thus it was that the Electors were members of the College of Princes, Brandenburg having as many as five votes, while Austria possessed three, Burgundy, although actually in Spanish possession,

Styria and Tyrol providing her qualifications. The balance between the religions favoured the Catholics, who were in the proportion of five to four even after several of the votes attached to the secularised bishoprics of North Germany had passed into Protestant hands in 1648. Of these Halberstadt, Kammin and Minden had fallen to Brandenburg,[1] Magdeburg to Saxony,[2] Ratzeburg to Mecklenburg - Strelitz, Hersfeld to Hesse - Cassel, Schwerin to Mecklenburg-Schwerin, and Bremen and Verden to Sweden.[3] Another foreign ruler was also a member of the College of Princes as the possessor of Holstein. Glückstadt provided the King of Denmark with a qualification, but Savoy had allowed her vote to lapse into abeyance. Among the possessors of more than one vote may be mentioned the Palatine Wittelsbachs who had five,[4] the various branches of the Brunswick family who had also five between them,[5] while a like number were held by the Ernestine Saxons. Baden, Hesse and Mecklenburg had three apiece, and Würtemberg two, for Mömpelgard (Montbeliard) and Stuttgart.

Least in importance was the remaining College of the Diet, that of the Free Imperial Cities. It might have been thought that the constant quarrels between the two other Colleges would have been turned to good use by the third. The Princes were always bitterly jealous of the privileges of the Electors, and friction was frequent. But the Cities were in no position to profit by this. It was only at the Peace of Westphalia that the old dispute as to the value of their vote had been settled in their favour, and that it had been agreed that they should possess the *Votum decisivum* and not merely the *Votum Consultativum*. Even then the parallel questions, whether the Cities should be called upon to decide when the Electors and Princes disagreed and whether the Electors and Princes combined could carry a point against the Cities, had been left to the next meeting of the Diet, to be decided in 1653–1654 in a manner which made the recognition of their claim to the

---

[1] Her other votes were for Cüstrin and Eastern Pomerania.

[2] On the death of its Saxon administrator, Augustus, son of John George I, in 1680, Magdeburg reverted, as duly arranged, to Brandenburg.

[3] The cession of Bremen and Verden to Hanover (1720) added two votes to those possessed by the Guelphs.

[4] For Lautern, Neuburg, Simmern, Veldenz and Zweibrücken.

[5] For Calenberg, Celle, Grubenhagen, Saxe-Lauenberg and Wolfenbüttel.

Votum decisivum a mere farce, for it was settled that the Cities should only be called upon to vote when the other two Colleges were agreed. But the reasons for the unimportance of the Cities lay deeper than any mere uncertainty as to their constitutional position. Their position was uncertain because they had already fallen from their high estate. Some of the " Free Imperial Cities " were no longer free, some were no longer Imperial but had passed under other masters, and some were not worthy of the name of "city." Their decline had begun with the changes in the distribution of commerce caused by the great geographical discoveries of the fifteenth century. Even without the Reformation and the Thirty Years' War, the German cities would have been hard hit by the opening of the new route to the East round the Cape of Good Hope, and by the great advance in shipbuilding which had made commerce oceanic and had freed traders from the necessity of creeping cautiously along the coast. Moreover, the altered conditions of national life in England and France affected German trade adversely. Consolidated kingdoms quickly developed a very definite commercial policy. Protective measures fostered the growth of national commerce and industries to the detriment of the foreigner. The Merchant Adventurers of England disputed the Hanseatic monopoly of the Baltic, and the legislation of Edward VI and Elizabeth dealt the League a crippling blow by depriving it of its privileges in England. And while the old trade-routes of the Middle Ages were being deserted, while the spices of the East were finding their way to the North of Europe by other lines than the traditional route of the Adriatic, the Alpine passes and the Rhine valley, political as well as economic conditions were fighting against the cities of Germany. With the consolidation of the power of the territorial Princes their appetite for the acquisition of valuable sources of revenue increased in proportion, and more than one important city found it impossible to resist the pressure of a powerful neighbour. Of concerted action on the part of the cities or joint resistance to would-be annexers there was no trace. Not, as a rule, individually large enough or wealthy enough to be able to stand alone, the cities were not sufficiently in union among themselves to act together. Had they been ready to give up some part of their independent powers and to place themselves in the hands of the Emperor, they might have managed to escape having to submit to lesser potentates; but they took no steps in that direction and the Hapsburgs showed no inclination to meet them half-way.   But vigorous resistance was hardly to be expected in the unhealthy state into which municipal life had fallen.   In most cities a narrow oligarchy had usurped the local government and completely controlled the municipal institutions.   Add to all this the tremendous upheaval of the Thirty Years' War, the utter disorganisation of social, commercial and industrial life which it had involved, the lawlessness and violence which followed in the train of war, and it is not surprising that the Free Cities emerged from that struggle as political nullities, and that in the course of the next half-century their political importance decreased rather than recovered itself.   In 1715 they still numbered about fifty, though many of the largest and most flourishing of them had failed to retain the independence of which much smaller places were still able to boast.   Thus Leipzig had become subject to the Elector of Saxony, while Ulm was still independent.   It was not by size or by importance that the question of freedom or subjection was determined, it was by the accident of the strength of the would-be annexer. Sometimes, indeed, a city retained its independence through being the object of conflicting claims.   Thus Erfurt, though never technically a Free City, had managed to enjoy a considerable independence for some time by playing off against each other the rival claimants, the Electors of Mayence and Saxony, until in 1664 the former managed to arrange a compromise with his opponent and by the aid of the Rhine League forced the city to submit.   Bremen, more fortunate, though compelled in 1654 to admit the suzerainty of Sweden, contrived to regain her independence twelve years later by the assistance of Cologne, Denmark and the Brunswick Dukes.

Those cities which at the beginning of the eighteenth century remained independent were for the most part very conservative, unprogressive even to stagnation, being in the hands of narrow and unenterprising oligarchies and quite devoid of any real municipal or industrial life.   Nuremberg, despite her sufferings in the siege of 1632, and Frankfort on Main may be mentioned as exceptions to the general rule of stagnation, while the Italian trade enabled Augsburg to retain some degree of prosperity and activity. Hamburg and Bremen had had the good fortune to be but little affected by the Thirty Years' War, but the greatness of the Hanseatic League was a thing of the past and in 1648 Lübeck was the only other member of the League which retained its status as a Free City, and even these three had lost much of their old commercial importance. Cologne also owed to her position on the Rhine a certain amount of trade, but the control which the Dutch exercised over the mouths of the Rhine proved a serious obstacle to the development of the trade of Western Germany. Another of the more flourishing cities of Germany had been lost to the Empire when, in 1681, perhaps the most high-handed of all the acts of Louis XIV deprived Germany of Strassburg. Outside the ranks of the Free Cities, Dresden, Münich and Berlin were gradually rising in importance with the consolidation of the powers of the territorial Princes, and though Vienna had suffered severely in the great siege of 1683, the Austrian capital was in some ways the most flourishing city in the Empire. But Germany was primarily a rural not an urban country; its cities were neither economically nor politically to be compared with those of Italy and the Netherlands, and the unimportance of the College of Free Cities accurately reflects the part which the towns played in German history in the eighteenth century.

It would not be going too far to assert that in none of the institutions of Germany was there anything which offered any prospect of the attainment of unity or real national life. Without a thorough reform of the constitution nothing could be done and of such a reform there was little chance. The Empire as such was moribund, and in no direction was any source of new life or strength to be found for it. To a certain extent the Hapsburgs had attempted in the years between the Peace of Westphalia and those of Utrecht and Rastatt to reassert the claims and pretensions which the Imperial title carried with it, but their success had been of the slightest. It might have been thought that opposition to the encroachments of Louis XIV would have served as a bond of union; that the necessity for common defence against so powerful and aggressive a neighbour would have rallied the country round its nominal head; that the seizure of Strassburg and the other places claimed by Louis in virtue of the verdicts of the *Chambres de Réunion*

would have called to life the dead or dormant national sentiment of Germany, would have brought home to the Princes
the need for co-operation and the dangers which they and
their neighbours were running through the pursuit of local and
particularist aims. If ever Germany was to be forced to
realise the need for unity, if ever a national movement was
to breathe fresh force into the old institutions and make the
German Kingdom something more than a mere name, one
might have expected this to have come about in the last
quarter of the seventeenth century. That something of the
sort was on foot is proved by the countless pamphlets, caricatures and squibs which flooded the country about that period,
among which the *Bedenken* of the great philosopher Leibnitz
are of more than mere ephemeral interest. In these he
pointed out with lucidity and force Germany's urgent need for
union and for proper preparation for war. But it was in vain
that he urged that the Emperor should put himself at the
head of the minor states, and that the Princes should join him
in securing that union of Germany which, according to the
writer, was the only security for the balance of power and for
the preservation of the peace of Europe. The Princes with
few exceptions showed no inclination to rally round the
Emperor, no disposition to make any sacrifices for the common
safety, or to abandon their purely particularist and selfish
policies. Louis xiv was fully aware of the merits of the
policy of *divide et impera* ; he saw that localism was a force
which he might use to paralyse and render impotent his
neighbour on the East, and he rarely failed to find among the
Princes of Germany men whose assistance, or at any rate
whose neutrality, could be purchased for a reasonable price.
Thus in 1658 Mazarin had founded the League of the Rhine,
and though the action of Louis in attacking the Spanish
Netherlands in May 1667 under the doubtful pretext of the
Jus Devolutionis seems to have so frightened the members
of the League that they allowed their alliances with him to
expire in 1668 and declined to renew them, he was able
when attacking Holland in 1672 to secure the neutrality of
Bavaria, the Elector Palatine, Treves and Würtemberg, and to
obtain the actual support of Cologne, of the Bishops of
Münster and Strassburg and of Duke John Frederick of
Hanover. It was the lukewarm support he received from the

Princes, notably Bavaria, Saxony and Brandenburg, which caused the Emperor Leopold to assent to the inglorious Peace of Nimeguen in 1679. It was largely because Brandenburg had enrolled herself among the paid retainers of France that Louis was able to set his *Chambres de Réunion* at work to carry out his annexations unopposed, and his successful retention of Strassburg was not merely due to the almost simultaneous troubles in Hungary and the outbreak of a new war with the Turks. The Emperor had to agree to the Truce of Ratisbon in 1684, because Frederick William of Brandenburg saw in the necessities of the Empire a chance for pressing his very dubious claims on Silesia, demanding terms so extravagant that Austria refused to grant them, with the result that the projected coalition fell through, it being realised that unless all Germany were united behind him it would be useless for Leopold to throw down the gauntlet to Louis. The League of Augsburg in 1688 included the majority of the principal states of Germany, and the deliberate devastation of the Palatinate went far to exasperate popular feeling against Louis; but the course of the war showed up not merely the utter inefficiency of the defensive arrangements of the Empire,[1] but also the lukewarm character of the support of many members of the Coalition. Those from whose territories the hostile armies were far distant exerted themselves but little on behalf of their compatriots on the frontier. From 1690 to February 1693 no contingent from Saxony took any part in the war, and only by bestowing on Hanover the largest bribe in his power, the coveted Electoral dignity, did the Emperor avert the formation of an alliance between the Brunswick Dukes, Brandenburg and Saxony, to bring the war to an end. Nor was Germany any more solid in its support of the Emperor in the War of the Spanish Succession. Duke Anthony Ulrich of Brunswick-Wolfenbüttel was only prevented from assisting the French by the prompt action of his cousins at Hanover and Celle, who occupied his territories and disarmed his troops, while the defection of the Wittelsbach Electors of Bavaria and Cologne threatened at one time to ruin the Grand Alliance by allowing the French to penetrate to Vienna and dictate terms to the Hapsburg in his capital.

Nor does the case appear any better when one turns to

[1] Cf. Erdmannsdörffer, ii. 25, and *Z.S.* ii. 41.

another important theatre and follows the course of the struggle with the still powerful and aggressive Moslem who was threatening Germany from the South-East. At no time was there a complete or a spontaneous rally for the defence of the Cross against the Crescent. Religious fervour and patriotism seemed equally extinct. Northern and Western Germany did little to beat back the tide of Turkish conquest in 1664, and the contingents of the Rhine League who shared in the victory at St. Gotthard on the Raab fought there at the bidding of their patron Louis XIV. In 1683, again, only two North German states were represented at the relief of Vienna, and the contingents of Hanover and Saxe-Weimar did not total two thousand men. Not a man from the Rhineland was there, and once again conditions which the Emperor could not accept were coupled with the protestations of zeal of which alone Brandenburg was lavish. Indeed, for any assistance the Emperor received in the task of ousting the Turk from Hungary a price, not a light one, had to be paid. The despatch of six thousand Hanoverians to the Danube in 1692, helped to earn the Guelphs the Electoral dignity; and when, in 1686, eight thousand Brandenburgers appeared on the Danube, it was because the Emperor had consented to cede Schwiebus to the Great Elector.

It may be argued that the Princes of Germany were thus lukewarm, because they felt that the reconquest of Hungary would be of little benefit to Germany as a whole, and mainly concerned the Hapsburgs and their dynastic interests. This is perhaps to some extent true; but no such plea can be advanced to exculpate those who not only failed to oppose the aggressions of Louis XIV, but were actually his accomplices and abettors. At the same time, it must be admitted that the Hapsburgs cannot escape the charge of having failed to do all they might have done. They were fatally hampered by the strong bias towards aggressive Roman Catholicism and the alliance with the Jesuits which made them objects of suspicion to the Protestant states, by the semi-Spanish traditions of the family, by their dynastic and non-German interests,—as, for example, the secret treaty of January 1668 with Louis XIV, providing for a partition in case the Spanish branch of the family should become extinct. Moreover, their autocratic traditions of government led them to repress rather than to encourage anything in the shape of a popular movement. Indeed, if they had made more of an effort to reassert themselves and make good their nominal position in Germany, the more vigorous elements in the German polity would have been found opposed to them; for these elements, such as they were, took the shape of the efforts of the larger principalities at territorial independence and aggrandisement. The rise of Brandenburg-Prussia and Bavaria, their development from local divisions of Germany into minor European Powers, fatal though it was to anything like unity in Germany, certainly testified to the existence in those states of some degree of strength and activity. Thus it is that when one attempts to trace the history of Germany during the eighteenth century, one is at once met at the outset by the fact that Germany as a whole hardly has any history; in its place one has the history of the various states of Germany, international not national affairs hardly to be distinguished from the history of Europe as a whole, since France and Russia and England were all more or less directly concerned with the rivalries of the different minor states. At the most, the history of Germany can be said to deal with the complete decay of the constitutional life of the Holy Roman Empire and of the national life of the German Kingdom. Even the modified national existence which had still existed at the end of the fifteenth century[1] had disappeared. A distinguished authority on Romano-Germanic law, Michael Munchmayer, wrote in 1705 that it would have been about as possible to produce unity among Germans as to wash a blackamoor white. Indeed, the disintegration had gone to such lengths that it is really rather remarkable that the forms of unity and of a constitution should still have been retained.

To have put an end to the nominal as well as to the practical existence of the Empire would doubtless have been logical, but politics are not ruled by logic; and while there was no special reason why the process of disintegration should have been carried to its logical conclusion, for no one in particular stood to profit greatly by that event, there were excellent reasons why it should have been left incomplete. To the maintenance of the forms of the Empire as a hollow sham there were two possible alternatives, reconstruction and im-

[1] Cf. Professor Tout's chapter in vol. i. of the *Cambridge Modern History*.

mediate dissolution. Reconstruction was out of the question; even if there had been any real wish for it in Germany, of which there were even fewer indications in 1715 than in 1648, the other Powers of Europe would not have cared to see the Empire so remodelled as to become a reality. Immediately after 1648 an attempt at reconstruction would have met with determined opposition from France and Sweden; in 1715, if Sweden was no longer a force to be regarded, and France was temporarily incapable of active interference, disintegration had gone so far that the diplomatic support of France would have probably been sufficient to enable Brandenburg or Bavaria to wreck the scheme. But, on the other hand, the dissolution of the Empire was about the last thing which anyone desired. The Hapsburgs were not the men to make great changes prematurely; the formal dissolution of the Empire would probably have been the signal for the immediate outbreak of a struggle of the most fearful description, which could hardly have failed to surpass even the horrors of the Thirty Years' War; a scramble among the stronger states for the possessions of the territories of those of their neighbours who lacked the power to defend their independence; a carnival of greed, violence and aggression; the universal application to the petty principalities of Germany of the rule that might is right. This the continued existence of the Empire did at least avert: the semblance of law and order was maintained, private war and armed strife among its members were checked, if not altogether prevented. The existence of the Empire protected the Principality of Anhalt against the danger of forcible annexation to Brandenburg; it made it useless for the ruler of Hesse-Darmstadt to cast covetous eyes on the Counties of Isenburg or Solms; it restrained Würtemberg from attempting to incorporate the Free City of Reutlingen and Bavaria from compelling the Franconian Knights to admit themselves her subjects as she was to try to do at the eleventh hour of the Empire's life.[1] In a way, the very subdivision which made the Empire so weak and unity so unattainable prevented the Empire from being dissolved. As Napoleon declared, " If the Germanic Body did not exist, we should have to create it." Its existence was at least better than the anarchy which dissolution would have brought in its train. The three

[1] Cf. pp. 467-468.

hundred and sixty-five states of one description and another which were included within it were, for the most part, too small and too insignificant to be capable of independent existence.   Not even the strongest of the minor states now rising into practically independent sovereign powers was ready as yet for the actual dissolution of the Empire.   The substance of independence was as much as Saxony and Würtemberg wanted, and it they certainly already enjoyed.   Having obtained ample freedom from the control of the Empire, they had no wish to complete its ruin ; and, ruin as it was, there was yet enough potential utility in the old fabric for Austria to find it worth the trouble of its maintenance.   The Imperial position, with its great, albeit shadowy, traditions, with its claims, disputed and obsolescent though they might be, might not be worth attaining at a heavy cost, but it was not to be lightly discarded.   If Louis XIV had found it worthy of his candidature, Ferdinand III had had good reason for keeping it if he could. Possibilities still lurked in it ; it was not even yet beyond all chance of revival.   Joseph I had done not a little to reassert the Imperial claims and to raise the Imperial prestige and authority when he was suddenly cut off early in life : had he survived, there would have been a very different end to the Spanish Succession War and the Empire would have occupied a very different position in 1715.   And even then there was a chance that at a more favourable season the old machinery might be put into working order, the old constitution might again prove capable of being turned to good account.   So for nearly a century after the Peace of Baden the Empire survived, at once in the ideas it embodied the symbol of the German unity which had once existed, and in its actual condition the most striking example of that disintegration and disunion of Germany which is the main theme of these pages.

CHAPTER II

THE GERMAN STATES IN 1715

AMONG the three hundred and sixty-five states which together made up the German Kingdom the territories ruled by the Hapsburg family deserve the first place, even apart from their long standing connection with the Empire, since both in area and in population they exceeded all the others. "Austria," if by this convenient though somewhat anachronistic term one may describe the multifarious dominions of the Hapsburgs, was a conglomerate of provinces fortuitously brought together, differing greatly in race and language, in history and traditions, in social and political conditions, with little to connect them save the rule of a common dynasty, but for the most part geographically adjacent. Thus while no foreign territory intervened between Austria strictly so called and the group of provinces in which Bohemia was the chief and Moravia and Silesia the satellites, the territories attached to the Archduchy, Carniola, Carinthia, Styria and Tyrol, formed a connected group, and, to the South-Eastward, Hungary with Croatia and Transylvania continued the Hapsburg dominions in unbroken succession down the great highway of the Danube almost to the gates of Belgrade. Till 1715, Hungary and its dependencies had been the only non-German territories under the rule of the Austrian Hapsburgs, and from 1648 to 1683 Austrian Hungary had included but a small portion of the old Magyar kingdom, so that the non-German element in the Hapsburg polity, which was destined to be of such doubtful benefit during the eighteenth century, was as yet comparatively insignificant. Indeed, in 1648 the only detached portions of territory which Austria possessed were calculated to interest her in the defence of Germany rather than to distract her attention to other quarters, as was the case after 1715. At the Peace of Westphalia she did indeed surrender to France the Sundgau and other portions of Alsace, but she retained

31

many scattered pieces of Swabia which may be comprehended under the title of "Further Austria" (*Vorder Ostreich*). Though separated from Austria by the Electorate of Bavaria and the Bishopric of Augsburg, these districts along the Upper Danube and in the Black Forest, among which the Breisgau and the Burgau were the most important, were within a very short distance of Austria's Alpine lands, Vorarlberg and Tyrol, and the Wittelsbach alliance with France may be understood when it is realised how these Austrian outposts in Swabia seemed to surround Bavaria with a cordon of Hapsburg territory, and to menace her with that annexation which she had been fortunate to escape during the Spanish Succession War. "Further Austria" might have served as stepping-stones to bring the Hapsburgs to the Middle Rhine, and enable them to assimilate the intervening territory just as Brandenburg's acquisitions in Westphalia [1] helped to plant her in secure possession of the Lower Rhine. The idea of acquiring Bavaria by annexation or exchange was one of the most constant factors in Austrian policy, the dream of Joseph II, the explanation and aim of many of Thugut's intrigues, not definitely abandoned till the need for obtaining Bavaria's help against Napoleon caused Metternich to agree to the Treaty of Ried in 1813.[2]

It would have been of the greatest benefit to Austria, whatever its effects on Germany as a whole, if, instead of conferring the Spanish Netherlands on the Hapsburgs the Treaties of Utrecht and Baden had carried out the project of giving them to the Wittelsbachs in exchange for Bavaria. Rich, fertile, thickly populated though they were, the Netherlands were a possession of little value to Austria. Lying far away from Vienna, they had not even Hungary's geographical connection with the "hereditary dominions." Hampered by the restrictions imposed by the Peace of Münster their trade and industries could not develop naturally, and though they had once been an integral part of the Empire, the folly of Charles VI in treating them as part of that Spanish inheritance he persisted in regarding as rightly his prevented the revival of the old connection. No real attempt was made to attach them either by interest or sentiment to their new rulers, and when the conquering armies of Revolutionary France threatened

[1] Cf. p. 21.   [2] Cf. p. 619.

to sever the connection between the Netherlands and the Hapsburgs Austria's defence of her provinces was so feeble and faint-hearted as to incur, almost to justify, suspicions that she desired to be rid of them.

Of the other acquisitions made by Austria in 1715, the Duchy of Milan also had once been subject to the Holy Roman Emperor, to whom it now returned ; but here again the determination of Charles VI to regard it and his other Italian possessions, the island of Sardinia and the kingdom of Naples, as belonging to him as King of Spain, prevented any assimilation of these Italian dominions by Austria. In a way the connection with Italy influenced Austria but little in the eighteenth century ; there was not much intercourse between Milan or Naples and the hereditary dominions, and it may be said that it was mainly because they excited the hostility of Spain and so helped to involve Austria in wars with the Bourbon powers, that these possessions affected her. It was only later on, when Austria had abandoned all efforts to reassert her position in Germany, that she turned to Italy to seek her compensation there.

Racial divisions and jealousies, the great problem which confronts the Hapsburgs at the present day, had not yet become a pressing question in 1715. The provinces were too loosely connected, too little in touch with one another, to trouble much about their relations with each other. The connection between them had to become effective before it could be felt to be oppressive. The sense of nationality was dormant, or, at any rate, inarticulate and without influence. The Government was everywhere in the hands of the nobles, who were but little affected by racial sentiment, except perhaps in Hungary. The nationalist movement in Bohemia in the nineteenth century has been largely a popular movement, the outcome in a sense of the great upheaval of the French Revolution. In 1715 there was not the least indication of anything of the sort. Hungary, it is true, clung resolutely to all its privileges and constitutional rights, and in the fifty years that followed the reconquest of Hungary from Turkish rule, the Hapsburgs found their relations with their Magyar subjects a frequent source of trouble. Hungarian disloyalty was a source of weakness to Austria which Louis XIV knew well how to turn to his advantage : in 1703, when Villars and Elector Maximilian of Bavaria threatened Vienna, from the Upper Danube, Hungarian insurgents were in the field lower down the river, and not until January 1711 was the insurrection finally suppressed and the authority of the Hapsburgs completely re-established in Hungary and Transylvania. One of the principal causes of this disloyalty was the mistaken religious policy of Leopold I, whose bigotry had prevented him from utilising the opportunity afforded by the reconquest from the Turks. Had wiser counsels prevailed when, after a century and a half (1541–1686), Buda-Pesth was delivered from Turkish rule, it might have been possible to attach the Hungarians to the Hapsburg dynasty. Religious concessions were all that were needed, for the so-called "Nationalist" party formerly headed by Tököli had been discredited by its alliance with the Turks and the townsfolk were very hostile to the nobles. But the influence of the Jesuits carried the day, and a fierce persecution of the Protestants was set going which caused the Hungarians to identify the Hapsburg dynasty with Roman Catholic intolerance. Not till Joseph I abandoned this impolitic persecution and granted toleration to the Protestant religion was the insurrection brought to an end, or the foundations laid for that reconciliation of the Magyars to their rulers which Maria Theresa was afterwards to complete.[1] Thus in 1715, Hungary was hardly a great source of strength to Austria, and the almost complete autonomy which the country possessed helped to keep them apart. The constitutional relations between Hungary and the Hapsburgs had been put on a definite footing in 1687, when, at a Diet held at Pressburg, the succession to the Hungarian monarchy had been declared hereditary in the Hapsburg family. The Emperor had on this occasion shown a praiseworthy moderation : he had not insisted on his rights as conqueror, but had only introduced one other important modification of the Constitution, the abolition of Clause 31 in the Bull of Andrew II, which had established the right of armed resistance to unconstitutional government, a privilege similar to that of "confederation," which was to prove so potent a factor in the ruin of Poland. These concessions paved the way for the work Maria Theresa was to do, but the recognition of Hungary as a quite independent kingdom established that "dualism" which the twentieth

[1] Cf. p. 182.

century finds as a force more powerful than ever, and which has served as an effective barrier against the amalgamation of Hungary with Austria.

Regarding the dominions of the Hapsburgs as a whole, one might fairly say that the dynasty was almost the only bond between the groups of provinces subject to it. The germs of a common administration existed at Vienna in the Conference,[1] in the Aulic Chamber (*Hofkammer*), which was occupied with financial and commercial questions, and the War Council; but the existence of this machinery was hardly enough by itself to balance the all but complete autonomy of the provinces. Thus the War Council's task of organising an efficient standing army was made all but impossible by the excessive powers of the local authorities, each province having a separate budget and negotiating separately with the central authority as to its contribution towards the common defence. Bohemia had actually its own Chancery, which was at once judicial and administrative, being the supreme court of justice for Bohemia and its dependencies, and also the channel of communication between the local officials at Prague and the Emperor. The great need of the Hapsburg dominions was centralisation, and in dealing with the Austrian and Bohemian groups of territory, steady progress had been made by Ferdinand III and his sons. Joseph I was doing much when his sudden death deprived Austria of the ruler who seemed about to restore the authority of the Emperor and to weld together his disunited provinces. The change from local autonomy to centralised despotism was no doubt bitterly opposed by those who found themselves deprived of their cherished privileges, but in clipping the wings of the local Estates and wresting from the local nobles who filled those bodies their exclusive control over administrative and financial affairs, the Hapsburgs were following a policy which had every justification. The feudal aristocracies who controlled the provincial Estates administered local affairs with little regard either to the welfare of the whole state of which they formed a part, or to the interests of the mass of the population of the individual provinces. The general weal was sacrificed to a narrow particularism, the peasantry and burghers in each province were sacrificed to the selfish interests of the nobles.

[1] The Council of State had been reorganised under this name in 1709.

Provinces so disunited, feudal oligarchies so incapable of taking any but the narrowest local view, or of considering the interests of any class but their own, needed to be disciplined by the strong hand of a despotic government. Before patriotism could replace localism and selfishness the provinces must be knit together by a common administration.

Next to the Hapsburg dominions, the territories of the Electors deserve notice. The three ecclesiastical members of the College, the Archbishops of Cologne, Mayence and Treves, form a class apart. In the domestic affairs of the Empire these three tended, as Catholics, to take the side of Austria, except that the traditional connection of the see of Mayence with the office of Arch Chancellor, and consequently with the duty of presiding in the College of Electors, usually disposed its occupant to place himself at the head of that party which may be described as that of the " Reich,"[1] and which was usually opposed to the Hapsburgs. Thus Mayence is often found opposing the Hapsburgs, and making special efforts to thwart any measures with a centralising tendency lest constitutional liberties should be infringed. Yet it might have been expected that the exposed position of these ecclesiastical Electorates would have made their holders support any reforms which tended to bind Germany together and to make the Empire less defenceless against its aggressive Western neighbour. Mayence, it is true, had but little territory West of the Rhine, for the bulk of her lands lay in the valley of the Lower Main, the chief outlying districts being Erfurt and the Eichsfeld in Thuringia. Cologne, too, held the duchy of Westphalia in addition to the long strip along the left bank of the Rhine from Andernach to Rheinberg, but the Electorate of Treves lay almost wholly in the Moselle valley and was much exposed to France. The accident that the territory along the frontier between France and Germany was not only much split up but was also for the most part in the hands of ecclesiastical rulers, had contributed in no small

---

[1] The distinction between the body of the Reich and its head the Kaiser is one for which there is no satisfactory English equivalent. To translate Reichs by " Imperial " almost involves translating Kaiserlich by " Austrian," which somewhat unduly exaggerates the reputed indifference of the Hapsburgs to the Reich ; but if one makes " Imperial " the equivalent to Kaiserlich, one is left without a word for Reichs : " national " would be misleading, " of the Empire " is a rather clumsy and not very clear way out of the difficulty.

degree to the weakness and disunion of Germany, and to make her a ready prey to Bourbon aggression. Had Cologne or Mayence been the seat of a hereditary Electorate in the hands of an able and ambitious house like the Hohenzollern, the history of the " Left Bank " would be very different reading. But ecclesiastical rulers, if on the whole their territories were not ill-governed, had not the urgent spur of the desire to found an abiding dynasty as an incentive to the energetic development of their dominions or to the promotion of the welfare of their subjects. Oppression by an ecclesiastical ruler was infrequent, energetic government rather rarer, reforms and progress almost unknown. Of the occupants of the ecclesiastical Electorates in 1715, Lothair Francis of Schönborn had been Elector of Mayence since 1693, and had distinguished himself by his patriotic conduct during the war of the Spanish Succession. Realising that the Hapsburgs alone could afford to maintain the institutions of the Empire, which he described " as a handsome but portionless bride whose support involves very heavy expenditure," he was, in defiance of the traditions of his see, a firm adherent of the Hapsburg family, and had played no small part in securing the election of Charles VI in 1711. As ruler of Mayence, he not only protected the city with elaborate fortifications, but devoted himself to its interests, and did much for its improvement and embellishment. His colleague at Treves, Charles of Lorraine, had only just been restored to his metropolitan city, which the French had evacuated on the conclusion of the peace. Before the year was out (Dec.) his sudden death at Vienna brought to a close his brief four years' tenure of his see, his successor being a member of the Neuburg branch of the Wittelsbach family, Francis Louis, who had been Bishop of Worms since 1694. The Elector of Cologne, Joseph Clement of Bavaria, had also just regained his Electoral dominions with the Peace of Baden. Though it had been his election to the see of Cologne which had been the nominal *casus belli* between Louis XIV and the Emperor in 1688, Joseph Clement had followed his brother, Maximilian Emmanuel, into the French camp in the Spanish Succession War, with the result that he had been driven from his Electorate, forced to take refuge in France, and had finally been put to the ban of the Empire in 1706. His reinstatement had been one of the concessions which England's desertion of the Coalition had enabled Louis XIV to exact; but it was not accomplished without some friction, for the Dutch, who were in possession of some of the fortresses of the Electorate, refused to quit Bonn unless the fortifications were destroyed, and finally had to be expelled by force. The incident, however, did not in the end prove serious, as an agreement was reached in August 1717 and the fortifications were duly destroyed, the same being done at Liège, of which, as well as of Hildesheim, Joseph Clement was the Bishop. In this plurality he was merely continuing a custom almost as traditional as that by which the Bavarian Wittelsbachs had supplied Cologne with an unbroken series.of Archbishops ever since the election of Ernest of Bavaria to the see in 1583.

Among the lay Electorates, Bohemia was in the hands of the Hapsburgs, and the King of Bohemia had become so completely merged in the Emperor that it was a question whether the validity of the Bohemian vote were to be any longer admitted. Saxony was held by the house of Wettin, Brandenburg by that of Hohenzollern, the ambitions of the Guelphs had recently been gratified by the creation for them of a ninth Electorate, that of Hanover, while the Wittelsbach family supplied two Electors, separate branches of the house ruling Bavaria and the Palatinate respectively. Frederick Augustus of Saxony was one of the three Electors who, in addition to their territories within the Empire, were rulers of kingdoms outside its boundaries. The connection of Saxony with Poland was certainly one which had brought no benefits to the Electorate, whatever its influence on the distressful partner with which Saxony had been linked since July 1696. It had deprived the Empire of the assistance of Saxony in the great war against Louis XIV. It had involved the Electorate in the wars which had troubled the Baltic ever since Charles XII of Sweden had opened his chequered career by his attack on Denmark in 1700. It had brought the victorious armies of the Swedish king to Alt Ranstadt, and had seemed at one time likely to prove a link between the Western and the Eastern wars. Indeed, in 1715 Saxon troops were actively engaged in the expulsion of the Swedes from German soil, an enterprise in which Saxony's own interests were but remotely concerned. Moreover, in order that no impediment should be offered to his election to the

Polish throne by his Protestantism—which, it must be admitted, sat but lightly upon him—Frederick Augustus had "received instruction" and had been admitted into the Roman Catholic Church, by which means the Roman Catholic majority in the College of Electors was still further increased. Yet it is not out of keeping with the other anomalies of the Germanic Constitution that despite this conversion the Wettin family retained the nominal leadership of German Protestantism traditional in their line. It was not thought necessary to transfer to another dynasty the headship of the *Corpus Evangelicorum*, the organised union of the German Protestants which had been officially recognised at the Peace of Westphalia. Prussia and Hanover both laid claim to it when in 1717 the Crown Prince of Saxony married the eldest daughter of the late Emperor, Joseph I, and became a Roman Catholic, but no change was made: religious differences were no longer the potent factor in German politics they had once been and the headship of the German Protestants carried with it no real political advantages. But it is not to this that the comparative unimportance of Saxony after 1715 is to be mainly attributed. The Electorate, though fairly populous and including some of the richest districts of Germany, suffered much through the accidental connection with a foreign country to which no ties of interest, sentiment, race, or religion bound it. Moreover, it was involved in further troubles by its geographical position between the two powers whose conflict is the chief feature of German history in the eighteenth century, while its rulers during the period were men of little ability or importance. Frederick Augustus I did, indeed, achieve a European reputation by his unparalleled profligacy, but he was an indifferent soldier and an incompetent ruler, and his son and successor, Frederick Augustus II, cuts but a sorry figure in the Austro-Prussian conflict. It was also unfortunate for Saxony that John George II (*ob.* 1656) had done for the Albertine branch of the Wettin family what had been done for the Ernestine line a hundred years earlier on the death of John Frederick II (1554). By partitioning his territories in order to establish separate cadet branches at Merseburg, Weissenfels and Zeitz [1] for his younger sons Christian, Augustus and Maurice, John George weakened the resources at the disposal of the main

[1] Extinct respectively in 1738, 1725 and 1746.

branch of the Wettin family. This process had been begun with the partition of 1485 between the Albertine and Ernestine branches, from which one may date the decline of the Wettin family, or, at any rate, the disappearance of the chance of making Saxony a compact and powerful state, able to exercise a controlling influence over the fortunes of Central Germany, but the will of John George carried it another stage forward.

Unlike the Wettin family, the Hohenzollern were destined to play a far more important part in Germany after 1715 than had hitherto fallen to their lot. The reign (1640–1688) of the so-called "Great Elector," Frederick William, marks the beginning of the advance of Brandenburg. Not only did the territorial acquisitions which he made at the Peace of Westphalia increase considerably the resources at his disposal, but they helped to connect the central mass of his dominions with his outlying possessions on the Rhine and beyond the Vistula. But far more important were the reforms which he introduced into the constitutional and administrative economy of his dominions. Though "unable to introduce complete uniformity of system and practice into the affairs of his several dominions," Frederick William did "impose the principle of his own supremacy on every official, and made it felt as a positive force throughout the whole frame of local polity." [1] The credit of having laid the foundations on which the power of Brandenburg-Prussia has been built up is clearly his. The reorganisation of the army on a professional basis, the arrangement by which the sums devoted to its upkeep were separated from the rest of the revenue and placed under the Minister of War, the subjection of the local Estates to the power of the Elector, the overthrow of the constitutional liberties and privileges which impaired his absolute authority, the encouragement by the State of all measures by which the material resources and prosperity of the country might be fostered and increased, are all to be found in the days of Frederick William. Personal control, rigid economy and the unsparing exaction of efficiency from officers and civil officials, were the leading features of his system of government; and though perhaps his work lacked the completeness and finish which his grandson, King Frederick William I, was to impart

[1] Tuttle, i. 224.

to it, it was well done, and did not fall to pieces when his guiding hand was removed.

In foreign policy also the "Great Elector" sketched the outlines of the policy which subsequent Hohenzollern rulers were to develope and complete. Of the patriotism and pan-Germanic ideals with which it has pleased some modern writers to credit him, it is hard to detect any traces among the shifts, the inconsistencies and the desertions which constitute his foreign policy: to him the aggrandisement at home and abroad of the House of Hohenzollern was the one and only end, and that end he pursued with an unflinching persistence and no small degree of success. Territorial acquisitions were what he above all desired, and he attained the great success of freeing East Prussia alike from Swedish and from Polish suzerainty. The Archbishopric of Magdeburg fell to him by reversion under the terms of the Peace of Westphalia (1680), he received Schwiebus in 1686 in return for the renunciation of a claim on Liegnitz, and 1666 saw a final division of the disputed Cleves-Jülich heritage. But despite the success of Fehrbellin (1675), Sweden still retained Western Pomerania and held the mouth of the Oder, and no territorial gain resulted from the policy of vassalage to France on which Frederick William embarked in 1679 after he had felt the weight of Louis XIV's hand in the Peace of St. Germain-en-Laye. His heir, Frederick III as Elector and I as King, has perhaps had less than justice done him by those who have done more than justice to the father. Less selfish and aggressive if less capable and energetic, he displayed a loyalty to the House of Hapsburg as head of the Empire which is in striking contrast to the shifting and tortuous policy of his predecessor. In the resistance of Germany to Louis XIV, the part played by Frederick I was certainly more consistent, more honourable, and, on the whole, more effective than that of the Great Elector. In domestic affairs he lacked his father's power of organising, his unsparing energy and his talent for rigid economy, but he did carry on the work which had been begun, and it would be foolish to dismiss as valueless that acquisition of the Prussian Crown with which his name will always be mainly associated. Personal vanity and pride, a love of titles and pomp, may have played their part in the acquisition, but it was an achievement of solid importance, which not only gave Frederick a better position in international affairs, but by enhancing the prestige and authority of the sovereign was of great use in assisting the consolidation of his scattered dominions. " The Crown " was no mere fad or whim, it was the logical conclusion to the " Great Elector's " work. Though based on Prussia, the Kingship extended over all the possessions of the Hohenzollern, and Frederick was " King in Prussia " not in Königsberg only, but in Cleves, in Minden and in Berlin.

One of the conditions upon which Austria had consented to recognise the new title was that Prussia should support the Emperor in his pretensions to the Spanish inheritance, and Prussian troops consequently played a prominent part in the campaigns of Marlborough and Eugene. Prussian contingents were to the fore at Blenheim, at Turin, at Oudenarde and at Malplaquet ; but it has been well said that " Prussia had a policy but no army in the North, she had an army but no policy in the West." Her poverty compelled her to hire out to the Maritime Powers the troops she could not herself afford to support, and this it is which explains why at the Peace of Utrecht, Prussia's gains were insignificant. Guelders, on which the Prussian monarch possessed a claim in virtue of his position as Duke of Cleves, was handed over to him, and the Powers recognised Prussia's right to those portions of the Orange inheritance which had come into Frederick's possession since the death of his cousin William III. Mors and Lingen he had held since 1702, Neuchatel since 1707. But by the time the Peace was signed (April 11th, 1713) the first " King in Prussia " was no more, and his place had been taken by his son Frederick William I (Feb. 25th, 1713).

Some account has already been given [1] of the process by which the Wittelsbach family, which had begun the Thirty Years' War with one Electorate in the family, ended it with two. Of the two, the Bavarian line was incontestably the more important. Maximilian I, whose reign of fifty-three years (1598–1651) may not unfairly be described as the period in which the foundations of the modern kingdom of Bavaria were well and truly laid, not merely had won for Bavaria the coveted Electoral dignity and the rich lands of the Upper Palatinate, but he had been one of the first of the rulers of

[1] P. 18.

the minor states of Germany to establish his autocracy at the expense of his Estates. The Princes wanted to be absolute in their dominions as well as independent of Imperial control, for where lay the benefit of being free from external interference if they were to be hampered by constitutional opposition at home? Everywhere there were contests over taxation between aggressive Princes and recalcitrant Estates, and nearly everywhere it was not the Princes who had to give way. This was partly because the Estates were not, as a rule, really representative and had no force behind them. The peasantry, unrepresented and inarticulate, accustomed to be oppressed and to obey, heavily taxed and in a miserable condition, were of no political importance; the towns had been hit too hard by the wars and the complete disorganisation of trade and industry to have any influence, and the nobles alone were unable to prevent the establishment of more or less absolute autocracies. In this work Maximilian I had been extremely successful; he had stamped out Protestantism in his dominions, he had suppressed the opposition of the Estates, and by his services to the Catholic cause in the early stages of the Thirty Years' War he had made himself the leader of the non-Austrian Catholics. It was their position as the only Catholic Princes capable of contesting the quasi-hereditary claim of the Hapsburgs to the Empire that gave the Bavarian house their special importance in international affairs, and caused them to be looked upon with favour by the power whose policy towards Germany was based on the maxim *Divide et impera*. The relations between France and Bavaria were of slow growth: Ferdinand Maria (1651–1679) had gone to the length of promising to support the candidature of Louis for the Empire (1670), but Maximilian Emmanuel (1679–1726) had at first rejected all the overtures of France, had been an energetic member of the League of Augsburg, and had only at length listened to the offers of Louis when the death (1698) of his son, the Electoral Prince, had taken away Bavaria's chief motive for alliance with Austria, the prospect of Austrian support for the Electoral Prince's claims on Spain. And there was always a reason for the Bavarian Wittelsbachs to look with some suspicion on Austria; for, if the Hapsburgs should ever succeed in obtaining a dominant position in Germany, it would not be long before they would discover adequate reasons for the incorporation in their own dominions of those Wittelsbach lands which intervened so inconveniently between Upper Austria and the Burgau.   Hence the alliance between Maximilian Emmanuel and Louis, and the chequered career of Bavaria in the Spanish Succession War, which afforded not less striking proofs of the advantages to France of possessing a client so favourably situated for forwarding her designs on Austria than of the utility to Bavaria of French protection against Hapsburg land-hunger.   It was to the good offices of France that Maximilian Emmanuel owed his restoration [1] to his hereditary dominions; and though the differences which kept France and Spain apart for the decade following the Peace of Utrecht tended to force Franco-Austrian hostility into the background for a time, the old policy was resumed by France when the Empire fell vacant in 1740.

The other branch of the Wittelsbach family was represented in 1715 by John William of Neuburg, the brother-in-law of the Emperor Leopold I and a constant adherent of the Hapsburgs.   He was the second of his line to rule in the Palatinate which had passed to his father, Philip William, in 1685 on the death of Charles, the last of the Simmern branch.   This branch had not long survived its restoration to the Electorate; [2] and though Charles Lewis (1648–1680), the eldest son of the " Winter King " by Elizabeth, daughter of James I, had done a good deal to restore prosperity to his diminished dominions, rebuilding the devastated Mannheim, refounding the University of Heidelberg, remitting taxation and giving all possible encouragement to commerce and agriculture, the celebrated devastation of the Palatinate by the French in 1674 and its repetition in 1689 had between them thrown back the work of restoration, besides contributing to embitter the relations between Germany and France.   The accession of the Neuburg line meant that another Electorate passed from Protestant into Roman Catholic hands, and Elector John William had been mainly instrumental in securing the inclusion in the Peace of Ryswick of the clause by which freedom of worship in the districts then restored by France was not to be allowed " where not expressly stated to the contrary." [3]

---

[1] It was not till 1717 that this restoration was finally completed.

[2] Cf. p. 18.

[3] This so-called " Ryswick clause " was used with effect against the Protestants

Moreover, despite the Compact of Schwabisch-Hall (May 1685), which had guaranteed freedom of worship to the Calvinist and Lutheran inhabitants of the Palatinate, Elector John William had inaugurated an era of rigorous persecution, which was only slightly mitigated by the intervention in 1705 of Frederick I of Prussia. In addition to the Lower Palatinate, the Neuburg line possessed the principality in the upper valley of the Danube from which they took their name, and the portion of the Cleves - Jülich inheritance which had fallen to their lot as representing one of the sisters of the last Duke of Cleves. This, as settled by the definite partition of 1666, included Jülich, Berg and Ravenstein, so that the rulers of the Palatinate possessed more territory in the Rhine valley than any other lay potentate. This exposed them to French hostility and may partly account for their loyal adherence to Austria; but the strained relations between the Neuburgs and their Bavarian cousins may also have tended to influence the attitude of the Palatinate in international affairs.

The balance of religions in the Electoral College, disturbed against the Protestants by the succession of the Neuburgs to the Palatinate and by the conversion of the Saxon Electors, had been to some extent redressed by the erection in 1692 of a new Electorate. The greater prominence of the Hohenzollern, and the misconceptions too often prevalent in England as to the true nature of the " beggarly Electorate " with which our country was so closely linked for over one hundred years, have contributed to somewhat obscure the real importance of the Brunswick family. Indeed, had it not been that the principle of indivisibility of territories was not adopted by the family till after the separation of the Dannenberg and Lüneburg lines (1569), and that the connection with Great Britain from time to time involved Hanover in quarrels with which she had little concern, it is hardly fanciful to imagine that Brandenburg might have found in Brunswick a rival quite capable of contesting with her the leading position among the North German states. But until just the end of the seventeenth century the lands of the Brunswick family were but little less divided than those of the Wittelsbachs or of the Ernestine Saxons, while partly

of some parts of Southern Germany in the early part of the eighteenth century. Cf. *Z.S.* ii. 134.

through this and partly through a premature disarmament the Brunswick Dukes had fared very badly at the Peace of 1648, when instead of sharing the Westphalian bishoprics with Brandenburg, they had had to content themselves with alternate nominations to Osnabrück.   However, by the year 1680 the various branches of the family had been reduced to four, the Dannenberg or "new Wolfenbüttel" line in the Duchy of Brunswick, the Lüneburg-Celle and Calenberg-Hanover branches of the "new Lüneburg" line, and the comparatively unimportant Dukes of Brunswick-Bevern, a cadet branch of the "new Wolfenbüttels." At this time George William of Lüneburg-Celle had only a daughter, the ill-fated Sophia Dorothea, while his brother Ernest Augustus of Calenberg-Hanover had only one son, George Lewis, afterwards George I of Great Britain.   A marriage between these two was therefore the natural method of giving effect to the principle of indivisibility adopted by the Lüneburg line in 1592, and in November 1682 the wedding took place, Ernest Augustus having been recognised two years previously by the Estates of Hanover as the destined successor of George William.   The will of Ernest Augustus, now "published by anticipation," laid down as the perpetual law of the family the principles of indivisibility and primogeniture. This arrangement was ratified by the Emperor in 1683 and duly came into force on the death (1705) of George William, undisturbed by the tragedy of the unlucky Sophia Dorothea (1694).[1]

But before this union of Lüneburg-Celle and Calenberg-Hanover, the dignity so ardently desired by the Guelphs as the consummation of their improved position had been acquired by Ernest Augustus.   In the necessities of the Emperor the Guelphs found a lever by which to lift themselves into the Electoral College.   Austria, occupied simultaneously with the recovery of Hungary from the Turks and the defence of Western Germany against Louis XIV, was in sore need of the considerable military force of which they could dispose; and when, in 1692, Leopold found that the Duke of Hanover

---

[1] In 1689 the Saxe-Lauenberg line, ruling the duchy of that name on the right bank of the Elbe above Hamburg, had become extinct; and, despite the opposition of several other claimants, among them John George III of Saxony, the Guelphs managed to secure possession of this valuable district, their right to which received Imperial recognition in 1716. Cf. Z.S. ii. 107.

was discussing with Sweden, with the Bishop of Münster, and with the malcontent Elector of Saxony [1] the formation of a "third party" within the Empire for the purpose of forcing the Emperor to come to terms with France, he had to give way. In March 1692 was signed the "Electoral Compact," by which the Emperor conferred the Electoral dignity on Ernest Augustus and his sons in return for considerable military assistance both on the Rhine and on the Danube.

The promotion of Ernest Augustus was received not with acclamations but with a chorus of protests, from the Electors jealous at the admission of an upstart into their ranks, from the Princes furious with the lost leader who had deserted them to gain the very privileges he had been foremost in attacking. However, by October 1692, Bavaria, Brandenburg, Mayence and Saxony had recognised the promotion, and most of the other states of Germany followed suit before very long. At the Congress of Ryswick the European Powers recognised Ernest Augustus as an Elector, and at length, in 1708, three years after the union of Celle and Hanover and ten years after the death of Ernest Augustus (1698), his son George obtained formal admission into the Electoral College. In 1714 he succeeded his cousin Anne as King of England, and from henceforward the fortunes of Hanover were destined to be affected by events on the Ganges and Mississippi, and by commercial quarrels in East and West Indies. To England also the connection was a doubtful advantage, though in many respects the Electorate compared less unfavourably with its ruler's new dominions than is usually assumed. If its population was only a little over a half a million as against the six millions of England and Wales, and its revenue only £300,000 as against £6,000,000, the Hanoverian army was but little smaller than the joint establishment of 31,000 men maintained in Great Britain, Ireland and the "plantations." Compared with the territories of their German neighbours, those of the Guelphs were fairly extensive, amounting to about 8500 square miles; but they were neither very populous nor very rich. Moorlands and sandy wastes formed a very large portion of the Electorate, which contained very few towns of any size, and was mainly agricultural, except for a few mining villages. Economically and socially alike the country was somewhat backward, its laws

[1] John George IV, *o.s.p.* 1694.

and system of government being mainly mediæval, local Estates retained enough vitality to prevent centralisation without being themselves efficient or energetic, while the peasantry were in a state of feudal subjugation and were extremely ignorant.

Outside the Electoral College the thirty-three ecclesiastical members of the College of Princes merit some attention. One of the Archbishoprics, Magdeburg, had passed into the possession of Brandenburg in 1680; the only other one, Salzburg, though nearly a fifth larger in area than any of the three Electorates,[1] consisted mainly of wild and unproductive mountainous country, and except in the river valleys its population was scanty.[2] Except that its holder presided in the College of Princes alternately with Austria one hears little of it. Of the Bishoprics, Trent (1650 square miles, 147,000 inhabitants) was chiefly important from its position between Austria and Italy; Bamberg (1400 and 180,000) and Würzburg (2100 and 250,000), which were situated in the fertile valley of the Main, were richer and more populous than the average; Liège (2300 and 220,000), also wealthy and populous, was still part of the Empire, and was generally held in common with Cologne, as was sometimes Münster also. This, the largest and most populous of all the ecclesiastical Principalities of Germany, its area being 4800 square miles and its population 380,000 persons, is less prominent in the eighteenth century than it had been in the last half of the previous century when ruled by that most unepiscopal but energetic prelate, Christopher Bernard von Galen, diplomatist, politician and warrior rather than ecclesiastic. Of the secularised Bishoprics of North Germany, Osnabrück (1200 square miles and 136,000 people), the largest of those so treated, was not wholly lost to the Roman Catholics, as it had been arranged at the Peace of Westphalia that it should be alternately in the hands of a Roman Catholic and of a Protestant "Administrator." For the rest, the College of Princes included the Grand Masters of the Teutonic Order and of the Knights of Malta, the Bishops of Augsburg, Basle, Brixen, Chur,

---

[1] It was over 3700 square miles, Cologne being 3100, Mayence and Treves both under 2700.

[2] The figures given in Z.S. (ii. 181) are Mayence 330,000 inhabitants, Treves 270,000, Cologne 240,000, Salzburg 190,000.

Constance, Eichstadt, Freisingen, Fulda, Passau, Ratisbon, Spires and Worms, and several Abbots.

Now that the Guelphs had attained to Electoral rank, the chief lay member of the College of Princes was perhaps the Duke of Würtemberg. This South German Protestant state is in some ways the most interesting of all the minor Principalities, since it possessed what most of its fellows lacked, a written constitution, established in 1514 when Duke Ulrich had concluded with his subjects the Treaty of Tübingen. In character it was somewhat democratic, for in Würtemberg there was hardly any aristocracy, most of the local nobles of Swabia being Imperial Knights, consequently the burgher element in the Estates was unusually powerful. The Estates owed their escape from suppression to the fact that the constitution gave them the power of the purse, and this they had managed to retain, so that the Duke found his authority much restricted by that of the Standing Committee of the Estates, and thus Würtemberg was a notable exception to the general rule of the establishment of princely absolutism on the ruins of local autonomy. Eberhard III (1623–1674) had lost his dominions in the Thirty Years' War but had regained them in 1648, when the little Principality of Montbeliard (Mömpelgard) passed to another branch of the family on the extinction of which (1723) it reverted to the senior line. Eberhard had made great and not unsuccessful efforts to heal the wounds which the ravages of the war had inflicted on his dominions, while the policy of supporting Austria which he had consistently followed was continued by his successors. In 1715, Würtemberg was under the rule of Duke Eberhard Louis (1677–1733), a man of considerable vigour and capacity, who had managed to obtain from the Estates the establishment of a small standing army, which enabled him to contest the authority of the Standing Committee and to be more tyrannical and extravagant than any of his predecessors. He had been able to do this because the Würtembergers had found that if the strict control the Standing Committee exercised over the Duke enabled his subjects to escape being sacrificed to the caprices of a ruling sovereign supported by military force, it also exposed them to injuries at the hands of their neighbours. *Das gute alte Recht* was no defence against the aggressions of Louis XIV, and Würtemberg suffered almost as heavily in the wars of

4

1688–1699 and 1702–1714 as in the Thirty Years' War itself. Hence the permanent army which the Duke was allowed to establish for the better defence of the 3500 square miles and the 660,000 inhabitants who owned his sway.

Between Würtemberg and the Rhine lay Baden, divided between the two branches of Baden-Baden and Baden-Durlach, ruled respectively in 1715 by Louis George (1707–1761), son and successor of that "Louis of Baden" who had played so prominent a part in the War of the Spanish Succession as the colleague of Marlborough and Eugene, and by Charles William of Durlach (1709–1738), chiefly noteworthy for having been, like his cousin, a warm supporter of Austria in the war of 1702–1714, but not over successful as a commander. Of the two, Baden-Baden was somewhat the larger, having an area of 770 square miles against 640 and 94,000 inhabitants against 73,000. Both branches of the family were Protestants, as were also the great majority of their subjects.

The territories of the House of Hesse resembled those of their Northern neighbours, the Guelphs, in being much sub-divided. The two main branches of the family sprang from the quadruple division which had followed the death of Landgrave Philip the Proud in 1567. Two of the lines then established had died out since then, Hesse-Rheinfels in 1583, Hesse-Marburg in 1604, the extinction of the last-named giving rise to a long contest for its territorities between the surviving branches, Hesse-Cassel and Hesse-Darmstadt. This had been decided at the Peace of Westphalia on the whole in favour of Hesse-Cassel, whose claims had been so warmly pressed by France and Sweden that the Emperor had been forced to cancel his original award in favour of his constant adherent Hesse-Darmstadt. Hesse-Cassel had also received the Abbey of Hersfeld and part of the County of Schaumburg, while its ruler, Landgrave William VI (1637–1677), had put a stop to all chance of further partitions by establishing the rule of primogeniture and indivisibility (1650). His son and successor, Landgrave Charles I, who was ruling Hesse-Cassel at the time of the Peace of Utrecht, merits certain attention as one of the first German Princes to turn his dominions into an establishment for the production and supply of mercenary troops. He had raised soldiers on a definitely and systemati-cally organised plan, which enabled him to dispose freely of a considerable force of excellent troops and thereby to earn large subsidies from Austria and the Maritime Powers, which subsidies, to his credit be it noted, he had spent on his country rather than on himself. One of the German Princes who profited by the expulsion of the Huguenots to welcome them to Cassel, to the great benefit of both sides to the bargain, Landgrave Charles had not adhered to the French alliance which had proved so useful to his family in 1648. Alarmed by the aggressions of Louis XIV, he had joined the so-called Magdeburg Concert of 1688 and had been one of the first German Princes to join the Grand Alliance, while Hessian troops had done excellent service under Marlborough and Eugene.

Considerably smaller and less populous than Hesse-Cassel it had 1750 square miles, mostly South of the Main, and 180,000 inhabitants as against an area of 2850 square miles and a population of 330,000—Hesse-Darmstadt followed a somewhat different policy. Like the Guelphs, it had been consistently Lutheran and consistently loyal to the Emperor ; whereas Hesse-Cassel was strongly and aggressively Calvinist and, though loyal enough from 1688 to 1715, had at one time been closely allied with France and Sweden. Its ruler in 1715, Landgrave Ernest Louis (1678–1739), was no exception to the traditions of the family ; the son of Louis VI, the founder of the University of Giessen, he had been a member of the Grand Alliance and had, like his cousin at Cassel, provided mercenaries for the Maritime Powers. Of the cadet branches of the House of Hesse those of Hesse-Rheinfels (new), Hesse-Rotenburg and Hesse-Eschwege sprang from Cassel; the Princes of Hesse-Homburg were an offshoot of the Darmstadt line dating from 1596.

But of all the families of Germany, perhaps the most subdivided was that of the Wittelsbachs ; for in addition to the two Electors of that house, it possessed several members of the College of Princes, their territories lying for the most part in the Upper Rhenish and Bavarian Circles. Of these lines and of the Electoral branches the common ancestor was Stephen, third son of Robert III, Elector Palatine from 1398 to 1410. On Stephen's death in 1459 his dominions had been divided between his sons Frederick and Louis, ancestors respectively of the Simmern and Zweibrücken lines, the former of which had succeeded to the Electorate in 1559 and had held it till 1685.

A cadet branch of the Zweibrücken line had been established at Veldenz in 1514, and on the death of Wolfgang of Zweibrücken (1569) his lands were divided afresh, three lines being thus established, the Birkenfeld, the Neuburg and the Zweibrücken. Yet another branch was founded in 1614 when the lands of Philip William of Neuburg were divided between his sons Wolfgang William, who took Neuburg, and Augustus, who received Sulzbach.[1] In 1715 the Neuburg branch had succeeded to the Palatinate,[2] Sulzbach[3] was ruled by Theodore (1708–1732), Veldenz[4] had passed to the Elector Palatine on the death of Duke Leopold Louis in 1694, Birkenfeld[5] was under Christian II (1654–1717). Zweibrücken had been divided by John I (*ob.* 1604) between his three sons, but, of the three branches thus established, only the Kleeberg line survived in 1715. To this, therefore, the Zweibrücken lands belonged, it being represented by Charles XII of Sweden, the great-grandson of John Casimir of Kleeberg by Christina of Sweden, daughter of Charles IX. On his death in 1718 the Zweibrücken lands passed to a cousin, Gustavus Leopold, from whom they passed in turn to Christian III of Birkenfeld (1717–1735) in 1731. Thus the multiplication of the Wittelsbach branches was gradually tending to be somewhat simplified; but these infinitesimal subdivisions deprived the family of the political weight it might have enjoyed had all its lands been united under one ruler. But even then they were so much scattered that even a common ruler could hardly have given coherence and cohesion to little parcels of territory distributed about on the Lower Rhine (Jülich and Berg), the Moselle, and between the Danube and the Main.

No other family in South Germany is important enough to merit special mention; but as one passes Northward from the Bavarian and Swabian Circles to the Franconian and Upper Saxon, one meets at Anspach and Baireuth cadet branches of the Hohenzollern. These Margraviates had come into the hands of Elector Joachim Frederick in 1603, when the

---

[1] Neuburg and Sulzbach had belonged to the Landshut branch of the Bavarian Wittelsbachs which had become extinct in 1503, whereupon a struggle for their inheritance occurred between the Zweibrücken line and Duke Albert II of Münich: the matter was settled by a compromise, which left Neuburg and Sulzbach to the Zweibrücken.   [2] Cf. p. 44.

[3] In the Upper Palatinate, which it divided in half.

[4] On the Moselle just below Treves.   [5] Just to the East of Treves.

Culmbach line established in them by the *Dispositio Achillea*
of Elector Albert Achilles (1473) had died out. Joachim
Frederick had bestowed them on his younger brothers, whose
descendants, William Frederick of Anspach (1702–1723,
brother of Caroline, wife of George II of England) and
George William of Baireuth (1712–1726), were ruling them
in 1715. Their joint area amounted to about 2600 square
miles and their population to over 360,000, rather above the
average for the whole country, although no town of much size
was included within their boundaries. The main importance
of these Franconian Hohenzollerns lay in the fact that they
provided their cousins at Brandenburg with a possible excuse
for interfering in South Germany, and of obtaining a foothold
South of the Main by the annexation of these Margraviates.

If the map of South-Western Germany may be described
as a mosaic of petty states, that of Thuringia easily bears off
the palm for bewildering intricacy of subdivision. What
with the Princes of Reuss, of Schwarzburg, of the various
branches of the Anhalt family, and the Counties of Mansfeld
and Hohenstein, Thuringian geography would have been complicated enough, even if all the territories of the Ernestine
Saxons had been united under one ruler. But the Ernestine
Wettins surpassed even their Albertine cousins in the subdivision of their territories and in the number of their cadet
branches; of these the most important were Saxe-Coburg,
subdivided at the death of the famous Ernest the Pious
(1605–1675) between his six sons, rulers respectively of
Saxe - Gotha, Saxe - Coburg, Saxe - Hildburghausen, Saxe-
Meinungen, Saxe - Saalfeld and Saxe - Eisenberg, and Saxe-
Weimar, whose Dukes had been much more moderate in
the creation of minor principalities, Saxe-Eisenach being the
only offshoot enjoying a separate existence in 1715.
Together the territories of the Ernestine Saxons amounted to
nearly 2000 square miles, peopled by some 360,000 persons,
the joint possessions of the Albertine line covering an area of
15,000 square miles and having a population of 1,700,000.

After the intricacies of Thuringia the affairs of Mecklenburg
seem almost simple. A disputed succession to the territories
of Gustavus of Mecklenburg-Güstrow, the last of the line
(*ob.* 1695), had given rise to certain complications, but had
been finally settled by the Treaty of Hamburg in 1701, which

established the two lines of Mecklenburg-Schwerin, with which went Güstrow itself and the vote, and Mecklenburg-Strelitz, to which was given the secularised Bishopric of Ratzeburg. By one of the most remarkable provisions even in that country of constitutional anomalies and curiosities, when Mecklenburg had originally been divided between the Dukes of Schwerin and of Güstrow the Estates of the two divisions had remained united,[1] with the result that the Estates had been able to utilise the division for their own benefit and to defend their aristocratic privileges against their Dukes with no small success.[2]   It might have been expected from the extensive seaboard which Mecklenburg possessed that she might have risen to influence and importance by means of commercial and maritime development, but the cession of Wismar to Sweden in 1648 and the admission of Sweden's claim to the tolls (*Licenten*) of the other ports of the country had spoilt this chance, and Mecklenburg remained a merely agrarian country, doomed to poverty and backwardness by the unfruitful character of her sandy soil, thinly populated, and of little weight in German affairs.   In 1715 the 300,000 inhabitants of the 5000 square miles of Mecklenburg - Schwerin were ruled by Charles Leopold (1713–1747), soon to make himself important by the complications introduced into Baltic affairs by his attempt to establish a more autocratic administrative system in his dominions.   Mecklenburg - Strelitz, not more than a fifth of the size or population of Schwerin, was under Adolphus Frederick II (1708–1749), a prince of no particular importance.

North-Westward of Mecklenburg lies a land whose story involves some of the very worst complications in all German history.   To get a clear idea of the relations between Schleswig-Holstein, Denmark and the Holy Roman Empire, it is necessary to go back even beyond the extinction of the old line of the Kings of Denmark in 1448, when the Danish crown was offered to Adolphus VII of Schleswig-Holstein, a member of the Schauenburg family and a subject of the Emperor as Count of Holstein.   The connection between Holstein, which admittedly formed part of the Holy

---

[1] Erdmannsdörffer, i. 73.

[2] The Estates were almost wholly composed of the local nobles, the peasantry being serfs, and the burghers devoid of any political power.

Roman Empire, and Schleswig, which no less certainly did not, had arisen through the cession of Schleswig to Count Gerhard of Holstein (1386) to be held as a fief of the Danish Crown. After various efforts by Denmark to recover immediate possession of Schleswig, it had been left in the hands of Adolphus of Schauenburg as a hereditary fief when Christopher of Bavaria had become King of Denmark (1439). When offered the Danish crown in 1448, Adolphus had declined it, but had suggested as a suitable choice his nephew, Christian of Oldenburg, who had then been offered the crown and had promptly accepted it. In 1459, Adolphus died childless, and Christian at once laid claim to Holstein as well as to Schleswig, claiming both as the nearest male heir of his uncle and Schleswig also as King of Denmark, the overlord to whom the fief should revert on the extinction of its holders. The Estates of the two provinces thereupon chose him as their ruler, but on the express conditions that they should be free for the future to select any of his descendants as their ruler, and should not have to take the King of Denmark.

The next landmark in the history of the Duchies was the division of Schleswig-Holstein made by Christian III of Denmark (1534—1558) in 1544, when the Duchies [1] were shared between Christian III and his brothers. This ultimately established two separate branches of the House of Oldenburg, the Glückstadt or royal line, and the Gottorp or ducal. Unfortunately for all concerned the division was not geographically symmetrical, but the possessions of the two branches were irretrievably intermingled, so that the Glückstadt line not merely ruled the Kingdom of Denmark, but also held portions of the Duchies, in virtue of which the King of Denmark enjoyed a seat in the College of Princes. As was only natural the relations between the two branches were not, as a rule, of the most friendly, for it was the constant endeavour of the Gottorp line to throw off altogether the ill-defined suzerainty which Denmark continued to assert and to attempt to make more definite and complete. To further their end the Dukes of Holstein-Gottorp are always to be found in alliance with Denmark's principal enemies, the Swedish Kings of the Vasa family, in whom they found willing protectors against

---

[1] Holstein had been erected into a Duchy in 1474, with a seat in the College of Princes.

Danish aggression.   Thus in the Baltic wars of the seventeenth century this debatable land between Denmark and Germany was both the scene of hostilities and the prize of victory, and not til! Sweden's day of greatness had come to an end at Pultowa and Friedrichshald [1] did Denmark achieve her principal object by the annexation of Schleswig (1721).   Meanwhile the successful *coup d'état* of 1660 in Denmark had introduced a new complication by making that kingdom an absolute and hereditary monarchy with female succession, while in Schleswig-Holstein the Salic law still prevailed.   In 1715 the Duke of Holstein-Gottorp was a minor, Charles Frederick, who had succeeded to the Duchies in 1703, his father Frederick IV having been killed when fighting for Charles XII at Klissow: the actual government of the Duchies was therefore in the hands of Christian Augustus of Holstein-Eutin, brother of the late Duke and head of the principal cadet branch of the family.

But in addition to the portions of Schleswig-Holstein which the Danish Kings had managed to keep, and which qualified them to rank as Princes of the Empire, they held other and larger territories in Northern Germany.   The branch of the House of Oldenburg which had retained possession of the ancestral Duchy on the West of the Weser when Denmark came into the possession of the family, had become extinct in 1667, and Oldenburg, with its appanages of Delmenhorst and Jever, had passed to the King of Denmark, a connection being thus established which was to last over a hundred years.   About half the size of Mecklenburg-Schwerin, Oldenburg was even more sparsely populated, having barely forty inhabitants to the square mile, and made practically no use of the possession of a seaboard to develop as a maritime state.   Possibly its Danish rulers would not have cared to see the Duchy embarking on such a career, but it had no industries on which to base any attempt at commercial enterprise.   Be that as it may, Danish rule, however, though mild and not oppressive, was never popular in Oldenburg and the termination of the connection was welcomed when it came by the inhabitants of the Duchy.[2]

Among his fellow-members of the College of Princes, the King of Denmark found his great rival in the Baltic, the King

---

[1] Cf. Chapter III.   [2] Cf. Chapter XVII.

of Sweden. In 1715 Sweden's hold on the possessions ceded to her at the Peace of Westphalia was all but shaken off; the Danes had occupied Bremen and Verden, Pomerania had been overrun by the joint forces of Prussia, Saxony - Poland and Hanover, and Stralsund was closely beset;[1] but technically these portions of the Empire were Swedish still, and even after the conclusion of that group of treaties of which the Peace of Nystad is the most important, part of Western Pomerania with Rügen and Wismar remained to the successors of Charles XII, who must therefore be reckoned among the Princes of Germany.

But while Sweden's constitutional relations with the Empire were clear enough, the same can hardly be alleged of the connection between the German *Reich* and the other foreign power which had taken a leading part in the Thirty Years' War. In 1648, France had received all the Imperial rights over the three Bishoprics, Metz, Toul and Verdun, of which she had been in actual possession since 1552, and also over the Landgraviates of Upper and Lower Alsace, the Sundgau and the town of Breisach, together with the provincial prefecture (*Landvogtei*) over the ten Imperial cities of Alsace, the so-called "Decapolis." But while the three Bishoprics, the Sundgau and Upper and Lower Alsace had been ceded in full sovereignty, this had not been the case with the "Decapolis." It would almost seem as if the uncertainty must have been deliberate, that the clauses of the Treaty of Münster dealing with the matter (Nos. 73, 74 and 87) were purposely worded so vaguely that both parties could interpret them as they wished.[2] Moreover, Alsace, like other parts of the Empire, was divided among many different rulers whose lands were inextricably confused, the possessions of the Hapsburgs being mixed up with territory belonging to the Bishoprics of Worms, Spires, Strassburg and Basle, to temporal Princes like Zwei-brücken, Baden and the Elector Palatine, to say no more of Counts and Imperial Knights. Formally these districts had not been ceded to France. Practically, however, they soon came to be as good as French; for though the Princes of the Empire who owned them were allowed to levy taxes from them, to nominate officials to govern them and to collect feudal dues and other items of revenue, they were not

[1] Cf. Chapter III.   [2] Cf. Erdmannsdörffer, i. pp. 39–47.

permitted to keep soldiers in these districts; any fortresses were occupied by French troops, only natives might be appointed to official posts, and the French taxed these districts just as they did those directly subject to the King of France. The towns of the Decapolis chose their own magistrates, and enjoyed local autonomy of a sort with exemption from some taxes; but a royal official was established in each of them to look after the interests of the King of France, and if the nominal connection with the Empire still existed, the events of Louis xiv's reign had left it hardly even a name.[1]   The work of the *Chambres de Réunion* had been in part undone at Ryswick and Utrecht, but Strassburg, the prize of the most flagrant of all the "acts of power" committed by Louis, was not recovered for Germany.

Westward of Alsace lay yet another portion of the Empire which was rapidly ceasing to be German.   Lorraine, long a debatable land between France and Germany, was in 1715 still in the hands of the descendants of Anthony the Good, the elder brother of the first Duke of Guise.[2]   Situated as it was, Lorraine had inevitably been involved in the complicated relations of France, Spain and the malcontent French nobility. Seized by Richelieu in 1634, it had not been restored to its Duke, Charles iii, till the Peace of the Pyrenees, and then France had reserved the right of free passage across the Duchy for her troops; and in subsequent wars Lorraine had been to all intents and purposes French.   Leopold Joseph (1690–1729), its ruler in 1715, had regained the Duchy at the Peace of Ryswick, subject as before to the French right of passage, and during the Spanish Succession War a French garrison occupied Nancy, though the neutrality of the Duchy was on the whole maintained, and its Duke was thus able to apply himself energetically and with some success to the arduous task of restoring order and prosperity to his much harassed dominions.

Of the remaining members of the College of Princes but little need be said.   Anthony Ulrich of Brunswick-Wolfen-büttel,[3] one of the few German Princes to join Louis xiv

---

[1] This information was derived from a course of lectures delivered by M. Rodolphe Reuss of the École des Hautes Études at Paris in 1898.

[2] Claude, *ob.* 1550.

[3] He had succeeded in adding the city of Brunswick to his dominions in 1671, and in 1679 acquired Thedinghausen from Sweden.

in 1702, when he had been promptly suppressed by the Hanoverian cousins he hated so bitterly, had died in 1714; his son and successor, Augustus William (1714–1731), was a man of little note. Anhalt, divided in 1603 between the Bernberg, Dessau, Kothen and Zerbst lines, and Aremberg had had *Virilstimmen* before 1648, but the Counts of Henneberg had been extinct since 1583, their lands had been partitioned between the various Saxon lines, Saxe - Weimar and the Electoral line giving the vote together. The vote formerly held by Savoy had lapsed through long disuse, that of Leuchtenberg had fallen to Bavaria, that of Saxe-Lauenberg to Hanover. But the College of Princes had from time to time been recruited by new creations, and seven new holders of *Virilstimmen* had appeared in 1653 and 1654, the Counts of Hohenzollern-Hechingen, Nassau-Dillenberg and Nassau-Hadamar, the Wildgrave of Salm, Barons Dietrichstein, Eggenberg and Lobkowitz, while subsequent additions had been the Counts of Auersberg (1664), East Friesland (1667), Fürstenberg (1667) and Schwarzenberg (1674).[1] Outside the ranks of these holders of individual votes were many other petty Princes, too numerous and too unimportant for individual mention, such as the Counts of Waldeck, Isenburg and Hohenlohe, who were only represented in the Diet through the *Curiatstimmen.*

Yet one numerous and important class requires description, the Imperial Knights, the rulers of the very pettiest states in all the mosaic of the infinite disunion of Germany. Lords of dominions which, as a rule, consisted of but a village or two, their position in the Empire approximated in some ways to the condition of subjects rather than of Princes. They had no footing in the Diet, not even a solitary *Curiatstimme* among the thousand members of their order. Indeed, in the greater part of the Empire, in Austria, in Bavaria and in North Germany, the lesser nobles, who roughly corresponded to the Knights in position and in the size of their holdings, had already been reduced to the footing of subjects. It was only in the Southern Circles in which there was no one predominant Prince that the Knights were numerous—in other words, that the lesser nobility had managed to become and remain sovereigns.

[1] These dates are those of the definite acquisition of the *Virilstimme.*

But they were sovereign only in that, holding immediately of the Emperor, they enjoyed rights of jurisdiction and taxation over their tenants, and were not subject to the Princes in whose territories their dominions were enclosed. If the majority of the petty states of Germany were much too small to be capable of developing that active political life which alone could justify their independent existence, much more was this the case with the Knights. Had the Princes been allowed to put a summary conclusion to the indefensible independence of this most anomalous class, it would have been a great boon to the unfortunate subjects of the Knights, and peace and order would have been much advanced. As it was, the territories of the Knights were as a rule Alsatias, to which robbers and broken men of every description commonly resorted. The robber Knights of the Middle Ages had disappeared, but things were still pretty bad, and no useful purpose was served by this independence. Indeed, it was most unfortunate that such a resident nobility, accustomed to local administration, a class which to some degree might have bridged the gap between Princes and subjects, should have been so completely ineffective for good. It was to the Emperor that the Knights owed their security against the Princes. To him they were of importance because the tax which they paid him, the *Charitätivsubsidien*, was one of the principal sources of his meagre income.[1] It was their affairs which provided the Imperial law courts with the bulk of their business, and the Knights were almost the only element in the Empire which, having no local or particularist interests, could be said to be members of the Empire, and to belong to it only. It might have been thought that on them and on the Cities the Emperor might have laid the foundations of a more national party by which to counteract the localism of the Princes; but the Knights were too weak and too scattered for united action, and in the eighteenth century the Hapsburgs had all but abandoned as hopeless the struggle against particularism. The Knights had, it is true, an organisation of their own, a Corpus composed of the "Knightly Circles" of Franconia,

---

[1] The Knights, being unrepresented in the Diet, always refused to pay the taxes voted by the Diet; nor did they contribute to the upkeep of the Imperial Chamber.

Swabia and the Rhine,[1] each of which was built up out of the "cantons" into which the Knights were divided; but for any practical political purpose this was of little value.

After this description of the political condition of Germany at the beginning of the eighteenth century, of the breakdown of the central institutions, of the want of union, of the utter absence of any national feeling, it will hardly be necessary to dwell at any great length on the social or the economic condition of the country. During the seventeenth century, Germany had been the theatre of more than one terrible and devastating conflict: for thirty years she had been the battle-ground of a war originally caused by bitter religious anta-gonisms and continued to satisfy the greed and ambition of foreign powers, a war waged mainly by mercenaries, soldiers of fortune whose main object was plunder and who were restrained neither by discipline nor by national sympathies from inflicting every variety of outrage and suffering on the wretched inhabitants of the countries they traversed. In the seventeenth century wars were not waged with kid gloves and neither commanders nor commanded were influenced for a moment by humanitarian scruples. And after thirty years of this there had come but a brief respite before the aggres-sions of Louis XIV had involved Germany in a new series of conflicts, which extended over forty-two years of which two-thirds were years of war. The double devastation of the unfortunate Palatinate and Marlborough's harrying of Bavaria were not calculated to heal the wounds left by the soldiers of Bernhard of Saxe-Weimar, of Tilly, of Pappenheim and of Condé. What wonder that Germany, which before the out-break of the Wars of Religion had been a rich and prosperous land, richer and more flourishing probably than any of its neighbours, had received injuries in these wars from which it is no exaggeration to say that it has taken her over two centuries to recover. From the Baltic to the Lake of Constance, from the Moselle to the Oder and the Moldau, the country had been fought over, plundered, ravaged and laid waste: in some places the population had fallen in 1649 to a tenth of what it had been in 1631, and there is probably no great exaggeration in the estimate which puts at a half the pro-portion of the population which perished in the savage and

---

[1] They stood quite outside the ordinary division into Circles.

devastating Thirty Years' War.[1] Since the Peace of Westphalia no doubt some progress had been made, but the wars
of the second half of the seventeenth century, if less brutal
and destructive than their predecessors, had retarded the
recovery of Germany and greatly hampered the efforts of those
of her rulers who had sought to encourage the revival of
population and prosperity. In 1715 the country was in a
much better condition than in 1648, but the recovery was a
slow and chequered process.

The effect of all this on agriculture, on manufactures, on
trade and commerce, can easily be understood. The Thirty
Years' War had brought them all to a stand-still; and though,
directly peace was concluded and order of a kind restored,
agriculture had soon recovered some degree of its old prosperity, thanks to the magnificent natural qualities of the soil,
the revival of trade and industry was a far slower process and
the end of the century found Germany very backward. The
skilled labourers had for the most part perished in the wars, or
had betaken themselves to the far more lucrative and attractive callings of the soldier and the bandit. Mines and
quarries had become unworkable through disuse. Means of
communication had fallen into disrepair: bridges had been
destroyed and not replaced. Moreover, the war had so
disturbed the country that the little capital which was available for employment was but cautiously ventured. More
settled political conditions must prevail before industry could
revive, certainly before men could again take up the more
difficult arts and crafts with any prospect of remunerative
employment. And it had been when Germany, thus stricken
by the Thirty Years' War, was just beginning to recover that
there had come the great development of French industries
and commerce under the fostering hand of Colbert. The
scientific tariff which he erected against the Dutch did not
spare Germany. England, too, was competing successfully
with the Dutch for their carrying-trade and for a share in the
commerce of the Baltic, so that in face of the strenuous rivalry
of these great commercial powers there was little chance of a
successful revival of the once mighty Hanseatic League.
Moreover, the political subdivision of the country was a great
barrier to its economic development. Different codes of law

[1] Cf. *Z.S.* i. pp. 41–45.

in different states, heavy taxation everywhere, internal tolls and taxes on commerce, a new customs-frontier every few miles, inefficient police arrangements, governmental and court establishments out of all proportion to the needs of the petty states, these were some of the many obstacles which the political complexity of Germany strewed in the path of industrial or economic progress.

Moreover, bad as were the political and economic conditions of the country, the state of moral and intellectual life was even worse. The horrors of the Thirty Years' War had produced a widespread demoralisation. Religious passions and animosities were temporarily exhausted but, as the next sixty years were too often to show, by no means extinct. Intolerance and persecution seemed the only means by which piety was displayed by the few rulers whom religious motives influenced in the least. Education had been thrown back centuries, schools were closed, the Universities flooded by the return of ex-students who had turned soldiers and now came back to an academical life for which their recent experiences had rendered them unfitted. The importation of the habits of the camp into the Universities was hardly calculated to make for intellectual progress, and the stagnation of German literature and thought during the greater part of the next century may be attributed in no small degree to the effects of the Thirty Years' War. Here and there some petty ruler, aping the *Grand Monarque*, might pose as a patron of the arts and letters, but usually it was in Paris or on French poets and painters that the taxes were spent which their lords and masters wrung from the miserable peasants of Germany. Yet even in this dead period a few great names are to be found, though not even Leibnitz can redeem the seventeenth century from the reproach which attaches to it in the intellectual history of Germany. The eighteenth century therefore opened with but faint hopes.

CHAPTER III

THE END OF THE NORTHERN WAR

NOT even when the conclusion of the Peace of Baden (Sept. 1714) finally closed the war which had arisen over the Spanish Succession was the whole of Germany at peace. The other great contest which had begun with the anti-Swedish coalition formed by Russia, Denmark and Saxony - Poland in 1699 had still several years to run. Charles XII, who had at one time threatened to interfere with decisive effect in the Western struggle, was no longer dominant in North-Eastern Europe. Within two years of the day when he set out Eastward from Alt Ranstadt his crushing defeat at Pultowa (June 26th, 1709) had sent him, a fugitive without an army, to seek the protection of the Turks, and marked the beginning of the end for Sweden's supremacy over the Baltic. The enemies Charles seemed to have crushed promptly had raised their heads again. Frederick Augustus of Saxony had denounced the Treaty of Alt Ranstadt directly he heard the news, and hastened to renew his alliance with Russia (Oct. 1709). Stanislaus Lecziński's tenure of the Polish throne had come to an abrupt conclusion, and the re-establishment of the Saxon dynasty at Warsaw had been effected without difficulty. Denmark, too, had repudiated the Treaty of Travendahl, unhindered by England and Holland, who were too well occupied elsewhere to be able to spare force to compel the Danes to respect their guarantee. Thus from all quarters the territories of the absent Swedish monarch had been attacked ; the provinces East of the Baltic were assailed by overpowering forces of Russians backed up by the new fleet which Peter was creating ; the Danes invaded Scania, and Sweden's one remaining field force, Krassau's, had to retire from Poland into Pomerania.

However, just as in the days of Charles' success the Western Powers had sought to prevent him from interfering

West of the Elbe, so after Pultowa it had been their object to make certain that his overthrow should not lead to the infringement of the neutrality of the Empire. Accordingly in March 1710 the Emperor and the Maritime Powers had signed a compact by which they agreed to guarantee the neutrality of Sweden's German possessions if Krassau would agree not to use them as a base for attacking Jutland or Poland. Welcomed by the Swedish Senate though repudiated by Charles, this " Neutrality Compact of the Hague" had on the whole been observed, for Russia, intending to direct her attacks on Finland and the Baltic provinces, was not disposed to contest it ; and though Frederick I of Prussia would have been glad to seize this chance of adding Pomerania to his dominions, he could not afford to offend his Dutch and English pay-masters. However, in August 1711, soon after the Peace of July 1711 had extricated Peter from his critical position on the Pruth, a force of 24,000 Russians, Poles and Saxons crossed Prussian territory on their way to Stralsund and Wismar, which they proceeded to besiege. Prussia's verbal protests met with little attention, and as she had no idea of embarking in the war on behalf of Sweden, she refrained from enforcing her words by blows.

Thus the Baltic war had spread to Germany ; and though Stralsund and Stettin successfully resisted their besiegers, a Danish force invaded Bremen and forced that province to swear allegiance to the King of Denmark (July to Sept. 1712), though George Louis of Hanover anticipated them in getting possession of Verden also by occupying it on the plea of sanitary precautions against the plague. For a time, indeed, matters went in favour of Sweden ; for Steenbock, landing in Rügen with 10,000 men (Sept.), raised the siege of Stralsund and then, taking the offensive against the Danes, won a brilliant victory over them at Gadebusch (Dec.) and drove them headlong into Holstein before their Russo-Saxon allies could come to their help.[1] But his success was only temporary ; pursuing his enemies into Holstein, he found himself surrounded by vastly superior numbers, driven under the guns of the neutral fortress of Tönningen and forced to capitulate (May

[1] The invaders of Scania had been defeated by Steenbock at Helsingborg (Feb. 1710) and had evacuated the province, thus enabling Steenbock to cross to Germany.

20th, 1713). Just before that, however, two important events had occurred. In February, Frederick I of Prussia had died, in April the Peace of Utrecht had been signed.

Neither the situation of his own kingdom nor that of Baltic affairs in general tempted Frederick William, the new " King in Prussia," to plunge at once into the. Northern war. Anxious as he was to acquire the coveted Western Pomerania, it was difficult to see by what path the desired goal might be best reached. Prussia required a period of rest, time in which to restore order to the entangled finances, to prepare for an intervention which might easily prove disastrous if undertaken prematurely. Moreover, the relations of the Baltic Powers were in so complicated a condition that it was by no means clear what line of policy was best suited to the requirements of Prussia; for little as the Hohenzollern liked the presence of Sweden at the mouth of the Oder, even Swedes were to be preferred to Russians or to Saxons.

The first opportunity of influencing the course of affairs which came to Frederick William was by means of a treaty with the Regent of Holstein-Gottorp. Christian Augustus of Holstein-Eutin, Administrator of the sequestrated see of Lübeck and guardian of the youthful Duke Charles Frederick, the heir presumptive of his childless uncle Charles XII of Sweden, was a person of no small importance; and in his minister, Görtz, he had at his side an active, restless in- triguer who hoped to suck no small advantage out of the position in which he found himself. Accordingly in June 1713 the Regent concluded a treaty with Frederick William by which Prussian and Holstein troops were to occupy Stettin, Wismar and the other Swedish possessions in order to secure their neutrality until the conclusion of peace, when they were to be restored to Sweden. Moreover, Prussia was to use her influence with Denmark to induce the Danes to evacuate Holstein-Gottorp and to agree to the succession of Charles Frederick to the Swedish throne. When he became King of Sweden, Charles Frederick was to hand over to Prussia Stettin and the Southern part of Swedish Pomerania. Thus Prussia hoped to obtain a hold on Swedish Pomerania which might prove exceedingly useful; but the whole scheme broke down because General von Meyerfeldt, the Governor of Stettin, declined to accept it without the assent of Charles XII.

Unable to obtain Stettin by negotiation with Sweden, Prussia had to fall back cn an agreement with Russia, whose troops proceeded to renew the siege of the town. For some months it held out, but in September 1713 the garrison had to capitulate, receiving a free passage to Sweden, while the town was handed over to the Prussians by the Russian general Mentschikov, with whom Frederick William concluded the Convention of Schwedt (Oct. 6th, 1713). This arranged for the occupation of Pomerania by the Prussians, who were to keep it neutral and prevent the Swedes using it as a base from which to attack the Allies. This convention marked the point at which Prussia found herself forced to cultivate better relations with Russia, of whom she had hitherto been extremely jealous and suspicious: it was mainly due to the conclusion of the Peace of Utrecht, which set the Maritime Powers free to interfere in the Baltic, in which case it was to be feared they might seek to bring about peace on the basis of *uti possidetis* before Prussia had had time to make any acquisitions. The next step in the Russo-Prussian alliance was a fresh convention, concluded in June 1714, by which Russia pledged herself to see Prussia secured in possession of Stettin and Pomerania to the Peene river, with the islands of Wollen and Usedom, Prussia undertaking a similar obligation towards Russia with regard to Carelia, Esthonia and Ingermannland.

But before this new alliance could lead to any definite result the situation was completely altered by the sudden reappearance of Charles XII, who arrived at Stralsund in November 1714 after an adventurous and circuitous journey from Turkey, while a few months earlier the death of Queen Anne had placed the British crown on the head of George Louis of Hanover and the British fleet at the disposal of the "Electoral" aims of the new King. Hitherto England had been absolutely neutral in the Baltic struggle, though her commercial interests in those quarters caused her to watch events there with great care. There had been a good deal of friction between England and Sweden over the capture by Swedish privateers of English merchantmen trading with Russia, and thereby infringing the "paper" blockade of the Russian coast which Sweden had declared.[1] England was therefore not merely serving an "Electoral"

[1] Cf. *England and Hanover* (A. W. Ward), p. 89.

policy when in 1715 she despatched a strong fleet to the Baltic. Indeed, but for the domestic complications of Anne's last few months, it is probable that ships would have been sent before the accession of George.

The object upon which George I was most keenly set was the acquisition of Bremen and Verden, districts which would add enormously to the strength of his Hanoverian possessions. Jealousy of Russia and Prussia, however, made him disinclined to take part with them against Sweden, and he tried hard to persuade Charles to cede the coveted territory to him as the reward for Anglo-Hanoverian assistance against the Czar and the King of Prussia. But Charles with equal obstinacy and blindness refused this offer, which though certainly not dictated by generosity or by a wish to help Sweden, did hold out to him better prospects than he could hope to secure if he rejected it. This refusal drove George I into joining the Russo-Prussian alliance, to which Denmark also acceded. In June 1715 the forces of the Coalition began the attack on Sweden's last transmarine possessions; the Hanoverians and Danes laid siege to Wismar, a mixed army of Danes, Russians and Saxons accompanied by a Danish squadron undertook the reduction of Stralsund, freedom from interruption by sea being secured by the presence of Norris and the English fleet, which could be relied upon to exercise a restraining influence over the Swedish naval forces.

The undertaking was no mere military promenade. The Swedes resisted stoutly, and not till they had been driven from the island of Usedom (July 31st) could the siege-train be brought up along the coast from Stettin. On August 22nd they were driven from their lines at Peenemünde, on September 25th the Danish ships forced the passage into the Rügen Sound. Even then Stralsund held out, and it was found necessary to obtain complete possession of Rügen, a task successfully accomplished by Leopold of Anhalt-Dessau on November 15th and 16th. At last it became obvious even to Charles that further resistance was hopeless, and on December 21st he made his escape by sea; three days later Stralsund capitulated and received a Danish garrison. In April 1716 the fall of Wismar deprived Sweden of her last foothold in Germany.

Had the Allies been in anything approaching to union,

the end of the war could not have been long delayed, but their quarrels and cross - purposes gave Charles time to protract his resistance for some years yet. Into the kaleidoscopic negotiations, schemes and intrigues of 1716–1718 it would be hopeless to enter: Görtz, Alberoni, the Scottish Jacobites, all conceivable alliances and arrangements fill the time. One or two things, however, are clear. Among the most important factors in the situation was the hostility of Hanover and Russia, which might even have brought about an alliance between Russia and Sweden when the death of the Swedish King, when attacking the Norwegian fortress of Frederickshald (Nov. 1718), ended his adventurous career and made the restoration of peace possible. Charles XII, despite all his triumphs in the field, had done more harm to his own country than to his enemies.

This hostility between George I and Peter became acute over the affairs of Mecklenburg and Schleswig - Holstein. When George made the arrangement with Denmark by which he received Bremen (1715), he had assented to the annexation by Denmark of Schleswig, against which the Duke of Holstein-Gottorp protested, being supported in this by Peter, who now championed the cause of Duke Charles Frederick and gave him his daughter Anne in marriage in 1716. Secondly, the Russian corps which had passed through Mecklenburg in the spring of 1716 on its way to Zealand to take part in a proposed descent on Southern Sweden, had had some share in the capture of Wismar, and Peter had therefore laid claim to the port. Much to his irritation his allies refused, not wishing to see him established so near the Elbe. Now as his troops returned from Zealand in the autumn of 1716, the descent having been abandoned, they halted in Mecklenburg and took up their winter-quarters there. In this way Peter was able to interfere in the constitutional quarrel then raging in Mecklenburg-Schwerin, where the Estates were resisting the efforts of their Duke, Charles Leopold, to alter the administrative system in the direction of absolutism. The Duke seized the chance of securing Russian aid, married Catherine, daughter of Peter's brother Ivan, and confiscated the lands of the nobles who had appealed to the Emperor. It was about this time that Peter was making overtures to France for an alliance in which Russia would have replaced Sweden as the Northern ally of the Bourbons.[1] England and France, however, were on the verge of concluding the alliance by which Stanhope and Dubois sought to maintain the situation established at Utrecht,[2] and Russia could obtain no more from France than a simple treaty of amity.   Another result of the Anglo-French treaty was that Peter found it expedient to evacuate Mecklenburg, though some of his troops remained there in the service of Charles Leopold.[3]

In response to the appeal of the Mecklenburg Estates, an Imperial rescript committed the task of restoring the old constitution to Hanover and Brunswick-Wolfenbüttel, who in February 1719 poured 13,000 troops ·into the Duchy, and despite a check at Waldemühlen on the Sudo (March), occupied the territory and carried out the decree of the Empire, Charles Leopold being thus suppressed despite Peter's patronage.

The death of Charles XII had led to considerable changes in Sweden: the fall of Görtz was one of the earliest, for there was no party in favour of the Duke of Holstein-Gottorp. Ulrica Eleanora and her husband Frederick of Hesse-Cassel secured the throne without much difficulty, though the nobles succeeded in recovering much of the power of which they had been deprived by Charles XI.   The new monarchs were not going to repeat Charles XII's folly in refusing any terms which involved the loss of territory.   They soon came to terms with George I, and in November 1719 the Peace of Stockholm recognised him as possessor of Bremen and Verden in return for a sum of 1,000,000 Reichsthalers. George now exerted himself to secure good terms for Sweden from her other foes.   By Carteret's mediation, Sweden recovered Stralsund, Rügen and Wismar from Denmark (July 1720), while Frederick William, though loath to make a peace in which Russia was not included, had already agreed to pay Sweden an indemnity of 2,000,000 dollars, but retained his conquests up to the Peene (Feb. 1720).   With regard to Poland, Sweden had only to abandon her unfortunate protégé Leczinski, for whom she could do nothing.

George I had thus so far attained his ends that he had

---

[1] Cf. Martin, xiv. pp. 81 ff.
[2] Anglo-French alliance signed November 28th, 1716.
[3] Cf. *England and Hanover*, p. 96.

isolated Russia—the only Power still hostile to Sweden—and England seemed .on the high road to a war against Russia on behalf of Sweden when the collapse of the South Sea Company and the financial crisis which followed involved the fall of the Stanhope-Sunderland section of the Whig party. With the accession of Walpole and his followers to office a new policy was introduced into the councils of England; all idea of active intervention in the Baltic was abandoned, and Sweden, left to her own resources, was not able to get very favourable terms from Russia. The Peace of Nystadt (Sept. 10th, 1721) marks the definite transfer of supremacy in the Baltic from Sweden to Russia. With the loss of Carelia, Esthonia, Ingermannland, Livonia and the islands of Dago, Moen and Oesel, Sweden's day of greatness came to an end, and Russia was firmly established as the dominant power in the North-East of Europe.

The twenty years of war which this Peace brought to an end afford in a way as striking an illustration of the weakness of Germany as does the treatment which the Empire received at Utrecht and Rastatt. Fought out though it was largely by German troops and on German soil, German interests played but little part in the struggle and received but little attention in the Peace. Prussia had, indeed, won the important city of Stettin and had gained control of the mouth of the Oder; the German districts of Bremen and Verden had passed from Sweden to one who was himself a German, even if he owed his acquisition in no small measure to non-German sources of strength, while the definite cession of Schleswig to Denmark (1721) was not without importance for the future. But the main result of the war was that though the Baltic had changed masters it was still under non-German control.

[Authorities for this chapter, besides Erdmannsdörffer and Zweidineck Südenhorst, articles in *E.H.R.* on "The Foreign Policy of England under Walpole," 1900 and 1901 f. ; Ward, *England and Hanover* ; Nisbet Bain, *Charles XII.*]

CHAPTER IV

PASSAROWITZ, SICILY AND THE PRAGMATIC SANCTION

A USTRIA had barely got rid of the great struggle for the Spanish inheritance when she found herself called upon to embark upon a new war against her hereditary foe in the South-East. Their success over the Russians in 1711 had much encouraged the Turks in their desire to retrieve the losses of Carlowitz, and they saw in the defenceless state of the Morea an opportunity for further gain. Both the Sultan Achmet and the new Grand Vizier, Damad Ali Pasha, were ambitious and aggressive, and they believed that the Venetian territories would prove an easy prey, and that the international situation would restrain the Great Powers from coming to the help of the Republic. They were both right and wrong. Right inasmuch as the Venetian hold on the Morea proved of the feeblest. Unprepared and unpopular, the Venetian garrisons were speedily swept out of the Peninsula, Cerigo followed suit, the Ionian Islands were in the gravest peril: only from Dalmatia were the Turks repulsed. Wrong because despite the critical condition of affairs in the North and despite the fear of possible complications in Italy—for Philip of Spain had never acquiesced in the arrangements of Utrecht, and would probably seize upon any embarrassment of Austria to interfere—the Emperor at the advice of Eugene decided to aid Venice.[1]

The first necessity was to send succour to Corfu, a point of great strategic importance, as its capture would enable the Turks to threaten Southern Italy and Sicily and would give their fleet a splendid base from which to operate in the Adriatic. Accordingly, by Eugene's advice an officer of great experience

---

[1] In April 1716 the Austro-Venetian treaty of 1684 was renewed, Venice promising her aid in case of a Spanish attack on the Italian possessions of Austria.

and capacity, John Matthias von Schulenburg, was sent to take command at Corfu (Dec. 1715), and his exertions were largely responsible for the fact that when the Turkish fleet threw 30,000 men into the island in July 1716, its defences and defenders were not found wanting.

Meanwhile Eugene, who was very anxious that the work which had been left unfinished at Carlowitz should be brought to completion, had been making great efforts to get ready an efficient army for the campaign on the Danube. As president of the War Council, Eugene was himself responsible for the readiness of the army; and though the chronic emptiness of the Treasury proved a serious hindrance to the mobilisation, he was able in July to collect 220 squadrons and 67 battalions, about 80,000 men in all, at Peterwardein. Meanwhile the Grand Vizier had assembled 200,000 men at Belgrade and advanced up the Danube. Eugene withdrew his men into the lines constructed at Peterwardein in the previous war by Caprara, and there gave battle (Aug. 5th). The fight was hotly contested; at one time the Austrian right became disordered owing to the difficulties of the ground, and the centre was also checked, but a dashing charge by Eugene and the heavy cavalry on the left restored the fortunes of the day and allowed the hard-pressed infantry to rally and recover their ground. Finally, after a most even struggle the Turks were overthrown with very heavy loss, the Grand Vizier being among the killed.

Eugene followed up his victory by laying siege to Temeswar, a strong and well-built fortress, which was so resolutely defended that there was time for a relieving army to be gathered together, though only to be beaten off on September 23rd. This sealed the fate of the town, which surrendered on October 13th after a bombardment, passing under Hapsburg rule after having been for a hundred and sixty-four years a Turkish possession. With it a large part of the Banat came into Austrian hands, including Pancsova and Mehadia. Another effect of the victory was that the besiegers of Corfu abandoned the attack on the hard-pressed fortress (Aug. 25th) on receiving the news of the battle, though no doubt the repulse of a grand assault they had delivered two days before contributed to induce them to retire.

With the Banat theirs, the next task for the Austrian

forces was to recover Belgrade, which they had lost in
1690 after a brief tenure. Early in June 1717 all was
ready for an advance. On the 14th, two corps from Peterwardein and from the Banat, including contingents from
Bavaria and Hesse-Darmstadt, united at Pancsova. Next
day the vanguard crossed the Danube by boats and constructed
bridges by which the main body crossed on the 19th
Belgrade was at once invested, but bad weather delayed the
siege operations, and it was not till July 22nd that the
bombardment could be begun. On that day the new Grand
Vizier, Chalil Pasha, had reached Semendria at the head
of a relieving army with which he proceeded to make a
raid into the Banat, and then, seeing that this would not
cause Eugene to relax his grip on the beleaguered city,
moved thither himself and took up a strong position with
his right on the Danube. Eugene, thus hemmed in, was
forced to hurl his troops directly against the Turkish camp,
strongly posted though it was (Aug. 16th). His scheme
for the attack [1] contemplated that his left should begin
the battle, but a heavy mist upset the plan. Some of
the troops went altogether astray and left a large gap
in the line, which had to be filled by bringing up part
of the second line. However, the attack proved a complete
success, the right outflanked the Turkish position, and after
two hours of fighting they were in complete flight, and
their camp in Austrian hands. At a cost of 1500 killed
and 3500 wounded, the victors had inflicted a loss of 20,000
on the Turks and decided the fate of Belgrade. Two
days after the battle the capitulation was signed, and on
the 22nd the Turks evacuated the town.

It might have been thought that two such campaigns would
have inspired the Emperor with a determination to push his
successes still further. The Turks had received two crushing
defeats from which it would be hard to rally. It seemed that
Austria had the ball at her feet, and that a vigorous prosecution of the war could hardly fail to give her secure possession
of the valley of the Lower Danube. But the opportunity
was allowed to pass and did not return again. For reasons
quite unconnected with the situation on the Danube, the
Emperor was ready to accept the proposals for peace

[1] Cf. *Z.S.* ii. 597.

which the new Vizier, Ibrahim, laid before Eugene. The contingency contemplated in the Austro-Venetian treaty had arisen. In August 1717 a Spanish squadron arrived off Cagliari and landed a force which occupied the island of Sardinia almost without any opposition.

The reasons for this move are not far to seek. Philip V of Spain had never abandoned his claim on the former possessions of the Spanish crown in Italy, just as Charles VI had adhered to his pretensions to be King of Spain. Moreover, his marriage with the intriguing and active Princess of Parma, Elizabeth Farnese, by whom he was all but exclusively influenced, had given him additional motives for desiring to upset the Utrecht arrangements. Elizabeth's great aim was to obtain separate establishments for her sons, since Philip's children by his first marriage would naturally succeed to Spain, and she hoped to do this by preventing the Emperor from carrying out his design of obtaining the reversion of the Imperial fiefs of Parma, Piacenza,[1] Tuscany[2] and Guastalla. With this attempt the name of Alberoni will always be associated, though here it would hardly be appropriate to relate the measures by which that able and enterprising minister sought to bring the undertaking to a successful conclusion. But it may be mentioned that the refusal of Great Britain to accept the highly advantageous offers of commercial concessions which Alberoni made in hopes of securing her support must in part be attributed to the German policy of George I as Elector of Hanover. It was not only his general policy of loyalty to the Empire, but the particular desire to get the Imperial sanction for his acquisition of Bremen and Verden, which bound George to the Austrian alliance. At the same time it would be inaccurate to regard these as the only causes of the rejection of Alberoni's offers. As long as Gibraltar and Minorca remained in British hands an alliance between England and Spain was not very probable. Moreover, in May 1716 the breach which the events of 1712–1713 had caused between Austria and England had been smoothed over by the Treaty of Westminster, by which the Whigs sought to revive the old alliance which Bolingbroke had abandoned.

[1] In the hands of Alessandro Farnese, last Duke of Parma.
[2] Gaston de Medici, the Duke, was childless.

This Anglo-Austrian Treaty, however, did not involve Austria in any connection with the United Provinces, once again joined to England by the treaty of January 1716, nor did the Anglo-French alliance, concluded in November 1716, at first include Austria. However, when Spain, provoked by the arrest (May 1717) of the Spanish Grand Inquisitor on his way through Lombardy, hastened into war with Austria, although Alberoni had only had two of the five years he had asked for in which to make his preparations, the Emperor appealed for help to the Triple Alliance, and the negotiation of the Convention of London (April 1718) was followed by the conclusion in August of the Quadruple Alliance.[1] But before this took place, the peace had been negotiated by which Austria turned back from the path which lay open before her, and for the sake of a transitory rule over Sicily, sacrificed the best chance she was ever to have of securing predominance in South-Eastern Europe at the expense of the Turk. The Peace of Passarowitz (July 21st, 1718), which was brought about by the efforts of England and Holland, accepted as its basis the principle of *uti possidetis*. This left to the Emperor the Banat, Northern Servia, including, of course, Belgrade, Wallachia as far as the Aluta, and a small district in Bosnia, but confirmed Candia and the Morea to the Turks. Venice, however, retained enough places on the Albanian and Dalmatian coasts[2] to have good security for the safety of the Ionian Islands. The Peace of Passarowitz is, it is true, the high-water mark of the tide of Austrian reconquest, and to that extent it may be reckoned among Austria's days of greatness, but from the point of view of what might have been done, it must be regretted as a half measure, or rather as a fatal mistake. That the Crescent still floats at Constantinople may be attributed in part to Charles VI's fatal preference for the former possessions of the Spanish crown once so nearly his. Had Austria pushed on in 1718, when Russia was so fully occupied with the Baltic War that she could not have interfered, the " Balkan question " might have been solved before it ever arose. And, indeed, it was hardly

---

[1] This included one treaty between the Emperor and England, France and Holland, and another between the Emperor and Victor Amadeus of Sicily.

[2] *e.g.* Butrinto, Prevesa, Vonizza.

necessary to have stopped Eugene's victorious progress for
the defence of Italy.   True, that the Spaniards followed up
their successful descent on Sardinia by an equally successful
descent on Sicily in 1718, that Palermo capitulated almost
at once (July), and that the ease with which the Spaniards
conquered the island was good evidence of the unpopularity
of the Savoyard rule.   But this success was of little avail
when Byng, by destroying the Spanish fleet off Cape Passaro
(Aug. 11th), asserted the British control of the Mediterranean
and severed the expeditionary forces from Spain.   France
and England combined were too much for the renascent power
of Spain, and Austria was able, not without some hard fighting
and one sharp check,[1] to recover Sicily.   Philip found himself compelled to give way, to dismiss Alberoni and to agree
to the terms proposed by the Quadruple Alliance.   Austria
obtained the coveted Sicily, in exchange for the valueless
Sardinia; Charles VI renounced his claims on Spain and the
Indies, Philip V his on Italy and the Netherlands; the
succession to Parma and Tuscany was promised to the
children of Elizabeth Farnese.[2]

With the Treaties of Passarowitz, of London, of Stockholm
and of Nystadt, one seems to have the questions which had
been agitating Europe settled on a basis which offered a
fair prospect of peace.   But this settlement was not in any
way final.   It was only the prelude to a series of conventions, coalitions, alliances, leagues and treaties which fill the
next decade.   Elizabeth Farnese and Charles VI between
them were to trouble the chanceries of Europe, not once
but many times in the next ten years, and if there were
to be few wars, that was not to be from want of "rumours
of war."

Yet at this time, as in 1648, the chief concern of the
states of Germany was with their internal affairs, and their
chief need was peace and quiet, financial reform, the restoration of order, and reorganisation in general.   Charles VI,
however, failed to realise this, failed to pay proper attention
to these urgent domestic needs, and unable to forget that
he had once been King of Spain, devoted himself to futile
efforts to reverse the arrangements of Utrecht, when the
internal condition of the Hapsburg dominions and of the

---

[1] At Francoville, June 1719.   Treaty of London, January 1720.

Empire afforded ample scope for all the energies of the most active and ambitious of statesmen.

One of the measures most characteristic of the way in which, renunciations or no renunciations, Charles VI could not bring himself to accept the rule of Philip V in Spain, was the maintenance of a separate government for his Italian and Belgian possessions, which he looked upon as his in virtue of his rights as King of Spain and, consequently, as quite unconnected with the other dominions over which he ruled. Thus he established a separate "Spanish Council" to administer their affairs, and governed them through Spaniards of the party which had remained faithful to him, a circumstance which partly contributed to the ease with which his South Italian possessions slipped out of his grasp in 1733. Moreover, it was unfortunate that his Spanish tastes caused him to pay great attention to the views of these exiles in other matters of state with which they were hardly qualified to deal. The existence, therefore, of this dual system went far to increase the want of unity which was the great weakness of the Hapsburg dominions and which in another way Charles was striving hard to check.

Between the disconnected dominions of the Hapsburgs, which had indeed a central financial authority in the *Hofkammer* and a central military authority in the *Hofkriegsrath*, but were in all other matters quite independent of each other, the dynasty was the only real link. Yet the dynasty itself was threatened with a failure of male heirs. Not only had Joseph died without a son, but Charles had none surviving, and there were no male descendants of younger sons of previous Emperors to take up the burden. The heir of the Hapsburgs must be a female. It was on this account that Leopold I had in 1703 attempted to regulate the succession by making a formal arrangement (*pactum mutuæ successionis*) that, in default of a male heir, females should succeed by primogeniture, the special proviso being added that Joseph's daughters should precede those of Charles.[1] At that time, however, the existence of two separate branches of the family had been contemplated, Joseph's at Vienna, that of Charles at Madrid, whereas since then Charles had

---

[1] Cf. *Z.S.* ii. 559, etc.; also A. Bachmann, *Die Pragmatische Sanction und die Erbfolgeordnung Leopold I's.*

succeeded to the whole Hapsburg heritage, and so might fairly claim that the case was altered and that the natural order of succession would place his own daughters before those of his brother.   Accordingly in 1713 he issued a family law altering the order of succession,—which, after all, he had as good a right to do as had Leopold or any other head of the family—and putting his own daughters before those of Joseph.   This done, he had to obtain the assent to this arrangement, known as the Pragmatic Sanction, of the daughters of Joseph and of the Estates of his various dominions, and also to induce the Powers of Europe to recognise it.

With the first two this was not hard.   He was able to extract an acceptance of the Pragmatic Sanction from the Archduchess Maria Josepha when she married the Electoral Prince of Saxony in 1719; a similar formal renunciation was made by his other niece, Maria Amelia, on her marriage to the Electoral Prince Charles Albert of Bavaria.   The assent to the arrangement of the Estates of Upper and Lower Austria, Bohemia, Carinthia, Moravia and Silesia was secured in 1720; Tyrol followed suit, but "saving its freedom and rights"; Croatia agreed in 1721, Hungary and Transylvania in 1722, the Netherlands in 1724.

To obtain its recognition by the Powers was, however, another matter, and was the guiding principle in all the foreign relations of the Emperor, determining his actions to the exclusion of other motives.   The first step to which it led him was a somewhat remarkable change of front.   An international congress was opened at Cambrai in 1722 to try to settle outstanding difficulties, but its negotiations broke down over the commercial quarrels of the Maritime Powers with the Emperor and with Spain.   Elizabeth Farnese found that her Italian schemes would receive no support from England and France, the Spanish ministers, who set the prosperity of their country before the interests of the dynasty, found England unyielding on the question of the West Indian trade, and the Emperor, annoyed at the opposition of the Maritime Powers to his favourite commercial scheme, the Ostend East India Company, drew nearer his old enemy, Philip of Spain. Through the instrumentality of Ripperda, a Dutch adventurer in the Spanish service, the League of Vienna was concluded in May 1725. The keynote of this surprising arrangement was the proposal for a double marriage between the two daughters of the Emperor and the two sons of Elizabeth Farnese, the idea being that Don Carlos as the husband of the elder sister should be elected King of the Romans, while Don Philip and the Archduchess Maria Anna should receive the Italian possessions of the family. Renunciations were exchanged by the Emperor and the King; and while Austria promised her good offices towards obtaining Minorca and Gibraltar for Spain, Philip V recognised the Pragmatic Sanction and promised his support to the Ostend Company, which was to be put on the same footing in West Indian waters as England and Holland.

This Ostend Company was the result of the adoption by Prince Eugene and the Emperor of a scheme, begun by private enterprise, to develope the trade of the Austrian Netherlands and to utilise the natural advantages of their geographical position, hitherto restrained and hampered by the artificial trammels of the Peace of Münster and the Barrier Treaty. So much success had attended the first efforts of the enterprise that Dutch hostility was greatly excited, and they proceeded to seize Belgian vessels and treat them as good prize. Upon this the Emperor took the enterprise under his protection, and the Ostend Company was formed in June 1722, to trade with the East and West Indies and with Africa. The Company established factories at Canton, in Bengal and on the Coromandel Coast; and its progress was soon such as to excite the jealousy of the Maritime Powers. It was not merely its commercial success which alarmed the eager traders of Amsterdam, for whose benefit Spain had been forbidden to trade to the Indies from Belgium in 1648.[1] It was not merely that Ostend promised to become a great trading centre, as Trieste was doing in the Adriatic; complete success would have made the Emperor much less dependent on the naval strength of Maritime Powers. Hence England supported the Dutch in their opposition to the Company; while France, though less concerned in the affairs of the Ostend Company

---

[1] The Emperor's contention was that the Netherlands had been thus restricted by the Treaty of Münster, because in Spanish hands they had ceased to be part of the Empire with which they were now reunited, so that the restrictions had ceased to apply to them. Cf. *Z.S.* ii. 622.

and anxious to avoid a war with Austria and Spain, followed
—without enthusiasm—in the lead of England.

The result was that while Russia, Bavaria, Cologne,[1]
Treves[2] and the new Elector Palatine, Charles Philip
of Neuburg, who had succeeded his brother, John William,
in 1716, adhered to the League of Vienna, a counter-
coalition was formed by Townshend in the shape of the
League of Herrnhaüsen (Sept. 1725), which included
England, Holland, France and Prussia.[3] With Europe
thus arrayed in two hostile camps, a great war seemed
imminent. But except for Elizabeth Farnese, no one really
desired war: the unnatural Austro-Spanish alliance was
already showing signs of weakness, since neither partner
displayed any intention of carrying out the pledges they had
undertaken. Ripperda's unpopularity forced the Queen to
discard him in favour of Patinol in May 1726. There was a
strong party at Vienna, led by Eugene and Stahremberg,
which was opposed to the idea of the Spanish match; and
though the Spaniards undertook a fruitless siege of Gibraltar,
while England blockaded Porto Bello and stopped the West
Indian trade, the war did not spread to Germany or become
general. In March 1728 the Convention of the Pardo brought
the Anglo-Spanish war to an end, and in the summer a
Congress was opened at Soissons.

The upshot of the Congress of Soissons was that in
November 1729, Spain came to terms with England, France
and Holland. The uncertainty as to the succession in France,
the chief cause of the hostility which had, since 1715, prevailed
between Spain and her natural ally France, and which had
driven her into allying with her chief rival in Italy, was
removed by the birth of the Dauphin (1729), and with the
anti-Spanish party gaining the ascendant at Vienna and the
Austro-Spanish marriage proposals obviously abandoned, Spain
was ready enough to throw over the Emperor and the Ostend

---

[1] Clement Augustus, Archbishop-Elector and Bishop of Osnabrück, Paderborn,
Münster and Hildesheim, a Bavarian Wittelsbach, elected in 1723.

[2] Archbishop-Elector Francis Louis, also a Wittelsbach, elected in 1716.

[3] Subsequent additions to this coalition were Hesse-Cassel (March 1726),
Denmark (April 1727) and Sweden (1727), though in October 1726 Count
Seckendorf detached Prussia from the League and bound her to the Emperor by
the Treaty of Wüsterhausen, which promised Jülich and Berg to Prussia, Frederick
William guaranteeing the Pragmatic Sanction.

Company, and to fulfil the commercial clauses of the Peace of Utrecht in return for a guarantee of the Italian Duchies to Don Carlos. To obtain the Emperor's assent to the Treaty of Seville was a more difficult task. Townshend had been successful in breaking up the League of Vienna without a war; he was anxious to avoid having to join France, Spain and Holland in forcing terms upon Charles VI, who had drawn closer his alliance with Russia in December 1728. And when ministerial changes in England resulted in Townshend's resigning his Secretaryship of State (May 1730), thereby giving place to William Stanhope, Lord Harrington, it was the pacific Walpole who was left at the head of the government. He was very anxious to maintain good relations with France and Spain, mainly for commercial reasons, but he saw in the Pragmatic Sanction a way of escape from the dilemma in which he was placed. George II guaranteed it both as King of England and as Elector of Hanover, and this induced the Emperor to give way on points on which he had hitherto resisted. By the Second Treaty of Vienna (March 16th, 1731) he abolished the Ostend Company, promised that Don Carlos should succeed to the Italian Duchies, and agreed to the occupation of several towns in Parma and Tuscany by Spanish troops.[1] This arrangement was, however, only secured at the cost of a rift within the lute of the Anglo-French alliance, for Fleury was very loath to guarantee the Pragmatic Sanction, and declined to follow England's lead, though Holland did do so. The truth was that the exceptional circumstances which had brought about the Anglo-French alliance were ceasing to exist: France and Spain were no longer necessary enemies, Chauvelin was using his influence against England, trade rivalries were forcing themselves to the front, and the question of Dunkirk was a fruitful source of disagreement.

The Second Treaty of Vienna marks the close of one distinct period of alliances and combinations. It did not give Europe the peace which Walpole desired, but the quarrel which was to bring about a renewal of war two years later may be more

---

[1] This took place, 6000 Spaniards being escorted to Leghorn by the English fleet and quartered in Parma and Tuscany, much to the disgust of Duke Gaston de Medici. In 1732, the Duke of Parma being dead, Don Carlos obtained possession of the territories of the Farnese, which the Emperor had actually occupied on the Duke's death.

justly regarded as the prelude to the War of the Austrian Succession than as part and parcel of the efforts to upset the Peace of Utrecht. The so-called War of the Polish Succession began, it is true, in that international storm-centre, but it owes its importance to having been the first attack of the Bourbon Powers, reunited by the first of the Family Compacts, upon the Hapsburg dominions.

It must certainly be admitted that in all these negotiations and coalitions, one has heard little of German powers and nothing of Germany. Charles was to some extent acting as head of the Empire in his attempts to give the trade of Germany an outlet to the ocean through his own dominions, but the real importance to Germany of all these diplomatic variations lies in the underlying attempt to get the Pragmatic Sanction recognised by the Powers. And in this Charles had been fairly successful. Spain had been the first to give her guarantee (in May 1725), Russia came next (August 1726), then (September 1st) the four Wittelsbach Electors, Bavaria, Cologne, the Palatinate and Treves, followed in October by Prussia at the Treaty of Wüsterhausen. The Elector of Mayence, the Duke of Brunswick, and various other minor Princes were also secured; and though Charles Albert of Bavaria, who had succeeded Maximilian Emmanuel in February 1726, withdrew his recognition on the ground that the terms of the treaty of 1726 had never been fulfilled, and assisted by Saxony and the Palatinate obstructed the Emperor's efforts to obtain the assent of the Diet, this was secured in 1732, just after the concessions to Don Carlos and the abandonment ot the Ostend Company had won the recognition of the Pragmatic Sanction by England, Hanover and the United Provinces. Still, as the event was to prove, these guarantees were little more than paper, and it would have been better if Charles VI had devoted his time to the constructive reforms which might have given his dominions the unity and coherence which they so badly needed and which would have been a far surer safeguard.

CHAPTER V

PRUSSIA UNDER FREDERICK WILLIAM I

IF the minor Powers of Germany play but unimportant parts in international affairs in the years following on the Peace of Utrecht, it must be admitted that, apart from the troubles to which the retention of the "Ryswick clause" in the Peace of Baden gave rise, their internal affairs equally fail to afford much material for history. One is not accustomed to attribute to religious motives a very important influence on international affairs after 1648, but what had happened in that year was that the religious differences had been slurred over rather than settled, and so the strife continued, though in a somewhat different form. In the latter half of the seventeenth century, Roman Catholicism had been stronger and more aggressive than Protestantism; it had made marked progress among the upper classes, to whom it offered better social and financial prospects than did the rival creeds. Poverty and ambition had been effective missionaries in the leading Protestant families. Two[1] of the children of the "Winter-King" himself had been among the converts. Christian Louis of Mecklenburg-Schwerin had changed his faith in order to get a divorce which would let him marry one of the Montmorenci family; Ernest of Hesse-Rheinfels endeavoured by this means to gain the Imperial support in his disputes with his cousins at Hesse-Cassel. Of the conversion of Frederick Augustus of Saxony and of the change in the religion of the Elector Palatine with the accession of the Neuburgs, mention has already been made;[2] but it is important to notice that some authorities go so far as to call these religious differences the principal cause of the weakness and disunion of Germany at this period.[3] Be that as it may,

[1] Edward, who married Anne of Gonzaga-Nevers, and Louise, a nun, *o.s.p.* 1709.
[2] Cf. pp. 39 and 44.
[3] *e.g.* de Broglie, *Frederic II et Marie Thérèse*, i. 250. Cf. Erdmannsdörffer, bk. iii. ch. 5.

religious dissensions did continue to give much trouble and to provide the Diet with the greater part of its occupation ; such a question, for instance, as the objection raised by the Protestants to the reduction in the " matricular " contribution of Cologne on the score that the falling off in the trade and revenue of that city was due to the oppression of its Protestant inhabitants.

Among those on whom the " Ryswick clause " bore most heavily were the Protestant subjects of the Elector Palatine. John William had been largely responsible for the clause, and he put it into force with unsparing vigour.   An era of persecution set in ; the churches and estates of the Calvinists were confiscated on the most flimsy pretexts, their freedom of worship was seriously hindered ; the Jesuits were greatly encouraged, and, despite all pledges to the contrary, were allowed to obtain control of the Faculty of Philosophy in the University of Heidelberg with disastrous results to the University.   By way of bringing pressure to bear on John William, Frederick I of Prussia, a sturdy and consistent Evangelical, who had refused to make concessions to the Catholics even to gain the coveted "Crown,"[1] had threatened to levy reprisals on his Catholic subjects in Westphalia, and had thereby induced the Elector to withdraw some of his edicts ; but John William's successor, Charles Philip (1716–1742), continued the policy of persecution.   In 1719 he forbade the use of the Heidelberg Confession of 1563, and refused to let the Calvinists share any longer in the use of the chief church of Heidelberg, that of the Holy Ghost. At this point Hanover, Hesse-Cassel and Prussia intervened and by making reprisals on their Catholic subjects forced Charles Philip to give way sulkily (Feb. 1720), one manifestation of his discontent being his removal of his official residence from Heidelberg to Mannheim.

A rather better known episode in this persecution is the treatment of the Protestants who formed a majority among the inhabitants of the Archbishopric of Salzburg.   Their Protestantism was of the staunchest, and nothing could induce them to forsake it.   From 1668 to 1687 they had suffered grievously from Archbishop Maximilian Gandulph von Kuenburg, but since his time peace had prevailed until the election

---

[1] Cf. E. Berner, *Auf den Briefwechsel König Friedrichs von Preussen und seiner Familie.*

of Leopold von Firmian as Archbishop in 1727. He at once instituted a vigorous persecution only to meet with a stubborn resistance. The Archbishop declared his subjects rebels, and called in Austrian troops to " dragonnade " them into submission ; and finally, in October 1731, he compelled them to leave their homes at the very shortest notice, not allowing the statutory three years' grace promised at Osnabrück. This proved Frederick William's opportunity, just as the Revocation of the Edict of Nantes had been his grandfather's. East Prussia had been depopulated and reduced almost to the condition of a desert by the ravages of cattle-disease and the plague, especially in 1709 and 1710, and Frederick William saw that the exiles would prove most desirable colonists. He therefore issued an edict (Feb. 1732) in which he offered a welcome to the Salzburgers, most of whom found their way to this haven of refuge ; some stopped on the way in Franconia and Swabia, others pushed on to the Netherlands, a few wandered as far afield as North America. Though attended with great difficulties, the settlement in East Prussia was on the whole a great success, and Frederick William managed to extort from the Archbishop compensation for the confiscated property of the emigrants.

But the recolonising of East Prussia with the Salzburgers is but a small item in the work which Frederick William I did for the Hohenzollern monarchy. His is not an attractive or an edifying personality, but his place in the history of Prussia is one of the greatest importance. If the Great Elector had laid the foundations, it was not everyone who could have built upon them with such sureness and success, who could have so filled up the gaps in the original design and improved upon it. The twin pillars on which the success of Frederick II's foreign policy rested, the highly efficient army and the centralised bureaucracy under the exclusive direction of the autocratic head of the State, were the work of Frederick William. Intensely practical, hard-working, unsparing of himself or others, harsh, narrow-minded, in some points petty, but thoroughgoing in every respect, Frederick William preached the gospel of hard work and efficiency, and did not fail to practise what he preached. As in the Great Elector's, so in Frederick William's political creed, absolutism was the chief article. He had a great idea of the kingly office, of its duties no less than of its rights and privileges. Regarding his position as held from God, he accepted the fullest responsibility for all the acts of the administration, no detail being too petty to escape his supervision, while even when immersed in details he did not lose sight of the principles involved.

From the moment of his accession it became obvious that the Prussian state was on the verge of sweeping changes. The gorgeous funeral which Frederick William gave to his father may be regarded as emblematic of the obsequies of the ceremonious and extravagant order which had prevailed under the first King in Prussia. A complete reform of the Court establishment ushered in the new system. The household was cut down to a fifth of what it had been, the salaries of the few officials who escaped being dismissed were greatly reduced, luxury was banished, an almost Spartan simplicity and economy became the order of the day. Similarly, all branches of the administration were subjected to a relentless purging of sinecures and abuses. Peculation and corruption were severely punished, inefficiency was stamped out, a new spirit and a new discipline infused into the public service. Moreover, measures of organic reform were introduced with a promptitude which showed that they had for the most part been devised in advance.

Thus in August 1713 there appeared an edict regulating the affairs of the royal Domains. The King took them completely into his own control, only letting them out on short terms, raised the rents wherever it was possible, took every opportunity of increasing the Domains by purchase, invested any surplus in this way, and declared the whole Domain inalienable. The success of all these reforms may best be judged from the fact that the revenues of the Domains, which in 1713 amounted to 1,800,000 thalers, had risen to 3,300,000 thalers by 1740, a sum all but equal to the 3,600,000 thalers produced by the General War Fund. Together with this went reforms in the administration. Hitherto the Domains' revenues, with those of the Mint, Post Office and Customs, had been under one set of officials, the direct taxes—specially allotted to the Army—being under the Military Board.[1] Frederick William worked up this system further: a General Directory was organised to supervise the local officials responsible for the Domains

---

[1] Erdmannsdörffer, ii. 486 ff.

and indirect taxes, a Director of the War Commission (*Generalkriegscommissariat*) was put over the "war taxes" (*Kriegsgefälle*); but as this arrangement seemed to produce two Finance Ministers, the Finance Chamber (*Generalrechenkammer*) was established in 1714 to control both.   However, this plan proved productive of much confusion and friction, and in 1723 Frederick William carried out a most radical change, abolishing the dual system, and substituting for it a central administrative body.   Of this new General Directory, formed by the amalgamation of the two existing branches, and organised in five departments each under a Minister, the King was himself the head.   To this central authority the local officials were completely subordinated, this arrangement practically doing away with the last shreds of local autonomy.

Corresponding to these changes in the financial administration was the supersession of the Privy Council, which had proved altogether too large for efficiency, as the chief engine of government.   The King's personal activity was largely responsible for this, but the definite allotment of business to the separate Ministers had much to do with it.   A leading feature in this whole scheme of reform was the delocalisation of the administration.   Vacancies were never filled by a native of the district in which they occurred, for Frederick William meant the officials to be his servants, looking only to him as their master, indifferent to any interests but his, a hierarchy working automatically as his delegates.   This, of course, involved the complete subordination of the local and municipal government to the central administration, the culmination of victory of the Prince (*Fürstenthum*) over the Estates (*Ständethum*).   The *Landtag* (Diet) completely lost its powers, the nobles, who retained their great social privileges, being reconciled to the new order by being almost identified with the army, to whose interests all other considerations were postponed.   On one occasion only was constitutional opposition offered.   This was in 1717, when Frederick William introduced a scheme for doing away with tenure by military service, substituting a tax of fifty thalers per annum on each knight's fee (*Ritterpferd*) to be paid to the war chest.   This aroused the nobles of East Prussia and Magdeburg, who objected greatly to being put on the same footing as the peasantry and townsfolk; but though the Magdeburg knights went so far as to appeal to the Emperor, who listened favourably to their complaints, Frederick William really triumphed. He granted the reduction of the tax from fifty to forty thalers as a concession to the Emperor, but this was a cheap price for the establishment of the principle. Equally successful was his attack on the municipal government. The towns were under petty oligarchies which kept the majority of the townsfolk out of any share in the government, so that the burghers benefited on the whole by being deprived of the relics of what had once been autonomy. The management of their finances was taken away from the towns and transferred to the central government, which also obtained control over justice and police, and in this way the old local oligarchies were really quite broken up, the royal tax-collector (*Steuer-rath*) in each town becoming the real head of the administration. If this government by the central authorities was oppressive and heavy, it was at least even-handed, economical and efficient.

The condition of judicial affairs afforded another field for the King's reforming activities. Almost immediately after his accession (June 1713), Frederick William adopted many of the reforms which Bartholdi, the Minister of Justice, had urged upon Frederick I in the previous year. He gave orders for the compilation of a code of Prussian law, of which an instalment was published by von Cocceji in 1721, though it was not till nearly the close of the century that the code was completed. Much was also done by von Cocceji at the head of the Court of Appeal in the way of clearing off arrears of work and accelerating the speed of judicial procedure so as to keep pace with new cases.

It was rather more difficult to obtain success when Frederick William turned his attention to the improvement of industrial conditions, as the fact that the old order continued to prevail over the border in Saxony and Hanover interfered considerably with his legislation as to the guilds, though an edict published in 1732 (*Handwerksgesetzgebung*) did subject them to State supervision and alter and adapt their bye-laws to new conditions. The object which Frederick William had before him in this branch of legislation was the development of the resources of the country. A system of rigid protection laid prohibitory duties on foreign competition and gave every encouragement to home manufactures. To aid the wool-weavers the export of wool and the import of English cloth were forbidden, while the whole army was clothed in local products.   Recognising that he had plenty of other occupation without dabbling in colonial expansion, Frederick William abandoned the ill-fated African enterprise of the Great Elector, and not even the acquisition of Stettin tempted him to try to develop an oversea commerce.   He sought to improve the social, and economic conditions of his subjects, but for a very definite purpose.   His aim was to improve their condition " not by lightening their burdens, but by increasing their capacity for bearing burdens."   For in all these reforms, in the centralising of the administration, in the increase and improvement of the Domains, in the accumulation of a great reserve war fund, in the bureaucratic organisation of the State under an autocratic ruler, Frederick William's great aim was to enable Prussia to support that large army, so out of all proportion to her territory and her population, which could alone give her weight in the councils of Europe.   It was as a military state that Prussia was organised, to the Army that everything else was sacrificed, military power that was the object for which the Prussian kingdom existed.   He is, perhaps, chiefly remembered on account of his favourite corps, the celebrated but not very serviceable " Potsdam Grenadiers " ; but it would be a grave error to let the solid merit of his military achievements be concealed behind their ranks.   It is a remarkable fact that Frederick William, one of the most successful organisers of an army there has ever been, should have been one of the most pacific and least belligerent of rulers.   His military fame must rest upon the army he built up and bequeathed to his son, not on what he himself did with it ; and yet that is a secure enough foundation for any reputation.   If he cannot be reckoned more than " a very good peace general," it is because he did not attempt to test the weapon he had forged, not because he tried and failed.

The Prussian army at the accession of Frederick William I mustered some 38,000 men.[1]   The new King's first step was to raise seven more regiments, and every political

---

[1] There was also a reserve in the shape of a Land Militia about 10,000 strong for home service or garrison duty, but it was before long disbanded as of little military value.

incident or complication was eagerly used as an excuse for fresh additions. By 1725 the army had been increased to 60 battalions of infantry and 100 squadrons of cavalry, a total, with garrison troops, of 64,000 men, of whom about 10,000 depôt and garrison troops were not available for field service. By 1740 its numbers had risen to 89,000, the field army comprising 66 battalions, 114 squadrons, including 9 of hussars, 6 companies of field and 4 of fortress artillery, and a Life Guard of 2500, the famous " Potsdam Grenadiers." But it was not merely its numbers which gave it importance. No effort was spared to increase its efficiency. A harsh and stern system of discipline was introduced and rigorously maintained. The utmost care was devoted to the exercising and training of the troops. Their drill was revolutionised by the introduction of a cadenced step and the reduction of the depth of formation from six ranks to three, both due to Leopold of Anhalt-Dessau. In all manœuvres a high standard was set up and reached, thus enabling the Prussian regiments to change from one formation to another with a rapidity and precision which was the wonder of the age. The movements of the parade-ground were accurately reproduced on the battlefield in a way which gave the Prussian generals a great advantage over less flexible and mobile opponents, who found it a matter of the greatest difficulty to change a position which they had once taken up, as their troops, being less carefully drilled, were apt to fall into confusion when they attempted to manœuvre in face of an enemy. Moreover, better discipline meant better fire-discipline, and the introduction of iron ramrods allowed a greater rapidity of fire. As a potent factor in producing a high state of efficiency the well-developed regimental system must not be forgotten. Of the value of *esprit de corps* Frederick William had a high opinion, and in his distribution of rewards and punishments he laid great stress upon it. Moreover, the partial territorialisation of the army encouraged a local feeling which helped to foster this regimental spirit.

To keep this great army up to its established strength was no very easy task, seeing that in population Prussia stood as low as twelfth among the countries of Europe, and that the army had to be raised by voluntary enlistment. It was found necessary, therefore, to supplement the local recruits by sending out recruiting-officers into the neighbouring countries, especially into the Imperial Cities. The Prussian recruiters made themselves notorious from Scandinavia to Transylvania, and from the Liffey to the Niemen; they were a constant source of friction with the authorities of other states, besides being a heavy expense.[1]

It was the difficulty and the great expense[2] of keeping up a voluntary army of the size which the King desired which at last decided Frederick William to adopt a system of modified conscription. In September 1733 he issued his famous "cantoning scheme," by which the country was divided into cantons, to which regiments were assigned for recruiting purposes, a regiment of infantry being allotted 6000 "hearths," one of cavalry 1800. Universal liability to service was recognised though with very liberal exemptions in favour of the nobles, the professional classes and certain trades which it was desired to specially encourage. This provided a fairly regular supply of recruits, but it was eked out by the enlistment of mercenaries on a large scale, so much so, indeed, that in 1768 only about half the army was composed of native Prussians, and at times during the Seven Years' War the proportion must have sunk even lower. One object in thus hiring foreigners was to let the native subjects of Frederick devote themselves to productive pursuits such as agriculture and manufactures, so that they might not be withdrawn from increasing the resources and tax-paying capacities of the kingdom. In time of peace, too, the native conscripts were only with the colours for a quarter of the year, being on unpaid furlough for the remaining nine months. The presence of the large proportion of foreigners of doubtful allegiance, together with the great harshness of the discipline and the many hardships of the soldier's lot, provides a sufficient explanation of the great prevalence of desertion in the Prussian army.

With the double purpose of bringing the nobles into closer touch with the Crown through the army, and of fostering

[1] A quarrel of this kind in 1729 nearly brought about a war between Prussia and Hanover, some Prussian recruiters having been arrested in Hanover, where the shelter given by the Prussian army to Hanoverian deserters was much resented.

[2] Out of the 7,000,000 thalers to which the total revenue amounted in 1740, no less than 5,000,000 were expended on the Army.

among them discipline and the military spirit, Frederick
William drew his officers almost exclusively from the native
nobility, who had hitherto held somewhat aloof from the service.
The exaggerated militarism so characteristic of the Prussian
"Junker" is due in large measure to this move on his part,
while the great social gulf between officers and men made it
easier to maintain that strict discipline and that rigid subordination of the lower ranks which were such marked features
of the Prussian system.   At the same time, it was made very
clear that the army was the King's army, that the officers were
the King's servants and their men the King's men rather than
theirs.   There was a struggle before the King could gain the
complete control over the appointment of the officers and over
the internal administrative economy of the regiments, but in the
end he prevailed, and the completeness of his victory marked
a great stride forwards towards absolutism.

With so strong a force at his disposal the unimportant
part played by Frederick William in international affairs is
a little surprising.   This was partly due to his natural caution
and self-control.   Unless he saw the issues clearly, he would
not let ambition or adventurousness plunge him into any
hazardous or uncertain enterprise.   Moreover, he was never
presented with such an opportunity as that which Charles vi's
death placed before Frederick ii.   Frederick William liked to
know how far he was committing himself, and preferred to
gain his ends by peaceful means, or, at any rate, with the
minimum outlay of blood or money.   It was most characteristic
of him that in his one warlike enterprise, his share in the
Northern War, he was fairly successful without acquiring
thereby anything of a military reputation.   With his other
great object, the acquisition of Jülich and Berg, he was less
fortunate than with his designs on Pomerania ; but it is nevertheless the key to his policy, more especially to his relations
with the Emperor.

The truth of the matter was that Prussia was not on good
terms with the majority of her neighbours, more especially
with Saxony and Hanover, the other leading Protestant Powers
of Germany with whom she might have been expected to be
friendly.   But Saxony through her connection with Poland
was the possessor of the coveted West Prussia, while between
Hanover and the Hohenzollern there were many causes of

hostility. Hanover had utilised the Mecklenburg affair [1] to plant herself firmly in that territory, and did not evacuate it until some time after the Emperor had deposed Duke Charles Leopold and replaced him by Christian Louis, his brother (May 1728), and declared the Imperial edict (*Reichexecution*) void, her defence for the continued occupation being that the costs of the execution had not been paid.[2] East Frisia, where the Cirksena family was on the point of dying out, was another open question. Hanover claimed it under a "blood-brotherhood" made in 1693; Prussia's claims upon it had been admitted by the Emperor at the time of the restitution of Schwiebus in 1692. But beyond this there was personal ill-feeling between the two reigning families: George I had not been on good terms with Frederick William, and George II's feelings towards his brother-in-law were exceedingly hostile, though at the time of the League of Herrenhaüsen (1725), Townshend so far overcame the hostility between George I and Frederick William as to enlist Prussia on the same side as Hanover.[3]

But the adherence of Prussia to the Maritime Powers was not of long duration. In October 1726, Frederick William, finding that he could get nothing from England and France but vague promises of support in the matter of Jülich and Berg, and having no intention of being involved in a war with

[1] Cf. p. 69.

[2] Christian Louis obtained control of Mecklenburg, though not without difficulty, and finally succeeded his brother as Duke in 1747.

[3] It is important to notice that to the English Ministers Prussia seemed a natural ally. This may be traced all through the relations of Prussia with England and Hanover; those English Ministers who hoped to hold their enemies, whether Spain or France, in check by alliances with the German Powers, looked upon securing the alliance of Prussia as an essential step. Thus one finds Sir Thomas Robinson endeavouring to reconcile Maria Theresa to the robber of Silesia, while Walpole favoured an alliance with Prussia for political and commercial reasons, but found himself opposed by Hanoverian prejudices and hatred of Prussia. Horace Walpole (the elder) writes to point out the importance of gaining Prussia to the side of the Maritime Powers (*Trevor MSS.*, Hist. MSS. Commission, p. 50; cf. p. 51: "Europe, England, and Hanover want a political union and intimacy, and as the safety of England depends on the balance of Europe, I think I can demonstrate that the security of Hanover depends on both: here I fix my point of view, and shall date the duration of our apparent friendship with Berlin upon the measures pursued for this end"). But "His Majesty (George II) continues very averse to do anything that squints in the least towards favouring the King of Prussia" (*ibid.* p. 5). Again, Hanoverian hostility to Prussia plays a part, though it has to give way in the end, in the negotiations which culminated in the Treaty of Westminster of 1756; cf. pp. 186 ff.

Austria and Russia in defence of Hanover, allowed Count
Seckendorff to win him over to the side of Austria; and the
Emperor promised to try to induce the Sulzbach branch of
the Wittelsbachs to agree to the compromise which Frederick
William was ready to accept.[1] The matter stood in this state:
Charles Philip of Neuburg, the Elector Palatine, who held
Jülich and Berg in virtue of the 1666 compact, had no son,
his brother, Francis Louis, Elector of Treves, was, of course,
unmarried, so that the next heir was Theodore, Count Palatine
of Sulzbach (1708-1732).[2] The Hohenzollern therefore
claimed that Jülich and Berg should fall to them on the failure
of the males of the Neuburg line; but Joseph of Sulzbach,
eldest son of Theodore, put in a claim both on his own
behalf as descended from the Dukes of Cleves and in virtue
of his wife, Elizabeth, the eldest daughter of Charles Philip.[3]
The Emperor also had something of a claim, his mother having
been a sister of Charles Philip; but this he declared himself
ready to waive, resigning Jülich to the Sulzbachs, Berg and
Ravenstein to Prussia, if both would agree.[4] Upon this
the treaty of 1726 with Prussia was converted into a
definite alliance, Prussia guaranteeing the Pragmatic Sanction
and pledging her support to the Emperor, more particularly
to the husband of Maria Theresa, who would be the natural
Hapsburg candidate for the next vacancy in the Empire.
But the pledges which Austria gave to Prussia on this subject
were of a rather vague and indefinite character; the Hapsburgs
had no great wish to see the Hohenzollern in these Duchies
rather than the Sulzbachs who were Catholics, and it must
be admitted that Charles vi played fast and loose with
Prussia in the matter; for in the hope of obtaining the assent
of the Sulzbachs to the Pragmatic Sanction the Emperor
endeavoured to come to terms with them over Jülich and
Berg, and to mollify them by inducing Prussia to assent to
a compromise decidedly in their favour. Thus the matter
lingered on till, in February 1738, Austria, England, France
and Holland presented identical notes calling upon Prussia
and the Sulzbachs to submit the question to a conference.
To this Frederick William refused to agree, and conscious of
his isolation and of Austria's preference for the Sulzbachs, he

[1] Cf. *Z.S.* ii. 628.
[2] Cf. Wittelsbach Genealogy, p. 707.
[3] *Ibid.*
[4] Erdmannsdörffer, ii. 427.

decided to make overtures to France and so secure a means
of putting pressure on the Emperor. Fleury, with the
prospect of being involved in the impending Anglo-Spanish
war, was glad of the chance of securing himself against
Prussia's hostility, as he feared she might be subsidised to
take part with England. In April 1739 a treaty was
signed by which France promised to induce Charles Philip
to agree to a partition which would leave most of Ravenstein
and Berg to Prussia, while compensating the Sulzbachs with
the remainder of the territory in dispute. A secret article
further pledged Prussia to closer co-operation with France.
But had it been the father and not the son who was on the
Prussian throne at the moment when the death of Charles VI
opened a question of the most momentous importance to
Germany, it would hardly have been in accord with the whole
tenor of Frederick William's policy to have allowed this
treaty to commit him to anything like the action which
Frederick II took. Not even the treatment he had received
over Jülich and Berg would have quite induced the cautious
Frederick William to bring French armies into the heart of
Germany.

CHAPTER VI

THE LAST WARS OF CHARLES VI

IT is only from the study in disorganisation and misfortune presented by the Hapsburg monarchy in the last two wars in which the luckless Charles VI engaged, that one can fairly estimate the perilous nature of the crisis which his death precipitated. The Emperor's own shortcomings as a ruler had no doubt much to answer for, but they were aggravated by the persistent misfortune which followed him throughout his career.

At the moment when the death of Frederick Augustus of Saxony-Poland (Feb. 1733) opened the ever thorny question of the succession to that realm of troubles, the old system which had united Austria, the Maritime Powers and the minor states of Germany against France and Spain seemed about to be revived. The bonds of the Anglo-French alliance were slackening, and anyone with a less purely insular attitude than Walpole must have seen that the change in the relations of France and Spain brought about by the birth of the Dauphin must materially affect the footing on which England stood towards her old enemy but present ally. To some extent the old relations between England and Austria had been restored by Walpole's guarantee of the Pragmatic Sanction, and Hanoverian traditions made George II favour supporting the Emperor.

However, when through the old connection between France and Poland the succession question developed into a general European war, the Anglo-French alliance proved strong enough yet to keep England out of the strife. The new Elector of Saxony, Augustus III as Elector but Frederick Augustus II as King of Poland, came forward at once as a candidate for the Polish throne, and succeeded in securing Austria's support by guaranteeing the Pragmatic Sanction, and abandoning for himself and his wife, the eldest daughter of Joseph I, all claims on the Hapsburg dominions. Russia

7

he won over by a promise to cede Courland to Count Biron, Catherine's favourite. Russia and Austria had not at first meant to support the Saxon, and had actually agreed with Prussia to adopt as their candidate Prince Emmanuel of Portugal.[1] But when the time came Emmanuel was found to be most unsuitable, and, moreover, Russia had never ratified the treaty. Thus, much to the disgust of Frederick William, to whom the presence of the Saxon line at Warsaw was most distasteful, the Löwenwolde arrangement was thrown over, and with it slipped away the chance that something might be done for Augustus William, Frederick William's second son. The opposition to Augustus of Saxony came from the elements which were opposed to Russian influence, the "National" party, which adopted with enthusiasm the cause of the ex-King Stanislaus Leczinski, who was put forward by his son-in-law, Louis XV. So large indeed was the party in Leczinski's favour that it carried the day at the election (Sept. 1733), but the intervention of a Russian army put the adherents of Stanislaus to flight, and enabled the Saxon party to proclaim Augustus as King (Oct. 5th). Stanislaus did indeed reach Dantzic, and stood a siege there; but France was unable to send him any effective aid, fearing to arouse English and Dutch jealousy by sending a squadron into the Baltic, and in July 1734 Dantzic had to surrender.

However, if Austria and Russia had carried the day in Poland, the entanglement of Austria in the Polish war gave France and Spain an opportunity too tempting to be allowed to pass. As a diversion in favour of Stanislaus, France had overrun Lorraine in the summer of 1733, and Marshal Berwick had laid siege to Kehl, taking it on October 28th; the defenceless state of Austrian Italy, denuded of troops for the war in Poland, proved an irresistible attraction to the covetous Elizabeth Farnese, and Charles Emmanuel III of Savoy eagerly grasped at so good a chance of further acquisitions in Lombardy at the expense of Austria. Chauvelin therefore found little difficulty about negotiating treaties between France and Savoy,[2] and between Spain and France;[3] but the jealousy which the Savoyards entertained towards Spain prevented these two alliances being combined in a

---

[1] Treaty of Löwenwolde (1732).
[2] Turin (Sept. 1733).   [3] The Escurial (Nov. 1733).

triple alliance.   The Emperor thus found himself threatened in
Italy and in Germany with a Franco-Spanish attack, but the
Allies from whom he might have hoped to receive assistance
failed him in his hour of need.   Walpole allowed Fleury's
promise that the neutrality of the Austrian Netherlands
should be respected to lure him into leaving the Emperor in
the lurch, a piece of short-sightedness which was to cost his
country dear before ten years had passed.   It would not be
too much to say that if the Maritime Powers had come to
the aid of Austria in 1733 the question of the Austrian
Succession might have never led to a war.   It was very
largely the failure of Austria in this war, and in the disastrous
Turkish war which she undertook partly in the hope of obtaining compensation for the loss of Naples, which encouraged
her enemies to entertain the idea of partitioning her dominions
in 1741.   Nor did Walpole's pacific policy in 1733 achieve
his object by ultimately averting the war with Spain over
the West Indies.   In the war of the Austrian Succession,
England had to carry on a maritime and colonial war and at
the same time to assist Maria Theresa to check a career of
conquest on the part of the House of Bourbon, which might
never have been begun had a revived Grand Alliance successfully withstood France and Spain in 1733–1734.   Moreover, in 1733, Frederick William, and not, as in 1740, his
more ambitious and grasping son, was on the Prussian throne,
and it would not have been very difficult to obtain with English
subsidies the assistance of that Prussian army which was to
deal Austria more than one stab in the back between 1740
and 1745.   Eugene, too, was still alive, and with proper
support might still have done good service.   And if Austria
had not been humiliated and beaten between 1733 and 1738,
if she had not suffered the losses of those years, and if her
weakness had not been thereby exposed, Frederick II might
well have hesitated before he dashed at Silesia in December
1740.   It was because he saw that Austria was weaker than
France that he seized upon Silesia, upon which he had no
claim, rather than on Jülich and Berg, to which he certainly had
some right.   And that Austria was weak and a tempting prey
to the spoilers was in large measure due to the fact that Walpole
had preferred a temporary continuance of an insecure peace to
opening his eyes to the true facts of the European situation.

One ally Charles might have secured : Frederick William of Prussia offered to lead his whole army to the Rhine, but only on condition of receiving an almost absolutely free hand, terms which even Eugene was somewhat unwilling to grant him. The Diet, it is true, did declare war (Jan. 1734) on France, but the utility of this declaration was diminished by the refusal of the three Wittelsbach Electors, Bavaria, Cologne and the Palatinate, to join in the resistance to the French.[1] That the campaign on the Rhine in 1734 should have gone altogether in favour of the French was therefore not surprising. A detached corps secured Treves and Trarbach, while the main army under Berwick besieged Philipsburg. Eugene was given the command of the force designed to relieve it, but neither the quantity nor the quality of his forces gave him any satisfaction; his auxiliaries were very slow to arrive, and when, Berwick having been killed in the trenches (June 12th), the Austrian commander did move up to attempt the relief of the fortress, the faint-hearted von Wutgenau surrendered (July 18th), almost under the eyes of the relievers. The new French commander, d'Asfeld, then moved on Mayence, but Eugene interposed so as to cover the city, and d'Asfeld relapsed into inactivity. Next year things went no better. The Elector of Bavaria mobilised his forces in rear of the Imperial army, and his hostile attitude prevented Eugene from doing anything beyond covering Mayence and the passes over the Black Forest. Even when 12,000 Russians reached Heidelberg (August), all that could be done was to force Charles Albert of Bavaria to dismiss his troops. Had the French been more energetic they might have repeated with every prospect of success the stroke which Marlborough had foiled in 1704, but their inactivity was partly due to a desire not to rouse the minor states of South-West Germany into active measures of defence. The operations on the Rhine were only important inasmuch as they diverted Austria's attention from Italy. There the success of the Allies had been even more pronounced; the French and Sardinians gradually drove the Austrians out of Lombardy, and, despite Mercy's stubborn resistance at Parma (June 29th, 1734) and Königsegg's victory on the Sesia (Sept. 15th, 1734),

[1] Good relations between the Bavarian and Palatine branches had been restored by the conclusion of a family compact in 1724.

forced them after a defeat at Guastalla (Sept. 19th, 1734) to fall back into the Tyrol and leave Mantua exposed: meanwhile the Spaniards overran the Two Sicilies with consummate ease. Almost without a blow they possessed themselves of Naples; by the end of 1733 only Capua remained in Austrian hands and nearly all Sicily had been lost, the rest following suit early in 1734. It was only the quarrels of the Allies that prevented them from ousting the Austrians altogether from Italy in 1735; but the rivalry of Sardinia and Spain proved the salvation of Mantua, and allowed Khevenhüller and Neipperg to maintain their positions on Lake Garda and the Adige.

By the autumn of 1735 even Charles VI had to confess himself worsted: deserted by his allies, slackly supported by the rest of Germany, at the end of his resources, and with a Turkish war impending, he had no option but to make peace. The Preliminaries of Vienna were signed with France in October 1735, and ratified in November,[1] though it was not till 1739 that the definite assent of Spain and of Sardinia was obtained. France abandoned Leczinski's candidature for Poland, but as a compensation he received the Duchy of Bar, with a promise of Lorraine; this he was to obtain as soon as the death of the last Medici should have set Tuscany free to be handed over to Francis Stephen of Lorraine as a compensation for the loss of his ancestral dominions. At Leczinski's death his possessions were to pass to France. It was a severe blow to the Empire, though severer to Francis Stephen, from whom a reluctant consent was purchased by his marriage to Maria Theresa (Feb. 1736), while Fleury had the satisfaction of having associated his name with one of the most important of the territorial acquisitions of France. The Emperor also had to cede the Two Sicilies to Don Carlos, and Novara and Tortona to Charles Emmanuel, but he recovered Parma and Piacenza. Naples was a serious loss, since its wealth had made it a very valuable and profitable possession; but the South Italian dominions had been isolated and very difficult to defend, and the territories left to Austria in the valley of the Po were much more compact. Finally, the Empire recovered Kehl, Philipsburg, Treves and Trarbach, and Charles VI obtained from France a recognition, though a recognition so conditioned and safeguarded as to be quite

---

[1] The definite peace between France and Austria was signed on Nov. 8th, 1738.

ambiguous, of the Pragmatic Sanction. It is also noteworthy that the " Ryswick clause," the abolition of which had been demanded by those Protestant members who voted for the war, was not mentioned in the 1738 treaty; and this was taken by the Protestants to be equivalent to cancellation, a view in which the Catholics practically acquiesced.

Shortly after the preliminaries had been ratified Eugene died (April 21st, 1736). Though not himself of German birth, he had been in peace almost as much as in war the mainstay of the Empire under the last three Emperors. He had just outlived the marriage of Maria Theresa to Francis Stephen; he must be considered fortunate in that he did not live to see the work of his last great victory undone in the unfortunate Turkish war of 1737–1739, in which Charles now became involved.

It was partly in fulfilment of his obligations to Russia, undertaken when Catherine guaranteed the Pragmatic Sanction in 1726, but also with the idea of recouping his losses in Italy at the expense of Turkey, that, at a time when peace, financial retrenchment and careful reorganisation were the crying needs of the Hapsburg monarchy, Charles VI embarked in a fresh war. Russia had declared war on Turkey in 1735 on the pretext that the Tartars, when attacking Persia, had violated the neutrality of Russian territory. Not being altogether successful in the campaigns of 1735–1736, she called upon Austria for the assistance which the Treaty of 1726 pledged the Hapsburgs to send. There were great debates as to the course which Austria should adopt; she might content herself with sending 30,000 men as auxiliaries and yet remain neutral as a whole, as Seckendorff and Palffy, the Palatine of Hungary, suggested; or she might embark upon the war as a full partner in the enterprise. Bartenstein, now coming to the front as Secretary to the Austrian Conference, was in favour of the latter plan; and it would appear that it was to this that Charles VI himself inclined. The position of a mere auxiliary was hardly consonant with his Imperial dignity, and therefore, though Poland and Venice held aloof, though his German vassals failed to support him, and in some cases absolutely refused to help, though hardly any part of the aid which the Diet voted ever reached the Emperor's coffers, though the condition of the Austrian army, administration and finances certainly did not warrant any such enterprise, he resolved to take part with his whole force in the campaign of 1737.

The military operations began with a fair measure of success. Seckendorff invaded Servia and took Nissa (July 23rd); but undue division of forces, failure to keep touch between the different corps, and the quarrels and jealousies of the commanders, produced the natural result, the Turks got the best of some minor affairs, and their successes spread to the main operations. Saxe-Hildburghausen was forced back from Banjaluka in Bosnia to Gradiska on the Save; Khevenhüller failed in an attempt on Widdin; and Nissa, the sole prize of the campaign, was lost within two months of its capture. Seckendorff, who as a Protestant and a foreigner was unpopular with the other generals and had little control over them, was rather unfairly made the scapegoat for the general failure: he was court-martialed and imprisoned; but his successor, Königsegg, did little better in 1738. He did defeat the Turks at Mehadia, and force them to evacuate Orsova, but he was unable to take Widdin; and far from following up a success he won at Cornia in July, by the end of the year he had been driven in under the walls of Belgrade, and, like Seckendorff, was removed from the command. However, the new general, Wallis, brought no change of fortune. Instructed to fight a decisive battle, he did so at Crozka, near Belgrade (July 23rd), with singular ill success, for his bad choice of ground more than nullified the good behaviour of the troops, with the result that after losing 20,000 men, he had to leave Belgrade to its fate and retire on Pancsova. All he could do was to begin negotiations with the Turks which his successor, Neipperg, completed. The Peace of Belgrade (signed Sept. 18th, 1739) was a sad contrast to Passarowitz and Carlowitz. Once again Western Wallachia and Servia, including Belgrade, passed under Turkish rule, and the boundary of Bosnia was restored to its position in 1699, the Danube and the Save forming the frontier. Thus Austria, which had embarked on the war in the hope that she might make gains to set off against her Italian losses, found herself involved in even greater humiliation. The war was in every way a failure. Its cost was great in men and in money alike. The reputation of the Austrian army received a severe blow; its unpreparedness, indiscipline and inefficiency were displayed to all the world, its most reputed and trusted generals were found wanting. Wallis . and Neipperg shared the fate of Seckendorff; they were court-martialed both for their conduct of the military operations and still more for their precipitation in concluding peace. But such treatment was a little unfair to the generals, the fault lay rather with the government as a whole, and with the unsound condition of the Hapsburg dominions at that moment. Painstaking, anxious to do good, capable of seeing what it would be well to do, but quite incapable of the moral courage and hard work needed to carry the task through, Charles VI was persistently unfortunate throughout his reign, and in nothing so much as in its abrupt end. His death (Oct. 20th, 1740) was by no means expected. Only fifty-six years old, he might well have lived another fifteen or even twenty years ; and it was confidently expected that he would survive his wife, Elizabeth Christina of Brunswick-Wolfenbüttel, who was very ill, in which case a second marriage might have produced the male heir of whom the Hapsburg dynasty stood in such great need.[1] He had, it is true, obtained the assent of nearly all the Powers to the Pragmatic Sanction, though Bavaria and the Elector Palatine had withdrawn that given in 1726; but, as Eugene had warned him, paper promises were to prove of far less value than a full treasury and an efficient army. He had also apparently solved the question of Jülich and Berg in favour of the Sulzbachs by a secret treaty with France in January 1739 ; but Fleury, feeling that the cards were in his hands, was just about to make a somewhat similar compact with Prussia.[2] No moment could have been more unfortunate than that at which Charles VI actually died. Austria was of all countries the least fitted for the troubles of a disputed succession ; above all things she needed ten years of rest and recuperation, while, little though it was anticipated, the death of Frederick William of Prussia (May 31st, 1740) was destined to be of enormous importance to her. It was early in October when Charles was taken ill at his hunting-box at Schönborn and died in a few days, leaving to his successor a sea of troubles for many of which it is difficult not to hold him responsible.

---

[1] It was probably for some such reason as this that he neglected to secure the election of Francis Stephen of Lorraine as King of the Romans.

[2] Cf. p. 96.

CHAPTER VII

MARIA THERESA AND HER ENEMIES

IT was not merely the special circumstances of the moment at which Charles VI died, not merely the fact that his heir and successor was a young and inexperienced woman, which made the Hapsburg dominions in 1740 so tempting a prey to the would-be spoilers: the constitution of the disunited and incoherent realm and the relations between its different parts seemed to promise an easy success to the grasping claimants who were proposing to divide them. The accumulation of territories to which Maria Theresa succeeded was not a nation, it was not even organised as a federation. Under Charles VI little had been done towards binding together by administrative or judicial reforms the three main groups, the Austrian, the Bohemian and the Hungarian, which still remained in all essentials separate, while the outlying dependencies, in the Netherlands and Italy, tended rather to absorb the attention of their rulers and draw them away from the task, difficult enough already, of welding together the central dominions. The constitutional and administrative arrangements had undergone few changes since 1715. To a certain extent the Imperial authority had gained ground at the expense of local officials, but the progress of centralisation had been slow. The recognition of the Pragmatic Sanction, however, had done something to bind the provinces together; it had established a common principle of succession accepted and acknowledged all through the Hapsburg dominions, and though Charles VI had shrunk from attempting to push the process, further signs were not altogether wanting of a tendency towards the work Maria Theresa was to accomplish when she fused the separate Bohemian and Austrian Chancelleries and brought all the German dominions of the Hapsburgs under the same judicial and administrative system. But in 1740 these changes were still to come, and at that time, as far as constitution went, Austria might still be said to have barely emerged from the Middle Ages; her government was still largely feudal in character, and in efficiency and organisation was far behind the other countries of Western Europe.[1]

In each province of the Hapsburg dominions the old constitutional forms lingered on, retaining enough vitality to hamper and impede the action of the central government, to diminish its authority and its control over the resources of the state, but devoid of the compensating advantages which might have been derived from a system of real and adequate representative government, since they had their roots in feudal privileges rather than in real and active constitutional life and liberties. In these assemblies (*Landtäge*) the power lay with the nobles; for while the burghers had few votes and less influence, it was only in the Tyrol that the peasantry were represented at all. And at this period, as they were soon to show, the Austrian nobility were sadly lacking in patriotism, in public spirit and in self-sacrifice. Charles VI had made great efforts to attach them to the Hapsburg dynasty, but his over-anxiety had defeated its own ends. Unduly lavish concessions and favours had only whetted their appetites and made them ask for more. Selfish and parochial, they looked to their own personal ends, or at the utmost to the interests of their provinces, rather than to those of the dynasty and the state. Still they were not merely an idle privileged caste, as was the case in France. If they enjoyed the benefits of their feudal position, they discharged its duties, officering the Army and controlling local government. Neither burghers nor peasantry were of much account. The cities differed in constitutions, in rights and privileges, and utterly lacked combination, either political or industrial. Those which stood on the lands of nobles paid them dues and performed services just as the peasants did. Inside the towns the power was usually in the hands of a narrow oligarchy, often a guild which had become obsolete and inefficient. Charles VI had made some praiseworthy efforts to sweep away the cramping relics of these mediæval institutions, but he had not had much success, and trade and industry were still subject to their blighting influence. To this must be attributed the comparative failure of the public works, of the encouragement to commerce, and of the

[1] Cf. Chapter II. pp. 35–36.

other efforts which Charles VI made to promote the material prosperity of his subjects. In the German districts there was no serfdom, but in Bohemia the peasants were still unfree, the chattels of their lords; and that all was not well with them may be judged from the agrarian revolts which had broken out in Bohemia in 1680, in Moravia as late as 1717. A great part of the land was in the hands of the clergy, who were numerous and powerful, and not by any means a factor towards progress. Though somewhat on the wane, the influence of the Jesuits was still considerable enough to be deleterious. The state of the judicial organisation and administration urgently required reform, while even more complete chaos prevailed in the finances. The Court was wasteful, the taxes were at once oppressive and unproductive, the revenue, which stood at about 30 million thalers, was quite insufficient for the Army and the administration. All Charles VI's efforts to reform the finances had broken down, and the two recent and most disastrous wars seemed to have utterly exhausted the resources of the country. The Treasury was practically empty, and the heaviness of the taxation had made the people discontented and disaffected. Nowhere were the effects of the financial disorders and constitutional chaos more pernicious than in their influence on the condition of the Army. In the first place, it suffered from the division of control between the War Council, which attended to the levying of the troops, and the local Estates, which provided the funds for their maintenance. A certain amount had been done of late years to improve the Army, but its organisation left an enormous amount to be desired. Facilities for training the officers and exercising the troops were lacking, and its whole tone and prestige were suffering from the disastrous Turkish war. Nominally fairly strong—the establishment for 1734 was fixed at 150,000—the actual numbers bore little resemblance to the paper strength; and of the 60,000 men to which the Army actually amounted on a peace footing, the majority were in Hungary, Lombardy, or the Netherlands, and only very few were to be found in the central provinces.

Nor had Maria Theresa much better cause for satisfaction and confidence in the advisers on whom she had to rely. The Turkish war had left all her most famous generals under a cloud, and not one of the ministers who composed the " Conference" could be described as a pillar of strength. With hardly any exceptions they were over seventy years of age, and though they had once done good service, that day was past. Age had brought irresolution; prejudices, timidity and indolence had warped their judgment and diminished their powers; the work was too much for them physically as well as morally. The Chancellor, Philip Louis Sinzendorff, was worn out, and quite unfit for his post; Alois Harrach, the Land Marshal of Lower Austria, lacked vigour and capacity; his brother Joseph, who was President of the War Council from Königsegg's fall in 1738 till 1764, was younger than the rest of the Conference, but not much more efficient, being indolent and slow. Philip Kinsky, the Chancellor of Bohemia, was dominated by local and particularist ideas; he was devoid of any wider patriotism, and his sole object seems to have been to assist Bohemia to avoid bearing her proper burdens The Finance Minister, Gundacker Stahremberg, was perhaps the most capable member of the Conference; he came of a family eminent for its good services, and his own record was honourable; but he was feeling the weight of his years, and he was hardly fitted to cope with such a crisis as that of 1740. Under these circumstances it was not unnatural that the Secretary to the Conference, Bartenstein (1689–1757), an energetic, rather opinionated man of considerable capacity in some respects, but quite devoid of the higher qualities of a statesman, should have enjoyed a rather greater share of Maria Theresa's confidence in the early days of her reign than he did later on, when experience enabled her to judge more for herself, both of men and of policies.

That at this particular crisis Bartenstein's judgment was much at fault cannot be denied. He relied blindly on the good intentions of France, not seeing that the concessions Charles VI had made in the hope of securing Fleury's good offices had only brought the weakness and helplessness of Austria before the notice of her enemies.

And when Maria Theresa looked round upon the Powers of Europe, it must have been as probable enemies rather than possible allies that the majority of them appeared to her. True that they had almost all guaranteed the Pragmatic Sanction,[1] but faithful observance of the most solemn treaty

[1] For list, see Erdmannsdörffer, bk. vii. ch. 5, and cf. p. 83.

engagements was hardly a characteristic feature of European statesmen in the eighteenth century.[1] Most of the Powers did return favourable replies to the circular which Maria Theresa addressed to them on her accession, announcing that she had succeeded under the terms of the Pragmatic Sanction, and claiming the fulfilment of their promises; but these replies also were mere paper securities of which the worthlessness was soon to be proved.

Of the claims which Maria Theresa had to fear, those of Bavaria and Saxony were undoubtedly the strongest. The Elector of Bavaria and the King of Saxony were in the first place the husbands of those daughters of the Emperor Joseph I who had been deprived of the succession to the Hapsburg dominions in favour of Maria Theresa.[2] Charles Albert of Bavaria had, moreover, a claim on his own behalf as a descendant of Anne, daughter of Ferdinand I of Austria. By the will of that Emperor, in case the descendants of his sons (Maximilian II and Charles of Styria) failed, those of Anne were to succeed. According to the Bavarian contention, Anne's heirs were to come in on the failure of the *male* line; but as the Austrians contended, and as was proved by the production of the authentic will from the archives at Vienna, it was on the failure of "legitimate" heirs that the contingency was to arise.[3] Still Charles Albert did not hesitate to claim the succession directly Charles VI died; and though his own resources were not sufficient to make him formidable, in the Polish Succession War the old relations between France and Bavaria had to some extent been renewed,[4] so that it was the support of France rather than the strength of Bavaria which made the Wittelsbach claim a danger. Moreover, there was in the Austrian dominions a faction which was decidedly favourable to the Bavarian claim, the party that had objected to the marriage of Maria Theresa to Francis Stephen of Lorraine; and this disaffection largely accounted for the feeble resistance of Upper Austria to the invaders in 1741, and for the discreditable readiness with which many of the nobles and officials of that province and of Bohemia submitted to the Bavarian and accepted office under him.

[1] Cf. Sorel, *Europe et la Révolution Française*, i. 24.   [2] Cf. pp. 78–79.
[3] Cf. von Arneth, *Maria Theresa*, vol. i. p. 97, and Wolf's *Austria*, bk. i. ch. i.
[4] Cf. p. 100; also *Instructions aux Ambassadeurs de France—Bavière*.

Augustus of Saxony-Poland ought, if gratitude had any influence over his policy, to have supported Austria, to whom he mainly owed his Polish crown. He did at first recognise the Pragmatic Sanction,[1] and place himself on Austria's side ; but before long the successes of Maria Theresa's enemies, the influence of Marshal Belleisle and of Montijo, the Spanish Ambassador at Dresden, and the rejection of the concessions he demanded as the price of his support,[2] caused Augustus to drift over to the other side and finally to participate in the attack on Bohemia.

Spain and Sardinia also made more or less formal claims on the Hapsburg territories, but their claims were of that class which would be amply met by a dividend of a shilling in the pound, and with a maritime war against England already engaging her resources, Spain would hardly have done anything unless France gave her a definite lead. And France procrastinated over her reply, making excuses of a formal nature, and waiting to see what was going to happen in the hope that she might direct events to her own advantage.

England, the United Provinces and Russia were thus about the only Powers from whom Maria Theresa had nothing to fear ; but unfortunately for her the course of affairs in Russia following on the death of the Empress Anne Ivanovna (Oct. 28th, 1740) resulted in the temporary supremacy of Münich and Ostermann, who were hostile to Austria, and thus deprived Maria Theresa of the assistance from that quarter which she might have hoped.

It seemed, therefore, that all depended on the action of France. Fleury is generally credited with a wish to preserve the peace of Europe, and is held to have been forced into a war he disliked by the importunities of a younger and more enterprising generation, just as Walpole was driven into the Spanish war. It would appear, however, that the acquisition of Lorraine by France under his auspices had whetted his appetite for further territorial gains, and that if he resisted Belleisle's proposals that France should seize this splendid opportunity of partitioning the Hapsburg dominions and so completing

---

[1] Von Arneth, i. 101.

[2] Namely, a strip of territory in Silesia giving military communication between Saxony and Poland, the royal title for Saxony, *i.e.* a kingdom within the Empire, together with those portions of Lower Lusatia which Prussia held as fiefs of the Bohemian Crown. Cf. von Arneth, i. 207.

the work of Mazarin and Louis XIV, it was rather from jealousy of the proposer than from dislike of the proposal, and also because France seemed at the moment on the verge of being involved in the Anglo-Spanish war.   He had told the Elector of Bavaria that the French guarantee of the Pragmatic Sanction would not be observed if any third party should prove to have a better right to the Hapsburg dominions than Maria Theresa had; and, in the words of a contemporary,[1] to say that " the Queen of Hungary has a right to her possessions not in prejudice to the rights of others . . . is a door to evade the whole obligation."

But it was by might, not by right, that the question was to be decided.   While every one was watching France, the blow fell from a very different quarter.   The young monarch who had ascended the Prussian throne on the death of Frederick William I a few months earlier was burning for an opportunity to make a name for himself.   He would have no more of the cautious policy of neutrality and inaction which had made men sneer at the military monarch who never let his parade-ground soldiers fire a shot in real earnest.   He was, moreover, a true Hohenzollern in his desire for territorial gains, and in his determination to seek them along the line of least resistance. Energetic, ambitious, anxious to use the fine weapon his father had left him and which he had at the very outset begun to increase, adding no less than 16,000 men at once, he had already given proof of his aggressive and imperious character by his action in the Herstal affair.   Herstal was one of those fragments of the Orange inheritance which had finally been adjudged to Frederick William I when the quarrel between him and Louis XV over that point was compromised in 1732. The Bishop of Liége also laid claim to it, and had tried to prevent the Prussian recruiters enlisting men there.   Frederick William, when no friendly settlement could be arranged, had let the matter alone.   Frederick II at once took forcible action, marched troops into the district, exacted a contribution and compelled the inhabitants to support the force in occupation, disregarding absolutely the Emperor's orders to him to retire from the territory.   It was a minor matter, but it was typical. Regardless of forms or rights, Frederick II used force unsparingly to gain his ends, and paid heed to no commands that had not force at their back.

[1] Robert Trevor to H. Walpole, *Trevor MSS.*, Hist. MSS. Com. p. 66.

Such a monarch was not likely to let slip the promising opportunity which the state of the Austrian dominions at Charles VI's death laid before him. Nor was it hard to find precedents for aggression. Included in the Austrian province of Silesia were the Duchies of Liegnitz, Wohlau and Brieg, which had passed into the direct rule of the Hapsburgs on the death in 1675 of George William, last Duke of Liegnitz. In that year the Great Elector had advanced a claim to these Duchies on the strength of an *Erbverbrüderung* or "heritage fraternity" entered into in 1537 by the then Elector of Brandenburg, Joachim II, and Duke Frederick of Liegnitz. However, not only had the arrangement never received the sanction of the Emperor, whose rights it undoubtedly infringed, but Charles V had protested against it at the time; while in 1546 Ferdinand I, interfering as King of Bohemia and immediate overlord of Liegnitz, compelled the Duke to cancel the treaty. That technically Brandenburg had any case at all is difficult to believe,[1] though the Hohenzollern seem to have acted on the principle that a claim acquires validity from mere frequency of assertion. It was partly because the Emperor had taken possession of the Liegnitz inheritance in 1675, as being fiefs which naturally lapsed to their overlord on failure of heirs, and had flatly refused Frederick William any compensation, that the Great Elector had concluded in October 1679 a treaty which enrolled Brandenburg among the clients of France—a curious proceeding for a prince in whom some later historians have endeavoured to discover a champion of Germany against French aggression. In 1686 the matter had gone a stage further. Alarmed by the strongly anti-Protestant attitude of Louis XIV, and perhaps made uneasy by the Truce of Ratisbon (1684), which confirmed Louis in the possession of Strassburg, for which he must have felt himself in no small measure responsible, Frederick William began to seek opportunities of drawing nearer to Austria, offering his aid against the Turks and eventually against France—on conditions. These conditions, however, were more than the Emperor and most of his advisers were disposed to grant, for Frederick William suited his demands to the measure of the necessity of Austria. Ultimately, after much haggling, a treaty was signed in March 1686, by which in return for considerable subsidies and the

---

[1] Cf. von Arneth, *Maria Theresa*, i. 105.

cession of the little district of Schwiebus and a guarantee of the Lichtenstein claim on East Friesland, which had now passed to the Hohenzollern, the Great Elector despatched 8000 men to the seat of war in Hungary and abandoned all further claims on the Silesian Duchies.

But unfortunately this was not the end of the Silesian question. At the same time that this negotiation was concluded, the Emperor's envoy, Baron Fridag, concluded a secret treaty with the Electoral Prince, who pledged himself to restore Schwiebus to the Emperor on succeeding to the Electorate. The facts with regard to this negotiation are disputed, and the truth is not clear. The account given on the Prussian side[1] is that the Austrians represented to the Electoral Prince, who was one of the leaders of the anti-French party in Brandenburg, that the French party at the Court were insisting on the cession of Schwiebus to prevent an understanding between Austria and Brandenburg. The Austrian account, on the other hand, represents the proposal to surrender Schwiebus as coming from Frederick, who hoped thereby to secure the Emperor's good offices in the matter of his father's will. The Great Elector was at this time much under the influence of his second wife, Dorothea of Holstein-Glücksburg, who had induced him to bequeath to the four sons she had borne him, separate territorial appanages out of the lands he had acquired. Thus Minden was to go to Prince Philip William, Halberstadt and Reinstein to provide a territorial establishment for his brother Albert Frederick. That such an arrangement would have tended to weaken the power of the family seems certain, for there is little reason to suppose that its results would have differed from those which followed in Saxony from the very similar dispositions made by John George I.[2] Carefully as the Great Elector sought to reserve for his successor as Elector military and diplomatic control over the territories of the cadet-branches, even their partial independence must have proved a fatal obstacle to the completeness of King Frederick William I's administrative reforms. Under the terms of the will, the Emperor was appointed executor, and had he chosen to support the claims of the younger sons of the Great Elector, Frederick I might have found them difficult to resist. Thus, when the death of Frederick

[1] Cf. Droysen, *Geschichte der Preussischen Politick*, Part iv. vol. 4, pp. 154–204.
[2] Cf. pp. 39–40.

8

William brought the question forward, the surrender of Schwiebus was the price for the Emperor's consent to the setting aside of the will. On making the restoration, Frederick declared that he resumed his claims on the Silesian Duchies; somewhat unjustifiably, for if it happened that the district received by Frederick William as compensation for the abandoned claim coincided with the price paid by his successor for the very definite service of quashing the Great Elector's will, one may fairly regard that service as the real compensation for the none too strong claim, a fairly ample *quid pro quo*. Subsequent events, then, make it appear more probable that of the two versions the Austrian is nearer the truth.[1]

That the surrender of Schwiebus does not affect the Prussian claim on the Duchies may therefore be admitted, and at the same time it may be pointed out that the resumption of the claim by Frederick I cannot be regarded as in the least making up for its original invalidity. The claim on Jaegerndorf was hardly any stronger when put to the test of facts. This Duchy had once been in the possession of John George of Brandenburg, second son of the Elector Joachim Frederick (1598–1608), though the Hohenzollern title to it had never received Imperial recognition. In 1622, John George of Jaegerndorf was put to the ban of the Empire for assisting Frederick V of the Palatinate in his attempt to deprive the Hapsburgs of Bohemia. The Duchy was accordingly forfeited with all due formalities and annexed by Ferdinand II, and had remained in Hapsburg hands at the Peace of 1648. Thus according to the laws and customs of the Empire the Hohenzollern title to Jaegerndorf was valueless, and indeed the only right which Frederick II possessed over Silesia was the right of the stronger.

When it is further remembered that in 1728 Prussia had formally guaranteed the Pragmatic Sanction, that Frederick II himself admitted that in his place Frederick William would have kept his word, the only thing that is surprising is that Frederick should ever have taken the trouble to produce any so-called "justification" for his action; but it certainly is not a little striking to reflect that but for Charles VI there would have been no Frederick II in existence in 1740. It was largely the Emperor's intervention, ill-timed indeed in the

[1] Cf. *Z.S.* ii. 21.

interests of his family, which had caused the irate Frederick William to refrain from executing the sentence of death pronounced against the then Crown Prince for his attempted desertion (1730). The return which Frederick II now made gives one some idea of the standards of international morality, public faith and private gratitude upon which he acted.

As a justification for the seizure of Silesia, it has been urged that if Prussia was to keep her position in Europe she must have more territory and population to support her disproportionate army, and that therefore she had to make what acquisitions she could;[1] an argument whose barefaced appeal to force is fully in keeping with the high-handed Prussian traditions, but which is not worth serious consideration. That Prussia had been ill-treated by Austria in the matter of Jülich and Berg[2] is undeniable, but that hardly gave Frederick a valid claim on Silesia; though if he had chosen to forcibly assert his claim to Jülich and Berg, and had marched troops into them in order to obtain security that they would fall to him on the death of their holder, his action would not have been liable to the censure which one cannot but pass on his utterly unjustifiable seizure of Silesia. But the truth was that he was afraid of France—afraid that if he were to seize Jülich and Berg, Fleury might adopt the cause of the Catholic Sulzbachs and dispossess him, afraid that France might not like his presence at so important a point on the Rhine. Moreover, Silesia was richer, larger, more populous, more conveniently situated with regard to Brandenburg, and the easier prey. Frederick knew that he was not the only vulture gathered round the carcase of the apparently moribund Hapsburg monarchy; he knew that there were others as greedy as himself, and that he could rely on being imitated and probably supported, that Maria Theresa was beset by possible enemies, that France would probably view with approbation the humiliation of the Power which had struggled so hard to defend Germany against her, and he preferred plundering a woman in distress to incurring the displeasure of the Bourbon monarchy. The pretext that Maria Theresa was threatened with an attack from Saxony—which had recognised its guarantee—and from Bavaria—which could not dispose of more than 20 to 30,000 men—was the merest subterfuge: even had it been true it would hardly

[1] Cf. *E.H.R.* 1889, p. 586.   [2] Cf. p. 95.

have justified a Power on friendly terms with its neighbour in taking forcible and uninvited possession of one of that neighbour's provinces because it has selected it as the reward for services not yet rendered. But there was about as much truth in the assertion as there was in the proclamation which Frederick published when he crossed the frontier, declaring that the step was taken in concert with Maria Theresa, with whom he was negotiating.

The invasion of Silesia was as successful as it was unexpected. The province was all but without a garrison; and even had it been at its full peace establishment of 13,000 men, that force would have been outnumbered by two to one by the 5000 cavalry and 22,000 infantry of whom Frederick took command at Crossen on December 14th, to say nothing of the 10,000 more troops who were a few days' march in rear. All that the Governor of the province, Count Wallis, could do was to throw the few troops he had into the fortresses of Brieg, Glogau and Neisse, which were hastily prepared for defence. Breslau, the capital of the province, refused to admit a garrison, and declared that it would be responsible for its own defence. Luckily for the Austrians, bad weather delayed the Prussian movements, and Frederick, as yet unaware of the value of promptitude, wasted six valuable days in an unnecessary delay at Herrendorf, five miles from Glogau (Dec. 22nd to 28th). This gave time for Brieg and Neisse to be put into such a condition that they could stand a siege. On December 28th the King's column resumed its march up the Oder on Breslau, leaving part of the reserve division to blockade Glogau, while Schwerin and the right wing, who had moved parallel up the Bober, occupied Liegnitz. The people of Breslau behaved with a culpable lack of patriotism and courage, tamely opening their gates on January 2nd on condition that they should not be forced to receive a Prussian garrison. Indeed, with the exception of the three fortresses of Brieg, Glogau and Neisse, and one or two minor places like Namslau and Ottmachau, the whole province submitted to the invader almost without firing a shot, nobles, townsfolk and peasantry displaying an apathy which did them little credit. By the end of January these three fortresses alone held out. The time which Frederick had wasted had been turned to good effect; and he was now learning the value of rapid movements, for his army was unable to go into winter-quarters but had to maintain the blockades of these towns.   If the Austrians could gather a relieving army with anything like reasonable speed, the Prussian position might prove hazardous.   And Maria Theresa was sparing no effort to avenge the injury which Frederick had done her, and to make him pay dearly for his insolent assumption of a victor's airs, his taking it for granted that she would not be able to regain Silesia.   This attitude was an insult above all to the Austrian army, which looked upon the Prussians as mere soldiers of the parade-ground, and relied confidently on its own experience of real war to give it the victory over these troops who had never seen a shot fired, in anger.[1]   The Queen of Hungary therefore rejected with scorn the proposals made to her through Baron Götter, offering her Frederick's assistance against other enemies, and promising his vote at the Imperial election to Francis Stephen of Lorraine if she would cede the Silesian Duchies.   The Chancellor, Sinzendorf, and one or two of the other ministers were for yielding; but Maria Theresa would not hear of concessions, and Bartenstein and Stahremberg were equally firm for " no surrender."   Moreover, it looked as though she were going to find a friend in need in George II.   In vain Walpole contended that what Great Britain required was the settlement of the differences between Austria and Prussia : in vain he opposed the action of George II in proceeding to Hanover in May 1741 to put himself at the head of the force he was collecting there ; the English nation was full of sympathy for Maria Theresa, and for once the King had the unusual experience of sharing the sentiments of his subjects.   Walpole had to propose in Parliament a subsidy of £300,000 for the Queen of Hungary, and George II planned to take the field at the head of a considerable force, including, besides Dutch and British, 12,000 Danes and Hessians to be secured by a British subsidy, and 15,000 Hanoverians, 3000 at his expense as Elector, 12,000 in British pay.   So threatening, indeed, was his attitude, that many of the Prussian reinforcements destined for Silesia had to be diverted to join the force which Frederick placed near Magdeburg under command of Leopold of Anhalt-Dessau to hold Hanover and Saxony in check, for Augustus III

[1] Cf. von Arneth, i. 219.

also, alarmed at the success of his Prussian neighbour, for whom he had no special love, was negotiating with Maria Theresa. It should also be mentioned that on March 2nd a treaty, amicably regulating various disputed points as to their boundaries, was signed between Austria and the Porte, the Turk thus displaying a very different spirit from the Christian neighbours who sought to profit by the embarrassments of Maria Theresa.

Meanwhile the army which Neipperg was bringing up through Moravia was drawing near the scene of action. Luckily for Frederick, the weakness of the Austrian army and the utter inefficiency of its administration combined with Neipperg's failure to appreciate the necessity for rapid action to make its movements as slow as Frederick's own had been in December. Thus the Prussians were able to storm Glogau (March 9th) and to bring up its besiegers to join the King at Schweidnitz long before Neipperg appeared on the Silesian side of the *Riesengebirge*.

Had Neipperg been a man of any real capacity, and had he made proper use of his excellent irregular cavalry to conceal his own movements and to acquaint him with the dispositions of the Prussians, he might have brought the military career of Frederick to an abrupt and inglorious conclusion. The Prussian troops were unduly scattered and out of supporting distance from each other, when Neipperg, moving from Olmütz by Freudenthal on Neisse, burst into the midst of their cantonments (April 2nd). Frederick happened to be at Jaegerndorf with some 4000 men, and might easily have been cut off and taken, but the Austrian was utterly unaware of the chance before him. He pushed straight on to Neisse, which he reached on April 4th, letting Frederick retire from Jaegerndorf by Steinau, where he rallied Kalkstein and 10,000 men, Friedland (April 6th), and Michelau, where he crossed to the left of the Neisse (April 8th), to Pogarell, where the detachment which had been blockading Brieg joined him (April 9th). Meanwhile Neipperg, having relieved Neisse, had moved on towards Brieg and Breslau, to which last place he was actually nearer than Frederick was; but once again his slowness and his total ignorance of his adversary's movements cast away the advantage on which he had stumbled. On the night of the 9th he reached Mollwitz, seven miles to the North-Westward of Pogarell, and here he was resting his troops when, about midday on the 10th, news was brought to him that the Prussian army was marching against him in full battle array.

The armies which were to fight the first battle of the war were of approximately equal strength, roughly 20,000 men each; but while the Prussians had but 4000 cavalry, Neipperg had 8600 of much better quality. On the other hand, Frederick had an overwhelming superiority in artillery, having sixty guns to eighteen.[1] Both armies were drawn up in the same style, in two lines with the infantry on the centre and the cavalry on the wings. Owing to a mistake of their commander, Schulenberg, the Prussian cavalry on the right did not extend outwards as far as they should have done. Crowding in unduly on the centre, they threw the infantry next to them into such confusion that three battalions had to fall back and take up their position at right angles to the rest, thus covering the space between the two lines of infantry. It was largely by this accident that the fate of the battle was decided; for when the Austrian left wing of cavalry, sweeping down upon the Prussian right, broke them at the first shock and drove them from the field, it was these three battalions which checked the victors when they turned against the Prussian centre. But for these battalions having been so posted as to cover the exposed flank of the infantry, the Austrian horsemen would have caught the Prussian infantry as they faced to the right to meet the charge at a great disadvantage, from which even their steadiness and excellent fire-discipline might have failed to extricate them. As it was, Römer and his cavalry could not break the steady lines of the Prussian foot, though they charged repeatedly, even attacking the second line in rear and forcing it to face right about to repulse the attack. Neipperg had meanwhile pushed his infantry forward to support the advantage gained by their cavalry, for the Austrian right had been no less successful than their comrades of the left, but the rapid fire of the Prussian infantry backed up by their superiority in artillery was more than the Austrian infantry could face, and they wavered, ceased to advance, and halted. For a time the fire-duel continued, then Schwerin—left in command when Frederick, thinking the battle lost by the defeat of his cavalry, had joined in their headlong

---

[1] Oncken (*Zeitalter Friedrichs der Grosse,* i. 323) gives the Prussian force as 35 squadrons and 31 battalions, the Austrian as 86 squadrons and 18 battalions.

flight—gave the order to advance. The Austrians at once gave way and fell back in some disorder towards Neisse, the Prussians making no attempt to pursue.

Such was the battle of Mollwitz, an action of far more importance than many in which much greater forces have been engaged. In military history it is remarkable as a display of the possibilities of really well-trained and disciplined infantry. Before Mollwitz and between armies of equal strength the better chance would have been held to be possessed by the side which had a two to one superiority in cavalry: Mollwitz showed the impotence of cavalry even when excellent against steady infantry whose fire-discipline was good. It was a victory for the army, not for its commander. Schwerin did much to encourage his men, but the victory was not due to superiority in generalship or in tactics. It was the lucky accident which placed the three battalions in the decisive position on the right flank of the centre which, combined with the years of hard work on the parade-grounds of Potsdam, won the battle. One might almost fancy that the spirit of Frederick William cannot have been far away when the army that he had trained was put to its first real test and came through it so victoriously. Frederick II's share in the success is not so easy to find.

As far as immediate military results went the victory was rather barren. Brieg was now bombarded, and on May 4th it fell; but Neipperg remained unmolested in his camp at Neisse, against which the Prussians made no advance. Thus if defeated at Mollwitz and unsuccessful in his endeavour to sweep the Prussians from Silesia, Neipperg had at least checked the conquest of the province and had recovered some lost ground; in August, indeed, he made a dash on Breslau which Schwerin just forestalled by occupying the town with 8000 men; and when at last the Austrians withdrew from Silesia and left Neisse to its fate, it was not because Frederick had forced them. In a sense it was his work, immediately it was the appearance of another enemy on the scene.

The political results of Mollwitz had been far more decisive than the military. Even before the end of March the "forward party" at Versailles had already so far carried the day that Marshal Belleisle set out to visit the minor Courts of Germany, and to win by persuasion and by bribery the support of the various Electors and Princes to the Bavarian candidature for the Empire; but it cannot be doubted that an Austrian victory at Mollwitz would have greatly altered the complexion of affairs. Mollwitz seemed to promise victories for the other claimants. Austria's incapacity to defend herself was published to the world, and Bavarian, Saxon and Spanish land-hunger received a powerful stimulant. Had Frederick been defeated, had Austria shown herself capable of defending her rights and of making good her title to her provinces at the point of the bayonet, these Powers might have found it advisable to reconsider their proposed policy. Fleury's conscientious scruples might have been awakened, he might have hailed it as an argument for combating Belleisle's policy, and have used this means of recovering the control of affairs now slipping away from him. As it was, France believed more than ever that the day had come for the final overthrow of the Hapsburgs and for the consummation of the work of the House of Bourbon. Belleisle did not, indeed, at once succeed in bringing about a definite agreement with the victor of Mollwitz. His first interview with Frederick, which took place before Brieg towards the end of April, left matters rather as they stood. Indeed Frederick, instead of welcoming the alliance which the French envoy proposed, rather sought to use the mediation of England to arrange an accommodation with Maria Theresa. Meanwhile Belleisle hastened to negotiate a treaty (May 28th) by which Spain and Bavaria, the principal claimants to the Hapsburg heritage, settled on their respective shares, while France by the Treaty of Nymphenburg (May 18th) pledged herself definitely to support the Bavarian on the understanding that she should keep her own gains.[1]

Spain was already stirring and preparing to forcibly assert Don Philip's claims on Lombardy. Charles Emmanuel of Sardinia and his ambitious minister, d'Ormea, were on the

---

[1] There is much difference of opinion as to what exactly was arranged : Droysen (*Friedrich der Grosse*, vol. i. pp. 273 ff.), with whom Oncken (*AG*, iii. 8, vol. i. p.355) agrees, would seem to believe that the treaty usually ascribed to May 18th is a fabrication, that the Franco-Bavarian alliance dated from the secret treaty of 1727, and that Belleisle merely negotiated the Spanish-Bavarian treaty : von Arneth (*Maria Theresa*, i. p. 193) and Ranke take the view adopted in the text : the essential point is that Bavaria accepted French aid in her attack upon Austria and in her candidature for the Empire, and that Belleisle arranged for a joint attack of Maria Theresa's enemies upon her. Cf. also Wolf, p. 31.

alert, balancing the inability of Austria to defend herself against the danger of undue acquisitions by the Spanish Bourbons.   Augustus III of Saxony, anxious not to find himself on the weaker side, was negotiating with Belleisle, and in July a promise of Moravia and Upper Silesia secured his support for the Bavarian claims.   The minor Powers followed this lead.   The Elector Palatine, no longer at feud with his Bavarian cousins, and Clement Augustus o f Cologne,[1] brother of the "bold Bavarian" himself, were anxious to see the Imperial dignity in their family.   Philip Charles of Eltz-Kempten, Elector of Mayence since 1734, was on the whole inclined to favour Austria, but let himself be guided by his nephew Count d'Eltz into accepting Belleisle's overtures, though without enthusiasm.[2]   Francis George of Schönborn at Treves (1729–1756) followed the lead given him by his neighbours, while Würtemberg imitated the larger states around her by advancing claims upon parts of the Hapsburg dominions.

But even with these dangers impending, Maria Theresa resolutely resisted the efforts of the English envoys to induce her to come to terms with Frederick.   All that the arguments and entreaties of Sir Thomas Robinson could win from her was an offer of Limburg; not an inch of Silesia would she yield. Her obstinacy may have been impolitic, it would perhaps have been wiser to swallow the insult to her pride involved in making up her mind to the loss of Silesia and accepting Frederick's assistance against her other enemies.   A coalition such as the English ministers desired, of Austria, England and Hanover, Holland and Prussia, might have proved victorious over the Bourbons and Bavaria, but it is impossible not to sympathise with Maria Theresa's indignant rejection of the idea; and what she thus lost is to some extent compensated for by the moral advantage involved in her magnificent and courageous obstinacy.   The appeal she was able to make to her subjects did awaken their slumbering patriotism and sense of what one may call "Austrian nationality": it would have been but a weak appeal that she could have made to any sentiment if she had stood forward as the ally of the man who had dealt with her so treacherously and insolently.

Frederick therefore, finding Maria Theresa obdurate, accepted

---

[1] Archbishop-Elector, 1723–1761.
[2] Cf. *Frédéric II and Marie Thérèse*, i. 295 ff.

the offered French alliance.   By the Treaty of Breslau (June 5th, 1741),France guaranteed Breslau and Lower Silesia to Frederick; he in return gave up all claim on Jülich and Berg in favour of the Sulzbachs, and promised his vote and his help to the Elector of Bavaria.   Such a treaty must effectually deny to Frederick any claim to have had the interests of Germany at heart.   He placed himself at the disposal of the Power which had for over a hundred years been the greatest foe to Germany and German nationality.   To argue that Austria drove him into the arms of France is ridiculous.   There was another alternative : he might have held on to Silesia, rejecting the French alliance, and wait- ing till the advance of the Franco-Bavarians forced Maria Theresa to come to terms with him to save Vienna.   The fact that he would have preferred to make terms with Maria Theresa is itself an indication that he realised that the intervention of France was contrary to the best interests of Germany, and it was only his own aggression and rapacity which made it impossible for the Queen of Hungary to seek the alliance of the rising North German Power to resist the insidious attempt of France to still further weaken and disunite her Eastern neighbour.

For a discussion of the wisdom of the policy of France this is hardly the place, yet it should be noticed that a different course of action might have suited France better.   A statesman of keener perceptions than Fleury, a man of more political insight and broader ideas than Belleisle, might have seen that it was not from Austria that France had anything to fear.   If it was to the interest of France that Germany should continue weak and disunited, there was much to be said for seeking to induce Austria to make slight concessions to Bavaria, Spain, Sardinia and Saxony, even perhaps to cede part of the Austrian Netherlands to France herself ; but by assisting her against this new enemy France might have earned Maria Theresa's gratitude, and have separated her from England.   It would be fatuous to urge that Fleury ought in 1740–1741 to have foreseen Sedan and the loss of Alsace-Lorraine, but the promptitude and decision of Frederick's action, the evidence of his strength afforded by Mollwitz, his obvious self-confidence and ambition, might well have made Fleury pause.   If it was his object to prevent the rise in Germany of any Power capable of giving France trouble, he might well have asked himself whether it was good policy to assist a monarch so evidently capable of helping himself.

CHAPTER VIII

THE AUSTRIAN SUCCESSION WAR

TO THE TREATY OF WORMS

IT seems to have been at a meeting of the *Conseil du Roi* on July 11th that Louis XV and his Ministers decided what help they would send to their German allies. While one army under Belleisle himself was to join the Elector of Bavaria in yet another thrust down the Danube valley at Vienna, a second, to be commanded by Marshal Maillebois, was to cross the Rhine into Westphalia and so hold in check the "Pragmatic Army" which George II was collecting in Hanover. But for the present France abstained from a formal declaration of war against Austria, announcing that she was merely acting as an ally of the Elector of Bavaria, not as a principal, and that her troops were to be considered as mere "auxiliaries" of the Bavarians.[1]

When, on August 15th, the leading division of the French crossed the Rhine near Fort Louis, hostilities had already been begun with the Bavarians' seizure of Passau on the last day of July. However, it was not till September 11th that their combined forces, 50,000 strong of whom 34,000 were French, broke up from Scharding and advanced down the Danube. On September 14th they reached Linz which made no resistance, for the partisans of Bavaria were numerous in Upper Austria, and nobles and burghers flocked to take the oaths of allegiance to Charles Albert and to acknowledge him as their ruler. Had the Franco-Bavarians pushed on towards Vienna with any vigour, it is difficult to see how they could have failed to take the city. Its fortifications were not strong, its garrison was weak, and there was no quarter from which any help could

---

[1] A convention regulating the relations and status of these "auxiliaries" was signed at Versailles by d'Amelot and the Bavarian envoy Grimberghen on August 9th.

be obtained, for the only armies of Austria were that of
Neipperg, far away at Neisse, and the force with which Traun
was preparing to defend Lombardy against the threatened
Spanish attack.   But not only did Charles Albert spend nearly
three weeks in useless inaction at Linz, not moving on till
October 5th, but when he had reached St. Polten on October
21st and was almost within sight of Vienna, he suddenly
changed his plan, retraced his steps up the Danube to Maut-
hausen, crossed to the left bank (Oct. 24th) and moved
thence by Freystadt upon Budweis in Bohemia.   The reasons
for this remarkable move are hard to understand.   That
Charles Albert was afraid that his communications with
Bavaria might be cut by Austrian troops recalled from Italy
seems unlikely, in any case it was not a serious danger; that
he had no siege-guns is not a sufficient explanation, for he was
in communication by river with the arsenals of Ingolstadt and
other fortresses; more probably he did not trust either his
Saxon or his Prussian ally, and believed that only by moving
in person to Bohemia could he prevent one or other of those
two friends from forestalling him by annexing the province.
The responsibility for this fatal mistake, which Charles Albert
adopted at General Törring's advice, must be borne by the
Elector himself; but Belleisle, though absent at Frankfort at the
time, owing to the preparations for the Imperial election, approved of it, since he wished to draw nearer Frederick of whose
sincerity he had suspicions which were only too well grounded.

    Maria Theresa had faced the Bavarian attack with fortitude
and resolution.   Ten regiments were recalled from Italy, every
effort was made to raise recruits and bring together all available
soldiers, while her famous appeal to the loyalty and patriotism
of her Hungarian subjects really proved a remarkable success,
even though the "insurrection" was only decreed by the Diet
at Pressburg after the Queen had made considerable constitutional concessions and restored many political privileges.   Her
courage in throwing overboard the traditional suspicion and
distrust with which the German ministers of the Hapsburgs had
always regarded the Hungarians, was justified by the altered
attitude of that people.   But even though the "insurrectionary"
levy flocked to the Austrian standards, time must elapse before
it could be ready for battle, and meanwhile the danger was
pressing and the need great.   From one quarter only could

Vienna be saved, for George II, Austria's only faithful ally, had been forced by the approach of Maillebois to conclude a treaty of neutrality (Sept. 27th), by which he pledged himself to abstain from assisting Maria Theresa or from giving his vote to Francis Stephen of Lorraine. Neipperg's army was the one force which could save Vienna, and Neipperg's army could only be set free by accepting Frederick's terms. It was a bitter humiliation for Maria Theresa, but there was no alternative. In vain she offered West Flanders to Louis XV, the Milanese and Tuscany to Bavaria, Lusatia to Saxony. England continually pressed her to come to terms with Frederick in order that she might devote all her energies to the only object about which the English cared, the defeat of France. Unable to fight both Frederick and the Franco-Bavarians, she was compelled to free herself of one enemy, and on October 9th the secret Convention of Klein-Schellendorf relieved her of the active hostility of Prussia at the sacrifice of Lower Silesia and of Neisse which was surrendered to the enemy after a mock siege. Frederick was glad to come to terms. His men had been in the field for ten months, and badly needed rest. To be spared the loss of life and the trouble of taking Neisse was no small gain. Moreover, he distrusted France, and had no wish to see her too successful.

Neipperg, who had been largely reinforced, accordingly broke up from Neisse on October 16th, his march being directed upon Prague, now threatened by 20,000 Saxons under Rutowski,[1] and by a division of French and Bavarians under Polastron from Amberg and Pilsen as well as by their main body from Budweis. Like Silesia, Bohemia was not in a good state to meet an attack; the province had been all but swept bare of troops, and even so important a point as Prague was weakly held. Once again a fatal slowness characterised Neipperg's movements. Not till November 7th did he reach Znaym, where Francis Stephen joined and took command. By November 17th the army reached Neuhaus, where it halted for four days, a mistake of the greatest importance, for a rapid advance would have brought them to Prague in time, the enemy being still widely separated. As it was, the delay allowed the Franco-Bavarians to concentrate under the walls

---

[1] A natural son of Augustus II, and half-brother of the more famous Maurice de Saxe.

of Prague on the 23rd, the Austrians being then at Tabor, over fifty miles to the Southward.   At the advice of Rutowski, whom Maurice de Saxe strongly supported, an assault was at once attempted, and, brilliantly conducted by Maurice, it proved a complete success (night of Nov. 24th to 25th).

· Too late to save Prague, a failure for which he had only his own slowness to blame, Francis Stephen and his 40,000 men fell back from Beneschau to a position in the rough country between Neuhaus and Tabor, and there stood at bay.   For the time both sides were inactive and operations at a standstill, the only move, an Austrian attack on Pisek (Dec. 26th), being easily repulsed by de Broglie, who had just (Dec. 20th) taken over the command from Belleisle, the latter retaining his diplomatic functions for the election was now at hand.

So far both sides had shown up but ill.   Both had moved with a culpable indifference to the value of time; but the Elector's errors in strategy were not confined to slowness alone. Instead of striking at Vienna, the great seat of his enemy's power, when he had it almost in his grasp, he had concentrated his whole strength upon taking a relatively unimportant town in Bohemia, whose capture must have been involved in the fall of the Hapsburg capital.   He had mistaken his objective; he had struck at the branches not at the trunk of the tree, and in so doing he had exposed Bavaria.

For while the campaign in Bohemia had resulted in a deadlock, Maria Theresa had managed to collect at Vienna a second army, the nucleus of which was formed by 4000 cavalry and 8000 regular infantry from Italy, with 14,000 wild irregulars from Hungary and the border countries, Croats, Pandours, Tolpatches and all the other light cavalry, who had no superiors in Europe in the arts of the raider and the forager.   And luckily for Maria Theresa she had available in Khevenhüller a general who possessed no small degree of that promptitude, resolution and energy so lacking in Neipperg and Francis Stephen.

It was on December 31st that Khevenhüller advanced up the Danube with 16,000 men, Bärenklau with 10,000 more, mainly irregulars, co-operating by moving on Münich through Tyrol.   The move was an instant success: Upper Austria was recovered, Bavaria overrun and laid waste by Bärenklau's moss-troopers.   Ségur with the French troops left behind on the

Danube, some 10,000 strong, was driven in on Linz and cooped up there. Unable to escape, he was forced to capitulate on Jan. 24th, Törring, who tried in vain to save him, being beaten by Bärenklau at Scharding (Jan. 17th) and driven back to Ingolstadt. It was a remarkable coincidence that the very day that Ségur surrendered and that Passau also fell into Austrian hands, Charles Albert was being elected Emperor at Frankfurt as Charles VII.[1] Similarly, on the day of the new Emperor's coronation (Feb. 12th), his capital, Münich, was concluding a capitulation to save itself from being plundered by Menzel's hussars. With the exception of Ingolstadt and one or two other strong places, all Bavaria was in Austrian hands.

But Maria Theresa's successes had alarmed Frederick, and just as he had concluded the Convention of Klein-Schellendorf behind the backs of his allies, so now he proceeded to break it when it was no longer convenient to keep it. It had served his purpose: his men were refreshed by four months' rest, and he had obtained Neisse without fighting for it. His allegation that Austria had failed to keep the convention secret was a palpable untruth: Austria's interest was to keep it dark, and it does seem that Austria had tried to do so; whereas within three weeks of signing it Frederick had signed a treaty with France, Bavaria and Saxony for a partition of the Austrian dominions,[2] a fairly sufficient test of his sincerity. Frederick and his allies, however, found it harder to decide upon a plan of campaign than upon the terms of their proposed partition of Maria Theresa's dominions. Even before the news of the fall of Linz arrived there had been great debates. De Broglie, supported by Maurice de Saxe, was very anxious for a move due South to save Bavaria by a direct attack on the Austrian main army. This force was lying between Iglau, Neuhaus, Budweis and Tabor, itself inactive but materially assisting Khevenhüller's operations by protecting them from any interference by de Broglie. Frederick, on the other hand, favoured an invasion of Moravia, by which he would turn the right flank of the Austrians and threaten Vienna. But his allies objected to his proposals as

---

[1] The Elector Palatine managed to purchase with his vote the renunciation of the Hohenzollern claim on Jülich and Berg in favour of the Margrave of Sulzbach.

[2] Von Arneth, i. p. 335; cf. ii. p. 28.

they would have involved his using their troops to carry out
his plan.[1]   Finally, they consented to let their left under
Polastron assist Frederick's invasion of Moravia by attacking
Iglau.   The Prussians had already crossed the frontier of
Moravia before the end of December and had occupied Glatz
and Olmutz, and when Frederick started from Wirchau on
February 5th, he was almost unopposed.   However, when the
news of Ségur's capitulation arrived, Polastron was at once
recalled, though Frederick pushed on, furious at what he
styled this " desertion."   His advanced guard got within forty
miles of Vienna and Ziethen's cavalry penetrated even nearer, but
Brünn, to which he had laid siege, resisted stoutly, de Broglie
refused to move, the Saxons failed to bring up a promised siege-
train, and with Hungarian irregular cavalry menacing his communications with Silesia Frederick had no alternative but to
retreat.   By April 17th he was at Chrudim in Bohemia, very
ill-content with de Broglie, though the latter after Klein-
Schellendorf had no reason to trust Frederick too far, and
might fairly plead that his original plan had been the better,
since the enemy's army was the true objective, while his own
corps was hardly in condition for much hard work.   Indeed,
it was partly with the idea of securing his own retreat that
about this time de Broglie occupied Eger and thereby opened
communications with Harcourt, who had just reached the
Upper Danube with some reinforcements from France.

Meanwhile the Austrians, now under Prince Charles of
Lorraine, were about to take the offensive.   The Saxons had
already been driven back into Bohemia, while three regiments
of cavalry, four of infantry and 13,000 Croats, whom Khevenhüller had rather unwillingly detached (Feb. 19th) from
his army, came up from Bavaria.   On May 10th, 30,000
Austrians[2] were at Saar on the Sasawa, moving on Prague
with the double object of cutting in between Frederick and
de Broglie, and of falling on the latter before his reinforcements
could arrive.   But the move took them right across Frederick's
front ; and though the failure of his intelligence department
and the unduly scattered positions of his troops caused him
to miss his best chance, he did succeed in concentrating

---

[1] Cf. Maurice's letter to Frederick, comparing the latter's behaviour at Mollwitz
with that of de Broglie at Pisek, *Frédéric II et Marie Thérèse*, ii. 196.

[2] 12 regiments of cavalry, 13 of infantry and the Croats.

28,000 men at Chrudim on the 13th. On the 15th he moved forward to Kuttenberg, which he reached next day, Leopold the younger of Anhalt-Dessau and his rear division arriving at Chotusitz.

Charles of Lorraine had planned to surprise the Prussian force near Chotusitz on the morning of May 17th, but the night march by which he attempted to carry out this scheme went wrong, and Leopold, learning his danger, was able to warn the King in time for him to bring back his division from Kuttenberg before 8 a.m. As at Mollwitz, both sides were drawn up in two lines with the cavalry on the wings. On the Prussian right Büddenbrock's cavalry overlapped their opponents, on their left Waldow's horsemen should have rested on a park wall, but to do this they were somewhat unduly extended, so that the Austrian cavalry here charged and routed them, while their infantry, outflanking the Prussian centre, attacked and captured part of Chotusitz. Büddenbrock, however, had overthrown Bathyanny's cavalry, only to be checked by von Thüngen's infantry, and routed and driven off by the cavalry of the second line. It was at this critical moment that Frederick, arriving from Kuttenberg with the reserve, restored the day. He seized the chance given him by the fact that the Austrian cavalry were chasing Büddenbrock off towards Kuttenberg and had thus left the flank of their infantry exposed, to shake their cohesion by a heavy cannonade and then to hurl his division upon the unprotected flank. His vigorous attack forced the Austrian left and centre to retire. This decided the day; for Chotusitz was still in dispute, and unfortunately for the Austrians the cavalry of their right were pillaging Leopold's camp to the neglect of their duties. Prince Charles was able to draw his men off in good order, for with the Prussian cavalry practically destroyed Frederick could not pursue. The stout fight made by the Austrians who, if their total losses were nearly 7000 had inflicted some 5000 casualties on the Prussians, including 2000 killed, and had practically annihilated the Prussian cavalry, made no small impression on Frederick. "It was a Prussian victory, but hardly an Austrian defeat," says von Arneth; and there is some truth in the judgment, for Frederick remained absolutely inactive and allowed Charles of Lorraine to reinforce Lobkowitz unmolested. Lobkowitz, moving down the Moldau on Prague as Charles of Lorraine moved forward to Chotusitz, had been attacked by de Broglie at Sahay (May 26th) and had retired again to Budweis ; but Frederick's inaction enabled the Austrians, who outnumbered the French by two to one, to resume the advance and drive them in on Prague after some sharp fighting.   Unable to hold Frauenberg, de Broglie retired to Pisek, thence to Pilsen, and finally to Prague, hard pressed by the Croats, and utterly unassisted by Frederick (June 4th to 13th); the garrisons he left behind were promptly cut off and taken, and the fall of Pilsen severed the communications between the French armies of Bohemia and Bavaria.

The explanation of Frederick's inaction is simple enough. Chotusitz had been fought for political reasons, as a move in the diplomatic game.   Distrusting his allies, alarmed at the prospect of the active intervention of England on behalf of Maria Theresa, for in February Walpole had fallen and in the new ministry Carteret was in charge of foreign affairs, and discouraged by his failure in Moravia, Frederick was thinking of leaving France and the Emperor in the lurch.   It was from him that the first overtures came ; and if the Austrians had some difficulty in believing in his sincerity, they soon saw it was to their interest to close with him.   On June 11th the Preliminaries of Breslau promised Frederick Glatz and Upper and Lower Silesia— with the exception of Troppau and Tetschen—and on July 28th a definite peace was signed at Berlin.   Notwithstanding his protestations of devotion to the cause of his allies, Frederick had not hesitated to desert them when he found he could get what he wanted from Maria Theresa.   His assertion that he only anticipated France in this treaty seems unsupported by the facts ; so far from being about to come to terms with her, France was steadily refusing all Maria Theresa's offers.[1]

Frederick's desertion, coupled with that of Saxony, which under the influence of Great Britain definitely acceded to the Peace of Berlin on September 7th, left the French army of Bohemia in a perilous position.   Not only was it weakened by a long campaign, by hard work and the privations due to the inefficient management of its supplies, but Belleisle, who had resumed the command, found himself exposed to greatly superior forces, absolutely isolated and "in the air."   It helped

[1] *Frédéric II et Marie Thérèse*, ii. 340.

him but little that Harcourt with 10,000 men from France
had reinforced the Bavarians and was holding Khevenhüller's
diminished forces in check; for if Harcourt could "contain"
Khevenhüller he could do no more, and had he attempted
to move across the Böhmer Wald to the relief of Prague
he would have given the enterprising Austrian an
admirable opportunity for using his light troops to full
advantage.

The interest of the situation was now centred at Prague,
where the French garrison was holding out courageously.
Maria Theresa was most anxious to secure them as prisoners;
their unconditional surrender would be some compensation for
the injury France had done her, and would be a valuable
diplomatic asset. Her idea was to obtain an equivalent for
Silesia, and for that purpose Bavaria seemed well adapted, in
which case it would be left to France to compensate the
Elector. France was equally set on rescuing Belleisle's army,
and as the task was beyond Harcourt's means, it was decided
to utilise the force on the Lower Rhine with which Maillebois
had till now been overawing Hanover. By the end of August
Maillebois was on the move, by September 12th he was at
Amberg in the Upper Palatinate, whereupon the Austrians by
orders from Vienna raised the siege and moved Westward to
meet him, leaving 9000 light horse to continue the blockade.

As Maillebois approached the French division from
Bavaria, now under Maurice de Saxe, moved up to join
him, which it did at Bramahof in September. Khevenhüller,
executing a parallel march, joined the Grand Duke of
Tuscany, who was at Heyd barring the road to Prague, on
September 27th. His departure from the Danube allowed
Seckendorff to recover Bavaria. On October 7th the
Bavarians reoccupied Münich. Bärenklau, too weak to hold
his ground, fell back behind the Inn, leaving garrisons in
Passau and Schärding.

Neither of the main armies was directed with much energy
or skill, for Saxe alone among the commanders was anxious
for battle. Not till October 6th did Maillebois advance from
Bramahof to Eger (8th) and Karden (10th); he apparently
hoped that this would allow the French from Prague to move
out towards Leitmeritz and so join him; but though the
garrison could easily have made their way out through the

cordon of disorderly and inefficient irregulars, Broglie and Belleisle held on to Prague, hoping that Maillebois would come through to them, and that Bohemia would yet be theirs.

But Maillebois was doing nothing of the sort. Bad roads, bad weather, tired and ill-fed troops, dismayed and disheartened him : beaten without a battle, he fell back to Eger, from there to Neustadt (Oct. 27th), and then moved slowly away to Bavaria, where he took up his winter-quarters (Nov.). Only a thoroughly inefficient and over-cautious commander like the Grand Duke of Tuscany could have let slip the chance afforded by this retreat; instead of falling on Maillebois as he retired, Francis Stephen let him get away unfought and unimpeded. Lobkowitz was sent back to take Leitmeritz, thereby isolating Prague of which he then resumed the siege, while the main army moved slowly South, parallel with Maillebois, like him crossing to the right bank of the Danube, at Braunau (Nov. 12th), and going into winter-quarters. It is difficult to say which commander showed least enterprise and least appreciation of the real needs of the situation and of those first principles of strategy, which concentrate attention on the importance of bringing one's enemy to action and rendering him incapable of doing damage rather than on out-manœuvring and evading.

At Prague Belleisle was now in sole command, for de Broglie had escaped just before communications were cut. The garrison might easily have held out some weeks longer ; but Belleisle, seeing no hope of relief, decided to attempt to break out. To Chevert he entrusted the task of getting what terms he could for the 6000 invalids and details who were left behind, and on the night of December 16th/17th, 3000 horse and 11,000 infantry pierced Lobkowitz's lax blockade and after a trying march, which cost them 1500 men in ten days, reached Eger on the 27th. Lobkowitz, who ought never to have let them get through, also failed to pursue properly, but his culminating error was in allowing Chevert to capitulate with the honours of war (Jan. 3rd) and to retire to Eger. Chevert and his invalids could never have held the town against an assault ; but Lobkowitz, a Bohemian nobleman who had much property in Prague, allowed Chevert's threats to burn the town to frighten him into granting such easy terms.

Still even if Belleisle and most of his shattered regiments

had managed to slip through Maria Theresa's hands, Prague was once more under the Austrian rule, Bohemia, with the exception of Eger and one or two other posts, was free from the French, and Belleisle's great scheme had failed completely. If it had benefited any one it was Frederick II, who had used Belleisle and the French as the catspaw with which he had secured Maria Theresa's reluctant consent to his possession of Silesia. But the French had not done with Germany yet: 1743 had more disasters in store for them and their luckless Bavarian client. The year opened with the death (Jan. 29th) of the aged Cardinal on whom so large a share of the responsibility for the war must rest; latterly Fleury had shown a desire to come to terms with Austria, even to anticipate 1756, and his death removed the chief influence in favour of peace; for though Belleisle was discredited, the man who now came to the front as the director of foreign affairs, the Duc de Noailles, urged a vigorous prosecution of the war. Cardinal Tencin, who came nearer than the other ministers to succeeding Fleury as First Minister, was more inclined towards throwing the strength of France into the scale on the side of Spain in the West Indian war then raging, but he did not oppose de Noailles' war policy in Germany.

During the winter there was much negotiating. England instigated Austria to offer terms to the Emperor, hoping so to detach him from the French alliance and to add him to a coalition against France. But as the Emperor held out for the complete restoration of Bavaria, and would not agree to the compensation elsewhere which Maria Theresa proposed, the negotiations were broken off. The only military event of the winter was the relief of Eger by du Chayla (April); the garrison ought to have been withdrawn, but was foolishly reinforced and replenished, though no military advantage could be hoped for from leaving it there.

It was at the beginning of May that the Austrians took the offensive on the Danube. The French and Bavarians were not on good terms: de Broglie's corps was in a thoroughly bad condition, its 67 infantry battalions mustered hardly 27,000 men, and 91 squadrons barely reached 10,000 sabres, there were many sick, and its equipment was deficient; moreover, he was opposed to the Emperor's proposal to take the offensive, and the result was that the Bavarians at Simbach and elsewhere found themselves exposed to the Austrian attack. Simultaneous attacks from North and East cut off the Simbach detachment; on May 9th it had to surrender, a few fugitives alone escaping to Braunau out of a force of over 6000. As the Austrians pushed on West the French recoiled across the Isar. A garrison which they left in Dingolfing was attacked and expelled by Daun (May 17th), and before the advance of the Austrians down the Isar Landau was evacuated. Crossing to the Northern bank of the Danube, Charles of Lorraine carried Deggendorf by storm, having first thrust three battalions in between the garrison and their bridge and so intercepted their retreat. Lobkowitz was now moving on the Danube from the Upper Palatinate, and to his attention Charles left the French, recrossing the river to deal with the Bavarians (June 6th). They proved unable to make a stand, but retired to Ingolstadt and thus exposed Münich which surrendered to Bärenklau, June 9th.

By this time de Broglie had abandoned all idea of defending Bavaria, and he now (June 7th) proposed an immediate retreat to join de Noailles, who was holding King George and the Pragmatic Army in check on the Main. It may fairly be surmised that this plan was not unconnected with Maurice de Saxe, for it certainly offered the best course of action under the circumstances; and despite despatches from France which ordered de Broglie to hold on to Ingolstadt, the Emperor's entreaties and the arrival of some 15,000 reinforcements, de Broglie steadily refused to resume the offensive, retiring on June 23rd to Donauwerth and declaring he would retreat to the Rhine. On the 26th a despatch of June 22nd arrived authorising a retreat but not a move to join de Noailles, nevertheless it was towards the Main that de Broglie moved. Had de Noailles waited for him, the extra numbers might have turned the scale at Dettingen and victory would have condoned disobedience, but the day after de Broglie left Donauwerth, Noailles gave battle and was beaten (June 16th to 27th). On hearing of this de Broglie moved straight to the Rhine; before the end of July he regained the left bank near Spires. His action was typical of the French disgust for the German campaign; the regiments ordered thither had nearly mutinied when they heard their destination, and as an English envoy wrote,[1] "the discourse among the French at Frankfort is,

[1] *Montagu House MSS.* (Hist. MSS. Com.) p. 404.

'What business have we here?'—they are very sick of Germany."

Left in the lurch by de Broglie, Charles Albert fled to Augsburg, while Seckendorff, who with the relics of the Bavarian army was at Rain, began negotiations with the Austrians, which resulted in the Convention of Niederschonfeld (end of June). This allowed him and his army to retire into Franconia and become neutral. Braunau, though defended by 4000 men, had already fallen. Ingolstadt held out stubbornly, but was at last forced to capitulate to Bärenklau on September 30th, Eger having surrendered three weeks earlier.

The force upon the Main, which de Broglie had proposed to join, was an army which had been collected on the Moselle earlier in the year to prevent the march of the so-called "Pragmatic Army" up the Rhine from intercepting de Broglie's retreat. One of the first-fruits of the fall of Walpole had been the more active part which England now prepared to play in the Continental War. In April 1742, British troops had begun to cross to Belgium, and by the middle of summer some 16,000 men[1] had been collected there under Lord Stair. This was not a very imposing force, but it was all that, thanks to Walpole's unwise economy, the country had at her disposal. Walpole had not merely neglected and starved the Army,[2] but he had not even attempted to remedy this weakness by hiring the mercenaries who formed the staple commercial product of so many of the minor states of Germany. Stair, a veteran of Marlborough's wars, united diplomatic with his military functions. The policy he favoured may be described as that of the "Grand Alliance." Maria Theresa must devote her whole resources to the expulsion of the French from Germany, and to following up their retreat by an invasion of France: in this Stair proposed to co-operate from the Netherlands. It is needless to add that this policy involved the abandonment of Silesia to Prussia, and when Maria Theresa at last gave way and signed the Preliminaries of Breslau, Stair's opportunity seemed to have come. The perilous position of the French in Bohemia called off Maillebois,

---

[1] 4 troops of Household Cavalry, 8 regiments of Horse and Dragoons, 3 battalions of the Guards, and 12 of the Line.

[2] Cf. J. W. Fortescue, *History of the British Army*, vol. ii. bk. vii., especially chs. i. and ii.

hitherto equally favourably placed for a blow at the Netherlands or at Hanover, into the interior of Germany and seemed
to lay the thinly guarded North-Eastern frontier of France
open for a blow down the Oise on Paris. Had the Hanoverian
army at once hastened to join Stair, who had 14,000 Austrians
as well as his 16,000 British, there was practically nothing
between him and Paris but a corps of some 12,000 men at
Dunkirk. The plan, if daring, was sound enough in idea;
for even if Stair had failed to take Paris, he might have fallen
back into Normandy and re-established communications with
England by sea. But George II hung back: he developed
scruples, he was not at war with Louis XV, he was only the
ally of the Queen of Hungary and Louis the ally of the
Elector of Bavaria, and thus a fine chance was allowed to
escape.

For 1743 the Austrians were anxious to bring the
Pragmatic Army into Germany, hoping in this way to bring
pressure to bear on the minor Powers and influence them in
favour of Austria, even if France were not thereby induced to
come to terms.[1] George II was well disposed to this plan,
and about the middle of February the British troops began
their move Eastward to the Rhine and then South up that
river.[2] On the way 16,000 Hanoverians joined them; on
the Main, which Stair reached early in May, they were
overtaken by 12,000 Austrians from the Netherlands, whose
places in the fortresses had been taken by Hessians in British
pay. The march had frightened Frederick of Prussia, he
protested vehemently against the English entering the
Empire; but his threats to intervene do not seem to have
received much attention or to have checked the advance for
a moment

On the Main, however, a halt was called, much to the
disgust of Stair, who was anxious to repeat 1704 by pushing
forward to the Upper Danube to make sure of intercepting
de Broglie's retreat. But this move was too daring for
George II, and the halt gave France time to collect an army of
some 70,000 men under de Noailles, which crossed the Rhine

---

[1] Cf. *Trevor MSS.* p. 85.

[2] The march is described in great detail by Colonel Charles Russell of the
1st Guards in the *Checquers Court MSS.* (Hist. MSS. Com.), from which source
much information as to the whole campaign may be obtained.

near Worms unopposed (May 25th), for George would not let Stair cross to the South of the Main. Ségur was first pushed forward to reinforce de Broglie, and then de Noailles took post to oppose the further advance of the Pragmatic Army.[1]

The refusal of George II to allow Stair to retain any of the posts he had occupied South of the Main soon made its bad effects felt. It left the whole of the left bank free to the French foragers, and they also crossed to the right bank and drew supplies from that side. Straitened for supplies, the Pragmatic Army pushed up the Main to Aschaffenburg and just forestalled the French in the occupation of the passage there (June 7th to 18th). Two days later the King joined the army, which, through no fault of Stair's, began to find itself in great straits for food. The French barred the route to Bavaria higher up the river, and their foragers plundered the North bank freely between Aschaffenburg and Frankfurt. The only alternative to starvation was a retreat on the magazines at Hanau, where George hoped to be joined by 6000 Hessians in British pay and 6000 "Electoral" Hanoverians.[2]

The French commander saw his chance; five brigades crossed at Aschaffenburg to press on the rear of the Allies, Militia battalions and batteries of guns lined the Southern bank of the river, while 23,000 of his best troops under his nephew de Grammont took post on the Northern bank to bar the retreat. De Grammont's position was behind the little Beck which flows into the Main just East of Dettingen, while the wooded hills at whose foot the river runs seemed an effective obstacle to an escape Northward. Indeed the Allies were in a very perilous position. Raked by the batteries which inflicted heavy loss on their columns,[3] they had halted and front-faced to the South near Klein Ostheim, when de Grammont's corps was detected at Dettingen. Stair appears now to have intervened, and under cover of the cavalry

[1] De Noailles' army was of very mixed quality; it included the *Maison du Roi* and some regiments which had been in garrisons in the South and West, but the bulk of it consisted of the units which had escaped from Prague hastily reformed with Militia recruits of poor quality.

[2] *i.e.* in his pay as Elector.

[3] The bulk of the losses of the Austrians and Hanoverians were incurred in this way.

of the right wing (British and Austrian) a new front was formed facing de Grammont.   On the right next the hills were four cavalry regiments, then an Austrian infantry brigade, then seven British battalions with another cavalry regiment next the river.   A second line of five cavalry regiments and nine battalions, five British, four Hanoverian, was drawn up in rear.   Farther away to the right rear the British Guards were posted on a height which covered a path over the wooded hills Northward.   Probably because he saw this move of the Guards and concluded that the force in front of him was a rearguard seeking to cover a retreat, partly also because his men were being galled by Stair's guns, de Grammont suddenly anticipated attack by moving forward and crossing the Beck, a step which threw his troops into some disorder.   The Allies also advanced, and a sharp fire-fight between the opposing infantries saw the French centre recoiling in disorder, when their cavalry, coming up on the right, fell upon the exposed flank of the British infantry near the river, where only a weak regiment of dragoons [1] covered it.   For a time they were successful, but the steadiness and heavy volleys of the British infantry checked them, and the British and Austrian cavalry from the other wing came up to the rescue.   The first few regiments behaved none too well and were routed, but the arrival of reinforce-ments turned the scale; the *Maison*, beaten off by the infantry, gave way before a charge by the 4th and 6th Dragoons and two Austrian regiments.   This allowed the Allies' infantry to advance against the second line of French foot, " in high spirits at having repulsed the French cavalry." There was a sharp fight, but the murderous volleys of the British infantry—Marshal Neipperg " never saw such a firing " —were too much for the French.   They were falling back in complete disorder, flocking down to the bridges, and Stair seemed on the point of annihilating de Grammont's broken corps when George II intervened to stop pursuit.   His inter-vention was attributed by the British army to Hanoverian influence,[2] for Stair certainly seems to have strongly urged

---

[1] Bland's, now 3rd Hussars.

[2] " Nothing but a Hanoverian was listened to or regarded " (Colonel Russell). " The King halted, and the scene of action and military ardour was at once turned into a Court circle " (Colonel C. V. Townshend's *Memoirs of Marquess Townshend,*

a pursuit, and to have protested against the undue haste with which George pressed on to Hanau, leaving his wounded on the field to the care of de Noailles. Here he found the 12,000 Hessians and Hanoverians, but even so remained utterly inactive; and only when Charles of Lorraine came up to Cannstadt (July 9th) and Durlach (25th) did de Noailles retire behind the Rhine, crossing at Turckheim (July 17th) and occupying the Lauterburg lines.[1]

The failure to utilise the victory was almost as discreditable to George II as were the blunders which had made the Pragmatic Army fight at such a disadvantage. When at length Charles of Lorraine arrived much time was wasted over concerting a plan of operations, for Charles did not wish to be second in command, and therefore objected to George's proposals for a junction. Finally, the Pragmatic Army crossed the Rhine above Mayence (Aug. 24th) and moved to Worms (29th), de Noailles retiring to Landau. A little more vigour and a decisive success might have been gained: the French were intimidated, and reinforcements, including a Dutch contingent and four British regiments, had come up by way of Treves, but the Pragmatic Army remained inactive at Worms till September 24th, while the Austrians seeking to force a passage over the Rhine near New Breisach were beaten off (Sept. 3rd). Early in October the Allies dispersed, the Pragmatic Army returning to the Netherlands, the Dutch, the "Electoral" Hanoverians and the Hessians to their respective homes, the Austrians taking up winter-quarters in the Vorderland. If the campaign had not proved quite as brilliant a success as better handling of the Pragmatic Army might have made it, the Allies had reason to be fairly satisfied. The French had been expelled from Germany, and it seemed as though the next year might see the tables turned and Alsace and Lorraine invaded.

To some extent diplomatic considerations may account

p. 29); the Guards bitterly resented being put under the Hanoverian General von Ilten, whom they called "the confectioner of the Household Brigade—because he preserves them."

[1] The losses at Dettingen were heavy on both sides; the Allies had about 750 killed, 1600 wounded—800 being British, 550 Hanoverians, 1000 Austrians: the estimates of the French loss vary from 17,000 to 8000, of which the more moderate (cf. *Trevor* and *Montagu House MSS.*) seems more reasonable, though many were drowned in the Main.

for the sluggishness of the Pragmatic Army after Dettingen, though George II's want of strategic capacity and his failure to work harmoniously with Charles of Lorraine were more immediately important. The truth was that George II and Carteret did not see eye to eye with Maria Theresa. Looking to the humiliation of France rather than to the satisfaction of Maria Theresa as the principal object, they put pressure upon her to strengthen the Coalition by concessions to Bavaria and to Sardinia which she was ill-disposed to make. Thinking that France had been more completely beaten than was really the case, Maria Theresa was now determined to recover her husband's family land, Lorraine; and reluctant as she was to let Charles VII off so lightly, it is possible that she would have agreed to restore Bavaria to him and to recognise him as Emperor had Carteret been able to procure from the English Parliament the subsidies which he demanded as the price of his adhesion to the Coalition. But Carteret had little influence in Parliament and could not command subsidies: the old cry was raised that he was sacrificing England's maritime and colonial interests to Hanover, and Parliament was reluctant to support one so recently the client of France as Charles VII. Thus the "Project of Hanau" resulted in failure, and Carteret found himself compelled to give way. His policy was really one of using the King's Hanoverian predilections to assist his own European policy, a policy of "conquering America in Germany" which one of his bitterest assailants was one day to carry out triumphantly; but he had no party behind him, and could not combat the "Revolution Families" with success. In one quarter, however, he did succeed in gaining his ends, and the Treaty of Worms, signed September 13th, did bind the slippery Charles Emmanuel of Sardinia to the Allied cause.

If the course of events in Italy does not concern the history of Germany as closely as do the campaigns on the Elbe, the Oder, the Rhine and the Danube, it forms too important a part of the Austrian Succession War to be passed over hastily. The keynote to its varied fortunes is to be found in the double relations of Sardinia to Austria and to the House of Bourbon. Charles Emmanuel, the able and unscrupulous ruler of "the Prussia of Italy," and his minister, d'Ormea, while determined to reap all the advantage they could out of Maria Theresa's embarrassment, viewed with great hostility Elizabeth Farnese's schemes for her second son Don Philip. Lombardy, which she proposed to conquer for him, was the last place in which the Sardinians could with equanimity see Bourbons established. The instinct for holding the balance between the rivals drove Charles Emmanuel over to the side of Austria as being the weaker, and though he negotiated simultaneously with both parties, it was with Austria that he came to terms in February 1742. This treaty, arranged by English mediation, was of a provisional nature. Charles Emmanuel was to support Maria Theresa, while the thorny question of concessions was to be settled later.[1]

It was fortunate for Maria Theresa that she thus obtained the help of Sardinia, for she needed it badly. Escorted by the French Toulon fleet, whose superiority in force had deterred the English Mediterranean squadron under Haddock from attempting to dispute their passage, 15,000 Spaniards from Barcelona had landed at Orbitello in December 1741. Had the Neapolitans joined them at once Traun, who had had to detach most of his troops from Milan to save Vienna,[2] would have had a difficult task; as it was, their delays saved him. By the time that the Spaniards and Neapolitans united at Pesaro (Feb. 1742) the arrangement with Sardinia had been concluded and some reinforcements had returned from Austria. With 12,000 Austrians[3] and some 20,000 Sardinians, Traun took the offensive, invaded the territory of Modena, whose Duke (Francis III of Este) had just declared for the Bourbons, besieged and took (June 28th) that town, and generally displayed so bold a front that the Spanish commander Montemar fell back to Foligno. Here the Neapolitans left him, recalled home by the demonstration

---

[1] Charles Emmanuel demanded the Ticino as his Eastern boundary with Stradella and Finale: this last district had been sold to Genoa by Charles VI and Maria Theresa indignantly refused to rob Genoa by cancelling the sale. Its importance lay in giving the continental dominions of Sardinia direct access to the sea. It was Spain's refusal to let Charles Emmanuel have all Lombardy, a demand to which France was favourable, which caused the breaking off of the negotiations.

[2] Cf. p. 127.

[3] The Austrians relied entirely on German and Hungarian troops in Italy, they did not even hire Swiss mercenaries; and though their government was by no means unpopular and hatred of Sardinia would certainly have secured the fidelity of a Milanese militia, they had not raised any local troops.

of Commodore Martin's English squadron off Naples (Aug.
22nd), which had forced Don Carlos to retire from the
Coalition.   Traun was, however, prevented from overthrowing
Montemar by the return home of the Sardinians.   A Spanish
force under Don Philip passing overland through France, for
the English fleet under Matthews had severed communications
by sea between Spain and Italy, was threatening Piedmont.   It
was repulsed (Sept.), but it brought Traun to a standstill.

Hoping to take advantage of this diversion, Elizabeth
Farnese now directed Gages, who had replaced Montemar,
to try a winter-campaign.   Moving against Finale, however,
he was checked by Traun at Buonoporto, and fell back to
Campo Santo on the Panaro.   Here on the afternoon of
February 8th, 1743, Traun attacked Gages, and by skilful
handling of his reserves at a critical moment won a handsome
victory.   But various causes prevented him from making full
use of his success.   He was in disfavour at Vienna, being
accused of maladministration of the Italian provinces and of
wasteful expenditure.   Therefore, expecting to be recalled,
he took no steps towards pushing home his advantage.
Charles Emmanuel had come to the conclusion that it would
be well to come to a definite settlement as to the concessions
he was to receive before Austria gained any further success,
and the war languished, the only quarter in which much
activity was displayed being at sea.

The negotiations about the concessions were long and
complicated.   Maria Theresa at last agreed to the demands
of Sardinia, but sought to make them conditional on her
recovering Silesia.   Charles Emmanuel would not hear of
anything but an immediate cession, and England objected to
the reopening of the Silesian question, still hoping to bring
Frederick into line with herself and Austria against France.
In the end a threat that, if she did not yield, Charles
Emmanuel would come to terms with France, extorted from
Maria Theresa a reluctant consent to the Treaty of Worms
(September 13th, 1743).   By this she ceded to Sardinia
Parma, Piacenza and the districts of Anghiara and Vigevano,
the last strips of Austrian territory West of the Ticino.
Charles Emmanuel abandoned all claims on the Milanese,
but received the reversion of Austria's rights over Finale.   It
was agreed that the Bourbons should be expelled from Italy;

to this end Maria Theresa was to provide 30,000 men and to receive Naples and the Tuscan ports, Charles Emmanuel's 40,000 men were to win him back Sicily. England undertook to provide subsidies and the assistance of her fleet.

It is certainly open to question whether Maria Theresa was well advised in concluding this treaty. It was a direct challenge to France and Spain and, while France was heartily tired of the war in Germany, the threat of an Austrian invasion of Alsace, the danger of losing the acquisitions of 1738 and the wish to wipe out the humiliations of Belleisle's failure by victories in the Netherlands combined to arouse warlike enthusiasm and violent anti-Austrian feeling in France. To have taken the head of a German crusade to recover Alsace and Lorraine would have been a policy worthy of the best traditions of the Hapsburg House; but for such a policy England and Sardinia would have cared but little, and to organise a German league against France with the titular head of Germany a fugitive under French protection and the strong military power of Prussia indifferent if not actively hostile was impossible. It would certainly appear that Maria Theresa would have done well to have come to terms with France, to have acknowledged Charles VII as Emperor, and thus to have isolated Frederick. She could have counted on Hanoverian hostility to Prussia and the needs of the maritime and colonial war to keep England neutral, she might have even won the assistance of the Bourbons by some such concession as the cession of Tuscany to Louis XV's son-in-law Don Philip, she would have been better able to resist Sardinia's demands for concessions. France had no immediate object in continuing the war save the restoration of her military prestige. The attempt to partition the Hapsburg dominions had failed, and it is not a little difficult to see why the war should have gone on.

An explanation is perhaps to be found in the continued presence of Frederick II in Silesia. This was the real obstacle to peace on the Continent. Until she had recovered that province or obtained some territorial compensation for its loss, Maria Theresa would not rest content. But where was such compensation to be obtained? Bavaria seemed the most attractive alternative, but France could not look on and see her Imperial client deprived of his hereditary dominions, and such a solution would have aroused Prussia's fears and opposition. To win Lorraine or Naples and Sicily from the Bourbons and compensate the Elector of Bavaria by an exchange might have been more generally acceptable, but this scheme involved their conquest, which was sure to be no easy task. The deciding factor in the situation was Maria Theresa's poverty: she could do nothing without English subsidies, and she therefore had to fall in with the policy agreeable to England. And while England under Carteret's guidance was seeking to revive the Continental coalition against the Bourbons as the best means of combating their ascendency, the reaction had already begun in France, and the trend of feeling in favour of an active prosecution of the war was marked by the conclusion, on October 25th, 1743, of the Treaty of Fontainebleau, the Bourbon counterblast to the Treaty of Worms. By this famous treaty, the second of the so-called "Family Compacts," France recognised the rights of Don Philip to the Milanese, Parma and Piacenza. She also undertook to help Spain to recover Gibraltar and Minorca from England, and promised to definitely declare war on Austria and England.

CHAPTER IX

THE AUSTRIAN SUCCESSION WAR—*concluded*

TO THE TREATY OF AIX-LA-CHAPELLE

THE change in character which the war had undergone was marked by the first moves attempted by the French in 1744. The policy of intervening in Germany to assist the Emperor was discarded in favour of a direct attack on England by Saxe and 15,000 men from Dunkirk, who were to be escorted across the Channel by de Roquefeuil and the Brest fleet, and of a vigorous offensive in Italy, to allow of which it would be necessary to raise the blockade established by Matthews over Toulon when the Spanish fleet had taken refuge there in 1742. Both plans miscarried; de Roquefeuil was only saved by a lucky shift of the wind from destruction at the hands of Norris and the Channel Fleet;[1] while the famous "miscarriage off Toulon" on February (11th O.S.) 22nd, which threw so much discredit on the British Navy, showed that even a drawn battle was sufficient to foil de Tencin's schemes for gaining control of the Mediterranean as a preliminary to driving the Austrians out of Italy.

Far different was the case with their invasion of the Netherlands. When early in May 80,000 French troops, well equipped and accompanied by the King himself, crossed the frontier into the Austrian Netherlands, they found the Allies weak,[2] absolutely unready for war, at feud amongst themselves, with no recognised commander-in-chief. It was

[1] A French account in the *Gentleman's Magazine* for March 1744 makes it clear that had not the wind dropped, Norris would have brought on an action on the morning of February 24th ; but the ebb tide forced him to anchor, and the violent gale which came on that evening proved the salvation of the French, who escaped under its cover to Brest.

[2] Only 55,000 of all nationalities.

hardly wonderful, therefore, if for a time the invaders were quite unchecked. Courtrai (May 18th), Menin (June 5th), Ypres (June 25th) and Furnes (July 11th), in bad repair and indifferently held,[1] provided a series of facile triumphs. The country between the Lys and the sea had passed into their hands, and they were about to attack Ostend, when they were suddenly forced to change their plans. This was not due to their immediate opponents, though the Allies had at last collected a respectable force round Brussels,[2] but to the news of the Austrian invasion of Alsace. To meet this danger a strong division of the army of Flanders was at once detached to the Upper Rhine, and Maurice de Saxe had to adopt a defensive attitude with the remainder. That he succeeded in maintaining his position, and with it all the conquests of the early summer, is partly to be ascribed to his admirable defensive tactics, but even more to the quarrels, disunion and aimless proceedings of the Allies. The Dutch had not yet declared war on France, and the party which favoured a French rather than an English alliance was strong. As Colonel Russell wrote: " If we end by having a pacific campaign it will be owing to the Dutch, who will by all means avoid declaring war with France." Still there was no little reason for their complaints that George II was not doing enough in his capacity as Elector of Hanover.[3] The Hanoverian troops in the field ought to have been paid by Hanover and not by England, whose subsidies should have been used to hire Hessians and other neutrals; as it was, George II as King was hiring troops from himself as Elector, " one's right hand paying one's left," Robert Trevor calls it, and he put the matter succinctly when he wrote: ". . . nothing would so much contribute to save Europe, encourage the Empire and strengthen the Ministry's hands . . . as our Royal Master's drawing his Electoral sword and his Electoral purse-strings gallantly and unreservedly in support of our common cause."

Meanwhile the Austrians on the Upper Rhine under

---

[1] The Dutch had shamefully neglected these " Barrier Fortresses "; they failed to find the required garrisons and conducted the defence without zeal or endurance.

[2] By the end of May the Austrians had failed to produce more than 3000 men. The Dutch were equally backward, and loud complaints were heard at the absence of the " ungrateful Hessians."

[3] Cf. *Trevor MSS.* p. 106.

Prince Charles of Lorraine, though somewhat late in beginning operations, seemed in a fair way to possess themselves of Alsace. They had forced a passage at Germersheim on the last day of June, the Bavarian corps posted there, the relics of the army of the Emperor, being somewhat negligent, and Marshal Coigni, who lay to the North, having his attention diverted by a corps which crossed the river at Mayence, thanks to the Elector's connivance. Advancing to Lauterburg and Weissenburg, the Austrians took these posts and all but cut Coigni off from Alsace. He managed to retake Weissenburg and so push through to his province, but he was driven back to Haguenau and thence to Strassburg, and the route over the Vosges into Lorraine was left open. It was this critical situation which brought the King and de Noailles with 25,000 men from Flanders up to Metz at full speed. At Metz their progress was checked by the sudden illness of Louis, whose death was hourly expected (Aug.). Uncertain whether he would be in favour with the Dauphin, de Noailles betrayed a hesitation and indecision in his conduct of military affairs which might have proved serious had the Austrians displayed greater activity. Not till the King was out of danger did de Noailles advance, enter Alsace by way of Willer and join Coigni near Strassburg (Aug. 17th). A week later he had the pleasure of "assisting" at the repassage of the Rhine at Beinheim by the Austrians, an operation he altogether failed to hinder or harass, for the feeble attack which he did deliver upon their rearguard was easily beaten off and the difficult undertaking was accomplished in good order, a matter not a little creditable to Prince Charles and his chief adviser Marshal Traun.

But it was not the arrival of de Noailles on the scene which was primarily responsible for the Austrian evacuation of Alsace. The credit for having ruined the best chance the eighteenth century was to see of reuniting that province to the Empire is due to Frederick II. His fear that he might be disturbed in his possession of Silesia outweighed with him the natural satisfaction which every patriotic German should have felt at the prospect of seeing Alsace recovered from the Bourbons. Where Frederick William I or even the Great Elector would probably have welcomed the chance of wreaking the Empire's vengeance on its most formidable enemy,

Frederick II preferred to deal Austria yet one more stab in the back for the benefit of Louis XV.

That it would not be to his advantage if the Emperor were driven out of Germany and compelled to take refuge in France, Frederick was well aware. As early as the spring of 1743 he had been contemplating an alliance of the neutral Powers of Germany to bring about peace on terms favourable to the Emperor rather than to Maria Theresa, but he had preferred remaining in quiet possession of Silesia to risking anything for his nominal overlord. Since then many things had occurred which had awakened his suspicions. The Treaty of Berlin had not been in the list of treaties guaranteed at Worms; a treaty had been concluded between Austria and Saxony guaranteeing without specification *all* the possessions of Austria; it seemed possible that the hopelessness of his situation might induce Charles VII to come to terms with Maria Theresa and allow her to incorporate Bavaria in her dominions on giving him in exchange Alsace-Lorraine, Naples or the Netherlands. Frederick would have had no objection to seeing Austria take Naples for herself, but Maria Theresa, like Joseph II, aimed rather at re-establishing Hapsburg predominance in Germany than at fresh acquisitions elsewhere; there was even a prospect that the Electors—for not only Hanover, but Saxony and the Ecclesiastical Electors were now on her side—might be induced by Maria Theresa to set aside the election of Charles VII as invalid and to choose Francis Stephen as Emperor in his place. One may or may not believe in the genuineness of Frederick's alarm on behalf of the German constitution, but it cannot be denied that he had reason to tremble for Silesia; still one may fairly ask whether Maria Theresa would not have reconciled herself to the loss of Silesia and have acknowledged Charles VII as Emperor if the Union of Frankfurt had turned the scale against France and enabled her to wrest Alsace and Lorraine from the heir of Louis XIV?

The Union of Frankfurt was the league which Frederick with the assistance of Chavigny, the French envoy at Münich, organised in May 1744. It included, besides Charles VII, the new Elector Palatine, Charles Theodore of Sulzbach, who had succeeded to all the possessions of the Neuburg line, including Jülich and Berg, on Charles Philip's death in 1742, Landgrave

Frederick I of Hesse-Cassel and other Princes. Its objects were to restore the lawful constitution of the Empire, and to maintain the Emperor in his rights; to recover for Charles VII his hereditary dominions, and on this basis and with the guarantee of Silesia to Frederick to re-establish peace in Germany. By a secret article France guaranteed this compact, while some weeks later another secret treaty with the Emperor promised to Prussia large concessions in Bohemia, and to France fortresses in the Netherlands.

Good relations between France and Prussia had not been very easy to restore. With good cause each distrusted the other's sincerity. Voltaire's mission to Berlin in July 1743 had for this reason proved a fiasco, and not·until Frederick saw France thoroughly committed to the war, both formally by having declared it and practically by having invaded Flanders, did he conclude an arrangement with Louis XV's government (June 5th, 1744). The possible hostility of Russia, where there was a strong anti-Prussian party led by Bestuchev, he had already to some extent neutralised by arranging for the marriage of Sophia of Anhalt-Zerbst (afterwards Catherine II) to Duke Peter, the heir of the Czarina Elizabeth.[1]

The first result of this alliance was that on August 15th, eight days after his ultimatum had been presented at Vienna, Frederick's troops streamed across the Saxon frontier on their way to Bohemia, and on September 2nd united before Prague with a column which had come from Silesia through Glatz. It was the presence of Frederick's 80,000 men in Bohemia which brought Charles of Lorraine back from the Rhine to repel this new attack. Prague, as in 1741, was weakly held; but it resisted for a fortnight, falling on September 16th, after which Frederick pushed up the Moldau with the intention of intercepting the Austrian retreat and catching them between his army and the Franco-Bavarians, whom he somewhat hastily concluded to be following hard upon their tracks.

This, however, was not the case. While the Austrians, marching with a celerity which was as commendable as it was unusual on their part, reached Donauwerth on September 10th and Waldmünchen on the border between Bavaria and

---

[1] He was grandson of Peter the Great, being the son of his daughter Anne and Duke Charles Frederick of Holstein-Gottorp.

Bohemia a fortnight later, de Noailles and the main body of
the French had turned aside to besiege Freiburg in Breisgau.
This was a move it is impossible to justify: they had given no
specific pledge to Frederick, but common sense might have
shown de Noailles that it would be well to co-operate with an
ally so capable of lending useful help, while the obvious
strategy was to press hard upon the Austrian retreat and
bring them to action. The siege of Freiburg, which was
begun on September 18th, had no definite strategical object,
and served no really useful purpose.   Probably the real reason
why de Noailles forbore to send more than twenty battalions
under Ségur forward into Bavaria with Seckendorff and the
Imperial army, was that he did not wish to commit himself to
a repetition of the fate that had befallen the last invasion of
Germany; that lively recollections of their experiences in those
quarters made his officers and men loath to revisit them, and
that neither de Noailles nor the French government felt
inclined to risk anything to the chance of Frederick's sincerity
in co-operation.

Be that as it may, Frederick found that his move South-
Westward had brought him into considerable danger.   He
had to recoil hastily from Budweis to Frauenberg, which he
reached on the day (Oct. 2nd) that Prince Charles and Traun
joined Bathyanny and 20,000 men recalled from Bavaria at
Mirstitz. This compelled Frederick to retire precipitately
behind the Sasawa, for his communications with Prague were
threatened.   Once more Maria Theresa had appealed to the
Hungarians, and in reply clouds of their light horsemen were
rallying to the Austrian standard and were making their
presence felt by the Prussians, whose stragglers and foragers
and outposts they harassed with great persistence and success.

Traun, though joined by a Saxon contingent on October
22nd, steadily declined to be brought to the pitched battle by
which Frederick hoped to extricate himself from his troubles.
Not even the most careful feints would tempt him.   On
November 4th, Frederick retired to Kolin, the Austrians
moving up to Kuttenberg.   Frederick next crossed to the
North-East of the Elbe, intending to take up his winter-
quarters behind that river; but the Austrians suddenly
became active, pushed across the river at Teinetz, and so cut
him off from Prague (Nov. 19th).   The King had no alternative

but to retire as best he could to Silesia: he was fortunate in that the Austrians did not move quickly enough to profit more by the scattered state of his troops, but his army suffered much and lost heavily on their retreat. The garrison of Prague evacuated the town and also made their way to Silesia after a disastrous march. Traun followed the Prussians into Upper Silesia early in the New Year, but the bitter weather made a winter campaign impossible, and he withdrew almost at once to Bohemia. He had the satisfaction of having—as Frederick himself quite admitted—altogether out-manœuvred the King of Prussia, but he had perhaps carried caution too far, and might have risked a battle when the Prussians had once begun to be demoralised by continually retreating. But a price had to be paid for the deliverance of Bohemia from the Prussians, and this was the expulsion of Bärenklau from Bavaria. With only 20,000 men to oppose the 32,000 of Seckendorff and Ségur, he had had to evacuate Münich (Oct. 15th) and retire behind the Inn, retaining possession, however, of Passau, Salzburg and Braunau. Freiburg meanwhile after a gallant defence had succumbed to the French on November 24th.

Two events of great importance marked the winter of 1744–1745. In November the Marquis d'Argenson became Foreign Minister of France. On January 20th the Emperor Charles VII died.

The foreign policy of d'Argenson presents a curious mixture of the obsolete and the premature. In his idea of establishing in Italy an independent federation under the hegemony of Sardinia, he was as much in advance of his times as he was behind them in thinking the humiliation of the Hapsburgs the chief object of French policy towards Germany. In his desire to accomplish this end, to put in practice the policy of *divide et impera*, he never seems to have stopped to consider whether the Prussian alliance might not prove a two-edged weapon. Opposed as he was to England and anxious to revive the French Marine, he failed to see that the hostility of Austria and Prussia might be relied upon to paralyse Germany and to keep her neutral in the Anglo-French contest for the seas which was of no immediate concern to Hapsburg or Hohenzollern.

The death of Charles VII involved the collapse of the

Union of Frankfurt, and opened up the question of the succession to the Empire. Even before the Emperor's death the Franco-Bavarian alliance had been showing signs of weakness. German feeling was anti-French; the Empress, an Austrian Archduchess, favoured a reconciliation with Austria; and the Emperor's best general, Seckendorff, distrusting the prospects of successfully holding Bavaria, was quite ready to come to terms. So averse was he to the war, that when in January an Austrian division attacked the French posts at Amberg, he refused to stir to its aid. Ségur attempted the relief, but was badly beaten, whereupon the town capitulated. Just about this time a refusal to comply with the Emperor's urgent appeal for reinforcements was received from Louis XV, and it is not too much to say that this was the final blow to Charles VII. "The Bold Bavarian," who must have found the Imperial dignity a very disappointing possession, was only forty-eight at his- death (Jan. 1745). Led away by a not unnatural ambition and by the promises of French and Prussian assistance, he had embarked upon a course from which he had reaped no advantage, and which had exposed his unhappy subjects to great sufferings. It is hardly possible to keep pace with the number of times Bavaria changed hands. This ill-fortune was a warning to any who might aspire to the Empire. Charles Albert had tried to gain the headship of Germany by the aid of Germany's old enemy. It would be hard to condemn him for falseness to an all but non-existent German nationality and patriotism, but in letting himself be the puppet of France and his candidature be the cloak for French aggressions on Germany, he cannot be said to be free from responsibility for the misfortunes which befell him.

The death of Charles VII opened up to Maria Theresa an opportunity for attaining one of the principal objects of her ambition, her husband's election as Emperor. Nor was it easy to see where a candidate could be found to oppose Francis Stephen. Maximilian Joseph, the new Elector of Bavaria, was a mere youth and, even had he been willing to subject his country again to the perilous honour of having the Emperor for its ruler, his candidature could hardly have had any chance. As Protestants, if for no other reasons, George of Hanover and Frederick of Brandenburg were impossible. The Elector Palatine was on personal grounds quite out of the question, and there only remained Augustus III of Saxony, who had recently come to terms with Austria and Russia,[1] and therefore declined the offers of France and Prussia. Notwithstanding this, d'Argenson continued to hanker after the idea of inducing Augustus III to stand; and he urged that as a means to exercise influence over the Imperial election, France should once again assume the offensive on the Danube and join Frederick in Bohemia. This would entail standing on the defensive in the Netherlands, which he regarded as quite unimportant, and would prevent France lending much aid to the Spanish Bourbons in Italy, thereby withdrawing France from an alliance his feelings towards which are well expressed in his famous aphorism, " le destin de l'Espagne est toujours de nous ruiner."

But meanwhile Maria Theresa, acting with a remarkable decision and promptitude, had hurled a strong force under Bathyanny on the scattered Franco-Bavarian forces in Bavaria. He crossed the Inn on March 21st, took Landshut, Straubing and Dingolfing almost unopposed, drove Ségur in on Donauwerth, sent the Elector flying to Augsburg, and in a fortnight the unlucky Bavaria had once more suffered a change of masters.

The Elector had no alternative but to accept the offers Maria Theresa now made through her cousin the Empress Dowager. In vain Chavigny fought to keep Maximilian Joseph true to an ally who made no effort to succour him. On April 22nd, 1745, the Treaty of Füssen restored him to his dominions on his guaranteeing the Pragmatic Sanction, promising neutrality in the war,[2] and pledging his vote to Francis Stephen at the Imperial election.

This treaty, to which Hesse-Cassel and Würtemberg hastened to accede, was a great triumph for Maria Theresa and a corresponding blow to Frederick and France. Deprived of the moral support of her alliance with Bavaria, it is rather difficult to see what reasons France had for continuing the war. Probably the successes of 1744 in Flanders had whetted Louis XV's attitude for conquest : to make peace as matters then stood would be a somewhat humiliating confession of failure, and d'Argenson, who was a firm supporter

---

[1] The Treaty of Warsaw was arranged in January, but not ratified till May 18th.
[2] A secret article placed 12,000 troops at the disposal of the Maritime Powers on hire.

of the Prussian alliance, was possessed by the belief that he would be able to induce Augustus III to stand for the Empire. It was therefore resolved to adopt a vigorous offensive in Italy and the Netherlands as the means of extorting a good peace from Maria Theresa.

This decision was not palatable to Frederick. He had urged upon France an attack upon Hanover which should cut that country off from the ecclesiastical electorates and, as in 1741, intimidate the Electoral College, while another army should advance through Bavaria into Bohemia; but France had had enough of campaigning in Germany, and did not care enough about the choice of an Emperor to sacrifice to that object the chance of territorial aggrandisement in Italy and the Netherlands. The measure of Frederick's annoyance may be gathered from the fact that he offered to vote for Francis Stephen if Silesia were guaranteed to him. Short of money and other resources, he found himself threatened with the hostility of Saxony and of Saxony's patron Russia, the third party to the Treaty of Warsaw.[1]

Thus, while 50,000 Austrians under Bathyanny moved Westward after the conclusion of the Treaty of Füssen and establishing themselves near Frankfurt covered the meeting of the Electoral College, France instead of reinforcing Coigni, who had moved to the Middle Rhine after the fall of Freiburg, was devoting her principal efforts to the Netherlands. A magnificent army of 90,000 men under Marshal Saxe converged upon Tournay and laid siege to that important fortress (April 19th). To save it the Duke of Cumberland, who had been appointed commander-in-chief of the Allied Forces, collected some 50,000 men near Brussels and, moving up to its relief,[2] engaged Saxe at Fontenoy on May 11th (N.S.). Cumberland, whose daring blow at the most vulnerable point of the French line was hardly the mixture of stupid courage and ignorant incompetence described by some writers, was only baulked of success by the misconduct of the Dutch on

[1] This guaranteed the succession to Poland to the son of Augustus III, promised to reconquer Silesia for Maria Theresa and reduce Prussia to its original limits: Augustus III was to vote for Francis Stephen. As far as Russia was concerned it was the work of Bestuchev, who favoured Austria.

[2] Of this force, 53 battalions and 90 squadrons, the Dutch provided 26 and 40, the British 22 and 26, the Hanoverians 5 and 16, the Austrians only 8 squadrons, d'Aremberg having taken 24,000 men to the Main to join Bathyanny.

his left. They completely failed to second the efforts of the British and Hanoverian infantry, whose conduct on this day has probably never been surpassed and rarely equalled. Had the Dutch only engaged the attention of the French right and prevented Saxe bringing up troops from that quarter to hurl upon Cumberland's column, the French could not have averted defeat; as it was, Saxe was able to throw in all his reserves and win.[1]

Ten days after the battle the Dutch garrison of Tournay surrendered after a feeble defence, and Cumberland, unable to cover both Ghent and Brussels, had the mortification of seeing the former taken by the French on July 11th (N.S.). He had to retire to Vilvorde between Antwerp and Brussels, but he was unable to make any attempt to interfere with Saxe's operations against West Flanders, for he received orders to send back to England first ten battalions of infantry, and finally his whole army save five regiments of horse and one of foot. The reason for their recall was that on July 25th Prince Charles Edward Stuart had landed in Scotland. The connection between the " Forty-Five " and the course of affairs on the Continent, more especially in Germany, may perhaps seem remote, but it was the recall of Cumberland and his army quite as much as the slackness of the Dutch, the extreme efficiency of Saxe's engineers and artillerymen, or the absence of the Austrians, which was responsible for the ease with which the French in the latter half of 1745 overran West Flanders.

The absence of the Austrians from the Netherlands was due to their presence at Frankfurt for the Imperial election. From the moment the French crossed the frontier of Flanders, Francis Stephen's election was assured. Together, Frederick and France might have perhaps overcome the reluctance of Augustus III, but the futile negotiations which the untiring d'Argenson was conducting with Saxony merely prevented any chance of the French army on the Rhine taking the offensive, as d'Argenson supposed Augustus would not wish to push his candidature home with French bayonets.[2] When

---

[1] For Fontenoy, see the Hon. J. W. Fortescue's *History of the British Army*, ii. pp. 109–120; the *Trevor MSS.* p. 116; the *Gentleman's Magazine* for June and July 1745; the reports of Saxe and Ligonier, *E.H.R.*, 1897, pp. 524–527; pp. 51–70 of the *Life of Marquess Townshend*; and pp. 395–429 of de Broglie's *Marie Thérèse Impératrice*, vol. i.

[2] De Broglie, *Marie Thérèse Impératrice*, ii. 94.

d'Aremberg's corps arrived from the Netherlands and 20,000 Frenchmen were called up from the Rhine to fill the gaps which Fontenoy had made in Saxe's army, only forms remained to be gone through. On September 13th the Grand Duke of Tuscany was elected Emperor under the title of Francis I, the Empire returned to the Hapsburgs, and Marie Theresa had obtained one of her two main objects.[1]

From attaining the other, the recovery of Silesia, she was, however, as far removed as ever. After the abortive invasion of Upper Silesia in January, the Austrian main body had remained inactive on the Bohemian side of the mountains, their light cavalry scouring the country and pushing their raids over Silesia. Not till May was Frederick, who had to refit and rest his shattered army, able to deal effectively with them. Then Winterfeldt and Ziethen, now making his first appearance of any importance, routed and dispersed a large body of Austrian irregulars near Jaegerndorf. But it was the Austrians and not the Prussians who took the offensive in the campaign. On May 31st, Prince Charles of Lorraine left Landshut, intending to move upon Breslau down the Striegauwasser and cut the town off from Frederick and the main Prussian army, 70,000 strong, who were lying round Schweidnitz and Jauernik in the valley of the Schweidnitzwasser. Frederick made no attempt to defend the passes, and the Saxons, who formed the Austrian vanguard, were as far forward as Striegau before he moved Westward from Schweidnitz and, under cover of a sharp skirmish between his right and the Saxons, crossed to the left bank of the Striegauwasser on the evening of June 3rd. His object in thus delaying had been to make certain of a battle: had he defended the passes, the Austrians might not have pushed their attack home.

Had Prince Charles of Lorraine kept sufficiently close to the Saxons it is possible that the battle of June 4th might have had a very different ending, for the Prussian rearguard, which was to form their left, did not manage to arrive at the appointed time, having been delayed by the breakdown of a bridge over the Striegauwasser. Thus, when on the morning of June 4th Charles at length arrived on the field from Hohenfriedberg, the Saxons had already attacked Striegau,

---

[1] Frederick II abstained from voting, as did the Elector Palatine, but the validity of the Bohemian vote was acknowledged.

had been repulsed, and then thrown into confusion by a counter-attack of the Prussian cavalry, but Frederick's line was not yet formed. However, Charles hesitated, and hesitating gave Ziethen time to push his belated cavalry across a ford and throw himself into the gap in the Prussian line. At the same time the Prussian right advanced to turn the flank of the Austrian left, exposed by the rout of the Saxons, and the Austrians giving way all along the line fell back towards the passes. Had Frederick pursued vigorously he might have converted the Austrian defeat into a disaster; as it was, they straggled through the hills in some disorder, leaving 2500 prisoners behind, besides losing some 9000 killed and wounded. The Prussians, whose loss amounted to under 5000, were too much fatigued by their night march to profit by the enemy's discomfiture at once, but Frederick soon followed the retreating Austrians into Bohemia. Before his advance Prince Charles at first retired, but standing at bay at König-gratz brought Frederick to a standstill (July 20th). For about six weeks Frederick remained inactive on the Elbe: he could not drive the Austrians from their lines, and his own position was somewhat precarious. At the end of his resources, with no prospect of obtaining assistance from France either in men or money, he was really anxious to extract a peace which would leave him Silesia, and hoped by this bold offensive to lend weight to the representations George II was making to Maria Theresa. However, the country, as in 1744, was bitterly hostile to him: Austrian light troops swarmed upon his flanks and rear, cut off his convoys and foragers and so straitened him for supplies that when, on September 16th, the capture of Neustadt cut his line of retreat through that town to Glatz, he at once decided to retire on the other line, by Landshut and the Schatzlar Pass, while it was still open, and on September 18th he set out for Silesia.

So slow, however, was his retreat that Charles of Lorraine was able to get in between him and the Schatzlar Pass and to bar the retreat at Sohr. On the morning of September 29th, Frederick suddenly found the Austrians moving in battle array upon his unsuspecting camp. His cavalry outposts had served him badly, and it was only by his own extraordinary exertions and by the good drill and discipline of his men that he was able to form them up in time to meet the attack. The key to the

Prussian position was a hill upon their right which the Austrian left wing at once seized and, planting 28 guns on it, proceeded to enfilade their enemy. Quick to see the importance of this point, Frederick concentrated all his efforts on its capture, and "refusing" his left, assailed the hill vigorously with the bulk of his infantry, while Büddenbrock and the cavalry of the right supported the attack by charging the Austrian cavalry opposite them and driving them back into some broken ground in their rear. At the second attempt the Prussians mastered the hill and then turned to succour their left and centre, which were hard pressed, the village of Burghersdorf in the centre being in great danger of falling into the Austrian hands. The intervention of the Prussian right proved decisive, the Austrians drew off, and Frederick found himself able to continue his march to Silesia unmolested. If he had died before 1756 the battle of Sohr would be his chief claim to reputation as a tactician. Surprised though he was, the promptitude with which he formed up his men, the quickness with which he realised the importance of the hill, the resolution and courage with which he concentrated all his efforts on this critical point, his good judgment in refusing his left, make Sohr as peculiarly his victory as Mollwitz had been his soldiers'. The Austrians threw away the great advantage with which they began the battle by their fatal slowness and want of vigour. An immediate and headlong attack before the Prussians could form up was all that was needed. Precision should have been sacrificed to promptitude, exactness to energy. But Charles of Lorraine could not shake off the trammels of his pedantic training, and energy was a stranger to him.

Just before the battle, Frederick had concluded with George II a treaty of great importance. Always anxious to bring the Silesian war to an end, and if possible to bring Prussia into line with Austria and the Maritime Powers against France, George II had at this moment an unusually urgent reason for wishing to achieve this end. The same cause which had paralysed Cumberland's defence of the Netherlands, the Jacobite insurrection in Scotland, was filling George with alarms for the safety of his beloved Hanover, which he saw exposed to a French attack. Accordingly he hastened to come to terms with Frederick, whom he found ready enough to listen to his overtures. On August 26th, 1745, by the Convention of Hanover the two Powers exchanged guarantees of each other's possessions, Silesia being definitely included among those of Prussia. Frederick further promised not to vote against Francis Stephen, and it was agreed that Maria Theresa should be allowed to accede to the treaty any time within the next six weeks.

But Maria Theresa did not require six minutes in which to decide. Indignantly refusing to accede to the Convention, she turned to France and, through the mediation of Saxony, made overtures which, in the light of the terms arranged at Aix-la-Chapelle, France was very ill-advised to refuse. Maria Theresa would have surrendered the greater part of the French conquests in the Netherlands—which after all concerned the Maritime Powers rather than Austria—in return for peace and the recognition of Francis as Emperor. But Louis xv's appetite for military glory and d'Argenson's equally infatuated adherence to the idea of the Prussian alliance caused the rejection of this chance of a substantial territorial gain. Maria Theresa fell back on the alternative of a joint attack upon Brandenburg in concert with her Saxon ally. Relying on Russia's intimation to Frederick that she would assist Saxony if the Elector were attacked by Prussia, Maria Theresa planned an advance down the Elbe by Rutowski's Saxons supported by an Austrian division, to be covered by an advance of the Austrian main body into Lusatia. This, if only it were executed with the necessary dash and secrecy, was by no means an unpromising scheme : it would have cut off Frederick in Silesia from his hereditary dominions. Secrecy, however, the indispensable condition of success, was not observed. Count Brühl indiscreetly let out the scheme to the Swedish Ambassador at Dresden, and by this means—for Sweden was on good terms with Frederick, whose sister Ulrica had married Adolphus Frederick of Holstein, the heir to Sweden—the Prussians were warned in time to make preparations. Accordingly, when Charles of Lorraine entered Lusatia on November 20th by the valley of the Lusatian Neisse, Frederick had already concentrated 35,000 men at Liegnitz, while the presence of 30,000 more at Halle under Leopold of Anhalt-Dessau checked the Western advance. On November 21st, Frederick moved West, thinking to fall upon the Austrian rear and cut

them off from Bohemia. But on this occasion their slowness
proved a positive advantage. It was on their van, not, as he had
expected, on their rear that Ziethen hurled himself at Hennersdorf on November 24th. The Saxons, a mere brigade of barely
3000 strong, were surprised and cut to pieces; but the check,
slight as it was, sufficed to cause Charles to change his plan.
He fell back hastily to Zittau and thence by the pass of Gabel
to Aussig on the Elbe, moving from there down the Elbe to
the assistance of Rutowski and Grüne, against whom Leopold
of Anhalt-Dessau was advancing. It is possible that Charles
may have hoped to draw Frederick after him, and thereby
prevent him from assisting his general by involving the
Prussian main body in the hills; but Frederick was not
tempted, and moved Westward by Bautzen on the bridge over
the Elbe at Meissen.

Meanwhile Leopold was moving on Dresden, somewhat
too slowly for Frederick's satisfaction, for his delays allowed
Rutowski to concentrate and Grüne to join the Saxons. The
campaign thus resolved itself into a race between Leopold, the
Austrians and Frederick. Would Leopold be able to defeat
Rutowski before Lorraine could arrive, or would Lorraine be
up in time for his army to unite with Rutowski and crush
Leopold before Frederick could succour him? As usual,
Charles of Lorraine was very slow, and had not arrived when,
on December 15th, Leopold came up to the strong position
occupied by Rutowski and Grüne at Kesselsdorf, a few miles
North of Dresden. The position, however, had the grave
defect that the stream and ravine at the foot of the hill on
which the Austrians, who formed the right, were posted, while
making that wing all but impregnable, would hinder the delivering of a counter-attack. Accordingly the old general
massed his troops opposite Kesselsdorf, where the Saxons had
thirty guns well entrenched. Twice he hurled his men at the
battery, twice they were repulsed, but the imprudence of the
Saxon counter-attack gave Leopold the chance he wanted.
His cavalry fell upon the Saxons and overthrew them. The
infantry rallying under cover of this diversion came on again,
entered Kesselsdorf on the heels of the Saxons and carried
the great battery, whose fire the counter-attack had masked.
This decided the day; the Saxons gave way in disorder, and
though the Austrians beat off an attack and got away safely

to rejoin Prince Charles, Dresden opened its gates at once and the Elector had to fly.

Leopold's victory proved really decisive. Even Maria Theresa could no longer resist. Not only did Saxony come to terms with Frederick and accept the Convention of Hanover, but England threatened to cease paying her subsidies unless she made peace with Prussia. In vain Harrach negotiated with Vaulgrenant, the French Minister at Dresden : Louis XV and d'Argenson were not prepared to effect a complete revolution in foreign policy at the moment when d'Argenson's schemes for detaching Sardinia from Maria Theresa's side seemed on the point of success and the expulsion of the Hapsburgs from the Italian peninsula appeared only a question of days.[1] Reluctantly she gave way, and on December 25th the Treaty of Dresden definitely gave up Silesia and Glatz to Frederick. In return he recognised Francis I as Emperor, and guaranteed the Pragmatic Sanction.

It must be admitted that Frederick was decidedly fortunate in being able to obtain from Maria Theresa all he desired when he was practically at the end of his resources. It was all very well for him to declare that Marshal Saxe's victory at Fontenoy was of no more use to him than a victory on the Scamander. There can be no doubt that the French successes in the Netherlands and Italy had great influence over Maria Theresa, for had Fontenoy been a victory for the Allies or the campaign in Italy different in its result, Frederick might have found her as unyielding as before. Indeed, he had good reason to be grateful to Charles Edward and the Scottish Jacobites, for that diversion was the principal cause of the Convention of Hanover, to say nothing of its influence on the campaign in the Netherlands. The Highlanders contributed in no small measure to the acquisition of Silesia by Prussia. Above all, it was fortunate for Frederick that the Czarina, on whose co-operation Austria and Saxony had confidently relied, should have so suddenly grown cool in the cause and have failed to do what was expected. It would not have been safe for Prussia to count on her continued neutrality, and her intervention in earnest would have turned the tables completely.

But if it was largely to the efforts of France and the other enemies of Austria that Frederick owed his success in capturing

[1] Cf. p. 164.

and keeping Silesia, his own share in this important acquisition was not small.   The decision, the promptitude and the energy which he displayed form a striking contrast to the hesitation of Fleury, the helplessness of Charles VII, the tergiversations of Augustus III, and the dilatoriness of Neipperg and Charles of Lorraine.   Frederick's policy was undoubtedly determined by an unscrupulous ambition and an unbridled selfishness; it was contrary to loyalty to the interests of Germany, it did not look beyond the aggrandisement of the Hohenzollern.   But it had the merit of being consistent and resolute, and so far it deserved to be successful.   Moreover, if Fortune threw many opportunities in Frederick's way, it was not every one who would have been able to turn these chances to such striking advantage.

With the Treaty of Dresden the purely German phase of the Austrian Succession War came to an end; the battles of the three years which the war had still to run were to be fought in other lands than Germany.   In Italy Austria was undoubtedly fighting to obtain some compensation for the territorial loss she had undergone in Germany; in the Netherlands the French were seeking among other things to retrieve that military reputation which their performances on the Elbe and the Danube had tarnished; but though German troops were largely employed in both these theatres of war, and though Austrian territories were the scene of operations, it is the results rather than the events of these years which concern German history.

It has already been mentioned that the peril of her Italian possessions was one of the contributing causes of Maria Theresa's reluctant assent to the Treaty of Dresden.   To be in danger of being expelled from Italy was indeed a striking contrast to the high hopes which she had entertained when she signed the Treaty of Worms; but things had not gone well for the Allies in 1744, and 1745 saw the Austrians apparently on the point of being ousted from the Milanese.   Of all the losses which the Hapsburg monarchy had sustained in recent years, that of the rich lands of Naples was perhaps the most grievous, and the task allotted to Traun's successor, Lobkowitz, was to attempt to recover it.   Spanish rule was most unpopular in Naples, and it was hoped that a popular rising against Don Carlos would certainly follow if the Austrian forces were once to appear on Neapolitan soil. But Lobkowitz had not penetrated beyond Monte Rotondo in the Campagna when the Spanish army of North Italy, aided by a French division under Conti, created a diversion by assailing Piedmont from Dauphiné (July 1744) and laying siege to the fortress of Coni. In great alarm Charles Emmanuel recalled his contingent with Lobkowitz's force, from which Maria Theresa also detached a regiment, that her slippery ally might have no cause to complain that he was being left in the lurch. Thus weakened, Lobkowitz had no alternative but to retire into winter-quarters behind the Metaurus (Nov.), and thence early in the next year to Modena. Meanwhile Leutrum's gallant defence of Coni had proved successful, the Franco-Spaniards raising the siege and retiring into Dauphiné, though they retained possession of both Savoy and Nice.

With the spring of 1745 matters took a turn even more unfavourable to the Allies. Genoa, annoyed by English interference with her commerce and indignant at the proposed cession of Finale to Sardinia, definitely threw in her lot with the Bourbons, and so opened the Riviera route for a junction between the Spaniards from Naples and the Franco-Spanish force under Don Philip, with whom was now associated Marshal Maillebois (April). Unable to dispute the passage of the Apennines against considerable numerical superiority, the Austro-Sardinians retired to Bassignano, whence the Austrians were before long called off by an advance of the Spaniards into the Milanese from Pavia. The Sardinians, left isolated at Bassignano, were attacked by the French and badly beaten (Sept. 27th), the whole country South of the Tanaro passing into the hands of the Franco-Spaniards, while the Austrians found themselves pressed back towards Tyrol by the Spaniards under Gages, who occupied Milan almost unopposed on December 19th. The only weak point in the military position of the victorious Bourbons was that in their eagerness to possess themselves of the Milanese the Spaniards allowed themselves to become somewhat widely separated from their allies.

It was now that the persevering but visionary d'Argenson threw himself into the task of concluding a separate peace with Charles Emmanuel, as the necessary preliminary to his favourite project of the federation of Italy. The negotiations

of Turin proved abortive in the end, because the jealousy of
Spain and Sardinia caused delays of the utmost importance
which gave time for the conclusion of the Treaty of Dresden
and the despatch of Austrian reinforcements to Italy.
Charles Emmanuel was probably genuine enough in opening negotiations with d'Argenson: if Maria Theresa could
not defend her own possessions, it was not his place or policy
to risk his dominions for her sake.   But the delays due to
Spain's refusal to agree to the terms for which Sardinia held
out gave the situation time to change so much that the shifty
King, who feared the Bourbons more than he did the Hapsburgs,
finally used the negotiations to lull Maillebois into a false
security from which he was rudely awakened when, early in
March, the Piedmontese troops were suddenly put in motion
against the scattered Franco-Spaniards.   Within a very short
time Maillebois was driven back to Novi and the Austrians,
returning, ousted Gages and Don Philip from the Milanese.
Indeed, it was only by a brilliant counterstroke, a daring
offensive return to the North of the Po, which drew the Austro-
Sardinians after him, that Maillebois finally managed to save
himself and his allies from being severed from France by a
Sardinian attack on their communications.   Even as it was
the Franco-Spaniards had to retire behind the Var (Sept.
17th), leaving Genoa to be besieged and taken by the
Austrians.   The turn of fortune was complete; the more
so because, on July 9th, Philip v of Spain had died, and with
his death Elizabeth Farnese's influence had ceased to be
predominant at Madrid.   The new King, Ferdinand vi, was
not prepared to sacrifice Spain to his stepmother's dynastic
ambitions, and did not intend to risk much in Italy.

Masters of Italy, and with their ally Charles Emmanuel no
longer in any danger, the Austrians would have moved against
Naples had not the English insisted upon their undertaking
an invasion of Provence.   This enterprise resulted in failure,
for a rising at Genoa forced the Austrian garrison to evacuate
the town after several days of savage street-fighting (Dec.
5th to 10th), and the invaders had to fall back behind the Var
(Feb. 2nd, 1747) in order to cover the siege of Genoa which
was vigorously conducted by the Austrians with the aid of
Admiral Medley and the English Mediterranean squadron.
To relieve Genoa, Belleisle undertook as a diversion an invasion

of Piedmont by the Col d'Assiette, which resulted, indeed, in a disastrous repulse from the strong position of Exilles (July 19th), but succeeded in drawing off the Piedmontese contingent from Genoa and so forcing the Austrians to raise the siege. With the repulse at Exilles the operations of the war in Italy were practically at an end, for, though the Austrians resumed the siege of Genoa in the next year, they were unable to take the town. As far as Italy was concerned, Maria Theresa had been successful: she had not only come through the war with undiminished territories, but was actually in possession of those of the Duke of Modena. That at the conclusion of peace she was unable to retain this conquest, but, on the contrary, had to sacrifice Parma and Piacenza, was due to the turn the war had taken in another theatre. Italy had to pay the debts of Flanders.

It was not so much the defeat at Fontenoy, but the Jacobite insurrection in Scotland which had left Flanders at the mercy of Maurice de Saxe. After the recall of Cumberland and his army Saxe found the Eastern Netherlands an easy prey. With England fully occupied at home and Austria comparatively indifferent to the fate of the Netherlands, the burden of defence was left mainly to the Dutch, whose adhesion to their allies was extremely faint-hearted. Indeed they went so far as to open negotiations for a separate peace ; and, though these fell through, it would have been quite easy for France to detach the United Provinces from England and Austria had d'Argenson only listened to the advice of Saxe and permitted that general to make Holland the objective of his campaign. Had this been done there is little doubt that the Dutch would have hastened to make peace, in which case, with Ostend lost and Holland neutral, England would have had no landing-place near the scene of operations, and would have found co-operation with the Austrians exceedingly difficult. But d'Argenson was afraid of provoking an anti-French reaction in Holland, and therefore Saxe had to devote himself to the reduction of the Eastern Netherlands.

In this enterprise Saxe was able to avail himself of another French army, that of Conti, to which had been entrusted the task of demonstrating along the frontiers of the Empire in order to overawe the minor Princes of South and Western Germany and prevent Maria Theresa from recruiting the Coalition among

them.   But to do this there was no need of an army.   The
despatch of a French envoy to the Diet of Ratisbon to promise
that France would respect the neutrality of the Empire was
quite sufficient.   Würtemberg and the Elector Palatine were
decidedly favourable to France; and though Bavaria hired out
6000 troops to the Maritime Powers, the influence of Maurice
de Saxe over his half-brother induced Augustus III to
declare for the Empire remaining neutral, a policy which was
cordially supported by the three ecclesiastical Electors whose
principal desire was to keep the war out of their coasts.
Thus Conti's army could be safely diverted from the Middle
Rhine to the Netherlands, where it speedily reduced Mons
(July 11th) and laid siege to Charleroi.   Saxe had opened
operations in January by a successful dash at Brussels, which
had fallen after a three weeks' siege (Feb. 20th): he then
dislodged the Allies from the Demer, forced them back into
Holland and detached Clermont to form the siege of Antwerp,
which he covered with his main body.   Antwerp fell on May
31st, by which time a considerable force of Allies was
beginning to collect at Breda to take the field; Culloden
(April 16th) had set free a small English corps and the
6000 Hessians who had been sent across to Scotland in
February, and Charles of Lorraine had come up from Austria
with large reinforcements.   Towards the end of July the
Allies made an attempt to relieve Charleroi but were too late,
its fall occurring (Aug. 1st) before they could get much
beyond the Mehaigne.   They then took post to cover Namur
but were dislodged by the capture of Huy, which imperilled
their communications and forced them to withdraw East of
the Meuse.   Namur was promptly besieged and fell before
the end of September, while Lorraine was equally unsuccessful
in an attempt to save Liége, being ousted by Saxe from his
position at Roucoux after a sharply - contested action
(Oct. 11th).

Thus 1746 closed with the Middle Meuse in the hands
of Saxe, and only Maastricht left to cover Holland from
attack.   Nor was 1747 any more satisfactory to the Allies.
Cumberland replaced Charles of Lorraine as commander-in-
chief; but though he collected over 90,000 troops of all
nationalities, he was unable to prevent the reduction of the
mouth of the Scheldt by Saxe's trusted lieutenant Löwendahl,

who took Sluys and Cadzand, and was only prevented from adding Zealand to his conquests by the timely arrival of a British squadron with reinforcements (April to May). Then, when Cumberland had succeeded in drawing Saxe from his lines between Malines and Louvain by moving up the Meuse to attack a detached corps under Clermont, he found himself anticipated by Saxe in an attempt to secure the Herdeeren heights just South-West of Maastricht (July 1st), and was defeated in the battle which was fought next day for that position. Lauffeldt was a repetition of Fontenoy, for the traditional immobility of the Austrians allowed Saxe to neglect them and concentrate his attack on the British and their German auxiliaries; and in this quarter of the field the misconduct of the Dutch at a very critical moment sacrificed the fruits of the splendid behaviour of the British, the Hessians and the Hanoverians. The Allies were able to save Maastricht, but Saxe could safely detach Löwendahl to besiege and take (Sept. 16th) the great fortress of Bergen-op-Zoom, with which most of Dutch Brabant fell into French hands.

Thus by the end of 1747 all but a very small part of the Austrian Netherlands had been conquered for Louis XV; and though, as d'Argenson had predicted, the French violation of Dutch territory had produced a reaction in Holland against the Francophil "Burgher party," the upshot of which was the practical restoration of the monarchical element with the election (May 1747) of William of Nassau-Dillenberg as Stadtholder and Captain-General of the Netherlands, this revolution was of more political than military importance, for the Dutch defence of their territories was extremely weak, not to say culpably negligent and indifferent.[1] But if the Maritime Powers had no reason to wish for another campaign on land, the pressure of England's supremacy at sea, now satisfactorily reasserted by the victories of Anson (May 3rd) and Hawke (October 14th) in the Bay of Biscay, was exerting an equally powerful influence over Louis XV in the direction of peace. Austria possibly would have liked to try another campaign in Italy, where she might have hoped to achieve something at the expense of Naples or Genoa, but England and France were both thoroughly weary of the war, and the negotiations of Aix-la-Chapelle, begun early in 1748, produced a definite

[1] Cf. *Checquers Court Papers*, Hist. MSS. Commission, pp. 376-391.

result on April 30th, when the representatives of England, France and Holland signed the preliminaries of peace. Maria Theresa's was almost the only voice to be raised in opposition to peace, for she had recently (May 1746) secured the promise of Russian assistance on a considerable scale, and she was afraid that the compensations which peace was bound to make necessary would have to be provided at her expense. In the hopes of getting better terms out of France by a separate negotiation, she instructed Kaunitz, her representative at Aix, to try to arrange a treaty with Louis xv; but France was simultaneously negotiating with the Maritime Powers, and as their naval supremacy made their hostility more formidable than was Maria Theresa's, it was with England and Holland that the preliminary treaty was signed.

Not till nearly six months later, however, was the definite treaty signed—six months of every kind of intrigue and bargaining. In the end, Maria Theresa found herself compelled to accede to the treaty by the fact that she could do nothing if deserted by England and Sardinia, while they were independent of her. At length, on October 16th, the plenipotentiaries of England, France and Holland affixed their signatures to the treaty; Spain followed suit on October 20th, Austria on November 8th, Sardinia on November 20th. From the point of view of German history the most important clauses were those which guaranteed Silesia and Glatz to Frederick II, which recognised Francis II as Emperor, and which guaranteed the Pragmatic Sanction except as regarded Silesia and Parma and Piacenza. To Maria Theresa and the Hapsburgs the evacuation by France of the Austrian Netherlands, the restoration of the Barrier-fortresses to the Dutch, who had done so little to defend them, the cession of Parma and Piacenza to Don Philip of Spain, and of the Ticino boundary in Lombardy to Charles Emmanuel,[1] and the restoration of Francis of Modena to his dominions, were also of great importance. The reciprocal restitution of conquests by England and France shows that the peace marks not an end but a pause in the great struggle for the sea, which affected Germany indirectly not a little and directly still more through the Anglo-Hanoverian connection.

If, then, it be asked what Power had gained most by the

[1] He had to give up Finale to Genoa, but recovered Nice and Savoy.

war, it would not be difficult to answer. By promptly taking
advantage of the embarrassments of allies and enemies alike,
Frederick of Prussia had gained territory and a reputation : he
was still to have to fight for his share in the spoils, but of all
the vultures which had gathered round the carcase of the
Hapsburg monarchy he alone had succeeded in appeasing his
appetite. It was not much consolation to France for all her
efforts, her vast expenditure in men and money, her hard-won
victories in the Netherlands, to have established Don Philip
in Parma and to have materially assisted the rise of Prussia.
As for Bavaria and Saxony, they had gained nothing, but they
had been detached from the French alliance and were, for the
immediate future at any rate, to be faithful allies of Austria.
Sardinia had made another step forward. Spain, now that
Elizabeth Farnese's power was no more, could follow under
Ferdinand VI the dictates of national policy untrammelled
by a dynastic attraction to Italy. Russia had made another
appearance in the European area. England had retrieved
a bad start at sea and, despite Fontenoy and Lauffeldt, had
largely contributed to preventing France from retaining the
Netherlands ; she might also claim to have helped the Hapsburg monarchy not a little to weather the storm which had
threatened to engulf it, even if her actions had been prompted
rather by her own interests than by the dictates of mere
disinterestedness. Holland's part in the war had been but
feeble and her power was obviously on the decline, while the
bonds which bound her to the English alliance were as
obviously becoming relaxed.

Finally, the question must be answered, how had Austria
come through this time of trial ? Thanks largely to her own
magnificent courage and resolution, to an endurance which had
never failed, and to a determination which had been proof
against all trials, Maria Theresa had brought her inheritance
safely through a sea of formidable dangers, lessened, it is true,
by the loss of Silesia and Parma, but strengthened in ways
which amply compensated for those losses. Her dominions
had been welded together by the war, which had done much to
excite the loyalty and patriotism of the heroic Queen's subjects.
It was not in Hungary only that Maria Theresa's appeals had
touched an answering chord, though it was a great thing to
have converted that source of weakness into a source of

Map to illustrate THE CAMPAIGN OF MOLLWITZ.

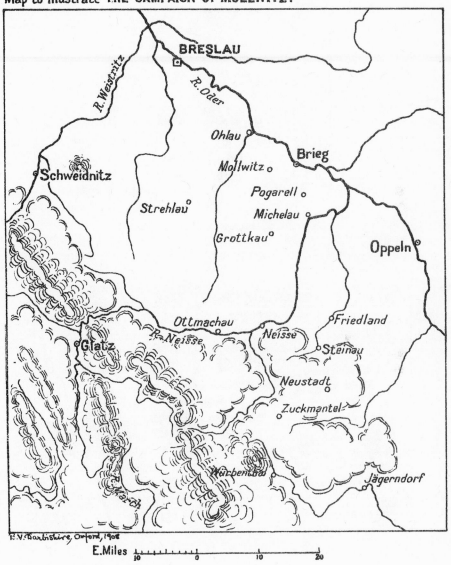

BRESLAU

R. Weistritz

R. Oder

Ohlau

Brieg

Schweidnitz

Mollwitz

Pogarell

Michelau

Strehlau

Oppeln

Grottkau

Ottmachau

R. Neisse

Friedland

Neisse

Glatz

Steinau

Neustadt

Zuckmantel

March

Würbenthal

Jägerndorf

P.V. Barbishire, Oxford, 1908

E. Miles

10   0   10   20

SOHR Sep. 30th 1745.

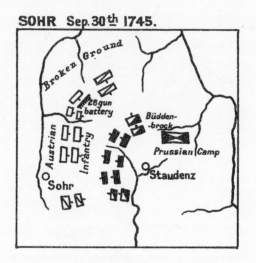

CHOTUSITZ or CZASLAU May 17th 1742.

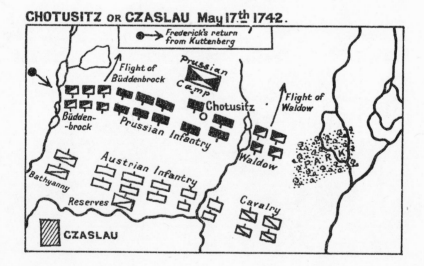

strength. The Imperial dignity had been won back and secured to the new line of the Hapsburgs. If clear signs were not wanting that the old Anglo-Austrian alliance had been strained almost to the breaking-point, Bavaria, hitherto an enemy and a client of France, and Saxony were now among Austria's allies; the Russian alliance of 1746, even if it be held to have been in itself undesirable, did strengthen her hands against Prussia, and the attitude of the Bourbon Powers was by no means uncompromisingly hostile. With one Power only were Maria Theresa's relations of an unfriendly nature. The guarantee of Silesia which she had at last given grudgingly and reluctantly was a pledge by which she could hardly be expected to abide. Other accidental circumstances had combined to prevent Austria doing herself justice in the struggle for Silesia: meanwhile the army had improved greatly during the war, and peace would permit of further increases and improvements, and a chance might come when the conditions would favour Austria more.

It was for these reasons, because Maria Theresa, far from being reconciled to the loss of Silesia, was still planning all possible means of recovering it, and also because the Anglo-French quarrel was undecided, that the Peace of Aix-la-Chapelle was a truce not a real peace, and that the settlement of the two great questions at issue was merely postponed until 1756–1763.

CHAPTER X

MARIA THERESA'S REFORMS AND THE DIPLOMATIC REVOLUTION

MARIA THERESA had agreed to the Peace of Aix-la-Chapelle with the less reluctance because even she had become convinced that peace was necessary, and that she had more to gain from it than from prolonging the war. She saw that the road to the recovery of Silesia lay rather through allowing her resources to recuperate and through reforms in her army and her administration than through a war which offered little prospect of a satisfactory issue. "Peace, retrenchment and reform" was therefore her programme on the morrow of Aix-la-Chapelle; and she was the better able to set about such a task because—as she herself put it—"Providence had relieved her by death of councillors too prejudiced to give useful advice, too respectable and too meritorious to be dismissed."

Of the septuagenarians of whom the Conference had consisted in October 1740, Sinzendorff had died in 1742, Gundacker Stahremberg in 1745, Philipp Kinsky in 1748. To Sinzendorff had succeeded Count Ulefeld, a well-meaning, honest but incapable man, unequal to the important position of Chancellor, which he owed in no small degree to the influence of Bartenstein. This latter, Secretary to the Conference since 1727, was virtually Minister of Foreign Affairs from 1740 to 1753. He had won Maria Theresa's confidence by supporting such favourite projects of hers as the proposal that Francis Stephen should be co-Regent, but his blind belief in Fleury's good intentions had somewhat shaken his credit. More of a lawyer than a statesman, narrow-minded and unprogressive, somewhat obstinate and self-satisfied, his influence declined as that of Kaunitz rose, and when the latter was summoned to office in 1753, Bartenstein practically retired from the administration. At the same time Ulefeld exchanged the Chancellorship for an office more adapted to his capacities, that of Grand Chamberlain (*Obersthofmeister*). The vacancy in the Chancellorship was filled by the man whose name must always be associated with that of Maria Theresa, whose chief minister he was and under whom he may be said to have almost ruled Austria. Wenceslaus Anthony von Kaunitz was in 1753 a man of forty-two years of age, who had served Austria as the Emperor's representative with the Diet at Ratisbon, as envoy at several Italian courts, as chief minister to the Archduchess Maria Anna in the Netherlands, as Ambassador at St. James', and as plenipotentiary at Aix-la-Chapelle. From 1750 to 1753 he was Ambassador to the Court of Versailles, and after laying the foundations for the Franco-Austrian reconciliation during this period he returned to Austria to become Chancellor in 1753. His principal contribution to the reforms which the Empress-Queen was now undertaking was the separation between the State Chancery (*Staatskanzlei*) and the purely Austrian Court Chancery (*Hofkanzlei*). Under him the State Chancery was transformed into a Ministry of Foreign Affairs to which was entrusted also the control of the affairs of Lombardy and the Netherlands. But while principally concerned with foreign policy, Kaunitz, whose authority completely surpassed that of his colleagues, exercised no small influence over domestic affairs. In the Moravian troubles of 1777 his voice was uplifted in favour of conciliation, and being a somewhat lukewarm adherent of the Catholic doctrine he was able to moderate the extreme measures to which a religious fervour verging on intolerance at times inclined Maria Theresa.

More immediately responsible for the domestic reforms were Count Frederick William Haugwitz (1700–1765), a Silesian nobleman who had adhered to the Austrian cause, Count Rudolf Chotek (1706–1771), a member of one of the oldest families in Bohemia, and Count Charles Hatzfeldt (1718–1793), another Bohemian noble. Of these three Haugwitz was probably the ablest, and it was in him that Maria Theresa found her most efficient assistant in the task of reform. When the Court Chancery was separated from the State Chancery in 1753 it was he who was placed at the head of what was henceforward to be virtually a Ministry of the Interior. In this capacity he was the founder of the centralised bureaucracy which Maria Theresa endeavoured to substitute for the semi-feudal system of government she had inherited. Haugwitz succeeded in abolishing the exemption of the nobility from taxation, brought the somewhat recalcitrant Estates under the control of the central government through the bureaucracy, introduced a new system of taxation, and centralised the administration. Chotek, first prominent as the negotiator of the Peace of Füssen,[1] reorganised the administration of Tyrol, Trieste and Further Austria between 1747 and 1748, became head of the Indirect Taxation Bureau (*Banco-Prësident*) in 1749 and President of the Treasury (*Hofkammer*) in 1759, thus obtaining complete control over the whole finances. In 1762 he succeeded Haugwitz at the Ministry of the Interior. His chief work was in connection with indirect taxation and the development of the resources of the country ; its trade, manufactures, roads and bridges came under his control. More aristocratic in sentiments than Haugwitz, he was more in sympathy with the Estates, and not uncommonly there was friction between the two Ministers. Hatzfeldt, best known as President of the Council of State, succeeded in reconciling the nobles and clergy to the policy of centralisation in which he was a firm believer. Education was his principal care, but he did 'much during the Seven Years' War to obtain money. In 1765 he became President of the Treasury, on Chotek's death in 1771 Minister of the Interior, which post he resigned in the same year to Count Henry Blümegen in order to become head of the new Council of State (*Staatsrath*).

Another minister whose influence was considerable, though hardly so beneficial, was Count Joseph Harrach, who for twenty-four years (1739–1762), and to the disadvantage of the Austrian army, was President of the War Council. Incapable and quite past his work, he was an encumbrance on the efficiency of the Council and the army, and it would have been well for Maria Theresa had she made up her mind to dismiss him in 1756, when he was already seventy-eight years of age, instead of waiting till the end of the war, in which his incapacity cost Austria so dear.

The key to the reforms of Maria Theresa is to be found in her wish to free the authority of the central government

[1] Cf. p. 154.

from the trammels which the continued existence of what had once been a feudal constitution imposed upon it. She sought to make the State supreme over the Estates, to put the whole before the parts, the welfare of the Austrian monarchy and all the peoples subject to it before the local and provincial interests which had shown themselves so strong in Upper Austria and in Bohemia in 1741. Maria Theresa was not attacking real constitutional liberties when she endeavoured to sweep away the constitutional powers of the nobles and clergy and to take from them their immunity from taxation. The objects of her attack were mere relics of a past stage of development, now become obsolete and a danger to the higher interests of the State as a whole. " Despotic " though her actions may have been, in spirit she was far from Louis XV or even Frederick II. She had a real wish for the welfare of her subjects, and her efforts to benefit the peasantry and improve their position show that it was not merely to increase the tax-paying capacity of her dominions so that they might support a vast army that she undertook these reforms.

The first and most important step was to deprive the provincial Estates of the authority they still possessed over the army. Before the army could be made a really efficient instrument for war, it was necessary to do away with the pernicious system of dual control by which the supply of funds for its maintenance depended on the fluctuating votes of the local Estates, which in each case strove continually to shift the burden of national defence on to the shoulders of the other provinces. Indeed the army was provincial rather than royal. Each province raised and maintained its own contingent mainly by taxes in kind. Uniformity of organisation was lacking, and the central government practically had to negotiate every year with each province for the support of the various contingents. Haugwitz's scheme, the so-called Ten Years' Recess, was intended to do away with this inefficient and cumbrous system. A fixed sum was demanded from each province, and to set the whole matter on a firm basis it was voted for a period of ten years, thus practically taking the army completely out of the control of the Estates. So new a departure could not fail to arouse considerable opposition from the nobility, more especially as their cherished privilege of immunity from taxation was at the same time taken away, all classes being liable to the new taxes which replaced the old payments in kind. In the Conference itself Count Frederick Harrach assumed the leadership of the opposition, but his colleagues did not support him, and Maria Theresa was able to carry her point, and with the aid of Haugwitz and Chotek to induce the Estates to pass the required vote.

The reorganisation of the Austrian army which was thus made possible took for its model the Prussian system. The Army was brought completely under the control of the Sovereign, uniformity and system were introduced into its establishments, uniforms, pay, weapons and interior economy. A much more careful military training was introduced with a new drill and the iron ramrod of the Prussian infantry. Camps of exercise were started, manœuvres were held. Officers were given a chance of studying their profession though the restriction of commissions to men of noble birth was maintained. A modified conscription based on the lines of the Prussian cantoning system assured the means of keeping the regiments up to their establishment, and measures were adopted for the improvement of discipline, especially that of the Irregular troops. One important step was the regimentation of the Frontier Forces (*Grenzsoldaten*),[1] whose turbulence and excesses had done much to neutralise their efficiency as soldiers. In no department was so much improvement effected as in the artillery. In this branch Austria had no need to fear comparisons with other armies, though it may be questioned whether the very efficiency of their artillery did not somewhat defeat its own object by increasing their immobility and their love for strong positions and defensive tactics. It may be held, however, with as much plausibility that this preference for the defensive caused such great importance to be attached to the improvement of the artillery. One reform, however, which would have been of great service was not carried out. The War Council, of which the aged Count Joseph Harrach was the head, was organised as a civilian and not as a military board.[2] It was

---

[1] These *Grenzsoldaten* were a special institution : the whole population of the frontier districts from the Adriatic to Transylvania were organised on military lines, and were specially liable to service.

[2] It was in 1753 divided into three departments, dealing respectively with military organisation, discipline and supply.

not till the evils of this arrangement had exercised their pernicious influence in the Seven Years' War that Maria Theresa at last (1762) dismissed Harrach, replaced him by Daun, and substituted Generals for the civilians of whom the Council had till then been mainly composed. Khevenhüller and Traun, the two commanders who had done most to distinguish themselves in the War of the Austrian Succession, had not survived till the peace;[1] but Neipperg did better at the War Council than in the field, and to Wenceslaus Liechtenstein, Director General of Ordnance since 1744, belongs most of the credit for the great improvement of the artillery.

But the reorganisation of the Army was only one branch of the reforms which were introduced. Almost more important was the amalgamation of the Court Chanceries (*Hofkanzleis*) of Austria and Bohemia, whose separate existence had hitherto been a great stumbling-block in the path of administrative unity and efficiency. While the Chanceries were relieved of all judicial work, which was transferred to a High Court of Justice erected at Vienna for Austria and Bohemia in 1749, they were fused in a *Directorium* which was the chief instrument through which the central government exercised control over local administration. In each province there was a subordinate court (*Representation*), which was the channel of communication between the *Directorium* and the District Councils (*Kreis-Ämter*) which were entrusted with the supervision of local affairs. Their sphere of influence included the control of municipal government and the enforcement of the decrees of the central government; but Maria Theresa left the actual work of local government very largely in the hands of the local nobility, who, unlike the French noblesse, did identify themselves with the country districts and did serve the State in all its various departments.

Pressure of work upon the *Directorium* caused all business connected with the finances to be altogether transferred in 1762 to the Treasury (*Hofkammer*), on which the old name of "joint Chancery of Bohemia and Austria" was restored to the *Directorium*,[2] and its head again became Court Chancellor (*Obersthofkanzler*). Subordinate to the Treasury were the *Banko-Deputation*, an office which dealt especially with the indirect taxes, the Ministry of Commerce,

---

[1] Khevenhüller died in 1744, Traun early in 1748.   [2] Wolf, p. 96.

12

the local financial chambers (*Landkammern*), and a special department for the management of the public debt and loans (*Hofrechenkammer*) not to mention Revenue and Customs officials.

In the management of the finances great improvements were effected, principally by Chotek, though the strain of the Seven Years' War completely upset the equilibrium between revenue and expenditure which he seemed to be reaching during the peace. Heavy taxes had to be imposed, and as the nobles were not taxed at the same rate as the peasants, even when their exemption had been abolished, the improvement in the financial administration added to the burdens on the taxpayers rather than reduced them. Much was done to increase the indirect revenue by giving encouragement to trade and manufactures. A rigidly protective tariff formed part of the system ; but internal tolls between province and province were much reduced and this hindrance to unity partly removed, though as Hungary remained outside this fiscal system, "dualism" was extended from the political to the economic sphere.

The reform of the judicial system was another task which engaged the attention of Maria Theresa and her councillors. A code of law was very much needed on account of the great differences between the various parts of the Hapsburg dominions, but it must be admitted that the Civil Code produced in 1767 was not one of the most successful efforts of the Theresian epoch. Long, unwieldy and somewhat unsystematic, under Joseph II it had to be replaced by a new codification. Better success attended the compilation of a Criminal Code. This "*Nemesis Theresiana*" of 1769, though it retained the rack and branding, and contained clauses dealing with sorcery and witchcraft, was yet a decided step in advance, and was improved by the abolition of torture in 1776. In 1788, Joseph's code superseded it.

In like manner, attempts were made to improve education. The Universities were subjected to sweeping reforms and taken over by the government as a State department, not perhaps with altogether the best results to education. Great attention was paid to the schools, both secondary and primary. Van Swieten, one of the most trusted advisers of the Empress, was principally responsible for this branch, and his reforms embraced technical as well as intellectual education, and must be regarded as a very remarkable contribution to the regeneration of Austria.

In the main, then, Maria Theresa's efforts to establish unity and a centralised system of government were successful. One hears little in her reign of the hostility between Slav and Teuton, between German and Czech. Her personal popularity was great, her courage and steadfastness in the time of danger had won the admiration and devotion of many of her subjects, and the strain and trials of the war served to show the different provinces that they had higher interests than merely seeking their own advantage, and that, after all, even their particular interests might be best served by union with their neighbours. Common perils surmounted safely helped to give unity. Indeed, after 1748 one may fairly look upon the epithet " Austrian " as implying more than merely " subject to Hapsburg rule," one may regard the phrase " Austrian nationality " as something more than a mere contradiction in terms when applied to Bohemians and Styrians. But there were still parts of the Hapsburg dominions which remained distinct and isolated. The " dualism " of Austria and Hungary was still a weak point in the Hapsburg monarchy, geographical even more than political and racial considerations prevented the Netherlands and Lombardy from ever becoming anything more than accidental additions to the central mass. Maria Theresa was too statesmanlike, too practical and too tactful to attempt to try to apply to these outlying provinces, devoid as they were of any connection with Austria and its immediate dependencies, the same reforms she was introducing elsewhere. She was able to see what escaped the notice of her doctrinaire son, that differences in circumstances necessitate differences in methods. She preferred to govern the Netherlands in the way best suited to their conditions, and her rule never provoked revolt in Belgium. They were left in the enjoyment of their federal Constitutions. The laws and privileges of the provinces, of which the *Joyeuse Entrée* of Brabant is typical, were left untouched. The Estates enjoyed local autonomy tempered only by the presence at Vienna of a Netherlands Council[1] and at Brussels of a Governor

[1] From 1757 on it was a department of the State Chancery.

of the Netherlands, usually a member of the dynasty with some capable nobleman as his chief minister. Thus Eugene had been Governor from 1714 to 1725; Archduchess Maria Elizabeth, sister of Charles VI, had succeeded him; Charles of Lorraine and his wife had held the post jointly, and after her death Charles retained it, though generally absent in Austria, till 1758. In his absence Königsegg, Kaunitz and others had acted as deputies, and from 1753 to 1770 Charles Cobenzl was virtual ruler of the provinces. All was not well, however, with the Netherlands. Though after 1748 their peace was untroubled, they were heavily taxed for the Seven Years' War, the government was corrupt and at once slack and oppressive; the Barrier-fortresses were allowed to fall into complete disrepair, and the natural development of the country was greatly hindered by the cramping fetters of the Peace of Münster. Still, if sluggish and unprogressive, the forty years during which Maria Theresa ruled the Netherlands were to be preferred to the stormy season which came in with Joseph II.

In Lombardy somewhat similar conditions prevailed. The Italian Council at Vienna[1] and the Governor-General at Milan administered a " paternal despotism " of an uneventful type, which smothered the original Spanish sympathies of the inhabitants without creating any strong loyalty for Austria. From 1754 till 1771 Duke Francis III of Modena, who had been reconciled to the Hapsburgs by the betrothal of his grand-daughter and heiress to one of Maria Theresa's sons, acted as Governor-General, with Beltrame Christiani and Charles Firmian as his ministers. These enlightened ministers carried out reforms of the same nature as those introduced by Turgot in France. Education was encouraged, the Inquisition abolished, and the right of the State to control the Church successfully asserted. Trade was relieved from restrictions, the possession of land made free, the numerous clergy compelled to bear a share of the public burdens. Thus even under the idle and wasteful Francis Lombardy prospered, and in 1771 the Archduke Ferdinand took over the government and continued to rule the country on the same lines.

With Hungary matters were rather different. It has been said that " Austria had an administration, but no constitution. Hungary a constitution, but no administration," and this is not

[1] Made a department of the State Chancery in 1757.

far from the truth.   The Diet, composed of two houses, one of
the magnates and higher clergy, the other of lesser nobles and
deputies of the cities, controlled taxation, had an important
share in legislation and could veto the levying of troops.
National feeling was strong and by no means favourable to
Austria, so that any reform coming from that quarter was
likely to provoke opposition, whatever its merits.   The control
of the country was in the hands of the nobles, for the burghers
had little influence and the peasantry and their goods were
practically the property of their lords.   The nobles paid no
taxes, had great political, social and legal privileges, including
even freedom from arrest and imprisonment, and formed a
numerous, haughty and turbulent aristocratic caste.

Maria Theresa's appeal to Hungarian loyalty in 1741,
and the concessions by which she obtained very valuable
assistance, have already been mentioned.   The Queen had
managed to evade the demands for the nationalising of
the administration and for complete Home Rule in financial
and military matters, but she had had to guarantee the
exemption of the nobility from taxation and to promise to
treat Transylvania as appertaining to Hungary.   Even after
1741 the Hungarian army was weak [1] and its annual cost,
two and a half million florins, was only half of what
Bohemia, though much smaller, paid for the same purpose;
while of the annual revenue of 20 millions only four were
devoted to the general purposes of the whole State.   In 1751,
therefore, Maria Theresa tried to induce the Diet to vote
an increase in the contribution.   To this proposal the lesser
nobles offered a bitter resistance, though the magnates
supported the Crown.   In the end (June 30th) a vote of three
and a half millions was carried.   In the Seven Years' War,
Hungary put considerable forces into the field but contributed
little in money, while in 1764 a Diet refused to allow the
organisation of the " Insurrection " in regiments but did vote
an additional 600,000 florins.   A third subject which Maria
Theresa broached at this meeting, a measure for the amelioration of the condition of the peasantry, met with unanimous resistance, but nevertheless she issued in 1766 an ordinance regulating their position, fixing their obligations, giving them a legal
status and means of redress.   At the same time she gave up

---

[1] Only six regiments.

summoning the Diet, appointed Joseph co-Regent, and replaced the Palatine, a national quite as much as a royal official, by a Stattholder and Captain-General, a post conferred on Duke Albert of Saxe-Teschen. To this extent Maria Theresa managed to bring Hungary under her control, and she was successful on the whole in conciliating the principal families; but as the dualism was too strong to be overthrown, she, with her usual wisdom, refrained from directly attacking it. Local autonomy she found too flourishing to be brought under a centralised system, and so she left it alone. She did manage to curb and control the lesser nobles, but without diminishing their strength, as Joseph II was to find to his cost.

Meanwhile, changes no less important were taking place in the foreign policy of Austria. Not only was Maria Theresa doing all she could to build up her own military and financial resources in order to resume some day the struggle for Silesia, she was also seeking allies who would work with her for the abasement of the upstart Hohenzollern. Naturally she looked first to the other signatories of the Treaty of Warsaw which had been reaffirmed and re-enforced in 1746 by the addition of Russia; while England, still possessed by the old idea of holding France in check by utilising the traditional rivalry between Hapsburg and Bourbon, gave a general adhesion to the treaty in 1750, though not to the secret clauses which contemplated the dismemberment of Prussia. But this old Anglo-Austrian alliance was not quite the firm union it had been. The war had strained it almost to breaking point. England's steadfast refusal to help her against Frederick, England's share in wringing from her the Treaties of Berlin and Dresden, England's attempts to force her to unite with the robber of Silesia against the Bourbon from whom she had suffered so much less, and England's support to the demands of Sardinia, had made Maria Theresa feel that her English ally had done her as much harm as her French foe.

It was with this idea in her mind that shortly after the Peace of Aix-la-Chapelle, Maria Theresa requested the members of the Conference to submit in writing their views on the political situation, and their advice as to the policy most advantageous to Austria. The majority, including Marshal Königsegg, Colloredo, the Vice-Chancellor, and the Emperor himself,

while admitting that the action of England had been selfish in
the extreme, were not prepared to recommend any change in
the old system of alliances.   Very different, however, were the
proposals of Kaunitz, the most recent addition to the Conference.
Premising that under existing circumstances the Maritime
Powers, Russia and Saxony were the natural allies of Austria
and France, Prussia and Turkey the natural enemies, he
pointed out that the traditional enemies, France and Turkey,
were far less formidable than the new enemy within the
Empire, especially as in the case of danger from France
Austria could confidently rely on that English assistance
which had not been and could not be reckoned upon against
Prussia.   But as Prussia was the chief danger, as, apart from
all idea of regaining the lost Silesia, Austria must for the
future be on her guard against another unprovoked attack,
Kaunitz boldly proposed to try to win the alliance of France
and to secure, if not indeed her assistance, at any rate her
neutrality in the event of another Silesian war.   The price
which he proposed to pay was one which would be no real loss
to Austria, cessions of territory in the Netherlands to Don
Philip of Parma, son-in-law of Louis xv.

For a revolution so radical in her foreign relations, Maria
Theresa was hardly prepared.   It was true that the idea of
coming to terms with France had already crossed her mind;
more than once, notably towards the end of 1745, she had
attempted to effect a reconciliation.   It was true that the
hostility between France and Austria no longer rested on any
necessary basis.   With a Bourbon on the throne of the
Spanish Hapsburgs, with Germany so disunited that a pan-
German crusade to recover the conquests of Louis xiv was
quite out of the question, with France made secure on her
North-Eastern and Eastern borders by the acquisition of a
scientific frontier and occupied mainly with her colonial and
maritime rivalry with England, the relations of Bourbon and
Hapsburg were altogether different from what they had been
when Henri iv and Richelieu had striven to free France from
the " Hapsburg net " which then threatened her.   That object
had been long ago accomplished; France had nothing to fear
from Austria, and in England and Prussia the two Powers had
new rivals and new dangers to meet.   However, the old
traditions were still so strong that Maria Theresa and her

husband, while regarding Kaunitz's project as a possible alternative, looked upon it mainly as a means of bringing pressure to bear on England in the adjustment of the differences which threatened to sever the old alliance. At the same time they thought it well to seek to promote more friendly relations with France, and with that object Kaunitz was sent to Paris as Ambassador in 1750. During his residence there (1750–1753) he laboured steadily at laying the foundations for the future alliance; and if the seed seemed at first to have fallen on barren ground, if he failed to prevent France supporting Prussia's opposition to the election of Joseph as King of the Romans in 1752, he made a beginning. Among others, Madame de Pompadour was won round to the new policy, and when Kaunitz returned to Vienna to take up the office of State Chancellor his successor Stahremberg continued his work.

Still Kaunitz himself would seem to have for the time abandoned his idea, and to have even urged that Maria Theresa should reconcile herself to the loss of Silesia and add Prussia to the Anglo-Austrian alliance. George II, however, hated Frederick and would not hear of it, while Maria Theresa was equally unyielding. It might perhaps have been the wiser policy in the end, but it would be unreasonable to blame Maria Theresa for her refusal to come to terms with the Power which had behaved so treacherously to her, and which in its dealings with Bavaria and France had shown itself no less fickle and untrustworthy as an ally than formidable as a foe. She could have no guarantee that at some crisis Frederick would not leave her in the lurch.

Thus between 1750 and 1755 only one real change in the diplomatic position of Europe occurred. This was the Treaty of Aranjuez in 1752, by which Austria and Spain came to terms with regard to Italy, guaranteeing the existing territorial conditions. Naples, Parma and Sardinia adhered to this treaty, and thus the tranquillity of Italy was secured for nearly forty years, and one obstacle in the way of Franco-Austrian reconciliation removed.[1] But the Anglo-Austrian

---

[1] Ferdinand VI, under the influence of his Queen, Barbara of Portugal, and his chief minister, Wall, an Irish refugee, was following a policy of peaceful commercial and industrial development and had more or less broken away from the French alliance. As long as he remained on the throne, Spain was neutral in the Anglo-French quarrel.

alliance was growing weaker. While Austria complained bitterly of England's action and policy in the late war, especially in the matter of Silesia, which had been guaranteed to Prussia by the Convention of Hanover, England could point with about equal justice to the way in which Austria had neglected the defence of the Netherlands. The suppression of the Ostend Company [1] was still a sore point with the Hapsburgs, and England's refusal in 1748 to have the Barrier Treaty abrogated had greatly irritated Maria Theresa: she now refused to pay the annual subsidy due to the Dutch or to repair the half-dismantled fortresses. Moreover, though England and Hanover had supported the candidature of the Archduke Joseph for King of the Romans, Hanover had backed up the claims advanced by the Elector Palatine for compensation from Austria for the losses he had suffered in the war.[2] Thus, altogether, Maria Theresa though still loyal to the old alliance, felt far from inclined to make any sacrifices and run any risks for the sake of England.

It was when matters were in this state that the great quarrel between England and France in North America over the valleys of the Ohio and Mississippi and all that their possession involved came to a head with the conflict between the French and Colonel Washington's Virginian militia on the Monongahela (July 1754). From that moment the two countries drifted steadily into war; for though it was not till nearly two years later that the formal declaration was issued (May 1756), hostilities on a considerable scale began with the despatch of Braddock's expedition in January 1755. That the declaration was so long postponed was due to the indecision and irresolution which marked the proceedings of both home governments.

The struggle for the "hinterland" of the North American colonies of France and England does not seem at first sight to

---

[1] Cf. pp. 80–82.

[2] Conferences were held at Hanover in August 1750 to see how the Archduke's election could best be secured. The Electors of Bavaria and Cologne took the opportunity to demand certain financial concessions from Austria, while Charles Theodore of Sulzbach, Elector Palatine, claimed territorial indemnification. Of this Austria would not hear, since Charles Theodore had been a partisan of France. Prussia then refused to admit that a mere majority among the Electors was sufficient for the election of a King of the Romans. France, represented by Vergennes, was prepared to support Prussia and, after dragging on for two years, the whole negotiations came to an utterly inconclusive end.

have more than an indirect connection with the affairs of Germany. The issue of the conflict could not, of course, fail to alter the balance of maritime and colonial power, and to that extent must affect the political equilibrium of Europe, but that would hardly appear enough to have involved Austria and Prussia in the war. The connecting link between the Ohio and the Oder was supplied by the Personal Union between England and Hanover, and by the fact that in Hanover George II was particularly vulnerable. In Hanover he could be attacked by the French Army without the interposition of the guns of the British Navy or of the waves of the English Channel, and at this time the French Army was sufficiently influential at the Court of Versailles to override any arguments which the Marine Department might put forward through Machault in favour of making the war exclusively naval. Briefly stated, it was because the French Army would not agree to the neutralisation of Hanover, which Frederick urged upon them, that Frederick came to terms with England and agreed to defend Hanover, a step which left France no alternative but to come to terms with Austria, if not necessarily to commit herself to assisting Austria to recover Silesia. It was the French who tried to " conquer America in Germany," and so caused Pitt to meet them and beat them with their own weapons.

From the very first it was obvious that unless one side or the other would give way over the American quarrel—and if neither government seemed resolved on war, neither would bring itself to make the necessary concessions—France would attack England through Hanover. George II therefore set about providing for the defence of his Electorate in the old way; he sought to obtain the help of Austria, and through his alliance with her to hire soldiers from those minor Princes of Germany whose armies were always at the disposal of the highest bidder. He was ready to make an agreement with Russia for the purpose of keeping Prussia in check, but to join the anti-Prussian coalition was rather more than he was prepared to do.

George II therefore [1] called upon Austria to fulfil her obli-

---

[1] It is rather remarkable to notice how every one seems to have assumed that in case of an Anglo-French war the first step France would take would be an invasion of the Austrian Netherlands, and how one has England far more solicitous about their defence than is their own ruler, Maria Theresa.

gations for the defence of the Netherlands and in June 1755 the Hanoverian ministers Münchhaüsen and Steinberg drew up the famous "Project of Herrenhaüsen," whose failure may be taken as the parting of the ways between England and Austria. By this project George II was to unite with Austria and Saxony-Poland to maintain an army for the defence of Hanover, Saxony and the German dominions of Austria: this with the help of Russia would set free 30,000 Austrians to defend the Netherlands, in which task they were to be assisted by 6000 British and 14,000 Bavarians and Hessians in British pay. The project, however, was based on obtaining the requisite subsidies from the British Parliament, and it was here that it broke down. It represented George's policy as Elector of Hanover, and the refusal of Pitt to hear of so indefinite an extension of the system of subsidies caused its rejection; a Hanoverian policy, in fact, was sacrificed to the wishes of England.

George had therefore to fall back on such definite subsidy-treaties as he could get Parliament to accept. He was able to arrange for 12,000 Hessians, and he also suggested that if Austria would increase her forces in the Netherlands he would make a treaty with her ally Russia. Kaunitz had already (June) offered to send some 12,000 men to the Netherlands if England would take her share in their defence; but he now (August) flatly refused to send a man, alleging that the despatch of reinforcements at so critical a moment would merely precipitate war. Austria, indeed, no longer stood firm to the British alliance, she was ready to leave the Netherlands to their fate. She felt, and very rightly, as Holland did also, that the American question was not a matter of such concern to her as to justify her in involving herself in a war with France. With Russia, however, George was more successful, and in September a treaty was concluded by which Elizabeth promised to provide 55,000 men to defend Hanover against either the French or Frederick.

But if Frederick II had no great love for England or for George II he had no wish at so critical a moment in his fortunes to let his French alliance involve him in a war with England. As early as 1753 the treachery of one Mentzel, a clerk in the Saxon Chancery, had disclosed to him the secret articles of the Treaty of 1746, and he knew what he had to expect. If he were to attack Hanover on behalf of France, it would not only give Austria and her friends the opportunity they wanted, but it would cause England, which had hitherto refused to furnish Russia with the subsidies needed for the purposes of an attack on Prussia, to definitely array herself on the anti-Prussian side. Nor was the prospect of what might happen if he stood neutral while France attacked Hanover much more promising. His relations with Russia were not such as to make him welcome the introduction of 55,000 Muscovite troops into the heart of Germany to defend Hanover against a French attack. He therefore urged his French allies strongly to leave Hanover alone, to consent to its being neutralised. He was the more anxious to persuade the French not to attack Hanover because to reach it they must cross the Westphalian provinces of Prussia, and would probably want to use Wesel and the other Prussian fortresses on the Rhine as their base. Keenly awake to the possibilities of the situation, Frederick now began to cultivate better relations with his Hanoverian cousins, an object which was not a little advanced by a visit paid by his sister, the Duchess of Brunswick-Wolfenbüttel, to George II at Hanover.

His overtures were well received. When the Austrians refused to send troops to the Netherlands (Aug.), Münch-haüsen invited the good offices of the Duke of Brunswick towards obtaining a promise of Prussian neutrality in the case of a French attack on Hanover. Frederick, without actually rejecting these overtures, hastened to put himself in communication with the Court of Versailles, asking that the Duc de Nivernais, a friend of his and a warm partisan of the Franco-Prussian alliance, might be sent to Berlin to arrange matters. The French Government, however, with a most culpable negligence and indecision did nothing to make sure of Frederick's alliance. They still hoped that the American question might be settled without war and, while doing little or nothing to facilitate a peaceful solution by keeping their local representatives in America under control, they were still carrying on secret negotiations with England.

Unable to get any reply from France, Frederick did not neglect the other string to his bow. Through the Prussian Secretary of Legation in London, Frederick became aware of the definite terms of the Anglo-Russian treaty of September, which were hardly to his liking.   At the same time he learnt that the proposed Anglo-Prussian treaty of neutrality would give him satisfaction in the case of some Prussian merchant-men which had been seized in the late war, would remove his fears as to Russia and renew England's guarantee of Silesia.   Accordingly on December 7th he gave his assent to a convention which took the shape (Jan. 16th, 1756) of the Convention of Westminster.   By this most important treaty England and Prussia expressed their desire to maintain peace in Germany and guaranteed its neutrality, though not that of the Netherlands; agreed to oppose the entrance into Germany or the passage through it of any foreign army; and guaranteed each other's possessions.

It has been said of this treaty that " the action of Frederick II stung the supine and pacifically disposed Govern-ment of Louis XV into taking the first step that made the second inevitable. . . . The anxiety of King George II to safeguard the Hanoverian frontier was the final cause of the Franco-Austrian agreement." [1]   To describe as " pacifically disposed " a government which, like that of Louis XV, was pursuing " a policy of pin pricks " in North America, seems hardly accurate, " supine " it was; but surely the true " final cause " of the Franco-Austrian agreement, of the special character which it assumed and of the consequent course of the war, was the outvoting of those in France who were prepared to let Hanover be neutralised by those who sought to gain compensation for losses at sea and in the colonies by conquests on the Weser, in a word, of Machault and the Marine Department, by the more influential Army.

The true character of the Anglo-Prussian agreement may be seen from the fact that both England and Prussia regarded it as quite in keeping with their existing alliances.   England explained it to Austria as a step towards an Austro-Prussian reconciliation.[2]   Frederick continued to point out to France the advantages to her in her maritime war of the neutralisation of Germany.   This was not the light in which France regarded the news, which arrived almost simultaneously with the English rejection of the French ultimatum.   France was furious, some-

---

[1] *England and Hanover*, p. 181.

[2] The exclusion of the Netherlands from the guarantee of neutrality was intended to force Austria to join England and Prussia against France.

what unreasonably, for she only had herself to blame for it, at her ally's conclusion of a treaty with her enemy behind her back. Frederick's behaviour rather than the terms of the treaty infuriated Louis XV and his ministers, and caused them to regard with favour the proposals Austria was now putting forward again.

When the Anglo-Austrian negotiations broke down in August 1755, Kaunitz had revived his former project and had suggested through Stahremberg that France should join a great coalition to be formed against Frederick for the double purpose of recovering Silesia for Maria Theresa and of securing her and the other neighbours of Frederick against future unprovoked aggressions on his part. As a compensation, France might receive a rectification of her frontier towards the Netherlands, including the important fortress of Mons, the rest of the Netherlands might go to Don Philip of Parma in return for the reversion to Austria of his Italian duchy. Accordingly, in September 1755, Stahremberg and the Abbé Bernis met at La Babiole, but France, while quite ready for some form of alliance with Austria, was not prepared to do all Austria wanted. A counter-proposal from France for a guarantee of the possessions of Austria, France and Prussia, which was to leave France free to attack Hanover while Maria Theresa was to prevent Russia hiring out her troops for the defence of Hanover, was not at all what Austria desired. Matters were lingering on and a decision seemed distant, when the conclusion of the Convention of Westminster revolutionised the situation. Austria was still negotiating with Keith while France had recalled Nivernais from Berlin, so she had now the trump card in the alternative of an alliance with England and Prussia: the French ministry would have only had their own indecision to thank if England had united Austria and Prussia in a great continental coalition against France. It was therefore France which was the keener on concluding a treaty and from whom concessions must come.

The negotiations were long, intricate and delicate, neither quite liking to break with an old ally. At last Austria promised that if France would take active measures against Prussia, she would on obtaining Silesia and Glatz take similar steps against England. At a meeting of the French ministry a defensive treaty on these lines was agreed upon as a preliminary to a

closer union. It is interesting to notice that Belleisle, the
Comte d'Argenson and the rest of the military party in France
were so far from regarding this decision as bellicose that they
opposed it steadily, fearing that it would secure peace and so
prevent the French army from seeing service on the Continent.[1]

The first treaty of Versailles, which was concluded on May
1st, 1756, included three things : a Convention of Neutrality, a
Defensive Alliance and a Secret Convention. The first pledged
Maria Theresa to neutrality in the Anglo-French war, Louis XV
binding himself to respect the Netherlands frontier in attacking Hanover. The Defensive Alliance was the most important section of the treaty. Both parties agreed to uphold
the Peace of Westphalia and other treaties since concluded
between them, guaranteed each other's actual possessions in
Europe against attack, except as regarded the Anglo-French
war already in progress, and promised to assist each
other, if attacked by a third party, with 24,000 men or
an equivalent in money. Finally, the Secret Convention
promised Maria Theresa's aid to Louis should any Power
attack French territory as an ally of England, Louis undertaking a parallel obligation. It also declared the Emperor
(for Tuscany), Naples, Parma, Spain, or any other Power whose
adhesion might be considered desirable, to be eligible for
admission to the alliance ; and both signatories agreed not to
make any fresh treaty without communication with the other
party.

Such was the famous treaty of May 1st, 1756. That it
was more to the advantage of Austria than of France is not to
be denied ; she was not involved in the war against England
which France pledged herself to continue as long as Austria and
Prussia were at war, and France was only to receive her compensation when Austria had regained Silesia and Glatz.[2] It was
probably the ever-present fear that England might in the end
unite Austria, Prussia and Russia, an unlikely but not impossible
alliance for which Newcastle was still hoping, which induced
Bernis to recede in this way from his demand for reciprocity.
Shortly before the conclusion of the treaty, Maria Theresa had
the satisfaction of hearing from St. Petersburg that Elizabeth
would accede to the Franco-Austrian alliance, and would
contribute 80,000 troops to the attack on Prussia, promis-

[1] Waddington, i. 329.   [2] *E.H.R.* (1898), p. 793.

ing to continue the war until Maria Theresa had regained Silesia and Glatz. In the partition of the Prussian dominions, East Prussia was to go to Poland, which would in return cede Courland to Russia; Magdeburg was to fall to the lot of Saxony, Pomerania to Sweden.[1]

For France the treaty was the first step on a path which was to lead to humiliation and defeat, to loss of prestige and of position, which was to bring her appreciably nearer the Revolution; but it does not necessarily follow that the treaty was a mistake. In the first place, nothing can be clearer than the fact that the object of the French ministry in concluding this treaty was to secure the peace of Europe, to administer a snub to Frederick and show him plainly that he was by no means indispensable to France. That the French guarantee would prove insufficient to keep Prussia quiet never crossed the minds of Rouillé and his colleagues. In the meantime they hoped in the negotiations for a closer alliance which were now to be set on foot to obtain concessions in the Netherlands for France and for Don Philip as the price not of French aid to Maria Theresa's anti-Prussian schemes, but of French neutrality. To Frederick and to the other Courts of Europe who were unaware of the impending developments of the treaty it appeared that all that France was doing was to secure herself against continental complications which could divert her attention from the colonial and naval war. Indeed, had not Frederick by his unexpected attack on Saxony provided the *casus fœderis* of the third clause of the Defensive Alliance and of the first of the Secret Convention, it is at least doubtful whether France would have been among his immediate opponents.

That France and Austria were throwing over their traditional policy is undeniable; but Austria had not found England so satisfactory an ally in the matter of Silesia that it was not to her advantage to discard the old alliance for a new and more promising combination. France also had more to fear from England and from Prussia than from Austria. There was no necessary hostility between Bourbon and Hapsburg: it was as a stronger Power whose strength threatened her independence that France had first fought Austria

---

[1] Cf. von Arneth, v. 46. The best account of these negotiations is that given in M. Waddington's *Louis XV et le Renversement des Alliances*, especially chs. v.–viii.

and no one could say now that France was in any danger from a Hapsburg preponderance. Nor had the results of the policy of 1741 been such as to encourage France to adhere to her alliance with a monarch so regardless of anything but his own interests as was Frederick. The real causes of the French disasters lay not in putting an end to an obsolete traditional policy, but in making the war continental by persisting in the attack on Hanover—but for which France need never have exceeded the limits of the assistance to which she pledged herself in 1756—in allowing Austrian interests to direct the war, and above all, in the utter inefficiency of Army, Navy and government which the war displayed, and of which neither it nor the treaty was the cause.

13

CHAPTER XI

THE SEVEN YEARS' WAR

TO THE END OF 1757

BUT it was not only Maria Theresa who had been turning to good use the years of peace since Aix-la-Chapelle. Frederick II had never deluded himself with the belief that he could count on the undisturbed enjoyment of Silesia; he knew that he must be prepared to make good his title to it by the means by which he had acquired it, and one of the chief reasons for his readiness to make peace in December 1745 was that he was then at the end of his resources, and imperatively needed a period of rest and recuperation. During the peace he had introduced many reforms, in the administration, in finance, in the domestic economy of the kingdom, in the judicial system.[1] The burden of taxation had hardly been lightened in the least; but while money had flowed freely into his depleted treasury, the strictest economy had been practised, and in 1756 he had a reserve fund of eighteen million thalers. Even more important were the measures which he had taken to increase and improve the army with which the very existence of the Prussian kingdom was so closely bound up. To increase it was his first object, and by 1756 it mustered 155,000 men. Garrison duty absorbed 27,000 of these; for the repairing and strengthening of many fortresses, especially in the newly-acquired Silesia, had made a considerable increase in the garrison-battalions necessary. The rest, 126 battalions and 210 squadrons, formed a highly efficient field army, which an iron discipline, a careful training on the parade-ground and in the manœuvres and camps of exercises which were held every year had made a force even more formidable than that which Frederick William had bequeathed to his son. In staff work, in organisation, in preparations for

---

[1] Cf. Chapter XIV.

mobilisation, great improvements had been made. No efforts had been spared to collect vast reserves of clothing, weapons, provisions and military stores of every kind. But it may be doubted whether it was not even more to the King and commander than to the soldiers that these years were so useful. There was not the same room for improvement in the Prussian army as there was in its commander. Frederick had learnt a good deal about the art of war on the battlefields of Bohemia and Silesia, and he devoted the peace to a careful study of the profession of arms. It was now that he devised and worked out the system of attacking in oblique order, which was to win so conspicuous a triumph at Leuthen. Many of the greatest qualities of a general he already possessed, resolution, decision, a readiness to take risks, promptitude, tenacity, unbounded self-confidence; but it was in handling large masses of men in the manœuvres that he learnt to really understand his weapon, on the drill-ground that he was able to test and improve his system of tactics, in peace that he prepared for war.

As has been already explained, Frederick did not regard the Convention of Westminster as a complete breach with France, and still expected her to agree to the neutralisation of Germany. Even the negotiations between France and Austria caused him no anxiety; for he, like his minister Knyphaüsen, looked upon them as merely intended to secure the neutrality of the Netherlands. The movements of the Austrian and Russian troops, however, were of a character to arouse his suspicions, and when on June 22nd he received from his minister at Dresden, Maltzahn, a copy obtained by Mentzel of a despatch from Fleming, the Saxon representative at St. Petersburg, to Count Brühl, speaking openly of Russia's hostile intentions towards Prussia, he saw at once that war was inevitable.[1] The mobilisation of the army began at once, and, in opposition to the advice of Podewils and of Prince Henry, Count Klinggraeffen, the Prussian envoy at Vienna, was instructed to lay before Maria Theresa a request for an explanation of the movements of her armies (July 26th). Maria Theresa's reply led Frederick to present an ultimatum (Aug. 20th), pressing for more explicit explanations, and for a definite statement that she did not mean to attack him

[1] Cf. Frederick's letter to Wilhelmina of Baireuth, June 22nd, 1756.

either that year or in the coming year. Maria Theresa answered that no offensive alliance against Prussia was in existence, and she threw upon Frederick all the responsibility for the armaments and for the military precautions she had been forced to take. On August 25th, Frederick received this answer; on the 26th he instructed Maltzahn to demand from the Elector of Saxony free passage through his dominions for the Prussian troops on their way to Bohemia; on the 28th he left Berlin, and on the 29th he crossed the Saxon frontier.

That in thus acting Frederick was only anticipating attack is true; there was a design on foot for a great coalition against Prussia, even if it was still in an inchoate condition; but it may be doubted whether he might not have gained more by waiting to be attacked; he threw away the moral advantage of being the defender and failed to achieve the military results he had hoped to win by adopting the offensive. And by attacking Bohemia through Saxony he enabled Maria Theresa to call upon France to fulfil her treaty obligations, and made it impossible for France to remain neutral. But for this he might not have had to reckon with more than the malevolent neutrality of France. Unless Frederick gained very striking military successes, unless he was able to destroy the coalition against him before it could really get to work, the moral and diplomatic advantage to Maria Theresa of being able to point once again to the unwarrantable aggressions of her ambitious neighbour would be enormous.

It would appear that in taking the offensive Frederick calculated—not without good reason—upon an easy success over the weak and not very efficient Saxon army.[1] After obtaining military possession of Saxony he would press on into Bohemia, and hoped to dictate a peace under the walls of Vienna which would leave Saxony in his possession and compensate Augustus III with Bohemia.[2] Nor were the prospects unpromising. He had for his main army some 70,000 men,[3] who converged upon the Saxon capital from Halle through Leipzig and Chemnitz, straight up the Elbe by Torgau and from Lusatia, while an independent corps under Schwerin, 27,000 strong, entered Bohemia by Glatz and

---

[1] Though 50,000 strong on paper, it was much below strength; and with some regiments absent in Poland, the available force was hardly 20,000.

[2] Cf. Waddington, i. 521–533.   [3] 101 squadrons and 67 battalions.

Nachod, moving on Königgratz. On paper Austria should have had in Bohemia and Moravia nearly 90,000 men to oppose to the invaders; but many corps had not yet arrived, and others were below strength, so that the force which General Browne collected at Kolin at the end of August only mustered 7000 horse and 25,000 foot, while Piccolomini in Moravia had no more than 22,000 men, 5000 being cavalry. The Austrian mobilisation was very far from complete, which may be taken as evidence that no immediate attack on Prussia had been intended, and at so late a season no help could be expected from France or Russia.

When Frederick crossed the Saxon frontier Augustus at first offered to be neutral and to hand over certain fortresses as a guarantee; but this did not satisfy Frederick who demanded also that the Saxon army should be incorporated in his own, or at least disarmed. Augustus would not agree to this, and it was decided to make a stand in the strong position of Pirna, where the Saxon army had been collected. The only alternative was a retreat into Bohemia for which Augustus was hardly prepared, as he feared Frederick would take the opportunity to annex the Electorate. By the middle of September, therefore, the Saxons were surrounded in the Pirna position, and Frederick, who had not expected anything of the sort, found his plans for the invasion of Bohemia suspended. He could not move on and leave the Saxons unmasked in his rear, while if he left behind a force sufficient to contain the Saxons, he would not be strong enough to besiege Prague or undertake any similar operation. The unexpected action of the Saxons therefore disarranged his whole plan; and had not Augustus and Brühl neglected to make an adequate provision of food and other supplies, so that the Saxons were unable to hold out till an Austrian army strong enough to effect their release could be collected, the invasion of Saxony might have ended disastrously for Frederick. The Saxon camp, protected by a brook and marsh in its front, resting on the Elbe and on the strong fortresses of Lilienstein and Königstein and well fortified, would have been almost impossible to storm. But that the inefficiency of the Saxon government displayed itself in the collection of supplies for four weeks only instead of four months, the sudden resolve of Augustus to stand at Pirna might have been attended by complete success.

As things were, General Browne, an able officer of Irish birth who commanded the Austrian forces in Bohemia, had only a very short time in which to effect the relief. Though inferior in force to the Prussians, and hardly prepared for instant action, he did not hesitate but pushed forward to Budin on the Eger to see if he could get into touch with the Saxons (Sept. 29th).

Frederick had already pushed Marshal Keith forward into Bohemia with a covering force, which had driven an Austrian detachment out of Aussig (Sept. 13th); and on hearing of Browne's advance he moved up and joined Keith (Sept. 29th), leaving some 40,000 men to blockade Pirna. On the 30th, Browne, who had had to wait for his guns and pontoons, moved from Budin to Lobositz, the Prussians also moving forward and occupying the hills of Lobosch and Homolka, just North of Lobositz, the same day. On the morning of October 1st the Croats, pushing out from Lobositz, found the Prussians in position.

The two forces were of nearly equal strength,[1] but in position the Prussians had an advantage, holding the hills on either side of the road from Lobositz to Welmina, while the Austrian right in and around Lobositz was cut off from the centre and left, which were behind the Morell Brook. The battle began with an advance of the Prussian cavalry in the centre; but though at first successful they were repulsed by the heavy fire of the Austrian infantry and of the guns behind the Morell Brook. Their supports then joined them, but were charged and routed by the Austrian cavalry. Browne now reinforced his right, and sent it forward against the hill of Lobosch; but Frederick parried this stroke by bringing up the second line of his right, which he could safely do as the Morell Brook covered that wing from a counter-attack by the Austrian left. There was a sharp struggle for the Loboschberg; but on the fall of their commander, Lacy, the Austrians gave way and retired through Lobositz, which the Prussians occupied. Beyond that they did not attempt to press their advantage, for Browne's centre and left were still intact, and his force drew off in excellent order, falling back next day to

---

[1] The Austrians had 34 battalions of infantry to 29, and were equal in cavalry, each side having 70 squadrons; but the Prussian establishments were rather higher.

Budin. Inasmuch as they had checked Browne's advance on Pirna and had forced him to evacuate Lobositz, the Prussians could claim the victory; but their losses, 3300 all told, somewhat exceeded the Austrian, 2300 killed and wounded and 700 prisoners, and they had had to fight very hard for their success. Frederick could not but realise that he had a different enemy to deal with than the comparatively inefficient Austrian army of 1741–1745.

Browne's check had by no means been fatal to the relief of Pirna. He had, on the contrary, drawn off Frederick and a large part of his army and thereby reduced the pressure; and on October 6th he started off with 8000 picked men, and by forced marches by Kamnitz and Schluckenau reached Mitteldorf, only three miles from Schandau, on the afternoon of the 11th. Had the Saxons been ready to co-operate promptly and to take advantage of the helping hand Browne thus held out, the greater part of their army might have got away; but the pontoons were in the wrong place, much time was wasted, and when at last the crossing began (11.30 p.m. Oct. 12th) every possible mistake was made. The utmost confusion prevailed, the camp was evacuated too soon, the crossing was not properly covered against attacks in rear. Moreover, the delay had allowed Winterfeldt to reinforce the division facing Browne; and when, about 4 o'clock next afternoon, (13th) the bridge broke down the Saxon army found itself cooped up between Lilienstein and the Elbe in a position commanded by Prussian cannon, and from which all the exits were blocked by Prussian troops. To persist was hopeless, surrender was inevitable, and very reluctantly Augustus had to agree. He himself managed to get away to Warsaw, but nearly 18,000 troops had to lay down their arms (Oct. 16th). Browne, who had done his share, held on at Lichtenhayn till late on the 14th, but then finding that the crossing had failed had no alternative but to retire. By October 20th he was back at Budin.

Thus Frederick obtained possession of Saxony, which he proceeded to mulct in large sums of money, besides forcing his Saxon prisoners to enlist in his army;[1] but the

[1] They took the first opportunity to desert, as the dislike for the Prussians in Saxony was very strong. By February over 2500 had gone over to Austria, and early in the next year three whole regiments deserted and made their way to Poland.

comparative success obtained at Pirna and Lobositz must not hide the fact . that Frederick's plans as a whole had failed. The resistance of the Saxons had saved Bohemia by detaining Frederick until Browne had time to get his army together. By the time Pirna fell it was too late to attempt another move. The Prussians from Lobositz were back in Saxony by October 28th, and Schwerin, who had been held in check at Königgratz by Piccolomini's inferior force, retired to Silesia.

To trace in detail the complicated negotiations between Austria and her French and Russian allies which filled the winter of 1756–1757 would be an endless task. What is quite clear, however, is that Maria Theresa took a very different view of the aims of the treaty of May 1756 from that held at Versailles. While France was by no means pleased with the subordinate part which the strict fulfilment of that treaty would have assigned to her, and was anxious to put her whole force into the field against Hanover, Maria Theresa would have been quite content with the punctual execution of the obligations France had then assumed, with the despatch of an auxiliary corps by the Danube to Bohemia or Moravia. She was very anxious to avoid making the war general, lest she should give the appearance of truth to the accusations Frederick hurled at her, that she was introducing the French into the Empire and involving all Germany in war. She did not wish to do anything to alarm Holland or the Protestant Powers of North Germany, and would have been glad if it had been possible to neutralise Hanover; for, as she pointed out to the French ministers, she had no quarrel with England and was not concerned in the quarrel over America, which was altogether distinct from the treaty into which France and Austria had entered for the recovery of Silesia and the debasement of Prussia—an end, she hinted, quite as much to be desired by France as by Austria. France, she pointed out, was definitely pledged to assist Austria at the time that Frederick's attack on Saxony provided a *casus belli*; Austria had undertaken no such obligations towards the war which had previously broken out in America.

Thus, though at the outset France, irritated by Frederick's attack on Saxony in defiance of her guarantee, prepared to send the 24,000 men according to the treaty, and began collecting them at Metz, by October 2nd Stahremberg was writing to announce that the despatch of the auxiliary corps had been postponed for the present. France, indeed, had no wish to confine herself to the despatch of these auxiliaries so far afield as Moravia, where they would be out of her control, and would not be available for her designs on Hanover. She therefore prepared to take the field on a much larger scale, and d'Estrées was sent off to Vienna to arrange a scheme of operations.

It would appear that d'Argenson, Rouillé, Paris-Duverney, and their friends opposed the idea of playing a merely secondary rôle in the German war, because they feared that if they did this the war would be indefinitely protracted; their idea was to seize Hanover as a set-off against possible losses in the colonies, and then to operate on the Middle Elbe against Frederick in conjunction with the Austrians from Bohemia. As the first step, they proposed to assemble an army of observation on the Lower Rhine. However, they did consent that Austria should attempt to negotiate the neutrality of Hanover, an idea which had been mooted by the Hanoverian ministers as early as September 1756, and upon which Maria Theresa, anxious to prevent Frederick from identifying his cause with that of the North German Protestants, was keenly set. Hanover, indeed, was anti-Prussian, and would gladly have come to terms with the Empress; and England, though she did not intend to desert Frederick, would have liked to escape from the necessity of undertaking the defence of Hanover. But the proposal to extend the neutrality of Hanover to Brunswick and to Hesse-Cassel, practically to establish a line of demarcation which the French troops would have to respect, broke down when the French held out for *transitus innoxius*—in other words, freedom to use this neutral sphere for an attack on Prussia.

A great deal also turned on the question of " reciprocity "; when and on what conditions was Maria Theresa to hand over the Netherlands to France or to Don Philip? Austria was afraid of alarming England and the United Provinces, France wanted to force on a complete breach between Austria and her old ally. Despatch after despatch passed between Vienna and Versailles. On February 21st, Maria Theresa wrote to Stahremberg declaring her readiness to hand over the Netherlands on getting back Silesia and Glatz even if Frederick were no further reduced, while as the hopes of neutralising Hanover faded away, the idea of localising the war became more and more impossible of realisation. Finally, exactly a year after the conclusion of the First Treaty, the Second Treaty of Versailles was signed on May 1st, 1757. France promised to send to Maria Theresa's aid 24,000 French troops as auxiliaries, with 10,000 subsidised South Germans, also to put 105,000 men into the field on her own account. She also agreed to pay 12 million gulden a year, in monthly instalments, and not to make peace till Austria's possession of Silesia and Glatz had been admitted by Frederick and his allies. Austria's contingent was to be 80,000 men; she was to hand over Ostend and Nieuport to France as a security when the first instalment of the subsidy was paid, to hand over Mons, Ypres and several other towns on obtaining Silesia and Glatz, and to give the rest of the Netherlands to Don Philip when the proposed partition of Prussia should have taken place. By this Halberstadt, Halle and Magdeburg were to go to Saxony, Sweden was to recover the portion of Pomerania lost in 1720, Cleves and Guelders to be divided between the United Provinces and the Elector Palatine should they join the Coalition; Crossen was to be added to Maria Theresa's share. Louis XV promised to use his influence to get Joseph elected King of the Romans, while the treaty also included several less important clauses relating to Italy.

As finally arranged, the treaty was greatly in Maria Theresa's favour, for France had given way on several points, notably with regard to the payment of the subsidies. But it does not therefore follow that it represented a complete triumph for Austrian interests over French. Probably France would have been better advised had she confined herself to the despatch of the 24,000 auxiliaries; but it was rather in the practical execution of the policy than in the policy itself that she was to do herself so much damage. Maria Theresa must, of course, answer the charge of having so far sacrificed the Empire to her own ends that she was introducing French armies into the heart of Germany to compass the destruction of a leading German state. Yet it was not as much as Frederick had done when he accepted French aid in 1741; and there was no small difference between Maria Theresa's action in invoking French help to enable her to recover a province wrested from her by force, and Frederick's in calling in France in support of a policy of pure aggression. Maria Theresa's action was retributive, if not indeed defensive—after her experience in 1741 no one can blame her if she felt insecure as long as Frederick was free to act as he pleased.

Simultaneously with the Franco-Austrian negotiations similar negotiations were going on between Austria and Russia. Here Esterhazy, the Austrian Ambassador, found himself opposed by the Chancellor Bestuchev who, if not fond of Prussia, was now in the pay of England;[1] while Woronzov the Vice-Chancellor inclined to favour Prussia, but was open to conviction. Olsuviev, the other influential minister, was frankly for Austria. In Russia as in France the news of the attack on Saxony aroused great indignation: it quite decided the attitude of Elizabeth, and with hers Woronzov's also. A difficulty was then caused by the question of territorial readjustment. Russia coveted Courland and Semigallia; but the traditional policy of France had been to support Poland against Russia and it might be difficult to get Louis XV to agree. A solution was found in the compensation of Poland with East Prussia; on November 13th, Maria Theresa agreed to considerable modifications in the Convention of April, and on January 11th, 1757, Russia notified her adhesion to the Defensive Treaty of Versailles. On February 2nd an Austro-Russian Convention was drawn up, and on May 19th ratifications were exchanged. But this was far from exhausting the list of Austria's allies. In January 1757 the Diet of the Empire declared its adhesion to the anti-Prussian cause, its aid being more valuable morally than materially, for it disproved Frederick's assertions that the war was a quarrel between religions, and it gave to the Coalition such constitutional sanction as the obsolescent forms could convey. Frederick, at any rate, could hardly plead that he was the champion of the Imperial constitution. Hanover had done its best to keep the Empire neutral, and it had been supported by Brunswick, by Hesse-Cassel, by Saxe-Weimar and by Baireuth; but the majority of sixty to twenty-six by which the vote was carried included many Protestant states, notably Zweibrücken, Hesse-Darmstadt, Baden-Durlach and even the Anspach

[1] Cf. *Buckinghamshire Papers* (R.H.S.), and Waddington, i. 508.

Hohenzollern themselves. Maria Theresa received a promise of assistance from Wurzburg, which offered 6000 men, while Bavaria (4000), Cologne (1800), the Palatinate (6000), and Würtemberg (6000) hired considerable forces to France.[1] Sweden, another Protestant state, in which the Senate now in power was much under French influence and bitterly opposed to Prussia, to whom the monarchical party looked for support, was induced to join the Coalition by a promise of the restoration of Pomerania to the conditions of 1679.

Frederick was thus left with only England and Hanover and a few of the North German states on his side, for Denmark and Spain were resolved to keep out of the conflict, and the fact that the Orange faction favoured Prussia made the " Burgher party " in the United Provinces prefer neutrality. England, though taken by surprise by Frederick's sudden attack on Saxony, decided to support him steadily. To aid in the defence of Hanover, the corps of Hessians and Hanoverians, which had been brought over to defend England when the fears of an invasion were at their height, were sent back to Germany (Dec. 1756) to form the nucleus of an army to be concentrated on the Lippe, and Pitt obtained a vote of £200,000 from the House of Commons for the defence of the Electorate. This army, reinforced by 10,000 Prussians and by contingents from Brunswick, Hesse-Cassel and Saxe-Weimar, was also to defend the Prussian provinces on the Rhine, and hold in check the French " army of observation " should that force exchange a passive for an active policy.

For the campaign of 1757 both sides had made great preparations. Frederick by impressing unwilling recruits in Saxony had raised his forces to nearly 200,000 of whom depôts and garrisons absorbed about a quarter. Of the field army, he had only allotted 20,000 to East Prussia and 10,000 to the Rhenish provinces, so that including Schwerin's corps (12,000 horse and 32,000 foot) in Silesia he had over 120,000 available for an attack on Bohemia. His original intention would seem to have been to remain on the defensive and await attack, as he had done at the beginning of 1745 ; but this would have played into the hands of the Austrians,

---

[1] The attempts of Prussian officers to enlist recruits in the territory of Mecklenburg-Schwerin had resulted in a violent quarrel with its Duke, Frederick (1756–1785), and ranked the former among the supporters of Austria.

whose best policy obviously was to put off a decisive engagement until the advance of their French and Russian allies on either flank could make itself felt, and at length Frederick, yielding to Winterfeldt's representations, resolved to take the offensive. Four columns were accordingly directed upon Prague, the army of Silesia by Trautenau, Gitschin and Brandeis, Augustus William of Brunswick-Bevern with 5000 horse and 18,000 foot from Zittau by Reichenberg and Münchengratz, the main body under the King moving straight up the Elbe from Dresden and Maurice of Anhalt-Dessau from Chemnitz. The latter after being checked in a move on Eger joined the main column at Linay on April 24th, bringing it up to a strength of 15,000 horse and 45,000 foot.[1] This converging movement, of course, enabled the Prussians to move with much greater celerity than if they had all been concentrated upon one line of advance; but to plan the junction of these columns under the walls of a fortified town forty leagues from their base was, as Napoleon has pointed out, an exceedingly risky movement. Luckily for Frederick the situation of the Austrians was not such as to enable them to turn this chance to good advantage. General Browne had originally intended to take the offensive; he had collected large magazines near the frontier, and his dispositions, though not ill-adapted for an advance, proved most unsatisfactory when he was superseded by Prince Charles of Lorraine and that incarnation of indecision and undue caution resolved to assume a defensive attitude.

Thus when between April 18th and 20th the Prussian columns set out for Bohemia their enemies were too near the frontier and dangerously separated. On the right was Serbelloni (27,000) at Königgratz, Königsegg with 23,000 confronted Bevern, at and around Prague stood Browne with 39,000, on the left, at Eger, d'Aremberg had about 20,000. Frederick's plan was to keep Browne occupied upon the line of the Eger while Schwerin and Bevern fell on Königsegg, crushed him, captured his magazines, and came up on the right flank of Browne by Brandeis.

This scheme proved only partially successful. Königsegg checked Bevern at Reichenberg April 21st, and when Schwerin

---

[1] Waddington's figures are rather different; he gives Schwerin as 41,000, Bevern 18,000, Frederick 39,000, and Maurice 19,000; ii. 282.

endeavoured to intercept his retreat, slipped away across that general's front to Brandeis. Schwerin and Bevern united at Münchengratz on the 26th and moved rather slowly upon Prague, being delayed at Brandeis by the fact that Königsegg's rearguard had burnt the bridge over the Elbe. Meanwhile Charles of Lorraine, who had taken over command of the Austrians at Tuchomierschitz on April 30th, had withdrawn to Prague instead of adopting Browne's advice and giving battle on the line of the Eger at Budin. His action was characteristically over-cautious. A man of any dash or any real strategic insight would have seen that, with Schwerin and Frederick divided by the Elbe and several days apart, the true policy for the Austrians was to concentrate on one bank or the other, breaking down all bridges by which the Prussians could get across, and to fall either on Frederick or his lieutenant in force. This would have been fairly easy, for d'Aremberg had joined Browne and Königsegg was much nearer his main body than was Schwerin to Frederick.

The retreat of the Austrians allowed Frederick to move up to Prague unopposed, his van arriving on the White Mountain on May 2nd. Schwerin was still some marches away,—he did not cross the Elbe at Brandeis till the evening of May 5th, —and a more energetic commander than Prince Charles might have seized the chance of hastening Königsegg's movements and forcing an action on Frederick. But Charles was contemplating a further retreat to join Serbelloni, and was only dissuaded from doing so by Browne's urgent representations that such a move would be most disastrous to the prestige of the Austrians. Had Serbelloni shown moderate energy, had he used his cavalry to delay Schwerin, or pushed forward fast enough to reach Prague before Schwerin could reinforce his master, the stand would have been wise. As things turned out, by giving battle at Prague the Austrians had to fight Frederick and Schwerin combined with the nearest of Serbelloni's 27,000 no nearer than Aruval, eight and a half miles from the nearest point of the battlefield.

It was on the morning of May 6th that Frederick, leaving Keith with 30,000 men on the White Mountain, took 38 squadrons and 20 battalions across to the right of the Moldau and joined Schwerin. He did this unmolested by the Austrians, who were drawn up in position along the hills East of Prague, facing North, their left on the steep Ziscaberg, their centre and right on the rather more accessible Schanzenberg and Taborberg. In their front the marshy valley of the Roketnitz served to strengthen the position, the village of Hloupetin on the far side, which served as bridge-head to a road up a ravine giving access to the plateau near Hortlozes, having been occupied by a detachment. Had Frederick carried out his original intention of a direct attack, the Prussians would have had an extremely difficult task; but fortunately for his army he allowed Schwerin to prevail upon him to push the Prussian left wing round to the South, so that they could attack the easier Eastern slopes of the plateau by Sterbohol. This move outflanked the Austrian right and forced that division to alter its position hastily, its right moving from near Hostawitz to Sterbohol, its left coming up to the East of Maleschitz. Thus the Austrian line presented a salient angle somewhat insufficiently protected in the direction of Hostawitz. About 10 a.m. Schwerin having reached Potschernitz deployed his men into line, the cavalry on the left, the infantry in two columns under Winterfeldt and Bevern, and began climbing the slopes. He met with a stout resistance, and the swamps at the foot of the slopes proved difficult to cross. On the left his cavalry after being twice repulsed were reinforced by Ziethen and obtained the mastery over Lucchesi, whose horsemen they routed and chased from the field, thus neglecting their duty of succouring the hard-pressed Prussian infantry. Winterfeldt's men, checked by the artillery fire, were routed by a charge of some grenadiers whom Browne brought up, and Schwerin himself perished in the attempt to rally them. The Austrians pursuing too far got somewhat out of hand, for Browne had been badly wounded, and they had to retire when Schwerin's reserve gave Winterfeldt a point on which to rally. In falling back the Austrians were taken in flank by Bevern, whose men, separated by a spur of the hill from Winterfeldt's, had not shared in their comrades' disaster. Just at this moment the Prussian right, having carried Hloupetin, began to push up the ravine towards Hortlozes. This move was due to Mannstein, and was well seconded by Ferdinand of Brunswick, who planted a large battery on the hills by Hloupetin. Simultaneously Prince Henry of Prussia's division of the centre pushed across the

Roketnitz brook from Kyge and assailed the Taborberg, thus thrusting itself into the gap at the salient angle of the Austrian position, which had been left open by the advance of the left division of the right from Maleschitz to repulse Bevern. Prince Henry's appearance near Maleschitz decided the struggle on the right; Bevern, who had been checked, was able to carry Maleschitz, and the whole right and centre of the Austrian army was now in complete disorder. Their left, hitherto hardly engaged at all, now fell back in good order to Prague, its retirement being covered by some regiments of cuirassiers, who charged home with great effect against the Prussian infantry and prevented Frederick's cavalry from molesting their retreat.

The battle thus ended about 3 p.m. with the retreat of the Austrian army within the walls of Prague. Some 15,000 men, mainly the routed cavalry of Lucchesi's division, got away to the Southward, but 33 guns were left on the field and the killed, wounded, and prisoners amounted at least to 15,000. Frederick on his side lost 5 guns, captured from Winterfeldt by Browne's grenadiers, and the official return gave his losses as nearly 13,000. The move round the right of the Austrian position was the decisive stroke, as it forced the Austrians to alter their front in a great hurry, and to give battle in a position whose defects were shown when the counter-attack of their right exposed the salient angle of their line. At the same time the sudden illness of Prince Charles, who had been seized with a fit when trying to rally Lucchesi's cavalry, and the fall of Browne had contributed not a little to give the Prussians the victory by leaving the Austrians without a commander.

But though he had within a fortnight overrun Northern Bohemia, driven his enemies in on Prague, captured the valuable magazines they had collected, beaten them in a pitched battle, and cooped up nearly 50,000 of them within the walls of the Bohemian capital, Frederick had a heavy task still before him. Prague was now strongly fortified and well garrisoned, and was not likely to prove the easy prey it had been in 1741 and 1745. Unless the garrison showed unexpected faintheartedness or the Austrian government displayed a lack of energy in collecting a relieving force, Frederick might find himself in an awkward position. Nevertheless he set himself down to the siege of the Bohemian capital, pushing out Bevern with 2000 cavalry and 5000 infantry in the direction of Kolin, whither Daun and the corps formerly under Serbelloni had withdrawn on hearing of the battle of May 6th.

Daun retired as Bevern approached, falling back towards Czaslau. He was in no hurry for a battle, as the fugitives from Prague, many of whom had joined him, were in no condition for immediate action, and considerable reinforcements were coming up from Moravia and elsewhere. Moreover, it would be to his advantage to draw Bevern away from the Prussian main body.

The Prussians conducted the attack on Prague with no little vigour, and by May 28th the batteries were ready for the bombardment. Much damage was done to the town, but the injury inflicted on its defences was but slight, and a violent storm quenched the fires caused by the Prussian shells and, causing the Moldau to rise rapidly, carried away Frederick's bridges of boats. For forty-eight hours Keith's division on the left bank was in great peril, but the Austrian commanders, though they could have thrown 40,000 men upon his 15,000, their bridge being intact, let this fine opportunity escape. Luckily for Maria Theresa the general in command of the relieving army was a man of more capacity and enterprise than Charles of Lorraine, for had the fate of Prague depended on that Prince its fall would have been only a question of time. By the first week in June, Daun had collected a force of over 50,000 men, a third being cavalry, and on June 12th he moved forward on Kuttenberg. Bevern had received various reinforcements from time to time, but he was much weaker than Daun and was driven in on Kolin (June 13th) after some sharp fighting. The danger to his lieutenant forced Frederick to come up himself and join Bevern at Kaurzim (June 13th) with fresh reinforcements, which brought the covering army up to 34,000, 16,000 being cavalry. Frederick entertained but a poor opinion of Daun and his army, which he regarded as a rabble of raw recruits, not exactly "stiffened" by the runaways of May 6th, and he expected an easy victory, which would enable him to press the siege to a successful issue. He therefore resolved to attack at once despite his inferiority in numbers and the strength of the Austrian position (June 18th).

14

Daun had posted his army along the Kamhayek hills which slope up gradually to the South of the road from Planian to Kolin. His left at Radenin and Podborz was covered by a brook which served as the connection between a chain of large pools, and this with a swamp in rear secured him against a flanking movement. His right rested on the village of Kreczor at the opposite end of the heights, a corps of cavalry under Nadasky being thrown forward on the lower ground in front of Kreczor across the road to Kolin. The first reconnaissance showed Frederick that a frontal attack on the left or left centre would be most unwise but that a better chance offered on the right. Accordingly, repeating the manœuvre which had been so successful at Prague, he moved across the Austrian front to assail their right flank. This time, however, the manœuvre did not cause the Austrians to shift their position, and in moving across the enemy's front the Prussians were galled by the Austrian guns on the heights and the Croat sharpshooters lying in the cornfields at their foot.

Ziethen and the cavalry of the Prussian vanguard began well by driving Nadasky off to the South-East while the infantry, seven battalions under Hülsen, wheeling to the right when past Kudlirz, assaulted and carried Kreczor. Here, however, they were checked by a battery of twelve guns Daun had posted on the left of the village and by Wied's infantry and some Croats in an oak-grove to the South-West of it. This last obstacle also checked Ziethen's pursuit of Nadasky, and Hülsen, though reinforced by three battalions, could get no farther. According to the original plan he should have been supported by the infantry of the left under Maurice of Dessau, who were to have followed in his tracks, but this division found itself instead committed to a frontal attack on Brzisti just West of Kreczor. Frederick, anxious to get it forward, ordered it to face to the right long before it reached the proper turning-place, and losing his temper when Maurice expostulated, gave the order "forward" without adding the words "half left," which would have sent it to Hülsen's aid. Hülsen, indeed, used the diversion to push on and carry the battery behind Kreczor, but Daun brought up two infantry divisions from the second line to hold him and Maurice in check, four battalions of grenadiers recovered the oak-grove from Hülsen and pouring a flanking

fire into Ziethen's ranks forced him to retire before the rallied
squadrons of Nadasky. Meanwhile on the Prussian centre
things had gone altogether wrong. Mannstein, whose division
was following Maurice's along the road, was so much worried
by the Croat skirmishers that he wheeled a battalion to the
right to disperse them. The Croats stood their ground and
were reinforced, Mannstein also reinforced his men, and before
long his whole division was committed to a frontal attack on
Chotzemitz which made little progress. The arrival of the
reinforcement from the second line quickly restored the balance
on the Austrian right. Pennavaire's cavalry division attempting to assist Hülsen was foiled by a fine charge by two Saxon
cavalry regiments, more Austrian cavalry were thrown into the
fight, and at last the divisions of Hülsen and Maurice gave back
in disorder, their example being followed by Mannstein, whose
men lost heavily under artillery fire. On the Austrian left
Puebla's infantry came down from the heights above Breczsan
and, vigorously supported by Stampa's cavalry, assailed the
eight battalions under Bevern which formed the one intact
division of the Prussian army. Luckily for Frederick these
battalions made a gallant resistance, and at the cost of nearly
3000 men kept the road towards Planian clear for the fugitives
of the left and centre to stream past behind them.

Daun had won a great victory to which he had contributed largely himself. His excellent choice of the position,
his judicious handling of his well-served artillery, and his
promptitude and decision in reinforcing the threatened points,
had as much to do with the victory as the error in the
directions given to Maurice, or the blunder of marching the
Prussian army across the Austrian front within range of
their guns, which had led to Mannstein's becoming prematurely
engaged. Ziethen also must be held partly responsible, since
he failed to support Hülsen properly; but when all is said
and done the chief cause of the defeat was that Frederick
did not, after the victory outside Prague, at once push out
against Daun and destroy his detachment. On the morrow
of May 6th he would have had little to fear from the
demoralised army of Charles of Lorraine: 25,000 men
could have held them in check with ease. But Frederick,
underestimating Daun and the defensive capacities of Prague,
had tried to reduce in six weeks a fortress capable of holding

out much longer, and the defeat of Kolin was the result of his error of judgment.

Leaving Bevern and Maurice to withdraw the relics of the covering army over the Elbe at Nimburg, Frederick hastened back to Prague [1] to raise the siege. On the 20th of June the retreat began, the Austrians sallying out in time to fall on Keith, who was covering the movement, and inflict on him severe losses, including five guns and most of his baggage. More might perhaps have been done, but Charles of Lorraine was not the man to make the most of his chances. It was a great misfortune for Austria that Charles should have so far recovered his health as to be able to take command of the united armies which joined forces at Podschernitz on June 26th. A really vigorous pursuit ought to have clinched the success of Kolin by cutting off one of the two retreating columns, either the besiegers who moved by Budin to Leitmeritz, or the Kolin force, now under Prince Augustus William of Prussia, which had reached Bohm Leipa on July 7th. It was against this force that Daun and Lorraine turned, crossing the Elbe at Brandeis (July 1st) and moving by Münchengratz (July 7th) and Liebenau to threaten Augustus William's communications with Zittau and Gabel. On July 15th they took Gabel, which forced Augustus to retire to Zittau by the roundabout route through Raumburg. The Austrians had only twenty-five miles to cover against forty, and might have anticipated the Prussians at Zittau and cut them off completely. However, their ineradicable slowness once again let the Prussians be first at the critical spot, and Augustus William, whose men had suffered great privations and had deserted freely, finally reached a haven of refuge at Bautzen on July 27th. His failure to maintain his position had involved the retreat of Keith's corps from Leitmeritz to Bohemia, after which Frederick, leaving Maurice of Dessau on the Elbe, brought all available troops across to Bautzen to join the Kolin army and try to retrieve all by forcing a battle on Lorraine. But Lorraine stood firm in a strong position near Zittau, and Frederick had to retire in disappointment to Ostritz (Aug. 19th). Thus the invasion

[1] The Prussian loss was about 13,500, of which 12,000 were among the infantry, who were thus reduced to a third of their original strength; they left 45 guns and 5000 prisoners in Daun's hands. The Austrian losses slightly exceeded 8000.

of Bohemia, from which so much had been hoped and which had begun so well, ended in failure, and Frederick found himself at the end of August in the same position as he had occupied in April, only with his most trusted lieutenant dead and his army nearly ruined.

Nor was it very cheerful intelligence which reached him from the forces covering his flanks against the allies of Maria Theresa. Had not the Russian commanders, Apraxin and Fermor, been deterred by political considerations in addition to natural slowness and incapacity they could have done far more against the weak force opposed to them. As it was, their headquarters did not reach Kovno till June, and not till July 5th did the fall of Memel allow Fermor to rejoin the covering force under Apraxin. Even after this their movements were so slow and apparently meaningless that despite the great disparity of numbers the Prussian commander Lehwaldt ventured to attack them at Gross Jaegerndorf (Aug. 30th). A sharp fight resulted in a victory for the big battalions, Lehwaldt losing 4500 men and 28 guns; but if tactically a defeat, strategically it was a Prussian victory, for Apraxin made no effort to follow it up, but fell back to Tilsit and from there to Memel, pleading that he was too short of supplies to do anything further (Sept.). His retreat allowed Lehwaldt to move across into Pomerania, which the Swedes were overrunning, to drive them out of it, take Anclam and Demmin, and coop them up in Stralsund and Rügen. The true causes for Apraxin's strange conduct were not military but political: the Czarina was supposed to be at the point of death, and the admiration of the heir, Grand Duke Peter, for the Prussian King was notorious. Apraxin had no wish to make himself impossible by overthrowing his future master's hero.

Very different was the course of events in Western Germany. The Prussian corps on the Rhine had found it hopeless to attempt to hold Cleves and Mark against the vast army gathering to attack them. The French mustered 127 squadrons (at 160) and 107 battalions (at 720), a force imposing on paper, but overburdened with a vast staff of general officers, far larger than could be of any use, and accompanied by an enormous baggage-train. The troops were not in the best condition, the discipline and tone of the French army was bad, the administration defective and corruption rampant in the supply service. On April 8th d'Estrées occupied Wesel, but not till May 21st were the contractors, of whom Paris-Duverney was the chief, able to provide enough transport and supplies to permit a further advance. Against so large a force Cumberland, who at Frederick's request had taken command of the army which George II had collected for the defence of Hanover,[1] could do nothing but retire. He concentrated at Bielefeldt by June 12th and retired behind the Weser, the French moving slowly forward by Münster (June 1st) and Rheda (June 14th) to Bielefeldt (June 18th). Here they halted till July 8th, after which Contades with 20,000 men was detached against Cassel, which was duly occupied, the main body preparing to cross the Weser at Hoxter. This move at once threatened Cumberland's left, and covered the operations of a new corps it was proposed to put into the field between the Lahn and Main. The stroke roused Cumberland. To protect Hanover he broke up from Afferda and moved upstream to Hastenbeck, coming into contact with the French on July 24th. It was on July 26th that the French moved forward against Cumberland's position at Hastenbeck. It was fairly strong, a hill on the right, the Sintelberg, gave a good post for the 29 battalions and 30 squadrons of that wing. The centre, 22 battalions, was in rear of Hastenbeck, forming a connecting link with the 8 battalions of the left on the Scheckenberg. The only weak spot seemed to be a ravine in the left centre between Hastenbeck and the mountain, but this had been secured by the erection of three large batteries. However, it was against the left that d'Estrées directed his main attack, delivered by the gallant Chevert and 12 battalions. Despite a fog and the difficulties of the ground, Chevert accomplished his task, while d'Armentières in the right centre carried one of the three batteries but failed to keep Chevert and the centre in touch, so that Anlazy's division[2] had to be put in before another battery could be won or Hastenbeck carried by Contades. About 11.30 both these tasks had been accomplished. Cumberland's centre was pierced, his left seemed going to be cut off by

---

[1] Waddington, ii. 195.
[2] Partly composed of Austrians from the Netherlands.

Chevert, who was advancing to roll up the Hanoverian line, when the troops to his left were suddenly attacked and disordered by Breitenbach and the Hanoverian Guards. Two regiments under de Lorges gave way completely and the disorder spread to Anlazy's Austrians and Swiss. But the effort was too late; Cumberland had already given orders to retire, and Breitenbach's bold stroke only served to secure an unmolested retreat. Out of a force of 40,000, Cumberland had lost about 1500 of all ranks with 12 guns; but he had the satisfaction of inflicting on the enemy, who were superior by half his force, a loss of 1000 killed and 1300 wounded. He was a little precipitate in ordering the retreat, but Chevert's success had completely compromised his position. He made no attempt to stand before reaching Nienbourg on the Weser, where he rallied his men, moving thence to Verden (Aug. 8th), which he evacuated on August 23rd for Stade.

Meanwhile d'Estrées had been superseded by the Duc de Richelieu on August 3rd. This was the outcome of intrigues at Paris and had the effect of temporarily paralysing the activity of the French. However, the effects of the victory were considerable enough as it was. Hanover, Minden and Hameln capitulated without delay, the Duke of Brunswick came to terms with the victors and placed his duchy at their disposal (Aug. 10th). On August 20th, Richelieu, whose force had been considerably reinforced and included 4 Austrian battalions and 10 from the Palatinate, resumed his advance from Nienbourg on Stade. On August 21st he received from Cumberland a proposal for a suspension of hostilities, on the ground that there was no war between Hanover and France; but this he declined, although it seems to have suggested to him the notion of utilising the intervention of Denmark to make some arrangement of the sort. Before his appointment in place of d'Estrées it had been proposed to give him command of a new corps to operate between the Lahn and Main, and he was very anxious to be able to devote himself to his proper objective, Magdeburg. The retreat of Cumberland had drawn the French away from that point, and Richelieu found the prospect of sitting down before Stade most distasteful. The siege was likely to be difficult and unhealthy, the country was poor and ill-provided with roads, and if the defence was stubborn an English force which was believed to be at sea might arrive and raise the siege. Accordingly Richelieu availed himself of Danish mediation to conclude the famous Convention of Kloster Zeven (Sept. 8th). By this Cumberland agreed to send his auxiliaries to their homes, to canton the Hanoverians, who were not to be regarded as prisoners of war, on the farther bank of the Elbe, except for 4000 men who were to hold Stade under a Danish guarantee of its neutrality; while the French were to occupy Bremen and Verden. The motives which led the Duke of Cumberland to conclude this unfortunate arrangement and the tale of its reception by King George II belong properly to the biography of the ill-fated commander. If his tactics at Hastenbeck had not been of the most skilful, he cannot be held solely responsible for the Convention: it is quite clear that in concluding a convention of neutrality he was not exceeding his powers. He had orders to save the army at any price: on August 11th full powers to conclude a peace for Hanover had been sent to him, and it was not till September 16th, a week after the Convention had been signed, that new orders were sent, directing him to retire on Magdeburg.[1] This alteration was caused by George II discovering that his scheme for a separate peace for Hanover would not be acceptable at Vienna. The episode is really the last phase of that conflict between British and Hanoverian interests in which the Electorate was at last sacrificed to its partner.

As things turned out it was not only George II who was annoyed with the Convention. In France it was thought by no means satisfactory, as it did not secure the disbandment or disarmament of the Hanoverians; but the French were prepared to accept it. George II was unreasonably furious with Cumberland, and only refrained from denouncing the Convention because he assumed that the troops had been dispersed according to its terms and would be at the mercy of the French. On learning, therefore, that this had not been the case, and that a hitch over the details connected with the Hessians had caused delay in its execution, he decided to refuse to ratify it (Oct. 5th). The British

[1] Cf. Waddington, ii. ch. ix.

ministry had all along refused to be bound by it, and had declared that they would continue to support Frederick: they now (Oct. 7th) decided to take the Hanoverian army also into British pay.

George was able to tear up the Convention in this way because, directly it had been concluded, Richelieu had moved off from the mouth of the Elbe to Brunswick (Sept. 20th), and thence to Halberstadt (29th), Ferdinand of Brunswick's Prussian division retiring before him. Beyond Halberstadt, on which he had fixed as his winter-quarters, he refused to go, declaring, not without truth, that it would ruin the army, which, indeed, was in a bad condition, for Richelieu had been scandalously lax as to discipline. Austria urged that he should make one more effort, that something should be done in co-operation with Soubise and the Imperial army which had come up to the Saale. Had Richelieu been enough of an officer ·to keep his men in hand, and enough of a strategist to grasp the supreme importance of maintaining the advantage Soubise's advance had won, he would not have contented himself with the despatch of de Broglie with 17 squadrons and 20 battalions to reinforce Soubise but would have brought up every available man. Richelieu's inactivity at Halberstadt was largely responsible for the disastrous end of the campaign on the Saale.

The Franco-Imperial force on that river represented the junction of the original " auxiliary corps," [1] with the motley and half-organised army of the Empire which had been collected at Nüremberg by the Prince of Saxe-Hildburg-hausen. This force, a strange mosaic of detachments of half-trained and undisciplined militiamen, drawn from all the petty states of South-Western Germany, was without proper transport, commissariat and other administrative services. To take such a rabble into the field would be to court disaster, and it is not surprising if Soubise displayed considerable anxiety to avoid that contact with the Prussians for which Saxe-Hildburghausen was so zealous. His own corps should have included the 10,000 Bavarians and Würtembergers in French pay, but they had already been pushed forward to join the main Austrian army, and had been replaced by 8000 men drawn from Richelieu's army. With some 22,000 men (32

[1] Cf. p. 200.

squadrons and 31 battalions) Soubise set out from Strassburg at the beginning of August, and on the 25th joined at Erfurt the army of the Empire, which had left Nüremberg a fortnight earlier.

To settle the direction of their next move Soubise and his colleague found difficult, but the question was settled for them by Frederick, who, though everybody was expecting him to keep his force concentrated, suddenly broke up (Aug. 25th) from his position in Lusatia. Taking 12,000 men with him, and picking up Maurice of Dessau at Dresden on the way, he pushed across Saxony to Erfurt, which he reached on September 13th after a march of 170 miles. Before his approach Soubise recoiled into the hilly country round Eisenach, where he halted (Sept. 15th). Frederick made no attempt to force him to fight, but remained inactive at Erfurt until October 11th. This inactivity might have cost him dear against somewhat more enterprising opponents, but he was probably right not to push on against Soubise, who might have drawn him farther away from his other divisions by a continued retreat.

Frederick's move to the Saale had decided the problem of their next step, which had been troubling the Austrian generals. Not unnaturally, Maria Theresa was dissatisfied with the inaction into which the main army had relapsed after its success in Bohemia, and it had been decided to send a corps into Silesia to attempt the recovery of that province; but nothing had been settled as to its strength or objective, as no one could tell what Frederick would be likely to do. His move gave them two alternatives, either to follow him and try to catch him between themselves and the Franco-Imperial army, a policy which would in many ways have been the wisest, or to fall on Bevern and the corps left opposite them in Lusatia. It was on this second course that they decided, and accordingly Daun and Lorraine moved down the Neisse, but found Bevern in so strong a position at Ostritz that they hesitated to attack. One Prussian corps, however, offered more favourable chances to an assailant. This was Winterfeldt's division of 10,000 men, which stood at Moys on the right bank of the Lusatian Neisse, covering Bevern's left and protecting his communications with Silesia. Against this corps Lorraine detached Nadasky and d'Aremberg, and they falling upon Winterfeldt defeated him completely. He himself was killed, and his corps had 2000 casualties and lost

5 guns (Sept. 7th).   This reverse dislodged Bevern from
Ostritz (Sept. 9th).   He retired North-East to Bunzlau (Sept.
15th), and thence to Liegnitz (18th), covering Silesia, but
sacrificing his communications with Frederick.   He might
easily have been cut off from Silesia had Lorraine handled
his cavalry with any skill, or even succeeded in triumphing
over the difficulties of road and rain to the same extent as
Bevern did ; but it is hardly necessary to state that the cautious
and unenterprising Lorraine failed completely to anticipate
Bevern, and when a bombardment forced the Prussians from
their position at Liegnitz they were allowed to get away to
Breslau in comparative safety by a fine forced march, despite
the great numerical superiority of the Austrian cavalry.
Bevern was actually able to cross to the right of the Oder,
and gain Breslau along that bank (Oct. 1st) quite unmolested.

    Slowly the Austrians followed to Breslau, where they
found Bevern, with the Lohe Brook and several fortified
villages in his front, sheltering almost under the guns of the
fortress.   An attack was proposed ; but Daun objected that,
even if successful, it would merely drive the Prussians back
into Breslau, which could not be taken without long-range siege
guns.   It was therefore decided that the main body should
take post near Breslau to cover the siege of Schweidnitz by
Nadasky and 20,000 men from any possible interruption by
Bevern.   It was a weak policy, for it kept the main Austrian
army uselessly inactive until the fall of Schweidnitz (Nov.
12th) set Nadasky free for further operations ; but it was not
so serious an error as the failure to intercept and defeat Bevern.
On November 19th Nadasky rejoined Lorraine, upon which it
was decided to try the attack on Bevern which had till then
been deemed inadvisable.   If they delayed much longer,
Frederick, who had won a great victory at Rossbach a fortnight before, would be back to help Bevern.   This was indeed
what he was attempting, hoping to be in time to save
Schweidnitz, and to catch the Austrians in flank and rear if
they fulfilled his expectations and retired on Bohemia before
Bevern's advance.

    Bevern's position was one of considerable strength.   The
Oder and some marshy ground where the Lohe flowed into it
covered his right, and a row of fortified villages, Pilsnitz on
the right, Klein Mochber and Schmiedefeld in the centre,

Grabischen and Kleinburg on the left, with the Lohe as wet ditch in their front, made his line strong. It had, however, the defect of being over long for his numbers.[1] Under cover of a heavy cannonade the Austrians threw bridges across the Lohe and advanced to the attack (Nov. 22nd). Nadasky at first carried Kleinburg, but was driven out of it again and brought to a standstill. At the other end of the line there was a desperate and equal struggle for the village of Pilsnitz. In the centre, however, the battle was decided. A division under General Sprechor stormed the Prussian battery at Klein Mochber, pushed on to Grabischen and threatened the rear of the villages of Schmiedefeld and Hoefichen against the front of which d'Arberg was advancing. The combined attack rolled the Prussian centre back in disorder on Klein Gandau and this success forced Bevern's right to fall back to avoid being cut off, indeed the Austrian cavalry did catch and ride down several of the retiring battalions. Had Nadasky's attack proved as successful as that of the centre, the Prussians must have been cut off from Breslau, to which they now fell back, leaving 6000 killed and wounded, 3000 prisoners and 42 guns on the field. Next day the relics of the army crossed hastily to the Northern bank of the Oder and began retiring on Glogau. Bevern himself, reconnoitring the Austrian position, fell into the hands of the enemy and was taken (Nov. 21st). A garrison of 5000 men had been left in Breslau, but it was mainly composed of impressed Saxons and Silesians who had no inclination to fight for Prussia, and General Lestewitz had to surrender two days after the battle. His men almost without exception took service with the Austrians gladly; and if the Silesian population had shown indifference to the Austrian cause in 1741, there could be no doubt about their feelings now. Fifteen years of Prussian rule had been quite enough, and the re-establishment of the Austrian government was decidedly popular.

But if the victory of November 22nd had given the Austrians possession of most of Silesia their hold was not to pass unchallenged long. Frederick had secured himself against any further danger from Western Germany, and leaving Leipzig on November 13th, had reached Bautzen on the 21st. Three days later, at Naumburg on the Queiss, he

[1] 100 squadrons and 40 battalions, 35,000 men, as against nearly 80,000 Austrians.

heard of Bevern's defeat.   On the 28th he halted at Parchwitz, having covered 180 miles in fifteen days, a very fine march indeed in November.   The Austrians decided not to await Frederick's coming at Breslau but to move out against him, and accordingly they took post across the great road from Liegnitz to Breslau, their right at Nypern, their centre at Leuthen, their left resting on the Schweidnitzwasser, though the cautious Daun strongly urged that the right bank of this stream would prove a much better and stronger position.

The action on the Saale which had enabled Frederick to turn back to the help of Bevern had come about through a raid against Berlin by Hadik and 3000 men from the Austrian division in Lusatia.   The news of this raid, which resulted in the Austrians levying a contribution of 225,000 thalers on Frederick's capital and then retiring safely with their booty, brought Frederick back from Erfurt to Torgau (Oct. 14th to 19th).   With the enemy removed from their front, Saxe-Hildburghausen and Soubise were at liberty for an offensive movement, for which the Imperial commander was anxious, but the Frenchman, who had little confidence in the military qualities of his allies, disinclined.   Saxe - Hildburghausen, however, prevailed on Soubise to advance against the some-what exposed Prussian corps left to face them under Keith. Before their advance it fell back on Leipzig (Oct. 23rd); but Frederick at once turned back to its aid, calling up Ferdinand of Brunswick from Halle and recalling the divisions sent back to Berlin.   On October 28th, having concentrated some 45 squadrons and 27 battalions, between 20,000 and 25,000 men, at Leipzig, he moved out against the French and Imperialists, who had recoiled behind the Saale and picked up de Broglie and the reinforcements from Richelieu's army at Merseburg.

On October 31st the Prussian divisions reached the Saale to find the passages at Weissenfels, Halle and Merseburg held against them.   Had the Franco-Imperialists stood their ground, Frederick's task would have been difficult in the extreme, but they fell back in some haste to Mücheln and took post at the mouth of the defile through the hills by Merseburg (Nov. 2nd).   The Prussians, thus given an unopposed passage, reconnoitred the position on the 4th, but finding it too strong to make a direct attack advisable, remained halted opposite it, their right at Bedra, their left at Rossbach. Their inactivity encouraged Saxe-Hildburghausen to plan a bold move to the South-East, his idea being to circle round their left so as to get in their rear, cut their communications and drive them into the river.

A division under St. Germain was left at Mücheln to make a show and keep Frederick occupied while the turning movement was in progress. This started about 11 a.m., but the careful arrangements and rapid movement which might have earned success were conspicuous by their absence. Believing the Prussians to be retreating, they pushed on without sending out scouts, without adopting anything like a battle formation, without even leaving haversacks and kettles behind. Two regiments of Austrian cavalry and the cavalry of the Circles led, the infantry followed in three columns, supported by 10 French squadrons and covered on the left by 12 more.[1] Expecting nothing less than an attack, they were pushing on steadily Eastward when, about 3.30, the Prussians suddenly appeared on their flank. A low ridge which runs East and West from Leiha and culminates in the Janus Hill, the point for which the Allies were making, had completely concealed Frederick's movements and enabled him to surprise the over-confident Allies. The Prussian attack was led by Seydlitz, who, wheeling to the right on reaching the Polzen Hill and circling round, came sweeping down on the vanguard of cavalry. The cavalry of the Circles gave way at once, but the Austrian cuirassiers offered a gallant resistance which temporarily checked Seydlitz's charge and gave time for the five regiments of French cavalry which were in support to come up on the right near Reichartswerben. However, Seydlitz hurled his left against them, while his right engaged the Austrian cavalry, and his vigorous onslaught made them all give way : they rallied on four more regiments of French which Soubise brought up from the left, and even checked the Prussian front line, but a charge of Seydlitz's reserve sent them all to the right-about. Meanwhile a Prussian battery of 18 field and 4 heavy guns on the Janus Berg was pouring a heavy fire into the surprised columns, and Frederick's left wing of infantry, 12 battalions under his brother Henry, was coming on over the slopes to the right of the battery. Hastily the Allied infantry

---

[1] The total Franco-Imperialist force was 51 squadrons and 65 battalions, of which 16 and 10 formed St. Germain's division.

endeavoured to deploy and to advance against the Prussian positions, but the disorder in which they had marched produced hopeless confusion. The regiments of Piedmont and Mailly, the leaders of the two columns which now formed the right of the deployed lines, and those of Poitou and Rohan of the reserve, which had marched so fast as to get in between the two columns and so practically form a third line, behaved well and advanced steadily. However, they were met by a tremendous fire from infantry and artillery, and as they wavered Seydlitz's squadrons, which after putting the hostile cavalry to the rout had re-formed in a hollow near Tagewerben, came charging in on their right flank and rear. The second (actually the third) line gave way at once, and in a moment all was hopeless disorder. The troops of the Circles made no attempt to resist, and though one or two isolated French regiments stood their ground well, they were ridden down. By 4.30 all was over. Some cavalry from the French left intervened and their charge gave the fugitives some respite, but in the end St. Germain's division was the only body to leave the field in orderly formation: it acted as rearguard, and covered the retreat by Langensalza (Nov. 7th) to Hanau. Frederick made no attempt to pursue; he was well content with the advantage he had gained, and with good reason. With only 22,000 men against 36,000 French and 10 to 12,000 Imperialists, he had inflicted on his enemies a loss of about 3000 killed and wounded, 5000 prisoners and 67 guns. But the moral effects of the victory were even greater. It is difficult to say whether the blunders of the Allied commanders or the misbehaviour of the troops was the more discreditable. That of the Army of the Circles might have been anticipated by any one acquainted with its organisation and utter want of training and discipline. It is not necessary to attribute it to disaffection, or to pretend that the Darmstadters and Wurz-burgers found it impossible to fight against the " champion of German nationality." The Imperial army behaved as raw troops of indifferent quality are likely to do when taken by surprise. But that the bulk of the French should have behaved so ill is indeed remarkable, and speaks volumes for the demoralisation of their army. Maurice de Saxe's victories had temporarily restored its tone, but its state in 1757 was worse than it had ever been before. On the Prussian side

Frederick showed great coolness in letting the enemy commit themselves thoroughly to their turning movement before he launched his men at them ; but the good discipline and efficiency of the Prussian army, as shown in the rapidity with which they broke up their camp and were ready for action almost directly they got their orders, the excellent fire-discipline of the infantry, the good work done by the Prussian artillery in combination with the other arms, and above all the splendid way in which Seydlitz handled his horsemen and utilised to the full the chances afforded by what was an ideal piece of ground for cavalry manœuvres, had even more to do with the result.

Thus freed from anxiety as to his right flank, Frederick could and did retrace his steps to Silesia. Too late to save Breslau, he halted at Parchwitz and there picked up the battered remnant of Bevern's corps, which the slackness of Charles of Lorraine had allowed to get away unmolested. Vigorous and stringent measures did something to restore the tone of the beaten army. Exhortations to do their duty, the example of the King's high spirit and determined courage, appeals to their *esprit de corps* and lost prestige raised in them the desire to do some deed to be named with Rossbach, and the army followed Frederick cheerfully when on December 4th he moved to Neumarkt and thence next morning against the Austrian position across the road to Breslau.

In thus bringing on a battle, Frederick was running great risks, for the Austrian position was fairly strong, and their force probably half as large again as his.[1] On the right, Lucchesi's corps stretched from Nypern to Leuthen, with an outpost at Börne in its front and its flank covered by peat-bogs and a wood. In the centre was the reserve under d'Aremberg, on the left Nadasky's corps, part of which from Sagschütz to the Schweidnitzwasser was drawn up *en potence*.[2] In front, South-West of Sagschütz, was the Kiefer Berg, a hill on which a large battery was posted under the protection of three Würtemberg battalions which were not altogether trustworthy.

Leaving Neumarkt about 5 a.m. Frederick fell on

---

[1] The Prussians had 128 squadrons, about 13,000 men, and 48 battalions, 24,000 bayonets, on the field. Lorraine's army mustered 144 squadrons and 84 battalions, and its units were rather stronger than Frederick's ; but something must be deducted for the garrisons of Breslau and Liegnitz.

[2] *i.e.* wheeled back at an oblique angle to the main line so as to cover it.

Lucchesi's outpost at Börne just about daybreak and drove it out. This made Lorraine imagine that the Prussians intended to attack his right, which he too promptly reinforced from his reserves. The morning mists were still heavy, and the rolling ground in front also helped to conceal the movements of the Prussians, who, leaving a small force to feint against Nypern and so attract Lorraine's attention thither, were moving to their right in the famous "oblique order" which was Frederick's great contribution to the drill-book. They had been marching in four columns, the two outer ones composed of cavalry, the inner of infantry. The infantry now formed two lines, commanded by Maurice of Dessau and General Retzow, while Ziethen's horse (43 squadrons) took post on the right, Driesen's (40 squadrons) on the left, each having 10 squadrons of hussars in support, the rest of the cavalry forming a general reserve under Eugēne of Würtemberg. A detachment of 6 battalions of infantry was in close support of Ziethen. The infantry of the first line after deploying formed half-right and advanced in that direction, the movement taking them obliquely across the front of the Austrian position so as to bring them into action against Nadasky's corps. When opposite Sagschütz (about 1 p.m.), Ziethen wheeled to the left and advanced against the refused part of Nadasky's line, but the Austrian commander was ready and hurled his cavalry upon Ziethen with success, the Prussian was driven back in disorder and only saved by his infantry supports, who checked Nadasky's charge. Meanwhile Wedel with the leading battalions of the Prussian main body had attacked the Würtembergers at the angle of the Austrian line. The mistake of confiding this important post to untrustworthy troops was now apparent. As Wedel came on, covered by a heavy cannonade, for the Prussians of Bevern's corps having lost their field-guns at Breslau had been furnished with heavy guns from the fortifications of Glogau,[1] the Würtembergers broke and fled, and Wedel pushing on stormed the 14-gun battery on the Kiefer Berg. Maurice of Dessau seconded Wedel's efforts, and as Nadasky's horse had fallen back on Gohlau when checked by the infantry, the whole Austrian left rolled back Northward. Lorraine now exerted himself to rally them, and the gallant resistance of the battalions in

---

[1] These were 12-pounders, the usual field-guns of the day being 6-pounders, or more often 3-pounders.

15

Leuthen village checked the Prussian advance long enough[1] for a new line to be formed behind the village, running from North of West to South of East at an angle of $75°$ to the old position. This charge was covered by the fire of a battery on some hillocks to the North of Leuthen which threw the left of the Prussian infantry (Retzow's division) into disorder, while Maurice of Dessau in the centre and Wedel, who with the six battalions attached to Ziethen now formed the right of the line, were held up by the Austrians in Leuthen, now reinforced from their original right. Lucchesi's cavalry also came up from the same quarter and were just charging in on the exposed flank of Retzow's infantry when Frederick delivered the decisive stroke by hurling Driesen's horse of the left wing from Radaxdorf on the flank and rear of Lucchesi. The Austrian cavalry were routed, and their flight exposed the flank of the new line, which Driesen promptly attacked. The whole Austrian army gave way in disorder, the defenders of Leuthen being cut off and taken, though their resistance checked the pursuit and gave time for the fugitives of the right and centre to get away. Similarly Nadasky's rallied cavalry covered to some extent the rout of the left, but the defeat was complete, and the Austrians had to thank the darkness that they were able to get away and rally next day behind the Lohe. They had lost too heavily to think of facing another battle, even if they had stood in Bevern's old position at Breslau where they could have utilised the heavy guns, which to their cost they had not taken to Leuthen. But one Leuthen had been enough; they had lost 27,000 in killed, wounded and prisoners; they had left 116 guns behind, and their fighting capacities were for the time annihilated. An additional 10,000 men were left to hold Breslau, in other words, to swell the numbers of the prisoners, for the garrison, quite demoralised, surrendered on the 21st after a very poor resistance, and Lorraine withdrew with the rest of his shaken army to Königgratz, which they reached after a terrible and exhausting march. Liegnitz copied Breslau's example at the interval of a week, and with its fall Schweidnitz became the only Silesian fortress still in Austrian hands.

Frederick, in whose military career Leuthen may fairly be regarded as the masterpiece, had lost some 6000 men, but

[1] 2.30 to 3.30 p.m.

Silesia was his.   His daring in attacking such superior numbers had been amply justified by success.   The feint against Nypern to divert attention from the true attack, the refusing of Driesen's horse till the moment when they could be used with telling effect, the skill with which the ground and the mists were used to conceal the risky move to the right, the able way in which the Prussian artillery was handled in support of the infantry attack are much to his credit, even if it be remembered that it was only with the most highly trained and drilled troops that manœuvres demanding such exactitude in execution could be successfully practised.   And once again it may be remarked that the Austrian love for the defensive and the want of enterprise betrayed by their commanders had contributed to the Prussian success.   As Moltke has pointed out,[1] they chose a position with a river behind them, extended their lines unduly, were taken in by the feint on their right, and let themselves be beaten in detail.   Proper scouting should have warned them of the direction in which the Prussians were moving, and the ineptitude which allowed Frederick to move across their front without a counter-attack being made is only paralleled by the unwisdom of their move out to Leuthen, which forced them to leave behind a third of their guns, including the heavier pieces of which such good use had been made at Breslau.

But though this brilliant victory allowed Frederick to end the campaign of 1757 in possession of practically as much territory as he had held at the beginning of the year,[2] it must be confessed that the outlook was not promising.   If his tremendous exertions, his three victories, his heavy losses in officers and men—that of Schwerin and Winterfeldt alone meant much to him—had only sufficed to ward off dangers and leave him where he had begun, what would happen in the next year if Austria were to discover a general capable of doing more than merely defend, if Russia were to take a serious part in the campaign, if the French intervention were to be directed with some approach to capacity?   Neither in men nor in money were Prussia's resources very great; and even with Saxony to draw upon another such year might find Frederick near the limits of his endurance.

[1] Cf. Waddington, ii. 718.
[2] The Westphalian provinces were the only losses.

CHAPTER XII

THE SEVEN YEARS' WAR—*continued*

THE CAMPAIGNS OF 1758 AND 1759

DISMAYED only for a moment by the disaster of Leuthen,[1] Maria Theresa was soon busy with schemes for retrieving the failure of 1757. Vigorous measures were taken to increase and equip the broken army now rallying in Bohemia and to make it fit for service again, and the Empress proceeded to discuss with her allies a concerted plan of operations by which the isolated and disjointed efforts of the previous year might be combined with happier result.

In Russia there was greater keenness on the prosecution of the war than in the previous year. Elizabeth had been ill but had recovered, Duke Peter had been somewhat reconciled to Austria by the fact that Bestuchev, who had been intriguing against his succession, had been dismissed and replaced by Woronzov; and Apraxin's misconduct of the campaign had brought him before a well-deserved court-martial. After much correspondence it was agreed that the Russian main army should advance upon Posen, in which district it would threaten both Brandenburg and Silesia, and would cover the operations of a detached corps in Pomerania.

France was more inclined to repent of the war, and there seemed some chance that she might withdraw from it. Bernis was talking of peace; irresolution personified, he was quite overcome by the duties of a post altogether beyond his limited capacities. But Louis XV and Madame de Pompadour were set on a vigorous prosecution of the war in which the King felt his prestige to be involved. He might have been better advised to content himself with the mere furnishing of the auxiliary corps to Maria Theresa, but to tamely accept Rossbach and retire from the war would be too humiliating

[1] Cf. Waddington, ii. 734.

228

PRAGUE May 6th 1757.

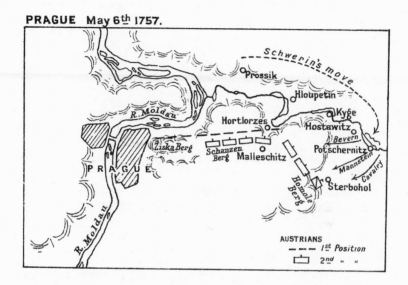

Schwerin's move

Prossik

Hloupetin

Kyğe

Hostawitz

Hortlorzes

Bevern

R.Moldau

Ziska Berg

Schanzen Berg

Malleschitz

Potschernitz

Mannstein

Cavalry

P R A G U E

Homole Berg

Sterbohol

R.Moldau

AUSTRIANS
- - - 1st Position
☐ 2nd " "

KOLIN June 18th 1757.

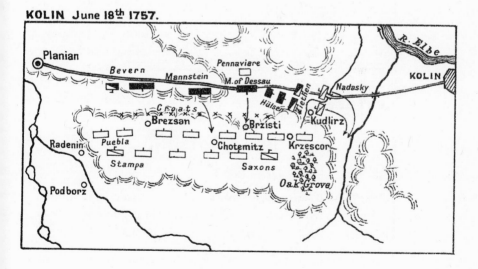

R.Elbe

Planian

Bevern

Pennaviare

Mannstein

M.of Dessau

Nadasky

KOLIN

Hülsen

Ziethen

Croats

Brezsan

Brzisti

Kudlirz

Radenin

Puebla

Chotemitz

Krzescor

Stampa

Saxons

Podborz

Oak Grove

ROSSBACH Nov. 5th 1757.

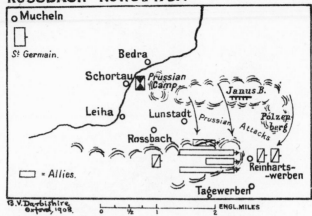

Mucheln

St Germain.

Bedra

Schortau · Prussian Camp

Leiha

Lunstadt · Prussian

Rossbach

Janus B.

Polzen-berg

Prussian Attacks

Reinharts--werben

☐ = Allies.

Tagewerben

B.V.Darbishire
Oxford, 1908.

0   ½   1   2   ENGL.MILES

BRESLAU Nov. 22nd 1757.

R. Oder

BRESLAU

Pilsnitz

Klein Gandau

Klein Mochber

Kleinburg

Schmiede--feld

Hoefichen

Grabischen

d'Arberg

R. Lohe

Sprechor

Wadasky's attack

LEUTHEN Dec. 5th 1757.

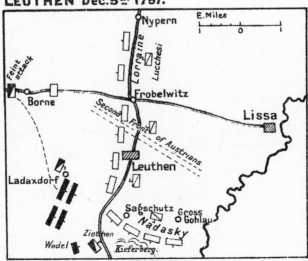

Nypern

E.Miles

Lorraine
Lucchesi

Feint attack

Borne

Frobelwitz

Lissa

Second Front of Austrians

Ladaxdorf

Leuthen

Saßschutz
Gross Gohlau

Nadasky

Ziethen

Wedel

Kieferberg

and Louis was resolved to go on. To decide on a plan of operations was more difficult, though both French and Austrians looked upon the destruction of the Hanoverian army as a necessary prelude to any attempt by the French and Imperial armies to move to the assistance of the Austrians either in Saxony or in Silesia. The idea of detaching Hanover from Frederick by a separate treaty had been put forward again by Kaunitz, but had met with a very decided rebuff from George II, who was now (Feb. 1758) growing extremely bellicose, and had quite abandoned the idea of following separate lines in his dual capacities as Elector and King. George's rejection of the suggested mediation of Denmark[1] went far to restore Frederick's confidence in his ally, a confidence which had been somewhat shaken by the refusal of the English ministry to employ their own troops in the continental war, or to send a squadron into the Baltic.[2] Suspicion of England's motives, a fear that this refusal to appear in the Baltic was prompted by a wish to keep on good terms with Russia, and a dislike of the appearance of subordination involved in the acceptance of a subsidy, at first caused Frederick to decline England's offers of financial assistance; but irksome though it was to him to admit it, he could not conceal from himself the fact that his own resources were by no means capable of meeting the demands upon them, and in March he announced his readiness to accept the proffered subsidy even though England remained obdurate against the despatch of a naval force to the Baltic.

So it was that on April 11th the lengthy and intricate negotiations between England and Prussia were brought to a satisfactory conclusion by the signature of a new treaty. Both parties pledged themselves to make no separate peace or truce without consulting their ally, and England placed an annual subsidy of £670,000 at the disposal of Frederick to be devoted to the maintenance and augmentation of the forces he was employing in the common cause.[3] Simultaneously George II undertook to apply to Parliament for the supplies needed to maintain an army of 50,000 German troops for the defence of Hanover and Western Germany. The whole Hanoverian army had already been taken into British pay (Oct. 1757), and with the addition of contingents from Hesse

[1] Cf. Waddington, iii. 201 ff.   [2] *Ibid.* iii. 195.   [3] *Ibid.* iii. 208.

and Brunswick, and vigorous recruiting in Hanover, it was found possible to place 50,000 men at the disposal of Prince Ferdinand of Brunswick, the general whom Frederick, at the request of King George, had sent to take command of the army of Western Germany. Ferdinand combined in an unusual degree the qualities of daring and of prudence so indispensable to a general. His task as the commander of this army of Germans in British pay, which had to face the simultaneous attacks from West and South of greatly superior numbers of French, was one of enormous difficulty. Outnumbered always, he nevertheless frequently managed to be in superior force at the critical point, and his campaigns are brilliant examples of a defence carried on largely by means of the counter-offensive. Quick to take advantage of his adversaries' mistakes, he was not cast down by occasional reverses or over-boldened by success. He was patient, calm, a good administrator as well as a capable strategist and a skilful tactician, and England is to be accounted fortunate that she was able to borrow from her ally the services of one of the very few generals of the day capable of discharging with success the very difficult and important task she had undertaken as her contribution to the common cause, the defence of Western Germany against the French. Both to England and to Prussia Ferdinand's services were of almost incalculable value. One has only to consider how hopeless Frederick's plight would have been if at the time of Hochkirch or of Kunersdorf a French army had been in the same position as that in which Richelieu's found itself in October 1757, even after the none too skilfully conducted operations of that year, to be able to estimate what it meant to Frederick to be relieved of all further anxiety as to his right flank and rear. After the beginning of 1758, Frederick was quite secure in that quarter. To England, Ferdinand's work was not less useful. The army with which England was protecting her ally against French attacks was at the same time playing an indirect but still most important part in the struggle for America and India and maritime supremacy. It was preventing the French from "conquering America in Hanover," it was diverting their attention and their resources away from the sea and the colonies to the hills and rivers of Westphalia and Hesse; Montcalm and Lally were left almost unassisted in their gallant struggles in order that there might be men and money for Soubise, Contades and Broglie, with which they might acquire for themselves and for the French arms a tarnished prestige and diminished reputation. Nor did Pitt fail to grasp the opportunity. He had been so far consistent in that opposition to England's embarking on a large scale in continental warfare by which he had achieved notoriety in his younger days that, much to Frederick's chagrin, he steadily refused to employ British troops in Germany. In April 1758 he made the concession of occupying Embden, which the French had just evacuated, with a British garrison; but this would seem [1] to have been mainly intended as a concession to Newcastle. Ferdinand's victories opened his eyes and produced a complete change of attitude, none the less commendable if it certainly was an inconsistency. Crefeld showed him that he had in Ferdinand a general in whose hands British troops could be employed to the very great advantage of the special interests of Britain as well as of the common cause, and the result was the decision (June 27th) to despatch 2000 British cavalry to the Continent, a force almost immediately augmented to 9000 horse and foot. In August this contingent joined Prince Ferdinand at Coesfeld,[2] providing his army with an element which, if it caused him occasional uneasiness in camp and on outposts,[3] was perhaps its most efficient and valuable portion in the day of battle.

Ferdinand's appearance on the scene was not slow to produce important results. Long even before the French and Austrians could mature their plans for the coming campaign the initiative had passed out of their hands. The hitch in the carrying out of the Convention of Kloster Zeven had given rise to much correspondence between Richelieu and the Hanoverian commander von Zastrow. In consequence there had been great delay. The French general, who had retired from Halberstadt upon Hanover, had actually given way about the Hessians, and had agreed that they should be allowed to go home without being disarmed. This, however, had not been done, and when the Brunswickers endeavoured to depart (Nov. 19th) they were forcibly prevented by the Hanoverians. Five days later Ferdinand of Brunswick reached Stade, took over the command of the Hanoverians and their allies and announced to Richelieu (Nov. 28th)

[1] Cf. Waddington, iii. 207.   [2] Fortescue, ii. 341.   [3] *Ibid.* ii. 559.

the rupture of the armistice. Operations were promptly begun again by the bombardment of the French post at Harburg. Richelieu, whose disposable forces, 25 squadrons and 35 battalions, barely amounted to 17,000 men, was not only unable to move to its relief but even to hold on at Lüneburg. He fell back to Celle (Dec. 3rd) and drew in his outlying detachments, so that by December 13th, when the Hanoverians appeared, he had 28,000 men, 52 squadrons and 54 battalions, with him and was ready to accept battle if Ferdinand offered it Ferdinand's army, however, needed rest and refitting, and was hardly in a fit state for a winter-campaign, so he prudently decided to fall back to Lüneburg and there take up winter-quarters. This allowed Richelieu to remain on the Aller and Broglie to occupy Bremen, though Harburg fell on December 30th after a brave defence. On January 22nd Richelieu was recalled to France. He left his command in a thoroughly bad condition; discipline was practically non-existent, the equipment of the troops was most defective, their pay greatly in arrears, they plundered freely and committed every possible misdemeanour, resembling rather a horde of brigands than a regular and disciplined army. In numbers the army was still formidable, its 131 battalions gave over 60,000 men present, its 123 squadrons could horse nearly 14,000 sabres, but it was not concentrated or in any way posted with a view to resuming operations. Moreover, Clermont, who replaced Richelieu, though well-meaning and honest, had even less capacity than his predecessor, in whose military character negligence, greed and want of devotion to duty rather than want of strategic insight or resolution were the most important defects. Thus when, towards the end of February, Ferdinand of Brunswick, after giving his troops the rest and refitting they so much needed, broke up from his winter-quarters and advanced against Clermont's cantonments, it was with an unready and demoralised enemy that he had to deal. Taken completely by surprise, Clermont recoiled in such confusion over the Weser that Ferdinand resolved to push his successes further. By dislodging the French from Hoya (Feb. 23rd) he forced St. Germain to evacuate Bremen (Feb. 24th), and moving on against Clermont he caused that general to retire from Hanover (Feb. 28th) to Hameln. Minden, which was held by some 4000 men, delayed Ferdinand nearly a fortnight, but on March 14th it fell, and four days later the advance was resumed, Clermont, who had rallied about 30,000 men and contemplated an attempt to save Minden, abandoning the idea of a stand and retiring hastily towards Wesel. In the beginning of April the French army of Westphalia recrossed the Rhine at Wesel, having been ignominiously hustled out of Germany in less than six weeks. De Broglie also, who had replaced Soubise, was unable to maintain his position East of the Rhine and had to follow Clermont's example, quitting Cassel on March 21st and retiring to Düsseldorf, while the detachment till then in occupation of East Friesland regained the left bank of the Rhine at Emmerich on March 27th.

Meanwhile in Bohemia the Austrians had been making great efforts to reinforce their main army, which, when Daun took command of it at Königgratz, March 12th, mustered 13,000 regular cavalry, 37,000 infantry, and 13,000 irregulars. The choice of Daun in place of Charles of Lorraine was a wise step. His military capacities were distinctly superior to those of his predecessor in command, and though he, too, was much hampered by the preference for the defensive and by the want of enterprise, which were the chief faults of the Austrian army, he was a tactician of resource and as yet commanded the confidence of his allies.

However, it was Frederick who was the first to move. During the winter he had achieved marvellous results in the difficult task of refitting his army, filling its depleted ranks and training his new recruits into efficient soldiers. Schweidnitz had been more or less blockaded all the winter, and on April 2nd the blockade was converted into a siege. General Thürheim made a gallant defence, and when on the 16th a successful assault on the all-important Gallows Fort forced the fortress to surrender, its garrison of 8000 men had been reduced to 5000. Daun had found it impossible to come to its relief; his preparations for a move were not complete, and Loudoun, who was in command of the advanced detachments near Branau, was driven in by superior forces on Potisch and prevented from attempting any diversion in favour of the garrison. With Silesia thus cleared of Austrians, Frederick resolved upon an invasion of Moravia, which, if successful, would allow him to threaten Vienna, which in any case would bring him into fertile and unexhausted country and would draw the Austrians away from the Oder, in which direction the Russians were to be expected. Accordingly in the last week of April the Prussians moved off to Neisse and entering Moravia in two columns by Troppau and Jaegerndorf, united before Olmütz on May 5th. The move created great alarm in Vienna, where it was believed [1] that Frederick would merely mask Olmütz and push on to the capital itself; and it was quite unlooked for by Daun, who was expecting Frederick to invade Bohemia in co-operation with Prince Henry and the 30,000 Prussians in Saxony. Thus it was not till April 29th that the Austrian main body concentrated at Skalitz and moved into Moravia, 20,000 men under General Harsch being left to guard Bohemia. On May 5th Daun took post at Leutomischl near the Bohemio-Moravian boundary, and there remained sometime, using the light troops under von Jahnus and Loudoun to harass the Prussian communications, in which they displayed untiring energy and skill.

Urged on by orders from Vienna that Olmütz must be relieved, Daun at length moved up to Gewitsch, where he was only two marches from the fortress (end of May). Now began a somewhat intricate series of manœuvres; Daun kept on shifting from one camp to another, hoping thus to occupy the Prussian covering army and, if possible, induce it to attack him in one of the strong positions he loved, or, at any rate, to distract it and prevent the rapid advance of the siege-works. These were not progressing very rapidly. Not till May 20th did the siege artillery arrive, and the trenches were not opened till eight days later. The Prussians did not shine in siege-craft; their engineers were bad, and the activity of the Austrian light troops on the lines of communication proved a useful aid to the dash and energy with which Marshall and his garrison made sorties. It was felt that much would depend on the safe arrival of a vast convoy of 3000 waggons, bringing ammunition and all kinds of military stores, which set out from Neisse on June 21st escorted by 8000 men, recruits, convalescents, drafts from Silesian garrisons and other details.

To intercept this all-important train Loudoun, who had some 4000 men, was ordered to take post on its line of route,

[1] Waddington, iii. 222

another 5000 men under Siskovitch being detached from
Daun's main body to join him.   On June 27th Loudoun was
at Sternberg, not far from the Domstadtl Pass, and next morning
the unwieldy convoy advancing from Bautsch found its passage
disputed near Guntersdorf.   There was a sharp fight.   At first
the Austrians had the upper hand, but Siskovitch had gone
astray and his failure to appear allowed Colonel Mosel to thrust
the Austrians aside, and that evening the convoy straggled
into Neudorffl, where it found Ziethen, who had been sent
out with 3000 men to bring it in.   But it had been so
much shaken by the rough handling it had received that it
needed rest and could not resume its march till the 30th ; and
then as its leading waggons were reaching the Domstadtl Pass,
Siskovitch, whom the day's delay had allowed to retrace his
steps, assailed it on the left, Loudoun joining in from the right.
Some 200 waggons managed to get through, the rest were
forced to halt and laager, and ultimately fell into Loudoun's hands
after a stubborn fight, which cost the Austrians over 1000
men but made the relief of Olmütz a certainty.   Not only had
the Prussians lost over 4000 men killed, wounded and taken,
while Ziethen had had to fall back on Troppau to avoid being
taken and was thus severed from the King, but the stores the
convoy was bringing had been absolutely essential to the
success of the siege.

If Frederick must be held largely responsible for the loss
of the convoy, which he had done practically nothing to assist,
allowing Daun to occupy his attention, it was a bold move he
took in this extremity.   The road back to Silesia was beset by
the Austrians, but against a move into Bohemia they were not
so well prepared, and it would take him through their country
in which he could exist at their expense.   Accordingly on
July 2nd he moved away West, Keith leading one column by
Littau and Trubau, the King taking the road by Konitz to
Zittau.   The siege-train had for the most part to be left
behind, as to have taken it would have impeded the rate of progress and allowed Daun to intercept the march on Königgratz.
Daun's manœuvres to draw Frederick off from aiding the convoy had brought him to the South-East of Olmütz when the
siege was raised, and he failed to begin the pursuit till the 7th,
thus giving Frederick so much start that despite all the efforts
of Loudoun and Buccow and the light troops to check their

march, the Prussians reached Königgratz on July 14th, Daun being still several marches in rear.

At Königgratz the Prussians remained for ten days, Daun though decidedly superior in numbers[1] not feeling inclined to hurl his men against the strong entrenchments he had himself constructed earlier in the year. In this he was probably wise, but he certainly ought to have brought Frederick to action when the news that the Russians were nearing the Oder forced the King to evacuate Königgratz (July 25th). Daun had beset the three main roads to Silesia, but Frederick tricked him by taking instead the bad road by Skalitz, Nachod and Grüssau to Landshut (Aug. 9th). When he saw the Prussians in full retreat, Daun ought certainly to have risked something on a battle which might ruin the Prussian army, since even victory could only give them a free retreat.

But even when Frederick had left Landshut (Aug. 11th) with 15,000 men and was pushing across Lusatia to the assistance of his hard-pressed lieutenant on the Oder, Dohna, Daun's movements still left much to be desired. If it was useless to try to follow Frederick—and it probably was, for Daun was never a rapid marcher—he might at least have crushed the 40,000 Prussians left in Silesia under Keith. But this had been tried in 1757 and the result had been Leuthen; Daun therefore preferred to move to Saxony and see if, with the assistance of the Austrian corps in Northern Bohemia and of the reorganised but still somewhat indifferent Imperial army now, under the command of the Duke of Zweibrücken, which had come up to the frontier of Saxony, he could drive Prince Henry and his 30,000 Prussians out that country. This plan if carried out with energy and resolution promised well enough; but Daun not only moved at the rate of only nine miles a day,[2] but he left large detachments inactive in Silesia to watch Keith, from whom no forward movement was to be feared; and when he did gain touch with the Imperial army which had forced Prince Henry back on Gahmig near Dresden, he failed to attack but stood tamely on the defensive at Stolpen and Rädeburg, covering Bohemia against an attack with which it was not threatened. This extraordinary strategy

---

[1] Waddington (iii. 242) gives the Austrian force as 70,000, the Prussian as 40,000.

[2] Frederick did twenty-two miles a day when moving back to Saxony after Zorndorf.

was not the high road to the recovery of Silesia, but it should not be laid at the door of the authorities at Vienna, who urged in strong terms the need for prompt and vigorous action. If Daun had brought up every available man, even if he still shrank from a direct assault on the strong position at Gahmig, he ought to have been able to detach a corps against Dresden, by which means he would have given Prince Henry the choice between the equally distasteful alternatives of losing Dresden and of fighting a battle to save it against a very much stronger force. But Daun as little realised the importance of concentrating his forces to secure any particular object as he did the value of promptitude and decision in action. He failed to concentrate all the troops available, he equally failed to employ those he had with him to turn his opportunities to account.

Very different was Frederick's conduct at this crisis. If in the Third Silesian War his strategy was not always above criticism, if he owed much to the extraordinary blunders of his opponents, in energy and in resolution at least he was never deficient. He never hesitated about striking a blow in season ; he never allowed the prospect of losing men to deter him from purchasing important advantages at the cost of a few hundred lives. And rarely did he show as brilliant an example of determination and energy as in the critical month of August 1758. Realising that Fermor's advance must not only be promptly checked, but that a decisive victory over the Russians was very essential to Prussia at that juncture, he hastened by forced marches to Dohna's assistance. Nine days after leaving Landshut he reached Frankfort on the Oder (Aug. 20th). On the 21st he joined Dohna, who had fallen back behind the river to Gorgast, just opposite Cüstrin, which the Russians had been attacking since the 15th.

So far Fermor had shown himself but little improvement on Apraxin. After occupying East Prussia in January without encountering any serious opposition, he had spent the next five months in all but total inaction. Not till the beginning of July had the Russians at last advanced to Posen, ravaging the country they passed through with equal thoroughness and brutality. Still, though they thus inflicted much injury on their enemies, they made these districts quite useless to them-selves as a possible source of supplies. It is equally impossible to perceive the object of Fermor in attacking Cüstrin. Observance of the elementary rules of strategy might have shown him that his proper objective was the army under Dohna, which had fallen back as he advanced, and was now on the left bank of the Oder. Similarly a move into Pomerania, which would have enabled him to co-operate more effectively with the Swedes, might have resulted in the reduction of Colberg and Stettin, and so obtained a base in Eastern Pomerania which would have given the Russians speedy communication by sea with their capital, and enabled them to escape the long overland journey across the miserable roads of Poland. By sitting down before Cüstrin, Fermor played into the hands of Frederick, especially as he at the same time detached 12,000 men under General Rumanjev to occupy Stargard and establish communications with the Swedes.

Frederick was not slow to act; directly his own division came up, although in ten days they had covered 150 miles, he at once set his whole army in motion and, after feinting against the Russians' bridge at Schaumburg, established a pontoon bridge at Gusteliese, 10 miles below Cüstrin, and there transferred his troops to the right bank of the Oder (Aug. 22nd to 23rd). The evening of the 23rd found him at Klossow, the Prussians having thus interposed themselves between Fermor and Rumanjev's detached division. Next day Frederick advanced to Neu Damm on the Mietzel and was successful in securing the passage of that river at that place, though the Cossacks managed to forestall him at Darmietzel and Kütsdorf and to destroy those bridges. Meanwhile Fermor had raised the siege of Cüstrin and moved up to Quartschen just South of the Mietzel (Aug. 23rd), apparently expecting a direct attack across that stream.

However, this was far from being Frederick's intention. A direct attack across the Mietzel would have in any case been a most difficult and risky operation; it would, moreover, have robbed him of the advantages he might hope to gain from his superiority in cavalry. In this arm he was very strong, his 83 squadrons giving him 12,000 horsemen, nearly double the numbers of the Russian cavalry, even when to Fermor's 3300 regulars are added the 3000 Cossacks. For cavalry operations the ground in rear of the Russian position, the wide and open plain to the South of Zorndorf and Wilkersdorf was far better adapted and it was there that Frederick meant to engage. But to gain access to this country it was necessary to embark on one of the wide turning movements which had succeeded so well at Leuthen and at Prague. Accordingly at dawn on August 25th the Prussian army, 12,000 cavalry and 25,000 infantry (38 battalions) crossed the Mietzel at Neu Damm, well to the East of the Russian position, and, covered from the Russian scouts by the forest of Massin, pushed Southward till they emerged in the open again at Balzlow. Thence they continued their move till past Wilkersdorf, when a turn to the right enabled them to deploy for battle in the position Frederick had selected, the open ground South of Zorndorf. With this lengthy movement the Russians made practically no attempt to interfere, although to an enterprising adversary it offered many promising opportunities for a brisk counter-stroke. But Fermor would appear to have been too much occupied with altering his own dispositions to venture on anything so spirited, and he thus tamely allowed Frederick to unopposed take up a position in which he was at once in touch with his own base, Cüstrin, and between the Russian main body and its baggage at Klein Cammin. It is possible that, as some authorities have argued, this success should have contented Frederick. Fermor, once his baggage had fallen into Prussian hands, could not have retained his position, but must have either attacked or retired at once. But Frederick above all wanted a victory in a pitched battle, and he attacked promptly, strong as the Russian position proved to be, because delay would have allowed Fermor to reinforce his 42,000 men by the 12,000 troops detached under Rumanjev.

The formation of the Russian army at Zorndorf has given rise to much controversy. They had certainly spent the night in one of those square formations in which they were accustomed to encounter Tartars and other mounted enemies whose mobility enabled them to change the point of attack with a celerity greater than that with which the indifferently trained Russians could face about to meet them. For such warfare it had great advantages, but against artillery it provided an ideal target, and it was, of course, most cumbrous and liable to become disordered, and it seems improbable that in the battle it was really the formation adopted by Fermor.[1] Probably the Russians had changed front from North to South but had left a few battalions covering the ends of the two lines in which the bulk of the infantry were formed. The cavalry were posted behind the infantry, who were closely massed on a narrow front on the sandy plateau North of Zorndorf, the Western end of which is marked by the ravine of the Zabergrund, the Eastern or left end by the village of Zicher just beyond the similar ravine of the Langerbruck or Doppel-grund. Yet a third of these ravines down which marshy brooks flowed to the Mietzel, the Galgengrund, divided the Russian right from their centre.

The Prussians opened the action with a brisk and effective cannonade of about an hour's duration, after which the infantry of their left advanced against the Russian right on the Fuchsberg. The 8 battalions of the advance-guard, East Prussians under Manteuffel, led the way, with the left wing of the first line, 10 battalions under Kanitz, in support. Unluckily for the Prussians, the flames and smoke from the burning village of Zorndorf, to which the retreating Cossacks had set fire, interposed between Manteuffel and Kanitz and caused them to diverge, so that Kanitz instead of acting as a support to Manteuffel came up on his right flank. Thus the Prussian attack, which should have been delivered by a fairly solid mass, developed into the advance of a long and thin deployed line which was soon brought to a standstill by the heavy fire poured into it by the Russians. A charge by the cavalry of Fermor's right sent Manteuffel's wavering battalions flying back in disorder behind Zorndorf, the greater part of Kanitz's division becoming involved in their flight. Had it not been for the Prussian cavalry, with which Seydlitz and Maurice of Dessau hastened to the rescue, it would have gone hard with Manteuffel, even with this prompt succour he lost 26 guns. Still the success of the Russian right was a double-edged triumph; as their infantry pressed forward after the fugitives of Manteuffel and Kanitz, Seydlitz's heavy cavalry came thundering in upon them, while Maurice and his dragoons routed and drove off the Russian cavalry. Taken at a great disadvantage and in considerable disorder, the Russian infantry made a desperate but hopeless resistance.

[1] Waddington, iii 263.

After a horrible carnage they were all but exterminated, and only some broken remnants managed to escape.

But the battle was far from finished. Behind the Galgengrund the Russian centre stood firm, and their left held unshaken hold of the ground between the Langerbruck and Zicher. Against this last quarter of the enemy's position Frederick now prepared to advance, hoping to hurl the Russians back upon the unfordable Mietzel, now doubly impassable because the bridges had all been burnt. As before, he paved the way for his infantry attack by a cannonade, and between one and two o'clock his intact right, supported on the left by those of Kanitz's battalions which had managed to rally, moved forward to the attack. A counter-attack by the Russian cuirassiers, at first brilliantly successful, was checked by the Prussian dragoons; but the Russian infantry not merely offered a stubborn resistance but put to flight the greater part of the Prussian infantry, who fled back to Wilkersdorf and refused to be led forward again.[1] Fortunately for Frederick the battalions he had brought with him from Silesia stood firm when their comrades fled, and their desperate prowess aided by the repeated charges of the Prussian cavalry at last succeeded in shattering the Russian left and driving its fragments back upon the Mietzel, though even then the Russian centre remained firm in its position behind the Galgengrund and was still unshaken when night and exhaustion put an end to the stubborn conflict. Both armies had fought to a standstill, and the arrival of only a small reinforcement for either side would probably have turned the doubtful into a victorious issue.

However, no reinforcements appeared, and after the two armies had spent the next day (Aug. 26th) in watching each other without attempting to renew the engagement, Fermor slipped away during the night of August 26th to 27th, passing to the South of the Prussians, who made no effort to

---

[1] The majority of these men would seem to have belonged to East Prussia, which province, it should be mentioned, had passed into the hands of the Russians after a remarkably feeble resistance, greatly to Frederick's disgust (cf. Waddington, iii. 249). The troops who had accompanied Frederick from Silesia, whose conduct was so very different, seem to have included several battalions of the territorial regiments of the Oder valley, so that their steadfast resistance must be partly attributed to a desire for revenge on the Russian devastators of their homes, for evidence of the Russians' handiwork was only too prominent.

interrupt the movement. His retreat was a tacit admission of defeat, but it allowed him to rejoin his baggage at Klein Cammin, whence a few days later he retired to Landsberg. There Rumanjev rejoined him; but this reinforcement, whose presence on the 26th would have probably enabled Fermor to turn the tables on his conquerers, was too late to effect anything decisive. Frederick having gained his victory had gone off again to Lusatia, but he left Dohna with a force strong enough to hold Fermor in check; at least Zorndorf had deprived the Russian commander of all wish for another battle, even against Dohna, and he remained practically inactive until the beginning of November when the Russians set their faces homeward, having rather shown what they might do against Prussia, if only they were properly handled, than managed to obtain any very substantial gain for the cause of the Allies.

Thus Zorndorf, evenly contested as it had been and narrow as was the margin which had interposed between Frederick and failure, must be accounted a real victory for Prussia. Out of an army of 37,000, nearly a tenth were killed (3600) and the wounded and missing numbered almost 8000 more, so that it is not wonderful that the Prussians found themselves incapable of interfering with Fermor's move on Klein Cammin on the day after the battle. The Russian losses were even heavier, 5000 killed and prisoners, 13,000 wounded, with no less than 103 guns, though they had, it is true, captured 26 pieces from Manteuffel. The Prussian victory was mainly due to the cavalry and to the infantry which Frederick had brought with him; but the conduct of the infantry as a whole shows that the strain of the war was beginning to be felt, the gaps which Kolin and Breslau had made had been filled after a fashion, but the quality was not the same. Frederick could no longer rely quite so confidently on his troops to retrieve any errors he might make, and he had had an object-lesson in the endurance and determination of the Russians. Clumsy in manœuvring, lacking something of drill and discipline, their fighting power and tenacity made them formidable enemies.

It had not been part of Frederick's purpose to pursue the Russians. A more urgent task called him elsewhere. By forced marches he hastened back to the succour of Prince

Henry, and on September 12th he was again in touch with his brother. He had to thank Daun's undue caution that Prince Henry was there to welcome him, for the Austrian general, especially after his junction with the 40,000 men of the Army of the Empire, had been in ample force to have crushed the Prince. But he had delayed ; and though urgent orders from Vienna had at last brought him to the point of being about to deliver the belated blow, the arrival of Frederick caused him to relapse into a strict defensive from which Frederick was unable to lure him. Firmly posted at Stolpen, Daun had his left at Pirna covered by the Elbe, while on the other wing he had Loudoun at Bautzen. Meanwhile an Austrian corps under Harsch was pressing hard upon Neisse, and Frederick, growing anxious for that fortress, moved out to Bischofswerda, pushing Retzow on ahead to Hochkirch, which caused Loudoun to retire from Bautzen (Oct. 1st). Supposing the movement to be aimed at his own magazines at Zittau, Daun thereupon evacuated Stolpen (Oct. 5th) and retired by Neustadt to Kittlitz, hoping thereby to cut Frederick's communications with Silesia. It was a risky move to undertake in such close proximity to the Prussian army along whose front it was necessary to pass, but Lacy's staff work and arrangements were so admirable that the movement was practically complete before Frederick perceived it.

At Kittlitz, Daun covered both the road to Silesia by Görlitz and that to Bohemia by Zittau. Frederick came up to Bautzen on the 7th, and then, being increasingly anxious for Neisse, moved on to Hochkirch (Oct. 10th), meaning to push on across Daun's front, gain his flank, and so interpose between him and Silesia. However, he could not at once carry out this daring scheme, for he found it necessary to remain halted at Hochkirch for three days, probably in order to allow his provision trains to come up and rejoin him. This halt gave Daun an opportunity of which he for once did not fail to avail himself. The Hochkirch position was dominated by a hill to the North-East, the Stromberg, which Retzow had neglected to occupy and which was in possession of a strong Austrian detachment. Notwithstanding this Frederick proceeded to pitch his camp almost under its guns, despite the repulse by the Austrians of an attempt to gain possession of the hill (Oct. 11th). Further, with an access of over-confidence which was to cost him dear, he allowed Retzow and the vanguard (10,000 men) to push on beyond the Lobau-wasser to the Weissenberg, and thus to put a gap of fully four miles between them and the nearest support, Keith's division, which lay between Lauska and the King's headquarters at Rodewitz, while the rearguard, which in the battle formed the right, was at Hochkirch, some two miles to the South of Rodewitz.

Daun, it is true, was the very personification of caution, but for once Frederick had overestimated his enemy's lack of enterprise; and though warned by more than one of his lieutenants of the risk he was running, he refused to alter his position; his belief that Daun feared him far too much to ever contemplate taking the offensive against him was only increased by the elaborate fortification of the Austrian camp, which in reality served as the cover for preparations for an attack. During the night of October 13th/14th the Austrian measures were carried out with unusual secrecy and despatch: Loudoun led the left round to the South-West of Hochkirch, so that it outflanked the Prussian right, the Austrian centre stood ready to fall on Hochkirch from the South-East, while d'Aremberg and their right prepared to join in by attacking Lauska and Kotitz as soon as the battle was fairly begun. Thus even if Baden-Durlach and the Austrian reserve from Reichenberg should fail to keep Retzow and the Prussian van occupied, d'Aremberg would interpose between that division and Keith's. The woods which covered the hills on which the Austrians were posted hid their preparations from the Prussians, and the narrow space which separated the armies was all in favour of a surprise.

As the bells of the village clock-towers struck five o'clock the Austrian left advanced to the attack. Their success was immediate. The thin line of Prussian outposts was crushed in and the Austrians, falling on the enemy as they gathered hastily from their bivouacs, drove them back into Hochkirch in disorder, stormed a battery erected to cover the village, and, pressing on, hurled themselves against the houses and gardens among which the Prussians were endeavouring to rally. To a certain extent the fog and mist which had contributed to the surprise of the Prussians now proved of assistance to them by helping to disorder the Austrians and to conceal from them the full extent of their success. At any rate their first rush was stayed, and Frederick, warned by the thunder of the Austrian guns that this was not the mere affair of outposts he had at first supposed it, hastened to bring up battalions from the centre and left to the succour of his endangered right. Thus when the Austrians resumed the assault of Hochkirch they met with a most resolute resistance, and for a couple of hours an even and desperate contest raged in and around the village. Keith perished in a gallant effort to recapture the lost 20 gun battery, and the Austrians following up his repulse made themselves masters of the greater part of Hochkirch. Maurice of Dessau brought forward his division only to be repulsed in his turn, and though a charge by Ziethen's cavalry saved his battalions from destruction, the rescuers were in turn thrown back in disorder by O'Donnell and some Austrian cavalry and Maurice himself went down in a desperate attempt to turn the fortunes of the day.

Meanwhile, on the extreme Austrian left, Loudoun's Croats routed the cavalry who were seeking to cover the right of Maurice's infantry and, supported by a detached brigade of the force which had assailed Hochkirch, they pressed on against Pomritz, engaging the Prussian reserves and even threatening their line of retreat. D'Aremberg also was beginning to push forward against Kotitz, although a little behind his appointed hour. Repulsed at the first attempt, he was more successful on renewing it, carrying a battery of 30 guns which had checked his first onset, forcing the defile of Kotitz and compelling the Prussians to recoil towards Rodewitz. By this time (about 9 a.m.) the long struggle for Hochkirch had gone definitely in favour of the Austrians, a last effort by the Prussian infantry having been worsted by Lacy charging at the head of some squadrons of heavy cavalry. However, thanks to their artillery, who sacrificed themselves to cover the retreat of the rest of the army, the Prussians were able to fall back to Pomritz, where the right and centre rallied on a couple of battalions brought up from the left, Bülow also checking Colloredo's attacks on Ziethen. The rallied infantry then began their retreat through the pass of Drehsa, a great battery collected by Frederick from all quarters of the field and established on the Drehsa heights managing to hold Loudoun at bay. In the end the guns were lost, a fate shared by those near Rodewitz, which had at first repulsed d'Aremberg only to be carried at his second attempt. Had Baden-Durlach not allowed Retzow to slip away from Weissenberg and come to the succour of his King, it might have been all over with the Prussian army. But Retzow was able to make his way to Drehsa and cover the retreat of the main body through the defile, the Austrians with an unnecessary prudence making hardly any effort to push home their success. They might well have renewed the attack. Their losses did not amount to more than 6000 all told; the greater part of Baden-Durlach's corps had not fired a shot; even in the left and centre 18 battalions out of 52 had hardly been engaged, and the captured guns might have been turned on their old owners. But Daun was just the man to be content with "having done very well":[1] satisfied with having won a great victory, with having punished Frederick's temerity and carelessness, with having captured his camp and most of his artillery and inflicted on him very heavy losses,[2] he let the Prussians draw off unimpeded to Doberschutz where they rallied in an excellent position behind the Lesser Spree. Not an attempt was made to follow up the great advantage which had been established, and thus Frederick was not only able to lie undisturbed in his new quarters until he had refitted and encouraged his beaten troops, supplied himself with fresh artillery, and called Prince Henry and 8 battalions from Dresden to his assistance but in the words of a French envoy in the Austrian camp, he was able "to behave as if he had forgotten the battle he had lost," to actually resume and carry out his original plan. Breaking up from Bautzen on the evening of the 24th he marched quite unobserved round Daun's position, for Daun supposed him to be retiring on Glogau, and pushing on to Görlitz he placed himself between Neisse and the Austrian main body.

Twenty-four hours late Daun started in pursuit of his daring adversary (Oct. 26th a.m.), but a reconnaissance of the Prussian position quite deprived him of any inclination to attack, and on October 29th he had recourse to the doubter's expedient, a council of war. It was obvious, he pointed

---

[1] Cf. Mahan's *Nelson*, i. 169.

[2] These probably amounted to 9000 all told, more than half being killed, taken or missing.

ZORNDORF Aug.25ᵗʰ 1758.

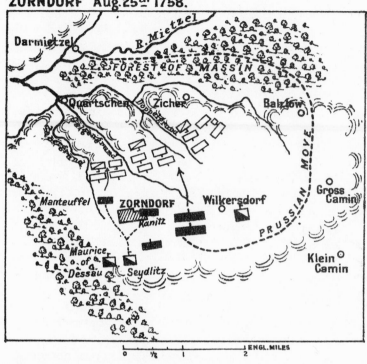

Darmietzel

R. Mietzel

FOREST OF MASSIN

Quartschen   Zicher   Balzow

Gross Camin

Manteuffel   ZORNDORF   Wilkersdorf

Ranitz

Maurice of Dessau   Seydlitz

Klein Camin

PRUSSIAN MOVE

0   ½   1   2   ENGL. MILES

HOCHKIRCH Oct. 14ᵗʰ 1758

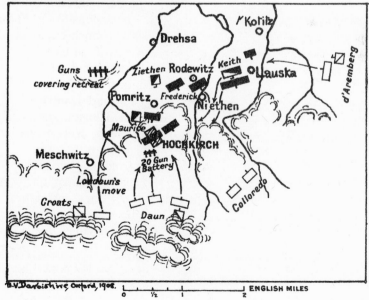

Kotitz

Drehsa

Guns covering retreat

Ziethen   Rodewitz   Keith   Lauska

d'Aremberg

Pomritz   Frederick

Niethen

Maurice

HOCHKIRCH

Meschwitz

20 Gun Battery

Loudoun's move

Croats

Daun

Colloredo

B.V. Darbishire Oxford, 1908.

0   ½   1   2   ENGLISH MILES

out to his officers, that if the King of Prussia moved to the
relief of Neisse he could not be stopped: it would be unreasonable to expect the Austrians to move with the same
celerity that Frederick always found possible, and it would be
equally impossible for Harsch to hold his own during the
three days which must elapse before the Austrian main body
could come to his aid.   Daun therefore proposed that as soon
as Frederick started for Neisse, Loudoun, O'Kelly and Bela
with the light troops should follow hard upon his rear, so as
to give him the impression the whole army was after him,
whereas the Austrian main body should really take the opposite
direction, rejoin the Imperial army in Saxony and fall on
Finck and the small Prussian corps in that province, destroy
it and retake Dresden.   But this plan, though put into force
when Frederick left Görlitz for Silesia (Oct. 30th), proved a
total failure.   Daun did actually cover the distance from
Jauernik and Dresden between November 4th and 9th, but
he failed to cut off from Dresden the weak Prussian force in
Saxony, 18 battalions under Finck ; a feeble attack upon
the city was checked by Schmettau's setting fire to the Pirna
suburb; whereupon Daun, not wishing to cause the destruction
of the capital of an ally of Austria, gave up the attack,
fell back to Rodewitz and there waited helplessly till Frederick
came back to Saxony.   Frederick, though much harassed by
his pursuers, had relieved Neisse (Nov. 7th), Harsch sending
his guns safely over the mountains and then following himself
when the King drew near.   Neisse safe, Frederick retraced his
steps.   On the 18th he was back at Bautzen; on the 20th he
regained Dresden to find Daun in full retreat on Bohemia by
Pirna, and the Imperial army gone to Chemnitz after an
unsuccessful attempt on Torgau, foiled by the arrival of
Wedel and Dohna from Pomerania.   Once again, therefore,
Frederick, despite a great defeat, was able to end the campaign
in no worse condition, save as regards his resources in men
and money, than he had begun it.   His generalship was
often faulty: for the defeat of Hochkirch he had his own
incredible rashness to blame; at Olmütz he let Daun and
Loudoun out-manœuvre him, and he might have avoided the
carnage of Zorndorf, for he might have forced the Russians
to retire if he had seized their baggage and supply trains at
Klein Cammin on the 24th.   But against these errors he can

point to the fine march into Bohemia after Olmütz, the decision and energy of the marches from Landshut to the Oder, from Zorndorf to Saxony, and from Silesia back to Saxony in November; above all, to the resolution unshaken by defeat and to the inexhaustible energy with which he retrieved the losses of Hochkirch. If there was one thing in which Frederick shone pre-eminent, it was his thorough appreciation of the cardinal rule of strategy, that "the advantage of time and place in all martial actions is half a victory, which being lost is irrecoverable." Daun, on the other hand, had failed to utilise his chances and had spoilt all by adopting Fabian tactics when they were least advisable. Austria's resources, when backed up by those of her allies, were much greater than those of Frederick; her troops were improving rapidly, those of her enemy had begun to deteriorate; it was to her interest to force the fighting, to pursue a policy of attrition; the waiting game was to Frederick's advantage, since it enabled him to save his soldiers and husband his resources. As for the Russians, they had once again neutralised by their utter want of strategy their good fighting capacities and the advantages of their position on Frederick's left flank. They had inflicted heavy losses on Prussia, both in men and in resources, but they had altogether failed to achieve results commensurate with their opportunities.

It was in no small measure due to Frederick's ally, England, and the army she was maintaining in Western Germany, that the issue of the campaign of 1758 had been as satisfactory as it had proved. Ferdinand of Brunswick had not failed to follow up his success in driving Clermont out of Germany. Resuming operations before his enemy had had time to finish refitting his troops or to make good his losses, Ferdinand crossed the Rhine at Emmerich (June 1st), boldly disregarding the neutrality of Dutch territory which Holland was quite unable to enforce. Clermont, his left thus turned, fell back to Rheinberg, but finding a stand there impossible, retired to Meurs (June 13th) and thence towards Neuss (June 16th), evacuating the province of Cleves and leaving the important fortress of Wesel quite isolated. Ferdinand could only spare men enough to blockade Wesel, not to attack it, but he pushed on against Clermont, whom he found on June 23rd strongly posted at Crefeld and ready to give battle. Ferdinand had only 33,000 men to oppose to 47,000 ; but nevertheless he attacked, demonstrating against Clermont's front and right in order to keep him occupied until the real attack, a turning movement round the French left to gain their rear, should have developed. With numbers so inferior the stroke was most venturesome, almost rash, but it proved a brilliant success. After a sharp action, in which the French lost 3 guns and had over 4000 casualties as against the 1700 of the Allies, Clermont was dislodged from his position and fell back precipitately to Cologne, which he reached on June 28th. His retreat exposed Düsseldorf which was promptly attacked. Its garrison, mainly troops in the service of the Elector Palatine, made but a feeble defence and on July 7th the town capitulated.

Indeed it seemed for a moment as if even Cologne would have to be evacuated ; but this was to prove unnecessary. Contades replaced the unlucky Clermont, considerable re-inforcements were hastily sent to his succour, and as a diversion the auxiliary corps under Soubise destined for Bohemia was called up from Hanau to the Rhine. Thus, thanks to the operations of Ferdinand, no help could be sent to Austria by France in this campaign.

These measures proved sufficient to stop Ferdinand. Soubise was successful in an action at Sondershausen near Cassel (July 23rd) against Isenburg and the Hessian corps on which Ferdinand was relying for the protection of his com-munications. The success was not followed up, since Soubise spent the next three weeks in inaction at Cassel, but it was enough to alarm Ferdinand, and with the enemy in his front growing rapidly stronger he saw that it was out of the question for him to maintain himself West of the Rhine. Accordingly, outwitting and outmarching Contades, he fell back to his bridge of boats at Rees. This had been attacked for a few days by a column under Chevert despatched from Cologne for the purpose of destroying the bridge and so cutting off Ferdinand's retreat, but in a sharp action at Meers (Aug. 5th) Imhoff and the division acting as bridge guard repulsed Chevert with loss. Even then Ferdinand's position was none too secure, for floods made the approaches to the bridge impracticable, and it had to be shifted down stream to Griethuysen and reconstructed there to enable the Allies to cross. However, this difficult operation was so quickly and successfully performed that by the evening of August 11th the Allied army found itself once more East of the Rhine, not a man nor a waggon having been lost in the passage. Contades followed Ferdinand across the river, crossing at Alpen a few days later; but the somewhat negative success of having forced the Allies to evacuate the left bank seemed for the time to quite content him, for after establishing his headquarters at Recklinghausen on August 21st and posting his troops along the left of the Lippe, he remained inactive for nearly seven weeks, unable to lure Ferdinand from his position behind that river and, though superior in numbers by three to two, unwilling to risk a direct attack. It was during this period that the British contingent of 6 cavalry regiments and 6 battalions of infantry joined Ferdinand (Aug. 21st); and thanks to this and to other reinforcements Ferdinand was able to maintain his position through the remainder of the campaigning season. Soubise alone gave him cause for anxiety by a not too energetic advance against Göttingen (Sept. 9th), which Ferdinand parried by thrusting Oberg and Isenburg forward against Cassel (Sept. 27th). A little more energy on Oberg's part, and Cassel might have been wrested from its feeble garrison, mainly composed of ill-disciplined and untrustworthy Würtembergers; but Soubise just got back in time and, reinforced by Chevert and a division lent by Contades (Oct. 8th), he brought Oberg to action on October 10th, successfully dislodging him from his position on the Lutterberg and driving him back in some disorder on Munden. But notwithstanding this victory Ferdinand's position remained unshaken; Lippstadt and Münster were secure, and with the arrival of November Contades fell back to the left bank of the Rhine to take up his winter-quarters, while Soubise broke up from Cassel and retired behind the Lahn. Thus Ferdinand could justly congratulate himself on having with inferior forces retained possession of the provinces he had wrested from Clermont earlier in the year. Of all the principal commanders engaged in the campaign of 1758 Ferdinand had most enhanced his reputation by its results.

In some ways the most important event of the winter months was the fall of Bernis. He had long ago come to favour a peace-policy and had been steadily losing ground at Court, so that his dismissal was no surprise. To him succeeded de Stainville, formerly French envoy at Vienna and now (Oct. 1758) Duc de Choiseul. He signalised his accession to power by negotiating a new treaty between France and Austria (Dec. 31st) by which the obligations of France were appreciably modified. She continued to pay large subsidies,[1] but she was no longer pledged to continue the war till Silesia should be recovered; she promised instead to do her best to win back the lost province. Similarly, France had to modify her demands; nothing more was heard of cessions in the Netherlands.

As usual, the winter was spent by both sides in arduous and energetic preparations for the coming campaign, while Frederick made desperate but unsuccessful efforts to embroil Turkey with Russia[2] and to intrigue with malcontents both in Sweden and Russia. The Allies also devoted much time and labour to preparing a plan for the operations of the summer, hoping to effect by a proper co-operation that complete overthrow of their adversary which 1758 might have seen had their efforts only been better arranged. One project which was for some time entertained, was that the Austrian forces should be divided into two quite independent armies, one to co-operate on the Elbe with the Imperial army and with the French auxiliary corps, the other to effect a junction in Upper Silesia with 40,000 Russians who were to reach that district by a march across Poland, the rest of the Russian army assisting the Swedes in Pomerania. However, two reasons prevented it from being adopted. In the first place, the French flatly declined to detach any auxiliary force to Saxony until they had crushed Ferdinand and his Anglo-Hanoverian army. Secondly, the Russians were most unwilling to divide their main body, but wished to act independently rather than as Austria's auxiliaries. Moreover, if they moved into friendly country like Poland they would not be able to provide for their troops by their usual fashion of making war support war, only in a hostile country could they indulge in wholesale requisitioning. Accordingly they proposed to wait till the grass had grown and then move against Stettin. But this proposal did not please the Austrians and a voluminous correspondence followed, the

---

[1] 288,000 gulden a month, together with 250,000 in lieu of the auxiliary corps of 24,000 men.

[2] Cf. Waddington, iv. 113.

final decision being that the Russian army should concentrate at Posen and move forward to the Middle Oder where it was to be joined by the Austrians, who were to devote themselves to keeping Frederick occupied on the frontiers of Saxony and Silesia until such time as the Russians were ready.

The result of the adoption of this plan was that the real opening of the campaign was very much delayed, and that a longer time than usual was available for the raising and training of recruits and for other preparations. But though both main armies remained long inactive, raids and forays were numerous, the Prussians being specially active and ubiquitous in gathering in supplies and in destroying those of their enemies. Once they ventured as far as Bamberg in Franconia (May), and a damaging blow was struck at the Army of the Circles which was forced to recoil with much disorder and loss to Nüremberg. Still for the first time since the beginning of the war Frederick adopted the defensive at the outset of a campaign. The days in which he could risk taking the offensive were past. His men were no longer the soldiers of 1756, or he would hardly have allowed Daun to lie inactive and undisturbed in his cantonments in Northern Bohemia while the slow-moving Russians were gradually concentrating at Posen.

The drain of war had made a very great difference in the quality of the Prussian army, while the fighting capacities of their enemies were rather improving. Zorndorf had taught Frederick not to despise the Russians, and Hochkirch would hardly have been possible to the Austrian army of the First or Second Silesian Wars. The fact that Frederick found himself compelled to increase the strength of his artillery until his guns reached the high proportion of $4\frac{1}{2}$ per 1000 men of the field army,[1] is an indication of the changing situation.

But if it was necessary for Frederick to remain strictly on the defensive, for Daun to adopt such a course was hardly sound strategy. Outnumbering the 130,000 men of whom Frederick could dispose by 30,000 Austrians alone, even when the 20,000 men of the Army of the Circles are omitted and the 25,000 whom Frederick had to detach against the Russians and Swedes are included in the King's total, Daun had no need to wait for the Russians. With numbers so superior the

---

[1] Compare Napoleon's action in 1813, when he stiffened his young conscripts with an exceptionally powerful artillery.

true strategy for him was to force an action, to compel Frederick to fight and use up his resources. But after moving up from Schurtz near Münchengratz, where he had lain so long inactive, to Marklissa on the Upper Queiss (June 28th to July 0th), Daun once more relapsed into inaction, fearing to hurl his 90,000 men against the strong position near Landshut where Frederick had entrenched the 50,000 who composed his main body. Not till the end of July were serious operations begun, and by that time the Russians had at last carried out their share of the compact.

It cannot be alleged that the Russians had shown any remarkable alertness in their movements. About the middle of June they had begun to concentrate at Posen, but for some time their force at that point was so weak that if Dohna, to whom Frederick had again entrusted the defence of his Eastern provinces, had known what a chance lay before him he might have attacked Posen with a very fair prospect of success. However, Dohna though reinforced by 10,000 men under Hulsen detached from Prince Henry's corps, failed to seize the opportunity and by the end of June the Russian army, over 50,000 strong, was duly concentrated at Posen. It was under the command of the veteran Soltikov, who superseded Fermor without thereby bringing to the direction of the Russian arms the resolution and determination which had been so conspicuously lacking in the superseded commander.

Soltikov began his march to the Oder by quitting Posen on July 7th and advancing by Tarnovo to Goltzen, where on July 20th he entered the province of Brandenburg. His opponent had sought to check the Russian advance by threatening their communications with the Vistula, but, finding his threat disregarded, fell back from Obornik to Zullichau. There on July 22nd General Wedel joined the Prussian army, having been sent by Frederick to replace Dohna with whose conduct the King was most discontented. Wedel's orders directed him to arrest the march of the enemy by bringing them promptly to action; but he was not fortunate in the manner in which he carried them into effect, and the battle which he fought at Paltzig (July 23rd) resulted in a severe defeat for the Prussians. Out of some 30,000 men they lost over 8000, a quarter of whom with 13 guns were left in the hands of the Russians, whose casualties did not exceed

5000. Even more serious was the demoralised condition in which the defeated army was left. Several regiments had behaved none too well in the action ; one battalion composed of recruits forcibly enlisted by the Prussians in the Austrian province of Upper Silesia revenged itself by deserting in a body to the Russians,[1] and, as its conduct on a more important battlefield a few weeks later was to show only too plainly, the army of East Prussia was no very solid bulwark for the Hohenzollern dominions. Quite unable to face his enemy again Wedel put the Oder between them and his broken corps (July 24th), and the Russians after occupying Crossen on the 25th pushed on to Frankfort and possessed themselves almost unopposed of that important town with its well-supplied magazines (July 31st).

The Russians had thus executed their share of the programme, and it was Daun's turn to perform his. He did not, indeed, propose to move his main body to the Oder ; it remained on the Queiss to hold Frederick in check, while some 18,000 men under Loudoun pushed across from Rothenburg past Priebus, where Hadik joined him (July 29th), and Sommerfeld (July 30th) to Zilchendorf on the Oder, where on August 2nd he established communications with the Russians. Much to Loudoun's annoyance, however, he found it impossible to induce Soltikov to cross to the left bank of the Oder, and he was in the end forced to transfer himself and his troops to the right bank in order to avoid being attacked and driven into the river by the Prussians who were now approaching.

Frederick had been prevented from intercepting Loudoun's march to the Oder by the celerity of his movements, a quality most unusual in the Austrian army, but he had lost no time in following him to that river, being well aware that the essential thing for him was to defeat the Russians.[2] Accordingly he called up Prince Henry to Schmottseifen to take command of the troops destined to defend Silesia and keep Daun in check (July 29th), he himself with some 35 squadrons and 20 battalions leaving Sagan on August 1st and pushing across to Müllrose on the Oder and Spree Canal, where on August 6th he effected a junction with Wedel and his broken troops. It was this move which forced Loudoun to

[1] Waddington, iv. 139.
[2] Cf. letter of July 25th to Prince Henry, *Correspondance Politique*, xviii. 449.

put the Oder between himself and the Prussians, and Frederick also had the satisfaction of forcing Hadik, who was following more slowly in Loudoun's track, to suspend his move and to fall back to join Daun in order to escape being cut off, a fate which did befall his rearguard at Spermberg (Aug. 3rd). Three days after the junction with Wedel, Frederick was reinforced by a division under Finck which he had summoned up from Torgau and which performed no inconsiderable feat in covering 160 miles in 9 days. The Prussian army was thus brought up to a strength of 106 squadrons and 63 battalions, well supplied with artillery. This concentration was made possible by exposing a dangerously weak force to Daun, and the Austrian commander was much at fault in not punishing his adversary's temerity, but Frederick knew the man he was dealing with, and risked a disaster in Silesia with impunity.

But it was not everywhere that this impunity was to attend Frederick. The enemies he had to face were not to be lightly estimated on the battlefield if their strategy was such as to justify him in calculating on their making mistakes. Determined to bring the Russians to battle, he proceeded to throw two bridges over the Oder at Goritz, 15 miles below Frankfort (Aug. 10th to 11th), and on the 12th he pushed up to Bischoffsee, ready to attack the formidable position which the Austro-Russians were fortifying on the heights of Kunersdorf just East of Frankfort. This step was exactly what Loudoun was hoping for. That energetic commander had been urging Soltikov to cross the river and force Frederick to fight, but he found the Russian most unwilling to commit himself to so venturesome a step, and it was with the utmost difficulty that Loudoun extracted from him a conditional promise to do so. Indeed, the Austrian was not a little afraid that the sole result of the Russian advance to the Oder would be their return to Posen as soon as they came to the end of their supplies and had collected all the plunder on which they could lay their hands. It was therefore a great relief to him when Frederick took the decision out of Soltikov's hands by crossing to the right bank and preparing to attack.

The position which the Russians and their allies had taken up on the heights which starting at Frankfort run North-East-ward from the Oder, was one of considerable strength in itself, and had been carefully fortified by them. Against attacks from the West it was protected by a wide extent of swampy ground, the Elsbusch, so that the Allies, whose line as a whole faced East, had no reason to be nervous for their rear. The ridge was crossed at right angles by several narrow ravines, thus being divided into several quite independent heights, each capable of being separately defended. Thus the Northernmost part of the ridge, the Mühlberg, which formed the left of the Allied position, was separated from the Kuhberg by one depression, the Kuhberg in turn was cut off from the central part of the ridge by the Kuhgrund and Tiefe Weg, and between the central mass and the Southern portion, the so-called Judenberg, intervened the rather wider ravine now known as Loudoun's Grund. These three main divisions roughly corresponded to the left, the centre, and the right of the Russians' position, Fermor's division of 18 battalions being posted on the Judenberg with Loudoun's infantry (14 battalions) in support, the divisions of Villebois and Rumanjev (33 battalions) holding the central mass and the Spitzberg, a hill which projected from it so as to form a salient on which guns could be most advantageously placed, while Galitzin and the reserve (14 battalions) held the Mühlberg and Kuhberg, their left being thrown back at right angles so as to face North against a flanking attack. The cavalry were for the most part in reserve, though some were extended beyond Fermor's right. At the Eastern end of the Kuhgrund was the village of Kunersdorf, the greater part of which had been burnt to make it useless as cover, while from it a line of large ponds stretched Eastward to the forest which ran parallel with the ridge. A deep ravine, down which the swampy brook of the Huhnerfleiss flowed into the marsh, served as a wet ditch to the Mühlberg, and separated it from the hills to the North which supplied the Prussians with good positions for their artillery. Altogether it was a formidable position, as the forest hindered the march of an attacking army, and a general might well have hesitated before he launched his troops against it, even if the proportions had been reversed and the assailants had outnumbered the defenders by four to three. As it was, Frederick was attacking some 18,000 Austrians and 48,000 Russians with a force which certainly did not amount to 50,000.[1] Both sides were well supplied with artillery, but here again the Allies had the advantage with 300 pieces to

[1] Cf. Waddington, iv. 157-159.

240, and as about half Frederick's infantry consisted of the East Prussian troops who had been beaten at Paltzig and who had behaved none too well at Zorndorf, he could hardly claim a superiority in quality. However, confident as usual of success, he did not hesitate to attack, since to desist would be a confession of inferiority.

From the first things failed to go right. Compelled by the ground to attack from the Eastward, the Prussians had to make a long march before they could get into position; and as Frederick intended to deliver his attack with his left wing against the centre of the Allied line, the troops had to be set in motion at 2 a.m. (Aug. 12th). The manœuvre was similar in character to that which had been adopted at Prague and at Zorndorf, and it was to be covered by the Prussian right, which had to demonstrate against the Mühlberg and to make a show of attacking that point in order to draw the enemy's attention. However, the march through the forest proved more difficult than had been expected; the passage of the Hühnerfleiss caused great delays, the artillery stuck and floundered among the swamps, and the whole operation was so much retarded that Frederick altered his plan, ordered his columns to swerve to their right and to direct their march against the Mühlberg, instead of pushing on past the pools which run East from Kunersdorf in order to attack the Spitzberg. This change of plan caused more confusion, but about mid-day the advance-guard debouched from the woods and prepared to attack. An hour or so earlier the action had been begun by the Prussian artillery, which was cannonading Galitzin's position from the hills now known as the Fincksberg and Kleistberg.

The first rush of the Prussian infantry was completely successful: undeterred by the salvoes of grape poured into them at short range, they scaled the slopes, closed with the Russian infantry and after a savage struggle drove them off the Mühlberg into the ravine at its foot, capturing 40 guns and many prisoners. But there were no cavalry at hand to take advantage of this success, to charge the flying Russians as they streamed across the low ground between the Mühlberg and the next part of the ridge, so that they were able to rally and form up across the ridge ready to withstand the next attack. Moreover, it proved impossible to turn the

17

captured guns on their late owners, and only 4 pieces could be got into position on the Mühlberg which were heavy enough to reach the opposite slope, where Soltikov had plenty of heavy guns and used them with effect. Meanwhile the infantry of the Prussian left and the majority of the cavalry were still struggling through the forest on their way to Kunersdorf; and though Finck and his 8 battalions managed to push across the Hühnerfleiss and come up on the right of the advance-guard, a brigade of the right wing went astray and was out of action for over an hour.

About 2 p.m. the Prussians advanced again, and once more with success. Though reinforced by Austrian grenadiers whom Loudoun brought up, the Russians were ousted from the Kuhberg and driven behind the Kuhgrund. Here another sharp fight took place, till after the missing brigade of the Prussian right had arrived and after the capture of the cemetery of Kunersdorf had allowed the defenders of the Kuhgrund to be taken in flank, the Allies were forced back to their next line of defence, the Tiefe Weg. But by this time the gallant regiments of the Prussian advance-guard and right wing were almost exhausted. They had been marching and fighting for thirteen hours and more, without food, in exceedingly hot weather, and their losses had been enormous. They had accomplished wonders, but the Russian hold on the ridge was hardly shaken; they replaced their broken units with fresh battalions from their centre and right, a numerous and powerful artillery posted on the Spitzberg swept the narrow space between Kunersdorf and the Tiefe Weg, where alone the Prussians could hope to gain access to the plateau. But Frederick would not listen to those who urged him to be content with the partial success he had achieved; to have wrested half the field of battle from the enemy was not enough for him, they must be driven into the Oder.

By this time his left, mainly composed of Wedel's troops, had at last come up, and while the cavalry pushed through the intervals in the line of ponds under a heavy fire from the hostile artillery in order to hurl themselves against the Spitzberg, the infantry of this division made their way up the steep and narrow slope from Kunersdorf. Their efforts were not less valiant than those of their comrades of the right, but they were equally unsuccessful. Brigade after

brigade was pushed up the slope in close formations through
which the hostile cannon ploughed lanes of dead and wounded :
one and all were unable to gain their end. The cavalry
suffered the same fate and, as they were reeling in confusion,
a well-timed counter-charge by Loudoun's cavalry completed
their overthrow and drove their shattered remnants into the
shelter of the woods, after which the Austrians falling on
the infantry thus exposed cut them to pieces. All hope of
victory was now gone, but Frederick attempted to exact from
the relics of his right yet one last charge of which. they
were quite incapable. Then at last the Allies took the
offensive and swept the Prussians back all along the line,
back past the Kuhgrund, back past the Kuhberg; back till they
made a sort of rally on the Mühlberg. They even repulsed
the first assault of the Russians on this refuge ; but when
Soltikov brought up some of his still intact right, the
Mühlberg, with the guns and most of the prisoners Galitzin
had lost earlier in the day, passed again into Russian hands.
With this the murderous struggle ended ; the Prussian army,
scattered in headlong flight through the forest, was only saved
from complete destruction by the failure of the victors to
pursue. All order was lost, the bonds of discipline were
relaxed, nearly every gun was left behind and the whole
army was a helpless mob. Luckily for the fugitives night
soon fell, the exhaustion of the Austrian and Russian cavalry
prevented a pursuit, while the Cossacks who had played but
little part in the battle devoted themselves to plunder. Had
they attended to their proper task it must have gone hard
with Prussia ; indeed Frederick, believing all was lost, prepared
to commit suicide. He had known defeat before but not
such a disaster. Even from Kolin his army had got away
in some semblance of order, but this seemed irreparable.
Nearly 8000 had fallen, 5000 prisoners were left in the victors'
hands, as many more wounded filled the hospitals of Goritz
and Cüstrin, while at least 2000 deserters failed to rejoin the
Prussian standards. The Russian losses were far from slight,
amounting in all to some 15,000, while the Austrian casualties
came to over 2000 ; but heavy as these were, the inactivity of
the victors was inexcusable. Had Soltikov realised how far
worse was the condition of the Prussians, he would not have
allowed the fatigue of his troops to prevent him from falling

on their rallied relics as they recrossed the Oder by the bridge of boats at Reitwein next day. But he remained inactive and the exhausted Prussians carried out the passage unimpeded. Not till the 16th did Soltikov cross the river and with that he declared the Austrians must be content; he and his army had done their share, it was now for Daun to play his part.

The respite afforded him by the delays of the victors gave Frederick's courage time to revive. Within a few days all thought of suicide was past and he was making every effort to retrieve the disaster. Hardly ever were his great powers of organisation, his resolution and his tenacity more strikingly displayed. He fell back towards Berlin, called to his aid the division under Kleist from Pomerania, trusting to the normal inefficiency of the Swedes for the safety of that province, scraped together from depôts and fortresses every man and every gun that could possibly be spared, and before very long had again collected quite a respectable force. But remarkable as his exertions were, it was really to his adversaries that he owed his escape. Had they pressed their advantage the Prussian monarchy, reeling under the shock it had received, could hardly have survived. But the ineptitude of Daun and Soltikov passes comprehension. A finer chance they could not have hoped for, a feebler use of it Frederick could not have desired.

Under the circumstances it did not perhaps matter very much what Daun did as that he should act promptly and vigorously. Had he marched direct on Berlin, had he fallen on Prince Henry and the comparatively weak force opposite him at Schmottseifen, had he directed his blow against Fouqué and the still weaker force in Upper Silesia, or had he adopted the really sound strategy of attacking Frederick and endeavouring to repeat Kunersdorf at Fürstenwalde whither the King had now retired, he could hardly have failed to be successful, and his superior numbers would have secured him against a reverse. But as usual his lack of energy was fatal. Even a Kunersdorf could not rouse him from the caution and indecision which had become habitual with him. Though Maria Theresa saw clearly that Frederick was the trunk whose fall would bring all the branches down with it,[1] she could not

[1] Cf. Waddington, iv. 189.

induce Daun to realise that a blow at the Prussian army would do far more to recover Silesia than all the skilful manœuvrings proper to the warfare of positions to which he clung so tenaciously.   It is easy to imagine what Frederick or Ferdinand of Brunswick would have done in Daun's place, and one can picture the energetic Loudoun chafing as he saw the fruits of the victory he had done so much to win slipping through the nerveless grip of his over-cautious superior.

While Daun and Soltikov were wasting time in futile discussion the favourable moments slipped by.   Frederick's forces were gradually regaining respectable dimensions, and when at last, after many delays, Daun moved to Spermberg (Sept. 9th) in order to co-operate with Soltikov in the attack on Frederick which should have been made three weeks earlier, he allowed himself to be diverted from this object by 30,000 men.   Prince Henry had been lying at Schmottseifen since the end of July, successfully braving the risks of being attacked by Daun and his 50,000, and had moved up to Sagan (Aug. 28th) in the hope of effecting a junction with his brother.   Finding that the Austrian and Russian main bodies were so posted as to render this all but impossible, he changed his plan.   Leaving Sagan on September 5th he marched up the Bober to Kunzendorf, destroyed the Austrian magazines at Friedland and caused de Ville to retire hastily from Görlitz to Bautzen, thereby exposing Bohemia to Prince Henry. This had the desired effect of drawing Daun off from -Frederick's neighbourhood.   The news of Prince Henry's move reached Daun at Spermberg just as the tardy blow against Frederick seemed at last about to be delivered.   He was alarmed not only for his magazines but for the safety of Dresden, which had capitulated to the Army of the Circles on September 4th. This force had bestirred itself when at the end of July the departure first of Prince Henry's corps for Sagan and then of Finck's for the Oder had left Saxony denuded of Prussian troops, and the Duke of Zweibrücken had without much difficulty possessed himself of Leipzig, Torgau and Wittenberg before moving against Dresden in conjunction with an Austrian force under Brentano and Maguire.   But these successes had not been longlived.   Frederick had been able, thanks to Daun's inactivity, to detach Wunsch and Finck to the Elbe, and these officers had defeated St. André and

10,000 of the Imperial army and had recovered Torgau and Leipzig. Daun therefore, being most anxious not to lose Dresden again, hastened after Henry when he heard of the latter's move Westwards, even though this involved abandoning the proposed co-operation with Soltikov. On September 13th Daun joined de Ville at Bautzen, Prince Henry taking post at Görlitz till the 23rd, when he set out for the Elbe, drawing after him Daun in some fear for Dresden. By forced marches the Austrians reached Kesselsdorf on the 29th and got into touch with the Army of the Circles. Meanwhile Henry, content with having drawn Daun still farther away from the Russians, fell back towards Strehla, at which place he on October 4th effected a junction with Finck, so that he now had 40,000 men under his orders.[1] Daun, whose 75 squadrons and 64 battalions made him superior to his adversary by 10,000 men, endeavoured to bring him to battle; but Henry had little difficulty in avoiding the snares laid for him, and even inflicted a sharp check on a division under d'Aremberg which was seeking to cut his communications (Oct. 29th). However, Daun was pressing somewhat closely on Prince Henry when the news that Frederick, now free from all fear of the Russians, was on his way to the Elbe caused the Austrian to recoil to Wilsdruf (Nov. 14th) where he took post in the hope of being able to cover Dresden.

Frederick had been set free to devote his attention to Saxony by the departure of Soltikov for the Vistula. When Daun had turned back from Spermberg to follow Henry to Bautzen the Russians, now reinforced by some 10,000 more Austrians, moved into Silesia to form the siege of Glogau. But Frederick, though his available force only mustered 24,000, mostly survivors of Paltzig and Kunersdorf, hastened to its succour, outmarched Soltikov, and barred his path at Neustadtl (Sept. 24th). The Russian refused to attack, fell back across the Oder (Sept. 30th) and announced his intention of withdrawing to his winter-quarters with the middle of October, a measure he actually carried out at the end of the month. Loudoun's Austrians, thus cut off from their friends, had to regain Moravia by a long and painful detour by Czenstochov and Cracow. Thus by the middle of November the situation had undergone a complete change,

[1] 103 squadrons and 53 battalions.

and Frederick, passing from deepest depression to the opposite extreme, was contemplating taking the offensive against Daun just though Kunersdorf had never been fought and lost. Much encouraged by the remissness of his enemies, which had allowed him time to rally and retrieve his position, he had returned to his old faults of over-confidence in himself and undervaluing his enemy. Before the end of October he had detached some 30 squadrons and 18 battalions to reinforce Prince Henry, and on November 14th he himself took command of the Prussian forces in Saxony and at once embarked on an elaborate movement by which he expected to drive Daun out of the Electorate.

The measure by which he proposed to effect this was not a frontal attack on the strong position at Plauen to which Daun had now recoiled, but a turning movement round the left flank of the Austrian position directed against their communications with Bohemia. This task Frederick entrusted to one of his most capable lieutenants, Finck, to whom he gave some 35 squadrons of cavalry and 18 battalions of infantry, in all about 14,000 men. Finck's instructions were to move from Nossen by Dippoldiswalde to Maxen, where he would be on Daun's line of communications with Bohemia and could thrust out flying columns against the Austrian magazines. But this position in rear of the Austrian camp was one of peril, and it was essential that Finck should be supported by an advance of the Prussian main body against Daun's front. This was not forthcoming, for Frederick would seem to have expected that the mere appearance of Finck in Daun's rear would be enough to send the Austrian army back in confusion to Bohemia. He was to be grievously disappointed. Daun had already detached Brentano's division to oppose Finck and he now moved on Dippoldiswalde with that of Sincere, over 19,000 strong (Nov. 19), and occupying that point placed himself across the line by which Finck had advanced and by which he would have to retreat if checked by the forces ahead of him. These included Brentano's division to the Northward, a brigade under Palffy across his line of advance Eastward at Dohna, and 7000 men of the Army of the Circles to the South-East. Trapped between these vastly superior forces, Finck's position was hopeless. Early on November 20th the triple attack began, from North, from East, and from South-

West. It was from this last quarter that the principal attack came, and before the advance of Sincere's troops, directed by Daun himself, the Prussians soon had to give way, they were driven in disorder from the heights near Maxen to Schmorsdorf. Here they rallied, but Daun and Brentano got into touch and pushing on expelled the Prussians from their refuge. Flying headlong to Bloschwitz they found their way barred by the Imperial Army and by Palffy's brigade. An attempt of the cavalry to escape under cover of night proved unsuccessful, and with the morning surrender came. The entire force had to lay down its arms as prisoners of war, a success purchased by the Austrians at the cost of some 1000 casualties. Finck must not be blamed for the disaster, he had done all he could, and the responsibility must rest with Frederick, who despatched so weak a force on so difficult an errand and then failed to give his unfortunate lieutenant timely or adequate support.

It might have been expected that a blow like that of Maxen would have been turned to good use by the victorious general, but Daun once again failed to profit by his success or to act against Frederick with the same energy and promptitude with which he had utilised Finck's isolation. He did fall on another Prussian detachment, Diericke's at Meissen, and drove it over the Elbe with a loss of 1500 men and 8 guns (Dec. 3rd), but he made no move against Frederick, who was reduced to making a despairing appeal to Ferdinand of Brunswick for the help he could expect from no other source. But though Ferdinand promptly sent off 12,000 men, who arrived at Freyberg on December 28th, they could not have reached Frederick in time if Daun had been prepared to risk anything. No doubt the weather made operations difficult and a failure might have involved the loss of Dresden; but, important as was the safe retention of that city by the Allies, it was but a sorry result for a campaign which had seen Frederick brought to the brink of ruin at Kunersdorf. The three critical weeks of August which Soltikov and Daun had so failed to use must be reckoned as one of the greatest dangers the Prussian monarchy has ever encountered; and, seeing how near he had been to total disaster, Frederick had more cause to congratulate himself on the outcome of the campaign than the Allies had. Still, when in January the enemies retired into their winter-

quarters the outlook for the Prussian King was unpromising.
He had for the first time in the war lost territory, and despite
the marvellous way in which he had recovered from the
staggering blow of Kunersdorf his military reputation had
not been enhanced by the events of the year. For Maxen,
as has been said, the responsibility was mainly his, and at
Kunersdorf he had attempted a task beyond the capacities of
his army and had sacrificed the solid if partial advantage of
the capture of the Mühlberg in the desperate endeavour to
carry the whole position.

Once again he had good reason to congratulate himself on
the skill and success with which his right flank had been protected during this critical year. Once again the French had
been prevented from lending a helping hand to their ally
by the interposition of the Anglo-German army of Western
Germany so efficiently commanded by Ferdinand of Brunswick.
Though always opposed by greatly superior forces, Ferdinand
handled his troops so skilfully and judiciously that he was
able to hold his own and the campaign saw him successful in
the principal battle of his career.

Much to the annoyance of the French, who had no
intention of beginning their operations till June, Ferdinand
was in the field before March was out. Collecting some 30,000
men at Cassel he opened the campaign by falling on the
cantonments of the Army of the Circles in Franconia,
inflicting considerable losses upon it and practically putting it
out of action for some months. Then returning to Fulda
(April 7th), he made a rapid march Southward, hoping to
recover Frankfort-on-Main of which Soubise had possessed
himself somewhat treacherously soon after the New Year.
But he did not succeed in catching Soubise's successor, de
Broglie, napping and on April 13th he found his way barred
by a slightly superior force at Bergen, a few miles north
of Frankfort. A sharply contested action followed, turning
mainly on the village of Bergen, which formed the key to the
French position and was bravely held by 8 battalions of
Swiss and Germans in the French service, while on the French
left was posted the Saxon contingent attached to de Broglie's
army. Repeated attacks somewhat insufficiently supported
by Ferdinand's artillery failed to wrest Bergen from the
possession of the French, and after these had been repulsed the

action developed into a cannonade which lasted till nightfall. Ferdinand's stroke had failed, he had lost between 2000 and 3000 men with 5 guns, and there was nothing for him but a retreat into Hesse. By April 23rd he had established himself at Ziegenhayn near Cassel, the French having made hardly any effort to pursue. At Ziegenhayn he remained till May 15th, when he moved to Lippstadt, leaving a division under Imhoff to cover Hesse.

Ferdinand had moved to Lippstadt because he expected the attack of Contades and the Army of the Rhine to be delivered against either that fortress or Münster; but in this he was mistaken. When Contades took the field it was on Giessen that he moved from Düsseldorf, and near Giessen that he was joined by the available portions of the Army of the Main (June 1st). With 100 battalions and 80 squadrons at his disposal, Contades advanced northwards into Hesse-Cassel; on June 10th de Broglie occupied the town of Cassel. Too weak to risk a battle to save Hesse, Ferdinand had to call Imhoff to him and take post at Büren, leaving Wangenheim and a Hanoverian division to protect Westphalia, which was menaced by the 20,000 Frenchmen left on the Lower Rhine under d'Armentières. Ferdinand had by this time been joined by Lord George Sackville and the British contingent who had not taken part in the dash against Frankfort. However, the position proved untenable and Ferdinand fell back to Lippstadt, while on June 29th Contades resumed his advance and once more Ferdinand had to retreat as the French general kept on pushing his right wing on ahead so as to turn Ferdinand's left. Unable to get a chance of dealing a blow at the outflanking wing, for Contades and the main body were never out of supporting distance, Ferdinand had to keep on retreating.

One of the principal objects of the French movement was to isolate Ferdinand from the Prussians, and it was for this reason that it was his left which was always turned. On July 9th, by the surprise of Minden, Contades secured a passage over the Weser, a success of great importance, for it placed it in his power to secure possession of other passages lower down the river, and by thus preventing Ferdinand from crossing to the right bank, to cut him off from all chance of communicating with Frederick. The only means of avoiding this open to Ferdinand, who at that moment was at Osnabrück, was to retire down the Weser and so secure the passages. This, however, involved risking the all-important fortress of Münster on which largely depended Ferdinand's communications with England through Embden.   It had just been left exposed to d'Armentières and the Army of the Lower Rhine by the calling up of Wangenheim's division to the main army, which even when thus reinforced was inferior to that of Contades. However, there was no help for it, and Ferdinand fell back to Stolzenau on the Lower Weser, where he took post (July 14th).   Meanwhile Contades had halted at Minden waiting till d'Armentières, who had formed the siege of Münster, should have also reduced Lippstadt.   Only by forcing on a battle could Ferdinand hope to save the fortresses, and with this object in view he detached a small force of men under the Hereditary Prince of Brunswick to seize Gohfeld, and so threaten the French communications with Cassel (July 31st).

However, Contades did not now need to be forced to fight.   Much encouraged by the news that Münster had fallen (July 25th), and that d'Armentières was about to attack Lippstadt, he had resolved to profit by the apparent dispersion of his enemies ; for while the division at Gohfeld seemed too far away to take part in any action, another portion of Ferdinand's army had been pushed forward to Todtenhausen so as to protect convoys coming up from the Lower Weser, and seemed dangerously exposed.   Accordingly he resolved to quit the strong position behind the Bastau brook, in which he might have awaited an attack with the greatest confidence, to advance against Ferdinand and drive him off.   Very early on the morning of August 1st, therefore, he put his troops in motion, crossing the Bastau and deploying in front of Minden.

The ground on which the battle was to be fought was a more or less triangular piece of open country, very suitable for the movements of cavalry.   On the East ran the Weser, on which the French right under de Broglie was to rest, to the South-West the Minden Marsh covered the French left, while to the North-West an affluent of the Bastau and the forest of Heisterholz served to cover the movements of Ferdinand. That general's force was divided into two ; he himself with 31 battalions and 42 squadrons, which in the battle formed his right and centre, lay between the villages of Hille and

Fredewald, Wangenheim with the 19 squadrons and 15 battalions of the left wing holding the villages of Todtenhausen and Kutenhausen on the edge of the forest and somewhat in advance of the rest. Contades' scheme was that his right, de Broglie's corps supported by the infantry divisions of Nicolai and St. Germain, should advance against Todtenhausen and capture it: under cover of this the rest of the army should deploy on a semicircular front, its left, composed of infantry, resting on the marsh, more infantry on the right keeping touch with de Broglie's corps, while the bulk of the cavalry, drawn up in three lines, formed the centre. Had these movements been carried out promptly they might well have proved successful, but de Broglie hesitated, not wishing to attack till Nicolai's arrival should secure his flank, and the delay was turned to good account by Ferdinand. He hastened the deploying of his troops to such purpose that by 8 a.m. it had been completed without any intervention on the part of the French, while on his extreme right he was able to secure the village of Hahlen and so establish in an excellent position several batteries of artillery who played with much effect on the French. Moreover, by the time that de Broglie began to press his attack on Todtenhausen, touch had been established between Wangenheim and the left of the main body.

The artillery of both sides had been busily employed for some time, when suddenly to the general surprise the 6 British and 3 Hanoverian battalions which formed the right of Ferdinand's infantry began to advance straight to their front against the cavalry who formed the French centre. The reason for this unexpected move was that an order of Ferdinand's that the advance, when made, should be with drums beating, was misinterpreted as a direction to the division to advance immediately " on sound of drum." It certainly took the French completely by surprise, and had the most astonishing results. The French cavalry promptly charged, but were thrown back in disorder: the second line fared little better, it shook the infantry for a moment but was itself routed. In vain the French batteries poured in a heavy fire: they could not stop "that astonishing infantry." In vain the third line of French cavalry hurled itself upon them. Though it broke through some of the battalions in the front line, it failed to shake the second, which Ferdinand, quick to utilise the advantage accident had given him, had promptly reinforced with 6 battalions. As the third line of squadrons reeled back a splendid opportunity was presented to the Allied cavalry of turning the French defeat into an overwhelming disaster. But in an evil hour for his reputation, Lord George Sackville, who commanded the 24 squadrons, 15 of them British, of the Allied right, failed to obey the repeated orders of his commander-in-chief: it is only too probable that his disobedience was deliberate, and that he sacrificed the public service to his own personal spite against Ferdinand.

Still even without Sackville's cavalry the plight of the French was pitiable. Their centre was completely broken, the efforts of Beaupreau's infantry to succour the cavalry by storming Maulbergen had failed, and the division was cut to pieces by some Hessian squadrons. Before the advance of Imhoff and the Prince of Holstein's cavalry, Nicolai had to give way: his guns were taken. On the French left the infantry, more than half of whom were Saxons, recoiled in disorder when attacked by the English infantry and by the Hanoverians of Scheele and Wutgenau. The Anglo-German artillery, admirably served, wrought havoc among the flying masses, and had not de Broglie's intact corps intervened to cover the retreat a complete disaster could hardly have been avoided. As it was, Sackville's inaction and the steadiness of de Broglie's wing allowed the French to recross the Bastau and the Allies, content with their success, halted outside the fortifications of Minden.

Indeed they had achieved a remarkable success. Though inferior by at least 12,000 to the 81 squadrons and 80 battalions of Contades, the Anglo-German army had at a cost of less than 3000 inflicted on their enemies one of 8000 at the lowest estimate, while 10,000 would probably be nearer the mark. Of their own casualties, one-half occurred among the 6 British battalions who had played so conspicuous and important a part in the action, the 3 Hanoverian battalions who had shared in the charge getting off more lightly with 300. Forty-three guns were among the prizes of victory, and as the division at Gohfeld had simultaneously fallen on the French at Hervorden, beaten them and cut their communications with Paderborn, Contades had to recoil promptly up the Weser upon Cassel.

Ferdinand certainly owed his victory mainly to the 9 battalions whose advance almost unsupported against the French cavalry was certainly the most brilliant and remarkable feat accomplished by any infantry in the war. The high proportion of their losses shows how large a share of the fighting fell on them. But Ferdinand's own contribution to the success of the day was not inconsiderable. The clever manœuvres by which he induced Contades to leave his formidable position and give battle on ground which was far more favourable to his adversaries, was only less meritorious than the promptitude with which he seized the unexpected chance given him by the advance of the 9 battalions. Instead of being disconcerted by so surprising a turn of events, Ferdinand at once supported the advancing infantry with great skill, handling his artillery so as to materially assist the advance, and sending up fresh battalions to their help. Had Sackville only done his duty, Minden would probably have been a more complete rout than Rossbach.

Ferdinand cannot, however, escape criticism for his conduct immediately after the battle. A prompt pursuit could hardly have failed to be successful, and it ought to have been possible to anticipate the French at Cassel, for the line by which they retired was not of the most direct, and their march, hampered by a great quantity of baggage, was very slow, ten days being spent in covering 110 miles. But Ferdinand hardly attempted to pursue, and on the 12th, when the French main body crawled into Cassel after a tedious and painful march through a difficult and unfriendly country, during which a good many of the Saxons took the opportunity to desert, his headquarters had not got beyond Stadtberg. At Cassel, Contades regained touch with d'Armentières, who had raised the siege of Lippstadt. However, his stay at Cassel was not to be long. Extremely afraid of being cut off from the Rhine, he fell back to Marburg directly the appearance of part of Ferdinand's army at Corbach (Aug. 18th) seemed to indicate a turning movement against the French left. Nor did Marburg afford more than a temporary resting-place. On September 4th it also was evacuated and a retreat made to Giessen, where a halt was called behind the Lahn. Ferdinand, whose move on Wetzlar had caused this retreat, followed to the Lahn, and took post on the north bank, having first taken Marburg (Sept.

11th). He made no attempt to force the French position, for his army had been considerably reduced by the detachments he had had to make, notably for the siege of Münster. This was a slow affair; but when the Prince of Lippe Bückeburg[1] replaced General Imhoff in command of the besiegers (Nov.) matters progressed more rapidly till, on November 21st, the garrison found themselves forced to capitulate. However, it was then too late for Ferdinand to undertake any serious operations, especially as in response to Frederick's urgent appeals he had detached (Dec. 9th) a strong division to Saxony to the succour of the hard-pressed King of Prussia. Indeed the chief breach in the inaction of the two armies which faced each other across the Lahn from September to the beginning of December came from the French. In November the command of the army was transferred from Contades to de Broglie, and the new commander, having at his disposal a corps of some 10,000 Würtembergers whose Duke had just concluded a new convention with France, employed this reinforcement to threaten Ferdinand's left flank by pushing them forward to Fulda (Nov. 20th). But this exposed them to a counter-stroke, and on November 30th the Hereditary Prince of Brunswick surprised the Würtembergers, who had scattered to pillage, inflicted on them over 1500 casualties and drove them back in great disorder. This reverse, combined with the news of the fall of Münster, induced de Broglie to withdraw from Giessen to Friedberg (Dec. 5th), though on the retreat of Ferdinand to his winter-quarters the French reoccupied their old cantonments on the Lahn (Jan. 1760), the Saxons and Würtembergers being between Hanau and Würzburg, and the Army of the Lower Rhine, now under de Muy, to the West of that river. Ferdinand's men were distributed between Westphalia and Hesse, some being posted from the Lahn to the Werra so as to cover Hesse from the South, the rest extending from Münster to the Upper Weser. Thus closed a campaign in which, despite their superior numbers, the French had completely failed to maintain the ground they had gained in the opening stages: Ferdinand's tenacity, resolution and skilful manœuvring and the excellent fighting qualities of his English and Hanoverians had brought him safely out of a very awkward situation, and

[1] Cf. p. 372.

he could congratulate himself on having driven the invaders out of the territories it was his task to guard, and inflicted on the French the severest defeat their principal army suffered during the war. Moreover, he had been able to detach to the aid of the King of Prussia a really considerable reinforcement. It is easy to picture the plight in which Frederick would have found himself had Minden been a French victory. He could hardly have survived Kunersdorf.

The months of inaction which followed the long-drawn-out campaign of 1759 were as usual spent by Austria and her allies in recriminations over the disasters of the past year, and in planning schemes for accomplishing in the coming campaign all that had not been achieved in the last. France, not without reason, was much discouraged, and would have been glad to come to terms with England, for Minden was not the only blow which the Bourbon monarchy had suffered at the hands of King George. Lagos, Quebec and Quiberon were quite enough for one year, and the only ray of hope in the situation was the accession of the inveterate enemy of England, Don Carlos of the Two Sicilies, to the Spanish throne left vacant by the death (Aug. 1759) of Ferdinand VI. But in the end, after much correspondence and negotiating, France remained true to her alliances, and the only important change was a modification of the Austro-Russian treaty by which it was agreed that East Prussia was to fall to the share of Russia and not to be given to Poland.

CHAPTER XIII

THE SEVEN YEARS' WAR—*concluded*

FOR the campaign of 1760 two alternative schemes were proposed. Daun was in favour of that of Lacy, which contemplated a defensive attitude until the Russians should arrive; Loudoun, on the contrary, pleaded for a vigorous offensive which would not give Frederick time to recover the heavy losses of the previous year, a proposal with which Kaunitz on the whole concurred. Finally, though Soltikov induced the Czarina to refuse the request that an auxiliary Russian corps should be detached to join Loudoun, it was decided to adopt a modification of the latter's scheme. While the main Austrian army in Saxony was to watch Frederick, Loudoun was to assemble a second army, 40,000 strong, in Bohemia and attempt Silesia, the Russians co-operating by crossing the Oder at Frankfurt and besieging Breslau.

At the end of May, Loudoun moved forward from Königgratz to Frankenstein, where he took post (May 31st). Opposed to him was General Fouqué at Landshut, with some 12,000 men, Prince Henry having moved up from Sagan to the Wartha to check the Russian advance from Posen. Loudoun's real objective was the fortress of Glatz, but he had first to dispose of Fouqué. By feinting at Breslau he induced Fouqué to leave Landshut, to which place he promptly pushed forward his advanced guard, himself taking post at Pischwitz and forming the blockade of Glatz. Frederick thereupon (June 14th) ordered Fouqué to reoccupy Landshut. It was a disastrous order: the Prussian's advance was checked on the ridge behind Landshut and Loudoun came up with large reinforcements. On the early morning of June 23rd a converging attack was delivered on Fouqué's unfortunate force. The two principal redoubts were carried after nearly two hours' fighting, and by 9 a.m. the survivors of the division had laid down their arms. Some few escaped, but 1500 were

18

killed and 8300 taken, mostly wounded, the Austrians having some 3000 casualties in a force of 30,000.

To retrieve this disaster, Frederick set off for Silesia himself; but Daun moved by Bautzen and Görlitz over the Queiss at Naumburg and united with Loudoun, whom he had called up to the Katzbach, on July 7th, Lacy being with a separate corps at Bischofswerda, Frederick in an interior position at Bautzen. Finding his road to Silesia barred by the junction of Daun and Loudoun, the King fell back on his other alternative. Turning round he dashed at Lacy (July 8th) but missed him, for that general slipped away back across the Elbe and joined the Army of the Empire at Gross-Sedlitz. Frederick thereupon assailed Dresden only to meet with a stubborn resistance from the valiant Maguire, the commander of the garrison. It was in vain that a siege-train specially brought up from Magdeburg bombarded the city (July 18th); Maguire held out most stubbornly until Daun returned to his assistance. Daun had waited to let Frederick really commit himself to the attack on Dresden before he started (July 15th) to its relief. On the evening of the 18th he fell on a Prussian post near Weissig with complete success and was thus able to get into communication with Maguire. Frederick had to raise the siege and draw off (July 29th) to Zehren below Meissen, and there cross to the East of the Elbe. Daun, who was considerably superior in numbers, once again neglected a good chance by not forcing on a battle.

Meanwhile Loudoun had returned from the Katzbach to Glatz, and pushed on the siege with such vigour that on the 21st the trenches were ready and on July 26th, after a redoubt and the covered way had been stormed, the fortress surrendered. Loudoun promptly pushed on to Breslau, arriving there July 31st, and at once began preparing to bombard it. Luckily for Prussia, General Tauenzien, the officer in command of the 7 weak battalions which with numerous convalescents formed the 4000 men of the garrison, was a soldier of great resolution, who held out stoutly although Loudoun bombarded the city with great effect. In making this dash at Breslau the Austrian general had counted on the assistance of Soltikov who had promised to leave Posen on July 23rd and to be at Breslau in ten days. Loudoun quite reasonably expected that his Russian colleague would give occupation to Prince Henry and prevent him interfering with the siege, and it was much to his disgust that he learnt on August 2nd that whereas Prince Henry, who had made a rapid march from Landsberg on the Wartha, was pressing on his outposts, Soltikov was still East of the Oder and would not reach Breslau for another week. Compelled to raise the siege, Loudoun fell back to Striegau (August 7th) to avoid losing his communications with Daun. Meanwhile Frederick had started for Silesia on August 3rd, and on the 7th he reached Bunzlau, having covered 100 miles in five days. Daun, moving parallel more slowly, though far faster than his usual pace, was at Bautzen on the 3rd, at Schmottseifen on the Queiss on the 7th. Frederick's object was now to effect a junction with his brother before the Russians, who were now quite close to Breslau, could fall on Henry and overwhelm him. Accordingly he moved on (August 9th) to the Katzbach, and on the 10th reached Liegnitz by the left bank of the river, Daun moving along the right. At Liegnitz, Frederick found himself beset by enemies; a move across the Katzbach proved unavailing, and on the 13th he returned to Liegnitz. To the South lay Daun at Jauer, to the South-West, at Goldberg, Lacy, forming Daun's rearguard, to the East, Loudoun at Koischwitz. To cover the despatch of his transport trains to Glogau to replenish his supplies from that ample magazine, Frederick evacuated Liegnitz, leaving all his fires burning (p.m. Aug. 14th), and advanced to the Pfaffendorf Heights, where he meant to encamp and there to await the return of his convoy before pushing through by Parchwitz to join Prince Henry. His men had barely reached the position when about 3 a.m. (August 15th) they were suddenly attacked from the Eastward. The assailants were Loudoun's corps, which in accordance with a scheme already arranged was moving up to seize the same heights and so bar the way to Glogau ; at the same time Daun was to fall on the Prussians from the Southward and Lacy to assail them in flank from Goldberg. Frederick's change of position had upset this scheme, but Loudoun was not the man to draw back. Though taken by surprise, he boldly attacked Frederick's position, which rested on the right on the Katzbach at Panten and was covered on the left by the Hummel Wood. His men had hardly been prepared for the case shot with which they were greeted as they came up in close order, but Loudoun rose to the emergency. He extended his lines to the right and gradually forced the Prussian left back, though they managed to prevent him from turning their flank. Had Daun come up on the Prussian rear at this time and fallen on Ziethen and Wedel, who lay behind the Schwarzwasser, Frederick's position would have been precarious ; but neither Daun nor Lacy put in an appearance. Repeated attacks by Loudoun could thus be met by fresh troops from the Prussian reserves. At last about 6 a.m., seeing no signs of his colleagues, Loudoun drew off in excellent order, having lost 10,000 all told out of some 30,000. It was not his fault that the scheme for the annihilation of the Prussians had miscarried. Indeed, Daun and Lacy were very much to blame. Deceived by Frederick's stratagem of leaving the fires burning in his old camp, they had not discovered his departure till about 2 a.m. They then moved very slowly, never heard the sound of Loudoun's guns as the wind was blowing from the West, and came up to the Schwarzwasser about 5 a.m. to find Ziethen drawn up to receive them. A mild attack by Daun's vanguard was so warmly received by Ziethen, that when Frederick's columns appeared in his support Daun drew off, while Lacy, who had been detached to cross the river higher up, failed to do so. Superior in numbers as he was, Daun ought to have brought Frederick to action. He had been somewhat remiss in letting Frederick get away unobserved ; but his failure to succour Loudoun need not be ascribed to jealousy of his more capable subordinate, his conduct was too much of a piece with his habitual deliberation and want of enterprise to justify that suspicion, but it was a serious error not to have forced on a battle.

Frederick utilised his success with the utmost promptitude. Within four hours of the end of the battle he was moving off towards Parchwitz, having sent a peasant with a message to Prince Henry which he was instructed to let fall into Russian hands. The Russian vanguard under Czernitchev, already across the Oder, alarmed at the prospect of being attacked simultaneously by Henry and Frederick, fell back at once to the safety of the right bank, while Frederick pushed on to Breslau, encamping near that city on the evening of the 19th. Liegnitz had, however, been an escape rather than a victory ;

and, as before, if the Austrians and the Russians had combined vigorously they might have gained a decisive advantage.   But after Loudoun's experience of Daun's co-operation on August 15th, the Russians were very chary of trusting overmuch to the Austrian commander, and he, preferring to out-manœuvre his enemy rather than force him to fight, wasted time on manœuvres which were useless because their object was not the only object which could have been of any real benefit, a decisive pitched battle.   The inactivity of the Russians allowed Frederick to leave 12,000 men under General von Göltz to observe them and to call up the rest of Prince Henry's corps to join him (August 29th), and with his force thus increased to 50,000 men, he was able to foil all Daun's efforts to form the siege of Schweidnitz.   But this was all he could achieve and meanwhile in other quarters the Prussian arms were not over successful.   In Saxony, von Hülsen had been beaten by the much improved Imperial army which had taken Torgau and Wittenberg and practically driven him out of the country.   In Pomerania, Colberg was sore beset by sea and land by a joint force of Swedes and Russians, though towards the end of September a detachment from the corps of von Göltz managed to raise the siege.

It was not much to the credit of Soltikov that von Göltz should have been able to make this detachment in safety, but the Russian general was busy planning a raid on Berlin by 5000 men under Tottleben, supported by Czernitchev's corps.   In this Daun decided to co-operate, and Lacy from near Bunzlau was pushed up by Cottbus to Berlin (Sept. 28th to Oct. 7th).   He found that after a futile bombardment Tottleben had fallen back on the arrival of a corps under Eugene of Würtemberg.   Next day, however, Czernitchev arrived, and despite Hülsen's reinforcing Eugene with his corps from Saxony, the Prussian troops had to evacuate Berlin, which capitulated (Oct. 9th), and to retire to Spandau.   Heavy contributions were exacted from the city, but the raid proved for all practical purposes as barren as that of Hadik in 1757; for on a rumour of Frederick's approach the Allies took their departure, Lacy for Torgau, the Russians for the Oder.

Frederick had indeed broken up from Bunzelwitz on October 7th, and had moved on Berlin, his movements being, as usual, quite unimpeded by the over-cautious Daun; but at Güben he heard that Berlin had been evacuated. He then left von Göltz, reinforced to 20,000 men, in Silesia and moved rapidly into Saxony. He reached the Elbe near Wittenberg (Oct. 26th), crossed and picked up the divisions of Hülsen and Eugene (14,000) next day. Before his approach the Army of the Empire had fallen back from Wittenberg on Leipzig, while Daun had left his old positions (Oct. 7th) and moved to the Elbe by Naumburg (10th) and Ullersdorf. On the 22nd Daun joined Lacy near Torgau and then crossed to the left bank so as to get nearer the Army of the Empire. On the 27th he was at Eilenburg, Frederick moving to Düben (Oct. 29th) and pushing Hülsen out to Leipzig (Oct. 31st), from which the Imperial army retired. Daun thereupon fell back upon his magazines at Torgau (Nov. 1st). Here Frederick resolved to attack him. The Austrian army was ranged between the Suptitz heights, where their right and right-centre lay, and the town of Torgau, which was on their left. In front of the left, formed by Lacy's corps, was a large pond, connected with the Suptitz heights by a stream, the so-called Rohrgraben. For defence against a frontal attack from the South the position was extremely strong, so Frederick, despite the fact that he had under 50,000 men to oppose to Daun's 63,000 with 360 guns, decided on a double attack. Ziethen (18,000) was to advance up the great road from Schilda to Suptitz and attack the heights in front, timing his movements so as to coincide with the appearance on the right rear of the Austrians of the Prussian centre and left, as the result of a wide sweeping movement through the woods to the West by Weidenhayn and Elsnig. Ziethen, having a far shorter distance to go than the turning columns, should have delayed until Frederick was ready; but Frederick was behind time, and the Prussian right coming into touch with Lacy's out-posts swerved to the right towards Torgau and became pre-maturely engaged, only to be beaten off with heavy loss. Meanwhile Daun, whose light troops had informed him of Frederick's flanking movement, had altered his dispositions to meet the attack, forming a new front facing North-West and well provided with guns from the reserve artillery park at Grosswig. Frederick's own division, the innermost of the three columns engaged in the turning movement, was the first to come up, and though alone it advanced to the attack about 2 p.m.; but the heavy fire of the Austrian guns played havoc with the Prussian grenadiers and the attack failed. Hülsen coming up about 3 p.m. was put in with no better success, his men failing to face the guns. Meanwhile nothing had been heard of Frederick's extreme left, which was blundering about in the woods. It arrived about 4.30, just in time to check the Austrians who were following up the repulse of Hülsen's foot, but this success was only temporary. Daun rallied his men, brought up new regiments from his reserve, and when about 7 p.m. he was wounded and had to leave the field, it was with the full assurance of victory. But at last Ziethen came up against the Suptitz heights, on which he should have directed his attack much earlier, and renewed the fight. The Austrians, disordered by their victory and surprised by this unexpected attack, repulsed Ziethen once but he came on again: an undefended causeway over the Rohrgraben was found, and about 8 p.m. the Prussians were in possession of the Weinberg behind Suptitz village and the Austrians were in retreat on Torgau. Both sides had lost heavily, the Prussians somewhat the most, as the failure of their early attacks had cost them in addition some 3000 prisoners. It was a curious action. Frederick's original plan failed because he had not allowed enough time, and because Ziethen did not obey orders. His own attack was premature and disastrous, and, finally, it was only Ziethen's renewed attack in the dusk which turned an imminent defeat into a victory. The Austrians allowed victory to be wrested from them through unsteadiness in the hour of success. Torgau, however, failed to shake the Austrian hold on Saxony. They did retire across the Elbe, but Frederick was in no position to follow up his success, and the end of the campaign saw them in their old positions round Dresden, Frederick wintering at Meissen. In his absence from Silesia nothing had been achieved; the departure of the Russians, the badness of the weather, and his inability to bring von Göltz's corps to action had prevented Loudoun from taking Cosel. Farther North, Werner after relieving Colberg had had a slight success over the Swedes at Pasewalk, which was quite enough to paralyse any Swedish attack on Berlin.

In this year Ferdinand of Brunswick had for once not been able to hold the ground he had won in the previous campaign. Reinforced before the campaign opened by 5 regiments of cavalry and 8 infantry battalions from England, he took the field in May, taking post at Fritzlar with his main body, a detached corps being at Kirchhain on the Ohm and the troops guarding Westphalia between Coesfeld and Hamm. Not till the middle of June did the French, who had a great superiority in numbers, move up from the Main by Giessen. Ferdinand moved South to meet them, but the failure of General Imhoff to hold the pass of Homberg in front of Kirchhain allowed de Broglie to force this barrier and reach Neustadt (June 24th). The French commander now endeavoured to hold Ferdinand in check while St. Germain and the Army of the Rhine were coming up to Corbach to join the Army of the Main. On July 7th de Broglie also marched off towards Corbach, upon which Ferdinand endeavoured to get in between him and his colleague, seize the Sachsenhausen Pass, and so prevent their junction : St. Germain was too swift for him, and Ferdinand's attack was beaten off with considerable loss (July 10th). He fell back to Sachsenhausen, called up Spörcke from Westphalia to Volksmarsen on the Diemel and remained facing the French, who lay to the Westward of him at Corbach. A move against his left he foiled at Emsdorff, where a British dragoon regiment [1] greatly distinguished itself (July 16th); but more serious threats against his communications forced him back to Kalle, on which de Broglie pushed out a corps under de Muy, St. Germain's successor, to Warburg on the Diemel to cut Ferdinand off from Westphalia. This was Ferdinand's chance : he fell on de Muy's corps at Warburg (July 31st) and routed it completely, with a loss of 8000 men, a charge by Lord Granby and the British cavalry deciding the day. He had, however, to evacuate Cassel and take post North of the Diemel covering Westphalia. Here he held de Broglie in check ; but that marshal's superior numbers allowed him to detach strong corps to threaten Brunswick and Hanover along the right bank of the Weser, while Ferdinand could not move against him without exposing the important fortress of Lippstadt. Accordingly as a diversion, Ferdinand detached

[1] 15th Light Dragoons.

MINDEN Aug. 1st 1759

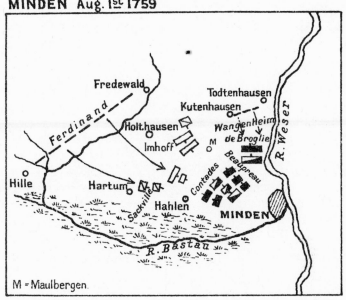

M = Maulbergen.

TORGAU Nov. 3rd. 1760

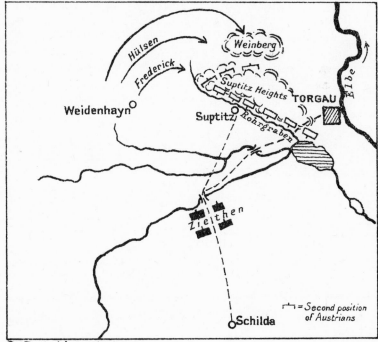

⌐ = Second position of Austrians

B.V. Darbishire, Oxford, 1908.

KUNERSDORF   Aug. 13th 1759.

Finck's Berg
Finck's attack
Kleist Berg
First attack of Prussians
Eisbruch
Mühl Berg
Galitzin
KUNERSDORF
Kuh Berg
Kuh Grund
Tiefe Weg
Willebois
Wedels attack
Prussian Cavalry
Loudoun's Cavalry Stroke
Rumänjev
Spitz Berg
Loudoun's Grund
Fermor
Juden Berg
Loudoun

----Final position of Allies.
+++   "   "   " Prussians
ENGLISH MILES
½   0   1

his nephew, the Hereditary Prince of Brunswick, Prince Charles William Ferdinand, the "Brunswick" of Valmy and Auerstadt, with 47 battalions, 10 of them British, and 30 squadrons, 8 of which were British, to attack the French base, Wesel (Sept. 23rd). The investment of Wesel (Sept. 30th) had the desired effect, for de Broglie detached 32 squadrons and 31 battalions under de Castries to its relief. Crossing at Cologne, October 12th, after a very fine forced march, de Castries came up to Rheinberg (Oct. 15th), and thus forced the Prince, who had only 22 squadrons and 21 battalions available, to move out against him with. A rash attempt to surprise the French at Klostercampen miscarried, and after a sharp fight (Oct. 16th) the Prince found himself compelled to recross the Rhine, raise the siege of Wesel and take post in Westphalia to cover Lippstadt and Münster. Ferdinand thus found himself unable to shake de Broglie's hold on Hesse, and the campaign closed with the Anglo-German army lying North of the Diemel, with Göttingen in French hands and Hanover and Brunswick exposed to their attacks through their possession of the passage of the Weser at Münden.

After a winter which had been spent in the usual abortive discussions about making peace, Daun was once again, much to the annoyance of the Allies, placed in command of the Austrian forces for the campaign of 1761. There was indeed no alternative, for the senior officers of the army would have all refused to serve under one as much their junior as Loudoun or even Lacy, so that these two were both impossible. As before, Daun's plan of campaign was purely defensive; the main army, 100,000 strong, was to gather in Saxony and to confine itself to observing Frederick, while the subsidiary corps under Loudoun in Silesia, reduced to 30,000 men, was to protect Glatz against recapture and to cover Bohemia and Moravia from attack. Loudoun protested vigorously against so preposterous a plan. He saw clearly that it was not "masterly inactivity" but a vigorous offensive which was the true line, that Frederick could be beaten by attrition even if he could not be beaten in the field. His views were warmly supported by Kaunitz; and as Buturlin, the new Russian commander, seemed most anxious for an energetic prosecution of the war, it was arranged that Daun and the main army should "contain"

Frederick in Saxony, while Loudoun with a second army was to operate in Silesia with the assistance of the Russian main body. Colberg was, as before, to be attacked by the Russian fleet and by a detached corps by land. Hardly had this plan been adopted when Frederick, leaving 30,000 men in Saxony under Prince Henry, hurried to Silesia with the rest of his available forces to join von Göltz, whom he thus saved from Loudoun. It seems probable that one of Peter's adherents in the Russian Council had betrayed the plan of campaign to the Grand Duke's favourite hero. Loudoun, however, contrary to expectation, was not compelled to leave Glatz to its fate but maintained his post. With some difficulty he obtained reinforcements from Daun, until by July 19th he had nearly 60,000 men. With these he set out by Frankenstein and Münsterberg, intending to join the Russians, who were creeping up slowly to the Oder along the Polish frontier. Frederick by a rapid march planted himself across Loudoun's path at Neisse (July 23rd), but the Austrian induced his Russian colleague to push on down the Oder and to cross below Breslau, which he did on August 12th. A rapid march brought Loudoun to Liegnitz, and on the 19th a junction was effected near that town. Out-manœuvred in the attempt to prevent the junction, Frederick was reduced to a purely defensive attitude, and took post at Bunzelwitz near Schweidnitz (Aug. 20th). Loudoun urged Buturlin to attack at once before the Prussians could fortify their position; and as the Austrians and Russians had more than double Frederick's force,[1] a prompt attack would have had excellent chances of success. But while Buturlin hesitated, Frederick entrenched himself with feverish haste and the favourable moment passed. Buturlin's hesitation was not unconnected with political considerations. Elizabeth was in a most precarious state of health, at any moment the news might arrive from St Petersburg that she was dead, and it would not be exactly a passport to the new Czar's favour to have just assisted to destroy the last army of Prussia. Accordingly, Loudoun had the mortification of seeing the favourable opportunity escape; and he must have been heartily relieved when, on September 9th, Buturlin departed homewards but left a corps under Czernitchev 16,000 strong behind

[1] Oncken, ii. 326, gives Austrians 83,000, Russians 42,000, Prussians 50,000 : von Arneth, vol. vi., does not put Loudoun above 60,000.

him. Loudoun's enemies had profited by his failure to achieve success even when he had 60,000 men under him to complain bitterly and intrigue against him, and orders had been sent to him to detach 40,000 men to Saxony to enable Daun to take up winter-quarters in Lusatia, when he was able to confront his critics with the capture of Schweidnitz. Want of provisions had forced Frederick to leave Bunzelwitz about September 23rd. He had moved as though to invade Moravia, but he could not draw Loudoun off from Schweidnitz. Detaching light troops to follow and harass Frederick, Loudoun moved on Schweidnitz with 15,000 men and assaulting its somewhat dilapidated works at five places (p.m. Sept. 30th), carried it by storm. By 7 a.m. October 1st, Schweidnitz was for the second time in the war in Austrian hands.[1] This blow checked Frederick's stroke at Moravia, he fell back to Strehlen to cover Breslau, Brieg and Neisse. Loudoun should now have been reinforced by every available man from Daun's army; but instead of this the former plan was carried out on a modified scale, and Loudoun had to detach over 10,000 men to Saxony. Here it is hardly necessary to say Prince Henry had found little difficulty in "containing" the much superior forces of Daun and the Imperial army under Serbelloni. Not even when Loudoun's men came up was he as much as expelled from Saxony. His manœuvres were skilful and did him great credit, but it was to Daun's want of strategic insight that he really owed his escape. One success only the Allies did gain. Colberg, closely blockaded by the Russian fleet, and hard pressed by Rumanjev with 35,000 men, was forced to surrender (Dec. 16th) after Eugene of Würtemberg had failed in a gallant attempt to relieve it. With Colberg much of Pomerania passed into Russian hands.

From the Western theatre of war came news which must have cheered Frederick. An advance into Hesse in February

---

[1] In connection with this episode von Arneth points out how unfair it is to attribute all the non-success of the Austrian arms to the interference of the *Hofkriegsrath* at Vienna with the operations of the generals. That body was concerned with raising recruits and providing supplies for the army, with its administration not with its operations. It was the generals, especially Daun, who continually referred important points to the decision of Maria Theresa and Kaunitz, though they begged the commanders not to do so but to act on their own initiative. Loudoun in this instance acted on his own initiative; and though he thus interfered with a plan arranged at Vienna was not reprimanded in any way.

by which Ferdinand attempted to surprise the French in their winter-quarters, met with great success for a time; but in pressing on to reach a district in which he could feed his troops as he went, he was forced to leave large detachments behind to besiege Cassel and Marburg, and de Broglie concentrating a considerable force at Giessen defeated the Hereditary Prince of Brunswick at Grünberg (March 21) and forced Ferdinand back behind the Diemel. Here he had to await reinforcements and to refresh his exhausted men, while Soubise collected 100,000 men at Wesel and prepared to advance Eastward through Westphalia, de Broglie with 60,000 coming up from Hesse. Not till June 13th did Soubise cross the Rhine, whereon Ferdinand, his army refreshed by ten weeks' rest, moved boldly West to Dortmund to threaten the French communications. This move, indeed, left open the road by which the two French armies could unite; but it startled Soubise, who made no attempt to turn on his enemy, but hastened to Soest to unite with his colleague (July 10th). Their joint force mustered over 100,000; Ferdinand, even after Spörcke's Hanoverians, who had been forcing de Broglie, joined him, had only 60,000; but he stood firm on the Southern bank of the Lippe at Vellinghausen, and the French, finding that before they could take Lippstadt they must beat Ferdinand, attacked him (July 15th to 16th) there, only to be defeated with heavy loss. The brunt of the battle fell on the Allied left, where Granby's corps, mainly British, was posted; but the failure of Soubise to support de Broglie was the chief cause of the defeat. Discontented with each other, the French generals then separated, Soubise returning to Wesel, followed by the Hereditary Prince, de Broglie moving East to threaten Hanover, with Ferdinand after him. As soon as the two marshals were well apart, Ferdinand struck at de Broglie's communications with Frankfort (Aug. 10th), a blow which brought him back from Hameln and Göttingen to Cassel; a second move across the Weser against Hanover was frustrated in the same way (Sept.), while later on again a corps which de Broglie detached to Brunswick (Oct.) was headed back, though he did retain Göttingen. Meanwhile Soubise moved into East Friesland, took Embden and threatened Bremen, but was forced to retire by the Hereditary Prince. Thus for all their twofold superiority in numbers the French achieved nothing in yet another campaign.

But if Frederick had once again reached the end of a campaign without being destroyed, his plight was of the worst. His resources were strained to the utmost, and he had nothing to which he could point as a set-off against Colberg and Schweidnitz. On the other hand, Choiseul's bellicose views were things of the past and he was seeking to bring about peace by means of separate negotiations between England and France. Indeed, he had gone to the length of drawing up a draft treaty with John Stanley, the English agent at Paris, when Stahremberg reminded him that such a treaty, if it left England free to prosecute the war on behalf of Prussia, would be contrary to the most recent Franco-Austrian agreement, that of 1758. This produced a warm conflict between the Allies, Kaunitz having little difficulty in showing that Choiseul's conduct, whether the right policy for France or not, was a breach of her obligations. He would, however, have raised no objection if the peace had debarred both France and England from assisting their old allies, but the negotiations never reached this point. For some time past the relations between England and Spain had been of a strained character, and Choiseul's fertile brain saw in this a chance of throwing the weight of Spain into the colonial and maritime struggle which had gone so badly for France. Pitt, fully aware of the Franco-Spanish negotiations,[1] was anxious to bring matters to a crisis, and placed before his colleagues the definite issue of peace or war. They seized the opportunity of getting rid of him, though it is probable that they were for the most part genuinely convinced of Spain's good intentions. They were undeceived, however, when Spain, the Plate Fleet once safely in, adopted so uncompromising a tone that England had no option but to declare war (Jan. 5th, 1762), whereupon the Anglo-French negotiations were broken off. Choiseul, hoping that the aid of Spain would enable France to retrieve the losses she had sustained, was once more as bellicose as ever, and when Austria made tentative inquiries as to the attitude of France towards a peace, she found her ally inclined to go on with the war. Austria herself was not disinclined to peace. Her resources had been strained to their limits. Every possible financial expedient had been tried, an income-tax, a 10 per cent.

---

[1] The secret treaty was signed August 16th, 1761, but the Spanish declaration of war was deferred until the treasure-ships from Spanish America should be in.

succession-duty, heavy poll-taxes on a graduated scale.[1]   But even so the expenditure far exceeded the revenue, and, much against Lacy's wishes, before the campaign of 1762 every regiment had to be cut down by two companies.

Pitt's fall (Oct. 5th, 1761) was in itself something of an encouragement to Austria.   The new King, George III, had boasted that he was no Hanoverian but "gloried in the name of Briton," and his new minister, Bute, wished to take advantage of the national dislike for paying heavy subsidies to German Princes by getting rid of the continental war.   But any advantage that Austria might have gained in this way was more than balanced by the death, on January 5th, 1762, of the Czarina Elizabeth.   Nothing could have been more timely for Frederick.   The failure of the Russian armies to accomplish all that might have been hoped from them was in no degree due to lack of goodwill or keenness on the part of Elizabeth.   It is partly to be attributed to the inefficient state of the Russian army, especially of its administration, but still more to the fact that the Russian generals were well acquainted with the Grand Duke Peter's enthusiastic admiration for Frederick.[2]   To this admiration Peter proceeded to give practical expression, first by concluding an armistice with Prussia and recalling Czernitchev's corps from Loudoun's army (March), then by making a definite peace (May), evacuating East Prussia altogether without any demand for compensation —which caused much discontent in Russia,—and guaranteeing Silesia to Frederick.   He in return guaranteed Holstein to Peter.   Sweden, whose part in the war had been neither prominent nor very satisfactory to herself, followed her neighbour's example and concluded (May) the Treaty of Hamburg, which restored the *status quo ante bellum*.   The only compensating feature of the situation—from an Austrian point of view—was that all the arguments of the Prussian agents failed to induce Lord Bute to obtain from Parliament a renewal of the subsidy for the King of Prussia.

For the campaign of 1762, Austria gathered two armies, that in Silesia being once again entrusted to Daun, that in Saxony, which was to co-operate with the Army of the Empire,

---

[1] Cf. von Arneth, vi. pp. 255 ff.

[2] Peter III was the son of Anna, daughter of Peter the Great and Charles Frederick of Holstein-Gottorp.

to Serbelloni. But neither the latter nor his Imperialist colleague, Stolberg, proved a match for Prince Henry, who managed to separate them and drive the Imperial army back upon Franconia. Meanwhile Daun was confining his efforts to covering Schweidnitz and Glatz against Frederick, now reinforced by the release, by Peter's orders, of all the Prussian prisoners in Russian hands, and by the return of Czernitchev's corps which Peter declared it was his duty as a Lieutenant-General in the Prussian service to place at Frederick's disposal. When Czernitchev joined him at the end of June, Frederick took the offensive, feinting at Daun's left as though about to invade Bohemia. An attempt by Wied to seize the Adelsdorf position (July 2nd) was parried by Daun, and after some more futile manœuvres Frederick resolved to assault the Austrian positions South of Schweidnitz, between Burkersdorf and Dittmannsdorf. A corps under Wied moved round to the East to attack the Austrian right at Burkersdorf in rear, Möllendorf attacking in front (July 20th). Daun was somewhat remiss in looking after his rear and Brentano, sent up to save Leuthmannsdorf, arrived too late and failed to retake it, the result of which was that Daun fell back towards the Bohemian frontier and left Schweidnitz to its fate. In the action of July 21st, Czernitchev had played a passive but important part: his corps had manœuvred with the rest of Frederick's force, and its conduct had not given any reason to suppose that it was going to move away homewards next day. But yet another change had taken place in Russia. Peter's Germanising tendencies had offended the army and the clergy, his surrender of East Prussia had aroused Russian patriotism and, above all, his treatment of Catherine had offended her so bitterly that she placed herself at the head of a conspiracy which resulted in the deposition (July 9th) and murder (July 19th) of the unfortunate Czar. Catherine, though on the whole favourable to Austria, went no farther than to recall Czernitchev, otherwise she accepted the treaty of May; but short as Peter's reign had been he had managed to do a great deal for Frederick, and among the causes which enabled Prussia to surmount the dangers which threatened her Peter's assistance must take a high place. Entrusting the siege of Schweidnitz, which was begun on August 4th, to General Tauenzien, Frederick took post between Peterswaldau and Seitendorf to cover it. Daun made one attempt to raise the siege, but the failure of Lacy and Brentano to adequately support Beck's headlong onslaught on Bevern's corps at Peilau (Aug. 16th) convinced him that the task was impossible, and he fell back to the Bohemian frontier. Schweidnitz made a resolute defence, and the Prussians lacking skill in siege-craft it was not till October 9th that it surrendered. Daun was much to blame for his inactivity during this period. Exhausted as Austria was, Prussia was equally far spent; and had Daun pushed against Berlin and burnt it, or joined Serbelloni in Saxony and forced a battle on Henry, he might have even at that late hour turned the fortunes of the war, or at the least relieved Schweidnitz. In Saxony there had been a last flicker of military activity. At the end of August the Imperial army which had retired to Baireuth came back to Dresden through Eger and Chemnitz and joined the Austrians. Their advance forced Henry to leave his camp at Pretzchendorf and retire to Rossen (West of Dresden) on October 22nd, but Henry, catching the Army of the Empire isolated at Freiberg (October 29th), inflicted a severe defeat upon it which drove it back to Dippoldiswalde. It was perhaps appropriate that the last battle of the war should have been so typical of the utter collapse of the Imperial fabric, which the Silesian wars had reduced to a condition of all but complete decay.

One set of operations remains to be mentioned. The campaign of 1762 was not the least creditable of those fought by Ferdinand of Brunswick and his able English lieutenant, Granby. As usual, the French had two armies in the field, that of the Main under Soubise (80,000) posted from Altenkirchen by Cassel to Langensalza, that of the Rhine under Condé (30,000) between Cleves and Cologne. Ferdinand was first in the field, moving up to the Diemel early in June; and when Soubise came up to Wilhelmsthal and pushed de Castries forward in front of his right to Carlsdorff, Ferdinand moved against him. The French were already retiring when Granby, coming up from Warburg, fell on the corps of de Stainville, which sacrificed itself to cover the retreat of the main body, and cut it to pieces (June 24th). Soubise retired across the Fulda and took post between Cassel and Lutternberg, but Ferdinand again attacked him (July 24th) with success, and by pressing against his communications drove him out of Hesse before the end of August. Condé now coming up from the Rhine, joined Soubise (Aug. 30th) after beating off the Hereditary Prince, who had followed his movements. The French then moved on Cassel to cut Ferdinand off from that town; but he was too quick for them and, hastening up the Lahn, headed them off at Wetter (Sept. 15th). They fell back and took post along the Ohm, their left at Marburg, their right at Homberg, Ferdinand taking post opposite them. They made one attempt to force a passage by the bridge of Amöneburg (Sept. 21st); but though the attack was pushed home bravely, Granby's division (2 cavalry regiments and 8 infantry battalions) came up to the succour of Zastrow's Hanoverians and beat off every attack. It was the last offensive movement of the French in the war. Cassel, blockaded by Ferdinand as he moved South, was now (Oct. 16th) regularly invested. On November 1st it fell, and in a fortnight came the news that an armistice had been concluded.

When it became obvious that not only was no more help to be expected from Russia, but that France was going to conclude a peace with England upon terms which would leave Maria Theresa isolated, even the Empress Queen resigned herself to relinquishing the attempt to recover the province filched from her in 1741. Glatz, it is true, was still in her hands; but she recognised that its retention was not worth the expense of another campaign, and while much of Saxony was still in Frederick's hands, the French had thrown away the trump-card in the diplomatic struggle by evacuating Prussia's Rhenish provinces without handing them over to Austria. It was a step of which Maria Theresa had good right to complain, for the advantages which the Allies had won were thus sacrificed without any equivalent. About the same time that preliminaries were signed at Fontainebleau between England and the Bourbon Powers, negotiations were opened between Austria and Prussia through the channel of Augustus III, the King of Poland being empowered to take advantage of Austria's pacific dispositions to get such terms as he could for his distressed Electorate. Under this cloak, Austrian dignity was to some extent spared the humiliation involved in the evacuation of Glatz, on which Frederick absolutely insisted. Finally, after long negotiations the Peace of Hubertsberg (Feb. 15th, 1763) restored the arrangements of the

19

Berlin Treaty of 1745. Saxony recovered her lost territories, but Maria Theresa's efforts to regain Silesia had proved altogether unsuccessful. The only concession that could be extorted from Frederick was a promise of the Brandenburg vote at the election of a King of the Romans to Maria Theresa's eldest son, Joseph.

Thus in the end Prussia emerged without any territorial loss from a war in which with better management the Austrian schemes against her might have easily been brought to a successful conclusion, a war in which the star of the Hohenzollern monarchy had seemed on several occasions to be about to be permanently eclipsed; the great struggle left her exhausted and heavily burdened indeed, but with the prestige of having beaten off the attacks of an apparently invincible coalition. The credit for this result belongs very largely to Frederick himself. His only right to the possession of Silesia lay in his power to take and to keep it ; but in enforcing the doctrine that might is right he had displayed a vigour, a tenacity, a courage in the most desperate extremities, which go far towards redeeming his case. If he could not plead, as Maria Theresa had been able to plead in 1741, that he was being attacked without just cause, he could at least claim the sympathy that naturally attaches to the weaker side, even though had he succumbed in the struggle he would have only had himself to thank for having originally provoked the contest. If his strategy and tactics were by no means free from serious error, and if he owed his escape very largely to the deficiencies of his enemies ; their errors, their slowness, their hesitation, their failure to bring on the pitched battles by which alone the contest could be decided, only serve to show up in favourable light the opposite qualities of resolution, promptitude and vigour which marked the operations of Frederick. One man alone upon the Austrian side can be put upon a level with the Prussian King, and Loudoun never had the opportunity to give full scope to the talents which he was able to show that he possessed. He almost alone among the opponents of Frederick seems to have realised that a vigorous offensive would reduce the Prussian monarch to his last gasp far sooner than all the out-manœuvring in the world ; that a policy of attrition by pitched battles was the true strategy ; that the Allies could better afford to lose men or

battles than Frederick could. Time after time Frederick was
allowed to recover from blows which if promptly followed up
must have been fatal. Moreover, Frederick was better served
by his allies than was Maria Theresa by hers. If Daun
deserves to be called slow and unenterprising, what is to be
said of Apraxin and Fermor? Soltikov too, if an improvement on his predecessors, was quite as much to blame as
Daun for the failure of the Allies' plans. Nevertheless, despite
the inefficiency of her generals, Russia did actually play the
deciding part in the war. Elizabeth's death was without
question the decisive event of the long struggle: had she
lived Frederick, if deprived of England's subsidy, could hardly
have survived the campaign of 1762. As it was, Peter's short
reign was just long enough for him to save Frederick, if in
so doing he brought about his own fall. The part of France in
the continental war was inglorious and ineffectual. Her armies
received check after check from the altogether inferior forces
of Ferdinand of Brunswick, whose reputation was as much
enhanced by the war as that of Loudoun himself. Not one
of her generals rose above mediocrity, most fell much below
that level. Richelieu failed to pursue the advantages won in
the only pitched battle of the war which resulted in a French
success, but he did just enough to show the vast importance
to Frederick of the work of the Anglo-Hanoverian army of
Western Germany. In bringing that force together, maintaining it in the field, paying and supplying it, England, though
at the same time achieving ends of her own, did Frederick
a service of incalculable value. The rancour with which
Frederick regarded his former ally and paymaster may be
taken as some measure of the importance to him of Bute's
departure from the policy of Pitt.[1] Indeed, paradoxical and
somewhat exaggerated as the statement may sound, it may
almost be said that it was France which saved Frederick by

[1] The question of Bute's policy towards Frederick belongs rather to the English
side of the Seven Years' War. For refusing to continue the subsidy Bute had a fair
case, especially in view of the intervention of Spain, and after the death of the
Czarina Frederick was no longer in danger. But Frederick had some reason for his
belief that Bute had meant to leave him in the lurch, and in the course of the Anglo-
French negotiations the relations between England and Prussia became greatly
strained. In the end, however, it was England which secured the restoration to
Frederick of his Westphalian territories, and such cause for complaint as Frederick
had was rather against the manner in which Bute had conducted his measures than
against his actual actions.

taking an active part in the coalition against him. It was because France was attacking Hanover that England had to take active steps on behalf of Frederick. Had Hanover been neutralised and the French share in the war confined to the fulfilment of the obligations contracted in 1756, it is not likely that a single English soldier would have set foot on German soil, or that English money would have found its way into Frederick's coffers.

But if Frederick must be considered fortunate in having weathered the storms of the Third Silesian War, his prestige and the whole position of Prussia not only in Germany but in Europe were enormously enhanced by the result. If Prussia was still second to Austria in Germany, her position far more nearly approached to that of Austria than it did to that of Bavaria, or Hanover, or Saxony. She was not only a practically independent state, for so were they to all intents and purposes, but she was a factor of principal importance in the affairs of Europe, while they were only subordinates, accessories, minor members of alliances. Austria's position in Germany had not indeed been directly assailed by Prussia. Frederick had not sought to substitute the Hohenzollern for the Hapsburgs as the leading power in Germany. It can hardly be said that there was any " German " side to his policy. He aimed at independent political existence. In his relations with the minor states of Germany he sought at the most to prevent Austria reviving the old Imperial forms with which she was still invested. It may be argued that in a way he was fighting the battle of the German Princes, inasmuch as success in the humiliation and partition of Prussia would have altogether altered the footing on which Austria stood in relation to the other members of the Empire; but even so to fight for the independence of the German Princes was not to fight for Germany or for German nationality. On the contrary, it still further increased, if possible, the disunion of Germany and the decay of the Empire. To a certain extent, no doubt, German sentiment rejoiced in the defeat of the French at Rossbach. That rejoicing, however, was mainly due to the misconduct of the French, whose indiscipline, exemplified in rapacity and marauding, made them hateful to the inhabitants of the countries they visited. There were no such rejoicings over Leuthen or Torgau. The re-establishment of

Austrian rule in Silesia was not unpopular, nor did the Silesian peasantry indulge in guerilla warfare against the Austrians. The Prussian plundering incursions into Thuringia and other parts of the Empire roused the bitterest resentment and dislike, and if the army of the Empire failed to do any damage to the Prussian cause, it is not necessary to attribute that to goodwill towards Frederick. The Würtemberg contingent in the Austrian army in 1757 was notorious for the desertions from its ranks, but they deserted to avoid taking part in a war about which they did not care, not because they saw in Frederick the champion of oppressed German nationality. Desertion was rife in both armies, and was hardly ever, except in the case of the Saxons forcibly drafted into the Prussian ranks,[1] sentimental or political. It was always practical, due to want of food, to want of pay, to hardships of one sort or other. The only real effect of the war on Germany was to complete the utter disintegration of the German kingdom which had suffered so much through its association with the Holy Roman Empire. Germany was yet to drain the cup of humiliation to the dregs ; but that Germany was trampled under foot by the Corsican upstart until at last her sufferings aroused the slumbering sense of German nationality and German unity, was in no small measure due to the fact that the Silesian wars had destroyed all possibility of the Hapsburg House reuniting Germany under its leadership or breathing new life into the moribund fabric of the Empire, and that the Revolution found her a mere geographical expression, no less devoid of unity than Italy itself.

[1] Cf. p. 199, footnote.

CHAPTER XIV

AUSTRIA AND PRUSSIA AFTER THE WAR AND THE PARTITION OF POLAND

ON the restoration of peace the first object to which Frederick turned was the repairing of the ravages of the war. It was no light task. Not only had the provinces which had been the theatre of war been plundered and swept bare by the contending armies, but even the districts which had escaped the presence of the belligerents had been drained dry of men and money to enable the King to prosecute the struggle. Frederick promptly dismissed some 30,000 of his troops, sending them back to till the fields; he disposed of his cavalry and artillery horses to the farmers; the war-chest which had been replenished by great efforts for the campaign he had not had to fight disgorged its contents, which were sparingly and prudently distributed to relieve the most pressing needs. The war had, of course, been paid for in large part by the contributions exacted from countries he had overrun, above all from the luckless Saxony, by the large subsidies from England, by depreciating the coinage, which was now redeemed at only one-fifth of its face value, and by withholding their salaries from the civil servants of the state. They had been paid in promissory notes, which Frederick now proceeded to pay off in the depreciated currency at its nominal not its real value. It was a characteristic act, a gross piece of injustice which meant ruin to a good many overworked and underpaid officials, but a successful stroke, for it materially reduced the claims upon the Prussian exchequer.

The measures which Frederick took at this time to promote agriculture and industry, to attract colonists to the depopulated provinces, to increase home products and make Prussia independent of foreign countries, especially of Polish corn, do not differ in kind from the similar steps taken by his father.[1]

Cf. Chapter V.

Roads, bridges, canals and other public works were undertaken. Extensive reclamations of waste and swampy lands added nearly 1500 square miles to the cultivatable area of the kingdom. A rigid policy of protection unsparingly enforced did much to establish in Prussia industries hitherto unknown. The production and manufacture of silk and cotton goods, the promotion of the woollen industry by prohibiting the export of the raw material, while sheep farming was encouraged by the introduction of Spanish sheep, the offer of bounties to attract the skilled workmen of other countries to Prussia, were all part of an economic policy based on the principles of the Mercantile System and enforced with a thoroughness few other monarchs could rival. Commerce it was not Frederick II's policy to foster. In his eyes the future of Prussia was not on the sea; and although Embden, acquired in 1744, was made a free port and the tolls on the Oder were lowered for the benefit of Stettin, he looked rather to the creation of a self-centred, self-sufficing State, producing a large revenue and capable of supporting a large army. The effect of his economic policy on the social conditions of the kingdom served to accentuate the spirit of militarism he did so much to foster. Apart from the *Ritterpferd* which he maintained [1] the nobles were as a class exempt from taxation; and this distinction did much to perpetuate class barriers, to keep down the townsfolk and the peasantry, whom Frederick looked upon merely as tax and recruit producers, and to prevent them from uniting. Moreover, the political condition of Prussia assisted to repress the tax-paying classes. Absolutism had been made the guiding principle by Frederick William I; Frederick II did not in the least diminish his hold on power. Not even the nobles shared to any extent in the administration of the country. It was in the hands of a well-organised, centralised bureaucracy, efficient but unsympathetic. Throughout the country, from the bailiffs who administered the Domains through the *Landräthe*, who, like the Sheriffs in mediæval England, kept the peace, attended to the levy of contributions and acted as the King's agent in their district, and the tax commissioners who were responsible for the excise and the police, to the members of the General Directory itself, all the officials were the King's

[1] In 1745 he allowed it to be capitalised and redeemed.

servants, owing their appointments to him, responsible to him alone. The defects of the system were not, of course, apparent, whilst the man on whom the supreme direction of affairs devolved was as resolute, as vigorous and as efficient as Frederick, but the burden he could bear was too much for a less capable successor. His ministers, depending entirely on him and accustomed to look to him for orders rather than decide even minor points on their own responsibility, were clerks and subordinates rather than administrators, and the removal of his guiding hand was followed by the breakdown of the system he had inherited from his father and had handed on unchanged in the main though improved in details. He had been vigilant and strong enough to check corruption and peculation, but those inherent defects of an over-centralised and underpaid bureaucracy proved too much for an inefficient wielder of the central power.

In the organisation established in 1723 Frederick II did not make many changes. The Directory, originally organised in four departments on a territorial basis, was increased by separate departments for trade and manufactures and for military affairs. The Provincial Chambers formed the links between the Directory and the local *Landräthe* and tax commissioners. Foreign affairs were entrusted to an altogether separate department, · including usually two or three ministers, one of whom was of special importance, and may be looked upon as the chief. Similarly the War Council (*Geheime Kriegs Rath*) was quite a distinct body. In the reform of justice and the judicial system, Frederick did rather more. Aided by von Cocceji, head of the Department of Justice since 1738, he sought to grapple with the expenses and delays of litigation, the collusion and corruption of solicitors and assessors, and the overcrowded state of the judicial bench. In 1746 the control over justice, hitherto exercised by the Directory, was transferred to the special legal Department. Procedure was abridged to expedite litigation. The number of the judges was reduced, and good jurists appointed at adequate salaries. Arrears of work were systematically tackled by Cocceji, province by province, and were cleared off. The Common Law was codified, and the confusion arising from the mixture of Roman, Teutonic, and barbarian laws materially reduced, the new code being based on Roman law, but modified to suit the social system of Prussia. Subordinated to the Department of Justice was the *Consistorium*, a body which looked after education and religious affairs; but Frederick, himself practically a Free Thinker, was not the kind of man to pay overmuch attention to the latter subject. The only important step he took in this respect was the establishment of religious toleration for practically all creeds, the Jews alone being still subjected to very considerable restrictions.

Frederick's system was one which bore heavily on most classes of his subjects. Taxation was heavy, and the partial exemption enjoyed by the nobles therefore all the more emphasised their position as a separate caste marked off from the rest of the nation by social and fiscal privileges. The lot of the peasantry was far from easy. If not exactly slaves, they were certainly not free, being *ascripti glebæ* and as such liable to change masters with the estates to which they belonged. Not only had they to pay a quite disproportionate share of the taxes, but it was from them that the recruits were drawn under the cantonment system. They had to spend much of their time working for their lords, to hand over to them a large part of the produce of their labour, and to perform personal and menial services. Nor was it, as a rule, possible for a peasant to better his station in life. Frederick, while realising to some extent the evils of the situation, refrained from making any attempt to alter them, for fear apparently of in any way subverting the rigid discipline on which the Prussian state was based.

This rigid discipline was felt as much by civilian officials as by soldiers. The Civil Service was so harshly and vigorously treated that it was not wonderful that it was not popular. The absolutism of the King and the cramping fetters of official routine left no scope for the development of individual initiative and efficiency. The machine of the Prussian administration happened to be efficient under Frederick II, but the efficiency was due to external impulses and not to any inherent quality. Lacking in organic vitality, it derived its efficiency from the King's vigilant and inspiring personality; left to itself it was bound to perish under the weight of its own routine. It has been well described as

" an organised bureaucracy with a numerous personnel, with roots and branches shooting in every direction, with a code of procedure that provided for nearly every problem that might arise and a system of discipline that kept all the parts in a state of harmonious subjection." Yet with all these good qualities it was a mere machine, it needed a master hand to guide it.

Not dissimilar were the conditions which prevailed in the Army. Here again there was a rigidly enforced uniformity, a highly organised administration, a system which, in the thirty years of peace that intervened before it was again engaged in any serious war, was allowed to become the end in itself and not the means. The parade-ground was allowed to obscure the battlefield, and when Lord Cornwallis visited the Prussian manœuvres in 1785 he found that the practical had been sacrificed to a precision carried to the verge of pedantry.[1] The deep gulf fixed between officers and men might help to make the maintenance of due subordination more easy, but it was detrimental to true cohesion, and the savage discipline needed to keep in proper subjection an army mainly composed of foreign mercenaries to a certain extent defeated its own ends. Worst of all was the fact that so large a proportion of the men were not subjects of the King they served. This made the Army non-national; and though Frederick II, who had the gift of leadership and of getting the last ounce of work out of all his subordinates, Ministers of State and privates of foot alike, did manage to keep his men together by a belief in him and by the glamour of his reputation, his successors had no such qualities. But after 1763 the Prussian army was resting on its well-earned laurels. There was no other army on the Continent which could compare with it, and the defects which were to prove fatal to it in 1792 and 1806 had yet to develope to their full extent.

Like her enemy Frederick, Maria Theresa was also engaged on the task of reconstruction. She had failed in the purpose she had set before her, she had been forced to leave Silesia in Prussian hands and to acquiesce in the failure of the plans so carefully laid and matured. Yet in some respects Austria's position in 1763 was not as bad

[1] Cf. his letter to Colonel Ross, *Cornwallis Correspondence*, i. 212.

as might have been expected. The war had cost her dear in men and in money, but a large part of the expense had been defrayed by the French subsidies, and since the abortive invasion of Moravia in 1758 the Austrian territories had escaped being the theatre of war. Her provinces were therefore, at any rate when compared with the miserable condition of Saxony, East Prussia, Silesia and Westphalia, in a fairly flourishing state, and when once the excessive burdens imposed during the war were removed their condition improved rapidly.

But the war had been a severe trial to the civil and military organisation of Austria, and in several directions further changes in the system remodelled by Haugwitz were shown to be necessary. Of these the most important was the establishment (1758), at the suggestion of Kaunitz, of a Council of State to advise the sovereign, and so secure a more efficient supervision of the whole administration than the Directory had so far provided. This Council was to be composed of leading men of great experience and influence in the state rather than merely of the heads of the various departments of the government, though the Chancellor was to be a member *ex officio*. It was to advise and supervise, not to execute, and foreign and military affairs did not come within its province, while the non-German provinces were not subjected to it.[1] Haugwitz, whom Chotek succeeded as Court Chancellor (*Obersthofkanzler*), and Count Henry Blümegen, afterwards to be one of Joseph II's principal subordinates, were the chief members of the new Council, and the young Archduke Joseph was constantly present at its discussions.

Soon after the Peace of Hubertsburg the election of Joseph as King of the Romans, defeated on a former occasion by Prussian opposition, was brought to a successful conclusion. Frederick was pledged to vote for Joseph by the terms of the Peace, Hanover had all along favoured his election, the ecclesiastical Electors could easily be secured by a small outlay, and Saxony was the close ally of Austria. Any opposition that Bavaria or the Palatinate felt inclined to offer was removed by various promises and slight concessions, and the election was unanimous.

Despite the disappointment of the high hopes Maria

[1] Wolf, p. 96.

Theresa had based upon the new alliance with the House of Bourbon, it was now one of her principal objects to maintain that alliance, and if possible to draw it closer by a series of marriages between members of the Bourbon and the Hapsburg families. Thus Joseph had married Isabella of Parma, and on her death at the early age of twenty-one, in November 1763, it was suggested that he should marry another Princess of the same family, while three of the Archduchesses were married to Bourbon Princes, Caroline to Ferdinand of Naples in April 1768, Amelia to Ferdinand of Parma in 1769, Marie Antoinette to the Dauphin, afterwards Louis XVI of France, in 1770. Even more political importance attached to the marriage of the Archduke Leopold, the second surviving son of the Empress, to the Infanta Louise, daughter of Charles III of Spain, as it was agreed that the Emperor should hand over to Leopold the Duchy of Tuscany, all claims on which Joseph resigned. The wedding had only just been celebrated at Innsbruck when, on August 18th, 1765, the Emperor was suddenly smitten by an apoplectic seizure and died. Francis Stephen of Lorraine is a man who plays a prominent part in history through the accident of his marriage to Maria Theresa rather than by reason of his own very mediocre capacities. Neither as a statesman nor as a general did he distinguish himself, and Maria Theresa's excessive grief and extravagant praise of his virtues cannot hide the fact that he had never been in himself a person of much weight. The Empress seems for a time to have contemplated retiring into a convent and handing all power over to her son, who styled himself Emperor from the moment of his father's death, and whom she now took into partnership with her as joint ruler (Dec. 1765). But this idea did not last long, and Maria Theresa soon again assumed the reins of government, though sharing her power with her son and to a great extent with Kaunitz. Seeing how completely Joseph's views on most questions of importance differed from his mother's, she conservative, religious to the verge of bigotry, aristocratic in sentiment, well versed in affairs and well acquainted with men, he an ardent reformer, tolerant and broad-minded, almost indifferent in religious matters, a tactless doctrinaire unable to distinguish the practical from the unwise, it is much to his credit that they should have worked together as smoothly as they did and should have got on so well. Causes of friction were frequent, several big differences occurred, but Joseph always preferred to give way to his mother's opinion rather than cause a deadlock by persisting in his own, even when thoroughly convinced of its justice. Kaunitz, too, had a difficult task. The strongest ties of regard, affection and gratitude bound him to the mistress he had served so faithfully and by whom he had always been implicitly trusted. To have to intervene as a third party between the Empress and her son, especially as on many matters he agreed with Joseph, was no pleasant task, but on the whole he came out of the ordeal with great success.

Joseph was not slow about setting out on a career of reforms. He cut down the establishment, the ceremonial and the expenses of the Court, gave up the vast hunting establishment left by his father, turned the Prater into a public park, devoted the private fortune bequeathed to him by his father to assist in the conversion of the debt and the reduction of the interest from five to four per cent. Such were the economies he effected that by 1775 the revenue not only balanced the expenses, but there was actually a surplus of five and a half million gulden, a condition of affairs almost unprecedented in Austria.

In the ranks of the Ministers several changes occurred about this time. Haugwitz had died in 1765, Chotek, his successor as *Hofkanzler*, in 1771, on which Hatzfeldt became the minister next in importance to Kaunitz. Kolowrat succeeded Hatzfeldt at the Treasury; and when, in the hope of securing unity in the administration, Hatzfeldt was made President of the Council of State, the post of *Hofkanzler* was given to Henry Blümegen. In the reform of the army, Joseph was keenly interested. Daun had already in 1762 replaced Joseph Harrach at the head of the War Council, and did good service till his death in 1765. Joseph thereupon appointed Lacy to the vacant post, thereby passing over some thirty other officers, among them Loudoun, certainly Lacy's superior on the field of battle. But administration was Lacy's province, and he did excellent work in improving the organisation, drill and equipment of the army, establishing a definite General Staff, attending to fortifications and bringing the Supply Department properly under the control of the War Council. These reforms were of the greatest benefit to the army, but they led to collisions with the civil authorities and even with the Emperor, and in 1774 Lacy retired, being replaced by Andreas Hadik.

But while doing all this as head of the Hapsburg dominions, Joseph was at heart even more anxious to revive the Empire and to galvanise it into fresh life. The task was an all but hopeless one, but it does seem that there is no small truth in the remark that " Joseph was a Lorrainer, not a Hapsburg." If that saying implies that Joseph's great desire was to be able to restore the Empire to a really active and working condition, it is probably right. A study of his foreign policy [1] does seem to show that it was on the Upper rather than on the Lower Danube that his hopes centred. Bavaria meant more to him than the Balkans. But the Aulic Council (*Reichshofrath*) was a poor weapon with which to effect great reforms, and the Imperial Court (*Hofgericht*) was dilatory and negligent and treated its office as a mere source of profit. The condition of the *Reichskammergericht* at Wetzlar was no better. Hopelessly corrupt and inefficient, it had let cases accumulate till in 1772 over 60,000 were waiting to be decided: one case in particular had been going on for a hundred and eighty-eight years. Joseph ordered a Visitation (May 1767), the first since 1588, but it could do little good. It was not of much use to dismiss indolent and corrupt officials when the root of the matter lay in the complete collapse of the Empire. It had practically ceased to exist, and in its stead were numerous small states more or less independent, too small for any real national life of their own, too independent to allow of any united national life, while the more powerful among them devoted all their energies towards self-aggrandisement in every possible way. It may be argued that under Joseph II Austria was just as ready to grasp at any scrap of territory on which she could lay her hands as was any other Power. The accusation is in large measure true; but in seeking to increase his dominions in Germany, Joseph was acting as Emperor, as representative of the unity—such as it was—of Germany, not merely as the head of his family, or even as one among the "great

[1] Cf. Chapter XV,

Powers" of Europe. He was striving to restore reality to the historic position which he held.

The first country whose affairs claimed the attention of Germany after the close of the Silesian Wars was its unhappy neighbour on the East, Poland. In October 1763, Augustus II of Saxony-Poland had died. Neither as the enemy nor as the ally of Austria had he had much success. His Electorate, the buffer state between the contending forces of the Hapsburgs and the Hohenzollern, had suffered enormously in the wars: his Kingdom had served as the base for the operations of the Russians, and its condition was but little better. His death was probably accelerated by the disasters and disappointments he had gone through, and it was followed in December by that of his successor, Frederick Christian. Thus, not only was the Polish throne vacant, but the Saxon House was unable to put forward a candidate for the vacancy, since the heir to Saxony, Augustus, son of Elector Frederick Christian, was only twelve years old. Austria now found herself in an awkward situation. She strongly approved of the presence of the Saxon dynasty at Warsaw, since her interests were best served when the Polish throne was occupied by a Prince independent of Russia and not over friendly with Prussia. Despite the alliance with France, she rather distrusted the extraordinary intrigues by which Louis XV sought to obtain the Polish throne for the Prince de Conti. Still she was unable to find a suitable candidate to oppose to Stanislaus Poniatowski, the Polish nobleman whom Russia with the support of Prussia now put forward. Poniatowski's candidature was not altogether popular in Poland. The Czartoriski family with which he was connected was the main strength of the Russophil faction, and the opponents of this faction would probably have been prepared to resist his election had Austria and France shown themselves ready to support such resistance. But Maria Theresa had had enough of war: she did not mean to appeal to arms again if she could help it, and her diplomacy was henceforward greatly hampered by this unwillingness to fight. Austria and France accordingly had to content themselves with the empty protest of withdrawing their representatives from Warsaw, and in September 1764, Poniatowski was duly elected. His election was really a triumph for Russia, for Frederick had played a somewhat subordinate part, and the overtures he before long made to Austria may be interpreted as a recognition of the dangers with which Germany was threatened by the undue aggrandisement of her formidable Eastern neighbour. It was clearly Russia's policy to absorb Poland if she could, failing that to subject the Republic completely to her influence. Neither of these courses would have been to Frederick's liking, since both would put barriers in the way of his acquisition of the coveted district of West Prussia. But apart from this, it was certainly not to his advantage or to Austria's that Russia should become predominant in Poland. Had Austria and Prussia combined to set the Polish constitution on a rational basis and to help Poniatowski, who showed himself less amenable to Russian authority than had been expected, to assert and maintain his independence, Poland might have been made an efficient " buffer state " against the Russian advance; but Silesia barred the way to a reconciliation and Frederick's aims were to be attained by the disintegration of Poland rather than by its revival. Moreover, Maria Theresa's religious bigotry caused her to look with disfavour on the proposal to remove the disabilities of the Dissidents, one of the main causes of Polish disunion. She would have been glad to unite with France to guarantee the integrity of Poland, but she distrusted Frederick too much to co-operate with him in anything and she was specially anxious to prevent him gaining any influence over Joseph, who was already somewhat inclined to hold sceptical and cynical views of political and religious affairs.

Meanwhile the troubles of Poland culminated in conflicts between the adherents of the Greek Church and of the Catholic religion. The attempt of Stanislaus to abrogate the *Liberum Veto* was foiled by Russian opposition (Nov. 1766), and in the following year the Russophil party formed the Confederation of Radom, terrified the Diet into accepting certain modifications of the constitution and appointed Catherine its guardian. In reply, the Catholics, led by Marshall Krasinski, formed the Confederation of Bar. Religious riots on a large scale followed, and practically the whole country was plunged into civil war. Russian troops intervened on behalf of their partisans and, in pursuing some Polish fugitives, violated the frontier of Turkey. France had already been urging the Porte to send assistance to the Poles, and the Turks were not slow to declare war (Oct. 1768). One important result was that Austria, wishing to observe strict neutrality, guarded her frontier with a strong military cordon, while to prevent disputes the frontier was marked out by a line of posts bearing the Austrian eagles. The opportunity was taken to include inside these limits the district of Zips, formerly part of Hungary which had been pledged to Lladislaus Jagellon by the Emperor Sigismund. The reoccupation of this district, geographically part of Hungary since it took Poland over the Carpathians, was carried out with Stanislaus Poniatowski's full agreement; but at Joseph's orders the line of demarcation included Sandez, Neumarkt and Csorsztyn, which were also claimed as part of Hungary.

The situation called forth from Kaunitz a characteristically ingenious plan for the recovery of Silesia. An alliance was to be formed between Austria, Prussia and Turkey to save Poland and check the Russian advance. Poland was to provide the "satisfaction" for Prussia, which in return for her good offices was to receive Courland and West Prussia but to surrender Silesia to Austria, while Turkey would find her share of the benefits of the alliance in getting safely through a war which from the very start had gone ill with her. This plan, however, was too revolutionary and too chimerical to commend itself; Maria Theresa and even Joseph hated the notion of any alliance with Prussia. Still, Kaunitz saw that if Austria did not mean to give actual support to Turkey, and of this there was no intention, the only possible course was joint action with Prussia; and as the result of his persistent advocacy of this course there occurred the celebrated interviews between Joseph and Frederick at Neisse in August 1769 and at Neustadt in the following year. Frederick used all the arts of which he was master to flatter and cajole the young Emperor, whose admiration for the re-nowned Prussian King was far from being to the liking of Maria Theresa. No immediate results followed, however, except that Frederick saw he need not fear Austrian opposition.

Meanwhile the danger of war was increasing. The Russian successes against the Turks continued, and Austria collected a large force in Hungary ready to fall on the communications of the Russians should they advance across the Danube. In July 1771, Thugut, Austria's representative at Constantinople, con-

20

cluded a convention with Turkey by which Austria undertook
to save Turkey from a peace on humiliating terms. In return
she was to receive Little Wallachia and a large subsidy.
Maria Theresa objected strongly to the transaction, for which
Joseph and Kaunitz were really responsible. She refused to
ratify it, feeling that it compromised Austria's dignity, took
an unfair advantage of a Power which had acted most
honourably in Austria's hour of need in 1741, and also fearing
that it would lead to war. It was to this prospect that
Frederick also objected. He did not wish to be involved in a
war against Austria and Turkey on behalf of Russia, nor was
he anxious to see Austria and Russia arrive at an understanding. It was quite a possibility that Austria might induce
Russia to content herself with moderate gains, and might
obtain these concessions from Turkey, and that then Russia
and Austria might firmly oppose any partition of Poland,
thereby preventing Frederick from acquiring the much-coveted
West Prussia. For a partition was the expedient by which
Frederick sought to extricate the three Powers from their
dilemma. It would hardly be profitable to follow the complicated intrigues, proposals and counter-projects in detail.
The idea of a partition was not, of course, new. Maximilian II
in 1573, Charles X of Sweden in 1657, Alberoni, even
Augustus II of Saxony in 1733, had suggested schemes for it;
but Frederick and his brother Prince Henry[1] were responsible
for bringing it forward now. Catherine disliked it as preventing her from absorbing all Poland; it was only with real and
sincere reluctance that Maria Theresa at last listened to the
urgent advocacy of it by Kaunitz and Joseph. Russia had
forborne to push her successes across the Danube for fear of
Austrian intervention; she was ready to relinquish Moldavia
and Wallachia if compensation could be found in Poland.
But when Austria proposed that the Czarina should, in consideration of Austria's mediation of a peace between her and
Turkey, support Austria in resisting any division of Poland,
Catherine declined to accept the proposal, and Kaunitz found
that the Czarina and Frederick were already in practical
agreement, and that they had no intention of letting go those
portions of Poland which they had resolved to annex. It would
appear that this had been settled as early as February 1771

[1] Cf. Mirabeau, *Secret History of the Court of Berlin*, i. 312.

when Prince Henry visited Catherine. In November, Frederick informed van Swieten, the Austrian envoy to Berlin, that Russia intended to take compensation for the Danubian Principalities at the expense of Poland. In December, Austria learnt definitely that Frederick meant to annex West Prussia as his share. The only problem, since it was out of the question for Austria to prevent the Partition, as Choiseul had fallen and England was fully occupied across the Atlantic, was whether she should join the spoilers or mark her disapproval of their action by protests. There was no question in the minds of Joseph and Kaunitz. Their "land hunger" was almost worthy of a Hohenzollern. The balance of power must be maintained; Austria could not afford to stand aside when her neighbours were making territorial gains. The doctrine of compensation by equivalents was a specious cloak for greed. Even Maria Theresa would have raised no objection to the annexation of West Prussia if Frederick would have resigned Glatz and part of Silesia, a concession he refused to contemplate. To sharing in the Partition she was strongly opposed, and indignantly repudiated the charge that Austria had begun the spoliation of Poland by the occupation of Zips. Superficially, of course, this would seem to be the case, but there was a great difference between the reoccupation of a small piece of territory, Poland's right to which was certainly disputable, and wholesale annexations amounting to a third of the whole country. At the same time it was unfortunate that the pretext should have been given to people who knew how to use it as well as Frederick and Catherine did.

In February 1772 the Russian Ambassador definitely invited Austria's co-operation in the treaty of partition arranged by Frederick and Catherine, intimating that Austria's action would in no case affect the resolve of these two contracting parties. At this Maria Theresa yielded with the greatest reluctance and unwillingness, whereupon it was discovered that Galicia had formerly been part of Hungary, and a formal claim was produced. Kaunitz as usual claimed more than he dreamt of getting in order not to get less than he hoped; but Joseph, taking over the direction of the affair, marched troops into the districts he meant to have, and thus secured what he wanted. On August 2nd, 1772, the treaty of partition was signed at St. Petersburg, and on September 26th Austria published a proclamation annexing Galicia. Poland was powerless to resist, and in September 1773 bribery coupled with threats of violence wrung from the reluctant Diet its consent to the scheme. Kaunitz would have been glad to take the opportunity to make certain reforms in the Polish constitution, notably the abolition of the *Liberum Veto*, and to add to the Royal revenues by secularising certain bishoprics; but these suggested improvements of the condition of the Republic were not at all to the liking of Russia and Prussia, and though in the next fifteen years a certain number of minor reforms were effected, to maintain the weakness of Poland was a cardinal point in the designs of Catherine and of Frederick.

Of the three participators in this high-handed action, Russia took the largest share, advancing her Western frontier to the Dwina and Druck. To Austria there fell Lemberg, Belz and parts of Cracow and Sandomir, a district which contained valuable salt mines. Prussia, which contented herself with Pomerelia, Marienburg and Ermeland, with the larger portions of the Palatinates of Kulm, Posen and Gniezno, obtained the territorial connection with East Prussia which had so long been coveted by the Hohenzollern; and her share, if the smallest in area, was of far more advantage to her than was Austria's to Austria, even if the all-important Dantzic still remained unabsorbed.

The Partition of Poland is an action which it is much easier to condemn in the strongest terms than to extenuate in the least. It is the typical example of the "land hunger," which so dominated the rulers of Europe in the 18th Century as to make them quite impervious to the dictates of common fairness. It is an action quite in keeping with Frederick's previous career; and the only reason why Catherine's share in it excites surprise is that Russia would so obviously have preferred to keep Poland undivided in the hope of wholesale annexation; but one is not prepared to find Maria Theresa in such company or sharing in so discreditable an action. The truth would seem to be that Joseph and Kaunitz between them were too much for her.

That the dismembered provinces, those at least which fell into the hands of Austria and Prussia, profited materially by the exchange, hardly affords in itself a sufficient justification for their annexation. Indeed, it rather lends force to the argument that by stopping short of a complete partition the three Powers had deprived themselves of their only defence. Had they pleaded, as they might reasonably have pleaded, that the condition of Poland was so bad that partition was the only remedy, that reform was out of the question, the plea might be admitted, but the admission only makes the partial partition the more inexcusable. A complete partition would have involved conflicts that might have ended in war, and the partners preferred to avoid that.

Joseph proceeded to carry his point as to the administration of his new province. Galicia was treated like one of the regular Austrian provinces, and a Chancery was established for it at Vienna instead of its being placed directly under the control of the State Chancery as were Lombardy and the Netherlands, or, as the Hungarians desired, incorporated as Zips had been in Hungary. In 1775 it was given Estates after the pattern of the German provinces; but their functions were to advise rather than to decide, and the question they had to settle was not " whether " but " how " taxes should be raised. On the whole, Austrian rule soon became fairly popular, though the nobles regretted the exemption from taxation and the greater licence to please themselves which they had enjoyed under Polish rule.

Meanwhile one result of Austria and Russia agreeing upon joint action in Poland had been to avert all danger of a collision between them on the Danube. Russia agreed to restore Moldavia and Wallachia to Turkey, and this she did when, after an abortive congress at Fokschau, brought together under the auspices of the ministers of Austria and Prussia (August 1772), had failed to bring about peace, repeated defeats caused Turkey to conclude the disastrous Peace of Kainardji in July 1774. It is not exactly to Joseph's credit, nor to that of Kaunitz either, that Austria, pretending that she had fulfilled her share of the 1771 compact in inducing Russia to relinquish the Danubian Principalities, retained possession of the Bukovina district [1] which her troops had occupied at the time of the Austro-Turkish convention. The district was maintained under military rule till 1786, being under the General commanding at Lemberg subject to the supervision of the War Council; it was then united to the adjacent province of Galicia.

[1] Northern Moldavia, formerly part of Transylvania but lost to the Turks in the 15th Century.

CHAPTER XV

THE FOREIGN POLICY OF JOSEPH II

THE share of Austria in the Partition of Poland is not least interesting as affording evidence that the direction of the foreign policy of the Hapsburgs was passing from the hands of Maria Theresa to those of her ambitious and energetic son. It was Joseph whose desire for territorial acquisitions had brought Austria into line with the holder of Silesia, Joseph who must be held responsible for the unworthy subterfuges by which a cloak of right was given to the retention of Bukovina, an action which was a poor return for Turkey's conduct in 1741. And in the next international incident in which Austria was involved it was again Joseph who was the principal mover: Maria Theresa's part was limited to that of a commentator.

If there was any district in Germany upon which a Hapsburg was likely to look with covetous eyes it was the country to the West of him, not very much farther up the Danube. The importance of Bavaria to Austria is one of the commonplaces of strategical geography: the years 1703–1704 and 1741–1744 tell their own tale. Moreover, to acquire even a part of Bavaria would enormously strengthen Austria's political prestige in the Empire, enable her to exercise a far greater influence in Southern Germany, and afford some compensation for the diminution which the German element in the Hapsburg dominions had suffered in the loss of Silesia. For these reasons, if for no others, Joseph took no small interest in the succession to Maximilian Joseph, the childless Elector of Bavaria. As to the immediate heir, indeed, there was no doubt. Charles Theodore of Sulzbach, Elector Palatine since 1742, was the next representative of the common ancestor of the Bavarian and

Palatinate branches of the House of Wittelsbach.[1] But Charles Theodore was also without legitimate heirs; he cared very little for Bavaria; took no account of the wishes of the Bavarians or of his heir presumptive, Charles II of Zweibrücken-Birkenfeld,[2] in whose hands the scattered possessions of the Landsberg, Kleeberg, Zweibrücken and Bischweiler branches[3] had become united. So far as he cared for anything except the gratification of his own pleasures, Charles Theodore was interested in the dominions he already possessed on the Rhine, and was especially anxious to preserve Jülich and Berg from falling into the hands of Frederick II of Prussia, whom he suspected of designs upon them. It was not very difficult, therefore, for Joseph to come to an agreement with him. Negotiations for an Austrian guarantee of Jülich and Berg in return for the Elector's recognition of the claims on Bavaria which Austria had no difficulty in finding when a pretext was wanted, had begun in 1776 and were in progress when, in December 1777, Maximilian Joseph died.

Maria Theresa was opposed to the line of action upon which Joseph and Kaunitz had resolved. It rather too much resembled the treatment she had herself received in 1741 to find favour in her eyes. To bring up an old 15th Century arrangement by which the Emperor Sigismund had granted Lower Bavaria to Albert V of Austria as a female fief[4] and to claim Lower Bavaria on the extinction of the main Wittelsbach line in virtue of this former ownership, was only veiling mere greed for territory under a transparent covering of legality. For the claim on parts of the Upper Palatinate as fiefs of the Bohemian Crown there was perhaps a rather better case, and the Emperor had the right to sequester a vacant fief of the Empire, though to annex it to his hereditary dominions would exceed his powers. However, despite the Empress-Queen's disapproval, Joseph and Kaunitz proceeded to conclude a convention with Charles Theodore (January 2nd, 1778) by which the Elector recognised Austria's right to

---

[1] This was Lewis II, Duke of Bavaria (1253–1294) and Elector Palatine; at his death (1294) his territories had been divided, Bavaria going to Lewis III, Emperor 1314–1347, the Palatinate to the latter's brother Rudolf.

[2] A distant cousin, descended from Wolfgang of Zweibrücken (1532–1569), the common ancestor of the Neuburg, Sulzbach, Birkenfeld and Zweibrücken lines.

[3] Cf. genealogy (p. 707) and p. 52.

[4] Albert had sold it to the Duke of Bavaria.

Lower Bavaria, to Mindelheim in Swabia, and to certain Bohemian fiefs with which last alone he was to be invested. The prospect of arranging an exchange for the whole country was also held out, for Austria was already contemplating getting rid of a distant province which was a burden rather than a benefit to her, the Netherlands. On the ratification of this convention, Austrian troops promptly occupied the Upper Palatinate (Jan. 16th, 1778).

However, this merely served to provoke an agitation in Bavaria against the project of division, and the Duchess Marianne, widow of Duke Clement of Bavaria,[1] put herself at the head of the party which desired to preserve the integrity of the Electorate. Charles of Zweibrücken had expressed in general terms his acquiescence in the scheme; but when he found Frederick II inclined to support him, he issued a protest against the violation of his rights as heir-apparent. Frederick, fearing the aggrandisement of Austria, at once refused to recognise Austria's claims. Saxony had a claim on the allodial property in Bavaria, and was anything but friendly to Austria; while Hanover, though on the whole favouring the Austrian claim, did not go beyond benevolent neutrality.[2]

Now was the time when the Franco-Austrian alliance on which Kaunitz and Maria Theresa set so much store, and which they had spared no pains to maintain, was to be put to the test. But it was Joseph's distrust of the alliance, not Maria Theresa's confidence in it which was to be justified. Vergennes was now in power in France and from him no support to the aggrandisement of Austria was to be expected; even if France, inspired by the news of Saratoga, had not been on the point of renewing the struggle with England for the dominion of the seas, Vergennes would never have consented to take any steps on behalf of the Hapsburgs. Nor did Russia's attitude correspond to Joseph's hopes; on the contrary, she inclined to support Frederick.[3]

Negotiations continued through the early part of 1778. Charles Theodore would have gladly exchanged Bavaria against the Netherlands; but the "Old Bavarian" party was opposed to this, and though Frederick did propose conditions

---

[1] The younger brother of Maximilian Joseph, who had predeceased the Elector.
[2] Cf. Ward, *England and Hanover*, p. 200.   [3] Wolf, p. 176.

upon which he would have agreed to the annexation of Eastern Bavaria by Austria, they were so exorbitant[1] that Joseph refused them. Accordingly, on July 3rd Frederick issued an ultimatum, declaring that Austria had no just claims upon Bavaria, and two days later he crossed the Bohemian frontier near Nachod.

The chief feature of the War of the Bavarian Succession is its utter absence of military interest. Practically there was no fighting, beyond a certain amount of skirmishing, and but little manœuvring. Both armies were numerous rather than efficient. In both the administration and equipment were somewhat deficient; and while the Austrians for political motives adopted the defensive Frederick was not prepared to attack. Indeed, both sides displayed not a little nervousness and a decided wish not to risk anything on the chances of a general action, the more so because negotiations were still proceeding. Maria Theresa, thinking Joseph was prepared to give way, had despatched Thugut to Berlin to renew them (July). However, nothing came of this attempt to avert hostilities. Both sides regarded the pretensions of the other as exorbitant, and neither was ready to abate its own. In August, Frederick advanced somewhat farther into Bohemia, Loudoun recoiling before him; but the difficulty of getting supplies and the ravages of disease effectually checked the Prussian advance. The Austrian position at Königgratz was too strong to be attacked, and in September Frederick retreated. He had not done anything to add to his military reputation in this, his last, campaign.

Maria Theresa was now using all her influence in favour of peace, and with Russia, guided by Panin whom Potemkin, the Czarina's favourite, had won over to Prussia's side, threatening to support Frederick unless peace were made directly, and no prospect of any help from France, even Kaunitz and Joseph realised the hopelessness of securing Bavaria. An armistice put an end to the minor warfare which had continued with but little result through the winter; in March a congress met at Tetschen, and the upshot of its deliberations was a peace signed on May 13th, 1779. By this Austria agreed to

---

[1] Mindelheim, Swabia, and part of the Upper Palatinate to go to Saxony, which should hand Lusatia over to Prussia, while Charles Theodore was to receive Guelders or Limburg in return for the cessions made to Austria.

cancel the Convention of January 1778, but received the strip of territory between the Danube on the North, the Inn on the West, and the Salza on the South and East, a district some 850 square miles in size and containing 60,000 inhabitants. As a settlement of its claim on the allodial property Saxony received 6,000,000 gulden and the little district of Schönberg, while Prussia's right to absorb the Franconian margraviates of Anspach and Baireuth[1] was to pass unopposed. The Duke of Mecklenburg-Schwerin, who had also advanced a claim on the Bavarian inheritance, was bought off with the privilege "de non appellando." This peace was guaranteed by France and Russia, and in the following February it was accepted by the Empire.

Of the Powers concerned in the Peace of Tetschen, Russia had undoubtedly gained most in influence. She rather than France had held the balance in her hands: her decision as to the exchange of the Franconian margraviates against Lusatia and as to the amount of compensation for Saxony had been accepted: it was really the very decided line she had taken which had foiled Austria's attempt on Bavaria. Had she supported Austria's claims, as Joseph seems to have expected she would, there would have been a very different story to tell. Prussia also had gained, but rather indirectly than materially. The war had cost her 29 million thalers and 20,000 men, but Frederick was able to represent his action as a disinterested intervention on behalf of the Princes of the Empire against an Emperor bent on turning to his own advantage such relics of a constitution as survived. Such a description of Joseph's policy is not altogether fair. It would not have been to the disadvantage of Germany if the tide of French conquest, so soon to overwhelm her, had found her a little less weak and disunited, had found an Empire which was not practically extinct, and an Emperor whose authority did mean something; but Joseph does appear in the light of one prepared to seize every opportunity of profiting by his neighbours' necessities to increase his territories. Rather different was the action of Maria Theresa. That peace

[1] The Baireuth Hohenzollern had become extinct in 1769 with Frederick, 6th Margrave: his territories passed to the Anspach line. In 1792, by arrangement between Frederick William II and Christian Frederick, 9th Margrave of Anspach, the Franconian margraviates were incorporated with Prussia.

was so soon restored was largely due to her influence. Had her advice been followed throughout, Austria would have been spared the humiliation of a check for which 850 square miles were hardly an adequate compensation. It was almost the last episode in the career of the great Empress, for her health was beginning to fail. One last collision, however, was to take place between her and her lifelong enemy Frederick, and one is glad to be able to relate that in this last encounter Maria Theresa triumphed. The contest was over the election of a Coadjutor to the Elector of Cologne.[1] This office Maria Theresa succeeded in obtaining for her youngest son, Maximilian, Frederick's efforts on behalf of Joseph Hohenlohe being frustrated (August 1780).

But her failing strength would not much longer enable her to continue the daily round of duties in which she still persisted. In November she became rapidly worse, and on the 29th she died. What she did for Austria it is hard to overestimate. Her indomitable courage and perseverance carried her dominions through an almost unexampled danger and made the surmounting of that very danger a source of union and strength. She did much to reconcile Hungary to the Hapsburg dynasty, to reform the administration and the social, financial and political conditions of the countries over which she ruled. A woman of the highest character, a true mother of her people, a " benevolent despot " in the very best sense of the words, she had the tact and sympathy to see what was possible and suitable, and to avoid the errors into which her more impetuous, more theoretical and more self-centred son fell. In all the annals of the House of Hapsburg, there is hardly any name which can be put on the same level as that of Maria Theresa.

The importance of the part played by Russia in the affair of the Bavarian Succession is best attested by the eagerness with which Joseph now sought to secure the friendship of the Czarina. Even before the death of Maria Theresa, Joseph had made a journey to Russia, had had an interview with Catherine at Mohilev in Lithuania (August 1780), and had subsequently visited Moscow and St. Petersburg. Maria Theresa, who was not unnaturally prejudiced against Catherine

---

[1] This was Maximilian of Rottenfels, Dean of Cologne 1756–1761, elected Archbishop in succession to Clement Augustus of Bavaria, April 1761.

as a person, had disliked this journey very much, but Joseph found the Czarina most anxious for better relations with Austria.

The alliance between Russia and Prussia, first concluded in 1764 and renewed in 1772, had expired in 1780 and had not been renewed, for Frederick did not by any means desire to see Russia's power further increased, and Catherine had not found Prussia a very satisfactory or cordial ally. She was now occupied with schemes for ousting the Turks from Europe and establishing a Christian kingdom under Russian protection on the Bosphorus ; and in carrying out such aims it was far more important to secure the alliance, or at least the neutrality, of Austria than that of Prussia. Accordingly, after much correspondence an arrangement was made between Austria and Russia in May 1781 by which both Powers guaranteed each other's possessions, while Joseph promised to join Russia within three months should she go to war with the Porte, and also guaranteed Oldenburg to the younger branch of the House of Holstein. Catherine for her part promised to assist Austria in case of a Prussian attack, while in the course of the year Joseph announced his adhesion to the "Armed Neutrality" in the war between England and her Bourbon enemies, an alliance of which Catherine was the chief bulwark. It was not to be long before the Czarina was to have an opportunity of making use of the Austrian alliance. Disturbances among the Tartars of the Crimea in the course of 1782 threatened to lead to serious trouble with the Porte ; but though Joseph was not prepared to join the Czarina in using this *casus belli* to begin the crusade for the dismemberment of the Ottoman Empire on which her wishes were set, he was able to help her to force Turkey to give way. A large force was collected on the frontiers of Hungary to lend weight to the diplomatic representations of Joseph on behalf of the Russian claims to suzerainty over the Tartars, and it was very largely the prospect of having to face Austria as well as Russia which caused the Turks in January 1784 to accept a convention[1] which secured the Crimea and the Kuban to Russia. Austria's only gain from this treaty was the opening of the Danube to commerce ; but Joseph now reckoned confidently on the support of Russia for the various projects which he was hoping to realise.

[1] That of Ainali Karak.

Mention has already been made of the anomalous relations in which the Netherlands stood to their Austrian rulers, and also of the great obstacles to the development of the Netherlands, the Barrier Treaty of 1715 and the closing of the Scheldt in accordance with the Peace of Münster.   Maria Theresa had succeeded in reducing the annual subsidy paid to the Dutch garrisons from a million gulden to half a million, but she had been unable to get rid of the Dutch, whose presence was a constant source of friction.   It was after a journey in Belgium in 1781 that Joseph, realising the full extent of these encumbrances, decided to seize the favourable opportunity of the war between England and the United Provinces to get rid of them.   He confined himself at first to announcing to the Dutch that they could withdraw their garrisons, as he intended to "slight" the majority of the towns in question.   The more important question of the Scheldt he did not at this time raise, herein giving way to Kaunitz, who believed that it would almost certainly provoke a war with France.   The Dutch found that they had no alternative but to withdraw their troops, and with the exception of Luxemburg, Ostend and the citadel of Antwerp, the fortifications were demolished.   The Barrier Treaty had also contained certain agreements as to territorial cessions which had never been properly carried out, and Joseph, taking advantage of a technical infraction of the Belgian frontier by Dutch troops, denounced the treaty as null and void, and demanded a readjustment of the frontier.   At the same time he raised the question of the opening of the Scheldt to commerce.[1]   A Belgian vessel had been fired upon while in Belgian waters (Oct. 1783), and this served as the occasion for Joseph to demand the slighting of the Dutch forts on the Scheldt, the removal of the guardships and the surrender of Maastricht and its dependencies.   These demands were based on the terms of a convention made in 1673 between Holland and Spain.   To enforce his claim, Joseph collected some 20,000 troops; but they were ill-supplied with artillery, and were without the pontoon-train so urgently needed in a country so much intersected by watercourses as Holland, and the Dutch, by opening the sluices and inundating the frontier districts, made military operations impossible.   However, it was not military difficulties but the attitude of France which made

[1] Cf. Oncken's *Frederick*, vol. ii. p. 824.

Joseph draw back. Had Holland stood alone, Joseph might have obtained his demands, but the Anglo-Dutch war had led to a renewal of the old alliance between France and the democratic party in Holland. This, the so-called " Burgher party," had been revived by the influence of de Vauguyon, French envoy at The Hague since 1776, and Vergennes was not prepared to allow Holland to fall away from the new connection, as would probably happen if France by failing to support her forced her to fall back on England's aid. Accordingly, when negotiations were broken off after Fort Säftingen had fired upon a brigantine flying the Emperor's colours and had forced it to strike (Oct. 1784), Joseph found the influence of France thrown into the scale against him. Russia, it is true, favoured Joseph's action, and neither England nor Prussia seemed prepared to intervene in favour of Holland; but the resolute language of Vergennes convinced Joseph that the risks were too great. The question seems to have been with him to a large extent one of dignity. He did not greatly care for the welfare of his Belgic provinces, but he resented the restrictions imposed upon them as a slight on his prestige.[1] Therefore, when he found that to persevere with his plans would involve the ruin of the Franco-Austrian alliance, he fell back upon another and more promising project.

If the Netherlands could not be freed from the encumbrances which prevented the development of their natural resources and made them so unsatisfactory a possession, it might be possible to exchange them for a country of far greater value to Austria, the Electorate of Bavaria. The idea of the exchange was not altogether new, but Joseph thought the moment favourable for realising it. By making concessions to France in the matter of the Scheldt he might induce her to sacrifice Bavaria for the sake of Holland, for to Vergennes at least it seemed better for France to have a Wittelsbach than a Hapsburg as her neighbour in Belgium. The support of the Czarina, Joseph hoped he had won by pointing out to her how much the acquisition of Bavaria and the consequent improvement of Austria's resources and military position would increase her ability to assist Russia's schemes in the East. The Elector, Charles Theodore, cared very little for his Bavarian subjects, to whom no real ties bound him; if the exchange could be

[1] Cf. F. Magnette, *Joseph II et la liberté de l'Escant.*

arranged on terms which would gratify his personal interests he was quite prepared to sacrifice the wishes of the Bavarians and the interests of his Zweibrücken cousin.   All that seemed really necessary was to secure the consent of Charles of Zweibücken to the agreement.   But, somewhat unexpectedly, when the Russian Ambassador to Bavaria approached the Duke on this matter, he was met by the most uncompromising reply : rather, Charles declared, would he be buried under the ruins of Bavaria.   Such an answer could mean one thing only ; it was dictated from Potsdam, and the Duke had received trust-worthy assurances that he could count upon the assistance of Frederick II.   This was indeed the case.   As jealous as ever of Austria, alarmed by her alliance with Russia, whose power he had had such good cause to appreciate, determined to thwart her wherever possible and to prevent her from recovering influence or authority over the minor Princes of Germany, Frederick had been playing skilfully on the distrust which Joseph's attempts to assert his rights as Emperor and his efforts to increase his hereditary dominions had caused among the petty sovereigns of Southern and Western Germany.   Quite without any general patriotism, oblivious of anything but their own per-sonal and dynastic interests, even the more enlightened and unselfish among them were bitterly hostile to the Imperial pretensions, and the decay of the Imperial institutions had already proceeded so far that they were practically past re-viving.   Had Joseph been able to come forward with a definitely Imperial programme it is just possible that he might have done something, but as things stood it was impossible to prevent the suspicion that under the cloak of the interests of the Empire he was seeking to aggrandise the Hapsburg-Lorraine dynasty : the " Imperial " could not be distinguished from the " Austrian."   But while Joseph had not the power to do what Ferdinand II, though with much better chances and with Wallenstein behind him, had failed to accomplish, or to enforce unity on Germany, nothing could have been more alien to his principles or his practice than an appeal to the people, to the spirit of German nationalism which was not yet awake ; he would have been glad to regain the powers his predecessors had lost, but he had no idea of replacing the moribund Empire by something new.

It was therefore easy for Frederick to form a confederation

of German Princes for the defence of their rights against the Emperor's encroachments. In effect much the same as the Union of Frankfort of 1744, since both were aimed against Austria, in theory the *Fürstenbund* was somewhat different, since its avowed objects were anti-Imperial, while the earlier league had been formed to defend the then Emperor. But Frederick was only inconsistent on the surface: he sought in both cases to extend Prussian influence over Southern and Western Germany at the expense of the Hapsburgs. The project of the formation of such a confederation was set forth in a memorandum addressed to the Prussian ministers von Finckenstein and Hertzberg in October 1784. In this the King of Prussia spoke of resisting the Emperor's attempts to bestow all vacant sees on his nephews from Tuscany and Modena, and by then secularising the sees to gain a permanent Hapsburg majority in the College of Princes—a danger about as chimerical as the other peril against which this protector of the German constitution was ready to invoke foreign aid, namely, that the Emperor should convert the Diet at Ratisbon and the Imperial Chamber at Wetzlar into the instruments of a tyrannical despotism.[1]

Joseph was, it is true, making somewhat futile efforts to restore the Aulic Council and the Imperial Chamber to some measure of efficiency, but these were hardly enough to justify Frederick's extravagant fears. In the matter of the *Panis-briefe*, a claim that the Emperor should appoint a lay canon in every ecclesiastical corporation, he was seeking to revive a right which had not been exercised since the 14th Century, and he was undoubtedly anxious to get his candidate elected whenever any sees fell vacant, as, for example, the choice of the Archduke Maximilian as Coadjutor in Cologne and Münster. That he also entertained designs upon the Cities, the ecclesiastical dominions and the minor states of South Germany in general is probable enough; it is also probable that incorporation in Austria would have brought to the peasants and artisans in these petty principalities considerable material benefits, which might perhaps have been set off against the infringement of the rights of the rulers and upper classes. If the attainment of German unity was desirable in any way, there is no reason to blame Joseph for having wished to reassert

[1] Oncken's *Frederick*, vol. ii. p. 834.

the claims of the Empire as against those local lords whose disregard of the Imperial authority had received the sanction of prescription bestowed upon them by many centuries.

No such league had actually been formed, when in January 1785 Charles of Zweibrücken appealed to Frederick for assistance in the matter of the Bavarian exchange. This was the opportunity Frederick wanted, and in March Hertzberg and von Finckenstein laid before the King projected articles of association of a Union of Princes of the Empire to guarantee and maintain the existing constitution and territorial arrangements of Germany. Its members were to act together in the election of a new King of the Romans or in the creation of a new Electorate. No distinction was to be made between religions, and it was definitely stated that armed resistance could be offered to the proposed exchange of Bavaria. July 23rd, 1785, may be taken as the date of the definite formation of the Union, as it was then that the terms of association were signed by the Electors of Brandenburg, Hanover and Saxony. In October the Elector of Mayence, the Dukes of Saxe-Weimar, Saxe-Gotha, Zweibrücken and Brunswick declared their adhesion to it ; their example was followed in November by the Margrave of Baden and the Landgrave of Hesse-Cassel, and gradually by most of the other members of the Empire, the only dissentients being Cologne, Treves, Hesse-Darmstadt, Oldenburg and Würtemberg.[1] This body thus commanded a majority in the Electoral College, and as the Elector of Bavaria had hastened to withdraw his consent to the exchange as soon as he found how matters were going—in February 1785 he denied that any such scheme was in existence—Joseph's plan was again foiled.

Moreover, his failure was not confined to Bavaria alone. To obtain French assent to the exchange he had withdrawn most of the claims he had made upon Holland. He had accepted French mediation and this practically implied the abandonment of his designs upon the Scheldt. To the great disgust of his Belgian subjects, who saw the high hopes of commercial prosperity they had based on Joseph's demands thus irretrievably disappointed, he gradually abandoned claim after claim. Finally, in November 1785 the Treaty of

---

[1] These last two were connected with Russia ; Hesse-Darmstadt was consistently on the Austrian side.

Fontainebleau reaffirmed the Peace of Münster and maintained the closing of the Scheldt, though some of the forts were handed over to the Emperor, others " slighted," and the frontier restored to its condition in 1664. Maastricht remained in Dutch hands, but ten million gulden, of which France paid four and a half, were handed over to the Emperor as a pecuniary compensation. Thus Joseph received a decided rebuff, and at the hands of France. The support of Russia had not passed much beyond words, and the discontent of the Belgian population at the way in which their interests had been sacrificed was destined to lead to further trouble. So complete a surrender after such protestations smacked of insincerity and gave good grounds for complaints that Belgian interests were altogether disregarded by the Emperor. The internal troubles so soon to convulse the Austrian Netherlands,[1] may be traced in part to the failure of Joseph's designs on Bavaria.

After these disappointments it was not unnatural that Joseph should have asked himself whether the Russian alliance had proved as beneficial as he had hoped. It was not to Austria's interests to assist Russia's advance upon Constantinople unless Russian influence were going to obtain for her corresponding advantages in Germany. But with France decidedly unfriendly, and with the minor Princes of Germany leagued together under Prussian influence, it seemed that the only alternative to the Russian alliance was complete isolation, and for this Joseph was not altogether prepared.

However, in the year following the formation of the *Fürstenbund,* the death of Frederick II [2] seemed to make a new policy possible. The generation which had known Silesia as part of the Hapsburg dominions had passed or was passing away. Joseph for his part had never entertained that intense and personal feeling of hostility to the Hohenzollern which had animated his mother, and he seems to have contemplated a reconciliation with Frederick William II. The new King, the son of the unfortunate Augustus William whose conduct of the retreat from Bohemia had so annoyed Frederick II in 1757, was of a very different calibre to his famous uncle. He had none of the calm self-command, of the cold-blooded calculation, of the clear-sightedness, of the acute judgment, of the initiative,

---

[1] *Vide infra*, pp. 340 ff.　　　　　　　　[2] August 17th, 1786.

energy and resource, of the capacity for sustained efforts, of the power to work himself and to exact work from others, which had made Frederick II so successful a ruler. Frederick William's talents were mediocre ; he had neither the will nor the capacity to be a really efficient ruler, or to effectively control and supervise the elaborate governmental machine of which as King he was the pivot, and the decay of Prussia under his rule must be in large measure attributed to his utter failure to fill his uncle's place. Personally he was the slave of his passions, extremely self-indulgent, yet mingling superstition with sensuality and a kind of morbid religious devotion with his debaucheries, a strange mixture which recalls Louis XV but has nothing in common with the Atheistic cynicism and deliberate selfishness of Frederick II.

It was not unnatural that Joseph should have entertained the project of a Prussian alliance. As he explained to Kaunitz, Austria and Prussia if united would have nothing to fear from any other Power, and might be able to secure a lasting peace. A common nationality and a common language would provide a bond of union which ought to be able to obliterate old prejudices and hostility, and, if Austria could forget the past and forgive Silesia, it should have been possible to present to the growing influence of Russia that barrier which the Silesian question had hitherto prevented the two leading Powers of Germany from forming. But it was not to be. Joseph's doubts of the value of the Russian alliance were not shared by Kaunitz, who could not be expected to get rid of his distrust of the Power he had sought so hard to humble, and he pleaded strongly against the proposed overtures to Prussia. Moreover, Frederick William retained as his Foreign Minister the man who represented the traditions of hostility to Austria which had been the foundation of his uncle's policy, and as long as Hertzberg was in power at Berlin a reconciliation between Austria and Prussia was out of the question. Accordingly Joseph, not without misgivings, accepted Catherine's invitation to visit her and in May 1787 undertook a visit to Russia. With the Russian Court he journeyed through the newly-acquired provinces on the Black Sea, and it would seem that in the course of this progress he pledged himself to support the schemes of aggrandisement at the expense of Turkey which Catherine entertained. However that may have been, in August 1787 the Sultan, alarmed by the unconcealed preparations of Russia, startled the world by suddenly arresting the Russian Ambassador and issuing a declaration of war. By the Treaty of 1781, Joseph's obligations were limited to an auxiliary corps of 30,000 men; but he was ambitious of military fame and anxious to obtain a share in the direction of the war by taking a principal's part in it, and accordingly he collected in Southern Hungary an army of 130,000, and in February 1788 declared war.

The results of this step fell very far short of Joseph's anticipations. The failure owing to fog of the attempt to surprise Belgrade, which Joseph had made even before the declaration of war, was typical of the Austrian performances. For the campaign of 1788 the principal force under Joseph himself was to attempt the invasion of Servia, while a subsidiary force on the right under Loudoun assailed Bosnia, and another on the left under Coburg co-operated with the Russians in Moldavia. Loudoun was fairly successful, capturing Dubitza, Novi and Schabatz, while despite the late arrival of the Russians, Coburg did take Choczim on the Dniester (September) and so pave the way for an advance into Wallachia. But the main army not only was unable to attempt the siege of Belgrade, it failed to prevent the Turks invading and ravaging the Banat; and though Joseph, hurrying thither, forced them to retire, this was at best a negative success. The truth was that Joseph had not the qualities needed by a successful general. Though a keen soldier, he was deficient in strategical insight; and as he never knew where to draw the line between a commander-in-chief's due supervision of his subordinates and meddlesome interference, his lieutenants altogether lacked confidence in him. Moreover, the army suffered terribly from disease, and in November Joseph himself had to return to Vienna very much out of health.

It was not only the ill-success of the campaign which caused Joseph anxiety. Prussia, as usual finding her opportunity in the embarrassments of her neighbours, was on the alert, eager to utilise the Austro-Turkish war to make good her own designs on the much-coveted Polish towns of Dantzic and Thorn. Hertzberg and Frederick William II had just secured no slight advantages by their intervention in Holland on behalf of the House of Orange. The old struggle between the Stadtholder and the burgher aristocracy of Amsterdam had come to a head in 1786. An armed rebellion had forced William V and his wife Wilhelmina, Frederick William's sister, to fly from The Hague and appeal to England and Prussia for assistance. This the two Powers were very ready to grant, Prussia largely for dynastic reasons, England in order to detach Holland from her new connection with France, on whose support the Burgher party were relying. But at the critical moment (Feb. 1787) Vergennes died, and France, without a minister capable of controlling her or following a consistent foreign policy, looked on feebly while England and Prussia interfered to suppress the insurrection, restored the Stadt-holderate and concluded an alliance in which Holland was included. This successful episode greatly increased the prestige of Prussia, though no doubt the ease with which it was accomplished may have contributed to the utterly false estimate which Frederick William formed of the possibilities of intervening in a not dissimilar situation in France five years later. The formation of the Triple Alliance (June 1788) seemed to provide Hertzberg with a powerful influence which he could bring to bear upon the situation in the East of Europe. His idea was to offer to mediate between Turkey and her enemies, and so manipulate the terms of peace as to induce or compel Austria to resign Galicia to Poland, which would then reward Prussia's good offices by the cession of Dantzic and Thorn, now as ever the key to all Prussia's intrigues. There was at least no uncertainty about Prussia's objects. As a compensation, Austria was to keep Moldavia and Wallachia, while Russia might bring her boundary up to the Dniester. Should Prussia's mediation be refused, a threat of armed inter-ference would, Hertzberg hoped, prove efficacious, especially if he had the Maritime Powers at his back. They also were ready for intervention, but their objects were not quite the same as Hertzberg's. Trade interests, both in the Baltic and in the Levant, made Pitt anxious for the restoration of peace; beyond that he was not prepared to go.

Joseph was so far alarmed by the attitude of Prussia, which besides encouraging the Porte was in communication with the Hungarian malcontents[1] and was fostering the growing trouble in Belgium, that he at first thought to

[1] Cf. p. 345.

checkmate Prussia by a prompt peace with Turkey, with or without Russia. Kaunitz, however, dissuaded him strongly from this, and neither Russia nor Turkey seemed inclined to peace. The only result of the negotiations, therefore, was that the opening of the campaign of 1789 was much delayed. During the winter, Suvorov had stormed the great fortress of Oczakov on the Black Sea (Dec. 7th, 1788), while the death of the Sultan, Abdul Hamid (April 27th), had placed on the Turkish throne Selim III, a keen and energetic ruler, bent on the active prosecution of the war. His first step was to disgrace the Grand Vizier and replace him at the head of the army by the Pasha of Widdin. However, the new commander received two severe defeats at the hands of Coburg and Suvorov;[1] while Loudoun, who replaced the worn-out Hadik in command of the main Austrian army (August), also took the offensive with success. Breaking up from Semlin he crossed to the south of the Save and laid siege to Belgrade (Sept. 18th). The suburb was stormed on September 30th, and eight days later the town capitulated. Its fall was followed by the surrender of the fortresses between the Drina and the Timok, Semendria, Kladowa and others. Bosnia, Moldavia, half Servia and the greater part of Wallachia were in Austrian hands, and Austria seemed on the verge of great successes when the news of the outbreak of trouble in Belgium (August) and the threatening attitude of Prussia paralysed her advance. The greater part of the Austrian troops had to be transferred to Bohemia, leaving on the Danube forces hardly adequate to maintain the ground already won, while little help was to be expected from Russia, whose attention had been diverted to the Baltic to meet the vigorous attacks of Gustavus III of Sweden.

For this intervention, Hertzberg was mainly responsible. It was not to Austria only that he was hostile, his attitude towards Russia was equally antagonistic. Thus he fostered and abetted the Swedish King's hostility to Russia, and by addressing himself to the anti-Russian faction in Poland seemed to have secured control of that country. It appeared certain that the spring of 1790 would see the sword of Prussia thrown into the scales on the side of Turkey, when in February 1790

---

[1] On July 31st at Foksani and in September at Martinestyi on the Rymnik, both places just West of Galatz.

the situation was completely altered by the death of Joseph II and the accession of a more practical and competent statesman in Leopold II.

Ever since the campaign of 1788 Joseph had been in very bad health, and the constitutional troubles in Hungary and the outbreak of rebellion in Belgium, where he had hoped all was settled, had naturally aggravated the physical and mental strain. In great bodily pain, he had the misfortune to see his cherished schemes leading to failure and disaster everywhere, his reforms misunderstood, his efforts to increase his dominions frustrated, Belgium in open rebellion, Hungary seething with discontent, similar troubles impending in Tyrol, a powerful coalition apparently about to intervene to take advantage of his domestic and foreign embarrassments. So black was the outlook, so formidable the crisis which he seemed to be going to leave to his successor, that Joseph could not persevere on his chosen course. In January 1790 he gave way to the constitutional opposition of Hungary, cancelled all his edicts save only those in favour of the serfs, and restored the administrative system to the footing on which it had stood at Maria Theresa's death. It was with the greatest reluctance that he did this, but there seemed no alternative. One other step which he took just before his death was to re-establish a special Conference to deal with foreign affairs, which included Kaunitz and Lacy and the Treasurer, Count Rosenberg, while Count Hatzfeldt was put in charge of domestic affairs. On February 20th Joseph died at the early age of forty-eight (born March 1741).

CHAPTER XVI

MARIA THERESA AND JOSEPH II

(DOMESTIC AFFAIRS)

IF from the time of the Partition of Poland, Joseph II had begun to exercise the predominant influence in the direction of the foreign affairs of Austria, this was as much the case in domestic policy; for though Joseph treated his mother with great deference and paid much attention and respect to the ideas and suggestions of Kaunitz, he had made up his own mind on many important points and was determined to push through without delay the reforms which he desired. Both Maria Theresa and Kaunitz found the pace which Joseph set too hot for their liking. Well-intentioned, energetic, a very hard worker, keenly and genuinely anxious to benefit his subjects, Joseph was too much of a doctrinaire, too little of a practical man to distinguish between the possible and the ideal and to be able to adapt to his extraordinary complicated collection of dominions measures better suited to a Utopia. The problem of Austria was one which Joseph failed to look at from an Austrian point of view: he was too detached, too little acquainted with the feelings of his subjects, too little touched by the local patriotism and provincial *esprit de corps* which animated them. He could not see the parts for the whole, they could not see the whole for the parts. Thus wise and salutary as many of his schemes were in themselves, they were applied to situations and circumstances so unsuitable that the good often became evil. Want of tact, want of patience, want of knowledge of men, want of sympathy with other men's views, all these played a large part in the comparative failure of the reforms of Joseph II.

Among the institutions which needed reform, the Church stood out prominently. It was rich, powerful, numerous, but backward, negligent and superstitious. It was still in the

16th Century, and as there was little chance that it would be reformed from within, the State had to undertake the task. Joseph I had done something in this way, Charles VI had also dabbled with the question, while the second decade of Maria Theresa's reign had seen the Church courts regulated, the increase of clerical estates checked and the condition of those already in Church hands improved by their administration being put under the supervision of the Chancery (1750). It was between 1770 and 1780, however, that more radical measures were taken, and for these Joseph was mainly responsible. Austria was strongly Catholic, but the reforming movement of the period enjoyed the support of public opinion, since it did not touch the teaching or dogma of the Church, but only affected it as a social and political institution. It is true that the number of fast- and feast-days was curtailed, but that was done for an economic reason, to diminish the interference of such religious ceremonies with labour and industry. In the same way the efforts to combat the many superstitious and semi-pagan rites and practices which still prevailed hardly affected the real tenets of the Church. The more important reforms related to the jurisdiction of the clergy over the laity, into which a commission inquired between 1765 and 1780, with the result that the laity were only subjected to ecclesiastical courts in matrimonial affairs, to the property of the Church, which was made liable for a fair share of the ordinary taxes on landed property, and to the monasteries, whose powers and privileges were much reduced, while the abuses with regard to their acquisition of property were checked by monks being forbidden to witness wills, and so exercise undue influence over dying testators. The amount of property a novice might bring in on being admitted was also regulated, and the purchase of lands by monastic bodies was subjected to State control. Other useful measures were the limitation of the right of asylum (1775) and the redistribution of the Bishoprics, as the mediæval scheme was now quite obsolete. Maria Theresa founded new sees at Görz, Leitmeritz, Königgratz and Brünn, and erected Olmütz into an Archbishopric. Joseph II created six more sees, transferred three others to new places, and managed to detach those districts which while politically part of Austria belonged to non-Austrian sees from the dioceses to which they belonged. Thus Linz, one of his own foundations, and Vienna, a see created by Charles VI, shared the portions of Upper Austria hitherto subject to Passau.[1] These arrangements were completed by 1783, and, though only after some demur, were duly accepted and ratified by the Pope.

That reforms so extensive should have led to a conflict with the Papacy was only natural, for they certainly infringed the privileges and pretensions of the Pope. It would seem that Joseph had studied the famous pamphlet, *De statu Ecclesiæ et legitima potestate Romani pontificis*, by means of which Febronius had exercised so much influence over Catholic Germany in the 18th Century, expressing views which were widely held. Something had already been done in this direction, for in 1755 an order had been published directing that all excommunications should be made known to the government, and in 1767 old ordinances were revived which forbade the promulgation of Papal Bulls without the leave of the State. Joseph himself would probably have gladly gone a good deal further than this in the direction indicated by Febronius. His views were, to say the least, Erastian in the extreme, and there were those who accused him of being a freethinker and could make out a plausible case in support of their charge. However, though he may have contemplated emulating Henry VIII in breaking the bonds of Rome, that was a step for which Austria was certainly not prepared. Public opinion had been mainly on Joseph's side in his quarrel with the Papacy over his reforms; and the famous " Ems Punktuation" of 1786, by which the four German Archbishops reduced the Papal authority over Germany to quite narrow limits,[2] shows that the anti-Papal· feeling in Germany was not confined to the laity; but a complete breach between the Papacy and the Holy Roman Empire was out of the question. Moreover, the wisdom of the Popes in making timely concessions assisted to disarm hostility. The relations between Austria and Clement XIII (1758–1769) had at times been very much strained, but Clement XIV (1769–1774) gave way on most of the points at issue, and Pius VI (1774–1799) yielded to the unimpeachable orthodoxy of Maria Theresa what he would never have conceded to Joseph, whom he regarded as little better than an Atheist.

In some ways, however, the most important feature in the

<hr />

[1] Cf. Wolf, p. 259.　　　　　　　　　　[2] Cf. Fisher, p. 10.

relations between Church and State during this period was the part played by Austria in a movement common to almost all Europe, the attack on the Jesuits. This was of special importance in Austria, since it involved the liberation of education from the hands of the Jesuits who had till then enjoyed an almost complete control of it. In Austria the Jesuit Order was wealthy and powerful and most unpopular, and it was not only the lay officials, but the Bishops who disliked them and were anxious for their overthrow. Maria Theresa had at first held back from the general attack, regarding the abolition of the Order as a purely ecclesiastical affair, which ought therefore to be left solely to the Pope. However, on the publication of the Bull abolishing the Society of Jesus, she did not hesitate to put it into execution. A commission was appointed to look after their affairs, which issued its report in January 1774. The property of the Order was confiscated, but it was appropriated to the objects to which it had been, theoretically at least, devoted, pious works and education.

The fall of the Jesuits opened the way to really consider-able reforms in education.[1]   Over 200 *Gymnasia* were in their hands, and they practically controlled the Universities through being supreme in the Philosophical and Theological Faculties. The education they gave was still the education of the 16th Century. Nothing had been done to keep in touch with modern developments; all modern studies were neglected, and their scholars could hardly write their own language. The leader of the attacks on the educational system of the Jesuits was the celebrated Viennese physician, Gerhard van Swieten, a man who enjoyed a considerable share of Maria Theresa's confidence. Under his leadership the great Medical School of Vienna was founded, while Philosophy and Theology, released from Jesuitical trammels, made great strides. The Legal Faculty had already (1753–1754) been reformed, and it was kept up to date; while the University was brought under State control, not, perhaps, the ideal chance for its development, but still an improvement on its complete subjugation to the Church. The *Gymnasia* were also reformed, Professor von Gaspari being mainly responsible for the new measures. Modern subjects like History and Geography

---

[1] Cf. Wolf, Bk. ii. ch. 2.

were introduced into the curriculum; and though it was impossible to establish complete uniformity, or from want of qualified teachers to dispense altogether with ex-Jesuits as instructors, a great deal was done to reduce confusion to order and to establish State control. The reform of the elementary schools (*Volkschülen*) presented fewer difficulties. Here again what was actually accomplished fell short of what was aimed at, but primary education on a fairly liberal scale was provided under the ordinances of 1774. Finally, in 1778 the educational Commission which had been established in 1760 was put under the direction of the Chancery.

After the death (Nov. 29th, 1780) of Maria Theresa, Joseph carried his Church reforms still further, and between 1781 and 1784 many very important measures were added. He was bitterly opposed by the Papal Nuntios and by the Archbishops of Gran, Olmütz and Vienna; but he had at his back a strong reforming party, including Kaunitz, the younger van Swieten, Vice-Chancellor Greiner, and the Bishops of Laibach and Königgratz. The first point of attack was the relations of the Austrian clergy with Rome. Joseph began (March 1781) by renewing the *Placitum Regium* of Maria Theresa, by forbidding any communication between monastic Orders in Austria and their headquarters at Rome or their branches in other countries and by cutting out of the Service-book the Bulls *Unigenitus* and *In Cœna Domini* (claiming dispensing power for the Pope). He followed up these steps by attacking the monasteries. Austria teemed with monastic establishments,[1] many of them in a bad condition, some on the verge of bankruptcy. All that Maria Theresa had done was to impose on them a share in taxation and regulate their liability to ecclesiastical law. Joseph went further, he sought to diminish their number. In 1781 the monasteries devoted to the speculative[2] life were closed, and the funds thus obtained were devoted to the local clergy, whose numbers and position Joseph sought to improve. In 1782 the assault fell on the Carthusians, Augustinians, Carmelites, Capuchins and Franciscans: their convents and monasteries were shut, the inmates being pensioned off. It was in vain that Pius VI came to Vienna (March 22nd to

---

[1] In 1781 there were 2163 in Austria with 65,000 inmates.　　[2] *Beschaulich.*

April 24th, 1782) to expostulate; his visit had little effect beyond lowering his own prestige. He could not go very far, for he was much afraid of a schism; and if the Pope adopted an unconciliatory attitude, Joseph would have had a good excuse for trying to nationalise the Roman Catholic Church in Austria and to assert its independence of Rome. He always supported the Bishops whenever they were in opposition to the Pope, and he exacted from them an oath to the Emperor which bound them not to do anything contrary to the interests of the State.

Such being Joseph's attitude towards the Church, it is hardly remarkable to find that under his rule Austria was well ahead of the rest of Europe in the matter of religious toleration. This had not been so under Maria Theresa. Her devotion and her real piety included not a little of the spirit of bigotry and intolerance. Her hand had fallen very heavily upon the Protestants. They were excluded from all offices, not allowed to have freedom of worship, except in Hungary where they were very numerous, over three millions, and they had to have their marriages blessed by a Roman Catholic priest; and Joseph had great difficulty in checking a fierce persecution of the Moravian converts to Protestantism in 1777. The condition of the Jews was even worse: they were not allowed to own houses in Vienna, and the Ordinance of the Jews of 1753 imposed upon them a series of restrictions of a similarly galling nature.

But under Joseph things were very different. Lutherans, Calvinists and the Greek Church enjoyed freedom to worship, might build prayer-houses and schools, own land and houses, enter the professions and hold municipal, civil and military offices. Thus it was hardly wonderful that the Protestants in Austria, who had only numbered 74,000 in 1782, had reached 157,000 in 1787, many who had conformed outwardly to Roman Catholicism now professing their real beliefs. The Jews also shared in the benefit of Joseph's reforms. To make them more useful citizens he removed some restrictions, allowing them to attend schools and universities, and giving them some measure of freedom. This toleration was not shared by all Joseph's Ministers. It was most distasteful to Hatzfeldt, the President of the Council of State, and Blümegen (Court Chancellor), while a good many more officials, notably in Bohemia, were dismissed on account of their persistent opposition to the policy. But while Joseph thus did much which provoked the opposition of the Church, it would be most unjust to regard him as its enemy. He was a Catholic and not an Atheist, he was not even a Free-mason or a " Voltairian." If he freed education from Church control and made it secular, if he made the State altogether independent of the Church, it was because he sought the good of the State, that wider whole of which the Church formed a part.

In other directions Joseph took up and extended the reforms initiated by Maria Theresa. In codifying the civil and criminal law, in introducing greater simplicity into the laws relating to marriages (published 1783) and to suc-cession and inheritance (1786), he did good work. The property law of 1786 and the penal code of 1787 show a distinct advance and are quite modern. Much that was barbarous was removed from the penal code; the property of a person under a charge but as yet unconvicted was respected; duelling was treated as murder.

In another sphere Joseph had pushed on further even in Maria Theresa's lifetime than she was herself prepared to go. This was the agrarian question. Maria Theresa was sincerely anxious for the well-being of the peasantry, to protect them against oppression and undue exactions on the part of their lords, but she herself was at heart one of the old aristocracy of Austria. With her, good treatment of the lower orders was a matter of the heart, not, as with Joseph, of the head, an obligation which the ruler must observe, not a right which the subjects could demand. She was utterly untouched by the theories and principles which dominated him. However, she made no opposition to his schemes for the regulation of the " Robot."[1] The condition of the peasantry differed considerably with the provinces. In the Sclavonic lands they were much worse off than in the German districts; in Hungary they were unfree, and weighed down by heavy burdens which the lesser nobility among the Magyars stoutly defended against Joseph's efforts to remove them. In Austria itself and in Tyrol the peasantry were best off, though the Bohemian nobles were the best farmers and landowners in the

[1] Services due from the peasants to the landowners.

Hapsburg dominions, and did much to improve their estates and the conditions under which their tenantry existed, rebuilding villages, draining swamps and looking after the forests. In the lands along the Drave the peasantry were attached to the soil, but enjoyed a fair amount of personal freedom. They could acquire personal property and dispose of it by will, and were not fettered by restrictions as to marriage. In Carinthia and Styria only Catholics were allowed to own houses and the population was as a whole backward, though cases occurred of peasants leaving as large a fortune as 30,000 gulden.

The chief aims of Joseph's reforms were the abolition of serfdom, or, where he could not actually effect this, to render fixed and definite the uncertain claims of the lords. His first efforts in these directions provoked strenuous opposition on the part of the Estates, and even to some extent from the administration, which in composition and in sympathies was very largely aristocratic. In 1770 an Ordinance was published for Bohemia, which forbade the lords to forestall or to press labour or exact dues on marriages or on the purchase of land by their tenants. After much opposition and trouble it was decided that the matter should be left to be settled by arrangement between the lords and their subjects ; but though this was done on the Royal domains, elsewhere it remained for the most part a dead letter, with the result that in 1775 the peasants, losing all hope of getting relief by any other way, endeavoured to extort it by an insurrection. The troops, however, were quite untouched by popular sympathies and the revolt was suppressed without difficulty.

In no way deterred by this revolt, Joseph pushed on with his schemes of agrarian reform. He regarded those who had opposed his measures as responsible for the rising, and in August 1775 he induced Maria Theresa to grant a " Robot patent " by which the services due were fixed so as not to exceed three days' work a week, while it was possible to commute this for money or produce on a settled system. The relative contributions of the vassal and the lord to the land-tax were also fixed, and in 1778 a supplementary edict defined the normal " Robot " as two days. Altogether this was a marked advance on previous conditions, but Joseph was not content. Soon after he became sole ruler, he published an edict abolishing personal serfdom (Jan. 15th, 1781). The sixth article of this document promised the peasants freedom to marry as they would, freedom to move their residence, the right to the products of their labour, and abolished several other of the more oppressive "incidents" of their vassalage. However, the peasant was not even now withdrawn from all dependence on the lord. He was still responsible to him, attended at his court, and had to perform the services due according to the "Robot," unless he had already commuted them. But these services were now fixed, and the peasantry could obtain legal redress in cases of infringement of the arrangements. In September 1781 another edict greatly reduced the criminal jurisdiction of the lords, and took the peasantry under the protection of the State, which appointed public advocates in all the provinces to act as counsel for the peasants. The result of these reforms is well summed up by Wolf.[1] "Before the time of Joseph II, the peasantry formed a class of the people: after Joseph they were again an estate (*Stand*), with public rights and duties."

Closely connected with all this was the reassessment of the land-tax, for Joseph was most anxious to reduce the burden on the peasants, declaring that unless the peasantry were prosperous the kingdom could not be. It was a work of great difficulty, for when a reassessment was ordered in April 1785 nobles, clergy, Estates and even many of the ministers themselves protested and offered all the opposition they could. In September 1789, however, the new rates were published. Houses were to pay 10 per cent. of their rent, agricultural land $12\frac{1}{4}$ per cent. of its gross produce, the communities being made responsible for the tax. The peasantry had in addition to pay $17\frac{3}{4}$ per cent. to their landlords. But this system proved a failure. The work had been done rather too hastily and had been somewhat scamped, the rate being fixed a good deal too high; and as the whole plan was most unpopular Leopold I rescinded it on his accession.

It was not merely over these matters of the position of the peasantry and over the land-tax that Joseph came into collision with the nobility, who still held a most important

[1] P. 287.

and influential position in the Hapsburg dominions. They still retained under their control, minor justice, police and the supervision of the schools, they had great power and influence locally, they had never been detached from the land and made mere satellites of the Court as their contemporaries in France had been. Moreover, they had in the Estates of the various provinces a constitutional means of making their views known, so that the efforts which Joseph made at every favourable opportunity to restrict the sphere of activity of the Estates were really attacks on the aristocratic element in the government and constitution. His great idea was to promote the happiness of the many by diminishing the powers of the few, and it was with this object that he attacked social and fiscal privileges, as in the matter of the "robot" and land-tax or the political powers of the nobles, as in forbidding in 1782 all payments by the Estates which the government had not authorised. But this policy was far from being popular, even with those most closely associated with the Emperor and holding the principal offices under him. Zinzendorf, then President of the Debt Commission (*Hofrechenkammer*), declared in February 1787 that neither the ministers nor the Council of State were competent to decide upon a new system of taxation, and that it should be referred to an assembly of " Notables." Joseph accordingly sought to recruit his bureaucracy independently of class distinctions; but while the bureaucrats too often displayed a want of the zeal, single-mindedness and self-sacrifice which Joseph somewhat over-confidently expected, the Emperor was much at fault in seeking to impose on Austria a system she was not fitted to receive. Conscious of his own sincerity and of his zeal for the welfare of his subjects, Joseph could not understand that the old distinctions of provinces and classes which he yearned to sweep away, the old constitutional forms and rights which marred the completeness of his bureaucratic absolutism and in which he could only see the obsolete relics of an unenlightened past, did not appear in the same light to other people, that it was possible to differ from him and his policy honestly and without bad motives. Thus it was that he failed to appreciate the opposition he aroused, sought to override rather than to conciliate it, out-

22

stripped even those of his ministers and subjects who on the whole approved of his policy, never gave his measures time to live down opposition by successful working, and was always " taking the second step before the first."

Joseph, indeed, was by no means as absolute and autocratic as was, for example, his neighbour Frederick II. In Austria the personality of the ministers still was of great importance, especially when there was among them such a man as Kaunitz. President of the Council of State, Chancellor, Minister of the Interior,[1] he exercised an enormous influence over domestic and foreign affairs alike. Methodical, precise, a trifle slow, he was quite the reverse of the more erratic and impetuous Joseph; and on many points, notably the treatment of Hungary and the Netherlands, they were at variance, while Kaunitz clung with the utmost tenacity to the system of foreign policy he had introduced in 1756; and not until the French Revolution had developed into a danger to all Europe, and Frederick II was dead, did he so far overcome his habitual distrust of Prussia as to advocate an alliance with the Court of Berlin.

No one else among the Austrian ministers could compare in authority with Kaunitz. Henry Blumegen, Court Chancellor from 1771 to 1781; Leopold Kolowrat, his successor in that office; Count Seilern, the Minister of Justice; Rudolf Chotek, nephew of Maria Theresa's Minister and assistant to Kolowrat till 1789, were all thoroughly competent as subordinates, but not capable of doing much independently. Trained for the most part in the Theresian school, they tended to be conservative: Blumegen resigned when, in 1781, Joseph united the financial and political administration; Chotek, though a strong advocate of the supremacy of the Crown, was too much of an aristocrat to accept the abolition of serfdom: he resigned in 1789 as a protest against the new system of taxation. Zinzendorf, a man of great financial and commercial knowledge, and a keen supporter of Joseph's Church policy, disliked the agrarian reforms and was much opposed to the suppression of all constitutional forms. Kolowrat, Zinzendorf's predecessor as President of the Debt Commission (1771 to 1782) and subsequently Director of the united financial and political administration, had strong aristocratic and constitutional sympathies which made him a half-hearted agent for Joseph.

[1] Wolf, p. 224.

Moreover, Joseph was not able to allay the rising discontent by the most effective of all palliatives, reduction of taxation. His reforms were for the most part expensive: a bureaucracy, especially if it is to be honest and efficient, must be adequately paid; it was impossible to cut down the sums devoted to the army, and with hospitals, sanitation and charitable institutions all making great demands Joseph had rather to increase than to diminish taxation. He also sought to readjust the burden, as, for example, by reassessing the land-tax, and so make it easier to be borne, and to increase the tax-producing capacities of his dominions by public works, by fostering industries and manufactures, and by encouraging trade. Under Zinzendorf as Governor Trieste made great progress: in 1782 it had an import trade of $8\frac{1}{2}$ million gulden and exported 13 millions' worth. In 1790 the number of vessels visiting the port had risen from the 4300 of 1782 to 6750 6 per cent. being Austrian. However, on the whole Joseph's efforts to make income and expenditure balance were not very successful. Whenever careful economy had produced a surplus, some shift of foreign policy was sure to swallow it up and leave a considerable deficit. Thus in 1783 the revenue reached 78,000,000 gulden and exceeded the expenses by nearly four millions; but the question of the Scheldt sent up the outgoings to 84 millions, 87 millions and $85\frac{3}{4}$ millions in the next three years. In 1787 there was again a surplus, the revenue reaching 92 millions, the expenditure $85\frac{1}{3}$; but the Turkish War proved most costly, and at Joseph's death there was a deficit of nearly 28 millions and a debt of no less than 370. Still he did effect great reforms in the financial administration, swept away a great many obsolete and unnecessary posts, allowed several unproductive old taxes to expire, and found new sources of revenue in stamps, newspapers and the tobacco monopoly. Tariff reform was another important sphere in which Joseph did good work, although he failed to get rid of the customs-boundary between Austria and Hungary. He was a strong Protectionist, and the tariff of 1784 was mainly designed to keep out foreign competition, though subsequently it underwent considerable modifications.

Joseph's difficulties, great enough when confined to the problems arising out of Austria, Bohemia and their dependencies, were multiplied enormously by Hungarian autonomy, and by the resistance of the Netherlands to the reforms he sought to introduce into that isolated portion of his dominions. In both these countries, reforms were urgently needed, but in both the old constitutional forms were strong enough to serve as the nucleus for the resistance of all those vested interests which Joseph had attacked and offended.

The Netherlands were, as a rule, governed by some member of the Imperial family, assisted by a Minister Plenipotentiary. Up till 1780 Charles of Lorraine acted as Stadtholder, and on his death Albert of Saxe-Teschen and his wife, the Arch-duchess Marie Christina, youngest daughter of Maria Theresa, succeeded to the office; but Joseph treated them more as representatives of the dynasty than as responsible for the government, which was mainly in the hands of Count George Adam Stahremberg. The latter, however, resigned in 1783 as he found his advice neglected by the Emperor, and Count Belgiojoso succeeded him.

The reforms which Joseph proposed to introduce into the Netherlands were of much the same kind as those attempted in Austria. Trade was in a bad condition, owing largely to the closing of the Scheldt,[1] the administration was neither very efficient nor very honest, justice was proverbially tedious, the economic and social condition of the country unsatisfactory, the defences inefficient, and the Church wealthy and influential. It was the Church, therefore, that Joseph first attacked. He applied to the monks in the Netherlands the same measures as he had applied in Austria (1782), and with fair success; for while the clergy offered bitter opposition, the mass of the people acquiesced. In 1786 further trouble was caused by the foundation of a Seminary at Louvain to give the clergy a rather more liberal education than that which they were receiving in the Episcopal schools. This measure the Papal Nuntio, Zondaderi, and the Archbishop of Malines, Count Frankenberg, resisted so stoutly that the latter had to be recalled to Vienna and the former sent back to Rome. Thus Joseph alienated the clergy completely, while the provinces as a whole, disappointed at the failure of his efforts to free the Scheldt, had not appreciated the proposed exchange against Bavaria, and not unreasonably cared but little about a ruler who admittedly wanted to get rid of them. Accordingly, when

[1] Cf. p. 322.

in January 1787 Joseph published edicts abolishing the
Council of State, the Privy Council, the Secretariat and the
Financial Council, which were all to be replaced by a Council
of the Governor-General of the Netherlands, remodelling the
judicial arrangements completely, taking away the privileges
and special jurisdictions of the nobility, dissolving the old provincial boundaries and constitutions and dividing the land into
nine " Circles " each under an Intendant, it was the clergy who
fanned the flame of discontent into resistance.

Joseph's proposals aimed at unity, coherence and centralisation of administration; but the Belgians adhered to their
cherished autonomy and regarded the establishment of absolutism as a tyrannical outrage.   They preferred their feudal and
federal arrangements, even if they were in Joseph's eyes quite
indefensible.   Moreover, equality before the law was a breach
of each man's rights to the privileges of his class ; the burghers
hated the conscription and the Austrian criminal procedure,
and the nobles were especially hostile to the scheme.
When the Estates of Brabant met (April 1787) the opposition
soon found its voice and gave vent in no measured terms to
its disapproval of the new measures. Belgiojoso was vigorously
denounced ; and the Viceroys, after vainly trying to quell the
discontent, were compelled to withdraw the obnoxious edicts
and cancel the new arrangements in order to avert an actual
outbreak (May 30th).   Joseph, however, determined to persist,
and to overcome opposition by force if necessary.   Convinced
as he was of the excellence of his reforms, and that they could
not fail to prove beneficial, he could not conceive that honest
opposition could be offered to them and totally failed to com-
prehend the feelings of his Belgian subjects.   Much against
the advice of Kaunitz he refused to make any concessions,
replaced Belgiojoso by Trautmansdorf, and gave the command
in the Netherlands to d'Alton, superseding General Murray,
who had hitherto averted a conflict by concessions, notably by
withdrawing the troops from Brussels.

With Trautmansdorf really in the place of the Viceroys
and the rough and stern d'Alton at Trautmansdorf's elbow,
the reign of coercion was not far off.   Nevertheless, 1788 on
the whole passed off quietly enough, though arbitrary arrests,
the suppression of the Press, and the prevention of public
meetings served rather to muzzle than to stamp out the

spreading disaffection. When the taxes for 1789 had to be voted, the first two orders of the Estates of Brabant consented to vote them, but the Third Estate refused, and its example was followed in Hainault. Joseph determined to use force. In June a new ordinance was published, suppressing the *Joyeuse Entrée*, the principal charter of Belgian liberties, abolishing the Council of Brabant,[1] doing away with the Estates, and establishing an entirely new system of local administration and a new High Court of Justice. To force the Belgians replied with force. A Revolutionary Committee assembled at Breda to direct the insurrection, which spread like wildfire. The troops, few in number and somewhat disaffected, were unable to hold their own. All Flanders had to be evacuated. Brabant rose, and the troops had to be concentrated at Brussels, and to confine their efforts to holding out there and maintaining the line of communications by Namur and Luxembourg. Two distinct parties were now taking shape in the insurgent ranks. One, aristocratic and conservative, led by Van der Noot, was contemplating appealing to the Triple Alliance to which the recent (1787) intervention of England and Prussia in Holland[2] had given birth. The other, guided by the able but uncompromising Vonck, was frankly democratic, and looked for help to France, where revolutionary principles were gaining ground rapidly; and it was this party which took the lead in the attack on the troops. The insurrection had occurred at a time most unfavourable to Joseph. He was deeply implicated in the perennial Eastern Question, and his relations with the other Powers, notably with Prussia, were somewhat strained. He was therefore in no position to continue his coercive policy, especially as he feared that Prussia might take the part of the insurgents and intervene in Belgium. Accordingly he revoked his ordinances, promised to dissolve the Louvain Seminary, restored the *Joyeuse Entrée*, issued a general amnesty, and sent the Vice-Chancellor, Philip Cobenzl, to the Netherlands (Nov. 26th). But these concessions were interpreted as merely signs of weakness, and the insurgents, much encouraged, attacked Brussels and forced

---

[1] The High Court of Justice, which had important political functions as guardian of the constitution.

[2] Cf. p. 325.

d'Alton to evacuate it (Dec. 12th) and fall back to Luxembourg. Flushed with success, they declared that the Emperor had forfeited his sovereign rights, and in January 1790 deputies from the revolted provinces met at Brussels and proclaimed their independence as the United States of Belgium. It might have been predicted, however, that unless one of the Great Powers recognised this new State its independent existence would be shortlived. France was not unwilling, but the Belgian constitution was too aristocratic for her, and early in 1790 France was not in a position to take a very active line in foreign affairs, while Prussia could not act alone; and though the threat to recognise the Belgian Republic was an effective card in the diplomatic game, it was not very seriously intended. Thus, though Joseph did not live to see it, as soon as Austria's hands had been more or less freed by the Convention of Reichenbach and the subsequent Peace of Sistova, the Belgian Republic was called upon to defend itself and failed to answer to the challenge.

Belgium, however, was not the only part of the Hapsburg dominions in which the discontent aroused by Joseph's reforms became a really serious matter. Hungary, despite the reforms of Maria Theresa, who had exercised a practically absolute power over it from 1765 to 1780, was still a feudal state, almost untouched by modern changes. Since 1764 no Diet had been summoned. The office of Palatine had been replaced by those of Stadtholder and Captain-General, posts conferred on Albert of Saxe-Teschen; but Hungary retained a great deal of autonomy, the local officials being for the most part elective, and the strength of the lower nobility was still very great. Moreover, the various abuses on which Joseph was waging war everywhere flourished with special vigour in Hungary. The judicial system was obsolete, education in the hands of a wealthy but rather ignorant clergy, the nobles controlled the government and did nothing, the peasants were unfree and weighed down with heavy burdens. Here as elsewhere the Church was the first institution to experience Joseph's attacks; but though the granting of toleration to Jews and Protestants, the suppression of the monasteries and the exaction of a new oath from the Bishops were all declared to be breaches of the constitution, they were as a whole accepted quietly enough, and it was not till after Joseph's visit to Hungary in 1784 that trouble really began.

To a proud and sensitive race like the Magyars it was an insult that German should have been proclaimed to be the official language, as was done in 1784, another decree announcing that in future only German-speaking persons would be appointed to official posts. An even more serious grievance was Joseph's interference in the social and economic arrangements of the country. In August 1785 an edict was published abolishing serfdom. It met with bitter opposition from the serf-owning territorial magnates, and as a matter of fact remained a dead letter. In Transylvania the disappointment of the peasants resulted in a social rising which developed into a " Jacquerie." Many landowners were murdered, many castles and houses pillaged and burnt before the insurrection was ruthlessly and sternly repressed. Both sides put the blame on Joseph. The peasants felt that he had deserted them and had not fulfilled his promises: the nobles looked on his reforms as the cause of the trouble and were indignant with his leniency towards the insurgents. But further measures were to come, amounting to a widespreading alteration of the constitution, including the re-division of the land into ten Circles, each under a Commissary, a royal official who was to be responsible for public order, for raising taxes, levying recruits and similar work. This was an interference with local government, hitherto the province of the nobles, higher and lower, and caused much dissatisfaction. But Joseph paid no heed to the rising opposition, nor attempted in the least to conciliate it or to give his reforms time to make themselves more acceptable in practice. He hurried on from one reform to another. The conscription, introduced in 1785, was bitterly resented as an attempt to supersede the national " Insurrection." A census was taken in 1785 as the preliminary to a reform of the land-tax, from which by the rescript of February 10th, 1786, nobles and clergy were to be no longer exempt. In December 1786 an Imperial rescript announced a complete change in the administration which would have the effect of subjecting it completely to the Emperor's control.

However, foreign complications made it impossible to put all these new arrangements into force. The outbreak of the Turkish War, actually begun in December 1787, though not formally declared till February 1788, made it necessary to demand a vote of men and money, and in Hungary the principle that "redress of grievances should precede supply" was well understood.   The nobles and the other bodies to which the Emperor applied demanded that the Diet should be summoned.   Joseph steadily refused, fearing that the Diet would be more than he could control.   Opposition accordingly grew stronger, and so did the pressure of the financial needs. Moreover, as in old days, there was a small party in Hungary which was ready to appeal to external assistance against the sovereign.   The quarter to which this section looked was no longer Constantinople but Berlin.   Frederick William II when invited to guarantee the freedom of Hungary did not show himself prepared to go quite to that length.   He and his influential minister, Hertzberg, were glad to use the threat of supporting discontent in Hungary to forward their objects on the Vistula, but they had no intention of going any further. Moreover, Hungary as a whole was quite loyal to the dynasty ; the cause of discontent was the reforms which might be withdrawn, there was no real wish for independence.   However, the danger of Prussian intervention added yet another anxiety to the load of troubles under which Joseph was fast giving way.   Bitterly disappointed as he was at the results of his well-meant reforms, at the ingratitude with which his efforts for the good of his subjects had been met, at the failure of his schemes for the revival of the Empire and of his ambitious foreign policy in general, his health, never of the best, was breaking down completely.   It was a final blow that in January 1790 he found himself obliged to concede almost all that Hungary demanded.   He cancelled his reforms and restored the old arrangements, but even now he refused to call a Diet.   Whether he would have had to do so in the end is a question which his death (Feb. 20th) left unanswered.

Many different verdicts have been pronounced on Joseph II. If he was deficient in judgment and in the power of suiting his policy to his circumstances, if he failed to appreciate the ideas of his subjects or to make allowances for their prejudices, there are few monarchs of whom it can so confidently be asserted that their chief care was the public good, and fewer still who have been so consistently unfortunate.

He set up a high ideal of duty, and practically killed himself in trying to carry out a policy which was dictated by the best motives. Shortlived as were many of his reforms, unsuccessful as were many of his schemes, he yet did accomplish much. He got rid of much that was effete and obsolete, aroused a new spirit in Austria, and enunciated principles on which others were to base their work.

CHAPTER XVII

LEOPOLD II AND THE EASTERN QUESTION

L EOPOLD, the third son of Maria Theresa, was forty-three
years of age when Joseph's death called him from
Florence to Vienna. In 1765 he had been given his father's
Grand Duchy of Tuscany of which he had taken over the
direct rule in 1770, it having till then been in the hands of the
Marquis Botta d'Adorno and, since 1776, of Count Orsini-
Rosenberg. Under Leopold's rule, Tuscany had been orderly,
peaceful and prosperous; and he had carried out, though on a
smaller scale and with rather more success, much the same
measures of domestic reform that Joseph II had attempted in
Austria. Where, however, Leopold differed from Joseph was
in possessing strong constitutionalist sympathies, which enabled
him to appreciate far more fairly the opposition which Joseph
could not understand. Though admirably loyal to Joseph, he
felt that his brother had gone too far in the matter of Hungary,
and he was inclined to make really considerable concessions
to the Belgian insurgents. To coercion and arbitrary action
he was on principle opposed, for he looked upon monarchs as
delegates and representatives of their subjects; indeed, he had
gone so far as to contemplate the introduction into Tuscany of
some form of representative government, but had abandoned
the project on account of the lukewarmness of the nobility and
the obstructionist attitude of the clergy.

Leopold came to the Austrian throne with the fixed
determination to make peace as soon as possible, since he saw
that it was badly wanted and was an essential preliminary to
putting the internal affairs of his dominions on a sound basis.
Moreover, it was clear that the Turkish war was not by any
means the " walk over " for which Joseph II had hoped, and
that, in view of Prussia's evident hostility, Austria would do
well to make peace before she suffered any serious disaster on
the Danube. Already Austria had been forced to mass nearly

150,000 men on the frontiers of Poland and Prussia, and on March 29th, 1790, Hertzberg completed the negotiation of a treaty with Poland by which Prussia promised in return for Dantzic and Thorn to obtain Galicia from Austria for Poland, guaranteed the Polish constitution and pledged herself to assist Poland, if she were attacked, with 18,000 men. This treaty was certainly a breach of Prussia's engagements to Austria and Russia, but its provisions were never carried into effect. In the first place, financial considerations made it impossible for Prussia to act without the support of the Maritime Powers, and they were anxious for peace, more especially as Leopold had hinted to England that unless he got help somewhere he would have to surrender Belgium to France. Pitt had no liking for the ambitious and aggressive policy of Frederick William, and the maintenance of Austrian authority in Belgium was one of the cardinal points of his policy, so that Leopold's overtures were well received, and when two Austrian envoys arrived at the Prussian headquarters at Reichenbach (June 26th, 1790) the ministers of the Maritime Powers insisted on being present at the conference and pronounced decisively in favour of the maintenance of existing arrangements. Hertzberg's schemes were thus completely upset. Moreover, Frederick William, who was so determined not to be the tool of his responsible ministers that he was absolutely controlled by irresponsible favourites like Lucchesini, rather distrusted Hertzberg and was already feeling a little nervous about the spread of democratic principles in France. Poland also would not give up Dantzic and Thorn unless she got adequate compensation, and nothing short of an overwhelming defeat would induce Austria to give up Galicia. In so unpromising a state of affairs Frederick William decided to come to terms with Leopold, in whose political creed hostility to Prussia was not, as it was with Kaunitz, the principal tenet. Indeed, Leopold had fathomed the true condition of things in Prussia, and realising the divergence of opinion between Hertzberg and his master, with great adroitness addressed himself directly to Frederick William and his confidants, Bischoffswerder and Lucchesini. The result was that an agreement was soon reached, both monarchs being ready to facilitate the restoration of peace by renouncing all idea of territorial gain. Austria was somewhat loath to give up all her recent acquisitions, especially as Alexinez and Orsova had been taken (April), and Clerfayt had gained a considerable victory over the Turks at Kolafat (June 26th). However, Loudoun's death (July 14th) damped the ardour of the bellicose, and so on July 27th, the same day that Clerfayt gained another victory on the Danube, at Florentin, the Treaty of Reichenbach was signed. It was really a triumph for Leopold, who by clever diplomacy escaped from a rather awkward position. The Triple Alliance guaranteed the restoration of Austrian authority in Belgium, and promised to bring about peace with Turkey. As to the cession of Galicia to Poland not a word was said, and Prussia had, for the time being at any rate, to forego the coveted Dantzic. Frederick William also pledged his support to Leopold's candidature for the Empire. Six weeks later the armistice of Giurgevo (Sept. 19th) put an end to the hostilities between the Austrians and Turks, and in December a congress was opened at Sistova to settle the terms of peace.

Leopold was thus able to devote his energies to the resettlement of Hungary and to the reassertion of Austrian authority in Belgium. In Hungary he had a far from easy task. The whole country was in a turbulent and disorderly condition. Conciliatory measures were interpreted as confessions of impotence, and when the Diet was opened at Ofen on June 8th the most extravagant claims were advanced and a strenuous opposition offered to Leopold's proposals. The Diet actually went to the length of proposing that the constitution should be guaranteed by Prussia; upon which Leopold, who had already carried conciliation to the extreme limit of reasonableness, prepared to use force. It was this domestic difficulty, however, which caused him to modify his tone at Reichenbach, as Prussia held a strong card in the. diplomatic game in the threat to acknowledge the Belgian Republic or to assist the Hungarians. Fortunately Leopold's firmness produced the desired result. The clergy and the burghers were now on his side, and the Diet, deprived of the hope of Prussian intervention by the conclusion of the Treaty of Reichenbach, gave way. On November 15th, Leopold was crowned at Pressburg. This did not end all troubles, for the Diet went in detail into the land question, the organisation of the administration and of justice, and the question of the position of the Protestants. Not a jot of their privileges and rights could the nobles be induced to give up, and the result was that Hungary, to which Joseph's reforms would have opened the door to progress, relapsed into and remained in a condition of stagnation. Though no longer serfs, the peasantry were still unfree. The townsfolk were without power or influence. The nobles, free from taxation and from military service, retained their position as a privileged and dominant aristocracy. But at this price Leopold had succeeded in restoring peace and order to the most troublous portion of his dominions. Had he lived it is quite likely he might have attempted, in some form or other, the much-needed reforms which for the time being he had had to sacrifice.

About the same time a Diet was held in Transylvania. Here the problems were much simpler. Things had been at once restored (March 1790) to the condition which had existed before Joseph's innovations, and the Emperor now (Feb. 1791) decided upon the separation of the Transylvanian from the Hungarian Chancery. He also succeeded despite the opposition of the local nobility in securing the abolition of serfdom.

In the case of the Netherlands, the chief danger was that of foreign intervention, but the idea that England would take the side of the rebels was always a mere chimera. France was too well occupied at home to do anything, and the Treaty of Reichenbach removed all anxiety as to Prussia, although a Prussian officer, von Schönfeld, had been given the post of commander-in-chief by the Clerical section among the insurgents. This party, led by Van der Noot, had gained the upper hand in a fierce struggle with the democratic section, the Vonckists, who were more inclined to approve of the reforms in general and were therefore prepared to listen to the pacific overtures of Leopold. The Emperor was most anxious to avoid bloodshed, but the Clericals would not hear of a compromise. The Bishops preached a crusade against him, and were ready to throw themselves into the arms of France, though no help was forthcoming from that quarter, partly because Pitt had let it be understood that in case of a French intervention he would assist Austria. Finally, in November, no surrender having been made by the appointed time (Nov. 21st), an Austrian corps of 33,000 men was put in motion. On the 26th Namur fell, on the 30th Brussels was reached, on

December 2nd it opened its gates. Practically no resistance was made and the country as a whole welcomed the Emperor's troops. This success was used with the utmost mildness. Leopold declined to exercise the rights of a conqueror. He issued a general amnesty, dissolved the hated Seminary, restored the University of Louvain, allowed the Church free disposal of its revenues and made no attempt to get hold of the ringleaders. Indeed, the Vonckists were the only people who had any cause to grumble. They had hoped to see something in the way of democratic reforms, and in their disappointment they began to plan a new rising, in which they hoped for the support of France, now rapidly passing under the control of the democratic party.

But though the discontent excited by Joseph's well-meant reforms had nowhere else reached so high a pitch as in Hungary and the Netherlands, it was by no means non-existent in the "hereditary dominions." Leopold had begun by repealing Joseph's land-tax and new laws as to land-tenure (March 1790). He then summoned assemblies in the various provinces to discuss further measures. It is interesting to notice that while the demands of the various assemblies included a share in legislation for the Estates, their general tenor was retrograde rather than Radical. They did not attack the absolutist régime as such, and where they did desire modifications of the existing state of things, it was rather in the direction of feudalism than of democratic representative government. In Moravia 1628 was taken as the golden time to which the Estates wished to return : Joseph's land-tenure system was denounced as "derogatory to the nobles and the State." In Styria the nobles bitterly opposed a proposed increase in the representation of the cities. In Bohemia local autonomy was demanded. In Carinthia the upper classes condemned the encouragement of education as dangerous and subversive of order. In Tyrol alone it was the peasants and burghers who offered opposition ; but Tyrol was con-stitutionally quite different from the other provinces, and even there the demand was for freedom from the conscription and restriction of official posts to local men.

The truth was that in all these districts feudalism was making a last effort to assert itself against the enlightened absolutism which Maria Theresa and Joseph had planted so strongly that it could not be completely overthrown. There was no feeling in favour of any really constitutional movement, and Leopold was able to restore order and reassert his authority without abandoning any very valuable rights. What was done in the way of alteration or reform was done by the authority of the head of the State through the bureaucracy, which Leopold strove hard to keep up to a high standard of efficiency.

The best means of judging fairly the work of Maria Theresa and her sons is to compare the Austria of 1792 with the Austria of Leopold I. In population and material prosperity there had been an enormous advance. Bohemia alone had 2,700,000 inhabitants as against 800,000 in 1648. Manufactures and industry were if anything too carefully fostered by the State. If Joseph had not done all he desired for the peasantry, they and the burghers had received considerable encouragement from the efforts of their rulers on their behalf. They had been taught self-respect; more enterprise, ambition and industry had been instilled into them. The Jesuit monopoly of education had been broken down, and thought freed from the trammels hitherto imposed on it. One effect of this was the great intellectual activity of the period, in literature, in the theatrical and musical worlds.[1] In music the period was of special importance, for Vienna served as a half-way house between Italy and Northern Germany. Mozart was prominent at the Court of Maria Theresa, Haydn was a native of Lower Austria, and Beethoven took up his residence at Vienna in 1792, and gave a new impetus to musical life there. It was during this period that Vienna developed its character of a gay and lively capital, much frequented by the German nobility and even by the leading Magyar nobles, who maintained great state and spent money freely. A good deal was done for the improvement of the capital by Leopold I and succeeding rulers, especially for sanitation, which needed reform very badly, for between 1770 and 1782 the death-rate was as heavy as 40 in the 1000.[2] It may have been partly owing to the social amenities of Vienna that its inhabitants concerned themselves but little with politics. They might protest, as in

---

[1] Cf. Wolf, pp. 415 ff.

[2] The population was about 250,000, Paris at the time having 700,000 people, London, 900,000.

1789, against the heaviness of the taxation, but they did not trouble about Joseph's ecclesiastical reforms ; and even the storm and stress of the Napoleonic wars did not affect them to anything like the same extent as it did the North Germans. They neither suffered as much nor felt the degradation of Napoleon's domination as keenly, so that even the enthusiasm of the War of Liberation left them comparatively untouched.

Even the Treaty of Reichenbach had not got rid of the Eastern Question. It had only made a provisional arrangement by which the war was prevented from spreading further ; peace had yet to be made, and it was by no means certain that it would be possible to arrange it on terms satisfactory to all concerned. However, one result of the treaty was that no opposition was offered to Leopold's candidature for the Empire. It was felt desirable in view of the state of affairs in France that the interregnum should be brought to an end as soon as possible, and on September 30th, 1790, Leopold was unanimously elected. His first important act as Emperor was to issue a protest (Dec. 14th) against the decrees of the French Assembly of August 4th, 1789, abolishing feudalism and its appendages, on the ground that they violated the treaty rights of those members of the Empire who held lands in Alsace. But this protest was a mere paper form, and was only important as an indication of future trouble ; for the time being Leopold's most pressing task was to bring about peace with Turkey, and to put his relations with Prussia and Russia on a satisfactory footing.

Though disposed to establish good relations with Prussia, Leopold had no intention of throwing Russia over altogether ; and Russia, if relieved by the Peace of Verela (Aug. 1790) from the hostility of the still respectable naval power of Sweden, was yet afraid of a coalition between the Triple Alliance, Poland and Turkey, and therefore desired to retain the Austrian alliance, although negotiations for peace between Austria and the Porte had begun at Sistova in December 1790. These at first failed to produce any satisfactory result. The Turks demanded that Austria should not merely give up her recent conquests but Bukovina also, a proposal Austria absolutely refused to entertain, so that the negotiations were broken off (Feb. 10th). It seemed as if Leopold's efforts to avert a general European war would be unsuccessful, for Pitt

23

had committed himself to forcing Russia to relax her grip on Oczakow, and in conjunction with Prussia he was preparing to present an ultimatum to Catherine. Leopold had no wish to embark in a war against England and Prussia in order that Russia should keep Oczakow, but the failure to arrange terms with Turkey made his position very awkward. It might have been difficult for him to avoid supporting Russia against the Triple Alliance had not relief come from England (March). Public opinion proved absolutely hostile to the proposed intervention on behalf of Turkey, and Pitt found himself compelled to abandon the idea. Prussia showed no disposition to take up arms alone on behalf of Turkey, Russia's position was enormously improved and the Turks found themselves compelled to modify their attitude towards Austria. Negotiations were accordingly resumed (May), and after several hitches, were finally brought to an end by the Peace of Sistova (Aug. 4th, 1791). This renewed the Peace of Belgrade and the subsequent Austro-Turkish commercial treaties. Austria restored the conquests she had made since February 1788, but a separate treaty ceded to her Old Orsova and a small strip of territory in Croatia.[1] The Russo-Turkish War was brought to a close about the same time by a preliminary treaty at Galatz, which was completed by the definite Peace of Jassy in January 1792.

The real importance of the cessation of the Turkish War was that it removed one of the principal obstacles to those better relations between Austria and Prussia for which, mainly on account of the state of affairs in France, both Leopold and Frederick William were anxious. Kaunitz, of course, was still opposed to anything in the way of an alliance, but the Vice-Chancellor, Philip Cobenzl, received Bischoffswerder when he visited Vienna early in 1791 to convey Frederick William's overtures to Leopold. The truth was that both in Austria and in Prussia the monarchs were taking the direction of affairs from the ministers who had till then guided them; and while despite the prejudices of Kaunitz, who could never forget Silesia and 1740, Leopold was coming to favour a reconciliation with Prussia, Frederick William, without actually dismissing Hertzberg, was abandoning the traditions of the system of Frederick II which Hertzberg represented.

[1] Cf. Wolf, p. 383.

In June 1791, Bischoffswerder revisited Leopold, then at Milan, and acquainted him with Frederick William's desire for a personal interview. Leopold was not long about deciding. On June 18th he informed Bischoffswerder that he approved of the project of an alliance and would be glad to have an interview with Frederick William. It was arranged that this should be held in Saxon territory at Pillnitz, and in the course of the summer; and with this Bischoffswerder departed (June 24th). The foundation of the First Coalition had been laid.

CHAPTER XVIII

GERMANY AND THE FRENCH REVOLUTION

AMONG the causes of Leopold's anxiety for peace with Turkey, even on terms hardly in keeping with the military successes Austria had gained in the war, was his wish to have his hands free to deal with France. Few things are more remarkable than the way in which the earlier stages of the movement which was to exercise so enormous an influence over every branch of German life were overshadowed by the Eastern Question. Far from engaging the attention of Germany or of Europe as a whole, the French Revolution was, until the year 1791, regarded as a purely French concern, important to the rest of Europe only because it prevented France from taking her usual part in international politics. It was looked upon as likely to paralyse the power of France, to weaken her, to engage her in civil and domestic strife, and to make her a negligible quantity in the calculations of the Foreign Ministries of Europe. Leopold had, of course, to take into consideration the chances of the complication of the situation in Belgium by the intervention of French revolutionaries; but when the Belgian insurrection had been suppressed, and the Bishop of Liége, in virtue of a decree of the Imperial Chambér of April 1790, had been restored to his dominions and to his ancient rights, there seemed no immediate likelihood of trouble.[1]

The causes to which the intervention of the Powers of Europe in the affairs of France is most commonly assigned, the support of monarchical principles against a militant and subversive democracy and Leopold's anxiety to succour his sister and his brother-in-law, were not perhaps the most important

[1] An insurrection had broken out in Liége in the autumn of 1789, the Bishop, a Count von Hoensbrook, had been forced to fly to Treves, upon which Prussia marched troops into the Bishopric to restore order. This intervention was mainly designed to give Prussia a foothold in the Netherlands, but on the restoration of better relations between her and Austria she abandoned the Liègois and withdrew her troops.

factors in embroiling France with Europe in 1791–1792. These motives did exist, and did influence Leopold and Frederick William II, though neither of these monarchs was animated merely, as was the Swedish knight-errant King, Gustavus III, by a chivalrous desire to come to the assistance of the imperilled Bourbons; nor did their notions of propriety and orderliness receive the same shock that the excesses of the Revolutionists inflicted upon the order-loving mind of George III. Leopold can have known but little of his sister; and the Franco-Austrian alliance, which he is supposed to have wished to preserve, had been practically non-existent ever since Vergennes had first obtained the direction of the affairs of France. Frederick William II interfered rather more as the champion of absolutist and monarchical principles; but he was a true Hohenzollern and in his eyes the strongest argument in favour of intervention was the prospect of obtaining territorial acquisitions at the expense of the weakened France, torn by internal dissensions, with which he expected to have to deal. Quite apart from these questions, however, there were two points over which a collision between France and the Empire was inevitable, the rights of those Princes of the Empire who held land in Alsace, and the support and shelter given by the Princes of Western Germany to the bands of French *emigrés* who were collecting along the Eastern frontier of France and breathing vengeance on the enemies from whom they had fled.

Of the many anomalies in the constitution of Germany in the 18th Century, the relations which existed between Alsace and the Empire were about the most remarkable.[1] Alsace had been ceded in full sovereignty to France in 1648, but " saving the rights of the Empire." What this exactly meant was never clear—probably it was never meant to be clear. In any case the important fact was that many Princes of the Empire, including among others the Elector Palatine, the Electors of Treves and Mayence and the Bishop of Worms, held lands in Alsace by feudal tenure and had thus been affected by the decrees of August 4th, 1789, abolishing feudalism altogether. They had protested vigorously against this infringement of the rights secured to them by the Peace of Westphalia, but they had not been able to get the National Assembly to see eye to eye with them in the matter. Just before Joseph's death the

[1] Cf. pp. 57–58.

deputies of the Upper Rhenish Circle had petitioned him to protect their rights in Alsace, and Leopold's election capitulations had pledged him to see justice done. In December 1790 the Emperor took the matter up, addressing to the French Assembly a request for the restoration of the old conditions, to which that body returned no answer. The question was then referred to the Diet ; but no further steps were taken beyond the publication of a decree (*Reichsschluss*) upon the subject. Meanwhile the emigration had begun, and French nobles were beginning to cross the frontier and to collect in the cities along the Rhine, where they were for the most part welcomed by the local authorities, who looked with great disfavour on the Revolutionary principles now beginning to make themselves felt beyond the French frontiers.

As a whole, Germany was so very different from France, socially, politically and intellectually, that the ideas of the Revolution gained but little ground even in the more advanced parts of the country, and the influence which the Revolution exercised was one of reaction rather than of attraction. Split up into petty principalities, Germany lacked the homogeneity and uniformity which made France strong, compact, and concrete in thought, which enabled the Revolution to identify itself with the country, to overthrow the Bourbons by accusing them of being dynastic rather than national, and to make *incivisme* the worst of crimes. It was not merely political unity that Germany lacked. Socially and economically there were far greater differences between districts only a very small distance apart than there were between provinces at one end of France and those at the other. This was partly due to the want of homogeneity in administration ; but other causes affected it also. Differences in religion were reflected by marked differences in condition between Catholic and Protestant states. On the whole, the former were backward, poor and ignorant; the latter, more wealthy, enlightened and prosperous.[1] Even in the intellectual sphere the same effects were to be traced. It was want of unity in Germany which tended to make thought abstract, to build up separate literary schools which gloried in their independence and isolation. Where the unity of France made it possible to establish a so-called "equality," the localism and particularism

---

[1] Cf. Mirabeau, *Royaume de Prusse.*

of Germany kept classes apart and prevented fusion not merely between the higher and the lower, but also between corresponding strata in different states. If the French Revolution gave birth to German nationalism, it did it by first strengthening local patriotism. The subjects of an Imperial Knight had to become Würtembergers or Bavarians before they could become Germans. The substitution of states of moderate size for the multitude of petty principalities whose existence was so strong a barrier to unity of interests or of ideas, seemed a stopping short on the road to the unification of Germany, but it was an essential preliminary to the attainment of any approach to that end. The process was one of degrees. Good government and the abolition of the abuses of the *ancien régime* were more desired by the peoples of Germany than self-government was. For that they were not prepared—they were in too backward a stage of political development. They looked to their rulers to play the part of the enlightened despot and to effect for them the reforms they needed. Thus, where the dynasty rose to the occasion and identified itself, as in Prussia, with the adaptation of the French Revolution to local needs and aspirations, it gained enormously in prestige and influence from a movement which had overthrown the ancient monarchy of France.

It was a curious circumstance that the first impulse given by the clearing away of the old system through French influence was in the direction of getting rid of French influences, especially over language and thought. The first of the " rights of man " was the right to be a German, and this made itself apparent in poetry, in philosophy and in art. The French tastes, education and ideas which had ruled the courts of Germany were gradually ousted. No German Prince had been more under French influence than Frederick II. The Louis XIV of Prussia, French in language and utterly without national feeling, though alive to the advantage of posing as the defender of Germany and the champion of German interests, it was a little curious that he should have done something to revive German feelings by his victory at Rossbach over an army mainly composed of Germans, and representing the only bond between the various parts of Germany, the Empire. The truth was that great as was the power and influence of France over Germany, so far as the elements of a national feeling existed hostility and opposition to France were its principal ingredients. The formidable

Western neighbour was a constant menace to Germany. If the generations had long since passed away which had seen the Palatinate devastated, Heidelberg laid in ruins, Mannheim given to the flames, there must have been many Hessians and Westphalians who retained vivid recollections in 1792 of the performances of the soldiery of "Père la Maraude"[1] and his successors in the Seven Years' War. The loss of Lorraine was only half a century old, and the centenary of the seizure of Strassburg must have recalled the bitter memory of Germany's helplessness in the face of the *Chambres de Reunion* to every patriotic German, if indeed any German living in 1792 had a claim to that description. The German Princes might outrage their patriotic sentiments by assisting in the aggrandisement of France at the expense of Germany, but their insulted national pride could only be healed by a corresponding increase in the compensation they must receive. Frederick II might stoop to accept the help of France in robbing another German Power of one of its provinces, Charles of Bavaria might condescend to owe his precarious tenure of the Imperial throne to the heir of Louis XIV, but one and all professed to look upon France as a foreigner even when receiving benefits at her hands, one and all were ready, if it suited the momentary exigencies of their policy, to invoke the name of Germany, to allege German national interests and to pose as the watchful defenders of Germany against France.

But although the condition of Germany in 1792 was such that there was but little likelihood of resistance to French aggression, Germany was not as accessible to the influence of the new French propaganda as were Belgium and Holland and Italy. It would not, of course, be true to represent Germany as quite untouched by sympathy with the Revolution. The high ideals of some of the men of 1789 were fully in keeping with the doctrines of the *Illuminati*; the notion of Liberty, Fraternity and Equality, the appeal to the "rights of man," the tendency to regard all humanity as one, all these were eagerly welcomed by the cosmopolitan "intellectuals" to whom patriotism was at best only a heroic weakness. Schiller and Goethe raised no protest against the advance of the French frontier to the banks of the Rhine; Kant and Fichte welcomed the overthrow of privilege, of class distinctions, of feudal restrictions as steps

[1] The Duc de Richelieu.

towards the millennium of liberty and the rule of the intellect, they did not stop to reflect that reforms effected by a foreign conqueror have but an uncertain guarantee. Yet the men who welcomed the Revolution were politically of little weight. Trees of liberty were planted at Hamburg, in several places the taking of the Bastille was celebrated; but this was of scarcely any political significance. The governments of Germany saw in the new movement a danger to be closely watched and suppressed; and even if men like Thugut had not been on the alert to prevent the Republican propaganda from taking hold, the country offered an unfruitful soil to the seed. The inhabitants of Southern and Western Germany had but little in common with the French, they received laws and constitutions from France without being in any way assimilated.

The reasons for this are not hard to discover. In Germany there was nothing to correspond to the French *bourgeoisie*, no class capable of throwing off the yoke of the nobles. Feudalism had still so strong a hold upon German society that the idea of achieving political independence hardly seems to have entered into the minds of the peasantry: they were still too much under the authority of their lords, and the lords, on their part, were identified with their estates and with the local administration in a way which France with her idle and absentee *noblesse* could not parallel. Thus, except where the mediæval state of things had begun to pass away, the Revolution in Germany was not a root and branch affair, for in most places the mediæval system retained sufficient vitality to stand being reformed. In a few places only was it already so far advanced towards decadence that it could be swept completely away. Among these the territories on the left bank of the Upper Rhine had advanced about the furthest. Here the inhabitants were for the most part vine-growers, more alert, more excitable and more vigorous than the sluggish and submissive agricultural population lower down the river. Round Mayence there really existed the nucleus of a German Republican party, a *Tiers-État* in embryo. The peasantry in this part were proprietors, and having much more civil liberty than was the case elsewhere in Germany, were sufficiently advanced to desire still more.

It was a district without political traditions, very much split up, largely in the hands of ecclesiastical rulers who, expecting that before long the threatened secularisation of the ecclesiastical territories would deprive them of the duty of governing, were therefore preparing themselves for the loss of their administrative functions by neglecting them. Nor were the lay rulers much more formidable barriers to French influence. The Palatinate branch of the Wittelsbach family governed indifferently, the Zweibrücken branch distinctly ill. The Imperial Cities had no real municipal life or patriotism : the oligarchies which ruled them were weak and discredited. Any movement towards democracy among the lower classes was bound to tell in favour of France, and there was nothing whatever to check French aggression or even annexation. Förster and the rest of the Republican party at Mayence would probably have preferred a Cisrhenane Republic under French protection to direct incorporation, but civil and social liberty, good government and the abolition of feudal abuses were quite enough to reconcile the districts West of the Rhine to annexation. To a modified degree this was true of most of South and Western Germany. The application of the Napoleonic system brought great material benefits, received through the local dynasties which had accepted French protection. It was only when this came to involve the rigid enforcement of the Continental System and a heavy drain of conscripts to fight in a quarrel which did not concern the states from which they were drawn, that French protection was found to be a yoke too heavy to be borne and that Napoleon's arbitrary rearrangement of the map of Germany excited opposition. Nothing so clearly illustrates the weakness of the resistance of Germany to the French in the war against the First Coalition as the very gradual way in which South and Western Germany deserted the failing fortunes of the Emperor in 1813. The difference between the attitude of Prussia, which had received no material benefits, but only insults and injuries from Napoleon, and that of Baden or Würtemberg, which would not join the Allies until Austria and Prussia had promised to respect the reorganisation effected under French influence, is typical of the state of Germany between 1792 and 1814. The "national" movement of 1813–1814 was made possible by France and by France alone. It was not merely that she neutralised the material benefits of her rule by the even greater material injuries of the conscription and the Continental System, it was not merely that Napoleon's actions betrayed his selfishness and his lack of consideration for German interests, and that his arbitrary and oppressive rule brought home to the client-states the fact that their "protector" was in truth a tyrant and an oppressor. By suppressing the material obstacles which had till then prevented the union of the German peoples, by concentrating the petty states and uniting them in medium-sized states, France opened avenues to that national life which her propaganda, no less than the example of the national resistance of England, Spain and Russia, had fomented. The overthrow of the relics of the Empire left the ground clear for the construction of something not intimately associated as the Empire was with disunion, localism and *Kleinstaaterei.*

But as things stood in 1792 the action of Germany was bound to be determined rather by the relations of the various members of the Empire to one another, than by any national feeling. Disunited, without an army, almost without a con-stitution, for the Diet, which was the sole bond of union between the states of Germany, had fallen into such disrepute that only 14 Princes out of 100 eligible to send representatives and only 8 cities out of 51 troubled to be represented at Ratisbon in 1788, Germany cannot be said to have adopted any attitude towards the French Revolution, because no "Germany" capable of adopting an attitude really existed. In place of Germany stood Austria and Prussia, whose opposition was to soon reassert itself despite the temporary reconciliation between their rulers, and the whole host of minor states, lay and ecclesiastical, each following its own local and dynastic policy without any glimpse of a wider patriotism. Yet disunited, distracted and divided as Germany was, there still existed a German idea, a confused notion of Germany as a whole, a sense of unity and nationality which the neighbours and enemies of Germany had always sought to suppress, and which not even the Germans themselves had done anything to arouse. The intellectual revival which was making itself felt throughout Germany in the latter half of the 18th century had not taken a national line, even where it had touched political or social grievances. It had done much to arouse intellectual activity, to make people think, to pave the way for the reception of new ideas, but the idea of German nationality was not one to which the leaders of German thought had as yet paid any attention. If the German idea existed it was in a state of suspended animation.

Of the domestic situation of Austria and of Prussia enough

has already been said; but seeing that the war which was about to break out affords the classical example of the utter disintegration of Germany, it may be well to make a brief survey of the principal minor states and their rulers, and trace the chief changes which had taken place among them since 1715. To follow their history in detail is impossible: in those where there is any history to be followed it is but little connected with the general course of affairs outside of which it lies. Too small for the most part to develope very marked differences either socially, economically, or intellectually, the minor states of Germany tend to lack individuality, and it is only by means of their rulers that one can distinguish between them. When it has been said that the 18th Century was the age of the "benevolent despots," and that in some of the minor Princes of Germany the benevolent predominated and in others the despotic, one has said almost all that is to be said.

Next to the Hapsburgs and the Hohenzollerns, the family which in 1792 held most land ,in Germany was that of the Wittelsbachs. The extinction of the Neuburgs in 1742 had brought the Lower Palatinate[1] into the possession of the Sulzbach branch, who already held the principality of that name in the Upper Palatinate together with the part of the Cleves-Jülich inheritance assigned to them in 1666.[2] On the extinction in 1777 of the Bavarian line the Elector Palatine had succeeded to the 14,000 square miles and the 1,100,000 subjects of his cousins at Münich, while his heir, the Duke of Zweibrücken, ruled some 70,000 people inhabiting a district of under 900 square miles. On the accession of Maximilian Joseph of Zweibrücken to Bavaria and the Palatinate in 1799, the representative of all these Wittelsbach lines was the ruler of the third largest accumulation of territories in Germany, in all 21,000 square miles with about 2½ million inhabitants, which had an additional importance from their strategical position on the Upper Danube, which gave Bavaria the power of being either Austria's stoutest bulwark or the most useful ally of her enemies. Charles Theodore, the reigning Elector in 1792, was on the whole a good administrator, though by no means popular. He was a somewhat bigoted Roman Catholic, and his readiness to acquiesce in Joseph II's designs on Bavaria did

---

[1] 5300 square miles, with about a million inhabitants.
[2] Some 660 square miles and 50,000 people.

not much recommend him to his Bavarian subjects. In the Palatinate he was far better liked. There he felt at home: there he did a good deal for education and for the encouragement of art and literature. Heidelberg and Mannheim were both embellished and improved under his direction, Mannheim becoming the best and most famous theatrical centre in Germany.

In inhabitants the territories of the Wettin dynasty in Saxony exceeded the Wittelsbach lands; but in the valleys of the Saale and the Middle Elbe population was far denser than on the Upper Danube and along the foothills of the Alps, despite even the ravages in which the Silesian struggle had involved the unhappy Saxons. Frederick Augustus III had been a minor under the regency of his uncle Xavier for the first five years of his rule (1763–1768), and it was just as well for Saxony that he therefore did not come forward as a candidate for that Polish crown which had brought so little advantage either to Saxony or to its rulers. Under his wise and enlightened rule Saxony had enjoyed peace which had permitted the return of some degree of prosperity, education, agriculture and forestry all coming in for much encouragement and protection.

Of the other territories of the Wettin family the Electoral line had recovered Merseburg, Weissenfels and Zeitz on the extinction of the three cadet branches established by the partition of 1656, but there still existed in 1792 several small principalities belonging to the Ernestine line of which Saxe-Weimar alone merits special notice.

Under the beneficent and wise rule of Duke Charles Augustus (succeeded 1758, a minor till 1775) it was the intellectual centre of Germany. Goethe had settled at Weimar in response to a special invitation from the Duke, and the University of Jena was one of the most flourishing and vigorous in the whole country. Schiller was one of its most popular teachers, Wieland and Herder completed the quartette whose presence made Weimar famous. But Charles Augustus was not so much addicted to the intellectual as to be unmindful of the material side of life. The finances of the little state were in good order; agriculture, mining and industries flourished; public works of importance and benefit were undertaken. Politically the Duke was an adherent of Prussia: he had been active in negotiating the formation of the League of Princes in

1785, and he was to take part in the campaigns of 1792 and 1806 as a Prussian General.

After the close of the Seven Years' War one hears but little the British partner in the " Personal Union " had had some of the Electorate of Hanover.[1]   If under George I and George II cause to complain that its interests were sacrificed to those of Hanover, under George III, who prided himself on his freedom from the Hanoverian prejudices of his predecessors, the tables were completely turned.   Hanoverian battalions had shared in Elliott's successful defence of Gibraltar (1779-1783), and in Murray's scarcely less honourable capitulation at Minorca (1782). At this very moment (1792) the 14th and 15th Hanoverian regiments formed part of the British forces in India,[2] a quarter in which by no stretch of the imagination could Hanover be said to be much concerned.   But if no longer given the first place in the affections of its ruler, Hanover was not badly governed, though the administration was altogether in the hands of an unprogressive aristocracy, which not only filled the Privy Council, the body by which the government was administered, but also controlled the local Estates.   These were of more importance than they would otherwise have been owing to the absence of any general assembly for the whole Electorate.   Thus every new tax had to be agreed to by all these Estates, which caused constant delays and hindrances. This absence of centralisation was not overcome by any special energy or activity on the part of the Privy Council, whose authority was restricted by the existence of a separate department for the domains, mines and forests, and of an equally independent War-Chancery.   Still the government if unenterprising was mild and unoppressive; and if in some parts the peasantry were still serfs, they were on the whole fairly prosperous.   Politically, Hanover tended to act with Brunswick-Wolfenbüttel and with Prussia, though the old hostility to the Hohenzollern was by no means extinct.   It still lingered among some of the leading men; but at the time of Joseph's attempt to exchange the Netherlands for Bavaria, Hanover adhered to the League of Princes.

---

[1] Hanover had during the 18th century acquired the County of Bentheim, pawned to it in 1753, and the little districts of Blumenthal (1741) and Seyn Altenkirchen (1782).

[2] Cf. Cornwallis Correspondence.

The Duchy of Brunswick-Wolfenbüttel, though little more than a sixth of the size of the Electorate, its area being not much over 1500 square miles, was in proportion more populous and wealthy; but along with the rest of North-Western Germany it had suffered a good deal during the Seven Years' War. On the extinction of the "new" Dannenberg line with Duke Louis Rudolf in 1735, the Duchy had passed to Ferdinand Albert of Brunswick-Bevern, the head of a cadet branch established in 1666. He died in the same year, and was succeeded by his eldest son Charles, who ruled the Duchy for forty-five years and did it great service. The great Ferdinand of Brunswick, who died in 1792, was the second son of Duke Ferdinand Albert, while other members of the family were also closely identified with the Prussian service. Duke Charles was another of those Princes who did a good deal for education and for literature. The celebrated Lessing was given the post of Ducal Librarian in 1770, the *Collegium Carolinum* was founded at Brunswick, a Museum was established, and the schools were thoroughly reformed. But the Duke was an extravagant ruler, and contracted debts which the limited revenues of his territories[1] did not suffice to discharge. Thus he was very glad of the opportunity which England's American troubles afforded to him as to the other needy owners of Germany's principal article of export, mercenaries, for filling his coffers and finding occupation for his men. In January 1776 he concluded a subsidy treaty by which in return for 110,000 thalers a year and a lump sum of 50 thalers a head, 4300 Brunswickers were taken into British pay.[2]

Duke Charles was succeeded by his eldest son Charles William Ferdinand, "the Hereditary Prince" of Crefeld and Minden, the "Brunswick" of Valmy and Auerstadt, who proved no less benevolent and careful as a ruler than gallant as a soldier. Under him the Duchy made considerable advances: the burden of taxation was reduced, the poor-laws were improved, and the country well-governed. Following his father's policy, he adhered firmly to the Prussian alliance, and

---

[1] They amounted to about 1,500,000 thalers per annum: Oncken, *Zeitalter Friedrich der Grosse*, ii. 709.

[2] This force was sent to Canada, and shared in Burgoyne's gallant but ill-fated expedition.

commanded the Prussian force which made the unopposed promenade to Amsterdam in 1787.

But as a provider of mercenaries, Brunswick was quite eclipsed by Hesse-Cassel. Of the 29,000 Germans whose services England hired in 1776–1777, Hesse-Cassel provided nearly 17,000. From the days of Landgrave Charles I (1676–1730), Hesse-Cassel had been pre-eminently a military State. His sons Frederick I (1730–1751)[1] and William VII (1751–1760) had followed in his steps, the latter supplying a large contingent to the army in English pay with which Ferdinand of Brunswick disputed Western Germany with the French. Of this war Hesse-Cassel was so unfortunate as to be one of the principal theatres: it endured great hardships and was much thrown back, so that the chief task of Landgrave Frederick II (1760–1785), an energetic and careful ruler, was to foster in every possible way the restoration of his dominions to a prosperous condition. He introduced the cultivation of the potato, reformed the land-laws and the system of weights and measures. He established a cantoning system after the Prussian model, and maintained his forces at a high level of efficiency. At the same time, he was not behind the other Princes of the day in encouraging the arts and education. His son William IX, the builder of the famous castle of Wilhelmshöhe, followed the same policy. While Hesse-Cassel had continued throughout the 18th Century to adhere to the Prussian alliance, which was one of the family traditions, Hesse-Darmstadt had been no less loyal to her traditional policy of fidelity to the Emperor. Its rulers during the period, Ernest Louis (1678–1739), Louis VIII (1739–1768), Louis IX (1768–1790), and Louis X (1790–1830), were always on the side of Austria, and in the Seven Years' War Hesse-Darmstadt was distinguished by its antagonism to Prussia, the patron and ally of Hesse-Cassel.[2] Louis IX is best known in connection with his military establishment at Pirmasens, held by a special regiment of grenadiers to whose training he had devoted much time. In contrast to the other Princes of the day, he steadily refused to hire out his men to foreign Powers, and it was not his

[1] King of Sweden (from 1720–1751) in virtue of his marriage with Ulrica Eleanore, sister of Charles XII.

[2] It may perhaps be worth mentioning that in 1866 it was Hesse-Cassel which was annexed to Prussia ; Hesse-Darmstadt has retained its separate existence.

subjects who acquired for the name of " Hessian " so unfavourable a reputation in the American War.[1]

In extent the possessions of the House of Mecklenburg were more considerable than those of families of greater importance in German history; but one does not hear much of either Mecklenburg-Strelitz or Mecklenburg-Schwerin except for the quarrel between Duke Charles Leopold and his Estates, which had so nearly involved England and Hanover in a war with Russia.[2] Both duchies had been so fortunate as to lie outside the theatre affected by the Seven Years' War, in which they had remained somewhat apathetically neutral, failing to profit economically by the sufferings of their neighbours. The most noticeable feature with regard to Mecklenburg was the definite constitutional acknowledgment in 1755 of the free condition of the peasants, whose condition had been steadily growing worse since the Thirty Years' War. They were not merely bound to the soil, but were actually serfs. The whole district was one of the poorest and most backward in all Germany, and neither Frederick Francis I of Schwerin (1785–1837) nor Charles of Strelitz (1794–1816) played at all a prominent part in the Revolutionary epoch.

Not long after the end of the Seven Years' War an important change had taken place in one of the states of North-Western Germany. The Duchy of Oldenburg had, as has been already stated, been under Danish rule since 1666, but the Holstein-Gottorp family had never admitted Denmark's right to hold it, and in 1773 Paul of Russia,[3] now the representative of the main line of the Holstein-Gottorp family, managed to arrange a compromise. He renounced his claims on Holstein in favour of Denmark, which thereupon ceded Oldenburg to the Czar's cousin, Duke Frederick Augustus of Holstein-Eutin, Prince-Bishop of Lübeck, a grandson of Christian Albert of Gottorp, the great-great-grandfather of Paul.[4] This change was much appreciated by the Oldenburgers, who found in Frederick Augustus a mild and beneficent ruler, while on his death (1785) his nephew Peter Frederick Louis, who acted as Regent for the imbecile heir, Peter Frederick William, governed on very similar lines.

---

[1] Cf. Trevelyan, *American Revolution*, Part II.   [2] Cf. pp. 69–70, 84, 94.

[3] Peter III of Russia was a Holsteiner on his father's side, Charles Frederick of Holstein having married Anna, daughter of Peter the Great.

[4] Cf. p. 56.

24

Baden, divided since 1536 between the Baden-Baden and the Baden-Durlach lines, had been reunited twenty years before the outbreak of the Revolution on the extinction, in 1771, of the Baden-Baden line. Augustus George, who had succeeded to his brother Louis George in 1761, was, like his brother, childless, and in January 1765 he concluded with his cousin of Baden-Durlach the compact which came into operation in 1771. Charles Frederick of Baden-Durlach, who thus reunited the old territories of the House of Zahringen, had succeeded his grandfather Charles William (1709–1738), chiefly noticeable as a warm supporter of Austria in the Spanish Succession War, when only ten years of age, and in the eighty-three years (1738–1821) in which he ruled he saw great changes in the fortunes of Baden. As the ruler of territories coterminous with France, he was naturally much concerned by the events taking place over the border, and was most anxious to prevent Baden having again, as in 1688–1697 and 1702–1714, to bear the brunt of the war and to be once more reduced to a condition of devastation and ruin. He saw a prospect that all the good work he had done would be undone in one campaign, and his conduct in the coming wars was directed largely by this fear.

Of all the minor states of Germany there are few which have so individual a character as Würtemberg. Even into the 18th Century it retained enough of a constitution[1] to distinguish it from the other states. But, as has been explained,[2] the necessities of a more effective defence against the French than the enjoyment of constitutional liberties had altered the position of affairs, and forced the Würtembergers to allow the Duke to strengthen his position greatly by raising a standing army. Thus Eberhard Louis was far more autocratic than any Duke since 1514. Under him Würtemberg experienced the evils of French influence in peace as well as of French hostility in war. The extravagance of his Court, his efforts to ape the " Grande Monarque," to make the Ludwigsburg vie with Versailles, his subjection to the notorious Countess Christina von Gravenitz, brought much harm on his subjects. His successor Charles Alexander, a cousin, who had till then ruled over the territory of Winnenden, acquired by Eberhard III in 1668, was not much of an improvement. He had gone over to Roman Catholicism in 1712 partly from pique at the

[1] Cf. pp. 245–246.   [2] Chapter II.

refusal of the Committee to increase his appanage, and had not his rule (1733–1737) been abruptly closed by his sudden death he would have attempted to overthrow the constitution by a *coup d'état* in which he hoped for Austrian aid. His eldest son, Charles Eugene, was a minor, and did not take over the government till 1744, having been educated in the meantime at the Court of Berlin. He was at first a faithful adherent of Prussia, but his extravagant ways and his love for the theatre, for indulging his architectural fancies, for keeping up a considerable state and a luxurious mode of living, involved him in financial necessities. To extricate himself he concluded a subsidy-treaty with Louis XV in 1752 by which he placed 6000 men at the disposal of France. In the Seven Years' War he fulfilled his obligations by forcibly impressing five regiments of 1000 men each in deliberate disregard of the constitution; a most unpopular measure, as the indifferent behaviour of the Würtemberg regiments at Leuthen [1] proved. The Committee protested against this action and appealed in July 1764 to the Aulic Council, accusing the Duke of levying heavy poll-taxes without the consent of the authorised representatives of the taxpayers, of ill-treating the Church, and generally of denying justice. The Aulic Council, acting with a most unusual precipitation, declared in favour of the Estates within two months of receiving the appeal, and in 1766 the Duke had to dismiss his minister Montmartin. In 1770 a compromise was arranged, and till the Duke's death in 1793 [2] Würtemberg enjoyed a period of peace and comparative prosperity, his encouragement of culture and intellectual life generally, his foundation of a large library and of the so-called "Carlsacademie" going hand in hand with the usual measures by which a "benevolent despot" sought to improve the manufactures, agriculture, trade and revenues of his dominions.

Of the other minor states there are not many which call for special remark. The Franconian branch of the Hohenzollern had ceded its territories to its cousins at Berlin just before the outbreak of war in 1792. The Anhalt-Zerbst line became extinct in 1793, and its territories were divided between the other branches of the family at Bernberg, Dessau and Köthen.

---

[1] Cf. p. 226, and Oncken, *Friedrich der Grosse*, ii. 162.
[2] Charles Eugene was succeeded by his son, Louis Eugene, who died in May 1795, S.P.M.

Count William of Lippe-Schaumburg deserves mention as the founder of the famous military school at Wilhelmstein, at which Scharnhorst was educated. A typical soldier-prince, he did with his peasants in Lippe-Bückeburg on a small scale what the Landgrave of Hesse-Cassel did on a larger, and he is also notable for his reorganisation of the Portuguese army after his campaign in Portugal in 1762.[1] The two lines of the House of Reuss, raised to the rank of Princes in 1778 and 1790 respectively, the Schwarzburg family, divided between Schwarzburg-Sondershausen and Schwarzburg-Rudolstadt in 1681, Waldeck and Hohenlohe were among the larger of those infinitesimal principalities which complicate the map of Germany in 1792 and whose pretensions to independence and to sovereign rights contributed so much to the disunion and defencelessness of Germany. One family also deserves mention, more because of its connection with the United Provinces than on account of its part in the affairs of Germany, that of Nassau. After a variety of changes[2] the position of head of the family had passed to the Nassau-Dietz branch, which had recovered the Stadtholderate of the United Provinces in 1747.[3] Of the ecclesiastical states, the Free Cities, and the Imperial Knights, it might be enough to say that they were in 1792 fully ripe in the annexations they were shortly to undergo. Only the jealousy and rivalry of the larger states had prevented a general scramble for these tempting morsels

---

[1] Cf. Oman, *Peninsular War*, ii. p. 208.

[2] The House of Nassau had split up into two branches in 1255, Walram II and Otto I, the sons of Henry II, obtaining respectively the territories South and North of the Lahn. In 1627, on the death of Louis II, his three sons divided the lands of Walram's branch into the Idstein, Saarbrück-Usingen and Weilburg lines. Between 1718 and 1775, Charles of Nassau-Usingen reunited the Idstein territories with Saarbrück and Usingen, and his sons Charles William (1775–1803) and Frederick Augustus (1803–1816) obtained acquisitions of territory at Lunéville and ruled their lands in common with those of their cousin Frederick William of Nassau-Weilburg (1788–1816), the Duchy of Nassau being formed by the union of the two lines in 1816. Meanwhile Otto's line, of which the Orange-Nassau line in the Netherlands was an offshoot, had similarly split up into three branches on the death of John VI (1606), the Hadamar (extinct 1711), Dillenburg (extinct 1789), and Dietz lines. This last branch had by 1792 reunited all the possessions of the line, so that William V of Holland (1751–1806) was also a member of the Empire as Prince of Nassau.

[3] On the death of William III of England (1702), John William Friso of Nassau-Dietz had inherited his Netherlandish possessions, and it was his son William IV (1711–1751) who was chosen as Hereditary Stadtholder in 1747.

taking place long ago. Directly the French Revolution produced the necessary disturbance in the political equilibrium of Germany, the secularisation of the Bishoprics, the "mediatisation" of the Knights and the annexation of the Cities were bound to come. In 1792 four Archbishops (the three Ecclesiastical Electors and Salzburg), sixteen Bishops and about thirty other prelates were represented in the Diet, not to mention secularised Bishoprics such as Paderborn and Osnabrück.

The three Ecclesiastical Electors in this year were Frederick Charles Joseph of Erthal at Mayence (elected 1774), Clement Wenceslaus of Saxony (son of Augustus II, elected 1768) at Treves, and the Archduke Maximilian Joseph of Austria (elected 1785) at Cologne. The Elector of Mayence was also Bishop of Worms; the Elector of Treves held Freising, Ratisbon and Augsburg in addition to his Electorate; Maximilian of Cologne had been Bishop of Münster since 1780. More important in some ways than any of these Electors was Charles Dalberg, Coadjutor to the Elector of Mayence, who managed, thanks to the Elector's official position as Chancellor of the Empire, to exercise a considerable influence over German politics. For the rest, the Bishops and Abbots were for the most part scions of noble houses, often good and honest rulers, but as a rule too much hampered by their Chapters to do much even when zealous for reform, so that the ecclesiastical states were on the whole very backward.

Fifty-one[1] Free Cities maintained an independent existence in 1789, but many of them, especially among the thirty-one in the Swabian Circle, were of no importance whatever. Of the once-powerful Hanseatic League, Bremen, Lübeck and Hamburg still maintained a commercial union; but of the others which had been represented at the last Hansetag at Lübeck in 1669 only Cologne remained a Free City. Brunswick had been forced to submit to the Duke of Brunswick. Minden was in Prussian, Dantzic in Polish hands. Osnabrück had succumbed to its Prince-Bishop, Rostock to the Duke of Mecklenburg-Schwerin. Frankfurt on Main with 60,000 inhabitants, Nüremberg with 80,000, Augsburg and Ulm with

---

[1] The matricular list of 1521 gives a total of eighty-four cities, since when several (e.g. Basel and Metz) had been annexed by foreign Powers and others (e.g. Donauwörth) incorporated by neighbouring states.

between 30,000 and 40,000 were still of comparative importance; but even in them there was little real municipal life, still less any political union between one and another. Had the Emperor been able to bind the Free Cities to him, had they and the Imperial Knights been willing to sacrifice the shadow of a useless independence for a real union under the head of the Empire, it might have been possible to make "Germany" something more than a geographical expression; but not only was the jealousy of the other states certain to thwart any move from one side or the other, the narrow and obstinate localism of the Cities caused them to cling to their privileges and their separate existence and condemned them to decadence and impotence.

Indeed it was with edged tools that the Emperor and Frederick William II were playing in 1792 when by associating themselves with the cause of the Bourbons they gave an excuse for an attack on Germany to the rising tide of French national feeling with which the Revolution was soon to become identified. Disunited, worse than disunited, distracted by jealousy and localism, Germany could ill afford to give a foothold within her borders to the compact force which the Republic for all its internal commotions wielded as a factor in the European situation.

CHAPTER XIX

THE FIRST COALITION

AS has been already mentioned, it was over the questions of Alsace and of the *emigrés* rather than through the connection between the Hapsburgs and the Bourbons that the Revolution actually came into conflict with the European Powers, though the hostility of the Revolutionary party in France towards Austria was largely due to their fear of intervention. It is quite true that the first steps towards interference taken by Leopold were of the nature of an intervention in the cause of monarchy. The Note issued to the monarchs of Europe in May 1791 did not do more than call attention to the fact that the situation of the King of France was a matter of concern to the other Powers, and at the time Leopold was honestly trying to keep the Comte d'Artois and the rest of the *emigrés* in check. He was by no means anxious to intervene and, although ready to do what he could by diplomatic means, dreaded having to use force. The flight to Varennes (June 1791) was undertaken against his advice, and its failure forced his hand. While negotiations with Prussia were carried on in hopes of arriving at an alliance on definite terms, Leopold issued the " Declaration of Padua " (July 6th), explaining to the other monarchs the steps he proposed to take. These included the recall of his Ambassador, the collection of troops on the frontiers, and the summoning of a conference. This circular excited great indignation in France and made popular feeling, already aroused by shelter and support given to the *emigrés* by the Rhenish Princes, very hostile towards Austria. In August 1791 Leopold and Frederick William met at Pillnitz on the Elbe, a few miles above Dresden, and the Declaration which they issued (Aug. 27th), inviting the co-operation of Europe in helping the King of France to "lay the bases of a monarchical government in liberty," served to still further fan the flame of resentment and hostility to Austria. " It is difficult and dangerous," wrote Lord Auckland to Mr. Pitt,[1] "for sovereigns possessing an absolute authority to become the armed mediators of a free constitution and a moderated monarchy to France," and the anger of the French found expression in Isnard's declaration that "if the cabinets of foreign Courts try to stir up a war of Kings against France, we will stir up for them a war of peoples against Kings" (Nov. 1791). This was one of the first expressions of that revolutionary propagandism which the French were to make their main instrument of attack against the existing European system.

For the time, however, the crisis seemed averted; for on September 21st Louis XVI accepted the revised constitution, and Leopold hailed this as an excuse for taking no further steps. But things had really gone too far already. The war-feeling in France was growing daily stronger. The Legislative Assembly, which had on October 1st replaced the Constituent, was dominated by the more extreme party. One section, it is true, desired a war with the Ecclesiastical Electors and with Austria over the question of the *emigrés*, because they hoped it might show up the necessity for a strong executive and thereby force the Assembly to increase the powers and authority of the King. But this "limited liability" war which Narbonne[2] and the "Feuillants" in general desired was not the object of the Girondins. Led by Brissot and Vergniaud they wanted a real war against Austria, a war which would force Louis to choose definitely between acquiescing in the Revolution and declaring himself its enemy. He would either have to place himself at the head of the anti-Austrian feeling which was gaining ground in France, or he would have to show that the accusations of *incivisme*, of disloyalty to France, of preferring the *emigré* and the foreigner to the nation, were really well-grounded.

In November 1791, Louis, at the bidding of the Assembly, formally demanded that Leopold should disperse the *emigré* forces, while the Elector of Treves was given a month in which to comply with a similar request. But instead of taking any steps to meet the wishes of the French, Leopold laid before the Assembly the Resolution (*Reichsschluss*) of the Diet, that the action of France with regard to Alsace had violated the Peace

[1] *Dropmore Papers, Hist. MSS. Commission*, vol. ii. p. 159.
[2] Appointed War Minister in December.

of Westphalia (Dec. 3rd). On December 24th he not only refused to disperse the *emigrés*, but complained of the efforts of the French to propagate sedition and discontent within the Empire, and more especially in Belgium. It was hardly likely that the Legislative Assembly would accept such a rebuke quietly, and their announcement that Leopold's failure to give them satisfaction before March 1st would be regarded as a declaration of war might easily have been predicted. With such attitudes on the various sides war was only a question of time. On January 17th, 1792, the Austrian Conference decided to present an ultimatum to the French, demanding that the orders to assemble three armies on the frontiers should be cancelled, and that compensation should be given to the Pope for the loss of Avignon and to the Alsatian Princes. A week later, orders were given to mobilise 40,000 men to reinforce the garrisons in the Netherlands and in Further Austria. Nor did the Emperor neglect the chances of obtaining the assistance of other Powers. On February 7th an offensive and defensive alliance was concluded between Austria and Prussia, pledging both parties to assist each other if attacked, or in case of internal troubles, to guarantee the integrity of Poland and a "free constitution" for that country, and finally to promote a European Concert for the settlement of French affairs. All was thus in train for the formation of a coalition against France, when, on the last day of February, Leopold was suddenly seized with a severe chill, and on March 1st he died. His premature death was a great blow to Austria—indeed to Europe. Had he been at the head of the Coalition, the foolish and offensive proclamation which heralded Brunswick's invasion would probably have never been issued. A statesman of experience and capacity, he would have restrained the *emigrés*, and would have had far more chance of keeping the Coalition together than any other monarch could have had. As it was, the Coalition went to pieces at once for want of a real leader. Francis II, Leopold's heir and successor, did in the end do good service to Austria and to Europe; but he had not the strength of mind or the experience to prevent Thugut from wrecking the Second Coalition, and still less was he fitted in 1792 to cope with such a problem as that of the French Revolution. So far as the First Coalition had any leader, it was Frederick William II, who was neither a great soldier nor a great statesman, though he fancied himself both, and who, moreover, having always one eye fixed on the chances of aggrandisement in Poland, was unable to devote exclusively to the affairs of France even the very slender capacities as a statesman and a leader with which he was endowed. Meanwhile, Leopold's answer had brought about the overthrow of the Feuillant ministry, and in their place Louis had been forced to accept a ministry drawn from the Girondin party, of which the leading member was Dumouriez (March 1792). The policy on which Dumouriez pinned his faith was that of detaching Prussia from the side of Austria by reviving the old friendly relations between Paris and Berlin. Hoping to isolate Austria, he sent Custine to Berlin and Talleyrand to London, while he spared no effort to keep the minor states of Germany from making common cause with the Emperor.

When, in April 1792, a reply was received from Austria, in which Kaunitz definitely refused to diminish the warlike preparations, and alleged as his reason the menace to Belgium of the Jacobin propagandism, only one course was possible. On April 20th the Assembly declared war on "the King of Hungary and Bohemia,"[1] and Belgium was at once attacked by four converging columns. The invasion proved a complete fiasco, not because the Austrian preparations for defence were specially efficient, but through the disorderliness, insubordination and utter inefficiency of the Volunteers who composed a large part of the invading forces. But the Austrians were in no condition to profit by the disorderly retreat of their adversaries. They had also to wait for their Prussian allies, and the slowness with which the Prussian mobilisation was being carried out was a proof of the decline in the efficiency of the Prussian army.

The failure of the invasion of Belgium had produced wild excitement and much disorder at Paris. Accusations of treachery were brought against the Court and the generals, and it was just this moment that Louis XVI chose for refusing to sign a decree against those priests who had not accepted the Civil Constitution of the Clergy, and to dismiss his Girondin ministry. The result was the riot of June 20th, while three

---

[1] Francis II. was not elected Emperor till July 14th, and the French hoped to keep the Empire out of the war by thus treating Francis merely as the head of the Hapsburgs and make it possible for its members to remain neutral ; which, with the exception of Hesse-Cassel, they all did.

weeks later, on July 11th, the Assembly declared the country in danger.

By this time the Austrians and Prussians were at last ready to take the field. The principal attack was committed to the Duke of Brunswick with 42,000 Prussians, who was to advance into Champagne from Coblence, supported on the left by 14,000 Austrians from the Breisgau and 10,000 *emigrés* and Hessians. On his right another Austrian corps (15,000) was to advance against Thionville, while yet a third under Albert of Saxe-Teschen proceeded to lay siege to Lille. The Allies heralded their advance by publishing in the name of the Duke of Brunswick the famous proclamation of July 27th, which completed the rage and exasperation of the French at this intervention in their affairs. It was really the work of the *emigrés*,[1] approved by Frederick William, accepted by Francis II without enthusiasm and by Brunswick with great misgivings.

It was in the last days of July that the invasion began. On paper the invading armies made a great show, but in the field they were much less formidable. Both Austrians and Prussians suffered from insufficient organisation, bad staff-work and all but non-existent administrative services. The commissariat was especially inefficient, and if the Prussians maintained the rigid regimental discipline of Frederick's days, routine and parade had with them usurped the place of practice. The Austrians, as in 1741, had had more recent experience of war but had not turned its lessons to much profit. Nor did the commander's merits make up for the shortcomings of his army. Brunswick, anxious not to compromise his reputation, was not altogether inclined to an advance on Paris. He would have preferred the systematic reduction of the fortresses on the Meuse; but Frederick William, relying quite unjustifiably on the assurances of the *emigrés* that France would really welcome the invaders, overruled this cautious plan. The Prussians began well enough. A cavalry skirmish on August 19th saw the advance-guard of the French army of the Centre driven back in confusion. On the 20th, Longwy was summoned; on the 23rd it surrendered. Verdun capitulated on September 2nd after an equally feeble resistance. This seemed to open the road to Paris, and on September 5th the Prussians crossed the Meuse on their way to Chalons. To

[1] Cf. Lord E. Fitzmaurice's *Life of Brunswick*.

oppose them Dumouriez hurried to the front and took command of the troops collected at Sedan. With them he took post in the wooded hills of the Argonne and occupied the passage of Les Islettes by which Brunswick intended to cross. Meanwhile Kellermann was pushing up from Metz with the 22,000 men of the Army of the Centre to join his colleague. Brunswick displayed a great want of energy. Instead of forcing the Les Islettes position and so bringing Dumouriez to battle before Kellermann could join, he tried to turn the position by seizing another of the passes of the Argonnes, and thus let Dumouriez fall back behind the Aisne and take up a position near St. Menehould, threatening the Prussian flank should they continue their advance on Paris. On September 19th Kellermann arrived, and next day occurred the celebrated skirmish which has been dignified by the name of the "battle" of Valmy. The action was confined to a cannonade, in which the excellence of the French artillery and the firm attitude of the old troops of the Line, who formed the bulk of their army,[1] brought Brunswick to a standstill. Finding the French position too strong for a direct attack, he had not enough confidence in himself or his army to continue his advance and risk leaving the French on his line of communications. He came to a halt at La Lune and waited there for a fortnight, the condition of his army becoming daily worse. The administration broke down completely under the strain of war; the troops, excellent as they were on the parade - ground, proved quite unfitted for the practical work of a campaign, sickness decimated their ranks, and Brunswick was in the end lucky to secure an unmolested retreat. This he achieved by means of negotiations with Dumouriez, who, a politician quite as much as a soldier, still clung to his hopes of detaching Prussia from Austria. Thus he was ready to let Brunswick withdraw from a really very perilous position in return for the evacuation of Longwy and Verdun. This arrangement also enabled Dumouriez to transfer himself and his army to the Austrian Netherlands. The Austrians had already raised the siege of Thionville, and on October 7th the Duke of Saxe-Teschen abandoned his futile attack on Lille and fell back to Mons, ready to dispute the invaders' advance along a line from Mons by Charleroi to Namur. On November 6th Dumouriez,

[1] Cf. Hauterive, *L'Armée sous la Révolution*, pp. 245–246, and Chuquet, *Les Guerres de la Révolution*, ii. 247 ff.

following him up, attacked and carried his main position at Jemappes, a stubborn fight resulting in the complete defeat of the Austrians. The results of the victory were enormous. Mons (Nov. 7th), Brussels (Nov. 13th), Malines, Liége, Namur, Antwerp capitulated one after another almost without resistance. Saxe-Teschen withdrew the relics of his forces towards Liége. The people welcomed the French as deliverers. On November 16th a decree of the Legislative Assembly declared the Scheldt open to commerce, thus defying the Barrier Treaty and the Treaty of Münster, to say nothing of more recent compacts. On the 19th another decree promised fraternity and assistance to any nation engaged in recovering its liberty; but it throws a rather curious light on these professions that, much to the consternation of its people, on December 13th Belgium was declared part of France, as Savoy and Nice had been a month earlier. Austrian rule was most unpopular in the Netherlands; but the Clericals, who had so vigorously opposed Joseph's reforms, were hardly the people to welcome the Rights of Man and the reign of Reason. Meanwhile, on the Middle Rhine Custine, with the Army of the Vosges, had been carrying all before him, spreading alarm all through the states of Southern Germany. On September 30th he entered Spires. Five days later Worms and Philipsbourg were occupied. Encouraged by the news of the check to Brunswick, Custine resolved to push on into Germany. Mayence surrendered at the first summons (Oct. 21st), and the French crossing the Rhine were received warmly at Frankfort. Only the timely arrival of the contingent of Hesse-Cassel saved Coblence from falling into French hands (Oct. 26th).

It was in this part of Germany that there was most chance for the Revolutionary propaganda to obtain a firm foothold. Custine announced that he was making war on the despots, not on the people; that he had come to make them free, to let them choose their own form of government, and to help them throw off the oppressive yoke under which they were groaning. At first these declarations were believed and the population welcomed the French; for it was only the richer classes, the clergy, the nobles and the big merchants who had to suffer anything at their hands. A Convention was summoned to meet at Mayence to settle the government of the conquered territory, and under the influence of George Förster, one of those Germans in whom the Revolution had awakened sentiments akin to those expressed in England by Charles James Fox, it hastened to vote the union of the country between the Queich and the Nahe with France (March 18th, 1793). The idea of extending France to her "natural frontiers" had by now taken firm hold of the French imagination, and the delegates of the National Convention of Rhenish Germany received a hearty welcome at Paris.

By this time events had moved apace. On the day of the affair of Valmy the National Convention had met at Paris and declared France a Republic. On January 21st the Republican party had burnt its boats by the execution of the King, and on February 1st it had followed this act up by declaring war on England and Holland, which until then had maintained a strict neutrality. It was not merely the execution of the King which alarmed Europe and united practically all the Powers, Denmark, Sweden and Switzerland alone standing aloof, in a Coalition to oppose the Republic. The violent actions and language of the Assembly, its obvious disposition to ignore the received rules of international relations, its interference with the affairs of its neighbours, its open adoption and propagation of revolutionary doctrines, the encouragement given to the discontented and disaffected in every state, the disregard displayed for all treaties and conventions, all these drove the alarmed monarchs of Europe into taking arms in defence of their thrones and their territories.

As might have been expected, the relations between Austria and Prussia had not been improved by the events of 1792. Prussia complained that Austria had failed to fulfil her promises; Austria that Brunswick had secured an unmolested retreat at the expense of his ally. Moreover, events in Eastern Europe had served to increase their dissatisfaction. The patriotic party in Poland had in May 1791 introduced a new and revised constitution, abolishing the elective monarchy, the *liberum veto*, and the various other anomalies which had contributed so much to the decadence of the nation. This was accepted by the Diet at Warsaw, but not without opposition, and the malcontents, forming themselves into the Confederation of Targovitsa, appealed to Russia as the guarantor of the old constitution (May 1792). Catherine, eagerly grasping at the pretext for intervention, sent Suvorov and a large army to the aid of the Confederates. Austria might have intervened on behalf of the new constitution, which offered a chance of rescuing Poland from the grip of Russia, if she could have got Prussia to join her; but Frederick William would not hear of it, and Austria, paralysed by the death of Leopold and the troubles with France, had no alternative but to conclude a treaty with Russia (July 1792), guaranteeing the old constitution of Poland. Russian troops now poured into Poland and put down the patriotic party, while Catherine concluded a treaty with Prussia (Jan. 23rd, 1793) for the Second Partition of Poland. By a mixture of force and bribery the Diet was forced to give way to the demands of the invading Powers: on July 22nd it signed a treaty with Russia and on September 25th that which allotted to Prussia 2000 square miles of Polish territory, mainly in Posen and Great Poland, but including the much coveted Dantzic and Thorn. It is this which explains the very small part taken by Prussia in the West during 1793. The certainty of territorial aggrandisement in the East was irresistible and drew Frederick William away from a quarter in which his hopes of acquisitions were rapidly growing fainter; but this neglect of the West for the East was in no small measure responsible for the loss of the Prussian territories West of the Rhine a couple of years later.

Dumouriez opened the campaign of 1793 in February by an advance into Holland, moving by Dortrecht upon Leyden and so for Amsterdam. On his right, Miranda laid siege to Maastricht, while Valence took up a position on the Roer to cover these operations against any interference from the Austrians. At first things went well. Breda fell after a somewhat feeble defence. Dumouriez took Gertruydenberg and was on the point of entering Holland when the news reached him (March 3rd) that the Austrians under the Prince of Coburg-Saalfeld had fallen on Valence near Aix-la-Chapelle, beaten him badly and driven him in on Liége in disorder. Miranda, thus exposed, had to raise the siege of Maastricht and to retire by Tongres on Louvain, while a Prussian corps secured Venloo. Dumouriez, his communications thus endangered, fell back behind the line of the Demer with his army in a state of confusion and demoralisation. The practice of the French "liberators" of Belgium had not altogether corresponded to their professions, and their misconduct and exactions had alienated even their own partisans. The discipline of the army was in a deplorable condition, and the general, who had long been at odds with the Convention and with the Ministry of

War, was already contemplating desertion. One last effort he made, attacking the Austrian positions at Neerwinden on March 18th. It was a desperate fight, but the defeat of Miranda on the French left decided the battle against Dumouriez. Beaten again in another action near Louvain three days later, he fell back behind the Scheldt and, failing in his efforts to get his army to declare against the Convention, finally deserted to the Austrians on April 5th. Thus left in the lurch, his army withdrew behind the frontier. Now was the time for a really vigorous effort by the Allies, and Brunswick strongly urged Frederick William to co-operate heartily with the Austrians to secure the Netherlands and break through the French defences. But Frederick William cared far more for Poland than for the French war, and failed to support Austria with all his strength. The declaration of war by the Diet of the Empire (March 22nd) did not add materially to the strength of the Coalition, and neither the operations in the Alps nor in the Pyrenees exercised any real influence on the fate of the campaign. Holland proved an ally of little value, and the unwise economy which had led Pitt to cut down the peace establishment of Great Britain almost to vanishing point prevented England from putting into the field a force adequate to the emergency. It is a platitude to say that had the Coalition displayed in 1793 anything approaching the resolution and vigour the Powers of Europe were to show in 1814 and 1815, the successful march to Paris might have been anticipated by twenty years. For France was in utter confusion. The army seemed to have lost all cohesion ; there was no real executive ; the Royalists had risen at Toulon, at Lyons, and in La Vendée ; the Girondins were taking arms in Normandy and Guienne. Anarchy, administrative chaos and civil strife seemed to leave France helpless at the feet of the Coalition. It was not in the Netherlands only that things had gone badly. Before the end of 1792 Brunswick had recovered Frankfort, and in March Custine, who had taken post on the Nahe between Bingen and Kreuznach, was outflanked and driven from his positions by the Prussians, who had crossed the Rhine (March 27th) lower down at St. Goar. He fell back to Worms and thence to Landau (April 1st), completely abandoning all his conquests save Mayence, which made a desperate resistance. The siege was begun in April, but not till July 23rd did the brave garrison capitulate and evacuate the city, taking with them those of the inhabitants who had espoused their cause. Meanwhile in the Netherlands the Anglo-Austrians had stormed the French camp at Famars (May 25th) and driven them back to Bouchain. This success allowed Coburg to besiege and take Condé (July 12th) and Valenciennes (July 28th).

The Allies had the ball at their feet. Had their statesmen succeeded in subordinating individual ambitions to the common end, had their commanders looked to more than immediate and local advantage, had they displayed any grasp of the general strategic situation, it would have gone hard with France. But it was a war of governments, not of peoples. There was no enthusiasm for the war in Germany. Even the prospect of recovering Alsace and Lorraine from France failed to arouse any keenness or interest. It mattered little to the inhabitants of the left bank of the Rhine what yoke they laboured under. The Southern states supported the war but languidly, and it was being fought too far away from Austria and from Prussia for its importance to be realised in those countries. Even the rulers and their ministers, who might have been expected to understand the issues involved, failed to grasp the importance of cohesion and of loyal and energetic co-operation. Thus the jealousies, the divisions, the delays and the mistaken strategy of the Allies saved France, and gave the Committee of Public Safety time to get firmly seated in power, to provide a really strong executive, to build up and reorganise a most efficient army out of the relics of the really excellent troops of the *ancien régime*, the enthusiastic " Volunteers of '91 and '92," who only needed discipline and experience, and the vast hordes of men placed at their disposal by the *levée en masse*. During this critical time the Allies were engaged in the pleasing but illusory task of dividing between themselves the acquisitions they were to make from France. Thugut, who had replaced Philip Cobenzl as the principal minister of Francis II, when the latter was dismissed on account of the Second Partition of Poland, which he had failed to prevent or to turn to Austria's profit, was keenly set on extending the Netherlands to the Somme, or annexing Bavaria to compensate Austria for Prussia's gains in Poland—the Elector was to receive Alsace-Lorraine, which the Prussians were to conquer. England thought more of securing her commerce by capturing Dunkirk than of the

25

defeat of the main armies of the enemy. Prussia, more concerned for her own acquisitions in Poland than for the success
of the common cause, was negotiating with France behind
the back of her allies; for the party which favoured the policy
of a Franco-Prussian alliance numbered among its adherents
Prince Henry, Count Haugwitz, General Mollendorf and the
King's favourite Lucchesini, while Brunswick himself so far
favoured the idea as to lend but a languid support to the operations of Würmser's Austrians in Alsace.

Thus the critical month of August slipped past   The
Anglo-Hanoverians separated from Coburg to lay siege to
Dunkirk after clearing the enemy from their path at Lincelles
(Aug. 18th), Coburg and the main body, though within 160
miles of Paris, set about besieging the comparatively unimportant Le Quesnoy, while Brunswick remained inactive in
the Palatinate, never utilising the chance which the disorganisation of the French Armies of the Rhine and the Moselle
offered him.   This gave Carnot time to reinforce the armies
charged with the defence of the French frontiers and to place
more efficient officers at their heads.   Between September 6th
and 8th Houchard cleared away the Hanoverians and Dutch
who at Hondschoote and Menin were covering the Duke of
York's operations against Dunkirk, though he failed to prevent
the safe retreat of the besiegers to Furnes.   A little later the
Austrians, who after taking Le Quesnoy (Sept. 11th) had
laid siege to Maubeuge, were attacked by Houchard's successor, Jourdan, at Wattignies, and after two days of fierce
fighting (Oct. 15th to 16th) were driven from their position,
forced to raise the siege and to retire behind the Sambre
to join the Duke of York.   An advance into West Flanders, however, proved less successful.   Nieuport beat off all
attacks, and in November the French retired behind their own
frontier.

Meanwhile the position on the Middle Rhine had undergone
great changes.   The necessity of taking Mayence had prevented
the Allies from following up Custine's retreat, and when its fall
set them free the want of harmony between the Austrians and
the Prussians came to the assistance of the French.   Würmser,
the Austrian commander, was most anxious to advance into
Alsace; but Brunswick refused to co-operate, having no intention
of conquering Alsace from France to restore it to the rule of

the Hapsburgs. At last Würmser advanced alone against the Army of the Rhine, and pushing Southward drove it from the Weissembourg lines (Oct. 13th) and forced it back over the Lauter in confusion. Had Brunswick supported Würmser properly they might have had Strassburg on which the French had retired; but neither Brunswick nor Frederick William would agree to a winter campaign in Alsace, and the favourable moment slipped by. St. Just and Le Bas, the commissioners sent by the Assembly to purge and reform the Army of the Rhine, set about the restoration of discipline with a vigour which soon produced satisfactory results. In Pichégru it received a commander of quite a different stamp from the incompetent officers till then at its head; and with the not less brilliant Hoche sent by Carnot to command the Army of the Moselle a change was not long in coming. The Allied forces, spread out in a long and straggling line from Kaiserslautern to Haguenau, gave Hoche and Pichégru the chance they wanted. Attempting to relieve Landau by a direct attack on the Prussians, Hoche was checked at Kaiserslautern (Nov. 28th to 30th) and forced to change his plan. Pichégru had taken advantage of Hoche's diversion to advance against Würmser, and Hoche, instead of operating by himself, moved Southward to help Pichégru by falling upon Würmser's right. Several days of severe fighting (Dec. 15th to 24th) saw the Austrians driven from Haguenau and Frœschwiller in upon their lines in front of Landau. The culminating battle was on December 26th, when the two French armies, united under the command of Hoche, managed to storm the Geisberg, the key to the Austrian position. Only the arrival of Brunswick, whose inactivity had allowed Hoche to ĵoin Pichégru unhindered and was therefore the chief cause of the disaster, enabled the Austrians to avoid a complete rout. As it was, the French relieved Landau and recovered Worms and Spires, the Austrians recrossed the Rhine at Philipsburg (Dec. 30th), the Prussians fell back to Oppenheim to cover Mayence, and the Palatinate West of the Rhine passed again into French hands.

For these reverses the Coalition had chiefly itself to thank. The slackness of the Prussians, Thugut's greed for territorial acquisitions, Coburg's want of energy and strategic insight, the unreadiness of England for war, the feebleness of the efforts made by most of the members of the Empire, were preventable causes, even if the energy of the Committee of Public Safety, the organising powers of Carnot, the enthusiasm of the Revolutionary armies, and the talents of the young generals to whom a great career had been opened were factors outside the control of the Allies. But even now they had not learnt their lessons. Unity of purpose, energy and sincere co-operation were as conspicuous by their absence in 1794 as in 1793. All Pitt's efforts could not induce Prussia to do her duty by her allies. Already Frederick William, tired of the war and anxious to have his hands free to deal with Poland, declared that he would withdraw from the Coalition unless the Empire undertook to support his army. For the Empire to do so was obviously impossible; but England concluded a subsidy-treaty with Prussia in May by which the King promised to put 62,000 men at the disposal of Great Britain, a promise which he did not fulfil in the spirit. With Brunswick and with Hesse-Cassel, Pitt also concluded subsidy-treaties; but he was to have only too clear proof that it is the very falsest economy which so reduces a country's forces in peace that in war-time she must depend on raw recruits and hired foreigners to fight her battles. The Austrian army also was not in as good a condition as it might have been. The Emperor was in nominal command, but he had no military capacity; and though several of the other generals were good divisional leaders, there was no really competent commander-in-chief and bad Staff-work was responsible for an absence of accuracy and precision in carrying out the plans decided upon. In Thugut, Francis possessed a minister who had at least the merits of determination and resolution; but he was most unpopular with the great nobles who held the chief places at the Court of Vienna, and the internal condition of the affairs of Austria[1] was hardly a source of strength to the Coalition.

The plan adopted by the Allies for 1794 was the work of an Austrian officer whose name was to become unpleasantly familiar to British ears before his errors and misfortunes reached their climax at Ulm. General Mack's scheme[2] was that the main body, 85,000 strong, under Saxe-Coburg, should advance between the Sambre and the Scheldt and open a path into Picardy by the capture of Landreçies. It was to be supported

[1] Cf. *Dropmore MSS.* ii. pp. 614–636.
[2] *Ibid.* ii. p. 505, cf. p. 525.

on its flanks by smaller corps, that on its right under Clerfayt stretching from the Scheldt to the sea, that on its left under Kaunitz and Beaulieu from the Sambre to the Moselle, while 50,000 more troops under Saxe-Teschen were to be collected on the Moselle in the hopes of the Prussian aid which the Anglo-Prussian convention seemed to have secured for the Allies. To oppose them Carnot gave Pichégru command of the Army of the North, and arranged for the organisation of a new army, with that of the Ardennes as its nucleus, to co-operate with him. After some skirmishing the siege of Landreçies was begun on April 17th; but a simultaneous advance of the French against both flanks resulted in Pichégru's turning the right of the Allies, driving in Wallmoden from Courtrai, forcing Clerfayt back on Tournai, and taking Menin. Despite this, Landreçies fell on April 30th; but the efforts of the Allies to catch the invaders of West Flanders between simultaneous attacks from the North, to be made by Clerfayt from Tielt, and from the East, to be made by the main army, miscarried. After heavy fighting round Turcoing on May 17th and 18th, of which the brunt fell on the British columns under Abercromby and the Duke of York, the Allies fell back behind the Scheldt; and though Pichégru's counter-attack (May 22nd) was repulsed, he was able to besiege and take Ypres (June 1st to 17th) and then to lay siege to Ostend and Nieuport, taking post on the left of the Scheldt to cover the operation. But the Allies were in no condition to interfere. Clerfayt had fallen back to Ghent, and the successful advance of Jourdan now compelled Saxe-Coburg to turn Eastward. Jourdan had brought up 50,000 men from the Moselle to reinforce the Army of the Ardennes, till then held in check behind the Sambre and unable to cross, had forced the passage of the river and laid siege to Charleroi (June 18th), Beaulieu recoiling on Namur. Too late to save Charleroi, which fell on June 25th, Coburg could not withdraw without a battle, and Jourdan's hard-won victory at Fleurus (June 26th) decided the fate of the Netherlands. The Allies retired, the Duke of York to Malines, the Austrians to Louvain. Ostend, Mons, Tournay, Ghent and Brussels fell into the hands of the French. The Army of the North joined hands with Jourdan's of the Sambre and Meuse, and before their joint advance the British, Dutch and Hanoverians fell back to Breda to cover Holland; the Austrians retired by Tirlemont and

Liége across the Meuse, leaving the remaining fortresses of the Netherlands to make what resistance they could. By September nearly all were in French hands.

The timely reinforcement which Jourdan had brought up from the Moselle to decide the campaign in the Netherlands, had been allowed to leave its original station by the inactivity of the Prussians on the Middle Rhine.[1] Prussia had accepted a heavy subsidy from England, in return for which she had pledged herself to place troops at the disposal of England to aid in the defence of the Netherlands. But far from actively sharing in this task, Prussia failed also to contribute to it by means of a diversion elsewhere. Saxe-Teschen had crossed near Mannheim during May and driven Michaud behind the Queich; but unsupported the Austrian commander could get no farther, and in July the French resumed the offensive, drove Möllendorf's Prussians from Kaiserslautern (July 15th), and forced Saxe-Teschen to recross the Rhine. In September, Jourdan, following up his success at Fleurus, turned Eastward to the Meuse. His right under Scherer secured Namur, and driving Clerfayt's 60,000 men before it, won a great victory near Jülich (Oct. 2nd). Kléber then besieged Maastricht, which fell on November 4th; while Jourdan moving Southward, cleared the left bank of the Rhine of the Austrians, capturing Cologne, Andernach and Coblence. At this point he got into touch with the Army of the Moselle, which had taken Treves on October 8th, and Mayence was again besieged. Meanwhile the Armies of the Alps and of the Pyrenees had been winning successes in their turn. The "natural boundaries" had been reached on all sides; and if the English had defeated the Brest Fleet on June 1st, they had been driven from Toulon and had not done anything for La Vendée.

But the most conspicuous of the successes of the French was yet to come. The position of the English and their auxiliaries on the Waal was seriously threatened by the disaffection of a very large section of the Dutch. There had always been a Francophil party in Holland, and the Committee of Public Safety was counting on this when they rejected all the efforts of the Stadtholder to arrange a peace and sent orders to their generals to push on with the conquest of Holland, even in the depth of a most severe winter. Helped by the memorable

[1] Cf. *Dropmore MSS.* ii. p. 577.

frost which had frozen all the wonted water defences of the United Provinces, Pichégru set his forces in motion towards the end of December. The British and Hanoverians fought well, but the numbers of the French and the lukewarmness of the Dutch were too much for them, and the Hanoverian Count Wallmoden, who was in command, after repulsing one French attack on the line of the Lech, had to withdraw his right to Amersfoort, and thus to expose Utrecht and Amsterdam to the French (Jan. 14th). In fearful weather the British retired Eastward upon Bremen, the Hanoverians and Hessians homeward, while the dramatic capture of the frozen fleet in the Texel by a handful of cavalry under Moreau put the final touch to the conquest of Holland. The foundation of the Batavian Republic and a treaty with France which placed the Dutch navy at the service of its new ally marked the beginning of the end of the Coalition.

For, indeed, the Coalition was fast perishing, not merely by reason of the French successes, but of its own divisions. 1795 saw Spain, Tuscany and other non-German states withdraw from its ranks; and the more important defection, that of Prussia, was no more than might have been expected. Even without Poland to distract the attention of Prussia, the standing jealousy between the Hohenzollern and the Hapsburgs would probably have prevented anything like a sincere co-operation; and all along there had been at the Court of Berlin a party which advocated making friends with the Mammon of militant democracy in the hopes of thereby obtaining advantages greater than those to be gained by opposing it. Once the monarchical crusade against the Revolution and its subversive principles had failed, once it became clear that France must be beaten before she could be partitioned, this party had steadily grown in influence. France, too, was ready for peace. With the repulse of the invasion and the complete success of the French arms the need for an internal government as violent and repressive as that of the Committee of Public Safety had ceased. A reaction against the excesses of the Terror had set in, and the " revolution of Thermidor" had placed in power men of moderate views who had no wish to remain at war with all Europe.[1] Even those among them who, like Rewbell, wished to continue the war against the "hereditary enemies," Austria

[1] Cf. speech of Merlin of Douai to the Convention, Dec. 4th, 1794.

and England, were fully awake to the advantage of detaching Prussia and the rest of the Coalition from the side of their enemies. In January 1795 negotiations were begun at Basel in which Barthélemy represented France, and von Goltz and, after his death (Feb. 6th), Hardenberg acted for Prussia. France demanded the recognition of the Republic and of the Rhine frontier as the boundary of France. This involved the surrender by Prussia of her territory West of the Rhine, Cleves, Upper Guelders and Mors. These, however, Prussia was ready to give up in return for the recognition by France of the neutrality of Germany North of the Main, and the promise that at the conclusion of a general peace Prussia should be compensated for her losses. On these terms a peace was before long arranged, and on April 5th, 1795, it was signed by the plenipotentiaries of the two Powers. The arrangements about compensation were embodied in secret articles, which also translated the promise of the formal treaty that France would accept the good offices of the King of Prussia in favour of those German states which should claim his protection into a definite recognition of their neutrality under a Prussian guarantee. It was further arranged that should Hanover refuse to accept this neutrality, Prussian troops should occupy the Electorate; but Hanover so far disassociated herself from the action of Great Britain as to acquiesce in the arrangement, and not till 1801 did the Prussians take possession of the country.[1]

Few actions have been more criticised than that of Prussia in making peace with France in 1795. In the light of subsequent events it is easy to see that the path on which Prussia thus entered was to lead to Jena and Auerstädt, to the humiliation of Tilsit, and the degradations of 1808–1812. It is easy to see now that England and Austria can plead an ample justification for their refusal to make peace in 1795; that the professions of pacific intentions with which the new system in France was inaugurated were belied by the continued instability of the French Government at home and by the disregard of treaties and of international obligations which the Directory no less than the Convention exhibited in dealing with other nations; that the final outcome of the recurrent constitutional crises in France was the establishment of the

[1] Cf. Chapter XXXV.

most formidable military despotism the world has yet seen. But it may be urged that the pacific intentions of France were never given a fair chance; that the continuation of the war involved financial and domestic troubles which made a military despotism inevitable; that peace would have freed the Directory from the difficulties which finally overthrew it; that it was the Italian campaign of 1796 which gave Bonaparte his first real start on the road to supreme power; that without the Italian campaign of 1796 he would never have had a chance, and that if England and Austria had followed Prussia's example and made peace in 1795 no campaign would have been fought in Italy in 1796. Between these two views it is not easy to adjust the balance of probabilities. For each there is much to be said. It is clear that Pitt at least was anxious to grasp the opportunity offered by the establishment of the Directory, and to test the sincerity of their pacific professions by opening negotiations.[1] But his overtures fell on unfruitful soil, and rather encouraged the bellicose element in the Directory. The fatal thing was Prussia's isolated action. If she was right to make peace, she was not right to make peace alone. England and Austria may have let the best chance slip early in 1795 when the tone of the French was fairly moderate, but Prussia's desertion was an important factor in raising the demands of the Directory, which, when Pitt made his overtures, had reached a point far beyond that to which either England or the Emperor was prepared to go. Perhaps one may say that Prussia's action was stultified by the line adopted by England and Austria, but that the course of events fully bore out their expectations. After all, the question whether, if a general peace had been made in 1795 the Directory could or could not have provided France with a stable government capable of living in harmony with its neighbours, concerns French rather than German history. It must, moreover, be admitted that Prussia made the Peace of Basel not so much from a desire to restore peace to Europe, or even to Germany, as from more selfish motives. The establishment of a line of demarcation,[2] behind which the North German states were to enjoy neutrality, was again

---

[1] Cf. "France and the First Coalition before the Campaign of 1796": J. H. Rose in *E.H.R.*, April 1903.

[2] The line of demarcation ran up the Ems to Münster, thence by Coesfeld and Borken to the Duchy of Cleves. It then followed the Rhine as far as Duisburg, and

dictated by Hardenberg's wish to revive the Prussian influence over these principalities, rather than by a desire to minimise the area afflicted with war; loyalty to the Empire, into which it introduced a new division, had nothing to do with his action. It was for Prussia's benefit that Brunswick and Waldeck were to enjoy peace, not for their own sake. Austria may have played a feeble part in the war, may have been an inefficient and unsatisfactory ally, Thugut's greed may have contributed largely to the failure of the Coalition, but after all from the point of view of German interests it is impossible not to pronounce Austria's conduct as more praiseworthy than Prussia's. By setting the example of desertion, Prussia shattered the Coalition; by separating the Northern from the Southern members of the Empire she split up what was left of the Holy Roman Empire. After having been foremost in preaching the monarchical crusade against the iniquities of the Revolution, she gave the signal for capitulating when France showed that she would not prove a second Poland.

Austria would, indeed, have been glad to make peace. She does seem to have offered to sacrifice the left bank if France would agree to her annexing Bavaria; but this was after Prussia had already left Germany in the lurch. In July also the Emperor, acting on behalf of the Diet, made overtures through Denmark which were rejected; but Austria would not submit without a further struggle to the terms Prussia had no difficulty in accepting. She did at least continue to resist the annexation by the Republic of the debatable lands between France and Germany, and refused to admit that "the German Rhine" is the natural and proper boundary of France. Prussia had made no effort to hold out for these things. She had tamely acquiesced in the French claims, and proposed to indemnify herself at the expense of weaker Powers who had given her at least no cause for complaint, even if it be admitted that they had practically nothing to plead in defence of the independence they enjoyed. The remaining states of Germany may have condoned and even approved Prussia's action by following her example, but this condemns them rather than excuses

---

went up the Main, crossing to the Neckar, which it followed to Wimpfen. Thence it skirted the frontiers of Bavaria and Bohemia so as to include the Franconian and Upper Saxon Circles. Cf. Haüsser, ii. pp. 6 ff.

Prussia.[1] Austria, no doubt, was fighting for her own hand, but so far as there was a " Germany " in 1795, so far as there was a German national cause or national feeling, Austria rather than Prussia was its champion.

[1] Hesse-Cassel made peace in August 1795, Würtemburg in September. Baden followed suit in July 1796, the Swabian Circle in August, while Bavaria concluded an armistice in September. All these treaties reserved the Diet's ratification, but that was practically assured by the action of the individual voters. Thus Prussia found plenty of imitators whose isolated surrender destroyed all chance of arranging the more satisfactory peace that their joint action might have secured.

CHAPTER XX

FROM BASEL TO CAMPO FORMIO

THE ineffective part played by Prussia in resisting the tide of French conquest can be partially explained, though the explanation is no exculpation, by the fact that her heart was never in the task. As in 1793, so in 1794 the Vistula rather than the Rhine was the point upon which Prussia's hopes and interest were concentrated. The Second Partition had not put an end to the troubles of Poland : it had roused up an intense feeling against Prussia, whose conduct in allying with Poland in 1790 and then not only abandoning her in 1792, but actually joining Russia to despoil her former ally, was looked upon by the Poles as the basest treachery, while even Russia's own partisans seem to have been surprised at the Czarina's cynical rapacity. Some of the authors of the Constitution of 1791 had fled to Saxony, and from that refuge had begun a nationalist agitation. This spread rapidly over Poland and in March 1794 culminated in the outbreak of an insurrection at Cracow. Though disavowed by the King the rebels were at first successful. Their gallant leader Kosciuzsko routed a Russian force at Raclawice (April 4th), and aided by the inhabitants expelled the Russian garrison from Warsaw (April 17th). But his successes were not to be long-lived. Russia put a large force into the field and retook Vilna (Aug. 22nd). Thugut had no intention of letting Austria be again left out of the distribution of spoils which was sure to follow the suppression of the rebellion ; he was, moreover, anxious to renew good relations with Catherine. Austria therefore declared against the Poles and occupied Polish Galicia, and in July 50,000 Russians advanced to Warsaw and laid siege to the town. An insurrection in the provinces acquired by Prussia in 1793 forced Frederick William to raise the siege (Sept. 6th) ; but Suvorov, the best Russian general of the day, advanced steadily West, defeating the Poles in several encounters, of which that at Macejowice (Oct. 10th) was the most important,

and stormed the Praga suburb of Warsaw on Nov. 4th.   With
the fall of Warsaw five days later the independence of Poland
passed away.   The jealousies and intrigues of the three partners
in the overthrow of the Republic protracted the negotiations
over the Partition for nearly a year.   Russia, which had done
the lion's share of the suppression of the rebellion, held the
best cards and was disposed to favour Austria rather than
Prussia, so as to preserve the balance between them.   Once
the terms arranged between Catherine and Thugut (Jan. 1795)
had been at a favourable moment (Aug. 9th) communicated to
Prussia the end was not far off.   Unsatisfactory as the division
was to him, Frederick William could not oppose Russia's decision, and on October 25th the treaties were signed which
divided the unhappy country among its covetous neighbours.
Warsaw and the greater part of the Palatinate of Cracow fell
to the share of Prussia, Cracow itself, Lublin, Sandomir and
part of Masovia to Austria, the remainder to Russia.   In extent
the territories which Prussia and Austria thus acquired exceeded
those they were losing to France beyond the Rhine, and geographically the new provinces were more advantageously situated
than were those for which they were in some measure a compensation ; but Prussia had already as large a Slavonic element
in her population as she desired, and even the Belgians had
more in common with the Austrians than Poles had.   Though
the anarchy, the selfishness and the want of patriotism which
had made the Polish Republic a byword may be said to have
to some extent justified the treatment Poland received, it is not
unsatisfactory to reflect that the Partition profited its authors
very little.   The real gainer by the Polish troubles was the
French Republic, which owed its great successes on the Meuse
and Rhine in no small measure to the preoccupation of Austria
and Prussia in playing jackal to Russia's lion in Poland.

Meanwhile hostilities were about to be resumed on the Rhine.
Here, as was only natural, Prussia's defection had been the
signal for a storm of abuse and bitter recrimination.   But it
was a little absurd for states, most of which had not made any
conspicuous efforts in their own defence or in the defence of
their neighbours, to talk of Prussia's "treachery," "breach of
oaths and obligation," to make the belated discovery that
Germany was one state with one head, not a federation of
independent Powers.   The hollowness of the outcry was shown

by the action of the individual members of the Empire. The states whose territories were covered by the proposed line of demarcation readily grasped the chance of being left undisturbed ; with the fortunes of the rest of the Empire they did not concern themselves. To Prussia's credit it must be admitted that she did not at once give up all hopes of expanding the Peace of Basel into a general peace. To facilitate this she sought to induce France to modify her terms and to give up the demand for the left bank. But of doing this France had not the least intention; all she would concede was that it should be open to any member of the Empire to accede to the Peace of Basel within the next three months.

When the Prussian envoy communicated this offer to the Diet (April), the Emperor replied by an appeal to the states to keep together and not play into the hands of France by acting singly. He proceeded to show the line he intended to adopt by concluding a fresh treaty with England (May 4th), by which he undertook in return for a loan of £4,600,000 to put into the field a force of 200,000 men. At the same time, he was in full agreement with the decree of July 3rd, which announced the anxiety of the Diet to conclude a joint and general peace according to the constitution of the Holy Roman Empire and preserving its full territorial integrity. Indeed, the Emperor went so far as to empower Denmark to make peace proposals to France on behalf of the Empire. These were duly made, but they did not prevent the resumption of hostilities and about the end of October the proposals were definitely rejected by France.

After the conquest of Holland and the expulsion of the Allied field forces from the left bank of the Rhine, military operations had languished, being indeed quite subordinated to diplomatic requirements. Moreover, even the victorious French needed time to reorganise and refit, and so throughout the greater part of 1795 they contented themselves with the sieges of the few places on the left bank, such as Mayence and Luxembourg, which still resisted their attacks.

For the defence of the right bank a considerable army had been got together under the command of Clerfayt ;[1] but he made no effort to relieve Luxembourg, as Thugut had come to regard Belgium as definitely lost and hoped to gain more from

[1] 250 squadrons and 137 battalions.

the plots for a Royalist counter-revolution in France, which were at this time on foot. In these Pichégru, the commander of the Army of the Rhine and Moselle, was to some extent implicated. His army, some 90,000 strong, lined the Upper Rhine from Huningen to Mayence; and according to Carnot's plan of campaign it was to co-operate with Jourdan and the 85,000 men of the Sambre and Meuse Army, who were on the Middle Rhine, stretching from Coblence to Cleves. Set free to resume the offensive by the fall (June 25th) of Luxembourg, Jourdan put his troops in motion in September, crossed the Rhine at Neuss and Düsseldorf, and by the simple expedient of violating the neutrality of the "line of demarcation," outflanked Clerfayt's right, thus forcing the Austrians to abandon the lines of the Sieg and the Lahn and to retire behind the Main. Meanwhile Mannheim had surrendered to Pichégru at the mere threat of a bombardment (Sept. 20th), and that general's forces were pushing across the Palatinate towards Heidelberg, driving before them Würmser, who commanded the left wing of the Austrian army. The surrender of Mannheim, like that of Düsseldorf a few days earlier, was attributed by the Austrians to treachery on the part of the Elector Palatine. Charles Theodore was on the point of coming to terms with France, and the charge seems to have had some foundation. Indeed, the attitude of Germany as a whole was hardly creditable. The appearance of the French on the right bank and the extension to it of both the official requisitions and the even more exacting unofficial plundering, which had swept the left bank all but bare, were quite enough to check any democratic sympathies. However, instead of uniting in a determined effort to repulse the invader, the Princes of Western Germany sought security in separate understandings with the enemy. Hanover and the North German Princes as a whole gladly availed themselves of the shelter of the "line of demarcation." The Saxon contingent in the Army of the Empire was recalled "to defend Saxony against the dangers which threaten it." Hesse-Cassel had already made peace with France (Aug. 29th); Würtemberg followed suit in September.

But Clerfayt was soon able to put a different complexion upon affairs. Deceiving Jourdan into a belief that he was going to respect the neutral line which Jourdan himself had disregarded, the Austrian commander suddenly crossed the

Main above Frankfurt (Oct. 11th), and moving upon Bergen rolled up the French line from its left. The Army of the Sambre and Meuse went completely to pieces and fell back to the left bank in great confusion, the peasantry whom its ravages and plundering had provoked retaliating in kind on its stragglers and sick. Clerfayt then turned his steps to Mayence, which had been for some time closely beset, and was hemmed into the Westward by strong lines of circumvallation. Against these he delivered, early in the morning of October 29th, a well-planned and well-conducted sortie. Their centre pierced and their left turned, the French had to fall back behind the Pfriem, to cover the line from Worms to Donnersberg. On the same day Würmser, who had checked on September 24th the French advance on Heidelberg at Neuenheim, stormed Pichégru's position on the Galgenberg outside Mannheim. These successes allowed Clerfayt to interpose between the Army of the Rhine and Moselle and that of the Sambre and Meuse. The former was driven back behind the Queich, and then Würmser was left to keep Pichégru in check, while Clerfayt, turning Northward, frustrated Jourdan's efforts to come to his colleague's help, and forced him back to the Moselle. Mannheim was retaken on November 22nd,[1] and on December 21st an armistice was concluded with Pichégru which brought hostilities to a close.

Thus the campaign in Germany ended somewhat more favourably for Austria than had any since the war began. This was mainly due to the failure of Pichégru to co-operate properly with Jourdan; but though Clerfayt's critics declared that a man of more resolution and decision would have achieved even greater victories,[2] his generalship had had a good deal to do with the successful issue of the campaign, and it was a bad thing for Austria that Thugut's omnipotence required the general's dismissal before the next campaign. The all-powerful minister could not brook any independence or any opposition on the part of the generals, much less the outspoken and well-grounded criticism which Clerfayt had bestowed upon the indifferent military administration and on the general

---

[1] Oberndorf, the officer responsible for the capitulation of September 20th, and Salabert, the minister of Zweibrücken, were by Thugut's orders arrested on a charge of treason and kept in prison. This " outrage " on the subjects of a member of the Electoral College was much resented in the Empire, and even the Hapsburg Elector of Cologne joined in the outcry against the action of Austria.

[2] Cf. *Dropmore MSS.* iv. p. 7.

policy of the minister.   Moreover, Clerfayt was on bad terms
with Würmser, who was in high favour at Court, and despite
his victories he was removed from the command.[1]   It was an
unfortunate step; for although his successor, the Archduke
Charles, was a man of not less capacity, his supersession was a
victory for the little "War Office ring," which under the general
direction of Thugut endeavoured with the most scanty success
to conduct campaigns from Vienna.

During this period negotiations had still been going on, but
all efforts to arrange a general peace proved futile.   Neither
the Emperor nor the Directory would give way, and the
negotiations of Russia with France were as far as ever from
bringing about any definite result.   Hardenberg was already
beginning to feel uneasy.   He saw the dangers to Prussia
involved in continued French successes, and he went as far as
to point out to his King that the justification of the Peace of
Basel would be removed if it failed to serve as the basis for a
general peace; but it was not to be expected that Prussia
would sacrifice the immediate benefits of neutrality for a rather
remote general interest, and so, despite the misgivings her line
of action excited in the minds of some of her more clear-sighted
ministers, Prussia adhered to the path she had chosen at Basel.

For the campaign of 1796 the Directory proposed a three-
fold attack upon the hereditary dominions of Austria: Jourdan
with the refitted Army of the Sambre and Meuse was to
advance by the Main; Moreau, who had succeeded to Pichégru's
command, was to push down the Danube; while their joint
operations were to be assisted by those of the Army of Italy
under an officer who had yet to win his spurs in independent
command, Napoleon Bonaparte.   In the original plan the
Italian campaign, though important, was really secondary to
the far less famous operations on the Rhine.   Only 50,000 men
were allotted to it, as against Jourdan's 76,000 and Moreau's
80,000; but the genius of the young commander of the Army
of Italy altered their relative importance.   Massena's victory
at Loano in the previous autumn had been too late in the year
(Nov. 24th) to be followed up at once, but it had cut off the
Austro-Sardinians from the sea, and had opened the way for
the brilliant operations by which Bonaparte, breaking through
the centre of the Austro-Sardinian positions along the Apen-

[1] Cf. Haüsser, ii. p. 45.

26

nines, thrust Beaulieu's Austrians back upon Milan, and forced the Sardinians, thus separated from their allies, to make peace at Cherasco on the terms he dictated (April 28th). Thus freed from the Sardinians, Bonaparte pushed on Eastward, drove the Austrians out of the Milanese, compelled Beaulieu to take refuge in Tyrol, and laid siege to Mantua, the last bulwark of Austrian rule in Italy. Even before the campaign on the Rhine opened 25,000 men had had to be detached from the Southern wing of the Austrian army in Germany to attempt to check his victorious progress.

This left the Archduke Charles with some 140,000 men to oppose to the combined advance of Jourdan and Moreau. This total included the garrisons of Mayence, Ehrenbreitstein and other fortresses, and the relics of Würmser's wing, now under Latour, an officer hardly fit for an independent command, but more suited to his subordinate position than a self-asserting colleague like Würmser. At the beginning of June, Kléber at the head of Jourdan's left wing pushed across the Rhine at Düsseldorf and, supported by his chief, who crossed at Neuwied, drove the Austrians back towards the Lahn. At Wetzlar the Archduke, who had come up with reinforcements, barred the French advance, and a sharp fight (June 14th) saw the French compelled to retire by the turning of their left. Kray pursued Kléber closely and suffered some loss in an action with his rearguard at Altenkirchen (June 19th); but Jourdan had to recross the Rhine (June 21st), and for the time Franconia was cleared.

But Jourdan had occupied the Archduke's attention, and so allowed Moreau to utilise the chance given him by Würmser's defective dispositions, which the Archduke had had no time to alter. A feint on Mannheim (June 20th) drew Latour off to his right, thereby enabling Moreau to force a passage at Kehl, weakly defended by 7000 Swabians (June 24th). This severed the 10,000 men in the Breisgau from Latour's centre and right, which took post behind the Murg. The news of Moreau's passage of the Rhine brought the Archduke South again. He left Wartensleben with some 40,000 men to "contain" Jourdan, and hurried up to the Murg, only to be attacked by Moreau near Malsch (July 10th) and beaten in a well-contested action. He fell back to Pforzheim and thence behind the Neckar to Cannstadt, thus leaving the road into

Swabia by Stuttgart open to Moreau.   On July 22nd the
French attacked his positions behind the Neckar, but their
assaults were repulsed.   However, the news that Wartensleben
was retreating before Jourdan and had left Würzburg on the
22nd, decided the Archduke to retire towards the Danube,
where he took up a position, its left resting on the river near
Gunzburg, while the right extended through Neresheim to
Nördlingen.   Here he remained halted some days, holding
Moreau in check and recovering touch with the division from
the Breisgau which was retreating down the right bank of the
Danube.   His chief concern was to retain touch with Wartensleben and by keeping the interior position between the two
French armies to be able at the right moment to concentrate
all his forces against whichever of the opposing armies he could
attack with most prospect of success.

No better example can be found of the way in which
particularism and selfish local feelings dominated Germany, to
the exclusion of the national idea and of all sense of community
of interest, than the conduct of the minor Powers at this time.
The outrages, exactions and excesses of the French armies
were enough to have stung the most slack and selfish into
activity and to have roused the fiercest opposition ; but, as in
1794 and 1795, the states which found themselves threatened
by the advance of Jourdan and Moreau hastened to make the
best terms they could with the invader, each for itself, without
ever realising that the only protection or security worth having
was that which was not to be obtained except by showing the
enemy that they were capable of defending themselves and
each other.   Localism was no less strong in Spain, while the
excesses of the Armies of the Sambre and Meuse and of the
Rhine and Moselle were hardly surpassed by the Napoleonic
armies in the Peninsula ; but in Spain the separate provinces
never attempted to gain their own security by betraying the
others, and though, if unaided by regular forces, the guerilla
bands would have failed to expel the invaders, the Spanish
peasantry did retaliate very effectively upon the plunderers of
Cordova and the stormers of Saragossa.   But as the French
armies approached their territories in 1796 the minor Princes
of Germany sought safety in tame surrenders and in the security
of a promised "protection."   The Swabian Circle set the
example of negotiating with Moreau, and withdrew its troops

from the Archduke's army; Würtemberg did the same, concluding an armistice in July and converting it into a definite
peace a month later (Aug. 15th); and Baden concluded a
treaty on practically the same terms (Aug. 22nd). Both
Powers abandoned to France all their possessions on the left
bank;[1] both declared themselves ready to receive ecclesiastical
territory as a "compensation"; both promised not to lend any
help to any Power which was hostile to France. The Saxon
contingent, as in 1795, departed homeward, and the Elector
concluded a convention of neutrality. The three Ecclesiastical
Electors took refuge in the interior of Germany, and many of
the minor Princes followed the example their flight had set.
But while these states were to find the promised protection
a very shadowy affair, they had to pay both in money and
in contributions in kind sums which would have amply sufficed
to defend their territories against the French. The Franconian
Circle had to pay 6 million francs in cash and to provide
goods to the value of 2 millions more; Baden may be held
to have got off lightly with 2 millions; while the Swabian
ecclesiastical territories were heavily taxed with 7 millions.
About the same time the negotiations between Prussia and
France which had been dragging on for some months were
brought to a conclusion, and on August 5th a new treaty was
signed. A new line of demarcation was arranged, while in the
secret articles all pretence about the "integrity of the Empire"
was abandoned, and the principle of compensation at the expense of the ecclesiastical states for territorial losses on the left
bank was accepted. Among other proposed changes the House
of Orange-Nassau was to receive Bamberg and Würzburg as a set-
off against the United Provinces, Prussia thus agreeing that Germany should provide the compensation for a loss of non-German
territory; an arrangement which may be explained by the relation
existing between the families of Orange and Hohenzollern.

Meanwhile the retrograde movements of Wartensleben and
the Archduke had brought them nearer together. With less
than 40,000 men Wartensleben had no chance of arresting
the advance which Jourdan resumed towards the end of June.
He was driven back up the Main, Frankfort, Würzburg and
Bamberg falling one after another into French hands. From

[1] These included Mömpelgard, Hericourt and Ostheim belonging to Würtemberg;
Sponheim, Herspring and Beinheim belonging to Baden.

Bamberg, which he evacuated on August 2nd, Wartensleben fell back Eastward by Nüremberg towards Amberg (Aug. 12th), fearing to expose to Jourdan the magazines collected along the Bohemian frontier should he continue his movement Southward to join the Archduke. This step might have been fatal, as it gave Jourdan a chance of interposing between the Archduke and Wartensleben by a rapid advance to the Danube. But Jourdan was a little slow to grasp his chance. He halted his men at Nüremberg from August 13th to 16th, and at this crisis the Archduke acted with a decision and a calculated daring which entitle him to a high place among commanders. He had by a hard fought action at Neresheim (Aug. 11th) secured an unmolested retreat to Donauwerth, and now, leaving Latour with a comparatively thin screen of troops to hide his movements from Moreau, he crossed to the right bank of the Danube with the bulk of his corps (Aug. 15th), marched downstream to Ingolstadt and recrossed there (Aug. 16th). Jourdan had resumed his advance on the 17th, had driven Wartensleben back before him to the river Naab, and had thrust a division under Bernadotte out to his right towards Neumarkt. It was on this division, less than 10,000 strong, that the Archduke fell with three times as many men on August 22nd. Bernadotte was crushed, and his defeat parried Jourdan's thrust at the Danube and forced him to fall back to Amberg. Here on August 24th the united forces of the Archduke and his lieutenant, over 60,000 in all, attacked Jourdan's 40,000. A fiercely-contested battle ended in the disorderly retreat of the Army of the Sambre and Meuse by Nüremberg to the Main. By a great effort Jourdan so far rallied his men as to stand at Würzburg and offer battle (Sept. 1st) in the hope that Moreau might help him ; but Moreau was before the gates of München, and on September 3rd an Austrian attack drove Jourdan from his position. His situation was critical. Pursued by superior forces, with the peasantry turning out to harass his retreat and cut off stragglers, his army was fast degenerating into a rabble, when it was saved from destruction by the interposition of Marceau and a force drawn from the besiegers of Mayence and Ehrenbreitstein. At Altenkirchen (Sept. 20th), Marceau sacrificed his life, but he secured the safe retreat of the relics of Jourdan's broken army behind the shelter of the Rhine.

This set the Archduke free to attend to the Army of the Rhine and Moselle. Moreau had crossed the Danube at Dillingen on August 19th, had forced the passage of the Lech five days later despite Latour's gallant resistance, and had pushed forward into Bavaria, which till then had not been touched by the war. The presence of his plundering hordes completed the distaste which the Bavarians already felt for the war. Distrusting Austria, fearing with only too good reason that she had not relinquished her designs on their country, the Bavarians and their ruler had never been enthusiastic for the war, and now that they found themselves experiencing the horrors of a French invasion they at once began negotiating. Still the Treaty of Pfaffenhofen (Sept. 7th) can only be regarded as the *ne plus ultra* of localism, the carrying to its logical conclusion of that independence of the sovereign Princes of Germany which had been established at Westphalia. Despite the fact that Jourdan was known to have been beaten and to be in full retreat before the Archduke, that Moreau's position was thereby rendered most perilous, Bavaria pledged herself to neutrality, withdrew her contingent from the Archduke's army, paid an indemnity of 10 million livres and a large contribution in kind, and promised to facilitate in every way the retreat of Moreau to the Rhine.

It was largely to this pusillanimous action on the part of Bavaria that Moreau owed his escape from a dangerously exposed position, though his own skilful and well-ordered dispositions contributed to it in no small measure. It must also be allowed that he owed much to the want of harmony among the Austrian forces engaged in harassing the retreat, while the Archduke cannot escape censure for not having hastened sooner to transfer himself, ahead of his forces, from the Main to the Danube in order to give to the pursuit that co-ordination which it lacked from the absence of a single will to direct all the forces engaged in it. Thus when Moreau, who had fallen back to the Iller on hearing of Jourdan's retreat, quitted Ulm (Sept. 27th) and retired upstream to avoid being cut off by the forces moving against his line of communications with the Rhine, divergence of opinion between the Austrian commanders came to his aid. Latour wished to follow him closely, but Nauendorf, who commanded a separate corps at Ulm, was for marching across the chord of the arc by Tübingen to join Petrasch's corps on the Upper Neckar and bar the passage of the Black Forest. Unable to agree, they separated. Latour attacking with only 20,000 men was so badly beaten at Biberach (Oct. 2nd) that he was quite incapable of molesting the retreat further. Thus the French were able to cross the Black Forest by the Höllenthal in safety (Oct. 7th to 15th). Too late the Archduke arrived and took supreme command; he could only check a move downstream on Kehl (Oct. 19th), and was unable to prevent the French recrossing the Rhine at Hüningen unmolested (Oct. 25th).

The popular movement in South Germany which the French invasion had aroused was one of great possibilities had Austria known how to turn it to advantage. The Elector of Bavaria refused to ratify the Treaty of Pfaffenhofen. Other Powers which had made terms for themselves endeavoured to explain their action.[1] But with a man at the head of the Austrian ministry as narrow as Thugut and as incapable of inspiring or feeling confidence, it was not likely that such a chance would be properly used. And peace was as far off as ever. It was useless for England to send Lord Malmesbury to Paris to negotiate in the hope that the expulsion of the French from Germany would have lowered their tone and disposed them to peace, when France could point to victories such as those of Bonaparte in Italy as a set-off against her reverses in Germany, and when the addition of Spain to the allies of France led to the evacuation of the Mediterranean by the British navy.

Since the conquest of the Milanese and Beaulieu's retreat into Tyrol the Italian campaign had centred at Mantua, and had consisted of repeated efforts to relieve that gallantly defended fortress. In July Würmser's advance had forced Bonaparte to raise the siege for a moment; but the victories of Lonato (Aug. 3rd) and Castiglione (Aug. 5th) had sent Würmser back to Tyrol and allowed Bonaparte to resume the blockade, though the fortress had been replenished and the French siege-train destroyed. A second effort in September resulted in Würmser making his way from the Brenta to Mantua and reinforcing the garrison, but at the expense of being cut off from Tyrol and himself besieged. A new army, mainly composed of raw recruits and half-trained Croats, was gathered by Alvinzi, and in November it renewed the attempt. Checked

[1] Cf. Haüsser, ii. p. 91.

408 GERMANY IN THE EIGHTEENTH CENTURY [1796-7

at Caldiero (Nov. 12th), Bonaparte won a victory at Arcola four days later (Nov. 16th) which threatened Alvinzi's communications and drove him back to the mountains. In January a final attempt was made. The main body came down the Adige from Tyrol only to suffer defeat at Rivoli (Jan. 14th), and a second column under Provera, moving Westward from the Brenta, penetrated to the suburbs of Mantua merely to be crushed in its turn (Jan. 16th). This decided the fate of Mantua. Its fall (Feb. 2nd, 1797) marked the end of Hapsburg predominance in Italy. Though not exactly oppressive, the rule of Austria had been far from popular. The steady drain of money to Vienna from the rich and productive plains of Lombardy had excited resentment. The old traditions of Guelph and Ghibelline had just sufficient existence to make it easy for the enemies of Austria to appeal to time-honoured prejudices. The democratic propaganda of the French Republic had fallen on fruitful soil in the valley of the Po, and the invaders had been welcomed as deliverers from the "German" yoke.

Bonaparte was now free for an advance against the hereditary dominions of Austria. Only some 30,000 dejected and dispirited troops, the survivors of many defeats, were in his way; and though the Archduke Charles was sent to Illyria in the hope that he might stay Napoleon's advance, the task was beyond his powers. Three divisions under Massena advancing along the foot of the mountains turned the right flank of each line of defence in succession, the Piave, the Tagliamento and the Isonzo, as Napoleon advanced against it in front. Fierce fighting left the all-important Col di Tarvis in French hands, and the Archduke beat a hurried retreat. By the end of March, Bonaparte was in Illyria; on the 25th he occupied Laibach. At Neumarkt and again at Unzmarkt the Archduke was beaten, and by the 5th of April the French headquarters were at Jüdenberg in Styria, their vanguard at Leoben within 80 miles of the Hapsburg capital. Bonaparte's advance produced a panic in Vienna and lent weight to the advice of that party which had for some time past been counselling peace. Thugut, supported by the British Ambassador, Morton Eden, still urged resistance. His hopes of inducing Russia to throw in her lot with the Coalition had been disappointed when on the very verge of success[1] by the sudden death of Catherine (Nov. 17th, 1796), for her successor

[1] Cf. *Dropmore MSS.* iii. pp. 246, 261.

Paul favoured a Prussian rather than an Austrian alliance; but he had still good arguments on his side. Bonaparte's position at Leoben was not without its perils. He was a long way from his base; communication even with Joubert's corps in Tyrol was uncertain, for the peasantry were in insurrection, and neither the Army of the Rhine and Moselle nor that of the Sambre and Meuse could give him any effective assistance.[1] It was at least possible that a last effort might have forced even the victorious Bonaparte to recoil to Italy. But Thugut was too unpopular to rally a nation to an effort of the required description, and too distrustful of popular movements to wish to do so. At the same time, his credit had been somewhat shaken by recent disasters, by Pitt's profession of inability to comply with the rather exorbitant Austrian demands for pecuniary help,[2] and by the failure of the negotiations with Russia. The pacific counsels were therefore well received by the Emperor, and it was decided to accept Bonaparte's offer of terms. On April 13th negotiations were begun, on the 18th they resulted in the Preliminaries of Leoben. It was arranged that a congress should be held to make peace between the French Republic and the Empire on the basis of the "integrity" of the Empire, and Austria ceded Belgium to France on condition of receiving an equitable indemnity elsewhere. This indemnity was defined in secret articles by which the Emperor gave up all his territory West of the Oglio, receiving in return the Venetian territory between the Oglio, the Po and the Adriatic; the Venetian Republic obtaining in exchange Bologna, Ferrara and Romagna. Compensation in Germany was also promised to the Duke of Modena, whom a democratic rising had ousted from his duchy. The conclusion of these preliminaries did not bring negotiations to an end. They dragged on through the summer of 1797, Bonaparte threatening and blustering, Thugut procrastinating in the hope that a revolution in France, which seemed quite within the bounds of possibility, might put the control of affairs into the hands of a more moderate party.[3] During this time both sides went on with their preparations for war as though hostilities

---

[1] Hoche, who had replaced Jourdan, did, it is true, cross the Rhine at Neuwied on April 18th, and he had driven the Austrians back behind the Nidda when the news of the armistice arrived, but he could have done little to help Bonaparte had a determined stand been made and the latter's communications attacked.

[2] Cf. *Dropmore MSS.* iii. pp. 270 ff.

[3] Cf. Haüsser, ii. p. 123.

were quite likely to be resumed, for Austria was most anxious to avoid having to fulfil the obligations of Leoben and hoped to be able to do something for the Empire. However, the tangled skein of diplomacy was rudely broken when the *coup d'état* of "Fructidor" (Sept. 4th) put an end to all chance of a reaction in France. Bonaparte, now feeling that he was treading on firm ground, went to the length of addressing an ultimatum to Thugut; peace must be made by October 1st or hostilities would be resumed. Thugut had no alternative but to send Count Louis Cobenzl—one of the leaders of the pacific party—to Udine to conduct the negotiations. Bonaparte had no wish to press Austria severely, for his aim was to separate Austria from England by making peace acceptable to her, rather than to humiliate her, as the Directory, now in a Jacobinical and ultra-democratic mood, wished to do. The Treaty of Campo Formio, signed on October 17th, was thus by no means unfavourable when looked upon in the light of the dynastic interests of the Hapsburgs, although they had to purchase these advantages by conditions most disadvantageous to the Empire of which Francis II was the nominal head. Austria gave up Lombardy[1] and the Netherlands. In return she was to receive Dalmatia, Istria and the other mainland possessions of Venice, the Adige thus forming the Western boundary of her Italian possessions. The Ionian Islands, which Thugut had sought to obtain for Austria, went to France. The dispossessed Duke of Modena was to receive the Breisgau as a compensation, thus establishing a cadet branch of the Hapsburg family at the head waters of the Danube. The arranging of a peace between the Holy Roman Empire and the French Republic was to be entrusted to a congress which was to meet for the purpose at Rastatt. More important in some ways than these published conditions were the secret articles[2] by which the Emperor promised to secure for France the Rhine as a frontier from Switzerland as far as Andernach, thence the boundary was to ascend the Nette, cross to the Roer, and descend

[1] This with Modena, Bologna, Ferrara and Romagna formed the Cisalpine Republic.

[2] These secret articles were subsequently a stumbling-block to a renewal of good relations between Austria and England, as Pitt and Grenville believed that they contained stipulations prejudicial to the interests of Great Britain (cf. *Dropmore MSS.* iv. p. 91) and therefore requested that Thugut would disclose the terms of the agreement. Haüsser, ii. pp. 130–131.

that river to its junction with the Meuse. The object of this was to leave Prussia her old possessions on the left bank, and so deprive her of all claim to compensation on the right bank. Furthermore, as a "compensation" for Belgium, Austria was to receive the Archbishopric of Salzburg and the part of Bavaria between the Inn, the Salza, Tyrol and Salzburg. The Emperor gave up all his own claims upon Italy, and promised that the Empire would do the same. Those Princes who would lose territory through the annexation of the left bank to France, including among others the three ecclesiastical Electors, Bavaria, Zweibrücken, Baden, the two Hesses, Nassau-Saarbrücken and Würtemberg, were to be compensated on the right bank.

Thus Austria, despite her defeats, only lost provinces never very easy to hold or to govern. Belgium was a possession she would have given up gladly any time during the last twenty years, if she could only have obtained a reasonable substitute, and certainly Salzburg and the promised district of Bavaria were in every respect more desirable possessions. Geographically they were adjacent to the hereditary dominions, and therefore their defence fell in with the general scheme of defensive preparations. Their population was closely akin to that of Upper Austria, and would be an addition to the German element among the subjects of the Hapsburgs. Politically there would be no need to set up an entirely separate government for them. In Italy also Venetia with its seaboard was a far more useful possession than the more distant Milanese, and it might be hoped that its acquisition would mark the beginning of a new era in the maritime history of Austria. But these acquisitions did not increase Austria's prestige. The spoliation of Venice was an act of the same class as the seizure of Silesia and the partitions of Poland. Moreover, the adoption of the plan of compensation by secularisation was nothing more or less than making the weakest pay the costs of the settlement, and the concessions included in the secret articles amounted to the abandonment of the rights of that Empire of which Austria posed as the champion. It is true that the suzerainty over Italy still nominally vested in the Holy Roman Empire had for centuries been nothing but a name, but the surrender of this time-honoured form at the bidding of an upstart Republic could not fail to deal a hard blow at an Empire whose very existence was a form. The surrender of the left bank to that same Republic was a not less severe blow to the German Kingdom; but worst of all was the voice which France was to have in the arrangement of the "compensation." One justi..ication and one only Austria can urge for her abandoning the defence of the Empire: the selfishness and utter want of patriotism displayed by every other member of the Empire from Prussia and Bavaria to Lippe-Detmold and Schwarzburg-Sondershausen. She did not abandon the Empire until the example had been set and almost universally followed. Still for the moment Germany was so glad to be rid of the war at any cost that the peace was almost popular.

The Peace of Campo Formio marks the complete failure of the attempt of monarchical Europe to interfere in the affairs of Revolutionary France. By it Austria followed the example of Prussia in making terms with the formidable Power whose hostility their intervention had provoked. England, the only Power which continued the war, had not shared in the intervention on behalf of the Bourbons, and the struggle between her and the French Republic was only another phase of the old maritime struggle she had waged with the French Monarchy. But Austria and Prussia had embarked on the war in a different spirit, and the situation in which they found themselves at the end of it might well have induced their rulers to question the wisdom of the policy they had pursued and to reflect seriously on its lessons for the future.

The ease with which the resources of Austria had stood the strain of the war was no small testimony to the soundness of the work of reform carried on by Maria Theresa and her son, but in many respects Austria was slipping back into old bad grooves of the days before Maria Theresa. She was in sore need of another Haugwitz to guide her internal affairs into more healthy channels, and of another Kaunitz to direct her foreign policy. This was largely due to the fact that Francis II, though careful and observant, anxious to do his duty by his subjects, and anything but a bad man or a bad king, was not strong enough for the task before him. Drastic reforms were urgently needed, but Francis II could neither realise the need nor be persuaded by those who, like the Archduke Charles, were alive to the evils of the situation. Rather narrow-minded, lacking vigour and real statesmanship, his very carefulness degenerated into pedantry and formalism, his painstaking anxiety to do his work left him immersed in unimportant details of routine and unable to take a broad view, his caution made him so over-suspicious that he did not trust his ministers enough. Nor were his ministers the men to compensate for his defects. Kaunitz, old, worn out, and no longer able to exercise his once pre-dominant influence over the affairs of the country, had given up the Chancellorship in August 1792; and with all his faults none of his successors came up to his level as a statesman. Lehrbach was an intriguer, whose only idea was to obtain Bavaria for Austria by fair means or foul; he was a mere instrument in Thugut's hands. Louis Cobenzl, though in-dependent of Thugut, was no statesman. Well versed in intrigue, well acquainted with Court backstairs, he was a man of little capacity. Indeed, Thugut himself was the only man who stood head and shoulders above the mediocrities around him, and his supremacy was hardly to the advantage of his country. Head of the State Chancery since 1793, he had replaced Philip Cobenzl at the Foreign Office in 1794, and he practically ruled the army through his friends and creatures in the War Council. Energetic, resolute, cool and clear-headed, he was utterly unscrupulous, cynical and un-principled. Absolutely without popular sympathies despite his humble origin, he was an ideal minister for a despot, the typical upholder of feudal and religious absolutism against the assaults of Liberalism or democracy. This was best seen in his harsh and severe domestic policy, in the highly-organised and extensive system of espionage which he maintained, in the atmosphere of distrust and suspicion he communicated to all branches of the government, in the rigid centralisation he maintained, in the harsh press censorship, and in the obtrusive police system. In a word, the internal troubles of Austria which culminated in 1848 may be in no small measure attributed to the reactionary and repressive turn which Thugut gave to the Hapsburg government. Nothing could have been further removed from the spirit of Maria Theresa and of Joseph II than the attitude of harshness guided by suspicion which he imparted to the dealings of the rulers of Austria with their subjects.

Under such a man it was not unnatural that Austria fell into a stagnant condition. Routine was everything. All changes were distrusted as such, apart from their merits. Useful developments were prevented or cramped. Reform was looked upon as playing with fire, as likely to lead to revolution, as Jacobinical. Much of Joseph's best work, especially in the religious and educational spheres, was abolished or altered, while his bureaucracy remained and flourished, uninspired by its author's zeal for efficiency, for honesty and for progress. It was to his hold on to the reins of domestic government that Thugut owed his continued tenure of office, for his foreign policy was rather too adventurous for the less enterprising Francis II. In his hatred for Prussia he recalled the days of Maria Theresa; in his adherence to the English alliance and his opposition to France he went back to Leopold I and the Grand Alliance. It was a policy for which there would have been much to be said had it not been marred by a fatal defect. His insatiable desire for territorial gain was published by his designs on Bavaria and Poland, by his readiness to sacrifice the integrity of the Empire for the sake of Venetia. His eagerness to turn to the advantage of Austria the upheaval of Europe caused by the Revolution outweighed his desire to restore the European equilibrium by the reduction of the power of France. Certainly he made it hard for an ally to put much trust in him. And when all this went hand in hand with the methods by which he sought his ends, with his lack of scruple and almost of honesty, it is hardly wonderful if for all his ability his policy went far towards wrecking the Coalition. It may be perhaps an exaggeration to say with von Sybel, "to him France owed her victory in the Revolutionary War," but he must ever be typical of the way in which diplomatic skill may overreach itself, and in which too much cleverness may recoil on itself while simpler methods succeed by reason of their straightforwardness.

Nor was the condition of Austria's great rival any more healthy. Frederick William II had withdrawn from the Coalition partly in the hope that thereby he might allow the finances of Prussia to recuperate, and might be able to cure the abuses which had grown up in the Prussian administration. Moreover, Prussia had a task of no small difficulty to tackle, the assimilation of the million or so of Poles who had just become her unwilling subjects. An even-handed, capable and firm treatment on the lines of Frederick II's administration might have gone far towards reconciling the Polish peasantry to the loss of a national independence which had never meant good government or given them justice or material prosperity, but their discontent was only augmented by an oppressive, exacting and corrupt rule, by lavish and unwise grants of Polish land to Prussian favourites. Nor were the nobles any better pleased with the results of annexation to Prussia. More than any other class they resented the suppression of Poland's national existence, since to them it had meant cherished privileges.

The failure to achieve in the assimilation of the new shares of Poland even as much success as Frederick II had obtained in dealing with the provinces acquired in 1773, is typical of the general decline in the efficiency of the Prussian State. The administration was full of corrupt and indolent officials, zeal and energy were conspicuous by their absence. Here and there individual officials, as, for example, Baron Stein, at this time practically in charge of the administration of the Westphalian provinces of Prussia,[1] were exceptions to an all but universal rule. But patriotism, self-sacrifice, discipline, devotion to the State, seemed all to have disappeared with Frederick II. The nobles were tending to become a more privileged order, the lower classes, groaning under heavy taxation, were indifferent to the welfare of the country, since their lot was in no way improved, however matters might stand.

In the way of Army Reform a certain amount had been accomplished by a War Directory of which Brunswick and Möllendorf were the leading members. It had added to the establishment of officers, had made some amelioration in the conditions of service, and had improved the equipment of the troops. These, however, were but palliatives and could not cure the deep-seated evils which 1792 had displayed.[2] The Army was living in a fool's Paradise on its old reputation, and was doing nothing to keep itself in touch with the changes in tactics and strategy which the Revolution had brought in its train.

The tone of society was not only bad, but, following the example of the Court, it was hypocritical. Frederick William II might try to cloak his immorality behind a show of devotion, his imitators in Prussian society did not trouble themselves with that amount of concession to the proprieties. At the same time

[1] Cf. Seeley, vol. i. bk. i. 2.
[2] Cf. Chuquet's chapter on the Prussian Army, *Les Guerres de la Révolution*, vol. i. ch. iii.

there was much interference with opinion, almost amounting to a religious persecution of a petty and futile description, an attempt to impose on every one a flabby and formal orthodoxy.

In the finances the effects of this decline in efficiency were most marked. Once the bureaucracy lost that automatic precision and punctuality imparted by the iron discipline maintained under Frederick II, the task of making both ends meet proved altogether too much for it. The reserve fund left by Frederick II had been spent; the tobacco monopoly, abolished with so much parade at Frederick William II's accession, had been reimposed in 1797; but the revenue could not nearly balance the expenses.

With the death of Frederick William II in November 1797, certain changes were made, but only in degree, not in kind: [1] Prussia continued to follow the same paths both in domestic and in foreign policy. Free from his father's combination of mysticism, superstition, hypocrisy and immorality, Frederick William III was too narrow-minded and too diffident to pull Prussia out of the mire in which she was becoming involved. By himself he could do little, he needed some really great statesman to help him. Simple, pious and straightforward, but rather stupid, he was lacking in vigour and in decision, and though he did impart to the administration rather more order and economy, he was not the man to carry out wide reforms or to insist upon and obtain administrative efficiency by means of close personal supervision. Nor were his ministers more likely to do this. Haugwitz, in whom love of power was so strong that he was ready to sacrifice any principles or personal convictions which might have proved inconvenient to his master, if only he could thereby indulge his ruling passion, had since 1792 been mainly responsible for the conduct of foreign affairs. Lombard, a clever but untrustworthy man, was all-influential in domestic policy. From them reforms were not to be expected, negligence in discharge of duties went almost unpunished. The selfish and short-sighted policy of peace which Prussia followed to her own undoing was only one manifestation of the thoroughly unsound condition into which the country had fallen. Whatever arguments might have been urged in defence of the Peace of Basel when it was first concluded, the experiences of the years which followed it should have shown a statesman capable of grasping

---

[1] The "immediate" departments which had hitherto been independent of the General Directory were incorporated with it.

the essential features of the state of Europe how dangerous a policy Prussia was pursuing. Pitt had seized the occasion of the accession of the new King to attempt by the aid of the Duke of Brunswick to oust from office Haugwitz, whom he regarded as mainly responsible for the Peace of Basel and the subsequent inaction of Prussia. But Brunswick, though alive to the dangers of continued neutrality and personally hostile to Haugwitz,[1] was too afraid of the consequences of a breach with the Republic to urge any such departure; and though, as the negotiations of the winter of 1797–1798 showed,[2] it was no longer Haugwitz who was the main obstacle to a change of policy, the advocates of neutrality led by Schulemberg and Prince Henry were still strong enough to carry the day. All that Prussia would offer England was that in return for a considerable subsidy she would mobilise her troops in order to preserve the neutrality of the line of demarcation; and as England was not prepared "to pay an extravagant price for what we think of little value,"[3] Prussia, despite the misgivings which haunted several of her wisest statesmen, adhered to the policy of the Peace of Basel. Between the alternatives of joining the rest of Europe in resisting French aggression and of frankly throwing in her lot with France, she was endeavouring to pursue a middle course which combined some of the disadvantages of both. Mischievous as her conduct was in its influence over Germany, in assisting the spirit of division which it was the aim of France to foster, in offering to the minor Powers "the specious appearance of peace and neutrality,"[4] while Austria was seeking to induce them to join her in a war which concerned them no less than her, Prussia herself was no gainer by her policy. By refusing a definite alliance with France she showed her suspicion and fear of the Republic's successes, and thus failed to obtain any return for the considerable services she was rendering to the Republic by holding aloof from the Coalitions. She earned contempt rather than gratitude; and when she at last realised in 1806 the true tendencies of French policy, France had no reason to spare the country by whose short-sightedness and indecision she had profited so much.

---

[1] Cf. *Dropmore MSS.* iv. 405.   [2] *Ibid. passim.*
[3] T. Grenville to Lord Grenville, *ibid.* p. 514.   [4] *Ibid.* p. 490.

CHAPTER XXI

RASTATT AND THE SECOND COALITION

IN concluding secret compacts with France in the hope of purchasing her good offices at the coming Congress, Austria and Prussia had not been alone. Indeed, most of the minor Powers had sought to safeguard their interests by this expedient, from which it might have been foreseen that France rather than any German Power would play the chief part at Rastatt, and that her interests would prevail in the resettlement of Germany. Her diplomatists were not slow to grasp the opportunity which the estrangement of Austria and Prussia gave them, and by insinuating to each Power in turn that only the opposition of its rival prevented the realisation of its own desires they managed to still further widen the breach between these two leading German states. At the same time, the French sought to excite the alarms of the minor states, to instil into them distrust of Hapsburg and Hohenzollern alike, and teach them to look across the Rhine for protection. By showing herself well disposed to the Princes and to their claims for compensation, France divided them from the Bishops, at whose cost alone compensation could be provided. Indeed, abortive though the Congress was, the foundations of the Confederation of the Rhine were laid at Rastatt.

The principal questions which occupied the attention of the Congress were those of the Left Bank and of "compensation." On the first point, the French envoys adopted from the outset a most peremptory tone, declaring that the assistance and shelter given to the *emigrés* by the Princes of that district had been one of the chief causes of the war. The Austrians had carried out the Convention of December 1st, and their evacuation of the fortresses as they departed homeward proved conclusively that Austria had made up her mind not to resist, and no other state was likely to oppose the cession. Even the Ecclesiastical Electors were more concerned with the chances of avoiding secularisation than with saving the Left Bank.   There was no one to speak on behalf of the Empire, which would receive no compensation for the 25,000 square miles and the $3\frac{1}{2}$ million inhabitants which it was losing, however skilfully the territorial cards were shuffled.   Dynasties might obtain complete compensation, might even gain, but some one had to bear the loss, and it was upon the helpless and inarticulate corporate body to which they belonged that the dynasties of Germany managed to shift the burden of the loss.   In January 1798 the incorporation of the Left Bank with France, its division into departments, and its complete subjection to French codes and arrangements, took place, though nearly two months more elapsed before the deputation appointed by the Diet formally agreed to the cession (March 11th).

The question of compensation and the closely connected problem of secularisation provided the Congress with ample material for discussion and for intrigues of every kind during the remainder of its existence.   Into these it is unnecessary to go, since the renewal of hostilities brought its deliberations to an abortive close.   The problem was one which if tackled by men who really had the interests of Germany at heart, might perhaps have resulted in a real reform of the Empire, might have given it a new constitution and a new lease of life.   There were not wanting optimists who hoped that the beginning of a new era for Germany might be dated from the Congress of Rastatt.   Such a result, however, difficult to reach under any circumstances, was quite out of the question when the predominant partner in the Congress was the Power to whose interests a real revival of Germany was most inimical.   Even now, if Austria and Prussia could have agreed to sink their differences and to make a stand against the policy of the Directory, it might have been possible to turn the Congress to a useful end.   However, co-operation was as far off as ever. Haugwitz was as much an object of aversion and suspicion at Vienna as was Thugut at Berlin.   The old hostility, the old jealousy and the old suspicions survived in great strength and frustrated the efforts of those who sought to bring the old rivals together; and France spared no efforts to keep the breach between them open.[1]   Both favoured or opposed each proposal, each suggested territorial rearrangement according as it was

[1] Cf. P. Bailleu, *Preussen und Frankreich, 1795–1806.*

more or less disadvantageous to the other. Prussia would give up her claims on compensation if Austria were to receive nothing. Austria was prepared to do without Salzburg if Prussia made no new acquisitions. Moreover, the designs which Thugut entertained on Bavaria were a stumbling-block in the path of any possible understanding.

The Left Bank once lost, the question of secularisation was inevitably brought forward. By secularisation alone could the necessary " compensation " be provided. But it was not without some misgivings that Germany approached the problem. Every one saw that the secularisation of the ecclesiastical states would be the beginning of the end of the old constitution and of the old order of things, but nobody could tell where the process would end, and all felt not a little nervous about the future. Hanover and Saxony, for example, shared Austria's wish to confine any secularising to very limited dimensions. Their rivals would profit more by it than would they themselves, therefore they opposed any wide-sweeping measures. But the smaller states as a whole, those large enough to be sure of getting some morsel of ecclesiastical land, some abbey or priory, clamoured keenly for secularisation as " the only way to restore efficiency to the Empire "[1] — in other words, the only thing likely to benefit them individually.

In May the deliberations of the Congress were rudely enlivened by the production by the French emissaries of an entirely new series of demands. The Rhine was to be free to traffic, all tolls were to be abolished, Kehl and Castel were to be handed over to France, Ehrenbreitstein was to be " slighted," the islands in the river were to be allotted to the Republic. From June onwards the Congress spent its time in making a futile opposition to these and other equally new demands. But it was rapidly becoming more certain that a fresh appeal to the sword was imminent, for the aggressive and disingenuous policy of the Directory allowed little hope of a stable peace ever being reached by negotiation.

In their dealings with Germany the Directors had all along shown themselves tainted with that same disregard for treaties, for the most solemn promises and the most definite agreements, which had characterised the Convention. French emissaries had been sedulously spreading the Revolutionary propaganda

[1] Cf. Haüsser, ii. p. 164.

throughout South Germany, stirring up the peasantry, fomenting social discontent. The Directory did, indeed, disavow these agitators, but their conduct was exactly the same as the line its agents were pursuing in Switzerland and in the Papal States, where democratic discontent was excited, to be used as a pretext for intervention. Similarly, in the matter of Ehrenbreitstein they hardly even pretended to abide by the conditions of the armistice arranged between Hoche and Werneck in April 1797. The fortress was held by an Austrian garrison which was allowed to periodically reprovision itself, though not to increase its supplies beyond the amount in stock when the armistice was concluded. When, in December 1797, the Austrians withdrew, 2500 men in the service of the Elector of Treves replaced them; but the French in deliberate violation of the armistice resumed the close blockade of the fortress. Not content with this, they kept on raiding the Right Bank, levying forced contributions and subjecting the inhabitants to all manner of violence. Such conduct was by itself sufficient indication of the intentions of the French, and an ample justification for breaking off negotiations. Moreover, their behaviour went far to alienate even their strongest supporters in the Rhine lands. The annexation of all ecclesiastical and monastic property, the introduction of the French codes of law, calendar and tables of weights and measures, the appointment of Frenchmen to all the new posts and offices, the abolition of the old German education, briefly, the contrast between the promised liberty and the practical oppression roused a very strong anti-French feeling in the Rhine valley.

In April 1798 relations between France and Austria were still further strained by an incident which took place at Vienna. Bernadotte, the French Ambassador, had been sent there with the definite object of mixing himself up in the internal politics of Austria and endeavouring to overthrow Thugut, or at least to undermine the position of that strenuous opponent of France. On April 13th he provoked a riot by displaying a Tricolour on his house. The mob, enraged by this, stormed the house and tore down the flag. Bernadotte made all the political use he could of this incident. He demanded his passports and even quitted Vienna. This might have been followed by war, but that the provocation came from France before the financial or military situation of Austria had improved sufficiently to enable her to defy the Republic, and the Emperor humbled himself to make a concession to France which for the time averted a rupture : Thugut gave up his post as Foreign Minister (May 1st) and confined himself to domestic affairs, Louis Cobenzl, a strong advocate of peace with France, replacing him. The change was seen in the private negotiations between the Hapsburgs and the French, which now took place at Selz near Rastatt; for Francis was anything but bellicose, and Cobenzl would have been glad to avert a renewal of hostilities by coming to terms with France. But the French were not prepared to bid high enough for Austria's neutrality, and even Cobenzl had to admit that with such a Power it was almost impossible to come to terms. By the middle of July Thugut was back in office, Cobenzl going off on a special embassy to Berlin with the object of inducing Prussia to come into line with Austria and Russia to resist further French aggressions, for events elsewhere were moving rapidly towards the now inevitable war.

The intervention of the Directory in the affairs of Switzerland (April 1798) has already been mentioned (p. 421). The annexation of Biel, Geneva and Mühlhausen to France might be defended on geographical grounds, but it was an arbitrary and rapacious act, extremely disconcerting to the other neighbours of the Republic. The appropriation of the contents of the treasuries of Berne, Lucerne and Zürich—16 million francs in cash besides goods of about equal value—to the purposes of Bonaparte's Egyptian expedition was an utterly unjustifiable example of high-handed violence, and showed that the Helvetic Republic was little more than a vassal of France—in other words, that the strategical situation had been materially altered to Austria's disadvantage, as her armies in Swabia would no longer have their left flank protected by the neutrality of the territory to the South. About the same time (March 1798) the intervention of the Directory in the internal affairs of the Batavian Republic gave an example of the real meaning of the liberty and independence enjoyed by the states under the protection of France. Nor were these outrages confined to the valley of the Rhine. The mixture of treachery and force displayed by Bonaparte's treatment of the Knights of St. John and his seizure of Malta had the important effect of enraging the Czar Paul, already alarmed by the progress of French arms and principles and anxious to test the armies of Holy Russia against the conquerors of the rest of Europe. Austria, finding it likely that she would have the zealous support of Russia if she took up arms, was growing more bellicose, and her warlike dispositions were increased by the action of France in Italy, where the arrangements made at Campo Formio, on the whole not unfavourable to Austria and her friends, were being radically altered. The assassination of the French envoy at Rome, Duphot, served as a pretext for Berthier to attack Rome, drive out Pope Pius VI, and proclaim the Roman Republic (Feb. 1798); and when the King of the Two Sicilies, encouraged by Nelson's victory at the Nile to measure his strength with the Power which was so rapidly subjugating all Italy, rashly attacked this unwelcome new neighbour and occupied Rome (Nov. 29th), Championnet not only promptly expelled the Neapolitans, but followed up his success by invading their territory. The Court took refuge in Sicily, and France added the Parthenopean Republic to the list of her clients (Jan. 1799). Nor was this all. In December 1798, Charles Emmanuel of Savoy was forced to abandon his continental for his insular dominions, and a Prince of the Hapsburg House, Archduke Ferdinand of Tuscany, was forcibly dispossessed of his Duchy.

Such a series of outrages, of violations of treaties, of unprovoked aggressions, could have but one result: indeed, it is only remarkable that the Powers of Europe were so long about uniting to withstand the Directory. It was no fault of England's, for, since the beginning of 1798, Pitt had been seeking to bring together a new coalition. But while acrimonious disputes over the repayment of money lent to the Emperor in the previous war prevented cordial co-operation between Austria and Great Britain, the extravagances and eccentric conduct of Paul of Russia made Francis II more than usually cautious about committing himself to any course of action in which he might find himself left suddenly in the lurch through the vagaries of his unstable Eastern neighbour. The return of Thugut to office (July 1798), the conclusion of a convention with Russia (Aug. 10th) promising military aid to the Emperor, the signature of an Anglo-Russian Treaty (Dec. 29th, 1798), mark stages in the slow progress by which at last Austria came to draw the sword. Her declaration of war (March 12th, 1799) would have been more efficacious had it been launched six months earlier, when France was still staggering under the news of destruction of her Mediterranean fleet at the Nile. The delay is to be attributed to her desire to give her shattered resources time to recuperate, and to the need for more military preparations.

From the Second Coalition, which comprised Austria, England, Naples and Russia, one Power was absent which, both for her own interests and for those of Europe, ought to have been prominent in its ranks. Not the least important causes of the renewal of hostilities was the utterly unreasonable rapacity displayed by the French at Rastatt. Their conduct towards Germany had been too unblushingly aggressive for any German statesman with any claim to foresight or national spirit, or even to a correct appreciation of the interests of his own particular state, to overlook the serious menace to the independence of Germany. Yet Frederick William III clung obstinately to his father's policy of neutrality, which had already been weighed in the balance and found wanting. One may explain, one may to some extent excuse the Peace of Basel; 1806 is the best comment on the inglorious inaction of 1799.

Prussia's continued neutrality was a great disappointment to the Allies. Every effort was made to bring her into line with the other Powers. Her relations with France were not of the most cordial, and Austria and Russia hoped to use this to enlist her on their side. Haugwitz himself had begun to realise how dangerous to Prussia was the supremacy of France, and to see that Prussia had more in common with Austria and Russia than with the Republic; in fact, Prussia had gone so far as to reject the overtures of Siéyès for a definite alliance with France (May 1798). Alvensleben, indeed, foretelling the collapse of the Prussian military system, did argue that the French alliance was the only road to safety, since it would enable Prussia to turn the resettlement of Germany to her own benefit and the disadvantage of Austria;[1] but the King was not well disposed towards such a step. Yet Prussia could not or would not see that for once there was no safety in the middle path. It was in vain that representatives of the four principal Powers of Europe met at Berlin (May 28th) to discuss the formation of an alliance; in vain that England and the Czar sought to induce Prussia to join in a Quadruple Alliance for the reduction of France to her old limits, the restoration of the House of Orange to Holland, and the re-establishment of the integrity of Germany. Beguiled by Talleyrand's assurances that France would respect

[1] Cf. Bailleu, *Preussen und Frankreich.*

the neutrality of North Germany, Frederick William failed to see that the success of France would place Germany at the mercy of the Republic, and that, if the Coalition were victorious, Prussia's voice would not be listened to when the affairs of Europe were resettled unless she had shared in earning the fruits of victory. Hesitation and indecision governed her policy, and there could be no better illustration of her endeavour to run with the hare and hunt with the hounds than the advice she gave to the new Elector of Bavaria, Maximilian Joseph of Zweibrücken. This Prince succeeded to the Wittelsbach inheritance on the death (Feb. 1799) of his cousin Charles Theodore. Bavaria's position was critical. Thugut's designs on the Electorate were an open secret. The events of 1795 [1] had not been forgotten by Austria; it was thought more than probable that Austria's hostility would leave Maximilian no alternative but to rely on French assistance. However, neither the new Elector himself nor his chief minister, the Savoyard Montgelas, regarded the friendship of France with much confidence, and once again, as in 1786, it was to Prussia that Maximilian turned for protection.[2] But Prussia could do no more for Bavaria than advise her most emphatically to do nothing that could give the Coalition reasonable grounds for taking offence. Thus left in the lurch, Maximilian Joseph had only one expedient remaining by which to avert the hostility of the Coalition. He knew that Thugut was doing all he could to incite the Czar against him, for the head of the Holy Roman Empire was so reduced that he dared take no step except with the consent of the monarch who claimed to be the heir of Byzantium, by representing to Paul that Bavaria was a partisan of France and a nursery of Jacobin intrigue. Maximilian therefore threw in his lot with the Coalition, and Bavaria was one of the few minor states of Germany which took an active part in the war. The conduct of the German Princes as a whole was not very creditable either to their patriotism or to their sense. Not even yet awakened to a full understanding of the meaning of French supremacy, they would have much preferred to see the completion of a settlement based on the secularisation of the ecclesiastical states and dictated by France, to the renewal of the attempt to confine the power of France within reasonable bounds.

[1] Cf. p. 399.   [2] Cf. *Der Krieg von 1799*, i. pp. 102 ff.

By the beginning of 1799 it was certain that hostilities would be resumed as soon as the season made operations possible. The gallant defenders of Ehrenbreitstein were compelled to surrender before January was over; for, though Austria was making preparations for war on a considerable scale, the relief of the fortress was out of the question. The Archduke Charles, with a perhaps undue caution, put off the opening of hostilities, although delay was, had he only realised it, even more useful to the French than to their enemies,[1] and in the end it was the French who on March 1st opened the campaign by crossing the Rhine.

The peculiarity of the campaign of 1799 is the prominence of Switzerland as a theatre of operations. Despite the difficulties of moving, feeding and manœuvring armies among its mountains and in its narrow valleys, its position between Italy and Germany made its possession of vital importance to the combatants, since it served as the pivot on which the campaign turned. From it as from a bastion, blows could be struck against the flanks of the forces contending in the valleys of the Po and of the Danube; it would be exceedingly difficult to defend Swabia against a French advance from Alsace if at any moment the defenders might be taken in flank and rear by forces debouching from Switzerland. Through it also ran the most direct routes by which reinforcements might be detached from one wing to the other. Unless Switzerland were wrested from Masséna's possession Archduke Charles in the valley of the Danube would be unable to communicate with Suvorov in Italy except by most circuitous routes: the French would hold the interior position and be able to direct their blows against either enemy as they would.

Thus while Scherer with 60,000 men took post along the line of the Adige to cover the Cisalpine Republic against the 60,000 Austrians of Kray, and Jourdan with 48,000 advanced across the Black Forest to Rottweil and Tuttlingen to contend with Archduke Charles (70,000) for the upper valley of the Danube, Masséna with 30,000 men pushed forward through Switzerland across the Upper Rhine in the hope of driving the Austrians from the Vorarlberg back into Tyrol, and thereby completely severing their communications and menacing their flanks should their wings be successful.

[1] Cf. Hüffer, *Der Krieg von 1799*, i. pp. 19, 20.

It was about March 6th that Masséna began his advance. The Austrians, some 26,000 men under a general of Swiss birth, the gallant Hotze, extended from Bregenz to Chur. On the left Masséna's vigorous attacks, well conceived and well executed, drove them back into the Engadine. Almost simultaneously Lecourbe forced his way from Bellinzona to Thusis, and pushing on thence by the Julier Pass drove back into Tyrol the detachments of Bellegarde's unduly scattered corps (March 6th to 17th). Dessolles, coming up the Valtelline, forced his way after heavy fighting into the Münsterthal and inflicted on the Austrians a severe reverse at Taufers (March 25th), for which Bellegarde's own carelessness was responsible. Only on their right at Feldkirch did the Austrians manage to maintain their ground; but the end of March saw the French firmly established on the upper waters of the Inn and of the Adige; the Engadine and the Grisons were in their hands; the Austrians, despite considerable numerical superiority, had suffered a loss of 10,000 men, and the communications between Vorarlberg and Southern Tyrol were cut.

On the flanks, however, fortune had been very different. Archduke Charles, whose headquarters were at the moment at Friedberg, was better prepared for attack than was Bellegarde in Tyrol or Auffenberg in the Grisons; and when Jourdan, in obedience to definite orders from Paris but against his own better judgment, advanced again and took post behind the Osterach, the Archduke, though too late to fulfil his intention of forestalling the French at this river, had little difficulty in forcing them to retreat (March 21st). Profiting by the leisurely nature of the Austrian pursuit, Jourdan turned suddenly to bay at Stockach, and as the Austrians reconnoitred his position, delivered a furious counter-attack (March 25th). His principal effort was on his left, where St. Cyr, reinforced by d'Hautpoult and Soult, drove Merveldt's Austrians back in disorder from Liptingen, while the Austrian centre and left had the greatest difficulty in maintaining their position at Stockach. Victory seemed in Jourdan's grasp, and he was aiming a turning movement against the enemy's line of retreat when, just in time, the Archduke brought up reinforcements and quite turned the tables by a successful stroke at the French centre. His success was decisive: the French were driven back and their line cut in half; and though the Archduke failed to make the renewed attack next morning which might have clinched his victory, Jourdan fell back across the Black Forest (March 29th to 30th) without attempting to defend its passes.   His army, ill-disciplined and ill-provided, went completely to pieces, and could have been annihilated had the pursuit been hotly pressed. Still even if Jourdan was lucky to escape, the Archduke had achieved no inconsiderable success.

Not only was Jourdan compelled to recross the Rhine in order to cover Alsace against the attack which was expected, but Bernadotte, who had advanced up the Neckar, levying contributions and plundering in the usual style, hastily fell back also ; and, save for the garrisons of Kehl and Mannheim, the Right Bank was free from the French.   Moreover, their forces in Italy had also suffered disaster.   Schérer, somewhat too old for his work, was less successful in the field than as a Minister of War, and his attempt to defeat Kray before the promised Russian reinforcements could arrive ended in complete disaster. After repulsing the attacks of the French between Legnago and Pastrengo (March 26th), and thwarting an effort they made to cross the Adige near Verona, Kray, a Wallachian of no little talent, popular with his men and trusted by them if not by the little clique which ruled the Austrian War Council, took the counter-offensive with success.   Only the energy and skill of Moreau, Schérer's second in command, saved the French army from complete ruin at Magnano, just South of Verona (April 5th). Even so they had to abandon the lines of the Mincio and Oglio, and only about 25,000, not half Schérer's original force, could be rallied behind the Adda.   Meanwhile Suvorov had arrived with the first contingent of his Russians (April 15th) and taken command of the Allies.

The veteran Russian general, though nearly seventy, was full of a youthful vigour which was conspicuous by its absence among the slower and more methodical officers of Austria. His enterprise and dash, combined as they were with a power of endurance and a calm resourcefulness not often met with in a nature so impetuous, made him resemble the generals of the Revolutionary school rather than those brought up in the more precise traditions of Frederick II and Marshal Lacy.   Keenly alive as he was to the importance of rapidity, of concentrating his troops to strike a decisive blow, he startled the Austrian generals as much by his proposal to push forward, leaving Mantua untaken in his rear, as he annoyed them by compelling their troops to practise the bayonet exercise all day. Nor was it wonderful that he came into collision with the Austrian War Council. Suvorov was not the man to spare criticism where it was as well deserved as it was by the inefficient administration of Thugut and his clique. Moreover, the Council actually went so far as to issue direct orders to the Austrian troops which had been placed under his command, an interference he angrily resented. When it is also added that the policy of Thugut, which included designs on Piedmont and Genoa, differed materially from that of Suvorov and his master and led to violent quarrels, it is not the defeats but the successes of the Allies that excite surprise. Favourable as the opportunity seemed for overthrowing France, with her best general locked up in Egypt, her armies falling back defeated and in confusion towards her frontiers, pursued by the hatred of the populations they had maltreated, her home government discredited and a prey to factions, it was not by a disunited Coalition that her defeat was to be accomplished. When Prussia and most of the other Powers of Germany held aloof, and Austria and Russia entertained antagonistic views as to the policy to be pursued, France had not really much to fear.

Meanwhile the Congress of Rastatt had been continuing its sessions. Long after more than sufficient reasons had been given for the rupture of negotiations, Francis II had clung to the hopes of arranging a satisfactory settlement at Rastatt, and the lesser members of the Empire were too much engrossed in the intrigues and bargains of the Congress to pay any heed to events in Italy or Switzerland. Even after Austria's declaration of war (March 12th), only Lehrbach and Metternich left the Congress. The majority of the minor states eagerly accepted the assurance of the French that they would not be molested unless they supported Austria, for the French never missed a chance of sowing dissension between the Emperor and the Empire. With this object they disclosed the secret arrangements of Campo Formio, and the deliberations of the Congress were only interrupted by the arrival of Austrian troops, who surrounded the town and compelled the plenipotentiaries to disperse, as the Emperor had formally declared the Congress dissolved. The French envoys were given passports ordering them to quit Rastatt within twenty-four hours (April 28th); but delaying their departure until evening, they found the gates closed and did not get out until 10 p.m. They had hardly left the town before they were beset by a party of Austrian hussars, attacked and cut down; two of them, Bonnet and Roberjot, being killed on the spot and the third, de Bry, left for dead. The French version of the affair is that it was intentional, that it was done by Thugut's orders to make the breach with France insuperable, or perhaps to destroy the evidence of Austrian negotiations with France. However, there seems no reason whatever for laying the blame at Thugut's door. He was much too clever a man to have planned an act so brutal, so useless, and so calculated to excite horror and disapproval.[1] It seems rather more probable that the military authorities, well aware that the French had abused their ambassadorial office for purposes of espionage, intended to seize their papers, though no personal injury to the Ambassadors was contemplated,[2] but that the officer entrusted with the affair misinterpreted and exceeded his instructions with disastrous results.[3] It is, of course, possible that the outrage may have been the work of French *emigrés* in the Austrian service;[4] but the evidence is on the whole unfavourable to this theory, though the Austrians endeavoured to get it accepted. Whatever explanation be accepted, the incident was most discreditable to Austria, and Thugut would have done more to clear himself of the suspicion of complicity had more been done to punish the authors of an outrage worthy of the worst days of Revolutionary excess.

One result of the Allied successes in Italy and on the Danube was that the French were unable to retain their advanced position in Tyrol. Lecourbe had to fall back to Chur, and Dessolles to follow suit. Chiavenna was evacuated; Loison failed to maintain his position in the Valtelline and had to retire by the Splügen Pass into the Rhine valley; and Hotze carrying the Luciensteg (May 14th) at a second attempt, the French were expelled from Eastern Switzerland. Greater successes might have been obtained but for the highly culpable slackness of Bellegarde;[5] and, moreover, when the Grisons had been cleared of the French he refused to push on to the St. Gotthard and seize that pass, though this would enable him to cut off the retreat of the French divisions from the Italian

---

[1] Cf. *Der Krieg von 1799*, ch. iii. *passim*.   [2] *Ibid.* i. p. 79.
[3] *Ibid.* i. p. 96.   [4] *Ibid.* i. p. 72.   [5] *Ibid.* i. pp. 57–60.

lakes, but took instead the road to Italy by the Splügen and Como, alleging that his instructions bade him reinforce Suvorov. Even more unfortunate was it that during this period the Archduke should not merely have done nothing to follow up his successes against Jourdan, but made no move against Masséna either. Switzerland after her bitter experiences as one of the daughter Republics with which France had surrounded herself, would have welcomed the once-hated Austrians as deliverers. Masséna with barely 30,000 men in the midst of a hostile population could hardly have hoped to maintain his position against Hotze's 20,000, together with the 40,000 troops of whom the Archduke could have disposed, even if some portions of the Austrian force must have been left to watch Jourdan. To a certain extent this inaction was caused by Bellegarde's defeats, and the Archduke's own health was so bad that for several weeks he was unable to discharge his duties. He himself attributed his inactivity to the insufficiency of his force and to the deficiencies in his equipment and supplies—in other words, to the bad administration of the War Council; but the principal reason[1] was the resolve of the Emperor and Thugut, influenced not a little by political considerations, to wait for the arrival of the large Russian reinforcements which were on their way. The Archduke himself would have resumed operations about the middle of April, but orders from Vienna held him back.[2] The time thus lost by the Allies was of incalculable value to France. Masséna spared no effort to improve his position and to reorganise and refit his troops, and to repress the tentative efforts of the Swiss to rise and free themselves from the yoke of the invaders; while Bernadotte, transferred to the Ministry of War, exhibited wonderful energy and great administrative capacity in getting together a new army 100,000 strong out of the new levies whom the law of the Conscription (Sept. 23rd, 1798) had placed at his disposal.

Not until the end of May were hostilities resumed. Even then the efforts of the Austrian main army were designed mainly to assist Hotze's operations in Eastern Switzerland. The Archduke advanced South against Masséna's positions in the district between the Thur, the Glatt and the Limmat, Hotze moving East from St. Gallen to co-operate with him. Dashing

[1] Cf. *Der Krieg von 1799*, i. p. 107.   [2] *Ibid.* p. 109.

at the Archduke, who had crossed the Rhine near Schaffhausen on May 23rd, Masséna was repulsed (May 25th) after heavy fighting, and the Austrians were able to unite and to force the French steadily back on Zürich (May 27th to 29th). To hold this town, important as the point on which many roads converged, Masséna took up a strong position stretching North-Westward from the lake to the Glatt. Here on June 4th he gave battle to the Archduke. On their left the Austrian columns penetrated to the suburbs of Zürich, but were there checked; in the centre neither the column which assailed the Zürich Berg nor that under Hotze which tried to storm the Geisberg was able to gain any decisive advantage; while an equally indecisive result was reached on the right wing in the direction of Afholtern. But Masséna saw that he would not be able to hold his own against the renewed attack which the Archduke was preparing, and accordingly he evacuated Zürich and retired to a strong position behind the Lower Reuss. Meanwhile Lecourbe, who was endeavouring to hold the St. Gotthard against Bellegarde, had been forced back to 'Altorf at the head of the Lake of Lucerne and the shortest line of communications between the German and Italian theatres of war was once more in Austrian hands. Had the Archduke only pushed forward the Austrians might have gained a real success; they were superior in numbers, and the population of Eastern Switzerland was strongly in their favour. But once again political complications proved fatal to the cause of the Coalition. Thugut was very anxious to get Suvorov out of Italy, lest the Russian general should interfere with his schemes for the disposal of the territory reconquered from the French. While Russia looked upon the restoration to Charles Emmanuel of the mainland possessions of the House of Savoy as one of the principal objects of the Coalition, Thugut had other designs for Piedmont, alleging that only if it were in Austria's hands could it be made a satisfactory bulwark against French aggression, and assuming that Charles Emmanuel had forfeited all claims upon the Allies by deserting them in 1796. Accordingly he readily agreed to a scheme which the English ministry put forward with the Czar's consent, by which Suvorov was to come up from Italy with his Russian corps, unite with the Archduke and with a Russian corps under Korsakov, now on its way to Switzerland, and advance into France. Suvorov was not ill-disposed to this scheme. Considerable as were the successes he had gained in Italy, he found himself continually thwarted by the interference of the Austrian War Council; the Emperor insisted on treating him as though completely at his disposal, and his plans were constantly upset and altered by Thugut. The refusal of the Austrians to co-operate in an invasion of Provence, since they wished to complete the conquest of Italy, increased Suvorov's desire to turn North and join Korsakov in Switzerland.

During the five months which had elapsed since he had taken over the command of the Allied forces in Italy, Suvorov had achieved much. He had begun by capturing Brescia (April 21st) and Cremona, and forcing the passage of the Adda behind which the French, encouraged by the substitution of Moreau for the discredited Schérer, had attempted a stand. But not even Moreau could stem Suvorov's advance. The Austrians of Ott's division forced their way across the river by Cassano (April 27th), and the advantage was pressed home. Moreau, his centre thus pierced, was thrust back Southward, and completely severed from his left under Sérurier higher up the river. The confused retreat of the French resulted in the capture of Sérurier and the bulk of his division, and on April 29th the Russian general entered Milan. Luckily for Moreau, however, Suvorov abandoned his first intention of following hard after the French and cutting them off from Genoa, to turn aside into Piedmont where the population welcomed him as a deliverer. On May 25th he was before Turin, which opened its gates to him two days later. Meanwhile Moreau fell back across the Apennines towards Genoa, not a little fortunate in that he escaped the pursuit which must have ruined the remnants of his army. Arrived at Genoa (June 6th), he covered his communications with France and held out a hand to Macdonald, who after collecting from Tuscany, Rome and Naples the various divisions of the French army in those quarters, some 36,000 in all, had abandoned Southern Italy to its fate and was coming up the Via Æmiliana towards Piacenza, a march which seemed to threaten an attack on the left flank and communications of the Allies.

The situation of the Allies was one of no small peril. They were so much scattered that the main body was little over 20,000 strong; but Suvorov rose to the occasion. Con-

28

centrating some 36,000 troops at Alessandria (June 12th), he set off Eastward on the 15th; and so rapid were his movements, that as Macdonald was forcing back Ott's Austrians from the Trebbia to the Tidone (June 17th), Suvorov's vanguard suddenly planted itself across his path and checked the French advance. A fierce struggle was ended about 3 p.m. by the arrival of the Allied main body, headed by the Russian veteran in person. Two more days of desperate and strenuous fighting on the banks of the Trebbia followed. In vain Macdonald sought to cut his way through to Tortona, the place appointed for his junction with Moreau. So stubborn was the resistance of Russians and Austrians alike, that at the end of the third day (June 21st) the French army, broken and demoralised, began a disorderly but unmolested retreat across the Apennines into Tuscany. But that Suvorov had to dash back to Tortona to succour Bellegarde, the lieutenant he had left behind to keep Moreau in check, and was therefore unable to pursue, things might have gone very ill with Macdonald. As it was, he managed to extricate himself from a perilous position by making his way over indifferent roads to the Riviera, thus regaining touch with Moreau, who had fallen back from Tortona (June 25th) the moment Suvorov drew near.

But though the Allies had an excellent chance of expelling the French from Italy, they failed to improve the occasion. As in 1793, the victorious field army was dispersed to besiege Mantua and other fortresses, the direct interference of the Austrian War Council thus wrecking Suvorov's plans when they seemed on the point of success.' Clearly as Suvorov realised that if Moreau were once beaten out of Italy the fate of the garrisons he had left behind would be sealed, he could not collect his forces for the pitched battle which alone could give decisive victory till July had been frittered away in sieges of minor importance, and the Directory had been able to send Joubert with large reinforcements to take command of the Army of Italy. Not till August 5th, however, was the new commander free to start to the relief of the beleaguered fortresses, and by that time both Alessandria (July 21st) and Mantua (July 29th) had fallen, and the besieging forces were on their way to rejoin Suvorov. Thus Joubert's advance ended in disaster. Near Novi he found his way barred by Suvorov with superior forces (Aug. 14th), and only after some hesitation did he decide to stand and fight. Next day the battle was begun by an advance of Kray's Austrians on the Allied right, and Joubert hurrying to the spot was hit and killed. Moreau succeeded to the command, and by supreme exertions held his ground against the repeated attacks of Kray of the Russians in the centre. But with the afternoon there arrived on the scene a fresh division of Austrians under Melas, and their intervention—a direct attack on the French right at Novi combined with an outflanking movement more to the Southward—decided the sixteen hours' struggle in favour of the Allies. In complete disorder the French fell back on Genoa. Want of transport prevented an immediate pursuit by the Allies. Tortona was still untaken, and the Austrian corps of Klenau was detached into Tuscany by the War Council instead of supporting Suvorov. Accordingly the Russian general determined to transfer himself to Switzerland, and about the middle of September his columns began to make their way past Bellinzona up the Leventina valley towards the St. Gotthard.

The diversion of Suvorov's corps from Italy to Switzerland was not in itself a mistaken move. Had Archduke Charles remained on the Limmat holding Masséna in check, the appearance of the Russian veteran on the St. Gotthard in the French general's right rear would have seriously endangered his position. But the Archduke with 36,000 of his 60,000 men had moved away down the Rhine long before Suvorov arrived. He was well aware of the danger of leaving Hotze and Korsakov with little over 50,000 men to face the 80,000 men now under Masséna, but he had not the moral courage or the resolution to defy Thugut and refuse to carry out the task allotted to him. There was some idea that by attacking Alsace he would materially assist the efforts of the Anglo-Russian expedition to North Holland, which had just (Aug. 27th) effected a successful landing at the Helder: possibly Thugut was anxious to have Austrian troops in close proximity to the Netherlands in case the efforts of England and Russia should induce Prussia to throw in her lot with the Allies; always jealous of Prussia, he may have desired to be able to prevent her making acquisitions on the Lower Rhine. Be that as it may, the Archduke's operations had no influence whatever over the fighting along the Zuyder Zee; and though he managed to relieve Philipsburg, on which the French were pressing closely (Sept. 12th), and stormed their position at Mannheim with complete success, the operations of his 36,000 men had practically no effective influence over the results of the campaign. Though there was a good deal of spasmodic fighting going on along the Rhine, the French making raids, the peasantry supported by small parties of regulars resisting with fair success, it was of quite minor importance. Albini, the chief minister of the Elector of Mayence, had taken advantage of these efforts of the peasantry to organise their resistance, his example had been imitated elsewhere, and fair success had been achieved, so that the Archduke was not wanted on the Neckar and his presence was badly needed on the Limmat.[1]

Masséna was not the man to neglect such a chance as the Archduke's departure gave him. Already, during the middle of August, Lecourbe had resumed the offensive against the Austrian left in the valleys of the Upper Reuss and Upper Rhone. He had managed to regain possession of the Simplon and St. Gotthard passes, and thus, when Suvorov came up from Bellinzona he found the pass in possession of the enemy. Between the 19th and the 26th of September the fate of the campaign was decided. After a series of desperate struggles in which every step of the way was fiercely contested, Suvorov forced his way over the St. Gotthard to the Devil's Bridge and over the Devil's Bridge (Sept. 24th) to Altdorf at the head of the Lake of Lucerne (26th). Thence he turned East, pushed through the Schachenthal (Sept. 27th) and over the Kinzig Kulm into the valley of the Muotta (29th), to find in his front at Schwytz, not Korsakov, whom he hoped to meet, but Masséna. For while Suvorov was struggling over the St. Gotthard, Masséna had concentrated 40,000 men round Zürich, had crossed the Limmat, and hurled Mortier's corps on Korsakov's front while Oudinot outflanked him and threatened his retreat. Two days' hard fighting ended in the complete defeat of the Russian army (Sept. 25th to 26th), the relics

---

[1] The Archduke wanted to use Albini's organisation to found a permanent *Landsturm* in South Germany. The chance was fair; for, if one may judge its quality by the verbal expressions it found, there was a very violent anti-French feeling in South Germany, and the Franconian and Swabian Circles, Bavaria, Würtemberg and other Powers were raising contingents. However, such a step was entirely opposed to Thugut's policy, and nothing came of the idea.

of which only escaped having to surrender by a prodigious effort which carried them through the encircling French. Simultaneously Soult had forced the passage of the Linth, defeated and killed Hotze, and driven the left wing of the Austro-Russian army back into the Vorarlberg by St. Gall.

Thus Suvorov found that all his efforts had been in vain. His feat in extricating his 16,000 exhausted men from their perilous position and bringing them in safety to the right bank of the Upper Rhine was the supreme achievement of his career; but Switzerland was none the less lost, for the relics of Korsakov's forces had put the Rhine and the Lake of Constance between them and the victorious Masséna.

Thus the campaign of 1799 had ended in defeat and disappointment for the Coalition. In Italy, Liguria alone was left to the French, for Championnet's attempt to profit by Suvorov's departure to recover possession of Piedmont had resulted in the defeat of the Army of Italy by Melas near Genoa (Nov. 4th). Similarly the right bank of the Rhine was clear of all but raiding parties of French; but Switzerland was again in their possession, and the next campaign was to show how great was the strategic advantage they were to derive from this. Moreover, failure had attended the Anglo-Russian campaign in Holland. Not really beaten in the field, the Duke of York had found it impossible to advance in a country so much cut up by canals and marshes with an army largely composed of raw recruits from the Militia, and with Allies as unsatisfactory and untrustworthy as Hermann and his Russians. Moreover, the expedition had been misdirected from the first. When it was first proposed, it had been expected that Prussia would join the Coalition, in which case the true policy would have been to land the troops on the East of the Zuyder Zee, in Gröningen and Friesland, the strongholds of the Orange party, not in North Holland, the most Republican part of the whole country. In Gröningen the Allies would have been in a friendly country and in easy communication with Hanover; and if at the same time a Prussian army had crossed the Rhine to recover Cleves and Guelders, the chances of the Coalition would have been enormously improved. At the root, then, of the failure in North Holland was Prussia's selfish, shortsighted and most reprehensible neutrality. Her refusal to join caused the expedition to be hurried to sea without any definite aim in order to do something, and to this want of definite purpose may be attributed the failure.[1]

With Austria and Russia on decidedly strained terms, and the relations between Russia and England not much better, the fortunes of the Coalition were already on the wane, even before the return of Bonaparte to France (Oct.) and the improvement in her military effectiveness involved in the establishment of the firm and centralised government of the Consulate on the ruins of the Directory (Nov. 1799). Indeed, the Coalition was on the point of dissolving. The exchange of projects for the next campaign only brought Austria and Russia into more violent conflict. On October 22nd, Paul announced his secession from the Coalition; in December the Russian troops started homeward. This destroyed the last chance of inducing Prussia to join the Allies. Earlier in the year, Russia had put strong pressure on her to join. There were not wanting men who proclaimed the unwisdom of the policy of neutrality. Brunswick was among them; and Haugwitz, now realising the dangers of French predominance in Europe, went so far as to explain to Otto, the French Minister at Berlin, that it had not been Prussia's idea, when agreeing to the Peace of Basel, that Holland should remain permanently in the occupation of France. But Frederick William was not to be persuaded to change his policy, and France procrastinated and put off answering until the critical moment was past. Nor did the rest of Germany show much more forwardness in the common cause. When the Diet met, Sweden urged that the Empire should take part in the war; but though the breaking off of the Congress at Rastatt had left the Empire at war with France, there were the usual unending delays about the voting of supplies or contingents, the usual forms and ceremonies, and the vote of 100 Roman months, which the Diet finally passed, was not ratified till October 31st when the campaign was over. Indeed, it is not a little remarkable to find that, despite all Austria's efforts to rouse the German Princes to take part in the struggle against the aggressions of the intrusive foreigner, Bavaria was the only one of the minor states to display any keenness.

---

[1] Cf. Dunfermline's *Life of Sir Ralph Abercromby*, especially pp. 141–159; Bunbury's *Narrative of the Campaign in North Holland*; and *W. O. Original Correspondence* (Public Record Office), vols. 62–65.

Maximilian Joseph's zeal can hardly have been to the liking of Thugut. The Austrian minister would have rather seen the Elector adopt a line which would have borne out the charges of Francophil tendencies which had been brought against him. He had hoped to be able to denounce Maximilian to the Czar as a traitor to the Empire, and with the Czar's consent to have deposed him and carried out that annexation of the Wittelsbach lands to the Hapsburg dominions after which he so hankered. But this was impossible when Maximilian's ardour disarmed all hostility, and when he concluded a treaty in October 1799 by which he promised in return for a British subsidy to put 20,000 men into the field.

CHAPTER XXII

MARENGO, HOHENLINDEN AND LUNÉVILLE

AFTER the failures in Holland and Switzerland, and the consequent estrangement between Russia and her allies, the prospects of the Coalition for the year 1800 were not of the brightest. Nevertheless, when Bonaparte, with a great parade of his desire for peace, offered Austria the same terms which she had obtained at Campo Formio, she rejected them without much hesitation. When there was hardly a Frenchman on the right of the Rhine, and when the forces of the Republic seemed on the point of being expelled from Italy, it was the height of presumption and arrogance to offer terms Austria had reluctantly accepted when Bonaparte was at Leoben and Hoche at Wetzlar. Her achievements in 1799 might not unreasonably have increased her confidence in her own military prowess, and, moreover, Great Britain had not only arranged subsidy-treaties with Bavaria, Mayence and Würtemberg for 12,000, 3200 and 3200 men respectively, but was proposing to take an active part in the continental war. The expedition to North Holland had at least shown that she was at last coming into possession of a respectable military force, the want of which had hampered her so fatally at the beginning of the war, and the scheme of Sir Charles Stuart for a descent on the Riviera by 15,000 British was one which offered great possibilities.[1] The troops existed, and had the British administration been equal to despatching to the Mediterranean in February 1800 the force which it collected off Cadiz in October, the fall of Genoa might have been hastened by some weeks, and Masséna's gallant resistance might not have given Napoleon the chance he used so well. As it was, the government accepted the plan, but failed to act with the required promptitude: long before the expedition could arrive, the fate of the campaign had been decided.

The Austrian plan comprised a vigorous offensive in Italy as

[1] Cf. Bunbury, *Some Passages in the War with France*, pp. 57-78.

the prelude to an invasion of the South of France, while on the Rhine Kray was to maintain a defensive attitude. The fatal defect in this scheme, however, was that the possession of Switzerland enabled the French to attack either portion of the Austrian forces in flank, and the concentration of the Army of Reserve at Dijon put into Bonaparte's hands a formidable weapon, equally available for employment in Germany or in Italy. His original idea was to unite with Moreau and strike from Schaff-hausen at Kray's left flank and rear, and by placing the French army on his line of communications, to cut him off from Vienna and leave him " in the air." But seeing that Moreau was unlikely to prove a satisfactory colleague, Bonaparte changed his plan ; he resolved to transfer the Army of Reserve [1] to Italy, where, at the beginning of April, Masséna (40,000 men) was standing on the defensive along the Riviera, covering Genoa against Melas. With his usual keen appreciation of the strategical situation, Bonaparte saw that a descent from Switzerland upon Turin or Milan would place him in a commanding position on the Austrian line of communications with Tyrol, if only Masséna could hold out long enough and keep Melas occupied while the Army of Reserve crossed the Alps. Melas meanwhile had put his 60,000 available men in motion early in April. By the 19th, Masséna's line had been pierced, his left under Suchet, 10,000 strong, had been driven back across the Var by Melas with 28,000; he himself with 28,000 men, over half of them sick and wounded, had been cooped up in Genoa, to which Ott (24,000) laid siege (April 21st). Early in May the Army of Reserve started on its way to the Great St. Bernhard. On May 15th the passage began ; on the 20th Ivrea in the valley of the Dora Baltea was occupied by the advance-guard under Lannes. A week later, Bonaparte, while feinting with his right at Turin, was pushing Eastward over the Sesia, the Agogna and the Ticino on Milan. This daring stroke had completely changed the situation. But, while it is unfair to represent Melas as having been surprised by Bonaparte's irruption into the valley of the Po,[2] for it is clear that as far back as May 1st he was expecting such a move, he cannot escape the responsibility for the negligence which left scattered and unconcentrated the 30,000 Austrians in Piedmont.[3] Had

---

[1] Cf. Hermann, *Marengo*, pp. 83 ff. [2] Cf. *ibid*. p. 106.
[3] *Ibid*. p. 110.

they been collected in good time, they might have prevented the French from debouching from the passes; as it was, they were swept away before Bonaparte's advance. On the 1st of June, the French forced the passage of the Ticino at Turbigo and occupied Milan. The next week saw them secure the passages of the Po from Pavia to Piacenza, while 15,000 men under Moncey, detached from the Army of Germany by Bonaparte's orders, came down over the Simplon and the St. Gotthard (May 26th to 27th) to Milan. This reinforcement had been set free by Moreau's successes against Kray in the Danube valley, which had driven the Austrian Army of Germany in behind the Iller.

Meanwhile Melas was at last concentrating his forces at Alessandria. It would have been wiser to have raised the siege of Genoa and hurried North with every available man directly he heard the first news of Bonaparte's movement. But he was expecting to be attacked from the Var, and his forces were so much scattered, and moved so slowly, that he could not even attempt to defend the passage of the Po. His position was perilous, but by no means hopeless; for Bonaparte, departing from the sound strategy of concentration of which he was as a rule the truest prophet, had thrust out divisions far to the East to chase the Austrian garrison of Milan behind the Oglio, and had barely 30,000 men at hand. By this time Melas could dispose of the besiegers of Genoa, for on June 4th Masséna's heroic defence had come to an end, not before it had enabled Bonaparte to carry out his brilliant plan and to place himself in a situation of overwhelming strategic advantage. Ott moved up from Genoa by Novi and Voghera, intending to seize Piacenza and so recover a line of communication with Tyrol; but on June 9th he encountered Lannes and the French advanced guard near Montebello, and was driven back on Alessandria with the loss of 4000 men. Bonaparte, anxious to put the finishing touch to his strategic success by victory in a pitched battle, had crossed the Po on the 8th, intending to bring Melas to action, and now pushed on from Stradella towards Alessandria. On the 13th he drove the Austrian outposts in from Marengo behind the Bormida, and posted Victor with two divisions at Marengo to bar Melas's route to Pavia. At the same time, fearing that the Austrian general might attempt to escape by the Riviera round the French left, he sent off Desaix with a division to Novi to block that route. On the Northern bank of the Po there were two detached divisions on which Bonaparte relied to prevent Melas breaking through the net in which he found himself.

This dispersion of his forces was nearly fatal to Bonaparte. It left him much weaker than Melas; and when on the morning of June 14th the Austrians sallied out across the Bormida and opened the battle by falling on Victor, numbers eventually told. Lannes hurried up to Victor's aid, and prolonged the line on his right in the direction of Castel Ceriolo. The Austrians were checked, but soon came on again. The fight was stubbornly contested, the strength of the French position making up for the Austrian superiority in numbers. The action had already been in progress nearly three hours, when Ott and the left column of the Austrians wheeled to the right after carrying Castel Ceriolo, thereby outflanking Lannes. Almost at the same moment (1.30 p.m.) a renewed attack by the Austrian grenadiers carried Marengo. The French fell back in some confusion. Bonaparte brought up fresh troops under Monnier and St. Cyr, and restored the position for a time. However, Ott drove Monnier back; and as the Austrian main column pressed forward, Victor's two divisions, which had been fighting hard since 9 a.m., fell into disorder. It was in vain that the Consular Guard planted itself in Ott's path; it also was overwhelmed and forced to retreat (3.30 p.m.). The fortunes of the day seemed to have definitely gone in favour of the Austrians, and the French retreat was rapidly degenerating into a rout. Melas, worn out by fatigue, for he was over seventy, and by a slight wound, returned to Alessandria in the full belief that the victory was won. It was an unfortunate step, for if the victory had been won, the situation called imperatively for an energetic and close pursuit. But the failure to follow hard on the heels of the retreating French was typical of the worst vices of the Austrian military system, their slowness, formalism and pedantry.[1] Moreover, the greater part of the cavalry had been wasted during the action, and barely 2000 horse were available. Even so, it was inexcusable that the pursuit should have been so leisurely that touch had been quite lost with the French, when, between 5 and 6 p.m., Desaix suddenly appeared in their front near San Guiliano. He

[1] Cf. Hermann, p. 168,

had been delayed in his march on Novi by the flooding of the Scrivia, and so received Bonaparte's orders recalling him before he had gone too far to be able to reach the battlefield in time.[1]   He flung his division across the path of the Austrians, advancing somewhat carelessly in the confidence of victory along the high road.   Marmont, by a great effort, collected eighteen guns, and his salvoes of case shot and the musketry of Desaix's division checked and staggered the Austrian grenadiers.   But it would seem[2] that not even this would have proved decisive by itself. The Austrians rallied, and were coming on again[3] when Kellermann, acting entirely on his own responsibility, delivered the decisive stroke.   He hurled his rallied cavalry on the flank of their infantry, unprotected for the dragoons, who should have covered it, had fallen behind.   The change of fortune was complete.   Surprised by this unexpected resistance, the Austrians fell into disorder.   A panic set in, their cavalry disgraced themselves by taking to flight, and in a short time the all but victorious column was being swept back to Marengo in total rout, while Ott and the other flank detachments had some difficulty in recrossing the Bormida in safety. The defeat was too much for Melas.   Had he held out in Alessandria, he might have played the part of Masséna in Genoa; for if he had lost 10,000 men, at least 8000 French had fallen.[4]   But his nerve was gone, his men were demoralised, and the state of the fortresses was such as to make the success of resistance very doubtful.[5]   On June 15th he signed the Convention of Alessandria, by which he undertook to evacuate all Italy West of the Adige and South of the Po, with the exception of Ancona, Borgoforte and Tuscany.   Thus at one blow all the conquests of 1799 were lost; Italy passed from Hapsburg under French domination, and Bonaparte, mainly through the lucky accident of Desaix's timely return, obtained as the prize of his Pyrrhic victory results quite out of keeping with the evenly-balanced fighting.   That other alternatives were open to Melas seems certain.   If he did not fancy the prospects of a move to Genoa, whence by the aid of the English fleet he

---

[1] Cf. Hermann, p. 136.   [2] Cf. *ibid*. ch. vii.
[3] *Ibid*. p. 183.   [4] Cf. *ibid*. ch. viii.
[5] For this the blame must be divided between the Austrian War Council and Thugut and his protégé, Zach, the Austrian Chief of the Staff: cf. a narrative of the action (probably written by Radetzky) in Hüffer, pp. 352-367.

might have made his way to Tuscany, there seems good reason to suppose that Bonaparte could not have checked him had he attempted to force his way through the weak and scattered French divisions on the Northern bank of the Po.[1] So tame a surrender was certainly uncalled for, and indicates how unfit Melas was for his command, and how unsound the Austrian military system which could allot such a task to one so unsuited for it, and who, to do him justice, was himself well aware of his incapacity.[2]

Nor had the campaign in Germany redressed the balance in favour of Austria. Whereas in previous years the contending forces of France and Austria had faced each other on either side of the straight course of the Rhine below Basel with the neutral territory of Switzerland covering their Southern flanks, the French occupation of Switzerland and their success in maintaining their grip on it in 1799 had quite altered the situation. Their right wing could be extended from Basel to Schaffhausen so that it outflanked the Austrians along the Black Forest, and could take that defensive position in rear by a descent into the Danube valley by Stockach and Moeskirch. The Austrians had either to expose themselves to an attack on their communications by this route, or if they fell back to the more defensible line of the Iller, to abandon to the enemy Baden, Würtemberg and a large part of the Swabian Circle. Of these alternatives Kray had chosen the former, hoping to cover the large magazines which had been collected at Engen, Stockach and other places, but his 100,000 men were over much extended. His right stretched from the Main to the Rench, and on his left the corps in the Vorarlberg under the Prince of Reuss was dangerously far from the main body at Villingen and Donaueschingen. Moreau, on the other hand, had the 100,000 men of whom he could dispose concentrated in four corps at Strassburg, Breisach, Basel and Schaffhausen. Bonaparte had urged him to concentrate the whole force between Schaffhausen and Lake Constance for a direct blow at Ulm, but Moreau had a plan of his own on which he was so much set that Bonaparte gave way. This was to feint with his left (Ste. Suzanne) and left centre (Gouvion St. Cyr) against the passages over the Black Forest by the valley of the Kinzig and the Hollenthal, while his right centre (his own corps),

---

[1] Cf. Hermann, ch. ix.　　　　[2] Cf. Hüffer, p. 261.

profiting by this diversion, crossed at Basel and united with the right (Lecourbe), which was to cross at Schaffhausen. Ste. Suzanne was to recross the river as soon as he had drawn Kray's attention, to ascend the left bank to Breisach, cross again there and come up by Freibourg on the left of St. Cyr, who was to push forward by St. Blazien to the Wutach, where he would regain touch with the Reserve and Lecourbe. This plan was perhaps better under the circumstances than Bonaparte's more brilliant design, especially as it was to be executed by Moreau and not by Bonaparte. It profited more by the dispersion of the Austrians, since the feint against their right confirmed them in their fears for that wing, and so delayed their concentration; also it utilised more points of passage over the Rhine. To throw the whole force across between Schaffhausen and the lake would have taken time, possibly so much that Kray would have discovered his danger and concentrated in time. It is true that Moreau risked defeat in detail in case Kray concentrated his forces to fall on St. Cyr or Lecourbe before they had got into touch with the Reserve and with each other; but this was not likely with so dispersed and slow-moving a force as the Austrians.

In the main the scheme, which was well executed by Moreau and his subordinates, proved successful. On April 25th Ste. Suzanne opened the move; by May 2nd, after much marching and manœuvring and some fighting, Moreau had concentrated three of his corps between the Aach and the Wutach, and Ste. Suzanne had come through the Höllenthal and was at Neustadt on the flank of the Austrians, who were endeavouring to concentrate between Stockach and Geisingen. In this, however, they were unsucessful, for Lecourbe pushing up the Aach fell on their left at Stockach (May 3rd), routed it, and captured the vast magazines there. Meanwhile Kray bringing up his main body from Geisingen came into conflict with St. Cyr at Zollhaus and with Moreau's Reserve at Engen. The battle was stubbornly contested; Kray on the whole held his own, and only the bad news from Stockach caused him to fall back to Tuttlingen lest Lecourbe's advance on Moeskirch should cut him off from Ulm. Moreau, having let St. Cyr and the Reserve be drawn into battle to his left, could not reinforce Lecourbe and so secure a decisive success, and thus Kray was able to reach

Moeskirch in safety (May 4th). Driven from Moeskirch by the French attack next day, he rallied his men and thrust his right forward to cover the retreat of an isolated division from Tuttlingen; but though successful in this and in checking Lecourbe's advance, he had to fall back to the North of the Danube to avoid being cut off by Ste. Suzanne, who was coming down the Danube from Donaueschingen. By May 12th Kray was back at Ulm, where he rallied some 60,000 men. He had lost nearly 30,000 as well as the magazines for which he had risked so much; but Moreau, having had to detach Moncey's corps to Italy, was in no position to press home his success at once, and was for some time detained by Kray's stand at Ulm. Once he tried to turn the position by thrusting his right across the Iller higher up; but Kray fell on the detached corps left in front of Ulm to cover the French communications with Schaffhausen and brought Moreau back to its succour (May 16th). Undeterred, the French commander renewed the attempt a fortnight later. This time the "containing" corps, left between the Danube and Iller to protect the French communications with the Rhine, held its own against all Kray's attacks, and Moreau's right pushed out to Augsburg. Thence it pressed on to the Danube at Lavingen and Blenheim, the centre preparing to cross at Gunzburg. The French success in securing a passage at Blenheim (June 19th) made Ulm untenable. With his communications imperilled and his retreat along the left bank alone open to him, Kray fell back by Heidenheim to Nördlingen (June 23rd), and passing across the front of the French regained the Danube below them (June 26th), thus placing himself between them and Vienna. Moreau, however, returning South of the Danube overran Bavaria up to the Isar, profiting greatly by the comparatively unexhausted state of the country. On July 15th an armistice put a temporary stop to hostilities, Kray in accordance with its terms retiring behind the Inn.

This want of success in both theatres of war was a powerful argument for those persons at Vienna who desired to accept Bonaparte's renewed proposals for peace. The only real obstacle was that a new subsidy-treaty had just been concluded with England by which Austria received £2,000,000, promising in return not to conclude a separate peace before February 28th, 1801. Thus as Bonaparte declined to admit

England to a peace conference, except on terms England would not contemplate, namely, that he might relieve Malta and Egypt, Austria could only obtain peace by abandoning her obligations to England. The armistice should have expired on September 20th, but it was renewed for another six weeks from that date, a concession which Austria purchased by surrendering Ulm, Ingolstadt and Philipsburg. This had a rather disastrous influence over some of Austria's German allies, who believed that the Emperor was sacrificing the interests of the Empire to the security of his hereditary dominions. The Elector of Cologne, for example, went so far as to obtain passports from the French for the withdrawal of his troops from Ulm to Münster, where they sheltered behind the neutrality of the line of demarcation.[1] Still Austria needed the respite badly. She was making great efforts to resume hostilities if necessary, reinforcing and re-equipping the army, but her preparations were still incomplete. The peace party was, moreover, steadily gaining ground, which was in itself no indistinct indication that Thugut's unpopularity was increasing. He was held responsible for the disasters of the war; and though, indeed, his inefficiency as an administrator was in large measure to blame, it was not on this that public resentment fixed, but on his policy of resistance to France. He was accused, with little reason, of making the interests of Austria subservient to those of England. He was not accused, as he might well have been, of wrecking the campaign of 1799 by his undue haste to reap the fruits of victory without troubling to make success certain by vigorous and whole-hearted co-operation with his allies. It was obvious that his fall was imminent. On October 8th his resignation of the Ministry of Foreign Affairs was announced, and Louis Cobenzl was appointed a member of the Conference and Vice State Chancellor to direct the Court, State and Cabinet Chanceries, Lehrbach taking the Home Office.

Cobenzl's first act was to go in person to Lunéville in Alsace to discuss terms with Joseph Bonaparte. The sole obstacle to peace was Austria's refusal to agree to England's exclusion from the peace congress. Cobenzl would have even been prepared [2] to make a secret treaty with France not

[1] Cf. Hüffer, *Quellen zur Geschichte des Krieges, 1799–1800*, ii. 414.
[2] Cf. Haüsser, ii. 308.

to be divulged until Austria's obligation to England was at an end, but nothing had been settled when on November 26th the armistice came to an end and hostilities were resumed.

Austria had made good use of the armistice. She had brought up her army on the Danube to 130,000, including 12,000 Bavarians in British pay. Of this force 30,000 under Klenau were on the left bank, 20,000 under Hiller in Tyrol, the rest, now under the command of the Emperor's fifth brother, the eighteen year old Archduke John, held the line of the Inn. Similarly in Italy, Bellegarde had replaced Melas and was strongly posted between the Mincio and the Adige, relying on the fortresses of the "Quadrilateral." Opposite them stood Moreau in Bavaria with 100,000 men flanked by 12,000 under Lecourbe in Western Tyrol and 20,000 more under Augereau North of the Danube. In Italy, Brune threatened Bellegarde's front, while a column under Macdonald, crossing the Splügen Pass in the depth of winter, forced its way by the Valtelline into the upper valley of the Adige, and after tremendous perils and sufferings captured Trent (end of December), thus interposing between Hiller and Bellegarde's connecting link, his extreme right under Loudon.

Meanwhile the Austrians in Germany had taken the offensive, had crossed the Inn the day the armistice expired (Nov. 26th), and were moving against Moreau. This action, somewhat rash, since the Austrian troops were not only inferior in numbers to the French veterans, but were mainly composed of raw recruits and were but ill-equipped, is to be explained by the young Archduke's belief that the previous defeats of the Austrians had been due to their excessive caution. This may have been true, but undue temerity was no improvement on undue caution, especially as rain and the bad state of the roads combined with the inefficiency of the Archduke's Staff to so delay the Austrian movements that the original plan of an advance past Moreau's left by Braunau and Landshut on Munich had to be abandoned for a direct blow at the French left.[1] Near Ampfing on December 1st the Archduke fell on Grenier

---

[1] Nothing stands out more clearly from a study of the documents dealing with the campaign from the Austrian side than the imprudence of the Archduke and his chief advisers, Weyrother and Lauer. The original plan of outflanking the French left might have worked well if executed in good weather and by a well-organised army with an efficient Staff. Under existing circumstances the advance was a piece of almost criminal folly. Cf. Hüffer, *op. cit.* pp. 415-426.

and the three divisions (33,000 men) who formed his corps. Taken by surprise and outnumbered, the French fell back fighting stubbornly on Hohenlinden, being succoured in their retreat by Grouchy's division of the centre; but they left 6 guns and nearly 1000 prisoners behind, and the Austrians were much elated by their success.[1] Hohenlinden lies in a clearing of the Forest of Ebersberg, and though the excellent high-road from Muhldorf to München leads through it, the woods are so close to the road as to convert it into a regular defile, while the side-roads and forest paths on either flank are but ill-fitted for military manœuvres. Yet on December 3rd the Archduke plunged gaily into the defile with 16,000 men, two columns under Latour (11,000) and Keinmayer (16,000) moving parallel with him on his right; while to the Southward Riesch with 13,000 pushed forward on Albaching, intending to outflank the right of Grenier's position at Hohenlinden. The despatch in which Zweibrücken, the commander of the Bavarian contingent,[2] announced to his Electoral master[3] that "your Highness' troops have been sacrificed by ignorance and ineptitude," is a scathing commentary on the Austrian Staff. No proper precautions were taken to secure the simultaneous co-operation of the different columns, the flanks were not protected by patrols, no reserve was told off, and the artillery and baggage were allowed to take the road before it had been properly secured by the capture of Hohenlinden. The culminating complaint was that at the moment the movement began the Archduke and the whole Headquarter Staff were comfortably asleep. Therefore it is hardly surprising that disaster followed.

Utterly uncombined and ill-timed, the Austrian columns came into action one by one. The Archduke, moving faster than his supporters, since his road was the best, engaged Ney and Grouchy around Hohenlinden about 8 a.m. Gradually Latour and Keinmayer came up, but neither could make much impression on Bastoul and Legrand. But it was on the left that matters went most amiss. Riesch, delayed by the bad road and the falling snow, went astray in the woods, and never reached his appointed place. This exposed the left flank of the main column to an attack from the French right at Ebersberg, and Moreau pushed Durutte and Decaen up to

---

[1] Cf. Hüffer, p. 428.
[2] William of Zweibrücken-Birkenfeld, brother-in-law of the Elector.
[3] Cf. Hüffer, p. 452.

St. Christopher to hold Riesch at bay, while under cover of this he hurled Richepanse against the Bavarian division which formed the rear of the Archduke's long column on the high-road. Hampered by the guns and waggons which cumbered the road, the Bavarians could not deploy properly, and simultaneously with Richepanse's onslaught Ney made a counter-attack on the head of the column, outflanking it on both wings. Before this double assult the Archduke's men gave way in disorder. Only the intervention of Lichtenstein's cavalry saved the column from complete destruction. Their defeat was decisive; Riesch had to fall back, and the Austrian right had the mortification of having to do the same just as they were beginning to gain ground.[1]

Leaving 17,000 killed and prisoners behind them, the Austrians recrossed the Inn (Dec. 5th) in a state of demoralisation and exhaustion. Energetically pursued by Moreau, they failed to stand behind either the Salza, the Traun or the Enns, although Archduke Charles, to whom the War Council had turned in its alarm, took over the command and made every effort to rally them. Only when he had outmarched the forces on his flanks did Moreau check his pursuit. North of the Danube, Augereau was pressing Klenau back from Aschaffenburg to Ingolstadt. In Italy, Macdonald's adventurous march had outflanked Bellegarde and enabled Brune to cross the Mincio at Pozzolo and the Adige at Bussolengo, and to take Verona. On neither quarter was there any hope for Austria. Hohenlinden had finally damped the bellicose ardour of the Elector of Bavaria. Defeat had revived his distrust of the Hapsburgs, and had,thrown him under the influence of Prussia. So anxious was he for peace that he was prepared to forego the payments due from England, and on December 8th he wrote to recall the relics of the subsidiary corps.[2] So hopeless was the military situation,[3] so broken and dejected the Austrian troops, who had ceased to bear any resemblance to an army and had become a mass of fugitives,[4] that Archduke Charles could only counsel surrender, and on December 25th he had to agree to the Armistice of Speyer, which handed Würzburg and the fortresses of Bavaria over to the French, provided for the evacuation of Tyrol, Carinthia and the Grisons, dismissed the Tyrolese " insurrection " to their homes, and pledged Austria to make peace apart from England.[5] Harsh and exceedingly disgraceful as the terms

---

[1] Cf. Hüffer, pp. 437–480.
[3] *Ibid.* pp. 490–492. [4] *Ibid.* p. 495.
[2] *Ibid.* p. 481.
[5] *Ibid.* pp. 508–511.

were, there was no alternative but a defeat which would have left Austria absolutely at the mercy of the enemy.[1] In January an armistice was signed at Treviso for the Italian armies.

Little time was lost in converting these armistices into a definite peace. Bonaparte could name his conditions, and on those conditions he insisted inexorably. Cobenzl made no attempt to obtain the admission of England to the negotiations : his efforts were directed to trying to get Modena and Tuscany restored to their rulers, and to save part of Lombardy for Austria. But the Adige frontier was all that the First Consul would grant; he was prepared to compensate Tuscany with the Legations, but Modena's compensation must be in Germany, and it was imperatively demanded that the Emperor should cede the Left Bank at once in his capacity as head of the Empire. Unpalatable as these demands were, and strenuously as Cobenzl fought point after point, it was not of much use resisting Bonaparte, especially as he had by this time bound the Baltic Powers, including Prussia, to him in the shape of the "Armed Neutrality." Moreover, the spectacle of South Germany, helpless and at the mercy of the French armies, increased the Emperor's readiness for peace. If the discipline and behaviour of the armies of the Consulate was an improvement on that of the troops of the Directory, their presence was sufficiently burdensome and oppressive. There was no appeal against the plunderings of the rank and file when all they did was to follow the example of their generals. With no small part of his own hereditary dominions in French hands, Francis II was most anxious to come to terms. Fear of a Franco-Russian coalition, for Paul was by now as keen an admirer of Napoleon as he had been a bitter opponent of the Republic three years before, made him abandon hope of saving even the ecclesiastical Electorates from being secularised, and on February 9th, 1801, the Peace of Lunéville was signed.

The Peace of Campo Formio was accepted as the basis of the territorial rearrangements, but subject to certain not unimportant modifications. The Emperor signed the peace on behalf of the Empire, openly ceding the Left Bank to France, and no longer attempting to hide this surrender in a secret article.

It was agreed that the rulers thus dispossessed should be "compensated" for their losses by means of secularisation, a provision which practically amounted to the destruction of the existing constitution of the Empire. While France obtained

[1] Archduke Charles to Emperor. Hüffer, p. 513.

MARENGO June 14th 1800.

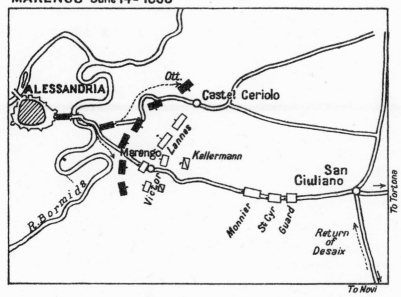

HOHENLINDEN Dec. 3rd 1800.

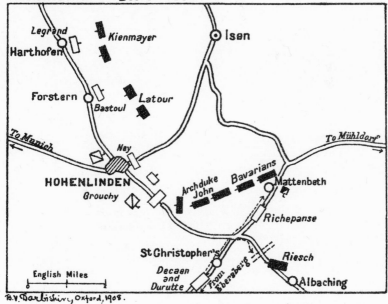

B.V. Darbishire, Oxford, 1908.

recognition from the Emperor of the client Republics with which she was surrounded, the Batavian, the Cisalpine, the Helvetian and the Ligurian, Austria's clients in Italy, her cadet branches at Florence and Modena, lost their lands, and were added to the long list of persons deserving compensation at the expense of the Empire. Tuscany went to the dispossessed Prince of Parma[1] as the kingdom of Etruria, a change of rulers which was not to its advantage; Modena was swallowed up in the Cisalpine, soon (Feb. 1802) to become the Italian Republic. The King of the Two Sicilies was restored to his dominions, but Charles Emmanuel IV did not recover Piedmont. No stipulations were made in the treaty as to its fate, but in April 1801 it was divided into departments; and in September 1802 it was formally annexed to France. Thus with the Adige as Austria's frontier in Italy the peninsula was completely dominated by France.

Still the peace was not altogether disadvantageous to Austria. If it be compared with Campo Formio she really gained in territory, for the secularised bishoprics of Brixen and Trent were a more than ample set-off against the loss of a small strip between the Po and the Adige; and if she gave up the Breisgau, it was to a connection of her own House, the Duke of Modena.[2] Thugut's designs on Bavaria were not realised, but the cession of the Archbishopric of Salzburg to Archduke Ferdinand, the ex-Grand Duke of Tuscany, was most acceptable to the Hapsburgs. To the Empire Lunéville was a severe blow. The definite cession of 25,000 square miles and 3½ millions of people[3] was an absolute loss. The Empire could not comfort itself with the reflection which consoled Austria for the loss of Belgium, that it was losing a source of weakness and gaining a better strategical frontier. The Left Bank territories were an integral and a valuable part of the Empire, and the Rhine had not proved a very strong frontier either in 1796 or in 1800. Moreover, it was only on condition that their fortifications should be "slighted" that the French had evacuated the towns they held on the right of the river.[4]

---

[1] Ferdinand, son of Don Phillip of Spain and Marie Louise, daughter of Louis xv.

[2] (1780–1803), father-in-law of Ferdinand, son of Maria Theresa and Duke of Modena-Breisgau (1803–1806).

[3] Haüsser, ii. 328.

[4] Haüsser, of course, reckons in *German* miles, which are equal to 4·6 or 4·7 English miles: thus the German square mile is, roughly speaking, 22 times as large as the English.

To the inhabitants of the Left Bank the definite separation from Germany came as in some way a relief. In hardly any other part of Germany were the characteristics of German disunion so pronounced. The Left Bank was divided into the most minute parcels; there was not even as large a state as Baden or Oldenburg to give some approach to unity, and the only independent states which exceeded the infinitesimal were precisely those in which there was the least approach to a vigorous localism, ecclesiastical Principalities. The separation from Germany was not likely to be unpopular among people bound to Germany neither by practical nor sentimental considerations. The Empire had been incapable of defending them against the exactions and excesses of the French; as the subjects of the Republic they would at least have a claim to preferential treatment. Nor were German patriotism and national sentiment so strongly rooted among them but that they could be effaced by a few years of careful, honest and appropriate administration. And this they did obtain from the Consulate. Even under the Directory they had been better off than under ecclesiastical or Palatinate rule, and now that, under the direction of Jean Bon St. André, a permanent organisation was substituted for the temporary arrangements of the last ten years, the Left Bank enjoyed a material prosperity which went far to reconcile it to incorporation in France.[1] It was not till France itself began to weary under the burdens which the extension of the Napoleonic supremacy imposed upon her, not till Napoleon's oppression of Germany beyond the Rhine had begun to drive home into Bavarian and Westphalian, into Prussian and Würtemberger, the consciousness that union is strength and that only by a joint effort could Germany free herself of the conscription and the Continental System, that the Left Bank became alive to the fact that the Rhine was a German river, and not the boundary between France and Germany. And not even then was there any strong desire in the Rhineland for separation from France. The return to German rulers was accepted, not welcomed. Had Bonaparte managed to keep the treaties of Lunéville and Amiens, and avoided the continual aggressions which bound Europe together against him, Mayence and Cologne might have become as French as were Metz and Strassburg in 1870.

[1] Cf. Fisher's chapter on the Rhine Departments.

CHAPTER XXIII

THE RESETTLEMENT OF 1803

I N the whole history of German disunion[1] and particularism
there are few pages more discreditable than that which
narrates the protracted negotiations which followed the Peace
of Lunéville. The spectacle of the Princes of Germany vying
with one another in currying favour with Napoleon, of the
bribery, the intrigues, the utter selfishness, the want of any
appeal to patriotism or national feeling, is one which has
few parallels. It gave Napoleon an idea of the lengths to which
it would be possible to carry that principle of *Divide et impera*
on which he based his dealings with the Germans. His policy
after all was only the policy of Richelieu, Mazarin and
Louis XIV attuned to the altered circumstances. Germany
must not be allowed to unite. No Power must be allowed to
grow strong enough to rally the other states in defence of their
common interests. The estrangement between Austria and
Prussia must be cultivated and fostered. Austria must be
isolated, and at the same time Prussia must not be allowed to
make good her pretensions to be the champion of the minor
states and their protector against Austria. This was an office
to be reserved for France. If the Confederation of the Rhine
did not formally take shape till 1806, the bonds which held it
together were being forged all through the negotiations of
1801 and 1802.

It might perhaps have been supposed that the territorial
resettlement of the Empire was a matter to be left to the Diet
to arrange. But the Diet was quite incapable of discharging
such a task. The conditions which had contributed to the loss
of the Left Bank made it impossible to setttle on the " compensation " for that loss without the intervention of the Power
which had carried off the spoils. The first step in the process
was, it is true, taken with a celerity altogether foreign to the

---

[1] Cf. Haüsser, ii. pp. 333 ff. ; also Fisher, pp. 38–47.

habits of the Diet. By signing the Peace of Lunéville on behalf of the Empire, Francis II had encroached on the province of the Diet; but that body hastened to condone his action, announced to them on February 25th, 1801, by ratifying the Treaty on March 7th.

The loss of the Left Bank having been thus accepted, together with the principle of compensation by means of secularisation, it remained to arrange a scheme of redistribution, and to settle to whom the drawing up of the scheme should be entrusted. Saxony proposed that the whole Diet should discuss the matter, but the lay states were not inclined to give their ecclesiastical victims a voice in deciding the fate which was to befall them. Bavaria suggested that the Emperor should act as reporter, and should submit a plan to the Diet; a proposal he promptly declined, though he would have been prepared to accept the suggestion of the ecclesiastical states that the entire matter should be entrusted to him without appeal to the Diet. But such a plan was not to the liking of Prussia or Bavaria or any of the other larger lay states who hoped to see as extensive a secularisation as possible. The Emperor would certainly have spared the ecclesiastical Electors, usually his firm adherents, and he would probably have sought to restrict the secularisation even more. Hence a majority in the College of Princes favoured Bavaria's proposal, and the Elector of Mayence, or rather his coadjutor, Charles von Dalberg, a clever but unstable statesman destined to play a leading part in putting Germany at Napoleon's disposal, came round to their side and so carried the proposal through the College of Electors (April 30th). However, the Emperor flatly refused to entertain a proposal which promised him all the invidious work without the satisfaction of the decisive voice. Thus the wearisome discussion and disputes dragged on almost interminably. Not till October 2nd was a Deputation of eight members appointed to arrange a settlement. It was composed of four members from the College of Electors, Bohemia, Brandenburg, Mayence and Saxony, and four from the College of Princes, Baden, Bavaria,[1] Würtemberg and the Grand Master of the Teutonic Order. It was with the aid of France to draw up a scheme to be presented to the Diet for approval. More than ten months, however, elapsed before the Deputation began its labours at Ratisbon

---

[1] The Elector had a seat in the College of Princes as Duke of Bavaria.

on August 24th, 1802. In the meantime projects without number had been put forward, only to be found unsatisfactory and rejected. Every member of the Empire sought to secure the favour of the all-powerful First Consul for himself or for his friends. Austria pushed the claims of the Grand Dukes of Modena and Tuscany; Prussia was urgent for another non-German claimant, the Prince of Orange, who was connected by marriage with the Hohenzollern family. Not a scrap of ecclesiastical territory but was claimed by many competitors. Each state struggled for its own hand, of common action there was none ; and though a few people, among them Stadion, an Imperial Knight who was Austrian representative at Berlin, did try to reconcile Austria and Prussia in the hope of thereby preventing France and Russia from having things their own way, these efforts proved quite abortive.

At the very outset of the negotiations there had been an opportunity which the Emperor might have utilised to settle the matter without the interference of France. Bonaparte was still at war with England, and the Armed Neutrality of the Baltic Powers on which he had counted so much had broken down before the double blow of the murder of the Czar (March 25th, 1801), and of Nelson's victory at Copenhagen. Bonaparte thus lost the Russian alliance which had allowed him to assume airs of domination, and he had to somewhat modify his tone. At this time Bavaria and the other minor states had not been won over to France by separate treaties, and the relations of Prussia with France were rather strained. This was due to Prussia's share in the Armed Neutrality. The Prussian merchant marine was of sufficiently respectable dimensions to have suffered a good deal through the rigorous maritime code which the English applied to all neutrals. Partly for this reason, partly from a wish not to be left isolated, Prussia had adhered to the Armed Neutrality in December 1800, and when Denmark occupied Hamburg and Lübeck on behalf of the Armed Neutrality (March 1801), Prussia did likewise with Bremen, Hanover and Oldenburg. In so doing, Prussia probably only anticipated France; at any rate her action was interpreted in this way in Hanover and in England, and no opposition was offered. She gave out that her sole object was to preserve the neutrality of North Germany. At the same time, in the general scramble for territory there was no harm in having so valuable an asset occupied by her troops.

458 GERMANY IN THE EIGHTEENTH CENTURY [1801-

It was on this that Napoleon worked. He did not wish to see Prussia in possession of the Franconian bishoprics she coveted so much as a foothold in Southern Germany. He therefore urged Prussia to keep Hanover, to which Prussia would not agree unless England's consent could be obtained. Another suggestion, that Prussia should resign Hanover to France, and receive Bamberg and Würzburg, was flatly rejected. Hence there was some coolness between France and Prussia, an opportunity Austria would have done well to seize. Unluckily a quarrel over the sees of Cologne and Münster, left vacant by the death of the Elector Archduke Maximilian (July 27th), created a new breach between the chief Powers of Germany. Prussia proposed that pending the resettlement no election should be made; and when Austria proceeded to use her influence with the Chapters to get Archduke Anthony, the Emperor's youngest brother, elected in his uncle's place (at Münster, Sept. 9th, at Cologne, Oct. 7th), she declined to recognise the election. The Emperor thereupon issued a strongly-worded proclamation condemning Prussia's action.

With Austria and Prussia thus at variance, with all Germany in confusion and disorder, it was not wonderful if the minor Princes appealed to one so firm, so decided and so strong as Bonaparte. Bavaria, after contemplating a scheme put forward by Austria which would have practically allowed her to absorb all the petty states, lay and ecclesiastical alike, of Swabia in return for the cession of most of the Upper Palatinate to Austria, returned to the policy of 1703 and concluded a separate treaty with France as early as August 1801, and confirmed it in the following May. This was indeed the method by which Bonaparte achieved his aims. A series of separate treaties between France and the various Powers of Germany arranged the details of the compensation. These treaties had a double object. On the one hand, they bound the middle states of Germany to Bonaparte, to whom they owed their gains; on the other, by enriching the friends of Russia in Southern Germany, notably Baden, the home of Alexander's wife, and Würtemberg, his mother's country, they conciliated the Czar. Before the Deputation met four of its members had thus pledged themselves, and Dalberg, quick to see that not Austria, nor Prussia, but Bonaparte was the dispenser of patronage and the only Power by whose aid he could hope to save something in the secularisation, was now completely at the First Consul's service.

Thus though the Deputation's deliberations produced no result, the matter was being settled out of court, and all that the Deputation could do was to accept the Franco-Russian proposals. On December 6th the scheme was laid before the Diet without even waiting to obtain the Emperor's assent. Bonaparte might fairly excuse the abruptness of his action by the utter failure of the Empire to arrive at any conclusion as the result of a year's deliberations. If he had not intervened, nothing would ever have been settled. The Diet had no choice but to accept, and Bonaparte, not anxious to drive Austria to extremities when war with England was threatening and when a change of ministry in Russia had substituted the unfriendly Woronzov for Gallophils in Kurakin and Kotschubev, secured the Emperor's assent by concessions. He agreed to let Salzburg go to Archduke Ferdinand, the dispossessed Duke of Tuscany, while the other Hapsburg claimant for compensation, the Duke of Modena, was to receive the Breisgau and Ortenau, Austria obtaining instead the Bishoprics of Brixen and Trent.[1]

Certain slight modifications were made by the Diet in the scheme submitted to it, but on the whole the " Recess " of February 25th, 1803, reproduced the proposals which France and Russia had laid before the Deputation on September 8th, 1802. The final step, the ratification by the Emperor, took place on April 27th, 1803.

The changes thus sanctioned by the Diet really amounted to the destruction of the old order and the dissolution of the Holy Roman Empire. It was veiled under a thin veneer of decency and formality, inasmuch as the execution of the scheme was left to the Diet itself, and a principle was found on which the annexation of the Church lands could be defended. This principle was that of heredity, and as hereditary rulers the Counts and Imperial Knights whose existence contributed so much to the territorial intricacies of South and Western Germany escaped molestation.[2] But with three exceptions the ecclesiastical states disappeared, and the balance of power in the Diet was altogether altered. Moreover, the Imperial villages were mediatised, and their fate was shared by all but six of the Free Cities,

[1] Haüsser, ii. 391. [2] Cf. Seeley's *Stein*, i. 124.

Augsburg, Bremen, Frankfurt, Hamburg, Lübeck and Nüremberg alone retaining their old independence. Their neutrality
was indeed guaranteed with full judicial independence and
territorial sovereignty, they even obtained slight gains of territory;
but even so they must have felt their position none too secure.

Though so much had been said about compensation, in the
actual redistribution there was no attempt to make losses and
gains proportionate. Thus while Bavaria, which had lost more
territory on the Left Bank than any other Power, including
Simmern, Jülich, Zweibrücken and part of the Palatinate,
obtained about 6400 square miles in return for the 4800 which she
lost; Prussia, whose losses only amounted to a little over 1000
square miles, received nearly 5000; Würtemberg was paid four-
fold for the 150 square miles of Mompelgard, and Baden's gain
of 1300 square miles was out of all due proportion to the 180
she relinquished. Bonaparte used the spoils of the Church not
to do justice to the dispossessed, but to buy himself partisans in
South Germany.

The net result of the redistribution was to build up a
number of medium - sized states with some approach to
geographical homogeneity. The separation and division of
even the pettiest states, which had been so strong a barrier to
administrative unity, to good government, and to the growth
of common interests, was to some extent removed. The minor
lay states remained but the arguments which had been used to
justify the suppression of the abbeys and Free Cities might
be urged with equal force against the continued independent
existence of the Counts and Knights. The idea of rounding
off the dominions of a middle state by the incorporation of the
independent parcels which broke up its homogeneity was new,
but it was readily accepted. The expediency and propriety of
simplifying the political map commended itself strongly to those
who survived the process and profited by it. The land-hunger
of Bavaria and Würtemberg could be represented as the only
chance of political salvation for the scattered districts of
Swabia, too small to justify independence, too petty and poor
to support the separate court and the complex administration
with which every minor potentate surrounded himself. Stein
might protest against the incorporation of his hereditary
dominions in as small a state as Nassau,[1] but it must be

---

[1] Cf. Seeley's, *Stein*, i. 126.

admitted that in many respects the growth of middle states like Baden and Hesse-Cassel was an advance on the system it replaced. As long as the pettiest Prince claimed an independence which was real enough to prevent the internal union of Germany but a mere farce from an international standpoint, the aggrandisement of the middle states was not without justification. Small as they were, they had possibilities of being healthy and efficient polities which their physical limitations denied to the pettier units. Indeed, if the process had only been carried a little further, it would be easier to justify it. Had all the minor Princes like the Arembergs, the Salms, Thurn und Taxis and the branches of the House of Reuss, been absorbed into larger entities, while only the Electorates and these larger states which like the Hesses or Mecklenburg-Schwerin could pretend to Electoral rank were permitted to maintain their independence, the process might have been represented as an attempt to meet the true needs of Germany. But it was not the interests of Germany, but those of the dynasties which were being consulted, to say nothing of those of the powerful and none too friendly Western neighbour with whom the decision really rested.

Bavaria as the principal loser actually gained most. She received seventeen Imperial cities and villages of which Ulm and Nördlingen were the most important, together with twelve abbeys and priories, mostly in the Franconian and Swabian Circles. There also fell to her lot the Bishoprics of Augsburg, Freisingen, Bamberg and Würzburg—which Prussia especially coveted—and parts of Passau and Eichstadt, which she shared with Salzburg. She lost nearly 800,000 subjects, and a revenue of 5,800,000 gulden, but received 850,000 people producing 6,600,000 gulden of revenue. More than this, her gains lay in the most fertile and cultivated part of South Germany; geographically they were part and parcel of her, and so helped to round her off and to give her a compactness of enormous advantage. Hitherto her rather disconnected condition had given some plausibility to Thugut's schemes for annexing parts of the Electorate to Austria and compensating its ruler elsewhere. Bavaria had now obtained the districts which might naturally have been selected as this compensation, and she had not had to cede anything to Austria. Her aggrandisement was a sufficient answer and barrier to Thugut's designs.

Baden was another state which was treated on the most favoured footing, thanks largely to Charles Frederick's relation to the Czar. The Margrave became an Elector, and his dominions were enlarged by the Bishopric of Constance, by the portions of those of Basel, Strassburg and Spires which lay to the East of the Rhine, and by part of the Palatinate, hitherto Bavarian, including Heidelberg and Mannheim. A population of a quarter of a million and a revenue of 1,250,000 gulden was an ample recompense for the 25,000 people and 250,000 gulden lost with the Left Bank. Würtemberg also owed much to her Russian connection. Nine Imperial cities and about as many abbeys in Swabia fell to the lot of Duke Frederick II, now advanced to the rank of Elector. This increased the number of his subjects by 110,000 and the annual revenue of his state by 700,000 gulden, his losses only amounting to 14,000 people and 350,000 gulden per annum. Würtemberg, moreover, gained greatly in compactness through the disappearance of the petty states which had interrupted her continuity.

Only one other state in South-Western Germany deserves mention. This was the new Duchy erected out of the Austrian possessions on the Rhine for the dispossessed Duke of Modena. In accordance with the treaty between Bonaparte and the Emperor of December 26th, 1802, Duke Ferdinand received the Breisgau and Ortenau, Austria being compensated for her loss by obtaining the secularised Bishoprics of Brixen and Trent, which if somewhat smaller and less populous, were richer, easier to defend, and geographically much more desirable.

Proceeding northward, the next state which deserves mention is the Landgraviate of Hesse-Darmstadt, one of the states which had profited most by the redistribution. In return for certain cessions which only amounted to some 300 square miles inhabited by 40,000 people, the Landgrave received the old Duchy of Westphalia, hitherto part of the Electorate of Cologne, a few abbeys and villages, the Free City of Friedberg, and portions of the Archbishopric of Mayence, of the Palatinate and of the Bishopric of Worms, a long and narrow strip from the Lippe to the Neckar over 2000 square miles in extent, with 120,000 inhabitants and a revenue of 800,000 gulden.

Hesse-Cassel, on the other hand, received much less territory than she had hoped to get. As the Landgrave had had no possessions at all on the Left Bank, he perhaps obtained all he deserved when he got the Free City of Gelnhausen and the dignity of Elector. But even this hardly consoled him for seeing the ex-Stadtholder of Holland, William V of Orange, of the Nassau-Dillingen line, endowed out of the districts for which he himself had hoped with a Principality composed of the Bishoprics of Fulda and Corvey and the Free City of Dortmund, a scattered holding, but amounting in all to 1000 square miles with a revenue of a million gulden. The other branches of the Nassau line, Weilburg and Usingen, received between them a considerable stretch of territory between the Rhine, the Main and the Lahn, formerly belonging to the ecclesiastical Electors, more than equivalent to their losses on the Left Bank.[1] The cousins, Dukes Frederick Augustus of Usingen (1803–1816), and Frederick William of Weilburg (1788–1816), had agreed to treat their possessions as one Duchy, and ruled it in common.

A little higher up the Main came a new state, the principality created for Dalberg, now as Arch Chancellor of the Empire and Primate of Germany, the only survivor of the ecclesiastical Electors. He obtained Aschaffenburg and district, formerly parts of Mayence and Würzburg, the Cities of Wetzlar and Ratisbon, the secularised Bishopric of Ratisbon, and three abbeys. The revenue of 600,000 gulden which these possessions were calculated to produce was to be supplemented by 400,000 gulden secured on the tolls of the Rhine. Dalberg was now definitely enrolled among the partisans of Bonaparte. Hitherto he had endeavoured to carry on the old traditions of the see of Mayence as the leader among the German Princes, he had wavered between Austria and Prussia: in 1801 he had at first struggled hard to save the Bishoprics, but, realising this was impossible, he devoted himself most zealously to furthering the interests of Bonaparte, as he saw in this the only royal road to security.[2]

In North-Western Germany the principal question of interest was the fate which would befall the rich Westphalian Bishoprics. It was here that Prussia was to find compensation for her loss of Cleves, Guelders and Mors. It was not quite what she had wanted. Hardenberg had been very anxious to see Bamberg and Würzburg in Prussian hands; Bonaparte was not merely determined to keep Prussia out of Franconia, but he

---

[1] Saarbrücken and Saarwerden.   [2] Cf. Seeley's *Stein*, ii. 365 ff.

would have liked to make her take Mecklenburg as her share, transplanting the Dukes of Schwerin and Strelitz to Westphalia and Franconia. But the refusal of the Dukes to leave their ancestral dominions frustrated this attempt to thrust Prussia back to the East of the Elbe, and Bonaparte was forced to agree to let her take the Bishoprics of Paderborn and Hildesheim, a large part of that of Münster, the town of that name, the Thuringian possessions of Mayence, Erfurt and the Eichsfeld, together with six abbeys and three Cities. These amounted in all to 5000 square miles against a loss of 1050, with a population of 500,000 against a quarter of that number, and a revenue of four millions against one of one and a half. Rich and fertile for the most part, these acquisitions gave Prussia a dominant position in North-Western Germany, since there was only one other state of any importance in that quarter. This was Hanover, which gained but little in the redistribution, having to surrender her rights over Sayn - Altenkirchen to Nassau, over Wildeshausen to Oldenburg, to which there also fell a fragment of the Bishopric of Münster. In return, Hanover obtained Osnabrück permanently.[1] Of other states in this part of Germany, Brunswick-Wolfenbüttel received a couple of abbeys, while various minor dynasties, notably Salm and Aremberg, divided the rest of Münster. Saxony was unconcerned in the redistribution, and the only other features of importance were the survival of the Teutonic Order, of which the Archduke Charles was now Grand Master, and of the Knights of St. John, and the erection of the Archbishopric of Salzburg into an Electorate for the Grand Duke of Tuscany.

Minor potentates like the Princes of Isenburg, Löwenstein, and Thurn und Taxis also survived the storm, and were more or less fairly compensated for their losses. The compensation of the Counts was a more difficult matter, since the estates of the Swabian prelates did not suffice for the purpose,[2] while the promise of compensation with which the Imperial Knights had to content themselves was at the best a dubious guarantee.

Territorial changes so far-reaching naturally involved great political changes. Except that nothing new was substituted, the Recess might be described as the end of the Holy Roman Empire. The Diet and the Imperial Chamber at Wetzlar survived, but their possibility of usefulness was gone. What

---

[1] Cf. p. 46.　　　　　　　　[2] Cf. Haüsser, ii. 415.

relics of the old federal institutions remained, such as the Circles, were quite incompatible with the new arrangements. Moreover, the disappearance of the ecclesiastical states and the transfer of votes to the lay Princes who had received the secularised prelacies had entirely altered the balance of power in the Diet. The Protestants were now in the majority, for of the 82 voters to which the loss of the Left Bank and the disappearance of the joint votes of the Rhenish and Swabian prelates had reduced the College of Princes, 52 were now Protestant and 30 Catholic.[1] One result of the change was that Austria's influence in the Diet was much decreased. She had usually been able to reckon on the clerical voters, but most of their votes were now in the hands of her enemies.[2]

With the disappearance of the ecclesiastical states the secular element gained the upper hand in Germany completely, even to the extent of the subjection of ecclesiastics to secular jurisdiction. Their disappearance was in so far a benefit that on the whole they had been in a bad condition, and greatly needed the reforms they were more likely to get from their new than from their old rulers. Similarly, not even in their most flourishing days had most of the mediatised towns ever been large enough to justify their territorial independence, and in 1803 they were for the most part much decayed. If the type of administration introduced in the new middle states of Germany under the influence of Napoleonic France tended to be oppressively inelastic and on unduly rigid lines, it was still a great improvement on what it replaced. But what is remarkable about these changes, is the fact that they were effected without apparently exciting any great movement of public opinion. They had been from first to last the work of the dynasties, not of their subjects.

They were accepted with a positive apathy almost everywhere. The inhabitants of the Left Bank, who since 1797 had enjoyed the advantages of being regularly incorporated in France, showed no desire to return to their old allegiance, and accepted readily enough the theory of Görres, that Nature had

---

[1] The vote of the Westphalian Counts alternated ; this reckons it as Catholic.

[2] In the College of Princes, Prussia (formerly 8) had now 11 votes. Bavaria (6) had 9, Hanover (6) 7, Baden (3) 6, the Ernestine Saxons 6, Nassau (2) 4, Mecklenburg-Schwerin 3, Austria 3, Salzburg 3, Oldenburg, Würtemburg and Hesse-Cassel 2 each ; four groups of Counts and 20 single votes made up the total of 82.

30

created the Rhine to serve as the boundary of France. Material benefits had followed annexation, and the state of these departments was certainly superior to that of their neighbours on the Eastern bank of the river.

The German Revolution, for so it may be described, though in part the effect of the great popular upheaval in France, was not in the least a popular movement. Instead of welding a nation together by destroying barriers between classes and provinces, the German Revolution reinforced and fortified particularism. At the same time, the incorporation of the smallest states in the larger was an example which might be pushed further. The system of rounding off a territorial unit by assimilating the petty states enclosed in it might be greatly extended. The new grouping of Germany paved the way to unification, even while destroying most of the old outward forms of German unity. The greed of the German Princes had destroyed the Holy Roman Empire ; the oppression of Napoleon was to build up in its place the German national feeling which the Empire had suggested rather than aroused.[1]

---

[1] Haüsser's chapter (Book III. ch. vii.), *Der Reichsdeputations Hauptschluss*, has been my principal authority for this account of the resettlement of Germany. Compare also Fisher, ch. ii., and Maps xi. and xii. in the *Clarendon Press Atlas*.

CHAPTER XXIV

THE CAUSES OF THE THIRD COALITION

UNSATISFACTORY as the resettlement of 1803 must have
been to all patriotic Germans, it was not in itself doomed
to inevitable failure. The Recess was not carried out without
conflicts between the stronger Powers—Austria and Bavaria, for
example, nearly came to blows over Burgau[1]—or protests from
the weaker states, who appealed to the protection of the First
Consul. But with Austria and Prussia on bad terms, and the
middle states bound to Napoleon by gratitude for past favours
and the stronger tie of hope of future benefits, an equilibrium
seemed to have been established in Germany which was not
likely to be disturbed from within if Napoleon only took
reasonable precautions to keep on good terms with the
Continental Powers. A little moderation, a little regard for the
fears and susceptibilities of Austria and Russia, such as true
statesmanship would surely have dictated, might have prevented
the growth of that Third Coalition, which is rather to be ascribed
to Napoleon's aggressions, to his failure to abide by the conditions he had himself laid down, than to the insidious influence
of " Pitt's gold."[2] Napoleon was himself Great Britain's best
recruiting sergeant and the most influential advocate of the
Third Coalition.

The complete decay of the Holy Roman Empire is perhaps
best illustrated by the treatment received by the Imperial
Knights during the years 1803 and 1804. That their position
was anomalous, that their independence was theoretically unjustifiable, cannot be denied. The contention of Prussia, that the
privileges of the Knights were usurpations which had grown up
under ecclesiastical rule, but which must be restricted now that

---

[1] Cf. Haüsser, ii. 439.
[2] Cf. Rose's *Napoleon*, vol. ii. pp. 5, 6, and also a volume of the Royal Historical
Society's Transactions dealing with *The Third Coalition against France: 1804–
1805*, edited by Dr. Rose.

secular government had replaced ecclesiastical,[1] had perhaps a little more historical accuracy than characterised the proclamation published by the Elector of Bavaria on October 9th, 1803, which roundly declared that the Knights were mere local landholders who had thrown off the authority of their overlords. Both views, however, were in deliberate violation of the clause in the Peace of Westphalia which recognised the Knights as a component part of the German polity, and guaranteed their enjoyment of their rights and privileges.[2] That their territories were on the whole ill-governed, backward in every way, an incubus on trade and commerce, a menace to public order and security as being the resort of gipsies, vagrants and criminals, was more or less true ; but their suppression was a matter which should have been effected by legal forms, by the authority of the Diet, and not merely by the right of the stronger.

This, however, was what Bavaria was trying to do. The Elector collected a committee of the Franconian Knights, had himself proclaimed their overlord, ordered the magistrates to join the Electoral courts of justice, and directed that the taxes due to the Knights should be paid into the Electoral coffers. The committee was compelled to admit themselves to be the Elector's subjects, and to pay to him the sums hitherto paid to the Emperor.

His action found many imitators, foremost among them Hesse-Cassel, Hesse-Darmstadt and the Princes of the House of Nassau. Petty Princes like the rulers of Leiningen and Isenburg were not restrained from using violence against their defenceless neighbours by the reflection that their own possessions might with equal justification be subjected to a similar process. Saxony and Baden alone refrained from the game of "grab," which in some places, where more than one claimant attempted to seize the same village, resulted in bloodshed. In vain the Knights appealed to Napoleon. He would not alienate more useful clients for the sake of these helpless applicants for his protection. The Emperor, however, did bestir himself upon their behalf, and an Imperial Commission of the Aulic Council pronounced in favour of the Knights (Jan. 1804), and ordered restoration of the previous state of things. The Emperor, the Arch Chancellor, Baden and Saxony were appointed guardians of the rights of the Knights.

[1] Cf. Haüsser, ii. 485.   [2] Cf. Turner, p. 122.

Bavaria now found herself isolated, for Napoleon was not disposed to intervene on her behalf and to embroil himself with Austria just when the unexpected firmness of the Addington Cabinet had involved him, before he was ready, in a fresh war with England. Accordingly on February 19th the Elector intimated to the Diet his willingness to withdraw. His action had been somewhat over-hasty, but it was typical of the way in which the middle states were seeking to assert their authority over their new acquisitions, and to build up on a small scale autocracies after the Napoleonic model. Bureaucratic centralisation, an extensive and active system of police, complete control over the finances, uniformity in organisation and administration, were the objects aimed at. When the interests of the subject were the chief care of the ruler, as was the case in Baden, where education was fostered by the revival of Heidelberg University, and all possible means were taken to promote good government, this had a good side. In Würtemberg one sees the reverse side of the shield, a caricature of the Napoleonic system, an oppressive rule, sacrificing the interests of the governed to the whim of a selfish ruler, heedless of his subjects. But it is in Bavaria that one has the most typical case of the conflict between the old and the new. In the last days of Elector Charles Theodore, things had not been well with Bavaria. Mistresses, monks and favourites had held sway over an extravagant, corrupt and inefficient government. Taxation had been oppressive, the debt heavy, trade and industry had languished under the blighting influence of monopolies and privilege. Justice was conspicuous by its absence, the administration was at once oppressive and lax. Education was neglected, superstition universal. With Maximilian Joseph a new era had begun. Modern, alert, and if rather lacking in force of character still genuinely anxious to introduce reforms, he found a congenial minister in the gifted Savoyard Montgelas. Together they assailed privilege, priestcraft and feudalism, introduced reforms into the Army, the Church, the administration of justice and of police, into the position of the peasants and the rights of the landowners. It was an assistance to them that Bavaria's acquisitions in 1803 were rich and in many important respects ahead of the rest of Germany. Some indication of the liberal tendencies of the Elector and his minister is given by their grant of toleration to Protestants (Sept. 1800), by their suppression of superfluous monasteries, by their refusal to allow Franciscans and Capuchins to recruit their numbers, by their assuming control of Church property, and placing all schools in the hands of the State.

Meanwhile Napoleon, not content to let well alone, was making peace as impossible for the Continental Powers as he had already made it for Great Britain. His interference in the internal affairs of Holland (Sept. 1801) and of Switzerland (Sept. 1802), his annexations of Piedmont and of the Valais, his election as First Consul of the Italian Republic (Jan. 1802), could not but excite unrest and uneasiness at Vienna and at St. Petersburg, even if they failed to bring home to the dull mind of Frederick William III the dangers of the path he had chosen. And yet he had seen nearer home an act "just such as Prussia might have entreated Napoleon to commit in order to give her an occasion of showing the difference between a policy of non-intervention and a policy of mere passiveness."[1] This was the French occupation of Hanover.

As in 1756 so in 1803 Hanover was the link that bound the maritime and colonial war between England and France to the affairs of the Continent. Through Hanover Napoleon hoped to strike at England, little though either George III or his people concerned themselves with the fate of the monarch's German subjects. But as an inlet by which English commerce might find its way into Europe, Hanover had its importance even to England, and the occupation of Hanover was the first step in that policy of controlling the Continent in order to keep out English trade which led Napoleon on to Moscow.

At the end of May 1803 20,000 French troops under General Mortier crossed the frontier of Hanover. The army of the Electorate was neither very large nor very efficient. Since the Peace of Basel, Hanover had enjoyed the shelter of the "line of demarcation," and the army had been reduced accordingly. Still, if the administration had chosen to make a stand, the Hanoverian troops might have resisted as weak a corps as Mortier's with good prospects of success. But the Electorate was under the lax and placid rule of a bureaucratic aristocracy, too mild to arouse popular discontent and make the invaders welcome, too slack and inert to arouse popular resistance based on patriotic feeling. Thus no preparations for resistance were

[1] Seeley, i. 230.

made till the invaders were on the move. Some trusted to the protection of the Holy Roman Empire, some to the equally futile Prussian guarantee of neutrality.

As early as March 1803 Napoleon had sent Duroc to Berlin to explain that to secure the flank of the Grand Army against an English attack he would have to occupy Hanover. Rather feebly Prussia sought to dissuade Napoleon from a step so inimical to her interests, so derogatory to her prestige, so detrimental to her trade, since it was certain that England would reply to the occupation by a blockade of the Elbe and Weser. But while Prussia hesitated and attempted to mediate between England and France, while the Hanoverian ministry displayed equal hesitation and indecision and only definitely appealed to Prussia when it was too late, Napoleon carried out his plan. It seems probable that had Prussia taken Lord Hawkesbury's hint to Jacobi and, as in 1801, forestalled Napoleon by herself occupying Hanover, England would have taken no official notice of what after all did not concern her, while Napoleon would most likely have acquiesced rather than alienate Prussia. But prompt and decided action of any nature was not to be expected from Prussia. At last (May 25th) a proposal was adopted by which Russia and Prussia were to guarantee the neutrality of Hanover, a payment being made by the Electorate to France, and the Duke of Cambridge acting as Stadtholder; but by this time Mortier's men were on the point of crossing the frontier, and Talleyrand informed Lucchesini that Napoleon intended to occupy "the British possessions on the Continent," though he hinted that his master was well disposed towards a Franco-Prussian alliance which might leave Hanover in Prussian hands.

It was on May 30th that Mortier entered Hanover. He met with no opposition. A *levée en masse* had been ordered but countermanded, and the Hanoverian troops fell back on Suhlingen, while emissaries from the Privy Council attempted to negotiate with Mortier. Neither civil nor military authorities had any idea of resisting, and on June 3rd a Convention was signed at Suhlingen which placed the whole Electorate, with its fortresses and revenues, at the disposal of the French. The Hanoverian army undertook to retire across the Elbe and not to bear arms against France unless exchanged. This, however, did not satisfy Napoleon. He insisted that the army should surrender as prisoners of war, wishing to exchange them against the French sailors on the English prison-hulks whom his fleet so sorely needed. The British ministry not unaturally declined to meet his wishes. Thereupon he refused to ratify the Convention, and bade Mortier disarm the Hanoverian troops. To this Wallmoden, the Hanoverian commander, would not agree, and for a time it seemed as though Hanover would after all resist. But the troops were in bad condition, their discipline was relaxed, they did not understand what was happening, and when the Estates of Calenberg - Celle demanded that the troops should submit, Wallmoden gladly grasped at this excuse for capitulation. Mortier waived the demand that the men should become prisoners of war, and the troops then laid down their arms and dispersed to their homes (July 5th). No small number of them, however, keenly sensitive to the disgrace to the honour of their army, took advantage of the fact that the oath of neutrality had not been administered to them to escape through Holstein to England, there to be formed into that King's German Legion which was to do such good service to the cause of England and of Europe, which was to serve in Denmark and in Portugal, in Sicily and in Spain, and to end a glorious career by playing a prominent part in the "crowning mercy" of Waterloo.[1]

In this way Hanover passed into the power of France: the first district of Germany East of the Rhine to suffer the lot of subjugation to Napoleon, which sooner or later was meted out to the whole country. It exchanged a government which, with all its faults, could not be called exacting or tyrannical, for the heavy burden of a military occupation aimed at draining dry the resources of the country. Not much change was made in the administration, but an Executive Commission was appointed on which fell the task of wringing out of the unfortunate Electorate the sums Napoleon demanded. The normal annual revenue of the country was little over 12,000,000 francs, but nearly 18,000,000 were extorted between July 5th and December 23rd, 1803. Moreover, the French troops had to be supplied and given quarters at the

---

[1] Beamish's *History of the King's German Legion* contains a full and interesting account of the Legion and its services: for the French occupation of Hanover, see Fisher, ch. iii., and *England and Hanover*, pp. 203 ff.

expense of the inhabitants. In June 1804, when Bernadotte replaced Mortier, matters improved slightly. His yoke was rather milder, his extortions less crushing, the discipline he maintained rather better. Yet even so the Electorate was burdened and taxed unmercifully, while the threat of a like fate wrung from the neighbouring city of Hamburg an unwilling "loan" of three million marks in November 1803.

From the other Powers of Germany no redress was to be looked for by the unfortunate Hanoverians. The Emperor accepted the occupation as a fact: he was as ready to see the French there as the Prussians. Prussia meanwhile put up with the check as best she might. She did, indeed, send Lombard to Brussels (July 1803) to ask Napoleon's intentions and complain about his seizure of Cuxhaven, which belonged to Hamburg. The mission only committed Prussia more and more to France. Lombard returned declaring that Napoleon only meant to respect the rights of neutrals, and that his action had been forced upon him by England's illegalities.[1] A proposal made by Prussia to get Russia to guarantee the neutrality of the Continent so as to secure Napoleon against the foundation of a new coalition by British gold, Napoleon rejected. He had no wish to see Russia and Prussia on good terms, but intended to keep Prussia isolated and so at his mercy. It was a sense of this isolation which caused Prussia in the course of 1804 to make tentative efforts to build up a new League of Princes on the lines of the *Fürstenbund* of 1785. The idea came to nothing; for Duke Charles Augustus of Saxe-Weimar, when sounded by Prince William of Brunswick, did not prove enthusiastic, while Prussia was equally unwilling to let the Duke of Weimar draw her into a league with Austria. The relations of the two leading Powers of Germany were as usual strained, and not even the outrage on the Empire, on treaty rights, international law and public opinion involved in the abduction of the Duc d'Enghien (March 1804) from the shelter of his refuge at Baden, could make them unite to protect the Empire against so flagrant and forcible an outrage. Indeed, it is a striking commentary on the state of Germany that the most strenuous protests should have come not from Austria or Bavaria or Prussia, but from England, Russia

---

[1] She had blockaded the mouths of the Elbe and Weser, and the trade of Hamburg and Bremen was feeling the effects of the blockade.

and Sweden. The conduct of the Elector of Baden was pusillanimous and ignominious in the extreme. Far from bringing the case before the Diet himself, he endeavoured to prevent Russia from moving in the matter at all[1] (July), asking the Diet to let it drop lest a greater evil should follow. Hanover, however, refused to do this, and called on the Emperor to demand satisfaction and redress for the double breach of the rights of the Empire committed by Napoleon in this matter and in the occupation of Hanover. To avoid having to vote on the question, most of the representatives left Ratisbon before the end of July.[2]

Not long after the abduction and murder of the only member of the House of Bourbon on whom he could conveniently lay his hands, Napoleon assumed the Imperial title (May 18th, 1804). This was not quite to the liking of Austria. The new title was felt to reflect in some way on that of Francis. It seemed to hint at a new competitor for the Imperial throne quite capable of ending the Hapsburg monopoly. Moreover, the changes of 1803 had given the Protestants a clear majority in the Electoral College, and it was to make certain that in some form or other the Imperial title should continue in his line that Francis resolved upon the erection of his own immediate dominions into an hereditary Empire.[3] It was on August 14th, 1804, that the decree was published by which this was done: but not before negotiations for the reciprocal recognition of the two titles had for some time been keeping Paris and Vienna in constant correspondence.[4]

[1] Russia at first seems to have contemplated an immediate rupture with France, but decided in favour of the " more circumspect" course of appealing to the members of the Empire to co-operate with the Czar in " restraining the ambition of France" and defending their rights and liberties (*The Third Coalition*, p. 5). However, as Napoleon took offence at Russia's protests against the execution of the Duc d'Enghien, and complained bitterly that Russia was interfering in matters which did not concern her, relations rapidly became strained, and in August 1804 the Russian Minister at Paris, after presenting an ultimatum with the terms of which Napoleon altogether failed to comply, left France altogether. This rupture of diplomatic relations did not, however, immediately lead to war. *Ibid.* pp. 30–32.

[2] Cf. Fisher, pp. 67–75 ; Haüsser, ii. pp. 497 ff.

[3] Some contemporary documents use the title "the Emperor of Germany" in speaking of Francis II (cf. *The Third Coalition*, passim), but it was not, of course, his official title.

[4] Austria's recognition of Napoleon's Imperial title gave much offence to the Czar (*The Third Coalition*, p. 36), and despite the efforts of England to promote a good understanding between Vienna and St. Petersburg, Russia at first actually

Partly with the object of publishing to the world his claim to be regarded as the successor of Charlemagne, partly in order to acquaint himself thoroughly with his new Rhenish provinces, Napoleon undertook in September 1804 a tour through the recent annexations on the left bank of the Rhine. At Aix-la-Chapelle, Charlemagne's old capital, he received the Austrian envoy sent to formally recognise the new Imperial title. Thence he proceeded by Cologne (Sept. 13th) to Mayence, where he was greeted by a large and subservient assembly of German Princes and envoys, including two Electors. The presence of the Elector of Baden was a lurid commentary on that Prince's attitude in the matter of the Duc d'Enghien; the attendance of Dalberg in the city of Mayence was a humiliating proof of the great change in that prelate's policy since the days when he had desired to reconcile the *Fürstenbund* of 1785 to the Hapsburgs, even more since the days when he had urged Archduke Charles to ' assume the powers of a dictator over Germany. Formerly the stoutest champion of the Empire, Dalberg had at least made a complete change when he turned his coat, and Napoleon had not now a keener supporter. The see of Mayence had always been associated with the Imperial traditions ever since the days of Elector Berthold of Henneberg,[1] and even before his day, and Dalberg was now ready to continue his advocacy of Imperialism, but with Napoleon as his Emperor.

The meeting at Mayence though indicative of future developments, did not see any definite steps towards the organisation of the Confederation of the Rhine. It served to familiarise the minor Princes of Germany with the notion of a German union under the benevolent protection of France, which would secure them against the aggressions of Austria and Prussia. Such a plan had indeed been suggested earlier in the year by Waitz, the principal minister of the Elector of Hesse, but it had been put aside by Napoleon as likely to interfere with the Prussian alliance he was anxious to secure.

refused to recognise the title of "Hereditary Emperor of Austria" (p. 54); this with differences of opinion as to the policy to be pursued towards Turkey (p. 47), and the reluctance of the Austrian ministers, more especially of Cobenzl, the leading man amongst them, to undertake the risks of defying Napoleon, kept the two Courts from forming that alliance by which England hoped to rally Europe against Napoleon until 1805 was far advanced.

[1] Cf. C.M.H. i. pp. 300 ff.

Napoleon was anxious for a Prussian alliance, because he was well aware of the growing hostility of Russia;[1] nor could he overlook the fact that, though men like Cobenzl might be well disposed to him, or at least so much afraid of his displeasure that they would do nothing to provoke it, the old Austrian aristocracy with all its traditions could not so readily accept the mushroom Bonapartist Empire, or forget what Austria had suffered at the Corsican upstart's hands. In view of the hostility of Austria and Russia, it would be most unwise to alienate Prussia. England must not be allowed to unite all the three leading Continental Powers in a great coalition.

But as long as Prussia maintained her policy of neutrality, Napoleon could not feel quite secure of her. Though recent events had rather shaken his belief in passive neutrality, Frederick William III lacked the decision, the courage and the energy for definitely throwing in his lot either with France, as Haugwitz and Lombard on the whole advised, or with her enemies, whose cause was pleaded by the patriotic Queen Louise and by the King's enterprising cousin, Prince Louis Ferdinand. He still clung to his idea of a Russo-Prussian guarantee of the neutrality of the Continent, in return for which Napoleon would evacuate Hanover. He thus quite overlooked the fact that Russia was already more than half-way to an alliance with England, and much more disposed to force Prussia into line with the rest of Europe by threats and menaces than to buy her support with concessions;[2] that it was most unlikely that Napoleon would give up so valuable a pawn in the diplomatic game as Hanover, and that the neutrality Prussia offered was not of the least value to France. What Napoleon wanted was to force Prussia, like the middle states, into an alliance with him which should keep Austria and

---

[1] Russia had begun negotiating with Great Britain as far back as November 1803, when the occupation of Naples by French troops seemed to herald French intervention in the Morea and attempts on the integrity of Turkey (cf. Rose, *Napoleonic Studies*, pp. 364–367); but her anxiety to avoid throwing Austria or Prussia or the minor German states into the arms of France by a too precipitate declaration of policy (*The Third Coalition* (R.H.S.), p. 12), had prevented any immediate action resulting from the negotiations. England and Russia were, however, in substantial accord as to the necessity of putting some check on Napoleon's aggressions.

[2] Cf. *The Third Coalition*, pp. 101 ff.: England seems to have been far keener about securing Prussia's friendship; Russia, to have thought it would be easier to intimidate than to encourage Frederick William into an alliance.

Russia in check and abate their bellicose tendencies. But he was rather too impatient: by trying to force Frederick William to a decision he alarmed that essentially deliberate monarch, who was endeavouring to play Russia and France off against each other. The Czar, however, losing patience with Prussia's indecision, did not attempt to conceal his opinion of the Prussian King's policy, and Alexander's openly expressed contempt made Frederick William incline towards France. This disposition received something of a check through a fresh outrage on the part of Napoleon, the seizure of Sir George Rumbold, the British agent at Hamburg (Oct. 24th, 1804). This violation of neutral territory was possibly partly intended as a reply to Russia's protests about the abduction of d'Enghien;[1] anyhow it was an insult to Frederick William, who was Director of the Lower Saxon Circle, and for once he showed some decision. His indignant protests induced Napoleon to release Rumbold as a concession, not to international law, but to the King of Prussia. For the moment Napoleon did not wish to play into the hands of the bellicose party in Prussia, which seemed to have gained ground by recent changes in the ministry. During the summer of 1804 Haugwitz, without actually resigning, handed over the control of the Foreign Office to Hardenberg and retired to his Silesian estates. From time to time, however, he returned to Berlin and took part in ministerial conferences, a most anomalous arrangement which led to great confusion. The expected change in foreign policy did not follow. Hardenberg, much as he distrusted Napoleon, was not prepared to advocate a complete change, and Prussia continued her futile efforts to keep on good terms with both sides.

But by this time war was becoming inevitable. Napoleon's repeated infringements of the Peace of Lunéville had convinced Alexander of the unwisdom of the policy which had assisted Napoleon to rise to so dangerous a strength. The occupation of Naples and Hanover in order to exclude British goods from the Continent, the spectacle of Spain's dependence on the Emperor,— she became involved in Anglo-French war in December 1804,—above all, the murder of the Duc d'Enghien further excited his resentment. In August 1804 the Russian Ambassador at Paris, Count Oubril, had demanded his pass-

[1] Cf. *The Third Coalition*, p. 57.

ports, and though war had not immediately followed it could not be long delayed. Nor was Austria any better pleased with the situation. Only the memories of Marengo and Hohenlinden and the great need for the reorganisation of army administration and finances acted as a check on bellicose leanings.[1] Archduke Charles was too well aware of the deficiencies of the army to desire war, and Cobenzl's knowledge of the internal condition of the realm made him equally pacific. Yet Napoleon's actions in Italy and elsewhere could not fail to arouse resentment and suspicion, and in November 1804 Stadion concluded on behalf of Austria a defensive alliance with Russia, providing for the co-operation of Austria and Russia in case of further outrages by Napoleon. This was followed (April 11th, 1805) by an Anglo-Russian treaty, the objects of which were the expulsion of the French from North Germany, the restoration of the independence of Holland, Switzerland and Italy, and the restoration of the House of Savoy. Sweden had already concluded similar compacts with both Powers, with England in December 1804, with Russia in January 1805; but the rather inconsiderate zeal of Gustavus IV threatened to embroil him with Prussia over Pomerania,[2] and so to impede the attempts of the Coalition to enlist Prussia on their side.

To relate the action and discuss the motives of Frederick William and his advisers is a monotonous task. Hardenberg, Haugwitz and Frederick William were all pessimistic as to the Coalition's chances of overthrowing Napoleon. Russia's ill-timed efforts to force Prussia and Bavaria into an anti-French alliance had only the opposite effect. Prussia hoped to combine the advantages of both policies by adopting neither, and Napoleon's skilful dangling of the bait of Hanover before her kept her undecided. About the end of July 1805 he replied to Lucchesini's complaints about his recent action in Italy by an

---

[1] The despatches of Lord Harrowby, Sir J. B. Warren, and others, printed in Dr. Rose's *Third Coalition* (R.H.S.), contain frequent references to the poverty and financial exhaustion of Austria as the main reason for her reluctance to resume the struggle against Napoleon. It is also clear that Cobenzl's influence was steadily exercised against the "forward party," while the bad relations between Archduke Charles and Thugut forbade the recall to office of that energetic minister, who, with all his faults, at least was the sincere and convinced opponent of Napoleon; *e.g.* p. 69.

[2] Cf. Haüsser, ii. 543.

offer of Hanover,[1] appealing not merely to Frederick William's greed, but to his love of peace also by declaring that Prussia's open adhesion to the side of France would probably keep the Coalition from making war. Even Hardenberg was caught by this prospect of plunder. The Duke of Brunswick,[2] believing that a Franco-Prussian alliance would dissolve the Coalition at once, favoured the annexation of Hanover, and when Duroc came to Berlin at the end of August 1805 all indications pointed to the success of his mission. The dictatorial and minatory tone Russia was assuming had offended Prussia, and seemed likely to drive her into an alliance with Napoleon. But even at this late hour, when the Grand Army was already well on its way from the Channel to the Danube, Frederick William clung to the idea of mediating between the contending forces and so averting war. The natural result of his culpable indecision was that neither side would listen to his proposals, and that both treated Prussia "with a reckless contempt which shows that nothing was hoped, and at the same time nothing was feared from her wooden immobility." [3]

Meanwhile the war had come. The announcement in the *Moniteur* of March 17th, 1805, that the Italian Republic had offered the Iron Crown of Lombardy to Napoleon, was naturally interpreted as a deliberate challenge to the Coalition. The conversion of the Batavian Republic into a kingdom for Louis Bonaparte, the grant of Piombio and Lucca to Elise Bonaparte as a Principality, the annexation of Parma, Piacenza, Guastalla and the Ligurian Republic (June 9th) to France, merely added fuel to the flames. Even Prussia's placid acquiescence in Napoleon's aggressions received a shock which caused the Cabinet of Berlin to recognise the possibility that it might find it necessary to change its policy with regard to France.[4] The Russian envoy who was on his way to lay the last demands of the Allies before Napoleon received orders from the Czar bidding him suspend his journey. Austria's hesitations gave place to a firmer and more resolute tone and to a protest against the last outrage on the liberties of Europe. To

---

[1] Cf. Bailleu, *Preussen und Frankreich*, vol. ii. pp. 354 ff.

[2] Cf. Haüsser, ii. 600 ff.   [3] Seeley, i. 235.

[4] Cf. Novosilzov to Woronzov (quoted in *The Third Coalition*, p. 187). The whole attitude of Germany towards Napoleon is altering; he is "no longer a guardian angel," but a monster who will "swallow up Germany if she persists in a policy of inaction."

this Napoleon answered that he should consider Austria's action as a declaration of war; but the protest was not withdrawn. Hostilities did not at once follow. Indeed, it was not till August 9th that Austria signed the treaty by which she formally adhered to the Russo-British alliance of April 11th.[1] In the interval Napoleon had sent an envoy to warn Austria against the insidious designs of Russia and Britain, to profess his own pacific intentions, and to complain of Austria's unreasonably hostile attitude. At the critical moment of his great design against his arch-enemy England, when he was hoping every day to hear that Villeneuve had released Ganteaume and the Brest fleet from Cornwallis' vigilant blockade, and that the combined squadrons of Brest and Toulon were sweeping up the Channel on their way to Boulogne, Napoleon did not wish to precipitate matters with Austria. If he could put off the breach long enough to allow him to cross the Channel, he expected to be able to dictate terms to a dismayed Europe from the conquered capital of George III.

[1] Owing to difficulties raised by Russia with regard to Malta and to the English Maritime Code, it was not till July 28th that this treaty was ratified. The delay thus caused and that due to the reluctance of Austria to commit herself to war as long as any prospect, however faint, of a peaceful settlement still remained, had no slight share in producing the disasters of the campaign.

CHAPTER XXV

ULM AND AUSTERLITZ

AUSTRIA did not embark on a fresh war without serious misgivings. There were not wanting prophets who declared that the time was not ripe, and that neither her political nor her military situation was favourable. Indeed as patriotic a German and as keen an enemy of Napoleon as Gentz despaired of success as long as the administration was in the hands of Cobenzl, Colloredo and their school.[1] The military preparations were in a backward state. In March a complete change had been made in the administration. Archduke Charles, who for some time had been losing his hold on his brother's confidence, had resigned the Presidency of the War Council to Latour, Schwarzenberg becoming Vice-President, and Mack replacing von Duca as Quartermaster-General. This was more than a change of persons, it implied the overthrow of the incompetent gang who had been misusing the Archduke's ill-bestowed favour to let the efficiency of the army decline. Mack, a soldier who had risen from the ranks, was well fitted for his new post. Energetic, painstaking, not without administrative capacity, he was " a good peace general " even if his performances in the field were destined to prove disastrous, and in a short time he did succeed in effecting great reforms. He managed to collect a really considerable force; but the troops were for the most part raw, their equipment was far from complete, and the men were unknown to their officers. Moreover, the flagrant strategical errors of his plan of campaign more than neutralised his good services as an organiser, and the disturbance caused by his reforms had not had time to settle down. The machinery was put to the severest of tests before it could be properly adjusted to its work.

If there was any step which the Austrians, seeing how unprepared they were, ought to have avoided, it was risking

[1] Cf. Haüsser, ii. 556.

31

a pitched battle with Napoleon before their Russian allies could join them. Yet this was precisely what Mack did. Though the first Russian troops did not cross the border of Galicia till the middle of August, and could not possibly reach the Inn until nearly the end of October, the Austrians actually took the offensive, and advanced into Bavaria before the middle of September. Not only this, but the army which made this rash move was not the principal Austrian force. Only 90,000 men were allotted to the Danube, while 140,000 were to be gathered on the Mincio and Adige for a campaign in Italy, another 30,000 in Tyrol forming a connecting link. More-over, Austria's foremost soldier, Archduke Charles, who with all his defects was a man of tried capacity, received the com-mand in Italy, that on the Danube being nominally entrusted to Archduke Ferdinand, the son of the Grand Duke of Salzburg, though his appointment left the real direction of the army completely to Mack. Those who bethought them of Mack's performances in the field in 1798 can hardly have been filled with confidence.

It was not merely because the Russians could take no part in it that the advance into Bavaria was so unwise. The fate of Mack's army shows clearly how completely the framers of the plan failed to appreciate either the strategical or the political situation. By advancing to the Black Forest they hoped to forestall Napoleon in gaining military possession of South-Western Germany. But in thinking to surprise Napoleon they lent themselves to being completely surprised. They had quite overlooked the strategic possibilities of the position of the Grand Army along the Channel and in Hanover. They had not realised that the Grand Army need not pass through Alsace on its way from Boulogne to the Danube, that it might just as well direct its march towards Frankfort and the Main as towards the Upper Rhine and Strassburg, and that an army which advanced to meet an anticipated French attack on the line of the Black Forest would expose its Northern flank to Bernadotte from Hanover and to Marmont from Holland. Politically, their calculations were almost as much at fault. They hoped that their forward movement would cause the States of South-Western Germany to declare in their favour; but Napoleon, foreseeing the certainty of war, had been beforehand in securing the alliance of Bavaria, Würtemberg and Baden. Maximilian Joseph of Bavaria hesitated a little before accepting the proposals laid before him (March 1805), which took the shape of an offensive and defensive alliance between France and Bavaria to be cemented by the marriage of his eldest daughter to Napoleon's stepson Eugene. But jealousy and dread of Austria, and the knowledge that he must choose one side or the other, outweighed his wife's arguments in favour of the Austrian alliance, and caused him to come down on the same side of the fence as the stronger battalions. On August 24th he signed a provisional treaty with France. A fortnight later (Sept. 6th) he received an ultimatum from Austria requiring him to join his forces to hers or be treated as an enemy. Not without hesitation the Elector fled to Würzburg to seek the protection of the advancing French for himself and his army. On October 12th he confirmed the provisional treaty, though the French envoy Otto, in order to give colour to Napoleon's assertion that the Elector had been driven from his territories by a wanton act of aggression, and that the Emperor was merely coming to the assistance of an injured ally, deliberately altered the date of the draft from August 24th to September 23rd. Baden had shown much less hesitation. The Treaty of Ettlingen (Sept. 2nd) bound the Elector to supply a contingent of 3000 men to the French army. Frederick II of Würtemberg made rather more parade of needing compulsion. His connection with Russia and England on the whole inclined him to the Coalition, and the project he laid before Bavaria, Baden, Hesse-Darmstadt and Prussia for an armed neutrality which should exclude both belligerents from the territories of the contracting parties, probably does represent the policy he would have preferred. The failure of this project and the appearance of French troops at the gates of his capital removed his scruples; on October 8th he signed a treaty committing himself to the French alliance and promising the help of 10,000 troops. Of the four Powers whom Napoleon intended to unite in his projected Germanic Confederation, Hesse-Darmstadt alone stood neutral, looking to Berlin for a lead which that hesitating Court failed to give until Austerlitz had left her hardly any choice. The attitude of the Diet was even more pitiable. Occupied with appeals and verdicts arising out of the Recess of February 25th,

1803, with the case of the Knights whom Austria was prepared to abandon if her demand for the admission of enough new Catholic votes into the College of Princes to secure equality between the religions were admitted, the Diet was quite unprepared to cope with such an emergency as this, and when Napoleon claimed that he was acting as its champion and defending the right of the Princes, the Diet's silence could be represented as a tacit admission of his contention.

Thus the Austrian advance into Swabia not merely thrust the head of their army into the lion's jaws, not merely exposed Mack and his men to destruction long before their Russian allies could reach the Inn, also it drove Bavaria over to Napoleon's side. Moreover, Mack capped the original blunder of an advance with the additional error of choosing the line of the Iller rather than that of the Black Forest, the true position for an army seeking to carry out the task on which he believed his to be engaged of repelling an invasion coming from Alsace. So, too, he failed to use his numerous cavalry to gain and keep touch with the enemy. That his forces were unduly dispersed was only in keeping with his other errors. When the storm broke upon him on October 8th, he had men all along the Danube from Neuburg and Ingolstadt to the Iller and even farther Westward.

Meanwhile Napoleon was taking full advantage of the chance Mack's rashness had placed in his hands. Not till August 22nd, when the news reached him that Villeneuve, despairing of his task of raising the blockade of Brest, had turned Southward for Cadiz on August 15th, had the Emperor finally abandoned the idea of invading England and adopted the alternative of a blow at England's continental allies. That for some time past he had been contemplating such a change of plan is practically certain. He saw, none clearer, that the army at Boulogne might easily be diverted to the Danube, and he was ready for either effort. Had the longed-for opportunity of crippling the Coalition by a blow at its heart come to him, he would hardly have been deterred from taking it by the knowledge that 60,000 Austrians were moving slowly up the Danube and that by the end of October 40,000 Russians might be expected on the Inn; but the chance never came, and he turned to a hardly less dramatic if less decisive success. With the beginning of September the Grand Army started on its

famous march to the Danube. Its left, Bernadotte from
Hanover and Marmont from Holland, moved towards the
Main, Davoût's corps was directed on Spires, Soult's on
Mannheim, the Guards, Murat's cavalry, Lannes and Ney
made for Strassburg. Before the end of the month they were
crossing the river, after marches performed with wonderful
celerity and precision. Pushing on through Swabia, their
movements covered from the Austrians by their cavalry, the
French were on the Danube from Donauwörth to Ingolstadt
before Mack had discovered their object. Convinced that
their main attack would be delivered against the line of
the Iller, he had been completely taken in by such feints
as had been made in that direction. Bernadotte's presence
at Würzburg, where he joined the Elector of Bavaria on
September 27th, Mack dismissed as a mere feint to divert
his attention from the true attack; and not even when, on
October 8th, he heard that Murat had seized Donauwörth
and driven Kienmayer's division back upon München did he
realise his danger or take the prompt and decisive steps
which alone might have extricated his army from its imminent
peril.

At the moment when Murat and Soult secured the passage
at Donauwörth (a.m., Oct. 7th), the bulk of the Austrian forces
were on the Iller and at Ulm, only some 20,000 men lining
the Danube from Gunzburg to Ingolstadt. Thus the French
were able to sever Mack from his base with but little trouble.
Pushing out two corps only towards the Isar to thrust
Kienmayer Eastward and to keep the Russians in check should
they arrive in time to attempt a diversion, Napoleon directed
the rest of the Grand Army on Ulm, seeking to close every
possible avenue of escape. Soult after seizing Augsburg
(Oct. 9th) was pushed out to the Southward to secure the
road to Tyrol through Memmingen. Murat and Lannes,
supported by Marmont, took the direct road to Ulm up the
right bank of the Danube, meeting and defeating at Wertingen
an Austrian division which was making Eastward to recover
Donauwörth (Oct. 8th). Ney moved parallel along the left
bank to close the line of retreat which Kray had taken in
June 1800.[1]

Mack was thus in the toils; but had he adopted the

[1] Cf. p. 447.

Archduke Ferdinand's proposal, and at once endeavoured to cut his way out through Nördlingen across the communications of the Grand Army, he might have got away, more especially as, through some misunderstanding, Murat had brought two of Ney's three divisions over to the right bank (Oct. 10th). The third division, that of Dupont, was thus left isolated, and advancing alone on Ulm, was defeated and cut to pieces at Albeck (Oct. 11th). But Mack failed to avail himself of this chance of escape. Beguiled by a false rumour that Napoleon had been recalled to the Rhine by a rising at Paris, he stuck fast to Ulm, and only Werneck's division moved out on the 13th to the comparative safety of Heidenheim. Thus when, on the 14th, Riesch followed, it was too late. Ney by a brilliant stroke secured the bridge of Elchingen, planted his corps in the path of the Austrians, and thrust them back on Ulm. This success allowed the French to close the Northern road again; and with Soult at Memmingen, from which place he had driven Jellachich back into Tyrol (Oct. 13th), the Southern line also was blocked. Archduke Ferdinand with 1500 mounted men did manage to push through by Aalen and Ottingen to Nüremberg and so to Eger, but the rest of Mack's army were less fortunate. Ney's capture of the Michaelsberg, a strong position north of the town, made Ulm almost untenable, and Mack's brave words about dying in the last ditch came down on the 17th to a promise to capitulate if not relieved within a week, and on the 20th to an immediate surrender, which set the whole of the French army except Ney's corps free for further operations. Had he managed to delay Napoleon a week so as to give the Russians time to fall on the screen containing them, he would have done something to mitigate the disaster his rashness, his short-sightedness and his obstinacy had produced. Almost the only Austrian who comes creditably out of the affair is Werneck, who made a gallant but unsuccessful attempt at a diversion by falling on Ney's rear on the 14th, instead of getting away Northward. His mistimed loyalty involved him in the disaster, for Murat overtook him and forced him to surrender at Trochtelfingen (Oct. 16th), so that nothing was left of Mack's whole army but Kienmayer's division and the fugitives who had gained Bohemia with Archduke Ferdinand or Tyrol with Jellachich.

Napoleon was not the man to leave unimproved such a success as Ulm. The line of the Lech was made the French base for the next phase of the campaign, and within four days of the fall of Ulm the French columns were again on the move. Between Napoleon's victorious host and Vienna there were only some 35,000 Russians who had just reached the Inn, and about 20,000 Austrians, Kienmayer's division with various details. Such a force could not hope to stop Napoleon, and orders had to be sent to Archduke Charles to abandon the Italian campaign and return with all speed to save Vienna. Thus Napoleon was able to cross in succession the Southern tributaries of the Danube, beginning with the Inn (Oct. 28th). While his main body moved down the river, Ney's corps and the Bavarians were detached into Tyrol to obtain touch with Masséna's Army of Italy, which, despite a sharp check at Caldiero (Oct. 31st), was following the Austrians as they retreated. Had the Austrians known how to use them, there were in Tyrol the elements for an effective diversion. If the various corps, Hiller in South Tyrol, Jellachich in Vorarlberg, Archduke John in the valley of the Inn, had been properly combined and supported by the Tyrolese "insurrection," which would have given the Austrians 20,000 good shots and hardy mountaineers, an effective blow might have been struck at the French communications. But the opposite was done. There was no cohesion: Jellachich was cut off and taken (Nov. 13th), Archduke John evacuated Tyrol and, moving over the Brenner and down the Pusterthal, joined the Army of Italy in Carinthia, and the French were able to seize the Brenner and to get into touch with Masséna.

Meanwhile Kutusov had retired from one river to another, steadily refusing to fight, a policy much resented by his Austrian colleague Merveldt. The disagreement led to the Austrians taking a Southerly direction after leaving the Inn, with the idea of gaining touch with Archduke Charles. Altering his plan, however, Merveldt moved down the Enns to rejoin Kutusov at St. Pölten, only to encounter, at Steyer, Marmont on his way to Leoben (Nov. 8th), and a sharp fight resulted in the annihilation of the Austrians. This put out of Kutusov's head any idea he may have had of fighting a battle for Vienna. He was already feeling nervous for his communications with the second Russian army now on the frontier of Moravia, for

Napoleon had detached three divisions under Mortier to the left bank, and they were moving down the river. Kutusov therefore evacuated the strong St. Pölten position and fell back across the Danube at Mautern (p.m., Nov. 8th). This allowed Napoleon to push on past St. Pölten to Vienna, where there was only a weak garrison some 13,000 strong ; but it gave Kutusov a chance of falling on Mortier's isolated force. As Mortier's divisions moved through the difficult defile of Dürrenstein one Russian division barred their path and another intercepted their retreat (Nov. 11th). Gazan's division was annihilated, and the whole corps nearly destroyed. Still sharp as was the check which Kutusov had the satisfaction of having inflicted on the French, it had little influence on the fortune of the campaign: nothing was done to follow it up, and meanwhile Napoleon had seized Vienna (Nov. 13th) and obtained possession of the great bridge over the Danube.

Kutusov and the garrison of Vienna now fell back Northward, Napoleon's effort to intercept the retreat of the Russians from Krems being foiled by Bagration at Hollabrünn (Nov. 16th), so that they made their way safely through Znaym to Brünn. The Russians were thus able to unite with their second army near Olmütz (Nov. 20th). Napoleon had pushed out as far as Brünn in the hopes of cutting them off; but finding his effort unsuccessful, he came to a halt. The truth of the matter was, that despite his success in seizing his enemy's capital his position was none too secure. The force which he had available—the Guards, Murat's cavalry, and the corps of Soult and Lannes—was not much more than 60,000 men, while the joint armies of Kutusov, Büxhowden and the Austrians were well over 80,000, and a force at least as large was threatening Vienna from the South. This was the united corps of the Archdukes Charles and John, now at Marburg on the Drave. Between these forces Napoleon had indeed the interior position, but his long line of communications had absorbed the greater portion of his force. Two corps (Ney and Augereau) were in Tyrol, one (Marmont) was in Styria, the greater part ot another (Davoût) in and round Vienna, Mortier and the contingents of Baden and Würtemberg higher up the Danube, and the only troops within reach were Bernadotte's corps at Znaym on his left and one of Davoût's divisions a little way to the right rear. Had the Allies only refrained from risking all on an immediate action, had they even waited for the reinforcements Archduke Ferdinand was rallying in Bohemia and for those which were still on their way from Russia, the delay would have been all in their favour.

Moreover, there was another and a greater danger threatening Napoleon. On his march through Franconia, Bernadotte's corps had violated the neutrality of the Prussian province of Anspach. The infringement appears to have been deliberate. Had Bernadotte made a detour to avoid Anspach, his arrival on the Danube would have been delayed by at least a day, and Napoleon seems never to have imagined that Prussia's apparently inexhaustible capacity for submitting to insults would not be equal to this additional slight.[1] But it awoke in Frederick William and in Prussia an explosion of furious wrath, which was increased rather than assuaged by the off-hand manner in which Napoleon treated the matter as a mere bagatelle. Prussia began to arm. Hanover, evacuated by Bernadotte, was occupied by Prussian troops, and the resentment which had recently been excited by the Czar's efforts to coerce Prussia into joining the Coalition was now diverted against Napoleon. Alexander hastened to Berlin to arrange in person for the adhesion of Prussia to the Coalition; and though the first news which greeted him there was the tidings of the disaster at Ulm, his influence proved sufficient to keep Frederick William firm in his determination to join the Allies. The opposition of the Francophil party had been revived by the news from the Danube, but Frederick William felt that he had gone too far to recede, and on November 3rd he signed the Convention of Potsdam. By this Prussia was to offer Napoleon certain terms; and if within four weeks he had not accepted them was to join the Allies with 180,000 men.[2] These terms amounted to the independence of all Europe outside the " natural boundaries " of France. The King of Sardinia was to obtain Parma, Piacenza and Genoa in lieu of Piedmont; Austria was to have the Mincio as her boundary in Italy. The question which more than any other had contributed to keep Prussia from joining the Allies, that of Hanover, was relegated to a secret article. Alexander promised to use his good offices with England to obtain not only subsidies on the usual scale, but the cession of Hanover to Prussia. That Pitt should have absolutely refused to con-

---

[1] Cf. Haüsser, ii. 611.   [2] Cf. *The Third Coalition*, pp. 221 ff.

template the proposal was only natural; it was also one of the causes which made Frederick William finally draw back at the eleventh hour.

It is hardly necessary to suppose that Frederick William was guilty of bad faith in the extraordinary way in which he followed up this treaty. Though there was probably much truth in the Duke of Wellington's opinion, that "the Prussians fancied . . . they could fall upon the rear of Bonaparte in a moment, but I knew that the King of Prussia could not have his troops on the Danube under three months,"[1] this was hardly the King's opinion. Yet he selected Haugwitz as the bearer of this all-important ultimatum to Napoleon, though Haugwitz was the typical representative of the policy whose unwisdom Prussia was now learning. Moreover, Haugwitz delayed his departure till November 14th, and did not arrive at Brünn till November 28th, so that as Napoleon was to be given a month in which to give his answer, Prussia's intervention could not have taken place till practically two months after the Treaty of Potsdam. This need not be ascribed to treachery on Frederick William's part. He could hardly be expected to act with promptitude and decision even when the fate of Europe depended on his action.

Meanwhile the decisive battle had been fought. The heavy responsibility for fighting at Austerlitz must be laid at Alexander's door. The strategic situation made a premature decision the height of folly, for an English force under Lord Cathcart was landing in Hanover and was about to join hands with the Swedes from Pomerania and a Russian corps, another Anglo-Russian expedition was preparing a great diversion in Italy, Bennigsen's Russians were only a few marches away, and Napoleon could hardly have forced on the battle he so sorely needed if the Allies had adopted Fabian tactics. But the Czar was blind to all this. Supremely confident in Russian invincibility, anxious to prove that Napoleon's successes were due to his never having encountered Russia's bayonets, Alexander listened to the advice of his aide-de-camp, Peter Dolgorucki and of a few other hot-headed young men, and rejecting the sounder but less attractive proposals of the cautious Kutusov, determined to fight. He failed to see that any mishap to the Coalition would be sure to exercise an enormous influence over the

[1] Cf. Maxwell's *Wellington*, i. 75.

vacillating hesitation and cautious self-seeking of Prussia. Moreover, Francis II was almost as anxious for battle as Alexander, though Schwarzenberg was against fighting. An effort was made to induce Napoleon to come to terms, but he asked too much, and the only result of the negotiations was to inflame Dolgorucki's zeal for battle by convincing him that Napoleon desired to avoid it.

On November 27th the Allies began their move on Brünn, driving in the French outposts from Wischau (28th), and coming up to Austerlitz by the evening of December 1st. Napoleon had made great efforts to concentrate all available troops, and was able to put nearly 70,000 men into the field against 80,000 Allies. His position behind the little Goldbach was at right angles to the high road from Brünn to Austerlitz on which his left rested. His right was covered by the marshy lakes of Mennitz and Satschan, and found a source of strength in the villages of Sokelnitz and Tellnitz. It was against this flank that the Allies intended to direct their attack, hoping to drive in Napoleon's right, and so sever his communications with Vienna. Kienmayer's Austrians were to lead the way with three Russian corps in support, some 35,000 men in all being detailed for this move. In the centre stood the plateau and village of Pratzen. Here under Kutusov's own direction Kollowrat's Russians and a few Austrians formed a weak connecting link with Lichtenstein's cavalry, 18 Austrian and 30 Russian squadrons, Bagration's Russian corps and the Russian Imperial Guard, who formed the Allied right. Napoleon had realised the Allied plan when he saw their masses concentrating on their left. Entrusting to Davoût the task of holding the turning movement in check, opposing Murat and Lannes to Bagration and Lichtenstein, he launched Soult with Oudinot in support against the Southern part of the heights of Pratzen, Bernadotte moving forward on his left against Brasowitz. Just as Kutusov at the express orders of the Czar was moving to the support of the turning movement, Soult delivered his attack. Kutusov promptly formed his men to their front to contest the possession of the Pratzen plateau, and a division of Bernadotte's corps had to come to the help of Soult. There was heavy fighting for a couple of hours, a great cavalry contest between the cavalry of the Russian Guard and those of Napoleon's Guard under Rapp and Bessières, which ended in the success of the French, frequent efforts on the part of the Russians to recover the plateau, determined opposition on the part of Soult and Bernadotte. At last success turned definitely to the French, the Russian centre was pierced, and the victorious French, turning to their right, fell in full force on the flank of the Allied left which had been unable to crush Davoût or do more than thrust him back. Caught between Davoût in their front and Soult on their flank, the Russians were driven in upon the Littawa, a stream which runs into the Goldbach below Tellnitz at an acute angle. A few got away across the bridge of Anjesd before it broke, some escaped by the strip of land between the two lakes of Mennitz and Satschan, some over the ice, but the slaughter was tremendous. The ice broke in many places ; and though a few battalions sacrificed themselves to save the rest, the columns engaged in the turning movement were practically annihilated.

On the right the fight had been fairly even, inclining in favour of the French, for Lannes' infantry had beaten back the repeated charges of the Russian and Austrian horse; but there the Allies drew off in good order. Their losses had been enormous : 30,000 men and nearly 200 guns is probably no exaggerated figure. Their army, completely disorganised and demoralised by so overwhelming a disaster, withdrew in a South-Easterly direction, as though making for Hungary; but Austerlitz had banished all ideas of further resistance from the mind of Francis II. His willingness to treat for peace was perhaps a little premature. Had Prussia not entrusted her ultimatum to a man to whom the news of Austerlitz cannot have been exactly distasteful, had she intervened even at the eleventh hour, when the army of Archduke Charles was still intact and there was an excellent chance of raising North Germany round the nucleus formed by Cathcart's corps, even Austerlitz need not have been decisive. But Francis had had enough. Resolution was not his most salient characteristic, nor was he the man to make great sacrifices for an idea. He acquiesced in his defeat, and was ready to make peace on bad terms lest a prolongation of the struggle should bring even sterner conditions. On December 6th an armistice was signed between Napoleon and Francis, a contribution of 100,000,000 francs being imposed on the Hapsburg dominions, and the Russian army promptly departing for its own territories.

This meant the collapse of the Coalition. Austria's defection

absolved Prussia from the obligations of November 3rd, while
Haugwitz hastened to explain away the ultimatum, to congratulate Napoleon on his victory, and to sign, almost at a
moment's notice, the Treaty of Schönbrunn, which placed
Prussia at Napoleon's disposal (Dec. 15th). This abdication of
the mediatory position she had assumed obtained for Prussia
the coveted Hanover. In return she ceded Anspach to Bavaria,
Neufchatel and Wesel to France, and Cleves to an unnamed
Prince of the Empire. If she had made a treaty with France
on these terms in July, her policy might have been open to
criticism, but there would be less occasion to condemn her
conduct. But to receive as a gift from the man against whom she
had been fulminating a province belonging to a friendly Power
from whom she was actually demanding subsidies that she
might avenge—among other things—the wrongs committed by
that same man in seizing this very province, such an action
could not but destroy any shreds of reputation which yet
lingered round the Prussian name. The possession of Hanover
gave compactness to her territories in North Germany, it had
been one of her principal desires for many years, but it was
destined to prove a gain as temporary as it was discreditable.
Haugwitz has a heavy burden of responsibility to bear. His
slowness in travelling to the Danube, his utter incapacity to deal
with Napoleon, his failure to even present his ultimatum,
played into Napoleon's hands and contributed very largely to
the humiliating situation in which Prussia found herself.

Meanwhile the Treaty of Schönbrunn had deprived the
Austrian diplomatists, who were striving hard to obtain good
terms from the conqueror, of their last ray of hope. On
December 26th, Austria signed the Peace of Pressburg, by which
she had to accept and acknowledge the constitutional and
territorial changes made by Napoleon since the Peace of
Lunéville, and to purchase peace by great cessions of territory.
To the Kingdom of Italy she had to cede Venetia, Istria and
Dalmatia. Baden and Würtemberg divided between them the
Breisgau and the other Austrian possessions in Swabia. Brixen,
Trent and the other gains of 1803 went now to Bavaria, and
the bitterest blow of all was to be compelled to abandon
Tyrol and its gallant mountaineers to the tender mercies of
Maximilian Joseph. After this an indemnity of 40 million
gulden was a minor aggravation.

Austria did obtain a little territory in return, Berchtesgaden and the Archbishopric of Salzburg, the Elector being compensated with Würzburg, which Bavaria resigned. However, her Imperial position in Germany received a *coup de grâce* in the celebrated fourteenth article of the Peace, which not only mediatised these Imperial Knights whose dominions were situated in the territories of Baden, Bavaria and Würtemberg, but declared that these three Powers should enjoy complete and undivided sovereignty over their states. This formal recognition of their practical independence was completed by the elevation of the Electors of Bavaria and Würtemberg to the rank of Kings, of the Elector of Baden and the Landgrave of Hesse-Darmstadt to that of Grand Dukes. The policy Rewbell had enunciated in 1797, when he declared " il faut reléguer l'Empereur dans ses états héréditaires et la dépouiller de tout la reste,"[1] seemed to have been carried to a successful conclusion. Indeed, Napoleon might justly claim to have realised the object of Richelieu and of Mazarin, to have effected what neither Francis I nor Louis XIV had been able to accomplish, the humiliation of the House of Hapsburg. Whether in imposing such harsh terms on Austria Napoleon was not a little short-sighted may well be doubted. Austria, annoyed with Russian dilatoriness, angry with England's failure to lend more effective help, furious above all with Prussia's vacillation, might have been won over to Napoleon in 1805, and bound to him by a less galling chain than the alliance of 1811. Talleyrand, indeed, urged upon Napoleon the wisdom of a return to Choiseul's Franco-Austrian alliance, suggesting that by compensating Austria with the Danubian principalities, France might alienate her so completely from Russia that she would be bound to the French alliance.[2] Napoleon's rejection of this suggestion was probably due to his wish to induce Russia and Prussia to accede to the " Continental System," by which he hoped to cripple England completely by excluding her commerce from Europe. If he gave the Danubian principalities to Austria, he would create an insuperable breach between France and Russia. Hence he adopted a policy towards Austria which allowed her in 1809 to identify herself with the cause of German national resistance to his tyranny, which did much to unite the different

[1] Cf. Bailleu, *Preussen und Frankreich.*
[2] Cf. Haüsser, ii. 653, and Rose, ii. 47-48.

races which owned the Hapsburg rule by the bond of common sufferings, which probably went far to decide Austria's course at the crisis of the great struggle in 1813. Had Napoleon wanted to base his power over Europe on a sure foundation, he might have compensated Austria for her loss of influence in South-West Germany by undoing the work of 1741. A Franco-Austrian alliance founded on the restoration of Silesia to Austria need not have alienated Russia, and one may judge by 1806 of the scanty chance of success with which the successors of Frederick II would have resisted a revival of the alliance of fifty years earlier.

CHAPTER XXVI

THE CONFEDERATION OF THE RHINE AND THE OVERTHROW OF PRUSSIA

AUSTERLITZ had in all but in name destroyed the Holy Roman Empire; but as Napoleon had once said, "it was necessary to create something in its place," and it was on this task that he was occupied during the earlier part of the year 1806. That some reconstruction was impending was notorious. It was impossible for a constitution to continue in which the Diet stood mute while some of the Electors made war upon the Emperor. Projects for reform were put forward on all sides, and the wildest rumours were current throughout Germany. That that reconstruction would come from Paris was certain, and all eyes were directed thither. The French troops were still in occupation of Southern Germany; and even if the principal states had not already pledged themselves to Napoleon, his *fiat* could not have been resisted. Moreover, he was beginning that dynastic policy which, on the one hand, erected new principalities for his relations or imposed them on the thrones of older houses, and, on the other, bound the old dynasties to his by marriages. Thus, while a new Duchy was erected on the Rhine for Murat out of Berg (March), which Bavaria gave up, Eugene Beauharnais was married to the daughter of the King of Bavaria, and the Electoral Prince of Baden, to whom she had been betrothed, had to accept in her stead Eugene's cousin Stephanie.

Meanwhile the old game was being played at Paris. Intrigue and bribery were rife once more, only that "mediatisation" had replaced "compensation" as the convenient formula under which the plunder of the weaker by the stronger was being disguised. Scheme after scheme was drafted and placed before Napoleon before he could be satisfied. At last, early in July a plan was adopted, though its publication had to be deferred until the steps necessary to secure the military hold of France on Southern

Germany had been taken. On July 17th the treaty establishing a Confederation of the Rhine was laid before the envoys of the various German states then at Paris. It provided for the union of some sixteen states in a Confederation, under the protection of the Emperor of the French and quite independent of the Holy Roman Empire. The various members were to retain full sovereignty and independence in domestic affairs, while a Diet sitting at Frankfurt was to regulate their foreign affairs, to settle quarrels between members, and discuss matters of common interest. This Diet was to consist of two Colleges, that of Kings, which was to include the Arch Chancellor, the Kings of Bavaria and Würtemberg, and the Grand Dukes of Baden, Berg and Hesse-Darmstadt; and that of Princes, composed of the ten other members of the Confederation, the Princes of Nassau-Usingen, Nassau-Weilburg, Hohenzollern-Hechingen, Hohenzollern-Sigmaringen, Lichtenstein, Salm-Salm, Salm-Kyrburg, Isenburg, the Duke of Aremberg, and the Count de la Leyen. When the two Colleges sat together, the Arch Chancellor, henceforward to be called Prince Primate, was to preside. The dependence of the Confederation on Napoleon was secured by a proviso that the nomination of a successor to the Prince Primate should be entrusted to the Emperor. One article bound the members not to take service except in the Confederation or with its allies, another established a close alliance between the French Empire and the Confederation, which was pledged to take part in every war in which France chose to engage; while yet another fixed the contingents to be supplied by the members.[1] The Confederation was not much more than a military and political union, since the Diet was not empowered to interfere with the domestic affairs of the members, could not legislate, and was not really more than " a political congress in which equals with common interests discuss those interests amicably and agree upon measures for the common utility."[2]

The majority of the articles of the constituting document dealt with a matter of the very greatest interest to the German Princes, the territorial question. Briefly, an enormous simplification was to be effected in the map of Germany by the mediatisation of all the petty states which had the misfortune to find their

---

[1] France was to provide 200,000, Bavaria 30,000, Würtemberg 12,000, Baden 8000, Berg 5000, Darmstadt 4000, the College of Princes 4000.

[2] Cf. Fisher, p. 165.

32

territories enclosed in the dominions of their larger neighbours. At one stroke the four benches of Counts, the Grand Masters of the Maltese and Teutonic Orders, many princely families which had collective votes, and at least eight which held individual votes, among them Lobkowitz, Thurn und Taxis, Orange-Fulda and Dietrichstein, in all some sixty-seven immediate *Herr-schaften*, were reduced to the rank of subjects. With them the Imperial Knights lost their independent sovereignty, though all the Princes thus mediatised retained their patrimonial property and all non-sovereign rights, while in the matter of taxation they were to be placed on the same footing as members of reigning houses. The magnitude of the change can be best appreciated from the fact that the suppressed states amounted to over 12,000 square miles, and contained 1,200,000 inhabitants. It was a highly necessary change had it only been brought about in a different way. The statelets which thus disappeared were obstacles to good government and to material prosperity. They were the scenes of extravagant efforts to vie with larger Courts; their independent existence had made Germany a complex, involved tangle, in which national life was impossible; and if Napoleon was aiming at his own advantage in thus destroying the forms of a constitution which had kept Germany weak and disunited, if his work of destruction was only unintentionally the necessary preliminary to Bismarck's work of construction, and was only accidentally the means of his own undoing, he had at least cleared away the obsolete débris of the old organisation which had hitherto prevented the growth of a new and vigorous institution.

The members of the new Confederation did not all receive it with enthusiasm; even Dalberg, who had gone further than any man in his desire to see Napoleon's authority over Germany formally established, at first declared that he had not meant to abolish the Germanic Constitution;[1] but his qualms of conscience were shortlived. The ratifications were speedily exchanged, and on August 1st four Electors and twelve Princes announced to the Diet at Ratisbon that they had ceased to belong to the Holy Roman Empire. Had Stadion, now Foreign Minister of Austria in Cobenzl's place, had his way, there would have been no Holy Roman Empire for them to desert. He had urged Francis to abandon the title of his own initiative before he was

[1] Cf. Fisher, p. 121.

forced to do so. But Francis had been slow to act, and it was not till August 6th that his proclamation renouncing his title of Holy Roman Emperor elect, and formally declaring the links between himself and the Empire dissolved, brought to an end even the nominal existence of the great institution which Charlemagne had founded.[1]

This action on the part of Francis II amounted to a tacit acknowledgment of Napoleon's new creation. Austria would accept the accomplished fact : after all, her strength had not depended on her connection with the Empire, she was following a policy very much like that Pufendorf had suggested for her.[2] And where Austria acquiesced, it was hardly to be expected that the Power which had concluded the Treaty of Schönbrunn and had accepted its subsequent developments, would do otherwise.

Haugwitz's action in signing the Treaty of Schönbrunn had provoked an indignant outcry at Berlin, especially in the more bellicose circles. The Council of State, however, was not prepared to go to the length of disowning him even though it disliked the terms and wanted to get them modified. The Prussian Ministers wanted to get Hanover, but without committing themselves to hostility to George III. They still clung to the notion that they might mediate a peace between England and Napoleon, and obtain the coveted Electorate as the reward for their good offices. Thus, true to the Prussian tradition of sitting on the fence, they neither accepted nor rejected the treaty. They proposed to take Hanover and hold it on deposit until a general peace should settle all questions at issue in Europe; and accordingly on the departure (Feb.) of Cathcart's expeditionary force, Prussian troops at once reoccupied the Electorate without waiting for Napoleon to signify his assent. But it was a dangerous game to play with Napoleon. His answer was to occupy Anspach and Baireuth, and to point out to the Prussian envoy that as the treaty had not been ratified, Prussia was at war with France. This argument was the more cogent because in a fit of ill-advised economy Prussia had already begun to demobilise her troops. Meanwhile the Emperor, though offering Hanover to Prussia, was also intending to use it

---

[1] For the Confederation of the Rhine, cf. Haüsser, ii. pp. 691 ff. ; Zwiedineck-Südenhorst, *Deutsche Geschichte*, 1806–1871, vol. i. pp. 9–12 ; also Fisher, ch. v.

[2] Cf. p. 8.

in the negotiations with the Whig Ministry which had just come into power in England through Pitt's death (Jan. 23rd, 1806). Prussia thus found herself compelled by a threat of immediate war to sign a treaty pledging her to unqualified hostility against England.[1] This treaty, signed by the unfortunate Haugwitz on February 15th and ratified on March 3rd, gave Prussia Hanover, but at the price of barring the Elbe and Weser to British ships, of giving up Anspach to Bavaria without receiving any compensation and of consenting to the expulsion of the Bourbons from Naples. The extent of Prussia's submissiveness may be judged from the fact that French officers accompanied the Prussians to Hanover to see that the exclusion of the English was complete, that Hardenberg was practically dismissed, under the form of unlimited leave of absence, Haugwitz replacing him in charge of foreign affairs, and that Prussia was promptly involved in war with England, who replied to the exclusion of her goods by blockading the mouths of the Elbe and Weser (April 5th), seizing over 300 Prussian merchantmen, and declaring war on Prussia (April 20th). Napoleon had certainly been successful in sowing dissension between England and Prussia; for, as Fox's letter of April 16th to Talleyrand[2] shows, the action of Prussia in the matter was far more bitterly resented in England than was the part played by France; it was only to be expected that France—an open and avowed enemy—should seek to injure England by all the means in her power. Prussia, on the other hand, was at peace with England, and her conduct was "viewed with pain and disgust."

But if Prussia found herself in the somewhat humiliating position of one of the client states of the French Empire, this was little more than was to be expected from the thoroughly unsatisfactory condition of the country. The King, well-meaning but weak, a mediocrity himself and content with mediocrity in those around him, has been well described as "the most respectable but the most ordinary man that has reigned over Prussia."[3] He was quite incapable of carrying out the reforms that were so urgently needed by Prussia, and Lombard, Haugwitz and even Hardenberg all failed to rouse him to a more vigorous policy. The most capable man among the Prussian ministers

[1] Cf. Seeley, i. 239.
[2] Cf. Coquelle, *England and Napoleon*, p. 89.　　　　[3] Seeley, i. 195.

was undoubtedly the Freiherr von Stein, an Imperial Knight who had entered the Prussian service in 1780, had done well in various administrative posts, notably in charge of the Prussian acquisitions in Westphalia, which had been entrusted to him in September 1802, while in 1804 he had been called to the Ministry of Manufactures and Commerce. Yet not even Stein could do much under the circumstances which prevailed. The chief object of his attacks was the so-called Cabinet, a body composed not of the heads of the various departments, but of the King's personal advisers, who without responsibility or practical connection with the details of administration really decided on the policy of the country.[1] Thus the ministers who carried out the details of the policy had little share in forming it, and the Cabinet intervened between them and the King. The system had grown up under Frederick William II, the Cabinet, originally established by his grandfather as a committee for foreign affairs,[2] superseding the old Ministry of State.

But this was not all. Society was in an unhealthy condition; it had grown wealthy and luxurious, and with increased luxury it had lost the martial and Spartan tone given it by Frederick II. The Court was frivolous and foolish. An overbearing military set, domineering and bumptious, was living on the reputation of past victories it had not helped to win. It was this party which called insistently for war. Its better elements were summed up in the gallant but erratic Prince Louis Ferdinand, whose lack of self-restraint and steadiness impaired the example of his high courage and enthusiasm. Typical of its baser elements were the arrogant young nobles who boastfully sharpened their swords on the steps of the French Embassy before marching out to Jena.

The Prussian army, in which the whole country reposed a confidence as profound as it was soon to be proved baseless, was still in all essentials the army of Frederick II. It had failed to keep pace with recent changes. A fine army on the parade-ground, in the field it represented an obsolete tradition. When Napoleon's system of requisitions was making war support war, it still depended in a fertile country on magazines at fixed points. It had no co-ordinated divisions of all three arms. Its officers

---

[1] Cf. Seeley, i. pp. 267 ff.

[2] Hence the name " Cabinet Minister " often applied to the Foreign Minister.

were for the most part ignorant of their profession, and the veterans of Frederick's school knew only how to obey. The rank and file were drawn from the lowest classes. Both conscript and long service at once, since the numerous exemptions made twenty years the term of service, the army rested neither on the sound moral basis of universal compulsion nor on the hardly less sound foundation of voluntary patriotic efforts. It was not even national, for its ranks included a very large proportion of foreigners. These and other defects had not escaped the notice of many observers. Gebhard von Scharnhorst, a Saxon by birth who had learnt the military art under the Count of Lippe-Buckeburg,[1] and had served with distinction in the Hanoverian army before joining that of Prussia in 1801, had made some effort to introduce reforms; but the infallibility of the Frederician tradition was still sacrosanct. Nor was it even numerically in a satisfactory state. Nominally nearly 240,000 strong,[2] of whom 186,000 should have formed the field army, it was not able at the critical moment to put more than 120,000 in the field, Silesia and the new acquisitions in Poland and Westphalia absorbing large forces which were not even mobilised. And for economy's sake in each company of infantry some twenty-six men were allowed to be absent on furlough, and their efficiency was more than doubtful. Yet with this army Hohenlohe and Brunswick cheerfully committed themselves to an offensive campaign against Napoleon and the Grand Army.

At the price of a quarrel with England, Prussia had obtained Hanover. She also found herself involved in a conflict with Sweden for Pomerania, which Napoleon was prepared to let her take if she would cede Mark to the new Grand Duchy of Berg. But Prussia was very far from feeling satisfied with her position; she could not but realise that she held these new possessions by the good pleasure of Napoleon. Had he failed to grasp the meaning of her action in 1805? Prussia could not tell whether his professions of friendship were sincere, and she looked with a distrustful and suspicious glance upon the formation of the Confederation of the Rhine. Napoleon cast out suggestions for the foundation of a North German Confederation with Prussia as head; he even hinted at an Imperial crown for the Hohenzollern. But, strangely enough, the other

---

[1] Cf. p. 371.

[2] 255 squadrons, 546 batteries, 174 field and 58 garrison battalions.

Powers of North Germany did not accept the idea with enthusiasm: it made them eye Prussia rather suspiciously, which was perhaps what Napoleon intended. But the truth would seem to be that the Emperor was not paying much heed to Prussia during the early months of 1806; the organisation of the Confederation of the Rhine and negotiations with England and Russia were more than sufficient to occupy his attention.[1] There are no grounds for supposing that his policy was deliberately designed to drive Prussia into war. For the moment it was the question of Naples and Sicily which was uppermost in his mind.[2] Stuart's brilliant success over Reynier at Maida (July 4th, 1806) had imperilled the stability of Joseph Bonaparte's new kingdom of Naples, and it was in the hopes of inducing the British to evacuate Sicily that Napoleon took the step which finally goaded the supine Frederick William to take up arms. Not the least important effect of the failure of the great expedition to the Weser on which Pitt had founded such high hopes, and which Austria's defeat and Prussia's submission had made vain and hopeless, was that it had served as a final blow to the most persistent of Napoleon's opponents. Pitt's death (Jan. 23rd, 1806) opened the way to office to the Whig politician whose partiality for France had outlived even the establishment of a military despotism on the ruins of Liberty, Fraternity and Equality, and in the negotiations which Fox had promptly (Feb. 20th) set on foot in the hopes of restoring peace, Napoleon found Hanover a very useful asset. On August 6th the King of Prussia received a letter from Lucchesini, his Ambassador at Paris, informing him that Napoleon had offered to restore Hanover to George III if the British would withdraw from Sicily and agree to the compensation of the Neapolitan Bourbons with the Balearic Islands.

Such an insult was more than even Frederick William could endure. Public opinion in Prussia found vent in the most violent expressions of feeling. There was a loud cry for the dismissal of Haugwitz, but Frederick William would not comply with it; and this unfortunate loyalty to the man who was identified with the Treaty of Schönbrunn prevented England and Russia from reposing full confidence in Prussia's desire for war, contributed very largely to keep Austria neutral, and was hardly calculated to inspire in the nation at large a strong belief

[1] Cf. Seeley, i. 244.   [2] Cf. Rose, ii. pp. 79 ff.

in the King's zeal for the cause. The Queen, Prince Louis Ferdinand, Generals Rüchel and Phull, Hardenberg, Stein and other leaders of the patriotic party did what they could to arouse national feeling, and Napoleon materially assisted to fan the flame of hostility to France by his execution of the Nüremberg bookseller Palm (Aug. 25th). A pamphlet, entitled, "Germany in her deep Humiliation," had been published at Vienna. It was a protest against the brutal conduct of the French army of occupation in the "allied" kingdom of Bavaria, where their exactions rivalled the days of the Thirty Years' War. Palm, who was proved to have sold copies of this publication, was arrested, carried off to Braunau, an Austrian town occupied by French troops, tried by court-martial and shot. This brutal act was intended to terrorise Germany. Its effect was quite the reverse. It excited violent indignation, and made Frederick William for the moment the spokesman of German national feeling, when he demanded that Napoleon should withdraw his armies behind the Rhine.

During this period negotiations had been going on between Napoleon and the Czar. In July, Napoleon had induced the Russian envoy Oubril to sign a treaty, but the Czar's refusal to ratify it had left the two Powers still at war. Hence in challenging Napoleon, Prussia could hope for Russian support; but no steps had been taken to concert a plan of common operations, and the fatuous strategy of the Prussians exposed them to a disaster even more complete than Mack's. Inferior in numbers though they were to the 190,000 men whom Napoleon rapidly concentrated in Northern Bavaria, the Prussians resolved to advance across Thuringia upon Mayence, thinking to fall on Napoleon's communications, and so force him to evacuate Southern Germany to recover the line of the Rhine. It is needless to point out how this exposed their own interior flank to a crushing blow which completely intercepted their retreat to Berlin.

This advance would have been justifiable in one event only, if all North Germany had risen on behalf of the cause. But North Germany did not rise. William VIII of Hesse-Cassel, Elector since 1803, viewed with alarm the aggrandisement of Napoleon, but nevertheless all efforts to induce him to join Prussia failed. However his conduct during the critical period was somewhat ambiguous, and his failure to demobilise his army or to exclude the Prussians from his nominally neutral territory brought down on him the wrath of Napoleon. Brunswick, of course, took part with Prussia, since its Duke was in command of the Prussian army; but a more important if less willing ally was found in Saxony. The Elector Augustus Frederick was a pacific but rather feeble Prince. Since 1796 he had maintained a consistent neutrality, fear of Prussia and dislike of France alternately ruling him. His action in joining Prussia in 1806 was to be ascribed more to the pressure put on him by the near presence of the Prussian army than to any keenness in the cause. He had to choose between joining Prussia and fighting her; and as at the moment no French were at hand to help him, he had no alternative but to join Prussia.

With the addition of the 20,000 men of whom the Saxon army consisted, Brunswick and his colleague Hohenlohe could dispose of about 140,000 troops. Concentrated behind the Elbe or even between the Saale and Elster near Jena and Gera, this force might have effected something; but the impatience of the army to show the victors of Marengo and Austerlitz that the successors of Frederick II were prepared to keep up the traditions of Rossbach had a good deal to do with the decision to advance beyond this good defensive position. Moreover, it was hoped by taking the offensive and covering the territories of Hesse-Cassel to induce the Elector to throw in his lot with Prussia. But Hohenlohe and Brunswick could not even agree on a plan. Brunswick, wishing to threaten Mayence, wanted to feint at Fulda with his extreme right, but to move his main body forward on Hildburghausen and Meiningen, Hohenlohe with his corps moving parallel on the left by Saalfeld. Hohenlohe would have preferred a move against the French centre and right, but his plan would have equally committed the Prussians to an advance with the army in two parts, separated by the Thuringian Forest. The net result was that October 4th found the Prussians scattered over a front of 85 miles, when news of Napoleon's advance forced them to suspend their westward move. Rüchel with 25 squadrons and 12 battalions was far forward on the way to the Rhine; Brunswick with the 90 squadrons and 60 battalions of the main army, 70,000 strong, was between Gotha and Erfurt; Hohenlohe's corps lay in the valley of the Upper Saale, its advance-guard at Saalfeld, the Saxons near Gera, the bulk of the corps on the left of the Ilm, near Hochdorf.

Against a force thus divided and leaders without a real plan, Napoleon was on the point of dealing a tremendous blow. He had his whole army so admirably concentrated on a front of 38 miles that the whole force could be collected at any point under 48 hours. Three roads led Northward from the points at which he had concentrated his army for an advance. Soult (IVth corps) and Ney (VIth), forming the right, took the road by Baireuth on Hof; Bernadotte (Ist), Davoût (IIIrd), the Guards and Murat's cavalry that in the centre on Saalburg by Bamberg and Kronach; on the left, Lannes (Vth) and Augereau (VIIth) moved through Coburg on Saalfeld. The rapidity and certainty of the French moves contrasted sharply with the somewhat aimless operations of the Prussians. Napoleon had seen the weak spot in their armour, and his blow at their communications brought them hurrying back to avoid being cut off from the Elbe. But Napoleon was much too quick for them. On October 9th, Murat and Bernadotte drove Tauentzien with Hohenlohe's vanguard out of Schleiz, Soult reached Hof, Lannes on the left getting to Grafenthal. On the 10th, Prince Louis Ferdinand, making a stand at Rudolstadt to cover Hohenlohe's return to the Saale, was defeated by Lannes. He himself fell in the action, but Hohenlohe managed to concentrate the Saxons, Tauentzien and his own main body near Jena. The bulk of Napoleon's army was now over the Thuringian Forest, the centre having pushed on as far as Auma, while on the right Soult had reached Plauen. Advancing to Gera next day and meeting with no opposition Napoleon realised that he had got between the Prussians and the Elbe : he therefore thrust his centre forward to Naumburg, which Davoût secured on the morning of the 12th, while he called in the right by the cross-road from Plauen to Gera. On the same day, the 12th, Lannes moved down the left bank of the Saale on Jena, where Hohenlohe was standing inactive and wasting precious time. Had he pushed forward against the French he might have caught them more or less dispersed, but he stood still with the idea of covering the main body under Brunswick, who were moving by Weimar on Auerstadt and Naumburg. This inactivity on his part continued next day. Not an effort did he make to dispute the all-important position of the Landgrafenberg, which Lannes secured and with it the passage of the Saale at Jena. Meanwhile Napoleon was concentrating the corps of Soult, Ney and Augereau at Jena, Davoût was moving forward from Naumburg to seize the defile of Kosen, Bernadotte was making for Dornberg to secure that passage and to connect up Napoleon with Davoût, who from being the centre had become the extreme right of the French. Brunswick also was moving on Kosen; but the division detailed to secure that point failed to achieve its purpose. Rüchel following in rear of Brunswick reached Weimar.

Thus the French on the East of the Saale threatened to interpose between the Prussians and their base, and were prepared to dispute any attempt by Brunswick to recover his line of communications. Had the Prussian commander known their situation, which he does not seem to have done, he might have retreated straight to Magdeburg and there crossed the Elbe; but such a move would have left Berlin and Dresden equally open to Napoleon's attacks.

Of the twin battles of October 14th, that of Jena was no disgrace to the Prussian army, for Hohenlohe's 50,000 men made a very gallant resistance to the 90,000 whom Napoleon brought against them. Their commander was not a little to blame for his failure to drive Lannes off the Landgrafenberg on the previous afternoon; for if, instead of having their leading corps already in position on the Eastern edge of the plateau which commands the passage of the Saale, the French had had to force their way up its steep slopes, the issue of the day might have been very different. But Hohenlohe, intending to retreat as soon as he had covered Brunswick's march from a flank attack, had remained inactive, and the French by great exertions had succeeded in bringing guns and reinforcements up the precipitous path from the valley below. Early on the 14th Lannes opened the battle by falling on Hohenlohe's vanguard at Closwitz. There was sharp fighting in the fog but by 10 a.m. Lannes had secured the line from Lutzeroda to Closwitz, and had gained sufficient room for the other corps to deploy into line as they came up on to the plateau. Soult's leading division had already pushed up the Rauthal, but was closely engaged with a Prussian detachment from Rödingen; while Augereau, taking the line of the Muhlthal and Schneckethal, was in action with the Saxons who formed Hohenlohe's right: Ney, following Lannes, thrust his leading division forward between those of Lannes, and the French front line now advanced against the Vierzehn Heiligen-Isserstadt position just as Hohenlohe delivered a counter-attack. This was about 11 a.m., and for a couple of hours the battle was evenly contested, till two more of Soult's divisions coming up advanced on the right of Gazan's division of Lannes and began to press back the Prussian left. At the same time another of Ney's divisions reinforced the centre, and the Guards moved forward against Vierzehn Heiligen. In vain Hohenlohe hurled his cavalry in fruitless charges against the advancing French; attacking without proper combination, making spasmodic and not united efforts, even their furious on-slaughts could not stem the advance, while the Prussian infantry, already shaken by the fire of the French artillery, gave way as the French advanced. It was at this moment that Rüchel's battalions came up from Weimar. The wisest course would have been to employ them to cover the retreat, but Hohenlohe, not content with this, made a counter-attack on Ney's leading division, a rash and ill-advised stroke which involved Rüchel in the general disaster. Beaten all along the line, Hohenlohe's army fell back in disorder on Weimar, pursued by Murat's cavalry, which had just arrived on the scene. Still though beaten the Prussians had fought well. The precision and accuracy of their manœuvres had excited the admiration of their enemy, even if their lines had smacked too much of the parade-ground and had proved no match for the heavy columns, preceded by dense clouds of skirmishers, in which the French attacked. Hohenlohe rather than his army had been principally at fault; his failure to fall on Lannes on the 13th had allowed the French to gain access to the Landgrafenberg on the 14th, the men had fought well against superior numbers, and but for the tame surrenders and the complete military collapse to which Jena was the prelude, the Prussian army would have no cause to be ashamed of their performance there.

Meanwhile a fight of a very different nature had been raging a few miles to the Northward. About 8 a.m. Brunswick's vanguard under Schmettau came into contact with Davoût's leading division near Hassenhausen. Brunswick hurried to the front to try to secure the hills on his right and to sweep Davoût from his path, while Blücher's cavalry assailed the French on the other wing. But Davoût's infantry stood firm, and beat off

AUSTERLITZ Dec 3rd 1805.

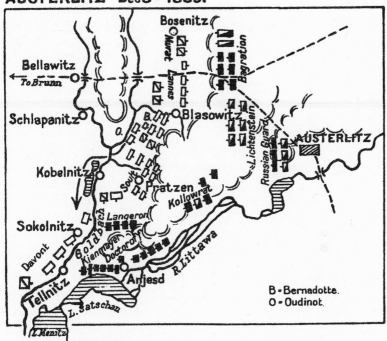

Bosenitz

Murat

Lannes

Bagration

Bellawitz

To Brunn

Schlapanitz

O.

B.

Blasowitz

AUSTERLITZ

Lichtenstein

Russian Guard

Kobelnitz

Soult

Pratzen

Kollowrat

Sokolnitz

Langeron

Goldbach

Kienmayer

Doctoroff

Davont

R. Littawa

Anjesd

Tellnitz

L. Satschan

L. Menitz

B - Bernadotte.
O - Oudinot.

JENA. Oct. 14th 1806

Rödingen.

Soult

Rautks

Vierzehn
Heiligen

Lützerode

Closwitz

Ney

Lannes

Landgrafen Berg

Isserstadt

Gospoda

Guard

Rüchel's
arrival

Augereau

Schuecke
Thal

Mühl Thal

JENA

Saale R.

II Position of Prussians

Saxons

ENGLISH MILES

0   1   2

B.V. Darbishire, Oxford, 1905.

all Blücher's attacks. Brunswick brought up reinforcements to renew the effort, but fell mortally wounded; and his fall spread confusion through the Prussian ranks. This gave time for the second division of Davoût's corps, that of Friant, to come up and to take up its position on the right of its hard-pressed comrades of Gudin's division. Again and again the Prussians attacked, but their superior numbers failed to shake Davoût. There was a want of co-ordination about the Prussian efforts, since there was no commander-in-chief; and when about noon, when Morand brought up the third division and began to extend to the Southward of Hassenhausen, Davoût actually ventured a counter-attack, though altogether he had only 27,000 to at least 40,000 Prussians. Outflanked by the cavalry of Vialannes, the Prussian left fell back in confusion; and the right followed its example, though in much better order, both taking the road to Weimar, a direction which before long brought them into contact with the fugitives of Hohenlohe's army fleeing from Murat. On that Brunswick's corps also went to pieces. All cohesion was lost, and the energetic pursuit of the French cavalry completed what the battle had begun. Möllendorf with 10,000 men surrendered at Weimar on the 15th; 16,000 under Kalkreuth laid down their arms at Erfurt next day. Eugene of Würtemberg, standing at bay at Halle to let the rest of the army cross the Elbe, was cut to pieces by Bernadotte (Oct 17th). And while the relics of the Prussian armies were being thrust North and West in utter demoralisation, making for Magdeburg, Napoleon had secured a shorter route to the Prussian capital, and Davoût's corps had secured the passage of the Elbe at Wittenberg and was marching upon Berlin with all speed (Oct. 20th).

But Jena and Auerstadt were as nothing to the disgraces which were in store for the Prussian army. Fortress after fortress, well supplied, strongly garrisoned and capable of a good defence, surrendered tamely on the first summons without firing a shot. Had strong places like Spandau, Cüstrin and Magdeburg made as good a defence as did Blücher at Lübeck, to which distant spot the old veteran managed to draw two French corps in pursuit of the 20,000 men he had rallied, the French might have been detained till the Russians could reach the Oder. Their feeble surrender is almost without a parallel in history.

Hohenlohe had by October 20th collected about 45,000 men

at Magdeburg, but they were completely demoralised. The administration had broken down, the men were without pay and without food, their organisation and discipline had gone to pieces. Accordingly the news that Soult, Ney, Bernadotte and Murat were within a day's march of Magdeburg drove Hohenlohe from the town. Leaving over 20,000 men behind him, he started for Stettin through Rathenow and Ruppin; but before he could reach the Oder he was headed off by Murat and Lannes, who on October 28th barred his path at Prenzlau, not 30 miles from Stettin. With 10,000 dispirited and broken men he surrendered. Spandau (Oct 25th) had already opened its gates; Davoût occupied Berlin on the 25th, Napoleon arriving there next day; Stettin surrendered upon a mere summons by Lasalle's light cavalry on the 29th; and though Blücher, who was following Hohenlohe with 20,000 men, managed to make his way to Lübeck, he was forced to lay down his arms to Soult and Bernadotte on November 7th. A day later Magdeburg, a fortress which should have been capable of a longer defence, capitulated to Ney. For once in a way a bulletin of Napoleon's was in prosaic agreement with the facts when on November 12th he announced " the whole of the Prussian monarchy is in my power." But for the garrisons in Silesia, Eastern Pomerania and the Polish provinces, the famous Prussian army had been swept out of existence, while Prussia's one ally in Northern Germany had been detached from her cause by Napoleon's adroit courtesy to his Saxon prisoners. Well aware of the dilemma with which the Prussian ultimatum had confronted Frederick Augustus, Napoleon saw that in the Court of Dresden he might find a useful ally. On October 21st he announced that there would be no more hostilities against the Saxons; and though the Electorate and the Saxon Duchies were taken in charge by French officials and remained in French occupation till the end of the war, being subjected to the payment of an indemnity of 25 million francs and to equally heavy contributions in kind, Napoleon had little difficulty in separating Saxony from Prussia and securing her adherence to the Confederation of the Rhine. This body had already (Sept.) been enlarged by the adhesion of the Elector of Würzburg; it now had not only the Elector of Saxony added to its numbers with the title of King (Dec. 11th), but the five Dukes of the Ernestine line followed his example (Dec. 15th). Contingents amounting in all to over 25,000 [1] were thus placed at Napoleon's disposal, while the deposition of the Elector of Hesse (Nov. 4th), of the House of Brunswick—the old Duke died of his wounds shortly after Auerstadt and was succeeded by his son Frederick William, who fell at Quatre Bras nine years later—and of William Frederick of Orange, who thus lost the Principality of Fulda-Corvey he had received in 1803, placed much territory in North-Western Germany at Napoleon's disposal.

From the point of view of German history the subsequent events of the campaign of 1806–1807 are of less importance than the effects of the collapse of Jena, Auerstadt, Prenzlau and Magdeburg on the government of Prussia. A Prussian corps played an honourable part in a campaign fought out in territory German by rule if Polish by geography, but its part was little more than that of the auxiliary of the Russians; and when the defeat of Friedland decided the Czar to come to terms with Napoleon, Prussia had to acquiesce in the terms which her Eastern neighbour was prepared to accept for her. The first effect of the defeats was a change in the Prussian ministry. Haugwitz retired to ponder at leisure on the fruits of the Treaty of Schönbrunn. His post as Foreign Minister was offered to Stein (Nov. 29th), with which an intricate negotiation began. Stein and his friends sought to use the opportunity to induce the King to abandon his Cabinet [2] in favour of a Council composed of the responsible Ministers. The King went so far in the direction of compliance that he agreed to appoint Rüchel War Minister, von Zastrow Foreign Minister, and Stein Finance Minister; but he desired to retain Beyme as Secretary of this new Cabinet Council, and on this rock the negotiations foundered. Stein would not tolerate Beyme; the King refused to dispense with him. Finally, on January 3rd Stein was dismissed. On his refusal to take office, von Zastrow, Voss and Schrötter formed a ministry, Beyme acting as Secretary and Hardenberg attending its meetings. Mainly through the influence of the Czar, who preferred Hardenberg to Zastrow, the former became First Cabinet Minister in April 1807, while in addition to the control over foreign affairs, domestic affairs were also entrusted to his charge, so that he was practically Premier. [3]

---

[1] Würzburg 2000, King of Saxony 20,000, Saxon Dukes 3300.   [2] Cf. p. 501.
[3] Cf. Seeley, i. 291, 339, etc. ; also Zwiedineck-Südenhorst, i. p. 59.

The substitution for Haugwitz of members of the party which favoured opposition to Napoleon had done something to restore public confidence, which was also encouraged by the rejection of Napoleon's offer of an armistice. It would have bound Prussia but not him, and the terms which he offered Prussia were too humiliating. Frederick William, therefore, rather than purchase peace at the price of surrendering his provinces West of the Elbe and joining Napoleon in a close alliance against Russia, resolved to continue the struggle as best he might, with the resources of his Eastern provinces and relying on Russian support.

CHAPTER XXVII

FRIEDLAND, TILSIT AND ERFURT

THE utter failure of the Prussian fortresses to detain 'the French after Jena made it quite impossible for Frederick William to attempt to maintain the line of the Oder. With barely 20,000 men, all whom Kalckreuth and Lestocq had managed to collect from the Eastern provinces, he fell back across Poland towards his Russian allies; and Napoleon, pushing Eastward with the bulk of the Grand Army, found himself on the Vistula before the end of November. On the 30th, Murat secured Warsaw, the Russians under Bennigsen retiring up the Narew, while Lestocq's Prussians on the right evacuated Thorn, which Ney occupied. The first half of December saw the French establish themselves on the Vistula, one corps under Jerome moving up the Oder into Silesia to reduce that province, another under Mortier remaining in Mecklenburg and Pomerania to secure the coast fortresses. During this period reinforcements joined Bennigsen and emboldened him to advance from Ostrolenka to Pultusk, pushing Lestocq forward to regain Thorn. Napoleon determined to fall upon him, and about December 20th he set his army in motion. On the right Davoût and Lannes advanced against Bennigsen's position at the confluence of the Narew and Bug; in the centre Soult and Augereau, with Bernadotte in support, moved on Buxhowden's corps, which was along the Ukra; on the left Ney tackled Lestocq. Between December 22nd and 26th there was some heavy fighting. Napoleon's effort to surround the enemy resulted in his thrusting out his wings too far apart; and when Lannes tried to intercept at Pultusk the retreat of the Russian centre from Golymin (Dec. 26th), Bennigsen thrust him aside, and Galitzin, though roughly handled by Davoût and Augereau at Golymin, managed to get away. With the retreat of the Russians towards the Niemen, operations came to a standstill. The Grand Army wanted rest, and the state of the country was such as to make operations impracticable. The Polish mud had baffled Napoleon's well-laid plans.

About a month later, operations were resumed. Bennigsen made an advance against the corps on the French left which were covering the siege of Dantzic. This was being carried on by Lefebvre with the contingents of the Confederation and the Poles, who had flocked to Napoleon's standard in the hopes that he would undo the work of 1772 and 1795. One of the covering corps, Ney's, had just anticipated the Russian advance by a dash at Königsberg. However, Lestocq had repulsed it at Bartenstein (Jan. 20th to 23rd), and if Bennigsen had moved with greater speed Ney might have been cut off. As it was, the Russian advance miscarried. Bernadotte checked it in front along the Passarge, while Napoleon swung up his centre and right to the help of the left. The French corps were posted from Ostrolenka on the Narew by Neidenberg to Osterode, and their Northward movement threatened Bennigsen's interior flank. Only by a prompt retreat could he save his communications from being severed. Murat, pressing forward, managed to bring the Russian rearguard to action at Hof on February 6th, upon which Bennigsen turned to bay at Eylau. Two days of desperate and even fighting and terrible slaughter ended with the arrival of Lestocq's Prussians just in time to paralyse Davoût's turning movement against the Russian left, whereby the unmolested retreat of the Russians to Königsberg was secured. Napoleon, left in possession of the field, had to content himself with making the most he could on paper out of this Pyrrhic victory. His position was none too satisfactory. The numbers of the Grand Army had been reduced by nearly a half by losses in battle and by disease. Its discipline had become relaxed; the difficulties of making war support war in a country as poor, as thinly peopled, and as roadless as Poland were enormous and taxed to the utmost the powers of the Emperor. He had to put forth all his great powers of organisation to restore the Grand Army to an efficient condition, to collect adequate reserves and make ready for a fresh advance; and meanwhile he had to continue the sieges of Dantzic, of Colberg, so bravely defended by Gneisenau, and of the Silesian fortresses.

This juncture was Austria's opportunity. If Francis II had thrown his sword into the scale in April 1807, his intervention might have been decisive. But even in 1809 Austria was hardly ready, and in 1807 the reforms of Archduke Charles had had no time to bear fruit, so that his voice was strong for the maintenance of peace, while even Stadion shrank from the prospect of war. What had alarmed Austria and threatened to rally her to the Allies was Napoleon's encouragement of the aspirations of the Poles; but Napoleon hastened to assure Francis that he would do nothing to cause trouble in Austrian Poland, and with this assurance Francis was unwisely content.

Thus during the critical spring months of 1807, Austria adhered to the same line of action which had ruined Prussia in 1805. There was another Power whose conduct was scarcely less short-sighted. England did indeed join the alliance which Russia and Prussia reaffirmed at Bartenstein (April 26th), but too late (June 27th) to make her share in the league of any practical value. When 40,000 or even 25,000 men flung ashore in Hanover or Pomerania in rear of the Grand Army might have been of the greatest service, for Hesse and Hanover were ripe for revolt,[1] and Stralsund in Swedish Pomerania would have formed an effective base for an attack on Mortier's corps, the "Ministry of All the Talents" had confined itself to empty promises of aid. Much might have been done to succour Dantzic and Colberg and enable them to prolong their defence, but no effective steps were taken. With the advent of the Portland Ministry to power (April), Canning assumed charge of the Foreign Office, Castlereagh of the administration of the Army, and a better era seemed to have dawned; but before this more vigorous ministry could give effect to its policy of sending active help to our allies, the Third Coalition had received its death-blow.

Bennigsen would have been well advised had he adhered to his original plan of campaign for 1807 and stood on the defensive behind the Pregel until reinforcements could join him from the interior of Russia, until England and Sweden might make an effective diversion in Pomerania, or Austria be induced to join the Allies. But Bennigsen was a strange mixture of vigour and indecision. He was tempted by the exposed position of Ney's corps at Gutstadt on the Alle to try again the stroke that had failed in January. But it was really too late. Neisse had fallen, and of all the Silesian fortresses only Kosel and Glatz were

[1] *Castlereagh Correspondence*, vi. pp. 169, 211, etc.

holding out. Dantzic's brave defence had come to an end on May 26th, which had set the French left free to advance. Nevertheless, Bennigsen took the offensive. Ney retired before him; higher up the Passarge, Soult and Bernadotte held their ground, and the Emperor set all his forces in motion to utilise the chance Bennigsen's rash move had given him, Hastily the Russian general fell back along the right bank of the Alle, the French pushing forward along the opposite bank in hopes of cutting off his retreat to Königsberg. At Heilsberg (June 10th), Soult and Murat brought him to action; but so savage a stand did the Russians make that only the arrival of Lannes prevented the battle from ending in a French defeat. From Heilsberg, Bennigsen continued his march along the right bank of the Alle, which here makes a great bend to the East and North, so that the French, moving across the chord while he followed the arc, were able to outstrip him. On the 13th he crossed to the left bank only to find his way barred by the corps of Lannes. Friedland was a battle Bennigsen should never have fought. It would have been wiser to have fallen back behind the Pregel and united there with Lestocq's corps, which had been moving parallel with the Russians but nearer the sea. Better even to have abandoned Königsberg than to have given Napoleon the opportunity to dictate terms at Tilsit as the result of his victory at Friedland. For Friedland removed from Alexander's mind the last inclination to continue resisting. Dislike for England, which had done so little for her allies and yet enforced against them a most stringent maritime code,[1] admiration for Napoleon, and a real hatred of war, all went for much with him. The party at the Russian Court which had all along favoured peace, Czartoriski, the Grand Duke Constantine, Kurakin and others, was now in the ascendant. A week after the battle the armistice of Tilsit was concluded. Four days later (June 25th), Napoleon and Alexander had their famous interview, and on July 9th the Peace of Tilsit restored peace to the Continent and placed North Germany at the mercy of Napoleon. The Czar did indeed insist on certain concessions in favour of his unfortunate ally, but the peace which Prussia had no option but to accept reduced the kingdom of the Hohenzollerns to half its former dimensions. Not only were the acquisitions of 1803 lost, but also everything else West of the Elbe, including

[1] Cf. Rose, ii. 127.

East Frisia which went to Holland, all that was left of Prussia's share in the Cleves-Jülich inheritance, all the gains made at the Peace of Westphalia and at the Peace of Utrecht. Not even the interposition of Queen Louise could induce the conqueror to leave Magdeburg to his victim. Moreover, the shares of Poland acquired in 1793 and 1795 were transformed into a new state, the Duchy of Warsaw. Dantzic became independent; but as it was occupied by a French garrison, it was really a French city. To sow dissension between Russia and Prussia a so-called "rectification of frontiers" gave the Prussian district of Bialystock to the Czar, while Saxony was also made an accessory to the partition of Prussia by receiving Cottbus. One Power alone Napoleon forgot to conciliate: he consented to restore Silesia to Frederick William when he might have won Austria's gratitude by handing it over to her. Prussia was thus reduced to the lands between the Elbe and the Oder with Eastern Pomerania, East and West Prussia, and Silesia, about ·62,000 square miles, with rather under five million inhabitants. Her losses were the more serious because the lands West of the Elbe were richer and more productive than those she retained. It was some advantage that the kingdom in its reduced form was at least geographically united: there were no outlying detached provinces, hard to defend, even harder to unite with the central mass.

But territorial loss was by no means the only humiliation inflicted on Prussia. Napoleon had never imposed a peace on a conquered enemy which did not reimburse him for the expenses of the conquest, and Prussia was not to escape the common lot. Moreover, while the Convention of July 12th made the evacuation of Prussia by the French troops depend on the payment of an indemnity, it somewhat strangely failed to fix the amount to be paid. Of this omission the usual explanation is negligence on the part of Kalckreuth, the Prussian negotiator; but it is at least probable that he was tricked into it by Napoleon's orders, for nothing could have suited the Emperor better. While the debt remained unpaid, Prussia was absolutely at his mercy and could not even enjoy such shreds of independence and initiative as Alexander's good offices had seemed to have secured her. That it was such a hold over Prussia which Napoleon wanted even more than the money, was seen when at last, in September 1808, he finally fixed the indemnity. The sum which he named, 154,000,000 francs, was altogether beyond what Prussia with her diminished resources could hope to pay for a long time, and she seemed to have before her a prospect of many years of dependence. What that would mean might be judged from the dismissal of Hardenberg and Rüchel at the bidding of Napoleon, and by the enforced adhesion of Prussia to Napoleon's great scheme for the ruin of England. In common with the rest of Germany, Prussia had to close her ports to British ships and to fulfil punctually the requirements of the Berlin and Milan Decrees. But there was a touch of irony in the fact that among the men whom Napoleon nominated to fill the vacant offices, Zastrow, Schulenburg and Stein, there should have been one who was destined to prove a far more dangerous foe to the Napoleonic régime than ever Hardenberg had been.

The arrangements made at Tilsit embraced a good deal more than the terms on which Napoleon was prepared to permit Prussia to continue a maimed existence. In the alliance between France and Russia which was there concluded, Napoleon took care that the balance of advantage should be on his side; that while he avoided pledging himself to do anything for the Czar, Russia was committed to the Continental System and to making the rest of Europe fall into line with Napoleon's anti-British crusade. Russia had also to accept the alterations which Napoleon was making in Northern Germany. The principal change which the Emperor proposed was the erection of a new kingdom out of the territory which his despoiling of Prussia and his deposition of the rulers of Brunswick, Hesse-Cassel and Orange-Nassau had placed at his disposal. This Kingdom of Westphalia, the largest and the most important of the new states created by Napoleon in Germany, was formed out of the Prussian provinces West of the Elbe, the Duchy of Brunswick-Wolfenbüttel, the Electorate of Hesse-Cassel together with Corvey and Osnabrück, the Southern portions of Hanover,[1] and smaller districts taken from Saxony. From an area of rather over 15,000 square miles and a population of about a couple of million, it supplied a contingent of 25,000 men to the Confederation of the Rhine. Following the example he had set with the Grand Duchy of Berg, Napoleon bestowed this new creation not on any of the existing dynasties of Germany, but on one of his own relations, his youngest brother, the clever but idle and self-indulgent Jerome.

[1] *i.e.* Grübenhagen and Göttingen.

Next in size and importance to Westphalia came Berg. Originally formed for Murat in March 1806 out of Berg, which Bavaria ceded in exchange for Anspach, and the portions of Cleves on the right bank of the Rhine, Prussia being compensated with Hanover, it was largely increased after Tilsit at the expense of Prussia, receiving Mark, Tecklenberg, Lingen and the Prussian share of Münster, though Murat had to let the important fortress of Wesel be incorporated in the French department on the opposite bank of the Rhine. At its greatest extent it amounted to nearly 9000 square miles and contained 1,200,000 inhabitants, its contingent to the Confederation's army, originally 5000 men, being increased to 7000 on the addition of Münster and Mark.

These creations disposed of the bulk of the North German lands in the occupation of Napoleon. They had on coming into his hands been divided into seven military governments (Oct. to Nov. 1806), and Fulda, Erfurt and the coast districts of Hanover remained in this condition for varying periods after the other governments had been incorporated in the more highly organised states of Westphalia and Berg. In these military governments the old local organisation and customs remained more or less unchanged; but a superstructure of French rule was imposed upon them, the general in command being assisted by an inspector and a receiver to control the finances of the district, and to drain it dry in the attempt to meet Napoleon's insatiable requirements.[1] Fulda after some two years of French rule was given to Dalberg (Feb. 1810) in exchange for Ratisbon. Hanover itself and the greater part of the Principality of Lüneburg were added to Westphalia in January 1810, but the remaining portions of the Electorate[2] were incorporated in the four new departments which Napoleon added to France in December 1810. These were formed out of the Duchies of Oldenburg and Aremberg, of the Hanseatic towns, of the Principality of Salm and the Northern portions of Westphalia[3] and of Berg.[4] His object in making this arrangement was to bring the North Sea coast-line under his own immediate rule for the better enforcement of the Continental System, which even his own brothers could not

---

[1] Cf. Fisher, pp. 154 ff.
[2] The old bishoprics of Bremen and Verden, the County of Hoya and Saxe-Lauenberg.
[3] The Department of the Weser.   [4] The Department of the Ems.

be trusted to carry out as he desired. To these districts, whether as military governments or in their later state of French departments, Napoleon gave strong government, a modern code of law, the benefits of the social changes of the Revolution; but the oppression of his tax-gatherers, the hardships entailed by the Continental System, and the demands of the conscription more than sufficed to crush out any gratitude these reforms may have earned him.

Meanwhile a large number of the minor Princes of Germany had averted mediatisation by a timely adhesion to the Confederation of the Rhine. In April 1807 the three branches of the ducal House of Anhalt, the four Princes of Reuss, the two of Schwarzburg, the two of Lippe, and the Prince of Waldeck had become members of Napoleon's new creation. In 1808 it was further increased by Mecklenburg-Strelitz (Feb.), Mecklenburg-Schwerin (March), and Oldenburg (Oct). This completed the reconstitution of Germany. The Imperial cities of Frankfurt and Nüremberg shared the fate of the less distinguished members of their order. They were mediatised, Frankfurt being given to Dalberg, Nüremberg to Bavaria. Thus with the exception of Prussia, Swedish Pomerania[1] and the German dominions of the Hapsburgs, all Germany was either annexed to France or united to her through adhesion to the Confederation of the Rhine. Napoleon, the "protector" of the Confederation, was the real master of Germany. So secure, indeed, did he feel of his position in Central Europe that he turned all his attention to the prosecution of his anti-English designs; to compelling Sweden and Portugal to close their markets to English goods, to which course Austria was forced to pledge herself by the Convention of February 28th, 1808. It was largely with a view to furthering his chances in the great contest with England by strengthening his hold on the Mediterranean, that he embarked on that Spanish venture which was to prove so important a factor in bringing about his overthrow. The events of July and August 1808 did not merely throw into confusion Napoleon's great

---

[1] This province had been invaded by the French in the course of 1807, and by September Gustavus IV had been compelled to evacuate Stralsund and Rügen; but though occupied by the French it was ultimately restored to Sweden in January 1810, when Charles XIII, the successor of Gustavus, came to terms with Napoleon and adhered to the Continental System.

schemes for the partition of Turkey and the subjugation of England by an overland attack on India, they were the first checks which Napoleon's domination over Europe had received, the first intimation to the people who were beginning to feel and to resent the heaviness of his rule, to the nations he had conquered and humiliated, that his power was not invincible. Austria, arming herself for the attempt to undo the work of Austerlitz and Pressburg, was inspired with fresh resolution and hope by the news of Baylen and Vimiero. Germany saw the spectacle of a nation hardly less split up than herself by local and provincial jealousies and differences, animated nevertheless by a common spirit of resistance to the same Power which had dictated terms to the Hapsburg and the Hohenzollern, and which numbered the Wettin and the Wittelsbach among its dependent allies. The example of Spain might prove contagious. Napoleon could not commit himself to the subjugation of the Iberian Peninsula as long as there was a danger that Austria might seize the opportunity of his absence on the Ebro to renew the struggle in the Danube valley. But since the Spaniards had dared to resist his selection of a monarch for their benefit, subdue them Napoleon must, even if he must first secure Germany by a new arrangement with Russia in which the conditions would not be so much in his favour as they had been at Tilsit. Negotiations had been going on all the year between the signatories of the Peace of Tilsit, but no definite settlement had yet been reached. The two sovereigns therefore agreed to meet at Erfurt in September to settle their future relations.

Among other causes of friction between Alexander and Napoleon must be mentioned the treatment Napoleon had meted out to Prussia. Alexander, though beguiled with the prospect of a great expedition to the East, with the idea of acquiring the Danubian Principalities, and by the notion of accomplishing the overthrow of England, was aggrieved by the manner in which Napoleon was grinding down his former ally Prussia, for whom he believed himself to have secured good treatment at Tilsit. He felt his honour to some extent implicated.

Napoleon's treatment of Prussia had been anything but gentle. After naming 112,000,000 francs as the amount of the indemnity (March 1808), he raised it to 154,000,000 on account of some hostile expressions in an intercepted letter of Stein's, though even the first sum would have been more than sufficient to keep Prussia in the position of a debtor for many years to come, and therefore to postpone indefinitely his evacuation of the principal Prussian fortresses which he held as security for payment. All attempts to get him to modify these terms had failed; Prince William's mission to Paris (Jan. 1808) was as unsuccessful as Queen Louise's pleading for Magdeburg. Stein therefore, finding that the indemnity must be paid, devoted himself to the task of raising the money. Taxation was greatly increased, notably by introducing an income-tax after the English model, 70 millions were raised by mortgages on the Royal domains, over 50 more by bills which bankers were induced to accept. One proposal which all Prussians joined in disliking, was that Prussia should surrender Royal domains to the value of 50 millions; but this provision Stein had succeeded in evading when he induced Daru, Napoleon's financial representative at Berlin, to sign a convention (March 9th, 1808) by which the French agreed to receive pledges as a guarantee for the payment of some 50 millions.[1] Napoleon, however, gave no orders for the departure of the French troops until Baylen and Vimiero created a demand for their presence elsewhere.[2] Negotiations were then begun which resulted in the Convention of September 8th, 1808, by which the French evacuated all Prussia except the fortresses of Cüstrin, Glogau and Stettin, which were to be held as security for the payment of the arrears of the indemnity. Heavy as this price was, an even greater humiliation was in store for Prussia. The Convention

[1] Haüsser, ii. 138.

[2] It may be worth mentioning that besides the French troops whom Napoleon withdrew from Germany to the Peninsula, he called upon his German clients to provide troops for that service. One division of infantry was required from the Confederation of the Rhine, Baden, Hesse-Darmstadt and Nassau each supplying two battalions and Frankfort one. Westphalia was called upon to provide a separate contingent of an infantry brigade and a regiment of light cavalry. Moreover, there were in the Peninsula several of the German corps already in Napoleon's service: he had, for example, raised a Hanoverian Legion in 1803 which formed part of the army which invaded Portugal under Junot: most of the men of this corps took service with the English after the capitulation of Cintra. Another corps had been raised out of the Prussian prisoners in 1806, so that with the King's German Legion in the British service, Germany was well represented in the Peninsula. Cf. Oman's *History of the Peninsular War*, especially the appendices; Balagny, *Napoléon en Espagne*, and *Les Allemands sous les Aigles Françaises*.

fixed the establishment of her army at 42,000, and forbade the organisation of a Militia, or of anything in the shape of a *levée en masse*.[1]

At the end of the month which saw these galling restrictions imposed upon Prussia, occurred the famous conference at Erfurt (Sept. 27th to Oct. 13th). It was a brilliant gathering. Most of the Kings and Princes who formed the Confederation of the Rhine were gathered to grace their " protector's " triumph. The presence of Goethe and his interview with Napoleon, from whom he accepted the Cross of the Legion of Honour on the anniversary of the battle of Jena, have added a peculiar interest. Goethe was the literary representative of the cosmopolitanism and lack of patriotism which had enabled Napoleon to attain to his predominant position ; the coming literary movement was to be typified by men such as Fichte and Arndt, leaders of one side of that national movement in which the reaction against the triumph of Erfurt culminated.

But the triumph of Erfurt was of a delusive character. Napoleon was not in a position to dictate to Alexander, and he could not succeed in inducing Alexander to assist him in compelling Austria to disarm and to recognise Joseph Bonaparte as King of Spain. Alexander was not prepared to complete the destruction of a Power which he might find useful in the future, though he declared himself ready to assist Napoleon should Austria take the offensive. But this was only purchased by Napoleon's grudging consent to the acquisition by Russia of the Danubian principalities. That Napoleon was not altogether satisfied with his ally was evident from his refusal to make the concessions to Prussia which Alexander asked of him : he absolutely refused to evacuate the fortresses on the Oder, and only consented to reduce the indemnity by 20,000,000 francs. Indeed, in the negotiations of Erfurt more than one hint was given of the coming rupture between France and Russia. The Convention merely reasserted their hostility to England, it accentuated rather than removed the causes of discord. " Napoleon," it has been well said, " used the great pageant of Erfurt to extricate himself from a dangerous position. In the event of a rupture with Austria . . . at least the neutrality of Russia was indispensable." This he had secured,

---

[1] Cf. Oncken, *Allegemeine Geschichte*, part iv. vol. i. pp. 407–408 ; also Haüsser, ii. pp. 185–190.

at the price of giving Russia a free hand against the Danubian principalities, a concession he made with some reluctance. Moreover, he did not completely relax his hold on Prussia, and to that he owed in no small measure his success in weathering the storms which were to beset him in 1809.

CHAPTER XXVIII

AUSTRIA'S EFFORT TO OVERTHROW NAPOLEON

I F in his dealings with Germany Napoleon reached a pinnacle of power far beyond that to which Louis XIV ever attained, it must nevertheless be admitted that the Bourbon shows to greater advantage in his dealings with Germany than does the Corsican. Bent on a purely personal aggrandisement, consistent with neither the interests, the welfare, nor the ambitions of his French subjects, Napoleon had since 1805 been striving to establish on the twin pillars of military force and centralised autocratic government an entirely new order of things, violating nationality and geography alike. Where Louis XIV had sought to profit by the decay of the old constitution of Germany rather than to destroy it and impose a new one in its stead, where he had aimed at influencing rather than commanding, where he had left the task of keeping Germany disunited to the jealousies of the individual states, Napoleon's reforms had removed many obstacles to the union of Germany, while his oppressions and his aggressions had supplied a motive power to the tendencies towards unity. The example of national resistance given by Spain, the chance afforded to England to intervene on the Continent with effect, the specimen of his conduct presented at Bayonne, were useful lessons to the German Powers. It was obvious that no confidence could be placed upon Napoleon's promises, that no amount of subservience would make a dependent state secure even of its existence if it should suit him to decide otherwise.

But while even the states on which Napoleon had conferred benefits were liable to have their constitutions or territories changed at any moment by the caprice of their "protector," there was one state which had special reason to view with alarm and distrust the spectacle of his aggressions on Spain and Portugal, of his interference in the affairs of the Balkans, of his occupation of the Papal States, and of the harsh measure he meted out to Prussia. Napoleon had beaten Austria in 1805, and he had treated her in a way she could not forgive. Since then he had forced the Continental System on her, and had demanded a recognition of Joseph Bonaparte as King of Spain; but at the same time he had not left her so utterly crushed that she could not hope to rise again. And ever since the Treaty of Pressburg great efforts had been made in Austria to prepare for an appeal against the verdict of 1805 by a renewal of the struggle against Napoleon.[1]

In few countries had a few years produced a greater change than in Austria. Under the vigorous and enlightened leadership of Count Stadion a new spirit was spreading through the Hapsburg dominions. An Imperial Knight by origin, Stadion, after leaving the Austrian diplomatic service in 1793 for a post under the Bishop of Würzburg, had returned to the Austrian service in 1801, had acted as Ambassador at Berlin for two years,[2] at St. Petersburg for two more, and had been called to the Ministry of Foreign Affairs in 1806. Keen and energetic as he was, his want of administrative training and of acquaintance with the internal affairs of Austria to some extent neutralised his good work in arousing a national feeling of hostility to Napoleon. He did indeed succeed in making the war thoroughly popular: the troops fought in 1809 with a keenness and a tenacity which had been lacking in 1805, and the Hungarian Diet of 1808 displayed a rather unexpected bellicose feeling. It voted new levies for the line regiments, agreed to the formation of a Reserve, and placed in the Emperor's hands the right to summon an "insurrection" without the leave of the Diet at any period in the next six years.

Stadion was warmly seconded in his efforts by Archduke Charles. From the misfortunes of 1805 his reputation had emerged unscathed, and his appointment as Commander-in-Chief (Feb. 10th, 1806) gave him, as he was also President of the War Council and Minister of War, a splendid opportunity for carrying out the reforms which he knew to be essential to the efficiency of the Austrian army. Incompetent and indolent officers were dismissed, encouragement was given to those who really desired to study their profession. The treatment and terms of service of the rank and file were improved, the drill was revised, and no effort was spared to make the Austrian troops capable of coping

---

[1] Cf. Lanfrey's *Napoleon*, iv. pp. 480–482.   [2] Cf. p. 457.

with the French. Most important was the Imperial Patent of June 9th, 1808, which created a *Landwehr*, composed of all men between nineteen and forty years of age. Still, though much had been effected, much more remained to be done. The Staff was inadequate, the artillery and engineers weak, the transport and commissariat departments deficient, while the higher ranks of the army were to prove singularly barren of men capable of commanding even a corps. The worst deficiencies lay in the finances and civil administration,[1] but the tremendous expenses of an armed peace made either war or disarmament imperative; and Stadion, though himself free from the bad traditions of the repressive and illiberal system of Thugut and Cobenzl, had not the power or the influence to remodel the old Austrian administration and infuse it with his own patriotic enthusiasm.

The efforts which Austria was making to rebuild her military power had not escaped the notice of Napoleon. As has been already described,[2] one of the objects of the interview of Erfurt had been to induce the Czar to join him in requiring Austria to disarm. But Alexander had been too wary to aid Napoleon by destroying a Power which might some day be a useful ally for Russia, and he had refused to do more than promise his help if Austria should attack Napoleon.[3] Meanwhile Austria had steadily continued her preparations, much hampered and delayed by her financial embarrassments. It was mainly these embarrassments which had made it impossible for Austria to seize what was in some ways a more favourable moment for a rising than that which she actually took, the moment when Baylen, Cintra and the retreat of Joseph to the Ebro made it imperative that Napoleon should forthwith proceed to Spain. At that time North Germany seemed ripe for revolt, and even Napoleon would have found it hard to direct a war on the Danube at the same time that he was conducting his great movements for the re-conquest of Spain. That this occasion could not be used, had been partly due to the action, or rather the inaction, of Prussia, still more to the attitude of Alexander: to lay the blame on Austria[4] is most unfair.

The bellicose party at Vienna had hoped not only for a rising in North-West Germany, for Hessians, Hanoverians and

---

[1] Cf. *Deutsche Geschichte*, 1806–1871, i. p. 137.   [2] Cf. p. 523.
[3] Cf. Rose, ii. 179–182.
[4] Cf. *Deutsche Geschichte*, 1806–1871, i. 135.

Brunswickers were all showing symptoms of restiveness, but also for the assistance of Prussia where a strong party favoured war. About the most anxious to make common cause with Austria against Napoleon's yoke had been Stein: in the autumn of 1808, when a rupture between France and Austria seemed imminent, he had thrown all his influence into the scale on the side of an insurrection. To conciliate the Poles he would even have given up all claim on Prussia's lost Polish provinces. However, Austria had been hardly ready for an immediate breach, and when Hardenberg despaired of the chances of a rising it was hardly wonderful that Frederick William had turned a deaf ear to Stein's advice. The King's own leanings were as usual against desperate measures. As always, he distrusted Austria; and thus, when Alexander on his way to Erfurt had visited Frederick William at Königsberg and sought to dissuade him from joining Austria, the Czar had found his cause half gained already, and Austria, with no hope of Prussia's help and with Russia pledged to keep the peace of Central Europe, had been forced to wait. Thus Napoleon had time to overthrow the Spaniards on the Ebro, to reinstate Joseph at Madrid, and to return to Paris before Austria moved.

In the meantime Stein had fallen. Frederick William's rejection of his proposals made his fall inevitable. Napoleon had already declared against him by publishing in the *Moniteur* of Sept. 8th an intercepted letter in which Stein's hostility to the Emperor was openly expressed, but in deference to Alexander he did not at once press for dismissal. However, Frederick William, having decided against an insurrection, soon made up his mind to part with Stein. On November 24th the Minister was dismissed, Dohna becoming Minister of the Interior, Golz Foreign Minister, von Altenstein Minister of Finance. Almost the only opponent of Napoleon left in office in Prussia at the end of 1808 was Scharnhorst, who was at the head of the War Office.

But though the most favourable moment for a breach with Napoleon had passed, she had gone too far to draw back, and even though Archduke Charles at the Conference of Feb. 8th, 1809, gave his vote against war the majority decided to take the risks. Archduke John was as keen on war as his brother was against it. Stadion urged strongly that the favourable opportunity should not be allowed to slip: he hoped for much from a rising in North Germany, which could hardly be expected unless the Austrians took the offensive. Metternich, too, pointed out that if Austria did not anticipate Napoleon she would merely be leaving him to choose the favourable moment for his attack; he had no illusions as to Austria's attitude and would not fail to attack her when it suited him; Austria must either strike at once or submit.

For the campaign the Austrian army was organised in eleven corps in all, amounting to 240,000 men, with the *Landwehr* and the Hungarian "insurrection," forces which may be estimated at 100,000 more, behind the first line. Two corps, nearly 50,000 men, were told off as the Army of Inner Austria or of Italy under Archduke John. Another of 30,000 was allotted to Galicia to keep the Grand Duchy of Warsaw in check, the rest were given to Archduke Charles for the campaign on the Danube.

By the spring of 1809 the French troops in Germany had been considerably reduced, so that Davoût was only able to concentrate a field force of some 54,000 men at Würzburg. To reinforce him, four divisions on their way to Spain were diverted to the Iller; to which river the contingents of Baden and Hesse were also directed, those of Bavaria and Würtemberg being ordered to collect on the Danube between Ratisbon and Ulm. These forces mustered in all some 120,000 men, behind which large reserves were rapidly prepared. Expecting the Austrians to take the offensive, Napoleon first ordered Berthier to concentrate the army behind the Lech, with the right under Masséna at Augsburg, the centre at Donauwörth, and the left at Ratisbon, but with detachments stretching as far as Ingolstadt. Then, as the Austrian advance was somewhat delayed, he altered his plan. Ratisbon was to be the principal point of concentration, only a small force assembling at Augsburg. Berthier, however, so far confused the plans that by the 16th of April Davoût and the left were at or near Ratisbon, seventy-six miles from Augsburg where the corps of Masséna and Oudinot were concentrating. Communication between these two wings depended on the Bavarians under Lefebvre, who had been thrust back from the Isar by the Austrian advance and were retiring towards the Danube between Kelheim and Neustadt, where they expected the support of Vandamme's Würtembergers. The position was one of considerable peril had the Archduke risen to the opportunity.

34

The original Austrian plan of campaign had been that the main body should advance from Bohemia to the Main, catching Davoût in flank as it moved, and driving him behind the Rhine, while two corps were to co-operate in Bavaria and South Germany. By operating in force on the Main it was hoped to cover the expected insurrection of North Germany. This plan had its defects; but what was essential was sufficient rapidity in its execution to profit by the dispersion of the French forces. Nothing could have been more fatal than the belated change of plan, which wasted ten invaluable days, threw the commissariat arrangements into disorder, and allowed the French to continue their concentration unimpeded. The new scheme threw the main body of the Army of the Danube upon Bavaria. Six corps were to advance up the right bank, push the Bavarians from the Isar, and then turning North to catch Davoût at Ratisbon between themselves and Bellegarde, who with the two remaining corps was to descend upon the Upper Palatinate from Bohemia. It was in some ways a better plan, as it did not expose the main body to being cut off from Vienna by a rapid advance of Napoleon down the Danube to gain the interior flank of the Austrian army on the Main; but its advantages did not in the least compensate for the invaluable time wasted over the transfer of the Archduke's main body from Pilsen in Bohemia, where it had concentrated, through Linz to the Inn.

Not till April 10th did the Austrians get started on this new advance, and the slowness of their movements wasted even more time. It took them eight days to get from the Inn to the Isar, bad weather, bad roads and bad commissariat arrangements delaying them. After a stout resistance the Bavarians were driven in on Neustadt and Kelheim; but the delays allowed Davoût to concentrate 40,000 men at Ratisbon by April 19th, though, had he made due haste, Bellegarde might have seized that town on the 14th, on which day only one of Davoût's divisions would have been there. Moreover, Napoleon had time to arrive at Dillingen. He promptly remedied Berthier's error by calling Davoût up from Ratisbon to Ingolstadt by Neustadt, and pushing Masséna and Oudinot up from the Lech to Pfaffenhofen. The move was not without danger, for it took Davoût across the front of the enemy, but it restored touch between the dangerously separated French wings.

The Archduke's failure to pierce the enemy's centre by crushing Lefebvre's Bavarians on the Isar had greatly diminished the chances of an Austrian success. His next move was scarcely less unfortunate. Had he even now fallen with his whole force on Lefebvre, he might have cut off Davoût from the Emperor, and been able to concentrate upon the French left when thus isolated. If Lefebvre and Vandamme had been so badly handled as to be even temporarily *hors de combat*, Davoût would have been in great peril, for Masséna and Oudinot were still too far away to help him. But the Archduke moved North with his right and centre upon Ratisbon (April 19th). As this exposed his communications, he had to leave the two corps which formed his left, those of Hiller and Archduke Louis, on the Abens river to cover the operation. Nor was this move well managed. Had his force been properly concentrated he might have checked Davoût's move up stream to join Lefebvre. As it was, Hohenzollern's isolated corps (the left centre) met Davoût near Dinzling, and lost 5000 men in an attempt, unsuccessful because unsupported, to prevent him forcing his way past. Meanwhile by nightfall Masséna had come up to Pfaffenhofen, so that on the morning of the 20th Napoleon was able to hurl Lefebvre, Vandamme and a new corps under Lannes on the Austrian containing force along the Abens, while Davoût stood firm on his left near Dinzling and Masséna and Oudinot pushed forward against Landshut. The result of a day's heavy fighting all along the Abens was that the Austrian left wing, outnumbered and outflanked, had to fall back to the Isar, every step it took removing it farther from the Archduke's main body, which had wasted the day in the comparatively useless capture of Ratisbon. The campaign might yet have been retrieved had the Archduke fallen on Davoût on the 21st while Napoleon was pursuing Hiller and Archduke Louis from Landshut to Neumarkt; but this last chance went the way of the others, and Napoleon did not give him any more. Realising that the Austrian main body was not in front of him, but must be near Ratisbon, Napoleon left the pursuit of Hiller to Bessières, and wheeling 80 battalions and 80 squadrons round to the left moved Northward. The Archduke now moving South with the idea of threatening the French communications, met him next day (April 22nd) just South of Ratisbon along the line Abbach - Eckmühl. The brunt of

Napoleon's attack fell on the corps of Rosenberg, which formed the Austrian left. It held on to Eckmühl most gallantly; but the Archduke failed to support it, though nearer to the Danube his right was hardly engaged at all. After three hours Rosenberg was forced back to Eggloffsheim, and the Austrians were in no small danger of being driven pell-mell into the river. But Napoleon for once paid more attention to the fatigue of his men than to the utilisation of his victory, and his failure to press on allowed the Archduke's army to escape to the North bank (April 23rd), to unite with Bellegarde, and to retire safely along that side of the Danube. Hiller meanwhile had turned on his pursuers at Eggenfelden (April 24th), beaten them and opened himself a road to Dingolfing and Deggendorf; but the Archduke's defeat at Eckmühl made it impossible to reunite so far up the Danube, and Hiller had therefore to make for Linz. Taking the Burghausen road in preference to the better road by Schärding, he could not avoid being overtaken; and though his rearguard did stand at Ebelsberg (May 3rd) and sacrifice itself to let him escape, he only managed to bring 16,000 men across the river at Mautern (May 8th).

Thus the campaign in Bavaria which had promised so well ended in disaster. It was not the rank and file of the Austrian army who had been at fault. They had fought far better than their predecessors in 1805, and had suffered heavier losses before giving way. The failure to obtain that initial success which alone could have roused North Germany and induced Prussia to reconsider her policy was partly due to the shortcomings of the Austrian military administration, but mainly to the errors of Archduke Charles. His initial mistake in changing the whole plan had caused much delay; more time was wasted by the slowness of the move from the Inn to the Isar, which allowed Napoleon to arrive before the errors of his lieutenant had become irreparable; finally, the failure to keep the various Austrian corps concentrated exposed them to defeats in detail. The Archduke's strategy was certainly open to criticism, but it was his execution of his schemes which was so deplorably weak. It certainly contrasts most unfavourably with his 1796 campaign, in which he had shown a far truer appreciation of the importance of keeping his divisions in hand and not exposing them to be defeated one by one. As for lack of mobility, that was a traditional failing of the Austrian army which nothing seemed

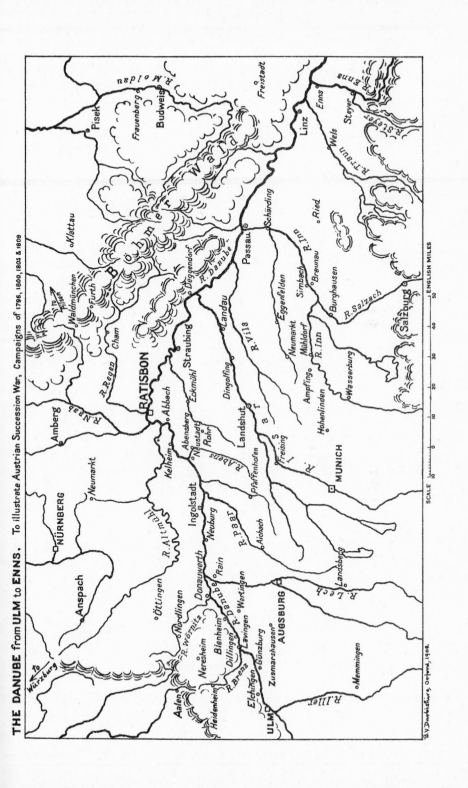

THE DANUBE from **ULM** to **ENNS.** To illustrate Austrian Succession War, Campaigns of 1796, 1800, 1805 & 1809

SCALE

ENGLISH MILES

B.V.Darbishire, Oxford, 1908.

able to eradicate.   And it was not only the Austrian offensive campaign which thus failed.   Germany would not rise to aid a defeated Power, Prussia would not risk anything when the venture would only involve her in Austria's overthrow.   Thus the attempts at insurrection which had been made during these critical days remained isolated expressions of a general feeling, heroic efforts of desperate individuals to achieve what could only be accomplished by a joint effort.

These attempts, however, have no small importance as indications of the growth of a national feeling in Germany. Though Napoleon's rule had not yet begun to press half as heavily on Germany as it was to do before the Continental System succumbed to its own inherent defects, it had already provoked widespread opposition.   He had forcibly interfered in the affairs of every portion of Germany; he had overthrown old established dynasties and replaced them with his own upstart relations; he had torn provinces from their old allegiance to transfer them to foreign rulers.   The abortive risings in Westphalia under von Dörnberg, in the Alt Mark of Brandenburg under Katt, at Marburg in Hesse, at Hanover, at Ziegenhayn, effected little but were eloquent of much.   Had Archduke Charles adopted the bold policy some suggested after Eckmühl, marched into North-West Germany and raised it to fall on Napoleon's communications, he might have failed, he might not even have checked the Emperor's advance on Vienna, but it would hardly have been because Westphalia and Hesse preferred their new masters to their old.   If the hardships which the Napoleonic rule was to inflict upon Germany had not yet begun to bear so heavily on every class of society that the Westphalian burghers and peasants were ready to rise, universal sympathy was felt for the insurgents.   No one but officials and soldiers attempted to stop Schill or Brunswick.   At the best, the new régime was tolerated on account of the material benefits it had brought: it had not attached any one to it or obtained any popular favour.[1]   The exploits of Schill and Brunswick leave little doubt as to the attitude of the country.   The Westphalian kingdom, the Confederation of the Rhine itself, rested on one thing only, on the continued military predominance of Napoleon.

Ferdinand von Schill, the colonel of a Prussian Hussar

[1] Cf. Fisher, pp. 249-258.

regiment quartered at Berlin, had been privy to the conspiracy in Westphalia, and expected to be denounced when it failed. Accordingly he decided to call his regiment out on behalf of the insurrection, declaring that he was acting with the King's assent (April 28th). The regiment followed him readily enough, and he was also joined by over 100 men from the Berlin garrison and by many volunteers. At their head he moved by Potsdam and Wittenberg to Dessau. Here on May 4th he learnt not only of Austrian defeats on the Danube, but that Dörnberg's rising had miscarried, and that the King of Prussia, instead of declaring war on Napoleon, had disowned all connection with his own enterprise. He might have moved into Bohemia and taken service with Austria, but he still claimed to be acting as a loyal Prussian, and he set out for the coast, intending to seize some port and hold it till help arrived. Milhaud, the French commander at Magdeburg, sent a column out to intercept him; but Schill brushed it aside (May 5th), and made his way by Domitz on the Elbe to Stralsund (May 25th). Had he at once taken ship he and his men could have escaped, but he decided to stand an attack—a hopeless enterprise, for the townspeople though favourable to him were not prepared to emulate Saragossa, and the fortifications were weak. May 31st saw 6000 Danes, Dutch and Holsteiners gathered before Stralsund. Schill, who had not more than a quarter of the number, was unable to prevent them entering by a weakly held gate which was in bad repair. Street fighting ended in the death of Schill and most of his party. Their effort had been premature, but they had not met a hero's death in vain. They set Germany an example of patriotism and self-sacrifice which the rulers of Prussia might perhaps have done well to follow.

One German ruler, indeed, did profit by the example. Frederick William of Brunswick, third son of the man who had fallen at Auerstadt, had been given the Duchy of Oels in Silesia as compensation for his lost ancestral dominions. In February 1809 he had concluded a treaty with Austria by which he undertook to raise a Free Corps to assist Austria. With this corps, the famous "Black Legion," 1700 men vowed to fight to the death for the liberation of Germany, aided by an Austrian division, he invaded Saxony from Bohemia. At first he was brilliantly successful. The Westphalians and Rivaud's division of Junot's corps who hurried to the help of the King of Saxony proved powerless to prevent the seizure of Leipzig and Dresden. Junot was checked at Bamberg, but King Jerome recovered Dresden (July 1st), and the armistice of Znaym (July 12th) put an end to the operations of the Austrians. But Brunswick preferred emulating Schill to a tame retreat into Bohemia along with the Austrians. The Black Legion was ready to follow him on the daring errand of a raid into Brunswick to raise his father's old subjects. On July 24th he moved from Zwickau by Halle, and after a desperate but victorious encounter with a Westphalian regiment at Halberstadt reached Brunswick on the 31st. He was cordially received, but the prospects of a successful rising were desperate. The Brunswickers had seen previous efforts at insurrection suppressed. French troops were gathering round him. The English army he had hoped to see landed in Hanover had not appeared, and there was nothing to be done but for the Duke and his Black Legion to cut their way through Rewbell's division to the mouths of the Weser, where friends in need in the shape of an English squadron received them. Thus carried to Ireland the Black Legion passed into the pay of Great Britain, its cavalry as the Brunswick Hussars, its infantry as the Brunswick Oels Light Infantry.[1]

Meanwhile on the Danube Napoleon had pressed on to Vienna, Hiller's retreat over the Danube having cleared the path. On May 10th the French were before the walls of the Austrian capital. Archduke Maximilian offered an ineffectual resistance for two days, which resulted in considerable damage to property and the evacuation of the city on the 13th. Napoleon thus for the second time found himself master of Vienna. His success in the principal theatre of operations had already exercised a great influence on the course of events elsewhere. The Army of Inner Austria under Archduke John had crossed the frontier into Italy on April 11th, had turned Eugene's position on the Tagliamento, brought him to action at Sacilio (April 16th), and inflicted a severe defeat on him, a fifth of his 50,000 men being killed or taken. This

---

[1] This battalion was sent to Portugal in October 1810, and after serving for a time in the famous Light Division, from which it unfortunately had to be removed for misconduct and a propensity to desertion, formed part of the Seventh Division from March 1811 till the end of the war, being present at Salamanca, at Vittoria, at the battles of the Pyrenees, and at Orthez. The Brunswick Hussars did good service in the Mediterranean and on the East Coast of Spain, especially distinguishing themselves in Bentinck's affair with Suchet near Villafranca in September 1813.

defeat caused the French to evacuate all Istria; and the Viceroy would have abandoned the Adige and fallen back to Mantua had not Macdonald induced him to stand at Caldiero. Two days' indecisive fighting (April 29th and 30th) saw the French left endangered by the appearance of Chasteler's Austrians at Rovoredo, and the French had no alternative save retreat.

Chasteler's force was part of a corps, the Eighth, which had been detached from Carinthia into Tyrol to aid the peasants to throw off the unpopular Bavarian rule which had been imposed on them at Pressburg. The reforms of Montgelas had irritated all classes by necessitating higher taxes; they had been specially irksome to the clergy on account of their anti-clerical bias. The old hatred of Bavaria, the old local feeling and love of independence thus inflamed, brought the peasants in thousands from their homes and drove the Bavarian garrisons out of the valleys of Tyrol. On April 12th the Tyrolese recovered Innsbrück, on the 14th a Bavarian column under General Brisson pushing through the Wippthal to Innsbrück was hemmed in and forced to capitulate. German Tyrol passed into Austrian hands in a very few days, and Chasteler moving South over the Brenner drove the French division under d'Hilliers out of Italian Tyrol.

This favourable situation was altogether changed by the news from the Danube. Archduke John had to retreat, for Marmont was in Dalmatia and threatening his communications. It was suggested that the Archduke should throw himself into Tyrol and assist the peasants, with whom he was very popular, to defend their fortress-like country; but in the end the Army of Inner Austria retired over the Piave (May 8th) and took post along the frontier of Carinthia to defend the passes over the mountains. Several days' sharp fighting, signalised by some heroic exploits on the part of small bodies of Austrians, saw the Archduke forced back into Styria. He had to retire by Klagenfurt upon Gratz (May 16th to 20th). This left the high road to Vienna down the Mur open to Eugene and cut off the Archduke from Tyrol. There the insurgents had meanwhile been hotly attacked by Lefebvre's Bavarians, whom Napoleon had detached against Tyrol after Eckmühl. They were abandoned by the majority of the Austrian regulars, Chasteler moving down the Drave to Villach to rejoin the Archduke, and Lefebvre retook Innsbrück on May 19th; but the peasantry nevertheless continued with no small success their desperate resistance.

Napoleon's first object on obtaining possession of Vienna was to secure a passage to the North bank of the Danube, if possible, before Archduke Charles could arrive on the Marchfeld. His first effort at Nussdorf and Jedler-Aue (May 16th) was checked by the arrival of Hiller's corps from Korneuburg: on the 16th the Archduke's army began to arrive; by the 19th 146 squadrons and 116 battalions, in all some 105,000 men, were in position on the Marchfeld. For effecting a passage, Napoleon had available part of the Guard, Bessières' cavalry reserve, Oudinot's grenadiers, and the corps of Lannes, Davoût and Masséna, in all 120 squadrons and 149 battalions, some 115,000 men, with 300 to 400 guns. Vandamme's Würtembergers and Bernadotte's corps of Saxons, Nassauers and other Confederates guarded the communications, and had just repulsed an attempt on Linz by Kollowrat's Austrian corps from Bohemia (May 17th).

Resolved to bring the Archduke to action before he could gather reinforcements, Napoleon seized the island of Lobau, which the Austrians had neglected to occupy (May 15th), and threw bridges across from it to the left bank. On May 20th Masséna's corps began the passage, and occupied the villages of Aspern and Essling, which provided an admirable bridge-head for the protection of the passage of the rest of the army. But next morning (May 21st), long before this difficult operation could be completed, the covering divisions were furiously attacked by five converging Austrian columns. The heaviest fighting was on the Austrian right, where Hiller (VIth corps), Bellegarde (Ist) and Hohenzollern (IInd) joined in attacking Aspern. The village was carried by their first attack; but Masséna retook it and by supreme efforts held it against repeated assaults. Similarly on the French right Lannes, who had followed Masséna across, maintained his hold of Essling. When the attention of the French was mainly occupied in the effort to hold these villages at the ends of their line, the Archduke advanced against their centre, depleted to reinforce the wings. To check him, Bessières' cavalry had to be thrown into line to connect the two villages, since the breakdown of the bridges was causing delay in the arrival of reinforcements. Bessières made several dashing charges on the Austrian infantry opposite him, but they stood their ground with un-precedented firmness and repulsed all his charges. Towards evening the Archduke hurled Hiller and Bellegarde in a last attack on Aspern; Molitor's division of Masséna was all but destroyed, and the Austrians managed to obtain possession of half the village before nightfall put an end to the struggle. Next morning (May 22nd) opened with the expulsion of the Austrians from Aspern, Masséna putting Carra St. Cyr's fresh division into the fight. Davoût's corps was now (7 a.m.) coming across the restored bridges into Lobau, and Napoleon prepared to deal a great blow at the enemy's centre with Oudinot's grenadiers, Bessières' cavalry and St. Hilaire's division of Davoût. The Austrians resisted desperately, and were only being forced back towards Breitenlee after very heavy fighting, when the sudden collapse of the great bridge over the main stream of the Danube altered the complexion of affairs. The pressure of the logs and tree trunks brought down by the rising river was too much for the bridge.[1] It gave way, and not only cut off most of Davoût's corps but also the sorely needed reserve of ammunition. Just at this moment (8 a.m.) the Archduke brought up his reserve of grenadiers, and before them the French recoiled to the ridge between Aspern and Essling. Along this and around the two villages the fight was contested with desperate valour on both sides. About 3 p.m., after the sheer exhaustion of the combatants had caused a lull of nearly two hours in the battle, the pressure of the Austrians on the French flanks became so serious that the Emperor had to give orders for a retreat. A Transylvanian regiment finally gained possession of Aspern, and only the Young Guard kept Rosenberg out of Essling, and covered the withdrawal of the exhausted corps of Lannes and Masséna into the island of Lobau. Minimise the defeat as he might, ascribe it if he would to the breaking of the bridges, Aspern was a battle of a very different character from any Napoleon had yet fought. He had not merely, as at Eylau and Heilsberg, failed to defeat his enemy, he had been forced to retreat with a loss of over 30,000 against 24,000 which he had inflicted on the enemy. The Austrians had displayed a remarkable resolution and tenacity. Repulsed from the villages time after time, they had as often returned to the

---

[1] The Austrians seem to have sent heavily-laden barges down the stream to increase the pressure on the bridge.

attack, until at last they had had the satisfaction of seeing the Grand Army retreat before them.

But would Austria be able to utilise the advantage she had won? Much depended on the action of Archduke Charles, even more on the movements of the Army of Inner Austria under Archduke John. If it could prevent the Army of Italy and Marmont from Dalmatia from reinforcing Napoleon, Aspern might prove decisive.

But neither of the Austrian leaders proved equal to the occasion. It would be unreasonable to expect that the exhausted victors of Aspern should have renewed their exertions without some rest,[1] but too many troops had been left to cover Bohemia and menace ineffectually the French communications; and though before Wagram Kollowrat rejoined the main army, the failure to concentrate every available man at the decisive spot was to cost Austria dear. Chasteler's divisions, for instance, which might have kept Bernadotte back from Wagram had they joined the Tyrolese, who fell on the Bavarians with renewed vigour in the week after Essling and drove them in disorder back into their own country, merely wasted their time in futile skirmishes round Klagenfurt with Rusca's Italians, who were keeping open Macdonald's communications with Italy. Archduke Ferdinand in Galicia gained some successes over Poniatowski's Poles, even forcing them to evacuate Warsaw; but the presence of half his 30,000 men on the Marchfeld might have turned the scales on July 6th. Much in the same way the Army of Inner Austria was not turned to proper account. On the day of Aspern Archduke John was at Gratz in Styria, waiting for Jellachich's division to come in from Radstadt on the Upper Salza. Jellachich, however, a thoroughly incompetent officer, moved very slowly and failed to keep a proper lookout, with the result that he could not avoid an action against Eugene at St. Michael on the Mur (May 25th), which resulted in his total defeat, and allowed Eugene to get through to Bruck and so establish communication with Napoleon. This decided Archduke John

---

[1] Thus Oncken (*Allgemeine Geschichte*, part iv. vol. i. p. 426) is perhaps too hard on the Archduke's inaction after May 22nd: his troops had suffered severely and were almost as unfit for action as the French; but still it is undeniable that the failure of the Archduke to follow up his success showed a great want of enterprise and of insight into the situation.

to move into Hungary. On June 1st he reached Körmend, where his troops found reinforcements and supplies. Meanwhile the Hungarian " insurrection " was gathering at Raab, and on June 7th Archduke John, in obedience to orders from his brother, left Körmend to join them. Moving down the Raab by Papocz he reached Raab on June 13th; but he found the " insurrection " had only produced 20,000 raw and untrained recruits instead of the expected 40,000, and detachments for various purposes had so weakened his own force that he found himself much inferior to the four divisions which Napoleon had sent out against him under Eugene, and by which he was attacked on June 14th. The battle of Raab ended in the total defeat of the Army of Inner Austria. The horsemen of the " insurrection " on the Austrian left were thrown into disorder by the French artillery, and gave way before Grouchy's cavalry; their flight uncovered the infantry, who were maintaining a stubborn fight in the centre. With the loss of over 7000 men the Archduke fell back to Komorn. His force was to all intents no longer to be reckoned with: at any rate, he could not hope to bring up to the Marchfeld a reinforcement large enough to turn the scale, which might have been the case had his movements been better arranged and more rapid. He had tried to do too much at once, and had dispersed forces which if properly concentrated might have held Eugene at bay at the Semmering. For the unwise move from Körmend to Raab which brought him within easy reach of Eugene Archduke Charles must be held responsible; had he directed his brother to move by Stuhlweissenberg and Gran, the move would have taken longer, but would have probably meant the arrival of 30,000 men on the Marchfeld, since the corps on the Croatian frontier under Banus Giulay could have joined him. But Archduke John was himself to blame for not falling on the two divisions under Macdonald which had followed him from Carniola and had only regained touch with Eugene on the day of the battle of Raab. Here as at other periods of the campaign it was the want of good leadership which told so heavily against the Austrians. The " insurrectionary " levies had not done much at Raab, but nothing could have been better than the conduct of the disciplined troops of the Line, and even of the *Landwehr*.

The net result of all this was that while Napoleon, who did

realise the importance of concentrating every available man at the critical point, was able to collect nearly 170,000 men in and near Lobau by the end of June, the Austrians had only two men to his three. Napoleon had brought up Bernadotte's Saxons from Linz, replacing them by a Bavarian division re-called from Tyrol; the two corps of Eugene and Macdonald had arrived from Italy, and that of Marmont from Dalmatia, besides minor reinforcements. The corps of Kollowrat was the only real addition to the army of Archduke Charles, though on July 2nd he did send off a despatch to Archduke John bidding him bring up his corps from Pressburg, where it then stood. Received on the evening of July 4th, this order was too late to bring Archduke John up to the Marchfeld before 5 p.m. on the 6th, and by then the decisive action had been fought and lost.

The Austrians since the end of May had retained hold of Aspern and Essling, and so strong was their position that Napoleon realised that the passage to the left bank could not be effected there. Under cover, therefore, of a heavy cannonade and feints against this point, the French made their way over the Lobau branch of the Danube by five bridges flung over it on the Eastern side of the island. Begun about 10 p.m. on July 4th by Oudinot's corps (formerly that of Lannes, who had been mortally wounded on May 22nd), the movement was so far ad-vanced by 6 a.m. on the 5th that the corps of Masséna on the left then moved against Gross Enzersdorf; Davoût on the right attacked Wittau, Oudinot formed the centre. The Austrians made little resistance, evacuating their advanced position (Aspern, Essling, Enzersdorf, Wittau) and falling back to the stronger line of Neusiedel, Baumersdorf, Deutsch - Wagram, Gerasdorf, Stammersdorf. The left of this position was covered by the Russbach, and the right rested on the Danube at Jedlersdorf, to which Klenau's corps (late Hiller's) had retired from Aspern: its chief defect was that its re-entrant angle at Wagram gave the French the interior position, and the total front was so long that orders took nearly four hours to get from flank to flank. It was also exposed on the left, where Archduke John was expected; but he was still many hours away.

The retreat of the Austrians from their advanced position encouraged Napoleon to try a direct attack on the evening of the 5th. He hoped to drive in their left from its position behind the Russbach and so interpose between the main army and the corps of Archduke John : he therefore held the Austrian centre and right in check with his left, Masséna's (IVth) corps, and opposed Bernadotte, Eugene, Oudinot and Davoût to the three corps of Bellegarde, Hohenzollern and Rosenberg, which formed the Austrian left. Bernadotte carried Wagram, only to be driven out again, and as the corps on his right were repulsed from Baumersdorf and Neusiedel the attack proved an expensive failure. Encouraged by this, Archduke Charles decided to take the offensive next morning without waiting for his brother. His plan was for his right, Klenau and Kollowrat, to push forward Eastward, threatening to outflank Napoleon's left and cut him off from Aspern ; but his centre, his Grenadier reserve, and left centre, Bellegarde and Hohenzollern, were also to advance on Aderklaa to keep touch with the right. Napoleon, too, intended his principal effort to be on his right : he meant to storm the heights behind the Russbach and to pierce the Austrian centre by Aderklaa and Wagram ; but he had the great advantage of having his troops concentrated to meet badly timed converging attacks. For the Austrian left moved too soon and had already been repulsed from Glinzendorf by Davoût, when at length Klenau fell on Masséna as the latter came up from Breitenlee to support Bernadotte. The leading division of the IVth Corps, Carra St. Cyr's, was repulsed from Aderklaa, its rear, Boudet, was driven in on Aspern. In vain Masséna tried to make head against the Austrians with Legrand and Molitor : he was pressed back in some disorder, Kollowrat moving forward on Klenau's left caught Bernadotte in flank, while d'Aspre's Grenadier reserve and Bellegarde advancing from Wagram on Aderklaa assailed him in front. By 10 a.m. the French left and left centre were in retreat, and the battle seemed in a fair way to be lost. But Napoleon never rose higher than at so critical a moment. He saw that a successful blow at the Austrian centre would paralyse the advance of their right by cutting it off from their left, and while he checked Klenau and Kollowrat with such cavalry and artillery as he had at hand, he collected a great body of infantry for the deciding stroke. Soon after midday he launched this column against Aderklaa. It was headed by Macdonald's corps and followed by a Bavarian division of Lefebvre's with cavalry on its wings. Simultaneously Eugene renewed the attack on Wagram, Oudinot pushed forward against Hohenzollern's front, Davoût, with Montbrun's cavalry covering his flank, made a turning movement by Neusiedel, driving Rosenberg in before him.

But it was in the centre that the battle was decided. The way had been prepared for Macdonald by the great battery Napoleon had collected, and the Army of Italy, though suffering heavy losses, did pierce the Austrian centre and drive it in on Gerasdorf. The simultaneous success of Eugene against Wagram and of Oudinot and Davoût farther to the right, clinched this advantage. In good order the Austrians drew off all along the line. They maintained a front firm enough to secure them against pursuit; indeed, the French were too exhausted to press on, and the arrival of Archduke John's belated corps at Ober-Siebenbrünn far to the Eastward spread a panic through the French ranks which showed what his appearance earlier might have effected. As far as losses went, the honours of the day were evenly divided. If the Austrians left 8500 prisoners behind them, besides 25,000 killed and wounded, they had inflicted a loss of 30,000 on the French, and could point to 11 guns and 12 eagles as trophies against the 9 guns and 1 colour of which the French could boast. Had their wings only combined their movements better, had Archduke John and his 15,000 men been in time to take up their appointed place and cover the exposed Austrian left, had he played Blücher to his brother's Wellington, Wagram might have been an enlarged edition of Aspern, or might have anticipated Waterloo.

But Napoleon's downfall was not to be achieved by Austria alone. The Archduke who had fallen back on Znaym, where he concentrated 60,000 men by July 10th, was anxious for an armistice. Napoleon had had too strong a taste of the chances of defeat to refuse his overtures. After an indecisive action on the 11th, in which Marmont and Masséna failed to dislodge Bellegarde from his position at Znaym, an armistice was arranged. The military situation hardly made this necessary. Archduke John might have got together 30,000 to 40,000 regulars and as many Hungarian levies for a diversion South of the Danube, and there was still a chance that Prussia might take up arms, or England make an effective if belated diversion in North Germany. However, the opponents of Stadion had gained influence, Wagram had converted the opportunist Metternich into an advocate of peace, and the resignation of Archduke Charles (July 23rd) rather than dismiss his adjutant Count Grünne was a blow to the war party. With him the Archdukes John and Joseph threw up their commands, while Metternich replaced Stadion as Foreign Minister.[1] Count Lichtenstein, who became Commander-in-Chief, was the leader of those who desired peace ; and as Russia remained obstinately neutral and Prussia refused to rise unless Austria would denounce the armistice, which Austria declined to do unless Prussia would first take up arms, even the bellicose gradually abandoned hope. England, too, by sending her great expedition not to the Weser but to the Scheldt, destroyed all lingering chance of an insurrection in North Germany. The troops who perished of fever in the Walcheren marshes ought to have been landed in Hanover in June—the Hanoverian population had welcomed Cathcart in 1805[2] and four years of Napoleon's rule had not increased its popularity, — but the quarrel in the ministry between Castlereagh and Canning was largely responsible for the delays through which the splendid opportunity was allowed to slip away ; when it finally sailed, there was perhaps as much to be gained by a blow at Antwerp as by landing in North Germany after the best chance was past. The failure of the expedition was due not so much to its destination, as to the feeble execution of the scheme, for which Lord Chatham must be held responsible.

The final blow came when Prussia declined to stir unless she were put on exactly the same footing in Germany as Austria. Rather than this Francis preferred peace with Napoleon, and Lichtenstein was despatched to negotiate a treaty in personal communication with the Emperor. The terms were harsh, but Napoleon was in a position to dictate. Austria ceded to France Trieste, Carniola, Istria, Fiume, Monfalcone, Dalmatia, the circle of Villach in Carinthia, and all her possessions on the right of the Save down to the Bosnian frontier. She abandoned all claims on Salzburg, Berchtesgaben and the Innviertel, which Napoleon handed over to his Bavarian client. Another vassal state, the Grand Duchy of Warsaw, was enlarged by West

---

[1] Stadion offered his resignation July 8th, but Metternich did not finally take over the position from him till October.

[2] *War Office Original Correspondence*, vol. lxviii., Hanover.

ASPERN May 21ˢᵗ & 22ⁿᵈ 1809 (second day)

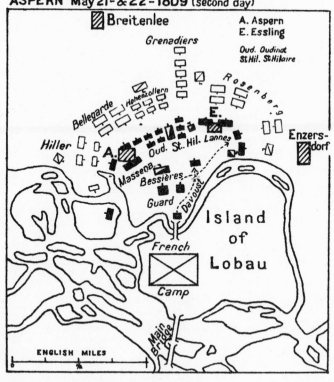

Breitenlee

A. Aspern
E. Essling

Oud. Oudinot
St. Hil. St Hilaire

Grenadiers

Rosenberg

Bellegarde Hohenzollern

Hiller A. Oud. St. Hil. Lannes Enzersdorf

Massena Bessières

Guard Davoust

Island of Lobau

French Camp

Main Bridge

ENGLISH MILES

WAGRAM July 5ᵗʰ & 6ᵗʰ (Second Day)

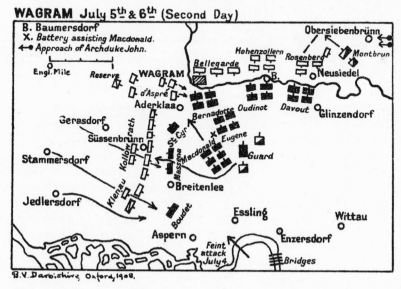

B. Baumersdorf
X. Battery assisting Macdonald.
←● Approach of Archduke John.

Obersiebenbrünn

Engl. Mile Reserve WAGRAM Hohenzollern Rosenberg Montbrun

d'Aspré Bellegarde B. Neusiedel

Gerasdorf Aderklaa Bernadotte Oudinot Davout Glinzendorf

Süssenbrunn St. Cyr Macdonald Eugene

Stammersdorf Kollowrath Massena Guard

Jedlersdorf Klenau Breitenlee

Boudet

Aspern Essling Wittau

Enzersdorf

Feint attack July 4 Bridges

B.V. Darbishire, Oxford, 1908.

Galicia and Cracow, Austria's share in the 1795 partition, while Russia received the South-Eastern corner of Old Galicia. Austria had, moreover, to acquiesce in the abolition of the Teutonic Order, to accept the Continental System, to limit her army to 150,000 men, and pay an indemnity of 85,000,000 francs. Her loss of inhabitants was 3,500,000, of territory over 40,000 square miles. The Treaty of Schönbrunn (Oct. 14th) thus marked the lowest point to which the power of the Hapsburgs had yet sunk. Cut off from the sea, compelled to submit to Napoleon almost as completely as must Baden or Lippe-Detmold, Austria had the added mortification of having to abandon the gallant Tyrolese. Even after Wagram and Znaym they had continued their heroic but hopeless resistance, and had again repulsed the Bavarians when they for the third time advanced against them (August). The conclusion of peace allowed large forces to be directed against the mountaineers, up the Inn, up the Salza, and from Italy. Still the Tyrolese refused to submit. But this time numbers were too much even for them. By the end of December all was over except the executions. The gallant Hofer met his fate in February 1810, and with him ends one of the most romantic incidents in all German history. South Tyrol now went to the Kingdom of Italy, part of Eastern Tyrol to the Illyrian provinces, the rest to the detested Bavarians.

Moreover, Stadion's resignation marked the abandonment of Austria's effort at a truly patriotic policy. Stadion had made her the champion of German nationality, but the effort had been premature. Her defeat had been in no small measure due to the inaction of some German states and to the active hostility of others, those members of the Confederation of the Rhine whom gratitude to Napoleon or a sense that their gains and new titles would not survive the overthrow of their author made faithful to his cause, since as yet he had not sacrificed their material prosperity to his hatred of England. With Stadion's fall disappeared the popular policy he had advocated. Austria under Metternich was once again subject to the suspicion-ridden system of Thugut and Cobenzl. Had she won in 1809 under the leadership of Stadion and Archduke Charles, Austria could hardly have gone back from the principles they had enunciated, could hardly have abandoned their more Liberal policy to become the chief stronghold of reaction. The failure

35

of 1809 was therefore of momentous importance to her future. But if one of its lessons may have been that Austria should have put all other considerations aside to assist Russia and Prussia in 1807, the conduct of Prussia in 1799 and 1805 was even more responsible for Germany's humiliation and Napoleon's triumph.

CHAPTER XXIX

GERMANY AT NAPOLEON'S MERCY

IT would be one of the gravest errors to regard Austria's failure to overthrow Napoleon as having merely postponed the day of reckoning and involved a change in the conditions under which it was to come about. If one reads the story of 1809 in the light of 1813, if one looks back on Wagram through Waterloo, Leipzig, Vittoria and the Beresina, one is in danger of misreading it. The lesson of 1809 is that Germany had not yet been welded into one by Napoleon's oppression; indeed, Austria owed her defeat in no small measure to the assistance given to Napoleon by his German vassals, and to the apathy or selfishness or timidity of Prussia and the other states to whom she had looked for support. To the South-West of Germany Napoleon was still a benefactor rather than an oppressor, the protector of Bavarian and Franconian against the Hapsburg and the Hohenzollern, the author of manifold ameliorations in the social and material circumstances of the mass of the population; while even in the North-West, in Westphalia and in the Hanoverian districts still under military rule, his yoke was not yet so galling that those who bore it were ready to risk all in the attempt to throw it off. It was in the years between Wagram and the retreat from Moscow that the attitude of the people of Germany towards Napoleon finally crystallised into one of uncompromising hostility, precisely because it was in these years that the pressure of the Continental System on every German household brought home to Hessians, to Brunswickers, to Saxons, to burghers of the Hanseatic towns, of Rhenish cities like Düsseldorf, and of Baltic ports like Dantzic, the fact that the new Charlemagne was prepared to sacrifice their interests and their welfare to his struggle with the Mistress of the Seas. The enforcing of the Continental System, Napoleon's great weapon against Great Britain, was at the root of his aggressions on Germany, of the arbitrary territorial alterations which gave offence to the Princes, of the financial extortions and the interference with trade and industry which inflicted such widespread suffering on the peoples, of the Spanish and Russian campaigns for which the conscription took its toll not from French families only, but from Dutch, German and Italian homes ; finally, his failure to enforce this system on Russia and on Spain brought about that military situation which made the successful rising of 1813 possible.

But in 1809 these things were still in the future. If the modern investigator can see clearly in the Franco-Russian alliance the signs of its coming dissolution, they were not quite so obvious when it had just sufficed to keep Russia's neutrality proof against the temptation of Aspern. With Austria humbled, Prussia's helplessness proclaimed by her inaction, North-West Germany occupied by his troops or carved up into new principalities of his own creation, and the states of South-West Germany his faithful allies, Napoleon might reasonably feel satisfied with the state of affairs in Germany. If he could have induced England to make peace on terms which acknowledged his territorial resettlement of Europe, it is more than possible that his organisation might have endured, at least that it might have lasted his lifetime. But to overcome England he was driven into courses which deprived him of the benefit of much of what he had done for Germany. The destroyer of the *ancien régime*, of social and economic privilege, became lost in the author of the Continental System, and in the master whose servants the conscribing officials were. Gratitude was before long forgotten, and submerged by hatred.

Yet, as 1813 was to prove, the intensity of the hostility to Napoleon varied enormously in different states. It was strongest in Prussia, which had only received insult and injury at his hands, since the remodelling of the institutions of the country on the lines he had laid down elsewhere, the benefits of the abolition of feudalism and privilege, came not from him, but from the Hohenzollern and their ministers. It was weaker in the North-West, which suffered greatly from the Continental System, which had been bandied about from one of his puppets to another, but which had still received from him and his nominees the benefits of an orderly, systematic and modern rule. It was weakest in the South-West, where states like Bavaria and Würtemberg represented the realisation by his help of traditional ideas, were developments, not new creations, and possessed some other justification for their existence than the mere *fiat* of the conqueror. They, too, were sacrificed to the Continental System, their contingents perished for the Emperor in Russia and in Spain; but they owed Napoleon no small debt, and it was only when the Allies guaranteed them the continued enjoyment of the boons he had conferred on them that their German patriotism overpowered Napoleon's hold on their allegiance.

Among these states, Bavaria owed as much to Napoleon as did any other. She had resumed the position she had held in Louis XIV's time of the principal client state of France. This had caused her a great increase of territory, the annexations of 1809 bringing her area up to nearly 40,000 square miles, and her population to over 3,000,000. But her territorial development was of less importance than the work of Maximilian Joseph and Montgelas in building up a well-organised, strongly centralised modern state. More fortunate than his Austrian namesake, Joseph II, the King of Bavaria was able to utilise the ideas and methods of the French Revolution to carry out a revolution from above for which his subjects were by no means prepared. The Liberal principles of the King and his minister were not altogether popular, especially with the Catholic inhabitants of the numerous small towns and with the Tyrolese peasantry, who bitterly resented the interference with their religious rites and customs, the dissolution of their Estates, and the confiscation of Church property. Outside Tyrol, however, a Bavarian nationality was really created. The old constitution was swept away, and a new order established in its place (May 1808). The nobles, while retaining their social privileges, were compelled to pay taxes; personal freedom was guaranteed to all persons and classes. That an army based on conscription was among the innovations, that the *Code Napoléon* was introduced, the administration organised on French lines, and that the country was divided after the French model into fifteen departments [1] named after the rivers, need hardly be mentioned. The government may be best described as a Liberal bureaucratic absolutism, for the representative element in the constitution was so small and unimportant as to be practically negligible. The

---

[1] Tyrol provided three of these.

chief difficulty was financial: Napoleon's demands on his allies were not easily appeased, nor could a modern administration be provided without considerable outlay: moreover, Maximilian Joseph was not less extravagant than the majority of his family, if he never imitated the wilder performances of some of the later Wittelsbachs.[1]

In Baden a very similar state of things prevailed, though on a somewhat smaller scale. Duke Charles Frederick deserves credit for having endeavoured to spare his subjects as far as possible from the burden of the expense of the increased military establishment. To this end he effected great economies at his Court, while endeavouring to bring the financial system into line with modern requirements. Here also one meets an administration organised on the French pattern: a Council with the five departments of Finance, Justice, the Interior, War, and Foreign Affairs subordinated to it; a Legislative Council of ministers and nominees; an enlightened autocracy governing in the interests of subjects who were hardly allowed any voice in the settlement of their affairs.

Frederick of Würtemberg presents a rather different aspect. If Würtemberg had retained more of its mediæval constitution longer than its neighbours, the change it now underwent was the more complete. An oppressive absolutism was substituted for "*das gute alte Recht*," the nobles found themselves powerless to resist the loss of most of their cherished privileges, and all classes were equally compelled to submit to the interference of the monarch in every sphere of activity. Napoleon secured the allegiance of his German clients by consulting the interests of the sovereigns, not those of the subjects, and the destruction of the old liberties of Würtemberg was typical of the removal of all such obstacles which marred the completeness of his vassal monarchs' control of their principalities, since the more absolute the vassal, the more completely could the overlord dispose of the resources of the subject states. Local liberties were a hindrance, and must therefore be swept away. But with the Napoleonic absolutism Würtemberg received the *Code Napoléon* and the abolition of many of the cramping relics of feudalism which had so much impeded the social and economic development of the country. Frederick has been described as "an inconsiderate despot who oppressed the noble Swabian people

[1] Cf. *Deutsche Geschichte, 1806-1871*, vol. i. pp. 94 ff.

with disgraceful disregard ";[1] but for all that he was the real
creator of the Kingdom of Würtemberg; he brought the country
safely through the perils of the Napoleonic era, and out of "a
collection of odds and ends" built up a compact and well-organised monarchy with an efficient army which, if out of all proportion to the size of the kingdom, was yet the best guarantee that
it should be respected by its neighbours.   Himself a Protestant,
Frederick was the first sovereign of Würtemberg to secure for
Roman Catholics the toleration hitherto denied to them by the
bigotry of the Lutheran clergy, who had in past time carried
their intolerance to the point of refusing to receive the
Huguenot refugees because they were Calvinists.[2]

Saxony resembled the states of the South-West, inasmuch
as it also had an old dynasty which Napoleon had bound to his
cause by favours and concessions instead of deposing it: it
differed from them, however, in being but little affected by the
reforming movement which was making itself so strongly felt
elsewhere.   Very conservative himself, Frederick Augustus was
supported in his opposition to reform by his ministers, Marcolini
and Hopfzarten, who would not hear of any changes in the
internal administration, cumbrous and unworkable though it
was, and did not even attempt to tax the nobles.   Not till 1811
did the increased expense of a larger army necessitate some
readjustment of the system of taxation.   Saxony thus was less
affected by the changes of the time than any other part of
Germany, though the Grand Duchy of Warsaw which had been
placed under her King by the Peace of Tilsit was organised on
the usual French lines, with six departments, a two-chamber
Assembly whose functions were practically nominal, and a
Council of five to whom the government was entrusted.   Baron
Senfft, the Saxon Foreign Minister, would have gladly made
the union between Saxony and Poland closer, hoping to crush
Prussia between them, but this was not what Napoleon seems
to have intended.   The hold of the King of Saxony on the
Grand Duchy was little more than a convenient cloak for
French predominance in its affairs, under which the Poles
might hope for a more complete restoration than it had as
yet been convenient for Napoleon to give them.   The connection
with Saxony remained therefore little more than nominal.

[1] *Deutsche Geschichte, 1806–1871*, i. 435.
[2] Cf. A. Pfister, *König Friedrich von Würtemberg und seine Zeit.*

In the North-West of Germany some of the old dynasties remained, in Mecklenburg and in Oldenburg and in Hesse-Darmstadt, where Landgrave Louis X, now Grand Duke, was so wedged in between two of Napoleon's new creations as to be powerless for harm even if he had been hostile to Napoleon, and not, as he was, one of the Emperor's most faithful adherents. Of the new states, the Grand Duchy of Würzburg, given (1806) in exchange for Salzburg to Archduke Ferdinand, who had then for the second time been dispossessed, needs but a brief mention. Admitted to the Confederation of the Rhine in September 1806, he had had to send his contingent of 2000 men to support Napoleon in 1809, but the improved relations between France and Austria inaugurated by Metternich and crowned by the marriage of Marie Louise to Napoleon (April 1810), removed all danger of a collision of interests.

The Grand Duchy of Frankfort, the principality with which the unstable Dalberg was now invested, is a more interesting study. Originally given the Free Cities of Frankfort and Ratisbon with the Principality of Aschaffenburg, Dalberg had had after Wagram to agree (Feb. 16th, 1810) to a modification which gave Ratisbon to Bavaria and compensated him with Hanau and Fulda. His dominions thus formed a curiously shaped strip some 2200 square miles in extent, all but a very small portion being situated on the North bank of the Main. A population of some 300,000, marked by many diversities of race, occupation and religion, was given some measure of unity by having to submit to the same laws and the same administrative system, both borrowed from France, and to provide a contingent of 4200 to the Confederation's army. The abolition of the different local and municipal institutions and the establishment of legal and fiscal unity were but a poor compensation for the heavy taxation, the loss of trade with England, the confiscation and destruction of colonial goods which had been imported through that country. Education was, it is true, encouraged, the administration of justice enormously improved, the position of the Jews in some degree ameliorated, the substitution of the French Penal Code for the *Carolina*, a penal law so barbarous as to be practically obsolete, was a great advantage; but against that the trade of Frankfort was practically ruined, and large numbers of the men of the Duchy met their death in the service of the Emperor for a

cause which could not benefit them or their countrymen.[1]
Had Napoleon maintained his supremacy, the Duchy was to
have passed to Eugene Beauharnais on Dalberg's death; but
its existence was anomalous and unjustifiable, a violation of
history and geography alike, and it did not survive the fall
of its founder.[2]

A rather larger state, the Grand Duchy of Berg,[3] was formed
with part of the much-disputed Cleves-Jülich inheritance as
its nucleus.   Cleves, which had gone to Prussia, and Berg, which
had passed through the Neuburg Wittelsbachs into the hands
of Maximilian Joseph of Zweibrücken and Bavaria, thus came
together again under the rule of Murat.[4]   Murat received a
seat in the College of Kings, and on the formation of the
Confederation of the Rhine the possessions of William Frederick
of Nassau, the ex-Stadtholder of the United Provinces,[5] were
added to the Grand Duchy on the refusal of their ruler to join
the Confederacy; while the overthrow of Prussia led to its being
further increased by receiving Mark, also part of the Cleves-
Jülich inheritance, Tecklenberg, Lingen and the Prussian
portion of Münster—an addition of 3200 square miles and
360,000 people.[6]   The Grand Duchy thus included the valleys
of the Sieg, Ruhr and Lippe, all tributaries of the Rhine,
and the upper waters of the Ems, covering in all some 12,000
square miles, with a population of 1,200,000, and including
some of the chief manufacturing towns of Germany.   "It was
the Birmingham and Sheffield, the Leeds and Manchester
of Germany rolled into one."[7] inasmuch as iron and steel
works, textile manufactures, the cloth, the cotton, the silk and
the wool industries flourished side by side.   But its prosperity
depended on the ready importation of raw material and on
finding a market for its finished products, so the continental
blockade and the rigid protective system of France caught

---

[1] A battalion from Frankfort was in Leval's German division of the Second Corps
which entered Spain in the autumn of 1808; it was badly mauled at Talavera, and
was one of the corps which came over to the British during the fighting round
Bayonne in December 1813.

[2] Fisher, ch. xiv., gives a most interesting account of the Grand Duchy of
Frankfort.

[3] Cf. Fisher, chs. ix. and x.   [4] March 1806.

[5] Cf. p. 372.

[6] At this time the fortress of Wesel, hitherto part of the Grand Duchy, was handed
over to France.

[7] Fisher, p. 206.

the Grand Duchy between the upper and the nether millstones. By 1812 its exports had declined to a fifth of what they had been in 1807, since its markets across the ocean had been lost to it by British commercial and maritime supremacy, and the French Empire was surrounded with an insurmountably high tariff-wall. The Grand Duchy was so far advanced on the road to commercial ruin that in 1811 a deputation was actually sent to Paris to petition for incorporation in the French Empire.

Thus here again the Continental System uprooted any gratitude which the reforms introduced by the French might have earned. But this was not all. Instead of the light taxation which had been the rule before the creation of the Grand Duchy, its inhabitants found themselves borne down by a heavy burden. It was not merely the introduction of the French fiscal system; that might have been expected to increase the revenue somewhat without really increasing its burdensomeness. But instead of the 3,000,000 francs which the Grand Duchy might have provided with ease, in 1813 no less a sum than 10,000,000 was extorted from its taxpayers. And it is easy to appreciate where all the money went and how much benefit its unfortunate inhabitants derived from their exertions, when one sees that between 4 and 5 millions were annually devoted to the army, when one meets with four battalions from Berg fighting Napoleon's battles in Catalonia, and reads of the 6000 men with the Grand Army of 1812 and of the 4000 recruits demanded from her to fill the gaps which the Russian disaster had made.

But in many ways Berg benefited by the French rule. Count Beugnot, the Imperial Commissioner by whom the government of the Grand Duchy was carried on, was one of the best of the officials employed by Napoleon. Honest, painstaking and zealous, under his auspices the French administration was a model of order, method and definition: it was bureaucratic and absolute, it did nothing to teach the people to govern themselves, but it was systematic, diligent, careful, prompt and decided. The French substituted good and simple laws for the chaos of conflicting, obsolete customs and statutes which had hitherto prevailed. They abolished caste privileges, broke down the monopoly of land possessed by the gentry, made all trades and professions free to all to enter, and enormously improved the social and economic situation of the peasantry.[1] Public works, education, religious toleration, the jury system, the French codes, the French judicial system, were among the benefits of French rule, and the abuses which they had swept away were exorcised once and for all. Thus though Murat ceded Berg to Napoleon in July 1808, and the Grand Duchy remained without a sovereign till, in March 1809, Napoleon suddenly conferred it on his five year old nephew, Napoleon Louis, son of the King of Holland; though in January 1811 the Grand Duchy was deprived of the portions North of the Lippe, which were then annexed to the French Empire as the Departments of Lippe and Ems Supérieur, it needed all the grinding tyranny of the conscription and the Continental System to provoke the riots which preceded the arrival of the delivering Cossacks in November 1813.

The largest and most important of Napoleon's new creations was that erected for his brother Jerome. Its constitution, promulgated on November 15th, 1807, was a marked advance on anything which the Hessians who formed so large a part of Jerome's new subjects had yet known. Besides the four ministers to whom the departments of the administration were entrusted,[2] and a Council of State nominated by the King to give advice on administrative matters, draft laws and act as a court of appeal, the kingdom was given elected Estates which would really seem to have been something more than a mere form. That the kingdom was divided into departments, of which there were eight, and subdivided into districts and cantons, that the Civil Code was introduced, the old seigneurial jurisdiction swept away to make room for a judicial hierarchy on the French model, that the Church was subordinated to the State and no small portion of its revenues diverted to other purposes, some beneficial others the reverse, that education was carefully organised, that feudalism was abolished, labour services done away with or made commutable for money-payments, all this was the natural result of the application of French principles of government to Westphalia. Life was made easier and simpler in many respects, personal freedom

---

[1] Cf. Fisher, pp. 202–205.

[2] Namely, Justice and the Interior ; War ; Finance, Commerce and the Treasury, and a Minister of State.

and practical equality before the law were great boons. Commerce was freed from the barriers and restrictions which had hitherto impeded it, and the substitution of one system of finance, and that system thoroughly modern and enlightened, for the complications which had hitherto prevailed in the different provinces from which the kingdom had been made up was a great improvement. Exemptions disappeared, with them went a multitude of minor imposts, difficult and trouble-some to collect, and unproductive at the best. Import and export duties were so arranged as to permit the normal development of the resources of the country. If the Kingdom of Westphalia had been in fact what it was in name, a free and independent state, it might have arrived at no small pitch of prosperity. Had the districts which separated it from the sea been added to it, it might have become what the House of Brunswick-Lüneburg might have created but had failed to create, a strong and united state, to be in North-Western Germany what Bavaria was in the South-West. If the Hessians seem to have regretted their old rulers, the Brunswickers were reconciled to the new order by the advantages it brought them, and Prussia had not apparently made herself so dear to her Westphalian provinces that they found the separation hard to bear. But the interests of the Westphalian peoples had not been the object for which the kingdom had been created. Napoleon had only his own benefit in view when he built it up: the selection of Jerome as its king was in itself a sufficient proof of this.

At first energetic and active, Jerome was by nature too indolent, too self-indulgent, too easy-going for the assiduous devotion to his duties which his position demanded. Self-sacrifice and hard work were not to be looked for from him. He had able ministers: von Bülow, a Prussian, looked after the finances with skill and integrity, and when he incurred Napoleon's displeasure and was dismissed (April 1811), Malchus, his successor, proved as able, if harsher and less honest. In the Baron de Wolffradt, Jerome possessed a capable Minister of the Interior, formerly a faithful servant of the Duke of Brunswick, who had taken service with his new master at the request of his old.

Idle, vicious, and devoid of moral strength as Jerome was, ill-suited for the position he occupied, the harm he brought upon his subjects was a mere trifle compared with the mischief wrought by the heavy hand of Napoleon. To one ignorant of the circumstances under which the kingdom of Westphalia came into existence, and judging by the treatment it received from Napoleon, it would hardly seem that the country owed its creation to the Emperor of the French. Rather one might suppose that it was a kingdom on which he desired to avenge himself for some signal slight or injury. Westphalia was compelled to keep up an army of 25,000 men, half of whom were Frenchmen, an army which fought Napoleon's battles in Spain[1] at the expense of Westphalia, instead of paying its way by being hired to foreign Powers, after the manner of that of Hesse-Cassel in times past. Moreover, Jerome's kingdom had to support a permanent charge on the royal domains of 7,000,000 francs in favour of France; and it started its career with the heavy incubus of a debt of 30,000,000 francs, representing the indebtedness incurred by the Elector of Hesse for all his rigid parcimony; another of 8,000,000, the cost of the French occupation during 1807; and worst of all, of a war indemnity of 26,000,000 more.

To support such a burden was quite beyond the capacities of the kingdom and even Napoleon had to admit this, and to consent to modify the terms. In January 1810 a new treaty handed over to Westphalia most of the rest of Hanover, and reduced the indemnity to the more moderate dimensions of 16,000,000 francs, and extended the time within which it had to be paid from eighteen months to ten years. Still even this relief was only partial. Westphalia had to maintain 18,500 Frenchmen in addition to her own army of 25,000 men, and Napoleon demanded the annual payment of 4,500,000 francs from the Hanoverian domains for a term of ten years. The negotiations over the cession were still far from complete when, in December 1810, the exigencies of enforcing the Continental System led to the annexation by Napoleon of the coast districts of Germany from the Ems to Lübeck. Napoleon's object in bringing these lands under his more immediate control was to enforce the decrees of Fontainebleau (Oct. 1810), which established special

---

[1] There was a Westphalian division with St. Cyr in Catalonia in 1809, mustering over 5000 men ; by June 1st, 1810, it had been reduced to four battalions. A Westphalian cavalry regiment also formed part of the main invading army in 1808.

tribunals to try persons suspected of introducing prohibited goods, and to check the extensive system of smuggling by which his attempt to keep out British goods was being circumvented. The districts thus forcibly incorporated in the French Empire included the Hanseatic towns which had been in French occupation since the end of 1806,[1] and their fate was shared by the Duchy of Oldenburg, the Principalities of Aremberg and Salm, and not avoided even by Napoleon's own creations, Berg and Westphalia. The Northern part of Hanover was thus withdrawn from Jerome, and with it went the greater part of the Westphalian department of the Weser.[2] In vain Jerome protested: in the end he was lucky to obtain the reduction of the French troops whom he had to support to their old number of 12,500; in the territorial rearrangement he had to acquiesce with the best grace he could muster.

Where Napoleon treated his own creations with such severity, it was not likely that the lot of Prussia would be particularly happy. Of the means by which Napoleon continued to hold Prussia down, of the great indemnity he had extorted from her, and of his interference with the composition of the Prussian ministry, some account has already been given.[3] That despite all this, and despite the hostility and suspicion with which Napoleon regarded the country he had injured so sorely, Prussia should have carried out in these years of distress social and military reforms of the utmost importance, makes the achievement all the more remarkable. The names which must always be associated with this work are those of Stein and Scharnhorst. The latter's share in the regeneration of Prussia, though of the utmost importance, was of a more restricted character than that of Stein, although when one seeks to estimate their relative work for Prussia it must be remembered that Stein was only in office from the October of 1807 till the following December, that much of the necessary preliminaries to his great measures had been done by others, and that his work was continued by others after he had to fly from the wrath of Napoleon. Still it is Stein who best represents the new Prussia. Himself an Imperial Knight, his position as a Prussian patriot and minister is

---

[1] Cf. Fisher, ch. xv.
[2] Roughly corresponding to the bishopric of Osnabrück.
[3] Cf. Chapter XXVII.

typical of the way in which the rising tide of German national feeling was to make for the future aggrandisement of Prussia.   Indeed, it is a remarkable fact that nearly all the men who played the chief parts in the regeneration of Prussia were not Prussians by birth.   Mecklenburg gave her Blücher, to Hanover she owed Hardenberg and Scharnhorst, Gneisenau was a Saxon.   But a common hatred of Napoleon seems to have caused them, as it were instinctively, to seek the service of the one German state which owed Napoleon nothing but injuries, and was to that extent marked out as a likely disciple of the gospel of vengeance.

Roughly speaking, the work of Stein was to adapt to the requirements of Prussia the work of the French Revolution. Prussia already possessed highly centralised institutions and all the machinery needed for a benevolent despotism : the Hohenzollern family was identified with the traditions of a vigorous and active personal rule, and Frederick William III, even if deficient in the promptness and decision of Frederick William I, or of Frederick II, did not altogether fail to carry out his task : his share in the reform of his kingdom is more often unduly depreciated than exaggerated.   Briefly stated, what Stein did for Prussia and for the Hohenzollern was to inaugurate a series of important social reforms and to identify the dynasty with this work.   He did not create the Prussian bureaucracy, but he reformed it, swept away inefficiency and corruption, and infused it with fresh vigour.

It is with the reform of the administration that Stein is most peculiarly connected : that was his special work.   When he came into office the General Directory had practically gone to pieces, the King relied on his Cabinet Secretaries, the departments were without proper correlation or supervision. This increased the trouble caused by its want of unity, by the cross division between departments whose clashing produced great confusion.

Stein's plan included the erection of a Council of State to control the administration, audit the accounts of the ministers, decide disputes between the departments, and legislate.   It was to include the ministers and ex-ministers, all Princes of the blood over the age of eighteen, and other persons specially appointed.   For purposes of administration the Council was to be divided into five departments, th › of Foreign Affairs, War, Justice, Finance,[1] and the Interior.[2] This plan was not carried out in its entirety, but the edicts of December 18th reforming the central administration, and of the 26th reforming the provincial government, were almost identical with Stein's unratified edict of November. The Council of State did not come into existence till 1810, and even then it did not control the administration; but on the whole Stein's ideas were accepted.

In local government, Stein abolished the War and Domains Chambers, which, originally merely financial bodies, had become administrative and judicial also. He now divided the provinces into districts (*Bezirke*), in each of which "deputations" corresponded to the departments of the Directory. The old provincial arrangements were so far kept up that Superior Presidents were appointed to exercise a general supervision over groups of districts, and to deal with special emergencies. Justice was separated from administration, rural tribunals being created for minor judicial work.

Stein's aims did not stop at mere reforms in degree. He was anxious to introduce in some form or another representative institutions, possibly a national Parliament. It is as a step in this direction that the Municipal Reform Edict, published in November 1808,[3] is most interesting. The towns of Germany had in the 18th Century fallen into great decay. True municipal life hardly existed. Narrow oligarchies controlled the few towns where the forms of self-government had not given place to the rule of royal officials, appointed quite regardless of their fitness for the posts they held. This edict gave the townsfolk control of their property, the State only interfering to see that its own rights were respected and its laws observed; it placed in their hands local government, justice and police; it freed them from their manorial lords, and placed them all in the same relation to the State, the only distinctions it observed being those of size.[4] This grant of municipal self-government was a free gift, in no sense a concession; indeed it was given to

[1] Including the Treasury and the commissions for managing the Taxes and the Domains and Forests.

[2] Under this head were comprised Education, Public Health, Mining, Police and Trade.

[3] Cf. Seeley, ii. 238–243.

[4] Towns with over 10,000 inhabitants were classed as "great," those having from 3500 to 10,000 as "medium," those with from 800 to 3500 as "small."

people not always well prepared or anxious for it. " The people were commanded, not allowed, to govern themselves." [1]

With this Municipal Reform must be connected the famous Emancipating Edict of October 9th, 1807.[2] This great measure had been discussed by an Intermediate Commission in July 1807. The Report of August 17th showed how urgent was the necessity for free trade in land ; how the impoverished landowners could not sell part of their estates and so obtain the money they needed, because the middle-class capitalists who had the money to invest were not allowed to purchase noble land (*Rittergut*). Hardenberg's Memorandum of September 17th drew an outline of the measures embodied in the edict, and it would seem that the idea of establishing free trade in land originated with Schön, while the work of drafting the edict was performed by Stägemann : still Stein took up the project warmly, supported it with all his might, made it of universal application, and it was he who carried it through.[3]

The edict was fully in accord with his principle of removing all artificial hindrances in the way of the full development of the country. Divided as the population of Prussia was into distinct classes, separated as into water-tight compartments by the strictest lines of caste, nobles, citizens and peasants had hardly anything in common ; for while the peasantry did come into contact with the nobles as landlords and as officers in the army, the citizens were not even brought into line with their fellow-subjects through the army, being non-military in the extreme. What Stein did was that he managed to abolish caste in persons and in land ; for the division extended not merely to the owners but to their estates.[4] Prussia had hitherto been divided into manors, with a primitive and rigid organisation : the peasants were subject to heavy burdens, but they were at least secure against the caprice and arbitrary punishments of their landlords. They had a secure tenure and a definite status. But this was restrictive as well as protective : they could not rise beyond their status. Stein's object was to open all careers to every one, and the Edict of Emancipation made the occupation of the peasants voluntary and no longer obligatory.[5] This celebrated edict [6] abolished personal serfdom,

[1] Seeley, ii. 244.   [2] *Ibid.* i. 430.
[3] *Ibid.* i. 446.   [4] *Ibid.* i. 437.
[5] *Ibid.* ii. 185.   [6] For the text, cf. Seeley, i. 443 ff.

and especially menial services, together with forced labour ; but it did not free the peasants from the obligations by which they were bound as free persons through the possession of an estate or by special contracts. To these they continued to be liable ; and the opponents of the measure attacked it vehemently, because it put the peasants at the mercy of their creditors, and by encouraging them to sell their land, took away the fixity of tenure their definite status had hitherto secured to them.

What amount of force there was in this charge had more validity against the edicts by which after Stein's dismissal Hardenberg[1] completed his work. These followed on the lines Stein had laid down. That of November 1810 was based on the principle that no one should have the power to close a trade against any man. By this and by the more celebrated Edict of September 1811,[2] which freed leasehold and copyhold alike from all services, and established alienability and free disposition of property, Hardenberg wrought a great change in Prussia, His solution of the land question took the form of a compromise. The peasantry were divided into two classes, leaseholders and those who had hereditary or life claims on their tenements. It was proposed to let the landlords buy out the first class by giving them half their holdings, for compensation in money was altogether out of the question from the want of cash in the country. Finally, copyholders for life were subjected to the same arrangement, hereditary tenants compensating their land-lords by surrendering a third of their tenements. This system had been anticipated by Stein when, in July 1808, he had relieved the needs of the peasantry on the royal domains in Prussia, among whom serfdom had been abolished as long ago as the reign of Frederick William I. He had adopted a scheme of Schrotter's,[3] which allowed the peasants to possess their holdings as their own, subject to land-tax and to the resumption by the State of various rights and concessions. At the same time, much was done in the way of abolishing monopolies; for instance, that of making and selling millstones and building mills, hitherto in the hands of the Government, was abolished by Stein for Prussia only in the spring of 1808, for the whole kingdom by Hardenberg in the two following years.

Reforms in the judicial system, aiming at even and speedy

[1] Recalled to office as Chancellor in 1810.
[2] Cf. Seeley, ii. 185.   [3] *Ibid.* ii. 192.

justice, with equality before the law, financial measures, including the imposition of an income tax (Sept. 1811), the abolition of that exemption from taxation which the nobles had hitherto enjoyed, the establishment of a State Bank, and the introduction of a paper currency, were among the objects with which Hardenberg was occupied during his tenure of the Chancellorship. In this capacity he did Prussia excellent service, even if he seemed to have abandoned the cause of opposition to Napoleon and dissembled his hatred of the Emperor so well that even Stein distrusted him.[1] But to secure the success and continuity of these reforms something more was wanting. It was useless to introduce reforms unless provision could be made that there should be men to work them, and to work them in the right way. It had not been the machinery but the *morale* of Prussia which had failed her in 1806, and one of the most pressing needs was a thorough reform of the system of education, both primary and secondary. The rising generation must be taught the necessity of patriotism and civic duty, the *gymnasia* must be reformed, and something done to repair the loss inflicted on Prussian education by the cession of Halle and its University to Westphalia. With this branch of the regeneration of Prussia the name of William von Humboldt will always be associated. Appointed Minister of Public Instruction in 1809, he was largely responsible for the foundation in the August of that year of the University of Berlin, supported by the State with a grant which must have been a severe tax on its already burdened exchequer. The share of this University in keeping alive the spirit of opposition to foreign rule and in identifying Prussia with the growing feeling of German nationality was destined to be no small one, and in 1811 a sister University was established at Breslau to help in the work.

Parallel with the civil and social reorganisation of Prussia, went the reform of that army on whose traditions and past glories Prussia had relied with such fatal effect in 1806. Reform was essential, but there was still a school of military thought which adhered to its belief that a dead lion was superior to any number of living animals of other species, and therefore resisted all attempts at departure from the Frederician system. On the Military Reorganisation Commission, of which Scharnhorst had been appointed President, both schools were represented,

[1] Cf. Seeley, ii. 462.

the Frederician being stronger in numbers, the more modern school powerful through the character of its representatives. Scharnhorst himself, Gneisenau the brave defender of Colberg, and von Grolmann, a young major of great zeal and capacity. These three were in full accord as to the essential needs, the formation of a reserve outside the standing army, the nationalisation of the army by uniting all classes in its ranks, and the substitution of a discipline of reason and humanity for the savage rule by terror which was the ideal of the Frederician school.[1] These proposals provoked much opposition, both in the Commission and in the army as a whole; but the King was heartily with the reformers, remodelled the Commission so as to give them the upper hand, and supported them in most of the changes they introduced.

Naturally the first steps taken were in the direction of getting rid of the inefficient and incompetent officers who had been responsible for the shameful surrenders of 1806, of dismissing the foreigners of whom there had always been so large a number in the army since the practice of enlisting them had been introduced by Frederick II, of opening the commissioned ranks to non-nobles, of improving the *morale* of the troops by ameliorating the conditions and the terms of their service. But these were only details compared with the great change Scharnhorst desired to introduce. Frederick William I had established the principle that a subject is by the fact of his allegiance bound to serve his master; but the exemptions so freely granted and the large enlistment of foreigners had made it almost a dead letter. Scharnhorst desired to make national defence the primary duty of every citizen, to cause it to be regarded as a privilege not a burden, and he favoured the establishment of a national militia which would also serve as a bond of political union. This was more than Frederick William was quite prepared for; he rather dreaded the political effects of the arming of the masses, while the Radicals feared that military training would destroy culture. But it was Napoleon who forced a decision by the famous clause in the Convention of September 8th, 1808, which fixed the strength of the Prussian Army at 42,000 and forbade the organisation of a militia. Accordingly, Scharnhorst adopted the plan of passing through the ranks as large a number of men as possible, letting them serve for such a period only as

[1] Cf. *Deutsche Geschichte, 1806-1871,* i. pp. 223 ff.

was necessary to give them an adequate military training, and then dismissing them to their homes. This "furlough system," established by a Cabinet Order of August 6th, 1808, provided for a steady stream of recruits coming forward to replace the men dismissed to their homes; and thus, despite Napoleon's conditions, a reserve of trained men was built up. These men on furlough were maintained in an efficient condition by secret drilling, sergeants being sent round the country for the purpose, by which means Napoleon's refusal to allow the formation of a *Landwehr* was circumvented.

Scharnhorst, however, did not escape Napoleon's notice. When, in 1810, on the fall of Stein's successor, Altenstein, Hardenberg was with Napoleon's consent called to office,[1] the Emperor insisted that Scharnhorst should be dismissed. This, of course, took place; but Scharnhorst did not have to imitate Stein in flying from Prussia: he remained in the kingdom, and took a very large share in the work of military reorganisation nominally carried on by his successor, Hake.

But though in these various ways and at the expense of many of the old traditions of the Frederician system a new Prussia was being built up out of the ruins of the edifice which had collapsed at Jena, Prussia had still to drain the cup of humiliation to the dregs. She had remained inactive in 1809; but when, in 1812, Central Europe was once more plunged into war by Russia's refusal to continue to enforce the Continental System, it was not with inaction that Napoleon was content. Prussia's last humiliation was the Convention of February 24th, 1812, which made her little more than the advanced base of the French invasion of Russia. Not only did she have to send a contingent of 20,000 to Napoleon's army, she had to collect vast magazines of supplies for his use, and to place the country and all its fortresses and resources at his disposal.

For between 1809 and 1812 a great change had come over Napoleon's foreign relations. Russia was no longer the ally, Austria no longer the enemy. With the substitution of the reactionary and opportunist Metternich for Stadion, Austria had abandoned her championship of German nationalism, and had readily accepted Napoleon's overtures. Metternich was utterly unaffected by sentimental considerations. The traditions of the Holy Roman Empire were nothing to him; he was only

---

[1] *Deutsche Geschichte, 1806–1871*, i. 264.

moved by the new feeling of German nationality inasmuch as it aroused his suspicions and dislike. Anything in the way of a popular movement was sure to arouse the bitterest hostility in him. A reactionary, narrow and suspicious, he hated Napoleon as the man who had humiliated Austria and deprived her of provinces and prestige, not as the representative of military despotism or as the oppressor of Germany. But when Napoleon showed signs of a wish to make friends with Austria, the hope of future favours made Metternich only too ready to overlook past injuries.

The outward sign of these better relations was Napoleon's marriage to Archduchess Marie Louise, celebrated at Vienna not nine months after the battle of Wagram (March 11th, 1810). The haughty Hapsburgs thus descended almost to the level of the Wittelsbachs and the other families with whom the Bonapartes had been pleased to form marriage alliances. Nevertheless, Metternich failed even to secure the concessions he had hoped to obtain; for Napoleon hurried Prince Schwarzenberg, the Austrian Ambassador at Paris, into signing the convention (Feb. 7th), so that he might be able to counter the Czar's rejection of the overtures he had made for the hand of a Russian Princess by the accomplished fact of his Austrian match.

This was one of the causes of disagreement between Napoleon and his ally of Tilsit. More serious was the Continental System. Russia found her interests and her commercial prosperity injured by her faithful fulfilment of Napoleon's demands. Alexander could not help recalling the circumstances of his father's death: why should he sacrifice the trade of Russia to a quarrel which was not his own? Moreover, Napoleon's measures for the enforcement of the Continental System were going beyond Alexander's powers of endurance. The annexation of the German coast-lands from the Ems Eastward (Dec. 13th, 1810) was a high-handed act which would, however, hardly have aroused Alexander's wrath so much had it not involved the suppression of the Grand Duchy of Oldenburg, held by his cousin, Duke Peter. Russia's reply to this was the ukase of December 31st, 1810, imposing heavy taxes on French wines, and permitting the importation of colonial products under a neutral flag. This was practically a defiance of Napoleon; and though the rupture was delayed for more than another year, it was henceforward inevitable.

To come to blows with Russia there was only one road which Napoleon could take, and that lay through Germany, so that the conflict was bound to be of vital importance to Germany even if the question at issue had not really been the continuation of Napoleon's predominance over Europe. But as Germany stood in 1812, the choice of the line to be taken was not hers to make. The states which formed the Confederation of the Rhine were pledged to assist Napoleon, even though the Continental System which Russia was refusing to endure any longer pressed even more heavily on them than on the subjects of the Czar. In Russia there were no interfering French Custom-house officers to make domiciliary visits: no Russian shop-keeper need fear to be dragged off to the galleys for the heinous crime of possessing goods of English origin. Yet to these and similar infringement of their liberty the Germans had been liable ever since the Fontainebleau decrees ; and while the export trade of Germany was practically at a standstill, tobacco, coffee, tea and sugar, luxuries so common as to be practically necessities, could only be obtained with great difficulty and at famine prices. Germany was under a tyrant against whom she could hope for no redress, and her sufferings in this way only emphasised her helplessness. Austria also was about to send a contingent to aid Napoleon. The hope of obtaining some return for her services combined with jealousy of Russia's success in the Balkans to bring about this result. Metternich, indeed, was able to represent this action as unavoidable. To take the side of Russia was out of the question, neutrality without mobilisation would be perilous, armed neutrality too expensive to be considered : Austria must therefore take part in the invasion, but her part in the campaign was typical of her real sentiments. The 30,000 men of whom her contingent consisted took care to do as little as possible for their ally : they formed a separate corps and thus preserved the appearance of inde-pendence; while the assistance they gave Napoleon was of no serious importance, chiefly consisting of letting Chichagoff's forces slip unmolested past their front on their way from the Lower Danube to the Beresina.

Prussia in like manner had to decide between the desirable and the possible, between defying her oppressor by throwing in her lot with Russia, and submitting to Napoleon's requirements. The question was soon settled. Krusemarck's convention was hailed by the "patriots" as the death-blow to their hopes. "We have signed our own death-warrant," wrote Gneisenau, and he and Boyen and Clausewitz resigned their commissions in disgust and left the country. "All is lost, and honour with it," was Blücher's comment; but the alternative was impossible. If Prussia joined Russia, the Russian forces would have to deprive themselves of an ally far more valuable than even the regenerated Prussian army, the physical difficulties which their country would place in an invader's way. Alone, Prussia could do nothing: for the Russians to advance beyond the Niemen would only invite a repetition of 1807. The Convention of February 24th was a humiliation, but it was the necessary corollary of Prussia's previous policy.

Thus all Germany stood on Napoleon's side as he advanced Eastward. In the army which invaded Russia there were almost as many Germans as Frenchmen.[1] Thus the whole VIth Corps (28,000 men) was composed of Bavarians, the VIIth (19,000) of Saxons, the VIIIth (19,000) of Westphalians. The contingents of Baden, Mecklenburg and Hesse-Darmstadt formed part of Davoût's huge Ist Corps; in the IInd Corps were included the men of the Hanseatic towns; the Würtembergers marched under Ney in the IIIrd Corps, the men of Berg and the minor states came up later with Victor. Macdonald's Xth Corps included the Prussian contingent and a mixed division of Bavarians, Westphalians and Poles. In like manner four of Murat's eleven cavalry divisions were made up of Germans and Poles. In all some 150,000 men from the Confederation of the Rhine formed part of the Grand Army, about a quarter of the total, while among the 200,000 "Frenchmen" in its ranks a small number must have come from the departments on the left bank of the Rhine, formerly part of the Holy Roman Empire. Indeed, if one includes in the reckoning the Austrian and Prussian contingents, the German element in the army of invasion was probably larger than any German army ever collected by the rulers of Germany for an enterprise in which the interests or the aspirations of Germany were concerned. Napoleon had united Germany in a way her own Princes and peoples had never united her before. But the heart of Germany was not in the invasion. It was with the utmost reluctance that the Prussian contingent

[1] Cf. H. B. George, *Napoleon's Invasion of Russia*, which is also very useful for the attitude and policy of Austria and Prussia at this period.

marched against the forces on whom the last hopes of Prussia rested; how little zeal for the cause inspired the Austrians has already been described; and if in the contingents of the Confederation there were many who had good reason to be grateful to Napoleon for the benefits his rule had brought them, there were also many who had been dragged from their homes to serve. Yet there was no approach to disaffection or treachery among the Germans in the Grand Army.[1] The poor success which attended the efforts of Stein and the Duke of Oldenburg to organise a German Legion out of them is a testimony to the hold which Napoleon had over his vassals. Few of the prisoners enlisted, fewer still deserted the Grand Army to join the Legion; and even if the privations they had endured may have accounted for their unwillingness to undergo new hardships under new colours, it also shows that the long-suffering Germans were not yet fully roused against Napoleon, or lacked the courage and the determination to risk anything for Germany. But so far as German nationalism was a real thing and had a real existence, it was all against Napoleon.

And to some degree cosmopolitanism and localism were beginning to give way to a national feeling. The period is one of the utmost importance in German literature; and though for the most part the great writers of the day pursued their own lines of intellectual development, quite regardless of the political situation of their country, some few did turn towards it. The *Tugendbund*, founded at Königsberg in 1808 for the revival of "morality, religion and public spirit," and suppressed at Napoleon's instance in the following year, was in the main the work of these same "intellectuals" who had hitherto held aloof from politics; and even if it and the secret societies to which its suppression gave rise really effected but little, their formation is an indication of the new order of things. The career of the philosopher Johann Gottlieb Fichte is typical of this change from the cosmopolitan to the national ideal. His *Grundzügen des Zeitalters* of 1806 has only to be compared with the *Reden an die Deutschen Krieger*, written two years later. Patriotism and the fate of his country were nothing to him before 1806, but that autumn of misfortune and disgrace changed his attitude. He now urged on his hearers at Berlin the adoption of a national system of education as the only way to cure the evils of localism

---

[1] Cf. George, pp. 49–50.

and lack of union: he preached a gospel of self-sacrifice for the national welfare, and called on all Germans to sink local differences in striving for a common end.

Another writer who exercised a great influence over his fellow-countrymen, rousing them to a sense of their common interests and common sufferings, was the poet Heinrich von Kleist. Keenly alive to the degradation and humiliating position of Germany, he read the present into the past: his *Hermanns-schlact* is really prophetic, not historic; anti-Gallicanism inspires it; to him the Romans are Frenchmen, and Frenchmen only.

The rise of this feeling was assisted by the great development of universities all over Germany. In Bavaria Maximilian Joseph abolished the Jesuit schools at Bamberg and Dillingen, freed München and Würzburg from clerical control, and called in North German professors of great repute. In Baden von Reizenstein, the enlightened minister of the Grand Duke, did much to revive Heidelberg University, and the Theological Faculty in that body played an important part in rousing national feeling. Of the University of Berlin and von Humboldt, mention has already been made; but great as was the direct service to education which Humboldt thus gave, of even more importance was the indirect result of his work. Till now the great intellects of Germany had been cosmopolitan in their outlook, non-national if not actively anti-national in their ideas. What Humboldt did was to enlist culture on the side of the State, to turn the intellectual movement into a patriotic channel, to reconcile the widely different schools of thought represented by Goethe and Stein.

Thus, despite the great reception which Napoleon held at Dresden on his way to the Niemen, despite the good service done by the German troops in his army—some idea of this may be gathered from the fact that there were no less than 186 Westphalian officers in the casualty list at Borodino,[1] and that one Bavarian light cavalry regiment could only muster 2 officers and 30 men at the close of the day[2]—Germany as a whole waited for the fate of the expedition with feelings in which anxiety for her sons was mixed with hopes for her oppressor's failure.

[1] Cf. Fisher, p. 305.   [2] *Deutsche Geschichte, 1806–1871*, i. 289.

GERMANY in 1811.

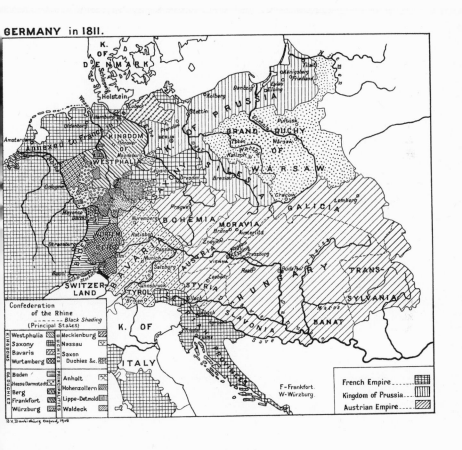

Confederation
of the Rhine
- - - - - - Black Shading
(Principal States)

KINGDOMS			DUCHIES	
	Westphalia			Mecklenburg
	Saxony			Nassau
	Bavaria			Saxon
	Wurtemberg			Duchies &c.

DUCHIES			PRINCIPALITIES	
	Baden			Anhalt
	Hesse Darmstadt			Hohenzollern
	Berg			Lippe-Detmold
	Frankfort			Waldeck
	Würzburg			

F = Frankfort.
W = Würzburg.

French Empire........	
Kingdom of Prussia....	
Austrian Empire.....	

B. V. Darbishire Oxford 1908

CHAPTER XXX

THE WAR OF LIBERATION, I

COMPLETELY as Napoleon's great invasion of Russia had failed his repulse had by no means settled the question of his supremacy over Central Europe. His yoke was too firmly fixed upon Germany, Italy and the Netherlands to be thrown off in a moment, and after only one defeat; and the completeness of his control of France may be estimated by the prodigious efforts he was able to command from France to retrieve his lost prestige. Though the shattered and demoralised relics of the Grand Army which had straggled back across the Niemen in December 1812 hardly mustered a sixth of the mighty host which had crossed it on the Eastward way, it was far from certain that 1813 might not see the attack renewed by a new Grand Army. Napoleon, who had hurried off to Paris, had thrown himself with characteristic energy into the Herculean task of reorganisation, and never were his great talents as an administrator more conspicuously displayed. Russia, on the other hand, was much exhausted by her exertions; she had worsted Napoleon, but it had been at no light cost that such a victory could be achieved over the master of Western Europe. Many of her generals and statesmen, among them Kutusov himself, were strongly opposed to the idea of risking anything in an attempt to follow up the success of the defensive campaign. They judged, and rightly, that all depended on the action of Austria and Prussia. Unless Russia could rely on the co-operation of those two Powers, to advance across the Niemen would merely court disaster.

And as yet neither Austria nor Prussia saw the way clear before them. Much as Frederick William longed to throw off the yoke of Napoleon, he could not at first nerve himself to the desperate step of defying the Emperor, not even when Metternich opened negotiations and showed himself anxious to turn Napoleon's misfortunes to the advantage of his unwilling allies.[1]

[1] Cf. *Deutsche Geschichte, 1806–1871*, i. 299, also *La Defection de la Prusse.*

And Metternich was only preparing to run with the hare in case hunting with the hounds should prove too dangerous a policy. Jealousy of Russia was with him a far stronger motive than hostility to France: he had no intention of shaking Napoleon's supremacy off Central Europe only to substitute that of the Czar. Public opinion in Austria might be strongly in favour of the bolder policy, but Metternich had no desire for a conflict with Napoleon; all he wanted was an opportunity of establishing an equilibrium in Europe which should secure the independence of Central Europe by balancing West against East; he wanted a peace in which Napoleon would for once not dictate, but accept terms. Schwarzenberg, it is true, went to the length of disobeying Eugene's orders to assist him in holding the line of the Vistula, and withdrew with the Austrian auxiliary corps into Galicia (January); but no immediate breach in the alliance between Austria and Napoleon followed: Metternich was waiting on events. However, while the governments were hesitating, the control of events was taken out of their hands by men who had a more accurate appreciation of the possibilities of the case.

Among these the place of honour must be given to General Yorck, the commander of the Prussian corps which had formed part of Marshal Macdonald's command. With that officer Yorck had soon quarrelled, and as early as October the Russians were making overtures to him in the hope that he would join them and help them to cut off the retreat of the Grand Army. Yorck had acquainted his King with these offers; but as he had received no new instructions, but only orders to assume the Governorship of East Prussia, he had taken no further step. However, when, in December, Macdonald ordered a retreat, Yorck deliberately allowed[1] Wittgenstein's Russians to interpose between himself and Macdonald, and, under the plea of being isolated, proceeded to enter into negotiations with the Russians. On December 30th, acting entirely on his own responsibility, he took the momentous step of concluding the Convention of Tauroggen. By this the Prussian troops under Yorck were to take post in the territory between Memel, Tilsit and the Haff, which was to be neutralised. Should the convention be repudiated either by the Czar or by the King of Prussia, they were to be free to depart, but were not to serve against Russia before March 1st.

The immediate result of this was that Macdonald found it

[1] *La Defection de la Prusse*, pp. 115–118,

impossible to maintain himself at Tilsit, and retired from Königsberg to Dantzic.   However, the political importance of Yorck's
action in thus disassociating a Prussian force from the alliance
with France was far greater than the mere military results of the
step.   What would the King do? would he ratify his general's
bold action by declaring against Napoleon? would he treat Yorck
as guilty, as technically he certainly was, of high treason, and
disown him?   At first the chances seemed to favour this second
alternative.   To take arms against Napoleon was by no means
so simple a matter as it might seem to those who had no thought
for anything but the sufferings and the humiliation which
Prussia had endured at his hands.   The overthrow of Napoleon,
even when accomplished, would merely bring up new difficulties.
Napoleon had made too many changes in the political complexion of Germany for the removal of his yoke to restore
Germany to the condition in which it had been before its subjection to his influence.   The fate of the Confederation of the Rhine
promised a superfluity of contentious matter, and it was only
one among several problems.   Thus Frederick William with the
idea of appeasing Napoleon did actually disown Yorck and
order his arrest; but Wittgenstein prevented the written order
reaching Yorck's quarters, Bülow in West Prussia acknowledged
him as Governor of East Prussia, and his summons to the *levée
en masse* of East Prussia was obeyed with an alacrity and an
enthusiasm which left no doubt as to the attitude of the population.   In Eastern Germany the peasantry had not received at
Napoleon's hands those benefits which his rule had brought to
Westphalians and Swabians: to them he was only the enemy
and the oppressor, the author not of the Code, but of the Continental System.

It was fortunate for the patriotic party in Germany that at
this moment Stein should have been in Alexander's confidence.
More accessible to the influence of ideas than was Francis II or
Frederick William III, the Czar listened to Stein's advice, and,
caught by the notion of associating his name with the liberation
of Germany, decided to come forward as the champion of the
cause Stein had so much at heart.   Thus with insurrection
already on foot in East Prussia, the Czar committed to a forward
policy, and Austria letting it be known that she would not oppose
it since her aim was a peace which could ensure Europe against
Napoleon's undue predominance, with Hardenberg supporting

Scharnhorst's pleadings in favour of a bolder policy, Frederick William's doubts were solved for him. But it was only gradually that the decision was reached. The first step was taken when Frederick William retired from Berlin to Breslau, partly in order to be more out of the way, and so better able to avoid a collision with Napoleon, partly because he had some idea of trying to keep Silesia neutral by denying it to both parties. But when, on February 12th, the troops in Pomerania and Silesia were mobilised, and volunteers were called for to bring them up to establishment, recruits flocked in with a zeal and a keenness which went far to decide Frederick William's mind. So insistent was the popular clamour and the demand to be led against the French, that on February 27th a treaty was negotiated at Kalisch which definitely committed Prussia to hostility to Napoleon, and confirmed the decision the King had made four days earlier. This treaty pledged Russia to continue the war until Prussia regained the territories she had possessed before 1806; but it was understood that the restoration should not include Hanover, and that Prussia would give up her claims to the greater part of the acquisitions she had made from Poland in 1793 and 1795. These reservations were most necessary: without the second, Prussia could not hope to secure the indispensable Russian aid, while her claim on Hanover had contributed as much as anything to the ruin of the Third Coalition, and if persisted in now could not fail to lead to trouble with Great Britain, whose help was no less important.

Meanwhile both sides were straining every nerve to get ready for the coming campaign. While the relics of the Grand Army had been thrown into the fortresses of Poland and Prussia and were endeavouring to hold the line of the Vistula, and so keep the Russians at bay, Napoleon was devoting all his marvellous energy and powers of organisation to the creation of an even vaster army with which to wipe out the memories of his defeats. The raw material he had ready to hand.[1] Over 130,000 of the conscripts of 1813 had already been called out, and had been drilling at the depôts since November 1812. A decree of the Senate of January 11th, 1813, placed at his disposal 100,000 men belonging to the classes of past years who had hitherto escaped service, and also anticipated the conscription of 1814 by calling up 150,000 men not due till that year. The

[1] Cf. Friedrich, i. pp. 59-70.

National Guard had already provided 80,000 men, the so-called
"Cohorts," who had already been under arms for a year and
were now formed into regiments of the Line, another 80,000 of
the same force being called upon a little later to fill their places.
For a leaven by which these masses of recruits might be turned
into efficient soldiers, Napoleon was so fortunate as to have
among the survivors of the Grand Army some 20,000 more
officers and under-officers than were needed by the units under
Eugene and in the fortresses on the Vistula. Without these invaluable veterans the campaign of 1813 would have been impossible. Had the news of the decision to retire from Moscow found
Prussia prepared to rise in Napoleon's rear and so to intercept
the retreat of the Grand Army, she could have paralysed the
military resources of France and averted the awful loss of life
in the campaigns of 1813 and 1814. Such a step was, however,
impossible. Prussia was too securely held down under
Napoleon's heel, and the famished remnant of the Grand Army
was on the Niemen before the full extent of the disaster was
realised throughout Germany. The Emperor also recalled from
every battalion of the army in Spain 150 men to serve as the
nucleus of the new units; he summoned from retirement every
half-pay officer, every veteran still capable of service; he stripped
his useless fleets of marines and of seamen to provide his new
army with artillerymen. By these means he succeeded in
getting together an enormous force. Nor was it only on France
alone that he made these vast demands. His vassal states had
to provide their contingents, and no small number of Germans
were called upon to do battle to keep Germany in subjection
to Napoleon. Thus Westphalia had to put into the field
close upon 30,000 men,[1] while from Berg over 4000 were
demanded.

Numbers alone do not make an army; and while time was
needed to drill, train and equip the new levies, their *morale* and
readiness to fight were considerations of even greater importance. On the whole, there was no fault to be found with the
spirit shown by the French recruits. Many, of course, deserted;
but the great traditions of the French army, the magic of the
Emperor's personality, the warlike spirit of the nation, were not
slow to assert themselves. With the recruits of the vassal states
things were naturally rather different; but it was noticeable that

[1] Cf. Fisher, p. 305.

though the Italian and Illyrian recruits deserted in large numbers and the Bavarians hung back, the contingents of Baden, Würtemberg and other minor states came forward readily enough. A Thuringian battalion raised by the petty Princes of that district who belonged to the Confederation of the Rhine did, it is true, desert as a body to the Prussians just before Lützen, and two battalions were formed by the Prussians from deserters coming from the former provinces of Prussia West of the Elbe;[1] but the South and West of Germany was as a whole still loyal to Napoleon, partly, no doubt, from necessity, but in no small measure from choice.

To meet these vast preparations the Allies had also to make a great effort. The Russians had suffered very heavily indeed in 1812; and though large reserves were on their way Westward, they had far to travel and the force at the front was but weak. Much, therefore, depended on Prussia and in Prussia on the measure of success which should attend Scharnhorst's plans when put to the proof. Thanks to the system of rapidly passing through the ranks a succession of trained men, he had little difficulty in bringing up to their full establishment the 46 battalions and 80 squadrons to which Napoleon had restricted the Prussian army. Indeed, the reservists came forward in such strength that it was possible to organise 42 new battalions.[2] But this was by no means all: volunteers also flocked to the colours in numbers, full of enthusiasm and patriotism, anxious to throw off Napoleon's yoke, many of them belonging to the classes hitherto exempt from military service. These for the most part formed themselves into Free Corps, providing their own uniforms and equipment, doing little drill, and relying mainly on their shooting. Some of them were formed in companies and attached to the regulars for skirmishing work, while others were organised as separate units, of which Lützow's is the best known. In partisan warfare, in raids against French communications, in cutting off messengers and stragglers, these corps did no small service. However, Scharnhorst wisely desiring a more solid reserve for the troops of the Line than these somewhat tumultuary organisations, brought forward a measure based on the *Landwehr* organisation adopted by

[1] Friedrich, i. 41.
[2] These were known as "Reserve Regiments," and must not be confused with the *Landwehr*.

Austria in 1809.[1] A royal proclamation of February 9th declared national defence to be a duty incumbent on the whole
nation, another of March 17th authorised the levy of 120,000 men
by conscription. Lots were to be drawn among the men between
17 and 40 years of age, while the upper classes were brought
into connection with the scheme through the measures adopted
for providing the equipment. Behind this force were to stand
as a last resource the *Landsturm*, armed with such weapons as
they could get, and carrying out somewhat miscellaneous duties.
The poverty of Prussia and the exhausted state of the country
made the equipment of all these recruits a very difficult matter.
Had better weapons been forthcoming much more could have
been done and a larger force placed in the field; but though a
certain amount of help in money and stores was received from
England, that country, whose action in Germany was, of course,
much influenced by its connection with Hanover, looked rather
towards rousing an insurrection in the old territories of the
Guelphs, and was making the equipment of an Anglo-German
design in that quarter its chief effort.[2] Prussia was thus thrown
mainly on her own resources; and great as was the readiness of
the whole nation to contribute all it could scrape together, not
even the patriotism and self-sacrifice which all classes displayed
could create resources which did not exist. Thus though troops
of a sort were forthcoming to blockade the French garrisons,
there were not many more than 60,000 Prussians ready for the
field in April, without including Free Corps. The *Landwehr*
for the most part were too ill-supplied to be fit for field service.

It was on March 15th that Frederick William issued simultaneously his declaration of war and his appeal to his subjects
to support him in his struggle for liberty. Four days later,
Nesselrode and Stein acting for Russia, and Hardenberg and
Scharnhorst for Prussia, drew up the Convention of Kalisch. In
this, in the spirit of their denunciation of the Confederation of
the Rhine as the work of the foreign tyrant, they provided that
any German Prince who within a certain prescribed time should
not have joined the Allies, should be liable to be deprived of
his territory.[3] At the same time, arrangements were made for

---

[1] The *Landwehr* produced some 149 battalions of infantry, averaging nearly 700,
with 116 squadrons of cavalry, rather under 100 strong.
[2] Cf. Friedrich, i. 19.
[3] *Deutsche Geschichte, 1806–1871*, i. pp. 323–324.

the administration of such portions of North Germany as might come into the hands of the Allies.

As yet the actual outbreak against Napoleon in Germany was confined to Prussia, though the feelings which prompted it were no less strong in other quarters. In Austria there was a strong nationalist movement. An influential party, headed by Archduke John and recalling the ideas of Stadion, earnestly desired to join the opponents of Napoleon and to recover Tyrol and the other provinces of which he had despoiled the Hapsburgs. This party aimed at an *Alpenbund*, an alliance between Tyrol, Illyria, Switzerland, Salzburg and the Vorarlberg which would serve as the nucleus for a South German rising against Napoleon.[1] But its views were very far from finding favour in Metternich's eyes. Much as he hated Napoleon's predominance, he hated democracy and Liberalism more, and he was most anxious to prevent anything in the way of a popular movement. If he could manage it, the reduction of the undue greatness of France should be achieved by the governments, not by the peoples.[2] Moreover, he knew that neither the financial nor the military situation of Austria[3] was such as to make war desirable, he distrusted Russia and was determined to thwart her schemes of self-aggrandisement, while he was little better disposed to Prussia. A neutral position was therefore what he desired to adopt, since it offered most prospect of settling the whole matter by diplomacy without an appeal to arms. For it was this which was his chief object. Neither the Austrian minister nor his master seems to have contemplated joining Napoleon, not even when he attempted to bribe them with Silesia and Illyria (March 27th). If they departed from their attitude of neutrality it would be to join Napoleon's opponents; but their hope was to avoid having to take this step. Accordingly, though Metternich went so far in the direction of joining the Allies as to conclude a convention with Russia which suspended hostilities and allowed Schwarzenberg to withdraw unmolested, he announced to Narbonne that his master desired " peace, and nothing but peace," and would

---

[1] *Deutsche Geschichte, 1806–1871*, i. p. 329.   [2] *Ibid.* p. 325.
[3] After the disasters of 1809 the Austrian army had been restricted to a strength of 150,000 men and its regiments were exceedingly weak, so that much time was needed before they could be brought up to war strength by levies of recruits; cf. Friedrich, i. 52–55.

assume a mediatory position, mobilising her forces to procure respect for her mediation. Meanwhile, to prove that Austria had no intention of raising the banner of insurrection in Germany, he induced the Emperor to have Archduke John arrested and sent to his estates, by representing to the jealous Francis that his brother was aiming at erecting for himself an independent kingdom of " Rhaetia."[1]

The attitude of Bavaria was largely influenced by that of Austria, since nothing was more certain than that Austria would seek to recover Tyrol. A premature rising of the Tyrolese would make relations between Austria and Bavaria very awkward. Thus when Prussia sought to induce Bavaria to join the Allies, or at least to send no assistance to Napoleon, offering as an inducement to resign all claims on Anspach and Baireuth, Bavaria was hardly prepared to desert Napoleon. Montgelas was not altogether ill-disposed to the notion, but he disliked the Prussian appeal to the people, fearing that it would lead to anarchy : he was also very much afraid of Napoleon and was alarmed by the rumours of his vast preparations. Thus a Bavarian contingent was in the end to be found under Napoleon's colours, though her zeal for the cause was decidely evanescent.

Somewhat similar was the plight of Saxony. Prussia's hostility to her Southern neighbour was notorious, and directly war was declared by Prussia, Blücher seized Cottbus[2] in the name of his King. Austria, however, was much more kindly disposed: indeed, Metternich was almost ready to promise Saxony compensation for the Duchy of Warsaw, which Alexander was resolved to annex, and in April a convention was concluded between Austria and Saxony, the latter promising to support Austria in her efforts to bring about a peace. The Allies were by this time advancing into Saxony ; and before their approach King Frederick Augustus, uncertain what course to pursue, fled first to Plauen and then to Ratisbon. In his absence the people of Saxony received the Allies with great enthusiasm, though the officials were hostile, and the Saxon army was kept concentrated at Torgau by its commander, Thielmann, well out of the way.

In the meantime the campaign had begun. Eugene's effort to hold the line of the Vistula had been frustrated by Schwarzenberg, who evacuated Warsaw without fighting and withdrew to

[1] Cf. Friedrich, i. pp. 20 ff.   [2] Cf. p. 517.

Galicia, which compelled the Viceroy to quit Posen (Feb. 12th) for Frankfort on the Oder, by which Rapp at Dantzic and the other French garrisons on the Vistula were left isolated. But the line of the Oder was in its turn abandoned when raiding parties of Cossacks crossed the river and began to threaten the French communications, one band actually penetrating to Berlin. By the first week in March, Eugene had fallen back to the Elbe, establishing his headquarters at Magdeburg. He had left garrisons in the principal fortresses on the Oder which it would have been better to have kept with the field-army, for the Allies, disregarding these obstacles, pressed on after him, the Russian advanced guard reaching Berlin (March 11th) about a week after he had left it, while on the left the Prussians from Silesia under Blücher moved on Dresden; and farther North, Tettenborn's Russian light troops occupied Hamburg (March 18th), which Carra St. Cyr had evacuated.

As Wittgenstein continued his advance on Magdeburg (April 2nd), he fell in a little to the East of that town with Eugene, who had taken the offensive in the hope of catching the Allies unconcentrated. The effort proved a failure, for a sharp action between Nedlitz and Möckern (April 5th) ended in the retreat of the French, who fell back across the Elbe to the Saale, which allowed the Russians to move up the Elbe to Dessau, cross there (April 9th), and gain touch with Blücher who, after occupying Dresden, from which the French had withdrawn, had pushed on to the Mulde.

It was a critical situation for Napoleon, for had the Allies pressed on resolutely they might have fallen upon the troops he was concentrating to support Eugene—and organising and training, too, simultaneously with their concentration—before they could be ready to go into action. Scharnhorst pleaded urgently for such a move, but the Allies were not prepared to run the risk until Miloradovitch's Russian corps could come up; and this was not three days behind, as it should have been, but fourteen. Thus the critical moments slipped by, and on April 24th Napoleon arrived at Erfurt and was within supporting distance of the Viceroy's troops on the Saale. The Emperor had with him about 80,000 men, comprising the Guard and the corps of Ney (III.), Bertrand (IV.), Marmont (VI.), and Oudinot (XII.), all of which were mainly composed of raw recruits, hastily formed into battalions and imperfectly trained and equipped. He was very weak in cavalry, having barely 8000 horsemen, for it was in this arm that it was most difficult to fill the gaps which 1812 had made; and though well supplied with artillery, his army was one with which only a most daring general would have ventured to undertake a bold offensive movement.

Yet such was Napoleon's design. Dresden was the point on which he was moving, though Leipzig was his immediate objective. He aimed at executing the converse movement to that which had led to the brilliant success of Oct. 1806, that is, he wished to fall on the right flank of his enemy, crush it, and so push through to the Elbe and place himself between them and Prussia.[1] Wittgenstein also meant to take the offensive. He had concentrated the field army of the Allies, including the Prussians of Blücher[2] and Yorck[3] and some 40,000 Russians, partly under his own command, partly under Winzingerode, in all about 90,000 men, to the South of Leipzig. Despite his inferior numbers, he resolved on a daring stroke, a flank attack on the French as they moved forward on Leipzig.

Napoleon had reached Weimar on the 28th of April, and next day an advance to Weissenfels brought his columns into touch with Eugene's men, who came up to Merseburg.[4] From the Saale Napoleon pushed forward towards Leipzig by Markranstädt and Lindenau. Meanwhile Wittgenstein moved from behind the Elster by Pegau on Lützen, hoping to fall on Napoleon's right flank and rear, and by surprising the young French troops to throw them into confusion.

It was about midday on May 2nd, while Napoleon was watching his advanced guard, Lauriston's corps, drive Kleist's Prussians in upon Leipzig, that Wittgenstein delivered his attack. To cover the movements of the rest of the army against any interruption from the Southward, Napoleon had left Ney's corps on his right flank, and it was on this corps, posted between the villages of Gross Görschen and Starsiedel, that Wittgenstein's blow fell. Though outnumbered, Ney offered an obstinate resistance, clinging resolutely to the villages, and only being

---

[1] Cf. Yorck von Wartenburg, ii. 247.

[2] 52 squadrons and 38 battalions.

[3] 16 squadrons and 19 battalions.

[4] Eugene's force comprised the corps of Lauriston (V.), composed of the regiments formed out of the "cohorts" of the National Guards, Reynier (VII.) and Macdonald (XI.), these last two representing the reserves of the Grand Army which had escaped the disaster of 1812 : he had in all some 70,000 men.

forced back from the Görschens and Rahna to Kaja after very heavy fighting. This gave Napoleon time to alter his dispositions, to divert to their right Macdonald and the Guard, who had been following Lauriston, and to hasten back to Ney's succour. Had Ney been unsupported he must have been overpowered, but Marmont's corps came up on his right and relieved the pressure on him by occupying Starsiedel; and of this village the French retained possession all day, Bertrand arriving about 4 p.m. and supporting Marmont. Wittgenstein had to devote all his Russians to the contest in this quarter, and thus he had no troops left to support Blücher, whose success in driving in Ney from the villages to which he clung so tenaciously could not be followed up. Indeed, he was unable to maintain the ground he had won; for Napoleon, judging the situation critical, sent the Young Guard and one of Marmont's divisions forward against Kaja, retook it and the other villages, and hurled the Prussians back. The arrival of some Russian reinforcements was more than neutralised by that of Macdonald, who pushed forward over the Flossgraben against the Allied right and decided the day. Had Napoleon had any cavalry available for the pursuit, he might have done much; as it was, the Allies were strong enough in this arm to secure an unmolested retreat. They had lost no guns and very few prisoners, and the 15,000 casualties they had suffered were exceeded by the losses they had inflicted on the French, which probably amounted to 25,000.[1] Still the battle was a great triumph for the young soldiers of France, more especially for their officers, who had in so short a time made their raw conscripts capable of facing the Allies in a pitched battle. Discipline they had not yet acquired, and it was largely because his army was neither physically nor morally capable of great exertions immediately after a battle that Napoleon was unable to follow up the battle of Gross Görschen as he had followed up Jena. He did, it is true, push on in the wake of the retreating Allies to Dresden, which he occupied on the 8th, the Allies retiring behind the Elbe; but his want of cavalry prevented his pursuit from doing them any serious damage.

Having reoccupied the Saxon capital, Napoleon's next step was to send an ultimatum to the King of Saxony demanding that he should do his duty as a Prince of the Confederation of

[1] Rousset, *La Grande Armée de 1813*, p. 90.

the Rhine. Frederick Augustus, impressed by the spectacle of
Napoleon again victorious, obeyed, and his troops took the
position assigned to them as the 24th and 25th Divisions in
Reynier's (VII.) corps. Meanwhile Vandamme moved North
against the Allied force which, after occupying Hamburg, had
crossed the Elbe into Hanover and inflicted a defeat on Morand's
division at Lüneburg (April 2nd). The nucleus of the Allied
force in this quarter consisted of some Russian troops under
Tettenborn; but Swedish help was expected, and it was to this
district that the Russo-German Legion, organised out of the
German prisoners taken in 1812, was sent. But in addition to
these forces, much was done in the way of raising battalions
among the inhabitants of North-Western Germany who had
suffered so much from Napoleon's Customs officials. In this
work England played a prominent part, providing arms and
equipment and sending over to Germany some 500 men of the
King's German Legion to stiffen the new levies, while the 3rd
Hussars and two artillery batteries of that force together with
an English rocket battery of the Royal Artillery were also
added to this very miscellaneous corps, which was placed under
the command of a Hanoverian general, Count Wallmoden. The
arrival of the French reinforcements quite changed the situation
on the Lower Elbe. After some sharp fighting the Allies had
to retire to the right bank of the river, and Hamburg was reoccupied by the French (May 30th). Bülow also, who had come
up to Magdeburg and Wittenberg, fell back to Berlin, and the
whole line of the Elbe from the Bohemian frontier to the sea
was again in French hands.

Napoleon did not spend more time than he could help at
Dresden. The victory of May 2nd had been far from decisive,
and he was most anxious to bring the Allies to battle again.
They made no attempt to dispute the line of the Elbe, and on
the 12th Napoleon began to transfer his army to the right bank.
He believed that the Russians had separated from the Prussians,
and that the latter were retreating on Berlin, their allies up the
Oder to Breslau. Accordingly he divided his own forces, directing Ney with the IIIrd, Vth and VIIth Corps against Berlin,
advancing himself with the Guards, the IVth, VIth, XIth
and XIIth Corps into Lusatia.

But his idea that the Allies had adopted divergent lines of
retreat was quite erroneous. On the contrary, they had received

considerable reinforcements, including 14,000 Russians under Barclay de Tolly and some Prussian reserves, and had taken up a strong position behind the Spree at Bautzen, and were quite prepared for battle. Here it was that Napoleon found them when he pushed forward into Lusatia, expecting to drive the Russians before him. As soon as he discovered that they meant to give battle, he sent orders to Ney to change his route and to come back to the aid of the main body, directing him to move on Drehsa in the right rear of the Allies' position in order to outflank them, cut them off from Silesia, and compel them to retreat, not on Breslau but against the Bohemian frontier. Ney received these orders at Hoyerswerda on the 19th of May, on which day the rest of the army was assembled to the West of Bautzen.

The position of the Allies was one of some strength: they were drawn up on the heights behind the Spree, their right—Barclay's Russians—thrown back from Plieskowitz to Gleina, where it rested on the Blösa, an affluent of the Spree. Blücher's corps formed the right centre, Yorck being on his left, the main body of the Russians beyond that. Somewhat in front of the main line were Kleist's Prussians at Burk, and Miloradovitch's Russians in and to the left of Bautzen itself. This was a strong position, but it had the grave defects of being intersected by the narrow valley of the Blösa and of being rather too long for the numbers available. Moreover, the Allies were seriously handicapped by the want of a proper commander-in-chief; Wittgenstein's control over their operations was little more than nominal, for Alexander had practically taken the direction of affairs out of his hands, and the Czar had no pretensions to match himself against Napoleon.

Wishing to deceive the Allies into the belief that he was aiming rather at turning their left flank than their right, and at cutting them off not from Silesia but from Bohemia, Napoleon began his attack on the 20th with Oudinot's corps, which formed his extreme right. Oudinot crossed the Spree at Grubschütz and forced the Russians back with some success, while Macdonald and Marmont advanced against Bautzen and the IVth Corps assailed Kleist's position. The fighting was well contested, but at length a division of Marmont's corps (VI.) carried Bautzen, and by outflanking Kleist forced him also to retire from the heights of Burk to the second line. Oudinot on the right had been

checked, but the result of the day's fighting was on the whole
favourable to the French.   Ney had hardly been engaged: he
had had some sharp fighting on the 19th at Königswartha
against Barclay who had been pushed out thither to check him;
but though the Allies gained some successes at first, Ney had
in the end forced them back behind the Spree.   On the evening
of the 20th his leading brigade reached the left bank of the Spree
at Klix.

Next morning (May 21st) the Emperor decided to defer the
serious frontal attack until Ney's turning movement had
developed sufficiently to really threaten the Allied retreat; but
that Marshal, after forcing Barclay back from Malschwitz to
Preititz by 10 a.m., forbore to push forward, partly because he
misinterpreted Napoleon's order to be in Preititz by 11 o'clock
into a command not to be beyond Preititz at that hour, partly
because he thought he had the Russian Guards in front of him,
though they were in reality already engaged with the French
centre round Baschütz.   As soon as the sound of Ney's guns
had told the Emperor that the turning movement had really
begun he had committed his troops to the frontal attack.   On
the Allied left St. Priest's Russians had some success against
Oudinot, but the advance of the IVth Corps by Nieder Gurick
and of the VIth on Basankwitz compelled Blücher and Yorck,
who came to his help, to fall back from Kreckwitz behind the
Blösa.   Had Ney been as far forward as Napoleon hoped he
would be, the Prussians would probably have found it impossible
to extricate themselves; but Kleist had managed to regain
Preititz, and though thrust from it when Reynier's Saxons and
Lauriston reinforced Ney, he so far delayed the turning movement that the Allies were able to escape from the net Napoleon
had cast for them.   But with their right driven in, their retreat
endangered, and Macdonald and Oudinot pressing hard upon
St. Priest and the Russian Guards, they had no alternative but
to go back all along their line.   By abandoning the contest
before they had really been defeated, and by using their
numerous cavalry to protect their retirement, they got away in
good order, leaving but few prisoners and hardly any guns
behind.   It was then that Napoleon felt most bitterly the want
of the squadrons he found it so hard to create out of his new conscripts and his untrained horses.   If he could have overwhelmed
the Allied cavalry, their retreat might have been changed into a

disastrous rout, and Bautzen might have ranked with Austerlitz and Marengo. As it was, the Allies retired in good order by Bunzlau to Liegnitz and by Löwenberg on Goldberg, thence turning Southward to Schweidnitz.

The reason of the Allies for turning away from the Oder and placing themselves in the triangle formed by Glatz, Neisse and Schweidnitz, were, in the first place, that they wished to keep touch with Austria in case that Power should, as they fervently desired, throw in her lot with them; secondly, that a retreat behind the Oder, the only other alternative, would have been an enormous incentive to Napoleon. Had the Allies given so clear a proof of their discouragement, he would hardly have made the fatal blunder of an armistice. But the decision was taken in opposition to the wishes of the Russian generals, especially of Barclay, who had succeeded to the command which Wittgenstein laid down in disgust.

The Allied army, indeed, was in no condition for another action. Their losses at Bautzen had been lower than those of the French, who must have had at least 18,000 casualties,[1] but still the two defeats had shaken their *morale* considerably, especially that of the Russians, and had produced a good deal of friction between the Allies. Directly after Bautzen Barclay declared that the condition of his army was such that it was imperative for him to retire behind the Oder to recruit and refresh his men; and indeed their numbers, equipment, discipline and general tone did leave a good deal to be desired.[2] But the Prussians were aghast at so fatal a proposal. To abandon to Napoleon so fertile and productive a district as Silesia would be most harmful. Their troops were in rather better condition than were the Russians: recruits were coming in freely, and they felt, not without good reason, that so retrograde a movement would be the beginning of the end. It would perhaps bring Barclay's weakened forces nearer the reinforcements they so badly needed, but it would deliver the greater part of Prussia over to Napoleon, would as much discourage the national move-ment in the parts of Germany still under his rule as it would encourage his troops and confirm in their allegiance to his cause those who were wavering. Moreover, it would greatly increase the difficulties of co-operating with Austria if Francis II. should be induced to declare against Napoleon.[3]

[1] Cf. Rousset, p. 96.　　[2] Cf. Friedrich, i. 3.　　[3] *Ibid*. i. 2.

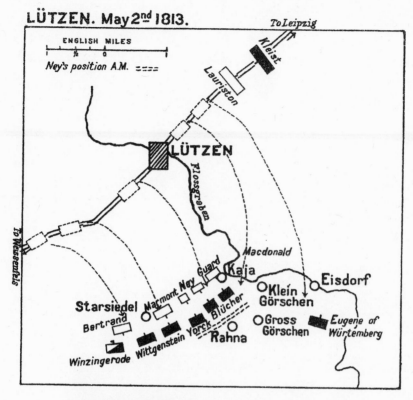

LÜTZEN. May 2nd 1813.

ENGLISH MILES

Ney's position A.M. ====

To Leipzig

Kleist

Lauriston

To Weissenfels

Flossgraben

LÜTZEN

Macdonald

Kaja

Klein Görschen

Eisdorf

Starsiedel

Bertrand

Marmont Ney Guard

Wittgenstein Yorck

Blücher

Rahna

Gross Görschen

Eugene of Würtemberg

Winzingerode

BAUTZEN May 20th & 21st 1813.

BAUTZEN

× Positions of French on the 20th

Namschütz

Macdonald

BURK

Marmont

Basankwitz

Bertrand

Nieder Gurick

Spree R.

Oudinot

Plieskowitz

Klix

Miloradovich

Kreckwitz

Yorck Blücher

Barclay

Basthutz

Ney

St Priest

Klein Bautzen

Prevtitz

Gleina

Retreat of Allies

Kleist

Prussian Guards

Barclay's

Reynier

Lauriston

Baruth

Engl. Miles

W. Darbishire, Oxford, 1908.

The divergence between the views of the Allies might have had serious consequences, indeed the Russians were within measurable distance of separating from the Prussians when the intervention of Austria resulted in the Armistice of Poischwitz.[1] Austria's action at this critical moment was of the utmost importance. Metternich may not have been a man of high principle, his policy and aims may have been reactionary, illiberal and opportunist, but he handled the diplomatic situation with great acuteness and skill. He saw that were Austria now to assist Napoleon to make good his threatened predominance in Europe, she would merely rivet the chains more firmly on her own neck; but he was determined to avoid encouraging the popular movement in Germany, and he desired as little change in the existing territorial arrangements as might prove compatible with the secure independence of Austria and the restoration to the Hapsburgs of at any rate the provinces they had lost in 1809. Further, knowing as he did the state of the Austrian finances and of the Austrian army, he was anxious to avoid having recourse to arms if he could possibly gain his ends by any other means. He was therefore well pleased when the mission of Stadion to the headquarters of the Allies and of Bubna to Napoleon's camp resulted, despite all Napoleon's bluster and threats, in the conclusion of an armistice (June 4th). At the moment Napoleon's headquarters were at Neumarkt, his left wing was nearing Breslau, his right close to Schweidnitz, the Allies being concentrated between Strehlen and Nimptsch. Oudinot, after one success against the Prussian force covering Berlin at Hoyerswerda (May 28th), had been repulsed when he again attacked Bülow at Lückau (June 4th), and had fallen back to the Black Elster. Victor had relieved Glogau, and Davoût had reoccupied Hamburg and got into touch with the Danes. The line of demarcation, therefore, which was now arranged had to correspond to this situation. Leaving Hamburg and Lübeck in French hands, it ran up the Elbe to Magdeburg, thence followed the frontier between Saxony and Prussia to the Oder, which it reached at Müllrose. From there it ascended the Oder to the Katzbach, where it divided, the French having to keep behind the Katzbach, the Allies behind the Striegau Wasser, the intervening space being declared neutral. During the suspension of hostilities, beleaguered fortresses might be supplied

[1] Cf. *Deutsche Geschichte, 1806–1871*, i. 348.

from outside but must not increase their stock of provisions, and no troops were to cross the lines of demarcation. This last provision was none too well observed by some of the irregulars attached to the Prussian army, notably the well-known Free Corps under Lützow, which after raiding Erfurt and the Saxon Duchies was brought to action by Arrighi's cavalry at Kitzen near Leipzig and destroyed (June 17th).

In agreeing to this armistice, Napoleon played into the hands of his enemies. Military and political considerations alike should have induced him to reject the proposals. Lützen and Bautzen had cost him dear, and the exertions his young soldiers had made had nearly exhausted them; but for all that the campaign had so far gone in his favour, the Allies could hardly have hoped to avert defeat in another battle, and it was at least doubtful whether the Russo-Prussian alliance would survive another defeat. Even if the Allies remained true to their alliance, great military advantages might have been gained by pushing forward to the Lower and Middle Oder; beleaguered fortresses might have been relieved, and the veterans who formed their garrisons would have been a welcome stiffening to Napoleon's young conscripts. Moreover, to accept an armistice would publish to the world the fact that all was not well with the Emperor's position; why otherwise should he halt in a career of victory? Austria and other waverers were more likely to rally to his cause if he showed himself confident of victory, than if he confessed himself unable to follow up the advantages he had secured.

But the campaign in Saxony had shown Napoleon some weak points in his armour, above all his want of cavalry, and he was in sore need of time in which to supply his deficiencies in that arm. Moreover, his raw troops were hardly fit for another desperate struggle like that of Bautzen. Munitions and supplies were nearly exhausted, his communications with the Rhine and with France were being harassed by the Free Corps, which were playing the part which Spanish guerillas and Portuguese militia had played in the Peninsula, his men were worn out and in bad need of rest. But the Emperor failed to see that useful as delay would be to him, the respite which the armistice would give might be turned to even better use by the Allies, that their need of a breathing space in which to refresh and reorganise their forces was even greater than his; that their resources if more distant were larger. Yet, though it was largely because he

wanted time in which to refit and increase his forces that he
concluded the armistice, there can be little doubt that the fear of
Austrian invention was also most influential with him.   The
retreat of the Allies towards the Austrian frontier seemed to
point to an understanding between them and the government at
Vienna, and at the moment the Emperor was not inclined to
face the Austrians as well as the Russians and Prussians.   It
was mainly the great strategic advantage of their position in
Bohemia which made the Austrians so formidable : posted across
his flank, they could sever his communications with France by a
move down the Elbe.   To neutralise this Napoleon was relying
on the demonstration which the Army of Italy was to make
against Carniola, and at the end of May the Army of Italy was
only just beginning to take shape under Eugene.

In his appreciation of the political situation, Napoleon was
even more at fault ; if it was a serious blunder to have accepted
the armistice, it was an even graver error not to have accepted
the very favourable terms Austria suggested.   But just as he
could not believe that he could fail to overthrow the Allies, even
if Austria threw in her lot with Russia and Prussia, so, too, he
seems to have failed to grasp the policy of Metternich, and to
have relied too much on the influence of his marriage to Marie
Louise,[1] almost expecting it to blind Austria to her own interests :
he never imagined that a judicious mixture of threats and bribes
would fail to bring Austria to heel.

But Metternich gauged the situation too acutely to be
caught by the bait of Illyria and Silesia and the redistribution
of Germany to the disadvantage of Prussia.   Napoleon's word
was but a poor security for the punctual performance of the
promises made to Austria in his hour of need : once he had
overthrown the renascent power of Prussia and hurled Russia
back behind the Niemen by Austrian aid, the Hapsburgs might
wait in vain for their wages.   Much as Metternich disliked
Prussia, he was not prepared to indulge his hatred of the
Hohenzollern at the heavy price of re-establishing Napoleon's
supremacy over Europe : he preferred maintaining a balance of
power by helping Prussia to regain her old position to receiving
even Silesia as the vassal of Napoleon.   The only effect of
Napoleon's victories was, therefore, to convince Metternich that
Austria must draw nearer the Allies lest Alexander should lose

[1] Cf. *EHR, 1887*, p. 391.

heart and accept the overtures which Napoleon was making to him through Caulaincourt. By the time the Congress of Prague was arranged Metternich had come to the conclusion that the only course open to Austria was to take arms against Napoleon; and he seems to have welcomed the Congress, because he expected that it would convince Francis II that no other solution was possible. Francis was more inclined to cling to peace, more anxious to build a golden bridge across which Napoleon could retire without any humiliation to his pride; but Metternich was able to bring the Emperor round to his own views, and to induce him to agree to the convention which was the result of the negotiations with the Czar on which Metternich now embarked. This convention, signed at Reichenbach on June 27th, laid down certain indispensable conditions upon which Austria would insist as the basis of her mediation. They were the abolition of the Grand Duchy of Warsaw and its partition between its three former owners, the liberation of the Hanseatic towns and of the rest of the German coast-lands seized in 1810, the restoration of Illyria to Austria, and the evacuation by the French of the Polish and Prussian fortresses still in their hands. If by July 21st Napoleon should not have accepted these terms, Austria pledged herself to join the Allies and declare war against the Emperor of the French.[1]

The first result of Austria's interposition was that Napoleon, after vainly attempting to bully Metternich into submission, agreed (June 30th) to accept her mediation and that a Peace Congress should forthwith be held at Prague. To allow time for the deliberations of this Congress, it was agreed that the armistice should be extended to August 10th.

The negotiations of the Peace Congress, which duly met at Prague on July 10th, were felt from the first to be a mere form: Napoleon showed no indication of intending to treat them seriously, and, indeed, he was far more occupied with preparing his forces for the great campaign which was to humble Austria as well as Russia and Prussia. Similarly, on the side of the Allies it is the discussion of the plans for the coming operations which are of real interest and importance.

In these discussions a prominent part was played by Bernadotte. Greatly to Napoleon's disgust his former Marshal, who had been chosen as Crown Prince of Sweden in 1810 and

---

[1] Cf. Friedrich, i. 30.

had at first applied the Continental System most rigorously, had not remained true to the French alliance. By no means a devoted adherent of Napoleon, and anxious above all things to identify himself with his adopted country, Bernadotte had not hesitated to relax the Continental System when he found what disastrous effects it was having on Sweden. Infuriated by this, Napoleon had (Feb. 1812) reoccupied Swedish Pomerania, which had only been restored to Sweden in 1810. Thereupon Bernadotte concluded the Peace of Abo with Russia (April 1812) and bestirred himself to reconcile the Czar with Great Britain. He had followed up his success in this diplomatic endeavour by concluding treaties with England (March 3rd, 1813) and Prussia (April 22nd), pledging him to hostility to Napoleon; but his demand that Sweden should be indemnified with Norway for the loss of Finland to Russia had caused a hitch in his negotiations with that Power and with Prussia. His proposal to compensate Denmark with the Hanseatic towns and other parts of North Germany had not unnaturally been disliked by Prussia, and Frederick William had at first refused to ratify the treaty of April 22nd. However, Lützen and Bautzen forced the Czar and Frederick William to change their tone and to fall in with Bernadotte's proposals. It was agreed that 35,000 Russians and 27,000 Prussians should be put under his orders and should join the 18,000 Swedes with whom he landed at Stralsund on May 24th. This, of course, decided the action of Denmark, which promptly threw in her lot with Napoleon's, concluding a treaty (July 10th) of no small influence on the fortunes of Germany, as it removed all possibility of the creation of a strong Danish state on the Lower Elbe.[1] The assistance of some 12,000 Danes, who joined Davoût at Hamburg, went far to secure that important position, the extreme left of the line Napoleon was now taking up on the Elbe.

Meanwhile the utmost efforts were being made on all sides to put into the field every available man. Napoleon's officers had to teach their recruits the elements of drill and discipline as they marched across Germany to the Elbe. From the interior of Russia large reinforcements were slowly pushing Westward. In June England concluded subsidy treaties with Russia and Prussia, agreeing to pay them respectively over a million and half a million sterling. Munitions, too, were

---

[1] Cf. Friedrich, i. pp. 11–18.

shipped in considerable quantities to Stralsund and Colberg, and, thanks largely to this source of supply, it was found possible to equip the *Landwehr* for field service. Muskets were served out to them instead of the pikes with which so many of them had till then been armed ; they were formed into battalions and squadrons, and were now brigaded with the older troops, whose depleted ranks had again been brought up to full strength by vigorous recruiting.

At the same time the arrangement of a plan of campaign was being steadily pushed forward. Long before the Peace Congress had begun to display its futility by meeting, Austrian generals had been framing schemes in consultation with the Allies. The eagerness with which this was being done was itself a proof that no one regarded the chances of a pacific settlement as worth considering. Still none of the plans gave universal satisfaction, and the want of a Commander-in-Chief was badly felt. Scharnhorst had been badly wounded at Lützen, but despite his wound he had gone to Prague to consult with the Austrians. However, he became suddenly worse, and died on June 28th, not having lived to see Prussia reap the harvest of vengeance on Napoleon which his hard work had sowed. His death left von Knesebeck as Prussia's principal representative in the councils of the Allies, Toll and Barclay being Russia's spokesmen, Schwarzenberg and his able Chief of Staff, Joseph Radetzky, Austria's. Into the details of the various schemes it is impossible to go ; [1] they illustrate the divergent interests and points of view inevitable in a coalition, but at length the Russian and Prussian headquarters decided on a plan by which three armies were to be formed, one in the Mark of Brandenburg under Bernadotte to cover Berlin, one in Silesia under a Prussian commander, which would serve to maintain the communications of the main army in Bohemia with Russia by way of Poland. This main army was to be formed by the union of the greater part of the Russo-Prussian forces near Schweidnitz with the Austrians. Submitted to the Austrians, the idea met on the whole with their approval ; but they proposed that the main army should adopt a defensive attitude, leaving the initiative to Napoleon, and that the Swedo-Russian Army of the North, with the aid of Bülow's corps, should alone on the Allied side take the offensive. [2]

[1] Cf. Friedrich, i. 71–86.   [2] *Ibid.* i. 87–88.

However, Bernadotte's assent had to be obtained, and he had some time before this been pressing for a personal interview with the Allied monarchs as the only possible means of reaching any satisfactory decision: this meeting now took place, the Czar, Frederick William and the Crown Prince of Sweden coming together at the Castle of Trachenberg near Breslau (July 9th). A conference of some three days resulted in the adoption of the plan of campaign generally known as the Compact of Trachenberg, a plan which on the whole followed the lines laid down by the Crown Prince, and which, having been submitted to the Austrians, was by them adopted with some modifications [1] which Radetzky suggested.[2]

The keynote of the scheme of operations finally accepted by the Allies was the employment of a policy of attrition. Instead of the combined offensive operations suggested by Toll the Allies were to adopt a defensive strategy, to refuse Napoleon the chance of fighting a pitched battle until marches and counter-marches against one point after another in the surrounding semicircle of hostile armies, which always retired as he approached, should have so diminished his numbers and worn out his men as to let the Allies attack them with every prospect of victory. But while a pitched battle with the main army of the enemy was to be avoided, any isolated or detached corps was to be brought to action and destroyed. The three armies which were to be formed—Bernadotte's in the North; Blucher's in Silesia, consisting of his own Prussian corps with that of Yorck and the Russians of Langeron and Sacken; the main 'army in Bohemia, which was to be reinforced by the greater part of the Russo-Prussians from Schweidnitz—were all to adopt the same strategy: each was to retire before Napoleon if he advanced against it, to advance and threaten the French flanks and communications should Napoleon move against either of the others. Thus, should the Emperor, as was expected, invade Bohemia, the main army would draw back up the Elbe; Bernadotte, leaving 20,000 men to contain the Danes and Hamburg, would move against the Middle Elbe, aiming at Leipzig; Blücher and the Army of Silesia was to push forward to the Elbe, cross the river between Dresden and Torgau, and obtain touch with the Army of the North.[3]

This strategy is one which has been criticised as a reversion

[1] Cf. Friedrich, i. 89-92.   [2] *Ibid.* i. 94-96.   [3] *Ibid.* i. 96-99.

38

to the dilatory and over-methodical operations of the 18th Century; as a failure to appreciate or to practise the cardinal principle of strategy of which Napoleon had been so brilliant an exponent, the principle of concentrating all available forces against the enemy's main force to decide the issue once and for all by a pitched battle.[1] Pertinent as this criticism is, it is nevertheless one-sided : the strategy of the Allies had as its ultimate objective a pitched battle; they wanted to make Napoleon do their work for them by wearing out his young troops through constant but fruitless exertions, to refuse him the chance of a general action would exasperate and annoy him, and in the end, when the work of attrition had been done, the offensive would be taken.

Meanwhile about the time of the conference at Trachenberg good news had reached the Allied Headquarters. Napoleon's efforts to conceal or minimise the tidings from Spain had been unsuccessful, and the letter of Francis II to Bernadotte of July 9th [2] is only one of many instances of the encouraging effect of the news of Vittoria. Wellington's great victory (June 21st) was a battle of far more than local importance; it was not merely that the French had been driven headlong out of the Peninsula, and that the "intrusive King" had looked for the last time on his Spanish dominions. Any lingering doubts in Austria's mind were now dispelled. The Allies already seemed to see Germany delivered from Napoleon's rule as Spain had been. The Czar ordered the performance of the first *Te Deum* that the Russian Court had sung for a victory gained by other than Russian troops.[3] Moreover, now that France was threatened with invasion not another man could be withdrawn from the Bidassoa to the Elbe, and Napoleon had to send Soult, the Marshal most capable of exercising an independent command, to try to restore affairs in the Peninsula : not many days were to pass before he would feel his absence from Saxony.

By this time the end of the armistice was close at hand, and the deliberations at Prague had produced no tangible result. Austria asked more than Napoleon would give, and neither side would give way, for each expected success as the result of an appeal to the sword. Thus the time limit was reached and passed. On August 11th the Prussians from Silesia set foot as allies on Bohemian soil, and next day Austria published her declaration of war.

[1] Cf. Friedrich, i. 99.   [2] Cf. Rose, ii. 321.   [3] *Ibid.*

CHAPTER XXXI

THE WAR OF LIBERATION—TO THE BATTLE OF KULM

THE good use which Napoleon had made of the armistice may best be estimated from the fact that at its conclusion the forces under his command on German soil alone amounted to nearly 600,000 men, a total hardly inferior to that of the great host collected sixteen months before for the invasion of Russia. Not that all these were available for active operations in the field. The fortresses to the Eastward still holding out for the Emperor absorbed 50,000 men, survivors for the most part of the Grand Army of 1812; another 25,000 garrisoned the fortresses along the Elbe, and about the same number maintained the line of communications with France through Erfurt and Würzburg. Far away on the Emperor's left Davoût at Hamburg had some 40,000, 12,000 of whom were Danes, ready for field operations. In like manner on the extreme right Wrede's Bavarian corps, 25,000 strong, watched the Austrians under Count Reuss on the Danube. Two incomplete corps, one of cavalry under Milhaud, one of infantry under Augereau, which were being formed at Mayence and Würzburg, amounted to 15,000 more. But when all these deductions had been made there remained 400,000 available for the main operations which the Emperor intended to conduct himself. He was well provided with artillery, having over 12,000 guns, and on paper he had made good his dangerous weakness in cavalry, having brought together 380 squadrons or, about 70,000 sabres. Even so, however, he was much outnumbered in this arm by the Allies, and the difficulty of improving cavalry was to be emphasised on many occasions by the indifferent work and conduct of these hastily raised squadrons. This main body of the Emperor's forces comprised the Guard, the kernel of the whole army, 60,000 strong, five corps of cavalry and eleven of infantry together with independent divisions at Magdeburg, to keep open the communications with Davoût, and at Leipzig.

But this great force was by no means entirely composed of Frenchmen. One corps, the VIIIth, was exclusively composed of Poles; five infantry divisions and some odd battalions were provided by the Confederation of the Rhine, the Kingdom of Italy supplied one whole division and parts of others. Naples was represented by a brigade, while among the troops nominally French were Dutch, Belgians, Swiss, Germans from the Rhinelands and the shores of the North Sea, and many Italians.[1] Thus, as in 1809, it was with an army which included no small number of Germans that Napoleon prepared to reassert his claims to dominate Germany: much would depend on the loyalty of his German vassals to him and of their subjects to them. Would the sentiment of German unity and nationality be strong enough to overpower the bonds of military discipline and local patriotism, if Napoleon were successful? would military discipline and localism be strong enough to resist the seductions of German sentiment, if fortune inclined to the side of the Allies?[2]

But enormous as were the French forces, the efforts of the Allies had produced an even larger total. Apart from their

[1] No less than three whole infantry divisions usually described as French came from the North Italian departments of the Empire.

[2] My principal authority for the composition of Napoleon's Army of 1813 is Major Friedrich's valuable work on *The Autumn Campaign of 1813*, to which I shall have constant occasion to refer throughout this chapter. His appendices (III. V. VI. and VII.) give the details as to the contingents provided by the Confederation of the Rhine. Out of the 502 battalions of the field army, 65 came from the Confederation, Saxony supplying 19, Bavaria 15, Würtemberg 11, Westphalia and Hesse 6 apiece, Baden 4, Würzburg and the Saxon Duchies 2 each. In the cavalry the proportion was rather larger, a sixth, 63 squadrons out of 372, being German. Here again Saxony had the largest contingent, 17 squadrons, Westphalia sending 10, Würtemberg 8, Bavaria and Berg 6 apiece, Baden 5, Hesse and Mecklenburg 4 each, Anhalt 2, and Würzburg 1. Sixteen batteries of artillery were also provided by the Confederation, and it must be remembered that among the garrisons of the fortresses there was a considerable proportion of German troops. For example, Dresden was held by 5 Westphalian battalions and some Saxon garrison artillery (p. 450). Unfortunately, Major Friedrich does not give the composition of the garrisons, nor is this to be found in M. Camille Rousset's *La Grande Armée de 1813* (Paris), to which I have referred for the statistics about the corps of Augereau (IX.) and Davoût (XIII.). The former's 23 battalions included 4 belonging to the 113th of the Line, a regiment raised at Genoa ; the rest of the corps and all Davoût's 28 battalions were Frenchmen. As a rough estimate, a seventh of Napoleon's army may be said to have been Germans.

three main armies, those of Bohemia, Silesia, and the North, there were the miscellaneous levies which Wallmoden was opposing to Davoût;[1] there were the troops, mainly *Landwehr*, occupied in blockading the fortresses in French hands; there were the Free Corps and other irregular forces, detachments which would probably not be overestimated at 100,000.[2] Of the three main armies that of Bohemia was the largest. In addition to the Austrians, some 117 squadrons and 107 battalions, not less than 125,000 in all, it included 109 squadrons and 92 battalions of Russians under Barclay de Tolly, rather over 80,000 men; the second Prussian Army Corps under Kleist, 44 squadrons and 41 battalions amounting to 37,000; and the 7000 men, 8 squadrons and 6 battalions, of the Prussian Guards. In accordance with the scheme arranged at Reichenbach, these forces had moved from Silesia into Bohemia by way of Glatz and Schweidnitz, had crossed to the left of the Elbe and joined the Austrians on the Eger (August 16th) the day before the six days' grace over and above the armistice expired.

Next in size was Bernadotte's Army of the North in which the Prussians, 72,000 strong, outnumbered the combined Russians (30,000) and Swedes (23,000). One of the two Prussians corps, Tauentzien's, 29 squadrons and 48 battalions, was almost entirely composed of *Landwehr*; the other, Bülow's, 42 squadrons and 40 battalions, was the most efficient portion of the whole army, as the Swedes had had little experience of warfare, and over a quarter of Winzingerode's Russians were Cossacks, who were of little value in battle. Really the Army of Silesia, though weaker by nearly 20,000 men, was a much more efficient force; it included Yorck's Prussian corps, 48 squadrons and 43 battalions, 38,000 strong, and the two Russian corps of Sacken and Langeron, which between them amounted to 67 squadrons and 74 battalions, or nearly 70,000 men.

All told, the three armies mustered about 480,000, roughly speaking a fifth again as large as Napoleon's main body. But against that the Emperor could set the advantages of a central position and of unity of command, considerations which went far to neutralise his numerical inferiority.

---

[1] Friedrich, i. 58.

[2] Major Friedrich (i. 59) puts the forces of the Allies not in the first line at the gigantic total of 350,000; but this includes not only reserves, depôts and garrisons, but the Austrian corps facing Eugene in Italy and Wrede in Bavaria.

The choice of a Commander-in-Chief had been a matter of great difficulty to the Allies. Alexander would readily have taken the post himself, but his military capacities were altogether inadequate and Metternich would have opposed the suggestion. Bernadotte had yet to earn the full confidence of his new allies, and Moreau, who hurried over from America to place his services at their disposal, had not the necessary position or authority. The Allies had indeed at their disposal a general whose reputation stands at the present day far higher than that of any other possible candidate, but at that time Archduke Charles was still under the clouds of Wagram, and, moreover, he was on very bad terms with his brother and with Metternich. Accordingly, Austria put forward as her candidate for the command of the army of Bohemia, Prince Schwarzenberg, who had commanded the Austrian auxiliary corps in the invasion of Russia. He was a man of considerable military experience and of respectable capacities, though of altogether insufficient calibre to be matched against Napoleon. He was too cautious, too anxious, too wanting in self-confidence, decision and energy to be a great general, but the unfavourable verdicts so often passed upon him fail to do justice to what he did accomplish. He had not merely to direct the movements of an enormous army and to combine his operations with those of two other armies which were practically independent, but he was the general of a coalition, and he had at his headquarters the three Allied monarchs whose presence could not fail to be a serious handicap. Add to this his many vigorous and opinionated colleagues and the multitude of counsellors of great experience, including besides Barclay de Tolly and Moreau, Radetzky, Toll and Jomini, always ready with the best conflicting advice, and Schwarzenberg's achievements seem not so very poor after all. No one would pretend that it was Schwarzenberg's strategy which was the chief cause of Napoleon's overthrow. Bernadotte rather than the Austrian general was the author of the plan Schwarzenberg had to carry out, and all that there is to be urged on his behalf is the rather negative praise that no great strategical blunder is to be laid to his door; his errors were errors of omission not of commission, he did not do anything much and therefore did little wrong. Still in keeping the Allies together, and preserving good relations between them, his tact and diplomacy were of the utmost value;

it may certainly be questioned whether the Allies could have improved upon the choice.

Still the operations of the Allies lacked the accurate co-ordination which could only be given by a Commander-in-Chief of really great capacity and authority, whose office was a good deal more than a name, and who could plan a campaign and rely on having his plan put into execution in the manner he intended. On the whole the scheme arranged at Trachenberg was faithfully adhered to, but it cannot be maintained that it was by superior strategy that the Allies succeeded in ousting the French from Germany. They owed their victory largely to the comparatively indifferent quality of the French army, especially of the cavalry, to whose inefficiency may be attributed the failure to obtain accurate information which did so much to ruin Napoleon's plans, largely to the errors and misfortunes of Napoleon's subordinates, partly it must be admitted to Napoleon's own errors,[1] but in great measure to the waning fidelity of his long-suffering allies and vassals. Austria had given the example of rejecting the Emperor's specious offers, it remained to be seen whether Bavaria and Saxony and Würtemberg would do the same. It was the uncertainty of the political situation which did so much to paralyse the Emperor's movements. In 1812 he had had little reason to fear for his communications with France, even when he had won the Pyrrhic victory of Borodino in the heart of Russia. After Bautzen and after Dresden he could not feel sure of the far shorter line from the Elbe to the Rhine. Germany was seething with disloyalty in his rear; and though as yet the states of the Confederation were bound to his cause by their uncertainty as to the Allies' intentions towards them, individuals began to desert even before the tide of success turned against the Emperor. As early as August 22nd the two Westphalian Hussar regiments which formed the cavalry brigade of the IInd Corps, Victor's, came over to the Allies,[2] and at the critical moment in the battle of Leipzig it was the defection of a Saxon division which secured the French defeat.

---

[1] Count Yorck von Wartenburg in his *Napoleon as a General* is very, but not perhaps unduly, severe in his criticisms on the Emperor's strategy in this campaign, especially on his failure to concentrate his forces at the decisive point, and his neglect to strike at the enemy's main army.

[2] Friedrich, i. 173.

The end of the armistice found the greater part of the French army on the right bank of the Elbe, in a position, therefore, which gave them the advantage of being able to operate on interior lines against the converging forces of their enemies. Yet despite this it did not see Napoleon putting his whole force in motion for one of the bold offensive movements usually so characteristic of his strategy. Such a stroke, whether directed against the Army of Silesia or against the Austrians in Bohemia, could only prove successful if it resulted at once in a decisive battle. Should the force assailed evade an action by retreat, the Emperor would only expose his flanks and rear to the other Allied forces if he allowed himself to be drawn into a pursuit, while he could not call on troops so young and raw as the majority of his were for the great efforts in marching by which alone a reluctant enemy might be compelled to stand and fight. The adoption of the defensive was therefore the policy which his circumstances made advisable. To await in his central position in Lusatia the advance of his enemies, until one or the other came near enough to let him dash at it, bring it to battle, crush it, and turn against the other, was the strategy which promised the best results. But Napoleon was impatient; he longed to reassert his supremacy and encourage his young troops by a speedy victory; he could not reconcile himself to the mere defensive, to accommodating his movements to those of the enemy. And with good reason he feared the bad effects on the fidelity of his allies and the *morale* of his troops which were bound to result from the spectacle of his inactivity. Accordingly, while he took post on the Elbe and in Lusatia with the greater part of his army, ready to parry any advance of the Allies from Silesia or Bohemia,[1] he decided to take the offensive against Bernadotte's Army of the North, whose fighting capacities he somewhat underestimated.

His scheme was that three corps of infantry, those of Bertrand (IV.), Reynier (VII.) and Oudinot (XII.), with Arrighi's cavalry, should advance Northward on Berlin, Davoût co-operating by a move Eastward from Hamburg against Bernadotte's communications with Stralsund. The defeat of Bernadotte would, so Napoleon calculated, secure his threatened hold on North Germany, especially Westphalia, and would also allow him to relieve the beleaguered garrisons of Cüstrin, Stettin and even

[1] Cf. Friedrich, i. 116.

Dantzic. By obtaining command of the Lower Oder the French would outflank the Army of Silesia and threaten its communications with Russia. However, by detaching 70,000 men against Berlin, Napoleon seriously diminished the forces he had available to meet the combined advance of the Allies from Bohemia and Silesia, the foes from whom he had most to fear, and over whom alone a decisive victory could be won.[1] It might have been wiser, as St. Cyr and Marmont advised,[2] to be content with holding Bernadotte in check, and to concentrate as large a force as possible against the main armies of the Allies. At the same time, in the hands of Soult or Davoût with 100,000 of the better troops at Napoleon's disposal, the move might have proved a success; but it would have necessitated the adoption of the strictest defensive in Silesia, and as it was the Emperor did not choose the right general or detach a force sufficient either in numbers or in quality to secure success. Oudinot, though a brave soldier and a capable subordinate, was hardly fitted for so important an independent command, and his troops, even if Girard's divisions at Magdeburg and Wittenberg be included in the total, only mustered 84,000, while the Army of the North came to half as many again. Moreover, they were of rather indifferent quality, a mixture of nationalities, with hardly any good French troops among them. A third of his infantry (35 battalions out of 106) and over half his cavalry (35 squadrons out of 67) were Germans from the Confederation of the Rhine, troops whose loyalty to the Emperor would be subjected to a severe strain; another division (14 battalions) was drawn from the kingdom of Italy; and three of the four "French" divisions were French in name only, being recruited from the Italian provinces of the Empire; while the remaining one, Durutte's, was mainly composed of "disciplinary" regiments.[3] Arrighi's cavalry were mostly French, but even they were of little value, a collection of single squadrons of different regiments, raw recruits indifferently mounted, hardly able to perform the simplest manœuvres, and quite incompetent to conceal the movements of their own army or discover those of their enemy.[4] Moreover, to add to Oudinot's difficulties, Davoût had his hands too full with Wallmoden to be able to carry out his proposed diversion against Bernadotte's communications with Stralsund.

---

[1] Cf. Friedrich, i. 128–130.
[2] *Ibid.* i. 133–135.
[3] *Ibid.* i. 367.
[4] *Ibid.* i. 367 ff.

While Oudinot was collecting his forces for the attack on Berlin, Napoleon was by no means inactive. Acting upon the mistaken impression that the force which had moved from Silesia to join the Austrians in Bohemia only consisted of Wittgenstein's Russians, and was 40,000 not, as was really the case, 125,000 strong, the Emperor directed his attention to the Army of Silesia, imagining that Blücher rather than Schwarzenberg was at the head of the principal army of the Allies. The troops upon whom he was relying to keep the Army of Silesia in check were Sebastiani's cavalry and the infantry of Ney (IIIrd Corps), Lauriston (Vth) and Macdonald (XIth). These were posted along a line which rested its right on the Riesengebirge near Friedeberg, and its left on the Oder near Parchwitz. Similarly Kellermann's cavalry and Poniatowski's Poles (the VIIIth Corps) faced Southwards towards Bohemia on the right bank of the Elbe, and in conjunction with St. Cyr's infantry (XIVth Corps) and L'Heritier's cavalry on the left bank covered Saxony and Lusatia against the Army of Bohemia. The Guard in and around Görlitz, Vandamme's corps (Ist) at Bautzen, Victor's infantry (IInd) and Latour-Maubourg's cavalry between Görlitz and Zittau with Marmont's corps (VIth) at Bunzlau formed the central reserve, available for service on either front.

The Emperor's original idea seems to have been to push forward into Bohemia up the right bank of the Elbe; possibly he hoped so to catch Wittgenstein in flank before he could execute his bold march across the French front. However, it was soon discovered that the Austrians and their allies were all on the left bank,[1] and Napoleon, still under the impression that the Army of Silesia, which had just (August 17th) begun to press in upon the French corps in its front, was the principal force of the Allies, decided to turn against it and to defer the invasion of Bohemia until after the destruction of the Army of Silesia, when he would be able to use the Lusatian passes for an advance against Schwarzenberg. He saw that an advance even to Prague would be a blow wasted on the air unless it brought on a decisive action, and that even a victory over Schwarzenberg would leave him in a difficult position if in the meantime his communications with Lusatia through Zittau and Görlitz were to be severed by Blücher driving Ney's containing

[1] Cf. Friedrich, i. 189.

force in upon Dresden. Accordingly the Emperor left Victor and Vandamme to support Poniatowski and Kellermann and to keep touch with St. Cyr at Dresden by means of the bridges at Pirna and Königstein ; and having thus, as he thought, provided against any move Schwarzenberg was likely to make, he hastened (Aug. 20th) with the rest of the reserve to the assistance of Ney's "Army of the Bober," against which the Army of Silesia was beginning to push forward. Blücher's advance had forced Ney to fall back rather rapidly from the Katzbach to the Bober (Aug. 17th to 20th), and the Army of Silesia was about to follow up its success by an attack on the French positions between Bunzlau and Löwenberg when the arrival of Napoleon and his reserves was announced to the Prussian commander (Aug. 20th). For an action against one of Napoleon's lieutenants the Army of Silesia was ready and even anxious, but to fight the Emperor himself was a very different matter, and in accordance with the fixed principle which governed the Allies' operations, Blücher decamped hastily Eastward rather than give Napoleon the chance of a pitched battle, a decision for which Lützen, Bautzen and Dresden afford ample justification. Napoleon pursued vigorously, and there was some sharp rearguard fighting in which the Allies suffered severely; but they made good their escape behind the Katzbach, and Napoleon had to admit that they had evaded him. He could press the pursuit no further, for urgent messages reached him from St. Cyr that the Army of Bohemia had crossed the Erzgebirge and was threatening Dresden. Accordingly Napoleon had to turn back towards the Elbe to St. Cyr's assistance, taking with him the Guards, Marmont and Latour - Maubourg, and leaving Macdonald with his own corps and those of Ney (now under Souham), Lauriston, and Sebastiani to contain Blücher (Aug. 23rd).

Thus the French army, instead of being concentrated in superior force against one of its three opponents, had become separated into three or rather four portions, one opposing each of the Allied armies, and Napoleon with the central reserve hurrying back across Lusatia to save Dresden from Schwarzenberg. The position was critical, but Napoleon hoped for the best. If only his lieutenants proved equal to the tasks allotted to them, if, for example, St. Cyr could keep the Allies at bay until Napoleon could cross the Elbe at Pirna and fall in force on the communications of the Army of Bohemia, the most brilliant success might be looked for.

But Napoleon's lieutenants were destined to disappoint their master's expectations grievously. Oudinot had concentrated his army round Baruth by August 18th, and next day began his advance on Berlin. His road lay through the belts of wooded and swampy country which lie to the South of the Prussian capital, and which offer many good positions to a defending force, besides making very difficult lateral communications between columns moving forward parallel along the main roads. Still at first he made good progress. On the 21st he came into touch with the Army of the North between Trebbin and Zossen, and drove in its outposts after some sharp fighting, so that by the evening of the 22nd, despite the difficulties of the country, he had won his way through the worst part, and all that remained was to attack the main position of the Army of the North. This force was standing at bay with its right at Gütergotz and its left—Tauentzien's *Landwehr*—at Blankenfelde. Bernadotte, indeed, being for political reasons very anxious to avoid all risks of a defeat, would have preferred not to give battle South of the Spree at all, but to have retired across that river so as to make use of the defensive capacities of the country to the North of it, which was admirably adapted for the policy he wished to adopt of keeping the enemy at bay without allowing him to force on a battle. However, the protection of Berlin had been one of the tasks assigned to his army at Trachenberg, and Bülow was urgent in his demands that a battle should be risked for the Prussian capital. For this purpose the position Bernadotte selected was well adapted; it was fairly strong, and it covered the three main roads which converge on Berlin from the Southward. The French, having still some woods to pass through, were moving in three columns quite independently and not expecting a battle. This, with the indifferent scouting of their cavalry, was the main cause of the disaster which befell them. Their attacks were not delivered simultaneously, and their left column, Oudinot's own corps and Arrighi's cavalry, was so much behind that it practically took no part in the action. Thus though Reynier, moving by the central road, carried Gross Beeren at the first attack, and maintained himself there from 3 p.m. till after 7, he received no assistance from his colleagues, and could only oppose 18,000

men to Bülow, who had double that number.[1] Even so the
VIIth Corps did very well, and Sahr's Saxon division, though
exposed to a heavy cannonade, held on most tenaciously to
Gross Beeren until simultaneously taken in flank by Borstell's
Pomeranians and assailed in front by the three other Prussian
divisions. Gross Beeren was lost, and Durutte's French division became involved in Sahr's overthrow. Lecoq's Saxons
then intervened and endeavoured to retrieve the day by an
advance against Bülow's right; but they were checked by
some Swedish light infantry, and Reynier's whole corps went to
its rear in confusion, leaving over 3000 men behind. Too late
Oudinot's own vanguard reached the field: the rout of the
centre compelled it to retreat. Bertrand meanwhile had
opened the action with some success against Tauentzien, who
was barring the Eastern road at Blankenfelde; but he had failed
to push his advantage home and now had to conform to the
retrograde movement. By September 2nd Oudinot was back
at Wittenberg, the *morale* and the physical condition of his
troops badly shaken. His defeat had led to a further disaster,
for Girard, moving up from Magdeburg to cover Oudinot's left,
had found himself dangerously exposed by the Marshal's retreat,
and in endeavouring to regain touch with his colleagues he
was brought to action by Hirschfeld's *Landwehr* at Hagelberg,
and totally defeated after an action of very varying fortune
(Aug. 27th).

Nor was this the only bad result of Gross Beeren. Wallmoden, whose operations have a special interest for English
readers, inasmuch as his force included the only British troops
which played an active part in this momentous campaign,[2] had
some 25,000 to 30,000 men at his disposal. However, Davoût,
despite a check at Kammin (Aug. 21st) was forcing him to
retire Eastward, had himself advanced to Schwerin and had
pushed Loison's division as far as Wismar, forcing Vegesack's
Swedes back to Rostock, when the news of Gross Beeren compelled him to retire to the Stecknitz and adopt a defensive
attitude.

In like manner Macdonald had come to grief. As already

---

[1] Friedrich, App. IV. and V.

[2] He had the 2nd battalion of the 73rd Regiment, one of six sent out to garrison
Stralsund in July 1813, a Rocket Troop and two batteries of the Royal Horse
Artillery, and the 3rd Hussars of the King's German Legion.

mentioned, Blücher had fallen back from the Bober just in time to avoid an action with Napoleon and had retreated by forced marches to Jauer (Aug. 22nd to 24th), thus returning to the positions from which he had advanced at the end of the armistice. The weather had been very bad, the roads difficult and supplies often short, so that what with the long marches, many of them at night, the want of rest, the hardships and privations they had undergone, the constant rearguard actions and the apparent uselessness of all their exertions, the Army of Silesia was rapidly being reduced to a wreck. Yorck protested violently against operations which had brought his *Landwehr* battalions almost to the point of disbanding,[1] and had cost his corps not only 4000 men in action, but many more through the toils of the march.[2] The state of the Russians was little better, and Blücher, realising that to continue to carry out his orders to keep close touch with his opponents and yet avoid a battle would mean the ruin of his army, at length decided to fight. He was moving back from Jauer to the Katzbach when he met the French advancing to meet him (Aug. 26th).

Macdonald had received orders from Napoleon to drive the Army of Silesia back beyond Jauer, and then take up a position behind the Bober to cover the principal operations against Bohemia from interruption by Blücher.[3] The order was unwise, for Macdonald was hardly strong enough to put out of action an enemy as numerous as was the Army of Silesia, and Napoleon's rear might have been as efficiently protected against Blücher without the advance to Jauer. But the Marshal had learnt that the enemy were somewhat disorganised by their sufferings, and he seems to have been to some extent counting on this. It was rather to his surprise, therefore, that he found Blücher moving towards him. His dispositions had been made for a fight at Jauer, and were none too well adapted for immediate action. Souham's corps on the left had started late and was some distance behind, and two divisions, one of Lauriston's and one of Macdonald's own, had been detached to the right to contain St. Priest's Russians near Hirschberg who were keeping touch between the Army of Silesia and Bohemia. Thus Macdonald had under 50,000 men at hand with whom to engage the 80,000 Allies in front of him.

The position of the Allies was divided in two by the Roaring

---

[1] Friedrich, i. 41.   [2] *Ibid.* i. 286–289.   [3] *Ibid.* i. 202, cf. 295.

(*Wüthende*) Neisse, on the left of which stood Langeron's Russians, their right touching the river at Schlaupe, their left resting on the high hill of the Monchswald. On the other bank Yorck's Prussians with Sacken's Russians beyond them were drawn up between the villages of Bellwitzhof, Eichholtz and Ober Hochkirch, some way back from the edge of the plateau which rises abruptly Eastward from the Neisse. Macdonald pushed Lauriston forward on his right through Seichau against Langeron and sent his own corps and Sebastiani's horsemen over the Katzbach at Kroitsch, over the Neisse at Nieder Crayn and Weinberg and up the slopes beyond. It was raining and the rivers were rising rapidly; but Macdonald attacked nevertheless in this somewhat precipitate manner, when he would have done better to wait for the arrival of Souham, or until the enemy should attack.

On the French right things went well enough. Lauriston not only drove in the Russian front, crossing the two small streams which protected it, and carrying the village of Hennersdorf, but pushed some battalions in between Langeron's flank and the Monchswald, and by thus turning his left drove him back on Peterwitz. But in the centre Macdonald's infantry and Sebastiani's cavalry had become much mixed; they got in each other's way, and their attacks, delivered in disorder and without cohesion, soon came to a standstill. Yorck's corps then advanced to deliver a counter-attack, and for some time the struggle was evenly contested until a flank attack by Sacken's Russians on the French left sent cavalry, infantry and artillery in headlong confusion down the steep slopes and into the swollen and rising rivers. This quite decided the day; for Souham's own division, which had just arrived and was endeavouring to assist its comrades, became involved in the general rout, and Blücher was enabled to send his reserves to the assistance of Langeron and so to bring Lauriston to a standstill. Too late to do any good, two more of Souham's divisions appeared on the extreme left, and engaged Sacken; but the battle was lost, and though Lauriston held on to Hennersdorf till nightfall and beat back Langeron's repeated attacks, he could do no more than retire in fair order. The retreat was a terrible experience: Macdonald's corps went completely to pieces and became a huddled mass of fugitives; Lauriston and Souham managed to preserve some measure of order, but the weather was most inclement, and Gneisenau pressed the pursuit with relentless energy, though hampered by the continual rains and the swollen mountain torrents in his way. By the 1st of September the relics of the Army of the Bober were behind the Queiss, a rabble rather than an army; discipline had lost its hold over the men, whole divisions had been cut to pieces, over 100 guns and 18,000 prisoners had fallen into the hands of the Allies, while as many more had perished. But for the moment the condition of their pursuers was little better: Yorck's ill-equipped *Landwehr* regiments had dwindled in some cases to a tenth of their establishment, and the exertions and hardships of the pursuit had been so great that it could not be pressed any further.[1] Moreover, news had come from Dresden which made Blücher pause.

If the advance of the Army of Bohemia had been conducted with rather more energy and definiteness of purpose a great deal more success might have been obtained. But the roads over the mountains were in a very bad condition, and the Staff of the army was hardly equal to moving so large a force. Nor was the object of the advance very clear. Schwarzenberg was somewhat loath to embark upon it, he would have preferred to leave to the enemy the difficulties of crossing the mountains in order to bring on a battle. However, Napoleon showed no disposition to fall in with this desire, and the main army could not afford to remain idle while Blücher and Bernadotte might be being beaten in detail. Accordingly on August 19th the Allies set out Northward with the idea of striking a blow at Napoleon's communications by seizing Leipzig. Moving in four columns they crossed the watershed on August 22nd, and made for Chemnitz; but finding that only on the right (Wittgenstein's Russians) was any resistance offered, and that an advance to Leipzig would not bring them into contact with any of their enemies, they had to alter their plans. At a council of war held at Zöplitz on the 22nd, it was decided to turn North-Eastward against Dresden, which was known to be but weakly held. It was this advance of which the news reached Napoleon at Görlitz on the evening of the 23rd, and brought him back in haste to the Elbe.[2]

On the afternoon of August 25th the vanguard of the Allies appeared before Dresden. Marshal St. Cyr had fallen back before them with three of his four infantry divisions, a force which even when the 5000 troops of the garrison be added to it cannot have much exceeded 25,000. His remaining division was

[1] Cf. Friedrich, i. 327.   [2] *Ibid.* i. 209.

at Königstein seeking to keep open that line for Napoleon's projected advance. Marshal Vandamme, whose corps was the
nearest to Dresden, and might have been in that city by the
evening of the 24th,[1] had not moved from Rumburg and New-
stadt, and Victor was still farther away. Thus, if the Allies had
attacked at once, it is probable that they would have captured
the town. It is true that less than half of their total force had
arrived, but the 80,000 on the spot ought to have been more than
sufficient for the task : the garrison was less than a third of their
strength, and the extensive fortifications, too large for so small a
force, were hastily constructed and weak. But the Allies hesitated,
and let the opportunity escape. The responsibility for this
grievous oversight has been repudiated on behalf of all the
principal persons on the Allied side. Jomini and others have
blamed Schwarzenberg for the delay, whereas that general's bio-
grapher, Prokesch, claims that he was anxious to attack ; and it
would seem that really it was the Czar who was responsible
for the inaction of the Allies, and that Schwarzenberg allowed
Alexander to overrule his own better judgment.[2]

Be this as it may, the delay saved Dresden. That evening
the garrison were able to see on the Eastern horizon the distant
bivouac fires of the returning Guards ; and when, about six o'clock
next morning (Aug. 26th), the Allies did at last attack, the
assault was not directed with much vigour. On the Allied right,
Wittgenstein's Russians made some headway along the low
ridge running along the Elbe from the Blasowitz woods to the
city. Next to them Kleist's Prussians effected a lodgment in
the Grosse Garten, the public park on the South-East of the
town, while the Austrians on the left centre carried the village
of Plauen only to be repulsed from the Wildsruffer suburb.
Beyond the little river Weisseritz also the Austrians made much
headway, carrying Lobtau and driving the French back into the
Friedrichstadt ; but in no one quarter was the attack pressed
home, and every minute brought the reinforcements from Lusatia
nearer. It was between one and two in the afternoon that the
leading regiments of the Young Guard hurled themselves into
the fight on the extreme French left, dislodging the Russians
who had begun to make their way into the Pirna suburb. From
that moment a continuous stream of troops came pouring across
the great bridges over the Elbe, and Dresden was safe.

[1] Cf. Friedrich, i. 208.　　　　　　　[2] *Ibid.* i. 179–181.

39

It was when all real chance of success was gone and they would really have done better to be preparing to retreat, that the Allies suddenly launched their belated attack in force against the town. It was everywhere repulsed. Mortier on the left drove Wittgenstein back beyond Striesen. Pirch and Ziethen by a great effort carried the Grosse Garten, and reached the suburb behind, only to be hurled back by another division of the Young Guard. On their left another Prussian brigade went reeling back in disorder to Strehla, and even Colloredo's Austrians, who had made a lodgment in one of the French batteries and were pressing on, were driven from the ground they had so hardly won by the bayonets of the Old Guard. All along the line the Allies had to go back. West of the Weisseritz their attacks had made little further advance, and about 6 p.m. Murat headed a sortie which drove them back to Lobtau and the adjacent villages. By nightfall the French had not only recovered all the ground they had lost, but were well posted for following up their success by a counter-attack next day. The Allies would have been well advised if they had retired: there was nothing to be gained by retaining their positions, especially as their supplies were beginning to run short. But Frederick William felt that it would be too much of a confession of weakness to retire, and it was largely due to him that they remained to tempt their fate.

The principal effort of the French on the next morning was directed against the Allied right. Here Mortier with two divisions of the Young Guard and Nansouty's cavalry outflanked the Russians, and pushing them back towards the South and West gained possession of Seidnitz and Gross Dobritz, thus driving them off from the Pirna road. St. Cyr advancing from the Grosse Garten deprived the Prussians of Strehla, while Marmont, who continued the line to the Westward, kept the Austrians opposite him in play. Beyond the Weisseritz, Victor attacked and carried the heights between Dolzschen and Wolffnitz, while under cover of his operations Murat was directing Latour-Maubourg's cavalry and an odd brigade of Vandamme's corps in a sweeping movement round by Burgstadtel which was to roll up the Austrian left. About midday the battle rather languished. Mortier carried Reick, but could get no farther, for the Russian reserve cavalry outnumbered Nansouty by three to one and menaced his flank. Similarly, St. Cyr could not obtain secure possession of Leubnitz. It was on the left of the Weisseritz that the decisive stroke was dealt. Soon after Victor had carried Ober Gorbitz, thereby cutting off part of Alois Lichtenstein's division and forcing that of Weissenwolff to retire, Teste's infantry and Chastel's cavalry appeared in rear of the Austrian left at Pennrich. The rest of Murat's horsemen were quickly thrown into the fight. Ten Austrian battalions were cut off and taken to a man, the rest of their left wing fell back in complete confusion along the Kesselsdorf road with Murat's troopers at their heels.

After this there could be no question as to the retreat of the Allies: to stay on would play into Napoleon's hands, and, moreover, Vandamme, though stoutly opposed by the Russian corps under Eugene of Würtemberg, which had been left at Pirna to keep open the road to Töplitz, was beginning to make his presence felt. Luckily for the Allies, Napoleon did not press home his attacks on the afternoon of the 27th; his men had had a full share of marching and fighting, and were tired out, and he was also waiting to let Vandamme's operations develope. Thus the Allies maintained their positions till the evening and withdrew under cover of night, Barclay with the Russians and Kleist being given the road by Peterswalde to Töplitz, the Austrians of the centre that by Dippoldiswalde to Brux, Klenau's unengaged reserve and the relics of the left wing taking the road through Tharandt to Freiberg. Thus the 28th found the Army of Bohemia in full retreat across the Erzgebirge. Worn out by their exertions and hardships, ill-clad, short of food, ill-equipped, their columns, even though but leisurely pursued, left numbers of stragglers and prisoners behind as they toiled in inclement weather along the indifferent mountain roads. The Poles in the Austrian ranks deserted freely, and some of the Prussian *Landwehr* battalions lost all cohesion. A more vigorous pursuit might have turned the retreat into a rout, and if Vandamme had been able to forestall the Allies in reaching Töplitz their plight would have been perilous. But Vandamme, partly owing to the gallant resistance of Eugene of Würtemberg, partly owing to the mistakes made by the other pursuing columns, partly to the accident that Barclay's disobedience of his orders brought Kleist's corps unexpectedly to Fürstenwalde on the evening of the 29th, failed to accomplish his task. He had with him nearly 40,000 men, all his own corps save a few battalions, a division of St. Cyr's (Mouton's), a brigade of Victor's and a light cavalry division (Corbineau's) of Latour-Maubourg's corps. He had crossed at Königstein on the 26th, had been sharply engaged with Eugene most of that day, finally gaining possession of the Pirna plateau, and by the 28th he had obtained a position which flanked the great road to Töplitz and threatened to prevent Eugene retiring by that way.

Eugene, however, was fully alive to the importance of not letting Vandamme secure undisputed possession of this all-important road, so on the 28th instead of falling back to Maxen in obedience to Barclay's orders, which would have left the road to Töplitz open to Vandamme, he determined to push past the Ist Corps and get between it and Töplitz. To do this he made an attack on Vandamme's lines with his own corps, under cover of which Ostermann's division of the Russian Guards got across the front of the French. He achieved his purpose but at a heavy cost, for his corps was dispersed, and Vandamme came pressing hard on his heels. At Priesten, in front of the last pass over the mountains, Eugene stood at bay next day, and after a fierce and stubbornly-contested action, which brought his losses up to 6000 out of his 15,000 men, he had the satisfaction of keeping off Vandamme until the simultaneous arrival of reinforcements and nightfall stopped the fight. By the next morning (Aug. 30th), when Vandamme renewed his attempts, such large reinforcements had arrived that Eugene was not only able to maintain his hold upon Priesten and so keep the French right and centre in check, but three Austrian divisions pushed forward through Karbitz against Vandamme's left. They were gradually gaining ground; and as none of his efforts could shake the Russian hold on Priesten, the prospects of success for Vandamme were becoming very faint, when his failure was suddenly converted into disaster by the arrival of Kleist's Prussians in his rear. This corps, delayed by Barclay's action in taking the Dippoldiswalde road in preference to that by Peterswalde, in consequence of which the road became overcrowded, had reached Fürstenwalde on the evening of the 29th and had there received an urgent summons to the help of Eugene. Moving in answer to this appeal, Kleist did not make straight for Priesten, but took a South-Easterly direction across the hills to Nollendorf. Much to his surprise and relief he found no French troops on the road ; for Napoleon, hearing that the Allies were retiring South-West, had diverted the XIVth Corps, which was to have followed Van-

to Bautzen
R. Elbe

Blasowitz

Nansouty

Friedrich-stadt

MURAT

L.M. Victor

Cotta

DRESDEN

Striesen

Mortier

Grosser

Y.G.

Wittgenstein

städtel

Giulai & Bianchi

Marmont

St. Eyl

Garten

Seidnitz

Löbtau

O. G.

Gross

Dobritz

Wölfnitz

Räcknitz

Austrians

Miloradovitch

R & P
G.

Kleist

Strehlen

Reick

Gorbitz

Plauen

Leubnitz

Prohlis

Doltzschen

Kaitzbach

Pesterwitz

1   Engl. Mile   0   1

damme, towards Maxen, and Pajol, who commanded St. Cyr's cavalry, had formed an erroneous impression as to Kleist's route, and had gone astray to the Westward.

When he perceived his peril, Vandamme made a most vigorous attempt to extricate himself. His artillery sacrificed themselves in an endeavour to keep the Russians at bay, while a strong column of infantry backed by Corbineau's cavalry hurled themselves on the Prussians. At the same time eight infantry battalions took post at Arbesau, and their stubborn resistance prevented the Austrians from completing their outflanking movement and joining the Prussians. In and around Vorder Tellnitz there was a tremendous struggle. The desperate energy of Vandamme's attack was more than the Prussians could stand. The *Landwehr* gave way by battalions, and the whole corps was shattered and rent asunder. But the French had spent themselves in the effort, and on finding their path barred at Jungferndorf, a few miles farther North, by a brigade which Kleist had pushed out thither to secure his rear, many of those who had made their way through Tellnitz laid down their arms in sheer exhaustion. Still a good many escaped, including most of the cavalry; while Mouton, whose division formed the extreme right of the French line, seeing that retreat through Kulm along the high road was out of the question for him, took at once to the hills and so got away to Ebersdorf and Fürstenwalde. Still the Ist Corps as a fighting force had ceased to exist, 10,000 men were killed and wounded, as many more were taken together with their commander and 82 guns. It was a disaster of enormous importance. Not merely had Napoleon's plan for reaping the fruits of Dresden miscarried entirely, but the Army of Bohemia, which on the 28th had been retiring in the deepest dejection and depression, could now claim a victory won almost under the eyes of Napoleon. Not much had been wanted to convert the failure of the blow at Dresden into a disaster, now the tables were turned and the fears that the Emperor might reply to that stroke by a victorious march on Prague need no longer be entertained. Indeed, even before the news of Kulm, Napoleon had been forced to abandon all idea of an immediate invasion of Bohemia by hearing of the defeats of Oudinot and Macdonald, and to some extent the successes of Blücher and Bernadotte contributed to that of August 30th by calling off the Emperor's attention from the pursuit. Had he been giving his undivided mind to its direction, it is hard to believe that he would have lost touch with Kleist or left Vandamme altogether unsupported. One reason no doubt for his failure to utilise his victory at Dresden was that he overestimated it, believing it another Jena and not understanding the great difference in the *morale* of his opponents since 1806. Thus, Dresden notwithstanding, these critical last ten days of August had gone emphatically in favour of the Allies. Gross Beeren, the Katzbach and Kulm were an ample set-off against their one repulse, and in mere numbers the French losses exceeded those of the Allies. But the moral advantages of their success outweighed its material result. If Napoleon himself had not yet been beaten, it had been conclusively proved that his lieutenants were not invincible, and that even he could not altogether disregard the loss of half a million of soldiers. He had not managed to secure even the partial success of the spring campaign; his hold on Germany had been challenged and the challengers had survived the conflict. A decisive success for Napoleon at Dresden might have confirmed the Confederation of the Rhine in its adherence to his cause, the partial success of the Allies went far to shake the allegiance of his German vassals and to encourage those who yearned to be free from his heavy yoke.

CHAPTER XXXII

THE WAR OF LIBERATION—LEIPZIG AND HANAU

EVEN after the disaster of Kulm, Napoleon could not bring himself to a mere defensive. To adopt a passive attitude would be a confession of failure, an admission that the initiative had passed from his hands, an invitation to his wavering vassals to desert the cause of one whose own actions proclaimed him no longer master of the situation. But notwithstanding the object-lesson he had received of the inherent viciousness of the plan of operating offensively against superior numbers in several quarters simultaneously, Napoleon failed to return to the sounder strategy of concentrating all available forces against the enemy's main army. Adhering to his error, he sent Ney to take command of Oudinot's force and resume the attack on Berlin, at the same time that he himself moved Eastward to the succour of Macdonald and to force an action on Blücher, taking with him the Guard, Latour-Maubourg's cavalry and Marmont's infantry. But as before, Blücher's hasty retreat prevented the Emperor from winning the much desired victory over the Silesian Army; and as the Army of Bohemia, which he believed to be quite out of action for the time being, was, on the contrary, actually threatening Dresden, he had once more to return to the Saxon capital (Sept. 3rd).

Meanwhile Ney had taken command of the Army of Berlin at Wittenberg (Sept. 3rd) and was advancing Northward. At Zahna he was stoutly opposed by Tauentzien's *Landwehr* (Sept. 5th), and not until Bertrand came to the assistance of the XIIth Corps were the Prussians forced back to Juterbogk. Tauentzien's corps had fought very well, and it left 3000 dead behind it and Ney under the impression that he had had the whole Army of the North in action against him. He therefore took no precautions to discover where Bülow and Bernadotte might be, and moved forward next morning, believing the enemy to be in full retreat. But when Bertrand neared Dennewitz he came into contact with Tauentzien, who was moving Westward to regain touch with Bülow. The French at once attacked. An even and well-contested struggle had just been decided in favour of the French by the arrival of Reynier, when Bülow came up to Tauentzien's help. His fresh divisions, moving up by Niedergorsdorf on the right of the hard-pressed *Landwehr*, fell upon an Italian division of the IVth Corps and routed it. Reynier intervened and stayed the Prussian advance, but reinforcements joined Bülow and he succeeded in driving the French out of Golsdorf. Next Oudinot appeared on the scene from Ohna, and engaged and drove back Bülow. However, Tauentzien was pressing so hard on Bertrand's right, a division of Würtembergers, at Rohrbeck, that Ney, instead of pushing home the advantage he had gained against Bülow, disengaged Oudinot and transferred him to the right to reinforce Bertrand. This left Reynier alone to face Bülow ; and before the renewed attacks of the Prussians his Saxons and disciplinary battalions, outflanked and outnumbered, had to give back. Just as they were driven from Golsdorf, Bertrand's corps gave away also, and in its disorderly retreat from Rohrbeck Oudinot became involved. In hopeless confusion the French fell back on Torgau ; and had the pursuit been pressed with real energy, Ney's whole army might have been annihilated. As it was, the remnants of it which rallied behind the Elbe were in the most deplorable state. Its losses amounted to 29,000, of whom 15,000 were prisoners, and the discipline, equipment, and moral and physical condition of those who remained with the colours left much to be desired. The Germans now began to desert in numbers: it was not only defeat which was too much for their loyalty to Napoleon, the even stronger incentive of hunger bade them depart. The country had been eaten bare of food, and with partisan bands growing increasingly active on the French communications rations began to be scanty and irregular.

After Dennewitz there was somewhat of a lull in the operations. After his return to Dresden from Silesia (Sept. 6th) the Emperor moved South again, hoping to engage Schwarzenberg ; but once more he was baulked of his desire, not indeed because Schwarzenberg retired, for after the outposts had fallen back to the main position the Austrian commander stood his ground, but because of the impassable state of the roads over the

KATZBACH Aug. 26th 1813

English Miles

Oberhochkirch
Sacken
Eichholtz
Flank attack
Bellwitzhof
Wütende Neisse
Yorck
Peterwitz
Katzbach
Souham
Sebastiani
Macdonald
Schlaupe
Langeron
Weinberg
Lauriston
Russians driven back
Kroitsch
Nieder Crain
Hennersdorf
Seichau
Mönchswald

DENNEWITZ, Sept. 6th 1813 (On Oudinot's Arrival)

English Miles

The numbers denote divisions
"Arr" = Part of Arrighi's Cavalry Corps

JÜTERBOGK
TAUENTZIEN
(Wurtembergers)
BERTRAND
38
Swedes
Rohrbeck
Thümen
15
Arr.
Saxons
W
Nieder-Görsdorf
12
Dennewitz
Krafft
Ü
REYNIER
32
Arrighi
Borstell
B
L
Homburg
Arr.
Ohna
Hesse
R
24
14
OUDINOT
13
(Saxons)
25
Gohlsdorf
29 (Bavarians)

B.V. Darbishire, Oxford, 1902.

Erzgebirge.[1] Napoleon therefore had again to return to Dresden (Sept. 12th). Another advance towards Nollendorf and Kulm had the same result (Sept. 17th to 19th), it prevented Schwarzenberg from carrying out a stroke he was aiming at Napoleon's communications in the direction of Leipzig; but though there was some sharp fighting round Kulm, no general action followed, and the only result was that Blücher was able to press Macdonald in on Dresden.

Once again, therefore, Napoleon dashed at Blücher (Sept. 22nd to 24th), but as before without result. His weakness in cavalry made it difficult for him to keep touch with his enemies; an even heavier handicap was the want of stamina of his troops, which diminished their mobility and to that extent detracted from the advantages of the central position, while the growing difficulty of obtaining supplies in a country so exhausted and impoverished as Saxony seriously increased his troubles. Indeed the Emperor's position was growing most unsafe, and common prudence would have dictated a retreat behind the Saale, for the position of the Austrians in Bohemia outflanked the line of the Elbe and made it strategically most unsafe. But a retreat behind the Saale would have abandoned Saxony, and the evacuation of that kingdom would have been the beginning of the end for the Confederation of the Rhine. To keep up his waning prestige, political and military, Napoleon must show a bold front; but as days slipped past and the great victory he so much needed still remained to be won, his hold on his half-willing allies grew weaker. His movements during this critical period display hesitation and indecision most unusual in him: plan after plan was formed, begun and abandoned incomplete. One great reason was the insecurity of his communications. Turn whichever way he would, he must expose his flanks and rear; and, above all, warnings were not wanting that he could not rely on the fidelity of the states which lay between him and France.

Indecisive as were the military operations upon which the month of September 1813 was spent, that month saw an event of the very greatest diplomatic importance, the negotiation of the Treaty of Töplitz (Sept. 9th). Hitherto Southern and Western Germany had remained faithful to Napoleon; but not so much from love of him as from fear of the Allies, and from a belief that the triumph of Austria and Prussia would be the

[1] Yorck von Wartenburg, ii. 315.

death-knell of the independence of the minor states. This fear was now removed, and a door was opened by which Napoleon's vassals might desert him. The Treaty of Töplitz provided, it is true, for the restoration to Austria and Prussia of the dominions they had held in 1805, the friendly co-operation of the Allies in deciding the fate of the Grand Duchy of Warsaw, the re-establishment of the House of Brunswick-Lüneburg in its old territories, and, above all, for the dissolution of the Confederation of the Rhine; but it guaranteed the independence of the members of that body.

This treaty was a great triumph for Metternich over the party which desired a complete reconstruction of Germany, and therefore urged that the partisans of Napoleon ought to be involved in their master's overthrow. Metternich's success undoubtedly contributed to the speedy expulsion of the French from Germany; for had Bavaria and Würtemberg felt that their independent existence was bound up with the cause of Napoleon, they would have made strenuous efforts on his behalf instead of deserting his standard. Where Stein's uncompromising policy would have driven the clients of France to desperation, Metternich's opportunism cut the ground from under Napoleon's feet. That this at the same time greatly delayed anything in the way of the unification of Germany cannot be denied; but seeing what the relations and aims of Austria and Prussia were, a thorough reconstruction would hardly have been possible without an appeal to the sword, for which neither Hapsburg nor Hohenzollen was prepared.

The first result of the Treaty of Töplitz was the defection of Bavaria from the side of Napoleon. Bavaria was not prepared to continue the struggle on the Emperor's behalf and to risk the hostility of Austria when such a way of escape lay open to her. And though the withdrawal of Augereau's corps, which had been called off to Saxony, had left the Wittelsbach kingdom with barely 40,000 men to meet an Austrian attack, Austria was ready to forego the chance of profiting by the exposed condition of Bavaria if she could thereby secure her Western neighbour for the side of the Allies. In Bavaria, Montgelas favoured neutrality but General Wrede and the Crown Prince saw that the surest way to avoid being involved in the overthrow of Napoleon was to associate Bavaria as closely as possible with the work of bringing about the tyrant's downfall. They therefore pleaded for joining the alliance, and carried their point. By the Treaty of Ried (Oct. 8th), Bavaria committed herself to the side of the Allies : she promised to restore to Austria such territory as might be needed for the rounding off of Austria's dominions, including, of course, Tyrol, but she was promised an adequate compensation. Reuss's Austrians, who had been opposing Wrede, now joined him, and the joint force prepared to intercept Napoleon's communications with the Rhine.[1]

Meanwhile the decisive movements of the campaign in Saxony had begun. By the end of September, Napoleon had come to the conclusion that he must abandon the right bank of the Elbe, and he had drawn in the greater part of his army to Dresden and its neighbourhood, though he had had to send Marmont and Latour-Maubourg back to the Mülde to support Ney. That general was occupied in reorganising the army beaten at Dennewitz in order to dispute the passage of the Elbe should Bernadotte, now on the right bank between Zerbst and Wittenberg, attempt to cross. Further afield an action of some importance had been fought by Wallmoden, which began the isolation of Davoût's corps. That Marshal had detached a division towards Magdeburg to clear the intervening district of the Allies and secure his communications with the main army of the French. Thereupon Wallmoden, having collected some 6 regiments of cavalry and 15 battalions of infantry, crossed the Elbe at Dömitz (Sept. 15th) and, pushing forward to Dannenberg, brought the French to action near the Göhrde Forest (Sept. 19th). A smart contest ended in the defeat and retreat of the French, the one British infantry battalion present, the 2nd battalion of the 73rd Foot, distinguishing itself by the capture of a battery from which a German corps had been repulsed.[2] Thus Wallmoden not only checked Davoût's move on Magdeburg, but established himself on the left bank of the Elbe, thereby encouraging the inhabitants of Hanover and Brunswick to take arms, Davoût the while remaining inactive, and eventually (end of October) retiring into Hamburg.

Thus the line of the Elbe which Napoleon was endeavouring to maintain could no longer be said to be in his hands, and his delay in the dangerously advanced position of Dresden became

[1] The Bavarian contingent with Napoleon's field-army, already much reduced by its losses in action and by desertion, now withdrew from his ranks, returning homeward.

[2] Cf. Beamish's *King's German Legion.*

daily more inexpedient. His repeated failures to bring one or other of the Allied armies to battle had only served to exhaust his troops and reduce their numbers. Every day that passed without the decisive success in a pitched battle which alone could have saved Napoleon made that decisive success more unlikely, for the ranks of the Austrians and Prussians were being replenished with recruits, and the Russian Army of Reserve under Bennigsen, 60,000 strong, was daily drawing nearer. Napoleon, on the contrary, had but few reinforcements to expect. Augereau was bringing up the newly organised IXth Corps to Leipzig, though his march was harassed by partisan corps, by Platof's Cossacks, and by an Austrian light division under Maurice Lichtenstein which had pushed forward from the extreme left of the Army of Bohemia ; but even this corps and the cavalry of Milhaud who accompanied it, some good regiments from the Army of Spain, did not between them amount to more than 20,000. Yet the Emperor would not fall back behind the Saale although the danger to his communications kept on compelling him to detach portions of his army farther and farther West to keep the line open.

September 27th saw the decisive movements begin. On that day Blücher, leaving 20,000 men to threaten Dresden from Bautzen, started North-Westward to join Bernadotte, and simultaneously the Army of Bohemia began a movement to its left, under cover of the divisions which were observing Dresden from the Southward. The object of these joint movements was that the Allies should concentrate behind the Saale and so interpose between Napoleon and France, and force on the battle it was no longer their object to avoid. One thing only could have saved Napoleon, a rapid concentration behind the Saale, followed by prompt blows against the converging forces of the Allies before they could unite. But such a course was unlikely, partly because the quality of the French troops was such that their mobility was low, partly because Napoleon was badly served by his cavalry and seems to have been ill supplied with news of his enemies' movements, but also because when he moved from Dresden he failed to first concentrate his army before trying to bring his enemies to action.

Blücher took with him some 65,000 men, Yorck's Prussians and the Russians of Langeron and Sacken. By October 3rd he was at the confluence of the Elbe and Black Elster, where he set about attempting a passage. Simultaneously Bernadotte advanced against the bridges of Acklow and Rosslau lower down the river, in order to occupy the left wing of the French Army of the North and prevent Reynier, whose corps had charge of those passages, coming to the aid of Bertrand who was opposing Blücher's crossing.[1]

Bertrand made an obstinate resistance and inflicted no small loss on Yorck, but the latter's numbers were too much for him, and enabled Blücher to force his way across at Bleddin on Bertrand's right. Accordingly the IVth Corps fell back towards Düben and Bitterfeld, on which places Reynier also retired, having failed to prevent Bernadotte from forcing the passages at Acklow and Rosslau. Thus October 4th saw both the Army of the North and that of Silesia established on the left bank of the Elbe, and three days later their forces came into touch between the Mülde and the Saale, threatening Leipzig from the North, while from the South Schwarzenburg was moving upon that city, having put his troops in motion on September 26th. Meanwhile Napoleon had at last left Dresden. On October 7th he had announced his intention of evacuating Dresden and falling back to the Mülde, where he meant to adopt a central position at Würzen, from which he could assist either the corps holding the passages of the Middle Elbe or those covering Leipzig against Schwarzenberg. These had been placed under Murat, and included Victor, Lauriston, Poniatowski and L'Heritier's cavalry, in all about 40,000. By the evening of the 8th the move had been carried out and the Guard, Sebastiani and Macdonald were at Würzen, giving a central force of 64,000 men, Marmont and Latour-Maubourg with 25,000 more being in easy reach at Taucha. But this force should have been nearly 30,000 stronger had not Napoleon, with an unwisdom almost incredible in one who had written,[2] "Whenever one wishes to fight a battle, one should not divide but concentrate all one's forces," left St. Cyr with his own corps and the remnants of the Ist, now under Lobau, to hold on to Dresden, a position which had ceased to have any great strategical value the moment the line of the Elbe was abandoned.

---

[1] After Dennewitz, Oudinot's corps (XIIth) was so much reduced that the remnants of it were incorporated in the IVth and VIIth Corps, which mustered between them about 20 to 25,000 men, instead of the 65,000 these three had totalled before Gross Beeren. The two Saxon divisions of Reynier were amalgamated at the same time.

[2] Napoleon to Berthier, Dec. 6th, 1811.

The Emperor's next move was to the Northward, yet another attempt to catch the wary foe who had so frequently escaped, but once again Blücher evaded the action which Napoleon sought to force on him. To do this he had indeed to sacrifice his communications, but he was successful in slipping away Westward across Napoleon's front and placing himself behind the Saale in touch with Bernadotte. That commander, nervously apprehensive of the political consequences of a defeat, would have been glad to withdraw from such dangerous proximity to the Emperor, but the representations of Charles Stewart, the English representative with the Army of the North, induced him to abandon his intention of retiring to the comparative safety of the right bank of the Elbe, and thus the joint armies of Silesia and the North took post on the left of the Saale, menacing Leipzig from the North-West, and ready to move in upon it as soon as Schwarzenberg's cautious advance from the South-East should make co-operation possible.

The result of Blücher's Westward move, a step probably taken by the advice of his Chief of Staff, Gneisenau, was that Napoleon on pushing forward to the Elbe found no one but Tauentzien's *Landwehr* in his front (Oct. 9th to 11th). Thus the Emperor's scheme for driving Blücher and Bernadotte out of reach of their allies miscarried completely. In vain he secured the passages over the Elbe and drove Tauentzien back with some loss; the news of Schwarzenberg's advance on Leipzig stayed his advance further. The Austrian commander was pushing steadily forward, forcing Murat back before him; and even Napoleon could not venture to attempt any of the hazardous projects of a dash on Berlin, or of a move up the right bank of the Elbe to Torgau to recross there and strike at Schwarzenberg's rear, which he contemplated only to lay aside.

Accordingly, on October 12th the Emperor gave orders for the troops under his immediate command to return to Leipzig. This decision was undoubtedly correct. Now that Schwarzenberg was really placing the Army of Bohemia within the Emperor's reach, the only chance of victory lay in Napoleon's being able to defeat him before Blücher or Bernadotte could intervene. Every available man should have been set on the road to Leipzig; and it was a grievous error to have let Reynier, who had crossed to the right bank of the Elbe on the 11th, push his pursuit of Tauentzien further on the 12th. Leipzig was the critical spot, and

Map to illustrate Movements between **DRESDEN & LEIPZIG**

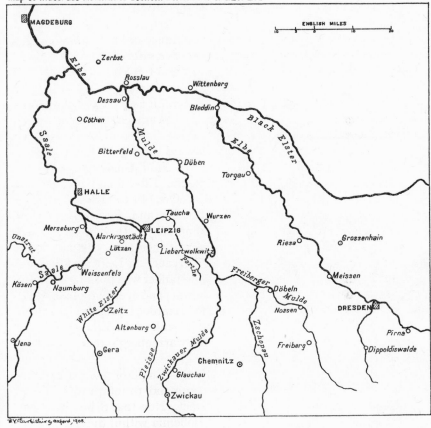

Leipzig was in some peril, for Schwarzenberg had driven Murat right in on the town; and though a sharp action around Wachau and Liebertwolkwitz on the 14th had resulted in the repulse of the Allies, the French counter-attack had failed.

By the evening of the 15th Napoleon had concentrated round Leipzig between 170,000 and 180,000 men, though several divisions, including one of the IIIrd Corps (Ney's) and all Reynier's (VII.), were still absent. Schwarzenberg, though actually superior in numbers, had not so large a proportion of his army with him, and unless the Army of Bohemia were supported by its allies from beyond the Saale there seemed a chance that Napoleon might snatch a victory at this eleventh hour. But nothing short of complete victory would suffice. Failure to defeat Schwarzenberg would mean that the ultimate victory was only a question of when the Allies' reinforcements would be up.

Napoleon's main body lay to the South of Leipzig: its right, Poniatowski's Poles (VIII.), on the Pleisse between Connewitz and Mark Kleeberg. Next them stood Victor (II.) at Wachau, and Lauriston (V.) at Liebertwolkwitz, with Augereau's IXth Corps, recently arrived from Bavaria, flung back so as to cover the left flank of the line and holding Zuckelhausen and Holzhausen. In support of these infantry were the cavalry corps of Kellermann at Dösen, of Latour-Maubourg at Zweinaundorf, and of Sebastiani in support of Augereau. When the battle began Macdonald (XI.) was at Taucha moving up towards Holzhausen, and Souham with two of Ney's divisions (III.) had reached Mockau. To the North of the town Marmont (VI.) was between Breitenfeld and Möckern, Bertrand (IV.) at Eutritzsch, Arrighi's cavalry in support. The Guards were at Reudnitz and Crottendorf as a general reserve, and Reynier (VII.) was on his way from Düben. Had the Emperor decided there and then to engage Schwarzenberg, the chances would have been in favour of the French; for Blücher, who was on the road from Halle, had not got beyond Gross Kugel, and Bernadotte at Zölbig and Oppen was still farther away. However, the Emperor, never believing that Blücher or Bernadotte would be able to interfere in the least with his operations next day, let the valuable hours slip by unused, making all preparations to concentrate every man South of Leipzig next morning to fall on Schwarzenberg.

But next morning (Oct. 16th), when Marmont prepared to move from the North of the Parthe to Liebertwolkwitz to support the great attack on the Austrians which the Emperor had planned, he found Blücher pressing in so close upon him that he had to face about, taking post from Möckern on his left to Widderitsch on his right, where Ney's divisions were beginning to arrive. Meanwhile to the South the main action had begun. Here the Army of Bohemia was moving forward on both sides of the Elster and of the Pleisse. Schwarzenberg's plan was that Giulai's Austrians should push down the left bank of the Elster from Markranstadt on Lindenau, with the twofold object of getting into touch with the Army of Silesia, and securing the great road from Leipzig by Lützen and Erfurt to Mayence, the road along which the French must retire if defeated. On Giulai's right the Austrians of Merveldt and Alois Lichtenstein were to push forward between the Elster and the Pleisse, to cross the latter river at Connewitz and turn the French right flank, some 38,000 men being in all allotted to these tasks. The rest of the Army of Bohemia stretched from the Pleisse to the Kolmberg, Kleist's Prussians (30,000) being next the river and opposite Mark Kleeberg, Eugene of Würtemberg at Gossa opposite Wachau, Gortschakoff beyond him opposing Lauriston, the Austrians of Klenau (25,000) on the right again. In reserve were the Russian and Prussian Guards, the whole force being over 130,000. The first stages of the day's fighting went somewhat in favour of the Allies, who forced the French to give ground, though they failed to carry the villages, to which Victor, Poniatowski and Lauriston clung with stubborn determination. About midday the Emperor had all ready for a counter-attack. Macdonald replaced Augereau on the left, and the IXth Corps pushed across to the Pleisse to fall into line between the Poles and Victor; the Young Guard supported Lauriston, Drouet massed a great battery near Wachau, and Murat collected all the available cavalry in order to hurl them on the Allied centre.

For a time all went well. Macdonald with Mortier and some of the Young Guard supporting him stormed the Kolmberg and drove Klenau back by threatening his right flank: on the other wing Augereau pushed forward to Crostewitz and wrested it from Kleist, Victor aided by two divisions of the Young Guard under Oudinot stormed Auenhayn; only at Güldengossa did the Allies manage to hold the French at bay, and there Gortschakoff had the greatest difficulty in repulsing Lauriston. About three o'clock Murat delivered his great charge, launching some 12,000 horsemen on the Allied batteries near Güldengossa, where there was a gap between Eugene of Würtemberg's right and Gortschakoff's left only filled by a few Russian cavalry. The French squadrons reached and captured the guns, but the timely arrival of the Allied reserves saved the day. The Austrian Reserve came up from Zobigker, assisted Kleist to make head against Augereau and even to regain lost ground. Latour-Maubourg was wounded, and the French cavalry, their horses spent by their charge, failed to press the advantage they had gained, wavered and finally gave way before the attacks of the cavalry of the Russian and Prussian Guards. A Russian Grenadier division came to Eugene's aid and, after a stubborn contest, retook Auenhayn and forced Victor to retreat, while Klenau, rallying his corps, managed to hold Macdonald in check and prevent him executing the flanking movement in which he had not received the expected assistance of Ney's corps.

Thus all along the line the French had to recoil, and evening found them in the positions they had occupied in the morning, reduced in numbers and much exhausted. The timely intervention of the Austrian Reserve had been the decisive point in the engagement, and had prevented Napoleon from gaining the victory which had seemed in his grasp. But the Army of Silesia also had had an important influence over the action to the South of Leipzig, for it was its pressure on the French to the North of the city which had prevented the expected supports from that quarter from joining in Macdonald's turning movement by Seiffertshayn.

The command of the French forces in this quarter had been entrusted to Marshal Ney, who had under him Bertrand, Marmont, Arrighi's cavalry, and, when they should arrive, his own corps, now under Souham, and that of Reynier. But the Emperor was so far from anticipating any attack by the Army of Silesia that he had ordered Marmont to move to the assistance of Lauriston, an order Marmont was unable to fulfil because he found himself attacked by the Army of Silesia, and spent the rest of the day in a desperate struggle for the villages of Möckern and Widderitsch. In like manner Bertrand's corps, which Ney despatched to Liebertwolkwitz in place of Marmont's, had to be diverted elsewhere before it could reach the Southern scene of action, for Giulai was pressing in on Lindenau, and threatened to close the French line of retreat. Souham also started to

40

support Macdonald but never got into action, being recalled to the North of the city to succour the hard-pressed Marmont, so that he spent the day in fruitless countermarches between one battlefield and the other, as d'Erlon was to do on the day of Ligny.

Meanwhile Marmont was very hard pressed. His left rested on Möckern and the Elster, in front of his centre he held Lindenthal, his right was at Widderitsch. With some 20,000 men available he had to face treble his numbers, for the whole Army of Silesia attacked him: but his troops were of better quality than most of the French, 17 of his 42 battalions being Marines. Yorck assailed Möckern; Sacken carried Lindenthal and came up in support of Yorck; Langeron attacked Widderitsch and carried it, only to lose it again when the belated third division of the IIIrd Corps arrived from Düben and succoured Marmont's right. The fighting on this side was about the most obstinate of the day. Möckern and Widderitsch were taken and retaken repeatedly. Nightfall found Marmont actually in possession of Möckern; but his corps had suffered so heavily and been so much reduced, that under cover of darkness he fell back over the Parthe, having lost 8000 men and 53 guns which he could not remove.

Indeed it was only to the South-West that the French had gained any real advantage. Hampered by the difficulties of the ground in which they were operating, Merveldt and Lichtenstein had achieved nothing and had failed to cross the Pleisse; while Bertrand not only recovered Lindenau, to which Giulai had penetrated, but by driving the Austrians back as far as Klein Zschocher kept open the line of retreat.

October 17th saw but little fighting. Both sides were spent by their exertions; the French had lost over 25,000 men, the Allies at least half as many again, so that they had good reason to wait, for every hour brought their reinforcements nearer. Colloredo's Austrians reached Cröbern that evening, Bennigsen and the Russian Army of Reserve were not far behind, and the 60,000 men of the Army of the North came up to Breitenau in the course of the day. This force, indeed, might have taken part in the fighting of the 16th had Bernadotte displayed rather more eagerness for battle;[1] but Sir Charles Stewart's entreaties had not availed to move the Crown Prince forward from Halle.

[1] Cf. Cathcart, *War of 1812-1813*, pp. 314-318.

The inaction of the Allies was not turned to good account by Napoleon. There can be little doubt that after the drawn battle of the 16th, he should have endeavoured to extricate himself from his dangerous position before the net closed in completely on him. He does seem to have contemplated a retreat, but did nothing to prepare for it, an omission which was to cost his army dear two days later. All that the Emperor did was to draw the army in nearer to Leipzig, so that on the morning of the 18th their positions formed a semicircle from the Elster at Dölitz, where Poniatowski and Augereau stood, through Probstheida, held by Victor, Stötteritz and Mölkau, defended by Macdonald, Paunsdorf where Reynier took post on arriving from Düben, to the Parthe at Schönfeld which Souham held. Marmont covered the left flank by taking post behind the Parthe, Lauriston was in second line behind Victor and Macdonald, the cavalry and the Guards formed a general reserve, while Bertrand was thrust out along the road to Weissenfels to secure the defile of Kösen.

Meanwhile the Allies had made their dispositions for the attack. Schwarzenberg is at least open to criticism for not having done more to intercept the Emperor's line of retreat Westward; what he seems to have feared most was that Napoleon would make a desperate attempt to break out through the circle which was closing in on him in the direction of the Elbe, through the gap in the Allied line which Bernadotte was to close with the Army of the North. The main attack thus took the shape of an advance of the Army of Bohemia and Bennigsen's reserves in three columns against the French right wing. Giulai so far from being strongly reinforced, was actually called upon to send back one of his divisions from the West of the Elster to reinforce the attack on Lossnig.

It was about 7 a.m. that the attack was begun. Hesse-Homburg's Austrians, pressing forward along the right bank of the Pleisse, carried Dölitz and Dosen after heavy fighting but could not wrest Connewitz from the Poles. On their right Kleist and Wittgenstein assailed Probstheida; but Victor would not be dislodged and repulsed repeated attacks. The third column under Klenau, which attempted to wrest Holzhausen from Macdonald, had at first little success; but about 2 p.m. Bennigsen came up to his help and Holzhausen was carried, though even then their efforts to take Stötteritz were less fortunate, and

Bennigsen, swerving more to his right in order to get into touch with the Army of the North, could not get beyond Engelsdorf for Reynier's Saxons, who formed the right of the force with which Ney was prepared to oppose Bernadotte, held on firmly to Mölkau and Paunsdorf. Thus the attack of the Army of Bohemia came to more or less of a standstill, the strong and stoutly defended position of Stötteritz-Probstheida, with Lauriston and much reserve artillery supporting its defenders, defying their assaults. Both these villages remained in French hands till nightfall, Kleist and Wittgenstein suffering heavily in their unsuccessful attempts on Probstheida, while Klenau and Ziethen's Prussians, less closely engaged, lost fewer men but achieved no more against Macdonald.

But meanwhile the battle was being decided elsewhere. Not, indeed, by Blücher, who had detached Langeron to co-operate with Bernadotte, and thus had only Yorck and Sacken with whom to engage Marmont. He was successful in driving in the French outposts from Gohlis and Pfaffendorf, but their main position behind the Parthe proved too much for him: at one time he managed to force a passage, and even to gain possession of Reudnitz, but the Emperor sent up reinforcements and recovered the lost ground. It was the arrival of the Army of the North which really decided the battle. About midday Bernadotte's vanguard reached Taucha and got into touch with Langeron, who had crossed the Parthe at Mockau to assist the Crown Prince's operations. Langeron then advanced against Ney's left at Schönfeld, while Winzingerode pushed across to Paunsdorf to establish communications with Bennigsen, thus closing the gap between the left of the Army of Silesia and the right of that of Bohemia.

Encouraged by the prospect of the arrival of the Army of the North, Bennigsen's troops resumed their attacks on Reynier's position at Mölkau and Paunsdorf. As Bubna's Austrians also pressed forward, the troops opposed to them, instead of resisting their advance, came over in a body and threw in their lot with the Allies. These deserters were the Saxons, who formed so large a part of Reynier's corps, and their defection was followed by that of a Würtemberg cavalry brigade nearly 1500 strong. Even apart from the moral effect on the Allies and on the French alike of so striking an incident, so public a proclamation of Napoleon's failure to retain the fidelity of his allies, the desertion of the Saxons was of great immediate and practical importance, for Reynier's remaining division gave way before Bubna's attack, and the Austrians occupied Paunsdorf. To the success of this attack the presence with Winzingerode's cavalry of the one unit which represented England in this great "battle of the nations" contributed appreciably. Captain Bogue's rocket-troop of the Royal Artillery played a most effective part in aiding Bubna's advance, its novel missiles doing much execution and creating quite a sensation.

Ney hastened to Reynier's assistance with such reserves as he had at hand and temporarily recovered Paunsdorf; but before the steady pressure of the advance of the Army of the North even Ney had to recoil and to content himself with extricating Reynier's remnant. In vain Nansouty brought the cavalry of the Guard to Ney's help. Bülow's arrival forced Ney back on Reudnitz, and Langeron returning to the attack after several repulses at last wrested Schönfeld from its defenders. Thus all round the line the French were being pressed back into Leipzig; and even Napoleon could no longer conceal from himself the fact that retreat was inevitable. Fortunately for him the road to the West still presented a way of escape; for Giulai, his force reduced to one division by the recall of the second to succour Hesse-Homburg, had been unable to hold his own against Mortier and two divisions of the Young Guard, who had thrust him aside and cleared the road to France.

But hardly any preparations had been made for a retreat. No extra bridges had been laid over the Elster and Pleisse, the troops were in great disorder and disorganisation, and the utmost confusion prevailed. Had Schwarzenberg made better arrangements for hindering the retreat, the entire French army might have been cut off. As it was, the orders intended for Bianchi, who had replaced Hesse-Homburg, never reached him, and his column instead of crossing the Elster and supporting Giulai remained near Leipzig on the 19th. Blücher had started Yorck, whose men had been in reserve all the 18th, off towards the Unstrutt on the evening of that day; but he had to make a detour by Halle, and only came up with the rear of the French as they were crossing at Freiburg on the 22nd, while Bertrand was able to keep Maurice Lichtenstein and Giulai at bay near Kösen. A very large number of prisoners were certainly taken by the Allies, but this was due to Napoleon's neglect to make proper arrangements for the retreat and to the premature destruction of the bridges over the Elster, rather than to the efforts of the Allies. They devoted themselves on the morning of the 19th to assaulting the various gates of the city, which were stoutly defended by the contingents of the vassal states, the Poles, the Italians, the handful of Spaniards, the Illyrians, the Dutch-Belgians, the Swiss, and such Germans as had not yet deserted, while the French were filing out of the city Westward. In all about 80,000 troops managed to make their way to Markranstädt by the evening of the 19th; but the Allies secured with the city of Leipzig not less than 250 guns and 50,000 prisoners, of whom over 20,000 were wounded. In killed and wounded they had themselves probably lost almost as heavily as the French;[1] but the capture of so large a number of prisoners made all the difference, reducing the Grand Army to less than half of its strength before the battle.

There was no thought now among the French of a stand East of the Rhine. The Grand Army had one object only, to place that river between themselves and their enemies: only behind its shelter could they feel safe, there only could they find reinforcements and succour. Germany was lost irrevocably; for great as the military success of the Allies had been, that was nothing when compared with the political results of Leipzig. It completed the collapse of the tottering Confederation of the Rhine. The minor states hastened to follow the lead of Bavaria. French rule disappeared from Berg and from Westphalia amid an outburst of popular enthusiasm. Benefits were forgotten in the general hurry to be rid of Napoleon's yoke. The general joy at the overthrow of the Emperor found expression in patriotic poems and songs, notably in Arndt's demand that the Rhine should once again become a German river. Popular feeling ran high, nationalist sentiments were openly expressed, other Liberal ideas not less distasteful to Metternich were current everywhere. He saw with alarm Germany on the verge of being thrown into the melting-pot of "reconstruction": he had good reason to dread the turn which events might take unless something were speedily done to check the flow of the tide. There were two things he detested with about equal fervour: Liberalism and Nationalism. By admitting Napoleon's vassals to terms he

[1] *Deutsche Geschichte, 1806–1871*, i., gives their losses as: Austrians, 15,000; Prussians, 16,000; Russians, 22,000.

LEIPZIG. Oct. 16th to 19th, 1813.

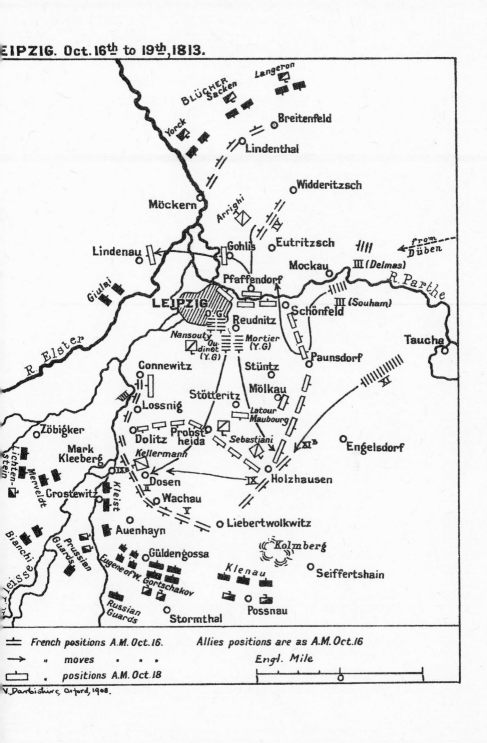

Langeron

BLÜCHER Sacken

Yorck

Breitenfeld

Lindenthal

Widderitzsch

Möckern

Arrighi

Gohlis

Eutritzsch

Mockau

from Düben

III (Delmas)

R. Parthe

Lindenau

Pfaffendorf

Giulai

LEIPZIG

O. G.

Reudnitz

Schönfeld

III (Souham)

Taucha

R. Elster

Nansouty

Oudinot (Y.G.)

Mortier (Y.G.)

Paunsdorf

XI

Connewitz

Stüntz

Mölkau

Stötteritz

VII

Lossnig

Latour Maubourg

Zöbigker

Probst heida

Dolitz

Sebastiani

LXI B

Engelsdorf

Mark Kleeberg

Lichtenstein

Kellermann

IX

Holzhausen

Merveldt

IX

Dosen

Crostewitz

Kleist

Wachau

V

Bianchi

Auenhayn

Liebertwolkwitz

Kolmberg

Prussian Guards

Güldengossa

Eugene of W.

Klenau

Seiffertshain

Gortschakov

R. Pleisse

Russian Guards

Stormthal

Possnau

French positions A.M. Oct. 16. Allies positions are as A.M. Oct. 16.

„ moves „ „ „ Engl. Mile

„ positions A.M. Oct. 18.

V. Darbishire, Oxford, 1908.

hoped to checkmate both, to prevent the reconstruction on Liberal lines which he was determined to avoid. His hatred of reconstruction was in large measure inspired by his dislike of Prussia. Reconstruction must involve a definite settlement of the relation between Austria and Prussia, and Metternich did not intend to allow this to come to pass. Hence he seized the earliest possible opportunity of coming to terms with the South German Princes: Frederick I of Würtemberg was no less anxious to be admitted to terms, hoping thus to secure the gains he had made by Napoleon's help by bringing them under the shelter of an Austrian recognition. A champion of particularism and a bitter enemy of German nationalism, he desired to escape the fate which had befallen Saxony and which was threatening his dominions, of being seized and administered by the Allies as a "common possession." The Treaty of Fulda (Nov. 2nd) saved Würtemberg from being treated in this way, from being taxed and requisitioned to the limits of its capacity to defray the expenses of the Allies. Würtemberg, like Bavaria, not only received official sanction for her existence, but promised to send a contingent of 12,000 men to assist Austria. Her action was imitated by Baden, by Nassau, by the Saxon Duchies and by Hesse-Darmstadt. The last-named concluded a military convention with Austria (Nov. 2nd) which three weeks later was expanded into a definite treaty of alliance. Even more effective as a check on the popular movement and the nationalist spirit than the recognition of these states which owed so much to Napoleon and had been his vassals so long, was the recall of the old rulers, whose dominions had gone to make up those creations of Napoleon's which were bound to fall with him. To Brunswick, Electoral Hesse, Hanover and Oldenburg their dispossessed sovereigns came back in the spirit of the most uncompromising *emigré*, determined to restore the old *régime* and as far as possible to obliterate the immediate past, to slur over the reforms effected in their absence and which were in so strong a contrast to their own negligent rule.

But the immediate task of the Allies was not to reconstitute Germany, but to complete the work of Leipzig. There were two things to be done: Napoleon must be pursued, cut off if possible, driven over the Rhine if he should escape capture; secondly, the fortresses still held by his troops must be blockaded or taken. Klenau's Austrians and Bennigsen's Russians had therefore to be left on the Elbe to attend to the French strongholds on that river, Dresden, Torgau, Magdeburg and Wittenberg; Kleist's Prussians with the assistance of Winzingerode's Russians took charge of Erfurt; Bernadotte moved North to assist Wallmoden against Davoût and the Danes. Wallmoden, encouraged by his success at the Göhrde, had begun to pass his troops over to the left bank of the Elbe soon after that action, and had pushed them forward to Bremen and Hanover, stirring up insurrections in those districts, with the result that Davoût had been quite cut off from his master. Bernadotte's arrival compelled the Marshal to retire into Hamburg, where he maintained himself for the rest of the war, while the Danes, driven back into Holstein and pursued by Wallmoden, were forced to conclude the Treaty of Kiel in January 1814. By that time several of the fortresses had fallen, Dresden and Torgau having succumbed early in November, Stettin, Wittenberg and Dantzic before the end of the year, and the garrisons of the remainder, closely beset by the Army of the North, now broken up, and by the *Landwehr*, who came forward in great numbers, were condemned to a useless inactivity.

In the other part of their task, the interception and capture of the retreating Grand Army, the Allies were less successful. Napoleon had reached Weissenfels on the evening of October 20th and had hastened to cross to the left bank of the Saale, thus leaving the main road up the right bank by Naumburg for fear that the difficulties of getting through the narrow defile of Kösen would afford opportunities to his enemy. The change of road took the French through hilly country, and so far delayed them that Yorck caught up their rearguard just as the main body had got across the Unstrutt, and inflicted some loss on it. However, even so the Prussians failed to check the retreat; and as Bertrand kept Lichtenstein and Giulai at bay at Kösen, the relics of the Grand Army regained the high road at Buttelstadt and arrived at Erfurt in safety on October 23rd. Here a short stay was made, and Napoleon was able to do something to refit and reorganise his shattered army. But advantageous as the position of Erfurt would have been for a stand had Napoleon adopted it earlier when his army was still intact, the time for a stand was past: not even with the Harz Mountains to cover his left and the Thuringian Forest to protect his right,[1] did he contemplate another action. With Southern Germany rising

[1] Cf. Cathcart, pp. 274-276.

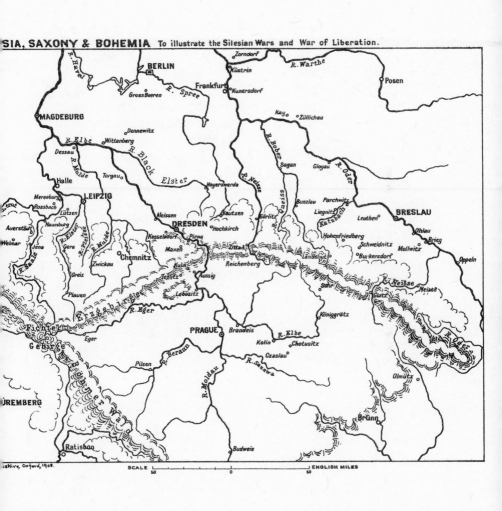

SIA, SAXONY & BOHEMIA To illustrate the Silesian Wars and War of Liberation.

BERLIN
Zorndorf
R. Warthe
Küstrin
Frankfurt
Kunersdorf
Posen
Gross Beeren
R. Spree
R. Havel

MAGDEBURG
Kay
Züllichau
Dennewitz
R. Elbe Wittenberg
Dessau R. Mulde
R. Bober
Sagan
Glogau
R. Oder
Torgau
R. Black
Halle
Elster
Hoyerswerda
R. Neisse
Bunzlau
Parchwitz
Merseburg
LEIPZIG
Meissen
Bautzen
Liegnitz
Leuthen
BRESLAU
Rossbach
Lützen
Naumburg
DRESDEN
Görlitz
Katzbach
Ohlau
Auerstädt
R. Elster
Kesselsdorf
Hochkirch
Hohenfriedberg
Brieg
Weimar
Jena
Gera
R. Neisse
Mulde
Maxen Pirna
Zittau
Schweidnitz
Mollwitz
Chemnitz
Landshut
Burkersdorf
Oppeln
Greiz
Zwickau
Jeschzi
Reichenberg
R. Neisse
R. Saale
Plauen
Erzgebirge
Aussig
Suhr
Neisse
R. Eger
Lobositz
Glatz
Fichtel
Königgrätz
Gebirge
Eger
PRAGUE
Brandeis
R. Elbe
Kolin
Chotusitz
Pilsen
R. Berann
Czaslau
R. Moldau
R. Sazawa
Olmütz
UREMBERG
Budweis
Brünn
Ratisbon

ishire, Oxford, 1908.

SCALE 50 — 0 — 50 ENGLISH MILES

against him in his rear, with the North-West seething with hostility, with the structure he had raised collapsing around him, and the main body of the Allies in pursuit, he had no option but to fall back, and on October 25th he resumed his retreat towards Frankfort.

The Allies were moving in two main bodies, Schwarzenberg taking the road by Jena on Weimar, Blücher with Langeron and Yorck moving by Merseburg and Freiburg on Langensalza. But for the intercepting of Napoleon they relied mainly on Wrede, who with his own Bavarian corps and the Austrians of Prince Reuss had come up from Anspach by Würzburg to Hanau (Oct. 28th) and was blocking the high road to France. Expecting that Wrede's intervention would force the French to turn aside and seek to regain the left bank of the Rhine at Coblence, Blücher changed his course and made for Giessen and Wetzlar, thus losing touch with the French. His move enabled Napoleon to win a last victory on German soil. On October 30th the French vanguard found Wrede's 40,000 men drawn up on the North bank of the Kinzig, in front of Hanau, barring their road to France. There was some sharp and even fighting, but finally a great attack by all the cavalry that Nansouty and Sebastiani could collect was directed against Wrede's left, the way having been paved for it by Drouet, who massed a great battery against that point. The Allied flank was beaten in and the road cleared, Wrede's men retiring across the Kinzig. Next day Napoleon attacked them in their new position, employing the corps of Bertrand and Marmont, which fought uncommonly well considering all they had recently been through. By this means he occupied Wrede's attention and gained time for his rearguard, the Young Guard under Oudinot, to get past Hanau, whereupon the rest of the French retired also. On November 2nd the columns of the Grand Army were trailing safely over the Rhine at Mayence. It was not Wrede's fault that the Emperor had got away. The pursuit after Leipzig was none too well managed, though a little more energy might have saved the losses of the next year's campaign. It would have been far better to send every available sabre and bayonet straight after the Grand Army rather than to pay so much attention to reducing fortresses, whose fate was but a secondary affair. But here, as always, the lack of an effective Commander-in-Chief hampered the operations of the Allies.

CHAPTER XXXIII

1814 AND THE TREATY OF PARIS

THUS at last was Germany freed from Napoleon's rule; but, successful as the efforts of the Allies had been, 1813 had no more ended the struggle than had 1812. Just as the advance into Germany had been needed to reap the fruits of the repulse of the invasion of Russia, so the liberation of Germany could only be made secure by following up the expulsion of Napoleon from German soil. For the man whose rule was founded on victory could not afford to acquiesce in defeat, not even a Leipzig would induce him to accept the highly favourable terms on which the Allies would gladly have given him peace. He at least had not had enough of fighting, though France, exhausted by the prodigious efforts she had made in response to his demands, had neither the capacity nor the inclination to repeat her useless sacrifices. Napoleon hoped that the prospect of invasion would produce a reaction in his favour, would provoke a popular movement against the foreigner similar to that of 1792; but although twelve days before Napoleon left Leipzig a victorious enemy had already crossed the frontier of France, Wellington's men when they crossed the Bidassoa (Oct. 6th and 7th, 1813) found themselves among a population who displayed nothing like the hostility which the French peasantry had shown to the Austrians and Prussians twenty years before. France had begun to realise that Napoleon was making her fight his battles and not hers, and her response to his appeal was but half-hearted.

The campaign of 1814 was one which ought never to have been fought. Politically, France had nothing to gain; from the military point of view Napoleon had nothing to hope for. With barely 80,000 men to oppose to the overwhelming forces of the Allies even he could not expect to win: the weight of numbers was bound to crush him; despite the marvellous exhibition of skill and resource which he gave, despite the repeated blunders of his enemies, he was in the end overpowered by numbers. That he persisted in fighting was largely because pride and obstinacy would not let him admit defeat, because self-confidence bade him expect victory, but mainly because, not without good reason, he trusted to the dissensions of his enemies.

That there was no small divergence between the views of Austria and of Prussia Napoleon was well aware. He knew that Metternich's hostility to him had its limits, and that rather than favour anything likely to provoke a Jacobinical reaction, as, for example, the restoration of the Bourbons, the Austrian minister would be prepared to let him retain the throne of France. Indeed, the excellent terms offered to Napoleon in November 1813, the so-called "Proposals of Frankfort," may be taken as embodying the views of Austria rather than of her allies. To give France the Rhine, the Alps and the Pyrenees as her boundaries would have been distasteful to England, which much disliked leaving Antwerp and all Belgium in her hands; the mere restoration of the former rulers in Italy, Holland and Germany, and the recognition by Napoleon of the unconditional independence of Germany and Italy would have been far from satisfying the desire for revenge which animated Prussia and Russia; but the Allies agreed to the offer, and it was from Napoleon that the rejection came. He demanded instead the fortresses of Wesel, Kehl and Cassel, a kingdom for Jerome in Germany, and compensation in Italy for Eugene, who would be deprived of his reversion of the Grand Duchy of Frankfort. If Napoleon had wished to make peace impossible he could hardly have adopted more successful means. His obstinacy compelled the Allies to subordinate their discords to the one thing they had in common, their desire to compass his overthrow.

But though resolved not to let the fruits of their victory escape them, the Allies found some difficulty about settling on a plan of campaign. Radetzky and Gneisenau advocated an immediate invasion, judging that it would be better to undergo the hardships of a winter campaign than to give Napoleon time to build up a new army. This was opposed by von Knesebeck, who was in great favour with the King of Prussia, and who with the support of his master and of the Austrian von Duka declared that the fortresses on the Rhine must be taken before an invasion could be attempted. Schwarzenberg, however, so far departed from his usual policy as to reject this cautious plan and to declare for an advance. He did not, however, adopt Gneisenau's suggestion that the Army of Silesia with part of that of the North should invade France through Belgium, while the Army of Bohemia moved on Paris by Mayence and Metz. The plan which Schwarzenberg and Radetzky preferred was that the Army of Bohemia should move through Switzerland, thereby turning the lines of the Rhine and Vosges, and descend on Paris from the plateau of Langres, a country which had long been spared the horrors of war and was therefore well adapted to support and supply an advancing army. Blücher with the Army of Silesia and part of that of the North was to move due West from the Middle Rhine, crossing the river between Mannheim and Coblence. The rest of the Army of the North was either operating against Davoût under Bernadotte or blockading the fortresses the Allies were leaving untaken in their rear, or assisting Sir Thomas Graham and an English corps of some 8000 men to expel the French from Holland.[1]

The Allies had not less than 300,000 men available for the invasion. Their main army amounted to 90,000 Austrians,[2] 50,000 Russians,[3] 29,000 Bavarians under Wrede, a corps from Würtemberg 14,000 strong, and the 6000 men of the Prussian Guards, in all not far short of over 200,000 men. Blücher had Yorck's Prussian corps and the Russians of Sacken and Langeron, in all about 80,000, while a reserve army was being collected in South Germany from the states whose contingents only a year before had been flocking to Napoleon's banner: it included 19,000 Hessians from Cassel, the so-called IVth "German League Corps," 9000 from Nassau, Berg, Waldeck and other minor states (Vth Corps), a Hesse-Darmstadt corps (the VIth) brought up to 10,000 by contingents from Würzburg, Reuss and Frankfort, and one from Baden (the VIIth) of 10,000 men. When one adds to these numbers the forces in the Netherlands, those left behind in Germany, the Austrian Army of Italy which was steadily wresting that peninsula from its Viceroy, Eugene, not forgetting the 90,000 British and Portuguese at whose head Wellington was pushing forward irresistibly through the South-West of France, one has some conception of the mighty effort needed to free Europe from Napoleon's

---

[1] Cf. *Der Feldzug 1814 in Frankreich*, by Lieutenant-General von Janson.
[2] 4 corps and 2 light divisions.
[3] Their Guards and 2 corps under Wittgenstein and Barclay de Tolly.

dominion. The forces the Grand Alliance had put into the field a century earlier to repel the aggressions of Louis XIV seem insignificant in comparison.

To oppose them Napoleon had a field-force of little more than a quarter of the total available for the invasion. His Guard, reorganised in three corps under Ney, Oudinot and Mortier, mustered 35,000; the relics of the Grand Army provided some 12,000 cavalry and four skeleton corps of infantry amounting to 23,000. Behind these were forming new battalions of conscripts, National Guards and others, most of which were drawn into the fighting line as the campaign proceeded, but which were not available when the invasion began.

The main interest of the campaign of 1814 lies in a subject which does not call for very detailed treatment here, the marvellous skill with which Napoleon kept the overwhelming forces of his enemies at bay. The proceedings of the Allies, their quarrels, mistakes and failures, need rather more attention, and to them must partly be attributed Napoleon's success in maintaining the unequal struggle so long. As the armies of the Allies neared the frontier of France their fear of Napoleon, the common interest which had hitherto held them together, began to give place to hopes of individual advantages to be gained by his overthrow; the cohesion of the Coalition began to show signs of weakening, differences of aim to exercise their influence over the actions of the Allies.

It was at the end of December that the Austrians began their march through Switzerland; by January 18th the Allied Headquarters reached Langres and began descending the valleys of the Seine, Aube and Marne: Wrede had turned aside to Alsace to secure that province with the assistance of the VIth and VIIIth German League Corps. Blücher meanwhile having detached part of Yorck's corps to seize Luxembourg, Metz and Thionville, and left Langeron to besiege Mayence, had found himself too weak to do much independently, and was moving Southward to gain touch with the main army. This exposed him to Napoleon, and on January 29th the Emperor, who had concentrated 33,000 men at Vitry on the 25th, fell on the Prussian commander at Brienne sur Aube and drove him back up the river. Following in pursuit, Napoleon again engaged the Prussians at La Rothière (Feb. 1st). The battle might have gone against them had not an Austrian division despatched by Schwarzenberg to Blücher's help succoured the Prussian left, while at the critical moment Wrede brought up his Bavarians from Joinville, a movement undertaken entirely on his own initiative. This gave the Allies so great a numerical superiority that Napoleon had to fall back to Arcis sur Aube. Meanwhile Yorck had been in action with Macdonald near Chalons (Feb. 2nd to 3rd) and had forced him back down the Marne. In the hope of profiting by this success to separate Macdonald and Napoleon, Blücher now moved to join Yorck, taking with him also Kleist and Langeron, who had come up from the rear. On February 8th he began a march down the Marne on Paris, relying on the Army of Bohemia to move down the Seine, and so contain Napoleon who had fallen back to Nogent.

Blücher's move was so conducted as to afford Napoleon a splendid opportunity. In the attempt to get between Macdonald and the Emperor the Prussian commander allowed his divisions to become widely separated, with the result that Napoleon fell with 30,000 men on Olsuviev's Russians at Champaubert (Feb. 10th) and cut the Army of Silesia in two, Yorck at Chateau-Thierry and Sacken at Montmirail being thus separated from the headquarters near Vertus. But instead of retreating promptly to the right of the Marne, Blücher made a desperate effort to concentrate on the left bank. The result was that while Marmont kept Blücher in check at Vauchamps, Sacken (on the 11th) was defeated at Montmirail and driven back on Yorck, and the two corps were bundled across the Marne in a shattered condition. Blücher, who had wasted two days in inaction at Vertus (Feb. 11th and 12th), expecting Yorck and Sacken to join him, was then in turn assailed by Napoleon and badly beaten (Feb. 13th). By February 16th the Army of Silesia, weaker by 16,000 men than it had been six days earlier and not a little demoralised and shaken, was at Chalons, and Napoleon dashed off Southward, fell on the Würtembergers at Montereau (Feb. 18th) and thus paralysed Schwarzenberg's tardy advance. The Austrian commander's delay may be explained, though not excused, by the fact that he had been expecting the negotiations then in progress at Chatillon to result in the conclusion of peace. The Allies indeed had, after much debate, agreed to accept Caulaincourt's suggestion of an armistice, and the Army of Bohemia had made but little progress, and so was quite unable to assist

Blücher in any way. The 21st saw it back at Troyes, and when Blücher moved across to Méry on the Seine to communicate with his ally, all Schwarzenberg could suggest was a retreat to Langres, since Augereau from Lyons was threatening his communications, and he had had to make large detachments for their protection. Napoleon, meanwhile, believing that victory had returned to him, was now forming the wildest schemes and forbidding Caulaincourt to accept anything short of the proposals of Frankfort.

Fortunately for the Allies, the troops of Bülow and Winzingerode, which belonged to the army under Bernadotte, were at this moment within easy reach, and, mainly at the instigation of Lord Castlereagh, it was decided to risk offending Bernadotte by disregarding the orders he had given to his subordinates, and summoning them to march at once to the assistance of the main body. To co-operate with Bülow, Blücher was to move North, the Army of Bohemia standing on the defensive and "containing" Napoleon while Blücher and Bülow took the offensive. The move was risky; once again the Allies failed to concentrate and force on a battle under conditions which would allow them to utilise their numerical superiority, once again they gave Napoleon the chance of defeating them in detail. Marching by La Ferté and Meaux Blücher exposed himself to Napoleon: an attempt on Meaux (Feb. 28th) saw Sacken and Kleist repulsed by Mortier, while Napoleon, leaving Macdonald and Oudinot to keep Schwarzenberg occupied, hastened after Blücher. On hearing of this Blücher had to make for the Aisne in the hopes of joining Bülow before Napoleon could overtake him. All turned on Soissons. It had been taken by the Russian Winzingerode, but Mortier had recovered it and placed a garrison in it. If this garrison could have held out it would have kept Bülow and Blücher from uniting, and so have allowed Napoleon to catch Blücher's corps, exhausted by constant marching and frequent fighting, with the Aisne at their backs.[1] Soissons, however, capitulated tamely on March 3rd, and Blücher was able to reach the comparative safety of the North bank of the Aisne. Without attempting to dispute the passages of the Aisne, the Allies

---

[1] Cf. Wolseley, *Decline and Fall of Napoleon*, pp. 100–103. *Deutsche Geschichte, 1806–1871* (i. 478), denies that Blücher was in danger, alleging that he could have bridged the Aisne.

retired to Craonne. Driven thence by Napoleon's attacks (March 7th), they fell back to Laon, where Napoleon again assailed them two days later. This time he was less successful. On the left, where he himself opposed Bülow and Winzingerode, the French carried the village of Ardon but could get little farther. Marmont on the right drove Yorck and Kleist back some way, but was checked by Langeron and Sacken, who reinforced the Prussians. The day thus ended indecisively; but in the night Ziethen's cavalry surprised Marmont's bivouacs, and thus threatened Napoleon's retreat to Craonne. But the advantage was not followed up. Blücher was incapacitated by illness, and Gneisenau, who succeeded to the command, seems to have lost his head. He displayed an extraordinary vacillation and confusion, and with the Prussian army thus relapsing into inaction Napoleon was able to slip away unpursued under cover of an attack on Bülow's corps, and to hurry back to the Seine to meet Schwarzenberg's renewed advance. Unimpeded by the Army of the North, which remained stationary on the Aisne for over a week, with Blücher ill and Yorck and Gneisenau at furious feud, Napoleon moved by Rheims, where he surprised and routed St. Priest's Russians (March 13th), and La Fere Champenoise (March 18th) to the Aube, joined Macdonald, who was withstanding Schwarzenberg's renewed advance with barely 30,000 men (March 20th), and on the 21st delivered an attack on the Allies at Arcis sur Aube. Including the troops he had brought from Rheims, a corps of 10,000 which had joined him from Paris and Macdonald's command, the Emperor had little more than 50,000 men, the Allies being enormously superior, as Schwarzenberg was concentrating all his outlying divisions. This superiority in numbers gave the Allies the victory in what was in some ways the decisive battle of the campaign. Had Schwarzenberg been beaten there can be little doubt but that he would have fallen right back to Langres, leaving Blücher and Bülow in the lurch. But in the end the French were badly beaten. Even the interior position could not compensate for the odds against them. Wrede's Bavarians thrust Ney back from Torcy. Giulai's Austrians at the other end of the line drove the French right from Vilette, the Russians in the centre gained ground steadily, and by the end of the day the French had had to retire over the Aube, and were in full retreat Northward towards Sézanne.

The reason for Schwarzenberg's concentration is to be found in the determination of the Allies to put an end to the struggle. Though after La Rothière Napoleon had agreed to a conference at Chatillon, his object had not been to conclude peace but to separate Austria from her Allies—a possibility always present to his mind. He played the game of procrastination with some temporary success, but with the final result of convincing the Allies that his overthrow was indispensable if peace were to be secured.[1] Alexander was now keen upon his deposition, and the Allies were in accord on that point, if there seemed little prospect that, when they had got rid of him, they would be able to agree as to his successor. The Treaty of Chaumont, concluded mainly through Castlereagh's influence (March 1st), brought them a stage nearer unity. France was to be restored to her ancient limits, her vassals were to be set completely free, and Germany was to be reconstructed as a Federal Union.

After Napoleon's repulse at Arcis sur Aube the Allies held a council of war, which came, not without misgivings, to the all-important decision to press on straight to Paris and so force a conclusion of the whole matter. They had just had the good fortune to intercept a despatch from Napoleon to Marie Louise in which the Emperor announced his resolve to try the effect of a blow at the communications of the Allies, a desperate move by which he hoped to paralyse the advance on Paris which he found himself unable to stem ; he still hoped to cajole or intimidate Austria into deserting the Coalition, and the move would also allow him to gather reinforcements from the fortresses of the Eastern frontier. Accordingly he moved from Sézanne on Vitry and St. Dizier, defeated a Russian corps at the latter place on the 28th, and then learnt that the main army of the Allies, instead of being, as he hoped, in full retreat for the Rhine, was moving on Paris. He hastened Westward, but it was already too late; he had only reached Fontainebleau when the news came that Paris was already in the hands of the Allies.

The idea of disregarding communications and pushing on to Paris originated with the Russian Toll. Alexander took it up

---

[1] M. Fournier (*Der Congress von Chatillon : die Politik im Kriege von 1814*) shows that it was the capture by the Allies of the letter to Caulaincourt, written by Napoleon on March 19th, which finally persuaded Francis II that Napoleon was playing fast and loose with him, and could not be trusted to abide by any concessions which might be extorted from him. Thus Napoleon's efforts to work on Austria's jealousy of Russia and Prussia, which had at one time seemed to be bearing fruit, came to nothing.

41

at once with great warmth, and Schwarzenberg and Frederick William acquiescing, the Army of Bohemia had started for Paris as Napoleon moved East (March 20th). The Army of Silesia had resumed its march on the 18th, pushing the corps of Marmont and Mortier back before it. These detachments had fallen back to Vertus when Napoleon summoned them Eastward to join him. In obeying his orders they met the Army of Bohemia at La Fere Champenoise (March 25th), were beaten and driven in on Paris. By the 29th the Army of Bohemia, which had moved by Melun and Corbeil, was at Charenton, Blücher had come up by Meaux to St. Denis. On March 30th there was sharp fighting outside Paris. Only at a heavy cost did the Allies wrest Montmartre, Montreuil and Vincennes from Marmont's corps; but the positions were gained, and Paris, exposed without appeal to a bombardment, could only avert that disaster by opening its gates. March 31st saw the Allies enter Paris in triumph, and even Napoleon had to confess himself beaten, for his army would not follow him to a campaign behind the Loire. On April 6th he agreed to abdicate, and on the 11th a provisional treaty was signed between him and the Allies. Napoleon renounced the throne of France and retired to Elba, and with the conclusion of the definite Treaty of Paris (May 30th), by which France was left with the frontier she had possessed in 1792, his overthrow seemed accomplished; and the problem before Europe, and especially before Germany, was no longer to destroy the structure he had reared, but to rebuild something stable out of its ruins.

The Treaty of Paris was a sad disappointment to those who had hoped to have their revenge upon France for the injuries inflicted upon Germany under Napoleon's auspices. The Allies by adopting the principle that Napoleon alone was responsible and that France must not be punished, had refused to satisfy those—and there were many of them in Germany—who had desired an eye for an eye and a tooth for a tooth, who clamoured for a war indemnity, territorial cessions, safeguards against future aggression. Had the leaders of the great popular movement in Germany had their way, had the views expressed by Arndt been shared by those in authority, France would not have got off lightly. But in the conclusion of the Treaty of Paris the preponderating influence was that of the Czar: it was he rather than Frederick William or Francis II who had the last

word, and his zeal for the emancipation of Germany was already
dying down and being replaced by a generous wish to spare the
defeated French.   Stein was losing his influence over him, and
Talleyrand, adroitly utilising the Czar's weakness for a principle,
had enlisted him on behalf of the Legitimism in which the
astute Frenchman had divined the best defence that France
could oppose to those who wished to despoil her.   The Allies,
while professing to restore the state of things which had existed
before the Revolution, could hardly deprive France of Alsace
and Lorraine.   England was not less warm in supporting the
Legitimist principle, and Castlereagh defended the restoration
to France of most of her colonies as being likely to incline her
to peace by giving her no cause for dissatisfaction.   Austria,
despite Metternich's quarrel with the Czar over the violation of
Swiss neutrality, was not disposed to press France hard.   She
wanted to avoid change as much as possible, to limit the area
affected by the inevitable but distasteful reconstruction, and she
had no reason to fear a restoration of the Bourbon monarchy to
the full extent of its old dominions.   There remained only
Prussia; but neither Frederick William nor Hardenberg had
fully identified themselves with the aspirations of the national
party in Germany, nor were they likely to oppose the unanimous
voice of their allies.   German nationalism might desire that
not only the annexations which Napoleon had made on the left
bank of the Rhine should be taken from France, but that the
opportunity should be taken to recover the provinces lost to
Louis XV and Louis XIV; but the Irridentist spirit found
opponents rather than champions in the men who would speak
for Germany at the coming congress.   Dynastic not national
considerations were to regulate the settlement.   The thorny
problem of building up a really united Germany was avoided
by statesmen who saw that the autocracy of the Princes, their
masters, was absolutely incompatible with union on nationalist
and popular lines.   It would be impossible to adopt the principle
of nationalism and at the same time to stifle the dreaded voices
of Liberalism and democracy.

CHAPTER XXXIV

THE CONGRESS OF VIENNA

EVEN before the meeting of Congress which was to recast the political map of Europe, enough had happened to make it abundantly clear that the reconstruction would be the work of the princes, not of the peoples, and that the main object of the negotiations would be to confine the necessary changes within the narrowest possible limits. Thus the projects for the reconstruction of Germany, with which every publicist was busy from Cologne to Königsberg and from Münich to Hamburg, hardly received even a nominal consideration from Metternich and his fellows. Stein alone among the plenipotentiaries present at Vienna was in sympathy with the aspirations of the nationalist party in Germany; and Stein was present, not as the representative of any German state, but among the Russian deputation; and even in that capacity he was far less influential than he had been twelve months earlier, when he had enjoyed a greater share of the Czar's confidence.

But not even Stein himself seems to have contemplated anything like the German Empire of the present day; he had no idea of excluding Austria from Germany, but apparently wished to see a federation under the leadership of Austria, in which Prussia and Austria were to co-operate on terms of practical equality. Now as always, he was the bitter opponent of the middle-sized states, in which he saw the main obstacles to the unification of Germany. The Bavaria or the Baden of 1814 could make out a far better case for its independent sovereignty than had been possible to the Bavaria or Baden of 1794. To obtain some degree of unification and of subjection of the middle states to the central organisation, Stein at one time proposed the resuscitation of the Holy Roman Empire. This was only what had been proposed by the Treaty of Kalisch when Prussia and Russia had announced their intention of

" re-establishing the venerable Empire" to afford "effective protection and defence" to the people of Germany. But since March 1813 things had changed. The popular movement to which the sovereigns had then appealed was now the force they were endeavouring to curb and control, and the Kalisch appeal, which had contemplated a reconstruction effected by the joint action of princes and peoples, had become one of the things best forgotten. But the idea of a revived Empire was by no means without support: in advocating it Stein did but agree with one of the many projects which were being put forward in unofficial circles. This was the scheme of the Professor of Civil Law in the University of Halle, Christian Daniel Voss. He declared that legally the Holy Roman Empire still existed, since it had never been dissolved; but he differed greatly from Stein in going on to propose that, in order to maintain a due equality between Austria and Prussia, the head of the House of Nassau should be chosen Emperor with Frankfort as his capital. But this proposal, like that which would have given Bavaria the headship of the revived Empire, and another which would have made the Imperial dignity rotate between half a dozen of the leading Houses, was altogether out of the range of practical politics, and Austria's absolute refusal to have the Empire restored, except on terms which none of the other Powers would ever have contemplated, proved decisive. It was hardly wonderful that Austria should have taken this line. The nominal headship over states which did all they could to make that headship still less effective, which took every chance of hampering and obstructing the authority of the head, had no attractions for the Hapsburgs. It would be not unfair to say of Metternich what has been said with far less truth of Joseph II, that he neglected the German for the dynastic interests of the Hapsburgs. He saw a chance of establishing Austrian supremacy over Italy, and to secure that he made no attempt to recover the ground Austria had lost in Germany. Thus although Austria's intervention may be said to have decided against Napoleon the struggle for the liberation of Germany, Austria made no attempt to profit by it to reassert her claims or strengthen her influence over Germany. Stadion and the Archdukes Charles and John might have managed to identify Austria with the national revolt against French domination, but unfortunately for Austria it was by the spiritual heir of Thugut that her policy was guided at the critical moment.

Thus though unofficial writers like Grüner of Coburg might point out that what Germany needed was the "union of its forces to preserve freedom and independence, homogeneity of administration through the subjection of individual states to a common system of law," the realisation of this desired unity was bound to be prevented by the fact that a centralised organisation, if it were to be effective, must involve the partial suppression of the internal independence which the middle-sized states had secured under Napoleon's rule. The Princes would not surrender sovereign rights on which they set as much store as they did on that of making treaties with other Powers, still less would they agree to submit their domestic affairs to the supervision of the officials of the Confederacy, and yet unless some means were provided by which the Confederacy could secure the due performance of their duties by its members, its existence would soon be as much of a fiction as that of the Empire had ever been.

But the constitutional reconstruction of Germany was not the only task which awaited the Congress when it assembled at Vienna on October 1st, 1814. An even harder task was that of territorial redistribution. Differences of opinion over the constitution had the effect of making it more negative, since the less definite the constitution the less acute the differences: hence they were somewhat of the nature of an academic discussion, and not likely to lead to a serious conflict. Quarrels over the constitution could always be averted by adopting a solution so indefinite as to really amount to the shelving of the disputed point ; quarrels over territory were far more important: there was something tangible at stake, and but for the return of Napoleon from Elba it is possible that the map of Europe would not have been settled without an actual collision between the former allies.

The plenipotentiaries assembled at Vienna had not an absolutely free hand. Their deliberations were bound to take account of the arrangements already made by the four Treaties of Kalisch, Töplitz, Chaumont and Paris, which have been well described as "the preamble to the Congress of Vienna."[1] These had removed from the path two of the old obstacles on which European coalitions had come to grief. At Töplitz, Prussia had renounced all claims on Hanover, the stone on which the Third

[1] Rose, p. 325.

Coalition had stumbled, while a corollary of the same agreement, the Treaty of Ried, had seen Austria renounce her more extensive designs on Bavaria in the hope of compensation in Italy, though she recovered Tyrol, Salzburg and the other acquisitions which Bavaria had made from her by Napoleon's aid. Two very important questions remained: the fate of Poland and—closely connected with the Polish question—the treatment of Saxony. There was no idea of undoing the work of secularisation effected in 1803 and the subsequent "mediatisation" which had between them reduced the "sovereign" states of Germany from the 300 of 1786 to the 39 of 1815; but even so in the three states more particularly identified with Napoleon which had shared his overthrow, Westphalia and the Grand Duchies of Berg and Frankfort, and in the recovered districts West of the Rhine, there was ample store of plunder out of which every German dynasty hoped to make acquisitions to be veiled under the blessed name of "compensation."

But these four treaties had settled certain other things which marked out the lines along which the discussions were to run. At Kalisch, Prussia had been promised an Eastern frontier connecting Silesia with West Prussia, and compensation in Northern and Western Germany for her surrender of the rest of her Polish possessions to Russia. At Töplitz the German Princes between the Elbe and the Rhine had been promised "full and unconditional independence." At Chaumont a federal alliance had been selected as the most satisfactory form for the reconstituted Germany. Finally, by the Treaty of Paris, Italy was to be divided between Austria and the various Houses which Napoleon had dispossessed, the House of Orange was to receive an accession of territory, and the ex-departments of Mont Tonnerre, Sarre, Rhin et Moselle and Roer were to be divided between Prussia and the minor states of Germany.

October 1st found the plenipotentiaries assembled at the Austrian capital, but it was decided to postpone the opening of the actual negotiations for a month to allow the preparation of *agenda*. All the principal statesmen of Europe were present. Austria had as her principal representative Metternich, whose voice carried as much if not more weight in the deliberations than that of any other negotiator, and whose position was appropriately recognised by his election as President of the Congress; he was assisted by the able and energetic von Wessemberg-

Amfingen, and by von Gentz who acted as Secretary to the Congress. From England came Lords Cathcart and Castlereagh,[1] with Count Münster as the envoy of Hanover. France sent Talleyrand, who was to display his diplomatic prowess to the greatest advantage. Prussia entrusted her interests to Hardenberg and von Humboldt. Most of the minor sovereigns of Germany were present in person, and all were represented, even down to the various "benches" of Counts suppressed at the time of the great mediatisation. Russia characteristically sent two foreigners, the German Stein and the Italian Capo d'Istria, among the colleagues of her Foreign Minister, Nesselrode, while the Czar was also present. It was generally felt that Alexander's share in the Congress would be no small one; but those who feared or distrusted Russia might take comfort in the evident signs of antagonism between him and Metternich. This opposition, partly personal, accentuated by the action of Austria in 1814 and over the violation of Swiss neutrality, had had its origin in Metternich's successful opposition to the Czar's wish to assume the command of the Allied forces in 1813. The Polish question, if no other, seemed bound to provoke a conflict between them.

The question of German reconstruction, the least contentious of the problems before the Congress, but still bound to be a lengthy affair, had begun to be discussed by a committee a fortnight before the Congress opened.[2] Stein and Hardenberg had come forward with a project, based on the Treaty of Chaumont, for the management of German affairs by a Directory composed of Austria, Bavaria, Hanover and Prussia. This was to include commercial union, with no internal tariffs against other German states, an Assembly which should include representatives of local Estates, and a federal revenue to be derived from Customs and from an *octroi* on the Rhine. An alternative suggestion of Hardenberg's was that the new federation should exclude all Prussian territory East of the Elbe, and

[1] In January the latter had to return home for the opening of Parliament, and the Duke of Wellington took his place.

[2] The work of the Congress was mainly conducted by separate committees appointed to consider each individual question (*e.g.* the reorganisation of the Swiss Confederation), while the envoys of the Powers which had assisted to conclude the Peace of Paris, Austria, France, Great Britain, Portugal, Prussia, Russia, Spain and Sweden, formed a "Committee of Eight," which for all practical purposes was the effective part of the Congress.

all that of Austria save Berchtesgaden, Salzburg, Tyrol and the Vorarlberg. For the rest of their territory, Austria and Prussia would stand outside the federation, merely concluding close alliances with it and guaranteeing its integrity and independence.

But neither of these schemes found much favour with the Congress, and in the end Hardenberg acquiesced in the Twelve Articles which Metternich put forward,[1] and which were submitted to the consideration of a special committee (Oct. 16th). On this committee Austria, Bavaria, Hanover, Prussia and Würtemberg were represented, but it soon became evident that its deliberations were not likely to produce any satisfactory result. The scheme drawn up under Metternich's direction would have divided Germany into Circles, two to be directed by Austria, two by Prussia and one each by Bavaria, Hanover and Würtemberg; it would also have established two Councils, one composed of the Heads of the Circles, and another of the other members. The Council of Heads was to represent Germany in foreign affairs, decide on peace and war, and to act as a legislative chamber in conjunction with the Council of Members. The Heads were also to be charged with the execution of the decisions of the Confederation and with the conduct of military affairs. The right of secession was secured to the individual states, and they were to enjoy full sovereignty except where expressly limited. There was to be no formal head of the Confederation, but Austria was to preside in both Chambers.[2]

But this scheme did not commend itself to Bavaria and Würtemberg. They protested vigorously against the loss of the right to conclude alliances and to make war on their own account. Moreover, a clause which pledged the individual states to govern constitutionally and to give constitutional rights to their subjects, excited their most strenuous opposition. They argued with no small force that to apply to the minor states of Germany institutions which larger states had gained as the result of long struggles, would be altogether premature and out of keeping with the state of political development at which Germany had arrived.

The clause was certainly one which it is surprising to find in any scheme drawn up under the auspices of Metternich. It was not exactly in accord with his professions or his practice, and

---

[1] Cf. *Deutsche Geschichte, 1806–1871*, i. 527 ff.   [2] *Ibid.* i. 527–529.

might be thought to have been inserted to produce dissension. Anyhow, the committee's labours proved fruitless: Würtemberg declared (Nov. 16th) that it would be impossible to arrange the affairs of the Confederation until the boundaries had been settled, and therefore withdrew from the committee, which in consequence suspended its sittings, although Metternich, Hardenberg and some of the other plenipotentiaries continued, more or less informally, to draft and discuss schemes of reorganisation. Meanwhile the representatives of the minor states had been meeting and discussing the situation. They talked vaguely of reviving the Empire, but showed no inclination to do anything to make a revived Empire an effective institution, or to give the Emperor the powers without which his position could be nothing but a farce. Stein, who had not yet abandoned all hope of seeing a constitution adopted which would permit the development of that national feeling on which almost every other German statesmen looked with so much distrust, did what he could to encourage the idea, but it was out of the question. A Brunswick Privy Councillor, von Schmidt, went so far as to submit to Count Münster, the chief Hanoverian representative, a memorandum which laid down four functions as the proper sphere for the Emperor's authority; but these involved concessions Austria could never have obtained from the Princes, and without the power to superintend the execution of the decisions of the Confederation, without the control of the administration of justice and of the defensive system of the Empire, the right of presiding over the meeting of the Confederation would have been worthless. Münster, indeed, could only reply to von Schmidt that he had himself urged Austria to revive the Empire, but that he found her determined to stand by the clause in the Treaty of Chaumont, which prescribed a federative alliance as the new constitution for Germany. Thus it was in the end as a federative alliance, not as a united nation, that Germany emerged from the Congress, when in March the sudden escape of Napoleon from Elba and his return to France precipitated a settlement. This took the shape suggested by Metternich, who resolutely refused any revival of the old Empire. He saw that Austria's own dominions were enough in themselves to form an Empire, and that the loose and indefinite relations which would prevail under a Confederation would be better adapted for maintaining Austrian influence over the South

German states than any accurately defined constitution. Nor was there any Power in Germany which felt disposed to champion the cause of that national sentiment which the struggle of 1813 had aroused, but which, now that it had served its purpose, was muzzled and impotent. Nothing could have been further from the minds of Prussia's representatives in 1814 than the idea of trying to oust Austria from Germany in order to identify Prussia with this national sentiment of which fifty-six years later the Hohenzollern were to make such excellent use.

Thus the Germanic Confederation, to the formation of which the representatives of the states of Germany formally agreed on June 15th, 1815, was little more than the Confederation of the Rhine, with the addition of Austria and Prussia, and without Napoleon as " Protector." Five Kingdoms, Bavaria, Hanover, Prussia, Saxony and Würtemberg ; eight Grand Duchies, Baden, Hesse-Cassel, Hesse-Darmstadt, Luxemburg (which belonged to the King of the Netherlands), Oldenburg, Mecklenburg-Schwerin, Mecklenburg - Strelitz and Saxe - Weimar ; eight Duchies, Anhalt - Bernburg, Anhalt - Dessau, Anhalt - Köthen, Brunswick, Holstein and Lauenburg (which belonged to the King of Denmark), Nassau, Saxe-Gotha and Saxe-Hildburghausen ; twelve Principalities, Hesse-Homburg, Hohenzollern-Hechingen, Hohenzollern-Sigmaringen, Liechtenstein, Lippe-Detmold, Saxe-Coburg, Saxe-Meiningen, Schaumburg-Lippe, Schwarzburg-Rudolstadt, Schwarzburg-Sondershausen, Reuss and Waldeck ; and four Free Cities, Bremen, Frankfort, Hamburg and Lübeck, were included in the Confederation, whose affairs were entrusted to the control of a Diet under the presidency of Austria. To this body were delegated the tasks of providing the Confederation with the fundamental laws the Congress had not the time to lay down, and also that of arranging the details of the military and other organisations which had to be erected. It was to have two Chambers, an ordinary Assembly sitting permanently at Frankfort and consisting of 17 members, and a General Assembly of 69 members, summoned intermittently when more important matters called for discussion. But the control of the Diet over the members of the Confederation was neither very complete nor very effective ; private war between members was forbidden, but in domestic affairs each might go his own way. One of the clauses of the Act of Federation did indeed declare that a constitution should be established in each state, but nothing was done to enforce this provision, and in the absence of a " sanction " it was in most cases a dead letter from the very first. This was in no small measure due to Metternich : he desired to allow the minor states to enjoy the utmost possible independence, and therefore made Austria the champion of localism. Prussia had shown herself less unfavourable to the proposals for the unification of Germany, and Bavarian and Saxon particularists were beginning to look on her as the chief danger to their independence. Hence Austria's rôle was now to be that of the guarantor of the rights of the minor states ; Metternich was to make her the supporter of the very principles which had brought about the failure of her efforts to unite Germany. It was a strange inversion of parts, but the work of disintegration had been completely done, too thoroughly to allow any prospect that it could be undone, and Metternich thought that more might be gained by keeping on good terms with the South German states and devoting the efforts of Austria to securing control over Italy. Thus it was Metternich who succeeded in so amending Humboldt's " Fourteen Articles " that the Council of the Confederation, instead of being an efficient and vigorous executive, found its sphere of activity so much curtailed and its initiative so much cramped that it was all but powerless.

Lengthy as the negotiations over the constitution had been, those over the territorial redistribution excited far more interest and feeling. Of all the members of the Confederation of the Rhine the King of Saxony had adhered with most fidelity to Napoleon in 1813. Taken prisoner after Leipzig, he had not been able to secure himself or his dominions by such a compact as those made by Würtemberg at Fulda and by Hesse-Darmstadt, so Prussia proceeded to claim the kingdom as hers by right of conquest and in compensation for the losses she was prepared to suffer farther East. Alexander for his part was firmly resolved to have Poland, not merely the Russian shares of the three partitions, but if possible the whole country. He desired to rebuild Poland as a kingdom to be united to Russia by a personal tie such as that between Great Britain and Hanover. Influenced by Czartoriski, he hoped to rally Polish national feeling to him by this means. If he could gain this end he was prepared to see Saxony pass to Prussia, while Austria was to be left to recoup herself as best she could in Italy. This would have involved a division by no means acceptable to the other members of the Congress, and least of all to Castlereagh, whose policy, following in the lines laid down by Pitt, was to restore as far as possible that distribution of territory which had the authority of tradition. That Russia's efforts in the cause of Europe entitled her to the lion's share of the Grand Duchy of Warsaw was generally admitted, but there was not the same disposition to include as a corollary Prussia's preposterous claim to the whole of Saxony. At first, however, England contemplated letting Prussia have Saxony : not free from suspicions of Russia, she had no wish to see her unduly strong, and hoped by reconciling Austria and Prussia to make the Germanic Confederation a powerful factor in European politics. Were they united the rest of Germany must follow them, and Russia would find herself balanced by her neighbour on the West. To this end Castlereagh would have reluctantly sacrificed Saxony ; but Metternich, though he had no desire to press Austria's claims on Poland, was full of distrust of Alexander, even if he had not been bitterly opposed to the extension of Prussian influence. However, it was in Talleyrand that Saxony found her most effective ally. That astute diplomatist had no intention of letting France be kept out of her share in the councils of Europe: he argued that it was Napoleon, not France, that had been the universal enemy; it was therefore unfair to punish the Bourbon for the wrong-doings from which he also had suffered; France ought not to be treated as a pariah, but as a friend. The claim was one the Powers could not but admit. At the same time, Talleyrand had been doing all he could to establish good relations between France and the smaller states. A better opportunity of acting as their champion than that afforded by the case of Saxony he could not have desired. The project was exceedingly unpopular in Saxony, where no element of the population was prepared to be handed over from its old rulers to the detested Hohenzollern, nor was it much better liked in other parts of Germany. Bavaria and the other Princes, vigorously supported by Talleyrand, protested that without a free and independent Saxony there could be no stable federal Germany, and the French minister had little difficulty in persuading England and Austria to adopt this view.

Alexander and Frederick William were furious. They were in military possession of Saxony, and declared that they would not give it up. For a time it seemed as if it might come to a question of force, and Austria, England and France went to the length of concluding a defensive alliance (Jan. 3rd, 1815) with a view to this possibility. With all the rest of Germany on its side, for outside Prussia public opinion as expressed by the journalists and writers was strongly in favour of Saxony, this coalition was a strong incentive to a more reasonable attitude on the part of Russia and Prussia, and after a period of considerable tension Metternich managed to arrange a compromise which was accepted. Saxony escaped wholesale annexation at the price of a partition (Feb. 11th) which left the greater part of the country to its King, and handed over to Prussia Lower Lusatia, including Cottbus, the greater part of Upper Lusatia, and the North-Western portion of the Electorate, including Wittenberg, Torgau and Merseburg. All the efforts of Hardenberg, however, failed to obtain for Prussia the much-coveted Leipzig, and the portions which the House of Wettin retained, though only little more than half the area of the kingdom as it had been in 1812, contained 1,200,000 inhabitants out of 2,000,000 and included the richer as well as the more populous districts. At this heavy price Saxony was saved. A reluctant consent was extracted from Frederick Augustus (April 6th), on which the Prussians proceeded to evacuate the territory they had hoped to make their own. It is, however, open to question whether from the French point of view it might not in the long-run have been better to let Prussia take Saxony and to compensate the dispossessed monarch with a kingdom on the Rhine made up out of the old ecclesiastical Electorates with Cleves-Jülich and Zweibrücken. The majority of the subjects of such a kingdom would have shared their ruler's religion, whereas on the Elbe the Catholic Wettins ruled a Protestant population. There would also have been no slight advantage to France in keeping Prussia well to the Eastward, and in giving her Saxony with its traditional connection with Poland, thereby making it more likely that she would be brought into conflict with Russia than with France. By being established on the Rhine, Prussia became ultimately identified with the ideas embodied in the popular poem *Die Wacht am Rhein*: should a new Napoleon arise in France it would be Prussia which would bar his path into Germany. Moreover, the elements which the Rhenish provinces brought into the Prussian polity gave her more in common with the Catholics of the South than she had hitherto possessed, and made her leadership less unpalatable to the rest of Germany than it would have been had she been concentrated to the Eastward, apart from and outside the districts in which the ideas of the revolutionary epoch had taken root and on which the Napoleonic administration had left its mark. The more scattered the territories of Prussia, the more diverse the racial and social elements included within her dominions, the easier it would be for her to identify herself with Germany. The acquisition of the Rhenish provinces was a great step on the way to a distant but wider concentration, the annexation of Saxony would have given an immediate concentration at the probable sacrifice of the future. In the hands of the Hohenzollern Cologne, though separated from Berlin by a wide extent of non-Prussian territory, was an outpost which when the time should come would serve to make easy the absorption of the intervening independent states. But in 1815 not even Talleyrand's astuteness could have been expected to see so far into the future.

This solution of the question of Saxony removed the principal difficulty : it allowed that of Poland to be settled also. The lion's share, 37,000 square miles, with 2,500,000 people, fell to Russia, Austria contenting herself with recovering Galicia,[1] and letting Cracow become an independent Republic. Prussia kept her share of the original partition, West Prussia, Ermeland and the Netze District, and also Dantzic, Thorn and Posen out of the territories she had annexed in 1793, but she gave up the greater part of that share and all the gains of 1795. It was therefore out of the kingdom of Westphalia and the Rhenish provinces that she received the bulk of her "compensation." Of her old possessions she relinquished East Friesland, Goslar, Lingen, Osnabrück and part of Münster to Hanover, while Anspach and Baireuth remained in Bavarian hands ; but the rest of her lost territories were restored to her, including the Altmark, Cleves, Halberstadt, Guelders, Mark and Ravensberg, Magdeburg, Minden, Paderborn and most of Münster. Not less important were the new acquisitions, the greater part of the three ecclesiastical Electorates, the long-coveted Berg and Jülich, to which the Electors of Brandenburg had first laid claim more than two hundred years earlier, some portions of Nassau, Thuringia and Westphalia, and, last but not least, Swedish Pomerania, with Rügen and the much-desired Stralsund. These acquisitions enormously improved and strengthened

---

[1] The frontier was not quite identical with that of 1773, but what she now held corresponded approximately to her share of the First Partition.

Prussia's position. In actual extent she covered less territory than in 1806; but for what she lost in the way of Polish wastes and swamps the rich, fertile and thickly-populated Rhenish and Westphalian districts were a more than ample compensation. As in 1806, her territories were scattered and disconnected, though less so than before, and the dispersion was not an unmixed evil.

Of the territory remaining disposable, after Hanover had been reinstated in its old possessions with some additions, the bulk went to Bavaria in return for the provinces she had restored to Austria. Aschaffenburg and part of Fulda from the suppressed Grand Duchy of Frankfort, the Grand Duchy of Würzburg, given up by Archduke Ferdinand who returned to Tuscany, together with Anspach and Baireuth, were her principal acquisitions East of the Rhine, while it was only appropriate that a considerable share of the former Rhenish departments should go to the head of the Wittelsbach family under the name of the Bavarian Palatinate. Hesse-Darmstadt obtained the left bank lands between Bingen and Worms as a compensation for losses in Westphalia; Oldenburg received Birkenfeld, and Saxe-Coburg the little district of Lichtenberg; Mecklenburg-Strelitz, which had some claims on the left bank of the Rhine, was brought out and became a Grand Duchy, as did Oldenburg, Saxe-Weimar and Mecklenburg-Schwerin. William IX of Hesse-Cassel obtained part of Fulda and the now meaningless title of "Elector." Minor rectifications of frontier were too numerous to merit separate mention. Mayence became a Federal fortress with a mixed garrison of Austrians and Prussians, while some of the territory of the old Electorate went to the Duchy of Nassau, at this time held jointly by Frederick Augustus of Nassau-Usingen and Frederick William of Nassau-Weilburg. This Duchy also received part [1] of the territories of Orange-Nassau, the rest of which [2] went to Prussia in return for some portions of Guelders which were incorporated in the new kingdom of the United Netherlands. This new state, to which geographical unity was to prove unable to give permanence in face of racial, political and religious differences, although ruled over by a German prince, and composed of states once part of the Holy Roman Empire, was quite unconnected with Germany except through Luxemburg, which at the same time sent

---

[1] *Deutsche Landes und Provinzial Geschichte*, p. 176.
[2] Siegen and the district on the right bank opposite Bonn and Coblence.

deputies to the Estates General of the Netherlands and representatives to the Diet, since it formed part of the new Germanic Confederation by whose troops its fortresses were garrisoned. The cession of Swedish Pomerania to Prussia in return for a sum of 2,000,000 dollars severed the connection between one Scandinavian kingdom and Germany, a connection which had brought no good either to Sweden or to Germany since the fall of Gustavus at Lützen. The other Scandinavian kingdom, however, did remain bound to Germany by its complicated relations with Schleswig-Holstein, to which was now added the little Duchy of Lauenburg. Frederick of Denmark had hoped for better terms when he consented to cede Norway to Sweden; he had expected to receive Swedish Pomerania, but he had to pay the penalty for his loyalty to Napoleon.

The only other territorial readjustments which deserve mention were the acquisitions in Italy with which Austria sought to recompense herself for her neglect of Germany. Not only did she recover Istria and Dalmatia,[1] for which geography provides some justification, but Venetia and the Milanese, in which now were included Napoleon's annexations of Bormio, Chiavenna and the Valtelline, were formed into a kingdom, while Austrian bayonets were the true foundation of the power of the Hapsburg or kindred dynasties now restored in Modena, Tuscany and Parma.[2] Why Austrian rule over Italy, accepted placidly enough in the 18th Century, should have been so unendurable to the 19th Century Italians, is a problem which belongs to the history of Italy rather than to that of Germany; but that Austria should have sought her gains here rather than lower down the Danube valley does not give Metternich much claim to foresight or to appreciation of the situation in the Italian peninsula and of the changes which twenty years of Napoleon's rule had wrought in the sentiments of the Italians.

Throughout these arrangements nothing had been heard of the wishes of the populations thus bandied about from one dynasty to another. Racial divisions, traditions, sentiment, even geographical considerations, had to give way to the selfishness of

---

[1] She also, besides recovering from Bavaria Tyrol, Salzburg, Vorarlberg and parts of Upper Austria, regained possession of Carinthia, Carniola and the other districts which France had ruled directly under the name of the Illyrian Provinces, including the territories of the Republic of Ragusa. This gave her a much larger seaboard than she had hitherto possessed.

[2] Given to Marie Louise, Napoleon's wife.

42

the princes. The territorial rearrangement was a fitting counter-part to the constitutional settlement. Both served rather to postpone than to forward the realisation of that German unity of which so much had been heard in the opening months of 1813. The peoples of Germany might have then discovered that they were one and the same nation, poets and orators might have applauded unity, the rulers of Germany collected at Vienna were determined that the outcome of the "War of Liberation" should be a very different thing from that which the popular leaders had sought. Repression, not emancipation, was the watchword of the governments in 1815. And this could the more easily be accomplished since the nationalist and Liberal forces, practically without leaders or organisation, were powerless. To a certain extent they had wrought their own undoing by reinforcing the hands of their rulers in the struggle against Napoleon. To throw off the French yoke popular enthusiasm had had to ally itself with the governments. Patriotic fervour had played no small part in the successes of 1813, but it had been compelled to flow along the official channels. By submitting to military dis-cipline the popular movement had given up the control over itself to the princes and their ministers and generals. It was thus powerless to defend itself against the measures now taken to retain it under control. Its ally had become its master. At the same time the general weariness of war and strife made people ready to acquiesce in the decisions of the Congress, and there was no small truth in the argument of the Bavarian delegates [1] that Germany was not yet qualified to receive representative institutions and constitutional government. Before unity could be achieved there was much still to be done. The middle states, Bavaria, Würtemberg, Saxony and the rest, had to continue by themselves the work of consolidation begun under Napoleon's influence. Prussia had to reorganise the provinces she had re-covered from France and her vassals, and to assimilate her new acquisitions. Above all, there was yet another round to be fought out in the great struggle between Austria and Prussia. Germany could not be united until the question had been settled under whose hegemony the union was to take place. While that remained undecided no rearrangement of Germany, territorial or constitutional, could be other than temporary and a makeshift. Indeed, when the Act of Federation was signed (June 18th), it

[1] Cf. p. 649.

THE SOUTH WESTERN STATES IN 1815

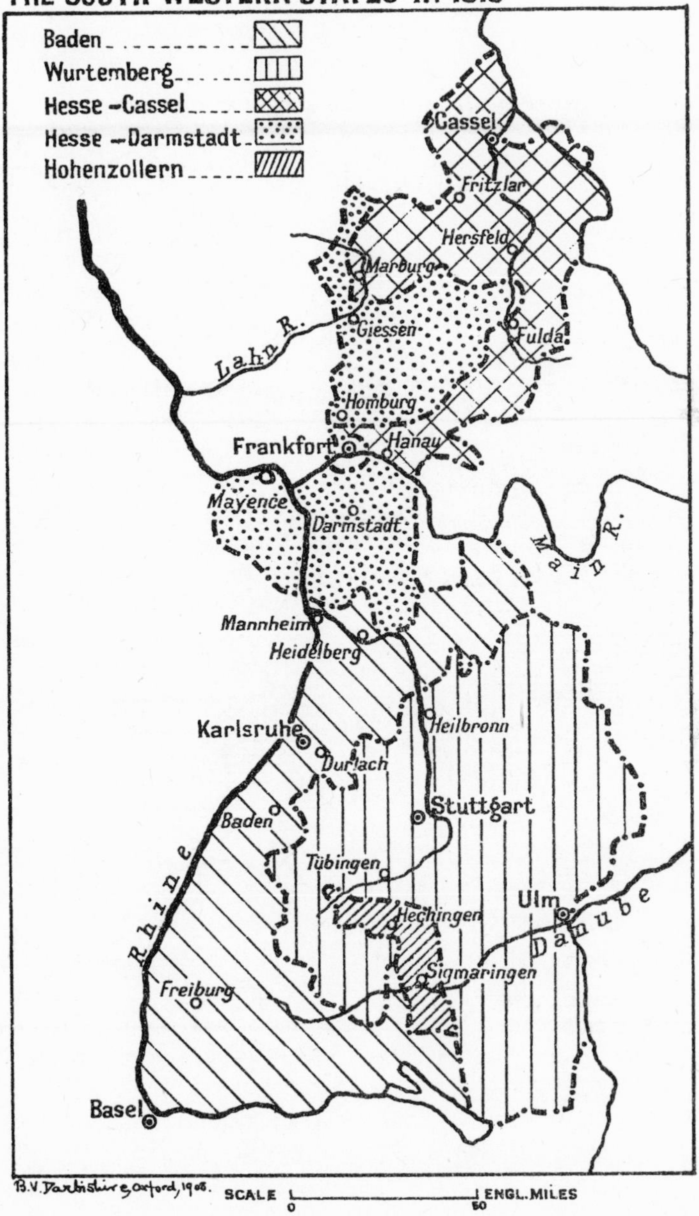

Baden _ _ _ _ _ _ _ _ _

Wurtemberg _ _ _ _ _ _ _

Hesse –Cassel _ _ _ _ _

Hesse –Darmstadt _

Hohenzollern _ _ _ _ _

Cassel

Fritzlar

Hersfeld

Marburg

Lahn R.

Giessen

Fulda

Homburg

Frankfort

Hanau

Mayence

Darmstadt

Main R.

Mannheim

Heidelberg

Karlsruhe

Heilbronn

Durlach

Rhine

Baden

Stuttgart

Tübingen

Ulm

Hechingen

Danube

Sigmaringen

Freiburg

Basel

B.V. Darbishire, Oxford, 1908.   SCALE

0   50   ENGL. MILES

Kingdom of HANOVER in 1801 showing gains of 1803 & 1815

was still uncertain whether its provisions would not be subjected to a complete revision at the hands of the founder of the Confederation of the Rhine. Had Napoleon been victorious at Waterloo the work of the Congress of Vienna would hardly have escaped radical modification.

CHAPTER XXXV

THE HUNDRED DAYS

NAPOLEON may have been quite sincere in the desire for peace with the rest of Europe which he professed on his return from Elba, but it was hardly to be expected that the Allies would take him at his word. They could not afford to overlook the promises he had made and broken in the past, they could not trust him even if he were speaking the truth, for circumstances he could not control must have driven him into an attempt to retrieve the defeats of 1813 and 1814. His Empire was founded on victory and military prestige, and the reputation of the French arms required that Leipzig and Vittoria should be wiped out; moreover, once his expulsion of the Bourbons had challenged the settlement of 1814, it was inevitable that, sooner or later, he would have to tear up the Treaty of Paris and seek to recover at the least the "natural boundaries" of France. Indeed, the Allies had no alternative but to take up their arms again and endeavour to repeat the work of 1814. Less than a week after the news of the Emperor's escape reached Vienna (March 7th), the representatives of the eight Powers which had signed the Treaty of Paris issued a declaration that Napoleon had forfeited all rights by his breach of the arrangements made with him and was consequently delivered over to public justice (March 13th). A fortnight later (March 27th), Austria, England, Prussia and Russia renewed the Treaty of Chaumont, the minor states adhering to the anti-Napoleonic alliance, though without much enthusiasm. Even Napoleon's faithful partisan Denmark did not stir on his behalf; and though the King of Saxony procrastinated, hoping to obtain some modification of the harsh treatment which was being meted out to his kingdom, in the end he, too, joined the Coalition (May 27th). Naples was the only exception, and Murat took up arms not so much with the idea of assisting his old master, as in the hope of rousing a national insurrection in Italy against Austria and Sardinia, and of driving those Powers out of the peninsula as the champion of Italian nationalism and unity.[1]

The attitude of Germany towards Napoleon in 1815 was rather different from what it had been two years earlier. Then he had been the foreign tyrant, the oppressor whose alien yoke the nations of Europe were yearning to throw off. The opposition he encountered in 1815 was one of governments, not of peoples. Conservatism took arms to repel the attacks of militant Revolution. It was the "crowned Jacobin" whom Metternich dreaded: when everything seemed satisfactorily settled the return of Napoleon threatened to throw reconstructed Germany back into the melting-pot and to provoke an explosion of the forces Metternich thought he had managed to stifle and keep down. Prussia's point of view was different. Prussia was the only German state in which there was real enthusiasm for the war. To Prussia more than to any other of his enemies Napoleon had been the oppressor; in Prussia the hatred of him was deepest and bitterest and the cry for revenge strongest and most insistent. Moreover, his return threatened Prussia's recent acquisitions on the Rhine, and the nation was unanimous in its determination to retain them. The King appealed to the nation, and volunteers flocked forward in reply. But if in the other states which formed the alliance there was less keenness against Napoleon, one and all prepared to take their part in the task of carrying out the sentence pronounced against him.

For the moment, however, it was impossible to undertake active operations. The only troops immediately available were some 30,000 Prussians who formed the army in occupation of the new territories allotted to Prussia on the Rhine, 10,000 British, the troops who had made the campaign of 1814 in the Netherlands under Sir Thomas Graham and still remained in that country,[2] 14,000 Hanoverians belonging like the British to the army which was occupying the Netherlands pending the conclusion of the Congress of Vienna, and the greater part of the King's German Legion, which had been collected in Brabant on its way from the South of France to Hanover, where it was to be disbanded. It supplied about 3200 cavalry, 600 artillery and 4000 infantry, while another 8000 men must

---

[1] Cf. R. M. Johnston, *Napoleonic Empire in Southern Italy.*

[2] Some 15 battalions of infantry, for the most part very weak, and, as they were second battalions, mainly composed of raw recruits.

be added for the available forces of the Kingdom of the Netherlands. The total of these forces amounted even on paper to only about 70,000, and they were so heterogeneous and so utterly unprepared for a campaign that an immediate move was out of the question. Thus it was impossible to crush Napoleon there and then; and while the Allies were gradually collecting their forces from all quarters, the Austrians from the Theiss and Danube, the Russians from the distant Don and Dnieper, the British from as far West as North America, to which quarter the flower of the Peninsular army had been sent, Napoleon had time to organise an effective army out of the veterans whom the peace had released from their confinement in Germany, England and Russia.

Wellington was at once nominated to the command of the Allied army in the Netherlands, which was reinforced by all the available troops from Great Britain and Hanover, by a Brunswick contingent rather over 6000 strong, by a brigade of 2800 men from Nassau, and by considerable forces of Dutch-Belgians. At the same time the Prussian army was rapidly augmented to a strength of over 100,000; but it included a strong contingent of Saxons who were anything but well affected to the Allied cause, and whose disaffection resulted before the campaign opened in open mutiny, while the population of the Rhenish districts recently annexed to Prussia contained a considerable Francophil faction.[1] Behind this army, which was placed under the command of Blücher, was being collected a Prussian army of reserve, which would eventually provide about 70,000 men, but would not be ready to take the field for some time. Two other armies were also to be put into the field, one of Russians, which was making its way across Germany in three columns, amounting in all to 160,000 men; another under Schwarzenberg, composed of a nucleus of Austrians together with the contingents of Bavaria, Würtemberg and the other South German states, was gathering on the Upper Rhine.[2]

---

[1] Cf. Houssaye, *Waterloo*, p. 85.

[2] Lord Cathcart, the English representative at Vienna, made great endeavours to have the contingents of Hesse-Cassel, Hesse-Darmstadt and several other states placed under Wellington's command; but this was resolutely opposed by von Knesebeck, who for political reasons wished them to serve with the Prussians. In the end the Hesse-Darmstadt contingent, 8000 strong, was attached to Schwarzenberg's Army of the Upper Rhine, most of that of Hesse-Cassel was allotted to the garrison of Mayence, while Baden (16,000), Bavaria (60,000) and Würtemberg (25,000)

But these two last-mentioned armies could not possibly be ready to begin operations till the end of June, and therefore the Allies had to choose between giving Napoleon all that time in which to organise the resources of France and, if they preferred to attack him while his preparations were far from complete, doing so with only a small part of the great force they would eventually have at their disposal. Wellington at first favoured a prompt attack, and suggested May 1st for beginning operations, a proposal which the enterprising Blücher cordially supported. Austria and Russia, however, refused to entertain the idea, and it was therefore abandoned.[1] Gneisenau then put forward a plan closely resembling that which the Allies had adopted in 1813. By it three armies should assemble on the Upper Rhine, the Lower Rhine and in the Netherlands, with a central reserve behind them, and should move concurrently but independently on Paris. If Napoleon fell on one of these three it was to retire on the reserve and the other two were to press forward, so that Napoleon would have to give up the pursuit of the one he was attacking and turn aside to protect his flanks and communications.[2] Weighty objections were urged against this scheme; but as it was never put into force they need not be discussed, for it was decided to wait until the Russians and Schwarzenberg were ready to co-operate with Wellington and Blücher, a choice which let the initiative pass from the Allies to Napoleon.

To have adopted a defensive attitude would have fitted in best with the peaceful professions Napoleon had made on his return from Elba: had he waited for the Allies to assume the offensive, he could have represented that the Powers were assailing the liberties and independence of France, and could have appealed to the sentiments of 1792. But he did not quite trust the French democracy, and he preferred to make his appeal to the military spirit and to the national love of glory and conquest with which he had identified his Empire, rather than to Republican traditions. Moreover, the initiative was more in keeping with his active and enterprising genius than was the

supplied about half Schwarzenberg's army. Thus the German element in Wellington's army was smaller than it should have been. Cf. Wellington's *Supplementary Dispatches*, vol. x. pp. 11-14 and 117-120.

[1] Cf. *Deutsche Geschichte, 1806-1871*, i. 567; and Houssaye, pp. 90-92.
[2] Cf. *Supplementary Dispatches*, x. 172.

tamer defensive; he hoped by a speedy success over the English and their allies in the Netherlands to rally Belgium to his standard, and to meet the main armies of the Coalition with all the prestige of restored victory. Who could say what influence the defeat of Wellington and Blücher might exercise on the old members of the Confederation of the Rhine, or even on Austria? Accordingly, Napoleon decided to take the offensive before the middle of June, and to throw the 125,000 men who formed his available field-army on the point where the left of Wellington's cantonments touched the right of Blücher's.

This critical point was, roughly speaking, defined by the great road from Charleroi to Brussels, and it was between Avesnes and Philippeville to the South of Charleroi that the French were concentrated by the evening of June 14th. Napoleon's design was to attack the two armies of Blücher and Wellington separately before they could unite, and by interposing between them and thrusting forward on Brussels, to push them apart as he had the Austro-Sardinians in 1796. He calculated that Blücher, if beaten, would retire Eastward, towards the Meuse, and that Wellington's only way of escape from disaster would be a rapid retreat to his base, Ostend.

The Waterloo campaign is a subject so thorny and so bristling with difficulties that one naturally shrinks from the attempt to tell again the story of the eventful four days (June 15th to 18th) which saw Napoleon, despite his initial success over the Prussians at Ligny, utterly and completely beaten when those same Prussians, whom he believed that he had put out of action, came back to the aid of the English and their allies. Still the campaign was of vital importance to Germany; and even if it is to be told mainly from the point of view of the Prussian army and its share in the campaign, it is impossible to attempt even that without relating the doings of Wellington's army, more especially of the Germans under his command, or without discussing to some extent the plans and the actions of Napoleon.

In the first place, it must be pointed out that the success of Napoleon's plan depended mainly on the promptitude and precision with which it was put into force, that the attack on the Allied centre placed Napoleon at the point at which it was easiest for both Allied armies to come into action, that there is a good deal to be said for Wellington's view that the Emperor would have done better to make that attack on the English communications, which the Duke so much feared. Had he done so, Wellington must either have retreated Northward, abandoning his direct communications with Ostend,[1] or have given battle on the 16th, probably somewhere between Ath and Hal, without any chance of Blücher coming to his aid in force.[2] By attacking at the point of contact, Napoleon made it essential that he should destroy and not merely defeat the army on which his first attack fell, and that he should lose no time about following up the advantages he might gain.

At the moment Napoleon delivered his attack, the Allied armies were certainly dangerously extended. Both Wellington and Blücher were misled by receiving intelligence from France that Napoleon would adopt the defensive, and the French concentration was certainly admirably conducted, inasmuch as hardly any accurate information about it seems to have leaked across the frontier. Thus June 15th found Wellington's headquarters and his reserve (25,000 men) at or near Brussels; his cavalry corps (10,000) between Ninove and Grammont; Hill's corps (27,000) distributed between Ghent, Ath, Oudenarde and Alost; that of the Prince of Orange (30 000) between Mons, Seneffe, Braine le Comte, Nivelles and Genappe.[3]

---

[1] It should be remembered that at the moment the campaign opened Wellington was receiving continual reinforcements from England by way of Ostend. Thus Sir John Lambert's brigade, two old Peninsula battalions, 1/4th and 1/40th, and one which had seen service on the East coast of Spain, 1/27th, only reached the field of Waterloo during the action, having come up from Ghent by forced marches; the 7th, 29th and 43rd, three strong battalions which had been among the best of the whole Peninsula army, landed at Ostend on June 18th, June 13th and June 16th respectively, indeed the 29th actually got near enough to hear the guns of Waterloo.

[2] A containing force of the strength of that detached under Grouchy after Ligny would have sufficed to keep at bay the corps of Ziethen, which would have been all the Prussian commander could have brought up on the 16th. Pirch and Thielmann, who only reached Sombreffe about 11 a.m. and 1 p.m. respectively on the 16th, could not have exercised much influence over a battle Westward of Nivelles on that day.

[3] Of this force about 69,000 were infantry, the British providing 29 battalions with a total of 20,310, the King's German Legion 8 battalions (3285 men), the Hanoverians 23 battalions (13,788 men), the Brunswickers 8 battalions (5376 men), the contingents of Nassau and Orange-Nassau 8 battalions (7100), 5 of which were included in a Dutch-Belgian division, the Dutch-Belgian contingent of 33 battalions being 19,674 strong. The cavalry came to 14,500, 5913 of whom (16 regiments) were British, 5 regiments mustering in all 2560 belonged to the King's German Legion, 3 were Hanoverians, one and a squadron of Uhlans came from Brunswick, 7 were Dutch-Belgians. The army included 32 batteries of

Blücher had his headquarters at Namur, his army being divided into four corps, of which that of Ziethen was nearest to the threatened point, being distributed between Thuin, Charleroi, Marchienne, Moustiers and Fleurus. The next corps, that of Pirch, was at Namur, with portions at Heron, Huy and Hannut. Thielmann's corps, distributed between Ciney, Dinant and Huy, was a good deal farther from the critical spot; and Bülow's, at and around Liége, was not less than 45 miles from the place appointed for the concentration. This was Sombreffe, about 14 miles from Namur and the same distance from Charleroi, to which place it must be pronounced to have been dangerously near, seeing how widely the Prussian cantonments were scattered. If Wellington's cantonments also were too far apart, he did not commit the mistake of selecting as the point of concentration a position so far advanced as Sombreffe: Blücher must be accounted lucky in that Napoleon did not, by attacking a little earlier on the 16th, overthrow Ziethen's corps before those of Pirch and Thielmann could arrive.

The Prusssian army was rather larger than that underWellington. Three of its four corps averaged about 31,000, the fourth, that of Thielmann, being only 24,000 strong. This was due to the mutiny of the Saxon troops originally belonging to it. These troops, when it had been proposed to allot the soldiers individually to the Prussian or to the Saxon service in conformity with the distribution of the districts they came from between Prussia and Saxony, had broken out into open revolt, "declaring that

---

artillery, 18 British, 3 K. G. L., 2 Hanoverian, 2 Brunswick and 7 Dutch-Belgian : these varied from 4 to 8 guns, and in all provided 204 pieces. This did not complete Wellington's force, as he had under his command, though not in the fighting line, von der Decken's Hanoverian Reserve Corps, 13 battalions or 9000 men, while 6 British battalions on garrison duty amounted to 3200 more. Of these troops the British and King's German Legion were by far the best, 18 battalions and 12 cavalry regiments of the British having served in the Peninsula, as had also 5 battalions and all the cavalry of the German Legion, though even these corps had a good many recruits in their ranks. The Hanoverians were nearly all young troops, and most of them *Landwehr ;* and much the same was the state of the Brunswickers. Three of the Nassau battalions had served in Spain, but on Napoleon's side, they being the troops which had come over to Wellington before Bayonne in December 1813. The Dutch-Belgians were the least efficient part of the army : many of them, including practically all the officers, had been in the French service, and their zeal for the Allied cause was worse than doubtful. Their conduct during the campaign was such as to make them an element of weakness rather than of strength to their commander, and Wellington would have gained could he have exchanged them for a much smaller number of British troops or even of Hanoverian *Landwehr.*

they were the soldiers of the King of Saxony, and would serve no other cause."[1] The mutiny was repressed, the Saxon Guards and the two Grenadier battalions implicated were disbanded, several of the ringleaders were shot; and as the whole body of the Saxon troops, 15,000 men in all, continued unanimous in their opposition to the transfer, it was finally decided to send them all back to Westphalia.[2] Thus Thielmann's corps was short of the 4500 to which the brigade it had been proposed to form out of the transferred Saxons should have amounted. In support of the Prussian army a corps of some 20,000 men was being collected at Treves, composed of the contingents of Mecklenburg, Anhalt, Reuss, Lippe and other minor states of North Germany; but it was not called upon to take any active part in the campaign.

The concentration of the French had not been effected without some indication of it reaching the Allies, but the information which Wellington received on June 14th from the Belgian van der Merlen at Binche, and from Major-General von Dörnberg who commanded the British cavalry brigade in front of Mons, was not sufficiently definite to do more than put him on the alert. The news that French columns were massing in the direction of Avesnes, and that they seemed to be withdrawing from opposite Wellington's right, might only be an elaborate blind to conceal the stroke against his communications which the British commander feared. Meanwhile Blücher hearing from Ziethen late on the 14th that the French were gathering in his front, sent orders to Pirch to move to Sombreffe, to Thielmann to come up to Namur, and to Bülow to concentrate at Hannut.

Next morning (June 15th) the French advance began. Napoleon had collected a force superior in average quality to either of the armies opposed to him, but one which, as M. Houssaye shows,[3] was as little to be relied upon in some ways as it was formidable in others. In numbers it was superior to either of its enemies, inferior to the two combined in the proportion of 3 to 5.[4] It included the Guard, over 20,000 strong, four corps of cavalry amounting to 13,000 men, and five of infantry varying from the 25,000 of Reille's corps to the 11,000

---

[1] *Supplementary Dispatches*, x. p. 220.
[2] *Ibid*. x. pp. 238–240, 245, and 266.   [3] P. 83.
[4] Wellington's army may be put at about 90,000 effectives, Blücher's at 115,000, Napoleon's at 125,000.

of Lobau's. It was much better supplied with artillery than was Wellington, and somewhat better than were the Prussians.

On June 15th the French got on the move about daybreak, marching in three columns on Marchienne au Pont, on Charleroi, and on Châtelet. Very early they came into contact with Ziethen's outposts, which gave way before them not without some brisk skirmishing. Between 9 and 10 a.m. the French columns reached the Sambre, Reille's vanguard under Bachelu at Marchienne, Pajol, who led the centre column, at Charleroi. Here they were checked for a time; but about midday both passages were secured, and Steinmetz from Thuin and Pirch II from Charleroi were retiring by Gosselies and Fleurus on Ligny, where the other two divisions of Ziethen's corps were concentrating.[1] The French plans had been somewhat upset by Vandamme's lateness in starting, a delay due to his orders not having reached him, and similarly d'Erlon and Gérard failed to carry out punctually the movements prescribed to them. Thus Steinmetz was able to make good his retreat to Fleurus, despite Reille's efforts to intercept him. To this success Pirch II's stubborn stand at Gilly from about 2 to 6 p.m. contributed materially, as he prevented Pajol's cavalry from pushing forward along the direct road to Fleurus. However, when Vandamme at last delivered his attack, the division had some difficulty in extricating itself and retiring to Fleurus. As the Prussians started to go to the rear they were assailed by the French cavalry; one battalion was ridden over and cut to pieces, another escaped only by forming square and cutting its way through its assailants into the shelter of the woods. Yet, badly as the division was mauled, Ziethen's corps had certainly done well in withdrawing from its extended positions and concentrating between Ligny and St. Amand with the loss of only 1200 men killed, wounded and prisoners. It had performed its task of delaying the French advance with very fair success, the time gained was of great value, but it was unfortunate that Ziethen should have neglected the principal duty of the commander of an outpost screen such as that formed by his corps, namely, that of forwarding complete and prompt information of what is going on at the front to the commanders of the main forces whose

---

[1] Each Prussian corps was made up of four so-called "brigades," corresponding in strength rather to the divisions of the Anglo-Dutch army, so that it is less misleading to describe them as "divisions."

concentration he was covering. He had, it is true, sent off a messenger to Blücher directly the first shots were heard in his front (5 a.m.), and a message seems to have been sent to Wellington about 8 a.m.;[1] but to Ziethen's neglect to send any further news must be mainly attributed the slowness of the British concentration. Wellington, hearing no more of the attack on Ziethen, had no reason to suppose that it was more than a feint, and still believed that the real attack would come on his right. The Prince of Orange arrived about 3 p.m. with news that the Prussian outposts were falling back, but he had left the front about 10 a.m. before the French attack had thoroughly developed, and his information was hardly conclusive; thus orders for the concentration of the army at Nivelles were not given till after 7 p.m., when at last a despatch saying that all was quiet on the side of Mons arrived from Dörnberg. The latter's share of the responsibility for the delay in the concentration is no small one, for his failure to send earlier information in conjunction with Ziethen's neglect left the Duke uncertain as to the true line of the advance. Certainly some valuable hours might have been saved had Ziethen done his duty in sending full and constant information so as to show Wellington that the attack near Charleroi was the real thing.

Meanwhile the IInd Prussian Corps had by the evening of the 15th come up almost to Sombreffe and was at hand to support Ziethen; while Thielmann, who had reached Namur, was only about 15 miles away. Bülow, however, largely through Gneisenau's fault,[2] had failed to do more than make arrangements to concentrate at Hannut on the morning of the 16th, which had made it certain that the IVth Corps would take no part in any action that might be fought on the 16th.

Thus at nightfall on June 15th the position of the Allies was none too satisfactory. Wellington's concentration had not begun; Blücher had only two of his corps together, and they were in dangerous proximity to the French. Luckily for the Allies, however, the French movements had not been all that the Emperor desired. Bad Staff work had been the cause of several delays; Vandamme, d'Erlon and Reille had all started behind time, and thus Napoleon's intention of occupying Quatre

---

[1] *Dispatches*, xii. 473.

[2] Cf. J. von Pflugk - Harttung, *Vorgeschichte der Schlacht der Belle - Alliance*, pp. 252 ff.

Bras and Fleurus had not been accomplished. On the right, where Grouchy was in command, the vanguard of cavalry was just short of Fleurus, with Vandamme a little way behind. Gérard's corps was not yet over the Sambre. In the centre, Lobau had still to cross the river, the Old Guard was between Charleroi and Gilly, the Young Guard had reached Gilly. On the left the cavalry had not got beyond Frasnes; Reille's infantry were between Mellet, Wangenies and Gosselies; d'Erlon had two divisions nearly up to Gosselies, but two still on the Sambre. What had happened in this quarter was that after Steinmetz had cleared his way past Gosselies to Heppignies and Fleurus by a bold counter-attack on the advance-guard of Reille's corps,[1] Ney, who commanded the left wing of the French, had not pushed on in force towards Quatre Bras, judging reasonably enough that it would be inexpedient to thrust forward too far in front of the rest of the army. Thus only some cavalry had got as far as Frasnes which they found occupied by a battalion of the 2nd Regiment of Nassau. This battalion stood firm, and the French had to send back for infantry support. The delay allowed Prince Bernhard of Saxe-Weimar to bring the regiment of Orange-Nassau up from Genappe,[2] and so bold was the front he showed that, after some skirmishing, Ney decided not to attempt to capture Quatre Bras that evening.[3] Thus though the day had on the whole favoured the French, though they had established themselves in close proximity to the line on which the Allies proposed to carry out their still incomplete concentration, they had not made all the progress needed to assure success. The morning of the 16th found them anything but ready for an immediate attack either on the Prussians or on Wellington, and the six hours' delay which followed was all-important in deciding the fortunes of the campaign.

Indeed it was not till June 16th was well advanced that further fighting took place. Vandamme did not bring his corps up into position opposite the Prussians till after 10 a.m., and

---

[1] *Circa* 3 p.m.   [2] About 6.30 p.m.

[3] Prince Bernhard, who had acted on his own responsibility, had only anticipated the orders of General Perponcher, the divisional commander ; and it would seem that Quatre Bras had been named as the point for the brigade to concentrate, for another battalion of the 2nd Nassau came up independently from Bezy (Siborne, p. 117); but nevertheless the Prince's action and that of Major Normann and his battalion of the 2nd Nassau deserve much credit. Though officially part of the Dutch-Belgian army, these troops should rather be regarded as Germans.

Gérard was three hours behind him. About 11 a.m. Napoleon arrived on the scene from Charleroi. The scheme which he had formed overnight was based on the assumption that the retreat of the Prussian outposts to the North-East pointed to an intention to retire towards their base, Liége and Maastricht, and to abandon the attempt to combine with Wellington, who the Emperor concluded must be in full retreat on Antwerp or Ostend. Thus he did not expect any serious fighting on the 16th; he meant to push his right forward as far as Gembloux, driving in any rearguard the Prussians might leave at Sombreffe and then to transfer his central reserve to the left wing and reinforce Ney, who was meanwhile to have adopted a waiting attitude at Quatre Bras. This done, Napoleon meant to advance straight on Brussels, which he expected to reach in the morning of the 17th. This plan was completely upset by Blücher's resolve to stand at Ligny, a resolve to which the Prussian commander clung even when he discovered that Bülow's disobedience would deprive him of over a quarter of his force. Nor does the decision appear to have been prompted by any hope, much less by any definite promise, of help from Wellington.[1] Blücher certainly hoped Wellington would arrive, but his mind had been made up long before his interview about noon with the Duke, whose promise of help was purely conditional on his not being attacked himself.

The Emperor thus found that instead of a rearguard action with a force trying to cover the Prussian retreat, he would have to fight a battle on a considerable scale, for which he was not yet ready. Though Ziethen's corps alone was actually in position between Ligny and St. Amand, Pirch's was just arriving; and Thielmann, who had left Namur at 7 a.m., came up shortly after midday, though it was not till between two and three that his whole force arrived. Still, even with only Ziethen in his front, the Emperor was not prepared to attack without a rather larger force than the 24,000 to which Vandamme and the cavalry of Pajol and Excelmans amounted. Accordingly the

---

[1] The attempt of Herr Delbrück in his Life of Gneisenau to prove that Blücher was relying on Wellington's assistance, and would not otherwise have fought at Ligny, is quite unsuccessful. Cf. Houssaye, p. 142; also *Vorgeschichte der Schlacht der Belle-Alliance*, by J. von Pflugk-Harttung, quite the most judicial and unbiassed German account of these events; the instalment of the *Geschichte der Befreiungs Krieg*, which deals with 1815, Herr von Lettow-Vorbeck's *Napoleons Untergang*, unfortunately reproduces the Prussian "legend of Waterloo" in its most extreme form.

attack had to be put off till Gérard's corps had deployed into line, and its leading columns did not appear till after one. The delay was of the utmost value to the Prussians, for long before the attack was delivered Pirch had taken up his position in support of Ziethen, and most of Thielmann's men had arrived, and thus Blücher's uncovered left had been secured.

The Prussian position was not one of any great strength. It consisted of the heights of Bry, Sombreffe and Tongrines, which lie along the Northern bank of the Ligny brook; on its right it was bounded by a ravine down which a smaller rivulet flows into the stream, and a similar ravine flowing from the village of Botey into the Ligny brook marked the natural limit of the position on the left. The Ligny brook, however, does not flow in a straight line, but, after running to the North-East through St. Amand and Ligny, bends due East at the hamlet of Mont Potriaux just South of Sombreffe, and then curving round to the South past Tongrines at one time actually flows South-Westward. Near the village of Boignée, however, it bends again to the East, to end by joining the Ormeau near Mazy, the spot where the Namur-Nivelles road crosses that tributary of the Sambre. The centre, therefore, of an army taking post on the Northern bank of this stream is much "refused," the wings being thrust forward, especially the right wing at the Western end of the position. Dotted all over these heights and along the course of the Ligny brook and its affluents are various villages and hamlets, some, like Ligny and St. Amand, of fair size, others, as, for example, Balâtre and Tongrenelles, quite small. These provided much cover for a defending force, and were the pivots on which the action was bound to turn.

Part of Ziethen's corps, which formed the Prussian right, was flung back *en potence* along the line of the rivulet which joins the larger brook at St. Amand, so as to face South-West and protect St. Amand and Ligny against a flank attack. This face of the position, with the villages of Hameau St. Amand, Wagnelée and St. Amand la Haye, was entrusted to Steinmetz's division. St. Amand itself was held by 3 battalions of Jägow's, the other 6 of which were being in reserve; in Ligny were 4 battalions of Henckel, whose other 2 were on the slopes behind the village, Pirch II's division being in reserve near Bry and the mill of Bussy. The cavalry on being driven in from the front took post between Jägow and Pirch.

The importance which Blücher attached to his right may be judged from the fact that the entire IInd Corps, Pirch I's, was drawn up in support of Ziethen along the Namur-Nivelles road just west of Sombreffe. The centre was formed by Börcke's division of Thielmann, posted near Sombreffe with a battalion at Mont Potriaux, the rest of the IIIrd Corps being more to the left, with battalions in Tongrines, Tongrenelles, Boignée and Balâtre, and the cavalry under von Hobe covering the extreme left of the position.

Unfortunately for Blücher the slopes south of the Ligny brook were slightly higher than those on which his army was posted, so that it was very difficult to conceal his movements from the enemy, and his reserves were throughout exposed to a cannonade : to get cover he must have posted them so far back that they would have found it almost impossible to lend timely support to the fighting line along the brook. The ground certainly was most unfavourable from a tactical point of view, it provided practically no cover ; and the defects in the posting of the Prussian army did not escape the notice of Wellington, who about noon came over from Quatre Bras to consult with Blücher. In vain he urged his colleague to alter his dispositions ; Blücher would not hear of it, with the result that Wellington's curt comment to Hardinge, " If they fight here they will be damnably mauled," was proved only too true a prophecy before the day was out. Besides this, the position was too long for the numbers available to defend it, and being without any definite boundary to its right rear was liable to be turned from the direction of Frasnes.

About 2.30 p.m. the attack was begun. Vandamme assailed St. Amand, Gérard hurled Pecheux's division upon Ligny, Grouchy's cavalry supported by another of Gérard's divisions engaged the Prussian left and by demonstrations against Balâtre and Tongrines kept a large part of Thielmann's corps occupied. The struggle for the villages was long, desperate and even. Time after time the French were forced back only to return to the assault. At the fourth attack on Ligny, Pecheux, supported by a brigade of the remaining division of the IVth Corps, obtained possession of the portion of the village which lies on the upper or South bank of the stream. In vain Henckel's reserve battalions joined in the fight, the French pressed on and effected a lodgment on the farther bank, only

43

to be driven back across the stream when Jägow brought up the greater part of the Third Division. More and more reinforcements were thrown into the fight on both sides: Krafft of the IInd Corps replaced Henckel's broken battalions, Gérard hurled Vichery's remaining brigade at Lower Ligny and gradually gained ground. In despair Krafft appealed for reinforcements, but for the moment Blücher had none to send (*circa* 5 p.m.).

Meanwhile Vandamme had begun by ousting the three battalions of Jägow's division from St. Amand. Succoured by Steinmetz they returned to the charge, and Vandamme had to deploy Berthézéne's division on the left of Lefol's and to send Girard's of the IInd Corps, which had come up from Ransart to join in the attack, against the villages which lie to the North-West of St. Amand. These villages, La Haye, Hameau St. Amand and Wagnelée, Girard carried at the first rush; a success which filled Blücher with anxiety, for he attached the utmost importance to preventing the French from turning his right and so severing his communications with Wellington. He therefore hurled the last unengaged division of Ziethen's corps, that of Pirch II, directly against Girard, and prepared to turn his flank by sending against Wagnelée, Tippelskirch's division of the IInd Corps supported by Jürgass with Pirch I's cavalry.

Pirch II had some success. He shook Girard's hold on La Haye, and only by a prodigious effort did the French general rally his troops and recover the village, perishing himself just as the Prussians gave way. The flanking movement was less successful. Surprised in column of march before they could deploy, Tippelskirch's infantry were thrown back in disorder, and Jürgass was unable to effect anything in face of Domon and the light cavalry of Vandamme's corps.

Now it was (about 5 o'clock) that Blücher himself hurried to his right, rallied Pirch II, supported him with battalions from the IInd Corps, and sent him forward again against La Haye, at the same time relieving Steinmetz, whose efforts to recover St. Amand had resulted in the complete exhaustion of his division, and rallying Tippelskirch. These efforts were rewarded by the recapture of La Haye, from which the relics of Girard's division were again driven ; but at Hameau St. Amand they rallied and made a stand. More reinforcements were needed, and Blücher had to fetch up the last reserves of the IInd Corps, several battalions of which had become involved in the carnage in Ligny. The repeated calls on his reserve had reduced it to vanishing point, and to fill the position in front of Sombreffe, left vacant by Langen's division (of the IInd Corps) moving to the right to join in the struggle for St. Amand, part of Thielmann's corps had to move up from the left. It would certainly seem that the Prussian commander was overhasty in throwing in his reserves and in withdrawing battalions to the rear before their condition became absolutely desperate, unless, indeed, he had not the same confidence in his men's endurance that Wellington had in the staying powers of his British and Legionaries. Certainly the last Prussian reserves were utilised at a far earlier period in the battle of Ligny than was to be the case with the Anglo-Allied army at Waterloo two days later. Wellington no doubt posted his men better, and thereby exposed them less and demanded rather less from them; but Blücher was certainly rather precipitate in utilising his reserves. Nor has the Prussian general's use of his reserves escaped well-merited censure.[1] Situated as he was, offensive tactics were hardly suitable until Bülow or some portion of Wellington's army came to his succour. Yet instead of confining himself to the defensive and beating off the attacks of the French, Blücher had resolved to take the offensive with his right. Accordingly, just before 6 o'clock, Tippelskirch and Jürgass advanced again by Wagnelée against the French flank, and Pirch II supported by Brause and some of Krafft's battalions assailed St. Amand and the other villages. Girard's division, reduced to less than half its original strength, fell back from Hameau St. Amand. Lefol and Berthézéne were unable to maintain their hold on St. Amand itself, for the sudden appearance of strange columns in the direction of Mellet had caused a panic among their men.

It was the approach of this unknown quantity and the consequent retreat of Vandamme before the attacks of Brause and Pirch which compelled Napoleon to suspend the decisive blow he had been on the point of delivering. He had not failed to notice that Blücher had diverted every available bayonet to the Prussian right, and that the Prussian reserves were practically all engaged, and he was preparing to launch the Guard and Milhaud's cuirassiers against Blücher's weakened centre, when

[1] Cf. Siborne, p. 257.

the news from his left forced him to desist, and to send Duhesme with the Young Guard and three regiments of the Middle Guard to the help of Vandamme.

But the strangers were not, as had at first been imagined, Wellington's men coming to complete a victory over Ney by playing a decisive part in the contest at Ligny. It was the corps of d'Erlon whose unexpected appearance in that quarter had so disconcerted its comrades. The Ist Corps had been late starting from its bivouacs South of Gosselies, and its leading columns had not yet reached Frasnes when, about 4.15 p.m., Colonel Forbin-Janson handed to d'Erlon the Emperor's order, sent off at 3.30 p.m., directing him to move towards St. Amand. Had d'Erlon been as far forward as the Emperor supposed him to be, a move on St. Amand would have brought him up in rear of the Prussian right; as it was, his direct route to St. Amand involved his appearing in Vandamme's rear. But the misfortunes of the Ist Corps were not yet at an end. Forbin-Janson had failed to proceed to Ney's headquarters and to acquaint the Marshal with the change in d'Erlon's orders, and Ney only heard of the movement from one of d'Erlon's Staff officers without receiving any explanation of it from the Emperor. Accordingly he hastened to recall d'Erlon towards Quatre Bras; and his messenger overtaking d'Erlon about 6.30, caused the Ist Corps to retrace its steps, Napoleon making no effort to retain it within his sphere of operations.[1]

Thus the Ist Corps disappeared from the field of Ligny without taking any part in the action except on the extreme left; there Jacquinot's light cavalry engaged some Prussian cavalry who were threatening to outflank Girard's much-harassed division. The chief effect of d'Erlon's appearance was to delay by over an hour Napoleon's intended attack on the Prussian centre, and that delay was to prove a factor of the utmost importance. Meanwhile the movements and counter-movements of the Guard seem to have made Blücher believe the French were on the point of retiring, and that victory was in his grasp. Rallying his right therefore, which had given back before the Young Guard, he prepared for a final stroke. He gathered together the relics of Tippelskirch, whom Duhesme

[1] Even if, as Houssaye (p. 177) argues, it was too late for a wide turning movement on Bry, d'Erlon might have been directed towards Wagnelée in support of Vandamme's left.

had sent back behind Wagnelée, of Brause, whom Girard's much-enduring men had driven again out of Hameau St. Amand and La Haye, and of Pirch II, from whom Lefol and Berthézéne had recovered St. Amand: to these he added a few battalions of Langen's, the division of Steinmetz which had been out of action since 5 o'clock, and finally Stulpnägel from near Sombreffe. But even this last effort failed. Duhesme's battalions were too much for it, and at the same moment Napoleon launched the Old Guard at the Prussian centre. This stroke was a brilliant success. As the Guard advanced Gérard's men made a final and successful effort, driving the defenders of Ligny out of the shattered village and up the slopes in rear. In vain Langen and Krafft sought to rally their men: Milhaud's cuirassiers following close in the wake of the Guard were upon them. In vain Blücher hurled the Prussian cavalry at the advancing French: the infantry of the Guard beat off every charge of Röder's squadrons. Now was the time when a reserve would have been invaluable, but even Thielmann was too hotly engaged on the left to have a man to spare. Only the darkness and the exhaustion of the French troops on whom the brunt of the action had fallen, prevented Ligny from being a victory such as Napoleon needed to ensure the success of his plan of campaign. He had a considerable intact reserve in the shape of Lobau's corps, and with another hour of daylight much might have been done. As it was, the piercing of the Prussian centre ended the active part of the day's operations. The bulk of the defenders of Ligny got away through the darkness to Bry, where Pirch II and his division made a stand which enabled them to rally. Some other battalions halted nearer Sombreffe, into which village Stulpnägel's division threw itself. Farther to the Prussian right Jürgass covered the withdrawal of Ziethen and Pirch I towards Tilly, a movement conducted with remarkably little difficulty. On the other wing Thielmann's men held on unmolested to Tongrines and Mont Potriaux until 3 o'clock next morning. The French spent the night on the slopes to the north of Ligny and St. Amand, which had formed the position of the Prussian main body during the day. With the field of battle they found themselves also in possession of 21 guns which the Prussians had failed to carry off; but their victory lacked completeness, and the fact that the Prussians contrived to retire unmolested after so close and fierce an engagement is the best testimony to the impression, physical and moral, their stubborn defence, their repeated rallies, their constant efforts to recover the lost villages, had made on their victors.

It would be no exaggeration to say that it was in the twelve hours which followed the close of the battle of Ligny that the Waterloo campaign was decided. The French had lost some chances through delays ; but had they promptly followed up the success of Ligny as they had followed up that of Jena, the campaign would have probably been a triumphant success. But Napoleon let his prey slip through his grasp, and with the unmolested and unobserved retreat of the Prussians the best chance of a French victory slipped away. Badly though it had been mauled, the Prussian army was still " in being," and quite capable of playing its part in the further developments of the campaign. Directly the troops had been got into order again, Gneisenau gave directions for a further retreat, though not towards Liége and Namur, the bases on which it would have been natural for the beaten Prussians to retire. The direction given was Northward towards Wavre,[1] so that they might not lose touch with Wellington's army, which the Prussian retreat would force to withdraw from its position at Quatre Bras, a position it had been fortunate enough to maintain against all Ney's attacks throughout the 16th, but which became dangerously exposed by Blücher's retreat from Ligny. Only the leading incidents of the battle of Quatre Bras need mention here. Ney's orders from the Emperor [2] contemplated the Marshal remaining more or less inactive about Quatre Bras till Napoleon, having settled with the Prussians opposing Grouchy and the right, should transfer himself with his reserve to the left and begin the advance on Brussels. Partly therefore, lest a premature advance on his part should dislocate Napoleon's plans, and partly because the brave show made by Perponcher with his Nassauers and Dutch-Belgians imposed upon him, Ney did not attack the force in front of him till nearly 2 p.m. The French had then just driven Perponcher's men back into the wood of Bossu, and were on the point of seizing Quatre Bras when the arrival of Picton with the British brigades of Kempt and Pack, and the Hanoverians of Best saved the situation (2.40 p.m.). Next, part of the

---

[1] The part Gneisenau played on the morning of the 18th must not be allowed to diminish the credit due to him for this courageous and important resolve.

[2] Cf. Siborne, pp. 136–138.

Brunswick corps arrived and took up their ground between
Picton's right, East of the Charleroi-Nivelles road, and the wood
of Bossu. Seeing the French infantry advancing in column,
Wellington met them in the old Peninsula style with an advance
of Picton's division in line, with the result that the French
columns were driven back in much confusion. However, the
French cavalry now advanced to the attack, and though their
charge failed to shake the Peninsula veterans of Picton's division,
it broke through the raw Brunswick levies, who fled headlong to
the rear, cavalry and infantry involved in the same confusion.
In the effort to rally his men Duke Frederick William was
mortally wounded, and only the stubborn defence of Picton's
squares repelled the French attack. It was renewed almost at
once by Kellermann, who had just arrived with a division of
cuirassiers. Again the British infantry beat off the charges; and
though one of Best's Hanoverian *Landwehr* battalions was
caught by a body of lancers and ridden down before it could
form square, the rest of the brigade stood their ground. About
five o'clock Alten's division came up to the assistance of Picton,
the Brunswickers rallied on the arrival of two belated battalions
of their corps, and after another onset by the French cavalry
had been beaten back, Kielmansegge's Hanoverians of Alten's
division behaving no less steadily than did Picton's veterans, the
British Guards came up and secured Wellington's right by
recovering the wood of Bossu, from which the Dutch-Belgians
had been driven. This enabled Wellington to order a general
advance before which Ney gave way, retiring to the heights in
front of Frasnes where d'Erlon joined him about 9 o'clock.

The nature of the struggle at Quatre Bras may be best understood from the respective losses of the units engaged on the
Allied side. The British had some 2300 casualties out of rather
over 11,000 engaged, Picton's two brigades losing between them
30 per cent. of their numbers. The Brunswick corps also lost
heavily, its 800 casualties representing about a seventh of its
strength, and the Hanoverians with under 400 casualties among
the 5700 present got off comparatively lightly. In Perponcher's
division there were some 1000 killed, wounded and missing out of
7500, but the comparatively high proportion of the latter dimin-
ishes the merits of their performance. The French, whose
numbers at the end of the fight were considerably inferior to
those opposed to them, confessed to over 4000 casualties among

21,000 engaged: at the same time it should be remembered that the Allied force did not outnumber Ney's until Alten arrived, and that even then about a third of Wellington's 26,000 consisted of Dutch-Belgians on whom but little reliance could be placed. Foy's admission that "conceal it as we may, Quatre Bras was a defeat for us," is no more than the truth. Ney's attacks had been repulsed with loss, and as the arrival during the night of the greater part of the British cavalry supplied the deficiency in that arm which had so hampered Wellington during the day, there is no reason to suppose that if the Marshal had done what some of his critics would have had him do and renewed his attack early on the 17th, he would have been much more fortunate than on the 16th. But for the delay in attacking on the 17th it is hardly Ney who should be held responsible.

Knowing what force he had before him, and anxious to do nothing which should in any way compromise the Emperor's movements, Ney forbore from any movement on his own initiative, waiting for orders. Not till midday did Napoleon send off a messenger to Ney, bidding him attack the English at once and adding that he was himself on his way to Quatre Bras to assist him. But by this time even the English cavalry who formed the rearguard were quitting the position.

Wellington had been left without any news from his Prussian allies, as the only messenger Gneisenau sent him was intercepted by the French. Hence the delay of the Allied forces in their somewhat exposed position. However, the inaction of Napoleon averted the peril thus risked. The Emperor's conduct on the morning of June 17th has been criticised and explained times without number. His neglect to move at once to Quatre Bras directly he received, at 7.30 a.m., Ney's account of the previous day's operations was an error far less serious than the failure to keep touch with the Prussians, or to discover the true direction of their retreat. Very early on the 17th Wellington had patrols out, and was thoroughly on the alert. From one of these patrols, which had pushed as far as Tilly and communicated with Ziethen's rearguard, he heard about 7.30 that the Prussians were retiring on Wavre, so that directly the French showed signs of being about to attack he could have set his troops in motion rearward. As it was, the infantry moved off about 10 a.m. and reached the position of Mont St. Jean, where Wellington had decided to make his stand if only one corps of

LIGNY   June 16th 1815

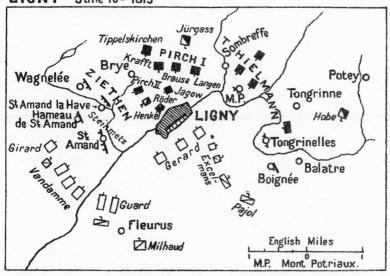

PRUSSIAN GAINS WEST OF THE ELBE IN 1815

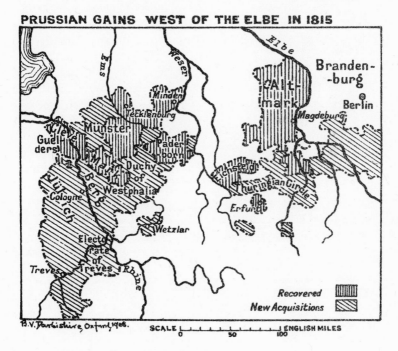

the Prussian army would join him, without being in the least pressed. Similarly Lord Uxbridge and the cavalry who covered the retreat, though closely pursued by Napoleon, had little difficulty in performing their task without much loss, a sharp skirmish at Genappe, in which the French lancers repulsed the 7th Hussars but were routed by the much heavier Life Guards, being the only important incident of the retreat.

Thus the evening of the 17th found Wellington with the bulk of his forces, 67,600 men with 150 guns,[1] along the ridge which runs from the château of Hougoumont past the farm of La Haye Sainte towards Ohain; one Anglo-Hanoverian division[2] and some 10,000 Dutch-Belgians being posted at Hal to protect the Duke's communications with the sea and, in case of need, assist to cover a retreat to the North-Westward. Napoleon with the Guard and the cavalry of Milhaud, Kellermann, Domon and Subervie, and the corps of d'Erlon, Reille and Lobau, in all some 74,000 men with 240 guns, lay opposite to him. At the same time Grouchy with the 33,000 men entrusted to him for the purpose of pursuing the Prussians and completing their defeat[3] had not got beyond Gembloux. This is not the place for an adequate discussion of Grouchy's proceedings and of his share of the responsibility for the results of the campaign. That he showed a lack of energy and initiative is not to be denied, even by those who regard the master rather than the subordinate as mainly to blame for the disaster which befell the French. Grouchy's orders certainly contemplated a pursuit of the Prussians away from the English, though they admitted the possibility that the Allies might seek to reunite to cover Brussels. There was nothing in his instructions about rejoining the Emperor to fight a battle against Wellington; and even the orders sent off by Napoleon at 10 a.m. on the 18th, which speak of co-ordinating the movements of the detached force with those of the main body, direct the Marshal to continue his move on Wavre. Such information as Napoleon had at 11 p.m. on the 17th coincided with his own belief, a belief to which perhaps the wish was father, that the Prussians were retiring towards the Meuse. Pajol

---

[1] Of these 24,000 were British, 15,000 being infantry, 6000 cavalry and 3000 artillery; the King's German Legion had 2000 cavalry, 500 gunners and 3300 infantry: of Hanoverians there were about 11,000, 1000 being cavalry and artillery, the Brunswick contingent was a little under 6000, the Nassauers of Kruse and Prince Bernhard were somewhat stronger, and the rest, nearly 14,000, were Dutch-Belgians.

[2] Colville's.   [3] Cf. Houssaye, p. 225.

had sent in word that his light cavalry had found guns, waggons and stragglers on the road to Namur, and the French vedettes near Tilly and Gentinnes had failed to notice or to announce the retreat of the Prussians from those villages or the direction which it had taken. The true causes of Grouchy's failure to prevent the Prussians from coming to the aid of their allies at Waterloo were firstly, Napoleon's assumption, warranted perhaps by the general principles of strategy but partially based on a false estimate of the success he had gained on the previous day,[1] that Namur or Maastricht would prove to be the point on which the beaten Prussians had fallen back, and secondly, the Emperor's extraordinary inactivity on the morning of the 17th. The touch which was then lost with Blücher's retreating forces, the hours that were then wasted, contributed far more to bring about the defeat of Waterloo than Grouchy's resolve to continue his march from Sart a Walhain to Wavre instead of striking to his left across the Dyle towards Planchenoit and the sound of the guns. And even had Grouchy resolved to depart from his orders and make a move for which he had no authority, it is still most unlikely that any appreciable fraction of his corps could have arrived on the battlefield in time. The physical difficulties which retarded Bülow and Ziethen would have been no less potent to delay the French. The passage of the Dyle would have been no simple or rapid operation when 33,000 men with 116 guns had only a wooden bridge at Moustier and a stone bridge at Ottignies by which to cross. In short, as Mr. Hereford George has remarked in his just and trenchant criticism of Judge O'Connor Morris' *Campaign of 1815*,[2] " it is only upon the map, not on the real ground, that Grouchy could have saved Napoleon from defeat."

Meanwhile the Prussian army had managed to get away unhindered and almost unobserved from the dangerous position in which the timely advent of night had found it on June 16th. Under cover of the friendly darkness the Prussians had rallied in a manner which speaks volumes for their discipline and for the spirit by which they were animated. Despite the fact that their losses in killed, wounded and prisoners amounted to nearly 12,000,[3] and that many members of the contingents drawn from the Rhenish and Westphalian provinces lately annexed to Prussia had hastened to disassociate themselves from a cause

[1] Cf. Houssaye, p. 315.   [2] Cf. *E.H.R. 1900*, p. 816.   [3] Houssaye, p. 184.

for which they had no zeal by a headlong flight towards Aix-la-Chapelle and Liége, the bulk of the army rallied directly the action ceased. There seems to have been great disorder in the centre and considerable confusion on the left, but the troops of Ziethen and Pirch I withdrew in very fair order[1] and a rear-guard of the Ist Corps held Bry till daybreak, Sombreffe being in like manner occupied by a portion of Thielmann's corps, the bulk of which remained almost in their battle positions till 3 a.m. on the 17th, when they withdrew to Gembloux.

For the decision to retire by Tilly and Mont St. Guibert on Wavre, Gneisenau was responsible. Blücher had been unhorsed and badly injured in the closing stages of the battle, and did not resume control of the army's operations until 11 a.m. on the 18th. In thus retiring Northward Gneisenau did not absolutely sacrifice his communications. If he abandoned the lines of retreat by Namur and Liége, those by Tirlemont or Louvain on Maastricht or Wesel were still open to him, and his action on the 18th makes it clear that he had by no means subordinated everything to the chance of joining Wellington.

The retreat was effected with very little difficulty. Ziethen moving from Tilly by Mont St. Guibert established his troops on the left bank of the Dyle soon after midday. Pirch I from Gentinnes after halting at Mont St. Guibert to cover Ziethen's passage of that defile, followed through it in his turn and bivouacked between St. Anne and Aisemont on the right bank of the river. Thielmann after remaining stationary at Gembloux from 6 a.m. to 2 p.m., a piece of most culpable imprudence, which only escaped the severest punishment through Napoleon's equally extraordinary laxity in pursuing the defeated Prussians, arrived at Wavre late in the evening. Most of his corps crossed the Dyle and encamped at La Bavette, but his rearguard remained on the right bank. Finally, Bülow, whose troops had advanced no farther than Baudeset on the evening of the 16th, where his orders found him about 9.30 a.m. next day, arrived at Dion le Mont after a somewhat leisurely march by Walhain and Corroy. Detachments under Colonels Lebedur and Sohr were left to cover the main army and to keep a lookout for the advance of the French, and patrols were thrust out on the left bank of the Dyle to collect intelligence of Wellington's army and their opponents.

[1] Houssaye, p. 181.

It was not long after his arrival at Wavre that Blücher received Wellington's message, sent off at 9.30 a.m., in which the Duke announced that if he could be secure of the assistance of, at any rate, one Prussian corps he would give battle in front of Waterloo on the following morning. This assurance Blücher was in a position to send him ; for, very fortunately, the Prussian reserve ammunition park had arrived safely at Wavre in the course of the afternoon, and the corps of Pirch and Ziethen were thus able to replenish their exhausted pouches and limbers, and so to put themselves in a fit condition for another action.

The facility with which the retreat of the Prussians had been accomplished had been partly due to the negligence of the French outposts near Tilly and Gentinnes; partly to the fact that Pajol's cavalry, thrust out to their right to seek for the retreating enemy, had found enough traces of fugitives to make them believe the line chosen was that towards Namur and Liége ; partly to Berton's cavalry failing to send full information back to headquarters, when, pushing out to Gembloux about 9 a.m. they found that village still occupied in force by Thielmann, and again neglecting to observe the Prussians closely when they did retire. Nightfall found Grouchy at Gembloux under the impression that though a portion of the Prussians might be making for Wavre with the idea of joining Wellington, part were certainly retiring Eastward to Namur while the bulk of their army was on its way to Liége through Perwez.

It was not, however, by this impression that his proceedings on the next morning were governed. His letter to Napoleon, written at 6 a.m., regards the Prussians as concentrating at Wavre in order to fall back on Brussels ; but he omitted to consider that they might as easily move to their flank towards Ohain as to their rear towards Brussels. The only way to make certain of their movements was to close with them as early as possible, and Grouchy's delay on the morning of the 18th was a most serious error for which he cannot evade the responsibility. Not till after 7 a.m. did Vandamme's corps set out, and Gérard was two hours later in starting. Thus Grouchy had not got beyond Walhain when, a little before midday, the distant sound of cannon became audible. A sharp discussion between Grouchy and Gérard resulted in the Marshal deciding to continue his move on Wavre and rejecting his lieutenant's appeal to him to march towards the sound of the guns. He had just heard from his cavalry that they had fallen in with the Prussian rearguard near Wavre, and before he left Walhain he received the despatch sent off by Napoleon at 10 o'clock bidding him move on Wavre.

Between 9 and 10 a.m. (June 18th) Excelmans' cavalry had reached the wood of La Huzelle and sighted Prussian troops on the heights between them and Wavre. However, Excelmans made no effort to engage, but withdrew his main body to Corbais. This allowed Ledebur and the detachment left at Mont St. Guibert, whose retreat was in danger of being cut off, to force their way through the French outposts and take up a position at the Southern end of the defile made by the road from Gembloux to Wavre in passing the wood of La Huzelle. To force this defile the French had to wait for Vandamme's infantry. These did not appear till after 3 p.m., and it was already near 4 o'clock when the French having pushed through the wood, from which Ledebur had withdrawn, prepared to attack Wavre. By this time the rearguard of the IInd Corps had already crossed the Dyle by the bridge of Bierge, which they destroyed behind them. Indeed, the whole Prussian army was in motion towards Waterloo, a few detachments excepted. The appearance of the French forced Thielmann to retrace his steps, and in obedience to Blücher's orders the IIIrd Corps took up a position on the left bank of the Dyle to dispute the passage of the river and thereby cover the movement of the rest of the army towards Waterloo from any interruption—a task which it performed with complete success despite the superior numbers Grouchy was able to bring against it.

The movement which it was Thielmann's task to cover was that to which Blücher had pledged himself on the previous evening, and on which Wellington was relying, when, with an army somewhat inferior in numbers and certainly very inferior in average quality, he faced Napoleon at Waterloo. It cannot be said that the move was executed with as much promptitude or skilful management as is usually represented. As it was all-important that the Prussian reinforcements should be at Wellington's disposal as early in the day as possible, one would naturally have expected that the corps detailed to lead the way would have been one of the two which had bivouacked on the nearer side of the Dyle. But instead of choosing Thielmann, who at La Bavette was only six miles from St. Lambert, the point on which Bülow was in the first instance directed, or

Ziethen, who at Bierge was about half a mile nearer, the Prussian commander—or more probably his Chief of Staff, Gneisenau—selected Bülow's corps, which not only had nearly nine miles to cover, but had to pass through Wavre on the way, in doing which it was considerably delayed by a fire in the main street. Bülow's corps had, of course, not been engaged on the 16th, and it was natural to select it rather than the shaken corps of Ziethen and Pirch; but Thielmann had not suffered at all heavily at Ligny, and it is difficult to understand why his corps should not have headed the movement. From La Bavette to Ohain is barely seven miles, and if Thielmann had set out at 8 o'clock his corps ought to have been at Ohain well before midday. Bülow and Pirch could have covered the move of Thielmann and Ziethen quite as effectively as the Ist and IIIrd Corps covered the advance of the IInd and IVth; while if Pirch, who was ordered to follow Bülow, had only been allowed to precede him, the IInd Corps, having more than two miles less to cover, might have been at St. Lambert soon after 10 o'clock. As things were managed, Bülow's vanguard was at St. Lambert about 11; but the bulk of the corps was much later, and the rearguard did not arrive there till nearly 3 p.m. Pirch's men were under arms from 7 a.m. until midday, when at last they left their bivouacs at Aisemont; at 2 o'clock half the corps had not yet crossed the Dyle. Similarly, Ziethen's men only began their march towards Ohain about midday; and the fact that the arrangements which directed Ziethen on Smohain and Pirch on St. Lambert involved additional delay through these corps crossing each other's path, has been justly but severely criticised by Clausewitz.[1] More than this, Bülow's advance-guard halted directly it had crossed the defile of the Lasne, and remained inactive in the Wood of Paris for some hours. And yet there are those who represent the late arrival of the Prussians at Waterloo as due merely to the bad roads over which they had to move. Undoubtedly the roads were bad, and the passage of the defile of the Lasne was a matter of great difficulty, especially for the guns, and was partly responsible for the delay, but the physical difficulties do not adequately explain the fact that it was after 4 o'clock before a shot was fired by any of the Prussian army, when at daybreak the most distant portion of it, Bülow's corps at Dion le Mont, was less than thirteen miles from Mont St. Jean.

[1] *Der Feldzug von 1815*, p. 110.

Gneisenau's notorious distrust of Wellington must be taken into account in dealing with the Prussian movements on June 18th. He seems to have feared that the British general would retire without fighting, and thereby expose to the joint attacks of Napoleon and Grouchy the Prussian detachments which were on their way towards Waterloo. Moreover, injured and shaken as Blücher was, it seems only reasonable to ascribe to Gneisenau more responsibility for the arrangements of the Prussian movement than would otherwise have been the case. The intervention of the Prussians was, of course, the decisive factor in the day's fighting; but it was in no sense an accident due merely to Grouchy's negligence: their co-operation was an essential feature in the scheme on which the battle was fought; it was as much part of Wellington's calculations as were the movements of his own divisions; the Prussians were behind their time and so endangered his left, which was his weak spot.[1] Indeed it seems certain that the Duke looked for the arrival of the Prussians at quite an early hour; that he must have almost expected the corps for which he had asked to be up in its place on the left of his line before the French attack began. It is not too much to say that if Wellington had not received a definite promise of assistance he would never have given battle at Waterloo. The delay, of course, added to the dramatic effect of the intervention. Wellington's coolness, steadfastness and tactical skill, and the courage and endurance of his troops had been taxed to a very high degree before at last the pressure of Bülow upon the French right and the arrival of Ziethen at Ohain afforded the long-desired succour; but had the Prussian Staff work in managing their movement been better done, or had Gneisenau had a little more of that confidence in his colleague which induced Wellington to risk being defeated by Napoleon before his tardy allies appeared, the resisting powers of the Allied army would never have been exposed to so great a strain.

Numerous as are the criticisms which have been urged against the strategy of Wellington in the Waterloo campaign, little fault has been found with his tactics in the great contest which raged between Hougoumont and Papelotte on that momentous Sunday from before midday till after 8 o'clock. The failure to adequately support Major Baring and the 2nd Light Battalion of the German Legion, who maintained so splendid a

[1] Cf. Sir Harry Smith's *Memoirs*, p. 276.

defence of La Haye Sainte till after 6 o'clock, is the only serious blot in the Duke's management of the battle. His admirable dispositions enabled him to utilise to the full the advantages of the ground to cover his men from the French cannonade, his employment of his reserves was judicious and timely. He was nobly seconded by his subordinates and by the troops under his command. It may perhaps not be out of place to say something of the individual parts played in the battle by the various German contingents. First and foremost among them the King's German Legion deserves mention. Waterloo is perhaps the brightest page in its history. The five cavalry regiments charged again and again, and the two infantry brigades behaved with a steadiness none could surpass. Of these two Ompteda's brigade was posted on the right of the high road from Charleroi to Nivelles, having Kielmansegge's Hanoverians on their right and Picton's division on their left on the other side of the road. It was to this brigade that Baring's battalion belonged, as did also the two unfortunate battalions, the 5th and 8th Line, which having at separate times been rashly deployed by the express orders of the Prince of Orange to drive off the French skirmishers, were caught by the French cavalry and practically destroyed.[1] The other brigade, Duplat's, which belonged to Clinton's division, was in reserve behind the right wing at the beginning of the action, but was moved up into the front line about 5 o'clock during the attacks of the French cavalry, and took post to the East of Hougoumont. Portions of it also shared in the defence of Hougoumont. Of the four Hanoverian brigades present in the action, those of Vincke and Best were posted on the extreme left of the line, beyond Picton's British brigades, that of Kielmansegge was in the right centre between Ompteda and Colin Halkett's British brigade, that of William Halkett was in reserve till nearly 6 o'clock, when it moved forward on the right, two battalions supporting Duplat, the other two taking post on the Nivelles road to prevent any turning movement by Piré's light cavalry. Of these brigades that of Kielmansegge unquestionably underwent the severest ordeal; its heavy losses, over 33 per cent. of its strength, testify to the strain put upon it. The solitary Hanoverian cavalry regiment present, the Cumberland Hussars, hardly came out of the battle as creditably as did its comrades of the infantry. On being

---

[1] Cf. Siborne, pp. 460 and 480.

brought forward by Lord Uxbridge to support the infantry of the centre, the entire corps abandoned the not very exposed position in which the Earl had placed them, and, disregarding alike his orders and expostulations, went solidly to the rear to spread panic and false rumours of defeat through Brussels.

The Brunswickers behaved upon the whole in a most creditable fashion: one battalion took part in the great struggle for Hougoumont, and the greater part of the division was employed on the right to fill the gap caused by Byng's Guards reinforcing the defenders of Hougoumont, in which position they resisted with great steadiness the charges of the French cavalry. About 7.30, at the time of the last great French attack, Wellington moved five battalions of the Brunswickers more to the centre, placing them in the front line between Kruse's Nassauers and Colin Halkett. On coming under a very heavy fire from the advancing French the young Brunswick battalions gave way and fell back in disorder, in which the brigades of Kruse, Kielmansegge and Ompteda became involved. This was the most critical moment in the battle, for the Guard was then ascending the slopes just to the East of Hougoumont, and d'Erlon's men were making their final effort. By great efforts Wellington rallied the Brunswickers, who re-formed and checked the French just in time; then, when Vivian brought up his Hussars in their support, they moved forward again, the Germans of Kielmansegge and Ompteda also rallying and advancing, so that the Third Division once again resumed its ground, sending the French back down the hill. Kruse's brigade, whose loyalty to the Allied cause was by no means above suspicion, since the battalions had served in Spain under the French colours, came out of the ordeal well. When the Brunswickers gave way Kruse's men did the same, and were only prevented from breaking by the 10th Hussars, who blocked their way to the rear; but the Nassauers rallied like the rest of the right centre. Prince Bernhard's brigade defended Papelotte with great steadiness, and the detachments of the 2nd Nassau in Hougoumont took their full share in the defence of the post. As to the Dutch-Belgians, Bylandt's brigade had some excuse for breaking when d'Erlon charged, as they had been much exposed to the French artillery; but Chassé's division could plead no such extenuation for the high percentage of

44

"missing" among their casualties.[1] Trip's cavalry declined to face the French, and the small losses suffered by Ghigny and van Merlen show how insignificant was their part in the fight.

The services of the Prussians can hardly be explained without some narrative of the leading features of the action. It may be divided into six stages. The first of these is from the opening of the cannonade between 11.30 and 12 to the advance of d' Erlon just before 2 p.m. Of this stage Reille's attack on Hougoumont and the cannonade which paved the way for d'Erlon's assaults were the principal features. The second stage is that of the great attack of d'Erlon's corps on the Allied left centre. This was checked by Picton's infantry and converted into a disastrous repulse by the charge of the Household and "Union" cavalry brigades. Meanwhile most of Reille's corps had become absorbed in the desperate struggle for Hougoumont. The third stage, beginning about 3 o'clock and lasting till nearly 6, is that of the repeated attacks of the French cavalry against the British and German squares to the West of the high road. These charges were varied by a heavy cannonade, and by the attacks of the numerous skirmishers whom the French thrust forward. However, neither artillery nor cavalry nor skirmishers succeeded in breaking a single square, for the 8th Line Battalion of the German Legion, which was caught in open order by French cavalry and cut to pieces, had been foolishly deployed by the Prince of Orange. During this period d'Erlon more than once renewed his attacks on the British and Hanoverians to the East of the high road, but with no better success than before, while the struggles for Hougoumont and La Haye Sainte continued to rage with unabated fury. However, all Reille's attacks were repulsed, and Baring maintained his hold on La Haye Sainte. The fourth stage was marked by the advance of Bachelu's division of Reille's corps with a brigade of Foy's of the same corps between Hougoumont and the high road. It seems to have been then, about 6 o'clock, that Wellington brought up the brigades of Duplat and Adam to aid his hard-pressed right, and apparently it was largely by them that Bachelu and Foy were repulsed.[2] However, at this

[1] The claim of Dittmer's brigade to have repulsed the Imperial Guard is one which, despite M. Houssaye's support, I cannot admit to be borne out by the evidence; cf. *Quarterly Review*, June 1900, for a criticism of M. Houssaye's account.

[2] Cf. *Waterloo Letters*, accounts of Adam's brigade.

moment success finally rewarded the assaults of the French on La Haye Sainte, and the importance of the capture of the post was at once seen from the vigour and success with which the French skirmishers pressed forward against Alten's division in the right centre and against Lambert and Kempt to the East of the road. To drive off the skirmishers, the Prince of Orange ordered Ompteda to deploy the 5th Line Battalion of the Legion into line ; Ompteda, obeying against his better judgment, for he knew that French cavalry were close at hand, led the battalion forward only to have his forebodings verified : a regiment of cuirassiers charged in upon its right flank and cut the unfortunate battalion to pieces, Ompteda himself being among those who perished. However, though La Haye Sainte was lost Hougoumont was still untaken, and the steadfast squares of infantry, reduced though some were to mere handfuls, kept their ground unflinchingly. A fresh effort was needed if the French were to win. Their cavalry had spent themselves in their repeated charges, all the attacks of d'Erlon and Reille had been repulsed. But there remained the Guard, and the fifth stage of the great battle came when, about 7.30, this last reserve was thrown into the scale.[1] As the Guard advanced the persevering infantry of d'Erlon came on again—Allix and Marcognet on the East of the high road, Donzelot to the West of it pushing forward against Alten's shattered division. This Wellington had just reinforced with five battalions of Brunswickers from the right. It was at this moment that the Brunswickers on coming under the heavy fire of Donzelot's infantry were seized by the temporary panic

---

[1] According to M. Houssaye only five battalions of the Guard took part in this attack, though it seems most doubtful whether, as he alleges (p. 369), the 4th Chasseurs had lost so heavily at Ligny as to have been reduced to one battalion (cf. Professor Oman's article in *E.H.R. 1904*, p. 689), and one may fairly put the force engaged in this attack at six battalions at least. All eight battalions of the Young Guard and two of the Old had been diverted to Planchenoit : one was at Caillou guarding the military chest, two halted at Rossomme as a reserve, while four were not sent forward to the attack, but held in reserve to be pushed forward " if all went well "—Houssaye, p. 402. If this was actually the case, it is difficult to understand what the Emperor can have expected to achieve by sending only 3000 men against a position from which nearly double that number (*i.e.* Foy and Bachelu) had just been repulsed. If the Guard were to be put in at all, every available battalion should surely have been utilised. It is, of course, possible that the old version of the attack of the Guard in two columns is after all not so inaccurate as has been represented, and that two or three of these apparently unemployed battalions did actually move forward in support of their comrades only to be caught in flank and destroyed by the 52nd.

which threatened to produce a disaster;[1] but they rallied, and aided by the rest of the division recovered the position they had so nearly lost. To the East of the road Pack brought his battalions back into the front line on the left of Kempt and Lambert,[2] and between them they sent Allix and Marcognet back in disorder down the slopes. It was at this moment— 7.45 p.m.—that the cry went up from the French ranks, "The Guard recoils"; for, confronted by the brigades of Maitland and Colin Halkett, caught in flank by Colborne, who wheeled the 52nd up into line, a masterly stroke in which he was copied by the rest of Adam's brigade, and with Duplat's Legionaries and William Halkett's Hanoverians pressing forward more to the right, the forlorn hope of the French gave way and fell back in disorder. And as Adam's men with the light cavalry of Vivian and Vandeleur pressed forward on the heels of the defeated Guard, the battle passed into its sixth and final stage, that of the counter-attack.

Long before this, of course, the approach of the Prussians had begun to make itself felt.[3] Indeed, even before d'Erlon's first and most formidable attack, while the cannonade was still paving the way for that effort, Napoleon's attention had been called to the presence of troops far out on his right flank in the direction of St. Lambert. It was at first supposed that these might be Grouchy's men, but the capture of a prisoner belonging to the Silesian Hussars proved them to be Bülow's vanguard. However, they did not advance, and Napoleon contented himself with pushing out the cavalry of Domon and Subervie to observe their movements, at the same time instructing Lobau to support this cavalry screen. But for this it is possible that the VIth Corps would have been used to renew the attack on the left and left centre which d'Erlon had made with such little success. It is not to be denied that this second attack, which d'Erlon made about 3 or 3.30 p.m.[4] with his own men only, would have had far more chance of success if the 8000

---

[1] v.s. p. 689; cf. Siborne, pp. 515-517.

[2] After the repulse of d'Erlon's first attack, when Lambert's 2000 fresh bayonets arrived, Pack's brigade had been withdrawn to the second line ; cf. *Waterloo Letters*.

[3] Unquestionably the best summary of the questions as to the Prussian co-operation at Waterloo is the chapter on the subject in Dr. J. H. Rose's *Napoleonic Studies*, which was published after the first draft of this chapter was written, but which I have consulted when revising my account of the campaign.

[4] Cf. *Waterloo Letters*, pp. 354 and 404.

bayonets of the VIth Corps had at the same time pushed forward by Papelotte and turned the left flank of the Allied line. The Prussians remained inactive, but the menace of their presence at Chapelle St. Lambert was enough to "contain" Lobau, and d'Erlon's attack failed completely, being beaten back by the British infantry without much difficulty or the intervention of the cavalry. This was the first point at which the Prussians in the least influenced the battle. It is also possible that their presence at St. Lambert may have induced Napoleon to support instead of suspending the cavalry charges which Ney began somewhat prematurely about 4 p.m.[1]

Blücher, who had left Wavre about 11 o'clock, seems to have caught up the bulk of Bülow's corps about two hours later. It was then still on the Eastern side of the miry valley of the Lasne, the two battalions and the cavalry regiment which formed the advance-guard having alone crossed and taken position in the Wood of Paris.[2] However, far from at once pushing forward to Wellington's assistance, it was not till he learnt from his scouts that there was no prospect of any French troops interfering with his passage of the defile that Blücher set his men in motion towards Planchenoit. By that time it was nearly 2 o'clock.[3] Such were the difficulties of the passage, particularly for the artillery, that the two miles between Chapelle St. Lambert and the Wood of Paris took fully two hours to cover, and only by the greatest exertions were the guns brought across the stream. Thus it was not till half-past four that Bülow's two leading divisions at last debouched from the Wood of Paris and advanced along the road to Planchenoit, driving before them Domon and Subervie. To meet them Napoleon moved Lobau's corps to the right, and the 8000 infantry of the divisions of Jannin and Simmer advanced against the oncoming Prussians and drove them, superior in numbers though they were, back upon the Wood of Paris. But Blücher had reserves at hand and about 5.30 p.m. the two remaining divisions of Bülow advanced from the Wood of Paris and joined in. Lobau had to recoil towards Planchenoit, against which Blücher thrust forward Hiller's division with Ryssel and the cavalry of the corps under Prince Augustus William of

[1] Cf. Houssaye's note, p. 357.
[2] It was these troops whom Napoleon first perceived about 1 or 1.15.
[3] Houssaye, p. 366.

Prussia in support, while with Losthin and Hacke he assailed Lobau in front. Only one brigade of the VIth Corps could be spared for the defence of Planchenoit, and outnumbered and assailed in front and flank, it was ousted from the village after a severe struggle (6 p.m.). The other three brigades, posted to the North of the Planchenoit-St. Lambert road, kept the Prussians at bay, but the capture of the village at once threatened Lobau's flank and the line of retreat of the whole French army. The recovery of Planchenoit was therefore imperative, and Napoleon directed Duhesme thither with the eight battalions of the Young Guard. Attacking with great dash they thrust Hiller's division out of Planchenoit. However, the Prussians were at once reinforced and returned to the attack, and Duhesme's men, though fighting most obstinately, had to give way before the superior numbers of their assailants.

It was then about 7 o'clock. Though sorely tried and much reduced in numbers Wellington's line was still unbroken, and Napoleon, having used up all the rest of his army in his fruitless efforts to drive the Allies from their positions, found himself forced to play his last card and send forward the veterans of the Old and Middle Guard to see if they would succeed where their comrades of the Line had failed. But at the moment that he was preparing to launch this magnificent reserve against Wellington's line, the pressure of the Prussians on his right compelled him to detach two battalions to Planchenoit which Bülow's renewed assault had just succeeded in wresting from Duhesme.

The intervention of the Old Guard, however, was more than Bülow's men could stand. They gave way before the veterans, who, pushing forward, retook the village. Encouraged by their assistance the troops of Duhesme and Lobau rallied, and once more Bülow was thrust back all along the line. However, the corps of Pirch I was now beginning to arrive in Bülow's rear, and behind the Allied left Ziethen was at last putting in a belated appearance. His advance-guard, indeed, consisting of three regiments of cavalry and four battalions of infantry, had arrived at Ohain over an hour before, but harassed by conflicting orders,[1] had not pushed on until sent forward by Ziethen himself, a delay which, seeing how valuable every man was to Wellington at that moment—he had even called up Chassé's Dutch-Belgians from Braine l'Alleud—might have

[1] Rose, *Napoleonic Studies*, p. 297 ; but cf. Houssaye, p. 387.

proved most disastrous. However, the fact that Ziethen was at hand allowed Wellington to withdraw from his extreme left the light cavalry of Vandeleur and Vivian and part of Vincke's Hanoverians, thus stiffening his shattered right centre at a most critical juncture.[1]

The final attack of the Guard, if incomparably the most dramatic moment in the battle of Waterloo, was hardly the decisive point. Once Bülow had begun to seriously menace the French retreat, and once Ziethen had come within reach, the French had lost any real chance of victory. It is possible that if all the Old Guard had been put in when Bachelu and Foy advanced on the West of the high road just after 6 p.m., about which time Duhesme was driving Bülow from Planchenoit, Napoleon might have utilised the chance given him by the tardiness of the Prussians, and broken the English line before their allies could arrive. At 7 o'clock it would probably have been wiser to use the Guard to cover a retreat.[2] The Guard, whatever the number of battalions that took part in the attack, could hardly have hoped to succeed. Maitland, Adam, and Colin Halkett between them must have had 3000 bayonets remaining, not to mention Duplat's Legionaries and William Halkett's *Landwehr*. But at the time (7.30–8 p.m.) that Napoleon put into the fray his last reserves, Ziethen's columns were debouching by Smohain and Papelotte against Durutte on d'Erlon's extreme flank, and his men had got into touch with the flanking parties Bülow had thrown out towards Frischermont. Simultaneously Bülow moved forward again, with Pirch's leading brigades to help him. Tippelskirch led the attack on Planchenoit supported by Hiller and Ryssel : Bülow's right wing, connected with his left by the cavalry of the IInd and IVth Corps, moved forward against Lobau. Thus the advance of the Guard coincided with the final and most formidable attack of the Prussians on the forces covering the right flank of the French array. Even had the veterans broken Wellington's line the success could hardly have been followed up with three Prussian corps at last at hand. However, despite the vigour of the Prussian attack, Lobau and Duhesme stood their ground with splendid tenacity. The struggle for Planchenoit was especially desperate, the two battalions of the Old Guard which had flung themselves into that village held on to the churchyard with the greatest determination, repelling

[1] Cf. p. 689, and Siborne, p. 515.   [2] Cf., however, Houssaye, p. 388.

every frontal attack until at length the Prussians succeeded in outflanking the village. By this time (8.30 p.m.) all was over. The Guard had been repulsed. With Ziethen's corps close at hand Wellington had been able to take the risk of a check since reinforcement was certain; and seeing the whole French army staggering under the blow of the failure of the Guard, he had at once followed up his advantage by pushing forward against its retreating masses Adam's infantry and the all but intact cavalry brigades of Vivian and Vandeleur. These troops had made a vigorous counter-attack, forcing their way into the French centre, compelling the reserves of the Guard to retire, and thus threatening Reille's right and d'Erlon's left. But these divisions also were retiring; and as the relics of the Allied army advanced all along the line, the French fell into great disorder. The bonds of discipline seemed to become unloosed. The army degenerated into a rabble. Ziethen's leading brigade began to press heavily on Durutte and to drive his division back. Its retreat uncovered the left flank and rear of Lobau's corps which had till then held its ground against Bülow. As Ziethen's men fell on its flank the VIth Corps gave way and became involved in the universal confusion, in which even the last reserves of the Old Guard were swallowed up. Pelet's men, recoiling from Planchenoit, with difficulty beat off the attacks of the Prussian cavalry who were now crowding forward to take up the pursuit. On the ridge which had formed the main position of the French, Wellington halted his exhausted men (8.30 or 8.45 p.m.). To pursue was beyond their power, but the Prussians of Pirch and Ziethen were comparatively fresh, and Gneisenau's chase of the beaten army was as vigorous and relentless as Napoleon's pursuit of the fugitives from Jena and Auerstadt. Not till he reached the heights of Frasnes did he desist from the chase, and not till they had put the Sambre between them and the Prussians did the beaten troops of France rally to any appreciable extent.

The completeness of the overthrow of the French at Waterloo is to be in part ascribed to the very lateness of the Prussians in arriving, which has given rise to the impression, in Germany and elsewhere, that their arrival "saved the English army from destruction." In a sense, of course, this statement is true, but it is so partial and one-sided a version of the truth as to be relatively false. If Wellington's command was in danger of destruc-

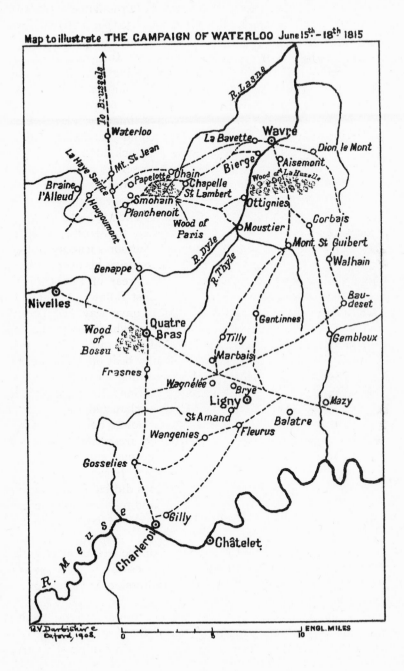

Map to illustrate **THE CAMPAIGN OF WATERLOO** June 15th.–18th 1815

tion, that was mainly due to the lateness of the Prussians in appearing, a lateness which has already been shown to have been anything but unavoidable. That Wellington would have been defeated had he given battle to Napoleon and his 74,000 men with only his own motley host and altogether unaided by the Prussians, is no more to be denied than it is to be supposed that Wellington would ever have given battle at Waterloo if he had not expected Prussian co-operation, and that at an earlier hour than it actually arrived. If when the Prussians intervened their allies were nearly at the end of their tether, the fact is hardly as creditable to the late-comers as it is to the troops whose endurance had been so sorely tried and had stood the test so well. No doubt the delay of the Prussians encouraged Napoleon to go on attempting to defeat Wellington before his allies could arrive, when the more prudent course would have been to have disengaged his army and withdrawn. Had a Prussian corps arrived at Ohain between 12 and 1, when Wellington seems to have expected them to appear,[1] it would have been fairly easy for Napoleon to draw off with his forces practically intact, and the indifferent manœuvring capacities of the Allied army would have made a counter-attack on intact troops very risky. By 7 o'clock both French and Allies had got very near the limits of their powers of endurance, and consequently the intervention of the Prussians was proportionately more decisive.

The losses of the combatants are most instructive. The British had over 7000 casualties, roughly 30 per cent. of their total strength. The King's German Legion suffered almost as heavily, having 1600 casualties among under 6000 men. The Brunswickers, Hanoverians and Kruse's Nassauers lost respectively 11, 14, and 22 per cent. The Dutch-Belgians had 4000 casualties among about 18,000 men,[2] but of these 4000 nearly a third were "missing." The Prussian losses were very heavy in proportion to the time during which they were actively engaged. In about four hours Bülow had nearly 6000 casualties out of 30,000 men. This figure includes about 1200 "missing," probably stragglers who had failed to keep up with the long marches the corps had

---

[1] M. Houssaye (p. 351) seems to follow Muffling in putting the hour at which Wellington expected the Prussians as between 2 and 3; but, amongst other things, it seems probable from the Duke's dispositions that he was counting on the Prussian corps, whose succour Blücher had promised, to take post on his left, and so secure that somewhat weak wing, at quite an early hour. But it was after noon when Ziethen started.

[2] If Prince Bernhard's brigade be included among them.

made since leaving Hannut; but even when these men are deducted the Prussian losses bear eloquent testimony to the stubbornness of the resistance offered by the 15,000 Frenchmen who withstood their attacks, and also to the superiority of the line over the column : the Prussians drawn up in the solid columns common to the Continental armies suffered losses out of all proportion to those of the British, who when opposed to the hostile infantry fought in line. Ziethen and Pirch had between them 600 casualties, a third of whom were "missing."[1]

The rest of the campaign is soon told. Grouchy had begun attacking Thielmann's position about the time that Bülow first advanced on Planchenoit. A sharp action saw the Prussian rearguard driven over the Dyle, but the French failed to force the passage at Bierges or to make their way across from the suburb on the right bank into the town on the left. However, Pajol and Teste carried the bridge of Limale, more than a mile higher up, and supported by two divisions of Gérard's corps established themselves on Thielmann's right flank before night put an end to the conflict. Next morning the battle was resumed, and was going in favour of Grouchy, who had forced Thielmann to abandon Wavre and fall back towards Louvain, when, about 10.30, an officer brought him news of the total defeat of the Emperor. A hasty retreat on Namur was the only course open to him; and this he successfully accomplished, though Pirch I was pushed out to intercept him, and was actually at Mellery, six miles nearer to Gembloux than Grouchy was, when the Marshal began his retreat. Pirch did not advance beyond Mellery on the 19th; and though next day he overtook Grouchy as the latter was about to cross the Sambre at Namur, his efforts to intercept the retreat were beaten off, and he and Thielmann's cavalry, who had also come up, suffered a loss of 1500 men in trying to storm Namur, which Teste and Grouchy's rearguard defended with great success.

But Grouchy's escape could not alter the fortunes of the campaign. The main army made some efforts to rally, but it could not face the Allies again or arrest their steady advance on Paris. On June 24th Colville's division stormed Cambray ; three days later Ziethen's advance-guard secured the bridge of Compiègne, and on the 29th Blücher reached St. Denis. To intervene between Paris and the arrival of any assistance from the

[1] Siborne, pp. 587–592.

South (July 2nd), he next crossed the Seine and established himself at Meudon and Chatillon, Wellington's army taking post at
St. Denis. This move of Blücher's would have been most risky
and dangerous if Paris had meant to fight, but Napoleon's
efforts to get France to rally to his side had proved unsuccessful; Fouché and Talleyrand were in the ascendant, and France
would not stir. July 4th saw a convention signed at St. Cloud
which placed Paris in the hands of the Allies, the French troops
retiring behind the Loire. Napoleon had already fled, after
abdicating in favour of his son, and on July 8th, the day that
the Emperor embarked at Rochefort, hoping to get away to
America, Louis XVIII re-entered Paris.

But before peace could be finally restored or the affairs of
Europe definitely settled, much remained to be done. A provisional Government had established itself at Paris with Fouché
at its head, while on July 10th the Allied monarchs arrived at
the French capital. A certain number of the fortresses on the
North-Eastern and Eastern frontiers had refused to surrender or
to accept the suspension of hostilities, and operations thus went
on in some places for a couple of months and more after the fall
of Napoleon. The Prussians, whose political views caused them
to impart more vigour to their operations than was displayed by
the other Allies, managed to possess themselves of about a
dozen French fortresses; but the main army of the Allies under
Schwarzenberg[1] after some sharp fighting with Rapp and the
corps detailed for the defence of Alsace, concluded a suspension
of hostilities on July 24th.

The activity of the Prussians in besieging and reducing the
French fortresses is to be attributed to the bitter feelings by
which Blücher and his compatriots were animated: it was their
ardent desire to make France drink to the dregs the cup of
humiliation which she had compelled Prussia to drain after Jena
and Friedland. But in this animosity to the vanquished Prussia
stood alone among the Allies. Wellington's conduct in his
march on Paris had been very different from that of his
colleague. His troops had paid their way, pillaging and plunder
had been strictly prevented, and the fortresses which surrendered
to him were occupied in the name of Louis XVIII, since it was
not against France but against Napoleon that England was

---

[1] This included besides Austrians the contingents of Bavaria, Saxony, Hesse-
Darmstadt, Würtemberg and several minor states.

fighting. Similarly when the Allies reached Paris, Blücher was only prevented from blowing up the Pont du Jéna by Wellington placing an English picquet on guard over that bridge. Blücher, however, carried his point when he demanded that the trophies and spoils taken from Berlin to adorn the French capital should be handed over to their original owners, and in this the other nations whose treasures Napoleon had annexed imitated him.

When it came to settling the terms of peace the same discrepancy was evident. Prussia clamoured for extensive cessions of territory and a heavy war indemnity: England declared she had taken part in the war as an ally of the King of France, and that she would never agree to such treatment of her ally. Prussia's proposals voiced the opinion of Germany, which favoured the severest measures; France must be treated as a conquered state, the annexations of Louis xv and Louis xiv must be taken from her, at least she must make good the damage she had inflicted on Germany under Napoleon's rule. The Crown Prince of Würtemberg urged that for the protection of South Germany France should be deprived of Alsace. When Capodistria suggested that a pecuniary indemnity would be sufficient, Hardenberg declared that at least the frontier fortresses must be handed over, and von Knesebeck, the mouth-piece of the King of Prussia, took the same line. But the deciding voice in the affairs of Europe and among them of Germany was to be that of the Czar.

Alexander had not been altogether pleased with the fact that the great victory had been won and Napoleon overthrown without his presence: he was equally annoyed by Blücher's action in concluding the Convention of July 4th, considering that the matter should have been referred to him. Hence there was a coolness between Prussia and Russia which Metternich, always on the lookout for a chance to isolate Prussia, assiduously fomented. Alexander had long ago thrown over his ideas of freeing Germany, and much influenced by his semi-mystical religious views he had come to look on Napoleon as the embodiment of irreligion and sin, and to desire to make his overthrow the basis for the resettlement of Europe on Christian lines. Universal peace, the union of Christian nations in one family, the overthrow of heathendom by the expulsion of the Turks from Europe, these were among his projects, and in accomplishing these he thought the re-establishment of France would be more useful to him than the aggrandisement of Prussia, either at the expense of France or by any rearrangement of Germany on lines calculated to increase her influence. Moreover, he had no intention of doing anything to strengthen a Power which might be troublesome to him, as Prussia might, in Poland. Austria was as little disposed to do anything to assist Prussia or to humiliate France. All she desired was a satisfactory settlement of the affairs of Italy, for Frimont's victory over Murat at Tolentino (May 2nd) had laid the peninsula at her feet, and marked the beginning of Austrian predominance in Italy. Accordingly Prussia, finding herself unsupported by any of the other Great Powers, and by no means unanimously supported by the minor German states, several of whom had good reasons of their own for preferring the restoration of France to her pre-Revolution position to the predominance of Prussia, had to give way.

The Second Treaty of Paris (Nov. 20th), with its exaction of an indemnity of 700,000,000 francs, its arrangements for the division of that indemnity and for the occupation of the principal fortresses of France by an Allied army of 150,000 men in order to provide security against such another disturbance of the peace of Europe, touches on German history mainly through the rectification of frontier, which was the principal penalty inflicted on France for her share in the Hundred Days. Bouillon, Marienburg and Philippeville on the North-East, Landau and Saarbrück on the East, were taken from her, the frontier of Rhenish Bavaria was moved up to the Lauter, and the little county of Gex was given to Geneva. The fortifications of Hüningen were to be destroyed, and no new fortress erected within a radius of three leagues. At the same time, some changes were made in the redistribution of Germany, Bavaria giving up the Innviertel to Austria and obtaining Landau instead.

With the Second Treaty of Paris the end of one great epoch in the history of Germany is reached, though the treaty marks only the end of the first act of the great drama which had begun with the dissolution of the Holy Roman Empire and was to end at Versailles in 1871. Indeed, in some ways 1806 is a better dividing line than 1815. In the history of Prussia this is certainly the case, but up till 1815 the history of Prussia is only a part of the history of Germany. What happened in 1815 was that in the resettlement following the final overthrow of Napoleon, and with him of the structure he had raised in Germany, Austria made no effort to resume the nominal headship which she had laid down in 1806. She now definitely adopted a line of policy which drew her away from Germany and from the German traditions of the Holy Roman Empire. Yet she did not so completely withdraw herself from Germany as to allow of the establishment of a new organisation which could hope to be permanent.

Thus it is that while the liberation of Germany from the yoke of Napoleon may be regarded as the final act of the drama which was begun in 1792 by the intervention of Austria and Prussia in the internal affairs of France, yet it also belongs to the history of nineteenth-century Germany. The forces which Napoleon called into being, both by his reforms and by his oppression, were to be the influences which actuated and agitated Germany until unity, though a not quite complete unity even then, was at last achieved under the leadership of Prussia, until a "German Empire" was created which is neither the Holy Roman Empire nor the mediæval Kingdom of Germany. But in 1815 those forces, let loose though they had been when Germany rose to shake off the yoke of Napoleon, had for the time been put under restraint. With Metternich at the helm and the "Holy Alliance" an accomplished fact, Europe and with it Germany had slipped for a time into a backwater of reaction.

I. THE HOUSE OF HAPSBURG

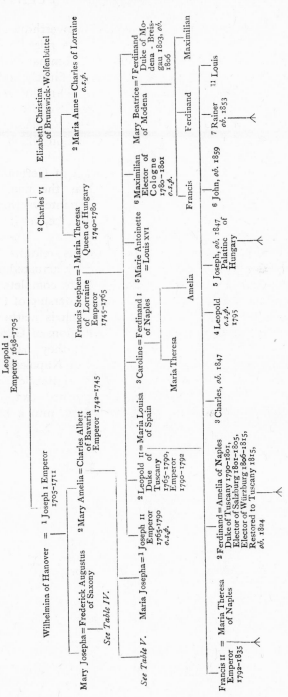

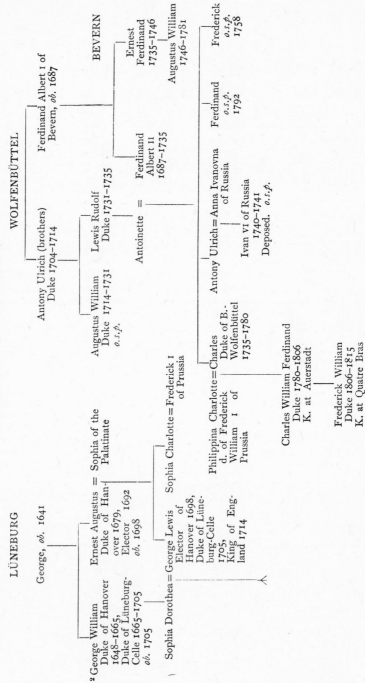

II. THE HOUSE OF BRUNSWICK

III. HOUSE OF HOHENZOLLERN

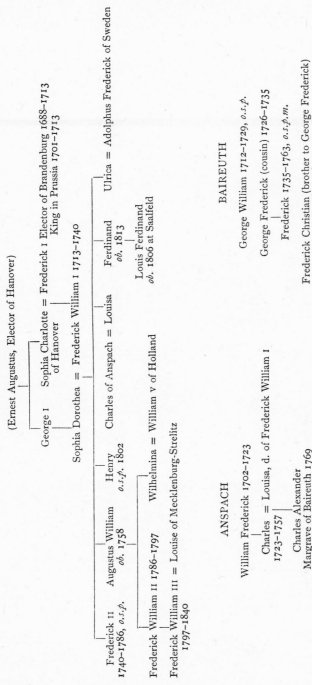

(Ernest Augustus, Elector of Hanover)

George I

Sophia Charlotte = Frederick I Elector of Brandenburg 1688–1713
of Hanover   King in Prussia 1701–1713

Sophia Dorothea = Frederick William I 1713–1740

Charles of Anspach = Louisa

Ferdinand
ob. 1813

Louis Ferdinand
ob. 1806 at Saalfeld

Ulrica = Adolphus Frederick of Sweden

Frederick II
1740–1786, o.s.p.

Augustus William
ob. 1758

Henry
o.s.p. 1802

Wilhelmina = William v of Holland

Frederick William II 1786–1797

Frederick William III = Louise of Mecklenburg-Strelitz
1797–1840

ANSPACH

William Frederick 1702–1723

Charles = Louisa, d. of Frederick William I
1723–1757

Charles Alexander
Margrave of Baireuth 1769
Resigned territories to Prussia 1791

BAIREUTH

George William 1712–1729, o.s.p.

George Frederick (cousin) 1726–1735

Frederick 1735–1763, o.s.p.m.

Frederick Christian (brother to George Frederick)
1763–1769, o.s.p.

Common ancestor of all three branches is John George of Brandenburg, 1571–1598, whose eldest son, Joachim Frederick, succeeded him in Brandenburg [Elector 1598–1608], and whose younger sons, Joachim Ernest and Christian, obtained Anspach and Baireuth respectively.

45

IV. HOUSE OF WETTIN (ELECTORAL BRANCH ONLY)

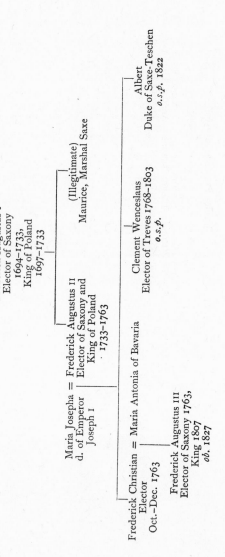

Frederick Augustus I
Elector of Saxony
1694–1733,
King of Poland
1697–1733

Maria Josepha = Frederick Augustus II
d. of Emperor   Elector of Saxony and
Joseph I   King of Poland
                              · 1733–1763

(Illegitimate)
Maurice, Marshal Saxe

Frederick Christian = Maria Antonia of Bavaria
Elector
Oct.–Dec. 1763

Frederick Augustus III
Elector of Saxony 1763,
King 1807
ob. 1827

Clement Wenceslaus
Elector of Treves 1768–1803
o.s.p.

Albert
Duke of Saxe-Teschen
o.s.p. 1822

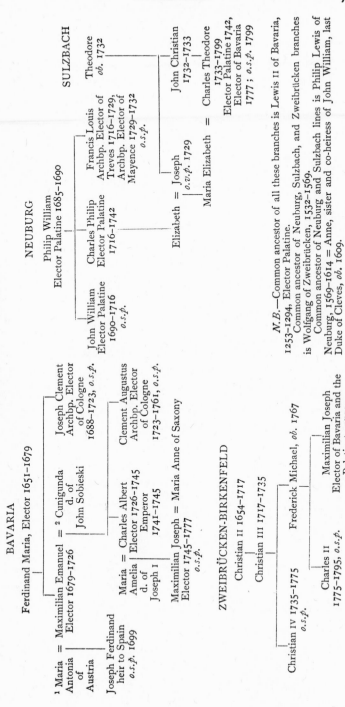

V. HOUSE OF WITTELSBACH

INDEX

ABENS, battle of the (1809), 531
Achmet, Sultan of Turkey (1703–1730), 72
Adolphus Frederick of Holstein, 160
Adolphus Frederick II, Duke of Mecklenburg-Strelitz (1708–1749), 54
Agrarian reforms of Joseph II, 334–338
Ainali Karak, Convention of (1784), 316
Alberoni, Cardinal, 69, 75–77
Albini, Francis Joseph von (chief minister of Elector Charles Joseph of Mayence), 436
Alessandria, Convention of (1800), 444
Alexander I (Czar of Russia), cf. 474 n. ; grows hostile to Napoleon, 477 ff. ; responsibility for defeat of Austerlitz, 490, 504 ; makes peace of Tilsit, 516 ; alliance with Napoleon, 517–518, 521 ; at Erfurt (1808), 522 ; policy of, 1808–1809, 527 ; quarrel with Napoleon, 566–568 ; attitude in 1813, 573 ; champions German movement against Napoleon, 570, Chapters XXX.-XXXII. passim ; anxious to command Allies, 598 ; delays attack at Dresden, 609 ; keen on deposing Napoleon, 641 ; decisive influence over Treaty of Paris (1814), 642 ; at Vienna, 648 ; antagonism to Metternich, 648 ; designs on Saxony and Poland, 652–655 ; has decisive voice in settlement of 1815, 700
Alten, Sir Charles, at Quatre Bras, 679 ; at Waterloo, 691
d'Alton, Count (Austrian general), 341
Alsace, ceded to France in 1648, 31 ; condition of, etc., in 1715, 57 ; affected by French Revolution, 353, 357, 376
Alvensleben (Prussian general), foretells collapse of Prussia, 424
Amberg, battle of (1796), 405
Anhalt, 59, 371, 520 ; contribution to Napoleon's army (1813), 596 n. ; Princes of, 651
Cf. Leopold of Anhalt-Dessau
Anna (daughter of Peter the Great), 69, 150 n., 369 n.
Anna Ivanovna, Empress of Russia (1727–1740), 110

Anspach Hohenzollern, 52 ; absorb Baireuth, 314 n. ; Prussia's right to, admitted, 314 ; line extinct (1792), 371, 519, 656 ; Bernadotte crosses territory en route to Danube (1805), 489.
Anthony Ulrich, Duke of Brunswick-Wolfenbüttel (1704–1714), 26, 58 ; cf. genealogy, 704
Apraxin, Stephen (Russian general), 203 ; court-martialed, 228
Arcis sur Aube, battle of (1814), 640
Aremberg, Princes of, 59, 461, 464 ; join Confederation of the Rhine, 496 ; territories annexed to France, 519.
d'Argenson, Marquis de, Foreign Minister of France, 152, 154, 156, 162 ; negotiates with Sardinia, 164 ; 166
"Armed Neutrality" (of 1800–1801), 457, 458
Armistice of Poischwitz (1813), 587
Arndt, Ernst Moritz (German poet), 523, 630, 642
Aschaffenburg, principality of, 497, 552
Aspern, battle of (1809), 537–538
Auerstadt, battle of (1806), 508, 509
Augereau, Pierre François (French Marshal), 451, 488 ; in campaign of 1806, 506–510, 513 ; of 1813, 619 ; of 1814, 639
Augsburg, Peace of, 3
League of (1688), 26
Bishopric of, 48 ; annexed by Bavaria, 461
Augustus Frederick I of Saxony (Augustus I of Poland), election to Poland, 19, 39, 97, 706
Augustus Frederick II of Saxony and of Poland (1733–1763), elected King of Poland, 98 ; claim on Austria, 109 ; in Austrian Succession War, Chapters VII.-IX. ; joins Bavaria, 122 ; makes peace with Austria, 131 ; in Second Silesian War, 151–161, 167 ; joins Austria in 1756, 196 ; beset in Pirna, 197–199 ; escapes to Warsaw, 199 ; negotiates peace (1763), 289 ; death (1763), 303 ; 706
Augustus III (Frederick) of Saxony ;

succeeds as Elector (1763), 303; 365; joins Prussia in 1806, 503; makes peace, 510; becomes King, 510; Grand Duke of Warsaw, 551; attitude in 1813, 579; joins Napoleon, 583; taken prisoner, 652; accepts Allies' terms (1815), 654; 706

Augustus George, last Margrave of Baden-Baden (1761–1771), 370

Augustus William, Duke of Brunswick-Wolfenbüttel (1714–1731), 59, 83; 704

Augustus William of Prussia, 98, 212; 705

Augustus William, Duke of Brunswick-Bevern (1746–1781), 205–212, 322; 704

Aulic Chamber (*Hofkammer*), 35, 78

Aulic Council (*Reichshofrath*), Imperial Chamber of Justice, 8; its history, 15 ff., 302, 320, 371

Austerlitz, battle of (1805), 490

Austria, possessions and condition of, in 1715, 31–36; failures in Italy and Turkey, Chapter VI.; condition of, in 1740, 105–107; reforms of Maria Theresa, 175–182; of Joseph II, 328–339; condition of, in 1792, 352; conduct of, in 1795, 394; makes peace with France (1797), 410 ff.; conduct of, 412; under Thugut, 413–414; made an Hereditary Empire, 474; attitude to Napoleon, 476 ff.; joins Russia and Great Britain, 480; in campaign of 1805, Chapter XXV.; losses at Pressburg, 493; Napoleon's policy towards, 494–495; inaction in 1807, 515; accepts Continental System, 520; attitude in 1808, 521; changes in, 1805–1809, 526–527; quarrel with Napoleon, 528 ff.; losses in 1809, 544–545; reaction in, 545, 565; alliance with Napoleon, 566, 567; attitude in 1813, 572, 578, 586; negotiates armistice of Poischwitz, 587–590; concludes Convention of Reichenbach, 590; joins the Allies, 594; attitude to Napoleon, 635; views as to reconstruction, Chapter XXXIV. *passim*, esp. 645, 652; renounces designs on Bavaria, 619, cf. 647; gains and losses in 1815, 657; attitude in 1815, 702

Austrian Army, condition in 1740, 103; reformed, 176; condition in 1756, 199; in 1792, 379, 443, 478; changes in command of (1805), 481–482; reforms in, 526, 527; in 1813, 578 n.

Bachelu (French general) in Waterloo campaign, 690

Baden, Peace of, 1

Baden-Baden [cf. Louis of, Louis George (1707–1761), Augustus George (1617–1771)], extent of, 50; united to Baden-Durlach, 370; conduct in 1796, 395 n.,

404; connection with Russia, 458; gains and losses in 1803, 462; becomes Electorate (1803), 462, 469; assists Napoleon (1805), 483, 488; Grand Duchy, 494; joins Confederation of the Rhine, 497; contingent in Spain, 522 n.; assists Napoleon (1809), 529 ff.; development of, 550; sends contingent to Grand Army of (1812), 568; of 1813, 596 n.; defection from Napoleon, 631; assists Allies (1814), 636, 651; contingent of, in 1815, 662 n.

Baden-Durlach, extent of, 50; united to Baden-Baden, 370 *n.s.*

Cf. Charles William of (1709–1735), Charles Frederick of (1738–1821)

Bagration, Prince Peter (Russian general), in 1805, 488, 491–492

Baireuth Hohenzollern, 53, 203; line becomes extinct (1769), 314; territories pass to Prussia (1792), 371; to Bavaria, 519, 656: cf. 705

Bamberg, Bishopric of, 48; annexed by Bavaria (1803), 463

Banko-Deputation (Austria), 177

Bar, Confederation of (1767), 304

Barclay de Tolly, Prince (Russian general), spring campaign of 1813, 584–588, 592; autumn campaign of 1813, 597–633

Bärenklau (or Bernklau, Austrian general), 127; takes München, 135, 152

Baring, Major (K.G.L.), defends La Haye Sainte, 687–688, 690

Bartenstein, John Christopher (Austrian minister), 102, 108, 117, 172

Bartenstein, Treaty of (1807), 515

Bassignano, battle of (1745), 164

Batavian Republic, established (1795), 391; French interference in (1798), 422, 437; made into a kingdom, 479

Bautzen, battle of (1813), 584–586

Bavaria, relations with Louis XIV, 26, 36, 43; with Austria, 32; its territories, policy, etc., in 1715, 42–44; allied with France and Spain (1741), 121; invaded by Khevenhüller, 127 ff.; in 1743, 135, 152; comes to terms with Austria (1745), 154; Joseph II's designs on, 310–314, 318–319; condition in 1792, 364; conduct in 1796, 406; Thugut's designs on, 420, 425, 439; supports Second Coalition (1799), 425, 436 n., 439; action in 1801, 456–458; gains and losses (1803), 460, 461; attacks Imperial Knights, 467–468; condition of, in 1803, 469–470; joins Napoleon (1805), 483; obtains Tyrol, 493; made a Kingdom, 494; joins Confederation of the Rhine, 497; receives Nüremberg, 520; assists Napoleon against Austria, 529–544;

gains in 1809, 545; development of, 549–550; sends contingent to Grand Army 1812, 568, 570; attitude of, in 1813, 579; contribution to Napoleon's army (1813), 596 n.; deserts Napoleon, 618; concludes Treaty of Ried (1813), 619; tries to intercept Napoleon's retreat, 633; assists Allies (1814), 636–642, 647; views, etc., of, at Vienna, 649, 651; supports Talleyrand over Saxony, 653; gains, etc., in 1815, 656; contingent of, in 1815, 662; affected by Second Treaty of Paris, 701

Bavaria, cf. Maximilian I (1598–1651), Ferdinand Maria (1651–1679), Maximilian Emanuel (1679–1726), Joseph Clement, Charles Albert (1726–1745), Clement Augustus, Maximilian Joseph (1745–1777), Charles Theodore (1777–1799), Maximilian Joseph (1799–1825) Genealogy, 707
    Cf. also Montgelas, Seckendorff, Wrede

Beauharnais, Eugene, 496, 535; victorious at Raab, 540; at Wagram, 541–548; 553, 572; spring campaign of 1813, 579–588; sent to Italy, 589, 635

Beauharnais, Stephanie, 496

Belgians. See Dutch-Belgians

Belgiojoso, Count (Austrian minister), Governor of the Netherlands, 340, 341

Belgrade, captured by Eugene (1717), 74; lost to Turkey (1739), 103; captured by Loudoun, 326
    Peace of, 103

Bellegarde, Count Henri de (Austrian general), in 1799, 427, 430, 434; in 1800, 449; in 1809, 530–544

Belleisle, Count Charles Louis (French Marshal), 110; embassy to Germany, 121, 123; escapes from Prague, 133, 165

Bennigsen, Count (Russian general), 490; campaign of 1806–1807, 513–516; of 1813, 620, 626

Berg, ceded to Neuburg Wittelsbachs (1666), 45; Prussian claim on, 93, 95, 128 n.; made a Grand Duchy (1806), 496; joins Confederation of the Rhine, 497; increased, 519; its development, 553–555; contingent in Spain, 554; in Russia, 568; in 1813, 596 n.; 647

Bergen, battle of (1759), 265

Bernadotte, Jean, beaten at Amberg (1796), 405; at Vienna, 421, 428; Minister of War, 431; 473, 485, 488–491; campaign of 1806, 505–510; of 1809, 529–544; Crown Prince of Sweden, 590; declares against Napoleon, 591, 593, 598; autumn campaign of 1813, 602–631 (esp. 604, 626, 628), 632, 636

Bernis, Abbé (French minister), 190, 228; retires, 250

Berthier, Louis (French Marshal), 529 ff.

Berthold of Henneberg, Elector of Mayence (1484–1504), 14, 475

Bertrand, Henri Gratien, Count (French general), in spring campaign of 1813, 580–585; autumn, 600–633
    Cf. Gross Beeren, Dennewitz

Berwick, Marshal, 98, 100

Bessières (French Marshal), 491

Bestuchev, Count Alexis (Russian minister), 150, 155, 203; dismissed, 228

Beyme, K. von (Prussian minister), 511

Birkenfeld branch of Wittelsbach family, 52, 707; district ceded to Oldenburg (1815), 656

Bischoffswerder, Johann Rudolf (Prussia), 348, 354

"Black Legion," 534–535

Blücher, Gebhardt, Marshal, campaign of 1806, 506–510, 559, 579; spring campaign of 1813, 580–588, 593; autumn campaign of 1813, 597–633, esp. Katzbach, 620–622; pursues Napoleon, 633; in campaign of 1814, 636–642; in 1815, Chapter XXXV. passim, esp. 666; battle of Ligny, 671–678, 683; moves on Waterloo, 687–689; at Waterloo, 693 ff.; keen for revenge, 699, 700

Blümegen, Count Henry (Austrian minister), 299, 301, 333, 338

Bohemia and the Thirty Years' War, 4, 13 n.; its Chancery, 35; the Bohemian vote, 38; condition of, 334

Borodino, battle of (1812), 570

Brandenburg, Electorate of, office of Arch Butler attached to it, 19; territories and policy, 40–42
    Cf. Hohenzollern; Prussia

Brause (Prussian general), at Ligny, 674–677

Breisgau, 32; transferred to Duke of Modena, 410, 453, 462; divided by Baden and Würtemberg (1805), 493

Bremen, city of, 23, 460, 651

Bremen (Archbishopric of, cf. also Verden), passes to Sweden, 21; ceded to Hanover, 68

Brentano (Austrian general), 261, 263–264, 287

Breslau, 116; battle of (1757), 219–220; taken by Austrians, 220; retaken by Frederick, 226

Brieg, 116; falls (1741), 120

Brienne sur Aube, battle of (1814), 637

British troops employed in Germany (1743), 136–140; at Fontenoy, 156, 167–168; sent to join Ferdinand of Brunswick (1758), 250, 266; at Minden, 268–269, 280, 284, 288; in

Netherlands (1793–1795), 386 ff. ; in Germany in 1805, 490 ; in 1813, 605, 619 ; at Leipzig, 629 ; in 1815, 661 ; at Waterloo, 688–697

Brixen, Bishopric of, 48 ; annexed by Austria, 453, 462

Broglie, Comte de (French Marshal), 127, 128, 131 ; evacuates Bavaria (1743), 135

Broglie, Duc de (French general), replaces Soubise, 233 ; campaign of 1759, 265–271 ; of 1760, 280–281 ; of 1761, 284

Browne, Count Ulysses (Austrian general), campaign of 1756, 197–200 ; campaign of 1757, 205

Brühl, Count (Saxon minister), 160, 195, 197

Brunswick-Bevern, Augustus William of (Prussian general), 205–210 ; in command in Silesia (1757), 218–220. Ferdinand Albert II of, succeeds to Brunswick-Wolfenbüttel (1735), 367 Cf. genealogy, 704

Brunswick Hussars, 535 n.

Brunswick-Lüneburg, cf. Electorate of Hanover

Brunswick Oels, Frederick William of, his rising in 1809, 534–535 ; restored to Brunswick-Wolfenbüttel (1813), 631 ; killed at Quatre Bras, 679 ; 704

Brunswick Oels Light Infantry, 535 n.

Brunswick-Wolfenbüttel, Duchy of, for neutrality in 1757, 203 ; submits to Richelieu, 215 ; in 1792, 367, 464 ; confiscated by Napoleon, 511 ; part of Kingdom of Westphalia, 518 ; old dynasty restored, 1813, 631 ; contingent of, in 1815, 665 n. ; at Quatre Bras, 679 ; at Waterloo, 689, 691.
Cf. also Anthony Ulrich, Augustus William, Charles, Charles William Ferdinand, Ferdinand, Ferdinand Albert, Frederick William, Lewis Rudolf
Genealogy, 704

Bukovina, acquired by Austria, 309

Bülow, Friedrich (Prussian general), 573 ; spring campaign of 1813, 584–588 ; autumn campaign, 597–633 (cf. Gross Beeren, Dennewitz) ; campaign of 1814, 639–642 ; of 1815, Chapter XXXV. passim, esp. 667 ; absence from Ligny, 671 ; reaches Wavre, 683 ; move on Waterloo, 685–687 ; at Waterloo, 693

Bute, Earl of, 286, 293 n.

Buturlin, Alexander (Russian general), 281 ff

Buxhowden, Count Frederick William (Russian general), 513

Bylandt, General (Dutch-Belgian), at Waterloo, 689

Caldiero, battle of (1805), 487

Calvinists and the Thirty Years' War, 4 ; in Palatinate, 45 ; in Würtemberg, 551

Cambrai, Congress of (1722), 79

Campo Formio, Peace of (1797), 410, 411

Campo Santo, battle of (1743), 143

Canning, George, becomes Foreign Secretary, 515 ; 544

Carlos, Don (= Charles III of Spain), 80 ; obtains Parma, 82 ; obtains the Two Sicilies, 101, 143 ; succeeds to Spain, 272

Carniola, 30 ; ceded to Napoleon, 544 ; restored to Austria (1815), 657 n.

Carteret, John, Lord (afterwards Earl Granville), 70, 131 ; attempts to revive the Grand Alliance, 140–141, 145

Castiglione, battle of (1796), 407

Castlereagh, Lord, takes office, 515, 544, 639 ; at Chaumont, 641, 643 ; at Vienna, 648 ; attitude on Saxon question, 653

Castries, de (French general), campaign of 1760, 280 ; of 1762, 288

Cathcart, Lord, expedition to the Weser (1805), 490, 499 ; at Vienna (1815), 648, 662 n.

Catherine I of Russia (1725–1727), 102

Catherine II of Russia (1762–1796), 287 ; share in Partition of Poland, 306–309 ; brings about Peace of Tetschen, 313 ; Balkan policy, 315, 316 ; alliance with Joseph II, 322–323 ; war with Turkey (1787–1792), 324–326, 354 ; Second Partition of Poland, 382 ; Third Partition, 396–397 ; death (1796), 408

Chalil Pasha (Grand Vizier of Turkey), 74

Champaubert, battle of (1814), 638

Charles, Duke of Brunswick (1735–1780), 367, 704

Charles I, Landgrave of Hesse-Cassel (1676–1730), 50, 368

Charles VI, Emperor (1711–1740), his attitude to the Peace of Utrecht, 33 ; acquires Sicily, 77 ; issues Pragmatic Sanction, 79, 80 ; and the Jülich-Berg question, 95 – 96 ; his last wars, Chapter VI. ; death, 104, 114 ; 703

Charles XII of Sweden, his relations with Saxony-Poland, 38 ; connection with Zweibrücken, 52 ; share in the Northern War (1699–1721), Chapter III. ; death, 69

Charles Albert of Bavaria (1726–1745), 79, 83 ; in Polish Succession War, 100 ; claim on Austria, 109 ; in Austrian Succession War, Chapters VII. and IX. ; mistaken strategy, 125 ; elected Emperor as Charles VII, 128 ; death (1745), 152 ; 707

Charles of Austria, Archduke, succeeds Clerfayt, 401; campaign of 1796, 402–407; of 1797, 408; political views, 412; campaign of 1799, 426–428, 431–432, 435–436; of 1800, 451, 464; disinclined to fight (1804), 478; resigns Presidency of War Couucil, 481; campaign of 1805, 487–488, 515; military reforms of, 526–527; against war (1809), 528; campaign of 1809, 529–544; strategy criticised, 532, 539 n.; resigns, 544; not employed in 1813, 598; 645; 703

Charles Alexander, Duke of Würtemberg (1733–1737), 371

Charles Augustus, Duke of Saxe-Weimar (1758–1828), 321, 365–366, 473, 510

Charles Emmanuel III of Sardinia (1730–1773), 98, 121; concludes Treaty of Worms (1743), 141, 163–165, 169

Charles Emmanuel IV of Sardinia (1796–1802), 423, 432, 453

Charles Eugene, Duke of Würtemberg (1737–1793), 154, 167, 203, 371

Charles Frederick, Margrave of Baden-Durlach (1738–1821), 203; at Hochkirch, 224, 226; joins *Fürstenbund*, 321; acquires Baden-Baden, 370; connection with Russia, 458; becomes Elector (1803), 462, 468; attitude towards abduction of Duc d'Enghien, 473–475; supports Napoleon (1805), 483; becomes Grand Duke, 494, 550; 570; deserts Napoleon, 631

Charles Frederick of Schleswig-Holstein (1703–1739), 56, 66, 69, 150, 369 n.

Charles Leopold, Duke of Mecklenburg-Schwerin (1713–1747), 54; quarrel with Estates, 69 ff.; deposed, 94, 369

Charles Lewis, Elector Palatine (1648–1680), 18, 44

Charles of Lorraine, Elector of Treves (1711–1716), 37

Charles of Lorraine (Austrian general); campaign of 1742, 129–131; of 1743, 135–140; of 1744, 148–152; of 1745, 157–161; in Netherlands, 167, 180; campaign of 1757, 205–208, 212, 218–220; death (1780), 340

Charles Philip of Neuburg, Elector Palatine (1716–1742), 81, 83; persecutes Protestants, 85, 95, 128; death, 149

Cf. Wittelsbach genealogy, 707

Charles of Simmern, Elector Palatine (1680–1685), extinction of Simmern Wittelsbachs at his death, 19

Charles Theodore of Sulzbach, succeeds as Elector Palatine (1742), 128, 149, 154, 157, 167, 185 n.; supports Maria Theresa in 1756, 203, 249; claim on Bavaria, 310; succession to Bavaria,

311–314, 318, 321, 357, 364; makes peace with France, 399; death (1799), 425

Cf. Wittelsbach genealogy, 707

Charles II of Zweibrücken - Birkenfeld (1775–1795), 311, 319, 321, 362, 364, 707

Charles William, Margrave of Baden-Durlach (1709–1738), 50, 370

Charles William Ferdinand, Hereditary Prince of Brunswick-Wolfenbüttel, in campaign of 1759, 269–271; in 1760, 281; in 1761, 284; of 1762, 289, 325; succeeds to Duchy (1780), 367; invades France (1792), 379–380, 384, 387, 415, 417, 438, 479; supports Prussia in 1806, 505; campaign of 1806, 505–509; death, 511; 704

Chasteler, John Gabriel (Austrian general), 536, 539

Chatillon, Conference of, 641

Chaumont, Treaty of (1814), 641; renewed (1815), 660

Chauvelin, Count Louis (French diplomat), 98

Chavigny (French envoy at Münich), 149, 154

Chemnitz, Philip Boguslaw (= Hippolytus a Lapide), 7

Cherasco, Peace of (1796), 402

Chevert (French general), 133; at Hastenbeck, 214, 249

Choiseul, Duc de, becomes Foreign Minister of France (1758), 251, 285; fall of, 307

Chotek, Count Rudolf (Austrian minister), 173, 178, 299

Chotek, Rudolf (the younger) (Austrian minister), 338

Chotusitz, battle of (also called Czaslau), 1742, 129–131

Christian Augustus of Holstein-Eutin, Bishop of Lübeck (1705–1726), Regent of Schleswig-Holstein, 56, 66

Christian Louis, Duke of Mecklenburg-Schwerin (1747–1756), 84, 94

Church in Austria, 328–330

Circles, the, 13

Clement III (Pope), 330

Clement XIV (Pope), 330

Clement Augustus of Bavaria, Elector of Cologne (1723–1761), 81, 122; 707

Clement Wenceslaus of Saxony, Elector of Treves (1768–1803), 373, 376, 421; 706

Clerfayt, Joseph (Austrian general), victory at Kolofat, 349; campaign of 1794, 389–390; of 1795, 398–400; quarrels with Thugut, 400

Clermont, Comte de (French general), campaign of 1758, 232–233, 248–249

Cleves - Jülich, inheritance, 41, 45;

Prussia loses her share, 392, 517; regains it at Vienna (1815), 655
Closter Seven, Convention of (1757), 216; broken off, 231
Coalition, the First (1792–1797), Chapters XIX. and XX., esp. 385; collapse of, 391
Coalition, the Second (1798–1801), Chapters XXI. and XXII.; formation, 424; Prussia's abstention, 424; Russia withdraws, 438; collapse of, 448
Coalition, the Third (1805–1806), causes of, Chapter XXIV.; its formation, 478–480: cf. Chapter XXV.
Cobenzl, Charles, 180
Cobenzl, Louis, 413, 422; replaces Thugut, 448; at Lunéville, 449, 475; favours peace (1804), 478, 481; replaced by Stadion, 498
Cobenzl, Philip, Vice - Chancellor of Austria, 342, 354; dismissed, 385, 413
Cocceji, Samuel von (Prussia), 89, 296
Coigni, Marshal (French), 148, 155
Colberg, 238; besieged (1760), 277; taken by Russians (1761), 283; siege of (1807), 514
Colloredo, Jerome (Austrian general), at Leipzig, 626–628
Colloredo, Joseph (Austrian general), 245
Colloredo, Rudolf (Vice-Chancellor of Austria), 182
Cologne, Electorate of, office of the Arch Chancellor of Italy attached to, 19; its territories and position, 36, 48; in 1791, 372; fate in 1803, 462
Cologne, Electors of; cf. Joseph Clement of Bavaria (1688–1723):
    Clement Augustus of Bavaria (1723–1761), 81, 83, 100, 122, 167, 185, 204
    Maximilian Joseph of Austria (1780–1801), 315, 320, 321, 373, 448, 459
    Maximilian of Rottenfels (1761–1780), 315, 321
Comitial rechte, 9
Committee of Public Safety, 385
Confederation of the Rhine, 455; formed (July 1806), 497; enlarged, 510; assists Napoleon (1807), 514; enlarged, 520; contingents in Spain, 522 n.; its contribution to Napoleon's army (1813), 596; loyalty wavering, 599; collapses after Leipzig, 630
Conference, the (Austrian Council of State), 35; its members in 1740, 108
Consulate (France), established, 438
Contades, Marquis de (French general), 214; campaign of 1758, 249–250; of 1759, 266–271; superseded, 271
Conti, Prince of, candidate for Poland (1763), 303

"Continental System," the, 518, 520, 547–548, 567
Corfu, attacked by Turks, 72
Cornwallis, Admiral, 480
Cornwallis, Lord, 298
Cottbus, given to Saxony (1807), 517, 579; restored to Prussia, 655
Crefeld, battle of (1758), 249
Crozka, battle of (1739), 103
"Cumberland Hussars" at Waterloo, 688
Cumberland, William Augustus, Duke of, campaign of 1745, 155, 166; campaign of, 1747, 168; campaign of 1757, 214–216
Custine, Comte Philip de (French general), 378, 381, 384
Custrin, 21 n.; attacked by Russians (1758), 237, 510; garrisoned by French (1808), 522
Cuxhaven, occupied by Napoleon (1803), 473
Czartoriski, Adam (confidant of Alexander I), 516
Czartoriskis (Polish nobles), 303
Czernitchev (Russian general), 277, 282, 286–287

Dalberg, Charles, Coadjutor to Elector of Mayence, 373, 456, 458; made Arch Chancellor and Primate, 463; 475; joins Confederation of Rhine as Prince Primate, 497; receives Fulda, 519; receives Frankfurt, 520, 552
Dalmatia, annexed by Austria, 410; ceded to Napoleon, 549; restored to Austria (1815), 657
Damad Ali Pasha, Grand Vizier of Turkey, 72
Dantzic, 309, 325, 373; acquired by Prussia, 383; siege of (1807), 514; falls, 516; fate in 1807, 517; besieged in 1813, 580; falls, 632; regained by Prussia (1815), 655
Daru, Count Pierre (French minister), 522
Daun, Count Philip, Marshal, 177; replaces Serbelloni, 209; wins Kolin, 210–211; invades Silesia, 218–220; given chief command (1758), 233; campaign of 1758, 233–237, 243–248; campaign of 1759, 252, 260, 264; campaign of 1760, 273–279; of 1761, 281–283; of 1762, 287–288; President of War Council (1762), 301; death, 301
Davoût, Louis Nicolas, Marshal, 485, 488, 491–492; campaign of 1806, 505–510, 513; of 1809, 529–544; of 1813, 587, 591, 595, 601, 605; after Leipzig, 632
Defenestratio of Prague, 4

Denmark, connection with College of Princes, 21 ; with Schleswig-Holstein (*q.v.*), 55-56 ; connection with Oldenburg, 56 ; exchanges it against Holstein, 369 ; negotiates Convention of Closter Seven, 216 ; joins Napoleon (1813), 591 ; makes peace at Kiel (1814), 632 ; loses Norway, 657

Dennewitz, battle of (1813), 616

Desaix, Joseph (French general), wins Marengo, 444

Dettingen, battle of (1743), 138-140

Diet, the, its origin and organisation, 17 ff. ; supports Maria Theresa in 1757, 203 ; in 1801, 455 ; after 1803, 465

Diet of Cologne (1512), 13
of Ratisbon (1653), 14, 20
of Pressburg (1687), 34

Directorium (Austria), 177

Directory (France), established, 391 ; policy towards Austria and Prussia, 392 ; replaced by Consulate (1799), 438

Dissertatio de ratione status in Imperio nostro Romano Germanico, 7

Dohna, Christopher (Prussian general), 236-238, 242, 247, 252

Domstadtl Pass, 235

Dornberg, Major-General von, in 1815, 667

Dresden, 24 ; occupied by Leopold of Anhalt-Dessau (1745), 162 ; Treaty of, 162 ; occupied by Prussians (1756), 197 ; captured by Imperial Army, 261, 274, Napoleon at (1812), 570 ; captured by French (1813), 582 ; battle of (1813), 608-611 ; held by St. Cyr, 621-622 ; falls, 632

Drouet (French general) at Leipzig, 624 ; at Hanau, 633

Dubois, Cardinal, 70

Dumouriez, Charles Francis, 378 ; at Valmy, 380 ; invades Holland, 383 ; deserts to Allies, 384

Dunkirk, English attack on (1793), 385

Duplat, Colonel (K.G.L. Brigadier), at Waterloo, 688, 692, 695

Dürrenstein, battle of (1805), 488

Dutch, in Austrian Succession War, 147, 166-168 ; war with Joseph II, 317-318, 386 ; disaffected (1794), 390 ; submit to France (1795), 391 (= Batavian Republic)

Dutch-Belgian troops assist French (1809), 534 ; at Leipzig, 630 ; in 1815, 665 n. ; at Waterloo, 689-690 ; at Quatre Bras, 678-679

East Friesland, 113 ; ceded to Holland (1807), 517 ; to Hanover (1815), 656

Ebelsberg, battle of (1890), 532

Eberhard III of Würtemberg (1623-1674), 49

Eberhard Louis of Würtemberg (1677-1733), 49, 370

Eckmühl, battle of (1809), 531-532

Edict of Restitution, 6

Elchingen, battle at (1805), 486

Electorate of Bohemia, office of Arch Butler attached to, 18 ; vote in abeyance, 19

Electorate of Brandenburg, office of Arch Chamberlain attached to, 18
Cf. Hohenzollern, Prussia

Electorate of Cologne, office of Arch Chancellor of Italy attached to, 19 ; fate in 1803, 462

Electorate of Hanover, created in 1692, 19
Cf. Brunswick-Lüneburg, Hanover

Electorate of Mayence, office of Arch Chancellor of Germany attached to, 19 ; its traditional policy ; fate in 1803, 462 ; 464

Electorate of Saxony, office of Arch Marshal attached to, 18 ; connection with *Corpus Evangelicorum*, 19

Electorate of Treves, office of Arch Chancellor of Burgundy attached to, 19 ; fate in 1803, 462, 464

Electors, College of, 18-20

Elizabeth of Russia (1740-1762), 150 ; treaty with George II, 187 ; joins Franco-Austrian alliance, 191, 203, 213, 228, 282 ; death, 286, 291

Elizabeth Farnese (Queen of Spain), 75, 79, 81, 98, 142

" Emancipating Edict," 561

Emperor, history of office, powers and position in 1715, 9-10
Cf. also Charles VI, Charles VII, Francis I, Joseph II, Leopold II, Francis II

Empire, Holy Roman, condition of in 1715, 2 ; how affected by Peace of Westphalia, 4 ; end of (1806), 498 ; proposals for reconstruction (1814-1815), Chapter XXXIV. *passim*

Enghien, Louis Duc de (ob. 1804), abducted and executed, 473

Erfurt, interview of (1808), 523-524

Erlon, Jean Comte de (French Marshal), in Waterloo campaign, 668 ; on June 16th, 676 ff., 680

Ernestine Saxons, divisions of, 53 ; 365, 510
Cf. Saxe-Coburg, Saxe-Gotha, Saxe-Weimar

Ernest Augustus of Hanover, 19, 47

Ernest Louis, Landgrave of Hesse-Darmstadt (1678-1739), 51, 368

Essling, battle of (1809), 537 ff.

Estrées, Louis Charles de (French general), campaign of 1757, 214

Eugene ; cf. Beauharnais

Eugene of Savoy, Prince, 12; in the Turkish War (1715–1717), 72–75, 80, 99; campaign of 1734, 100; death, 102

Eugene of Würtemberg, Prince; in Prussian service (1806), 509; in Russian (1813), 610–612; at Leipzig, 624 ff.
 Cf. also Frederick Eugene (Duke, 1763–1795), Prussian general in Seven Years' War

Eylau, battle of (1807), 514

Febronius, 330
Fehrbellin, battle of (1675), 41
Ferdinand I (Emperor), 112
Ferdinand II (Emperor), 7, 114
Ferdinand, Archduke (son of Maria Theresa), marries heiress of Modena, 180, 409; receives the Breisgau, 410, 453, 459, 462; dispossessed (1805), 493
 Cf. genealogy, 703
Ferdinand, Archduke (son of Ferdinand of Modena), in nominal command (1805), 482, 486, 489; 539
Ferdinand of Brunswick, at battle of Prague, 207, 217, 221; given command in Western Germany (1758), 230; campaign of 1758, 230–232, 248–250; campaign of 1759, 265–272; of 1760, 280–281; of 1761, 283–284; of 1762, 288–289; death (1792), 367
 Cf. Brunswick Genealogy, 704
Ferdinand VI, King of Spain (1746–1759), 165, 184; death, 272
Ferdinand of Tuscany (second son of Leopold II), receives Tuscany, 347; dispossessed by French, 423; receives Salzburg, 453, 459; transferred to Würzburg (1805), 494, 510, 552; regains Tuscany, 656
Fermor, William (Russian general), 213; in campaign of 1758, 237–241; superseded, 253; at Kunersdorf, 256
Fichte, Johann Gottlieb, 360, 523, 569
Finck, Frederick Augustus (Prussian general), 247; at Kunersdorf, 258, 261; at Maxen (1759), 263–264
Firmian, Charles, 180
Firmian, Leopold von, Archbishop of Salzburg, 85
Fleurus, battle of (1794), 399
Fleury, Cardinal, 82, 96, 101, 104; policy in 1740, 110, 123; death, 134
Fontenoy, battle of (1745), 155
Förster, George, 362, 381
Fouqué, Henry Augustus (Prussian general), 260, 273
Fox, Charles James, 382, 503
Foy, Maximilian (French general), on Quatre Bras, 680; at Waterloo, 690, 691 n.

Francis Stephen, Duke of Lorraine, 101; campaign of 1741, 126–127; elected Emperor as Francis I, 157, 182; death and character; 300, 707
Francis II (Emperor, 1792–1835): succeeds Leopold II, 377; intervenes in France, 379; character, 402; accepts Peace of Lunéville, 456; recognises Napoleon as Emperor and assumes title "Emperor of Austria," 474 n.; at Austerlitz, 490; comes to terms with Napoleon, 492, 515, 590; in 1814, 641 n.
Francis III of Este, Duke of Modena (1737–1780), 142; restored to dominions, 169; governs Lombardy, 180
Francis George of Schönborn, Elector of Treves (1729–1756), 122, 167
Francis Louis of Neuburg, Elector of Treves (1715–1729), 37, 81, 95; Elector of Mayence (1729–1732), 83, 707
Frankenberg, Count (Archbishop of Malines), 340
Frankfort, Grand Duchy of, created for Dalberg (1803), 463, 552–553; contingent in Spain, 552 n. and 553 n., 635, 647; suppressed (1815), 656
Frankfort am Main, given to Dalberg, 520; fate in 1815, 651
Frankfort, proposals of (1813), 635
 Union of (1744), 149
Frankfort on Oder, taken by Russians (1759), 254
Frederick I of Hesse-Cassel (Landgrave, 1730–1751), succeeds to Sweden (1720), 70; joins Union of Frankfurt, 150, 368
Frederick II of Hesse-Cassel (1760–1785), 321, 368
Frederick IV of Holstein-Gottorp (ob. 1703), 56
Frederick, Duke of Mecklenburg-Schwerin (1756–1785), 204
Frederick V, Elector Palatine, 5, 6, 84
Frederick I of Prussia, 19, 41; dies (1713), 66; 85
Frederick II of Prussia (1740–1786), 94; action in 1740, 99, 115; seizes Herstal, 111; his claim on Silesia, 112 ff.; in the first Silesian War, 116–131; makes Convention of Klein Schellendorf, 126; breaks it, 128; makes Peace of Berlin, 131; organises Union of Frankfort (1744), 149; in Second Silesian War, 150–161; makes Peace of Dresden, 162, 187; treaty with George II, 188–190; responsibility for Seven Years' War, 192; reforms during peace, 194–195; campaign of 1756, 196–200; of 1757, 204–212, 218–227; of 1758, 233–248; of 1759, 252–265;

of 1760, 273–279; of 1761, 281–283; of 1762, 287–288; position in 1763, 291; reforms, etc., after war, 294–298; policy towards Poland, 303–309; interference in Bavarian Succession, 312–314; forms *Fürstenbund* (1786), 320; death of (1786) and character, 322, 359
Cf. Hohenzollern genealogy, 705
Frederick, Duke of Würtemberg (1797–1816), becomes Elector (1803) 462; 469; joins Napoleon (1805), 483; becomes King (as Frederick I), 494; joins Confederation of Rhine, 497; the maker of Würtemberg, 550–551; deserts Napoleon, 631
Frederick Charles, Elector of Saxony (1763, Oct.–Dec.), 303
Frederick Eugene of Würtemberg (Duke, 1795–1797), serves as Prussian general in Seven Years' War, 225–226, 277–278, 283; 404
Frederick William, Elector of Brandenburg, his relations with Louis XIV, 26; with Leopold I, 27; his character and work, 40–41, 112
Frederick William I of Prussia (1713–1740), succeeds, 66; takes part in the Northern War, Chapter III.; guarantees Pragmatic Sanction, 81; protects Protestants, 85; military and domestic reforms, 86–93; foreign policy, 95–96, 99; death, 104; 564; 705
Frederick William II of Prussia; succession of, 1786, 322; character, 323; intervenes in Holland (1787), 325; foreign policy, 345, 348; relations with Austria, 354; attitude to French Revolution, 356 ff., 375, 377; Second Partition of Poland, 382; slackness in opposing France, 383–390; makes peace (1795), 392; Third Partition, 396–397; Prussia under his rule, 414–416; death (1797), 416; 705
Frederick William III of Prussia; succession (1797) and character, 416; continues neutral, 417; abstention from Second Coalition, 424, 437–438, 470; attitude to France (1803–1804), 476 ff.; is offered Hanover, 479; roused by Napoleon's violation of Prussian neutrality, 489; signs Convention of Potsdam, 489; character, 500; breach with Napoleon (1806), 503–504, 513, 515, 528; share in Stein's reforms, 559; attitude in 1813, 571, 573, 577, 591, 610, 643; designs on Saxony, 653–655; gains in 1815, 655; 705
Frederick William, Duke of Brunswick-Wolfenbüttel; receives Oels, 534; his rising, 534–535; restored, 631; killed at Quatre Bras, 689; 704

Free Cities, College of, 21–23; in 1792, 363, 373; fate of, in 1803, 460
Freiberg, battle of (1762), 288
Freiburg in Breisgau, siege of (1744), 151
French Revolution, becomes a European concern, 356; influence on Germany, 358–363
Friedland, battle of (1807), 516
Fulda, given to William V of Holland, 463; confiscated, 511; given to Dalberg, 519; 552, 656
Fürstenbund (1786), 320, 473, 475

Gadebusch, battle of (1712), 65
Gages (Spanish general), 143, 164
Gahmig, Prince Henry at (1758), 236
Galicia, claimed by Austria, 307; under Austrian rule, 309; divided (1809), 545; restored to Austria, 655
Galitzin, Alexander (Russian general), 256
General Directory (Prussia), 87 ff., 296, 416, 559
Genoa, joins Bourbons (1745), 164; Masséna's defence of (1800), 441–442
Gentz, Frederick von, 481; at Congress of Vienna, 648
George William of Luneburg-Celle, 46
George Lewis of Hanover (George I of England), his succession to Hanover, 47; to England, 19; share in Northern War, Chapter III.; refuses Alberoni's offers, 75
George II of England, 82; policy in 1741, 117, 124, 126, 137; in campaign of 1743, 138–141, 159, 184; relations with Austria, 185–187; treaty with Prussia, 189; denounces Convention of Closter Seven, 216–217; treaty with Prussia (1758), 229
George III of England, 286, 321, 470
Gérard, Etienne, Comte de (French Marshal), in Waterloo campaign, 668, 669; at Ligny, 673–678; with Grouchy, 684–685
Germanic Confederation, established by Congress of Vienna, 651–652
"German League Corps" (1814), 636; in 1815, 662 n.
Girard, Jean, Baron (French general), 601; defeated at Hagelberg, 605; at Ligny, 672–677
Girondins, 376, 384
Glatz, ceded to Prussia, 162; taken by Loudoun (1760), 274; given up to Prussia, 289
Gneisenau, Count Augustus (Prussian general), defends Colberg (1807), 514, 559, 564, 568, 607, 622, 635, 640; plan of campaign (1815), 663, 678; responsible for retreat to Wavre, 683,

for lateness of Prussians at Waterloo, 684 – 685 ; pursuit after Waterloo, 967

Goethe, Johann von, 360 ; at Wiemar (1808), 365, 523, 570

Göhrde, action at the (1813), 619

Golymin, battle of (1806), 513

Gortschakov, Prince Peter (Russian general), at Leipzig, 626–630

Gortz (Swedish minister), 66, 70

Gottorp ; vide Holstein

Graham, Sir Thomas, 636, 661

Granby, Marquis of, 280, 284, 288

Grand Army of 1812, Germans in, 568,570

Grand Army of 1813, 574–576 ; Germans in, 576 n. and 596 n., 616, 617

Gross Beeren, Oudinot defeated at (1813), 604–605

Gross, Görschen (=Lutzen), battle of (1813), 581–582

Grouchy, Emmanuel, Marshal, 450 ; in 1815, Chapter XXXV. passim, esp. 681–682 (his pursuit of Blücher), 684–685 (conduct on June 18th), 698–699 (battle of Wavre and retreat)

Guard, Napoleon's, at Dresden, 609–610 ; at Leipzig, 624–630 ; at Ligny, 675–677 ; at Marengo, 443 ; 602 ; at Waterloo, 691 n., 694–696

Guastalla, battle of (1734), 101

Gustavus III of Sweden, 326, 357

Gustavus IV of Sweden, keenly hostile to France, 478, 520

Gute alte Recht, das, 49, 550

Halberstadt, Bishopric of, passes to Bradenburg, 21

Halkett, Colin ·(British brigadier), at Waterloo, 688, 689, 695

Halkett, William (Hanoverian brigadier), at Waterloo, 688, 692, 695

Hanau, battle of (1813), 633

Hanover (cf. Brunswick-Luneburg), raised to Electorate, 19, 27, 45, 47 ; its territories, etc., in 1715, 47–48 ; troops of, at Dettingen, 137–140, 147 ; at Fontenoy, 156, 167–168 ; attitude in 1756, 201 ; troops of, in Seven Years' War, Chapters XI.–XIII. passim, esp. 204, 214–216, 268–269, 288 ; condition in 1792, 366 ; troops of, in India and at Gibraltar, 366, in Netherlands (1793–1795), 387 ff. ; accepts Peace of Basle, 392, 464 ; occupied by French (1803), 470–472 ; offered to Prussia, 479 ; occupied by Prussia, 489 ; given to Prussia at Schonbrünn, 493, 499 ; offered to England, 500, 503 ; partitioned, 518 ; arrangements as to 1813, 574, 617, 647, 651 ; extent, etc., in 1815, 655–656 ; contingent of, in 1815, 661,

656 n. ; at Quatre Bras, 678–679 ; at Waterloo, 688–696 ; losses, 697

Hanover, Convention of (1745), 160

Hanseatic League, decline of, 22, 373, 457 ; fate of, in 1807, 518, 558, 568, 590, 651

Harcourt, Comte de (French general), 129, 132

Hardenberg, Prince Charles Augustus (Prussian minister), negotiates Peace of Basle, 392 ; suspicions of France, 401, 463 ; in charge of foreign affairs (1804), 477 ; anxious to get Hanover, 478 ; out of office, 500 ; "First Cabinet Minister," 511 ; dismissed, 518, 528, 559 ; his reforms, 562–563 ; urges war (1813), 573, 577, 643 ; at Congress of Vienna, 648–659

Harrach, Joseph (Austrian minister), 108, 174, 301

Harsch (Austrian general), 234 ; besieges Neisse (1578), 243, 247

Hastenbeck, battle of (1757), 214

Hatzfeldt, Charles (Austrian minister), 173 ; Hofkanzler (1771), 301, 327, 333

Haugwitz, Christian Henry (Prussian minister), favours peace with France, 386, 416, 417, 419, 424 ; changing policy, 438 ; favours France, 476 ; losing ground, 477 ; sent with ultimatum to Napoleon, 490 ; signs Treaty of Schonbrünn (1805), 493 ; action criticised, 499 ; again in office, 500, 503 ; retires, 510

Haugwitz, Frederick William (Austrian minister), 173, 174, 176, 299 ; death, 301

Heilsberg, battle of (1807), 516

Henckel (Prussian general) in Waterloo campaign, 672–675

Henry of Prussia, Prince, 195 ; at battle of Prague, 207 ; at Rossbach, 222, 234, 236, 243, 246, 254, 260–263, 273–279, 287–288, 306, 386, 417, cf. 705

Herrnhausen, League of (1725), 79, 81 ; project of (1755), 187

Hersfeld, Bishopric of, passes to Hesse-Cassel, 21, 50

Herstal, seized by Frederick II, 111

Hertzberg, Count Frederick (Prussian minister), 320, 323, 325–326, 345 ; treaty with Poland (1790), 348, 354

Hesse-Cassel, extent of, 50 ; troops of, in British pay (1743–1748), 138–140, 147 n., 167, 168 ; (1756–1762), 204, 216, 231, 249, 269 ; for neutrality in 1757, 203 ; during Seven Years' War, Chapters XI.–XIII. passim ; joins Furstenbund, 321 ; in 1792, 368 ; hires troops to England (1777–1782), 368–369, (1793–1795), 388 ; makes peace with France, 395 ; gains and losses in

1803, 462 ; becomes Electorate, 463, 504 ; confiscated by Napoleon, 518 ; part of Kingdom of Westphalia, 518 ; risings in (1809), 533 ff. ; old government restored, 631 ; assists Allies (1814), 636, 651, 656 ; in 1815, 662 n. Cf. Charles I, Frederick I and II, William VI, VIII, IX

Hesse-Darmstadt, extent of, etc., 50 ; accedes to Treaty of Füssen, 154 ; supports Maria Theresa in 1757, 203, 321 ; condition in 1792, 368 ; gains and losses in 1803, 462 ; neutral in 1805, 483 ; joins Confederation of the Rhine, 497 ; sends contingent to Spain, 522 n. ; to Russia, 568, 552 ; contribution to Napoleon's army (1813), 596 n. ; deserts Napoleon (1813), 631 ; assists Allies (1814), 636, 651, 656 ; in 1815, 662 n. Cf. Ernest Louis (1678-1739), Louis VIII (1739-1768), Louis IX (1768-1790), Louis X (1790-1830)

Hildesheim, Bishopric of, 48 ; annexed by Prussia, 464

Hill, General Lord, in Waterloo campaign, 665 ff.

Hiller, Johann, Baron von (Austrian general), campaign of 1809, 531-544

Hiller (Prussian general), at Waterloo, 693-696

Hippolytus a Lapide = Ph. Boguslaw Chemnitz, 7

Hoche, Lazare (French general), 387, 409 n., 421

Hochkirch, battle of (1758), 243

Hofer, Andreas, 545

Hofgericht, 16, 302

Hofkammer (Austrian Treasury), 35, 78, 107, 177

Hofkriegsrath, 78, 283 n.

Hohenfriedberg, battle of (1745), 157

Hohenlinden, battle of (1800), 449-451

Hohenlohe, Frederick Louis, Prince of (Prussian general), 502 ; campaign of Jena, 505-510

Hohenzollern, family of, genealogy, 705 Cf. Anspach, Baireuth, Brandenburg, Prussia

Hohenzollern-Hechingen, 497, 651

Hohenzollern-Sigmaringen, 497, 651

Holland, adheres to League of Herrnhausen, 81 ; attitude in 1759, 204 ; conflict with Joseph II, 317-318 ; troubles in (1787-1788), 325 ; conquered by French (1795), 390 ; becomes Batavian Republic, 391 ; Anglo-Russian expedition to (1799), 435, 437 ; obtains E. Frisia, 517

Holstein (cf. Schleswig-Holstein), 54-56, 316 ; exchanged against Oldenburg, 369 ; 651, 657

Cf. Adolphus Frederick, Charles IV, Charles Frederick, Paul of Russia

Holstein-Eutin, Christian Augustus of, 56, 66

Holstein-Eutin, Frederick Augustus of, becomes Duke of Oldenburg (1773-1785), 369

Holstein-Eutin, Peter Frederick Louis ; Regent of Oldenburg (q.v.), 369, 569 Peter Frederick William, Duke of Oldenburg (1785-1823), 369, 566

Hotze, Frederick (Austrian general), 427-430 ; killed, 437

Houchard, Jean Nicolas (French general), 386

Hulsen (Prussian general), 210-211 ; 277-279

Humbolt, William von, Minister of Public Instruction, Prussia, founds University of Berlin, 563, 570 ; at Congress of Vienna, 648-659, esp. 652

Hungary, connection with Austria, 31, 33 ; supports Maria Theresa, 125, 151 ; condition of, under Maria Theresa, 180-182 ; discontent in, 325, 327, 334, 343-345 ; Leopold I's settlement, 349, 540

Illyrian provinces, 545, 590 ; restored to Austria (1815), 657

Imhoff (Hanoverian general), 249, 266, 280

Imperial Army, its composition and condition in 1715, 10-12 ; in the Rossbach campaign, 217, 221-222 ; in 1758, 236 ; in 1759, 252 ; captures Dresden (1759), 261 ; at Maxen, 263 ; in 1760, 277-278 ; 288

Imperial Chamber (cf. Kanmergericht or Reichskammergericht), 464

Imperial Court (cf. Hofgericht)

Imperial deputation, 13

Imperial Knights, their position, 59, 374 ; escape suppression in 1803, 459, 464 ; treatment of (1803-1805), 467-468 ; mediatised, 494, 496

Imperial revenue, 13, 59

"Inn-Viertel," ceded to Austria (1779), 314 ; transferred to Bavaria (1809), 544 ; restored to Austria (1815), 701

Italy, Kingdom of, 479 ; receives Venice and Dalmatia, 493 ; receives South Tyrol, 545

Jaegerndorf, Prussian claim on, 114

Jägow (Prussian general), at Ligny, 672-679

Jellachich, Baron Francis von (Austrian general), 486-487, 539

Jena, University of, 365 ; battle of (1806), 507-508

Jerome Bonaparte (King of Westphalia), 513, 535, 555-558, 635

Jesuits, 331

John, Archduke (sixth son of Leopold II), commands at Hohenlinden, 449–451; in Tyrol 1805), 487; bellicose (1809), 528; campaign of 1809, 535–544; beaten at Raab, 540; too late at Wagram, 543; resigns, 544; attitude in 1813, 578, 645; 703

John George II of Saxony (ob. 1656), his disposition of his territories, 39, 113

John Frederick, Duke of Hanover, 25

John William of Neuburg, Elector Palatine (1690–1716), his policy, 44–45; persecutes Protestants, 85; 707

Joseph I, death of, a turning point in German history, 1, 30; and Hungary, 34

Joseph II (Emperor 1765–1790), 178, 182; election as King of the Romans, 184, 185, 202, 290; elected, 299; becomes Emperor, 300; inaugurates reforms, 301–302; share in Partition of Poland, 305–309; foreign policy of, Chapter XV. (cf. Bavaria, Netherlands, Catharine II); death and character, 327, 346; ecclesiastical policy, 328–334; educational policy, 331–332; legal reforms, 334; agrarian reforms, 334–336; and his ministers, 338; economic policy, 339; provokes insurrection in Netherlands, 340–343; and Hungary, 343–345

Joseph of Austria (fifth son of Leopold II), Archduke, 544, 703

Joseph Bonaparte, 448; King of Naples, 503; of Spain, 528

Joseph of Sulzbach, 95, 707

Joseph Clement of Bavaria, Elector of Cologne (1688–1723), 37–38, cf. 707

Joubert, Barthélemy (French general), 409; killed at Novi (1799), 435

Jourdan, Jean Baptiste, Marshal, wins Fleurus (1794), 389, 390, 399, 401; campaign of 1796, 402–407; of 1799, 426–428

Joyeuse Entrée, 179, 342

Jülich (cf. Berg), 45, 81, 94 ff., 128; annexed to France, 460; to Prussia (1815), 655

Jürgass (Prussian general), at Ligny, 672–677

Kalisch, Treaty of (1813), 574, 647; Convention of, 577

Kalckreuth, Count (Prussian general), 513, 517

Kammergericht (Imperial Chamber of Justice), 8; how supported, 13; its composition and history, 14, 302, 320, 464

Kammerzieler (=Chamber Terms), 13

Kanitz (Prussian general), 240

Kant, Immanuel, 360

Katzbach, battle of the (1813), 606–608

Kaunitz, Wenceslaus Anthony, Count, 169, 172–173; foreign policy, 180, 182–184; becomes Chancellor, 184; renews project for French alliance, 190, 229, 283 n., 285, 299; share in Partition of Poland, 304–309; opposes overtures to Prussia, 323, 326; ecclesiastical policy, 332, 341; hostile to Prussia, 354; resigns (1793), 413

Keith, James Francis Edward (Prussian Marshal), 198, 206, 209, 235; killed at Hochkirch (1758), 245

Kellermann, Francis Christopher, Duc de Valmy (French Marshal), at Valmy, 380

Kellermann, Francis Stephen (French general), at Marengo, 444; in 1813, 602, 623; in 1815, 679

Kempt, Sir John, at Quatre Bras, 678; at Waterloo, 691

Kesselsdorf, battle of (1745), 161

Khevenhüller, Louis (Austrian general), 101, 103; campaign in Bavaria (1741–1742), 127 ff., 177

Kielmansegge (Hanoverian general), at Quatre Bras, 679; at Waterloo, 688–689

Kienmayer, Baron Michael (Austrian Marshal), at Hohenlinden, 450; 488–489; at Austerlitz, 491

" King's German Legion," formation of (1803), 472; 522 n., 583, 605; in 1815, Chapter XXXV. passim, esp. 661, 665 n.; at Waterloo, 688

Kinsky, Philip (Chancellor of Bohemia), 108, 172

Klein Schellendorf, Convention of (1741), 126; denounced by Frederick, 128

Kleist, Emilius Friederich (Prussian general), in autumn campaign of 1813, 597–633, esp. 612

Kleist, Heinrich von (poet), 570

Kleist (Prussian general), 260

Klenau, Johann (Austrian general), 435, 449, 451; at Wagram, 541–543; in 1813, 611, 624–628

Knesebeck, von (Prussian Marshal), 592, 635, 662 n., 700

Knyphausen, Henry (Prussian minister), 195

Kolafat, battle of (1790), 349

Kolin, battle of (1757), 210–211

Kolowrat, Leopold (Austrian minister), 301 (Chancellor), 338

Kolowrat (Austrian general), in 1809, 537, 539, 542

Königgratz, 235

Königsegg (Austrian general), 100, 103, 180, 182

Königsegg (Austrian general), the younger, 205, 206

Korsakov, Michaelovitch (Russian general), 432, 435–437

Kosciuzsko, Thaddeus (Polish patriot), 396

Krafft (Prussian general), at Ligny, 672–677

Krasinski, Marshal (Poland), 304

Kray, Baron Paul (Austrian general), 402, 426, 428, 435; campaign of 1800, 441, 442, 445–447

Kruse, Colonel (Nassau), 681 n., 689

Kulm, battle of (1813), 611–613; its effects, 614

Kunersdorf, battle of (1759), 225–259

Kurakin, Count (Russian minister), 459, 516

Kutusov, Prince Michael (Russian general), campaign of 1805, 487–496, 571

Lacy, Count Joseph Maurice (Austrian general), at Lobositz, 198; at Hochkirch, 245; plan for 1760, 273; campaign of 1760, 274–279, 287; President of War Council, 1765–1774, 301, 327, 428

La Fere Champenoise, battle of (1814), 640

La Haye Sainte (cf. Waterloo), 688, 690–691

Lambert, Sir John, 665 n.; at Waterloo, 691

Landshut, Fouqué defeated at (1760), 273

Langen (Prussian general), at Ligny, 675–677

Langeron, Count (Russian general), 593, 597; autumn campaign of 1813, 606–633, esp. Katzbach, Leipzig; of 1814, 636–642

Lannes, Jean (Franch Marshal), 441, 485, 491–492; campaign of 1806, 505–510, 513; campaign of 1809, 531–538

Laon, battle of (1814), 640

La Rothière, battle of (1814), 637

Latour-Maubourg, Marquis de (French general), autumn campaign of 1813, 602–633

Lauffeldt, battle of (1747), 168

Lauriston, Marquis de (French Marshal), spring campaign of 1813, 580–588; autumn campaign, 602–633

League of the Rhine (1658), 25, 27

League of Vienna (1725), 79

Leczinski, Stanislaus, 64; candidature for Poland, 98 ff.; receives Lorraine, 101

Lefebvre, Francis Joseph (French Marshal), besieges Dantzic, 514; commands Bavarians (1809), 529–544

Lehrbach, Louis Conrad (Austrian minister), 429, 448

Lehwaldt (Prussian general), beaten at Gross Jaegerndorf (1757), 213

Leibnitz, Gottfried Wilhelm, his reply to Pufendorf, 8; his *Bedenken*, 25

Leipzig, battle of (1813), 623–629

Leipzig, city of, 23, 654

Leoben, preliminaries of (1797), 409

Leopold II (Emperor, 1790–1792), becomes Grand Duke of Tuscany (1765), 300, 336; succeeds Joseph II, 347; concludes Treaty of Reichenbach, 348–349; settlement of Hungary, 349; suppresses Belgian insurrection, 350; reforms, 351–352; attitude to French Revolution, 353; makes peace with Turkey, 353; negotiations with Prussia, 354; intervention in France, 375–376; death, 377; 703

Leopold of Anhalt-Dessau, Prince (the elder), 68, 91, 117, 160–162

Leopold of Anhalt-Dessau, Prince (the younger), 130

Leopold Joseph, Duke of Lorraine (1690–1729), 58

Lestocq, Anton von (Prussian general), 513–516

Leuthen, battle of (1757), 224–227

Lichtenstein, Prince, 544

Liége, Bishopric of, 48, 111
City of, taken by Saxe, 167
insurrection in (1789), 356

Liegnitz, Prussian claim on, 112; battle of (1760), 275, 276

Ligny, battle of 1815, 671–677

Linz, seized by Franco-Bavarians (1741), 124, 537; see of, 329

Lippe, Princes of, 520, 651

Lippe-Schaumburg or Lippe-Bückeburg, William of, 371, 502

Lobau, Count (French general), in Waterloo campaign, 668, 677; at Waterloo, 695, 696

Lobau, island of, 537–541

Lobkowitz, Count (Austrian general), 130; allows Belleisle to escape from Prague, 133; in Italy, 163

Lobositz, battle of (1756), 198

Lombardy, Austrian rule in, 142 n., 300, 408; ceded to France, 409; restored to Austria, 657
Cf. Milanese

Lorraine, 58, 98; ceded to Stanislaus Leczinski, 101, 360

Lothair Francis of Schönborn, Elector of Mayence (1693–1729), 37

Loudoun, Gideon Ernest (Austrian general), at siege of Olmütz, 234–236; at Hochkirch, 243–245; in campaign of 1759 (Kunersdorf), 254–259, 262; campaign of 1760, 273–279; takes

Schweidnitz (1761), 283, 291, 313; campaign of 1788 (Danube), 324; of 1789, 326; death (1790), 349

Louis of Austria, Archduke (eleventh son of Leopold II), 531; 703

Louis IX, Landgrave of Hesse-Darmstadt (1768–1790), 368

Louis X, Landgrave of Hesse-Darmstadt (1790–1830), 368, 483, 497; faithful to Napoleon, 552, 631, 651, 656

Louis XIV, aggressions against Germany, 2, 24; and the League of the Rhine (1658), 25; and Hungary, 33; policy towards Germany compared with Napoleon's, 525

Louis XV, 98; supports Bavaria, 124, 126, 148, 154; supports war policy (1758), 228; policy towards Poland, 303

Louis XVI, 376, 378; executed, 382

Louis of Baden-Baden, Margrave (1677–1707), 12, 50

Louis, Dauphin, born (1729), 81

Louis Eugene, Duke of Würtemberg (1793–1795), 371 n.

Louis Ferdinand of Prussia, Prince, anti-French, 476; leads war party, 501, 504; death, 506; 705

Louis George of Baden-Baden, Margrave (1707–1761), 50, 370

Louise, Queen of Prussia, hostile to France, 476, 504, 517; 705

Löwenwolde, Treaty of (1732), 98

Lucchesi (Austrian general), 207–224

Lucchesini, Jerome, Marquis de (Prussia), 348; favours peace with France, 386, 471, 478, 503

Lunéville, negotiations at, 448; peace of (1801), 452–453

Lutterberg, battle of (1758), 250

Lützen, battle of (1813), 581–582

Lützow's Free Corps, 576, 588

Luxemburg, Grand Duchy of, 651, 656

Macdonald, Marshal (French), in Italy (1799), 433–434; in 1800, 449, 451; campaign of 1809, 536–544; campaign of 1812, 568, 572; spring campaign of 1813, 581–588; autumn campaign, 602–633 (esp. cf. Katzbach); of 1814, 637–642

Mack, Charles (Austrian general), 388; appointed Quarter-Master General, 481; in campaign of 1805, 482–486

Magdeburg, Bishopric of, passes to Brandenburg, 21; taken from Prussia (1807), 517; restored in 1815, 655

Maillebois, Marshal (French), 124, 126, 132, 164

Maltzahn (Prussian minister), 195

Mannstein (Prussian general), at Prague, 207; at Kolin, 210–211

Manteuffel (Prussian general), 240

Mantua, 101, 402; siege of (1796–1797), 407–408; taken by Austrians (1799), 434

Marengo, battle of (1800), 443–444

Maria Amelia, Archduchess, marries Charles Albert of Bavaria, 79, 109, 154; 703, 707

Maria Anna, Archduchess, 80, 173, 180; 703

Maria Josepha, Archduchess, marries Electoral Prince of Saxony, 79, 109; 703, 706

Maria Theresa, 45; marriage of, 101; succeeds Charles IV (1740), 105; and her enemies, Chapter VII.; in the Austrian Succession War, Chapter VIII. and IX.; appeal to Hungarian loyalty, 125; has to make peace, 169; military and domestic reforms, 174–182; foreign policy, 182–185; action in 1756, 195–196; in the Seven Years' War, Chapters XI.–XIII.; agrees to peace (1763), 289; reforms, etc., after the war, 298–301; policy towards Poland, 304–309; overruled by Joseph II, 310, 313; death (1780) and character, 315, 317; ecclesiastical policy, 329–330

Cf. Hapsburg genealogy, 703

Marie Louise, Archduchess, marries Napoleon, 552; 566, 657 n.; 703

Marmont, August (French Marshal), 444, 487, 488, 536; spring campaign of 1813, 581–588, 601; autumn campaign, 601–633, esp. Dresden; Leipzig, of 1814, 636–642

Masséna, André (French Marshal), 401; in Switzerland (1799), 426–427, 431–437; defence of Genoa (1800), 440–442; commands in Italy (1805), 487; campaign of 1809, 529–544

Matthews (English admiral), 143, 146

Maurice of Anhalt-Dessau (Prussian general), 205, 210–211, 218, 225–226, 240, 244–245

Maurice de Saxe (Marshal Saxe), 127, 147, 166–168, 223; 706

Maxen, Finck capitulates at (1759), 263–264

Maximilian I (Emperor), 3, 14, 16

Maximilian II (Emperor), 16

Maximilian of Austria, 315, 320; Elector of Cologne (1785–1801), 373, 400 n., 448; death of, 458; 703

Maximilian of Austria, Archduke (son of Ferdinand of Modena), 535

Maximilian I of Bavaria (1598–1651), his character and achievements, 42–43

Maximilian Emanuel of Bavaria (1679–1726), his policy in the Spanish Succession War, 19, 43, 83

Maximilian Joseph of Bavaria (1745–1777), 153; makes Peace of Füssen, 154; supports Austria in Seven Years' War, 203; death of, 310–311; 707

Maximilian Joseph of Zweibrücken, 364, 409 n.; becomes Elector of Bavaria (1799), 425; supports Second Coalition, 425, 439, 451, 456, 468–470; joins Napoleon (1803), 483, 493; becomes King, 494, 497, 520, 529, 549–550, 553, 570; 707

Maximilian of Rottenfels, Elector of Cologne (1761–1785), 315, 321

Mayence, city of, taken by French (1792), 381; recovered (1793), 385, 387, 390, 398; siege of, raised (1795), 400; Napoleon at (1804), 475; a Federal fortress (1815), 656

Mayence, Electorate of, connection with Arch Chancellorship of Germany, 19; its traditional policy, etc., 36, cf. 463; its extent, 36, 48; in 1792, 373, 454; fate in 1803, 462, 464; in 1815, 655–656

Mayence, Electors of, Lothair Francis of Schönborn (1695–1729), 37
Francis Louis of Neubourg (1729–1732), 83, 95; 707
Philip Charles of Eltz-Kempten (1732–1743), 122
John Frederick of Ostein (1743–1763), 167
Emeric Joseph of Breidbach (1763–1774)
Frederick Charles Joseph of Erthal (1774–1803), 321, 357, 373, 436, 456
Cf. Dalberg

Mazarin, Cardinal, his policy towards Germany, 25, 455

Mecklenburg, divisions of, 53; affairs of, 69; condition of, in 1792, 369; contingent of, in Grand Army of 1812, 568; of 1813, 576 n.; 656; 667

Mecklenburg-Schwerin, Dukes of:
Charles Leopold of (1713–1747), 54, 69–70, 94
Christian Louis of (1747–1756), 84, 94
Frederick of (1756–1785), 204, 314
Frederick Francis I of (1785–1837), 369, 464; joins Confederation of the Rhine, 520, 568, 596, 651; becomes Grand Duke, 656

Mecklenburg-Strelitz, Dukes of:
Adolphus Frederick II (1708–1749), 54
Charles Louis (1749–1752)
Adolphus Frederick III (1752–1794)
Charles (1794–1816), 369, 464; joins Confederation of the Rhine, 520, 568, 596 n., 651; becomes Grand Duke, 656

"Mediatisation," 498

Melas, Michel, Baron de (Austrian general), at Novi, 435; defeats Championnet, 437; campaign of 1800 (Marengo), 441–445

Mentzel, Frederick William (Saxony), 187, 195

Metternich, Prince Clement Wenceslaus, at Rastatt, 429; advocates peace, 544; becomes Foreign Minister, 544; his internal policy, 545, 552; alliance with Napoleon, 565–566; attitude in 1813, 572, 578, 579, 587, 598; negotiates Treaty of Töplitz, 618, 630, 635; not revengeful, 643; policy in 1814, 645 ff.; presides over Congress of Vienna, 647; champions minor states, 652; attitude on Saxon question, 653; attitude towards Napoleon in 1815, 661; fosters Russo-Prussian disagreements, 700; 702

Milan, Duchy of, ceded to Austria (1715), 33; lost at Campo Formio, 410; restored to Austria, 657

Minden, battle of (1759), 268–270
Bishopric of, 42, 655

Möckern, battle of (1813), 580

Modena, added to Cisalpine Republic, 453; Hapsburgs restored in, 657
Cf. Francis III of Este; Ferdinand

Moldavia, occupied by Russia, 306; restored to Turkey, 309

Möllendorf, Joachim Henry (Prussian general), 386, 415; surrenders at Weimar (1806), 509

Mollwitz, battle of (1741), 118

Mömpelgard (Montbéliard), 21; acquired by Würtemberg (1723), 49, 404 n.; lost (1803), 460

Montereau, battle of (1814), 638

Montgelas, Count Max von (Bavarian minister), 425, 469, 536, 549, 579; favours neutrality, 618

Montijo (Spanish Ambassador at Dresden), 110

Montmartin (Würtemberg), 371

Montmirail, battle of (1814), 638

Monzambano, Severin de, cf. Pufendorf

Moreau, Jean Victor (French general), campaign of 1796, 401–403; of 1799, 433; of 1800, 440, 445–447; victory at Hohenlinden, 450; joins Allies (1813), 598

Mors, acquired by Brandenburg (1702), 42; lost to France, 392, 463

Mortier, Edouard (French Marshal), invades Hanover (1803), 470, 473, 488, 513, 610; in 1814, 636–642

Moys, Winterfeldt defeated at (1757), 218

Münchhäusen, Baron Gerlach Adolf von (Hanoverian minister), 187

Munchmayer, Michael, on the German Constitution, 28

Münich, Marshal (Russia), 110

"Municipal Reform Edict," 560

Münster, Bishopric of, 48 ; fate in 1803, 464 ; in 1807, 519 ; in 1815, 655

Münster, Count von, Hanoverian representative at Vienna, 648, 650

Murat, Joachim (Marshal), 485, 586, 490–492 ; obtains Grand Duchy of Berg, 496 ; campaign of 1806, 505–510 ; of 1807, 514–516, 553 ; transferred to Naples as King, 555 ; 568 ; at Dresden, 610–611 ; at Leipzig, 622–626 ; action in 1815, 660 ; beaten at Tolentino, 701

Nadasky, Francis Leopold (Austrian general), 210–211, 218–220, 224

Naples, Kingdom of, ceded to Austria (1715), 33 ; to Don Carlos, 101, 163 ; joins Second Coalition (1798), 423, 503 Cf. Two Sicilies, Murat

Napoleon, influence of on Germany, 362 ; Italian campaign of 1796, 401–402, 407–408 ; at Leoben, 408 ; returns to France (1799), 438 ; campaign of 1800, 441–444 ; imposes conditions on Austria, 452, 454 ; policy towards Germany, 1801–1803, 455–460 ; true author of Third Coalition, 465 and Chapter XXIV. *passim* ; assumes Imperial title, 474 ; visits Mayence (1804), 475 ; moves against Austria, 480 ; campaign of 1805, Chapter XXV. ; policy of, 494–495 ; forms Confederation of the Rhine, 497–498 ; offers Hanover to England, 503 ; execution of Palm, 504 ; campaign of 1806–1807, 505–516 ; makes peace of Tilsit, 516–518 ; creates new states in Germany, 518–520 ; starts Continental System, 520 ; relations with Alexander I, 521–524 ; with Austria, 521 ; at Erfurt (1808), 523 ; policy towards Germany, 525–526 ; compared with Louis XIV, 526 ; in Spain, 528 ; campaign of 1809, 530–543 ; dictates Peace of Schönbrunn, 544–545 ; attitude of Germany to, 547–549, 567 ; changed relations with Austria, 565–566 ; quarrels with Russia, 566–568 ; efforts of, in 1813, 571, 574–576 ; spring campaign of 1813, 580–588 ; agrees to armistice, 587 ; his error, 588–589 ; misled by Metternich, 589 ; preparations for autumn campaign, 595–596 ; strategy in autumn campaign, 600–601, cf. 615 ; autumn campaign, 602 ff. ; position at end of August, 614 ; retires from Dresden, 621 ; defeated at Leipzig, 622–629 ; retreats to

France, 630 and 632 ; victory of Hanau, 633 ; campaign of 1814, 634–642 ; abdicates, 642 ; escapes from Elba (1815), 660 ; attitude of Powers towards him, 661 ; his professions and preparations, 663–665 ; plan of campaign (1815), 664 ; his army, 667–668 ; plan on June 16th, 671 (cf. Ligny); delay on June 17th, 680, cf. 682 ; at Waterloo, 687–696 ; abdicates, 699

Narbonne, Comte Louis de (French War Minister), 376

Nassau, in 1715, 59 ; in 1792, 372 and n. (=Orange-Nassau), 404, 460, 463, 497, 656 ; confiscated, 511 ; contingent in Spain, 522 n. ; assists Napoleon (1809), 537 ; restored, 631 ; assists Allies, 636, 651, 655 ; contingent of, in 1815, 665 n., 670 ; at Waterloo, 681, 689

Nassau-Dillenberg, William of, elected Stadtholder of United Provinces, 1747, 168 ; cf. William v

Neerwinden, Dumouriez defeated at (1793), 384

Neipperg, William, Marshal, 101 ; campaign of 1741, 118–120, 126, 139, 163, 177

Neisse, 116 ; surrenders to Frederick II, 126 ; interview between Frederick and Joseph at (1769), 305 ; besieged (1807), 515

Nemesis Theresiana (Austrian Criminal Code), 178

Nesselrode, Charles Robert (Russian minister), 577 ; at Vienna (1814), 648

Netherlands, 36 ; relations to Austria, 105, 179–180, 201 ; under Joseph II, 317–318, 322 ; troubles in, 327, 342–343 ; rebellion suppressed, 350 ; conquered by French (1794), 390 ; surrendered by Austria, 410, 453 ; Kingdom of, 656 ; its troops in 1815, 662, cf. Dutch-Belgians

Neuburg, Philip William of, cf. Philip William, Elector Palatine

Neuchatel, acquired by Brandenburg (1707), 92

Newcastle-under-Lyme, Thomas, first Duke of, 191

Ney, Michel, Marshal, at Hohenlinden, 450–451 ; campaign of 1805, 485–496 ; of 1806, 506–510 ; of 1807, 514–516 ; 568 ; spring campaign of 1813, 580–588 ; autumn campaign, 602–633, esp. 615–616 ; campaign of 1814, 636–642 ; in Waterloo campaign, 670, 676–680

Noailles, Duc de, 134 ; at Dettingen, 137–140, 148

Norris, Admiral Sir John, 68, 146

North, Army of the (1813), 597, 600 ; at Gross Beeren, 604–605 ; at Dennewitz, 615–616, 622; at Leipzig, 626–629

Novi, battle of (1799), 435

Nystadt, Peace of (1721), 71

Oldenburg, connection with Denmark, 56; guaranteed to Holstein family, 316; ceded to Frederick Augustus of Holstein-Eutin (1773), 369; gains in 1803, 464; annexed by Napoleon (1810), 518, 520, 558, 566, 651; becomes Grand Duchy, 656

Olmütz, besieged by Frederick II, 234; relieved, 236

Olsuviev (Russian general), 638

Olsuviev (Russian minister), 203

Ompteda, Colonel von (K.G.L.), at Waterloo, 688–689, 691

Orange, House of, 59, 169, 463, 631, 647

Orange, Prince William of, in 1815, 665, 669; at Waterloo, 688, 690–691

Orsova, ceded to Austria (1791), 354

Osnabrück, Bishopric of, 46, 48, 464; forms part of Westphalian kingdom, 518; restored to Hanover (1815), 655

Ostend East India Company, 79–80; suppressed, 82, 185

Ostend, Wellington's base in 1815, 665

Ott, Baron von (Austrian general), 433–435, 441–444

Otto, Louis (French minister at Berlin), 438

Oubril, Count (Russian Envoy at Paris), 478

Oudinot, Charles Nicolas, Marshal, 436; campaign of 1809, 529–544; spring campaign of 1813, 580–588; autumn campaign, 600–633 (cf. esp. 601; Gross Beeren, Dennewitz); campaign of 1814, 636–642

Pack, Sir Denis, in Waterloo campaign, 678

Paderborn, Bishopric of, 48; acquired by Prussia (1803), 464

Pajol (French general), in Waterloo campaign, 666, 684

Palm, Johann Philip, execution of, 504

Paltzig, battle of (1759), 253

Panin, Count (Russian minister), 313

Pardo, Convention of the, 81

Paris, surrenders to Allies (1814), 642
    Treaty of (1814), 642
    Second Treaty of (1815), 701
    occupied by Allies (1815), 699

Paris-Duverney (French minister), 202, 213

Parma (see also Elizabeth Farnese), passes to Don Carlos; battle at (1734), 100; restored to Austria, 101; ceded to Don Philip, 169; annexed

to France, 479; restored to Bourbons, 657

Passaro, Cape, battle of (1718), 77

Passarowitz, Peace of (1718), 75

Patinol, Don José, 81

Paul I of Russia, renounces claim on Holstein, 369; joins Second Coalition, 423–425; withdraws from it, 438; supports Napoleon, 452; murdered (1801), 457

Peace of Carlowitz (1699), 73
    Passarowitz (1718), 75
    Nystadt (1720), 71
    Stockholm (1720), 70
    Vienna (1738), 101
    Belgrade (1739), 103
    Berlin (1742), 131
    Aix-la-Chapelle (1748), 169
    Hubertsberg (1763), 289
    Fontainebleau (1763), 289
    Kainardji (1774), 309
    Tetschen (1779), 313
    Sistova (1791), 354
    Verela (1792), 352
    Jassy (1792), 354
    Basel (1795), 392
    Cherasco (1796), 402
    Lunéville (1801), 452
    Pressburg (1805), 493
    Tilsit (1807), 516–518

Perponcher, Count William (Dutch-Belgian general), in 1815, 670, 678

Peter the Great, 65–71

Peter III of Russia, 150, 213, 228, 282; succeeds, 286; assists Frederick, 286; deposed, 287, 291

Peter Frederick Louis of Holstein-Eutin, Regent, and later Duke of Oldenburg 369, 566, 569

Peterwardein, battle of (1716), 73

Pfaffenhofen, Treaty of (1796), 406–407

Philip V of Spain, attacks Sicily and Sardinia, 75 ff., 79; guarantees Pragmatic Sanction, 80; death of (1746), 165

Philip Charles of Eltz-Kempten, Elector of Mayence (1734–1743), 122

Philip, Don (son of Elizabeth Farnese), 142, 144, 145, 164; obtains Parma, 169; 183

Philip William of Neuburg, Elector Palatine (1685–1690), succeeds to Palatinate, 19; 707

Phull (Prussian general), 504

Piccolomini (Austrian general), 197, 200

Pichégru, Charles (French general), 387, 389, 391, 399–400

Picton, Sir Thomas, in Waterloo campaign, 678–679, 690

Piedmont, annexed to France, 453; Thugut's designs on, 432; attitude in 1799, 433

Pillnitz, Declaration of (1791), 375
Pirch I (Prussian general), in 1815, at Ligny, 671–677, 686; at Waterloo, 695
Pirch II (Prussian general), in 1815, 668, 671–679
Pirna, Saxons besieged at, 197–200
Pitt, William (Earl of Chatham), 186, 204; employs British troops in Germany, 231; falls, 286
Pitt, William, foreign policy, 325, 348, 350, 354, 376; share in First Coalition, 384; subsidy treaties, 388, 393, 409, 417, 467; refuses to let Russia take Hanover, 489; death (1806), 500, 503
Pius VI (Pope), 330; visits Vienna, 333, 423
Planchenoit (cf. Waterloo), 693–696
Poland, connection with Saxony, 19; share in Northern War (1700–1721), Chapter III.; affairs of, 303–309; First Partition (1773), 308; Second Partition (1793), 382–383; Third Partition (1795), 385, 396–397; rally to Napoleon, 514; fate of, discussed at Vienna, 652–655; redistribution of (1815), 655
Pomerania, Western, Southern portion passes to Prussia (1720), 70; Swedish, 520 n.; ceded to Prussia (1815), 655
Poniatowski, Prince Joseph, in French service, 539; autumn campaign of 1813, 602–630
Poniatowski, Stanislaus, elected King of Poland, 303; 304, 396
Portland Ministry (1807–1809), 515
Posen, ceded to Prussia (1773), 308, 655
Potemkin, Prince Gregory (Russia), 313
Potsdam, Convention of (1805), 489
Pragmatic Sanction, issued by Charles VI, 79; recognised by Philip V, 80; guaranteed, 83; the Powers, and after Charles VI's death, 108–114, 162
Prague, taken by Franco-Bavarians (1741), 127; retaken by Austrians, 133; taken by Frederick II, 150; evacuated, 152; battle of (1757), 206–208; besieged, 208–212; Congress of (1813), 592–594
Princes, their interests as affected by the Reformation, 4; their relations with the Imperial Courts of Justice, 9; College of, 20–21; Ecclesiastical members of, 48; minor lay members, 59; escape suppression, 460; in 1803, 465
Protestantism, its political importance, 4; persecution of, 34, 85; in Austria, 333; in majority in Diet, 465
Prussia, condition of, government, etc., 41–42, 86–93; share in Northern War, 66–71, 81 n.; foreign policy of, 94–

96; in Austrian Succession War, 111–163; 170; in Seven Years' War, Chapters XI.–XIII., 294–298; and Poland, 303–308; opposes Joseph II over Bavaria, 312–314; forms Fürstenbund, 319–320, 322; intervenes in Holland, 324–326; in Hungary, 326, 345, 348; ineffective part in First Coalition, Chapter XIX., esp. 390; makes peace at Basel, 392–395; under Frederick William II and III, 414–416; policy of neutrality, 417, 424; in 1799, 437–438; joins Armed Neutrality (1800), 457, 458–459; gains in 1803, 460, 463–464; alarmed by French occupation of Hanover (1803), 471–472; conduct in the Austerlitz campaign, 489–492; draws back after Austerlitz, 493; quarrel with Napoleon, 499–500; embroiled with England, 500; unsatisfactory condition of, in 1805, 500–502; mistaken strategy, 504; ministerial changes, 511; war with Napoleon, 504–516; losses at Tilsit, 516–518; Napoleon's harshness to, 521; has to accept Convention of Sept. 1808, 522; inaction in 1809, 534, 544; reforms of Stein and others, 558–565; assists Napoleon against Russia, 565; anti-Napoleonic movement (1813), 572–573; declares against Napoleon, 574; anxious for revenge, 635, 643; views on reconstruction, 647–650; designs on Saxony, 652–655; attitude towards Napoleon in 1815, 661; bitterness of, against France, 699; isolation of, 701; cf. Frederick William I, II and III; Frederick I and II; Stein, Hardenberg, etc.
Prussian Army, reformed by Frederick William I, 90–93; condition in 1756, 194; in Seven Years' War, Chapters XI.–XIII.; (esp. 224, 241 n., 242, 252); after the war, 294, 298; in 1792, 379, 415; collapse foretold, 424; condition in 1805, 501–502; collapse in Jena campaign, 505–511; reformed by Scharnhorst, 563–565; in 1813, 576 ff.; in 1814, 636–640; in 1815, 661–662; at Ligny, 672–677; retreat to Wavre, 682–683; late arrival at Waterloo, 684–685; share in Waterloo, 692–696; losses, 697
Pufendorf (=Severin de Monzambano), his views on the German constitution, 8, 499
Pultowa, battle of (1709), 64
Pultusk, battle of (1806), 513

Quadruple Alliance (1718), 76
Quatre Bras, 669; skirmish at, 670; battle of, 678–680

Raab, battle of (1809), 540
Radetzky, Joseph, 444 n. ; Austrian Chief of Staff (1813), 592, 635
Radom, Confederation of (1767), 304
Rapp, Jean, Comte de (French general), at Dantzic (1813), 580; in 1815, 699
Rastatt, Congress of (1798–1799), 418–420, 429; envoys murdered at, 430
Ratisbon, Truce of (1684), 26, 112
Reformation, effect of, on Holy Roman Empire, 2; effect of, on German Kingdom, 3
Reichenbach, Congress of (1790), 348; Treaty of, 349
Reichsarmee. See Imperial Army
Reichshofrath (" Aulic Council "), 8; its origin and position, 15, 302
Reichskammergericht, 16, 302
Reille, André Charles, Count (French general), in Waterloo campaign, 688; at Quatre Bras, 678–679, 681; at Waterloo, 690
" Reserved Rights," 9
Retzow (Prussian general), 225–226, 243
Reuss, Princes of, 59, 372, 461, 520, 651
Reynier, Claude (French general), beaten at Maida, 503; spring campaign of 1813, 581–588; autumn campaign, 600–633
   Cf. Gross Beeren, Dennewitz, Leipzig
Rhine, Confederation of (1806–1815)
   Cf. Confederation of the Rhine
Rhine League of 1658
   Cf. League of the Rhine
Rhinelands, attitude of, in 1792, 361–362; annexed to France, 410, 454; fate in 1815, 654 ff.; attitude to Napoleon, 662
Richelieu, Louis Armand, Duc de, campaign of 1757, 215–217; recalled, 232, 360
Ripperda, Baron Willem von (Spain), 79; dismissed, 81
Robinson, Sir Thomas, 122
Rocket Troop, R.A., with Wallmoden, 605; present at Leipzig, 629
" Roman Months," 10
Rossbach, battle of (1757), 221–222
Rottweil, seat of *Hofgericht*, 16
Roucoux, battle of (1746), 167
Rouillé (French minister), 192, 201
Rüchel, Ernst Friedrich von (Prussian general), 504–510, 511, 518
Rumanjev, Count Peter (Russian general), 238, 242, 256
Rumbold, Sir George, seizure of, 477
Russia, in Northern War, Chapter III.; joins League of Vienna (1725), 81; guarantees Pragmatic Sanction, 83; in Polish Succession War, 98 ff.; calls for Austrian help against Turkey, 102; in 1740, 110; concludes treaty of War-

saw, 154, 155, 160; 169; treaty with George II (1755), 187; with Maria Theresa, 191, 203; in Seven Years' War, Chapters XI.–XIII. *passim*, esp. 213, 237–242, 251, 253–262, 273, 275, 277, 281–283; changes of government in (1762), 286–287, 291; share in First Partition of Poland, 303–309; negotiates Peace of Tetschen, 313; alliance with Joseph II, 315–316, 319, 322–326, 348, 353–354; connection with Oldenburg, 369; share in Second Partition of Poland, 382–383; share in Third Partition, 396–397; hostile to France (1798), 422; joins Second Coalition, 423–438 (cf. Suvorov); withdraws, 438, 452; forms Armed Neutrality (1800), 457; and the reconstruction of 1803, 458–459; alarmed by Napoleon, 474; alliance with Austria (1804), 478; with Great Britain, 478; in campaign of 1805, Chapter XXV.; assists Prussia (1806–1807), 513–516; makes peace at Tilsit, 516; receives Old Galicia, 545; quarrel with Napoleon, 565–566, 568; assumes offensive in 1813, 571–573; in War of Liberation, Chapters XXX.–XXXII. *passim*, esp. 576, 594, 641; gains in 1815, 647, 653, 655; 648; action in 1815, 660, 662, 700
Russo-German Legion (1813), 583
Rutowski, Count (Saxon general), 126, 160
Ryssel (Prussian general), at Waterloo, 693–696
" Ryswick Clause," the, 44, 102

Sacilio, battle of (1809), 535
Sacken, Count (Russian general), 593, 597; autumn campaign of, 1813, 602–633 (esp. Katzbach, Leipzig); in 1814, 636, 638–640
Sackville, Lord George, in campaign of 1759, 266–268
St. Amand, St. Amand la Haye, Hameau St. Amand; cf. Ligny
St. Cyr, Gouvion (French Marshal), in 1800, 445–446; in autumn campaign of 1813, 602–633
St. Germain, Count (French General), at Rossbach, 221–222, 232
St. Germain-en-Laye, Peace of (1679), 41
Salabert (of Zweibrücken) surrenders Mannheim (1795), 400 n.
Salzburg, Archbishopric of, extent of, 48; persecution of Protestants in, 85; promised to Austria (1797), 411; transferred to Archduke Ferdinand, 453–459; becomes Electorate (1803), 464; transferred to Austria (1805), 494; to Bavaria (1809), 544; restored to Austria (1815), 657 n.

Sardinia, overrun by Spaniards, 76; exchanged for Sicily, 77
Cf. Charles Emmanuel, Piedmont

Savoy, Prince Eugene of. See Eugene

Saxony, connection with Poland, 19; policy of, 1690–1693, 26; its territories and condition in 1715, 38–40; share in Northern War, Chapter III.; in Austrian Succession War, Chapters VIII.–IX.; in Seven Years' War, Chapters XI.–XII.; attitude to Prussia, 299; condition in 1763, 303; in 1792, 365; conduct in 1796, 404, 464; supports Prussia in 1806, 505; detached by Napoleon and joins Confederation of Rhine as a Kingdom, 510; obtains Cottbus, 517; assists Napoleon (1809), 529–544; development of, 550; contingent in 1812, 568; attitude in 1813, 579; decides for Napoleon, 583; contribution to his army (1813), 596 n.; Saxon troops in 1813 at Gross Beeren, 604–605; at Dennewitz, 616; their defection at Leipzig, 628: treatment of, in 1813, 631; fate of, discussed at Vienna, 647, 652–655; joins Coalition 1815, 660, 666; cf. Augustus Frederick I, II and III, John George II: cf. Wettin genealogy, 706

Saxe-Coburg, 53, 510, 651, 656

Saxe-Coburg-Saalfeld, Josias of (Austrian general), 324, 326, 383

Saxe-Hildburghausen, 53, 651
Prince Ernest Frederick of, commands Imperial Army at Rossbach, 217, 221–222

Saxe, Maurice de, cf. Maurice

Saxe-Meiningen, 53, 651

Saxe-Merseburg, 39, 365

Saxe-Teschen, Albert of, 182, 338, 343, 379–381, 389; 706

Saxe-Weimar, 53, 365–366; joins Confederation of the Rhine, 511, 651; becomes Grand Duchy, 656
Cf. Charles Augustus, Duke of Bernhard, Prince of, in 1815, 670 n., 689

Saxe-Weissenfels, 39, 365

Saxe-Zeitz, 39, 365

Scharnhorst, Gebhard von (Prussian general), 372, 502, 528, 559; reforms Prussian army, 563–565; in 1813, 576–577; death, 592

Scheldt, opening of the, 317

Scherer, Barthélemi (French general), 426; superseded, 433

Schill, Ferdinand von, his rising (1809), 533–534

Schiller, Friedrich, 360, 365

Schleswig, ceded to Denmark (1721), 70, 657
Cf. Holstein

Schleswig-Holstein, affairs of, 54–56
Cf. Holstein

Schmidt, von (Bavaria), at Vienna, 648

Schulenberg, John Matthias, defends Corfu, 72

Schwabisch-Hall, compact of (1685), 45

Schwarzenberg, Prince Charles Philip, 481, 566, 572, 579, 592; chosen as Commander-in-Chief (1813), 598; his character and achievements, 598; autumn campaign of 1813, 599–633 (esp. 609); decides to invade France, 636; plan of campaign, 1814, 636; invasion of France, 637–642; in 1815, 662 and n., 699

Schwedt, Convention of (1713), 67

Schweidnitz, captured by Nadasky (1758), 219; retaken by Prussians, 233; taken by Loudoun, 283; retaken (1762), 288; Allies retire on (1813), 586

Schwerin, Christopher, Marshal (Prussian), 116; at Mollwitz, 119; in 1756, 196, 200; in 1757, 204–207; killed at Prague, 207

Schwiebus; ceded to Brandenburg, 27, 41, 113

Sebastiani, François (French general), in autumn campaign of 1813, 602–633, esp. Katzbach

Seckendorff, Count Frederick Henry, 81; fails against Turks, 103; in Bavarian service, 132; makes Convention of Rain (1743), 136, 151, 152

Ségur, Comte de (French general), 127, 151, 154

Selim III, Sultan (1789–1807), 326

Senfft, Baron (Saxon Foreign Minister), 551

Serbelloni (Austrian general), 205–206, 283, 287

Servia, acquired by Austria (1718), 75; lost (1739), 103; invaded (1788), 324

Sérurier, Comte de (French general), 433

Sesia, battle on the (1733), 100

Seven Years' War, Chapters XI.–XIII.; summary of results, 290–293

Seydlitz, Frederick William (Prussian general), at Rossbach, 222; at Zorndorf, 240

Sicily, transferred from Savoy to Austria, 77; transferred to Don Carlos, 101, 503

Silesia, 31; Prussian claim on, 112–115; invaded by Frederick II, 116 ff.; ceded to Frederick (Klein Schellendorf), 126, 131; invaded by Austrians, 152, 157–158; guaranteed to Frederick by George II (1745), 160; definitely ceded by Austria, 162; during Seven Years' War, Chapters XI.–XIII. passim, esp. 220; left to Prussia (1763), 290, 305; left to Prussia (1807), 517, 574

Silesia, Army of (1813), 597; autumn campaign of 1813, 602–633, esp. 606–608, 620–621, 625

Sinzendorff, Philip Louis, Chancellor of Austria, 108, 117, 172

Sistova, Congress of (1790), 349, 353; Peace of (1791), 354

Sohr, battle of (1745), 159

Soissons, Congress of, 81
Blücher's danger at (1814), 639

Soltikov, Peter (Russian general), campaign of 1759, 253–262; of 1760, 275, 277, 291

Sombreffe, 672 ff.

Sondershausen, battle of (1758), 249

Sophia Dorothea of Lüneburg-Celle, 46, 704

Soubise, Prince de (French general), campaign of, 1757, 217–218, 221–222; campaign of 1758, 249–250; of 1761, 284; of 1762, 288

Souham, Joseph (French general), in autumn campaign of 1813, 602–633; esp. Katzbach

Soult, Nicholas Jean (French Marshal), 427, 437, 485, 488, 491–492, 506–510, 513; sent off to Spain (1813), 594

Spain, Napoleon's intervention in, 520; German troops in, 522 n., 552 n., 557 n.

Speyer, Armistice of (1801), 452

Stadion, Count Philip Charles, Austrian minister at Berlin, 457; negotiates Austro-Russian defensive alliance, 478; 498, 515; leads opposition to Napoleon, Chapter XXVIII., esp. 526; resigns, 544; 545, 587, 645

Stahremberg, Count George Adam, succeeds Kaunitz at Paris, 190; negotiates Second Treaty of Versailles, 201–212, 285, 340

Stahremberg, Gundacker, 81, 108, 117, 172

Stair, John, second Earl of, 136–140

Stanhope-Sunderland Ministry (England), fall of (1721), 71

Stanhope, William (Lord Harrington), 82

Steenbock, Magnus (Swedish general), 65 ff.

Stein, Henry Frederick Charles, Freiherr von, early career of, 501; anti-French, 504; in office, 511; retires, 511; restored to office, 518; desires alliance with Austria, 528; his reforms, 558–562; 569, 577, 618, 643; ideas for reconstructing Germany, 644; at Vienna, 648, 650

Steinmetz (Prussian general), in 1815, 669, 670; at Ligny, 673–677

Stettin, lost to Sweden (1713), 67; surrenders (1806), 510; garrisoned by French, 522; in 1813, 600; falls, 632

Stockach, battle of (1799), 427

Stockholm, Peace of (1719), 70

Stralsund, capitulation of (1715), 68; restored to Sweden, 70; Schill at (1809), 534; ceded to Prussia (1815), 655

Strassburg seized by Louis XIV (1681), 24

Stuart, Prince Charles Edward, 156, 162

Stulpnägel (Prussian general), at Ligny, 677

Suhlingen, Convention of (1803), 471

Sulzbach branch of Wittelsbachs, acquire Jülich and Berg, 45; 52; 95
Cf. genealogy, 707

Sundgau ceded to France (1648), 31

Suvorov, Peter Alexis (Austrian general), takes Oczakov, 326; suppresses Poles (1792), 383; captures Warsaw (1794), 397; Italian campaign of (1799), 428–429, 433–435; move into Switzerland, 432–433, 435–437

Sweden, has seat in College of Princes, 21; territories in Germany, 57; assailed by coalition, Chapter III.; joins coalition against Prussia (1757), 203; ineffective operations, 213; withdraws from war (1762), 286; action in 1804–6, 478, 490, 502, 515; 520; joins Allies against Napoleon (1813), 591; loses Pomerania, 657
Cf. Gustavus III and IV, also Bernadotte, Charles XII

Switzerland, interference of French in, 421–422; strategical importance of, 426; Allies move through (1813–1814), 636–637

Talleyrand-Perigord, Charles Maurice de, 378, 424, 471; proposed policy of, 494, 500; influences Alexander I, 643; at Congress of Vienna, 648–659, esp. 653

Tauentzien, Count Boguslav (Prussian general), 506–510; autumn campaign of 1813, 597–633, esp. 515, 604, 622

Tauroggen, Convention of (1812), 572

Temesvar, taken by Eugene, 73

Theodore of Sulzbach (1708–1732), 52, 95; 707

Thielmann, John Adolphus, General, commands Saxon army, 599; commands a corps in 1815, Chapter XXXV. passim, esp. 666, 669, 683; left at Wavre, 685; battle of Wavre, 698–699

Thugut, Francis, Baron von, Austrian minister at Constantinople, 305, 313, 377; becomes Chief Minister, 385, 388; joins in Third Partition of Poland, 396, 398, 400 n.; quarrels with Clerfayt, 400–401, 407; opposes peace, 408–410; policy and character of, 413–414, 419; designs on Bavaria,

420, 439, 461 ; 422 ; 425 ; 429 ; designs on Piedmont, 430, 432 ; 444 n. ; dismissed (1800), 448 ; 478, 545, 645

Thurn und Taxis, Princes of, 59, 461, mediatised, 498

Tilsit, Peace of (1807), negotiated, 516 ; terms of, 517–518

Tippelskirch (Prussian general), at Ligny, 674–677

Toll, Charles Ferdinand (Russian general), 592 ; advocates direct move on Paris (1814), 641

Töplitz, Treaty of (1813), 617, 646

Torgau, battle of (1760), 278–279

Törring, Count (Bavarian general), 125, 128

Tournay besieged (1745), 155

Townshend, Charles, second Viscount, 82, 94

Trachenberg, Compact of (1813), 593 ; criticised, 594

Transylvania, 34 ; troubles in, 344 ; separated from Hungary, 350

Traun, Otto, Marshal, 125 ; Italian campaigns of, 142–143 ; campaign of 1744, 148–152, 177

Trautmansdorf, Count (Governor of Netherlands), 341

Treaties of the Crown (1701), 19
of Westminster (1716), 75
of London (1720), 77
of Wüsterhausen (1726), 81
of Vienna (1731), 82
of Löwenwolde (1732), 98
of Turin (1733), 98
of the Escurial (1733), 98
of Nymphenburg (1741), 121
of Breslau (1741), 123
of Worms (1743), 141, 143
of Fontainebleau (1743), 145
of Füssen (1745), 154
of Warsaw (1745), 154
of Dresden (1745), 162
of Aranjuez (1752), 182
of Hamburg (1762), 286
of Fontainebleau (1785), 322
of Reichenbach (1790), 349
of Pfaffenhofen (1796), 349
of Campo Formio (1797), 410
of Ettlingen (1805), 483
of Schönbrunn (1805), 493
of Schönbrunn (1809), 545
of Kalisch (1813), 574, 646
of Töplitz (1813), 617, 646
of Ried (1813), 32, 619, 647
of Fulda (1813), 631
of Kiel (1814), 632
of Chaumont (1814), 641, 646
of Paris (1814), 641, 646
of Paris (1815), 701

Trebbia, Suvorov's victory on the (1799), 434

Trent, Bishopric of, 48 ; annexed to Austria, 453

Treves, Electorate of, connection with Arch Chancellorship of Burgundy, 19 ; its extent, etc., 37, 48 ; occupied by French (1734), 100 ; restored, 101 ; taken by French (1794), 390 ; annexed to France, Chapter XXIII. ; passes to Prussia (1815), 655
Electors of :
Charles of Lorraine (1711–1716), 37
Francis Louis of Neuburg (1716–1729), 37, 81, 95
Francis George of Schönborn (1729–1756), 83, 122, 197
John Philip of Walderdorff (1756–1768)
Clement Wenceslaus of Saxony (1768–1803), 357, 373, 421

Trieste, development of, 80, 339 ; ceded France (1809), 544 ; recovered by Austria (1815), 657

Triple Alliance (1788), 325

Tugendbund, the, 569

Turkey, war with Austria and Venice, Chapter IV. ; with Austria and Russia (1735–1739), 102–103 ; at war with Russia (1768–1773), 304–309 ; relations with Russia, 316 ; war with Austria and Russia (1787–1791), 324–326, 347–349

Tyrol, 32, 334, 351 ; handed over to Bavaria (1805), 493 ; insurrection in (1809), 536 ; subdued and partitioned, 545 ; restored to Austria, 657

Ulefeld, Count (Austrian Chancellor), 172

Ulm, Kray at (1800), 447 ; Mack capitulates at, 485–486

Ulrica Eleanora, Queen of Sweden (1718–1741), 70

Utrecht, Peace of, turning point in German history, 1

Uxbridge, Lord, at Waterloo, 689

Valmy, battle of (1792), 380

Vandamme, Count Dominique (French general), commands Würtemberg contingent (1809), 529–544 ; spring campaign of 1813, 583–588 ; autumn campaign, 602–614, esp. Kulm ; in Waterloo campaign, 668, 672–677, 684–685

Van der Noot (Belgium), 342, 350

Veldenz, 52

Vellinghausen, battle of (1761), 284

Venice, war with Turkey, Chapter IV. ; partitioned (1797), 410 ; transferred to Kingdom of Italy, 493 ; annexed to Austria (1815), 657

Verden, 21, 68

Vergennes, Charles, Comte de, 185, hostile to Hapsburgs, 312 ; supports

Dutch against Joseph II, 317 ; death, 325

Vergniaud, Pierre (France), 376

Versailles, First Treaty of (1756), 191, 200 ; Second (1757), 201–203

Victor, Claude, Duc de Belluno (French Marshal), autumn campaign of 1813, 601–633

Vienna, in 1715, 24 ; League of, 82 ; Treaty of (1731), 82 ; Peace of, (1738), 101 ; see of, 330 ; under Leopold I, 352 ; occupied by Napoleon (1805), 488 (1809), 535 ; Congress of ; (1814–1815), 646–659

Vimiero, battle of (1808), 521, 522

Vincke, General (Hanoverian brigadier), at Waterloo, 688, 695

Vittoria, battle of (1813), effect of, 594

Vivian, Sir Hussey, General, at Waterloo, 689, 695, 696

Vonck (Belgium), 342, 350

Voss, Christian Daniel, 645

Wagram, battle of (1809), 541–543

Waitz (minister of Hesse Cassel), 475

Walcheren, English expedition to (1809), 544

Waldemühlen, 70

Wallenstein, Albert von, 6

Wallmoden, Louis George, Count (Hanoverian), 391 ; concludes Convention of Suhlingen (1803), 472 ; in 1813, 583, 597, 601, 605 ; action at the Gohrde, 619, 632

Walpole, Sir Robert, 71, 82 ; policy in 1733, 99 ; fall of, 131, 137

Warburg, battle of (1762), 288

Warsaw, Grand Duchy of, created (1807), 517, 529, 544 ; connection with Saxony, 550, 618 ; fate in 1815, 653

Wartensleben (Austrian general), 402–407

Washington, George, 185

Wedel, Charles Henry (Prussian general), at Rossbach, 225–226 ; beaten at Paltzig (1759), 253, 254 ff.

Wellington, Duke of, victory at Vittoria, 594 ; invades France (1813), 634, 636 ; at Congress of Vienna, 648 ; campaign of 1815, Chapter XXXV. *passim*, esp. his strategy, 669 ; his army, 665 and n., also 681 ; criticises Blucher's dispositions, 673 ; at Quatre Bras, 678–680 ; retires to Waterloo, 681 ; expects Prussians early on June 18th, 686 ; at Waterloo, 687–696 ; treatment of France, 699

Werneck (Austrian general), 486

Westminster, Convention of (1756), 189

Westphalia, Kingdom of, created (1807) for Jerome Bonaparte, 518 ; sends contingent to Spain, 522 n., 557 n. ; risings in (1809), 533–535 ; develop-

ment of, 555–558 ; contingent to Grand Army (1812), 568 ; of 1813, 596, 647 ; greater part given to Prussia (1815), 655

Westphalia, Peace of, a turning point in German history : its results, Chapter I. *passim*.

West Prussia, 95 ; acquired by Frederick II (1773), 305–308 ; 517, 655

Wettin, family of, genealogy, 706
Cf. Saxony, Saxe-Coburg, Gotha, Weimar

Wilhelmina of Prussia (sister of Frederick William II), 325, 705

William VI, Landgrave of Hesse-Cassel (1637–1663), 50

William VIII, Landgrave of Hesse-Cassel (1751–1760), for neutrality in 1757, 203 ; hires troops to George II, 368

William IX, Landgrave of Hesse-Cassel (1785–1830), 368 ; makes peace (1795), 395 n. ; becomes Elector, 463, 475 ; ambiguous conduct in 1806, 504 ; deposed, 511 ; restored, 631 ; acquisitions in 1815, 656, 662 n.

William V of Holland, 168, 325, 372 ; receives Nassau, 463 ; deposed (1806), 511

William of Lippe-Schaumburg, 371

Winterfeldt, Hans (Prussian general), 199, 205, 207 ; defeated and killed (1757), 218

Winzingerode, Ferdinand, Baron von (Russian general), spring campaign of 1813, 580–588 ; autumn campaign, 597–633 ; in 1814, 639

Wittelsbach, family of, genealogy, 707 ; cf. Bavaria, Palatinate, Neuburg, Zweibrücken ; minor branches of, 51–52, 364–365

Wittgenstein, Prince Louis (Russian general), 572 ; spring campaign of 1813, 580–588 ; autumn, 602–633

Wolffradt, Baron, 556

Woronzov, Count Michael (Russian minister), 203 ; Chancellor, 228
Count Simon (Russian minister), takes office (1802), 459

Wrede, Prince Charles von (Bavarian general), 595, 597 n. ; favours joining Allies (1813), 618 ; intercepts Napoleon's retreat, 633 ; in campaign of 1814, 636–642, esp. 638

Wurmser, Dagobert (Austrian Marshal), campaign of 1793, 386–387 ; of 1795, 400 ; in Italy (1796), 407

Würtemberg, Duchy of, 49–50 ; policy of, in 1741, 122, 154, 167 ; assists Maria Theresa, 203 ; contingent at Leuthen, 224–226, cf. 250 ; in 1759, 271, 292 ; history of, in 18th century, 371 ; comes to terms with France

(1795), 395 ; in 1796, 404 ; connection with Russia, 458 ; gains and losses in 1802, 460, 462, 469, 483 ; becomes Kingdom, 494 ; 497 ; assists Napoleon (1809), 529–544 ; development of, 550–551 ; sends contingent to Grand Army (1812), 568 ; of 1813, 596 n., 616, 628 ; assists Allies (1814), 636, 638 ; views of, at Congress of Vienna, 649–650 ; attitude in 1815, 662, 699, 700 ; part of Germanic Confederation, 651
 Cf. Eberhard Louis (1677–1733) ; Charles Alexander (1733–1737) ; Charles Eugene (1737–1793); Louis Eugene (1793–1795); Frederick Eugene (1795–1797) ; Frederick II (and I) (1797–1816)
Würzburg, Bishopric of, 48 ; annexed by Bavaria, 461 ; made an Electorate for Ferdinand of Salzburg, 494 ; joins Confederation of Rhine, 511, 552 ; contingent of, in 1813, 596 n. ; assists Allies (1814), 636
Wüsterhausen, Treaty of (1726), 81

Xavier of Saxony, Regent for Frederick Augustus III, 365

Yorck von Wartenburg, Count (Prussian general), concludes Convention of Tauroggen, 572 ; spring campaign of 1813, 581–588, 593 ; autumn campaign of 1813, 597–633 (esp. Katzbach, Leipzig) ; in campaign of 1814, 636–642

York, Frederick, Duke of, 386, 437

Zach (Austrian officer), 444
Zahna, battle of (1813), 615
Zastrow, General (Prussian minister), 511, 518
Ziethen, Count Hans Joachim (Prussian general), in Austrian Succession War, 129, 157, 161 ; in Seven Years' War, 207, 225–226, 235, 278
Ziethen, Count Hans Ernest von (Prussian general), in 1815, Chapter XXXV. passim, esp., 668–689 ; move on Waterloo, 686–687 ; at Waterloo, 694
Zinzendorf, Carl von (Austrian minister), 337–339
Zips occupied by Austria (1768) 305
Znaym, armistice of (1809), 543
Zondaderi, Cardinal, Papal Nuntio in Netherlands, 340
Zorndorf, battle of (1758), 239–241
Zürich, first battle of (May 1799), 432 ; second (September 1799), 436
Zweibrücken, subdivisions of, 52 ; annexed to France, 460 ; cf. genealogy, 707
 Birkenfeld, Charles II (1775–1795), claim on Bavaria, 311, 319, 321, 362, 364 ; 707
 Christian IV, Duke of, commands Imperial Army (1758), 236 ; (1759), 261 ; 707
 Maximilian Joseph of, succeeds to Bavaria and Palatinate (1799), 364 ; cf. Maximilian Joseph

Fodor's

W9-AWC-162

ITALY

Where to Stay and Eat
for All Budgets

Must-See Sights
and Local Secrets

Ratings You Can Trust

Fodor's Travel Publications   New York, Toronto, London, Sydney, Auckland
www.fodors.com

FODOR'S ITALY
Editor: Matthew Lombardi

Editorial Production: Tom Holton
Editorial Contributors: Peter Blackman, Jeff Booth, Ryan Bradley, Linda Cabasin, Robin S. Goldstein, Cristina Gregorin, Denise Hummel, Madeleine Johnson, Dana Klitzberg, Gerry Madigan, Ann Reavis, Chris Rose, Patricia Rucidlo, Pamela Santini, Megan K. Williams
Maps: David Lindroth, *cartographer;* Bob Blake and Rebecca Baer, *map editors.* Additional cartography provided by Henry Colomb, Mark Stroud, and Ali Baird, Moon Street Cartography; and by Mapping Specialists Ltd.
Design: Fabrizio La Rocca, *creative director,* Chie Ushio, Guido Caroti, Siobhan O'Hare, Tina Malaney, Brian Ponto
Photography: Melanie Marin, *senior picture editor*
Production/Manufacturing: Colleen Ziemba
Cover Photo (Piazza Santo Stefano, Bologna): Atlantide S.N.C./age fotostock

SPECIAL SALES
This book is available for special discounts for bulk purchases for sales promotions or premiums. Special editions, including personalized covers, excerpts of existing books, and corporate imprints, can be created in large quantities for special needs. For more information, write to Special Markets/Premium Sales, 1745 Broadway, MD 6-2, New York, New York 10019, or e-mail specialmarkets@randomhouse.com.

AN IMPORTANT TIP & AN INVITATION
Although all prices, opening times, and other details in this book are based on information supplied to us at press time, changes occur all the time in the travel world, and Fodor's cannot accept responsibility for facts that become outdated or for inadvertent errors or omissions. So **always confirm information when it matters,** especially if you're making a detour to visit a specific place. Your experiences—positive and negative—matter to us. If we have missed or misstated something, **please write to us.** We follow up on all suggestions. Contact the Italy editor at editors@fodors. com or c/o Fodor's at 1745 Broadway, New York, NY 10019.

THIS 2007 EDITION PRINTED IN THE UNITED STATES OF AMERICA

10 9 8 7 6 5 4 3 2 1

Your opinion matters. It matters to us. It matters to your fellow Fodor's travelers, too. And we'd like to hear it. In fact, we *need* to hear it.

When you share your experiences and opinions, you become an active member of the Fodor's community. That means we'll not only use your feedback to make our books better, but we'll publish your names and comments whenever possible. Throughout this guide, look for "Word of Mouth" excerpts of unvarnished feedback.

Here's how you can help improve Fodor's for all of us.

Tell us when we're right. We rely on local writers to give you an insider's perspective. But our writers and staff editors—who are the best in the business—depend on you. Your positive feedback is a vote to renew our recommendations for the next edition.

Tell us when we're wrong. We're proud that we update our Italy guide every year. But we're not perfect. Things change. Hotels cut services. Museums change hours. Charming cafés lose their charm. If our writer didn't quite capture the essence of a place, tell us how you'd do it differently. If any of our descriptions are inaccurate or inadequate, we'll incorporate your changes in the next edition and will correct factual errors at fodors.com *immediately.*

Tell us what to include. You're bound to have some fantastic experiences that haven't made it in this guide—Italy's that kind of place. Why not share them with a community of like-minded travelers? Maybe you chanced upon a palazzo or a trattoria that you don't want to keep to yourself. Tell us why we should include it. And share your discoveries and experiences with everyone directly at fodors.com. Your input may lead us to add a new listing or highlight a place we cover with a "Highly Recommended" star or with our highest rating, "Fodor's Choice."

Give us your opinion instantly at our feedback center at www.fodors.com/feedback. You may also e-mail editors@fodors.com with the subject line "Italy Editor." Or send your nominations, comments, and complaints by mail to Italy Editor, Fodor's, 1745 Broadway, New York, NY 10019.

You and travelers like you are the heart of the Fodor's community. Make our community richer by sharing your experiences. Be a Fodor's correspondent.

Buon viaggio! (Or simply: Happy traveling!)

Tim Jarrell, Publisher

CONTENTS

PLANNING YOUR TRIP

About This Book 9
What's Where 10
When to Go .17
Quintessential Italy 18
If You Like 20
Great Itineraries 26
On the Calendar 38

ITALY

1 VENICE 39
Piazza San Marco 52
Dorsoduro 58
San Polo & Santa Croce 63
Castello & Cannaregio 67
San Giorgio Maggiore & the Giudecca . .74
Islands of the Lagoon 75
Where to Eat 78
Where to Stay 87
Nightlife & the Arts 96
Sports 99
Shopping 99
Venice Essentials 102

2 THE VENETIAN ARC 109
Padua 114
Vicenza 121
Verona 130
Treviso & the Hillside Towns 137
Friuli-Venezia Giulia 145
Venetian Arc Essentials 155

3 THE DOLOMITES: TRENTINO–ALTO
ADIGE 157
Trentino 162
Bolzano (Bozen) 174

Alto Adige & Cortina 179
Heart of the Dolomites 189
Dolomites Essentials 194

4 MILAN, LOMBARDY &
THE LAKES 197
Milan 202
Pavia, Cremona & Mantua 229
Lake Garda 236
Lake Como & Bergamo 242
Lake Maggiore & Lake Orta 252
Milan, Lombardy & the Lakes
Essentials 256

5 PIEDMONT & VALLE D'AOSTA . .261
Turin 266
The Colline & Savoy Palaces 281
The Monferrato & the Langhe 286
Valle d'Aosta 292
Piedmont & Valle d'Aosta
Essentials 302

6 THE ITALIAN RIVIERA 305
Riviera di Levante 310
Genoa 330
Riviera di Ponente 344
Italian Riviera Essentials 352

7 EMILIA-ROMAGNA 357
Emilia 362
Bologna 378
Ferrara 389
Romagna .394
Ravenna 400
Emilia-Romagna Essentials 405

8 FLORENCE 407
The Duomo to the Ponte Vecchio 412
San Lorenzo to the Accademia 422

Santa Maria Novella to the Arno 433
The Oltrarno 435
Santa Croce 439
Where to Eat 442
Where to Stay 452
Nightlife & the Arts 458
Shopping 460
Side Trips From Florence 465
Florence Essentials 468

9 TUSCANY 471
Northwestern Tuscany 476
Lucca 481
Pisa 487
Chianti 491
Hill Towns Southwest of Florence . . .497
Siena 503
Arezzo & Cortona 512
Southern Tuscany 517
Tuscany Essentials 524

10 UMBRIA & THE MARCHES 527
Perugia 532
Assisi 538
Northern Umbria 546
Spoleto 552
Southern Umbria 556
The Marches 563
Umbria & the Marches Essentials . . .568

11 ROME 571
The Vatican 576
Baroque Rome 594
Piazza Venezia to the Spanish
   Steps .600
Monti & San Giovanni 603
Il Quirinale to Piazza della
   Repubblica 606

ITALY IN FOCUS

VENICE
Cruising the Grand Canal 45
THE VENETIAN ARC
Palladio Country 125
MILAN, LOMBARDY & THE LAKES
The Fashionista's Milan 224
PIEDMONT & VALLE D'AOSTA
On the Trail of Barolo 289
THE ITALIAN RIVIERA
The Cinque Terre 313
EMILIA-ROMAGNA
Emilia, One Taste at a Time 373
FLORENCE
Who's Who of Renaissance Art 423
TUSCANY
Siena's Piazza del Campo & the Palio . . .506
UMBRIA & THE MARCHES
Assisi's Basilica di San Francesco 541
ROME
Ancient Rome: Glories of the Caesars . . .584
NAPLES & CAMPANIA
Ancient Pompeii, Tomb of a
   Civilization .719
SICILY
Sicily's Valle dei Templi 836

Villa Borghese to the Ara Pacis 608
The Ghetto, Tiberina Island &
   Trastevere 611
The Catacombs & Via Appia Antica . .617
Where to Eat 619
Where to Stay 632
Nightlife & the Arts 644
Sports & the Outdoors 651

CONTENTS

Shopping 651
Rome Essentials 658

12 SIDE TRIPS FROM ROME 663
Ostia Antica 667
The Etruscan Seaboard 670
Tuscia 675
Tivoli, Palestrina & Subiaco 679
Sermoneta, Ninfa & Sperlonga 682
Rome Side Trips Essentials 684

13 NAPLES & CAMPANIA 687
Naples 692
The Phlegrean Fields 713
Herculaneum, Vesuvius & Pompeii . .718
Caserta & Benevento 728
Ischia & Procida 729
Capri 733
Sorrento & the Amalfi Coast 739
Naples & Campania Essentials 755

14 THE MEZZOGIORNO 759
Bari & the Adriatic Coast 764
Gargano Promontory 771
The Trulli District 774
Salento & Ports of the Heel 778
Basilicata 784
Calabria 789
Mezzogiorno Essentials 799

15 SICILY 803
The Ionian Coast 808
Siracusa 823
The Interior 830
Agrigento & Western Sicily 833
Palermo 845
The Tyrrhenian Coast 856
The Aeolian Islands 858
Sicily Essentials 862

16 SARDINIA 865
Cagliari & the Southern Coast 869
Su Nuraxi to the Costa Smeralda 877
Sardinia Essentials 888

ITALIAN VOCABULARY 892
MENU GUIDE 897
SMART TRAVEL TIPS 904
INDEX 930
ABOUT OUR WRITERS 944

CLOSEUPS

Wading through the Acqua Alta 58
Venice's Scuola Days 65
Let's Get Lost 73
Venetian Masks Revealed 101
The World's Most Elegant Taxi 104
Traveling the Veneto's Wine
   Roads 143
Trieste's Caffè Culture 151
Enrosadira & the Dwarf King 170
Hiking the Dolomites 190
Calcio Crazy 223
The Olympic Legacy in Turin 279
The Art of the Pesto Pestle 341
Cooking alla Bolognese 388
Talking Politics 393
San Marino, a Country on a Cliff 399
Florence's Trial by Fire 431
What Tripe! .450
Bacchus in Tuscany 518
Sorry, Vasari 521
Truffle Trouble 554
Hiking the Umbrian Hills 563
A Morning with the Pope 580

Roman Baroque 597
Pizza, Roman Style 628
Entertainment Alfresco 645
Uncovering the Etruscan Past 673
Neapolitan Art in the Present
    Tense 705
Folk Songs à la Carte 706
A Stop on the Way to Hell 717
Sweet Sicily 818
Prizzi's Honor 844
Sardinia by Rail 882

MAPS

Italy 12–13
Venice .40–41
Piazza San Marco 53
Dorsoduro 59
San Polo & Santa Croce 64
Cannaregio .68
Castello 69
Venetian Lagoon 77
Where to Stay & Eat in Venice 82–83
The Venetian Arc 110–111
Padua 116
Vicenza 122
Verona 131
Treviso & the Hillside Towns 138
Friuli-Venezia Giulia 146
The Dolomites: Trentino–Alto
    Adige 158–159
Trentino 163
Bolzano 175
Alto Adige & Cortina 181
Milan, Lombardy & the
    Lakes 198–199

Milan 205
The Po Plain & Lake Garda 230
The Western Lakes & Bergamo 243
Piedmont & Valle d'Aosta 262–263
Turin 268
Piedmont 282
Valle d'Aosta 293
The Italian Riviera 306–307
Riviera di Levante 311
Genoa 332–333
Riviera di Ponente 345
Emilia-Romagna 358–359
Emilia 365
Bologna 379
Romagna 395
Ravenna 402
Florence 408–409
Florence Sights 416–417
Where to Stay & Eat in
    Florence 446–447
Tuscany 472–473
Northwestern Tuscany 477
Lucca 482
Pisa 488
Chianti & the Hill Towns Southwest
    of Florence 492
Siena 504
Arezzo, Cortona & Southern
    Tuscany .514
Umbria & the Marches 528–529
Perugia 533
Assisi 539
Northern Umbria 547
Spoleto 553
Southern Umbria 557

CONTENTS

The Marches 565

Rome 572–573

The Vatican 578

Baroque Rome 595

Piazza Venezia to the Spanish
  Steps 602

Monti & San Giovanni 605

Il Quirinale to Piazza della
  Repubblica 607

Villa Borghese to the Ara Pacis 610

The Ghetto & Trastevere 613

Catacombs & Via Appia Antica 618

Where to Eat in Rome 622–623

Where to Stay in Rome 634–635

Rome Metro & Suburban Railway . . .659

Lazio 664–665

Ostia Antica 668

Side Trips from Rome 671

Naples & Campania 688–689

Naples .694–695

The Bay of Naples 714

Capri 735

Sorrento & the Amalfi Coast 741

The Mezzogiorno 760–761

Puglia 767

Basilicata & Calabria 785

Sicily 804–805

Eastern Sicily & the Aeolian
  Islands 809

Ortygia Island, Siracusa 826

Western Sicily 841

Palermo 847

Sardinia .867

Exploring Sardinia 874

ABOUT THIS BOOK

Organization

The first part of this book is designed to give you the lay of the land and help you decide where to go. **What's Where** describes Italy's regions, including their pleasures and pitfalls for travelers. **If You Like . . .** identifies some classic Italian experiences and tells you where you can have them.

Jump to the back pages for **Smart Travel Tips,** a section of nuts-and-bolts planning information. Topics are arranged in alphabetical order. Some won't apply to you, but many will.

The remainder of the book consists of our region-by-region listings—the places to go and things to do—interlaced with history, background, and tips from our on-the-spot writers. Chapters appear in geographical order, beginning at the top of the boot and working south.

Our Ratings

Anything we list in this guide, whether it's a museum, a ruin, or a restaurant, has our recommendation. Naturally, not every place is going to be for everyone. Our goal is to provide the information you need to make choices that are right for you.

A black star next to a listing means it's **Highly Recommended.** Year in and year out, travelers of all stripes

have great experiences at these spots.

Orange stars indicate our highest rating, **Fodor's Choice.** These are the places we think you'll be telling your friends about when you return home—places where you stand a good chance of making a memory. Some selections you'll expect, but others might surprise you. They're all truly special and uniquely Italian. When you have your own Fodor's Choice experience, let us know about it at www.fodors.com/feedback.

Deciphering the Listings

For the most part, our listings are self-explanatory, but a few details are worth mentioning.

For attractions, we give standard adult admission fees; reductions for children, students, and senior citizen are rare (unless you're an EU citizen). Hotel and restaurant price categories are defined on the charts found in each chapter. Unless otherwise indicated, restaurants are open for lunch and dinner daily. We mention dress at restaurants only when there's a specific requirement and reservations only when they're essential or not accepted. Hotels have private bath, phone, TV, and air-conditioning unless other-

wise indicated. We list facilities but not whether you'll be charged extra to use them, so when pricing accommodations, find out what's included.

Want to pay with plastic? **AE, DC, MC, V** following restaurant and hotel listings indicate whether American Express, Diner's Club, MasterCard, and Visa are accepted.

Many Listings

★	Fodor's Choice
★	Highly recommended
☾	Family-friendly
⊠	Physical address
⊠	Branch address
✛	Directions
⊕	Mailing address
☎	Telephone
🖷	Fax
⊕	On the Web
✉	E-mail
🎫	Admission fee
☉	Open/closed times
Ⓜ	Metro stations
▭	Credit cards
⇨	See also

Hotels & Restaurants

🏨	Hotel
⇦	Number of rooms
⚲	Facilities
¶⦿⦿	Meal plans
✕	Restaurant
⇧	Reservations
🏛	Dress code
⤸	Smoking
♙⧣	BYOB
✕🏨	Hotel with restaurant that warrants a visit

WHAT'S WHERE

VENICE 	Venice is one of the world's most novel cities, with canals where streets should be and an atmosphere of faded splendor that practically defines the word *decadent*. Once a great seafaring power, Venice now lives for tourism, prompting cynics to compare it to Disneyland. It's true that Piazza San Marco, the magnificent main square, is often packed with sightseers, and there are plenty of kitschy souvenirs for sale in the heavily trafficked area around the Rialto Bridge. But Venice is no Mickey Mouse affair: it has a rich history, it's packed with artistic treasures accumulated over a thousand years, and despite the crowds it remains inescapably romantic. If you give the city a few days and spend time wandering the quieter neighborhoods, it's hard not to succumb to Venice's allure.
THE VENETIAN ARC 	The green plains stretching west of Venice hold three of northern Italy's most appealing midsize cities: Padua, Vicenza, and Verona. Each has notable artistic treasures and an attractive historic center; Padua is famous for its Giotto frescoes, Vicenza for its Palladian villas, and Verona for its ancient arena. Farther north, Alpine foothills are dotted with small, welcoming towns and some of Italy's most distinguished vineyards. To the east, the region of Friuli–Venezia Giulia has a split personality, half Italian and half Central European. In the main city, Trieste, you can feel the influences of both Venice and Vienna.
THE DOLOMITES 	The Dolomites are Italy's finest mountain playground, with stupefying cliffs, curiously shaped peaks, charming meadows, and crystal-clear lakes. The skiing, hiking, and mountain drives are comparable to what you'll find in the Austrian Alps just to the north, at better prices and with an Italian sensibility. There's a definite Austrian influence here as well; most of the area is bilingual, with German sometimes prevailing. Notable cities are the lively university town of Bolzano, history-rich Trento, the spa center Merano, and the chic ski resorts of Cortina d'Ampezzo and Madonna di Campiglio.
MILAN, LOMBARDY & THE LAKES 	The variety of natural beauty in Italy is remarkable, and the region of Lombardy makes a significant contribution to the mix with its gorgeous lakes, Como Garda, and Maggiore. Their deep-blue, Alps-fed waters have been drawing accolades since the days of ancient Rome. In more recent times, regal villas, voluptuous gardens, and pretty resort towns have taken up positions along their shores. At the center of Lombardy is Milan, Italy's second-largest city and its business cap-

	ital. The Milanese are criticized for being too businesslike—for not knowing how to relax and enjoy life the way their countrymen do. But the city's wealth has brought with it some sophisticated pleasures, including Italy's most renowned opera house and its most stylish shopping district.
PIEDMONT & VALLE D'AOSTA	On lists of Italian superlatives, these two regions in the northwest corner of the country almost always find themselves one spot down from the top. The mountains are unquestionably impressive, but for hiking and skiing they rate just below the Dolomites. The French-influenced cuisine is a pleasure, but isn't as heralded as Emilia-Romagna's. The city of Turin ranks second to Milan in urban sophistication and business clout. And the wine-producing hills aren't quite as alluring as their counterparts in Tuscany—though the wine itself is second to none. So, there are two reasons to visit this area: first, all those runner-up honors mean you can have a variety of great experiences; second, you'll be off the main tourist circuit.
THE ITALIAN RIVIERA	The region of Liguria (known to pleasure-seekers as the Italian Riviera) has northern Italy's most attractive stretch of coastline. Though there are some good beaches, the main appeal is the beauty of the seaside cliffs and coves, and of the small towns interspersed among them. The most celebrated of these is tiny but glamorous Portofino, though these days it gets competition from the even tinier villages of the Cinque Terre, famous for the hiking paths that run between them. Smack in the middle of the coast is Genoa, Italy's busiest port. It holds the region's main cultural attractions, intermixed with some port-city grit.
EMILIA-ROMAGNA	Emilia-Romagna doesn't have the striking natural beauty of its neighboring regions—instead, it wins your heart through your stomach. Many of Italy's signature food products come from here, including Parmigiano-Reggiano cheese (aka Parmesan), prosciutto di Parma, and balsamic vinegar. The pasta is considered Italy's finest—a reputation the region's chefs earn every day. But food isn't Emilia-Romagna's be-all and end-all. Attractive cities dot the map: Bologna is the principal cultural and intellectual center, with rows of street arcades winding through grandiose towers. The mosaics in Ravenna are glittering treasures left from the era of Byzantine rule, and Ferrara, Parma, and Modena all reward you for your attention.

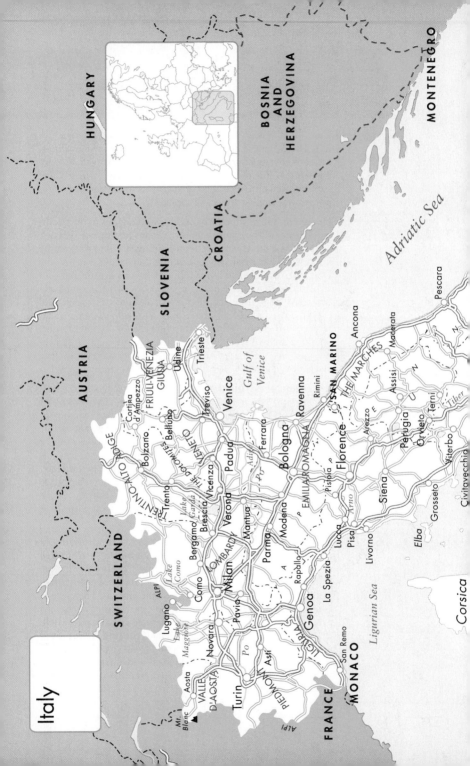

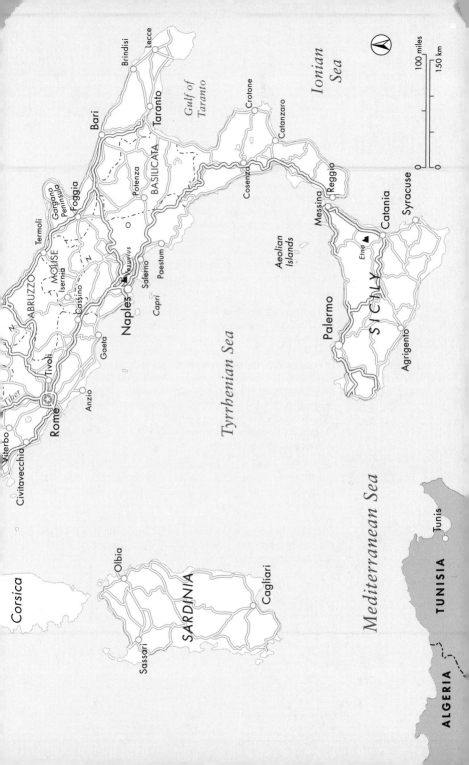

WHAT'S WHERE

FLORENCE 	It's hard to think of a place that's more closely linked to one specific historical period than Florence. In the 15th century the city was at the center of an artistic revolution, later labeled the Renaissance, that changed the way people see the world. Five hundred years later the Renaissance remains the reason people see Florence—the abundance of treasures is mind-boggling. Present-day Florentines have a somewhat uneasy relationship with their city's past; the never-ending stream of tourists is something they seem to tolerate more often than embrace. Still, they pride themselves on living well, and that means you'll find exceptional restaurants and first-rate shopping to go with all that amazing art.
TUSCANY 	Nature outdid herself in Tuscany, the central Italian region that has Florence as its principal city. Descriptions and photographs can't do the landscape justice—the hills, draped with woods, vineyards, and olive groves, may not have the drama of mountain peaks or waves crashing on the shore, yet there's an undeniable magic about them. Aside from Florence, Tuscany has several midsize cities that are well worth visiting, but the greatest appeal lies in the smaller towns, often perched on hilltops and not significantly altered since the Middle Ages. Despite its popularity with fellow travelers, Tuscany remains a place you can escape to.
UMBRIA & THE MARCHES 	Umbria was the first region in Italy to be dubbed by travel writers "the next Tuscany," a term that's since been applied to locations all up and down the boot. There's some sense to the comparison—like Tuscany, Umbria has beautiful rolling hills with attractive old towns sitting on top of them. There's no city with the size or significance of Florence, but a number of the smaller cities, particularly Assisi, Perugia, Spoleto, and Orvieto, have lots to hold your interest. Umbria's Roman past is much in evidence—expect to see Roman villas, aqueducts, theaters, walls, and temples. To the east, in the region of the Marches, the main draw is the town of Urbino, where the Ducal Palace reveals more about the artistic energy of the Renaissance than a shelf of history books.

ROME	Rome is a large, busy city that lives in the here and now, yet there's no other place on Earth where you'll encounter such powerful evocations of a long and spectacular past. Take a few steps from a piazza designed by Michelangelo and you're looking down upon the ruins of ancient Rome, with the Colosseum as your backdrop. Exit a church housing a masterpiece by Caravaggio, turn the corner, and find yourself face to face with the Pantheon. From there a short walk takes you across the River Tiber to the world headquarters of the Roman Catholic Church, with its grandest cathedral and a massive, spectacular art collection, topped off by the Sistine Chapel. If there's a downside to Rome's abundance, it's that you can find yourself feeling overwhelmed. It pays to prioritize, pace yourself, and accept the fact that you won't see it all.

LAZIO	The region surrounding Rome has appealing places to visit if you're looking for a break from the hubbub of the city. In fact, people have been doing just that for almost as long as Rome has existed. The worthwhile, generally undervisited sights include papal palaces, landscaped gardens, medieval hill towns, beaches, and antiquities both Etruscan and Roman.
NAPLES & CAMPANIA	Campania is the gateway to southern Italy—and as far south as many travelers get. The region's happy combination of spectacular geology and rich cultural heritage makes it a popular place both to unwind—on the pint-size island of Capri or the resorts of the Amalfi Coast—and to explore the past—at the archaeological ruins of Pompeii, Herculaneum, and Paestum. In the middle of everything is Naples, a chaotic metropolis that people love and hate in nearly equal measure, though after a decade of urban renewal the lovers now appear to be in the majority. On a good day it's Italy's most fun and friendly large city. On a bad one it's a giant traffic jam, filled with crooked cabbies and purse-snatching kids on scooters.
THE MEZZOGIORNO	The southernmost regions of the peninsula—Puglia, Basilicata, and Calabria—are known informally as the *mezzogiorno*. The name translates literally as "midday," and it's meant to evoke the blazing sun that presides over the medieval villages, shimmering seas, and varied landscapes. The coastline of Puglia, along the heel of Italy's boot, is popular with beachgoers, but for the most part you're off the beaten path here, with all the pleasures and challenges that entails. You'll find fewer English-

WHAT'S WHERE

	speakers but more genuine warmth from the people you encounter. The most distinctive attractions are the *sassi* (cave dwellings in the Basilicata village of Matera) and *trulli* (mysterious conical-roof dwellings found in abundance in the Puglia town of Alberobello). Both are UNESCO World Heritage sites.
SICILY 	The architecture of Sicily reflects the island's centuries of successive dominion by the Greeks, Byzantines, Arabs, Normans, and Spaniards. Baroque church–hopping could be a sport in the cacophonous streets of Palermo and seafaring Siracusa. The breezes are sultry, and everyday life is without pretense, as witnessed in the workaday stalls of the fish markets all along the ports of the Tyrrhenian and Ionian coasts, bursting with tuna, swordfish, and sardines. Greek ruins stand sentinel in Agrigento's Valley of the Temples, blanketed in almond, oleander, and juniper blossoms. All over the island the ins and outs of life are celebrated each day as they have been for centuries—over a morning coffee, at the family lunch table, and in the evening *passeggiata*.
SARDINIA 	Too distant from imperial and papal Rome to be influenced by the character of the mainland, Sardinia is as unique as its weatherworn landscape. Although the indigenous culture is one of Italy's most interesting, many travelers opt to explore the high-profile Costa Smeralda, a chic resort developed by the Aga Khan, who discovered its charms when his yacht took shelter from a storm. Intrepid travelers head for the *nuraghi,* cyclopean stone defensive structures that are among prehistory's enigmas. Severely beautiful Sardinia is a prime destination if you're looking for a vacation getaway—whether of the chic or rugged variety.

WHEN TO GO

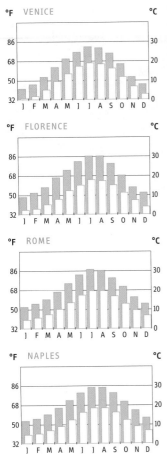

The main tourist season runs from April to mid-October. The so-called low season from fall to early spring may be cooler and rainier, but it has its rewards: less time waiting in line and more time for unhurried views of what you want to see.

Tourists crowd the major art cities at Easter, when Italians flock to resorts and to the country. From March through May, busloads of schoolchildren take cities of artistic and historical interest by storm. You don't want to be on an Italian beach in August because of the crowds. June and September are best; July can be crowded at the major resorts.

Climate

The best months for sightseeing are April, May, June, September, and October, when the weather is mild. The hottest months, July and August, can be unpleasant. Winters are relatively mild in most places on the main tourist circuit but always include some rainy spells.

In general, the northern half of the peninsula and the Adriatic Coast down to Puglia are rainier than elsewhere. Except for Taormina and some towns on the Italian Riviera, coastal resorts usually close up tight from October through Easter.

🔁 **Forecasts Weather Channel Connection** ☎ 900/9328437, 95¢ per min ⊕ www.weather.com.

QUINTESSENTIAL ITALY

Il Caffè (Coffee)

The Italian day begins and ends with coffee, and more cups of coffee punctuate the time in between. To live like the Italians do, drink as they drink, standing at the counter or sitting at an outdoor table of the corner bar. (In Italy, a "bar" is a coffee bar.) A primer: *caffè* means coffee, and Italian standard issue is what Americans call espresso—short, strong, and usually taken very sweet. *Cappuccino* is a foamy half-and-half of espresso and steamed milk; cocoa powder *(cacao)* on top is acceptable, cinnamon is not. If you're thinking of having a cappuccino for dessert, think again—Italians drink only caffè or caffè *macchiato* (with a spot of steamed milk) after lunchtime. Confused? Homesick? Order caffè *americano* for a reasonable facsimile of good old filtered joe.

Il Calcio (Soccer)

Imagine the most rabid American football fans—the ones who paint their faces on game day and sleep in pajamas emblazoned with the logo of their favorite team. Throw in a dose of melodrama along the lines of a tear-jerking soap opera. Ratchet up the intensity by a factor of 10, and you'll start to get a sense of how Italians feel about their national game, soccer—known in the mother tongue as *calcio*. On Sunday afternoons throughout the long September-to-May season, stadiums are packed throughout Italy from tip to toe. Those who don't get to games in person tend to congregate around television sets in restaurants and bars, rooting for the home team with a passion that feels like a last vestige of the days when the country was a series of warring medieval city-states. How calcio mania affects your stay in Italy depends on how eager you are to get involved. At the very least, you may notice an eerie Sunday-af-

If you want to get a sense of contemporary Italian culture and indulge in some of its pleasures, start by familiarizing yourself with the rituals of daily life. These are a few highlights—things you can take part in with relative ease.

ternoon silence on the city streets, or erratic restaurant service around the same time, accompanied by occasional cheers and groans from a neighboring room. If you want a memorable, truly Italian experience, attend a game yourself. Availability of tickets may depend on the current fortunes of the team in the town where you're staying, but they often can be acquired with some help from your hotel concierge.

Il Gelato (Ice Cream)

During warmer months, *gelato*—the Italian equivalent of ice cream—is a national obsession. It's considered a snack rather than a dessert, bought at stands and shops in piazzas and on street corners, and consumed on foot, usually at a leisurely stroll. (*See* La Passeggiata, *below.*) Gelato is softer, less creamy, and more intensely flavored than its American counterpart. It comes in simple flavors that capture the essence of

the main ingredient. (You won't find Chunky Monkey or Cookies 'n' Cream.) At most gelaterias standard choices include pistachio, nocciola (hazelnut), caffè, and numerous fresh-fruit varieties. Quality varies; the surest sign that you've hit on a good spot is a line at the counter.

La Passeggiata (Strolling)

A favorite Italian pastime is the *passeggiata* (literally, the promenade). In the late afternoon and early evening, especially on weekends, couples, families, and packs of teenagers stroll the main streets and piazzas of Italy's towns. It's a ritual of exchanged news and gossip, window-shopping, flirting, and gelato eating that adds up to a uniquely Italian experience. To join in, simply hit the streets for a bit of wandering. You may feel more like an observer than a participant, until you realize that observing is what la passeggiata is all about.

IF YOU LIKE...

Ancient Civilizations

Heavily colonized by the ancient Greeks, and later the center of the Roman Empire, Italy has a wealth of classical sites, many of them in an excellent state of preservation. Rome the city was, of course, capital of Rome the empire, and a number of ancient sites remain there today, seemingly plunked down in the middle of the modern metropolis.

Campania, too, is full of important classical landmarks from both the Greek and Roman eras. Farther south, Sicily was a center of trade and culture in the Hellenic world, and the island is still richly blessed with remarkable Greek temples—and fantastic Roman mosaics, too. Sardinia, meanwhile, is dotted with *nuraghi,* mysterious prehistoric stone fortresses. Italy's classical highlights include:

- **Ancient Rome.** The Roman Forum, the Capitoline Hill, and the unforgettable Colosseum and Pantheon are the best preserved ruins of the Empire's epicenter. At every turn you'll behold the crumbling remains of an ancient civilization—with motor scooters whizzing blithely past.

- **Pompeii and Herculaneum.** The eruption of Mt. Vesuvius in AD 79 left these two Roman cities buried in the volcanic ash and mud that famously preserved buildings and objects of everyday life. To walk their streets is to travel back in time.

- **Valley of the Temples, Agrigento.** This valley on the southern coast of Sicily, awash in almond blossoms, is considered by many to have the finest and best-preserved Greek temples anywhere—including Greece.

Renaissance Art

Travel veterans will tell you that the seemingly countless masterpieces of Italian art can cause first-time visitors—eyes glazed over from a heavy downpour of images, dates, and names—to lean, Pisa-like, on their companions for support. After a surfeit of Botticellis and Raphaels, even the miracle of the High Renaissance may begin to pall. The secret is to act like a tortoise, not a hare, and take your sweet time.

Instead of trotting after brisk tour guides, allow the splendors of the age to unfold slowly. Don't stop at the museums; get out and explore the chapels, palaces, and town squares for which Italy's marvelous art was conceived centuries ago and where much of it remains. Take in Michelangelo's *David* in Florence's Accademia, but then meander down the nearby 15th-century street where the sculptor was born.

Those caveats aside, here are the places to go when you're ready for an art feast:

- **Galleria degli Uffizi, Florence.** Allow the better part of a day to explore the world's greatest collection of Italian Renaissance art.

- **Musei Vaticani, Rome.** To gaze up at the impossible brushstrokes forming Michelangelo's Adam into muscular perfection at the zenith of the Sistine Chapel is to confront the divine—however you define it.

- **Basilica di San Francesco, Arezzo.** Piero della Francesa's *Legend of the True Cross* merits a pilgrimage to this Tuscan town.

Monumental Churches

Few images are more identifiable with Italy than the country's great churches, stunning works of architecture that often took one or even two centuries to build. And just as every Italian town has its main piazza, every town also has its duomo, often rising above that piazza.

Duomo literally means "dome," but is used to refer to the principal church of any given town or city. Generally speaking, the bigger the city, the more splendid its duomo. Still, some impressive churches inhabit some unlikely places—in the Umbrian hill towns of Assisi and Orvieto, for example.

Across the boot you'll find churches whose architecture ranges from flying-buttressed medieval Gothic to rococo and fanciful baroque. In Venice you'll see Byzantine influences, in Palermo you'll see Arab-Norman flair, and in Alto Adige (Südtirol) don't be surprised to see onion-bulb towers and Germanic spires.

- **Duomo, Milan.** The largest Gothic cathedral in Italy dates back to 1386; it is regal and arrogant, its spire rising high over fashionable Milan.

- **Duomo, Florence.** Brunelleschi's beautiful dome is the most recognizable in Italy, an unequaled feat of 15th-century engineering.

- **Basilica di San Pietro, Rome.** You've probably seen the Catholic Church's mother ship a thousand times on TV, but the imposing splendor of the Vatican can't be captured by the small screen.

- **Duomo, Siracusa.** Italy's classical past is on display at this cathedral, which incorporates the columns of a 6th-century BC Greek temple.

Driving

If you associate Italian roads with unruly motorists, impenetrable road signage, and endless traffic nightmares, you're only partly right. You'll attract headlight-flashing tailgaters if you plod along at 120 kph in the left lane, but Italy's network of fast *autostrade* (toll highways) is well maintained, with excellent service stations.

More rewarding, though, are the rural back roads, along which you might stop, on a lark, to take pictures of a crumbling farmhouse, have a coffee in a time-frozen hill town, or enjoy an epic lunch at a rustic *agriturismo* inaccessible to public transportation. Driving, in short, is the best way to see Italy. Winding rural roads with beautiful scenery crisscross the country, but here are three of the most memorable drives:

- **SS48 (Grande Strada delle Dolomiti).** This legendary mountain ascent takes you through the so-called "Heart of the Dolomites," the famous Passo di Sella, and into the Val Gardena, passing some of Europe's most unforgettable, craggy-peaked views.

- **SS1 (Via Aurelia).** Every time the A1 autostrada tunnels through the mountains, this smaller road stays out on the jagged coastline of the Italian Riviera, passing palm-filled winter gardens, terraced vineyards, cliff-hanging villages, and shimmering seas.

- **SS222 (Strada Chiantigiana).** This back road between Florence and Siena meanders through classic Tuscan landscapes: rolling hills and vineyards in the heart of the Chianti wine region. Take the drive slowly, stopping at wineries and local *enoteche*.

IF YOU LIKE...

Rustic Cooking

Italian cuisine all comes back to *la cucina di casa* (home cooking). From Genoa's handmade pasta twists with garden-fresh pesto to a simply grilled whole fish drizzled with olive oil anywhere along Italy's coastline, the finest plates are often the simplest. The emphasis is on exceptionally good *materie prime* (primary ingredients) handled with skill and with respect for the foods themselves and for the traditional methods of preparing them.

Each region of Italy has its own distinct, time-tested cuisine that's a source of local pride, and even sophisticated restaurants often maintain an orthodox focus on gen-erations-old recipes. Chefs revere even the most humble ingredients, devoting the same attention to day-old bread that they do to costly truffles. Here are a few places where the simplest food will take your breath away:

- **Da Michele, Naples.** There are only two items on the menu here—a margherita and a marinara—but the transcendent pizza at this 130-year-old establishment by itself justifies a trip to Italy.

- **Trattoria Casareccia, Lecce.** In Italy's warm and welcoming deep south, this white-walled house could be your Italian grandmother's. Their *purè di fave e cicoria* (puree of fava bean with chicory) is peasant food at its best.

- **Su Gologone, Nuoro, Sardinia.** There is a deep commitment to centuries-old recipes at this rural guesthouse and restaurant strikingly situated within Sardinia's wild interior.

Alta Cucina

Even with the strong peasant traditions of Italian cooking, French-influenced haute cuisine, or *alta cucina* in Italian, has blossomed at certain top-end restaurants around the boot. Sophisticated recipes take tradi-tional techniques and give them a creative twist that often shows influences from beyond Italian borders, but Italy's commit-ment to top primary ingredients remains a signature.

To partake of alta cucina, you should be prepared to journey off the beaten path. Many of Italy's most heralded—and best—restaurants are located in the countryside, in small, otherwise unexceptional towns. These are places of pilgrimage, where you can plan to escape the city and indulge in a long, opulent meal free from outside dis-tractions. Here are a few:

- **Ambasciata, Quistello, Lombardy.** Chef Ro-mano Tamani's food isn't just world-class—it's something unique in the world, deeply in touch with rural Ital-ian tradition (and the town of Quis-tello is about as rural as it gets).

- **San Domenico, Imola, Emilia-Romagna.** In the Italian region most dedicated to food worship, this is a gourmet's tem-ple improbably located in a town known for auto racing.

- **Ristorante Graziano, Villafrati, Sicily.** Nino Graziano is the chef that put Sicily on the alta cucina map, and this is the groundbreaking restaurant in the countryside south of Palermo where he did it.

Hiking

Even if you don't fancy yourself a disciple of Reinhold Messner (the favorite son of the Dolomites and the first man to reach the peak of Everest without oxygen), you'll find great summer hiking aplenty all over Italy.

First and foremost is the mountainous region of Trentino–Alto Adige, whose Dolomites are striped with well-marked trails on every level. But it doesn't end there. The Apennines are a highlight farther south. The well-established Club Alpino Italiano (CAI) is an excellent resource that can point you to mountain refuges all over Italy.

- **Vie Ferrate (Iron Paths), Trentino–Alto Adige.** Reinforced trails through the mountains, once forged by the Italian and Austro-Hungarian armies, feature ladders, bridges, and safety cables; they're a great way to get off the beaten path in the Dolomites.

- **Cinque Terre, Italian Riviera.** They're not undiscovered, as they once were—you'll hear English spoken everywhere—but these five villages clinging to the cliffs of the Riviera di Levante are still spectacular, and they're all connected by invigorating hiking trails with memorable views of the towns, the rocks, and the Ligurian Sea.

- **The Paths of St. Francis, Umbria.** Outside Assisi, an easy half-hour walk takes you from the town of Cannara to Pian d'Arca, site of St. Francis's sermon to the birds. It takes a bit more effort to make the walk from Assisi to the Eremo delle Carceri; from there you can head up to the summit of Monte Subasio, where you have views for miles in every direction.

Shopping

"Made in Italy" is synonymous with style, quality, and craftsmanship, whether it refers to high fashion or Maserati automobiles. The best buys are leather goods of all kinds (from gloves to bags to jackets), silk goods, knitwear, ceramics, and, of course, the country's world-famous food products, from artisanal pasta sauces to world-class wine to extra-virgin olive oil.

Every region has its specialties. Venice is known for glassware, lace, and velvet; Milan and Como for silk; and the Dolomites and the mountains of Calabria and Sicily for hand-carved wooden objects. Bologna and Parma are known for their cheeses and hams; Modena for its balsamic vinegar; Florence for straw goods, gold jewelry, leather, and paper products (including beautiful handmade notebooks); Assisi for embroidery; and Deruta, Gubbio, Vietri, and many towns in Puglia and Sicily for ceramics.

- **Quadrilatero, Milan.** Italy's fashion capital is shop-happy, and the streets of the Quadrilatero district display the cutting edge of European design—but come with a full wallet. End-of-season discounts go into effect in mid-January and mid-July.

- **Piazza di Spagna, Rome.** You can join the throngs shopping for high fashion in the shadow of the Spanish Steps—or hit the Via del Corso for more than a mile of stores of all varieties.

- **Tamburini, Bologna.** Be overwhelmed by the smells of all that is good about the legendary food of Emilia-Romagna—and of Italy. Then, vacuum-pack it all and take it home with you.

IF YOU LIKE...

Nightlife

In the big cities, generic techno clubs hop with activity on Friday and Saturday. But the cutting-edge nightlife in Rome and Milan is exclusive, expensive, and evanescent. You'd do best to ask a model or soccer star where the scene is that particular week—then see if you can get in.

Outside the very largest cities, Italy is an eminently seasonable place, and partying happens mostly during *ferragosto* (August vacation), when Italians flock to beaches all over the country's extensive coastline and partake of up to a month of nonstop revelry that dwarfs the nightlife at any other time of year. Prominent party towns include:

- **Rimini, Emilia-Romagna.** It's not for everyone, but as far as many young Italians are concerned, this murky-water Adriatic beach town hosts the best summer party, anywhere, anytime.

- **Capri.** You may come to this island to admire its rocky cliffs and *Grotta Azzurra*, but the Italians come in August to admire each other. On a late summer evening the island's picture-perfect piazzas burst at the seams with beautiful young things.

- **Catania, Sicily.** Many tourists think of the island's youngest and liveliest city as dirty and dangerous, but it's neither. Catania has become a nerve center of youth culture in southern Italy, with an exploding live music scene, microbrewed beer, and nightclubs to rival those of the cities of the north—without the exclusivity.

Wine

For years, most Italian wine production was mass-export jug wine, much of it from the flat southern vineyards. Unfortunately, many wine drinkers identified Italy more with this low-quality *vino sfuso* than with the country's prestigious D.O.C.G. ("Denominazione di Origine Controllata") appellations, which include Barolo and Barbaresco (tannic, age-worthy Piedmontese wines), Brunello di Montalcino (a Tuscan wine made with Sangiovese), and Amarone (the deep, dark pride of the Veneto).

Recent decades have seen the emergence of the "Super Tuscans." Dubbed *vini di tavola* (table wines) or "I.G.T." *(indicazione geografica tipica),* these nontraditional blends have powerful flavors suited to the tastes of the modern wine world.

Regions such as Umbria and Sicily are following in the footsteps of the Super Tuscans, creating their own newfangled upscale blends at lower prices. Many results have been exciting. Wines to look for include:

- **Ca' del Bosco.** No winery in Italy has won more acclaim from the wine press than this Lombardy house, for both its bruts and reds.

- **Cerviolo.** One of the more affordable ways to taste a Super Tuscan, this wine is as interesting and potent as bottles costing two or three times as much.

- **Feudi di San Gregorio.** This winery has emerged as the pride of Campania, making fresh but complex whites and deep, dark, spicy, and full-bodied reds, including the masterful Patrimo.

Skiing

Italy may not have Europe's most challenging ski areas, but the views of the Alps and Dolomites along the slopes in the northern regions of Valle d'Aosta and Trentino–Alto Adige are peerless, and Italian ski passes are cheaper than Swiss or Austrian ones. There's little snowmaking here, so slopes are often not viable until mid-February—but thereafter they're frequently blanketed with wonderful fresh powder.

Italian recreational skiers favor a full-week stay (*settimana bianca*), during which they tend to keep a relaxed ski schedule—10 or 11 AM until 3 or 4 PM. (If you're an early riser, you'll have the snow to yourself.) Perhaps unsurprisingly, the Italians have perfected the art of après-ski; grappa, the king of Italian digestifs, is in its finest form when enjoyed in front of a ski-lodge fire after a day on the lifts.

- **Courmayeur, Valle d'Aosta.** Monte Bianco, or Mont Blanc, is one of Europe's most famous mountains, but Courmayeur's slopes are fairly tame. Take your passport for the jaw-dropping cable-car ride over to Chamonix on the French side of the mountain.

- **Cortina d'Ampezzo, Alto Adige.** Probably the best town in Italy for après-ski, Cortina is the grand old Dolomites resort town with the region's best hotels and liveliest bars. The nearby Sella Ronda is Italy's best ski circuit.

- **Mt. Etna, Sicily.** Believe it or not, you can actually ski this active volcano, and while the trails are unremarkable, they make for great scenery—and a great story.

Il Dolce Far Niente

"The sweetness of doing nothing" has long been an art form in Italy. This is a country in which life's pleasures are warmly celebrated, not guiltily indulged. Of course, doing "nothing" doesn't really mean nothing. It means doing things differently. It means lingering over a glass of wine for the better part of an evening just to watch the sun slowly set. It means coming home from wherever you are at midday, whether you're a suited businessman or a third-grade schoolgirl, just to have lunch at the family table.

It means savoring a slow and flirtatious evening passeggiata along the main street of a little town, a procession with no destination other than the town and its streets. And it means making a commitment—however temporary—to thinking, feeling, and believing that there is nowhere that you have to be next, that there is no other time than the magical present.

- **Ravello.** This quiet, stunningly positioned hilltop village above the Amalfi Coast is the quintessential small Italian town—and a perfect place to gaze out at the Gulf of Salerno and *far niente*.

- **Bellagio.** Italy's enchanting Alpine lakes are icons of relaxation. Meander through stately villa gardens, dance on the wharf, or just watch the boats float by in the shadow of the Alps.

- **Gondola ride, Venice.** There is still nothing more romantic than a glide along Venice's canals in a gondola, your escorted trip to nowhere, watched over by Gothic palaces with delicately arched eyebrows.

GREAT ITINERARIES

ROME, FLORENCE, VENICE & HIGHLIGHTS IN BETWEEN

This itinerary and the ones that follow are designed for maximum impact—they'll keep you moving. Think of them as rough drafts for you to revise according to your own interests and time constraints.

Day 1: Venice

Arrive in Venice's Marco Polo Airport (there are some direct flights from the United States), take the boat across the lagoon to Venice, check into your hotel, then get out, and get lost in the back canals for a couple of hours before dinner. If you can get a reservation, Osteria da Fiore would make a memorable first meal in Italy; it's an unforgettable place for sweet, delicate Adriatic seafood.

Logistics: At the airport, follow signs for water transport and look for Alilaguna, which operates the soothing one-hour, boat trip into Venice. The boats stop at the Lido and finally leave you near Piazza San Marco; from there you can get to your hotel on foot or by vaporetto. The water taxis are much more expensive and aren't really worth the cost, although they'll take you directly to your hotel.

Day 2: Venice

Begin by skipping the coffee at your hotel and have a real Italian coffee at a real Italian coffee shop. Spend the day at Venice's top few sights, including the Basilica di San Marco, Palazzo Ducale, and Galleria dell'Accademia. Stop for lunch, perhaps sampling Venice's traditional specialty, *sarde in saor* (grilled sardines in a mouthwatering sweet-and-sour preparation that includes onions and raisins), and be sure to

check out the ancient fish market, Rialto Bridge, and sunset at the Zattere before dinner. Later, stop at one of the pubs around the Campo San Luca or Campo Santa Margarita, where you can toast to freedom from automobiles.

Logistics: Venice is best seen by wandering. The day's activities can be done on foot, with the occasional vaporetto ride.

Day 3: Ferrara/Bologna

Get an early start and head out of Venice on a Bologna-bound train. The ride to Ferrara—your first stop in Emilia-Romagna—is about an hour and a half. Visit the Castello Estense and Duomo before lunch; a panino and a beer at one of Ferrara's prim and proper cafés should fit the bill. Wander Ferrara's cobblestone streets before hopping on the train to Bologna (a ride of less than an hour). In Bologna, check into your hotel and take a walk around Piazza Maggiore before dinner. At night, you can check out some of northern Italy's best nightlife.

Logistics: In Ferrara, the train station lies a bit outside the city center, so you'll want to take a taxi into town (check your luggage at the station). Going out, there's a taxi stand near the back of the castle, toward Corso Ercole I d'Este. In Bologna the walk into town from the station is more manageable, particularly if you're staying along Via dell'Indipendenza.

Day 4: Bologna/Florence

After breakfast, spend the morning checking out some of Bologna's churches and piazzas, including a climb up the leaning

See this itinerary with full-color photos at fodors.com

Torre degli Asinelli for a red rooftop–studded panorama. After lunch, head back to the train station, and take the short ride to Florence. You'll arrive in Florence in time for an afternoon siesta and an evening passeggiata.

Logistics: Florence's Santa Maria Novella train station is within easy access to some hotels, farther from others. Florence's traffic is legendary, but taxis at the station are plentiful; make sure you get into a licensed, clearly marked car that's outside in line.

Day 5: Florence

This is your day to see the sights of Florence. Start with the Uffizi Gallery (reserve your tickets in advance), where you'll see Botticelli's *Primavera* and *Birth of Venus*. Next, walk to the Piazza del Duomo, the site of Brunelleschi's spectacular dome, which you can climb for an equally spectacular view. By the time you get down, you'll be more than ready for a simple lunch at a laid-back café. Depending on your preferences, either devote the afternoon to art (Michelangelo's *David* at the Galleria dell'Accademia, the magnificent Medici Chapels, and perhaps the church of Santa Croce) or hike up to Piazzale Michelangelo, overlooking the city. Either way, finish the evening in style with a traditional *bistecca*

alla fiorentina (a grilled T-bone steak with olive oil).

Day 6: Lucca/Pisa

After breakfast, board a train for Lucca. It's an easy 1½-hour trip on the way to Pisa to see this walled medieval city. Don't miss the Romanesque Duomo, or a walk in the park that lines the city's ramparts. Have lunch at a local trattoria before continuing on to Pisa, where you'll spend an afternoon seeing—what else—the Leaning Tower, along with the equally impressive Duomo and Battistero. Walk down to the banks of the Arno River, contemplate the majestic views at sunset, and have dinner at one of the many inexpensive local restaurants in the real city center—a bit away from the most touristy spots.

Logistics: Lucca's train station lies just outside the walled city, so hardier travelers may want to leave the station on foot; otherwise, take a taxi. Check your luggage at the station. Pisa's train station isn't far from the city center, although it's on the other side of town from the Campo dei Miracoli (site of the Leaning Tower).

Day 7: Orvieto/Rome

Three hours south of Pisa is Orvieto, one of the prettiest and most characteristic

GREAT ITINERARIES

towns of the Umbria region, conveniently situated right on the Florence–Rome train line. Check out the memorable cathedral before a light lunch accompanied by one of Orvieto's famous white wines. Get back on a train bound for Rome, and in a little more than an hour you'll arrive in the Eternal City in time to make your way to your hotel and relax for a bit before you head out for the evening. When you do, check out Piazza Navona, Campo de' Fiori, and the Trevi Fountain—it's best in the evening—and take a stand-up *aperitivo* (Campari and soda is the classic) at an unpretentious local bar before dinner. It's finally pizza time; you can't go wrong at any of Rome's popular local pizzerias.

Logistics: To get from Pisa to Orvieto, you'll first catch a train to Florence and then get on a Rome-bound train from there. Be careful at Rome's Termini train station, which is a breeding ground for scam artists. Keep your possessions close at hand, and only get into a licensed taxi at the taxi stand.

Day 8: Rome

Rome took millennia to build, but unfortunately on this whirlwind trip you'll only have a day and a half to see it. In the morning, head to to the Vatican Museums to see Michelangelo's glorious *Adam* at the Sistine Chapel. See St. Peter's Basilica and Square before heading back into Rome proper for lunch around the Pantheon, followed by a coffee from one of Rome's famous coffee shops. Next, visit ancient Rome—first see the magnificent Pantheon, and then head across to the Colosseum, stopping along the way along Via dei Fori Imperiali to check out the Roman Forum from above. From the Colosseum, take a

taxi to Piazza di Spagna, a good place to see the sunset and shop at stylish boutiques, Take another taxi to Piazza Trilussa at the entrance of Trastevere, a beautiful old working-class neighborhood where you'll have a relaxing dinner.

Day 9: Rome/Departure

Head by taxi to Termini station and catch the train ride to the Fiumicino airport. Savor your last cup of the world's richest coffee at one of the coffee bars in the airport before boarding.

Logistics: The train from Termini station to the airport is fast, inexpensive, and easy—for most people, it's preferable to an exorbitantly priced taxi ride that, in bad traffic, can take twice as long.

TIPS

1. The itinerary can also be completed by car on the modern autostrade, although you'll run into dicey traffic in Florence and Rome. For obvious reasons, you're best off waiting to pick up your car on Day 3, when you leave Venice.

2. Among trains, aim for the reservation-only Eurostar Italia—it's more comfortable and faster.

3. The sights along this route are highly touristed; you'll have a better time if you make the trip outside the busy months of June, July, and August.

THE COURTLY NORTH

Day 1: Genoa

Fly into Genoa's pint-size Aeroporto Internazionale Cristoforo Colombo, pick up your rental car, and drive to your hotel (try to get a place near Piazza de Ferrari, the gateway to the *centro storico*). Leave your car there for the rest of the day. Spend the afternoon wandering the old city's ancient streets—*vicoli*—some of which are so narrow that lovers on upper floors would leap across to each other's rooms. Don't miss the Porta Soprana, the fortified portal to Europe's largest medieval city; the black-and-white-striped San Lorenzo cathedral; Via Garibaldi, lined with some of northern Italy's most impressive palazzi; and a ramble around the old port, site of Europe's largest aquarium. Do some window-shopping during the evening passeggiata along Via XX Settembre, then sample the city's culinary delights—the fresh fish with a water view at Antica Osteria del Bai, for example (you'll want to take a taxi there), or *trofie al pesto* (stubby, dense pasta twists with pesto, potatoes, and green beans) anywhere in town. Genoa is the birthplace of pesto—and focaccia, too.

Logistics: Alitalia's international flights to Genoa connect through Milan, Rome, or, if you're on a European carrier, other European cities including Zürich, Paris, London, and Munich. Try to get in as early in the morning as possible. Genoa is a vertical city, implausibly sandwiched between the mountains and the sea. Maps have a hard time conveying this third dimension, so be sure to ask your hotel for detailed driving and parking directions.

Day 2: Riviera di Levante/Cinque Terre

Heading out of Genoa, cross your fingers for good weather, and spend the morning driving one of Italy's most scenic roads, the Via Aurelia, in the direction of La Spezia (along the Riviera di Levante, or the "Riviera of the Rising Sun"). This road hugs the coast for hours. Stop for a brief wander around one or two of the many idyllic villages you pass; good candidates include Camogli and Santa Margherita Ligure, less than an hour outside Genoa. Portofino is on a promontory framed by those two towns; it's a bit more of a detour, but its allure is unmistakable. When you arrive in the Cinque Terre, check into a hotel in Riomaggiore or Vernazza; the latter is perhaps the most beautiful of these fishing ports that cling implausibly to the cliffs. From there, hike some of the impressive paths that connect the towns, including the Via dell'Amore between Manarola and Riomaggiore. Eat in whichever town you end up in at dinnertime, then take the train back to your hotel.

Logistics: The Via Aurelia (SS1) first heads out of town past the Genoese neighborhoods of Quarto, Quinto, and then Nervi. If you're not in view of the water, you're probably on the wrong road. From there it's a slow but beautiful drive to the Cinque Terre. If you're running short on time, switch over to the parallel A10 autostrada.

Day 3: Parma

Your next stop will be the stately food capital of Parma. When you arrive, check out the city's harmonious piazzas and medieval architecture. Shop for Parmigiano-

GREAT
ITINERARIES

Reggiano cheese and prosciutto di Parma (Parma ham)—where better?—or simply acquaint yourself with the *dolce far niente* (sweetness of doing nothing), perhaps browsing the city's stately boutiques with breaks for coffee (order simply "caffè"), gelato, or an aperitivo. When night comes, seize the occasion to welcome yourself to Italy with an elaborate meal. There are many fine restaurants in this food town, but perhaps none finer than La Greppia.

Logistics: From the Cinque Terre, take the Via Aurelia to La Spezia, where you'll head north on the A15—it's no more than an hour up to Parma on this fast highway.

Day 4: Verona

After breakfast, depart from Parma for Verona, which might be the most quintessentially Italian city on this itinerary. Standing along the side of the fast-flowing River Adige, gazing at the rows of old palazzi along its banks and the rolling hills of cypress beyond, you'll find it hard not to fall in love with this city of Romeo and Juliet. Spend your morning wandering the city's medieval piazzas. Skip the touristy so-called "House of Juliet," but don't miss Verona's stunning Roman Arena, the Castelvecchio (old castle), and San Zeno Maggiore, possibly Italy's finest Romanesque church. Accompany your dinner with a bottle of the Amarone wine for which the region is known. If it's summer and you plan things right, you might even time your day in Verona to coincide with an opera performance in the Arena.

Logistics: Take the A1 autostrada and then turn onto the A22 after about 50 km (31 mi), before you hit Modena. The A22 heads straight north past Mantua to Verona. Once there, park your car and go it on foot; Verona is definitely a walking city.

Day 5: Trento/Bolzano

Head north on the highway after breakfast, stopping for lunch and a walk around Trento's castle and Piazza del Duomo with its beautifully crenellated Palazzo Pretorio. After lunch, it's back on the road north. If you're not familiar with the region, you may be surprised, upon reaching beautiful Bolzano, to discover that everybody is speaking German. This is Alto Adige, also known as Südtirol, a semiautonomous region of Italy in which Italian is only one of the two official languages. The feel of the town, with its dim beer halls and elegant Piazza Walther, is positively Germanic. Not to be missed in town is the archaeological museum and a face-to-5,300-year-old-face visit with its amazingly preserved Iceman. Have a casual dinner of grilled meats and microbrewed beer at the young and laid-back Hopfen & Co, or gorge yourself with rich Tirolean mountain food at the more formal Zür Kaiserkron.

Logistics: Trento is due north of Verona on the A22 autostrada. It shouldn't take more than an hour and a half to get there. Continue north on the A22 to reach Bolzano—it's only another 50 km (31 mi).

Day 6: Padua/Venice

Leave bright and early and head back to the Veneto, where you'll be stopping in Padua, a wondrous university town full of bicycles and beautiful medieval architecture. The drive should take about two hours. Stop to see Giotto's unbelievable fresco cycle in the Cappella degli Scrovegni before continuing into the centro storico, parking wherever you can, and wandering through the streets of the old town (watch out for those bikes!). After lunch, drive straight to Venice (less than an hour), return your rental car, check into your hotel, and if all goes well, you'll still have time for some afternoon sight-

seeing. Get lost in the city's back canals for a couple of hours before finding your way to a seafood dinner. Afterward, consider having a nightcap around the Campo San Luca or Campo Santa Margarita.

Logistics: This day really requires an early start. Head south on the A22—back through Verona—and then east on the A4. Padua is on the way to Venice on the A4. When you arrive in Venice, return your car at Piazzale Roma, where most major companies have a garage. Then at the Piazzale Roma vaporetto stop, buy 72-hour vaporetto "travel cards," and take the vaporetto to your hotel. If you're not in the mood for such a hectic day, then skip Padua.

Day 7: Venice

Begin with a morning vaporetto cruise along the Grand Canal. Proceed with a visit to Piazza San Marco, the Byzantine splendor of the Basilica di San Marco, and the imposing Palazzo Ducale. Stop for lunch, perhaps at a traditional Venetian *bacaro* (wine bar). Next, take the Accademia footbridge across the Grand Canal, and see the Gallerie dell'Accademia, Venice's most important art gallery. Wander through the Dorsoduro neighborhood, finishing up with a romantic sunset walk around the Zattere before proceeding to dinner.

Day 8: Venice/Departure

Have breakfast at your hotel and head by vaporetto to San Marco, where you'll transfer to the airport boat. Savor your last çup of the world's richest coffee at the airport's coffee bar before boarding.

Logistics: Alilaguna operates the one-hour, €10 boat trip from Venice to the airport. Water taxis are much more expensive but they pick you up at your hotel.

TIPS

❶ The itinerary can also be done by train. All these stops are well connected by Italy's rail network, and none of the trips will take more than a couple of hours. In most cases you'll want to take a taxi from the train station to your hotel. The only tricky parts will be on Days 5 and 6, when you'll be stopping for lunch in Trento and Padua, respectively. You can check your luggage at the train station.

❷ Winter is not the time for this trip. Northern Italy can get very cold in December, January, and especially February.

GREAT ITINERARIES

CLASSICS OF CENTRAL ITALY

Day 1: Florence

If you're coming in on an international flight, you'll probably settle in Florence in time for an afternoon stroll or siesta (depending on your jet-lag strategy) before dinner.

Logistics: On your flight in, read through the restaurant listings in this guide and begin anticipating the first dinner of your trip. Look for a place near your hotel, and when you arrive, reserve a table (or have your concierge do it for you). Making a meal the focus of your first day is a great way to ease into Italian life.

Day 2: Florence

Begin your morning at the Uffizi Gallery (reserve your ticket in advance). The extensive collection will occupy much of your morning. Next, take in the neighboring Piazza della Signoria, Florence's most impressive square, then head a few blocks north to the Duomo. There, check out Ghiberti's famous bronze doors on the Battistero, and work up an appetite by climbing the 463 steps to the cupola of Brunelleschi's splendid cathedral dome, atop which you'll experience a memorable vista. Spend the afternoon relaxing, shopping, and wandering Florence's medieval streets; or, if you're up for a more involved journey, head out to Fiesole to experience the ancient amphitheater and beautiful views of the Tuscan countryside.

Day 3: Florence

Keep the energy level up for your second full day in Florence, sticking with art and architecture for the morning, trying to see most of the following: Michelangelo's *David* at the Galleria dell'Accademia, the Palazzo Pitti and Boboli Gardens, the Medici Chapels, and the churches of Santa Maria Novella and Santa Croce. If it's a clear day, spend the afternoon on a trip up to the Piazzale Michelangelo, high on a hill above Florence, for sweeping views of the idyllic Florentine countryside. Given all the walking you've been doing, tonight would be a good night to recharge by trying the famed *bistecca alla fiorentina* (a grilled T-bone steak with olive oil).

Logistics: You can get up to the Piazzale Michelangelo by taxi or by taking Bus 7 from Santa Maria Novella. Otherwise, do your best to get around on foot; Florence is a brilliant city for walking.

Day 4: San Gimignano

Now that you've been appropriately introduced to the bewildering splendor of Renaissance Italy, it's time for a change of pace—and time for a rental car, which will enable you to see the back roads of Tuscany and Umbria. After breakfast, pick up your car, and head out. On a good day the lazy drive from Florence to San Gimignano, past vineyards and typical Tuscan landscapes, is truly spectacular. The first thing that will hit you when you arrive at the hill town of San Gimignano will be the towers everywhere. The medieval skyscrapers of Italy, they also once occupied the role now played by Ferraris or Hummers: they were public displays of wealth. After finding your way to a hotel in the old town, set out on foot and check out the city's turrets and alleyways, doing your best to get away from the trinket shops, and later have a leisurely dinner with the light but delicious local white wine, Vernaccia di San Gimignano.

Logistics: Some hotels might be able to co-ordinate with some rental-car agencies so that your car can be brought to your hotel for you. Once you navigate your way out of Florence (no easy task), San Gimignano is only 57 km (35 mi) to the southwest, so it's an easy drive; you could even take a detour on the SS222 (Strada Chiantigiana), stop at one of the Chianti wine towns, and visit a winery along the way.

Day 5: Siena

In the morning, set out for nearby Siena, which is known worldwide for its Palio, a festival that culminates in an elaborate horse race competition among the 17 *contrade* (medieval neighborhoods) of the city. Because of the enormous influx of tourists, especially in summer, Siena isn't everyone's cup of tea, but it's still one of Tuscany's most impressive sights; however many tourists you have to bump elbows with, it's hard not to be blown away by the city's precious medieval streets and memorable fan-shape Piazza del Campo. Not to be missed while in town are the spectacular Duomo, the Battistero, and the Spedale di Santa Maria della Scala, an old hospital and hostel that now contains an underground archaeological museum.

Logistics: It's a short and pretty drive from San Gimignano to Siena, but once there, parking can be a challenge. Look for the *stadio* (soccer stadium), where there's a parking lot that often has space.

Day 6: Arezzo/Cortona

Get an early start, because there's a lot to see today. From Siena you'll first head to Arezzo, home to the Basilica di San Francesco, which contains important frescoes by Piero della Francesca. Check out the Piazza Grande along with its beautiful Romanesque church of Pieve di Santa Maria. Try to do all of this before lunch (La Torre di Gnicche is a good choice), after which you'll head straight to Cortona. If Arezzo didn't capture your imagination, Cortona, which dates back to the 5th century BC, will. Olive trees and vineyards give way to a medieval hill town with views over ridiculously idyllic Tuscan countryside and Lake Trasimeno. Cortona is a town for walking and relaxing, not sightseeing, so enjoy yourself, wandering through the Piazza della Repubblica and Piazza Signorelli, perhaps doing a bit of shopping.

Logistics: Siena to Arezzo is 63 km (39 mi) on the E78. From Arezzo to Cortona, it's just 30 km (18 mi)—take S71.

Day 7: Assisi

Today you'll cross over into Umbria, a region just as beautiful as Tuscany but still

GREAT
ITINERARIES

less trodden. Yet another impossibly beautiful hill town, Assisi, is the home of St. Francis and host to the many religious pilgrims that come to celebrate his legacy. Going here is the most treasured memory of many a traveler's visit to Italy. Upon arriving and checking into your lodging, head straight for the Basilica di San Francesco, which displays the coffin of St. Francis and a bevy of unbelievable frescoes. From there take Via San Francesco to Piazza del Commune and see the Tempio di Minerva before a break for lunch; Osteria Piazzetta dell'Erba would be a fine and relaxed choice. After lunch, see San Rufino, the town cathedral, and then go back through the piazza to Corso Mazzini and see Santa Chiara. If you're a true Franciscan, you could instead devote the afternoon to heading out 16 km (10 mi) to Cannara, where St. Francis delivered his sermon to the birds.

Logistics: From Cortona take the S71 to the A1 autostrada toward Perugia. After about 40 km (24 mi), take the Assisi exit (E 45), and it's another 14 km (8 mi) to Assisi.

Day 8: Spoleto

This morning will take you from a small Umbrian hill town to a slightly bigger one: Spoleto, a walled city that's home to a world-renowned arts festival each summer. But Spoleto needs no festival to be celebrated. Its Duomo is wonderful. Its fortress is impressive. And the Ponte delle Torri, a 14th-century bridge that separates Spoleto from Monteluco, is a marvelous sight, traversing a gorge 260 feet below and built upon the foundations of a Roman aqueduct. See all these during the day, stopping for a light lunch of a panino or salad, saving your appetite for a serious last dinner in Italy: Umbrian cuisine is excellent everywhere, but Spoleto is a memorable culinary destination. Do your best to sample black

truffles, a proud product of the region; they're delicious on pasta or meat.

Logistics: One school of thought would be to time your visit to Spoleto's world-renowned arts festival that runs from mid-June through mid-July. Another would be to do anything you can to avoid it. It all depends on your taste for big festivals and big crowds. The trip from Assisi to Spoleto is a pretty 47-km (29-mi) drive (S75 to the S3) that should take you less than an hour.

Day 9: Spoleto/Departure

It's a fair distance from Spoleto to the Florence airport, your point of departure. Depending on your comfort level with Italian driving, allow at least 2½ hours to reach Florence's airport. If your flight out is at midday or before, this will mean getting an early start.

Logistics: An alternative possibility would be to try to get a flight out of Perugia's tiny airport, which is a lot closer to Spoleto than Florence. It offers connections to Milan and Rome (Ciampino)—but not many. Otherwise, just get an early start and drive to Florence along the A1 autostrada.

TIP

Because of spotty train service to Tuscan hill towns, this itinerary is extremely difficult to complete without a car. Driving is easy and relaxing in the region, whose roads can be windy but are generally wide, well kept, well marked, and not too crowded. If you absolutely don't want to drive, buses are the best way to go, but you'll often have to change buses in hubs like Florence, and it would be best to cut out some of the smaller Tuscan hill towns and spend extra time in Siena and Spoleto.

THE SULTRY SOUTH

Day 1: Naples

Fly into Naples's Aeroporto Capodichino, a scant 8 km (5 mi) from the city. Naples is rough around the edges and may be a bit jarring if you're a first-time visitor, but it's classic Italy, and most visitors end up falling in love with the city's alluring waterfront palazzi and spectacular pizza. First things first, though: recharge with a nap and, after that, a good caffè—Naples has some of Italy's best. Revive in time for an evening stroll down Naples's wonderful shopping street, Via Toledo—it's quintessential Italy—before dinner and bed.

Logistics: Under no circumstances should you rent a car for Naples. Take a taxi from the airport—it's not far, or overly expensive—and you should face few logistical obstacles on your first day in Italy.

Day 2: Naples

Start the day in Piazza Gesù, and head east along Spaccanapoli through the very heart of old Naples, stopping at the churches of Gesù Nuovo and Santa Chiara. Farther up Spaccanapoli, try to check out Cappella Sansevero and the Duomo, before heading left on Via Foria to the Museo Archeologico Nazionale. From there take a taxi to Da Michele, and begin your afternoon with the best pizza in the world. Post pizza, check out the harbor and the Castel Nuovo; then head past the Teatro San Carlo to the enormous Palazzo Reale. Walk 15 minutes south to the Castel dell'Ovo in the Santa Lucia waterfront area, one of Naples' most charming neighborhoods. Then it's back up to Via Caracciolo and the Villa Comunale, before heading back to your hotel for a short

rest before dinner and perhaps a night out at one of Naples's lively bars or clubs.

Logistics: This entire day is easily done on foot, with the exception of the taxi for your midday pizza. Naples is one of the best walking cities in Italy.

Day 3: Pompeii/Sorrento

After breakfast, pick up your rental car, pack in your luggage, and drive from Naples to Pompeii, one of the true archaeological gems of Europe. If it's summer, be prepared for an onslaught of sweltering heat as you make your way through the incredibly preserved ruins of a city that was devastated by the whims of Mt. Vesuvius nearly two thousand years ago. You'll see the houses of noblemen and merchants, brothels, political graffiti, and more. From Pompeii, get back in your car and it's on to Sorrento, your first taste of the wonderful peninsula that marks the beginning of the fabled Amalfi Coast. Sorrento is touristy, but it may well be the Italian city of your imagination: cliff-hanging, cobblestone-paved, and graced with an infinite variety of fishing-port and coastal views. There, have a relaxing dinner of fish and white wine before calling it a day.

Logistics: Naples to Pompeii is all about the A3: a short 24 km (15 mi) brings you to this archaeological gem. From Pompeii it's a short ride back on the A3 until the exit for Sorrento; from the exit, you'll take the S145 to reach Sorrento.

Day 4: Positano/Ravello

Your stay in Sorrento will be short, as there's much of the Amalfi Coast still to

GREAT
ITINERARIES

see: Positano, your next stop, is a must. It's one of the most visited towns in Italy for good reason: its blue-green seas, stairs "as steep as ladders," and white Moorish-style houses make for a truly memorable setting. Walk, gaze, and eat (lunch), before heading on to the less-traveled, even-higher-up town of Ravello, your Amalfi Coast dream come true, an aerie that is "closer to the sky than the sea." Don't miss the Duomo, Villa Rufolo, or Villa Cimbrone before settling in for a dinner in the sky.

Logistics: Sorrento to Positano is just a 34-km (21-mi) jaunt, but the winding roads will draw it out for the better part of an hour—a scenic hour. From Positano, Ravello is another slow 40 km (24 mi) to the east, perched high above the rest of the world. Be prepared to use low gears if you're driving a stick shift (as you almost surely will be).

Day 5: Matera

It will take a bit of a drive to get to Basilicata from the Amalfi Coast; leaving Campania and entering Basilicata is generally a lonely experience. Little-traveled roads, wild hills, and distant farms are the hallmarks of this province, which produces deep, dark aglianico wines and has perfected the art of peasant food. You'll spend a while in your car to make it to Matera, a beautiful, ancient city full of Paleolithic *sassi* (cavelike dwellings hewn out of rock)—but it's worth it. Traversing the city is like taking a voyage through time. Spend the afternoon exploring the sassi, but take care not to miss the new part of the city, too. Then enjoy a relaxing dinner at one of Matera's excellent restaurants—just decide whether you want flavorful local beef (Le Botteghe) or a flurry of Basilicatan tapas (Lucanerie). Basilicata, you'll soon discover, is full of unrivaled values at restau-

rants, and with such options you'll be guaranteed to sleep well in the sassi.

Logistics: It's a long haul from your starting point, Ravello, to Matera. It's a good thing Basilicata's landscape is so pretty. Once in Matera, if you're staying in the sassi, get extra-detailed driving and parking instructions from your hotel beforehand—navigating through thousand-year-old alleyways can be challenging.

Day 6: Lecce

This drive will take a good three hours, so get an early start. The baroque city of Lecce will mark your introduction to Puglia, the heel of Italy's boot. It's one of Italy's best-kept secrets, as you'll soon find out upon checking out the spectacular church of Santa Croce, the ornate Duomo, and the harmonious Piazza Sant'Oronzo. The shopping is great, the food is great, and the evening passeggiata is great. Don't miss the opportunity, if you wind up at a bar or café in the evening, to chat with Lecce's friendly residents—unfazed by tourism, the welcoming Leccesi represent southern Italians at their best.

Logistics: It's not far from Matera to Lecce as the crow flies, but the trip is more involved than you might think; patience is required. The best route is via Taranto—don't make the mistake of going up through Bari.

Day 7: Bari

The trip from Lecce to Bari is a short one. Check into the pleasant Hotel Palace and spend the morning and afternoon wandering through Bari's centro storico. The wide-open doors of the town's humble houses and apartments, with bickering families and grandmothers drying their pasta in the afternoon sun, will give you a taste of the true flavor of the mezzogiorno, Italy's deep

south. Don't miss Bari's castle and the walk around the ridge of the ancient city walls, with views of wide-open sea at every turn. Finish the day with a good fish dinner, and celebrate your last night in Italy by checking out one of the city's multitude of lively bars—Bari boasts one of southern Italy's most hopping bar scenes.

Logistics: This is one of your most straightforward, if not quickest, drives: just take the coastal S16 for 154 km (95 mi) until you hit Bari. They're two-lane highways, though, so don't be surprised if the trip takes two hours or more. If you get tired, beautiful Ostuni (the "città bianca," the white city) is a perfect hilltop pit stop halfway there.

Day 8: Bari/Departure

Bad news: this is your wake-up-and-leave day. Bari's Aeroporto Palese is small but quite serviceable. Exploit its absence of crowds and easy access and use it as your way out of Italy. Connections through Rome or Milan are more frequent than you might think. Plan on leaving with southern Italy firmly established in your heart as the best way to see the Italy that once was—and be thankful that you were able to see it while it is still like this.

Logistics: Bari hotels offer easy airport transfers; take advantage of them. Return your

rental car at the Bari airport; you won't have to arrive at the airport more than an hour or so before your flight.

TIPS

① Alitalia usually doesn't mark up openjaw trips. However, VolareWeb (www.volareweb.com) has inexpensive domestic air service, and is now operating Milan (Linate)–Naples and Bari–Milan (Linate) routes. Alpi Eagles (www.alpieagles.com) also has service along those routes. If you're able to find a deep-discount round-trip fare from your home to Milan plus those two flights on low-cost carriers, you might save some money. (The Malpensa–Linate connection can be done on regularly scheduled buses.)

② Also look at low-cost carriers that shuttle passengers between London and southern Italy; you can often save the most money of all by combining two such one-way fares with a round-trip discount fare to London; however, beware of inconvenient airport connections in London (Luton, for example).

ON THE CALENDAR

	The Italian calendar is filled with festivals and holidays. These are the biggest ones—those that could play a part in your trip planning.
WINTER February 12– February 21	A big do in the 18th century and revived in the latter part of the 20th century, Carnevale in Venice includes concerts, plays, masked balls, fireworks, and indoor and outdoor happenings of every sort. It is probably Italy's most famous festival, bringing in hundreds of thousands.
SPRING April 8	Needless to say, the Messa di Pasqua al Vaticana (Easter Mass at the Vatican) in Rome is long, intense, and packed, with many people attending in elaborate holiday costumes.
Late April– Early July	Maggio Musicale Fiorentino (Florence May Music Festival) is the oldest and most prestigious Italian festival of the performing arts.
SUMMER/FALL Mid-June– November	In odd-numbered years (including this one, 2007), the Biennale Exhibition of Contemporary Art dominates Venice's cultural scene throughout summer and into fall.
Mid-June– Mid-July	The Festival dei Due Mondi (Festival of Two Worlds), in Spoleto, is perhaps Italy's most famous performing arts festival, bringing in a worldwide audience for concerts, operas, ballets, film screenings, and crafts fairs. Plan well in advance.
July 2 & August 16	The world-famous Palio in Siena is a bareback horse race with ancient Sienese factions showing their colors and participants competing for a prized *palio* (banner).
Early July– Late August	The Arena di Verona Stagione Lirica (Verona Arena Outdoor Opera Season) heralds spectacular productions in Verona's 16,000-seat Roman amphitheater.
July	The Umbria Jazz Festival, in Perugia, brings in many of the biggest names in jazz each summer.
July 21	Venice's Festa del Redentore (Feast of the Redeemer) is a procession of gondolas and other craft commemorating the end of the plague of 1575. The fireworks over the lagoon are spectacular.
Late August–Early September	The Festival di Venezia (Venice Film Festival), the oldest of the international film festivals, takes place mostly on the Lido.

Venice

Gondola

WORD OF MOUTH

"There's no way to adequately describe the uniqueness, the beauty, and the charm that is Venice. It's like the Grand Canyon. It doesn't matter how many pictures you've seen, until you've come face to face with her, you can't begin to imagine her splendor."

—dcd

WELCOME TO VENICE

Gondola navigating a side canal

TOP 5
Reasons to Go

1. **Basilica di San Marco:** Whether its opulence seduces you or overwhelms you, it's a sight to be seen.

2. **Gallerie dell'Accademia:** It only makes sense that you find the world's best collection of Venetian paintings here.

3. **Santa Maria Gloriosa dei Frari:** Of Venice's many gorgeous churches, this one competes with San Marco for top billing.

4. **Cruising the Grand Canal:** Whether seen by gondola or by water bus, Venice's Main Street is something from another world.

5. **Snacking at a bacaro:** The best way to sample genuine Venetian cuisine is to head for one of the city's classic wine bars.

Getting Oriented

Seen from the window of an airplane, central Venice looks like a fish laid out on a blue platter. The train station at the western end is the fish's eye, and the Castello *sestiere* (neighborhood) is the tail. In all, the "fish" consists of six sestieri—Cannaregio, Santa Croce, San Polo, Dorsoduro, San Marco, and Castello. More sedate outer islands swim around them—San Giorgio Maggiore and the Giudecca just to the south, beyond them the Lido, and to the east Murano, Burano, and Torcello.

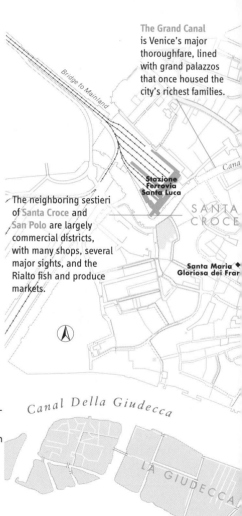

The Grand Canal is Venice's major thoroughfare, lined with grand palazzos that once housed the city's richest families.

The neighboring sestieri of Santa Croce and San Polo are largely commercial districts, with many shops, several major sights, and the Rialto fish and produce markets.

Santa Maria della Salute

Piazza San Marco

1

Cannaregio is short on architectural splendor, but it provides some of the prettiest canal-side walks in town. **The Fondamenta della Misericordia** is a nightlife center, and the **Jewish Ghetto** has a fascinating history and tradition all its own.

CIMITERO SAN MICHELE

0   20 mi
0   20 km

CANNAREGIO

Fond. d. Misericordia

THE JEWISH GHETTO

Canal Grande   Ca' d'Oro

ande

SAN POLO

Campo Santi Giovanni e Paolo

CASTELLO

Basilica di San Marco

Piazza San Marco

Palazzo Ducale

SAN MARCO

Canal Grande

Gallerie dell'Accademia

Peggy Guggenheim Collection

Santa Maria della Salute

DORSODURO

Zattere promenade

SAN GIORGIO MAGGIORE

Castello, along with Cannaregio, is home to most of the locals. It's the sestiere that's least influenced by Venice's tourist culture—except when the Biennale art festival is on.

Piazza San Marco, called by Napoleon "the world's most beautiful drawing room," is the heart of Venice and the location of its two most distinctive sights, the **Basilica di San Marco** and the **Palazzo Ducale.**

0   1/4 mile
0   400 meters

Rio di Palazzo

Dorsoduro is an elegant residential area that's home to the **Gallerie dell'Accademia** and the **Peggy Guggenheim Collection.** The Zattere promenade is one of the best spots to stroll with a gelato or linger at an outdoor café.

The sestiere of **San Marco,** in the city's center, is one of Italy's most expensive neighborhoods. Its streets are lined with fashion boutiques, art galleries, and grand hotels.

VENICE PLANNER

Making the Most of Your Time

A great introduction to Venice is a ride on *vaporetto* (water bus) Line 1 from the train station all the way down the Grand Canal. If you've just arrived and have luggage in tow, you'll need to weigh the merits of taking this trip right away versus getting settled at your hotel first. (Crucial factors: your mood, the bulk of your bags, and your hotel's location.)

Seeing Piazza San Marco and the sights bordering it can fill a day, but if you're going to be around awhile, consider holding off on your visit there—the crowds can be overwhelming, especially when you're fresh off the boat. Instead, spend your first morning at Santa Maria Gloriosa dei Frari and the Scuola Grande di San Rocco, then wander through the Dorsoduro sestiere, choosing between visits to Ca' Rezzonico, the Gallerie dell'Accademia, the Peggy Guggenheim Collection, and Santa Maria della Salute—all A-list attractions. End the afternoon with a gelato-fueled stroll along the Zattere boardwalk. Then tackle San Marco on day two.

If you have more time, make these sights your priorities: the Rialto fish and produce markets; Ca' d'Oro and the Jewish Ghetto in Cannaregio; Santa Maria dei Miracoli and Santi Giovanni e Paolo in Castello; and, across the water from Piazza San Marco, San Giorgio Maggiore. (In Venice, there's a spectacular church for every day of the week, and then some.) A day on the outer islands of Murano, Burano, and Torcello is good for a change of pace.

Getting Around

It's true: there are no cars whatsoever in Venice. You get around primarily on foot, with occasional trips by boat on the famous canals that lace through the city. These are your basic boat-going options:

■ **Vaporetto.** Water buses run up and down the Grand Canal, around the city, and out to the surrounding islands. They're Venice's primary means of public transportation.

■ **Gondola.** Traveling by gondola is a romantic, pricey joy ride (rather than a way to get from one place to another). You pay by the hour. Be sure to agree on the fare before boarding, and ask to be taken down smaller side canals.

■ **Traghetto.** There are only three bridges across the Grand Canal. Traghetti are gondola-like ferries (rowed by gondoliers in training) that fill in the gaps, going from one bank to the other in eight spots. They can save a lot of walking, and they're a cheap (€.50), quick taste of the gondola experience.

■ **Water taxi.** A more accurate name might be "water limousine"—sky-high fares make taxis and indulgent way to get from place to place.

For details on getting around, see "Essentials" at the end of this chapter.

KNOWING WHERE YOU'RE GOING

Be sure to arrive in Venice with precise directions to your hotel (usually available on the hotel Web site). Getting lost in Venice can be a charming adventure, but the charm level drops to zero when you're hauling around luggage.

Venetian Vocabulary

Venetians use their own terms to describe their unique city. In fact, they have their own dialect; if you have an ear for Italian, you'll notice a distinct difference in the language. Here are some key words to know:

Sestiere: A neighborhood in central Venice. (There are six of them.)

Rio: A small canal.

Riva: A street running along a canal.

Fondamenta: Another name for a riva.

Calle: A street not running along a canal.

Campo: A square—what elsewhere in Italy would be called a piazza. (The only piazza in Venice is Piazza San Marco.)

Bacaro: A wine bar.

Ombra: A glass of wine served at a bacaro.

Cicchetto (pronounced "chick-ay-toh")**:** A snack served at a bacaro—roughly the Venetian equivalent of tapas.

How's the Weather? 1

One thing Venice has in common with much of Italy: spring and fall are the best times to visit. Summers are hot, sticky, and crowded. Winters are relatively mild and tourist-free, but there are frequent rainy spells, and at the beginning and end of the season there's the threat of *acqua alta*, when tides roll in and flood low-lying parts of the city, including Piazza San Marco.

Festivals to Build a Trip Around

■ Venice's most famous festival is **Carnevale**, drawing revelers from all over the world. For 10 days leading up to Ash Wednesday, it takes over the city—think Mardi Gras meets Casanova.

■ The prestigious **Biennale** is a century-old international art festival held in late summer and early fall of odd-numbered years. It's spawned several other festivals, including the **Biennale Danza, Biennale Musica,** and, most famously, **Biennale Cinema**, also known as the Venice Film Festival, held every year at the end of August.

■ The **Festa Redentore** (Feast of the Redeemer), on the third Sunday in July, is the biggest celebration of the year among locals, who float out in boats on Bacino San Marco and watch midnight fireworks displays.

■ There are three noteworthy annual contests of Venetian-style rowing: the **Regata delle Bafane**, on January 6; **Vogalonga** (long row), on a Sunday in May; and **Regata Storica**, on the first Sunday in September.

Zattere

TOP PASSEGGIATA

With its streets given over to pedestrians, all of Venice is in a state of perpetual passeggiata, but Fondamenta delle Zattere, along the southern end of Dorsoduro, is a particularly prime spot.

IT'S CALLED LA SERENISSIMA, "the most serene," a reference to the majesty, wisdom, and monstrous power of this city that was for centuries the unrivaled mistress of trade between Europe and the Orient and the bulwark of Christendom against the tides of Turkish expansion. "Most serene" could also describe the way lovers of this miraculous city feel when they see it, imperturbably floating on its calm blue lagoon.

Built entirely on water by men who defied the sea, Venice is unlike any other town. No matter how many times you've seen it in movies or on TV, the real thing is more dreamlike than you could ever imagine. Its landmarks, the Basilica di San Marco and the Palazzo Ducale, seem hardly Italian: delightfully idiosyncratic, they are exotic mixes of Byzantine, Gothic, and Renaissance styles. Shimmering sunlight and silvery mist soften every perspective here, and you understand how the city became renowned in the Renaissance for its artists' rendering of color. It's full of secrets, inexpressibly romantic, and at times given over entirely to pleasure.

You'll see Venetians going about their daily affairs in *vaporetti* (water buses), aboard the *traghetti* (traditional gondola ferries) that carry them across the Grand Canal, in the *campi* (squares), and along the *calli* (narrow streets). They are nothing if not skilled—and remarkably tolerant—in dealing with the veritable armies of tourists from all over the world who fill the city's streets for most of the year.

EXPLORING VENICE

Updated by
Pamela Santini

Many of Venice's major churches and museums are organized into two groups that coordinate hours and admissions fees. Fifteen art-filled churches are known as the **Chorus churches** (☎ 041/2750462 ⊕ www. chorusvenezia.org): Santa Maria del Giglio, Santo Stefano, Santa Maria Formosa, Santa Maria dei Miracoli, Santa Maria Gloriosa dei Frari, San Polo, San Giacomo dell'Orio, San Stae, Sant'Alvise, Madonna dell'Orto, San Pietro di Castello, Santissimo Redentore, San Sebastiano, Gesuati, and San Giovanni Elemosinario. They're open to visitors all day except Sunday morning, and usually someone there can provide information and a free leaflet in English. Postcards and booklets about the sights are on sale. Single church entry costs €2.50, or you can visit them all with an €8 Chorus pass. The price of the pass includes audio guides except in the Frari, where they cost an additional €1.60. The artwork in Chorus churches is labeled, and the staff can show you where to switch on lighting for selected paintings.

Eleven museums make up Venice's **Musei Civici** (☎ 041/2715911 ⊕ www. museicivicivenezian.it). A museum pass costing €18 and valid for three months lets you make one visit to each museum. A Museum Card, good only at the Piazza San Marco museums—Palazzo Ducale, Museo Correr, Museo Archeologico, and Biblioteca Nazionale Marciana—costs €12.

CRUISING THE GRAND CANAL

THE BEST INTRODUCTION TO VENICE IS A TRIP DOWN MAIN STREET

Venice's Grand Canal is one of the world's great thoroughfares. It winds its way in the shape of a backward "S" from Ferrovia (the train station) to Piazza San Marco, passing 200 palazzos born of a culture obsessed with opulence and fantasy. There's a theatrical quality to a boat ride on the canal: it's as if each pink- or gold-tinted façade is trying to steal your attention from its rival across the way.

The palaces were built from the 12th to 18th centuries by the city's richest families. A handful are still private residences, but many have been converted to other uses, including museums, hotels, government offices, university buildings, a post office, a casino, and even a television station.

It's romantic to see the canal from a gondola, but the next best thing, at a fraction of the cost, is to take the Line 1 *vaporetto* (water bus) from Ferrovia to San Marco. The ride costs €5 and takes about 35 minutes. Invest in a Travel Card (€12 buys 24 hours of unlimited passage) and you can spend the better part of a day hopping on and off at the vaporetto's 16 stops, visiting the sights along the banks. Either way, keep your eyes open for the highlights listed here; those with numbered bullets have fuller descriptions later in this chapter.

FROM FERROVIA
TO RIALTO

Santa Maria di Nazareth

Ponte di Scalzi

R. Di BIASIO

FERROVIA

Stazione Ferrovia Santa Lucia

As you head out from Ferrovia, the baroque church immediately to your left is **Santa Maria di Nazareth**. Its shoeless friars earned it the nickname Chiesa degli Scalzi (Church of the Barefoot).

The first of only three bridges over the Grand Canal is the **Ponte di Scalzi**. The original version was built of iron in 1858; the existing stone bridge dates from 1934.

After passing beneath the Ponte di Scalzi, ahead to the left you'll spy **Palazzo Labia** **22**, one of the most imposing buildings in Venice, looming over the bell tower of the church of San Geremia.

A hundred yards or so further along on the left bank, the uncompleted façade of the church of **San Marcuola** gives you an idea of what's behind the marble decorations of similar 18th-century churches in Venice. Across the canal, flanked by two *torricelle* (side wings in the shape of small towers) and a triangular *merlatura* (crenellation), is the **Fondaco dei Turchi**, one of the oldest Byzantine palaces in Venice; it's now a natural history museum. Next comes the plain brick **Depositi del Megio,** a 15th-century granary—note the lion marking it as Serenissima property—and beyond it the obelisk-topped **Ca' Belloni-Battagia.** Both are upstaged by the **Palazzo Vendramin-Calergi** **24** on the opposite bank: this Renaissance gem was built in the 1480s, at a time when late-Gothic was still the prevailing style. A gilded banner identifies the palazzo as site of Venice's casino.

Palazzo Vendramin-Calergi

The German composer Richard Wagner died in Palazzo Vendramin-Calergi in 1883, soon after the success of his opera *Parsifal*. His room has been preserved—you can visit it on Saturday mornings by appointment.

Ca' d'Oro

Ca' d'Oro means "house of gold," but the gold is long gone—the gilding that once accentuated the marble carvings of the façade has worn away over time.

Church of San Marcuola

S. MARCUOLA ▲

Ca' Belloni-Battagia

S. STAE ▲

Ca' Pesaro

Fondaco dei Turchi

Depositi del Megio

San Stae Church

▲ CA' D'ORO

Ca' Corner della Regina

Pescheria

The pescheria has been in operation for over 1,000 years. Stop by in the morning to see the exotic fish for sale—one of which may wind up on your dinner plate. Produce stalls fill the adjacent *fondamenta*, and butchers and cheesemongers occupy the surrounding shops.

Fondaco dei Tedeschi

Ca' dei Camerlenghi

▲ RIALTO

The white, whimsically baroque church of **San Stae** ⑰ on the right bank is distinguished by a host of marble saints on its façade. Further along the bank is another baroque showpiece, **Ca' Pesaro** ⑯, followed by the tall, balconied **Ca' Corner della Regina.** Next up on the left is the flamboyant pink-and-white **Ca' d'Oro** ㉕, arguably the finest example of Venetian Gothic design.

Across from Ca' d'Oro is the loggia-like, neo-Gothic **pescheria**, Venice's fish market, where boats dock in the morning to deliver their catch.

The canal narrows as you approach the impressive Rialto Bridge. To the left, just before the bridge, is the **Fondaco dei Tedeschi**. This was once the busiest trading center of the republic—German, Austrian, and Hungarian merchants kept warehouses and offices here;

today it's the city's main post office. Across the canal stands the curiously angled **Ca' dei Camerlenghi**. Built in 1525 to accommodate the State Treasury, it had a jail for tax evaders on the ground floor.

FROM RIALTO TO THE PONTE DELL' ACCADEMIA

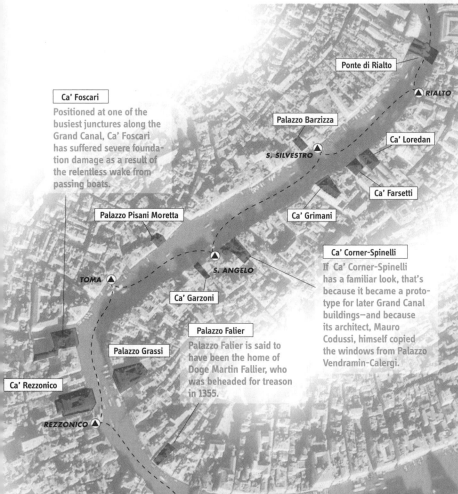

Ponte di Rialto

▲ RIALTO

Ca' Foscari

Positioned at one of the busiest junctures along the Grand Canal, Ca' Foscari has suffered severe foundation damage as a result of the relentless wake from passing boats.

Palazzo Barzizza

Ca' Loredan

S. SILVESTRO

Ca' Farsetti

Ca' Grimani

Palazzo Pisani Moretta

Ca' Corner-Spinelli

If Ca' Corner-Spinelli has a familiar look, that's because it became a prototype for later Grand Canal buildings—and because its architect, Mauro Codussi, himself copied the windows from Palazzo Vendramin-Calergi.

S. ANGELO

TOMA ▲

Ca' Garzoni

Palazzo Falier

Palazzo Falier is said to have been the home of Doge Martin Fallier, who was beheaded for treason in 1355.

Palazzo Grassi

Ca' Rezzonico

REZZONICO ▲

ACCADEMIA ▲

Gallerie dell'Accademia

Until the 19th century, the shop-lined **Ponte di Rialto** ⑭ was the only bridge across the Grand Canal.

Rialto is the only point along the Grand Canal where buildings don't have their primary entrances directly on the water, a consequence of the two spacious *rive* (waterside paths) once used for unloading two Venetian staples: coal and wine. On your left along Riva del Carbon stand **Ca' Loredan** and **Ca' Farsetti**, 13th-century Byzantine palaces that today make up Venice's city hall. Just past the San Silvestro vaporetto landing on Riva del Vin is the 12th- and 13th-century facade of **Palazzo Barzizza**, an elegant example of Veneto-Byzantine architecture that managed to survive a complete renovation the 17th century. Across the water, the sternly Renaissance

Ca' Grimani has an intimidating presence that seems appropriate for today's Court of Appeals. At the Sant'Angelo landing, the vaporetto passes close to another massive Renaissance palazzo, **Ca' Corner-Spinelli**.

Back on the right bank, in a salmon color that seems to vary with the time of day, is elegant **Palazzo Pisani Moretta**, with twin water entrances. To your left, four-storied **Ca' Garzoni**, part of the Universita di Venezia Ca' Foscari, stands beside the San Toma *traghetto* (gondola ferry), which has operated since 1354. The boat makes a sharp turn and, on the right, passes one of the city's tallest Gothic palaces, **Ca' Foscari**.

The vaporetto passes baroque **Ca' Rezzonico** ⑦ so closely that you get to look inside one of the most fabulous entrances along the canal. Opposite stands the

Grand Canal's youngest palace, **Palazzo Grassi**, commissioned in 1749. Just beyond Grassi and Campo San Samuele, the first house past the garden was once Titian's studio. It's followed by **Palazzo Falier**, identifiable by its twin loggias (windowed porches).

Approaching the canal's third and final bridge, the vaporetto stops at a former church and monastery complex that houses the world-renowned **Gallerie dell'Accademia** ⑪.

> The wooden pilings on which Venice was built (you can see them at the bases of the buildings along the Grand Canal) have gradually hardened into mineral form.

ARCHITECTURAL STYLES ALONG THE GRAND CANAL

BYZANTINE: 12th and 13th centuries.
Distinguishing characteristics: high, rounded arches, relief panels, multicolored marble.
Examples: Fondaco dei Turchi, Ca' Loredan, Ca' Farsetti, Palazzo Barzizza (and, off the canal, Basilica di San Marco).

GOTHIC: 14th and 15th centuries.
Distinguishing characteristics: Pointed arches, high ceilings, and many windows.
Examples: Ca' d'Oro, Ca' Foscari, Ca' Franchetti, Palazzo Falier (and, off the canal, Palazzo Ducale).

RENAISSANCE: 16th century.
Distinguishing characteristics: classically influenced emphasis on order, achieved through

symmetry and balanced proportions.
Examples: Palazzo Vendramin-Calergi, Ca' Grimani, Ca' Corner-Spinelli, Ca' dei Camerlenghi (and, off the canal, Libreria Sansoviniana on Piazza San Marco and the church of San Giorgio Maggiore).

BAROQUE: 17th century.
Distinguishing characteristics: Renaissance order wedded with a more dynamic style, achieved through curving lines and complex decoration.
Examples: churches of Santa Maria di Nazareth and San Stae, Ca' Pesaro, Ca' Rezzonico (and, off the canal, the church of Santa Maria della Salute).

FROM THE PONTE DELL'ACCADEMIA TO SAN ZACCARIA

Ca' Franchetti

Until the late 19th century, Ca' Franchetti was a *squero* (gondola workshop). A few active squeri remain, though none are on the Grand Canal. The most easily spotted is Squero di San Trovaso, in Dorsoduro on a small canal near the Zattere boat landing.

Ca' Barbaro

Monet, Henry James, and Cole Porter are among the guests who have stayed at Ca' Barbaro. Porter later lived aboard a boat in Giudecca Canal.

Ponte dell' Accademia

ACCADEMIA ▲

Casetta Rossa

Ca' Pisani-Gritti

S. M. DEL GIGLIO ▲

Ca' Barbarigo

Palazzo Venier dei Leoni

SALUTE ▲

Palazzo Salviati

S. Maria della Salute

Ca' Dario

The wooden Ponte dell'Accademia, like the Eiffel Tower (with which it shares a certain structural grace), wasn't intended to be permanent. Erected in 1933 as a quick replacement for a rusting iron bridge built by the Austrian military in 1854, it was so well liked by Venetians that they kept it. (A perfect replica, with steel bracing, was installed 1986.)

You're only three stops from the end of the Grand Canal, but this last stretch is packed with sights. The lovely **Ca' Franchetti**, with a central balcony made in the style of Palazzo Ducale's loggia, dates from the late Gothic period, but its gardens are no older than the cedar tree standing at their center.

When she was in residence at Palazzo Venier dei Leoni, Peggy Guggenheim kept her private gondola parked at the door and left her dogs standing guard (in place of Venetian lions).

Ca' Barbaro, next door to Ca' Franchetti, was the residence of the illustrious family who rebuilt the church of Santa Maria del Giglio.

Farther along on the left bank, a garden, vibrant with flowers in summer, surrounds **Casetta Rossa** (small red house) as if it were the centerpiece of its bouquet. Across the canal, bright 19th-century mosaics on **Ca' Barbarigo** give you some idea how the frescoed facades of many Venetian palaces must have looked in their heyday. A

However tilted Dario might be, it has outlasted its many owners, who seem plagued by misfortune. They include the Italian industrialist Raul Gardini, whose 1992 suicide followed charges of corruption and an unsuccessful bid to win the America's Cup.

few doors down are the lush gardens within the walls of the unfinished **Palazzo Venier dei Leoni**, which holds the **Peggy Guggenheim Collection** ⑫ of contemporary art.

Lovely, leaning **Ca' Dario** on the right bank is notable for its colorful marble façade.

Past the landing of Santa Maria del Giglio stands the

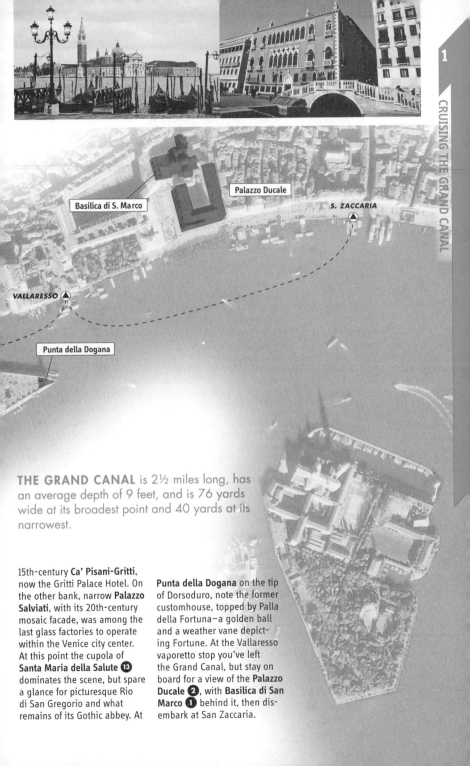

Basilica di S. Marco

Palazzo Ducale

S. ZACCARIA

VALLARESSO

Punta della Dogana

THE GRAND CANAL is 2½ miles long, has an average depth of 9 feet, and is 76 yards wide at its broadest point and 40 yards at its narrowest.

15th-century **Ca' Pisani-Gritti**, now the Gritti Palace Hotel. On the other bank, narrow **Palazzo Salviati**, with its 20th-century mosaic facade, was among the last glass factories to operate within the Venice city center. At this point the cupola of **Santa Maria della Salute** ⓭ dominates the scene, but spare a glance for picturesque Rio di San Gregorio and what remains of its Gothic abbey. At **Punta della Dogana** on the tip of Dorsoduro, note the former customhouse, topped by Palla della Fortuna—a golden ball and a weather vane depicting Fortune. At the Vallaresso vaporetto stop you've left the Grand Canal, but stay on board for a view of the **Palazzo Ducale** ❷, with **Basilica di San Marco** ❶ behind it, then disembark at San Zaccaria.

Piazza San Marco

One of the world's most evocative squares, Piazza San Marco (St. Mark's Square) is the heart of Venice, a vast open space bordered by an orderly procession of arcades marching toward the fairy-tale cupolas and marble lacework of the Basilica di San Marco. Perpetually packed by day with people and fluttering pigeons, it can be magical at night, especially in winter, when mists swirl around the lampposts and the Campanile.

If you face the basilica from in front of the Correr Museum, you'll notice that rather than being a strict rectangle, this square opens wider at the basilica end, creating the illusion that it's even larger than it is. On your left, the long, arcaded building is the Procuratie Vecchie, built in the early 16th century as offices and residences for the powerful procurators (magistrates) of San Marco.

On your right is the Procuratie Nuove, built half a century later in a more-grandiose classical style. It was originally planned by Venice's great Renaissance architect, Sansovino, to carry on the look of his Libreria Sansoviniana (Sansovinian Library), but he died before construction on the Nuove had begun. Vincenzo Scamozzi (circa 1552–1616), a neoclassicist pupil of Andrea Palladio (1508–80), completed the design and construction. Still later, the Procuratie Nuove was modified by architect Baldassare Longhena (1598–1682), one of Venice's baroque masters.

When Napoléon (1769–1821) entered Venice with his troops in 1797, he called Piazza San Marco "the world's most beautiful drawing room"— and promptly gave orders to redecorate it. His architects demolished a 16th-century church with a Sansovino facade in order to build the Ala Napoleonica (Napoleonic Wing), or Fabbrica Nuova (New Building), which linked the two 16th-century procuratie and effectively enclosed the piazza.

Piazzetta San Marco, the "little square" leading from Piazza San Marco to the waters of Bacino San Marco (St. Mark's Basin), is a *molo* (landing) that was once the grand entryway to the republic. It's distinguished by two columns towering above the waterfront. One is topped by the winged lion, a traditional emblem of St. Mark that became the symbol of Venice itself; the other supports St. Theodore, the city's first patron, along with his dragon. Between these columns the republic traditionally executed convicts.

Timing

It takes a full day to take in everything on the piazza thoroughly; so if time is limited you'll have to prioritize. Plan on 1½ hours for the basilica and its Pala d'Oro, Galleria, and Museo di San Marco. You'll want at least two hours to appreciate the Palazzo Ducale. Do take time to enjoy the piazza itself from a café table, or on a clear day, from atop the Campanile.

The Main Attractions

❶ **Basilica di San Marco.** An opulent synthesis of Byzantine and Romanesque styles, Venice's gem is laid out in a Greek-cross floor plan and topped with five plump domes. It didn't become the cathedral of Venice until 1807, but its role as the Chiesa Ducale (doge's private chapel) gave it

Fodor's Choice
★

Basilica di
San Marco **1**

Campanile **3**

Museo Correr . . . **4**

Palazzo
Ducale **2**

Torre dell'
Orologio **5**

Piazza
San Marco

immense power and wealth. The original church was built in 828 to house the body of St. Mark the Evangelist. His remains, filched from Alexandria by the doge's agents, were supposedly hidden in a barrel under layers of pickled pork to sneak them past Muslim guards. The escapade is depicted in the 13th-century mosaic above the door farthest left of the front entrance, one of the earliest mosaics on the heavily decorated facade; look closely to see the church as it appeared at that time.

A 976 fire destroyed most of the original church. It was rebuilt and reopened in 1094, and for centuries it would serve as a symbol of Venetian wealth and power, endowed with all the riches admirals and merchants could carry off from the Orient, to the point where it earned the nickname Chiesa d'Oro (Golden Church). The four bronze horses that prance and snort over the doorway are copies of sculptures that victorious Venetians took from Constantinople in 1204 after the fourth crusade (the originals are in the Museo di San Marco). The rich, colorful exterior decorations, including the numerous different marble columns, all came from the same source. Look for a medallion of red porphyry in the floor of the porch inside the main door. It marks the spot where, in 1177, Doge Sebastiano Ziani orchestrated the reconciliation between Barbarossa—the Holy Roman Emperor—and Pope Alexander III. Dim lighting, galleries high above the naves—they served as the *matroneum* (women's gallery)—the *iconostasis* (altar screen), and the single massive Byzantine chandelier all seem to wed Christianity with the Orient, giving San Marco its exotic blend of majesty and mystery.

The basilica is famous for its 43,055 square feet of mosaics, which run from floor to ceiling thanks to an innovative roof of brick vaulting. Many of the original windows were filled in to make room for even more artwork. At midday, when the interior is fully illuminated, the mosaics truly come alive, the shimmer of their tiny gold tiles becoming nothing short of magical. The earliest mosaics are from the 11th and 12th centuries, and the last were added in the early 1700s. One of the most recent is the *Last Judgment,* believed to have been designed by Tintoretto (1518–94), on the arch between the porch and the nave. Inside the main entrance, turn right on the porch to see the Book of Genesis depicted on the ceiling. Ahead through a glass door, 13th-century mosaics depict St. Mark's life in the **Cappella Zen** (Zen Chapel). The **Cappella della Madonna di Nicopeia,** in the left transept, holds the altar icon that many consider Venice's most powerful protector. In nearby **Cappella della Madonna dei Mascoli** the life of the Virgin Mary is depicted in fine 15th-century mosaics, believed to be based on drawings by Jacopo Bellini (1400–71) and Andrea Mantegna (1431–1506).

In the **Santuario** (Sanctuary), the main altar is built over the tomb of St. Mark, its green marble canopy lifted high on carved alabaster columns. Perhaps even more impressive is the **Pala d'Oro,** a dazzling gilt silver screen encrusted with 1,927 precious gems and 255 enameled panels. Originally commissioned in Constantinople by Doge Orseolo I (976–978), it was enlarged and embellished over four centuries by master craftsmen and wealthy merchants. The bronze door leading from the sanctuary into the sacristy is by Jacopo Sansovino (1486–1570). In the top left corner the artist included a self-portrait, and above that, he pictured friend and fellow artist Titian (1485–1576). The **Tesoro** (Treasury), entered from the right transept, contains many treasures carried home from conquests abroad.

Climb the steep stairway to the **Galleria** and the **Museo di San Marco** for the best overview of the basilica's interior. From here you can step outdoors for a sweeping panorama of Piazza San Marco and out over the lagoon to San Giorgio. The displays focus mainly on the types of mosaic and how they have been restored over the years. But the highlight is a close-up view of the original gilt bronze horses that were once on the outer gallery. The four were most probably cast in Rome and taken to Constantinople, where the Venetians pillaged them after sacking that city. When Napoléon sacked Venice in 1797, he took them to Paris. They were returned after the fall of the French Empire, but came home "blind"—their big ruby eyes had been sold.

Be aware that guards at the basilica door turn away anyone with bare shoulders or knees; no shorts, short skirts, or tank tops are allowed. If you want a free guided tour in English during summer months (less certain in winter, as the guides are volunteers), look for groups forming on the porch inside the main door. You may also arrange tours by appointment. ✉ *Piazza San Marco* ☎ *041/5225205 basilica, 041/*

2702421 for free tours Apr.–Oct. (call Tues. or Thurs. morning) ✉ *Basilica free, Tesoro €2, Santuario and Pala d'Oro €1.50, Galleria and Museo di San Marco €3* ☉ *May–Sept., Mon.–Sat. 9:45–5:30, Sun. 2–4; Oct.–Apr., Mon.–Sat. 9:45–4:30, Sun. 2–4; last entry ½ hr before closing* Ⓥ *Vallaresso/San Zaccaria.*

★ ❷ **Palazzo Ducale** (Doge's Palace). Rising above the Piazzetta San Marco, this Gothic-Renaissance fantasia of pink-and-white marble is a majestic expression of the prosperity and power attained during Venice's most glorious period. Some architectural purists find the building top-heavy—its hulking upper floors rest upon a graceful ground-floor colonnade—but the design is what gives the palace its distinctive identity; it's hard to imagine it any other way. Always much more than a residence, the palace was Venice's White House, Senate, torture chamber, and prison rolled into one.

Though a fortress for the doge stood on this spot in the early 9th century, the building you see today was begun in the 12th century, and like the basilica next door was continually remodeled over the centuries. Near the basilica you'll see the ornately Gothic **Porta della Carta** (Gate of the Paper), where official decrees were traditionally posted, but visitors enter under the portico facing the water. You'll find yourself in an immense courtyard with the **Scala dei Giganti** (Stairway of the Giants) directly ahead, guarded by Sansovino's huge statues of Mars and Neptune. Though ordinary mortals must use the central interior staircase, its upper flight is the lavishly gilded **Scala d'Oro** (Golden Staircase), also by Sansovino. It may seem odd that you have to climb so many steps to reach the government's main council rooms and reception halls, but imagine how this extraordinary climb must have impressed, and perhaps intimidated, foreign emissaries.

The palace's sumptuous chambers have walls and ceilings covered with works by Venice's greatest artists. Visit the **Anticollegio,** a waiting room outside the Collegio's chamber, where you'll see the *Rape of Europa* by Veronese (1528–88) and Tintoretto's *Bacchus and Ariadne Crowned by Venus.* Veronese also painted the ceiling of the adjacent **Sala del Collegio.** The ceiling of the **Sala del Senato** (Senate Chamber), featuring *The Triumph of Venice* by Tintoretto, is magnificent, but it's dwarfed by his masterpiece *Paradise* in the **Sala del Maggiore Consiglio** (Great Council Hall). A vast work commissioned for a vast hall, this dark, dynamic piece is the world's largest oil painting (23 by 75 feet). The room's carved, gilt ceiling is breathtaking, especially with Veronese's majestic *Apotheosis of Venice* filling one of the center panels. Around the upper walls, study the portraits of the first 76 doges, and you'll notice one picture is missing near the left corner of the wall opposite *Paradise.* A black painted curtain, rather than a portrait, marks Doge Marin Falier's fall from grace; he was beheaded for treason in 1355, which the Latin inscription bluntly explains.

A narrow canal separates the palace's east side from the cramped cell blocks of the **Prigioni Nuove** (New Prisons). High above the water arches the enclosed marble **Ponte dei Sospiri** (Bridge of Sighs), which earned its name from the sighs of those being led to their fate. Look out its windows to see the last earthly view these prisoners beheld.

VENICE THROUGH THE AGES

Up from the Muck. Venice was founded in the 5th century when the Veneti, inhabitants of the mainland region roughly corresponding to today's Veneto, fled their homes to escape invading Lombards. The unlikely city, built atop wooden posts driven into the marshes, would evolve into a great maritime republic. Its fortunes grew as a result of its active role in the Crusades, beginning in 1095 and culminating in the Venetian-led sacking of Constantinople in 1204. The defeat of rival Genoa in the Battle of Chioggia (1380) established Venice as the dominant sea power in Europe.

Early Democracy. As early as the 7th century, Venice was governed by a participatory democracy, with a ruler, the doge, elected to a lifetime term. Beginning in the 12th century, the doge's power was increasingly subsumed by a growing number of councils, commissions, and magistrates. In 1268 a complicated procedure for the doge's election was established to prevent nepotism, but by that point power rested foremost with the Great Council, which at times numbered as many as 2,000 members.

Laws were passed by the Senate, a group of 200 elected from the Great Council, and executive powers belonged to the College, a committee of 25. In 1310 the Council of Ten was formed to protect state security. When circumstances dictated, the doge could expedite decision making by consulting only the Council of Ten. To avoid too great a concentration of power, these 10 served only one year and belonged to different families.

A Long Decline. Venice reached its height of power in the 15th and 16th centuries, during which time its domain included all of the Veneto region and part of Lombardy. But beginning in the 16th century, the tide turned. The Ottoman Empire blocked Venice's Mediterranean trade routes, and newly emerging sea powers such as Britain and the Netherlands ended Venice's monopoly by opening oceanic trading routes. The republic underwent a slow decline. When Napoleon arrived in 1797, he took the city without a fight, eventually delivering it to the Austrians, who ruled until 1848. In that tumultuous year throughout Europe, the Venetians rebelled, an act that would ultimately lead to their joining the Italian Republic in 1866.

Art Stars. In the 13th through 15th centuries the influence of Gothic architecture resulted in palaces in the Florid Gothic style, for which the city is famous. Renaissance sensibilities arrived comparatively late. Early Venetian Renaissance artists—Carpaccio, Giorgione, and the Bellini brothers, Giovanni and Gentile—were active in the late 15th and early 16th centuries. Along with the stars of the next generation—Veronese, Titian, and Tintoretto—they played a key role in the development of Western art, and their best work remains in the city.

Like its dwindling fortunes, Venice's art and culture underwent a prolonged decline, leaving only the splendid monuments to recall a fabled past. The 18th-century paintings of Canaletto and Tiepolo were a glorious swan song.

The palazzo's "Secret Itinerary" tour takes you to the doge's private apartments, through hidden passageways to the interrogation (torture) chambers, and into the rooftop *piombi* (lead) prison, named for its lead roofing. Venetian-born writer and libertine Giacomo Casanova (1725–98), along with an accomplice, managed to escape from the piombi in 1756, the only men ever to do so. ⊠ *Piazzetta San Marco* ☎ *041/2715911, 041/5209070 "Secret Itinerary" tour* ⊠ *Piazza San Marco museum card €12, Musei Civici museum pass €18, "Secret Itinerary" tour €12.50* ⊙ *Apr.–Oct., daily 9–7; Nov.–Mar., daily 9–5; last tickets sold 1 hr before closing. English "Secret Itinerary" tours in morning; reservations advisable* Ⓥ *Vallaresso/San Zaccaria.*

NEED A BREAK?

Caffè Florian (☎ 041/5205641), located in the Procuratie Nuove, has served coffee to the likes of Casanova, Charles Dickens, and Marcel Proust. It's Venice's oldest café, continuously in business since 1720 (though you'll find it closed Wednesday in winter). Counter seating is less expensive than taking a table, especially when there's live music. In the Procuratie Vecchie, **Caffè Quadri** (☎ 041/5289299) exudes almost as much history as Florian across the way, and is similarly pricey. It was shunned by 19th-century Venetians when the occupying Austrians made it their gathering place. In winter it closes Monday.

Also Worth Seeing

❸ Campanile. Venice's famous brick bell tower (325 feet tall, plus the angel) had been standing nearly 1,000 years when in 1902, practically without warning, it collapsed, taking with it Jacopo Sansovino's 16th-century marble loggia at the base. The crushed loggia was promptly restored, and the new tower, rebuilt to the old plan, reopened in 1912. In the 15th century, clerics found guilty of immoral behavior were suspended in wooden cages from the tower. Some were forced to subsist on bread and water for as long as a year, and others were left to starve. The stunning view from the tower on a clear day includes the Lido, the lagoon, and the mainland as far as the Alps but, strangely enough, none of the myriad canals that snake through the city. ⊠ *Piazza San Marco* ☎ *041/5224064* ⊠ *€6* ⊙ *Apr.–Sept., daily 9:30 AM–5:30; Oct.–Mar., daily 9:30–4:30; last entry ½ hr before closing* Ⓥ *Vallaresso/San Zaccaria.*

❹ Museo Correr. Exhibits in this museum of Venetian art and history range from the absurdly high-soled shoes worn by 16th-century Venetian ladies (who walked with the aid of a servant) to the huge *Grande Pianta Prospettica* by Jacopo de' Barbari (circa 1440–1515), which details in carved wood every nook and cranny of 16th-century Venice. The city's proud naval history is evoked in several rooms through highly descriptive paintings and numerous maritime objects, including ships' cannons and some surprisingly large iron mast-top navigation lights. The Correr has a room devoted entirely to antique games, and its second-floor **Quadreria** (Picture Gallery) has works by Venetian, Greek, and Flemish painters. The Correr exhibition rooms lead directly into the **Museo Archeologico** and the **Stanza del Sansovino,** the only part of the **Biblioteca Marciana** open to visitors. ⊠ *Piazza San Marco, Ala Napoleonica* ☎ *041/2405211* ⊠ *Piazza San Marco museum card €12, Musei Civici*

Wading Through the Acqua Alta

YOU HAVE TO WALK almost everywhere in Venice, and where you can't walk, you go by water. Occasionally you walk *in* water, when normally higher fall and spring tides are exacerbated by falling barometers and southeasterly winds. The result is *acqua alta*—flooding in the lowest parts of town, especially Piazza San Marco, which lasts a few hours, until the tide recedes.

Work has begun on the Moses Project, a plan that would close off the lagoon when high tides threaten, but it's a much-debated response to an emotionally charged problem. Protecting Venice and its lagoon from high tides—as well as high use and the damaging wave action caused by powerboats—is among the city's most contentious issues.

museum pass €18 ⊘ *Apr.–Oct., daily 9–7; Nov.–Mar., daily 9–5; last tickets sold 1 hr before closing* Ⓥ *Vallaresso/San Zaccaria.*

NEED A BREAK?

If you'd like to attend happy hour with the ghosts of Ernest Hemingway, Aristotle Onassis, and Orson Welles, head to **Harry's Bar** (☎ 041/5285777). Walk out Piazza San Marco near the Correr Museum and turn left at Calle Vallaresso; you'll find the legendary hangout right at the vaporetto landing. Harry's still boasts Venice's driest martinis and freshest Bellinis (white peach juice and sparkling *prosecco* wine).

❺ Torre dell'Orologio. Five hundred years ago, when this enameled clock was built, twin Moor figures would strike the hour, and three wise men with an angel would walk out and bow to the Virgin Mary on Epiphany (January 6) and during Ascension Week (40 days after Easter). An inscription on the tower reads HORAS NON NUMERO NISI SERENAS ("I only count happy hours"); if that's true, perhaps happy hours will return to Venice when they finally fix the clock. It's been under restoration for years and may resume functioning sometime in 2007. You can visit the three wise men in the Palazzo Ducale, where they are on display. ⊠ *North side of Piazza San Marco.*

Dorsoduro

The sestiere Dorsoduro (named for its "hard back" solid clay foundation) is across the Grand Canal to the south of San Marco. It is a place of monumental churches, meandering canals, the city's finest art museums, and a boardwalk called the Zattere, where on sunny days you'll swear half the city is out for a *passeggiata*, or stroll. The eastern point of the peninsula, Punta della Dogana, has one of the best views in town. The Stazione Marittima, where in summer cruise ships line the dock, lies at the western end. Midway between these two points, just off the Zattere, is the Squero di San Trovaso, where gondolas have been built and repaired for centuries.

Dorsoduro is also home to the Gallerie dell'Accademia, which has an unparalleled collection of Venetian painting, and Ca' Rezzonico, the

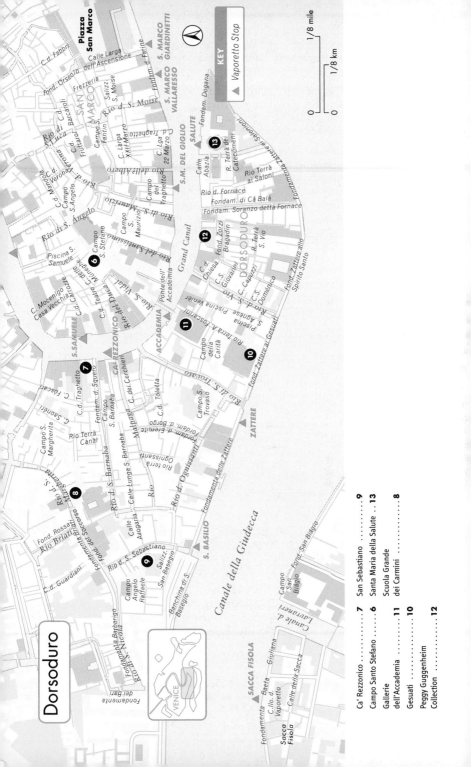

Dorsoduro

SAN MARCO

Piazza
San Marco

S. MARCO
GIARDINETTI

S. MARCO
VALLARESSO

SALUTE

DORSODURO

S.M. DEL GIGLIO

Grand Canal

S.SAMUELE

CA' REZZONICO

ACCADEMIA

ZATTERE

S. BASILIO

Canale della Giudecca

SACCA FISOLA

KEY

▲ Vaporetto Stop

0   1/8 km

0   1/8 mile

VENICE

Ca' Rezzonico **7**

Campo Santo Stefano **6**

Gallerie
dell'Accademia **11**

Gesuati **10**

Peggy Guggenheim
Collection **12**

San Sebastiano **9**

Santa Maria della Salute .. **13**

Scuola Grande
dei Carmini **8**

Museo del Settecento Veneziano. Another of its landmark sites, the Peggy Guggenheim Collection, has a fine selection of 20th-century art.

Timing

The Gallerie dell'Accademia demands a few hours, but if time is short an audio guide can help you cover the highlights in about an hour. Give yourself at least 1½ hours for the Guggenheim Collection. Ca' Rezzonico deserves a couple of hours.

The Main Attractions

★ ➐ **Ca' Rezzonico.** Designed by Baldassare Longhena in the 17th century, this palace was completed nearly 100 years later by Giorgio Massari and became the last home of English poet Robert Browning (1812–89). Elizabeth Taylor and Richard Burton danced in the baroque ballroom in the 1960s. Today Ca' Rezzonico is the home of the **Museo del Settecento** (Museum of Venice in the 1700s). Its main floor is packed with period furniture and tapestries in gilded salons (note the four Tiepolo ceiling frescoes) and successfully retains the feel of an old Venetian palazzo. Upper floors contain hundreds of paintings, most from Venetian schools of artists. There's even a restored apothecary, complete with powders and potions. ⊠ *Fondamenta Rezzonico, Dorsoduro 3136* ☎ *041/2410100* 🔖 *€6.50; museum card €8, includes Palazzo Mocenigo and Casa Goldoni; Musei Civici museum pass €18* ☉ *Apr.–Oct., daily 10–6; Nov.–Mar., daily 10–5; last entry 1 hr before closing* Ⓥ *Ca' Rezzonico.*

★ ⓫ **Gallerie dell'Accademia.** Napoléon founded these galleries in 1807 on the site of a religious complex he'd suppressed, and what he initiated now amounts to the world's most extraordinary collection of Venetian art. Jacopo Bellini is considered the father of the Venetian Renaissance, and in Room 2 you can compare his *Madonna and Child with Saints* with such later works as *Madonna of the Orange Tree* by Cima da Conegliano (circa 1459–1517) and *Ten Thousand Martyrs of Mt. Ararat* by Vittore Carpaccio (circa 1455–1525). Jacopo's son Giovanni (circa 1430–1516) draws your eye not with his subjects but with his rich color. Rooms 4 and 5 are full of his Madonnas; note the contrast between the young Madonna and child and the neighboring older Madonna after the crucifixion—you'll see the colors of dawn and dusk in Venice. Room 5 contains *Tempest* by Giorgione (1477–1510), a work that was revolutionary in its time and has continued to intrigue viewers and critics over the centuries. It depicts a storm approaching as a nude woman nurses her child and a soldier looks on. The overall atmosphere that Giorgione creates is as important as any of his figures.

In Room 10, *Feast in the House of Levi,* commissioned as a Last Supper, got Veronese dragged before the Inquisition over its depiction of dogs, jesters, and German (therefore Protestant) soldiers. The artist saved his neck by simply changing the title, so that the painting represented a different biblical feast. Titian's *Presentation of the Virgin* (Room 24) is the collection's only work originally created for the building in which it hangs. Don't miss Rooms 20 and 21, with views of 15th- and 16th-century Venice by Carpaccio and Gentile Bellini (1429–1507), Giovanni's brother—you'll see how little the city has changed.

Booking tickets in advance isn't essential but helps during busy seasons and costs only an additional €1. Booking is necessary to see the **Quadreria,** where additional works cover every inch of a wide hallway. A free map names art and artists, and the bookshop sells a more informative English-language booklet. In the main galleries a €4 audio guide saves reading but adds little to each room's excellent annotation. ⊠ *Campo della Carità, Dorsoduro 1050* ☎ *041/5222247, 041/5200345 reservations* ⊕ *www.artive.arti.beniculturali.it* ✆ *€6.50, €11 includes Ca' d'Oro and Museo Orientale* ۩ *Tues.–Sun. 8:15–7:15, Mon. 8:15–2* Ⓥ *Accademia.*

NEED A BREAK?

There's no sunnier spot in Venice than **Fondamenta delle Zattere,** along the southern edge of Dorsoduro. It's the city's gigantic public terrace, with bustling bars and gelato shops; come here to stroll, read in the open air, and play hooky from sightseeing. The Zattere's most decadent treat is found at **Gelateria Nico** (⊠ Dorsoduro 922 ☎ 041/5225293)—order their famous *gianduiotto,* a nutty slab of chocolate ice cream floating on a cloud of whipped cream, and relax on the big, welcoming deck.

ⓒ **⑫ Peggy Guggenheim Collection.** A small but choice selection of 20th-century painting and sculpture is on display at this gallery in the heiress Guggenheim's former Grand Canal home. Through wealth and social connections, Guggenheim (1898–1979) became a serious art patron, and her collection here in Palazzo Venier dei Leoni includes works by Picasso, Kandinsky, Pollock, Motherwell, and Ernst (at one time her husband). The museum serves beverages, snacks, and light meals in its refreshingly shady, artistically sophisticated garden. On Sunday at 3 PM the museum offers a free tour and art workshop for children 12 and under. ⊠ *Fondamenta Venier dei Leoni, Dorsoduro 701* ☎ *041/2405411* ⊕ *www.guggenheim-venice.it* ✆ *€10* ۩ *Wed.–Mon. 10–6* Ⓥ *Accademia.*

> **WORD OF MOUTH**
>
> "Personally, I liked the garden and the villa itself at the Peggy Guggenheim museum better than the art."
>
> –Dayle

⑬ Santa Maria della Salute. The view of La Salute (as this church is commonly called) from the Riva degli Schiavoni at sunset or from the Accademia Bridge by moonlight is unforgettable. Baldassare Longhena was 32 years old when he won a competition to design a shrine honoring the Virgin Mary for saving Venice from a plague that killed 47,000 residents. Outside, this simple white octagon is adorned with a colossal cupola lined with snail-like buttresses and a Palladian-style facade; inside are a polychrome marble floor and six chapels. The Byzantine icon above the main altar has been venerated as the Madonna della Salute (of health) since 1670, when Francesco Morosini brought it here from Crete. Above it is a sculpture showing Venice (left) on her knees while the plague (right) is driven from the city. The **Sacrestia Maggiore** contains a dozen works by Titian, including his *San Marco Enthroned with Saints* altarpiece. You'll also see Tintoretto's *The Wedding at Canaan,* and on special occasions the altar displays a 15th-century tapestry depicting the Pentecost. For the Festa della Salute, held November 21, Venetians make a pilgrimage here and light candles in thanksgiving for another year's health. ⊠ *Punta della Dogana, Dorsoduro* ☏ *041/5225558* 🖃 *Church free, sacristy €1.50* ◷ *Apr.–Sept., daily 9–noon and 3–6:30; Oct.–Mar., daily 9–noon and 3–5:30* Ⓥ *Salute.*

NEED A BREAK? Filled with cafés and restaurants, **Campo Santa Margarita** also has produce vendors, pizza by the slice, and benches where you can sit and eat. For more than a portable munch, bask in the sunshine at popular **Il Caffé** (☏ 041/5287998), commonly called Caffé Rossa for its bright red exterior. It's open past midnight, serving drinks and light refreshment every day except Sunday.

Also Worth Seeing

❻ Campo Santo Stefano. In Venice's most prestigious residential neighborhood, you'll find one of the city's busiest crossroads just over the Accademia bridge; it's hard to believe this square once hosted bullfights, with bulls (or oxen) tied to a stake and baited by dogs. For centuries the campo was grass except for a stone avenue called the *liston*. It was so popular for strolling that in Venetian dialect *"andare al liston"* still means "go for a walk." A sunny meeting spot popular with Venetians and visitors alike, the campo also hosts outdoor fairs during Christmas and Carnevale seasons. Check out the 14th-century **Chiesa di Santo Stefano** and its ship's-keel roof, created by shipbuilders. You'll see works by Tintoretto and the tipsiest bell tower in town—best appreciated from nearby Campo San Angelo. ⊠ *Campo Santo Stefano, San Marco* ☏ *041/2750462 Chorus* 🖃 *€2.50, Chorus pass €8* ◷ *Mon.–Sat. 10–5, Sun. 1–5* Ⓥ *Accademia.*

❿ Gesuati. When the Dominicans took over the church of Santa Maria della Visitazione from the suppressed order of Gesuati laymen in 1668, Giorgio Massari was commissioned to build this structure. It has a score of works by Giambattista Tiepolo (1696–1770), Giambattista Piazzetta (1683–1754), and Sebastiano Ricci (1659–1734). ⊠ *Zattere, Dorsoduro* ☏ *041/2750462 Chorus* 🖃 *€2.50, Chorus pass €8* ◷ *Mon.–Sat. 10–5, Sun. 1–5* Ⓥ *Zattere.*

❾ San Sebastiano. Paolo Veronese (1528–88) established his reputation while still in his twenties with the frescoes at this, his parish church, and for decades he continued to embellish them with amazing trompel'oeil scenes. Don't miss his altarpiece *Madonna in Glory with Saints.* Veronese is buried beneath his bust near the organ. ⊠ *Campo San Sebastiano, Dorsoduro* ☏ *041/2750462 Chorus* 🖃 *€2.50, Chorus pass €8* ◷ *Mon.–Sat. 10–5, Sun. 1–5* Ⓥ *San Basilio.*

❽ Scuola Grande dei Carmini. When the order of Santa Maria del Carmelo commissioned Baldassare Longhena to build Scuola Grande dei Carmini in the late 1600s, their brotherhood of 75,000 members was the largest in Venice and one of the wealthiest. Little expense was spared in the decorating of stuccoed ceilings and carved ebony paneling, and the artwork was choice, even before 1739, when Tiepolo painted the **Sala Capitolare.** In what many consider his best work, Tiepolo's nine great canvases vividly transform some rather unpromising religious themes into flamboyant displays of color and movement. ⊠ *Campo dei Carmini, Dorsoduro 2617* ☎ *041/5289420* 💳 *€5* 🕙 *Daily 10–5* Ⓥ *Ca' Rezzonico.*

San Polo & Santa Croce

The two smallest of Venice's six sestieri, San Polo and Santa Croce were named after their main churches, though the Chiesa di Santa Croce was demolished in 1810. The city's most famous bridge, the Ponte di Rialto, unites sestiere San Marco (east) with San Polo (west). San Polo has two other major sites, Santa Maria Gloriosa dei Frari and the Scuola Grande di San Rocco, as well as some worthwhile but lesser-known churches.

Shops abound in the area surrounding the Rialto Bridge. On the San Marco side you'll find fashions, on the San Polo side food. Chiesa di San Giacometto, where you see the first fruit vendors as you come off the bridge on the San Polo side, was probably built in the 11th and 12th centuries, about the time the surrounding market came into being. Public announcements were traditionally read in the church's campo; its 24-hour clock, though lovely, has rarely worked.

Timing

To do the area justice requires at least half a day. If you want to take part in the food shopping, come early to beat the crowds. Bear in mind that a *metà kilo* is about a pound and an *etto* is a few ounces. The campo of San Giacomo dell'Orio, west of the main thoroughfare that takes you from the Ponte di Rialto to Santa Maria Gloriosa dei Frari, is a peaceful place for a drink and a rest. The museums of Ca' Pesaro are a time commitment—you'll want at least two hours to see them both.

The Main Attractions

★ ⑭ **Ponte di Rialto** (Rialto Bridge). The competition to design a stone bridge across the Grand Canal (replacing earlier wooden versions) attracted the late-16th-century's best architects, including Michelangelo, Palladio, and Sansovino, but the job went to the less-famous but appropriately named Antonio da Ponte. His pragmatic design featured shop space and was high enough for galleys to pass beneath; it kept decoration and cost to a minimum at a time when the republic's coffers were low due to continual wars against the Turks and the opening of oceanic trade routes. Along the railing you'll enjoy one of the city's most famous views: the Grand Canal vibrant with boat traffic. Ⓥ *Rialto.*

⑳ **Santa Maria Gloriosa dei Frari.** This immense Gothic church of russet-color brick, completed in the 1400s after more than a century of work, is deliberately austere, befitting the Franciscan brothers' insistence on spirituality and poverty. However, *I Frari* (as it's known locally) contains some of the most brilliant paintings in any Venetian church. Visit the sacristy first, to see Giovanni Bellini's 1488 triptych

Fodor's Choice
★

Campo
San Polo **19**

Ca' Pesaro **16**

Ponte di
Rialto **14**

San Giacomo
dell'Orio **18**

San Giovanni
Elemosinario . . **15**

San Stae **17**

Santa Maria
Gloriosa
dei Frari **20**

Scuola Grande di
San Rocco **21**

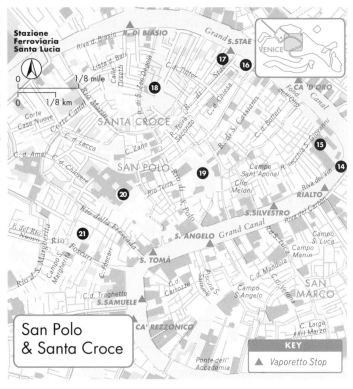

Madonna and Child with Saints in all its mellow luminosity, painted for precisely this spot. The Corner Chapel on the other side of the chancel is graced by Bartolomeo Vivarini's (1415–84) 1474 altarpiece *St. Mark Enthroned and Saints John the Baptist, Jerome, Peter, and Nicholas,* of similar exquisite detail and color. There is also a fine sculpture of St. John the Baptist here by Jacopo Sansovino. You can see the rapid development of Venetian Renaissance painting by contrasting Bellini and Vivarini with the heroic energy of Titian's *Assumption,* over the main altar, painted only 30 years later. Unveiled in 1518, this work was not initially accepted by the church, precisely because of the innovative style and bright colors, especially Titian's trademark red, which would make it famous.

Titian's beautiful *Madonna di Ca' Pesaro,* in the left aisle, was modeled after his wife, who died in childbirth. The painting took almost 10 years to complete, and in it Titian totally disregarded the conventions of his time by moving the Virgin out of center frame and making the saints active participants. On the same side of the church look at the spooky, pyramid-shape monument to the sculptor Antonio Canova (1757–1822). Across the nave is a neoclassical 19th-century monument to Titian, executed by two of Canova's pupils. ⊠ *Campo dei Frari, San Polo* ☎ *041/ 2728618, 041/2750462 Chorus* ⊠ *€2.50, Chorus pass €8* ⊗ *Mon.–Sat. 9–6, Sun. 1–6* Ⓥ *San Tomà.*

CLOSE UP

Venice's Scuola Days

1

AN INSTITUTION you'll inevitably encounter from Venice's glory days is the *scuola* (plural *scuole*). These weren't schools, as the word today translates, but an important network of institutions established by different social groups—enclaves of foreigners, tradesmen, followers of a particular saint, and parishioners.

For the most part secular despite their devotional activities, the scuole concentrated on charitable work, either helping their own membership or assisting the city's neediest citizens. The tradesmen's and

servants' scuole formed social security nets for elderly and disabled members. Wealthier scuole assisted orphans or provided dowries so poor girls could marry. By 1500 there were more than 200 major and minor scuole in Venice, some of which contributed substantially to arts and crafts guilds. The republic encouraged their existence—the scuole kept strict records of the names and professions of contributors to the brotherhood, which helped when it came time to collect taxes.

NEED A BREAK?

On a narrow passage between the Frari and San Rocco, **Gelateria Millevoglie** ([Thousand Desires]; ☎ 041/5244667) has pizza slices, calzones, and gelato so popular it backs up traffic. It's closed December and January, but it's open seven days a week—10 AM to midnight in summer and until 9 PM October–March.

Just off of Campo San Tomà is the decadent **Vizio Virtù** (☎ 041/2750149). If it's too cold for a gelato, have a hot chocolate to go or choose from a selection of gourmet chocolate creations.

㉑ **Scuola Grande di San Rocco.** St. Rocco's popularity stemmed from his miraculous recovery from the plague and his care for fellow sufferers. Throughout the plague-filled Middle Ages, followers and donations abounded, and this elegant example of Venetian Renaissance architecture was the result. Although it is bold and dramatic outside, its contents are even more stunning—a series of more than 60 paintings by Tintoretto. In 1564 Tintoretto edged out competition for a commission to decorate a ceiling by submitting not a sketch, but a finished work, which he moreover offered free of charge. *Moses Striking Water from the Rock, The Brazen Serpent,* and *The Fall of Manna* represent three afflictions—thirst, disease, and hunger—that San Rocco and later his brotherhood sought to relieve. ⊠ *Campo San Rocco, San Polo 3052* ☎ *041/5234864* ⊕ *www. scuolagrandesanrocco.it* ◪ *€5.50; students up to 26 €4; children up to 18 free if accompanied by parent* ☉ *Apr.–Oct., daily 9–5:30; Nov.–Mar., daily 10–5; last entry ½ hr before closing* Ⓥ *San Tomà.*

NEED A BREAK?

The bridge behind Scuola Grande di San Rocco leads to a bustling little student area of bars and restaurants. **Café Noir** (⊠ Calle Crosera, Dorsoduro 3805 ☎ 041/710925) has a good selection of sandwiches. It's open until 2 AM but closed Sunday morning.

Pasticceria Tonolo (✉ Calle Crosera, Dorsoduro 3764 ☎ 041/5237209) has been fattening up Venetians since 1886. During Carnevale it's still the best place in town for *fritelle*, fried doughnuts (traditional raisin or cream-filled); during *acqua alta* flooding, the staff dons rubber boots and keeps working. The place is closed Monday, and there's no seating anytime.

Also Worth Seeing

⓳ **Campo San Polo.** Only Piazza San Marco is larger than this square, where not even the pigeons manage to look cozy, and the echo of children's voices bouncing off the surrounding palaces makes the space seem even more cavernous. Not long ago Campo San Polo hosted bull races, fairs, military parades, and packed markets, but now it only really comes alive on summer nights, when it hosts the city's outdoor cinema. The **Chiesa di San Polo** has been restored so many times that little remains of the original 9th-century church, and sadly, 19th-century alterations were so costly that the friars sold off many great paintings to pay bills. Though Giambattista Tiepolo is represented here, his work is outdone by 16 paintings by his son Giandomenico (1727–1804), including the *Stations of the Cross* in the oratory to the left of the entrance. The younger Tiepolo also created a series of expressive and theatrical renderings of the saints. Look for altarpieces by Tintoretto and Veronese that managed to escape auction. San Polo's bell tower remained unchanged through the centuries—don't miss the two lions guarding it, playing with a disembodied human head and a serpent. ✉ *Campo San Polo* ☎ *041/2750462 Chorus* ✉ *€2.50, Chorus pass €8* ☾ *Mon.–Sat. 10–5, Sun. 1–5* Ⓥ *San Tomà.*

⓰ **Ca' Pesaro.** Baldassare Longhena's grand baroque palace is the beautifully restored home of two impressive collections. The **Galleria Internazionale d'Arte Moderna** has works by 19th- and 20th-century artists such as Klimt, Kandinsky, Matisse, and Miró. It also has a collection of representative works from Venice's Biennale art show that amounts to a panorama of 20th-century art. The **Museo Orientale** has a small but striking collection of Oriental porcelains, musical instruments, arms, and armor. ✉ *San Stae, Santa Croce 2076* ☎ *041/5240662 Galleria, 041/5241173 Museo Orientale* ✉ *€5.50 includes both museums* ☾ *Apr.–Sept., Tues.–Sun. 10–6; Oct.–Mar., Tues.–Sun. 10–5* Ⓥ *San Stae.*

⓲ **San Giacomo dell'Orio.** It was named after a laurel tree *(orio)*, and today trees give character to this square. Add benches and a fountain (with a drinking bowl for dogs), and the pleasant, oddly shaped campo becomes a welcoming place for friendly conversation, picnics, and neighborhood kids at play. Legend has it the **Chiesa di San Giacomo dell'Orio** was founded in the 9th century on an island still populated by wolves. The current church dates from 1225; its short unmatched Byzantine columns survived renovation during the Renaissance, and the church never lost the feel of an ancient temple sheltering beneath its 15th-century ship's-keel roof. In the sanctuary, large marble crosses are surrounded by a bevy of small medieval Madonnas. The altarpiece is *Madonna with Child and Saints* (1546) by Lorenzo Lotto (1480–1556), and the sacristies contain works by Palma il Giovane (circa 1544–1628). ✉ *Campo*

San Giacomo dell'Orio, Santa Croce ☎ *041/2750462 Chorus* 🖂 *€2.50, Chorus pass* €8 ⊙ *Mon.–Sat. 10–5, Sun. 1–5* Ⓥ *San Stae.*

🚯 **San Giovanni Elemosinario.** Storefronts make up the facade, and the altars were built by market guilds—poulterers, messengers, and fodder merchants—at this church intimately bound to the Rialto Market. It's as rich inside as it is simple outside. During San Giovanni Elemosinario's restoration, workers stumbled upon a frescoed cupola by Pordenone (1484–1539) that had been painted over centuries earlier. Don't miss Titian's *St. John the Almsgiver* and Pordenone's *Sts. Catherine, Sebastian, and Roch,* which in 2002 were returned after 30 years by the Gallerie dell'Accademia, a rare move for an Italian museum. ✉ *Rialto Ruga Vechia San Giovanni, Santa Croce* ☎ *041/2750462 Chorus* 🖂 *€2.50, Chorus pass* €8 ⊙ *Mon.–Sat. 10–5, Sun. 1–5* Ⓥ *San Silvestro/Rialto.*

🚯 **San Stae.** The most renowned Venetian painters and sculptors of the early 18th century—known as the Moderns—decorated this church with the legacy left by Doge Alvise Mocenigo II, who's buried in the center aisle. A broad sampling of these masters includes works by Tiepolo, Ricci, Piazzetta, and Lazzarini. ✉ *Campo San Stae, Santa Croce* ☎ *041/ 2750462 Chorus* 🖂 *€2.50, Chorus pass* €8 ⊙ *Mon.–Sat. 9–5, Sun. 1–5* Ⓥ *San Stae.*

Castello & Cannaregio

Twice the size of tiny San Polo and Santa Croce, Castello and Cannaregio combined spread east to west from one end of Venice to the other. From working-class shipbuilding neighborhoods to the world's first ghetto, here you see a cross section of city life that's always existed beyond the palace walls. There are churches that could make a Renaissance pope jealous and one of the Grand Canal's prettiest palaces, Ca' d'Oro, as well as detour options for leaving the crowds behind.

Timing

Visiting both sestieri involves a couple of hours of walking, even if you never enter a building, and there are few chances to hop a boat and save your legs. Some sights have restricted hours, making it virtually impossible to see everything even in a full day. Your best bet is to choose a few sights as priorities, time your tour around their open hours, and then drop in at whatever others happen to be open as you're passing by. If you're touring on Friday, keep in mind that synagogues close at sunset.

The Main Attractions

🚯 **Arsenale.** The Venetian Republic never could have thrived without the Arsenale shipyard. Today it belongs to the Italian Navy and isn't regularly open to the public, but it opens for the Biennale and for Venice's festival of traditional boats, held every May. If you're here during those times, don't miss the chance for a look inside. At other times, it's still worthwhile to walk by and observe the place from the outside.

The Arsenale is said to have been founded in 1104 on twin islands. The immense facility that evolved was given the old Venetian dialect name *arzanà,* borrowed from the Arabic *darsina'a,* meaning "workshop." At

Ca' d'Oro **25**

Gesuiti **26**

Jewish
Ghetto **23**

Palazzo
Labia **22**

Palazzo
Vendramin-
Calergi **24**

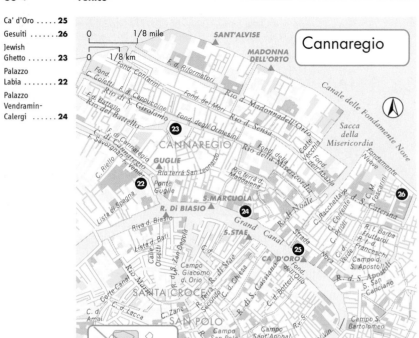

Cannaregio

KEY

▲ Vaporetto Stop

times it employed as many as 16,000 *arsenalotti,* workers who were among the most respected shipbuilders in the world. (Dante immortalized these sweating men armed with pitch and boiling tar in his *Inferno.*) Their diligence was confirmed time and again—whether building 100 ships in 60 days to battle the Turks in Cyprus (1597) or completing one perfectly armed warship—start to finish—while King Henry III of France attended a banquet.

The Arsenale's impressive Renaissance **gateway** (1460) is guarded by four lions, war booty of Francesco Morosini, who took the Peloponnese from the Turks in 1687. The 10-foot-tall lion on the left stood sentinel more than 2,000 years ago near Athens, and experts say its mysterious inscription is runic "graffiti" left by Viking mercenaries hired to suppress 11th-century revolts in Piraeus. If you look at the winged lion above the doorway, you'll notice that the Gospel at his paws is open but lacks the customary *Pax* inscription; praying for peace perhaps seemed inappropriate above a factory that manufactured weapons. ⊠ *Campo dell'Arsenale, Castello* Ⓥ *Arsenale.*

★ ㉕ **Ca' d'Oro.** This exquisite Venetian Gothic palace was once literally a "Golden House," when its marble traceries and ornaments were embellished with pure gold. Created in 1434 by the enamored patrician

Arsenale **34**

Museo Storico
Navale **35**

Ospedaletto . . . **31**

Querini-
Stampalia **29**

San Francesco
della Vigna . . . **33**

San Pietro di
Castello **36**

Santa Maria dei
Miracoli **27**

Santa Maria
Formosa **28**

Santi Giovanni
e Paolo **30**

Scuola di San
Giorgio degli
Schiavoni **32**

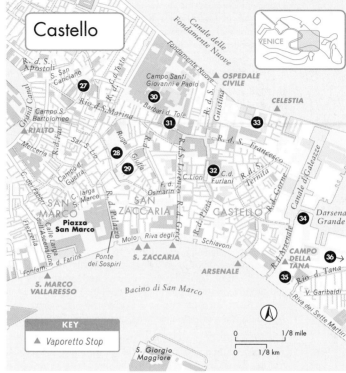

Castello

Marino Contarini for his wife, Ca' d'Oro became a love offering a second time when a 19th-century Russian prince gave it to Maria Taglioni, a celebrated classical dancer who collected palaces along the Grand Canal. The last proprietor, perhaps more taken with Venice than with any of his lovers, left Ca' d'Oro to the city, after having had it carefully restored and filled with antiquities, sculptures, and paintings that today make up the **Galleria Franchetti**. Besides Andrea Mantegna's celebrated *St. Sebastian* and other first-rate Venetian works, the Galleria Franchetti contains the type of fresco that once adorned the exteriors of Venetian buildings (commissioned by those who could not afford a marble facade). One such detached fresco displayed here was made by a young Titian for the (now grayish-white) facade of the Fondaco dei Tedeschi, now the main post office. ✉ *Calle Ca' d'Oro, Cannaregio 3933* ☎ *041/ 5200345* 💶 *€5, €11 includes Gallerie dell'Accademia and Museo Orientale* ☉ *Tues.–Sun. 8:15–7, Mon. 8:15–1; last entry ½ hr before closing* Ⓥ *Ca' d'Oro.*

㉓ **Jewish Ghetto.** The neighborhood that gave the world the word *ghetto* is today a quiet warren of backstreets that is still home to Jewish institutions, a kosher restaurant, a rabbinical school, and five synagogues. Though Jews may have arrived earlier, the first synagogues weren't built and a cemetery wasn't founded until the Askenazim, or Eastern

European Jews, came in the late 1300s. Dwindling coffers may have prompted the republic to sell temporary visas to Jews, but over the centuries they were alternately tolerated and expelled. The Rialto commercial district, as vividly recounted in Shakespeare's *The Merchant of Venice,* depended on Jewish merchants and moneylenders for trade, and to help cover ever-increasing war expenses.

In 1516 relentless local opposition forced the Senate to confine Jews to an island in Cannaregio, named for its *geto* (foundry), which produced cannons. Gates at the entrance were locked at night, and boats patrolled the surrounding canals. The German accents of early residents changed the soft g sound of "geto" (zheto) into the hard g in "ghetto." Jews were allowed only to lend money at low interest, operate pawnshops controlled by the government, trade in textiles, or practice medicine. Jewish doctors were highly respected and could leave the ghetto at any hour when on duty. Though ostracized, Jews were nonetheless safe in Venice, and in the 16th century the community grew considerably, with refugees from the Near East, southern and central Italy, Spain, and Portugal. The ghetto was allowed to expand twice, but it still had the city's densest population and consequently ended up with the city's tallest buildings (nine stories); notice the slanting apartment blocks on Campo del Ghetto Nuovo. Although the gates were pulled down after Napoléon's 1797 arrival, the Jews realized full freedom only in the late 19th century with the founding of the Italian state. On the eve of World War II there were about 1,500 Jews left in the ghetto: 247 were deported by the Nazis; 8 returned.

The area has Europe's highest density of Renaissance-era synagogues, and visiting them is a unique cross-cultural experience. Though each is marked by the tastes of its individual builders, Venetian influence is evident throughout. Women's galleries resemble those of theaters from the same era, and some synagogues were decorated by artisans who were simultaneously active in local churches.

The small but well-arranged **Museo Ebraico** highlights centuries of Jewish culture with splendid silver Hanukkah lamps and torahs, and handwritten, beautifully decorated wedding contracts in Hebrew. Tours of the ghetto in Italian and English leave hourly from the museum. ⊠ *Campo del Ghetto Nuovo, Cannaregio 2902/b* ☏ *041/715359* ⊕ *www. museoebraico.it* ☎ *Museum €3, museum and synagogues €8.50* ⊘ *June–Sept., Sun.–Fri. 10–7, last tour 5:30; Oct.–May, Sun.–Fri. 10–5:30, last tour 4:30* Ⓥ *San Marcuola/Guglie.*

You might complete your circuit of Jewish Venice with a visit to the **Antico Cimitero Ebraico** (Ancient Jewish Cemetery) on the Lido, full of fascinating old tombstones half hidden by ivy and grass. The earliest grave dates from 1389; the cemetery remained in use until the late 18th century. ⊠ *Via Cipro, Lido* ☏ *041/715359* ☎ *€8.50* ⊘ *Tours Apr.–Oct., Sun. 2:30; call for arrangements* Ⓥ *Lido–S.M.E.*

★ ㉗ **Santa Maria dei Miracoli.** Tiny yet perfectly proportioned, this early Renaissance gem is sheathed in marble and decorated inside with exquisite marble reliefs. Architect Pietro Lombardo (circa 1435–1515) miraculously compressed the building into its confined space, then created the illusion of greater size by varying the color of the exterior, adding extra pilasters on the building's canal side, and offsetting the arcade windows to make the arches appear deeper. The church was built in the 1480s to house *I Miracoli,* an image of the Virgin Mary that is said to perform miracles—look for it on the high altar. ⊠ *Campo Santa Maria Nova, Cannaregio* ☎ *041/2750462 Chorus* 🎫 *€2.50, Chorus pass €8* ⊙ *Mon.–Sat. 10–5, Sun. 1–5* Ⓥ *Rialto.*

★ ㉚ **Santi Giovanni e Paolo.** This massive Dominican church, commonly called San Zanipolo, contains a wealth of art. The 15th-century stained-glass window near the side entrance is breathtaking for its brilliant colors and beautiful figures, made from drawings by Bartolomeo Vivarini and Gerolamo Mocetto. The second official church of the republic after San Marco, San Zanipolo is the Venetian equivalent of London's Westminster Abbey, with a great number of important people, including 25 doges, buried here. Artistic highlights include an outstanding polyptych by Giovanni Bellini (right aisle, second altar); Alvise Vivarini's *Christ Carrying the Cross* (sacrestia); and Lorenzo Lotto's *Charity of St. Antonino* (right transept). Don't miss the *Cappella del Rosario* (Rosary Chapel), off the left transept, built in the 16th century to commemorate the 1571 victory of Lepanto, in western Greece, when Venice led a combined European fleet to defeat the Turkish navy. The chapel was devastated by a fire in 1867 and restored in the early years of the 20th century with works from other churches, among them the sumptuous Veronese ceiling paintings. However quick your visit, don't miss the Pietro Mocenigo tomb to the right of the main entrance, a monument built by the ubiquitous Pietro Lombardo and his sons. ⊠ *Campo dei Santi Giovanni e Paolo, Castello* ☎ *041/5235913* 🎫 *€2.50* ⊙ *Mon.–Sat. 9–6, Sun. 1 PM–6 PM* Ⓥ *Fondamente Nuove/Rialto.*

NEED A BREAK?

To satisfy your sweet tooth head for Campo Santa Marina and the family-owned and -operated **Didovich Pastry Shop** (☎ 041/5230017). It's a local favorite, especially for Carnevale-time *fritelle* (fried doughnuts). There is limited seating inside, but in the warmer months you can sit outside. **Bar ai Miracoli** (☎ 041/5231515) in Campo Santa Maria Nova is a good place to grab a quick bite and gaze across the canal at Maria dei Miracoli, Lombardo's miracle in marble.

Also Worth Seeing

㉖ **Gesuiti.** Extravagantly baroque, this 18th-century church completely abandons classical Renaissance straight lines in favor of flowing, twisting forms. Its interior walls resemble brocade drapery, and only touching them will convince skeptics that rather than paint, the green-and-white walls are inlaid marble. Over the first altar on the left the *Martyrdom of St. Lawrence* is a dramatic example of Titian's feeling for light and movement. ⊠ *Campo dei Gesuiti, Cannaregio* ☎ *041/5286579* ⊙ *Daily 10–noon and 4–6* Ⓥ *Fondamente Nuove.*

㉟ **Museo Storico Navale** (Museum of Naval History). The boat collection here includes scale models such as the doges' ceremonial *Bucintoro,* and full-size boats such as Peggy Guggenheim's private gondola complete with romantic *felze* (cabin). There's a range of old galley and military pieces, and also a large collection of seashells. ⊠ *Campo San Biagio, Castello 2148* ☎ *041/5200276* ✉ *€1.55* ⏱ *Weekdays 8:45–1:30, Sat. 8:45–1* Ⓥ *Arsenale.*

③ **Ospedaletto.** This 16th-century "little hospital" was one of four church foundling homes that each had an orchestra and choir of orphans. Entering through **Santa Maria dei Derelitti** (St. Mary of the Destitute) you'll see a large gallery built for the young musicians. The orphanage is now a home for the elderly; its beautiful 18th-century **Sala della Musica** (Music Room) is the only one of its kind to survive. On the far wall the fresco by Jacopo Guarana (1720–1808) depicts Apollo, god of music, surrounded by the orphan musicians and their maestro, Pasquale Anfossi. ⊠ *Calle Barbaria delle Tole, Castello 6691* ☎ *041/2719012* ✉ *€2* ⏱ *Thurs.–Sat. 3:30–6:30* Ⓥ *Fondamente Nuove/Rialto.*

② **Palazzo Labia.** Once the home of 18th-century Venice's showiest family, this palace is now the Venetian headquarters of the Italian media giant RAI—modern broadcasting goes baroque. In the **Tiepolo Room,** the Labia's gorgeous ballroom, the final flowering of Venetian painting is seen in Giambattista Tiepolo's playful frescoes of Antony and Cleopatra among dwarfs and Barbary pirates. You have to call ahead to arrange a visit here. ⊠ *Campo San Geremia, Cannaregio 275* ☎ *041/781277* ✉ *Free* ⏱ *Wed.–Fri. 3–4, by appointment* Ⓥ *Ferrovia.*

② **Palazzo Vendramin-Calergi.** This Renaissance classic with an imposing carved frieze is the work of Mauro Codussi (1440–1504). You can see some of its interior by dropping into the **Casinò di Venezia.** Fans of Richard Wagner (1813–83) might enjoy visiting the **Sala di Wagner,** the room (separate from the casino) in which the composer died. Though rather plain, it's loaded with music memorabilia. ⊠ *Cannaregio 2040* ☎ *041/5297111, 041/2760407 Fri. AM to reserve Wagner Room tours* ✉ *Casino €10, tour €5 suggested donation* ⏱ *Slots 2:45 PM–2:30 AM, tables 3:30 PM–2:30 AM, Wagner Room Sat. AM by appointment* Ⓥ *San Marcuola.*

② **Querini-Stampalia.** The art collection at this Renaissance palace includes Giovanni Bellini's *Presentation in the Temple* and Sebastiano Ricci's triptych *Dawn, Afternoon, and Evening.* Portraits of newlywed Francesco Querini and Paola Priuli were left unfinished on the death of Giacomo Palma il Vecchio (1480–1528); note the groom's hand and the bride's dress. Original 18th-century furniture and stuccowork are a fitting background for Pietro Longhi's portraits. Nearly 70 works by Gabriele Bella (1730–99) capture scenes of Venetian street life. Admission Friday and Saturday includes concerts with antique instruments at 5 and 8:30. ⊠ *Campo Santa Maria Formosa, Castello 5252* ☎ *041/2711411* ⊕ *www.querinistampalia.it* ✉ *€8* ⏱ *Tues.–Thurs. and Sun. 10–6, Fri. and Sat. 10–10* Ⓥ *San Zaccaria.*

③ **San Francesco della Vigna** (St. Francis of the Vineyard). Legend says this is where an angel awakened St. Mark the Evangelist with the famous words, "Pax tibi Marce Evangelista meus" (Peace to you, Mark, my Evangelist), which became the motto of the Venetian Republic. The land was given in 1253 to the Franciscans, who kept the vineyard but replaced the ancient church. Bring some €0.20 coins to light up the Antonio Vi-

CLOSE UP

Let's Get Lost

1

GETTING AROUND VENICE presents some unusual problems: the city's layout has few straight lines; house numbering seems nonsensical; and the *sestieri* (six districts) of San Marco, Cannaregio, Castello, Dorsoduro, Santa Croce, and San Polo all duplicate each other's street names. The numerous vaporetto lines can be bewildering, and often the only option for getting where you want to go is to walk. Yellow signs, posted on many busy corners, point toward the major landmarks—San Marco, Rialto, Accademia, etc.—but don't count on finding such markers once you're deep into residential neighborhoods. Even buying a good map at a newsstand—the kind showing all street names and vaporetto routes—

won't necessarily keep you from getting lost.

Fortunately, as long as you maintain your patience, getting lost in Venice can be a pleasure. For one thing, being lost is a sign that you've escaped the tourist throngs. And although you might not find the Titian masterpiece you'd set out to see, instead you could wind up coming across an ageless bacaro or a quirky shop that turns out to be the highlight of your afternoon. Opportunities for such serendipity abound. Keep in mind that the city is nothing if not self-contained: sooner or later, perhaps with the help of a patient native, you can rest assured you'll regain your bearings.

---

varini (circa 1415–84) triptych of Sts. Girolamo, Bernardino da Siena, and Ludovico, which hangs to your right as you enter the main door, and Giovanni Bellini's *Madonna with Saints* inside the Cappella Santa. Antonio da Negroponte's glittering gold *Madonna Adoring the Child*, near the side door, is an inspiring work of the late 15th century. Here you'll see the transition from formal Gothic rigidity to naturalistic Renaissance composition and detailed decoration. Two cloisters open out from the left aisle, paved entirely with VIP tombstones. ⊠ *Campo San Francesco della Vigna, Castello* ☎ *041/5206102* ✉ *Free* ☉ *Daily 8–12:30 and 3–7* Ⓥ *Celestia.*

㊱ **San Pietro di Castello.** This church's stark campanile, the first in Venice built from marblelike Istrian stone, stands out against the picturesque, workaday slips along the Canale di San Pietro and the Renaissance cloister, which for years was a squatters' colony. The Veneti settled on the island where the church is located years before Venice was officially founded, but today it's a sleepy, almost forgotten place, with little to suggest that for 1,000 years the church was Venice's cathedral—until the Basilica di San Marco superseded it in 1807. The interior has some minor 17th-century art and San Pietro's ancient *cattedra* (throne). ⊠ *Campo San Pietro, Castello* ☎ *041/2750462 Chorus* ✉ *€2.50, Chorus pass €8* ☉ *Mon.–Sat. 10–5, Sun. 1–5* Ⓥ *San Pietro di Castello/Giardini.*

㉘ **Santa Maria Formosa.** Guided by his vision of a beautiful Madonna, 7th-century St. Magno is said to have followed a small white cloud and built a church where it settled. Gracefully white, the marble building you see today dates from 1492, built by Mauro Codussi on an older foundation. The interior is a blend of Renaissance decoration, a Byzantine cupola, barrel vaults, and narrow-columned screens. Of interest are two fine paintings: *Our Lady of Mercy* by Bartolomeo Vivarini and *Santa Barbara* by Palma il Vecchio. The surrounding square bustles

with sidewalk cafés and a produce market on weekday mornings. ✉ *Campo Santa Maria Formosa, Castello* ☎ *041/5234645, 041/ 2750462 Chorus* 🖅 *€2.50, Chorus pass €8* ⊗ *Mon.–Sat. 10–5, Sun. 1–5* Ⓥ *Rialto.*

③② **Scuola di San Giorgio degli Schiavoni.** Founded in 1451 by the Dalmatian community, this small scuola was, and still is, a social and cultural center for migrants from what is now Croatia. It's dominated by one of Italy's most beautiful rooms, lavishly yet harmoniously decorated with the *teleri* (large canvases) of Vittore Carpaccio. A lifelong Venice resident, Carpaccio painted legendary and religious figures against backgrounds of Venetian architecture. Here he focused on saints especially venerated in Dalmatia: St. George, St. Tryphone, and St. Jerome. He combined observation with fantasy, a sense of warm color with a sense of humor (don't miss the priests fleeing St. Jerome's lion, or the body parts in the dragon's lair). ✉ *Calle dei Furlani, Castello 3259/a* ☎ *041/ 5228828* 🖅 *€3* ⊗ *Apr.–Oct., Tues.–Sat. 9:30–12:30 and 3:30–6.30, Sun. 9:30–12:30; Nov.–Mar., Tues.–Sat. 10–12:30 and 3–6, Sun. 10–12:30; last entry ½ hr before closing* Ⓥ *Arsenale/San Zaccaria.*

San Giorgio Maggiore & the Giudecca

Beckoning travelers across St. Mark's Basin, sparkling white through the mist, is the island of San Giorgio Maggiore, separated by a small channel from the Giudecca. A tall brick campanile on that distant bank perfectly complements the Campanile of San Marco. Beneath it looms the stately dome of one of Venice's greatest churches, San Giorgio Maggiore, the creation of Andrea Palladio.

You can reach San Giorgio Maggiore via vaporetto Line 82 from San Zaccaria. The next three stops on the line take you to the Giudecca. The island's past may be shrouded in mystery, but today it's about as down to earth as you can get and one of the city's few remaining neighborhoods that feels truly Venetian.

Timing

A half day should be plenty of time to visit the area. Allow about a half hour to see each of the churches, and an hour or two to look around the Giudecca.

The Main Attractions

Giudecca. The island's name is something of a mystery. It may come from a possible 14th-century Jewish settlement, or because 9th-century nobles condemned to *giudicato* (exile) were sent here. It became a pleasure garden for wealthy Venetians during the republic's long and luxurious decline, but today, like Cannaregio, it's largely working class. The Giudecca provides spectacular views of Venice and is becoming increasingly gentrified. While here, visit the **Santissimo Redentore** church, designed by Palladio and built to commemorate a plague. The third weekend in July it's the site of the Venetians' favorite festival, Redentore, featuring boats, fireworks, and outdoor feasting. Thanks to several bridges, you can walk the entire length of the Giudecca's promenade, relaxing at one of several restaurants or just taking in the lively atmosphere. Accommodations run the gamut from youth hostels to the city's most exclusive hotel, Cipriani. ⊠ *Fondamenta San Giacomo, Giudecca* ☎ *041/5231415, 041/2750462 Chorus* ✍ *€2.50, Chorus pass €8* ⊙ *Mon.–Sat. 10–5, Sun. 1–5* Ⓥ *Redentore.*

San Giorgio Maggiore. There's been a church on this island since the 8th century, with a Benedictine monastery added in the 10th century (closed to the public). Today's refreshingly airy and simply decorated church of brick and white marble was begun in 1566 by Palladio and displays his architectural hallmarks of mathematical harmony and classical influence. *The Last Supper* and the *Gathering of Manna,* two of Tintoretto's later works, line the chancel. To the right of the entrance hangs *The Adoration of the Shepherds* by Jacopo Bassano (1517–92); his affection for his foothills home, Bassano del Grappa, is evident in the bucolic subjects and terra-firma colors he chooses. The monks are happy to show Carpaccio's *St. George and the Dragon,* hanging in a private room, if they have time. The campanile is so tall that it was struck by lightning in 1993. Take the elevator to the top for some of the finest views in town. ⊠ *Isola di San Giorgio Maggiore* ☎ *041/5227827* ✍ *Church free, campanile €3* ⊙ *Daily 9–12:30 and 2:30–6* Ⓥ *San Giorgio.*

Islands of the Lagoon

The perfect vacation from your Venetian vacation is an escape to Murano, Burano, and sleepy Torcello, the islands of the northern lagoon. Torcello offers greenery, breathing space, and picnic opportunities (remember to pack lunch). Burano is a toy town of houses painted in a riot of colors—blue, yellow, pink, ocher, and dark red. Visitors still love to shop here for "Venetian" lace, even though the vast majority of it is machine-made in Taiwan. Murano is renowned for its glass, but also notorious for the high-pressure sales on its factory tours, even those organized by top hotels. Vaporetto connections to Murano aren't difficult, and for the price of a boat ticket you'll buy your freedom and more time to explore. The Murano "guides" herding new arrivals follow a rotation so that factories take turns giving tours, but you can avoid the hustle by just walking away.

Timing

Hitting all the sights on all the islands takes a full day. If you limit yourself to Murano and San Michele, a half day will suffice. In summer San Zaccaria is connected to Murano by express vaporetto Line 5; the trip takes 25 minutes. In winter the local Line 41 takes about 45 minutes.

The boat leaves San Zaccaria (in front of the Savoia e Jolanda hotel) every 20 minutes, circling the east end of Venice and stopping at Fondamente Nuove before making the 5-minute hop to the San Michele island cemetery and then heading on to Murano. To see glassblowing, get off at Colonna; the Museo stop will put you near the Museo Vetrario.

Line LN goes from Fondamente Nuove direct to Murano, Burano, and Torcello every 30 minutes, and the full trip takes 45 minutes each way. To get to Burano and Torcello from Murano, pick up Line LN at the Faro stop (Murano's lighthouse), which runs to Burano before continuing on to Torcello, only five minutes away.

The Main Attractions

★ ➌➒ **Burano.** Cheerfully painted houses line the canals of this quiet village where lace making rescued a faltering fishing-based economy centuries ago. As you walk the 100 yards from the dock to Piazza Galuppi, the main square, you pass stall after stall of lace vendors. These good-natured ladies won't press you with a hard sell, but don't expect precise product information or great bargains—real handmade Burano lace costs $1,000 to $2,000 for a 10-inch doily.

The **Museo del Merletto** (Lace Museum) lets you marvel at the intricacies of Burano's lace making. It's also a skills center—more sewing circle than school—where on weekdays you'll usually find women carrying on the tradition. They sometimes have authentic pieces for sale privately. ⊠ *Piazza Galuppi 187* ☎ *041/730034* ⊠ *€4, €6 with Museo Vetrario; Musei Civici pass €18* ☉ *Apr.–Oct., Wed.–Mon. 10–5; Nov.–Mar., Wed.–Mon. 10–4* Ⓥ *Burano.*

> **WORD OF MOUTH**
>
> "A ferry ride (cheap) to Burano is a great way to see how the average person outside the city lives and works. Yes, lace is very expensive, but you can always just look, and you can even watch a woman making it by hand in a store window. Pretty, colorful homes, more canals. Have lunch on a canal. It's laid back and just darn nice."
>
> −Carole

☾ ➌➑ **Murano.** As in Venice, bridges here link a number of small islands, which are dotted with houses that once were workmen's cottages. In the 13th century the republic, concerned about fire hazard, moved its glassworks to Murano, and today you can visit the factories and watch glass being made. Many of them line the Fondamenta dei Vetrai, the canal-side walkway leading from the Colonna vaporetto landing.

Before you reach Murano's Grand Canal (a little more than 800 feet from the landing) you'll pass **Chiesa di San Pietro Martire.** Reconstructed in the 16th century, it houses Giovanni Bellini's *Madonna and Child* and Veronese's *St. Jerome.* ⊠ *Fondamenta dei Vetrai* ☎ *041/739704* ☉ *Mon.–Sat. 9–noon and 3–6, Sun. 3–6* Ⓥ *Colonna.*

The collection at the **Museo Vetrario** (Glass Museum) ranges from priceless antiques to only slightly less-expensive modern pieces. You'll see authentic Venetian styles and patterns, including the famous Barovier wedding cup (1470–80). ⊠ *Fondamenta Giustinian 8* ☎ *041/739586*

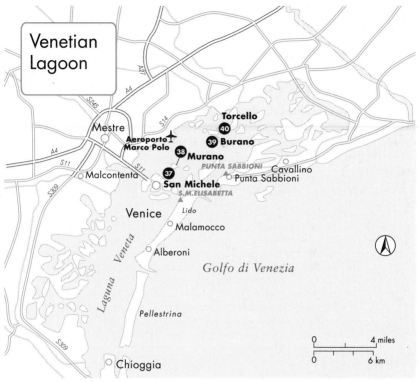

Venetian Lagoon

Mestre

Aeroporto Marco Polo

Torcello ⓐ

39 Burano

38 **Murano**

PUNTA SABBIONI Cavallino

Malcontenta

37 **San Michele** Punta Sabbioni

S.M.ELISABETTA

Venice *Lido*

Malamocco

Alberoni

Golfo di Venezia

Laguna Veneta

Pellestrina

0   4 miles

0   6 km

Chioggia

🏛 *€4, €6 with Museo del Merletto; Musei Civici pass €18* ☉ *Apr.–Oct., Thurs.–Tues. 10–5; Nov.–Mar., Thurs.–Tues. 10–4; last tickets sold ½ hr before closing* Ⓥ *Museo.*

The **Basilica dei Santi Maria e Donato,** just past the glass museum, is among the first churches founded by the lagoon's original inhabitants. The elaborate mosaic pavement includes the date 1140; its ship's-keel roof and Veneto-Byzantine columns add to the semblance of an ancient temple. ⊠ *Fondamenta Giustinian* ☎ *041/739056* 🏛 *Free* ☉ *Mon.–Sat. 8–noon and 4–6, Sun. 2–6* Ⓥ *Museo.*

★ ⓐ **Torcello.** In their flight from barbarians 1,500 years ago, the first Venetians landed here, prospering even after many left to found the city of Venice. As malaria took its toll and the island's wool manufacturing was priced out of the market, Torcello became a ghost town. In the 16th century there were 10 churches and 20,000 inhabitants; today you'll be lucky to see one of the island's 16 permanent residents.

Santa Maria Assunta was built in the 11th century, and Torcello's wealth at the time is evident in the church's high-quality Byzantine mosaics. The massive *Last Judgment* shows sinners writhing in pain, while opposite, above the altar, the Madonna looks calmly down from her field of gold. Ask to see the inscription dated 639 and a sample of mosaic pavement from the original church. The adjacent **Santa Fosca** church, added when the body of the saint arrived in 1011, is still used for religious services. It's worth making the climb up the adjacent **Campanile** for an incomparable view of the lagoon wetlands. ⊠ *Torcello* ☎ *041/730119* ✈ *Santa Maria Assunta €3, Campanile €3* ☉ *Basilica Mar.–Oct., daily 10:30–6; Nov.–Feb., daily 10–5. Campanile Mar.–Oct., daily 10:30–5:30; Nov.–Feb., daily 10–4:30. Last entry ½ hr before closing* Ⓥ *Torcello.*

NEED A BREAK?

Locanda Cipriani (☎ 041/730150), closed Tuesday and January, is famous for good food and its connection to Ernest Hemingway, who often came to Torcello seeking solitude. Today the restaurant (not to be confused with the Giudecca's Cipriani hotel) is busy, with well-heeled customers speeding in for lunch (dinner also on weekends). Dining is pricey, but you can relax in the garden with just a glass of prosecco.

Also Worth Seeing

㊲ San Michele. This cypress-lined island is home to the pretty Renaissance church of **San Michele in Isola**—and to some of Venice's most illustrious deceased. The church was designed by Codussi; the graves include those of poet Ezra Pound (1885–1972), impresario and art critic Sergey Diaghilev (1872–1929), and composer Igor Stravinsky (1882–1971). Surrounded by the living sounds of Venice's lagoon, this would seem the perfect final resting place. However, these days newcomers are exhumed after 10 years and transferred to a less-grandiose location. ☎ *041/7292811* ✈ *Free* ☉ *Apr.–Sept., daily 7:30–6; Oct.–Mar., daily 7:30–4* Ⓥ *San Michele.*

WHERE TO EAT

Updated by Jeff Booth

The catchword in Venice, at both fancy restaurants and holes-in-the-wall, is fish, often at its tastiest when it looks like nothing you've seen before. How do you learn firsthand about the catch of the day? An early-morning visit to the Rialto's *pescheria* (fish market) is more instructive than any book.

There's no getting around the fact that Venice has more than its share of overpriced, mediocre eateries that prey on tourists. Avoid places with cajoling waiters standing outside, and beware of restaurants that don't display their prices. At the other end of the spectrum, showy *menu turistico* (tourist menu) boards make offerings clear in a dozen languages, but for the same 15–20 euros you'd spend at such places you could do better at a *bacaro* (the local version of a wine bar) making a meal of *cicchetti* (savory snacks).

Dining options in Venice range from the ultrahigh end, where jackets and ties are required, to the supercasual, where the clientele (almost all of them tourists) won't notice if you're wearing shorts. Some of Venice's swankiest restaurants—the ones that usually have only male waiters wearing white jackets and bow ties—trade on long-standing reputations and might seem a little stuffy and faded. The food at such places tends toward interpretations of international cuisine and, though often expertly prepared, can seem as old-fashioned as the waiters who serve it. On the other hand, mid-

1

range restaurants are often more willing to break from tradition, incorporating ingredients such as ginger and wasabi in their creations.

Budget-conscious travelers, and those simply looking for a good meal in unpretentious surroundings, might want to stick to trattorias and bacari. Trattorias often serve less-highfalutin versions of classic Venetian dishes at substantially reduced prices; bacari offer lighter fare, usually eaten at the bar (though sometimes tables are available), and wine lists that offer lots of choices by the glass.

WHAT IT COSTS In euros					
	$$$$	**$$$**	**$$**	**$**	**¢**
AT DINNER	over €45	€35–€45	€25–€35	€15–€25	under €15

Prices are for a first course (primo), second course (secondo), and dessert (dolce).

Cannaregio

$$–$$$ ✕ **A la Vecia Cavana.** The young, talented kitchen staff here creates a highly refined menu of Italian and Venetian dishes. Look for *filetti di pesce a cottura differenziata* (fish fillet, cooked on one side and quickly seared on the other), tender baby cuttlefish, and, among desserts, *gelato al basilico* (basil ice cream). The 18th-century *cavana* (boathouse) maintains its original low columns, arches, and brick walls, but has been decorated with contemporary flair. ⊠ *Rio Terà SS. Apostoli, Cannaregio 4624* ☎ *041/5287106* ▭ *AE, DC, MC, V* ⊘ *Closed Mon., 2 wks in Jan., and Aug.* Ⓥ *Rialto/Ca' d'Oro.*

★ **$$–$$$** ✕ **Vini da Gigio.** A friendly, family-run trattoria on the quay side of a canal just off the Strada Nova, da Gigio is very popular with Venetians and other visiting Italians. They appreciate the affable service; the well-prepared homemade pasta, fish, and meat dishes; the imaginative and varied wine cellar; and the high-quality draft wine. It's good for a simple lunch at the tables in the barroom. ⊠ *Fondamenta de la Chiesa, Cannaregio 3628/a* ☎ *041/5285140* ▭ *DC, MC, V* ⊘ *Closed Mon. and Tues., 2 wks in Jan., and 3 wks in Aug.* Ⓥ *Ca' d'Oro.*

$–$$$ ✕ **Algiubagiò.** A waterfront table is still relatively affordable here on Venice's northern Fondamente Nuove, where you can gaze out toward San Michele and Murano—on a clear day, you can even see the Dolomites. Algiubagiò has a dual personality: pizzas and big, creative salads at lunch; elegant secondi such as Angus fillets and duck with prunes and rosemary at dinner. (There are no fish on the dinner menu.) The young, friendly staff also serves ice cream, drinks, and *tramezzini* (sandwiches) all day. A table here is worth the walk. ⊠ *Fondamente Nuove, Cannaregio 5039* ☎ *041/5236084* ▭ *MC, V* Ⓜ *Fondamente Nuove.*

$$ ✕ **Anice Stellato.** Hidden away on one of the most romantic fondamente of Cannaregio, this family-run bacaro-trattoria is the place to stop for fairly priced, great-tasting food in a part of town that doesn't teem with restaurants. The space has plenty of character: narrow columns rise from the colorful tile floor, dividing the room into cozy booths. Traditional Venetian fare is enriched with such offerings as *carpacci di pesce* (thin

EATING WELL IN VENICE

VENETIAN CUISINE is based on seafood—*granseola* (crab), *moeche* (soft-shell crab), and *seppie* or *seppioline* (cuttlefish) are all prominently featured, and trademark dishes include *sarde in saor* (fried sardines with olive oil, onions, pine nuts, and raisins) and *baccalà mantecato* (cod creamed with milk and olive oil). When served whole, fish is usually priced by the *etto* (100 grams, about ¼ pound) and can be quite expensive. Antipasti may take the form of a seafood salad, prosciutto, or pickled vegetables. As a first course, Venetians favor risotto, the creamy rice dish, prepared with vegetables or shellfish. Pasta, too, is paired with seafood sauces: *pasticcio di pesce* is pasta baked with fish, usually baccalà, and *bigoli* is a strictly local pasta shaped like short, thick spaghetti, usually served with *nero di seppia* (squid-ink sauce). A classic first course is pasta *e fagioli* (thick bean soup with pasta). Polenta (creamy cornmeal) is another pillar of regional cooking;

it's often served with *fegato alla veneziana* (calf's liver and onions).

Though it originated on the mainland, tiramisu is Venice's favorite dessert, a heavenly concoction of mascarpone (a rich, soft double-cream cheese), espresso, chocolate, and *savoiardi* (ladyfingers). Local wines are the dry white tocai and pinot grigio from the Friuli region and bubbly white prosecco, a naturally fermented sparkling wine that is a shade less dry. Popular red wines include merlot, cabernet, raboso, and refosco. You can sample all of these in Venice's *bacari* (little watering holes), a great Venetian tradition. For centuries, locals have gathered at these neighborhood spots to chat and have a glass of wine (known as an *ombra* in Venetian dialect) accompanied by *cicchetti* (snacks such as marinated fish, deep-fried vegetables, and meatballs), often substantial enough for a light meal.

slices of raw tuna, swordfish, or salmon dressed with olive oil and fragrant herbs), tagliatelle with king prawns and zucchini flowers, and several tasty fish stews. Meat dishes are also served, including a tender beef fillet stewed in Barolo wine with potatoes. ⊠ *Fondamenta de la Sensa, Cannaregio 3272* ☎ *041/720744* ▤ *MC, V* ☉ *Closed Mon., Tues., and Aug.* Ⓥ *S. Alvise.*

★ $ ✕ **Alla Vedova.** This warm trattoria not far from the Ca' d'Oro (it's also known as Trattoria Ca' d'Oro) was opened as a bacaro by the owner's great-grandparents. A Venetian terrazzo floor, old marble counter, and rustic furnishings lend a pleasant authenticity that's matched by the food and service. Cicchetti include tender *seppie roste* (grilled cuttlefish), *polpette* (meatballs), and *baccalà mantecato* (cod creamed with milk and olive oil). The house winter pasta is the *pastisso de radicio rosso* (lasagna with sausage, radicchio, and béchamel sauce). In spring the chef switches to pastisso *de asparagi* (with asparagus). ⊠ *Calle del Pistor, Cannaregio 3912* ☎ *041/5285324* ▤ *No credit cards* ☉ *Closed Thurs. No lunch Sun.* Ⓥ *Ca' d'Oro.*

Castello

★ $$$$ ✕ **Alle Testiere.** A strong local following can make it tough to get one of the 22 seats at this tiny trattoria near Campo Santa Maria Formosa. With its decidedly unglamorous ceiling fans, the place feels as informal as a bistro (or a saloon); the food, however, is much more sophisticated. Chef Bruno Gavagnin's dishes stand out for lightness and balance: try the *gnocchetti con moscardini* (little gnocchi with tender baby octopus) or the linguine with *coda di rospo* (monkfish), or inquire about the carpaccio of the day. The well-assembled wine list is particularly strong on local whites. ✉ *Calle del Mondo Novo, Castello 5801* ☎ *041/5227220* ⌨ *Reservations essential* 🞕 *MC, V* ⊙ *Closed Sun. and Mon., 3 wks in Jan. and Feb., and 4 wks in July and Aug.* Ⓥ *Rialto/San Zaccaria.*

$$$$ ✕ **Do Leoni.** The Two Lions, in the Hotel Londra Palace, is a sumptuous candlelit setting in which to sample Venetian and other Italian cuisine. The kitchen turns out creative dishes like millet soup with bacon; the seven-course €85 tasting menu utilizes such non-Italian ingredients as vanilla and ginger. The summer terrace occupies a good portion of the Riva. ✉ *Riva degli Schiavoni, Castello 4171* ☎ *41/2700680* ⌨ *Reservations essential* 🞕 *AE, DC, MC, V* Ⓥ *San Zaccaria.*

★ $-$$ ✕ **Corte Sconta.** You're close to seafood heaven at this firm favorite on the Venetian dining scene. Simple wooden tables are arranged around an open courtyard with outdoor seating in summer. You could make a meal of the seafood antipasti alone, but you'd miss out on such delights as spaghetti *neri alle capesante e zucchine* (cuttlefish-ink pasta with scallops and zucchini) and *vongole veraci spadellate allo zenzero* (clams sautéed in ginger). The house dessert is a warm zabaglione with Venetian cookies, and the house pour is a smooth, still prosecco, backed up by a good range of bottled wines. ✉ *Calle del Pestrin, Castello 3886* ☎ *041/5227024* ⌨ *Reservations essential* 🞕 *MC, V* ⊙ *Closed Sun. and Mon., 4 wks in Jan. and Feb., and 4 wks in July and Aug.* Ⓥ *Arsenale.*

$-$$ ✕ **Da Remigio.** Locals almost always fill this place, especially on the weekend (you'll need to book ahead), and it's easy to see why: the food is good, the service prompt (if sometimes rushed), and the atmosphere lively. The *canocchio bollite* (boiled, then chilled mantis shrimp) is a perfect starter, particularly when paired with an effervescent local white wine. Though the menu is strong on fish (fish risotto for two is particularly creamy), Da Remigio also turns out respectable alternatives such as the spaghetti *con porcini* (with mushrooms) and grilled meats. ✉ *Salizzada dei Greci, Castello 3416* ☎ *041/5230089* ⌨ *Reservations essential* 🞕 *AE, DC, MC, V* ⊙ *Closed Tues., 2 wks in July and Aug., and 4 wks in Dec. and Jan. No dinner Mon.* Ⓥ *Arsenale.*

Dorsoduro

$$$-$$$$ ✕ **Ai Gondolieri.** If you're tired of fish, this is the place to come—meat and food of the mainland are menu mainstays. Despite the tourist-trap name, it's a favorite with Venetians. Feast on *filetto di maiale con castraure* (pork fillet with baby artichokes), duck breast with apple and sweet onion, or more-traditional dishes from the Veneto hills such as horse meat and game, gnocchi, and polenta. The wine list is above average in

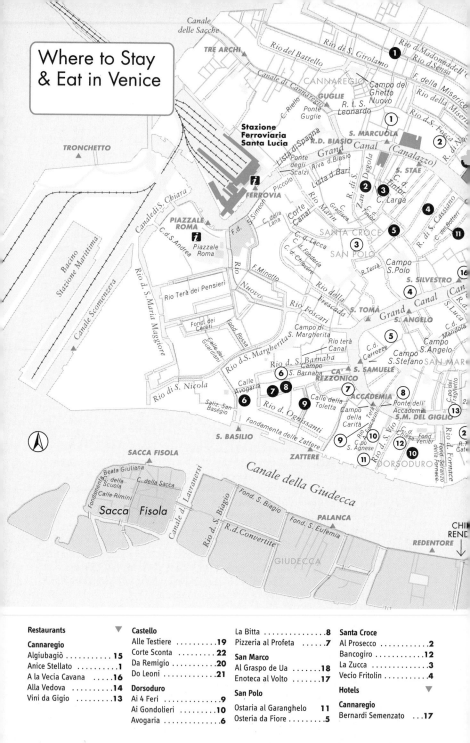

Where to Stay & Eat in Venice

Restaurants ▼

Cannaregio
Algiubagiò **15**
Anice Stellato **1**
A la Vecia Cavana **16**
Alla Vedova **14**
Vini da Gigio **13**

Castello
Alle Testiere **19**
Corte Sconta **22**
Da Remigio **20**
Do Leoni **21**

Dorsoduro
Ai 4 Feri **9**
Ai Gondolieri **10**
Avogaria **6**

La Bitta **8**
Pizzeria al Profeta **7**

San Marco
Al Graspo de Ua **18**
Enoteca al Volto **17**

San Polo
Ostaria al Garanghelo . . **11**
Osteria da Fiore **5**

Santa Croce
Al Prosecco **2**
Bancogiro **12**
La Zucca **3**
Vecio Fritolin **4**

Hotels ▼

Cannaregio
Bernardi Semenzato . . . **17**

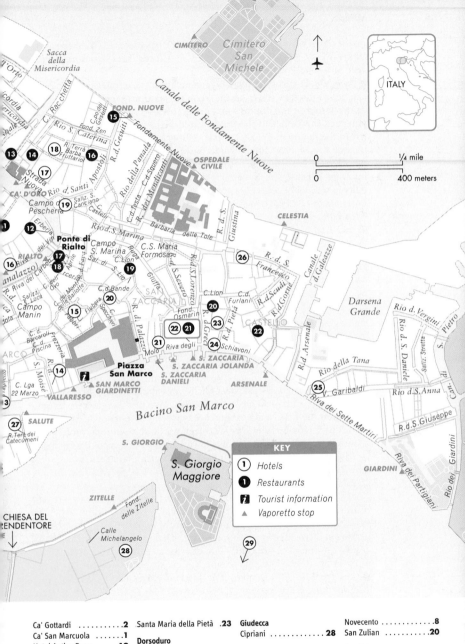

Ca' Gottardi **2**
Ca' San Marcuola **1**
Hotel Antico Doge **19**
Palazzo Abadezza **18**

Castello
Ca' Formenta **25**
Danieli **21**
Hotel Londra Palace . .**22**
Metropole **24**
Palazzo Contarini **26**

Santa Maria della Pietà .**23**

Dorsoduro
Agli Alboretti **9**
American–Dinesen **12**
Ca' Maria Adele **27**
Ca' Pisani **10**
Hotel Pausania **6**
La Calcina **11**
Pensione Accademia
Villa Maravege **7**

Giudecca
Cipriani **28**

Lagoon
San Clemente Palace . . .**29**

San Marco
Albergo San Samuele **5**
Gritti Palace **13**
Il Palazzo at the Bauer . .**14**
Locanda Orseolo **15**

Novecento **8**
San Zulian **20**

San Polo
Ca' Angeli **4**
Oltre il Giardino **3**
Sturion **16**

quality and variety. ✉ *Fondamenta dell'Ospedaletto, Dorsoduro 366* ☎ *041/5286396* ▭ *AE, DC, MC, V* ⊙ *Closed Tues. No lunch in July and Aug.* Ⓥ *Accademia.*

★ **$$$–$$$$** ✕ **Avogaria.** In terms of both food and architecture, ultrafashionable Avogaria lends modern flavor to the Venice restaurant scene. The clean, elegant design of the dining room and garden leaves no doubt that here, you're in the Venice of the present, not the past. The cuisine is Pugliese (from the region in the heel of Italy's boot); highlights among the primi include *orecchiette* (small, round pasta) with turnip tops, and zucchini *involtini* (roll-ups) made with fresh stracciatella cheese. Pugliese cooking, like Venetian, reveres fresh seafood, and you can taste this sensibility in the slow-cooked, sesame-encrusted tuna steak. ✉ *Calle Avogaria, Dorsoduro 1629* ☎ *041/2960491* ▭ *AE, DC, MC, V* ⊙ *Closed Tues.*

★ **$$** ✕ **La Bitta.** The decor is more discreet, the dining hours longer, and the service friendlier and more efficient here than in many small restaurants in Venice—and the creative nonfish menu is a temptation at every course. You can start with a light salad of Treviso radicchio and crispy bacon, followed by smoked-beef carpaccio or *gnocchetti ubriachi al Montasio* (small marinated gnocchi with Montasio cheese). Then choose from secondi such as lamb chops with thyme, *anatra in pevarada* (duck in a pepper sauce), or Irish Angus fillet steak. Secondi are served with vegetables, which helps bring down the price. The restaurant is open only for dinner, but serves much later than most, continuously from 6:30 to 11. ✉ *Calle Lunga San Barnaba, Dorsoduro 2753/A* ☎ *041/5230531* ▭ *No credit cards* ⊙ *Closed Sun. No lunch* Ⓥ *Ca' Rezzonico.*

$–$$ ✕ **Pizzeria al Profeta.** Though Pizzeria al Profeta offers more than 100 types of pizza, their real strength is massive portions of roast and grilled meats and, on occasion, fresh fish. Two or three people can split the baked pie filled with Angus beef, porcini mushrooms, and radicchio. For a wonderfully medieval feeling, sit at a wooden table in the spacious, simple garden and use both hands to tear into a large leg of lamb. Sharing an ample dish can make this a great value. ✉ *Calle Lunga San Barnaba, Dorsoduro 2671* ☎ *041/5237466* ▭ *AE, DC, MC, V* ⊙ *Closed Tues. in winter.*

$ ✕ **Ai 4 Feri.** The paper tablecloths and cozy, laid-back ambience are part of this small restaurant's charm. The menu varies according to what's fresh that day; imaginative combinations of ingredients in the primi— herring and sweet peppers, salmon and radicchio, giant shrimp and broccoli (with pumpkin gnocchi)—are the norm. A meal here followed by after-dinner drinks at Campo Santa Margarita, a five-minute walk away, makes for a lovely evening. The kitchen closes early on weekdays. ✉ *Calle Lunga San Barnaba, Dorsoduro 2754/a* ☎ *041/5206978* ▭ *No credit cards* ⊙ *Closed Sun. and June* Ⓥ *Ca' Rezzonico.*

San Marco

$$$$ ✕ **Al Graspo de Ua.** Opened in the 19th century as a small osteria, the "Bunch of Grapes" became the meeting place of artists and movie stars back in the 1960s. Today it serves a faithful clientele of wealthy Italians. The decor is a miscellany of plants, sculpture, candlelight, and paintings set against brick and white-stucco walls. The owner, Lucio Zanon,

VOICES OF ITALY

Lino & Sandra Gastaldi
bacaro owners, Dorsoduro

Husband and wife Lino and Sandra Gastaldi run the *bacaro* (wine bar) Cantinone Già Schiavi, on Fondamenta Nani, across from the *squero* (gondola workshop), in Dorsoduro. Following the bacaro tradition, they serve *cicchetti*–distinctly Venetian snacks–with their wine. Lino pours and handles distribution, while Sandra makes exquisite panini and crostini. The couple works seven days a week, with assistance from three sons.

All in the family. "We have been here since 1949," Lino explains. "My father took over from the Schiavi family–we kept the name. Soon I'll retire and my sons will take over. It's always been a family-run business, and I hope it stays that way. Over the years we've continued to grow, and we have a wide range of customers–regulars who come in every day at the same time, university students who stop in for a bite before class, as well as an increasing number of foreign visitors."

Cicchetti and ombre. "I love bacari and fight to keep the tradition alive," Sandra says. "There aren't many left in Venice that still follow the tradition of cicchetti and ombre, which has been around for more than 500 years. *Il cicchetto* was the typical break taken by Venetians at about 10 o'clock in the morning. In past centuries, workers would stop and have a sandwich or piece of cheese with a small glass of wine in the shade of the bell tower in Piazza San Marco. The term *ombra*, which means shade or shadow in Italian, is the name for a glass of wine in Venetian dialect. Nowadays people come in throughout the day–it's busiest at lunchtime and early in the evening.

"Some typical Venetian cicchetti are *baccalà mantecato*, whipped codfish served on bread, chunks of *mortadella* or salted pork meat with peppers, hard-boiled eggs served with onion, *folpeti*–tiny octopus–and *polpette*, which are deep-fried meatballs. And I love creating new cicchetti–like my tuna-and-leek spread or crostini with cheese and figs."

The bacaro state of mind. Sandra surveys Cantinone and declares, "*This* is bacaro." Her husband and sons hustle at the counter; behind them, the wall is lined with wine bottles. Customers sip, snack, and chat, creating a pleasant buzz. "People come to socialize. That's the real bacaro–you come in, have a cicchetto, and talk. It's like you're part of the family."

Despite the sociable atmosphere, bacari aren't meant for lingering–they're places for a quick bite, taken standing at the counter. "Many visitors don't understand this, and they go all the way to our storage room at the back looking for a table, or sit outside on the steps of the San Trovaso bridge. This is a definite faux pas."

But as the population of native Venetians declines, such bacaro traditions are slowly eroding. Few places meet Sandra's standards. "The only traditional bacaro is Do Mori, near the Rialto market. It's run by the Schiavi family who used to own Cantinone. The bacaro there dates back to the 15th century."

speaks fluent English and will introduce you to a wide-ranging menu of fresh pastas, seasonal risottos, and meat and seafood. A treat in late spring is the thick white asparagus from Bassano, which, with a couple of fried eggs, is eaten as a main course. Desserts are all homemade. ⊠ *Calle dei Bombaseri, San Marco 5094* ☎ *041/5223647* ▭ *AE, DC, MC, V* ☉ *Closed Mon. and 1 wk in Jan.* Ⓥ *Rialto.*

¢–$ ✕ **Enoteca al Volto.** A short walk from the Rialto Bridge, this bar has been around since 1936; the fine cicchetti and primi have a lot to do with its staying power. Two small, dark rooms with wooden tables and chairs are the backdrop for the enjoyment of simple fare. The place prides itself on its considerable wine list of both Italian and foreign vintages; if you stick to the *panini* (sandwiches) and a cicchetto or two, you'll eat well for relatively little. If you opt for one of the primi of the day, the price category goes up a notch. ⊠ *Calle Cavalli, San Marco 4081* ☎ *041/5228945* ▭ *No credit cards* ☉ *Closed Sun.* Ⓥ *Rialto.*

San Polo

★ $$$$ ✕ **Osteria da Fiore.** Tucked away on a little calle off the top of Campo San Polo, Da Fiore is a favorite among high-end diners for its superbly prepared Venetian cuisine and refined yet relaxed atmosphere. A superlative seafood lunch or dinner here might include delicate hors d'oeuvres of soft-shell crab, scallops, and tiny octopus, followed by a succulent risotto or pasta *con scampi e radicchio* (with shrimp and radicchio), and a perfectly cooked main course of *rombo* (turbot) or *tagliata di tonno* (tuna steak). A jacket is not required, but is highly recommended. ⊠ *Calle del Scaleter, San Polo 2202* ☎ *041/721308* ⌨ *Reservations essential* ▭ *AE, DC, MC, V* ☉ *Closed Sun. and Mon., Aug., and Dec. 24–Jan. 15* Ⓥ *San Silvestro/San Stae.*

$–$$ ✕ **Ostaria al Garanghelo.** Superior quality, competitive prices, and great ambience means this place is often packed with Venetians, especially for lunch and an after-work *ombra* (small glass of wine) and cicchetti. Chef Renato takes full advantage of the fresh ingredients from the Rialto market, located a few steps away, and prefers cooking many dishes *al vapore* (steamed). The spicy *fagioli al uciletto* (literally beans, bird-style) has an unusual name and Tuscan origins; it's a perfect companion to a plate of fresh pasta. Don't confuse this centrally located restaurant with one of the same name in Via Garibaldi. ⊠ *Calle dei Boteri, San Polo 1570* ☎ *041/721721* ▭ *MC, V* ☉ *Closed Sun.*

Santa Croce

$$$ ✕ **Vecio Fritolin.** At this tidy bacaro *con cucina* (with kitchen) you can have a traditional meal featuring such dishes as *bigoli in salsa* (thick spaghetti with anchovy sauce), baked fish with herbs, and ravioli with scampi and chicory. The name, which translates as "Old Fry Shop," refers to a bygone Venetian tradition of shops selling fried fish "to go," like in London, except paired with polenta rather than chips. For €8, you can still get a paper cone of *fritto* here. ⊠ *Calle della Regina, Santa Croce 2262* ☎ *041/5222881* ▭ *AE, DC, MC, V* ☉ *Closed Mon.* Ⓥ *San Stae.*

$–$$$
Fodor's Choice
★
× **Bancogiro.** Come to this casual spot in the heart of the Rialto market in a 15th-century loggia for a change from standard Venetian food. Yes, fish is on the menu, but offerings such as mousse *di gamberoni con salsa di avocado* (shrimp mousse with an avocado sauce) and Sicilian-style *sarde incinte* (stuffed, or "pregnant," sardines) are far from typical fare—though portions can be small. The wine list and cheese plate are both divine. There are tables upstairs in a carefully restored room with a partial view of the Grand Canal; when it's warm you can sit outdoors and get the full canal view. ⊠ *Campo San Giacometto, Santa Croce 122 (under the porch)* ☎ *041/5232061* ▭ *No credit cards* ☉ *Closed Mon. No dinner Sun.* Ⓥ *Rialto.*

$–$$
× **La Zucca.** The simple place settings, latticed-wood walls, canal window, and mélange of languages make this place feel as much like a typical vegetarian restaurant as you could expect to find in Venice. Though the menu does have superb meat dishes such as the *piccata di pollo ai caperi e limone con riso* (sliced chicken with capers and lemon served with rice), more attention is paid to dishes from the garden: try the *radicchio di Treviso con funghi e scaglie di Montasio* (radicchio with mushrooms and shavings of Montasio cheese) or the *finocchi piccanti con olive* (fennel in a spicy tomato-olive sauce). ⊠ *Calle del Tintor, Santa Croce 1762* ☎ *041/5241570* ⋏ *Reservations essential* ▭ *AE, DC, MC, V* ☉ *Closed Sun. and 1 wk in Aug.* Ⓥ *San Stae.*

¢–$$
× **Al Prosecco.** Locals stream into this place, down an order of "spritz bitter" (a combination of white wine, Campari, and seltzer water), and continue on their way. Or they linger over a glass of one of the numerous wines on offer, perhaps also tucking into a tasty panino, such as the *porchetta romane verdure* (roasted pig, Roman style, with greens). Proprietors Davide and Stefano preside over a young and friendly staff who reel off the day's specials with ease. There are a few tables in the enticing back room, and when the weather's warm you can eat outside on the beautiful campo. ⊠ *Campo San Giacomo dell'Orio, Santa Croce 1503* ☎ *041/5240222* ▭ *No credit cards* ☉ *Closed Sun.* Ⓥ *San Stae.*

WHERE TO STAY

Most of Venice's hotels are in renovated palaces, but space is at a premium—and comes for a price—with all Venice lodging. The most exclusive hotels are indeed palatial, although even they may have some small, dowdy rooms. In lower-price categories rooms may be cramped, and not all hotels have lounge areas. Because of preservation laws, some hotels are not allowed to have elevators. In summer you might suffer the heat but unless specified otherwise, all hotels listed here have air-conditioning. Although the city has no cars, it does have boats plying the canals and pedestrians chattering in the streets, even late at night, so ask for a quiet room if noise bothers you. In summer don't leave your room lights on at night *and* your window wide open: mosquitoes can descend en masse. If you find that these creatures are a problem, ask at your hotel's desk for a Vape, a plug-in antimosquito device.

It is *essential* to know how to get to your hotel when you arrive, as transport can range from arriving in a very expensive water taxi or gondola to wandering alleys and side streets—luggage in hand—with relapses of déjà vu. Many hotels accept reservations online; the handy Web site ⊕ www.veniceinfo.it offers free information (with photographs) about most hotels in town. It's advisable to book well in advance. If you don't have reservations, try **Venezia Sì** (☎ 39/0415222264 from abroad, 199/173309 from Italy, Mon.–Sat. 9 AM–11 PM ☎ 041/5221242 ⊕ www.veneziasi.it), which offers a free reservation service over the phone. It's the public relations arm of **AVA** (Venetian Hoteliers Association) and has booths where you can make same-day reservations at **Piazzale Roma** (☎ 041/5231397 ⊗ Daily 9 AM–10 PM), **Santa Lucia train station** (☎ 041/715288 or 041/715016 ⊗ Daily 8 AM–9 PM), and **Marco Polo Airport** (☎ 041/5415133 ⊗ Daily 9 AM–10 PM).

Prices

Venetian hotels cater to all tastes and come in all price ranges. Rates are about 20% higher than in Rome and Milan, but can be reduced by as much as half off-season (November–March, excluding Christmas and Carnevale, and also to some degree in August).

	WHAT IT COSTS In euros				
	$$$$	$$$	$$	$	¢
FOR 2 PEOPLE	over €290	€210–€290	€140–€210	€80–€140	under €80

Prices are for two people in a standard double room in high season.

Cannaregio

★ **$$$–$$$$** 🖼 **Hotel Antico Doge.** The delightful palazzo that was once home to Doge Marino Falier has been completely modernized in elegant Venetian style, with a wealth of textiles and some fine original furnishings. Some rooms have *baldacchini* (canopied beds) and views; all have fabric walls and hardwood floors. The location is only minutes away from San Marco and the Rialto Bridge. An ample buffet breakfast is served in a room with a frescoed ceiling and a Murano chandelier. ✉ *Campo SS. Apostoli, Cannaregio 5643, 30131* ☎ *041/2411570* ☎ *041/2443660* ⊕ *www.anticodoge.com* ➘ *20 rooms, 1 suite* ♨ *In-room safes, minibars, cable TV, in-room data ports, bar* ⊟ *AE, DC, MC, V* ⊗ *Closed 3 wks in Jan.* ⦿⦙ *BP* Ⓥ *Ca' d'Oro.*

$$$–$$$$ 🖼 **Palazzo Abadessa.** At this palace dating to the late 16th century, you sense the passion for precious materials and luxury that's part of Venice's heritage. You ascend a majestic staircase to enter rooms decorated with antique furniture, frescoed ceilings, original stuccoes, paintings, and silk fabrics. In summer breakfast is served in the garden. ✉ *Calle Priuli off Strada Nova Cannaregio 4011, 30131* ☎ *041/2413784* ☎ *041/5212236* ⊕ *www.abadessa.com* ➘ *6 rooms, 7 suites* ♨ *Cable TV, minibars, in-room safes, Wi-Fi, laundry, dry cleaning* ⊟ *DC, MC, V* ⦿⦙*BP* Ⓥ*Ca' d'Oro.*

★ **$$** 🖼 **Ca' Gottardi.** Ca' Gottardi is one of a new generation of small hotels that dusts off traditional Venetian style and mixes in some contemporary design. The entrance, on the second floor of a Renaissance palace, is done in white marble and glass, making a graceful contrast to the Murano chandeliers and wall brocades of the guest rooms. Bathrooms are large and modern, and a rich breakfast is served in a salon that's pleasantly full of light. Location is another plus: it's just off the Grand Canal, near the Ca' d'Oro and across the canal from the Rialto markets. ⊠ *Strada Nova, Cannaregio 2283, 30121* ☎ *041/2759333* 🖷 *041/2759421* ⊕ *www. cagottardi.com* ⇋ *10 rooms, 1 suite* ⚲ *Minibars, in-room data ports, cable TV, Internet, bar, babysitting* ▤ *DC, MC, V* ⏐◎⏐ *BP* Ⓥ *Ca' d'Oro.*

$ ⊡ **Bernardi Semenzato.** This is a particularly inviting little place just off Strada Nova and near the gondola ferry to the Rialto market. Some rooms have exposed ceiling beams, and some have rooftop or garden views. Practical pluses include in-room coffee- and tea-making facilities. All rooms are very basic, but those in the nearby *dipendenza* (annex) are larger with newer amenities. ⊠ *Calle dell'Oca, Cannaregio 4366, 30121* ☎ *041/ 5211052* 🖷 *041/5222424* ⊕ *www.hotelbernardi.com* ⇋ *24 rooms, 20 with bath* ⚲ *In-room safes, cable TV, Internet, some pets allowed, no-smoking rooms* ▤ *AE, DC, MC, V* ⊗ *Closed Jan.* ⏐◎⏐ *BP* Ⓥ *Ca' d'Oro.*

$ ⊡ **Ca' San Marcuola.** Opened in 2002 in a busy area of shops, trattorias, and wine bars frequented by Venetians and tourists alike, this family-owned hotel stands out for its relaxed and familiar atmosphere. The comfortable rooms, all full of light and with spacious bathrooms, are furnished in a quiet Venetian mode with delicate pastel colors. An elevator that provides access to all floors and a very convenient location close to a water-bus stop on the Grand Canal make this a good choice for those with limited mobility. ⊠ *Campo San Marcuola, Cannaregio 1763, 30121* ☎ *041/716048* 🖷 *041/2759217* ⊕ *www.casanmarcuola. com* ⇋ *14 rooms* ⚲ *In-room safes, minibars, in-room data ports, cable TV, bar, Internet, concierge* ▤ *AE, DC, MC, V* ⊗ *Closed 4 wks in Dec. and Jan.* ⏐◎⏐ *BP* Ⓥ *San Marcuola.*

Castello

$$$$ ⊡ **Danieli.** You'll feel like a doge in Venice's largest luxury hotel, a complex of newer buildings and a 14th-century palazzo. Sumptuous Venetian decor prevails from the moment you set foot in the soaring atrium with its sweeping staircase. Long favored by world leaders and movie stars, Danieli is predictably expensive and very elegant. The rooftop terrace restaurant has a heavenly view but unexceptional food. May through October, you have access to the pool, tennis courts, and beach of the Hotel Excelsior on the Lido via a private (free) launch running on the hour. ⊠ *Riva degli Schiavoni, Castello 4196, 30122* ☎ *041/ 5226480, 041/2961222 reservations in English* 🖷 *041/5200208* ⊕ *www. starwoodhotels.com/danieli* ⇋ *221 rooms, 12 suites* ⚲ *Restaurant, room service, in-room safes, minibars, cable TV, in-room data ports, bar, babysitting, dry cleaning, laundry service, concierge, Internet, business services, meeting rooms, some pets allowed, no-smoking rooms* ▤ *AE, DC, MC, V* ⏐◎⏐ *EP* Ⓥ *San Zaccaria.*

$$$$ ⊡ **Hotel Londra Palace.** A wall of windows overlooking the lagoon and the island of San Giorgio makes this the hotel of choice for soaking up that extraordinary lagoon view—sweeping all the way from the Salute to the Lido. The downstairs restaurant is all glass, light, and water views,

and 34 rooms offer the same spectacle. The view must have been pleas-.ing to Tchaikovsky, who wrote his 4th Symphony here in 1877. Neo-classical public rooms, with splashes of blue-and-green glass suggesting the sea, play nicely off guest rooms, which have fine fabric, damask drapes, Biedermeier furniture, and Venetian glass. The staff is top-notch, as are the restaurant and the bar. ⊠ *Riva degli Schiavoni, Castello 4171, 30122* ☎ *041/5200533* 🖷 *041/5225032* ⊕ *www.hotelondra.it* ✒ *36 rooms, 17 suites* ⚘ *Restaurant, room service, in-room fax, in-room safes, minibars, cable TV, in-room data ports, Wi-Fi, piano bar, wine bar, babysitting, dry cleaning, laundry service, concierge, Internet, business services, meeting room* ☰ *AE, DC, MC, V* ⵏⵓⵍ *BP* Ⓥ *San Zaccaria.*

$$$$ 🏨 **Metropole.** Eccentrics, eclectics, and fans of Antonio Vivaldi (who taught music here) love the Metropole, a labyrinth of unusual spaces furnished with antiques and jammed with cabinets displaying some very unusual collections indeed. The owner, a lifelong collector of odd objects, displays enough antiques to fill a dealer's shop—some of which furnish the beautifully appointed rooms. The best rooms here are up in the roof—two with spacious roof-top terraces—but only six of the standard double rooms offer lagoon views. The restaurant receives high accolades. ⊠ *Riva degli Schiavoni, Castello 4149, 30122* ☎ *041/5205044* 🖷 *041/ 5223679* ⊕ *www.hotelmetropole.com* ✒ *43 rooms, 26 suites* ⚘ *Restaurant, room service, in-room safes, minibars, cable TV, in-room data ports, bar, babysitting, dry cleaning, laundry service, concierge, meeting room, some pets allowed* ☰ *AE, DC, MC, V* ⵏⵓⵍ Ⓥ *San Zaccaria.*

$$$$ 🏨 **Palazzo Contarini della Porta di Ferro.** Formerly the residence of the Contarinis, one of the most powerful families of Venice, this late-14th-century palace has been a hotel since 2001. The building's aristocratic past shows in the elegant inner courtyard with a majestic marble staircase. All differently furnished, the spacious, light-filled rooms have high wood-beamed ceilings, while the apartments include a kitchen, dining room, and open mezzanine. The large Torcello Suite also has a wooden roof terrace from which you can take in a spectacular view of the city. On the *piano nobile* (main floor) is a large, well-appointed hall overlooking the garden; private dinners, meetings, and small conferences are sometimes held here. In sunny weather breakfast is served in the small garden. The hotel has an elevator and a private dock for boats. ⊠ *Salizzada S. Giustina, Castello 2926, 30122* ☎ *041/2770991* 🖷 *041/ 2777021* ⊕ *www.palazzocontarini.com* ✒ *9 apartments* ⚘ *In-room safes, minibars, cable TV, in-room data ports, room service, babysitting, dry cleaning, Internet, concierge, some pets allowed* ☰ *AE, MC, V* ⵏⵓⵍ *BP.*

$$–$$$ 🏨 **Ca' Formenta.** You're in residential rather than tourist Venice here, but the front rooms still have a wonderful lagoon view. Dating from the 15th century, the simple building underwent a complete makeover before opening in 2003 as a hotel with high-quality services, an elevator, and a canal-side entrance for guests arriving by water taxi. The 15-minute stroll along the waterfront between Piazzo San Marco and this friendly gem of a hotel is through a genuinely "local" part of the city, with plenty of cafés and restaurants. One of the rear rooms has direct access to a pleasant rooftop terrace with tables. ⊠ *Via Garibaldi, Castello 1650, 30122* ☎ *041/5285494* 🖷 *041/5204633* ⊕ *www.hotelcaformenta.it* ✒ *14 rooms* ⚘ *In-room safes, minibars, cable TV, in-room data ports,* *laundry service, some pets allowed* ⊟ *AE, DC, MC, V* |◉| *BP* Ⓥ *Arsenale/Giardini.*

$ 🏨 **Santa Maria della Pietà.** There's more space—both public and private—in this *casa per ferie* (vacation house) than in many four-star hotels in Venice. It occupies two historic palaces and opened as a hotel in 1999. Completely restored with Venetian terrazzo floors throughout, it has big windows and a huge rooftop terrace with a coffee shop, a bar, and unobstructed lagoon views. On top of all this, it is excellently situated—just 100 yards from the main waterfront and about 10 minutes' walk from St. Mark's—meaning you'll have to book early to stay here. The spartan rooms have only beds and wardrobes, but the shared bathrooms are plentiful, spacious, and scrupulously clean. Some family rooms with up to six beds are available. ⊠ *Calle della Pietà, Castello 3701, 30122* ☎ *041/2443639* 🖷 *041/2411561* 🛏 *15 rooms* ⚍ *Coffee shop, bar, lounge; no room phones, no room TVs* ⊟ *No credit cards* |◉| *BP* Ⓥ *San Zaccaria/Arsenale.*

Dorsoduro

$$$$ 🏨 **Ca' Maria Adele.** Venice's most elegant small hotel is a mix of classic style—terrazzo floors, dramatic Murano chandeliers, antique furnishings—and touches of modern design, found in the African-wood reception area and breakfast room. Five "concept rooms" take on themes from Venetian history; the Doge's Room is draped in deep red brocades, while the Oriental Room is inspired by the travels of Marco Polo. Ca' Maria Adele's location is a quiet spot near the church of Santa Maria della Salute. ⊠ *Campo Santa Maria della Salute, Dorsoduro 111, 30123* ☎ *041/5203078* 🖷 *041/5289013* ⊕ *www.camariaadele.it* 🛏 *12 rooms, 2 suites* ⚍ *Bar, room service, cable TV, in-room data ports, in-room safes, minibars, babysitting, laundry service, dry cleaning, some pets allowed* ⊟ *AE, DC, MC, V* |◉| *BP* Ⓥ *Salute.*

FodorsChoice
★

$$$$ 🏨 **Ca' Pisani.** Here's a breath of fresh air: a Venetian hotel with no brocades and chandeliers to be found. Instead there's a tasteful mix of modern design and well-chosen antique pieces. The entrance hall has marble floors and an interesting play of colors and lights; the rooms contain original art deco pieces from the 1930s and '40s (every bed is different). The no-smoking wine bar La Rivista serves light meals all day, and upstairs are a Turkish bath and a wooden rooftop terrace where you can take the sun. ⊠ *Rio Terà Antonio Foscarini, Dorsoduro 979/a, 30123* ☎ *041/2401411* 🖷 *041/2771061* ⊕ *www.capisanihotel.it* 🛏 *25 rooms, 4 suites* ⚍ *Restaurant, room service, in-room safes, minibars, cable TV with movies, in-room data ports, Turkish bath, wine bar, dry cleaning, laundry service, concierge, Internet, some pets allowed, no-smoking floor* ⊟ *AE, DC, MC, V* |◉| *BP* Ⓥ *Accademia.*

$$$-$$$$ 🏨 **American–Dinesen.** This quiet, family-run hotel has a yellow stucco facade typical of Venetian houses. A hall decorated with reproduction antiques and Oriental rugs leads to a breakfast room reminiscent of a theater foyer, with red velvet chairs and gilt wall lamps. Rooms are spacious and tastefully furnished in sage-green and delicate pink fabrics, with lacquered Venetian-style furniture throughout. Some front rooms have terraces with canal views. A 2002 overhaul has made the place sparkle, though the four-story building still has no elevator. ⊠ *San Vio, Dorso-*

duro 628, 30123 ☎041/5204733 🖷041/5204048 ⊕*www.hotelamerican. com* 🛏 *28 rooms, 2 suites* ⚹ *In-room safes, minibars, cable TV, in-room data ports, babysitting, Internet, no-smoking rooms, laundry service, some pets allowed* ▤ *AE, MC, V* ⦿| *BP* ▾ *Accademia/Salute.*

$$–$$$ 🏠 **Hotel Pausania.** From the moment you ascend the grand staircase rising above the fountain of this 14th-century palazzo, you sense the combination of good taste and modern comforts that characterizes Hotel Pausania. Light-colored rooms are spacious, with comfortable furniture and carpets strewn with rugs. Some rooms face the small canal (which can become a bit noisy early in the morning) in front of the hotel, whereas others look out over the large garden courtyard. ⊠ *Fondamenta Gherardini, Dorsoduro 2824, 30123* ☎ *041/5222083* 🖷 *041/5222989* ⊕ *www.hotelpausania.it* 🛏 *26 rooms* ⚹ *Minibars, cable TV, Internet, bar, babysitting, dry cleaning, concierge, some pets allowed* ▤ *AE, MC, V* ⦿| *BP* ▾ *Ca' Rezzonico.*

$$–$$$
Fodor's Choice
★
🏠 **Pensione Accademia Villa Maravege.** A secret garden awaits just beyond an iron gate, complete with a mini Palladian-style villa, flower beds, stone cupids, and verdant trees—all rarities in Venice. Aptly nicknamed "Villa of the Wonders," this patrician retreat once served as the Russian embassy and was the residence of Katharine Hepburn in the movie *Summertime.* Conservative rooms are outfitted with Venetian-style antiques and fine tapestry. The location is on a promontory where two side canals converge with the Grand Canal, which can be seen from the garden. Book well in advance. ⊠ *Fondamenta Bollani, Dorsoduro 1058, 30123* ☎ *041/5210188* 🖷 *041/5239152* ⊕ *www.pensioneaccademia. it* 🛏 *27 rooms* ⚹ *In-room safes, minibars, cable TV, bar, babysitting, dry cleaning, laundry service* ▤ *AE, DC, MC, V* ⦿| *BP* ▾ *Accademia.*

$$ 🏠 **Agli Alboretti.** The Alboretti is one of the many hotels clustered at the foot of the Ponte dell'Accademia. Its unpretentious, rather small rooms are blessed with plenty of light. Their nautical decor, with original pieces taken from old ships' cabins, goes well with the cries of seagulls living along the nearby Giudecca Canal. In warm weather, breakfast is served in an inner courtyard under a rose bower and a small terrace with potted plants is open. The elevator is a welcome convenience for weary travelers. ⊠ *Rio Terà Foscarini, Dorsoduro 884, 30123* ☎041/5230058 🖷 *041/5210158* ⊕ *www.aglialboretti.com* 🛏 *23 rooms* ⚹ *Restaurant, cable TV, bar, Wi-Fi, laundry service, concierge, some pets allowed, no-smoking rooms* ▤ *AE, MC, V* ⦿| *BP* ▾ *Accademia.*

★ $–$$ 🏠 **La Calcina.** The Calcina sits in an enviable position along the sunny Zattere, with front rooms offering views across the wide Giudecca Canal. You can sunbathe on the *altana* (wooden roof terrace) or enjoy an afternoon tea in one of the reading corners of the lounge with flickering candlelight and barely perceptible classical music. A stone staircase (no elevator) leads to the rooms upstairs, which have parquet floors, original art deco furniture and lamps, and firm beds. Besides full meals at lunch and dinner, the Piscina bar and restaurant offers drinks and freshly made snacks all day in the elegant dining room or on the wooden waterside terrace out front. ⊠ *Zattere, Dorsoduro 780, 30123* ☎ *041/5206466* 🖷 *041/5227045* ⊕ *www.lacalcina.com* 🛏 *27 rooms, 26 with bath; 5 suites* Restaurant, in-room safes, minibars, cable TV ▤ AE, DC, MC, V ⦿| BP ▾ Zattere.

1

Giudecca

$$$$ ⊞ **Cipriani.** It's impossible to feel stressed in this oasis of stunning rooms and suites, some with garden patios. The hotel launch whisks you to Giudecca from San Marco and back at any hour; those dining at the exceptional restaurants can use it as well. Rooms of extraordinary luxury are available both in the main building and in the adjoining 16th-century-style annexes, Palazzo Vendramin and Palazzetto, which offers view across to Piazza San Marco. Prices are high even by Venetian standards, but this is the only place in town with such extensive facilities and services, from an Olympic-size pool and tennis courts to cooking courses, a beauty-and-wellness center, fitness programs, and even a vineyard. ⊠ *Giudecca 10, 30133* ☎ *041/5207744* 🖷 *041/5207745* ⊕ *www.hotelcipriani.it* 🛏 *46 rooms, 58 suites* ⌂ *4 restaurants, room service, in-room safes, minibars, cable TV, Wi-Fi, Internet, tennis court, saltwater pool, health club, massage, sauna, spa, bar, babysitting, dry cleaning, laundry service, concierge, meeting room* ☰ *AE, DC, MC, V* ☾ *Main hotel closed Nov.–Mar.; Palazzo Vendramin and Palazzetto closed 4 wks in Jan. and Feb.* ❘⊙❘ *BP* Ⓥ *Zitelle.*

Lagoon

$$$$ ⊞ **San Clemente Palace.** If you prefer wide-open spaces to the intimacy of Venice, this is your hotel. It occupies an entire island, about 15 minutes from Piazza San Marco by (free) shuttle launch, with acres of parkland, a swimming pool, tennis courts, a wellness center, and three restaurants. The 19th-century buildings are on the site of a 12th-century monastery, of which only the chapel remains. They form a large quadrangle and contain spacious, modern rooms. The view back to Venice with the Dolomites behind on a clear day is stunning. This hotel, opened in 2003, offers all the five-star comforts: it even has three holes of golf. ⊠ *Isola di San Clemente 1, San Marco, 30124* ☎ *041/2445001* 🖷 *041/2445800* ⊕ *www.sanclemente.thi.it* 🛏 *107 rooms, 96 suites* ⌂ *3 restaurants, coffee shop, in-room safes, minibars, cable TV, in-room data ports, 3-hole golf course, 2 tennis courts, pool, exercise equipment, health club, hair salon, hot tub, massage, sauna, spa, bars, shop, laundry service, convention center, meeting rooms, some pets allowed, no-smoking rooms* ☰ *AE, DC, MC, V* ❘⊙❘ *BP.*

San Marco

$$$$ ⊞ **Gritti Palace.** Queen Elizabeth, Greta Garbo, and Winston Churchill all made this their Venetian address. The feeling of being in an aristocratic private home pervades this legendary hotel replete with fresh flowers, fine antiques, sumptuous appointments, and old-style service. The dining terrace on the Grand Canal is best enjoyed in the evening, when the boat traffic dies down. May through October you have access to the pool, tennis courts, and beach of the Hotel Excelsior on the Lido via a private (free) launch. ⊠ *Campo Santa Maria del Giglio, San Marco 2467, 30124* ☎ *041/794611* 🖷 *041/5200942* ⊕ *www.starwoodhotels.com/grittipalace* 🛏 *84 rooms, 6 suites* ⌂ *Restaurant,* *room service, in-room safes, minibars, cable TV with movies, in-room data ports, bar, babysitting, dry cleaning, laundry service, concierge, Internet, Wi-Fi, business services, meeting rooms, some pets allowed, no-smoking rooms* ▤ *AE, DC, MC, V* ⦿ *BP* ☑ *Giglio.*

$$$$ ⌂ **Il Palazzo at the Bauer.** Il Palazzo, under the same management as the larger Bauer Hotel, is the ultimate word in luxury. Bevilacqua and Rubelli fabrics cover the walls, and no two rooms are decorated the same. What they have in common, however, are high ceilings, Murano glass, marble bathrooms, and damask drapes. Many have sweeping views. Breakfast is served on Venice's highest terrace, appropriately named Il Settimo Cielo (Seventh Heaven). The outdoor hot tub, also on the 7th floor, offers views of La Serenissima that won't quit. ✉ *Campo San Moisè, San Marco 1413/d, 30124* ☎ *041/5207022* 🖷 *041/5207557* ⊕ *www.ilpalazzovenezia.com* ⇆ *36 rooms, 40 suites* ⦿ *Restaurant, room service, in-room fax, in-room safes, some in-room hot tubs, minibars, cable TV with movies, in-room data ports, golf privileges, health club, outdoor hot tub, massage, sauna, Turkish bath, dock, bar, babysitting, dry cleaning, laundry service, concierge, Wi-Fi, some pets allowed, no-smoking rooms* ▤ *AE, DC, MC, V* ⦿ *EP* ☑ *Vallaresso.*

$$$ ⌂ **Locanda Orseolo.** This small hotel just behind Piazza San Marco has a friendly staff and comfortable, well-appointed rooms. Classic Venetian design is given a Carnevale theme, with each room dedicated to a traditional mask. The friendly atmosphere pervades at breakfast, where it's common to get engrossed in conversation with the other guests. ✉ *Corte Zorzi (off Campo San Gallo), San Marco 1083, 30124* ☎ *041/5204827* 🖷 *041/5235586* ⊕ *www.locandaorseolo.com* ⇆ *15 rooms* ⦿ *In-room safes, minibars, cable TV, in-room data ports, Wi-Fi, babysitting, dry cleaning, some pets allowed* ▤ *AE, DC, MC, V* ⦿ *BP* ☑ *Vallaresso.*

★ $$$ ⌂ **San Zulian.** A minimalist entrance hall leads to rooms that are a refined variation on the Venetian theme, with lacquered 18th-century-style furniture and parquet floors. Room 304 is on two levels and has its own delightful covered veranda. Two ground-floor rooms have bathrooms equipped for people with disabilities. The handy location near San Marco and the Rialto and the top-notch staff make a stay here eminently enjoyable. ✉ *Campo della Guerra, San Marco 534/535, 30124* ☎ *041/5225872 or 041/5226598* 🖷 *041/5232265* ⊕ *www.hotelsanzulian.com* ⇆ *22 rooms* ⦿ *In-room safes, minibars, cable TV, some pets allowed* ▤ *AE, DC, MC, V* ⦿ *BP* ☑ *Vallaresso/San Zaccaria.*

$$–$$$ ⌂ **Novecento.** In a quiet street just a 10-minute walk from St. Mark's Square is this small family-run hotel, opened in 2002. Inspired by the style of Mariano Fortuny, the early-1900s artist and fashion designer, the intimate rooms are a surprisingly elegant mélange of multiethnic and exotic furnishings. The Mediterranean, Indian, and Venetian fabrics, silverware, chandeliers, and furniture create a sensual turn-of-the-20th-century atmosphere. In fine weather breakfast is served in the inner courtyard. ✉ *Calle del Dose (Campo San Maurizio), San Marco 2683/84, 30124* ☎ *041/2413765* 🖷 *041/5212145* ⊕ *www.novecento.biz* ⇆ *9 rooms* ⦿ *In-room safes, minibars, cable TV, in-room data ports,* *bar, dry cleaning, laundry service, Wi-Fi* ⊟ *AE, DC, MC, V* ⏀⏀ *BP* ☑ *Santa Maria del Giglio.*

$ ⊞ **Albergo San Samuele.** Near the Grand Canal and Palazzo Grassi, this friendly hotel has clean, sunny rooms in surprisingly good shape for the price. Five of the bathrooms are relatively new, with white-and-gray-blue tiles, and the walls are painted in crisp, pleasant shades of pale pink or blue. Curtains and bedspreads are made from antique-looking fabrics, and although the furniture is of the boxy modern kind, the owners are gradually adding more-interesting-looking pieces. ⊠ *Salizzada San Samuele, San Marco 3358, 30124* ☎ *041/5228045* ⤳ *10 rooms, 7 with bath* ⟰ *Fans, some pets allowed, no-smoking rooms; no a/c, no room TVs* ⊟ *No credit cards* ⏀⏀ *EP* ☑ *San Samuele.*

San Polo

$$–$$$$ ⊞ **Oltre il Giardino—Casaifrari.** It's easy to overlook (and a challenge to find) this quiet house, sheltered by a brick wall near the Frari church. Especially in high season, the six-room hotel with a pleasant garden is an oasis of peace. The prevalent white-and-pastel color scheme and elegant, understated decor contribute to the relaxed environment. The house was once the residence of Alma Mahler, widow of composer Gustav Mahler and a fascinating woman in her own right; today it still conveys her style and charm. ⊠ *San Polo 2542, 30125* ☎ *041/2750015* ⊞ *041/795452* ⊕ *www.oltreilgiardino-venezia.com* ⤳ *6 rooms* ⟰ *Cable TV, minibars, safes, in-room data ports, babysitting* ⊟ *DC, MC, V* ⏀⏀ *BP* ☑ *San Tomà.*

$$$ ⊞ **Sturion.** At the end of the 13th century this building housed foreign merchants selling their wares at the Rialto, and the painter Vittore Carpaccio depicted it in his 1494 *Miracle of the Cross* (on view at the Accademia). Now it's decorated in 18th-century Venetian style and run with great care by a Venetian family. Rooms (two with views of the Grand Canal) are done in red-and-gold brocade; there's also a small but inviting breakfast room. Two rooms comfortably sleep four and are perfect for families. All rooms have coffee- and tea-making facilities, an uncommon feature for Italy. Be warned that the stairs are steep here (the hotel is on the 4th and 5th floors), and there's no elevator. ⊠ *Calle del Sturion, San Polo 679, 30125* ☎ *041/5236243* ⊞ *041/5228378* ⊕ *www. locandasturion.com* ⤳ *11 rooms* ⟰ *In-room safes, minibars, Internet, some pets allowed, no-smoking rooms* ⊟ *MC, V* ⏀⏀ *BP* ☑ *San Silvestro/Rialto.*

$$–$$$ ⊞ **Ca' Angeli.** The former residence of a Venetian architect, located on the top floor of a palace along the Grand Canal, has been transformed by his heirs into a small, elegant hotel. It retains the classic style of its former owner—most of the furniture was his, including an 18th-century briar-wood bureau, an original icon, and 18th- and 19th-century art. A rich breakfast, including select cheese and ham from local producers, is served in a room overlooking the Grand Canal. ⊠ *Calle del Tragheto della Madoneta 1434, 30125, San Polo* ☎ *041/5232480* ⊞ *041/2417077* ⊕ *www.caangeli.net* ⤳ *7 rooms* ⟰ *In-room safes, minibars, in-room data ports, babysitting* ⊟ *DC, MC, V* ⏀⏀ *BP* ☑ *San Silvestro.*

NIGHTLIFE & THE ARTS

The Arts

A Guest in Venice, a monthly bilingual booklet free at most hotels, is your most accessible, up-to-date guide to Venice happenings. It also includes information about pharmacies, vaporetto and bus lines, and the main trains and flights. You can visit their Web site, ⊕ www.aguestinvenice.com, for a preview of musical, artistic, and sporting events. *Venezia News,* available at newsstands, has similar information but also includes in-depth articles about noteworthy events. The tourist office publishes *Leo* and *Bussola,* bimonthly brochures in Italian and English listing events and updated museum hours. *Venezia da Vivere* is a seasonal guide listing nightspots and live music. Several Venice Web sites allow you to scan the cultural horizon before you arrive; try ⊕ www.ombra.net (which has a fantastic map function to find any address in Venice), ⊕ www.veniceonline.it, and ⊕ www.venicebanana.com. Last but not least, don't ignore the posters you see everywhere in the streets. They're often the most up-to-date information you can find.

Carnevale

The first historical evidence of Carnevale (Carnival) in Venice dates from 1097, and for centuries the city marked the days preceding *quaresima* (Lent, the 40 days of abstinence leading up to Palm Sunday) with abundant feasting and wild celebrations. The word *carnival* is derived from the words for meat (*carne*) and to remove (*levare*), as eating meat was prohibited during Lent. Venice earned its international reputation as the "city of Carnevale" in the 18th century, when partying would begin right after Epiphany (January 6) and the city seemed to be one continuous decadent masquerade. With the republic's fall in 1797, the city lost a great deal of its vitality, and the tradition of Carnevale celebrations was abandoned.

Carnevale was revived in the 1970s when residents began taking to the calli and campi in their own impromptu celebrations. It didn't take long for the tourist industry to embrace the revival as a means to stimulate business during low season. The efforts were successful. Each year over the 10- to 12-day Carnevale period (ending on the Tuesday before Ash Wednesday) more than a half million people attend concerts, theater and street performances, masquerade balls, historical processions, fashion shows, and contests. **A Guest in Venice** (⊕ www.aguestinvenice.com) gives free advertising to public and private event festivities and is therefore one of the most complete Carnevale guides. For general Carnevale information, contact **Consorzio Comitato per il Carnevale di Venezia** (✉ Santa Croce 1714, 30135 ☎ 041/717065, 041/2510811 during Carnevale 🖷 041/5200410 ⊕ www.carnevale.venezia.it). The **Tourist Office** (☎ 041/5298711) has detailed information about daily events.

If you're not planning on joining in the revelry, you'd be wise to choose another time to visit Venice. Enormous crowds clog the streets (which become one-way, with police directing foot traffic), bridges are designated "no-stopping" zones to avoid gridlock, and prices absolutely skyrocket.

The view from Ravello, high above the Amalfi Coast.

(top) Young priests stroll along Venice's Grand Canal. *(bottom)* The Regata Storica, a race of traditional Venetian boats, held the first weekend in September. *(opposite page, top)* Fashion is a passion in Milan. *(opposite page, bottom)* The Piazza del Duomo, in the heart of Florence.

(top) The peaks of the Dolomites. *(bottom)* Riomaggiore, one of five towns that make up the Italian Riviera's Cinque Terre.

(top) Assisi, one of Umbria's definitive hill towns. *(bottom)* The café scene outside Verona's ancient arena.

(top left) Rome's Bocca della Verità. *(top right)* Italy's national game, played in front of the Palazzo Reale in Naples. *(bottom)* The Colosseo, Rome. *(opposite page, top)* Beachgoers on the Golfo di Orosei, Sardinia. *(opposite page, bottom)* Rome's Vatican Museums.

Greek ruins at Selinunte, Sicily.

Festivals

The **Biennale** (⊕ www.labiennale.org) cultural institution organizes events year-round, including the Venice Film Festival, which begins the last week of August. The Biennale international exhibition of contemporary art is held in odd-numbered years, usually from mid-June to early November, at the Giardini della Biennale, and in the impressive Arsenale.

The third weekend of July, the **Festa del Redentore** (Feast of the Redeemer) commemorates the end of a 16th-century plague that killed about 47,000 city residents. Just as doges have done annually for centuries, you too can make a pilgrimage across the temporary bridge connecting the Zattere to the Giudecca. Venetians take to the water to watch fireworks at midnight, but if you can't find a boat, the Giudecca is the best place to be. Young people traditionally greet sunrise on the Lido beach while their elders attend church.

Music

Although there are occasional jazz and Italian pop concerts in clubs around town, the vast majority of music you'll hear is classical, with Venice's famed composer, Vivaldi, frequently featured. A number of churches and palazzi regularly host concerts, as do the Ca' Rezzonico and Querini-Stampalia museums. You'll find these events listed in publications such as *A Guest in Venice*; also try asking the tourist information office or your concierge. The **Vela Call Center** (☎ 041/2424 ⊗ Daily 8–8) has information about musical events, and you can buy tickets at Vela sales offices in Piazzale Roma, Ferrovia, and Calle dei Fuseri (a 10-minute walk from San Marco). (When busy, the Vela Call Center number doesn't give a signal, but instead is silent.)

The travel agency **Kele & Teo** (⊠ Ponte dei Bareteri, San Marco 4930 ☎ 041/5208722) has tickets for a number of venues and is conveniently located midway between Rialto and San Marco.

Opera

Teatro La Fenice (⊠ Campo San Fantin, San Marco ☎ 041/786511 ⊕ www.teatrolafenice.it), one of Italy's oldest opera houses, has witnessed many memorable premieres, including the 1853 first-night flop of Verdi's *La Traviata*. It's also had its share of disasters, the most recent being a terrible fire, deliberately set in January 1996. It was completely and luxuriously restored, and reopened to great fanfare in 2004. Visit the Fenice Web site for a schedule of performances and to buy tickets.

Nightlife

Piazza San Marco is a popular meeting place in nice weather, when the cafés stay open late and all seem to be competing to offer the best live music. The younger crowd, Venetians and visitors alike, tends to gravitate toward the area around Rialto Bridge, with Campi San Bartolomeo and San Luca on one side and Campo Rialto Nuovo on the other. Especially popular with university students are the bars along Cannaregio's Fondamenta della Misericordia and around Campo Santa Margarita and San Pantalon. Pick up a booklet of *2Night* or visit their Web site ⊕ www.2night.it for nightlife listings and reviews.

Bars

L'Olandese Volante (⊠ Campo San Lio near Rialto ☎ 041/5289349) is a popular hangout for many young Venetians. Nothing special by day, **Bar Torino** (⊠ Campo San Lucaz ☎ 041/5223914) is one of Venice's liveliest nightspots, open late and spilling out onto the campo in summer. **Bácaro Jazz** (⊠ Across from Rialto Post Office ☎ 041/5285249) has music (not usually live) and meals until 2 AM, and its gregarious staff is unlikely to let you feel lonely. The **Martini Scala Club** (⊠ Campo San Fantin, San Marco 1983 ☎ 041/5224121), the Antico Martini restaurant's elegant bar, has live music from 10 PM to 3:30 AM. Full meals are served until 2 AM.

One of the newest and hippest bars for the late-night chill-out crowd, **Centrale** (⊠ Piscina Frezzeria, San Marco 1659/B ☎ 041/2960664) is in a former movie theater—and the crowd does look more Hollywood than Venice. Excellent mojitos and other mixed drinks, black-leather couches, and dim lighting strike a loungey note, and the DJ keeps the beats cool.

Campo Santa Margarita is a student hangout all day and late into the night. Try **Orange** (⊠ Campo Santa Margarita, Dorsoduro 3054/a ☎ 041/5234740) for piadine sandwiches, drinks, and soccer games on a massive screen. The bohemian **Il Caffè** (⊠ Campo Santa Margarita, Dorsoduro 2963 ☎ 041/5287998), also known as Caffè Rosso for its red exterior, is especially popular in nice weather.

Casinos

The city-run gambling casino in the splendid **Palazzo Vendramin-Calergi** is a classic scene of well-dressed high-rollers playing French roulette, Caribbean poker, chemin de fer, 30–40, and slots. You must be 18 to enter, and men must wear jackets; no tennis shoes allowed. ⊠ *Cannaregio 2040* ☎ *041/5297111* 🎫 *€10 entry includes €10 in chips* ☉ *Slots 2:45 PM–2:30 AM, tables 3:30 PM–2:30 AM* Ⓥ *San Marcuola*.

Mestre's **Ca' Noghera** casino, near the airport, has slots, blackjack, craps, poker, and roulette. Minimum age is 18. There's a free shuttle bus from Piazzale Roma from 4:05 PM until closing. ⊠ *Via Triestina 222, Tessera, Mestre* ☎ *041/5297111* 🎫 *€10 entry includes €10 in chips* ☉ *Slots 11 AM–3:30 AM, tables 3:30 PM–3:30 AM*.

Nightclubs

Dancing and clubbing is a hard find on the Venetian islands, so your best bets are on the *terra firma*. **Magic Bus** (⊠ Via delle Industrie, 118, 2nd Industrial Zone, Marcon ☎ 041/5952151) is an alternative rock club with pop art walls and zebra-stripe floors. It showcases new and established European acts every weekend.

Claiming to be Venice's only "real" disco club, **Casanova** (⊠ Lista di Spagna, Cannaregio 158/a ☎ 041/2750199) undeniably has the largest dance floor. With Internet points, student-night specials, and no cover charge, it attracts mostly foreign students and some young Venetians.

SPORTS

Beaches

Those looking for a cooling break in summer should head for the **Lido** (🔽 S. M. Elisabetta). Large sections of the long, narrow beach are private, renting chairs and umbrellas and offering toilets, showers, and restaurants. If your hotel has no beach rights, you can pay for entry. The free beach areas, with no facilities, are generally crowded unless you head south by bus toward Malamocco and Alberoni.

Running

The most scenic running route (6–7 km [4–4½ mi] long) heads east from Piazza San Marco and skirts the lagoon along the Riva degli Schiavoni to the pinewood of Sant'Elena. You can return by way of the picturesque neighborhood of Castello and the island of San Pietro di Castello. This route can get packed with pedestrians from spring through fall, so if you don't want to run a slalom course, try the Lido beach or the area around the Zattere.

SHOPPING

Updated by
Pamela Santini

Alluring shops abound in Venice. You'll find countless vendors of trademark Venetian wares such as glass and lace; the authenticity of some goods can be suspect, but they're often pleasing to the eye regardless of their place of origin. For more-sophisticated tastes (and deeper pockets), there are jewelers, antiques dealers, and high-fashion boutiques on a par with those in Italy's larger cities but often maintaining a uniquely Venetian flair. There are also some interesting craft and art studios, where you can find high-quality, one-of-a-kind articles, from handmade shoes to decorative lamps and mirrors.

It's always a good idea to mark on your map the location of a shop that interests you; otherwise you may not be able to find it again in the maze of tiny streets. Regular store hours are usually 9–12:30 and 3:30 or 4–7:30; some stores are closed Saturday afternoon or Monday morning. Food shops are open 8–1 and 5–7:30, and are closed Wednesday afternoon and all day Sunday. Many tourist-oriented shops are open all day, every day. Some shops close for both a summer and a winter vacation.

Food Markets

The morning open-air fruit-and-vegetable market at **Rialto** offers animated local color and commerce. On Tuesday through Saturday mornings the **fish market** (adjacent to the Rialto produce market) provides an impressive lesson in ichthyology, with species you've probably never seen before. In the Castello district you'll find a lively food market weekday mornings on **Via Garibaldi.**

Shopping Districts

The **San Marco** area is full of shops and couture boutiques such as Armani, Missoni, Valentino, Fendi, and Versace. **Le Mercerie,** along with the Frezzeria and Calle dei Fabbri, leading from Piazza San Marco, are some of Venice's busiest shopping streets. Other good shopping areas surround Calle del Teatro and Campi San Salvador, Manin, San Fantin, and San Bartolomeo. Less-expensive shops are between the Rialto Bridge and San Polo.

Specialty Stores

Glassware

Glass, most of it made in Murano, is Venice's number one product, and you'll be confronted by mind-boggling displays of traditional and contemporary glassware, much of it kitsch. Take your time and be selective. You will probably find that prices in Venice's shops and the showrooms of Murano's factories are pretty much the same. However, because of competition, shops in Venice with wares from various glassworks may charge slightly less.

Domus (⊠ Fondamenta dei Vetrai, Murano 82 ☎ 041/739215) has a selection of smaller objects and jewelry from the best glassworks.

For chic, contemporary glassware, Carlo Moretti is a good choice; his designs are on display at **L'Isola** (⊠ Campo San Moisè, San Marco 1468 ☎ 041/5231973 ⊕ www.carlomoretti.com). **Marina Barovier** (⊠ Calle delle Botteghe off Campo Santo Stefano, San Marco 3216 ☎ 041/5236748 ⊕ www.barovier.it) has an excellent selection of contemporary collectors' glass.

Go to Michel Paciello's **Paropàmiso** (⊠ Frezzeria, San Marco 1701 ☎ 041/5227120) for stunning Venetian glass beads and traditional jewelry from all over the world. **Pauly** (⊠ Piazza San Marco 73, 77, and 316; Ponte dei Consorzi ☎ 041/5209899 ⊕ www.paulyglassfactory.com) has four centrally located shops with an impressive selection of glassware at better prices than for Murano. **Venini** (⊠ Piazzetta dei Leoncini 314, San Marco ☎ 041/5224045 ⊕ www.venini.com) has been an institution since the 1930s, attracting some of the foremost names in glass design.

Lace & Fabrics

Much of the lace and embroidered linen sold in Venice and on Burano is really made in China or Taiwan. However, at **Il Merletto** (⊠ Sotoportego del Cavalletto, under the Procuratie Vecchie, Piazza San Marco 95 ☎ 041/5208406), you can ask for the authentic, handmade lace kept in the drawers behind the counter. This is the only place in Venice connected with the students of the Scuola del Merletto in Burano, who, officially, do not sell to the public. Hours of operation are daily 10 to 5. A top address for linen is **Jesurum** (⊠ Cannaregio 3219, Fondamenta della Sensa ☎ 041/5242540 ⊕ www.jesurum.it).

Go to **Lorenzo Rubelli** (⊠ Palazzo Corner Spinelli, San Marco 3877 ☎ 041/5284411 ⊕ www.rubelli.it) for the same brocades, damasks, and cut velvets used by the world's most prestigious decorators. **Venetia**

Venetian Masks Revealed

IN THE TIME OF THE REPUBLIC, the mask trade was vibrant—Venetians wore masks all year to go about town incognito. Napoléon suppressed their use, a by-product of his effort to end Carnevale, and when Carnevale was revived in the late 1970s, mask making returned as well. Though many workshops use centuries-old techniques, none has been in business for more than 30 years.

A landmark date in the history of Venetian masks is 1436, when the *mascareri* (mask makers) founded their guild, but masks were popular well before then. Laws regulating their use appeared as early as 1268, intended to prevent wearers from carrying weapons and masked men disguised as women from entering convents to seduce nuns.

In the 18th century, masks started being used by actors playing the traditional roles of the commedia dell'arte. Inexpensive papier-mâché versions of these masks can be found everywhere. The character Arlecchino has the round face and surprised expression, Pantalone is the one with the curved nose and long mustache, and Pulcinella has the protruding nose.

The least-expensive mask is the white Bauta, smooth and plain with a short, pointed nose intended to disguise the wearer's voice; in the 18th century it was commonly accompanied by a black three-cornered hat and a black cloak. The pretty Gnaga, which resembles a cat's face, was used by gay men to "meow" proposals to good-looking boys. The basic Moretta is a black oval with eyeholes. The Medico della Peste (the Plague Doctor) has a beaklike nose and glasses; during the plague of 1630 and 1631, doctors wore masks with herbs inside the nose intended to filter infected air and glasses to protect the eyes.

Studium (✉ Calle Larga XXII Marzo, San Marco 2403 ☎ 041/5229281 ✉ Calle Larga XXII Marzo, San Marco 723 ☎ 041/5229859 ⊕ www. venetiastudium.com) sells silk scarves, bags, and cushion covers, as well as the famous Fortuny lamps.

Lamps

The studio **A Mano** (✉ Rio Terà, San Polo 2616 ☎ 041/715742), near the Frari, is worth hunting down. Alessandro Savadori makes imaginative table, wall, and ceiling lamps that may well cross the boundary from craft into art.

Masks

Guerrino Lovato, proprietor of **Mondonovo** (✉ Rio Terà Canal, Dorsoduro 3063 ☎ 041/5287344 ⊕ www.mondonovomaschere.it) is one of the most respected mask makers in town. He was called on to oversee reconstruction of reliefs and sculptures in Teatro La Fenice after it burned to the ground in 1996.

Shoes

Fine shoes and boots are handmade to order at **Daniela Ghezzo, Segalin a Venezia** (✉ Calle dei Fuseri, San Marco 4365 ☎ 041/5222115), operated by one of the city's two female shoemakers. Ghezzo carries on the tradition established by the renowned Rolando Segalin.

Giovanna Zanella (✉ Calle Carminati, Castello 5641 ☎ 041 5235500) creates custom-made footwear with daring color combinations and unique styles. Her accessories make a statement as well.

VENICE ESSENTIALS

Transportation

BY AIR

Venice's Aeroporto Marco Polo is served by domestic and international flights, including connections from 21 European cities, plus direct flights from Moscow and New York's JFK. In addition, Treviso Airport, some 32 km (20 mi) north of Venice, receives daily arrivals from London's Stansted Airport.

A shuttle bus or 10-minute walk takes you from Marco Polo's terminal to a dock where public and private boats are available to deliver you directly to Venice's historic center. For €10 per person, including bags, Alilaguna operates regularly scheduled service from predawn until nearly midnight. It takes about an hour to reach the landing near Piazza San Marco, stopping at the Lido on the way. A *motoscafo* (water taxi) carries up to four people and four bags to the city center in a sleek, modern powerboat. The base cost is €80, and the trip takes about 25 minutes. Each additional person, bag, and stop costs extra, so it's essential to agree on a fare before boarding.

Blue ATVO buses take 20 minutes to make the nonstop trip from airport to Piazzale Roma; from here you can get a vaporetto to the landing nearest your hotel. The ATVO fare is €3, and tickets are available on the bus when the airport ticket booth (open daily 9 to 7:30) is closed. Orange ACTV local buses (Line 5) leave for Venice at 10 and 40 minutes past every hour (hourly service after 11:10 PM) and take 30 minutes; before boarding, you must buy a €2 ticket at the airport tobacconist-newsstand, open daily 6:30 AM to 9 PM, or from the ATVO/ACTV booth in the arrivals hall on the ground floor. During rush hour, luggage can be a hassle on the local bus. A land taxi from the airport to Piazzale Roma costs about €40.

🛈 Airport Information **Aeroporto Marco Polo** ✉ Tessera, 10 km (6 mi) north of the city on the mainland ☎ 041/2609260 ⊕ www.veniceairport.it.

🛈 Taxis & Shuttles **Alilaguna** ☎ 041/5235775 ⊕ www.alilaguna.it. **ATVO** ☎ 0421/383672 ⊕ www.atvo.it. **Motoscafo** ☎ 041/5222303 airport transfers. **Radio Taxi** ☎ 041/5952080.

BY BOAT & FERRY

BY GONDOLA   It's hard to believe that Venice could get any more beautiful, but as your gondola glides away from the fondamenta, a magical transformation takes place—you've left the huddled masses behind to marvel at the city as visitors have for centuries before you. To some it feels like a Disney ride, and some complain about flotsam, jetsam, and less-than-pleasant odors, but if you insist that your gondolier take you winding through the tiny side canals, you'll get out of the city's main salon and into her intimate chambers, where only private boats can go. San Marco is loaded with gondola stations, but to get off the circuit, and maybe even have a canal to yourself, try the San Tomà or Santa Sofia (near Ca' d'Oro) stations. The price of a 40-minute ride is supposed to be fixed at €75 for up to six passengers, rising to €95 between 7:30 PM and 8 AM, but these are minimums and you may have difficulty finding a gondolier who will work for that unless the city is empty. Bargaining can help, but in any case come to terms on cost and duration before you start, and make it clear that you want to see more than just the Grand Canal.

BY TRAGHETTO Many tourists are unaware of the two-man gondola ferries that cross the Grand Canal at numerous strategic points. At €0.50, they're the cheapest and shortest gondola ride in Venice, and they can save a lot of walking. Look for TRAGHETTO signs and hand your fare to the gondolier when you board.

BY VAPORETTO ACTV water buses serve several routes daily and after 11 PM provide limited service through the night. Some routes cover the length of the Grand Canal, and others circle the city and connect Venice with the lagoon islands. Landing stages are clearly marked with name and line number, but check before boarding to make sure the boat is going in your direction.

Line 1 is the Grand Canal local, calling at every stop and continuing via San Marco to the Lido. The trip takes about 35 minutes from Ferrovia to Vallaresso, San Marco. Circular Line 41 (the odd number indicates it goes counterclockwise) will take you from San Zaccaria to Murano, and Line 42 (clockwise) makes the return trip. Likewise, take Line 42 from San Zaccaria to Giudecca's Redentore, but Line 41 to return. Line 51 (counterclockwise) runs from the station to San Zaccaria via Piazzale Roma, then continues to the Lido. From the Lido, Line 52 circles clockwise, stopping at San Zaccaria, the Zattere, Piazzale Roma, the station, Fondamente Nuove (connect to northern lagoon islands), San Pietro di Castello, and back to the Lido. From San Zaccaria, Line 82 (same number both directions) loops past Giudecca and the Zattere, then stops at Tronchetto (parking garage) on the way to Piazzale Roma and the station. From the station, Line 82 becomes the Grand Canal express to Rialto, with some boats continuing to Vallaresso (San Marco) and in summer going all the way to the Lido beaches. Line N runs from roughly midnight to 6 AM, stopping at the Lido, Vallaresso, Accademia, Rialto, the train station, Piazzale Roma, Giudecca, and San Zaccaria, then returning in the opposite direction.

BY WATER TAXI A motoscafo (water taxi) isn't cheap; you'll spend about €60 for a short trip in town, €65 to the Lido, and €85 per hour to visit the outer islands. The fare system is convoluted, with luggage handling, waiting time, early or late hours, and even ordering a taxi from your hotel adding expense. Always agree on the price first.

FARES & SCHEDULES An ACTV water bus ticket for all lines costs €5 one-way (Children under four ride free.) Another option is Travel Cards: €12 buys 24 hours and €25 buys 72 hours of unlimited travel on ACTV boats and buses. For travelers between 14 and 29, the 72-hour pass is €15 with the Rolling

The World's Most Elegant Taxi

MORE THAN WINGED LIONS or Carnevale masks, gondolas are the symbol of Venice, re-created en masse as plastic toys, snow globes, and virtually every other tchotchke known to man. But if you look beyond the kitsch, you'll find an austerely beautiful, elegantly designed boat that has evolved over centuries to meet Venice's unique needs.

The gondola is the most enduring of numerous flat-bottomed craft that were developed to navigate the lagoon's shallow waters. The first written reference to a gondolas dates to the 11th century, and images of them appear in Venetian art as early as the 1300s. At the height of their popularity in the 17th century, more than 5,000 were active on Venice's waterways. (There are now around 500.) They were made slim to maneuver the narrowest canals and topped with *felzi*, small cabins that allowed a city full of Casanovas to travel incognito.

The republic's economic decline triggered experiments in gondola construction that would allow the boats to be handled by one gondolier rather than two. Boat-builder Domenico Tramontin perfected the design in the late 1800s, creating an ingenious asymmetrical hull that keeps the gondola traveling straight even though it's being rowed by a single oar. This would be the last genetic modification to one of the world's loveliest dinosaurs—for within fifty years, the gondola would be driven to the brink of extinction by engine-driven boats.

Gondolas are made and repaired in a workshop called a *squero*. Starting with well-seasoned wood, builders can construct a gondola body in about a month, but embellishments can take much longer. The finishing touch is the *ferro*, the ornament that adorns the bow. According to common wisdom, the ferro's graceful "S" curve is meant to mimic the bends of the Grand Canal, its six prongs represent Venice's six sestieri, and its rounded top echoes the shape of the doge's hat. This explanation was most likely invented by gondoliers to impress their passengers, but it's ingenious enough to have become part of gondola lore.

The most conspicuous squero of the few that remain is at San Trovaso, just down the small canal near the Zattere boat landing. Not far from there is another squero, **Domenico Tramontin and Sons** (⊠ Dorsoduro 1542, Fondamente Ognissanti, near Giustinian Hospital 🖼️🖼️ 041/5237762 ⊕ www.tramontingondole.it), where Domenico's great-grandson Roberto and grandson Nedis continue to practice the family trade. Tours with a translator can be arranged by contacting Roberto via fax or through the Web site. North Carolinian Thom Price came to Venice with a fellowship to study gondola making and never went back. At his **Squero Canaletto** (🖼️🖼️ 041/2413963 ⊕ www.squero.com) he not only builds boats but also conducts weeklong workshops on gondola construction and Venetian rowing.

The shapely *forcola* (oarlock) used in Venetian-style rowing is itself a work of refined engineering. To see *forcole* being made, visit the shop of **Saverio Pastor** (⊠ Fondamenta Soranzo, Dorsoduro 341 🖼️ 041/5225699 ⊕ www.forcole.com), open weekdays 8–6. There you can buy a forcola for yourself; architects I. M. Pei and Frank Gehry are among those who have taken one home.

Venice card. Ask for the card (€4) before buying your tickets. A shuttle ticket allows you to cross a canal, one stop only, for €2.

Line information is posted at each landing, and complete timetables for all lines are available for €0.60 at ACTV/Vela ticket booths, located at most major stops. Buy tickets before getting on the boat and remember to validate them in the yellow time-stamp machines. Tickets are also sold on the boat; you must ask to buy one immediately upon boarding, which can be a hassle. When inspectors come aboard, ticketless riders are fined, as are those who haven't validated their tickets. Ignorance will not spare you; the fine is €25, and getting fined can be embarrassing. The law says you must also buy tickets for dogs, baby strollers left unfolded, and bags more than 28 inches long (there's no charge for your bag if you have a Travel Card), but this is generally enforced only for very bulky bags. The telephone number for ferry information listed below has assistance in English.

🚹 **Boat & Ferry Information ACTV** ☎ 041/2424 ⊕ www.hellovenezia.it or www.actv. it. **Water taxi** ☎ 041/5415084 or 041/5222303.

BY BUS
From Venice's Piazzale Roma terminal, buses connect with Mestre, the Brenta Riviera, Padua, Treviso, Cortina d'Ampezzo, and other regional destinations as well as many major European cities.

FARES & SCHEDULES ACTV buses to Mestre (€1) are frequent, and there's night service; ACTV buses to Padua (€3.80) leave at 25 and 55 minutes past each hour and stop along the Brenta River. ATVO has daily buses to Cortina (€11) June–September and throughout the Christmas–New Year holidays. Buses leave Venice at 7:50 AM and depart from Cortina at 3:15 PM. Service is available only on weekends September–May.

🚹 **Bus Information ACTV** ☎ 041/2424 ⊕ www.actv.it. **ATVO** ☎ 0421/383671 ⊕ www. atvo.it. **Bus Terminal** ✉ Piazzale Roma across Grand Canal from train station, Santa Croce.

BY CAR
Venice is on the east–west A4 autostrada, which connects with Padua, Verona, Brescia, Milan, and Turin. If you bring a car to Venice, you will have to pay for a garage or parking space.

You can take your car to the Lido; the car ferry (Line 17) makes the half-hour trip about every 50 minutes from a landing at Tronchetto, but in summer there can be long lines. It costs €10–€20, depending on the size of the car.

PARKING Warning: don't be waylaid by illegal touts, often wearing fake uniforms, who may try to flag you down and offer to arrange parking and hotels; drive on to one of the parking garages. Parking at Autorimessa Comunale costs €20 for 24 hours. The private Garage San Marco costs €20 for up to 12 hours and €26 for 12–24 hours. You can reserve a space in advance at either of these garages; you'll come upon both immediately after crossing the bridge from the mainland. Another alternative is Tronchetto parking (€20 for 1–24 hours); watch for signs for it coming over the bridge—you'll have to turn right before you get to Piazzale Roma. Many hotels have negotiated guest discounts with San

Marco or Tronchetto garages; get a voucher when you check in at your hotel and present it when you pay the garage. Line 82 connects Tronchetto with Piazzale Roma and Piazza San Marco and also goes to the Lido in summer. When there's thick fog or extreme tides, a bus runs to Piazzale Roma instead. Avoid private boats—they're a rip-off. There's a luggage-check office, open daily 6 AM–9 PM, next to the Pullman Bar on the ground floor of the municipal garage at Piazzale Roma.

🚗 Garages **Autorimessa Comunale** ⊠ Piazzale Roma, Santa Croce, End of S11 road ☎ 041/2727211 ⊕ www.asmvenezia.it. **Garage San Marco** ⊠ Piazzale Roma 467/f, Santa Croce, Turn right into bus park ☎ 041/5232213 ⊕ www.garagesanmarco.it. **Tronchetto** ☎ 041/5207555.

BY TRAIN

Venice has rail connections with every major city in Italy and Europe. Some Continental trains do not enter Venice but stop only at the main-land Mestre station. All trains traveling to and from Venice Santa Lucia stop at Mestre, and it's just a 10-minute hop on the next passing train. If you change from a regional train to an Intercity or Eurostar, you'll need to upgrade with a *supplemento* (extra charge) or be liable for a hefty fine. You'll also be fined if before boarding you forget to validate your train ticket in one of the yellow machines found on or near platforms.

🚆 Train Information **Stazione Ferroviaria Santa Lucia** ⊠ Grand Canal, northwest corner of the city, Cannaregio ☎ 041/785670, 892021 Trenitalia train information ⊕ www. trenitalia.com. **Stazione Ferroviaria Venezia-Mestre** ⊠ Mestre, 12 km [7 mi] north-west of Venice ☎ 041/784498, 892021 Trenitalia train information ⊕ www.trenitalia.com.

Contacts & Resources

EMERGENCIES

The U.K. Consulate can recommend doctors and dentists, as can your hotel or any pharmacy. The nearest pharmacy is never far, and they take turns staying open nights, Saturday afternoons, and Sunday; the list of after-hours pharmacies is posted on the front of every pharmacy and appears in daily newspapers.

🚑 Emergency Services **General Emergencies** ☎ 113. **Ambulance** ☎ 118. **Carabinieri** ☎ 112. **U.K. Consulate** ⊠ Piazza Donatori di Sangue 2, Mestre ☎ 041/5055990.

TOURS

BOAT TOURS Boat tours to the islands of Murano, Burano, and Torcello, organized by Serenissima Motoscafi and Bucintoro Viaggi, leave from various docks around Piazza San Marco daily. The 3½-hour trip cost €19 per person with Serenissima Motoscafi. Bucintoro Viaggi charges €20 for a four-hour boat ride. Both can be annoyingly commercial, often em-phasizing glass-factory showrooms and pressuring you to buy at prices even higher than normal. Trips depart at 9:30 and 2:30 April–October, at 2:30 November–March.

More than a dozen major travel agents in Venice have grouped together to provide frequent, good-quality tours of the city. Serenaded gondola trips, with or without dinner (€74, €36), can be purchased at any of their offices or at American Express. Nightly tours leave at 7:30 and

8:30 April–September, at 7:30 only in October, and at 3:30 November–March.

American Express ⊠ Salizzada San Moisè, San Marco 1471 ☎ 041/5200844 🖷 041/5229937. **Bucintoro Viaggi** ⊠ Campo San Luca 4267 ☎ 041/5210632 🖷 041/2411619 ⊕ www.bucintoroviaggi.com. **Serenissima Motoscafi** ☎ 041/5224281.

PRIVATE GUIDES Cooperativa Guide Turistiche Autorizzate has a list of more than 100 licensed guides. Tours lasting about two hours with an English-speaking guide start at €124 for up to 30 people. Agree on a total price before you begin, as there can be some hidden extras. Guides are of variable quality.

Cooperativa Guide Turistiche Autorizzate ⊠ San Marco 750, near San Zulian ☎ 041/5209038 🖷 041/5210762.

TOURS OF THE REGION Various agencies offer several excursions in the Veneto region of the Venetian Arc. A boat trip to Padua along the Brenta River with Il Burchiello makes stops at three Palladian villas, and you return to Venice by bus. The tours run three times a week (Tuesday, Thursday, and Saturday) from March to October and cost €62 per person (€86 with lunch); bookings need to be made a few days in advance.

Bassani offers excursions as well as personalized travel through the Veneto and other Italian cities.

Fees & Schedules Avventure Bellissime ⊠ San Marco 2442/A ☎ 041/5208616 🖷 041/2960282 ⊕ www.tours-italy.com. **Bassani** ⊠ San Basilio, Santa Marta, Fab. 17 ☎ 041/5203644 🖷 041/5204009 ⊕ www.bassani.it. **Il Burchiello** ⊠ Via Orlandini 3 ☎ 049/8206910 🖷 049/8206923 ⊕ www.ilburchiello.it

WALKING TOURS More than a dozen major travel agents offer a two-hour walking tour of the San Marco area (€30), which ends with a glassblowing demonstration daily (no Sunday tour in winter). From April to October there's also an afternoon walking tour that ends with a gondola ride (€40). Venicescapes, an Italo-American cultural association, offers several themed itineraries focusing on history and culture as well as tourist sights. Their three- to seven-hour tours are private, and groups are small (generally six to eight people). Reservations are recommended during busy seasons, and prices start at €240 for two people. Walks Inside Venice also does several themed tours for small groups starting at €70 per hour and lasting up to three hours.

Fees & Schedules Alba Travel ⊠ Calle del Magazin, San Marco 4538 ☎ 041/5210123 🖷 041/5200781 ⊕ www.albatravel.it. **Oltrex Viaggi** ⊠ Castello 4192 ☎ 041/5242840 🖷 041/5221986 ⊕ www.oltrex.it. **Venicescapes** ⊠ Campo San Provolo, Castello 4954 ☎☎ 041/5206361 ⊕ www.venicescapes.org. **Walks Inside Venice** ☎🖷 041/5202434 ⊕ www.walksinsidevenice.com.

VISITOR INFORMATION

The train-station branch of the Venice Tourist Office is open daily 8–6:30; other branches generally open at 9:30.

The Rolling Venice pass, costing €4 and valid throughout a calendar year, buys visitors ages 14–29 discounts on 72-hour vaporetto passes and admission to lots of museums, and at assorted hotels, restaurants, and shops. Just show your passport or ID at Vela ticket offices (major vaporetto stops), at the Assessorato alla Gioventù (weekdays 9:30–1, plus Tuesday and Thursday afternoons 3–5), or at the Associazione Italiana Alberghi per la Gioventù (Monday through Saturday 8–2). The Rolling Venice card allows you to avoid lines at city museums and prepays for vaporetti and municipal toilets. Order online or by phone and pay cash when you pick up the card. Price depends on how many days you're staying; though convenient, it's not a significant discount.

🏗 **Assessorato alla Gioventù** ✉ Corte Contarina, San Marco 1529, behind Piazza San Marco post office ☎ 041/2747651. **Associazione Italiana Alberghi per la Gioventù** ✉ Calle Castelforte, San Polo 3101, near San Rocco ☎ 041/5204414. **Rolling Venice** ☎ 041/5298711 or 041/2424 ⊕ www.venicecard.it.

Venice Tourist Offices ☎ 041/5298711 ⊕ www.turismovenezia.it ✉ Marco Polo Airport ✉ Train Station, Cannaregio ✉ Procuratie Nuove, San Marco 71/f, near Museo Correr ✉ Venice Pavilion, near Giardini Reali, San Marco ✉ Garage Comunale, Piazzale Roma ✉ S. Maria Elisabetta 6/a, Lido ☉ Summer only.

Villa Cordellina Lombardi

WORD OF MOUTH

"Verona and Vicenza are both stunningly beautiful cities that we liked very much. Vicenza is smaller and seems to have more green space. It's also less touristy. Verona gives you the 'Romeo and Juliet' thing. Although I personally did not find any one attraction in Verona that impressive, the city as a whole stole my heart."

–Jocelyn P

WELCOME TO THE VENETIAN ARC

Villa Barbaro, Maser

TOP 5
Reasons to Go

1 Giotto's frescoes in the Capella degli Scrovegni: At this chapel in Padua, Giotto's innovative painting techniques helped to launch the Renaissance.

2 Villa Barbaro in Maser: Master architect Palladio's most gracious Renaissance creation meets Veronese's opulent paintings in a one-time-only collaboration.

3 Opera in Verona's ancient arena: Even if the music doesn't move you, the spectacle will.

4 The Scenery of Asolo: Few places in Italy more perfectly embody the countryside hilltown than Asolo, once the stomping grounds of Robert Browning and Eleonora Duse.

5 The wine roads north of Treviso: A series of routes take you through beautiful hillsides to some of Italy's finest wines.

The elegant art city of Vicenza, nestled on the green plain reaching inland from Venice's lagoon, bears the signature of the great 16th-century architect Andrea Palladio. The **Corso Palladio**, a main road through the center of town, is lined with palaces he designed.

Shakespeare placed Romeo, Juliet, and a couple of gentlemen in Verona, one of the oldest, best-preserved, and most beautiful cities in Italy. Try to catch *Aida* at the gigantic Roman arena.

Arena, Verona

Treviso

Getting Oriented

The Venetian Arc is the sweep of land curving north and east from the Adige River to the Slovenian border. It's made up of two Italian regions—the Veneto and Friuli–Venezia Giulia—that were once controlled by Venice, and the culture is a mix of Venetian, Alpine, and central European sensibilities.

Juliet's House, Verona

Asolo (the City of a Hundred Horizons) is the most prominent in a series of charming towns that dot the wine-producing hills north of Treviso.

Set between the Adriatic and Slovenia in the eastern corner of Italy, **Friuli–Venezia Giulia** is a region where menus run the gamut from gnocchi to goulash.

Home to the mighty tiramisu, known to dessert lovers everywhere, **Treviso** is a busy town with a touch of Venetian style.

The port city of **Trieste** has a mixed Venetian-Austrian heritage. It's filled with belle-époque cafés and palaces once favored by Habsburg royalty.

A city of both high-rises and history, **Padua** is most noted for Giotto's frescoes in the **Capella degli Scrovegni**, where you can marvel at the first painted blue skies in Western art.

Wine Cellar, Spessa Friuli

THE VENETIAN ARC PLANNER

Making the Most of Your Time

The towns of the Veneto region should be on your itinerary if you're doing a tour of northern Italy, and they're good day-trip options if you're making an extended stay in Venice. Lined up in a row west of Venice are Padua, Vicenza, and Verona—three well-to-do towns, each with its own appealing character and worthwhile sights. Verona has the greatest charm, and it's probably the best choice for a base in the area (though this is no secret—Verona also draws the most tourists).

The hills north of Venice make for good drives. Treviso, the largest town, is worth a stop, but you're more likely to fall for the smaller towns of Asolo and Bassano del Grappa and the visitor-friendly wine country that surrounds them.

East of the Veneto, the region of Friuli-Venezia Giulia is off the main tourist circuit. You probably won't go here on a first trip to Italy, but by your second or third visit you may be drawn by its caves and castles, its battle-worn hills, and its mix of Italian and central European culture. The port city of Trieste, most famous for its elegant cafés, has quiet character that some people find dull and others find intriguing. (Famed travel writer Jan Morris's book in praise of the city is tellingly titled *Trieste and the Meaning of Nowhere*.) The vineyards of the Collio area on the Slovenian border have smaller yields than other Italian wine regions, but the quality of the final product is very high.

Getting Around

Padua, Vicenza, and Verona are neatly arranged on the highway and train line between Venice and Milan. Seeing them without a car isn't a problem, and having a car can complicate matters. The cities sometimes limit access, permitting only cars with plates ending in an even number on even days, odd on odd, or prohibiting cars altogether on weekends. There's no central source for information about these sporadic traffic restrictions; the best strategy is to check with your hotel before arrival for an update. On the other hand, you'll need a car to get the most out of the hill country that makes up much of the Venetian Arc. For details about getting around, see "Essentials" at the end of this chapter.

Prime Picnicking

One of the pleasures of this mellow region is buying provisions at an open-air market or *salumeria* (the Italian version of a deli) and relaxing over a picnic. In the countryside, good picnicking spots are countless. If you're limiting your trip to the cities, consider these two locations:

■ In Verona, the Ponte Scaligero footbridge across the Adige River, just behind the Castelvecchio, has a lookout area at the halfway point that's excellent for picnicking. You can find everything you need at the exceptional Salumeria Albertini.

■ Padua's Basilica di Sant'Antonio is one of the rare churches in Italy that welcomes picnickers—it even provides the tables. For supplies, head to the Palazzo della Ragione food market.

Planning Ahead

Three of the top sights in the region demand advance planning:

■ Reservations are required to see the Giotto frescoes in Padua's Cappella degli Scrovegni—though if there's space, you can "reserve" on the spot.

■ Outside Vicenza, Villa La Rotonda, one of star architect Palladio's master-pieces, is open to the public only on Wednesday from mid-March through October. (Hours for visiting the grounds are less restrictive.)

■ Another highly acclaimed Palladian villa, Villa Barbaro near Maser, is open from March through October on Tuesday, Saturday, and Sunday afternoons. For the rest of the year, it's only open on week-ends.

For details about Cappela degli Scrovegni, look in this chapter under "The Main Attractions" in Padua. For the villas, see "Palladio Country."

In the Cards

If you're planning to see more than a sight or two in Padua, Verona, or Trieste, it pays to pick up one of the tourist cards each city offers. For one price, you get admission to most sights and unlimited use of public transportation. Specifics are listed at the beginning of the city write-ups in this chapter.

Finding a Place to Stay

There's a full range of accommodations throughout the region. It's a trend for hotels to renovate and subsequently hike their prices, but good low-cost options can still be found. Ask about weekend discounts, which are often available at hotels catering to business clients. Rates tend to be higher in Padua and Verona than in the rest of the region. Agriturismo (farm stay) information is available at local tourist information offices and sometimes on the offices' Web sites.

Dining & Lodging Price Categories

WHAT IT COSTS in Euros					
	$$$$	**$$$**	**$$**	**$**	**¢**
Restaurants	over €45	€35–€45	€25–€35	€15–€25	under €15
Hotels	over €220	€160–€220	€110–€160	€70–€110	under €70

Restaurant prices are for a first course (primo), second course (secondo), and dessert (dolce). Hotel prices are for two people in a standard double room in high season, including tax and service.

How's the Weather?

The ideal times to visit are late spring and early summer (May and June) and in September and October. If you're an opera buff, it's worth tolerating the summer heat in order to see a performance at the Arena di Verona (where the season runs from July through September). Winter is a good time to avoid travel to the region: foggy conditions and wet, bone-chilling cold are not unusual from November through March.

TOP PASSEGGIATA

An evening walk along Via Mazzini between Piazza dei Signori and Piazza Bra captures the essence of Verona's appeal. On nights when there's a performance, you can sit in one of Piazza Bra's cafés and make out strains of opera coming from the arena next door.

Piazza dei Signori

Updated by
Robin
Goldstein

THE ARC AROUND VENICE—stretching from Verona to Trieste, encompassing the Veneto and Friuli–Venezia Giulia regions—falls under the historical and spiritual influence of its namesake city. Whether seaside or inland, the emblem of Venice, St. Mark's winged lion, is emblazoned on palazzos or poised on pedestals, and the art, architecture, and way of life all reflect the splendor of La Serenissima.

The area is primarily flat green farmland. As you move inland, though, you encounter low hills, which swell and rise in a succession of plateaus and high meadows, culminating in the snowcapped Alps. Much of the pleasure of exploring here comes from discovering the variations on the Venetian theme that give a unique character to each of the towns. Some, such as Verona, Treviso, and Udine, have a solid medieval look; Asolo, dubbed "the town of a hundred horizons," has an idyllic setting; Bassano del Grappa combines a bit of both of these qualities. Padua is ennobled by Giotto's frescoes, Vicenza by the villas of Palladio. In Friuli–Venezia Giulia, Udine is a genteel, intricately sculpted city that's home to the first important frescoes by Giambattista Tiepolo. In Trieste, just a stone's throw from Slovenia, there's a youthful buzz, and the aroma of freshly roasted coffee fills the city center.

PADUA

Bustling with bicycles and lined with frescoes, Padua has long been one of the major cultural centers in northern Italy. It's home to the peninsula's—and the world's—second-oldest university, founded in 1222, which attracted the likes of Dante (1265–1321), Petrarch (1304–74), and Galileo Galilei (1564–1642), thus earning the city the sobriquet *La Dotta* (The Learned). Padua's Basilica di Sant'Antonio, begun not long after the university in 1234, is dedicated to St. Anthony, the patron saint of lost-and-found objects, and attracts grateful pilgrims in droves, especially on his feast day, June 13.

> **WORD OF MOUTH**
>
> "To me, Padua, even more than Venice, is evocative of the 'old' Italy. In the old city *(città vecchia)*, the maze of tiny streets is just the thing for wandering around and getting lost."
>
> –Wayne

Three great artists—Giotto (1266–1337), Donatello (circa 1386–1466), and Mantegna (1431–1506)—left great works here, with Giotto's Scrovegni chapel one of the best-known, and most meticulously preserved, works of art in the country. Today, cycle-happy students rule the roost, flavoring every aspect of local culture. Don't be surprised if you spot a *laurea* (graduation) ceremony marked by laurel leaves, mocking lullabies, and X-rated caricatures.

Exploring Padua

Padua is a pedestrian's city, and you'll want to spend your time in the city on foot (or bike). If you arrive by car, leave your vehicle in one of the parking lots on the outskirts, or at your hotel. The *Padova Arte* ticket (€14), valid for 48 hours, is a good deal if you plan to visit several of

THE VENETIAN ARC, PAST & PRESENT

Long before Venetians had made their presence felt, Ezzelino III da Romano (1194-1259), a larger-than-life scourge who was excommunicated by Pope Innocent IV, laid claim to Verona, Padua, and the surrounding lands and towns. After he was ousted, powerful families such as Padua's Carrara and Verona's della Scala (Scaligeri) vied throughout the 14th century to annex these territories. With the rise of Venetian rule came a time of relative peace, when noble families from the lagoon and the mainland commissioned Palladio to design their palazzos and enlisted the three Ts—Titian, Tintoretto, and Tiepolo—to decorate their interiors. This opulent legacy, superimposed upon medieval castles and fortifications, is central to the identities of present-day Padua, Vicenza, and Verona.

Friuli-Venezia Giulia has a diverse cultural history that's reflected in its architecture, language, and cuisine. It's been marched through, fought over, hymned by patriots, and romanticized by James Joyce, Rainer Maria Rilke, and Jan Morris. It's seen Fascists and Communists, Romans, Habsburgs, and Huns. It survived by forging sheltering alliances—Udine beneath the wings of San Marco (1420), Trieste choosing Duke Leopold of Austria (1382) over Venetian domination.

Some of World War I's fiercest fighting took place in Friuli-Venezia Giulia, where memorials and cemeteries commemorate hundreds of thousands who died before the arrival of Italian troops in 1918 finally liberated Trieste from Austrian rule. During World War II one of Italy's two concentration camps, still visitable, was in Trieste. After the war, Trieste enjoyed a period as an independent republic, but ultimately, thousands of ethnic Slav residents bore the brunt of Fascist persecution, and in Istria Italian residents suffered Yugoslavia's retaliation. When peace was declared in other parts of Europe, Trieste became a subject of Cold War conflict between Zone A and Zone B—the free-world Allies versus Tito's socialism. Only in 1976 was the "Trieste question" finally resolved with Treaty of Osimo: Italy retained the city but surrendered the entire Istrian Peninsula, now part of Croatia. With Slovenia's 1991 declaration of independence from Yugoslavia, confrontation again flared along the border, but the 2004 admission of Slovenia to the European Union may ultimately end the area's bloody legacy.

the town's principal sights: it allows entry to the Cappella degli Scrovegni, Musei Civici degli Eremitani, Palazzo della Ragione, Battistero, Scoletta del Santo, Musei Antoniani, and the Orto Botanico. It is available from the tourist office and at some museums.

The Main Attractions

★ ❼ **Basilica di Sant'Antonio.** Thousands of worshipers throng to Il Santo, a cluster of Byzantine domes and slender, minaret-like towers that gives this huge basilica an Asian-inspired style reminiscent of San Marco in Venice. The interior is sumptuous, too, with marble reliefs by Tullio Lom-

Basilica di Sant'-
Antonio **7**

Battistero del
Duomo **6**

Cappella degli
Scrovegni **1**

Museo Civici
degli Eremitani . . **2**

Orto
Botanico **8**

Palazzo del Bo' . **3**

Palazzo della
Ragione **4**

Piazza dei
Signori **5**

Villa Pisani **9**

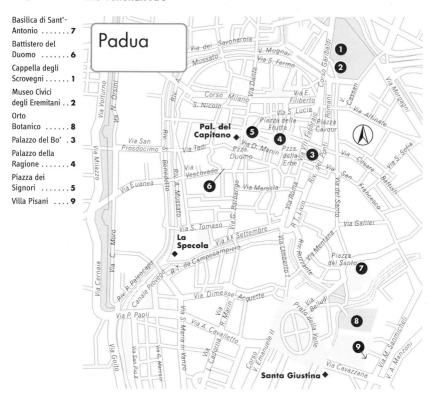

bardo (1455–1532), the greatest in a talented family of marble carvers who decorated many churches in the area, among them Venice's Santa Maria dei Miracoli. The artistic highlights here, however, bear Donatello's name; the 15th-century Florentine master did the remarkable series of bronze reliefs illustrating the life of St. Anthony. The **Cappella del Santo** was built to house the green marble tomb of the saint and is now filled with votive offerings. Reconstructed in the 16th century, it shows Italian High Renaissance at its best. The **Cappella del Tesoro** (☉ Daily 8–noon and 2:30–7) holds the not-so-pristine tongue of the saint in a 15th-century reliquary. In front of the church is Donatello's powerful statue of the *condottiere* (mercenary general) Erasmo da Narni, known by the nickname Gattamelata. Cast in bronze—a monumental technical achievement in 1453—the statue had an enormous influence on the development of Italian Renaissance sculpture. ✉ *Piazza del Santo* ☎ *049/8789722* ⊕ *www.santantonio.org* ☉ *Daily 6:30 AM–7 PM.*

❶   **Cappella degli Scrovegni.** This chapel, the second most famous in Italy
FodorśChoice   after the Sistine, was erected by wealthy Paduan Enrico Scrovegno to
★   atone for the usury practiced by his deceased father, Reginaldo. Giotto and his assistants were commissioned to decorate the interior; they worked from 1303 to 1305 on a magnificent fresco cycle illustrating the lives of Mary and Christ. In typical medieval comic-strip fashion,

the 38 panels are arranged in tiers intended to be read from left to right. Opposite the altar is a powerful *Last Judgment,* where Enrico offers his chapel to the Virgin. The depth and perspective in these frescoes—which include the first blue skies in Western painting—were revolutionary. Mandatory reservations, available by Web or phone, are for a specific time and are nonrefundable. In order to preserve the artwork, doors are opened only every 15 minutes. A maximum of 25 visitors at a time must spend 15 minutes in an acclimatization room before making a 15-minute chapel visit. You can see fresco details as part of a virtual tour at Musei Civici degli Eremitani. A good place to get some background before visiting the chapel is the multimedia room, which offers films and interactive computer presentations. Entrance is only by reservation, which you should make at least two days ahead. It is usually possible to buy your admission on the spot—although you might have to wait a while until there's an opening. Visits are scheduled every 20 minutes, and punctuality is essential. Get to the chapel at least ½ hour before your reservation time. ⊠ *Piazza Eremitani 8* ☎ *49/2010020 for reservations* ⊕ *www.cappelladegliscrovegni.it* ⊡ *€12 including Musei Civici, or €1 with Padova Card* ⊙ *Daily 9* AM*–10* PM.

★ ❹ **Palazzo della Ragione.** Also known as Il Salone, this spectacular, arcaded palace, which divides the Piazza delle Frutta from the Piazza delle Erbe, is the most memorable architectural image of the city. In the Middle Ages the building was the seat of Padua's government; today, its street-level arcades shelter shops and cafés. Art shows are often held upstairs in the frescoed **Salone,** at 85 feet high one of the largest and most architecturally pleasing halls in Italy, where there's an enormous 15th-century wooden replica of Gattamelata's bronze steed sculpted by Donatello. ⊠ *Piazza della Ragione* ☎ *049/8205006* ⊡ *Salone €8* ⊙ *Tues.–Sun. 9–7.*

❺ **Piazza dei Signori.** Some fine examples of 15th- and 16th-century buildings line this square. On the west side, the **Palazzo del Capitanio** has an impressive **Torre dell'Orologio,** with an astronomical clock dating from 1344. The **Duomo,** just a few steps away, is not the most interesting church in town.

⟳ ❾ **Villa Pisani.** Extensive grounds with rare trees, ornamental fountains, and garden follies surround this extraordinary 18th-century palace in Stra, 13 km (8 mi) southeast of Padua. It was one of the last of many stately residences constructed along the Brenta River from the 16th to 18th century by wealthy Venetians for their *villeggiatura*—vacation and escape from the midsummer humidity. Tiepolo's trompe-l'oeil frescoes on the ballroom ceiling alone are worth the visit. If you have youngsters in tow surfeited with old masters, explore the gorgeous **park** and **maze.** To get here from Venice, you can take the Brenta River bus that leaves from Piazzale Roma. ⊠ *Via Doge Pisani 7, Stra* ☎ *049/502074* ⊡ *Villa, maze, and park €5; maze and park only €2.50* ⊙ *Apr.–Sept., Tues.–Sun. 9–7; villa and park only Oct.–Mar., Tues.–Sun. 9–4; last entry 1 hr before closing.*

Also Worth Seeing

❻ **Battistero del Duomo** (Cathedral Baptistery). The often-overlooked 12th-century baptistry contains mid-1370s frescoes depicting scenes from the

Book of Genesis. They're the greatest work of Giusto de' Menabuoi, who further developed Giotto's style of depicting human figures naturally, using perspective and realistic lighting. The building is a refreshingly cool retreat from the city. ⊠ *Piazza Duomo* ☎ *049/656914* ⬚ *€2.50 or Padova Card* ⊗ *Daily 10–6.*

❷ **Musei Civici degli Eremitani** (Civic Museum). What was once a monastery now houses works of Venetian masters, as well as fine collections of archaeological pieces and ancient coins. Notable are the Giotto Crucifix, which was once in the Scrovegni Chapel, and the *Portrait of a Young Senator* by Bellini. ⊠ *Piazza Eremitani 10* ☎ *049/8204551* ⬚ *€10, €12 with Scrovegni Chapel, or Padova Card* ⊗ *Tues.–Sun. 9–7.*

❽ **Orto Botanico** (Botanical Garden). The Venetian Republic ordered the creation of Padua's botanical garden in 1545 to supply the university with medicinal plants. You can stroll the arboretum and wander through hothouses and beds of plants that were first introduced to Italy in this Renaissance garden, which still maintains its original layout. A St. Peter's palm, planted in 1585, stands protected in its own private greenhouse. ⊠ *Via Orto Botanico 15* ☎ *049/8272119* ⊕ *www.ortobotanico. unipd.it* ⬚ *€4 or Padova Card* ⊗ *Apr.–Oct., daily 9–1 and 3–6; Nov.–Mar., Mon.–Sat. 9–1.*

❸ **Palazzo del Bo'.** The University of Padua, founded in 1222, centers around this 16th-century palazzo with an 18th-century facade. It's named after the Osteria del Bo' (*bo*' means "ox"), an inn that once stood on the site. It's worth a visit to see the exquisite and perfectly proportioned anatomy theater and a hall with a lectern used by Galileo. You can enter only as part of a guided tour. Most guides speak English, but it is worth checking ahead by phone. ⊠ *Via VIII Febbraio* ☎ *049/ 8273044* ⬚ *€3* ⊗ *Mon., Wed., and Fri. at 3:15, 4:15, and 5:15; Tues., Thurs., and Sat. at 9:15, 10:15, and 11:15.*

Where to Stay & Eat

$$$$ ✕ **Antico Brolo.** In a 16th-century building not far from central Piazza dei Signori, charming Antico Brolo is one of Padua's top restaurants. The outdoor area has a simpler menu; the indoor restaurant is more elaborate. Pastas are uniformly excellent; seasonal specialties prepared with flair might include starters such as tiny flans with wild mushrooms and herbs or fresh pasta with zucchini flowers. The wine list doesn't disappoint. ⊠ *Corso Milano 22* ☎ *049/664555* ⊕ *www.anticobrolo.it* ⊟ *AE, MC, V* ⊗ *No lunch Mon.*

$$$ ✕ **La Vecchia Enoteca.** The ceiling is mirrored, the shelves are filled with books and wine, the silver service on which your meal arrives once belonged to a shipping line, and the flower displays are extravagant. In this luxurious ambience enjoy *branzino in crosta di patate* (sea bass with a potato crust) or beef with rosemary and balsamic vinegar, followed by a homemade dessert such as *crema catalana* (cream caramel). Reservations are advised. ⊠ *Via Santi Martino e Solferino 32* ☎ *049/8752856* ⊟ *MC, V* ⊗ *Closed Sun. and 1st 3 wks in Aug. No lunch Mon.*

$–$$$ ✕ **Bastioni del Moro.** The genial owner devises his own recipes according to season, with vegetarians and calorie watchers in mind, although

EATING WELL IN THE VENETIAN ARC

With the decisive seasonal changes of the Venetian Arc, it's little wonder many restaurants shun printed menus. Some of the region's defining culinary elements are from the field and the forest, and are only available at certain times of year: in spring, highlights include white asparagus and wild herbs; in autumn, chestnuts, radicchio, and wild mushrooms. Any time of the year, you're sure to find Italian families and friends indulging in the Sunday tradition of lunching out; equally certain is the likelihood of finding nothing more than bar snacks open from 3 until 8 PM.

The catch of the day is always a good bet. The shellfish of the Adriatic are sweet and succulent, and lake fish from Garda to the north can also be excellent. Inland, meat prevails: pork and veal standards are supplemented with lamb and rabbit, and goose, duck, and guinea fowl are all common poultry options. North around Asolo, snails are popular. In Verona, a tradition of eating horse meat dates to a bloody 19th-century skirmish, when a starving populace created *pastisada*, a stew made with the animals killed in battle. In Friuli–Venezia Giulia, menus show the influences of Austria, Hungary, Slovenia, and Croatia. You may find

wild deer and hare on the menu, as well as Eastern European–style goulash and beer, *cjalzòns* (ravioli made from flour-and-water-only dough, stuffed with spinach, apple, pear, or cheese, and topped with melted butter and cinnamon), and such unusual treats as *nervetti* (cubes of gelatin from a cow's knee with onions, parsley, oil, and lemon). And you can't get out of Treviso without eating the ubiquitous radicchio, found in soup, salad, pasta, and even dessert.

For starches, the Veneto dines on *bigoli* (thick, whole wheat pasta), and risotto is wine-saturated with Amarone in Verona and prosecco in Conegliano. You'll encounter gnocchi made with pumpkin or plums in Udine, strudel filled with *bruscandoli* (wild greens) in Cormòns. Polenta is everywhere, varying from a stiff porridge topped with Gorgonzola or stews, to a patty grilled alongside meat or fish.

Austrian-style pastries will sweeten your stay in Trieste, and Verona scoops some of the best gelato. Treviso claims to have invented the area's signature dessert, tiramisu, but chefs in virtually every kitchen believe they hold the secret to making the best version.

---

carnivores are well cared for, too. Gnocchi, eggplant, artichokes, and pumpkin all appear on the menu in different guises. For starters, you could try *tagliolini gratinati con prosciutto* (thin ribbons of egg noodles with prosciutto) or *gnocchi con capesante e porcini* (gnocchi with scallops and porcini mushrooms). The garden is put to good use in summer. Reservations are recommended. ⊠ *Via Pilade Bronzetti 18* ☎ *049/8710006* ⊕ *www.bastionidelmoro.it* ▭ *AE, DC, MC, V* ⊗ *Closed Sun. and 2 wks in Aug.*

★ **$–$$** ✕ **L'Anfora.** Sometimes you stumble across an *osteria* (tavernlike restaurant) that is so infused with local character that you wonder why every meal can't be this atmospheric, this authentically local, this effortlessly delicious. With dark wooden walls and typically brusque service, L'Anfora, in Padua's old center, is just such a gem. Skip the fried appetizers, which can get soggy as they sit, and start with some cheese: a nearly perfect piece of *mozzarella di bufala campana* (water-buffalo mozzarella from the Campania region) or, even better, an impossibly creamy *burrata* (similar to mozzarella, wrapped in herbs). After that, you might move on to *tagliatelle* (flat noodles) with fresh seasonal mushrooms, or perhaps a plate of simply grilled artichokes and potatoes. The place is packed at lunchtime, so expect a wait. ✉ *Via Soncin 13* ☎ *049/656629* 🖃 *AE, V* ☉ *Closed Sun. except Dec.; closed 1 wk in Aug.*

$ ✕ **Gigi Bar.** Simple and unpretentious: yellow walls and tablecloths brighten this inexpensive restaurant where high ceilings open up a second-floor seating area. The central kitchen is behind a counter low enough for the convivial owner-chef Ferruccio to see and supervise the equally friendly dining-room staff. The terrific and popular fish soup is one of the affordable seafood dishes that keep locals queuing up. There are also tasty steaks, salads, vegetable plates, and pizzas with a surprisingly light crust. ✉ *Via Verdi 18/20* ☎ *049/8760028* 🖃 *DC, MC, V* ☉ *Closed Tues., 2 wks in July.*

¢–$ ✕ **Hostaria Ai Do Archi.** Frequented by an older neighborhood crowd, this is nothing more—or less—than a Padovan version of the *bacari* that are so typical of the Veneto: wine bars where people sit and stand all day long, sipping wine, tasting local snacks, and talking politics. It's a true experience. ✉ *Via Nazario Sauro 23* ☎ *049/652335* 🖃 *No credit cards* ☉ *Closed Tues. No lunch.*

$$$ 🏨 **Plaza.** In a town without many downtown hotels, this is one of the few comfortable options. Even if its design seems trapped in a 1960s modernist fantasy, that's not necessarily a bad thing; the giant globes that illuminate the sidewalk in front of the hotel add a little dreaminess to an otherwise nondescript block of apartments and office buildings. Rooms are spacious, modern, and comfortable, and it's only a five-minute walk to the city center. ✉ *Corso Milano 40, 35139* ☎ *049/656822* 🖷 *049/ 661117* ⊕ *www.plazapadova.it* ⇆ *130 rooms, 9 suites, 7 apartments* ⚒ *Restaurant, bar, WiFi, in-room safes, minibars, gym, meeting rooms, parking (fee)* 🖃 *AE, DC, MC, V* ⦿ *BP.*

★ **$$$** 🏨 **Villa Pisani.** The spacious high-ceiling rooms in this enormous 16th-century villa are furnished entirely with period pieces—some units even have fully frescoed walls. All rooms look out over stunning formal gardens and beyond to a 15-acre park with rare trees, a chapel, a theater, and a concealed swimming pool. You have access to three big *sale* (lounges), where you can chat with the few other lucky guests and Signora Scalabrin, who shares her patrician living areas, music, and books. With breakfast served on silver platters, this is a bed-and-breakfast that outstrips almost all the hotel competition. ✉ *Via Roma 19, 35040 Vescovana, 30 km (19 mi) south of Padua, off Hwy. A13* 🖷 *0425/ 920016* ⊕ *www.villapisani.it* ⇆ *7 rooms, 1 suite* ⚒ *Pool, horseback riding, convention center, free parking, some pets allowed, Internet* *room; no a/c in some rooms, no room phones, no TV in some rooms, no smoking* ☰ *AE, DC, MC, V* ⚫ *BP.*

★ **$$–$$$** ▦ **Majestic Toscanelli.** The elegant entrance, with potted evergreens flanking the steps, sets the tone in this stylish, central hotel close to the Piazza della Frutta. It's easily the best-located hotel in the city, but beside that the rooms and service justify the price. Plants feature strongly in the breakfast room, and the charming bedrooms are furnished in different styles from 19th-century mahogany and brass to French Empire. Your very welcoming hosts offer discounts to seniors, AAA members, and those carrying Fodor's guidebooks. ⊠ *Via dell'Arco 2, near Piazza della Frutta, 35122* ☎ *049/663244* 🖨 *049/8760025* ⊕ *www.toscanelli. com* 🛏 *26 rooms, 6 suites* ⚫ *Café, some in-room safes, minibars, cable TV with movies, in-room data ports, bar, meeting room, parking (fee), some pets allowed (fee), no-smoking floor, WiFi* ☰ *AE, DC, MC, V* ⚫ *BP.*

$ ▦ **Al Fagiano.** Some rooms in this peaceful hotel have views of the spires and cupolas at Basilica di Sant'Antonio. Facilities are modest, and rooms simply furnished, but an amiable staff and central location make this a pleasant and convenient place to stay. Breakfast is available for €6. ⊠ *Via Locatelli 45, 35100* ☎ *049/8750073* 🖨 *049/8753396* ⊕ *www. alfagiano.it* 🛏 *29 rooms* ⚫ *Restaurant, cable TV, in-room data ports, bar, parking (fee), some pets allowed* ☰ *AE, DC, MC, V* ⚫ *EP.*

Cafés & Wine Bars

Since 1831 **Caffè Pedrocchi** (⊠ Piazzetta Pedrocchi ☎ 049/8781231) has been a place to sip and snack while musicians play jazz and intellectuals debate. An innovative bistro menu means you can now enjoy coffee-flavor pasta, or share zabaglione made from Pedrocchi's 150-year-old recipe. This neoclassical cross between a museum and stage set is open Sunday–Wednesday 9–9, and until midnight Thursday–Saturday.

One of Padua's greatest traditions is the outdoor en-masse consumption, most nights in decent weather, of **aperitifs:** *spritz* (a mix of Aperol or Campari, soda water, and wine), *prosecco* (sparkling wine), or wine. It all happens in the Piazza delle Erbe and Piazza delle Frutta, where several bars provide drinks in plastic cups to masses of people, who then take the drinks outside and consume them standing up. The ritual begins at 6 PM or so, at which hour you can also get a snack from one of the outdoor seafood vendors; on weekends, the open-air revelry continues into the wee hours, transitioning from a lively cocktail hour to a wine-soaked bash.

VICENZA

Vicenza bears the distinctive signature of the 16th-century architect Andrea Palladio, whose name has been given to the "Palladian" style of architecture. He gracefully incorporated elements of classical architecture—columns, porticoes, and domes—into a style that reflected the Renaissance celebration of order and harmony. His elegant villas and palaces were influential in propagating classical architecture in Europe, especially Britain, and later in America—most notably at Thomas Jefferson's Monticello.

Palazzo
Chiericati **11**

Palazzo Leoni
Montanari **12**

Piazza
dei Signori . . . **13**

Teatro
Olimpico **10**

Villa
Valmarana
ai Nani **14**

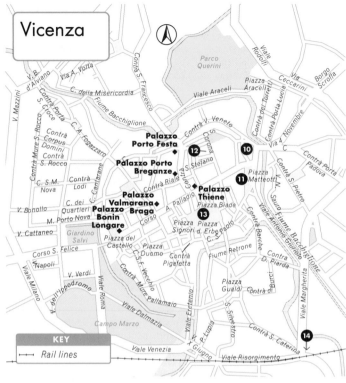

In the mid-16th century Palladio was commissioned to rebuild much of Vicenza, which had been greatly damaged during wars waged against Venice by the League of Cambrai, an alliance of the papacy, France, the Holy Roman Empire, and several neighboring city-states. He made his name with the Basilica, begun in 1549 in the heart of Vicenza, then embarked on a series of lordly buildings, all of which adhere to the same classicism.

Exploring Vicenza

Many of Palladio's works join the Venetian Gothic and baroque palaces that line Corso Palladio, an elegant shopping thoroughfare where Vicenza's status as one of Italy's wealthiest cities is evident.

The Main Attractions

★ ⑩ **Teatro Olimpico.** Palladio's last, and perhaps most exciting, work was completed after his death by Vincenzo Scamozzi (1552–1616). Based closely on the model of an ancient Roman theater, it represents an important development in theater and stage design and is noteworthy for its acoustics and the cunning use of perspective in Scamozzi's permanent backdrop. The anterooms are frescoed with images of important figures in Venetian history. ⊠ *Piazza Matteotti* ☎ *0444/222800* ✉ *€8, includes*

admission to Palazzo Chiericati ⊙ *Sept.–June, Tues.–Sun. 9–5;*
July and Aug., Tues.–Sun. 9–7.

| Villa La Rotonda | See Page 128 |

2

Also Worth Seeing

⑪ Palazzo Chiericati. This exquisite and unmistakably Palladian palazzo houses Vicenza's **Museo Civico.** The museum's Venetian collection includes paintings by Tiepolo (1696–1770) and Tintoretto (1519–94). ⊠ *Piazza Matteotti* ☎ *0444/321348* ⌑ *€8, includes admission to Teatro Olimpico* ⊙ *Sept.–June, Tues.–Sun. 9–5; July and Aug., Tues.–Sun. 9–6.*

⑫ Palazzo Leoni Montanari. In a city dominated by Palladio, this distinctly baroque building is often overlooked, as are its galleries. On display are more than 500 Orthodox icons dating back to the 13th century, making this one of the most significant such collections outside Russia. A second gallery of Veneto art includes paintings by Longhi (1702–85), Canaletto (1697–1768), and Francesco Guardi (1712–93). ⊠ *Contrà Santa Corona 25* ☎ *800/578875* ⊕ *www.palazzomontanari.com* ⌑ *€3.50* ⊙ *Fri.–Sun. 10–6.*

⑬ Piazza dei Signori. At the heart of Vicenza sits this square, which contains the **Palazzo della Ragione,** commonly known as Palladio's basilica, though it wasn't a church at all but originally a courthouse and public meeting hall. Palladio made his name by successfully modernizing the medieval building, grafting a graceful two-story exterior loggia onto the existing Gothic structure. Take a look also at the **Loggia del Capitaniato,** opposite, which Palladio designed but never completed. Note that the palazzo and its loggia are open to the public only when there's an exhibition: ask at the tourist office.

⑭ Villa Valmarana ai Nani. Inside this 18th-century country house a series of frescoes by Tiepolo depict fantastic visions of a mythological world, including one of his most stunning works, the *Sacrifice of Iphigenia.* The neighboring *foresteria* (farmworkers' dormitory) is also part of the museum; it contains more frescoes showing 18th-century Veneto life at its most charming by Tiepolo's son Giandomenico (1727–1804). You can reach the villa on foot by following the same path that leads to Palladio's Villa la Rotonda. ⊠ *Via dei Nani 2/8* ☎ *0444/544546* ⌑ *€6* ⊙ *Mid-Mar.–Oct., Wed., Thurs., and weekends 10–noon and 3–6, Tues. and Fri. 10–noon.*

> ### WORD OF MOUTH
>
> Vicenza is fairly small and very quaint. I loved it as a base. We could walk to the train station to catch a train to Venice. We rented a car and that is how we explored some of the other cities in the area."
>
> –Eurotraveller

Where to Stay & Eat

$$$ ✕ **Antico Ristorante agli Schioppi.** Veneto country-style decor, with enormous murals, matches simple yet imaginative cuisine in this family-run restaurant established in 1897. Begin with the Parma ham served with eggplant mousse and Parmesan. The *baccalà* (salt cod) is a delicacy, as are the *petto d'anitra all'uva moscata e indivia* (duck breast with muscat grapes and endive) and *coniglio alle olive nere* (rabbit with black olives). Desserts include ever-so-light fruit mousse and a pear cake with red-wine sauce. ✉ *Contrà del Castello 26* ☎ *0444/543701* ⊕ *www. ristoranteaglischioppi.com* ⊟ *AE, DC, MC, V* ⊘ *Closed Sun., last wk of July–mid-Aug., and Jan. 1–6. No dinner Sat.*

$$–$$$ ✕ **Dai Nodari.** Seven restaurant veterans—with a shared passion for good food and hard work—opened this exciting restaurant in January 2005. They must also share a flare for the dramatic: a silent film shows in the bar and Dante's Inferno plays in the men's room. Appetizers include interesting cheeses, such as *bastardo del drappa* (aged 60 days), and dishes like tuna marinated in orange. Move on to fish or steak, or try rabbit roasted with juniper berries. There are also several pasta and salad choices. ✉ *Contrà do Rode 20* ☎ *0444/544085* ⊟ *AE, DC, MC, V.*

★ **$–$$** ✕ **Ponte delle Bele.** With all the pine furniture and lacy lamps, you may feel like you've stumbled into an Alpine cabin, so it's no surprise when your homemade pasta resembles dumplings or spaetzle. At this friendly *Tyrolese* (Tirolean) restaurant, your prosciutto might be made from wild deer or boar, and venison in blueberry sauce is not usually found this far south of the mountains. Try guinea fowl roasted with white grapes, or the local cheese plate served with honey and preserves (but take care with the tough rye cracker-bread, which only a dentist could love). ✉ *Contrà Ponte delle Bele 5* ☎ *0444/320647* ⊕ *www.pontedellebele. it* ⊟ *AE, DC, MC, V* ⊘ *Closed Sun. and 2 wks in mid–Aug.*

¢–$ ✕ **Righetti.** After staking out seats, line up (with elbows ready) at the self-service food counters here. There's a daily pasta, a risotto, and a hearty soup such as *orzo e fagioli* (barley and bean) on the menu. Vegetables, salads, and baccalà are standards; at dinner, meats are grilled to order. Once you have your meal on your tray, help yourself to bread, wine, and water. Sharing tables is the norm. After you've finished, tell the cashier what you had and he'll total your (very reasonable) bill. Low prices and simple, enjoyable food has generated a loyal following. ✉ *Piazza Duomo 3* ☎ *0444/543135* ⊟ *No credit cards* ⊘ *Closed weekends and Aug.*

$$ ⊞ **Giardini.** The hotel Giardini is in good company near Palladio's Teatro Olimpico and Palazzo Chiericati, off the central Piazza Matteotti. Rooms have a modern Italian style, with sleek, mid-tone wood floors and multicolor bedspreads; two rooms are equipped for guests with disabilities. ✉ *Viale Giurioli 10, 36100* ☎ *0444/326458* ⊕ *www. hotelgiardini.com* ⥲ *17 rooms* ♣ *In-room safes, minibars, cable TV, bar, meeting room, free parking* ⊟ *AE, DC, MC, V* ⊘ *Closed Dec. 23–Jan. 2 and 3 wks in Aug.* ⊺◯⫿ *BP.*

$ ⊞ **Due Mori.** Antiques fill the rooms at the 1883 hotel Due Mori, one of the oldest in the city. Loyal regulars favor the place because it's light

Continued on page 130

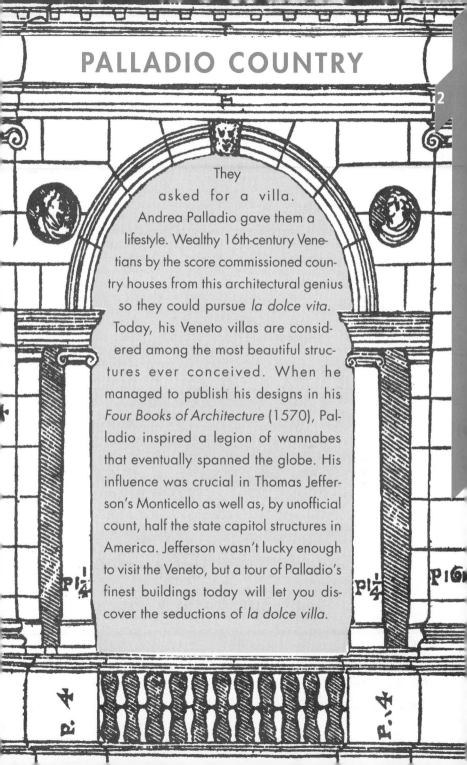

PALLADIO COUNTRY

They asked for a villa. Andrea Palladio gave them a lifestyle. Wealthy 16th-century Venetians by the score commissioned country houses from this architectural genius so they could pursue *la dolce vita*. Today, his Veneto villas are considered among the most beautiful structures ever conceived. When he managed to publish his designs in his *Four Books of Architecture* (1570), Palladio inspired a legion of wannabes that eventually spanned the globe. His influence was crucial in Thomas Jefferson's Monticello as well as, by unofficial count, half the state capitol structures in America. Jefferson wasn't lucky enough to visit the Veneto, but a tour of Palladio's finest buildings today will let you discover the seductions of *la dolce villa*.

TOWN & COUNTRY

Although the villa, or "country residence," was still a relatively new phenomenon in the 16th century, it quickly became all the rage once the great lords of Venice turned their eyes from the sea toward the fertile plains of the Veneto. They were forced to do this once their trade routes had faltered when Ottoman Turks conquered Constantinople in 1456 and Columbus opened a path to the riches of America in 1492. In no time, canals were built, farms were laid out, and the fashion for *villeggiatura*—the attraction of idyllic country retreats for the nobility—became a favored lifestyle. As a means of escaping an overheated

Rome, villas had been the original brainchild of the ancient emperors. But emperors, after all, required palatial, not rustic, lodgings—so it was no accident that Palladio zeroed in on this style of country residence. His process of evaluating the standards, and standbys, of ancient Roman life through the eye of the Italian Renaissance, combined with Palladio's innate sense of proportion and symmetry, became the lasting foundation of his art. In turn, Palladio threw out the jambalaya of styles prevalent in Venetian architecture—Oriental, Gothic, and Renaissance—for the pure, noble lines he had found in the buildings of the Caesars.

PALLADIO, STAR ARCHITECT

Andrea Palladio (1508–1580)

"Face dark, eyes fiery. Dress rich. His appearance that of a genius." So was Palladio described by his wealthy mentor, Count Trissino. In a brilliant bit of brand marketing, Trissino encouraged the young student to trade in his birth name, Andrea della Gondola, for the catchy Palladio, derived from Pallas, Greek deity of wisdom. He did, and it proved a wise move indeed. Born in Padua in 1508, Andrea moved to nearby Vicenza in 1524 and was quickly taken up

2

THE OLD BECOMES NEW

La Malcontenta

Studying ancient Rome with the eyes of an explorer, Palladio created a style that linked old with new—but often did so in unexpected ways. Just take a look at Villa Foscari, nicknamed "**La Mal-contenta**" (Mira, 041/5470012, www.lamalcontenta.com € 5.15. Open May–Oct., Tues. and Sat. 9–noon; from Venice, take an ACTV bus from Piazzale Roma to Mira or opt for a boat ride up on the Burchiello). Shaded by weeping willows and mirrored by the Brenta Canal—the Beverly Hills of 16th-century Venice—"The Unhappy" was built for Nicolò and Alvise Foscari and is the quintessence of Palladian poetry. Its nickname was presumably coined for the recalcitrant wife of one of the original owners, as she had misbehaved so scandalously in Venice that she was kept locked up here. In revolutionary fashion, Palladio applied the ancient Roman public motif of a temple facade to a private, domestic dwelling, topped off by a pediment, a construct previously used exclusively for religious structures. Inside, he used the technique of vaulting seen in ancient Roman baths to enhance the spatial flow. With giant windows and immense white walls ready-made for the colorful frescoes painted by Zelotti, the resulting effect almost feels like a spacious New York City loft.

by the city's power elite. But he experienced a profound revelation on his first trip, in 1541, to Rome. Foregoing his earlier impulse to turn his adopted city, Vicenza, into a Gothic-mannered Venice, he decided instead to turn it into another Rome. This turnaround led to his spectacular conversion of the city's Palazzo della Ragione (1545) into a basilica modeled after the great meeting halls of antiquity. In years to come, after relocating to Venice, he created some memorable churches, such as S. Giorgio Maggiore (1564). Despite these varied projects, Palladio's unassailable position as one of the world's greatest architects is tied to the country-side villas, which he spread across the Veneto plains like a firmament of stars. Nothing else in the Veneto illuminates more clearly the idyllic beauty of the region than these elegant residences, their stonework now nicely mellowed and suntanned after five centuries.

VICENZA, CITY OF PALLADIO

Palazzo della Ragione

La Rotonda

To see Palladio's pageant of palaces, head for Vicenza, 53 km (33 mi) to the northwest of Mira's Malcontenta. His **Palazzo della Ragione**, or "Basilica," landmarks the city's heart, the Piazza dei Signori. This is where Palladio most brilliantly adopted the Serliana motif, an open arch framed by columns and circular windows. Across the way is his redbrick **Loggia dei Capitaniato**. One block past the Loggia is Vicenza's main street, appropriately named Corso Andrea Palladio. Just off this street is the Contrà Porti, where you'll find the **Palazzo Porto Barbaran** (1570) at No. 11, with its fabulously rich facade erupting with Ionic and Corinthian pillars. Today, this is the Centro Internazionale di Studi di Architettura Andrea Palladio (0444/323014, www.cisapalladio.org), a study center which mounts impressive temporary exhibitions. At No. 12 is Palladio's **Palazzo Thiene** (1558) while No. 21 is **Palazzo Porto Festa**, which he started. Contrà Reale leads to Corso A. Fogazzaro, where Palladio's **Palazzo Valmarana Braga** is found at No. 16, its grand facade ornamented with gigantic pilasters. A family cartouche once surmounted the roofline and was illuminated at night—à la Trump. Return to Corso Palladio and head left for five blocks to Piazza Mattotti and the **Palazzo Chiericati** (1550)—now the Museo Civico—Palladio's take on an imperial Roman loggia. Across the piazza the **Teatro Olimpico**, one of his final works (begun in 1579–80), reveals Palladio's knowledge of ancient Roman theaters. For a suitably grand finale, nothing will satisfy but a visit to one of the greatest buildings in all of Europe, **Villa La Rotonda** (Via della Rotonda 29, 0444/321793; villa €10, grounds €5. Villa open mid-Mar.–Oct., Wed. 10–noon and 3–6. Grounds mid-Mar.–Oct., Tues.–Sun. 10–noon and 3–6; Nov.–mid-Mar., Tues.–Sun. 10–noon and 2–5. Getting to the villa is a pleasant 20-minute walk from the city center, or take Bus 8 from Viale Roma. Created for papal prelate Paolo Almerico, La Rotonda seems less a villa than a Roman temple, which was precisely the architect's intention. Take sufficient time to admire it from all sides; you'll realize Palladio just repeated the temple portico on all four faces, to take advantage of the idyllic views. Inspired by the hillside site on Monte Berico and topped by a dome like Rome's Pantheon, La Rotonda is Palladio's only freestanding, centralized design, because it was intended to be a showplace, not a working farm. Still owned by the Counts Valmarana, La Rotonda's interior is rarely open. But it's no loss, as it's awash in florid frescoes Palladio would have detested.

THE "WINGED DEVICE"

Villa Barbaro

One of Palladio's most gracious Renaissance creations lies 48 km (30 mi) northeast of Vicenza: his **Villa Barbaro** (Via Cornuda 7, 0423/923004, www. villadimases.it, €5. Open Apr.–Oct., Tues. and weekends 3–6; Nov.–Mar., weekends 2:30–5; or by reservation; closed Dec. 24–Jan. 6). Near Asolo and built just outside the town of Maser in 1549 for the two Barbaro brothers, this villa spectacularly illustrates Palladio's famous "winged device"—using a villa's outlying wings, which often housed granaries, to frame the main building, and linking them together with graceful loggias (the 16th-century answer to air-conditioning). With this one stroke,

he brought everything together, making the parts subservient to the whole. His dramatic frontal designs have led historians to compare these facades to theater stages and to term his sense of space scenographic. Inside the cool halls of the villa, painted courtiers provocatively peek out behind frescoed doors. Legend has it that these famous paintings of Paolo Veronese were the cause of a rift, since Palladio felt these trompe l'oeil scenes distorted the purity of his architectural design. Today, the villa is still owned by Barbaro descendants, and its enduring beauty ensures that future generations of architects will continue to shape and enrich the Palladian style.

ALONG THE BRENTA CANAL

During the 16th century the Brenta was transformed into a landlocked version of Venice's Grand Canal with the building of nearly 50 waterside villas. Back then, boating parties viewed them in "*burchielli*"–beautiful boats. Today, the Burchiello excursion boat (Via Orlandini 3, Padua,

049/8206910, www.ilburchiello.it) makes an all-day villa tour along the Brenta, from March to November, departing from Padua on Wednesday, Friday, and Sunday and from Venice on Tuesday, Thursday, and Saturday; tickets are €62 and can also be bought at American Express at Salizzada San

Moisè in Venice. You visit three houses, including the Villas Pisani and Foscari, with a lunchtime break in Oriago. Another canal excursion is run by the Battelli del Brenta (www.battellidelbrenta.it). Note that most houses are on the left side coming from Venice, or the right from Padua.

and airy (with tall ceilings and pale walls), yet at the same time cozy (with substantial wood beds). This comfortable, convenient bargain is off the Piazza dei Signori. ⊠ *Contrà Do Rode 24, 36100* ☎ *0444/ 321886* 📠 *0444/326127* ⊕ *www.hotelduemori.com* 🛏 *30 rooms* ⚲ *Bar, some free parking, some pets allowed; no a/c, no room TVs* ▤ *AE, MC, V* ⊗ *Closed last 2 wks July* ⑪ *BP.*

Nightlife & the Arts

The **Teatro Olimpico** (⊠ Piazza Matteotti ☎ 0444/222801 ⊕ www. comune.vicenza.it) hosts a jazz festival in May, classical concerts in June, and classical drama performances in September. Even if your Italian is dismal, it can be thrilling to see a performance in Palladio's magnificent theater.

VERONA

On the banks of the fast-flowing River Adige, 60 km (37 mi) west of Vicenza, enchanting Verona has timeless monuments, a picturesque town center, and a romantic reputation as the setting of Shakespeare's *Romeo and Juliet*. With its lively Venetian air and proximity to Lake Garda, it attracts hordes of tourists, especially Germans and Austrians. Tourism peaks during summer's renowned season of open-air opera in the Arena and during spring's Vinitaly, one of the world's most important wine expos. For five days you can sample the wines of more than 3,000 wineries from dozens of countries. (Book months in advance for hotels during approximately the second week in April.)

Verona grew to power and prosperity within the Roman Empire as a result of its key commercial and military position in northern Italy. After the fall of the Empire, the city continued to flourish under the guidance of barbarian kings such as Theodoric, Alboin, Pepin, and Berenger I, reaching its cultural and artistic peak in the 13th and 14th centuries under the della Scala dynasty. (Look for the *scala*, or ladder, emblem all over town.) In 1404 Verona traded its independence for security and placed itself under the control of Venice. (The other recurring architectural motif is the lion of St. Mark, symbol of Venetian rule.) Verona remained under Venetian protection until 1797, when Napoléon invaded. In 1814 the entire Veneto region was won by the Austrians it wasn't reunited with Italy until 1866.

Exploring Verona

If you're going to visit more than a sight or two, it's worthwhile to purchase a Verona Card, available at museums, churches, and tobacconists for €8 (one day) or €12 (three days). You get a single admission to most of the city's significant museums and churches, and you can ride free on city buses. A €5 Chiese Vive Card is sold at Verona's major churches and gains you entry to the Duomo, San Fermo Maggiore, San Zeno Maggiore, and Sant'Anastasia. Do note that Verona's churches strictly enforce their dress code: no sleeveless shirts, shorts, or short skirts.

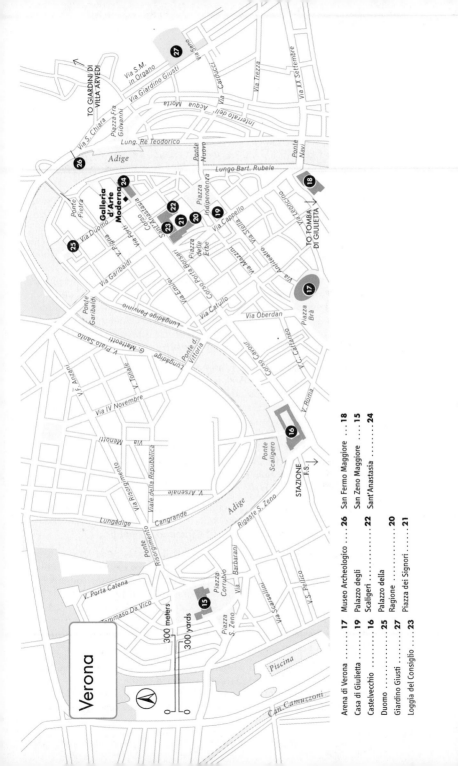

Verona

Arena di Verona **17**
Casa di Giulietta **19**
Castelvecchio **16**
Duomo **25**
Giardino Giusti **27**
Loggia del Consiglio ... **23**

Museo Archeologico **26**
Palazzo degli
Scaligeri **22**
Palazzo della
Ragione **20**
Piazza dei Signori **21**

San Fermo Maggiore ... **18**
San Zeno Maggiore **15**
Sant'Anastasia **24**

The Main Attractions

Arena di Verona. Only the Colosseum in Rome and the arena in Capua can outdo this amphitheater in size. Just four arches remain of the arena's outer arcade, but the main structure is so complete that it takes little imagination to picture it as the site of the cruel deaths of countless gladiators, wild beasts, and Christians. Today you can visit the arena year-round; in summer, audiences of up to 16,000 pack the stands for Verona's famously spectacular open-air opera productions. ⊠ *Arena di Verona, Piazza Brà 5* ☏ *045/8003204* ⊕ *www.arena.it* ⊠ *€5 or VeronaCard, €1 1st Sun. of month* ⊘ *Mon. 1:30–7:15, Tues.–Sun. 8:30–7:15, on performance days 8–3:30; last entry 45 mins before closing.*

Castelvecchio (Old Castle). This crenellated, russet brick building with massive walls, towers, turrets, and a vast courtyard was built for Cangrande II della Scala in 1354. It presides over a street lined with attractive old buildings and palaces of the nobility. To really appreciate the massive castle complex, go inside the **Museo di Castelvecchio,** which gives you a good look at the vaulted halls and the collections of Venetian art and medieval weapons and jewelry. For the benefit of sightless visitors, some paintings have been rendered in plastic relief and have recorded explanations. Behind the castle is the Ponte Scaligero, a public walkway spanning the River Adige. ⊠ *Corso Castelvecchio 2* ☏ *045/8062611* ⊠ *€4 or VeronaCard, free 1st Sun. of month* ⊘ *Mon. 1:30–7:30, Tues.–Sun. 8:30–7:30; last entry 6:45.*

Duomo. Verona's cathedral is an amalgamation of religious buildings, the earliest dating back to 380; it's ornately Romanesque but also shows Venetian and even Byzantine influences. Noteworthy inside are carvings of Oliver and Roland, two of Charlemagne's knights, guarding the main entrance, and Titian's *Assumption* gracing the first chapel on the left. Unlike in most Italian cities, this Duomo is tucked off in one of the quieter parts of town. ⊠ *Via Duomo* ☏ *045/592813* ⊕ *www.chieseverona.it* ⊠ *€2.50, €5 for combined churches ticket, or VeronaCard* ⊘ *Nov.–Feb., Tues.–Sat. 10–4, Sun. 10–5; Mar.–Oct., Mon.–Sat. 10–5:30, Sun. 1:30–5:30.*

Loggia del Consiglio. This graceful structure, built in the 12th century as a site for city council meetings, still serves as seat of the provincial government. ⊠ *Piazza dei Signori* ⊘ *Closed to the public.*

Palazzo degli Scaligeri. The iron-fisted della Scalas ruled Verona from this medieval stronghold. Though the palazzo is closed to the public, you can gaze into the adjacent **Arche Scaligere,** site of the suitably impressive marbled Gothic tombs of family members Cangrande I ("Big Dog"), Mastino II ("Mastiff"), and Cansignorio ("Top Dog"). ⊠ *Via Arche Scaligere* ⊠ *€4* ⊘ *Arche Scaligere visible at all times from the outside; inside open to walk among the tombs, Mon. 1:30–7:30, Tues.–Sun. 8:30–7:30; last entry 30 mins before closing.*

Palazzo della Ragione. An elegant pink marble staircase leads up from the *mercato vecchio* (old market) courtyard to the magistrates' chambers in the 12th-century palace also known as the Palazzo del Comune. The building is undergoing renovation and will be turned into a conference center. You can get the highest view in town from atop the attached 270-foot-tall **Torre dei Lamberti,** which is open during reconstruction. Taking the elevator costs only slightly more than walking up the 368 steps for the panoramic view—but the burned calories are priceless. ⊠ *Piazza dei Signori* ☎ *045/8032726* 💳 *€2, €3 with elevator* ☉ *Mon. 1:30–7:30, Tues.–Sun. 8:30–7:30; last entry 6:45.*

★ **Piazza delle Erbe.** A Roman forum once bustled on this site and until recently it housed the daily fruit-and-vegetable market. Many of the stalls have now gone (you still have a wide choice of trinkets, postcards, and snacks), perhaps adding charm to the medieval square. The surrounding frescoed town houses, the fountains, and the buzz of people and vendors all combine to make this one of northern Italy's most memorable city squares.

㉑ **Piazza dei Signori.** Verona's most impressive piazza, the center of things for more than 1,000 years, is today lorded over by a pensive statue of Dante, often as not with a pigeon on his head. His back is toward the Loggia del Consiglio and his left hand points toward the Palazzo degli Scaligeri. He faces Palazzo del Capitanio (to his left) and Palazzo della Ragione (to his right). All these buildings are closed to the public except those on government business.

⑱ **San Fermo Maggiore.** From its humble Benedictine beginnings, San Fermo grew through the centuries, in part as a result of rebuilding after floods from the nearby River Adige. The tomblike lower church, dating from the 8th century, became usable again when the Adige was reengineered to stay within its banks. The mammoth upper church completed in the 14th century has the Veneto's oldest and perhaps finest ship's-keel ceiling, decorated with paintings of 400 saints. ⊠ *Stradone S. Fermo* ☎ *045/592813* ⊕ *www.chieseverona.it* 💳 *€2.50, €5 for combined churches ticket, or VeronaCard* ☉ *Nov.–Feb., Tues.–Sat. 10–1 and 1:30–4, Sun. 1–5; Mar.–Oct., Mon.–Sat. 10–6, Sun. 1–6.*

★ ⑮ **San Zeno Maggiore.** Possibly Italy's finest Romanesque church, San Zeno stands between two medieval bell towers. A 13th-century rose window depicts the wheel of fortune, and bronze doors from the 11th and 12th centuries are decorated with scenes from the Bible and from the life of Verona's patron saint, Zeno, who's buried in the crypt. Look for the statue *San Zeno Laughing* to the left of the main altar—the unknown artist, or perhaps the saint himself, must have had a sense of humor. A *Madonna and Saints* triptych by Andrea Mantegna (1431–1506) hangs over the main altar, and a peaceful cloister lies to the north (left) of the nave. ⊠ *Piazza San Zeno* ☎ *045/592813* ⊕ *www.chieseverona.it* 💳 *€2.50, €5 for combined churches ticket, or VeronaCard* ☉ *Nov.–Feb., Tues.–Sat. 10–4, Sun. 1–5; Mar.–Oct., Mon.–Sat. 8:30–6, Sun. 1–6.*

㉔ **Sant'Anastasia.** Verona's largest church, completed in 1481, is a fine example of Gothic brickwork and has a grand doorway with elaborately carved biblical scenes. The finest of its numerous frescoes is the pastel *St. George and the Princess* by Pisanello (1377–1455) above the Pellegrini Chapel right off the main altar, where the saint appears more gentleman than warrior. As you come in, look for the *gobbi* (hunchbacks) supporting holy-water stoups. ✉ *Vicolo Sotto Riva 4* ☎ *045/592813* ⊕ *www.chieseverona.it* ✆ *€2.50, €5 for combined churches ticket, or VeronaCard* ☾ *Nov.–Feb., Tues.–Sat. 10–4, Sun. 1–5; Mar.–Oct., Mon.–Sat. 9–6, Sun. 1–6.*

Also Worth Seeing

⑲ Casa di Giulietta (Juliet's House). The small courtyard balcony evokes Shakespeare's play, even if it is part of a 20th-century remodel. Despite historians' belief that the famous lovers had no real-life counterparts, thousands of visitors refuse to let truth get in the way of a good story. ✉ *Via Cappello 23* ☎ *045/8034303* ✆ *€4* ☾ *Mon. 1:30–7:30, Tues.–Sun. 8:30–7:30; last entry 6:45.*

㉗ Giardino Giusti. In 1570 Agostino Giusti designed these formal gardens on the hillside behind his villa. Though the toothy mask halfway up the hill no longer breathes flames, little has been changed of Giusti's maze, fountains, or stalactite grotto. And though Verona might no longer be recognizable to Johann Wolfgang von Goethe (1749–1832), you can still enjoy the terrace views that inspired this German poet and dramatist to record his impressions. ✉ *Via Giardino Giusti 2* ☎ *045/8034029* ✆ *€5* ☾ *Apr.–Sept., daily 9–8; Oct.–Mar., daily 9–7.*

㉖ Museo Archeologico. The views of the city from this museum housed in an old monastery are even better than its archaeological exhibits. It sits high above the Teatro Romano, near the Arena di Verona. ✉ *Rigaste del Redentore 2* ☎ *045/8000360* ✆ *€3, free 1st Sun. of month* ☾ *Mon. 1:30–7:30, Tues.–Sun. 8:30–7:30; last entry 6:45.*

Out of Town: Amarone & Valpolicella Wine Country

Touring wineries near Verona is a good way to see, and taste, the lush countryside of the Veneto. Be aware that at Italian wineries you need to call ahead to arrange a visit.

Allegrini, one of the top producers in the region, is also one of the friendliest; at their Fumane estate, less than half an hour's drive from downtown Verona, you can tour the facility and watch a video of their story, which goes back to 1854. Of course, you can also taste their wines, including an award-winning Amarone Classico and a spectacular, full-bodied wine, La Poja, made from 100% Corvina grapes. To get here from Verona, follow the *super strada* toward Sant'Ambrogio and San Pietro in Cariano, then head north on SP33 to reach Fumane. ✉ *Via Giare 7, Fumane* ☎ *045/6832011* ⊕ *www.allegrini.it* ✆ *Free* ☾ *By appointment.*

Serègo Alighieri ages some of its wines in cherrywood, a virtually unheard-of practice. Wondering about that name? Legend has it that the poet Dante Alighieri finished his *Paradiso* while living out several years of his exile in the castle here. One of his direct descendents, a count, owns Castel dei Ronchi (now an inn and convention center) and makes delicious Amarone. He operates in partnership with Masi, another extremely important producer; at the shop you can taste Masi as well as Alighieri wines, and buy vintages going back to the 1980s. The winery is 20 km (12 mi) from Verona: take the super strada toward Sant'Ambrogio and head west on SP4. ✉ *Gargagnano di Valpolicella* ☎ *045/7703622* ⊕ *www.seregoalighieri.it* ✆ *Tours €8, wines ₵50–€2.50 per* taste ☉ Wine shop Mon.–Sat. 10 AM–6 PM; tours by appointment 3 days in advance.

Where to Stay & Eat

★ **$$$$** ✕ **Il Desco.** *Cucina dell' anima* (food of the soul) is how Chef Elia Rizzo describes his cuisine, which preserves natural flavors through quick cooking and a limit of three ingredients per dish. He spares no expense in selecting those ingredients, and you pay accordingly. Dishes like *petto di faraona con purea di topinambur, salsa al ll'aceto balsamico e cioc-colato* (breast of guinea fowl with Jerusalem artichoke purèe and a chocolate and balsamic vinegar sauce) are standouts. For a real splurge, order the tasting menu (€110), which includes appetizers, two first courses, two second courses, and dessert. Decor is elegant, if overstated, with fine tapestries, paintings, and an impressive 16th-century lacunar ceiling. ☒ *Via Dietro San Sebastiano 7* ☏ *045/595358* ⌯ *Reservations essential* ▭ *AE, DC, MC, V* ☉ *Closed Sun. and Mon., Dec. 25–Jan. 8, and June 6–25. Closed Sun. and Mon.*

$$$$ ✕ **Dodici Apostoli.** Vaulted ceilings, frescoed walls, and a medieval ambience make this an exceptional place to enjoy classic regional dishes. Near Piazza delle Erbe, it stands on the foundations of a Roman temple. Specialties include gnocchi *di zucca e ricotta* (with squash and ricotta cheese) and *vitello alla Lessinia* (veal with mushrooms, cheese, and truffles). ☒ *Vicolo Corticella San Marco 3* ☏ *045/596999* ⊕ *www.12apostoli.it* ▭ *AE, DC, MC, V* ☉ *Closed Mon.; no dinner Sun. Closed Jan. 1–10 and June 15–30.*

★ **¢–$** ✕ **Antica Osteria al Duomo.** You'd think, from the name of the place, that this would be a tourist trap. Quite the contrary—the side-street eatery lined with old wooden walls and ceilings, and decked out with musical instruments, serves Veronese food to a Veronese crowd; they come to quaff the local wine (€1–€3 per glass) and to savor northern dishes like *canederli con speck, burro fuso, e rosmarino* (dumplings with bacon, melted butter, and rosemary) and *stracotto di cavallo con polenta* (horse meat with polenta). ☒ *Via Duomo 7/a* ☏ *045/8004505* ▭ *AE, MC, V* ☉ *Closed Thurs. Oct.–Mar., Sun. Apr.–Sept.*

¢ ✕ **Du de Cope.** Il Desco's star chef decided to branch into pizza making and the result is four-star, wood-fired pizza at one-star prices. Toppings like buffalo mozzarella and Parmigiano Reggiano cheese cover the lightest crust that ever hovered on a plate. Notice how well modern drop lighting merges with old-fashioned, blue-and-white tile walls; place mats quilt the hardwood tables and burlap tapestries decorate the walls. ☒ *Galleria Pellicciai 10* ☏ *045/595562* ▭ *AE, DC, MC, V* ☉ *Closed Tues. No lunch Sun.*

★ **¢** ✕ **Osteria al Duca.** Folks jam this place at lunchtime, sharing tables, wine, and conversation in a building that legend claims to have been Romeo's birthplace. Beneath low-slung ceilings, generous portions of local specialties are served for a very reasonable fixed price along with a wine list that belies the simplicity of the surroundings. Try Gorgonzola served with polenta, vegetarian eggplant with mozzarella, or homemade *bigoli al torchio,* a thick spaghetti forced through a press. This may be some of the best food available for the price in town. ⊠ *Arche Scaligere 2* 🕾 *045/594474* 🖃 *MC, V* ☾ *Closed Sun. and mid-Dec.–mid-Jan.*

★ **$$$$** ✕🖸 **Villa del Quar.** Leopoldo and Evelina Montresor spared no expense when converting part of their 16th-century villa into a sophisticated luxury property with antiques and marble bathrooms. The Relais & Chateaux hotel is surrounded by gardens and vineyards, 15 minutes by car from Verona's city center. Service is both familiar and impeccable, whether at the poolside bar or in the acclaimed Arquade restaurant ($$$$). One of the top places to dine in northern Italy, it occupies a softly lighted converted chapel and a beautiful outdoor terrace. Chef Bruno Barbieri's creative menu might include inspired preparations of lobster, scampi, and foie gras, but simpler dishes, such as a platter of steamed fish, meet with equal success. The wine list, needless to say, is magnificent, and the hotel can help you organize a visit to some of Valpolicella's best wineries. ⊠ *Via Quar 12, 37020 Pedemonte di San Pietro in Cariano, 10 km (6 mi) northwest of Verona* 🕾*045/6800681* 🖃*045/6800604* ⊕*www.hotelvilladelquar. it* ➹ *18 rooms, 10 suites* ⟂ *Restaurant, in-room safes, minibars, cable TV, in-room data ports, pool, health club, massage, 2 bars, meeting room, helipad, free parking, some pets allowed, no-smoking rooms, Internet room* 🖃*AE, DC, MC, V* ☾*Closed Jan.–mid-Mar. Restaurant closed Mon. Oct.–May. No lunch Tues.* 🍽 *BP.*

$$ 🖸 **Hotel Europa.** The third generation of this inn-keeping family, which has operated the Europa since 1956, welcomes you to a convenient downtown hotel. Expect hardwood floors and pastel *marmarino* (Venetian polished plaster) walls. Rooms are comfortable and up-to-date, and the breakfast room on the ground floor is exceptionally bright. ⊠ *Via Roma 8, 37121* 🕾 *045/594744* 🖃 *045/8001852* ⊕ *www. veronahoteleuropa.com* ➹ *46 rooms* ⟂ *In-room safes, minibars, cable TV, parking (fee), no-smoking rooms* 🖃 *AE, DC, MC, V* 🍽 *BP.*

$ 🖸 **Torcolo.** It may not look like much from the outside, but this hotel boasts several advantages: a warm welcome from owners Diana Castellani and Silvia Pomari, pleasant rooms decorated unfussily, and a central location close to Piazza Brà and the Arena. Breakfast, which costs an extra €7–€12, is served outside on the front terrace in summer. ⊠ *Vicolo Listone 3, 37121* 🕾 *045/8007512* 🖃 *045/8004058* ⊕ *www. hoteltorcolo.it* ➹ *19 rooms* ⟂ *Breakfast room, in-room safes, minibars, cable TV, bar, parking (fee), some pets allowed* 🖃 *AE, DC, MC, V* ☾ *Closed mid-Jan.–mid-Feb.* 🍽 *EP.*

Opera

Of all the venues for enjoying opera in the region, pride of place must go to the **Arena di Verona** (Box office ⊠ Via Dietro Anfiteatro 6/b 🕾 045/8005151 ⊕ www.arena.it ☾ Box office weekdays 9–noon and 3:15–5:45, Sat. 9–noon. June 21–Aug. 31, 10–9 on performance days and 10–5:45 on nonperformance days 🎫 Tickets start at €22). During its summer opera season (July–September) audiences of as many as 16,000 sit on the original stone terraces or in the modern cushioned stalls. The best operas are the big, splashy ones, like *Aïda,* that demand huge choruses, lots of color and movement, and, if possible, camels, horses, or elephants. But the experience is memorable no matter what's play-

FodorśChoice
★

ing. Order tickets by phone or online: if you book a place on the cheaper terraces, be sure to take or rent a cushion—four hours on a 2,000-year-old stone bench can be an ordeal. Sometimes you can even hear the opera from Piazza Brà cafés.

Shopping

Food & Wine

Salumeria Albertini (⊠ Corso S. Anastasia 41 ☎045/8031074) is Verona's oldest delicatessen: look for the prosciutto and salami hanging outside. **De Rossi** (⊠ Corso Porta Borsari 3 ☎ 045/8002489) sells baked bread and cakes, pastries, and biscotti that are lusciously caloric.

Markets

On the third Saturday of every month an antiques and arts-and-crafts market fills **Piazza San Zeno.** The city's main general market takes place at the **Stadio** on Saturday 8:30 AM–1 PM.

TREVISO & THE HILLSIDE TOWNS

In this area directly north of Venice, market towns cling to the steep foothills of the Alps and the Dolomites alongside streams raging down from the mountains. Villa Barbaro, one of Palladio's most graceful country villas, is here, as are the arcaded streets and romantic canals of undiscovered Treviso and the graceful Venetian Gothic structures of smaller hill towns.

Marostica

28 *26 km (16 mi) northeast of Vicenza, 93 km (58 mi) northwest of Venice.*

From the 14th-century Castello Inferiore, where the town council still meets, an ancient stone wall snakes up the hill to enclose the Castello Superiore, with its commanding views. Marostica's most celebrated feature is the checkerboard-like square made with colored stone, Piazza Castello.

☾ A game of human-scale chess known as **Partita a Scacchi** is acted out in Piazza Castello by players in medieval costume on the second weekend in September in even-number years. There's a game presented Friday–Sunday evenings and there's a Sunday-afternoon show. Tickets go on sale in April; the tourist office can help with bookings.

Where to Stay

★ **$–$$** ⚏ **Due Mori.** Recessed lighting adds to the modern, minimalist design at this historic inn, which has been this medieval town's only refuge for travelers since the 18th century. Warm wooden floors and soft-beige marble bathrooms are all made of local materials. Some windows look out onto the city walls or olive tree–filled terraces, but rooms 7, 8, 11, and 12 have picture-perfect views of the upper castle. There's a comfortably chic restaurant ($$) downstairs. ⊠ *Corso Mazzini 73, 36063* ☎ *0424/471777* 🖷 *0424/476920* ⊕ *www.duemori.com* 🛏 *12 rooms* ⚐ *Restaurant, minibars, cable TV, in-room data ports, free parking, some pets allowed, no-smoking rooms* ▤ *AE, DC, MC, V* ☾ *Closed 1st wk Jan., 1 wk mid-Aug.* ⦿ *BP.*

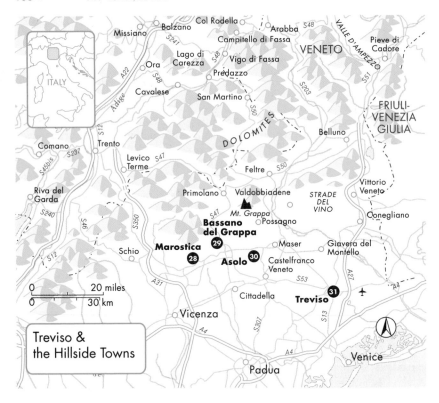

Treviso & the Hillside Towns

Bassano del Grappa

29 *7 km (4½ mi) east of Marostica, 37 km (23 mi) north of Venice.*

Nestled at the base of the Mt. Grappa massif (5,880 feet), with the mountain-fresh Brenta River sluicing through, this town seems to be higher in the mountains than it actually is. Bassano has old streets lined with low-slung buildings adorned with wooden balconies and pretty flowerpots. Bright ceramic wares produced in the area are displayed in shops along byways that curve uphill toward a centuries-old square and, even higher, to a belvedere with a good view of Mt. Grappa and the beginning of the Val Sugana.

Bassano's most famous landmark is the **Ponte degli Alpini,** a covered bridge named for Italy's Alpine soldiers. There's been a bridge spanning the Brenta here since 1209, but floods and wars have required repeated rebuilding. The present version was constructed by Alpine soldiers following World War II. They used Andrea Palladio's 16th-century design, which astutely calls for easily replaceable wood as the building material.

Almost as famous as Bassano's bridge is the nearby bar and liquor shop ★ **Nardini** (✉ Ponte Vecchio 2 ☎ 0424/527741 ☉ Closed Mon. Oct.–May). The shop draws locals for after-work *aperitifs,* such as the trademark mix of grappa and *chino* (a lighter bittersweet spirit). Stop in before 9 PM for a sip in view of the bridge or to buy a bottle of the house *invecchiata* (aged grappa).

Grappa was once considered by alchemists to have supernatural qualities, and its distillation techniques, you might say, were half science, half black magic. A few steps uphill from Ponte degli Alpini, the noted grappa producer Poli has set up the **Poli Grappa Museum** (⊠ Ponte Vecchio ☎ 0424/524426 ⊴ Free ⊙ Daily 9:30 AM–9 PM). Most interesting are the old grappa stills, their glass tubes twisting every which way into improbably shaped coils. You can taste almost all of Poli's numerous grappas (for free) and take home a bottle or two (not for free).

Where to Stay & Eat

★ **$$–$$$** ✕ **Al Sole da Tiziano.** With the personable Franco Chiurato in the dining room, you can't help but leave here satisfied. Within these walls, which are decorated with hefty, ornamental ceramic whistles (of the sort once used to warn of enemy approaches), Bassano home cooking flirts with the international: duck ends up in pomegranate, pheasant in cognac, and cauliflower and cheese hand-stuffed into luscious pasta pillows. ⊠ *Via Vittorelli 41/43* ☎ *0424/23206* ☐ *AE, DC, MC, V* ⊙ *Closed Mon. and 3 wks late July–mid-Aug.*

$–$$ ✕ **Osteria Terraglio.** The creative modern menu here focuses on absolute freshness, from the wonderful array of savory snacks to the big, crisp *insalatone* (main-course salads with tuna or various cheeses), and the steak fillet, cut to order. Special tasting sessions of local delicacies such as asparagus, cold-pressed olive oil, and fine wines are a regular feature. October through May there's live jazz on Tuesday evening. ⊠ *Piazza Terraglio 28* ☎ *0424/521064* ☐ *AE, DC, MC, V* ⊙ *Closed Mon.*

$$$ ✕▥ **Ca' Sette.** Were it not for an engraving showing Napoléon's troops massed in the courtyard, you'd never guess the great age of this hotel, which has an ultramodern interior. Each room has a different tasteful design in local wood and marble. Light sleepers should request a room that doesn't face the rather busy road. **Ca' 7** restaurant ($$$–$$$$) is among the best in the area. From Chef Alex Lorenzon's menu you might choose a dish in which you dig into a deep-fried, bread crumb–covered egg yolk to find it bursts golden cream over your plate of polenta, fresh mushrooms, and Asiago cheese. ⊠ *Via Cunizza da Romano 4, 36061* ☎ *0424/383350* ⊟ *0424/393287* ⊕ *www.ca-sette.it* ⊲ *17 rooms, 2 suites* ⊲ *Restaurant, in-room safes, minibars, in-room data ports, bicycles, free parking, some pets allowed, no-smoking rooms* ☐ *AE, DC, MC, V* ⊙ *Restaurant closed Mon., 1st wk in Jan., and 2 wks mid-Aug. No dinner Sun.* ⍢ *BP.*

$$ ▥ **Hotel Belvedere.** This 15th-century hotel, now a member of the Bonotto chain, has richly decorated public rooms with period furnishings and Oriental rugs; the lounge has an open fireplace and a piano. Guest rooms are decorated in traditional Venetian or contemporary style. Two restaurants provide a choice between light, inexpensive dishes and full-course regional meals. ⊠ *Piazzale G. Giardino 14, 36061* ☎ *0424/529845* ⊟ *0424/529849* ⊕ *www.bonotto.it* ⊲ *83 rooms, 4 suites* ⊲ *2 restaurants, cable TV with movies, some in-room data ports, piano bar, meeting rooms, parking (fee), some pets allowed (fee), no-smoking* *rooms, Internet room, WiFi* ▤ *AE, DC, MC, V* ⊘ *Restaurant closed Sun.* ⊘I *BP.*

$ ▦ **Al Castello.** In a restored town house at the foot of the medieval Torre Civica, the Cattapan family's Castello is a reasonably priced, attractive choice. The simply furnished rooms all differ in shape and size, some have wood beam ceilings. Request a room at the front for a small balcony with a view of the charming square below. ⊠ *Piazza Terraglio 19, 36061* ▦▦ *0424/228665* ⊕ *www.hotelalcastello.it* ⥲ *11 rooms* ⚑ *Breakfast room, bar, Internet room* ▤ *AE, MC, V* ⊘I *EP.*

Asolo

30 *11 km (7 mi) east of Bassano del Grappa, 33 km (20½ mi) northwest*
Fodor'sChoice *of Treviso.*
★

The romantic, charming hillside hamlet of Asolo was the consolation prize of an exiled queen. At the end of the 15th century, Venetian-born Caterina Cornaro was sent here by Venice's doge to keep her from interfering with Venetian administration of her former kingdom of Cyprus, which she had inherited from her husband. To soothe the pain of exile she established a lively and brilliant court in Asolo. Through the centuries, Venetian aristocrats continued to build gracious villas on the hillside, and in the 19th century Asolo once again became the idyllic haunt of musicians, poets, and painters. And it's no wonder why—this aerie is one of Italy's most strikingly situated villages, combining views across miles of mountainous countryside with a slow-paced, fortified-hilltown feel. Here, you can stroll past villas once inhabited by Robert Browning and the actress Eleonora Duse. Be warned that the town's charm vaporizes on holiday weekends when the crowds pour in. Asolo hosts a two-day antiques market on the second Sunday of every month except July and August.

Renaissance palaces and antique cafés grace **Piazza Maggiore,** Asolo's town center. In the piazza, the frescoed 15th-century Loggia del Capitano contains the **Museo Civico,** which displays memorabilia—Eleonora Duse's correspondence, Browning's spinet, portraits of Caterina Cornaro, manuscripts—of Asolo's dead coterie. ⊠ *Piazza Maggiore* ☎ *0423/952313* ⊠ *€4* ⊘ *Sat. and Sun. 10–noon and 3–7 and by reservation.*

▌ **NEED A BREAK?** While away some idle moments at **Caffè Centrale** (⊠ **Via Roma 72** ☎ **0423/952141** ⊕ **www.caffecentrale.com** ⊘ **Closed Tues.**), which has overlooked the fountain in Piazza Maggiore and the Duomo since about 1700. It's open until 1 AM.

Several cathedrals have stood on the spot now occupied by the **Duomo,** which was built in 1747. This was once the location of Roman baths, and it is said that the first of the Duomo's predecessors was erected here in 590. For the 18th-century rendition Caterina Cornaro donated the baptismal font, and Jacopo Bassano (circa 1510–92) and Lorenzo Lotto (1480–1556) painted *Assumption* altarpieces. ⊠ *Piazzetta S. Pio X 192* ☎ *0423/952376* ⊘ *Daily 7–noon and 3:30–6:30.*

Walking along Via Browning takes you past smart shops, Browning's house at No. 153, and the enoteca **Alle Ore** (⊠ Via Browning 183

2

☎ 0423/952070), where you can sample the local wine and grappa. It's closed Monday. Heading uphill from Piazza Maggiore, you'll pass Caterina Cornaro's ruined **Castello** (✉ Piazzetta E. Duse), whose theater was transported to Florida in 1930. The castle is closed to the public. Above the Castello stands the imposing **Villa Pasini** (closed to the public), with its grand stairways and its ground floor still occupied by the signora Pasini. After a healthy, winding, half-hour climb to the summit, you'll reach the medieval **Rocca** (fortress). The hilltop site affords a view of Asolo's "hundred horizons," but it closes when the weather turns bad. ✉ *Monte Ricco* ☎ *0423/529046 tourist office* 💶 *€1.50* ☉ *Apr.–Oct. daily 10–7; Nov.–Mar. daily 10–5; July–Aug. daily 10–12:30 and 3–7.*

Where to Stay & Eat

$$$–$$$$ ✕ **Ca' Derton.** Opposite the entrance to the castle, Ca' Derton is pleasantly old-fashioned, with early photos of Asolo and bouquets of dried flowers. Proprietor Nino and his wife, Antonietta, serve both local and international dishes, and take pride in their homemade pasta, bread, and desserts. From November through April, try the bean soup or the *sopa coada,* a local pigeon-and-bread soup that takes two days to prepare; the recipe is several centuries old. ✉ *Piazza Gabriele D'Annunzio 11* ☎ *0423/529648* ⊕ *www.caderton.com* 🖃 *AE, DC, MC, V* ☉ *Closed Sun. and Feb. No lunch Mon.*

¢–$ ✕ **Al Bacaro.** Since 1892 this osteria has been a second home to Asolani laborers and craftsmen. Whether you eat downstairs in the bar with hanging copper kettles or upstairs in the dining room lighted by lacy lamps, you get affordable wines and pastas and home-style food. Take the leap and have goulash or a dish with stewed game, tripe, or snails. If you can't go there, choose from the tempting selection of big open-face sandwiches generously topped with fresh salami, speck, or other cold cuts. ✉ *Via R. Browning 165* ☎ *0423/55150* 🖃 *AE, DC, MC, V* ☉ *Closed Wed. and 2 wks in Aug.*

$$$$ 🏨 **Villa Cipriani.** On a hillside just below the center of Asolo, a roman-
Fodor'sChoice tic garden surrounded by gracious country homes is the setting for this
★ historic villa, now part of the Starwood chain. The setting is one of the most beautiful in Italy, and the experience is opulent from start to finish, with every creature comfort accompanied by impeccable service. Past guests have included Prince Philip, Aristotle Onassis, and Queen Juliana. Superior-class rooms and above have views; the two suites with private terraces are very expensive but absolutely stunning. The restaurant ($$$$) has its own terrace overlooking the garden and hills, a perfect place to sip an aperitif. ✉ *Via Canova 298, 31011* ☎ *0423/523411* 🖷 *0423/952095* ⊕ *www.starwood.com/italy* ➥ *31 rooms* ♺ *Restaurant, in-room safes, minibars, in-room data ports, cable TV, bar, in-room broadband, parking (fee), meeting room, some pets allowed (fee), no-smoking floor* 🖃 *AE, DC, MC, V* ⊠ *BP.*

★ **$$$–$$$$** 🏨 **Al Sole.** The smell of the polished wood floor greets you as you enter this 1920s pink-washed hotel overlooking the main square. This was once actress Eleonora Duse's preferred haunt, and her favorite room has been preserved. All the rooms are large and furnished in antique style. The more expensive superior rooms enjoy great views over the town, while the back rooms have leafy, rural views; a few rooms are set up for mobility-impaired guests. Decoratively tiled, the bathrooms come equipped with hydro-massage showers, which might come in handy if you take advantage of the hotel's golf discount. From the pleasant terrace of the summer-only restaurant ($$$) you can gaze out upon picturesque Asolo as you have dinner or a sunset drink. ⊠ *Via Collegio 33, 31011* ☎ *0423/951332* 🖷 *0423/951007* ⊕ *www.albergoalsole. com* ⟲ *22 rooms, 1 suite* ⌂ *Restaurant (Apr.–Oct.), in-room safes, minibars, cable TV, Internet room, gym, massage, bar, some pets allowed (fee)* ⊟ *AE, MC, V* ⑩ *BP.*

$$ 🏠 **Duse.** A spiral staircase winds its way up this narrow, centrally located building to rooms with a view of the town square. The scene gets lively on antique fair weekends, but if the sights don't make up for the sounds, ask for the larger and quieter attic room—skylights instead of windows mean your only view is the stars. Furnishings, such as slip-covered chairs and small tables with pastel table cloths, are simple and well tended. Some rooms are smallish, but for Asolo, the price is a real deal. ⊠ *Via Browning 190, 31011* ☎ *0423/55241* 🖷 *0423/950404* ⊕ *www. hotelduse.com* ⟲ *14 rooms* ⌂ *Minibars, cable TV, in-room data ports, bar, parking (fee), meeting room; no smoking* ⊟ *AE, MC, V* ⑩ *EP.*

Treviso

③ *35 km (22 mi) southeast of Maser, 30 km (19 mi) north of Venice.*

Treviso has often been dubbed "Little Venice." Even though the town's peaceful canals can't possibly compete with Venice's spectacular network, Treviso indeed has a unique charm that La Serenissima can't touch, with an authentic Italian atmosphere and a beautiful medieval historic center.

The description "painted city" is more apt: practically everywhere you look you'll see frescoes on the outside of buildings. Together with the arcaded streets and the mossy banked canals, where weeping willow fronds trail in the water, the frescoes help to create an appealing town center. There are fashionable shops and boutiques at every turn in this busy commercial hub, which was well established long before Venetian influence spread here in the late 14th century. Minting its own coins as early as the 8th century, Treviso became a center for literary and artistic excellence by the 13th. Modern structures popped up after a bombing raid on Good Friday, 1944, destroyed about half the city (black-and-white photos of the damage hang under the arcades in the Palazzo dei Trecento), but Treviso has not lost the feel of its old town. Through the years the city has meticulously maintained its narrow, timeworn streets while also integrating the shopping and *caffè* culture of a more modern Italy.

The **Piazza dei Signori** is the center of medieval Treviso and still the

> **WORD OF MOUTH**
>
> "If you do stay in Treviso, make sure you have a cappuccino in Piazza dei Signori—the best place to people watch and enjoy the ambience!"
>
> –Paulareg

CLOSE UP

Traveling the Wine Roads

YOU'D BE HARD-PRESSED to find a more stimulating and varied wine region than northeastern Italy. From the Valpolicella, Bardolino, and Soave produced near Verona to the superlative whites of the Collio region, wines from the Veneto and Friuli–Venezia Giulia earn more Denominazione di Origine Controllata (DOC) seals for uniqueness and quality than those of any other area of Italy.

You can travel on foot, by car, or by bicycle over hillsides covered with vineyards, each field nurturing subtly different grape varieties. On a casual trip through the countryside you're likely to come across wineries that will welcome you for a visit; for a more organized tour, check at local tourist information offices, which have maps of roads, wineries, and vendors. (If you find yourself in Bassano del Grappa, stop by Nardini distillery to pick up some grappa, the potent liquor made from grape husks.) Be advised that Italy has become more stringent about its driving regulations; seat belts and designated drivers can save fines, embarrassment, or worse.

One of the most hospitable areas in the Veneto for wine enthusiasts is the stretch of country north of Treviso, where you can follow designated wine roads—tours that blend a beautiful rural setting with the delights of the grape. Authorized wine shops where you can stop and sample are marked with a sign showing a triangular arrangement of red and yellow grapes. There are three routes to choose from, and they're manageable enough that you can do them all comfortably over the course of a day or two.

MONTELLO & ASOLO HILLS

This route provides a good balance of vineyards and non–wine-related sights. It winds its way from Nervesa della Battaglia, 18 km (10 mi) north of Treviso, past two prime destinations in the area, the lovely village of Asolo and the Villa Barbaro at Maser. Asolo produces good prosecco, whereas Montello favors merlot and cabernet. Both areas also yield pinot and chardonnay.

PIAVE RIVER

The circular route follows the Piave River and runs through orchards, woods, and hills. Among the area's gems are the DOC Torchiato di Fregona and Refrontolo Passito, both made according to traditional methods. Raboso del Piave, renowned since Roman times, ages well and complements local dishes such as beans and pasta or goose stuffed with chestnuts. The other reds are cabernet, merlot, and cabernet sauvignon. As an accompaniment to fish, choose a Verduzzo del Piave or, for an aperitif, the lovely warm-yellow Pinot Grigio del Piave.

PROSECCO

This route runs for 47 km (29 mi) between Valdobbiadene and Conegliano, home of Italy's first wine institute, winding between knobby hills covered in grapevines. These hang in festoons on row after row of pergolas to create a thick mantle of green. Turn off the main route to explore the narrower country lanes, most of which eventually join up. They meander through tiny hamlets and past numerous family wineries where you can taste and purchase the wines. Spring is an excellent time to visit, with no fewer than 15 local wine festivals held between March and early June.

2

town's social hub, with outdoor cafés and some impressive public buildings. One of these, the Palazzo dei Trecento, has a small alley behind it that leads to the *pescheria* (fish market), on an island in one of the small canals that flow through town.

The most important church in Treviso is **San Nicolò**, an impressive Gothic structure with an ornate vaulted ceiling and frescoes of the saints by Tommaso da Modena (circa 1325–79); the depiction of *St. Agnes* on the north side is particularly charming. More remarkable are Tommaso's astoundingly realistic portraits of 40 Dominican friars in the seminary next door. They include one of the earliest-known paintings of a subject wearing glasses. ⊠ *Seminario Vescovile, Via San Nicolò* ☎ *0422/ 3247* ⊘ *Daily 8–noon and 3:30–7.*

Inside Treviso's seven-domed **Duomo,** the Malchiostro Chapel contains an *Annunciation* by Titian and frescoes by Pordenone (1484–1539), including an *Adoration of the Magi.* The crypt has 12th-century columns. ⊠ *Piazza del Duomo* ⊘ *Daily 8–noon and 3:30–7.*

**OFF THE
BEATEN
PATH**

CONEGLIANO – The town of Conegliano, 23 km (14 mi) north of Treviso, is in wine-producing country. The town itself is attractive, with Venetian-style villas, frescoed houses, and an elegant 14th-century Duomo, but the real draw is the wine, particularly the effervescent prosecco, sold in local wine bars and shops.

Where to Stay & Eat

★ **$–$$** ✕**Antica Osteria al Cavallino.** What will be on the handwritten menu tonight is anyone's guess at this centuries-old dining mecca. Maybe risotto *ai funghi porcini* (with porcini mushrooms) or tagliolini with lobster. Surely it will include a fresh fish of the day. Without a doubt, everything will be superbly prepared from the day's ingredients, and served with deeply personal attention. Parts of the incredible palazzo, such as the outdoor terrace built into the wall of the ancient city, date back to 1540. Inside, dark wood walls are adorned with old oil paintings. It would be hard to find a more authentic evening of ancient *trevigiano* tradition. ⊠ *Borgo Cavour 52* ☎ *0422/412801* ⊟ *AE, DC, MC, V* ⊘ *No lunch Aug.*

★ **$–$$** ✕**Osteria Ponte Dante.** What could be more romantic than dining alfresco, at the junction of two quiet canals, in a spot once described by Dante? You can do it here, and, incredibly, the food lives up to the setting. The kitchen turns out great, simple local dishes like ravioli *ai porcini e ricotta affumicata* (with porcini mushrooms and smoked mozzarella) and a classic *fritto misto di pesce* (mixed fried fish), all at reasonable prices. ⊠ *Piazza Garibaldi 6* ☎ *0422/582924* ⊟ *No credit cards* ⊘ *Closed Sun.*

$–$$ ✕**Toni del Spin.** Wood-paneled and styled with 1930s decor, this place oozes delightful, old-fashioned character. Locals love the friendly and bustling feel as well as the wholesome food. The menu changes twice a week and is chalked on a hanging wooden board: try the filling *zuppa d'orzo e fagioli* (barley and bean soup) or the pasta e fagioli, delivered with panache and care. They also do a nice job with *branzino* (Mediterranean sea bass). Don't leave without quaffing a glass or two of prosecco. ⊠ *Via Inferiore 7* ☎ *0422/543829* ⊕ *www.ristorantetonidelspin.com* ⌦ *Reservations essential* ⊟ *AE, MC, V* ⊘ *Closed Sun. No lunch Mon.*

\$\$\$ 🏨 **Carlton Hotel.** Pass the river flowing outside, walk through a lobby that's seen better days, and seek out the huge terrace right on top of the old city wall. Even the parking lot has a view from here. The hotel has a time-frozen, decades-old feel, but that's part of the charm. Above the Embassy cinema, five minutes from the train station, and five minutes from the heart of Treviso, it is very convenient for touring—that is, if you're not too busy using the gym, enjoying free golf at Asolo, or tasting wine in the vineyards nearby. ⊠ *Largo di Porta Altinia 15, 31100* ☎ *0422/411661* 🖷 *0422/411620* ⊕ *www.hotelcarlton.it* 📲 *93 rooms* ☖ *Restaurant, in-room safes, minibars, cable TV, golf privileges, gym, bicycles, bar, meeting room, free parking, some pets allowed* ⊟ *AE, DC, MC, V* ☉ *Restaurant closed Sun.* ❙◯❙ *BP.*

★ **\$** 🏨 **Il Focolare.** Spitting distance from the back of the Palazzo dei Trecento, in the very heart of Treviso's *centro storico*, Il Focolare has the kind of spectacular location enjoyed by precious few *trevigiano* hotels. It's also a pleasant enough place to stay, with tidy, if smallish, rooms and a bright, welcoming reception area. ⊠ *Piazza Ancilotto 4* ☎ *0422/42256601* 🖷 *0422/4319900* ⊕ *www.ilfocolare.net* 📲 *14 rooms* ☖ *Minibars, bar* ⊟ *AE, DC, MC, V* ❙◯❙ *BP.*

FRIULI–VENEZIA GIULIA

The peripheral location of the Friuli–Venezia Giulia region in Italy's northeastern corner makes it easy to overlook, but with its ethnic mix of Italian, Slavic, and central European cultures, along with a legendary wine tradition, it's a fascinating area to explore. Venetian culture crept northward until it merged with northern European into the Veneto-Byzantine style evident in places like the medieval city of Udine. The Cividale del Friuli and the Collio wine regions around Cormòns are a short hop away from Udine, and the old Austrian port of Trieste was once an important symbol of Italian nationalism.

Udine

32 *94 km (58 mi) northeast of Treviso, 127 km (79 mi) northeast of Venice.*

Udine, the largest city on the Friuli side of the region, has a more provincial, genteel atmosphere than Venezia-Giulia's sprawling Trieste. Give the old center a day of your strolling time, and you'll find unevenly spaced streets bursting with fun little wine bars, open-air cafés, and gobs of Friulian character. The city sometimes seems completely unaffected by tourism or even modernity. Commanding a view from the Alpine foothills to the Adriatic Sea, Udine stands on a mound that, according to legend, was erected so Attila the Hun could watch the burning of Aquileia, an important Roman center to the south. In the Middle Ages Udine flourished, thanks to its favorable trade location and the right granted by the local patriarch to hold regular markets.

★ There is a distinctly Venetian architectural feel to the medieval city, noticeable in the large main square, the **Piazza della Libertà.** The Palazzo del Comune, a typical 15th-century Venetian palace, built in imitation of the Palazzo Ducale in Venice, dominates the square. Opposite stands

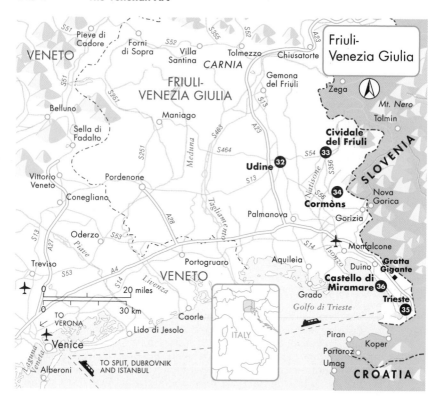

the Renaissance Porticato di San Giovanni and the Torre dell'Orologio, a clock tower complete with naked *mori* (the Moors who strike the hours) on the top. Inspired by the Torre d'Orologio in Piazza San Marco, the tower is another reference to Venice.

West of Piazza Libertà, **Piazza Matteotti,** surrounded on three sides by arcades and on the fourth by the church of San Giacomo, is the central piazza of Udine. The balcony of San Giacomo has an outside altar, which was built so that Mass could be said while business went on uninterrupted in the market below.

From the hilltop **Castello** panoramic views extend to Monte Nero (7,360 feet) in neighboring Slovenia. Here Udine's civic museums of art and archaeology are centralized under one roof. Particularly worth seeing is the national and regional art collection in the **Galleria d'Arte Antica,** which has canvases by Venetians Vittore Carpaccio (circa 1460–1525) and Giambattista Tiepolo. ⊠ *Castello di Udine* ☎ *0432/271591* ⊕ *www. museiprovinciaud.it* ✉ *€3, €1 Sun.* ☉ *Tues.–Sat. 9:30–12:30 and 3–6, Sun. 9:30–12:30.*

One of the true legends of the grappa world, **Nonino** has operated in the little town of Percoto, 13 km (8 mi) south of Udine, since 1897. The grappa giant offers tours of its distillery and tastings at its shop. Take Viale Pal-

2

manova (SS56) south out of town and bear left onto SP2. Go through the town of Pavia di Udine and continue south until you see signs for Nonino. Call in advance to schedule a visit. ⊠ *Via Aquileia 104* ☎ *0432/ 676331* ⊕ *www.nonino.it* 🖃 *Free* ☉ *By appointment only.*

Where to Stay & Eat

★ $$$–$$$$ ✕ **Vitello d'Oro.** Udine's very elegant, landmark restaurant is the one re-served by most local people for special occasions. The big terrace in front is popular for alfresco dining in summer. The menu features both meat and fish in classic regional dishes as well as more innovative creations. You might start with an antipasto of assorted raw shellfish, including the impossibly sweet Adriatic *scampi,* followed by the fresh fish of the day. Service is impeccable, as is the Friuli-focused wine list. Perhaps the best way to go is the multicourse tasting menu. ⊠ *Via Valvason 4* ☎ *0432/508982* ⊕ *www.vitellodoro.com* ⚘ *Reservations essential* 🖃 *AE, DC, MC, V* ☉ *Closed Sun. July–Sept. and Wed. Oct.–June.*

★ $–$$ ✕ **Osteria Al Vecchio Stallo.** Hidden away in a narrow alley, this popu-lar osteria bursts with trinkets and character, its beautiful courtyard shaded by grape arbors. The menu includes a bevy of the most traditional Friuli specialties with unpronounceable spellings, including sweet *cjalzòns* (ravioli stuffed with spinach, apple, pear, or cheese, and topped with butter and cinnamon). More challenging are the *nervetti* (gelatinous cubes of veal's knee), which you probably won't find anywhere west of here. There's a great selection of wines by the glass, and the gregarious chef-owner is a gracious host. ⊠ *Via Viola 7* ☎ *0432/21296* 🖃 *No credit cards* ☉ *Closed Sun. and Wed.*

★ $$–$$$ 🏨 **Hotel Clocchiatti.** Not satisfied to rest on their laurels, the owners of this converted late-19th-century city mansion added the "Next" wing, whose groundbreaking modern design and comfort is unequalled in all of Friuli. Starkly angular suites come equipped with flat-panel TVs; ir-regularly shaped suites have sunken Japanese baths and gardens; and rooms integrate modern art into the beds and nightstands. Overlook-ing the garden's centuries-old trees, a terrace provides a peaceful place. High-design chaises surround a swimming pool that's done entirely in black (it keeps the water warmer). ⊠ *Via Cividale 29, 33100* ☎ *0432/ 505047* ⊕ *www.hotelclocchiatti.it* 📞 *13 rooms* ⚘ *In-room safes, mini-bars, pool, bicycles, bar, in-room broadband, WiFi, laundry service, free parking, some pets allowed* 🖃 *AE, DC, MC, V* ⧖ *BP.*

Cividale del Friuli

㉝ *17 km (11 mi) east of Udine, 144 km (89 mi) northeast of Venice.*

Cividale was founded in AD 53 by Julius Caesar, then commander of Roman legions in the area. Locals say their Ponte del Diavolo, bridging the Nati-sone River, is supported by rocks the devil tossed down during a tantrum. Here you can find Celtic and Roman ruins alongside Venetian Gothic buildings, including the Palazzo Comunale. Cividale's Renaissance **Duomo** contains a magnificent 12th-century silver gilt altarpiece. ⊠ *Piazza Duomo* ☎ *0432/731144* ☉ *Apr.–Oct., Mon.–Sat. 9:30–noon and 3–7, Sun. 3–7; Nov.–Mar., Mon.–Sat. 9:30–noon and 3–6, Sun. 3–6.*

The **Tempietto Longobardo,** perched above the meandering river, is a little gem of a Lombard church. It has an archway with a vine motif, guarded by an 8th-century procession of female figures. The fine carved wooden stalls date from the 14th century. ⊠ *Via Monastero Maggiore* ☎ *0432/ 700867* ⊕ *www.museiprovinciaud.it* ✏ *€2* ☉ *Apr.–Sept., Mon.–Sat. 9:30–12:30 and 3–6:30, Sun. 9:30–1 and 3–7:30; Oct.–Mar., Mon.–Sat. 9:30–12:30 and 3–5, Sun. 9:30–12:30 and 2:30–6.*

Where to Eat

$　✕ **Ai Tre Re.** Here, legend says, three kings once divided up the countryside, and since the 1500s the Three Kings has refreshed travelers within its stone-wall garden or beside its 6-foot-square woodstove. Beneath the beamed ceiling everything is homemade, including the bread of wheat and *maize* (corn). Try pumpkin gnocchi with smoked ricotta, followed by sausage in cream sauce or cheese grilled with wild herbs. ⊠ *Via Stretta San Valentino 31* ☎ *0432/700416* ⊟ *MC, V* ☉ *Closed Tues., 2 wks in June, and 1 wk in Oct.*

Cormòns

㉞ *18 km (11 mi) south of Cividale del Friuli, 51 km (32 mi) northwest of Trieste.*

Southeast of Udine, in the rolling hills of Friuli–Venezia Giulia, Cormòns is the epicenter of the Collio region. A small, pretty, and walkable jumble of red roofs and little piazzas, the town lies amidst hills and vineyards, producing exceptional white wine. Route 356, just west of the Slovenian border, winds through miles of vineyard-covered hills. Residents boast that Ribolla grapes have grown here for 1,000 years, the region's Tocai grape vines may be the original source for Hungary's famous Tokay wine. Local Picolit grapes are said to have been the source of papal communion wine for centuries, and it is still made here by the Sovereign Military Order of Malta.

The region has changed hands in bloody battles since the days of imperial Rome. Following World War II, international arbitrators determined whose farms would be part of Italy and whose would end up within Tito's Yugoslavia. It's no surprise that many residents here speak Slovenian in their homes and have relatives or cultivate fields across the border. In May 2004 the border effectively dissolved when Slovenia was welcomed into the European Union.

Where to Stay & Eat

★ $$$–$$$$　✕ **La Cacciatore de la Subida.** Set among the Collio's vineyards, La Cacciatore serves food that reflects the region's Slovenian-Austrian-Italian cultural blend: *zlikrofi* is a cross between ravioli and tortellini, and gnocchi are made with plum and with butter and cinnamon instead of savory ingredients. You may even find wild *sambuco* (elderflowers) and *dragoncello* (tarragon) in the desserts. The prix-fixe menu (€48–€55) provides a consistently delicious meal. The restaurant is the centerpiece of La Subida country lodging. ⊠ *La Subida, Località Monte 22* ☎ *0481/ 60531* ⊕ *www.lasubida.it* ✐ *Reservations essential* ⊟ *MC, V* ☉ *Closed Tues., Wed., and July 1–10. No lunch weekdays.*

VOICES OF ITALY

Josko Gravner
wine maker, Collio region

Josko Gravner's Friuli home looks across a shallow valley into Slovenia, and his vineyards straddle the national divide, literally half-Italian and half-Slovene. The area has been racked by political turmoil; it also produces exceptional white wines. "These hills here are drier," Josko explains. "The grapes are stressed, robbed. They suffer." Such conditions result in small yields but a rich final product.

Josko is one of the Italian wine world's leading innovators and iconoclasts—a reputation he cemented in the mid-1990s by becoming its most staunch traditionalist. He swapped his modern press for an antiquated model—"one that presses the grapes, instead of chewing them." He was labeled a madman when he replaced his refrigerated tanks with terra-cotta amphorae from the Kakheti province of Georgia, where the first wine is thought to have been made 5 millennia ago. These 3,000-liter (nearly 800-gallon) vessels—pointed at the bottom, 7 feet tall, 5½ feet across at their widest—are buried in the ground, and the wine settles in them, making filtration unnecessary.

Josko describes his approach in straightforward terms. "It isn't a science, it's a philosophy. I have to make wine that I like." He forgoes chemical fertilizers, fortifiers, and clarifiers, and he bottles under a waning moon. "I don't have the goal to get rich but to make good wine, natural wine, as simple as possible. One is rich when one is content."

In this idyllic region along the Isonzo River, contentment has been hard to come by. In Friuli, 300,000 residents consider themselves ethnic Slovenes. "Mussolini's people closed my grandfather's trattoria because he would not join the Fascist party," Josko recalls. "After World War II, the border was drawn in London. It was possible to have the house in one country and the barn in another." The Slovene language was banned, but Josko, born in 1952—"after the war, but before the peace"—grew up speaking it nonetheless. So did his wife, Maria, the Yugoslavian girl next door.

Much has changed, to say the least, in recent years. May 2004 marked Slovenia's admission into the European Union, a telltale sign of the culture's growing acceptance among its neighbors. The change can be felt locally as well. Now, according to Miha, Josko's youngest son and wine-making partner, "When you interview for a job, you don't get it if you don't speak Slovene."

Meanwhile, the Gravners are earning accolades from those who once doubted Josko's sanity. According to Gambero Rosso, Italy's leading organization of wine critics, "Gravner's wines are exploring ways forward that are as exciting as their maker's personality. The amphorae are no mere exotic curiosities. They are serious cellar tools that produce stunningly rounded wines."

The Gravners welcome visitors when time allows. Try contacting Josko by e-mail at joskogravner@libero.it. Proprietors of La Subida in Cormòns can also help arrange a visit.

2

★ $$$ ⊞ **Castello Formentini.** Count Formentini's stunning castle has been ancestral property for five centuries. The restored complex today includes a winery, sports facilities, and superb accommodations that blend antique furnishings with modern conveniences. Not only is breakfast included, but there's complimentary wine, beer, and grappa, as well as a daylong buffet of antipasto and sweets. About once a month the hotel hosts a medieval banquet in the massive hall—complete with sword fights, fire-eaters, 15th-century recipes, and no forks. Though such events can feel contrived and tacky, here they pull it off with style; it's the closest thing there is to time travel. ✉ *Via Oslavia 2, 34070 San Floriano del Collio, 20 km (12 mi) northeast of Cormòns* ☎ *0481/884051* 🖶 *0481/884052* ⊕ *www.golfhotelformentini.com* ➥ *14 rooms, 1 suite* ♿ *Snack bar, minibars, 9-hole golf course, tennis court, pool, bar, meeting room, free parking, some pets allowed, no-smoking rooms; no a/c in some rooms* ▤ *AE, DC, MC, V* ⊘ *Closed Dec. 20–Feb.* ⦿| *BP.*

$–$$ ⊞ **La Subida.** Josko and Loredana Sirk's painstakingly created country refuge has 13 rustic-yet-modern cottages. Wooden beams and white lace lend nostalgia to the lodgings. Wood is delivered to the rooms each day so you can enjoy the *fogolar,* a traditional Friulian fireplace. Be sure to dine in the noteworthy restaurant, La Cacciatore; there is also the less-formal (and less-expensive) Osteria La Subida on-site. ✉ *Località Monte 22, 34071* ☎ *0481/60531* 🖶 *0481/61616* ⊕ *www.lasubida.it* ➥ *13 cottages* ♿ *2 restaurants, kitchenettes, cable TV, tennis court, pool, bicycles, horseback riding, bar, some pets allowed; no a/c* ▤ *MC, V* ⊘ *Closed 3 wks in Feb. Osteria closed Thurs. and Nov.* ⦿| *EP.*

Trieste

③⑤ *51 km (32 mi) southeast of Cormòns, 163 km (101 mi) east of Venice.*

Surrounded by rugged countryside and the beautiful Adriatic, Trieste is built on a mere fringe of coast and the rugged Karst plateau above. This town was once the chief port of the Austro-Hungarian Empire, but its quays now serve as parking lots, and the container port has moved to the south side of Trieste. In recent years, the city has undergone a degree of rejuvenation and has become something of a center for science and the computer industry. Having absorbed new waves of Slavic and Eastern European immigrants, Trieste now balances the tattered romance of wars past with the offbeat ambience of a remote frontier town.

Italian revolutionaries of the early 1800s rallied their battle cry around Trieste, because of what they believed was foreign occupation of their rightful motherland. After World War II, the sliver of land including Trieste and a small part of Istria became an independent, neutral state that was officially recognized in a 1947 peace treaty. Although it was actually occupied by British and American troops for its nine years of existence, the Free Territory of Trieste issued its own currency and stamps. In 1954 a Memorandum of Understanding was signed in London, giving civil administration of Trieste to Italy and the rest of the former Free Territory to Yugoslavia, but it was not until the 1975 Treaty of Osimo that the territory was finally formally divided.

CLOSE UP

Trieste's Caffè Culture

TRIESTE IS JUSTLY FAMOUS for its coffee, and so it is perhaps no coincidence that its former mayor Riccardo Illy (now serving as President of the Friuli–Venezia Giulia region) is an heir to the Illycaffè dynasty, supplier of top-quality caffeine fixes throughout Italy and the world. The elegant civility of Trieste plays out beautifully in a caffè culture rivaling that of Vienna. In Trieste, as elsewhere in Italy, ask for a *caffè* and you'll get a thimbleful of high-octane espresso. Your cappuccino here will also come in an espresso cup, with only half as much frothy milk as you'll find elsewhere and a dollop of whipped cream. Many cafés are part of a *torrefazione* (roasting shop), so you can sample a cup and then buy beans to take with you.

Few cafés in Italy—or in the world—can rival **Antico Caffè San Marco** (✉ Via Battisti 18 ☎ 040/363538) for its art deco style and bohemian atmosphere. After being destroyed in World War I, it was rebuilt in the 1920s and became a meeting place for local intellectuals. **Cremcaffè** (✉ Piazza Carlo Goldoni 10 ☎ 040/636555) isn't the ideal place to sit and read the paper, but its downtown location and selection of 20 coffee blends make it one of the busiest cafés in town. Founded in 1830, classic **Caffè Tommaseo** (✉ Piazza Tommaseo 4/c ☎ 040/362666) is a comfortable place to linger, especially on weekend evenings and Sunday morning when there's live music. For a great view of the great piazza, you couldn't do better than **Caffè Degli Specchi** (✉ Piazza dell'Unità d'Italia 7 ☎ 040/365777), where the many mirrors heighten the opportunities for people-watching. The atmosphere is more modern than old-world at **I Paesi del Caffè** (✉ Via Einaudi 1 ☎ 040/633897), which brews and sells beans of top international varieties, including Jamaica Blue Mountain.

2

Like Vienna's coffeehouses, Trieste's belle epoque cafés are social and cultural centers and much-beloved refuges from winter's bitter *bora* (wind from the north). Though often clogged with traffic, the spacious streets hold a lively mix of monumental, neoclassical, and art nouveau style architecture, granting an air of stateliness to the city.

★ The sidewalk cafés on the vast seaside **Piazza dell'Unità d'Italia** are popular meeting places in the summer months. The memorably imposing square, completely ringed by grandiose facades, is similar to Piazza San Marco in Venice; both are focal points of architectural interest and command fine views of the water. On the inland side of the piazza is the majestic, Viennese **Palazzo Comunale** (Town Hall). Steps behind it lead uphill, tracing Trieste's upward expansion from its roots as a Roman fishing port.

A statue of Habsburg emperor Leopold I looks out over **Piazza della Borsa,** which contains Trieste's original stock exchange, the **Borsa Vecchia,** a neoclassical building now serving as the chamber of commerce.

The 1st century AD amphitheater **Teatro Romano** ruins, opposite the city's *questura* (police station), were discovered during 1938 demolition work. Its statues are now displayed at the Museo Civico and the space that once held 6,000 spectators is filled with grass and flowers. ⊠ *Via del Teatro Romano.*

The 14th-century **Cattedrale di San Giusto** contains remnants of two previous churches built on the same ground, the earliest dating from the 5th century. The exterior includes fragments of Roman tombs and temples, adding to the jumble of styles: the pillars of the main doorway are the most conspicuous Roman element. Inside, don't miss the 12th-century gold mosaic behind the main altar. ⊠ *Piazza della Cattedrale 2* ☎ *040/309666* ☉ *Apr.–Sept., Mon.–Sat. 8–noon and 3:30–7:30, Sun. 8–1 and 3:30–8; Oct.–Mar., Mon.–Sat. 8–noon and 2:30–6:30, Sun. 8–1 and 3:30–8.*

The hilltop **Castello di San Giusto** was built on the ruins of the Roman town of Tergeste. Given the excellent view, it's no surprise that 15th-century Venetians turned the castle into a shipping observation point; the structure was further enlarged by Trieste's subsequent rulers, the Habsburgs. Due to structural instability, the castle and the museum within are temporarily, and indefinitely, closed to the public.

On the hill near the Castello is the **Civico Museo di Storia ed Arte,** an eclectic history and art museum with statues from the Roman theater and artifacts from Egypt, Greece, and Rome. There's also an assortment of glass and manuscripts. The **Orto Lapidario** (Lapidary Garden) has classical statuary, pottery, and a small Corinthian temple. ⊠ *Via Cattedrale 15* ☎ *040/310500* ▱ €*3* ☉ *Tues. and Thurs.–Sun. 9–1, Wed. 9–7.*

The **Civico Museo Revoltella e Galleria d'Arte Moderna** was founded in 1872, when the city inherited the palazzo, library, and art collection of shipping magnate Baron Pasquale Revoltella, vice president of the consortium that built the Suez Canal. The gallery holds one of the country's most important collections of 19th- and 20th-century art, with Italian artists particularly well represented. Hours vary for special exhibits, but don't miss a summer evening at the museum's rooftop café, where the view rivals the artwork. ⊠ *Via Armando Diaz 27* ☎ *040/6754350* ▱ €*5* ☉ *Sept.–July 18, Mon. and Wed.–Sat. 9–1:30 and 4–7, Sun. 10–7; July 19–Aug., Mon. 9–2, Wed.–Sat. 9–2 and 4–midnight, Sun. 10–7.*

Ⓒ At Trieste's **Museo del Mare** (Museum of the Sea) you can learn how Venetian galley rowers managed to sit three abreast and not smash one another with their oars. Displays include lots of boat models and a diorama with *casoni* (fishermen's grass huts) and submerged *seragi* (fishnet traps). Outside is a park with giant anchors and shady benches. ⊠ *Via di Campo Marzio 5* ☎ *040/304987* ▱ €*3* ☉ *Tues.–Sun. 8:30–1:30.*

Where to Stay & Eat

★ **$$$–$$$$** ✕ **Al Bagatto.** At this warm little seafood restaurant near the Piazza Unità, chef-owner Giovanni Marussi will personally shepherd your meal from start to finish. The best way to eat here is to leave things in his hands with a tasting menu. Its many little courses might include such Adriatic wonders as *scampi crudi* (raw scampi) and delicate treatments of *aragosta* (similar to lobster). Giovanni's preparations often integrate nouvelle ingredients without overshadowing the freshness of whatever local fish that

2

he has bought in the market that morning. ✉ *Via F. Venezian 2* ☎ *040/301771* ⌕ *Reservations essential* ▭ *AE, DC, MC, V* ⊗ *Closed Sun.*

$$ ✕ **Suban.** Head for the hills—to the landmark trattoria operated by members of the hospitable Suban family since 1865. Sit by the dining room fire or relax on a huge terrace and watch the sunset. This is fish-free Italian food with a Slovene, Hungarian, and Austrian accent. Start with *jota carsolina* (a rich soup of cabbage, potatoes, and beans), and then you might order a steak grilled and sliced at your table. Lighter fare includes *insalatine tiepide* (warm salads with smoked pork or duck) and a locally smoked beef that is truly special. To get here you can take Bus 35 from Piazza Oberdan. ✉ *Via Comici 2* ☎ *040/54368* ▭ *AE, DC, MC, V* ⊗ *Closed Tues., 1st 3 wks in Aug., and 1 wk in early Jan. No lunch Mon.*

★ **$** ✕ **Antipastoteca di Mare.** Hidden away halfway up the hill to the Castello di San Giusto, Roberto Surian's simple little restaurant is well worth seeking out during the day and booking for the evening. You'll find here some of the tastiest of hot and cold seafood combinations, from calamari and barley salad to scallops, mussels, and *sardoni in savor* (big sardines with raisins, pine nuts, and caramelized onions). The extraordinary fish soup of sardines, mackerel, and tuna, sprinkled with lightly fried, diced garlic bread and polenta, won Roberto first prize in Trieste's prestigious Sarde Day competition. Fish is everything here, accompanied only by a simple salad, potatoes, and house wine. ✉ *Via della Fornace 1* ☎ *040/309606* ▭ *No credit cards* ⊗ *Closed Mon. and 1–2 wks in Aug. No dinner Sun.*

★ **¢–$** ✕ **Trattoria da Giovanni.** The trattoria's *fritto misto di pesce* is an elemental masterpiece, crisped by a feathery batter that preserves every drop of moisture within and casting a spotlight on the freshness of the fish that flops into the kitchen straight from the Adriatic. Elegant, acidic, and equally deferential to the seafood is a simple side dish of chicory; don't forget to drizzle it with local oil. The space, too, is an object lesson in simplicity, more like an osteria than a trattoria. Familiar service and outdoor tables along one of Trieste's more evocative streets add to the effect. ✉ *Via San Lazzaro 14* ☎ *040/639396* ▭ *No credit cards* ⊗ *Closed Sun. and Aug.*

★ **$$$$** ⌂ **Duchi d'Aosta.** On the spacious Piazza Unità d'Italia, this hotel, beautifully furnished in Venetian-Renaissance style, has come a long way since its original incarnation as a 19th-century dockers' café. Each of the rooms is decorated in elegant "one-off" style, with dark-wood antiques, rich carpets, and plush fabrics. One of northern Italy's most impressive indoor pool-spa complexes, done up in the basement, below sea level, reflects the style of ancient Roman baths. Steam is scented, lights fade from one color into the next, and one gently rocking cradle even simulates weightlessness. On the hotel's ground floor is Harry's Grill ($$$$), one of the city's most select restaurants. ✉ *Piazza Unità d'Italia 2/1, 34121* ☎ *040/7600011* 🖷 *040/366092* ⊕ *www.grandhotelduchidaosta.com* ↯ *51 rooms, 2 suites* ⌂ *Restaurant, minibars, indoor pool, hot tub, spa, bar, meeting rooms, parking (fee), some pets allowed* ▭*AE, DC, MC, V* �ⓞ*BP.*

$$ ⌂ **Alla Posta.** The reading lounge—with its high-back armchairs, parquet floor, and potted plants, plus a roaring fire in winter—will entice you into this elegant, central hotel. Upstairs, stylishly decorated guest rooms are outfitted with high-tech controls for amenities such as heating, air-conditioning, and wake-up calls. The spacious bathrooms are done in Italian marble. ⊠ *Piazza Oberdan 1* ☎ *040/365208* 🖷 *040/ 633720* ⊕ *www.albergopostatrieste.it* ➼ *47 rooms* ⚏ *In-room safes, minibars, in-room data ports* ▤ *AE, DC, MC, V* ⦿❘ *BP.*

$$ 🏨 **Riviera & Maximilian's.** Seven kilometers (4 miles) north of Trieste, this lovely hotel commands stunning views across the Golfo di Trieste to Castello di Miramare. There's no sand on this stretch of coast, but an elevator leads to the hotel's own private bathing quay below, as well as to a children's area. Room decor varies from modern design to vintage wood, with some balconies and kitchenettes. The restaurant and the breakfast room also face the stunning panorama. ⊠ *Strada Costiera 22, 34010* ☎ *040/224551* 🖷 *040/224300* ⊕ *www.hotelrivieraemaximilian. com* ➼ *56 rooms, 2 suites, 9 apartments* ⚏ *Restaurant, minibars, in-room data ports, pool, beach, bar, WiFi, meeting rooms, free parking, some pets allowed; no a/c in some rooms* ▤ *AE, DC, MC, V* ⦿❘ *BP.*

$ 🏨 **Filoxenia.** The location on the city waterfront, and the reasonable prices, make this small hotel a choice accommodation. Members of Trieste's Greek community run the Filoxenia, and there's a good Greek restaurant on-site. The staff makes up in friendliness for what it might lack in professionalism. Rooms are simple and fresh, with white walls and two single beds covered in Mediterranean blue–stripe spreads; family rooms sleep four (€120). ⊠ *Via Mazzini 3, 34121* ☎ *040/3481644* 🖷 *040/ 661371* ⊕ *www.filoxenia.it* ➼ *20 rooms* ⚏ *Restaurant, in-room safes, bar, meeting rooms, no-smoking rooms; no a/c in some rooms* ▤ *DC, MC, V* ⦿❘ *BP.*

Castello di Miramare

★ ⚅ 🟤 *7 km (4½ mi) northwest of Trieste.*

Archduke Maximilian of Habsburg, brother of Emperor Franz Josef and retired commander of the Austrian navy, built this seafront extravaganza in the 19th century. It has ship's-keel wooden ceilings, marine-blue furnishings, and windows onto the wide, open Adriatic. His peaceful retirement was interrupted in 1864 when he reluctantly became Emperor of Mexico; he was killed three years later by a Mexican firing squad. The castle was later owned by Duke Amadeo of Aosta, who renovated in the rationalist style and installed modern plumbing in his art deco bathroom. Within the 54-acre garden surrounding the castle, the **Tropical Park** greenhouse is populated by butterflies and birds and has a café-bar. Bus 36 from Piazza Oberdan in Trieste leaves for here every half hour. Guided tours in English are available by reservation. The castle makes a good morning or afternoon jaunt from Trieste, or you can stop on your way into or out of the city. ⊠ *Viale Miramare, off SS14, Miramare* ☎ *040/224143* ⊕ *www.castello-miramare.it* 🎫 *Castle €4, guided tour €3.50, park free, greenhouse €6.50* ⊙ *Castle daily 9–7, last entry 30 mins before closing. Park daily Apr.–Sept., 8–7; Nov.–Feb., 8–5; Mar. and Oct., 8–6. Greenhouse daily Apr.–Oct., 9–6; Nov.–Mar., 10–5.*

VENETIAN ARC ESSENTIALS

Transportation

BY AIR

The main airport serving the Venetian Arc, Aeroporto Marco Polo, is 10 km (6 mi) north of Venice and handles international and domestic flights to the region. Aeroporto Catullo di Verona–Villafranca, 11 km (7 mi) southwest of Verona, is served by European and domestic airlines such as Alitalia, Alpi Eagles, Air Dolomiti, Iberia, Air France, British Airways, Meridiana, and Lufthansa. A regular bus service connects the airport with Verona's Porta Nuova railway station.

Aeroporto di Treviso, 5 km (3 mi) southeast of Treviso, 32 km (19 mi) north of Venice, has become something of a hub for the European low-cost carrier Ryanair (⊕ www.ryanair.com), which offers service between Treviso and the United Kingdom, Germany, Belgium, Spain, and elsewhere. From here, an ACTT local bus leaves for Treviso every 30 minutes during the day (until 9 PM), or a taxi will come to the airport to pick you up. There are domestic and some European flights (including a daily Ryanair London service) to Aeroporto Ronchi dei Legionari, 35 km (22 mi) northwest of Trieste, linked with the Trieste's Piazza della Libertà bus terminal (beside the railway station) by regular APT bus service, or you can take a convenient *servizio navetta* (shuttle).

🛈 Airport Information **Aeroporto Marco Polo di Venezia** ☎ 041/2606111 ⊕ www. veniceairport.it. **Aeroporto Catullo di Verona–Villafranca** ☎ 045/8095666 ⊕ www. aeroportoverona.it. **Aeroporto Ronchi dei Legionari di Trieste** ☎ 0481/773224 ⊕ www. aeroporto.fvg.it. **Aeroporto di Treviso** ⊕ www.trevisoairport.it ☎ 0422/315131.

BY BUS

There are interurban and interregional connections throughout the Veneto and Friuli. Local tourist offices may be able to provide details of timetables and routes; otherwise contact the local bus station or, in some cases, the individual bus companies operating from the station, listed below.

🛈 Bus Information **ACTT buses** ✉ Piazzale Duca D'Aosta 25, Treviso ☎ 0422/3271. **ACTV buses** ✉ Piazzale Roma, Venice ☎ 041/24240 buses to Brenta Riviera ⊕ www. actv.it. **AMT buses** ✉ Via Torbido 1, Verona ☎ 045/8871111 ⊕ www.amt.it. **APTV buses** ✉ Autostazione di Verona Porta Nuova, Piazzale XXV Aprile, Verona ☎ 045/8057911 ⊕ www.aptv.it. **ATVO buses** ✉ Piazzale Roma, Venice ☎ 0421/383671 ⊕ www.atvo. it. **FTV buses** ✉ Piazzale della Stazione near Campo Marzio, Vicenza ☎ 0444/223115 ⊕ www.ftv.vi.it. **SITA buses** ✉ Piazzale Boschetti, Padua ☎ 049/8206844 ⊕ www. sita-on-line.it. **TT buses** ✉ Piazza della Libertà, Trieste ☎ 800/016675 ⊕ www. triestetrasporti.it.

BY CAR

The two main access roads to the Venetian Arc from southern Italy are both linked to the A1 (Autostrada del Sole), which connects Bologna, Florence, and Rome. They are the A13, which culminates in Padua, and the A22, which passes through Verona running north–south. Linking the region from east to west is the A4, the primary route from Milan to Trieste, skirting Verona, Padua, and Venice along the way. The distance from Verona to Trieste via A4 is 263 km (163 mi), with one break in the autostrada near Venice/Mestre. Branches link the A4 with Treviso (A27), Pordenone (A28), and Udine (A23).

EMERGENCY ACI Emergency Service offers 24-hour roadside assistance.
SERVICES ⚑ **ACI dispatchers** ☎ 803/116.

BY TRAIN
Trains on the main routes from the south stop almost hourly in Verona, Padua, and Venice. From northern Italy and the rest of Europe, trains usually enter via Milan or through Porta Nuova station in Verona. Treviso and Udine both lie on the main line from Venice to Tarvisio, from which Eurocity trains continue to Vienna and Prague.

To the west of Venice, the main line running across the north of Italy stops at Padua (30 minutes from Venice), Vicenza (1 hour), and Verona (1½ hours); to the east is Trieste (2 hours). Local trains link Venice to Bassano del Grappa (1 hour), Padua to Bassano del Grappa (1 hour), Vicenza to Treviso (1 hour), and Udine to Trieste (1 hour).
⚑ **Train Information Trenitalia** ☎ 892021 ⊕ www.trenitalia.com.

Contacts & Resources

EMERGENCIES
For first aid, dial the general emergency number (118) and ask for *pronto soccorso* (first aid). Be prepared to give your address. (If you can find a concierge or some other Italian-speaker to call on your behalf, do so, as not all operators speak English.) All pharmacies post signs on the door with addresses of pharmacies that stay open at night, on Saturday afternoon, and on Sunday.
⚑ **Ambulance** ☎ 118, **Police** ☎ 113.

VISITOR INFORMATION
⚑ Tourist Information **Asolo** ✉ Piazza Garibaldi, 31011 ☎ 0423/529046 ⊕ www.asolo.it. **Bassano del Grappa** ✉ Largo Corona d'Italia 35, 36061 ☎ 0424/524351 ⊕ www.vicenzae.org. **Marostica** ✉ Piazza Castello 1, 36063 ☎ 0424/72127 ⊕ www.marosticaonline.it. **Padua** ✉ Padova Railway Station, 35100 ☎ 049/8752077 ✉ Galleria Pedrocchi, 35135100 ☎ 049/8767927 ⊕ www.turismopadova.it. **Treviso** ✉ Piazza Monte di Pietà 8, 31100 ☎ 0422/547632. **Trieste** ✉ Piazza dell Unità d'Italia 4/b, 34100 ☎ 040/3478312 ⊕ www.triestetourism.it. **Udine** ✉ Piazza I Maggio 7, 33100 ☎ 0432/295972 ⊕ www.turismo.fvg.it. **Verona** ✉ Piazza Brà, 37100 ☎ 045/8068680 ✉ Porta Nuova Railway Station ☎ 045/8000861 ⊕ www.tourism.verona.it. **Vicenza** ✉ Piazza Giacomo Matteotti 12, 36100 ☎ 0444/320854 ✉ Piazza dei Signori 8 ☎ 0444/544122 ⊕ www.vicenza.org.

The Dolomites

Trentino

WORD OF MOUTH

"There are so many beautiful valleys and mountains, it's hard to choose. My favorite drive is through the Val Gardena from north of Bolzano to Cortina. The area around Cortina, especially to the west, is full of great little villages."

—Wayne

WELCOME TO THE DOLOMITES

Merano

TOP 5
Reasons to Go

1 Cortina d'Ampezzo: The former hangout of the ultra hip has aged gracefully into the Grand Dame of Italian ski resorts.

2 Museo Archeologico dell'Alto Adige, Bolzano: The impossibly well-preserved body of the iceman Ötzi, the star attraction here, provokes countless questions about the meaning of life 5,000 years ago.

3 Hiking: No matter your fitness level, there's a memorable walk in store for you here.

4 Trento: A graceful fusion of Austrian and Italian styles, this breezy, frescoed town is famed for its imposing castle.

5 Grande Strada delle Dolomiti (Great Dolomites Road): Your rental Fiat will think it's a Ferrari as it wends its way along this gorgeous drive through the Heart of the Dolomites.

At the spa town of Merano you can soak in hot springs, take the "grape cure," and stroll along lovely walkways.

AUSTRIA

40

Glorenza
Spondigna

Merano

SWITZ. 38

Parco Nazionale dello Stelvio

Bormio

PIEMONTE

42

Madonna di Campiglio

Mezzolombardo

TRENTINO

Trento

237

12

Rovere

Trentino

Butterfly-shaped Trentino province is Italy with a German accent. Its principal city, history-rich **Trento**, is situated at the center. To the northwest are **Madonna di Campiglio**, Italy's most fashionable ski resort, and **Bormio**, another notable skiing destination that doubles as a gateway to the **Parco Nazionale dello Stelvio**.

Getting Oriented

Shadowed by the Dolomite mountains—whose other-worldly pinnacles Leonardo depicted in the background of his *Mona Lisa*—the northeast Italian provinces of Trentino and Alto Adige are centered around the valleys of the Adige and Isarco rivers, which course from the Brenner Pass south to Bolzano.

Alto Adige

The Alto Adige region was a part of Austria until the end of World War I, and Austrian sensibilities still predominate over Italian.

AUSTRIA

Brenner Pass

12

49

Brúnico

Bressanone

49

Dobbiaco

ALTO ADIGE

Cortina d'Ampezzo

VAL GARDENA

Sella Mt. Range

48

38 Bolzano

Grande Strada delle Dolomiti

12

Col Rodella

Canazei

VAL DI FASSA

Predazzo

48

The spectacular Sella mountain range and the surrounding Val di Fassa and Val Gardena make up the area known as the **Heart of the Dolomites.** It's distinguished by great views and great mountain sports, both summer and winter. At the town of **Canazei,** the cable car 3,000 feet up to the Col Rodella lookout packages the vast panorama perfectly.

Strigno

Lago di Caldonazzo 47

Bolzano, Alto Adige's capital, is the Dolomites' most lively city. Look for high-gabled houses, wrought-iron signs, and centuries-old wine cellars.

20 mi

20 km

Bolzano

Canazei

THE DOLOMITES PLANNER

Making the Most of Your Time

For a general pleasure tour (as opposed to a skiing- or hiking-intensive vacation), your best choice for a base is vibrant Bolzano, where you'll get a sense of the region's contrasts—Italian and German, medieval and ultramodern. The Archaeological Museum shouldn't be missed. After a day or two in town, venture out to history-laden Trento or the lovely spa town of Merano; both are viable day trips from Bolzano and good places to spend the night as well.

If you have more time in the region, you're going to want to get higher into the mountains. The trip on the Grande Strada delle Dolomiti (Great Dolomites Road) through the Heart of the Dolomites to Cortina d'Ampezzo is one of Italy's most spectacular mountain drives. You can either spend a full day on the road and return to Bolzano, splurge on a night in Cortina, or bed down in one of the homier towns along the way.

Getting Around

Driving is easily the most convenient way to travel in the Dolomites. It's also the most exhilarating, as you rise from broad valleys into mountains with narrow, winding roads straight out of a sports car ad. In summer there are several sight-seeing bus tours through the mountains. There's also regular bus service to most towns, but if you're aiming for anywhere beyond the major destinations, you'll need great patience or great luck catching the infrequent runs. Bressanone, Bolzano, Trento, Rovereto, and Morano are accessible by train. For more about car, bus, and train travel, see "Essentials" at the end of this chapter.

Speaking the Language

Alto Adige is the only region in Italy with two official languages: Italian and German. In Bolzano, Merano, and environs, street signs, menus, city names, and street chatter are completely bilingual. Trentino, Madonna di Campiglio, and Cortina d'Ampezzo are Italian-speaking, but there's a distinctive regional accent—notice the "r," which is guttural rather than rolled.

Hitting the Slopes

The Dolomites have some of the most spectacular downhill skiing in Europe, with the facilities to match. The most comprehensive centers are the upscale resorts of Cortina d'Ampezzo and Madonna di Campiglio, which draw an international clientele with impressive terrain, expansive lift systems, and lively après-ski. For traditional Tirolean *Gemütlichkeit* (congeniality), try one of the more rustic resorts: in the Val di Fassa or Val Gardena your liftmate is more likely to be a schoolteacher from a neighboring town than a businessman from Milan (or Tokyo). Both major resorts and out-of-the-way villages have well-marked trails for *sci di fondo* (cross-country skiing). With the exception of the main bargain period known as *settimane bianche* (white weeks) in January and February, the slopes are seldom overcrowded.

Hitting the Trails

Walking and hiking options are appealing, varied, and abundant. Whether on an hour's stroll in the foothills of Merano or a weeklong trek high above Ortisei and Canazei, you'll experience a pleasant climate and captivating vistas that have been attracting visitors to the Dolomites for centuries. The region is also a major draw for hardcore climbers—it's not surprising that Reinhold Messner, the first person to reach the summit of Everest without oxygen, is a lifelong resident.

Local tourist offices are the places to find maps and descriptions of hiking trails, as well as expert advice.

■ **The Club Alpino Italiano** (CAI), the world's oldest organization of its kind, is an excellent resource for more ambitious adventures. www.cai.

it. Bolzano: Piazza delle Erbe 46, 0471/981391; Merano: Corso della Libertà 188, 0473/448944; Trento: Via Manci 57, 0461/981871.

■ **The Scuole di Alpinismo** (Mountaineering Schools) in Madonna di Campiglio and

Cortina d'Ampezzo offer guided mountain trips for fit hikers of any experience level. Madonna di Campiglio: www.guidealpinecampiglio.it, 0465/442634. Cortina d'Ampezzo: www.guidecortina.com, 0436/868505.

Finding a Place to Stay

Classic Dolomite lodging options range from restored castles to chalets to stately 19th-century hotels. Small villages often have scores of places to stay, many of them inexpensive. Hotel information offices at train stations and tourist offices can help if you've arrived without reservations. The Bolzano train station has a 24-hour hotel service, and tourist offices will give you a list of all the hotels in the area, arranged by location and price. Hotels at ski resorts cater primarily to longer stays at full or half board: you should book ski vacations as packages in advance. Nearly all rural accommodations close from early November to mid- or late December, as well as for a month or two after Easter.

Dining & Lodging Price Categories

WHAT IT COSTS in Euros					
	$$$$	**$$$**	**$$**	**$**	**¢**
Restaurants	over €45	€35–€45	€25–€35	€15–€25	under €15
Hotels	over €220	€160–€220	€110–€160	€70–€110	under €70

Restaurant prices are for a first course (primo), second course (secondo), and dessert (dolce). Hotel prices are for two people in a standard double room in high season, including tax and service.

How's the Weather?

The Dolomites are a two-season destination: winter and summer. Most ski resorts are open from mid-December through April, but snowfall in early winter is unreliable, and the best conditions often aren't seen until late February. Hiking trails can remain icy well into June, and mountain temperatures drop sharply in September. Spring and autumn are quiet—many of the mountain tourist facilities close down entirely. It can still be a pleasant time to visit; in the fall, cozy taverns serve up the new wine and roasted chestnuts.

TOP PASSEGGIATA

A stroll on Merano's Passeggiata Tappeiner is as relaxing as any of the town's spa treatments.

3

THE VAST, MOUNTAINOUS DOMAIN of northeastern Italy, unlike other celebrated Alpine regions, has remained relatively undeveloped. Strange, rocky pinnacles jut straight up like chimneys, looming over scattered, pristine mountain lakes. Below, rivers meander through valleys dotted with peaceful villages and protected by picture-book castles. In the most secluded Dolomite vales, unique cultures have flourished: the Ladin language, an offshoot of Latin still spoken in the Val Gardena and Val di Fassa, owes its unlikely survival to centuries of topographic isolation.

The more accessible parts of Trentino–Alto Adige, on the other hand, have a history of near-constant intermingling of cultures. The region's Adige and Isarco valleys make up the main access route between Italy and central Europe, and as a result the language, cuisine, and architecture are a blend of north and south. Whereas the province of Trentino is largely Italian-speaking, Alto Adige is predominantly Germanic: until World War I, the area was Austria's South Tirol. As you move north toward the famed Brenner Pass—through the prosperous valley towns of Rovereto, Trento, and Bolzano—the Teutonic influence is increasingly dominant; by the time you reach Bressanone, it's hard to believe you're in Italy at all.

TRENTINO

Until the end of World War I, Trentino was Italy's frontier with the Austro-Hungarian Empire, and although this province remains unmistakably Italian, Germanic influences are tangible in all aspects of life here, including architecture, cuisine, culture, and language. Visitors are drawn by historical sights reflecting a strategic position at the intersection of southern and central Europe: Trento was the headquarters of the Catholic Counter-Reformation; Rovereto the site of an emblematically bloody battle during the Great War. Numerous year-round mountain resorts, including fashionable Madonna di Campiglio, are nestled in the wings of the butterfly-shape region.

Trento

❶ *51 km (32 mi) south of Bolzano, 24 km (15 mi) north of Rovereto.*

Trento is a prosperous, cosmopolitan university town that retains an architectural charm befitting its historical importance. It was here, from 1545 to 1563, that the structure of the Catholic Church was redefined at the Council of Trent. This was the starting point of the Counter-Reformation, which brought half of Europe back to Catholicism. The word *consiglio* (council) appears everywhere in Trento—in hotel, restaurant, and street names, and even on wine labels.

Today the Piazza del Duomo remains splendid, and its enormous medieval palazzo dominates the city landscape in virtually its original form. The 24-hour Trento Card (€9) grants admission to all major town sights and can be purchased at the tourist office or any museum. A 48-hour card (€14) is also available, and includes entrance to the modern art museum in Rovereto. Both cards provide a number of other perks, including free public transportation, wine tastings, and the cable car ride to Belvedere di Sardagna.

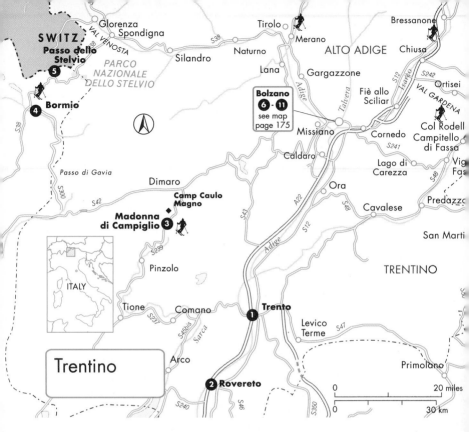

Guided tours of Trento depart Saturday from the **tourist office.** You can meet at 10 AM for a visit to the Castello del Buonconsiglio (€6, including admission to the castle), or at 3 PM for a tour of the city center (€3). Reservations are not required. ⊠ *Via Manci 2* ☎ *0461/983880* ⊕ *www. apt.trento.it.*

The massive Romanesque **Duomo,** also known as the Cathedral of San Virgilio, forms the southern edge of the Piazza del Duomo. Locals refer to this square as the city's *salotto* (sitting room), as in fine weather it's always filled with students and residents drinking coffee, enjoying an aperitif, or reading the newspaper. A baroque **Fontana del Nettuno** presides over it all. When skies are clear, pause here to savor the view of the mountaintops enveloping the city.

Within the Duomo, unusual arcaded stone stairways border the austere nave. Ahead is the *baldacchino* (altar canopy), a copy of Bernini's masterpiece in St. Peter's in Rome. In the small **Cappella del Crocifisso** (Chapel of the Crucifix) to the right is a mournful 15th-century crucifixion, with the Virgin Mary and John the Apostle. This crucifix, by German artist Sixtus Frei, was a focal point of the Council of Trent: each decree agreed on during the two decades of deliberations was solemnly read out in front of it. Outside, walk around to the back of the cathedral to see an exquisite display of 14th-century stonemason's art, from the small porch to the intriguing knotted columns on the graceful apse. ⊠ *Piazza del Duomo* ☎ *0461/980132* ⊗ *Daily 6:30–noon and 2–8.*

★ The crenellated **Palazzo Pretorio,** situated so as to seem like a wing of the Duomo, was built in the 13th century as the fortified residence of the prince-bishops, who enjoyed considerable power and autonomy within the medieval hierarchy. The remarkable palazzo has lost none of its original splendor. The crenellations are not merely decorative: the square pattern represents ancient allegiance to the Guelphs (the triangular crenellations seen elsewhere in town represent Ghibelline loyalty). The Palazzo now houses the **Museo Diocesano Tridentino,** where you can see paintings showing the seating plan of the prelates during the Council of Trent; early-16th-century tapestries by Pieter van Aelst (1502–56), the Belgian artist who carried out Raphael's 15th-century designs for the Vatican tapestries; carved wood altars and statues; and an 11th-century sacramentary, or book of services. These and other precious objects all come from the cathedral's treasury. Accessible through the museum, a subterranean **archaeological area** reveals ancient ruins of a 6th-century Christian basilica and a gate dating from the 9th century. ⊠ *Piazza del Duomo 18* ☎ *0461/234419* ⊠ *€4, includes archaeological area* ⊗ *Wed.–Mon. 9:30–12:30 and 2–5:30.*

NEED A BREAK? | **Scrigno del Duomo** (⊠ Piazza del Duomo 30 ☎ 0461/220030) serves more than 30 wines by the glass, with an excellent selection of local cheeses to match, in a building with some of the oldest frescoes in town. Salads and regional specialties are also available; the *canederli* (seasoned bread balls in broth) are especially flavorful here. If you walk downstairs to the wineshop, you can see excavated Roman-era walls—this was the level of the ancient square that became Piazza del Duomo.

Many sessions of the Council of Trent met at the Renaissance church **Santa Maria Maggiore.** Limited light enters through the simple rose window over the main door, so you have to strain to see the magnificent ceiling, an intricate combination of stucco and frescoes. The church is off the northwest side of the Piazza del Duomo, about 200 yards down Via Cavour. ⊠ *Via Cavour* ⊗ *Daily 8–noon and 2:30–6.*

Locals refer to **Via Belenzani** as Trento's outdoor gallery because of the frescoed facades of the hallmark Renaissance palazzi. It's an easy 50-yard walk up the lane behind the church of Santa Maria Maggiore.

The **Torre Vanga** is a 13th-century tower near the Adige River and one of the bridges that crosses it, the Ponte San Lorenzo. You can take a cable car up to the **Belvedere di Sardagna,** a lookout point 1,200 feet above medieval Trento. The trip is free if you have a Trento Card. *Cable car* ⊠ *Ponte San Lorenzo* ☎ *0461/983627* ⊠ *€2 round-trip* ⊗ *Daily 7–5.*

★ The **Castello del Buonconsiglio** (Castle of Good Counsel) was once the stronghold of the prince-bishops; its position and size made it easier to defend than the Palazzo Pretorio. Look for the evolution of architectural styles: the medieval fortifications of the Castelvecchio section (on the far left) were built in the 13th century; the more decorative, Renaissance Magno Palazzo section (on the far right) wasn't completed until 300 years later. Part of the Castello now houses the **Museo Provinciale d'Arte,** where permanent and visiting exhibits of art and archaeology hang in frescoed medieval halls or under Renaissance coffered ceilings. The 13th-century **Torre dell'Aquila** (Eagle's Tower) is home to the castle's artistic highlight, a 15th-century *ciclo dei mesi* (cycle of the months). The four-wall fresco is full of charming and detailed scenes of medieval life in both court and countryside. To get to the tower, follow signs to the small office, and wait—you need a guide to accompany you up. ⊠ *Via Bernardo Clesio 5* ☎ *0461/233770* ⊕ *www.buonconsiglio.it* 🖼 *Museo €6, Torre dell'Aquila €1 extra* ☉ *June–Oct., Tues.–Sun. 10–6; Nov.–May, Tues.–Sun. 9:30–5.*

The **Museo Storico in Trento** (Trento Historical Museum), housed in the former joiner's shop inside the castle walls, has been undergoing restoration and is scheduled to reopen in 2007. The focus is modern Trentino history, with dioramas and displays about the region from the unification of Italy in 1861 through World War II. ⊠ *Via Bernardo Clesio 3* ☎ *0461/230482* ⊕ *www.museostorico.tn.it.*

The **Torre Verde** (Green Tower) is part of Trento's 13th-century fortifications, standing alongside other fragments of the city walls. You can't go inside, but the exterior is worth a look. ⊠ *Piazza Raffaello Sanzio near the castle.*

The **Museo d'Arte Moderna e Contemporanea di Trento** is installed in the Palazzo delle Albere, a Renaissance villa on the Adige River. Works in the permanent collection date from the 19th and 20th centuries, but the real focus here is the rotating exhibitions of contemporary artists. ⊠ *Palazzo delle Albere, Via Roberto da Sanseverino 45* ☎ *0461/234860* ⊕ *www.mart.tn.it* 🖼 *€5* ☉ *Tues.–Sun. 10–6.*

About 20 km (12 mi) southeast of Trento in the Val Sugana, **Levico Terme** is a medieval spa town with thermal waters. This valley enclave was inhabited by the Celts and then conquered by the Romans; the Latin-derived Ladin dialect is still spoken today. Two weeks advance booking is recommended for the spa services at **Palazzo delle Terme.** ⊠ *Viale Vittorio Emanuele, 38056 Levico Terme* ☎ *0461/706481* 🖶 *0461/707722* ☉ *Mid-Apr.–Oct., Mon.–Sat. 7–12:30.*

Where to Stay & Eat

★ **$$$** ✕ **Le Due Spade.** This Tirolean tavern has been around the corner from the Duomo since the Council of Trent. Able servers bring superb local dishes to you amid the coziness created by the wood paneling and an antique stove. You can sample traditional *gnocchetti di ricotta* (miniature ricotta cheese dumplings) and such savory second courses as *tagliata di Angus alla griglia* (grilled slivers of beef) served with an aromatic herb sauce. Given the restaurant's deserved popularity with locals and the limited seating, reservations are a must. ⊠ *Via Rizzi 11* ☎ *0461/234343* 🍽 *Reservations essential* 🟰 *AE, DC, MC, V* ☉ *Closed Sun. No lunch Mon.*

$$ ✕ **Chiesa.** Near the castle, a 15th-century building conceals a bright, modern restaurant that attracts romancing couples and power lunchers

EATING WELL IN THE DOLOMITES

Everything in Alto Adige (and, to a lesser extent, Trentino as well) has more than a tinge of the Teutonic—and the food is no exception. Germanic influence can be seen in the profusion of pastry shops, lively beer halls, and wood-paneled Tirolean *Stuben* (pubs) serving hearty meat-and-dumpling fare. Although the early dining schedule you'll find in Germany or Austria is somewhat tempered here, your options for late-night meals are more limited than in southern Italy, where la dolce vita has a firmer grip. Thankfully, the coffee is every bit as good as in parts south.

Local dishes vary from one isolated mountain valley to the next; one universal is the thinly sliced *speck tirolese* (smoked ham). Other specialties include *canederli* (also known as *Knoedel*), seasoned bread balls with many variations, served either in broth or with a sauce; *Würste* (sausages) and sauerkraut; ravioli made from rye flour, stuffed with spinach, and fried; and apple or pear strudel. *Alimentari* (food shops) stock a bounty of regional cheeses, pickles, salami, and smoked meats—perfect for picnics—and bakeries turn out a wide selection of crusty dark rolls and caraway-studded rye breads. The best of the cheeses are the mild Asiago and *fontal* and the more pungent *puzzone di Moena* (literally, "stinkpot").

Not to be missed are the outdoor Wurst carts, even (or perhaps especially) in colder weather. After placing your order at these movable sausage stands you'll get a sheet of wax paper, followed by a dollop of mustard, a hard Kaiser roll, and your chosen Wurst. You can sometimes make your selection by pointing to whatever picture seems most appealing; if not, pass on the familiar-sounding *Frankfurter* and try the local *Meraner*. The carts can reliably be found in Bolzano (try Piazza delle Erbe, or in front of the archaeological museum) and Merano (Piazza del Grano, or along the river).

alike. Ubiquitous apple imagery and excellent risotto *alle mele* (with apples) celebrate the local produce—there's even a set meal featuring apples in every course. Otherwise, the food is traditional: specialties are *maccheroncini con salsiccia e verze* (short, narrow pasta tubes with sausage and cabbage) and *tonco de Pontesel* (a stew of mixed meat made according to a 15th-century recipe). ⊠ *Via San Marco 64* ☎ *0461/238766* ▤ *AE, DC, MC, V* ⊗ *Closed Sun.*

$ ✕ **Pizzeria Laste.** Owner Guido Rizzi is a deserving national pizza-making champion; he invented pizza Calabrese, a white pizza with garlic, mozzarella, and hot red-pepper flakes. Each of his 35 pies—including the *sedano* (mozzarella, celery root, aged Parmesan cheese, oregano)—is delectable. Save room for desserts like the pizza *dolce* (sweet), which is made with bananas, strawberries, kiwi, and caramel. In a pleasant hilltop villa above the city center, the pizzeria is a bit hard to reach, but worth it. ⊠ *Via alle Laste 39* ☎ *0461/231570* ▤ *MC, V* ⊗ *Closed Tues.*

$–$$ ✕⊡ **Castel Pergine.** A 13th-century castle, appropriated by Trento's prince-bishops in the 16th century, is now skillfully managed by Theo Schneider, an Austrian architect, and his charming Swiss wife, Verena Neff (a former translator). Amid the labyrinth of stone and brick chambers, prisons, and chapels are sparse, rustic rooms with carved-wood trim, lace curtains, and heavy wooden beds, some canopied. The grounds host a different modern-art installation each year. The popular candlelit restaurant serves ages-old seasonal recipes from Trento in lighter guises: risotto with lemon and rosemary, for example. ⊠ *Via al Castello 10, 38057 Pergine Val Sugana, 12 km (7½ mi) east of Trento* ☎ *0461/531158* 🖷 *0461/531329* ⊕ *www.castelpergine.it* 🖙 *21 rooms, 14 with bath* ⚿ *Restaurant, horseback riding, bar, library; no a/c, no room TVs* ▭ *AE, MC, V* ☉ *Closed Nov.–Mar. No lunch Mon.* ⓇⓄⒾ *MAP.*

$$$–$$$$ ⊡ **Imperial Grand Hotel Terme.** For spa treatments and luxe comforts, choose the graciously restored, golden yellow palace in the nearby spa town of Levico Terme. It's not hard to imagine yourself as Austrian nobility (for whom this was once home) while you idle in the beautiful swimming pool set in a restful garden, or dine at one of the elegant restaurants. Your room may even have a frescoed ceiling. In summer a poolside bar and grill is open. ⊠ *Via Silva Domini 1, 38056 Levico Terme, 20 km (12 mi) east of Trento* ☎ *0461/706104* 🖷 *0461/706350* ⊕ *www. imperialhotel.it* 🖙 *69 rooms, 12 suites* ⚿ *4 restaurants, in-room safes, minibars, cable TV, 2 pools (1 indoor), gym, spa, billiards, 2 bars, babysitting, meeting rooms, some pets allowed (fee)* ▭ *AE, DC, MC, V* ☉ *Closed Nov.–mid-Mar.* ⓇⓄⒾ *BP.*

$$–$$$ ⊡ **Boscolo Grand Hotel Trento.** Its contemporary rounded facade amid ancient palaces makes this hotel on Piazza Dante an anomaly. Inside the lush, modern appointments include marble and woodwork in the lobby and lounges to the Clesio restaurant's rich drapery. Rooms are ample, with thick carpets and clubby, wood-trim furniture. ⊠ *Via Alfieri 1, 38100* ☎ *0461/271000* 🖷 *0461/271001* ⊕ *www.grandtrento.boscolohotels. com* 🖙 *126 rooms, 10 suites* ⚿ *Restaurant, in-room safes, minibars, cable TV, massage, sauna, bar, laundry service, business services, meeting rooms* ▭ *AE, DC, MC, V* ⓇⓄⒾ *EP.*

★ $$ ⊡ **Accademia.** This friendly hotel occupies an ancient, character-filled house in the historic center of Trento, close to Piazza del Duomo. Enter through a beautiful arched passage; the public rooms also retain the original vaulting. Bedrooms have comfortable beds and handsome lithographs of the town. In warm weather, you can enjoy a meal or a drink in the courtyard garden. ⊠ *Vicolo Colico 4/6, 38100* ☎ *0461/233600* 🖷 *0461/ 230174* ⊕ *www.accademiahotel.it* 🖙 *41 rooms, 2 suites* ⚿ *Restaurant, in-room safes, minibars, bar, meeting rooms* ▭ *AE, DC, MC, V* ☉ *Closed Dec. 24–Jan. 6* ⓇⓄⒾ *BP.*

$$ ⊡ **Buonconsiglio.** Near the train station, this efficient hotel has well-kept, sizable, and sound-resistant, rooms. Both singles and doubles are available. The prompt service also helps make Buonconsiglio ideal for the business traveler. Modern art decorates the public spaces. ⊠ *Via Romagnosi 18, 38100* ☎ *0461/272888* 🖷 *0461/272889* ⊕ *www. hotelbuonconsiglio.it* 🖙 *46 rooms, 1 suite* ⚿ *In-room safes, minibars, cable TV, bar, meeting rooms, parking (fee)* ▭ *AE, DC, MC, V* ☉ *Closed 2 wks mid-Aug.* ⓇⓄⒾ *BP.*

$ ⊡ **Aquila d'Oro.** A prime location, steps from Piazza del Duomo, is a main selling point for the Aquila d'Oro. The friendly owner gives good suggestions about what to see, do, and eat while in town. Most rooms have nondescript contemporary veneer furniture. ⊠ *Via Belenzani 76, 38100* ☎ *0461/986282* ⊟ *0461/986292* ⊕ *www.aquiladoro.it* ⇆ *19 rooms* ⚬ *Minibars, cable TV, in-room data ports, bar* ⊟ *AE, DC, MC, V* ⊘ *Closed late Dec.–mid-Feb.* ⊠ *BP.*

Nightlife & the Arts

I Suoni delle Dolomiti (The Sounds of the Dolomites; ☎ 0461/839000 ⊕ www.isuonidelledolomiti.it) festival is held in July and August every year. This series of free concerts is held at refuges high in the hills of Trentino: you'll enjoy chamber music played in grassy meadows, echoing through the mountain air. Wine buffs can take part in the **Vinum Bonum** (☎ 0461/822820) with music and wine tastings for €8 at different cellars in Trentino July and August, each Tuesday, Thursday, and Friday from 4:30 to 7.

Townspeople don medieval clothing in honor of their patron saint during **Festive Vigiliane,** a spectacular weeklong pageant in the Piazza del Duomo, culminating on June 26.

In late April or early May, Trento hosts a celebration of movies about mountains, the **Città di Trento Film Festival** (☎ 0461/986120 ⊕ www. mountainfilmfestival.trento.it).

Since 1936 the late-May wine festival, **Mostra dei Vini** (☎ 0461/497371), has attracted wine lovers of every stripe; farmers from surrounding hillside towns bend elbows with sommeliers from all over Italy. The weeklong festival includes tastings, tours, and prizes.

The **Festivale di Musica Sacra** (Sacred Music Festival; ☎ 0462/983880) is a monthlong series of concerts in May and June held in Trentino's churches.

Shopping

A number of pleasant souvenir shops and glassware outlets line **Via Manci,** near the church of Santa Maria Maggiore. You can pick up meats, cheeses, produce, local truffles, and porcini mushrooms at the small morning market in **Piazza Alessandro Vittoria.** The **Enoteca di Corso** (⊠ Corso 3 Novembre 54 ☎ 0461/916424) is an extraordinary shop laden with local products, including cheese, salami, and wine.

Galleria Trentino Art (⊠ Via Belenzani 43/45 ☎ 0461/263721) sells the widest selection of traditional Trentino handicrafts. **Il Laboratorio** (⊠ Via Roma 12 ☎ No phone) specializes in terra-cotta pieces molded by local artists. You can buy excellent handcrafted wooden objects at **Il Pozzo** (⊠ Piazza Pasi 14 ☎ No phone).

Rovereto

➋ *24 km (15 mi) south of Trento, 75 km (47 mi) south of Bolzano.*

Some of the fiercest fighting of World War I took place in the wooded hills around the medieval town of Rovereto, with Italian and Austrian troops bogged down in prolonged and costly conflict. Every evening at nightfall you're reminded of the thousands who died by the ringing of the *Campana dei Caduti* (Bell of the Fallen). Today, Rovereto is Trentino's peaceful second city. Its 15th-century castle looks down on winding streets, long-shadowed piazzas, and crumbling pastel-color villas.

The **Museo Storico Italiano della Guerra** (Italian Historical War Museum) was founded after World War I to commemorate the conflict—and to warn against repeating its atrocities. An authoritative exhibition of military artifacts is displayed in the medieval castle perched above Rovereto; the views alone warrant a visit. From May through November you can also see a collection of artillery from the Great War housed in a former air-raid shelter. ⊠ *Via Castelbarco 7* ☎ *0464/438100* ⊕ *www. museodellaguerra.it* ☑ *€5.50* ☉ *July–Sept., Tues.–Fri. 10–6, weekends 9:30–6:30; Oct.–June, Tues.–Sun. 10–6.*

NEED A BREAK?

Weathered wine barrels serve as tables at **Bacchus** (⊠ **Via Garibaldi 29** ☎ **No phone**), which has an excellent selection of local wines by the glass. Better yet, find a spot at the bar and ask for a bitter *negroni sbagliato* to be ladled out of the largest wine glass you've ever laid eyes upon. In addition to the usual Campari, gin, and vermouth, this "mistaken" negroni also employs vodka, oranges, and a few undisclosed ingredients.

The paintings of native son Fortunato Depero (1892–1960), a prominent futurist, can be found throughout town. There's a good selection of his work at the **Museo D'Arte Moderna e Contemporanea.** ⊠ *Corso Bettini 43* ☎ *0464/438887* ⊕ *www.mart.tn.it* ☑ *€8* ☉ *Tues.–Thurs., Fri. 10–9, weekends 10–6.*

Where to Stay & Eat

$$$$ ✕ **Ristorante Al Borgo.** Renowned throughout Italy for its creative cuisine, Al Borgo has a modernist take on classics. Trentino specialties on the seasonal menu may include *strangola preti* (literally "priest-chokers," dumplings with a texture so heavy that they were considered unsuitable for the delicate throats of the clergy). You could try the simple *tagliolini ai frutti di mare* (long ribbons of pasta with shellfish), or in fall, you might choose *polentina* (soft, creamy polenta) with a fondue of Trentino cheeses and truffle. The restaurant's interior is elegant and calm, with attractive art adorning the walls. ⊠ *Via Garibaldi 13* ☎ *0464/ 436300* ⌖ *Reservations essential* ⊟ *AE, DC, MC, V* ☉ *Closed Sun., Mon., 3 wks in July.*

$$–$$$ ✕▥ **Hotel Rovereto.** Brothers Marco and Fausto Zani preside over welcoming public spaces and warm-color guest rooms at the modern, central Hotel Rovereto. Their mother, Wanda, oversees the kitchen at the candlelit Ristorante Novecento ($$), one of the city's most appealing restaurants. Luscious dishes, paired with local wines, include *tortelli con fonduta di formaggi* (pasta squares stuffed with spinach and ricotta in a butter sauce) and *quaglia con finferli e polenta* (quail with wild mushrooms and polenta). ⊠ *Corso Rosmini 82/d, 38068* ☎ *0464/435222* 🖷 *0464/439644* ⊕ *www.hotelrovereto.it* ➥ *49 rooms* ⌂ *Restaurant, in-room safes, minibars, cable TV, meeting rooms, parking (fee)* ⊟ *AE, DC, MC, V* ☉ *Restaurant closed Sun. and Aug.* ⑃ *BP.*

Enrosadira & the Dwarf King

THE DOLOMITES, the inimitable craggy peaks Le Corbusier called "the most beautiful work of architecture ever seen," are never so arresting as at dusk, when the last rays of sun create a pink hue that languishes into purple. In the Ladin language, spoken only in the isolated valleys below, this magnificent transformation has its own word—the *enrosadira*. You can certainly enjoy this phenomenon from a distance, but one of the things that makes the Dolomites such an appealing year-round destination is the multitude of options for getting onto the mountains themselves. Whether you come for a pleasant stroll or a technical ascent in summer, to plunge down sheer faces or glide across peaceful valleys in winter, or to brave narrow switchbacks in a rented Fiat, your perspective, like the peaks around you, can only become more rose colored.

The enrosadira is so striking that it's prompted speculation about its origins. The French nobleman and geologist Déodat Guy Silvain Tancrède Gratet de Dolomieu (1750–1801) took the scientific approach: he got his

name applied to the range after demonstrating that the peaks have a particular composition of stratified calcium magnesium carbonate which generates the evening glow. For those unconvinced that such the phenomenon can be explained by geology alone, Ladin legend offers a compelling alternative.

Laurin, King of the Dwarfs, became infatuated with the daughter of a neighboring (human) king, and captured her with the aid of a magic hood that made him invisible. As he spirited her back to the mountains, the dwarf king was pursued by many knights, who were able to track the kidnapper after spotting his beloved rose garden. Laurin was captured and imprisoned, and when he finally managed to escape and return home, he cast a spell turning the betraying roses into rocks—so they could be seen neither by day nor by night. But Laurin forgot to include dusk in his spell, which is why the Dolomites take on a rosy glow just before nightfall. (This story is the subject of frescoes in the bar of Bolzano's Park Hotel Laurin.)

Madonna di Campiglio

❸ *89 km (56 mi) northwest of Rovereto, 88 km (55 mi) southwest of Bolzano.*

The chichi winter resort of Madonna di Campiglio has surpassed Cortina d'Ampezzo as the most fashionable place for young Italians to ski and be seen in the Dolomites. Madonna's popularity is well deserved, with more than 130 km (80 mi) of well-groomed ski runs served by 39 lifts. The resort itself is a modest 5,000 feet above sea level, but the downhill runs, summer hiking paths, and mountain-biking trails venture high up into the surrounding peaks (including Pietra Grande at 9,700 feet). Madonna's cachet is evident in its well-organized lodging, skiing, and trekking facilities.

The stunning pass at **Campo Carlo Magno** (5,500 feet) is 3 km (2 mi) north of Madonna di Campiglio. This is where Charlemagne is said to have stopped in AD 800 on his way to Rome to be crowned emperor. Stop here to glance over the whole of northern Italy. If you continue north, take the descent with caution—in the space of a mile or so, hairpin turns and switchbacks deliver you down more than 2,000 feet.

Where to Stay & Eat

★ $$$ ✕ **Cascina Zeledria.** This remote, rustic mountain restaurant near Campo Carlo Magno is not accessible by car; in winter, you'll be collected on a motorized Sno-Cat and ferried up the slopes. After the 10-minute ride, sit down to grill your own own meats and vegetables over stone griddles; the kitchen-prepared mushrooms and polenta are also house specialties. Although the majority of meals in Madonna are taken in resort hotels, Italians consider an on-mountain dinner to be an indispensable part of a proper ski week. Call in advance to reserve a table—and arrange for transportation. ⊠ *Località Zeledria* ☎ *0465/440303* ⌁ *Reservations essential* ▤ *No credit cards* ⊘ *Closed May, June, Oct., and Nov.*

$$$$ ▦ **Golf Hotel.** You need to make your way north to the Campo Carlo Magno pass to reach this grand hotel, the former summer residence of Habsburg emperor Franz Josef. A modern wing has been added, but old-world charm persists: Rooms 114 and 214 retain the lavish imperial style, and the rest of the resort is replete with verandas, Persian rugs, and bay windows. In summer the golf course attracts a tony crowd. ⊠ *Via Cima Tosa 3, 38084* ☎ *0465/441003* ▤ *0465/440294* ⊕ *www.golfhotelcampiglio.it* ⟿ *107 rooms, 8 suites* ⌁ *Restaurant, minibars, cable TV, 9-hole golf course, gym, spa, bar, convention center, free parking* ▤ *AE, DC, MC, V* ⊘ *Closed mid-Apr.–June and Sept.–Nov.* ▮◯▮ *MAP.*

$$$$ ▦ **Grifone.** A comfortable Alpine lodge sits catching the sun with a distinctive wood facade and flower-bedecked balconies. Contemporary singles, doubles, and triples have views of the forested slopes. The restaurant serves home cooking as well as international dishes. The hotel is south of the lake, a bit out of town, but the Spinale cable car is nearby. Half or full board is required. ⊠ *Via Vallesinella 7, 38084* ☎ *0465/442002* ▤ *0465/440540* ⊕ *www.hotelgrifone.it* ⟿ *38 rooms, 2 suites* ⌁ *Restaurant, in-room safes, cable TV, spa, bar, free parking; no a/c* ▤ *AE, DC, MC, V* ⊘ *Closed May, June, and Sept.–Nov.* ▮◯▮ *MAP.*

★ $$$$ ▦ **Savoia Palace.** This central hotel is also Madonna's most traditional, full of carved-wood and mountain-style furnishings. Two fireplaces blaze away in the bar, where you can relax as you recall the day's exploits on the ski slopes. The elegant restaurant serves a mixture of local specialties and rich dishes combining Italian and Austrian influences. Full or half board is required. ⊠ *Viale Dolomiti di Brenta 18, 38084* ☎ *0465/441004* ▤ *0465/440549* ⊕ *www.savoiapalace.com* ⟿ *55 rooms* ⌁ *Restaurant, in-room safes, minibars, cable TV, bar; no a/c* ▤ *AE, DC, MC, V* ⊘ *Closed Apr.–June and Sept.–mid-Dec.* ▮◯▮ *MAP.*

Nightlife

For lively, family-friendly après-ski, head to the homey **Stube Franz Joseph** (⊠ Viale Dolomiti di Brenta ☎ 0465/440875). Fashionable **Bar Suisse** (⊠ Piazza Righi 5 ☎ 0465/441023) is the most popular (and crowded) spot for predinner drinks, and the attached **Cantina del Suisse** (☎ 0465/442632) offers live music until midnight.

Sports & the Outdoors

GOLF The 9-hole **Campo Carlo Magno** (✉ Via Cima Tosa 15, near Golf Hotel ☎ 0465/440622) course is one of the highest in Europe, at 5,500 feet. It's open July–September.

HIKING & CLIMBING The Madonna di Campiglio **tourist office** (✉ Via Pradalago 4 ☎ 0465/447501 ⊕ www.campiglio.to) has maps of a dozen trails leading to waterfalls, lakes, and stupefying views. Climbing and trekking adventures are organized by Madonna's **Scuola di Alpinismo** (Mountaineering School; ✉ Piazza Brenta Alta 16 ☎ 0465/442634 ⊕ www.guidealpinecampiglio.it). The cable car to 6,900-foot **Punta Spinale** (Spinale Peak; ✉ Off Via Monte Spinale ☎ 0465/447744 🚡 Cable car €8 round-trip ⊗ Mid-July–early Sept., daily 8:30–5:30) offers skiers magnificent views of the Brenta Dolomites in winter, and also runs during peak summer season.

SKIING Miles of interconnecting ski runs—some of the best in the Dolomites—are linked by the cable cars and lifts of **Funivie Madonna di Campiglio** (Main cable car ✉ Off Via Presanella, across from Piazza Righi ☎ 0465/447744 ⊕ www.campiglio.to). Advanced skiers will delight in the extremely difficult terrain found on certain mountain faces, but there are also many intermediate and beginner runs, all accessible from town. There are also plenty of off-piste opportunities. Ski passes (€35 per day) can be purchased at the main *funivia* (cable car) in town.

EN ROUTE The route between Madonna di Campiglio and Bormio (2½ hours) takes you through a series of high mountain passes. After Campo Carlo Magno, turn left at Dimaro and continue 37 km (23 mi) west through Passo del Tonale (6,200 feet). At Ponte di Legno, turn north on S300. You pass the *Lago Nero* (Black Lake) on your left just before the summit. Continue on to Bormio through the Passo di Gavia (8,600 feet).

Bormio

❹ *97 km (60 mi) northwest of Madonna di Campiglio, 100 km (62 mi) southwest of Merano.*

At the foot of Stelvio Pass, Bormio is the most famous ski resort on the western side of the Dolomites, with 38 km (24 mi) of long pistes and a 5,000-plus-foot vertical drop. In summer its cool temperatures and clean air entice Italians away from cities in the humid Lombard plain. This dual-season popularity supports the plentiful shops, restaurants, and hotels in town. Bormio has been known for the therapeutic qualities of its waters since the Roman era, and there are numerous spas.

Ancient Roman baths predate the wonderland of thermal springs, caves, and waterfalls now known as the **Bagni Vecchi** (Old Baths); Leonardo da Vinci soaked here in 1493. ✉ *Strada Statale Stelvio* ☎ *0342/910131* ⊕ *www.bagnidibormio.it* 🚡 *Weekdays €35, weekends €38* ⊗ *Tues. and Thurs. 10–11; Wed. and Fri.–Mon. 10–8.*

Modern facilities and comprehensive spa treatments are available at **Bormio Terme**. ✉ *Via Stelvio 14* ☎ *0342/901325* ⊕ *www.bormioterme.com*

🗊 *Day pass, including thermal baths and hot tub €16; total mud treatment €24* ⊘ *Jan.–Mar., July, and Aug., Thurs. and weekends 9–8; Mon.–Wed. 9–10; Fri. 9–midnight.*

Bormio makes a good base for exploring the Alps' biggest national park, the **Parco Nazionale dello Stelvio,** spread over 1,350 square km (520 square mi) and four provinces. Opened in 1935 with the express intent to preserve flora and protect fauna, today it thrives, with more than 1,200 types of plants, 600 different mushrooms, and more than 160 species of animals, including the chamois, ibex, and roe deer. There are many entrances to the park, and nine visitor centers that are open at different times of the year. ⊠ *Off SS38 and SS42* ⊕ *www.parks.it/parco. nazionale.stelvio* 🗊 *Free.*

Where to Stay & Eat

$$ ✕ **Kuerc.** This central restaurant building was for centuries where justice was publicly served to accused witches, among others. These days, things are rather more refined: enjoy local specialties like *brasaola* (salted, air-dried beef) with lemon and olive oil, or *pizzoccheri* (buckwheat pasta) with garlic and winter vegetables. ⊠ *Piazza Cavour 7* ☎ *0342/904738* 🍽 *MC, V* ⊘ *Closed Tues.*

$$$ 🏨 **Nazionale.** Bordering the Stelvio National Park, the Nazionale caters to both the winter and summer crowds. Behind the Alpine exterior, rooms are small but have solid wood furniture, minibars, and balconies on all floors except the top one. The hotel operates a shuttle bus to the cable cars. ⊠ *Via al Forte 28, 23032* ☎ *0342/903361* 🖷 *0342/905294* ⊕ *www.hotelnazionale.info* ⤴ *48 rooms* ♨ *2 restaurants, in-room safes, minibars, indoor pool, hot tub, sauna, bar, recreation room, shops; no a/c* 🍽 *AE, DC, MC, V* ⊘ *Closed mid-Sept.–Nov. and mid-Apr.–mid-June* ⊺◉ *BP.*

$$$ 🏨 **Posta.** The Ostelli della Posta stagecoach inns are a time-honored tradition in northern Italy. The warm reception at this town-center hotel helps to temper the winter cold, as does the rustic decoration, with its warm wood detail in the low-vault areas. Rooms are cozy and comfortable, with heavy drapery and bed linens. Perks include a small health club with a pool, sauna, gym, and Turkish bath—and a shuttle bus to the slopes. ⊠ *Via Roma 66, 23032* ☎ *0342/904753* 🖷 *0342/904484* ⊕ *www.hotelposta.bormio.it* ⤴ *50 rooms* ♨ *Restaurant, in-room safes, cable TV, indoor pool, health club, sauna, Turkish bath, pub; no a/c* 🍽 *AE, DC, MC, V* ⊘ *Closed May, June, and Sept.–Nov.* ⊺◉ *BP.*

Sports

SKIING You can buy a ski pass (€32 per day) and pick up a trail map at the base **funivia** (cable car; ☎ 0342/901451 ⊕ www.skipassaltavaltellina. it) in the center of town to connect to the Bormio 2000 station (6,600 feet) on Vallecetta, the main resort mountain. From there, you can ski down intermediate trails (which comprise the majority of Bormio's runs), use the extensive lift network to explore secondary ski areas, or get another funivia up to the Cima Bianca station (9,800 feet) for more challenging terrain. These cable cars are more for skiing than hiking.

Passo dello Stelvio

★ ❺ *20 km (12 mi) north of Bormio, 80 km (48 mi) west of Merano.*

At more than 9,000 feet, the Passo dello Stelvio is the second-highest pass in Europe, connecting the Valtellina in Lombardy with the Val Venosta in Alto Adige. The view from the top is well worth the drive; looking north you can see Switzerland. The pass is open from May or June to October, depending on weather conditions. Stelvio itself is a year-round skiing center, with many of its runs open in summer.

EN ROUTE Between the Stelvio Pass and the town of Spondigna, 30 km (19 mi) of road wind down 48 hair-raising hairpin turns. The views are spectacular, but this descent is not for the faint of heart. In Spondigna keep to the right for the road to Naturno.

BOLZANO (BOZEN)

32 km (19 mi) south of Merano, 50 km (31 mi) north of Trento.

Bolzano (Bozen), the capital of the autonomous province of Alto Adige, is tucked in among craggy peaks in a Dolomite valley just 77 km (48 mi) from the Brenner Pass and Austria. Tirolean culture dominates Bolzano's language, food, architecture, and people. It may be hard to remember that you're in Italy when walking the city's colorful cobblestone streets and visiting its lantern-lighted cafés, where·you may enjoy sauerkraut and a beer among a lively crowd of blue-eyed German-speakers. However, fine Italian espresso, fashionable boutiques, and reasonable prices will help remind you where you are. With castles and steeples topping the landscape, this quiet city at the confluence of the Isarco (Eisack) and Talvera rivers has retained a provincial appeal. Proximity to fabulous skiing and mountain climbing—not to mention the world's oldest preserved mummy—make it a worthwhile, if undiscovered, tourist destination. And its streets are immaculate: with the highest per capita earnings of any city in Italy, Bolzano's residents enjoy a standard of living that is second to none.

> **WORD OF MOUTH**
>
> "Bolzano is a fairly big town, a college town, lots of stores and places to eat. There are many gondolas to take, the tourist office has a great little book with about 10 walks/hikes. It's such a beautiful city, right in the middle of the mountains."
>
> –Susanna

Exploring Bolzano

The Main Attractions

❽ **Chiesa dei Domenicani.** The 13th-century Dominican Church is renowned as Bolzano's main repository for paintings, especially frescoes. In the adjoining **Cappella di San Giovanni** you can see works from the Giotto school, one of which is a *Triumph of Death* (circa 1340). Despite its macabre subject, this fresco shows the birth of a pre-Renaissance sense

Chiesa dei
Domenicani **8**

Duomo **7**

Museo
Archeologico
dell'Alto
Adige **11**

Museo Civico ..**10**

Piazza delle
Erbe **9**

Piazza
Walther **6**

of depth and individuality. ✉ *Piazza Domenicani* ☎ *0471/973133* ⊙ *Mon.–Sat. 9:30–5, Sun. noon–5.*

❼ Duomo. A lacy spire looks down on the mosaic-like roof tiles of the city's Gothic cathedral, built between the 12th and 14th century. Inside are 14th- and 15th-century frescoes and an intricately carved stone pulpit dating from 1514. Outside, don't miss the **Porta del Vino** (Wine Gate) on the northeast side; decorative carvings of grapes and harvest workers attest to the long-standing importance of wine to this region. ✉ *Piazza Walther* ☎ *0471/978676* ⊙ *Weekdays 10–noon and 2–5, Sat. 10–noon and 2–4, Sun. 1–5.*

⓫ Museo Archeologico dell'Alto Adige. This museum has gained international

Fodor'sChoice fame for Ötzi, its 5,300-year-old iceman, discovered in 1991 and the

★ world's oldest naturally preserved body. In 1998 Italy acquired it from Austria after it was determined that the body lay 100 yards inside Italy. The iceman's leathery remains are displayed in a freezer, preserved along with his longbow, ax, and clothing. The rest of the museum relies on models and artifacts from nearby archaeological sites (an eloquent English audio guide is €2) to lead you not only through Ötzi's Copper Age, but also into the preceding Paleolithic and Neolithic eras, and the Bronze and Iron ages that followed. ✉ *Via Museo 43* ☎ *0471/*

320100 ⊕ *www.iceman.it* ☒ €8 ⊙ *Tues., Wed., and Fri.–Sun. 10–6; Thurs. 10–8; last admission 1 hr before closing.*

❾ **Piazza delle Erbe.** A bronze statue of Neptune, which dates back to 1745, presides over a bountiful fruit-and-vegetable market in this square. The stalls spill over with colorful displays of local produce; bakeries and grocery stores showcase hot breads, pastries, cheeses, and delicatessen meats—a complete picnic. Try the *speck tirolese* (a thinly sliced smoked ham) and the apple strudel.

❻ **Piazza Walther.** This pedestrian-only square is Bolzano's heart; in warmer weather it serves as an open-air living room where locals and tourists alike can be found at all hours sipping a drink (such as a glass of chilled Riesling). In the center stands Heinrich Natter's white-marble, neo-Romanesque **Monument to Walther,** built in 1889. The piazza's namesake was the 12th-century German wandering minstrel Walther von der Vogelweide, whose songs lampooned the papacy and praised the Holy Roman Emperor.

Also Worth Seeing

Castel Mareccio (Schloss Maretsch). This castle, tucked below mountains and enveloped by vineyards, dates from the 13th century. It's been pressed into service as a modern conference center. You can only view the frescoes inside by calling ahead and joining a free guided tour on Tuesday (in German or Italian). ☒ *Lungotalvera, Bolzano; head north along the river* ☎ *0471/976615* ☒ *Free* ⊙ *Tues. by appointment.*

Castel Roncolo (Schloss Runkelstein). The green hills and farmhouses north of town surround the meticulously kept castle with a red roof. It was built in 1237, destroyed half a century later, and then rebuilt soon thereafter. There's a beautifully preserved cycle of medieval frescoes inside. A **tavern** in the courtyard serves excellent local food and wines. ☒ *Via San Antonio 1, Number 12 bus from Piazza Walther, or 20-min walk from Piazza delle Erbe: head north along Via Francescani, continue through Piazza Madonna, connecting to Via Castel Roncolo* ☎ *0471/ 329808 castle, 0471/324073 tavern* ⊕ *www.comune.bolzano.it/roncolo* ☒ €8 ⊙ *Tues.–Sun. 10–6.*

❿ **Museo Civico.** Bolzano's municipal museum has a rich collection of traditional costumes, wood carvings, and archaeological exhibits. It's scheduled to reopen, following renovations, in 2008. ☒ *Via Cassa di Risparmio 14* ☎ *0471/974625.*

Passeggiata del Guncina. An 8-km (5-mi) botanical promenade dating from 1892 ends with a panoramic view of Bolzano. ☒ *Entrance near Vecchia Parrocchiale, in Gries, across river and up Corso Libertà.*

Vecchia Parrocchiale (Old Parish Church). Visit this church, said to have been built in 1141, to see its two medieval treasures: an 11th-century Romanesque crucifix and an elaborately carved 15th-century wooden altar by Michael Pacher—a true masterpiece of the Gothic style. ☒ *Via Martin Knoller, in Gries, across river and up Corso Libertà* ☎ *0471/ 283089* ⊙ *Apr.–Oct., weekdays 10:30–noon and 2:30–4.*

Off the Beaten Path

Renon (Ritten) Plateau. The earth pyramids of Renon Plateau are a bizarre geological formation where erosion has left a forest of tall, thin, needle-like spires of rock, each topped with a boulder. To get here, take the Soprabolzano funicular from Via Renon, about 300 yards left of the Bolzano train station. At the top, switch to the electric train that takes you to the plateau, which is in Collalbo, just above Bolzano. The two rides take about 12 minutes. ⊠ *Via Renon, Collalbo* ☎ *0471/978479* ⊠ *€7 round-trip* ⊗ *Daily 7–7.*

3

Where to Stay & Eat

★ **$$$** ✕ **Zür Kaiserkron.** Traditional Tirolean opulence and attentive service set the stage for some of the best food in town. Appetizers might include potato blini with salmon caviar, and marinated artichokes with butter (not to be missed if available). Main dishes, such as veal with black truffle–and–spinach canederli make use of ingredients from the local valleys. This place is popular with dignified local businesspeople. ⊠ *Piazzetta Mostra* ☎ *0471/970770* ☰ *AE, DC, MC, V* ⊗ *Closed Sun. No dinner Sat.*

$–$$ ✕ **Alexander.** Typical Tirolean dishes are served at this convivial city-center restaurant. The venison ham and the lamb cutlets *al timo con salsa all'aglio* (with thyme and garlic sauce) are particularly good, but make sure to leave room for the rich chocolate cake. ⊠ *Via Aosta 37* ☎ *0471/918608* ☰ *MC, V* ⊗ *Closed Sat.*

★ **$–$$** ✕ **Batzenhausl.** Locals hold animated conversations over glasses of local wine in a modern take on the traditional Weinstube (wine tavern, often abbreviated to "stube"). Tasty South Tirolean specialties include speck tirolese and *mezzelune casarecce ripiene* (house-made stuffed half-moons of pasta). If you're seeking a quiet meal, ask for a table on the second floor, near the handsome stained-glass windows of this medieval building. ⊠ *Via Andreas Hofer 30* ☎ *0471/050950* ☰ *MC, V.*

$ ✕ **Cavallino Bianco.** Ask a local for a restaurant recommendation in Bolzano, and you're likely to be pointed toward this dependable favorite near Via dei Portici. A wide selection of Italian and German dishes is served in a spacious, comfortable dining room, where there are usually many extended families enjoying their meals together. ⊠ *Via Bottai 6* ☎ *0471/973267* ☰ *No credit cards* ⊗ *Closed Sun. No dinner Sat.*

¢–$ ✕ **Hopfen & Co. (Bozner Bier).** Fried white *Würstel* (sausages), sauerkraut, and grilled ribs complement the excellent home-brewed Austrian-style pilsner and wheat beer at this lively pub-restaurant. There's live music on Thursday night, attracting Bolzano's students and young professionals. ⊠ *Piazza delle Erbe 17* ☎ *0471/300788* ☰ *MC, V.*

★ **$$$–$$$$** ✕🏨 **Park Hotel Laurin.** An exercise in art nouveau opulence, Park Hotel Laurin is considered the finest lodging in all of Alto Adige, with art-filled modern guest rooms and handsome public spaces (the frescoes in the bar tell the legend of the dwarf King Laurin). The hotel presides over a large park in the middle of town. Its history is speckled with visits from Europe's grand nobility, including Archduke Franz Ferdinand (whose murder in Sarajevo sparked World War I). Restaurant Laurin is superb, bringing an international sensibility to rustic regional dishes. ⊠ *Via Laurin 4, 39100* ☏ *0471/311000* 🖷 *0471/311148* ⊕ *www.laurin.it* ⇆ *88 rooms, 8 suites* ⚐ *Restaurant, in-room safes, minibars, cable TV, pool, bar, convention center, parking (fee), no-smoking rooms* ▭ *AE, DC, MC, V* ¶Ⓞ|*BP.*

$$$–$$$$ 🏨 **Hotel Greif.** Even in a hospitable region, the Greif is a rare gem. This
FodorśChoice small central hotel has been a Bolzano landmark for centuries, and a
★ beautiful renovation has set a standard for modernity in Alto Adige. In-room computers with ISDN Internet and private whirlpool baths are just a few of the perks. Public spaces are airy and immaculate; each guest room was designed by a different local artist—contemporary installations are thoughtfully paired with 19th-century paintings and sketches. The clean-line modern furnishings contrast with views of the Gothic cathedral across the square. ⊠ *Piazza Walther 1, 39100* ☏ *0471/318000* 🖷 *0471/318148* ⊕ *www.greif.it* ⇆ *33 rooms* ⚐ *In-room safes, in-room hot tubs, minibars, cable TV, in-room broadband, parking (fee)* ▭ *AE, DC, MC, V* ¶Ⓞ|*BP.*

★ $$$–$$$$ 🏨 **Schloss Korb.** A romantic 13th-century castle hotel, with crenellations and a massive tower, perches in a park amid vine-covered hills. Much of the ancient character is preserved, and the public rooms are filled with antiques, elaborate wood carvings, paintings, and attractive plants. The guest rooms have solid, rustic, pine beds with pillow-top mattresses; some in the tower have striking Romanesque arched windows. It's well worth the 5-km (3-mi) drive west from Bolzano to get here. ⊠ *Via Castel d'Appiano 5, 39050 Missiano* ☏ *0471/636000* 🖷 *0471/636033* ⊕ *www. schlosskorb.com* ⇆ *57 rooms, 5 suites* ⚐ *Restaurant, 2 tennis courts, 2 pools (1 indoor), sauna, bar, parking (fee); no a/c* ▭ *No credit cards* ☉ *Closed Nov.–Mar.* ¶Ⓞ| *MAP.*

$$ 🏨 **Luna-Mondschein.** This central yet secluded hotel in a tranquil garden dates from 1798. The comfortable rooms have wood paneling throughout; those overlooking the garden have balconies, others have good views of the mountains. First-rate dining is available in both the cozy, convivial Tirolean stube and the art nouveau Ristorante Van Gogh, one of the city's best. ⊠ *Via Piave 15, 39100* ☏ *0471/975642* 🖷 *0471/975577* ⊕ *www.hotel-luna.it* ⇆ *85 rooms* ⚐ *Restaurant, Weinstube, meeting rooms, parking (fee); no a/c* ▭ *AE, DC, MC, V* ¶Ⓞ|*BP.*

Nightlife & the Arts

Concerts & Theater

There's a lively performance scene in town. A weekly schedule of what's on is available at the tourist office. Note that theater performances may be in German.

For opera information and schedules, call **Friends of Opera** (☏ 0471/913223). Orchestral concerts are held at **Haus der Kultur** (⊠ Via Sciliar 1 ☏ 0471/977520).

A frequently used theater venue is the imposing **Nuovo Teatro Comunale** (⊠ Piazza Verdi 40 ☏ 0471/304130 ⊕ www.ntbz.net). **Cortile Theater im Hof** (⊠ Piazza delle Erbe 37 ☏ 0471/980756) specializes in children's theater.

Nightlife

A centuries-old tradition of late-night merriment carries on at **Hopfen & Co.** (✉ Piazza delle Erbe 17 ☎ 0471/300788), a beer hall and restaurant. A modernization of the ground floor of ancient tavern **Batzenhausl** (✉ Via Andreas Hofer 30 ☎ 0471/050950) into a sleek wine-bar has only increased its popularity among locals, who have gathered here for centuries. The bar at **Vögele** (✉ Via Goethe 3 ☎ 0471/973938) stays open until 1 AM, serving an outstanding selection of wines by the glass in a relaxed setting. The **Park Hotel Laurin Bar** (✉ Via Laurin 4 ☎ 0471/311000) hosts jazz combos on Friday and a jazz pianist all other nights.

Sports & the Outdoors

Biking

If you're in decent shape, a great way to see some of the surrounding castles, lakes, and forested valleys of the Dolomites is by bike. **Alp Bike** (☎ 0471/280795 ⊕ www.alpbike.it) leads different guided excursions almost every day, at all levels, but you must reserve a week or more ahead for the more ambitious trips.

Hiking

Club Alpino Italiano (✉ Piazza delle Erbe 46 ☎ 0471/981391 ⊕ www.cai.it) provides helpful information on area hiking and rock climbing.

Shopping

Local Crafts

The long, narrow arcades of **Via dei Portici** house shops that specialize in Tirolean crafts and clothing. The largest store for locally made handcrafted goods is **Artigiani Atesini** (✉ Via Portici 39 ☎ 0471/978590).

Markets

From the end of November to Christmas Eve there's a traditional **Christkindlmarkt** (Christmas market) in Piazza Walther, with stalls selling all kinds of Christmas decorations and local handcrafted goods. An outdoor fruit-and-vegetable market takes over the central **Piazza delle Erbe** Monday–Saturday 8–1. A weekly flea market takes place Saturday morning in **Piazza della Vittoria.**

Wine

Walk down a small alleyway near Piazza delle Erbe to discover **Il Baccaro** (✉ Via Argentieri 17 ☎ 0471/971421), a tiny *enoteca* (wine bar) and wineshop. It's invariably filled with older men engrossed in conversation—you can't go wrong buying a bottle of whatever they're drinking. On Saturday in October the **Bacchus Urbanus** program leads guided excursions to vineyards near Bolzano; contact the tourist office for details.

ALTO ADIGE & CORTINA

Prosperous valley towns (such as the famed spa center Merano) and mountain resorts (including the archetypal Cortina d'Ampezzo) entice those seeking both relaxation and adventure. Alto Adige (Südtirol) was for centuries part of the Austro-Hungarian Empire, only ceded to Italy at the end of World War I. Ethnic differences led to inevitable tensions in the 1960s and again in the '80s, though a large measure of provincial autonomy has, for the most part, kept the lid on nationalist ambitions. Today Germanic and Italian balance harmoniously, as do medieval and modern influences, with ancient castles regularly playing host to contemporary art exhibitions.

Naturno (Naturns)

⑫ *44 km (27 mi) northwest of Bolzano, 61 km (38 mi) east of Passo dello Stelvio.*

Colorful houses covered with murals line the streets of Naturno (Naturns), a sunny horticultural center. Art lovers will appreciate the church of **San Procolo**; the frescoes inside are some of the oldest in the German-speaking world, dating from the 8th century. It's northeast of the town center, off S38. ⊠ *Via San Procolo* ☎ *0471/667312* ⊗ *Easter–Nov., Tues.–Sun. 9:30–noon and 2:30–5:30.*

A five-minute drive west of Naturno, in the hills above the hamlet of Stava, is the 13th-century **Castel Juval**, since 1983 the home of the South Tirolese climber and polar adventurer Reinhold Messner—the first man to conquer Everest solo and the first to reach its summit without oxygen. Part of the castle has been turned into a museum, showing Messner's collection of Tibetan art, mountaineering illustrations, and masks from around the world. ⊠ *Viale Europa 2* ☎ *0473/221852* 💳 *€7* ⊗ *Apr.–June and Sept.–mid-Nov., Thurs.–Tues. 10–4.*

Where to Eat

$$ ✕ **Schlosswirt Juval.** Below Castel Juval, Reinhold Messner's restored farmhouse is home to an old-style restaurant serving Mediterranean standards and traditional local dishes. Not to be missed are the smoked hams and flavorful cheeses provisioned from the farm outside; they are well paired with the estate's Castel Juval wine. Dinner is often accompanied by live jazz. ⊠ *Via Municipio 1* ☎ *0473/668238* ☐ *No credit cards* ⊗ *Closed Wed., July and Aug., and Nov.–Easter.*

EN ROUTE The source of the full-flavor beer served throughout the region is the striking **Forst Brewery** (⊠ Via Venosta 8, Lagundo ☎ 0473/447727), on the road connecting Naturno and Merano. Tours are possible in summer (roughly June–August, daily 2–4), but you need to call ahead for reservations. You can turn up any time of year to sample the product line. In warm weather, cross a covered, flower-lined bridge to reach the delightful beer garden.

Merano (Meran)

★ ⑬ *16 km (10 mi) east of Naturno, 24 km (15 mi) north of Bolzano.*

The second-largest town in Alto Adige, Merano (Meran) was once the capital of the Austrian region of Tirol. When the town and surrounding area were ceded to Italy as part of the 1919 Treaty of Versailles, Inns-

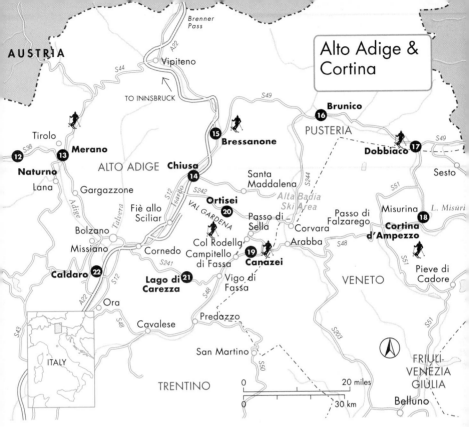

Alto Adige & Cortina

bruck became the capital. Merano, however, continued to be known as a spa town, attracting European nobility for its therapeutic waters and its grape cure, which consists simply of eating the grapes grown on the surrounding hillsides. Sheltered by mountains, Merano has an unusually mild climate, with summer temperatures rarely exceeding 80°F (27°C) and winters that usually stay above freezing, despite the skiing that is within easy reach. Along the narrow streets of Merano's old town, houses have little towers and huge wooden doors, and the pointed arches of the Gothic cathedral sit next to neoclassical and art nouveau buildings. Merano serves as a good respite from mountain adventures, or from the bustle of nearby Trento and Bolzano.

The 14th-century Gothic **Duomo**, with a crenellated facade and an ornate campanile, sits in the heart of the old town. The Capella di Santa Barbara, just behind the cathedral, is an octagonal church containing a 15th-century pietà. ⊠ *Piazza del Duomo* ⊙ *Easter–Sept., daily 8–noon and 2:30–8; Oct.–Easter, daily 8–noon and 2:30–7.*

The thermal baths at the **Terme di Merano** reopened in 2005 after an expansive renovation: a sprawling hotel and spa complex has 25 pools (including a brine pool with underwater music) and eight saunas (with an indoor "snow room" available for cooling down). Along with the usual spa treatments, personalized services include traditional cures using local products, such as grape-based applications and whey baths. ⊠ *Piazza Terme 9* ☎ *0473/252000* ⊕ *www.termemerano.it* ⊡ *€8.50 (2 hrs in thermal baths) to €20 (full day's use of all baths and saunas); additional treatments extra* ☉ *Daily 9 AM–10 PM. Saunas women-only Thurs.*

Castel Trauttmansdorff, a Gothic castle 2 km (1 mi) southeast of town, was restored in the 19th century, and now serves as a museum, celebrating 200 years of tourism in South Tirol. Outside, a sprawling garden has an extensive display of exotic flora organized by country of origin. ⊠ *Via S. Valentino 51a* ☎ *0473/235730* ⊕ *www.trauttmansdorff.it* ⊡ *€9.50* ☉ *Apr.–mid-May and mid-Sept.–mid-Nov., daily 9–6; mid-May–mid-Sept., daily 9–9.* Overlooking the town atop Mt. Tappeinerweg is a castle that was the home of poet Ezra Pound from 1958 to 1964. Still in the Pound family, the castle now houses the **Museo Agricolo di Brunnenburg**, devoted to Tirolean country life. Among its exhibits are a blacksmith's shop and, not surprisingly, a room with Pound memorabilia. To get there, take Bus 3, which departs every hour on the hour, from Merano to Dorf Tirol (20 minutes). ⊠ *Via Castello 17, Brunnenburg* ☎ *0473/923533* ⊡ *€3* ☉ *Apr.–Oct., Wed.–Mon. 10–5.*

FodorśChoice ★ A stroll along one of Merano's well-marked, impossibly pleasant **promenades** may yield even better relaxation than a spa treatment. **Passeggiata Tappeiner** (Tappeiner's Promenade) is a 3-km (2-mi) path with panoramic views from the hills north of the Duomo, and the exceptionally mild climate gives way to diverse botanical pleasures along the walk. **Passeggiata d'Estate** (Summer Promenade) runs along the shaded south bank of the Passirio River, and the **Passeggiata d'Inverno** (Winter Promenade), on the exposed north bank, provides more warmth and the Wandelhalle—a sun trap decorated with idyllic paintings of surrounding villages. The popular Austrian Empress Sissi (Elisabeth of Wittelsbach, 1837–98) put Merano on the map as a spa destination; a trail named in her honor, the **Sentiero di Sissi,** (Sissi's Walk) follows a path from Castel Trauttmansdorff to the heart of Merano.

NEED A BREAK? **Cafe Saxifraga** (⊠ Passeggiata Tappeiner ☎ 0473/237249) occupies an enviable position overlooking Merano and the peaks enveloping the town; an extensive selection of teas and other beverages can be enjoyed on the patio, which has panoramic views. You can enjoy a rich hot chocolate or a cold beer above a gurgling waterfall at **Cafe Glif** (⊠ Passeggiata Glif 51 ☎ 0473/234701), at the northeast edge of the Passeggiata d'Inverno.

Where to Stay & Eat

★ $$$ ✕ **Sissi.** In this relaxed, light-filled restaurant just off Via dei Portici, rustic regional dishes are prepared with the precision of haute Italian cooking. Menu choices may include risotto *alle erbe* (with herbs) and *filetto di vitello con salsa di alloro* (veal fillet with bay-leaf sauce); a set menu (about €60) provides a complete five-course dinner. ⊠ *Via Galilei 44* ☎ *0473/231062* ⚏ *Reservations essential* ▤ *MC, V* ☾ *Closed Mon. and Jan. and Feb.*

$$ ✕ **Haisrainer.** Among the rustic wine taverns lining Via dei Portici, this one is most popular with locals and tourists alike; a menu in English is available for the latter. Warm wooden walls provide a comfortable setting for Tirolean and Italian standards: try the *zuppa al vino bianco* (stew with white wine) or the seasonal risottos (with asparagus in spring, or Barolo wine in chillier months). ⊠ *Via dei Portici 100* ☎ *0473/237944* ▤ *MC, V* ☾ *Closed Sun.*

$–$$ ✕ **Sieben.** Young Meraners crowd the hip bar on the ground floor of this modern bistro, in the town's central arcade. Upstairs, a more mature crowd enjoys the contemporary cooking and attentive service in the jazz-theme dining room. Don't miss the Blues Brothers, poised over the staircase. ⊠ *Via dei Portici 232* ☎ *0473/210636* ▤ *MC, V* ☾ *No lunch Sun.*

¢–$ ✕ **Vinoteca-Pizzeria Relax.** If you have difficulty choosing from the long list of appetizing pizzas here, ask the friendly English-speaking staff for help with the menu—and the wine list. You're unlikely to find a better selection, or a more pleasant environment for sampling. You can also buy bottles of the locally produced vintage to take home. ⊠ *Via Cavour 31, opposite Grand Hotel Palace* ☎ *0473/236735* ▤ *AE, MC, V* ☾ *Closed Sun. and 2 wks in late Feb.*

★ $$$$ ▥ **Grand Hotel Palace.** Merano's finest hotel is an old-world institution in an extensive garden. The art nouveau touches present in the public spaces—Tiffany glass, marble pillars, and high ceilings—spill over into the spacious guest rooms. The renowned spa has baths, massages, mud treatments, and other cures that attract fatigued soccer stars and others in search of renewal. Rooftop suites have balconies with stunning views of Merano's steeples and the surrounding mountains. ⊠ *Via Cavour 2, 39012* ☎ *0473/271000* ☐ *0473/271100* ⊕ *www.palace.it* ⇆ *125 rooms, 12 suites* ⚏ *2 restaurants, minibars, cable TV, pool, spa, bar, wineshop, meeting rooms, free parking* ▤ *AE, DC, MC, V* ⦿ *BP.*

$$$–$$$$ ▥ **Castello Labers.** The red-tile gables, towers, and turrets give this castle its unmistakably Tirolean style, as it sits on a hilltop amid forested slopes. Ceiling beams, painted fresco decorations, and crossed halberds on the walls complete the look inside. The hospitable Stapf-Neubert family owns the hotel and takes an active part in its management. ⊠ *Via Labers 25, 39012, 3 km (2 mi) northeast of Merano's center* ☎ *0473/234484* ☐ *0473/234146* ⊕ *www.labers.it* ⇆ *32 rooms, 1 suite* ⚏ *Restaurant, in-room safes, tennis court, pool; no a/c* ▤ *AE, DC, MC, V* ☾ *Closed mid-Nov.–mid-Apr.* ⦿ *BP.*

$ ▥ **Conte di Merano.** If you don't feel like paying for one of Merano's resorts, this simple central hotel is a good alternative. Steps away from Via dei Portici and open year-round, it's an efficient base for exploring the town. Rooms have spartan furnishings, but are clean and comfortable. ⊠ *Via delle Corse 78, 39012* ☎ *0473/490260* ☐ *0473/490261* ⊕ *www.grafvonmeran.com* ⇆ *23 rooms* ⚏ *Restaurant, in-room safes, cable TV, bar* ▤ *AE, DC, MC, V* ⦿ *BP.*

Nightlife

Merano is a quiet town after dark, but there is no shortage of pleasant watering holes. Younger Meraners favor **Bar Piccolo** (⊠ Corso Libertà 5 ☎ 0473/236765). Mellow cafés such as **Cafe Darling** (⊠ Passeggiata Inverno 5 ☎ 0473/237221) line the promenade along the river.

Shopping

Merano's main shopping street, the narrow arcaded **Via dei Portici** (Laubengasse), runs west from the cathedral. There are regional products—wood carvings, Tirolean-style clothing, embroidery, cheeses, salami, and fruit schnapps—for sale, along with more standard clothing-boutique shopping. You can taste a selection of locally grown varietals at the retail outlet of winemaker **Burggräfler** (⊠ Via dei Portici 218 ☎ 0473/237147). From the end of November until Christmas Eve, Merano holds a traditional **Christkindlmarkt** in the main square.

Chiusa (Klausen)

⑭ *30 km (19 mi) northeast of Bolzano.*

Beautiful narrow streets are lined with houses built in the 15th and 16th centuries in Chiusa (Klausen), the main town in the Val Isarco. Geraniums and begonias fill window boxes beneath the carved wooden shutters. From here you can catch a bus east to Val di Funes, where the church of Santa Maddalena is spectacularly hemmed in by the Geisler Peaks.

Above the town of Chiusa is the Benedictine monastery of **Saviona** (Saeben), built as a castle in the 10th century but occupying a site that was fortified in Roman times. The monastery buildings date from the late Middle Ages and are a mixture of Romanesque and Gothic architecture surrounded by walls and turrets. Guided visits to Saviona are organized by the Chiusa **tourist office** (⊠ Piazza Tinne 6 ☎ 0472/847424).

Bressanone (Brixen)

⑮ *14 km (9 mi) north of Chiusa, 40 km (25 mi) northeast of Bolzano.*

Bressanone (Brixen) is an important artistic center and was the seat of prince-bishops for centuries. Like their counterparts in Trento, these medieval administrators had the delicate task of serving two masters—the pope (the ultimate spiritual authority) and the Holy Roman Emperor (the civil and military power), who were virtually at war throughout the Middle Ages. Bressanone's prince-bishops became experts at tact and diplomacy. The imposing **Duomo** was built in the 13th century but acquired a baroque facade 500 years later; its 14th-century cloister is decorated with medieval frescoes. Free guided tours (in German or Italian) are available between April–October, Monday–Saturday at 10:30 and 3. ⊠ *Piazza Duomo* ☉ *Daily 6–noon and 3–6.*

The Bishop's Palace houses the **Museo Diocesano** (Diocesan Museum) and its abundance of local medieval art, particularly Gothic wood carvings. The wooden statues and liturgical objects were all collected from the cathedral treasury. During the Christmas season, curators arrange the museum's large collection of antique Nativity scenes; look for the shepherds wearing Tirolean hats. ✉ *Palazzo Vescovile 2* ☎ *0472/830505* ⊕ *www. dioezesanmuseum.bz.it* 🎫 *€6, Nativity scenes €4* ☉ *Museum Mar. 15–Oct., Tues.–Sun. 10–5; Nativity scenes only Dec. and Jan., daily 2–5.*

From the end of November until January 6, there is a traditional **Christkindlmarkt** in Piazza Duomo, with stalls selling Christmas decorations and local handcrafted goods.

Abbazia di Novacella. They've been making wine at this Augustinian abbey (founded 1142) for at least nine centuries. In the tasting room, you can sample varietals produced in the Isarco Valley; Novacella is most famous for the delicate stone-fruit character of its dry white Sylvaner. You can also wander the delightful grounds; note the progression of Romanesque, Gothic, and baroque building styles. Guided tours of the abbey depart on the hour. ✉ *Località Novacella 1, 39040 Varna, 3 km (2 mi) north of Bressanone* ☎ *0472/836189* 🖶 *0472/ 837305* ▭ *AE, MC, V* 🎫 *Grounds and tasting room free, guided tours €4.50* ☉ *Grounds Mon.–Sat. 10–7, tasting room Mon.–Sat. 9–noon and 2–6, guided tours 10–4.*

Where to Stay & Eat

$$ ✕ **Fink.** Try the *carré di maiale gratinato* (pork chops roasted with cheese and served with cabbage and potatoes) or the *castrato alla paesana*, a substantial lamb stew, here. In addition to hearty Tirolean specialties, there's an affordable daily set menu, as well as international dishes. The rustic wood-paneled dining room is upstairs in this restaurant under the arcades of the pedestrian-only town center. ✉ *Via Portici Minori 4* ☎ *0472/834883* ▭ *MC, V* ☉ *Closed Wed., July 1–14, and Feb. 1–14. No dinner Tues.*

★ **$$$** 🏨 **Elephant.** This cozy inn, one of the region's best, takes its name from the 1551 visit of King John III of Portugal, who stopped here while leading an elephant (a present for Austria's Emperor Ferdinand) over the Alps. Each room is unique, many with antiques and paintings. Housed on the park property is the separate Villa Marzari, with 14 rooms. A rustic three-room stube serves decent fare. ✉ *Via Rio Bianco 4, 39042* ☎ *0472/832750* 🖶 *0472/836579* ⊕ *www.hotelelephant.com* 🛏 *44 rooms* 🔧 *Restaurant, minibars, cable TV, 2 tennis courts, pool, gym, sauna, bar, Internet* ▭ *DC, MC, V* ☉ *Closed early Jan., Feb., and Nov.* ⦿ *BP.*

$ 🏨 **Croce d'Oro** (Goldenes Kreuz). A five-century-old tradition of hospitality is still practiced by the Reiserer family at this central, pink hotel. Interior styles range from a modern reception area to a tavern-style bar; guest rooms are spacious, with sturdy wood appointments. The hotel is open year-round. ✉ *Bastioni Minori 8, 39042* ☎ *0472/836155* 🖶 *0472/834255* ⊕ *www.goldeneskreuz.it* 🛏 *75 rooms* 🔧 *Restaurant, in-room safes, cable TV, spa, bar; no a/c* ▭ *No credit cards* ⦿ *BP.*

Brunico (Bruneck)

★ **⑯** *33 km (20 mi) east of Bressanone, 65 km (40 mi) northwest of Cortina d'Ampezzo.*

With its medieval quarter nestling below the 13th-century bishop's castle, Brunico (Bruneck) is in the heart of the Val Pusteria. This quiet and quaint town is divided by the Rienza River, with the old quarter on one side and the modern town on the other.

The **Museo Etnografico dell'Alto Adige** (Alto Adige Ethnographic Museum) re-creates a Middle Ages farming village, built around a more modern 300-year-old mansion. The wood-carving displays are most interesting. The museum is in the district of Teodone, northeast of the center. ⊠ *Via Duca Diet 27, Teodone* ☎ *0474/552087* ⊕ *www.provincia.bz.it/ volkskundemuseen* 🎫 *€5* ⊙ *Mid-Apr.–Oct., Tues.–Sat. 9:30–5:30, Sun. 2–6.*

Where to Stay

$$$ ⊞ **Post.** The Von Grebmer family maintains a traditional, homey hotel in an 1880s building, and provides efficient service. This is the most central, appealing lodging choice in town, especially if you've got a sweet tooth: the attached pastry shop is as popular with locals as with international guests. The hotel has its own parking, an unusual perk in the pedestrian-only center. ⊠ *Via Bastioni 9, 39031* ☎ *0474/555127* 🖨 *0474/551603* ⊕ *www.hotelpost-bruneck.com* 🛏 *54 rooms, 45 with bath* ⌂ *Restaurant, café, in-room safes, minibars, cable TV, spa, Weinstube, shop, laundry service, some pets allowed (fee); no a/c* ⊟ *AE, MC, V* ⦿ *BP.*

Sports

The **Alta Badia ski area** (☎ 0471/836176 ⊕ www.altabadia.org) can be reached by heading 30 km (19 mi) south on S244 from Brunico. It's less expensive—and more Austrian in character—than other, more-famous ski destinations in this region.

Dobbiaco (Toblach)

⓱ *25 km (16 mi) east of Brunico, 34 km (21 mi) north of Cortina d'Ampezzo.*

In Dobbiaco (Toblach), Italian is spoken grudgingly, and the place seems more Germanic than Austria itself. Gustav Mahler (1860–1911), the great Austrian composer, came here often for inspiration. The same mountain vistas and pleasant climate that attracted Mahler continue to draw tourists to Dobbiaco, as does its proximity to low-key alternatives to the Dolomites' better-known resorts.

Where to Stay

$$$ ⊞ **Cristallo.** Wood beams and paneling lend an Old Tirolean patina to this small hotel in a garden outside town. The architecture and furnishings reflect the local preference for combining traditional chalet design with functional, comfortable modern furniture. You can relax in the cozy and informal stube. ⊠ *Viale S. Giovanni 37, 39034* ☎ *0474/972138* 🖨 *0474/972755* ⊕ *www.hotelcristallo.com* 🛏 *30 rooms* ⌂ *Restaurant, in-room safes, cable TV, indoor pool, sauna, bar; no a/c* ⊟ *MC, V* ⊙ *Closed mid-Mar.–May and mid-Oct.–mid-Dec.* ⦿ *MAP.*

★ **$$** ⊞ **Alpenhotel Ratsberg.** To reach this traditional chalet you can drive up by car, or take the 10-minute cable-car ride from Santa Maria (5 km [3 mi] northwest of Dobbiaco) to Monte Rota (Ratsberg). Front rooms have balconies and stunning mountain views; those in the back look out over the dense mountain forest. The many windows, along with light-color furnishings, make the rooms feel open. You needn't take the cable car back down for sustenance: the hotel has a good restaurant, a bar, and a Tirolean-style stube. ⊠ *Monte Rota 12, 39034 Monte Rota* ☎ *0474/972213* 🖷 *0474/972916* ⊕ *www.alpenhotel-ratsberg.com* ↳ *30 rooms ⌂ Restaurant, cable TV, tennis court, indoor pool, sauna, bar; no a/c ⊟ No credit cards ⊙ Closed mid-Mar.–May and mid-Oct.–late Dec.* ⊺⊙⊺ *BP.*

Sports

SKIING Groomed trails for **cross-country skiing** (usually loops marked off by the kilometer) accommodate differing degrees of ability. Inquire at the local tourist office. Downhill skiing can be found at the modest **Monte Elmo** (☎ 0474/710355 ⊕ www.helmbahnen.com), 10 km (6 mi) southeast of Dobbiaco.

Cortina d'Ampezzo

18 *30 km (19 mi) south of Dobbiaco.*

Fodor'sChoice
★

Cortina d'Ampezzo has been the Dolomites' mountain resort of choice for more than 100 years; a half century before Turin, the Winter Olympics were held here in 1956. Although its glamorous appeal to younger Italians may have been eclipsed by steeper, sleeker Madonna di Campiglio, Cortina remains, for many, Italy's most idyllic incarnation of an Alpine ski town.

Surrounded by mountains and dense forests, the "The Pearl of the Dolomites" is in a lush meadow 4,000 feet above sea level. The town hugs the slopes beside a fast-moving stream, and a public park extends along one bank. Higher in the valley, luxury hotels and the villas of the rich are identifiable by their attempts to hide behind stands of firs and spruces. The bustling center of Cortina d'Ampezzo has little nostalgia, despite its Alpine appearance. The tone is set by smart shops and cafés as chic as their well-dressed patrons, whose corduroy knickerbockers may well have been tailored by Armani. Unlike neighboring resorts that have a strong Germanic flavor, Cortina d'Ampezzo is unapologetically Italian and distinctly fashionable.

On Via Cantore, a winding road heading up out of town to the northeast (becoming S48), you can stop and see the **Pista Olimpica di Bob** (Olympic Bobsled Course), a leftover from the 1956 Winter Games.

Where to Stay & Eat

$$$ ✕ **Tavernetta.** Near the Olympic ice-skating rink, this popular restaurant has Tirolean-style, wood-paneled dining rooms and a local clientele. Here you can try Cortina specialties such as *zuppa di porcini* (porcini mushroom soup), ravioli *di cervo* (stuffed with venison), and game. ⊠ *Via Castello 53* ☎ *0436/868102* ⊟ *AE, DC, MC, V* ⊙ *Closed Nov.*

$$$$ ✕▥ **De la Poste.** Loyal skiers return year after year to this lively hotel;

Fodor'sChoice
★

its main terrace bar is one of Cortina's social centers. De la Poste has been under the careful management of the Manaìgo family since 1936. Each unique room has antiques in characteristic Dolomite style; almost all have wooden balconies. A refined main dining room—with high ceilings and large chandeliers—serves nouvelle cuisine and superb soufflés; there's also a more informal grill room with wood paneling and the family's pewter collection. Sporadic off-season bed-and-breakfast rates can be a bargain. ⊠ *Piazza Roma 14, 32043* ☎ *0436/4271* ⊟ *0436/868435* ⊕ *www.delaposte.it* ⇨ *83 rooms* ⌂ *2 restaurants, minibars, cable TV, bar, free parking; no a/c* ⊟ *AE, DC, MC, V* ⊘ *Closed Apr.–mid-June and Oct.–mid-Dec.* ⵔ *MAP.*

$$$$ ⊡ **Corona.** Noted ski instructor Luciano Rimoldi, who has coached such luminaries as Alberto Tomba, runs a cozy Alpine lodge. Modern art adorns small but comfortable pine-paneled rooms; the convivial bar is a pleasant place to relax. The hotel is a 5-minute walk—across the river—from the center of town, and a 10-minute ride from the lifts (a ski shuttle stops out front). ⊠ *Via Val di Sotto 12, 32040* ☎ *0436/3251* ⊟ *0436/867339* ⊕ *www.cortina.dolomiti.com/alberghi/corona* ⇨ *44 rooms* ⌂ *Restaurant, cable TV, bar, free parking; no a/c* ⊟ *AE, DC, MC, V* ⊘ *Closed Apr.–June and Sept.–Nov.* ⵔ *MAP.*

$$$$ ⊡ **Miramonti Majestic.** This imposing and luxe hotel, more than a century old, has a magnificent mountain-valley position about 1 km (½ mi) south of town. A touch of formality comes through in the imperial Austrian design, and the interior reflects the period style throughout. There's always a roaring fire in the splendid bar, and the hotel's recreation rooms are lined with windows overlooking mountain vistas. The history of Cortina is intricately tied to the Miramonti, and you can feel a part of it all here. ⊠ *Località Peziè 103, 32043* ☎ *0436/4201* ⊟ *0436/867019* ⊕ *www.cortina.dolomiti.org/hmiramonti* ⇨ *105 rooms* ⌂ *Restaurant, minibars, cable TV, 9-hole golf course, 2 tennis courts, indoor pool, gym, sauna, bar, meeting rooms, free parking; no a/c* ⊟ *AE, DC, MC, V* ⊘ *Closed Apr.–June and Sept.–mid-Dec.* ⵔ *MAP.*

Nightlife & the Arts

At the **VIP Club** inside the Hotel Europa (⊠ Corso Italia 207 ☎ 0436/3221) you can mingle with the couture set; nonguests are welcome, but don't expect to spend less than €30.

Sports

BOBSLEDDING Cortina Adrenalin Center's **Taxi-Bob** offers visitors the chance to don bodysuits and hurtle down a 4,000-foot Olympic bobsled course at more than 70 mph; two paying passengers wedge between a professional pilot and brakeman. ⊠ *Località Ronco* ☎ *0436/860808* ⊕ *www.adrenalincenter.it* ⊡ *€80 per person* ⊘ *Dec. 15–Feb. 15.*

HIKING & CLIMBING Hiking information is available at the excellent local **tourist office** (⊠ Piazzetta San Francesco 8 ☎ 0436/3231 ⊕ www.cortina.dolomiti.com).

Cortina's **Scuola di Alpinismo** (Mountaineering School; ⊠ Corso Italia 69 ☎ 0436/868505 ⊕ www.guidecortina.com) organizes climbing trips and trekking adventures.

SKIING Cortina's long and picturesque ski runs will delight intermediates, but advanced skiers might lust for steeper terrain, which can be found only off-piste. Efficient ski bus service connects the town with the high-speed chairlifts and gondolas that ascend in all directions from the valley.

The **Dolomiti Superski pass** (✉ Via Marconi 15 ☎ 0471/795397 ⊕ www.dolomitisuperski.com) provides access to the surrounding Dolomites (€38 per day)—with 450 lifts and gondolas serving 1,200 km (750 mi) of trails. Buy one at the ticket office next to the bus station. The **Faloria gondola** (✉ Via Ria de Zeta 8 ☎ 0436/2517) runs from the center of town. From its top you can get up to most of the central mountains.

Some of the most impressive views (and steepest slopes) are on **Monte Cristallo,** based at Misurina, 15 km (9 mi) northeast of Cortina by car or bus. The topography of the **Passo Falzarego** ski area, 16 km (10 mi) east of town, is quite dramatic.

3

HEART OF THE DOLOMITES

The area between Bolzano and the mountain resort Cortina d'Ampezzo is dominated by two major valleys, Val di Fassa and Val Gardena. Both share the spectacular panorama of the Sella mountain range, known as the Heart of the Dolomites. Val di Fassa cradles the beginning of the Grande Strada delle Dolomiti (Great Dolomites Road—S48 and S241), which runs from Bolzano as far as Cortina. This route, opened in 1909, comprises 110 km (68 mi) of relatively easy grades and smooth driving between the two towns—a slower, more scenic alternative to traveling by way of Brunico and Dobbiaco along S49.

In both Val di Fassa and Val Gardena, recreational options are less expensive, though less comprehensive, than in better-known resorts like Cortina. The culture here is firmly Germanic. Val Gardena is freckled with well-equipped, photo-friendly towns with great views overlooked by the oblong *Sasso Lungo* (Long Rock), which is more than 10,000 feet above sea level. It's also home to the Ladins, descendants of soldiers sent by the Roman emperor Tiberius to conquer the Celtic population of the area in the 1st century AD. Forgotten in the narrow cul-de-sacs of isolated mountain valleys, the Ladins have developed their own folk traditions and speak an ancient dialect that is derived from Latin and similar to the Romansch spoken in some high valleys in Switzerland.

Canazei

⑲ *60 km (37 mi) west of Cortina d'Ampezzo, 52 km (32 mi) east of Bolzano.*

Of the year-round resort towns in the Val di Fassa, Canazei is the most popular. The mountains around this small town are threaded with hiking trails and ski slopes, surrounded by large clutches of conifers. Four kilometers (2½ mi) west of Canazei, an excursion from Campitello di Fassa to the vantage point at **Col Rodella** is a must. A cable car rises some 3,000 feet to a full-circle vista of the Heart of the Dolomites, including the Sasso Lungo and the rest of the Sella range.

Where to Stay

$$ ☒ **Alla Rosa.** The view of the imposing Dolomites is the real attraction at this central hotel, so ask for a room with a balcony. The reception

CLOSE UP

Hiking the Dolomites

FOR MANY OVERSEAS VISITORS, the Dolomites conjure images of downhill skiing at Cortina d'Ampezzo and Madonna di Campiglio. But summer, not winter, is high season here; Italians, German-speaking Europeans, and in-the-know travelers from farther afield come here for clear mountain air and world-class hiking. Nature has done most of the work—impressive terrain, inspiring vistas, an impossibly pleasant climate—but the man-made facilities for enjoying the mountains are also exceptional.

On the trail, high in the Dolomites

PICKING A TRAIL

The Dolomites boast a well-maintained network of trails for hiking and rock climbing. As long as you're in reasonably good shape, the number of appealing hiking options can be overwhelming. Trails are well marked and designated by grades of difficulty: T for tourist path, H for hiking path, EE for expert hikers, and EEA for equipped expert hikers. On any of these paths you're likely to see carpets of mountain flowers between clutches of dense evergreens, with chamois and roe deer mulling about. If you're just out for a day in the mountains, you can leave the particulars of your walk open until you're actually on the spot; local tourist offices (especially those in Cortina, Madonna, and the Heart of the Dolomites) can help you choose the right route based on trail conditions, weather, and desired exertion level.

TRAVELING THE VIE FERRATE

If you're looking for an adventure somewhere between hiking and climbing, consider a guided trip along the Vie Ferrate (Iron Paths). These routes offer fixed climbing aids (steps, ladders, bridges, safety cables) left by Alpine divisions of the Italian and Austro-Hungarian armies and later converted for recreational use. Previous experience is generally not required, but vertigo-inducing heights do demand a strong stomach. Detailed information about Vie Ferrate in the eastern Dolomites can be found at ⊕ www.dolomiti.org. Capable tour organizers include Scuole di Alpinismo (Mountaineering Schools) in Madonna di Campiglio (☎ 0465/442634 ⊕ www.guidealpinecampiglio.it) and Cortina d'Ampezzo (☎ 0436/868505 ⊕ www.guidecortina.com).

BEDDING DOWN

One of the pleasures of an overnight adventure in the Dolomites is staying at a *rifugio*, one of the refuges that dot the mountainsides. There are hundreds of them, often in remote locations and ranging from spartan shelters to posh retreats. Most fall somewhere in between—they're cozy mountain lodges with dormitory-style accommodations. Pillows and blankets are provided (so there's no need to carry a sleeping bag), but you have to supply your own sheet.

Bathrooms are usually shared, as is the experience of a cold shower in the morning.

The majority of rifugi are operated by the Club Alpino Italiano (CAI) (⊕ www.cai.it). Contact information for both CAI-run and private rifugi are available from local tourist offices; most useful are those in Madonna di Campiglio (⊕ www. campiglio.to), Cortina d'Ampezzo (⊕ www.dolomiti.org), Val di Fassa (⊕ www.fassa.com), and Val Gardena (⊕ www.valgardena.it). Reservations are a must, especially in August, although Italian law requires rifugi to accept travelers for the night if there is insufficient time to reach other accommodations before dark.

EATING WELL

Food, true to Italian priorities, is as much a draw at rifugi as location. Although the dishes served are the sort of the rustic cuisine you might expect (salami, dumplings, hearty stews), the quality is uniformly excellent—an impressive feat, made all the more remarkable when you consider that supplies often have to arrive by helicopter. Your dinner may cost as much as your bed for the night—about €20 per person—and it's difficult to determine which is the better bargain.

Snacks and packed lunches are available for purchase, but many opt to sit down for the midday meal, to enjoy the camaraderie and diversity of their fellow explorers. Serving as both holiday hiking destination and base camp for difficult ascents, the rifugi welcome walkers and climbers of all stripes from intersecting trails and nearby faces. Multilingual stories are swapped, food and wine shared, and new adventures launched.

STUMBLING ON ÖTZI

It was at the Similaun rifugio in September 1991 that a German couple arrived talking of a dead body they'd discovered near a "curious pickax." This was to be the world's introduction to Ötzi, the oldest mummy ever found (now on display in Bolzano's Museo Archeologico dell'Alto Adige).

The couple, underestimating the age of the corpse by about 5,300 years, thought it was a matter for the police. World-famous mountaineers Reinhold Messner and Hans Kammerlander happened to be passing through the same rifugio during a climbing tour, and a few days later they were on scene, freeing the iceman from the ice. Ötzi's remarkable story was under way. You can see him on display, along with his longbow, ax, and clothes, at Bolzano's archaeological museum, where he continues to be preserved at freezing temperatures.

Ötzi as he was found.

area is spacious and welcoming, and guest rooms pleasantly blend rustic and modern elements. There's a modest restaurant serving local and international cuisine, and a cozy bar. ⊠ *Via del Faure 18, 38032* ☎ *0462/601107* 🖷 *0462/601481* ⊕ *www.hotelallarosa.com* 📤 *49 rooms* ♻ *Restaurant, minibars, cable TV, sauna, bar, recreation room, parking (fee); no a/c* ☰ *MC, V* ⫙ *MAP.*

EN ROUTE The **Passo di Sella** (Sella Pass) can be approached from S48, affording some of the most spectacular mountain vistas in Europe before it descends into the Val Gardena. The road continues to Ortisei, passing the smaller resorts of Selva Gardina and Santa Cristina.

Ortisei (St. Ulrich)

⑳ *28 km (17 mi) north of Canazei, 35 km (22 mi) northeast of Bolzano.*

Ortisei (St. Ulrich), the jewel in the crown of Val Gardena's resorts, is a hub of activity in both summer and winter; there are hundreds of miles of hiking trails and accessible ski slopes. Hotels and facilities are abundant—swimming pools, ice rinks, health spas, tennis courts, and bowling alleys. Most impressive of all is the location, a valley surrounded by formidable views in all directions.

For centuries Ortisei has also been famous for the expertise of its woodcarvers, and there are still numerous workshops. Apart from making religious sculptures—particularly the wayside calvaries you come upon everywhere in the Dolomites—Ortisei's carvers were long known for producing wooden dolls, horses, and other toys. As itinerant peddlers they traveled every spring on foot with their loaded packs as far as Paris, London, and St. Petersburg. Shops in town still sell woodcrafts. Fine historic and contemporary examples of local woodworking can be seen at the **Museo della Val Gardena.** ⊠ *Via Rezia 83* ☎ *0471/797554* 🎟 *€3* ⊙ *Feb.–mid-Mar., Tues.–Fri. 2:30–5:30; June and Sept.–mid-Oct., Tues., Thurs., and Fri. 2–6, Wed. 10–noon and 2–6; July and Aug., Tues.–Sat. 10–noon and 2–6, Sun. 2–6.*

Where to Stay

★ $$$$ 🏨 **Adler.** This hotel, the best in the valley, has been under the same family management since 1810. The original building has been enlarged several times, yielding spacious guest rooms (with wireless Internet access) and an expansive spa complex but retaining much of the old turreted-castle appeal. Most guests stay for a full week, picking up the busy schedule of activities (such as guided ski tours and snowshoe walks) when they arrive on Saturday evening. The same activities, at a slower pace, are available for children. ⊠ *Via Rezia 7, 39046* ☎ *0471/775000* 🖷 *0471/775555* ⊕ *www.hotel-adler.com* 📤 *123 rooms* ♻ *Restaurant, in-room safes, minibars, cable TV, Wi-Fi, indoor pool, health club, hair salon, sauna, spa, steam room, bar, children's programs (ages 4–12)* ☰ *MC, V* ⊙ *Closed Apr.–mid-May* ⫙ *MAP.*

$$$$ 🏨 **Cavallino Bianco.** The pink Cavallino Bianco looks like a gigantic dollhouse, with delicate wooden balconies and an eye-catching wooden gable. Beyond this facade lies a sprawling, all-inclusive modern resort, but the cozy bar—with its large, handcrafted fireplace—retains some of the charm of the old postal hotel it was. Guest rooms have upholstered furniture with cheery, large-scale plaids and honey-tone wood accents. The hotel is only a five-minute walk from the main ski facilities; ski guides are available. ⊠ *Via Rezia 22, 39046* ☎ *0471/783333* 🖶 *0471/797517* ⊕ *www.cavallino-bianco.com* ⊃ *184 rooms* ⚭ *Restaurant, coffee shop, in-room safes, minibars, cable TV, indoor pool, sauna, spa, mountain bikes, bar, dance club, children's programs (ages 2–12), Internet; no a/c* ▭ *AE, DC, MC, V* ⊘ *Closed mid–Apr.–mid-May* ⦿ *FAP.*

Sports

With almost 600 km (370 mi) of accessible downhill slopes and more than 90 km (56 mi) of cross-country skiing trails, Ortisei is one of the most popular ski resorts in the Dolomites. Prices are good, and facilities are among the most modern in the region. In warmer weather, the slopes surrounding Ortisei are a popular hiking destination, as well as a playground for vehicular mountain adventures: biking, rafting, even paragliding.

An immensely popular ski route, the **Sella Ronda** relies on well-placed chairlifts to connect 26 km (16 mi) of downhill skiing around the colossal Sella massif, passing through several towns along the way. You can ski the loop, which requires intermediate ability and a full day's effort, either clockwise or counterclockwise. Going with a guide is recommended. Chairlifts here, as elsewhere in the Dolomites, are covered by the €38-daily **Dolomiti Superski pass** (⊕ www.dolomitisuperski.com).

The **Val Gardena Tourist Office** (⊠ Via Dursan 81, Santa Cristina ☎ 0471/777777 ⊕ www.valgardena.it) can provide detailed information about sport-equipment rental outfits and guided-tour operators.

Gardena Mountain Adventures (☎ 335/6849031 ⊕ www.val-gardena.com/gma) outfits a particularly large choice of year-round mountain sport activities.

Lago di Carezza

㉑ *22 km (14 mi) west of Canazei, 29 km (18 mi) east of Bolzano.*

Glacial Lake Carezza is some 5,000 feet above sea level. The azure blue of the waters can at times change to magical greens and purples, reflections of the dense surrounding forest and rosy peaks of the Dolomites. You can hike down to this most quintessential of mountain lakes from the nearby village of the same name; there's a fountain with two marmots in the center of town.

Caldaro (Kaltern)

㉒ *45 km (28 mi) southwest of Lago di Carezza, 15 km (9 mi) south of Bolzano.*

A vineyard village with clear views of castles high up on the surrounding mountains represents the centuries of division that forged the unique character of the area. Caldaro architecture is famous for the way it blends Italian Renaissance elements of balance and harmony with the soaring windows and peaked arches of the Germanic Gothic tradition. The church of Santa Caterina, on the main square, is a good example.

Close to Caldaro's main square is the **Museo Provinciale del Vino,** with exhibits on how local wine has historically been made, stored, served, and worshipped. You can call ahead to reserve a wine tasting (€6) in the museum's cellar. ⊠ *Via dell'Oro 1* ☎ *0471/963168* ⊕ *www.provinz. bz.it/volkskundemuseen* 🖼 *€3* ⊘ *Apr.–mid-Nov., Tues.–Sat. 9:30–noon and 2–6, Sun. 10–noon.*

DOLOMITES ESSENTIALS

Transportation

BY AIR

The nearest airport, but the least well connected, is Aeroporto Bolzano Dolomiti (BZO), with scheduled service to Rome (FCO) and Milan Malpensa (MXP). A bit farther to the south, Verona (VRN) can be reached by plane from many European cities and is well connected by road and rail with the Dolomite area. Direct intercontinental flights are available into Milan Malpensa (MXP) to the southwest and Munich (MUC) to the north, both about a four-hour drive from Bolzano.

🔂 Airport Information **Aeroporto Bolzano Dolomiti** ☎0471/255255 ⊕www.abd-airport. it. **Aeroporto Milan Malpensa** ☎ 02/74852200 ⊕ www.sea-aeroportimilano.it. **Aeroporto Valerio Catullo di Verona Villafranca** ☎ 045/8095666 ⊕ www.aeroportoverona. it. **Munich International Airport** ☎ 049/8997500 ⊕ www.munich-airport.de.

BY BUS

Regular bus service connects larger cities to the south (Verona, Venice, and Milan) with valley towns in Trentino–Alto Adige (Rovereto, Trento, Bolzano, and Merano). You'll need to change to less-frequent local buses to reach resorts in the mountains beyond. For information, contact Trentino Trasporti or Alto Adige's SIT. A convenient bus service between Cortina d'Ampezzo and the Venice airport (€18 round-trip, complimentary at some hotels) is available on weekends from mid-December to March; bookings must be made through your hotel. DolomitiBus provides winter weekend service between Cortina and the Venice train station.

Local buses provide frequent service between the valley towns of Trento, Bolzano, and Merano. Although it's certainly possible to visit even the remotest villages without a car (if you're equipped with schedules and lots of time), most towns are designed for automobiles, and getting between your hotel, ski lifts, and après-ski locales without a vehicle can be very tricky. For detailed information on bus service within Trentino–Alto Adige, contact Trentino Trasporti or SIT. DolomitiBus serves the Eastern Dolomites, including Cortina d'Ampezzo.

🔂 Bus Information **DolomitiBus** ☎ 0437/217111 ⊕ www.dolomitibus.it. **SIT** (Servizio Integrato di Trasporto) ☎ 0471/415480 ⊕ www.sii.bz.it. **Trentino Trasporti** ☎ 0461/ 983627 ⊕ www.ttspa.it.

BY CAR

The most important route in the region is autostrada A22, the main north–south highway linking Italy with central Europe by way of the

Brenner Pass. It connects Innsbruck with Bressanone, Bolzano, Trento, and Rovereto, and near Verona joins autostrada A4 (which runs east–west across northern Italy, from Trieste and Venice to Milan and Turin). By car, Trento is 3 hours from Milan and 2½ hours from Venice. Bolzano is another hour's drive to the north (with Munich 4 hours farther on).

Driving definitely has its advantages when exploring the Dolomites; it can be difficult to reach the ski areas (or any town outside of Rovereto, Trento, Bolzano, and Merano) without a car. Caution is essential, especially in winter, when roads are often covered in snow and buffeted by high winds. Sudden closures are common, especially on high mountain passes, and can occur as early as November and as late as May. Even under the best conditions, expect to negotiate mountain roads at speeds no greater than 50 kph (30 mph). Call Autostrada Weather Information Service in Bolzano for information on weather-related closures.

EMERGENCY ACI Emergency Service offers 24-hour roadside assistance.
SERVICES   🚹**ACI dispatchers** ☎803/116. **Autostrada Weather Information Service** ☎0471/413810.

BY TRAIN
The rail line following the course of the Isarco and Adige valleys—from Munich and Innsbruck, through the Brenner Pass, and southward past Bressanone, Bolzano, Trento, and Rovereto en route to Verona—is well trafficked, making trains a viable option for travel between these towns. Eurocity trains on the Dortmund–Venice and Munich–Innsbruck–Rome routes stop at these stations, and you can connect with other Italian lines at Verona. Although branch lines from Trento and Bolzano do extend into some of the smaller valleys (including hourly service between Bolzano and Merano), most of the mountain attractions are beyond the reach of trains. Contact Trenitalia for more information.
🚹 Train Information **Trenitalia** ☎ 892021 ⊕ www.trenitalia.com.

Contacts & Resources

EMERGENCIES
For first aid, ask for *pronto soccorso,* and be prepared to give your address. Pharmacies take turns staying open late and on Sunday; for the latest information, consult the current list posted on the front door of each pharmacy or ask at the local tourist office.
🚹 **Ambulance** ☎ 118. **Polizia** ☎ 113 local police.

TOURS
Bus tours from Bolzano or Trento let you see the Dolomites without having to navigate the mountain roads. However, tours are offered only in the snow-free summer months.

In July and August, the SAD bus company's full-day mountain tours include a "Great Dolomites Tour" from Bolzano to Cortina and a tour of the Val Venosta that climbs over the Stelvio Pass into Switzerland. A tour of the Val Gardena and the Siusi Alps is available from April to October.

From June through September the Calderari e Moggioli travel agency offers a full-day guided bus tour of the Brenta Dolomites and its own

"Great Dolomites Tour," a full-day drive over the Pordoi and Falzarego passes to Cortina d'Ampezzo and Lake Misurina. The Trentino tourist office also organizes guided tours and excursions by train to castles in the region.

🎫 Fees & Schedules **Calderari e Moggioli** ✉ Via Manci 46 ☎ 0461/980275. **SAD** ✉ Via Conciapelli 60 ☎ 0471/450111 ⊕ www.sii.bz.it.

VISITOR INFORMATION

🎫 Tourist Information **Alto Adige Tourism** ☎ 0471/999999 🖶 0471/999800 ⊕ www. suedtirol.info. **Bolzano** ✉ Piazza Walther 8 ☎ 0471/307000 🖶 0471/980128 ⊕ www. bolzano-bozen.it. **Bormio** ✉ Via Roma 131/b ☎ 0342/903300 🖶 0342/904696 ⊕ www. valtellinaonline.com. **Bressanone** ✉ Via Stazione 9 ☎ 0472/836401 🖶 0472/836067. **Brunico** ✉ Piazza Municipio 7 ☎ 0474/555722 🖶 0474/555544. **Caldaro** ✉ Piazza Mercato 8 ☎ 0471/963169 🖶 0471/963469. **Canazei** ✉ Piazza Marconi 5 ☎ 0462/601113 🖶 0462/602502. **Chiusa** ✉ Piazza Tinne 6 ☎ 0472/847424 🖶 0472/847244. **Cortina d'Ampezzo** ✉ Piazzetta San Francesco 8 ☎ 0436/3231 🖶 0436/3235 ⊕ www.cortina. dolomiti.com. **Dobbiaco** ✉ Via Dolomiti 3 ☎ 0474/972132 🖶 0474/972730. **Dolomites Tourism** ☎ 0437/941148 🖶 0437/944202 ⊕ www.dolomiti.org. **Madonna di Campiglio** ✉ Via Pradalago 4 ☎ 0465/447501 🖶 0465/440404 ⊕ www.campiglio.to. **Merano** ✉ Corso Libertà 45 ☎ 0473/272000 🖶 0473/235524 ⊕ www.meraninfo.it. **Naturno** ✉ Piazza Municipio 1 ☎ 0473/666077 🖶 0473/666369. **Ortisei** ✉ Via Rezia 1 ☎ 0471/777600 🖶 0471/796749. **Rovereto** ✉ Corso Rosmini 6 ☎ 0464/430363 🖶 0464/435528. **Santa Cristina** ✉ Via Chemun 9 ☎ 0471/777800 🖶 0471/793198. **Selva Gardena** ✉ Via Mëisules 213 ☎ 0471/777900 🖶 0471/794245. **Trentino Tourism** ☎ 0461/839000 🖶 0461/260245 ⊕ www.trentino.to. **Trento** ✉ Via Manci 2 ☎ 0461/983880 🖶 0461/232426 ⊕ www.apt.trento.it. **Val Gardena Tourism** ☎ 0471/792277 🖶 0471/792235 ⊕ www.valgardena.it.

Milan, Lombardy & the Lakes

Lake Garda

WORD OF MOUTH

"Italy's Lake Maggiore is one of Europe's top vacation meccas for good reason. It's a long sliver of water ringed by Alpine scenery freckled with villas and resorts."

—PalQ

WELCOME TO MILAN, LOMBARDY & THE LAKES

Plaza and Duomo, Milan

TOP 5
Reasons to Go

1. **Lake Como:** Ferries crisscross the waters, taking you from stately villas to tiny towns.

2. **Leonardo Da Vinci's *Last Supper*:** Behold one of the world's most famous works of art.

3. **Bergamo Alta:** A funicular ride takes you up to the magnificent medieval city.

4. **Window shopping in Milan:** Italians' refined fashion sense is on full display in the famed *quadrilatero* shopping district.

5. **La Scala:** There's no better place to spend a night at the opera.

Getting Oriented

In Lombardy, jagged mountains and deep glacial lakes stretch from the Swiss border down to Milan's outskirts, where they meet the flat, fertile plain that extends from the banks of the River Po. Lake Como is north of Milan, while Lake Maggiore is to the northwest and Lake Garda is to the east. Scattered across the plains to the south are the Renaissance city-states of Pavia, Cremona, and Mantua.

La Scala, Milan

Lake Maggiore is smaller than Lake Garda and less famous than Lake Como, but with the Alps as a backdrop, it's impressively picturesque. One of the greatest pleasures here is exploring the lake's islands.

Stresa

Lago Maggiore Verbano

Varese

Orta San Giulio

Como

A26

A8

0   20 mi

0   20 km

PIEDMONT

Milan

Vigevano

Mortara

A7

Milan is Italy lived in the present tense. The country's leading city of commerce is also one of the world's fashion capitals, and there are cultural treasures here that rival those of Florence and Rome.

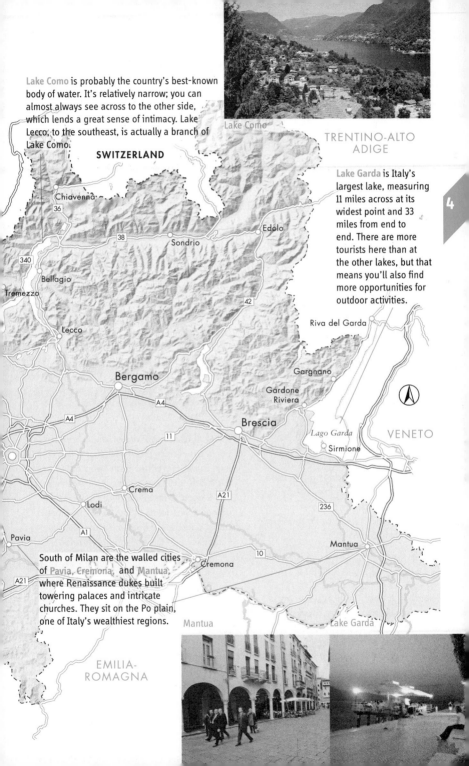

Lake Como is probably the country's best-known body of water. It's relatively narrow; you can almost always see across to the other side, which lends a great sense of intimacy. Lake Lecco, to the southeast, is actually a branch of Lake Como.

Lake Como

TRENTINO-ALTO ADIGE

SWITZERLAND

Lake Garda is Italy's largest lake, measuring 11 miles across at its widest point and 33 miles from end to end. There are more tourists here than at the other lakes, but that means you'll also find more opportunities for outdoor activities.

4

Chiavenna

36

Edolo

38

Sondrio

340

Bellagio

Tremezzo

42

Riva del Garda

Lecco

Gargnano

Bergamo

Gardone Riviera

A4

Brescia

Lago Garda

VENETO

A4

11

Sirmione

Crema

A21

236

Lodi

Pavia

A1

Mantua

10

South of Milan are the walled cities of Pavia, Cremona, and Mantua, where Renaissance dukes built towering palaces and intricate churches. They sit on the Po plain, one of Italy's wealthiest regions.

Cremona

A21

Mantua

Lake Garda

EMILIA-ROMAGNA

MILAN, LOMBARDY & THE LAKES PLANNER

Making the Most of Your Time

If you're visiting northern Italy, the odds are good you'll fly in and out of Milan's Malpensa airport, and for expediency you may end up spending your final night in Milan. Italy's capital of commerce isn't a top priority for most leisure travelers, but the city has a sophisticated urban appeal: its fashionable shops rival New York and Paris, its soccer teams are Italy's answer to the Yankees and the Mets, its opera performances set the standard for the world, and its art treasures are considerable. If that sounds appealing, think about giving Milan an additional day or two on your itinerary.

The biggest draw in the region, though, is the lake district. Lakes Como, Garda, Maggiore, and Orta all have long histories as travel destinations, and each has its own distinct character. If you're only spending a couple of days in the area, devote your time to the lake you think best suits your style, but if you have more time, make the rounds to two or three to get a sense of their contrasts.

Getting Around

Milan has an unmatched system of public transportation. Besides the trio of subway lines, there are dozens of bus and tram routes that connect all parts of the city. Buying an all-inclusive subway, bus, and tram pass good for 24 or 48 hours will save you the hassle of purchasing individual tickets. Taxis are expensive but reliable; they come in handy late at night.

Outside of Milan, driving is the best way to see the region. Getting almost anywhere is a snap, as several major highways intersect at Milan, all connected by the tangenziale, the road that rings the city. To get to the lakes you must exit onto well-maintained secondary roads, which have many places where you can stop and admire the view.

If you don't want to drive, you can still travel around Lombardy without a problem. Buses and trains both head out to the lakefront villages. Once you're there, you'll want to take one of the boats that crisscross the lakes themselves. For more about car, bus, and train travel, see "Essentials" at the end of this chapter.

A Night at the Opera

Attending a performance at the world's most venerated opera house, La Scala, is an unforgettable experience, regardless of whether you're an opera buff. Tickets go on sale two months in advance, and they sell out quickly. Your best bet is to order online at www.teatroallascala.org (phone orders aren't accepted). Once you're in Milan, you can check on ticket availability at the Scala box office, located in the Duomo metro station and open daily from noon to 6 PM. About 100 tickets for seats in the second gallery go on sale three hours before a performance—they're available at the ticket office of the theater itself.

Fashion Alerts

Milan becomes the world fashion capital par excellence four times a year, when the global fashion elite descend on the city for the ready-to-wear designer shows. The dates are late-February and late-September (for women) and late-June and mid-January (for men). The effect? Very little if you're outside the business, except that it's hard for mere mortals to get a taxi, a reservation in a top restaurant, or a hotel room.

Sales take place in early January and mid-July (dates set by law), with prices slashed by 30% to 50%. If you want the season's clothes as soon as they hit the shelves, plan your trip for January or early August.

Supper Reservations

Reservations are required to see Leonardo da Vinci's *The Last Supper,* housed in the refectory of Milan's Santa Maria delle Grazie church. You should call as far in advance as possible to make them, particularly if you're planning to go on a weekend. For details, see the Santa Maria delle Grazie listing in this chapter.

Finding a Place to Stay

The hotels in Italy's wealthiest region generally cater to a clientele willing to pay for extra comfort. Many are converted villas with well-landscaped grounds—they can be worth visiting, even if you don't stay the night. Most of the famous lake resorts are expensive; more reasonable rates can be found in the smaller towns. Local tourism offices can be an excellent source of information about affordable lodging. In Milan, reservations are recommended year-round.

Dining & Lodging Price Categories

	$$$$	$$$	$$	$	¢
WHAT IT COSTS in Euros					
RESTAURANTS					
	over €45	€35–€45	€25–€35	€15–€25	under €15
HOTELS					
in Milan	over €290	€210–€290	€140–€210	€80–€140	under €80
Elsewhere	over €220	€160–€220	€110–€160	€70–€110	under €70

Restaurant prices are for a first course (primo), second course (secondo), and dessert (dolce). Hotel prices are for two people in a standard double room in high season, including tax and service.

4

How's the Weather?

Early summer and early fall are the best times to see the area—though October can be chilly for swimming. The throngs that descend on the lakes in July and August, particularly on weekends, make reservations absolutely necessary—especially at Lake Como, the quintessential Italian lake resort. Fewer people visit in spring and fall, and in winter the lakeside towns are deserted. Note that many of the ferry services stop running in October and recommence in May.

Lake Como

TOP PASSEGGIATA

The small-town charm of Cernobbio, at the southern end of Lake Como, is in full force when families take their evening stroll through the piazza.

IT'S TEMPTING TO DESCRIBE LOMBARDY as a region that offers something for everyone. Milan is the country's business capital and the center for everything that's up-to-the-minute. The great Renaissance cities of the Po Plain—Pavia, Cremona, and Mantua—are stately and serene, embracing their past with nostalgia while at the same time keeping an eye on the present. Topping any list of the region's attractions are the lakes—glacial waters stretching out below the Alps—which have been praised as the closest thing to paradise by writers throughout the ages, from Virgil to Hemingway.

Millions of travelers have concurred: for sheer beauty, the lakes of northern Italy—Como, Maggiore, Garda, and Orta—have few equals. Along their shores are 18th- and 19th-century villas, exotic formal gardens, sleepy villages, and dozens of resorts that were once Europe's most fashionable, and still retain a powerful allure.

Milan can be disappointingly modern—a little too much like the place you've come to Italy to escape—but its historic buildings and art collections in many ways rival those of Florence and Rome. And if you love to shop, Milan is a mecca. It truly offers a fashion experience for every taste, from the broad Corso Buenos Aires, which has a higher ratio of stores per square foot than anywhere else in Europe, to elegant Via Montenapoleone, where a pair of cuff links can cost more than a four-course meal in a top-flight restaurant. Milan is home to global fashion giants such as Armani, Prada, and Trussardi; behind these famous names stands a host of smaller, less-renowned designers who help fill all those fabulous shops.

MILAN

Updated by
Madeleine
Johnson

Italy's business hub and crucible of chic is the country's most populous and prosperous city, serving as the capital of commerce, finance, fashion, and media. It's also Italy's transport hub, with the biggest international airport, the most rail connections, and the best subway system. Leonardo Da Vinci's *Last Supper* and other great works of art are here, as well as a spectacular Gothic Duomo, the finest of its kind. Milan even reigns supreme where it really counts (in the minds of many Italians), routinely trouncing the rest of the nation with its two premier soccer teams.

And yet, Milan hasn't won the battle for hearts and minds. Most tourists prefer Tuscany's hills and Venice's canals to Milan's hectic efficiency and wealthy indifference, and it's no surprise that in a country of medieval hilltop villages and skilled artisans, a city of grand boulevards and global corporations leaves visitors asking the real Italy to please stand up. They're right, of course. Milan is more European than Italian, a new buckle on an old boot, and although its old city can stand cobblestone for cobblestone against the best of them, seekers of Roman ruins and fairy-tale towns may pass. But Milan's new faces are hidden behind splendid beaux-arts facades and in luxurious 19th-century palazzi, and those lured by its world-class shopping and European sophistication enjoy the city's lively, cosmopolitan feel.

Virtually every invader in European history—Gaul, Roman, Goth, Longobard, and Frank—as well as a long series of rulers from France,

LOMBARDY THROUGH THE AGES

Lombardy has had a tumultuous history. Control by outsiders dates back more than 3,000 years, to when the Etruscans of central Italy first wandered north of the River Po. They dominated the region for centuries, to be followed by the Cenomani Gauls, then the Romans in the later days of the Republic. The region was known as Cisalpine Gaul ("Gaul this side of the Alps"), and under the rule of Augustus became a Roman province.

The decline of the Roman Empire was followed by invasion by Attila of the Huns and Theodoric of the Goths. These conquerors gave way to the Lombards, who then ceded to Charlemagne their iron crown, which became the emblem of his vast, unstable empire. Even before the bonds of the empire had begun to snap, the cities of Lombardy were erecting walls in defense against the Hungarians, and against each other.

These city-states formed the Lombard League, which in the 12th century finally defeated the German ruler Frederick Barbarossa. With the northern invaders gone, new and even bloodier strife began. In each city the Guelphs (bourgeois supporters of the popes) and the Ghibellines (noblemen loyal to the Holy Roman Empire) clashed. The city-states declined, falling under the yoke of a few powerful regional rulers. The Republic of Venice dominated Brescia and Bergamo. Mantua was ruled by the Gonzaga family, and the Visconti and Sforza families took over Como, Cremona, Milan, and Pavia.

The Battle of Pavia in 1525, in which the generals of Holy Roman Emperor Charles V defeated the French, brought on 200 years of occupation by the Spanish—who proved generally less cruel than the local tyrants. The War of the Spanish Succession in the early years of the 18th century brought in the Austrians.

Napoléon and his generals defeated the Austrians at the turn of the 19th century. The Treaty of Campoformio resulted in the proclamation of the Cisalpine Republic, which soon became the Republic of Italy and then the Kingdom of Italy—which lasted only until Napoléon's defeat brought back the Austrians. In March of 1848, demonstrations in Milan took on surprising force: the Austrians were driven out of the city, and a provisional government of Milan soon became a provisional government of Lombardy. In June of the same year, Lombardy united with Sardinia—the first step toward Italian unification in 1870.

The spirit of 1848 was rekindled in 1943. Discontent with Fascism provoked workers to strike in Turin and Milan, marking the beginning of the end of Fascist dominance. The Lombardy-based partisan insurrection against Mussolini and the German regime was better organized and more successful than in many other parts of the country. Indeed, Milan was liberated from the Germans by its own partisan organization before the Allied troops entered the city.

Dissatisfaction with the federal government is practically a given among Lombardy residents, and the prevailing attitude has been to ignore Rome and get on with business. It's an approach that's proven successful: Lombardy accounts for one-fifth of Italy's economy.

4

Spain, and Austria, took a turn at ruling the city. After being completely sacked by the Goths in AD 539 and by the Holy Roman Empire under Frederick Barbarossa in 1157, Milan became one of the first independent city-states of the Renaissance. Its heyday of self-rule proved comparatively brief. From 1277 until 1500 it was ruled by the Visconti and subsequently the Sforza dynasties. These families were known, justly or not, for a peculiarly aristocratic mixture of refinement, classical learning, and cruelty, and much of the surviving grandeur of Gothic and Renaissance art and architecture is their doing. Be on the lookout in your wanderings for the Visconti family emblem—a viper, its jaws straining wide, devouring a child.

> **WORD OF MOUTH**
>
> "What I loved about Milan was: attending a concert at La Scala and taking their backstage tour; walking amidst the marble spires on the roof of the Duomo on a sunny day, gazing at the Dolomites in the distance (a definite wow!); window-shopping in the too-chic-for-words Via Montenapoleone area; and seeing the *Last Supper*."
> –Maribel

The city center is compact and walkable, while the efficient Metropolitana (subway), as well as buses and trams, provides access to locations farther afield. Driving the streets of Milan is difficult at best, and parking can be downright miserable, so leave the car behind. The **tourist office** (✉ Via Marconi 1, near Piazza Duomo ☎ 02/72524301 ⊕ www.milanoinfotourist.com ☺ Mon.–Sat. 8:45–1 and 2–6, Sun. 9–1 and 2–5) in Piazza Duomo is an excellent place to begin your visit. It's tucked under the arches of one of the twin buildings designed in 1939 to complement the facade of the Galleria across the piazza. Free maps on a variety of themes are available. There is also a good selection of brochures about smaller museums and cultural initiatives. Pick up a copy of the English-language *Hello Milano* (ask, if it is not on display). This monthly magazine includes a day-to-day schedule of events of interest to visitors and a comprehensive map.

The Duomo & Points North

Milan's main streets radiate out from the massive Duomo, a late-Gothic cathedral that was started in 1386. Leading north is the handsome Galleria Vittorio Emanuele, an enclosed walkway that takes you to the world-famous opera house known as La Scala. Beyond are the winding streets of the elegant Brera neighborhood, once the city's bohemian quarter. Here you'll find one of Italy's leading art galleries, as well as the academy of fine arts. Heading northeast from La Scala is Via Manzoni, which leads to the *quadrilatero della moda*, or fashion district. Its streets are lined with elegant window displays from the world's most celebrated designers—the Italians taking the lead, of course.

Leading northeast from the Duomo is Corso Vittorio Emanuele. Locals and visitors stroll along this pedestrians-only street, looking at the shop windows, buying ice cream, or stopping for a coffee at one of the side-

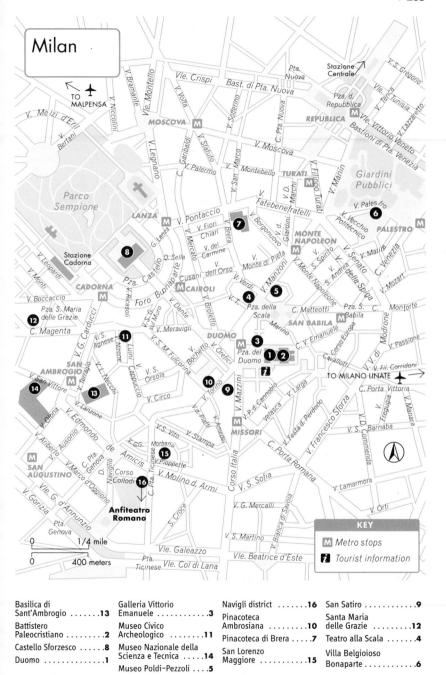

Milan

TO MALPENSA

MOSCOVA Ⓜ

Parco Sempione

LANZA Ⓜ

Stazione Cadorna

CADORNA Ⓜ

TURATI

Giardini Pubblici

MONTE NAPOLEON

PALESTRO Ⓜ

CAIROLI Ⓜ

DUOMO Ⓜ

SAN BABILA Ⓜ

SAN AMBROGIO

SAN AUGUSTINO Ⓜ

MISSORI Ⓜ

Anfiteatro Romano

Stazione Centrale

Pza. d. Repubblica

REPUBLICA

KEY

Ⓜ *Metro stops*

🛈 *Tourist information*

0   1/4 mile
0   400 meters

Basilica di
Sant'Ambrogio **13**

Battistero
Paleocristiano **2**

Castello Sforzesco **8**

Duomo **1**

Galleria Vittorio
Emanuele **3**

Museo Civico
Archeologico **11**

Museo Nazionale della
Scienza e Tecnica **14**

Museo Poldi-Pezzoli **5**

Navigli district **16**

Pinacoteca
Ambrosiana **10**

Pinacoteca di Brera **7**

San Lorenzo
Maggiore **15**

San Satiro **9**

Santa Maria
delle Grazie **12**

Teatro alla Scala **4**

Villa Belgioioso
Bonaparte **6**

walk cafés. Northwest of the Duomo is Via Dante, at the top of which is the imposing outline of the Castello Sforzesco.

The Main Attractions

★ ⑧ **Castello Sforzesco.** For the serious student of Renaissance military engineering, the Castello must be something of a travesty, so often has it been remodeled or rebuilt since it was begun in 1450 by the *condottiere* (hired mercenary) who founded the city's second dynastic family, Francesco Sforza, fourth duke of Milan. Though today the word "mercenary" has a pejorative ring, during the Renaissance all Italy's great soldier-heroes were professionals hired by the cities and principalities that they served. Of them—and there were thousands—Francesco Sforza (1401–66) is considered one of the greatest, most honest, and most organized. It is said he could remember the names not only of all his men but of their horses as well. His rule signaled the enlightened age of the Renaissance, but preceded the next foreign rule by a scant 50 years.

Since the turn of the 20th century, the Castello has housed municipal museums devoted variously to Egyptian and other antiquities, musical instruments, paintings, and sculpture. Highlights include the **Sala delle Asse,** a frescoed room still sometimes attributed to Leonardo da Vinci (1452–1519). Michelangelo's unfinished *Rondanini Pietà* is believed to be his last work—an astounding achievement for a man nearly 90, and a moving coda to his life. Reopened in 2005, after a four-year restoration project, the *pinacoteca* (picture gallery) features paintings from medieval times to the 18th century. The 230 paintings on display include works by Antonello da Messina, Canaletto, Andrea Mantegna, and Bernardo Bellotto. ✉ *Piazza Castello, Brera* ☎ *02/88463700* ⊕ *www. milanocastello.it* 🎟 *€3, free Fri. 2–5* ☉ *Tues.–Sun. 9–5:30* Ⓜ *Cairoli.*

★ ❶ **Duomo.** This intricate Gothic structure has been fascinating and exasperating visitors and conquerors alike since it was begun by Galeazzo Visconti III (1351–1402), first duke of Milan, in 1386. Consecrated in the 15th or 16th century, it was not completed until just before the coronation of Napoléon as king of Italy in 1809. Whether or not you concur with travel writer H. V. Morton's 1964 assessment that the cathedral is "one of the mightiest Gothic buildings ever created," there is no denying that for sheer size and complexity it is unrivaled. It is the second-largest church in the world—the largest being Saint Peter's in Rome. The capacity is reckoned to be 40,000. Usually it is empty, a sanctuary from the frenetic pace of life outside and the perfect place for solitary contemplation.

The building is adorned with 135 marble spires and 2,245 marble statues. The oldest part is the **apse.** Its three colossal bays of curving and counter-curved tracery, especially the bay adorning the exterior of the stained-glass windows, should not be missed. At the end of the southern transept down the right aisle lies the **tomb of Gian Giacomo Medici.** The tomb owes some of its design to Michelangelo but was executed by Leone Leoni (1509–90) and is generally considered to be his masterpiece; it dates from the 1560s. Directly ahead is the Duomo's most famous sculpture, the gruesome but anatomically instructive figure of **San Bartolomeo** (St. Bartholomew), whose glorious martyrdom consisted of being flayed alive. It is usually said the saint stands "holding" his skin, but this is not quite accurate. It would appear more that he is luxuriating in it, much as a 1950s matron might have shown off a new fur stole.

As you enter the apse to admire those splendid windows, glance at the **sacristy doors** to the right and left of the altar. The lunette on the right dates from 1393 and was decorated by Hans von Fernach. The one on the left also dates from the 14th century and is ascribed jointly to Giacomo da Campione and Giovanni dei Grassi. Don't miss the view from the Duomo's **roof**; walk out the left (north) transept to the stairs and elevator. Sadly, air pollution drastically reduces the view on all but the rarest days. As you stand among the forest of marble pinnacles, remember that virtually every inch of this gargantuan edifice, including the roof itself, is decorated with precious white marble dragged from quarries near Lake Maggiore by Duke Visconti's team along road laid fresh for the purpose and through the newly dredged canals.

Inspection and possible repair of 12 of the northern spires means the facade facing the piazza may be shrouded in scaffolding, although as individual sections are restored, some scaffolding comes down. The rest of the Duomo's intricate masonry and statuary, including the gleaming, emblematic **Madonnina** perched on the highest spire, remain unencumbered. ⊠ *Piazza del Duomo* ☎ *02/86463456* ⊕ *duomomilano. com* ⛱ *Stairs to roof €3.50, elevator €5* ☉ *Mid-Feb.–mid-Nov., daily 9–5:45; mid-Nov.–mid-Feb., daily 9–4:15* Ⓜ *Duomo.*

Exhibits at the **Museo del Duomo** shed light on the cathedral's history and include some of the treasures removed from the exterior for preservation purposes. ⊠ *Piazza del Duomo 14* ☎ *02/860358* ⛱ *€6, €7 including ticket for elevator to Duomo roof* ☉ *Daily 10–1:15 and 3–6.*

★ ❸ **Galleria Vittorio Emanuele.** This spectacular, late-19th-century glass-topped, barrel-vaulted tunnel is essentially one of the planet's earliest and most select shopping malls. Like its suburban American cousins, the Galleria Vittorio Emanuele fulfills numerous social functions. This is the city's heart, midway between the Duomo and La Scala. It teems with life, inviting people-watching from the tables that spill from the bars and restaurants, where you can enjoy an overpriced coffee. Books, records, clothing, food, pens, and jewelry are all for sale, and you'll also find here the venerable Savini restaurant.

The Galleria has undergone a refurbishment in recent years. Realizing that quality of the stores (except the Prada flagship store) and restaurants was not what the city wanted in its "parlor," city government and merchants' groups evicted some longtime tenants who had enjoyed anomalously low rents, in favor of Gucci, Tod's and Louis Vuitton.

Like the cathedral, the Galleria is cruciform in shape. Even in poor weather the great glass dome above the octagonal center is a splendid sight. And the floor mosaics are a vastly underrated source of pleasure, even if they are not to be taken too seriously. They represent Europe, Asia, Africa, and the United States; those at the entrance arch are devoted to science, industry, art, and agriculture. Be sure to follow tradition and spin your heels once or twice on the more-"delicate" parts of the bull beneath your feet in the northern apse; the Milanese believe it brings good luck. ✉ *Piazza del Duomo* Ⓜ *Duomo.*

NEED A BREAK?
One thing has stayed constant in the Galleria: the **Caffè Zucca,** known by the Milanese as Camparino. Its inlaid counter, mosaics, and wrought-iron fixtures have been welcoming tired shoppers since 1867. Enjoy a Campari or Zucca *aperitivo* (aperitif) as well as the entire range of Italian coffees, served either in the Galleria or in an elegant upstairs room.

❺ **Museo Poldi-Pezzoli.** This exceptional museum, opened in 1881, was once a private residence and collection, and contains not only pedigreed paintings but also porcelain, textiles, and a cabinet with scenes from Dante's life. The gem is undoubtedly the *Portrait of a Lady* by Antonio Pollaiolo (1431–98), one of the city's most prized treasures and the source of the museum's logo. The collection also includes masterpieces by Botticelli (1445–1510), Andrea Mantegna (1431–1506), Giovanni Bellini (1430–1516), and Fra Filippo Lippi (1406–69). ✉ *Via Manzoni 12, Brera* ☎ *02/794889* ∰ *www.museopoldipezzoli.it* 💷 €7 ⊗ *Tues.–Sun. 10–6* Ⓜ *Montenapoleone.*

★ ❼ **Pinacoteca di Brera** (Brera Gallery). The collection here is star-studded even by Italian standards. The entrance hall (Room I) displays 20th-century sculpture and painting, including Carlo Carrà's (1881–1966) confident, stylish response to the schools of cubism and surrealism. The museum has nearly 40 other rooms, arranged in chronological order—pace yourself.

The somber, moving *Cristo Morto* (*Dead Christ*) by Mantegna dominates Room VI, with its sparse palette of umber and its foreshortened perspective. Mantegna's shocking, almost surgical precision—in the rendering of Christ's wounds, the face propped up on a pillow, the day's growth of beard—tells of an all-too-human agony. It is one of Renaissance painting's most quietly wondrous achievements, finding an unsuspected middle ground between the excesses of conventional gore and beauty in representing the Passion's saddest moment.

Room XXIV offers two additional highlights of the gallery. Raphael's (1483–1520) *Sposalizio della Vergine,* with its mathematical composition and precise, alternating colors, portrays the betrothal of Mary and Joseph (who, though older than the other men gathered, wins her hand when the rod he is holding miraculously blossoms). *La Vergine con il Bambino e Santi* (*Madonna with Child and Saints*), by Piero della Francesca (1420–92), is an altarpiece commissioned by Federico da Montefeltro (shown kneeling, in full armor, before the Virgin); it was intended for a church to house the Duke's tomb. The ostrich egg hanging from the apse, depending on whom you ask, either commemorates the miracle of his fertility—Federico's wife died months after giving birth to a long-awaited male heir—or alludes to his appeal for posthumous mercy, the egg symbolizing the saving power of grace. ✉ *Via Brera 28* ☎ *02/722631* ∰ *www.brera.beniculturali.it* 💷 €5 ⊗ *Tues.–Sun. 8:30–7:15; last admission 45 mins before closing* Ⓜ *Montenapoleone.*

VOICES OF ITALY

Giampaolo Abbondio
gallery owner, Milan

Giampaolo Abbondio is a rising star in Milan's contemporary art scene. His **Galleria Pack** (✉ Foro Buonaparte 60 ☎ 02/86996395 ⊕ www.galleriapack.com), has attracted a number of important young artists to its stable. Giampaolo is a Milanese by birth, and unabashedly proud of what he calls "the least Italian city in Italy."

Q: Giampaolo, what exactly do you mean when you call Milan the least Italian city in Italy?

A: Well, it's not, of course. We're still Italians. But Milan has been a crossroads for many years, a meeting place from which Italy can access the rest of Europe, and from which the rest of Europe can be introduced to Italy. I think that has made Milan a little more European than other parts of the country. Some of that is good: we have excellent public transportation, stores that are open all day, things like that. And some of that is not so good: they say we work too much, we don't take the time to enjoy life like they do in the rest of Italy. But I'm sure that's clearer to Italians than from a foreigner's point of view. I mean, we still make an excellent risotto . . .

Q: Most people don't think of Milan when they're thinking of great Italian art; they think of places like Rome, Florence, and Venice. Are they making a mistake?

A: Of course! I mean, it's true that Milan isn't the most "artistic" place in Italy. It has a very strong private sector but a weak public sector, meaning there is not a lot of money for museums and other public cultural works. But it also means that there's a lot of private investment in art. Rome may have the museums, but Milan has the more fertile art scene.

Q: What features of Milan's contemporary art activities that a visitor to Milan should know about?

A: Well, the P.A.C., or **Padiglione di Arte Contemporanea** (✉ Via Palestro 14 ☎ 02/76009085 ⊕ www.comune.milano.it/pac). The P.A.C. is a public space that hosts a constantly changing series of temporary shows. It is a kind of city gallery that does four or five important shows a year. Another is the **Palazzo della Triennale** (✉ Via Alemagna 6 ☎ 02/724341 ⊕ www.triennale.it), which, like the Stazione Centrale, is interesting for its classic Fascist architecture no matter what's going on inside. And the Triennale is located in the middle of Parco Sempione, which has some important public artworks including a fountain by De Chirico and an amphitheater by Arman. And of course, at least as far as I'm concerned, no visit to Milan would be complete without a tour of the important contemporary art galleries! Besides my gallery, there are the **Emi Fontana** (✉ Viale Bligny 42 ☎ 02/58322237), **Salvatore & Carolina Ala** (✉ Via Monte di Pietà 1 ☎ 02/8900901), **Massimo De Carlo** (✉ Via Ventura 4 ☎ 02/70003987 ⊕ www.massimodecarlo.it), and **1,000 Eventi** (✉ Via Porro Lambertenghi 3 ☎ 02/45478297). This is the best way to avoid lines at the museums . . . you go see the art in a gallery before it gets too famous!

4

4 **Teatro alla Scala.** You need know nothing of opera to sense that, like Carnegie Hall, La Scala is closer to a cathedral than an auditorium. Here Verdi established his reputation and Maria Callas sang her way into opera lore. It looms as a symbol—both for the performer who dreams of singing here and for the opera buff who knows every note of *Rigoletto* by heart. Audiences are notoriously demanding and are apt to jeer performers who do not measure up. The opera house was closed after destruction by Allied bombs in 1943, reopened at a performance led by Arturo Toscanini in 1946, and closed again in 2002 for renovations. The massive reconstruction project, which left only the exterior shell standing, was completed in late 2004 and the opera house officially reopened on December 7, 2004—the traditional first night of the opera season, which coincides with the feast day of Saint Ambrose, Milan's patron saint.

If you are lucky enough to be here during the opera season, which runs for approximately six months, do whatever is necessary to attend. Tickets go on sale two months before the first performance, and are usually sold out the same day. Hearing opera sung in the magical acoustic of La Scala is an unparalleled experience. ⊠ *Piazza della Scala* ☎ *02/72003744* ⊕ *www.teatroallascala.org* Ⓜ *Duomo.*

At **Museo Teatrale alla Scala** you can admire librettos, posters, costumes, instruments, design sketches for the theater, curtains, and viewing box decorations, along with an explanation of the reconstruction project and several interactive exhibits. A highlight is the collection of antique gramophones and phonographs. ⊠ *Piazza della Scala* ☎ *02/43353521* ☞ *€5* ⊗ *Daily 9–noon and 1:30–5.*

Also Worth Seeing

2 **Battistero Paleocristiano.** Beneath the Duomo's piazza lies this baptistery ruin dating from the 4th century. Although opinion remains divided, it is widely believed to be where Ambrose, Milan's first bishop and patron saint, baptized Augustine. Tickets are available at the kiosk inside the cathedral. ⊠ *Piazza del Duomo, enter through Duomo* ☎ *02/86463456* ☞ *€1.50* ⊗ *Daily 9:30–5:15* Ⓜ *Duomo.*

★ **6** **Villa Belgioioso Bonaparte—Museo dell'Ottocento.** After three years of restoration, finished in March 2006, this museum, formerly known as the Galleria di Arte Moderna, is one of the city's most beautiful buildings. An outstanding example of neoclassical architecture, it was built between 1790 and 1796 as a residence for a member of the Belgioioso family. It later became known as the Villa Reale (royal) when it was donated to Napoléon, who lived here briefly with Empress Josephine. Its origins as residence are reflected in the elegance of its proportions and its private garden behind.

Likewise, the collection of paintings is domestic rather than monumental. There are many portraits, as well as collections of miniatures on porcelain. Unusual for an Italian museum, this collection derives from private donations from Milan's hereditary and commercial aristocracies. Among pieces on display are the collection left by prominent painter and sculptor Marino Marini and the immense *Quarto Stato* (Fourth Estate) which is at the top of the grand staircase. Completed in 1901 by Pellizza da

Volpedo, this painting of striking workers is an icon of 20th-century Italian art and labor history, and as such it has been satirized almost as much as the Mona Lisa.

This collection will not satisfy museumgoers seeking major Italian art. No matter, the best part is the building itself, with its delightful shell-color stucco decorations, splendid neoclassical chandeliers, pastel taffeta curtains, and garden view. It offers a unique glimpse of the splendors that the city hides behind its discreet and often stern facades. ⊠ *Via Palestro 16* ☎ *02/76340809* ⊕ *www.villabelgiojosobonaparte.it* ⊘ *Tues.–Sun. 9–1 and 2–5:30.*

The **Giardini Pubblici** (Public Gardens), across Via Palestro from the Villa Reale, were laid out by Giuseppe Piermarini, architect of La Scala, in 1770. They were designed as public pleasure gardens, and today they still are popular with families who live in the city center. Generations of Milanese have taken pony rides and gone on the miniature train and merry-go-round. The park also contains a small planetarium and the **Museo Civico di Storia Naturale** (The Municipal Natural History Museum).

Parents may want to visit the garden of the Villa Belgioioso-Bonaparte, on Via Palestro, which is entered from a gate to the building's left. Access to the garden, which has statuary and a water course designed in 1790 (the first English-style garden in Milan), is primarily for children accompanied by an adult. Adults without children wanting to see the garden are tolerated, as long as they do not linger in this protected area.

NEED A BREAK? If your energy is flagging after shopping or chasing children around the park, try some of Milan's best cappuccino and pastry at **Dolce In** (⊠ Via Turati 2/3 ⊘ Closed Mon.), which is equally close to Via della Spiga and the Giardini Pubblici. It's famous for its pastry and also serves sandwiches and cold plates at lunch. On Sunday mornings, classic-car enthusiasts meet informally here, parking their handsome machines out front while they have coffee.

South & West of the Duomo

If the part of the city to the north of the Duomo is dominated by its shops, the section to the south is famous for its works of art. The most famous is *Il Cenacolo*—known in English as *The Last Supper*. If you have time for nothing else, make sure you see this masterwork, which has now been definitively restored, after many, many, years of work. Reservations will be needed to see this fresco, housed in the refectory of Santa Maria delle Grazie. Make these before you depart for Italy, so you can plan the rest of your time in Milan.

There are other gems as well. Via Torino, the ancient road for Turin, leads to a half-hidden treasure: Bramante's Renaissance masterpiece, the church of San Satiro. At the intersection of Via San Vittore and Via Carducci is the medieval Basilica di Sant'Ambrogio, named for Milan's patron saint. Another lovely church southeast of Sant'Ambrogio along Via de Amicis is San Lorenzo Maggiore. It's also known as San Lorenzo alle Colonne because of the 16 columns running across the facade.

The Main Attractions

⓭ **Basilica di Sant'Ambrogio** (Basilica of St. Ambrose). Noted for its medieval architecture, the church was consecrated by St. Ambrose in AD 387 and is the model for all Lombard Romanesque churches. The church is often closed for weddings on Saturday. ⊠ *Piazza Sant'Ambrogio 15* ☏ *02/86450895* ⊘ *Mon.–Sat. 7–noon and 2:30–7, Sun. 3–8* Ⓜ *Sant'Ambrogio.*

NEED A BREAK?

A bit overcrowded at night, the **Bar Magenta** (⊠ Via Carducci 13, at Corso Magenta, Sant'Ambrogio ☏ 02/8053808) can be a good stop en route during the day. Beyond coffee at all hours, lunch, and beer, the real attraction is its casual but civilized, quintessentially Milanese ambience. It's open until 2 AM.

⓾ **Pinacoteca Ambrosiana.** This museum, founded in the 17th century by Cardinal Federico Borromeo, is one of the city's treasures. Here you can contemplate works of art such as Caravaggio's *Basket of Fruit*, prescient in its realism, and Raphael's awesome preparatory drawing for *The School of Athens* that hangs in the Vatican, as well as paintings by Leonardo, Botticelli, Luini, Titian, and Brueghel. The adjoining library, the Biblioteca Ambrosiana, dates from 1609, and is thought to be the oldest public library in Italy. Admission to the library these days is limited to scholars. ⊠ *Piazza Pio XI 2, near Duomo* ☏ *02/806921* ⊕ *www.ambrosiana.it* ▣ *€7.50* ⊘ *Tues.–Sun. 10–5:30* Ⓜ *Duomo.*

⓯ **San Lorenzo Maggiore.** Sixteen ancient Roman columns line the front of this sanctuary; 4th-century paleochristian mosaics survive in the Cappella di Sant'Aquilino (Chapel of St. Aquilinus). ⊠ *Corso di Porta Ticinese 39, Porta Ticinese* ☏ *02/89404129* ▣ *Mosaics €2* ⊘ *Daily 8:30–12:30 and 2:30–6:30.*

★ ⓽ **San Satiro.** First built in 876, this architectural gem was later perfected by Bramante (1444–1514), demonstrating his command of proportion and perspective, keynotes of Renaissance architecture. Bramante tricks the eye with a famous optical illusion that makes a small interior seem extraordinarily spacious and airy, while accommodating a beloved 13th-century fresco. ⊠ *Via Torino 9, near Duomo* ⊘ *Weekdays 7:30–11:30 and 3:30–6:30, weekends 9–noon and 3:30–7* Ⓜ *Duomo.*

★ ⓬ **Santa Maria delle Grazie.** Leonardo da Vinci's *The Last Supper*, housed in the church and former Dominican monastery of Santa Maria delle Grazie, has had an almost unbelievable history of bad luck and neglect—its near destruction in an American bombing raid in August 1943 was only the latest chapter in a series of misadventures, including, if one 19th-century source is to be believed, being whitewashed over by monks. Well-meant but disastrous attempts at restoration have done little to rectify the problem of the work's placement: it was executed on a wall unusually vulnerable to climatic dampness. Yet Leonardo chose to work slowly and patiently in oil pigments—which demand dry plaster—instead of proceeding hastily on wet plaster according to the conventional fresco technique. Novelist Aldous Huxley (1894–1963) called it "the saddest work of art in the world." After years of restorers' patiently shifting from one square centimeter to another, Leonardo's masterpiece is free of the shroud of scaffolding—and centuries of retouching, grime, and dust. Astonishing clarity and luminosity have been regained. *Reservations are required* to view the work; call several days ahead for weekday visits and several weeks in advance for a weekend visit. The reservations office is open 9 AM–6 PM weekdays and 9 AM–2 PM on Saturday. Viewings are in 15-minute slots.

Despite Leonardo's carefully preserved preparatory sketches in which the apostles are clearly labeled by name, there still remains some small debate about a few identities in the final arrangement. But there can be no mistaking Judas, small and dark, his hand calmly reaching forward to the bread, isolated from the terrible confusion that has taken the hearts of the others. One critic, Frederick Hartt, offers an elegantly terse explanation for why the composition works: it combines "dramatic confusion" with "mathematical order." Certainly, the amazingly skillful and unobtrusive repetition of threes—in the windows, in the grouping of the figures, and in their placement—adds a mystical aspect to what at first seems simply the perfect observation of spontaneous human gesture.

The painting was executed in what was the order's refectory, which is now referred to as the **Cenacolo Vinciano.** Take a moment to visit Santa Maria delle Grazie itself. It's a handsome church, with a fine dome, which Bramante added along with a cloister about the time that Leonardo was commissioned to paint *The Last Supper.* If you're wondering how two such giants came to be employed decorating and remodeling the refectory and church of a comparatively modest religious order, and not, say, the Duomo, the answer lies in the ambitious but largely unrealized plan to turn Santa Maria delle Grazie into a magnificent Sforza family mausoleum. Though Ludovico il Moro Sforza (1452–1508), seventh duke of Milan, was but one generation away from the founding of the Sforza dynasty, he was its last ruler. Two years after Leonardo finished *The Last Supper,* Ludovico was defeated by Louis XII and spent the remaining eight years of his life in a French dungeon. ⊠ *Piazza Santa Maria delle Grazie 2, off Corso Magenta, Sant'Ambrogio* ☎ *02/89421146 weekdays 9–6, Sat. 9–2* ✑ *€6.50 plus €1.50 reservation fee* ☉ *Tues.–Sun. 8–7:30; last entry 6:45* Ⓜ *Cadorna.*

Also Worth Seeing

⓫ **Museo Civico Archeologico** (Municipal Archaeological Museum). Housed in a former monastery, this museum has some enlightening relics from Milan's Roman past—from everyday utensils and jewelry to several fine examples of mosaic pavement. ⊠ *Corso Magenta 15, Sant'Ambrogio* ☎ *02/86450011* ✑ *€2, free Fri. 2–5* ☉ *Tues.–Sun. 9–5:30* Ⓜ *Cadorna.*

⍟ ⓮ **Museo Nazionale della Scienza e Tecnica** (National Museum of Science and Technology). This museum houses an extensive, eccentric collection of engineering achievements, from metal-processing equipment to full-size locomotives. But the highlights are undoubtedly the exhibits based on the inventive technical drawings of Leonardo da Vinci. On the second floor a collection of models based on these sketches is artfully displayed, with Leonardo's paintings offering striking counterpoint overhead. Explanations are not offered in English, leaving you to ponder possible purposes for the contraptions. On the ground level—in the hallway between the courtyards—is a room featuring interactive, moving models of the famous *vita aerea* (aerial screw) and *ala battente* (beating wing), thought to be forerunners of the modern helicopter and airplane, respectively. ⊠ *Via San Vittore 21, Sant'Ambrogio* ☎ *02/48555200* ⊕ *www. museoscienza.org* 🗋 *€7* ☉ *Tues.–Fri. 9:30–4:50, weekends 9:30–6:20* Ⓜ *Sant'Ambrogio.*

⑯ **Navigli district.** In medieval times, a network of *navigli,* or canals, crisscrossed the city. Almost all have been covered over, but two—Naviglio Grande and Naviglio Pavese—are still navigable. Once a down-at-the-heels neighborhood, the Navigli district has been gentrified over the last 20 years. Humble workshops have been replaced by trendy boutiques, art galleries, cafés, bars, and restaurants. The Navigli at night is about as close as you will get to more-southern-style Italian street life in Milan. On weekend nights, it is difficult to walk (and impossible to park) among the youthful crowds thronging the narrow streets along the canals. Check out the antiques fair on the last Sunday of the month. ⊠ *South of Corso Porta Ticinese, Porta Genova* Ⓜ *Porta Genova.*

Where to Eat

★ **$$$$** ✕ **Antica Osteria del Ponte.** Rich, imaginative seasonal cuisine composed according to the inspired whims of chef Ezio Santin is reason enough to make your way 20 km (12 mi) southwest of Milan to one of Italy's finest restaurants. The setting is a traditional country inn, where a wood fire warms the rustic interior in winter. The menu changes regularly; in fall, wild porcini mushrooms are among the favored ingredients. Various fixed menus (at 110 and 145 euros) offer broad samplings of antipasti, primi, and meat or fish; some include appropriate wine selections, too. ⊠ *Cassinetta di Lugagnano, 3 km (2 mi) north of Abbiategrasso* ☎ *02/9420034* 🍴 *Reservations essential* ▭ *AE, DC, MC, V* ☉ *Closed Sun. and Mon., Dec. 25–Jan. 12, and Aug.*

★ **$$$$** ✕ **Cracco-Peck.** When a renowned local chef (Carlo Cracco) joined forces with the city's top gourmet food store (Peck), the results were not long in coming. Within three years, Cracco-Peck boasted two Michelin stars. The dining room is done in an elegant style that favors cool earth tones. Specialties include Milanese classics revisited—Cracco's take on saffron risotto and breaded veal cutlet should not be missed. Be sure to save room for the light, steam-cooked tiramisu. If you can't decide, opt for the gourmet menu (€88 for six courses, excluding wine). ⊠ *Via Victor Hugo 4, near Duomo* ☎ *02/876774* 🍴 *Reservations essential* ▭ *AE, DC, MC, V* ☉ *Closed Sun., 10 days in Jan., and 2 wks in Aug. No lunch Sat. No dinner Sat. in July and Aug.* Ⓜ *Duomo.*

★ **$$$$** ✕ **Don Carlos.** One of the few restaurants open after La Scala lets out, Don Carlos, in the Grand Hotel et de Milan, is nothing like its indecisive operatic namesake (whose betrothed was stolen by his father). Flavors are bold, their presentation precise and full of flair: broiled red mullet floats on a lacy layer of crispy leek. Walls are blanketed with sketches of the theater, and the opera recordings are every bit as well chosen as the wine list, setting the perfect stage for discreet business negotiation or, better yet, refined romance. A gourmet menu costs €75 for six courses (two-person minimum), excluding wine. ⊠ *Grand Hotel et de*

EATING WELL IN LOMBARDY

Unlike most other Italian regions, Lombardy traditionally exhibits a northern European preference for butter rather than oil as its cooking medium, which imparts a rich and distinctive flavor to the cuisine. *Alla milanese*—Milanese-style cooking—usually means the food is dipped in egg and bread crumbs mixed with grated Parmesan, then sautéed in butter. One of the most popular specialties here, osso buco, is almost always paired with risotto, which the alla milanese preparation enriches with chicken broth and saffron.

The lakes are a good source of fish, particularly trout and pike. Gorgonzola, a strong, creamy, veined cheese, and panettone, a sweet yeast bread with raisins, citron, and anise, both hail from the Milan area and can be found throughout Lombardy. The most rewarding wines of the region, worth searching wine lists for, are the red Valtellina Superiore and Oltrepò Pavese, as well as the delicious light sparkling whites from the Franciacorta area.

4

Milan, Via Manzoni 29, Duomo ☎ *02/723141* ☖ *Reservations essential* ▤ *AE, DC, MC, V* ☉ *Closed Aug. No lunch* Ⓜ *Montenapoleone.*

$$$$ ✕ **Joia.** At this haute-cuisine vegetarian restaurant near Piazza della Repubblica, delicious dishes are artistically prepared by chef Pietro Leemann. The ever-changing menu offers dishes such as ravioli with basil, potatoes, pine nuts, and crisp green beans. (Fish also makes an appearance.) The dishes all have creative names, such as the onomatopoeic soup called "blub." In the depths of this thick mushroom-and-asparagus soup is an air bubble that makes a distinctive sound when it comes to the surface. Multicourse menus range from €55 to €95, excluding wine. ✉ *Via Panfilo Castaldi 18, Porta Venezia* ☎ *02/29522124* ▤ *AE, DC, MC, V* ☉ *Closed Sun., 3 wks in Aug., and Dec. 24–Jan. 7. No lunch Sat.* Ⓜ *Repubblica.*

$$$$ ✕ **La Terrazza.** An office building at the edge of the fashion district is home to this stylish eatery where contemporary design dominates both food and decor. Well-dressed business executives dine on inventive "Mediterranean sushi," which uses pearl barley instead of rice and incorporates pesto, blood oranges, or olive tapenade. There is a fixed-price meal for €62. In warmer weather, the scene shifts to the terrace, where you can see the treetops of the nearby Giardini Pubblici. There's a "happy hour" every day except Sunday; on Sunday, brunch is served. Takeout is also available. ✉ *Via Palestro 2, Quadrilatero* ☎ *02/76002277* ▤ *AE, DC, MC, V* ☉ *Closed last 3 wks in Aug.* Ⓜ *Turati, Palestro.*

$$$–$$$$ ✕ **Antica Trattoria della Pesa.** Fin-de-siècle furnishings, dark-wood paneling, and old-fashioned lamps still look much as they must have when this eatery opened 100 years ago. It's authentic Old Milan, and the menu is right in line, offering risotto, minestrone, and osso buco. Sample the *riso al salto con rognone trifolato,* which is fried rice with thinly sliced kidney. In winter, *polenta* is the best choice. ✉ *Viale Pasubio 10, Porta Volta* ☎ *02/6555741* ▤ *AE, DC, MC, V* ☉ *Closed Sun., Aug., and Dec. 24–Jan. 6* Ⓜ *Porta Garibaldi.*

$$$–$$$$ ✕ **Boeucc.** Milan's oldest restaurant, opened in 1696, is on the same square as novelist Alessandro Manzoni's house, not far from La Scala. With stone columns, chandeliers, Oriental rugs, and a garden, it has come a long way from its basement origins (*boeucc,* pronounced "birch," is old Milanese for *buco,* or "hole"). You'll savor such dishes as penne *al branzino e zucchini* (with sea bass and zucchini). For desert, try the *gelato di castagne con zabaglione caldo* (chestnut ice cream with hot zabaglione). ✉ *Piazza Belgioioso 2, Scala* ☎ *02/76020224* ⌣ *Reservations essential* ☰ *AE* ☽ *Closed Sat., Easter Sun. and Mon., Aug., and Dec. 24–Jan. 4. No lunch Sun.* Ⓜ *Montenapoleone, Duomo.*

$$$–$$$$ ✕ **Nobu.** From a minimalist corner of the Armani minimall, Milan's Nobu serves the same delicious Japanese-Peruvian fusion as its siblings in the world's other culinary capitals. Cocktails, appetizers, and beautiful people can be found at the ground-floor bar, well worth a visit even if you're not dining upstairs. Dinner can be a scene here; at lunch there is a fixed-price "box" for €25. ✉ *Via Pisoni, 1, corner of Via Manzoni 31, Quadrilatero* ☎ *02/72318645* ⌣ *Reservations essential* ☰ *AE, DC, MC, V* ☽ *No lunch Sun. and Mon.* Ⓜ *Montenapoleone.*

$$–$$$ ✕ **Il Brellin.** In front of this Milan classic is a sluice from the Naviglio (one of the canals that once crisscrossed the city) where the washerwomen who gave the street its name used to scrub the clothes of Milan's noble families. Now the Navigli area is filled with bars and restaurants, of which Il Brellin is one of the more serious. It offers a mix of homey classics, such as pasta *rustiga* and rigatoni sautéed with pancetta, as well as new twists on typical ingredients—a pumpkin tart as an appetizer. With its several small rooms with exposed beams, Il Brellin is cozy in winter. But on a nice Sunday, enjoy the brunch buffet at an outside table. ✉ *Vicolo dei Lavandai Navigli* ☎ *02/89402700* ☰ *AE, DC, MC, V* ☽ *No dinner Sun.*

$$–$$$ ✕ **La Libera.** Although this establishment in the heart of Brera calls itself a *birreria con cucina* (beer cellar with kitchen), locals come here for excellent evening meals in relaxed surroundings. A soft current of jazz and sylvan decor soothe the ripple of conversation. The creative cooking varies with the season, but could include linguine *al pescato* (with a fish sauce); *fritto di gamberi, zucchine e totanetti* (fried shrimp, zucchini, and baby squid); or *rognone alla senape* (veal kidneys cooked in mustard). ✉ *Via Palermo 21, Brera* ☎ *02/8053603 or 02/86462773* ☰ *AE, DC, MC, V* ☽ *No lunch* Ⓜ *Moscova.*

$$–$$$ ✕ **Paper Moon.** Hidden behind Via Montenapoleone and thus handy to the restaurant-scarce Quadrilatero, Paper Moon is a cross between neighborhood restaurant and celebrity hangout. Clients include families from this wealthy area, professionals, football players, and television stars. What the menu lacks in originality it makes up for in consistency—reliable pizza and *cotoletta* (veal cutlet). Like any Italian restaurant, it's not child friendly in an American sense—no high chairs or children's menu—but children will find food they like. Open until 12:30 AM. ✉ *Via Bagutta 1, Quadrilatero* ☎ *02/76022297* ☰ *AE, MC, V* ☽ *Closed Sun., 2 wks in Aug., and Dec. 25–Jan 7* Ⓜ *San Babila.*

FodorśChoice $$–$$$ ✕ **Trattoria Montina.** Twin brothers Maurizio and Roberto Montina have
★ turned this restaurant into a local favorite. Don't be fooled by the "trattoria" name—Chef Roberto creates exquisite modern Italian dishes such as warmed bruschetta with Brie and prosciutto, while Maurizio

moves around the restaurant chatting and taking orders. Try the *frittura impazzita*, a wild-and-crazy mix of delicately fried seafood. The warm chocolate-and-pear pie also comes highly recommended. ☒ *Via Procaccini 54, Procaccini* ☏ *02/3490498* ▱ *AE, DC, MC, V* ☉ *Closed Sun., Aug., and Dec. 25–Jan. 7. No lunch Mon.* Ⓜ *Trams 1, 19, 29, 33.*

★ **$–$$** ✕ **Da Abele.** If you love risotto, then make a beeline for this neighborhood trattoria. The superb risotto dishes change with the season, and there may be just two or three on the menu at any time. It is tempting to try them all. The setting is relaxed, the service informal, the prices strikingly reasonable. Outside the touristy center of town but quite convenient by subway, this trattoria is invariably packed with locals. ☒ *Via Temperanza 5, Loreto* ☏ *02/2613855* ▱ *AE, DC, MC, V* ☉ *Closed Mon., Aug., and Dec. 22–Jan. 7. No lunch* Ⓜ *Pasteur.*

$–$$ ✕ **La Bruschetta.** This tiny, bustling first-class pizzeria near the Duomo serves specialties from Tuscany and other parts of Italy. The wood oven is in full view, so you can see your pizza cooking in front of you, although there are plenty of nonpizza dishes available, too, such as spaghetti *alle cozze e vongole* (with clam and mussel sauce) and grilled and skewered meats. ☒ *Piazza Beccaria 12, Duomo* ☏ *02/8692494* ▱ *AE, MC, V* ☉ *Closed Mon., 3 wks in Aug., and late Dec.–early Jan.* Ⓜ *Duomo.*

¢–$$ ✕ **Joia Leggero.** In the Porta Ticinese area, and near the Navigli district, Joia Leggero (light) is a lower-priced, more-informal initiative of innovative chef Pietro Leemann, the man behind Joia. With a pleasant view of the church of St. Eustorgio and a few tables outside, this airy restaurant serves haute vegetarian food. "Leggero" does not necessarily refer to the calorie content; the offerings—especially the excellent desserts—are often satisfyingly rich. This is not typical sprouts-and-grains health food. Try the well-priced set meals (vegetarian lunch is €11, €14 with fish), which are attractively presented on Japanese-inspired trays. ☒ *Corso di Porta Ticinese 106, Porta Ticinese* ☏ *02/89404134* ▱ *AE, MC, V* ☉ *Closed Sun. and 3 wks in Aug. No lunch Mon.*

$–$$ ✕ **Al Rifugio Pugliese.** Just outside the center of town, this is a fun place to sample specialties from the Puglia region of southern Italy. These include homemade *orecchiette* (a small, ear-shape pasta) with a variety of sauces. There is a choice of 60 first courses, as well as plenty of vegetable and fish dishes. The lunch buffet is a good deal as are the fixed-price menus of €29 and €39 that can include wine, coffee, and after-dinner drinks. ☒ *Via Costanza 2, corner of Via Boni 16, Fiera* ☏ *02/48000917* ▱ *AE, DC, MC, V* ☉ *Closed Sun., Aug. 5–25, and Dec. 25–Jan. 7* Ⓜ *Wagner.*

¢–$ ✕ **Pizza Ok.** Pizza is almost the only item on the menu at this popular spot near Corso Buenos Aires, but it's very good and the dining experience will be easy on your pocketbook. Possibilities for toppings seem endless. ☒ *Via Lambro 15, Porta Venezia* ☏ *02/29401272* ▱ *No credit cards* ☉ *Closed Aug. and Dec. 24–Jan. 7. No lunch Sun.* Ⓜ *Porta Venezia.*

¢ ✕ **Bar Tempio.** This wine bar, not far from Giardini Pubblici and the shops of the Quadrilatero, was once so unprepossessing that it didn't have a name—but it turned out some of Milan's best panini. It's been renovated and given a name, but the same artist is still making the sandwiches. This is a lunch-only establishment, and you might have to wait your turn, as panini are made to order from a list (not in English, so bring your

4

phrase book). They feature cured prosciutto *di praga, cipolle* (onions), and various cheeses (including easily recognizable Brie). ✉ *Piazza Cavour 5 (enter from Via Turati), near Quadrilatero* ☎ *02/6551946* ✆ *No dinner* Ⓜ *Turati.*

¢ ✕ **Taverna Morigi.** This dusky, wood-panel wine bar near the stock exchange is the perfect spot to enjoy a glass of wine with cheese and cold cuts. At lunch, pasta dishes and select entrées are available; pasta is the only hot dish served in the evening. Platters of cheese and cold cuts are always available; if you're coming for a meal, a reservation is a good idea. ✉ *Via Morigi 8, Sant'Ambrogio* ☎ *02/86450880* ✉ *AE, DC, MC, V* ✆ *Closed Sun. and Aug. No lunch Sat.* Ⓜ *Cairoli.*

Where to Stay

$$$$ 🏨 **Carlton-Baglioni.** If you're in Milan to shop in the fashion district, this hotel is an ideal base. It's light and airy, with double-glazed windows, a parking garage, and lots of little touches such as complimentary chocolates and liqueurs to make up for the rather functional rooms. Some have terraces large enough for a table, a chair, and a shrub in a pot. The highly rated Baretto restaurant is a haunt of Milan's business and cultural elite. ✉ *Via Senato 5, Quadrilatero, 20121* ☎ *02/77077* 🖶 *02/783300* ⊕ *www. baglionihotels.com* ✆ *92 rooms* ⚭ *Restaurant, room service, minibars, cable TV, bar, laundry service, convention center, business center, parking (fee), no-smoking rooms* ✉ *AE, DC, MC, V* ⦿ *EP* Ⓜ *San Babila.*

$$$$ 🏨 **Four Seasons.** The Four Seasons has been cited more than once by the Italian press as the country's best city hotel—perhaps because once you're inside, the feeling is anything but urban. Built in the 15th century as a convent, the hotel surrounds a colonnaded cloister, and rooms added in a 2004 expansion have balconies giving onto a glassed-in courtyard. Everything about the place is standard Four Seasons (high) style, including a Brioni-decorated suite and a Royal Suite occupying its own floor. The Theater restaurant has some of Milanís best hotel dining. ✉ *Via Gesù 6–8, Quadrilatero, 20121* ☎ *02/7708167* 🖶 *02/ 77085000* ⊕ *www.fourseasons.com* ✆ *77 rooms, 41 suites* ⚭ *2 restaurants, room service, minibars, cable TV, Internet, bar, laundry service, business services, meeting rooms, no-smoking rooms, parking (fee), gym* ✉ *AE, DC, MC, V* ⦿ *EP* Ⓜ *Montenapoleone.*

$$$$ 🏨 **Grand Hotel et de Milan.** Only blocks from La Scala, this hotel, which opened in 1863, is sometimes called the "Hotel Verdi," because the composer lived here for 27 years. His apartment, complete with his desk, is now the Presidential Suite. In 2005 the entire hotel was refurbished. Moss-green and persimmon velvet enlivened the 19th-century look without sacrificing dignity and luxury. It's everything you hope for in a traditional European hotel; dignified but not stuffy, elegant but not ostentatious. The renovation also turned a former terrace into a small and airy glass-enclosed fitness center, which is a far cry from the usual, fluorescent-lighted basement den. The Don Carlos restaurant is one of Milan's best. ✉ *Via Manzoni 29, Scala, 20121* ☎ *02/723141* 🖶 *02/86460861* ⊕ *www. grandhoteletdemilan.it* ✆ *87 rooms, 8 suites* ⚭ *Restaurants, room service, minibars, cable TV, Wi-Fi, bar, laundry service, gym, parking (fee), no-smoking rooms* ✉ *AE, DC, MC, V* ⦿ *EP* Ⓜ *Montenapoleone.*

★ **$$$$** ▦ **The Gray.** At this small luxury hotel you get the best of everything, from location to amenities—all for a price. The interiors are decorated by famed Italian designer Guido Ciompi (who handles Gucci boutiques the world over). The atmosphere is trendy chic, from bottom-lighted tables in the hotel restaurant to patterns of laser light that play across the walls of the lobby. Rooms come equipped with everything from plasma TVs to specially designed oversize toiletries. The hotel does not have rooms with twin beds. Guests not staying in one of the two suites with private gyms may use the gym at sister Hotel de la Ville about three blocks away. ⊠ *Via San Raffaele 6, near Duomo, 20121* ☎ *02/7208951* 🖷 *02/ 866526* ⊕ *www.sinahotels.it* 🛏 *21 rooms, 2 suites* ⟁ *Restaurant, room service, minibars, cable TV, Wi-Fi, bar, laundry service, business services, no-smoking rooms* ▭ *AE, DC, MC, V* ¶⚬¶ *EP* Ⓜ *Duomo.*

★ **$$$$** ▦ **Principe di Savoia.** Milan's *grande dame* has all the trappings of an exquisite traditional hotel: lavish mirrors, drapes, and carpets, and Milan's largest guest rooms, outfitted with eclectic fin-de-siècle furnishings. Forty-eight "Deluxe Mosaic" rooms (named for the glass mosaic panels in their ample bathrooms) are even larger, and the three-bedroom presidential suite features its own marble pool. The Winter Garden is an elegant aperitivo spot, and the Acanto restaurant has garden seating. Lighter food is served in the Lobby Lounge. ⊠ *Piazza della Repubblica 17, Porta Nuova, 20124* ☎ *02/62301* 🖷 *02/653799* ⊕ *www.hotelprincipedisavoia.com* 🛏 *269 rooms, 132 suites* ⟁ *2 restaurants, room service, minibars, cable TV, Wi-Fi, health club, indoor pool, spa, bar, laundry service, business services, meeting rooms, convention center, no-smoking rooms* ▭ *AE, DC, MC, V* ¶⚬¶ *EP* Ⓜ *Repubblica.*

$$$–$$$$ ▦ **Hotel Spadari al Duomo.** That this hotel is owned by an architect's family shows in the details, including architect-designed furniture and a fine collection of contemporary art. The owner's idea of creating a hotel/gallery extends to the guest rooms, where paintings by young Milanese artists are on rotating display. For all the artistic accents, this is still a comfortable, homey hotel, with an inviting frescoed breakfast room and many rooms with private terraces. Personal touches, such as a collection of short stories on the turned-downed beds, abound. ⊠ *Via Spadari 11, near Duomo, 20123* ☎ *02/72002371* 🖷 *02/861184* ⊕ *www.spadarihotel.com* 🛏 *40 rooms, 3 suites* ⟁ *Minibars, cable TV, Wi-Fi, in-room broadband, bar, no-smoking rooms* ▭ *AE, DC, MC, V* ¶⚬¶ *BP* Ⓜ *Duomo.*

★ **$$–$$$** ▦ **Antica Locanda dei Mercanti.** On a quiet side street off Via Dante, this 14-room hotel is minutes—and light-years—away from Milan's bustling downtown. Rooms are on the second and third floors (four have private terraces), but you check in at ground-floor reception and take breakfast in the dining room—both added in 2006. Despite the renovations, prices at this hidden jewel remain in the same category. Reserve early for the terrace rooms. ⊠ *Via San Tomaso 6, Duomo, 20121* ☎ *02/8054080* 🖷 *02/8054090* ⊕ *www.lalocanda.it* 🛏 *14 rooms* ⟁ *Cable TV, Wi-Fi, bar* ▭ *MC, V* ¶⚬¶ *EP* Ⓜ *Cordusio.*

$$–$$$ ▦ **Ariston.** "Bio-architectural" principles prevail at this hotel near the Duomo, which was built using natural materials and has ionized air circulating throughout. As you might expect from such a progressive-minded place, the buffet breakfast includes organic foods. There's Internet access for free in the lobby (and for a fee in the rooms), and bicycles are available in summer. The location is close to the lively Porta Ticinese shops and restaurants and the young people's fashion mecca, Via Torino. Although a longish walk from the nearest subway stop, the Duomo, it is well served by tram. ⊠ *Largo Carrobbio 2, Duomo, 20123* 🕾 *02/ 72000556* 🖷 *02/72000914* ⊕ *www.aristonhotel.com* ⟆ *52 rooms* △ *Minibars, cable TV, in-room broadband, bicycles, bar, laundry service, parking (fee), no-smoking rooms* ▭ *AE, DC, MC, V* ⃝|*BP* Ⓜ *Duomo.*

\$\$–\$\$\$ 🖽 **Hotel Gran Duca di York.** This small hotel has spare but classically elegant and efficient rooms—four with private terraces. Built around a courtyard, the 1890s building was originally a seminary and still belongs to a religious institution. With an ideal location a few steps west of the Duomo, it offers exceptional value for Milan. ⊠ *Via Moneta 1/a, Duomo, 20123* 🕾 *02/874863* 🖷 *02/8690344* ⊕ *www.ducadiyork. com* ⟆ *33 rooms* △ *Minibars, cable TV, bar, laundry service, meeting rooms, parking (fee), no-smoking floor* ▭ *AE, MC, V* ⊗ *Closed Aug.* ⃝|*EP* Ⓜ *Cordusio.*

\$\$ 🖽 **Antica Locanda Leonardo.** Convenient to the church where you'll find *The Last Supper* and near the city center, this small hotel is in an inner courtyard, making it one step removed from the traffic outside. It's been run by the same family for more than 40 years, and the staff is welcoming and helpful. The rooms overlook the courtyard or the garden, which was renovated in 2006. ⊠*Corso Magenta 78, Sant'Ambrogio, 20123* 🕾*02/ 463317* 🖷 *02/48019012* ⊕ *www.anticalocandaleonardo.com* ⟆ *20 rooms* △ *Cable TV, Wi-Fi, bar, laundry service* ▭ *AE, DC, MC, V* ⊗ *Closed Dec. 31–Jan. 7 and 3 wks in Aug.* ⃝|*BP* Ⓜ *Sant'Ambrogio.*

\$–\$\$ 🖽 **Hotel Vittoria.** You'll forgive this hotel its baroque decor when you see how it reflects the owners' southern Italian approach to hospitality: they're eager to please, and they're proud of renovations that are bringing the telecommunications up to date and making rooms wheelchair accessible. Although out of the central tourist area (on a quiet residential street), the Vittoria is on the bus line from Linate airport and on other major tram lines. It's about a twenty-minute walk from the Duomo, and there's a good selection of restaurants nearby. English-speaking staff (not a given in smaller hotels) and spotless, comfortable rooms make this an attractive haven after a day out. ⊠ *Via Pietro Calvi 32, East Central Milan, 20129* 🕾 *02/5456520* 🖷 *02/55190246* ⊕ *www.hotelvittoriamilano.it* ⟆ *40 rooms* △ *In-room safes, minibars, cable TV, no-smoking rooms, parking (fee), meeting room* ▭ *AE, DC, MC, V* ⃝|*EP.*

★ \$–\$\$ 🖽 **London.** On a quiet side street just round the corner from the Castello Sforzesco, the London offers a good value and convenient access to Milan's main sights. Well-appointed rooms are in a 1960s-era building. ⊠ *Via Rovello 3, Castello, 20121* 🕾 *02/72020166* 🖷 *02/8057037* ⊕ *www. hotellondonmilano.com* ⟆ *29 rooms* △ *Cable TV, bar, laundry service, Internet* ▭ *MC, V* ⊗ *Closed Dec. 23–Jan. 6* ⃝|*EP* Ⓜ *Cairoli.*

\$ 🖽 **Gritti.** The Gritti is a bright, cheerful hotel with adequate rooms and good views (from the inside upper floor) of tiled roofs and the gold Madonnina statue on top of the Duomo, a few hundred yards away. ⊠ *Piazza Santa Maria Beltrade 4, north end of Via Torino, Duomo, 20123* 🕾 *02/ 801056* 🖷 *02/89010999* ⊕ *www.hotelgritti.com* ⟆ *48 rooms* △ *Minibars, cable TV, bar, laundry service, meeting room, parking (fee)* ▭ *AE, DC, MC, V* ⃝|*BP* Ⓜ *Duomo.*

Nightlife & the Arts

The Arts

For events likely to be of interest to non-Italian speakers, see *Hello Milano* (www.hellomilano.it.), a monthly magazine available at the tourist office on Via Marconi, or *The American* (www.theamericanmag.com), which is available at international bookstores and newsstands, and which has a thorough cultural calendar. The tourist office publishes the monthly *Milano Mese*, which also includes some listings in English.

MUSIC   The two halls belonging to the **Conservatorio** (⊠ Via del Conservatorio 12, Duomo ☎02/7621101 Ⓜ San Babila) host some of the leading names in classical music. The modern **Auditorium di Milano** (⊠ Corso San Gottardo, at Via Torricelli, Conchetta ☎ 02/83389201), known for its excellent acoustics, is home to the **Orchestra Verdi,** founded by Milan-born conductor Richard Chailly. The season, which runs from September to June, includes many top international performers. The **Teatro Dal Verme** (⊠ Via San Giovanni sul Muro 2, Castello ☎ 02/87905201 Ⓜ Cairoli) stages frequent classical music concerts from October to May.

OPERA   Milan's hallowed **Teatro alla Scala** (⊠ Piazza della Scala ☎ 02/86077 ⊕ www.teatroallascala.org) has undergone a complete renovation, with everything refreshed, refurbished, or replaced except the building's exterior walls. Special attention was paid to the acoustics, which have always been excellent. The season runs from early December to mid-June. Plan well in advance, as tickets sell out quickly.

THEATER   Milan's **Piccolo Teatro** (☎ 02/72333222 ⊕ www.piccoloteatro.org) is made up of three separate venues, each of which is noted for its excellent productions. The intimate **Teatro Paolo Grassi** (⊠ Via Rovello 2, Castello) is the traditional headquarters of the theater, and is named after its founder. The spacious, modern **Teatro Giorgio Strehler** (⊠ Largo Greppi 1, east of Piazzo Castello, Brera) takes its name from a famous Italian theater director. It hosts dance and musical performances as well as plays. The horseshoe-shape **Teatro Studio** (⊠ Via Rivoli 6, Castello) is a popular venue for experimental theater and music concerts.

Nightlife

BARS   Milan has a bar somewhere to suit any style; those in the better hotels are respectably chic and popular meeting places for Milanese as well as tourists. The bar of the **Sheraton Diana Majestic** (⊠ Viale Piave 42 ☎ 02/20581), which has a splendid garden, is a prime meeting place for young professionals and the fashion people from the showrooms of the Porta Venezia neighborhood. **El Brellin** (⊠ Vicolo Lavandai at Alzaia Naviglio Grande ☎ 02/58101351) is one of the many bars in the arty Navigli district. For a quiet drink in a sophisticated setting, try **Fiori Oscuri** (⊠ Via Fiori Oscuri 3 ☎ 02/45477057), in the heart of Brera. If you decide to stay for dinner, chefs Giovanni Valsecchi and Luca Marongiu will wow you with their creative Italian cuisine, savored with a fine wine from their cellar. Also in Brera, check out the **Giamaica** (⊠ Via Brera 32 ☎ 02/876723), a traditional hangout for students from the nearby Brera art school. On summer nights this neighborhood pulses with life; street vendors and fortune-tellers jostle for space alongside the outdoor tables.

For a break from the traditional, check out ultratrendy **SHU** (✉ Via Molino delle Armi, Ticinese ☎ 02/58315720), whose gleaming interior looks like a cross between *Star Trek* and Cocteau's *Beauty and the Beast*. The **Trussardi Bar** (✉ Piazza della Scala 5 ☎ 02/80688295) has an enormous plasma screen that keeps hip barflies entertained with video art. Open throughout the day, it's a great place for coffee.

Blue Note (✉ Via Borsieri 37, Garibaldi ☎ 02/69016888 ⊕ www. bluenotemilano.com), the first European branch of the famous New York nightclub, features regular performances by some of the most famous names in jazz, as well as blues and rock concerts. There's a popular jazz brunch on Sunday. Monday evenings are reserved for Italian musicians. For an evening of live music—predominantly rock to jazz—head to perennial favorite **Le Scimmie** (✉ Via Ascanio Sforza 49, Navigli ☎ 02/ 89402874 ⊕ www.scimmie.it). It features international stars, some of whom jet in to play here, while others, including Ronnie Jones, are longtime residents in Milan.

NIGHTCLUBS   **La Banque** (✉ Via Bassano Porrone 6, Scala ☎ 02/86996565 ⊕ www. labanque.it) is an exclusive and expensive bar, restaurant, and dance club, and is great for anything from an aperitivo to a night on the town. The dance floor starts hopping at 10:30 PM. The hip **Café l'Atlantique** (✉ Viale Umbria 42, Porta Romana ☎ 02/55193906 ⊕ www.cafeatlantique. com) is a popular place for dancing the night away and enjoying a generous buffet brunch on Sunday afternoon. **C-Side** (✉ Via Castelbarco 11, Porta Romana ☎ 02/58310682) is near Bocconi University. The music on the dance floor varies but includes Latin favorites.

Hollywood (✉ Corso Como 15/c, Centro Direzionale ☎ 02/6598996 ⊕ www.discotecahollywood.com) continues to be one of the most popular places for the sunglasses set. **Magazzini Generali** (✉ Via Pietrasanta 14, Porta Vigentina ☎ 02/55211313 ⊕ www.magazzinigenerali.it), in what was an abandoned warehouse, is a fun, futuristic venue for dancing and concerts.

Sports

Car Racing

Italy's Formula I fans are passionate about team Ferrari. Huge numbers of them converge on the second Sunday in September for the **Italian Grand Prix,** held 15 km (9 mi) northeast of Milan in Monza. The racetrack was built in 1922 within the **Parco di Monza** (⊕ www.monzanet.it).

Soccer

AC Milan and Inter Milan, two of the oldest and most successful teams in Europe, vie for the heart of soccer-mad Lombardy. For residents, the city is *Milano* but the teams are *Milan,* a vestige of their common founding as the Milan Cricket and Football Club in 1899. When an Italian-led faction broke off in 1908, the new club was dubbed Internazionale (or "Inter") to distinguish it from the bastion of English exclusivity that would become AC Milan (or simply "Milan"). Since then, the picture has become more clouded: although Milan prides itself as the true team

Calcio Crazy

FOR THE VAST MAJORITY of Italians, *il calcio* (soccer) is much more than a national sport—it's a way of life. The general level of passion for the game exceeds that expressed by all but the most die-hard sports fans in the United States. In 2005 there were no fewer than seven prime-time television shows and four major national newspapers dedicated to soccer—not to mention countless radio programs and local TV shows. In a country that's fine-tuned to nuance and inclined to see conspiracy around every corner, controversial referee calls can spark arguments that last weeks. In 2004, debate over questionable rulings in a match between Roma and Juventus (a perennial power from Turin) made it all the way to the floor of Parliament, where conflict between senators actually degenerated into a fistfight.

Nowhere is the passion more feverish than in big soccer cities, of which

Milan is the prime example. It's home to two of the country's dominant teams: AC Milan and F.C. Internazionale (aka, Inter Milan). On game days, it is not unusual to see boisterous bands of fans wandering the city center, team colors draped across their shoulders and rousing team choruses issuing from their mouths. At the stadium, even the most innocuous games are events where chants, insults, and creative banners make crowd-watching an appealing sideshow—especially the banners, which Italians affectionately refer to as *sfotto* ("razzings"). In the 2004 matchup between the Milanese teams, AC Milan fans silenced their rivals by unrolling an enormous banner that made fun of Internazionale's decade-long streak as runners-up, stating simply: "We live your dreams." Adding injury to insult, AC Milan took the game, three goals to one.

---

of the city and of its working class, Inter can more persuasively claim pan-Italian support.

AC Milan and Inter Milan share the use of **San Siro Stadium (Stadio Meazza)** (⊠ Via Piccolomini) during their August–May season. With more than 60,000 of the 85,000 seats appropriated by season-ticket holders and another couple of thousand allocated to visiting fans, tickets to the Sunday games can be difficult to come by. You can purchase advance AC Milan tickets at Cariplo bank branches, including one at Via Verdi 8, or at the club's **Web site** (⊕ www.acmilan.com). Inter tickets are available at Banca Popolare di Milano branches, including one at Piazza Meda 4, or at the club's **Web site** (⊕ www.inter.it). To reach San Siro, take subway Line 1 (red) toward Molino Dorino, exit at the Lotto station, and board a bus for the stadium.

If you're a soccer fan but can't get in to see a game, you might settle for a **stadium tour** (☎ 02/4042432 ⊕ www.sansirotour.com), which includes a visit to the Milan-Inter museum. Tours are available every half hour from Gate 21 from 10 AM to 5 PM, except on game Sundays; they cost €12.50. Call for reservations a few days before your visit.

THE FASHIONISTA'S MILAN

Opera buffs and lovers of Leonardo's *Last Supper,* skip ahead to the next paragraph. No one else should be dismayed to learn that clothing is Milan's greatest cultural achievement. The city is one of the fashion capitals of the world and home base for practically every top Italian designer. The same way art aficionados walk the streets of Florence in a state of bliss, the style-conscious come here to be enraptured.

It all happens in the *quadrilatero della moda,* Milan's toniest shopping district, located just north of the Duomo. Along the cobblestone streets, Armani, Prada, and their fellow *stilisti* sell the latest designs from flagship stores that are as much museums of chic as retail establishments. Any purchase here qualifies as a splurge, but you can have fun without spending a euro—just browse, window-shop, and people-watch. Not into fashion? Think of the experience as art, design, and theater all rolled into one. If you wouldn't visit Florence without seeing the Uffizi, you shouldn't visit Milan without seeing the quadrilatero.

FLORENCE HAS THE *DAVID*.

ROME HAS THE PANTHEON.

MILAN HAS THE CLOTHES.

On these pages we give a selective, street-by-street list of stores in the area. Hours are from around 10 in the morning until 7 at night, Monday through Saturday.

VIA DELLA SPIGA
(east to west)

Prada (No. 1)
☎ 02/76014448
www.prada.com
lingerie: for down-to-the-skin Prada fans

Dolce & Gabbana (No. 2)
☎ 02/795747
www.dolcegabbana.it
women's accessories

Agnona (No. 3)
☎ 02/76316530
www.agnona.com

women's clothes:
Ermenegildo excellence
for women

Gio Moretti (No. 4)
☎ 02/76003186
women's and men's
clothes: many labels, as
well as books, CDs,
flowers, and an art
gallery

Sergio Rossi (No. 5)
☎ 02/76390927
www.sergiorossi.com
men's shoes

Bulgari Italia (No. 6)
☎ 02/777001
www.bulgari.com
jewelry, fragrances,
accessories

cross Via Sant'Andrea

Sergio Rossi (No. 15)
☎ 02/76002663
www.sergiorossi.com
women's shoes

Fay (No. 16)
☎ 02/76017597
www.fay.it
women's and men's
clothes, accessories: a
flagship store, designed
by Philip Johnson

Prada (No. 18)
☎ 02/76394336
www.prada.com
accessories

Giorgio Armani (No. 19)
☎ 02/783511
www.giorgioarmani.com
accessories

Tod's (No. 22)
☎ 02/76002423
www.tods.com
shoes and handbags:
the Tod's flagship store

Dolce & Gabbana (No. 26)
☎ 02 76001155
www.dolcegabbana.it
women's clothes, in a
baroque setting

✔ **Just Cavalli** (No. 30)
☎ 02/76390893
www.robertocavalli.net
**Women's and men's
clothes, plus a café
serving big salads and
carpaccio. It's the
offspring of the Just
Cavalli Café in Parco
Sempione, one of the
hottest places in town
for drinks (with or
without dinner).**

Moschino (No. 30)
☎ 02/76004320
www.moschino.it
women's, men's, and
children's clothes: Chic
and Cheap, so they say

Roberto Cavalli (No. 42)
☎ 02/76020900
www.robertocavalli.net
women's and men's
clothes, accessories:
3,200 square feet of
Roberto Cavalli

Marni (No. 50)
☎ 02 76317327
www.marni.com
women's clothes

VIA MONTENAPOLEONE
(east to west)

Fratelli Rossetti (No. 1)
☎ 02/76021650
www.rossetti.it
shoes

Louis Vuitton (No. 2)
☎ 02/7771711
www.vuitton.com
leather goods, acces-
sories, women's clothes

Armani Collezioni (No. 2)
☎ 02/76390068
www.giorgioarmani.com
women's and men's
clothes: the "white label"

Tanino Crisci (No. 3)
☎ 02/76021264
www.taninocrisci.com
women's and men's
shoes, leather goods

Etro (No. 5)
☎ 02/76005049
www.etro.it
women's and men's
clothes, leather goods,
accessories

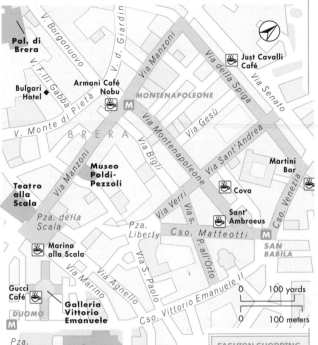

Bottega Veneta (No. 5)
☎ 02/76024495
www.bottegaveneta.com
leather goods: signature
woven-leather bags

Gucci (No. 5/7)
☎ 02/771271
www.gucci.com
women's and men's
clothes

Prada (No. 6)
☎ 02/76020273
www.prada.com
men's clothes

Prada (No. 8)
☎ 02/7771771
www.prada.com
women's clothes

cross Via Sant'Andrea

Armani Junior (No. 10)
☎ 02/783196
www.giorgioarmani.com
children's clothes: for the
under-14 fashionista

Versace (No. 11)
☎ 02/76008528
www.versace.com
everything Versace,
except Versus and
children's clothes

Corneliani (No. 12)
☎ 02/777361
www.corneliani.com

Versace in
Via Montenapoleone

men's clothes: bespoke
tailoring excellence

Cartier
corner Via Gesù
☎ 02/3030421
www.cartier.com

**FASHION SHOPPING,
ACCESSORIZED**

Milan's most ambitious
shops don't just want to
clothe you– they want
to trim your hair, clean
your pores, and put a
cocktail in your hand.
Some "stores with
more" in and around
the quadrilatero are
indicated by a ✔.

jewelry: precious stones,
fine gifts

Valentino
corner Via Santo Spirito
☎ 02/76020285
www.valentino.it
women's clothes: elegant
designs for special
occasions

Loro Piana (No. 27c)
☎ 02/7772901
www.loropiana.it
women's and men's
clothes, accessories:
cashmere everything

REFUELING

If you want refreshments and aren't charmed by the quadrilatero's in-store cafés, try **Cova** (Via Montenapoleone 8, ☎ 02 76000578) or **Sant'Ambroeus** (Corso Matteotti 7, ☎ 02 76000540). Both serve coffee, tea, aperitifs, sandwiches, and snacks in an ambience of starched tablecloths and chandeliers.

Cova's courtyard café

When the hurly-burly's done, head for the **Bulgari Hotel** (Via Fratelli Gabba 7b, ☎ 02/8058051), west of Via Manzoni, for a quiet (if pricey) drink, In summer, the bar extends into a beautiful, mature garden over an acre in size.

VIA SAN PIETRO ALL'ORTO
(east to west)

Versus (No. 10)
☎ 02/76014722
www.versace.com
women's, men's, and children's clothes:
Versace Jeans and Sport

Jimmy Choo (No. 17)
☎ 02/45481770
www.jimmychoo.com
women's and men's shoes

CORSO VENEZIA
(south to north)

Miu Miu (No. 3)
☎ 02/76001799
www.prada.com
women's clothes:
Prada's playful line

D&G (No. 7)
☎ 02/76002450
www.dolcegabbana.it
swimwear, underwear, accessories: Dolce & Gabbana diffusion

✔ **Dolce & Gabbana** (No. 15)
☎ 02/76028485
www.dolcegabbana.it
Men's clothes, sold in a four-story, early 19th-century patrician home. Added features are a barbershop (☎ 02/76408881), a beauty parlor (☎ 02/76408888), and the

Martini Bar, which also serves light lunches.

Borsalino
corner Via Senato
☎ 02/76017072
www.borsalino.com
hats: for people who want to be streets ahead

VIA VERRI
(south to north)

Ermenegildo Zegna (No. 3)
☎ 02/76006437
www.zegna.com.
men's clothes, in the finest fabrics.

Borsalino
Via Verri/corner Via Bigli
☎ 02/76398539
www.borsalino.com
hats

cross Via Bigli

Etro Profumi
corner Via Bigli
☎ 02/76005450
www.etro.it
fragrances

D&G in Via della Spiga

VIA SANT'ANDREA
(south to north)

✔ **Trussardi** (No. 5)
☎ 02/76020380
www.trussardi.com
Women's and men's clothes. The nearby flagship store (Piazza della Scala 5) includes the Trussardi Marino alla Scala Café (☎ 02 80688242), a fashion-forward bar done in stone, steel, slate, and glass. For a more substantial lunch, and views of Teatro alla Scala, head upstairs to the Marino alla Scala Ristorante (☎ 02 80688201), which serves creative Mediterranean cuisine.

Banner (No. 8/A)
☎ 02/76004609
women's and men's clothes: a multibrand boutique

Giorgio Armani (No. 9)
☎ 02/76003234
www.giorgioarmani.com
women's and men's clothes: the "black label"

Moschino (No. 12)
☎ 02/76000832
www.moschino.it
women's clothes: world-renowned window displays

BARGAIN-HUNTING AT THE OUTLETS

Milan may be Italy's richest city, but that doesn't mean all its well-dressed residents can afford to shop at the boutiques of the quadrilatero. Many pick up their designer clothes at outlet stores, where prices can be reduced by 50 percent or more.

Salvagente (Via Bronzetti 16, ☎ 02/76110328, www.salvagentemilano.it) is the top outlet for designer apparel and accessories from both large are small houses. There's a small men's department. To get there, take the 60 bus, which runs from the Duomo to the Stazione Centrale, to the intersection of Bronzetti and Archimede. Look for the green iron gate with the bronze sign, between the hairdressers and an apartment building. No credit cards.

DMagazine Outlet (Via Montenapoleone 26, ☎ 02/76006027, www.dmagazine.it) has bargains in the

✓ Gianfranco Ferré
(No. 15)
☎ 02/794864
www.gianfrancoferre. com
Everything Ferré, plus
a spa providing facials,
Jacuzzis, steam baths,
and mud treatments.
Reservations are
essential (☎
02/76017526), preferably
a week in advance.

Prada (No. 21)
☎ 02 76001426
www.prada.com
women's and men's
sportswear

VIA MANZONI
(south to north)

P-Box (No. 13)
☎ 02/89013000
www.aeffe.com
women's accessories,
shoes, bags: Aeffe group
labels, including Alberta
Ferretti, Philosophy, and
Narciso Rodriquez

Armani in Via Manzoni

✓ Armani Megastore
(No. 31)
☎ 02/72318600
www.giorgioarmani.com
The quadrilatero's most
conspicuous shopping
complex. Along with
many Armani fashions,
you'll find a florist, a
bookstore, a chocolate
shop (offering Armani
pralines), the Armani
Caffè, and Nobu (of the
upscale Japanese
restaurant chain). The
Armani Casa furniture
collection is next door at
number 37.

CORSO COMO
✓ 10 Corso Como
☎ 02/29000727
www.10corsocomo.com
Outside the quadrilatero,
but it's a must see for
fashion addicts. The
bazaar-like 13,000-
square-foot complex
includes women's and
men's boutiques, a bar
and restaurant, a
bookstore, a record shop,
and an art gallery
specializing in
photography. You can
even spend the night (if
you can manage to get a
reservation) at Milan's
most exclusive B&B,
Three Rooms (☎
02/626163). The
furnishings are a modern
design-lover's dream.

Prada store in the Galleria

**GALLERIA VITTORIO
EMANUELE**
(not technically part of
the quadrilatero, but
nearby)

✓ Gucci
☎ 02/8597991
www.gucci.com
Gucci accessories, plus
the world's first Gucci
café. Sit outside behind
the elegant boxwood
hedge and watch the
world go by.

Prada (No. 63-65)
☎ 02/876979
www.prada.com
the original store: look

for the murals
downstairs.

Louis Vuitton
☎ 02/72147011
www.vuitton.com
accessories, women's
and men's shoes,
watches

Tod's
☎ 02/877997
www.tods.com
women's and men's
shoes, leather goods,
accessories

Borsalino (No. 92
☎ 02/804337
www.borsalino.com
hats

Galleria Vittorio Emanuele

midst of the quadrilatero. Names on sale include Armani,
Cavalli, Gucci, and Prada.

DT-Intrend (Galleria San Carlo 6, ☎ 02/76000829)
sells last year's Max Mara, Max & Co, Sportmax, Marella,
Penny Black, and Marina Rinaldi. It's just 300 meters
from the Max Mara store located on Corso Vittorio
Emanuele at the corner of Galleria de Cristoforis.

At the **10 CorsoComo** outlet (Via Tazzoli 3, ☎ 02/29015130,
www.10corsocomo.com) you can find clothes, shoes,
bags, and accessories.

Fans of **Marni** who have a little time on their hands will
want to check out the outlet (Via Tajani 1, ☎ 02/70009735
or 02/71040332, www.marni.com). Take the 61 bus to the
terminus at Largo Murani, from which it's about 200 meters on foot.

Giorgio Armani has an outlet, but it's way out of town—
off the A3, most of the way to Como. The address is
Strada Provinciale per Bregnano 13, in the town of Verte-
mate (☎ 031 887373, www.giorgioarmani.com).

Shopping

The heart of Milan's fashion scene is the **quadrilatero della moda** district north of the Duomo. Here the world's leading designers compete for shoppers' attention, showing off their ultrastylish clothes in stores that are works of high style themselves. You won't find any bargains, but regardless of whether you're making a purchase, the area is a great place for window-shopping and people-watching. But fashion is not limited to one neighborhood. Wander around the **Brera** to find smaller shops with lesser-known names but with some interesting and exciting offerings. The densest concentration is along Via Brera, Via Solferino, and Corso Garibaldi.

Corso Buenos Aires, which runs northeast from the Giardini Pubblici, is a wide boulevard lined with boutiques. It has the highest concentration of clothing stores in Europe, so be prepared to give up half way. Avoid Saturday after 3 PM, when it seems the entire city is here looking for bargains.

Department Stores

Department stores, unlike all but the big Quadrilatero shops, are generally open all day and some evenings.

La Rinascente (⊠ Piazza del Duomo ☎ 02/88521) is Milan's most important department store, carrying everything from Armani cosmetics to Zegna men's suits over eight floors. An outstanding selection of household goods is found in the basement. Check out the restaurants on the top floor, where you can get everything from a quick sandwich to a gourmet meal, with prices to match.

The **Coin** stores, distributed around the city (⊠ Piazza Cinque Giornate 1/A, Piazza, Cantore 12, Corso Vercelli 30-32 and Piazzale Loreto 16 ☎ 02/55192083) have an impressive selection at moderate prices. Check out the handbags, accessories, and costume jewelry on the ground floor. The housewares in the basement are a good value. The eighth-floor Globe bar in the Cinque Giornate store is a fun place to have a drink.

Markets

Weekly open markets selling fruits and vegetables are still a common sight in Milan. Many also sell clothing and shoes. Bargains in designer apparel can be found at the huge **Mercato Papiniano** (⊠ Porta Genova) on Saturday and Tuesday from about 9 to 1. The stalls to look for are at the Piazza Sant'Agostino end of the market. It's very crowded—watch out for pickpockets.

Monday- and Thursday-morning markets in **Mercato di Via S. Marco** (⊠ Brera) cater to the wealthy residents of this central neighborhood. In addition to food stands where you can get cheese, roast chicken, and dried beans and fruits, there are several clothing and shoe stalls that are important stops for some of Milan's most elegant women. Check out the knitwear at Valentino, about midway down on the street side. Tasty

French fries and potato croquettes are available from the chicken stand at the Via Montebello end.

If you collect coins, stamps, or postcards, or if you just want to see Italian collectors in action, go on Sunday morning to the market at **Via Armorari** (⊠ Off Piazza Cordusio, near Duomo). Milan's most comprehensive antiques market is the **Mercatone dell'Antiquario,** held on the last Sunday of each month along the Naviglio Grande. The third Saturday of every month there's a major antiques and flea market on **Via Fiori Chiari,** near Via Brera.

PAVIA, CREMONA & MANTUA

4

Updated by
Denise
Hummel

Once proud medieval fortress towns rivaling Milan in power, these centers of industry and commerce on the Po Plain still play a key role in Italy's wealthiest, most populous region. Pavia is celebrated for its extraordinarily detailed Carthusian monastery, Cremona for its incomparable violin-making tradition. Mantua—the most picturesque of the three—was the home of the fantastically wealthy Gonzaga dynasty for almost 300 years.

Pavia

17 *41 km (25 mi) south of Milan.*

Pavia was once Milan's chief regional rival. The city dates from at least the Roman era and was the capital of the Lombard kings for two centuries (572–774). It was at one time known as "the city of a hundred towers," but only a handful have survived the passing of time. Its prestigious university was founded in 1361 on the site of a 10th-century law school, but has roots that can be traced to antiquity.

The 14th-century **Castello Visconteo** now houses the local **Museo Civico** (Municipal Museum), with an archaeological collection and a picture gallery featuring works by Correggio, Giovanni Bellini, Giambattista Tiepolo, and Vincenzo La Foppa, among others. ⊠ *Viale 11 Febbraio, near Piazza Castello* ☎ *0382/33853* ⊡ *€6* ☉ *Feb.–June and Sept.–Nov., Tues.–Sun. 10–5:45; last entry 5:15. Dec. and Jan., July and Aug., Tues.–Sun. 9–1:30; last entry 12:45.*

In the Romanesque church of **San Pietro in Ciel d'Oro** you can visit the tomb of Christianity's most celebrated convert, St. Augustine, housed in a Gothic marble ark on the high altar. ⊠ *Via Matteotti* ☎ *0382/303040* ☉ *Mon.–Sun. 7–noon and 3–7; Mass Mon.–Sat. 9 and 6:30, Sun. 9, 11, and 6:30.*

The main draw in Pavia is the **Certosa** (Carthusian monastery), 9 km (5½ mi) north of the city center. Its elaborate facade shows the same relish for ornamentation as the Duomo in Milan. The Certosa's extravagant grandeur was due in part to the plan to have it house the tombs of the family of the first duke of Milan, Galeazzo Visconti III (who died during a plague, at age 49, in 1402). The very best marble was used, taken undoubtedly by barge from the quarries of Carrara, roughly 240 km (150 mi) away. Though the floor plan may be Gothic—a cross

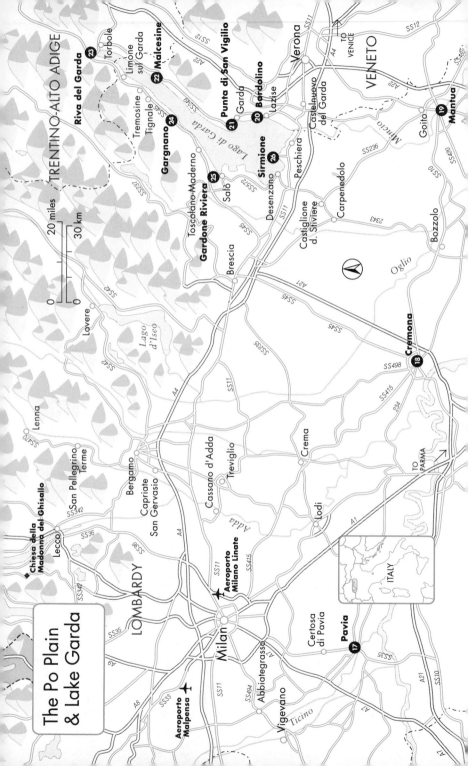

shape divided into a series of squares—the gorgeous fabric that rises above it is triumphantly Renaissance. On the facade, in the lower frieze, are medallions of Roman emperors and Eastern monarchs; above them are low reliefs of scenes from the life of Christ and from the career of Galeazzo Visconti III.

The first duke was the only Visconti to be interred here, and then only some 75 years after his death, in a tomb designed by Gian Cristoforo Romano. Look for it in the right transept. In the left transept is a more-appealing tomb—that of a rather stern middle-age man and a beautiful young woman. The man is Ludovico il Moro Sforza (1452–1508), seventh duke of Milan, who commissioned Leonardo to paint *The Last Supper.* The woman is Ludovico's wife, Beatrice d'Este (1475–97), one of the most celebrated women of her day, the embodiment of brains, culture, birth, and beauty. Married when he was 40 and she was 16, they had enjoyed six years together when she died while giving birth to a still-born child. Ludovico commissioned the sculptor Cristoforo Solari to design a joint tomb for the high altar of Santa Maria delle Grazie in Milan. Originally much larger, the tomb for some years occupied the honored place as planned. Then for reasons that are still mysterious the Dominican monks, who seemed to care no more for their former patron than they did for their faded Leonardo fresco, sold the tomb to their Carthusian brothers to the south. Sadly, part of the tomb and its remains were lost. ⊠ *Certosa, 9 km (5½ mi) north of Pavia* ☎ *0382/925613* ⊕ *www. comune.pv.it/certosadipavia* ⊠ *Free* ☉ *Tues.–Sun. 9–11:30 and 2:30–5.*

Where to Eat

$$$$ ✕ **Locanda Vecchia Pavia al Mulino.** At this sophisticated art nouveau restaurant 150 yards from the Certosa you'll find creative versions of traditional regional cuisine, including *risotto alla certosina* (rice with sturgeon eggs, frogs' legs, and river shrimp). *Casoncelli* (stuffed pasta), *petto d'anatra* (duck breast), and veal cutlet *alla milanese* are done with style, as are the imaginative seafood dishes. For dessert, consider the hot chocolate soufflé with white-chocolate sauce. ⊠ *Via al Monumento 5, Certosa* ☎ *0382/925894* ⊛ *Reservations essential* ▤ *AE, DC, MC, V* ☉ *Closed Mon., 3 wks in Aug., and 3 wks in early Jan. No lunch Wed.*

Cremona

⑱ *104 km (65 mi) east of Pavia, 106 km (66 mi) southeast of Milan.*

Cremona is where the world's best violins are made. Andrea Amati (1510–80) invented the modern instrument here in the 16th century. Though cognoscenti continue to revere the Amati name, it was an apprentice of Amati's nephew for whom the fates had reserved wide and lasting fame. In a career that spanned an incredible 68 years, Antonio Stradivari (1644–1737) made more than 1,200 instruments—including violas, cellos, harps, guitars, and mandolins, in addition to his fabled violins. Labeled simply with a small printed slip reading ANTONIUS STRADIVARIUS CREMONENSIS. FACIEBAT ANNO . . .—the date inserted in a neat italic hand—they remain the most coveted, most expensive stringed instruments in the world.

Strolling about this quiet, medium-size city, you cannot help noting that the violin making continues to flourish. There are, in fact, more than 50 *liutai,* many of them graduates of the Scuola Internazionale di Liuteria (International School of Violin Making). You are usually welcome to these ateliers, where traditional craftsmanship reigns supreme, especially if you are contemplating the acquisition of your own instrument; the tourist office can provide addresses.

Cremona's other claim to fame is *torrone* (nougat), which is said to have been created here in honor of the marriage of Bianca Maria Visconti and Francesco Sforza, which took place in October 1441. The new confection, originally prepared by heating almonds, egg whites, and honey over low heat and shaped and named after the city's tower, was created in symbolic celebration. The annual Festa del Torrone is held in the main piazza on the third Sunday in October.

The **Piazza del Comune,** surrounded by the Duomo, tower, baptistery, and city hall, is distinctive and harmonious: the combination of old brick, rose- and cream-color marble, terra-cotta, and old copper roofs brings Romanesque, Gothic, and Renaissance together with unusual success. Dominating Piazza del Comune is the **Torrazzo** (Big Tower), the city's symbol and perhaps the tallest campanile in Italy, visible for a considerable distance across the Po Plain. It's open to visitors, but in winter hours fluctuate depending on the weather. The tower's astronomical clock is the 1583 original. ⊠ *Piazza del Comune* ◫ €6 ⊗ *Daily 9–6.*

Cremona's Romanesque **Duomo** was consecrated in 1190. Here you'll find the beautiful *Story of the Virgin Mary and the Passion of Christ,* the central fresco of an extraordinary cycle commissioned in 1514 and featuring the work of local artists, including Boccacio Boccancino, Giovan Francesco Bembo, and Altobello Melone. ⊠ *Piazza del Comune* ⊗ *Daily 7:30–noon and 3:30–7.*

Legendary violin maker Antonio Stradivari lived, worked, and died near the verdant square at No. 1 **Piazza Roma.** According to local lore, Stradivari kept each instrument in his bedroom for a month before varnishing, imparting part of his soul before sealing and sending it out into the world. In the center of the park is **Stradivari's grave,** marked by a simple tombstone.

The **Museo Stradivariano** (Stradivarius Museum) in Palazzo Affaitati houses the city's collection of stringed treasures: a viola and five violins, including the golden-orange "Il Cremonese 1715" Stradivarius. Informative exhibits display Stradivari's paper patterns, wooden models, and various tools. ⊠ *Via Ugolani Dati 4* ☎ *0372/407770* ◫ €7 ⊗ *Tues.–Sat. 9–6, Sun. 10–6.*

Where to Stay & Eat

$–$$ ✕ **La Sosta.** This traditional Cremonese restaurant looks to the 16th century for culinary inspiration, following a time-tested recipe for a favored first course, gnocchi *Vecchia Cremona.* The homemade salami is also excellent. To finish off the evening, try the *semifreddo al torroncino* (chilled almond cake) and a dessert wine. ⊠ *Via Sicardo 9* ☎ *0372/456656* ▭ *AE, DC, MC, V* ⊗ *Closed Mon. and 3 wks in Aug. No dinner Sun.*

★ $ ✕ **Centrale.** Close to the cathedral, this old-style trattoria is a favorite among locals for traditional Cremonese fare, such as succulent *cotechino* (pork sausage) and *tortelli di zucca* (a small pasta with pumpkin filling), at moderate prices. ☒ *Vicolo Pertusio 4* ☎ *0372/28701* 🖃 V ⊘ *Closed Thurs. and July.*

$$–$$$ ⊞ **Delle Arti Design Hotel.** The name fits at this central hotel with elegant modern interiors and eclectic designer furniture. The contemporary feel provides a nice contrast to the surrounding historic center. ☒ *Via Bonomelli 8, 26100* ☎*0372/23131* 🖷*0372/21654* ⊕*www.dellearti.com* ⇗*33 rooms* ⌂ *Minibars, cable TV, gym, sauna, bar, meeting rooms, parking (fee), no-smoking rooms* 🖃 *AE, DC, MC, V* ⊘ *Closed Aug. 5–29* ⏵❘ *BP.*

$–$$ ⊞ **Hotel Continental.** This comfortable modern hotel is well equipped to satisfy its international business clientele. At the end of the road to the autostrade, on the periphery of the historic center, the Continental makes a convenient base for those wisely disinclined to navigate old Cremona by car. ☒ *Piazza Libertà 26, 26100* ☎ *0372/434141* 🖷 *0372/454873* ⊕ *www.hotelcontinentalcremona.it* ⇗ *62 rooms* ⌂ *Restaurant, minibars, cable TV, bar, meeting rooms, parking (fee), Internet* 🖃 *AE, DC, MC, V* ⏵❘ *BP.*

Nightlife & the Arts

At the end of May and the beginning of June, Cremona hosts an annual festival in honor of native composer Claudio Monteverdi, the great baroque pioneer of modern opera. For details, contact the **Teatro Ponchielli** (☎ 0372/22010 ⊕ www.teatroponchielli.it).

Shopping

For Cremona's specialty nougat, visit famed **Sperlari** (☒ Via Solferino 25 ☎0372/22346 ⊕www.fieschi1867.com). In addition to nougat, Cremona's best *mostarda* (a condiment made from preserved fruit served with meat and cheese) has been sold from this handsome shop since 1836; Sperlari and parent company Fieschi have grown into a confectionery empire. Look for the historical product display in the back.

Mantua

➒ *192 km (119 mi) southeast of Milan.*

Mantua stands tallest among the ancient walled cities of the Po Plain. Its fortifications are circled on three sides by the passing Mincio River, which long provided Mantua with protection, fish, and a steady stream of river tolls as it meandered from Lake Garda to join the Po. It may not be flashy or dramatic, but Mantua's beauty is subtle and deep, hiding a rich trove of artistic, architectural, and cultural gems beneath its slightly somber facade.

Although Mantua first came to prominence in Roman times as the home of Virgil, its grand monuments date from the glory years of the Gonzaga dynasty. From 1328 until the Austrian Habsburgs sacked the city in 1708, the dukes and marquesses of the Gonzaga clan reigned over a wealthy independent *commune,* and the arts thrived in the relative peace of that period. Raphael's star pupil Andrea Mantegna (1431–1506), who served as court painter for 50 years, was the best known of a succession of artists and architects who served Mantua through the years, and some of his finest work, including his only surviving fresco cycle, can be seen here. Giulio Romano (circa 1499–1546), Mantegna's apprentice, built his masterpiece, Palazzo Te, on an island in the river. Leon Battista Alberti (1404–72), who designed two impressive churches in Mantua, was widely emulated later in the Renaissance.

★ The 500-room **Palazzo Ducale,** the palace that dominates the skyline, was built for the Gonzaga family. Unfortunately, as the Gonzaga dynasty waned in power and prestige, much of the art within the castle was sold or stolen. The highlight is the Camera Degli Sposi—literally, the "Chamber of the Wedded Couple"—where Duke Ludovico and his wife held court. Mantegna painted it over a nine-year period at the height of his power, finishing at age 44. He made a startling advance in painting by organizing the picture plane in a way that systematically mimics the experience of human vision. Even now, more than five centuries later, you can sense the excitement of a mature artist, fully aware of the great importance of his painting, expressing his vision with a masterly, joyous confidence. The circular tromp l'oeil around the vaulted ceiling is famous for the many details that attest to Mantegna's greatness: the three-dimensional quality of the seven Caesars (the Gonzagas saw themselves as successors to the Roman Emperors and paid homage to classical culture throughout the palazzo); the self-portrait of Mantegna (in purple, on the right side of the western fresco), and the dwarf peering out from behind the dress of Ludovico's wife (on the northern fresco). Only 20 people are allowed at a time in the Camera Degli Sposi, and only for 10 minutes at a time. Read about the room before you enter so that you can spend your time looking up.

Walk-up visitors to Mantua's Palazzo Ducale may take a fast-paced guided tour conducted in Italian; signs in each room provide explanations in English. Alternatively, call the **tourist office** (⊠ Piazza Mantegna 6 ☎ 0376/328253) to arrange for English-language tours. ⊠ *Piazza Sordello* ☎ *0376/224832* ☑ *€6.50* ⊗ *Tues.–Sun. 8:45–7:15; last entry 6:30.*

Serious Mantegna aficionados will want to visit the **Casa di Andrea Mantegna,** designed by the artist himself and built around an intriguing circular courtyard, which is usually open to view. The interior can be seen only by appointment or during occasional art exhibitions. ⊠ *Via Acerbi 47* ☎ *0376/360506* ☑ *€3* ⊗ *Tues.–Sun. 10–12:30; also 3–6 during exhibitions.*

Mantegna's tomb is in the first chapel to the left in the basilica of **Sant' Andrea,** most of which was built in 1472. The current structure, a masterwork by the architect Alberti, is the third built on this spot to house the relic of the Precious Blood. The crypt holds two reliquaries containing earth believed to be soaked in the blood of Christ, brought to Mantua by Longinus, the soldier who pierced his side. They are displayed only on Good Friday. ⊠ *Piazza delle Erbe* ⊗ *Daily 8–12:30 and 3–6.*

★ **Palazzo Te** is one of the greatest of all Renaissance palaces, built between 1525 and 1535 by Federigo II Gonzaga. It is the mannerist masterpiece of artist-architect Giulio Romano, who created a pavilion where the strict rules of courtly behavior could be relaxed for libertine pastimes. Romano's purposeful breaks with classical tradition are lighthearted and unprecedented. For example, note the "slipping" triglyphs along the upper edge of the inside courtyard. Two highlights are the Camera di Amore e Psiche ("Room of Cupid and Psyche") that depicts a wedding set among lounging nymphs, frolicking satyrs, and even a camel and

> ### WORD OF MOUTH
>
> "The Palazzo Te in Mantua was awesome–amazing, vivid, huge, almost grotesque frescoes throughout. Well worth the visit in itself, if you are interested much in art/architecture. "
>
> –Hadley

an elephant; and the gasp-producing Camera dei Giganti ("Room of the Giants") that shows Jupiter expelling the Titans from Mount Olympus. The scale of the work is overwhelming; the floor-to-ceiling work completely envelops the viewer. The room's rounded corners, and the river rock covering the original floor, were meant to give it a cavelike feeling. It is a "whisper chamber" in which words softly uttered in one corner can be heard in the opposite one. For fun, note the graffiti from as far back as the 17th century. ⊠ *Viale Te* ☎ *0376/323266* ⊕ *www. centropalazzote.it* ⊡ *€8* ⊗ *Mon. 1–6, Tues.–Sun. 9–5:30.*

Where to Stay & Eat

★ **$$$$** ✕ **Al Bersagliere.** One of Lombardy's best restaurants is this rustic four-room tavern in the tiny riverside hamlet of Goito, 16 km (10 mi) north of Mantua on Route 236. It has been run by a single family for more than 150 years. The fish in particular is excellent, as is a Mantuan classic, frog soup. ⊠ *Via Goitese 260, Goito* ☎ *0376/60007* ⚑ *Reservations essential* ▤ *AE, DC, MC, V* ⊗ *Closed Mon. and Tues., and 3 wks in Aug.*

★ **$$$$** ✕ **Ambasciata.** Heralded by food critics the world over as one of Italy's finest restaurants, Ambasciata (Italian for "embassy") takes elegance and service to extremes that are rarely, if ever, achieved outside Europe. Chef Romano Tamani makes frequent appearances abroad (at New York's Le Cirque 2000, for one) but is at home in tiny Quistello, 20 km (12 mi) southeast of Mantua, where he offers to those willing to make the trek (and pay the bill) an ever-changing array of superlative creations such as *timballo di lasagne verdi con petto di piccione sauté alla crème de Cassis* (green lasagna with breast of pigeon and red currant). ⊠ *Via Martiri di Belfiore 33, Quistello* ☎ *0376/619169* ⚑ *Reservations essential* ▤ *AE, DC, MC, V* ⊗ *Closed Mon., Jan. 1–20, and Aug. 5–25. No dinner Sun.*

$$$–$$$$ ✕ **L'Aquila Nigra.** Down a small side street opposite the Palazzo Ducale, this popular restaurant is set in a former medieval convent, where frescoes grace the walls. Diners choose from such local dishes as *medaglione di anguilla all'aceto balsamico* (medallion of eel with balsamic vinegar), *saltarelli e frittata di zucchine* (lightly fried freshwater shrimp and zucchini), and *petto di faraona in pane grattinata con rosmarino* (breaded guinea fowl with rosemary). Reservations are recommended. ⊠ *Vicolo Bonacolsi 4* ☎ *0376/327180* ▤ *DC, MC, V* ⊗ *Closed 2 wks in Aug., Sun. (except for Sun. lunch in Apr., May, Sept., and Oct.), and Mon.*

$$–$$$ ✕ **Antica Osteria ai Ranari.** This mellow, inviting restaurant owned by the Giardi family serves such Mantuan specialties as *tortelli di zucca* (homemade pasta stuffed with sweetly spiced pumpkin in sage butter) and *ranne fritte* (fried frogs' legs). For dessert, try *sbrisolona*, which means "crumbs" in Mantuan dialect. This crumb cake with whole almonds and a deceptively large amount of butter is served warm and is meant to be eaten with the hands. ✉ *Via Trieste 11* ☎ *0376/328431* ⊟ *AE, D, MC, V* ⊘ *Closed Mon.*

$$–$$$ ✕ **Ristorante Pavesi.** Locals have been coming to this central restaurant for delicious food at reasonable prices since 1918. The menu changes every other month; homemade pasta is always a good bet. In warmer months you can dine on Mantua's handsome main square. ✉ *Piazza Erbe 13* ☎ *0376/323627* ⊟ *AE, DC, MC, V.*

$$$ ▥ **San Lorenzo.** As if spacious, comfortable rooms, authentic early-19th-century furnishings, and a prime location weren't enough, many rooms here have wonderful views overlooking Piazza Concordia, and some have private terraces. In summer, breakfast is served on the roof. ✉ *Piazza Concordia 14, 46100* ☎ *0376/220500* 🖷 *0376/327194* ⊕ *www.hotelsanlorenzo.it* ⤳ *32 rooms* ◌ *Minibars, cable TV, bar, meeting rooms, free parking* ⊟ *AE, DC, MC, V* ⦿ *BP.*

$–$$ ▥ **Hotel Broletto.** Here you'll get comfortable, clean digs in a perfect location. The furniture was new in the '60s and has stuck around long enough to come back in style. ✉ *Via Accademia 1, 46100* ☎ *0376/223678* 🖷 *0376/221297* ⤳ *16 rooms* ◌ *Minibars, cable TV* ⊟ *AE, DC, MC, V* ⊘ *Closed part of July and late Dec.* ⦿ *BP.*

LAKE GARDA

Updated by
Denise
Hummel

Lake Garda has had a perennial attraction for travelers and writers alike; even essayist Michel de Montaigne (1533–92), whose 15 months of travel journals contain not a single other reference to nature, paused to admire the view down the lake from Torbole, which he called "boundless."

Lake Garda is 50 km (31 mi) long, ranges roughly 1 km–16 km (½ mi–10 mi) wide, and is as much as 1,135 feet deep. The terrain is flat at the lake's southern base and mountainous at its northern tip. As a consequence, its character varies from stormy inland sea to crystalline Nordic-style fjord. It's the biggest lake in the region and by most accounts the cleanest. Drivers should take care on the hazardous hairpin turns on the lake road.

Bardolino

❷⓿ *24 km (15 mi) northeast of Sirmione, 157 km (97 mi) east of Milan.*

Famous for its red wine, Bardolino hosts the **Cura dell'Uva** (Grape Cure Festival) in late September–early October. It's a great excuse to indulge in the local vino, which is light, dry, and often slightly sparkling. (Bring aspirin, just in case the cure turns out to be worse than the disease.)

Bardolino is one of the most popular summer resorts on the lake. It stands on the eastern shore at the wider end of the lake. Here there are two handsome Romanesque churches: **San Severo,** from the 11th century, and **San Zeno,** from the 9th. Both are in the center of the small town.

Punta di San Vigilio

㉑ *6 km (4 mi) north of Bardolino, 163 km (101 mi) east of Milan.*

Just about everyone agrees that this is the prettiest spot on Garda's eastern shore. Punta di San Vigilio is full of cypresses from the gardens of the 15th-century **Villa Guarienti di Brenzone** (⊠ Frazione Punta San Vigilio 1); the villa itself is closed to the public.

Malcesine

㉒ *28 km (17 mi) north of Punta di San Vigilio, 190 km (118 mi) east of Milan.*

One of the loveliest areas along the upper eastern shore of Lake Garda, Malcesine is principally known as a summer resort with sailing and windsurfing schools. It tends to be crowded in season, but there are nice walks from the town toward the mountains. Six ski lifts and more than 11 km (7 mi) of runs of varying degrees of difficulty serve skiers. Dominating the town is the 12th-century **Castello Scaligero,** built by Verona's dynastic Della Scala family.

The futuristic *funivia* (cable car) zipping visitors to the top of **Monte Baldo** (5,791 feet) is unique because it rotates. After a 10-minute ride you're high in the Veneto, where you can stroll while enjoying spectacular views of the lake. You can ride the cable car down or bring along a mountain bike (or hang glider) for the descent. ⊠ *Via Navene Vecchia 12* ☎ *045/7400206* ⊕ *www.funiviamalcesine.com* 🎟 *€13 round-trip* ☉ *Daily 8–4.*

Riva del Garda

㉓ *18 km (11 mi) north of Malcesine, 180 km (112 mi) east of Milan.*

Set on the northern tip of Lake Garda against a dramatic backdrop of jagged cliffs and miles of beaches, Riva del Garda is the lake's quintessential resort town. The old city, set around a pretty harbor, was built up during the 15th century, when it was a strategic outpost of the Venetian Republic.

The heart of Riva del Garda, the lakeside **Piazza 3 Novembre** is surrounded by medieval palazzi. Standing in the piazza and looking out onto the lake you can understand why Riva del Garda has become a windsurfing mecca: air currents ensure good breezes on even the most sultry midsummer days.

The **Torre Apponale,** predating the Venetian period by three centuries, looms above the medieval residences of the main square; its crenellations recall its defensive purpose.

Where to Stay & Eat

$$$ ✕ **Castel Toblino.** A lovely stop for a lakeside drink or a romantic dinner, this castle is right on a lake in Sarche, about 20 km (12 mi) north of Riva toward Trento. The compound is said to have been a prehistoric, then Roman, village, and was later associated with the Church of Trento. Bernardo Clesio had it rebuilt in the 16th century in the Renaissance style. It's now a sanctuary of fine food, serving such local specialties as lake fish and guinea fowl. ⊠ *Via Caffaro 1, Sarche* ☎ *0461/864036* 🚘 *MC, V* ⊘ *Closed Tues. and mid-Nov.–Feb.*

$$$–$$$$ 🏨 **Hotel du Lac et du Parc.** Riva's most splendid hotel has elegance befitting its cosmopolitan name, with personalized service rarely found on Lake Garda since its aristocratic heyday. The airy public spaces include a dining room, bar, and beautifully manicured private garden leading to the public beach. The rooms are well appointed and comfortable; be sure to ask for air-conditioning. The outdoor pool has separate areas for adults and children. ⊠ *Viale Rovereto 44, 38066* ☎ *0464/566600* 🚘 *0464/566566* ⊕ *www.dulacetduparc.com* ⇥ *164 rooms, 5 suites* ⚖ *2 restaurants, minibars, cable TV, 2 tennis courts, 2 pools (1 indoor), gym, hair salon, sauna, Turkish bath, beach, bar, free parking* 🚘 *DC, MC, V* ⊘ *Closed Nov.–Mar.* ⁙⁙ *BP.*

$$$ 🏨 **Hotel Sole.** Within a lakeside 15th-century palazzo in the center of town, this lovely, understated hotel offers comfortable, affordable rooms. The terraced front rooms open to breathtaking views of the lake, and a secluded rooftop terrace is a perfect retreat from crowded beaches in summer. ⊠ *Piazza 3 Novembre 35, 38066* ☎ *0464/552686* 🚘 *0464/ 552811* ⊕ *www.hotelsole.net* ⇥ *52 rooms* ⚖ *Restaurant, room service, in-room safes, refrigerators, cable TV, sauna, bicycles, bar, parking (fee)* 🚘 *AE, DC, MC, V* ⁙⁙ *BP.*

$$–$$$ 🏨 **Luise.** This cozy, reasonably priced hotel has great amenities, including a big garden and a large swimming pool. The restaurant, La Limonaia, is recommended for its Trentino specialties. ⊠ *Viale Rovereto 9, 38066* ☎ *0464/550858* 🚘 *0464/554250* ⊕ *www.feelinghotelluise.com* ⇥ *68 rooms* ⚖ *Restaurant, minibars, cable TV, tennis court, pool, laundry facilities, no-smoking rooms* 🚘 *AE, DC, MC, V* ⁙⁙ *BP.*

Sports

Contact **Circolo Surf Torbole** (⊠ Torbole sur Garda ☎ 0464/505385 ⊕ www.circolosurftorbole.com) for news on windsurfing in the area.

EN ROUTE After passing the town of Limone—where it is said the first lemon trees in Europe were planted—take the fork to the right about 5 km (3 mi) north of Gargnano and head to Tignale. The view from the Madonna di Monte Castello church, some 2,000 feet above the lake, is spectacular. Adventurous travelers will want to follow this pretty inland mountain road to Tremosine; be warned that the road winds its way up the mountain through hairpin turns and blind corners that can test even the most experienced drivers.

Gargnano

㉔ *30 km (19 mi) south of Riva del Garda, 144 km (89 mi) east of Milan.*

This small port town was an important Franciscan center in the 13th century, and now comes alive in the summer months when German tourists, many of whom have villas here, crowd the small pebble beach. An Austrian flotilla bombarded the town in 1866, and some of the houses still bear marks of cannon fire. Mussolini owned two houses in Gargnano: one is now a language school and the other, Villa Feltrinelli, has been restored and reopened as a luxury hotel.

Where to Stay & Eat

$$$$ ✕ **La Tortuga.** This rustic trattoria is more sophisticated than it first appears, with an extensive wine cellar and nouvelle-style twists on local dishes. Specialties include *agnello con rosmarino e timo* (lamb with rosemary and thyme), *persico con rosmarino* (perch with rosemary), and *carpaccio d'anatra all'aceto balsamico* (goose carpaccio with balsamic vinegar). ✉ *Via XXIV Maggio at small harbor* ☎ *0365/71251* 🖷 *0365/71938* 🖃 *DC, MC, V* ☻ *Closed Tues. No lunch Dec.–Mar.*

$$$$ 🏨 **Villa Feltrinelli.** This 1892 art nouveau villa hotel, named for the Italian publishing family that used to vacation here, is immersed in private gardens and faces the lake. Meticulously restored, it has frescoed ceilings, wood paneling, and original tile floors. The rooms are spacious and equipped with every luxury (as befits the final bill). If you can afford it, take the tower room. There's an extensive library open to guests. ✉ *Via Rimembranza 38/40, 25084* ☎ *0365/798000* 🖷 *0365/798001* 🌐 *www.villafeltrinelli.com* ⟲ *21 rooms* 🍴 *Restaurant, room service, minibars, cable TV, pool, bar, laundry service, business services, no-smoking rooms* 🖃 *AE, DC, MC, V* ☻ *Closed late Oct.–Easter* ¶Ol *BP.*

¢ 🏨 **Hotel Bartabel.** This cozy hotel on the main street offers comfortable accommodations at a rock-bottom price. The restaurant has an elegant terrace overlooking the lake. ✉ *Via Roma 39, 25084* ☎ *0365/713300* 🖷 *0365/790009* ⟲ *10 rooms* 🍴 *Restaurant; no a/c* 🖃 *AE, DC, MC, V* ☻ *Closed mid- to late Nov.–late Dec. Restaurant closed Mon.* ¶Ol *EP.*

Sports & the Outdoors

The **Upper Brescian Garda Park** stretches over nine municipalities on the western side of the lake, from Salò to Limone, covering 380 square km (147 square mi). Call the **Limone Hotel Owners Association** (✉ Via Quattro Novembre 2/C ☎ 0365/954720) for trail and bicycle-rental information. They're also the people to contact if you'd like to take part in one of the free treks led by the Gruppo Alpini Limone every Sunday from June to September.

Gardone Riviera

㉕ *12 km (7 mi) south of Gargnano, 139 km (86 mi) east of Milan.*

Gardone Riviera, a once-fashionable 19th-century resort now delightfully faded, is the former home of the flamboyant Gabriele d'Annunzio (1863–1938), one of Italy's greatest modern poets. D'Annunzio's estate, **Il Vittoriale,** perched on the hills above the town, is an elaborate memorial to himself, filled with the trappings of conquests in art, love, and war (of which the largest is a ship's prow in the garden), and complete with an imposing mausoleum. ✉ *Gardone Riviera* ☎ *0365/296511* 🌐 *www.vittoriale.it* 🎟 *€11 for house or museum, €16 for both* ☻ *Grounds Apr.–Sept., daily 8:30–8; Oct.–Mar., daily 9–5. House and museum Apr.–Sept., Tues.–Sun. 9:30–7; Oct.–Mar., Tues.–Sun. 9–1 and 2–5.*

More than 2,000 Alpine, subtropical, and Mediterranean species thrive at the **Giardino Botanico Hruska.** ✉ *Via Roma* ☎ *0365/20347* 🎟 *€7* ☻ *Mar. 15–Oct. 15, daily 9:30–6:30.*

OFF THE
BEATEN
PATH

SALÒ MARKET – Four kilometers (2½ mi) south of Gardone Riviera is the enchanting lakeside town of Salò, which history buffs may recognize as the capital of the ill-fated Social Republic set up in 1943 by the Germans after they liberated Mussolini from the Gran Sasso. Every Saturday morning an enormous market is held in the Piazza dei Martiri della Libertà, with great bargains on everything from household goods to clothing to foodstuffs. In August or September a lone vendor often sells locally unearthed *tartufi neri* (black truffles) at affordable prices.

Where to Stay & Eat

★ $$$–$$$$ ✕ Villa Fiordaliso. The pink-and-white lakeside Villa Fiordaliso—once home to Claretta Petacci, given to her by Benito Mussolini—is a high-quality restaurant, but it also has seven tastefully furnished rooms, some overlooking the lake. The Claretta Suite is where Mussolini and Petacci were said to have carried on an affair. The art nouveau restaurant features seasonal ingredients such as zucchini flowers and porcini mushrooms, paramount in salads and soups. ⊠ *Corso Zanardelli 150* ☎ *0365/20158* 🖷 *0365/290011* ⊕ *www.villafiordaliso.it* ⇆ *6 rooms, 1 suite* ⚬ *Restaurant, cable TV, free parking* ☰ *AE, DC, MC, V* ⊘ *Closed mid-Nov.–mid-Feb. Restaurant closed Mon. No lunch Tues.* ⦿ *BP.*

★ $$$–$$$$ Villa del Sogno. A narrow winding road takes you from town to this imposing villa, which surveys the valley and the lake below it. The large hotel terrace and the quiet surrounding grounds create a sense of escape. You may think twice about a busy sightseeing itinerary once you've settled into position in the sun, cool drink in hand. ⊠ *Corso Zanardelli 107, 52083* ☎ *0365/290181* 🖷 *0365/290230* ⊕ *www.villadelsogno. it* ⇆ *26 rooms, 5 suites* ⚬ *Restaurant, tennis court, pool* ☰ *AE, DC, MC, V* ⊘ *Closed late Oct.–late Mar.* ⦿ *BP.*

$$–$$$$ Grand Hotel Fasano. A former 19th-century hunting lodge between Gardone and Maderno, the Fasano has matured into a seasonal hotel of a high standard. To one side you face the deep waters of Lake Garda; on the others you're surrounded by a 31,080-square-km (12,000-square-mi) private park where the original Austrian owners no doubt spent their days chasing game. Besides myriad activities on the water, there are two golf courses in the vicinity. All the rooms have a lake view. There are older rooms filled with antiques, but these lack air-conditioning. ⊠ *Corso Zanardelli 190, 25083* ☎ *0365/290220* 🖷 *0365/290221* ⊕ *www.ghf. it* ⇆ *68 rooms* ⚬ *Restaurant, minibars, cable TV, tennis court, indoor pool, beach, waterskiing, free parking; no a/c in some rooms* ☰ *No credit cards* ⊘ *Closed mid-Oct.–mid-May* ⦿ *BP.*

★ $$$ Gran Hotel Gardone. Directly facing the lake, this majestic 1800s palace is surrounded by an attractive landscaped garden. Nearly all the rooms look out over the water, and all bathrooms have been renovated in marble. The ground-floor Winnie's Bar, named after Winston Churchill, a frequent guest, envelopes you in charming art nouveau furniture and decorations. ⊠ *Via Zanardelli 84, 25083* ☎ *0365/20261* 🖷 *0365/ 22695* ⊕ *www.grangardone.it* ⇆ *143 rooms, 25 suites* ⚬ *Minibars, cable TV, pool, sauna, laundry service, meeting rooms, parking (fee)* ☰ *AE, DC, MC, V* ⊘ *Closed mid-Oct.–Mar.* ⦿ *BP.*

¢   Villa Maria Elisabetta. Many of the rooms in this charming hotel run by a group of hospitable nuns have views of Lago di Garda. You can sit in the hotel's garden or take one of the ground's trails down for a dip in the lake or a bask in the sun. ✉ *Corso Zanardelli 180, 25083* ☎ *0365/20206* 🖷 *0365/2020818* 🖶 *42 rooms* ⚐ *Restaurant, bar; no a/c, no room TVs* 🖃 *No credit cards* ⊗ *Closed Oct. 18–Dec. 18* ⦿ *BP.*

Nightlife & the Arts

Gardone's tranquillity is its greatest attraction, but that doesn't inhibit conviviality. Visitors and locals alike relish a *passeggiata* (stroll) along the lakefront, stopping perhaps to enjoy an ice cream or aperitif. **La Terrazza** (✉ Via Zanardelli 190 ☎ 0365/290220), in the Grand Hotel Fasano, is particularly elegant. Winston Churchill reputedly enjoyed more than a few brandies in the belle-epoque surroundings.

Sirmione

★ ❷ *138 km (86 mi) east of Milan.*

Dramatically rising out of Lake Garda is the enchanting town of Sirmione. "*Paene insularum, Sirmio, insularumque ocelle,*" sang Catullus in a homecoming poem: "it is the jewel of peninsulas and islands, both." The forbidding Castello Scaligero stands guard behind the small bridge connecting Sirmione to the mainland; beyond, cobbled streets wind their way through medieval arches past lush gardens, stunning lake views, and gawking crowds. Originally a Roman resort town, Sirmione served under the dukes of Verona and later Venice as Garda's main point of defense. It has now reclaimed its original function, bustling with visitors in summer. Cars aren't allowed into town; parking is available by the tourist office at the entrance.

Locals will almost certainly tell you that the so-called **Grotte di Catullo** (Grottoes of Catullus) was once the site of the villa of Catullus (87–54 BC), one of the greatest pleasure-seeking poets of all time. Present archaeological wisdom, however, does not concur, and there is some consensus that this was the site of two villas of slightly different periods, dating from about the 1st century AD. But never mind—the view through the cypresses and olive trees is lovely, and even if Catullus didn't have a villa here he is closely associated with the area and undoubtedly did have a villa nearby. The ruins are at the top of the isthmus and are poorly signposted: walk through the historic center and past the various villas to the top of the spit; the entrance is on the right. A small museum offers a brief overview of the ruins (on the far wall); for guided group tours in English, call 02/20421469. ✉ *Via Catullo Sirmione, Sirmione* ☎ *030/916157* 🖆 *€4* ⊗ *Mar.–mid-Oct., Tues.–Sun. 8:30–7; mid-Oct.–Feb., Tues.–Sun. 8:30–5.*

The **Castello Scaligero** was built, along with almost all the other castles on the lake, by the Della Scala family. As hereditary rulers of Verona for more than a century before control of the city was seized by the Visconti in 1402, they counted Garda among their possessions. You can go inside to take in the nice view of the lake from the tower, or you can swim at the nearby beach. ✉ *Piazza Castello, Sirmione* ☎ *030/916468* 🖆 *€4* ⊗ *Tues.–Sun 8:30–7.*

OFF THE
BEATEN
PATH

GARDALAND AMUSEMENT PARK – This park has more than 40 different rides and waterslides, making it Italy's largest amusement park. It's 12 km (8 mi) east of Sirmione. ☒ *Castelnuovo del Garda* ☎ 045/6449777 ⊕ *www.gardaland.it* 🖃 *€25.50 adults, €21.50 children* ☺ *July and Aug., daily 9* AM*–midnight; Apr.–June and Sept., daily 9–6:30; Oct., weekends 9–6:30.*

Where to Stay & Eat

$$$–$$$$ ╳ **La Rucola.** Next to Sirmione's castle, this elegant, intimate restaurant has a creative menu, with seafood and meat dishes accompanied by a good choice of wines. Three fixed-price menus are available. ☒ *Via Strentelle 3* ☎ 030/916326 ▤ *AE, DC, MC, V* ☺ *Closed Thurs. and Jan.–mid-Feb. No lunch Fri.*

$–$$ ╳ **Ristorante Al Pescatore.** Lake fish is the specialty at this simple, popular restaurant in Sirmione's historical center. Try grilled trout with a bottle of local white wine and settle your meal with a walk in the nearby public park. ☒ *Via Piana 20* ☎ 030/916216 ▤ *AE, DC, MC, V.*

★ $$$$ 🏨 **Villa Cortine.** This former private villa in a secluded park risks being just plain ostentatious, but it's saved by the sheer luxury of its setting and the extraordinary professionalism of its staff. The hotel dominates a low hill, and the grounds—a colorful mixture of lawns, trees, statues, and fountains—go down to the lake. The villa itself dates from the early part of the 19th century, although a wing was added in 1952: the trade-off is between the more-charming decor in the older rooms and the better lake views from the newer ones. In summer a three-night minimum stay and half board are required. ☒ *Via Grotte 6, 25010* ☎ 030/ 9905890 🖷 030/916390 ⊕ *www.palacehotelvillacortine.com* ⇘ 40 *rooms* ⚿ *Restaurant, minibars, cable TV, tennis court, pool, beach, bar, meeting rooms, free parking* ▤ *AE, DC, MC, V* ☺ *Closed late Oct.–mid-Apr.* �📍 *MAP.*

$$$–$$$$ 🏨 **Hotel Sirmione.** Just inside the city walls, near the Castello, this hotel and spa sits amid lakeside gardens and terraces. Rooms are furnished with comfortable Scandinavian slat beds, matching floral draperies and wall coverings, and built-in white furniture. Many guests have been returning for years, due largely to the homey feel and the attentiveness of the staff. ☒ *Piazza Castello 19, 25019* ☎ 030/916192 🖷 030/916558 ⊕ *www.termedisirmione.com* ⇘ *101 rooms* ⚿ *Restaurant, minibars, cable TV, pool, spa, 2 bars, parking (fee)* ▤ *AE, DC, MC, V* �📍 *BP.*

LAKE COMO & BERGAMO

Updated by
Denise
Hummel

For those whose idea of heaven is palatial villas, rose-laden belvederes, hanging wisteria and bougainvillea, lanterns casting a glow over lakeshore restaurants, and majestic Alpine vistas, heaven is Lake Como. In his *Charterhouse of Parma,* Stendhal described it as an "enchanting spot, unequaled on earth in its loveliness." Virgil called it simply "our greatest" lake. Though summer crowds do their best to vanquish the lake's dreamy mystery and slightly faded old-money gentility, they fail. Como remains a consummate pairing of natural and man-made beauty. The villa gardens, like so many in Italy, are a union of two landscape traditions: that of Renaissance Italy, which values order, and that of Victo-

The Western Lakes & Bergamo

rian England, which strives to create the illusion of natural wildness. Such gardens are often framed by vast areas of picturesque farmland—fruit trees, olive groves, and vineyards.

Lake Como is some 47 km (30 mi) long north to south and is Europe's deepest lake (almost 1,350 feet). If not driving, you arrive at the lake by pulling into the railway station at Como, a leading textile center famous for its silks. Many travelers hasten to the vaporetti waiting to take them to Bellagio and the *centro di lago,* the center region of the lake's three branches, and its most beautiful section. The 2,000-year-old walled city of Como should not be missed, however. Car ferries traverse the lake in season, making it easy to get to the other main towns, Cernobbio, Tremezzo, and Varenna.

Bergamo

🟢 *55 km (34 mi) west of Brescia, 52 km (32 mi) east of Milan.*

From behind a set of battered Venetian walls high on an Alpine hilltop, medieval Bergamo majestically surveys the countryside. Behind are the snowcapped Bergamese Alps, and two funiculars connect the ancient **Bergamo Alta** (Upper Bergamo) to the modern **Bergamo Bassa** (Lower Bergamo). A worthwhile destination in its own right, Bergamo Bassa's long arteries and ornate piazzas speak to its centuries of prosperity, but it's nonetheless overshadowed by Bergamo Alta's magnificence. The massive **Torre Civica** offers a great view of the two cities. ⊠ *Piazza Vecchia* ☎ *035/247116* 🎫 *€3* 🕙 *Apr.–Oct., Sun.–Tues. 9:30–7, Sat. 9:30–9:30; Nov.–Mar., Sat. 9:30–4:30, Tues.–Fri. by appointment only.*

Bergamo's **Duomo** and **Battistero** are the most substantial buildings in Piazza Duomo. But the most impressive is the **Cappella Colleoni,** with stunning marble decoration. ⊠ *Piazza Duomo* 🎫 *Free* 🕙 *Daily 10–12:30 and 2:30–5:30.*

In the **Accademia Carrara** you will find an art collection that is surprisingly rewarding given its size and remote location. Many of the Venetian masters are represented—Mantegna, Bellini, Carpaccio (circa 1460–1525/26), Tiepolo, Francesco Guardi (1712–93), Canaletto (1697–1768)—as well as Botticelli (1445–1510). ⊠ *Bergamo Bassa, Piazza Carrara 82* ☎ *035/247149* ⊕ *www.accademiacarrara.bergamo.it* 🎫 *€2.60* 🕙 *Daily 10–1:30 and 2:30–5:30.*

Where to Stay & Eat

★ **$$–$$$$** ✕ **Taverna Colleoni dell'Angelo.** Angelo Cornaro is the name behind the Taverna del Colleoni, on the Piazza Vecchia right behind the Duomo. He serves imaginative fish and meat dishes, both regional and international, all expertly prepared. ⊠ *Piazza Vecchia 7* ☎ *035/232596* 🝙 *AE, DC, MC, V* 🕙 *Closed Mon. and 1 wk in Aug.*

$$ ✕ **Da Ornella.** The vaulted ceilings of this popular trattoria on the main street in the upper town are marked with ancient graffiti, created by (patiently) holding candles to the stone overhead. Ornella herself is in the kitchen, turning out *casoncelli* (stuffed pasta) in butter and sage and platters of assorted roast meats. Three prix-fixe menus are available during the week, two on the weekend. Reservations are recommended. ⊠ *Via Gombito 15* ☎ *035/232736* 🝙 *AE, DC, MC, V* 🕙 *Closed Thurs.*

$$ ✕ **Vineria Cozzi.** The wine list at this romantic but informal *vineria* (wine bar) is exceptional, whether you order by the glass or the bottle. There's also an array of flavorful foods, from snacks to sumptuous full-course meals typical of the region. The atmosphere is warm and charming, harkening back to 150 years ago, when the age of the vineria reached its height. ⊠ *Via B. Colleoni, 22a Bergamo Alta* ☎ *035/238836* 🝙 *No credit cards* 🕙 *Closed Wed.*

$$ ✕ **La Trattoria del Teatro.** Traditional regional food tops the bill at this good-value restaurant in the upper town. The polenta is a silky delight, and game is recommended in season. Fettuccine *con funghi* (with mushrooms) is deceptively simple but a rich and memorable specialty. ⊠ *Piazza Mascheroni 3* ☎ *035/238862* 🝙 *No credit cards* 🕙 *Closed Mon. and 2 wks mid-July.*

$–$$ ✕ **Al Donizetti.** Find a table in the back of this central, cheerful *enoteca*
Fodor'sChoice (wine bar) before choosing local hams and cheeses to accompany your
★ wine (more than 800 bottles are available, many by the glass). Heartier
meals are also available, such as eggplant stuffed with cheese and salami,
but save room for the desserts, which are well paired with dessert wines.
⊠ *Via Gombito 17/a* ☎ 035/242661 ▤ *AE, MC, V.*

$$ ✕▥ **Agnello d'Oro.** A 17th-century tavern on the main street in Upper
Bergamo, with wooden booths and walls hung with copper utensils and
ceramic plates, Agnello d'Oro is a good place to imbibe the atmosphere
as well as the good local wine. Specialties are typical Bergamese risotto
and varieties of polenta served with game and mushrooms. The same
establishment has 20 modestly priced ($) rooms. ⊠ *Via Gombito 22*
☎ *035/249883* 🖷 *035/235612* ⟿ *20 rooms* ⅄ *Restaurant; no a/c*
▤ *AE, MC, V* ⊘ *Restaurant closed Mon. and Jan. 7–Feb. 5. No din-
ner Sun.* ❧❘ *EP.*

$$–$$$$ ▥ **Excelsior San Marco.** The most comfortable hotel in Lower Bergamo,
the Excelsior San Marco is only a short walk from the walls of the upper
town. The rooms are surprisingly quiet considering the central location.
You can breakfast on the rooftop terrace. ⊠ *Piazza della Repubblica 6,
24122* ☎*035/366111* 🖷*035/223201* ⊕*www.hotelsanmarco.com* ⟿*155
rooms* ⅄ *Restaurant, in-room safes, minibars, cable TV, bar, laundry
service, parking (fee), no-smoking rooms, Internet* ▤*AE, DC, MC, V* ❧❘*BP.*

Nightlife & the Arts

The annual summer **Festival Internazionale del Pianoforte** (International
Piano Festival) is held in Bergamo's **Teatro Donizetti** (⊠ Piazza Cavour
15 ☎ 035/4160602 ⊕ www.teatrodonizetti.it). Call the theater for information about drama, opera, and ballet events throughout the year.

EN
ROUTE
The Chiesa della Madonna del Ghisallo (Church of the Patroness of Bicyclists), open daily from March through November, is not far from the
shores of Lake Como and affords a fine view. You will often see cyclists
parked outside taking a breather after their uphill struggle, but many
come simply in homage to this unique Madonna. It's located 48 km (30
mi) northwest of Bergamo, on the road to Bellagio.

Bellagio

28 *30 km (19 mi) northeast of Como, 56 km (35 mi) northwest of Bergamo.*

Fodor'sChoice
★
Sometimes called the prettiest town in Europe, Bellagio always seems
to be flag-bedecked, with geraniums ablaze in every window and
bougainvillea veiling the staircases, or *montées,* that thread through the
town. At dusk Bellagio's nightspots—including the wharf, where an orchestra serenades dancers under the stars—beckon you to come and make
merry. It's an impossibly enchanting location, one that inspired French
composer Gabriel Fauré to call Bellagio "a diamond contrasting brilliantly with the sapphires of the three lakes in which it is set."

Boats ply the lake to Tremezzo, where Napoléon's worst Italian enemy,
Count Sommariva, resided at Villa Carlotta; and a bit farther south of
Tremezzo, to Villa Balbianello. Check with the **Bellagio tourist office**

(⊠ Piazza Mazzini [Pontile Imbarcadero] ☎ 031/950204 ⊕ www.
bellagiolakecomo.com) for the hours of the launch to Tremezzo.

★ **Villa Serbelloni,** a property of the Rockefeller Foundation, has celebrated
gardens on the site of Pliny the Elder's villa overlooking Bellagio. There
are only two guided visits per day, restricted to 30 people each, and in
May these tend to be commandeered by group bookings. ⊠ *Near
Palazza della Chiesa* ☎ *031/950204* ⊠ *€5* ⊙ *Guided visits Apr.–Oct.,
Tues.–Sun. at 11 and 4; tours gather 15 mins before start.*

The famous gardens of the **Villa Melzi** were once a favorite picnic spot
for Franz Lizst, who advised author Louis de Ronchaud in 1837: "When
you write the story of two happy lovers, place them on the shores of
Lake Como. I do not know of any land so conspicuously blessed by
heaven." The gardens are open to the public, and though you can't get
into the 19th-century villa, don't miss the lavish Empire-style family chapel.
The Melzi were Napoléon's greatest allies in Italy (the family has passed
down the name "Josephine" to the present day). ⊠ *Via Lungolago
Marconi* ☎ *031/951281* ⊠ *€5* ⊙ *Apr.–Oct., daily 9–6.*

Where to Stay & Eat

$$ ╳🏠 **La Pergola.** Try to reserve a table on the terrace at this popular lake-
side restaurant about 1 km (½ mi) from Bellagio, on the other side of
the peninsula. The best dining option is the freshly caught fish. You can
also stay in one of the inn's 11 rooms, all of which have baths. ⊠ *Pescallo,
Piazza del Porte 22021* ☎ *031/950263* 🖷 *031/950253* ⊕ *www.
lapergolabellagio.it* ⇗ *11 rooms* ⚫ *Restaurant* ⊟ *AE, MC, V* ⊙ *Restau-
rant closed Tues.* ⏲❘ *BP.*

$ ╳🏠 **Silvio.** At the edge of town, this family-owned trattoria with a
lakeshore terrace specializes in fresh fish. Served cooked or marinated,
with risotto or as a ravioli stuffing, the fish is caught by Silvio's family—
it's local cooking at its best. Many of the modestly priced guest rooms
have balconies and lake views. ⊠ *Lòppia di Bellagio, Via Carcano 10,
22021* ☎ *031/950322* ⊕ *www.bellagiosilvio.com* ⇗ *21 rooms, 9 apart-
ments* ⚫ *Restaurant, cable TV* ⊟ *MC, V* ⊙ *Closed Jan. and Feb.* ⏲❘ *BP.*

★ **$$$$** 🏠 **Grand Hotel Villa Serbelloni.** Designed to cradle nobility in high style,
this hotel is a refined haven for the discreetly wealthy, set within a
pretty park down the road from the Punta di Bellagio. The sense of 19th-
century luxury has not so much faded as mellowed: the rooms are im-
maculate and plush; public areas are gilt and marble with thick, colorful
carpets. The staff is unobtrusive and very knowledgeable about lake trans-
portation. Churchill's and John Kennedy's former rooms face the
Tremezzina, a group of towns across the lake. ⊠ *Via Roma 1, 22021*
☎ *031/950216* 🖷 *031/951529* ⊕ *www.villaserbelloni.it* ⇗ *81 rooms*
⚫ *2 restaurants, room service, minibars, cable TV, tennis court, 2 pools,
health club, hair salon, sauna, Turkish bath, laundry service, free park-
ing, no-smoking rooms, Internet* ⊟ *AE, DC, MC, V* ⊙ *Closed mid-
Nov.–early Apr.* ⏲❘ *BP.*

$$$ 🏠 **Du Lac.** In the center of Bellagio, by the landing dock, this comfortable,
medium-size hotel owned by an Anglo-Italian family has a relaxed and
congenial feel. Most rooms have views of the lake and mountains, and
there's a rooftop terrace garden for drinks or dozing. ⊠ *Piazza Mazzini*

32, 22021 ☏ 031/950320 🖷 031/951624 🛏 *48 rooms* ♨ *2 restaurants, minibars, cable TV, bar, free parking* ⊟ *MC, V* ⊘ *Closed Nov.–Mar.* ◐❙ *BP.*

$$–$$$ 🏨 **Hotel Florence.** This villa dating from the 1880s has an impressive lobby with vaulted ceiling and an imposing Florentine fireplace. Most of the rooms, furnished with interesting antiques, are large and comfortable and have splendid views of the lake. The restaurant and bar draw locals and visitors who appreciate the friendly and helpful staff. The hotel is across from the ferry stop. ✉ *Piazza Mazzini 46, 22021* ☏ *031/950342* 🖷 *031/951722* ⊕ *www.hotelflorencebellagio.it* 🛏 *30 rooms* ♨ *Restaurant, cable TV, spa, bar; no a/c* ⊟ *AE, MC, V* ⊘ *Closed Nov.–Mar.* ◐❙ *MAP.*

★ **$–$$$** 🏨 **Hotel Belvedere.** In Italian, Belvedere means "beautiful view," and it's an apt name for this enchanting spot. The hotel has been in the Martinelli-Manoni family since 1880, and the unbroken tradition of service makes it one of the best places to stay in town. Antique chairs and eye-catching rugs complement the modern rooms, many of which have balconies and view of the lake. The marble bathrooms are designed for comfort. Outstanding terraced gardens have replaced the vineyards that once surrounded the house. The restaurant is very good. ✉ *Via Valassina 31, 22021* ☏ *031/950410* 🖷 *031/950102* ⊕ *www.belvederebellagio. com* 🛏 *62 rooms* ♨ *Restaurant, cable TV, pool, bar, meeting rooms, free parking, no-smoking rooms; no a/c* ⊟ *AE, DC, MC, V* ⊘ *Closed Nov.–Mar.* ◐❙ *BP.*

Varenna

㉙ *6 km (4 mi) northeast of Bellagio, 56 km (35 mi) northwest of Bergamo.*

You can reach Varenna by ferry from Bellagio. The principal sight here is the spellbinding garden of the **Villa Monastero,** which, as its name suggests, was originally a monastery. Now it's an international science and convention center. ✉ *Varenna* ☏ *0341/295450* 🎫 *€2* ⊘ *Apr.–Oct., daily 9–7.*

Tremezzo

㉚ *34 km (21 mi) north of Cernobbio, 78 km (48 mi) north of Milan.*

If you're lucky enough to visit the small lakeside town of Tremezzo in late spring or early summer, you will find the magnificent **Villa Carlotta** a riot of color, with more than 14 acres of azaleas and dozens of varieties of rhododendrons in full bloom. The height of the blossoms is late April to early May. The villa was built between 1690 and 1743 for the luxury-loving marquis Giorgio Clerici. The garden's collection is remarkable, particularly considering the difficulties of transporting delicate plants before the age of aircraft. Palms, banana trees, cacti, eucalyptus, a sequoia, orchids, and camellias are counted among the more than 500 species.

> **WORD OF MOUTH**
>
> "We arrived in Varenna and almost immediately fell under the calming spell of Lake Como. It was so beautiful there words cannot describe it. Everything was slow, quiet and tranquil."
>
> –daria

According to local lore, one reason for the Villa Carlotta's magnificence was a competition between the marquis's son-in-law, who inherited the estate, and the son-in-law's archrival, who built *his* summer palace directly across the lake (Villa Melzi, in Bellagio). Whenever either added to his villa and garden, it was tantamount to taunting the other in public. Eventually the son-in-law's insatiable taste for self-aggrandizement prevailed. The villa's last (and final) owners were Prussian royalty (including the "Carlotta" of the villa's name); the property was confiscated during World War I.

The villa's interior is worth a visit, particularly if you have a taste for the romantic sculptures of Antonio Canova (1757–1822). The best known is his *Cupid and Psyche,* which depicts the lovers locked in an odd but graceful embrace, with the young god above and behind, his wings extended, while Psyche awaits a kiss that will never come. The villa can be reached by boats from Bellagio. ☎ *0344/40405* ⊕ *www. villacarlotta.it* ☜ *€7* ⊙ *Apr.–Sept., daily 9–6; Mar. and Oct., daily 9–11:30 and 2–4:30.*

Villa Balbianello may be the most magical house in all of Italy. It sits on its own little promontory, Il Dosso d'Avedo—separating the bays of Venus and Diana—around the bend from the tiny fishing village of Ossuccio. Relentlessly picturesque, the villa is composed of loggias, terraces, and *palazzini* (tiny palaces), all spilling down verdant slopes to the lakeshore, where you'll find an old Franciscan church, a magnificent stone staircase, and a statue of San Carlo Borromeo blessing the waters. The villa is most frequently reached by launch from Como and Bellagio. Check with the **Como tourist office** (☎ 031/269712) for hours. Visits are usually restricted to the gardens, but if you plan in advance it's also possible to tour the villa itself. You pay €30 for a guide—regardless of how many are in your party—and an additional €5 entrance fee. ⊠ *Il Dosso di l'Avedo* ☎*0344/56110* ☜*Gardens €5* ⊙ *Apr.–Oct., daily 10–6. Pedestrian entrance open Tues., Sat., and Sun., otherwise by boat only.*

Where to Stay

$$$$ ⊞ **Grand Hotel Tremezzo.** One hundred windows of this turn-of-the-20th-century building face the lake. The hotel, in the middle of a private park stretching over 12½ acres, has many creature comforts, from three heated swimming pools and private landing on the lake to a hillside bursting with flowers. The 18-hole Menaggio & Cadenabbia golf course is about five minutes away by car. ⊠ *Via Regina 8, 22019* ☎ *0344/42491* 🖶 *0344/40201* ⊕ *www.grandhoteltremezzo.com* ☜ *98 rooms, 2 suites* ⚲ *2 restaurants, room service, minibars, cable TV, tennis court, 3 pools, gym, hair salon, sauna, billiards, 3 bars, meeting room, free parking, no-smoking rooms* ⊟ *AE, DC, MC, V* ⊙ *Closed mid-Nov.–Feb.* ⫣⟊ *BP.*

$ ⊞ **Rusall.** On the hillside above Tremezzo in the midst of a large garden, this small and reasonably priced hotel offers quiet and privacy. You can lie out on the terrace and enjoy a nice view. Rooms are simple and comfortable. ⊠ *Via S. Martino 2, 22019* ☎ *0344/40408* 🖶 *0344/ 40447* ⊕ *www.rusallhotel.com* ☜ *23 rooms* ⚲ *Restaurant, tennis court, bar; no a/c in some rooms* ⊟ *AE, DC, MC, V* ⫣⟊ *EP.*

Cernobbio

31 *5 km (3 mi) north of Como, 53 km (34 mi) north of Milan.*

The legendary resort of Villa d'Este is reason enough to visit this jewel on the lake, but the town itself is worth a stroll. Despite the fact that George Clooney lunches here regularly, the place still has a neighborhood feel to it, especially on summer evenings and weekends when the piazza is full of families and couples taking their passeggiata.

Built over the course of roughly 45 years for fisherman-turned-cardinal Tolomeo Gallio, the **Villa d'Este** has had a colorful and somewhat checkered history since its completion in 1615, swinging wildly between extremes of grandeur and dereliction. Its tenants have included the Jesuits, two generals, a ballerina, Caroline of Brunswick—the disgraced and estranged wife of the future king of England, George IV—a family of ordinary Italian nobles, and, finally, a czarina of Russia. Its life as a private summer residence ended in 1873, when it was turned into the fashionable hotel it has remained ever since.

Where to Stay & Eat

$$ ✕ **Il Gatto Nero.** This restaurant in the hills above Cernobbio has a splendid view of the lake. Specialties include *filetto con aceto balsamico* (filet mignon with balsamic vinegar), *pappardelle al ragù di selvaggini* (pasta with wild game sauce), and lake fish. Save room for the warm chocolate tort with its delicious liquid chocolate center. Reservations are encouraged as this is a regular haunt of Italian soccer stars as well as the jet set. ✉ *Via Monte Santo 69, Rovenna* ☎ *031/512042* ▭ *AE, DC, V* ⊘ *Closed Mon. No lunch Tues.*

¢–$ ✕ **Pizzeria L'Ancora.** For the best pies in Como, and perhaps in the region, you won't want to miss this local haunt, run by a Neapolitan family that has been making pizza for three generations. Even Italians from out of town rave about the pizza here. Three sisters—Barbara, Grazie, and Linda—dish out hospitality as fine as the food. Their somewhat surly father (a dead ringer for Santa Claus) looks like he has enjoyed a pizza or two in his time. ✉ *Via Conciliazione 12, Tavernola* ☎ *031/340769* ▭ *No credit cards* ⊘ *Closed Wed.*

$$$$ ▨ **Villa d'Este.** One of the grandest hotels in Italy, the 17th-century Villa
Fodor'sChoice d'Este has long welcomed Europe's rich and famous, from Napoléon
★ to the Duchess of Windsor. The chandeliers in the vast lobby illuminate marble staircases leading to guest rooms furnished in the Empire style: walnut paneling, sofas in striped silk, and gorgeous antiques. A broad veranda sweeps out to the lakefront, where a swimming pool extends above the water. The fanciful pavilions, temples, miniature forts, and mock ruins make for an afternoon's walk of quietly whimsical surprises. ✉ *Via Regina 40, 22012* ☎ *031/3481* 🖷 *031/348844* ⊕ *www.villadeste. it* ⇥ *148 rooms, 13 suites* ₰ *3 restaurants, room service, minibars, cable TV, in-room broadband, 8 tennis courts, 2 pools (1 indoor), spa, sauna, squash, bar, nightclub, laundry service, free parking, no-smoking rooms* ▭ *AE, MC, V* ⊘ *Closed mid-Nov.–Feb.* ❙⦿❙ *FAP.*

Como

㉜ *5 km (3 mi) south of Cernobbio, 30 km (19 mi) southwest of Bellagio, 49 km (30 mi) north of Milan.*

Como, on the south shore of the lake, is only part elegant resort, where cobbled pedestrian streets wind their way past parks and bustling cafés. The other part is an industrial town renowned for its fine silks. If you're traveling by car, leave it at the edge of the town center in the clean, well-lighted underground parking facility right on the lake.

The splendid 15th-century Renaissance-Gothic **Duomo** was begun in 1396. The facade was added in 1455, and the transepts were completed in the mid-18th century. The dome was designed by Filippo Juvara (1678–1736), chief architect of many of the sumptuous palaces of the royal house of Savoy. The facade has statues of two of Como's most famous sons, Pliny the Elder and Pliny the Younger, whose writings are among the most important documents from antiquity. Inside, the works of art include Luini's *Holy Conversation,* a fresco cycle by Morazzone, and the *Marriage of the Virgin Mary* by Ferrari. ⊠ *Piazza del Duomo* ⊗ *Daily 7–noon and 3–7.*

At the heart of Como's medieval quarter, the city's first cathedral, **San Fedele,** is worth a peek, if only because it is one of the oldest churches in the region. ⊠ *Piazza San Fedele* ⊗ *Daily 7–noon and 3–7.*

If you brave Como's industrial quarter, you will find the beautiful church of **Sant'Abbondio,** a gem of Romanesque architecture begun by Benedictine monks in 1013 and consecrated by Pope Urban II in 1095. Inside, the five aisles of the church converge on a presbytery with a semicircular apse decorated with a cycle of 14th-century frescoes—now restored to their original magnificence—by Lombard artists heavily influenced by the Sienese school. In the nave the cubical capitals are the earliest example of this style in Italy. ⊠ *Via Sant'Abbondio* ⊗ *Daily 7–6.*

Exhibiting the path of production from silkworm litters to *moiré-*finishing machinery, the **Museo Didattico della Seta** (Silk Museum) is small but complete. The museum preserves the history of a manufacturing region that continues to supply almost three-fourths of Europe's silk. The friendly staffers will give you an overview of the museum; they are also happy to provide brochures and information about local retail shops. The museum's location isn't well marked: follow the textile school's driveway around to the low-rise concrete building on the left, and follow the shallow ramp down to the entrance. ⊠ *Via Velleggio 3* 🕿 *031/303180* ⊕ *www.museosetacomo.com* 🖃 €8 ⊗ *Tues.–Fri. 9–noon and 3–6. Tours in English available by reservation.*

Where to Stay & Eat

$$–$$$ ✕ **Raimondi.** This elegant restaurant in the Hotel Villa Flori (2 km [1 mi] toward Cernobbio) offers good value and a superb location, with a large terrace poised over the lake. The local freshwater fish is your best option, but a wide range of Italian dishes is capably prepared. The restaurant's season is longer than most, owing to its popularity with local residents. ⊠ *Via Cernobbio 12* 🕿 *031/338233* 🖃 *AE, DC, MC, V* ⊗ *Closed Mon. and Dec.–Feb. 14. No lunch Sat.*

★ **$$–$$$** ✕▦ **Terminus.** Commanding a panoramic view over Lake Como, this early-20th-century art nouveau building is the city's finest hotel. The marbled public spaces have an understated elegance, and the guest rooms are done in floral patterns and furnished with large walnut wardrobes and silk-covered sofas. In summer the garden terrace is perfect for relaxing over a drink. Bar delle Terme ($$), the candelit restaurant, is worth a trip. The cranberry-hue space, filled with plush velvet sofas, resembles a large living room. The food and service are as fine as the decor. Reservations are strongly advised, as there are only a few tables. It is closed Tuesday. ⊠ *Lungolario Trieste 14, 22100* ☎ *031/329111* 🖷 *031/302550* ⊕ *www.albergoterminus.com* ↪ *40 rooms* ⌂ *Restaurant, in-room safes, minibars, cable TV, in-room data ports, massage, sauna, meeting room, free parking, no-smoking rooms* ▭ *AE, DC, MC, V* ¶◎¶ *EP.*

$$–$$$ ▦ **Villa Flori.** Italian patriot Garibaldi spent his wedding night here, in a suite that now bears his name. The hotel enjoys a panoramic view of Lake Como and attracts locals with its highly acclaimed restaurant, Raimondi. ⊠ *Via Cernobbio 12, 22100* ☎ *031/33820* 🖷 *031/570379* ⊕ *www.hotelvillaflori.com* ↪ *45 rooms* ⌂ *Restaurant, minibars, cable TV, meeting room* ▭ *AE, DC, MC, V* ¶◎¶ *EP.*

$ ▦ **Tre Re.** This clean, spacious, welcoming hotel is a few steps west of the cathedral and convenient to the lake. Although the exterior gives away the age of this 16th-century former convent, the rooms are airy, comfortable, and modern. The moderately priced restaurant shares an ample terrace with the hotel. ⊠ *Via Boldoni 20, 22100* ☎ *031/265374* 🖷 *031/241349* ⊕ *www.hoteltrere.com* ↪ *41 rooms* ⌂ *Restaurant, cable TV, bar, free parking* ▭ *MC, V* ⊗ *Closed mid-Dec.–mid-Jan.* ¶◎¶ *BP.*

Sports & the Outdoors

The lake has many opportunities for sports enthusiasts, from windsurfing at the lake's northern end, to boating, sailing, and jet skiing at Como and Cernobbio. The lake is also quite swimmable in the summer months. For hikers there are lovely paths all around the lake. For an easy trek, take the funicular up to Brunate, and walk along the mountain to the lighthouse for a stunning view of the lake. For more information, contact the **tourist office** (⊠ Piazza Cavour 17 ☎ 031/269712).

Shopping

While in Como, seize the opportunity to shop for fine silk directly from its source. One of the biggest names is **Mantero** (⊠ Via San Abbondio 8 ☎ 031/321510), which supplies major design houses like Yves Saint Laurent, Nina Ricci, and Trussardi. Not far from the lake, good deals on ties, scarves, and shirts can be found at the factory store of **Binda** (⊠ Viale Geno 6 ☎ 031/3861629). **Frey** (⊠ Via Garibaldi 10 ☎ 031/267012) has a factory outlet on the western edge of the old town selling silk clothes and accessories. Another major name in silk production, **Ratti** (⊠ Via Per Cernobbio 19 ☎ 031/576000), has a factory store on the lake near Villa Flori.

On Saturday (except the first Saturday of every month), Piazza San Fedele holds a **local crafts market** from 9 to 7.

LAKE MAGGIORE & LAKE ORTA

Updated By
Denise
Hummel

Magnificently scenic, Lake Maggiore has its mountainous western shore in Piedmont, its lower eastern shore in Lombardy, and its northern tip in Switzerland. The lake stretches nearly 50 km (30 mi) and is up to 5 km (3 mi) wide. The better-known resorts are on the western shore, particularly Stresa, a tourist town that provided one of the settings for Hemingway's *A Farewell to Arms*. A mountainous strip of land separates Lake Maggiore from Lake Orta, its smaller neighbor to the west, in Piedmont. Orta attracts fewer visitors than the three larger lakes, and can be a pleasant alternative in summer.

Orta San Giulio

③ *76 km (47 mi) northwest of Milan.*

At the end of a small peninsula jutting out into Lake Orta, this charming town is full of 18th-century buildings adorned with wrought-iron balustrades and balconies. The shady main square looks out across the lake to the small island of San Giulio. There is nothing more relaxing than sitting at one of the piazza cafés and watching sailboats catch the breezes that blow across the languid waters.

Rising up behind Orta, **Sacro Monte** (Sacred Mountain) is an interesting hike. Pass the Church of the Assumption at the edge of the old town, and just ahead is a gateway marked Sacro Monte. This leads to a comfortable climb that takes about 40 minutes round-trip. As you approach the top, you pass no fewer than 20 17th-century chapels, all devoted to St. Francis of Assisi. Within them, life-size terra-cotta statues (almost 400 in all) illustrate the saint's life. The campanile of the last chapel provides a view over the lake and the town, about 350 feet below.

The island of **San Giulio** is accessible by hired boat for about €6 round-trip per boatload of up to four people. The island takes its name from the 4th-century St. Julius, who—like St. Patrick in Ireland—is said to have banished snakes from the island. Julius is also said to have founded the **Basilica** in AD 390, although the present building shows more signs of its renovations in the 10th and 15th centuries. Inside, there's a black-marble pulpit (12th century) with elaborate carvings, and a crypt containing relics of the saint. In the sacristy of the church is a large bone said to be from one of the beasts destroyed by the saint, but it actually resembles a whalebone.

Much of the area is occupied by private villas; it takes only a few minutes to walk around the parts of the island open to the public. The view to Orta, with Sacro Monte behind it, is memorable, particularly in the late afternoon when the light picks up the glint of the wrought-iron

> **WORD OF MOUTH**
>
> "If you are looking for a really cute village to stroll around in, nothing beats Orta San Giulio on Lago d'Orta. It's a nice place to stop for lunch and take in the views of the island basilica in the middle of the lake."
>
> —BelTib

traceries. Signs laud the virtues of silence and contemplation, and the island's quiet is broken only by the pealing of the basilica's bells.

Where to Stay & Eat

★ **$$$–$$$$** ✕ **Venus Ristorante.** The Restaurant overlooks the lake, with views from the terrace in summer, and from the upper floor in winter. The wine list consists of 800 choices and the manager, Paolo Guensi, will advise you of a fine food and wine pairing, or choose from the chef's tasting menu. Save room for his famous dessert *millefoglie di mele al rosmarino con crema al limone,* which consists of fine slices of apple surrounded by "a thousand" paper-thin layers of pastry and lemon cream, with the slightest scent of rosemary. ✉ *Piazza Motta 50* ☎ *0322/90362* ▤ *MC, V* ☾ *Closed Mon. Nov.–Mar.*

$$–$$$ ✕▤ **Hotel San Rocco.** Half the rooms in this converted 17th-century lakeside convent on the edge of town have views of the water, garden, and surrounding mountains; many also have balconies. The restaurant ($$$) serves international cuisine and has beautiful views of the lake. ✉ *Via Gippini 11, 28016* ☎ *0322/911977* 🖶 *0322/911964* ⊕ *www. hotelsanrocco.it* ⤴ *74 rooms* ⚬ *Restaurant, minibars, cable TV, pool, bar, parking (fee)* ▤ *AE, DC, MC, V* ❄ *BP.*

★ **$$$–$$$$** ▤ **Villa Crespi.** You'll be impressed before you set foot in Villa Crespi: the exterior looks like a Moorish palace, complete with a tall tower, and the parklike grounds descend to the lake. Inside, the Moorish theme continues—the original owner, Cristoforo Benigno Crespi, built the villa in 1879 after a visit to Persia. Guest rooms are lavishly decorated and well maintained, and the restaurant is a destination in itself for lovers of *alta cucina.* ✉ *Via Fava 18, 28016* ☎ *0322/911902* 🖶 *0322/911919* ⊕ *www. hotelvillacrespi.it* ⤴ *6 rooms, 8 suites* ⚬ *Restaurant, bar, Internet, cable TV, minibars* ▤ *AE, DC, MC, V* ☾ *Closed Jan.–mid-Mar.* ❄ *BP.*

Stresa

㉞ *16 km (10 mi) east of Orta San Giulio, 80 km (50 mi) northwest of Milan.*

Stresa, which has capitalized on its central lakeside position, has to some extent become a victim of its own success. The luxurious elegance that distinguished its heyday has faded; the grand hotels are still grand, but traffic now encroaches upon their parks and gardens. Even the undeniable loveliness of the lakeshore drive has been threatened by the roar of diesel trucks and BMW traffic. One way to escape is to head for the Isole Borromee (Borromean Islands) in Lake Maggiore.

As you wander around the palms and semitropical shrubs of **Villa Pallavicino,** don't be surprised if you're followed by a peacock or even an ostrich: they're part of the zoological garden and are allowed to roam almost at will. From the top of the hill on which the villa stands you can see the gentle hills of the Lombardy shore of Lake Maggiore and, nearer and to the left, the jewel-like Borromean Islands. In addition to a bar and restaurant, the grounds also have picnic spots. ✉ *Via Sempione 8* ☎ *0323/31533* ⊕ *www.parcozoopallavicino.it* ▣ *€6.70* ☾ *Early Mar.–Oct., daily 9–6.*

Boats to the **Isole Borromee** (www.borromeoturismo.it) depart every 15–30 minutes from the dock at Stresa's Piazza Marconi. Although you can hire a private boatman, it's cheaper and just as convenient to use the regular service. Make sure you buy a ticket allowing you to visit all the islands—Bella, Dei Pescatori, and Madre. The islands take their name from the Borromeo family, which has owned them since the 12th century.

Isola Bella (Beautiful Island) is the most famous of the three, and the first that you'll visit. It is named after Isabella, whose husband, Carlo III Borromeo (1538–84), built the palace and terraced gardens for her as a wedding present. Before Count Carlo began his project, the island was rocky and almost devoid of vegetation; the soil for the garden had to be transported from the mainland. Wander up the 10 terraces of the gardens, where peacocks roam among the scented shrubs, statues, and fountains, for a splendid view of the lake. Visit the palazzo to see the rooms where famous guests—including Napoléon and Mussolini—stayed in 18th-century splendor. *0323/30556 Garden and palazzo €10 Late Mar.–Oct., daily 9–5:30.*

Stop for a while at the tiny **Isola dei Pescatori** (Island of the Fishermen), less than 100 yards wide and only about ½ km (¼ mi) long. It's the perfect place for a seafood lunch before, after, or in between your visit to the other two islands. Of the 10 or so restaurants on this tiny island, the 3 worth visiting are Ristorante Unione (0323/933798), Ristorante Verbano (0323/30408), and Ristorante Belvedere (0323/32292). The island's little lanes strung with fishing nets and dotted with shrines to the Madonna are the definition of picturesque; little wonder that in high season the village is crowded with postcard stands. .

Isola Madre (Mother Island) is the largest of the three and, like Isola Bella, has a large botanical garden. Take time to see the profusion of exotic trees and shrubs running down to the shore in every direction. Two special times to visit are April (for the camellias) and May (for azaleas and rhododendrons). Also on the island is a 16th-century palazzo, where an antique puppet theater is on display, complete with string puppets, prompt books, and elaborate scenery designed by Alessandro Sanquirico, who was a scenographer at La Scala in Milan. *0323/31261 €9 Late Mar.–Oct., daily 9–5:30.*

For more information about the islands, contact the **Stresa tourist office** (Piazza Marconi 16 0323/30150) or ask at the docks (look for Navigazione Lago Maggiore signs).

Where to Stay

$$$$ Grand Hotel des Iles Borromées. This palatial establishment has catered to a demanding European clientele since 1863. And though it still has the spacious salons and lavish furnishings of the turn of the 20th century, it has been discreetly modernized. The bathrooms are luxurious. *Corso Umberto I 67, 28838 0323/938938 0323/32405 www.borromees.it 161 rooms, 11 suites Restaurant, room service, minibars, cable TV, in-room data ports, Wi-Fi, tennis court, indoor pool, spa, bar, laundry service, convention center, helipad, free parking AE, DC, MC, V BP.*

$ ⌧ **Primavera.** A few blocks up from the lake, Primavera has compact, simply furnished rooms in a 1950s building hung with flower boxes. Most rooms have balconies overlooking the streets of Stresa's old center. ✉ *Via Cavour 39, 28838* ☎ *0323/31286* ⊟ *0323/33458* ⤳ *34 rooms* ⚬ *Cable TV, bar, meeting rooms, parking (fee), Internet; no a/c* ⊟ *AE, DC, V* ⊘ *Closed mid-Nov.–mid-Mar.* ⏏ *BP.*

Verbania

③⑤ *16 km (10 mi) north of Stresa, 95 km (59 mi) northwest of Milan.*

Verbania, across the Gulf of Pallanza from Stresa, is known for the **Villa Taranto,** which has magnificent botanical gardens. The villa was acquired in 1931 by Scottish captain Neil McEachern, who expanded the gardens considerably, adding terraces, waterfalls, more than 3,000 plant species from all over the world, and broad meadows sloping gently down to the lake. In 1938 McEachern donated the entire complex to the Italian people. ✉ *Via Vittorio Veneto 111* ☎ *0323/404555* ⊕ *www.villataranto.it* ▱ *€8.50* ⊘ *Late Mar.–Oct., daily 8:30–7; last admission 1 hr before closing.*

OFF THE BEATEN PATH

SANTA CATERINA DEL SASSO BALLARO – Near the town of Laveno, this beautiful lakeside hermitage was constructed in the 12th century by a local merchant to express his gratitude for having been saved from the wrath of a storm. It's particularly striking as you approach it by boat or ferry. About 20 km (12 mi) farther north on the eastern side of the lake, you will find comfortable and charming Liberty-style lodgings at the family-run **Camin Hotel Luino** ($$). ✉ *Via Dante 35, 21016 Luino* ☎ *0332/530118* ⊟ *0332/537226* ⊕ *www.caminhotelluino.com* ⊟ *AE, DC, MC, V.*

Where to Stay & Eat

$–$$ ✕**Da Cesare.** Off Piazza Cadorna and close to the embarcadero, this restaurant serves tasty risotto *con filetti di persico* (with perch fillets) and typical Piedmontese meat dishes, such as beef braised in Barolo wine. ✉ *Via Mazzini 14* ☎ *0323/31386* ⊟ *AE, DC, MC, V.*

$$$ ✕⌧ **Il Sole di Ranco.** The same family has run this lakeside inn for more than 150 years. The present chefs, Davide Brovelli and his father, Carlo, do the family proud. Lake trout and perch find their way onto the menu, as do artichoke dishes in spring and eggplant in summer. Guest rooms ($$$–$$$$) are in two late-19th-century villas surrounded by a garden and overlooking the lake. Restaurant reservations are essential. ✉ *Piazza Venezia 5, Ranco, near Angera* ☎ *0331/976507* ⊟ *0331/976620* ⊕ *www.ilsolediranco.it* ⤳ *14 rooms* ⚬ *Restaurant, minibars, pool* ⊟ *AE, DC, MC, V* ⊘ *Closed Dec. and Jan. Restaurant closed Tues. No lunch Mon.* ⏏ *BP.*

Fodor's Choice
★

$ ⌧ **Il Chiostro.** Originally a 17th-century convent, this hotel expanded into the adjoining 19th-century textile factory, adding some conference facilities. Rooms are clean and functional. ✉ *Via Fratelli Cervi 14, 28900* ☎ *0323/404077* ⊟ *0323/401231* ⊕ *www.chiostrovb.it* ⤳ *100 rooms* ⚬ *Restaurant, cable TV, meeting rooms* ⊟ *AE, DC, MC, V* ⏏ *BP.*

MILAN, LOMBARDY & THE LAKES ESSENTIALS

Transportation

BY AIR

Aeroporto Malpensa (MXP), 50 km (31 mi) northwest of Milan, is the major northern Italian hub for intercontinental flights and also sees substantial European and domestic traffic. The smaller Aeroporto Milano Linate (LIN), 10 km (6 mi) east of Milan, handles additional European and domestic flights.

The Malpensa Express Train connects Malpensa airport to Cadorna station near downtown Milan. The 40-minute train ride costs €9 (€12 round-trip), leaving Cadorna every half hour from 5:50 AM to 8:20 PM and Malpensa every half hour 6:45 AM to 9:45 PM. Malpensa Express Buses make the trip outside of these hours. In addition, Malpensa Shuttle Buses (€5) go to and from Milan's central train station (Stazione Centrale). There are departures every half hour from about 5 AM to 10 PM, and the trip takes about 75 minutes.

From Linate, the municipal Bus 73 runs every 10 minutes to Piazza San Babila in the heart of the city. The trip takes approximately 20 minutes. Tickets cost €1 and are sold at the Arrivals lounge newsstand (by the pharmacy). You can go from Linate to Stazione Centrale on the STARFLY bus, which runs every half hour; tickets are €2.50 and are sold on board.

If you need to get from one airport to the other, you can take the shuttle bus Airpullman (€8), which runs every 90 minutes. The trip takes approximately 90 minutes.

The drive from Malpensa to Milan is about an hour; take Route S336 east to the A8 autostrada southeast. From Linate it's about 10 minutes into the central city; head west following the signs.

Taxis wait directly outside the arrival building doors at Malpensa, and will take you downtown for about €80. The fare from Linate is about €25.

Malpensa is closer to Lakes Como and Maggiore than to Milan itself. If that's where you're headed, it's perfectly feasible to skip the city altogether.
🛈 Airport Flight Information **Aeroporto Malpensa & Aeroporto Milano Linate** ☎ 02/74852200 ⊕ www.sea-aeroportimilano.it.

BY BOAT & FERRY

Frequent daily ferry and hydrofoil services link the lakeside towns and villages. Residents take them to get to work and school, while visitors can use them for exploring the area. There are also special round-trip excursions, some with (optional) dining service on board. Schedules and ticket price are available on the Navigazione Laghi Web site and are posted at the landing docks.
🛈 Boat & Ferry Information **Navigazione Laghi** ⊠ Via Ariosto 21, Milan ☎ 02/4676101 ⊕ www.navigazionelaghi.it. **Navigazione Lago di Como** ⊠ Via per Cernobbio 18, Tavernola, near Como ☎ 031/579211. **Navigazione Lago di Garda** ⊠ Piazza Mat-

teotti 2, Desenzano ☎ 030/9149511. **Navigazione Lago Maggiore** ✉ Viale Baracca 1, Arona ☎ 800/551801.

BY BUS

Bus service isn't a good option for travel between cities here—it's neither faster, cheaper, nor more convenient than the train. For those determined to travel by bus, Autostradale goes to Turin, Bergamo, and Brescia from its hub at Autostazione Garibaldi, north of Milan's city center. Reservations are required.

There's regular bus service between the small towns on the lakes. It's less convenient than going by boat or by car, and it's used primarily by locals (particularly schoolchildren), but sightseers can use it as well. The bus service around Lake Garda serves mostly towns on the western shore. Call the bus operator SIA for information.

🚌 Bus Information **Autostradale** ☎ 02/637901. **SIA** ☎ 030/3774237.

BY CAR

Although trains are often more convenient for intercity travel, driving is the best way to get a sense of Lombardy's varied landscape. Several major autostrada routes intersect at Milan, all connected by the *tangenziale,* the road that rings the city. The A4 runs west to Turin and east to Venice; A1 leads south to Bologna, Florence, and Rome; A7 angles southwest down to Genoa. A8 goes northwest toward Lake Maggiore, and A9 north runs past Lake Como and over the St. Gotthard Pass into Switzerland.

To get around the lakes, you have to follow secondary roads—often of great beauty. S572 follows the southern and western shores of Lake Garda, S45b edges the northernmost section of the western shore, and S249 runs along the eastern shore. Around Lake Como, follow S340 along the western shore, S36 on the eastern shore, and S583 on the lower arms. S33 and S34 trace the western shore of Lake Maggiore.

Milan is well served by public transit, and taxis are readily available, so there's little motivation for taking on city driving yourself. Also, there's no free street parking—an added disincentive. For car service, contact Autonoleggio Pini. English-speaking drivers are available.

🚗 Car Service **Autonoleggio Pini** ☎ 02/29400555 🖷 02/2047843 🌐 www.pini.it.

EMERGENCY SERVICES Your car-rental company should be your first resource if you had a problem while driving in Italy, but it's also good to know that the ACI, the Italian auto club, offers 24-hour roadside assistance (free for members, for a fee for nonmembers). Regularly spaced roadside service phones are available on the autostrade.

🚗 **ACI dispatchers** ☎ 803/116.

BY MILAN PUBLIC TRANSIT

Milan has an excellent system of public transit, consisting of three subway lines and 120 tram and bus routes. Tickets are valid for one trip on the Metropolitana (subway) or 75 minutes on buses and trams, and must be purchased before you board and then stamped in machines at station entrances or on poles inside trolleys and buses. Standard tickets cost €1 and can be purchased from news vendors, tobacconists, and—at larger stops—machines (some of which require exact change). All-inclusive subway, bus, and tram tickets cost €3 for 24 hours or €5.50 for 48 hours; they're available at Duomo Metro and Stazione Centrale Metro stations. Trains run from 6 AM to 12:30 AM. For more information, check the ATM Web site (which has an English-language version) or visit the information office at the Duomo stop.

🚹 **ATM (Azienda Trasporti Milanesi)** ⊕ www.atm-mi.it.

BY TAXI

Taxi fares in Milan are high compared to those in American cities, but drivers are honest. A short downtown ride will come to about €15. Taxis wait at stands, or can be called at one of the numbers listed below. Dispatchers may speak some English; they'll ask for the phone number you're calling from, and they'll tell you the number of your taxi and how many minutes your wait will be. If you're in a restaurant or bar, ask the staff to call a cab for you. It's not customary to flag taxis down in the street, but drivers do sometimes stop if you hail them.

🚹 **Taxi Companies** **Amicotaxi** ☎ 02/4000. **Autoradiotaxi** ☎ 02/8585. **Radiotaxi** ☎ 02/6969. **Taxiblu** ☎ 02/4040.

BY TRAIN

Stazione Centrale, 3 km (2 mi) northwest of Milan's Duomo, is one of Italy's major passenger-train hubs, with service to destinations throughout Italy and the rest of Europe, as well as frequent direct service within the region to Como, Bergamo, Brescia, Sirmione, Pavia, Cremona, and Mantua. Milan has several other railway stations; the one you're most likely to encounter is Cardorna, the central-city destination for the shuttle train from Malpensa airport. If you're traveling at off-hours, there's a chance you may have to venture to a suburban station—most notably Milano Lambrate for Bergamo.

For general information on trains and schedules, check with the FS–Trenitalia. The automated telephone line requires that you speak Italian, but the Web site has an English version.

🚹 **Train Information** **FS–Trenitalia** ☎ 892021 ⊕ www.trenitalia.com.

Contacts & Resources

EMERGENCIES

The nationwide ambulance number (118) connects you to the nearest emergency services provider. For first aid, ask for *pronto soccorso* and be prepared to give your address. Although the situation is gradually changing, do not expect emergency services workers to speak English, even at the highest levels. (A recent survey showed that only 10% of Italian doctors speak English.) It's wise to ask nonetheless, but even if the answer is yes, the level of proficiency is likely to be low. If you need the emergency services, try to find someone (such as a member of your hotel staff) who speaks both languages to assist you.

There are two national police forces, the *carabinieri* and the *polizia di stato*. If you need to report a theft, or need the police for any other matter, first try contacting the carabinieri, who are both more likely to have jurisdiction and more likely to have an English-speaking officer in their number.

Pharmacies in Milan are open from about 8:30 AM to 12:30 PM and then from 4 PM to 7 PM. The most central after-hours pharmacy is Farmacia Carlo Erba on the north side of Piazza del Duomo between the Galleria Vittorio Emanuele and Piazza Mercanti. Another option is Ambreck, in Piazza Argentina near Corso Buenos Aires. The pharmacy on the upper level of Stazione Centrale is open 24 hours a day throughout the year, though the station itself closes in the early-morning hours, at which time you need a police escort to get in. Throughout the region, pharmacies alternate late-night service. The address of the nearest open location is posted in every pharmacy window.

🚩 **Ambulance** ☎ 118. **Carabinieri** ☎ 112. **Police** ☎ 113.

🚩 24-Hour Pharmacies **Ambreck** ✉ Piazza Argentina, Milan ☎ 02/29526966. **Farmacia Carlo Erba** ✉ Piazza del Duomo, Milan ☎ 02/86464832. **Stazione Centrale** ✉ Piazza Duca D'Aosta, Milan ☎ 02/6690735.

TOURS

In Milan, a refurbished 1920s tram car operates a hop-on-hop-off tour of the city. Tickets (€20) are valid all day, and can be purchased on board. Departures are at 11 and 1 (also at 3, April–October) from Piazza Castello. The organization A Friend in Milan conducts walking tours of the city, including a visit to the *Last Supper*, day trips to the lakes, and shopping tours.

🚩 Resources **A Friend in Milan** ⊕ www.friendinmilan.co.uk.

TRAVEL AGENCIES

🚩 Local Agent Referrals **American Express Travel Agency** ✉ Via Larga 4, Duomo, Milan ☎ 02/721041. **Compagnia Italiana Turismo (CIT)** ✉ Via Dante 6, Castello, Milan ☎ 02/863701.

VISITOR INFORMATION

🚩 Tourist Information **Bellagio** ✉ Piazza Mazzini (Pontile Imbarcadero) ☎🖷 031/950204 ⊕ www.bellagiolakecomo.com. **Bergamo** ✉ Vicolo Aquila Nera at Piazza Vecchia, Upper Bergamo ☎ 035/242226 🖷 035/232730 ✉ Viale Vittorio Emanuele 20, Bergamo Bassa ☎ 035/210204 🖷 035/230184 ⊕ www.provincia.bergamo.it/turismo. **Cernobbio** ✉ Via Regina ☎🖷 031/510198. **Como** ✉ Piazza Cavour 17 ☎ 031/269712 🖷 031/240111 ⊕ www.lakecomo.org. **Cremona** ✉ Piazza del Comune 5 ☎ 0372/23233 🖷 0372/534080 ⊕ www.aptcremona.it. **Malcesine** ✉ Via Capitanato 6/8 ☎ 045/7400044 🖷 045/7401633 ⊕ www.aptgardaveneto.com. **Mantua** ✉ Piazza A. Mantegna 6 ☎ 0376/328253 🖷 0376/363292 ⊕ www.turismo.mantova.it. **Milan** ✉ Via Marconi 1, Piazza Duomo ☎ 02/72524301 🖷 02/72524350 ⊕ www.milanoinfotourist.com. **Pavia** ✉ Via Fabio Filzi 2 ☎ 0382/22156 🖷 0382/32221 ⊕ www.apt.pavia.it. **Riva del Garda** ✉ Giardini di Porta Orientale 8 ☎ 0464/554444 🖷 0464/520308 ⊕ www.gardatrentino.it. **Sirmione** ✉ Viale Marconi 2 ☎ 030/916114 🖷 030/916222. **Stresa** ✉ Piazza Marconi 16 ☎ 0323/30150 🖷 0323/32561 ⊕ www.distrettolaghi.it. **Tremezzo** ✉ Piazzale Trieste ☎ 0344/40493 ⊕ www.tremezzina.com.

Piedmont & Valle d'Aosta

Grape Harvest

WORD OF MOUTH

"Piedmont is way off the tourist track and as pretty as Tuscany. . . . Lots of wineries and wonderful undiscovered small towns."

—Barolo

"Valle d'Aosta is gorgeous. Old Roman ruins, neat towns, high peaks, rivers, and the day we were there, they had a festival for cows! . . . It's green and lush and just beautiful."

—Pat

WELCOME TO PIEDMONT & VALLE D'AOSTA

Landscape, Langhe

TOP 5
Reasons to Go

1 Sacra di San Michele: Explore one of the country's most spectacularly situated religious buildings.

2 Castello Fénis: This castle transports you back in time to the Middle Ages.

3 Monte Bianco: The cable car ride over the snowcapped mountain will take your breath away.

4 Turin's Museo Egizio: A surprising treasure—one of the word's richest collections of Egyptian art outside Cairo.

5 Regal wines: Some of Italy's most revered reds—led by Barolo, dubbed "the king wines"—come from the hills of southern Piedmont.

The mountains and valleys of Valle d'Aosta fairly cry out to be strolled, climbed, and skied. Here, the highest Alpine peaks— including **Monte Bianco** (aka Mont Blanc) and the **Matterhorn**—shelter resorts such as Breuil-Cervinia and Courmayeur and the great nature preserve known as the Gran Paradiso.

Gracing the Colline ("little hills") west of Turin are some opulent monuments of the 17th-century Piedmontese style, including the palace at **Stupinigi**, designed by Juvarra for the Savoy kings. Less worldly is the mesmerizingly medieval hilltop monastery of **Sacra di San Michele**.

Turin isn't just the car capital of Italy and home to the Holy Shroud. Neoclassical piazzas, shops filled with chocolates and chic fashions, and elegant baroque palazzos have all been prettied up for the 2006 Winter Olympics.

SWITZERLAND

Breuil-Cervinia

Courmayeur · Aosta · A5

VALLE D'AOSTA

A5

Susa · Sacra di San Michele · Turin

A32 · Stupinigi

23

Claviere

Pinerolo

FRANCE

Saluzzo

20 · A6

589 · Fossano

Cuneo

Mondovi

21

0 ——— 20 mi
0 ——— 20 km

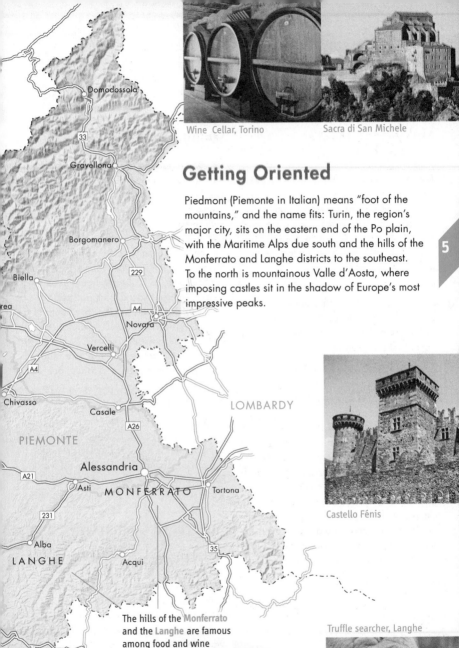

Wine Cellar, Torino

Sacra di San Michele

Getting Oriented

Piedmont (Piemonte in Italian) means "foot of the mountains," and the name fits: Turin, the region's major city, sits on the eastern end of the Po plain, with the Maritime Alps due south and the hills of the Monferrato and Langhe districts to the southeast. To the north is mountainous Valle d'Aosta, where imposing castles sit in the shadow of Europe's most impressive peaks.

Castello Fénis

The hills of the Monferrato and the Langhe are famous among food and wine connoisseurs. Asti gave the world Asti Spumante, Alba is known for its truffles and mushrooms, and the Langhe hills produce some of Italy's finest wines.

Truffle searcher, Langhe

PIEDMONT & VALLE D'AOSTA PLANNER

Making the Most of Your Time

The region is the site for the 2006 Winter Olympics, which is a good reason to pay a visit—and not just during the games. Lots of work, and many euros, have gone into development and renovation, the effects of which will linger well after the last medal has been handed out.

Turin is an underrated travel destination, and it's been polished to a shine for its role as Olympics host. If you like the idea of an Italian city with touches of Parisian sophistication, Turin is likely to strike your fancy.

Turin's residents will tell you how much it lifts their spirits when, on clear days, they have views of the surrounding mountains. In them you'll find exceptional hiking and climbing. Along the Piedmont–Valle d'Aosta border, the Gran Paradiso national park has beautiful, well-marked trails. Farther north is Monte Bianco, which should be a priority; you can ascend it by cable car, or, if you're an experienced climber, make a go of it with professional guides. If food and wine are your thing, also schedule a day or two on the less lofty slopes of the Langhe, south of Turin.

■ **The Truth about Turin's Shroud→→** When you hear the name Turin, the first thing that pops into your mind may be the Sacra Sindone (Holy Shroud), long held to be the burial shroud of Christ. Don't come to the city expecting to get a look at it—it's very rarely exhibited to the public, with the next appearance scheduled for 2025. Until then, you'll have to make do with a photocopy, on display in the Duomo.

Getting Around

Like any rugged, mountainous region, the Italian Alps can be tricky to navigate by car. Roads that look like superhighways on the map can be narrow and twisting, with steep slopes and cliff-side drops. Generally, roads are well maintained, but the sheer distance covered by all of those curves tends to take longer than you might expect, so it's best to figure in extra time for getting around. This is especially true in winter, when weather conditions can cause slow traffic and road closings. Check with local tourist offices, or in a pinch with the police, to make sure roads are passable and safe, and to find out whether you may need tire chains for snowy and icy roads.

Train service is extensive to the east of Turin along the Po plain. In the mountains, going by bus is the only public-transportation option; service is reliable, but slow. For more about car, bus, and train travel, see "Essentials" at the end of this chapter.

The French Connection

Napoleon's regime controlled Piedmont and Valle d'Aosta in the 19th century, and French influence remains evident in everything from traditional recipes redolent of mountain cheeses, truffles, and cream to Versailles-style gardens and wide, tree-lined boulevards. Well-dressed women in the cafés of Turin are addressed more often as *madama* than *signora*, and French is often spoken in the more remote mountain hamlets.

Hitting the Slopes

Skiing is the major sport in both Piedmont and Valle d'Aosta. Excellent facilities abound at resort towns such as Courmayeur and Breuil-Cervinia. The so-called Via Lattea (Milky Way)—five skiing areas near Sestriere with 400 km (almost 250 mi) of linked runs and 90 ski lifts—provides practically unlimited skiing. Lift tickets, running around €35 for a day's pass, are significantly less expensive than at major U.S. resorts.

To Italian skiers, a weeklong holiday on the slopes is known as a *settimana bianca* (white week). Ski resort hotels in the Piedmont and Valle d'Aosta encourage these getaways by offering six- and seven-day packages, and though they're designed with the domestic market in mind, you can get a bargain by taking advantage of the offers. The packages usually, though not always, include half- or full-board.

■ **Crossing Borders→→** You should have your passport with you if you plan to day-trip into France or Switzerland—though odds are you won't be asked to show it.

Finding a Place to Stay

High standards and opulence are characteristic of Turin's better hotels, and the same is true, translated into the Alpine idiom, at the top mountain resort hotels. The less-expensive hotels in cities and towns are generally geared to business travelers; make sure to ask if lower weekend rates are available.

Summer vacationers and winter skiers keep occupancy rates and prices high at the resorts during peak seasons. Many mountain hotels accept half- or full-board guests only and require that you stay for several nights; some have off-season rates that can reduce the cost by a full price category. If you're a skier, ask about package deals that give you a discount on lift tickets.

Dining & Lodging Price Categories

	$$$$	$$$	$$	$	¢
WHAT IT COSTS in Euros					
Restaurants	over €45	€35–€45	€25–€35	€15–€25	under €15
Hotels	over €220	€160–€220	€110–€160	€70–€110	under €70

Restaurant prices are for a first course (primo), second course (secondo), and dessert (dolce). Hotel prices are for two people in a standard double room in high season, including tax and service.

How's the Weather?

Snow conditions for skiing vary drastically year to year—there is nothing approaching the consistency of, say, the Rockies—so keep apprised of weather conditions. Some years there's good snow beginning in November, while others don't see much more than a flake or two until February.

The mountains to the north tend to shield the lowlands from the harshest winter weather, resulting in something resembling a Mediterranean climate. Spring starts early, fall lingers, and winter is mercifully short. Locals only complain about the steamy summers.

TOP PASSEGGIATA

Turin's Piazza San Carlo is one of the city's highlights, with arcaded walkways and distinguished cafés.

Updated by
Peter Blackman

A PAIR OF CONTRASTING CHARACTERISTICS define the appeal of northwest Italy's Piedmont and Valle d'Aosta regions: mountain splendor and bourgeois refinement. Two of Europe's most famous peaks—Monte Bianco (aka Mont Blanc) and Monte Cervino (the Matterhorn)—straddle Valle d'Aosta's borders with France and Switzerland, and the entire region is a magnet for skiers and hikers. To the south, the mist-shrouded lowlands skirting the Po River are home to Turin, a city that may not have the artistic treasures of Rome or the cutting-edge style of Milan, but has developed a sense of urban sophistication that makes it a pleasure to visit. You also taste a mountain/city contrast in the cuisine: the hearty peasant cooking served in tiny stone villages and the French-accented delicacies found in the plain are both eminently satisfying. Meals are accompanied by Piedmontese wines commonly held to be Italy's finest.

TURIN

Turin—Torino, in Italian—is roughly in the center of Piedmont/Valle d'Aosta and 128 km (80 mi) west of Milan; it's on the Po River, on the edge of the Po Plain, which stretches eastward all the way to the Adriatic. Turin's flatness and wide, angular, tree-lined boulevards are a far cry from Italian *metropoli* to the south; the region's decidedly northern European bent is quite evident in its nerve center. Apart from its role as northwest Italy's major industrial, cultural, intellectual, and administrative hub, Turin also has a reputation as Italy's capital of black magic and the supernatural. This distinction is enhanced by the presence of Turin's most famous, and controversial, relic, the Sacra Sindone (Holy Shroud), still believed by many Catholics to be the cloth in which Christ's body was wrapped when he was taken down from the cross.

Downtown Turin

Many of Turin's major sights are clustered around Piazza Castello, and others are on or just off the portico-lined Via Roma, one of the city's main thoroughfares, which leads 1 km (½ mi) from Piazza Castello south to Piazza Carlo Felice, a landscaped park in front of the train station. First opened in 1615, Via Roma was largely rebuilt in the 1930s, during the Mussolini era.

The Main Attractions

❶ Duomo di San Giovanni. The most impressive part of Turin's 15th-century cathedral is the shadowy, black marble–walled **Cappella della Sacra Sindone** (Chapel of the Holy Shroud), where the famous relic was housed before a fire in 1997. The chapel was designed by the priest and architect Guarino Guarini (1604–83), a genius of the baroque style who was official engineer and mathematician to the court of Duke Carlo Emanuele II of Savoy. The fire caused severe structural damage, and the chapel is closed indefinitely while restoration work proceeds.

The Sacra Sindone (Holy Shroud) is a 4-yard-long sheet of linen, thought by millions to be the burial shroud of Christ, bearing the light imprint of his crucified body. The shroud first made an appearance around the

PIEDMONT & VALLE D'AOSTA, PAST & PRESENT

Ancient History. Piedmont and Valle d'Aosta were originally inhabited by Celtic tribes, who over time were absorbed by the conquering Romans. As allies of Rome, the Celts held off Hannibal when he came down through the Alpine passes with his elephants, but they were eventually defeated, and their capital—Taurasia, the present Turin—was destroyed. The Romans rebuilt the city, giving its streets the grid pattern that survives today. (Roman ruins can be found throughout both regions and are particularly conspicuous in the town of Aosta.)

The Middle Ages and the Savoy. With the fall of the Roman Empire, the region suffered the fate of the rest of Italy and was successively occupied and ravaged by barbarians from the east and the north. In the 11th century, the feudal French Savoy family ruled Turin briefly; toward the end of the 13th century it returned to the area, where it would remain, almost continuously, for 500 years. In 1798 the French republican armies invaded Italy, but when Napoléon's empire fell, the house of Savoy returned to power.

Risorgimento. Beginning in 1848, Piedmont was one of the principal centers of the Risorgimento, the movement for Italian unity. In 1861 the Chamber of Deputies of Turin declared Italy a united kingdom. Rome became the capital in 1870, effectively marking the end of Piedmont's prominence in national politics.

Industry and Affluence. Piedmont became one of the first industrialized regions in Italy, and the automotive giant FIAT—the Fabbrica Italiana Automobili Torino—was established here in 1899. Today the region is the center of Italy's automobile, metalworking, chemical, and candy industries, having attracted thousands of workers from Italy's south. The FIAT company, led by the Agnelli family—roughly Italy's equivalent of the Kennedys—has been arguably the most important factor in the region's rise to affluence.

middle of the 15th century, when it was presented to Ludovico of Savoy in Chambéry. In 1578 it was brought to Turin by another member of the Savoy royal family, Duke Emanuele Filiberto. It was only in the 1990s that the Catholic Church began allowing rigorous scientific study of the shroud. Not surprisingly, results have bolstered both sides of the argument. On the one hand, three separate university teams—in Switzerland, Britain, and the United States—have concluded, as a result of carbon 14 dating, that the cloth is a forgery dating from between 1260 and 1390. On the other hand, they are unable to explain how medieval forgers could have created the shroud's image, which resembles a photographic negative, and how they could have had the knowledge or means to incorporate traces of Roman coins covering the eyelids and endemic Middle Eastern pollen woven into the cloth. Either way, the shroud continues to be revered as a holy relic, exhibited to the public on very rare occa-

268 <

Borgo
Medioevale ..**15**

Duomo di
San Giovanni ..**1**

Galleria
Sabauda **8**

Gran Madre
di Dio **12**

Mole
Antonelliana ..**11**

Museo dell'
Automobile ..**16**

Museo Egizio ..**9**

Palazzo
Carignano ...**10**

Palazzo
Madama **3**

Palazzo
Reale **2**

Parco del
Valentino **14**

Piazza
San Carlo **7**

Pinacoteca
Giovanni e
Marella
Agnelli **17**

San Carlo **5**

San Lorenzo ...**4**

Santa
Cristina **6**

Santa Maria
del Monte **13**

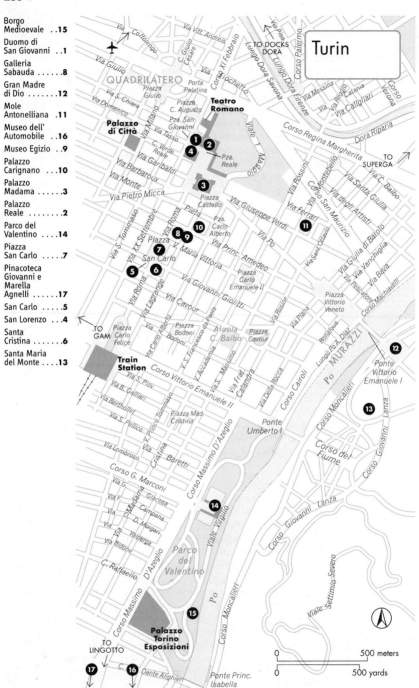

sions—the next official display is planned for 2025. In lieu of the real thing, a photocopy is on permanent display near the altar of the Duomo. ⊠ *Piazza San Giovanni, Centro* ☎ *011/4361540* ⊘ *Mon.–Sat. 6:30–noon and 3–7, Sun. 8–noon and 3–7.*

⑧ Galleria Sabauda. Some of the most important paintings from the vast collections of the house of Savoy are displayed here. The collection is particularly rich in 16th- and 17th-century Dutch and Flemish paintings: note the *St. Francis with Stigmata* by Jan Van Eyck (1395–1441), in which the saint receives the marks of Christ's wounds while a companion cringes beside him. Other Dutch masterpieces include paintings by Anthony Van Dyck (1599–1641) and Rembrandt (1606–69). *Tobias and the Angel* by Piero del Pollaiuolo (circa 1443–96) is showcased, and other featured Italian artists include Fra Angelico (circa 1400–55), Andrea Mantegna (1431–1506), and Paolo Veronese (1528–88). Along with the Egyptian Museum, the gallery is housed in the **Palazzo dell'Accademia delle Scienze,** a baroque tour de force designed by priest-architect Guarino Guarini. ⊠ *Via Accademia delle Scienze 6, Centro* ☎ *011/547440* 🖭 *€4, €8 with admission to Museo Egizio* ⊘ *Fri.–Sun. and Tues. 8:30–2, Wed. 2–5:30, Thurs. 2–7:30.*

★ ☾ ⑪ Mole Antonelliana. You can't miss the unusual square dome and thin, elaborate spire of this Turin landmark above the city's rooftops. This odd structure, built between 1863 and 1889, was originally intended to be a synagogue, but costs escalated and eventually it was bought by the city of Turin. In its time it was the tallest brick building in the world. You can take the crystal elevator to reach the terrace at the top of the dome for an excellent view of the city, the plain, and the Alps beyond. Also worth a visit is the Mole Antonelliana's **Museo Nazionale del Cinema** (National Cinema Museum, ⊕ www.museonazionaledelcinema.it), which embraces more than 34,000 square feet and houses many items of film memorabilia as well as a film library with some 7,000 titles. ⊠ *Via Montebello 20, Centro* ☎ *011/8125658* 🖭 *Museum €5.20, elevator €3.62, combination ticket €6.80* ⊘ *Museum Tues.–Fri. and Sun. 9–8, Sat. 9 AM–11 PM; ticket sales end 75 mins before closing; elevator Tues.–Fri. and Sun. 10–8, Sat. 10 AM–11 PM.*

⑨ Museo Egizio. The Egyptian Museum's superb collection includes statues of pharaohs and mummies and entire frescoes taken from royal tombs— all in all, it's one of the world's finest and largest museums of its kind. Look for the magnificent 13th-century BC statue of Ramses II and the fascinating Tomb of Kha. The latter was found intact with furniture, supplies of food and clothing, writing instruments, and a complete set of personal cosmetics and toiletries. Unfortunately, the museum's objects are not always displayed according to modern standards. Along with carefully constructed exhibits with detailed information in English

Fodor'sChoice ★

> **WORD OF MOUTH**
>
> "The highlights of our stay in Turin were walking under the grand arcades that run alongside miles of the streets downtown, window-shopping, and stopping for coffee, pastries, or chocolate at one of the many elegant cafés."   —Anne

and Italian you will also find rooms that resemble warehouses filled with objects, with little or no information identifying what they are. ✉ *Via Accademia delle Scienze 6, Centro* 🕾 *011/5617776* ⊕ *www.museoegizio. it* 🎫 *€6.50, €8 with admission to Galleria Sabauda* ☉ *Tues.–Sun. 8:30–7:30; ticket sales end 1 hr before closing.*

❸ Palazzo Madama. In the center of Piazza Castello, this castle was named for the Savoy queen Maria Cristina, who made it her home in the 17th century. The building incorporates the remains of a Roman gate with later-medieval and Renaissance additions. Filippo Juvarra (1678–1736) designed the castle's monumental baroque facade. Open to the public are the atrium; the large central room known as Il Voltone, where a glass floor reveals the castle's Roman foundations; Juvarra's splendid baroque staircase; and the Salone del Senato, where you'll find temporary art exhibitions. ✉ *Piazza Castello, Centro* 🕾 *011/4429912* ⊕ *www.comune. torino.it/palazzomadama* 🎫 *Free, exhibitions €3.50* ☉ *Tues.–Fri. and Sun. 10–8, Sat. 10 AM–11 PM.*

❼ Piazza San Carlo. Surrounded by shops, arcades, fashionable cafés, and elegant baroque palaces, this is one of the most beautiful squares in Turin. In the center stands a statue of Duke Emanuele Filiberto of Savoy, victor at the battle of San Quintino in 1557. The melee heralded the peaceful resurgence of Turin under the Savoy after years of bloody dynastic fighting. The fine bronze statue erected in the 19th century is one of Turin's symbols.

> **NEED A BREAK?**
>
> A chocolate lover's pilgrimage to Turin inevitably leads to **Al Bicerin** (✉ Piazza della Consolata 5, Centro 🕾 011/4369325 ⊕ www.bicerin.it ☉ Closed Wed.), which first opened its doors in 1763. Cavour, Nietzsche, Puccini, and Dumas have all sipped here, and if you order the house specialty, the *bicerin* (a hot drink with layers of chocolate, coffee, and cream), you'll understand why. Don't be surprised if the friendly and energetic owner, Marité Costa, also tries to tempt you with one of her flavored *zabajoni* (warm eggnogs). Chocolate goodies, including chocolate-flavor pasta, are on sale in the café store. The historic **Caffè San Carlo** (✉ Piazza San Carlo 156, Centro 🕾 011/532586) is usually lively with locals gathered at the marble-top tables under the huge crystal chandelier. Break-

A GOOD WALK: BAROQUE TURIN

When the Savoy moved the seat of their Duchy from France to Turin in 1563, they instituted a process of urban renewal that was to employ some of the most important baroque architects of the day. During 200 years of almost continuous development, Turin was transformed into an elegant European capital more than twice its original size, with new churches, palaces, public squares, and streets.

The first section of town to be developed was the *contrada nuova* (new district), to the southwest of the old medieval fortifications. It was surrounded by extensive walls, which no longer exist. Only the name of the present-day train station serves as a reminder of the *porta nuova* (new gate) that was once the main entrance to this part of town.

This walk, encompassing some of Turin's most important baroque monuments, begins in what was

fast and lunch, afternoon snack, and evening aperitifs are all served in this particularly elegant neoclassical setting.

❹ **San Lorenzo.** Architect Guarino Guarini was in his mid-sixties when he began this church in 1668. The masterful use of geometric forms and the theatrical control of light and shadow show him working at his mature and confident best. Stand in the center of the church and look up into the cupola to enjoy the full effect. ✉ *Piazza Castello, Centro* ☎ *011/4361527* ◷ *Daily 8:30–noon and 4–7.*

NEED A BREAK?

Baratti e Milano (✉ Piazza Castello 27, Centro ☎ 011/5613060), in the glass-roofed Galleria Subalpina near Via Po, is one of Turin's charming old cafés. It's famous for its exquisite chocolates—indulge your sweet tooth or buy some *gianduiotti* (hazelnut chocolates) or candied chestnuts to take home to friends. Light lunches are served at the tables to the rear of the café. The tiny café **Mulassano** (✉ Piazza Castello 15, Centro ☎ 011/547990), decorated with marble and finely carved wood panels, is famous for its *tramezzini* (small triangular sandwiches made with lightly toasted white bread), invented here in the 1920s. Popular with the pre- and post-theater crowd, the café also offers a unique roulette system for clients trying to decide on who pays the bill—ask the cashier for an explanation.

Also Worth Seeing

❿ **Palazzo Carignano.** A baroque triumph by Guarino Guarini (the priest who designed several of Turin's most noteworthy structures), this red-brick palace was built between 1679 and 1685 and would play an important role in the 19th-century unification of Italy. Vittorio Emanuele II of Savoy (1820–78), united Italy's first king, was born within these walls, and Italy's first parliament met here from 1860 to 1865. The palace now houses the **Museo del Risorgimento,** a museum honoring the 19th-century movement for Italian unity. ✉ *Via Accademia delle Scienze 5, Centro* ☎ *011/5621147* ⊕ *www.regione.piemonte.it/cultura/risorgimento* ▣ *€5* ◷ *Tues.–Sun. 9–7; ticket sales end 1 hr before closing.*

❷ **Palazzo Reale.** This 17th-century palace, the former Savoy royal residence, is an imposing work of brick, stone, and marble that stands on the site of one of Turin's ancient Roman city gates. In contrast to its sober ex-

designed to be the focal point of the contrada nuova, **Piazza San Carlo** ❼.
Developed in the style of the French *place royales* (royal square), Piazza San Carlo was not only the most important public space of this new part of the city, but also a symbol of the authority of the Savoy family. At the southwestern end are the twin baroque churches of **San Carlo** ❺ and **Santa Cristina** ❻, while some of Turin's most famous cafés are to be found beneath the porticoes that line each side of the square.

Beyond the northeast end of Piazza San Carlo is the imposing **Palazzo dell'Accademia delle Scienze,** begun by priest/architect Guarino Guarini in 1679. If you're in the mood for museums, devote an hour or two to the collections housed inside, the **Galleria Sabauda** ❽ and the **Museo Egizio** ❾.
To the east, across the street, is the graceful **Palazzo Carignano** ❿, united Italy's first parliament building and another of Guarino Guarini's architectural masterpieces in Turin. (As a brief detour, you can follow

terior, the palace's interior is swathed in luxurious, mostly rococo trappings, including tapestries, gilt ceilings, and sumptuous 17th- to 19th-century furniture. Behind the palace you can relax in the royal gardens. ⊠ *Piazza Castello, Centro* ☎ *011/4361455* 🎫 *Gardens free, palace €6.50* ⊙ *Palace Tues.–Sun. 8:30–6:15; guided visits depart every 40 mins. Gardens, daily 9–1 hr before sunset.*

The **Armeria Reale** (Royal Armory), in a wing of the Royal Palace, holds one of Europe's most extensive collections of arms and armor. It's a must-see for connoisseurs. ⊠ *Entrance at Piazza Castello 191, Centro* ☎ *011/ 543889* 🎫 *€4* ⊙ *Tues.–Sun. 10:30–7:30.*

❺ San Carlo. The ornate baroque facade of this 17th-century church was enhanced in the latter part of the 19th century to harmonize with the facade of neighboring Santa Cristina. ⊠ *Piazza San Carlo, south end of square, right corner, Centro* ☎ *011/5620922* ⊙ *Weekdays 8–noon and 4–6:30, Sat. 8–noon and 4–6, Sun. 9–12:45 and 4–6.*

❻ Santa Cristina. Built in the mid-17th century, this church received a baroque-style face-lift by Juvarra in 1715. ⊠ *Piazza San Carlo, south end of square, left corner, Centro* ☎ *011/539281* ⊙ *Daily 7–noon and 3–7.*

Off the Beaten Path

Galleria Civica d'Arte Moderna e Contemporanea (GAM). In 1863 Turin was the first Italian city to begin a public collection devoted to contemporary art. Housed in a modern building on the edge of downtown, a permanent display of more than 600 paintings, sculptures, and installation pieces provides an exceptional glimpse of how Italian contemporary art has evolved since the late 1800s. The futurist, pop, neo-Dada, and arte povera movements are particularly well represented, and the gallery has a fine video and art film collection. ⊠ *Via Magenta 31, Centro* ☎ *011/5629911* ⊕ *www.gamtorino.it* 🎫 *€7.50* ⊙ *Tues.–Sun. 9–7.*

Along the Po

The Po River is narrow and unprepossessing here in Turin, only a hint of the broad waterway that it becomes as it flows eastward toward the Adriatic. It's flanked, however, by formidable edifices, a park, and a lovely pedestrian path.

Via Principe, to the right of the palazzo, to see the eastern facade of the palace on Piazza Carlo Alberto.) Continue northeast on Via Accademia delle Scienze to reach **Piazza Castello.** The massive building occupying an entire block at the center of the square is **Palazzo Madama ❸**, parts of which are open to the public. Don't miss the dramatic baroque staircase, in the entrance hall, that was begun by Juvarra in 1718.

In the northwest corner of the same square is another example of Guarini's lively architectural vision, the church of **San Lorenzo ❹**. Near San Lorenzo is the entrance to the imposing **Palazzo Reale ❷**, where you can view some sumptuous rococo interiors and, in a separate wing to the east, the Armeria Reale. The gate, flanked by statues of Castor and Pollux, is thought by some to be a focal point of otherworldly powers. It marks the apex of two international triangles alleged to have magical significance, one formed by Turin, London, and San Francisco, the other by Turin, Lyon, and Prague.

The Main Attractions

⑮ Borgo Medioevale. Along the banks of the Po, this complex, built for a General Exhibition in 1884, is a faithful reproduction of a typical Piedmont village in the Middle Ages: craft shops, houses, a church, and stores cluster the narrow lanes, and in the center of the village the **Rocca Medioevale,** a medieval castle, provides the town's main attraction. ✉ *Southern end of Parco del Valentino, San Salvario* ☎ *011/4431701* ⊕ *www.borgomedioevaletorino.it* ✆ *Village free, Rocca Medioevale €5* ⊙ *Village Apr.–Oct., daily 9–8; Nov.–Mar., daily 9–7. Rocca Medioevale Tues.–Sun. 9–7; groups of no more than 25 enter the castle every ½ hr; ticket counter closes at 6:15.*

★ **⑯ Museo dell'Automobile.** No visit to car-manufacturing Turin would be complete without a pilgrimage to see perfectly conserved Bugattis, Ferraris, and Isotta Fraschinis. Here you'll get an idea of the importance of FIAT—and automobiles in general—to Turin's economy. There's a collection of antique cars from as early as 1896, and displays show how the city has changed over the years as a result of its premier industry. For the true automobile fan, there's even a section devoted to the history of car tires. ✉ *Corso Unità d'Italia 40, Millefonti* ☎ *011/677666* ⊕ *www.museoauto.it* ✆ *€5.50* ⊙ *Tues.–Sun. 10–6:30.*

⑭ Parco del Valentino. This pleasant riverside park is a great place to stroll, bike, or jog. Originally the grounds of a relatively simple hunting lodge, the park owes its present arrangement to Madama Maria Cristina of France, who received the land and lodge as a wedding present after her marriage to Vittorio Amedeo I of Savoy. With memories of 16th-century French châteaux in mind, she began work in 1620 and converted the lodge into a magnificent palace, the **Castello del Valentino.** The building, now home to the University of Turin's Faculty of Architecture, is not open to the general public. Next to the palace are botanical gardens, established in 1729, where local and exotic flora can be seen in a hothouse, herbarium, and arboretum. ✉ *Parco del Valentino, San Salvario* ☎ *011/6707446 botanical gardens* ✆ *Gardens €3* ⊙ *Gardens Apr.–Sept., weekends 9–1 and 3–7.*

⑰ Pinacoteca Giovanni e Marella Agnelli. This gallery was opened by Gianni Agnelli (1921–2003), the head of FIAT and patriarch of one of Italy's

Wrap up your walk by taking the passage to the left of the Palazzo Reale to reach Piazza San Giovanni and the **Duomo di San Giovanni** ①. This hushed, shadowy repository of the city's famed relic, the Shroud of Turin, is yet another Guarini creation.

most powerful families, just four months before his death. The emphasis here is on quality rather than quantity: 25 works of art from the Agnelli private collection are on permanent display, along with temporary exhibitions. There are four magnificent scenes of Venice by Canaletto (1697–1768), two splendid views of Dresden by Canaletto's nephew, Bernardo Bellotto (1720–80), several works by Manet (1832–83), Renoir (1841–1919), Matisse (1869–1954), and Picasso (1881–1973), and fine examples of the work of Italian Futurist painters Balla (1871–1958) and Severini (1883–1966). The gallery is located on the top floor of the **Lingotto,** a former FIAT factory that was completely transformed between 1982 and 2002 by architect Renzo Piano. The multilevel complex now contains two hotels, a shopping mall, several movie theaters, restaurants, and an auditorium. ⊠ *Via Nizza 230, Lingotto* ☎ *011/0062008* ⊕ *www. pinacoteca-agnelli.it* ⊒ *€4* ☉ *Tues.–Sun. 10–7.*

Also Worth Seeing

⑫ **Gran Madre di Dio.** On the east bank of the Po, this neoclassical church is modeled after the Pantheon in Rome. It was built between 1827 and 1831 to commemorate the return of the house of Savoy to Turin after the fall of Napoléon's empire. ⊠ *Piazza Gran Madre di Dio, Borgo Po* ☎ *011/8193572* ☉ *Mon.–Sat. 7:30–noon and 3:30–7, Sun. 7:30–1 and 3:30–7.*

⑬ **Santa Maria del Monte.** The church and convent standing on top of 150-foot Monte dei Cappuccini date from 1583. Don't be surprised if you find yourself in the middle of a wedding party, as couples often come here to be photographed. Next to the church is the tiny **Museo Nazionale della Montagna,** dedicated to mountains and to mountain climbing. ⊠ *Monte dei Cappuccini, above Corso Moncalieri, Borgo Po* ☎ *011/6604414 church, 011/6604104 museum* ⊕ *www.museomontagna.org* ⊒ *Church free, museum €5* ☉ *Church daily 9–noon, and 2:30–6; museum daily 9–7.*

Off the Beaten Path

Sassi–Superga Cog Train. The 18-minute ride from Sassi up the Superga hill is an absolute treat on a clear day. The view of the Alps is magnificent at the hilltop **Parco Naturale Collina Torinese,** a tranquil retreat from the bustle of the city. If you feel like a little exercise, you can walk back down to Sassi (about two hours) on one of the well-marked, wooded trails that start from the upper station. Other circular trails lead through the park and back to Superga, where mountain bikes are also available for rent. ⊠ *Piazza G. Modena, Sassi* ☎ *011/5764733 cog train, 011/8903667 bikes* ⊕ *www.gtt.to.it* ⊒ *Weekdays €1.55 one-way, weekends €2.58 one-way* ☉ *Hourly service Mon. and Wed.–Fri. 9–noon and 2–5; hourly service weekends 9–8; bus service replaces the train on Tues.*

Basilica di Superga. Since 1731, the Basilica di Superga has been the burial place of kings. Visible from miles around, the thoroughly baroque church was designed by Juvarra in the early 18th century, and no fewer than 58 members of the Savoia family are memorialized in the crypt. ⊠ *Strada della Basilica di Superga 73, Sassi* ☎ *011/8980083 basilica, 011/8997456 crypt* ⊒ *Free* ☉ *Basilica Apr.–Oct., daily 9–noon and 3–6; Nov.–Mar., daily 9–noon and 3–5. Crypt Apr.–Oct., Mon.–Thurs.*

9:30–1:30 and 2:30–6:30, weekends 9:30–7:30; Nov.–Mar., weekends
9:30–1:30 and 2:30–6:30.

Where to Eat

$$$$ ✕ **Al Garamond.** The ocher-color walls and the ancient brick vaulting
FodorśChoice set the stage in this small and brightly decorated restaurant. Traditional
★ and innovative dishes of both meat and seafood are prepared with creative flair; you might try the tantalizing *rombo in crosta di patate al barbera* (turbot wrapped in sliced potatoes and baked with Barbera wine).
For dessert, the mousse *di liquirizia e salsa di cioccolato bianco* (licorice
mousse with white chocolate sauce) is a must, even if you don't usually
like licorice. The level of service here is high, even by demanding Turin
standards. ✉ *Via G. Pomba 14, Centro* ☎ *011/8122781* 🍽 *AE, MC,
V* ✆ *Closed Sun., Jan. 1–6, and 3 wks in Aug. No lunch Sat.*

$$$$ ✕ **Del Cambio.** Set in a palace dating from 1757, this is one of Europe's
most beautiful and historic restaurants, with decorative moldings, mirrors, and hanging lamps that look just as they did when Italian national
hero Cavour dined here more than a century ago. The cuisine draws heavily on Piedmontese tradition and is paired with fine wines of the region.
Agnolotti with *sugo d'arrosto* (roast veal sauce) is a recommended first
course. ✉ *Piazza Carignano 2, Centro* ☎ *011/546690* 🍴 *Reservations
essential* 🎩 *Jacket and tie* 🍽 *AE, DC, MC, V* ✆ *Closed Sun., Jan. 1–6,
and 3 wks in Aug.*

★ **$$$** ✕ **Vintage 1997.** The first floor of an elegant town house in the center
of Turin makes a fitting location for this sophisticated restaurant. You
might try such specialties as *vitello tonnato alla nostra maniera* (roast
veal with a light tuna sauce) or *code di scampi con costolette di coniglio
su crema di scalogno* (shrimp and rabbit in a scallion sauce). For the es-
pecially hungry gourmet there's the *menu del Vintage,* a 13-course feast
that covers the full range of the restaurant's cuisine. There's an excel-
lent wine list, with regional, national, and international vintages well
represented. ✉ *Piazza Solferino 16/h, Centro* ☎ *011/535948* 🍽 *AE,
DC, MC, V* ✆ *Closed Sun. and 3 wks in Aug. No lunch Sat.*

★ **$$–$$$** ✕ **Savoia.** The enthusiasm of chef and owner Mario Ferrero permeates
three small rooms decorated with a few choice pictures and antique fur-
niture. His kitchen turns out creative takes on Piedmontese specialties
that change with the seasons. The bread and pasta are homemade, and
the wine cellar is tended with equal care. ✉ *Via Corta d'Appello 13, Cen-
tro* ☎ *011/4362288* 🍽 *AE, DC, MC, V* ✆ *Closed Sun. No lunch Sat.*

$$ ✕ **L'Agrifoglio.** This intimate local favorite has just 10 tables. Specialties change with the seasons, but you might find such delicacies as
risotto *al Barbaresco* (with Barbaresco wine) and *agnolotti dal plin al
sugo d'arrosto* (crescent-shape stuffed pasta with the pan juices of roast
veal) on the menu. L'Agrifoglio stays open late for the after-theater and
after-cinema crowd. ✉ *Via Accademia Albertina 38, Centro* ☎ *011/
837064* 🍽 *AE, DC, MC, V* ✆ *Closed Sun. and Mon. No lunch.*

$$ ✕ **Hosteria La Vallée.** Small and romantic, with elegant tableware and
linens, select pieces of antique furniture, and carefully designed light-
ing, this restaurant tucked away in a quiet section of central Turin has

EATING WELL IN PIEDMONT & VALLE D'AOSTA

The Piedmontese take their food and their wine very seriously, and although you will find a similar range of eating establishments here as in other regions of Italy, the number of formal restaurants, with elaborate service and extraordinary wine lists, exceeds the national average. This holds true both in cities and in the country, where even simply named trattorias may offer a *menu di degustazione* (a multicourse tasting menu) accompanied by wines appropriate to each dish. In Turin the ritual of the *aperitivo* has been finely tuned, and most cafés from the early evening onward provide lavish buffets that are included in the price of a cocktail—a respectable substitute for dinner if you are traveling on a limited budget. As a result, restaurants in Turin tend to fill only after 9 PM.

In Piedmont and Valle d'Aosta you will find rustic specialties from farmhouse hearths, fine cuisine with a French accent—and everything in between. The area's best-known dish is probably polenta, creamy cornmeal served with *carbonada* (veal stew), melted cheese, or wild mushrooms. Also at the top of the favorites list are *agnolotti dal plin,* crescent-shape stuffed pasta, served with the pan

juices of roast veal or with melted butter and shaved *tartufi bianchi* (white truffles) from Alba. Another regional specialty is *fonduta,* a local version of fondue, made with melted cheese, eggs, and sometimes grated truffles. Fontina and ham also often deck out the ubiquitous French-style *crepes alla valdostana,* served casserole style.

Throughout the region, though especially in Turin, you will find that most meals are accompanied by *grissini* (bread sticks). Invented in Turin in the 17th century to ease the digestive problems of little Prince Vittorio Amedeo II (1675–1730), these, when freshly made and hand-rolled, are a far cry from the thin and dry, plastic-wrapped versions available elsewhere. Napoléon called them *petits batons* and was, it seems, addicted to them.

Though desserts here are less sweet than in some other Italian regions, treats like *panna cotta* (a cooked milk custard), *torta di nocciole* (hazelnut torte), and *bonet* (a pudding made with hazelnuts, cocoa, milk, and macaroons) are delights. Turin is renowned for its delicate pastries and fine chocolates, especially for the hazelnut *gianduiotti.*

developed a devoted clientele. Recommended are *agnello scottato all'aglio e rosmarino* (lamb grilled with garlic and rosemary) followed by *sformato di cacao con cuore di fondente* (warm chocolate pudding). ⊠ *Via Provana 3b, Centro* ☎ *011/8121788* ⊟ *AE, MC, V* ☉ *Closed Sun., Jan. 1–7, and Aug. No lunch.*

$ ✕ **Locanda da Betty.** At this small and homey trattoria, traditional Piedmont cuisine is served to a usually packed house. The inexpensive four-course *menu di degustazione* (a multicourse tasting menu) is an especially good deal. ✉ *Via Bogino 17/e, Centro* ☎ *011/8170583* ▭ *MC, V* ☉ *Closed Sun.*

$ ✕ **Porto di Savona.** Look for this centuries-old tavern under the arcades of vast Piazza Vittorio Veneto, where it once served as a terminal for the Turin–Savona stagecoach line. The small street-level and upstairs dining rooms have a decidedly old-fashioned air; the marble stairs are well worn, and the walls are decked with photos of Old Turin. Customers sit at long wooden tables to eat home-style Piedmontese cooking, including gnocchi with Gorgonzola and *bollito misto* (mixed boiled meats, appropriately served only in winter). The Barbera house wine is good. ✉ *Piazza Vittorio Veneto 2, Centro* ☎ *011/8173500* ▭ *MC, V.*

Where to Stay

The **Turin Tourist Board** (✉ Via Bogino 8, Centro ☎ 011/8185011 🖷 011/883426 ⊕ www.turismotorino.org) provides a booking service for hotels and bed-and-breakfast–style accommodations in the city. In order to use the service, you must book hotels 48 hours in advance and B&Bs seven days in advance. The travel agency **Montagnedoc** (✉ Viale Giolitti 7/9, Pinerolo ☎ 0121/794003 🖷 0121/794932 ⊕ www.montagnedoc. it) provides help locating and booking vacation accommodations in the mountain valleys to the west of Turin.

$$$$ ▦ **Grand Hotel Sitea.** The finest of Turin's four-star hotels, the Sitea is ideally located in the city's historic center. Decorated in a warmly classical style, the public areas and guest rooms are elegant and comfortable. As might be expected from a first-rate hotel, top-notch service is provided by a courteous and efficient staff. Weekend rates ($$) are available. ✉ *Via Carlo Alberto 35, Centro, 10123* ☎ *011/5170171* 🖷 *011/548090* ⊕ *www.sitea.thi.it* ⤣ *110 rooms, 4 suites* ⌂ *Restaurant, minibars, cable TV with movies, in-room data ports, bar, Internet room, meeting rooms, parking (fee), some pets allowed* ▭ *AE, DC, MC, V* ❚⊘❙ *BP.*

$$$$ ▦ **Le Meridien Art+Tech.** Designed by architect Renzo Piano, this luxury hotel is part of the former Lingotto FIAT factory. The approach throughout is typically minimalist, with ultramodern fixtures and designer furniture decorating the rooms. The track on the roof, once used by FIAT to test its cars, is available to clients for jogging. Weekend rates ($$) are available. ✉ *Via Nizza 230, Lingotto, 10126* ☎ *011/6642000* 🖷 *011/6642001* ⊕ *www.lemeridien.com* ⤣ *141 rooms, 1 suite* ⌂ *Restaurant, in-room safes, minibars, cable TV with movies, in-room data ports, bar, Internet room, meeting rooms* ▭ *AE, DC, MC, V* ❚⊘❙ *BP.*

$$$ ▦ **Victoria.** Rare style, attention to detail, and comfort are the hallmarks of this boutique hotel furnished and managed to create the feeling of a refined town house. The newer wing has a grand marble staircase and individually decorated guest rooms. The same attention to detail is found in the refurbished rooms of the original wing, and the sitting room and breakfast room are particularly attractive. ✉ *Via Nino Costa 4, Centro, 10123* ☎ *011/5611909* 🖷 *011/5611806* ⊕ *www.hotelvictoria-torino. com* ⤣ *97 rooms, 9 suites* ⌂ *Pool, sauna, Turkish bath, meeting rooms, bicycles, bar, Internet room, parking (fee)* ▭ *AE, DC, MC, V* ❚⊘❙ *BP.*

Fodor'sChoice
★

5

$$–$$$ 🖾 **Genio.** The Genio, like many hotels in Turin, underwent a complete transformation in preparation for the Winter Olympics in 2006. Though steps away from the main train station, spacious and tastefully decorated rooms provide a quiet haven from the bustle of the city. Best of all is the service, which resembles that of a friendly family-run inn rather than a big-city business hotel. ⊠ *Corso Vittorio Emanuele II 47, Centro, 10125* 🖀 *011/6505771* 🖷 *011/6508264* ⊕ *www.hotelgenio. it* ⟟ *125 rooms, 3 suites* △ *Minibars, Wi-Fi, meeting rooms, parking (fee)* ⊟ *AE, DC, MC, V* ⦿| *BP.*

$$ 🖾 **Liberty.** The name of this small, conveniently located lodging comes from an Italian term for the art nouveau style, and the place is true to its name, with period-style furnishings and a stylish ambience. It's a favorite of academics, artists, and others who appreciate its solid, old-fashioned comfort and the Anfossi family's attentive courtesy. The hotel is on the upper floor of an otherwise poorly maintained building, so don't be put off by the shabby entrance and the rickety elevator. ⊠ *Via Pietro Micca 15, Centro, 10121* 🖀 *011/5628801* 🖷 *011/5628163* ⊕ *www.hotelliberty-torino. it* ⟟ *35 rooms* △ *Restaurant, bar* ⊟ *AE, DC, MC, V* ⦿| *BP.*

$$ 🖾 **La Maddalena.** It may be difficult to book a stay at this small B&B hotel (there are only three rooms), but it's worth a try. You'll be made to feel instantly at home by the proprietor, Maddalena Vitale, in this delightfully decorated and comfortably cluttered apartment not far from the main train station. One room has a double bed and en suite bathroom; the other two rooms have twin beds and private bathrooms across the hall. ⊠ *Via San Secondo 31, Centro, 10128* 🖀🖷 *011/591267* ⊕ *www.iam-maddalena.com* ⟟ *3 rooms* △ *In-room data ports; no a/c* ⊟ *No credit cards* ⦿| *BP.*

Nightlife & the Arts

The Arts

MUSIC Classical music concerts are held in the famous **Conservatorio Giuseppe Verdi** (⊠ Via Mazzini 11, Centro 🖀 011/8121268 ⊠ Piazza Bodoni, Centro 🖀 011/888470) throughout the year but primarily in winter. The **Settembre Musica Festival** (🖀 011/4424703), held for three weeks in September, highlights classical works. Traditional sacred music and some modern religious pieces are performed in the **Duomo** (⊠ Via Montebello 20, Centro 🖀 011/8154230) on Sunday evening; performances are usually advertised in the vestibule or in the local edition of Turin's nationally distributed newspaper, *La Stampa.* The Thursday edition comes with a supplement on music and other entertainment possibilities.

OPERA The **Teatro Regio** (⊠ Piazza Castello 215, Centro 🖀 011/8815557 ⊕ www.teatroregio.torino.it), one of Italy's leading opera houses, has its season from October to June. You can buy tickets for most performances (premieres sell well in advance) at the box office or on the Web site, where discounts are offered on the day of the show.

Nightlife

Two areas of Turin are enormously popular nightlife destinations: the Docks Dora, to the north of the city center, and the Murazzi embankment, near the Ponte Vittorio Emanuele I.

CLOSE UP

The Olympic Legacy in Turin

TURIN PLAYED HOST to the 20th Winter Olympics in 2006, and while the international spotlight has moved on, you can still sense the impact of the games. With the Olympics as an impetus (and further spurred by crises in the auto industry), Turin has worked to transcend its image as a city of industry and identify itself as a dynamic cultural and recreational travel destination.

The Olympics have brought about nothing less than a fundamental reorientation of the city. The central train station, Porta Nuova, and the nearby historical center have long been the focal points of activity, but the Olympics spurred development both to the west and along the city's north-south axis. The Olympic Village and Olympic skating rink are near a former FIAT factory, known as the Lingotto, to the south of the city core. For the games, the Lingotto train station, little used after the closure of the FIAT factory, was enlarged, and the industrial zone was largely transformed into a residential and commercial center, with new hotels and restaurants.

With the Olympics in mind, the city developed its first subway system; construction wrapped up on a section linking the Lingotto Olympic area with downtown Turin in late 2005. From the Porta Nuova station, the subway heads toward the now secondary Porta Susa station and then continues toward Turin's rapidly expanding western limits; the first stage of this plan was scheduled for completion in late 2006. Eventually Porta Susa will become Turin's principal train station and the Porta Nuova station will close, perhaps to be turned into a museum, like the d'Orsay train station in Paris.

The **Docks Dora** (⊠ Via Valprato 68, Madonna di Campagna ☎ 011/280251 ☾ Mon.–Sat. 9 PM–4 AM) is a complex of old warehouses that have been converted into artists' studios, gallery spaces, bars, cafés, and theaters. Live music and performances keep the area hopping, and the disco **Café Blue** serves up dance music all night long. Take the 51 bus from the Porta Susa train station or catch it heading north past the Duomo. On the Murazzi, near the Ponte Vittorio Emanuele I, is **Jammin's** (⊠ Murazzi del Po 17, Centro ☎ 011/882869 ☾ May–Sept., Mon.–Sat. 9 PM–4 AM), a popular disco with a mixed crowd; there's live music on Friday.

The center of town is also popular, especially earlier in the evening. With music, often live, that ranges from British pop and rock to punk, crossover, soul, and reggae, **Barrumba** (⊠ Via San Massimo 1, Centro ☎ 011/883322 ⊕ www.barrumba.it ☾ Thurs.–Sat. 10:30 PM–4:30 AM) is usually packed with a mix of young Turinese, university students, and visitors. A trendy meeting place for an aperitif or a pre-disco drink in the piazza at the end of Via Po is the wine bar **Caffè Elena** (⊠ Piazza Vittorio Veneto 5, Centro ☎ 011/8123341 ☾ Thurs.–Tues. 9 AM–2 AM). South of the main train station is **Rockcity** (⊠ Via Bertini 2, San Salvario ☎ 011/3184737 ☾ Thurs.–Sat. 10:30 PM–4 AM), where you'll find a smart crowd in their mid-twenties to mid-thirties listening to rock, techno, and commercial music.

Sports

Soccer

Turin's two professional soccer clubs, Juventus and Torino, play their games in the **Stadio delle Alpi** (⊠ 6 km [4 mi] northwest of city, Venaria). Juventus is one of Italy's most successful and most popular teams. There is fierce rivalry between its supporters and those of visiting clubs, especially Inter Milan and AC Milan. Home matches are usually played on Sunday afternoon during the season, which runs from late August to mid-May. It's possible to purchase tickets for Juventus and Torino games in any *tabaccheria* (tobacco shop) with a sign bearing a capital "T."

Shopping

Chocolate

The tradition of making chocolate began in Turin in the early 17th century. Chocolate at that time was an aristocratic drink, but in the 19th century a Piedmontese invention made it possible to further refine cocoa, which could then be used to create solid bars and candies. The most famous of all Turin chocolates is the gianduiotto (with cocoa, sugar, and hazelnuts), first concocted in 1867. The tradition of making these delicious treats has been continued at the small, family-run **Peyrano** (⊠ Corso Moncalieri 47, Centro ☎ 011/6602202 ⊕ www.peyrano.it), where more than 80 types of chocolates are concocted. **Stratta** (⊠ Piazza San Carlo 191, Centro ☎ 011/547920), one of Turin's most famous chocolate shops, has been in business since 1836 and sells confections of all kinds—not just the chocolates in the lavish window displays but also fancy cookies, rum-laced fudges, and magnificent cakes.

★

Markets

Go to the famous **Balon Flea Market** (⊠ Piazza Repubblica, Centro) on Saturday morning for excellent bargains on secondhand books and clothing and good browsing among stalls selling local specialties such as gianduiotti. (Be aware, however, that the market is also famous for its pickpockets.) The second Sunday of every month a special antiques market, appropriately called the **Gran Balon,** sets up shop in Piazza Repubblica.

Specialty Stores

Most people know that Turin produces more than 75% of Italy's cars, but they are often unaware that it's also a hub for clothing manufacturing. Top-quality boutiques stocking local, national, and international lines are clustered along Via Roma and Via Garibaldi. Piazza San Carlo, Via Po, and Via Maria Vittoria are lined with antiques shops, some—but not all—specializing in 18th-century furniture and domestic items.

Specialty food stores and delicatessens abound in central Turin. For a truly spectacular array of cheeses and other delicacies, try Turin's famous **Borgiattino** (⊠ Via Accademia Albertina 38/a, Centro ☎ 011/8394686). For hand-rolled *grissini* (bread sticks)—some as long as 4 feet—

the bakery **Bersano** (⊠ Via Barbaroux 5, Centro ☎ 011/5627579) is the best place in town. **Tabernalibraria** (⊠ Via Bogino 5, Centro ☎ 011/836515) is a delightful combination of *enoteca* (wineshop), delicatessen, and bookstore.

THE COLLINE & SAVOY PALACES

As you head west from Turin into the Colline ("little hills"), castles and medieval fortifications begin to pepper the former dominion of the house of Savoy and the Alps come into better and better view. In the region lie the storybook medieval towns of Avigliana, Rivoli, and Saluzzo; 12th-century abbeys; and, farther west in the mountains, the ski resorts of Bardonecchia and Sestriere, two of the venues used during the 2006 Winter Olympics.

Stupinigi

🔞 *8 km (5 mi) southwest of Turin.*

★ The **Palazzina di Caccia,** in the town of Stupinigi, was built by Juvarra in 1729 as a hunting lodge for the house of Savoy. More like a sumptuous royal villa, its many wings, landscaped gardens, and surrounding forests give a clear idea of the level of style to which the Savoy were accustomed. This regal aspect was not lost on Paolina Buonaparte, who briefly held court here during her brother Napoléon's reign over Italy. Today the Palazzina houses the **Museo d'Arte e Ammobiliamento** (Museum of Art and Decoration), a vast collection of paintings and furniture gathered from numerous Savoy palaces in the area. You can get there by taking Bus 41 from Turin's Porta Nuova train station. ⊠ *Via Principe Amedeo 7* ☎ *011/3581220* 💷 *€6.20* ⏰ *Apr.–Oct., Tues.–Sun. 10–7:30; Nov.–Mar., Fri.–Sun. 10–11:30 and 1:30–3:15.*

Rivoli

🔞 *16 km (10 mi) northwest of Stupinigi, 13 km (8 mi) west of Turin.*

The Savoy court was based in Rivoli in the Middle Ages. The 14th- to 15th-century **Casa del Conte Verde** (House of the Green Count) sits right in the center of town, and the richness of its decorations hints at the wealth and importance of the owner (and of Rivoli) during the period. Inside, a small gallery hosts temporary exhibitions. ⊠ *Via Fratelli Piol 8* ☎ *011/9563020* ⊕ *www.casadelconteverde.it* 💷 *Varies with exhibits* ⏰ *Varies with exhibits.*

★ The castle of Rivoli now houses the **Museo d'Arte Contemporaneo** (Museum of Contemporary Art). The building was begun in the 17th century and then redesigned but never finished by Juvarra in the 18th century; it was finally completed in the late 20th century by minimalist Turin architect Andrea Bruno. On display are changing international exhibitions and a permanent collection of 20th-century Italian art. To get to Rivoli from downtown Turin, take Tram 1 and then Bus 36. ⊠ *Piazzale Mafalda di Savoia* ☎ *011/9565222* ⊕ *www.castellodirivoli.org* 💷 *€6.50* ⏰ *Tues.–Thurs. 10–5, Fri.–Sun. 10–7.*

5

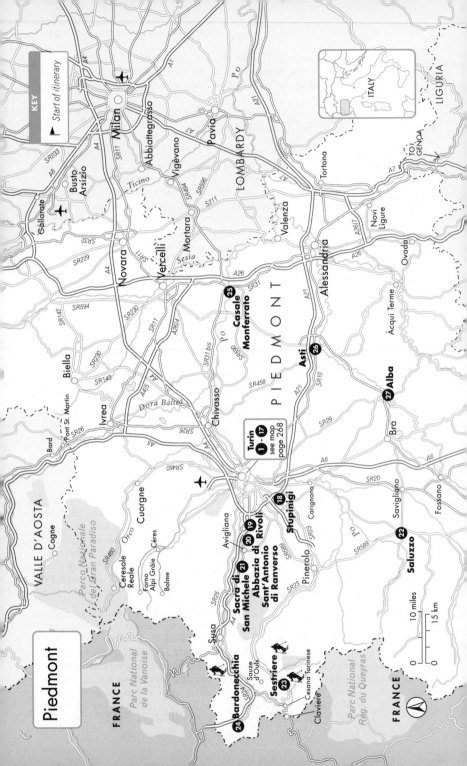

Abbazia di Sant'Antonio di Ranverso

㉒ *6 km (3½ mi) west of Rivoli, 23 km (14 mi) west of Turin.*

This abbey was originally a hospital, founded in the 12th century by the Hospitallers of St. Anthony to care for victims of St. Anthony's Fire, a painful medical condition brought on by consuming contaminated rye. Pilgrims came here over the centuries for cures and to offer thanks for a miraculous recovery. The 15th-century frescoes with their lifelike depictions of pilgrims and saints retain their original colors. ⊠ *Buttigliera Alta west of Rivoli, off SS25* 🕾 *011/9367450* 🖃 *€2.60* ☉ *Nov.–Mar., Tues.–Sun. 9–12:30 and 2–5; Apr.–Oct., Tues.–Sun. 9–12:30 and 2:30–6; last entrance ½ hr before closing.*

Sacra di San Michele

★ **㉑** *20 km (13 mi) west of Abbazia di Sant'Antonio di Ranverso, 43 km (27 mi) west of Turin.*

Unless you plan a 14-km (9-mi) hike from the town of Avigliana, a car is essential for an excursion to the Abbey of St. Michael, perhaps best known as inspiration for the setting of Umberto Eco's novel *The Name of the Rose.* San Michele was built on Monte Pirchiriano in the 11th century so it would stand out: it occupies the most prominent location for miles around, hanging over a 3,280-foot bluff. When monks came to enlarge the abbey they had to build part of the structure on supports more than 90 feet high—an engineering feat that was famous in medieval Europe and is still impressive today. By the 12th century this important abbey controlled 176 churches in Italy, France, and Spain; one of the abbeys under its influence was Mont-Saint-Michel in France. Because of its strategic position the Abbey of St. Michael came under frequent attacks over the next five centuries and was eventually abandoned in 1622. It was restored in the late 19th and early 20th centuries and can only be visited during accompanied tours.

From **Porta dello Zodiaco,** a splendid Romanesque doorway decorated with the signs of the zodiac, you climb 150 steps, past 12th-century sculptures, to reach the church. On the left side of the interior are 16th-century frescoes representing New Testament themes; on the right are depictions of the founding of the church. In the crypt are some of the oldest parts of the structure, three small 9th- to 12th-century chapels. Note that some sections of the abbey are only open on weekends. 🕾 *011/939130* ⊕ *www.sacradisanmichele.com* 🖃 *Weekends €4, weekdays €3.50* ☉ *Tours start every 30 min. Mar. 16–Oct. 15, Tues.–Sat. 9:30–12:30 and 3–6, Sun. 9:30–noon and 2:40–6; Oct. 16–Mar. 15, Tues.–Sat. 9:30–12:30 and 3–5, Sun. 9:30–noon and 2:40–5.*

Saluzzo

㉒ *58 km (36 mi) southwest of Turin.*

The russet-brick town of Saluzzo—a flourishing medieval center and later seat of a Renaissance ducal court—is a well-preserved gem with narrow, winding streets, frescoed houses, Gothic churches, and elegant Renaissance palaces. A map with instructions for a walking tour of the town's sights is available from the local **tourist information office** (⊠ Via Griselda 6 ☎ 0175/46710 ⊕ www.comune.saluzzo.cn.it). The older and more interesting part of the town hugs a hilltop in the Po Valley and is crowned by **La Castiglia,** a 13th-century castle that has served as a prison since the 1820s.

The exterior of the **Castello di Manta,** 4 km (2½ mi) south of Saluzzo, is austere, but inside are frescoes and other decorations of the period. Knights and damsels from an allegorical poem written by Marquis Tommaso III of Saluzzo, humanist lord of the castle, parade in full costume in the 15th-century frescoes of the **Sala del Barone.** The castle sometimes hosts exhibits, at which time higher admission is charged. *⊠ Via al Castello 14, Manta* ☎ *0175/87822* ✆ *€4.50* ☉ *Mar.–mid-Dec., Tues.–Sun. 10–1 and 2–6.*

Sestriere

㉓ *32 km (20 mi) east of Briançon, 93 km (58 mi) west of Turin.*

In the early 1930s, before skiing became a sport for commoners, the patriarch of the FIAT automobile dynasty had this resort built, with two distinctive tower hotels and ski facilities that have been developed into some of the best in the Alps. The resort lacks the charm of older Alpine centers, overdevelopment has added some eyesores, and the mountains don't have the striking beauty of those in Valle d'Aosta. But skiers have an excellent choice of trails, some of them crossing the border into France.

Where to Stay

$$$ 🏨 **Principi di Piemonte.** Large and elegant, this luxurious hotel sits on the slopes above the town, near the lifts and the town's golf course. Its secluded location heightens the sense of exclusivity, and though showing signs of age the hotel still attracts a stylish clientele. The restaurant and a cozy bar invite après-ski relaxation. *⊠ Via Sauze 3/B, 10058* ☎ *0122/7941* 🖶 *0122/755411* ⊕ *www.framon-hotels.com* 🛏 *96 rooms, 4 suites* ⌂ *Restaurant, indoor pool, hot tub, sauna, Turkish bath, bar, meeting rooms, some pets allowed* ▭ *AE, DC, MC, V* ☉ *Closed early Apr.–June and Sept.–Nov.* ⦿ *BP.*

$$$ 🏨 **Hotel Cristallo.** Half of the rooms at this hotel face the slopes of Sestriere, and the ski-lift station is just across the road. You'll find all the facilities you need for a stay in the mountains either in the hotel or just steps away from the lobby entrance. Rooms are elegantly and warmly furnished in the style of a modern ski lodge; ask for one with a terrace facing the view. *⊠ Via Pinerolo 5, 10058* ☎ *0122/750707* 🖶 *0122/ 755152* ⊕ *www.newlinehotels.com* 🛏 *40 rooms* ⌂ *Restaurant, minibars, gym, sauna, Turkish bath, bar, Internet room, parking (fee)* ▭ *AE, DC, MC, V* ⦿ *BP.*

$ 🏨 **Miramonti.** Nearly every room has a terrace at this pleasant, central, modern chalet. The ample, comfortable rooms are done in traditional mountain style, with lots of exposed wood and coordinated floral-print fabrics. *⊠ Via Cesana 3, 10058* ☎ *0122/755333* 🖶 *0122/755375*

VOICES OF ITALY

Ines Cavalcanti
Chambra d'Oc, Western Piedmont

Ines Cavalcanti is a member of Piedmont's Chambra d'Oc. The organization promotes the little-known language and culture of the Occitan peoples, inhabitants of the mountain valleys of western Piedmont, as well as much of southern France (including, naturally, the Languedoc region) and parts of northern Spain. Ines provides some background:

"All the mountain valleys at one time were filled with people, and all the villages, though small, were active communities. When the major industrialization of Italy began in the 1960s, people left the valleys to look for work in major towns like Turin. The population fell by more than 80%. Everything, practically everything, was abandoned.

"I come from a small village, Elva, more than 5,000 feet above sea level. Until I was 10 years old, I'd lived in Elva, and then my family came down from the valley—we emigrated to the towns in the Piedmont plains. In some ways, treated like foreigners in our new homes, we were worse off than we had been before.

"Until the 1970s, all the people of my generation spoke Occitan, with most people speaking only the one language. We weren't aware that, just across the Alps, 13 million people spoke exactly the same language! It wasn't until between about 1965 and 1970 that linguistic studies proved the language spoken in the valleys of western Piedmont was Occitan. When this happened, it was as though a new window opened for us. The knowledge that we belonged to a larger cultural group gave us a new perspective.

"Since 1999, a law guarantees the identity of all the minority cultures in Italy. But, our problem has been the fact that, until recently, the language was almost entirely oral, with no written tradition. The written language only began in the 1960s. It was actually started by Occitan poets who began to write down their poems. After the official recognition of Occitan as a language, there has been a boom in interest, and in the 1990s a commission was formed to standardize both the written and spoken language. We now have an Italian–Occitan dictionary and a newspaper, the *Occitano Vivo*. We also had a project—because all the valleys that were involved in the 2006 Winter Olympics are Occitan valleys—to give our culture a more visible presence during the games. Only a few people, though, realize an Occitan hymn was actually sung during the opening ceremonies. Our work goes on."

For more information about the language of Occitania, contact **Chambra d'Oc** (✉ Chamin Arnaud Daniel 18, 12020 Roccabruna ☎ 0171/918971). Though only in Italian and Occitan, the Web site www.jari.it/html/ousitanio.html provides maps indicating the extent of Occitania.

5

✍ *h.miramonti@tiscalinet.it* ➶ *30 rooms* ♨ *Restaurant, minibars, exercise equipment, bar, meeting rooms, some pets allowed* ▤ *AE, DC, MC, V* ¶◎¶ *BP.*

Sports & the Outdoors

SKIING At 6,670 feet, the ski resort of **Sestriere** (☎ 0122/799411 for conditions ⊕ www.vialattea.it) was built in the late 1920s under the auspices of Turin's Agnelli family. The slopes get good snow some years from November through May, other years from February through May. The **tourist office** (☎ 0175/46710 ⊕ www.comune.sestriere.to.it) in Sestriere provides complete information about lift tickets, ski runs, mountain guides, and equipment rentals, here and in neighboring towns such as Bardonecchia and Claviere. Its excellent Web site is also navigable in English. A quaint village with slate-roof houses, **Claviere** (⊹ 17 km [11 mi] west of Sestriere) is one of Italy's oldest ski resorts. Its slopes overlap with those of the French resort of Montgenèvre.

Bardonecchia

㉔ *36 km (22 mi) northwest of Sestriere, 89 km (55 mi) west of Turin.*

This sunny town is one of Italy's oldest winter ski resorts, attracting hardy sports enthusiasts from Turin since the 1920s. It's near the entrance to the Fréjus train and automobile tunnels.

Where to Stay

$$ ▦ **Des Geneys-Splendid.** One of the best hotels in the area sits in a pine-filled private park near the town center. The 1930s style is evident in the arched windows on the ground floor, the stucco walls, and the wrought-iron balconies. The public rooms are spacious and comfortable, and there's a playroom for children. ✉ *Via Einaudi 21, 10052* ☎ *0122/99001* 🖷 *0122/999295* ⊕ *www.desgeneys.it* ➶ *53 rooms, 4 suites* ♨ *Restaurant, gym, piano bar, meeting rooms* ▤ *AE, DC, MC, V* ⊘ *Closed mid-Apr.–mid-June and mid-Sept.–Nov.* ¶◎¶ *BP.*

★ $ ▦ **Asplenia.** Skiers love this small, modern version of a mountain chalet near the town center and the ski lifts. The ample rooms are comfortably furnished, with a small entryway and a balcony affording beautiful views. ✉ *Viale della Vittoria 31, 10052* ☎ *0122/999870* 🖷 *0122/901968* ⊕ *www.asplenia.it* ➶ *17 rooms, 4 suites* ♨ *Restaurant, some pets allowed* ▤ *AE, DC, MC, V* ¶◎¶ *BP.*

$ ▦ **Bucaneve.** Just a short walk from the ski lift, this small family-owned hotel is popular with the ski crowd. A cozy reading room and restaurant add to the allure of these affordable lodgings. ✉ *Viale della Vecchia 2, 10052* ☎ *0122/999332* 🖷 *0122/999980* ⊕ *www.hotelbucanevebardonecchia.it* ➶ *20 rooms, 4 suites* ♨ *Restaurant, bar, Internet room, some pets allowed; no a/c* ▤ *AE, MC, V* ⊘ *Closed Oct. and Nov.* ¶◎¶ *BP.*

THE MONFERRATO & THE LANGHE

Southeast of Turin, in the hilly wooded area around Asti known as the Monferrato and farther south in a similar area around Alba known as the Langhe, the rolling landscape is a patchwork of vineyards and dark woods dotted with hill towns and castles. This is wine country, producing some of Italy's most famous reds and sparkling whites. And hidden away in the woods are the secret places where hunters and their dogs unearth the precious, aromatic truffles worth their weight in gold at Alba's truffle fair.

Casale Monferrato

25 *42 km (26 mi) northeast of Asti, 75 km (46 mi) southwest of Milan.*

Casale Monferrato, strategically situated on the southern bank of the Po, was held by the Gonzaga, rulers of Mantua, before falling into the hands of the Savoy. The 16th-century **Torre Civica**, marking the heart of town in Piazza Mazzini, commands extensive views up and down the Po. It's open the second Saturday and Sunday of every month for free guided visits. In the second half of March the **Festa di San Giuseppe** brings artisans, musicians, and vendors of traditional sweets to the central Piazza del Castello.

Casale's most enlightening sight is the **Museo Israelitico** (Jewish Museum) in the women's section of its synagogue. Inside is a collection of documents and sacred art of a community that was vital to the prosperity of this mercantile city. The synagogue dates from the late 16th century, and neighboring buildings on the same street formed the Jewish ghetto of that period. ⊠ *Vicolo Olper 44, south of Torre Civica* ☎ *0142/71807* 🎫 *€4* ☉ *Mar.–Dec., Sun. 10–noon and 3:30–5:30; other times by appointment.*

Asti

26 *60 km (37 mi) southeast of Turin.*

Asti is best known outside Italy for its wines—excellent reds as well as the famous sparkling white spumante—but its strategic position on trade routes between Turin, Milan, and Genoa has given it a broad economic base. In the 12th century Asti began to develop as a republic, at a time when other Italian cities were also flexing their economic and military muscles. It flourished in the following century, when the inhabitants began erecting lofty **towers** (⊠ West end of Corso Vittorio Alfieri) for its defense, giving rise to the medieval nickname "city of 100 towers." In the center of Asti some of these remain, among them the 13th-century **Torre Comentina** and the well-preserved **Torre Troyana**, a tall, slender tower attached to the **Palazzo Troya**. The 18th-century church of **Santa Caterina** has incorporated one of Asti's medieval towers, the **Torre Romana** (itself built on an ancient Roman base), as its bell tower. Corso Vittorio Alfieri is Asti's main thoroughfare, running west–east across the city. This road, known in medieval times as Contrada Maestra, was built by the Romans.

The **Duomo** is an object lesson in the evolution of the Gothic architecture. Built in the early 14th century, it's decorated so as to emphasize geometry and verticality: pointed arches and narrow vaults contrast with the earlier, Romanesque attention to balance and symmetry. The porch on the south side of the cathedral facing the square was built in 1470 and represents Gothic at its most florid and excessive. ⊠ *Piazza Cattedrale* ☎ *0141/592924* ⊘ *Daily 8:30–noon and 3:30–5:30.*

The Gothic church of **San Secondo** is dedicated to Asti's patron saint, reputedly decapitated on the spot where the church now stands. Secondo is also the patron of the city's favorite folklore and sporting event, the annual Palio di Asti, the colorful medieval-style horse race (similar to Siena's) held each year on the third Sunday of September in the vast Campo del Palio to the south of the church. ⊠ *Piazza San Secondo, south of Corso Vittorio Alfieri* ☎ *0141/530066* ⊘ *Mon.–Sat. 10:45–noon and 3:30–5:30, Sun. 3:30–5:30.*

Where to Stay & Eat

$$$$ ✕ **Gener Neuv.** One of Italy's best restaurants, the family-run Gener Neuv is known for its rustic elegance. The setting on the bank of the Tanaro River is splendid. The menu of regional specialties may include agnolotti *ai tre stufati* (with a filling of ground rabbit, veal, and pork), and to finish, *composta di prugne e uva* (prune and grape compote). Fixed-price menus are available with or without the wine included. As you might expect, the wine list is first-rate. ⊠ *Lungo Tanaro 4* ☎ *0141/557270* ⊕ *www.generneuv.it* ⊟ *AE, DC, MC, V* ⊘ *Closed Aug. and Mon., closed Sun. Jan.–July. No dinner Sun.*

FodorśChoice
★

$$$ ✕ **L'Angolo del Beato.** Regional specialties such as *bagna cauda* (literally "hot bath," a dip for vegetables made with anchovies, garlic, butter, and olive oil) and *tagliolini al ragu di anatra* (pasta with a duck sauce) are the main attraction at this central Asti restaurant, housed in a building that dates back to the 12th century. There's also a good wine list. ⊠ *Via Guttuari 12* ☎ *0141/531668* ⊟ *AE, DC, MC, V* ⊘ *Closed Sun., last wk of Dec., 1st wk of Jan., and 3 wks in Aug.*

> ### WORD OF MOUTH
>
> "I love Piedmont. I just spent a week there, my second visit, and I can't get enough of the incredible trattorie in the region—not one bad experience, and what a fabulous range of foods, from local risotto, to Cuneo beef, antipasti to die for, fresh ravioli, so many cheeses, the list goes on and on."
>
> –Challicewell

$$ ⌂ **Reale.** This hotel in a 19th-century building is located on Asti's main square. The spacious rooms are somewhat eclectically decorated, with a mix of contemporary and period furniture. Though this is one of the oldest hotels in Asti, all the bathrooms have been modernized and are spotlessly maintained. ⊠ *Piazza Alfieri 6, 14100* ☎ *0141/530240* 🖨 *0141/34357* ⊕ *www.hotel-reale.com* ➯ *25 rooms, 2 suites* ⌂ *Cable TV, parking (fee), some pets allowed; no a/c* ⊟ *AE, DC, MC, V* ⦿⦿ *BP.*

$ ⌂ **Rainero.** An older hotel near the train station, the Rainero has been run by the same family for three generations. It's fitted with cheerful modern furnishings. Ask for one of the "green rooms," decked out in a green-and-white decor. ⊠ *Via Cavour 85, 14100* ☎ *0141/353866* 🖨 *0141/594985* ⊕ *www.hotelrainero.com* ➯ *53 rooms, 2 suites* ⌂ *Bar, Internet room, meeting rooms, parking (fee), some pets allowed* ⊟ *AE, V* ⊘ *Closed Jan. 1–15* ⦿⦿ *BP.*

Continued on page 292

ON THE TRAIL OF BAROLO

Picture yourself in the background of a grand medieval mural, and you won't be far off from what you experience driving through the idyllic wooded landscape south of Turin, in Piedmont's Langhe district.

The crests of the graceful hills are dotted with villages, each lorded over by an ancient castle. The gentle slopes of the valleys below are lined with row upon row of Nebbiolo grapes, the choicest of which are used to make Barolo wine. Dubbed "the king of wines and wine of kings" in the 19th century after finding favor with King Carlo Alberto, Barolo still wears the crown, despite stiff competition from all corners of Italy.

The Langhe district is smaller and surprisingly less visited by food-and-wine enthusiasts than Chianti and the surrounding areas of Tuscany, but it yields similar rewards. The best way to tour the Barolo-producing region is on day trips from the delightful truffle town of Alba—getting around is easy, the country roads are gorgeous, and the wine is fit for a king.

Above, Serralunga's castle
Right, bottles of old vintage Barolo

ALL ABOUT BAROLO

The Nebbiolo grapes that go into this famous wine come not just from Barolo proper (the area surrounding the tiny town of Barolo), but also from a small zone that encompasses the hill towns of Novello, Monforte d'Alba, Serralunga d'Alba, Castiglione Falletto, La Morra, and Verduno. All are connected by small but easy-to-navigate roads.

When wine lovers talk about Barolo, they talk about tannins—the quality that makes red wine dry out your mouth. Tannins come from the grape skins; red wine—which gets its color from the skins—has them, white wine doesn't. Tannins can be balanced out by acidity (the quality that makes your mouth water), but they also soften over time. As a good red wine matures, flavors emerge more clearly, achieving a harmonious balance of taste and texture.

A bottle of Barolo is often born so overwhelmingly tannic that many aficionados won't touch the stuff until it has aged 10 or 15 years. But a good Barolo ages beautifully, eventually spawning complex, intermingled tastes of tobacco, roses, and earth. It's not uncommon to see bottles for sale from the 1960s, 1950s, or even the 1930s.

WHERE TO DRINK IT

The word *enoteca* in Italian can mean a wine store, or a wine bar, or both. The words "wine bar," on the other hand—which are becoming increasingly trendy—mean just that. Either way, these are great places to sample and buy the wines of the Langhe.

An excellent enoteca in Alba is Vincafé (Via V. Emanuele, 12, Alba, 0173/364603). It specializes in tastes of Langhe wines, accompanied by *salumi* (cured meats), cheeses, and other regional products. More than 350 wines, as well as grappas and liqueurs, grace Vincafé's distinguished list. It's open from noon to midnight, and there's food until 9 pm.

In the fortfied hill town of Barolo, visit the Castello di Barolo (Piazza Falletti, 0173/56277, www.baroloworld.it) which has a little wine bar and a museum dedicated to Barolo.

HOW MUCH DOES IT COST?

The most reasonably priced, but still enjoyable Barolos will cost you €20 to €30. A very good but not top-of-the-line bottle will cost €40 to €60. For a top-of-the-line bottle you may spend anywhere from €80 to €200.

LABELS TO LOOK FOR

Barolo is a strictly controlled denomination, but that doesn't mean all Barolos are equal. Legendary producers include Prunotto, Aldo Conterno, Giacomo Conterno, Bruno Giacosa, Famiglia Anselma, Mascarello, Pio Cesare, and Michele Chiarlo.

WINE ESTATES TO VISIT

Right in the town of Barolo, an easy, if touristy, option for a visit is Marchesi di Barolo (Via Alba 12, Barolo, 0173/564400, www.marchesibarolo.com). In the estate's user-friendly enoteca you can taste wine, buy thousands of different bottles from vintages going way back, and look at display bottles, including an 1859 Barolo. Marchesi di Barolo's *cantine* (wine cellars, Via Roma 1, Barolo) are open daily 10:30–5:30. The staff here is used to catering to visitors, so you won't have to worry too much about endearing yourself to them.

From there you might want to graduate to Famiglia Anselma (Loc. Castello della Volta, Barolo, 0173/787217, www.anselma.it). Wine-maker Maurizio Anselma, in his mid-20s, is something of a prodigy in the Barolo world, and he's quite open to visitors. He is known for his steadfast commitment to produce only Barolo—nothing else—and for his policy of holding his wines for several years before release.

A good, accessible example of the new school of Barolo winemaking is Podere Rocche dei Manzoni (3, Loc. Manzini Soprano, Monforte d'Alba, 0173/78421, www.barolobig.com). The facade of the cantina is like a Roman temple of brick, complete with imposing columns. Rocche dei Manzoni's reds include four Barolos, one Dolcetto, one Langhe Rosso, two Langhe DOCs, and two Barbera d'Albas.

WINE TOUR TIPS

Keep in mind that visiting wineries in Italy is different from what you might have experienced in the Napa Valley or in France. Wherever you go, reservations are most definitely required, and you'll usually be the only person or group on the tour—so be sure to show up when you say you will, and keep in mind that it's impolite not to buy something in the end.

Wine buyers and wine professionals are the expected audience for tours. While this attitude is slowly changing and many winemakers are beginning to welcome interested outsiders, it's important to be humble and enthusiastic. You'll be treated best if you come in with an open mind, respect that the winemaker probably knows more about wine than you do, and make it clear that you aren't just looking to drink for free. It helps to speak Italian, but if you don't, the international language of effusive compliments can still go a long way.

BEYOND BAROLO

Neive, in the Barbaresco region

By no means do the fruits of the Langhe end with Barolo. The region boasts Italy's highest concentration of DOC (denominazione di origine controllata) and DOCG (denominazione di origine controllata e garantita) wines, the two most prestigious categories of appellation in Italy. The other DOCG in the Langhe is Barbaresco, which, like Barolo, is made from the Nebbiolo grape. Barbaresco is not quite as tannic as Barolo, however, and can be drunk younger.

Festivals

September is a month of fairs and celebrations in Asti, and the **Palio di Asti**, a horse race run through the streets of town, highlights the festivities. First mentioned in 1275, this annual event has been going strong ever since. After an elaborate procession in period costumes, nine horses and jockeys representing different sections of town vie for the honor of claiming the *palio*, a symbolic flag of victory. For 10 days in early September Asti is host to the **Douja d'Or National Wine Festival**—an opportunity to see Asti and celebrate the product that made it famous. During the course of the festival a competition is held to award "Oscars" to the best wine producers, and stands for wine tastings allow visitors to judge the winners for themselves. Musical events and other activities accompany the festival. Contact the **tourist office** (☎ 0141/530357 ⊕ www.atasti.it) for the schedule of events.

Shopping

The **Enoteca** on Piazza Alfieri, a square adjacent to Campo del Palio, is a wine center and shop, open Monday–Saturday 9–4:30, where you can try a range of Asti vintages, buy a bottle, and have a light snack. Be aware, though, that prices for spumante in Asti are not necessarily lower than those elsewhere.

Alba

㉗ *30 km (18 mi) southwest of Asti.*

This small town has a gracious atmosphere and a compact core studded with medieval towers and Gothic buildings. In addition to being a wine center of the region, Alba is known as the "City of the White Truffle" for the dirty little tubers that command a higher price per ounce than diamonds. For picking out your truffle and having a few wisps shaved on top of your food, expect to shell out an extra €16—which is well worth it. Visit in October for the Fiera del Tartufo (National Truffle Fair), Cento Torri Joust (a medieval jousting festival), and the Palio degli Asini (donkey races), held the first Sunday of the month.

> **WORD OF MOUTH**
>
> "I really like the Piedmont region in October. It is truffle season and there are many festivals going on! The Alba white truffles are heaven on earth." —SloJan

Where to Stay

$ ⊞ **La Meridiana.** If Alba strikes your fancy, consider a night at this reasonably priced belle epoque–style B&B, on a hill overlooking the historic center and surrounded by Dolcetto and Nebbiolo grapevines. ⊠ *Località Altavilla 9* ☎☎ *0173/440112* ✉ *cascinareine@libero.it* ⬐ *7 rooms, 2 apartments* ⌂ *Cable TV, pool, gym; no a/c in some rooms, no room phones* ═ *No credit cards* ⧇ *BP.*

VALLE D'AOSTA

The unspoiled beauty of the highest peaks in the Alps, the Matterhorn and Monte Bianco, competes with the magnificent scenery of Italy's old-

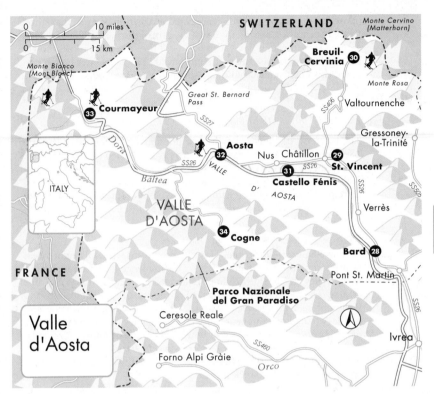

est national park in Valle d'Aosta, a semiautonomous, bilingual region tucked away at the border with France and Switzerland. Luckily, you don't have to choose—the region is small, so you can fit skiing, après-ski, and wild ibex into one memorable trip. The main Aosta Valley, largely on an east–west axis, is hemmed in by high mountains where glaciers have gouged out 14 tributary valleys, 6 to the north and 8 to the south. A car is very helpful here, but take care: though distances are relatively short as the crow flies, steep slopes and winding roads add to your mileage and travel time.

Coming up from Turin, beyond Ivrea the road takes you through countryside that becomes hillier and hillier, passing through steep ravines guarded by brooding, romantic castles. Pont St. Martin, about 18 km (11 mi) north of Ivrea, is the beginning of bilingual (Italian and French) territory.

Bard

28 *65 km (40 mi) north of Turin.*

A few minutes beyond the French-speaking village of Pont St. Martin you pass through the narrow Gorge de Bard and reach the **Forte di Bard** (closed to the public), a 19th-century reconstruction of a fort that stood for eight centuries, serving the Savoys for six of them. In 1800 Napoléon entered Italy through this valley and used the cover of darkness to get his artillery units past the castle unnoticed. Ten years later he remembered this inconvenience and had the fortress destroyed.

St. Vincent

㉙ *28 km (17 mi) north of Bard, 93 km (58 mi) north of Turin.*

The town of St. Vincent has been a popular spa resort since the late 18th century. Its main draw these days is the **Casinò de la Vallée,** one of Europe's largest gambling casinos. You must present identification and be at least 18 years old to enter. Dress is elegant, with jacket and tie requested at the French gaming tables. ⊠ *Via Italo Mus 1* ☎ *0166/ 5221* ⊕ *www.casinodelavallee.it* ☒ *€5* ⊗ *Sun.–Fri. 3* PM–*3:30* AM, *Sat. 3* PM–*4* AM.

Where to Stay & Eat

★ **$$$$** ✕ **Nuovo Batezar—da Renato.** This tiny restaurant with only eight tables ranks among the best in all of Italy. The ambience is rustic yet elegant, with arches and beamed ceilings enhanced by local antiques and fine crystal. The menu, which changes with the seasons, is Valdostana and Piedmontese, with creative variations. Mushrooms, fish, fresh game, and truffles often play prominent roles. As a starter, try the homemade pasta or the *pazzarella* (a small pizza with porcini mushrooms, mozzarella, and truffles). ⊠ *Via Marconi 1, near casino* ☎ *0166/513164* ⚒ *Reservations essential* ▤ *AE, DC, MC, V* ⊗ *Closed Wed., 3 wks in June, and Nov. 15–30. No lunch weekdays.*

$$$$ 🏨 **Billia.** A luxury belle epoque hotel with faux-Gothic touches, the Billia is in a park in the middle of town and connects directly to the casino by a passageway. Half the rooms are done in modern and half in period decor, but all have high ceilings, finely upholstered furniture, and well-stocked bathrooms. ⊠ *Viale Piemonte 72, 11027* ☎ *0166/5231* 🖷 *0166/ 523799* ⊕ *www.grandhotelbillia.com* ➭ *233 rooms, 7 suites* ⚴ *Restaurant, cable TV, in-room data ports, tennis court, pool, health club, sauna, bar, Internet room, convention center* ▤ *AE, DC, MC, V* ⊗ *BP.*

$ 🏨 **Elena.** A central location is the selling point of this hotel near the casino. The spacious rooms, some with balconies and king-size beds, are decorated in a comfortable modern style. ⊠ *Via Biavaz 2 (Piazza Zerbion), 11027* ☎ *0166/512140* 🖷 *0166/537459* ✉ *hotel.elena@libero.it* ➭ *46 rooms, 2 suites* ⚴ *Restaurant, minibars, gym, sauna, Turkish bath, bar, meeting rooms, parking (fee), no-smoking rooms; no a/c in some rooms* ▤ *AE, DC, MC, V* ⊗ *BP.*

Breuil-Cervinia/The Matterhorn

㉚ *30 km (18 mi) north of St. Vincent, 116 km (72 mi) north of Turin.*

Breuil-Cervinia is a village at the base of the **Matterhorn** (Monte Cervino in Italian; Mont Cervin in French). Like the village, the famous peak straddles the border between Italy and Switzerland, and all sightseeing and skiing facilities are operated jointly. Splendid views of the peak can be seen from **Plateau Rosa** and the **Cresta del Furggen,** both of which can be reached by cable car from the center of Breuil-Cervinia. Although many locals complain that the tourist facilities and condominiums in the village have changed the face of their beloved village, most would agree that the cable car has given them access to climbing and off-trail skiing in ridges that were once inaccessible.

Where to Stay & Eat

★ $$$ ╳▣ **Les Neiges d'Antan.** In an evergreen forest at Perrères, just outside Cervinia, this family-run inn is quiet and cozy, with three big fireplaces and a nice view of the Matterhorn. An excellent restaurant ($$$–$$$$) serves French dishes and local specialties such as *zuppa Valpellinentze* (a hearty soup of bread, cabbage, and fontina cheese) and an opulent antipasto (local salami, country pâté, *tomino* cheese, and much more). ⊠ *Località Perrères, 3½ km (2 mi) outside Cervinia, 11021* ☎ *0166/948775* 🖷 *0166/948852* ⊕ *www.lesneigesdantan.it* ⇝ *21 rooms, 3 suites* ⚴ *Restaurant, room TVs with movies, sauna, bar; no a/c* ▤ *MC, V* ☉ *Closed May, June, and mid-Sept.–Nov.* ⅚◎∥ *BP.*

$$ ╳▣ **Cime Bianche.** This calm, quiet mountain lodge offers commanding views of the Matterhorn and surrounding peaks from the balconies of its guest rooms. Wood-paneled rooms are simply furnished with the trekker in mind. The restaurant is one of the few dining spots (¢–$:) in town to offer regional Valdostana cuisine, serving *fonduta* (a local version of fondue, made with melted cheese, eggs, and sometimes grated truffles) polenta, and wild game in a rustic setting. The wood beams and tables are typical of a ski resort, but meals are produced with greater care than your average après-ski affairs. Reservations are highly recommended. ⊠ *Località La Vieille 44, near the ski lift 11021* ☎ *0166/949046* 🖷 *0166/948061* ⊕ *www.hotelcimebianche.com* ⇝ *15 rooms* ⚴ *Restaurant, bar; no a/c* ▤ *MC, V* ☉ *Closed Mon., and May and June* ⅚◎∥ *BP.*

★ $$$$ ▣ **Hermitage.** The entryway's marble relief of St. Theodolus reminds you that this was the site of a hermitage, but asceticism has given way to comfort and elegance at what is now one of the most exclusive hotels in the region. It has the look of a relaxed but posh family chalet, with rustic antiques, petit point upholstery, a fire always glowing in the enormous hearth, and a candlelit dining room. The bright bedrooms have balconies; suites have antique fireplaces and 18th-century furnishings. While here you can make use of Hermitage's extensive health and beauty facilities and play golf (for half price) at the Cervinia Golf Club. ⊠ *Via Piolet 1, Località Chapellette, 11021* ☎ *0166/948998* 🖷 *0166/949032* ⊕ *www.hotelhermitage.com* ⇝ *30 rooms, 6 suites* ⚴ *Restaurant, golf privileges, indoor pool, health club, massage, sauna, bar, Internet room, meeting rooms* ▤ *AE, DC, MC, V* ☉ *Closed May, June, Sept., and Oct.* ⅚◎∥ *BP.*

$$$ 🏨 **Bucaneve.** This small central hotel catering to longer stays is decorated in typical mountain style, with lots of wood paneling, cheery floral upholstery in spacious lounges, and terraces dripping with geraniums. Après-ski, there's a restaurant (half board is required) and a cozy bar with a big fireplace and pianist in the evening. ⊠ *Piazza Jumeaux 10, 11021* ☎ *0166/949119* 🖷 *0166/948308* ⊕ *www.hotel-bucaneve.it* ⇗ *20 rooms, 6 suites* ⚖ *Restaurant, gym, hot tub, sauna, piano bar, meeting rooms* ⊟ *AE, MC, V* ⊗ *Closed May–late June and Sept.–Nov., depending on weather* ⊺⊙⊦ *MAP.*

$$$ 🏨 **Chalet Valdotain.** About 2 km (1 mi) outside town on the road to Châtillon, this Alpine chalet has wooden balconies and snug rooms with terrific views of the Matterhorn. It's known for good food and a friendly atmosphere. ⊠ *Località Lago Bleu 2, 11021* ☎ *0166/949428* 🖷 *0166/948874* ⊕ *www.chaletvaldotain.it* ⇗ *35 rooms* ⚖ *Restaurant, pool, gym, sauna, Turkish bath, bar* ⊟ *AE, DC, MC, V* ⊗ *Closed May–mid-June and mid-Sept.–Oct.* ⊺⊙⊦ *BP.*

Sports & the Outdoors

CLIMBING   Serious climbers can make the ascent of the Matterhorn from Breuil-Cervinia after registering with the local mountaineering officials at the **tourist office** (⊠ Via Carrel 29 ☎ 0166/949136). This climb is for experienced climbers only. Less-demanding hikes follow the lower slopes of the valley of the River Marmore, to the south of town.

SKIING   Because its slopes border the Cervino glacier, this resort at the foot of the Matterhorn offers year-round skiing. Sixty lifts and a few hundred miles of ski runs ranging from beginner to expert make the area one of the best and most popular in Italy. Contact the **tourist office** (⊠ Via Carrel 29 ☎ 0166/949136) for information.

Castello Fénis

ⓒ ㉛   *11 km (7 mi) west of St. Vincent, 104 km (65 mi) north of Turin.*

Fodor'sChoice
★

The best-preserved medieval fortress in Valle d'Aosta, the many-turreted Castello Fénis was built in the mid-14th century by Aimone di Challant, a member of a prolific family related to the Savoys. The castle, which used a double ring of walls for its defense, is the sort imagined by schoolchildren, with pointed towers, portcullises, and spiral staircases. The 15th-century courtyard surrounded by wooden balconies is elegantly decorated with well-preserved frescoes. Inside you can see the kitchen, with an enormous fireplace that provided central heat in winter, the armory, and the spacious, well-lighted rooms used by the lord and lady of the manor. If you have time to visit only one castle in Valle d'Aosta, this should be it. ☎ *0165/764263* ⊠ *€5* ⊗ *Mar.–June, daily 9–6:30; July and Aug., daily 9–7:30; Sept., daily 9–6:30; Oct.–Feb., Wed.–Mon. 10–5; maximum of 25 people allowed to enter every ½ hr.*

⌐   EN ROUTE   The highway continues climbing through Valle d'Aosta to the town of Aosta itself. The road at this point is heading almost due west, with rivulets from the wilderness reserve Parco Nazionale del Gran Paradiso streaming down from the left to join the Dora Baltea River, one of the major tributaries of the Po and an increasingly popular spot for rafting. Be careful driving here in late spring, when melting snow can turn some of these streams into torrents.

Aosta

32 *12 km (7 mi) west of Castello Fénis, 113 km (70 mi) north of Turin.*

Aosta stands at the junction of two of the important trade routes that connect France and Italy—the valleys of the Rhône and the Isère. Its significance as a trading post was recognized by the Romans, who built a garrison here in the 1st century BC. At the eastern entrance to town, in the Piazza Arco d'Augusto and commanding a fine view over Aosta and the mountains, is the **Arco di Augusto** (Arch of Augustus), built in 25 BC to mark Rome's victory over the Celtic Salassi tribe. (The sloping roof was added in 1716 in an attempt to keep rain from seeping between the stones.) The present-day layout of streets in this small city tucked away in the Alps more than 644 km (400 mi) from Rome is the clearest example of Roman urban planning in Italy. Well-preserved Roman walls form a perfect rectangle around the center of Aosta, and the regular pattern of streets reflects its role as a military stronghold. St. Anselm, born in Aosta, later became archbishop of Canterbury in England.

The **Collegiata di Sant'Orso** is the sort of church that has layers of history in its architecture. Originally there was a 6th-century chapel on this site founded by the Archdeacon Orso, a local saint. Most of this structure was destroyed or hidden when an 11th-century church was erected over it. This church, in turn, was encrusted with Gothic, and later baroque, features, resulting in a jigsaw puzzle of styles, but, surprisingly, not a chaotic jumble. The 11th-century features are almost untouched in the crypt, and if you go up the stairs on the left from the main church you can see the 11th-century frescoes (ask the sacristan let you in). These restored frescoes depict the life of Christ and the apostles: although only the tops are visible, you can see the expressions on the faces of the disciples. Take the outside doorway to the right of the main entrance to see the church's crowning glory, its 12th-century **cloister**. Next to the church, it's enclosed by some 40 stone columns with masterfully carved capitals depicting scenes from the Old and New Testaments and the life of St. Orso. The turrets and spires of Aosta peek out above. ⊠ *Via Sant'Orso* ☎ *0165/40614* ☉ *Apr.–Sept., daily 9–5; Oct.–Mar., daily 10–5.*

The huge **Roman Porta Pretoria,** regally guarding the city, is a remarkable relic from the Roman era. The area between the massive inner and outer gates was used as a small parade ground for the changing of the guard. ⊠ *West end of Via Sant'Anselmo.*

The 72-foot-high ruin of the facade of the **Teatro Romano** guards the remains of the 1st-century BC amphitheater, which once held 20,000 spectators. Only a bit of the outside wall and 7 of the amphitheater's original 60 arches remain, and these are built into the facade of the adjacent convent of the sisters of San Giuseppe. The nuns will usually allow you in to see these arches (ask at the entrance). ⊠ *Via Anfiteatro 4.*

Aosta's **Duomo** dates from the 10th century, but all that remains from that period are the bell towers. The decoration inside is primarily Gothic, but the main attraction of the cathedral predates that era by 1,000 years: a carved ivory diptych portraying the Roman Emperor Honorius and dating from AD 406 is among the many ornate objects housed in the treasury. ⊠ *Via Monsignor de Sales* ☎ *0165/40251* ☉ *Duomo Easter–Sept. 7, Mon.–Sat. 6:30 PM–8 PM, Sun. 7 AM–8 PM; Sept. 8–Easter, Mon.–Sat. 6:30–noon and 3–7, Sun. 7–noon and 3–7. Treasury Apr.–Sept., Tues.–Sun. 9–11:30 and 3–5:30; Oct.–Mar., Sun. 3–5:30.*

Where to Stay & Eat

$ ✕ **Vecchio Ristoro.** Housed in a converted mill, this centrally located restaurant is furnished with antiques and a large ceramic stove. The chef-proprietor takes pride in creative versions of regional favorites, including *marbrè di bollito misto con bagnet verde* (terrine of mixed boiled meats with a parsley and anchovy sauce) and *carrè d'agnello gratinato alle erbe* (grilled loin of lamb in a pastry and herb crust). ⊠ *Via Tourneuve 4* ☎ *0165/33238* ⊟ *AE, DC, MC, V* ☉ *Closed Sun., June, and 1 wk in Nov. No lunch Mon.*

$ ✕ **Praetoria.** Just outside the Porta Pretoria, this simple and unpretentious restaurant serves hearty local dishes such as *crespelle alla valdostana* (crepes with cheese and ham). The pasta is made on the premises, and all of the menu offerings are prepared from traditional recipes. ⊠ *Via S. Anselmo 9* ☎ *0165/44356* ⊟ *AE, DC, MC, V* ☉ *Closed Thurs.*

¢   ✕ **La Brasserie du Commerce.** In the heart of Aosta, this small and lively eatery is near the Piazza E. Chanoux. On a sunny summer day try to snag a table on the terrace. Typical valley dishes such as fonduta are on the menu, as well as many vegetable dishes and salads. ⊠ *Via de Tillier 10* ☎ *0165/35613* ⌦ *Reservations not accepted* ⊟ *AE, DC, MC, V* ☉ *Closed Sun.*

$$$ 🖭 **Holiday Inn Aosta.** Attractive Provençal fabrics add some local color to this chain hotel's otherwise predictable amenities. The rooms, some equipped for people with disabilities, are modern and comfortable, and some have balconies overlooking the mountains. The central location is another plus. ⊠ *Corso Battaglione Aosta 30, 11100* ☎ *0165/236356* 🖷 *0165/236837* ⊕ *www.sixcontinentshotels.com* ⇆ *45 rooms, 5 suites* ⌂ *Restaurant, room TVs with movies, bar, business services, some pets allowed (fee), no-smoking rooms* ⊟ *AE, DC, MC, V* ⫟◯⫞ *BP.*

$$ 🖭 **Milleluci.** This small and inviting family-run hotel sits in an enviable position overlooking Aosta, 1 km (½ mi) north of town. A huge brick hearth and rustic wooden beams highlight the lounge. Bedrooms, some with balconies, are bright and charmingly decorated; all with splendid views of the city and mountains. Ten rooms are reserved for nonsmokers and some rooms are equipped for people with disabilities. ⊠ *Località Porossan Roppoz 15, 11100* ☎ *0165/235278* 🖷 *0165/235284* ⊕ *www.hotelmilleluci. com* ⇆ *26 rooms, 5 suites* ⌂ *Tennis court, pool, sauna, bar, Internet room, no-smoking rooms; no a/c* ⊟ *AE, DC, MC, V* ⫟◯⫞ *BP.*

FodorsChoice
★

$ 🖭 **Casa Ospitaliera del Gran San Bernardo.** Here's your chance to sleep in a 12th-century castle without emptying your wallet. In a monastery that Amedeo of Savoy gave to the Order of St. Bernard in 1137, this bargain-price lodging is still run by monks. Only 15 km (8 mi) north of Aosta, this simple pension is a good base for hikers and cross-country skiers. Hearty food is included in the full meal plan. ⊠ *Rue de Flassin 3, 11010 Saint-Oyen* ☎ *0165/78247* 🖷 *0165/789512* 🛏 *15 rooms* 🚫 *No a/c, no room phones, no room TVs* ⊟ *No credit cards* ⊘ *Closed May* �🍽 *FAP.*

Nightlife & the Arts

Each summer a series of **concerts** is held in different venues around the city. Organ recitals in July and August attract performers of world renown. Call the **tourist board** (⊠ Piazza E. Chanoux 8 ☎ 0165/236627) for information.

Shopping

Aosta and the surrounding countryside are famous for wood carvings and wrought iron. There's a permanent **crafts exhibition** in the arcades of Piazza E. Chanoux, in the heart of Aosta; it's a good place to pick up a bargain.

Courmayeur/Monte Bianco

★ ㉝ *35 km (21 mi) northwest of Aosta, 150 km (93 mi) northwest of Turin.*

The main attraction of Courmayeur is a knock-'em-dead view of Europe's tallest peak, **Monte Bianco** (Mont Blanc). Jet-set celebrities flock here, following a tradition that dates from the late 17th century, when Courmayeur's natural springs first began to draw visitors. The spectacle of the Alps gradually surpassed the springs as the biggest draw (the Alpine letters of the English poet Percy Bysshe Shelley were almost advertisements for the region), but the biggest change came in 1965 with the opening of the Mont Blanc tunnel. Since then, ever-increasing numbers of travelers have passed through the area.

Luckily, planners have managed to keep some restrictions on wholesale development within the town, and its angled rooftops and immaculate cobblestone streets maintain a cozy (if prepackaged) feeling. There is no train directly into Courmayeur, so if you don't have a car you'll need to bus it from nearby Pré-Saint-Didier, which is accessible by train from Aosta.

From La Palud, a small town 4 km (3½ mi) north of Courmayeur, you can catch the cable car up to the top of Monte Bianco. In summer, if you get the inclination, you can then switch cable cars and descend into Chamonix, in France. In winter you can ski parts of the route off-piste. The Funivie La Palud whisks you up first to the Pavillon du Mont Fréty—a starting point for many beautiful hikes—and then to the Rifugio di Torino, before arriving at the viewing platform at **Punta Helbronner** (more than 11,000 feet), which is also the border post with France. Monte Bianco's attraction is not so much its shape (much less distinctive than that of the Matterhorn) as its expanse and the vistas from the top.

The next stage up—only in summer—is on the **Télépherique de L'Aiguille du Midi,** as you pass into French territory. The trip is particularly impressive: you dangle over a huge glacial snowfield (more than 2,000 feet below) and make your way slowly to the viewing station above Chamonix. It's one of the most dramatic rides in Europe. From this point you're looking down into France, and if you change cable cars at the Aiguille du Midi station you can make your way down to Chamonix itself. The return trip covers the same route. Schedules are unpredictable, depending on weather conditions and demand; contact the **Courmayeur tourist office** (☎ 0165/842060 ⊕ www.courmayeur.net) for more information. ⊠ *Frazione La Palud 22* ☎ *0165/89925 Italian side, 00/ 33450536210 French side* ⊕ *www.montebianco.com* 🖼 *€11 roundtrip to Pavillon du Mont Fréty, €32 round-trip to Helbronner, €48 roundtrip to Aiguille du Midi, €75 round-trip to Chamonix* ⊗ *Call for hrs. Closed mid-Oct.–mid-Dec., depending on demand and weather.*

Where to Stay & Eat

★ **$$$** ✕ **Maison de Filippo.** Here you'll find country-style home cooking in a mountain house with lots of atmosphere, furnished with antiques, farm tools, and bric-a-brac of all kinds. There's a set menu only, which includes an abundance of antipasti and a tempting choice of local soups and pasta dishes. Cheese, dessert, and fresh fruit complete the meal. Reserve in advance, for it's one of the most popular restaurants in Valle d'Aosta. ⊠ *Entrèves* ☎ *0165/869797* 🔏 *Reservations essential* ⊟ *MC, V* ⊗ *Closed Tues., mid-May–June, Oct., and Nov.*

★ **$$$** ✕ **Cadran Solaire.** The Garin family made over the oldest tavern in Courmayeur to create a warm and inviting restaurant that has a 17th-century stone vault, old wooden floor, and huge stone fireplace. The menu offers seasonal specialties and innovative interpretations of regional dishes. The cozy bar is a popular place for a before-dinner drink. ⊠ *Via Roma 122* ☎ *0165/844609* 🔏 *Reservations essential* ⊟ *AE, MC, V* ⊗ *Closed Tues., May, and Oct.*

$$$$ ✕🖼 **Royal e Golf.** A longtime landmark in the center of Courmayeur, the Royal rises high above the surrounding town. With wide terraces and wood paneling, it is the most elegant spot in town. The cheery rooms have plenty of amenities. The hotel's restaurant ($$$–$$$$) is renowned for such culinary creations as frogs' legs in a basil fish broth. Reservations are required, as are a jacket and tie for men. The hotel caters to longer stays with half- or full-board service. ⊠ *Via Roma 87, 11013* ☎ *0165/831611* 🖼 *0165/842093* ⊕ *www.royalegolf.com* 🛏 *80 rooms, 6 suites* ⌂ *Restaurant, minibars, cable TV, in-room data ports, pool, health club, sauna, Turkish bath, bar, piano bar, meeting rooms, some pets allowed, no-smoking rooms; no a/c* ⊟ *AE, DC, MC, V* ⊗ *Closed wk after Easter–mid-June and mid-Sept.–Nov.* ⦿ *MAP.*

$$$$ 🖼 **Pavillon.** This modern take on an old-fashioned chalet comes complete with stylish furnishings and a clubby bar. Some stunning contemporary stained glass decorates the public areas and the well-equipped health center. Each room is individually decorated but all have the gold-hue wood paneling and solid furniture typical of mountain retreats. ⊠ *Strada Regionale 62, 11013* ☎ *0165/846120* 🖼 *0165/846122* ⊕ *www.pavillon.it* 🛏 *40 rooms, 10 suites* ⌂ *Restaurant, indoor pool, health club, hot tub, massage, sauna, steam room, bar, meeting room, some pets allowed; no a/c* ⊟ *AE, DC, MC, V* ⊗ *Closed end Apr.–June 15, Oct., and Nov.* ⦿ *FAP.*

$$$$ 🏨 **Villa Novecento.** Run with the friendly charm and efficiency of Franco
Fodor'sChoice Cavaliere and his son Stefano, the Novecento is a peaceful haven near
★ Courmayeur's otherwise busy center. In keeping with the style of a
comfortable mountain lodge, the lounge is warmed by a log fire in winter. Traditional fabrics, wooden furnishings, and early-19th-century
prints lend a soothing quality to the rooms. The restaurant ($$–$$$),
with only a few extra tables for nonguests, serves creative adaptations
of traditional cuisine; it's a good choice for a relaxed evening meal after
an active day on the slopes. ⊠ *Viale Monte Bianco 64, 11013* ☎ *0165/
843000* 🖷 *0165/844030* ⊕ *www.villanovecento.it* ➮ *24 rooms, 2
suites* ⌂ *Restaurant, gym, sauna, Turkish bath, bar, meeting rooms, some
pets allowed; no a/c* ☰ *AE, DC, MC, V* ⊗ *Closed May and Oct.* ⦿ *BP.*

$$$ 🏨 **Auberge de la Maison.** This modern hotel's stone-and-wood con-
struction, typical of this region, gives it the feeling of a country inn. Most
of the cozy rooms have views of Monte Bianco. Alpine prints on the
walls, plush fabrics, and wood-burning stoves make the accommoda-
tions very comfortable. A massage here can be the perfect ending to a
day of hiking or skiing. ⊠ *Via Passerin d'Entrèves 16, 11013* ☎ *0165/
869811* 🖷 *0165/869759* ⊕ *www.aubergemaison.it* ➮ *30 rooms, 3
suites* ⌂ *Restaurant, massage, sauna, Turkish bath, free parking; no a/c*
☰ *AE, MC, V* ⊗ *Closed May* ⦿ *BP.*

$$ 🏨 **Croux.** This bright, comfortable hotel is near the town center on the
road leading to Monte Bianco. Half the rooms have balconies, the other
half have great views of the mountains. The friendly staff goes out of
its way to make you feel welcome. ⊠ *Via Croux 8, 11013* ☎*0165/846735*
🖷 *0165/845180* ⊕ *www.hotelcroux.it* ➮ *33 rooms* ⌂ *Sauna, Turkish
bath, bar; no a/c* ☰ *AE, DC, MC, V* ⊗ *Closed mid-Apr.–mid-June and
mid-Sept.–mid-Dec.* ⦿ *BP.*

Sports & the Outdoors

SKIING Courmayeur pales in comparison to its French neighbor, Chamonix, in
both the number (it has only 24) and the quality of its trails. But with
good natural snow cover, the trails and vistas are spectacular. A huge
gondola leads from the center of Courmayeur to Plan Checrouit, where
gondolas and lifts lead to the slopes. The skiing around Monte Bianco
is particularly good, and the off-piste options are among the best in Europe. The off-piste routes from Cresta d'Arp (the local peak) to Dolonne,
and from the La Palud area into France, should be done with a guide.
Contact the **Funivie Courmayeur/Mont Blanc** (☎ *0165/846658*) for complete information about lift tickets, ski runs, and weather conditions.
For Alpine guide services contact the **Società delle Guide Alpine** (⊠ Strada
Villair 2 ☎ 0165/842064 ⊕ www.guidecourmayeur.com).

Cogne & the Parco Nazionale del Gran Paradiso

🟤 *52 km (32 mi) southeast of Courmayeur, 134 km (83 mi) northwest of
Turin.*

Cogne is the gateway to the Parco Nazionale del Gran Paradiso. This
huge park, once the domain of King Vittorio Emanuele II (1820–78) and
bequeathed to the nation after World War I, is one of Europe's most

rugged and unspoiled wilderness areas, with wildlife and many plant species protected by law. This is one of the few places in Europe where you can see the ibex (a mountain goat with horns up to 3 feet long) and the chamois (a small antelope). The park is open free of charge throughout the year and is managed by a park board, the **Ente Parco Nazionale Gran Paradiso** (⊠ Via della Rocca 47, 10123 Turin ☎ 011/8606211 Park Board, 0124/901070 visitor information center ⊕ www.pngp.it). Try to visit in May, when spring flowers are in bloom and most of the meadows are clear of snow.

Sports & the Outdoors

HIKING There's wonderful hiking to be done here, both on daylong excursions and longer journeys with overnight stops in the park's mountain refuges. The **Cogne tourist office** (⊠ Piazza E. Chanoux 36 ☎ 0165/74040 ⊕ www.cogne.org) has a wealth of information and trail maps to help.

PIEDMONT & VALLE D'AOSTA ESSENTIALS

Transportation

BY AIR

The region's only international airport, Aeroporto Torino Caselle, is 18 km (11 mi) north of Turin. It's notoriously foggy in winter, and many flights are diverted to Genoa, on the coast, with bus connections provided for the two-hour drive to Turin. From Aeroporto Caselle, local buses to Turin arrive at the bus station on Corso Inghilterra in the city center.

🚺 Airport Information **Aeroporto Torino Caselle** ☎ 011/5676361.

BY BUS

The Turin-based SADEM and SAPAV lines service the autostrada network to Milan and other destinations in Italy. SITA buses, part of the nationwide system, also connect Turin with the rest of Italy.

Turin's main bus station is on the corner of Corso Inghilterra and Corso Vittorio Emanuele. Urban buses and trams are operated by the agency ATM. SADEM and SAPAV bus lines both have service throughout Piedmont and Valle d'Aosta. SAVDA specializes in mountain service, providing frequent links between Aosta, Turin, and Courmayeur as well as Milan. There's also a major bus station at Aosta, across the street from the train station.

🚺 Bus Information **ATM** ⊠ Corso Turati 19/6, 10128 Turin ☎ 800/019152 ⊕ www.atm.to.it. **SADEM** ⊠ Via della Repubblica 14, Grugliasco, 10095 Turin ☎ 800801600. **SAPAV** ⊠ Corso Torino 396, 10064 Turin ☎ 800/801901 ⊕ www.sapav.it. **SAVDA** ⊠ Strada Ponte Suaz 6, 11100 Aosta ☎ 0165/361244. **SITA** ⊠ Via Cadorna 105, 50123 Florence ☎ 055/47821 ⊕ www.sita-on-line.it.

BY CAR

Italy's autostrada network links the region with the rest of Italy and neighboring France. Aosta, Turin, and Alessandria all have autostrada connections, with the A4 heading east to Milan and the A6 heading south to the Ligurian coast and Genoa. Turin is the hub of all the transportation systems in Piedmont, with autostrada connections to the north, south, and east.

For travel across the French, Swiss, and Italian borders in Piedmont and Valle d'Aosta, only a few routes are practicable year-round: the 12-km (7-mi) Mont Blanc tunnel connecting Chamonix with Courmayeur, the Colle del Gran San Bernardo/Col du Grand St. Bernard (connecting Martigny with Aosta on Swiss highway E27 and Italian highway SS27, with 6 km [4 mi] of tunnel), and the Traforo del Fréjus (between Modane and Susa, with 13 km [8 mi] of tunnel). There are other passes, but they become increasingly unreliable between November and April.

EMERGENCY SERVICES   If you have a breakdown on the road, you can walk to one of the roadside stations marked SOS and push the button. You'll be connected to the Automobile Club of Italy (ACI), which will come and assist you, for free if you have a membership card for the automobile club in your home country. (Otherwise, you must pay a fee.) For emergency road assistance, ACI can also be reached at the phone number below.

🔢 **ACI** ☎ 803/116.

BY TRAIN

Turin is on the main Paris–Rome TGV express line and is also connected with Milan, only 90 minutes away on the fast train. The fastest (Eurostar) trains cover the 667-km (400-mi) trip to Rome in about six hours, but most trains take about nine hours.

Services to the larger cities east of Turin are part of the extensive and reliable train network of the Lombard Plain. West of the region's capital, however, the train services soon peter out in the mountains. Continuing connections by bus serve these valleys; information about train-bus mountain services can be obtained from train stations and tourist information offices, or by contacting the Ferrovie dello Stato (FS), the Italian national train service.

🔢 Train Information **FS–Trenitalia** ☎ 892021 ⊕ www.trenitalia.com.

Contacts & Resources

EMERGENCIES

Pharmacies throughout the region take turns staying open late and on Sunday. Dial 192 for the latest information (in Italian) on which are open. The Farmacia Boniscontro in Turin takes a lunch break between 12:30 and 3 but is open all night.

🔢 **Ambulance service** ☎ 118. **Emergencies** ☎ 113. **Farmacia Boniscontro** ⊠ Corso Vittorio Emanuele II, 66, Turin ☎ 011/538271. **Police** ☎ 112.

TOURS

Turin's group and personally guided tours are organized by the city's tourist office. Here you can also get information about the Touristibus, a two-hour guided bus trip that leaves from Piazza Castello, at the corner of Via Po, every day but Tuesday at 2:30. Touristibus goes through the historic center of Turin, including Via Roma and Porta Nuova, and then out to view such locations as the Palazzina di Caccia in Stupinigi and the Parco Valentino.

PRIVATE GUIDES Alpine guides are not only recommended but essential if you're planning to traverse some of the dramatic ranges outside St. Vincent, Courmayeur, or Breuil-Cervinia. Before embarking on an excursion (however short) into the mountains in these areas, contact the representative of the CAI (Club Alpino Italiano) for information about hikes and the risks. Guides from the Alpine Guides Association can accompany you on treks and also lead skiing, canyoning, and ice-climbing excursions.

🚹 **Alpine Guides Association** ⊠ Strada Villair 2, Courmayeur ☎ 0165/842064. **CAI** ⊠ Piazza E. Chanoux 8, Aosta ☎ 0165/40194.

VISITOR INFORMATION

🚹 Tourist Information **Alba** ⊠ Piazza Medford 3, 12051 ☎ 0173/35833 ⊕ www.langheroero.it. **Aosta** ⊠ Piazza E. Chanoux 8, 11100 ☎ 0165/236627 ⊕ www.regione.vda.it/turismo. **Asti** ⊠ Piazza Alfieri 29, 14100 ☎ 0141/530357 ⊕ www.atasti.it. **Bardonecchia** ⊠ Viale Vittoria 44, 10052 ☎ 0122/99032 ⊕ www.comune.bardonecchia.to.it. **Breuil-Cervinia** ⊠ Via Carrel 29, 11021 ☎ 0166/949136 ⊕ www.cervinia.it. **Cogne** ⊠ Piazza E. Chanoux 36, 11012 ☎ 0165/74040 ⊕ www.cogne.org. **Courmayeur** ⊠ Piazzale Monte Bianco 13, 11013 ☎ 0165/842060 ⊕ www.courmayeur.net. **Novara** ⊠ Baluardo Quintino Sella 40, 28100 ☎ 0321/394059. **Saluzzo** ⊠ Via Griselda 6, 12037 ☎ 0175/46710 ⊕ www.comune.saluzzo.cn.it. **Sestriere** ⊠ Via Pinerolo 14, 10058 ☎ 0122/755444 ⊕ www.comune.sestriere.to.it. **Turin** ⊠ Atrium Torino, Piazza Solferino ☎ 011/535181 ⊠ Stazione Porta Nuova, 10121 ☎ 011/531327 ⊕ www.turismotorino.org. **Vercelli** ⊠ Viale Garibaldi 90, 13100 ☎ 0161/58002 ⊕ www.turismovalsesiavercelli.it.

The Italian Riviera

Portovenere

WORD OF MOUTH

"Vernazza, in the Cinque Terre, is so wonderful because everyone there is just hanging out doing nothing. People sit in cafés and sip drinks and gaze at the sea. Or they stroll down the main street and gaze at each other. That's it. And it's wonderful."

—daria

WELCOME TO THE ITALIAN RIVIERA

Hiking trail, Cinque Terre

TOP 5
Reasons to Go

1. **Walking the Cinque Terre:** Hike the famous Cinque Terre trails past gravity-defying vineyards, rock-perched villages, and the deep blue sea.

2. **Genoa's "Street of Gold":** Renaissance or rococo, the palaces of Via Garibaldi bear witness to the gilded heyday of Genoese splendor.

3. **Giardini Botanici Hanbury, Ventimiglia:** A spectacular natural setting harbors one of Italy's largest, most exotic botanical gardens.

4. **Portofino:** See the world through rose-tinted sunglasses at this glamorous little harbor village.

5. **Pesto:** The basil-rich sauce was invented in Liguria, and it's never been equaled elsewhere.

0 ———— 20 mi
0 ———— 20 km

Millesimo

Savona

29

PIEDMONT

Albenga

A10

Pieve
Di Teco

28

1

Riviera di Ponente

FRANCE

Ventimiglia

1

Imperia

San Remo

Bordighera

Palazzo San Giorgio, Genoa

The **Riviera di Ponente** (Riviera of the Setting Sun), reaching from the French border to Genoa, has protected bays and sandy beaches. The seaside resorts of **Bordighera** and **San Remo** share some of the glitter of their French cousins to the west.

Getting Oriented

The Italians perfected *il dolce far niente*—the sweet art of idleness—right here in the coastal region of Liguria, also known as the Italian Riviera. It's a collection of villages dedicated to the sea and the sun, running along a broad curve between France to the west and Tuscany to the east. Smack in the middle is Genoa, one of Italy's great port cities.

Riomaggiore

The pastel-hued town of **Portofino**, at the tip of the Portofino Promontory, has charmed generations of the rich and famous.

6

Genoa, birthplace of Christopher Columbus, is the urban anomaly among Liguria's charming villages. At its heart is Italy's largest historic district.

East of Genoa, the **Riviera di Levante** (Riviera of the Rising Sun) has minuscule bays and inlets that accent dramatic cliffs.

The five isolated villages of the **Cinque Terre** seem removed from the modern world—despite the many hikers who populate the trails between them.

Manarola   Sant Andrea Cloister, Genoa   Portofino

ITALIAN RIVIERA PLANNER

Making the Most of Your Time

Genoa or no Genoa—that's your first question. The city has been working hard to shed its reputation as a seamy port town, and the efforts have largely been successful. Genoa's artistic and cultural treasures are significant—you won't find anything remotely comparable elsewhere in the region—and the historical center is a pleasure to explore. Unless your goal is to avoid urban life entirely, consider a night or more in the city.

Your second decision, particularly with limited time, is between the two Rivieras. The Riviera di Levante, east of Genoa, is quieter and has a more distinctive personality; high-end Portofino and the rustic Cinque Terre are arguably the coast's most appealing destinations. The Riviera di Ponente, west of Genoa, is more of a classic European resort experience, with better beaches and more nightlife—similar to, but not as glamorous as, the French Riviera across the border.

Getting Around

Though the pace of life in the region is leisurely, getting around the Riviera is an expedient affair. Public transportation is excellent: trains connect all sights along the coast, and buses snake inland.

With the freedom of a car, you could drive from one end of the Riviera to the other on the autostrada in less than three hours. The A10 and A12 on either side of Genoa—engineering wonders with literally hundreds of long tunnels and towering viaducts—skirt the coast, avoiding the local traffic on the beautiful Via Aurelia, which was laid out by the ancient Romans. The Via Aurelia, also known as highway S1, connects practically all the towns on the coast.

For more about car, bus, and train travel, see "Essentials" at the end of this chapter.

Liguria by Boat

With so much coastline—350 km (217 mi)—and so many pretty little harbors, Liguria is a great place to get around by boat. You can take a boat tour of Genoa harbor with Cooperativa Battellieri del Porto di Genova, and excursion cruises between coastal towns are operated by the main ferry lines. But you can have as much fun (or more) negotiating a price with a boat owner at one of the smaller ports. You're likely to deal with someone who has a rudimentary command of English at best, but that's all you need to discuss price, time, and destination. For details about excursions, see "Essentials" at the end of this chapter.

Liguria by Foot

Walking the Italian Riviera's hilly terrain, with its abundance of gorgeous views, is a major leisure activity. The mild climate and laid-back state of mind can lull you into underestimating just how strenuous these walks can be. Wear good shoes, slather on the sun screen, and carry water—you'll be glad you did. Trail maps are available from tourist information offices, or upon paying admission to the Cinque Terre national park, the region's top hiking destination. Other walks worth considering:

■ On Portofino promontory, the relatively easy walk from Portofino to the Abbazia di San Fruttuoso is a popular choice, and there's a more challenging hike from Ruta to the top of Monte Portofino.

■ From Genoa, you can take the Zecca-Righi funicular up to Righi and walk along the ring of fortresses that used to defend the city, or ride the Genova–Casella railroad to one of the many rugged trailheads near the station stops.

Finding a Place to Stay

One argument against staying in Genoa is a general shortage of first-rate lodging options. Most hotels are in modern buildings (rather than the grand old restored villas you might expect), and the city gets noisy—so look for a place with windows that are *doppi vetri* (double-glazed). Lodging throughout Liguria can be pricey, especially in summer. At other times of year, ask for a *sconto bassa stagione* (low-season discount). Reservations are a particularly good idea because the coast is popular convention territory: if there's one taking place in the town where you're planning to stay, rooms can be hard to come by.

Dining & Lodging Price Categories

WHAT IT COSTS in Euros

	$$$$	$$$	$$	$	¢
Restaurants	over €45	€35–€45	€25–€35	€15–€25	under €15
Hotels	over €220	€160–€220	€110–€160	€70–€110	under €70

Restaurant prices are for a first course (primo), second course (secondo), and dessert (dolce). Hotel prices are for two people in a standard double room in high season, including tax and service.

How's the Weather?

Season is everything on the Italian Riviera. Shops, cafés, clubs, and restaurants stay open late in resorts during high season (at Easter and from June through August), but during the rest of the year they close early, if they're open at all. From October to February, the seaside towns go into hibernation, leaving little more than boarded-up cafés and waves crashing against the barren coast. April, May, and September may be the best times to visit: flowers are in bloom, the weather's mild, and the volume of tourist traffic is relatively low. October and November often bring torrential rains, and with them floods and landslides.

TOP PASSEGGIATA

In Nervi, just outside Genoa, the Passeggiata Anita Garibaldi runs along seaside cliffs, with deep blue water to one side, the lush gardens of the Parco Villa Grimaldi to the other, and great views of the city in the distance.

Updated by
Peter Blackman

LIKE THE FAMILY JEWELS that bedeck its habitual visitors, the Italian Riviera is glamorous, but in the old-fashioned way. The resort towns and coastal villages that stake intermittent claim on the rocky shores of the Ligurian Sea are the long-lost cousins of newer, overbuilt seaside paradises found elsewhere. Here the grandest palazzi share space with frescoed, angular, late-19th-century apartment buildings; high-rise glitz is far away. The rustic and elegant, the provincial and chic, the cosmopolitan and the small-town are blended together here in a sun-drenched pastiche that defines the Italian side of the Riviera.

Although the region bearing the name Liguria extends inland, its greatest charms are found on the coast, which has inspired poets and artists for centuries. Most famously, Percy Shelley praised the "soft blue Spezian bay," and his fellow Romantic poet, the daredevil Lord Byron, swam from Portovenere to Lerici. Today travelers escaping the stress of city living still head to the Italian Riviera. Mellowed by the balmy breezes blowing off the sea, they bask in the sun, explore the picturesque fishing villages, and pamper themselves at the resorts that dot this ruggedly beautiful landscape.

RIVIERA DI LEVANTE

Of the two Ligurian Rivieras, the Riviera di Levante, east of Genoa, is overall the wilder and more rugged, yet here you can also find towns like Portofino and Rapallo, world famous for their classic, elegant style. Around every turn of this area's twisting roads the hills plummet sharply to the sea, forming deep, hidden bays and inlets. Beaches on this coast are rocky, backed by spectacular sheer cliffs. The Portofino promontory has one sandy beach, on the east side, at Paraggi. From Chiavari to Cavi di Lavagna, the coast becomes a bit gentler, with a few sandy areas. Sailing conditions along the rugged coast from Sestri Levante down to Portovenere are good. Waterskiing, tennis, and golf are also popular. You may want to choose a base and take short day trips or explore the area by boat from the larger towns. You can anchor your boat in the relatively calm waters of small *ciazze* (coves) found all along the coast.

Lerici

❶ *106 km (66 mi) southeast of Genoa, 65 km (40 mi) west of Lucca.*

Near Liguria's border with Tuscany, this town is set on a magnificent coastline of gray cliffs and pine forests. Shelley was one of Lerici's best-known visitors and spent some of the happiest months of his life in the lovely white village of San Terenzo, 2 km (1 mi) away. After his death in 1822 the bay was renamed the Golfo dei Poeti, in his and Byron's honor.

Lerici once belonged to Tuscan Pisa, and the 13th-century Pisan **Castello di Lerici** has stood above the splendid bay for centuries. The castle now houses a museum of paleontology. ⊠ *Piazza S. Giorgio 1* ☎ *0187/ 969042* ⊕ *www.castellodilerici.it* ☎ *€5* ⊗ *Mar. 16–June and Sept.–Oct. 19, Tues.–Sun. 10:30–1 and 2:30–6; July and Aug., daily 10:30–12:30 and 6:30 PM–midnight; Oct. 20–Dec. 9 and Dec. 27–Mar. 15, Tues.–Fri. 10:30–12:30, weekends 10:30–12:30 and 2:30–5:30.*

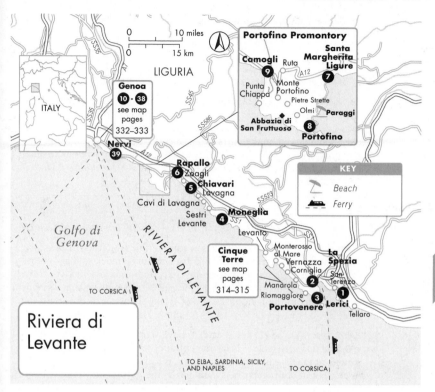

Where to Stay & Eat

$ ✕⌂ **Miranda.** Perched amid the clustered old houses in seaside Tellaro, 4 km (2½ mi) southeast of Lerici, the restaurant in this small family-run inn has become a gourmet's destination ($$$$) because of chef Angelo Cabani's imaginative way with Ligurian cooking. His unusual seafood menu changes daily, but might include *insalata di gamberoni e aragosta con finocchio* (shrimp and lobster salad with fennel) and risotto *mantecato con asparagi e gamberi* (with butter, asparagus, and shrimp). If you stay in one of the seven comfortable rooms with bath you have the option of half board at €180 for two people. ⌂ *Via Fiascherino 92, 19030 Tellaro* ☎ *0187/964012* 🖷 *0187/964032* ⊕ *www. locandamiranda.com* 🛏 *5 rooms, 2 suites* ⌂ *Restaurant; no a/c* ▭ *AE, DC, MC, V* ⊗ *Closed Jan. 12–Feb. 18; restaurant closed Mon.* ¶⊙ *BP.*

$$ ⌂ **Florida.** This seafront, family-run establishment is not the most beautiful from the outside, but it has bright rooms with all the extras you would expect in a higher category, including soundproofing and a balcony with a sea view. For an even better view, loll in one of the deck chairs on the roof terrace. The Florida overlooks a small beach area and is close to tennis courts and a golf course; a solarium is also on the premises. ⌂ *Lungomare Biaggini 35, 19032* ☎ *0187/967332* 🖷 *0187/967344* ⊕ *www.hotelflorida.it* 🛏 *40 rooms* ⌂ *In-room safes,* *minibars, beach, bar, Internet room* ⊟ *AE, DC, MC, V* ⊗ *Closed Dec. 20–Feb.* ⦿ *BP.*

La Spezia

❷ *11 km (7 mi) northwest of Lerici, 103 km (64 mi) southeast of Genoa.*

La Spezia is a large, industrialized naval port on routes to the Cinque Terre and to Portovenere. It lacks the quiet charm of the smaller towns. However, its palm-lined promenade, fertile citrus parks, and lively, balcony-lined streets make parts of La Spezia surprisingly beautiful. The remains of the massive 13th-century **Castel San Giorgio** now house a small museum dedicated to local archaeology. ⊠ *Via XX Settembre* ☎ *0187/751142* ⊠ *€5* ⊗ *Wed.–Mon. 9:30–12:30 and 2–5.*

Portovenere

★ ❸ *12 km (7 mi) south of La Spezia, 114 km (70 mi) southeast of Genoa.*

Portovenere's small colorful houses, some dating from the 12th century, were once connected to the 12th- to 16th-century citadel, so that in times of attack the villagers could reach the safety of the battlements. The town commands a strategic position at the end of a peninsula that extends southeast from the Cinque Terre and forms the western border of the Gulf of La Spezia.

Lord Byron (1788–1824) is said to have written *Childe Harold's Pilgrimage* in Portovenere. Near the entrance to the huge, strange **Grotto Arpaia,** at the base of the sea-swept cliff, is a plaque recounting the poet's strength and courage as he swam across the gulf to the village of San Terenzo, near Lerici, to visit his friend Shelley (1792–1822); the feat is commemorated as well by the name of the stretch of water, Golfo dei Poeti (Poets' Gulf). **San Pietro,** a 13th-century Gothic church open daily 7–6, is built on the site of an ancient pagan shrine, on a formidable solid mass of rock above the Grotto Arpaia. With its black-and-white-stripe exterior, it is a landmark recognizable from far out at sea.

Where to Stay & Eat

$$$–$$$$ ✕ **Da Iseo.** Try to get one of the tables outside at this waterfront restaurant with bistro accents and paintings of Portovenere. Seafood is the only choice, but it's fresh and plentiful. Pasta courses are inventive; try spaghetti *alla Giuseppe* (with shellfish and fresh tomato) or *alla Iseo* (with a seafood curry sauce). ⊠ *Waterfront* ☎ *0187/790610* ⊟ *AE, DC, MC, V* ⊗ *Closed Wed. and Jan. 15–Feb. 1.*

★ $$$ ▦ **Royal Sporting.** Appearances are deceptive at this modern hotel on the beach about a 10-minute walk from the village. From the outside, the stone construction seems austere, but the courtyards and interior—with fresh flowers, potted plants, and cool, airy rooms—are colorful and vibrant. The sports facilities are among the best in the area. ⊠ *Via dell'Olivo 345, 19025* ☎ *0187/790326* 🖷 *0187/777707* ⊕ *www.royalsporting.com* ⬪ *56 rooms, 4 suites* ⚲ *Restaurant, minibars, tennis court, saltwater pool, beach, bar, Internet room, meeting rooms, some pets allowed (fee)* ⊟ *AE, DC, MC, V* ⊗ *Closed Nov.–mid-Mar.* ⦿ *BP.*

THE CINQUE TERRE

Five remote villages make one must-see destination

"Charming" and "breathtaking" are adjectives that get a workout when you're traveling in Italy, but it's rare that both apply to a single location. The Cinque Terre is such a place, and this combination of characteristics goes a long way toward explaining its tremendous appeal.

The area is made up of five tiny villages (Cinque Terre literally means "Five Lands") clinging to the cliffs along a gorgeous stretch of the Ligurian coast. The terrain is so steep that for centuries footpaths were the only way to get from place to place. It just so happens that these paths provide drop-dead views of the rocky coast tumbling into the sea, as well as access to secluded beaches and grottoes.

Backpackers "discovered" the Cinque Terre in the 1970s, and its popularity has been growing ever since. Despite summer crowds, much of the original appeal is intact. Each town has maintained its own distinct charm, and views from the trails in between are as breathtaking as ever.

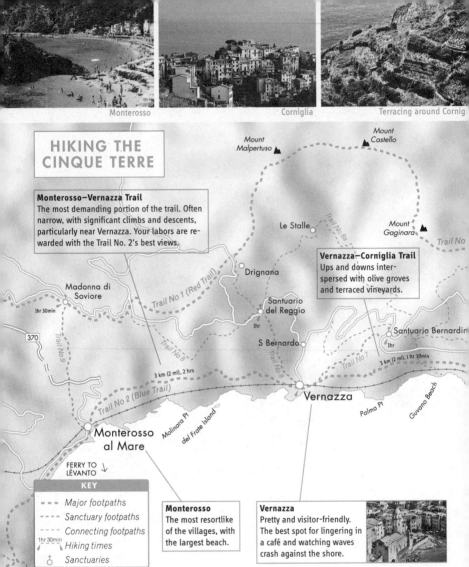

Monterosso

Corniglia

Terracing around Cornig

HIKING THE CINQUE TERRE

Monterosso–Vernazza Trail
The most demanding portion of the trail. Often narrow, with significant climbs and descents, particularly near Vernazza. Your labors are rewarded with the Trail No. 2's best views.

Mount Malpertuso

Mount Castello

Le Stalle

Mount Gaginara

Trail No

Trail No 8a

Vernazza–Corniglia Trail
Ups and downs interspersed with olive groves and terraced vineyards.

Drignana

Trail No 1 (Red Trail)

Madonna di Soviore

1hr 30min

Santuario del Reggio

Santuario Bernardin

370

1hr

Trail No 9

Trail No 6

S Bernardo

1hr

Trail No 7

3 km (2 mi), 1 hr 30min

3 km (2 mi), 2 hrs

Trail No 8

Trail No 2 (Blue Trail)

Vernazza

Palma Pt

Guvano Beach

Molinara Pt

del Frate Island

Monterosso al Mare

FERRY TO LÈVANTO ↓

KEY

- - - *Major footpaths*
- - - - *Sanctuary footpaths*
- - - - *Connecting footpaths*
1hr 30min *Hiking times*
⚲ *Sanctuaries*

Monterosso
The most resortlike of the villages, with the largest beach.

Vernazza
Pretty and visitor-friendly. The best spot for lingering in a café and watching waves crash against the shore.

THE CLASSIC HIKE

Hiking is the classic way to experience the Cinque Terre, and Trail No. 2, also known as the Sentiero Azzurro (Blue Trail), is the most popular path. It's perfect for a day trip: it's approximately 13 km (8 mi) in length, takes you to all five villages, and requires about five hours to complete. The best approach is to start at the east-

ernmost town of Riomaggiore and warm up your legs on the easiest segment of the trail. As you work your way west, the hike gets progressively more demanding. For a less strenuous experience, you can choose to skip a leg or two and take the inland train running between the towns instead. You'll miss out on some of the views, but your feet may thank you.

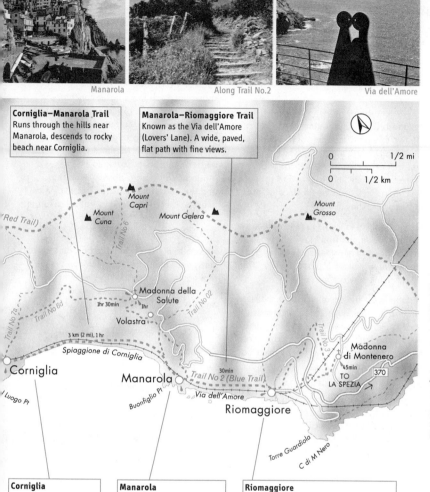

Manarola

Along Trail No.2

Via dell'Amore

Corniglia–Manarola Trail
Runs through the hills near Manarola, descends to rocky beach near Corniglia.

Manarola–Riomaggiore Trail
Known as the Via dell'Amore (Lovers' Lane). A wide, paved, flat path with fine views.

0   1/2 mi

0   1/2 km

Mount Capri

Mount Cuna

Mount Galera

Mount Grosso

(Red Trail)

Trail No 6

Trail No 7a

Trail No 60

Madonna della Salute

1hr 30min   1hr

Volastra

Trail No 02

3 km (2 mi), 1 hr

Spiaggione di Corniglia

Corniglia

l Luogo Pt

Manarola

Buonfiglio Pt

Trail No 2 (Blue Trail)

30min

Via dell'Amore

Riomaggiore

Trail No 3

Madonna di Montenero

45min

TO LA SPEZIA   370

Torre Guardiola

C di M Nero

Corniglia
Perched on a cliff high above the sea, reached by a switchback path (or by shuttle bus).

Manarola
The most photogenic of the villages, best seen from the cemetery a few minutes up the path toward Corniglia.

Riomaggiore
Cliff-clinging buildings are almost as striking as those in Manarola. Stairs to the left of the train station entrance cross over the tracks and lead to the trailhead.

BEYOND TRAIL NO.2

Trail No. 2 is just one of a network of trails crisscrossing the hills. If you're a dedicated hiker, spend a few nights and try some of the other routes. Trail No. 1, the Sentiero Rosso (Red Trail), climbs from Portovenere (east of Riomaggiore) and returns to the sea at Levanto (west of Monterosso al Mare). To hike its length takes from 9 to 12 hours; the ridge-top trail provides spectacular views from high above the villages, each of which can be reached via a steep path. Other shorter trails go from the villages up into the hills, some leading to religious sanctuaries. Trail No. 9, for example, starts from the old section of Monterosso and ends at the Madonna di Soviore Sanctuary.

VOICES OF ITALY

**Antonella Bongi &
Antonella Mariotti**
Cinque Terre

Antonella Bongi and Antonella Mariotti are the two energetic founders of La Spezia's Cooperativa Arte e Natura, which organizes guided walks, hikes, and visits to sites of interest in the Cinque Terre and La Spezia, as well as in the Province of Pisa, in Tuscany to the south.

Q: Most visitors to the Cinque Terre hike the standard route, the Trail No. 2, between Riomaggiore and Monterosso al Mare, and then leave to visit other places in Italy. What do you think they are missing?

Antonella B.: The entire *entroterra*, the hinterland that lies behind the coast. They miss coming into contact with the genuine part of the Cinque Terre that still exists, and they certainly miss contact with the real people who live here, the farmers and the wine-growers.

Antonella M.: You need a car or you can take the public bus, but a good way to start is to follow the SP 370, the Strada dei Santuari (the Road of the Sanctuaries), out of La Spezia. It climbs above the cliffs of the Cinque Terre and passes by each of the five sanctuaries that sit above each of the Cinque Terre towns. Did you know that each town has a sanctuary in the hills, that often predates the coastal town? There's the Madonna di Monte Nero above Riomaggiore, the Madonna della Salute above Manarola, San Bernardino above Corniglia, the Madonna di Reggio above Vernazza, and the Madonna di Soviore above Monterosso. There are walking trails that run up toward the sanctuaries as well—they're marked on the park's trail map.

Antonella B.: Yes, and there are some great viewpoints along the way. You can see the real nature of the landscape, with the #2 trail, the railway, the terraced vineyards, and the five villages far below. It's beautiful. The road goes through Groppo, where there's a wine cooperative . . .

Antonella M. (scandalized): But they give tastings in plastic cups!

Antonella B.: . . . and then continues through Volastra on the way to the other sanctuaries. (Antonella B. adds an aside:) How do you think they harvest the grapes on vines that are only 1 meter (3 feet) high on very narrow terraces? On their backs!

PRECAUTIONS

If you're hitting the trails, you'll want to carry water with you, wear sturdy shoes (hiking boots are best), and have a hat and sunscreen handy. ⚠ Check weather reports before you start out; especially in late fall and winter, thunderstorms can send townspeople running for cover and make the shelterless trails slippery and dangerous. Rain in October and November can cause landslides and close the trails. Note that the lesser-used trails aren't as well maintained as Trail No. 2. If you're undertaking the full Trail No. 1 hike, bring something to snack on as well as your water bottle.

ADMISSION

Entrance tickets for use of the trails, as well as tickets that combine use of the trails with unlimited use of the second-class trains or boats, are available at the Levanto, Monterosso, Vernazza, Corniglia, Manarola, Riomaggiore, and La Spezia train stations. For the price of your ticket you get trail maps, general information leaflets, and train and boat schedules. Prices: 1-day pass for footpaths €5, 1-day pass with train €6, 1-day pass with train and boat €15, 3-day pass with train €15, 7-day pass with train €20.

Working Cinque Terre's vertical vineyards

6

GETTING THERE & GETTING AROUND

The local train on the Genoa–La Spezia train line stops at each of the Cinque Terre. The train runs approximately every 30 minutes. A 24-hour Cinque Terre Tourist train ticket, which allows unlimited travel between the five towns, is available at the five train stations (€2.85).

Along the Cinque Terre coast two ferry lines operate. From June to September, Golfo Paradiso runs from Genoa and Camogli to Monterosso al Mare and Vernazza. The smaller, but more frequent, Golfo dei Poeti stops at each village from Portovenere (east of Riomaggiore) to Monterosso, with the exception of Corniglia, four times a day. A one-day ticket costs €11.50.

WHEN TO GO

The ideal times to see the Cinque Terre are September and May, when the weather is mild and the summer tourist season isn't in full swing.

SWIMMING & BEACHES

Each town has something that passes for a beach, but there are only two options where you'll find both sand and decent swimming. The more accessible is in Monterosso, opposite the train station; it's equipped with chairs, umbrellas, and snack bars. The other is the secluded, swimwear-optional Guvano Beach, between Corniglia and Vernazza. To reach it from the Corniglia train station, bypass the steps leading up to the village, instead following signs to an abandoned train tunnel. Ring a bell at the tunnel's entrance, and the gate will automatically open; after a dimly lit 10-minute walk, you'll emerge at the beach. Both beaches have a nominal admission fee.

Monterosso al Mare

THE TOWNS

Riomaggiore

At the eastern end of the Cinque Terre, Riomaggiore is the most accessible of the villages, reachable by car or train from La Spezia. It curves around a tiny harbor that's ringed with lively cafés and dotted with fishing boats, but doesn't have as much old-world charm as its sister villages—easy accessibility has brought traffic and more modern construction. According to legend, settlement along the narrow valley of the River Maior dates back to the 8th century, when Greek religious refugees came here to escape persecution by the Byzantine emperor.

Manarola

The enchanting pastel houses of Manarola spill down a steep hill overlooking a spectacular turquoise swimming cove and a bustling harbor. The whole town is built on black rock. Above the town, ancient terraces still protect abundant vineyards and olive trees. This village is the center of the wine and olive oil production of the region, and its streets are lined with shops selling local products.

Corniglia

The buildings, narrow lanes, and stairways of Corniglia are strung together amid vineyards high on the cliffs; on a clear day views of the entire coastal strip are excellent. The high perch and lack of harbor make this farming community the most remote of the Cinque Terre. On a pretty pastel square sits the 14th-century church of **San Pietro.** The rose window of marble imported from Carrara is impressive, particularly considering the work required to get it here. ⌧ *Main Sq.* ☎ *0187/ 3235582* ⊗ *Wed. 4–6, Sun. 10–noon.*

Vernazza

With its narrow streets and small squares, Vernazza is arguably the most charming of the five towns. Because it has the best access to the sea, it became wealthier than its neighbors—as evidenced by the elaborate arcades, loggias, and marblework. The village's pink, slate-roof houses and colorful squares contrast with the remains of the medieval fort and castle, including two towers, in the old town. The Romans first inhabited this rocky spit of land in the 1st century.

Today Vernazza has a fairly lively social scene. It's a great place to refuel with a hearty seafood lunch or linger in a café between links of the hike on Trail No. 2.

Monterosso al Mare

Beautiful beaches, rugged cliffs, crystal-clear turquoise waters, and plentiful small hotels and restaurants make Monterosso al Mare, the largest of the Cinque Terre villages (population 1,730), busiest in midsummer. The village center bustles high on a hillside. Below, connected by stone steps, are the port and seaside promenade, where there are boats for hire. The medieval tower, Aurora, on the hills of the Cappuccini, separates the ancient part of the village from the more modern part. The village is encircled by hills covered with vineyards and olive groves, and by a forest of scrubby bushes and small trees.

Monterosso has the most festivals of the five villages, starting with the Lemon Feast on the Saturday preceding Ascension Sunday, followed by the Flower Festival of Corpus Christi, celebrated yearly on the second Sunday after Pentecost. During the afternoon, the streets and alleyways of the *centro storico* (historic center) are decorated with thousands of colorful flower petals set in beautiful designs that the evening procession passes over. Finally, the Salted Anchovy and Olive Oil Festival takes place each year during the second weekend of September.

Thursday, the **market** attracts mingled crowds of tourists and villagers from along the coast to shop for everything from pots and pans and underwear to fruits, vegetables, and fish. Often a few stands sell local art and crafts as well as olive oil and wine. ⊠ *Old town center* ☉ *Thurs. 8–2.*

The **Chiesa di San Francesco,** was built in the 12th century in the Ligurian Gothic style. Its distinctive black stripes and marble rose window make it one of the most photographed sites in the Cinque Terre. ⊠ *Piazza Garibaldi* 🕾 *No phone* 🖃 *Free* ☉ *Daily 9–1 and 4–7.*

Main Square, Vernazza

WHERE TO STAY & EAT

Reservations are essential if you plan to stay in a hotel here in July or August. The area's numerous *affittacamere* (rooms for rent in private homes) are often indicated only by a simple handwritten sign on a front door. Tourist offices in Riomaggiore and Monterosso—a booking service is provided by the latter—have a list of officially licensed affittacamere. These rooms vary considerably in comfort, amenities, and cost.

Riomaggiore

$$–$$$ ✕ **Ripa del Sole.** Try some of the great local wine with one of the house specialties: *calamari con gran farro* (steamed squid with lemon sauce and barley), *tagliatelle fresche con scampi e tartufo bianco* (fresh pasta with scampi and white truffles), or *filetto di branzino al piatto rovente* (sea bass cooked on the griddle with herbs and garlic). In summer you can have your meal on the terrace. ✉ *Via de' Gaspari 282* ☎ *0187/920143* ☰ *AE, DC, MC, V* ⊘ *Closed mid-Jan.–mid-Feb. and Mon. Nov.–Mar.*

$ 🏨 **Due Gemelli.** Set above the sea, this small hotel has fabulous views of the turquoise water. The rooms have simple, mismatched furnishings, but they all have balconies, making them bright and airy. ✉ *Via Litoranea 1, 19017* ☎ *0187/ 920111* 🖷 *0187/920678* ⊕ *www. duegemelli.it* ⟿*14 rooms* ⚙ *Restaurant, bar; no a/c* ☰ *AE, DC, MC, V* ⏏*BP.*

Manarola

$ 🏨 **Ca' d'Andrean.** If you want to stay in one of the less crowded of the Cinque Terre, this tiny, simple hotel is one of your best options. White-tile floors cool off the rooms, some of which have balconies. In summer, breakfast, an optional extra at €6 per person, is served in a flower garden. ✉ *Via Discovolo 101, 19010* ☎ *0187/920040* 🖷 *0187/920452* ⊕ *www.cadandrean.it* ⟿ *10 rooms* ⚙*Bar; no a/c* ☰*No credit cards* ⊘*Closed mid-Nov.–mid-Dec.*

Corniglia

$–$$ ✕🏨 **Cecio.** On the outskirts of Corniglia, many of the spotless rooms at the family-run Cecio have spectacular views of the town clinging to the cliffs above the bay. The same memorable vista can be enjoyed from the hotel's restaurant, which serves inexpensive and well-prepared local seafood dishes. Try the delicious lasagna with pesto sauce as a first course. ✉*Via Serra 58, 19010, toward Vernazza* ☎*0187/812043* 🖷*0187/ 812138* ⟿*12 rooms* ⚙ *Restaurant; no a/c, no room phones, no TV in some rooms* ☰*DC, MC, V* ⏏*BP.*

Vernazza

$–$$$ ✕ **Gambero Rosso.** Relax on Vernazza's main square at this fine trattoria looking out at a church. Enjoy such delectable dishes as shrimp salad, vegetable torte, and squid-ink risotto. The creamy pesto, served atop spaghetti, is some of the best in the area. End your meal with Cinque Terre's own *sciacchetrà,* a dessert wine served with semisweet biscotti. Don't drink it out of the glass—dip the biscotti in the wine instead. ⊠ *Piazza Marconi 7* ☎ *0187/812265* ⊟ *AE, DC, MC, V* ⊗ *Closed Mon. Jan. and Feb.*

¢×▥ **Trattoria Gianni Franzi.** Order your pesto with *fagiolini* (green beans), a Ligurian specialty that somehow tastes better when you're eating it outside in a beautiful *piazzetta* (small square) with a view of the port, as you can here. Above the restaurant, a number of simply furnished, economical rooms are available. Your choice here is between the smaller, older rooms without private bathrooms, but with tiny balconies and great views of the port, or those in the newer section, with bathrooms but no view. ⊠ *Via G. Marconi 1, 19018* ☎ *0187/821003* ☒ *0187/812228* ⊕ *www.giannifranzi.it* ⤺ *20 rooms, 12 with bath* ⚥ *Restaurant, bar* ⊟ *AE, DC, MC, V* ⊗ *Closed Jan. 8–Mar. 8; restaurant closed Wed. early Mar.–mid-July and mid-Sept.–early Jan.* ⏍ *BP.*

Monterosso al Mare

$$$× **Il Gigante.** A good introduction to Ligurian seafood is the *zuppa di pesce* (fish soup) served at this traditional trattoria. It's usually served as a first course but is filling enough to be an entrée. Daily specials might include risotto *ai frutti di mare* (with a seafood sauce) and spaghetti with an octopus sauce. ⊠ *Via IV Novembre 9* ☎ *0187/817401* ⚤ *Reservations essential* ⊟ *AE, DC, MC, V* ⊗ *Closed Mon.*

★ **$$$**× **Miki.** Specialties here are anything involving seafood. The *insalata di mare* (seafood salad), with squid and fish, is more than tasty; so are the grilled fish and any pasta with seafood. If you're in the mood for a pizza, you can order that here as well. Miki has a beautiful little garden in the back, perfect for lunch on a sunny day. ⊠ *Via Fegina 104* ☎ *0187/817608* ⊟ *AE, DC, MC, V* ⊗ *Closed Nov. and Dec., and Tues. Sept.–July.*

$$ × **Il Pirata.** Bright and rustic, this trattoria near the port should be the first stop for lunch, especially if you make it in time to grab a seat at one of the long tables on the front porch. Specialties are those of the region, with a few surprising gourmet touches like the French wines lining the shelves and Maine lobster on the menu. Reservations are essential on weekends and in summer. ⊠ *Via Vittorio Emanuele 5* ☎ *0187/817536* ⊟ *No credit cards* ⊗ *Closed Thurs. and mid-Jan.–mid.-Feb.*

¢ × **Il Frantoio.** Some of the best focaccia on the coast is available here. It's a good place for a light lunch or a snack before heading out on the walk to Vernazza. ⊠ *Via Gioberti 1* ☎ *0187/818333* ⊟ *No credit cards.*

$$$–$$$$ ▥ **Porto Roca.** In a panoramic position above the sea, Porto Roca is set slightly apart, blessedly removed from the crowds. It has the look of a well-kept villa; its interiors have authentic antiques, and there are ample terraces. The rooms with views of the sea are bright and airy; avoid the back rooms, which are dark, dank, and without a view. ⊠ *Via Corone 1, 19016* ☎ *0187/817502* ☒ *0187/817692* ⊕ *www.portoroca.it* ⤺ *43 rooms* ⚥ *Restaurant, bar, some pets allowed* ⊟ *AE, MC, V* ⊗ *Closed Nov. 4–Mar. 27* ⏍ *BP.*

Moneglia

④ *34 km (21 mi) northwest of Monterosso al Mare, 56 km (35 mi) south-east of Genoa.*

The town of Moneglia, sheltered by the wooded hills of a nature pre-serve, faces a little bay guarded by ruined castles. An out-of-the-way al-ternative to fussier resorts, it's a quiet base for walks and excursions by boat, car, or train to Portofino and the Cinque Terre towns. A classical guitar festival is held here in September.

Where to Stay

$–$$ ⊞ **Villa Edera.** Ingeniously merging an older building on a verdant hill-side with a smart stone-and-glass wing, Villa Edera has a contemporary style. Terraces, a garden, luminous bedrooms, and lounges with stylish wicker armchairs are among the comforts. This hotel is owned by a fam-ily committed to personal attention; Mamma Ida's cooking is special, too. ⊠ *Via Venino 12, 16030* ☎ *0185/49291* 🖷 *0185/49470* ⊕ *www.villaedera.com* ⇆ *27 rooms* ⚖ *Restaurant, cable TV, Wi-Fi, pool, gym, sauna, bar, Internet room* ⊟ *AE, MC, V* ☉ *Closed Nov. 5–Feb.* ⊺⊙⊦ *BP.*

Chiavari

⑤ *19 km (12 mi) northwest of Moneglia, 38 km (23 mi) southeast of Genoa.*

Chiavari is a fishing town (rather than village) of considerable charac-ter, with narrow, twisting streets and a good harbor. Chiavari's citizens were intrepid explorers, and many emigrated to South America in the 19th century. The town boomed, thanks to the wealth of the returning voyagers, but Chiavari retains many medieval traces in its buildings.

In the town center, the **Museo Archeologico** displays objects from an 8th-century BC necropolis, or ancient cemetery, excavated nearby. The mu-seum closes the first and third Sunday of the month. ⊠ *Palazzo Costaguta, Via Costaguta 4, Piazza Matteotti* ☎ *0185/320829* ⊠ *Free* ☉ *Tues.–Sat. and the 2nd and 4th Sun. of the month 9–1:30.*

Shopping

The traditional, light—they weigh only 3 pounds—*campanine,* wood chairs made of olive or walnut, are still produced by a few Chiavari crafts-men. Macramé lace can also be found here.

Rapallo

⑥ *9 km (5½ mi) northwest of Chiavari, 28 km (17 mi) east of Genoa.*

Rapallo was once one of Europe's most fashionable resorts, but it passed its heyday before World War II and has suffered from the building boom brought on by tourism. Ezra Pound and D. H. Lawrence lived here, and many other writers, poets, and artists have been drawn to it. Today, the town's harbor is filled with yachts. A single-span bridge on the eastern side of the bay is named after Hannibal, who is said to have passed through the area after crossing the Alps.

The highlight of the town center, the cathedral of **Santi Gervasio e Protasio,** at the western end of Via Mazzini, was founded in the 6th century. ⊠ *Via Mazzini* ☎ *0185/52375* ☜ *Free* ☉ *Daily 6:30–noon and 3–6:30.*

The **Museo del Pizzo a Tombolo,** in a 19th-century mansion, has a collection of antique lace, a dying art for which Rapallo was once renowned. ⊠ *Villa Tigullio* ☎ *0185/63305* ☜ *Free* ☉ *Oct.–Aug., Tues., Wed., Fri., and Sat. 3–6, Thurs. 10–11:30 AM.*

Where to Stay & Eat

$$ ✕ **U' Giancu.** Owner Fausto Oneto is a man of many hats—don't be surprised if he wears six different ones during the course of a meal. Though original cartoons cover the walls and a children's playground is the main feature of the outdoor seating area, Fausto is completely serious about his cooking. Lamb dishes are particularly delicious, and the vegetables from his own garden provide the freshest of ingredients. Those who want to learn the secrets of Ligurian cuisine can attend lively morning cooking lessons. ⊠ *Via San Massimo 28, Località San Massimo, 3 km (2 mi) northwest of Rapallo* ☎ *0185/261212* ☰ *DC, MC, V* ☉ *Closed Wed. and mid.-Dec.–early Jan. No lunch.*

Fodor'sChoice ★

$–$$ ✕ **Da Mario.** Simply decorated and brightly lighted, this small and usually crowded trattoria serves some of the best seafood in Rapallo. Don't miss the spaghetti with seafood and tomatoes. A small terrace provides outdoor seating in summer. ⊠ *Piazza Garibaldi 23* ☎ *0185/51736* ⚭ *Reservations essential* ☰ *AE, DC, MC, V* ☉ *Closed Wed. and Oct. and Nov.*

$$$$ 🏨 **Grand Hotel Bristol.** This Victorian showcase outside Rapallo is set in lush gardens with a huge seawater pool. Spacious rooms, many with balcony overlooking the sea, are decorated in soft blues and greens in a smart, contemporary style and have extra-large beds. You can choose between a Rapallo view and a Portofino view. In summer, dinner is served on the roof terrace. ⊠ *Via Aurelia Orientale 369, 16035* ☎ *0185/273313* 🖷 *0185/55800* ⊕ *www.framon-hotels.com* ⇆ *80 rooms, 6 suites* ⚭ *2 restaurants, minibars, cable TV, saltwater pool, hot tub, sauna, billiards, bar, Internet room, meeting rooms, some pets allowed* ☰ *AE, MC, V* ☉ *Closed Nov.–Feb.* ⍢ *BP.*

Shopping

Guido Porati's aromatic shop, **Bottega dei Sestieri** (⊠ Via Mazzini 44 ☎ 0185/230530), sells Ligurian cheeses, wines, and other delicacies. For something truly regional, try the *trarcantu,* a cow's-milk cheese aged in grape skins. The store is on a narrow lane that runs parallel to Rapallo's waterfront.

The attractive coastal village of **Zoagli** (⊠ On S1, 4 km [2½ mi] east of Rapallo) has been famous for silk, velvet, and damask since the Middle Ages.

Santa Margherita Ligure

❼ *3 km (2 mi) south of Rapallo, 31 km (19 mi) southeast of Genoa.*

A beautiful old resort town favored by well-to-do Italians, Santa Margherita Ligure has everything a Riviera playground should have—plenty of palm

6

EATING WELL IN THE ITALIAN RIVIERA

Liguria's cooking might surprise you; it does employ all sorts of seafood—especially anchovies, sea bass, squid, and octopus—but it makes even wider use of vegetables and the aromatic herbs that grow wild on the hillsides, together with liberal amounts of olive oil and garlic. Basil- and garlic-rich pesto is Liguria's classic pasta sauce. You may also find *pansoti* (round pockets of pasta filled with a cheese mixture) and *trofie* (doughy, short pasta twists sometimes made with chestnut flour) with *salsa di noci*, an intense sauce of garlic, walnuts, and cream that, as with pesto, is ideally pounded with a mortar and pestle. Spaghetti *allo scoglio* is mixed with a tomato-based sauce containing an assortment of local *frutti di mare* (seafood). Fish is the best for a second course: the classic preparation is a whole grilled or baked whitefish—*branzino* (sea bass) and *orata* (dorado) are good choices—served with olives, potatoes, Ligurian spices, and a drizzle of olive oil. A popular meat dish is *cima alla Genovese*, veal roll stuffed with a mixture of eggs and vegetables and rolled, served as a cold cut. You should also try the succulent *agnello* (lamb), *coniglio* (rabbit), and fresh wild mushrooms foraged from the hills.

When you're hankering for a snack, turn to bakeries and small eateries serving focaccia, the flat bread that's the region's answer to the pizza. It comes simply salted and dribbled with olive oil; flavored with rosemary and olives; covered with cheese or anchovies; and even *ripiena* (filled), usually with cheese and/or vegetables and herbs. Local vineyards produce mostly light and refreshing whites such as Pigato, Vermentino, and Cinque Terre. Rossese di Dolceacqua, from near the French border, is the best red wine the region has to offer, but for a more robust accompaniment to meats opt for the more full-bodied reds of the neighboring Piedmont region.

trees and attractive hotels, cafés, and a marina packed with yachts. Some of the older buildings here are still decorated on the outside with the trompel'oeil frescoes typical of this part of the Riviera. This is a pleasant, convenient base, which for many represents a perfect balance on the Italian Riviera: bigger and less Americanized than the Cinque Terre; less glitzy than San Remo; more relaxing than Genoa and environs; and ideally situated for day trips, such as an excursion to Portofino.

Where to Stay & Eat

★ **$$$$** ✕ **Oca Bianca.** The menu at this small, excellent restaurant breaks away from the local norm—there is no seafood on the menu. Meat dishes are the specialty, and choices may include mouthwatering preparations of lamb from France or New Zealand, steak from Ireland or Brazil, South African ostrich, and Italian pork. Delicious antipasti, an extensive wine list, and the attentive service add to the experience. The Oca Bianca serves dinner until 1 AM. ⊠ *Via XXV Aprile 21* ☎ *0185/288411* ⌂ *Reservations essential* ▤ *AE, DC, MC, V* ⊘ *Closed Mon. and Jan.–mid-Feb. No lunch Tues.–Thurs. Sept.–Dec.*

$$$$ ✗ **La Stalla.** The breathtaking, hilltop views of Santa Margherita from this villa-turned-restaurant are worth the harrowing 3-km (2-mi) drive northwest to get here from Santa Margherita's port. Cesare Frati, your congenial host, is likely to tempt you with his homemade fettuccine *ai frutti di mare* (seafood) followed by the *pescato del giorno alla moda ligure* (catch of the day baked Ligurian style, with potatoes, olives, and pine nuts) and a delightfully fresh lemon sorbet to complete the feast. ✉ *Via G. Pino 27, Nozarego* ☎ *0185/289447* ▭ *AE, DC, MC, V* ✆ *Closed Mon. and Nov.*

$$$–$$$$ ✗ **Trattoria Cesarina.** This typical trattoria serves classic local fare—and that means seafood. The white interior is refreshingly free of bric-a-brac, allowing you to focus on your meal. Don't expect a menu; instead, allow the friendly staff to tell you what to eat. Among other treats, you may encounter a delectable antipasto of local frutti di mare, a seafood-theme pasta dish, and the catch of the day delicately grilled or baked in that laissez-faire Ligurian style. ✉ *Via Mameli 2/C* ☎ *0185/286059* ▭ *MC, V* ✆ *Closed Tues., and Dec. and Jan.*

$$$ ✗ **La Paranza.** From the piles of tiny *bianchetti* (young sardines) in oil and lemon that are part of the antipasto *di mare* (of the sea) to the simple, perfectly grilled whole sole, fresh seafood in every shape and form is the specialty here. Mussels, clams, octopus, salmon, or whatever else is fresh that day is what's on the menu. Locals say this is the town's best restaurant, but if you're looking for a stylish evening out, look elsewhere— La Paranza is about food, not fashion. It's just off Santa Margherita's port. ✉ *Via Jacopo Ruffini 46* ☎ *0185/283686* ✍ *Reservations essential* ▭ *AE, DC, MC, V* ✆ *Closed Mon. and Nov.*

★ **$$$$** ▦ **Grand Hotel Miramare.** Classic Riviera elegance prevails at this palatial hotel overlooking the bay south of the town center. Stroll through the lush garden, then take a dip in the curvaceous heated swimming pool or at the private swimming area on the sea. Antique furniture, such as crystal chandeliers and Louis XV chairs, fills the high-ceiling rooms, and there are marble bathrooms. ✉ *Via Milite Ignoto 30, 16038* ☎ *0185/ 287013* ☐ *0185/284651* ⊕ *www.grandhotelmiramare.it* ☜ *75 rooms, 9 suites* ♿ *2 restaurants, in-room safes, minibars, pool, beach, waterskiing, 2 bars, Internet room, meeting rooms, some pets allowed* ▭ *AE, DC, MC, V* ❙⊙❙ *BP.*

$$$$ ▦ **Imperiale Palace.** As Via Pagana climbs north out of Santa Margherita Ligure on its way toward Rapallo it passes this traditional luxury hotel. Set in an extensive park, the main building is a former villa built in 1889. Reception rooms with tall windows, plush chairs, and potted plants create a warm welcome. The rooms are furnished with antiques; many overlook the shore drive to the sea. ✉ *Via Pagana 19, 16038* ☎ *0185/288991* ☐ *0185/284223* ⊕ *www.hotelimperiale.com* ☜ *71 rooms, 18 suites* ♿ *Restaurant, in-room safes, minibars, pool, gym, beach, 2 bars, babysitting, meeting rooms* ▭ *AE, DC, MC, V* ✆ *Closed Nov.–Apr. 13* ❙⊙❙ *BP.*

$$$–$$$$ ▦ **Continental.** Built in the early 1900s, this stately seaside mansion with a columned portico stands in a lush garden shaded by tall palms and pine trees. The style is a blend of classic furnishings, mostly inspired by the 19th century, with some more functional pieces. There's also a modern wing. The hotel's own cabanas and swimming area are at the bottom of the garden. ✉ *Via Pagana 8, 16038* ☎ *0185/286512* ☐ *0185/*

6

284463 ⊕ *www.hotel-continental.it* ⊷ *68 rooms, 4 suites* ⚲ *Restaurant, in-room safes, minibars, Wi-Fi, bar, Internet room, meeting rooms, some pets allowed* ▤ *AE, DC, MC, V* ⓘⓄⓘ *BP.*

Portofino

❽ *5 km (3 mi) south of Santa Margherita Ligure, 36 km (22 mi) east of Genoa.*

One of the most photographed villages along the coast, with a decidedly romantic and affluent aura, Portofino has long been a popular destination for foreigners. Once an ancient Roman colony and taken by the Republic of Genoa in 1229, it has also been ruled by the French, English, Spanish, and Austrians, as well as by marauding bands of 16th-century pirates. Elite British tourists first flocked to the lush harbor in the mid-1800s. Some of Europe's wealthiest lay anchor in Portofino in summer, but they stay out of sight by day, appearing in the evening after buses and boats have carried off the day-trippers.

There's not actually much to *do* in Portofino other than stroll around the wee harbor, see the castle, walk to Punta del Capo, browse at the pricey boutiques, and sip a coffee while people-watching. However, weaving through picture-perfect cliff-side gardens and gazing at yachts framed by the turquoise Ligurian Sea and the cliffs of Santa Margherita can make for quite a relaxing afternoon. There are also several tame, photo-friendly hikes into the hills to nearby villages.

Unless you're traveling on a deluxe budget, you may want to stay in Rapallo or Santa Margherita Ligure rather than at one of Portofino's few very expensive hotels. Restaurants and cafés are good but also pricey (don't expect to have a beer here for much under €8). Trying to reach Portofino by bus or car on the single narrow road can be a nightmare in summer and on holiday weekends. No trains go directly to Portofino: you must stop at Santa Margherita and take the public bus from there (€1). An alternative is to take a boat from Santa Margherita, though even this can be a harrowing experience, as cruise ships also anchor here to disgorge their passengers for outings.

From the harbor, follow the signs for the climb to the **Castello di San Giorgio,** the most worthwhile sight in Portofino, with its medieval relics, impeccable gardens, and sweeping views. The castle was founded in the Middle Ages but restored in the 16th through 18th century. In true Portofino form, it was owned by Genoa's English consul from 1870 until its opening to the public in 1961. ⊠ *Above harbor* ☎ *0185/269046* ⤴ €3 ⊗ *Apr.–Sept., Wed.–Mon. 10–6; Oct.–Mar., Wed.–Mon. 10–5.*

The small church **San Giorgio,** sitting on a ridge, was rebuilt four times during World War II. It is said to contain the relics of its namesake, brought back from the Holy Land by the Crusaders. Portofino enthusiastically celebrates St. George's Day every April 23. ⊠ *Above harbor* ☎ *0185/269337* ⊗ *Daily 7–6.*

Pristine views can be had from the deteriorating *faro* (lighthouse) at **Punta Portofino,** a 15-minute walk along the point that begins at the southern end of the port. Along the seaside path you can see numerous impressive, sprawling private residences behind high iron gates.

The only sand beach near Portofino is at **Paraggi**, a cove on the road between Santa Margherita and Portofino. The bus will stop there on request.

OFF THE BEATEN PATH

ABBAZIA DI SAN FRUTTUOSO – On the sea at the foot of Monte Portofino, the medieval Abbey of San Fruttuoso—built by the Benedictines of Monte Cassino—protects a minuscule fishing village that can be reached only on foot or by water (a 20-minute boat ride from Portofino and also reachable from Camogli, Santa Margherita Ligure, and Rapallo). The restored abbey is now the property of a national conservation fund (FAI) and occasionally hosts temporary exhibitions. The church contains the tombs of some illustrious members of the Doria family. The old abbey and its grounds are a delightful place to spend a few hours, perhaps lunching at one of the modest beachfront trattorias nearby (open only in summer). Boatloads of visitors can make it very crowded very fast; you might appreciate it most off-season. Last entrance is 30 minutes before closing time. ✉ *15-min boat ride or 2-hr walk northwest of Portofino* ☎ *0185/772703* 🎟 *€4, €6 during exhibitions* ☉ *Mar.–Apr. and Oct., Tues.–Sun. 10–4; May–Sept., daily 10–6; Dec.–Feb., weekends 10–4.*

Where to Stay & Eat

$$$–$$$$ ✕ **Il Pitosforo.** A chic clientele, many from the luxury yachts in the harbor, gives this waterfront restaurant a high glamour quotient, which is augmented by outlandish prices. Spaghetti ai frutti di mare is recommended; adventurous diners might try *lo stocco accomodou* (dried cod in a sauce of tomatoes, raisins, and pine nuts). ✉ *Molo Umberto I 9* ☎ *0185/269020 or 0335/5615833* 🍴 *Reservations essential* 🖃 *AE, DC, MC, V* ☉ *Closed Mon. and Tues., and Jan.–mid-Feb. No lunch.*

$$$ ✕ **Ristorante Puny.** A table at this tiny restaurant is difficult to come by in summer, as the manager caters mostly to friends and regulars. If you are lucky enough to get in, however, the food will not disappoint you, nor will the cozy but elegant yellow interior. The unforgettable *pappardelle* (large, flat noodles) *al portofino* delicately blends two of Liguria's tastes, tomato and pesto. Ligurian seafood specialties include baked fish with bay leaves, potatoes, and olives as well as the inventive *moscardini al forno* (baked octopus with lemon and rosemary in tomato sauce). ✉ *P. Martiri dell'Olivetta 4–5, on the harbor* ☎ *0185/269037* 🍴 *Reservations essential* 🖃 *AE, DC, MC, V* ☉ *Closed Thurs., and Jan. and Feb.*

¢ ✕ **Canale.** If the staggering prices of virtually all of Portofino's restaurants put you off, the long line outside this family-run bakery indicates that you're not alone and that something special is in store. Here all the focaccia is baked on the spot and served fresh from the oven, along with all kinds of sandwiches, pastries, and other refreshments. The only problem is there's nowhere to sit—time for a picnic! ✉ *Via Roma 30* ☎ *0185/269248* 🖃 *No credit cards* ☉ *Closed Nov. and Dec. No lunch Jan.–Apr. and Oct.*

$$$$ 🛏 **San Giorgio.** If you decide to stay in Portofino, this is perhaps your best choice. Tucked away on a quiet backstreet with no views of the harbor, the San Giorgio offers rooms that are immaculate, comfortable, and soothingly designed with canopy beds, pastel walls, and ultramodern

6

bathrooms. Two small 19th-century town houses were joined to form the hotel, making the hallways seem like a labyrinth, but the level of service is high and the peaceful location—there's a secluded garden at the back—is a definite plus. ⊠ *Via Del Fondaco 11, 16034* 🕾 *0185/ 26991* 🖷 *0185/267139* ⊕ *www.portofinohsg.it* 🛏 *17 rooms, 1 suite* ⌂ *Bar, Web TV, Internet room, some pets allowed* ☰ *AE, DC, MC, V* ⊘ *Closed Dec.–Feb.* ⊚ *BP.*

$$$$ 🔲 **Splendido.** Arriving at this 1920s luxury hotel is so much like entering a Jazz Age film set that you'd almost expect to see a Bugatti or Daimler roll up the winding drive from the seaside below. There's a particular attention to color, from the coordinated floral linens in corals and gold to the fresh flowers in the reception rooms and on the large terrace. Even grander than the hotel are its prices (more than €500), and the large numbers of American guests smoking Cuban cigars. ⊠ *Salita Baratta 16, 16034* 🕾 *0185/267801* 🖷 *0185/267806* ⊕ *www.hotelsplendido. orient-express.com* 🛏 *31 rooms, 34 suites* ⌂ *Restaurant, tennis court, pool, gym, sauna, 2 bars, meeting rooms, some pets allowed* ☰ *AE, DC, MC, V* ⊘ *Closed mid-Nov.–late Mar.* ⊚ *BP.*

Sports & the Outdoors

HIKING If you have the stamina, you can hike to the Abbazia di San Fruttuoso from Portofino. It's a steep climb at first, and the walk takes about 2½ hours one-way. If you're extremely ambitious and want to make a day of it, you can hike another 2½ hours all the way to Camogli. Much more modest hikes from Portofino include a 1-hour uphill walk to Cappella delle Gave, a bit inland in the hills, from where you can continue downhill to Santa Margherita Ligure (another 1½ hours) and a gently undulating paved trail leading to the beach at Paraggi (½ hour). Finally, there's a 2½-hour hike from Portofino that heads farther inland to Ruta, through Olmi and Pietre Strette. The trails are well marked and maps are available at the tourist information offices in Rapallo, Santa Margherita, Portofino, and Camogli.

Camogli

★ ❾ *15 km (9 mi) northwest of Portofino, 20 km (12 mi) east of Genoa.*

Camogli, at the edge of the large promontory and nature reserve known as the Portofino Peninsula, has always been a town of sailors. By the 19th century it was leasing its ships throughout the continent. Today, multicolor houses, remarkably deceptive trompe-l'oeil frescoes, and a massive 17th-century seawall mark this appealing harbor community, perhaps as beautiful as Portofino but without the glamour. When exploring on foot, don't miss the boat-filled second harbor, which is reached by ducking under a narrow archway at the northern end of the first one.

> **WORD OF MOUTH**
>
> "Camogli was really charming—great seafood, ferries to various other towns along the coast, and a wonderful Fellini cast of characters along the passeggiata."
> —marktynenyc

The Castello Dragone, built onto the sheer rock face near the harbor, is home to the **Acquario** (Aquarium), which has tanks filled with local marine life built into the ramparts. ✉ *Via Isola* ☎ *0185/773375* 🎫 *€3* ⊘ *May–Sept., daily 10–noon and 3–7; Oct.–Apr., Fri.–Sun. 10–noon and 2:30–6, Tues.–Thurs. 10–noon.*

OFF THE
BEATEN
PATH

SAN ROCCO, SAN NICCOLÒ, AND PUNTA CHIAPPA – You can reach these hamlets along the western coast of the peninsula on foot or by boat from Camogli. They are more natural and less fashionable than those facing south on the eastern coast. In the small Romanesque church at San Niccolò, sailors who survived dangerous voyages came to offer thanks.

RUTA – The footpaths that leave from Ruta, 4 km (2½ mi) east of Camogli, thread through rugged terrain and contain a multitude of plant species. Weary hikers are sustained by stunning views of the Riviera di Levante from the various vantage points along the way.

Where to Stay & Eat

$$–$$$ ✕ **Vento Ariel.** This small, friendly restaurant serves some of the best seafood in town. Dine on the shaded terrace in summer months and watch the bustling activity in the nearby port. Only the freshest of seafood is served; try the spaghetti *alle vongole* (with clams) or the mixed grilled fish. ✉ *Calata Porto* ☎ *0185/771080* 🚇 *AE, DC, MC, V* ⊘ *Closed Wed. and Jan. 2–15.*

¢ ✕ **Pizzeria Il Lido.** As the name suggests, this popular spot is right across from Camogli's narrow beach, and the outside tables have great views of the sea. If you don't fancy one of the many varieties of pizza, you can choose one of the pasta dishes. ✉ *Via Garibaldi 133* ☎ *0185/ 770141* 🚇 *MC, V* ⊘ *Closed Tues.*

★ $$$–$$$$ ⊞ **Cenobio dei Dogi.** Perched majestically a step above Camogli, overlooking harbor, peninsula, and sea, Cenobio dei Dogi is indisputably the best address in town. Genoa's doges once summered here. Ask for one of the rooms with expansive balconies; though unimaginative in design, they have commanding vistas of Camogli's cozy port. You can relax in the well-kept park or enjoy a game of tennis. Cenobio dei Dogi can be crowded with business travelers and conventions. ✉ *Via Cuneo 34, 16032* ☎ *0185/7241* 🖨 *0185/772796* ⊕ *www.cenobio.it* ⇱ *102 rooms, 4 suites* ⟁ *Restaurant, Wi-Fi, tennis court, pool, gym, beach, bar, Internet room, business services, meeting rooms* 🚇 *AE, DC, MC, V* ⓘⓞⓘ *BP.*

$$ ⊞ **Hotel Augusta.** This friendly, family-run hotel is an economical choice in the center of Camogli. Though you won't have a view of the sea, it's just a short walk away. Quiet guest rooms, all with parquet floors, are bright and modern. A satisfying buffet awaits you in the breakfast room each morning. ✉ *Via Schiaffino 100, 16032* ☎ *0185/770592* 🖨 *0185/ 770593* ⊕ *www.htlaugusta.com* ⇱ *15 rooms* ⟁ *Restaurant, in-room safes, bar* 🚇 *AE, DC, MC, V* ⓘⓞⓘ *BP.*

Nightlife & the Arts

★ The highlight of the festival of San Fortunato, held on the second Sunday of May each year, is the **Sagra del Pesce,** a crowded, festive, and free-to-the-public feast of freshly caught fish, cooked outside at the port in a frying pan 12 feet wide.

GENOA

Genoa was the birthplace of Christopher Columbus, but the city's proud history predates that explorer by several hundred years. Genoa was already an important trading station by the 3rd century BC, when the Romans conquered Liguria. The Middle Ages and the Renaissance saw its rise into a jumping-off place for the Crusaders, a commercial center of tremendous wealth and prestige, and a strategic bone of international contention. A network of fortresses defending the city connected by a wall second only in length to the Great Wall of China was constructed in the hills above, and Genoa's bankers, merchants, and princes adorned the city with palaces, churches, and impressive art collections.

Known as *La Superba* (The Proud), Genoa was a great maritime power in the 13th century, rivaling Venice and Pisa in strength and splendor. But its luster eventually diminished, and the city was outshined by these and other formidable cities. By the 17th century it was no longer a great sea power. It has, however, continued to be a profitable port. Modern container ships now unload at docks that centuries ago served galleons and vessels bound for the spice routes. Genoa (Genova, in Italian) is now a busy, sprawling, and cosmopolitan city, apt to break the spell of the coastal towns in a hurry. Crammed into a thin crescent of land between sea and mountains, Genoa expanded up rather than out, taking on the form of a multilayer wedding cake, with churches, streets, and entire residential neighborhoods built on others' rooftops. Public elevators and funiculars are as common as buses and trains.

But with more than 2 millennia of history under its belt, magnificent palaces and museums, the largest medieval city center in Europe, and an elaborate network of ancient hilltop fortresses, Genoa may be just the dose of culture you are looking for. Europe's biggest boat show, the annual Salone Nautico Internazionale, is held here. Fine restaurants are abundant, and classical dance and music are richly represented; the Teatro Carlo Felice is the local opera venue, and where the internationally renowned annual Niccolò Paganini Violin Contest takes place.

With the occasional assistance of public transportation, the only way to visit Genoa is on foot. Many of the more interesting districts are either entirely closed to traffic, have roads so narrow that no car could fit, or are, even at the best of times, blocked by gridlock. Although it might seem a daunting task, exploring the city is made simple by its geography. The historical center of Genoa occupies a relatively narrow strip of land running between the mountains and the sea. You can easily visit the most important monuments in one or two days.

The Medieval Core & Points Above

The medieval center of Genoa, threaded with tiny streets flanked by 11th-century portals, is roughly the area between the port and Piazza de Ferrari. This mazelike pedestrian zone is officially called the Caruggi District, but the Genovese, in their matter-of-fact way, simply refer to the area as the place of the *vicoli* (narrow alleys). In this warren of narrow, cobbled streets extending north from Piazza Caricamento, the city's oldest churches sit among tiny shops selling antique furniture, coffee, cheese, rifles, wine, gilt picture frames, camping gear, and even live fish. The 500-year-old apartment buildings lean so precariously that penthouse balconies nearly touch those across the street, blocking what little sunlight would have shone down onto the cobblestones. Wealthy Genovese built their homes in this quarter in the 16th century, and prosperous guilds, such as the goldsmiths for whom Vico degli Indoratori and Via degli Orefici were named, set up shop here.

The Main Attractions

★ ㉓ **Cimitero Monumentale di Staglieno.** One of the most famous of Genovese landmarks is this bizarrely beautiful cemetery; its fanciful marble and bronze sculptures sprawl haphazardly across a hillside on the outskirts of town. A **Pantheon** holds indoor tombs and some remarkable works like an 1878 *Eve* by Villa. Don't miss Rovelli's 1896 **Tomba Raggio,** which shoots Gothic spires out of the hillside forest. The cemetery began operation in 1851 and has been lauded by such visitors as Mark Twain and Evelyn Waugh. It covers a good deal of ground; allow at least half a day to explore. It's difficult to locate; reach it via the number 480 and 482 buses from the Stazione Genova Brignole, the number 34 bus from Stazione Principe, or a taxi. ✉ *Piazzale Resasco, Piazza Manin* ☎ *010/870184* ⊕ *www.cimiterodistaglieno.it* ✆ *Free* ⊗ *Daily 7:30–5; entrance closes at 4:30.*

⑯ **Galleria Nazionale.** This gallery, housed in the richly adorned **Palazzo Spinola** north of Piazza Soziglia, contains masterpieces by Luca Giordano and Guido Reni. The *Ecce Homo,* by Antonello da Messina, is a hauntingly beautiful painting, of historical interest because it was the Sicilian da Messina who first brought Flemish oil paints and techniques to Italy from his sojourns in the Low Countries. ✉ *Piazza Pelliceria 1, Maddalena* ☎ *010/2705300* ⊕ *www.museigenova.it* ✆ *€4, €6.50 including Palazzo Reale* ⊗ *Tues.–Sat. 8:30–7:30, Sun. 1:30–7:30.*

⑲ **Palazzo Bianco.** It's difficult to miss the splendid white facade of this town palace as you walk down Via Garibaldi, once one of Genoa's most important streets. The building, completely restored in 2003–04, houses a fine collection of 17th-century art, with the Spanish and Flemish schools well represented. ✉ *Via Garibaldi 11, Maddalena* ☎ *010/ 2759185* ⊕ *www.stradanuova.it* ✆ *€7, includes Palazzo Rosso and Palazzo Doria Tursi* ⊗ *Tues.–Fri. 9–7, weekends 10–7.*

⑪ **Palazzo Reale.** Lavish rococo rooms provide sumptuous display space for paintings, sculptures, tapestries, and Asian ceramics. The 17th-century palace—also known as Palazzo Balbi Durazzo—was built by the Balbi family, enormously wealthy Genovese merchants. Its regal pretensions were not lost on the Savoy, who bought the palace and turned it into a royal residence in the early 19th century. The gallery of mirrors and the ballroom on the upper floor are particularly decadent. Look for works by Sir Anthony Van Dyck, who lived in Genoa for six years, beginning in 1621, and painted many portraits of the Genovese nobility. The formal gardens, which you can visit for €1, provide a welcome respite

Fodor'sChoice
★

6

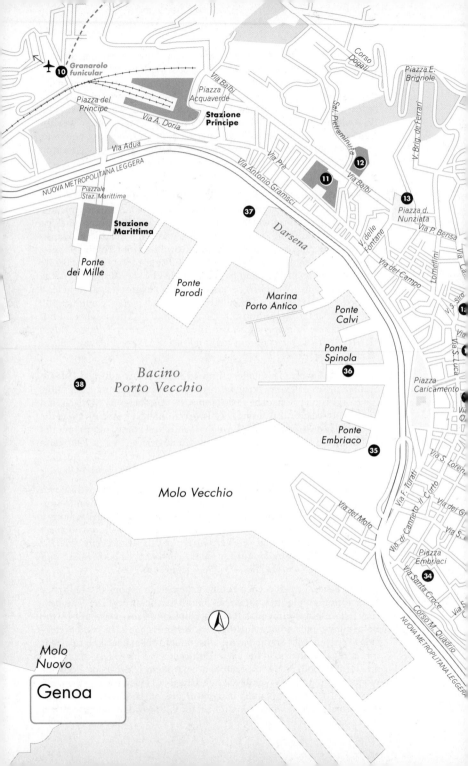

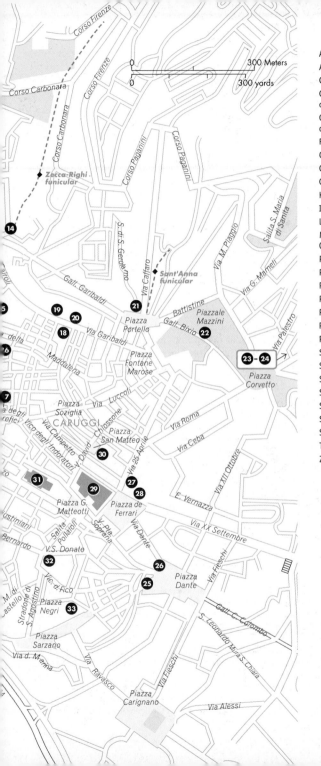

Accademia delle Belle Arti ...**28**
Acquario di Genova **36**
Castelletto **21**
Childhood home
of Christopher Columbus **26**
Cimitero Monumentale
di Staglieno **23**
Ferrovia Genova-Casella **24**
Galata Museo del Mare **37**
Galleria Nazionale **16**
Granarolo funicular **10**
Harbor **38**
Il Bigo **35**
Loggia dei Mercanti **17**
Museo d'Arte
Orientale Chiossone **22**
Palazzo Bianco **19**
Palazzo dell'Università **12**
Palazzo Ducale **29**
Palazzo Reale **11**
Palazzo Rosso **18**
Palazzo Doria Tursi **20**
Porta Soprana **25**
San Donato **32**
San Lorenzo **31**
San Matteo **30**
San Siro **15**
Sant'Agostino **33**
Santa Maria di Castello **34**
Santissima Annunziata **13**
Teatro Carlo Felice **27**
Zecca-Righi funicular **14**

from the bustle of the city beyond the palace walls, as well as great views of the harbor. ⊠ *Via Balbi 10, Pré* ☎ *010/27101* ⊕ *www. palazzorealegenova.it* ⊠ *€4, €6 including Galleria Nazionale* ⊙ *Tues. and Wed. 9–1:30, Thurs.–Sun. 9–7.*

⑱ Palazzo Rosso. This 17th-century baroque palace was named for the red stone used in its construction. It now contains, apart from a number of lavishly frescoed suites, works by Titian, Veronese, Reni, and Van Dyck. ⊠ *Via Garibaldi 18, Maddalena* ☎ *010/2759185* ⊕ *www.stradanuova. it* ⊠ *€7, includes Palazzo Bianco and Palazzo Doria Tursi* ⊙ *Tues.–Fri. 9–7, weekends 10–7.*

⑭ Zecca-Righi funicular. This is a seven-stop commuter funicular beginning at Piazza della Nunziata and ending at a high lookout on the fortified gates in the 17th-century city walls. Ringed around the circumference of the city are a number of huge fortresses; this gate was part of the city's system of defenses. From Righi you can undertake scenic all-day hikes from one fortress to the next. ⊠ *Piazza della Nunziata, Pré* ☎ *010/ 5582414* ⊕ *www.amt.genova.it* ⊠ *€1, free with bus ticket* ⊙ *Daily 6 AM–11:45 PM.*

Also Worth Seeing

㉑ Castelletto. One of Genoa's handy municipal elevators whisks you skyward from Piazza Portello, at the end of Galleria Garibaldi, for a good view of the old city. ⊠ *Piazza Portello, Castelletto* ⊠ *€1* ⊙ *Daily 6:40 AM–midnight.*

㉔ Ferrovia Genova–Casella. In continuous operation since 1929, the Genova–Casella Railroad runs from Piazza Manin in Genoa (follow Via Montaldo from the center of town, or take Bus 33 or 34 to Piazza Manin) through the beautiful countryside above the city, finally arriving in the rural hill town of Casella. On the way, the tiny train traverses a series of precarious switchbacks that afford sweeping views of the forested Ligurian hills. In Casella Paese (the last stop) you can hike, eat lunch, or just check out the view and ride back. There are two restaurants and two pizzerias near the Casella station; try local cuisine at Trattoria Teresin in Località Avosso. **Canova** (two stops from the end

---

A GOOD WALK: GENOA'S STREET OF GOLD

This walk starts from Piazza delle Fontane Marose and heads west along **Via Garibaldi,** one of Genoa's most famous streets. Between 1551 and 1558, three auctions sold off the lots of land along what was then known as the Via Aurea (Golden Street) to wealthy Genovese families, who proceeded to build the extravagant palaces you see there now. Several have become museums housing world-class collections. Many of the rest have courtyards open to the public.

Palazzo Cambiaso, at Via Garibaldi 1, is the first palace on the right, and like several of the other palaces along the street, it's now a bank. Built between 1558 and 1560 for Agostino Pallavicino, it is also one of the street's more traditionally designed buildings. The **Palazzo Gambaro,** at No. 2, is the first palace on your left. Perhaps fittingly, given that this building, too, is now a bank, the marble statues flanking the entrance represent Vigilance and Prudence. Number 3 is the **Palazzo Lercari Parodi,** built between 1571 and 1578. It's said that the broken noses of the figures on either side of the door

of the line) is the start of two possible hikes through the hills: one a two-hour, one-way trek to a small sanctuary, **Santuario della Vittoria,** and the other a more grueling four-hour hike to the hill town of **Creto.** Another worthwhile stop along the rail line is **Sant'Olcese Tullo,** where you can take a half-hour (one-way) walk along a river and through the **Sentiero Botanico di Ciaé,** a botanical garden and forest refuge with labeled specimens of Ligurian flora and a tiny medieval castle. For Canova and Sant'Olcese, inform your conductor that you want him to stop. The Casella railroad is a good way to get a sense of the rugged landscape around Genoa, and you may have it to yourself. The train runs about every hour. ⊠ *Piazza Manin* ☎ *010/837321* ⊕ *www. ferroviagenovacasella.it* ☒ *€4 round-trip Mon.–Sat., €6 Sun.* ☉ *Mon.–Sat. 7:30–7:30, Sun. 9–9.*

🐾 **⓾ Granarolo funicular.** Take a cog railway up the steeply rising terrain to another part of the city's fortified walls. It takes 15 minutes to hoist you from Stazione Principe, on Piazza Acquaverde, to **Porta Granarolo,** 1,000 feet above, where the sweeping view gives you a sense of Genoa's size. The funicular departs about every half hour. ⊠ *Piazza del Principe, San Teodoro* ☎ *010/5582414* ⊕ *www.amt.genova.it* ☒ *€1, free with bus ticket* ☉ *Daily 6 AM–10 PM, at 10:40 PM and 11:20 PM.*

⓱ Loggia dei Mercanti. This merchants' row dating from the 16th century is lined with shops selling local foods and gifts as well as raincoats, rubber boots, and fishing line. ⊠ *Piazza Banchi, Maddalena.*

㉒ Museo d'Arte Orientale Chiossone. In the Villetta di Negro park on the hillside above Piazza Portello, the Chiossone Oriental Art Museum has one of Europe's most noteworthy collections of Japanese, Chinese, and Thai objects. There's a fine view of the city from the museum's terrace. ⊠ *Piazzale Mazzini 4, Maddalena* ☎ *010/542285* ⊕ *www. museochiossonegenova.it* ☒ *€4* ☉ *Tues.–Fri. 9–1, weekends 10–7.*

⓬ Palazzo dell'Università. Built in the 1630s as a Jesuit college, this has been Genoa's university since 1803. The exterior is unassuming, but climb the stairway flanked by lions to visit the handsome courtyard, with its portico of double Doric columns. ⊠ *Via Balbi 5, Pré.*

are representative of Mengollo Lercari's penchant for cutting off the noses of prisoners. Note that the courtyard, rather than being centrally located, sits in front of the main portion of the building. At No. 4, the **Palazzo Carrega Cataldi,** built between 1558 and 1561 by Tobia Pallavicino, the "King of Alum" (a fixative used for dyeing cloth), is now home to Genoa's Chamber of Commerce. It was built on a relatively small lot, hence the claim that the architect, Giovanni Battista Castello (1509–69), *fece grande in poco spazio* (basically, did a lot with a little). In fact, there's a fair bit of theatricality to the design. For example, if the main entrance is open, you can see the grand double staircase that leads to the first floor. Only one side actually goes somewhere—the other is there simply for show. Farther down the street, at No. 5, is the **Palazzo Spinola,** one of many palaces built in Genoa by the fabulously wealthy Spinola family. It was built in 1558 for Angelo Giovanni Spinola, Genovese ambassador to the court of Spain and banker to Philip II. Rather austere on the outside, it's sumptuously stuccoed and frescoed within.

⑳ Palazzo Doria Tursi. In the 16th century, wealthy resident Nicolò Grimaldi had a palace built of pink stone quarried in the region. It's been reincarnated as Genoa's Palazzo Municipale (Municipal Building), and so most of the goings-on inside are the stuff of local politics and quickie weddings. You can visit the richly decorated **Sala Paganini,** where the famous Guarnerius violin that belonged to Niccolò Paganini (1782–1840) is displayed, along with the gardens that connect the palace with the neighboring Palazzo Bianco. ⊠ *Via Garibaldi 9, Maddalena* ☎ *010/ 2759185* ⊕ *www.stradanuova.it* 🏛 *€7, includes Palazzo Bianco and Palazzo Rosso* ⊙ *Tues.–Fri. 9–7, weekends 10–7.*

⑮ San Siro. Genoa's oldest church was the city's cathedral from the 4th to the 9th century. Rebuilt in the 16th and 17th centuries, it now feels a bit like a haunted house—imposing frescoes line dank hallways, and chandeliers hold crooked candles flickering in the darkness. ⊠ *Via San Luca, Maddalena* ☎ *010/22461468* ⊙ *Daily 7:30–noon and 4–7.*

⑬ Santissima Annunziata. Exuberantly frescoed vaults decorate the 16th- to 17th-century church, which is an excellent example of Genovese baroque architecture. ⊠ *Piazza della Nunziata, Pré* ☎ *010/297662* ⊙ *Daily 9–noon and 3–7.*

Southern Districts & the Aquarium

Inhabited since the 6th century BC, the oldest section of Genoa lies on a hill to the southwest of the Caruggi District. Today, apart from a section of 9th-century wall near Porta Soprana, there is little to show that an imposing castle once stood here. Though the neighborhood is considerably run-down, some of Genoa's oldest churches make it a worthwhile excursion. No visit to Genoa is complete, however, without at least a stroll along the harbor front. Once a squalid and unsafe neighborhood, the port was given a complete overhaul during Genoa's preparations for the Columbus quincentennial celebrations of 1992, and additional restorations in 2003 and 2004 have done much to revitalize the waterfront. You can easily reach the port on foot by following Via San Lorenzo downhill from Genoa's cathedral, Via delle Fontane from Piazza della Nunziata, or any of the narrow *vicoli* (alleyways) that lead down from Via Balbi and Via Pré.

The brothers Giovanni Battista and Andrea Spinola built the palace at No. 6, now the **Palazzo Doria.** In the atrium hangs a wrought-iron chandelier with the eagles symbolizing the Doria family, who bought the place in 1723. Moving along to No. 7, you reach the **Palazzo Podestà** (1559–66), named after one of Genoa's longest-sitting mayors, Andrea Podestà. In office almost continuously between 1866 and 1895, Podestà didn't have much of a commute to work—the town hall is right next door, at No. 9.

The **Palazzo Cattaneo Adorno,** at Nos. 8 and 10, was the last palace built on the land auctioned between 1551 and 1558. Shortly after the auction, the lot was resold, at an inflated price, to Lazzaro and Giacomo Spinola. Despite the homogeneous appearance of the facade, the building contains two separate palaces. Number 8 was purchased by a member of the Cattaneo family in 1875, while No. 10 passed to Giovanni Battista Adorno, Giacomo Spinola's son-in-law. It still belongs to the Adorno family. At No. 12 is the **Palazzo Campanella,** unfortunately considerably damaged during a World War II bombard-

The Main Attractions

★ ☾ **36** **Acquario di Genova.** Europe's biggest aquarium, second in the world only to Osaka's in Japan, is the third-most-visited museum in Italy and a must for children. Fifty tanks of marine species, including sea turtles, dolphins, seals, eels, penguins, and sharks, share space with educational displays and re-creations of marine ecosystems, including a tank of coral from the Red Sea. If arriving by car, take the Genova Ovest exit from the autostrada. Entrance is permitted every half hour and the ticket office closes 1½ hours before the aquarium. ☒ *Ponte Spinola, Porto Vecchio* ☎ *0101/ 23451* ⊕ *www.acquario.ge.it* ☜ *€14* ☽ *July and Aug., daily 9 AM–11 PM; Sept.–June, Mon.–Wed. and Fri. 9:30–7:30, Thurs. 9:30 AM–10 PM, weekends 9:30–8:30.*

37 **Galata Museo del Mare.** Devoted entirely to the city's seafaring history, this museum is probably the best way, at least on dry land, to get an idea of the changing shape of Genoa's busy port. Highlighting the displays is a full-size replica of a 17th-century Genovese galleon. ☒ *Calata De Mari 1, Ponte dei Mille* ☎ *010/2345655* ⊕ *www.galatamuseodelmare.it* ☜ *€10* ☽ *Mar.–Oct., daily 10–7:30; Nov.–Feb., Tues.–Fri. 10–6, and weekends 10–7:30; last entrance 1½ hrs before closing.*

6

38 **Harbor.** A boat tour gives you a good perspective on the layout of the harbor, which dates back to Roman times. The Genoa inlet, the largest along the Italian Riviera, was also used by the Phoenicians and Greeks as a harbor and a staging area from which they could penetrate inland to form settlements and to trade. The port is guarded by the Diga Foranea, a striking wall 5 km (3 mi) long built into the ocean. The **Lanterna,** a lighthouse more than 360 feet high, was built in 1544 at the height of Andrea Doria's career; it's one of Italy's oldest lighthouses and a traditional emblem of Genoa. Boat tours of the harbor (€6), provided by the Consorzio Liguria Viamare, launch from the aquarium pier and run about an hour. ☒ *Via Sottoripa 7/8, Porto Antico* ☎ *010/265712* ⊕ *www.liguriaviamare.it.*

29 **Palazzo Ducale.** This palace was built in the 16th century over a medieval hall, and its facade was rebuilt in the late 18th century and later restored. It now houses temporary exhibitions and a restaurant-bar serving fu-

ment. The facade has been restored, but the palace's claim to fame, the Salon of the Sun—a French-style room filled with mirrors and sculpture—is lost forever.

The largest of Via Garibaldi's palaces is at No 9. This is the **Palazzo Doria Tursi** **20**, built between 1565 and 1579 by the enormously wealthy banker Niccolò Grimaldi, nicknamed "the monarch." Later purchased by Giovanni Andrea Doria, the palace then passed on to his son Carlo, the Duke of Tursi, and now serves as Genoa's town hall. Directly opposite, at Nos. 14 and 16,

and set slightly back from the street, is the **Palazzo delle Torrette** (1562–66). Built by the Doria Tursi as a pendant to their main palace, the building also served as a passage to the workshops and other properties the family owned in the Caruggi District, just to the south. Next to the Palazzo Doria Tursi, and the last palace to the right on Via Garibaldi, is the **Palazzo Bianco** **19**, which was transformed in 1714 by Maria Durazzo Brignole Sale. It has a classical facade covered with white plaster (from which it gets its name). Maria Brignole

sion cuisine. Reservations are necessary to visit the dungeons and tower. Guided tours of the palace and its exhibitions are sometimes available. ⊠ *Piazza Matteotti 9, Portoria* ☎ *010/5574004* ⊕ *www.palazzoducale. genova.it* ☞ *Free* ⊙ *Tues.–Sun. 9–9.*

③¹ **San Lorenzo.** Contrasting black slate and white marble, so common in Liguria, embellished the cathedral at the heart of medieval Genoa—inside and out. Consecrated in 1118, the church honors St. Lawrence, who passed through the city on his way to Rome in the 3rd century. For hundreds of years the building was used for religious and state purposes such as civic elections. Note the 13th-century Gothic portal, fascinating twisted barbershop columns, and the 15th- to 17th-century frescoes inside. The last campanile dates from the early 16th century. The **Museo del Tesoro di San Lorenzo** (San Lorenzo Treasury Museum) housed inside has some stunning pieces from medieval goldsmiths and silversmiths, for which medieval Genoa was renowned. ⊠ *Piazza San Lorenzo, Molo* ☎ *010/2471831* ☞ *Cathedral free, museum €5* ⊙ *Cathedral daily 8–11:45 and 3–6:45, museum Mon.–Sat. 9–11:30 and 3–5:30.*

③³ **Sant'Agostino.** This 13th-century Gothic church was damaged during World War II, but it still has a fine campanile and two well-preserved cloisters that house an excellent museum displaying pieces of medieval architecture and fresco paintings. Highlighting the collection are the enigmatic fragments of a tomb sculpture by Giovanni Pisano (circa 1250–circa 1315). ⊠ *Piazza Sarzano 35/r, Molo* ☎ *010/2511263* ⊕ *www. museosantagostino.it* ☞ *€4* ⊙ *Tues.–Fri. 9–7, weekends 10–7.*

③⁴ **Santa Maria di Castello.** One of Genoa's most significant religious buildings, an early Christian church, was rebuilt in the 12th century and finally completed in 1513. You can visit the adjacent cloisters and see the fine artwork contained in the museum. Museum hours vary during religious services. ⊠ *Salita di Santa Maria di Castello 15, Molo* ☎ *010/ 2549511* ☞ *Free* ⊙ *Daily 9–noon and 3:30–6.*

Also Worth Seeing

②⁸ **Accademia delle Belle Arti.** Founded in 1751, the Academy of Fine Arts, as well as being a school, houses a collection of paintings from the 16th to the 19th century. Genovese artists of the baroque period are partic-

---

Sale gave the palace to the city of Genoa in 1884 on condition that it become an art gallery. The Brignole Sale also owned the last palace on the left-hand side of Via Garibaldi, the **Palazzo Rosso** ⑱, built between 1671 and 1677 with a red stone facade. It was also given by Maria Brignole Sale to the city of Genoa, in 1874. One block past the Palazzo Rosso, turn left onto Via 4 Canti di San Francesco and follow it down to Via della Madonna, where you turn right, and shortly thereafter left onto Via Pellicceria. Here stands perhaps the grandest of the Spinola family's palaces, the **Palazzo Spin-**

ola. Built for Grimaldi in 1593, it passed to the Spinola in the early 17th century. It was partially rebuilt and then turned over to the Italian State, which made it the **Galleria Nazionale** ⑯. In passing, don't miss the 15th-century sculpted doorway, with a relief of Saint George, across the street.

After this substantial dose of Genoa at its most luxurious, you can see another side of Genoa by dipping into the **Caruggi District,** the warren of medieval alleys positioned directly below, and only a few steps away from, Via Garibaldi's opulence.

ularly well represented. ⊠ *Largo Pertini 4, Portoria* ☎ *010/581957* ⊕ *www.accademialigustica.it* ⊡ *Free* ☺ *Mon.–Sat. 9–1.*

㉖ **Childhood home of Christopher Columbus.** The ivy-covered remains of this fabled medieval house stand in the gardens below the Porta Soprana. A small and rather disappointing collection of objects and reproductions relating to the life and travels of Columbus are on display inside. ⊠ *Piazza Dante, Molo* ☎ *010/2465346* ⊡ *€4* ☺ *Tues.–Sun. 9–5.*

㉟ **Il Bigo.** The bizarre white structure erected in 1992 to celebrate the Columbus quincentennial looks like either a radioactive spider or an overgrown potato spore, depending on your point of view. Its most redeeming feature is the **Ascensore Panoramico Bigo** (Bigo Panoramic Elevator), from which you can take in the harbor, city, and sea. Next to the elevator, in an area covered by sail-like awnings, there's an ice-skating rink in winter. ⊠ *Ponte Spinola, Porto Vecchio* ☎ *010/23451, 347/4860524 ice-skating* ⊡ *Elevator €3.30, skating rink €7.50* ☺ *Elevator Feb. and Nov., weekends 10–5; June–Aug., Tues., Wed., and Sun. 10–8, Thurs.–Sat. 10 AM–11 PM; Mar.–May and Sept., Tues.–Sun. 10–6; Oct., Tues.–Sun. 10–5; Dec. 26–Jan. 6, daily 10–5; skating rink Nov. or Dec.–Mar., weekdays 8 AM–9:30 PM, Sat. 10 AM–2 AM, Sun. 10 AM–midnight.*

㉕ **Porta Soprana.** A striking 12th-century twin-tower structure, this medieval gateway stands on the spot where a road from ancient Rome entered the city. It is just steps uphill from Columbus's boyhood home, and legend has it that the explorer's father was employed here as a gatekeeper. It's also known as Porta di Sant'Andrea (note the flags, with a red cross on a white background, flying atop the towers). ⊠ *Piazza Dante, Molo.*

㉜ **San Donato.** Although somewhat marred by 19th- and 20th-century restorations, the 12th-century San Donato—with its original portal and octagonal campanile—is a fine example of Genovese Romanesque architecture. Inside, an altarpiece by the Flemish artist Joos Van Cleve (circa 1485–1540) depicts the Adoration of the Magi. ⊠ *Piazza San Donato, Portoria* ☎ *010/2468869* ☺ *Mon.–Sat. 8–noon and 3–7, Sun. 9–12:30 and 3–7.*

㉚ **San Matteo.** This typically Genovese black-and-white-stripe church dates from the 12th century; its crypt contains the tomb of Andrea Doria (1466–1560), the Genovese admiral who maintained the independence of his native city. The well-preserved Piazza San Matteo was, for 500 years, the seat of the Doria family, which ruled Genoa and much of Liguria from the 16th to the 18th century. The square is bounded by 13th- to 15th-century houses decorated with portals and loggias. ⊠ *Piazza San Matteo, Maddalena* ☎ *010/2474361* ☺ *Mon.–Sat. 8–noon and 4–7, Sun. 9:30–10:30 and 4–5.*

㉗ **Teatro Carlo Felice.** The World War II–ravaged opera house in Genoa's modern center, Piazza de Ferrari, was rebuilt and reopened in 1991 to host the fine Genovese opera company; its massive tower has been the subject of much criticism. ⊠ *Passo Eugenio Montale 4, Piazza De Ferrari, Portoria* ☎ *010/53811* ⊕ *www.carlofelice.it.*

Where to Stay & Eat

$$$$ ✕ **Antica Osteria del Bai.** Look out from a large dark-wood-paneled room over the Ligurian Sea from this romantic upscale restaurant perched high on a cliff. A seaside theme pervades the art and menu, which might include black gnocchi with lobster sauce or ravioli ai frutti di mare. The restaurant's traditional elegance is reflected in its white tablecloths, dress code, and prices. ⊠ *Via Quarto 16, Quarto* ☎ *010/387478* 🏛 *Jacket and tie* ▭ *AE, DC, MC, V* ☺ *Closed Mon., Jan. 10–20, and Aug. 1–20.*

$$$$ ✕ **Gran Gotto.** Innovative regional dishes are served in this posh, spacious restaurant brightened by contemporary paintings. Try *cappellacci di borragine con vellutata di pinoli* (pasta with a pine-nut sauce) followed by *calamaretti brasati con porri e zucchine* (braised baby squid with leeks and zucchini), one of the many excellent second courses. Service is quick and helpful. ⊠ *Viale Brigata Bisagno 69/r, Piazza della Vittoria, Foce* ☎ *010/583644* 🖎 *Reservations essential* ▭ *AE, DC, MC, V* ☺ *Closed Sun. and Aug. 12–31. No lunch Sat.*

$$$$ ✕ **Zeffirino.** The five Belloni brothers share chef duties at a well-known restaurant full of odd combinations, including decor that has both rustic wood and modern metallic pieces. Try the *passutelli* (ravioli stuffed with ricotta cheese, herbs, and fruit) or any of the homemade pasta dishes. With a Zeffirino restaurant in Las Vegas and another in Hong Kong, the enterprising Bellonis have gone international. ⊠ *Via XX Settembre 20, Portoria* ☎ *010/591990* 🖎 *Reservations essential* 🏛 *Jacket required* ▭ *AE, DC, MC, V.*

$$–$$$ ✕ **Enoteca Sola.** Menus are chosen specifically to complement wines at Pino Sola's airy, casually elegant *enoteca* (wine bar) in the heart of the modern town. The short menu emphasizes seafood and varies daily but might include stuffed artichokes or baked stockfish. The real draw, though, is the wine list, which includes some of the winners of the *Tre Bicchieri* (Three Glasses) award denoting only the very best. ⊠ *Via C. Barabino 120/r, Foce* ☎ *010/594513* ▭ *AE, DC, MC, V* ☺ *Closed Sun. and Aug.*

$$ ✕ **Da Domenico.** Don't be dismayed by the labyrinth of rooms and wood passages that lead to your table at this restaurant in a quiet square near Piazza Dante—you've found one of those hidden corners that only the Genovese know. Traditional seafood and meat dishes make up most of the menu. ⊠ *Piazza Leonardo 3, Molo* ☎ *010/540289* 🖎 *Reservations essential* ▭ *AE, DC, MC, V* ☺ *Closed Mon.*

$–$$ ✕ **Bakari.** Hip styling and ambient lighting hint at this eatery's creative, even daring, takes on Ligurian classics. Sure bets are the spinach-and-cheese gnocchi, any of several carpaccios, and the delicate beef dishes. Reserve ahead, requesting a table on the more imaginative ground floor. ⊠ *Vico del Fieno 16/r, northwest of Piazza San Matteo, Maddalena* ☎ *010/291936* ▭ *AE, MC, V* ☺ *Closed Sun. No dinner Wed. or Fri.*

¢–$ ✕ **Exultate.** When the weather permits, umbrella-shaded tables spread out from this tiny eatery into the nearby square. Its selection popular with locals, the restaurant's inexpensive daily menu is presented on a chalk board for all to see, with elaborate salads and home-made desserts

The Art of the Pesto Pestle

YOU MAY HAVE KNOWN GENOA primarily for its salami or its brash explorer, but the city's most direct effect on your life away from Italy may be through its cultivation of one of the world's best pasta sauces. The sublime blend of basil, extra-virgin olive oil, garlic, pine nuts, and grated pecorino and Parmigiano Reggiano cheeses that forms *pesto alla Genovese* is one of Italy's crowning culinary achievements, a concoction that Italian food guru Marcella Hazan has called "the most seductive of all sauces for pasta." Unlike in the United States, where various versions of pesto bedeck everything from pizza to grilled-chicken sandwiches, Ligurian pesto is served only over spaghetti, gnocchi, lasagna, or—most authentically—*trenette* (a flat, spaghetti-like pasta) or *trofie* (short, doughy pasta twists), and then typically mixed with boiled potatoes and green beans. Pesto is also occasionally used to flavor

minestrone. The small-leaf basil grown in the region's sunny seaside hills is considered by many to be the best in the world, and your visit to Liguria affords you the chance to savor pesto in its original form. Pesto sauce was invented primarily as a showcase for that singular flavor, and the best pesto brings out the fresh basil's alluring aroma and taste rather than masking it with the complementary ingredients. The simplicity and rawness of pesto is one of its virtues, as cooking (or even heating) basil ruins its delicate flavor. In fact, pesto aficionados refuse even to subject the basil leaves to an electric blender; Genovese (and other) foodies insist that true pesto can be made only with mortar and pestle. Although satisfactory versions can surely be prepared less laboriously, the pesto purists' culinary conservatism is supported by etymology: the word *pesto* is derived from the Italian verb *pestare* (to pound or grind).

6

highlighting the list. ☒ *Piazza Lavagna 15/r, Maddalena* ☎ *010/2512605* 🗏 *MC, V* ⊗ *Closed Sun.*

$$$ 🏨 **Best Western City.** The location of this hotel can't be beat—it's in the heart of the city near Via Roma, the grand shopping street, and one block from Piazza de Ferrari, which divides new Genoa from old Genoa. A bland apartment-building exterior gives way to a polished lobby and light, modern rooms that are a bit small but very comfortable. Suites, on the top floor, have spectacular views, as do many of the standard rooms on the upper floors. A choice of pillows—firm and low, or fluffy and soft—and coffeemakers in all the rooms are pleasant added touches. ☒ *Via San Sebastiano 6, Portoria, 16123* ☎ *010/584707* 🖷 *010/ 586301* ⊕ *www.bwcityhotel-ge.it* 🛏 *63 rooms, 3 suites* 🍴 *Restaurant, in-room safes, in-room data ports, Wi-Fi, bar, Internet room, parking (fee)* 🗏 *AE, DC, MC, V* 🍽 *BP.*

★ **$$$** 🏨 **Bristol Palace.** The 19th-century grand hotel in the heart of the shopping district carefully guards its reputation for courtesy and service. Spacious guest rooms all have high ceilings and elegant wood wardrobes or headboards. Public spaces, all connected to the hotel's central oval staircase, are comfortable, small, and pleasantly discreet with paneled walls and soft lighting. ✉ *Via XX Settembre 35, Portoria, 16121* ☎ *010/592541* 🖷 *010/561756* ⊕ *www.hotelbristolpalace.com* ➲ *128 rooms, 5 suites* ⚭ *Restaurant, room TVs with movies, gym, bar, Internet room, meeting rooms, parking (fee), some pets allowed* ▤ *AE, DC, MC, V* ⦿ *BP.*

$–$$ ▦ **Cairoli.** This family-run hotel has an enviable location on a pedestrian street not far from the Acquario di Genova. The accommodations are plain, but three rooms open onto the pleasant rooftop terrace. A simple continental breakfast is served in a room off the lobby; an apartment with its own kitchen provides an economical choice for groups of up to seven people. ✉ *Via Cairoli 14/4, Maddalena, 16124* ☎ *010/2461454* 🖷 *010/2467512* ⊕ *www.hotelcairoligenova.com* ➲ *12 rooms, 1 apartment* ⚭ *Bar, gym* ▤ *AE, DC, MC, V* ⦿ *BP.*

$ ▦ **Agnello d'Oro.** The friendly owner at Agnello d'Oro does double duty as a travel agent: he's happy to help you with plane reservations and travel plans. Only a few of the simple, modern rooms have balconies, but a surprisingly varied continental breakfast awaits you in the morning. The hotel is about 100 yards from Stazione Principe, near the Palazzo Reale. ✉ *Vico delle Monachette 6, Pré, 16126* ☎ *010/2462084* 🖷 *010/2462327* ⊕ *www.hotelagnellodoro.it* ➲ *25 rooms* ⚭ *Restaurant, bar, parking (fee), some pets allowed; no a/c in some rooms* ▤ *AE, DC, MC, V* ⦿ *BP.*

Nightlife & the Arts

Especially in summer, the place for nightlife is on the waterfront near the *levante* (southeast) side of the city. From the center, take Corso Italia in the direction of Quarto, Quinto, and nearby Nervi to reach the outdoor nighttime hub. Several beachfront *bagni* (literally, baths) and their accompanying restaurants and bars in the area serve as nighttime summer hangouts.

Nightclubs

Makò. Big, well-known discotheques such as the famous Makò perch on a cliff about halfway to Nervi, attracting attention from Genovese twenty- and thirtysomethings. ✉ *Corso Italia 28/r, Quarto* ☎ *010/367652.*

Opera

Teatro Carlo Felice. Genoa's well-respected opera company, Fondazione Teatro Carlo Felice, stages lavish productions of old favorites and occasionally world premieres from October to May. ✉ *Passo Eugenio Montale 4, Piazza De Ferrari, Portoria* ☎ *010/5381304* ⊕ *www. carlofelice.it.*

Shopping

Liguria is famous for its fine laces, silver-and-gold filigree work, and ceramics. Look also for bargains in velvet, macramé, olive wood, and marble. Genoa is the best spot to find all these specialties. In the heart of the medieval quarter, Via Soziglia is lined with shops selling handicrafts and tempting foods. Via XX Settembre is famous for its exclusive shops. High-end shops line Via Luccoli. The best shopping area for trendy-but-inexpensive Italian clothing is near San Siro, on Via San Luca.

Clothing & Leather Goods

Bruno Magli. The Bologna-based designer makes an impeccable line of leather shoes, boots, handbags, and jackets. ⊠ *Via XX Settembre 135, Foce* ☎ *010/561890.*

Pescetto. Look for designer clothes, perfumes, and gifts at this fancy shop. ⊠ *Via Scurreria 8, Molo* ☎ *010/2473433.*

Jewelry

Codevilla. The well-established Codevilla is one of the best jewelers on a street full of goldsmiths. ⊠ *Via Orefici 53, Maddalena* ☎ *010/2472567.*

Wines

Vinoteca Sola. At this shop you can purchase the best Ligurian wines and have them shipped home. You can even buy futures for vintages to come. ⊠ *Piazza Colombo 13–15/r, near Stazione Brignole, Foce* ☎ *010/594513* ⊕ *www.vinotecasola.it.*

Side Trip from Genoa

Nervi

39 *11 km (7 mi) east of Genoa, 19 km (12 mi) west of Rapallo.*

★ The identity of this stately late-19th-century resort, famous for its seaside promenade, the **Passeggiata Anita Garibaldi** (1½ km [1 mi] long), its palm-lined roads, and its 300 acres of parks rich in orange trees, is given away only by the sign on the sleepy train station. Although Nervi is technically part of the city, its peace and quiet are as different from Genoa's hustle and bustle as its clear blue water is from Genoa's crowded port. From the centrally located train station, walk east along the seaside promenade to reach the beaches, a cliff-hanging restaurant, and the 2,000 varieties of roses in the public **Parco Villa Grimaldi,** all the while enjoying one of the most breathtaking views on the Riviera. Nervi—and the road along the way—is known for its nightlife in summer. Take one of the frequent trains for the 15-minute ride from Stazione Principe or Brignole (buy a ticket for Genova–Nervi), or take Bus 15 or 17 from Brignole or Piazza de Ferrari. Alternatively, a taxi from town center runs about €20 one-way.

WHERE TO
STAY & EAT
$–$$ ✕ **Marinella.** The impressive wrought-iron chandelier inside takes second billing to the great sea views from the dining room and the terrace. Try the *zuppa di pesce* (fish soup); main dishes change according to the day's catch. The restaurant, which perches on seaside shoals, has an inexpensive hotel, too. ⊠ *Passeggiata Anita Garibaldi 18/r* ☎ *010/3728343* ▤ *MC, V* ☉ *Closed Mon. and Nov.*

★ **$$$** ⊞ **Romantik Hotel Villa Pagoda.** In a 19th-century merchant's mansion modeled after a Chinese temple, this luxury hotel has a private park, access to the famed cliff-top walk, and magnificent ocean views. Request a tower room for the best vantage point. Villa Pagoda is the best of both worlds, as you can enjoy peace and quiet or be in bustling Genoa in 15 minutes. ⊠ *Via Capolungo 15, 16167* ☎ *010/3726161* ☎ *010/321218* ⊕ *www.villapagoda.it* ⊲ *13 rooms, 4 suites* ⚲ *Restaurant, in-room safes,*

6

minibars, tennis court, pool, piano bar, meeting room, some pets allowed ⊟ *AE, DC, MC, V* ⍩⍤ *BP.*

Extraordinarily popular with locals, **Senhor do Bonfim** (⊠ Passeggiata Anita Garibaldi ☎ 010/3726312), a nightclub along the water on Nervi's beautiful seaside promenade, has dancing every night and live music until late on weekends.

RIVIERA DI PONENTE

The Riviera di Ponente (Riviera of the Setting Sun) stretches from Genoa to Ventimiglia on the French border. For the most part it's an unbroken chain of beach resorts sheltered from the north by the Ligurian and Maritime Alps, mountain walls that guarantee mild winters and a long growing season—resulting in its other nickname, the Riviera dei Fiori (Riviera of Flowers). Actually, the name is more evocative than the sight of once-verdant hillsides now swathed in massive plastic greenhouses. Many towns on the western Riviera have suffered from an epidemic of overdevelopment, but most have preserved their old cores, usually their most interesting features. In major resorts, large, modern marinas cater to the pleasure-craft crowd. The Riviera di Ponente has both sandy and pebbly beaches with some quiet bays.

Pegli

40 *13 km (8 mi) west of Genoa.*

Once a popular summer home for many patrician Genovese families, Pegli has museums, parks, and some regal old homes with well-tended gardens. Two lovely villas—Villa Doria and Villa Durazzo Pallavicini—make Pegli worth an excursion. This suburb manages to maintain its dignity despite industrial development and the proximity of airport and port facilities. Pegli can be reached by convenient commuter train from Stazione Porta Principe in Genoa.

Villa Doria, near the Pegli train station, has a large park. The villa itself, built in the 16th century by the Doria family, has been converted into a **naval museum.** ⊠ *Piazza Bonavino 7* ☎ *010/6969885* ⊕ *www. museonavale.it* ⍨ *€4* ⊗ *Villa Tues.–Fri. 9–1, Sat. 10–1; park daily 9–noon and 2–6.*

Villa Durazzo Pallavicini, set in 19th-century gardens with temples and artificial lakes, contains an **archaeological museum.** ⊠ *Via Pallavicini 11* ☎ *010/6981048* ⍨ *€4* ⊗ *Tues.–Fri. 9–7, weekends 10–7.*

Albisola Marina

41 *30 km (19 mi) southwest of Pegli, 43 km (26 mi) west of Genoa.*

Albisola Marina has a centuries-old tradition of ceramic making. Numerous shops here sell the distinctive wares, and a whole sidewalk, **Lungomare degli Artisti,** has been transformed by the colorful ceramic works of well-known artists. It runs along the beachfront. The 18th-century

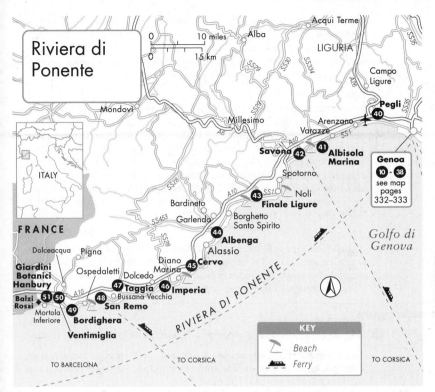

Riviera di
Ponente

ITALY

FRANCE

LIGURIA

Acqui Terme

Alba

Campo Ligure

Mondovì

Millesimo

Arenzano

Pegli
40

Varazze

Savona **42** **41** Albisola
Marina

Spotorno

Genoa
10 - **38**
see map
pages
332–333

Bardineto

43 Noli
Finale Ligure

Dolceacqua Pigna

Ospedaletti

Garlenda

Borghetto
Santo Spirito

44
Albenga
Alassio

*Golfo di
Genova*

6

Diano
Marina **45** **Cervo**

Dolcedo

47 **Taggia** **46** **Imperia**

**Giardini
Botanici
Hanbury**

**Balzi
Rossi** **51** **50**

Mortola
Inferiore

49

48 Bussana Vecchia
San Remo

Bordighera

Ventimiglia

RIVIERA DI PONENTE

TO BARCELONA

TO CORSICA

TO CORSICA

KEY

Beach

Ferry

Villa Faraggiana, near the parish church, has exhibits on the history of pottery. ☒ *Via dell'Oratorio* ☎ *019/480622* ☑ *Free* ☉ *Apr.–Sept., Wed.–Mon. 3–7.*

Shopping

Ceramiche San Giorgio (☒ Corso Matteotti 5 ☎ 019/482747) has been producing ceramics since the 17th century, and is known for both classic and modern designs. **Ernan** (☒ Corso Mazzini 77, Albisola Superiore ☎ 019/489916) sells blue-and-white patterns typical of the 18th century. **Mazzotti** (☒ Corso Matteotti 25 ☎ 019/481626) has an exclusive ceramics selection and a small museum.

Savona

42 *5 km (3 mi) southwest of Albisola Marina, 46 km (29 mi) southwest of Genoa.*

Savona is the fifth-largest seaport in Italy and handles vast oil and coal cargoes, as well as car and truck ferries. As it was considerably damaged during World War II, much of the town is modern and not very interesting, although a small austere older quarter near the harbor contains some fine homes of the town's merchant class. The large **Palazzo**

della Rovere (✉ Via Pia 28) was designed for Pope Julius II by the Florentine Giuliano da Sangallo in 1495. It is closed to the public. The 12th-century **Torre del Brandale** (✉ Piazza del Brandale 2 ☎ 019/821379), with its 14th-century annex, the **Palazzo degli Anziani,** and two other remaining medieval towers, is open by appointment.

Festivals

In even-numbered years, Good Friday fills Savona's streets with the Italian Riviera's most impressive **Easter parade.** Starting at 7:30 PM and throughout most of the night, 15 large wooden sculptural groups, representing the Passion of Christ, are carried through the town accompanied by two brass bands, three choirs, and a full orchestra. The rest of the year, you can see some of the sculptures in **Oratorio Nostro Signore di Castello** (✉ Via Manzoni 1 ☎ 019/804892 ☉ Sat. 4–7 and by appointment) and **Oratorio Cristo Risorto** (✉ Via Aonzo 1 ☎ 019/8386306 ☉ Sun. 8–noon, 4–7, and by appointment).

Shopping

Watch for shops selling crystallized fruit, a local specialty. In Millesimo, a town 4 km (2½ mi) west and 36 km (18 mi) inland from Savona, little rum chocolates known as *millesimi* are produced. Look for bargains, too, in wrought iron, copper, and carvings from local sandstone.

Finale Ligure

➍ *24 km (15 mi) southwest of Savona, 72 km (44 mi) southwest of Genoa.*

Finale Ligure is actually made up of three small villages: Finalmarina, Finalpia, and Finalborgo. The former two have fine sandy beaches and modern resort amenities. The most attractive of the villages is Finalborgo, less than 1 km (½ mi) inland, a hauntingly preserved medieval settlement, planned to a rigid blueprint, with 15th-century walls. The surrounding countryside is pierced by deep, narrow valleys and caves; the limestone outcroppings provide the warm pinkish stone found in many buildings in Genoa. Rare reptiles lurk among the exotic flora.

> ### WORD OF MOUTH
>
> "The pesto is incredible in Liguria. . . . We often would go to an alimentari and get pesto, bread, cheese, tomatoes (the best I've ever had) prosciutto, melon, etc. And relax."   –Skatterfly

Finalborgo is crowned by the impressive ruins of the huge **Castel Gavone.** ✉ *Via Beretta.*

The baroque church of **San Biagio** houses many works of art. ✉ *Piazza San Biagio, Finalborgo* ☎ *019/695617* ☉ *Daily 8–11:30 and 2:30–5.*

Enjoy the shade of the courtyard in the 14th- to 15th-century Dominican convent **Santa Caterina,** or step in to see the museum of local paleontology and natural history. ✉ *Museo Civico, Finalborgo* ☎ *019/690020* 🎟 *€2.60* ☉ *July–Oct., Tues.–Sat. 9–noon and 3–6, Sun. 9–noon; Nov.–June, Tues.–Sat. 9–noon and 2:30–4:30, Sun. 9–noon.*

NOLI – Just 9 km (5½ mi) northeast of Finale Ligure, the ruins of a castle loom benevolently over the tiny medieval gem of Noli. It's hard to imagine that this charming village was—like Genoa, Venice, Pisa, and Amalfi—a prosperous maritime republic in the Middle Ages. If you don't have a car, get a bus for Noli at Spotorno, where local trains stop.

Where to Stay & Eat

$$$–$$$$ ✕ **Ai Torchi.** You could easily become a homemade-pesto snob at this Finalborgo eatery. The high prices are justified by excellent inventive seafood and meat dishes and by the setting—a restored 5th-century olive-oil refinery. ⊠ *Via dell'Annunziata 12* ☎ *019/690531* ⊟ *AE, DC, MC, V* ⊘ *Closed Jan. 7–Feb. 10, and Tues. Sept.–July.*

Albenga

🄬 *20 km (12 mi) southwest of Finale Ligure, 90 km (55 mi) southwest of Genoa.*

Albenga has a medieval core, with narrow streets laid out by the ancient Romans. A network of alleys is punctuated by centuries-old towers surrounding the 18th-century Romanesque cathedral, with a late-14th-century campanile and a baptistery dating back to the 5th century.

BARDINETO – For a look at some of the Riviera's mountain scenery, make an excursion by car to this attractive village in the middle of an area rich in mushrooms, chestnuts, and raspberries, as well as local cheeses. A ruined castle stands above the village. From Borghetto Santo Spirito (between Albenga and Finale Ligure), drive inland 25 km (15 mi).

Where to Stay

$$$$ 🏨 **La Meridiana.** An oasis of hospitality and refinement occupies a handsome farmhouse compound surrounded by a garden. The interiors are those of a comfortable home, with brightly colored prints, freshly cut flowers, and a mix of traditional and period-style furniture in the common and guest rooms. Il Rosmarino restaurant ($$$$) serves fine wines and seafood dishes. You can enjoy privileges at the golf, tennis, and equestrian clubs nearby. ⊠ *Via ai Castelli, off A10, 17033 Garlenda, 8 km (5 mi) north of Albenga* ☎ *0182/580271* 🖷 *0182/580150* ⊕ *www.relaischateaux.com/meridiana* ⇥ *13 rooms, 15 suites* ⌂ *Restaurant, golf privileges, pool, sauna, bicycles, Ping-Pong, bar, Internet room, some pets allowed (fee)* ⊟ *AE, DC, MC, V* ⊘ *Closed Nov.–Mar.* ⦿ *BP.*

Cervo

🄳 *23 km (14 mi) southwest of Albenga, 106 km (65 mi) southwest of Genoa.*

Cervo is the quintessential sleepy Ligurian coastal village, nicely polished for the tourists who come to explore its narrow byways and street staircases. It's a remarkably well-preserved medieval town, crowned with a big baroque church. In July and August the square in front of the church is the site of chamber music concerts.

Imperia

46 *12 km (7 mi) west of Cervo, 116 km (71 mi) southwest of Genoa.*

Imperia actually consists of two towns: Porto Maurizio, a medieval town built on a promontory, and Oneglia, now an industrial center for oil refining and pharmaceuticals. Porto Maurizio has a virtually intact medieval center, an intricate spiral of narrow streets and stone portals, and some imposing 17th- and 18th-century palaces. There's little of interest in modern Oneglia, but the 1½-km (1-mi) trip northeast along the seafront from Porto Maurizio to Oneglia is worth taking for a visit to the olive-oil museum.

Imperia is king when it comes to olive oil, and the story of the olive is the theme of the small **Museo dell'Olivo.** Displays of the history of the olive tree, farm implements, presses, and utensils show how olive oil has been made in many countries throughout history. ⊠ *Via Garessio 11, Oneglia* ☎ *0183/720000* ⊕ *www.museodellolivo.com* ⊠ *Free* ☉ *Wed.–Mon. 9–noon and 3–6:30.*

Where to Eat

★ $ ✕ **Candidollo.** In this rustic country inn, with checkered tablecloths and worn terra-cotta floors, host Bruno Ardissone uses fresh, local ingredients to make traditional, seasonal recipes. The menu usually includes *coniglio al timo* (rabbit with thyme and other herbs) and *lumache all'agliata* (grilled snails in piquant sauce). It's well worth the detour to get to the village of Diano Borello, a mile or so north of Diano Marina. ⊠ *Corso Europa 23, Diano Borello, 6 km (4 mi) east of Imperia* ☎ *0183/43025* ⊟ *No credit cards* ☉ *Closed Tues. and Nov.–Mar. No lunch Mon.*

Taggia

47 *20 km (12 mi) west of Imperia, 135 km (84 mi) southwest of Genoa.*

The town of Taggia has a medieval core and one of the most imposing medieval bridges in the area. The church of **San Domenico,** with a small museum, was once part of a monastery founded in the 15th century that remained a beacon of faith and learning in Liguria for 300 years. An antiques market is held here, just south of Taggia, on the fourth weekend of the month. ⊠ *Piazzale San Domenico, Arma di Taggia* ☎ *No phone* ⊠ *Free* ☉ *Fri.–Wed. 9–5.*

San Remo

48 *10 km (6 mi) west of Taggia, 146 km (90 mi) southwest of Genoa.*

The self-styled capital of the Riviera di Ponente, San Remo is also the area's largest resort, lined with polished hotels, exotic gardens, and seaside promenades. Renowned for its royal visitors, glittering casino, and romantic setting, San Remo still maintains some of the glamour of its heyday from the late 19th century to World War II. Waterside palm fronds conceal a sizable old center that, unlike in other Ponente towns, is lively even in the off-season. Restaurants, wine bars, and boutiques are second in Liguria only to Genoa's, and San Remo's cafés bustle with afternoon activity.

The newer parts of San Remo suffer from the same epidemic of overbuilding that changed so many towns on the western Riviera for the worse. The Mercato dei Fiori, Italy's most important wholesale flower market, is held here in a market hall between Piazza Colombo and Corso Garibaldi and open to dealers only. More than 20,000 tons of carnations, roses, mimosa flowers, and innumerable other cut flowers are dispatched from here each year. As the center of northern Italy's flower-growing industry, the town is surrounded by hills where verdant terraces are now blanketed with plastic to form immense greenhouses. Consult the San Remo **tourist office** for information on the flowers and about events in town. ⊠ *Palazzo Riviera, Largo Nuvoloni 1* ☎ *0184/571571* ⊕ *www.sanremonet. com.*

Explore the warren of alleyways in the old part of San Remo, **La Pigna** ("the pinecone"), which climbs upward to Piazza Castello and a splendid view of the town.

The onion-domed Russian Orthodox church of **Cristo Salvatore, Santa Caterina d'Alessandria, e San Serafino di Sarov** testifies to a long Russian presence on the Italian Riviera. Russian empress Maria Alexandrovna, wife of Czar Alexander I, built a summerhouse here, and in winter San Remo was a popular destination for other royal Romanovs. The church was consecrated in 1913. ⊠ *Via Nuvoloni 2* ☎ *0184/531807* ⊗ *Daily 9:30–noon and 3–6.*

In addition to gaming, the art nouveau **San Remo Casinò** has a restaurant, a nightclub, and a theater that hosts concerts and the annual San Remo Music Festival. If you want to try your luck at the gaming tables, there's a €7.50 cover charge on weekends. Dress is elegant, with jacket and tie requested at the French gaming tables. ⊠ *Corso Inglesi 18* ☎ *0184/5951* ⊗ *Slot machines Sun.–Fri. 10 AM–2:30 AM, Sat. 10 AM–3:30 AM; tables Sun.–Fri. 2:30 PM–2:30 AM, Sat. 2:30 PM–3:30 AM.*

OFF THE BEATEN PATH

BUSSANA VECCHIA – In the hills where flowers are cultivated for export sits Bussana Vecchia, a self-consciously picturesque former ghost town largely destroyed by an earthquake in 1877. The inhabitants packed up and left en masse after the quake, and for almost a century the houses, church, and crumbling bell tower were empty shells, overgrown by weeds and wildflowers. Since the 1960s an artists colony has evolved among the ruins. Painters, sculptors, artisans, and bric-a-brac dealers have restored dwellings. ⊹ *8 km (5 mi) east of San Remo.*

Where to Stay & Eat

$ ✕ **Nuovo Piccolo Mondo.** Old wooden chairs dating from the 1920s,
Fodor'sChoice when the place opened, evoke the homey charm of this small, family-
★ run trattoria. The place has a faithful clientele, so get there early to grab
a table and order Ligurian specialties such as *sciancui* (a roughly cut flat
pasta with a mixture of beans, tomatoes, zucchini, and pesto) and *polpo
e patate* (stewed octopus with potatoes). ⊠ *Via Piave 7* ☎ *0184/509012*
▤ *No credit cards* ☉ *Closed Mon. No dinner Sun.*

$$$$ ☐ **Royal.** It's a toss-up whether this hotel or the Splendido in Portofino
is the most luxurious in Liguria. Rooms here have a mixture of modern amenities and antique furnishings and most have views of the sea.
The heated seawater swimming pool, open April–October, is in a large
tropical garden. On the terrace, candlelight dining and music are offered
each night in warm weather. Keep your eyes open for off-season discounts. The Royal is only a few paces from the casino and the train station. ⊠ *Corso Imperatrice 80, 18038* ☎ *0184/5391* ᵬ *0184/661445*
⊕ *www.royalhotelsanremo.com* ⤳ *114 rooms, 13 suites* ⚭ *2 restaurants, room service, in-room safes, cable TV, in-room data ports, Wi-
Fi, golf privileges, miniature golf, tennis court, saltwater pool, gym, hair
salon, beach, 2 bars, babysitting, playground, dry cleaning, laundry service, concierge, Internet room, convention center, meeting rooms* ▤ *AE,
DC, MC, V* ☉ *Closed Oct. 2–Dec. 17* ⍩ *BP.*

$–$$ ☐ **Paradiso.** A quiet palm-fringed garden gives the Paradiso an air of
seclusion in this sometimes hectic resort city. Rooms are modern and
bright; many have little terraces. The hotel restaurant has a good fixed-
price menu. This small central hotel is adjacent to a lush public park.
⊠ *Via Roccasterone 12, 18038* ☎ *0184/571211* ᵬ *0184/578176*
⊕ *www.paradisohotel.it* ⤳ *41 rooms* ⚭ *Restaurant, pool, bar, Internet room* ▤ *AE, DC, MC, V* ⍩ *BP.*

Bordighera

49 *12 km (7 mi) west of San Remo, 155 km (96 mi) southwest of Genoa.*

This garden spot was the first town in Europe to grow date palms, and
its citizens still have the exclusive right to provide the Vatican with palm
fronds for Easter celebrations. Bordighera, on a large, lush promontory,
wears its genteel past as a famous winter resort with unstudied ease. A
large English colony, attracted by the mild climate, settled here in the
second half of the 19th century and is still very much in evidence today;
you regularly find people taking afternoon tea in the cafés, and streets
named after Queen Victoria and Shakespeare. Thanks partly to its many
year-round English residents, Bordighera does not close down entirely
in the off-season like some Riviera resorts but rather serves as a quiet
winter haven for an older clientele. With plenty of hotels and restaurants, Bordighera makes a good base for exploring the region and is quieter and less commercial than San Remo.

Running parallel to the ocean, **Lungomare Argentina** is a pleasant promenade, 1½ km (1 mi) long, which begins at the western end of the town
and provides good views westward to the French Côte d'Azur.

Where to Stay & Eat

$$$$ ✕ **Le Chaudron.** A charming rustic interior, with ancient Roman arches, has the look of restaurants across the French border in Provence. Ligurian specialties are highlights on the predominantly seafood menu: try the cheese *pansoti con salsa di noci* (ravioli with walnut sauce) and the *branzino* (sea bass) with artichokes or mushrooms. ⊠ *Via Vittorio Emanuele 9* 🕾 *0184/263592* ⌁ *Reservations essential* 🖃 *DC, MC, V* ☺ *Closed Mon., 1st 2 wks in Feb., and 1st 2 wks in July.*

$$–$$$ ✕ **La Reserve.** This informal trattoria has access to the beach and excellent views from the dining room; there are even changing rooms for anyone who wants to take an after-lunch dip. Concentrate on the seafood here: specialties are seafood ravioli *al finocchio selvatico* (with wild fennel) and assorted grilled fish. La Reserve is part of the Hotel Parigi, 1½ km (1 mi) east of the center on the road to San Remo. ⊠ *Via Arziglia 20* 🕾 *0184/261322* 🖃 *AE, DC, MC, V* ☺ *Closed Mon. and mid-Nov.–mid-Dec. No dinner Wed.*

$–$$ ✕ **Piemontese.** Both the Ligurian seafood and the hearty cuisine of the neighboring Piedmont region served here are popular with locals. Risotto *al Barolo* is cooked with Barolo wine, sausage, and porcini mushrooms, and the winter specialty is *bagna cauda* (raw vegetables with a garlic, oil, and anchovy sauce). ⊠ *Via Roseto 8, off Via Vittorio Emanuele* 🕾 *0184/261651* 🖃 *AE, MC, V* ☺ *Closed Tues. and mid-Nov.–mid-Dec.*

$–$$ ✕ **Il Tempo Ritrovato.** A small wine bar and restaurant combine forces here on Bordighera's main street. Simple pasta dishes and a spectacular wine list make this a great choice. ⊠ *Via Vittorio Emanuele 144* 🕾 *0184/261207* 🖃 *AE, DC, MC, V* ☺ *Closed Sun. and Mon.*

Ventimiglia

50 *5 km (3 mi) west of Bordighera, 159 km (98 mi) southwest of Genoa.*

From its past life as a pre-Roman settlement known as Albintimilium, Ventimiglia retains some important archaeological remains, including a 2nd-century AD amphitheater. A vital trade center for hundreds of years, it declined in prestige as Genoa grew and is now little more than a frontier town that lives on tourism and the cultivation of flowers. (The Friday flower market, open to the trade only, creates traffic gridlock; it's best to avoid the town on that day.)

Ventimiglia is divided in two by the Roia River. The Città Vecchia is a well-preserved medieval old town on the western bank. Walk up Via del Capo to reach the ancient walls, which have fine views of the coast. The 11th-century **Duomo** has a Gothic portal dating from 1222. ⊠ *Piazza Cattedrale* 🕾 *0184/229507* ☺ *Thurs.–Tues. 8:30–noon and 3–5:30, Wed. 3–5:30.*

Where to Stay

$$ ▥ **La Riserva.** More than 1,100 feet above sea level is the village of Castel d'Appio, where you'll find this innlike establishment. Rooms are bright, airy, and simply decorated with contemporary furnishings and rich fabrics. The staff is very helpful, providing, for example, regular

FodorśChoice ★

lifts into town if you have no car. In addition to its excellent restaurant ($$$$), La Riserva has numerous activities and a lovely panoramic terrace for sunbathing, afternoon drinks, or candlelight dinners. Full-board rates are a good deal. ⊠ *Via Peidago 79, 18039 Castel d'Appio, 5 km (3 mi) west of Ventimiglia* ☎ *0184/229533* 🖷 *0184/229712* ⊕ *www.lariserva.it* ⇗ *16 rooms, 3 suites* ⚲ *Restaurant, pool, bicycles, billiards, Ping-Pong, bar, Internet room* ⊟ *AE, DC, MC, V* ⊘ *Closed mid-Oct.–Mar.* ⟨⊙⟩ *BP.*

EN ROUTE — From Ventimiglia, a provincial road swings 10 km (6 mi) up the Nervi River valley to a lovely sounding medieval town, Dolceacqua (its name translates as Sweetwater), with a ruined castle. Liguria's best-known red wine is the local Rossese di Dolceacqua. A farther 6 km (4 mi) along the road lies Pigna, a fascinating medieval village built in concentric circles on its hilltop.

Giardini Botanici Hanbury

★ ⑤ *6 km (4 mi) west of Ventimiglia, 165 km (102 mi) southwest of Genoa.*

Mortola Inferiore, only 2 km (1 mi) from the French border, is the site of the world-famous Giardini Botanici Hanbury (Hanbury Botanical Gardens), one of the largest in Italy. Planned and planted in 1867 by a wealthy English merchant, Sir Thomas Hanbury, and his botanist brother Daniel, the terraced gardens contain species from five continents, including many palms and succulents. There are panoramic views of the sea from the gardens. The ticket office closes one hour before the garden. ⊠ *Località Mortola* ☎ *0184/229507* 🗐 *€7.50* ⊘ *Mar.–June 15, daily 9:30–6; June 16–Sept. 15, daily 9:30–7; Sept. 16–last Sat. in Oct., daily 9:30–6; last Sun. in Oct.–Feb., Tues.–Sun. 10–5.*

OFF THE BEATEN PATH — **BALZI ROSSI** – Prehistoric humans left traces of their lives and magic rites in the Balzi Rossi (Red Rocks), caves carved in the sheer rock. You can visit the caves and a small museum displaying some of the objects found there. ⊠ *Via Balzi Rosso 9, 2 km (1 mi) west of Giardini Botanici Hanbury* ☎ *0184/38113* 🗐 *€2* ⊘ *Tues.–Sun. 8:30–5:30.*

ITALIAN RIVIERA ESSENTIALS

Transportation

BY AIR

There is daily air service between Genoa and Zürich (on Swiss International Air Lines), London (on British Airways), Paris (on Air France), Munich (on Air Dolomiti), and Milan and Rome (on Alitalia).

Aeroporto Internazionale Cristoforo Colombo is only 6 km (4 mi) from the center of Genoa. The nearest airports for direct U.S. flights are Nice, in France, about 2½ hours west of Genoa (an easy bus connection), and Milan's Linate and Malpensa, about 2 hours northeast.

Volabus services from Cristoforo Colombo Airport connect with Genoa's Stazione Brignole (35 minutes), stopping at Piazza Acquaverde

(Stazione Principe) on the way. Tickets cost €3 and may be purchased on the bus.

⚡ Airport Information **Aeroporto Internazionale Cristoforo Colombo** ✉ Sestri Ponente, Genoa ☎ 010/60151 ⊕ www.airport.genova.it.

⚡ Carriers **Air Dolomiti** ☎ 800/013366 ⊕ www.airdolomiti.it. **Air France** ☎ 848/884466 ⊕ www.airfrance.com. **Alitalia** ☎ 848/865641 ⊕ www.alitalia.com. **British Airways** ☎ 848/812266 ⊕ www.britishairways.com. **Swiss International Air Lines** ☎ 848/852000 ⊕ www.swiss.com.

⚡ Transfers **Volabus** ☎ 010/5582414.

BY BOAT & FERRY

Genoa, Italy's largest port, can be reached by sea from the United States as well as from other Italian and European ports, including Sardinia and Sicily. Ships berth in the heart of Genoa; ferries to various ports around the Mediterranean are operated by Tirrenia Navigazione, whose most popular destination is Sardinia (a 13-hour trip). Grimaldi Lines sends overnight ferries to Barcelona (an 18-hour trip) and Palermo, Sicily (a 20-hour trip). Corsica Ferries runs car ferries from Savona to Bastia and Ile-Rousse in Corsica.

Within Liguria, boat or ferry travel can be the most pleasant—and sometimes only—way to get from place to place. A busy network of local ferry lines, such as Servizio Marittimo del Tigullio and Alimar, connects many of the resorts. Golfo Paradiso lines run between Camogli, San Fruttuoso (on the Portofino promontory), and Recco, and in summer from the port of Genoa and Nervi to Portofino, Cinque Terre, and Portovenere, stopping in Recco and Camogli. Navigazione Golfo dei Poeti runs regular ferry services between Lerici, Portovenere, the Cinque Terre, Santa Margherita, and Genoa.

⚡ Boat & Ferry Resources, Interregional **Corsica Ferries** ✉ Calata Nord, Porto Vado, Savona ☎ 019/2155300 ⊕ www.corsicaferries.com. **Grimaldi Lines** ✉ Stazione Marittima, Ponte dei Mille, Genoa ☎ 010/589331. **Tirrenia Navigazione** ✉ Stazione Marittima, Ponte dei Mille, Genoa ☎ 010/2758041 ⊕ www.tirrenia.it.

⚡ Boat & Ferry Resources Within Liguria **Alimar** ✉ Calata Zingari, Molo, Genoa ☎ 010/256775. **Golfo Paradiso** ✉ Via Scalo 3, Camogli ☎ 0185/772091 ⊕ www.golfoparadiso.it. **Navigazione Golfo dei Poeti** ✉ Viale Mazzini 21, La Spezia ☎ 0187/732987 ⊕ www.navigazionegolfodeipoeti.it. **Servizio Marittimo del Tigullio** ✉ Via Palestro 8/1b, Santa Margherita Ligure ☎ 0185/284670 ⊕ www.traghettiportofino.it.

BY BUS & FUNICULAR

Generally speaking, buses are a difficult way to come and go in Liguria. Diana Tours provides service from the airport in Nice, but there's no bus service between Genoa and other major Italian cities such as Turin, Milan, Bologna, and Florence. Traveling from town to town by bus within Liguria is challenging due to the myriad bus companies servicing small segments of the region. There's no regular service connecting Genoa with the towns along the Riviera di Ponente. Things are somewhat easier along the Riviera di Levante where Tigullio Trasporti runs regular service.

6

The main bus station in Genoa is at Piazza Principe. Local buses, operated by the municipal transport company AMT, serve the steep valleys that run to some of the towns along the western coast. Tickets may be bought at local bus stations or at newsstands. (You must have a ticket before you board.) AMT also operates the funicular railways and the elevators that service the steeper sections of the city.

🚌 **Bus Information AMT** ✉ Piazza Acquaverde, Genoa ☎ 010/5582414 ⊕ www.amt.genova.it. **Diana Tours** ✉ Via G. Ardoino 151, Diano Marina ☎ 800/651931. **Tigullio Trasporti** ✉ Piazza Nostro Signore dell'Orto, Chiavari ☎ 0185/373234 ⊕ www.tigulliotrasporti.it ✉ Piazza Vittorio Veneto 1, Santa Margherita Ligure ☎ 0185/288834.

BY CAR

Autostrada A12 southeast from Genoa links up with the autostrada network for all northern and southern destinations; Rome is a six-hour drive from Genoa. The 150-km (93-mi) trip north to Milan on A7 takes two hours. Nice is 2½ hours of tunnels west on A10.

Two good roads run parallel to each other along the coast of Liguria. Closer to shore and passing through all the towns and villages is S1, the Via Aurelia, which has excellent views at almost every turn but gets crowded in July and August. More direct and higher up than S1 is the autostrada, A10 west of Genoa and A12 to the south. These routes save time on weekends, in summer, and on days when festivals slow traffic in some resorts to a standstill.

Be forewarned: driving in Genoa is harrowing and is best avoided whenever possible—if you want to see the city on a day trip, go by train; if you're staying in the city, park in a garage or by valet and go by foot and by taxi throughout your stay.

CAR EMERGENCIES If you break down on the highway, walk along the side of the road until you come to an emergency telephone. Call and the emergency highway road service comes to tow you to the nearest service station—for a hefty fee. On a smaller road, unless you have a cell phone you'd be better off walking to the nearest town or gas station (usually not too far) and calling ACI Emergency Service (a free call) from any pay phone. In order to describe where you are, be prepared to seek out the help of locals (*Dove siamo?*—Where are we?).

🚨 **Emergencies ACI** ☎ 803/116.

BY TRAIN

Frequent and fast train service by the Ferrovie dello Stato (Italian State Railways), also known as Trenitalia, connects Liguria with the rest of Italy. Genoa is 1½ hours from Milan and 5½–6 hours from Rome (4½ with the Eurostar). Many services from France (in particular, the French Riviera) pass along the Ligurian Coast on the way to all parts of Italy.

Within Liguria, it takes two hours for an express train to cover the entire coast; local trains make innumerable stops and take upward of five hours. Regular service operates from Genoa's two stations: departures from Stazione Principe travel to points west and Stazione Brignole to points east and south. All the coastal resorts are on this line.

🚆 Train Information **Ferrovie dello Stato** ☎ 892021 ⊕ www.trenitalia.com.

🚆 Train Stations **Stazione Brignole** ✉ Piazza Giuseppe Verdi, Foce, Genoa ☎ 892021. **Stazione Principe** ✉ Piazza del Principe, San Teodoro, Genoa.

EMERGENCIES

Europa and Ghersi are two late-night pharmacies in Genoa.

🚑 **Ambulance** ☎ 118. **Police** ☎ 112. **General emergencies** ☎ 113. **Europa** ✉ Corso Europa 676, Genoa ☎ 010/380239. **Ghersi** ✉ Corso Buenos Aires 18/r, Genoa ☎ 010/541661. **Ospedale Generale Regionale San Martino** ✉ Largo Rosanna Benzi 10, Genoa ☎ 010/5551.

TOURS

You can take a boat tour of Genoa harbor with Cooperativa Battellieri del Porto di Genova. The tour, which starts from the aquarium pier, costs €6, lasts about an hour, and includes a visit to the breakwater outside the harbor, the Bacino delle Grazie, and the Molo Vecchio (Old Port).

A bus tour of Genoa with an English-speaking guide is a good way to see the city and its panoramic upper reaches. A coach leaves every afternoon at 3 from Piazza Caricamento, by the port, and does the Giro Giro Tour, a two-hour narrated loop of the city (€15). It's operated by Genoa's municipal transport company in conjunction with the agency Macrame Viaggi.

Individual or group walking and hiking tours can introduce you to the lesser-known aspects of the region. For the Cinque Terre and the rest of the Province of La Spezia, the Cooperativa Arte e Natura is a good source for well-trained, English-speaking, licenced guides. A half day costs approximately €150.

🚢 Boat Tours **Cooperativa Battellieri** ✉ Stazione Marittima, Ponte dei Mille, Genoa ☎ 010/265712 ⊕ www.battellierigenova.it.

🚌 Bus Tours **Macrame Viaggi** ✉ Piazza Colombo 3, Maddalena, Genoa ☎ 010/5959779.

🚶 Walking Tours **Coopertiva Arte e Natura** ✉ Viale Amendola 172, La Spezia ☎ 0187/739410 🖶 0187/257391.

VISITOR INFORMATION

Most towns have a local tourist office, called either Agenzia di Promozione Turistica (APT) or Informazione ed Accoglienza Turistica (IAT), that can provide general information, and for a small fee can help you book accommodations Monday–Saturday 9–5. Note that the Terminale Crociere branch in Genoa is open only May–September, for the arrival of major ferries and cruise ships.

ℹ Tourist Information **Alassio** ✉ Viale Mazzini 62, 17021 ☎ 0182/647027 ⊕ www.inforiviera.it. **Albenga** ✉ Viale Martiri della Libertà 1, 17031 ☎ 0182/558444 ⊕ www.inforiviera.it. **Bordighera** ✉ Via Roberto 1, 18012 ☎ 0184/262322 ⊕ www.rivieradeifiori.org. **Camogli** ✉ Via XX Settembre 33, 16032 ☎ 0185/771066 ⊕ www.camogli.it. **Genoa** ✉ Stazione Principe, San Teodoro ☎ 010/2462633 ⊕ www.apt.genova.it ✉ Aeroporto Internazionale Cristoforo Colombo, Sestri Ponente ☎ 010/6015247 ✉ Via Roma 11

☎ 010/576791 ✉ Terminale Crociere, Ponte dei Mille ☎ No phone. **Imperia** ✉ Viale Matteotti 37, 18100 ☎ 0183/660140 ⊕ www.rivieradeifiori.org. **La Spezia** ✉ Via Mazzini 45, 19100 ☎ 0187/770900 ⊕ www.aptcinqueterre.sp.it. **Lerici** ✉ Via Biaggini 6, 19032 ☎ 0187/967346 ⊕ www.aptcinqueterre.sp.it. **Levanto** ✉ Piazza Cavour 12, 19015 ☎ 0187/808125 ⊕ www.aptcinqueterre.sp.it. **Monterosso** ✉ Via Fegina 38, 19016 ☎ 0187/817506 ⊕ www.aptcinqueterre.sp.it. **Portofino** ✉ Via Roma 35, 16034 ☎ 0185/269024 ⊕ www.apttigullio.liguria.it. **Rapallo** ✉ Lungomare V. Veneto 7, 16035 ☎ 0185/230346 ⊕ www.apttigullio.liguria.it. **Riomaggiore** ✉ Stazione Ferroviaria, 19017 ☎ 0187/920633 ⊕ www.aptcinqueterre.sp.it. **San Remo** ✉ Palazzo Riviera, Largo Nuvoloni 1, 18038 ☎ 0184/571571 ⊕ www.rivieradeifiori.org. **Santa Margherita Ligure** ✉ Via XXV Aprile 28, 16038 ☎ 0185/2929 ⊕ www.apttigullio.liguria.it. **Savona** ✉ Corso Italia 157/r, 17100 ☎ 019/8402321 ⊕ www.inforiviera.it. **Ventimiglia** ✉ Via Cavour 61, 18039 ☎ 0184/351183 ⊕ www.rivieradeifiori.org.

Emilia-Romagna

Duomo Square, Parma

WORD OF MOUTH

"Ah, Bologna . . . one of Italy's truly underrated gems. Sitting in an outdoor café in Piazza Maggiore is a true Italian experience."

—HowardR

"The cities in Emilia-Romagna are: (1) gastronomic heavens, (2) off the beaten tourist path, and (3) gastronomic heavens. Did I say that they were gastronomic heavens?"

—tdyls

WELCOME TO EMILIA-ROMAGNA

Tortellacci

TOP 5
Reasons to Go

1 The signature food of Emilia: This region's food—the prosciutto crudo, the Parmigiano-Reggiano, the balsamic vinegar, and perhaps above all, the pasta—alone makes the trip to Italy worthwhile.

2 Mosaics that take your breath away: The intricate tile creations in Ravenna's Mausuleo di Galla Placidia, in brilliantly well-preserved primary colors, depict pastoral scenes that transport you to another age.

3 Europe's oldest wine bar: You won't be the first to have a glass of wine at Osteria al Brindisi, in the heart of medieval Ferrara, beneath an apartment once inhabited by Copernicus—this venerable establishment has been continuously pouring since 1435.

4 The nightlife of Bologna: The red-roofed, left-leaning city of Bologna has the oldest student culture in Europe, and still one of the liveliest, from hopping Irish pubs to cutting-edge lounges.

5 The medieval castles of San Marino: The three castles are dramatically perched on a rock more than 3,000 feet above the flat landscape of Romagna.

A landscape of medieval castles and crumbling farmhouses begins just east of Milan, in Emilia, where you'll first find the delicious delights of **Parma,** with its buttery prosciutto, famous cheese, and crenellated palaces. Next along the road, continuing east, comes **Modena,** the city of bicycles and balsamic vinegar.

Piazza Grande, Modena
Cattedrale e Torre della Ghirlandina

Getting Oriented

Emilia-Romagna owes its beginnings to the Romans, who built the Via Emilia in 187 BC. Today the road bisects the flat, foggy region, paralleling the Autostrada del Sole (A1), making it easy to drive straight through. Bologna is in the middle of everything, with Piacenza, Parma, and Modena to the west, and Rimini to the east. Ferrara and Ravenna are the only detours—they're to the north of Via Emilia.

Ravenna

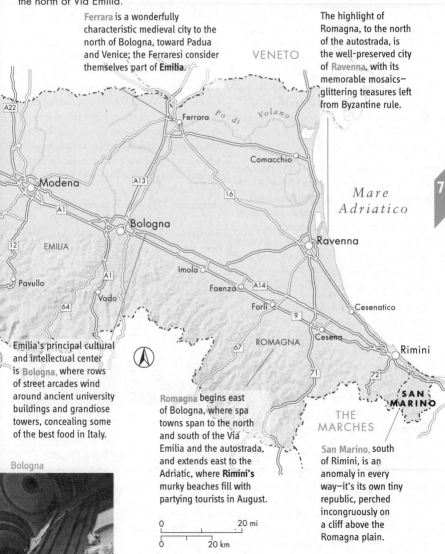

Ferrara is a wonderfully characteristic medieval city to the north of Bologna, toward Padua and Venice; the Ferraresi consider themselves part of Emilia.

The highlight of Romagna, to the north of the autostrada, is the well-preserved city of Ravenna, with its memorable mosaics—glittering treasures left from Byzantine rule.

Emilia's principal cultural and intellectual center is Bologna, where rows of street arcades wind around ancient university buildings and grandiose towers, concealing some of the best food in Italy.

Bologna

Romagna begins east of Bologna, where spa towns span to the north and south of the Via Emilia and the autostrada, and extends east to the Adriatic, where Rimini's murky beaches fill with partying tourists in August.

San Marino, south of Rimini, is an anomaly in every way—it's its own tiny republic, perched incongruously on a cliff above the Romagna plain.

0   20 mi
0   20 km

EMILIA-ROMAGNA PLANNER

Making the Most of Your Time

Plan on spending at least two days or nights in Bologna, the region's cultural and historical capital. The next two priorities should be the elegant food center of Parma and the wonderfully characteristic medieval city of Ferrara, followed—in this order—by Ravenna and its memorable Byzantine mosaics, and Modena with its bicycles, harmonious architecture, and famous balsamic vinegar.

If you only have a few days in the region, it's virtually impossible to do all five of those cities justice. If you're a dedicated gourmand, move from Bologna west along the Via Emilia (SS9), to Modena and Parma. If you're more interested in architecture, art, and history, choose the eastern route, heading north on A13 to Ferrara and then southeast on S16 to Ravenna.

If you have more time, you won't have to make such tough choices. You can start in Milan, go east, and finish on the Adriatic—or vice versa. Don't bother with the Adriatic beach resort of Rimini unless it's the peak of summer and you absolutely can't imagine not being on the beach.

Getting Around

Driving is the best way to get around Emilia-Romagna. Roads are wide, flat, and well-marked; distances are short, and beautiful farmhouses and small villages make for easily accessible detours. A car is particularly useful for visiting the spa towns of Romagna, which aren't well connected by train. With the exception of Bologna, the cities themselves are more or less navigable by car as well, although they're also easily walkable, so you may just want to park your car and get around by foot once you hit your hotel. Public transportation, too, is easy, aside from the Romagnan hilltowns. Trains are better than buses. They're fairly efficient and quite frequent, and most stations aren't too far from the center of town. For more about car, bus, and train travel in the region, see "Essentials" at the end of this chapter.

Seeing Through the Fog

Emilia-Romagna is famous for the low-lying fog that comes in from the Adriatic and blankets much of the region in fall and winter. In the cities, the mist can be ghostly and beautiful, but it can also be a driving hazard, with little visibility beyond about 10 yards. You should avoid driving at night in winter, but the problem can arise in the day, too. If it gets too bad, pull off at an Autogrill or café and wait for the fog to lift, and if you're on the road, keep your headlights on and don't exceed 60 km/h. Road signs throughout the region indicate speed limits in fog *(nebbia)*.

Tips for Foodies

Emilia-Romagna is famous for its food tradition. It's the region where tortellini, fettucine, and Parmesan cheese were invented, and it's justly famous worldwide for its balsamic vinegar and hams.

Along with these perfect primary ingredients, the region is dotted with spectacular, out-of-the-way restaurants with haute cuisine to rival any in Europe. These are places that might break your budget but are also likely to blow your mind. If you're moving east into Romagna, take time out to stop for a memorable meal at one of the region's top tables, either in Imola (near Dozza), or a Romagnan spa town such as Castrocaro Terme or Bagno di Romagna, where you might want to stay for the night after dinner—you won't want to drive after such a meal.

Finding a Place to Stay

Emilia-Romagna has a reputation for an efficiency uncommon in most of the rest of Italy. Even the smallest hotels are well run, with high standards of quality and service. Bologna is very much a businessperson's city, and many hotels there cater to the business traveler, but there are smaller, more intimate hotels as well. It's smart to book in advance—the region hosts many fairs and conventions that can fill up hotels even during "low season."

Though prices are high, you can expect an experience delightfully free of the condescending attitude and manipulative pricing schemes that sometimes mar Italy's tourist meccas. The one exception to the rule is Rimini, where numerous hotels have tourist-oriented full- and half-board packages. They overflow during July and August and close down for much of the off-season.

Dining & Lodging Price Categories

WHAT IT COSTS in Euros					
	$$$$	**$$$**	**$$**	**$**	**¢**
Restaurants	over €45	€35–€45	€25–€35	€15–€25	under €15
Hotels	over €220	€160–€220	€110–€160	€70–€110	under €70

Restaurant prices are for a first course (primo), second course (secondo), and dessert (dolce). Hotel prices are for two people in a standard double room in high season, including tax and service.

How's the Weather?

You would never visit Emilia-Romagna for the weather—so the season matters less here than it might in other regions. As elsewhere in Italy, fall and spring are best, especially in the Romagna countryside. Cold, gray winters can bring temperatures well below freezing, although the dense fog can be beautiful. It usually snows in the region a few times a year. Summers tend to be hot and humid.

7

TOP PASSEGGIATA

A walk down the Via delle Volte and around the cobble-stoned medieval district of Ferrara is a trip back through time.

Updated by
Robin S.
Goldstein

GOURMETS THE WORLD OVER claim that Emilia-Romagna's greatest contribution to humankind has been gastronomic. Birthplace of fettuccine, tortellini, lasagna, prosciutto, and Parmesan cheese, the region has a spectacular culinary tradition. But there are many reasons to come here aside from the desire to be well fed: Parma's Correggio paintings, Giuseppe Verdi's villa at Sant'Agata, the medieval splendor of Bologna's palazzos and Ferrara's alleyways, the rolling hills of the Romagna countryside, and, perhaps foremost, the Byzantine beauty of mosaic-rich Ravenna—glittering as brightly today as it did 1,500 years ago.

As you travel through Emilia, the western half of the region, you'll encounter sprawling plants of the industrial food giants of Italy, such as Barilla and Fini, standing side by side with the fading villas and farmhouses that have long punctuated the flat, fertile land of the Po Plain. Bologna, the principal city of Emilia, is a busy cultural capital, less visited but in many ways just as engaging as Italy's more famous tourist destinations—particularly given its acknowledged position as the leading city of Italian cuisine. The rest of the region follows suit: eating is an essential part of any Emilian experience. The area's history is replete with culinary legends, such as how the original *tortellino* (singular of tortellini) was modeled on the shape of Venus's navel and the original *tagliolini* (long, thin egg pasta) were served at the wedding banquet of Annibale Bentivoglio and Lucrezia d'Este—a marriage uniting two of the noblest families in the region. It's almost impossible to eat badly in Emilia, and everything is worth trying—Parma's famed prosciutto and Parmigiano Reggiano cheese, Modena's balsamic vinegar, and the best pasta in the world. The historical border between Emilia and Romagna lies near the fortified town of Dozza. East of there, Romagna gets hillier and more sparsely settled; finally, it flattens out into the low-lying marshland of the Po Delta, which meets the murky Adriatic Sea. Farther south, the down-market beach resort of Rimini draws hordes of Italian teenagers each summer. Each fall, in Romagna and Emilia alike, the region's trademark fog rolls in off the Adriatic to hang over the flatlands in winter, coloring cities and countryside alike with a spooky, gray glow.

EMILIA

The Via Emilia runs through Emilia's heart in a straight shot from medieval Piacenza, only 67 km (42 mi) southeast of Milan, to thoroughly modern Modena. On the way from the past to the present you encounter many of Italy's cultural riches—from the culinary and artistic treasures of Parma to the birthplace and home of Giuseppe Verdi and the mist-shrouded tangle of streets that make up Ferrara's old Jewish ghetto. It may be tempting to imitate Modena's Ferraris and zoom along the portion of the A1 highway spanning the region, but take time to detour into the countryside, with its decaying farmhouses and 800-year-old abbeys, and to stop for a taste of prosciutto.

EMILIA-ROMAGNA THROUGH THE AGES

Ancient History. Emilia-Romagna owes its beginnings to a road. In 187 BC the Romans laid out their Via Aemilia, a long highway running straight northwest from the Adriatic port of Rimini to the central garrison town of Piacenza, and it was along this central spine that the primary towns of the region developed.

Despite the unifying factor of what came to be known as the Via Emilia, the region has had a fragmented history. Its eastern portion, roughly the area from Faenza to the coast, known as Romagna, has looked first to the Byzantine east and then to Rome for art, political power, and, some say, national character. The western portion, Emilia, from Bologna to Piacenza, had a more northern, rather dour sense of self-government and dissent.

The principal city of Bologna was founded by the Etruscans and eventually came under the influence of the Roman Empire. The Romans established a garrison there, renaming the old Etruscan settlement Bononia. It was after the fall of Rome that the region began its fragmentation. Romagna, centered in Ravenna, was ruled from Constantinople. Ravenna eventually became the capital of the empire in the west in the 5th century, passing to papal control in the 8th century. Even today, the city is still filled with reminders of two centuries of Byzantine rule.

Family Ties. The other cities of the region, from the Middle Ages on, became the fiefs of important noble families—the Este in Ferrara and Modena, the Pallavicini in Piacenza, the Bentivoglio in Bologna, and the Malatesta in Rimini. Today all these cities bear the marks of their noble patrons. When in the 16th century the papacy managed to exert its power over the entire region, some of these cities were divided among the papal families—hence the stamp of the Farnese family on Parma, Piacenza, and Ferrara.

A Leftward Tilt. Bologna and Emilia-Romagna have established a robust tradition of rebellion and dissent. The Italian socialist movement was born in the region, as was Benito Mussolini—in keeping with the political climate of his home state, he was a firebrand socialist during the early part of his career. Despite having Mussolini as a native son, Emilia-Romagna did not take to fascism: it was here that the antifascist resistance was born, and during World War II the region suffered terribly at the hands of the Fascists and the Nazis.

Despite a long history of bloodletting, turmoil, and rebellion, the arts have always flourished. The great families financed painters, sculptors, and writers. (Dante found a haven in Ravenna after being expelled from his native Florence.) In modern times Emilia-Romagna has given to the arts such famous figures as painter Giorgio Morandi, filmmakers Michelangelo Antonioni and Federico Fellini, and tenor Luciano Pavarotti. Even since Bologna's emergence as a major tourist destination, the city has not lost its liberal feel, and it has been a locus of anti-Iraq war protests.

7

Piacenza

 66 km (41 mi) southeast of Milan, 150 km (94 mi) northwest of Bologna.

The city of Piacenza has always been associated with industry and commerce. Its position on the Po River has made it an important inland port since the earliest times; the Etruscans, and then the Romans, had thriving settlements on this site. As you approach the city today you could be forgiven for thinking that it holds little of interest. Piacenza is surrounded by ugly industrial suburbs (with particularly unlovely concrete factories and a power station), but forge ahead to discover that they surround a delightfully preserved medieval downtown and an unusually clean city. The prosperity is evidenced by the great shopping along Corso Vittorio Emanuele II.

The heart of the city is the **Piazza dei Cavalli** (Square of the Horses). The flamboyant equestrian statues from which the piazza takes its name are depictions of Ranuccio Farnese (1569–1622) and, on the left, his father, Alessandro (1545–92). Alessandro was a beloved ruler, enlightened and fair; Ranuccio, his successor, was less admired. Both statues are the work of Francesco Mochi, a master sculptor of the baroque period. Dominating the square is the massive 13th-century **Palazzo del Comune,** also known as the Palazzo Gotico. This two-tone, marble-and-brick, turreted and crenellated building was the seat of town government before Piacenza fell under the iron fists of the ruling Pallavicini and Farnese families.

Attached like a sinister balcony to the bell tower of Piacenza's 12th-century **Duomo** is a *gabbia* (iron cage), where miscreants were incarcerated naked and subjected to the scorn (and projectiles) of the crowd in the marketplace below. Inside the cathedral a less-evocative but equally impressive medieval stonework decorates the pillars and the crypt, and there are extravagant frescoes by Il Guercino (aka Giovanni Barbieri, 1591–1666) in the dome of the cupola. The Duomo can be reached by following Via XX Settembre from Piazza dei Cavalli. ⊠ *Piazza Duomo* ☎ *0523/335154* ⊗ *Daily 7:30–12:30 and 4–7:30.*

The **Museo Civico,** the city-owned museum of Piacenzan art and antiquities, is housed in the vast **Palazzo Farnese.** The ruling family had commissioned a monumental palace, but construction, begun in 1558, was never completed as planned. The highlight of the museum's rather eclectic exhibit is the 2nd-century BC Etruscan *Fegato di Piacenza,* a bronze tablet in the shape of a *fegato* (liver), with the symbols of the gods of good and ill fortune marked on it. By comparing this master "liver" with one taken from the body of a freshly slaughtered sacrifice, priests could predict the future. The collection also contains Botticelli's *Madonna with St. John the Baptist.* Reserve ahead for free one-hour guided tours. ⊠ *Piazza Cittadella 29* ☎ *0523/326981* ⊕ *www.musei.piacenza.it* 🎫 *€5.25* ⊗ *June–Sept., Tues.–Thurs. 9–1, Fri. and Sat. 9–1 and 3–6, Sun. 9:30–1 and 3–6; Oct.–May, Tues.–Thurs. 8:45–1, Fri. and Sat. 8:45–1 and 3–6, Sun. 9:30–1 and 3–6. Tours Tues.–Thurs. 10, Fri. 10 and 3:30; weekends 9:30, 11, 3, and 4:30.*

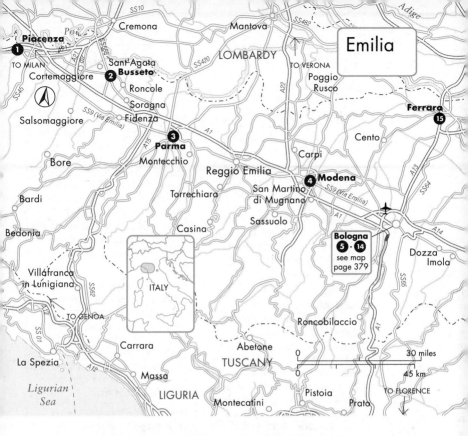

The **Galleria d'Arte Moderna Ricci Oddi** has been getting increasing attention for its unusually good collection of paintings from the 1800s and 1900s by luminaries from all over northern and central Italy—with a focus on Tuscany and Emilia. ⊠ *Via San Siro 13* ☎ *0523/320742* ⊕ *www.piacenzamusei.it* 🎟 *€4* ☉ *Tues.–Sun. 10–noon and 3–6.*

Where to Eat

★ **$$$$** ✕ **Antica Osteria del Teatro.** On a lovely little square in the center of town, this restaurant is one of the best in all Emilia-Romagna. The 15th-century building, with coffered ceilings and sober furniture, effuses elegance. The pricey, French-influence menu might be best described as haute Italian; some of the more nouveau flights of fancy might include, for example, a terrine of duck liver with marzipan-stuffed dates. The two tasting menus are an excellent way to sample the kitchen at its best. Service is excellent and the wine list impeccable. ⊠ *Via Verdi 16* ☎ *0523/323777* ⊕ *www.anticaosteriadelteatro.it* ⟨ *Reservations essential* ⊟ *AE, DC, MC, V* ☉ *Closed Sun. and Mon., Aug. 1–25, and Jan. 1–10.*

EATING WELL IN EMILIA-ROMAGNA

Emilia-Romagna's reputation as Italy's gourmet haven is well deserved. The specialties are nothing new in name, they're just better here, where they were born—for example, Parma's world-famous prosciuttos and crumbly Parmigiano Reggiano cheese. Bologna's pasta (especially tagliatelle) *al ragù* is in a heavenly, slow-cooked sauce of onions, carrots, minced pork and beef, milk, and (sometimes) fresh tomatoes. The rich, soft, garlicky mortadella has been reincarnated elsewhere to its detriment as "baloney."

Pasta Pillows. Among the many Emilian variations on stuffed pasta, *tortelli* and *cappellacci* are larger pasta pillows, about the size of a Brussels sprout, but with the same basic form as tortellini; they're often stuffed with pumpkinlike squash or spinach and cheese. Tortelloni are, in theory, even bigger, although their size varies. Stuffed pastas are generally served simply, with melted butter, sage, and (what else) Parmigiano Reggiano cheese, or *in brodo* (in beef or chicken broth), which brings out the subtle richness of the fillings.

Going Local. Look for the local specialties: *zampone* (a sausage made from pig's trotter) and *aceto balsamico* (balsamic vinegar) in Modena; risotto *in padella* (with fresh herbs and tomatoes) in Piacenza; *brodetto* (tangy seafood stew) in Rimini; ancient Roman *piadine* (chewy, flat griddle breads) in Romagna; *cappellacci di zucca* (large, squash-filled pasta pillows in a cream sauce with tomato, walnuts, and Parmesan) and *salama da sugo* (salty, oily aged sausage that is eaten cooked) in Ferrara; and everything in Bologna.

Also along the Adriatic coast, don't miss the simply grilled seafood: the *scampi* from the Adriatic, for instance, are a thin, shrimplike crustacean whose tender meat is so sweet that you may swear there's something added. (It's also great in tomato-based pasta sauce.) Razor clams, mussels, and little *noci* (tiny clamlike mussels) are among the sweet, warm-water shellfish available.

Parma is synonymous with prosciutto, but it's not alone in making the meat a specialty. Parma ham's even more prized, and pricey, cousin, is the sweet and flavorful *culatello di Zibello*, which is produced along the banks of the Po River, and is cured and aged for more than 11 months.

Wines. Emilia-Romagna's wines accompany the region's fine food rather than vying with it for accolades. The best known is Lambrusco, a sparkling red produced on the Po Plain that has some admirers and many detractors. It's praised for its tartness and condemned for the same quality. The region's best wines include Sangiovese di Romagna, which can be similar to Chianti, from the Romagnan hills, and Barbera, from the Colli Piacentini and Apennine foothills. Castelluccio, Bonzara, Zerbina, Leone Conti, and Tre Monti are among the region's top producers—keep your eyes out for their bottles. Stop at the Enoteca Regionale in Dozza for the best selection of wines from Emilia-Romagna anywhere in the region.

Busseto

② *30 km (19 mi) southeast of Piacenza, 25 km (15 mi) southeast of Cremona in Lombardy.*

Busseto's main claim to fame is its native son, master composer Giuseppe Verdi (1813–1901). The 15th-century **Villa Pallavicino** is where Verdi worked and lived with his mistress (and later wife) Giuseppina Strepponi. On display are the maestro's piano, scores, composition books, and walking sticks. At this writing the villa was closed for renovation with the reopening date uncertain. ⊠ *Via Provesi 36* ☎ *0524/92239* ⊕ *www.bussetolive.com.*

In the center of Busseto is the lovely **Teatro Verdi,** dedicated, as one might expect, to the works of the hamlet's famous son. Once inside the well-preserved, ornate 19th-century-style theater, use your imagination to get a feel for where he worked. Check with the Busseto tourist office for the performance schedule. Nonperformance visits are by appointment only. ⊠ *Piazza G. Verdi 10* ☎ *0524/92487* 🎫 *€4* ☉ *By appointment Mar.–Oct., Tues.–Sun. 9:30–12:30 and 3–6; Nov.–Feb., Tues.–Sun. 9:30–12:30 and 2:30–4:30.*

OFF THE
BEATEN
PATH

VILLA SANT'AGATA – For Verdi lovers, Sant'Agata (also known as Villa Verdi) is a veritable shrine. It's the grand country home Verdi built for himself in 1849, the place where some of his greatest works were composed. Tours are required, and you have to reserve a few days in advance by phone or on the Web. ⊠ *Via Verdi 22, Sant'Agata Villanova sull'Arda, 4 km (2½ mi) north of Busseto on S588, toward Cremona* ☎ *0523/830000* ⊕ *www.villaverdi.org* 🎫 *€6* ☉ *Jan. 6–26, Tues.–Sun. 9:30–11:30 and 2:30–4:30; Jan. 27–Mar., Tues.–Sun. 9:30–11:30 and 2:30–5:30; Apr.–Oct. 15, 9–11:45 and 2:30–6:45; Oct. 16–Dec. 15, 9:30–11:30 and 2:30–4:30.*

Parma

③ *40 km (25 mi) southeast of Busseto, 97 km (61 mi) northwest of Bologna.*

Dignified, delightful Parma stands on the banks of a tributary of the Po River. Much of the stately old center has been untouched by modern times, despite damage during World War II. Almost every major European power has had a hand in ruling Parma at one time or another. The Romans founded the city—then little more than a garrison on the Via Emilia—after which a succession of feudal lords held sway. In the 16th century came the ever-avaricious Farnese family (who are still the dukes of Parma) and then, in fast succession, the Spanish, French, and Austrians (after the fall of Napoléon). The French influence is strong. The novelist Stendhal (1783–1842) lived in the city for several years and set his classic *The Charterhouse of Parma* here.

Bursting with gustatory delights, Parma now draws crowds for its sublime cured ham, prosciutto *crudo di Parma* (known locally simply as prosciutto *crudo*). The pale yellow Parmigiano Reggiano cheese produced here and in nearby Reggio Emilia is the original—and best—of a class known around the world as Parmesan. The city's prosperity has long been tied to the Parmalat dairy empire, but at the end of 2003 the once-proud company was brought down by a huge corporate scandal. As the public learned of fictional $4 billion bank accounts and shell holding companies offshore, Parmalat went bankrupt (and even sold off the star players of Parma, the company-owned soccer team that wears trademark blue-and-yellow-striped shirts). The company is now run by a government-appointed administrator and the city has largely recovered from the ordeal, but the sting has not gone.

★ **Piazza Garibaldi** is at the heart of Parma. This square is where pedestrians and bicycles come together in a bustle of activity, where all ages sit together at big old cafés, and where the evening *passeggiata* begins. Strada Cavour, leading off the piazza, is Parma's prime shopping street. This square and its buildings, together with the nearby Piazza del Duomo, make up one of the most harmonious, tranquil city centers in Italy.

The delightful, 16th-century church of **Santa Maria della Steccata**, one of Parma's most recognizable domes, has a wonderful fresco cycle by Girolamo Parmigianino (1503–40). The painter took so long to complete it that his patrons imprisoned him briefly for breach of contract. ✉ *Piazza Steccata 9, off Via Dante near Piazza Garibaldi* ☎ *0521/234937* ⊕ *www.santuari.it/steccata* ☾ *Daily 9–noon and 3–6.*

The **Teatro Regio** opera house is a local landmark and the site of regular performances. ✉ *Via Garibaldi 16* ☎ *0521/039393* ⊕ *www.teatroregioparma.org* ✈ *€2* ☾ *Tours by reservation Mon.–Sat. 10:30–noon.*

The **Piazza del Duomo** contains the cathedral, the Battistero, the church of San Giovanni, and the palaces of the bishop and other notables. The magnificent 12th-century **Duomo** has two vigilant stone lions standing guard beside the main door. The arch of the entrance is decorated with a delicate frieze of figures representing the months of the year, a motif repeated inside the baptistery on the right-hand side of the piazza. Some of the church's original artwork still survives, notably the simple yet evocative *Descent from the Cross,* a carving in the right transept by Benedetto Antelami (1150–1230), a sculptor and architect whose masterwork is this cathedral's baptistery.

It is odd to turn from this austere work of the 12th century to the exuberant fresco in the dome, the *Assumption of the Virgin* by Antonio Correggio (1494–1534). The fresco was not well received when it was unveiled in 1530. "A mess of frogs' legs," the bishop of Parma is said to have called it. Today Correggio is acclaimed as one of the leading masters of mannerist painting. Note that the front facade of the Duomo is undergoing a major renovation and will likely remain hidden by scaffolding through 2006. ✉ *Piazza del Duomo* ☎ *0521/235886* ☾ *Daily 9–12:30 and 3–7; guided tours Sat. at 3.*

The impressive **Battistero** (Baptistry) has a simple pink-stone Romanesque exterior and an uplifting Gothic interior. The doors are richly decorated with figures, animals, and flowers, and the interior is adorned with figures carved by Antelami showing the months and seasons. ✉ *Piazza del Duomo* ☎ *0521/235886* 🎫 *€4* 🕙 *Daily 9–12:30 and 3–6:30.*

Once beyond the elaborate baroque facade of **San Giovanni Evangelista,** the Renaissance interior reveals several works by Correggio; his *St. John the Evangelist* (left transept) is considered the finest. Also in this church (in the second and fourth chapels on the left) are works by Girolamo Parmigianino—a contemporary of Correggio's and the spearhead of the mannerist art movement. Once seen, Parmigianino's swan-neck Madonnas are never forgotten: they pose with all the precious élan of today's fashion models. The church is next to the Battistero. ✉ *Piazzale San Giovanni 1, the Piazza del Duomo* ☎ *0521/235311* 🕙 *Daily 8–noon and 3–7:45.*

In the monastery adjoining the church of San Giovanni Evangelista is the **Spezieria di San Giovanni**—once a pharmacy where Benedictine monks mixed medicines and herbals. Although production stopped in 1881, the 16th-century decorations survive. ✉ *Borgo Pipa 1, off Piazzale San Giovanni* ☎ *0521/233309* 🎫 *€2* 🕙 *July, Aug. and Oct.–Apr., Tues.–Sun. 8:30–1:45; May, Tues.–Fri. 2–6, weekends 2–7; June and Sept., weekdays 8:30–6, weekends 8:30–7.*

Works by Parma's own Correggio and Parmigianino as well as Leonardo da Vinci (1452–1519), El Greco (1541–1614), and Bronzino (1503–72) hang at the **Galleria Nazionale.** The museum is on the ground floor of the rather grim-looking **Palazzo della Pilotta,** which was constructed on the riverbank in 1618. It's so big that from the air the building is Parma's most recognizable sight—hence the destruction it suffered from Allied bombs in 1944. Much of the building has been restored. The palazzo takes its name from the game *pilotta,* a sort of handball played within the palace precincts in the 17th century.

To enter the Galleria Nazionale you pass through the magnificent baroque **Teatro Farnese,** built in 1628 and based on Palladio's theater in Vicenza. Built entirely of wood, it was burned badly during Allied bombing but has been flawlessly restored. ✉ *Piazza Pilotta* ☎ *0521/233309* ⊕ *www.artipr.arti.beniculturali.it* 🎫 *€6, theater only €2* 🕙 *Tues.–Sun. 8:30–2.*

The **Camera di San Paolo** is the former dining room of the abbess of the Convent of St. Paul. It was extensively frescoed by Correggio, and despite the building's religious character the decorations aren't Christian but rather ravishingly beautiful depictions of mythological scenes—the *Triumphs of the Goddess Diana,* the *Three Graces,* and the *Three Fates.* ✉ *Via Melloni off Strada Garibaldi, near Piazza Pilotta* ☎ *0521/233309* 🎫 *€2* 🕙 *Tues.–Sun. 8:30–1:45.*

Where to Stay & Eat

$$$–$$$$ ✕ **La Greppia.** The most elegant, most talked-about restaurant in the city is also one of the best. Taste well-known chef Paola Cavazzini's innovative treats like the *anelli con cavolo nero e mostarda della Paola* (small ring-shape pasta with black cauliflower and caramelized fruits) and the *faraona al tartufo nero di Fragno* (guinea hen with black truffle and chestnut puree). Service is personal and friendly, thanks to the place's tiny size, and the unpretentious surroundings keep the focus on

the food. There's often a bargain set-price lunch for less than €30. ⊠ *Via Garibaldi 39/a* ☏ *0521/233686* ⌔ *Reservations essential* ⊟ *AE, DC, MC, V* ☾ *Closed Mon. and Tues., July, and Dec. 23–Jan. 5.*

$$$–$$$$ ✕ **Parizzi.** Named for its exciting young chef, Marco Parizzi, this restaurant rivals La Greppia for the title of Parma's finest. A stylish art nouveau interior with Persian rugs complements traditional Parma classics like stuffed *tortelli* (large tortellini) and sublime risotto with Parmigiano Reggiano and shaved white truffles (in season). Try antipasti such as *culatello di Zibello* (the most highly touted of Parma prosciuttos, aged more than 11 months). The wine list is top-notch. ⊠ *Strada Repubblica 71* ☏ *0521/285952* ⌔ *Reservations essential* ⊟ *AE, DC, MC, V* ☾ *Closed Mon., Aug., and Jan. 8–15.*

$$ ✕ **Osteria dei Mascalzoni.** Carefully placed mood lighting and expensive table settings exude romance: Osteria dei Mascalzoni is thoroughly refined in both conception and execution, yet the place remains somehow young and approachable. Meat dishes, such as the fillet of beef with a delicate cream of leek sauce, are good. The wine list is carefully chosen, with a particularly good selection from Sicily. Leave satisfied and charmed, if a bit poorer for your wine tab. The restaurant is usually open until 1 AM. ⊠ *Vicolo delle Cinque Piaghe 1* ☏ *0521/281809* ⌔ *Reservations essential* ⊟ *AE, DC, MC, V* ☾ *Closed Sun. and 3 wks in Aug. No lunch Sat.*

$–$$ ✕ **Parma Rotta.** In an old inn 2 km (1 mi) south of the center is an informal neighborhood trattoria with impressive culinary ambitions. Parma Rotta serves absolutely spectacular grilled steaks, spit-roast lamb, and other meats cooked on a wood-fire grill. The homemade pasta, which might include ravioli or tortelli, is no less impressive. Dine outdoors under a pleasant trellis in warm weather. ⊠ *Via Langhirano 158* ☏ *0521/966738* ⌨ *www.parmarotta.com* ⊟ *AE, DC, MC, V* ☾ *Closed Mon., Dec. 24–Jan. 14, and Sun. June–Aug.*

Fodor'sChoice
★

★ ¢ ✕ **Enoteca Antica Osteria Fontana.** Gregarious locals flock to the bright yellow, old-school *enoteca* (wine bar) that has a star-studded selection of wines at shockingly good prices. You have to queue up in anarchic fashion for a table—or eat at the bar—and service is brusque. But that's all part of the experience. The grilled *panini* (sandwiches), filled with Emilia's best *salumi* (cured meats), are delicious. Try the *coppa* (an interesting, full-flavor pork sausage) with artichokes, for example. The panini come quartered, so you can share. The place is the best take-out wine store in town, but it closes early (9 PM or before). ⊠ *Strada Farini 24/a, near the Piazza del Duomo* ☏ *0521/286037* ⌔ *Reservations not accepted* ⊟ *MC, V* ☾ *Closed Sun.*

$$$ ▦ **Hotel Stendhal.** The Stendhal is one of Parma's finest hotels. Rooms are smallish, but thickly carpeted and some have chandeliers and antique furniture. A few rooms have views of the Palazzo della Pilotta on the edge of the old center of town. The hotel is affiliated with the Jolly chain, but it's best to reserve through the property directly. ⊠ *Via Bodoni 3, 43100* ☏ *0521/208057* ☏ *0521/285655* ⌨ *www.hotelstendhal. it* ⇱ *62 rooms* ⚐ *Restaurant, minibars, cable TV, bar, meeting room, some pets allowed* ⊟ *AE, DC, MC, V* ⧗ *BP.*

$$$ ▦ **Palace Hotel Maria Luigia.** Top-quality and convenient to Old Parma and the train station, the Maria Luigia is popular with business travelers. Some of the traditional rooms, with heavy draperies and wood furniture, have lovely vistas of Parma. It's part of the Italian Sina Hotel chain. ✉ *Viale Mentana 140, 43100* ☎ *0521/281032* 📠 *0521/231126* 🌐 *www.sinahotels.com* 🛏 *93 rooms, 12 suites* ♻ *Restaurant, minibars, bar, meeting room* ▭ *AE, DC, MC, V* �‖ *BP.*

$$ 🏨 **Hotel Torino.** A warm reception and pleasant, relaxed surroundings welcome you to this former convent tucked away in a quiet pedestrian zone in the heart of town. Correggio reproductions hang on the walls of modern, compact rooms. If traveling by car, look online or fax ahead for a detailed map or directions—it's difficult to find. ✉ *Borgo Mazza 7, 43100* ☎ *0521/281046* 📠 *0521/230725* 🛏 *33 rooms* ♻ *Cable TV, bar, some pets allowed, Internet room* ▭ *AE, DC, MC, V* �‖ *BP.*

Nightlife & the Arts

Opera in Parma is taken just as seriously as in Milan, although tickets are a little easier to come by. Performances are staged at the landmark **Teatro Regio** (✉ Via Garibaldi 16 ☎ 0521/039399 🌐 www.teatroregioparma.org). The main opera season is December–May, and the Verdi festival is May–mid-June.

Modena

❹ *56 km (35 mi) southeast of Parma, 38 km (23 mi) northwest of Bologna.*

The area around Modena has gained recognition for three very contemporary names: the opera star Luciano Pavarotti comes from here, and so do the high-performance cars Maserati and Ferrari (sorry no public tours available). With apologies to the tenor and the Testarossa, however, it's Modena's syrupy balsamic vinegar, aged for up to 40 years, that may still be its greatest achievement. The town has become another Emilian food mecca, with delicious home cooking at every turn. Extensive modern industrial sprawl encircles the center; although the old quarter is small, it is filled with narrow medieval streets, pleasant piazzas, and typical Emilian architecture.

> ### WORD OF MOUTH
>
> "There are many permutations of artisanal balsamic vinegar without the *tradizionale* stamp that are less costly. Pricewise you will do much better in Modena or in Reggio Emilia, the two centers of production. For the best prices, pay a visit to the main markets in either city."
> –ekscrunchy

The 12th-century **Duomo,** also known as the Basilica Metropolitana, is a fine example of Romanesque architecture. The exterior is decorated with medieval sculptures depicting scenes from the life of San Geminiano, the city's patron saint, and fantastic beasts, as well as a realistic-looking scene of the sacking of a city by barbarian hordes—a reminder to the faithful to be ever vigilant in defense of the church. The bell tower is made of white marble and is known as **La Ghirlandina** (The Little Garland) because of its distinctive weather vane. The somber church interior is divided by an elaborate gallery carved with scenes of the Passion of Christ. The carvings took 50 years to complete and are by an anonymous Modenese master of the 12th century. The tomb of San Geminiano is in the crypt. ✉ *Piazza Grande* ☎ *059/216078* 🌐 *www.duomodimodena.it* ⊘ *Daily 7–12:30 and 3:30–7.*

7

Modena's principal museum is housed in the **Palazzo dei Musei,** a short walk from the Duomo. The collection was assembled in the mid-17th century by Francesco d'Este (1610–58), Duke of Modena, and the **Galleria Estense** is named in his honor. The gallery also houses the duke's **Biblioteca Estense,** a huge collection of illuminated books, of which the best known is the beautifully illustrated 15th-century *Bible of Borso d'Este.* A map dated 1501 was one of the first in the world to show Columbus's discovery of America. To get here, follow Via Emilia, the old Roman road that runs through the heart of the town, to Via di Sant'Agostino. ☒ *Piazza Sant'Agostino 337* ☎ *059/4395711* ⊕ *www.galleriaestense.it* ☒ *€4* ⊙ *Tues.–Sun. 8:30–7:30; last entrance at 7.*

At the **Consorzio Produttori Aceto Balsamico Tradizionale di Modena** you can do a tasting, have a tour of the small facility with the friendly staff, and, of course, buy their famous balsamic vinegar. ☒ *Strada Vaciglio Sud 1085/1* ☎ *059/395633* ⊕ *www.balsamico.it* ☒ *Free* ⊙ *By appointment.*

Where to Stay & Eat

$$$$ ✕ **Hosteria Giusti.** The ancient stone walls here are shared with what is reputedly the world's oldest deli, the Salumeria Giusti, founded in 1605. There are only four tables and a host of antique furnishings in the tiny room, where the kitchen turns out dishes like your Italian grandmother might have cooked—handmade tagliolini, *gnocco fritto* (fried dough) with salumi from next door, and items using Modena's famous balsamic vinegar. Reserve well ahead; it's an unforgettable Modena experience. ☒ *Vicolo Squallore 46* ☎ *059/222533* ⊕ *www.giusti1605.com* ⌂ *Reservations essential* ☐ *AE, DC, MC, V* ⊙ *Closed Sun. and Mon., Dec., and Aug. No dinner.*

$–$$ ✕ **Da Enzo.** This big, cheerful, well-patronized trattoria is in the old town's pedestrian zone, a few steps from Piazza Mazzini. All the classic Modenese specialties are represented, including *zampone* (bladder) and *cotechino* (creamy pork sausage). For starters, try the *tortelloni di ricotta e spinaci* (large tortellini stuffed with ricotta and spinach). Reserve ahead for Friday- and Saturday-night dining. ☒ *Via Coltellini 17* ☎ *059/225177* ☐ *AE, DC, MC, V* ⊙ *Closed Mon. and Aug. No dinner Sun.*

$$$ ⊞ **Canalgrande.** Once a ducal palace, the Canalgrande today has large, airy rooms appointed with ornate dark-wood and upholstered pieces. The garden has a fountain in back and breakfast is served on a pretty terrace there in summer. The hotel's restaurant, La Secchia Rapita ($$, closed August), gets rave reviews. ☒ *Corso Canalgrande 6, 41100* ☎ *059/217160* ☐*059/221674* ⊕*www.canalgrandehotel.it* ⌐*75 rooms, 3 suites* ⌂*Restaurant, in-room safes, minibars, bar* ☐ *AE, DC, MC, V* ⊙⊩ *BP.*

$–$$ ⊞ **Hotel Centrale.** The name says it all: this old-school hotel couldn't be more central, right around the corner from Piazza Grande. Rooms are basic and functional, with the classic feel of an Italian building whose layers of renovation don't quite cover up its aging design. The beige lobby is spiced up with cheery checkered floors. ☒ *Via Rismondo 55, 41100* ☎ *059/218808* ☐ *059/238201* ⊕ *www.hotelcentrale.com* ⌐ *40 rooms, 36 with bath* ⌂ *In-room safes, cable TV, bar, laundry service, parking (fee)* ☐ *AE, DC, MC, V* ⊩ *BP* ⊙ *Closed 3 wks in Aug.*

4 towns, dozens of foods, and a mouthful of flavors you'll never forget

Imagine biting into the silkiest prosciutto in the world or the most delectable homemade tortellini you've ever tasted. In Emilia, Italy's most acclaimed food region, you'll discover simple tastes that exceed all expectations. Beginning in Parma and moving eastward to Bologna, you'll find the epicenters of such world-renowned culinary treats as *prosciutto crudo*, Parmigiano-Reggiano, *aceto balsamico*, and tortellini. The secret to this region is not the discovery of new and exotic delicacies, but rather the rediscovery of foods you thought you already knew—in much better versions than you've ever tasted before.

TASTE 1 | PROSCIUTTO CRUDO

Quality testing

From Piacenza to the Adriatic, ham is the king of meats in Emilia-Romagna, but nowhere is this truer than in **Parma**.

Parma is the world's capital of *prosciutto crudo*, raw cured ham (*crudo* for short). Ask for *crudo di Parma* to signal its local provenance; many other regions also make their own crudo.

CRUDO LANGUAGE

It's easy to get confused with the terminology. Crudo is the product that Americans simply call "prosciutto" or the Brits might call "Parma ham." *Prosciutto* in Italian, however, is a more general term that means any kind of ham, including *prosciutto cotto*, or simply *cotto*, which means "cooked ham." Cotto is an excellent product and frequent pizza topping that's closer to (but much better than) what Americans would put in a deli sandwich.

Greasing the ham

Crudo is traditionally eaten in one of three ways: in a dry sandwich (*panino*); by itself as an appetizer, often with shaved butter on top; or as part of an appetizer or snack platter of assorted *salumi* (cured meats).

WHAT TO LOOK FOR

For the best crudo di Parma, look for slices, always cut to order, that are razor thin and have a light, rosy red color (not dark red). Don't be shy about going into a simple *salumeria* (a purveyor of cured meats) and ordering crudo by the pound. You can enjoy it straight out of the package on a park bench—and why not?

Fire branding

BEST SPOT FOR A SAMPLE

You can't go wrong with any of Parma's famed salumerie, but **Salumeria Garibaldi** (Via Farini 9) is one of the town's oldest and most reliable. You'll find not only spectacular prosciutto crudo, but also delectable cheeses, wines, porcini mushrooms, and more.

Quality trademark

LEARN MORE

For more information on crudo di Parma, contact the **Consorzio del Prosciutto di Parma** (Via Marco dell'Arpa 8/b, 0521/243987, www.prosciuttodiparma.com/eng).

Prosciutto di Parma

TASTE 2 PARMIGIANO-REGGIANO

Warming milk in copper cauldrons

From Parma, it's only a half-hour trip east to **Reggio Emilia**, the birthplace of the crumbly and renowned Parmigiano-Reggiano cheese. Reggio (not to be confused with Reggio di Calabria in the south) is a cute and characteristic little Emilian town that has been the center of production for this legendary cheese for more than 70 years.

SAY CHEESE

Grana is the generic Italian term for hard, aged, full-flavored cheese that can be grated. Certain varieties of Pecorino Romano, for example, or Grana Padano, also fall under this term, but Parmigiano-Reggiano is the foremost example.

Breaking up the curds

NOT JUST FOR GRATING

In Italy, Parmigiano-Reggiano is not only grated onto pasta, but also often served by itself in chunks, either as an appetizer—perhaps accompanied by local salumi (cured meats)—or even for dessert, when it might be drizzled with honey or Modena's balsamic vinegar.

MEET THE MAKERS

If you're a cheese enthusiast, you shouldn't miss the chance to take a free two-hour guided tour of a Parmigiano-Reggiano–producing farm. You'll witness the entire process and get to meet the cheesemakers. Tours can be arranged by contacting the **Consorzio del Formaggio Parmigiano-Reggiano** in Reggio Emilia (0522/506160, sezionere@parmigiano-reggiano.it, www.parmigiano-reggiano.it) at least 20 days in advance. (Ask specifically for an English-language tour if that's what you want.)

Placing cheese in molds

BEST SPOT FOR A SAMPLE

The production of Parmigiano-Reggiano is heavily controlled by the Consorzio del Formaggio, so you can buy the cheese at any store or supermarket in the region and be virtually guaranteed equal quality and price. For a more distinctive shopping experience, however, try buying Parmigiano-Reggiano at the street market on Reggio's central square. The market takes place on Tuesday and Friday from 8 AM to 1 PM year-round.

Aging cheese wheels

Parmigiano-Reggiano

EMILIA: ONE TASTE AT A TIME

7

TASTE 3 | ACETO BALSAMICO DI MODENA

Tasting tradizionale vinegar

Modena is home to *Aceto Balsamico Tradizionale di Modena*, a species of balsamic vinegar unparalleled anywhere else on Earth. The balsamic vinegar you've probably tried—even the pricier versions sold at specialty stores—may be good on salads, but it bears only a fleeting resemblance to the real thing.

HOW IS IT MADE?

The *tradizionale* vinegar that passes strict government standards is made with Trebbiano grape must, which is cooked over an open fire, reduced, and fermented from 12 to 25 or more years in a series of specially made wooden casks. As the vinegar becomes more concentrated, so much liquid evaporates that it takes more than 6 gallons of must to produce one quart of vinegar 12 years later. The result is an intense and syrupy concoction best enjoyed sparingly on grilled meats, strawberries, or Parmigiano Reggiano cheese. The vinegar has such a complexity of flavor that some even drink it as an after-dinner liqueur.

Wooden casks for fermenting

BEST SPOT FOR A SAMPLE

The **Consorzio Produttori Aceto Balsamico Tradizionale di Modena** (Corso Cavour 60, 059/236981, www.balsamico.it) offers tours and tastings by reservation only. The main objective of the consortium is to monitor the quality of the authentic balsamic vinegar, made by only a few licensed restaurants and small producers.

The consortium also limits production, keeping prices sky high. Expect to pay €50 for a 100-ml (3.4 oz) bottle of tradizionale, which is generally aged 12 to 15 years, or €80 and up for the older tradizionale extra vecchio variety, which is aged 25 years.

OTHER TASTES OF EMILIA

❏ **Cotechino:** a sausage made from pork and lard, a specialty of Modena

❏ **Culatello de Zibello:** raw cured ham produced along the banks of the Po River, and cured and aged for more than 11 months

❏ **Mortadella:** soft, smoked sausage made with beef, pork, cubes of pork fat, and seasonings

❏ **Ragù:** a sauce made from minced pork and beef, simmered in milk, onions, carrots, and tomatoes

❏ **Salama da sugo:** salty, oily sausage aged and then cooked, a specialty of Ferrara

❏ **Tortelli and cappellacci:** pasta pillows with the same basic form as tortellini, but stuffed with cheese and vegetables

WHERE TO EAT

In Modena, it's hard to find a bad meal. Local trattorie do great versions of tortellini and other stuffed pasta. If you can find *zampone* (a sausage made from stuffed pig's trotter), don't miss it—it's an adventurous Modena specialty. **Hosteria Giusti** (Vicolo Squallore 46, 059/222533, www.giusti1605.com) is a particularly good place to try local specialties; the adjacent **Salumeria Giusti** is reputedly the world's oldest deli, founded in 1605.

TASTE 4 | TORTELLINI

Making the dough

The venerable city of **Bologna** is called "the Fat" for a reason: this is the birthplace of tortellini, not to mention other specialties such as mortadella and ragù. Despite the city's new reputation for chic nightclubs and flashy boutiques, much of the food remains as it ever was.

You'll find the many Emilian variations on stuffed pasta all over the region, but they're perhaps at their best in Bologna, especially the native tortellini.

INSPIRED BY THE GODS

According to one legend, tortellini was inspired by the bellybutton of Venus, goddess of love. As the story goes, Venus and some other gods stopped at a local inn for the night. A nosy chef went to their room to catch a glimpse of Venus. Peering through the keyhole, he saw her lying only partially covered on the bed. He was so inspired after seeing her perfect navel that he created a stuffed pasta, tortellini, in its image.

Stretching the dough

ON THE MENU

Tortellini is usually filled with beef (sometimes cheese), and is served two ways: *asciutta* is "dry," meaning it is served with a sauce such as ragù, or perhaps just with butter and Parmigiano. *Tortellini in brodo* is immersed in a lovely, savory beef broth.

Adding the filling

BEST SPOT FOR A SAMPLE

Don't miss **Tamburini** (Via Drapperie 1, 051/234726), Bologna's best specialty food shop, where smells of Emilia-Romagna's famous spoils waft out through the room and into the streets.

Shaping each piece

WHERE TO EAT

The classic art deco restaurant **Rosteria Luciano** (Via Nazario Sauro 19, 051/231249, www.rosterialuciano.it) is a great place to try tortellini in brodo, one of the best choices on their fixed menu. A changing list of daily specials augments the menu. For a meat course it's usually best to order whatever special the kitchen has that day. The selection of local cheeses is also good. Please note that the restaurant is closed on Wednesday, the whole month of August, and Sunday from June through September.

Tortellini di Bologna

BOLOGNA

The centuries of wars, sackings, rebellions, and bombings that left such dramatic evidence in other cities of Emilia-Romagna have not taken their toll on Bologna's old city center. Narrow, cobblestone streets remain intact, as do the ancient churches, massive palaces, and medieval towers. Arcades line many of the main thoroughfares, shading the walkways to such an extent that you can stroll around town in a rainstorm for hours without feeling a drop.

Through its long history, first as an Etruscan city then a Roman one, then as an independent city-state in the Middle Ages, and ultimately as an epicenter of industry—manufacturing goods from silk to motorcycles—Bologna has always played a significant role in the north of Italy. Over the centuries the city has acquired a number of nicknames: Bologna the Learned, in honor of its venerable university, the oldest in the world; Bologna the Red, for its rosy rooftops and communist leanings; Bologna the Turreted, recalling the forest of medieval towers that once rose from the city center (two remarkable examples survive); and Bologna the Fat, a tribute to its preeminent position in the world of cuisine, the birthplace of mortadella, tortellini, and ragù.

Today one might also be tempted to dub it Bologna the Hip, for its position at the cutting edge of Italian culture. Recent years have brought an explosion of trendy *newyorkese* bars and lounges with postmodern music and Germanic track lighting, American brunches and California construction cuisine, and pricey boutiques in primary colors. The result is a jarring juxtaposition of leaning medieval towers and towering modernist fashion billboards. Unfortunately, the influx of people and industry that has accompanied these changes has also brought air and noise pollution, a further distraction from the city's architectural and culinary gems.

Although foreign tourists have lately begun to discover Bologna's special charm and arrive (along with Italians) in increasing numbers, the city's urban vitality still comes in large part from its student population. The university was founded in about the year 1088, and by the 13th century already had more than 10,000 students. It was a center for the teaching of law and theology, and it was ahead of its time in that many of the professors were women. Guglielmo Marconi, the inventor of the wireless telegraph, first formulated his groundbreaking theories in the physics labs of the university. Today the university has prominent business and medical faculties.

Exploring Bologna

Piazza Maggiore and the adjacent Piazza del Nettuno make up the core of the city. Arranged around these two squares are the imposing Basilica di San Petronio, the massive Palazzo Comunale, the Palazzo del Podestà, the Palazzo di Re Enzo, and the Fontana del Nettuno—one of the most visually harmonious groupings of public buildings in the entire country. From here, sights that aren't on one of the piazzas are but a short walk away, along delightful narrow cobbled streets or under the

Basilica di
San Petronio . . .**5**

Le Due Torri . . .**9**

Museo
Internazionale
della
Musica **12**

Palazzo
Comunale **6**

Palazzo del
Podestà **7**

Palazzo
Re Enzo **8**

Pinacoteca
Nazionale **14**

San
Domenico **10**

Santo
Stefano **11**

Università di
Bologna **13**

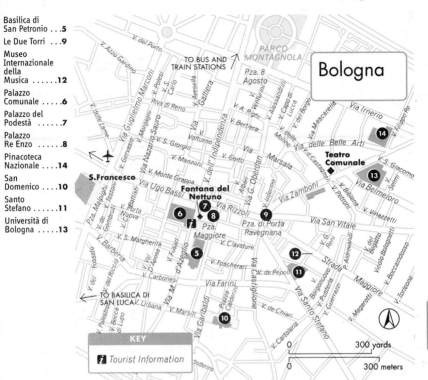

Bologna

KEY

i *Tourist Information*

0 — 300 yards

0 — 300 meters

ubiquitous arcades that double as municipal umbrellas. Take at least a full day to explore Bologna; it's compact and lends itself to easy exploration, but there is plenty to see.

The Main Attractions

⑤ Basilica di San Petronio. Construction on this cathedral began in the 14th century, and work was still in progress on this vast building some 300 years later. It's not finished yet, as you can see: the wings of the transept are missing and the facade is only partially decorated, lacking most of the marble face the architects had intended. The main doorway was carved by the great Sienese master of the Renaissance, Jacopo della Quercia. Above the center of the door is a Madonna and Child flanked by Saints Ambrose and Petronius, the city's patrons.

The interior of the basilica is huge: the Bolognans had planned an even bigger church—you can still see the columns erected to support the larger church outside the east end—but had to tone down construction when the university seat was established next door in 1561. The **Museo di San Petronio** contains models showing how the church was originally intended to look. The most important artworks in the church are in the left aisle, frescoes by Giovanni di Modena dating from the first years of the 1400s. ✉ *Piazza Maggiore* ☎ *051/225442* ✑ *Free* ☾ *Church*

Apr.–Sept., daily 7:30–1:15 and 2:30–6; Oct.–Mar., daily 7:30–1 and 2:30–6. Museum Mon.–Sat. 9:30–12:30 and 2:30–5:30, Sun. 2:30–5:30.

Fontana del Nettuno. Sculptor Giambologna's elaborate 1566 baroque monument to Neptune occupying Piazza Nettuno has been aptly nicknamed *Il Gigante* (The Giant). Its exuberantly sensual mermaids and undraped God of the Sea drew fire when it was constructed, but not enough, apparently, to dissuade the populace from using the fountain as a public washing stall for centuries. It's also known for another reason: walk behind Neptune and to his right for an infamously lewd angle on the statue. ⊠ *Piazza Nettuno, next to the Palazzo Re Enzo, Piazza Maggiore area.*

★ ❾ **Le Due Torri.** Two landmark towers, mentioned by Dante in *The Inferno*, stand side by side in the compact Piazza di Porta Ravegnana. Every family of importance had a tower as a symbol of prestige and power, and as a potential fortress; only 60 remain out of more than 200 that once presided over the city. **Torre Garisenda** (from the late 11th century), tilting 10 feet, was shortened to 165 feet for safety in the 1300s and is now closed to visitors. **Torre degli Asinelli** (circa 1109) is 320 feet tall. It leans an alarming 7½ feet off perpendicular. If you're up to a serious physical challenge—and you're not claustrophobic—you may want to climb the 500 narrow, wooden steps to get to the view over Bologna. ⊠ *Piazza di Porta Ravegnana, east of Piazza Maggiore* 🎫 €3 ⊙ *Torre degli Asinelli Apr.–Sept., daily 9–6; Oct.–Mar., daily 9–5.*

☺ ⓫ **Santo Stefano.** This splendid and unusual basilica actually contains between
Fodor'sChoice four and seven connected churches (authorities differ). Originally on this
★ site there was a 4th-century pagan temple to Iside, but the oldest remaining component is **Santi Vitale e Agricola,** which dates from the 8th century. It contains a 14th-century nativity scene much loved by Bologna's children, who come at Christmastime to pay their respects to the baby Jesus. Within the church of **San Sepolcro** (12th century) is the **Cortile di Pilato** (Courtyard of Pilate), named for the basin in its center said to be where Pontius Pilate washed his hands after condemning Christ. Also in the building is a **museum** displaying various medieval religious works and with a shop where you can buy sundry items such as honey, shampoo, and jam made by the monks. ⊠ *Via Santo Stefano 24, Piazza Santo Stefano, University area* ☎ *051/223256* 🎫 *Free* ⊙ *Daily 9–noon and 3:30–6.*

⓭ **Università di Bologna.** Take a stroll through the streets of the university area, a jumble of buildings, some dating as far back as the 15th century and most to the 17th and 18th. The neighborhood, as befits a college town, is full of bookshops, coffee bars, and cheap restaurants. None of them are particularly distinguished, but they're all characteristic of student life in the city. Try eating at the *mensa universitaria* (cafeteria) if you want to strike up a conversation with local students (most speak English). Political slogans and sentiments are scrawled on walls all around the university and tend to be ferociously leftist. Among the **university museums,** the most interesting are the **Musei di Palazzo Poggi,** which display scientific instruments and paleontological, botanical, and university-related artifacts. ⊠ *Via Zamboni 33, University area* ☎ *051/2099360* ⊕ *www.museopalazzopoggi.unibo.it* 🎫 *Free* ⊙ *Weekdays 10–1 and 2–4.*

Also Worth Seeing

⑫ Museo Internazionale della Musica. The music museum in the spectacular old Palazzo Aldini Sanguinetti, with its 17th- and 18th-century frescoes, offers among its exhibits a 1606 harpsichord and a collection of beautiful musical manuscripts going back to the 1500s. ⊠ *Strada Maggiore 34, University area* ☎ *051/2757711* ⊕ *www.museomusicabologna. it* 🖃 *€4* ⊙ *Jan.–May, Tues.–Sun. 10–5; June–July 14 and Sept. 16–Dec., Tues.–Thurs. 10–1:30, Fri.–Sun. 10–5.*

❻ Palazzo Comunale. A mélange of building styles and constant modifications characterize this huge palace dating from the 13th to 15th century. When Bologna was an independent city-state, this was the seat of government, a function it still serves today. Over the door is a statue of Bologna-born Pope Gregory XIII, most famous for reorganizing the calendar. There are good views from the upper stories of the palace. The first-floor **Sala Rossa** (Red Room) is open on advance request and during some exhibitions, while the **Sala del Consiglio Comunale** (City Council Hall) is open to the public during short hours in the late morning.

Within the palazzo there are also two museums. The **Collezioni Comunali d'Arte** exhibits paintings from the Middle Ages as well as some Renaissance works by Luca Signorelli (circa 1445–1523) and Tintoretto. The **Museo Morandi** is dedicated to the 20th-century still-life artist Giorgio Morandi; in addition to his paintings, there's a re-creation of his studio and living space. Underground caves and the foundations of the old cathedral can be visited by appointment made through the tourist office. ⊠ *Piazza Maggiore 6* ☎ *051/203111 Palazzo, 051/203526 Collezioni, 051/203332 Museo* ⊕ *www.museomorandi.it* 🖃 *Palace free, each museum €4, combined ticket €6* ⊙ *Sala del Consiglio Comunale Tues.–Sat. 10–1; Collezioni Tues.–Fri. 9–3, weekends 10–6:30; Museo Tues.–Fri. 9–3, weekends 10–6:30.*

The **Biblioteca Sala Borsa,** connected to the Palazzo Comunale, has an impressive interior courtyard surrounded by the library. ⊠ *Entrance from Piazza Nettuno, Piazza Maggiore area* ☎ *051/204400* ⊕ *www. bibliotecasalaborsa.it* 🖃 *Free* ⊙ *Mon. 2:30–8, Tues.–Fri. 10–8, Sat. 10–7.*

❼ Palazzo del Podestà. This classic Renaissance palace facing the Basilica di San Petronio was erected in 1484, and attached to it is the soaring **Torre dell'Arengo.** The bells in the tower have rung whenever the city has celebrated, mourned, or called its citizens to arms since 1453. ⊠ *Piazza Nettuno, Piazza Maggiore area* ☎ *051/224500* ⊙ *During exhibitions only.*

❽ Palazzo Re Enzo. King Enzo of Sardinia was imprisoned in this 13th-century medieval palace for 23 years, until his death in 1272. He had waged war on Bologna and was captured after the fierce battle of Fossalta in 1249. The palace has other macabre associations: common criminals received the last rites of the Church in the tiny courtyard chapel before being executed in Piazza Maggiore. The courtyard is worth peeking into, but the palace merely houses government offices. ⊠ *Piazza Re Enzo, Piazza Maggiore area* ☎ *051/224500* ⊙ *During exhibitions only.*

⑭ Pinacoteca Nazionale. Bologna's principal art gallery contains many works by the immortals of Italian painting, including the famous *Ecstasy of St. Cecilia* by Raphael. There's also a beautiful multipanel painting by Giotto, as well as *Madonna and Saints* by Parmigianino. ☒ *Via delle Belle Arti 56, University area* ☎ *051/4209411* ⊕ *www. pinacotecabologna.it* ☑ €4 ☉ *Tues.–Sun. 9–7.*

⑩ San Domenico. The tomb of St. Dominic, who died here in 1221, is called the **Arca di San Domenico** and is found in this church in the sixth chapel on the right. Many artists participated in its decoration, notably Niccolò di Bari, who was so proud of his contribution that he changed his name to Niccolò dell'Arca to recall this famous work. The young Michelangelo carved the angel on the right. In the right transept of the church is a tablet marking the last resting place of the hapless King Enzo, the Sardinian ruler imprisoned in the Palazzo Re Enzo. The attached **museum** displays religious relics and art. ☒ *Piazza San Domenico 13, off Via Garibaldi, south of Piazza Maggiore* ☎ *051/6400411* ☉ *Church daily 7:30–1 and 3:30–7:30; museum weekdays 10–noon and 3:30–6, Sat. 9:30–noon and 3:30–5:30, Sun. 3:30–5:30.*

Bologna walking tours. English-language "Discover Bologna" walking tours (€13) run by the tourist office in Piazza Maggiore depart at 10:30 AM Wednesday, Saturday, and Sunday. Tours by affiliated organizations also depart the office Monday and Friday at 11 AM and Tuesday, Thursday, and Saturday at 3 PM, also at a cost of €13 per person; bike tours cost €18 and leave Wednesday at 10 AM. ☒ *Tourist office, Piazza Maggiore 1* ☎ *051/246541* ⊕ *www.guidebologna.com.*

Off the Beaten Path

Basilica di San Luca. A spectacular one-hour walk (or 10-minute drive) leads uphill from Porta Saragozza to the Basilica di San Luca (follow Via Saragozza), an impressive church that's perched dramatically atop Monte della Guardia since 1160. The road is arcaded the entire way; you walk beneath 666 arches before arriving at the round basilica, which has a famous Madonna icon. But it's the sweeping views of the Emilian countryside and city from the 990-foot altitude that make the trip worthwhile—most of all in autumn, when the leaves of the hills on one side play off the blazing red rooftops of Bologna on the other. If you go by car (or, better yet, scooter), it's possible to ask for directions at the church and take an unmarked route back through the hills, winding past rustic Emilian restaurants before reentering the city center through Porta San Mammolo. ☒ *Via Saragozza, 3½ km (2 mi) southwest of Bologna* ☎ *051/6142339* ☉ *Oct.–Feb., Mon.–Sat. 7–12:30 and 2:30–5, Sun. 7–5; Mar., Mon.–Sat. 7–12:30 and 2:30–6, Sun. 7–6; Apr.–Sept., 7–12:30 and 2:30–7, Sun. 7–7.*

Museo del Patrimonio Industriale. Offering a refreshing change from all the art museums, this museum's displays document the development of Bologna's industries and industrial technologies from the 16th to 21st century, including fascinating examples of antique machinery, scientific devices, and cars. ☒ *Via della Beverara 123, Northwest of the city center* ☎ *051/6356611* ⊕ *www.comune.bologna.it/patrimonioindustriale* ☑ €4 ☉ *Jan.–Mar., Tues.–Thurs. 9–1, Fri. and Sat. 9–1 and 3–6, Sun.*

3–6; Apr., May, and Oct.–Dec., Tues.–Fri. 9–1, Sat. 9–1 and 3–6, Sun.
3–6; June–Sept., weekdays 9–1.

Where to Stay & Eat

$$$$ ✕**Al Pappagallo.** The well-known restaurant steps from Le Due Torri has
hosted just about everyone, including Alfred Hitchcock. Its long and storied past, which goes back to 1919, is documented in the many black-
and-white photos that line the tall, white walls. Al Pappagallo is formal
and expensive, but this is a classic Bologna experience. Menu options might
include the region's famed culatello di Zibello wonderfully paired with a
Parmesan mousse and tomato *mostarda* (like a chutney), a filled pasta in
an impossibly rich sauce of foie gras and cheese, or an interesting plate
of deep-fried meats and fruits. ⊠ *Piazza della Mercanzia 3/c, Piazza Maggiore area* ☎ *051/231200* ⊕ *www.alpappagallo.it* ⌂ *Reservations essential* ▭ *AE, DC, MC, V* ⊗ *Closed Sun. and Aug., and Sat. June–July.*

$$–$$$ ✕**Da Cesari.** It's the creative menu options—such as delicate squash gnoc-
chi, or a slowly braised veal cheek—that make Da Cesari truly memorable. Area standards such as veal cutlet Bolognese (with ham and
melted cheese) are also reasonably priced and well executed. Accompany your meal with wine made by the owner's brother: Cesari's Liano
is excellent. The gentle romantic buzz in the dining room is warm and
welcoming; the restaurant is in the very heart of the *centro storico* (historic center). ⊠ *Via de' Carbonesi 8, south of Piazza Maggiore* ☎ *051/
237710* ⌂ *Reservations essential* ▭ *AE, DC, MC, V* ⊗ *Closed Sun.,
Aug., and Jan. 1–7.*

★ **$$–$$$** ✕**Drogheria della Rosa.** This is not just a romantic little place to escape
from the city bustle; it's a complete experience. In the atmospheric wine
cellar below the restaurant, you can select from a large, uniformly excellent selection. If you want to try an old Barolo or Amarone, this is
the place to do it—but tell the staff a few hours beforehand so they can
let the wine breathe and prepare a meal to match. No matter what, you'll
eat fabulously here; chef Emanuele Addone, who's a real character, focuses above all on beautifully simple local ingredients in season; he might
prepare pasta with black truffle, or filet mignon with balsamic vinegar.
⊠ *Via Cartoleria 10, University area* ☎ *051/222529* ⊕ *www.
drogheriadellarosa.it* ▭ *AE, DC, MC, V* ⊗ *Closed Sun. No lunch.*

$$–$$$ ✕**Godot Wine Bar.** The buzzing, modern, bi-level Godot (open until 2
AM, full dinner menu until midnight) is equally popular with students
as with wine aficionados. This is the new face of Bologna. The extraordinary wine list is so diverse that you might be able to have, say, a scarce
Pugliese bottle that is impossible to find in Puglia. Although the food
may be the side attraction here, the basics are solid: they make a mean
tagliatelle *al ragù* (with a slow-cooked, tomato-based meat sauce), for
instance. ⊠ *Via Cartoleria 12, University area* ☎ *051/226315* ⊕ *www.
godotwine.it* ▭ *AE, MC, V* ⊗ *Closed Sun. and 3 wks in Aug.*

$$–$$$ ✕**Scacco Matto.** This extremely popular yet intimate and dimly lit restau-
rant specializes in food from Lucania (the traditional name for the
Basilicata region). That might mean *soppressata lucana* (a sausage from
Basilicata); *cavatelli* (small, thick homemade pasta twists) with tomato

7

and meatballs; or lamb with a wine sauce made from Aglianico, the typical grape from that region. ☒ *Via Broccaindosso 63/b, University area* ☎ *051/263404* ▭ *AE, DC, MC, V* ⊘ *Closed July 20–Sept. 1. No lunch Mon.*

$–$$ ✕ **Da Bertino.** Happy diners don't seem to mind the close quarters in the large, bustling space here. Maybe it's because of the low prices, or maybe it's because popularity hasn't spoiled this traditional neighborhood trattoria and its simple home-style dishes. Highlights are the homemade *paglia e fieno* (yellow and green, plain and spinach, pasta) with sausage and the choices on the steaming tray of *bollito misto* (boiled meats). Ask to be seated in the back, rather than the less-attractive room up front. ☒ *Via delle Lame 55, Porta San Felice* ☎ *051/522230* ▭ *AE, DC, MC, V* ⊘ *Closed Sun. and Aug. 5–Sept. 4. No dinner Sat. in July. No dinner Mon. Aug.–June.*

$ ✕ **Victoria.** It's not unusual for this unpretentious and charming trattoria-pizzeria off Via dell'Indipendenza to have lines, so reserve ahead. Locals come for the cheap pizzas, which are indisputably the highlight (*mozzarella di bufala*, buffalo mozzarella, is an excellent topping choice). Pastas and salads are less impressive. The back room has a lovely 17th-century painted wooden ceiling. ☒ *Via Augusto Righi 9/c, north of Piazza Maggiore* ☎ *051/233548* ▭ *AE, DC, MC, V* ⊘ *Closed Thurs.*

¢ ✕ **Cantina Bentivoglio.** This two-floor wine-jazz extravaganza is a classic place to relax by night. The ground floor is a dim, bottle-clad wine cellar; the cavernlike basement downstairs has live jazz. The extraordinarily reasonable wine list includes labels from many of Italy's lesser-known regions, and the menu lists pastas, meats, and interesting salads and lighter plates, such as *crostini* (toasted bread) with mozzarella, eggplant, tomato, and roasted peppers. Vegetarian options are plentiful. Doors stay open until 2 AM, and wine is also available to go. ☒ *Via Mascarella 4, University area* ☎ *051/265416* ⊕ *www.cantinabentivoglio.it* ▭ *AE, DC, MC, V* ⊘ *Closed Sun. Oct.–May. No lunch Sat.*

¢ ✕ **La Scuderia.** A bit of New York chic comes to Bologna via the cutting-edge café–wine bar–performance space in a stunning vaulted ballroom of an old palazzo. Next door to the university, La Scuderia serves as an informal meeting place for hip students and intellectuals. Salads, desserts, lunches, wines by the glass, and American-style Sunday brunch are options. You can just as easily drink coffee over a newspaper at breakfast as flirt over a piña colada in the evening. Many nights there's live jazz. ☒ *Piazza G. Verdi 2, off Via Zamboni, University area* ☎ *051/6569619* ▭ *AE, DC, MC, V* ⊘ *Closed Mon.*

¢ ✕ **Tamburini.** Smells of all that is good about Bolognese food waft through the room and out into the streets. Breads, numerous cheeses, salumi such as Parma and Bologna hams and prosciuttos, roasted peppers, inventive salads, balsamic vinegars, local olive oils, smoked salmon, and fresh pasta are among the delights. This upscale deli–cum–self-service buffet is *the* lunch spot. Tamburini also vacuum-packed foods for shipping or air travel. ☒ *Via Drapperie 1, Piazza Maggiore area* ☎ *051/234726* ▭ *AE, MC, V* ⊘ *No dinner.*

★ $$$$ ▦ **Corona d'Oro 1890.** A medieval printing house in a former life, this hotel is delightful—lyrically art nouveau in its reception and atrium, with enough flowers for a wedding. Guest rooms make opulent use of original 15th- and 16th-century decorations such as painted wood ceilings and Gothic-vault windows. The morning English breakfast buffet is worth getting up for. ⊠ *Via Oberdan 12, north of Piazza Maggiore, 40126* ☎ *051/7457611* 🖷 *051/7457622* ⊕ *www.bolognarthotels.it/corona* ⏎ *35 rooms* �'& *In-room safes, minibars, cable TV, in-room broadband, bicycles, bar, Internet room, meeting room, parking (fee), some pets allowed* ⊟ *AE, DC, MC, V* ☉ *Closed 1st 3 wks in Aug.* ⏏⏐ *BP.*

★ **$$$$** ⊡ **Grand Hotel Baglioni.** Sixteenth-century paintings and frescoes by the Bolognese Carracci brothers are rarely seen outside a museum or church, but in this 15th-century palazzo they provide the stunning backdrop for the public rooms and restaurant of one of Italy's most glamorous—and pricey—hotels. Lady Di slept here, and you may feel no less royal in a handsome room with antique furniture and brocaded walls. The highly regarded I Carracci restaurant serves top-notch food in regal, formal surroundings. ⊠ *Via dell'Indipendenza 8, north of Piazza Maggiore, 40121* ☎ *051/225445* 🖷 *051/234840* ⊕ *www.baglionihotels.com* ⏎ *116 rooms, 11 suites* ⚐ *Restaurant, some in-room faxes, in-room safes, minibars, cable TV, in-room data ports, Wi-Fi, bar, babysitting, laundry service, business services, meeting room, parking (fee)* ⊟ *AE, DC, MC, V* ⏏⏐ *BP.*

$$$–$$$$ ⊡ **Art Hotel Commercianti.** Rooms here were designed to retain the structural integrity of the 11th-century palace and tower the hotel occupies, and are therefore cozy and unique, with original wood beams built into the walls. Tower rooms and suites have balconies with magnificent views of San Domenico church; all are stylishly furnished with, among other things, Carrara marble desks custom-built following a 15th-century design. ⊠ *Via De' Pignattari 11, south of Piazza Maggiore, 40124* ☎ *051/7457511* 🖷 *051/7457522* ⊕ *www.bolognarthotels.it/commercianti* ⏎ *33 rooms, 2 suites* ⚐ *Dining room, in-room safes, minibars, in-room broadband, bicycles, bar, Internet room, parking (fee)* ⊟ *AE, DC, MC, V* ⏏⏐ *BP.*

★ **$$$–$$$$** ⊡ **Art Hotel Novecento.** A design-oriented hotel inspired by 1930s Europe, Novecento is at its core modern, modern, modern. Clean lines and elegant restraint are the hallmarks of the rooms, the lobby, and even the elevators. Breakfast is great, and happy hour comes with free wine and snacks. The hotel is in the middle of everything in downtown Bologna. Call ahead if you need a parking space, and be advised that the garage closes for the night. ⊠ *Piazza Gallilei, Piazza Maggiore area, 40126* ☎ *051/7457311* 🖷 *051/7457322* ⊕ *www.bolognarthotels.it/novecento* ⏎ *25 rooms* ⚐ *Dining room, in-room safes, minibars, in-room broadband, bar, Internet room, parking (fee)* ⊟ *AE, DC, MC, V* ⏏⏐ *BP.*

$$$–$$$$ ⊡ **Art Hotel Orologio.** Although occupying an old palazzo, which was originally a public building, the Orologio achieves a contemporary effect. A mid-level lounge and Internet room is a pleasant place to relax, and top-floor rooms have good views of Bologna's skyline. Under the same ownership as the other Art Hotels and the Corona d'Oro, this hotel is in a quiet pedestrian zone off Piazza Grande—an ideal sightseeing location. Fax ahead or check the Web site for driving directions. ⊠ *Via IV Novembre 10, Piazza Maggiore area, 40123* ☎ *051/7457411* 🖷 *051/7457422* ⊕ *www.bolognarthotels.it/orologio* ⏎ *33 rooms* ⚐ *Dining* *room, in-room safes, minibars, cable TV, in-room broadband, bicycles, Internet room, parking (fee), some pets allowed* ⊟ *AE, DC, MC, V* ⦿ *BP.*

$$ 🖵 **Accademia.** Looking for a mid-range, comfortable base for exploring the area? This small hotel is right in the center of the university quarter. The rooms are adequate, the staff friendly. Look for discounted prices on the Web site. A few more inexpensive rooms have a shared bath. ⊠ *Via delle Belle Arti 6, at Via delle Moline, University area, 40126* ☎ *051/ 232318* 📠 *051/263590* ⊕ *www.hotelaccademia.com* ⇨ *28 rooms, 24 with bath* ⚲ *Minibars, cable TV, bar, parking (fee), some pets allowed* ⊟ *MC, V* ⦿ *BP.*

$ 🖵 **San Vitale.** Modern furnishings and a garden distinguish this modest hostelry, about 1 km (½ mi) east of the center of town. The service is courteous, and rooms are clean and bright. There are private bathrooms, but facilities are very basic. ⊠ *Via San Vitale 94, University area, 40125* ☎ *051/225966* 📠 *051/239396* ⇨ *17 rooms* ⚲ *Internet room, parking (fee)* ⊟ *No credit cards* ⦿ *BP.*

Nightlife & the Arts

The Arts

Bologna's arts scene is one of the liveliest in Italy, reaching out not just to the traditional older crowds of operagoers and ballet fans, but also to younger generations and food lovers with regional festivals.

FESTIVALS   The first weekend in October crowds celebrate the **Festa di San Petronio** with bands, fireworks, and free mortadella sandwiches in Piazza Maggiore. Free movies are shown at the **Open-air Cinema** in the Arena Puccini, at Via Serlio near the train station, June–August. The tourist office has the schedule.

MUSIC & OPERA   The 18th-century **Teatro Comunale** (⊠ Largo Respighi 1, University area ☎ 199/107070 ⊕ www.comunalebologna.it) presents concerts by Italian and international orchestras throughout the year, but is dominated by the highly acclaimed opera performances November–May. Reserve seats well in advance. The ticket office is open Tuesday–Saturday 11–6:30.

Nightlife

As a university town, Bologna has long been known for its hopping nightlife. As early as 1300 it was said to have had 150 taverns. Most of the city's current 200-plus pubs and lounges are frequented by Italian students, young adults, and the international study-abroad crowd, with the university district forming the epicenter. In addition to the university area, the pedestrian-only zone on Via del Pratello, lined with a host of pubs, is also a hopping night scene, as is Via delle Moline, with cutting-edge cafés and bars. A more upmarket, low-key evening experience can be had at one of Bologna's many wine bars that are also restaurants, such as Cantina Bentivoglio and Godot Wine Bar. And then there are the hypertrendy bar-lounges that represent the newest, and most newyorkese, of Bologna's many faces; some of these joints make even Milan look old-school.

With live jazz staged every night (€4 cover), **Cantina Bentivoglio** (⊠ Via Mascarella 4/b, University area ☎ 051/265416) is one of Bologna's most appealing nightspots. You can light meals and nibbles as well. At **Le Stanze** (✉ Via del Borgo di S. Pietro 1, University area ☎ 051/228767) you can sip an *aperitivo* (aperitif) or a late-night drink at a modern bar under 17th-century frescoes in what was the private chapel of the 1576 Palazzo Bentivoglio. The adjoining avant-garde restaurant serves modern Italian fusion cooking. **The Loft** (✉ Via delle Moline 16/d, University area ☎ 320/5610963), one of Bologna's most cutting-edge spaces for drinking and dancing, is in a 15th-century convent. Featuring DJs and wine, the place hops on most nights; on Tuesday there are Latin dance lessons, and Friday and Saturday bring live music.

Balmoral (✉ Via de' Pignattari 1, Piazza Maggiore area ☎ 051/228694), a restaurant right near Piazza Maggiore, has good live music most nights, and a vague Middle Eastern theme. The casually hip **Divinis** (✉ Via Battibecco 4/c, University area ☎ 051/2961502) wine bar has a remarkable, if pricey, selection by the glass (as well as high-end food) served in chichi surroundings until 1:30 AM. A wine bar with romantic ambient lighting and a good draft beer selection, **Contavalli** (✉ Via Belle Arti 2, University area ☎ 051/268395) is a relaxing choice.

The elegant and trendy **Bar Calice** (✉ Via Clavature 13/a, at Via Marchesana, Piazza Maggiore area ☎ 051/264508) runs an indoor-outdoor operation year-round (with heat lamps); it's a cocktail and wine bar that's extremely popular with the see-and-be-seen thirtysomethings. The loud, modern, haywire **Nu Bar Lounge** (✉ Off Buco San Petronio, Via de' Musei 6, Piazza Maggiore area ☎ 051/222532 ⊕ www.nu-lounge. com) hosts a cocktail-sipping crowd.

Shopping

Books

Next to the Due Torri is the best bookstore in the region, **Feltrinelli** (✉ Piazza Ravegnana 1, east of Piazza Maggiore ☎ 051/266891 ⊕ www. lafeltrinelli.it), which capitalizes on the university town setting. Look at **Feltrinelli International** (✉ Via Zamboni 7/b, east of Piazza Maggiore ☎ 051/268070), one of Italy's best selections of English and other foreign-language books, and innumerable travel guides and maps.

Clothing

A host of small clothing and jewelry shops lines Via d'Azeglio in the center of town. For cheaper goods, Via dell'Indipendenza between the station and downtown is often lined with street vendors hawking bargain-basement clothing.

One of the most upscale malls in Italy, the **Galleria Cavour** (✉ Piazza Cavour, south of Piazza Maggiore) houses many of the fashion giants, including Gucci, Versace, and the jeweler and watchmaker Bulgari.

Wine & Food

Bologna is a good place to buy wine. Several shops have a bewilderingly large selection—to go straight to the top, ask the managers which wines were awarded the prestigious *Tre Bicchieri* (Three Glasses) award from Gambero Rosso's wine bible, *Vini d'Italia*.

Cooking alla Bolognese

A HOT TRAVEL TREND in Italy is spending a day at a cooking school to learn local recipes and techniques—and where better to do it than in Bologna the Fat? Barbara Bertuzzi, the author of a cookbook called *Bolognese Cooking Heritage*, teaches classes at **La Vecchia Scuola Bolognese** (the Old Bolognese Cooking School). Her four-hour sessions focus on pasta making and are offered daily; they begin at 9:30 AM and continue to lunchtime, when you can eat the fruits of your labor. Evening courses are available, and Bertuzzi also offers lunches and dinners by themselves. These tastings of traditional Bolognese recipes cost €30; Tuesday night is a traditional deep-fried meat, vegetable, and fruit dinner. The school is out toward the Ospedale Maggiore—take Bus 19 from Via Rizzoli near Piazza Maggiore, or a €15 taxi from the *centro storico*. ⊠ *Via Malvasia 49* ☎ *051/2240* ⊕ *www. lavecchiascuola.com* ✉ *€60 per person, €75 with meal.*

If you prefer your cooking classes in a truly regal setting, you might want to try **La Tavola della Signoria,** held in the spectacular 17th-century rooms of the **Palazzo Albergati** (www. palazzoalbergati.it). These classes are less frequent (offered only four or five times per month) and more expensive than some others, but they're also longer and more serious. Class starts at 8:30 AM and runs until 5:30 PM; you can choose between different modules, such as bread making, pasta making, desserts, and so on. For the true aficionados, two- and three-day fruit-and-vegetable courses are offered periodically. It's located 10 km (6 mi) west of the city center; to get there, take SS569, get off at the last Zona Predosa exit, and follow signs for the Palazzo Albergati. You can sign up online at the Web site. ⊠ *Via Masini 46* ☎ *051/750247* ⊕ *www. tavoladellasignoria.it* ✉ *€170–€200 per person for 1 day; up to €480 for 3 days.*

Repeatedly recognized as one of the best wine stores in Italy, **Enoteca Italiana** (⊠ Via Marsala 2/b, north of Piazza Maggiore ☎ 051/227132) lives up to its reputation with shelves lined with excellent selections from all over Italy at reasonable prices. Their delicious sandwiches with wine by the glass also make a great stand-up light lunch. Friendly owners run the midsize, down-to-earth **Scaramagli** (⊠ Strada Maggiore 31/d, University area ☎ 051/227132) wine store.

For fresh produce, meats, and other foods sold in traditional Italian markets, head to **Via Oberdan** (⊠ Piazza Maggiore area), the street just off Via dell'Indipendenza downtown. The **Mercato di Mezzo** (⊠ Via Peschiere Vecchie Piazza Maggiore area), which sells specialty foods, fruits, and vegetables, is an intense barrage of sights and smells; it's open daily 7–1 and 4:15–7:30, except on Thursday afternoons and Sunday. The **Mercato delle Erbe** (⊠ Via Ugo Bassi Piazza Maggiore area) is an equally bustling food market, open Monday, Tuesday, Wednesday, and Friday 7–1:15 and 5–7:30, Thursday and Saturday 7–1:15. The gargantuan **La Piazzola** city market (⊠ Piazza VIII Agosto off Via dell'Indipendenza, north toward the train station, Piazza Maggiore area) has vendors hawking wares of variable quality, including food, clothing, shoes,

books, and every imaginable household necessity. It's open Friday and
Saturday during daylight hours, and on some Sundays.

FERRARA

⑮ *47 km (29 mi) northeast of Bologna, 74 km (46 mi) northwest of
Ravenna.*

Today you are likely to be charmed by Ferrara's prosperous air and metic-
ulous cleanliness, its excellent local restaurants and fin-de-siècle coffeehouses, and its hospitable, youthful spirit: a boisterous mass of wine
drinkers gathers outside the Duomo on even the foggiest of weekend
evenings. Though Ferrara is a UNESCO world heritage site, the city still
draws amazingly few tourists—which only adds to its appeal. The legendary Ferrarese filmmaker Michelangelo Antonioni called his beloved
hometown "a city that you can see only partly, while the rest disappears
to be imagined," and perhaps he was referring to the low-lying mist that
rolls in off the Adriatic each winter and shrouds Ferrara's winding knot
of medieval alleyways, turreted pleasure palaces, and ancient wine
bars—once inhabited by the likes of Copernicus—in a ghostly fog. But
perhaps Antonioni was also suggesting that Ferrara's striking beauty often
conceals a dark and tortured past.

Although the site was first settled before the time of Christ and was once
ruled by Ravenna, Ferrara's history really begins with an ominous event—
the arrival of the Este in 1259. For more than three centuries the infamous dynasty ruled with an iron fist; brother killed brother, son fought
father, husband murdered wife. The majestic castle with moat, which now
guards the heart of Ferrara's old town in innocuous splendor, was originally built as a fortress to protect the ruthless Este dukes from their own
citizens; deep within the castle's bowels the Este kept generations of political dissidents in dank cells barely larger than a human body. The
greatest of the dukes, Ercole I (1433–1505), attempted to poison a nephew
who challenged his power, and when that didn't work he beheaded him.
Yet it is to this pitiless man that Ferrara owes its great beauty. In one of
his more empathetic moments, Ercole invited Sephardic Jews exiled from
Spain to settle in Ferrara, spawning half a millennium of Jewish history
that came to a spectacular end as Italy succumbed to Axis ideology. The
maze of twisting cobblestone streets that forms the old ghetto witnessed
the persecution of its Jews once fascist Italy came under the spell of Nazi
Germany, a tragedy documented in Giorgio Bassani's book and Vittorio
De Sica's canonical neorealist film, *The Garden of the Finzi-Continis.*

If you plan to explore the city fully, consider buying a museum card (€14)
at the Palazzo dei Diamanti or at one of the art museums around town;
it grants admission to every museum, palace, and castle in Ferrara. The
first Monday of the month is free at many museums.

The Main Attractions

Naturally enough, the building that was the seat of Este power domi-
★ nates the town: the massive **Castello Estense** is a perfectly preserved castle in the center of the city in Piazza Castello. The building was a suitable

symbol for the ruling family: cold and menacing on the outside, lavishly decorated within. The public rooms are grand, but deep in the bowels of the fortress are chilling dungeons where enemies of the state were held in wretched conditions—a function these quarters served as recently as 1943, when antifascist prisoners were detained there. In particular, the **Prisons of Don Giulio, Ugo, and Parisina** have some fascinating features, like 15th-century smoke graffiti protesting the imprisonment of the young lovers Ugo and Parisina, who were beheaded in 1425.

The castle was established as a fortress in 1385, but work on its luxurious ducal quarters continued into the 16th century. Representative of Este grandeur are the **Sala dei Giochi,** extravagantly painted with pagan athletic scenes, and the **Sala dell'Aurora,** decorated to show the times of the day. The tower, the terraces of the castle, and the hanging garden—once reserved for the private use of the duchesses—have fine views of the town and the surrounding countryside. You can cross the castle's moat, traverse its drawbridge, and wander through many of its arcaded passages at any time; in the still of a misty night, the experience is haunting. ✉ *Piazza Castello* ☎ *0532/299233* ⛓ *Castle €6, tower €1 extra* 🕐 *Castle Tues.–Sun. 9:30–5:30, tower Tues.–Sun. 10–4:45; ticket office closes at 4:45.*

★ The magnificent Gothic **Duomo,** a few steps away from the Castello Estense, has a three-tier facade of bony arches and beautiful carvings over the central door. It was begun in 1135 and took more than 100 years to complete. The interior was completely remodeled in the 17th century. ✉ *Piazza Cattedrale* ☎ *0532/207449* 🕐 *Mon.–Sat. 7:30–noon and 3–6:30, Sun. 7:30–12:30 and 3:30–7:30.*

The collection of ornate religious objects in the **Museo Ebraico** (Jewish Museum) bears witness to the long history of the city's Jewish community. This history had its high points—1492, for example, when Ercole I invited the Jews to come over from Spain—and its lows, notably 1624, when the papal government closed the **ghetto,** which was reopened only with the advent of a united Italy in 1859. The triangular warren of narrow, cobbled streets that made up the ghetto originally extended as far as Corso Giovecca (originally Corso Giudecca, or Ghetto Street); when it was enclosed, the neighborhood was restricted to the area between Via Scienze, Via Contrari, and Via di San Romano. The museum, in the center of the ghetto, was once Ferrara's synagogue. A guided tour is required to visit. ✉ *Via Mazzini 95* ☎ *0532/210228* ⛓ *€4* 🕐 *Guided tours Sun.–Thurs. at 10, 11, and noon.*

The **Palazzo dei Diamanti** (Palace of Diamonds) is so called because of the 12,600 small, pink-and-white marble pyramids ("diamonds") that stud the facade. The building was designed to be viewed in perspective—both faces at once—from diagonally across the street. Originally built in the 15th and 16th centuries, today the palazzo contains the **Pina-**

coteca Nazionale, which has an extensive art gallery and rotating exhibits. ⊠ *Corso Ercole I d'Este 19–21* ☎ *0532/205844* 🖼 *€4* ⊙ *Tues., Wed., Fri., and Sat. 9–2; Thurs. 9–7; Sun. 9–1.*

The oldest and most characteristic area of Ferrara is to the south of the Duomo, stretching between the Corso Giovecca and the city's ramparts. Here various members of the Este family built pleasure palaces, the most famous of which is the **Palazzo Schifanoia** (*schifanoia* means "carefree" or, literally, "fleeing boredom"). Begun in the 14th century, the palace was remodeled in 1466 and was the city's first Renaissance palazzo. The interior is lavishly decorated, particularly the **Salone dei Mesi,** with an extravagant series of frescoes showing the months of the year and their mythological attributes. The adjacent **Museo Civico Lapidario,** on Via Camposabbionario, has a collection of coins, statuary, and paintings. ⊠ *Via Scandiana 23* ☎ *0532/244949* ⊕ *www.comune.fe.it/musei-aa/ schifanoia/skifa.html* 🖼 *€ 5* ⊙ *Tues.–Sun. 9–6.*

One of the streets most characteristic of Ferrara's past, the 2-km-long (1-mi-long) **Via delle Volte,** is also one of the oldest preserved medieval streets in Europe. The series of ancient *volte* (arches) along the narrow cobblestone alley once joined the merchants' houses on the south side of the street to their warehouses on the north side. The street ran parallel to the banks of the Po River, which was home to the busy port of ancient Ferrara.

Also Worth Seeing

One of the best-preserved of the Renaissance palaces along Ferrara's old streets is the charming **Casa Romei.** Downstairs are rooms with 15th-century frescoes and several sculptures collected from destroyed churches. The house stands not far from the Palazzo del Paradiso, in the area behind Ferrara's castle. The schedule varies with exhibits. ⊠ *Via Savonarola 30* ☎ *0532/240341* 🖼 *€2* ⊙ *Tues.–Sun. 8:30–7:30.*

On the busy Corso Giovecca is the **Palazzina di Marfisa d'Este,** a grandiose 16th-century home that belonged to a great patron of the arts. The house has painted ceilings, fine 16th-century furniture, and a garden containing a grotto and an outdoor theater. ⊠ *Corso Giovecca 170* ☎ *0532/ 244949* ⊕ *www.comune.fe.it/musei-aa/schifanoia/marfi.html* 🖼 *€3* ⊙ *Tues.–Sun. 9–1 and 3–6.*

The grand but unfinished courtyard is the most interesting part of the luxurious **Palazzo di Ludovico il Moro,** a magnificent 15th-century dwelling built for Ludovico Sforza, husband of Beatrice d'Este. The palazzo contains the region's **Museo Archeologico,** a repository of relics of early man, Etruscans, and Romans found in the country surrounding the city. ⊠ *Via XX Settembre 124, near Palazzo Schifanoia* ☎ *0532/66299* 🖼 *€4* ⊙ *Tues.–Sun. 9–2.*

Where to Stay & Eat

★ $$$$ ✕ **Il Don Giovanni.** To find this elegant and secluded dining room, full of oranges, reds, yellows, and jazz vocals, is a challenge; look for the street sign that points you through a courtyard to the restaurant. Once inside, the high prices are justified by fireworks on the plate. Complex mozzarella di bufala is shockingly paired with raw shrimp so fruity it's like a dab of marmalade. Meltingly tender raw scallops reveal but a whisper of sweetness. Swallowing the raw, silver-skinned *sgombro*, like a smaller, milder version of mackerel, might remind you of the well-behaved dolphins at Sea World. Cooked fish is equally impressive: in an inspired combination, juicy, well-seasoned *branzino* (striped sea bass) sits daringly atop chili peppers. If you can't afford the restaurant, check out the less-expensive **La Borsa** wine bar, in the same complex (and with the same phone number), which has excellent cured meats, cheeses, sandwiches, and traditional dishes like *cappellacci di zucca* (squash-filled pasta pillows) and roast pork. ⊠ *Corso Ercole I d'Este 1* ☎ *0532/243363* ⊕ *www.ildongiovanni.com* ♨ *Reservations essential* ▭ *AE, DC, MC, V* ☉ *Closed Mon. No lunch.*

★ **$$$–$$$$** ✕ **Max.** A modern, minimalist restaurant steps from the Castello Estense is quietly turning the Ferrara dining scene on its head. Exciting *alta cucina* (haute cuisine) dishes at Max include an absolutely spectacular plate of raw shellfish from the nearby Adriatic. In the deconstructed eggplant parmigiana, pieces of eggplant are molded into an impossibly soft *sformatino* (soufflélike dish) with a béchamel sauce and sweet *scampi* (a Mediterranean shellfish); a whole crisped tomato sits off to the side. In spite of the restaurant's relative formality, the service is friendly. ⊠ *Piazza Repubblica 16* ☎ *0532/209309* ♨ *Reservations essential* ▭ *AE, DC, MC, V* ☉ *Closed Mon. and Aug. 15–31. No lunch Sun.*

$–$$$ ✕ **Trattoria La Romantica.** The former stables of a 17th-century merchant's house have been transformed into this casually elegant, welcoming restaurant, which is a great favorite among well-fed locals. Although the decor (warm light and wood-beam ceilings, incongruous prints, and a piano) seems to be in perpetual transition, the haute-rustic food is fully realized. Ferrarese specialties like cappellacci di zucca are served side by side with French oysters. ⊠ *Via Ripagrande 36* ☎ *0532/765975* ▭ *AE, DC, MC, V* ☉ *Closed Wed., Jan. 7–17, and Aug. 1–15.*

$–$$ ✕ **Antica Trattoria Volano.** Local businessmen often fill this white-wall, traditional-to-the-core neighborhood trattoria. The decor is rustic and the food includes such local treats as cappellacci di zucca and a good version of *salama da sugo*, a salty and oily boiled sausage, served over mashed potatoes. *Tris* is a first-course sampler of three pastas that change nightly. ⊠ *Via Volano 20* ☎ *0532/761421* ▭ *AE, DC, MC, V* ☉ *Closed Fri.*

$–$$ ✕ **Osteria del Ghetto.** Though the casually elegant *osteria* (tavernlike restaurant) is buried deep in the old Jewish ghetto, its seasonal menu is anything but old-fashioned. Dishes here represent the cutting edge of Ferrarese cooking: basmati rice torte with Colonnata lard and boletus mushrooms; eggplant flan with cold *grana* (aged, granulated cheese) cream; a lukewarm pheasant salad with balsamic vinegar. The dining room is modern and relaxing, with wood-beamed ceilings, a no-smoking section, and tables on the street in summer. ⊠ *Via Vittorio 26* ☎ *0532/ 764936* ▭ *AE, DC, MC, V* ☉ *Closed Tues.*

★ **¢** ✕ **Osteria Al Brindisi.** Ferrara is a city of wine bars, beginning with this, Europe's oldest, which began pouring in 1435. This might just be the most perfect place to drink wine in Italy—Copernicus, who once lived

Talking Politics

Emilia-Romagna might seem staid: city after city has immaculate streets filled with smartly dressed businessmen in impeccable shoes, covertly murmuring to each other through the winter fog over cups of coffee. But after dark, from Parma to Bologna, Piacenza to Ferrara, the middle managers are replaced on the streets by young, energetic would-be intellectuals, and the murmurs turn into impassioned political discussion—usually with a leftist slant—over jugs of table wine. If you enjoy this type of conversation, take time to stop for a drink after dinner in a student cafeteria, cozy café, or back-alley bar. Don't be afraid to join in—all ages are welcome, and divergent opinions, thoughtfully argued, are treated with respect. (Locals are usually happy to practice their English, which can often be quite good.) You'll experience another side of the region—a side that's important to understanding its culture and history.

---

upstairs, seemed to think so. Prices are low, the ambient lighting soft, and even the music (usually good jazz) somehow feels just right. There's a great selection by the glass, or you can choose from among the thousands of national and international bottles that line the ancient walls. A memorable spread of salumi and local cheeses is available, as well as tasty hot meals such as tortellini *in brodo* (in beef or chicken broth). ⊠ *Via degli Adelardi 11* ☎ *0532/209142* ▭ *AE, DC, MC, V* ☺ *Closed Mon.*

The **Prenotel hotel reservation hot line** (☎ 0532/462046), run by the city, allows you to make reservations at any of the accommodations listed below, among many others.

$$$ ⊡ **Annunziata.** The flower-covered minibalconies of this hotel could hardly be any closer to the castle and Ferrara's old town—this might just be the best location in the city. The building feels like an old private home, the lobby is inviting, and the pleasantly understated rooms have ceilings with old wooden beams. ⊠ *Piazza Repubblica 5, 44100* ☎ *0532/201111* 🖷 *0532/203233* ⊕ *www.annunziata.it* ⇦ *26 rooms* ⌂ *Room service, in-room safes, minibars, cable TV, Wi-Fi, bicycles, bar, parking (fee)* ▭ *AE, DC, MC, V* ⵙ *BP.*

$$–$$$ ⊡ **Hotel Ripagrande.** The courtyards, vaulted brick lobby, and breakfast
Fodor's Choice room of this 15th-century noble's palazzo retain much of their lordly
★ Renaissance flair. Rooms are decidedly more down-to-earth, but standard doubles and some of the enormous bi- and tri-level suites have faux-Persian rugs, tapestries, and cozy antique furniture; top-floor rooms and suites resemble a Colorado ski lodge, with terraces, and are roomy—especially good for families. Everything here, including the room service, is impeccable. The location is quiet but fairly convenient. ⊠ *Via Ripagrande 21, 44100* ☎ *0532/765250* 🖷 *0532/764377* ⊕ *www.ripagrandehotel.it* ⇦ *20 rooms, 20 suites* ⌂ *Restaurant, room service, in-room safes, minibars, cable TV, bar, meeting room, free parking* ▭ *AE, DC, MC, V* ⵙ *BP.*

$ ▣ **Hotel San Paolo.** On the edge of the old city, San Paolo is the best inexpensive choice in town. The 10-minute walk from the heart of Ferrara's medieval quarter is pleasant, and there are good restaurants in the vicinity. Singles are a particularly good value (about €65); triples are available. ⊠ *Via Baluardi 9, 44100* ☎ *0532/762040* ᕤ *0532/762040* ⊕ *www.hotelsanpaolo.it* ➪ *29 rooms* ⚲ *Cable TV, bicycles, some pets allowed; no a/c in some rooms* ⊟ *AE, DC, MC, V* ⎜Ⓞ⎜ *EP.*

$ ▣ **Locanda Borgonuovo.** This lovely bed-and-breakfast is in a 17th-century monastery on a quiet but central pedestrians-only street. It books up months in advance, partly because musicians and actors from the local theater make this their home away from home. Rooms are furnished with antiques, and one has its own kitchen for longer stays. Summer breakfasts are served in the leafy courtyard. ⊠ *Via Cairoli 29, 44100* ☎ *0532/211100* ᕤ *0532/246328* ⊕ *www.borgonuovo.com* ➪ *4 rooms* ⚲ *Dining room, in-room safes, some kitchens, minibars, bicycles, library, free parking* ⊟ *AE, MC, V* ⎜Ⓞ⎜ *BP.*

Bicycling

Cycling is extremely popular in Ferrara. **Pirana e Bagni** (⊠ Piazzale Stazione 2 ☎ 0532/772190) rents bicycles. Call **Cicloclub Estense** (☎ 0532/900931) to arrange a guided bike trip.

ROMAGNA

Anywhere in Emilia-Romagna, the story goes, a weary, lost traveler will be invited into a family's home and offered a drink. But the Romagnesi claim that he'll be served water in Emilia and wine in Romagna. The hilly, mostly rural, and largely undiscovered Romagna region has crumbling farmhouses dotting rolling hills, smoking chimneys, ancient Christian temples, and rowdy local bars dishing out rounds and rounds of *piadine* (flat griddle breads). Ravenna, the site of shimmering Byzantine mosaics, dominates the region, and Rimini is an overpopulated seaside resort.

Heading southeast out of Bologna, Via Emilia (SS9) and the parallel A14 Autostrada lead to the towns of Dozza and Faenza. From there, cut north to the Adriatic coast on the S71 to reach Ravenna, or continue on southeast on the A14 to reach Rimini. Alternatively, the slower S16 cuts a northwest–southeast swath through Romagna, directly connecting Ravenna and Rimini.

Imola

⓰ *42 km (26 mi) southeast of Bologna.*

The luxe town of Imola, with wide and stately avenues in the affluent, northern European mold, lies right on the border between Emilia and Romagna. It is best known for its Formula One auto-racing tradition; the San Marino Grand Prix has been held here in spring of every year since 1981 (it's now held in mid-April). The history of auto racing in Imola goes back to 1953, when, with the support of Enzo Ferrari, the racetrack just outside the city center was inaugurated. However, unless you happen to pop into town in mid-April for the race, you'll more likely

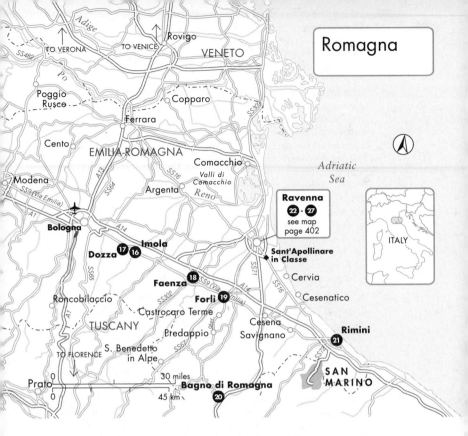

find yourself in Imola to shop for the well-known ceramics or to sample the town's world-class restaurant, San Domenico.

Where to Eat

$$$$ ✕ **San Domenico.** Some superstar restaurants come and go, but San
Fodor'sChoice Domenico has defended its position as one of Italy's most refined din-
★ ing destinations year after year. The majestic appointments complement celebrity chef Valentino Marcattilii's wondrous creations, like the
memorable *uovo in raviolo San Domenico,* in which one egg is stuffed
into a large ravioli and the yolk spills out and mixes with sweet Parmesan cheese, *burro di malga* (butter from an Alpine dairy farm), and sensational white truffles. Service is like a silent, perfectly choreographed
ballet, and the staggering wine list has more than 3,000 choices. Reserve
several days in advance. ⊠ *Via G. Sacchi 1* ☎ *0542/29000* ⊕ *www.
sandomenico.it* ⌔ *Reservations essential* ▤ *AE, DC, MC, V* ⊗ *Closed
Mon., Sun. June–Aug., 1 wk in Jan., and 1 wk in Aug. No lunch Sat.
June–Aug. No dinner Sun. Sept.–May.*

Dozza

🔟 *85 km (53 mi) southeast of Ferrara, 31 km (19 mi) southeast of Bologna.*

Dozza is a beautiful little fortified village just off the Via Emilia (SS9), to which artists from all over flock in September of odd years to take part in a mural competition. As a result, virtually every one of the town's buildings is covered with colorful scenes, executed with varying degrees of skill. The town makes a great lunch stop on the way between Bologna and Ferrara or Ravenna. If you arrive by car—and car is more or less the only way to arrive—you'll have to park in the lot down below the historical center and walk up a set of staircases,

> **WORD OF MOUTH**
>
> "Dozza was such a surprising, improbable combination of a traditional-looking medieval town and a unique offbeat art site. I was just amazed by it. Every two years artists paint murals on the houses and streets and other walls of the town. The works vary tremendously in style, but somehow the overall effect, though startling, is interesting rather than tacky."   –cmt

as only residents' vehicles are allowed in the center. At every turn once you're traipsing through Dozza's hilly streets, you'll catch panoramic glimpses of the rolling countryside below.

Dozza is crowned with a splendidly restored medieval castle museum, the **Rocca Sforzesca di Dozza.** ☎ *0542/678240* ☐ *€4* ☉ *Apr.–Sept., Tues.–Sat. 10–1 and 3–7, Sun. 10–1 and 3–7:30; Oct.–Mar., Tues.–Sat. 10–12:30 and 3–5, Sun. 10–1 and 2:30–6.*

The **Enoteca Regionale,** in Dozza's castle, is *the* wine shop for the region. In a series of cavernous rooms, along walls of ancient stone, lies an enormous selection of wines, all of them, remarkably enough, from Emilia-Romagna. Food products and olive oils are also available. Try Dozza's own Albana, a white wine that comes dry or sweet. For further consumption, the on-site wine bar is open Sunday afternoon 3–6:30; each Sunday features a different tasting theme. ⊠ *Rocca di Dozza* ☎ *0542/678089* ⊕ *www.enotecaemiliaromagna.it* ☉ *Tues.–Fri. 9:30–1 and 2:30–6, Sat. 10–1 and 2:30–6, Sun. 10–1 and 3–6:45.*

Where to Eat

★ ¢–$ ✕ **Piccola Osteria del Borgo.** Of tiny Dozza's few restaurants, this one is arguably the best loved by locals. It's set in a big, bustling room, where at least three-quarters of the patrons seem to be on a first-name basis with management. This is the place to try classics like *tagliatelle al ragù* (pasta ribbons with meat sauce) or tortellini; the darkly grilled *scamorza* cheese with greens is a good second course. There are also piadine on the menu. Skip the sweet, wimpy house wine and go for a bottle. ⊠ *Via XX Settembre 19, Imola* ☎ *0542/678200* ▭ *AE, DC, MC, V* ☉ *Closed Mon.*

Faenza

🔟 *23 km (14 mi) southeast of Dozza, 49 km (30 mi) southeast of Bologna.*

The renowned style of pottery called faience has been produced in Faenza, on the Via Emilia, since the 12th century. In the central **Piazza del Popolo** are dozens of shops selling the native wares. Faenza, not surprisingly, is home to the **Museo delle Ceramiche,** one of the largest ceramics museums in the world. During a renovation of indeterminate length, the 17th- to 19th-century pottery is not accessible. ⊠ *Viale Baccarini 19* ☎ *0546/697311* ⊕ *www.racine.ra.it/micfaenza* 🔄 €6 ⊙ *Apr.–Oct., Tues.–Sat. 9–7, Sun. 9:30–6:30; Nov.–Mar., Tues.–Fri. 9–1:30, weekends 9:30–5:30.*

Forlì

⑲ *16 km (10 mi) southeast of Faenza, 74 km (46 mi) southeast of Bologna.*

The biggest city on the Via Emilia between Bologna and Rimini is Forlì. It's a pretty, prosperous, provincial Romagnan city with a huge but harmonious piazza and duomo. Some of the true riches of Romagna lie along the smaller roads branching off to the north and south of Forlì.

Where to Eat

★ **$$$$** ✕ **La Frasca.** Chef Gianfranco Bolognesi is an artist with fresh Adriatic seafood, delectable fowl, and Romagnan produce. Expect far-fetched, haute-cuisine delights such as a pastry-crust quail stuffed with foie gras and black truffle. A set-price lunch menu is a relative bargain at €45 per person. In the warm weather you can dine in the garden. This elegant country restaurant is in the secluded spa town of Castrocaro Terme, a beautiful drive southeast of Forlì. ⊠ *Viale Mateotti 34, Castrocaro Terme, 11 km (7 mi) southeast of Forlì* ☎ *0543/767471* ⊕ *www. lafrasca.it* 🔷 *Reservations essential* ▭ *AE, DC, MC, V* ⊙ *Closed Tues., Jan. 1–21, and Aug. 15–30.*

Bagno di Romagna

⑳ *66 km (41 mi) southeast of Forlì, 81 km (51 mi) south of Ravenna.*

Bagno di Romagna is one of the spa hill towns that dot the bucolic Romagnan countryside. There's not a lot to see, but the hot springs in the center can be enjoyed year-round. You access the town's thermal waters through hotel spas, including the **Euroterme.** ⊠ *Via Lungosavio 2* ☎ *0543/911414* ⊕ *www.euroterme.com* 🔄 €17 for whole day, €9 for night session only ⊙ *Apr.–Oct., Mon.–Sat. 2:30–7 and 8:30–11, Sun. 10–7 and 8:30–11; Nov.–Mar., weekends 10–7, Tues. and Fri. 8:30–11.*

Where to Stay & Eat

★ **$$$$** ✕ **Paolo Teverini.** The chef-owner—and restaurant's namesake—is one of the star culinary personalities of the region. His relentlessly modern preparations are punctuated by essences, foams, gelatins, and reductions that display an almost conniving flair for drama, matched only by the outlandishly pink and posh decor. Most impressive of all is the voluminous wine list, which is like a gift from Paolo to the world: he offers Barolos and Barbarescos from the 1950s, 1960s, and 1970s at a fraction of what you'd pay at a wine store or auction. ⊠ *Piazza Dante 2* ☎ *0543/911260* ⊕ *www.paoloteverini.it* 🔷 *Reservations essential* ▭ *AE, DC, MC, V* ⊙ *Closed Mon. and Tues. Sept.–July.*

$$ ▦ **Tosco Romagnolo.** Right near Bagno di Romagna's thermal baths, the Tosco Romagnolo is in the same spa complex (and under the same ownership) as the inimitable Paolo Teverini restaurant. Rooms are reason-

7

ably priced (rates drop dramatically in winter), and suites, though more expensive, are top-notch. Ask for a room on one of the newer floors. ⊠ *Piazza Dante 2, 47021* ☎ *0543/911260* 🖷 *0543/911014* ⊕ *www. paoloteverini.it* ⟿ *45 rooms, 4 suites* ⚹ *2 restaurants, some in-room safes, minibars, pool, health club, outdoor hot tub, spa, bicycles, bar, meeting rooms, car rental* ⊟ *AE, DC, MC, V* ⧦ *BP.*

Rimini

㉑ *52 km (32 mi) southeast of Ravenna, 121 km (76 mi) southeast of Bologna.*

Rimini is the principal summer resort on the Adriatic Coast and one of the most popular holiday destinations in Italy, flooded with Italians and other Europeans. That said, the water is murky, the beaches are ugly and overcrowded, and the nightlife is largely a teenage pickup scene. Though there are hundreds of hotels—some very fine—with private beach turf, they all seem to be full in August. In the off-season (October–March) Rimini is a cold, windy fishing port with few places open. Any time of year, one of Rimini's least touristy areas is the port; rambling down the **Via Sinistra del Porto** or **Via Destra del Porto** past all the fishing boats, you would hardly know you were in a teen hookup hot spot.

Rimini's oldest monument is the **Arco d'Augusto,** now stranded in the middle of a square just inside the city ramparts. It was erected in 27 BC, making it the oldest surviving Roman arch. ⊠ *Largo Giulio Cesare.*

Where to Stay & Eat

★ ¢–$ ✕ **La Locanda di San Martino.** Patrons have been known to drive all the way from the Ligurian coast just for the seafood delights here. Dishes such as the *spaghettoni ai frutti di mare* (thick spaghetti with seafood sauce) and a grilled mixed seafood platter are uniformly fresh and superbly prepared; the mixed antipasto served with lunch is exquisite. An outdoor patio in the back is more romantic than the large main dining rooms. To get here take the road out of Rimini heading toward Bologna. ⊠ *Via Emilia 226* ☎ *0541/680127* ⊟ *AE, MC, V* ☽ *Closed Mon.*

¢ ✕ **Piada e Cassoni da Jonny.** Come here for the *piada* (grilled flat bread), one of the traditional specialties of Romagnan cooking. A brisk staff member fills the flat bread, or a *cassone* (a bigger pocket of bread, more like a calzone, but also grilled), with cheese, tomato, and meat or vegetables, to order while you wait. Don't expect to sit down at this bustling take-out place (open until about 9 PM daily), but Jonny also delivers. ⊠ *Via Giovanni XXIII 101* ☎ *0541/29675* ⊕ *www.piadajonny.com* ⊟ *No credit cards.*

★ $$$$ ⌂ **Grand Hotel.** This fin-de-siècle extravaganza, made famous by Fellini in his *Amarcord,* is grander than ever. The hyperluxe stage is set by enormous crystal chandeliers in the lobby and inlaid wood in the rooms that seem playful rather than formal. A spotless private beach, with a restaurant from June to September, completes the scene. Entourages and steamer trunks would not be out of place here; neither would it be a surprise to see a greyhound loping through the restaurant on her way to the pool with her owner. This is also one of the few hotels in the re-

San Marino, a Country on a Cliff

THE WORLD'S SMALLEST and oldest republic, as San Marino dubs itself, is landlocked entirely by Italy. It consists of three ancient castles perched high on cliffs of sheer rock rising implausibly out of the flatlands of Romagna, and a tangled knot of cobblestone streets below, lined with tourist boutiques, cheesy hotels and restaurants, and gun shops. The 45-minute drive from Rimini is easily justified, however, by the castle-top view of the countryside far below. The 1,000-meter-plus (3,300 feet and more) precipices will make jaws drop and acrophobes quiver.

San Marino was founded in the 4th century AD by a stonecutter named Marino who settled with a small community of Christians, escaping persecution by pagan emperor Diocletian. Over the millennia, largely because of the logistical nightmares associated with attacking a fortified rock, San Marino was more or less left alone by Italy's various conquerors, and continues to this day to be an independent country (population 26,000), supported almost entirely by its 3-million-visitors-per-year tourist industry.

San Marino's headline attractions are its **tre castelli** (three castles)—medieval architectural wonders that appear on every coat of arms in the city. Starting in the center of town, walk a few hundred yards past the trinket shops, along a paved cliff-top ridge, from the 10th-century **Rocca della Guaita** to the 13th-century **Rocca della Cesta** (which contains a museum of ancient weapons that's worthwhile mostly for the views from its terraces and turrets), and finally to the 14th-century **Rocca Montale** (closed to the public), the most remote of the castles. Every step of the way affords spectacular views of Romagna and the Adriatic; it is said that on a clear day you can see Croatia. The walks make for a good day's exercise but are by no means arduous. Even if you arrive after visiting hours, they're supremely worthwhile. ☎ *0549/882670* ⊕ *www. museidistato.sm* ✉ *Rocca della Guaita and Rocca della Cesta: €4.50* ⊘ *Sept. 21–Mar. 19, daily 8:50–5; Mar. 20–Sept. 20, daily 8–8.*

A must-see is the **Piazza della Libertà,** whose Palazzo Pubblico is guarded by soldiers in green uniforms. As you'll notice by peering into the shops along the old town's winding streets, the republic is famous for crossbows—and more: shopping for fireworks, firearms, and other items illegal for sale elsewhere is another popular tourist activity.

Visiting San Marino in winter—off-season—increases the appeal of the experience, as tourist establishments shut down and you more or less have the castles to yourself. In August, every inch of walkway on the rock is mobbed with sightseers. To get to San Marino by car, take highway SS72 west from Rimini. From Borgo Maggiore, at the base of the rock, a cable car will whisk you up to the castles and town. Alternatively, you can drive all the way up the winding road; public parking is available in the town itself. Don't worry about changing money, showing passports, and the like (although the tourist office will stamp your passport for €1); San Marino is, for all practical purposes, Italy—except, that is, for its majestic perch, its gun laws, and its reported 99% national voter turnout rate.

7

gion with kosher capabilities, and events are organized for Jewish holidays under rabbinical supervision. ✉ *Parco Federico Fellini, 47900* ☏ *0541/56000* 🖷 *0541/56866* ⊕ *www.grandhotelrimini.com* ⇱ *156 rooms, 12 suites* ♨ *Restaurant, minibars, tennis court, 2 outdoor pools, health club, hair salon, massage, sauna, beach, 2 bars, nightclub, meeting room* ▤ *AE, DC, MC, V* ⏧ *BP.*

EN ROUTE There are two auto routes between Ravenna and Rimini. The coastal road, S16, hugs the shoreline much of the way, passing through Cervia. Although its length of 52 km (32 mi) is not great, this scenic route is naturally slower (beware of fog in winter). The coast north of Rimini is lined with dozens of small resort towns, only one having any charm—the seaport of Cesenatico; the others are mini-Riminis, and in summer the narrow road is hopelessly clogged with traffic. A faster route is to take the S71 and the A14; the distance is 64 km (39 mi).

RAVENNA

A small, quiet city, Ravenna has brick palaces, cobbled streets, magnificent monuments, and spectacular Byzantine mosaics to remind you of its storied past. The high point in Ravenna's history was 1,500 long years ago, when it became the capital of the Roman Empire. The honor was short-lived—the city was taken by the barbarian Ostrogoths in the 5th century; in the 6th century it was conquered by the Byzantines, who ruled it from Constantinople.

Because Ravenna spent much of its past looking to the East, its greatest art treasures show that influence. Churches and tombs with the most unassuming exteriors contain within them walls covered with tiny, glittering tiles. The beautifully preserved Byzantine mosaics put an emphasis on nature—green pastures, sheep, and starry skies, for instance—not found in Italy's other ancient artistic treasures. Outside Ravenna, the town of Classe hides even more mosaic gems.

Exploring Ravenna

A combination ticket (available at ticket offices of all included sights) admits you to six of Ravenna's important monuments: the Mausoleo di Galla Placidia, the Basilica di San Vitale, the Battistero Neoniano, Sant'Apollinare Nuovo, the church of Spirito Santo, and the Museo Arcivescovile e Cappella Sant'Andrea. Start out early in the morning to avoid lines (reservations are necessary for the Mausoleo and Basilica in May and June). A half day should suffice to walk the town alone; allow an hour each for the Mausoleo, the Basilica, and the Museo Nazionale. Ticket offices often close 15–30 minutes before the sight themselves.

> **WORD OF MOUTH**
>
> "Much of Ravenna is car-free, so we were on foot. Many local people rode bicycles; some of them smoked as they rode. Bikes for hire are parked in blue holders. One rents a key, and can take a bike from any holder and leave it at any holder, like luggage carts at an airport." —smalti

The Main Attractions

㉓ Basilica di San Vitale. The octagonal church of San Vitale was built in AD 547, after the Byzantines conquered the city, and its interior shows a strong Byzantine influence. In the area behind the altar are the most famous works in the church, accurate portraits of the Emperor of the East, Justinian, attended by his court and the bishop of Ravenna, Maximian. Notice how the mosaics seamlessly wrap around the columns and curved arches on the upper sides of the altar area. Reservations are recommended from March through mid-June. ⊠ *Via San Vitale off Via Salara* ☎ *0544/541688 reservations, 800/303999 information* ⊕ *www. ravennamosaici.it* ✉ *Combination ticket €7.50* ☉ *Nov.–Feb. daily 9:30–5; Mar. and Oct. daily 9–5:30; Apr.–Sept. daily 9–7; ticket office closes 15 mins earlier.*

㉕ Battistero Neoniano. The baptistry, next door to Ravenna's 18th-century cathedral, is one of the town's most important mosaic sights. In keeping with the building's role, the great mosaic in the dome shows the baptism of Christ, and beneath that scene are the Apostles. The lowest band of mosaics contains Christian symbols, the Throne of God, and the Cross. Note the naked figure kneeling next to Christ—he is the personification of the River Jordan. The Battistero building is said to have been a Roman bath dating from the 5th century AD. ⊠ *Via Battistero* ☎ *0544/ 541688 reservations, 800/303999 toll-free information* ⊕ *www. ravennamosaici.it* ✉ *Combination ticket €7.50* ☉ *Nov.–Feb. daily 10–5; Mar. and Oct. daily 9:30–5:30; Apr.–Sept. daily 9–7; ticket office closes 15 mins earlier.*

㉒ Mausoleo di Galla Placidia. The little tomb and the great church stand side by side, but the tomb predates the Basilica di San Vitale by at least a hundred years. These two adjacent sights are decorated with the best-known, and most elaborate, mosaics in Ravenna. Galla Placidia was the sister of Rome's emperor, Honorius, the man who moved the imperial capital to Ravenna in AD 402. She is said to have been beautiful and strong-willed, and to have taken an active part in the governing of the crumbling empire. This tomb, constructed in the mid-5th century, is her memorial.

Fodor'sChoice
★

Outside, the tomb is a small, unassuming redbrick building; the exterior's seeming poverty of charm only serves to enhance by contrast the richness of the interior mosaics, in deep midnight blue and glittering gold. The tiny, low central dome is decorated with symbols of Christ and the evangelists and striking gold stars. Over the door is a depiction of the Good Shepherd. Eight of the Apostles are represented in groups of two on the four inner walls of the dome; the other four appear singly on the walls of the two transepts. Notice the small doves at their feet, drinking from the water of faith. Also in the tiny transepts are some delightful pairs of deer (representing souls), drinking from the fountain of resurrection. There are three sarcophagi in the tomb, none of which are believed to contain the remains of Galla Placidia. She died in Rome in AD 450, and there is no record of her body having been transported back to the place where she wished to lie. Reservations are required for the Mausoleo from March through mid-June. ⊠ *Via San Vitale off Via Salara* ☎ *0544/ 541688 reservations, 800/303999 toll-free information* ⊕ *www.*

7

Basilica di
San Vitale **23**

Battistero
Neoniano **25**

Mausoleo di Galla
Placidia **22**

Museo
Nazionale **24**

Sant'Apollinare
Nuovo **27**

Tomba di
Dante **26**

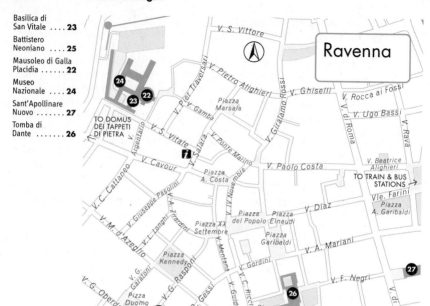

ravennamosaici.it ⌨ *€2 supplement in addition to obligatory €7.50 combination ticket Mar. 1–June 15* ⊘ *Nov.–Feb. daily 9:30–5; Mar. and Oct. daily 9–5:30; Apr.–Sept. daily 9–7; ticket office closes 15 mins earlier.*

㉗ Sant'Apollinare Nuovo. The mosaics displayed in this church date from the early 6th century, making them slightly older than the works in San Vitale. Since the left side of the church was reserved for women, it's only fitting that the mosaic decoration there is a scene of 22 virgins offering crowns to the Virgin Mary. On the right wall are 26 men carrying the crowns of martyrdom. They are approaching Christ, surrounded by angels. ⊠ *Via Roma at Via Guaccimanni* ☎ *0544/541688 reservations, 800/303999 toll-free information* ⊕ *www.ravennamosaici.it* ⌨ *Combination ticket €7.50* ⊘ *Nov.–Feb. daily 10–5; Mar. and Oct. daily 9:30–5:30; Apr.–Sept. daily 9–7; ticket office closes 15 mins earlier.*

Also Worth Seeing

Domus dei Tappeti di Pietra (Ancient Home of the Stone Carpets). This underground archaeological site was uncovered during the course of routine maintenance work by the city in 1993 and opened to the public in 2002. Below ground level (10 feet down) lie the remains of a 6th-century AD Byzantine palace, in which a beautiful and well-preserved network of floor mosaics display themes that are fascinatingly un-Christian.

✉ *Via Barbiani; enter through Sant'Eufemia* ☎ *0544/32512* ⊕ *www.ravennantica.it* ☑ *€3.50* ⏱ *Mar.–Oct., daily 10–6:30; Nov.–Feb., Mon.–Sat. 10–4:30, Sun. 10–6:30.*

㉔ **Museo Nazionale.** The National Museum of Ravenna, next to the Church of San Vitale, contains artifacts from ancient Rome, Byzantine fabrics and carvings, and pieces of early Christian art. The collection is housed in a former monastery, but is well displayed and artfully lighted. ✉ *Via Fiandrini* ☎ *0544/34424* ☑ *€4* ⏱ *Tues.–Sun. 8:30–7:30.*

㉖ **Tomba di Dante.** The tomb of Dante is in a small neoclassical building next door to the large church of St. Francis. Exiled from his native Florence, the author of *The Divine Comedy* died here in 1321. The Florentines have been trying to reclaim their famous son for hundreds of years, but the Ravennans refuse to give him up, arguing that since Florence did not welcome Dante in life it does not deserve him in death. The small **Museo Dantesco** has displays on the writer's life and the history of the tomb. ✉ *Via Dante Alighieri 4 and 9* ☎ *0544/30252* ☑ *Tomb free, museum €2* ⏱ *Tomb daily 9–noon and 2–5, museum Tues.–Sun. 9–noon.*

Off the Beaten Path

Sant'Apollinare in Classe. This church, about 5 km (3 mi) southeast of Ravenna, is landlocked now, but when it was built it stood in the center of the busy shipping port known to the ancient Romans as Classis. The arch above and the area around the high altar are rich with mosaics. Those on the arch, older than the ones behind it, are considered superior. They show Christ in Judgment and the 12 lambs of Christianity leaving the cities of Jerusalem and Bethlehem. In the apse is the figure of Sant'Apollinare himself, a bishop of Ravenna, and above him is a magnificent Transfiguration against blazing green grass, animals in skewed perspective, and flowers. ✉ *Via Romea Sud, Classe* ☎ *0544/473569* ☑ *€2* ⏱ *Mon.–Sat. 8:30–7:30, Sun. 1–7:30; ticket office closes ½ hr earlier.*

Where to Stay & Eat

$$ ✕ **Bella Venezia.** Graceful low archways lead into this attractive pink-and-white restaurant's two small, brightly lit dining rooms. Try the beans with olive oil and *bottarga* (cured roe) or the owner's special risotto with butter, Parmesan, cured ham, mushrooms, and peas to start. For the second course, the *fegato alla Veneziana* (grilled liver with onions) is a good choice. The outdoor garden is quite pleasant in season. ✉ *Via IV Novembre 16* ☎ *0544/212746* ⊕ *www.bellavenezia.it* ☰ *AE, DC, MC, V* ⏱ *Closed Sun. and 3 wks in Dec. and Jan.*

$–$$ ✕ **La Gardèla.** The kitchen seems to operate with an otherworldly efficiency, making this bright, bustling downtown restaurant extremely popular with the local business crowd—especially at lunch (always a good sign). The place is best for classics like tagliatelle al ragù and Adriatic fish, such as *sardoncini* (sardines, breaded and fried). ✉ *Via Ponte Marino 3* ☎ *0544/217147* ☰ *AE, DC, MC, V* ⏱ *Closed Thurs. and 10 days in Jan.*

★ **$–$$** ✕ **Locanda del Melarancio.** This contemporary establishment, on the second floor of a palazzo in the heart of the *centro storico*, is impossible not to like. Decor is minimalist without being stark, and modern artwork on the walls doesn't take away from the warm, traditional feeling. So, too, for the menu, which makes brilliant use of modern techniques to harness traditional Romagnan ingredients: *formaggio di fossa* (cheese aged in a cave) is made into a *sformato* (like a firm mousse) with julienned salami, honey, and balsamic vinegar, while cappellacci are filled with mascarpone and truffle under a sauce of porcini mushrooms. ⊠ *Via Mentana 33* ☎ *0544/215258* ⊕ *www.locandadelmelarancio.it* ⊟ *AE, DC, MC, V.*

★ $ ✕ **Ca' de Ven.** A vaulted wine cellar in the heart of the old city, the Ca' de Ven is great for a hearty meal. You sit at long tables with other diners and feast on platters of delicious cold cuts, flat breads, and cold, heady white wine. The tortelli *di radicchio e pecorino* (stuffed with radicchio and goat cheese) makes the best first course. ⊠ *Via C. Ricci 24* ☎ *0544/30163* ⊟ *AE, DC, MC, V* ⊘ *Closed Mon., 3 wks in Jan. and Feb., and 1st wk of June.*

$$–$$$ ▦ **Hotel Bisanzio.** Steps from San Vitale and the Tomb of Galla Placidia, this Best Western hotel is the most convenient lodging for mosaic enthusiasts. The exterior is drab, but rooms are comfortable and modern; the lobby's Florentine lamps add a touch of style. Ask to be on the top floor and you may get a view of the basilica. ⊠ *Via Salara 30, 48100* ☎ *0544/217111* 🖷 *0544/32539* ⊕ *www.bisanziohotel.com* 🛏 *38 rooms* ⚘ *Dining room, in-room safes, minibars, 2 bars, Internet room, meeting room, parking (fee)* ⊟ *AE, DC, MC, V* ⦿⦿ *BP.*

$$ ▦ **Sant'Andrea.** This simple bed-and-breakfast opened in 2005 offers an absolutely prime location, steps away from the Basilica di San Vitale. It's like staying in a well-appointed house—rooms are big, bright, and clean, done up in primary colors. The lobby is decked out with homey furniture, and breakfast can be taken in the breakfast room, or in the garden in good weather. Bathrooms are spotless and modern. A suite only costs €20 extra and can accommodate a family of four or five. ⊠ *Via Cattaneo 33, 48100* ☎🖷 *0544/215564* ⊕ *www.santandreahotel.com* 🛏 *12 rooms* ⚘ *In-room safes, minibars, bar, parking (fee)* ⊟ *AE, DC, MC, V* ⦿⦿ *BP.*

$ ▦ **Hotel Centrale Byron.** Tranquillity is assured here in the center of Ravenna's old town, because it's in a pedestrian zone. The old-fashioned, well-managed hotel has spotless if uninspired rooms. You can drop off your luggage at the door, but you have to park your car in one of the nearby garages or lots. ⊠ *Via IV Novembre 14, 48100* ☎ *0544/212225* 🖷 *0544/34114* ⊕ *www.hotelbyron.com* 🛏 *54 rooms* ⚘ *In-room safes, minibars, cable TV, bar, parking (fee)* ⊟ *AE, DC, MC, V* ⦿⦿ *BP.*

$ ▦ **Hotel Ravenna.** A functional stopover near the train station, the Ravenna is still only a few minutes' walk from the center. This modern hotel has smallish rooms; two rooms are equipped for people with disabilities. Service is friendly and helpful. ⊠ *Via Maroncelli 12, 48100* ☎ *0544/212204* 🖷 *0544/212077* ⊕ *www.hotelravenna.ra.it* 🛏 *26 rooms* ⚘ *Bar, parking (fee); no a/c* ⊟ *MC, V* ⦿⦿ *BP.*

Nightlife & the Arts

Friday evenings in July and August bring **Mosaics by Night,** when the Byzantine mosaic masterpieces in town are illuminated. The event is also held on certain Tuesdays; to check, call the tourist office, which also offers guided tours.

The **Ravenna Festival** is a musical extravaganza, held every year in June and July. Orchestras from all over the world come to perform in Ravenna's mosaic-clad churches and theaters.

EMILIA-ROMAGNA ESSENTIALS

Transportation

BY AIR

Bologna is an important business and convention center, well served by European airlines linking it with Italian cities and European capitals, including Rome and Milan (on Alitalia), Paris (on Air France), London (on British Airways and easyJet), Barcelona (on Iberia), Amsterdam (on KLM), and Frankfurt (on Lufthansa)—among others. Start-up airline EuroFly introduced the first nonstop service to the United States from Emilia-Romagna, with a direct New York (JFK)–Bologna route. At this writing, the service was limited to certain days of the week, and only operated May–September; check with the airline for the latest information. Otherwise, those wishing to fly direct often choose instead to fly into and rent a car at Milan Malpensa airport, a 45-minute drive on the A1 Autostrada from Piacenza and an easy two hours from Bologna. Alternatively, if your itinerary runs east to west, you might choose to fly into the Venice airport and rent a car there; it's about an hour's drive from Ferrara.

The main airport of the region, Guglielmo Marconi, is 10 km (6 mi) northwest of Bologna. Aerobus service (Bus 54, €5) connects Guglielmo Marconi with Bologna's central train station as well as a downtown stop. It runs every half hour from 6 AM to 11:30 PM.

🛈 Airport Information **Aerobus** ☎ 051/290290 ⊕ www.atc.bo.it. **Aeroporto Guglielmo Marconi di Bologna** ✉ Via Triumvirato 84, Bologna ☎ 051/6479615 ⊕ www.bologna-airport.it.

BY BUS

There's little reason to travel by bus in Emilia-Romagna. Trains are fast, efficient, and relatively inexpensive; they run frequently and connect most towns in the region. An ATR bus will get you to the smallest of towns, such as Bagno di Romagna, but given the inconvenience and limited schedules, it may not be worth the trip if you don't have a car.

🛈 Bus Information **ATR** ☎ 199/115577 ⊕ www.atr-online.it.

BY CAR

Entering Emilia-Romagna by car is as easy as it gets. Coming in from the west on the Autostrada del Sole (A1), Piacenza will be the first city you'll hit. It's a mere 45 minutes from Milan. On the other side of the region, Venice is about an hour from Ferrara by car on the A13.

Bologna is on the autostrada network, so driving between cities is a breeze. The Via Emilia (SS9), one of the oldest roads in the world, runs through the heart of the region. It's a straight, low-lying modern road, the length of which can be traveled in a few hours. Although less scenic, the A1 toll highway, which runs parallel to the Via Emilia from Bologna, to west Modena, Parma, and Piacenza, can get you where you're going about twice as fast. From Bologna, the A13 runs north to Ferrara, and the A14 takes you east to Ravenna and Rimini. Note that much of the historic center of Bologna is closed off to cars daily 7 AM–8 PM.

BY TRAIN

Bologna is an important rail hub for the entire northern part of Italy and has frequent, fast service to Milan, Florence, Rome, and Venice. Piacenza is less than an hour from Milan by train, Parma an hour and a half, and Bologna about two hours. The routes from Bologna to the south tend to go through Florence, which is only an hour away. The Eurostar takes 2½ hours to and from Rome; the same trip takes 4 hours on the Intercity train. On the northeastern edge of the region, Venice is an hour and a half east of Ferrara by train, and Trieste and Slovenia are not much farther.

Within the region, the railway line follows the Via Emilia (SS9). In Emilia, it's generally a half hour to 45 minutes from one major city to the next. To reach Ferrara or Ravenna, you'll usually have to change to a local train at the Bologna station. Trains run frequently, and connections are easy. Ferrara is a half hour north of Bologna on the train, and Ravenna is just over an hour.

⚡ Train Information **Ferrovie dello Stato (FS)** ☎ 892021 ⊕ www.trenitalia.com.

Contacts & Resources

EMERGENCIES

For first aid, call the police and ask for *pronto soccorso*. Be prepared to give your address. Pharmacies take turns staying open late and on Sunday; for the latest information, consult the current list posted on the front door of each pharmacy or ask at the local tourist office. ACI emergency service provides 24-hour roadside assistance.

⚡ **ACI** ☎ 803/116. **Carabinieri** ☎ 112. **Police, ambulance** ☎ 113. **Doctors and dentists** ☎ 113.

VISITOR INFORMATION

⚡ Tourist Information **Bologna** ✉ Guglielmo Marconi airport ☎ 051/246541 ✉ Stazione Centrale, 40121 ☎ 051/246541 ✉ Piazza Maggiore 1, 40124 ☎ 051/246541 ⊕ www.bolognaturismo.info. **Busseto** ✉ Comune, Piazza G. Verdi 10, 43011 ☎ 0524/92487 ⊕ www.bussetolive.com. **Dozza** ✉ Via XX Settembre, 40050 ☎ 0542/678052. **Faenza** ✉ Piazza del Popolo 1, 48018 ☎ 0546/691602. **Ferrara** ✉ Castello Estense, 44100 ☎ 0532/299303 ⊕ www.ferrarainfo.com ✉ Piazza Municipale 11, 44100 ☎ 0532/419474. **Modena** ✉ Piazza Grande 14, 41100 ☎ 059/2032660 ⊕ http://turismo.comune.modena.it. **Parma** ✉ Via Melloni 1/a, 43100 ☎ 0521/218889 ⊕ turismo.comune.parma.it. **Piacenza** ✉ Piazza Cavalli 7, 29100 ☎ 0523/329324 ⊕ www.provincia.pc.it/turismo. **Ravenna** ✉ Via Salara 8, 48100 ☎ 0544/35755 ⊕ www.turismo.ravenna.it. **Rimini** ✉ Piazzale Cesare Battisti, 47037 ☎ 0541/51331 ✉ Piazzale Fellini 3, Marina Centro, 47037 ☎ 0541/56902 ⊕ www.riminiturismo.it. **San Marino** ✉ Contra Omagnano 20, 47890 ☎ 0549/882400.

Florence

WORD OF MOUTH

"Michelangelo, Dante, Galileo. Gelato, red wine, amazing food. Some of the most wonderful art and architecture. Firenze is a magical city (and where my fiancé and I got engaged). It is an absolute gem."

–Kristin

WELCOME TO FLORENCE

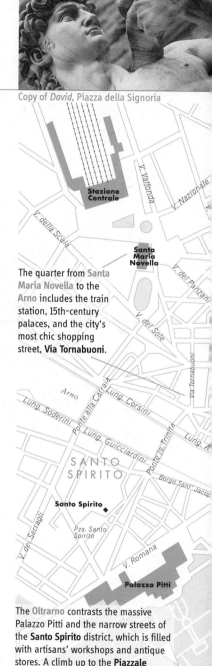

Copy of *David*, Piazza della Signoria

TOP 5
Reasons to Go

1 **Galleria degli Uffizi:** Italian Renaissance art doesn't get much better than this vast collection bequeathed to the city by the last Medici.

2 **The dome of the Duomo:** Brunelleschi's work of engineering genius is the city's undisputed centerpiece.

3 **Michelangelo's *David*:** One look and you'll know why this is the western world's most famous sculpture.

4 **The view from Piazzale Michelangelo:** From this perch the city is laid out before you. Being there at sunset heightens the experience.

5 **Piazza Santa Croce:** After you've had your fill of Renaissance masterpieces, hang out here and watch the world go by.

Getting Oriented

The historic center of Florence is flat and compact—you could walk from one end to the other in half an hour. In the middle of everything is the Duomo, with its huge dome towering over the city's terracotta rooftops. Radiating out from the Duomo are Renaissance-era neighborhoods identified by their central churches and piazzas. Though the majority of sights are north of the Arno River, the area to the south, known as the Oltrarno, has its charms as well.

The quarter from **Santa Maria Novella** to the **Arno** includes the train station, 15th-century palaces, and the city's most chic shopping street, **Via Tornabuoni**.

The **Oltrarno** contrasts the massive Palazzo Pitti and the narrow streets of the **Santo Spirito** district, which is filled with artisans' workshops and antique stores. A climb up to the **Piazzale Michelangelo** gives you a spectacular view of the city.

Piazza del Duomo

The blocks from the church of **San Lorenzo** to the **Accademia gallery** bear the imprints of the Medici family and of Michelangelo, culminating in his masterful *David*. Just to the north, the convent of San Marco is an oasis decorated with ethereal frescoes.

The area from the **Duomo** to the **Ponte Vecchio** is the heart of Florence. Among the numerous highlights are the city's greatest museum (the **Uffizi**) and an impressive square (**Piazza della Signoria**).

The **Santa Croce** district centers around its namesake basilica, which is filled with the tombs of Renaissance luminaries. The area is also known for its leather shops, some of which have been in operation since the 16th century.

MAP LABELS:

◆ San Marco
Pza. San Marco
Santissima Anunziata
V. Taddea
Galleria dell'Accademia
V. della Colonna
V. Canto de Nelli
Palazzo Medici Riccardi
V. degli Alfa...
San Lorenzo
V. Martelli
V. Bufalini
V. Cerretani
Battistero **Duomo**
Piazza del Duomo
V. dei Tosinghi
V. del Corso
Borgo degli Albizi
V. Dante Alighieri
V. Giuseppe Verdi
V. del Pepi
V. Porta Rossa
Pza. della Signoria
Via dell' Anguillara
V. dell' Agnolo
V. Vaccherecciа
Borgo dei Greci
Pza. Santa Croce
SANTA CROCE
V. Ghibellina
Galleria degli Uffizi
Santa Croce
Ponte Vecchio
Lung. Archibusieri
Corso Tintori
Arno
Lung. d. Grazie
Ponte alle Grazie
Lung. Torrigiani
OLTRARNO
Lung. Serristori

0 ¼ mile
0 400 meters

Ponte Vecchio

Santa Croce basilica

Ponte Vecchio

Santa Croce basilica

FLORENCE PLANNER

Making the Most of Your Time

With some planning, you can see Florence's most famous sights in a couple of days. Start off at the city's most awe-inspiring work of architecture, the Duomo, climbing to the top of the dome if you have the stamina. On the same piazza, check out Ghiberti's bronze doors at the Battistero. (They're actually high-quality copies; the Museo dell'Opera del Duomo has the originals.) Set aside the afternoon for the Galleria degli Uffizi, making sure to reserve tickets in advance.

On day two, visit Michelangelo's *David* in the Galleria dell'Accademia—reserve tickets here too. Linger in the Piazza della Signoria, Florence's central square, where a copy of *David* stands in the spot the original occupied for centuries, then head east a couple of blocks to Santa Croce, the city's most artistically rich church. Double back and walk across Florence's landmark bridge, the Ponte Vecchio.

Do all that, and you'll have seen some great art, but you've just scratched the surface. If you have more time, put the Bargello, the Museo di San Marco, and the Cappelle Medicee at the top of your list. When you're ready for an art break, stroll through the Boboli Gardens or explore Florence's lively shopping scene, from the food stalls of the Mercato Centrale to the chic boutiques of the Via Tornabuoni.

Getting Around

Florence's flat, compact city center is made for walking, but when your feet get weary, you can use the efficient bus system, which includes small electric buses making the rounds in the center. Buses also climb to Piazzale Michelangelo and San Miniato south of the Arno.

An automobile in Florence is a liability. If your itinerary includes parts of Italy where you'll want a car (such as Tuscany), pick the vehicle up on your way out of town. For more information on getting into, out of, and around Florence, see "Essentials" at the end of this chapter.

Titian's *Venus of Urbino*

Avoiding an Art Hangover

Trying to take in Florence's amazing art can be a headache—there's just too much to see. Especially if you're not a dedicated art enthusiast, remember to pace yourself. Allow time to wander and follow your whims, and ignore any pangs of guilt if you'd rather relax in a café and watch the world go by than trudge on sore feet through another breathtaking palace or church.

Florence isn't a city that can be "done." It's a place you can return to again and again, confident there will always be more treasures to discover.

Florentine Hours

Florence's sights keep tricky hours. Some are closed on Wednesday, some on Monday, some on *every other* Monday. Quite a few shut their doors each day (or on most days) by 2 in the afternoon. Things get even more confusing on weekends. Make it a general rule to check the hours closely for any place you're planning to visit; if it's somewhere you have your heart set on seeing, call to confirm.

Here's a selection of major sights that might not be open when you'd expect—consult the sight listings within this chapter for the full details. And be aware that, as always, hours can and do change.

■ The Uffizi and the Accademia are both closed Monday. All but a few of the galleries at Palazzo Pitti are closed Monday as well.

■ The Duomo closes at 3:30 on Thursday (as opposed to 5:30 on other weekdays, 4:45 on weekends). The dome of the Duomo is closed on Sunday.

■ The Battistero is open from noon until 7, Monday through Saturday, and on Sunday from 8:30 to 2.

■ The Bargello closes at 1:50 in the afternoon, and is closed entirely on alternating Sundays and Mondays.

■ The Cappelle Medicee are closed on alternating Sundays and Mondays.

■ Museo di San Marco closes at 1:50 on weekdays but stays open till 7 on weekends—except for alternating Sundays and Mondays, when it's closed entirely.

■ Palazzo Medici-Riccardi is closed Wednesday.

Making Reservations

At most times of day you'll see a line of people snaking around the Uffizi. They're waiting to buy tickets, and you don't want to be one of them. Instead, call ahead for a reservation (055/294883; reservationists speak English). You'll be given a reservation number and a time of admission—the further in advance you call, the more time slots you'll have to choose from. Go to the museum's reservation door at the appointed hour, give the clerk your number, pick up your ticket, and go inside. You'll pay €3 for this privilege, but it's money well spent.

Use the same reservation service to book tickets for the Galleria dell'Accademia, where lines rival those of the Uffizi. (Reservations can also be made for the Palazzo Pitti, the Bargello, and several other sights, but they aren't needed.) An alternative strategy is to check with your hotel—many will handle reservations.

How's the Weather?

The best times to visit Florence are in the spring and the fall. Days are warm, nights are cool, and the city is crowded, but not overly so. Avoid July and August if at all possible: the heat is unbearable, air-conditioning something of a rarity, mosquitoes are rampant, and so are tour groups. Those who want to find the city at its emptiest should consider visiting in November or January. It rains quite a bit and can get cold, but you'll spare yourself waits at museums and have reduced competition at restaurant tables.

8

Piazza Signoria

TOP PASSEGGIATA

Via dei Calzaiuoli, between Piazza del Duomo and Piazza della Signoria, is where Florence comes out for its evening stroll.

Updated by
Patricia Rucidlo

FLORENCE, THE CITY OF THE LILY, gave birth to the Renaissance and changed the way we see the world. For centuries it has captured the imagination of travelers, who come here to walk in the footsteps of Dante, Donatello, Botticelli, and Michelangelo. You'll find sublime art at almost every turn, but Florence (Firenze in Italian) isn't simply one large museum. Even if *David* and the Duomo didn't exist, you could still fall in love with the city for its winding streets, its earthy yet sophisticated food and wine, or the way the natives manage to lead thoroughly modern lives in a place that hasn't changed all that much since the 16th century.

Florence was "discovered" in the 1700s by upper-class northerners making the grand tour. It became a mecca for travelers, particularly the Romantics, who were inspired by the elegance of its palazzi and its artistic wealth. Today millions of modern visitors follow in their footsteps. When the sun sets over the Arno and, as Mark Twain described it, "overwhelms Florence with tides of color that make all the sharp lines dim and faint and turn the solid city to a city of dreams," it's hard not to fall under the city's spell.

EXPLORING FLORENCE

Most sights in Florence are concentrated in the relatively small historic center, and walking through its streets and alleyways is a discovery in itself. Today a handful of the more than 200 towers built in the 12th and 13th centuries survive; look for them them as you explore. The town has managed to preserve its predominantly medieval street plan and mostly Renaissance infrastructure while successfully adapting to the insistent demands of 21st-century life.

Centro Storico: The Duomo to the Ponte Vecchio

Florence's *centro storico* (historic center), stretching from the Piazza del Duomo south to the Arno, is as dense with artistic treasures as anyplace in the world. The churches, medieval towers, Renaissance palaces, and world-class museums and galleries contain some of the most outstanding aesthetic achievements of Western history.

Much of the centro storico is closed to automobile traffic, but you still must dodge mopeds, cyclists, and masses of fellow tourists as you walk the narrow streets, especially in the area bounded by the Duomo, Piazza della Signoria, Galleria degli Uffizi, and Ponte Vecchio.

The Main Attractions

★ ❼ **Bargello.** During the Renaissance, this building was headquarters for the *podestà*, or chief magistrate. It was also used as a prison, and the exterior served as a "most wanted" billboard: effigies of notorious criminals and Medici enemies were painted on its walls. Today it houses the **Museo Nazionale**, containing what is probably the finest collection of Renaissance sculpture in

> **WORD OF MOUTH**
>
> "I think the Bargello might be the most underrated museum in Florence, if not Italy."   –Jess

FLORENCE THROUGH THE AGES

Guelph vs. Ghibelline. Though Florence can lay claim to a modest importance in the ancient world, it didn't come into its own until the Middle Ages. In the early 1200s, the city, like most of the rest of Italy, was rent by civic unrest. Two factions, the Guelphs and the Ghibellines, competed for power. The Guelphs supported the papacy, the Ghibellines the Holy Roman Empire. Bloody battles—most notably at Montaperti in 1260—tore Florence and other Italian cities apart. By the end of the 13th century the Guelphs ruled securely and Ghibellines had been vanquished. This didn't end civic strife, however: the Guelphs split into the Whites and the Blacks for reasons still debated by historians. Dante was banished from Florence in 1301 because he was a White.

The Guilded Age. Local merchants had organized themselves into guilds by 1250. In that year they proclaimed themselves the "*primo popolo*" (literally, "first people"), and made an attempt at elective, republican rule. Though the episode lasted only 10 years, it constituted a breakthrough in Western history. Such a daring stance by the merchant class was a by-product of Florence's emerging economic power. Florentines were papal bankers; they instituted the system of international letters of credit; and the gold florin became the international standard currency. With this economic strength came a building boom. Palaces and basilicas were erected or enlarged. Sculptors such as Donatello and Ghiberti decorated them; painters such as Giotto and Botticelli frescoed their walls.

Mighty Medici. Though ostensibly a republic, Florence was blessed (or cursed) with one very powerful family, the Medici, who came to prominence in the 1430s and were the de facto rulers of Florence for several hundred years. It was under patriarch Cosimo il Vecchio (1389–1464) that the Medici's position in Florence was securely established. Florence's golden age occurred during the reign of his grandson Lorenzo de' Medici (1449–92). Lorenzo was not only an astute politician but also a highly educated man and a great patron of the arts. Called "Il Magnifico" (the Magnificent), he gathered around him poets, artists, philosophers, architects, and musicians.

Lorenzo's son, Piero (1471–1503), proved inept at handling the city's affairs. He was run out of town in 1494, and Florence briefly enjoyed its status as a republic while dominated by the Dominican friar Girolamo Savonarola (1452–98). After a decade of internal unrest, the republic fell and the Medici were recalled to power, but Florence never regained its former prestige. By the 1530s most of the major artistic talent had left the city—Michelangelo, for one, had settled in Rome. The now-ineffectual Medici, eventually attaining the title of grand dukes, remained nominally in power until the death of heirless Gian Gastone in 1737. (The last of the Medicis, Gian Gastone's sister Anna Maria Luisa, died equally childless in 1743.) With the demise of the Medicis, Florence passed from the Austrians to the French and back again until the unification of Italy (1865–70), when it briefly became the capital under King Vittorio Emanuele II.

8

Italy. The concentration of masterworks by Michelangelo (1475–1564), Donatello (circa 1386–1466), and Benvenuto Cellini (1500–71) is remarkable; they're distributed among an eclectic array of arms, ceramics, and enamels. For Renaissance-art lovers, the Bargello is to sculpture what the Uffizi is to painting.

In 1401 Filippo Brunelleschi (1377–1446) and Lorenzo Ghiberti (circa 1378–1455) vied for the most prestigious commission of the day: the decoration of the north doors of the baptistery in Piazza del Duomo. For the competition, each designed a bronze bas-relief panel depicting the Sacrifice of Isaac; both panels are displayed, together, in the room devoted to the sculpture of Donatello on the upper floor. The judges chose Ghiberti for the commission; see if you agree with their choice. ⊠ *Via del Proconsolo 4, Bargello* ☎ *055/2388606* ⊕ *www.polomuseale. firenze.it* ⌨ *€4* ⊘ *Daily 8:15–1:50. Closed 2nd and 4th Mon. of month and 1st, 3rd, and 5th Sun. of month.*

★ ❷ **Battistero** (Baptistery). The octagonal Baptistery is one of the supreme monuments of the Italian Romanesque style and one of Florence's oldest structures. Local legend has it that it was once a Roman temple of Mars; modern excavations, however, suggest that its foundations date from the 4th to 5th and the 8th to 9th century AD, well after the collapse of the Roman Empire. The round-arch Romanesque decoration on the exterior probably dates from the 11th century. The interior dome mosaics from the early 14th century are justly renowned, but—glittering beauties though they are—they could never outshine the building's famed bronze Renaissance doors decorated with panels crafted by Lorenzo Ghiberti. The doors—or at least copies of them—on which Ghiberti spent most of his adult life (1403–52) are on the north and east sides of the Baptistery, and the Gothic panels on the south door were designed by Andrea Pisano (active circa 1290–1348) in 1330. The original Ghiberti doors were removed to protect them from the effects of pollution and have been beautifully restored; some of the panels are now on display in the Museo dell'Opera del Duomo.

Ghiberti's north doors depict scenes from the life of Christ; his later east doors (dating 1425–52), facing the Duomo facade, render scenes from the Old Testament. Very different in style, they illustrate the artistic changes that marked the beginning of the Renaissance. Look at the far right panel of the middle row on the earlier (1403–24) north doors (*Jesus Calming the Waters*). Ghiberti captured the chaos of a storm at sea with great skill and economy, but the artistic conventions he used are basically pre-Renaissance: Jesus is the most important figure, so he is the largest; the disciples are next in size, being next in importance; the ship on which they founder looks like a mere toy.

The exquisitely rendered panels on the east doors are larger, more expansive, more sweeping—and more convincing. Look at the middle panel on the left-hand door. It tells the story of Jacob and Esau, and the various episodes—the selling of the birthright, Isaac ordering Esau to go hunting, the blessing of Jacob, and so forth—have been merged into a single beautifully realized street scene. Ghiberti's use of perspective suggests depth: the background architecture looks far more credible than on the north door panels, the figures in the foreground are grouped realistically, and the naturalism and grace of the poses (look at Esau's left leg and the dog next to him) have nothing to do with the sacred message being conveyed. Although the religious content remains, the figures and their place in the natural world are given unprecedented prominence and are portrayed with a realism not seen in art since the fall of the Roman Empire more than a thousand years before.

As a footnote to Ghiberti's panels, one small detail of the east doors is worth a special look. To the lower left of the Jacob and Esau panel, Ghiberti placed a tiny self-portrait bust. From either side, the portrait is extremely appealing—Ghiberti looks like everyone's favorite uncle—but the bust is carefully placed so that there is a single spot from which you can make direct eye contact with the tiny head. When that contact is made, the impression of intelligent life is astonishing. It is no wonder that these doors received one of the most famous compliments in the history of art from an artist known to be notoriously stingy with praise: Michelangelo himself declared them so beautiful that they could serve as the Gates of Paradise. ⊠ *Piazza del Duomo* 🕾 *055/2302885* ⊕ *www. operaduomo.firenze.it* 🎫 *€3* 🕙 *Mon.–Sat. noon–7, Sun. 8:30–2.*

❸ **Campanile.** The Gothic bell tower designed by Giotto (1266–1337) is a soaring structure of multicolor marble originally decorated with reliefs that are now in the Museo dell'Opera del Duomo. They have been replaced with copies. A climb of 414 steps rewards you with a close-up of Brunelleschi's cupola on the Duomo next door and a sweeping view of the city. ⊠ *Piazza del Duomo* 🕾 *055/2302885* ⊕ *www.operaduomo. firenze.it* 🎫 *€6* 🕙 *Daily 8:30–7:30.*

★ ❶ **Duomo** (Cattedrale di Santa Maria del Fiore). In 1296 Arnolfo di Cambio (circa 1245–circa 1310) was commissioned to build "the loftiest, most sumptuous edifice human invention could devise" in the Romanesque style on the site of the old church of Santa Reparata. The immense Duomo was not completed until 1436, the year it was consecrated. The imposing facade dates only from the 19th century; its neo-Gothic style complements Giotto's genuine Gothic 14th-century campanile. The real glory of the Duomo, however, is Filippo Brunelleschi's dome, presiding over the cathedral with a dignity and grace that few domes to this day can match.

> **WORD OF MOUTH**
>
> "The Duomo was a truly amazing cathedral. We visited it twice, once to attend mass (in English, which we appreciated), and once to look at its architecture and art and to climb up to the top. Although the climb is definitely a bit tiring, it was well worth it—the view from the top was incredible."   –Gina

Brunelleschi's **cupola** was an ingenious engineering feat. The space to be enclosed by the dome was so large and so high above the ground that traditional methods of dome construction—wooden centering and scaffolding—were of no use whatsoever. So Brunelleschi developed en-

8

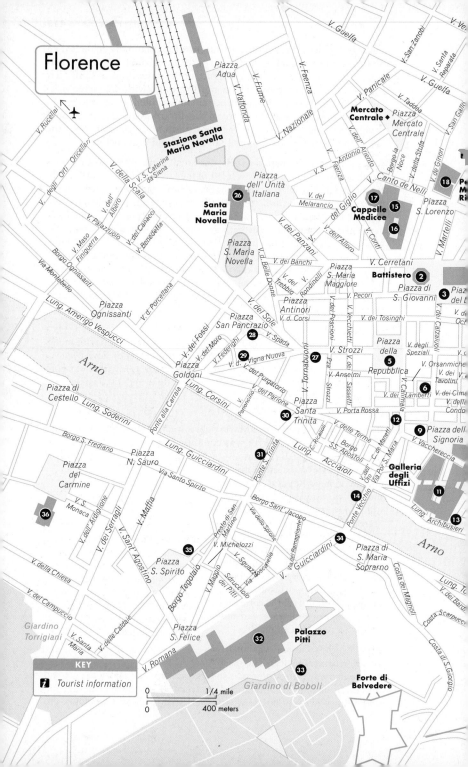

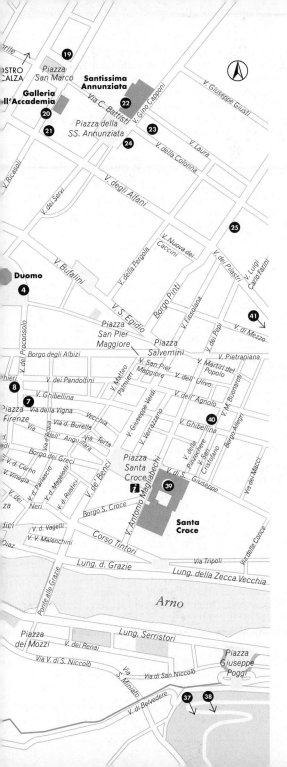

Badia Fiorentina **8**

Bargello (Museo Nazionale) **7**

Battistero **2**

Biblioteca Medicea
Laurenziana **16**

Campanile **3**

Cappelle Medicee **17**

Casa Buonarroti **40**

Duomo **1**

Galleria degli Uffizi **11**

Galleria dell'Accademia **20**

Giardino di Boboli **33**

Istituto e Museo di Storia
della Scienza **13**

Mercato Nuovo **12**

Museo Archeologico **23**

Museo dell'Opera
del Duomo **4**

Museo dell' Opificio delle
Pietre Dure **21**

Museo di San Marco **19**

Museo Marino Marini **28**

Orsanmichele **6**

Palazzo Medici-Riccardi **18**

Palazzo Pitti **32**

Palazzo Rucellai **29**

Palazzo Strozzi **27**

Palazzo Vecchio **10**

Piazza della Repubblica **5**

Piazza della Signoria **9**

Piazzale Michelangelo **38**

Ponte Santa Trinita **31**

Ponte Vecchio **14**

San Lorenzo **15**

San Miniato al Monte **37**

Santa Croce **39**

Santa Felicita **34**

Santa Maria del Carmine **36**

Santa Maria
Maddalena dei Pazzi **25**

Santa Maria Novella **26**

Santa Trinita **30**

Santissima Annunziata **22**

Santo Spirito **35**

Sinagoga **41**

Spedale degli Innocenti **24**

tirely new building methods, which he implemented with equipment of his own design (including a novel scaffolding method). Beginning work in 1420, he built not one dome but two, one inside the other, and connected them with common ribbing that stretched across the intervening empty space, thereby considerably lessening the crushing weight of the structure. He also employed a new method of bricklaying, based on an ancient Roman herringbone pattern, interlocking each course of bricks with the course below in a way that made the growing structure self-supporting. The result was one of the great engineering breakthroughs of all time: most of Europe's later domes, including that of St. Peter's in Rome, were built employing Brunelleschi's methods, and today the Duomo has come to symbolize Florence in the same way that the Eiffel Tower symbolizes Paris. The Florentines are justly proud, and to this day the Florentine phrase for "homesick" is *nostalgia del cupolone* (homesick for the dome).

The interior is a fine example of Florentine Gothic. Much of the cathedral's best-known art has been moved to the nearby Museo dell'Opera del Duomo. Notable among the works that remain, however, are towering equestrian frescoes honoring famous soldiers: *Niccolò da Tolentino,* painted in 1456 by Andrea del Castagno (circa 1419–57), and *Sir John Hawkwood,* painted 20 years earlier by Paolo Uccello (1397–1475); both are on the left-hand wall of the nave. A 10-year restoration, completed in 1995, repaired the dome and cleaned the vast and crowded fresco of the *Last Judgment,* executed by Vasari and Zuccaro, on its interior. Originally Brunelleschi wanted mosaics to cover the interior of the great ribbed cupola, but by the time the Florentines got around to commissioning the decoration, 150 years later, tastes had changed. Too bad: it's a fairly dreadful *Last Judgment* and hardly worth the effort of craning your neck to see it.

You can explore the upper and lower reaches of the cathedral. The remains of a Roman wall and an 11th-century cemetery have been excavated beneath the nave; the way down is near the first pier on the right. The **climb to the top of the dome** (463 steps) is not for the faint of heart, but the view is superb. ⊠ *Piazza del Duomo* ☎ *055/2302885* ⊕ *www. operaduomo.firenze.it* ✆ *Church free, crypt* €3, *cupola* €6 ۞ *Church Mon.–Wed. and Fri. 10–5, Thurs. 10–3:30, Sat. 10–4:45, Sun. 1:30–4:45, 1st Sat. of month 10–3:30. Crypt Mon.–Wed. and Fri. 10–5, Thurs. 10–3:30, Sat. 10–5:45, 1st Sat. of month 10–3:30. Cupola weekdays 8:30–7, Sat. 8:30–5:40, 1st Sat. of month 8:30–4.*

⑪ Galleria degli Uffizi. The venerable Uffizi Gallery occupies the top floor of the U-shape **Palazzo degli Uffizi** fronting on the Arno, designed by Giorgio Vasari (1511–74) in 1560 to hold the *uffizi* (administrative offices) of the Medici grand duke Cosimo I (1519–74). Later, the Medici installed their art collections here, creating what was Europe's first modern museum, open to the public (at first only by request) since 1591. Hard-core museum aficionados can pick up a complete guide to the collections at bookshops and newsstands.

Among the highlights are Paolo Uccello's *Battle of San Romano,* its brutal chaos of lances one of the finest visual metaphors for warfare ever

FodorsChoice
★

captured in paint; the *Madonna and Child with Two Angels,* by Fra Filippo Lippi (1406–69), in which the impudent eye contact established by the angel would have been unthinkable prior to the Renaissance; the *Birth of Venus* and *Primavera* by Sandro Botticelli (1445–1510), the goddess of the former seeming to float on air and the fairy-tale charm of the latter exhibiting the painter's idiosyncratic genius at its zenith; the portraits of the Renaissance duke Federico da Montefeltro and his wife, Battista Sforza, by Piero della Francesca (circa 1420–92); the *Madonna of the Goldfinch* by Raphael (1483–1520), which, though darkened by time, captures an aching tenderness between mother and child; Michelangelo's *Doni Tondo* (the only panel painting that can be securely attributed to him); a *Self-Portrait as an Old Man* by Rembrandt (1606–69); the *Venus of Urbino* by Titian (circa 1488/90–1576); and the splendid *Bacchus* by Caravaggio (circa 1571/72–1610). In the last two works, the approaches to myth and sexuality are diametrically opposed, to put it mildly. Six additional exhibition rooms opened in 2004, convoluting the way you exit the museum. Many of the more than 400 works now displayed would have been better left in storage.

> **WORD OF MOUTH**
>
> "The Uffizi has gorgeous high Renaissance art, but in my experience it is a user-unfriendly museum: lots of stairs, no captions or signs to speak of, no a/c. I was glad I went but I was also glad to leave. I'll go again, but with a headache tablet in hand."　　　–elaine

Late in the afternoon is the least crowded time to visit. For a fee, advance tickets can be reserved by phone or, once in Florence, at the Uffizi reservation booth at least one day in advance of your visit. If you book by phone, remember to keep the confirmation number and take it with you to the door at the museum marked "Reservations." Usually you're ushered in almost immediately. Come with cash, because credit cards are not accepted. When there's a special exhibit on, which is often, the base ticket price goes up to €9.50. ✉ *Piazzale degli Uffizi 6, near Piazza della Signoria* ☎ *055/2388651* ✉ *Advance tickets* ✉ *Consorzio ITA, Piazza Pitti 1, 50121* ☎ *055/294883* ⊕ *www.uffizi.firenze. it* 💶 *€6.50, reservation fee €3* ⊙ *Tues.–Sun. 8:15–6:50.*

NEED A BREAK?　Calling itself a "zupperia," **La Canova di GustaVino** (✉ Via della Condotta 29/r, near Piazza della Signoria ☎ 055/2399806) keeps several hearty, restorative soups on hand. Solid fare includes mixed cheese plates (both French and Italian), as well as *tomino con prosciutto* (mild cow's cheese, topped with thin slices of prosciutto) run under the broiler.

★ ❾ **Piazza della Signoria.** This is by far the most striking square in Florence. It was here, in 1497, that the famous "bonfire of the vanities" took place, when the fanatical friar Savonarola induced his followers to hurl their worldly goods into the flames; it was also here, a year later, that he was hanged as a heretic and, ironically, burned. A bronze plaque in the pavement marks the exact spot of his execution.

The statues in the square and in the 14th-century **Loggia dei Lanzi** on the south side vary in quality. Cellini's famous bronze *Perseus* holding the severed head of Medusa is certainly the most important sculpture in the loggia. Other works include *The Rape of the Sabine* and *Hercules and the Centaur,* both late-16th-century works by Giambologna (1529–1608), and, in the back, a row of sober matrons dating to ancient Roman times.

In the square, the Neptune Fountain, dating from between 1550 and 1575, wins the booby prize. It was created by Bartolomeo Ammannati (1511–92), who considered it a failure himself. The Florentines call it *Il Biancone,* which may be translated as "the big white one" or "the big white thing." Giambologna's equestrian statue to the left of the fountain pays tribute to Grand Duke Cosimo I. Occupying the steps of the Palazzo Vecchio are a copy of Donatello's heraldic lion of Florence, known as the *Marzocco* (the original is in the Bargello); a copy of Donatello's *Judith and Holofernes* (the original is inside the Palazzo Vecchio); a copy of Michelangelo's *David* (the original is now in the Galleria dell'Accademia); and Baccio Bandinelli's insipid *Hercules* (1534).

⑭ Ponte Vecchio (Old Bridge). This charming bridge was built in 1345 to replace an earlier bridge that was swept away by a flood, and its shops housed first butchers, then grocers, blacksmiths, and other merchants. But in 1593 the Medici grand duke Ferdinand I (1549–1609), whose private corridor linking the Medici palace (Palazzo Pitti) with the Medici offices (the Uffizi) crossed the bridge atop the shops, decided that all this plebeian commerce under his feet was unseemly. So he threw out the butchers and blacksmiths and installed 41 goldsmiths and eight jewelers. The bridge has been devoted solely to these two trades ever since.

Also Worth Seeing

⑧ Badia Fiorentina. This ancient church was rebuilt in 1285; its graceful bell tower, best seen from the interior courtyard, is beautiful for its unusual construction—a hexagonal tower built on a quadrangular base. The interior of the church was halfheartedly remodeled in the baroque style during the 17th century; its best-known work of art is the delicate *Vision of St. Bernard* by Filippino Lippi (circa 1457–1504), on the left as you enter. The painting—one of Lippi's finest—is in superb condition; note the Virgin Mary's beautifully rendered hands. ⊠ *Via Dante Alighieri 1, near Bargello* ☎ *055/264402* ⊠ *Free* ☉ *Mon. 3–6.*

⑬ Istituto e Museo di Storia della Scienza (Institute and Museum of the History of Science). Though it tends to be obscured by the glamour of the Uffizi, this science museum has much to recommend it: Galileo's own instruments, antique armillary spheres—some of them real works of art—and other reminders that the Renaissance made not only artistic but also scientific history. ⊠ *Piazza dei Giudici 1, near Piazza della Signoria* ☎ *055/265311* ⊕ *www.imss.fi.it* ⊠ *€5* ☉ *Oct.–May, Mon., Wed.–Sat. 9:30–5, Tues. 9:30–1; 2nd Sun. of month 10–1; June–Sept., Mon. and Wed.–Fri. 9:30–5, Tues. and Sat. 9:30–1; last Thurs. of June and Aug. 8–11, 1st Thurs. of July and Sept. 8–11.*

☾ ⑫ Mercato Nuovo (New Market). This open-air loggia was new in 1551. Beyond its slew of souvenir stands, its main attraction is a copy of

Pietro Tacca's bronze *Porcellino* (which translates as "little pig," despite the fact that the animal is, in fact, a wild boar) on the south side, dating from around 1612 and copied from an earlier Roman work now in the Uffizi. The Porcellino is Florence's equivalent of the Trevi Fountain: put a coin in his mouth, and if it falls through the grate below (according to one interpretation), it means that one day you'll return to Florence. ⊠ *Corner of Via Por Santa Maria and Via Porta Rossa, near Piazza della Repubblica* ☉ *Tues.–Sat. 8–7, Mon. 1–7.*

4 **Museo dell'Opera del Duomo** (Cathedral Museum). Ghiberti's original Baptistery door panels and the *cantorie* (choir loft) reliefs by Donatello and Luca della Robbia (1400–82) keep company with Donatello's *Mary Magdalen* and Michelangelo's *Pietà* (not to be confused with his more famous *Pietà* in St. Peter's in Rome). Renaissance sculpture is in part defined by its revolutionary realism, but in its palpable suffering Donatello's *Magdalen* goes beyond realism. Michelangelo's heart-wrenching *Pietà* was unfinished at his death; the female figure on the left was added by one Tiberio Calcagni (1532–65), and never has the difference between competence and genius been manifested so clearly. ⊠ *Piazza del Duomo 9* ☎ *055/2302885* ⊕ *www.operaduomo.firenze.it* ⫷ €6 ☉ *Mon.–Sat. 9–7:30, Sun. 9–1:40.*

6 **Orsanmichele.** This multipurpose structure began as an 8th-century oratory, then in 1290 was turned into an open-air loggia for selling grain. Destroyed by fire in 1304, it was rebuilt as a loggia-market. Between 1367 and 1380 the arcades were closed and two stories added above; finally, at century's end it was turned into a church. Within the church is a beautifully detailed 14th-century Gothic tabernacle by Andrea Orcagna (1320–68). The exterior niches contain copies of sculptures dating from the early 1400s to the early 1600s by Donatello and Verrocchio (1435–88), among others, that were paid for by the guilds. Though it is a copy, Verrocchio's *Doubting Thomas* (circa 1470) is particularly deserving of attention. Here Christ, like the building's other figures, is entirely framed within the niche, and St. Thomas stands on its bottom ledge, with his right foot outside the niche frame. This one detail, the positioning of a single foot, brings the whole composition to life. You can see the original sculptures inside, in the **Museo di Orsanmichele,** accessed via its own flight of stairs. ⊠ *Via dei Calzaiuoli (museum entrance at Via Arte della Lana), near Piazza della Repubblica* ☎ *055/284944* ⫷ *Free* ☉ *Weekdays 9–noon and 4–6, weekends 9–1 and 4–6. Closed 1st and last Mon. of month.*

10 **Palazzo Vecchio** (Old Palace). Florence's forbidding, fortresslike city hall, presumed to have been designed by Arnolfo di Cambio, was begun in 1299, and its massive bulk and towering campanile dominate the Piazza della Signoria. It was built as a meeting place for the elected guildsmen who governed the city at the time; over the centuries it has served lesser purposes, but today it is once again City Hall. The interior courtyard is a good deal less severe, having been remodeled by Michelozzo (1396–1472) in 1453; the copy of Verrocchio's bronze *puttino* (little child), topping the central fountain, softens the space.

8

Two adjoining rooms on the second floor supply one of the starkest contrasts in Florence. The vast **Sala dei Cinquecento** (Room of the Five Hundred) is named for the 500-member Great Council, the people's assembly established by Savonarola, which met here. The Sala was later decorated by Giorgio Vasari, around 1563–65, with huge—almost grotesquely huge—frescoes celebrating Florentine history; depictions of battles with nearby cities predominate. Continuing the martial theme, the Sala also contains Michelangelo's *Victory* group, intended for the never-completed tomb of Pope Julius II (1443–1513), plus other lesser sculptures.

The little **Studiolo** is to the right of the Sala's entrance. The study of Cosimo I's son, the melancholy Francesco I (1541–87), was designed by Vasari and decorated by Vasari and Bronzino (1503–72). It's intimate, civilized, and filled with allegorical art. ⊠ *Piazza della Signoria* ☎ *055/2768465* ▣ *€6* ☉ *By reservation Mon.–Wed. and Fri.–Sun. 9–7, Thurs. 9–2.*

❺ Piazza della Repubblica. This was the site of the ancient forum at the core of the original Roman settlement. The street plan in the area around the piazza still reflects the carefully plotted grid of the Roman military encampment. The Mercato Vecchio (Old Market), dating from the Middle Ages, was demolished and the piazza you see now was constructed between 1885 and 1895 as a neoclassical showpiece. The piazza is lined with outdoor cafés affording excellent spots to people-watch.

In Michelangelo's Footsteps: San Lorenzo to the Accademia

A sculptor, painter, architect, and even a poet, Florentine native son Michelangelo was a consummate genius, and some of his finest creations remain in his hometown. The Biblioteca Medicea Laurenziana is perhaps his most fanciful work of architecture. A key to understanding Michelangelo's genius can be found in the magnificent Cappelle Medicee, where both his sculptural and architectural prowess can be clearly seen. Planned frescoes were never completed, sadly, for they would have shown in one space the

> **WORD OF MOUTH**
>
> "Seeing *David* is a must. It is one of those magical moments in life."
> –JandaO

artistic triple threat that he certainly was. The towering yet graceful *David,* his most famous work, resides in the Galleria dell'Accademia.

After visiting San Lorenzo, resist the temptation to explore the market that surrounds the church. You can always come back later, after the churches and museums have closed; the market is open until 7 PM. Note that the Museo di San Marco closes at 1:50 on weekdays.

The Main Attractions

★ ⓱ Cappelle Medicee (Medici Chapels). This magnificent complex includes the **Cappella dei Principi,** the Medici chapel and mausoleum that was begun in 1605 and kept marble workers busy for several hundred years, and the **Sagrestia Nuova** (New Sacristy), designed by Michelangelo and so called to distinguish it from Brunelleschi's *Sagrestia Vecchia* (Old Sacristy).

Continued on page 429

WHO'S WHO OF RENAISSANCE ART

Michelangelo. Leonardo da Vinci. Raphael. The heady triumvirate of the Italian Renaissance is synonymous with artistic genius. Yet they are only three of the remarkable cast of characters whose work inspired the Renaissance, that extraordinary flourishing of art and culture in Italy, especially in Florence, as the Middle Ages drew to a close. The artists were visionaries, who redefined painting, sculpture, architecture, and even what it means to be an artist.

THE PIONEER. In the mid-14th century, a few artists began to move away the flat, two-dimensional painting of the Middle Ages. **Giotto**, who painted seemingly three-dimensional figures who show emotion, had a major impact on the artists of the next century.

THE GROUNDBREAKERS. The generations of **Brunelleschi** and **Botticelli** took center stage in the 15th century. **Ghiberti, Donatello, Uccello, Fra Angelico, Masaccio,** and **Filippo Lippi** were other major players. Part of the Renaissance (or "rebirth") was a renewed interest in classical sources—the texts, monuments, and sculpture of Ancient Greece and Rome. Perspective and the illusion of three-dimensional space in painting was another theme of this era, known as the Early Renaissance. Suddenly the art appearing on the walls looked real, or more realistic than it used to.

Roman ruins were not the only thing to inspire these artists. There was an incredible exchange of ideas going on. In Santa Maria del Carmine, Filippo Lippi was inspired by the work of Masaccio, who in turn was a friend of Brunelleschi. Young artists also learned from the masters via the apprentice system. Ghiberti's workshop (*bottega* in Italian) included, at one time or another, Donatello, Masaccio, and Uccello. Botticelli was apprenticed to Filippo Lippi.

THE BIG THREE. The mathematical rationality and precision of 15th-century art gave way to what is known as the High Renaissance. **Leonardo, Michelangelo,** and **Raphael** were much more concerned with portraying the body in all its glory and with achieving harmony and grandeur in their work. Oil paint, used sparingly and unknowingly up until this time, became more widely employed: as a result, Leonardo's colors are deeper, more sensual, more alive. For one brief time, all three were in Florence at the same time. Michelangelo and Leonardo surely knew one another, as they were simultaneously working on frescoes (never completed) inside Palazzo Vecchio.

When Michelangelo left Florence for Rome in 1508, he began the slow drain of artistic exodus from Florence, which never really recovered her previous glory.

A RENAISSANCE TIMELINE

IN THE WORLD

Black Death in Europe kills one
third of the population, 1347-50.

Joan of Arc burned
at the stake, 1431.

IN FLORENCE

Dante, a native of Florence, writes
The Divine Comedy, 1302-21.

Founding
of the Medici
bank, 1397.

Medici family
made official
papal bankers.

1434, Cosimo il Vecchio
becomes de facto ruler
of Florence. The Medici
family will dominate the
city until 1494.

1300

1400

IN ART

EARLY RENAISSANCE

Giotto fresoes in Santa Croce,
1320-25.

Masaccio and Masolino
fresco Santa Maria del
Carmine, 1424-28.

GIOTTO (ca. 1267-1337)

BRUNELLESCHI (1377-1446)

LORENZO GHIBERTI (ca. 1381-1455)

DONATELLO (ca. 1386-1466)

PAOLO UCCELLO (1397-1475)

FRA ANGELICO (ca. 1400-1455)

MASACCIO (1401-1428)

FILIPPO LIPPI (ca. 1406-1469)

Donatello sculpts his
bronze *David*, ca. 1440.

Fra Angelico frescoes
monks' cells in San Marco,
ca. 1438-45.

Uccello's *Sir John
Hawkwood*, ca. 1436.

1334, 67-year-old Giotto is appointed
chief architect of Santa Maria del
Fiore, Florence's Duomo (above). He
begins to work on the Campanile,
which will be completed in 1359,
after his death.

Ghiberti wins the
competition for the
Baptistery doors
(above) in
Florence, 1401.

Brunelleschi wins the
competition for the
Duomo's cupola (below),
1418.

Gutenberg Bible is
printed, 1455.

Columbus discovers
America, 1492.

Martin Luther posts his 95 theses on
the door at Wittenberg, kicking off the
Protestant Reformation, 1517.

Constantinople falls
to the Turks, 1453.

Machiavelli's *Prince*
appears, 1513.

Copernicus proves that the
earth is not the center of
the universe, 1530-43.

Lorenzo "il Magnifico"
(right), the Medici patron
of the arts, rules in
Florence, 1449-92.

Two Medici popes Leo X
(1513-21) and Clement VII
(1523-34) in Rome.

Catherine de'Medici
becomes Queen of France,
1547.

1450   **1500**   **1550**

HIGH RENAISSANCE   MANNERISM

Botticelli paints the
Birth of Venus, ca. 1482.

1508, Raphael begins
work on the chambers
in the Vatican, Rome.

Giorgio Vasari
publishes his first
edition of *Lives of
the Artists*, 1550.

1504, Michelangelo's
David is put on display
in Piazza della
Signoria, where it
remains until 1873.

Leonardo paints
The Last Supper in
Milan, 1495-98.

Michelangelo
begins to
fresco the
Sistine Chapel
ceiling, 1508.

BOTTICELLI (ca. 1444-1510)

LEONARDO DA VINCI (1452-1519)

RAPHAEL (1483-1520)

MICHELANGELO (1475-1564)

Fra Filippo Lippi's
*Madonna and
Child*, ca. 1452.

Giotto's *Death of St. Francis*   Donatello's *St. John the Baptist*   Ghiberti's *Gates of Paradise*

GIOTTO (CA. 1267-1337)

Painter/architect from a small town north of Florence.

He unequivocally set Italian painting on the course that led to the triumphs of the Renaissance masters. Unlike the rather flat, two-dimensional forms found in then prevailing Byzantine art, Giotto's figures have a fresh, life-like quality. The people in his paintings have bulk, and they show emotion, which you can see on their faces and in their gestures. This was something new in the late Middle Ages. Without Giotto, there wouldn't have been a Raphael.

In Florence: **Santa Croce; Uffizi; Campanile; Santa Maria Novella**

Elsewhere in Italy: **Scrovegni Chapel, Padua; Vatican Museums, Rome**

FILIPPO BRUNELLESCHI (1377-1446)

Architect/engineer from Florence.

If Brunelleschi had beaten Ghiberti in the Baptistery doors competition in Florence, the city's Duomo most likely would not have the striking appearance and authority that it has today. After his loss, he sulked off to Rome, where he studied the ancient Roman structures first-hand. Brunelleschi figured out how to vault the Duomo's dome, a structure unprecedented in its colossal size and great height. His Ospedale degli Innocenti employs classical elements in the creation of a stunning, new architectural statement; it is the first truly Renaissance structure.

In Florence: **Duomo; Ospedale degli Innocenti; San Lorenzo; Santo Spirito; Baptistery Doors Competition Entry, Bargello; Santa Croce**

LORENZO GHIBERTI (CA. 1381-1455)

Sculptor from Florence.

Ghiberti won a competition—besting his chief rival, Brunelleschi—to cast the gilded bronze North Doors of the Baptistery in Florence. These doors, and the East Doors that he subsequently executed, took up the next 50 years of his life. He created intricately worked figures that are more true-to-life than any since antiquity, and he was one of the first Renaissance sculptors to work in bronze. Ghiberti taught the next generation of artists; Donatello, Uccello, and Masaccio all passed through his studio.

In Florence: **Door Copies, Baptistery; Original Doors, Museo dell'Opera del Duomo; Baptistry Door Competition Entry, Bargello; Orsanmichele**

DONATELLO (CA. 1386-1466)

Sculptor from Florence.

Donatello was an innovator who, like his good friend Brunelleschi, spent most of his long life in Florence. Consumed with the science of optics, he used light and shadow to create the effects of nearness and distance. He made an essentially flat slab look like a three-dimensional scene. His bronze *David* is probably the first free-standing male nude since antiquity. Not only technically brilliant, his work is also emotionally resonant; few sculptors are as expressive.

In Florence: ***David*, Bargello; *St. Mark*, Orsanmichele; Palazzo Vecchio; Museo dell'Opera del Duomo; San Lorenzo; Santa Croce**

Elsewhere in Italy: **Padua; Prato; Venice**

Fra Angelico's *The Deposition* Masaccio's *Trinity* Filippo Lippi's *Madonna and Child*

PAOLO UCCELLO (1397-1475)
Painter from Florence.

Renaissance chronicler Vasari once observed that had Uccello not been so obsessed with the mathematical problems posed by perspective, he would have been a very good painter. The struggle to master single-point perspective and to render motion in two dimensions is nowhere more apparent than in his battle scenes. His first major commission in Florence was the gargantuan fresco of the English mercenary Sir John Hawkwood (the Italians called him Giovanni Acuto) in Florence's Duomo.

In Florence: *Sir John Hawkwood*, Duomo; *Battle of San Romano*, Uffizi; Santa Maria Novella

Elsewhere in Italy: Urbino

FRA ANGELICO (CA. 1400-1455)
Painter from a small town north of Florence.

A Dominican friar, who eventually made his way to the convent of San Marco, Fra Angelico and his assistants painted frescoes for aid in prayer and meditation. He was known for his piety; Vasari wrote that Fra Angelico could never paint a crucifix without a tear running down his face. Perhaps no other painter so successfully translated the mysteries of faith and the sacred into painting. And yet his figures emote, his command of perspective is superb, and his use of color startles even today.

In Florence: Museo di San Marco; Uffizi
Elsewhere in Italy: Vatican Museums, Rome

MASACCIO (1401-1428)
Painter from San Giovanni Valdarno, southeast of Florence.

Masaccio and Masolino, a frequent collaborator, worked most famously together at Santa Maria del Carmine. Their frescoes of the life of St. Peter use light to mold figures in the painting by imitating the way light falls on figures in real life. Masaccio also pioneered the use of single-point perspective, masterfully rendered in his *Trinity*. His friend Brunelleschi probably introduced him to the technique, yet another step forward in rendering things the way the eye sees them. Masaccio died young and under mysterious circumstances.

In Florence: Santa Maria del Carmine; *Trinity*, Santa Maria Novella

FILIPPO LIPPI (CA. 1406-1469)
Painter from Prato.

At a young age, Filippo Lippi entered the friary of Santa Maria del Carmine, where he was highly influenced by Masaccio and Masolino's frescoes. His religious vows appear to have made less of an impact; his affair with a young nun produced a son, Filippino (Little Philip, who later apprenticed with Botticelli), and a daughter. His religious paintings often have a playful, humorous note; some of his angels are downright impish and look directly out at the viewer. Lippi links the earlier painters of the 15th century with those who follow; Botticelli apprenticed with him.

In Florence: Uffizi; Palazzo Medici Riccardi; San Lorenzo; Palazzo Pitti
Elsewhere in Italy: Prato

Botticelli's *Primavera*

Leonardo's *Portrait of a Young Woman*

Raphael's *Madonna on the Meadow*

BOTTICELLI (CA. 1444–1510)
Painter from Florence.
Botticelli's work is characterized by stunning, elongated blondes, cherubic angels (something he undoubtedly learned from his time with Filippo Lippi), and tender Christs. Though he did many religious paintings, he also painted monumental, nonreligious panels—his *Birth of Venus* and *Primavera* being the two most famous of these. A brief sojourn took him to Rome, where he and a number of other artists frescoed the Sistine Chapel walls.
In Florence: *Birth of Venus, Primavera,* Uffizi; Palazzo Pitti
Elsewhere in Italy: Vatican Museums, Rome

LEONARDO DA VINCI (1452–1519)
Painter/sculptor/engineer from Anchiano, a small town outside Vinci.
Leonardo never lingered long in any place; his restless nature and his international reputation led to commissions throughout Italy, and took him to Milan, Vigevano, Pavia, Rome, and, ultimately, France. Though he is most famous for his mysterious *Mona Lisa* (at the Louvre in Paris), he painted other penetrating, psychological portraits in addition to his scientific experiments: his design for a flying machine (never built) predates Kitty Hawk by nearly 500 years. The greatest collection of Leonardo's work in Italy can be seen on one wall in the Uffizi.
In Florence: *Adoration of the Magi,* Uffizi
Elsewhere in Italy: *Last Supper,* Santa Maria delle Grazie, Milan

RAPHAEL (1483–1520)
Painter/architect from Urbino.
Raphael spent only four highly productive years of his short life in Florence, where he turned out made-to-order panel paintings of the Madonna and Child for a hungry public; he also executed a number of portraits of Florentine aristocrats. Perhaps no other artist had such a fine command of line and color, and could render it, seemingly effortlessly, in paint. His painting acquired new authority after he came up against Michelangelo toiling away on the Sistine ceiling. Raphael worked nearly next door in the Vatican, where his figures take on an epic, Michelangelesque scale.
In Florence: Uffizi; Palazzo Pitti
Elsewhere in Italy: Vatican Museums, Rome

MICHELANGELO (1475–1564)
Painter/sculptor/architect from Caprese.
Although Florentine and proud of it (he famously signed his St. Peter's *Pietà* to avoid confusion about where he was from), he spent most of his 90 years outside his native city. He painted and sculpted the male body on an epic scale and glorified it while doing so. Though he complained throughout the proceedings that he was really a sculptor, Michelangelo's Sistine Chapel ceiling is arguably the greatest fresco cycle ever painted (and the massive figures owe no small debt to Giotto).
In Florence: *David,* Galleria dell'Accademia; Uffizi; Casa Buonarroti; Bargello
Elsewhere in Italy: St. Peter's Basilica, Vatican Museums, and Piazza del Campidoglio in Rome

Michelangelo received the commission for the New Sacristy in 1520 from Cardinal Giulio de' Medici (1478–1534), who later became Pope Clement VII and who wanted a new burial chapel for his cousins Giuliano (1478–1534) and Lorenzo (1492–1519). The result was a tour de force of architecture and sculpture. Architecturally, Michelangelo was as original and inventive here as ever, but it is, quite properly, the powerful sculpture that dominates the room. The scheme is allegorical: on the tomb to the right are figures representing Day and Night, and on the tomb to the left are figures representing Dawn and Dusk; above them are idealized sculptures of the two Medici men, usually interpreted to represent the active life and the contemplative life. But the allegorical meanings are secondary; what is most important is the intense presence of the sculptural figures. ✉ *Piazza di Madonna degli Aldobrandini, near San Lorenzo* ☎ *055/294883 reservations* ⊕ *www.polomuseale.firenze.it* 💲 *€6* ⊙ *Daily 8:15–5. Closed 1st, 3rd, and 5th Mon. and 2nd and 4th Sun. of month.*

★ ⑳ **Galleria dell'Accademia** (Accademia Gallery). The collection of Florentine paintings here, dating from the 13th to the 18th century, is largely unremarkable, but the sculptures by Michelangelo are worth the price of admission. The unfinished *Slaves*, fighting their way out of their marble prisons, were meant for the tomb of Michelangelo's overly demanding patron, Pope Julius II (1443–1513). But the focal point is the original *David*, moved here from Piazza della Signoria in 1873. The *David* was commissioned in 1501 by the Opera del Duomo (Cathedral Works Committee), which gave the 26-year-old sculptor a leftover block of marble that had been ruined by another artist. Michelangelo's success with the block was so dramatic that the city showered him with honors, and the Opera del Duomo voted to build him a house and a studio in which to live and work.

Today *David* is beset not by Goliath but by tourists, and seeing the statue at all—much less really studying it—can be a trial, as it is surrounded by a Plexiglas barrier. Anxious Florentine art custodians determined not to limit the number of tourists (whose entrance fees help preservation), have suggested installing an "air blaster" behind *David* that would remove the dust and humidity that each tourist brings in. A two-year study is underway, and a decision will probably be reached sometime in 2007. The statue is not quite what it seems. It is so poised and graceful and alert—so miraculously alive—that it is often considered the definitive embodiment of the ideals of the High Renaissance in sculpture. But its true place in the history of art is a bit more complicated.

As Michelangelo well knew, the Renaissance painting and sculpture that preceded his work were deeply concerned with ideal form. Perfection of proportion was the ever-sought Holy Grail; during the Renaissance, ideal proportion was equated with ideal beauty, and ideal beauty was

> **WORD OF MOUTH**
>
> "I strongly recommend making reservations for both the Accademia and the Uffizi. We saved ourselves a ton of time. We walked right into the Accademia and right past the line of unreserved people."   –Ivy.

8

equated with spiritual perfection. But *David,* despite its supremely calm and dignified pose, departs from these ideals. Michelangelo did not give the statue perfect proportions. The head is slightly too large for the body, the arms are too large for the torso, and the hands are dramatically large for the arms. The work was originally commissioned to adorn the facade of the Duomo and was intended to be seen from below at a distance. Michelangelo knew exactly what he was doing, calculating that the perspective of the viewer would be such that, in order for the statue to appear properly proportioned, the upper body, head, and arms would have to be bigger, as they are farther away from the viewer's line of vision. But he also did it to express and embody, as powerfully as possible in a single figure, an entire biblical story. David's hands *are* big, but so was Goliath, and these are the hands that slew him. Save yourself a long and tiresome wait at the museum entrance by reserving your tickets in advance. ⊠ *Via Ricasoli 60, near San Marco* ☎ *055/294883 reservations, 055/2388609 gallery* ⊕ *www.polomuseale.firenze.it* ▨ *€6.50, reservation fee €3* ☉ *Tues.–Sun. 8:15–6:50.*

★ ⑲ **Museo di San Marco.** A former Dominican convent adjacent to the church of San Marco houses this museum, which contains many stunning works by Fra Angelico (circa 1400–55), the Dominican friar famous for his piety as well as for his painting. When the friars' cells were restructured between 1439 and 1444, he decorated many of them with frescoes meant to spur religious contemplation. His paintings are simple and direct and furnish a compelling contrast to those in the Palazzo Medici-Riccardi chapel. Whereas Gozzoli's frescoes celebrate the splendors of the Medici, Fra Angelico's exalt the simple beauties of the contemplative life and quiet reflection. Fra Angelico's works are everywhere in this complex, from the friars' cells to the superb panel paintings on view in the museum. Don't miss the famous *Annunciation* on the upper floor and the works in the gallery off the cloister as you enter. Here you can see his beautiful *Last Judgment*; as usual, the tortures of the damned are far more inventive and interesting than the pleasures of the redeemed. ⊠ *Piazza San Marco 1* ☎ *055/2388608* ⊕ *www.polomuseale. firenze.it* ▨ *€4* ☉ *Weekdays 8:15–1:50, weekends 8:15–6:15. Closed 1st, 3rd, and 5th Sun., and 2nd and 4th Mon. of month.*

⑮ **San Lorenzo.** The interior of this church, like that of Santo Spirito on the other side of the Arno, was designed by Filippo Brunelleschi around 1420. Both proclaim with ringing clarity the beginning of the Renaissance in architecture (neither was completed by Brunelleschi, and which he worked on first is unknown). San Lorenzo's most dramatic element is its floor grid of dark, inlaid marble lines. The grid makes the rigorous geometry of the interior immediately visible and is an illuminating lesson on the laws of perspective. If you stand in the middle of the nave at the church entrance, on the line that stretches to the high altar, every element in the church—the grid, the nave columns, the side aisles, the coffered nave ceiling—seems to march inexorably toward a hypothetical vanishing point beyond the high altar, exactly as in a single-point-perspective painting. Brunelleschi's **Sagrestia Vecchia** (Old Sacristy) has stucco decorations by Donatello; it's at the end of the left transept. The

Florence's Trial by Fire

One of the most striking figures of Renaissance Florence was Girolamo Savonarola, a Dominican friar who, for a moment, captured the conscience of the city. In 1491 he became prior of the convent of San Marco, where he adopted a life of austerity and delivered sermons condemning Florence's excesses and the immorality of his fellow clergy. Following the death of Lorenzo de' Medici, Savonarola was instrumental in the formation of the Grand Council, a representative body of 3,000 men, modeled after the council in Venice. In one of his most memorable acts, he urged Florentines to toss worldly possessions—from frilly dresses to Botticelli paintings—onto a "bonfire of the vanities" in Piazza della Signoria. Savonarola's antagonism toward church hierarchy led to his undoing: he was excommunicated in 1497, and the following year was hanged and burned on charges of heresy. Today, at the Museo di San Marco, you can visit Savonarola's cell and see his arresting portrait.

facade of the church was never finished. ⊠ *Piazza San Lorenzo* ☎ *055/ 290184* ⬚ *€2.50* ⊗ *Mon.–Sat. 10–5.*

Also Worth Seeing

⓰ **Biblioteca Medicea Laurenziana** (Laurentian Library). Begun in 1524 and finished in 1568, the Laurentian Library and its famous **vestibolo** (anteroom) and staircase express the idiosyncratic personal vision of Michelangelo the architect, who was every bit as original as Michelangelo the sculptor. Unlike Brunelleschi (the architect of San Lorenzo), he was obsessed not with proportion and perfect geometry but with experimentation and invention.

At this writing, the library was open only to scholars and the vestibule and stairs were temporarily closed. The strangely shaped anteroom has had experts scratching their heads for centuries. In a space more than two stories high, why did Michelangelo limit his use of columns and pilasters to the upper two-thirds of the wall? Why didn't he rest them on strong pedestals instead of on huge, decorative curlicue scrolls, which rob them of all visual support? Why did he recess them into the wall, which makes them look weaker still? The architectural elements here do not stand firm and strong and tall, like those inside the church next door; instead, they seem to be pressed into the wall as if into putty, giving the room a soft, rubbery look that is one of the strangest effects ever achieved by aping classical architecture. It is almost as if Michelangelo purposely set out to defy his predecessors, intentionally flouting the conventions of the High Renaissance to see what kind of bizarre, mannered effect might result. His innovations were tremendously influential and produced a period of architectural experimentation. As his contemporary Giorgio Vasari put it, "Artisans have been infinitely and perpetually indebted to him because he broke the bonds and chains of a way of working that had become habitual by common usage."

8

Nobody has ever complained about the anteroom's staircase (best viewed head-on), which emerges from the library with the visual force of an unstoppable lava flow. In its highly sculptural conception and execution, it's quite simply one of the most original and fluid staircases in the world. ✉ *Piazza San Lorenzo 9, entrance to left of San Lorenzo* 🕾 *055/210760* ⊕ *www.bml.firenze.sbn.it* 🖾 *Library free, special exhibitions €5* ⊙ *Daily 8:30–1:30.*

㉓ Museo Archeologico. Of the Etruscan, Egyptian, and Greco-Roman antiquities in this museum, the Etruscan collection is particularly notable—one of the largest in Italy. The famous bronze *Chimera* was discovered (without the tail, a reconstruction) in the 16th century. ✉ *Via della Colonna 38, near Santissima Annunziata* 🕾 *055/23575* ⊕ *www.comune. firenze.it/soggetti/sat/didattica/museo.html* 🖾 *€4* ⊙ *Mon. 2–7, Tues. and Thurs. 8:30–7, Wed. and Fri.–Sun. 8:30–2.*

㉑ Museo dell'Opificio delle Pietre Dure. Ferdinand I established a workshop in 1588 to train craftsmen in the art of working with precious and semi-precious stones and marble. Four hundred–plus years later, the workshop is renowned as a center for the restoration of mosaics and inlays in semiprecious stones. The little museum is highly informative and includes some magnificent antique examples of this highly specialized and beautiful craft. ✉ *Via degli Alfani 78, near San Marco* 🕾 *055/26511* 🖾 *€2* ⊙ *Mon.–Sat. 8:15–1:50.*

⑱ Palazzo Medici-Riccardi. The upper floor **Cappella dei Magi** is the main attraction of this palace begun in 1444 by Michelozzo for Cosimo il Vecchio. Benozzo Gozzoli's famous *Procession of the Magi* (finished in 1460) adorns the walls, it celebrates both the birth of Christ and the splendor of the Medici family. Gozzoli's gift was for entrancing the eye, not challenging the mind, and on those terms his success here is beyond question. The paintings are full of activity yet somehow frozen in time in a way that fails utterly as realism but succeeds triumphantly when the demand for realism is set aside. Entering the chapel is like walking into the middle of a magnificently illustrated children's storybook, and this beauty makes it one of the most enjoyable rooms in the entire city. ✉ *Via Cavour 1, near San Lorenzo* 🕾 *055/2760340* 🖾 *€4* ⊙ *Thurs.–Tues. 9–7.*

㉕ Santa Maria Maddalena dei Pazzi. One of Florence's hidden treasures, Perugino's (circa 1445/50–1523) cool and composed *Crucifixion* is in the chapter house of the monastery below this church. Here you can see the Virgin Mary and St. John the Evangelist with Mary Magdalen and Sts. Benedict and Bernard of Clairvaux posed against a simple but haunting landscape. The figure of Christ crucified occupies the center of this brilliantly hued fresco. Perugino's colors radiate—note the juxtaposition of the yellow-green cuff against the orange tones of Mary Magdalen's robe. ✉ *Borgo Pinti 58, near Santissima Annunziata* 🕾 *055/2478420* 🖾 *Donation requested* ⊙ *Mon.–Sat. 9–noon, 5–5:20, and 6–7; Sun. 9–noon and 5–6:20.*

㉒ Santissima Annunziata. Dating from the mid-13th century, this church was restructured in 1447 by Michelozzo, who gave it an uncommon (and lovely) entrance cloister with frescoes by Andrea del Sarto (1486–1530),

Pontormo (1494–1556), and Rosso Fiorentino (1494–1540). The interior is a rarity for Florence: an over-the-top baroque design. But it's not really a fair example, since it is merely 17th-century baroque decoration applied willy-nilly to an earlier structure—exactly the sort of violent remodeling exercise that has given baroque a bad name. The **Cappella dell'Annuziata,** immediately inside the entrance to the left, illustrates the point. The lower half, with its stately Corinthian columns and carved frieze bearing the Medici arms, was commissioned by Piero de' Medici in 1447; the upper half, with its erupting curves and impish sculpted cherubs, was added 200 years later. Each is effective in its own way, but together they serve only to prove that dignity is rarely comfortable wearing a party hat. ☒ *Piazza di Santissima Annunziata* ☎ *055/ 266186* ☉ *Daily 7:30–12:30 and 4–6:30.*

㉔ Spedale degli Innocenti. Brunelleschi designed this foundling hospital in 1419; it takes the prize for the very first Renaissance construction employing the two shapes he considered mathematically (and therefore philosophically and aesthetically) perfect—the square and the circle. Below the level of the arches the portico encloses a row of perfect cubes; above the arch level the portico encloses a row of intersecting hemispheres. The whole geometric scheme is articulated with Corinthian columns, capitals, and arches borrowed directly from antiquity. At the same time Brunelleschi was also designing the interior of San Lorenzo, using the same basic ideas, but the portico here was finished before the church. As exterior decoration, there are 10 ceramic medallions that depict swaddled infants, done in about 1487 by Andrea della Robbia (1435–1525/28). Inside there's a small museum devoted to lesser-known Renaissance works. ☒ *Piazza di Santissima Annunziata 12* ☎ *055/ 20371* ☒ *€4* ☉ *Mon.–Sat. 8:30–7, Sun. 8:30–2.*

Santa Maria Novella to the Arno

Piazza Santa Maria Novella, near the train station, suffers a degree of squalor, especially at night. Nevertheless, the streets in and around the piazza have their share of architectural treasures, including some of Florence's most tasteful palaces. Between Santa Maria Novella and the Arno is Via Tornabuoni, Florence's finest shopping street.

The Main Attractions

㉗ Palazzo Strozzi. The Strozzi family built this imposing palazzo in an attempt to outshine the Palazzo Medici. The design is based on a circa 1489 model by Giuliano da Sangallo (circa 1452–1516). Construction took place between 1489 and 1504 under Il Cronaca (1457–1508) and Benedetto da Maiaino (1442–97). The exterior is simple, severe, and massive: it's a testament to the wealth of a patrician, 15th-century Florentine family. The interior courtyard is another matter altogether. It is here that the classical vocabulary—columns, capitals, pilasters, arches, and cornices—is given uninhibited and powerful expression. Blockbuster art shows frequently take place here. ☒ *Via Tornabuoni, near Piazza della Repubblica* ☎ *055/2776461* ⊕ *www.firenzemostre.com* ☒ *Free except during exhibitions* ☉ *Daily 10–7.*

26 Santa Maria Novella. The facade of Santa Maria Novella looks distinctly clumsy by later Renaissance standards, and with good reason: it is an architectural hybrid. The lower half was completed mostly in the 14th century; its pointed-arch niches and decorative marble patterns reflect the Gothic style of the day. About a hundred years later (around 1456), architect Leon Battista Alberti was called in to complete the job. The marble decoration of his upper story clearly defers to the already existing work below, but the architectural motifs he added evince an entirely different style. The problem was to soften the abrupt transition between a wide ground floor and the narrow upper story. Alberti designed S-curve scrolls surmounting the decorative circles on either side of the upper story: this had no precedent in antiquity but set one in his time. Once you start to look for them, you see scrolls such as these (or sculptural variations of them) on churches all over Italy, and every one of them derives from Alberti's example here.

The architecture of the interior is, like the Duomo, a dignified but somber example of Florentine Gothic. Exploration is essential, however, because the church's store of art treasures is remarkable. Of special interest for its great historical importance and beauty is Masaccio's *Trinity,* on the left-hand wall, almost halfway down the nave. Painted around 1426–27 (at the same time he was working on his frescoes in Santa Maria del Carmine), it unequivocally announced the arrival of the Renaissance in painting. The realism of the figure of Christ was revolutionary in itself, but what was probably even more startling to contemporary Florentines was the barrel vault in the background. The mathematical rules for employing perspective in painting had just been discovered (probably by Brunelleschi), and this was one of the first works of art to employ them with utterly convincing success.

Other highlights include the 14th-century stained-glass rose window depicting the *Coronation of the Virgin* (above the central entrance); the Cappella Filippo Strozzi (to the right of the altar), containing late-15th-century frescoes and stained glass by Filippino Lippi; the Cappella Maggiore (the area around the high altar), displaying frescoes by Domenico Ghirlandaio (1449–94); and the Cappella Gondi (to the left of the altar), containing Filippo Brunelleschi's famous wood crucifix, carved around 1410 and said to have so stunned the great Donatello when he first saw it that he dropped a basket of eggs. Early, well-preserved frescoes painted between 1348 and 1355 by Andrea da Firenze are in the chapter house, or the **Cappellone degli Spagnoli** (Spanish Chapel). ⊠ *Piazza Santa Maria Novella* ☎ *055/210113* ✉ *Church €2.50, chapel €2.50* ☉ *Mon.–Thurs. and Sat. 9–5, Sun. 9–2.*

In the cloisters of the **Museo di Santa Maria Novella,** to the left of Santa Maria Novella, is a faded fresco cycle by Paolo Uccello depicting tales from Genesis, with a dramatic vision of the Flood. ⊠ *Piazza Santa Maria Novella 19* ☎ *055/282187* ✉ *€2.70* ☉ *Mon.–Thurs. and Sat. 9–5, Sun. 9–2.*

31 Ponte Santa Trinita. Take a moment to study the bridge down river from the Ponte Vecchio: it was designed by Bartolomeo Ammannati in 1567 (possibly from sketches by Michelangelo), blown up by the retreating Germans during World War II, and painstakingly reconstructed after the war. The view from Ponte Santa Trinita is beautiful, which might explain why so many young lovers hang out there. ⊠ *Near Ponte Vecchio.*

30 Santa Trinita. Started in the 11th century by Vallombrosan monks in Romanesque style, this church underwent a Gothic remodeling during the 14th century. (Remains of the Romanesque construction are visible on the interior front wall.) Its major work is the cycle of frescoes and the altarpiece in the Cappella Sassetti, the second to the high altar's right, painted by Domenico Ghirlandaio between 1480 and 1485. Ghirlandaio was a wildly popular but conservative painter for his day, and generally his paintings show little interest in the laws of perspective that other Florentine painters had been experimenting with for more than 50 years. But his work here has such graceful decorative appeal it hardly seems to matter. The frescoes illustrate the life of St. Francis, and the altarpiece, depicting the Adoration of the Shepherds, veritably glows. ⊠ *Piazza Santa Trinita, near Santa Maria Novella* ☎ *055/216912* ⊙ *Mon.–Sat. 8–noon and 4–6.*

Also Worth Seeing

28 Museo Marino Marini. One of the few 20th-century art museums in Florence is dedicated to Marino Marini's (1901–80) paintings, sculptures, drawings, and engravings. A 21-foot-tall Etruscanesque bronze of a horse and rider dominates the main gallery. The museum itself is an eruption of contemporary space in a deconsecrated 9th-century church, designed with a series of open stairways, walkways, and balconies that allow you to peer at Marini's work from all angles. ⊠ *Piazza San Pancrazio, near Santa Maria Novella* ☎ *055/219432* ⊠ *€4* ⊙ *Mon. and Wed.–Sat. 10–5; closed Sat. June–Aug.*

29 Palazzo Rucellai. Architect Leon Battista Alberti (1404–72) designed what is perhaps the very first private residence (built between 1455 and 1470) that was inspired by antiquity. A comparison between the Palazzo Rucellai's facade and that of the severe Palazzo Strozzi is illuminating. An ordered arrangement of elements is seen on both, but Alberti devoted a larger proportion of his wall space to windows, which lightens the appearance. He filled in the space with rigorously ordered classical details. Though still severe, the result is less fortresslike (Alberti is on record as saying that only tyrants need fortresses). Ironically, the Palazzo Rucellai was built some 30 years *before* the Palazzo Strozzi. Alberti's civilizing ideas had little influence on the Florentine palaces that followed. To Renaissance Florentines, power—in architecture, as in life—was as impressive as beauty. ⊠ *Via della Vigna Nuova, near Santa Maria Novella.*

The Oltrarno

A walk through the Oltrarno (literally "the other side of the Arno") takes in two very different aspects of Florence: the splendor of the Medici, manifest in the riches of the mammoth Palazzo Pitti and the gracious Giardino di Boboli; and the charm of the Oltrarno, a slightly gentrified but still fiercely proud working-class neighborhood with artisans' and antiques shops.

8

Farther east across the Arno, a series of ramps and stairs climbs to Piazzale Michelangelo, where the city lies before you in all its glory (skip this trip if it's a hazy day). More stairs (behind La Loggia restaurant) lead to the church of San Miniato al Monte. You can avoid the long walk by taking Bus 12 or 13 at the west end of Ponte alle Grazie and getting off at Piazzale Michelangelo; you still have to climb the monumental stairs to and from San Miniato, but you can then take the bus from Piazzale Michelangelo back to the

> **WORD OF MOUTH**
>
> "A good idea for Oltrarno: get lost between Borgo San Jacopo and Santo Spirito for wonderful antiques and restoration workshops. Extremely charming." –lcquinn2

center of town. If you decide to take a bus, remember to buy your ticket before you board.

The Main Attractions

Giardino di Boboli (Boboli Garden). The Italian gift for landscaping—less formal than the French but still full of sweeping drama—is displayed here at its best. The garden began to take shape in 1549, when the Pitti family sold the palazzo to Eleanora da Toledo, wife of the Medici grand duke Cosimo I. The initial horticultural plans were laid out by Niccolò Tribolo (1500–50). After his death, Vasari, Ammannati, Giambologna, Bernardo Buontalenti (circa 1536–1608), Giulio (1571–1635), and Alfonso Parigi (1606–56), among others, continued the work. The result was the most spectacular backyard in Florence. A copy of the famous *Morgante* statue, Cosimo I's favorite dwarf astride a particularly unhappy tortoise, is near the exit. Sculpted by Valerio Cioli (circa 1529–99), the work shows a perfectly executed potbelly. ⊠ *Enter through Palazzo Pitti* ☎ *055/294883* ⊕ *www.polomuseale.firenze.it* ⊠ *€4 combined ticket with Museo degli Argenti* ⊙ *Jan., Feb., Nov., Dec., daily 8:15–4:30; Mar. daily 8:15–5:30; Apr., May, Sept., Oct., daily 8:15–6:30; June, July, Aug., daily 8:15–7:30. Closed 1st and last Mon. of month.*

Palazzo Pitti. This palace is one of Florence's largest—if not one of its best—architectural set pieces. The original palazzo, built for the Pitti family around 1460, comprised only the main entrance and the three windows on either side. In 1549 the property was sold to the Medici, and Bartolomeo Ammannati was called in to make substantial additions. Although he apparently operated on the principle that more is better, he succeeded only in proving that more is just that: more. Today the palace houses several museums. The **Galleria Palatina** contains a collection of paintings from the 15th to the 17th century. High points include a number of portraits by Titian and an unparalleled group of paintings by Raphael, notably the double portraits of Angelo Doni and his wife, the sullen Maddalena Strozzi. The rooms here remain much as the Medici left them. The floor-to-ceiling paintings are considered by some to be Italy's most egregious exercise in conspicuous consumption, aesthetic overkill, and trumpery. Admission to the Galleria Palatina also allows you to explore the former **Appartamenti Reali,** containing furnishings from a remodel done in the 19th century. The **Museo degli Argenti** displays a vast collection of Medici household treasures; the **Galleria del Costume** showcases fashions from the past 300 years. In the **Galleria d'Arte Moderna** there's a collection of 19th- and 20th-century paintings, mostly Tuscan. ☒ *Piazza Pitti* ☏ *055/2388616* ☒ *Galleria Palatina €6.50, Museo degli Argenti combined with Giardino di Boboli €5, Galleria del Costume combined with Galleria d'Arte Moderna €5* ☉ *Tues.–Sun. 8:15–6:50. All but Galleria Palatina closed 2nd and 4th Sun. and 1st, 3rd, and 5th Mon. of month.*

38 Piazzale Michelangelo. From this lookout you have a marvelous view of Florence and the hills around it, rivaling the vista from the Forte di Belvedere. It has a copy of Michelangelo's *David* and outdoor cafés packed with tourists during the day and with Florentines in the evening. The **Giardino dell'Iris** (Iris Garden) off the piazza is in full flower in May. The **Giardino delle Rose** (Rose Garden) on the terraces below the piazza is only open when it blooms in May and June. ☒ *Lungarno South.*

36 Santa Maria del Carmine. Within the **Cappella Brancacci,** at the end of the right transept of this church, is a fresco cycle that forever changed the course of Western art. This masterpiece of Renaissance painting is the creation of three artists: Masaccio and Masolino (1383–circa 1440/47), who began it around 1424, and Filippino Lippi, who finished it some 50 years later, after a long interruption during which the sponsoring Brancacci family was exiled.

It was Masaccio's work that opened a new frontier for painting, as he was among the first to employ single-point perspective. He painted the *Tribute Money* on the upper-left wall; *St. Peter Baptizing* on the upper altar wall; the *Distribution of Goods* on the lower altar wall; and, most famous, the *Expulsion of Adam and Eve* on the chapel's upper-left entrance pier. If you look closely at the last painting and compare it with some of the chapel's other works, you see a pronounced difference. The figures of Adam and Eve have a startling presence, primarily due to the dramatic way in which their bodies seem to reflect light. Masaccio here shaded his figures consistently, so as to suggest a single, strong source of light within the world of the painting but outside its frame. In so doing, he succeeded in imitating with paint the real-world effect of light on mass, and he thereby imparted to his figures a sculptural reality unprecedented in his day. But his skill went beyond mere technical innovation. In the faces of Adam and Eve you see more than finely modeled figures. You see terrible shame and suffering depicted with a humanity rarely achieved in art. Tragically, Masaccio did not live to experience the revolution his innovations caused—he died in 1428 at the age of 27. Fire nearly destroyed the church in the 18th century; miraculously, the Cappella Brancacci survived almost intact.

Reservations to visit the church are mandatory, but can be booked on the same day. Your time inside is limited to 15 minutes—a frustration that's only partly mitigated by the 40-minute DVD about the history of the chapel you can watch either before or after your visit. ☒ *Piazza del Carmine, near Santo Spirito* ☏ *055/2768224 reservations* ☒ *€4* ☉ *Mon. and Wed.–Sat. 10–5, Sun. 1–5.*

③⑦ San Miniato al Monte. A fine example of Romanesque architecture, San Miniato al Monte dates from the 11th century. The lively green-and-white marble facade has a 12th-century mosaic topped by a gilt bronze eagle, emblem of San Miniato's sponsors, the Calimala (cloth merchants' guild). Inside are a 13th-century marble floor and apse mosaic. Spinello Aretino (1350–1410) covered the walls of the **Sagrestia** with frescoes on the life of St. Benedict. The adjacent **Cappella del Cardinale del Portogallo** is one of the richest Renaissance works in Florence. Built to hold the tomb of a Portuguese cardinal, Prince James of Lusitania, who died young in Florence in 1459, it has a glorious ceiling by Luca della Robbia, a sculptured tomb by Antonio Rossellino (1427–79), and inlaid pavement in multicolor marble. ⊠ *Viale Galileo Galilei, Piazzale Michelangelo, Lungarno South* ☎ *055/2342731* ⊗ *Apr.–Oct., daily 8:30–7; Nov.–Mar., Mon.–Sat. 8–noon and 3–5, Sun. 3–5.*

Also Worth Seeing

③④ Santa Felicita. This late-baroque church (its facade was remodeled 1736–39) contains the Mannerist Jacopo Pontormo's (1494–1556) tour de force, the *Deposition* (executed 1525–28), which is a masterpiece of 16th-century Florentine art and the centerpiece of the **Cappella Capponi.** The remote figures, which transcend the realm of Renaissance classical form, are portrayed in tangled shapes and intense pastel colors (well preserved because of the low lights in the chapel), in a space and depth that defy reality. Note, too, the exquisitely frescoed *Annunciation,* also by Pontormo, at a right angle to the *Deposition.* The granite column in the piazza was erected in 1381 and marks a Christian cemetery. ⊠ *Piazza Santa Felicita, Via Guicciardini, near Palazzo Pitti* ⊗ *Mon.–Sat. 9–noon and 3–6, Sun. 9–1.*

③⑤ Santo Spirito. The plain, unfinished facade gives nothing away, but the interior is one of a pair designed in Florence by Filippo Brunelleschi in the early 15th century (the other is San Lorenzo). It was here that Brunelleschi supplied definitive solutions to the two main problems of interior Renaissance church design: how to build a cross shape using architectural elements borrowed from antiquity, and how to reflect the order and regularity that Renaissance scientists (including himself) were discovering in the natural world around them at the time. Brunelleschi's solution to the first problem was brilliantly simple: turn a Greek temple inside out. To see this clearly, look at one of the stately arch-top arcades that separate the side aisles from the central nave. Whereas ancient Greek temples were walled buildings surrounded by classical colonnades, Brunelleschi's churches were classical arcades within walled buildings. This brilliant architectural idea overthrew the previous era's religious taboo against pagan architecture once and for all, triumphantly reclaiming that architecture for Christian use.

Brunelleschi's solution to the second problem—making the entire interior orderly and regular—was mathematically precise: he designed the church so that all its parts were proportionally related. The transepts and nave have exactly the same width; the side aisles are precisely half as wide as the nave; the little chapels off the side aisles are exactly half as deep as the side aisles; the chancel and transepts are exactly one-eighth the depth of the nave; and so on, with dizzying exactitude. For Brunelleschi, such a design technique would have been a matter of passionate conviction. Like most theoreticians of his day, he believed that mathematical regularity and aesthetic beauty were flip sides of the same coin, that one was not possible without the other. In the **refectory of Santo Spirito,** adjacent to the church, you can see the remains of Andrea Orcagna's fresco of the *Crucifixion.* ⊠ *Piazza Santo Spirito* ☏ *055/210030 church, 055/287043 refectory* ✉ *Church free, refectory €2.20* ☉ *Thurs.–Tues. 10–noon and 4–5:30, Sun. 11:30–noon.*

**NEED A
BREAK?**

Cabiria (⊠ **Piazza Santo Spirito 4/r** ☏ **055/215732), across the piazza from the church of Santo Spirito, draws a funky crowd in search of a cappuccino or a drink. When it's warm, sit outside on the terrace. Snacks and light lunches are also available.**

Santa Croce

The Santa Croce quarter, on the southeast fringe of the historic center, was built up in the Middle Ages outside the second set of medieval city walls. The centerpiece of the neighborhood was the basilica of Santa Croce, which could hold great numbers of worshippers; the vast piazza could accommodate any overflow and also served as a fairground and, allegedly since the middle of the 16th century, as a playing field for no-holds-barred soccer games. A center of leather working since the Middle Ages, the neighborhood is still packed with leather craftsmen and leather shops.

> **WORD OF MOUTH**
>
> "You can walk *anywhere* in Florence easily—it's one of my favorite cities because it is so compact. Every time I go I am surprised by how close all the major sights are." —Travelday

On June 24 each year, around the Festa di San Giovanni, the piazza hosts Calcio Storico, a medieval-style soccer tournament. Teams dress in costumes that represent the six Florence neighborhoods.

The Main Attractions

㊴
Fodor'sChoice
★

Santa Croce. Like the Duomo, this church is Gothic, but, also like the Duomo, its facade dates from the 19th century. As a burial place, the church probably contains more skeletons of Renaissance celebrities than any other in Italy. The tomb of Michelangelo is immediately to the right as you enter; he is said to have chosen this spot so that the first thing he would see on Judgment Day, when the graves of the dead fly open, would be Brunelleschi's dome through Santa Croce's open doors. The tomb of Galileo Galilei (1564–1642) is on the left wall; he was not granted a Christian burial until 100 years after his death because he produced evidence that Earth is not the center of the universe. The tomb of Niccolò Machiavelli (1469–1527), the political theoretician whose brutally pragmatic philosophy so influenced the Medici, is halfway down the nave on the right. The grave of Lorenzo Ghiberti, creator of

8

the Baptistery doors, is halfway down the nave on the left. Composer Gioacchino Rossini (1792–1868) is entombed at the end of the nave on the right. The monument to Dante Alighieri (1265–1321), the greatest Italian poet, is a memorial rather than a tomb (he is buried in Ravenna); it's on the right wall near the tomb of Michelangelo.

The collection of art within the complex is by far the most important of any church in Florence. The most famous works are probably the Giotto frescoes in the two chapels immediately to the right of the high altar. They illustrate scenes from the lives of St. John the Evangelist and St. John the Baptist (in the right-hand chapel) and scenes from the life of St. Francis (in the left-hand chapel). Time has not been kind to these frescoes; through the centuries, wall tombs were placed in the middle of them, they were whitewashed and plastered over, and in the 19th century they suffered a clumsy restoration. But the reality that Giotto introduced into painting can still be seen. He did not paint beautifully stylized religious icons, as the Byzantine style that preceded him prescribed; he instead painted drama—St. Francis surrounded by grieving friars at the very moment of his death. This was a radical shift in emphasis: before Giotto, painting's role was to symbolize the attributes of God; after him, it was to imitate life. His work is indeed primitive compared with later painting, but in the early 14th century it caused a sensation that was not equaled for another 100 years. He was, for his time, the equal of both Masaccio and Michelangelo.

Among the church's other highlights are Donatello's *Annunciation,* a moving expression of surprise (on the right wall two-thirds of the way down the nave); 14th-century frescoes by Taddeo Gaddi (circa 1300–66) illustrating scenes from the life of the Virgin Mary, clearly showing the influence of Giotto (in the chapel at the end of the right transept); and Donatello's *Crucifix,* criticized by Brunelleschi for making Christ look like a peasant (in the chapel at the end of the left transept). Outside the church proper, in the **Museo dell'Opera di Santa Croce** off the cloister, is the 13th-century *Triumphal Cross* by Cimabue (circa 1240–1302), badly damaged by the flood of 1966. A model of architectural geometry, the Cappella Pazzi, at the end of the cloister, is the work of Brunelleschi. ✉ *Pi-*

A GOOD WALK: FLORENTINE PIAZZAS

Y ou may come to Florence for the art, but once here you're likely to be won over by the vibrant, pedestrian-friendly street life played out on its numerous and wonderfully varied piazzas—which are often works of art themselves. This walk, designed for a beautiful day, takes you through many of them (but bypasses some of the most prominent ones you'll inevitably encounter while sightseeing). Stopping along the way for gelato, a caffè, or an aperitivo isn't mandatory, but when the urge strikes you, don't resist.

Start off in **Piazza Santa Maria Novella,** by the train station; note the glorious facade by Leon Battista Alberti decorating the square's church. Take Via delle Belle Donne, a narrow street running southeast from the piazza, and go left heading toward Via del Trebbio. Here you'll see a cross marking the site of a 13th-century street scuffle between Dominican friars and Patarene heretics. (The Dominicans won.) A right on Via Tornabuoni takes you to tiny **Piazza Antinori**; the 15th-century Antinori palace has been in the hands of its wine-producing namesake family for generations.

azza Santa Croce 16 🕾 *055/2466105* 🎟 *€4 combined admission to church and museum* ☉ *Mon.–Sat. 9:30–5:30, Sun. 1–5:30.*

❹ Sinagoga. Jews were already well settled in Florence by 1396, when the first money-lending operations were officially sanctioned. Medici patronage initially helped Jewish banking houses to flourish. Then in 1570, by decree of Pope Pius V (1504–72), Jews were required to live within the large ghetto, near today's Piazza della Repubblica. Construction of the modern Moorish-style synagogue, with its lovely garden, began in 1874 as a bequest of David Levi, who wished to endow a synagogue "worthy of the city." Falcini, Micheli, and Treves designed the building on a domed Greek-cross plan with galleries in the transept and a roofline bearing three distinctive copper cupolas. The exterior has alternating bands of tan travertine and pink granite, reflecting an Islamic style repeated in Giovanni Panti's ornate interior. Of particular interest are the cast-iron gates by Pasquale Franci, the eternal light by Francesco Morini, and the Murano glass mosaics by Giacomo dal Medico. The gilded doors of the Moorish ark, which fronts the pulpit and is flanked by extravagant candelabra, are decorated with symbols of the ancient Temple of Jerusalem and bear bayonet marks from vandals. The synagogue was used as a garage by the Nazis, who failed to inflict much damage in spite of one attempt to blow up the place with dynamite. Only the columns on the left side were destroyed, and, even then the women's balcony above did not collapse. Note the Star of David in black and yellow marble inlaid in the floor. The original capitals can be seen in the garden.

Some of the oldest and most beautiful Jewish ritual artifacts in all of Europe are displayed in the small **Museo Ebraico,** accessible by stairs or elevator. Exhibits document the Florentine Jewish community and the building of the synagogue. The donated objects all belonged to local families and date from as early as the late 16th century. Take special note of the exquisite needlework and silver objects. A small but well-stocked gift shop is downstairs. ✉ *Via Farini 4, near Santa Croce* 🕾 *055/2346654* 🎟 *€4* ☉ *Apr., May, Sept., and Oct., Sun.–Thurs. 10–5, Fri. 10–2; June–Aug., Sun.–Thurs. 10–6, Fri. 10–2; Nov.–Mar.,*

8

Continue south on Via Tornabuoni, stopping in **Piazza Strozzi** to admire (or recoil at) the gargantuan Palazzo Strozzi, a 15th-century palace designed specifically to dwarf Palazzo Medici. Step into the courtyard, which is as graceful as the facade is not. Next stop on Via Tornabuoni is lovely little **Piazza Santa Trinita.** Take a look into the church of Santa Trinita; in its Sassetti Chapel (right of the high altar), Ghirlandaio's 15th-century frescoes neatly depict the square where you were just standing.

Continue south to the Arno and cross it on the Ponte Santa Trinita, which affords an excellent view of the Ponte Vecchio upriver. Go south on Via Maggio, then make a right on Via Michelozzi, which leads to **Piazza Santo Spirito,** one of the loveliest—and liveliest—squares in Florence. Walking away from the piazza's church (heading south), make a left on Via Sant'Agostino, which quickly turns into Via Mazzetta. Stop briefly in **Piazza San Felice** and note Number 8, home of the English poets Elizabeth Barrett Browning and Robert Browning from 1849 to 1861.

From here Via Guicciardini takes you to the massive

Sun.–Thurs. 10–3, Fri. 10–2. English-guided tours 10:10, 11, noon, 1, 2 (no tour at 2 on Fri.).

Also Worth Seeing

40 **Casa Buonarroti.** Michelangelo Buonarroti the Younger, the grandnephew of the famed Michelangelo, turned his family house into a shrine honoring the life of his great-uncle. It's full of works executed by Michelangelo, including a marble bas-relief, the *Madonna of the Steps,* carved when Michelangelo was a teenager, and his wooden model for the facade of San Lorenzo. ☒ *Via Ghibellina 70, near Santa Croce* ☎ *055/241752* ⊕ *www.casabuonarroti.it* 🎫 €6.50 ☽ *Fri.–Wed. 9:30–2.*

WHERE TO EAT

Dining hours start at around 1 for the midday meal and at 8 for dinner. Many of Florence's restaurants are small, so reservations are a must. You can sample such specialties as creamy *fegatini* (a chicken-liver spread) and *ribollita* (minestrone thickened with bread and beans and swirled with extra-virgin olive oil) in a bustling, convivial trattoria, where you share long wooden tables set with paper place mats, or in an upscale *ristorante* with linen tablecloths and napkins. Follow the Florentines' lead and take a break at an *enoteca* (wine bar) during the day and discover some excellent Chiantis and Super Tuscans from small producers who rarely export.

WHAT IT COSTS In euros				
$$$$	**$$$**	**$$**	**$**	**¢**
AT DINNER over €45	€35–€45	€25–€35	€15–€25	under €15

Prices are for three courses *(primo, secondo, and dessert).*

The Duomo to the Ponte Vecchio

$–$$ ✕ **Frescobaldi Wine Bar.** Right around the corner from Palazzo Vecchio, this wine bar/restaurant showcases Frescobaldi wine, which the family has been making for centuries. Serious meals may be had in the lively

Piazza dei Pitti. Palazzo Pitti was intended to outstrip Palazzo Strozzi in size and ostentatiousness, and it certainly succeeds. Behind the palazzo is the Giardino di Boboli. Walking the straight axis to its top, you'll pass man-made lakes, waterfalls, and grottoes. Head for the 18th-century Giardino dei Cavalieri, then pause and admire the view. It's hard to believe the pastoral scene, complete with olive groves, is in the city center.

If you have a climb left in you, head back toward the Arno along Via Guicciardini. Just before the Ponte Vecchio, turn right onto Via de' Bardi. Stop for a moment in **Piazza Maria Sopr'Arno** and check out the eerie 20th-century sculpture of John the Baptist, patron saint of Florence. Continue along Via de' Bardi until it becomes Via San Niccolò. Make a right on Via San Miniato, passing through the city walls at Porta San Niccolò. Head up, steeply, on Via Monte alle Croci, and veer left, taking the steps of Via di San Salvatore al Monte. At the top is **Piazzale Michelangelo**, where your effort is rewarded with a breathtaking view of Florence below. Don't forget your camera.

color dining rooms with trompe l'oeil adorning the walls. Frescobaldino, the wine bar, serves lighter fare such as sumptuous salads and lovely cheese plates. Wine afficionados might like to try a flight or two from their wine tasting list. ⊠ *Via de'Magazzini 2–4/r, near Piazza della Signoria* ☎ *055/ 284724* ☐ *MC, V* ☉ *Closed Sun. No lunch Mon.*

$ ✕ **Coquinarius.** After seeing the Duomo, you can rest and replenish at this tranquil enoteca one block away. They serve tasty salads and sandwiches here, as well as clever pastas such as the *crespelle di farina di castagne con ricotta e radicchio* (chestnut pancakes stuffed with ricotta and radicchio). ⊠ *Via delle Oche 15/r, near Duomo* ☎ *055/2302153* ☐ *MC, V* ☉ *Closed Sun.*

San Lorenzo & Beyond

★ $$$–$$$$ ✕ **Taverna del Bronzino.** Want to have a sophisticated meal in a 16th-century Renaissance artist's studio? The former workshop of Santi di Tito, a student of Bronzino's, is now a restaurant with simple formality and white tablecloths. Lots of classic, superb Tuscan food graces the artful menu, and the presentation is often dramatic. Try the *i cappellacci al cedro* (round pasta pillows stuffed with ricotta and served in a citrus sauce). The wine list has solid, affordable choices. Book far ahead if you want to dine at the wine cellar's only table; the service is outstanding. ⊠ *Via delle Ruote 25/r, near San Marco* ☎ *055/495220* ⬧ *Reservations essential* ☐ *AE, DC, MC, V* ☉ *Closed Sun. and 3 wks in Aug.*

$–$$ ✕ **Le Fonticine.** Owner Silvano Bruci is from Tuscany, his wife, Gianna, from Emilia-Romagna; their ristorante near the train station combines the best of two Italian cuisines. Start with the mixed-vegetable antipasto plate and then move on to any of their house-made pastas. The feathery light *tortelloni nostro modo* is large stuffed tortellini with fresh ricotta, served with a tomato-and-cream sauce. The dining room, filled with the Brucis' painting collection, provides an upbeat space for this soul-satisfying food. Note that a 12% service charge may be automatically added to the bill. ⊠ *Via Nazionale 79/r, near San Lorenzo* ☎ *055/ 282106* ☐ *AE, DC, MC, V* ☉ *Closed Sun. and Mon., Nov. 24–Jan. 5, and July 25–Aug. 25.*

★ ¢–$ ✕ **Mario.** Florentines flock to this narrow family-run trattoria to feast on Tuscan favorites served at simple tables under a wooden ceiling dating from 1536. Genuine Florentine hospitality prevails: you're seated wherever there's room, which often means with strangers. Yes, there's a bit of extra oil in most dishes, which imparts calories as well as taste, but aren't you on vacation in Italy? Worth the splurge is *riso al ragù* (rice with ground beef and tomatoes). ⊠ *Via Rosina 2/r, at Piazza del Mercato Centrale, near San Lorenzo* ☎ *055/218550* ⬧ *Reservations not accepted* ☐ *No credit cards* ☉ *Closed Sun. and Aug. No dinner.*

¢ ✕ **Casa del Vino.** Most customers come here for the creative *panini* (sandwiches), such as *sgrombri e carciofini sott'olio* (mackerel and marinated baby artichokes), and the ever-changing list of significant wines by the glass. There's also a well-stocked collection of bottles to-go, at more than fair prices. ⊠ *Via dell'Ariento 16/r, near San Lorenzo* ☎ *055/ 215609* ☐ *MC, V* ☉ *Closed Sun.*

EATING WELL IN FLORENCE

A typical Florentine meal starts with an antipasto of *crostini* (grilled bread spread with various savory toppings) or cured meats such as prosciutto *crudo* (ham thinly sliced) and *finocchiona* (salami seasoned with fennel). *Primi piatti* (first courses) can consist of local versions of pasta dishes available throughout Italy. More distinctly Florentine are the vegetable-and-bread soups such as *pappa al pomodoro* (bread and tomato soup) and *ribollita* (minestrone thickened with bread and beans and swirled with extra-virgin olive oil), and, in summer, a salad called *panzanella* (tomatoes, onions, vinegar, oil, basil, and bread). Before they are eaten, these dishes are often christened with *un "C" d'olio*, a generous C-shape drizzle of the sumptuous local olive oil.

Unparalleled among the *secondi piatti* (second courses) is *bistecca alla fiorentina*—a thick slab of local Chianina beef, often grilled over charcoal, seasoned with olive oil, salt, and pepper, and served rare. Arista (roast loin of pork seasoned with rosemary) is also a local specialty, as are many other roasted meats that pair especially well with Chianti. A *secondo* is usually served with a *contorno* (side dish) of white beans, sautéed greens, or artichokes in season, all of which can be drizzled with more of that fruity olive oil.

Desserts in Florence are more or less an afterthought. The meal often ends with a glass of *vin santo* (literally, "holy wine"), an ocher-color dessert wine that pairs beautifully with *biscotti* ("twice-cooked" cookies).

Santa Maria Novella to the Arno

$$$ ✕ **Cantinetta Antinori.** After a rough morning of shopping on Via Tornabuoni, stop in this 15th-century palazzo and dine in the company of Florentine ladies (and men) who lunch. The kitchen reliably turns out Tuscan standards and a few unusual dishes like the *insalata di gamberoni con carciofi freschi* (shrimp salad with shaved raw artichokes). Most selections on the stellar wine list can be had by the glass, so that sampling Tignanello, the Super Tuscan that kicked off the entire Italian wine revolution, becomes affordable. ⊠ *Piazza Antinori 3, near Santa Maria Novella* ☎ *055/292234* ▤ *AE, DC, MC, V* ⊘ *Closed weekends, 20 days in Aug., and Dec. 25–Jan. 6.*

⟳ **$–$$** ✕ **Il Latini.** Although Il Latini may well be the noisiest, most crowded trattoria in Florence, it's also one of the most fun, precisely because of the liveliness. A genial Torello ("little bull") Latini presides over his four big, homey dining rooms. Ample portions of ribollita prepare the palate for the hearty meat dishes that follow. Florentines and tourists alike praise the *agnello fritto* (fried lamb), and the ravioli *con ricotta e spinaci* (stuffed with spinach and cheese) is so tasty that kids don't even realize they're eating greens. Though reservations are advised, there's always a wait anyway. ⊠ *Via dei Palchetti 6/r, near Santa Maria Novella* ☎ *055/210916* ⌲ *Reservations essential* ▤ *AE, DC, MC, V* ⊘ *Closed Mon. and 15 days at Christmas.*

Oltrarno

$–$$$ ✕ **Quattro Leoni.** The eclectic staff at this trattoria is an appropriate match for the diverse menu. Classics such as *taglierini con porcini* (long, thin, flat pasta with porcini mushrooms) are on the list, but so, too, are less-typical dishes such as the earthy cabbage salad with avocado, pine nuts, and drops of *olio di tartufo* (truffle oil). In cold weather, dine in one of two rooms with high ceilings; in summer you can sit outside. ⊠ *Piazza della Passera, Via dei Vellutini 1/r, near Palazzo Pitti* ☎ *055/218562* ☖ *Reservations essential* ▭ *AE, DC, MC, V* ☾ *No lunch Wed.*

$$ ✕ **Borgo Antico.** Perched on the beautiful piazza of Santo Spirito, this pizzeria-trattoria is almost always crowded with Florentines and tourists alike, seated outdoors in warm weather and at closely spaced indoor tables when it's chilly. The young staff expertly navigates this maze to bring tasty €7 pizzas (such as *prosciutto con funghi*) and large salads to the table. Plenty of grilled meats are on offer, as well as a *menu del giorno* (a menu of the day). ⊠ *Piazza Santo Spirito 6/r* ☎ *055/210437* ▭ *AE, MC, V.*

¢–$ ✕ **La Casalinga.** The nostalgic charm of a 1950s kitchen pervades "The Housewife" restaurant, and it has the Tuscan comfort food to match. If you eat ribollita anywhere in Florence, do so here—the soup couldn't be more authentic. The menu is long, portions are plentiful, and service is prompt and friendly. Save room for dessert: the *sorbetto al limoncello* (lemon sorbet) perfectly caps off the meal. Mediocre paintings clutter the semipaneled walls and tables are set close together in a place that is usually jammed. ⊠ *Via Michelozzi 9/r, near Santo Spirito* ☎ *055/218624* ▭ *AE, DC, MC, V* ☾ *Closed Sun., 1 wk at Christmas, and 3 wks in Aug.*

★ **¢** ✕ **Fuori Porta.** One of the oldest and best wine bars in Florence serves cured meats and cheeses, as well as daily specials such as the sublime spaghetti *al curry. Crostini* and *crostoni*—grilled breads topped with a mélange of cheeses and meats—are the house specialty; the *verdure sott' olio* (vegetables with oil) are divine. The friendly staff who wait on the rustic wooden tables set with paper place mats are only too happy to pour delicious wines by the glass or to discuss the beauties of the lengthy, comprehensive wine list. ⊠ *Via Monte alle Croci 10/r, near San Niccolò* ☎ *055/2342483* ▭ *AE, MC, V.*

¢–$ ✕ **Osteria Antica Mescita San Niccolò.** Always crowded, always good, and always cheap: this is simple Tuscan at its best. If you sit in the lower dining area, you're in what was once a chapel dating from the 11th century (the osteria is next to the church of San Niccolò). Such subtle but dramatic background plays off nicely with the food, such as *pollo con limone,* tasty pieces of chicken in a lemon-scented broth. In winter try the *spezzatino di cinghiale con aromi* (wild boar stew with herbs). ⊠ *Via San Niccolò 60/r,* ☎ *055/2342836* ☖ *Reservations essential* ▭ *AE, MC, V* ☾ *Closed Sun. and Aug.*

¢ ✕ **Le Volpi e l'Uva.** Just off Piazza Santa Trinita is an oenophile's dream: a little bar with a few stools, served by well-informed barmen who pour well-priced wine by the glass from lesser-known Italian vineyards and local favorites. Equally impressive are the cheeses and savory delights such as tiny truffled sandwiches. Something of a rarity among Floren-

8

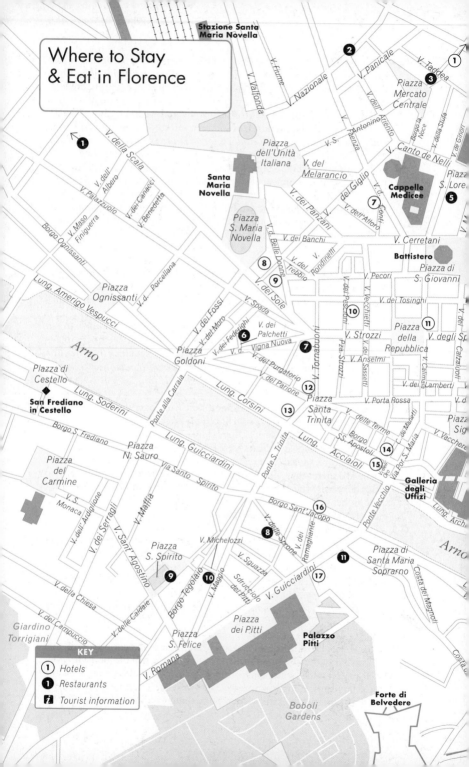

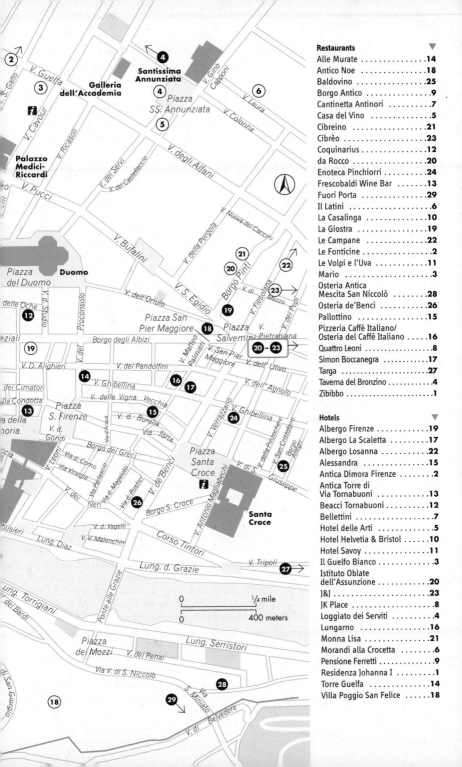

Restaurants ▼

Alle Murate **14**
Antico Noe **18**
Baldovino **25**
Borgo Antico **9**
Cantinetta Antinori **7**
Casa del Vino **5**
Cibreino **21**
Cibrèo **23**
Coquinarius **12**
da Rocco **20**
Enoteca Pinchiorri **24**
Frescobaldi Wine Bar **13**
Fuori Porta **29**
Il Latini **6**
La Casalinga **10**
La Giostra **19**
Le Campane **22**
Le Fonticine **2**
Le Volpi e l'Uva **11**
Mario **3**
Osteria Antica
Mescita San Niccolò **28**
Osteria de'Benci **26**
Pallottino **15**
Pizzeria Caffé Italiano/
Osteria del Caffé Italiano **16**
Quattro Leoni **8**
Simon Boccanegra **17**
Targa **27**
Taverna del Bronzino **4**
Zibibbo **1**

Hotels ▼

Albergo Firenze **19**
Albergo La Scaletta **17**
Albergo Losanna **22**
Alessandra **15**
Antica Dimora Firenze **2**
Antica Torre di
Via Tornabuoni **13**
Beacci Tornabuoni **12**
Bellettini **7**
Hotel delle Arti **5**
Hotel Helvetia & Bristol **10**
Hotel Savoy **11**
Il Guelfo Bianco **3**
Istituto Oblate
dell'Assunzione **20**
J&J **23**
JK Place **8**
Loggiato dei Serviti **4**
Lungarno **16**
Monna Lisa **21**
Morandi alla Crocetta **6**
Pensione Ferretti **9**
Residenza Johanna I **1**
Torre Guelfa **14**
Villa Poggio San Felice **18**

tine bars, this one offers wines and cheeses from France. The outdoor terrace opens in warmer weather. ⊠ *Piazza de'Rossi 1, near Palazzo Pitti* ☎ *055/2398132* ▤ *AE, MC, V* ⊗ *Closed Sun.*

Santa Croce

$$$$ ✕ **Alle Murate.** Few restaurants can boast that their staff includes an on-site art historian, but at this high-end eatery an expert will walk you around the site's medieval ruins and point out the building's lovely 14th-century frescoes. Along with a 2005 relocation to this space came a fresh new menu that's strong on Tuscan food with sophisticated variations: try the *tagliatelle all'olio nuovo, tonno fresco, e timo* (wide noodles with freshly pressed olive oil, tuna, and thyme). ⊠ *Via del Proconsolo near Santa Croce* ☎ *055/240 618* ⌖ *Reservations essential.* ▤ *MC, V* ⊗ *Closed Mon.*

$$$$ ✕ **Cibrèo.** From the crostini with a savory chicken-liver spread to the
Fodor'sChoice melt-in-your-mouth desserts, the food at this upscale trattoria is fantas-
★ tic and creative. If you thought you'd never try tripe—let alone like it—this is the place to lay any doubts to rest: the *trippa in insalata* (cold tripe salad) with parsley and garlic is an epiphany. If chef Fabio Picchi provides unsolicited advice, take it as a sign of his enthusiasm for cooking. Around the corner is Cibreino, Cibrèo's budget sibling. ⊠ *Via A. del Verrocchio 8/r, near Santa Croce* ☎ *055/2341100* ⌖ *Reservations essential* ▤ *AE, DC, MC, V* ⊗ *Closed Sun. and Mon., July 25–Sept. 5, and Dec. 31–Jan. 7.*

$$$$ ✕ **Enoteca Pinchiorri.** A sumptuous Renaissance palace—with high, frescoed ceilings and floral bouquets in silver vases—provides the backdrop for one of the most expensive restaurants in Italy. Some consider it one of the best, and others consider it a non-Italian rip-off; the kitchen is presided over by a Frenchwoman with sophisticated, yet internationalist, leanings. Interesting pasta combinations such as the *ignudi* (ricotta-and-spinach dumplings with a lobster-and-coxcomb fricassee) are always on the menu. Though portions are small, the holdings of the wine cellar are vast and service is top-notch. ⊠ *Via Ghibellina 87, near Santa Croce* ☎ *055/242777* ⌖ *Reservations essential* ▤ *AE, MC, V* ⊗ *Closed Sun. and Mon., and Aug. No lunch Tues. or Wed.*

$$$$ ✕ **Simon Boccanegra.** Florentine food cognoscenti flock to this place named for a *condottiere* (mercenary) hero in a Verdi opera. Under high ceilings, candles on every table cast a rosy glow; the fine wine list and superb service make a meal here a true pleasure. The young chef has a deft hand with fish dishes, as well as an inventive sense when it comes to reinterpreting such classics as risotto with chicken liver—he adds leek and saffron to give it a lift. Remember to save room for dessert. A less-expensive, less-formal wine bar serving a basic Tuscan menu is also on the premises. ⊠ *Via Ghibellina 124/r, near Santa Croce* ☎ *055/2001098* ⌖ *Reservations essential* ▤ *AE, DC, MC, V* ⊗ *Closed Sun. No lunch.*

★ $$$ ✕ **La Giostra.** The clubby La Giostra ("carousel") is owned and run by Prince Dimitri Kunz d'Asburgo Lorena, whose way with mushrooms is as remarkable as his charm. If you ask for an explanation of any of the unusually good pasta on the menu, Soldano, one of the prince's twin sons, will answer in perfect English. One favorite dish, *taglierini con tartufo* *bianco,* is a decadently rich, ribbonlike pasta with white truffles. To pair with the food, choose from the well-culled wine list. Do leave room for sweets, as this is the only show in town serving a sublime tiramisu *and* a wonderfully gooey Sacher torte. ⊠ *Borgo Pinti 12/r, near Santa Croce* ☎ *055/241341* ▤ *AE, DC, MC, V.*

★ **$–$$$** ✗ **Antico Noe.** If Florence had diners (it doesn't), this would be the best diner in town. The short menu at the one-room eatery relies heavily on seasonal ingredients picked up daily at the market. The menu comes alive particularly during truffle and artichoke season (don't miss the grilled artichokes if they're on the menu). Locals rave about the tagliatelle *ai porcini* (with mushrooms); the fried eggs liberally laced with truffle might be the greatest truffle bargain in town. The wine list is short but has some great bargains. ⊠ *Volta di San Piero 6/r, Santa Croce* ☎ *055/ 2340838* ▤ *AE, DC, MC, V* ⊗ *Closed Sun. and 2 wks in Aug.*

★ **$$** ✗ **Osteria de'Benci.** A few minutes from Santa Croce, this charming osteria serves grilled meats that are justifiably famous; the *carbonata* is a succulent piece of grilled beefsteak served rare. You might also try the *eliche del profeta* (a short pasta served with fresh ricotta, oregano, olive oil, tomatoes, and grated pecorino Romano cheese). When it's warm, you can dine outside with a view of the 13th-century tower belonging to the prestigious Alberti family. Next door, the Osteria de'Benci Caffè (¢) serves coffee, aperitifs, salads, and sandwiches 8 AM–midnight, as well as the osteria's menu. ⊠ *Via de'Benci 11–13/r, near Santa Croce* ☎ *055/2344923* ▤ *AE, DC, MC, V* ⊗ *No lunch Sun.*

☺ **$–$$** ✗ **Baldovino.** Here the standard pizzas delight the kids, and to satisfy the parents, there are pizzas with more sophisticated toppings, such as the *lombarda,* with potatoes, *taleggio* (soft, whole-milk cheese), and truffles. If pizza doesn't appeal, *primi* and *secondi* are available, including a taste bud–pleasing *petto di pollo ai broccoli e mandorle* (chicken breast with broccoli and almonds). ⊠ *Via San Giuseppe 22/r, near Santa Croce* ☎ *055/241773* ▤ *MC, V* ⊗ *Closed Mon.*

$ ✗ **Cibreino.** This intimate little trattoria, known affectionately to locals as "Cibreo povero" (loosely, the poor man's Cibrèo) shares its kitchen with that famed Florentine culinary institution. They share the same menu, too, though Cibreino's is much shorter. Start with *il gelatina di pomodoro* (tomato gelatine) liberally laced with basil, garlic, and a pinch of hot pepper, and then sample the justifiably renowned *passato in zucca gialla* (purèed yellow pepper soup) before moving on to any of the succulent second courses. Save room for dessert, as the pastry chef has a dangerous hand with chocolate tarts. To avoid sometimes agonizingly long waits, come early (7 pm) or late (after 9:30). ⊠ *Via dei Macci 118 near Santa Croce* ☎ *055/2341100* ✍ *Reservations not accepted* ▤ *No credit cards* ⊗ *Closed Sun. and Mon. Closed July 25–Sept. 5 and Dec. 31–Jan. 7.*

☺ **¢–$** ✗ **Pallottino.** With its tiled floor, photograph-filled walls, and wooden tables, Pallottino is the quintessential Tuscan trattoria. Hearty, heartwarming classics include *peposa alla toscana* (a beef stew laced with black pepper). The menu changes frequently to reflect what's seasonal; the staff is friendly, as are the diners, who often share a table and, eventually, conversation. They also do pizza here, as well as great lunch specials.

8

What Tripe!

WHILE IN FLORENCE, those with a sense of culinary adventure should seek out a tripe sandwich, which is just about as revered by local gourmands as the *bistecca alla fiorentina*—a thick slab of local Chianina beef, often grilled over charcoal, seasoned with olive oil, salt, and pepper, and served rare. In this case, however, the treasure comes on the cheap—sandwiches are sold from small stands found in the city center, topped with a fragrant green sauce or a piquant red hot sauce, or both. *Bagnato* means that the hard, crusty roll is first dipped in the tripe's cooking liquid; it's advisable to say *"sì"* when asked if that's how you like it. Sandwiches are usually taken with a glass of red wine poured from the tripe seller's *fiasco* (flask). If you find the tripe to your liking, you might also enjoy *lampredotto*, another, some say better, cut of stomach. For an exalted, high-end tripe treat, try Fabio Picchi's cold tripe salad, served gratis as an *amuse-bouche* at the restaurant Cibrèo. It could make a convert of even the staunchest "I'd never try *that*" kind of eater.

Tripe carts are lunchtime favorite of Florentine working men—it's uncommon, but not unheard of, to see a woman at a tripe stand. Afficionados will argue which sandwich purveyor is best; here are three that frequently get mentioned: **La Trippaia** (⊠ Via dell'Ariento, near Santa Maria Novella ☎ No phone ⊘ Closed Sun.). **Il Trippaio** (⊠ Via de'Macci, at Borgo La Croce, near Santa Croce ☎ No phone ⊘ Closed Sun.). **Nerbone** (⊠ Inside the Mercato Centrale, near Santa Maria Novella ☎ No phone ⊘ Closed Sun.)

⊠ *Via Isola delle Stinche 1/r, near Santa Croce* ☎ *055/289573* ▭ *AE, DC, MC, V* ⊘ *Closed Mon. and 2–3 wks in Aug.*

¢ ✕ **Pizzeria Caffè Italiano.** Locals swear by the pizzeria associated with the Osteria del Caffè Italiano, two doors down. Come early to grab one of the few tables, and ignore the intentionally rushed service. ⊠ *Via Isole delle Stinche, near Santa Croce* ☎ *055/289368* ▭ *No credit cards* ⊘ *Closed Mon.*

¢ ✕ **da Rocco.** At one of Florence's biggest markets you can grab lunch to go, or you could cram yourself into one of the booths and pour from the straw-cloaked flask (wine here is *da consumo,* which means they charge you for how much you drink). Food is abundant, Tuscan, and fast; locals pack in. The menu changes daily, and the prices are so right. ⊠ *In Mercato Sant'Ambrogio, Piazza Ghiberti, near Santa Croce* ☎ *No phone* ⚛ *Reservations not accepted* ▭ *No credit cards* ⊘ *Closed Sun. No dinner.*

Beyond the City Center

$$–$$$$ ✕ **Targa.** It looks and feels like California on the Arno at this sleek, airy restaurant a short ride from the city center. Owner-chef Gabriele Tarchiani has spent time in the United States, which shows in the plant-decorated interior. Creative touches on the frequently changing menu include combinations such as fusilli *al ragù di anatra e finferli* (with a minced duck and wild-mushroom sauce). The desserts are culinary master-

pieces. ✉ *Lungarno Colombo 7, east of center* ☎ *055/677377* ⚞ *Reservations essential* ▭ *AE, DC, MC, V* ⊙ *Closed Sun.*

$$–$$$ ✕ **Zibibbo.** Benedetta Vitali, formerly of Florence's famed Cibrèo, has a restaurant of her very own. It's a welcome addition to the sometimes claustrophobic Florentine dining scene—particularly as you have to drive a few minutes out of town to get here. Off a quiet piazza, it has two intimate rooms with rustic, maroon-painted wood floors and a sloped ceiling. *Tagliatelle al sugo d'anatra* (wide pasta ribbons with duck sauce) are aromatic and flavorful, and *crocchette di fave con salsa di yogurt* (fava bean croquettes with a lively yogurt sauce) are innovative and tasty. ✉ *Via di Terzollina 3/r, northwest of city center* ☎ *055/433383* ▭ *AE, DC, MC, V* ⊙ *Closed Sun.*

Cafés

Cafés in Italy serve not only coffee concoctions and pastries but also drinks and some light lunches as well. They open early in the morning and usually close around 8 PM.

The always-crowded **Caffè Giacosa/Roberto Cavalli** (✉ Via della Spada 10, near Santa Maria Novella ☎ 055/2776328), joined at the hip with a Florentine fashion designer's shop, is open for breakfast, lunch, tea, and cocktails—except on Sunday. Classy **Procacci** (✉ Via Tornabuoni 64/r, near Santa Maria Novella ☎ 055/211656) is a Florentine institution dating back to 1885; try one of the panini *tartufati* (a small roll with truffled butter) and swish it down with a glass of *prosecco* (a dry, sparkling white wine). It's closed Sunday.

Gran Caffè (✉ Piazza San Marco 11/r ☎ 055/215833) is down the street from the Accademia, so it's a perfect stop for a marvelous *panino* (sandwich) or sweet while raving about the majesty of Michelangelo's *David*. Perhaps the best café for people-watching is **Rivoire** (✉ Piazza della Signoria, Via Vaccherecchia 4/r ☎ 055/214412). Stellar service, light snacks, and terrific *aperitivi* (aperitifs) are the norm. Think twice, however, before ordering the more substantial fare, which is pricier than it is tasty.

Gelaterie & Pasticcerie

The convenient **Caffè delle Carrozze** (✉ Piazza del Pesce 3–5/r, near Piazza Signoria ☎ 055/2396810) is around the corner from the Uffizi; their gelati, according to some, are the best in the historic center. **Gelateria Carabe** (✉ Via Ricasoli 60/r, San Marco ☎ 055/289476) specializes in desserts Sicilian (including cannoli). Its *granità* (granular, flavored ices), made only in summer, are tart and flavorful—perfect thirst-quenchers.

Dolci e Dolcezze (✉ Piazza C. Beccaria 8/r, near Santa Croce ☎ 055/2345458), a *pasticceria* (bakery) in Borgo La Croce, probably has the prettiest and tastiest cakes, sweets, and tarts in town. It's closed Monday. Most visitors consider **Vivoli** (✉ Via Isola delle Stinche 7/r, near Santa Croce ☎ 055/292334) the best gelateria in town; Florentines find it highly overrated. It is closed Sunday. **Vestri** (✉ Borgo Albizi 11/r, near Santa Croce ☎ 055/2340374) is devoted to chocolate in all its guises, every day but Sunday. The small but sublime selection of chocolate-based gelati includes one with hot peppers.

8

Salumerie

Delicatessens and gourmet food shops specializing in fresh and cured meats and cheeses, *salumerie,* can be a great places to assemble a picnic or purchase dinner. Most are closed Sunday.

Looking for some cheddar cheese to pile in your panino? **Pegna** (⊠ Via dello Studio 8, near Duomo ☎ 055/282701) has been selling both Italian and non-Italian food since 1860. The cheese collection at **Baroni** (⊠ Mercato Centrale, enter at Via Signa, near San Lorenzo ☎ 055/289576) may be the most comprehensive in Florence. **Perini** (⊠ Mercato Centrale, enter at Via dell'Ariento, near San Lorenzo ☎ 055/2398306) sells everything from cured meats to sumptuous pasta sauces. They're generous with free samples. Hungry for lunch or a snack in the Oltrarno? Drop into **Azzarri Delicatesse** (⊠ Borgo S. Jacopo 27b/cr, near Santo Spirito ☎ 055/2381714) for a sandwich, meat for the grill, wine, or French cheeses.

WHERE TO STAY

Whether you are in a five-star hotel or a more modest establishment, one of the greatest pleasures of all is a room with a view, like the one made famous by E. M. Forster. Florence has so many famous landmarks that it's not hard to find lodgings with a panoramic vista. And the equivalent of the genteel pensions of yesteryear still exists, with the benefit of modern plumbing.

Florence's importance not only as a tourist city but as a convention center and site of the Pitti fashion collections throughout the year means a high demand for rooms. If you want to come during Pitti Uomo (early January), book well in advance, or you will be out of luck. Conversely, Florentine hotels often offer substantial deals in July, August, and February. If you find yourself in Florence with no reservations, go in person to **Consorzio ITA** (⊠ Stazione Centrale, near Santa Maria Novella ☎ 055/282893) to make a booking.

WHAT IT COSTS In euros				
$$$$	**$$$**	**$$**	**$**	**¢**
FOR 2 PEOPLE over €290	€210–€290	€140–€210	€80–€140	under €80

Prices are for a standard double room in high season.

Centro Storico

★ **$$$$** 🔳 **Hotel Helvetia & Bristol.** Painstaking care has gone into making this hotel in the center of town one of the prettiest and most intimate in Florence. From the cozy-yet-sophisticated lobby with its *pietra serena* (gray sandstone) columns to the guest rooms each decorated differently with antiques, the impression is one of a sophisticated manor house where you're spending the night. Osteria Bibendum, the restaurant ($$$$), serves sumptuous fare amid romantically tomato-red walls and cascading chandeliers. Top-notch staff make a stay here a real treat. ⊠ *Via dei Pescioni 2, Piazza della Repubblica, 50123* ☎ *055/26651* 🖨 *055/288353* ⊕ *www.hbf.royaldemeure.com* ⤴ *54 rooms, 13 suites* ⚑ *Restau-*

rant, room service, in-room safes, some in-room hot tubs, minibars, cable TV, in-room VCRs, Wi-Fi, bar, babysitting, dry cleaning, laundry service, concierge, meeting room, parking (fee), some pets allowed ⊟ *AE, DC, MC, V* †⊚† *EP.*

$$$$ ⊞ **Hotel Savoy.** On the outside, the Savoy is a paragon of the baroque style prevalent in Italian architecture at the turn of the 19th century. Inside, sleek minimalism and up-to-the-minute amenities prevail. Sitting rooms have a funky edge, their cream-color walls dotted with contemporary prints. Streamlined furniture and muted colors predominate in the guest rooms, many of which look out at the Duomo's cupola or Piazza della Repubblica. The deep marble tubs might be reason enough to stay here—but you may also appreciate the efficient and courteous staff. ⊠ *Piazza della Repubblica 7, 50123* ☎ *055/27351* 🖷 *055/ 2735888* ⊕ *www.roccofortehotels.com* ↩ *92 rooms, 11 suites* ⟋ *Restaurant, room service, in-room fax, in-room safes, minibars, cable TV with movies and video games, in-room VCRs, in-room data ports, Wi-Fi, exercise equipment, bar, children's programs (ages infant–12), dry cleaning, laundry service, concierge, business services, meeting rooms, parking (fee)* ⊟ *AE, DC, MC, V* †⊚† *EP.*

¢–$ ⊞ **Albergo Firenze.** A block from the Duomo, Albergo Firenze is on one of the oldest piazzas in Florence, and for the location, the place is a great bargain. Though the reception area and hallways have all the charm of a dormitory, the similarity ends when you enter the spotlessly clean rooms with tile floors and wood veneer. A good number of singles, triples, and quads make this an attractive alternative for families and budget travelers. ⊠ *Piazza Donati 4, near Duomo, 50122* ☎ *055/214203* 🖷 *055/ 212370* ⊕ *www.hotelfirenze-fi.it* ↩ *58 rooms* ⟋ *In-room safes, cable TV, parking (fee)* ⊟ *No credit cards* †⊚† *BP.*

San Lorenzo & Beyond

$$$ ⊞ **Morandi alla Crocetta.** Near Piazza Santissima Annunziata is a charm-
Fodor'sChoice ing and distinguished residence in which you're made to feel like priv-
★ ileged friends of the family. The former convent is close to the sights but very quiet, and is furnished comfortably in the classic style of a gracious Florentine home. One room retains original 17th-century fresco fragments, and two others have small private terraces. The Morandi is not only an exceptional hotel but also a good value. It's very small, so try to book well in advance. ⊠ *Via Laura 50, near Santissima Annunziata, 50121* ☎ *055/2344747* 🖷 *055/2480954* ⊕ *www.hotelmorandi.it* ↩ *10 rooms* ⟋ *In-room safes, minibars, cable TV, in-room data ports, Wi-Fi, dry cleaning, laundry service, concierge, parking (fee), some pets allowed* ⊟ *AE, DC, MC, V* †⊚† *EP.*

$$–$$$ ⊞ **Il Guelfo Bianco.** Though the 15th-century building has been retrofitted with all the modern conveniences, its Renaissance charm still shines, and though it is in the centro storico, it still feels somewhat off the beaten path. Rooms have high ceilings (some are coffered) and windows are triple-glazed to ensure quiet. Contemporary prints and paintings on the walls contrast nicely with classic furnishings. Larger-than-usual single rooms with French-style beds are a good choice if you are traveling alone. Take breakfast in the small outdoor garden when weather permits.

✉ *Via Cavour 29, San Marco, 50129* ☎ *055/288330* 🖶 *055/295203* ⊕ *www.ilguelfobianco.it* ⇆ *40 rooms* ♻ *In-room safes, minibars, cable TV, in-room data ports, Wi-Fi, babysitting, dry cleaning, laundry service, concierge, Internet room, business services, parking (fee), some pets allowed* 🟰 *AE, DC, MC, V* 🍽 *BP.*

$$ 🏨 **Hotel delle Arti.** If you're looking for a small hotel with lots of character, this place is perfect. Just down the street from Piazza Santissima Annunziata, one of Florence's prettiest Renaissance squares, the unobtrusive entrance (it looks like a well-appointed town house) leads to a reception room that feels like a small, intimate living room. Rooms are simply but elegantly furnished with pale, pastel walls, muted fabrics, and polished hardwood floors. Breakfast is taken on the top floor, and a small terrace provides city views. The highly capable staff is completely fluent in English. ✉ *Via dei Servi 38/a, near Santissima Annunziata, 50122* ☎ *055/2645307* 🖶 *055/290140* ⊕ *www.hoteldellearti.it* ⇆ *9 rooms* ♻ *Minibars, cable TV, dry cleaning, laundry service, business services, some pets allowed (fee)* 🟰 *AE, DC, MC, V* 🍽 *BP.*

$$ 🏨 **Loggiato dei Serviti.** Though the hotel was not designed by Brunelleschi, it might as well have been; it's a mirror image of the architect's famous Spedale degli Innocenti across the way. Occupying a 16th-century former convent building, this was once an inn for traveling priests. Vaulted ceilings, tester canopy beds, and rich fabrics help make this spare Renaissance building with modern comforts a find. The Loggiato is on one of the city's loveliest squares. ✉ *Piazza Santissima Annunziata 3, 50122* ☎ *055/289592* 🖶 *055/289595* ⊕ *www.loggiatodeiservitihotel.it* ⇆ *38 rooms* ♻ *In-room safes, minibars, cable TV, in-room data ports, bar, babysitting, dry cleaning, laundry service, parking (fee), some pets allowed* 🟰 *AE, DC, MC, V* 🍽 *BP.*

$–$$ 🏨 **Antica Dimora Firenze.** Each room in the intimate *residenza* (a residence property, this one opened in May 2004) is painted a different pastel color—peach, rose, powder blue. Simple, homey furnishings (that could be your grandmother's handmade quilt on the bed) and double-glazed windows ensure a peaceful night's sleep. You might ask for one of the rooms that has a small private terrace; if you contemplate a longer stay, one of their well-located apartments might suit. Coffee and tea, available all day in the sitting room, are on the house. Note that the staff goes home at 7 PM. ✉ *Via San Gallo 72, near San Marco, 50129* ☎ *055/4627296* 🖶 *055/4634450* ⊕ *www.anticadimorafirenze.it* ⇆ *6 rooms* ♻ *In-room safes, minibars, refrigerators, cable TV, in-room data ports, Wi-Fi* 🟰 *No credit cards* 🍽 *BP.*

$ 🏨 **Residenza Johanna I.** Savvy travelers and those on a budget know the Johanna I has a tremendous price-to-location ratio. Here you're very much in the centro storico. Rooms have high ceilings, traditional furniture (iron beds, wooden desks), and bedspreads done in pastel floral prints. Morning tea and coffee (but no breakfast) are taken in one's room. You're given a large set of keys to let yourself in, as the staff goes home at 7 PM. ✉ *Via Bonifacio Lupi 14, near San Marco, 50129* ☎ *055/481896* 🖶 *055/482721* ⊕ *www.johanna.it* ⇆ *11 rooms* ♻ *Fans, parking (fee); no a/c, no room phones, no room TVs* 🟰 *No credit cards* 🍽 *EP.*

FodorśChoice ★

Santa Maria Novella to the Arno

$$$$ 🖼 **JK Place.** Ori Kafri, the manager of this boutique hotel, refers to it
Fodor'sChoice as a house, and indeed it is a sumptuously appointed home away from
★ home. A library serves as the reception room; buffet breakfast is laid
out on a gleaming chestnut table in an interior atrium. Soothing earth
tones prevail in the rooms, some of which have chandeliers, others
canopied beds. A secluded rooftop terrace makes a perfect setting for
an aperitivo, as do the ground-floor sitting rooms with large, pillow-
piled couches. The Lounge restaurant ($$$–$$$$) offers Tuscan clas-
sics with a dash of fantasy. A stellar staff caters to every need. ⊠ *Piazza
Santa Maria Novella 7, Santa Maria Novella 50123* 📞 *055/2645181*
🖨 *055/2658387* 🌐 *www.jkplace.com* 🛏 *14 doubles, 6 suites* ⏦ *In-room
safes, minibars, cable TV, in-room VCRs, in-room data ports, Wi-Fi,
bar, babysitting, dry cleaning, laundry service, concierge, parking (fee),
some pets allowed* 🟰 *AE, DC, MC, V* 🍽 *BP.*

$$$ 🖼 **Antica Torre di Via Tornabuoni.** If you're looking for the proverbial view,
stop here, where just about every room has a window that frames the
awe-inspiring Duomo or the Arno (some even have small terraces). When
it's warm, you can sit on the rooftop terrace with a glass of wine and
enjoy a 360-degree panorama. The tastefully furnished rooms, with their
high ceilings and sweeping draperies, create a fine backdrop for historic
Florence. This is the perfect place if you desire luxe privacy; since it's a
residenza, the staff goes home at 7 PM. Charming host Jacopo d'Albasio
strives to ensure that all his guests are not only happy, but yearn to come
back. ⊠ *Via Tornabuoni 1, near Santa Maria Novella, 50122* 📞 *055/
2658161* 🖨 *055/218841* 🌐 *www.tornabuoni1.com* 🛏 *11 rooms, 1
suite* ⏦ *In-room safes, minibars, cable TV, in-room data ports, bar,
meeting rooms, parking (fee), some pets allowed* 🟰*AE, DC, MC, V* 🍽*EP.*

★ **$$–$$$** 🖼 **Beacci Tornabuoni.** Florentine pensioni do not come any more classic
than this one in a 14th-century palazzo. There's an old-fashioned grace,
and enough modern comforts. Wallpaper or tapestry-like wall hangings
make rooms inviting. The sitting room has a large fireplace, and the terrace has a tremendous view of some major Florentine monuments, such
as the church of Santa Trinita. On Monday, Wednesday, and Friday nights
May–October, the dining room ($$–$$$) opens to serve Tuscan special-
ties on a lovely, flower-strewn terrace. ⊠ *Via Tornabuoni 3, near Santa
Maria Novella, 50123* 📞 *055/212645* 🖨 *055/283594* 🌐 *www.
tornabuonihotels.com* 🛏 *28 rooms* ⏦ *Dining room, minibars, cable TV,
bar, babysitting, dry cleaning, laundry service, Internet room, parking
(fee), some pets allowed* 🟰 *AE, DC, MC, V* 🍽 *BP.*

$$ 🖼 **Torre Guelfa.** Enter this hidden hotel through an immense wooden door
on a narrow street, continue through the iron gate and up a few steps
to an elevator that takes you to the third floor. A few more steps and
you're in a 13th-century Florentine *torre* (tower) that once protected the
fabulously wealthy Acciaiuoli family. Now it's one of the best-located
small hotels in Florence. Each guest room is different—some with
canopied beds, some with balconies. Those on a budget might want to
consider one of the six less-expensive rooms on the second floor that
have no TVs. ⊠ *Borgo Santi Apostoli 8, near Santa Maria Novella, 50123.*
📞 *055/2396338* 🖨 *055/2398577* 🌐 *www.hoteltorreguelfa.com* 🛏 *24*

8

rooms, 2 suites ⚮ *Some in-room safes, Wi-Fi, babysitting, dry clean-ing, laundry service, parking (fee), some pets allowed; no TV in some rooms* ⊟ *AE, MC, V* ⦿ *BP.*

$–$$ 🏨 **Alessandra.** The building, known as the Palazzo Roselli del Turco, was designed in 1507 by Baccio d'Agnolo, a contemporary of Michelangelo's. Though little remains of the original design save for the high wood ceilings, there's still an aura of grandeur in the ample rooms. Several have views of the Arno; the sole suite is spacious. Friendly hosts Anna and Andrea Gennarini speak fluent English. The location, a block from the Ponte Vecchio, helps make this a good choice. ⊠ *Borgo Santi Apos-toli 17, near Santa Maria Novella, 50123* ☎ *055/283438* 🖷 *055/210619* ⊕ *www.hotelalessandra.com* 🛏 *26 rooms, 19 with bath; 1 suite; 1 apartment* ⚮ *In-room safes, some minibars, cable TV, in-room data ports, Wi-Fi, babysitting, dry cleaning, laundry service, parking (fee)* ⊟ *AE, MC, V* ⊗ *Closed Dec. 10–26* ⦿ *BP.*

$–$$ 🏨 **Bellettini.** You're in good hands at this small, three-floor pensione run by sisters Marzia and Gina Naldini and their husbands. Public rooms are simple but comfortable; the good-size guest rooms have Venetian or Tuscan provincial decor; bathrooms are bright and modern. The top floor has two rooms with a view, and a handful of triples and quadru-ples make this the perfect place for families or friends traveling to-gether. There's an ample buffet breakfast, including tasty homemade cakes. ⊠ *Via dei Conti 7, near Santa Maria Novella, 50123* ☎ *055/213561* 🖷 *055/283551* ⊕ *www.hotelbellettini.com* 🛏 *28 rooms* ⚮ *In-room safes, minibars, cable TV, in-room broadband, bar, parking (fee), some pets allowed* ⊟ *AE, DC, MC, V* ⦿ *BP.*

$ 🏨 **Pensione Ferretti.** Minutes away from Piazza Santa Maria Novella, this pensione has views onto the tiny piazza containing the Croce al Treb-bio, as well as easy access to the historic center. English-speaking owner Luciano Michel and his South Africa–born wife, Sue, do just about any-thing to make you feel at home (including providing 24-hour, free In-ternet access). Ceiling fans make warmer months more bearable. Though it's housed in a 16th-century palazzo, accommodations are no-frills. ⊠ *Via delle Belle Donne 17, near Santa Maria Novella, 50123* ☎ *055/2381328* 🖷 *055/219288* ⊕ *www.emmeti.it/Hferretti* 🛏 *16 rooms, 6 with bath; 1 apartment* ⚮ *Fans, Internet room, parking (fee), some pets allowed; no a/c, no room TVs* ⊟ *AE, DC, MC, V* ⦿ *BP.*

The Oltrarno

$$$$ 🏨 **Lungarno.** Many rooms and suites here have private terraces that jut out over the Arno, affording sumptuous views of the palaces that line the river. Four suites in the 13th-century tower retain details like exposed stone walls and old archways; they face onto a little square with a me-dieval tower covered in jasmine. The very chic decor approximates a breezily wealthy home, with lots of crisp white fabrics with blue trim. A wall of windows and a sea of white couches make the lobby bar one of the nicest places in the city to stop for a drink. The Lungarno Suites, across the river, are apartment-like lodgings that have kitchens. ⊠ *Borgo San Jacopo 14, Lungarno South, 50125* ☎ *055/27261* 🖷 *055/268437* ⊕ *www.lungarnohotels.com* 🛏 *60 rooms, 13 suites* ⚮ *Restaurant, in-room fax, cable TV with movies, in-room data ports, Wi-Fi, bar, babysit-*

ting, dry cleaning, laundry service, concierge, meeting rooms, parking (fee) ≣ *AE, DC, MC, V* ⦿I *BP.*

$$ 🖭 **Albergo La Scaletta.** For a tremendous view of the Boboli Garden, near the Ponte Vecchio and Palazzo Pitti, come to this exquisite pensione run by a mother-and-son team. It has simply furnished yet rather large rooms and a sunny breakfast room. In warm weather two flower-be-decked terraces are open, one with a stunning 360-degree view of Florence. ⊠ *Via Guicciardini 13, near Palazzo Pitti, 50125* ☎ *055/283028* 🖷 *055/289562* ⊕ *www.hotellascaletta.it* 🖙 *11 rooms, 10 with bath* ♿ *Cable TV, parking (fee), some pets allowed* ≣ *MC, V* ⦿I *BP.*

Santa Croce

★ $$$$ 🖭 **Monna Lisa.** Housed in a 15th-century palazzo, with parts of the building dating from the 13th century, this hotel retains some of its original wood-coffered ceilings from the 1500s, as well as its original marble staircase. Though some rooms are small, they are tastefully decorated, each with different floral wallpaper. The public rooms retain a 19th-century aura, and the intimate bar, with its red velveteen wallpaper, is a good place to unwind. ⊠ *Borgo Pinti 27, near Santa Croce, 50121* ☎ *055/2479751* 🖷*055/2479755* ⊕*www.monnalisa.it* 🖙*45 rooms* ♿ *In-room safes, mini-bars, cable TV, bar, babysitting, dry cleaning, laundry service, concierge, parking (fee), some pets allowed* ≣ *AE, DC, MC, V* ⦿I *BP.*

$$$–$$$$ 🖭 **J&J.** Cavernous suites in the 16th-century convent are ideal for honeymooners, families, and small groups of friends. Some are bi-level, and many are imaginatively arranged around the central courtyard. The smaller rooms are more intimate, some opening onto a little shared courtyard. Some bathrooms have been refitted with pale travertine tiles. The gracious owners enjoy chatting in the light and airy lounge; breakfast is served in a glassed-in Renaissance loggia or in the central courtyard. ⊠ *Via di Mezzo 20, near Santa Croce, 50121* ☎ *055/26312* 🖷 *055/240282* ⊕ *www.cavalierehotels.com* 🖙 *19 rooms, 7 suites* ♿ *Cable TV, in-room data ports, bar, babysitting, dry cleaning, laundry service, parking (fee)* ≣ *AE, DC, MC, V* ⦿I *BP.*

¢ 🖭 **Albergo Losanna.** Most major sights are within walking distance of this tiny pensione just within the Viale, the edge of the city center. Though dated and a little worn around the edges, the property is impeccably clean and the rooms have high ceilings; the mother and son who run the place are enthusiastic and cordial. Try to get a room facing away from the street; you won't have a view but you can get a quiet night's sleep. ⊠ *Via V. Alfieri 9, near Santa Croce, 50121* ☎🖷*055/245840* ⊕ *www.albergolosanna.com* 🖙 *8 rooms, 3 with bath* ♿ *Parking (fee); no a/c in some rooms, no room TVs* ≣ *AE, MC, V* ⦿I *BP.*

¢ 🖭 **Istituto Oblate dell'Assunzione.** Twelve nuns run this perfectly situated convent just minutes from the Duomo. Rooms are spotless and simple; some of them have views of the cupola, and others look out onto a carefully tended garden where guests are encouraged to relax. Several rooms have three and four beds. Curfew is at 11:30 PM, and those of you who want to attend Mass can do so every morning at 7:30. The nuns will provide half or full pension for groups of 10 or more. ⊠ *Borgo Pinti 15, near Santa Croce, 501201* ☎ *055/2480582* 🖷 *055/2346291* 🖙 *28*

8

rooms, 22 with bath ⌂ Parking (fee); no a/c in some rooms, no room phones, no room TVs ⊟ No credit cards ⏀ EP.

Outside the City

★ $$-$$$ ⊡ **Villa Poggio San Felice.** Livia Puccinelli Sannini, the descendant of a famed 19th-century Florentine hotelier, and her husband, Lorenzo Magnelli, have turned the family's former country villa (documented to the 15th century) into a lovely hotel 5 km (3 mi) southwest of the city limits. With only five rooms available, the villa still feels like a single-family dwelling. Some of the high-ceiling rooms have divine views of Brunelleschi's cupola below, others have working fireplaces. The landscaped gardens help make a stay here serene. Though there is daily shuttle service to the center of town, a car is vital. ⊠ Via San Matteo in Arcetri 24, Lungarno South, 50125 ☎ 055/220016 ⊟ 055/2335388 ⊕ www. villapoggiosanfelice.com ⇄ 4 rooms, 1 suite ⌂ Golf privileges, pool, wading pool, babysitting, laundry service, Internet room, free parking, some pets allowed ⊟ AE, MC, V ⊙ Closed Jan. 10–Feb. 28 ⏀ BP.

NIGHTLIFE & THE ARTS

The Arts

Florence is justifiably famous for its musical offerings. The annual Maggio Musicale attracts the best international talent. Theaters also host visiting American rock stars and cabaret performers. Opera, ballet, and concerts occur regularly throughout the year at different venues in town. Major traveling art exhibitions are mounted at Palazzo Strozzi throughout the year. There's a little publication available at bars and hotels called *Informacittà* (⊕ www.informacittafirenze.it): even though it's in Italian, it's pretty easy to read for event times and addresses.

Film

You can find movie listings in *La Nazione,* the daily Florentine newspaper. Note that most American films are dubbed into Italian rather than subtitled. The **Odeon** (⊠ Piazza Strozzi, near Piazza della Repubblica ☎ 055/214068 ⊕ www.cinehall.it) shows first-run English-language films on Monday, Tuesday, and Thursday at its magnificent art deco theater.

Concerts & Operas

The **Teatro Comunale** (⊠ Corso Italia 16, Lungarno North ☎ 055/213535) hosts the opera season September–December, as well as concerts, festivals, and dance performances throughout the year.

Teatro della Pergola (⊠ Via della Pergola 18/32, box office Via Alamanni 39, near Santissima Annunziata ☎ 055/2264316 ⊕ www.pergola. firenze.it) hosts classical concerts, Maggio Musicale events, and other dramatic performances.

★ The **Maggio Musicale Fiorentino** (☎ 055/213535 ⊕ www.maggiofiorentino. com) is a series of internationally acclaimed concerts and dance, ballet, and opera performances running May and June in venues across the city. Tickets can be purchased online and at the Teatro Comunale box office.

October to April is the concert season for the **Orchestra della Toscana** (✉ Via Alamanni 39, near Santa Croce ☎ 055/210804 ⊕ www.orchestradellatoscana.it), with performances staged at the Teatro Verdi. **Amici della Musica** (☎ 055/210804 ⊕ www.amicimusica.fi.it) organizes classical concerts at the Teatro della Pergola.

Nightlife

Florentines are rather proud of their nightlife. Most bars have some sort of happy hour, which usually lasts for many hours, often accompanied by substantial snacks. Dance clubs typically don't open until very late in the evening and don't get crowded until 1 or 2 in the morning. Cover charges are steep, but it's fairly easy to find free passes in trendier bars around town. Most clubs are closed either Sunday or Monday.

Bars

Zona 15 (✉ Piazza Brunelleschi, Via del Castellaccia 53–55/r, near Duomo ☎ 055/211678) is coolly chic with its pale interior, blond woodwork, and metallic surfaces. Lunch, dinner, cocktails, and brunch are on offer for Florentine cognoscenti and others. The oh-so-cool—bordering on pretentious—vibe at **La Dolce Vita** (✉ Piazza del Carmine 6/r, near Santo Spirito ☎ 055/284595) attracts Florentines and the occasional visiting American movie star.

Negroni (✉ Via dei Renai 17/r, near San Niccolò ☎ 055/243647) teems with well-dressed young Florentines at happy hour. **Zoe** (✉ Via dei Renai 13/r, near San Niccolò ☎ 055/243111) calls itself a café, and although coffee may indeed be served, twentysomething Florentines flock here for the fine (and expensive) cocktails.

i Visacci (✉ Borgo Albizi 80/r near Santa Croce ☎ 055/2001956) serves coffee and tasty panini throughout the day, and delivers cocktails with zing at aperitivo time.

Fusion Bar (✉ Vicolo dell'Oro 5, near Santa Maria Novella ☎ 055/27263) is the in-house bar of the Gallery Art Hotel. Beautiful folk come here to sip expensive cocktails and to snack on sushi. **Moyo** (✉ Via de'Benci 23/r, near Santa Croce ☎ 055/2479738) opened in December 2004; high ceilings, dramatic lighting, and superb aperitivi (with equally superb snacks) draw trendy Florentines. They also serve a respectable lunch until 5 PM. **Rex** (✉ Via Fiesolana 23–25/r, near Santa Croce ☎ 055/2480331) attracts a trendy, artsy clientele. **Sant'Ambrogio Caffè** (✉ Piazza Sant'Ambrogio 7–8/r, near Santa Croce ☎ 055/241035) has outdoor summer seating with a view of an 11th-century church (Sant'Ambrogio) directly across the street. When last call's come and gone and you're not finished with your evening, go where the bartenders unwind after their shift: **Loch Ness** (✉ Via de' Benci 19/r, near Santa Croce) pours drinks there until 5 AM. For a swanky experience lubricated with trademark Bellinis and fine martinis, head to **Harry's Bar** (✉ Lungarno Vespucci 22/r, Lungarno North ☎ 055/2396700).

8

Nightclubs

Yab (✉ Via Sassetti 5/r, near Piazza della Repubblica ☎ 055/215160) is one of the largest clubs; it attracts a young clientele. **Maracaná** (✉ Via Faenza 4, near Santa Maria Novella ☎ 055/210298) is a restaurant and pizzeria featuring Brazilian specialties; at 11 PM it transforms itself into a cabaret floor show and then it opens the floor to dancing. Book a table if you want to eat. If you had a transvestite grandmother, her home would look like **Montecarla** (✉ Via de' Bardi 2, near San Niccolò ☎ 055/2340259). On its two crowded floors people sip cocktails against a backdrop of exotic flowers, leopard-print chairs and chintz, and red walls and floors.

Jazz Club (✉ Via Nuova de' Caccini 3, at Borgo Pinti, near Santa Croce ☎ 055/2479700) puts on live music in a smoky basement.

SHOPPING

Since the days of the medieval guilds, Florence has been synonymous with fine craftsmanship and good business. Such time-honored Florentine specialties as antiques (and reproductions), bookbinding, jewelry, lace, paper products, leather goods, and silks attest to this. The various shopping areas are mostly a throwback to the Middle Ages, when each district supplied a different product. The Ponte Vecchio houses reputable but very expensive jewelry shops, as it has since the 16th century. The area around Santa Croce is the heart of the leather merchants' district. The fanciest clothing designers are mainly on Via Tornabuoni and Via della Vigna Nuova. There's a large concentration of antiques shops on Borgo Ognissanti and near Santo Spirito. Across the river in the Oltrarno, there's also a variety of artisans—goldsmiths, leather workers, and antique furniture restorers—plying their trade.

Shops are generally open 9–1 and 3:30–7:30 and are closed Sunday and Monday morning most of the year. Summer (June–September) hours are usually 9–1 and 4–8, and some shops close Saturday afternoon instead of Monday morning. When looking for addresses of shops, notice the two-color numbering system: the red numbers are commercial addresses; the blue or black numbers are residential.

Markets

Roam through the stalls under the loggia of the **Mercato Nuovo** (✉ Via Por Santa Maria and Via Porta Rossa, near Piazza della Repubblica) for cheery, inexpensive trinkets. In the huge, two-story **Mercato Centrale** (✉ Off Via Nazionale, near San Lorenzo ☉ Mon.–Sat. 7–2), food is everywhere, some of it remarkably exotic. The ground floor contains meat and cheese stalls, as well as some very good bars selling panini, and the second floor teems with vegetable stands. If you're looking for dill or mangoes in Florence, this is most likely where you'll find them. In the streets next to the church of San Lorenzo, shop for bargains at stalls full of clothing and leather goods that are part of the **Mercato di San Lorenzo**.

The flea market on **Piazza dei Ciompi** (✉ Sant'Ambrogio, near Santa Croce) takes place on the last Sunday of the month. An open-air produce and flea market is held in **Le Cascine park** (✉ Off Viale Fratelli

Rosselli, near Santa Maria Novella), just before the Ponte della Vittoria, every Tuesday morning.

Specialty Stores

Antiques

Giovanni Pratesi (✉ Via Maggio 13, near Santo Spirito ☎ 055/2396568) specializes in furniture, with some fine paintings, sculpture, and decorative objects turning up from time to time. Vying with Luigi Bellini as one of Florence's oldest antiques dealers, **Guido Bartolozzi** (✉ Via Maggio 18/r, near Santo Spirito ☎ 055/215602) sells predominately period Florentine pieces. **Galleria Luigi Bellini** (✉ Lungarno Soderini 5, Lungarno South ☎ 055/214031) claims to be Italy's oldest antiques dealer, which may be true, since father Mario Bellini was responsible for instituting Florence's international antiques biennial.

Books & Paper

Libreria d'Arte Galleria degli Uffizi (✉ Piazzale degli Uffizi 6, near Piazza della Signoria ☎☎ 055/284508) carries monographs on famous artists, some of whose work can be found in the Uffizi; it also carries scholarly works from both the Italian and anglophone worlds. Long one of Florence's best art-book shops, **Libreria Salimbeni** (✉ Via Matteo Palmieri 14–16/r, near Santa Croce ☎ 055/2340905) has an outstanding selection.

Alberto Cozzi (✉ Via del Parione 35/r, near Santa Maria Novella ☎ 055/294968) keeps an extensive line of Florentine papers and paper products. On-site artisans rebind and restore books and works on paper. One of Florence's oldest paper-goods stores, **Giulio Giannini e Figlio** (✉ Piazza Pitti 37/r ☎ 055/212621) is *the* place to buy the marbleized stock, which comes in many shapes and sizes, from flat sheets to boxes and even pencils. Photograph albums, frames, diaries, and other objects dressed in handmade paper can be purchased at **Il Torchio** (✉ Via dei Bardi 17, San Niccolò ☎ 055/2342862 ⊕ www.legatoriailtorchio.com). The stuff is of high quality, and the prices are lower than usual. **La Tartaruga** (✉ Borgo Albizi 60/r, Santa Croce ☎ 055/2340845) sells brightly colored, recycled paper in lots of guises (such as calendars and stationery), as well as toys for children.

Ceramics

The mother-daughter team of Antonella Chini and Lorenza Adami sell their Florentine-inspired ceramic designs, based on Antonella's extensive ceramics training in Faenza, at **Sbigoli Terrecotte** (✉ Via Sant'Egidio 4/r, near Santa Croce ☎ 055/2479713). They carry traditional Tuscan terra-cotta and ceramic vases, pots, and cups and saucers. **Rampini Ceramiche** (✉ Borgo Ognissanti 32/34, Lungarno North ☎ 055/219720) sells exquisitely crafted ceramics in various patterns, shapes, and sizes.

Clothing

The usual fashion gurus—such as Prada and Armani—all have shops in Florence; more and more of Via Tornabuoni resembles a giant *passarella* (catwalk). If you want to buy Florentine haute fashion while in Florence, stick to Pucci, Gucci, Ferragamo, and Roberto Cavalli, all of which call Florence home.

VOICES OF ITALY

Valentino Adami
ceramics shop owner,
Santa Croce area

Since 1970, Valentino Adami, a native of southern Tuscany who has lived all over the world, and his wife, Antonella Chini, a Florentine, have been owners of the ceramics shop Sbigoli Terrecotte. The operation is a family affair: Antonella studied in Faenza, the ceramics center in Emilia-Romagna, and daughter Lorenza holds two certificates in ceramics. Most days, they can be found in the back of the shop, painting vases. Valentino and daughter Chiara run the front of the store, two plain rooms bursting with colorful objects—vases, espresso cups, plates, and patio tables.

Valentino explains what makes Italian ceramics distinctive: "First of all, it's the type of clay we use. The clay we find here is softer. We fire it at a lower temperature, 950°C. You get better color if you fire it at a lower temperature."

The use of color is crucial. "The color of the sun, of the sea—it gives us confidence with color. Our colors are similar to what the Renaissance masters used, only we don't use lead. Like those Renaissance masters, we used to fire with wood. It would take three or four days. Now we use an electric kiln."

According to Valentino, works from major ceramics-making areas within Italy can be distinguished both by color and type of design. "The farther you go south, you'll find that the colors are stronger. Deruta [in Umbria] makes one kind of ceramics, and Montelupo [near Florence] another. The main difference in ceramics from Faenza is that they use faces and produce lots of hunting scenes. In Florence, it's more geometric. Our portraits are rougher compared to Faenza."

Florentine **Patrizia Pepe** (⊠ Piazza San Giovanni 12/r, near Duomo ☎ 055/2645056) has body-conscious clothes perfect for all ages, especially for women with a tiny streak of rebelliousness. For cutting-edge fashion, the fun and funky window displays at **Spazio A** (⊠ Via Porta Rossa 109–115/r, Piazza della Repubblica ☎ 055/212995 ⊕ www.aeffe.com) merit a stop. The shop carries such well-known designers as Alberta Ferretti and Narciso Rodriguez, as well as lesser-known Italian, English, and French designers. **Bernardo** (⊠ Via Porta Rossa 87/r, near Piazza della Repubblica ☎ 055/283333) specializes in men's trousers, cashmere sweaters, and shirts with details like mother-of-pearl buttons. At **L'essentiel** (⊠ Via del Corso 10/r, near Piazza della Signoria ☎ 055/294713) Lara Caldieron has spun her club-going years into fashion that also works well on the street and in the office. Though it may seem American, **Diesel** (⊠ Via dei Lamberti 13/r, near Piazza della Signoria ☎ 055/2399963) started in Vicenza; its gear is on the "must-have" list of many self-respecting Italian teens.

The aristocratic Marchese di Barsento, **Emilio Pucci** (⊠ Via Tornabuoni 20–22/r, near Santa Maria Novella ☎ 055/2658082), became an international name in the late 1950s when the stretch ski clothes he designed for himself caught on with the dolce vita crowd—his pseudopsychedelic prints and "palazzo pajamas" became all the rage. You can take home a custom-made suit or dress from **Giorgio Vannini** (⊠ Borgo Santi Apostoli 43/r, near Santa Maria Novella ☎055/293037), who also has a showroom for his prêt-à-porter designs. **Prada** (⊠ Via Tornabuoni 51–53/r, near Santa Maria Novella ☎055/267471 ⊠ Outlet ⊠ Levanella Spacceo, Estrada Statale 69, Montevarchi ☎055/91911) appeals to an exclusive clientele. Cognoscenti will drive or taxi about 45 minutes out of town to the Prada Outlet. Native son **Roberto Cavalli** (⊠ Via Tornabuoni 83/r, near Santa Maria Novella ☎055/2396226), whose outlandish designs appeal to Hollywood celebrities and those who want to look like more expensive versions of Britney Spears, has a corner shop with a trendy café attached.

Geraldine Tayar (⊠ Sdrucciolo de Pitti 6/r, Palazzo Pitti ☎055/290405) makes clothing and accessories of her own design in eclectic fabric combinations. **Piccolo Slam** (⊠ Via de'Neri 9/11r, near Santa Croce ☎055/214504) has classic styles for members of the junior set.

Embroidery & Linens

Sumptuous silks, beaded fabrics, lace, wool, and tweeds can be purchased at **Valli** (⊠ Via Strozzi 4/r, near Piazza della Repubblica ☎055/282485). It carries fabrics created by Armani, Valentino, and other high-end designers.

Antico Setificio Fiorentino (⊠ via Bartolini 4 Lungarno South ☎055/213 861) has been furnishing lavish silks to international royalty for years; a visit is well worth it, as is making an appointment beforehand.

Loretta Caponi (⊠ Piazza Antinori 4/r, near Santa Maria Novella ☎055/213668) is synonymous with Florentine embroidery, and her luxury lace, linens, and lingerie have earned her worldwide renown.

Food

Conti (⊠ Mercato Centrale, enter at Via Signa, near San Lorenzo ☎055/2398501) sells top-quality wines, olive oils, and dried fruits; they'll shrink-wrap the highest-quality dried porcini for traveling. **La Bottega dell'Olio** (⊠Piazza del Limbo 2/r, near Santa Maria Novella ☎055/2670468) sells a great collection of fine olive oil, as well as bath products made from olive oil. **Antico Salumificio Anzuini-Massi** (⊠Via de'Neri 84/r, near Santa Croce ☎055/294901) shrink-wraps their own pork products, making it a snap to take home some *salame di cinghiale* (wild boar salami).

Fragrances

Antica Officina del Farmacista Dr. Vranjes (⊠ Borgo La Croce 44/r, near Santa Croce ☎055/241748 ⊠ Via San Gallo 63/r, near San Marco ☎055/494537) makes aromatic oils and perfumes for people and for spaces. The essence of a Florentine holiday is captured in the sachets of the **Officina Profumo Farmaceutica di Santa Maria Novella** (⊠ Via della Scala 16, near Santa Maria Novella ☎055/216276), a

> **WORD OF MOUTH**
>
> "Officina Profumo di Farmaceutica Santa Maria Novella is the grandest perfume salon in the world."
> –ThinGorjus

turn-of-the-19th-century emporium of herbal cosmetics and soaps that are made following centuries-old recipes created by friars.

Jewelry

Carlo Piccini (⊠ Ponte Vecchio 31/r, near Piazza della Signoria ☎ 055/292030) has sold antique jewelry as well as made pieces to order for several generations; you can also get old jewelry reset. **Cassetti** (⊠ Ponte Vecchio 54/r, near Piazza della Signoria ☎ 055/2396028) combines precious and semiprecious stones and metals in contemporary settings.

Gatto Bianco (⊠ Borgo Santi Apostoli 12/r, near Santa Maria Novella ☎ 055/282989) has breathtakingly beautiful jewelry worked in semiprecious and precious stones; the look is completely contemporary. **Gherardi** (⊠ Ponte Vecchio 5/r, near Piazza della Signoria ☎ 055/211809), Florence's king of coral, has the city's largest selection of finely crafted pieces, as well as cultured pearls, jade, and turquoise.

Oro Due (⊠ Via Lambertesca 12/r, near Piazza della Signoria ☎ 055/292 143) sells gold jewelry the old-fashioned way: beauteous objects are priced according to the level of craftsmanship and the price of gold bullion that day. **Studio Ballerino** (⊠ Borgo Allegri 25/r, near Santa Croce ☎ 055/234 4658) has one-of-a-kind pieces crafted in semi-precious stone, gold, and silver. One of Florence's oldest jewelers, **Tiffany** (⊠ Via Tornabuoni 25/r, near Santa Maria Novella ☎ 055/215506), has supplied Italian (and other) royalty with finely crafted gems for centuries. Its selection of antique-looking classics has been updated with a choice of contemporary silver.

Shoes & Leather Accessories

Furla (⊠ Via Calzaiuoli 47/r, near Piazza della Repubblica ☎ 055/2382883) makes beautiful leather bags and wallets in up-to-the-minute designs. **Pollini** (⊠ Via Calimala 12/r, near Piazza della Repubblica ☎ 055/214738) has beautifully crafted shoes and leather accessories for those willing to pay that little bit extra. For sheer creativity in both color and design, check out the shoes at **Sergio Rossi** (⊠ Via Roma 15/r, near Duomo ☎ 055/294873) and fantasize about having a life to go with them.

Cellerini (⊠ Via del Sole 37/r, near Santa Maria Novella ☎ 055/282533) is a Florentine institution in a city where it seems that nearly everybody is wearing an expensive leather jacket. Born near Naples, the late Salvatore **Ferragamo** (⊠ Via Tornabuoni 2/r, near Santa Maria Novella ☎ 055/292123) earned his fortune custom-making shoes for famous feet, especially Hollywood stars'. The elegant store, in a 13th-century Renaissance palazzo, also displays designer clothing and accessories in addition to shoes. Though the Florentine family is no longer involved with the store that bears its name, **Gucci** (⊠ Via Tornabuoni 73/r, near Santa Maria Novella ☎ 055/264011) still manages to draw a crowd. **Il Bisonte** (⊠ Via del Parione 31/r, off Via della Vigna Nuova, near Santa Maria Novella ☎ 055/215722) is known for its natural-looking leather goods, all stamped with the store's bison symbol.

Madova (⊠ Via Guicciardini 1/r, near Palazzo Pitti ☎ 055/2396526) has a rainbow of high-quality leather gloves. **Paolo Carandini** (⊠ Via de' Macci

73/r, near Santa Croce ☎ 055/245397) works exclusively in leather, producing exquisite objects such as picture frames, jewelry boxes, and desk accessories. The **Scuola del Cuoio** (✉ Piazza Santa Croce 16 ☎ 055/244533 ⊕ www.leatherschool.com), in the former dormitory of Santa Croce, is a consortium for leather workers who ply their trade and sell their wares on the premises. **Giotti** (✉ Piazza Ognissanti 3–4/r, Lungarno North ☎ 055/294265) has a full line of leather goods and leather clothing.

SIDE TRIPS FROM FLORENCE

Gracious Gardens Around Florence

Like any well-heeled Florentine, you, too, can get away from Florence's hustle and bustle by heading for the hills. Take a break from city sightseeing to enjoy the gardens and villas set like jewels in the hills around the city. Villa di Castello and Villa La Petraia, both 6 km (4 mi) northwest of the center of town in Castello, can be explored in one trip. The garden at Villa Gamberaia is a quick 8-km (5-mi) jaunt east of the center near Settignano. Plan for a full-day excursion, picnic lunch included, if visiting all three. Spring and summer are the ideal times to visit, when flowers are in glorious bloom. For a taste of Medici living, venture farther afield to the family's Villa Medicea in Poggio a Caiano, south of Prato.

Villa di Castello

A fortified residence in the Middle Ages, Villa di Castello was rebuilt by the Medici in the 15th century. The Accademia della Crusca, the 400-year-old institution that is the official arbiter of the Italian language, occupies the palace, which is not open to the public. The gardens are the main attraction. From the villa entrance, walk uphill through the 19th-century park set above part of the formal garden. From the terrace, which affords a good view of the geometric layout of the Italian garden below, stairs on either side descend to the parterre.

Though the original garden design has been altered somewhat over the centuries, the allegorical theme of animals devised by Tribolo to the delight of the Medici in 1537 is still evident. The artificial cave, **Grotta degli Animali** (Animal Grotto), displays an imaginative menagerie of sculpted animals by Giambologna and his assistants. An Ammannati sculpture, a figure of an old man *Gennaio* (January), is at the center of a pond on the terrace overlooking the garden. Two bronze sculptures by Ammannati, centerpieces of fountains studding the Italian garden, can now be seen indoors in Villa La Petraia. Allow about 45 minutes to visit the garden; you can easily visit Villa La Petraia from here, making for a four-hour trip in total.

To get to Villa di Castello by car, head northwest from Florence on Via Reginaldo Giuliani (also known as Via Sestese) to Castello, about 6 km (4 mi) northwest of the city center in the direction of Sesto Fiorentino; follow signs to Villa di Castello. Or take Bus 28 from the city center and tell the driver you want to get off at Villa di Castello; from the stop, walk north about ½ km (¼ mi) up the tree-lined allée from the main road. ✉ *Via di Castello 47, Castello* ☎ *055/454791* ⊕ *www.polomuseale.firenze.it*

8

✉ €2, *includes entrance to Villa La Petraia* ⊙ *Garden Mar. and Oct., daily 8:15–6; Apr., May, and Sept., daily 8:15–7; June–Aug., daily 8:15–8. Closed 2nd and 3rd Mon. of month* ⌖ *Palace closed to public.*

Villa La Petraia

The splendidly planted gardens of Villa La Petraia lie high above the Arno Plain with a sweeping view of Florence. The villa was built around a medieval tower and reconstructed after it was purchased by the Medici sometime after 1530. Virtually the only trace of the Medici having lived here is the 17th-century courtyard frescoes depicting glorious episodes from the clan's history. In the 1800s the villa served as a hunting lodge for King Vittorio Emanuele II (1820–78), who kept his mistress here while Florence was the temporary capital of the newly united country of Italy.

The garden—also altered in the 1800s—and the vast park behind the palace suggest a splendid contrast between formal and natural landscapes. Allow 60–90 minutes to explore the park and gardens, plus 30 minutes for the guided tour of the villa interior. This property is best visited after the Villa di Castello.

To reach Villa La Petraia by car, travel as though you're going to Villa di Castello (head northwest from Florence on Via Reginaldo Giuliani), but take the right off Via Reginaldo Giuliani, following the sign for Villa La Petraia. You can walk from Villa di Castello to Villa La Petraia in about 15 minutes; turn left beyond the gate of Villa di Castello and continue straight along Via di Castello and the imposing Villa Corsini; take Via della Petraia uphill to the entrance. ✉ *Via della Petraia 40, Località Castello* ☎ *055/451208* ⊕ *www.polomuseale.firenze.it* ✉ *€2, includes entrance to Villa di Castello* ⊙ *Garden Mar. and Oct., daily 8:15–6; Apr., May, and Sept., daily 8:15–7; June–Aug., daily 8:15–8. Villa tours Oct.–Mar., daily at 9:15, 10, 10:45, 11:30, 12:10, 1:30, 2:20, 3, and 3:40; plus 4:45 in Apr., May, and Sept.; plus 4:45, 5:35, and 6:35 June–Aug. Closed 2nd and 3rd Mon. of month.*

Villa Gamberaia

Villa Gamberaia, near the village of Settignano on the eastern outskirts of Florence, was the rather modest 15th-century country home of Matteo di Domenico Gamberelli, the father of noted Renaissance sculptors Bernardo, Antonio, and Matteo Rossellino. In the early 1600s the villa passed into the hands of the wealthy Capponi family. They spared no expense in rebuilding it and, more important, creating its garden, one of the finest near Florence. Studded with statues and fountains, the garden suffered damage during World War II but has been restored according to the original 17th-century design. This excursion takes about 1½ hours, allowing 45 minutes to visit the garden.

To get here by car, go to Piazza Beccaria and turn onto Via Gioberti. This eventually becomes Via Aretino; follow the sign to the turnoff to the north to Villa Gamberaia, about 8 km (5 mi) from the center. To arrive by bus, take Bus 10 to Settignano. From Settignano's main Piazza Tommaseo, walk east on Via di San Romano; the second lane on the right is Via del Rossellino, which leads southeast to the entrance of Villa Gamberaia. The walk from the piazza takes about 10 minutes. ⊠ *Via del Rossellino 72, near Settignano* ☎ *055/697205* 🎟 *€10* ⊙ *Nov.–Mar., weekends 9–5; Apr.–Oct., daily 9–6.*

Fiesole

A half-day excursion to Fiesole, in the hills 8 km (5 mi) northeast of Florence, gives you a pleasant respite from museums and a wonderful view of the city. Fiesole began life as an ancient Etruscan and later Roman village that held some power until it succumbed to barbarian invasions. Eventually it gave up its independence in exchange for Florence's protection. The medieval cathedral, ancient Roman amphitheater, and lovely old villas behind garden walls are clustered on a series of hilltops. The trip from Florence by car or bus takes 20–30 minutes. Take Bus 7 from the Stazione Centrale di Santa Maria Novella, Piazza San Marco, or the Duomo. (You can also get on and off the bus at San Domenico.) There are several possible routes for the two-hour walk from central Florence to Fiesole. One route begins in residential Salviatino (Via Barbacane, near Piazza Edison, on the Bus 7 route), and after a short time you can peeks over garden walls of beautiful villas, as well as a panorama of Florence in the valley. A walk around Fiesole can take a couple of hours, depending on how far you stroll from the main piazza.

The **Duomo** reveals a stark medieval interior. In the raised presbytery, the **Cappella Salutati** was frescoed by 15th-century artist Cosimo Rosselli, but it was his contemporary the sculptor Mino da Fiesole (1430–84) who put the town on the artistic map. The Madonna on the altarpiece and the tomb of Bishop Salutati are fine examples of his work. ⊠ *Piazza Mino da Fiesole* ☎ *055/59400* ⊙ *Nov.–Mar., daily 7:30–noon and 2–5; Apr.–Oct., daily 7:30–noon and 3–6.*

Fiesole's beautifully preserved 2,000-seat **Anfiteatro Romano** (Roman Amphitheater) dates from the 1st century BC and is used for the summer concerts of the **Estate Fiesolana** (⊠ Teatro Romano ☎ 055/598720), a festival of theater, music, dance, and film that also utilizes the churches of Fiesole. To the right of the amphitheater are the remains of the **Terme Romane** (Roman Baths), where you can see the gymnasium, hot and cold baths, and rectangular chamber where the water was heated. A beautifully designed **Museo Archeologico,** an intricate series of levels connected by elevators, is built amid the ruins and contains objects dating from as early as 2000 BC. The nearby **Museo Bandini** is a small collection with a lot of interesting paintings. It's filled with the private collection of Canon Angelo Maria Bandini (1726–1803); he fancied 13th- to 15th-century Florentine paintings, terra-cotta pieces, and wood sculpture, which he later bequeathed to the Diocese of Fiesole. ⊠ *Via Portigiani 1* ☎ *055/59477* 🎟 *€8, includes access to archaeological park and museums (individual site admission €4)* ⊙ *Apr.–Sept., daily 9:30–7; Oct.–Mar., Wed.–Mon. 9:30–6.*

Via Vecchia Fiesolana is a narrow lane in use since Etruscan times; walk 4 km (2½ mi) back toward Florence on it to get to the church of **San Domenico.** Sheltered in the church is the *Madonna and Child with Saints* by Fra Angelico, who was a Dominican friar here. ☒ *Piazza San Domenico, off Via Giuseppe Mantellini* ☏ *055/59230* ☉ *Daily 9–noon.*

Where to Stay

$$$$ ☒ **Villa San Michele.** The cypress-lined driveway provides an elegant pre-amble to this incredibly gorgeous (and incredibly expensive) hotel nestled in the hills of Fiesole. The 16th-century building was originally a Franciscan convent designed by Santi di Tito. Not a single false note is struck in the reception area (formerly the chapel) or in the dining rooms (a covered cloister and former refectory). Tasteful antiques and art that decorate the rooms. Even seasoned travelers sometimes find the space cramped; do keep in mind that this was once a convent. The open-air loggia, where lunch and dinner are served, provides one of the most stunning views of Florence, which might compensate for the exorbitant prices. ☒ *Via Doccia 4, 50014* ☏ *055/5678200* ☎ *055/5678250* ⊕ *www.villasanmichele.com* ⇱ *21 rooms, 24 suites* ⚖ *Restaurant, room service, in-room fax, in-room safes, minibars, cable TV with movies, in-room VCRs, in-room data ports, Wi-Fi, pool, gym, mountain bikes (fee), 3 bars, piano bar, babysitting, dry cleaning, laundry service, concierge, free parking, some pets allowed* ⊟ *AE, DC, MC, V* ☉ *Closed mid-Nov.–mid Mar.* ⦿ *BP, MAP, FAP.*

$ ☒ **Fattoria di Maiano.** In the foothills of Fiesole you have all the pleasures of the country with Florence 5 km (3 mi) to the south. Here there are splendid views of olive tree groves (olive oil is produced by the Fattoria owners). The lovely apartments—wood floors, simple and sturdy furniture, and very modern kitchens—sleep 4–11 people and are rented by the week. ☒ *Via Benedetto da Maiano 11, 50016* ☏ *055/599600* ☎ *055/599640* ⊕ *www.fattoriadimaiano.com* ⇱ *13 apartments* ⚖ *Kitchenettes, pool, some pets allowed; no a/c* ⊟ *DC, MC, V* ⦿ *EP.*

FLORENCE ESSENTIALS

Transportation

BY AIR

Florence's Aeroporto A. Vespucci, commonly called Peretola, receives flights from Milan, Rome, London, and Paris. To get into the city center from the airport by car, take the A11. Tickets for the local bus service into Florence are sold at the airport's second-floor bar. Take Bus 62, which goes directly to the train station at Santa Maria Novella; the airport's bus shelter is beyond the parking lot.

Pisa's Aeroporto Galileo Galilei is the closest landing point with significant international service. It's relatively easy to get to Florence, as the SS67 leads directly there. For flight information, call the airport or Florence Air Terminal (which is an office at Santa Maria Novella, Florence's main train station). A train service connects Pisa's airport station with Santa Maria Novella, roughly a 1½-hour trip. Starting about 7 AM, several trains run from the airport and from Florence in the morning. Later service from both Pisa Aeroporto and Florence Santa Maria Novella is more sporadic, as only a handful of trains run from the late afternoon through the evening. You can check in for departing flights at the Florence Air Terminal, which is around the corner from train tracks 1 and 2.

🔰 Airport Information **Aeroporto Galileo Galilei** ✈ 12 km [7 mi] south of Pisa and 80 km [50 mi] west of Florence ☎ 050/849300 ⊕ www.pisa-airport.it. **Florence Air Terminal** ✉ Stazione Centrale di Santa Maria Novella ☎ 055/216073. **Peretola** ✈ 10 km [6 mi] northwest of Florence ☎ 055/373498 ⊕ www.airport.florence.it.

BY BIKE & MOPED

Brave souls (cycling in Florence is difficult at best) may rent bicycles at easy-to-spot locations at Fortezza da Basso, the Stazione Centrale di Santa Maria Novella, and Piazza Pitti. Otherwise try Alinari. You'll be up against hordes of tourists and those pesky *motorini* (mopeds). Le Cascine, a former Medici hunting ground turned into a large public park with paved pathways, admits no cars. The historic center can be circumnavigated via bike paths lining the *viali,* the ring road surrounding the historic center. If you want to go native and rent a noisy motorino, you may do so at Maxirent. However unfashionable, helmets are mandatory by law and you must rent one.

🔰 Rentals **Alinari** ✉ Via Guelfa 85/r, San Marco ☎ 055/280500 ⊕ www.alinarirental. com. **Maxirent** ✉ Borgo Ognissanti 155/r, Santa Maria Novella ☎ 055/265420.

BY BUS

Long-distance buses provide inexpensive if somewhat claustrophobic service between Florence and other cities in Italy and Europe. Lazzi Eurolines and SITA are the major lines; they have neatly divided up their routes, so there's little overlap.

Maps and timetables for local bus service are available for a small fee at the ATAF (Azienda Trasporti Area Fiorentina) booth, or for free at visitor information offices. Tickets must be bought in advance at tobacco shops, newsstands, from automatic ticket machines near main stops, or at ATAF booths. The ticket must be canceled in the small validation machine immediately upon boarding.

You have several ticket options, all valid for one or more rides on all lines. A €1 ticket is valid for one hour from the time it is first canceled. A multiple ticket—four tickets, each valid for 60 minutes—costs €3.90. A 24-hour tourist ticket costs €4.50. Two-, three-, and seven-day passes are also available.

🔰 Bus Information **ATAF** ✉ Next to train station; Piazza del Duomo 57/r, Santa Maria Novella ☎ 800/424500 ⊕ www.ataf.net. **Lazzi Eurolines** ✉ Via Mercadante 2, Santa Maria Novella ☎ 055/363041 ⊕ www.lazzi.it. **SITA** ✉ Via Santa Caterina da Siena 17/r, Santa Maria Novella ☎ 055/214721 ⊕ www.sita-on-line.it.

BY CAR

Florence is connected to the north and south of Italy by the Autostrada del Sole (A1). It takes about 1 hour of driving on scenic roads to get to Bologna (although heavy truck traffic over the Apennines often makes for slower going), about 3 hours to Rome, and 3–3½ hours to Milan. The Tyrrhenian Coast is an hour west on the A11. For help with car trouble, call the ACI (Automobile Club Firenze).

🔰 **ACI** ✉ Viale Amendola 36, outside town ☎ 055/2486246.

8

BY TAXI

Taxis usually wait at stands throughout the city (in front of the train station and in Piazza della Repubblica, for example), or you can call for one. The meter starts at €2.30, with a €3.60 minimum and extra charges at night, on Sunday, and for radio dispatch.

▮ Taxi Company **Taxis** ☎ 055/4390 or 055/4798.

BY TRAIN

Florence is on the principal Italian train route between most European capitals and Rome, and within Italy it is served frequently from Milan, Venice, and Rome by Intercity (IC) and nonstop Eurostar trains. Stazione Centrale di Santa Maria Novella, the main station, is in the center of town. Be sure to avoid trains that stop only at the Campo di Marte or Rifredi stations, which are not convenient to the center.

▮ Train Information **Stazione Centrale di Santa Maria Novella** ☎ 892021 ⊕ www. trenitalia.com.

Contacts & Resources

EMERGENCIES

You can get a list of English-speaking doctors and dentists at the U.S. Consulate, or contact the Tourist Medical Service. If you need hospital treatment and an interpreter, you can call AVO, a group of volunteer interpreters; it's open Monday, Wednesday, and Friday 4–6 PM and Tuesday and Thursday 10–noon. Comunale No. 13, a local pharmacy, is open 24 hours a day, seven days a week. For a complete listing of other pharmacies that have late-night hours on a rotating basis, dial 192.

▮ **AVO** ☎ 055/2344567. **Tourist Medical Service** ⊠ Via Lorenzo il Magnifico 59 ☎ 055/475411. **U.S. Consulate** ⊠ Lungarno Vespucci 38, Lungarno North ☎ 055/ 266951 ⊕ www.usembassy.it.

▮ Emergency Services **Ambulance** ☎ 118. **Emergencies** ☎ 113. **Misericordia** (Red Cross) ⊠ Piazza del Duomo 20 ☎ 055/212222. **Police** ⊠ Via Zara 2, near Piazza della Libertà ☎ 055/49771.

▮ 24-Hour Pharmacy **Comunale No. 13** ⊠ Stazione Centrale di Santa Maria Novella ☎ 055/289435.

TOURS

WALKING TOURS Licensed Abercrombie & Kent guides can take you to the highlights of Florence or create custom-tailored tours.

▮ Company **Abercrombie & Kent** ⊠ Via de' Fossi 13, near Santa Maria Novella ☎ 055/2648029.

VISITOR INFORMATION

The main Florence tourist office, APT, has locations next to the Palazzo Medici-Riccardi, in the main train station, and around the corner from the Basilica di Santa Croce. Its Web site is in Italian only. Fiesole's office is on the main piazza.

▮ Tourist Information **Fiesole** ⊠ Via Portigiani 3, 50014 ☎ 055/598720 ⊕ www.comune. fiesole.fi.it. **Florence** Agenzia Promozione Turistica (APT) ⊠ Via Cavour 1/r, next to Palazzo Medici-Riccardi, near San Lorenzo, 50100 ☎ 055/290832 ⊠ Stazione Centrale di Santa Maria Novella, 50100 ☎ 055/212245 ⊠ Borgo Santa Croce 29/r ☎ 055/2340444 ⊕ www.comune.firenze.it.

Tuscany

Montepulciano

WORD OF MOUTH

"The food in Tuscany, while simple and even rustic, can be some of the most satisfying in all of Italy. Wild boar ragu over papardelle pasta, tagliatelle with sauteed porcini mushrooms, and savory grilled sausages are just some of the dishes we lust after stateside."

—MLT

WELCOME TO TUSCANY

TOP 5 Reasons to Go

1. **Piazza del Campo, Siena:** Sip a cappuccino, lick some gelato, and take in this spectacular shell-shaped piazza.

2. **Piero della Francesca's *True Cross* frescoes, Arezzo:** If your holy grail is great Renaissance art, seek out these 12 silently enigmatic scenes.

3. **San Gimignano:** Grab a spot at sunset on the steps of the Collegiata church as swallows swoop in and out of the famous medieval towers.

4. **Wine-tasting in Chianti:** Sample the fruits of the region's gorgeous vineyards, at either the wineries themselves or the wine bars found in the towns.

5. **Leaning Tower of Pisa:** It may be touristy, but now that you can once again climb to the top, it's touristy fun.

Relaxed yet elegant Lucca is a little world of its own, surrounded by tree-bedecked 16th-century ramparts now used as delightful promenades.

Thanks to an engineering mistake, the name Pisa is instantly recognized the world over. The Leaning Tower, the cathedral, and the baptistery (above) are grouped together on the Piazza del Duomo.

Lucca

San Gimignano

0   20 mi

0   20 km

Getting Oriented

Hillsides blanketed with vineyards, silver-green olive groves, and enchanting towns are the essence of Tuscany, one of Italy's most beautiful landscapes. Little seems changed since the Renaissance: to the west of Florence, Pisa's tower still leans; to the south, Chianti's roads wind through cypress groves, taking you to Siena, with its captivating piazza.

In **Chianti,** the hillsides present a rolling pageant of ageless vineyards and villas. **Greve** is the area's hub.

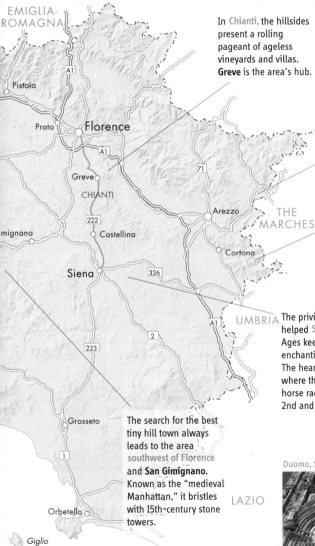

Chianti

Arezzo is best known for its sublime frescoes by Piero della Francesca.

Magnificently situated, the ancient stone town of **Cortona** sits high above the perfectly flat Valdichiana valley, offering great views of beautiful countryside.

The privileged hilltop site that helped **Siena** flourish in the Middle Ages keeps it one of Italy's most enchanting medieval towns today. The heart of the town is il Campo, where the frenzied 700-year-old horse race the Palio is held every July 2nd and August 16th.

The search for the best tiny hill town always leads to the area southwest of Florence and **San Gimignano.** Known as the "medieval Manhattan," it bristles with 15th-century stone towers.

Duomo, Siena

9

TUSCANY PLANNER

Making the Most of Your Time

Tuscany isn't the place for a jam-packed itinerary. One of the greatest pleasures here is indulging in rustic hedonism, marked by long lunches and show-stopping sunsets. Whether by car, bike, or foot, you'll want to get out into the glorious landscape, but it's smart to keep your plans modest. Set a church or a hill town or an out-of-the-way restaurant as your destination, knowing that half the pleasure is in getting there—admiring as you go the stately palaces, the tidy geometry of row upon row of grape vines, the fields vibrant with red poppies and yellow broom.

You'll need to devise a Siena strategy. The place shouldn't be missed; it's compact enough that you can see the major sights on a day trip, and that's exactly what most people do. Spend the night, and you'll get to see the town breathe a sigh and relax upon the day-trippers' departure. The flip side is, your favorite Tuscan hotel isn't likely to be in Siena. (See the comments under "Finding a Place to Stay.")

You face similar issues with Pisa and Lucca in the northwest. Pisa's famous tower is worth seeing, but ultimately Lucca has greater charms, making it a better choice for an overnight.

Getting Around

It's a tremendous advantage to have a car in Tuscany; driving is the only way (other than hiking or biking) to get to many of the small towns and vineyards. Roads are well maintained, but they're largely of the winding, two-lane variety—you need to be alert behind the wheel, and designated drivers are a must when wine tasting. The Strada Chiantigiana, also known as SR222, is the classic Tuscan drive.

If a car isn't an option, you can go by bus. Lines crisscross the region, connecting smaller towns and cities on the autostradas and superhighways. But making arrangements for bus travel, particularly for a non-Italian speaker, can be a test of patience. There's regular train service to the larger towns—most notably Pisa, Lucca, and Arezzo—but traveling by train makes it difficult to get a feel for the Tuscan countryside. For more about car, bus, and train travel, see "Essentials" at the end of this chapter.

Hidden Pleasures

These classic Tuscan experiences will take you away (sometimes far away) from the standard tourist path. And none of them will cost you a euro.

- Hang out in Greve on market day.
- Walk through the tiny town of Volpaia.
- Listen to Gregorian chants at Abbazia di Sant'Antimo, outside Montalcino.
- Visit the ruins of Abbazia di San Galgano.
- Take a dip in the Mediterranean at Biodola beach in Elba.
- Soak in the thermal waters of Saturnia.

Biking & Hiking

In spring, summer, and fall, bicyclists pedaling up and down Tuscany's hills are as much a part of the landscape as the cypress trees. Many are on weeklong organized tours, but it's also possible to rent bikes for jaunts in the countryside or to join afternoon or daylong rides.

Hiking is a simpler matter: all you need is a pair of road-worthy shoes. The tourist information offices in most towns can direct you on walks ranging from an hour to a full day in duration. You can also sign on for more elaborate guided tours.

■ **Italy by Design** (Via degli Artigiani 20, Panzano in Chianti; 055/852418 or 866-585-2418 in U.S.; www. italybydesign.com) provides you with bikes and hand-tailored itineraries, and will pick you up and drop you off at your hotel. The

Massachusetts-based ■ **Ciclismo Classico** (30 Marathon St, Arlington, MA 02474; 800/866-7314; www. ciclismoclassico.com) offers guided bike tours throughout Italy. ■ **Country Walkers** (Box 180, Waterbury, VT 05676; 802/244-1387 or 800/464-9255; www.

countrywalkers.com) conducts weeklong (and longer) trips throughout Tuscany in spring and fall. ■ **Italian Connection**, Walking & Culinary Tours (11 Fairway Dr. Suite 210, Edmonton, Alberta, Canada, 800/462-7911) offers itineraries to Tuscan hill towns.

Finding a Place to Stay

A visit to Tuscany is a trip into the country. There are plenty of good hotels in the larger towns, but the classic experience is to stay in one of the rural accommodations—often converted private homes, sometimes working farms or vineyards (known as *agriturismi*). Though it's tempting to think you can stumble upon a little out-of-the-way hotel at the end of the day, you're better off not testing your luck. Reservations are the way.

Dining & Lodging Price Categories

WHAT IT COSTS in Euros					
	$$$$	**$$$**	**$$**	**$**	**¢**
Restaurants	over €45	€35–€45	€25–€35	€15–€25	under €15
Hotels	over €220	€160–€220	€110–€160	€70–€110	under €70

Restaurant prices are for a first course (primo), second course (secondo), and dessert (dolce). Hotel prices are for two people in a standard double room in high season, including tax and service.

How's the Weather?

Spring and fall are the best times to visit Tuscany, when the weather is mild and the volume of tourists comparatively low. In summer try to start your days early and hit major sights first—that way you'll beat the crowds and the often-oppressive midday heat. Rising early isn't hard, as Tuscany is not about late nights; most restaurants and bars close well before midnight. Come winter, you'll meet with rain and chill. It's not a bad time to visit the cities—museums and monuments are uncrowded, and locals fill the restaurants. In the countryside, though, many restaurants and hotels close in November and reopen in the spring.

9

TOP PASSEGGIATA

Lucca's Passeggiata delle Mura is a pleasing walkway atop the thick walls that surround the old city.

Updated by
Patricia Rucidlo

MIDWAY DOWN THE ITALIAN PENINSULA, Tuscany (Toscana in Italian) is distinguished by rolling hills, snowcapped mountains, dramatic cypress trees, and miles of coastline on the Tyrrhenian Sea—which all adds up to gorgeous views at practically every turn. The beauty of the landscape proves a perfect foil for the region's abundance of superlative art and architecture. It also produces some of Italy's finest wines and olive oils. The combination of unforgettable art, sumptuous views, and eminently drinkable wines that pair beautifully with its simple food makes a trip to Tuscany something beyond special.

Many of Tuscany's cities and towns have retained the same fundamental character over the past 500 years. Civic rivalries that led to bloody battles centuries ago have given way to soccer rivalries. Renaissance pomp lives on in the celebration of local feast days and centuries-old traditions such as the Palio in Siena and the Giostra del Saracino (Joust of the Saracen) in Arezzo. Often, present-day Tuscans look as though they might have served as models for paintings produced hundreds of years ago. In many ways, the Renaissance still lives on in Tuscany.

NORTHWESTERN TUSCANY

In the shadows of the rugged coastal Alpi Apuane, where Michelangelo quarried his marble, this area isn't as lush as southern Tuscany—the hills flatten out, and there are hints of industry. It's well worth the effort to visit these spots, however—there's wonderful art, and there are some very fine restaurants with prices slightly lower than those in Florence.

Prato

❶ *17 km (11 mi) northwest of Florence.*

The wool industry in this city, one of the world's largest manufacturers of cloth, was known throughout Europe as early as the 13th century. It was further stimulated in the 14th century by a local cloth merchant, Francesco di Marco Datini, who built his business, according to one of his ledgers, "in the name of God and of profit." A €6 combination ticket provides admission to the Museo dell'Opera del Duomo, Museo di Pittura Murale, and the Castello.

Prato's Romanesque **Duomo** is famous for its **Pergamo del Sacro Cingolo** (Chapel of the Holy Girdle), to the left of the entrance, which enshrines the girdle of the Virgin Mary. It is said that the Virgin presented it to the apostle Thomas in a miraculous appearance after her Assumption. The Duomo also contains 15th-century frescoes by Prato's most famous son, Fra Filippo Lippi (1406–69), who executed scenes from the life of St. Stephen on the left wall and scenes from the life of John the Baptist on the right in the **Cappella Maggiore** (Main Chapel). ⊠ *Piazza del Duomo* ☎ *0574/26234* ☜ *€8* ⊙ *Mon.–Sat. 7–noon and 3:30–7, Sun. 7–12:30 and 3:30–8.*

Sculptures by Donatello (circa 1386–1466) that originally adorned the Duomo's exterior pulpit are now on display in the **Museo dell'Opera del**

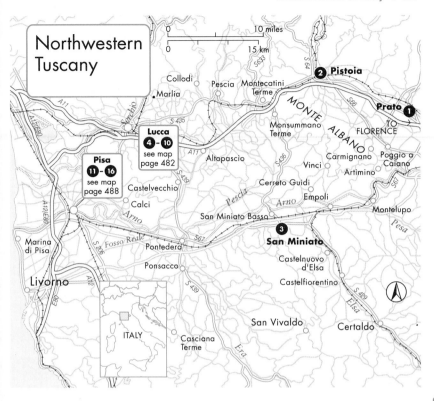

Northwestern Tuscany

10 miles
15 km

Collodi
Pescia Montecatini Terme
Marlia
Pistoia 2

Prato 1
TO FLORENCE

Lucca
4 - 10
see map page 482

Monsummano Terme
MONTE ALBANO
Poggio a Caiano
Carmignano
Vinci
Artimino

Pisa
11 - 16
see map page 488

Altopascio

Castelvecchio
Calci

Cerreto Guidi
Empoli
Montelupo

Pescia
Arno
San Miniato Bassa
3 **San Miniato**

Marina di Pisa
Fosso Reale
Pontedera

Castelnuovo d'Elsa

Ponsacco

Castelfiorentino

Livorno

ITALY

Casciana Terme

San Vivaldo
Certaldo
Elsa
Era

Duomo (Cathedral Museum). ⊠ *Piazza del Duomo 49* ☎ *0574/29339* 🎟 *€4* 🕙 *Mon. and Wed.–Sat. 9:30–12:30 and 3–6:30, Sun. 9:30–12:30.*

The permanent collection at the **Museo di Pittura Murale** (Museum of Mural Painting) contains frescoes from sites in and around Prato. There are also notable temporary exhibits. ⊠ *Piazza San Domenico 8* ☎ *0574/440501* 🎟 *€4* 🕙 *Sun., Mon, Wed., and Thurs. 9–1; weekends 9–1 and 3–6.*

The church of **Santa Maria delle Carceri** was built by Giuliano Sangallo in the 1490s and is a landmark of Renaissance architecture. ⊠ *Piazza Santa Maria delle Carceri off Via Cairoli, southeast of cathedral* ☎ *0574/27933* 🕙 *Daily 7–noon and 4–7.*

Though in ruins, the formidable **Castello** (Castle) built for Frederick II Hohenstaufen, adjacent to Santa Maria delle Carceri, is an impressive sight, the only castle of its type outside southern Italy. ⊠ *Piazza Santa Maria delle Carceri* ☎ *0574/38207* 🎟 *€2.50* 🕙 *Nov.–Mar., Wed.–Mon. 9–1; Apr.–Oct., Wed.–Mon. 9–1 and 4–7.*

OFF THE BEATEN PATH

VILLA MEDICEA – For a look at gracious country living Renaissance style, detour south of Prato to the Villa Medicea in Poggio a Caiano. Lorenzo "il Magnifico" (1449–92) commissioned Giuliano da Sangallo (circa 1445–1516) to redo the villa, which was lavished with frescoes by important Renaissance painters such as Andrea del Sarto (1486–1530) and Pontormo (1494–1557). You can also take a walk around the austerely ornamented grounds. Tours start every hour on the half hour beginning at 8:30; the last tour begins at 3:30. ⊠ *7 km (4½ mi) south of Prato, Poggio a Caiano* ☎ *055/877012* 💷 *€2* ⊙ *Sept. and Oct., daily 8:15–5:30; Nov.–Feb., daily 8:15–3:30; Mar., daily 8:15–4:30; Apr. and May, daily 8:15–5:30; June–Aug., daily 8:15–6:30.*

Where to Eat

★ **$$** ✕ **Da Delfina.** Delfina Cioni began cooking many years ago for hungry hunters, and now her son Carlo is proprietor. Dishes celebrate Tuscan food, with an emphasis on fresh local ingredients. *Secondi* (second courses) such as *coniglio con olive e pignoli* (rabbit sautéed with olives and pine nuts) are a real treat. The seasonal menu is complemented by a fine wine list, and service is gracious. From the restaurant's four comfortably rustic rooms you have a glorious view of the Tuscan countryside, including a Medici villa. ⊠ *Via della Chiesa 1, Artimino, 16 km (10 mi) southwest of Prato, 24 km (38 mi) north of Florence* ☎ *055/ 8718074* ⚠ *Reservations essential* ▭ *No credit cards* ⊙ *Closed Mon. and 2 wks in Aug. No lunch Tues. No dinner Sun. Oct.–May.*

¢ ✕ **La Vecchia Cucina di Soldano.** You could be sitting in your Italian grandmother's kitchen: the place is completely unpretentious, tablecloths are red-and-white-checked, and the servers are like old friends. Local Pratesi specialties include the odd but tasty *sedani ripieni* (stuffed celery), in which celery is pressed and stuffed with a minced veal and mortadella filling, then coated in flour and egg before being fried in olive oil and served with a meat sauce. Or you might enjoy the superb *tagliolini sui fagioli* (thin noodles with beans). The restaurant teems with locals. Clearly they, too, like the rock-bottom prices. ⊠ *Via Pomeria 23* ☎ *0574/34665* ▭ *No credit cards* ⊙ *Closed Sun.*

Shopping

Prato's biscotti (twice-baked cookies) have an extra-dense texture, making them excellent for submersion in coffee or *vin santo* (a dessert wine). The best in town are at **Antonio Mattei** (⊠ Via Ricasoli 20/22 ☎ 0574/25756).

The centuries-old tradition of selling fine textiles crafted into fine clothing continues in Prato. **Enrico Pecci di A. Pecci & C.** (⊠ Via del Pantano 16/e ☎ 055/89890) sells fabric by the meter.

Pistoia

➋ *18 km (11 mi) northwest of Prato, 36 km (22 mi) northwest of Florence.*

Pistoia can claim a Roman past, as well as a bloody history during the Middle Ages, when the town was rent by civil strife. Its historic center is a jewel—and little visited, which makes coming here all the more worthwhile. The **Cattedrale di San Zeno** in the main piazza houses the Dossale di San Jacopo, a magnificent silver altar. The two half figures on the left were executed by Filippo Brunelleschi (1377–1446). ⊠ *Piazza del Duomo* ☎ *0573/25095* 💷 *Illumination of altarpiece €2* ⊙ *Church daily 8:30–12:30 and 3:30–7; altar daily 10–noon and 4–5:45.*

The **Palazzo del Comune,** begun around 1295, houses the **Museo Civico,** with works by local artists from the 14th to 20th centuries. ⊠ *Piazza del Duomo 1* ☎ *0573/371296* ⊡ *€3.50, Sat. 3–7 free* ☉ *Apr.–Oct., Tues.–Sat. 10–6, Sun. 9–12:30; Nov.–Mar., Tues.–Sat. 10–5, Sun. 9–12:30.*

Founded in the 13th century and still a working hospital, the **Spedale del Ceppo** (literally, Hospital of the Tree Stump) has a glorious early-16th-century exterior terra-cotta frieze. Giovanni della Robbia (1469–1529) began the work on the frieze, and it was completed by the workshop of Santi and Benedetto Buglioni from 1526 to 1528. ⊠ *Piazza Ospedale, a short way down Via Pacini from Piazza del Duomo.*

An architectural gem in green-and-white marble, the medieval church of **San Giovanni Fuorcivitas** contains the terra-cotta sculpture *Visitation* by Luca della Robbia (1400–82), a painting attributed to Taddeo Gaddi, and a holy-water font that may have been executed by Fra Guglielmo around 1270. ⊠ *Via Cavour* ☎ *0573/24784* ☉ *Daily 8–noon and 5–6:30.*

Although it's not as grand as the silver altar in Pistoia's cathedral, Giovanni Pisano's powerfully sculpted pulpit (created 1298–1301) in the church of **Sant'Andrea** is considered by many the town's greatest art treasure. ⊠ *Via Sant'Andrea* ☎ *0573/21912* ☉ *Nov.–Mar., daily 8–12:30 and 3:30–6; Apr.–Oct., daily 8–12:30 and 3:30–7.*

☉ The **Giardino Zoologico,** a small zoo, is a 20-minute drive out of town. Take Bus 29 from the train station. ⊠ *Via Pieve a Celle 160/a* ☎ *0573/ 911219* ⊡ *€9.50* ☉ *Apr.–Sept., daily 9–7; Oct.–Mar., daily 9–5.*

Where to Eat

$ ✕ **La BotteGaia.** Jazz plays softly in the background as patrons sip wine at rustic tables in rooms with exposed brick-and-stone walls. In warm weather you can also dine alfresco with a splendid view of the Piazza del Duomo. Typical wine-bar fare, such as plates of cured ham and cheese, shares the menu with a surprisingly sophisticated list of daily specials. For example, you might try *insalatina con foie gras condita con vinaigrette* (foie gras with dressed greens). ⊠ *Via del Lastrone 17* ☎ *0573/ 365602* ⊛ *Reservations essential* ⊟ *AE, DC, MC, V* ☉ *Closed Mon. and 15 days in Aug. No lunch Sun.*

San Miniato

❸ *42 km (26 mi) southeast of Pisa, 43 km (27 mi) southwest of Florence.*

Dating from Etruscan and Roman times, San Miniato was so named when the Lombards erected a church here in the 8th century and consecrated it to the saint. The Holy Roman Empire had very strong ties to San Miniato. Today the pristine, tiny hill town's narrow, cobbled streets are lined with austere facades dating from the 13th to 17th centuries. Its artistic treasures are on a par with those of other similar-size towns in the area, but the real reason for a trip is simply that the place is so pretty—and that its most famous export, the white truffle, is sold around town and on many a restaurant menu.

TUSCANY THROUGH THE AGES

Etruscans & Romans. Tuscany was populated, at least by the 7th century BC, by the Etruscans, a mysterious lot who chose to live on hills—the better to see the approaching enemy—in such places as present-day Arezzo, Chiusi, Cortona, Fiesole, and Volterra. Some 500 years later, the Romans came, saw, and conquered; by 241 BC they had built the Aurelia, a road from Rome to Pisa that is still in use today. The crumbling of the Roman Empire and subsequent invasions by marauding Lombards, Byzantines, and Holy Roman Emperors meant centuries of turmoil. By the 12th century city-states were being formed throughout Tuscany in part, perhaps, because it was unclear exactly who was in charge.

Guelphs & Ghibellines. The two groups vying for power were the Guelphs and the Ghibellines, champions of the pope and the Holy Roman Emperor, respectively. They jostled for control of individual cities and of the region as a whole. Florence was more or less Guelph, and Siena more often than not Ghibelline. This led to bloody battles, most notably the 1260 battle of Montaperti, in which the Ghibellines roundly defeated the Guelphs.

Eventually—by the 14th century—the Guelphs became the dominant force. But this did not mean that the warring Tuscan cities settled down to a period of relative peace and tranquillity. The age in which Dante wrote his *Divine Comedy* and Giotto and Piero della Francesca created their incomparable frescoes was one of internecine strife.

Florentines & Sienese. Florence was the power to be reckoned with; it coveted its main rival, Siena, which it conquered, lost, and reconquered during the 15th and 16th centuries. Finally, in 1555, following in the footsteps of Volterra, Pisa, Prato, and Arezzo, Siena fell for good. They were all united under Florence to form the grand duchy of Tuscany. The only city to escape Florence's dominion was Lucca, which remained fiercely independent until the arrival of Napoléon. Eventually, however, even Florence's influence waned, and the 17th and 18th centuries saw the decline of the entire region as various armies swept across it.

In 1211 St. Francis founded San Miniato's **Convento e Chiesa di San Francesco** (Convent and Church of St. Francis), which contains two cloisters and an ornate wooden choir. For a dose of monastic living, you can stay overnight. ⊠ *Piazza San Francesco* ☎ *0571/43051* ☉ *Daily 9–noon and 3–7; or ring bell.*

Although the **Museo Diocesano** is small, the collection has a number of subtle and pleasant works of art. Note the rather odd Fra Filippo Lippi *Crucifixion, The Redeemer* by Verrocchio (1435–88), and the small but sublime *Education of the Virgin*, by Tiepolo (1696–1770). ⊠ *Piazza del Castello* ☎ *0571/418071* 💶 *€2.60* ☉ *Nov.–Mar., Tues.–Sun. 10–12:30 and 3–6; Apr.–Oct., Tues.–Sun. 9–noon and 3–6.*

Where to Stay & Eat

$–$$ ✕ **Il Convio.** A short drive down a steeply serpentine road from San Miniato brings you to a rustic country ristorante with sponged walls, stenciled decoration, and checkered tablecloths. The main courses are mostly Tuscan classics, such as *bistecca fiorentina* (a generous cut of grilled steak). White truffle, a local specialty, is showcased—you can get it with pasta, *crespelle* (thin pancakes filled with ricotta), tripe, eggs, beef fillet, and even pumpkin. There's a good selection of reasonably priced local wines, and service is courteous. ⊠ *Via San Maiano 2* ☎ *0571/408114* ⊟ *AE, DC, MC, V* ⊘ *Closed Wed.*

¢ 🏠 **Convento di San Francesco.** For a complete change of pace, stay at a 13th-century convent in the company of nine Franciscan friars. Rooms are simple, bordering on spartan, but are clean and quiet. You can participate in religious devotions or skip them altogether. All rooms have baths, and there are five larger rooms that accommodate up to six people. It's a 10-minute walk from the town center. Plan to arrive before 8 PM and they'll give you a set of keys—thus sparing the usually obligatory convent curfew. ⊠ *Piazza San Francesco, 56020* ☎ *0571/43051* 🖷 *0571/43398* ⟿ *30 rooms* ⚉ *No a/c, no room phones, no room TVs, no kids under 12* ⊟ *No credit cards* ⏉⦶ *EP.*

LUCCA

Ramparts built in the 16th and 17th centuries enclose a charming fortress town filled with churches (99 of them), terra-cotta-roof buildings, and narrow cobblestone streets, along which local ladies maneuver bikes to do their daily shopping. Here Caesar, Pompey, and Crassus agreed to rule Rome as a triumvirate in 56 BC. Lucca was later the first Tuscan town to accept Christianity, and it still has a mind of its own: when most of Tuscany was voting communist as a matter of course, Lucca's citizens rarely followed suit. The famous composer Giacomo Puccini (1858–1924) was born here; he is celebrated, along with his peers, during the summer Opera Theater and Music Festival of Lucca. The ramparts that circle the center city are the perfect place to take a stroll, ride a bicycle, kick a ball, or just stand and look down onto Lucca, both within and without.

9

Exploring Lucca

The historic center of Lucca, 51 km (31 mi) west of Florence, is walled, and motorized traffic is restricted. Walking and biking are the most efficient and most enjoyable ways to get around. You can rent bicycles, and the center is quite flat, so biking is easy. A combination ticket costing €6.50 gains you admission to both the Museo Nazionale di Villa Guinigi and the Pinacoteca Nazionale di Palazzo Mansi.

The Main Attractions

★ ❻ **Duomo.** The round-arched facade of the cathedral is an example of the rigorously ordered Pisan Romanesque style, in this case happily enlivened by a varied collection of small carved columns. Take a closer look at the decoration of the facade and of the portico below, which make for one of the most entertaining church exteriors in Tuscany. The Gothic interior contains a moving wood crucifix (called the *Volto Santo,* or Holy

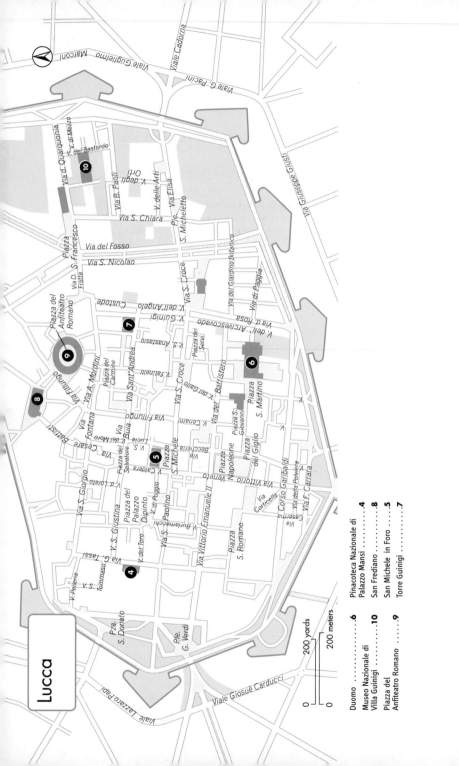

Lucca

Duomo 6
Museo Nazionale di
Villa Guinigi 10
Piazza del
Anfiteatro Romano 9
Pinacoteca Nazionale di
Palazzo Mansi 4
San Frediano 8
San Michele in Foro 5
Torre Guinigi 7

Face) brought here, legend has it, in the 8th century (though in fact it probably dates from between the 11th and early 13th centuries). The marble **tomb of Ilaria del Carretto** (1408) is the masterpiece of the Sienese sculptor Jacopo della Quercia (circa 1371–1438). ⊠ *Piazza del Duomo* ☎ *0583/490530* ☎ *Duomo free, tomb of Ilaria del Carretto €2* ⊙ *Duomo weekdays 7–5:30, Sat. 9:30–6:45, Sun. 11:30–11:50 and 1–5:30. Tomb Nov.–Mar., weekdays 9:30–4:45, Sat. 9:30–6:45, Sun. 11:30–11:50 and 1–5; Apr.–Oct., weekdays 9:30–5:45, Sat. 9–6:45, Sun. 9–10 and 1–5:45.*

★ ♨ **Passeggiata delle Mura** (Walk on the Walls). Any time of day when the weather is agreeable, you can find the citizens of Lucca cycling, jogging, strolling, or kicking a soccer ball in this large, unusual park atop the ring of ramparts that surrounds the city's *centro storico* (historic center). Sunlight streams through two rows of tall plane trees to dapple the walkway, a loop almost 5 km (3 mi) in length. Ten bulwarks are topped with lawns, many containing picnic tables, some with play equipment for children. One caution: there are no railings along the ramparts' edge and the drop to the ground is a precipitous 40 feet.

NEED A BREAK?

Gelateria Veneta (⊠ Via V. Veneto ☎ 0583/467037 ⊠ Via Beccheria ☎ 0583/496856) makes outstanding ice creams, sorbets, and ices (some sugar-free). The pièces de résistance are frozen fruits stuffed with their own creamy filling: don't miss the apricot-sorbet-filled apricot.

❾ Piazza del Anfiteatro Romano. A Roman amphitheater once stood on this spot; the medieval buildings constructed over the amphitheater retain its original oval shape and brick arches. It's a popular gathering place, with numerous cafés and some eclectic shops. ⊠ *Off Via Fillungo.*

♨ **❽ San Frediano.** The church contains a gorgeous sculpted polyptych by Jacopo della Quercia. The bizarrely lace-clad mummy of the patron saint of domestic servants, St. Zita, really seems to make kids shriek (usually in a good way) when they see her. ⊠ *Piazza San Frediano, Anfiteatro* ⊙ *Mon.–Sat. 8:30–noon and 3–5, Sun. 10:30–5.*

❺ San Michele in Foro. The facade of this church, slightly west of the centro storico, is even more fanciful than the Duomo's. Check out the superb panel painting of Sts. Girolamo, Sebastian, Rocco, and Helen by Filippino Lippi (1457/58–1504) in the right transept. ⊠ *Piazza San Michele, San Michele* ⊙ *Daily 7:40–noon and 3–6.*

♨ **❼ Torre Guinigi.** The tower of the medieval palace contains one of the city's most curious sights: six ilex trees have established themselves at the top, and their roots have grown into the room below. From the tower there's a magnificent view of the city and the surrounding countryside. ⊠ *Palazzo Guinigi, Via Sant'Andrea 42, Anfiteatro* ☎ *0583/583150* ☎ *€3.50* ⊙ *Mar. and Apr., daily 9:30–6; May–Sept., daily 9–midnight; Oct.–Feb., daily 9–5.*

Also Worth Seeing

❿ Museo Nazionale di Villa Guinigi. On the east end of the historic center, the museum houses an extensive collection of local Romanesque and

Renaissance art. ⊠ *Villa Guinigi, Via della Quarquonia, Lucca East* ☎ *0583/496033* 🎟 *€4* ⊘ *Tues.–Fri. 9–7, Sun. 9–1.*

❹ **Pinacoteca Nazionale di Palazzo Mansi.** Highlights at this art museum are the brightly colored *Portrait of a Youth* by Pontormo and portraits of the Medici painted by Bronzino (1503–72) and others. ⊠ *Palazzo Mansi, Via Galli Tassi 43, San Donato* ☎ *0583/55570* 🎟 *€4* ⊘ *Tues.–Sat. 9–7.*

Off the Beaten Path

Villa Reale. Napoléon's sister, Princess Elisa, once called Villa Reale home. Restored by the Counts Pecci-Blunt, the estate is celebrated for its spectacular gardens, which were originally laid out in the 16th century and redone in the middle of the 17th century. Gardening buffs adore the legendary **teatro di verdura**, a theater carved out of hedges and topiaries. The Lucca tourist office has information about the occasional concerts held here. ⊠ *Villa Reale, Marlia, 8 km (5 mi) north of Lucca* ☎ *0583/30108* 🎟 *€6* ⊘ *Mar.–Nov., guided visits Tues.–Sun. at 10, 11, noon, 3, 4, 5, and 6; Dec.–Feb., by appointment.*

Where to Stay & Eat

$$
Fodor'sChoice
★

✕ **Bucadisantantonio.** The staying power of Bucadisantantonio—it's been around since 1782—is the result of superlative Tuscan food brought to the table by waitstaff that doesn't miss a beat. The menu includes the simple-but-blissful, like *tortelli lucchesi al sugo* (meat-stuffed pasta with a tomato-and-meat-sauce), and more daring dishes such as roast *capretto* (kid) with herbs. A white-wall interior hung with copper pots and brass musical instruments creates a classy but comfortable dining space. ⊠ *Via della Cervia 3, San Michele* ☎ *0583/55881* ♣ *Reservations essential* ▤ *AE, DC, MC, V* ⊘ *Closed Mon., 2 wks in Jan., and 2 wks in July. No dinner Sun.*

$$
✕ **Il Giglio.** High ceilings, a large chandelier, and a big fireplace evoke the 19th century inside, and there is a terrace for dining outside in summer. Waiters in black double-breasted suits provide wise counsel on the wine choices, which complement the mostly Lucchesi dishes on the menu. Among the regional favorites are *farro garfagnino* (a thick soup made with emmer, a grain that resembles barley, and beans) and *coniglio con olive* (rabbit stew with olives). Save room for one of the desserts, such as *la frutta carmellata in forno con gelato di castagne* (caramelized fruit with chestnut ice cream)—wow! ⊠ *Piazza del Giglio 2, off Piazza Napoleone, Duomo* ☎ *0583/494058* ▤ *AE, DC, MC, V* ⊘ *Closed Wed. No dinner Tues.*

¢
✕ **i Santi.** This intimate little wine bar, just outside the amphitheater, offers a perfect place to have a light meal and a fine glass of wine. The extensive wine list has first-rate local and foreign (French) selections, and the menu has tasty things to go with it, such as *carpaccio di manzo affumicato* (thin slices of smoked beef served with celery and a fresh cheese made of cow's milk). Specials include a pasta of the day. In summer it is open throughout the day, meaning if you're hungry at 4 in the afternoon or at 11:30 at night (when just about everywhere else is closed), you're in luck. ⊠ *Via dell'Anfiteatro 29/a* ☎ *0583/496124* ▤ *AE, DC, MC, V* ⊘ *Closed Wed. Nov.–Mar.*

EATING WELL IN TUSCANY

Celebrating the Seasons. Just as the ancient Etruscans introduced cypress trees to the Tuscan landscape, their influence on regional food—in the use of fresh herbs—still lingers after more than 3 millennia. Simple and earthy, Tuscan food celebrates the seasons with a host of fresh vegetable dishes, wonderful bread-based soups, and savory meats and game perfumed with sage, rosemary, and thyme.

Saltless Tuscan bread is grilled and drizzled with olive oil *(crostino)*, spread with chicken liver *(crostino di fegatini)*, or rubbed with garlic and topped with tomatoes (bruschetta or *fettunta*). For their love of beans—particularly cannellini simmered in olive oil and herbs until creamy—Tuscans have been disparagingly nicknamed *mangiafagioli* (bean eaters) by Italians from other regions. Pecorino, a cheese made from sheep's milk, is particularly good in these parts—try it when it's young and in a soft, practically spreadable

state, as well as when it's *stagionato* (aged). At its best, it's the equal of the finest Parmesan. Relatively new to Tuscan cuisine is the reintroduction of dishes featuring *cinta senese*, a once nearly extinct pig.

Wines: Chianti & Beyond. Grape cultivation here also dates from Etruscan times, and particularly in Chianti vineyards are abundant. The resulting medium-body red wine is a staple on most tables; however, you can select from a multitude of other varieties, including such reds as Brunello di Montalcino and Vino Nobile di Montepulciano and such whites as Vermentino and Vernaccia. Super Tuscans, a fanciful name given to a group of wines by American journalists, now command attention as some of the best produced in Italy; they have great depth and complexity. The dessert wine *vin santo* is made throughout the region and is often sipped with biscotti (twice-baked cookies), perfect for dunking.

9

$$$$ ✕▦ **Locanda l'Elisa.** A stay here could evoke home for you—that is if home is a neoclassical villa with a lush garden and a caring staff that caters to your needs. Most rooms are suites, outfitted with fresh flowers, antiques, and fine fabrics. The restaurant il Gazebo is in a former Victorian conservatory. The Tuscan food-with-flair is deftly served by English-speaking waiters. Locanda l'Elisa is a short ride from the city. ⊠ *Via Nuova per Pisa 1952, 5 km (3 mi) southwest of town center, 55050* ☎ *0583/379737* ☐ *0583/379019* ⊕ *www.locandalelisa.com* ⤴ *3 rooms, 7 suites* ⬩ *Restaurant, in-room safes, minibars, cable TV, in-room data ports, pool, massage, bar, babysitting, dry cleaning, laundry service, concierge, Internet room, free parking* ▭ *AE, DC, MC, V* ⊗ *Closed Jan. 7–Feb. 11* ⦿⦾ *EP.*

$$$$ ▦ **Hotel Ilaria.** The former stables of the Villa Bottini have been transformed into a modern hotel within the historic center. A second-floor terrace, overlooking the villa, makes a comfortable place to relax. Rooms are done in a warm wood veneer. The availability of free bicycles is a great bonus in this bike-friendly city. Residenza dell'Alba, the hotel's annex across the street, was originally part of a 14th-century church; now it's a luxe accommodation with in-room hot tubs. ⊠ *Via del Fosso 26, Lucca East, 55100* ☎ *0583/47615* 🖷 *0583/991961* ⊕ *www.hotelilaria.com* ↩ *36 rooms, 5 suites* 🛆 *In-room safes, minibars, cable TV, bicycles, bar, babysitting, dry cleaning, laundry service, concierge, meeting room, free parking, some pets allowed (fee), no-smoking rooms* 🖃 *AE, DC, MC, V* ❑ *BP.*

★ $$$ 🏨 **Palazzo Alexander.** Lucchesi nobility would have felt at home at this small boutique hotel. The building, with its timbered ceilings and warm yellow walls, dates from the 12th century but has been completely restructured with 21st-century amenities. Brocade chairs adorn the public rooms, and the elegance is carried into the guest rooms, all of which have that same glorious damask upholstery and high ceilings. Top-floor suites have sweeping views of the town. The location is on a quiet side street, a stone's throw from San Michele in Foro. ⊠ *Via S. Giustina 48, San Michele, 55100* ☎ *0583/583571* 🖷 *0583/583610* ⊕ *www.palazzoalexander.com* ↩ *9 rooms, 3 suites, 1 apartment* 🛆 *In-room safes, minibars, cable TV, in-room data ports, bicycles, wine bar, dry cleaning, laundry service, concierge, parking (fee), no-smoking rooms* 🖃 *AE, DC, MC, V* ❑ *BP.*

$ 🏨 **Piccolo Hotel Puccini.** Steps away from the busy square and church of San Michele, this little hotel is quiet and calm—and a great deal. Wallpaper, hardwood floors, and throw rugs are among the handsome decorations. Paolo, the genial manager, speaks fluent English and dispenses great touring advice. ⊠ *Via di Poggio 9, San Michele, 55100* ☎ *0583/55421* 🖷 *0583/53487* ⊕ *www.hotelpuccini.com* ↩ *14 rooms* 🛆 *Fans, in-room safes, cable TV, bar, babysitting, dry cleaning, laundry service, parking (fee), some pets allowed, no-smoking floors; no a/c* 🖃 *AE, DC, MC, V* ❑ *EP.*

Nightlife & the Arts

The **Opera Theater of Lucca Festival,** sponsored by Lucca's opera company and the school of music of the University of Cincinnati, runs from mid-June to mid-July; performances are staged in open-air venues. Throughout summer there are jazz, pop, and rock concerts in conjunction with the **Estate Musicale Lucchese** music festival. The **Lucca Tourist Office** (⊠ Piazza Santa Maria Verdi 35, San Michele ☎ 0583/919931) has schedule and ticket information for many local events, including the Opera Theater and Estate Musicale Lucchese festivals.

From September through April you can see operas, plays, and concerts staged at the **Teatro del Giglio** (⊠ Piazza del Giglio, Duomo ☎ 0583/46531 ⊕ www.teatrodelgiglio.it).

Sports & the Outdoors

A splendid bike ride (rental about €12) may be had by circling the entire historic center along the top of the bastions—affording something of a bird's-eye view. **Barbetti Cicli** (⊠ Via dei Gaspari 83/r, Anfiteatro ☎ 0583/517073) rents bikes near the Piazza di Anfiteatro. **Poli Antonio**

Biciclette (✉ Piazza Santa Maria 42, Lucca East ☎ 0583/493787) is an option for bicycle rental on the east side.

Shopping

Lucca's justly famed olive oils are available throughout the city (and exported around the world). Look for those made by Fattoria di Fubbiano and Fattoria Fabbri—two of the best. On the second Sunday of the month there's a **flea market** in Piazza San Martino.

★ Chocoholics can get their fix at **Caniparoli** (✉ Via S. Paolino 96, San Donato ☎ 0583/53456). They are so serious about their sweets here that they do not make them from June through August because of the heat. Bargain hunters won't want to miss **Benetton Stock Outlet** (✉ Via Mordini 17/19, Anfiteatro ☎ 0583/464533), with its brightly colored garments at reduced prices.

PISA

When you think Pisa, you think Leaning Tower. Its position as one of Italy's most famous landmarks is a heavy reputation to bear, and it comes accompanied by abundant crowds and kitschy souvenirs. But the building *is* interesting and novel, and even if it doesn't captivate you, Pisa has other treasures that make a visit worthwhile. Taken as a whole, the Campo dei Miracoli (Field of Miracles), where the Leaning Tower, Duomo, and Baptistery are located, is among the most dramatic architectural ensembles in Italy.

Pisa may have been inhabited as early as the Bronze Age. It was certainly populated by the Etruscans and, in turn, became part of the Roman Empire. In the early Middle Ages it flourished as an economic powerhouse—along with Amalfi, Genoa, and Venice, it was one of the maritime republics. The city's economic and political power ebbed in the early 15th century as it fell under the domination of Florence, though it enjoyed a brief resurgence under Cosimo I in the mid-16th century. Pisa endured heavy Allied bombing—miraculously, the Duomo and Leaning Tower, along with some other grand Romanesque structures, were spared, though the Camposanto sustained heavy damage.

9

Exploring Pisa

Pisa is 84 km (52 mi) west of Florence. Like many other Italian cities, the town is best seen on foot. The views along the Arno are particularly grand and shouldn't be missed—there's a sense of spaciousness here that the Arno in Florence lacks. You should weigh the different options for combination tickets to sights on the Piazza del Duomo when you begin your visit. Combination tickets are sold at each sight (one monument costs €5, two monuments €6, up to €10.50 for all the main sights, excluding the Leaning Tower).

The Main Attractions

🔞 **Battistero.** The Gothic baptistery, which stands across from the Duomo's facade, is best known for the pulpit carved by Nicola Pisano in 1260.

Battistero **13**

Camposanto ..**14**

Duomo **12**

Leaning
Tower **11**

Museo
dell'Opera
del Duomo ...**15**

Museo
Nazionale di
San Matteo ...**16**

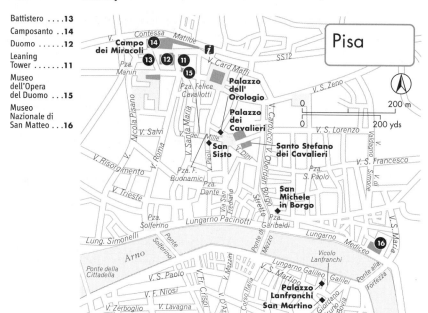

Ask one of the ticket takers if he'll sing for you inside the baptistery: the acoustics are remarkable (a tip of €3 is appropriate). ⊠ *Piazza del Duomo, Campo dei Miracoli* ☎ *050/3872210* ⊕ *www.opapisa.it* ⊠ *€5* ⊗ *Apr.–Sept., daily 8–8; Oct., daily 9–7; Nov.–Feb., daily 10–5; Mar., daily 9–6.*

🔟 **Duomo.** Pisa's cathedral was the first building to use the horizontal marble stripe motif (borrowed from Moorish architecture in the 11th century) common to Tuscan cathedrals. It's famous for the Romanesque panels depicting the life of Christ on the transept door facing the tower and for its expertly carved 14th-century pulpit by Giovanni Pisano. ⊠ *Piazza del Duomo, Campo dei Miracoli* ☎ *050/3872210* ⊕ *www.opapisa. it* ⊠ *€2, Oct.–Mar. free* ⊗ *Apr.–Sept., daily 10–8; Oct., daily 10–7; Nov.–Feb., daily 10–1 and 3–5; Mar. daily 10–6.*

★ ☾ 🔟 **Leaning Tower.** The final addition to the complex comprised of the Duomo, Baptistery, and the Camposanto was what is today known as the Torre Pendente (Leaning Tower). Construction started in 1174, and the lopsided settling was evident by the time work began on the third story. The tower's architects attempted to compensate by making the remaining floors slightly taller on the tilting side, but the extra weight only made the problem worse. The settling continued, to a point that by the end of the 20th century many feared it would simply topple over, despite all efforts to prop the structure up. In early 2000 the final step of restoring the tower to its original tilt of 300 years ago was executed, and it appears to have been successful. It has been firmly anchored to the earth and after years of being closed is once again open to the public for climbing. Legend holds that Galileo conducted an experiment on the nature of gravity by dropping metal balls from the top of the 187-foot-high tower; historians say this legend has no basis in fact (which is not quite to say that it is false). If you're visiting in low season (November–March), it's pretty easy to climb the tower without a reservation; if you come in high season, by all means book in advance. English-language tours are offered three times a day during high season. Tickets are available online 16–45 days in advance. ⊠ *Campo dei Miracoli* ☎ *050/3872210* ⊕ *www.opapisa.it* ✉ *€15* ☉ *Mar. 21–Sept., daily 8:30–8:30; Oct., daily 9–7; Nov.–Feb., daily 9:30–5; Mar. 1–Mar. 13, daily 9–6; Mar. 14–Mar. 20, daily 10–7.*

> **WORD OF MOUTH**
>
> "At Pisa we discovered a peaceful haven with relatively few tourists compared with Florence, and a magnificent lawn you could actually walk and sit on. I lay down in the lovely grass and slept in the sun until I was awakened by the cool shadow of the Leaning Tower. It was magic and peaceful and beautiful."
>
> –Jo

Also Worth Seeing

⓮ Camposanto. According to legend, this cemetery, a walled structure on the western side of the Campo dei Miracoli, is filled with earth from the Holy Land brought back by returning Crusaders. Contained within are numerous frescoes, notably the *Drunkenness of Noah* by Renaissance artist Benozzo Gozzoli and the disturbing *Triumph of Death* (14th century), whose authorship is disputed but whose subject matter shows what was on people's minds in a century that saw the ravages of the Black Death. ⊠ *Camposanto, Campo dei Miracoli* ☎ *050/3872210* ⊕ *www.opapisa.it* ✉ *€5* ☉ *Apr.–Sept., daily 8–8; Oct., daily 9–7; Nov.–Feb., daily 10–5; Mar., daily 9–6.*

⓯ Museo dell'Opera del Duomo. At the southeast corner of the sprawling Campo dei Miracoli, a marginally interesting museum holds numerous medieval sculptures and the ancient Roman sarcophagi that inspired the figures of Nicola Pisano (circa 1220–84). ⊠ *Via Arcivescovado, Campo dei Miracoli* ☎ *050/3872210* ⊕ *www.opapisa.it* ✉ *€5* ☉ *Apr.–Sept., daily 8–8; Oct., daily 9–7; Nov.–Feb., daily 10–5; Mar., daily 9–6.*

⓰ Museo Nazionale di San Matteo. On the north bank of the Arno, this museum contains wonderful early-Renaissance sculpture and a stunning reliquary by Donatello (circa 1386–1466). ⊠ *Lungarno Mediceo, Lungarni* ☎ *050/541865* ✉ *€5* ☉ *Tues.–Sat. 8:30–7:30, Sun. 8:30–1.*

Where to Stay & Eat

$$ ✕ **La Mescita.** Tall, vaulted ceilings and stenciled walls lined with wine bottles provide the simple background at this trattoria. There's nothing basic, however, about the inventive Tuscan dishes that chef-owner Elisabetta Bauti turns out. She draws inspiration—and fresh produce—from the market outside the door. *Tagliolini al sugo e piccolo ragù di salsiccia toscano,* thin noodles with sausage and a red-wine sauce, is one option you might find on the constantly changing menu. Desserts are not to be missed, especially the *ricotta montata col cioccolato fuso* (fresh sheep's milk cheese topped with chocolate sauce). ⊠ *Via Cavalca 2, Santa Maria* ☎ *050/544294* ⊟ *AE, DC, MC, V* ⊙ *Closed Mon., 3 wks in Jan., and last 3 wks in Aug. No lunch Tues.*

$–$$ ✕ **Osteria dei Cavalieri.** This charming white-wall *osteria* (a down-to-earth, tavernlike restaurant) has a versatile menu pleasing to carnivores and vegetarians alike. There are three reasonable, set price menus—from the sea, garden, and earth—or you can order à la carte. *Piatti veloci* (fast plates) are available at lunch only. The kitchen reliably turns out grilled fish, and the *tagliata* (thin slivers of rare beef) is a treat. A lemon sorbet bathed in *prosecco* (a dry sparkling wine) or chilled vodka makes a perfect finish to your meal—even if service can be a bit rushed. ⊠ *Via San Frediano 16, off Piazza dei Cavalieri, Santa Maria* ☎ *050/580858* ⊟ *AE, DC, MC, V* ⊙ *Closed Sun., July 25–Aug. 25, Dec. 29–Jan. 7. No lunch Sat.*

¢ ✕ **Vineria alla Piazza.** Translated, the name means, "wine store on the square," and the food here is just as straightforward: a simple blackboard lists two or three *primi* (first courses) and secondi. When the kitchen runs out of something, a choice is erased and a new one chalked in—a sure sign the food is made-that-moment fresh. The polenta *gratinata al gorgonzola* (mixed with Gorgonzola and run briefly under the broiler) is light as a feather. ⊠ *Piazza delle Vettovaglie 13, Santa Maria* ☎ *No phone* ⌔ *Reservations not accepted* ⊟ *No credit cards* ⊙ *Closed Sun.*

$$$$ ▦ **Hotel Relais dell'Orologio.** What used to be a private family palace opened as an intimate hotel in spring of 2003. Eighteenth-century antiques fill the rooms and public spaces; some rooms have stenciled walls and wood-beam ceilings. On the third floor, sloped ceilings add romance. A large shared sitting room, complete with fireplace, provides a relaxing spot to read or sip a glass of wine. ⊠ *Via della Faggiola 12/14, off Campo dei Miracoli, Santa Maria, 56126* ☎ *050/830361* ▤ *050/ 551869* ⊕ *www.hotelrelaisorologio.com* ⤴ *16 rooms, 5 suites* ⌔ *Dining room, room service, in-room safes, minibars, refrigerators, cable TV, in-room data ports, bar, babysitting, dry cleaning, laundry service, concierge, business services, meeting rooms, parking (fee), some pets allowed, no-smoking rooms* ⊟ *AE, DC, MC, V* ◍ *EP.*

$–$$ ▦ **Royal Victoria.** The Piegaja family has owned and operated the Royal Victoria since 1837—such dedication probably explains why Charles Dickens and Charles Lindbergh, among others, have stayed here in the past. The hotel faces the Arno, and though rooms are simply furnished and a bit dated, many have splendid river views. A fourth-floor terrace is a perfect spot for an *aperitivo* (aperitif) or postcard writing. The hotel's rental-car service helps provide easy access to beaches and points of interest outside town. From here it's a 10-minute walk to the Campo dei Miracoli. ⊠ *Lungarno Pacinotti 12, Lungarni, 56126* ☎ *050/940111* ▤ *050/940180* ⊕ *www.royalvictoria.it* ⤴ *48 rooms, 40 with bath*

♨ *Room service, some fans, cable TV, in-room data ports, bicycles (fee), bar, babysitting, dry cleaning, laundry service, concierge, parking (fee), some pets allowed; no a/c in some rooms* ▤ *AE, DC, MC, V* ⑩| *BP.*

Nightlife & the Arts

The **Luminaria** feast day on June 16 honors San Ranieri, the city's patron saint. Palaces along the Arno are lighted up, and there are plenty of fireworks; it's Pisa at its most beautiful.

Pisa has a lively performing arts scene, most of which happens at the 19th-century Teatro Verdi. Music and dance performances are presented from September through May. Contact **Fondazione Teatro di Pisa** (⊠ Via Palestro 40, Lungarni ☎ 050/941111 ⊕ www.teatrodipisa.pi. it) for schedules and information.

CHIANTI

Directly south of Florence is Chianti, one of Italy's most famous wine-producing areas; its hill towns, olive groves, and vineyards are quintessential Tuscany. Many British and northern Europeans have relocated here, drawn by the unhurried life, balmy climate, and charming villages; there are so many Britons, in fact, that the area has been nicknamed Chiantishire. Still, it remains strongly Tuscan in character, with drop-dead views of vine-quilted hills and elegantly elongated cypress trees.

The sinuous SS222 highway, known as the Strada Chiantigiana, runs from Florence through the heart of Chianti. Its most scenic section connects Strada in Chianti, 16 km (10 mi) south of Florence, and Greve in Chianti, whose triangular central piazza is surrounded by restaurants and vintners offering *degustazioni* (wine tastings), 11 km (7 mi) farther south.

Greve in Chianti

🐧 *40 km (25 mi) northeast of Colle Val d'Elsa, 27 km (17 mi) south of Florence.*

If there is a capital of Chianti, it is Greve, a friendly market town with no shortage of cafés, *enoteche* (wine bars), and craft shops lining its main square. The sloping, asymmetrical **Piazza Matteotti** is attractively arcaded and has a statue of Giovanni da Verrazano (circa 1480–1528), the explorer who discovered New York harbor, in the center. At one end of the piazza is the **Chiesa di Santa Croce.** The church contains works from the school of Fra Angelico (circa 1400–55). ⊠ *Piazza Matteotti* ☉ *Daily 9–1 and 3–7.*

OFF THE BEATEN PATH

MONTEFIORALLE – Just 2 km (1 mi) west of Greve, in the tiny hilltop town of Montefioralle, you'll find the ancestral home of Amerigo Vespucci (1454–1512), the navigator and mapmaker who named America and whose niece Simonetta may have been the model for Venus in Sandro Botticelli's (1445–1510) *Primavera.* Chianti's annual mid-September wine festival, **Rassegna del Chianti Classico,** takes place here.

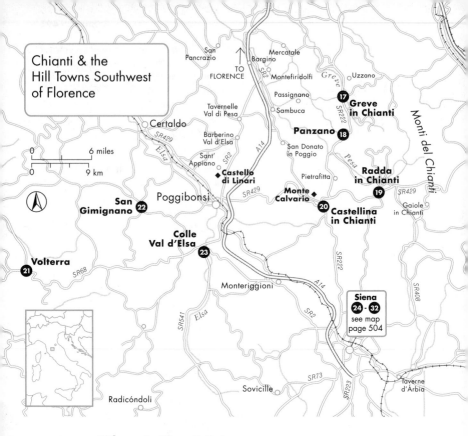

Where to Stay & Eat

★ $$$ ✕ **Osteria di Passignano.** Sophisticated country dining may not get better than at this deceptively simple restaurant next to a Vallombrosan abbey. A tiny sampling (maybe *sformatino di pecorino di fosso*, a flan made with aged pecorino) whets the appetite for what's to come. The young chefs in the kitchen can do traditional as well as whimsical Tuscan—and then divine things such as the *maccheroni del Martelli al ragù bianco di agnelli e carciofi morellini* (tubular pasta with a lamb and artichoke sauce), which really isn't Tuscan at all. The wine list is unbeatable, as is the service. ⊠ *Via Passignano 33, Località Badia a Passignano, 15 km (9 mi) east of Greve in Chianti* 🕾 *055/8011278* ▭ *AE, DC, MC, V* ⊙ *Closed Sun., Jan. 7–Feb. 1, and 15 days in Aug.*

★ $$ ✕ **Ristoro di Lamole.** Although off the beaten path (in this case, the SS222), this place is worth the effort to find—up a winding hill road lined with olive trees and vineyards. The view from the outdoor terrace is divine, as is the simple, exquisitely prepared Tuscan cuisine. Start with the bruschetta drizzled with olive oil or the sublime *verdure sott'olio* (vegetables marinated in oil) before moving on to any of the fine secondi. The kitchen has a way with *coniglio* (rabbit); don't pass it up if it's on the menu. ⊠ *Off SS222, Lamole in Chianti* 🕾 *055/8547050* ▭ *AE, DC, MC, V* ⊙ *Closed Jan. 6–Feb. 28.*

★ $ ✕ **Enoteca Fuoripiazza.** Detour off Greve's flower-strewn main square for food that relies heavily on local ingredients (especially those produced by nearby makers of cheese and salami). The lengthy wine list provides a bewildering array of choices to pair with *affettati misti* (a plate of cured meats) or one of their primi—the *pici* (a thick, short noodle) is deftly prepared here. All the dishes are made with great care. ✉ *Via I Maggio 2, Piazza Trenta* ☎ *055/8546313* ▭ *AE, DC, MC, V* ☺ *Closed Mon.*

★ $$$ ▦ **Fonte de' Medici.** The Antinori family has been making wine since 1180, and in 2001 they extended their efforts into an agriturismo—appropriately, each of the individually decorated rooms and apartments bears the name of a grape. All are decorated with sponged walls, some with canopy beds, most with fireplaces and deep bathtubs, and nearly all with views of the tranquil countryside. Rooms are scattered among three structures, the busiest being Santa Maria a Macerata, and the most remote Podere Vivaio. If you're after bliss in the middle of Chianti, look no further. ✉ *Via Santa Maria a Macerata 31, 50020 Montefiridolfi* ☎ *055/8244700* 🖷 *055/8244701* ⊕ *www.fontedemedici.com* ⟿ *7 rooms, 21 apartments* ⚒ *Restaurant, picnic area, BBQs, some fans, in-room safes, some kitchens, some microwaves, refrigerators, cable TV, in-room data ports, tennis court, pool, wading pool, exercise equipment, massage, sauna, steam room, mountain bikes, soccer, wine bar, babysitting, laundry facilities, laundry service, meeting rooms, free parking, some pets allowed (fee); no a/c in some rooms* ▭ *AE, DC, MC, V* ☺ *Restaurant closed Nov. and mid-Jan.–mid-Feb.* ⵊⵔ *BP.*

$$$$ ▦ **Villa Bordoni.** David and Catherine Gardner, expat Scots, have transformed a ramshackle 16th-century villa into a stunning little hotel nestled in the hills above Greve. Elaborate care has been given in decorating the rooms, no two of which are the same. All have stenciled walls; some have four-poster beds, others small mezzanines. Bathrooms are a riot of color, with tiles from Vietri. A public sitting room on the second floor, with comforting fireplace, is the perfect place for a cup of tea or a glass of wine. The hotel's restaurant has a young chef of notable talent. ✉ *Via San Cresci 31/32, Località Mezzuola, Greve* ☎ *055/8840004* 🖷 *055/8840005* ⊕ *www.villabordoni.com* ⟿ *8 rooms, 3 suites* ⚒ *Restaurant, minibars, in-room safes, in-room data ports, cable TV, Wi-Fi, pool, exercise equipment, mountain bikes (fee), babysitting, laundry service, free parking* ▭ *AE, DC, MC, V* ☺ *Closed Jan. and Feb.* ⵊⵔ *BP.*

FodorsChoice
★

$$–$$$ ▦ **Villa Vignamaggio.** The villa, surrounded by manicured classical Italian gardens, dates from the 14th century but was restored in the 16th. It's reputedly the birthplace of Mona Lisa, the woman later made famous by Leonardo da Vinci. There are guest rooms, suites, and apartments in the villa and other buildings, and a cottage on the grounds. The place also hosts tastings of its very fine wines: inquire at reception to organize one. Dinner can also be arranged sometimes. ✉ *Via Petriolo 5, 50022* ☎ *055/854661* 🖷 *055/8544468* ⊕ *www.vignamaggio.com* ⟿ *3 rooms, 4 suites, 13 apartments, 1 cottage* ⚒ *Dining room, minibars, cable TV, tennis court, 2 pools, mountain bikes, bar, babysitting, playground, laundry service, some pets allowed, no-smoking rooms* ▭ *AE, DC, MC, V* ☺ *Closed mid-Nov.–mid-Mar.* ⵊⵔ *BP.*

VOICES OF ITALY

Dario Cecchini,
butcher, Panzano

Dario Cecchini loves meat. At the half-century mark and standing more than 6 feet tall, he could be a poster boy for the beef industry. He breathes health, vitality, vigor.

By trade, Dario is a butcher, but his Antica Macelleria Cecchini is not your typical butcher shop. From its intimate confines at Via XX Luglio 11 in Panzano, he holds forth behind a counter teeming with luscious meats. Opera plays in the background; sometimes customers sing along. Dario quotes Dante as he offers up samples of his wares.

Dario calls himself *un artigiano* (an artisan)—an indication of the pride he takes in his work. His shop has been in the family since the late 1700s, and his father trained Dario in the craft. "At 13," he says, "my grandmother made me a butcher's jacket. My mother began to cry. I guess she hoped I'd choose something else." The same grandmother is responsible for Dario's habit of offering wine to his customers. "She said a glass of wine brings people together, and I like to bring people together."

In March 2001, when beef cuts near the spine were banned by the European Union due to fears of mad cow disease, he held a funeral for such cuts, and most of the town turned out to watch. A beef auction was part of the solemnities, with Sir Elton John the high bidder; proceeds went to a nearby children's hospital.

Dario is perhaps the world's greatest devotee of *bistecca*

fiorentina, the definitive Tuscan steak. To get one of his *bistecche*, you must request it seven days in advance. Ask him to halve its width, and you will incur this genial man's scorn. About its preparation, Dario brooks no compromises. "It must be very thick, seared on both sides, and very, very rare in the middle." If you prefer your steak well done? "You shouldn't order it." This is not to say that Dario is an unwavering traditionalist. One of his prized creations is sushi del Chianti, which took him five years to develop. After a taste of the coarsely ground raw beef, it can be difficult to stop eating.

What wine does Dario pair with his bistecca? "A young, simple, unstructured Chianti." If—heaven forbid—such a Chianti is not on the wine list? "Any young, honest red will do—no dallying in oak casks. Anything disliked by the *Wine Spectator*."

Where does Dario like to eat out these days? "Il Cipresso in Loro Ciuffenna (some 20 minutes northwest of Arezzo). Top-notch cooking with good seasonal ingredients."

As a lifelong resident of Chianti, Dario has a firm view on views. After a good meal, where should you go to contemplate the finest vista in Tuscany? "If I had only a short time, I'd say the hills around Volpaia (just outside Radda in Chianti). If I had more time, the Crete Senesi. It's *un luogo dell'anima*—a place to feed your soul."

Panzano

⑱ *7 km (4½ mi) south of Greve, 29 km (18 mi) south of Florence.*

The little town of Panzano, between Greve in Chianti and Castellina in Chianti, has inviting shops, and enoteche offering tastes of the local wine (in this case, Chianti). A walk up a steep incline brings you to the town's showpiece, the church of **Santa Maria Assunta**, where you can see an *Annunciation* attributed to Michele di Ridolfo del Ghirlandaio (1503–77). Your climb will also reward you with breathtaking views. ⊠ *Panzano Alto* ⊙ *Daily 7–noon and 4–6.*

Where to Stay & Eat

$$ ✕ **Oltre il Giardino.** An ancient stone farmhouse has been converted into a cozy dining area with a large terrace and spectacular views of the valley. Terra-cotta–color, stenciled walls, and simple wood tables provide the background for very tasty Tuscan food. The *peposo* (a beef stew laced with black pepper) is particularly piquant, the tagliatelle *sul piccione* (with a delicate squab sauce) delightfully fragrant. The wine list is particularly strong on the local variety, which in this case is Chianti Classico. ⊠ *Piazza G. Bucciarelli 42* 🖀 *055/852828* ▱ *AE, DC, MC, V* ⊙ *Closed Mon. and mid-Nov.–mid-Dec.*

$–$$ 🏨 **Villa La Barone.** Formerly the home of the Viviani della Robbia family, this 16th-century villa retains many aspects of a private home. The honor bar allows you to enjoy an aperitivo in the tile barroom or on the terrace while admiring the view, and there are views here in abundance, from the pool to the rose garden to the back of the villa. Guest rooms have tile floors, white walls, and timber ceilings. ⊠ *Via San Leolino 19, 50020* 🖀 *055/852621* 📠 *055/852277* 🛏 *30 rooms* ♿ *Dining room, Wi-Fi, tennis court, pool, babysitting, laundry service, concierge; no a/c in some rooms, no room TVs* ▱ *AE, MC, V* ⊙ *Closed Nov.–Easter* 🍽 *BP.*

Radda in Chianti

★ **⑲** *26 km (15 mi) south of Panzano, 52 km (32 mi) south of Florence.*

Radda in Chianti sits on a hill separating two valleys, Val di Pesa and Val d'Arbia. It's one of many tiny Chianti villages that invite you to stroll their steep streets; follow the signs pointing you toward the *camminamento*, a covered medieval passageway circling part of the city inside the walls. In Piazza Ferrucci, is the **Palazzo del Podestà** (or Palazzo Comunale), the city hall that has served the people of Radda for more than four centuries. It has 51 coats of arms embedded in its facade.

OFF THE BEATEN PATH

VOLPAIA – Perched atop a hill 10 km (6 mi) north of Radda is Volpaia, a fairy-tale hamlet that was a military outpost from the 10th to the 16th centuries and once a shelter for religious pilgrims. Every August, for the Festa di San Lorenzo, people come to Volpaia to watch for falling stars and a traditional fireworks display put on by the family that owns the adjacent wine estate and agriturismo lodging, **Castello di Volpaia** (⊠ Piazza della Cisterna 1, 53017 🖀 0577/738066).

9

Where to Stay & Eat

¢ ✕ **Osteria Le Panzanelle.** Nada Michelassi and Silvia Bonechi combined their accumulated wisdom in the hospitality industry to create this welcoming restaurant a few minutes outside Radda. The small but carefully crafted menu has typical tastes of Tuscany, such as the exquisite *trippa alla fiorentina* (tripe Florentine, with tomatoes, onions, and bay leaves), and unexpected treats like *crostone con salsiccia fresca* (toasted bread with fresh sausage). The wine list, equally well thought out, is particularly strong on the local Chianti Classicos and Super Tuscans. Two small, simple rooms and tables outdoors provide the setting for your meal. ✉ *Località Lucarellia 29* ☎ *0577/733511* 🗏 *MC, V* ⊘ *Closed Mon. and Nov.–Mar.*

★ $$$–$$$$ ✕🖾 **Relais Fattoria Vignale.** On the outside it's an unadorned manor house with an annex across the street. Inside it's refined country-house comfortable, with terra-cotta floors, sitting rooms, and nice stone- and woodwork. White rooms with exposed brick and wood beams contain simple wooden bed frames and furniture, charming rugs and prints, and modern white-tile bathrooms. The grounds, flanked by vineyards and olive trees, are equally inviting, with lawns, terraces, and a pool. The sophisticated Ristorante Vignale ($$$–$$$$) serves excellent wines and Tuscan specialties, such as Chianina beef; the *taverna* (wine bar) serves less-expensive fare. ✉ *Via Panigiani 9, 53017* ☎ *0577/738300 hotel, 0577/738094 restaurant, 0577/738012 enoteca* 🖶 *0577/738592* ⊕ *www. vignale.it* 🛏 *35 rooms, 5 suites* ⚖ *2 restaurants, in-room safes, minibars, cable TV, pool, bar, library, laundry service, concierge, free parking, no-smoking rooms* 🗏 *AE, DC, MC, V* ⊘ *Closed Jan.–Mar. Restaurant closed Thurs. and Jan.–Mar. Taverna closed Wed. and Jan.–Mar.* ⦿ *BP.*

$$$ 🖾 **Palazzo Leopoldo.** A contemporary interpretation of neoclassicism predominates at Palazzo Leopoldo. The former 15th-century palazzo on Radda's main street is now an invitingly intimate small hotel. Rooms have high ceilings and chandeliers—in the suites and in public rooms some are handcrafted 19th-century reproductions of Venetian Renaissance originals. The staff speaks English, and there's an inviting terrace. The tasty breads served at breakfast are made locally, and the restaurant has mostly Tuscan food; full and half board are options. ✉ *Via Roma 33, 53017* ☎ *0577/735605* 🖶 *0577/738031* ⊕ *www.palazzoleopoldo. it* 🛏 *8 rooms, 9 suites* ⚖ *Restaurant, room service, in-room safes, some kitchenettes, minibars, refrigerators, cable TV, Wi-Fi, indoor pool, hot tub, massage, sauna, spa, bar, babysitting, dry cleaning, laundry service, concierge, meeting room, free parking, some pets allowed, no-smoking rooms* 🗏 *AE, DC, MC, V* ⊘ *Closed Jan. and Feb.* ⦿ *BP.*

¢ 🖾 **La Bottega di Giovannino.** The name is actually that of the wine bar run by Giovannino Bernardoni; rentals are run by his children Monica and David in the house next door. This is a fantastic place for the budget-conscious traveler, as rooms are immaculate and beds comfortable. Most rooms have a stunning view of the surrounding hills. All have their own baths, though most of them necessitate taking a short trip outside one's room. ✉ *Via Roma 6–8, 53017* ☎ *0577/738056* 🛏 *10 rooms* ⚖ *Bar; no a/c, no room phones* 🗏 *MC, V* ⦿ *EP.*

Castellina in Chianti

20 *14 km (8 mi) west of Radda, 42 km (26 mi) south of Florence.*

Castellina in Chianti, or simply Castellina, is on a ridge above the Val di Pesa, Val d'Arbia, and Val d'Elsa, with beautiful panoramas in every direction. The imposing 15th-century tower in the central piazza hints at the history of this village, which was an outpost during the continuing wars between Florence and Siena.

Where to Stay & Eat

$$$–$$$$ ✕ **Alberghaccio.** The simple interior, with whitewashed walls and cypress-beam ceilings, stands in high contrast to the sophisticated meals that come from the kitchen at Alberghaccio. The chef pays attention to the seasons, with the menu reflecting what's freshest at the market. The *sformato di cavolo nero* (creamy polenta with Tuscan kale) is a highlight in fall and winter; the outstanding *arista* (roast pork with rosemary and sage) should not be missed. A comprehensive wine list has selections from all over the world. This upscale trattoria is a short walk from Castellina's tiny center. ⊠ *Via Fiorentina 63* ☎ *0577/741042* ⚑ *Reservations essential* ▤ *MC, V* ⊗ *Closed Sun.*

$$ ▥ **Collelungo.** One of the loveliest agriturismi in the area, Collelungo consists of a series of once-abandoned farmhouses that have been carefully remodeled. Set amid a notable vineyard (it produces internationally recognized Chianti Classico), the apartments—all with cooking facilities and dining areas—have exposed stone walls and typical Tuscan tile floors. The *salone* (lounge), which possibly dates from the 14th century, has satellite TV; adjacent to it is an honor bar. In high season a minimum three-night stay is required. ⊠ *Podere Collungo, 53011* ☎ *0577/740489* 🖷 *0577/741330* ⊕ *www.collelungo.com* ⚑ *12 apartments* ⚒ *BBQs, pool, bar, laundry service, free parking; no a/c, no room phones, no room TVs* ▤ *MC, V* ⊗ *Closed Nov.–Mar.* ▮⃝❙ *EP.*

$$ ▥ **Palazzo Squarcialupi.** This refurbished 15th-century palace on the main street in town is a pleasant, restful place to stay. Rooms have high ceilings, white walls, and tile floors; bathrooms are tiled in local stone. Many of the rooms have a view of the valley below. Common areas are elegant but comfortable, and the breakfast buffet is ample. The multilingual staff goes out of its way to be helpful. Though there's no restaurant, the hotel will arrange for a light lunch in the warmer months. ⊠ *Via Ferruccio 22, 53011* ☎ *0577/741186* 🖷 *0577/740386* ⊕ *www.palazzosquarcialupi.com* ⚑ *17 rooms* ⚒ *Minibars, cable TV, Wi-Fi, bar, babysitting, dry cleaning, laundry service, free parking, some pets allowed* ▤ *AE, DC, MC, V* ⊗ *Closed Nov.–Mar.* ▮⃝❙ *BP.*

HILL TOWNS SOUTHWEST OF FLORENCE

Submit to the draw of Tuscany's enchanting fortified cities that crown the hills west of Siena, many dating to the Etruscan period. San Gimignano, known as the "medieval Manhattan" because of its forest of stout medieval towers built by rival families, is the most heavily visited. This one-time Roman outpost, with its tilted cobbled streets and ancient buildings, can make the days of Guelph-Ghibelline conflicts palpable. Rising from

9

a series of bleak gullied hills and valleys, Volterra has always been popular for its minerals and stones, particularly alabaster, which was used by the Etruscans for many implements. Examples are now displayed in the exceptional and unwieldy Museo Etrusco Guarnacci.

Volterra

㉑ *48 km (30 mi) south of San Miniato, 75 km (47 mi) southwest of Florence.*

Unlike other Tuscan hill towns rising above sprawling vineyards and rolling fields of green, Volterra is surrounded by desolate terrain marred with industry and mining equipment. D. H. Lawrence described it as "somber and chilly alone on her rock" in his *Etruscan Places*. The fortress, walls, and gates still stand mightily over Le Balze, a distinctive series of gullied hills and valleys to the west that were formed by irregular erosion. The town has long been known for its alabaster, which has been mined since Etruscan times; today the Volterrans use it to make ornaments and souvenirs sold all over town. An €8 combined ticket is your only option for visiting the Museo Etrusco Guarnacci and the Pinacoteca e Museo Civico.

Volterra has some of Italy's best small museums. The extraordinarily large and unique collection of Etruscan artifacts at the **Museo Etrusco Guarnacci** is a treasure in the region. (Many of the other Etruscan finds from the area have been shipped off to state museums or the Vatican.) If only a curator had thought to cull the best of the 700 funerary urns rather than to display every last one of them. ⊠ *Via Don Minzoni 15* ☎ *0588/86347* ⊕ *www.comune.volterra.pi.it* ☜ *Combined ticket €8* ⊘ *Mar. 16–Nov. 3, daily 9–7; Nov. 4–Mar. 15, daily 9–1:30.*

The **Pinacoteca e Museo Civico** houses a highly acclaimed collection of religious art, including a *Madonna and Child with Saints* by Luca Signorelli (1445/50–1523) and a *Deposition* by Rosso Fiorentino (1494–1541) that is reason enough to visit Volterra. ⊠ *Via dei Sarti 1* ☎ *0588/87580* ⊕ *www.comune.volterra.pi.it* ☜ *Combined ticket €8* ⊘ *Mar. 16–Nov. 3, daily 9–7; Nov. 4–Mar. 15, daily 9–1:30.*

Next to the altar in the town's unfinished **Duomo** is a magnificent 13th-century carved-wood *Deposition*. Note the fresco by Benozzo Gozzoli (1420–97) in the Cappella della Addolorata. Along the left wall of the nave you can see the arrival of the Magi. ⊠ *Piazza San Giovanni* ☎ *0588/86192* ⊘ *Daily 9–1 and 3–6.*

Among Volterra's best-preserved ancient remains is the Etruscan **Porta all'Arco,** an arch dating from the 4th century BC now incorporated into the city walls. The ruins of the 1st-century BC **Teatro Romano,** a beautifully preserved Roman theater, are worth a visit. Adjacent to the theater are the remains of the **terme** (baths). The complex is outside the town walls past Porta Fiorentina. ⊠ *Viale Francesco Ferrucci* ☎ *0588/86347* ☜ *€2* ⊘ *Mar.–May and Sept.–Nov., daily 10–1 and 2–4; June–Aug., daily 10–6:45; Dec.–Feb., weekends 10–1 and 2–4.*

Where to Stay & Eat

$ ✕ **Il Sacco Fiorentino.** Start with the *porcini e fegatini di pollo saltati*—a medley of sautéed chicken liver and porcini mushrooms drizzled with balsamic vinegar. The meal just gets better when you move on to a dish like *filetto di maiale e cipolline,* pork medallions with pearl onions in a tangy mustard sauce. The wine list is a marvel, both long and affordably priced. Unremarkable white walls, tile floors, and red tablecloths are easily forgiven once the food starts arriving. ⊠ *Piazza XX Settembre 18* ☎ *0588/88537* ⊟ *AE, DC, MC, V* ⊙ *Closed Wed. and Jan. and Feb.*

$ 🏠 **Il Giardino di Venzano.** Terraced gardens bloom with native and exotic specimens: this agriturismo is run by two transplanted Australians with serious green thumbs. The grounds and buildings are what remains of an Augustinian monastery complete with Romanesque chapel. Three apartments, each sleeping two to four people, have high ceilings with light-color timbers, white walls and linens, and terra-cotta tile floors. Windows provide sweeping views of the surrounding countryside. A minimum one-week stay is required. ⊠ *Località Venzano, 56048 Mazzolla, 10 km (6 mi) south of Volterra* ☎ *0588/39095* ⊕ *www.venzanogardens.com* 🛏 *3 apartments* ⚖ *BBQs, fans, kitchens; no a/c, no room phones, no room TVs* ⊟ *No credit cards* ⊙ *Closed Nov. 1–Apr. 14* ⫿⊙⫿ *EP.*

$ 🏠 **San Lino.** Within Volterra's medieval walls, a convent-turned-hotel pairs wood-beam ceilings, archways, and terra-cotta floors in public spaces with modern-day comforts in your private domain. Hair dryers and some carpeting in the guest rooms accompany contemporary wood laminate furnishings and straight-line ironwork pieces. Sip a drink on the small terrace with tables, umbrellas, and potted geraniums; the pool area is framed on one side by a church with a stained-glass window of the Last Supper. The restaurant serves Tuscan classics and local specialties such as *zuppa alla volteranna,* a thick vegetable soup. ⊠ *Via San Lino 26, 56048* ☎ *0588/85250* ⊟ *0588/80620* ⊕ *www.hotelsanlino.com* 🛏 *43 rooms* ⚖ *Dining room, minibars, cable TV, pool, bar, dry cleaning, laundry service, concierge, parking (fee), some pets allowed, no-smoking rooms* ⊟ *AE, DC, MC, V* ⊙ *Closed Nov.–Jan.* ⫿⊙⫿ *BP.*

Shopping

A number of shops in Volterra sell boxes, jewelry, and other objects made of alabaster. The **Cooperativa Artieri Alabastro** (⊠ Piazza dei Priori 5 ☎ 0588/87590) has two large showrooms of alabaster pieces. At **Camillo Rossi** (⊠ Via Lungo le Mura del Mandorlo 7 ☎ 0588/86133) you can actually see craftspeople at work, creating alabaster objects for all tastes and budgets.

Anna Maria Molesini (⊠ Via Gramsci 45 ☎ 0588/88411) weaves scarves, shawls, jackets, throws, and jackets—mostly in mohair—on her loom in her small shop.

San Gimignano

㉒ *27 km (17 mi) east of Volterra, 57 km (35 mi) southwest of Florence.*

When you're high on its hill surrounded by centuries-old towers silhouetted against the blue sky, it's difficult not to fall under the medieval spell of San Gimignano. Today 15 towers remain, but at the height of the Guelph-Ghibelline conflict there was a forest of more than 70, and it was possible to cross the town by rooftop rather than street. The towers were built partly to defend the town—they provided a safe refuge and were useful for pouring boiling oil on attacking enemies—and partly to bolster the egos of their owners, who competed with deadly seriousness to build the highest tower in town. When the Black Death devastated the population in 1348, power and independence faded fast and civic autonomy was ultimately surrendered to Florence.

Today San Gimignano isn't much more than a gentrified walled city, amply prepared for its booming tourist trade but still very much worth exploring. Despite the remarkable profusion of chintzy souvenir shops lining its main drag, there's some serious Renaissance art to be seen here and an equally important local wine (Vernaccia, a light white) to be savored. Escape at midday to the uninhabited areas outside the city walls for a hike and a picnic, and return to explore the town in the afternoon and evening, when things quiet down and the long shadows cast by the imposing towers take on fascinating shapes. A €7.50 combination ticket covers the sights, except for the private Museo di Criminologia Medievale.

San Gimignano's most noteworthy medieval buildings are clustered around the central **Piazza del Duomo.** The imposing **Torre Grossa** is the tallest tower in town (177 feet), with views that are well worth the climb. ✉ *Piazza del Duomo 1* ☎ *0577/940008* *€5 (includes Palazzo del Popolo)* ⊙ *Mar.–Oct., daily 9:30–7; Nov.–Feb., daily 10–5:30.*

The **Palazzo del Popolo** houses the **Museo Civico,** featuring Taddeo di Bartolo's celebratory scenes from the life of San Gimignano. The town's namesake, a bishop of Modena, achieved sainthood by driving hordes of barbarians out of the city in the 10th century. Dante visited San Gimignano as an ambassador from Florence for only a single day in 1300, but it was long enough to get a room named after him, which now holds a *Maestà* by 14th-century artist Lippo Memmi. A small room (probably the private domain of the commune's chief magistrate) contains frescoes by Memmo di Filippuccio (active 1288–1324) depicting a young couple's courtship. ✉ *Piazza del Duomo* ☎ *0577/940008* *€5 (includes Torre Grossa)* ⊙ *Mar.–Oct., daily 9:30–7:30; Nov.–Feb., daily 10–5:30.*

★ The Romanesque **Collegiata** is a treasure trove of frescoes, including Bartolo di Fredi's cycle of scenes from the Old Testament on the left nave wall dating from 1367. Taddeo di Bartolo's otherworldly *Last Judgment,* on the arch inside the facade, depicts distorted and suffering nudes—avant-garde stuff for the 1390s. The New Testament scenes on the right wall, which may have been executed by Barna da Siena in the 1330s, suggest a more reserved, balanced Renaissance manner. The **Cappella di Santa Fina** contains glorious frescoes by Domenico Ghirlandaio (1449–94) depicting the story of this local saint. ✉ *Piazza del Duomo* ☎ *0577/940316* *€3.50* ⊙ *Apr.–Oct., weekdays 9:30–7:10, Sat. 9:30–5:10, Sun. 12:30–5:10; Nov.–Jan. 20 and Mar., Mon.–Sat. 9:30–4:40, Sun. 12:30–4:40.*

The **Museo di Criminologia Medievale** (Museum of Medieval Criminology) exhibits reproductions of medieval torture technology, along with operating instructions and a clear description of the intended effect.

Though scholars dispute the historical accuracy of many of the instruments, the final, very contemporary object—an electric chair imported from the United States—does give pause. ✉ *Via del Castello 1–3* ☎ *0577/942243* 🎟 *€8* ⊘ *Apr.–Sept, daily 10–8; Oct.–Mar., Mon.–Sat. 10–6, Sun. 10–7.*

Before leaving San Gimignano, be sure to see its most revered work of art: Benozzo Gozzoli's utterly stunning 15th-century fresco cycle depicts scenes from the life of St. Augustine in the church of **Sant'Agostino.** ✉ *Piazza Sant'Agostino, north end of town* ☎ *0577/907012* ⊘ *Nov.–Mar., daily 7–noon and 3–6; Apr.–Oct., daily 7–noon and 3–7.*

Where to Stay & Eat

$$ ✕ **La Mangiatoia.** Bright-color gingham tablecloths provide an interesting contrast to the 13th-century, rib-vault ceilings here—the lighthearted feminine touch might be explained by chef Susi Cuomo, who has been presiding over her kitchen for more than 20 years. The menu is seasonal: in autumn, don't miss her *sacottino di pecorino al tartufo* (little packages of pasta stuffed with sheep's cheese and truffles), and in summer enjoy lighter fare on the intimate, flower-bedecked terrace in the back. ✉ *Via Mainardi 5, off Via San Matteo* ☎ *0577/941528* ☰ MC, V ⊘ *Closed Tues., 3 wks in Nov., and Jan. and Feb.*

★ ¢ ✕ **Enoteca Gustavo.** The ebullient Maristella Becucci reigns supreme in this tiny wine bar (three small tables in the back, two in the bar, two bar stools) serving divine, and ample, crostini. The *crostino con carciofini e pecorino* (toasted bread with artichokes topped with semi-aged pecorino) packs a punch. The changing list of wines by the glass has about 16 reds and whites, mostly local, all good. The cheese plate is a bit more expensive than the crostini, but it's worth it. ✉ *Via San Matteo 29* ☎ *0577/940057* ⚶ *Reservations not accepted* ☰ AE, DC, MC, V ⊘ *Closed Tues. Oct.–Mar.*

$$$$ 🏨 **La Collegiata.** After serving as a Franciscan convent and then residence of the noble Strozzi family, the Collegiata has been transformed into a fine hotel. Antiques and precious tapestries furnish the rooms, and bathrooms have whirlpool tubs. A park surrounds the building: ask for a room with a private balcony to enjoy the view more closely. The restaurant occupies the deconsecrated church. ✉ *Località Strada 27, 53037, 1 km (½ mi) north of town center* ☎ *0577/943201* 🖷 *0577/940566* ⊕ *www.relaischateaux.com* ⇱ *20 rooms, 1 suite* △ *Restaurant, room service, in-room safes, some in-room hot tubs, cable TV, pool, bar, wine bar, meeting room, free parking, some pets allowed* ☰ AE, DC, MC, V ⊘ *Closed Jan. 7–Mar. 12* ⫿◎⫿ EP.

$–$$ 🏨 **Pescille.** A rambling farmhouse 4 km (2½ mi) outside San Gimignano has been transformed into a handsome hotel with understated contemporary furniture in the bedrooms. Country-classic motifs, such as farm implements hanging on the walls, dominate in the bar. From this charming spot you get a splendid view of San Gimignano and its towers. ✉ *Località Pescille, Strada Castel San Gimignano, 53037* ☎ *0577/940186* 🖷 *0577/943165* ⊕ *www.pescille.it* ⇱ *38 rooms, 12 suites* △ *Cable TV, Wi-Fi in some rooms, tennis court, pool, gym, bar, free parking; no a/c in some rooms* ☰ AE, DC, MC, V ⊘ *Closed Nov.–Mar.* ⫿◎⫿ BP.

9

Colle Val d'Elsa

㉓ *15 km (9 mi) southeast of San Gimignano, 50 km (31 mi) southwest of Florence.*

On the road from Florence to Siena, Colle Val d'Elsa rises dramatically along a winding road, its narrow streets lined with palazzi dating from the 15th and 16th centuries. For art enthusiasts, it's perhaps best known as the birthplace of Arnolfo di Cambio (circa 1245–1310), architect of Florence's Duomo. Once a formidable producer of wool, the town now produces glass and crystal sold in local shops. Colle has two distinct parts: the relatively modern and less-interesting lower town, Colle Bassa, and the older, upper town, Colle Alta.

Where to Stay & Eat

★ **$$$$** ✕ **Ristorante Arnolfo.** Food lovers with some money to spend should not miss Arnolfo, one of Tuscany's most highly regarded restaurants. Chef Gaetano Trovato sets high standards of creativity; his dishes straddle the line between innovation and tradition, almost always with spectacular results. The menu changes frequently and has two fixed-price options, but there are always plenty of fresh vegetables and herbs. You're in for a treat if *medaglioni di sogliola e gamberi rossi con finocchi allo zafferano* (sole and shrimp with fennel, flavored with saffron) is on the list. The restaurant is in a tranquil spot at the center of town. ⊠ *Piazza XX Settembre 52* 🖼 *0577/920549* ⊟ *AE, DC, MC, V* ☉ *Closed Tues. and Wed., mid-Jan.–mid-Feb., and 2 wks in Aug.*

★ **$$$$** 🏨 **La Suvera.** Pope Julius II once owned this luxurious estate in the valley of the River Elsa. The papal villa and adjacent building have magnificently furnished guest rooms and suites appointed with antiques and modern comforts. La Suvera's first-rate facilities, including drawing rooms, a library, an Italian garden, a park, and the Oliviera restaurant (serving organic estate wines), make it hard to tear yourself away. ⊠ *Pievescola (Casola d'Elsa) off SS541, 15 km (9 mi) south of Colle di Val d'Elsa, 53030* 🖼 *0577/960300* 🖼 *0577/960220* ⊕ *www.lasuvera. it* 🖺 *16 rooms, 16 suites* ⚼ *Restaurant, room service, in-room safes, minibars, cable TV, in-room broadband, tennis court, pool, exercise equipment, massage, Turkish bath, mountain bikes, bar, library, dry cleaning, laundry service, concierge, meeting room; no kids under 12* ⊟ *AE, DC, MC, V* ☉ *Closed Nov.–Easter* ⅠⓄⅠ *BP.*

$ 🏨 **Villa Belvedere.** The Conti-Iannone family, who have run this place since 1984, provide the intimacy that you might find in a family home. Some of the 17th-century villa's rooms have three beds (with an option for adding a fourth), making this a good choice for families. A classic garden provides a place to read or have a drink, and an on-site restaurant serves Tuscan specialties. On a good day you can glimpse San Gimignano from here, but there's a fair amount of traffic that goes by on the road in front of the hotel. Half board is available. ⊠ *Località Belvedere, 53034, 1½ km (1 mi) south on SS2* 🖼 *0577/920966* 🖼 *0577/92412* ⊕ *www.villabelvedere.com* 🖺 *15 rooms* ⚼ *Restaurant, cable TV, Wi-Fi, tennis court, pool, bar, free parking, some pets allowed; no a/c* ⊟ *AE, DC, MC, V* ⅠⓄⅠ *EP.*

SIENA

One of Italy's most enchanting medieval cities, Siena is the one place in Tuscany you should visit if you see no other. Florence's great historical rival was in all likelihood founded by the Etruscans. During the late Middle Ages it was both wealthy and powerful, for it saw the birth of the world's oldest bank, the Monte dei Paschi, still very much in business. It was bitterly envied by Florence, which in 1254 sent forces that besieged the city for more than a year, reducing its population by half and laying waste to the countryside. The city was finally absorbed by the grand duchy of Tuscany, ruled by Florence, in 1559.

Sienese identity is still defined by its 17 medieval *contrade* (neighborhoods), each with its own church, museum, and emblem. Look for streetlights painted in the contrada's colors, plaques displaying its symbol, and statues embodying the spirit of the neighborhood. The various contrade uphold ancient rivalries during the centuries-old Palio, a twice-yearly horse race (held in July and August) in the main piazza.

Exploring Siena

Practically unchanged since medieval times, Siena stretches over the slopes of three steep hills. The most interesting sights are in a fairly compact pedestrian-only centro storico, but leave some time to wander off the main streets.

If you have only one day in Siena, see the Piazza del Campo, the Duomo, the Cripta, and the Palazzo Pubblico. If you are seeing more sights, it's usually worthwhile to buy a combination ticket (valid for three days, €10), good for entrance to the Duomo's Biblioteca Piccolomini, the Battistero, and the Museo dell'Opera Metropolitana. If you can overnight here, by all means do so: the city is filled with day-trippers and tour buses, and in the late afternoon and evening it empties out. The *passeggiata* (evening stroll) along the main shopping streets should not be missed: Siena's medieval charm and narrow streets are thrown into high relief, and Piazza del Campo positively glows. Keep in mind that most shops are closed Sunday and museums have variable hours.

> **WORD OF MOUTH**
>
> "Wandering Siena's streets and alleys was a mystical experience, one our seven-year-old loved. It got his imagination going, thinking about centuries past. Bring a comfortable pair of shoes and lots of water!"
>
> —Jeff

Siena is 69 km (43 mi) south of Florence; there are two basic routes. The speedy, modern SS2 is good if you're making a day trip from Florence, as it's a four-lane divided highway. For a jaunt through Chianti, take the narrower and more meandering SS222, known as the Strada Chiantigiana. It's a gorgeous ride on only two lanes—patience is a necessity.

Battistero **28**

Duomo **26**

Duomo
Cripta **27**

Museo
dell'Opera
Metropolitana ..**29**

Palazzo
Pubblico **25**

Piazza del
Campo **24**

Pinacoteca
Nazionale **31**

San
Domenico **32**

Spedale di
Santa Maria
della Scala ...**30**

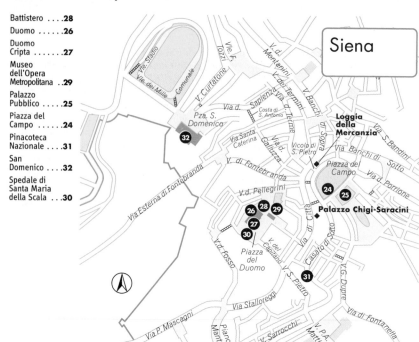

The Main Attractions

★ **26** **Duomo.** A few minutes' walk west of Piazza del Campo, Siena's Duomo is beyond question one of the finest Gothic cathedrals in Italy. The facade, with its multicolor marbles and painted decoration, is typical of the Italian approach to Gothic architecture, lighter and much less austere than the French. The cathedral as it now stands was completed in the 14th century, but at the time the Sienese had even bigger plans. They had decided to enlarge the building by using the existing church as a transept for a new one, with a new nave running toward the southeast. But in 1348 the Black Death decimated Siena's population, the city fell into decline, funds dried up, and the plans were never carried out. The beginnings of the new nave can be seen from the steps outside the Duomo's right transept.

The Duomo's interior, with its coffered and gilded dome, is striking. The magnificent inlaid marble floors took almost 200 years to complete (beginning around 1370); more than 40 artists contributed to the work, made up of 56 separate compositions depicting biblical scenes, allegories, religious symbols, and civic emblems. They are covered for most of the year for conservation purposes but are usually unveiled every September for the entire month. The Duomo's pulpit, also much appreciated, was carved by Nicola Pisano between 1266 and 1268; the life of Christ is depicted on the rostrum frieze. In the **Biblioteca Piccolomini,** a room painted by Pinturicchio (circa 1454–1513) between 1502 and 1509, frescoes show scenes from the life of native son Aeneas Sylvius Piccolomini (1405–64), who became Pope Pius II in 1458. They are in excellent condition and reveal a freshness rarely seen in Renaissance frescoes. ⊠ *Piazza del Duomo, Città* ☏ *0577/283048* 🎟 *Church free, Biblioteca Piccolomini €3* ⊙ *Mar.–May, Mon.–Sat. 10:30–7:30, Sun. 1:30–5:30; June–Aug., Mon.–Sat. 10:30–8, Sun. 1:30–6:30; Sept. and Oct., Mon.–Sat. 10:30–7:30, Sun. 10:30–7:30; Nov.–Feb., Mon.–Sat. 10:30–6:30, Sun. 1:30–5:30.*

㉗ Duomo Cripta. Rediscovered during routine excavation work, the crypt—
Fodor's Choice under the grand *pavimento* (floor) of the Duomo upstairs—was opened
★ to the public in fall of 2003. An unknown master executed the breathtakingly beautiful frescoes here sometime between 1270 and 1280; they retain their original colors and pack an emotional punch even given the sporadic paint loss. The *Deposition/Lamentation* gives strong evidence that the Sienese school could paint emotion just as well as the Florentine school, some 20 years before Giotto. Guided tours in English take place more or less every half hour and are limited to no more than 35 persons. ⊠ *Piazza del Duomo, Città* ☏ *0577/283048* 🎟 *€6* ⊙ *Mar.–May, daily 9:30–7; June–Aug., daily 9:30–8; Sept. and Oct., daily 9:30–7; Nov.–Feb., daily 10–5.*

> ㉔ Piazza del Campo, ㉕ Palazzo Pubblico   **See Page 507**

Also Worth Seeing

㉘ Battistero. The Duomo's 14th-century Gothic Baptistery was built to prop up one side of the Duomo. There are frescoes throughout, but the highlight is a large bronze 15th-century baptismal font designed by Jacopo della Quercia and adorned with bas-reliefs by various artists, including two by Renaissance masters: the *Baptism of Christ* by Lorenzo Ghiberti (1378–1455) and the *Feast of Herod* by Donatello. ⊠ *Piazza San Giovanni, Duomo* 🎟 *€3* ⊙ *Mar.–May, daily 9:30–7; June–Aug., daily 9:30–8; Sept. and Oct., daily 9:30–7; Nov.–Feb., daily 10–5.*

㉙ Museo dell'Opera Metropolitana. Built into part of the unfinished new cathedral's nave, the museum contains a small but important collection of Sienese art and the cathedral treasury. Its masterpiece is unquestionably the *Maestà* by Duccio (circa 1255–1318), painted around 1310 and magnificently displayed in a room devoted entirely to the artist's work. The tower inside the museum has a splendid view. ⊠ *Piazza del Duomo, next to Duomo, Città* ☏ *0577/283048* 🎟 *€6* ⊙ *Mar.–May, daily 9:30–7; June–Aug., daily 9:30–8; Sept. and Oct., daily 9:30–7; Nov.–Feb., daily 10–5.*

㉛ Pinacoteca Nazionale. The national picture gallery contains an excellent collection of Sienese art, including works by native sons Ambrogio

Continued on page 510

Climbing the 500 narrow steps of the **Torre del Mangia** rewards you with unparalleled views of Siena's rooftops and the countryside beyond.

The **Palazzo Pubblico**, Siena's town hall since the 14th century.

Something about the fan-shaped, sloping design of **Il Campo** encourages people to sit and relax (except during the Palio, when they stand and scream). The communal atmosphere here is unlike that of any other Italian piazza.

PIAZZA DEL CAMPO

24 The fan-shaped **Piazza del Campo,** known simply as il Campo (The Field),
Fodor'sChoice ★ is one of the finest squares in Italy. Constructed toward the end of the
12th century on a market area unclaimed by any contrada,
it's still the heart of town. The bricks of the
Campo are patterned in nine different sections—representing each member of the
medieval Government of Nine. At the
top of the Campo is a copy of the
Fonte Gaia, decorated in the early
15th century by Siena's greatest
sculptor, Jacopo della Quercia,
with 13 sculpted reliefs of biblical events and virtues. Those lining the rectangular fountain are
19th-century copies; the originals are in the Spedale di Santa
Maria della Scala. On Palio horse
race days (July 2 and August 16),
the Campo and all its surrounding
buildings are packed with cheering,
frenzied locals and tourists craning
their necks to take it all in.

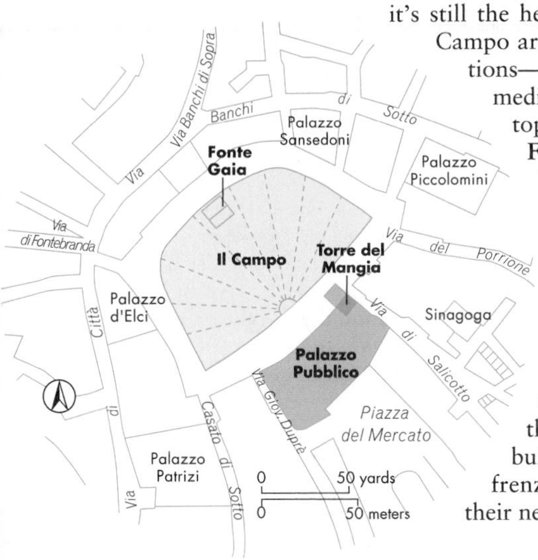

Map labels: Via Banchi di Sopra; Banchi di Sotto; Palazzo Sansedoni; Fonte Gaia; Via; Via di Fontebranda; Il Campo; Torre del Mangia; Palazzo d'Elci; Palazzo Patrizi; Palazzo Pubblico; Palazzo Piccolomini; Via del Porrione; Sinagoga; Via di Salicotto; Piazza del Mercato; Città; Via Giovanni Dupré; Casato di Sotto; Via

0 — 50 yards
0 — 50 meters

25 The Gothic **Palazzo Pubblico,** the focal point of the Piazza del Campo,
has served as Siena's town hall since the 1300s. It now also contains
the **Museo Civico,** with walls covered in early Renaissance frescoes. The
nine governors of Siena once met in the Sala della Pace, famous for Ambrogio Lorenzetti's frescoes called *Allegories of Good and Bad Government,* painted in the late 1330s to demonstrate the dangers of
tyranny. The good government side depicts utopia, showing first the
virtuous ruling council surrounded by angels and then scenes of a perfectly running city and countryside. Conversely, the bad government
fresco tells a tale straight out of Dante. The evil ruler and his advisers
have horns and fondle strange animals, and the town scene depicts the
seven mortal sins in action. Interestingly, the bad government fresco is
severely damaged, and the good government fresco is in terrific condition. The **Torre del Mangia,** the palazzo's famous bell tower, is named
after one of its first bell ringers, Giovanni di Duccio (called Man-
giaguadagni, or earnings eater). The climb up to the top is long and
steep, but the view makes it worth every step. ⊠ *Piazza del Campo 1,
Città* ☏ *0577/41169* ⌨ *Museo €7, Torre €6, combined ticket €10*
⊙ *Museo Nov.–Mar. 15, daily 10–6:30; Mar. 16–Oct., daily 10–7.
Torre Nov.–Mar. 15, daily 10–4; Mar. 16–Oct., daily 10–7.*

PIAZZA DEL CAMPO

9

THE PALIO

The three laps around a makeshift racetrack in Piazza del Campo are over in less than two minutes, but the spirit of Siena's Palio—a horse race held every July 2 and August 16—lives all year long.

The Palio is contested between Siena's contrade, the 17 neighborhoods that have divided the city since the Middle Ages. Loyalties are fiercely felt. At any time of year you'll see on the streets contrada symbols—Tartuca (turtle), Oca (goose), Istrice (porcupine), Torre (tower)—emblazoned on banners and engraved on building walls. At Palio time, simmering rivalries come to a boil.

It's been that way since at least August 16, 1310, the date of the first recorded running of the Palio. At that time, and for centuries to follow, the race went through the streets of the city. The additional July 2 running was instituted in 1649; soon thereafter the location was moved to the Campo and the current system for selecting the race entrants established. Ten of the contrade are chosen at random to run in the July Palio. The August race is then contested between the 7 contrade left out in July, plus 3 of the 10 July participants, again chosen at random. Although the races are in theory of equal importance, Sienese will tell you that it's better to win the second and have bragging rights for the rest of the year.

The race itself has a raw and arbitrary character—it's no Kentucky Derby. There's barely room for the 10 horses on the makeshift Campo course, so falls and collisions are inevitable. Horses are chosen at random three days before the race, and jockeys (who ride bareback) are mercenaries hired from surrounding towns. Almost no tactic is considered too underhanded. Bribery, secret plots, and betrayal are commonplace—so much so that the word for "jockey," *fantino,* has come to mean "untrustworthy" in Siena. There have been incidents of drugging (the horses) and kidnapping (the jockeys); only sabotaging a horse's reins remains taboo.

Above: The tension of the starting line. Top left: The frenzy of the race. Bottom left: A solemn flag bearer follows in the footsteps of his ancestors.

| AQUILA | BRUCO | CHIOCCIOLA |

17 MEDIEVAL CONTRADE

Festivities kick off three days prior to the Palio, with the selection and blessing of the horses, trial runs, ceremonial banquets, betting, and late-night celebrations. Residents don their contrada's colors and march through the streets in medieval costumes. The Campo is transformed into a racetrack lined with a thick layer of sand. On race day, each horse is brought to the church of the contrada for which it will run, where it's blessed and told, "Go little horse and return a winner." The Campo fills through the afternoon, with spectators crowding into every available space until bells ring and the piazza is sealed off. Processions of flag wavers in traditional dress march to the beat of tambourines and drums and the roar of the crowds. The *palio* itself—a banner for which the race is named, dedicated to the Virgin Mary—makes an appearance, followed by the horses and their jockeys.

The race begins when one horse, chosen to ride up from behind the rest of the field, crosses the starting line. There are always false starts, adding to the frenzied mood. Once underway, the race is over in a matter of minutes. The victorious rider is carried off through the streets of the winning contrada (where in the past tradition dictated he was entitled to the local girl of his choice), while winning and losing sides use television replay to analyze the race from every possible angle. The winning contrada will celebrate into the night, at long tables piled high with food and drink. The champion horse is guest of honor.

Reserved seating in the stands is sold out months in advance of the races; contact the Siena Tourist Office (⊠ Piazza del Campo 56 ☎ 0577/280551) to find out about availability, and ask your hotel if it can procure you a seat. The entire area in the center is free and unreserved, but you need to show up early in order to get a prime spot against the barriers.

CIVETTA	DRAGO
GIRAFFA	ISTRICE
LEOCORNO	LUPA
NICCHIO	OCA
ONDA	PANTERA
SELVA	TARTUCA
TORRE	VALDIMONTONE

PIAZZA DEL CAMPO

9

Lorenzetti (active 1319–48), Duccio, and Domenico Beccafumi (1486–1551). ✉ *Via San Pietro 29, Città* ☎ *0577/281161* 💳 *€4* ⊙ *Sun. and Mon. 8:30–1:30, Tues.–Sat. 8:15–7.*

㉜ San Domenico. In the church of San Domenico is the **Cappella di Santa Caterina,** with frescoes by Sodoma portraying scenes from the life of St. Catherine of Siena. Catherine was a much-respected diplomat, noted for ending the Great Schism by persuading the pope to return to Rome from Avignon. The saint's preserved head and finger are on display in the chapel. ✉ *Costa di Sant'Antonio, Camollìa* ☎ *0577/280893* ⊙ *Nov.–mid-Mar., daily 9–6; mid-Mar.–Oct., daily 7–7.*

㉚ Spedale di Santa Maria della Scala. A former *ospedale* (hospital) and hostel for weary pilgrims, built beginning in the late 9th century, continues to evolve into a grand exhibition space, hosting major contemporary art shows and housing, among other gems, some of the Fonte Gaia sculpted reliefs by Jacopo della Quercia (1371/74–1438). Even if you are not particularly taken with Etruscan objects, the subterranean archaeological museum contained within is not to be missed. Its interior design is sheer brilliance—it's beautifully lighted, eerily quiet, and an oasis of cool on hot summer days. ✉ *Piazza del Duomo, opposite front of Duomo, Città* ☎ *0577/224811* 💳 *€5.20* ⊙ *Mar. 17–Oct., daily 10–6; Nov.–Dec. 23, daily 10:30–4:30; Dec. 24–Jan. 6, daily 10–6; Jan. 7–Mar. 16, daily 10:30–4:30.*

Off the Beaten Path

Orto Botanico. Not far from the Duomo and the Pinacoteca, Siena's botanical garden is a great place to relax and enjoy views of the countryside. Guided tours in English are available with a reservation. ✉ *Via Pier Andrea Mattioli 4, Città* ☎ *0577/232874* 💳 *€8* ⊙ *Weekdays 8–12:30 and 2:30–5:30, Sat. 8–noon.*

Where to Stay & Eat

$$$ ✕ **Antica Trattoria Botteganova.** Chef Michele Sorrentino's cooking is all about clean flavors, balanced combinations, and inviting presentation. Look for inspiring dishes such as spaghetti *alla chitarra in salsa di astice piccante* (with a spicy lobster sauce). The dining room's interior, with high vaulting, is relaxed yet classy, and there's a small room for nonsmokers. Service is first rate. ✉ *Strada per Montevarchi (SS408) 29, 2 km (1 mi) north of Siena along road to Chianti* ☎ *0577/284230* 🚭 *AE, DC, MC, V* ⊙ *Closed Sun.*

$$–$$$ ✕ **Le Logge.** Bright flowers add a dash of color in this classic Tuscan dining room with stenciled ceilings. The wooden cupboards (now filled with wine bottles) recall the turn-of-the-19th-century food store it once was. A small menu, with four or five primi and secondi, changes regularly, but almost always includes *malfatti all'osteria,* ricotta and spinach dumplings in a cream sauce. Try inventive desserts such as *coni con mousse al cioccolato e gelato allo zafferano,* which is two diminutive ice-cream cones with chocolate mousse and saffron ice cream. ✉ *Via del Porrione 33, San Martino* ☎ *0577/48013* 🚭 *AE, DC, MC, V* ⊙ *Closed Sun. and 3 wks in Jan.*

★ **$-$$** ✕ **Osteria del Coro.** Chef-owner Stefano Azzi promotes local fare, uses age-old Sienese recipes, and backs up all his creations with a stellar wine list. His *pici con le briciole alla mio modo* (thick spaghetti with bread crumbs), liberally dressed with fried *cinta senese* (a local bacon), dazzles. The place was once a pizzeria, and it retains its unadorned, unpretentious nature—you certainly wouldn't come because of the decor. ✉ *Via Pantaneto 85–87, San Martino* ☎ *0577/222482* ⚠ *Reservations essential* ▱ *No credit cards.*

$ ✕ **La Taverna del Capitano.** Not far from the Duomo you can step into a comfortable little taverna that is simplicity itself. The *pici al pomodoro fresco,* thick noodles topped with a lively fresh tomato sauce and a bit of cheese dusted on top, proves that less can indeed be more. Tuscan specialties and flavorful primi are strong suits here. Waiters dash between the closely spaced tables and can speak knowledgeably about the fine wine list. ✉ *Via del Capitano 8, Città* ☎ *0577/288094* ▱ *AE, DC, MC, V* ☾ *Closed Tues.*

¢ ✕ **da Trombicche.** Wiped out from too much sightseeing? Consider an invigorating snack at this one-room eatery. Here they do tasty things with eggs (the frittata is exceptional), plates of cured meats, and made-to-order *panini* (sandwiches). The list of daily specials reflects the season, and the collection of *verdure sott'olio* (marinated vegetables) is refreshing. Anything you choose can be washed down with the inexpensive, eminently drinkable, house red. ✉ *Via delle Terme 66, Camollia* ☎ *0577/288089* ▱ *No credit cards* ☾ *Closed Sun.*

$$$$ ▥ **Certosa di Maggiano.** A former 14th-century monastery has been converted into an exquisite country hotel. The officious staff is a drawback, but rooms have the style and comfort of an aristocratic villa—with classic prints and bold colors such as a happy, daffodil yellow. Common spaces are luxurious, with fine woods and leather. In warm weather, breakfast is served on the patio next to the garden ablaze with flowers. Half board is required in high season. ✉ *Strada di Certosa 82, take the Siena Sud exit off superstrada, 53100* ☎ *0577/288180* ▤ *0577/ 288189* ⊕ *www.certosadimaggiano.it* ⇆ *9 rooms, 8 suites* ⚒ *Restaurant, minibars, cable TV, in-room data ports, tennis court, pool, exercise equipment, dry cleaning, laundry service, concierge, helipad, no-smoking rooms; no kids under 12* ▱ *AE, MC, V* ☾ *Closed mid.-Jan–mid Mar.* ⦿ *MAP.*

★ **$$-$$$** ▥ **Palazzo Ravizza.** There might not be a more romantic place in the center of Siena than this quietly charming pension, a 10-minute walk to the Duomo. Rooms exude a faded gentility, with high ceilings, antique furniture, big windows, and bathrooms done in hand-painted tiles. The restaurant serves Tuscan favorites, which, when it's warm, can be enjoyed outside in a lovely, tranquil garden complete with trickling fountain. ✉ *Pian dei Mantellini 34, near Porto San Marco, Città, 53100* ☎ *0577/280462* ▤ *0577/221597* ⊕ *www.palazzoravizza.it* ⇆ *40 rooms, 4 suites* ⚒ *Restaurant, some in-room safes, some minibars, cable TV, bar, laundry service, concierge, free parking, some pets allowed* ▱ *AE, DC, MC, V* ⦿ *BP.*

$$ ▥ **Antica Torre.** An old stone staircase, wooden beams, and original brick vaults here and there are reminders that the building is a 16th-century tower. The lodging is the work of a cordial couple who have carefully evoked a private home, with only eight simple but tasteful guest rooms. Antica Torre is a 10-minute walk from Piazza del Campo. ⊠ *Via Fieravecchia 7, San Martino, 53100* ☎ *0577/226102* 🖷 *0577/222255* ⊕ *www.anticatorresiena.it* ↩ *8 rooms* ♿ *Cable TV, parking (fee)* ☰ *AE, DC, MC, V* ¶❙ *EP.*

¢ ▦ **Alma Domus.** If you're after a contemplative, utilitarian experience, seek refuge at the former convent run by the committed parishioners of the Santurario Santa Caterina (Sanctuary of St. Catherine); it's around the corner from the church of San Domenico. Rooms are spartan and very clean. Many have a view of the Duomo and the rest of Siena, which might make the 11:30 curfew livable. A two-night minimum stay is required; the best way to reserve is by fax. ⊠ *Via Camporeggio 37, Camollìa, 53100* ☎ *0577/44177* 🖷 *0577/47601* ↩ *31 rooms* ♿ *No-smoking floors; no room phones, no room TVs* ☰ *No credit cards* ¶❙ *EP.*

Nightlife & the Arts

Music

During two weeks in July, Siena hosts the **Settimane Musicali Senesi,** a series of classical concerts held in churches and courtyards. The event is arranged by the **Accademia Musicale Chigiana** (⊠ Via di Città 89, Città ☎ 0577/22091 ⊕ www.chigiana.it), which also conducts master classes and workshops in July and August and sponsors concerts from November through April. Age-old venues such as Santa Maria della Scala and the church of Sant'Agostino provide the setting.

Shopping

Siena is known for its cakes and cookies, made from recipes of medieval origin—look for *cavallucci* (sweet spice biscuits), *panforte* (a densely packed concoction of honey, hazelnuts, almonds, and spices), and *ricciarelli* (almond-paste cookies). The best place in town to find Sienese baked goods, as well as to grab a cappuccino, is **Nannini,** located on the main drag north of the Campo (⊠ Banchi di Sopra 24, Camollìa ☎ 0577/236009).

Siena has excellent specialty wine and food shops. **La Bottega dei Sapori Antichi** (⊠ Via delle Terme 41, Camollìa ☎ 0577/285501) is a good option for local products. Italy's only state-sponsored enoteca, **Enoteca Italiana** (⊠ Fortezza Medicea, Camollìa ☎ 0577/288497), sells wines from all across Italy.

Siena Ricama (⊠ Via di Città 61, Duomo ☎ 0577/288339) has embroidered linens and other housewares for sale. Chiara Perinetti Casoni at **Bottega dell'Arte** (⊠ Via Stalloreggi 47, Città ☎ 0577/40755) creates high-quality copies of 14th- and 15th-century Sienese panel paintings using tempera and gold leaf.

AREZZO & CORTONA

The hill towns of Arezzo and Cortona carry on age-old local traditions—in June and September, for example, Arezzo's Romanesque and Gothic churches are enlivened by the Giostra del Saracino, a costumed medieval joust. Arezzo has been home to important artists since ancient times, when Etruscan potters produced their fiery-red vessels here. Fine examples of the work of Luca Signorelli are preserved in Cortona, his hometown.

Arezzo

33 *63 km (39 mi) northeast of Siena, 81 km (50 mi) southeast of Florence.*

The birthplace of the poet Petrarch (1304–74) and the Renaissance artist and art historian Giorgio Vasari, Arezzo is today best known for the magnificent Piero della Francesca frescoes in the church of San Francesco. The city dates from pre-Etruscan times and thrived as an Etruscan capital from the 7th to the 4th centuries BC. During the Middle Ages it was fully embroiled in the conflict between the Ghibellines (pro-emperor) and the Guelphs (pro-pope), losing its independence to Florence at the end of the 14th century after many decades of doing battle.

Urban sprawl testifies to the fact that Arezzo (population 90,000) is the third-largest city in Tuscany (after Florence and Pisa). But the old town, set on a low hill, is relatively small, and almost completely closed to traffic. Look for parking along the roads that circle the lower part of town, near the train station, and walk into town from there. You can explore the most interesting sights in a few hours, adding time to linger for some window-shopping at Arezzo's many antiques shops.

Fodor'sChoice ★ The remarkable frescoes by Piero della Francesca (circa 1420–92) in the **Basilica di San Francesco** were painted between 1452 and 1466. They depict scenes from the *Legend of the True Cross* on three walls of the *cappella maggiore,* or high altar choir. What Sir Kenneth Clark called "the most perfect morning light in all Renaissance painting" may be seen in the lowest section of the right wall, where the troops of the emperor Maxentius flee before the sign of the cross. A 15-year project restored the works to their original brilliance. Reservations are required to see the choir area with the frescoes. ✉ *Piazza San Francesco 6* ☎ *0575/ 352727* ⊕ *www.pierodellafrancesca.it* ✉ *Church free, choir €6* ☉ *Apr.–Oct., weekdays 9–6:30, Sat. 9–5:30, Sun. 1–5:30; Nov.–Mar., weekdays 9–5:30, Sat. 9–5, Sun. 1–5.*

Some historians maintain that Arezzo's oddly shaped, sloping **Piazza Grande** was once the site of an ancient Roman forum. Now it hosts a first-Sunday-of-the-month antiques fair as well as the **Giostra del Saracino** (Joust of the Saracen), featuring medieval costumes and competition, held here in the middle of June and on the first Sunday of September. Check out the 16th-century loggia designed by native son Giorgio Vasari on the northeast side of the piazza.

The curving, tiered apse on Piazza Grande belongs to **Pieve di Santa Maria,** one of Tuscany's finest Romanesque churches, built in the 12th century. Don't miss the Portale Maggiore (great door) with its polychrome figures representing the months; restored in 2002, they are remarkably vibrant. ✉ *Corso Italia* ☎ *0575/377678* ☉ *Daily 8–noon and 3–6:30.*

Arezzo's medieval **Duomo** (at the top of the hill) contains a fresco of a somber *Magdalen* by Piero della Francesca; look for it next to the large

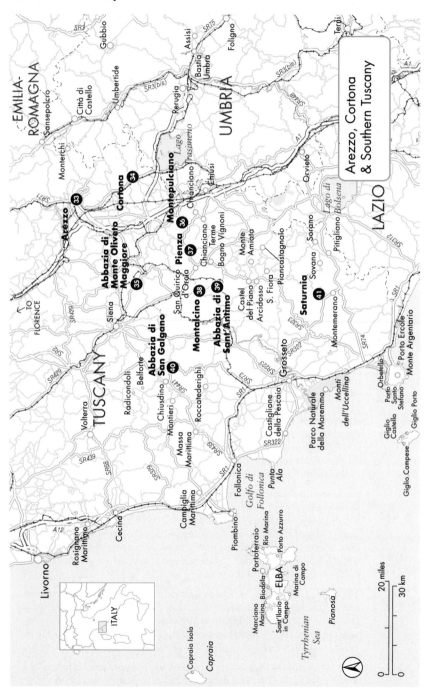

Arezzo, Cortona & Southern Tuscany

marble tomb near the organ. ✉ *Piazza del Duomo 1* ☎ *0575/23991* ⊙ *Daily 7–12:30 and 3–6:30.*

Italy's most famous art historian designed and decorated his private home, **Casa di Giorgio Vasari** in about the year 1540. ✉ *Via XX Settembre 55* ☎ *0575/409040* ▱ *€2* ⊙ *Mon. and Wed.–Sat. 8:30–6:30, Sun. 8:30–1:30.*

Where to Stay & Eat

¢ ✕ **La Torre di Gnicche.** Looking for Italian home cooking? Eating *ribollita* (a hearty, traditional Tuscan soup) here is a heightened experience, especially when accompanied by an affordable glass of red. The short menu includes assorted crostini, sensational vegetables marinated in oil, cheese plates, and an earthy *polpettone* (meat loaf). This one-room restaurant, seating about 30, is part of a Renaissance palazzo. ✉ *Piaggia San Martino 8* ☎ *0575/352035* ▭ *MC, V* ⊙ *Closed Wed.*

$$ ✕▦ **Castello di Gargonza.** Enchantment reigns at this tiny 13th-century hamlet in the countryside near Monte San Savino, part of the fiefdom of the aristocratic Florentine Guicciardini and restored by the modern Count Roberto Guicciardini as a way to rescue a dying village. A castle, church, and cobbled streets set the stage. A minimum two-night stay in any of the rooms is appreciated; apartments (sleeping 2–10 people) rent Saturday to Saturday. La Torre restaurant serves local fare, such as *zuppa di porcini* (a thick puree of porcini mushrooms). Follow with any of the superb grilled meats. Regional wines are well represented. ✉ *52048 Monte San Savino* ☎ *0575/847021* ▱ *0575/847054* ⊕ *www.gargonza. it* ⌨ *18 rooms, 11 apartments, 1 suite* ⌂ *Restaurant, minibars, pool, meeting room; no a/c, no room TVs* ▭ *AE, DC, MC, V* ⊙ *Closed 3 wks in Jan. and 3 wks in Nov. Restaurant closed Tues.* ⓞⅼ *BP.*

★ $ ▦ **Calcione Country and Castle.** The elegant Marchesa Olivella Lotteringhi della Stufa has turned her six-centuries-old family homestead into comfortable rental apartments. Think sophisticated rustic: many of the apartments have open fireplaces. The houses have a private pool (the apartments share the estate pool), and there are two nearby lakes for fishing and swimming. A stay here is restorative, since it's blissfully quiet. Calcione is convenient to Arezzo, Siena, San Gimignano, and the delights of Umbria. A one-week minimum stay is mandatory. ✉ *Lucignano, 52046* ☎ *0575/837100* ▱ *0575/837153* ⊕ *www.calcione.com* ⌨ *2 houses, 7 apartments* ⌂ *BBQ, 3 pools, lake, babysitting, some pets allowed; no a/c, no fans in some rooms, no room TVs, no room phones* ▭ *No credit cards* ⊙ *Closed Nov.–Mar.* ⓞⅼ *EP.*

Shopping

On the first Sunday of each month a colorful flea market with antiques and other less-precious objects for sale takes place in the **Piazza Grande.**

GOLD Gold production here is on an industrial scale. Uno-A-Erre is the largest of several factories supplying local shops. **Prosperi** (✉ Corso Italia 76 ☎ 0575/20746) works wonders in gold, silver, and platinum.

OUTLET MALLS Savvy shoppers head to the **Prada outlet** (✉ Località Levanella, SS69, Montevarchi, 29 km [18 mi] west of Arezzo ☎ 055/91901) for discounted Prada products. Go during the week—if a weekend is your only option,

9

remember that patience is a virtue. If you're on an outlet roll, continue north to **The Mall** (⊠ Via Europa 8, Leccio Reggello, 52 km [33 mi] northwest of Arezzo ☎ 055/8657775 ⊕ www.outlet-firenze.com), where discounts on lines such as Gucci, Yves Saint Laurent, Armani, Sergio Rossi—to name but a few—abound.

TEXTILES   At **Busatti** (⊠ Corso Italia 48 ☎ 0575/355295 ⊕ www.busatti.com), the Busatti-Sassolini family has been making sumptuous handwoven linen, wool, hemp, and cotton since 1842. Look for hand-stitched hems, embroideries, and lace.

Cortona

㉞ *29 km (18 mi) south of Arezzo, 79 km (44 mi) east of Siena, 117 km (73 mi) southeast of Florence.*

With olive trees and vineyards creeping up to its walls, pretty Cortona—popularized by Frances Mayes's *Under the Tuscan Sun*—commands sweeping views over Lake Trasimeno and the plain of the Valdichiana. Its two galleries and churches are rarely visited; its delightful medieval streets are a pleasure to wander for their own sake. The heart of town is formed by Piazza della Repubblica and the adjacent Piazza Signorelli, which both contain pleasant shops to browse through.

Cortona is considered one of Italy's oldest towns—popularly known as the "Mother of Troy and Grandmother of Rome." Tradition claims that it was founded by Dardanus, also the founder of Troy (after whom the Dardanelles were named). He was fighting a local tribe, so the story goes, when he lost his helmet (*corythos* in Greek) on Cortona's hill. In time a town grew up that took its name (Corito) from the missing headgear. By the 5th century BC the Etruscans had built the first set of town walls, whose cyclopean traces can still be seen in the 3-km (2-mi) sweep of the present fortifications.

The **Museo Diocesano** (Diocesan Museum) houses an impressive number of large and splendid paintings by native son Luca Signorelli, as well as a stunning *Annunciation* by Fra Angelico, a delightful surprise in this small town. ⊠ *Piazza del Duomo 1* ☎ *0575/637235* ⊠ €5 ⊗ *Nov.–Mar., Tues.–Sun. 10–5; Apr.–Oct., Tues.–Sun. 10–7.*

Where to Stay & Eat

$ ✕ **Osteria del Teatro.** Walls filled with photographs of theater stars provide the backdrop for a two-room restaurant much frequented by locals. They come for good reason: the food here is tasty and abundant. If you're lucky enough to be around during truffle season (fall and early winter), start with the *fonduta al tartufo* (truffle fondue), in this case made with melted pecorino served with little toast squares. The *fagottini di pollo con carciofi* (chicken-stuffed pasta) proves that it's possible to have divine, dairy-free filled pasta. ⊠ *Via Maffei 2, off Piazza del Teatro* ☎ *0575/ 630556* ⊟ *AE, DC, MC, V* ⊗ *Closed Wed. and 2 wks in Nov.*

$$$$ ✕🏠 **Il Falconiere.** The husband-and-wife team of Riccardo and Silvia
FodorśChoice   Baracchi run a hotel with rooms in an 18th-century villa, just minutes
★   outside Cortona. Suites are in the *chiesetta* (little church) that once belonging to an obscure 19th-century Italian poet and hunter. You can also

stay in the very private Le Vigne del Falco building at the end of the property, where suites have individual entrances and grand views of the plain. The restaurant's inventive menu is complemented by a wine list that's the product of Silvia's sommelier training. By all means sample their estate-produced olive oil. Weeklong cooking classes are available. ⊠ *Località San Martino 370, 52044* ☎ *0575/612679* 🖷 *0575/612927* ⊕ *www.ilfalconiere.com* ⇌ *13 rooms, 6 suites* ⌂ *Restaurant, room service, in-room safes, minibars, cable TV, in-room data ports, 2 pools, bar, babysitting, dry cleaning, laundry service, concierge, free parking, some pets allowed (fee), no-smoking rooms* ⊟ *AE, MC, V* ⊗ *Closed 3 wks in Jan. Restaurant closed Mon. Nov.–Mar.* ⦿ *BP.*

SOUTHERN TUSCANY

Along the roads leading south from Siena, soft green olive groves give way to a blanket of oak, cypress, and reddish-brown earth. Towns are small and as old as the hills. The scruffy mountain landscapes of Monte Amiata make up some of the wildest parts of Tuscany, and once you're across the mountains the terrain is still full of cliffs, like the one the town of Pitigliano perches on. Southern Tuscany has good wine (try Brunello di Montalcino or the exceptional, lesser-known Morellino di Scansano for a true treat), thermal baths at Saturnia, and Etruscan ruins.

Abbazia di Monte Oliveto Maggiore

35 *52 km (32 mi) southeast of Cortona, 37 km (23 mi) southeast of Siena.*

This Benedictine abbey, Tuscany's most visited religious house, is an oasis of olive and cypress trees amid the harsh landscape of a zone known as the Crete, where erosion has sculpted the hills starkly, laying open barren rock amid lush farmland. Surrounded by thick woodlands in the deep-cut hills south of Siena, it is accessible by car but not easily reached by bus.

Olivetans, or "White Benedictines," founded the abbey in 1313; this breakaway group sought to return to the simple ideals of the early Benedictine order. The monastery's mellow brick buildings in one of Tuscany's most striking landscapes protect a treasure or two. Only portions of the park and the main cloister are open to the public. In the main cloister, frescoes by Luca Signorelli and Sodoma depict scenes from the life of St. Benedict with earthy realism, a quality that came easily to Sodoma, described by Vasari as "a merry and licentious man of scant chastity." The wooden choir, with its intarsia designs, is an understated work of art that dates from 1503 to 1505. The monks make herbal liqueurs on-site. ⊠ *SS451 south of Asciano* ☎ *0577/707611* ⊗ *Daily 9:15–noon and 3:15–5:45.*

Montepulciano

36 *36 km (22 mi) southeast of Monte Oliveto Maggiore, 64 km (40 mi) southeast of Siena.*

Perched high on a hilltop, Montepulciano is made up of a cluster of Renaissance buildings set within a circle of cypress trees. At an altitude of

Bacchus in Tuscany

Tuscany produces some of Italy's finest wines. Here's a primer to help you navigate the region's wine lists, as well as its wine roads.

VARIETIES

The name **Chianti** evokes Tuscany as readily as gondolas evoke Venice, but if you think Chianti is about straw-covered jugs and deadly headaches, think again. This firm, full-bodied wine pressed from mostly Sangiovese grapes is the region's most popular, and it's easy to taste why. More difficult to understand is the difference between the many kinds of Chianti: there are seven subregions, including Chianti Classico, the oldest, whose wines have a *gallo nero* (black rooster) on the label. Each subregion has its own peculiarities, but the most noticeable—and costly—difference is between regular Chianti and the *riserva* stock, aged at least four years.

Beginning in the 1970s, some winemakers, chafing at the strict regulations for making Chianti, chose to buck tradition and blend their wines in innovative ways. Thus was born the **Super Tuscan** (a name coined by American journalists). These pricey, French oak-aged wines continue to be the toast of Tuscany.

The Etruscans were making wine in Montepulciano before the days of ancient Rome. **Vino Nobile di Montepulciano,** the "Noble Wine," gained its title by virtue of royal patronage: in 1669, England's William III sent a delegation to procure the highly regarded wine. Less noble but no less popular is **Rosso di Montepulciano,** a light, fruity red.

With its velvety black berries and structured tannins, **Brunello di Montalcino** is just as sophisticated as Vino Nobile. The strain of Sangiovese grape used to make it was developed in 1870 by a winemaker in need of vines that could cope with windy weather. The resulting wine was a hit. Brunello has a younger sibling, **Rosso di Montepulciano.**

Not all of Tuscany's great wines are reds; in fact, many give top honors to a white wine, **Vernaccia di San Gimignano.** This golden wine is made from grapes native to Liguria. Its name is thought to be a corruption of Vernazza, one of the Cinque Terre villages.

WINERY VISITS

The SS222 (aka the Strada Chiantigiana) running through the heart of Chianti and other Strade del Vino (Wine Roads) throughout the region will lead you to an abundance of producers. You can do preliminary research at www.terreditoscana. region.toscana.it (click on "Strade del Vino"). When you're on the ground, visit any tourist information center in wine country (Greve, Montalcino, and Montepulciano are the best places to start) for maps and guidance. Then hit the road. Many wineries—especially smaller producers—offer free tastings without an appointment. Larger producers usually charge a small fee for a three-glass tasting, and sometimes require a reservation for a tour. Remember: always have a designated driver. Vineyards are usually off narrow, curving roads. Sobriety is a must.

almost 2,000 feet, it's cool in summer and chilled in winter by biting winds that sweep the spiraling streets. Vino Nobile di Montepulciano, a robust red wine, is justifiably the town's greatest claim to fame. You can sample it in various wineshops and bars lining the twisting roads, as well as in most restaurants. The town is 13 km (8 mi) west of the A1 highway.

Montepulciano has an unusually harmonious look, the result of the work of three architects, Michelozzo (1396–1472), Antonio da Sangallo il Vecchio (circa 1455–1534), and Giacomo da Vignola (1507–73), who graced it with palaces and churches in an attempt to impose Renaissance architectural ideals on an ancient Tuscan hill town. The pièce de résistance is the **Piazza Grande,** a wide expanse of urban space lined with 15th-century family palazzi and the equally grand, but facadeless, Duomo. On the hillside below the town walls is the church of **San Biagio,** designed by Sangallo, a paragon of Renaissance architectural perfection considered to be his masterpiece. ⊠ *Via di San Biagio* ☎ *0578/ 7577761* ☉ *Daily 9–12:30 and 3:30–7:30.*

Where to Stay & Eat

★ $$$ ✕ **La Grotta.** You might be tempted to walk by La Grotta's innocuous entrance across the street from the Tempio di San Biagio (Church of San Biagio). Don't—the food is fantastic. The *tagliolini con carciofi e rigatino* (thin noodles with artichokes and bacon) is superb, as is the tagliatelle *di grano saraceno con asparagi e zucchine* (with asparagus and zucchini). Follow with any of the wonderful secondi, and wash it down with the local wine, which just happens to be one of Italy's finest—Vino Nobile di Montepulciano. ⊠ *Località San Biagio* ☎ *0578/757479* 🖃 *AE, MC, V* ☉ *Closed Wed. and Jan. 8–Feb. 28.*

★ $$$$ ✕🏠 **Locanda dell'Amorosa.** A 14th-century hamlet with its own chapel has been transformed into a romantic, refined place to rest your head. A cypress-lined drive leads to the main gate of this country inn outside Sinalunga. Owners Carlo and Alessandra Citterio live on-site and tend to every detail. Some rooms have stunning views, others a private garden or terrace; all are decorated with sumptuous fabrics. Color dominates the lusciously landscaped grounds in spring and summer. The restaurant, former horse stables, has candlelit tables, stone walls, and a menu grounded in Tuscan classics. ⊠ *Località Amorosa west of Valdichiana exit off A1, 53048 Sinalunga, 17 km (11 mi) north of Montepulciano* ☎ *0577/677211* 🖶 *0577/632001* ⊕ *www.amorosa.it* ⤳ *17 rooms, 8 suites* ⚑ *Restaurant, room service, in-room safes, minibars, cable TV, in-room data ports, pool, mountain bikes, wine bar, babysitting, dry cleaning, laundry service, concierge, meeting rooms, no-smoking rooms* 🖃 *AE, DC, MC, V* ☉ *Closed Jan. and Feb.* ⦿❙ *EP.*

$$$ 🏠 **Villa Poggiano.** Two kilometers (1 mi) west of Montepulciano's historic center, a delightful, intimate 18th-century villa has been lovingly restored by the Savini family and turned into a bed-and-breakfast. Though the villa is definitely in the country (a winding, narrow unpaved road takes you there), there's nothing rustic about the decor. This is sweet luxury all the way—tumbled marble tiles, rich upholstered headboards, hand-painted details, fluffy bathrobes. Most rooms are suites; enjoy the blissful silence while ensconced on your divan. A staff beautician gives manicures and massages by appointment. ⊠ *Va di Poggiano 7, 53045*

☎ 0578/758292 📠 0578/715635 ⊕ *www.villapoggiano.com* 🛏 *3 rooms, 6 suites* ♺ *In-room safes, minibars, cable TV, in-room data ports, pool, dry cleaning, laundry service, free parking, no-smoking rooms; no kids under 12* ▭ *MC, V* ⊘ *Closed Nov. 5–Mar.* †⊙† *BP.*

$$–$$$ 🏠 **Montorio.** A cluster of five apartments perched 1,980 feet above sea level, with a commanding view of San Biagio below, provides the perfect mix of country and city life. Each apartment, sleeping from two to four, is self-catering and has its own separate entrance. A housekeeper comes every day except Sunday to clean the kitchen and make the beds; a home-baked breakfast cake awaits you upon arrival. Stays usually run Saturday to Saturday, but three-night stays may be arranged. ✉ *Strada per Pienza 2, 53045* ☎ 0578/717442 📠 0578/715456 ⊕ *www.montorio. com* 🛏 *5 apartments* ♺ *Picnic area, some fans, kitchens, refrigerators, cable TV, massage, laundry facilities, free parking; no a/c* ▭ *AE, DC, MC, V* ⊘ *Closed Dec. 15–Jan. 31* †⊙† *EP.*

Nightlife & the Arts

The **Cantiere Internazionale d'Arte** (✉ Piazza Grande 7 ☎ 0578/757341 for tourist information office), held in July and August, is a festival of art, music, and theater, ending with a major theatrical production in Piazza Grande. The tourist office has information on scheduling and events.

Pienza

㊲ *15 km (9 mi) east of Montepulciano, 52 km (32 mi) southeast of Siena.*

Pienza owes its urban design to Pope Pius II, who had grand plans to transform his home village of Corsignano—the town's former name—into a model Renaissance town. The man entrusted with the project was Bernardo Rossellino (1409–64), a protégé of the great Renaissance architectural theorist Leon Battista Alberti (1404–74). His mandate was to create a cathedral, a papal palace, and a town hall (plus miscellaneous other buildings) that adhered to the humanist pope's principles. The result was a project that expressed Renaissance ideals of art, architecture, and civilized good living in a single scheme: it stands as a fine example of the architectural canon that Alberti formulated in the 15th century and emulated in many of Italy's finest buildings and piazzas. Today the cool nobility of Pienza's center seems almost surreal in this otherwise unpretentious village, though at times it can seem overwhelmed by the tourists it attracts. Pienza's pecorino, a sheep's-milk cheese, is a superior gastronomic experience.

The **Palazzo Piccolomini,** the seat of Pius II's papal court, was designed by Rossellino in 1459, using Florence's Palazzo Rucellai by Alberti as a model. You can visit the papal apartments, including a library, as well as the **Sala delle Armi,** with an impressive weapons collection. Look for the extravagant wooden ceiling in the music room. ✉ *Piazza Pio II* ☎ 0578/748503 🎟 *€3.50* ⊘ *Guided tours Tues.–Sun. 10–noon and 3–5:30. Closed 2nd half of Feb., mid-Nov.–mid. Dec.*

The interior of the **Duomo** is simple but richly decorated with paintings from the Sienese school. Begun in 1459 and finished in a record three years' time, the facade is divided into three parts. Renaissance pilasters

Sorry, Vasari

For many people, Tuscan art begins and ends with the art of Florence. There's no debating that Florence is littered with masterpieces, but the city's exalted status is due in no small part to the biases of Giorgio Vasari (1511–74), whose seminal book *Lives of the Artists* glorified the works of the Florentines above all others. In fact, even if Florence didn't exist, Tuscany would still be a place of phenomenal artistic achievement with a crucial role in the Renaissance. A few cases in point: Nicola Pisano (circa 1215/20–1278/84) carved a groundbreaking pulpit in Pisa, then worked with his son Giovanni on another in Siena. Giovanni carried the tradition to Pistoia. Ambrogio Lorenzetti (documented 1319–48) produced wonderful frescoes representing good and bad government in the Palazzo Pubblico in Siena. The frescoes of the *Legend of the True Cross* by Piero della Francesca (circa 1420–92) in Arezzo are among the 15th century's most stunning achievements. And Aeneas Silvius Piccolomini (1405–64), later Pope Pius II, carried out his vision of Renaissance ideals on a citywide scale in Pienza, his hometown.

on the facade draw attention to the pope's coat of arms encircled by a wreath of fruit, the papal tiara, and keys above it. ⊠ *Piazza Pio II* ☉ *Daily 8:30–1 and 2:30–7.*

Where to Stay & Eat

$–$$ ✕ **La Porta.** Montichiello is a hamlet minutes away from Pienza, where this wine bar is basically the only show in town. But what a show it is— from start to finish, the food is delicious. The menu changes regularly, but you can always count on top-quality cheeses (pecorino di Pienza, among others) and lively pasta dishes such as *tagliolini alla chianina* (thin noodles with a hearty minced-beef sauce). Second courses are just as strong; if rabbit's on the menu, don't miss it. Reservations are a good idea, especially in summer. ⊠ *Off SP88, Montichiello* ☎ *0578/755163* ⌁ *Reservations essential* ▤ *MC, V* ☉ *Closed Thurs. and Jan. 10–31.*

$ ✕ **La Chiocciola.** Enjoy typical Pienza fare, including homemade pici with hare or wild boar sauce, at a no-frills trattoria a few minutes' walk from the historic center. La Chiocciola's take on *formaggio in forno* (baked cheese), with assorted accompaniments such as fresh porcini mushrooms, is reason enough to come. ⊠ *Via Mencattelli 4* ☎ *0578/748683* ▤ *MC, V* ☉ *Closed Wed. and Jan.*

★ $–$$ ▦ **La Foce.** The former estate of noted Anglo-American historian Iris Origo and her husband, Antonio, has become an agriturismo with various farmhouses and apartments scattered about the property. Furnishings have a simple, rustic style—wood farm tables, sponged walls—and there are extraordinary views of rolling hills. Kitchens come fully equipped, and some of the rooms have working fireplaces. If you're searching for peace and quiet, look no further. From May through October, a minimum one-week stay is obligatory. ⊠ *Strada della Vittoria 61, Chianciano Terme, 53042* ☎☎ *0578/69101* ⊕ *www.lafoce.com* ⇗ *9 apartments, 6 farmhouses* ⚹ *Fans, kitchens, refrigerators, cable TV in*

9

some rooms, tennis court, 8 pools, playground, laundry facilities, laundry service, free parking; no a/c ⊟ *MC, V* ⦿ *EP.*

Montalcino

㊳ *24 km (15 mi) west of Pienza, 41 km (25 mi) south of Siena.*

Another medieval hill town with a special claim to fame, Montalcino is the source for Brunello di Montalcino, one of Italy's most esteemed red wines. You can sample it in wine cellars in town or visit one of the nearby wineries for a guided tour and tasting; you must call ahead for reservations—your hotel or the local tourist office can help with arrangements.

In the very heart of the centro storico is **Alle Logge,** a sophisticated wine bar where selections by the glass always include a significant Brunello. ⊠ *Piazza del Popolo* ☎ *0577/846186.*

The 14th-century **La Fortezza** has a tower you can climb and an enoteca for tasting wines. ⊠ *Via Panfilo dell'Oca* ☎ *0577/849211* 🎟 *€3.50* ⊙ *Nov.–Mar., weekdays 9–6, weekends 9–7:30; Apr.–Oct., daily 9–8.*

A Montalcino winery worth visiting is **Fattoria dei Barbi e del Casato.** The cellars date back to the 17th century. ⊠ *Località Podernuovi* ☎ *0577/ 841200* ⊕ *www.fattoriadeibarbi.it* 🎟 *Free* ⊙ *Weekdays 10–1 and 2:30–6.*

Where to Stay & Eat

$$$$ ✕ **Poggio Antico.** One of Italy's renowned chefs, Roberto Minnetti, abandoned his highly successful restaurant in Rome and moved to the country outside Montalcino. Now he and his wife, Patrizia, serve Tuscan cuisine masterfully interpreted by Roberto in a relaxed but regal dining room with arches and beam ceilings. The seasonal menu includes *pappardelle al ragù di agnello* (flat, wide noodles in a lamb sauce) and venison in a sweet-and-sour sauce. ⊠ *Località I Poggi, 4 km (2½ mi) southwest of Montalcino on road to Grosseto* ☎ *0577/849200* ⊟ *MC, V* ⊙ *Closed Mon. Nov.–Mar. and 20 days in Jan. No dinner Sun. Nov.–Mar.*

Abbazia di Sant'Antimo

★ ㊴ *10 km (6 mi) south of Montalcino, 51 km (32 mi) south of Siena.*

The pale stone of the 12th-century abbey sits amid the silvery green of an olive grove, making this Romanesque gem well worth a visit. The exterior and interior sculpture is outstanding, particularly the nave capitals, a combination of French, Lombard, and Spanish influences. According to legend, the **sacristy** (rarely open) formed part of the primitive Carolingian church (founded in AD 781), its entrance flanked by 9th-century pilasters. The small **vaulted crypt** dates from the same period. An unusual element is the ambulatory, with three radiating chapels (rare in Italian churches) that were probably copied from the French model. Throughout the day the monks fill this magnificent space with Gregorian chant. ⊠ *Castelnuovo dell'Abate* ☎ *0577/835659* ⊕ *www.antimo. it* ⊙ *Mon.–Sat. 10:15–12:30 and 3–5:30; Sun. 9:15–10:45 and 3–5.*

Abbazia di San Galgano

★ ⓐ *80 km (49 mi) northwest of the Abbazia di Sant'Antimo, 33 km (20 mi) southwest of Siena.*

This Gothic cathedral missing its roof is a hauntingly beautiful sight. The church was built in the late 12th century by Cistercian monks, who modeled it after churches built by their order in France. Starting in the 15th century it fell into ruin, declining gradually over the centuries. Grass has grown through the floor, and the roof and glass windows are gone. What's left of its facade and walls makes a grandiose and desolate picture. Behind it, a short climb up a hill brings you to the charming little church of San Galgano, with frescoes by Ambrogio Lorenzetti (active 1319–48), as well as a famous sword of local legend. As the story goes, Galgano, a medieval knight, had an epiphany on this spot and gave up fighting. He thrust his sword into a stone, where it remains to this day.

> **WORD OF MOUTH**
>
> "San Galgano is beautiful and worth the trip. A very romantic setting."
>
> —Nutella

Saturnia

④ *130 km (81 mi) southeast of Pimbino, 129 km (77 mi) south of Siena.*

Etruscan and pre-Etruscan tombs cut into the local rock can be seen in this town, a lively center in pre-Etruscan times. Today it is known for its hot sulfur thermal waters. You can soak for free at the tiered natural thermal pools of **Cascate del Gorello,** which get very crowded in August. ⊠ *2 km (1 mi) east on road to Montemerano* ☎ *No phone.*

There are four hot-spring pools at the **Terme di Saturnia**; it's attached to the hotel of the same name. ⊠ *Strada Saturnia–Pitigliano, 3 km (2 mi) east toward Montemerano* ☎ *0564/601061* ⊕ *www.saturnia-terme.it* ☑ *Full day €16, half day €12* ☉ *May–Sept., daily 9:30–7:30; Oct.–Apr., daily 9:30–5:30.*

Where to Stay & Eat

$$$$ ╳ **Da Caino.** Specialties include tomatoes and peppers on crisp phyllo dough, lasagna with pumpkin, and hearty dishes like *cinghiale lardolato con olive* (wild boar larded with olives) at this exceptional restaurant in the town of Montemerano. Prices are among the highest in the region; locals consider it a serious splurge. ⊠ *Via della Chiesa 4, Montemerano, 7 km (4½ mi) south of Saturnia* ☎ *0564/602817* ╱ *Reservations essential* ⊟ *AE, DC, MC, V* ☉ *Closed Wed., and Jan. and Feb. No dinner Thurs.*

$$–$$$ ╳ **I Due Cippi–Da Michele.** Owner Michele Aniello has a terrific restaurant with a lengthy and creative menu. Emphasis is placed on southern Tuscan specialties such as wild boar and duck—though there are other options as well; try the *tortelli di castagne al seme di finocchio*

9

(chestnut-stuffed tortelli with butter sauce and fennel seeds). In good weather you can enjoy your meal on a terrace overlooking the town's main square. ✉ *Piazza Veneto 26/a* ☎ *0564/601074* ♨ *Reservations essential* ▤ *AE, DC, MC, V* ⊗ *Closed Tues. Oct.–June, Dec. 20–26, and Jan. 10–25.*

$$$$ ⊞ **Terme di Saturnia.** Roam elegant public rooms in your bathrobe (provided in every room) between beauty treatments or on your way to take a dip into the 37.5°C (99.5°F) sulfurous thermal pools. Guest rooms have cherry-stained wood furnishings. Half and full board are options and should be considered, as the on-site restaurant is good. The multilingual staff can be helpful. ✉ *Strada Saturnia–Pitigliano, 3 km (2 mi) east toward Montemerano, 58050 Sinalunga* ☎ *0564/ 601061* ☏ *0564/601266* ⊕ *www.termedisaturnia.it* ⇆ *140 rooms, 10 suites* ⚴ *Restaurant, snack bar, room service, in-room safes, minibars, cable TV with movies, some in-room VCRs, in-room data ports, driving range, tennis court, 2 pools, 2 wading pools, health club, hair salon, sauna, spa, steam room, bar, piano bar, shops, dry cleaning, laundry facilities, concierge, helipad, some pets allowed* ▤ *AE, DC, MC, V* ⦿| *BP.*

$ ⊞ **Villa Garden.** Each of the nine rooms is charmingly furnished with comfortable beds, floral curtains and bedspreads, and tiled bathrooms. A few minutes from the center of town, it's a perfect place to stay if you want to take the waters without breaking the bank. The buffet breakfast is good and filling, the staff courteous and efficient. ✉ *Via Sterpeti 56, 58014* ☎☏*0564/601182* ⊕*www.laltramaremma.it/villa garden* ⇆9 *rooms* ⚴ *Minibars, cable TV, in-room data ports, bar, free parking, some pets allowed; no a/c in some rooms* ▤ *AE, DC, MC, V* ⦿| *BP.*

TUSCANY ESSENTIALS

Transportation

BY AIR

The largest airports in the region are Pisa's Aeroporto Galileo Galilei and Florence's Aeroporto Amerigo Vespucci, known as Peretola, which connects to Amsterdam, Brussels, Frankfurt, London, Munich, and Paris.

🖪 Airport Information **Aeroporto Galileo Galilei** ☎ 050/849300 ⊕ www.pisa-airport.com. **Peretola** ✉ 10 km [6 mi] northwest of Florence ☎ 055/315874 ⊕ www.airport.florence.it.

BY BUS

SENA connects Rome with Siena on several scheduled daily trips. When traveling to Tuscany from elsewhere in Italy, the train is almost always a better option than the bus; buses are subject to the vagaries of road traffic, and the seats are narrow and cramped.

Within Tuscany, bus service between towns is conducted primarily by two private companies, Tra-In and Lazzi.

🖪 Bus Information **CPT (Compagnia Pisana Trasporti)** ✉ Piazza Sant'Antonio 1, Pisa ☎☏ 050/505511 ⊕ www.cpt.pisa.it. **Lazzi Eurolines** ✉ Via Mercante 2, Florence

☎ 055/363041 ⊕ www.lazzi.it. **SENA** ⊠ Piazza Gramsci, Siena ☎ 0577/283203 🖨 0577/40731 ⊕ www.sena.it. **Tra-In** ⊠ Statale 73, Levante 23, Due Ponti, Siena ☎ 0577/204111.

BY CAR

The Autostrada del Sole (A1), northern and central Italy's major north–south highway, connects Florence with Bologna, 105 km (65 mi) to the north, and beyond that with Milan. Rome is 277 km (172 mi) south of Florence via the A1.

Within Tuscany, the cities west of Florence are easily reached by the A11, which leads to Lucca and then to the sea. The A1 takes you south from Florence to Arezzo and Chiusi (where you turn off for Montepulciano). Florence and Siena are connected by a superstrada and also the panoramic SS222, which threads through Chianti wine country. The hill towns north and west of Siena lie along superstrade and winding local roads—all are well marked, but you should still arm yourself with a good map.

Drivers should be prepared to navigate through suburban sprawl around Pisa and Arezzo, and to a lesser degree Lucca and Cortona; to reach the historic centers where most sights are, look for the CENTRO signs. In many small towns you must park outside the city walls.

EMERGENCY SERVICES If you have a breakdown on the autostrada, or any toll road, you will find along the side of the road "SOS" boxes placed every couple of kilometers. You push a button on the box, a green light pops on, and help is sent—you don't actually talk to a person. If you are on other roads, call ACI, the Italian Auto Club.
🚗 **ACI** ☎ 803/116.

BY TRAIN

Italy's main rail line, which runs from Milan in the north to Calabria in the toe of the boot, links Florence to Rome, Bologna, and numerous other Italian cities. Within Tuscany, trains on this line stop in Prato, Arezzo, and Chiusi as well as Florence. Another major line connects Florence with Pisa, and the coastal line between Rome and Genoa passes through Pisa and the Tuscan beach resorts (which, though popular with locals, aren't counted among the region's allures). There's also regular, nearly hourly service from Florence to Lucca via Prato, Pistoia, and Montecatini. If you want to visit other areas of Tuscany—Chianti, Montalcino, and Montepulciano, for example—you are better off going by bus or by car. Train stations in these towns, when they exist, are far from the historic centers, run infrequently, and are slow. Visit the Web site of FS, the Italian State Railway, for schedules and booking.
🚆 **Train Information FS** ☎ 892021 ⊕ www.trenitalia.com.

Contacts & Resources

EMERGENCIES

Pharmacies stay open at off-hours on a rotating basis. To find out who's open, check the schedule posted in all pharmacy windows.
🚑 **Ambulance, medical emergency** ☎ 118. **Police, fire** ☎ 113.

TOURS

From Florence, American Express operates one-day excursions to Siena and San Gimignano and can arrange for cars, drivers, and guides for special-interest tours in Tuscany.

⚡ Fees & Schedules **American Express** ✉ Via Dante Alighieri 22/r, Florence ☎ 055/50981.

VISITOR INFORMATION

⚡ Agritourist Information **Terranostra** ✉ Villa Demidoff 64/d, 50122 Florence ☎ 055/3245011 ⊕ www.terranostra.it.

⚡ Tourist Information **Arezzo** ✉ Piazza della Repubblica 28 ☎ 0575/377678 ⊕ www.apt.arezzo.it. **Colle Val d'Elsa** ✉ Via F. Campana 43 ☎ 0577/922791. **Cortona** ✉ Via Nazionale 42 ☎ 0575/630352 ⊕ www.cortonaweb.net. **Greve in Chianti** ✉ Piazza Ferrante Mori 1 ☎ 055/8546299 ⊕ www.chiantislowtravel.it. **Lucca** ✉ Piazza Santa Maria 35 ☎ 0583/919931 ⊕ www.luccatourist.it. **Montalcino** ✉ Costa del Municipio 1 ☎ 0577/849331 ⊕ www.prolocomontalcino.it. **Montepulciano** ✉ Piazza Don Minzoni 1 ☎ 0578/757341 ⊕ www.prolocomontepulciano.it. **Pienza** ✉ Corso Rossellino 51 ☎ 0578/8749071. **Pisa** ✉ Piazza del Duomo ☎ 050/560464 ⊕ www.pisa.turismo.toscana.it. **Pistoia** ✉ Palazzo dei Vescovi, Via Roma 1 ☎ 0573/21622 ⊕ www.pistoia.turismo.toscana.it. **Prato** ✉ Piazza delle Carceri 15 ☎ 0574/24112 ⊕ www.prato.turismo.toscana.it. **Radda in Chianti** ✉ Piazza Castello 1 ☎ 0577/738494. **San Gimignano** ✉ Piazza del Duomo 1 ☎ 0577/940008 ⊕ www.sangimignano.com. **San Miniato** ✉ Piazza del Popolo 1 ☎ 0571/42745 ⊕ www.cittadisanminiato.it. **Siena** ✉ Piazza del Campo 56 ☎ 0577/280551 ⊕ www.terresiena.it; www.comune.siena.it. **Volterra** ✉ Piazza dei Priori 20 ☎ 0588/87257 ⊕ www.volterratour.it.

Umbria &
the Marches

Norcia

WORD OF MOUTH

"I would suggest the Marches as a great, off-the-beaten-path region to visit. It has a very beautiful landscape and is just as central as Tuscany and Umbria (although, unlike Umbria, it has a coastline, and a nice one at that)."

–Jackie in Italy

WELCOME TO UMBRIA & THE MARCHES

Todi

TOP 5
Reasons to Go

1 **Palazzo Ducale, Urbino:** A visit here reveals more about the ideals of the Renaissance than a shelfful of history books.

2 **Assisi, shrine to St. Francis:** Recharge your soul in this rose-color hill town with a visit to the gentle saint's majestic Basilica, adorned with great frescoes.

3 **Spoleto, Umbria's musical Mecca:** Crowds may descend and prices ascend here during summer's Festival dei Due Mondi, but Spoleto's hushed charm enchants year-round.

4 **Tantalizing truffles:** Are Umbria's celebrated "black diamonds" coveted for their pungent flavor, their rarity, or their power in the realm of romance?

5 **Orvieto's Duomo:** Arresting visions of heaven and hell on the facade and brilliant frescoes within make this Gothic cathedral a dazzler.

Many Umbrian towns are set atop hills, providing magnificent views—none more so than from Assisi—sanctified by St. Francis—and from the Piazza della Signoria in medieval Gubbio, the "City of Silence."

Umbria's largest town, Perugia, is easily reachable from Rome, Siena, or Florence. Home to some of Perugino's great frescoes and a hilltop *centro storico*, it is also beloved by chocoholics: "Kisses"—the hazelnut Baci candies—were born here.

In southern Umbria, the town of **Orvieto** is famed for its cathedral, its dry white wines, and its spectacular hilltop location. To the east is the village of **Todi,** another historic jewel.

TUSCANY

Sansepolcro

Città Di Castello

E45

Lago Di Trasimeno

Perugia

71

UMBRIA

448

Todi

A1

Orvieto

LAZIO

Duomo , Orvieto   Perugia

Getting Oriented

Central Italy doesn't begin and end with Tuscany; the pastoral, hilly provinces of Umbria and the Marches pick up where the more famous neighbor leaves off. Divided by the Apennine range, both regions are studded with Renaissance-era villages and fortresses—a landscape hallowed by St. Francis and immortalized in the works of native son Raphael.

The steep, twisting roads of the **Marches** lead to well-preserved medieval towns before settling down to the sandy beaches of the Adriatic. Here you'll find **Urbino**, the best surviving example of the ideal Renaissance city.

Spoleto offers much more than Puccini on its Piazza del Duomo every summer: there are Filippo Lippi frescoes in the cathedral, a massive castle towering over the town, and a bridge across the neighboring valley that's an engineering marvel.

Filippo Lippi's frescoes, Spoleto

Ascoli Piceno

UMBRIA & THE MARCHES PLANNER

Making the Most of Your Time

Umbria is a nicely compact collection of character-rich hill towns; you can settle in one, then explore the others, as well as the countryside and forest in between, on day trips.

Perugia, Umbria's largest and most lively city, is a logical choice for your base, particularly if you're arriving from the north. If you want something a little quieter, virtually any other town in the region will suit your purposes; even Assisi, which overflows with bus tours during the day, is delightfully quiet in the evening and early morning. Spoleto and Orvieto are the most developed town to the south, but they're still of modest proportions.

If you have the time to venture farther afield, consider trips to Gubbio, northeast of Perugia, and Urbino, in the Marches. Both are worth the time it takes to reach them, and both make for pleasant overnight stays. In southern Umbria, Valnerina and the Piano Grande are out-of-the-way spots with the region's best hiking.

Getting Around

Umbria and the Marches are mountainous regions divided by the Apennines, Italy's backbone. The main geographic difference is that Umbria's valleys run north to south, while those in the Marches run east to west. As a result, travel through Umbria is much easier in a north–south direction; in the Marches, the only easy going north to south is along the coast. Crossing from valley to valley in either region involves slow, winding, sometimes treacherous roads that can occasionally be closed by snow in December and January.

Buses run throughout the region, but some routes in rural areas, especially in the Marches, are designed to serve as many destinations as possible, making for a slow trip. There's frequent train service to Orvieto (which is on the main Florence-Rome line), Perugia, and Assisi, and many towns are accessible on regional lines—though Gubbio and Urbino are not. For more about car, bus, and train travel, see "Essentials" at the end of this chapter.

What to Bring Home: Umbrian Ceramics

The most celebrated Umbrian export (and souvenir) is pottery, and Deruta, south of Torgiano on S3bis, is Umbria's pottery-making capital. Flamboyant designs fill the town's multitude of shops, and there's a fine museum displaying examples of ceramics dating back to the Renaissance. Gubbio also has a pottery tradition—its red glazes have been renowned since medieval times. The secret of the original glaze died with its inventor some 500 years ago, but the town's present-day potters produce a fair facsimile.

Festivals to Plan a Trip Around

Each summer Umbria hosts two of Italy's biggest music festivals. Spoleto's **Festival dei Due Mondi** (www. spoletofestival.it), from mid-June through mid-July, features classical music and also ventures into theater and the visual arts. Perugia is hopping for 10 days in July, when famous names in contemporary music perform at the **Umbria Jazz Festival** (www. umbriajazz.com).

If you want to attend either event, you should make arrangements in advance ... and if you don't want to attend, you should plan to avoid the cities during festival time, when hotel rooms and restaurant tables are at a premium. A similar caveat applies for Assisi during religious festivals at Christmas, Easter, the feast of St. Francis (October 4), and Calendimaggio (May 1), when pilgrims arrive en masse.

If you've got a sweet tooth and you're visiting during the fall, head to Perugia for the **Eurochocolate Festival** (www. eurochocolate. perugia.it) in the third week of October.

How's the Weather?

The forested hills of Umbria and the Marches are marked by rich fall colors and an explosion of greenery in spring, making those two seasons prime visiting time. Fall and winter are longer and colder here than in nearby Rome; you'll want to have warm clothes with you as early as October and as late as April. The consolation is that winter is the best season for the region's cuisine: January to April is truffle season in Norcia and Spoleto, and October to December brings a bounty of fresh local mushrooms. Summer, when the top of Monte Subasio and the Piano Grande are blanketed with wildflowers, is an excellent time for a hiking trip.

Finding a Place to Stay

Virtually every older town, no matter how small, has some kind of hotel. A trend, particularly around Gubbio, Orvieto, and Todi, is to convert old villas, farms, and monasteries into first-class hotels. The natural splendor of the countryside more than compensates for the distance from town—provided you have a car. Hotels in town tend to be simpler than their country cousins, with a few notable exceptions in Spoleto, Gubbio, and Perugia.

10

Dining & Lodging Price Categories

WHAT IT COSTS in Euros					
	$$$$	**$$$**	**$$**	**$**	**¢**
Restaurants	over €45	€35–€45	€25–€35	€15–€25	under €15
Hotels	over €220	€160–€220	€110–€160	€70–€110	under €70

Restaurant prices are for a first course (primo), second course (secondo), and dessert (dolce). Hotel prices are for two people in a standard double room in high season, including tax and service.

TOP PASSEGGIATA

Perugia's stately, palace-lined Corso Vannucci is where residents of Umbria's capital stretch their legs in style before dinner.

BIRTHPLACE OF SAINTS and home to some of the country's greatest artistic treasures, central Italy is a collection of misty green valleys and picture-perfect hill towns laden with centuries of history. Umbria and the Marches are the Italian countryside as you've imagined it: verdant farmland, steep hillsides topped with fairy-tale fortresses, winding country roads traveled by horses and FIAT 500s carrying crates of fresh olives. No single town here has the extravagant wealth of art and architecture of Florence, Rome, or Venice, but this works in your favor: small jewels of towns feel knowable, not overwhelming. And the cultural cupboard is far from bare. Orvieto's cathedral and Assisi's basilica are two of the most important sights in Italy, while Perugia, Todi, Gubbio, and Spoleto are rich in art and architecture.

East of Umbria, the Marches (Le Marche to Italians) stretch between the Apennines and the Adriatic Sea. It's a region of great turreted castles on high peaks defending passes and roads—a testament to the centuries of battle that have taken place here. Rising majestically in Urbino is a splendid palace, built by Federico da Montefeltro, where the humanistic ideals of the Renaissance came to their fullest flower, while the town of Ascoli Piceno can lay claim to one of the most beautiful squares in Italy. Virtually every small town in the region has a castle, church, or museum worth a visit—but even without them, you'd still be compelled to stop for the interesting streets, panoramic views, and natural beauty.

PERUGIA

The painter Perugino (the Perugian) filled his work with images of his home: soft hills with sparse trees, wide plains dotted with lakes. Despite the development of undistinguished modern suburbs, this peaceful landscape still survives, and venerable Perugia's medieval hilltop city remains almost completely intact. Perugia is the best-preserved hill town of its size; there are few better examples of the self-contained city-state that so shaped the course of Italian history. Little remains of Perugia's earliest ancestors, although the Arco di Augusto (Arch of Augustus) in Piazza Fortebraccio, the northern entrance to the city, is of Etruscan origin.

Exploring Perugia

The best approach to the city is by train—the station is in the unlovely suburbs, but there are frequent buses running directly to Piazza d'Italia, the heart of the old town. If you are driving, leave your car in one of the parking lots near the station and then take the bus or the escalator, which passes through subterranean excavations of the city's Roman foundations, from Piazza Partigiani to the Rocca Paolina. A half day is sufficient to visit the major sights in the center of town.

The Main Attractions

★ ➍ **Collegio del Cambio.** The series of elaborate rooms at Bankers' Guild Hall housed the meeting hall and chapel of the guild of bankers and money changers. The walls were frescoed from 1496 to 1500 by the most important Perugian painter of the Renaissance, Pietro Vannucci, better known

Collegio del
Cambio **4**

Duomo **1**

Galleria
Nazionale
dell'Umbria ...**3**

Museo
Archeologico
Nazionale **5**

Palazzo
dei Priori **2**

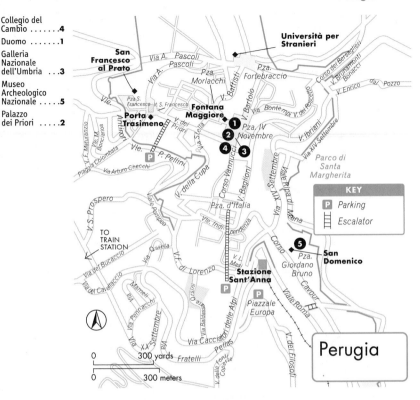

as Perugino (circa 1450–1523). The iconography prevalent in the works includes common religious themes, like the Nativity and the Transfiguration (on the end walls), but also figures intended to inspire the businessmen who congregated here. On the left wall are female figures representing the Virtues, beneath them the heroes and sages of antiquity. On the right wall are the prophets and sibyls. Perugino's most famous pupil, Raffaello Sanzio, or Raphael (1483–1520), is said to have painted here; experts say his hand is most apparent in the figure of Fortitude. On one of the pilasters is a remarkably honest self-portrait of Perugino, surmounted by a Latin inscription. The Collegio is on the ground floor of the Palazzo dei Priori, and is entered from Corso Vannucci. ⊠ *Corso Vannucci 25* ☎ *075/5728599* 🎟 *€2.60* ⏱ *Mon.–Sat. 9–12:30 and 2:30–5:30, Sun. 9–1.*

Corso Vannucci. The heart of the city is the broad stately pedestrian street that runs from Piazza d'Italia to Piazza IV Novembre. As evening falls, Corso Vannucci is filled with Perugians out for their evening *passeggiata,* a pleasant predinner stroll that may include a pause for an *aperitivo* (aperitif) at one of the many cafés that line the street.

❸ **Galleria Nazionale dell'Umbria.** On the fourth floor of the ⇨ **Palazzo dei Priori** is the region's most comprehensive art gallery. Well-placed infor-

UMBRIA THROUGH THE AGES

The earliest inhabitants of Umbria, the Umbri, were thought by the Romans to be the most ancient inhabitants of Italy. Little is known about them; with the coming of Etruscan culture the tribe fled into the mountains in the eastern portion of the region. The Etruscans, who founded some of the great cities of Umbria, were in turn supplanted by the Romans. Unlike Tuscany and other regions of central Italy, Umbria had few powerful medieval families to exert control over the cities in the Middle Ages—its proximity to Rome ensured that it would always be more or less under papal domination.

In the center of the country, Umbria has for much of its history been a battlefield where armies from north and south clashed. Hannibal destroyed a Roman army on the shores of Lake Trasimeno, and the bloody course of the interminable Guelph-Ghibelline conflict of the Middle Ages was played out here. Dante considered Umbria the most violent place in Italy. Trophies of war still decorate the Palazzo dei Priori in Perugia, and the little town of Gubbio continues a warlike rivalry begun in the Middle Ages—every year it challenges the Tuscan town of Sansepolcro to a crossbow tournament. Today the bowmen shoot at targets, but neither side has forgotten that 500 years ago its ancestors shot at each other. In spite of—or perhaps because of—this bloodshed, Umbria has produced more than its share of Christian saints. The most famous is St. Francis, the decidedly pacifist saint whose life shaped the Church of his time. His great shrine at Assisi is visited by hundreds of thousands of pilgrims each year. St. Clare, his devoted follower, was Umbria-born, as were St. Benedict, St. Rita of Cascia, and the patron saint of lovers, St. Valentine.

mation panels (in Italian and English) describe work by native artists—most notably Pinturicchio (1454–1513) and Perugino—along with others of the Umbrian and Tuscan schools. The gallery also exhibits frescoes, sculptures, and several superb painted crucifixes from the 13th and 14th centuries; other rooms are dedicated to Perugia itself, illustrating the evolution of the medieval city. The last entry is a half hour before closing. ⊠ *Corso Vannucci 19, Piazza IV Novembre* ☎ *075/5721009* ⊕ *www.gallerianazionaledellumbria.it* ⊠ *€6.50* ☉ *Daily 8:30–7:30; closed first Mon. of month.*

★ ❷ **Palazzo dei Priori.** The imposing palace, begun in the 13th century, has an unusual staircase that fans out into Piazza IV Novembre. The facade is decorated with symbols of Perugia's former power: the griffin is the city's symbol; the lion denotes Perugia's allegiance to the medieval Guelph (or papal) cause. Both figures support the heavy chains of the gates of Siena, which fell to Perugian forces in 1358. Most of the building now houses the town's municipal offices, which are not open to tourists, with access permitted only to the fourth floor ⇨ **Galleria Nazionale dell'Umbria.** ⊠ *Corso Vannucci 19* ☎ *075/5771.*

Also Worth Seeing

❶ Duomo. This church's prize relic is the Virgin Mary's wedding ring, stolen in 1488 from the nearby town of Chiusi. The ring, kept in a chapel on the left aisle, is the size of a large bangle and is kept under lock—15 locks actually—and key year-round except July 30 and the second-to-last Sunday in January. The first date commemorates the day the ring was brought to Perugia, the second, Mary's wedding anniversary. The cathedral itself is large and rather plain, dating from the Middle Ages but with many additions from the 15th and 16th centuries. There are some elaborately carved choir stalls, executed by Giovanni Battista Bastone in 1520. Precious objects associated with the cathedral are on display at the associated **Museo Capitolare**, including vestments, vessels, manuscripts, and gold work. An early masterpiece by Luca Signorelli (circa 1450–1523) is the altarpiece showing the Madonna with St. John the Baptist, St. Onophrio, and St. Lawrence (1484). Note that sections of the church may be closed to visitors during religious services and the last admission is a half hour before closing. ⊠ *Piazza IV Novembre* ☎ *075/5723832* ▧ *Duomo free, museum €3.50* ☾ *Duomo Mon.–Sat. 7–12:30 and 4–6:45, Sun. 8–12:30 and 4–6:45; museum daily 10–1 and 2:30–5:30.*

❺ Museo Archeologico Nazionale. Perugia was a flourishing Etruscan site long before it fell under Roman domination in 310 BC. This museum next to the imposing church of San Domenico contains an excellent collection of Etruscan artifacts from throughout the region. ⊠ *Piazza G. Bruno 10* ☎ *075/5727141* ⊕ *www.archeopg.arti.beniculturali.it* ▧ *€4* ☾ *Mon. 2:30–7:30, Tues.–Sun. 8:30–7:30.*

Where to Stay & Eat

$$ ✕ **La Taverna.** Medieval steps lead to a rustic two-story restaurant where wine bottles and artful clutter decorate the walls. Good choices from the regional menu include *caramelle al gorgonzola* (pasta rolls filled with red cabbage and mozzarella with a Gorgonzola sauce) and grilled meat dishes, such as the *medaglioni di vitello al tartufo* (grilled veal with truffles). ⊠ *Via delle Streghe 8, off Corso Vannucci* ☎ *075/5724128* ▭ *AE, DC, MC, V* ☾ *Closed Mon.*

$ ✕ **Il Falchetto.** Exceptional food at reasonable prices makes this Perugia's best bargain. Service is smart but relaxed in the two medieval dining rooms that put the kitchen and chef on view. The house specialty is *falchetti* (homemade gnocchi with spinach and ricotta cheese). ⊠ *Via Bartolo 20* ☎ *075/5731775* ▭ *AE, DC, MC, V* ☾ *Closed Mon. and last 2 wks in Jan.*

★ ¢ ✕ **Dal Mi' Cocco.** A great favorite with Perugia's university students, this is a fun, crowded, and truly inexpensive place to enjoy a multicourse fixed-price meal (€13). You may find yourself seated at a long table with other diners, but some language help from your neighbors could come in handy—the menu is in pure Perugian dialect. Meals change with the seasons, and each day of the week brings some new creation *dal cocco* (from the "coconut," or head) of the chef. ⊠ *Corso Garibaldi 12* ☎ *075/5732511* ◿ *Reservations essential* ▭ *No credit cards* ☾ *Closed Mon. and July 20–Aug. 15.*

10

EATING WELL IN UMBRIA & THE MARCHES

Central Italy is mountainous, and its food is hearty and straightforward, with a stick-to-the-ribs quality that sees hardworking farmers and artisans through a long day's work and helps them make the steep climb home at night. The region has made several important contributions to Italian cuisine. Particularly prized are winter's *tartufi neri* (black truffles) from the area around Spoleto and from the hills around the tiny town of Norcia. The delicacy shows up on menus stuffed in ravioli, layered in lasagna, and mixed with risotto. Local pasta specialties, such as thick, handmade *ciriole* (rough-shape, fat spaghetti) or *strangozzi*

(long, thin pasta)—also spelled *stringozzi* or *strengozzi*—are even better prepared *al tartufo*, enriched with excellent local olive oil and truffles. Norcia's pork products—especially sausages, salami, and *arista* (roast loin perfumed with rosemary)—are so famous that pork butchers throughout Italy are called *norcini*, and pork butcher shops are called *norcinerie*. Bakeries and storefronts sell *torta al testo* in Umbria, and *crescie* in the Marches. Both are traditional forms of flat, pitalike bread that can be filled to order with various combinations of meat, cheese, and vegetables, and make for delicious light meals.

$$$$ ⊞ **Brufani Palace.** A 19th-century palazzo has been turned into an elegant lodging choice, where public rooms and first-floor guest rooms have high ceilings and are done in grand belle epoque style. Second-floor rooms are more modern; many on both floors have a marvelous view of the Umbrian countryside or the city, as does the extensive rooftop terrace. Linen bedsheets and luxuriously equipped bathrooms make for a particularly comfortable stay, but breakfast (€32 per person) is not normally included in the price of a room. ⊠ *Piazza d'Italia 12, 06121* ☎ *075/5732541* 🖷 *075/5720210* ⊕ *www.brufanipalace.com* 🛏 *63 rooms, 31 suites* ⟁ *Restaurant, in room safes, cable TV, in-room data ports, Wi-Fi, indoor pool, gym, sauna, Turkish bath, bar, concierge, Internet room, meeting rooms, parking (fee)* ⊟ *AE, DC, MC, V* ⊺⊙⊺ *EP.*

$$$ ⊞ **Castello di Oscano.** A splendid neo-Gothic castle, a late-19th-century villa, and a converted farmhouse hidden in the tranquil hills north of Perugia offer a range of accommodations. Step back in time in the castle, where spacious suites and junior suites, all with high oak-beam ceilings, and some with panoramic views, are decorated with 18th- and 19th-century antiques. Standard rooms in the villa annex are smaller and more modern than those in the main building, while the apartments of the farmhouse, in the valley below the castle, provide kitchens and simple accommodation for two to five people. ⊠ *Strada Palaretta 19, 06134 Località Cenerente Oscano, 5 km (3 mi) north of Perugia* ☎ *075/584371* 🖷 *075/690666* ⊕ *www.oscano.it* 🛏 *24 rooms, 8 suites, 13 apartments* ⟁ *Restaurant, cable TV, pool, gym, bicycles, bar, library, Internet room, meeting rooms; no a/c in some rooms* ⊟ *AE, DC, V* ⊺⊙⊺ *BP.*

$$$ ⊞ **Locanda della Posta.** Reside at the center of Perugia's old district in an 18th-century palazzo. Renovation has left the reception and other public areas rather bland, but the rooms, all of which are carpeted, are tastefully and soothingly decorated in muted colors. Though sound-proofed, rooms at the front of the hotel face the busy Corso Vannucci and should be avoided in favor of those on the upper floors at the back of the building, which also have great views. ⊠ *Corso Vannucci 97, 06121* ☎ *075/5728925* 🖷 *075/5732562* ⤴ *38 rooms, 1 suite* ♨ *Minibars, bar, Internet room, parking (fee)* ☰ *AE, DC, MC, V* ⏮ *BP.*

$$ 🏨 **Hotel Fortuna.** The elegant furnishings in this friendly hotel comple-
FodorsChoice ment the 18th-century frescoes that decorate several of the rooms. Some
★ guest rooms have balconies, and a pleasant rooftop terrace affords panoramic views of the city. The building itself, just out of sight of Corso Vannucci, dates back to the 1300s and the sections of medieval walls exposed here and there throughout the structure are a fascinating fea-ture. A three-night stay is required during the Umbria Jazz and Euro-chocolate festivals and during a number of public holidays, including Christmas, New Year, and Easter. ⊠ *Via Bonazzi 19, 06123* ☎ *075/ 5722845* 🖷 *075/5735040* ⊕ *www.umbriahotels.com* ⤴ *51 rooms* ♨ *Some in-room hot tubs, minibars, in room safes, cable TV, bar, In-ternet room, meeting rooms, some free parking* ☰*AE, DC, MC, V* ⏮*BP.*

Nightlife & the Arts

The monthly *Viva Perugia* (sold at newsstands), with a section in Eng-lish, is a good source of information about what's going on in town. Summer sees several music festivals in Perugia. The **Festival delle Nazioni di Musica da Camera** (International Chamber Music Festival ⊠ On S3bis, 80 km [50 mi] north of Perugia, Città di Castello ☎ 075/8521142 🖷 075/8552461) is a two-week event held in late August and early Sep-tember. **Sagra Musicale Umbra** (☎ 075/5732800 ⊕ www.umbria.org/eng/ eventi) celebrates the traditional music of the region at performances
★ during 10 days in September. The **Umbria Jazz Festival** (☎ 075/5732432 🖷 075/572256 ⊕ www.umbriajazz.com), a world-famous concert se-ries, lasts for 10 days in July.

The third week in October is especially sweet, when Perugia hosts the **Eurochocolate Festival** (☎ 075/5732670 ⊕ www.eurochocolate.perugia. it) and the streets are filled with stands, sculptures, and—best of all—tastings.

Shopping

Judging by the expensive shops around the Corso Vannucci, Perugians are not afraid to part with their euros. Clothing shops selling Italian de-signers such as Gucci, Ferragamo, Armani, and Fendi line the streets. The town is also known for its famous Perugina chocolate, although the brand (a Nestlé company since the early 1990s) is easily found throughout Italy. *Cioccolato al latte* (milk chocolate) and *fondente* (dark chocolate) are sold in tiny jewel-like containers, and in giant boxes the size of serving trays, all over town. Round hazelnut-filled choco-late candies, *baci* (literally, "kisses"), come wrapped in silver foil and, like fortune cookies, contain romantic sayings in several languages, English included.

10

ASSISI

Assisi, 47 km (30 mi) north of Spoleto and 25 km (16 mi) east of Perugia, began as an Umbri settlement in the 7th century BC and was conquered by the Romans 400 years later, following the pattern of most towns in the region. It was Christianized by St. Rufino, its patron saint, in AD 238, but it is the spirit of St. Francis, patron saint of Italy, that is felt throughout the narrow medieval streets. Basilica di San Francesco, the famous 13th-century church built in his honor, was decorated by the greatest artists of the period. Assisi is pristinely medieval in architecture and appearance, due in large part to relative neglect from the 16th century until 1926, when the celebration of the 700th anniversary of St. Francis's death brought more than 2 million visitors. Since then, Assisi has become one of the most important pilgrimage destinations in the Christian world.

Exploring Assisi

The train station is 4 km (2½ mi) from town, with bus service about every half hour. The walled town is closed to outside traffic, so cars must be left in the parking lots at Porta San Pietro, near Porta Nuova, or beneath Piazza Matteotti. Frequent minibuses run between the parking lots and the center of town. You can see the major sights in Assisi in half a day, but set aside more time if you want to fully explore the town.

The Main Attractions

Eremo delle Carceri. In the caves on the slope of Monte Subasio, Francis and his followers established their first home, to which he returned often. The church and monastery—in dense woodlands—retain a tranquil, contemplative air. A narrow set of steps leads through the building to the areas where Francis slept and prayed. True to their Franciscan heritage, the friars here are entirely dependent on alms from visitors. ⊠ *Via Santuario delle Carceri, 4 km (2½ mi) east of Assisi* ☎ *075/812301* 🖃 *Donations accepted* ☉ *Nov.–Easter, daily 6:30–sunset; Easter–Oct., daily 6:30 AM–7:15 PM.*

❽ Santa Chiara. This striking red-striped 13th-century church is dedicated to St. Clare, one of the earliest and most fervent of St. Francis's followers and the founder of the Order of Poor Clares, in imitation of the Franciscans. The church contains the body of the saint, and in the **Cappella del Crocifisso** is the crucifix that spoke to St. Francis and led him to a life of piety. A heavily veiled member of St. Clare's order is stationed before the cross in perpetual adoration of the image. ⊠ *Piazza Santa Chiara* ☎ *075/812282* ☉ *Mar. 21–Oct., daily 6:30–noon and 2–7; Nov.–Mar. 20, daily 6:30–noon and 2–6.*

❻ Tempio di Minerva. Pieces of a Roman temple dating from the time of Augustus (63 BC–AD 14) make up this sanctuary, once dedicated to the goddess of wisdom, that was transformed into a Catholic church in the 16th century. The expectations raised by the perfect classical facade are not met by the interior, subjected to a thorough baroque assault in the 17th century, but both are worth a look. ⊠ *Piazza del Comune* ☎ *075/*

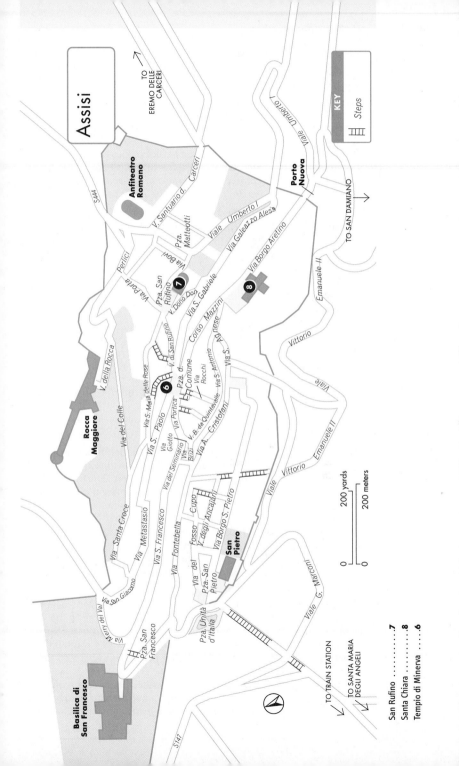

Assisi

Basilica di San Francesco

Rocca Maggiore

Anfiteatro Romano

TO EREMO DELLE CARCERI

Porto Nuova

TO SAN DAMIANO

San Pietro

TO TRAIN STATION

TO SANTA MARIA DEGLI ANGELI

S444

S147

V. della Rocca
Via del Colle
Via Santa Croce
Via S. Metastasio
Via S. Francesco
Via del Seminario
Via S. Paolo
Via S. Maria delle Rose
Pertici
Via del Porta
V. di San Rufino
Pza. San Rufino
V. Dono Doni
Via S. Gabriele
Corso Mazzini
Pza. del Comune
Via Portica
Via Giotto
Via Bizzi
V. B. da Quintavalle
Via A. Cristofani
Via Rocchi
Via S. Antonio
Via S. Ag nese
V. Santuario d. Carceri
Pza. Matteotti
Via Bovi
Viale Umberto I
Via Galeazzo Alessi
Via Borgo Aretino
Viale Umberto I
Viale Vittorio Emanuele II
Viale Vittorio
Viale
Via Merry del Val
Via San Giacomo
Pza. San Francesco
Via del Fosso
Via Fontebella
Cupo
V. degli Arcaiani
Via Borgo S. Pietro
Pza. San Pietro
Pza. Unità d'Italia
Viale G. Marconi

KEY

|||| Steps

0 — 200 yards
0 — 200 meters

San Rufino **7**
Santa Chiara **8**
Tempio di Minerva **6**

812268 ☉ *Mon., Wed., Thurs., and Sat. 7:15–7; Tues. and Fri. 7:15–2 and 5:15–7; Sun. 8:15–7.*

Also Worth Seeing

❼ San Rufino. St. Francis and St. Clare were among those baptized in Assisi's Duomo, the principal church in town until the 12th century. The baptismal font has since been redecorated, but it is possible to see the **crypt** of San Rufino, the martyred 3rd-century bishop who brought Christianity to Assisi. Admission to the crypt includes a look at the small **Museo Capitolare** and its detached frescoes and artifacts. ⊠ *Piazza San Rufino* ☎ *075/812283* 🎫 *Duomo free, crypt and museum €2.50* ☉ *Mar. 21–Oct., daily 8–1 and 3–7; Nov.–Mar. 20, daily 8–1 and 2–6.*

Santa Maria degli Angeli. The shrine here is much venerated because it was in the **Cappella del Transito,** then a humble cell, that St. Francis died in 1226. This baroque church is built over the **Porziuncola,** a chapel restored by St. Francis. It's on the outskirts of town, near the train station. ⊠ *Località Santa Maria degli Angeli* ☎ *075/80511* ☉ *Mar. 21–June and Oct., daily 6:15–7:45 PM; July–Sept., daily 6:15–7:45 PM and 9 PM–11 PM; Nov.–Mar. 20, daily 6:30–noon and 2–6.*

Off the Beaten Path

Cannara. A pleasant excursion 16 km (10 mi) southwest of Assisi leads to this tiny town; a half-hour walk then brings you to the fields of Pian d'Arca, the legendary site of St. Francis's sermon to the birds. The first week of September the town's *Sagra della Cipolla* (Onion Festival) is in full swing, with everything from soup to ice cream flavored with the town's favorite vegetable. *Pro Loco tourist office* ⊠ *Piazza Umberto I* ☎ *0742/72177.*

Where to Stay & Eat

Advance room reservations are absolutely essential if you are visiting Assisi between Easter and October or during Christmastime; latecomers are often left to choose from lodging in modern Santa Maria degli Angeli, 8 km (5 mi) out of town. Ask at the Assisi **tourist office** for a list of pilgrim hostels, an interesting and economical alternative to conventional lodgings. Private convents, churches, or other Catholic organizations run these *ostelli* (hostels) or *conventi* (convents). Rooms are on the spartan side, but you are virtually assured of a peaceful night's stay (€36–€68). ⊠ *Piazza del Comune 22, 06081* ☎ *075/812534* ☉ *Oct.–June, Mon.–Sat. 8–2 and 3–6, Sun. 9–1; July–Sept., Mon.–Sat. 8–2 and 3–6, Sun. 10–1 and 2–5* ⊕ *www.umbria2000.it.*

$$ ✕ **Buca di San Francesco.** In summer dine in a cool green garden; in winter under the low brick arches of the restaurant's cozy cellars: no wonder this central restaurant is Assisi's busiest. The food is first-rate, too. Try spaghetti *alla buca,* homemade pasta served with a roasted mushroom sauce. ⊠ *Via Brizi 1* ☎ *075/812204* ⊟ *AE, DC, MC, V* ☉ *Closed Mon. and July.*

$–$$ ✕ **La Fortezza.** Romans built parts of the walls that make up this family-run restaurant. The service is personable and the kitchen reliable. A particular standout is *anatra al finocchio selvatico* (duck with wild fen-

Continued on page 545

Basilica di San Francesco

ASSISI'S BASILICA DI SAN FRANCESCO

The legacy of St. Francis, founder of the Franciscan monastic order, pervades Assisi. Each year the town hosts several million pilgrims, but the steady flow of visitors does nothing to diminish the singular beauty of one of Italy's most important religious centers. The pilgrims' ultimate destination is the massive Basilica di San Francesco, which sits halfway up Assisi's hill, supported by graceful arches.

The basilica is not one church but two. The Romanesque **Lower Church** came first; construction began in 1228, just two years after St. Francis's death, and was completed within a few years. The low ceilings and candlelit interior make an appropriately solemn setting for St. Francis's tomb, found in the crypt below the main altar. The Gothic **Upper Church**, built only half a century later, sits on top of the lower one, and is strikingly different, with soaring arches and tall stained-glass windows (the first in Italy). Inside, both churches are covered floor to ceiling with some of Europe's finest frescoes: the Lower Church is dim and full of candlelit shadows, and the Upper Church is bright and airy.

VISITING THE BASILICA

THE LOWER CHURCH

The most evocative way to experience the basilica is to begin with the dark Lower Church. As you enter, give your eyes a moment to adjust. Keep in mind that the artists at work here were conscious of the shadowy environment—they knew this was how their frescoes would be seen.

In the first chapel to the left, a superb fresco cycle by Simone Martini depicts scenes from the life of St. Martin. As you approach the main altar, the vaulting above you is decorated with the *Three Virtues of St. Francis* (poverty, chastity, and obedience) and *St. Francis's Triumph*, frescoes attributed to Giotto's followers. In the transept to your left, Pietro Lorenzetti's *Madonna and Child with St. Francis and St. John* sparkles when the sun hits it. Notice Mary's thumb; legend has it Jesus is asking which saint to bless, and Mary is pointing to Francis. Across the way in the right transept, Cimabue's *Madonna Enthroned Among Angels and St. Francis* is a famous portrait of the saint. Surrounding the portrait are painted scenes from the childhood of Christ, done by the assis-

tants of Giotto. Nearby is a painting of the crucifixion attributed to Giotto himself.

You reach the crypt via stairs midway along the nave—on the crypt's altar, a stone coffin holds the saint's body. Steps up from the transepts lead to the cloister, where there's a gift shop, and the treasury, which contains holy objects.

THE UPPER CHURCH

The St. Francis fresco cycle is the highlight of the Upper Church. (See facing page.) Also worth special note is the 16th-century choir, with its remarkably delicate inlaid wood. When a 1997 earthquake rocked the basilica, the St. Francis cycle sustained little damage, but portions of the ceiling above the entrance and altar collapsed, reducing their frescoes (attributed to Cimabue and Giotto) to rubble. The painstaking restoration is ongoing. ⚠ The dress code is strictly enforced—no bare shoulders or bare knees. Piazza di San Francesco, 075/819001, Lower Church Easter–Oct., Mon.–Sat. 6:30 AM–6:50 PM, Sun. 6:30 AM–7:15 PM; Nov.–Easter, daily 6:30–5:40. Upper Church Easter–Oct., Mon.–Sat. 8:30–6:50, Sun. 8:30–7:15; Nov.–Easter, daily 8:30–5:40.

FRANCIS, ITALY'S PATRON SAINT

St. Francis was born in Assisi in 1181, the son of a noblewoman and a well-to-do merchant. His troubled youth included a year in prison. He planned a military career, but after a long illness Francis heard the voice of God, renounced his father's wealth, and began a life of austerity. His mystical embrace of poverty, asceticism, and the beauty of man and nature struck a responsive chord in the medieval mind; he quickly

attracted a vast number of followers. Francis was the first saint to receive the stigmata (wounds in his hands, feet, and side corresponding to those of Christ on the cross). He died on October 4, 1226, in the Porziuncola, the secluded chapel in the woods where he had first preached the virtue of poverty to his disciples. St. Francis was declared patron saint of Italy in 1939, and today the Franciscans make up the largest of the Catholic orders.

THE UPPER CHURCH'S ST. FRANCIS FRESCO CYCLE

The 28 frescoes in the Upper Church depicting the life of St. Francis are the most admired works in the entire basilica. They're also the subject of one of art history's biggest controversies. For centuries they were thought to be by Giotto (1267-1337), the great early-Renaissance innovator, but inconsistencies in style, both within this series and in comparison to later Giotto works, have thrown their origin into question. Some scholars now say Giotto was the brains behind the cycle, but that assistants helped with the execution; others claim he couldn't have been involved at all.

Two things are certain. First, the style is revolutionary, which argues for Giotto's involve-

ment. The tangible weight of the figures, the emotion they show, and the use of perspective all look familiar to modern eyes, but in the art of the time there was nothing like it. Second, these images have played a major part in shaping how the world sees St. Francis. In that respect, who painted them hardly matters.

Starting at the transept, the frescoes circle the church, showing events in the saint's life (and afterlife). Some of the best are grouped near the church's entrance—look for the nativity at Greccio, the miracle of the spring, the death of the knight at Celano, and, most famously, the sermon to the birds.

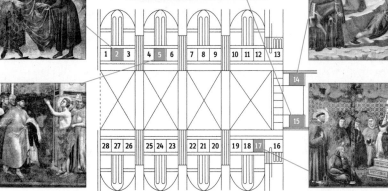

The St. Francis fresco cycle
1. Homage of a simple man
2. Giving cloak to a poor man
3. Dream of the palace
4. Hearing the voice of God
5. Rejection of worldly goods
6. Dream of Innocent III
7. Confirmation of the rules
8. Vision of flaming chariot
9. Vision of celestial thrones
10. Chasing devils from Arezzo
11. Before the sultan
12. Ecstasy of St. Francis
13. Nativity at Greccio
14. Miracle of the spring
15. Sermon to the birds
16. Death of knight at Celano
17. Preaching to Honorius III
18. Apparition at Arles
19. Receiving the stigmata
20. Death of St. Francis
21. Apparition before Bishop Guido and Fra Agostino
22. Verification of the stigmata
23. Mourning of St. Clare
24. Canonization
25. Apparition before Gregory IX
26. Healing of a devotee
27. Confession of a woman
28. Repentant heretic freed

Basilica di San Francesco

VOICES OF ITALY

Sister Marcellina,
Order of St. Bridget

Sister Marcellina of the Order of St. Bridget talks about her life in Assisi, where she and 11 other sisters live in a convent and guesthouse on the outskirts of the town:

"Before coming to Assisi, I lived in various countries. I've lived in India, and in England, and been to Holland, to Sweden, and to Finland, as well as lived in Rome. But Assisi is the place that I would never want to change for any other. I don't know, I think there is something very special about this place. I've been here 13 years now, and each year I pray that I won't be sent somewhere else. I'm very happy here.

"I like the atmosphere of Assisi, it's very friendly, and of course with St. Francis and St. Claire, but especially St. Francis, there is a simplicity to life that I like very much. Even though I'm in the Order of St. Bridget, living here I feel very much a part of Franciscan spirituality. There is also a very strong ecumenical feeling to Assisi and this is very nice. There are over 60 different religious communities, with people from all over the world. And even though they come from different religious backgrounds they still feel a part of Assisi. Living here, you don't see the people of Assisi, you see people who have come from all over the world.

"There is something you feel when you come to Assisi, something you feel in your heart that makes you want to come back. And people do return! They feel the peacefulness and tranquility. Not that there aren't other aspects, like the commercialism—but these things happen. People return for the simplicity of this place. People feel attracted to Assisi. There's always something that people feel when they come here—even the hard-hearted ones!"

Asked if she thinks Assisi is changing, Sister Marcellina answers, with laughter in her voice, "When they wanted to make all the changes in the year 2000, the Jubilee Year, our Lord said, 'I must stop everything.' They had lots of projects to build new accommodations to house the people coming for the Jubilee Year, but the Lord said, 'No!'"

nel). La Fortezza also has seven simple but clean guest rooms available. ⊠ *Vicolo della Fortezza 2/b* ☎ *075/812418* ⌛ *Reservations essential* ⊟ *AE, DC, MC, V* ⊘ *Closed Thurs. and Feb.*

★ $ ✕ **Osteria Piazzetta dell'Erba.** Avoid stodgy tourist eateries and come here for an informal meal or a light snack. There are two different *primi piatti* (first courses) every day, along with various salads and a good selection of fillings to go in the ever-present *torta al testo* (flat, pitalike bread that can be filled to order with various combinations of meat, cheese, and vegetables). The goat cheese is from Sardinia and is a delicious surprise. ⊠ *Via San Gabriele dell'Addolorata 15/b* ☎ *075/815352* ⊟ *MC, V* ⊘ *Closed Mon. and 3 wks late Jan.–mid Feb.*

¢ ✕ **La Stalla.** In a converted stable, a simple and rustic restaurant turns out hearty country fare. Meats grill and potatoes and onions bake on an open fire; for something light, try the torta al testo with your choice of local cheeses, salami, sausages, and vegetables. In summer take your meal outside under a trellis of vines and flowers. Though it's very popular with bus tours, the atmosphere and food make this an excellent stopover on your way to or from the Eremo delle Carceri. ⊠ *Via Santuario delle Carceri 8, 1 km (½ mi) east of center* ☎ *075/812317* ⊟ *No credit cards* ⊘ *Closed Mon. Oct.–June.*

¢ ✕▦ **La Pallotta.** One of the best hotels in its category and a great fam-
Fodor$Choice ily-run restaurant are found here under one roof. Upstairs, the beds are
★ firm, and some of the upper-floor rooms look out across the rooftops of town. Downstairs, with a separate entrance on the alley around the corner, Vicolo della Volta Pinta ($–$$) is a cozy trattoria with a fireplace and stone walls. The *menu di degustazione* (tasting menu) is a good way to sample the tasty local dishes, such as *strangozzi* (a long, thin pasta also spelled *stringozzi* and *strengozzi*) with *salsa di funghi* (mushroom sauce). ⊠ *Via San Rufino 6, 06081* ☎☎*075/812307 hotel* ☎*075/812649 restaurant* ⊕ *www.pallottaassisi.it* ⇝ *8 rooms* ⌂ *Restaurant, bar, Internet room; no a/c* ⊟ *AE, DC, MC, V* ⦿❘ *BP.*

$$$ ▦ **Castello di Petrata.** Built as a fortress in the 14th century, the Petrata
Fodor$Choice rightfully dominates its position—with Monte Subasio, Assisi, and the
★ distant hills and valleys of Perugia all in view. Every room is different from the last: wood beams and sections of exposed medieval stonework make up the background and comfortable couches and upholstered chairs turn each room into a delightful retreat. The bathrooms with tubs are considerably more spacious than those with showers. ⊠ *Località Petrata 22, 06081, 6 km (4 mi) east of Assisi* ☎ *075/815451* 🖷 *075/ 8043026* ⊕ *www.castellopetrata.com* ⇝ *21 rooms, 2 suites* ⌂ *Restaurant, minibars, pool, bar, Internet room, meeting rooms, some pets allowed; no a/c* ⊟ *AE, DC, MC, V* ⊘ *Closed Jan.–Mar.* ⦿❘ *BP.*

$$$ ▦ **Hotel Subasio.** The Subasio, housed in a converted monastery, has counted Marlene Dietrich and Charlie Chaplin among its guests. Some of the rooms remain a little monastic, but the splendid views, comfortable old-fashioned sitting rooms, flower-decked terraces, and lovely garden more than balance out a certain austerity in the furnishings. Ask for a room overlooking the valley. The hotel is close to the Basilica di San Francesco. ⊠ *Via Frate Elia 2, 06082* ☎ *075/812206* 🖷 *075/*

10

816691 ⊕ *www.hotelsubasio.com* 🖙 *54 rooms, 8 suites* ♨ *Restaurant, bar, parking (fee)* ☰ *AE, DC, MC, V* ❖ *BP.*

$$-$$$ ▦ **San Francesco.** You can't beat the location—the roof terrace and some of the rooms look out onto the Basilica di San Francesco, which is opposite the hotel. Rooms and facilities range from simple to homely, but you may be reminded that looks aren't everything by the nice touches like slippers, a good-night piece of chocolate, and soundproofing. Fruit, homemade tarts, and fresh ricotta make for a first-rate breakfast. ✉ *Via San Francesco 48, 06082* ☎ *075/812281* 🖷 *075/816237* ⊕ *www.hotelsanfrancescoassisi.it* 🖙 *44 rooms* ♨ *Restaurant, minibars, bar, Internet room, some pets allowed* ☰ *AE, DC, MC, V* ❖ *BP.*

$$ ▦ **Hotel Umbra.** A 16th-century town house is the setting for this charming hotel in a tranquil part of the city, an area closed to traffic and near Piazza del Comune. The rooms are arranged as small suites, each with tiny living room and balcony. Ask for an upper room with a view over the Assisi rooftops to the valley below. The restaurant, closed for lunch on Tuesday and Wednesday, has a charming vine-covered terrace leading to a secluded garden. ✉ *Via degli Archi 6, 06081* ☎ *075/812240* 🖷 *075/813653* ⊕ *www.hotelumbra.it* 🖙 *25 suites* ♨ *Restaurant, minibars, bar* ☰ *AE, DC, MC, V* ☽ *Closed mid-Jan.–mid-Mar.* ❖ *BP.*

NORTHERN UMBRIA

To the north of Perugia, placid, walled Gubbio watches over green countryside, true to its nickname, City of Silence—except for its fast and furious festivals in May, as lively today as when they began more than 800 years ago. To the south, along the Tiber River valley, are the towns of Deruta and Torgiano, best known for their hand-painted ceramics and wine—as locals say, go to Deruta to buy a pitcher and to Torgiano to fill it.

Gubbio

9 *48 km (30 mi) north of Assisi, 40 km (25 mi) northeast of Perugia.*

There is something otherworldly about this small jewel of a medieval town tucked away in a rugged, mountainous corner of Umbria. Even at the height of summer the cool serenity of the City of Silence's streets remains intact. Since medieval times Gubbio has been known for its red pottery. The town teeters on the slopes of Monte Ingino, and the streets are dramatically steep. Parking in the central Piazza dei Quaranta Martiri (40 Martyrs Square), named for 40 hostages murdered by the Nazis in 1944, is easy and secure, and it is wise to leave your car there and explore the narrow lanes on foot.

★ The striking Piazza Grande is dominated by the **Palazzo dei Consoli**, the 14th-century meeting place of Gubbio's parliament. The palace is the home of a small museum, famous chiefly for the *Tavole Eugubine* (Gubbio Tablets), seven bronze tablets written in the ancient Umbrian language, employing Etruscan and Latin characters and providing the best key to understanding this obscure tongue. Also in the museum are a captivating miscellany of coins, medieval arms, paintings, and majolica and

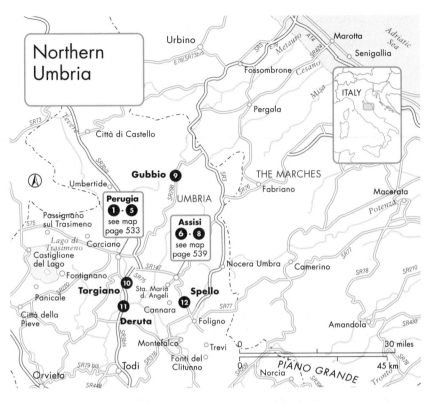

earthenware pots, not to mention the exhilarating views over Gubbio's roofscape and beyond from the lofty loggia. For a few days at the beginning of May the palace also displays the famous *ceri* (tall wooden pillars that ressemble candles) that are the focus of Gubbio's annual festivities. ⊠ *Piazza Grande* ☎ *075/9274298* ⊕ *www.gubbio-altochiascio. umbria2000.it* ⛶ *€5* ☉ *Apr.–Oct., daily 10–1 and 3–6; Nov.–Mar., daily 10–1 and 2–5.*

The **Duomo,** on a narrow street on the highest tier of the town, dates from the 12th century, with some baroque additions—in particular, a lavishly decorated bishop's chapel. Underneath the cathedral, a small museum, with an unexciting display of ecclesiastical objects and provincial art of the 14th to 16th century is more interesting for the glimpse it provides of the maze of crypts, chapels, and monastic chambers that form the foundations of the cathedral above. ⊠ *Via Federico da Montefeltro* ☎ *075/9272138 Duomo, 075/9220904 museum* ⛶ *Duomo free, museum €5* ☉ *Duomo, daily 9–6; museum, Mar. 21–Oct., daily 10–7; Nov.–Mar. 20, daily 10–6.*

The **Palazzo Ducale** is a scaled-down version of the Palazzo Ducale in Urbino (Gubbio was once the possession of that city's ruling family, the Montefeltro). Though virtually all of the original decorations have been removed—the inlaid wood panels of the duke's tiny study are in the Metropolitan Museum in New York—the sense of harmony and the carefully controlled proportions of the architectural elements faithfully reflect the Renaissance ideals of the palace in Urbino. A small collection of period furniture and paintings enlivens the rooms on the first and second floors, and the archaeological excavations, uncovering the foundations of the medieval buildings that once occupied the site, can also be visited. ⊠ *Via Federico da Montefeltro* ☎ *075/9275872* 🗂 *€2* ⊙ *Tues.–Sun. 8:30–7:30.*

Ↄ Outside Gubbio's walls at the eastern end of town, a **gondola** (actually a metal basket made for two) provides a bracing panoramic ride to the top of Monte Ingino. ⊠ *Via S. Girolamo, follow Corso Garibaldi or Via XX Settembre to end* ☎ *075/9273881* 🗂 *€5 round-trip* ⊙ *Nov.–Feb., Thurs.–Tues. 10–1:15 and 2:30–5; Mar., Mon.–Sat. 10–1:15 and 2:30–5:30, Sun. 9:30–1:15 and 2:30–6; Apr. and May, Mon.–Sat. 10–1:15 and 2:30–6:30, Sun. 9:30–1:15 and 2:30–7; June, Mon.–Sat. 9:30–1:15 and 2:30–7, Sun. 9–7:30; July and Aug., daily 9–8; Sept. 1–14, Mon.–Sat. 9:30–7 and Sun. 9–7:30; Sept. 15–30, Mon.–Sat. 9:30–1:15 and 2:30–7, Sun. 9–7:30; Oct., Mon.–Sat. 10–1:15 and 2:30–6, Sun. 9:30–1:15.*

Monte Ingino, along with its spectacular views, has the basilica of **Sant'Ubaldo,** repository of Gubbio's famous ceri. Statues of Sts. Ubaldo, George, and Anthony crown the three 16-foot pillars, which are transported to the Palazzo dei Consoli on the first Sunday of May in preparation for the race that takes place during the Festival of the Ceri. You can reach the church by car from the SP298, by hiking, or by taking a gondola. ⊠ *Top of Monte Ingino* ⊙ *Daily 9–noon and 4–7.*

Where to Stay & Eat

$$–$$$$ ✕ **Taverna del Lupo.** One of the city's most famous taverns, this popular restaurant seats 150 people and gets hectic on weekends and during the high season. Lasagna made in the Gubbian fashion—with ham and truffles—is an unusual indulgence, and the *coniglio di "Buon Ricordo,"* rabbit stew with herbs and spices, is a specialty. Peruse the extensive wine list and save room for the excellent desserts. ⊠ *Via Ansidei 21* ☎ *075/9274368* ▤ *AE, DC, MC, V* ⊙ *Closed Mon. Nov.–June.*

$–$$$ ✕ **Bosone Garden.** Succulent treats here include a two-mushroom salad with truffles, risotto *alla porcina* (with porcini mushrooms, sausage, and truffles), and leg of pork. This was once the stables of the palace that now houses the Hotel Bosone. A pleasant garden provides outdoor seating in summer. ⊠ *Via Mastro Giorgio 2* ☎ *075/9221246* ▤ *AE, DC, MC, V* ⊙ *Closed Mon. Nov.–June, and 2 wks in Jan.*

¢ ✕🏠 **Grotta dell'Angelo.** Angel's Grotto is a simple, rustic hotel and trattoria in the lower part of the old town, near the main square and tourist information office. Rooms are basic, with spare wood desks and chairs. Breakfast is optional at €4 per person. The restaurant ($–$$), with a few tables under a pergola in the hotel's garden, serves simple local specialties, including salami, stringozzi, and lasagna *tartufata* (with truffles). ⊠ *Via Gioia 47, 06024* ☎☎ *075/9273438* ⊕ *www.grottadellangelo.it* ➴ *18 rooms* ⚘ *No a/c* ▤ *AE, DC, MC, V* ⊙ *Closed 3 wks in Jan.* ❑ *EP.*

$$$ ☷ **Relais Ducale.** Three 15th-century town palaces unite to form this hotel with small, antiques-filled guest rooms. Ask for one on the upper floors to enjoy views of the town and valley. Especially impressive is the panorama from the hotel's hanging garden, where tables are set for breakfast during the summer months. The hotel is off Gubbio's Piazza Grande. ⊠ *Via Galeotti 19, 06024* ☎ *075/9220157* ☎ *075/9220159* ⊕ *www. mencarelligroup.com* ⇒ *20 rooms, 5 suites* ♿ *Bar, Internet room, meeting rooms* ⊟ *AE, DC, MC, V* ⭤ *BP.*

$$ ☷ **Hotel Bosone Palace.** Palazzo Raffaelli, a former palace, is home to the Hotel Bosone. Elaborate frescoes grace the ceilings of the two enormous suites, furnished with painted antiques, and top the hotel's small and delightful breakfast room. Standard rooms are comfortably though soberly decorated with heavy wooden furniture. Ask for a room facing the valley and away from the sometimes noisy street. ⊠ *Via XX Settembre 22, 06024* ☎ *075/9220688* ☎ *075/9220552* ⊕ *www. mencarelligroup.com* ⇒ *28 rooms, 2 suites* ♿ *Dining room, minibars, bar, Internet room* ⊟ *AE, DC, MC, V* ⊙ *Closed 3 wks in Jan.* ⭤ *BP.*

Nightlife & the Arts

★ ⟳   Gubbio explodes with exuberance every May 15 during the **Corsa dei Ceri** (Race of the Ceremonial Candles), held annually since 1151 in honor of St. Ubaldo, the town's patron saint. Teams race up Mount Ingino carrying three 16-foot poles, representing candles, elaborately decorated with statues of Sts. Ubaldo, George, and Anthony (representing three medieval guilds). Don't place any bets, though; Ubaldo always wins.

At Christmastime, kitsch is king in Gubbio. From December 7 to January 10, colored lights are strung down the mountainside in a tree pattern as the town stakes its claim as the home of the **world's largest Christmas tree.**

Sports & the Outdoors

⟳   A costumed medieval pageant with its roots in Gubbio's warring past, the Crossbow Tournament, **Palio della Balestra** (Gubbio tourist office ⊠ Via della Reppublica 6, 06024 ☎ 075/9220693), takes place on the last Sunday in May.

10

Torgiano

❿   *48 km (30 mi) southeast of Gubbio, 15 km (9 mi) southeast of Perugia.*

On the right bank of the Tiber River, Torgiano sits on a low-lying hill surrounded by the vineyards that have made the town famous since the Middle Ages. Even the town's coat of arms, a tower wrapped in a parchment covered with bunches of grapes, indicates the age-old importance of wine to the area.

Torgiano's **Cantine Lungarotti** winery is best known for Rubesco Lungarotti, San Giorgio, and chardonnay. ⊠ *Via Mario Angeloni 12* ☎ *075/ 9880348* ☷ *Free* ⊙ *Tours weekdays 8–1 and 3–6 by appointment.*

The **Museo del Vino** has a large collection of ancient wine vessels, presses, documents, and tools that tell the story of viticulture in Umbria and beyond. ⊠ *Corso Vittorio Emanuele 31* ☎ *075/9880200* ☷ *€4* ⊙ *Mar. 21–Oct., daily 9–1 and 3–7; Nov.–Mar. 20, daily 9–1 and 3–6.*

The **Osteria del Museo,** next door to the Museo del Vino, is a tavern devoted exclusively to the Lungarotti winery. You can buy the highly regarded wines there and, for €5–€10, take part in a tasting. ✉ *Corso Vittorio Emanuele 33a* 🕾🕾 *075/9880069* 🕓 *Mar. 21–Oct., daily 8–1 and 2:30–7:30; Nov.–Mar. 20, daily 8–1 and 2:30–6:30.*

Where to Stay & Eat

$$$ ✕🕮 **Le Tre Vaselle.** Four charming stone buildings, linked underground, house this hotel in the center of Torgiano. Its rooms are spacious, especially the suites, some of which have fireplaces; all have typical Tuscan red-clay floors and wood-beamed ceilings. The restaurant, Le Melagrane ($$$$), serves exquisite local specialties and has outdoor seating in summer. ✉ *Via Garibaldi 48, 06089* 🕾 *075/9880447* 🕾 *075/9880214* ⊕ *www.3vaselle.it* ⤴ *47 rooms, 13 suites* ⚭ *Restaurant, 2 pools (1 indoor), gym, sauna, bar, Internet room, meeting rooms, parking (fee)* ▤ *AE, DC, MC, V* 🍽 *BP.*

Deruta

⓫ *7 km (4 mi) south of Torgiano, 20 km (12 mi) southeast of Perugia.*

Deruta has been known for its ceramics since the 16th century. Notable in this medieval hill town are the 14th-century church of San Francesco and the Palazzo Comunale, but Deruta's main attraction is the magnificent ceramics collection in the **Museo Regionale della Ceramica.** ✉ *Largo San Francesco* 🕾 *075/9711000* ⊕ *www.museoceramicaderuta.it* 🎟 *€3* 🕓 *Apr.–June, daily 10:30–1 and 3–6; July–Sept., daily 10–1 and 3:30–7; Oct.–Mar., Wed.–Mon. 10:30–1 and 2:30–5.*

Shopping

Deruta has more than 70 ceramics workshops and boutiques. Start your browsing in the central Piazza dei Consoli.

Maioliche Cynthia (✉ Via Umberto I 1 🕾 075/9711255) specializes in reproductions of antique ceramic designs. **Ceramiche El Frate** (✉ Piazza dei Consoli 29 🕾 075/9711435) sells unusual ceramic tiles and jugs. The workshop at **Fabbrica Maioliche Tradizionali** (✉ Via Tiberina Nord 37 🕾 075/9711220) is open for visits weekdays 8:30–1 and 2:30–4:30 and also operates one of the largest shops in the area. **Maioliche Monotti** (✉ Via Tiberina Sud 276 🕾 075/972002) focuses on the colors used in traditional designs.

> **WORD OF MOUTH**
>
> "Best purchase *and* encounter with local people was going to a ceramic studio in Deruta. There are lots of places to buy ceramics, and a couple of places where there are true artists." —Marcy

Spello

⓬ *12 km (7 mi) southeast of Assisi, 32 km (24 mi) east of Deruta.*

Only a few minutes south of Assisi by car or train, the hill town of Spello, at the edge of Monte Subasio, makes an excellent base from which to explore the surrounding towns. Although it's half the size of Assisi, and has more than twice as many inhabitants, chances are you'll find the town relatively tourist-free. Spello's charms include a maze of quiet and picturesque backstreets, first-rate frescoes by Pinturicchio (1454–1513), and fine Roman ruins. The Romans called the town Hispellum, and traces remain of their walls, gates, amphitheater, and theater. Built, like Assisi, with pale pink stone from Monte Subasio, Spello is particularly attractive in the glowing light of an autumn sunset. The town is 1 km (½ mi) east of the train station, and buses run every 30 minutes for Porta Consolare; the dilapidated Roman gate at the south end of town and the best place to enter on foot. If you have a car, park in one of the lots outside the city walls and walk in.

★ Halfway up the main street that runs through town is the basilica of **Santa Maria Maggiore,** with vivid frescoes by Pinturicchio in the **Cappella Baglioni** (1501). From left to right are the *Annunciation* (with the artist's self-portrait on the far right), the *Nativity,* and the *Dispute at the Temple.* Rich colors, finely dressed figures, and complex symbolism place the frescoes among Pinturicchio's finest works, which already included the walls of the Sistine Chapel in the Vatican by the time he painted here. Two pillars on either side of the apse are decorated with frescoes by Perugino (circa 1450–1523), the other great Umbrian artist of the 16th century. ⊠ *Piazza Matteotti 18* ☎ *0742/301792* ⊙ *May–Sept., daily 8–12:30 and 2:30–7; Oct.–Apr., daily 8–12:30 and 2:30–6.*

Fodor'sChoice
★
The festival on the **Feast of Corpus Christi** (the ninth Sunday after Easter) is the region's most famous and most colorful. The streets of Spello are literally covered with *fiori* (flowers), arranged in vast canvases depicting religious subjects. Contact the tourist office for more information.

Where to Stay & Eat

$ ✕🏠 **La Bastiglia.** A renovated grain mill serves as home to a tidy hotel
Fodor'sChoice
★
where soft, light colors and a mix of antique and modern furnishings make the sitting rooms and bedrooms cozy. Ask for a top-floor room for a view. The terrace looks out onto the green and tranquil valley behind Spello and is used by the hotel's outstanding restaurant ($$$–$$$$). The refined and unusual menu changes with the season, but you might try the *costoletto di agnello in crosta di pistacchi* (pistachio encrusted lamb chops) followed by *rocciata di ananas con sorbetto di peperoncino* (pineapple strudel with a hot-pepper sorbet). ⊠ *Piazza Valle Gloria 17, 06038* ☎ *0742/651277* 🖷 *0742/301159* ⊕ *www.labastiglia.com* ↯ *31 rooms, 2 suites* ⚬ *Restaurant, some in-room hot tubs, pool, bar, Internet room* ⊟ *AE, DC, MC, V* ⊙ *Closed Jan. 7–Feb. 10* ⏣ *BP.*

$$–$$$ 🏠 **Palazzo Bocci.** Hints of this old town house's past are retained in the first-floor reading room, where vaulted ceilings and walls are decorated with bright trompe l'oeil frescoes. The solid colors and wooden furniture of the guest rooms are more modern. The staff here should win awards for their attentiveness. An ample buffet breakfast, with eggs in addition to cheese, cold cuts, and fruit, is a welcome change from standard Continental fare. ⊠ *Via Cavour 17, 06038* ☎ *0742/301021* 🖷 *0742/301464* ⊕ *www.palazzobocci.com* ↯ *19 rooms, 4 suites* ⚬ *Restaurant, bar, Internet room, meeting rooms* ⊟ *AE, DC, MC, V* ⏣ *BP.*

10

SPOLETO

For most of the year Spoleto is one in a pleasant succession of sleepy hill towns. But for three weeks every summer it shifts into high gear for its turn in the spotlight: the Festival dei Due Mondi, a world-class extravaganza of theater, opera, music, painting, and sculpture, where the world's top artists vie for honors and throngs of art aficionados vie for hotel rooms.

But there is good reason to visit Spoleto any time of the year. Roman and medieval attractions and superb natural surroundings make it one of Umbria's most inviting towns. From the churches set among silvery olive groves on the outskirts of town to the soaring Ponte delle Torri behind it, Spoleto has sublime views in every direction.

Exploring Spoleto

Spoleto is small, and its sights are clustered in the upper part of town, so it's best explored on foot. Several walkways cut down the hill, crossing the Corso Mazzini, which turns up the hill. Parking in Spoleto is always difficult; park outside the walls in Piazza della Vittoria. One day in Spoleto allows you to see the highlights and still have time for a leisurely lunch and a walk across the Ponte delle Torri.

The Main Attractions

🔟 **Duomo.** A Renaissance loggia, eight rose windows, and an early-13th-century gold mosaic of the Benedictory Christ lightens the church's rather dour 12th-century Romanesque facade. The contrast makes this one of the finest church exteriors in the region. Inside, the Duomo holds the most notable art in town, including the immaculately restored frescoes in the apse by Fra Filippo Lippi (1406–69), depicting the *Annunciation,* the *Nativity,* and the *Dormition of Mary,* with a marvelous *Coronation of the Virgin* adorning the dome. Be ready with a €0.50 coin to illuminate the masterpiece. The Florentine artist died shortly after completing the work, and his tomb—designed by his son, Filippino Lippi (1457–1504)—lies in the right transept. Another fresco cycle, including work by Pinturicchio, is in the **Cappella Eroli** off the right aisle. ⊠ *Piazza Duomo* ☎ *0743/44307* ☉ *Mar.–Oct., daily 8:30–12:30 and 3:30–7; Nov.–Feb., daily 8:30–12:30 and 3:30–6.*

★ 🔟 **Ponte delle Torri.** Spanning massively and gracefully across the gorge that separates Spoleto from Monteluco, this 14th-century bridge is one of Umbria's most-photographed sights, and justifiably so. Built by Gattapone over the foundations of a Roman-era aqueduct, it's 750 feet long and soars up to 262 feet above the forested gorge. Postcard valley views make a walk across the bridge a must, particularly on a starry night. Beyond are the slopes of Monteluco, where well-marked trails invite further exploration on foot. ⊠ *Via del Ponte.*

Also Worth Seeing

🔟 **Arco di Druso.** This arch was built in the 1st century AD by the Senate of Spoleto to honor the Roman general Drusus (circa 13 BC–AD 23), son

Arco di
Druro **18**

Casa
Romana **17**

Duomo **13**

La Rocca **15**

Ponte
delle Torri **16**

Sant'-
Eufemia **14**

Teatro
Romano **19**

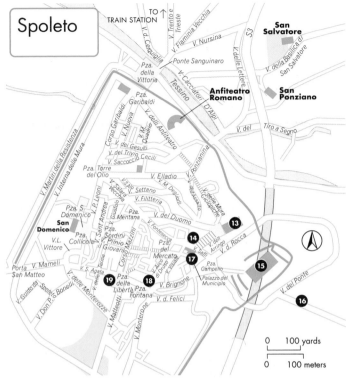

of the emperor Tiberius. It once marked the entrance to the Foro Romano (Roman Forum). ✉ *Piazza del Mercato.*

🄗 Casa Romana. The house excavated at the end of the 19th century is thought to have belonged to Vespasia Polla, the mother of the Roman Emperor Vespasian. The design is typical for houses of the 1st century AD, and some of the original decoration is still intact, including geometrically patterned marble mosaics and plaster moldings. ✉ *Palazzo del Municipio, Via Visiale 9* ☎ *0743/224656* 💶 *€2.50* ⊙ *June–Oct. 15, daily 10–8; Oct. 16–May, daily 10–6.*

🄖 La Rocca. The fortress built in 1359–63 by the Gubbio-born architect Gattapone dominates Spoleto. The structure served as a prison between 1860 and 1982 and now houses a small museum dedicated to medieval Spoleto. Plans for future development include an open-air theater and an international school for book restoration. You can admire the formidable exterior from the road that circles the extensive park beneath the castle. Tickets include a shuttle up to the entrance. Guided visits start on the hour; the last tour starts an hour before closing. ✉ *Via del Ponte* ☎ *0743/46434* 💶 *€6.50* ⊙ *Apr.–Oct. 15, daily 10–7; Oct. 16–Mar., weekdays 10–noon and 3–5, weekends 10–5.*

Truffle Trouble

UMBRIA IS RICH WITH TRUFFLES—more are found here than anywhere else in Italy—and those not consumed fresh are processed into pastes or flavored oils. The primary truffle areas are around the tiny town of Norcia, which holds a truffle festival every February, and near Spoleto, where signs warn against unlicensed truffle hunting at the base of the Ponte delle Torri. Although grown locally, the rare delicacy can cost a small fortune, up to $200 for a quarter pound—fortunately, a little goes a long way. At such a price there's great competition among the nearly 10,000 registered truffle hunters in the province, who use specially trained dogs to sniff them out among the roots of several types of trees, including oak and ilex. Despite one or two incidences of poisoning truffle-hunting dogs and importing inferior tubers from China, you can be reasonably assured that the truffle shaved onto your pasta has been unearthed locally.

⑭ Sant'Eufemia. Ancient and austere, this 11th-century church sits in the courtyard of the archbishop's palace. Its most interesting feature is the gallery, unique in Umbria, where female worshippers were required to sit. Enter through the attached **Museo Diocesano,** which contains paintings including a Madonna by Fra Filippo Lippi. ⊠ *Via Saffi between Piazza del Duomo and Piazza del Mercato* ☎ *0743/23101* ☒ *€3* ⊘ *Oct.–Mar., Wed.–Sat. and Mon. 10–12:30 and 3–6, Sun. 11–5; Apr.–Sept., Wed.–Sat. and Mon. 10–1 and 4–7, Sun. 10:30–1 and 3–6.*

⑲ Teatro Romano. The small but well-preserved Roman theater was the site of a gruesome episode in Spoleto's history. During the medieval struggle between Guelph (papal) and Ghibelline (imperial) factions for control of central and northern Italy, Spoleto took the side of the Holy Roman Emperor. And woe to those who disagreed: 400 Guelph supporters were massacred in the theater, their bodies burned in an enormous pyre. In the end, however, the Guelphs were triumphant, and Spoleto was incorporated into the states of the Church in 1354. Through a door in the west portico, the **Museo Archeologico** displays assorted artifacts and the *Lex Spoletina* (Spoleto Law) tablets dating from 315 BC. This ancient legal document prohibited the destruction of the *Bosco Sacro* (Sacred Forest), south of town on Monteluco, a pagan prayer site later frequented by St. Francis. The theater is used in summer for Spoleto's arts festival. ⊠ *Piazza della Libertà* ☎ *0743/223277* ☒ *€4* ⊘ *Daily 8:30–7:30.*

Off the Beaten Path

San Salvatore. The church and cemetery of San Salvatore seem very much forgotten, ensconced in solitude and cypress trees on a peaceful hillside, with the motorway rumbling below. One of the oldest churches in the world, it was built by eastern monks in the 4th century, largely of Roman-era materials. The highlight is the facade, with three exquisite marble doorways and windows, one of the earliest and best preserved in Umbria. It dates from a restoration in the 9th century and has hardly been touched since. ⊠ *Via della Basilica di San Salvatore, 1 km (½ mi) northeast of town, off Via Flaminia* ☉ *Nov.–Feb., daily 7–5; Mar., Apr., Sept., and Oct., daily 7–6; May–Aug., daily 7–7.*

Where to Stay & Eat

$$–$$$ ✕ **Il Tartufo.** As the name, the Truffle, indicates, dishes prepared with truffles are the specialty here—don't miss the risotto al tartufo—but there are also choices not perfumed with this expensive delicacy. Traditional fare is spiced up to appeal to the cosmopolitan crowd attending (or performing in) the summertime Festival dei Due Mondi. Incorporating the ruins of a Roman villa, the restaurant's decor is rustic on the ground floor; furnishings are more modern upstairs, and there's outdoor seating in warm weather. ⊠ *Piazza Garibaldi 24* ☎ *0743/40236* ⌛ *Reservations essential* ▤ *AE, DC, MC, V* ☉ *Closed Mon. and last 2 wks in July. No dinner Sun.*

$$ ✕ **Osteria del Trivio.** At this friendly trattoria serving up traditional Umbrian fare, everything is homemade and changes daily depending on what's in season. Dishes might include stuffed artichokes, pasta with *funghi sanguinosi* (a local mushroom) sauce, or chicken with artichokes. The homemade biscotti, for dunking in sweet wine, are a great dessert choice. There is a printed menu, but your effusive host will gladly explain the dishes in a number of languages. ⊠ *Via del Trivio 16* ☎ *0743/ 44349* ▤ *AE, DC, MC, V.*

$$ ✕ **Il Pentagramma.** A stable-turned-restaurant serves fresh local dishes such as *tortelli ai carciofi e noci* (artichoke-filled pasta with a hazelnut sauce) and lamb in a truffle sauce. It's quite central, off the Piazza della Libertà. ⊠ *Via Martani 4* ☎ *0743/223141* ▤ *DC, MC, V* ☉ *Closed Mon. No dinner Sun.*

$$ ✕ **Ristorante Panciolle.** In the heart of Spoleto's medieval quarter, this restaurant has one of the most appealing settings you could wish for: a small piazza filled with lemon trees. Dishes change throughout the year, and may include pastas served with asparagus or mushrooms, as well as grilled meats. When in season, more expensive dishes prepared with fresh truffles are also available. ⊠ *Vicolo degli Eroli 1* ☎ *0743/221241* ⌛ *Reservations essential* ▤ *AE, DC, MC, V* ☉ *Closed Wed.*

★ **$$** ▥ **Cavaliere Palace Hotel.** Turn into an arched passage off one of Spoleto's busy shopping streets and enter an elegant world through a quiet courtyard. Built in the 17th century for an influential cardinal, the rooms, particularly on the second floor, retain their sumptuously frescoed ceilings; care has been taken to retain a sense of old-world comfort throughout. In warm weather enjoy breakfast on a terrace and in a peaceful garden at the back of the hotel. ⊠ *Corso Garibaldi 49, 06049* ☎ *0743/220350* ▤ *0743/224505* ⊕ *www.cavalierehotels.com* ↪ *29 rooms, 2 suites* ⌖ *Restaurant, in-room safes, minibars, cable TV, bar, meeting rooms* ▤ *AE, DC, MC, V* ⏸◎⏸ *BP.*

$$ ▥ **Hotel San Luca.** The elegant San Luca is Spoleto's finest hotel, thanks to its commendable attention to detail: hand-painted friezes decorate guest-room walls, linen sheets cover firm beds, and some of the spacious rooms are wheelchair accessible. Enjoy an ample breakfast buffet, including homemade cakes, which is served in a pleasant room facing the

Fodor'sChoice ★

10

central courtyard. You can sip afternoon tea in oversize armchairs by the fireplace, and the hotel's rose garden provides a sweet-smelling backdrop for a walk or a nap. Service is cordial and prices are surprisingly modest. ☒ *Via Interna delle Mura 21, 06049* ☎ *0743/223399* 🖷 *0743/223800* ⊕ *www.hotelsanluca.com* 🛏 *33 rooms, 2 suites* ♿ *In-room safes, some in-room hot tubs, bar, laundry service, Internet room, parking (fee)* ▤ *AE, DC, MC, V* †◉| *BP.*

$$ 🖫 **Palazzo Dragoni.** Housed in the 15th-century palazzo of a Spoletan noble and decorated with antiques and frescoes, all the rooms of this hotel differ in size and aspect. Room 8 with a canopied bed and Room 10 with elegant picture windows are particularly beautiful. The plain tile bathrooms, although simple and functional, lack the charm of the rest of the building. Look out at the cathedral and the sloping rooftops of the town from the guest rooms that face the valley and from the loggia, where the buffet breakfast is served. ☒ *Via del Duomo 13, 06049* ☎ *0743/222220* 🖷 *0743/222225* ⊕ *www.palazzodragoni.it* 🛏 *15 rooms* ♿ *Wi-Fi, bar, meeting rooms, parking (fee), some pets allowed; no a/c in some rooms* ▤ *MC, V* †◉| *BP.*

$ 🖫 **Hotel Clitunno.** A renovated 18th-century building houses this pleasant hotel in the center of town. Cozy bedrooms and intimate public rooms, some with timbered ceilings, have the sense of a traditional Umbrian home—albeit one with a good restaurant. The hotel staff is glad to light the fireplace in Room 212 in advance of winter arrivals. Upper-floor rooms look over Spoleto's rooftops. ☒ *Piazza Sordini 6, 06049* ☎ *0743/223340* 🖷 *0743/222663* ⊕ *www.hotelclitunno.com* 🛏 *47 rooms* ♿ *Restaurant, minibars, bar, library, babysitting, laundry service, Internet room, meeting rooms; no a/c in some rooms* ▤ *AE, DC, MC, V* †◉| *BP.*

Nightlife & the Arts

Thousands of spectators flock to the **Festival dei Due Mondi** (Festival of Two Worlds ☒ Box office, Piazza Duomo 8 ☎ 800/565600 ⊕ www.spoletofestival.it), held mid-June–mid-July, to watch music, opera, and theater artists perform. Order tickets as far in advance as possible; full program information is available starting in February.

SOUTHERN UMBRIA

Orvieto, built on a tufa mount, produces one of Italy's favorite white wines and has one of the country's greatest cathedrals and most compelling fresco cycles. Nearby Narni and Todi are pleasant medieval hill towns. The former stands over a steep gorge, its Roman pedigree evident in dark alleyways and winding streets; the latter is a fairy-tale village with incomparable views and one of Italy's most perfect piazzas.

Todi

② *41 km (27 mi) northwest of Spoleto, 47 km (29 mi) south of Perugia.*

As you stand on **Piazza del Popolo**, it's easy to see why Todi is often described as Umbria's prettiest hill town. The square is a model of spatial harmony, with stunning views over the surrounding countryside. Nar-

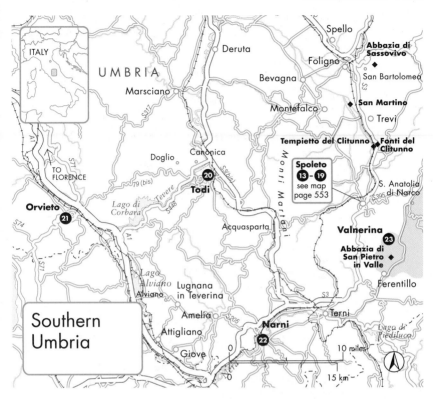

row cobblestone streets go winding around the hill, every so often finishing in a tiny quiet piazza. Todi's 12th-century Romanesque-Gothic **Duomo** is famed for its choir stalls by Antonio Bencivenni da Mercatello and his son Sebastiano, dating from 1530. Its simple square facade is echoed by the solid Palazzo dei Priori across the way. ⊠ *Piazza del Popolo* ☎ *075/8943041* ⊗ *Apr.–Oct., Mon.–Sat. 8:30–12:30 and 2:30–6:30, Sun. 8:30–12:30 and 2:30–5:30; Nov.–Mar., Mon.–Sat. 8:30–4:30, Sun. 8:30–12:30 and 2:30–5:30.*

The Renaissance church of **Santa Maria della Consolazione,** with an elegant pale-green dome, is a pleasant surprise on the outskirts of town. ⊠ *Via Menecali* ☎ *075/8948482* ⊗ *Apr.–Oct., Wed.–Mon. 9–1 and 2:30–6; Nov.–Mar., Wed.–Mon. 10–12:30 and 2:30–6.*

Where to Stay & Eat

★ **$$$** 🏨 **Tenuta di Canonica.** The affable hosts here, Daniele and Maria Fano, have retained the architectural integrity of this brick farmhouse and medieval tower in the Tiber Valley. You're bound to marvel at the exposed stone walls, high beamed ceilings, brick floors, and terra-cotta tiles—all in soothing earthy colors. Guest rooms are filled with family furniture and antique pieces. You can hike or ride on horseback through olive groves, orchards, and the forest on the grounds. ⊠ *Località La Canon-*

ica 75–76, 06059, 5 km (3 mi) northwest of center ☎ 075/8947545 📠 075/8947581 🌐 www.tenutadicanonica.com ⇆ 11 rooms, 2 apartments ♁ Dining room, pool, bar, library; no a/c, no room TVs ▭ MC, V 🍽 BP.

$$ ✕ Ristorante Umbria. Todi's most popular restaurant for more than four decades, the Umbria is reliable for sturdy country food, plus a wonderful view from the terrace. There's always a hearty soup simmering, as well as homemade pastas with truffles, game, and the specialty of the house, *palombaccio alla ghiotta* (roasted squab). ✉ *Via San Bonaventura 13 ☎ 075/8942737 or 075/8942390 ▭ AE, DC, MC, V ⊙ Closed Tues.*

$ 🏨 San Lorenzo Tre. Surrounded by antique furniture, paintings, and period knickknacks, you get the sense of a place more in tune with the 19th than the 21st century. The hotel doesn't pamper you with modern comforts; only four of the six rooms have private bathrooms, but all share a magnificent view over the valleys and hills to the north of town. A narrow alley off Todi's main square and a long flight of stairs lead up to this tiny guesthouse. ✉ *Via San Lorenzo 3, 06059 ☎📠 075/8944555 🌐 www.todi.net/lorenzo ⇆ 6 rooms, 4 with bath ♁ No a/c, no room phones, no room TVs ▭ MC, V ⊙ Closed Jan. and Feb. 🍽 BP.*

Orvieto

㉑ *30 km (19 mi) west of Todi, 81 km (51 mi) west of Spoleto.*

Carved out of an enormous plateau of volcanic rock high above a green valley, Orvieto has natural defenses that made the high walls seen in many Umbrian towns unnecessary. The Etruscans were the first to settle here, digging a honeycombed network of more than 1,200 wells and storage caves out of the soft stone. The Romans attacked, sacked, and destroyed the city in 283 BC; since then, it has grown up out of the rock into an enchanting maze of alleys and squares. Orvieto was solidly Guelph in the Middle Ages, and for several hundred years popes sought refuge in the city, at times needing protection from their enemies, at times from the summer heat of Rome.

WORD OF MOUTH

"When you go to Orvieto, stop first at the tourist information office across the piazza from the Duomo. Get tickets there to see the Signorelli frescoes inside the cathedral—they are stunning. Bring binoculars so you can get good close-up views, as many of them are high up." —nonnafelice

When painting his frescoes inside the Duomo, Luca Signorelli asked that part of his contract be paid in Orvietan wine, and he was neither the first nor the last to appreciate the region's popular white. In past times the caves carved underneath the town were used to ferment the Trebbiano grapes used in making Orvieto Classico; now local wine production has moved out to more traditional vineyards, but you can still while away the afternoon in tastings at any number of shops in town.

★ Orvieto's **Duomo** is a dazzling triumph of Romanesque-Gothic architecture. It was built to commemorate a local miracle: a priest in the nearby town of Bolsena suddenly found himself assailed by doubts about the transubstantiation—he could not bring himself to believe that the body of Christ was contained in the consecrated communion host. His doubts were put to rest, however, when a wafer he had just blessed suddenly started to drip blood onto the linen covering the altar. The pope certified the miracle and declared a new religious holiday—the Feast of Corpus Christi.

The stunning carved-stone church facade is the work of some of Italy's finest artists and took 300 years to complete. The bas-reliefs on the lower parts of the pillars by Lorenzo Maitani (circa 1275–1330), one of the Duomo's architects, show scenes from the Old Testament and some scary renderings of the *Last Judgment and Hell,* as well as a more tranquil *Paradise.*

Inside the cathedral you must cross a vast expanse to reach the major works, at the far end of the church in the transepts. To the left is the **Cappella del Corporale,** where the famous stained altar cloth is displayed in a modern casing. The cloth is carried outside the cathedral, for festive viewings, on Easter and on Corpus Christi (the ninth Sunday after Easter). It was originally stored in the golden reliquary that is also on display. Though often ignored, the old container, modeled after the cathedral and inlaid with transparent enamel images, deserves a closer look—it's one of the finest examples of this kind of 14th-century Italian workmanship in existence today. On the nearby chapel walls, frescoes executed by a trio of local artists depict the miracle. In the right transept, Signorelli's *Stories of the Antichrist and of the Last Judgement,* the artistic jewels of the Duomo, deck the walls of the **Cappella Nuova** (or Cappella di San Brizio; buy tickets in the tourist office across the square). In these delightfully gruesome works, the damned fall to hell, and lascivious demons bite off ears, step on heads, and spirit away young girls. Dante would surely have approved; his portrait accompanies *Scenes from Purgatorio.* Signorelli and Fra Angelico, who also worked on the chapel, witness the gory scene. ✉ *Piazza del Duomo* ☎ *0763/ 341167 Duomo, 0763/342477 Capella Nuova* ⊕ *www.opsm.it* 🖃 *Duomo free, Cappella Nuova €3* ☉ *Duomo, Nov.–Feb., daily 7:30–12:45 and 2:30–5:15; Mar. and Oct., daily 7:30–12:45 and 2:30–6:15; Apr.–Sept., daily 7:30–12:45 and 2:30–7:15. Capella Nuova, Nov.–Feb., Mon.–Sat. 9–12:45 and 2:30–5:15; Mar. and Oct., Mon.–Sat. 9–12:45 and 2:30–6:15; Apr.–Sept., Mon.–Sat. 9–12:45 and 2:30–7:15; Oct.–June, Sun. 2:30–5:45; July–Sept., Sun. 2:30–6:45.*

The **Museo Claudio Faina,** across the piazza from the Duomo, holds Etruscan and Roman artifacts. Its Roman coins, bronze pieces, and sarcophagi are accessible and interesting. ✉ *Piazza del Duomo 29* ☎ *0763/ 341511* ⊕ *www.museofaina.it* 🖃 *€4.50* ☉ *Apr.–Sept., daily 9:30–6; Oct. and Mar., daily 10–5; Nov.–Feb., Tues.–Sun. 10–5.*

There is no better way to get a sense of Orvieto's multilayered history than to take a tour of the maze of tunnels and chambers that make up
★ **Orvieto Underground.** Members of an Umbrian speleological club lead

small groups down below street level to explain the origins of the tufa plateau on which Orvieto sits and to reveal the fascinating purposes to which these hidden caverns where put. Tickets and information are available from the Orvieto Tourist Office, which also serves as the meeting place for tour groups. ☒ *Piazza Duomo 24* ☎ *0763/344891* ⊕ *www. orvietounderground.it* ☜ *€5.50* ☺ *Visits daily at 11, 12:30, 4, and 5:15.*

On Piazza Cahen, the **Fortezza,** built in the mid-14th century, encloses a public park with benches, shade, and an incredible view. The **Pozzo di San Patrizio** (Well of St. Patrick) was commissioned by Pope Clement VII (1478–1534) in 1527 to ensure a plentiful water supply in case of siege and its double spire of mule paths was clearly designed to avoid traffic jams. ☒ *Viale Sangallo, off Piazza Cahen* ☎ *0763/343768* ☜ *€4.50* ☺ *Oct.–Mar., daily 10–5:45; Apr.–Sept., daily 10–6:45.*

Where to Stay & Eat

$$$$ ✕ **Osteria dell'Angelo.** Come here for a decidedly nouvelle alternative to heavy Umbrian cuisine, in which tempting ingredients are delicately spiced and thoughtfully prepared. From the changing menu you might try the *animelle di carciofi con mousse di mele al calvados* (artichoke hearts with an apple-and-calvados mousse) as a starter, and continue with the *umbrichelli al sedano, limone, e burro del chianti* (local handmade spaghetti with a celery, lemon, and butter sauce). Desserts are spectacular, and the book-length wine list details an intoxicating array of producers and vintages. ☒ *Piazza XXIX Marzo 8/a* ☎ *0763/341805* ⌂ *Reservations essential* ☐ *AE, DC, MC, V* ☺ *Closed Sun. evening, Mon. and Tues. for lunch, and 2 wks in Jan. and in July.*

$$ ✕ **Le Grotte del Funaro.** This restaurant has an extraordinary location, deep in a series of caves within the volcanic rock beneath Orvieto. Once you have negotiated the steep steps, typical Umbrian specialties like tagliatelle *al vino rosso* (with red wine sauce) and grilled beef with truffles await. Sample the fine Orvieto wines, either the whites or the lesser-known reds. ☒ *Via Ripa Serancia 41* ☎ *0763/343276* ⌂ *Reservations essential* ☐ *AE, DC, MC, V* ☺ *Closed Mon. and 1 wk in July.*

¢ ✕ **Cantina Foresi.** For a light lunch of cheese, salami, bread, and salad accompanied by a glass of cool white wine, this small *enoteca* (wine bar) is hard to beat. The umbrella-shaded tables have one of the best views of the cathedral facade in town. ☒ *Piazza del Duomo 2* ☎ *0763/341611* ☐ *AE, DC, MC, V* ☺ *Closed Tues. Nov.–Mar.*

$$ ✕☷ **Villa Bellago.** Three farmhouses overlooking Lake Corbara have been completely renovated, resulting in a lodging with bright, spacious guest rooms and ample facilities. The hotel's fine restaurant ($$) specializes in imaginatively prepared Umbrian and Tuscan dishes, such as *umbrichelli alla norcina* (local handmade spaghetti with a cream-and-sausage sauce), and fresh fish is always on the menu. ☒ *On S448, 05023 Baschi, 7 km (4½ mi) south of Orvieto* ☎ *0744/950521* ☎ *0744/950524* ⊕ *www.argoweb.it/hotel_villabellago* ⇥ *19 rooms* ⌂ *Restaurant, minibars, tennis court, pool, gym, sauna, bar* ☐ *AE, DC, MC, V* ☺ *Restaurant closed Mon. and 3 wks in Feb.* ⦿| *BP.*

★ $$$$ ☷ **Hotel La Badia.** One of the best-known country hotels in Umbria occupies a 12th-century building—a former monastery. Vaulted ceilings and exposed stone walls establish the rustic elegance in the guest rooms, which have hand-knotted rugs and upholstered furniture. The rolling park around the hotel provides wonderful views of the valley and the town of Orvieto in the distance. ⊠ *Località La Badia, 05018 Orvieto Scalo, 4 km (2½ mi) south of Orvieto* ☎ *0763/301959* 🖷 *0763/305396* ⊕ *www.labadiahotel.it* 🛏 *21 rooms, 7 suites* ⚭ *Restaurant, 2 tennis courts, pool, bar, Internet room, meeting rooms* ▤ *AE, MC, V* ☯ *Closed Jan. and Feb.* ▢❙ *BP.*

$$ 🖼 **Palazzo Piccolomini.** Once a 16th-century palace, this is perhaps your best bet in central Orvieto for a pleasant stay. Though the entrance hall and bar are austere, the guest rooms, which vary in size, are modern and comfortable. Try for one of the larger rooms on an upper floor. Service is friendly and efficient. ⊠ *Piazza Ranieri 36, 05018* ☎ *0763/341743* 🖷 *0763/391046* ⊕ *www.hotelpiccolomini.it* 🛏 *29 rooms, 2 suites* ⚭ *Bar, Internet room* ▤ *AE, DC, MC, V* ☯ *Closed Jan. 15–31* ▢❙ *BP.*

Shopping

Excellent Orvieto wines are justly prized throughout Italy and the world. The whites pressed from the region's Trebbiano grapes are fruity, with a tart finish. Orvieto also produces its own version of the Tuscan dessert wine *vin santo*. It's darker than its Tuscan cousin and is aged five years before bottling. You can stop for a glass of vino at the **Wine Bar Nazzaretto** (⊠ Corso Cavour 40 ☎ 0763/340868), where there's also a good selection of sandwiches and snacks, and vin santo is for sale.

With a few small tables, a cheese counter that is second to none, a short menu, and a carefully chosen wine list, the specialty store **Carraro** (⊠ Corso Cavour 101 ☎ 0763/342870) is an excellent place for either a *degustazione* (tasting) of Orvietan cheese or a light lunch.

Orvieto artisans do particularly fine inlay and veneer woodwork. The Corso Cavour has a number of shops, the best known being the **Michelangeli family studio** (⊠ Via Michelangeli 3, at Corso Cavour ☎ 0763/342377), chock-full of imaginatively designed creations ranging in size from a giant *armadio* (wardrobe) to a simple wooden spoon.

Embroidery and lace making are not lost arts; **Duranti** (⊠ Corso Cavour 105 ☎ 0763/342222) is a good shop in which to find handmade *merletto* (lace).

10

Narni

㉒ *66 km (41 mi) southeast of Orvieto, 45 km (28 mi) southwest of Spoleto.*

At the edge of a steep gorge, Narni—like so many other towns in Umbria—is a medieval city of Roman origins. Below its finely paved streets and pretty Romanesque churches, excavations provide glimpses of an intriguing past. The **Lacus,** under **Piazza Garibaldi,** is an ancient Roman cistern with remnants of a Roman floor that was in use until the late Middle Ages. Two cisterns and assorted Roman fragments are visible in the crypt of the 8th-century church of **Santa Maria Impensole.** ⊠ *Via Mazzini* ☎ *0744/242226* 🎟 *Free* ☯ *Daily 9:30–noon and 4:30–6:30.*

A macabre note is struck by the symbols and dates on the walls of the rooms under the former church of **San Domenico,** inscribed by prisoners held there during the Inquisition. Tours are given in English. ✉ *Via Mazzini* ☎ *0744/722292* 🎫 *€5* ⊙ *Apr.–Oct., Sun. 10–1 and 3–6; Nov.–Mar., Sun. 11–1 and 3–5.*

You can take a unique tour of Narni's underground **Roman aqueduct**—the only one open to the public in all of Italy, but it's not for the claustrophobic. Contact Narni Sotterranea at least one week ahead to book a visit. ✉ *Narni Sotterranea, Via San Bernardo 12* ☎ *0744/722292* ⊕ *www.narnisotterranea.it* 🎫 *€5* ⊙ *Nov.–Mar., Sun. 11–1 and 3–5; Apr.–Oct., Sat. at 3 and at 6, Sun. 10–1 and 3–6; by appointment Mon.–Fri. for groups.*

Where to Eat

$$–$$$ ✕ **Il Cavallino.** Run by the third generation of the Bussetti family, Il Cavallino is a first-rate trattoria outside Narni. There are always several pastas to choose from, but it's the meat that makes this a worthy detour. Rabbit roasted with rosemary and sage and juicy grilled T-bone steaks are house favorites. The wine list has the best of what's local. ✉ *Via Flaminia Romana 220, 3 km (2 mi) south of center* ☎ *0744/761020* 🖃 *AE, DC, MC, V* ⊙ *Closed Tues. and Dec. 20–26.*

Valnerina

㉓ *Terni is 13 km (8 mi) northeast of Narni, 27 km (17 mi) southwest of Spoleto.*

The Valnerina (the valley of the River Nera, to the east of Spoleto) is the most beautiful of Central Italy's many well-kept secrets. The twisting roads that serve the rugged landscape are poor, but the drive is well worth the effort for its forgotten medieval villages and dramatic mountain scenery. You can head into the area from Terni on the S209, or on the SP395bis north of Spoleto, which links the Via Flaminia (S3) with the middle reaches of the Nera valley through a tunnel.

The **Cascata delle Marmore** are waterfalls engineered by the Romans in the 3rd century BC. To find them, drive east from Terni on the road to Lake Piediluco and Rieti. The waters are diverted on weekdays to provide hydroelectric power. On summer evenings, when the falls

> **WORD OF MOUTH**
>
> "I highly recommend a drive up the Valnerina. The highlight is the miraculous Piano Grande, which is an enormous and strange flat plain surrounded by mountains."
> –pfeldman

are in full spate, the cascading water is floodlighted. *Falls information office* ✉ *SP79, 3 km (2 mi) east of Terni* ☎ *0744/62982* 🎫 *Free* ⊙ *Light displays May, weekends 8 PM–10 PM; June–Aug., daily 8 PM–10 PM; mid-Mar.–Apr. and Sept., weekends 8 PM–9 PM.*

The Terni **tourist office** can provide information on the operating schedule of the Cascata delle Marmore, and on the region in general. ✉ *Viale Cesare Battisti 7/a, 05100* ☎ *0744/423047.*

Hiking the Umbrian Hills

MAGNIFICENT SCENERY makes the heart of Italy excellent walking, hiking, and mountaineering country. In Umbria, the area around Spoleto is particularly good; several pleasant, easy, and well-signed trails begin at the far end of the Ponte alle Torri bridge over Monteluco. From Cannara an easy half-hour walk leads to the fields of Pian d'Arca, the site of St. Francis's sermon to the birds. For slightly more arduous walks, you can follow the saint's path, uphill from Assisi to the Eremo delle Carceri, and then continue along the trails that crisscross Monte Subasio. At 4,250 feet, the Subasio's treeless summit affords views of Assisi, Perugia, far-off Gubbio, and the distant mountain ranges of Abruzzo.

For even more challenging hiking, the northern reaches of the Valnerina are exceptional; the mountains around Norcia should not to be missed. Throughout Umbria and the Marches, you'll find that most recognized walking and hiking trails are marked with the distinctive red-and-white blazes of the Club Alpino Italiano (CAI). Tourist offices are a good source for walking and climbing itineraries to suit all ages and levels of ability, while bookstores, *tabacchi* (tobacconists), and *edicole* (newsstands) often have maps and hiking guides that detail the best routes in their area. Depending on the length and location of your walk, it can be important that you have comfortable walking shoes or boots, appropriate attire, and plenty of water to drink.

Close to the town of Ferentillo is the outstanding 8th-century abbey of **San Pietro in Valle,** with fine frescoes in the church nave and a peaceful cloister. One of the abbey outbuildings houses an excellent restaurant with moderate prices. ⊠ *S209, 22 km (14 mi) northeast of Terni* ☎ *0743/54395.*

Norcia, the birthplace of St. Benedict, is better known for its Umbrian pork and truffles. Norcia exports truffles to France and hosts a truffle festival, the Mostra Internazionale del Tartufo Nero di Norcia, every November. The surrounding mountains provide spectacular hiking. ⊹ *67 km (42 mi) northeast of Terni.*

Piano Grande, a mountain plain 25 km (15 mi) to the northeast of the valley, is a hang glider's paradise, a wonderful place for a picnic or to fly a kite. It is also nationally famous for the quality of the lentils grown here, which are a traditional part of every Italian New Year feast.

THE MARCHES

Less touristed than Tuscany or Umbria, the Marches (Le Marche in Italian) have comparably diverse and attractive landscapes. Like those of its neighbors, the region's patchwork of hills is stitched with grapevines and olive trees producing delicious wine and oil. You're off the beaten path here and services tend to be less luxurious than in the regions to the west, but with a little luck you may have the place to yourself.

A car is recommended; train travel is slow and stops are limited, although you can reach Ascoli Piceno by rail. There is efficient bus service between the coastal town of Pésaro and Urbino, the principal tourist destinations of the region. Beyond the narrow coastal plain and away from major towns the roads are steep and twisting, but the only way to get around.

Urbino

24 *101 km (63 mi) northeast of Perugia, 107 km (66 mi) northeast of Arezzo.*

Majestic Urbino, atop a steep hill with a skyline of towers and domes, is something of a surprise—it's oddly remote—and it's humbling to reflect that it was once a center of learning and culture almost without rival in western Europe. The city takes great pride in its intellectual and humanistic heritage: it's home to the small but distinguished Università di Urbino, one of the oldest universities in the world. Very much a college town—with the usual bookshops, record stores, bars, and coffeehouses—during school term, Urbino's streets are filled with Italian students. In summer they are replaced by foreigners who come to study Italian language and arts at several prestigious academies.

Urbino's fame rests on the reputations of three of its native sons: Duke Federico da Montefeltro (1422–82), the enlightened warrior-patron who built the Palazzo Ducale; Raffaello Sanzio (1483–1520), or Raphael, one of the most influential painters in history and an embodiment of the spirit of the Renaissance; and the architect Donato Bramante (1444–1514), who translated the philosophy of the Renaissance into buildings of grace and beauty. Unfortunately, there's little work by either Bramante or Raphael in the city, but the duke's influence can still be felt strongly, even now, some 500 years after his death. The town looks much as it did in the glory days of the 15th century, a cluster of warm brick and pale stone buildings, all topped with russet-color tiled roofs.

Fodor'sChoice
★
The immense and beautiful **Palazzo Ducale** holds the place of honor in the city. In no other palace of its era are the tenets of the Renaissance better illustrated—in ideal form, it's a celebration of the nobility of man and his works, of the light and purity of the soul.

Today the palace houses the **Galleria Nazionale delle Marche,** with a superb collection of paintings, sculpture, and objets d'art, well arranged and properly lighted. Masterworks in the collection include Paolo Uccello's *Profanation of the Host,* Titian's *Resurrection* and *Last Supper,* and Piero della Francesca's *Madonna of Senigallia.* But the gallery's highlight is Piero's enigmatic masterpiece, long known as *The Flagellation of Christ.* Much has been written about this painting, and few experts agree on its meaning. It's one of the few works Piero signed (on the lowest step supporting the throne). The last tickets are sold 90 minutes before closing. ✉ *Piazza Duca Federico* ☎ *0722/322625* ⊕ *www.comune. urbino.ps.it* 🎫 *€4* ✆ *Apr.–Oct., Mon. 8:30–2, Tues.–Sun. 8:30* AM*–10* PM*; Nov.–Mar., Mon. 8:30–2, Tues.–Sun. 8:30–7:15.*

The **Casa Natale di Raffaello** is where the painter Raphael was born and, under the direction of his artist father, took his first steps in painting.

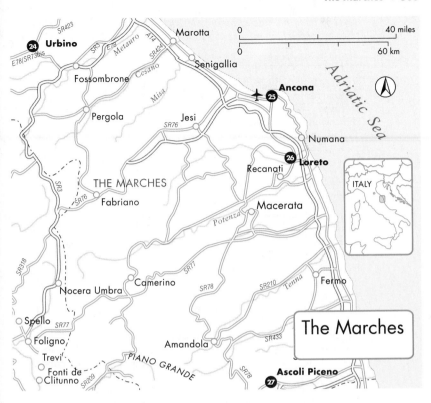

There is debate about the fresco of the Madonna here; some say it is by Raphael, whereas others attribute it to the father—with Raphael's mother and the young painter himself standing in as models for the Madonna and Child. ⊠ *Via Raffaello 57* ☎ *0722/320105* ⌛ *€3* ⊙ *Mar.–Oct, Mon.–Sat. 9–1 and 3–7, Sun. 10–1; Nov.–Feb., Mon.–Sat. 9–2, Sun. 10–1.*

Where to Stay & Eat

$–$$ ╳ **La Vecchia Fornarina.** Locals often fill the small, two-room trattoria near the Piazza della Repubblica to capacity. The specialty is meaty country fare, such as *coniglio* (rabbit) and *vitello alle noci* (veal cooked with walnuts) or *ai porcini* (with mushrooms). There's also a good selection of pasta dishes. ⊠ *Via Mazzini 14* ☎ *0722/320007* ⌛ *Reservations essential* ▭ *AE, DC, MC, V.*

$–$$ ▦ **Hotel Bonconte.** This classic dating from the beginning of the 20th century stands just inside the city walls, close to the Palazzo Ducale. Rooms, though somewhat small, are pleasantly decorated with some antiques and upholstered pieces; those at the front of the hotel have magnificent views of the valley below Urbino, although they also face the street. A terrace in the tranquil garden behind the hotel adjoins the cozy breakfast room and bar. ⊠ *Via delle Mura 28, 61029* ☎ *0722/2463* ▤ *0722/*

4782 ⊕ *www.viphotels.it/ita/hotel_bonconte.htm* ⇆ *23 rooms, 2 suites* △ *Bar, Internet room, meeting rooms* ⊟ *AE, DC, MC, V* ⦿ *BP.*

Shopping

Historically, Urbino has been a center for the production of fine majolica ceramic designs, and you can find pretty reproductions as well as contemporary designs at shops around town. A unique, though hard-to-carry, gift would be the Stella Ducale (Ducal Star), a complex three-dimensional decorative wooden star designed out of pyramid shapes by Renaissance mathematician Luca Pacioli.

Ancona

㉕ *87 km (54 mi) southeast of Urbino, 139 km (87 mi) northeast of Perugia.*

Set on an elbow-shape bluff (hence its name; *ankon* is Greek for "elbow") jutting out into the Adriatic, Ancona is one of Italy's most important ports. It's well served by trains, which makes it a good base for an excursion to Loreto or to Ascoli Piceno, farther south along the Adriatic coast. The city was the target of serious aerial bombing during World War II, and much was reduced to rubble, only to be rebuilt in a nondescript sprawl of boxy concrete. A few blocks from the main ferry terminal, what's left of the city's old center proves that Ancona was, and still is in parts, a lovely city. Narrow, cobbled streets wind steeply up from the waterfront, opening onto wide squares edged with handsome 19th-century brick-and-stucco buildings painted deep orange, pink, and ocher. The alleys leading downhill from central Piazza del Plebiscito are lined with chic shops selling everything from handmade linens to herbal cosmetics, and there are cafés and *pasticcerie* (pastry shops) aplenty to stave off hunger before your ferry leaves. There are enough sights to fill the longest layover, too.

The **Duomo di San Ciriaco,** built over a Greek temple, was redesigned in the 13th century to make it more visible to ships coming in to Ancona's port. ⊠ *Via Giovanni XXIII* ☎ *No phone* ☉ *Apr.–Sept., daily 8–noon and 3–7; Oct.–Mar., daily 8–noon and 3–6.*

Beginning in the 15th century the **Loggia dei Mercanti,** on the street of the same name, was Ancona's bazaar, where merchants and traders dealt in all manner of goods from the Far East. The Venetian Gothic building was restored in 2003 and is now used as a conference hall.

The 12th-century Romanesque church of **Santa Maria della Piazza** is built over a church from the 5th century; parts of the foundation and original hand-cut mosaic pavement are visible through handy glass cutouts in the floor. You can visit by appointment during the very irregular hours; call ahead. ⊠ *Via della Loggia* ☎ *071/200391.*

The 2nd-century **Arco di Traiano** (Trajan's Arch), out on the point at the end of Via Vanvitelli, is worth a look.

Where to Stay & Eat

$$–$$$ ✕ **La Moretta.** This family-run trattoria is on the central Piazza del Plebiscito, and in summer there's dining outside in the square. Among

the specialties here are *stoccafisso all'Anconetana* (cod baked with capers, anchovies, potatoes, and tomatoes) and the famous *brodetto* (fish stew). ⊠ *Piazza del Plebiscito 52* ☎ *071/202317* 🖃 *AE, DC, MC, V* ☾ *Closed Sun., Jan. 1–10, and Aug. 13–18.*

$$ ✕**Osteria del Pozzo.** The *antipasto di mare* (seafood appetizer), delicately flavored with a few drops of light olive oil and mixed with tiny pieces of seasonal fruit, is one reason the predominantly seafood restaurant is popular with locals. Pastas and main courses are equally delicious, and you should definitely finish with the restaurant's *sorbetto di limone* (lemon sorbet), served in a glass as a cool refreshing drink. This small, plain place is on a narrow cobblestone street between the port and Piazza del Plebiscito. ⊠ *Via Bonda 2* ☎ *071/2073996* 🖃 *AE, DC, MC, V* ☾ *Closed Sun., Jan. 6–15, and Aug. 7–31.*

$$–$$$ 🏨 **Grand Hotel Palace.** Widely held to be the best hotel in town, it's the extras here—slippers, bath salts, and shaving kits—that earn the ranking. Rooms are on the small side but beautifully furnished with French beds dressed in yellow damask, and half have a view directly over the port. Public rooms are grand and elegant, and the breakfast room is on the top floor with a panoramic view. ⊠ *Lungomare Vanvitelli 24, 60100* ☎ *071/201813* 🖷 *071/2074832* ⊕ *www.alberghiancona.it* ⤴ *39 rooms, 1 suite* ⚐ *Dining room, gym, bar, Internet room, meeting rooms* 🖃 *AE, DC, MC, V* ☾ *Closed Dec. 23–Jan. 1* ⧲ *BP.*

Loreto

㉖ *31 km (19 mi) south of Ancona, 118 km (73 mi) southeast of Urbino.*

★ Thousands of pilgrims come to Loreto every year to visit one of the world's best-loved shrines, the **Santuario della Santa Casa** (House of the Virgin Mary), within the basilica. According to legend, angels moved the house from Nazareth to this hilltop in 1295, when Nazareth fell into the hands of Muslim invaders. Excavations made at the behest of the Church have shown that the house did once stand elsewhere and was brought to the hilltop—either by crusaders or a family named Angeli (translated, "angels")—around that time.

Easter week and the Feast of the Holy House on December 10 are marked by processions, prayers, and a deluge of pilgrims; the rest of the year the shrine is relatively quiet. The house itself consists of three rough stone walls contained within an elaborate marble tabernacle; built around this centerpiece is the giant basilica of the Holy House, which dominates the town. The basilica was begun in Gothic style in 1468 and continued in Renaissance style through the late Renaissance with the help of some of the period's greatest architects: Bramante, Antonio da Sangallo (the Younger, 1483–1546), Giuliano da Sangallo (circa 1445–1516), and Sansovino (1467–1529).

The Holy Virgin of Loreto is the patroness of air travelers; in the church you can pick up Pope John Paul II's prayer for a safe flight—it's available in a dozen languages. ⊠ *Piazza della Madonna* ☎ *071/970104* ⊕ *www.santuarioloreto.it* ☾ *Apr.–Sept., daily 6:15–8 PM; Oct.–Mar., daily 6:45–7 PM.*

Ascoli Piceno

㉗ *74 km (38 mi) south of Loreto, 175 km (109 mi) southeast of Perugia.*

Ascoli Piceno is not a hill town; rather, it sits in a valley ringed by steep hills and cut by the fast-racing Tronto River. You can drive *around* the quaint old town, but much of the center of town is closed to traffic. This makes Ascoli Piceno one of the most pleasant large towns in the country for exploring on foot.

★ The heart of Ascoli Piceno is the majestic **Piazza del Popolo,** dominated by the Gothic church of **San Francesco** and the **Palazzo dei Capitani del Popolo,** a 13th-century town hall that contains a graceful Renaissance courtyard. The square functions as the city's living room: at dusk each evening the piazza fills with people strolling and exchanging news and gossip.

☼ Ascoli Piceno's **Giostra della Quintana** (Joust of the Quintana) is held on the first Sunday in August. Children love this medieval-style joust and the processions of richly caparisoned horses that wind through the streets of the old town. *Ascoli tourist office* ⊠ *Piazza del Popolo 1* ☎ *0736/253045.*

Where to Stay & Eat

★ **$–$$** ✕ **Ristorante Tornasacco.** At one of Ascoli Piceno's oldest restaurants you won't find nouvelle cuisine: the owners pride themselves on meaty local specialties such as olives *ascolane* (stuffed with minced meat, breaded, and deep-fried), *maccheroncini alla contadina* (homemade short pasta in a lamb, pork, and veal sauce), and *bistecca di toro* (bull steak). ⊠ *Piazza del Popolo 36* ☎ *0736/254151* ☰ *AE, DC, MC, V* ☼ *Closed Fri., July 15–31, and Dec. 23–28.*

$ ⊡ **Il Pennile.** Look for this modern, family-run hotel in a quiet residential area outside the old city center, amid a grove of olive trees. Rooms are functional singles, doubles, and triples; some have views of the city. ⊠ *Via G. Spalvieri, 63100* ☎ *0736/41645* 🖷 *0736/342755* ⊕ *www.hotelpennile.com* ⇗ *33 rooms* � *Minibars, gym, bar, Internet room* ☰ *DC, MC, V* ⸙⊙ *BP.*

UMBRIA & THE MARCHES ESSENTIALS

Transportation

BY AIR

Central Italy's closest major airports are in Florence, Rome, and Pisa— 2-, 2½-, and 3-hour drives, respectively. Perugia's tiny Aeroporto Sant' Egidio has daily flights to and from Milan, and seasonally scheduled flights to Paris, Copenhagen, and a small number of vacation destinations in the Mediterranean.

🛈 **Aeroporto Sant'Egidio** ☎ 075/592141 ⊕ www.airport.umbria.it. **Alitalia** ☎ 848/865642 ⊕ www.alitalia.it.

BY BUS

Perugia is served by the Sulga Line, with daily departures from Rome's Stazione Tiburtina and from Piazza Adua in Florence. Connections between Rome, Spoleto, and Urbino are provided by the associated bus companies Bucci and Soget, while Ascoli Piceno can be reached from Rome using the La Start company.

These same companies operate local bus service between all the major and minor towns within Umbria and the Marches. In addition, service between Loreto and Ancona is provided by the company Reni. Bus information is available from local tourist information offices or directly from area bus companies.

🚌 **Bus Information Bucci–Soget** ✉ Strada delle Marche 56, Pesaro ☎ 0721/32401 ⊕ www.autolineebucci.com. **Reni** ✉ Via Albertini 18, Ancona ☎ 071/8046504 ⊕ www. anconarenibus.it. **La Start** ✉ Viale Kennedy 22 ☎ 0763/263053 ⊕ www.startspa.it. **Sulga Line** ✉ Stazione Tiburtina, Rome ☎ 075/5009641 ⊕ www.sulga.it.

BY CAR

On the western edge of the region is the Umbrian section of the Autostrada del Sole (A1), Italy's principal north–south highway. It links Florence and Rome with Orvieto and passes near Todi and Terni. The S3 intersects with A1 and leads on to Assisi and Urbino. The Adriatica superhighway (A14) runs north–south along the coast, linking the Marches to Bologna and Venice.

The steep hills and deep valleys that make Umbria and the Marches so idyllic also make for challenging driving. Fortunately, the area has an excellent, modern road network, but be prepared for tortuous mountain roads if your explorations take you off the beaten track. Central Umbria is served by a major highway, the S75bis, which passes along the shore of Lake Trasimeno and ends in Perugia. Assisi is served by the modern highway S75; S75 connects to S3 and S3bis, which cover the heart of the region. Major inland routes connect coastal A14 to large towns in the Marches, including Urbino, Jesi, Macerata, and Ascoli Piceno, but inland secondary roads in mountain areas can be winding and narrow. Always carry a good road map, a flashlight, and, if possible, a cell phone in case of a breakdown.

🚗 **Car-Rental Agencies Avis** ✉ Sant'Egidio airport, Perugia ☎ 075/6929796 ✉ Stazione Ferroviaria Fontivegge, Perugia ☎ 075/5000395 ✉ Località S. Chiodo 164, Spoleto ☎ 0743/46272 ✉ Via XX Settembre 80/d, Terni ☎ 0744/287170. **Europcar** ✉ Via Ruggero d'Andreotto 7, Perugia ☎ 075/5731704 ✉ Via degli Artigiani 10, Terni ☎ 0744/817337 ✉ Raffaello Sanzio airport, Ancona ☎ 071/9162240. **Hertz** ✉ Via 7 Martiri 32/f, Orvieto ☎ 0763/301303 ✉ Piazza Vittorio Veneto 4, Perugia ☎ 075/5002439 ✉ Sant'Egidio airport, Perugia ☎ 075/5002439 ✉ Via Cerquiglia 144, Spoleto ☎ 0743/46703.

BY TRAIN

Frequent intercity trains link Florence and Rome with Perugia and Assisi, and local service to the same area is available from Terontola (on the Rome–Florence line) and from Foligno (on the Rome–Ancona line). Intercity trains between Rome and Florence make stops in Orvieto, and the main Rome–Ancona line passes through Narni, Terni, Spoleto, and

10

Foligno. Branch lines link Ancona with the inland towns of Fabriano and Ascoli Piceno. In Umbria, a small, privately owned railway operated by Ferrovia Centrale Umbra (FCU) runs from Città di Castello in the north to Terni in the south via Perugia. Note, train service is not available to either Gubbio or Urbino.

🚆 Train Information **Ferrovia Centrale Umbra** (FCU) ☎ 075/5729121 ⊕ www.fcu.it. **Ferrovie dello Stato** ☎ 892021 ⊕ www.trenitalia.com.

Contacts & Resources

EMERGENCIES

Emergency numbers are accessible from every phone, including cellular phones, all over Italy. If you have ongoing medical concerns, it's a good idea to make sure someone is on duty all night where you're staying—not a given in Umbria, less so in the Marches. As elsewhere in Italy, every pharmacy in Umbria and the Marches bears a sign at the door listing area pharmacies open in off-hours. Perugia, Spoleto, Assisi, Gubbio, and Urbino all have at least one so-called "night" pharmacy, but out in the countryside you may need a car to get to one. Try to bring extras with you of all medications you take regularly.

In car emergencies, call ACI for towing and repairs—you can ask to be transferred to an English-speaking operator; be prepared to tell the operator which road you're on, the direction you're going (e.g., "*verso* [in the direction of] Perugia") and the *targa* (license plate number) of your car. The great majority of Italians carry cellular phones, so if you don't have one, for help, flag down someone who does.

🚑 **ACI** ☎ 803/116. **Ambulance** ☎ 118. **Carabinieri** (Military Police) ☎ 112. **Emergencies** ☎ 113. **Fire** ☎ 115.

VISITOR INFORMATION

Turismo Verde, as well as local tourist offices, can provide you with information about *agriturismi* (farm stays) in the countryside. Though officially working farms, these range in style from rustic, with little more than a bed-and-breakfast, to luxury resorts with swimming pools and restaurants.

🛈 Tourist Information **Ancona** ✉ Via Thaon de Revel 4, 60100 ☎ 071/358991 ⊕ www. comune.ancona.it. **Ascoli Piceno** ✉ Piazza del Popolo 1, 63100 ☎ 0736/253045 ⊕ www.comune.ascoli-piceno.it/citta/infoindex.htm. **Assisi** ✉ Piazza del Comune 22, 06081 ☎ 075/812534 ⊕ www.assisi.umbria2000.it. **Gubbio** ✉ Via della Reppublica 6, 06024 ☎ 075/9220693 ⊕ www.gubbio-altochiascio.umbria2000.it. **Loreto** ✉ Via Solari 3, 60025 ☎ 071/970276 ⊕ www.turismo.marche.it. **Narni** ✉ Piazza dei Priori 3, 05035 ☎ 0744/715362 ⊕ www.umbria2000.it. **Orvieto** ✉ Piazza Duomo 24, 05018 ☎ 0763/341772 ⊕ www.orvieto.umbria2000.it. **Perugia** ✉ Piazza Matteotti 18, 06123 ☎ 075/5736458 ⊕ www.perugia.umbria2000.it. **Spoleto** ✉ Piazza della Libertà 7, 06049 ☎ 0743/238920 ⊕ www.spoleto.umbria2000.it. **Terni** ✉ Viale Cesare Battisti 7/a, 05100 ☎ 0744/423047. **Todi** ✉ Piazza Umberto I 6, 06059 ☎ 075/8943395 ⊕ www. todi.umbria2000.it. **Turismo Verde** ✉ Via Maria Angeloni 1, 06124 Perugia ☎ 075/ 5002953 🖷 075/5002956 ⊕ www.turismoverde.it. **Urbino** ✉ Piazza Duca Federico 35, 61029 ☎ 0722/2613 ⊕ www.turismo.marche.it.

Rome

Forum

WORD OF MOUTH

"There's something very powerful to being surrounded by all that history (and I'm not a history buff). It's not a place where you walk up, snap a picture, and say, 'All right I've seen it.' It's an imposing experience (in a good way). The effect is very strong. There are other beautiful scenic places in the world, but there's only one Rome."

—flatfeet

WELCOME TO ROME

St. Peter's Basilica

TOP 5
Reasons to Go

1. **The Pantheon:** Of ancient Rome's remains, this is the best preserved and most impressive.

2. **St. Peter's Square and Basilica:** The primary church of the Catholic faith is truly awe-inspiring.

3. **Galleria Borghese:** With a setting as exquisite as its collection, this small, elegant museum showcases some of the finest baroque and Renaissance art in Italy.

4. **A morning walk through Campo de' Fiori:** The city comes alive in this bustling square.

5. **Roman pizza:** Maybe it's the ovens, maybe the crust, maybe the cheese, but they just don't make it like this back home.

Getting Oriented

Rome is a sprawling city, but you'll likely spend all your time in and around the historic center. The area is split by the River Tiber (Tevere in Italian). To its west are the Vatican and the Trastevere neighborhood. To its east is everything else you've come to see: the Colosseum, the Pantheon, and scores of other exceptional sights, not to mention piazzas, fountains, shops, and restaurants. This is one of the most culturally rich plots of land in the world.

At the Vatican, headquarters of the Roman Catholic Church, everything is done in bold measures, from **St. Peter's Basilica** to the ceiling of the **Sistine Chapel.**

From Via del Corso to the Tiber, the cobblestone streets of Baroque Rome lead from one landmark to another, including the **Pantheon, Piazza Navona,** and **Campo de' Fiori.**

Trastevere residents pride themselves on being the most authentic Romans, and though the neighborhood has become trendy, it retains a tight-knit feel.

Villa Borghese

Villa Borghese is Rome's answer to Central Park. Within it is the exceptional **Galleria Borghese** art museum.

The **Spanish Steps**, rising up from the Piazza di Spagna, have been a popular gathering place for centuries. Radiating out from them is Rome's toniest shopping district.

The **Quirinale** area is filled with palaces, including the home of the Italian president, as well as several works by the baroque master Bernini.

The adjoining **Monti** and **San Giovanni** neighborhoods are home to several of Rome's most artistically rich churches.

Piazza Venezia, at the southern end of Via del Corso, is Rome's busiest crossroads.

The center of the present-day city was once the heart of **Ancient Rome**. The area of the forums and the **Colosseum** has been preserved as an archaeological treasure.

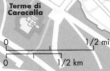

St. Peter's

ROME PLANNER

Making the Most of Your Time

"Roma, non basta una vita" (Rome, a lifetime is not enough): this famous saying should be stamped on the passport of every first-time visitor to the Eternal City. On the one hand, it's a warning: Rome is so packed with sights that it's impossible take them all in; it's easy to run yourself ragged trying to check off the items on your "must see" list. At the same time, the saying is a celebration of the city's abundance. There's so much here, you're bound to make discoveries you hadn't anticipated.

To conquer Rome, strike a balance between visits to major sights and leisurely neighborhood strolls. In the first category, the Vatican and the remains of ancient Rome loom the largest. Both require at least half a day; a good strategy is to devote your first morning to one and your second to the other. Leave the afternoons for exploring the neighborhood we label "Baroque Rome" and the shopping district around the Spanish Steps and Via del Corso.

If you have more days at your disposal, continue with the same approach. Among the sights, Galleria Borghese and the multilayered church of San Clemente are particularly worthwhile, and the neighborhoods of Trastevere and the Jewish Ghetto make for great wandering.

Getting Around

Most of Rome's sights are concentrated in the city center, but the area is too large to cover exclusively on foot. Transportation options are the metro (subway), bus, tram, and taxi—the pros and cons of each are detailed in the "Essentials" section at the end of the chapter. No matter what method you use to get around, try to avoid rush hours (8–9, 1–2:30, 7–8). Driving is always a mistake.

Expect to do lots of walking. Cobblestone streets call for comfortable shoes (though some natives seem willing to endure any pain in the name of fashion). Try to avoid the congestion and noise of major thoroughfares; plan routes along parallel side streets instead. Most hotels will give you a functional city map, and you can also pick maps up for free at tourist information booths. If you crave greater detail, purchase better maps at newsstands.

Safety Tips

Chances are your visit will be incident-free, but it's smart to be alert to the following:

■ The young pickpockets described under "Safety" in the Smart Travel Tips section at the back of this book are a common presence around Rome's major sights.

■ Pickpockets like to work public transit, particularly bus lines 64 and 40 Express between Termini station and St. Peter's. Gropers are also a presence on buses and subways. If you encounter one, react like the locals: forcefully and loudly.

■ Termini station is the site of numerous scams. Keep an eye on your belongings at all times.

■ They may not qualify as criminals, but the men who linger around the Colosseum in gladiator costume are con artists. They'll happily pose for a photograph with you, then demand a ridiculous fee.

Roman Hours

As you make your plans, keep in mind the following timing issues:

■ Most churches open at 8 or 9 in the morning, close from noon to 3 or 4, then reopen until 6:30 or 7. The notable exception is St. Peter's, which has continuous hours from 7 AM to 7 PM (6 in the fall and winter).

■ Many museums are closed on Monday, including the Galleria Borghese, the Etruscan Museum at Villa Giulia, and the museums of the Campidoglio.

■ The Vatican Museums are open on Monday but closed on Sunday, except for the last Sunday of the month (when admission is free and crowds are large). From November through mid-March, the museums close for the day at 1:45.

Piazza Navona

Reservations Required

You should reserve tickets for the following sights. See the listings within the chapter for contact information:

■ Galleria Borghese requires reservations. Visitors are admitted in two-hour shifts, and prime time slots can sell out days in advance, so it pays to plan ahead. You can reserve by phone or through the gallery's Web site.

■ In the ancient Rome archaeological area,

reservations for the Colosseum save you from standing in a ticket line that sometimes takes upward of an hour. You can reserve by phone or on the Web.

■ At the Vatican, you need to reserve several days in advance to see the gardens, and sev-

eral weeks in advance to see the necropolis. For information about attending a papal audience, see the CloseUp box "A Morning with the Pope" several pages into this chapter.

How's the Weather?

11

Not surprisingly, spring and fall are the best times to visit, with mild temperatures and many sunny days; the famous Roman sunsets are also at their best. Summers are often sweltering. In July and August, come if you like, but learn to do as the Romans do—get up and out early, seek refuge from the afternoon heat (nap if you can), resume activities in early evening, and stay up late to enjoy the nighttime breeze. Come August, many shops and restaurants close as natives head for the beach or the countryside. Roman winters are relatively mild, with persistent rainy spells.

Sistine Chapel

Updated by
Megan K.
Williams &
Dana Klitzberg
ROME IS A HEADY BLEND of artistic and architectural masterpieces, classical ruins, and extravagant baroque churches and piazzas—all of which serve as the backdrop to a joyful and frenetic street life. The city's 2,700-year-old history is on display wherever you look; the ancient rubs shoulders with the medieval, the modern runs into the Renaissance, and the result is a bustling open-air museum. Julius Caesar and Nero, the Vandals and the Popes, Raphael and Caravaggio, Napoléon and Mussolini—these and countless other political, cultural, and spiritual luminaries have left their mark on the city. More than Florence, more than Venice, Rome is Italy's treasure trove, packed with masterpieces from more than 2 millennia of artistic achievement. This is where a metropolis once bustled around the carved marble monuments of the Roman Forum, where centuries later Michelangelo painted Christian history in the Sistine Chapel, where Gian Lorenzo Bernini's nymphs and naiads dance in their fountains, and where an empire of gold was worked into the crowns of centuries of rulers.

Today Rome's formidable legacy is kept alive by its people, their history knit into the fabric of their everyday lives. Students walk dogs in the park that was once the mausoleum of the family of the emperor Augustus; Raphaelesque teenage girls zip through traffic on their *motorini*; priests in flowing robes walk through medieval piazzas talking on cell phones. Modern Rome has one foot in the past, one in the present—a fascinating stance that allows you to tip back an espresso in a square designed by Bernini, then hop on the metro to your hotel room in a renovated Renaissance palace. "When you first come here you assume that you must burrow about in ruins and prowl in museums to get back to the days of Numa Pompilius or Mark Antony," Maud Howe observes in her book *Roma Beata*. "It is not necessary; you only have to live, and the common happenings of daily life—yes, even the trolley car and your bicycle—carry you back in turn to the Dark Ages, to the early Christians, even to prehistoric Rome."

EXPLORING ROME

Updated by
Megan K.
Williams
Plan your day taking into account the varying opening hours of the sights you want to visit, which usually means mixing the ancient, classical, and baroque, museums and parks, the center and the environs. Keep in mind that an uncharted ramble through the heart of the old city can be just as satisfying as the quiet contemplation of a chapel or a trek through marbled museum corridors. The Rome Archeologia Card, a combination ticket for the Colosseum, Palatine, and the various branches of the Museo Nazionale Romano (Palazzo Altemps, Crypta Balbi, Terme di Diocleziano, Terme di Caracalla, Villa dei Quintili, the Tomba di Cecilia Metella, and Palazzo Massimo alle Terme), valid for seven consecutive days, is available at each participant's ticket office for €20—a good deal for ancient-history buffs.

The Vatican: Rome of the Popes

This tiny walled city-state, capital of the Catholic Church, draws millions every year to its wealth of treasures and spiritual monuments. You might visit the Vatican for its exceptional art holdings—Michelangelo's frescoes, rare archaeological marbles, and Bernini's statues—or you may want to appreciate the singular and grandiose architecture of St. Peter's Square. Many come here on pilgrimage, spiritual or otherwise, to see the seat of world Catholicism and the most overwhelming architectural achievement of the Renaissance, St. Peter's Basilica. At the Vatican Museums there are magnificent rooms decorated by Raphael, sculptures such as the *Apollo Belvedere* and the *Laocoön*, frescoes by Fra Angelico, paintings by Giotto and Leonardo, and the celebrated ceiling of the Sistine Chapel. The Church power that emerged as the Rome of the emperors declined gave impetus to a profusion of artistic expression and shaped the destiny of the city for a thousand years.

Allow yourself an hour to see the St. Peter's Basilica, 30 minutes for the Museo Storico, 15 minutes for the Vatican Grottoes, an hour for Castel Sant'Angelo, and an hour to climb to the top of the dome. Ushers at the entrance of St. Peter's Basilica and the Vatican Museums bar entry to people with "inappropriate" clothing—which means no bare knees or shoulders.

The Main Attractions

★ ❸ **Basilica di San Pietro.** The physical proportions of the sublime St. Peter's Basilica are staggering: it covers about 18,100 square yards, extends 212 yards in length, and carries a dome that rises 435 feet and measures 138 feet across its base. The church's history dates back to the year AD 319, when the emperor Constantine built a basilica over the site of the tomb of St. Peter (died AD 64). This early church stood for more than 1,000 years, undergoing a number of restorations, until it was on the verge of collapse.

In 1506 Pope Julius II (1443–1513) commissioned the architect Bramante to build a new and greater basilica, but construction would take more than 170 years. In 1546 Michelangelo was persuaded to take over the job, but the magnificent cupola was finally completed by Giacomo della Porta (circa 1537–1602) and Domenico Fontana (1543–1607). The new church wasn't dedicated until 1626; by that time Renaissance had given way to baroque, and many of the plan's original elements had gone the way of their designers. At the entrance, the 15th-century bronze doors by Filarete (circa 1400–69) fill the central portal. Off the entry portico, architect and sculptor Gianlorenzo Bernini's famous *Scala Regia,* the ceremonial entry to the Vatican Palace, is one of the most magnificent staircases in the world and is graced with Bernini's dramatic statue of Constantine the Great.

Entering the sanctuary, take a moment to adjust to the enormity of the space stretching in front of you. The cherubs over the holy-water fonts have feet as long as the distance from your fingertips to your elbow. It is because the proportions are in such perfect harmony that the vastness may escape you at first. The megascale was inspired by the size of the ancient Roman ruins.

Over an altar in a side chapel near the entrance is Michelangelo's *Pietà,* a sculpture of Mary holding her son Jesus's body after crucifix-

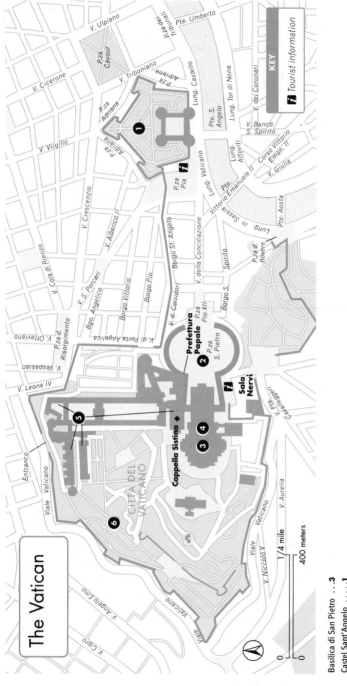

The Vatican

KEY

🛈 *Tourist information*

Basilica di San Pietro ...**3**
Castel Sant'Angelo **1**
Giardini Vaticani **6**
Musei Vaticani **5**
Piazza San Pietro **2**
Vatican Necropolis **4**

ion—the star attraction here other than the basilica itself. Legend has it that the artist, only 22 at the time the work was completed, overheard passersby expressing skepticism that such a young man could have executed such a sophisticated and moving piece. It's said that his offense at the implication was why he crept back that night and signed the piece—in big letters, on a ribbon falling from the Virgin's left shoulder across her breast.

Inlaid in the gorgeous marble pavement of the nave's central aisles are the names of the world's great cathedrals organized by church size—the message is clear, St. Peter's has them all beaten. At the crossing of the aisles four massive piers support the dome, and the mighty Bernini **baldacchino** (canopy) rises high above the papal altar, where the pope celebrates Mass. "What the barbarians didn't do, the Barberini did," 17th-century wags quipped when Barberini Pope Urban VIII had the bronze stripped from the Pantheon's portico and melted down to make the baldacchino (using what was left over for cannonballs). The bronze throne behind the main altar in the apse, the *Cathedra Petri* (Chair of St. Peter), is Bernini's work (1656), and it covers a wooden-and-ivory chair that St. Peter himself is said to have used. However, scholars contend that this throne probably dates only from the Middle Ages. See how the adoration of a million kisses has completely worn down the bronze on the right foot of the statue of St. Peter in front of the near-right pillar in the transept. Free one-hour English-language tours of the basilica depart Monday–Saturday at 10 and 3, Sunday at 2:30 (sign up at the little desk under the portico). St. Peter's is closed during ceremonies in the piazza. ⊠ *Piazza San Pietro* ⊕ *www.vatican.va* ⊙ *Apr.–Sept., daily 7–7; Oct.–Mar., daily 7–6.*

The **Grotte Vaticane** (Vatican Grottoes) in the basilica contain the tombs of many popes, including John Paul II, and the Tomb of St. Peter. The entrance is opposite the baldacchino, near a pillar where the dome begins. The only exit leads outside the church, so don't go down until you're finished elsewhere. ⊡ *Free* ⊙ *Apr.–Sept., daily 7–6; Oct.–Mar., daily 7–5.*

A small but rich collection of Vatican treasures is housed in the **Museo Storico** in St. Peter's Sacristy, among them precious antique chalices and the massive 15th-century sculptured bronze tomb of Pope Sixtus V (1520–90) by Antonio del Pollaiuolo (1431–98). ⊡ €9 ⊙ *Daily 8–5.*

The **roof** of St. Peter's Basilica, reached by elevator or stairs, provides a view among a landscape of domes and towers. An interior staircase (170 steps) leads to the base of the dome for a dove's-eye look at the interior of St. Peter's. Then, only if you are stout of heart and sound of lung should you attempt the taxing and claustrophobic climb up the remaining 330 steps to the balcony of the lantern, where the view embraces the Vatican Gardens and all of Rome. The up and down staircases are one-way; once you commit to climbing, there's no turning back. ☎ *06/69883462* ⊡ *Elevator €7, stairs €4* ⊙ *Daily 8–5.*

🅒 ❶ **Castel Sant'Angelo.** For hundreds of years this fortress guarded the Vatican, to which it is linked by the **Passetto**, an arcaded passageway. According to legend, Castel Sant'Angelo got its name during the plague of

A Morning with the Pope

The pope holds audiences in a large, modern hall (or in St. Peter's Square in summer) on Wednesday morning at 10. To attend, you must get tickets; apply in writing at least 10 days in advance to the **Papal Prefecture** (Prefettura della Casa Pontificia; ✆ 00120 Vatican City ☎ 06/69883273 📠 06/69885863), indicating the date you prefer, your language, and your hotel. Or go to the prefecture, through the Porta di Bronzo, the bronze door at the end of the colonnade on the right side of the piazza; the office is open Monday–Saturday 9–1, and last-minute tickets may be available. You can also arrange to pick up free tickets on Tuesday from 5 to 6:45 at the **Santa Susanna American Church** (✉ Via XX Settembre 15, near Termini ☎ 06/42014554); call first. For a fee, travel agencies make arrangements that include transportation. Arrive early, as security is tight and the best places fill up fast.

590, when Pope Gregory the Great (circa 540–604), passing by in a religious procession, had a vision of an angel sheathing its sword atop the stone ramparts. Though it may look like a stronghold, Castel Sant'Angelo was in fact built as a tomb for the emperor Hadrian (76–138) in AD 135. By the 6th century it had been transformed into a fortress, and it remained a refuge for the popes for almost 1,000 years. It has dungeons, battlements, cannon and cannonballs, and a collection of antique weaponry and armor. The lower levels formed the base of Hadrian's mausoleum; ancient ramps and narrow staircases climb through the castle's core to courtyards and frescoed halls, where temporary exhibits are held. Off the loggia is a café.

The upper terrace, with the massive angel statue commemorating Gregory's vision, evokes memories of Tosca, Puccini's poignant heroine in the opera of the same name, who threw herself off these ramparts with the cry, *"Scarpia, avanti a Dio!"* ("Scarpia, we meet before God"). On summer evenings a book fair with musical events and food stalls surrounds the castle. One of Rome's most beautiful pedestrian bridges, **Ponte Sant'Angelo** spans the Tiber in front of the fortress and is studded with graceful angels designed by Bernini. ✉ *Lungotevere Castello 50, San Pietro* ☎ *06/39967700* ⊕ *www.pierreci.it* 🎫 *€5* ⊙ *Tues.–Sun. 9–8.*

⑤ **Musei Vaticani** (The Vatican Museums). The Vatican Palace has been the papal residence since 1377; it's a collection of buildings covering more than 13 acres, with an estimated 1,400 rooms, chapels, and galleries. Other than the pope and his court, the occupant is the Musei Vaticani (Vatican Museums), containing some of art's greatest masterpieces. The Sistine Chapel is the headliner here, but in your haste to get there, don't overlook the Museo Egizio, with its fine Egyptian collection; the famed classical sculptures of the Chiaramonti and the Museo Pio Clementino; and the Stanze di Raffaello (Raphael Rooms), a suite of halls covered floor-to-ceiling in some of the master's greatest works.

Fodor'sChoice
★

On a first visit to the Vatican Museums, you may just want to see the highlights—even that will take several hours and a good, long walk. In peak tourist season, be prepared for at least an hour's wait to get into the museums and large crowds once inside. Getting there first thing in the morning is highly recommended. The collection is divided among different galleries, halls, and wings connected end to end. Pick up a leaflet at the main entrance to the museums to see the overall layout. The Sistine Chapel is at the far end of the complex, and the leaflet charts two abbreviated itineraries through other collections to reach it. An audio guide (€5.50, about 90 minutes) for the Sistine Chapel, the Stanze di Raffaello, and 350 other works and locations is worth the added expense. Phone at least a day in advance to book a guided tour (€16.50) through the Guided Visit to Vatican Museums.

The main entrance to the museums, on Viale Vaticano, is a long walk from Piazza San Pietro along a busy thoroughfare. Some city buses stop near the main entrance: Bus 49 from Piazza Cavour stops right in front; Buses 81 and 492 and Tram 19 stop at Piazza Risorgimento, halfway between St. Peter's and the museums. The Ottaviano–S. Pietro and the Cipro–Musei Vaticani stops on Metro A also are in the vicinity. Entry is free the first Sunday of the month, and the museum is closed on Catholic holidays, of which there are many. Last admission is an hour before closing. ⊠ *Main museum entrance, Viale Vaticano; guided visit office, Piazza San Pietro* ☎ *06/69883332, 06/69884676 guided visit reservations* 🖷 *06/69885100 guided visit reservations* ⊕ *www.vatican.va* 🖼 €12 ☉ *Mid-Mar.–Oct., weekdays 8:45–4:45, Sat. 8:45–2:45, last Sun. of month 8:45–1:45; Nov.–mid-Mar., Mon.–Sat. and last Sun. of month 8:45–1:45.*

Besides the galleries mentioned here, there are many other wings along your way—full of maps, tapestries, classical sculpture, Egyptian mummies, Etruscan statues, and even Aztec treasures. From the main entrance of the Vatican Museums take the escalator up to the **Pinacoteca** (Picture Gallery) on your right. This is a self-contained section, and it's worth visiting first for works by such artists as Leonardo, Giotto (circa 1266–1337), Fra Angelico (1387–1455), and Filippo Lippi (circa 1406–69), and Raphael's exceptional *Transfiguration, Coronation* and *Foligno Madonna.*

The **Cortile Ottagano** (Octagonal Courtyard) of the Vatican Museums displays some of sculpture's most famous works, including the 4th-century BC *Apollo Belvedere* (and Canova's 1801 *Perseus,* heavily influenced by it) and the 2nd-century *Laocoön.*

The **Stanze di Raffaello** (Raphael Rooms) are second only to the Sistine Chapel in artistic interest—and draw crowds comparable. In 1508 Pope Julius II employed Raphael, on the recommendation of Bramante, to decorate the rooms with biblical scenes. The result is a Renaissance tour de force. Of the four rooms, the second and third were decorated mainly by Raphael. The others were decorated by Giulio Romano (circa 1499–1546) and other assistants of Raphael; the first room is known as the Stanza dell'Incendio, with frescoes by Romano of the *incendio* (fire) in the Borgo neighborhood.

The frescoed **Stanza della Segnatura** (Room of the Signature), where papal bulls were signed, is one of Raphael's finest works; indeed, they are thought by many to be some of the finest paintings in the history of Western art. This was Julius's private library, and the room's use is reflected in the frescoes' themes, philosophy and enlightenment. A paradigm of High Renaissance painting, the works demonstrate the revolutionary ideals of naturalism (Raphael's figures lack the awkwardness of those painted only a few years earlier); humanism (the idea

that human beings are the noblest and most admirable of God's creations); and a profound interest in the ancient world, the result of the 15th-century rediscovery of classical antiquity. The *School of Athens* glorifies some of philosophy's greats, including Plato (pointing to Heaven) and Aristotle (pointing to Earth) at the fresco's center. The pensive figure on the stairs is thought to be modeled after Michelangelo, who was painting the Sistine ceiling at the same time Raphael was working here. Michelangelo does not appear in preparatory drawings, so Raphael may have added his fellow artist's portrait after admiring his work.

The tiny **Cappella di Nicholas V** (Chapel of Nicholas V) is aglow with frescoes by Fra Angelico, the Florentine monk whose sensitive paintings were guiding lights for the Renaissance. The **Appartamento Borgia** (Borgia Apartment) is worth seeing for the elaborately painted ceilings, designed and partially executed by Pinturicchio. Among the frescoes, look for the Borgia's family emblem, the bull, and for the blond Lucrezia, the Borgia pope's daughter, posing piously as St. Catherine.

In 1508, just before Raphael started work on his rooms, the redoubtable Pope Julius II commissioned Michelangelo to paint singlehandedly the more-than-10,000-square-foot ceiling of the **Cappella Sistina** (Sistine Chapel). The task cost the artist four years of mental and physical anguish. It's said that for years afterward Michelangelo couldn't read anything without holding it up over his head. The result, however, was the masterpiece that you now see, its colors cool and brilliant after restoration. Bring a pair of binoculars to get a better look at this incredible work (unfortunately, you're not allowed to lie down on the floor to study the frescoes above, the viewing position of choice in decades past). Tourists in the 19th century used pocket mirrors so as not to strain their necks.

The exhibition halls of the **Biblioteca Vaticana** (Vatican Library) are bright with frescoes and contain a sampling of the library's rich collections of precious manuscripts. The **Room of the Aldobrandini Marriage** (Room X) holds a beautiful Roman fresco of a nuptial rite, which deserves a look after you've seen the rest of the museum.

NEED A
BREAK?

You don't have to snack at the touristy joints outside the Vatican Museums; a short walk away are neighborhood restaurants catering to locals. Among them is the **Il Mozzicone** (⊠ Borgo Pio 180, near San Pietro), where you can fill up on solid Roman fare at moderate prices. **La Caravella** (⊠ Via degli Scipioni 32, at Via Vespasiano, off Piazza Risorgimento, near San Pietro) serves pizza at lunch every day but Thursday, when it's closed.

❷ Piazza San Pietro. As you enter St. Peter's Square you are officially entering Vatican territory. The piazza is one of Bernini's most spectacular masterpieces. It was completed in 1667 after 11 years' work, a relatively short time, considering the vastness of the task. The piazza can hold 400,000 people—as it did in the days following the death of Pope John Paul II. The piazza is surrounded by a curving pair of quadruple colonnades, topped by a balustrade and statues of 140 saints. Look for the two disks set into the pavement on either side of the obelisk at the center of the piazza. When you stand on either disk, a trick of perspective makes the colonnades seem to consist of a single row of columns. Bernini had an even grander visual effect in mind when he designed the square: the surprise of stepping into an immense, airy space after approaching it through a neighborhood of narrow, shadowy streets. The contrast was intended to evoke the metaphor of moving from darkness to light. But in the 1930s Mussolini spoiled the effect. To celebrate the "conciliation" between the Vatican and the Italian government under the Lateran Pact of 1929, he conceived of the Via della Conciliazione, the broad avenue that now forms the main approach to St. Peter's.

Remember to look for the Swiss Guards in their colorful uniforms; they've been standing at the Vatican entrances for the past 500 years.

Also Worth Seeing

❻ Giardini Vaticani (Vatican Gardens). Generations of popes have strolled in these beautifully manicured gardens, originally laid out in the 16th century. A two-hour guided tour, half by bus and half on foot, takes you through a haven of shady walkways, elaborate fountains, and exotic plants. Make reservations two or three days in advance and pick up your tickets in the Guided Visit to Vatican Museums Office at the museum entrance. If you have a reservation, you can skip the line (go in through the "Exit" door); the office window is inside the atrium. ⊠ *Viale Vaticano* ☎ *06/69884466 reservations* ⊕ *www.vatican.va* ☜ *€9* ⊘ *Tours Mon.–Sat. 10 AM, office Mon.–Sat. 8:30–7.*

❹ Vatican Necropolis. Visit the pre-Constantine necropolis under St. Peter's for a fascinating glimpse of the underpinnings of the great basilica, which was built over the cemetery where archaeologists believe they have found St. Peter's tomb. Apply in advance by sending a fax or e-mail with the name of each visitor, language spoken, proposed days for the visit, and a local phone number. Reservations will be confirmed a few days in advance. No children under 15 are admitted. Tickets are sometimes available for same-day tours; apply at the Ufficio Scavi (Excavations Office), on the right beyond the Arco delle Campane entrance to the Vatican, to the left of the basilica. Tell the Swiss Guard you want the Ufficio Scavi, and he will let you by. ⊠ *Piazza San Pietro* ☎ *06/69885318* 🖷 *06/69873017* ☜ *€10* ⊘ *Ufficio Scavi Mon.–Sat. 9–5.*

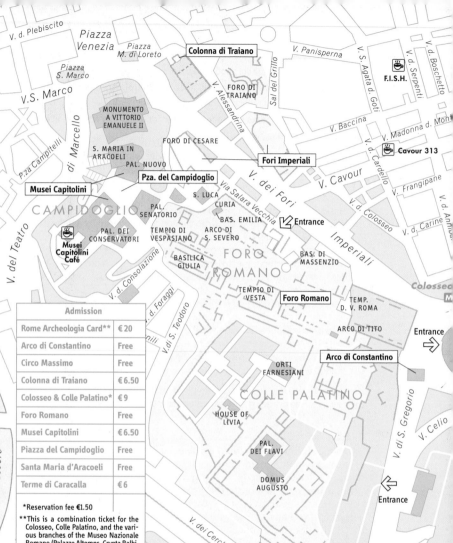

V. d. Plebiscito

Piazza Venezia

Piazza M. di Loreto

Piazza S. Marco

Colonna di Traiano

V. Panisperna

V. S. Agata d. Goti

V. d. Boschetto

V. d. Serpenti

☕ F.I.S.H.

V.S. Marco

MONUMENTO A VITTORIO EMANUELE II

FORO DI TRAIANO

V. Alessandrina

Sal. del Grillo

V. Baccina

V. Madonna d. Mont

☕ Cavour 313

V. d. Cardello

Pza Campitelli

di Marcello

S. MARIA IN ARACOELI

PAL. NUOVO

FORO DI CESARE

Fori Imperiali

V. dei Fori

V. Cavour

V. Frangipane

Pza. del Campidoglio

Via Salara Vecchia

Musei Capitolini

S. LUCA

CURIA

V. d. Colosseo

V. d. Carine

CAMPIDOGLIO

PAL. SENATORIO

BAS. EMILIA

↯ Entrance

Imperiali

V. d. Teatro

🍴 Musei Capitolini Café

PAL. DEI CONSERVATORI

TEMPIO DI VESPASIANO

ARCO DI S. SEVERO

V. d. Consolazione

BASILICA GIULIA

FORO ROMANO

BAS. DI MASSENZIO

Colosseo Ⓜ

V. d. Foraggi

V. d. S. Teodoro

TEMPIO DI VESTA

Foro Romano

TEMP. D. V. ROMA

Admission	
Rome Archeologia Card**	€ 20
Arco di Constantino	Free
Circo Massimo	Free
Colonna di Traiano	€ 6.50
Colosseo & Colle Palatino*	€ 9
Foro Romano	Free
Musei Capitolini	€ 6.50
Piazza del Campidoglio	Free
Santa Maria d'Aracoeli	Free
Terme di Caracalla	€ 6

*Reservation fee €1.50

**This is a combination ticket for the Colosseo, Colle Palatino, and the various branches of the Museo Nazionale Romano (Palazzo Altemps, Crypta Balbi, Terme di Diocleziano, Terme di Caracalla, Villa dei Quintili, the Mausoleo di Cecilia Metella, and Palazzo Massimo alle Terme), good for seven consecutive days.

ARCO DI TITO

Entrance ⇨

Arco di Constantino

ORTI FARNESIANI

COLLE PALATINO

V. di S. Gregorio

V. Celio

HOUSE OF LIVIA

PAL. DEI FLAVI

Tevere

DOMUS AUGUSTO

⇦ Entrance

V. dei Cerchi

Circo Massimo

Terme di Caracalla ↓

CAPITOLINE HILL: The original capitol hill. The seat of government in Rome since its founding now also holds the Capitoline Museums, chock-full of the treasures of antiquity.

ROMAN FORUM: Downtown Ancient Rome. People from all corners of the empire crowded into the Forum to do business, to hear the latest news, and to worship.

PALATINE HILL: Home of the empire's rich and famous. Luxurious villas lined Palatine Hill; emperors held court on its heights and vied with their predecessors for lasting renown.

CAMPIDOGLIO

FORO ROMANO

COLLE PALATINO

ANCIENT ROME
GLORIES OF
THE CAESARS

Time has reduced ancient Rome to fields of silent ruins, but the powerful impact of what happened here, of the genius and power that made Rome the center of the Western world, echoes across the millennia.

In this one compact area of the city, you can step back into the Rome of Cicero, Julius Caesar, and Virgil. Walk along the streets they knew, cool off in the shade of the Colosseum that towered over their city, see the sculptures that watched over their piazzas. At the end of a day of exploring, climb one of the famous seven hills and watch the sun set over what was once the heart of the civilized world.

Today, this part of Rome, more than any other, is a perfect example of that layering of historic eras, the overlapping of ages, of religions, of a past that is very much a part of the present. Christian churches rise from the foundations of ancient pagan temples. An immense marble monument to a 19th-century king shares a square with a medieval palace built by a pope. Still, the history and memory of ancient Rome dominate the area. It's fitting that in the aftermath of centuries of such pageantry Percy Bysshe Shelley and Edward Gibbon reflected here on the meaning of *sic transit gloria mundi* (so passes away the glory of the world).

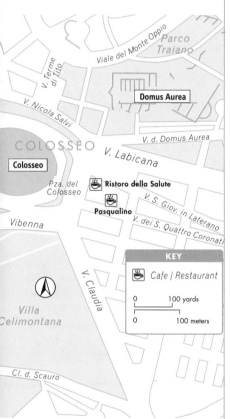

COLOSSEUM: Gladiators fought for the chance to live another day on the floor of the Colosseum, iconic symbol of ancient Rome.

CAMPIDOGLIO

⊙ **TIMING TIPS**

The Capitoline Museums are closed on Monday; admission is free on the last Sunday of the month. Late evening is an option for this area. Though the church is closed, the museums are open until 9 PM, and the views of the city lights and the illuminated Victor Emmanuel II monument and the Foro Romano are striking.

CLIMB MICHELANGELO'S DRAMATIC RAMP TO THE SUMMIT OF ONE OF Rome's seven hills, the Campidoglio (also known as Capitoline Hill), for views across the rooftops of modern Rome in one direction and across the ruins of ancient Rome in the other. Check out the stellar Musei Capitolini, crammed with a collection of masterpieces rivaled only by the Vatican museums.

★ **Piazza del Campidoglio.** In Michelangelo's piazza at the top of the Campidoglio stands a bronze equestrian statue of Marcus Aurelius (AD 121–180). A legend foretells that some day the statue's original gold surface will return, heralding the end of the world. Pending the arrival of that day, the original 2nd century statue was moved inside the Musei Capitolini; a copy sits on the piazza. Stand with your back to it to survey central Rome.

The Campidoglio, the site of the Roman Empire's first and holiest temples, had fallen into ruin by the Middle Ages and was called *Monte Caprino* (Goat Hill). In 1536 Pope Paul III (1468–1549) decided to restore its grandeur for the triumphal entry into the city of Charles V (1500–1558), the Holy Roman Emperor. He called upon Michelangelo to create the staircase ramp, the buildings and facades on the square, the pavement decoration, and the pedestal for the bronze statue.

The two buildings that make up the **Musei Capitolini** are on the piazza, flanking the **Palazzo Senatorio**. The Campidoglio has always been the seat of Rome's government; its Latin name is the root for the word capitol. Today, Rome's city hall occupies the Palazzo Senatorio. Head to the vantage points in the belvederes on the sides of the palazzo for great views of the ruins of ancient Rome.

★ **Musei Capitolini** (Capitoline Museums). This immense collection, housed in the twin Palazzi del Museo Capitolino and Palazzo dei Conservatori buildings, is a greatest hits collection of Roman art through the ages, from the ancients to the baroque.

The **Palazzi del Museo Capitolino** contains hundreds of Roman busts of philoso-

AN EMPEROR CHEAT SHEET

OCTAVIAN/AUGUSTUS (27 BC–AD 14)

After the death of Julius Caesar, Octavian gained control of Rome after a series of battles that culminated with the defeat of Antony and Cleopatra at Actium. Later known as Caesar Augustus, he was Rome's first emperor. His rule began a 200-year period of peace known as the Pax Romana.

Colle Palatino

CALIGULA (AD 37–41)

Caligula was tremendously popular when he came to power at the age of 25, but he very soon became infamous for his excessive cruelty, immorality, and erratic behavior. His contemporaries universally considered him to be insane. He was murdered by his own guard within four years.

phers and emperors—a fascinating Who's Who of the ancient world. Forty-eight Roman emperors are represented. Unlike the Greeks, whose portraits are idealized, the Romans preferred the warts-and-all school of representation. Other notable sculptures include the poignant *Dying Gaul* and the regal *Capitoline Venus*. In the Capitolino courtyard is a gigantic, reclining sculpture of Oceanus, found in the Roman Forum and later dubbed *Marforio*. This was one of Rome's talking statues to which citizens from the 1500s to the 1900s affixed anonymous satirical verses and notes of political protest. (Another talking statue still in use today sits at Piazza Pasquino, near Piazza Navona.)

Lining the courtyard of the **Palazzo dei Conservatori** are the colossal fragments of a head, leg, foot, and hand—all that remains of the famous statue of the emperor Constantine the Great, who believed that Rome's future lay with Christianity. These immense effigies were much in vogue in the later days of the Roman Empire. The renowned symbol of Rome, the *Capitoline Wolf*, a 6th-century

BC Etruscan bronze, holds a place of honor in the museum; the suckling twins were added during the Renaissance to adapt the statue to the legend of Romulus and Remus. The Palazzo also contains some of baroque painting's great masterpieces, including Caravaggio's *La Buona Ventura* (1595) and *San Giovanni Battista* (1602), Peter Paul Rubens's *Romulus and Remus* (1614), and Pietro da Cortona's sumptuous portrait of Pope Urban VIII (1627). When museum fatigue sets in, enjoy the view and refreshments on a large open terrace in the Palazzo dei Conservatoria. ☎ *06/39967800 or 06/67102475* ⊕ *www.pierreci.it* ☉ *Tues.–Sun. 9–8.*

Santa Maria d'Aracoeli. Seemingly endless, steep stairs climb from Piazza Venezia to the Santa Maria. There are 15th-century frescoes by Pinturicchio (1454–1513) in the first chapel on the right. ☉ *Oct.–May, daily 7–noon and 4–6; June–Sept., daily 7–noon and 4–6:30.*

NERO (AD 54–68)

Nero is infamous as a violent persecutor of Christians. He also murdered his wife, his mother, and countless others. Although it's not certain whether he actually fiddled as Rome burned in AD 64, he was well known as a singer and a composer of music.

Domus Aurea

DOMITIAN (AD 81–96)

The first emperor to declare himself "Dominus et Deus" (Lord and God), he stripped away power from the Senate. After his death, the Senate retaliated by declaring him "Damnatio Memoriae" (his name and image were erased from all public records).

Colle Palatino

FORO ROMANO

⊙ **TIMING TIPS**

It takes about an hour to explore the Roman Forum. There are entrances on the Via dei Fori Imperiali and near the Colosseum. Another hour's walk will cover the Imperial Fora. With exception of the overpriced stands along the avenue and cafés on Largo Corrado Ricci, there are few places nearby for food and drink, so bring a snack and water.

EXPERIENCE THE ENDURING ROMANCE OF THE FORUM. WANDER AMONG its lonely columns and great, broken fragments of sculpted marble and stone— once temples, palaces, and shops crowded with people from all corners of the known world. This was the heart of ancient Rome and a symbol of the values that inspired Rome's conquest of an empire.

★ **Foro Romano** (Roman Forum). Built in a marshy valley between the Capitoline and Palatine hills, the Forum was the civic core of Republican Rome, the austere era that preceded the hedonism of the emperors. The Forum was the political, commercial, and religious center of Roman life. Hundreds of years of plunder and the tendency of later Romans to carry off what was left of the better building materials reduced it to the series of ruins you see today. Archaeological digs continue to uncover more about the sight; bear in mind that what you see are the ruins not of one period but of almost 900 years, from about 500 BC to AD 400.

The **Basilica Giulia**, which owes its name to Julius Caesar who had it built, was where the Centumviri, the hundred-or-so judges forming the civil court, met to hear cases. The open space before it was the core of the forum proper and prototype of Italy's famous piazzas. Let your imagination dwell on Mark Antony (circa 81 BC–30 BC), who delivered the funeral address in Julius Caesar's honor from the rostrum left of the **Arco di Settimio Severo**. This arch, one of the grandest of all antiquity, was built hundreds of years later in AD 203 to celebrate the victory of the emperor Severus (AD 146–211) over the Parthians, and was topped by a bronze equestrian statuary group with six horses. You can explore the reconstruction of the large brick senate hall, the **Curia;** three Corinthian columns (a favorite of 19th-century poets) are all that remains of the **Tempio di Vespasiano**. In the **Tempio di Vesta**, six highly privileged vestal virgins kept the sacred fire, a tradition that dated back to the very earliest days of Rome, when guarding the community's precious fire was essential to its well-being. The cleaned and restored

AN EMPEROR CHEAT SHEET

TRAJAN (AD 98–117)
Trajan, from Southern Spain, was the first Roman emperor not born in Italy. He enlarged the empire's boundaries to include modern-day Romania, Armenia, and Upper Mesopotamia.
Colonna di Traiano

HADRIAN (AD 117–138)
He expanded the empire in Asia and the Middle East. He's best known for designing and rebuilding the Pantheon, constructing a majestic villa at Tivoli, and initiating myriad other constructions across the empire, including the famed wall across Britain.
Pantheon, in Baroque Rome

Arco di Tito, which stands in a slightly elevated position on a spur of the Palatine Hill, was erected in AD 81 to celebrate the sack of Jerusalem 10 years earlier, after the great Jewish revolt. A famous relief shows the captured contents of Herod's Temple—including its huge seven-branched menorah—being carried in triumph down Rome's Via Sacra. Making sense of the ruins isn't always easy; consider renting an audio guide (€4) or buying a booklet that superimposes an image of the Forum in its heyday over a picture of it today. Guided tours in English usually begin at 10:30 AM. In summer the Forum is sometimes open for midnight (guided) tours—look for signs at the entrance or ask at your hotel. ☎ 06/39967700 ⊕ *www.pierreci.it* ⊙ *Daily 9–1 hr before sunset.*

THE OTHER FORA
Fori Imperiali (Imperial Fora). These five grandly conceived squares flanked with columnades and temples were built by the emperors Caesar, Augustus, Vespasian, Nerva, and Trajan. The original Roman Forum, built up over 500 years of Republican Rome, had grown crowded, and Julius Caesar was the first to attempt to rival it.

He built the **Foro di Cesare** (Forum of Caesar), including a temple dedicated to himself and the goddess Minerva. Four later emperors followed his lead, creating their own fora. The grandest was the **Foro di Traiano** (Forum of Trajan) a veritable city unto itself built by Trajan (AD 53–117). The adjoining Mercati Traianei (Trajan's Markets), a huge multilevel brick complex of shops, walkways, and terraces, was one of the marvels of the ancient world. In the 20th century, Benito Mussolini built the Via dei Fori Imperiali directly through the Imperial Fora area. Marble and bronze maps on the wall along the avenue portray the extent of the Roman Empire and Republic, and many of the remains of the Imperial Fora lay buried beneath its surface.

Colonna di Traiano (Trajan's Column). The ashes of Trajan were buried inside the base of this column (the ashes have since been removed). Remarkable reliefs spiral up its sides, celebrating his military campaigns in Dacia (Romania). The column has stood in what was once the Forum of Trajan since AD 113. ☎ 06/69780532 ⊙ *Tues.–Sun. 9–4:30.*

MARCUS AURELIUS (AD 161–180)

Remembered as a humanitarian emperor, Marcus Aurelius was a Stoic philosopher and his *Meditations* are still read today. Nonetheless, he was an aggressive leader devoted to expanding the empire.

Piazza del Campidoglia

CONSTANTINE I (AD 306–337)

Constantine changed the course of history by legalizing Christianity. He legitimized the once-banned religion and paved the way for the papacy in Rome. Constantine also founded Constantinople, an Imperial capital in the East.

Arco di Constantino

COLLE PALATINO

⊙ **TIMING TIPS**

A stroll on the Palatino, with a visit to the Museo Palatino, takes about two hours. You can reserve tickets online or by phone—operators speak English. If you are buying tickets in person, remember that there are often shorter lines here than at the Colosseum and the ticket is good for both sights. The entrances are in the Roman Forum and on Via S. Gregorio.

IT ALL BEGAN HERE. IT IS BELIEVED THAT ROMULUS, THE FOUNDER OF ROME, lived on the Colle Palatino (Palatine Hill). It was an exclusive address in ancient Rome, and emperors built palaces upon its slopes. Tour the Palatine's hidden corners and shady lanes, take a welcome break from the heat in its peaceful gardens, and enjoy a view of the Circo Massimo fit for an emperor.

★ **Colle Palatino** (Palatine Hill). A lane known as the Clivus Palatinus, paved with worn stones that were once trod by emperors and their slaves, climbs from the Forum area to a site that historians identify with Rome's earliest settlement. The legend goes that the infant twins Romulus and Remus were nursed by a she-wolf on the banks of the Tiber and adopted by a shepherd. Encouraged by the gods to build a city, the twins chose this site in 735 BC, fortifying it with a wall that archaeologist Rudolfo Lanciani identified in the late 19th century when digging on Palatine Hill.

During the Republican era the hill was an important religious center, housing the Temple of Cybele and the Temple of Victory, as well as an exclusive residential area. Cicero, Catiline, Crassus, and Agrippa all had homes here. Augustus was born on the hill, and as he rose in power, he built libraries, halls, and temples here; the **House of Livia,** reserved for his wife, is best preserved. Emperor Tiberius was the first to build a palace here; others followed. The structures most visible today date back to the late 1st century AD, when the Palatine experienced an extensive remodeling under Emperor Domitian. His architects put up two separate palaces, the **Domus Augustana** and the **Domus Livia.** During the Renaissance, the powerful Farnese family built gardens atop the ruins overlooking the Forum. Known as the **Orti Farnesiani,** they were Europe's first botanical gardens. The **Museo Palatino** charts the history of the hill. Splendid sculptures, frescoes, and mosaic intarsia from various imperial buildings are on display. ☏ *06/39967700* ⊕ *www.pierreci.it* ⊙ *Tues.–Sun. 9–1 hr before sunset.*

THE RISE AND FALL OF ANCIENT ROME

218 BC

ca. 800 BC	Rise of Etruscan city-states.
510	Foundation of the Roman republic; expulsion of Etruscans from Roman territory.
343	Roman conquest of Greek colonies in Campania.
264–241	First Punic War (with Carthage): increased naval power helps Rome gain control of southern Italy and then Sicily.
218–200	Second Punic War: Hannibal's attempted conquest of Italy, using elephants, is eventually crushed.

NEAR THE COLLE PALATINO

Circo Massimo (Circus Maximus). Ancient Rome's oldest and largest racetrack lies in the natural hollow between Palatine and Aventine hills. From the imperial box in the palace on Palatine Hill, emperors could look out over the oval course. Stretching about 650 yards from end to end, the Circus Maximus could hold more than 300,000 spectators. On certain occasions there were as many as 24 chariot races a day, and competitions could last for 15 days. The central ridge was the sight of two Egyptian obelisks (now in the Piazza del Popolo and Piazza San Giovanni in Laterano). Check out the panoramic views of the Circus Maximus from the Palatine Hill's Belvedere. You can also see the green slopes of the Aventine and Celian hills, as well as the bell tower of Santa Maria in Cosmedin.

Terme di Caracalla (Baths of Caracalla). For the Romans, public baths were much more than places to wash. The baths also had recital halls, art galleries, libraries, massage rooms, sports grounds, and gardens. Even the smallest public baths had at least some of these amenities, and in the capital of the Roman Empire, they were provided on a lavish scale. Ancient Rome's most beautiful and luxurious public baths were opened by the emperor Caracalla in AD 217 and were used until the 6th century.

Taking a bath was a long and complex process, and a social activity first and foremost. Remember, too, that for all their sophistication, the Romans didn't have soap. You began by sweating in the *sudatoria*, small rooms resembling saunas. From these you moved on to the *calidarium* for the actual business of washing, using a *strigil*, or scraper, to get the dirt off. Next was the *tepidarium*, where you gradually cooled down. Finally, you splashed around in the *frigidarium*, the only actual "bath" in the place, in essence a cold water swimming pool. There was a nominal admission fee, often waived by officials and emperors wishing to curry favor with the plebeians. The baths' functioning depended on the slaves who cared for the clients and stoked the fires that heated the water. ☎ *06/39967700* ⊕ *www.pierreci.it* ☉ *Tues.–Sun. 9 AM–1 hr hour before sunset, Mon. 9–2.*

150 BC	Roman Forum begins to take shape as the principal civic center in Italy.
146	Third Punic War: Rome razes city of Carthage and emerges as the dominant Mediterranean force.
133	Rome rules entire Mediterranean Basin except Egypt.
49	Julius Caesar conquers Gaul.
44	Julius Caesar is assassinated.
27	Rome's Imperial Age begins; Octavian (now named Augustus) becomes the first emperor and is later deified. The Augustan Age is celebrated in the works of Virgil (70 BC–AD 19), Ovid (43 BC–AD 17), Livy (59 BC–AD 17), and Horace (65–8 BC).

44 BC

COLOSSEO

You can give the Colosseum a cursory look in about 30 minutes, but it deserves at least an hour. Make reservations by phone (there are English-speaking operators) or online at least a day in advance to avoid long lines. Or buy your ticket for the Colosseum at Palatine Hill, where the lines are usually shorter.

LEGEND HAS IT THAT AS LONG AS THE COLOSSEUM STANDS, ROME WILL stand; and when Rome falls, so will the world. No visit to Rome is complete without a trip to the crumbling oval that has been the iconic symbol of the city for centuries.

★ **Colosseo.** A program of games and shows lasting 100 days celebrated the opening of the massive and majestic Colosseum in AD 80. On the opening day alone, 5,000 wild beasts perished. More than 70,000 spectators could sit within the arena's 573-yard circumference, which had marble facing, hundreds of statues for decoration, and a *velarium*—an ingenious system of sail-like awnings rigged on ropes manned by imperial sailors—to protect the audience from the sun and rain. Before the imperial box, gladiators would salute the emperor and cry, "*Ave, imperator, morituri te salutant*" ("Hail, emperor, men soon to die salute you"); it is said that when one day they heard the emperor Claudius respond, "Or maybe not," they were so offended that they called a strike.

Originally known as the Flavian Amphitheater, it took the name Colosseum after a truly colossal gilt bronze statue of Nero that stood nearby. Gladiator combat and

staged animal hunts ended by the 6th century. The arena later served as a quarry from which materials were looted to build Renaissance churches and palaces. Finally, it was declared sacred by the Vatican in memory of the many Christians believed martyred here. (Scholars now maintain that Christians met their death elsewhere.) During the 19th century, romantic poets lauded the glories of the ruins when viewed by moonlight. Now its arches glow at night with mellow golden spotlights—less romantic, perhaps, but still impressive.

Expect long lines at the entrance and actors dressed as gladiators who charge a hefty fee to pose for pictures. Once inside you can walk around much of the outer ring of the structure and look down into the exposed passages under what was once the arena floor, now represented by a thin gangway and a small stage at one end. Climb the steep stairs for panoramic views in the Colosseum and out to the Forum and Arch of Constantine. A museum space on

THE RISE AND FALL OF ANCIENT ROME

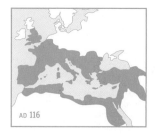

AD 116

43 AD	Rome invades Britain.
50	Rome is the largest city in the world, with a population of a million.
65	Emperor Nero begins the persecution of Christians in the Empire; Saints Peter and Paul are executed.
70–80	Vespasian builds the Colosseum.
98–117	Trajan's military successes are celebrated with his Baths (98), Forum (110), and Column (113); the Roman Empire reaches its apogee.

the upper floor holds temporary archaeological exhibits. ☎ 06/7005469, 06/39967700 *reservations* ⊕ *www.pierreci.it* ⊙ *Daily. 8:30–1 hr before sunset.*

Arco di Costantino. The largest (69 feet high, 85 feet long, 23 feet wide) and the best preserved of Rome's triumphal arches was erected in AD 315 to celebrate the victory of the emperor Constantine (280–337) over Maxentius (died 312). It was just before this battle that Constantine, the emperor who converted Rome to Christianity, had a vision of a cross in the heavens and heard the words "In this sign, thou shalt conquer."

NEAR THE COLOSSEO

Domus Aurea. Nero's "Golden House" is closed to visitors until at least late 2007, and possibly much longer, as preservationists struggle with how to slow its deterioration. The closure's unfortunate because the site gives a good sense of the excesses of Imperial Rome. After fire destroyed much of the city in AD 64, Nero took advantage of the resulting open space to construct a lavish palace so large that it spread over four of Rome's seven hills. It had a fa-cade of pure gold, seawater piped into the baths, decorations of mother-of-pearl, and vast gardens. Not much has survived of all this; a good portion of the building and grounds was buried under the public works with which subsequent emperors sought to make reparation to the Roman people for Nero's phenomenal greed. As a result, the site of the Domus Aurea itself remained unknown for many centuries. A few of Nero's original halls were discovered underground at the end of the 15th century. Raphael (1483–1520) was one of the artists who had themselves lowered into the rubble-filled rooms, which resembled grottoes. The artists copied the original painted Roman decorations, barely visible by torchlight, and scratched their names on the ceilings. Raphael later used these models—known as *grotesques* because they were found in the so-called grottoes—in his decorative motifs for the Vatican Loggia.

The palace remains impressive in scale, even if a bit of imagination is required to envision the original. ⊕ *www.pierreci.it.*

238 AD	The first wave of Germanic invasions penetrates Italy.
293	Diocletian reorganizes the Empire into West and East.
330	Constantine founds a new Imperial capital (Constantinople) in the East.
410	Rome is sacked by Visigoths.
476	The last Roman emperor, Romulus Augustus, is deposed. The Roman Empire falls.

Baroque Rome: Gold & Grandeur

The area between the Corso and the Tiber bend is one of Rome's most beautiful districts, filled with narrow streets bearing curious names, airy piazzas, and half-hidden courtyards. Some of Rome's most coveted residential addresses are nestled here. So, too, are the ancient Pantheon and the medieval square of Campo de' Fiori, but baroque design of the 16th and 17th centuries predominates.

Occupying the horn of land that pushes the Tiber westward toward the Vatican, this district has been an integral part of the city since ancient times, and its position between the Vatican and Lateran palaces, both seats of papal rule, put it in the mainstream of Rome's development from the Middle Ages onward. Craftsmen and shopkeepers toiled in the shadow of the huge palaces built to consolidate the power of leading figures in the papal court. Writers and artists, such as the satirist Aretino and the goldsmith-sculptor Cellini, made sarcastic comments on the alternate fortunes of the courtiers and courtesans who populated the area. Artisans and artists still live here, but their numbers are diminishing as the district becomes gentrified. Two of the liveliest piazzas in Rome, Piazza Navona and Piazza del Pantheon, are the lodestars in a constellation of cafés, trendy stores, restaurants, and wine bars.

The Main Attractions

★ ⓲ **Campo de' Fiori.** This bustling square is home to a famed market. Each morning, vendors fill temporary stalls with all manner of local produce, nuts, cheese, spices, flowers, and seafood; by early afternoon it's all gone, to reappear in the city's homes and restaurants at dinnertime. Cafés and bars where the city's hip, young professionals hang out at night border the market. Overseeing the action is a brooding statue of philosopher-monk Giordano Bruno (1548–1600), who along with many others from the Middle Ages, was burned alive in the square.

NEED A BREAK? Some of Rome's best pizza comes out of the ovens of **Il Forno di Campo de' Fiori** (☎ 06/68806662 ✉ Campo de' Fiori). Choose pizza *bianca*, topped with olive oil, or *rossa*, with tomato sauce. Move to the annex next door to have your warm pizza filled with prosciutto and figs, or other mouthwatering combinations.

⑨ **Largo di Torre Argentina.** In the middle of this busy piazza lies Rome's largest fully excavated Republican-era ruins. The **area sacra** (sacred area) has columns, altars, and foundations from four temples dating as far back as the 1st century BC. On the west side of the square lies the **Curia Pompeii**, the site where Caesar was slain in 44 BC. The frescoes on the taller brickwork are from the 12th-century church of San Nicola de' Cesarini, which was built into

> **WORD OF MOUTH**
>
> "My 'magic moment' had to be rounding the corner and coming upon the Pantheon without knowing it was coming up. I can't even describe it. This spot ended up becoming my favorite even after a month in Italy. The building just simply strikes me speechless."
>
> —reedpaints

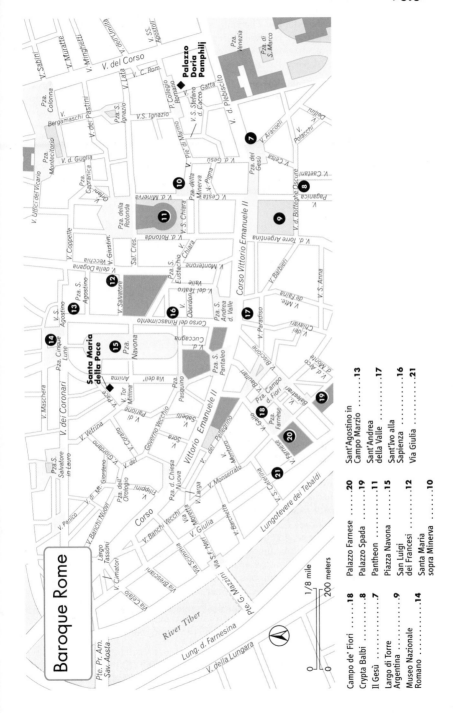

Baroque Rome

Campo de' Fiori **18**

Crypta Balbi **8**

Il Gesù **7**

Largo di Torre
Argentina **9**

Museo Nazionale
Romano **14**

Palazzo Farnese **20**

Palazzo Spada **19**

Pantheon **11**

Piazza Navona **15**

San Luigi
dei Francesi **12**

Santa Maria
sopra Minerva **10**

Sant'Agostino in
Campo Marzio **13**

Sant'Andrea
della Valle **17**

Sant'Ivo alla
Sapienza **16**

Via Giulia **21**

one of the temples. The ruins serve as a cat sanctuary for hundreds of the city's strays: take the staircase down to visit the cats and the cat ladies who look after them. Volunteer cat tenders are welcome, even for a few hours. ⊠ *Near Piazza Venezia.*

⑭ Museo Nazionale Romano. The ancient Roman and Egyptian sculptures in the **Palazzo Altemps,** part of the Museo Nazionale Romano, make up a terrific antiquities collection. Look for two works in the famed Ludovisi collection: the large, intricately carved Ludovisi Sarcophagus and *Galata,* a poignant work portraying a barbarian warrior who chooses death for himself and his wife rather than humiliation by the enemy. The 16th-century palazzo, with gorgeously frescoed ceilings and loggia, is an impressive home for the sculptures. This is a must-see for serious art buffs. ⊠ *Piazza Sant'Apollinare 46, near Piazza Navona* ☎ *06/39967700* 🔒 €6 ⊙ *Tues.–Sun. 9–7:45.*

⑪ Pantheon. One of Rome's most impressive and best-preserved ancient mon-

Fodor'sChoice
★

uments, the Pantheon is particularly close to the hearts of Romans. The emperor Hadrian designed it around AD 120 and had it built on the site of an earlier temple that had been damaged by fire. Although the sheer size of the Pantheon is impressive (until 1960 the dome was the largest ever built), what's most striking is its tangible sense of harmony. In large part this feeling is the result of the building's symmetrical design: the height of the dome is equal to the diameter of the circular interior. The oculus, or opening in the dome, is meant to symbolize the all-seeing eye of heaven; in practice, it illuminates the building and lightens the heavy stone ceiling. The original bronze doors have survived more than 1,800 years, centuries longer than the interior's rich gold ornamentation, which was plundered by popes and emperors. Art lovers can pay homage to the tomb of Raphael, who is buried in an ancient sarcophagus under the altar of Madonna del Sasso. ⊠ *Piazza della Rotonda, Pantheon* ☎ *06/68300230* 🔒 *Free* ⊙ *Mon.–Sat. 9–7:30, Sun. 9–5:30.*

★ ☺ ⑮ Piazza Navona. This famed piazza has the carefree air of the days when it was the scene of Roman circus games, medieval jousts, and 17th-century carnivals. Today it often attracts fashion photographers on shoots and Romans out for their *passeggiata* (evening stroll). Bernini's splashing **Fontana dei Quattro Fiumi** (Fountain of the Four Rivers), with an enormous rock squared off by statues representing the four corners of the world, makes a fitting centerpiece. Behind the fountain is the church of **Sant'Agnese in Agone,** an outstanding example of baroque architecture built by the Pamphilj Pope Innocent X. The facade—a wonderfully rich mélange of bell towers, concave spaces, and dovetailed stone and marble—is by Borromini, a contemporary and rival of Bernini, and by Carlo Rainaldi (1611–91). One story has it that the Bernini statue nearest the church, which represents the River Plate, has its hand up before its eye because it can't bear the sight of the Borromini facade. Though often repeated, the story is fiction: the facade was built after the fountain.

From early December through January 6 a Christmas market fills the square with games, Nativity scenes (some well crafted, many not), and multiple versions of the Befana, the ugly but good witch who brings candy

Roman Baroque

Flagrantly emotional, heavily expressive, and visually sensuous, the 17th-century artistic movement known as the baroque was born in Rome. It was the creation of three geniuses: the sculptor and architect Gianlorenzo Bernini (1598–1680), the painter and architect Pietro da Cortona (1596–1669), and the architect and sculptor Francesco Borromini (1599–1667). From the drama found in the artists' paintings to the jewel-laden, gold-on-gold detail of 17th-century Roman palaces, baroque style was intended both to shock and delight by upsetting the placid, "correct" rules of proportion and scale in the Renaissance. If a building looks theatrical—like a stage or a theater, especially with curtains being drawn back—it is usually baroque. Look for over-the-top, curvaceous marble work, tromp l'oeil, allusions to other art, and high drama to identify the style. Baroque's appeal to the emotions made it a powerful weapon in the hands of the Counter-Reformation.

and toys to Italian children on Epiphany. (Her name is a corruption of the Italian word for "epiphany," *Epifania*.)

⓬ **San Luigi dei Francesi.** The clergy of San Luigi considered Caravaggio's roisterous and unruly lifestyle scandalous enough, but his realistic treatment of sacred subjects—seen in three paintings depicting the life of St. Matthew in the last chapel—was too much for them. They rejected outright his first version of the altarpiece, and they weren't especially happy with the other two works. Thanks to the intercession of Caravaggio's patron, the influential Cardinal Francesco del Monte, the clergy were persuaded to keep them—a lucky thing, since the works are now thought to be among the artist's finest paintings. Have a few one-euro coins handy for the light machine. ⊠ *Piazza San Luigi dei Francesi, near Piazza Navona* ☎ *06/688271* ☉ *Fri.–Wed. 7–12:30 and 3:30–7.*

⓭ **Sant'Agostino in Campo Marzio.** Caravaggio's celebrated *Madonna of the Pilgrims*—which scandalized all Rome because it pictured pilgrims with dirt on the soles of their feet—can be found on the left over the first altar in this small church. Also of interest are Raphael's *Prophet*, on the first pilaster on the left, and the dozens of heart-shape ex-votos to *Madonna del Parto* (Mary of Childbirth) at the entrance. ⊠ *Piazza di Sant'Agostino, near Piazza Navona* ☎ *06/68801962* ☉ *Mon.–Sun. 7:45–12:30 and 4–7:30.*

Also Worth Seeing

❽ **Crypta Balbi** (Crypt of Balbus). After 20 years of excavation and restoration, these fascinating remains of a courtyard with a portico and theater built in 13 BC afford a unique look at Roman history. Rather than focus on one era, the crypt is displayed in such a way that it peels back the layers of the site, following the latest techniques in conservation. The well-explained exhibits (with text in English and Italian) give you a tangible sense of the sweeping changes that this spot—and Rome—underwent from antiquity to the 20th century. A partially restored wall provides an example of what marble and tufa constructions looked like before weather took its toll and medieval builders stripped the marble off for reuse. Copies of documents and reconstructed coins and other everyday objects found in drains, rubbish dumps, and tombs are a window into the world of the people who lived and worked here over the ages. ⊠ *Via Delle Botteghe Oscure 31, near Piazza Venezia* ☎ *06/39967700* ⊕ *www.pierreci.it* 🎫 *€6* ⊙ *Tues.–Sun. 9–7:45.*

❼ Il Gesù. Grandmother of all baroque churches, this huge structure was designed by the architect Vignola (1507–73) to be the tangible symbol of the Jesuits, a major force in the Counter-Reformation in Europe. It remained unadorned for about 100 years, but when it finally was decorated, no expense was spared: the interior drips with lapis lazuli, precious marbles, gold, and more gold. A fantastically painted ceiling by Baciccia (1639–1709) seems to merge with the painted stucco figures at its base. St. Ignatius's apartments, reached from the side entrance of the church, are also worth a visit (afternoons only) for the trompe-l'oeil frescoes and relics of the saint. ⊠ *Piazza del Gesù, near Piazza Venezia* ☎ *06/3613717* ⊙ *Daily 8:30–12:15 and 4–7:30, Sat. 8:30–12:15 and 4–10.*

㉑ Palazzo Farnese. The Farnese family rose to great power during the Renaissance, in part due to the favor Pope Alexander VI showed to the beautiful Giulia Farnese. The large palace was begun when, with Alexander's aid, Giulia's brother became cardinal; it was further enlarged on his election as Pope Paul III in 1534. The uppermost frieze decorations and main window overlooking the piazza are the work of Michelangelo, who also designed part of the courtyard (viewable through windows on Via Giulia), as well as the graceful arch over Via Giulia at the back. The facade on Piazza Farnese has geometrical brick configurations that have long been thought to hold occult meaning. When looking up at the palace from outside you can catch a glimpse of the splendid frescoed ceilings, including the **Galleria Carracci** vault painted by Annibale Carracci between 1597 and 1604—the second-greatest ceiling in Rome. For permission to view it from the inside, write several months ahead of time to the French Embassy, which now occupies the palace. Specify

A GOOD WALK: CARAVAGGIO'S ROME

Michelangelo Merisi—better known by the name of his birthplace, Caravaggio—may have been Rome's greatest painter. He certainly was one of its most notorious: he cultivated a reputation as a rebel, keeping company with prostitutes and local gangs. His nonconformist spirit found its way into his painting: his vibrant work was a major innovation in Western art. This walk introduces you to Caravaggio's art and his world. It covers about 1½ km (1 mi), including the final stretch to Piazza del Popolo.

Start at the **Palazzo Doria Pamphilj** ㉕, home to some of Caravaggio's most famous early works, including *Rest on the Flight to Egypt* and *Penitent Magdalene,* both from 1595. The latter created a scandal: Caravaggio used a real model for Mary Magdalene, something prohibited by the Church. To compound the sin, the model was his lover, the prostitute Maddalena Antonietti. It wouldn't be the last time Caravaggio used profane models for sacred subjects—later, his patrons drew the line at the *Death of Mary,* the model for which was said to be the drowned body of a prostitute.

the number in your party, when you wish to visit, and a local phone number for confirmation a few days before the visit. ⊠ *French Embassy, Servizio Culturale, Piazza Farnese 67, 00186* ☎*06/686011* ☎*Free* ☉*By appointment only.*

⑲ **Palazzo Spada.** A dazzling stuccoed facade on Piazza Capo di Ferro, west of Piazza Farnese, fronts an equally magnificent inner courtyard. On the southeast side of the inner courtyard, the gallery designed by Borromini creates an elaborate optical illusion, appearing to be much longer than it really is. On the first floor there are paintings and sculptures that belonged to Cardinale Bernardino Spada, an art connoisseur who collected works by Italian and Flemish masters. ⊠ *Piazza Capo di Ferro 13, near Campo de' Fiori* ☎ *06/6832409* ⊕ *www.galleriaborghese.it* ☎ *€5* ☉ *Tues.–Sun. 9:30–7:30.*

⑩ **Santa Maria sopra Minerva.** Michelangelo's *Risen Christ* and the tomb of the gentle 15th-century artist Fra Angelico are in practically the only Gothic-style church in Rome. Have some coins handy to light up the **Cappella Carafa** in the right transept, where exquisite 15th-century frescoes by Filippino Lippi (circa 1457–1504) are well worth the small investment. (Lippi's most famous student was Botticelli.) In front of the church, Bernini's charming elephant bearing an Egyptian obelisk has an inscription on the base stating that it takes a strong mind to sustain solid wisdom. ⊠ *Piazza della Minerva, Pantheon* ☎ *06/6793926* ☉ *Daily 7–noon and 4–7.*

⑰ **Sant'Andrea della Valle.** This huge 17th-century church looms mightily over a busy intersection. Puccini set the first act of his opera *Tosca* here; fans have been known to hire a horse-drawn carriage at night to trace the course of the opera from Sant'Andrea up Via Giulia to Palazzo Farnese—Scarpia's headquarters—to the locale of the opera's climax, Castel Sant'Angelo. Inside, above the apse are striking frescoes depicting scenes from St. Andrew's life by the Bolognese painter Domenichino (1581–1641). ⊠ *Corso Vittorio Emanuele II, near Campo de' Fiori* ☎ *06/6861339* ☉ *Daily 7:30–noon and 4:30–7:30.*

⑯ **Sant'Ivo alla Sapienza.** Borromini's eccentric church has what must surely be Rome's most unusual dome—topped by a golden spiral said

Exit the gallery and walk left along Piazza Collegio Romano, continuing on Via Piè di Marmo. The street bends right through Piazza Minerva, with its elephant obelisk, and continues alongside the Pantheon. In front of the Pantheon, walk around the fountain and take Via Giustiniani, extending left from the far left corner of the piazza. Follow it to the church **San Luigi dei Francesi** ⑫. Inside is the painting cycle of the Life of St. Matthew (1600), which shocked the public with its contemporary depiction of sacred subjects and thrilled the art world with its realism and use of light.

Leave the church, turn left along the piazza, then take the third right, Vicolo Vaccarella. Follow it until it ends, then turn left onto Vicolo Coppelle. This alley soon opens into Piazza Campo Marzio, with the entrance to the church of **Sant'Agostino** ⑬ on the right. Inside is the *Madonna of the Pilgrims* (1605), which caused another sensation for its depiction of filthy, ragged pilgrims, and for its model, once again the formidable Maddalena, dressed as the Mother of God. Exit the church and continue up Via Metastasio to Vicolo Divino Amore. At its corner with Vicolo San Biato have been inspired by a bee's stinger. ⊠ *Corso Rinascimento 40, near Piazza Navona* ⊙ *Sun. 10–noon.*

㉑ Via Giulia. Named after Pope Julius II and serving for more than four centuries as the "salon of Rome," this street is still the address of choice for Roman aristocrats and rich foreigners. Built with funds garnered by taxing prostitutes, the street is lined with elegant palaces, including the Palazzo Falconieri, and old churches (one, San Eligio, reputedly designed by Raphael himself). The area around Via Giulia is a wonderful place to wander in to get the feeling of daily life as carried on in a centuries-old setting—an experience enhanced by the dozens of antiques shops in the neighborhood.

Piazza Venezia to the Spanish Steps: Vistas & Views

Though it has a bustling commercial air, this part of the city also holds great visual allure, from the gaudy marble confection that is the monument to Vittorio Emanuele II to the theatrical Piazza di Sant'Ignazio. Among the things to look for are stately palaces, baroque ballrooms, and the greatest example of portraiture in Rome, Velázquez's incomparable *Innocent X* at the Galleria Doria Pamphilj. Highlights are the Trevi Fountain and the Spanish Steps, 18th-century Rome's most famous example of city planning.

The Main Attractions

★ ㉘ Fontana di Trevi (Trevi Fountain). The huge fountain designed by Nicola Salvi (1697–1751) is a whimsical rendition of mythical sea creatures amid cascades of splashing water. The fountain is the world's most spectacular wishing well: legend has it that you can ensure your return to Rome by tossing a coin into the fountain. It was featured in the 1954 film *Three Coins in the Fountain* and was the scene of Anita Ekberg's aquatic frolic in Fellini's *La Dolce Vita*. By day this is one of the most crowded sites in town; at night the spotlighted piazza feels festive. ⊠ *Off Via del Tritone, Piazza di Trevi.*

㉒ Monumento a Vittorio Emanuele II. Known as the Vittoriano, this vast marble monument was erected in the late 19th century to honor Italy's first king, Vittorio Emanuele II (1820–78), and the unification of Italy. Aes-

gio is the apartment where Caravaggio lived. It was here, on a mission from the irate landlady, that a debt collector discovered Caravaggio's secret method—he arranged glass and mirrors in order to create intense, focused light and shadow on subjects, which he then would view with a mirror as he painted.

Continue on Vicolo Divino Amore one block to Via Fontanella Borghese and turn left, then left again on to Via Pallacorda. The street was the site of a duel that changed Caravaggio's life. On May 29, 1606, the artist fought with and killed Ranuccio Tomassoni, a gang-

ster said to have been a contender for the favors of Maddalena. Condemned to death for the deed, Caravaggio fled Rome, never to return. He first went to Naples, then to Malta. He died near Porto Ercole, a coastal town in southern Tuscany, in 1610. From Via Pallacorda, continue north up Via Ripetta about 1 km (½ mi) to Piazza del Popolo and the church of **Santa Maria del Popolo** ㊾, at the far end of the piazza. The Cappella Cerasi there holds two more masterpieces.

thetically minded Romans have derided the oversize structure, visible from many parts of the city, calling it "the typewriter," "the wedding cake," or even "the urinal." Whatever you think of its design, the views from the top are unforgettable. Here also is the **Tomb of the Unknown Soldier** with its eternal flame. A side entrance in the monument leads to the rather somber **Museo del Risorgimento,** which charts Italy's struggle for nationhood. The red shirt and boots of revolutionary hero Giuseppe Garibaldi (1807–82) are among the mementos. Opposite the Vittoriano, note the name "Bonaparte" still visible on the enclosed wooden veranda fronting the palace on the corner of Via del Plebiscito and Via del Corso. Napoléon's mother had a fine view from here of the local goings-on for the many years that she lived in Rome. ⊠ *Entrance at Piazza Ara Coeli, near Piazza Venezia* ☎ *06/6991718* ⊕ *www.ambienterm. arti.beniculturali.it/vittoriano/index.html* 🗺 *Monument free, museum €5* ☉ *Tues.–Sun. 10–4.*

㉔ Palazzo Colonna. Inside the fabulous, private Palazzo Colonna, the 17th-century **Sala Grande**—more than 300 feet long, with bedazzling chandeliers, colored marble, and enormous paintings—is best known as the site where Audrey Hepburn met the press in *Roman Holiday.* The entrance to the picture gallery, the **Galleria Colonna,** hides behind a plain, inconspicuous door. The private palace is open to the public Saturday only; reserve ahead to get a free guided tour in English. ⊠ *Via della Pilotta 17, near Piazza di Trevi* ☎ *06/6784350* ⊕ *www.galleriacolonna. it* 🗺 *€7* ☉ *Sept.–July, Sat. 9–1.*

㉖ Sant'Ignazio. The interior dome in this sumptuous 17th-century church is a trompe-l'oeil oddity: the cupola is painted as, well, a cupola—but open at the top, and full of flying angels, saints, and heavenly dignitaries who float about in what appears to be a rosy sky above. To get the full effect of the illusionistic ceiling painted by Andrea del Pozzo (1642–1709), stand on the small disk set into the floor of the nave. The church also contains some of Rome's most splendid, jewel-encrusted altars. If you're lucky, you might catch an evening concert performed here (check with the tourist office). Step outside the church to look at it from Filippo Raguzzini's 18th-century piazza, where the buildings, as in much baroque art, are arranged resembling a stage set. ⊠ *Piazza Sant'Ignazio, near Pantheon* ☎ *06/6794406* ☉ *Daily 7:30–12:15 and 3–7:15.*

★ **㉚ Spanish Steps.** Both the steps and the Piazza di Spagna get their names from the Spanish Embassy to the Vatican on the piazza, though the staircase was actually built with French funds in 1723. In an allusion to the church of *Trinità dei Monti* (Trinity of the Mount), at the top of the hill, the staircase is divided by three landings (beautifully banked with azaleas from mid-April to mid-May). This area has always welcomed tourists: 18th-century dukes and duchesses on their Grand Tour, 19th-century artists and writers in search of inspiration—among them Stendhal, Balzac, Thackeray, and Byron—and today's enthusiastic hordes. The **Fontana della Barcaccia** (Fountain of the Old Boat) at the base of the steps is by Pietro Bernini, father of the famous Gianlorenzo. ⊠ *Piazza di Spagna.*

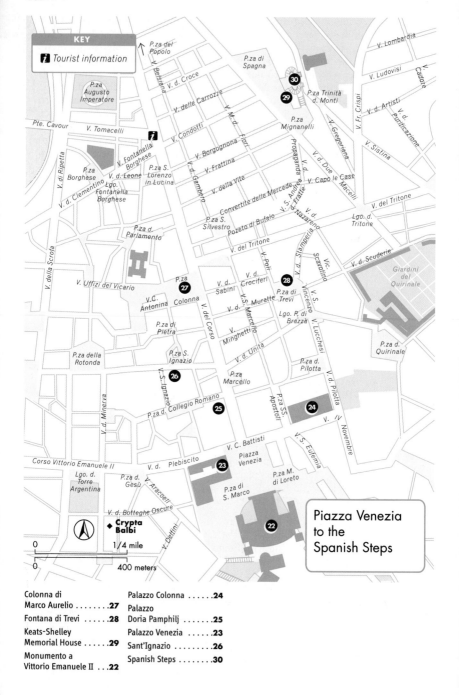

Piazza Venezia
to the
Spanish Steps

Colonna di
Marco Aurelio **27**

Fontana di Trevi **28**

Keats-Shelley
Memorial House **29**

Monumento a
Vittorio Emanuele II . . .**22**

Palazzo Colonna **24**

Palazzo
Doria Pamphilj **25**

Palazzo Venezia **23**

Sant'Ignazio **26**

Spanish Steps **30**

Also Worth Seeing

㉗ Colonna di Marco Aurelio. This ancient column, like the Colonna di Tra-iano, is an extraordinary stone history book. Its detailed reliefs spiral-ing up to the top illustrate the victorious campaigns of emperor Marcus Aurelius against the barbarians. It stands in front of a different kind of monument to power: the offices of the prime minister. ⊠ *Piazza Colonna, near Piazza di Spagna.*

㉙ Keats-Shelley Memorial House. English Romantic poet John Keats (1795–1821) once lived in what is now a (very small) museum dedicated to him and his great contemporary and friend Percy Bysshe Shelley (1792–1822). You can visit his tiny rooms, preserved as they were when he died here. ⊠ *Piazza di Spagna 26, next to the Spanish Steps* ☎ *06/ 6784235* ⊕ *www.keats-shelley-house.org* ⊠ *€3.50* ☉ *Weekdays 9–1 and 3–6, Sat. 11–2 and 3–6.*

㉕ Palazzo Doria Pamphilj. This bona fide patrician palace is still home to a princely family, which rents out many of its 1,000 rooms. You can visit the remarkably well preserved **Galleria Doria Pamphilj** (pronounced pom-*fee*-lee), a picture-and-sculpture gallery that gives you a sense of the sumptuous living quarters. Numbered paintings (the bookshop's mu-seum catalog comes in handy) are packed onto every available inch of wall space. Pride of place is given to the famous and strikingly modern portrait of the 17th-century Pamphilj pope Innocent X by Diego Velázquez (1599–1660), but don't overlook Caravaggio's affecting *Rest on the Flight into Egypt* or the formidable bust of Olympia, the pow-erful woman whose political brilliance launched the dynasty. The audio guide (included in admission) is narrated by the current Doria Pamphilj prince himself and gives a fascinating personal history of the palace. ⊠ *Pi-azza del Collegio Romano 2, near Piazza Venezia* ☎ *06/6797323* ⊕ *www.doriapamphilj.it* ⊠ *€8* ☉ *Fri.–Wed. 10–5.*

㉓ Palazzo Venezia. A Roman landmark on the city's busiest square, this palace is best known for the balcony over the main portal, from which Mussolini gave public addresses to crowds in Piazza Venezia during the dark days of Fascism. Today it's home to a haphazard collection of mostly early-Renaissance weapons, ivories, and paintings in its grand salons, some of which Il Duce used as his offices. The palace also hosts major touring art exhibits, so check to see what's currently showing. ⊠ *Pi-azza San Marco 49, near Piazza Venezia* ☎ *06/32810* ⊕ *www.ticketeria. it/palazzovenezia-eng.asp* ⊠ *€4* ☉ *Tues.–Sun. 8:30–7:30.*

Monti & San Giovanni: Centuries of Worship

Through the centuries, the development of Christian worship has shaped Rome's history; these monuments to Christianity, though less frequented today, are a living record of the faith and its expression in Rome. The city is home to hundreds of old churches, each with some-thing unique to offer visitors. Monti and San Giovanni, adjoining neighborhoods east of Rome's historic center, are packed with some of Rome's greatest art and architecture, executed for the glory of the Roman Catholic Church.

604 <   **Rome**

★ ㉜ **San Clemente.** A 12th-century church built on top of a 4th-century church, which in turn was constructed over a 2nd-century pagan temple to the god Mithras, San Clemente is an extraordinary archaeological site. The upper church, which you enter from street level, holds a beautiful early-12th-century mosaic showing a cross on a gold background, surrounded by swirling green acanthus leaves teeming with little scenes of everyday life. The marble choir screens, salvaged from the 4th-century church, are decorated with early Christian symbols: doves, vines, and fish. The **Cappella Castiglioni,** off the left aisle, holds frescos painted around 1400 by the Florentine artist Masolino da Panicale (1383–1440), a key figure in the introduction of realism and one-point perspective into Renaissance painting. Note the large Crucifixion and scenes from the lives of Sts. Catherine, Ambrose, and Christopher, plus an Annunciation (over the entrance). Before you leave the upper church, take a look at the pretty cloister—evening concerts are held here in summer.

From the right aisle, stairs lead down to the remains of the **4th-century church,** which was active until 1084, when it was damaged beyond repair during a siege of the neighborhood by the Norman prince Robert Guiscard. Its remains are largely intact, in part because it wasn't unearthed until the 19th century. (It was discovered by Irish Dominican monks; members of the order still live in the adjacent monastery.) The vestibule is decorated with marble fragments found during the excavations (which are still under way), and in the nave are colorful 11th-century frescoes depicting stories from the life of St. Clement. Another level down is the **Mythraeum,** a shrine dedicated to the god Mithras, whose cult spread from Persia and gained a hold in Rome during the 2nd and 3rd centuries. ✉ *Via San Giovanni in Laterano 108, San Giovanni* ☎ *06/70451018* 🎫 *€3* ⊗ *Mon.–Sat. 9–noon and 3–6, Sun. 10–12:30 and 3–6.*

㉛ **Santa Maria Maggiore.** One of Rome's four great pilgrimage churches was built on the spot where a 3rd-century pope witnessed a miraculous midsummer snowfall (reenacted every August 15). The gleaming mosaics on the arch in front of the main altar date from the 5th century, and the opulently carved wood ceiling is believed to have been gilded with the first gold brought from the New World. To view the elaborate 14th-century facade mosaics, inquire at the souvenir shop. ✉ *Piazza Santa Maria Maggiore, off Via Cavour* ☎ *06/483195* ⊗ *Daily 7 AM–8 PM.*

㉝ **Santi Quattro Coronati.** The 12th-century church of the Four Crowned Martyrs, part of a fortified abbey that provided refuge to early popes and emperors, is in an unusual corner of Rome, a quiet island that has resisted the tide of time and traffic flowing beneath its ramparts. Few places are so reminiscent of the Middle Ages. Don't miss the cloister with its well-tended gardens and 12th-century fountain. The entrance is the door in the left aisle; ring the bell if it's not open. You can also ring at the adjacent convent for the key to the **Oratorio di San Silvestro** (Oratory of St. Sylvester), with 13th-century frescoes. ✉ *Largo Santi Quattro Coronati, San Giovanni* ☎ *06/70475427* ⊗ *Easter–Christmas, daily 9:30–12:30 and 3:30–6; Christmas–Easter, daily 9:30–12:30.*

San Giovanni
in Laterano . . .**34**

San Clemente . **32**

Santa Maria
Maggiore **31**

Santi Quattro
Coronati **33**

Scala Santa . . **35**

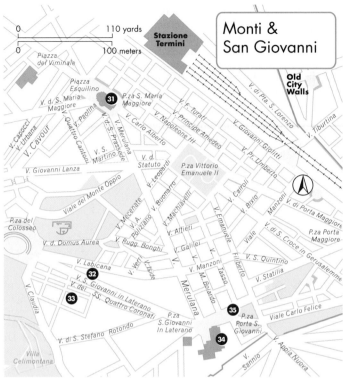

Also Worth Seeing

34 **San Giovanni in Laterano.** You may be surprised to discover that the cathedral of Rome is not St. Peter's but this church. (St. Peter's is in Vatican City, hence not technically part of Rome.) Dominating the piazza whose name it shares, this immense building is where the pope officiates in his capacity as bishop of Rome. The towering facade and Borromini's cool baroque interior emphasize the majesty of its proportions. The **cloister** is one of the city's finest, with beautifully carved columns surrounding a peaceful garden.

The adjoining **Palazzo Laterano** was the official papal residence until the 13th century, and is still technically part of the Vatican. It houses the offices of the Rome Diocese and the rather bland **Museo Storico Laterano** (Lateran Historical Museum). Behind the palace are the 4th-century octagonal **Battistero di San Giovanni** (St. John's Baptistery), forerunner of many similar buildings throughout Italy, and Rome's oldest and tallest obelisk, brought from Thebes and dating from the 15th century BC. ⊠ *Piazza San Giovanni in Laterano* ☎ *06/69886433* 🖾 *Church free, cloister €2.50, museum €4* ⊘ *Church Apr.–Sept., daily 7–7; Oct.–Mar., daily 7–6. Cloister 9–½ hr before church closing. Museum Sat. guided tours at 9:15, 10:30, and noon; 1st Sun. of each month 8:45–1. Baptistery daily 9–1 PM and 5 PM–1 hr before sunset.*

③⑤ Scala Santa (Sacred Stairs). A small building opposite the Palazzo Laterano houses what is claimed to be the staircase from Pilate's palace in
Jerusalem. The faithful climb it on their knees. ✉ *Piazza San Giovanni
in Laterano* ⊙ *Daily 6:15–noon and 3:30–6:30.*

Il Quirinale to Piazza della Repubblica: Palaces & Fountains

Near the Piazza della Repubblica you can see ancient Roman sculptures,
early Christian churches, and highlights from the 16th and 17th centuries, when Rome was conquered by the baroque—and by Bernini. Il
Quirinale is the highest of Rome's seven hills, and was once home to
the popes, housed in the massive Palazzo Quirinale, now Italy's presidential palace.

The Main Attractions

④⓪ Fontana del Tritone (Triton Fountain). The centerpiece of busy Piazza Barberini is Bernini's graceful fountain designed in 1637 for the sculptor's
patron, Pope Urban VIII. The pope's Barberini family coat of arms, featuring bees, is at the base of the large shell. Close by is the **Fontana delle
Api** (Fountain of the Bees), the last fountain designed by Bernini. ✉ *Piazza Barberini, near Via Veneto.*

④④ Palazzo Massimo alle Terme. This 19th-century palace in neobaroque style
holds part of the collections of antiquities belonging to the Museo
Nazionale Romano (also exhibited in the Palazzo Altemps). Here you
can see extraordinary examples of the fine mosaics and masterful paintings that decorated ancient Rome's palaces and villas. Don't miss the
fresco—depicting a lush garden in bloom—that came from the villa that
Livia, wife of Emperor Augustus, owned outside Rome. ✉ *Largo Villa
Peretti 1, near Termini* ☎ *06/480201* ⊕ *www.pierreci.it* ✉ €6
⊙ *Tues.–Sun. 9–7:45.*

③⑥ Il Quirinale. The highest of ancient Rome's seven hills, this is where ancient Romans, and later popes, built their residences in order to escape
the deadly miasmas and malaria of the low-lying area around the Forum.
The fountain in the square has ancient statues of Castor and Pollux rein-
ing in their unruly steeds and a basin salvaged from the Roman Forum.
The **Palazzo del Quirinale** passed from the popes to Italy's kings in the
19th century; it's now the official residence of the nation's president.
Every day at 4 PM the ceremony of the changing of the guard at the portal includes a miniparade complete with band. ✉ *Piazza del Quirinale,
near Piazza di Trevi* ☎ *06/46991* ✉ €5 ⊙ *Sept.–June, Sun. 8:30–noon.*

Directly opposite the main entrance of the Palazzo del Quirinale sits **Le
Scuderie Papale al Quirinale** (the Quirinal Stables), which once housed
more than 120 horses for the exclusive use of the pope and his guests.
The low-lying building was designed by Alessandro Specchi (1668–1729)
in 1722 and was among the major achievements of baroque Rome. The
stables were remodeled in the late 1990s by eminent architect Gae
Aulenti and now serve as a venue for touring art exhibits. ✉ *Piazza del
Quirinale, near Piazza di Trevi* ☎ *06/39967500 or 06/696271* ⊕ *www.
scuderiequirinale.it* ✉ €10 ⊙ *Sun.–Thurs. 10–7, Fri. and Sat. 10–9:30.*

Fontana del
Tritone **40**

Il Quirinale . . .**36**

Palazzo
Barberini **39**

Palazzo Massimo
alle Terme . . .**44**

Piazza della
Repubblica . . .**43**

San Carlino
alle Quattro
Fontane **38**

Santa Maria della
Concezione . . .**41**

Santa Maria della
Vittoria **42**

Sant'Andrea al
Quirinale **37**

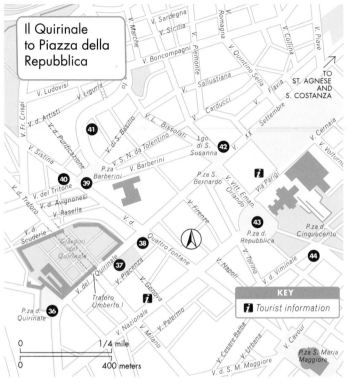

Il Quirinale
to Piazza della
Repubblica

KEY

🛈 *Tourist information*

🖑 **41** **Santa Maria della Concezione.** In the crypt under the main Capuchin church,
the bones of some 4,000 dead Capuchin monks are arranged in pecu-
liar decorative designs around the shriveled and decayed skeletons of
their kinsmen, a macabre reminder of the impermanence of earthly life.
Signs declare WHAT YOU ARE, WE ONCE WERE. WHAT WE ARE, YOU SOME-
DAY WILL BE. Although not for the easily spooked, the crypt is oddly beautiful. ⊠ *Via Veneto 27, Piazza di Spagna* ☎ *06/4871185* 💲 *Donation
expected* ⊙ *Fri.–Wed. 9–noon and 3–6.*

42 **Santa Maria della Vittoria.** The most famous feature here is Bernini's
baroque decoration of the **Cappella Cornaro,** an exceptional fusion of
architecture, painting, and sculpture in which the *Ecstasy of St. Teresa*
is the focal point. Bernini's audacious conceit was to model the chapel
after a theater: members of the Cornaro family—sculpted in white marble—watch from theater boxes as, center stage, St. Teresa, in the throes
of mystical rapture, is pierced by an angel's gilded arrow. To quote one
18th-century observer, President de Brosses: "If this is divine love, I know
it well." ⊠ *Via XX Settembre 17, Termini* ☎ *06/42740571* ⊙ *Mon.–Sat.
9–noon and 3–6, Sun. 3-6.*

Also Worth Seeing

③ Palazzo Barberini. Along with architect Carlo Maderno (1556–1629), Borromini helped make the splendid 17th-century Palazzo Barberini a residence worthy of Rome's leading art patron, Pope Urban VIII, who began the palace for his family in 1625. Inside, the **Galleria Nazionale d'Arte Antica** has some fine works by Caravaggio and Raphael, including the latter's portrait of his lover, *La Fornarina*. Rome's biggest ballroom is here; its ceiling, painted by Pietro da Cortona, depicts Immortality bestowing a crown upon Divine Providence escorted by a "bomber squadron"—to quote Sir Michael Levey—of mutant bees. (Bees featured prominently in the heraldic device of the Barberini.) ⊠ *Via Barberini 18, near Via Veneto* ☎ *06/328101* ⊕ *www.galleriaborghese.it* ⊡ *€6* ⊙ *Tues.–Sun. 8:30–7:30.*

㊷ Piazza della Repubblica. Smog-blackened porticoes, a subway station, and a McDonald's make this grand piazza feel a bit derelict. The racy **Fontana delle Naiadi** (Fountain of the Naiads), an 1870 addition to the square, depicts voluptuous bronze ladies wrestling happily with marine monsters. In ancient times, the Piazza della Repubblica served as the entrance to the immense **Terme di Diocleziano** (Baths of Diocletian), an archaeological site today. Built in the 4th century AD, these were the largest and most impressive of the baths of ancient Rome, with vast halls, pools, and gardens that could accommodate 3,000 people at a time. The *aula ottagonale* (octagonal hall) now holds a sampling of the ancient sculptures unearthed here, including two beautiful bronzes. ⊠ *Via Romita 8, near Termini* ☎ *06/4870690* ⊡ *Free* ⊙ *Tues.–Sat. 9–2, Sun. 9–1.*

The curving ancient Roman brick facade on one side of the Piazza della Repubblica marks the church of **Santa Maria degli Angeli,** adapted by Michelangelo from the vast central chamber of the colossal baths. Look for the sundial carved on the floor. ⊠ *Via Cernaia 9* ☎ *064880812* ⊕ *www. santamariadegliangeliroma.it* ⊙ *Mon.–Sat. 7–6:30, Sun. 7 AM–7:30 PM.*

㊳ San Carlino alle Quattro Fontane. In a church no larger than the base of one of the piers of St. Peter's, Borromini attained geometric architectural perfection. Characteristically, he chose a subdued white stucco for the interior decoration, so as not to distract from the form. Don't miss the cloister, which you reach through the door to the right of the altar. The exterior of the church is Borromini at his bizarre best, all curves and rippling movement. (Keep an eye out for cars whipping around the corner as you're looking.) Outside the *quattro fontane* (four fountains) frame views in four directions. ⊠ *Via del Quirinale 23, near Piazza di Trevi* ☎ *06/4883261* ⊙ *Daily 10–noon and 3–6 (closed Sat. afternoon).*

㊲ Sant'Andrea al Quirinale. This small but imposing baroque church was designed and decorated by Bernini, who considered it one of his finest works. ⊠ *Via del Quirinale, Piazza di Trevi* ☎ *06/4740807* ⊙ *Mon.–Sat. 8–noon and 3:30–7, Sun. 9–noon and 3:30–7.*

Villa Borghese to the Ara Pacis: Amid Sylvan Glades

Touring Rome's artistic masterpieces while staying clear of its hustle and bustle can be, quite literally, a walk in the park. Some of the city's finest sights are tucked away in or next to green lawns and pedestrian piazzas, offering a breath of fresh air for weary sightseers. Villa Borghese, one of Rome's largest parks, can alleviate gallery gout by offering an oasis in which to cool off under the ilex trees. If you feel like a picnic, have an *alimentare* (food shop) make you some *panini* (sandwiches) before you go; food carts within the park are overpriced.

The Main Attractions

51 **Ara Pacis Augustae** (Altar of Augustan Peace). This magnificent classical monument, with an exquisitely detailed frieze, was erected in 13 BC to celebrate Emperor Augustus's triumphant return from military conflicts in Gaul and Spain. It's housed in one of Rome's newest landmarks, a glass and travertine structure designed by American architect Richard Meier. The building was opened in 2006, after 10 years of delays and controversy, and early indications are that it's a triumph. Along the altar itself, the building holds a luminous museum overlooking the Tiber on one side and the imposing ruins of the marble-clad Mausoleo di Augusto (Mausoleum of Augustus) on the other. The result is a gloriously tranquil oasis in the center of Rome. ⊠ *Lungotevere in Augusta, near Piazza di Spagna* ☎ *06/82059127* ⊕ *www.arapacis.it* ☛ *€6.50* ☉ *Tues.–Sun. 9–6.*

45 **Galleria Borghese.** The palace that was completed in 1613 for Cardinal Scipione Borghese (1576–1633) is a monument to 18th-century Roman interior decoration at its most luxurious, dripping with porphyry and alabaster. Today it contains the art collection of the cardinal. The grand salons have ancient Roman mosaic pavements and statues of various deities, including one officially known as *Venus Victrix*. There has never been any doubt, however, as to the statue's real subject: Pauline Bonaparte, Napoléon's sister, who married Prince Camillo Borghese in one of the storied matches of the 19th century. Sculpted by Canova (1757–1822), the princess reclines on a chaise, bare-bosomed, her hips swathed in classical drapery, the very model of haughty detachment and sly come-hither. Pauline is known to have been shocked that her husband took pleasure in showing off the work to his guests. This coyness seems curious given the reply she is supposed to have made to a lady who asked her how she could have posed for the work: "Oh, but the studio was heated." Other rooms hold important sculptures by Bernini, including *David* and the breathtaking *Apollo and Daphne*. The picture collection has splendid works by Titian, Caravaggio, and Raphael, among others. Reservations are required, and the most popular time slots can sell out days in advance; you can book by phone or online. ⊠ *Piazza Scipione Borghese 5, off Via Pinciana, Villa Borghese* ☎ *06/8513979 information, 06/32810 reservations* ⊕ *www.galleriaborghese.it* ☛ *€10.50, audio guide or English guided tour €5* ☉ *Tues.–Sun. 9–7.*

Fodor'sChoice
★

Ara Pacis
Augustae 51

Explora II:
Il Museo dei
Bambini di
Roma 47

Galleria
Borghese 45

Museo Nazionale
Etrusco di Villa
Giulia 46

Piazza del
Popolo 50

Pincio 48

Santa Maria
del Popolo ...49

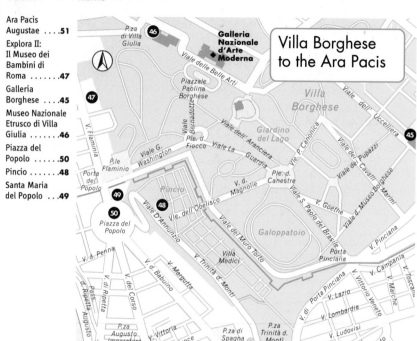

Villa Borghese
to the Ara Pacis

⑤⓪ Piazza del Popolo. Designed by neoclassical architect Giuseppe Valadier (1762–1839) in the early 1800s, this piazza is one of the largest in Rome, and it has a 3,000-year-old obelisk in the middle. Always a favorite spot for café-sitting and people-watching, the piazza is closed to motorized traffic. The bookend baroque churches **Santa Maria dei Miracoli** and **Santa Maria in Montesanto** are not, first appearances to the contrary, twins. On the piazza's eastern side, stairs lead uphill to the ⇨ **Pincio**. To the north, at the end of the square, is the 400-year-old **Porta del Popolo**, Rome's northern city gate, and next to it the church of Santa Maria del Popolo. The city gate was designed by Bernini to welcome the Catholic convert Queen Christina of Sweden to Rome in 1605. ⊠ *Near Villa Borghese.*

④⑨ Santa Maria del Popolo. This church next to the Porta del Popolo goes almost unnoticed, but it has one of the richest art collections of any church in Rome. Here is Raphael's High Renaissance masterpiece the **Cappella Chigi,** as well as two stunning Caravaggios in the **Cappella Cerasi.** Each December an exhibit of Christmas Nativity scenes is held in the adjacent building. ⊠ *Piazza del Popolo, near Villa Borghese* ☎ *06/3610836* ☉ *Mon.–Sat. 7–noon and 4–7, Sun. 7:30–1:30 and 4:30–7:30.*

Also Worth Seeing

🐾 ④⑦ **Explora: Il Museo dei Bambini di Roma.** Explore: the Museum for the Children of Rome is one of the few sights in the city geared specifically to kids. There are two floors of open space filled with hands-on activities and games for toddlers to 12-year-olds, and a child-friendly pizzeria. Steps from the car-free Piazza del Popolo and a short hike downhill from the playground in Villa Borghese, the museum is well suited to a kids' day in the neighborhood. Reservations are essential on weekends. You're let in for two-hour shifts. ✉ *Via Flaminia 82, near Villa Borghese* ☎ *06/3613776* ⊕ *www.mdbr.it/inglese* ✉ *€7 for children 3 and up, €6 for adults* ☉ *Tues.–Fri. admission at 9:30, 11:30, 3, and 5; weekend admission at 10, noon, 3, and 5.*

④⑥ **Museo Nazionale Etrusco di Villa Giulia** (National Etruscan Museum at Villa Giulia). Known for their sophisticated art and design, the Etruscans left a legacy of sarcophagi, bronze sculptures, terra-cotta vases, and stunning jewelry. (Unlike the Greeks, Etruscan women sat at the banquet tables with men and enjoyed displaying their wealth on their bodies.) Acclaimed pieces of statuary in the gallery include the *Goddess with Infant* and the *Sarcophagus of the Married Couple.* In the villa's courtyard visit the atmospheric underground **Ninfeo,** the remains of the Virgin's Aqueduct from the Augustan period. ✉ *Piazzale Villa Giulia 9, near Villa Borghese* ☎ *06/3226571* ⊕ *www.beniculturali.it* ✉ *€4* ☉ *Tues.–Sun. 8:30–7:30.*

> **NEED A BREAK?**
>
> **Caffè delle Arti** (✉ Viale delle Belle Arti 131, near Villa Borghese ☎ 06/32651236), an exquisite, light-filled space with towering ceilings and bronze statues, is inside the not-so-noteworthy Galleria Nazionale d'Arte Moderna, across the street from Villa Giulia. The menu includes tea with a variety of homemade pastries as well as Roman and Neapolitan dishes. In warm weather sit out on the huge terrace and take in the splendor of the surrounding Villa Borghese.

🐾 ④⑧ **Pincio.** At the southwestern corner of Villa Borghese, the Pincio belvedere and gardens were laid out by architect Giuseppe Valadier as part of his overall plan for Piazza del Popolo. Nineteenth-century counts and countesses liked to take their evening passeggiata here in the hope of meeting Pius IX (1792–1878), the last pope to go about Rome on foot. Nowadays you're more likely to see runners and in-line skaters, as well as throngs of Romans dressed in their best, out for a stroll. It's a good place to take in the summer concerts and New Year's fireworks staged in Piazza del Popolo below. ✉ *Piazza del Popolo.*

Crossing the Tiber: The Ghetto, Tiberina Island & Trastevere

Despite rampant gentrification, Trastevere remains about the most tightly knit community in the city, its natives proudly proclaiming their descent from the ancient Romans. The old Jewish Ghetto is a warren of twisting, narrow streets, where Rome's Jewish community was once confined, then deported, and now, barely, persists. Ancient bridges, the Ponte Fabricio and Ponte Cestio, link the Ghetto and Trastevere to Tiberina Island; this area is Rome's medieval heart.

The Main Attractions

⑤⑥ Fontana delle Tartarughe. The 16th-century Fountain of the Turtles in Piazza Mattei is one of Rome's loveliest. Designed by Giacomo della Porta (1539–1602) in 1581 and sculpted by Taddeo Landini (1550–96), the piece revolves around four bronze boys, each clutching a dolphin that jets water into marble shells. Several bronze tortoises, thought to have been added by Bernini, are held in each of the boys' hands and drink from the fountain's upper basin. The piazza is lined by a few interesting cafés and shops. It was named for the Mattei family, who built the **Palazzo Mattei** on Via Caetani. (The palace is not open to the public, but it's worth a peek at the sculpture-rich courtyard and staircase if the door is open.) ⊠ *Piazza Mattei, Ghetto.*

⑤⑨ Isola Tiberina (Tiberina Island) is where a city hospital stands on a site that has been dedicated to healing ever since a temple to Aesculapius was erected here in 291 BC. If you have time, and if the river's not too high, walk down the stairs for a different perspective on the island and the Tiber River. Every July, the city's Estate Romana hosts an open-air cinema on the island's paved shores. ⊠ *Ponte Fabricio and Ponte Cestio, near Ghetto.*

Jewish Ghetto. Rome has had a Jewish community since the 1st century BC, and from that time until the present its living conditions have varied widely according to its relations with the city's rulers. In 1555 Pope Paul II established Rome's Jewish Ghetto in the neighborhood marked off by the Portico d'Ottavia, the Tiber, and Via Arenula. The area quickly became Rome's most squalid and densely populated. At one point, Jews—who had engaged in many businesses and professions in Trastevere—were limited to the sale of used iron and clothing as a trade. The laws were rescinded around the time of the Italian unifications in the 1870s. German troops occupied Rome during World War II, and on October 16, 1943, many of Rome's Jews were rounded up and deported to Nazi concentration camps. In 1982 the synagogue here was attacked with grenades and machine guns by Palestinian terrorists, and in 1986, as a gesture of reconciliation, Pope John Paul II paid a visit to Rabbi Elio Toaff, becoming the first pope ever to pray in a Jewish synagogue. Today some of Rome's 15,000 Jewish residents still live in the area; there are a few Judaica shops and kosher groceries, bakeries, and restaurants—as well as linen and shoe stores run by Jewish families—especially on Via di Portico d'Ottavia. **Tours of the Ghetto** (€8, about two hours) that explore Rome's Jewish history can be booked through the SIDIC historical society. ⊠ *SIDIC Office, Via Garibaldi 28, Ghetto* ☎ *06/ 58333615* ⊕ *www.sidic.org.*

★ ⑥② Piazza di Santa Maria in Trastevere. This piazza is a popular spot for afternoon coffee and evening cocktails at its outdoor cafés. But the showpiece of the Piazza di Santa Maria is the 12th-century church of **Santa Maria in Trastevere.** The 13th-century mosaics on the church's facade—which add light and color to the piazza, especially at night when they are in spotlight—are believed to represent the Wise and Foolish Virgins. Inside, the enormous golden mosaic in the apse is the city's finest, a shining burst of Byzantine color and light set off by giant columns filched

Fontana delle
Tartarughe . . .**56**

Isola Tiberina .**59**

Palazzo
Corsini **65**

Piazza Bocca
della Verità . . .**52**

Piazza di Santa
Maria in
Trastevere **62**

San Francesco
a Ripa **61**

San Pietro in
Montorio **63**

Santa Cecilia
in Trastevere . .**60**

Sinagoga **58**

Teatro di
Marcello **55**

Tempio della
Fortuna Virilis **54**

Tempio di
Vesta **53**

Via del Portico
d'Ottavia **57**

Villa
Farnesina **64**

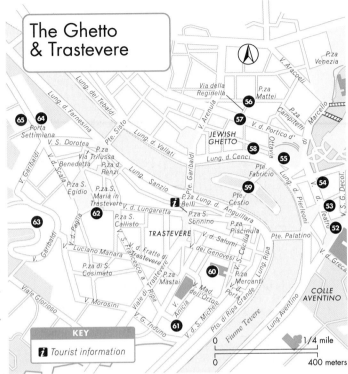

from an ancient Roman building. Make sure to look down at the splendid Cosmati work, a mosaic style from the 12th and 13th centuries in which tiny squares and triangles were laid with larger stones to form geometric patterns, in the church floors. In August, processions honoring the Virgin Mary gather at the church as part of Trastevere's traditional feast, called *Festa de Noantri* (Our Own Feast). ⊠ *Piazza di Santa Maria, Trastevere* ☎ *06/5814802* ☉ *Daily 7:30–1 and 4–7.*

58 **Sinagoga.** The imposing, square-dome synagogue on the Tiber is a Roman landmark. The **Museo Ebraico** documents the history of the Jewish community in Rome. Most of the decorative crowns, prayer books, holy chairs, and tapestries dating from the 17th century were donated by prominent Jewish families whose ancestors once lived in the Ghetto. The collection is a change of pace from the predominantly Christian art found elsewhere in Rome. ⊠ *Lungotevere Cenci 15, Ghetto* ☎ *06/68400661* ☒ *€7.50* ☉ *Oct.–May, Mon.–Thurs. 9–5, Fri. 9–2, Sun. 9–noon; June–Sept., Mon.–Thurs. 9–7:30, Fri. 9–4, Sun. 9–noon.*

55 **Teatro di Marcello.** The Teatro, hardly recognizable as a theater today, was originally designed to hold 20,000 spectators. It was begun by Julius Caesar; today, the 16th-century apartment building that sprouted out of its remains has become one of Rome's most prestigious residential addresses. The area south of the theater makes a grand stage for chamber music concerts in summer. ⊠ *Via del Teatro di Marcello, Ghetto* ☏ *06/87131590 concert information* ⊕ *www.tempietto.it* ⊘ *Open during concerts only.*

Trastevere. This area consists of a maze of narrow streets that is still, despite evident gentrification, one of the city's most authentically Roman neighborhoods. Literally translated, its name means "across the Tiber," and indeed Trastevere and the Trasteverini—the neighborhood's natives— are a breed apart. The area is hardly undiscovered, but among its self-consciously picturesque trattorias and trendy tearooms you can also find old shops and dusty artisans' workshops in alleys festooned with laundry hung out to dry. Stroll along Via dell'Arco dei Tolomei and Via dei Salumi, shadowy streets showing the patina of the ages. One of the least affected parts of Trastevere centers on Piazza in Piscinula, north of Via dei Salumi and south of the Ponte Cestio Fabricio, where the smallest medieval church in the city, San Benedetto, stands opposite the restored medieval Casa dei Mattei.

㊗ Via del Portico d'Ottavia. Along this street in the heart of the Jewish Ghetto are buildings where medieval inscriptions, ancient friezes, and half-buried classical monuments attest to the venerable history of the neighborhood. The old **Chiesa di Sant'Angelo in Pescheria** was built right into the ruins of the Portico d'Ottavia, which was a monumental area enclosing a temple, library, and other buildings within colonnaded porticoes. ⊠ *Ghetto.*

★ ㊽ Villa Farnesina. Money was no object to extravagant patron Agostino Chigi, a Sienese banker who financed many a papal project. His munificence is evident in his elegant villa, built about 1511. When Raphael could steal some precious time from his work on the Vatican Stanze and wooing Fornarina, he executed some of the frescoes, notably a luminous *Galatea*. Chigi delighted in impressing guests by having his servants cast precious dinnerware into the Tiber when it was time to clear the table. The guests didn't know of the nets he had stretched under the waterline to catch everything. ⊠ *Via della Lungara 230, Trastevere* ☏ *06/68027268* ⊕ *www.lincei.it/informazioni/villafarnesina/index.php* ⊡ *€5* ⊘ *Mon.–Sat. and 1st Sun. of month 9–1.*

Also Worth Seeing

㊺ Palazzo Corsini. This elegant palace holds the 16th- and 17th-century painting collection of the **Galleria Nazionale d'Arte Antica**; even if you're not interested in the paintings, stop in to climb the extraordinary 17th-century stone staircase, itself a drama of architectural shadows and sculptural voids. The adjacent Corsini gardens, now Rome's **Giardino Botanico,** offer delightful tranquillity, with native and exotic plants and a marvelous view at the top. ⊠ *Via della Lungara 10, Trastevere* ☏ *06/68802323* ⊕ *www.galleriaborghese.it* ⊡ *€4* ⊘ *Tues.–Sun. 8:30–1:30.*

㊲ Piazza Bocca della Verità. On the site of the Forum Boarium, ancient Rome's cattle market, this square was later used for public executions. Its name is derived from the marble **Bocca della Verità** (Mouth of Truth), a huge medieval drain cover in the form of an open-mouth face that is now set

VOICES OF ITALY

Dana Prescott
Artist/Arts Director, American Academy in Rome

For nearly two decades, Rome has been American artist Dana Prescott's home—and her muse. Between her painting and her work as Andrew Heiskell Arts Director of the venerable American Academy in Rome, she's immersed in the Eternal City's creative life. Dana shares some thoughts on the pleasures of her adopted hometown:

On Rome as inspiration: "I love Rome's ability to continue to surprise me. I bicycle around and keep falling in love with the shapes of things, the proportions, the sheer unfussy beauty of a city living and working amidst its monuments.

"As a painter, I tend to respond to things visually but somewhat randomly, so Rome is a perfect companion. From braided loaves of bread on a bakery shelf to the clutter of Porta Portese, from the polish on a Bernini sculpture to Italian moms wheeling kids around in baby carriages, from peeling facades to *ragazzi* on *motorini*, how ice cream is stacked in a gelateria, the twists on the end of a *bocconcino* of mozzarella, it's all a constant bombardment of visual stimulation."

On connecting with the ancient city: "Above all, take time in the Pantheon—not taking pictures there, just sitting. Feel the vast proportions, the amazing light, the swell of the floor. Move around; reconsider your position in time and space."

On her neighborhood, the Jewish Ghetto: "Its mesh of history, of humanity, of great food, its charming Turtle Fountain, *spoglie* (pieces of ancient stonework) tucked into facades, and its stories and legends all make the city instantly accessible."

On her favorite places: "I have so many. Sant'Ignazio, with its amazing anamorphic frescoes by Pozzo, how they change while you walk through the room. I love the botanical gardens (off Via della Lungara in Trastevere), especially the unmanicured edges of the park with bamboo and wildflowers sprawled all over the lawn. By far my favorite church is Santa Maria sopra Minerva, for its Filippino Lippi frescoes, the tomb of Saint Catherine, the Madonna of the Dowery by Antoniaccio Romano, the tomb of Fra Angelico—the patron saint for artists—and two—two!—Berninis and one Michelangelo. The list goes on and on: the Pantheon, Raphael's Galatea in the Villa Farnesina in Trastevere, Cavallino's scenes from the life of St. Mary at Santa Maria in Trastevere . . ."

On Rome's artistic spirit: "Every street corner reveals another trace of history or of a hand at work, a carving, a construction, a beautiful view. I don't need to go to a museum to see art and to feel its presence on a daily basis. Every fountain, church, roadway, facade—everything reveals the skill and labor of an artist or artisan. Rome humbles me."

into the entry portico of the 12th-century church of **Santa Maria in Cosmedin.** In the Middle Ages, legend had it that any person who told a lie with his hand in the mouth would have it chomped off. Today tour groups line up in this noisy, traffic-jammed piazza to give this ancient lie detector a go. ⊠ *Ghetto.*

61 **San Francesco a Ripa.** Ask the sacristan to show you the cell where St. Francis slept when he came to seek the pope's approval for his new order. Also in this church is one of Bernini's most dramatic sculptures, the figure of the *Blessed Ludovica Albertoni,* ecstatic at the prospect of entering heaven. ⊠ *Piazza San Francesco d'Assisi, Trastevere* ☎ *06/5819020* ☉ *Daily 7–noon and 4–7:30.*

63 **San Pietro in Montorio.** One of Rome's key Renaissance buildings, the **Tempietto,** stands in the cloister of this church built by order of Ferdinand and Isabella of Spain in 1481. Bramante built the Tempietto over the spot where St. Peter was thought to have been crucified. It's an architectural gem and was one of his earliest and most successful attempts to design a building in an entirely classical style. ⊠ *Via Garibaldi, Gianicolo, Trastevere* ☎ *06/5813940* ☉ *Church daily 8:30–noon and 1:30–5:30. Tempietto daily 8:30–noon and 3:30–5:30.*

60 **Santa Cecilia in Trastevere.** Mothers and children love to dally in the delightful little garden in front of this church. Duck inside for a look at the 9th-century mosaics and the languid statue of St. Cecilia under the altar. Fragments of a *Last Judgment* fresco cycle by Pietro Cavallini (circa 1250–1330), dating from the late 13th century, remain one of his most important works. Though the Byzantine-influenced fragments are obscured by the structure, what's left reveals a rich luminosity in the seated apostles' drapery and a remarkable depth in their expressions. A pretty cloister and remains of Roman houses are visible under the church. To see them, ask at the booth to the left of the main nave. ⊠ *Piazza Santa Cecilia, Trastevere* ☎ *06/5899289* ⊠ *Church free, frescoes €2.50* ☉ *Daily 9:30–12:30 and 4–6:30; frescoes Mon.–Sat. 10:15–12:15, Sun. 11:15–noon.*

54 **Tempio della Fortuna Virilis.** This rectangular temple devoted to "manly fortune" dates from the 2nd century BC and is built in the Greek style, as was the norm in the early years of Rome. For its age, its remains are remarkably well preserved, in part due to its subsequent consecration as a Christian church. ⊠ *Piazza Bocca della Verità, near Piazza Venezia.*

53 **Tempio di Vesta.** All but 1 of the 20 original Corinthian columns in Rome's most evocative small ruin remain intact. It was built in the 2nd century BC. Researchers now believe the temple was devoted to Hercules by a successful olive merchant. ⊠ *Piazza Bocca dell Verità, near Piazza Venezia.*

Off the Beaten Path

Colle Aventino (Aventine Hill). One of the seven hills of ancient Rome, Aventino is now a quiet residential neighborhood that most tourists don't see. It's home to some of the city's oldest and least visited churches and some appealing views. There's a wide panorama of the city from the walled park next to the church of **Santa Sabina,** off Via Santa Sabina. Peek through the keyhole in the gate to the **Garden of the Knights of Malta** for a surprise perspective of the dome of St. Peter's. ⊠ *Piazza Cavalieri di Malta, Colle Aventino.*

The Catacombs & Via Appia Antica

The early Christian sites on the ancient Appian Way are some of the religion's oldest. Catacombs, where early Christians (whose religion prohibited cremation) buried their dead and gathered to worship in secret, lie below the very road where tradition says Christ appeared to St. Peter. The Via Appia Antica, built 400 years before, is a quiet, green place to walk and ponder the ancient world. The Rome APT office provides an informative free pamphlet for this itinerary.

Resist any temptation to undertake the 1½-km (1-mi) walk between Porta San Sebastiano and the catacombs; it's a dull and tiring hike on a heavily trafficked cobblestone road, with stone walls the only scenery. Instead, hop on Bus 660 from the Colli Albani metro stop on Line A to the end of the line, at Via Appia Antica. (Bus 218 from San Giovanni in Laterano also passes near the catacombs, but you have to walk about ½ km [¼ mi] east from Via Ardeatina to Via Appia Antica.) A slightly more-expensive but hassle-free option is to take Bus 110 from Piazza Venezia; it's air-conditioned and allows you to hop on and off as you please.

The Main Attractions

67 **San Callisto.** A friar will guide you through the crypts and galleries of the well-preserved San Callisto catacombs. ⊠ *Via Appia Antica 110* ☎ *06/ 4465610* ⌨ €5 ⊗ *Mar.–Jan., Thurs.–Tues. 8:30–12:30 and 2:30–5.*

68 **San Sebastiano.** The 4th-century catacomb, named for the saint who was buried here, burrows underground on four levels. The only one of the catacombs to remain accessible during the Middle Ages, it's the origin of the term "catacomb," for it was in a spot where the road dips into a hollow, a place the Romans called *catacumbas* ("near the hollow"). Eventually the Christian cemetery that had existed here since the 2nd century came to be known by the same name, which was applied to all underground cemeteries discovered in Rome in later centuries. ⊠ *Via Appia Antica 136* ☎ *06/7850350* ⌨ €5 ⊗ *Mid-Nov.–mid-Oct., Mon.–Sat. 9–noon and 2–5.*

70 **Tomba di Cecilia Metella.** The circular mausoleum of a Roman noblewoman, who lived at the time of Julius Caesar, was transformed into a fortress in the 14th century. The tomb houses a tiny museum with sculptures from the Via Appia Antica and an interesting reconstruction of the area's geological and historical past. ⊠ *Via Appia Antica 161* ☎ *06/ 78021465 or 06/39967700* ⊕ *www.pierreci.it* ⌨ €2 ⊗ *Mon.–Sat. 9 AM–1 hr before sunset.*

Circo di
Massenzio ...**69**

San Callisto ..**67**

San
Sebastiano ...**68**

Tomba di Cecilia
Metella **70**

Via Appia
Antica **66**

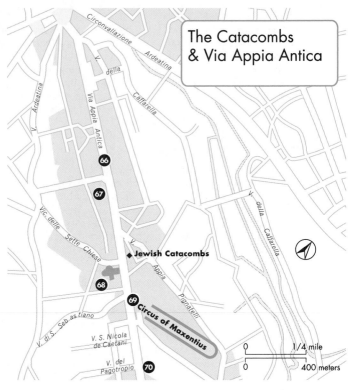

The Catacombs
& Via Appia Antica

Jewish Catacombs

66

67

68

69 Circus of Maxentius

70

0 — 1/4 mile
0 — 400 meters

★ **66** **Via Appia Antica.** This Queen of Roads, "Regina Viarium," was the most important of the extensive network of roads that traversed the Roman Empire, a masterful feat of engineering that made possible Roman control of a vast area by allowing for the efficient transport of armies and commercial goods. Completed in 312 BC by Appius Claudius, the road was ancient Europe's first highway, connecting Rome with Brindisi, 584 km (365 mi) away on the Adriatic coast. Part of the route exists as Via Appia (SS7), but it is a paved, modern highway. The stretch indicated here is closed to traffic; the ancient roadway passes through grassy fields and shady groves and by the villas of movie stars (Marcello Mastroianni and Gina Lollobrigida had homes here) and other VIPs. This part is still paved with the ancient *basoli* (basalt stones) over which the Romans drove their carriages—look for the wheel ruts. Taverns, houses, temples, and tombs flanked the ancient road, and the occasional lone statue, crumbling wall, or column is still visible, draped in ivy or alone in a patch of wildflowers. Pick a sunny day for your visit, wear comfortable shoes, and bring a bottle of water. You can take Bus 660 from the Colli Albani metro station Line A) for Via Cecilia Metella at Via Appia Antica. ⊠ *Exit Via Cristoforo Colombo at Circonvallazione Ardeatina, follow signs to Appia Antica parking lot.*

Also Worth Seeing

⑥⑨ Circo di Massenzio. On the east side of Via Appia Antica are the ruins where the obelisk now in Piazza Navona once stood. ⊠ *Via Appia Antica 153* ☎ *06/7801324* ▱ *€3* ◷ *Tues.–Sun. 9–1.*

WHERE TO EAT

Updated by
Dana Klitzberg

Rome has been known since ancient times for its great feasts and banquets, and though the days of the triclinium and the Saturnalia are long past, dining out is still the Romans' favorite pastime. The city is distinguished more by its good attitude toward eating out than by a multitude of world-class restaurants; simple, traditional cuisine reigns, although things are slowly changing as talented young chefs explore new culinary frontiers. Many of the city's restaurants cater to a clientele of regulars, and atmosphere and attitude are usually friendly and informal. The flip side is that in Rome the customer is not always right—the chef and waiters are in charge, and no one will beg forgiveness if you wanted *skim* milk in that cappuccino. Be flexible and you're sure to *mangiar bene* (eat well). Lunch is served from 12:30 to 2:30 and dinner from 8 until about 11, though some restaurants stay open later, especially in summer, when patrons linger at sidewalk tables to enjoy the parade of people and the *ponentino* (evening breeze).

WHAT IT COSTS In euros				
$$$$	**$$$**	**$$**	**$**	**¢**
AT DINNER	over €45	€35–€45	€25–€35	€15–€25	under €15

Prices are for a first course *(primo)*, second course *(secondo)*, and dessert *(dolce)*.

Campo de' Fiori

★ **$$-$$$$** ✕ **Osteria del Pesce.** The entrance to this restaurant looks like an upscale *pescheria* (fish market). Awaiting you inside is seafood from the coast south of Rome that's beautiful enough to display like aquatic jewels: from starters such as tuna or sea bass carpaccio, to seafood pasta dishes, to secondi of grilled or sautéed fish and crustaceans, all is simply prepared and of the highest quality. The space—hardwood floors, subtle lighting, and walls in royal blue and chili-pepper red—brims with energy. The extensive wine list has mostly whites; there are numerous after-dinner liqueurs available. ⊠ *Via di Monserrato 32, near Campo de' Fiori* ☎ *06/6865617* ▭ *AE, DC, MC, V* ◷ *Closed Sun. and 2 wks in Aug. No lunch.*

$-$$$ ✕ **Roscioli.** Marco Roscioli opened this restaurant (with an upscale deli counter and wine shop) around the corner from his famous *forno* (bakery). The menu has a mix of tasty and often uncommon Italian meats and cheeses, as well as pasta and fish dishes, all of which are meant to be paired with one of the 800 wines. Try the homemade pasta with duck prosciutto, the potato gnocchi with sea-urchin sauce, or splurge on the foie gras. If you book ahead you can get a table in the cozy, appealing wine cellar. ⊠ *Via dei Giubbonari 21/22, near Campo de' Fiori* ☎ *06/ 6875287* ▭ *AE, DC, MC, V* ◷ *Closed Sun.*

$–$$ ✕ **Grappolo d'Oro Zampanò.** This Campo area favorite has both a pizzeria and a restaurant, which serves eclectic regional Italian cuisine such as an eggplant flan with Gorgonzola sauce. Second courses include beef stewed in Sangiovese wine and a delicate grouper fillet oven-baked in foil with potatoes, tomatoes, and oregano. There's a well-selected (though not bargain-priced) wine list. ⊠ *Piazza della Cancelleria 80, near Campo de' Fiori* ☎ *06/6897080* ▭ *AE, MC, V* ⊗ *Closed Mon. and Aug.*

¢–$ ✕ **Acchiapafantasmi.** The name translates as "ghostbusters," after the restaurant's award-winning pizza shaped like a ghost with mozzarella, cherry tomatoes, and oregano. But the menu extends beyond pizza to spicy treats of the Commisso brothers' native Calabria, such as the spreadable *'nduja* sausage (half pork, half hot peppers) and an innovative version of eggplant parmigiana. The gelato, brought up from the southern town of Pizzo Calabria, is considered by some the best in Italy. ⊠ *Via dei Cappellari 66, near Campo de' Fiori* ☎ *06/6873462* ⌔ *Reservations not accepted* ▭ *AE, DC, MC, V* ⊗ *Closed Tues. and 1 wk in Aug.*

¢–$ ✕ **Le Piramidi.** Come here for great falafel, *schewerma* (spit-roasted meat, in this case veal), and other to-go Middle Eastern specialties. Sundry desserts are sure to include phyllo pastry, honey, and nuts. ⊠ *Vicolo del Gallo 11, Campo de' Fiori* ☎ *06/6879061* ▭ *No credit cards* ⊗ *Closed Mon.*

¢ ✕ **Il Forno di Campo de' Fiori.** Crowds fill this counter-service pizzeria throughout the day. Try the *farcita* (stuffed) pizza, filled with meats, cheeses, vegetables—even prosciutto and warm figs in season—at their adjacent sandwich bar. ⊠ *Piazza Campo de' Fiori 22* ☎ *06/66806662* ⌔ *Reservations not accepted* ▭ *No credit cards* ⊗ *Closed Sun.*

Piazza di Spagna

$–$$$ ✕ **Dal Bolognese.** The classic Dal Bolognese is both a convenient shopping-spree lunch spot and an in-crowd dinner destination. The tables on the expansive pedestrian piazza are prime people-watching real estate, and tables inside are perfectly spaced for table-hopping and lots of two-cheek kisses. As the name promises, the cooking here adheres to the hearty tradition of Bologna, with delicious homemade tortellini *in brodo* (in broth), fresh pastas in creamy sauces, and steaming trays of boiled meats. Among the desserts, try the *dolce della mamma* (a concoction of gelato, zabaglione, and chocolate sauce) and the fruit-shape gelato. ⊠ *Piazza del Popolo 1, near Piazza di Spagna* ☎ *06/3611426* ▭ *AE, DC, MC, V* ⊗ *Closed Mon. and Aug.*

$$ ✕ **Il Palazzetto.** At this small restaurant by the Spanish Steps is part of the International Wine Academy of Rome. Chef Antonio Martucci creates seasonal menus using traditional Roman ingredients, which he gives a unique "twist" to in preparation and flavor pairings. Stuffed calamari on an eggplant puree with sautéed baby peppers is a study in contrasting flavor and texture; homemade ricotta-filled gnocchi with sausage and asparagus hits all the right notes. It's wise to call in advance, both for reservations and to find out about regular prix fixe dinners, sometimes with guest chefs, focusing on wine-food pairings. ⊠ *Vicolo del Bottino 8, Piazza di Spagna* ☎ *06/6990878* ▭ *AE, DC, MC, V.*

$–$$ ✕ **GINA.** "Homey minimalism" isn't a contradiction at this whitewashed café with a modern edge (block seats, single flowers in mason jars, white chandeliers, mirrors). With a reasonable menu of salads, sandwiches, pastas, and American-style desserts, this is the perfect spot for a late lunch or a light dinner that won't break the bank despite the high-end neighborhood. Upscale picnic baskets are stocked and ready to pick up on the way to nearby Villa Borghese. For a relaxed Saturday evening, join the friendly owners for live jazz from 9:30 to midnight. ☒ *Via San Sebastianello 7A, near Piazza di Spagna* ☏ *06/6780251* ⊟ *AE, MC, V* ☺ *Closed Sun. and Aug.*

★ **$–$$** ✕ **Osteria della Frezza.** You can get regular tavern fare and service at this member of the 'Gusto restaurant empire (which dominates the surrounding block), or you can sample *cicchetti* (Venetian dialect for bar snacks). These are miniature portions of what's on the regular menu: cured meats and a head-spinning selection of cheeses; cooked meats like lamb chops and meatballs in tomato sauce; and pastas, including thick spaghetti with octopus, tomato, and pecorino cheese. Homemade desserts are also available in tiny portions. The wine list is full of interesting choices; trust the knowledgable staff to point you in the right direction. ☒ *Via della Frezza 16, near Piazza di Spagna* ☏ *06/3226273* ⊟ *AE, DC, MC, V.*

Piazza Navona & the Pantheon

$$$$
Fodor'sChoice
★

✕ **Il Convivio.** The Troiani brothers came to Rome in the late 1980s; since then they've been the leaders of a small circle of top Italian food elite. Their inventive fare can be characterized as Italian cuisine revisited— classic dishes made from the best ingredients, given a unique, elegant tweak. The raw "lacquered" tuna and the foie gras are luscious starters, and a delicious squid ink risotto has Asian touches of lemongrass and Thai basil. For secondi, the pigeon is exquisitely cooked, and the fish are all first-rate. Desserts are delicious, if a bit restrained, service is excellent, and the wine selection, although pricey, would impress any connoisseur. ☒ *Vicolo dei Soldati 31, near Piazza Navona* ☏ *06/6869432* ⌂ *Reservations essential* ⊟ *AE, DC, MC, V* ☺ *Closed Sun., 1 wk in Jan., and 2 wks in Aug. No lunch.*

★ **$$$–$$$$** ✕ **Myosotis.** Don't overlook the traditional Myosotis in favor of trendier choices in the area. Secondi include a hearty veal chop *alla Milanese,* breaded and panfried, as well as a delicate catch of the day in a garlic, olive oil, and tomato broth. A soup of whitefish, fava beans, and chicory is a study in bittersweet. The chocolate mousse in chocolate raspberry sauce is elegant in its simplicity. Bright and fresh, the space has parquet floors, creamy table linens, and walls sponge-painted the color of fresh fettuccine. Service is sometimes slow, but owners and staff obviously care about the food. ☒ *Vicolo della Vaccarella 3/5, near Piazza Navona* ☏ *06/ 6865554* ⊟ *AE, DC, MC, V* ☺ *Closed 2 wks in Aug.*

$$$–$$$$ ✕ **Romilo.** The name represents three locations where the owner wants to open a restaurant: Rome, Milan, and London. So far it's one out of three. Despite the cosmopolitan ambitions, Romilo does best with traditional Roman cuisine—the more-gimmicky dishes from chef Vito Specchia (formerly of Hotel de Russie and La Pergola) can fall flat. So stick to a delicious mushroom risotto, or a basic-but-satisfying fillet of beef with red-wine reduction and potato gratin. Desserts (almost exclusively frozen) are tasty, and the wine list has some interesting offerings

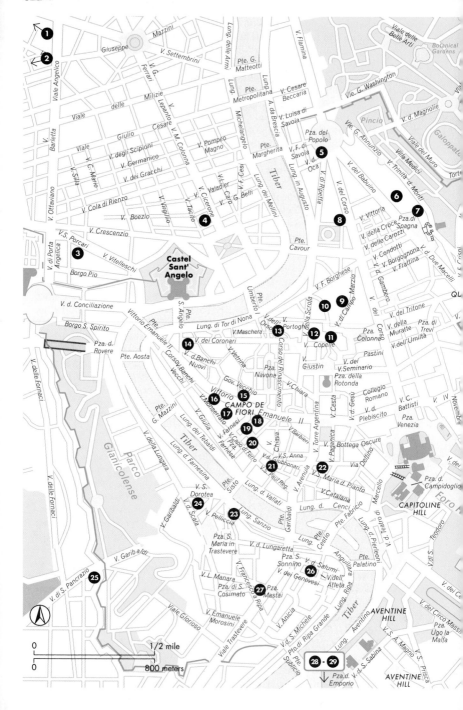

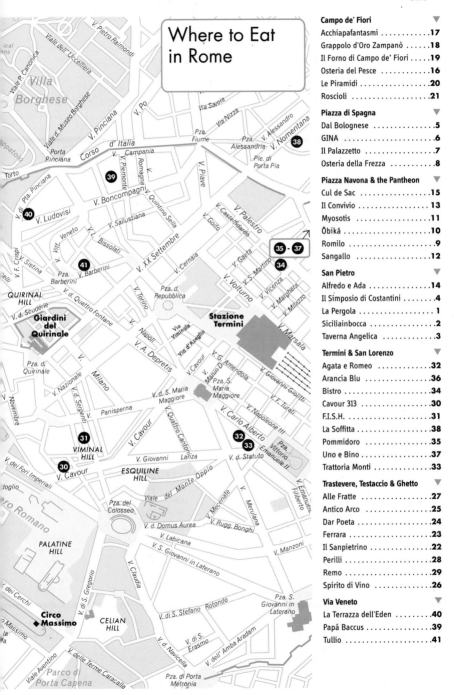

Where to Eat in Rome

Campo de' Fiori ▼
Acchiapafantasmi **17**
Grappolo d'Oro Zampanò **18**
Il Forno di Campo de' Fiori **19**
Osteria del Pesce **16**
Le Piramidi **20**
Roscioli **21**

Piazza di Spagna ▼
Dal Bolognese **5**
GINA **6**
Il Palazzetto **7**
Osteria della Frezza **8**

Piazza Navona & the Pantheon ▼
Cul de Sac **15**
Il Convivio **13**
Myosotis **11**
Ōbikà **10**
Romilo **9**
Sangallo **12**

San Pietro ▼
Alfredo e Ada **14**
Il Simposio di Costantini **4**
La Pergola **1**
Siciliainbocca **2**
Taverna Angelica **3**

Termini & San Lorenzo ▼
Agata e Romeo **32**
Arancia Blu **36**
Bistro **34**
Cavour 313 ....**30**
F.I.S.H. **31**
La Soffitta **38**
Pommidoro **35**
Uno e Bino **37**
Trattoria Monti **33**

Trastevere, Testaccio & Ghetto ▼
Alle Fratte **27**
Antico Arco **25**
Dar Poeta **24**
Ferrara **23**
Il Sanpietrino **22**
Perilli **28**
Remo **29**
Spirito di Vino **26**

Via Veneto ▼
La Terrazza dell'Eden **40**
Papá Baccus **39**
Tullio **41**

EATING WELL IN ROME

Roman cooking is simple, rustic cuisine, perfected over centuries. Dishes rarely have more than a few ingredients, and meat and fish are most often roasted, baked, or grilled. The best meat is often *abbacchio* (milk-fed lamb)—legs are usually roasted with rosemary and potatoes, and chops served *alla scottadito* (literally "burn your finger"—hot off the grill). Most Mediterranean fish are light yet flavorful, among them *spigola* (the Roman name for sea bass, more commonly called *branzino* elsewhere), *orata* (gilthead bream), and *rombo* (turbot). Romans swoon for batter-fried *baccalà* (cod).

The quintessential Roman pasta dishes are made with *guanciale* (cured pork cheek) and pecorino Romano cheese. *All'amatriciana* adds onion and tomato to the mix and is classically served with *bucatini* (a thick, hollow spaghetti); *alla carbonara* tosses the pork and cheese with egg yolk and black pepper; and *alla gricia* is amatriciana without tomatoes. Potato gnocchi with a tomato sauce and Parmesan or pecorino is a favorite for Thursday dinner.

Seasonal vegetables may not appear on the menu but are usually available. Romans love their greens—*cicoria* and *spinaci ripassati* (sautéed chicory and spinach) are perennial favorites—and many restaurants specialize in vegetable *fritto misto* (literally "mixed fried"). Rome is famous for *carciofi* (artichokes)—available from November to April—prepared *alla romana* (stuffed with garlic and mint and braised) or *alla giudia*

(fried whole, making each petal crisp). A springtime treat is *vignarola*, a mixture of tender peas, fava beans, artichokes, and guanciale.

Typical wines of Rome are from the Castelli Romani, the towns in the hills to the southeast: Frascati, Colli Albani, Marino, and Velletri. Though Roman tap water is the best in Italy, restaurants usually offer bottled water, either *gassata* or *frizzante* (sparkling) or *liscia* (still).

It was not so long ago that wine in Rome (and other towns) was strictly local; you didn't have to walk far to find an *osteria*, a tavernlike establishment where you could buy wine straight from the barrel or sit down to drink and nibble a bit, chat, or play cards. The tradition continues today, as many Roman wineshops are also open as *enoteche* (wine bars). Most have done away with the folding chairs and rickety tables in favor of designer interiors, chic ambience, and excellent menus. Shelves are lined with hundreds of bottles from all over the country, representing the best in Italian wine making, and many selections are available by the glass. Behind the bar you'll usually find a sommelier or at least a serious wine enthusiast.

at a fair markup. ⊠ *Via di Campo Marzio 13* ☎ *06/6893499* ▭ *AE, DC, MC, V* ☉ *Closed Sun.*

\$\$\$–\$\$\$\$ ✕ **Sangallo.** This quiet and intimate restaurant snuggled between Piazza Navona and the Pantheon serves high-quality seafood. The owner hails from Anzio, a coastal town south of Rome. The menu has some sophisticated touches, such as oysters tartare, snapper with foie gras, and pasta dishes made with toothsome *Gragnano* pasta (made in Gragnano of 100% Italian wheat, and dried to strict specifications). There are precious few tables in the tiny dining room, so make sure to book ahead. ⊠ *Vicolo della Vaccarella 11/a, near Piazza Navona* ☎ *06/6865549* ⌕ *Reservations essential* ▭ *AE, DC, MC, V* ☉ *Closed Sun., 1 wk in Jan., and 2 wks in Aug. No lunch Mon.*

\$–\$\$ ✕ **Ōbikā.** The owners of this concept restaurant are trying something original: a "mozzarella bar," with choices ranging from the familiar cow's-milk variety to delectable buffalo-milk mozzarella to sinfully rich *burrata* (fresh cow's-milk mozzarella encasing a creamy center of unspun curds). You can get cured meats, vegetables, sauces, and breads to accompany your cheese, and salads and pasta dishes, including interesting lasagnas, are also on the menu. The wines, like the mozzarella, tend to come from the southern Italian regions. ⊠ *Piazza di Firenze and Via dei Prefetti, near Pantheon* ☎ *06/6832630* ▭ *AE, DC, MC, V.*

★ \$ ✕ **Cul de Sac.** This is a classic Roman *enoteca* (wine bar), frequented by everyone from local soccer fans to the Fendi sisters. Quarters are cramped, both inside and out on the small piazza, but once you begin sipping the wine and sampling the food, you realize it's worth any discomfort. The selection of Italian regional cheeses and cured meats is vast, and the soups, pastas, and salads have homemade appeal. Especially refreshing are the international dishes: hummus, Greek salad, and pâtés that can be difficult to find in these parts. The wine list is tremendous and constantly changing. ⊠ *Piazza Pasquino 73, near Piazza Navona* ☎ *06/68801094* ▭ *AE, MC, V* ☉ *Closed 2 wks in Aug.*

San Pietro

\$\$\$\$ ✕ **La Pergola.** High atop Monte Mario, the Cavalieri Hilton's rooftop restaurant has a commanding view of the city below. Trompe-l'oeil ceilings and handsome wood paneling combine with low lighting to enhance the intimate dining experience. Celebrated wunder-chef Heinz Beck brings Rome its most polished example of Mediterranean *alta cucina* (haute cuisine): dishes are balanced and light (a perfectly cooked lobster) and presentation is striking (a plate of spiraling sea scallops and black truffles, each one the exact same size). For a window table reserve a month in advance; for others, two weeks. ⊠ *Cavalieri Hilton, Via Cadlolo 101, Monte Mario* ☎ *06/3509221* ⌕ *Reservations essential* 🎩 *Jacket and tie* ▭ *AE, DC, MC, V* ☉ *Closed Sun. and Mon., and 2 wks in Dec. No lunch.*

FodorśChoice ★

\$\$–\$\$\$\$ ✕ **Il Simposio di Costantini.** The most sophisticated wine bar in town is done in wood paneling and velvet, and has sculptured iron vines as decoration. Here you can choose from about 30 wines by the glass. Food is appropriately fancy: marinated and smoked fish, composed salads, top-quality salami and other cured meats, terrines and pâtés, vegetable dishes, and several inventive secondi, mostly meat-game selections. Finish off with a plate from an assortment of 80 cheeses grouped according to origin or type, and a well-balanced dessert menu. ☒ *Piazza Cavour 16, near San Pietro* ☎ *06/3211502* ☰ *AE, DC, MC, V* ☉ *Closed Sun. and last 2 wks of Aug. No lunch Sat.*

$$ ✕ **Alfredo e Ada.** Squeeze into a table at this lovable hole-in-the-wall and make yourself at home. There's no menu, just plate after plate of whatever Ada thinks you should try, from hearty, classic pastas to *involtini di vitello* (savory veal rolls with tomato) and homemade sausage. Sit back, relax, and enjoy—it's all good. By the time you leave you may have made some new friends, too. The cost depends on how many courses you eat and how much wine you consume, but an average meal might run around €25. Alfredo e Ada is across the river from Castel Sant'Angelo. ☒ *Via dei Banchi Nuovi 14, near San Pietro* ☎ *06/6878842* ☰ *No credit cards* ☉ *Closed weekends.*

$$ ✕ **Taverna Angelica.** The area surrounding St. Peter's Basilica isn't known for culinary excellence, but Taverna Angelica is an exception to the rule. The chef takes care with each dish, and the results are impressive: lentil soup with pigeon breast, duck in balsamic vinegar, and warm octopus salad on a bed of mashed potatoes with a basil-parsley pesto drizzle are all exquisitely executed. The narrow, candlelit dining room has plenty of space between tables; excellent service is icing on the cake. ☒ *Piazza A. Capponi 6, near San Pietro* ☎ *06/6874514* ✍ *Reservations essential* ☰ *AE, V.*

★ $–$$ ✕ **Siciliainbocca.** Looking for a straight-up, no-nonsense Sicilian restaurant? The owners, both Sicily natives, decided to open up Siciliainbocca after years of frustration at not finding a decent pasta *alla norma,* with eggplant, tomato sauce, and aged ricotta cheese. Try the risotto *ai profumi di Sicilia,* with lemon, orange, mozzarella, and zucchini. You might also opt for the delicious grilled swordfish, shrimp, or squid. Even in the dead of winter, Siciliainbocca's yellow walls and brightly colored ceramic plates are warming. There's outdoor seating in summer. ☒ *Via E. Faà di Bruno 26, near San Pietro* ☎ *06/37358400* ☰ *AE, DC, MC, V* ☉ *Closed Sun.*

Near Termini & San Lorenzo

★ $$$$ ✕ **Agata e Romeo.** The husband-and-wife team of Agata Parisella and Romeo Caraccio runs one of Rome's top restaurants. Agata puts an inspired twist on Roman cuisine with dishes such as crepes with chestnut flour and ewe's-milk ricotta, and breaded lamp chops. Romeo acts as maître d' and expert sommelier. The tasting menu, complete with wine, changes monthly to reflect seasonal dishes and allows you to try a range of specialties. Desserts are scrumptious and the wine list is excellent. ☒ *Via Carlo Alberto 45, near Termini* ☎ *06/4466115* ☰ *AE, DC, MC, V* ☉ *Closed weekends, 2 wks in July, and 2 wks in Aug.*

$$$–$$$$ ✕ **F.I.S.H.** The name stands for Fine International Seafood House, which sums up the kitchen's approach. This is fresh, fresh fish in capable and creative hands—from Italian fish-based pastas to a Thai mollusk soup with lemongrass and coconut milk that's a party for the senses. The menu is divided into three sections: sushi, Asian, and Mediterranean. Seating is limited, so book ahead. ☒ *Via dei Serpenti 16, Monti* ☎ *06/47824962* ✍ *Reservations essential* ☰ *AE, D, MC, V* ☉ *Closed Mon. and 2 wks in Aug.*

$$–$$$ ✕ **Bistro.** The high, pale-yellow arched ceilings, immense guilt mirrors, rich oak paneling, and wrought-iron bar counter here are all true to the art nouveau style. Chef Emanuele Vizzini serves fusion dishes such as fettuccine *al cabernet con scampi* (with red wine, shrimp, and vegetables) and *Nasdaq taglionini* (dollar-green pasta made with curaçao liqueur) topped with lobster. The wine list has 300 labels to choose from (12 available by the glass). ⊠ *Via Palestro 40, Termini* ☎ *06/44702868* ⊟ *AE, DC, MC, V* ☺ *No lunch Sun.*

$$–$$$ ✕ **Trattoria Monti.** The cuisine of the Marches region is underrepresented in Rome, especially considering that more Marchegiani live here than in the region itself. Trattoria Monti fulfills their desire for home cooking. The hearty dishes include soups and roasted meats and game. A selection of soufflés and timbales, generally vegetarian, changes seasonally. For dessert there are cheeses with dried fruits, nuts, and honey. The brothers who run the place are always welcoming. ⊠ *Via San Vito 13/a, Esquilino* ☎ *06/4466573* ⊟ *AE, DC, MC, V* ☺ *Closed Aug., 2 wks at Easter, and 10 days at Christmas.*

★ **$$** ✕ **Uno e Bino.** This restaurant in an artsy corner of the San Lorenzo neighborhood is popular with Romans from all over town. The kitchen turns out inventive cuisine inspired by the owner's Umbrian and Sicilian roots. Octopus salad with asparagus and carrots is a specialty, and perfectly prepared pigeon can satisfy the most critical foodies on an autumn night. ⊠ *Via degli Equi 58, San Lorenzo* ☎ *06/4460702* ⊟ *AE, D, MC, V* ☺ *Closed Mon. and Aug. No lunch.*

$ ✕ **Arancia Blu.** Owner-chef Fabio Passan has a mission—to prove that "vegetarian cuisine" isn't an oxymoron. He succeeds, with creative dishes that have won him a devoted omnivorous clientele. Start with a leek-and-almond quiche or lemon-ricotta ravioli with squash and sage, and move on to *polpettine vegetali* (meatless meatballs) with a tomato-and-coriander seed sauce. For dessert you might tickle your palate with a chocolate tasting: 14 chocolate wafers of different flavors and origins. Vegan and wheat-free dishes are available on request. ⊠ *Via dei Latini 65, San Lorenzo* ☎ *06/4454105* ⊟ *No credit cards* ☺ *No lunch.*

$ ✕ **Pommidoro.** Mamma's in the kitchen and the rest of the family greets, serves, and keeps you happy and well fed at this trattoria popular with artists, filmmakers, and actors. It's near Rome's main university in the countercultural San Lorenzo neighborhood, a short cab ride east of the Termini train station. The menu has especially good grilled meats and game birds as well as classic home-style cucina. You can dine outside in warm weather. ⊠ *Piazza dei Sanniti 44, San Lorenzo* ☎ *06/4452692* ⊟ *AE, DC, MC, V* ☺ *Closed Sun. and Aug.*

$ ✕ **La Soffitta.** This is Rome's hottest spot for classic Neapolitan pizza (thick-crusted, though crunchy on the bottom, rather than paper-thin and crispy like the Roman kind); it's one of the few pizzerias in town certified by the True Neapolitan Pizza Association. Desserts are brought in daily from Naples. You pay more here, but hey, it's imported. ⊠ *Via dei Villini 1/e, Termini* ☎ *06/4404642* ⌦ *Reservations not accepted* ⊟ *AE, DC, MC, V* ☺ *Closed Aug. 10–31. No lunch.*

★ **¢–$** ✕ **Cavour 313.** Wine bars are popping up all over the city, but Cavour 313 has been around for a while, and it's easy to understand its stay-

Pizza, Roman Style

PIZZA MAY HAVE BEEN invented somewhere else, but in Rome it's hard to walk a block without encountering it in one form or another. You'll see it in bakeries, usually made without cheese—either pizza bianca (just olive oil and salt) or pizza rossa (with tomato sauce). Many small shops specialize in pizza *al taglio* (by the slice), priced by the etto (100 grams, about 1/4 pound), according to the kind of topping. These places are great for a snack on the go any time of day.

But don't leave Rome without sitting down to a classic, wafer-thin, crispy Roman pizza in a lively, no-frills pizzeria. Most are open only for dinner, usually from 8 PM to midnight. Look for a place with a *forno a legna* (wood-burning oven), a must for a good thin crust on your plate-size Roman pizza. Standard models are the margherita (tomato, mozzarella, and basil) and the capricciosa (a little bit of everything, depending upon the "caprices" of the pizza chef: tomato, mozzarella, sausage, olives, artichoke hearts, prosciutto, even egg), and most pizzerias have a long list of additional options, including tasty mozzarella *di bufala* (made from buffalo milk).

---

ing power. Well-prepared food options include cured meats, cheeses, and salads. Choose from about 25 wines by the glass or uncork a bottle (there are more than 1,200) and linger. ⊠ *Via Cavour 313, Colosseo* ☎ *06/6785496* ▤ *AE, DC, MC, V* ☉ *Closed Aug. No lunch weekends. No dinner Sun. June 15–Sept.*

Trastevere, Testaccio & the Ghetto

$$–$$$$ ╳ **Ferrara.** What used to be a well-stocked wine bar with a few nibbles has expanded to become a full-fledged restaurant, wine bar, and gastronomic boutique—known as the "Ferrara block." It's a modernist destination with a frequently changing menu and tasty antipasti and primi. Consistency is neither the kitchen's nor the servers' strong point: you can have a wonderful experience one visit and a drawn-out, disappointing meal the next. The wine list never lets you down though, and the sinful desserts end things on a positive note. ⊠ *Via del Moro 1A, Trastevere* ☎ *06/58333920* ▤ *DC, MC, V* ☉ *Closed Tues. and 2 wks in Aug.*

$$$ ╳ **Il Sanpietrino.** Tucked away in a tiny corner of the Jewish Ghetto, this historic restaurant (named for the cobblestones that line its floors) serves fresh, simple preparations of Roman staples and a few more-distinctive dishes. Appetizers like the local Jewish-style fried artichokes are lip-smacking good, and homemade gnocchi with a white (tomatoless) rabbit ragu are light, fluffy pillows of potato heaven. ⊠ *Piazza Costaguti 15, Ghetto* ☎ *06/68806471* ▤ *AE, DC, MC, V* ☉ *Closed Sun. No lunch.*

$$–$$$ ╳ **Antico Arco.** Founded by three friends with a passion for wine and fine food, Antico Arco has won the hearts of foodies from Rome and beyond with its culinary inventiveness and high style. The menu changes with the season, but you may find such delights as *flan di taleggio con salsa di funghi* (cheese flan with mushrooms), or a *carré d'agnello* (rack of lamb) with foie-gras sauce and pears in port wine. Don't miss the chocolate soufflé with melted chocolate center: it's justly famous among chocoholics all over the city. ⊠ *Piazzale Aurelio 7, Trastevere* ☎ *06/ 5815274* ⌂ *Reservations essential* ☰ *AE, DC, MC, V* ☉ *Closed Sun. and 2 wks in Aug. No lunch.*

$$–$$$ ✕ **Spirito di Vino.** At this restaurant on the less-traveled side of Viale Trastevere, the food ranges from inventive (mini meatballs seasoned with coriander) to traditional (spaghetti with *cacio*, an aged sheep's milk cheese) to ancient (braised pork shoulder with apple and leeks—from a recipe by Apicius, Rome's first cookbook author). The dining room is welcoming and refined, with walls in tomato-red and dark wood. The proud owner is happy to explain every dish on the menu and give you the history of his wine cellar, where several ancient sculptures, now in the Vatican and Capitoline museums, were unearthed. ⊠ *Via dei Genovesi 31 A/B, Trastevere* ☎ *06/5896689* ☰ *AE, MC, V* ☉ *Closed Sun. and 2 wks in Aug.*

★ $–$$ ✕ **Alle Fratte.** Here staple Roman trattoria fare shares the menu with dishes that have a Neapolitan slant: spaghetti carbonara, as well as penne *alla Sorrentina*, with tomato, basil, and fresh mozzarella, for example. Try the pressed octopus carpaccio with arugula to start, followed by a mixed seafood pasta or a grilled sea bass with oven-roasted potatoes. Ask about daily specials, too—always worth a try. Boisterous owner Francesco, his American relatives, and their trusted waiter Peppe make you feel at home. ⊠ *Via delle Fratte di Trastevere 49/50* ☎ *06/5835775* ☰ *AE, DC, MC, V* ☉ *Closed Wed. and 2 wks in Aug.*

$–$$ ✕ **Perilli.** A bastion of authentic Roman cooking since 1911 (the decor has changed little), this trattoria is the place to go to try rigatoni *con pajata* (with calves' intestines)—if you're into that sort of thing. The pasta carbonara is also a classic. House wine is a hearty white from the Castelli Romani estate. ⊠ *Via Marmorata 39, Testaccio* ☎ *06/5742415* ☰ *AE, DC, MC, V* ☉ *Closed Wed.*

★ ¢–$ ✕ **Dar Poeta.** It's always crowded and lively at this innovative pizzeria, which serves both Roman style (paper-thin) and the thicker Neapolitan variety. Topping choices go beyond the usual: try the house specialty with sautéed zucchini, sausage, and hot pepper. There are several types of *bruschette* (grilled breads with toppings) and salads. A must-try: the dessert calzone, filled with ricotta cheese and chocolate-hazelnut Nutella. ⊠ *Vicolo del Bologna, Trastevere* ☎ *06/5880516* ☰ *AE, MC, V.*

¢–$ ✕ **Remo.** Expect a wait at this perennial favorite in Testaccio frequented by students and neighborhood locals. You won't find tablecloths or other nonessentials, just classic Roman pizza and boisterous conversation. ⊠ *Piazza Santa Maria Liberatrice 44, Testaccio* ☎ *06/5746270* ⌂ *Reservations not accepted* ☰ *No credit cards* ☉ *Closed Sun., Aug., and Christmas wk. No lunch.*

Via Veneto

$$$$ ✕ **La Terrazza dell'Eden.** The Hotel Eden's La Terrazza restaurant has an unparalleled view of Rome's seven hills and food that's just as spectacular. The culinary expertise of the well-traveled young chef is reflected in his refined touch with Mediterranean dishes and his pairing the finest primary ingredients with unusual accents like candied celery and pearl barley. If you're a wine enthusiast, ask the maître d' to let you view the restaurant's showcase cellar. ⊠ *Hotel Eden, Via Ludovisi 49, near Via Veneto* ☎ *06/47812752* ⌂ *Reservations essential* ▥ *Jacket and tie* ▭ *AE, DC, MC, V.*

★ **$$$–$$$$** ✕ **Papá Baccus.** Italo Cipriani takes his meat as seriously as any Tuscan, in fact imports what he serves here from his home region. Prized Chianina beef is used for the house-specialty *bistecca alla fiorentina,* a thick grilled steak left rare in the middle. Try the sweet and delicate prosciutto from Pratomagno or the *ribollita* (a traditional bread-based, minestrone-like soup). The welcome is warm, the service excellent. ⊠ *Via Toscana 36, near Via Veneto* ☎ *06/42742808* ▭ *AE, DC, MC, V* ☽ *Closed Sun. and 2 wks in Aug. No lunch Sat.*

$$$–$$$$ ✕ **Tullio.** For years members of the international business and the entertainment industries have frequented this upscale trattoria. The decor is basic—wood paneling and white linens—with the requisite older, often grumpy, waiters. But fresh seafood is available in abundance, as are greens such as *brocoletti* (broccoli florets), sautéed to perfection with garlic and olive oil. The menu is heavy on Tuscan classics such as ribollita and grilled steak; the wild-hare sauce, served over flat noodles, is delectable. The wine list favors robust Tuscan reds (for which you pay a hefty markup). ⊠ *Via San Nicola da Tolentino 26, off Piazza Barberini, near Via Veneto* ☎ *06/4745560* ▭ *AE, DC, MC, V* ☽ *Closed Aug.*

Cafés

Café-sitting is the most popular leisure-time activity in Rome, practiced by all and involving nothing more strenuous than gesturing to catch the waiter's eye. Cafés are meant for relaxing, chatting with a companion, and watching the passing parade, possibly within view of one of the city's spectacular fountains or churches. Part of the pleasure is resting your tired feet; you won't be rushed, even when the cafés are most crowded, just before lunch and dinner. (Be aware, though, that you pay for your seat—prices are higher at tables than at the counter.) Nearly every corner in Rome holds a faster-paced coffee bar, where locals stop for a quick caffeine hit at the counter. You can get coffee drinks, fruit juices, pastries, sandwiches, liquor, and beer there, too.

Pricey **Antico Caffè Greco** (⊠ Via Condotti 86, near Piazza di Spagna ☎ 06/6791700) is a national landmark popular with tourists; its red-velvet chairs and marble tables have hosted the likes of Byron, Shelley, Keats, Goethe, and Casanova. **Rosati** (⊠ Piazza del Popolo 5, near Piazza di Spagna ☎ 06/3225859) is Piazza del Popolo's premier people-watching spot. Tables on the car-free square fill up quickly on weekends, when it seems the whole city is here. **Ciampini** (⊠ Piazza San Lorenzo in Lucina 29, near Piazza di Spagna ☎ 06/6876606), in a jewel of a piazza off Via del Corso, is a prime spot for a predinner aperitivo. Be sure to ask for the free *assaggini* (Italian hors d'oeuvres). **Zoe Caffè** (⊠ Via della Colonna Antonina 42, near Pantheon ☎ 06/69380930) offers the usual café fare but also a lovely selection of sweets.

Antico Caffè della Pace (⊠ Via della Pace 3, near Piazza Navona ☎ 06/ 6861216) is ornate and old-fashioned. Inside, cozy candlelight is a treat, or you can sit outside by ivy-lined walls in warm weather. **Caffè Sant'Eustachio** (⊠ Piazza Sant'Eustachio 82, near Pantheon ☎ 06/6861309) makes one of the smoothest cappuccinos anywhere. The secret? *Crema di caffè* (coffee cream)—a rich, homemade addition slipped into each cup. If you want your *caffè* (espresso) without sugar, ask for it *amaro*. **Tazza d'Oro** (⊠ Via degli Orfani 84, near Pantheon ☎ 06/6789792) serves some of the best coffee in the city, as well as decadent *granita di caffè* (iced espresso) with a thick dollop of whipped cream mixed in.

Gelato & Pastry

For Italians, gelato is more a snack than a dessert. Romans are not known for having a sweet tooth, but there are few *pasticcerie* (pastry shops) in town that distinguish themselves with particularly good examples of regional desserts.

Gelateria Duomo (⊠ Largo Arenula 27, near Campo de' Fiori ☎ 320/ 1633871) specializes in artisanal, all-natural gelato. **Il Gelato di San Crispino** (⊠ Via della Panetteria 42, near Piazza di Trevi ☎ 06/6793924), closed Tuesday, is perhaps the most celebrated gelato in all of Italy, made without artificial colors or flavors. It's worth crossing town for.

Giolitti (⊠ Via Uffici del Vicario 40, near Pantheon ☎ 06/6991243), off Via Campo Marzio, has a quaint tearoom and delicious fruit-flavor gelato. **Fiocco di Neve** (⊠ Via del Pantheon 51 ☎ 06/6786025) is renowned for its zabaglione and *riso bianco* (white rice) ice cream.

Fonte della Salute (⊠ Via Cardinal Marmaggi 2, Trastevere ☎ 06/ 5897471), literally "fountain of health," serves frozen yogurt as well as traditional gelato. It's closed Tuesday in winter. **Forno del Ghetto** (⊠ Via del Portico d'Ottavia 1, Ghetto ☎ 06/6878637) preserves a tradition of Italian-Jewish sweets that cannot be found anywhere else. The ricotta cake (with sour-cherry jam or chocolate) is unforgettable. This hole-in-the-wall—no sign, no tables, just a take-out counter—is a neighborhood fixture. It's closed Friday at sundown, Saturday, and Jewish holidays. The apple strudel and Sacher torte at **Dolceroma** (⊠ Via del Portico d'Ottavia 20/b, Ghetto ☎ 06/6892196) may not be Italian, but this is a popular spot just the same. Prices have become a bit outrageous. It's closed Sunday afternoon, Monday, and four weeks in July and August.

Dagnino (⊠ Galleria Esedra, Via Vittorio Emanuele Orlando 75, near Termini ☎ 06/4818660) is an outpost of Sicilian sweets. The pastries, such as ricotta-filled cannoli and *cassata* (sponge cake with sheep's ricotta and candied fruit), as well as colorful marzipan candies, are exquisite. For decades, **Muse** (⊠ Via Eleanora Duse 1E, Parioli ☎ 06/ 8079300), popularly known as da Giovanni (after the owner), has been a mecca for Romans in the know. Winter flavors include chestnut and almond. It's closed Sunday.

WHERE TO STAY

Updated by
Dana Klitzberg

Appearances can be misleading in Rome: crumbling stucco facades may promise little from the outside, but they often hide interiors of considerable elegance. By the same token, elaborate reception areas may lead to surprisingly plain, even dilapidated, rooms. Generally, rooms tend to be small by U.S. standards. Many of the lower-priced hotels are actually old-fashioned *pensioni* (boardinghouses) set on one or several floors of a large building. One disadvantage of staying in central hotels in lower categories is noise; you can ask for an inside room if you are a light sleeper, but you may end up looking out on a dark courtyard. The grand monuments to luxury and elegance are around the major piazzas and Via Veneto.

Rome is a year-round destination, so you should always try to make reservations, even if only a few days in advance. Always ask about special rates, often available in both winter and summer if occupancy is low. If you arrive in Rome without reservations, try **Hotel Reservation Service** (☎ 06/6991000), with an English-speaking operator available daily 7 AM–10 PM, and with desks at Aeroporto Fiumicino and Stazione Termini. A list of all the hotels in Rome, with prices and facilities, is available from the main **APT information office** (✉ Via Parigi 5, Termini ☎ 06/48899255 ⊕ www.romaturismo.it).

WHAT IT COSTS In euros				
$$$$	**$$$**	**$$**	**$**	**¢**
FOR 2 PEOPLE over €290	€210–€290	€140–€210	€80–€140	under €80

Prices are for two people in a standard double room in high season.

Campo de' Fiori

$$$–$$$$ 🏨 **Hotel Ponte Sisto.** Staying near the pedestrian bridge that connects the Campo de' Fiori neighborhood to Trastevere provides the convenience of the city center and access to the trattorias and bars of Trastevere, an area popular with both Romans and expats. Once the palazzo of the noble Venetian Palottini family, the hotel now has clean and bright, if basic, rooms. Wall-to-wall carpeting and green-marble bathrooms add refinement, but the real draw is the large internal courtyard, where you can get sun, read beneath the shade of the enormous palms, and sip cocktails under the stars. ✉ *Off Ponte Sisto, Via dei Pettinari 64, Campo de' Fiori, 00186* ☎ *06/686310* 🖷 *06/68301712* ⊕ *www.hotelpontesisto. it* 🛏 *103 rooms, 4 suites* ♿ *Dining room, in-room safes, minibars, cable TV, bar, meeting rooms, parking (fee)* ⊟ *AE, DC, MC, V* ⓧ *BP.*

★ **$$–$$$** 🏨 **Residenza Farnese.** The Renaissance charm of this former priests' convent has been preserved—its landmark status prevents the owners from making too many changes. Room 309, believed to be a former chapel, has a ceiling fresco found during renovations; it's been professionally restored. Furnishings run from understated antiques and deep-blue fabrics to more-ornate hand-painted floral dressers and original artwork. All have hardwood floors and modern bathrooms with showers. There is a billiards room with a bar for socializing, and a large breakfast room where home-made breads and organic marmalades are served. ✉ *Via del Mascherone 59, Campo de' Fiori, 00186* ☎ *06/68891388* 🖷 *06/68210980* ✉ *residenzafarnese@libero.it* ⟿ *31 rooms* ♿ *In-room safes, minibars, cable TV, billiards, bar, meeting room, in-room data ports* ▭ *AE, MC, V* ⍾ *BP.*

\$ 🏨 **Hotel In Parione.** Smeraldo's sister hotel shines with marble—cream in the staircases and hallways, deeper reddish tones in the guest-room bathrooms. Celery-green fabrics and cherry-stain wood decorate the rooms, which are smallish, but very neat. Five floors above one of the bustling *vicoli* (small side streets) near the Campo de' Fiori, the roof garden provides a peek into the residential side of Roman living. ✉ *Via dei Chiavari 32, near Campo de' Fiori, 00186* ☎ *06/6892330* 🖷 *06/6834094* ⊕ *www.inparione.com* ♿ *Minibars, cable TV, in-room data ports, bar* ▭ *AE, DC, MC, V* ⍾ *EP.*

\$ 🏨 **Smeraldo.** The location, on a quiet side street a stone's throw from Campo de' Fiori, makes this an excellent choice in its price category. White marble floors, salmon-color bedding and curtains, and wooden bed frames and furniture decorate the guest rooms. Shiny bathrooms in green marble have showers or a combination bath and shower. The roof terrace has a nice view of the surrounding neighborhood. ✉ *Vicolo dei Chiodaroli 9, Campo de' Fiori, 00186* ☎ *06/6875929 or 06/6892121* 🖷 *06/68805495* ⊕ *www.smeraldoroma.com* ⟿ *25 rooms* ♿ *In-room safes, cable TV, bar* ▭ *AE, DC, MC, V* ⍾ *BP.*

Colosseo

\$\$\$–\$\$\$\$ 🏨 **47 Hotel.** The location of this office-building-turned-four-star-hotel is central to much of ancient Rome, and it offers a good quality-to-price ratio for the heart of the city, with fine service and modern amenities. The style of the place is comfortable modern-deco; muted earth tones and brickwork give it added warmth. The rooftop bar and restaurant offer excellent views over the Circus Maximus, Bocca della Verita, Teatro di Marcello, and the heart of *Roma antica.* ✉ *Via Petroselli 47, 00186* ☎ *06/6787816* 🖷 *06/69190726* ⊕ *www.fortysevenhotel.com* ⟿ *61 rooms* ♿ *Restaurant, in-room safes, minibars, cable TV, in-room data ports, bar, laundry, concierge, meeting rooms, no-smoking rooms* ▭ *AE, DC, MC, V* ⍾ *BP.*

\$\$\$–\$\$\$\$ 🏨 **Hotel Capo d'Africa.** Designed on a boutique hotel model, the Capo d'Africa has '60s-style furnishings in bright purple and orange, commissioned artwork on the walls, and quirky light fixtures. The 1903 building was originally a school, and as a result rooms are different sizes; all are done in earth tones and saffron, with marble-and-tile bathrooms. Two rooftop terraces, connected by the breakfast room, are a delightful bonus in warmer weather. ✉ *Via Capo d'Africa 54, near Colosseo, 00184* ☎ *06/772801* 🖷 *06/77280801* ⊕ *www.hotelcapodafrica.com* ⟿ *64 rooms, 1 suite* ♿ *In-room safes, minibars, cable TV, gym, bar, meeting rooms, parking (fee), no-smoking rooms, in-room data ports.* ▭ *AE, DC, MC, V* ⍾ *BP.*

\$\$ 🏨 **Duca d'Alba.** This elegant hotel has made a stylish contribution to the ongoing gentrification of the Suburra neighborhood, near the Colosseum and the Roman Forum. The tasteful neoclassical decor includes custom

Where to Stay in Rome

Near Campo de' Fiori ▼
Hotel In Parione **24**
Hotel Ponte Sisto **27**
Residenza Farnese **26**
Smeraldo **25**

Near Colosseo ▼
Duca d'Alba **33**
47 Hotel **31**
Hotel Capo d'Africa **32**

Near Piazza di Spagna ▼
Carriage **14**
D'Inghilterra **17**
Hassler **16**
Hotel Art **11**
Hotel de Russie **10**
Inn at the Spanish Steps **15**
Locarno **9**
Margutta **12**
Panda **13**

Trastevere ▼
Grand Hotel Gianicolo **30**
Hotel Santa Maria **29**
Hotel Trastevere House **28**

Near Piazza Navona ▼
Abruzzi **20**
Cesàri **21**
Coronet **23**
Fraterna Domus **18**
Raphaël **19**
Santa Chiara **22**

Near San Pietro ▼
Atlante Star **5**
Giulio Cesare **7**
Hotel Farnese **6**
Residenza Paolo VI **3**
San Giuseppe della Montagna . . .**2**
Sant'Anna **4**

Near Termini & Via Nazionale ▼
Adler **39**
The Beehive **41**
Britannia **38**
Des Artistes **43**
Exedra **40**
Hotel Venezia **42**
Mediterraneo **37**
Montreal **34**
Morgana **36**
Tempio di Pallade **35**

Near Via Veneto ▼
Aleph **46**
Eden **48**
La Residenza **47**
Rose Garden Palace **44**
Westin Excelsior **45**

Beyond the City Center ▼
Cavalieri Hilton **1**
Castello della Castelluccia **8**

furnishings such as inlaid wood headboards. All rooms are entirely soundproof. The breakfast buffet is ample. With its attentive staff and reasonable rates, Duca d'Alba is an exceptional value. ⊠ *Via Leonina 14, near Colosseo, 00184* ☎ *06/484471* 🖷 *06/4884840* ⊕ *www. hotelducadalba.com* ⌧ *27 rooms, 1 suite* ♵ *In-room safes, some kitchenettes, minibars, cable TV, in-room data ports, bar* ⊟ *AE, DC, MC, V* ⍾ *BP.*

Piazza di Spagna

$$$$ ⊞ **D'Inghilterra.** Legendary names like Liszt, Mendelssohn, Hans Christian Andersen, Mark Twain, and Hemingway litter the guest book here. With a residential feel and a staff that is as warm as the surroundings are velvety, this hotel near the Spanish Steps was once the guesthouse of the fabulously rich Prince Torlonia. Rooms are so full of carpets, gilt-frame mirrors, and cozy bergères, you hardly notice the snug dimensions. The chic Café Romano, with ocher walls and vaulted ceilings, serves eclectic cuisine and has tables on Via Borgogna. ⊠ *Via Bocca di Leone 14, near Piazza di Spagna, 00187* ☎ *06/699811* 🖷 *06/69922243* ⊕ *www.hoteldinghilterraroma.it* ⌧ *90 rooms, 8 suites* ♵ *Restaurant, in-room safes, minibars, cable TV, bar, laundry service, parking (fee), no-smoking rooms* ⊟ *AE, DC, MC, V* ⍾ *EP.*

$$$$ ⊞ **Hassler.** Enjoy sweeping views of Rome from the front rooms and the
Fodor'sChoice roof restaurant of the enchanting Hassler hotel, itself at the top of the
★ Spanish Steps; other rooms overlook the gardens of the Villa Medici. An extravagant 1950s elegance pervades the public spaces—especially the clubby winter bar and the summer garden bar. Luxe guest rooms are decorated in classic styles with rich fabrics and some ornate, hand-painted furniture; the fifth floor has stylized art deco rooms done in black and white. The penthouse suite, resplendent with antiques, has a huge terrace. ⊠ *Piazza Trinità dei Monti 6, near Piazza di Spagna, 00187* ☎ *06/699340* 🖷 *06/6789991* ⊕ *www.lhw.com* ⌧ *85 rooms, 15 suites* ♵ *Restaurant, in-room safes, minibars, cable TV, gym, hair salon, bar, laundry service, concierge, in-room data ports, Wi-Fi, parking (fee), no-smoking rooms* ⊟ *AE, DC, MC, V* ⍾ *EP.*

$$$$ ⊞ **Hotel Art.** Via Margutta has long been an artists' enclave, so it's fitting that this modern hotel is a favorite of creative types. In the futuristic lobby the check-in staff works within a glowing white, podlike fixture. Arches, vaults, and columns are painted in contrasting deep blue and white, defining the café-bar space. Each of the four floors has a corridor color (yellow, green, orange, and blue) that is mirrored in the guest rooms' bathroom tiles. Otherwise, the rooms—clean-line furnishings, high-quality linens, and sleek parquet floors—have a neutral palette. A central courtyard is a good lounging spot in warmer months. ⊠ *Via Margutta 56, near Piazza di Spagna, 00187* ☎ *06/328711* 🖷 *06/36003995* ⊕ *www.hotelart.it* ⌧ *44 rooms, 2 suites* ♵ *In-room safes, minibars, cable TV, gym, sauna, steam room, bar* ⊟ *AE, DC, MC, V* ⍾ *EP.*

$$$$ ⊞ **Hotel de Russie.** In the 19th century this hotel counted Russian princes among its guests; later Picasso and Cocteau leaned out the windows to pick oranges from the trees in the lush terraced garden. Famed hotelier Sir Rocco Forte has brought the de Russie to a superlative standard of accommodations and service today. Rooms are chic Italian contemporary in style, with Roman mosaic motifs in bathrooms. Many have garden views, and several suites have panoramic terraces. The spa is luxurious, but be warned: you have to dole out an extra €11 for health club privileges, an absurdity given the room cost. ✉ *Via del Babuino 9, off Piazza del Popolo, near Piazza di Spagna, 00187* ☎ *06/328881* 🖷 *06/32888888* ⊕ *www.rfhotels.com* 🛏 *130 rooms, 27 suites* ⚬ *Restaurant, in-room safes, minibars, cable TV, in-room data ports, health club, hair salon, spa, bar, meeting rooms* ▭ *AE, DC, MC, V* |○| *EP.*

$$$$ 🖼 **Inn at the Spanish Steps.** The name of this small, exclusive hotel tells it all. Staying here is like having your own little place on fabled Via Condotti, the elegant shopping street crowned by the Spanish Steps. The hotel occupies the upper floors of a centuries-old palazzo it shares with Caffè Greco. Rooms, all junior suites, are handsomely decorated with damask fabrics and antiques. ✉ *Via Condotti 85, near Piazza di Spagna, 00187* ☎ *06/69925657* 🖷 *06/6786470* ⊕ *www.atspanishsteps.com* 🛏 *22 suites* ⚬ *In-room safes, minibars, cable TV, airport shuttle, no-smoking rooms* ▭ *AE, DC, MC, V* |○| *BP.*

★ $$–$$$$ 🖼 **Locarno.** Art aficionados and people in the cinema have long appreciated this hotel's preserved fin de siècle charm, intimate feel, and central location off Piazza del Popolo. Wallpaper and fabric prints are coordinated in the rooms, and some rooms have antiques. Everything is lovingly supervised by the owners, a mother-daughter duo. The buffet breakfast is ample, there's bar service on the panoramic roof garden, and complimentary bicycles are available if you feel like braving the traffic. ✉ *Via della Penna 22, near Piazza di Spagna, 00186* ☎ *06/3610841* 🖷 *06/3215249* ⊕ *www.hotellocarno.com* 🛏 *64 rooms, 2 suites* ⚬ *Restaurant, in-room safes, minibars, cable TV, in-room data ports, bar, laundry service, no-smoking rooms* ▭ *AE, DC, MC, V* |○| *BP.*

$$$ 🖼 **Carriage.** The Carriage's location is its main appeal: it's two blocks from the Spanish Steps, in the heart of Rome. The decor of subdued baroque accents, richly colored wallpaper, and antique reproductions lends a touch of old-world charm. Some furniture has seen better days, and rooms can be pint-size, but several have small terraces. A roof garden adds to the appeal. ✉ *Via delle Carrozze 36, near Piazza di Spagna, 00187* ☎ *06/6990124* 🖷 *06/6788279* ⊕ *www.hotelcarriage.net* 🛏 *24 rooms, 3 suites* ▭ *AE, DC, MC, V* |○| *BP.*

$–$$ 🖼 **Margutta.** Looking for a decent value and friendly owner-managers? The Margutta's your place. The lobby and halls in this small hotel are unassuming, but rooms are a pleasant surprise, with tall windows, attractive wrought-iron bedsteads, and modern baths. Three rooms have private terraces. Though it's in an old building, there's an elevator. The location is on a quiet side street between the Spanish Steps and Piazza del Popolo. ✉ *Via Laurina 34, near Piazza di Spagna, 00187* ☎ *06/3223674* 🖷 *06/3200395* ⊕ *www.hotelmargutta.it* 🛏 *24 rooms* ⚬ *Cable TV, in-room data ports* ▭ *AE, DC, MC, V* |○| *BP.*

$ 🖼 **Panda.** Via della Croce is one of Piazza di Spagna's chic shopping streets, so it's refreshing to find a budget option (with an old pensione feel) in this decidedly nonbudget neighborhood. Guest rooms are outfitted in terra-cotta and wrought iron; they're smallish, but spotless and quiet, thanks to double-glaze windows. You can pay even less by sharing a bath—in low season, you may have it to yourself anyway. ⊠ *Via della Croce 35, Piazza di Spagna, 00187* ☎ *06/6780179* 🖷 *06/69942151* ⊕ *www.hotelpanda.it* ⤱ *20 rooms, 14 with bath* ⌂ *No a/c in some rooms, no room TVs* ▭ *MC, V* ⦿⦿ *BP.*

Trastevere

$$–$$$ 🏨 **Hotel Santa Maria.** All the ground-floor rooms at this lovely former convent surround a pebbled courtyard shaded by orange trees. Room furniture leans towards the standard American hotel style, with two double beds, but there are terra-cotta tile floors and a tub with shower in the bathrooms. In fair weather, breakfast or a drink in the courtyard is a real treat, with a backdrop of old Trastevere that seems more opera set than reality. ⊠ *Vicolo del Piede 2, behind Piazza Santa Maria, Trastevere, 00153* ☎ *06/5894626* 🖷 *06/5894815* ⊕ *www.htlsantamaria. com* ⤱ *18 rooms, 2 suites* ⌂ *In-room safes, minibars, cable TV, bar* ▭ *AE, DC, MC, V* ⦿⦿ *BP.*

$$ 🏨 **Grand Hotel Gianicolo.** Atop Janiculum Hill, one of the famed seven

Fodor'sChoice   hills of Rome, the Grand Hotel feels removed from the urban chaos.

★   It's a bargain, with many of the trappings standard at higher prices: beautifully manicured gardens, a pool, a rooftop terrace, conference rooms, and a clubby bar. Comfortable guest rooms have patterned wallpaper and draperies. The viewing point on the drive up has breathtaking, encompassing views of the Eternal City. ⊠ *Via delle Mura Gianicolensi 107, Trastevere, 00152* ☎ *06/58333405* 🖷 *06/58179434* ⊕ *www. grandhotelgianicolo.it* ⌂ *Café, in-room safes, some in-room hot tubs, minibars, cable TV, in-room data ports, pool, bar, babysitting, laundry service, concierge, meeting rooms, free parking, some pets allowed, no-smoking rooms* ▭ *AE, DC, MC, V* ⦿⦿ *BP.*

$ 🏨 **Hotel Trastevere House.** Close to the pizzerias and bars of Viale Trastevere, yet off the beaten path in an 18th-century house tucked onto a tiny street, this bed-and-breakfast is a find. The cozy rooms are done in traditional dark wood and deep-blue fabric, with wood-beam ceilings and terra-cotta floors. The owners have another hotel, Domus Tiberina, around the corner, complete with a suite with balcony. ⊠ *Vicolo del Buco 7, Trastevere, 00153* ☎☎ *06/5883774* ⊕ *www.trasterevehouse.it* ⤱ *10 rooms, 7 with bath* ⌂ *Cable TV; no a/c* ▭ *MC, V* ⦿⦿ *BP.*

Piazza Navona

$$$$ 🏨 **Raphaël.** Old-world European luxury is alive and well behind the vine-covered facade of Raphaël. An array of sculpture, hand-carved wood antiques, and original Picasso ceramics grace the lobby. Rooms—a few with minuscule proportions—are individually decorated, some with tapestries and columns. Bathrooms are finished with travertine marble or hand-painted tiles. A Richard Meier–designed wing adds a modern touch to this classic space. Arrange to have your meal on the bi-level Bramante Terrace for great city views. ⊠ *Largo Febo 2, near Piazza Navona, 00186* ☎ *06/682831* 🖷 *06/6878993* ⊕ *www. raphaelhotel.com* ⤱ *51 rooms, 7 suites, 10 apartments* ⌂ *Restaurant,* *cable TV, gym, sauna, bar, laundry service, parking (fee), in-room data ports* ▤ *AE, DC, MC, V* ⦿ *EP.*

$$ ⊞ **Abruzzi.** Look out from the windows of this little hostelry and the Pantheon is literally in your face. Though location is the main selling point, basic rooms are modern, and all have bathrooms with a shower or tub. The rooftop terrace has a great view over the remarkable dome and the piazza it dominates. ⊠ *Piazza della Rotonda 69, near Pantheon, 00186* ☎ *06/6792021* 🖷 *06/69788076* ⊕ *www.hotelabruzzi.it* ⇆ *26 rooms* ⟡ *In-room safes, minibars, cable TV* ▤ *AE, MC, V* ⦿ *BP.*

★ **$$** ⊞ **Cesàri.** The exterior of this 1787 hotel looks much as it did when Stendhal stayed here in the 1800s. Old prints of Rome embellish the cream-color guest room walls; soft-green drapes and bedspreads create comfort and serenity. Bathrooms are done in smart two-tone blue marble. Overall, Cesàri exudes a quiet elegance in a very central location on a traffic-free street. ⊠ *Via di Pietra 89a, near Pantheon, 00186* ☎ *06/6749701* 🖷 *06/67497030* ⊕ *www.albergocesari.it* ⇆ *47 rooms* ⟡ *Some in-room safes, some minibars, cable TV, bar, laundry service, parking (fee), some pets allowed, no-smoking floor* ▤ *AE, DC, MC, V* ⦿ *BP.*

★ **$$** ⊞ **Santa Chiara.** Three ancient buildings form a gracious hotel that has been in the same family for 200 years. The personal attention shows in meticulously decorated and maintained lounges and rooms. Each room has built-in oak headboards, a marble-top desk, and an elegant travertine bath. Double-glaze windows look out over the Piazza della Minerva. There are three apartments, for two to five people, with full kitchens. ⊠ *Via Santa Chiara 21, near Pantheon, 00186* ☎ *06/6872979* 🖷 *06/6873144* ⊕ *www.albergosantachiara.com* ⇆ *100 rooms, 4 suites, 3 apartments* ⟡ *Some kitchens, cable TV, bar* ▤ *AE, DC, MC, V* ⦿ *BP.*

$–$$ ⊞ **Coronet.** This small hotel occupies part of a floor in one wing of the vast Palazzo Doria Pamphilj; seven interior rooms overlook the family's lovely private garden court. Don't expect palatial ambience, but elaborate moldings in the carpeted halls and wood-beam ceilings in several rooms do lend a sense of age. The good-size rooms have oldish baths, some very small. Several rooms can accommodate three or four beds. ⊠ *Piazza Grazioli 5, near Piazza Venezia, 00186* ☎ *06/6792341* 🖷 *06/69922705* ⊕ *www.hotelcoronet.com* ⇆ *13 rooms, 10 with bath* ▤ *AE, MC, V* ⦿ *BP.*

¢ ⊞ **Fraterna Domus.** On a byway near Piazza Navona sits a guesthouse run by nuns, though you might not realize it because they don't wear religious habits. Rooms are spare, with single beds, but they have small private bathrooms. Three hearty meals a day are served in the dining room (dinner €12), and the curfew is 11 PM. ⊠ *Vicolo del Leonetto 16, Piazza Navona, 00186* ☎ *06/68802727* 🖷 *06/6832691* ✍ *domusrm@tin.it* ⇆ *20 rooms* ⟡ *Dining room; no a/c in some rooms, no room TVs* ▤ *DC, MC, V* ⦿ *BP.*

San Pietro

$$$–$$$$ ⊞ **Giulio Cesare.** An aristocratic town house with a garden in the residential but central Prati district, the Giulio Cesare is a 10-minute walk across the Tiber from Piazza del Popolo. It's beautifully run, with a friendly staff and a quiet luxury. The rooms are elegant, with chandeliers, thick rugs, floor-length drapes, and rich damasks in soft colors. Public rooms have Oriental carpets, old prints and paintings, marble fireplaces, and a grand piano. The buffet breakfast is a veritable banquet. ⊠ *Via degli Scipioni 287, near San Pietro, 00192* ☎ *06/3210751* 🖷 *06/3211736* 🖙 *90 rooms* ᗗ *Dining room, in-room safes, minibars, cable TV, in-room data ports* ☰ *AE, DC, MC, V* ❍❘ *BP.*

$$–$$$$ 🏨 **Atlante Star.** The lush rooftop-terrace garden café and the restaurant of this hotel have a knockout view of the basilica and the rest of Rome. The rooms in the distinguished 19th-century building are attractive, in striped silks and prints; many bathrooms have hot tubs. The friendly family management is attentive to your needs and takes pride in selling extra-virgin olive oil produced from their own trees in the country. A sister hotel around the corner, Atlante Garden, has larger rooms at slightly lower rates. ⊠ *Via Vitelleschi 34, near San Pietro, 00193* ☎ *06/6873233* 🖷 *06/6872300* ⊕ *www.atlantehotels.com* 🖙 *65 rooms, 10 suites* ᗗ *Restaurant, in-room safes, some in-room hot tubs, minibars, cable TV, bar, laundry service, concierge, parking (fee), no-smoking rooms* ☰ *AE, DC, MC, V* ❍❘ *BP.*

★ $$$ 🏨 **Hotel Farnese.** The intimate Farnese began life as a late-19th-century mansion. Today it's furnished with great attention to detail in belle epoque style: marble-top tables and curvaceous-wood or scrolled-iron headboards, for example. Fresco embellishments are lively; and the modern baths sparkle. A roof garden has tall hedges and umbrella-shaded tables for two. The hotel is not far from the metro. ⊠ *Via Alessandro Farnese 30, near San Pietro, 00192* ☎ *06/3212553* 🖷 *06/3215129* ⊕ *www.hotelfarnese.com* 🖙 *23 rooms, 2 suites* ᗗ *Minibars, cable TV, bar, laundry service, concierge, free parking* ☰ *AE, DC, MC, V* ❍❘ *EP.*

$$–$$$ 🏨 **Residenza Paolo VI.** The Paolo Sesto (Italian for Paul VI) is within the Vatican walls. Rooms in this former monastery are simple, with wood furniture, marble floors, and Persian rugs. The roof terrace, however, has a spectacular view of St. Peter's. Breakfast is an American-style buffet. ⊠ *Via Paolo VI 29, near San Pietro, 00193* ☎ *06/68134108* 🖷 *06/6867428* ⊕ *www.residenzapaolovi.com* 🖙 *29 rooms* ᗗ *In-room safes, minibars, cable TV, bar, laundry service, parking (fee), no-smoking rooms* ☰ *AE, D, MC, V* ❍❘ *BP.*

$$ 🏨 **Sant'Anna.** In the quiet Borgo neighborhood surrounding St. Peter's, this small hotel has done much with its limited size. The spacious attic rooms have their own tiny terraces, and some of the large bedrooms have coffered ceilings. Design accents are in navy, gold, and rose. Frescoes enliven the breakfast room, and the fountain in the courtyard is typically Roman. ⊠ *Borgo Pio 134, near San Pietro, 00193* ☎ *06/68801602* 🖷 *06/68308717* ⊕ *www.hotelsantanna.com* 🖙 *20 rooms* ᗗ *Minibars, cable TV, parking (fee)* ☰ *AE, DC, MC, V* ❍❘ *BP.*

¢ 🏨 **San Giuseppe della Montagna.** This convent is right outside the Vatican walls, near the entrance to the Vatican Museums. It's run by Catalan nuns, so unless you speak Italian or Spanish, you may have to work at communicating with the staff. The rooms are immaculate (no pun intended), though spare; some have three beds. Unusual for a convent is that there's no curfew; you are given keys. ⊠ *Viale Vaticano 87, near*

San Pietro, 00165 ☎ *06/39723807* 🖨 *06/39721048* 🛏 *15 rooms* ⚘ *No a/c, no room TVs* ▭ *No credit cards* ⍤ *BP.*

Termini & Via Nazionale

★ **$$$$** 🏨 **Exedra.** The opening of the luxurious, stately Exedra in December 2002 transformed a dilapidated piazza into a vibrant meeting place. Construction also unearthed additional baths of Diocletian, on view under glass outside the conference rooms on the lower floor. A red carpet leads to the arched entry; inside an attentive staff waits to attend your every need. Chandeliers hang from high ceilings that are detailed with stepped moldings or timbers, and king-size beds rest atop deep, soft carpets in neoclassical rooms. Marble adorns all bathrooms. A rooftop terrace contains the pool and a bar, and there's a world-class spa on-site. ⊠ *Piazza della Repubblica 47, near Via Nazionale, 00185* ☎ *06/489381* 🖨 *06/ 48938000* ⊕ *www.boscolohotels.com* 🛏 *262 rooms, 6 suites* ⚘ *3 restaurants, in-room safes, minibars, cable TV, pool, health club, spa, 2 bars, babysitting, dry cleaning, laundry service, concierge, meeting rooms, parking (fee), no-smoking rooms, Web TV, in-room data ports, Internet room* ▭ *AE, DC, MC, V* ⍤ *BP.*

$$$–$$$$ 🏨 **Mediterraneo.** Constructed in 1935—and operated as a hotel since 1940—the Mediterraneo is a service-oriented charmer. Though it lacks the slick modernities of a newly renovated hotel, it has clubby 1940s character. The lobby has a fireplace, and the breakfast room is done in green tile. Either parquet floors with Persian rugs or deep wall-to-wall carpeting lies underfoot in guest rooms, and velvet easy chairs wait for you to sink in. Double-glaze windows keep things surprisingly quiet. The rooftop terrace bar is open May–September. ⊠ *Via Cavour 15, near Termini, 00184* ☎ *06/4884051 or 800/2239832* 🖨 *06/4744105* ⊕ *www. romehotelmediterraneo.it* ⚘ *Restaurant, room service, in-room safes, minibars, cable TV, bar, laundry service, meeting rooms* ▭ *AE, DC, MC, V* ⍤ *BP.*

$$$ 🏨 **Britannia.** Owner Pier Paolo Biorgi has created a very special small
Fodor's Choice hotel. His influence is evident: the caring staff provides English-language
★ newspapers daily, and local weather reports are delivered to your room each morning. Planted palms and fluted columns adorn frescoed halls. Each guest room has a unique layout and is furnished with lush fabrics and original artwork. A heat lamp warms marble bathrooms. On the top floor, a light-filled suite opens onto a private terrace. ⊠ *Via Napoli 64, near Via Nazionale, 00184* ☎ *06/4883153* 🖨 *06/4882343* ⊕ *www.hotelbritannia.it* 🛏 *32 rooms, 1 suite* ⚘ *In-room safes, minibars, cable TV, babysitting, laundry service, free parking* ▭ *AE, DC, MC, V* ⍤ *BP.*

$$ 🏨 **Hotel Venezia.** Here's an old-fashioned, side-street hotel that's charming and, well, *pretty,* with 16th-century wood tables and sideboards set off by cozy matching armchairs and tapestries. Guest rooms are somewhat simpler but still a cut above many of the other hotels near the Termini station. There's even a "pillow menu" from which you can order the type of bed pillow you want. ⊠ *Via Varese 18, near Termini, 00185* ☎ *06/4457101* 🖨 *06/4957687* ⊕ *www.hotelvenezia.com* 🛏 *60 rooms* ⚘ *In-room safes, minibars, cable TV; no a/c in some rooms* ▭ *AE, D, MC, V* ⍤ *BP.*

$$ 🏨 **Morgana.** Apart from the fact it's near the central train station, nothing about this refurbished hotel screams Roman. Still, plaid wallcoverings, upholstered sofas, and soft chairs in the lobby reading room and the TV lounge are welcoming. The cozy public spaces belie the guestroom decor, which could be mistaken for that of a boutique hotel—slick and modern, in gray, black, and burgundy. Everything about the place (including the elevator) is compact, except for the breakfast room, where there's a big, full buffet. ⊠ *Via Filippo Turati 33, near Termini, 00185* ☎ *06/4467230* 🖷 *06/4469142* ⊕ *www.hotelmorgana.com* ↪ *103 rooms, 2 suites* ⚷ *In-room safes, minibars, cable TV, bar, laundry service, concierge, no-smoking rooms* ▭ *AE, DC, MC, V* �🍽 *BP.*

$-$$ 🏨 **Des Artistes.** The three personable Riccioni brothers have transformed their hotel into one of the best for its price range in the Termini train station neighborhood. They've lavished rooms with paintings, mahogany furnishings, and marble baths. The breakfast room doubles as a TV lounge with Internet access. One floor has 10 dorm-style rooms (six to eight beds per room, €20 per bed). ⊠ *Via Villafranca 20, near Termini, 00185* ☎ *06/4454365* 🖷 *06/4462368* ⊕ *www.hoteldesartistes. com* ↪ *40 rooms, 27 with bath* ⚷ *In-room safes, minibars, cable TV, in-room data ports, bar, concierge, parking (fee); no a/c in some rooms, no smoking* ▭ *AE, DC, MC, V* �🍽 *BP.*

$-$$ 🏨 **Montreal.** On a central avenue, three blocks from Stazione Termini, the compact Montreal occupies three floors of an older building. It's been totally renovated and has fresh-looking, though small, rooms. The owner-managers are pleasant and helpful, and the neighborhood has plenty of reasonably priced restaurants. ⊠ *Via Carlo Alberto 4, across from Santa Maria Maggiore, near Termini, 00185* ☎ *06/4457797* 🖷 *06/ 4465522* ⊕ *www.hotelmontrealroma.com* ↪ *27 rooms* ⚷ *In-room safes, minibars, cable TV, parking (fee)* ▭ *AE, DC, MC, V* �🍽 *BP.*

$ 🏨 **Adler.** This tiny pensione run by the same family for more than three decades provides a comfortable stay on a quiet street near the station for a very good price. Ideal for families, the Adler has six spacious rooms that sleep three, four, or five, as well as a single and a double. Rooms are basic but impeccably clean (owner Serena Biancalana sees to that). Worn but cozy chairs line the lobby, and in summer, breakfast can be taken on the leafy courtyard balcony. ⊠ *Via Modena 5, near Termini, 00184* ☎ *06/484466* 🖷 *06/4880940* ↪ *8 rooms* ⚷ *Cable TV, bar* ▭ *AE, DC, MC, V* ⌸ *BP.*

$ 🏨 **Tempio di Pallade.** This small hotel near Porta Maggiore is a good deal. Rooms are simple but elegant, done in blue and gold. The owners, Ranieri siblings, will be happy to make arrangements for you, from airport taxis to tours of the city to opera tickets. Triples and quads are available on request, as are group meals. ⊠ *Via Giolitti 425–427, near Termini, 00185* ☎ *06/70451521* 🖷 *06/70452758* ⊕ *www. hoteltempiodipallade.com* ↪ *50 rooms* ⚷ *In-room safes, minibars, cable TV, concierge* ▭ *AE, DC, MC, V* ⌸ *BP.*

★ ¢-$ 🏨 **The Beehive.** Linda Martinez-Brenner and Steve Brenner are the friendly American couple who run this funky B&B—as well as apartment rentals. Bright, clean rooms have ultramodern furniture and colorful artwork. One hostel-style room with eight bunk beds costs a mere

€20 per person. Downstairs, a café-lounge that serves drinks, light meals, and snacks. There's free Internet access and concierge service; have them book you a dinner reservation while you sit in the lobby's Phillipe Starck chairs and wonder how something so good can cost so little. ⊠ *Via Marghera 8, near Termini, 00185* ☎ *06/44704553* ⊕ *www.the-beehive. com* ⬐ *9 rooms without bath, 10 apartments* ♻ *Café, fans, concierge, Internet; no a/c, no room TVs, no smoking* ⊟ *No credit cards* ⍟| *EP.*

Via Veneto

★ **$$$$** ⊡ **Aleph.** Adam Tihany's upscale, boutique hotel design plays with the themes of heaven and hell: in the Paradiso spa, in the Angel lobby bar, in the flaming red Maremeto seafood restaurant. Guest rooms are done in a whimsical, modern Venetian style, with Murano-glass light fixtures, cream-and-deep-blue color schemes, and black-and-white accents—including full-wall photo blowups. ⊠ *Via San Basilio 15, near Via Veneto, 00187* ☎ *06/422901* ♻ *06/42290000* ⊕ *www.boscolohotels.com* ⬐ *94 rooms, 2 suites* ♻ *Restaurant, in-room safes, minibars, cable TV, gym, spa, 2 bars, laundry service, concierge, no-smoking rooms, in-room data ports* ⊟ *AE, DC, MC, V* ⍟| *EP.*

★ **$$$$** ⊡ **Eden.** This superlative hotel combines dashing elegance and stunning vistas of Rome with the warmth of Italian hospitality. The Eden was once a preferred haunt of Hemingway, Ingrid Bergman, and Federico Fellini. Antiques, sumptuous Italian fabrics, linen sheets, and marble baths are the essence of good taste. Views from the rooftop bar and terrace can take your breath away (as can the bill). The hotel's top-floor restaurant, La Terrazza dell'Eden, is one of the city's best. ⊠ *Via Ludovisi 49, near Via Veneto, 00187* ☎ *06/478121* ♻ *06/4821584* ⊕ *www. hotel-eden.it* ⬐ *112 rooms, 14 suites* ♻ *Restaurant, in-room safes, minibars, cable TV, gym, bar, laundry service, concierge, parking (fee), no-smoking rooms* ⊟ *AE, DC, MC, V* ⍟| *EP.*

$$$$ ⊡ **Rose Garden Palace.** The elegant Rose Garden Palace is a marriage of the classic (marble floors, velvet sofas, patterned curtains) and the contemporary (clean lines, modern wood). Guest rooms are done in calming tones of beige, slate blue, and terra-cotta. A state-of-the-art fitness room, pool, and sauna and steam room below ground are small but ideal. Friday nights, jazz musicians play in the bar, and in warm weather the bar opens into the rose garden. The hotel is behind the American Embassy. ⊠ *Via Boncompagni 19, near Via Veneto, 00187* ☎ *06/ 421741* ♻ *06/4815608* ⊕ *www.rosegardenpalace.com* ⬐ *59 rooms, 6 suites* ♻ *Restaurant, in-room safes, minibars, cable TV, indoor pool, gym, spa, bar, meeting rooms, parking (fee), no-smoking rooms* ⊟ *AE, DC, MC, V* ⍟| *BP.*

$$$$ ⊡ **Westin Excelsior.** Next door to the American Embassy, the Excelsior is the hotel of choice for visiting diplomats, American business conferences, and celebrities. It's of the breed that put the *luxe* in deluxe: every corner is lavished with mirrors, moldings, Oriental rugs, crystal chandeliers, and huge, baroque floral arrangements. Guest rooms have elegant drapery, marble baths, top-quality linens, and big, firm beds. ⊠ *Via Veneto 125, 00187* ☎ *06/47081* ♻ *06/4826205* ⊕ *www.westin.com* ⬐ *286 rooms, 35 suites* ♻ *Restaurant, in-room safes, minibars, cable*

TV, indoor pool, gym, bar, laundry service, concierge, no-smoking rooms ⊟ AE, DC, MC, V ⊚ EP.

$$ ⊞ **La Residenza.** Mainly Americans frequent this cozy hotel in a converted town house near Via Veneto. Rooms are basic and comfortable (although singles are windowless). The real charm is at the bar, on the terrace, and in the lounges (smoking and no-smoking), which have warm-colored wallpaper and love seats, a big-screen TV, a piano, and card tables. Rates include a generous American-style buffet breakfast and an in-house movie every night. ⊠ Via Emilia 22, near Via Veneto, 00187 ☎ 06/4880789 ⊟ 06/485721 ⊕ www.thegiannettihotelsgroup.com ⊅ 29 rooms ⚭ In-room safes, minibars, cable TV, bar, laundry service, parking (fee) ⊟ AE, MC, V ⊚ BP.

Beyond the City Center

$$$$ ⊞ **Cavalieri Hilton.** Though the Cavalieri is outside the city center, distance has its advantages, including the magnificent view from the hotel's hilltop position (ask for a room facing the city). This hotel is an island of quiet good taste with a distinctive Italian flair. If you can tear yourself away from the gardens and pools, a courtesy shuttle bus to downtown Rome leaves every hour. Don't miss the acclaimed rooftop restaurant, La Pergola. ⊠ Via Cadlolo 101, Monte Mario, 00136 ☎ 06/35091 ⊟ 06/35092241 ⊕ www.cavalieri-hilton.com ⊅ 357 rooms, 17 suites ⚭ 2 restaurants, cable TV, tennis court, 2 pools (1 indoor), health club, hair salon, spa, bar ⊟ AE, DC, MC, V ⊚ EP.

★ **$$$–$$$$** ⊞ **Castello della Castelluccia.** Removed from the hustle and bustle of Rome's city center, this beautifully renovated 12th-century castle is surrounded by a small wooded park. The original structure has been preserved, complete with watchtower (now a three-level suite); all that's missing is a medieval knight clinking down the echoing stone halls. Guest rooms are luxuriously appointed, with inlaid-wood antiques and four-poster beds; a few have marble fireplaces, and two have giant, tiled hot-tub alcoves. There's shuttle-bus service to central Rome. ⊠ Via Carlo Cavina, Località La Castelluccia, 00123, 16 km (10 mi) north of center ☎ 06/30207041 ⊟ 06/30207110 ⊕ www.lacastelluccia.com ⊅ 18 rooms, 6 suites ⚭ Restaurant, room service, some in-room hot tubs, minibars, cable TV, in-room data ports, pool, spa, horseback riding, bar, laundry service, meeting room, free parking, some pets allowed ⊟ AE, D, MC, V ⊚ BP.

NIGHTLIFE & THE ARTS

The Arts

Rome lacks the level of culture in some of Italy's other cities, but it is the capital, so performances from the worlds of music, dance, theater, and film are to be found. Consult one of the local publications for listings: in the back of the weekly *roma c'è* magazine (published Wednesday) there are comprehensive listings in English, along with handy bus and metro information. The monthly *Time Out Roma* gives event schedules, as well as editors' picks, that are mainly in Italian (with a small summary in English) but are easy to decipher. The monthly *Where* mag-

Entertainment Alfresco

11

Roman nightlife moves outdoors in summertime, and that goes not only for pubs and discos but for higher culture as well. Open-air opera in particular is a venerable Italian tradition; competing companies commandeer church courtyards, ancient villas, and soccer stadiums for performances that range from student-run mom-and-poperas to full-scale extravaganzas. The same goes for dance and for concerts covering the spectrum of pop, classical, and jazz. Look for performances at the Baths of Caracalla, site of the famous televised "Three Tenors" concert; regardless of the production quality, it's a breathtaking setting. In general, though, you can count on performances being quite good, even if small productions often resort to school-play scenery and folding chairs to cut costs. Tickets run about €15–€40. The more-sophisticated productions may be listed in newspapers and magazines such as *roma c'è* and *Wanted in Rome*, but your best sources for information are old-fashioned posters plastered all over the city, advertising classics such as *Tosca* and *La Traviata*.

azine is distributed free at hotels and restaurants. An English-language biweekly, *Wanted in Rome* (www.wantedinrome.com), is sold at central newsstands and has good listings of events and museum exhibitions. *Trovaroma* is the weekly entertainment guide published in Italian every Thursday as a supplement to the daily newspaper *La Repubblica*.

Concerts

Christmastime is an especially busy classical concert season in Rome. Many small classical concert groups perform in cultural centers and churches year-round; all performances in Catholic churches are religious music and are free. Look for posters outside the churches. Pop, jazz, and world music concerts are frequent, especially in summer, although they may not be well advertised. Many of the bigger-name acts perform outside the center, so it's worth asking about transportation *before* you buy your tickets (about €8–€30).

CLASSICAL   A year-round classical concert series is organized by the **Accademia di Santa Cecilia** (Concert hall and box office ✉ Via della Conciliazione 4, near San Pietro ☎ 06/684391). The **Accademia Filarmonica Romana** (✉ Via Flaminia 118, near Stadio Olimpico ☎ 06/3201752, 06/3265991 tickets) has concerts at the Teatro Olimpico. **Istituzione Universitaria dei Concerti** (✉ Aula Magna, Piazzale Aldo Moro 5, near San Lorenzo ☎ 06/3610051 ⊕ www.concertiiuc.it) presents small concerts with music ranging from swing to Bach. The internationally respected **Oratorio del Gonfalone series** (✉ Via del Gonfalone 32/a, Campo de' Fiori ☎ 06/6875952) focuses on baroque music. **Il Tempietto** (☎ 06/87131590 ⊕ www.tempietto.it) organizes classical music concerts indoors in winter and in the atmospheric settings of Teatro di Marcello and Villa Torlonia in summer.

The church of **Sant'Ignazio** (⊠ Piazza Sant'Ignazio, near Pantheon ☎ 06/6794560) often hosts classical concerts in its spectacularly frescoed setting.

ROCK, POP & JAZZ

Tickets for major music events are usually handled by **Orbis** (⊠ Piazza Esquilino 37, near Santa Maria Maggiore ☎ 06/4744776). **Box Office** (⊠ Viale Giulio Cesare 88, near San Pietro ☎ 06/37500375 ⊕ www. ticket.it/boxoffice.htm) sells rock, pop, and jazz concert tickets from Monday to Saturday. **Hello Ticket** (⊠ At Termini train station ☎ 06/47825710 ⊕ www.helloticket.it) sells tickets to concerts as well as theater and other cultural events. **Messaggerie Musicale** (⊠ Via del Corso 473, Piazza di Spagna ☎ 06/684401) is a huge, centrally located store that sells music, DVDs, books, and international magazines as well as concert tickets.

Dance

Modern dance and classical ballet companies from Russia, the United States, and Europe sporadically visit Rome; performances are at the Teatro dell'Opera, Teatro Olimpico, or one of the open-air venues in summer. Small dance companies from Italy and abroad perform in numerous venues.

The **Rome Opera Ballet** (☎ 06/48160255 tickets ⊕ www.opera.roma.it) performs at the Teatro dell'Opera, often with international guest stars.

Film

Movie tickets range in price from €4.50 for matinees and some weeknights up to €10 for reserved seats on weekend evenings. Check listings in *roma c'è* or *Trovaroma* (www.trovacinema.it). The **Metropolitan** (⊠ Via del Corso 7, off Piazza del Popolo, near Piazza di Spagna ☎ 06/32600500) has four screens, one dedicated to English-language films September–June. The five-screen **Warner Village Moderno** (⊠ Piazza della Repubblica 45–46, near Via Nazionale ☎ 06/47779202), close to the train station, usually has one theater with an English-language film.

Opera

The season for the **Opera Theater of Rome** (☎ 06/4817515 ⊕ www. opera.roma.it) runs from November or December to May. Main performances are staged at the Teatro dell'Opera in cooler weather and at outdoor locations, such as Piazza del Popolo in summer.

A GOOD WALK: TRASTEVERE BY NIGHT

For centuries home to Rome's artists and beggars, Trastevere has parlayed its bohemian appeal into a new life, as the place where Romans—and many visitors—step out at night. After dark, you'll have your choice of restaurants, bars, street performances, and the best people-watching in town. The neighborhood is a mix of the sacred and profane; follow this route in early evening for gelato, dinner, and a stroll—or stick around at night for a pub crawl with a cultural chaser. It covers about three-quarters of a mile.

From Piazza Sonnino, enter Trastevere by walking past the pharmacy on your right down Via Lungaretta. This street is Trastevere's main artery, jammed after dark with restaurants, bars, jewelry shops, street vendors, and revelers partying until the early hours. Continue on Via Lungaretta until it ends in **Piazza Santa Maria in Trastevere** ㉒. Bordered by two cafés and the swanky Sabatini restaurant (at No. 13), the piazza has a fountain in the center ringed by steps on which passersby join neo-hippies, grimy punks, and fresh-faced tourists for a front-row seat. On summer nights and weekends, jug-

Theater

Theater performances are staged throughout the year in Italian, English, and several other languages, depending on who is sponsoring the performance.

For comic theater in English, check out the **Miracle Players** (☎ 06/70393427 ⊕ www.miracleplayers.org), a group of English-speaking actors who write and produce free public performances every summer in the Roman Forum, presenting a perfectly balanced mix of the historical and the hilarious.

Venues

★ Rome's state-of-the-art **Auditorium-Parco della Musica** (✉ Via de Coubertin 15, Flaminio ☎ 06/80241350 ⊕ www.musicaperroma.it), a 10-minute tram ride from Piazza del Popolo, has three halls with excellent acoustics and a large courtyard used for concerts and other events—everything from chamber music to jazz to big-name pop, even film screenings and art exhibits.

Teatro Argentina (✉ Largo Argentina 52, near Campo de' Fiori ☎ 06/68804601), built in 1732 by the architect Theoldi, has been the home of the Teatro Sabile theater company since 1994. The theater has been renovated several times over the centuries, most recently in 2001. It's a beautiful, ornate structure, with velvet seats and chandeliers. The layout is more vertical than horizontal, creating a surprising number of seats, some at vertiginous heights. Teatro Argentina plays host to many plays, classical music performances, operas, and dance performances.

Both the city's ballet and opera companies, as well as visiting international performers, appear at the **Teatro dell'Opera** (✉ Piazza Beniamino Gigli 8, near Termini ☎ 06/481601, 06/48160255 tickets ⊕ www.opera.roma.it).

Teatro Valle (✉ Via del Teatro Valle 23A, near Pantheon ☎ 06/68803794) hosts dramatic performances of the same caliber as its neighbor, Teatro Argentina, but often with a more-experimental bent, particularly in fall. Dance and classical music are also presented here.

glers, flame-eaters, and magicians take turns wowing the crowds here. Bar del Marzio, next to Sabatini, has excellent gelato you can take with you out to the square. While you're there, stop into the church of Santa Maria in Trastevere, often open well into the evening in summer, for a look at the magnificent golden-tiled apse mosaic. Even if the church is closed, take a look at the fragments of ancient Roman graffiti salvaged from the city and plastered into the walls of the outer entryway.

Facing the church, follow the street leaving the piazza from the far right corner. It curves around to the right past several open-air restaurants, opening into Piazza Sant'Egidio. This lovely square is home to Rome's English-language Cinema Pasquino, a favorite with foreign residents. Next door are the outdoor tables of Ombre Rosse, where you'll find light meals, coffee, cocktails, the *International Herald Tribune,* and live music long, long into the night. Across the piazza, the Museo di Roma in Trastevere, open until 8, hosts Roman and international photography shows.

The ancient **Terme di Caracalla** (⊠ Via delle Terme di Caracalla 52, Aventino ☎ No phone) has one of the most spectacular and enchanting outdoor stages in the world.

Teatro Olimpico (⊠ Piazza Gentile da Fabriano 17, Stadio Olimpico ☎ 06/3265991) hosts both concerts and dance performances.

Nightlife

Rome's nightlife is decidedly more happening for locals and insiders who know whose palms to grease and when to go where. The "flavor of the month" factor is at work here, and many places fade into oblivion after their 15 minutes of fame. Smoking has been banned in all public areas in Italy (that's right, it actually happened); Roman aversion to clean air has meant a decrease in crowds at bars and clubs. The best sources for an up-to-date list of nightspots are the *roma c'è* booklet and *Where* magazine. Trastevere and the area around Piazza Navona are both filled with bars, restaurants, and, after dark, people. In summer, discos and many bars close to beat the heat (although some simply relocate to the beach, where many Romans spend their summer nights). The city-sponsored Estate Romana (Rome Summer) festival takes over, lighting up hot city nights with open-air concerts, bars, and discos. Pick up the event guide at newsstands.

Bars

So where do you go for a cocktail? **Bar della Pace** (⊠ Via della Pace 5, near Piazza Navona ☎ 06/6861216) has been the chic people-watching cocktail bar of choice since time immemorial. **Acqua Negra** (⊠ Largo Teatro Valle 9, Piazza Navona ☎ 06/97606025) packs in the twenty- to fortysomething crowd for aperitif, dinner, and postdinner drinks in a sexy, minimalist space. A hangout for scruffy-chic Romans sipping cocktails is **Société Lutéce** (⊠ Piazza di Montevecchio 17, off Via dei Coronari, Piazza Navona ☎ 06/6832361). **Freni e Frizioni** (⊠ Via de Politeama 4-6, Trastevere ☎ 06/58334210), another hot spot by the same owners, spills out onto its Trastevere piazza and down the stairs, filling the area around Piazza Trilussa with an attractive crowd of local mojito-sippers.

Continue on Via della Scala (with your back to Ombre Rosse, the street leaving from the piazza's far right corner). This narrow, pedestrian-only street has more bars and restaurants, all with street-side seating. At the end of Via della Scala, you'll see the Porta Settimiana, one of the city's ancient gates. Turning right here, follow Via San Dorotea to No. 19, once the home of La Fornarina, Raphael's Trasteverina lover.

Continue on Via San Dorotea across Piazza San Giovanni Malva to Piazza Trilussa and have a look at the Ponte Sisto crossing the Tiber. The original bridge dates to the 2nd century BC, although most of what you see now dates from a 15th-century renovation (and a 1999 cleanup). Heading back through Piazza Trilussa, follow Vicolo del Cinque past more bars and restaurants. If it's after midnight, you can stop at No. 40, Daniela Orecchia, for *cornetti caldi*, hot, sweet pastries fresh out of the oven. Continue up Vicolo del Cinque, leading back to Piazza Sant'Egidio. Here you can have a nightcap and then retrace your steps across Piazza Santa Maria in Trastevere and down Via Lungaretta to Piazza Sonnino, where there's a taxi stand.

Salotto 42 (✉ Piazza di Pietra 42, near Pantheon ☎ 06/6785804) is open morning until late; the cozy-sleek room reflects its owners' Roman–New York–Swedish pedigrees as it moves from daylight bar with smorgasbord to cocktail lounge–design den, complete with art books and local sophisticates.

English- and Irish-style pubs have long been a prominent part of the bar scene in Rome, among Italians and foreigners alike. **Trinity College** (✉ Via del Collegio Romano 6, near Piazza Venezia ☎ 06/6786472) is one of the best of these drinking halls.

Following the modern-design-bar trend, **Fluid** (✉ Via Governo Vecchio 46/47, near Campo de' Fiori ☎ 06/6832361) serves drinks to cool patrons seated on glowing ice cube–like chairs, as water streams down the walls. (As Fluid has gotten older, its clientele have gotten younger.) **La Vineria** (✉ Campo de' Fiori 15 ☎ 06/68803268) is the original bar on a square that's now full of them. It remains the truest example of an old-school Roman enoteca, always in style and great for watching the "scenery." **Crudo** (✉ Via Degli Specchi 6, Campo de' Fiori ☎ 06/6838989 ⊕ www.crudoroma.it) is a spacious, modern, New York–style lounge serving cocktails and *crudo* (raw) nibbles such as sushi and carpaccio. **Sloppy Sam's** (✉ Campo de' Fiori 10 ☎ 06/68802637) is an American-run pub on one of the city's busiest piazzas. Look for happy-hour specials and student discounts. For that essential predinner aperitivo, head for the buzzing **Friends** (✉ Piazza Trilussa 34, Trastevere ☎ 06/5816111) across the Tiber from the historic center. Late in the evening, head to **Stardust** (✉ Vicolo de' Renzi 4, Trastevere ☎ 06/58320875) for cocktails mixed up by an international bar staff and an ambience provided by eclectic music and local characters.

Music Clubs

Jazz, folk, pop, and Latin-music clubs are flourishing in Rome, particularly in Trastevere and Testaccio. Jazz clubs are especially popular, and talented local groups may be joined by visiting musicians from other countries. As admission, many clubs require that you buy a membership card, often valid for a month, at a cost of €6 and up. On weekend nights it's a good idea to reserve a table in advance no matter where you're going.

Behind the Vatican Museums, **Alexanderplatz** (✉ Via Ostia 9, near San Pietro ☎ 06/39742171), Rome's most famous jazz and blues club, has a bar and a restaurant. Local and internationally known musicians play nightly. **La Palma** (✉ Via Giuseppe Mirri 35, Tiburtina ☎ 06/43599029) is the venue favored by experimental jazz musicians. It's near the Tiburtina metro stop. **Big Mama** (✉ Vicolo San Francesco a Ripa 18, Trastevere ☎ 06/5812551) presents live blues, R&B, African, jazz, and rock. Latin rhythms are the specialty at **No Stress Brasil** (✉ Via degli Stradivari 35, Trastevere ☎ 06/5813249), where there's a Brazilian orchestra from Tuesday to Saturday. Monday is karaoke night.

Il Locale (✉ Vicolo del Fico 3, near Piazza Navona ☎ 06/6879075), closed Monday, pulls in a lively crowd for Italian rock. **The Place** (✉ Via Al-berico II 27–29, near San Pietro ☎ 06/68307137) has a mixture of live funk, Latin, and jazz sounds, accompanied by tasty fusion cuisine. In trendy Testaccio, **Caffè Latino** (✉ Via Monte Testaccio 96 ☎06/57288556) is a vibrant Roman locale that has live music (mainly Latin) almost every night, followed by recorded soul, funk, and '70s and '80s revival; it's closed Monday.

Nightclubs

Most dance clubs open about 10:30 PM and charge an entrance fee of about €20, which may include the first drink (subsequent drinks cost about €10). Clubs are usually closed Monday, and all those listed here close in summer, some opening instead at the beaches of Ostia or Fregene. The liveliest areas for clubs with a younger clientele are the grittier working-class districts of Testaccio and Ostiense. Any of the clubs lining Via Galvani, leading up to Monte Testaccio, are fair game for a trendy, crowded dance-floor experience—names and ownership of clubs change frequently, but the overall scene has shown some staying power.

The large **Art Café** (✉ Via del Galoppatoio 33, near Piazza di Spagna ☎ 06/36006578) has multiple levels, and there are theme nights (Tuesday fashion night, Thursday live jazz and dinner, Friday hip-hop), and *privé* (private) areas with a wading pool. **Supperclub** (✉ Via dei Nari 14, near Piazza di Spagna ☎ 06/68807207) is not only a place for reclined dining, but also a trendy club where DJs and live entertainment draw a sexy crowd. Most rooms are lined with big white beds and fluffy pillows, complete with roaming masseurs. Monday night is a laid-back hip-hop party organized by a former L.A. club promoter.

La Maison (✉ Vicolo dei Granari 4, near Piazza Navona ☎06/6833312), bedecked in purple velvet and chandeliers, has two distinct spaces and one main dance floor, with DJs dishing up the latest dance tunes. **Bloom** (✉ Via del Teatro Pace 29, near Piazza Navona ☎ 06/68802029) is a lounge-club in the city center, where Romans and visiting celebrities go to swill cocktails and dance in tight quarters. **Cabala** (✉ Via dei Soldati 23c, Piazza Navona ☎ 06/68301192), a multilevel disco–piano bar inside a gorgeous palazzo, can be uncomfortably packed on weekends. One of Rome's first discos, **Piper** (✉ Via Tagliamento 9, near Piazza Fiume ☎ 06/8414459), is still a magnet for young movers and shakers who favor disco and house beats and spectacular light effects. It's open Saturday and Sunday nights only.

Alibi (✉ Via di Monte Testaccio 39 ☎ 06/5743448) is a multilevel complex that caters to a mixed gay and straight crowd. The **Ex Magazzini** (✉ Via dei Magazzini Generali 8bis, Ostiense ☎ 06/5758040) is a happening disco bar that has a mix of live and DJ sets and hosts a vintage market on Sunday. **Goa** (✉ Via Libetta 13, Testaccio ☎ 06/5748277) is among Rome's trendiest clubs. In a Southeast Asian–inspired space you can listen to hip-hop, tribal, and house music played by some of Europe's most touted DJs.

SPORTS & THE OUTDOORS

Biking

You can rent a bike at **Collalti** (⊠ Via del Pellegrino 82, Campo de' Fiori ☎ 06/68801084), which is also a reliable bike-repair shop; it's closed Monday. **St. Peter Moto** (⊠ Via di Porta Castello 43, near San Pietro ☎ 06/6875714) is a good place to rent scooters as well as bikes.

Running

The best bet for running in central Rome is the **Villa Borghese** park, with a ⅔-km (½-mi) circuit of the Pincio, among the marble statuary. A longer run in the park itself might include a loop around Piazza di Siena, a grass riding arena. Although most traffic is barred from Villa Borghese, government and police cars sometimes speed through. Be careful to stick to the sides of the roads. For a long run away from all traffic, try the hilly and majestic **Villa Ada** in northern Rome, in the up-scale Parioli neighborhood. **Villa Doria Pamphilj** on Janiculum Hill is a beautiful spot for a run south of the city. History-loving runners should do as the chariot horses did and run at the old **Circus Maximus**. A standard oval track (dubbed "il biscotto" as it's shaped like a cookie) is in the park flanked by the **Via delle Terme di Caracalla.**

Soccer

Italy's favorite spectator sport stirs passionate enthusiasm. Games are usually held on Sunday afternoons fall–spring and can be seen at many sports bars around the city: just follow the fans' screams.

The two city soccer teams, Roma and Lazio, are both in Series A (the top division); they play home games at the **Stadio Olimpico** (⊠ Viale dello Stadio Olimpico ☎ 06/3237333), part of the Foro Italico complex built by Mussolini on the banks of the Tiber. There's a chance of Lazio soccer tickets being on sale at the box office before game time, but it's a better idea to buy them in advance from **Lazio Point** (⊠ Via Farini 34, near Termini ☎ 06/4826688) to see the Lazio team play. Go to **Orbis** (⊠ Piazza Esquilino 37, near Santa Maria Maggiore ☎ 06/4744776) to buy tickets to see the Roma play.

SHOPPING

Updated by
Dana Klitzberg

They say when in Rome to do as the Romans do—and the Romans love to shop. Stores are generally open from 9 or 9:30 to 1 and from 3:30 or 4 to 7 or 7:30. There's a tendency for shops in central districts to stay open all day, and hours are becoming more flexible throughout the city. Many places close Sunday, though this is changing, too, especially in the city center. With the exception of food stores, many stores also close Monday morning from September to mid-June and Saturday afternoon from mid-June through August. Stores selling food are usually closed Thursday afternoon.

You can stretch your euros by taking advantage of the Tax-Free for Tourists V.A.T. tax refunds, available at most large stores for purchases over €155. Or hit Rome in January and early February or in late July, when stores clean house with the justly famous biannual sales. There are so many hole-in-the-wall boutiques selling top-quality merchandise in Rome's center that even just wandering you're sure to find something that catches your eye.

Shopping Districts

★ The city's most famous shopping district, **Piazza di Spagna,** is conveniently compact, fanning out at the foot of the Spanish Steps in a galaxy of boutiques selling gorgeous wares with glamorous labels. Here you can ricochet from Gucci to Prada to Valentino to Versace with less effort than it takes to pull out your credit card. If your budget is designed for lower altitudes, you also can find great clothes and accessories at less-extravagant prices. But here, buying is not necessarily the point—window displays can be works of art, and dreaming may be satisfaction enough. Via Condotti is the neighborhood's central axis, but there are shops on every street in the area bordered by Piazza di Spagna on the east, Via del Corso on the west, between Piazza San Silvestro and Via della Croce, and extending along Via del Babuino to Piazza del Popolo.

Shops along **Via Campo Marzio,** and adjoining Piazza San Lorenzo in Lucina, stock eclectic, high-quality clothes and accessories—without the big names and at slightly lower prices. Running from Piazza Venezia to Piazza del Popolo lies **Via del Corso,** a main shopping avenue that has more than a mile of clothing, shoes, leather goods, and home furnishings from classic to cutting-edge. Running west from Piazza Navona, **Via del Governo Vecchio** has numerous women's boutiques and secondhand-clothing stores. **Via Cola di Rienzo,** across the Tiber from Piazza del Popolo, is block after block of boutiques, shoe stores, and department stores, as well as street stalls and upscale food shops. **Via dei Coronari,** across the Tiber from Castel Sant'Angelo, has quirky antiques and home furnishings. Via Giulia and other surrounding streets are good bets for decorative arts. Should your gift list include religious souvenirs, look for everything from rosaries to Vatican golf balls at the shops between Piazza San Pietro and **Borgo Pio.** Liturgical vestments and statues of saints make for good window-shopping on **Via dei Cestari,** near the Pantheon. On **Via Cola di Rienzo,** near San Pietro, there are stands selling everything from CDs to handicrafts, as well as many mid-level chain stores. **Via Nazionale** is a good bet for affordable stores of the Benetton ilk, and for shoes, bags, and gloves. The **Termini** train station has become a good one-stop place for many shopping needs. Its 60-plus shops are open until 10 PM and include a Nike store, the Body Shop, Sephora, Mango (women's clothes), a UPIM department store, and a grocery store.

Bargains

The market at **Via Sannio** (✉ Near San Giovanni) has lots of designer shoes and stalls selling new and used clothing at bargain prices; hours are weekdays 8–2, Saturday 8–5. The **Borghetto Flaminio** (✉ Piazza della Marina, Flaminio) market sells good-quality vintage clothing Sunday 9–2. The morning market in **Piazza Testaccio,** in the heart of the neighborhood of the same name, is known for stands selling last season's designer shoes at a third of the original price or less.

Romans and visitors alike flock to the **McArthurGlen Designer Outlet** (⊠ Via Ponte di Piscina Cupa, Castel Romano ☎ 06/5050050 ⊕ www.mcarthurglen.it), 10 km (6 mi) east of the city. Housed in a mock ancient Roman setting, the complex has more than 90 stores that sell major labels at prices 30% to 70% less than retail, from inexpensive Italian chains to designers such as Versace, Etro, and D & G. To get there, get on the Grande Raccordo Anulare ring road, take Exit 26 onto the Via Pontina (SS148) toward Pomezia, exit at Castel Romano, and follow the signs. The mall is open daily 10–10.

Department Stores & Malls

Italian department stores have little in common with their American cousins; most of them are much smaller and do not carry the same variety of merchandise, nor the recognizable brands. **Galleria Alberto Sordi** (⊠ Via del Corso and Viale Tritone, near Piazza di Spagna) is a mall with a café in the center of two corridors lined with shops. The star attractions are a large branch of Feltrinelli (a book and media store like Barnes & Noble), JAM (clothing and accessories, gifts and gadgets), and the women's affordable fashion mecca from Spain, Zara. **Rinascente** (⊠ Via del Corso 189, near Piazza di Trevi ☎ 06/6797691 ⊠ Piazza Fiume, Salario ☎ 06/8841231) sells only clothing and accessories in its main store. The Piazza Fiume branch also has furniture and housewares. Both stores are open seven days a week. **Oviesse** (⊠ Via Candia 74, near San Pietro ☎ 06/39743518 ⊂ other locations throughout the city) has moderately priced goods ranging from bathing suits to children's clothes.

Coin (⊠ Piazzale Appio 7, near San Giovanni ☎ 06/7080020 ⊠ Via Mantova 1/b, Salario ☎ 06/8416279) is somewhat trendier than other department stores; it carries a large collection of housewares as well as fashions for men and women. The mid-range chain store **UPIM** (⊠ Piazza Santa Maria Maggiore ☎ 06/4465579) is an institution in Italy; it sells clothing, bed linen, and contemporary kitchenware at reasonable prices. **Cinecittà Due** (⊠ Viale Palmiro Togliatti 2 ☎ 06/7220910) was the first of Rome's several megamalls (100 stores); take Metro A to the Subaugusta or Cinecittà stops.

Markets

Outdoor markets are open Monday–Saturday from early morning to about 1 PM (a bit later on Saturday), but get there early for the best selection. Remember to keep an eye on your wallet—the money changing hands draws Rome's most skillful pickpockets. And don't go if you can't stand crowds. Downtown Rome's most colorful outdoor food market is at **Campo de' Fiori**, south of Piazza Navona. The **Trionfale market** (⊠ Via Andrea Doria, near San Pietro) is big and bustling; it's about a five-minute walk north of the entrance to the Vatican Museums. There's room for bargaining at the Sunday-morning flea market at **Porta Portese**

(✉ Via Ippolito Nievo, Trastevere). Seemingly endless rows of merchandise includes new and secondhand clothing, bootleg CDs, old furniture, car stereos of suspicious origin, and all manner of old junk and hidden treasures.

Specialty Stores

Antiques & Prints

For old prints and antiques, **Tanca** (✉ Salita dei Crescenzi 12, near Pantheon ☎ 06/6875272) is a good hunting ground. Early photographs of Rome and views of Italy from **Alinari** (✉ Via Alibert 16/a, near Piazza di Spagna ☎ 06/69941998) make memorable souvenirs. **Nardecchia** (✉ Piazza Navona 25 ☎ 06/6869318) is reliable for prints. Stands in **Piazza della Fontanella Borghese.** (✉ Near Via del Corso) sell prints and old books.

Designer Clothing

All of Italy's top fashion houses and many international designers have stores near Piazza di Spagna. Buying clothes can be a bit tricky for American women, as sizes tend to be cut for a petite Italian frame. A size 12 (European 46) is not always easy to find, but the more-expensive stores should carry it. Target less-expensive stores for accessories if this is an issue.

D & G (✉ Piazza di Spagna 82 ☎ 06/69924999), a spin-off of the top-of-the-line Dolce & Gabbana, shows trendy casual wear and accessories for men and women. The flagship store for **Fendi** (✉ Largo Carlo Goldoni 419-421, near Piazza di Spagna ☎ 06/696661) is in the former Palazzo Boncompagni, renamed "Palazzo Fendi." It overlooks the intersection of famed Via Condotti and Via del Corso, and it's the quintessential Roman fashion house, presided over by the Fendi sisters. Their signature baguette bags, furs, accessories, and sexy separates are all found here. The **Giorgio Armani** (✉ Via Condotti 77, near Piazza di Spagna ☎ 06/6991460) shop is as understated and elegant as its designs. **Gucci** (✉ Via Condotti 8, near Piazza di Spagna ☎ 06/6783762) often has lines out the door of its two-story shop, testament to the continuing popularity of its colorful bags, wallets, and shoes in rich leathers. Edgy clothes designs are also available. Sleek, vaguely futuristic **Prada** (✉ Via Condotti 92, near Piazza di Spagna ☎ 06/6790897) has two entrances: the one for the men's boutique is to the left of the women's.

Rome's leading local couturier, **Valentino** (Valentino Donna ✉ Via Condotti 13, near Piazza di Spagna ☎ 06/6795862 ✉ Valentino Uomo ✉ Via Bocca di Leone 15, near Piazza di Spagna ☎ 06/6783656), is recognized the world over by the "V" logo. The designer has shops for the *donna* (woman) and the *uomo* (man) not far from his headquarters in Piazza Mignanelli beside the Spanish Steps. **Gianni Versace** (Versace Uomo ✉ Via Borgognona 24–25, near Piazza di Spagna ☎ 06/6795037 ✉ Versace Donna ✉ Via Bocca di Leone 26–27, near Piazza di Spagna ☎ 06/6780521) sells the rock-star styles that made the house's name.

Degli Effetti (✉ Piazza Capranica, near Pantheon ☎ 06/6791650) is a top-of-the-line boutique with men's and women's avant-garde fashion from the likes of Dries Van Noten, Miu Miu, Jil Sander, Martin Margiela, and Helmut Lang.

MEN'S CLOTHING   **Ermenegildo Zegna** (⊠ Via Borgognona 7/e, near Piazza di Spagna ☎ 06/6789143) has the finest in men's elegant styles and accessories. **Il Portone** (⊠ Via delle Carrozze 71, near Piazza di Spagna ☎ 06/69925170) embodies a tradition in custom shirt making. **Brioni** (⊠ Via Condotti 21, near Piazza di Spagna ☎ 06/6783428 ⊠ Via Barberini 79, near Piazza di Trevi ☎ 06/6783635) has a well-deserved reputation as one of Italy's top tailors. There are ready-to-wear garments in addition to impeccable custom-made apparel. **Davide Cenci** (⊠ Via Campo Marzio 1-7, near Pantheon ☎ 06/6990681) is famed for conservative clothing of exquisite craftsmanship. For something a little funkier, employing unusual cuts and lively colors, try Bologna designer **Daniele Alessandrini** (⊠ Corso Rinascimento 58, near Piazza Navona ☎ 06/6879664).

WOMEN'S CLOTHING   Come to the **Dress Agency** (⊠ 1B Via del Vantaggio, Piazza di Spagna ☎ 06/3210898) for designer-label consignment shopping: finds have included Prada sweaters and Gucci dresses, some pieces as low as €20. Although you never know exactly when you'll hit pay dirt, try right after the season changes and Roman women have cleaned out their closets to make room for new goodies. **Galassia** (⊠ Via Frattina 21, near Piazza di Spagna ☎ 06/6797896) has expensive, extreme, and extravagant women's styles by Gaultier, Westwood, and Yamamoto—this is the place for feather boas and hats with ostrich plumes. If you're in the market for luxurious lingerie, **La Perla** (⊠ Via Condotti 79, near Piazza di Spagna ☎ 06/69941934) is the place to shop.

If you're feeling flush, try **Nuyorica** (⊠ Piazza Pollarolla 36, Campo de' Fiori ☎ 06/68891243), which sells expensive, superchic designer pieces from Balenciaga, Chloe, and American favorite Marc Jacobs, among others. **Josephine de Huertas & Co.** (⊠ Via del Governo Vecchio 68, near Piazza Navona ☎ 06/6876586) is a precious little boutique with colorful, high-end stock from the likes of Paul Smith and lesser-known designers. **Ethic** (⊠ Via del Pantheon 46/47 ☎ 06/68803167) is a great reasonably priced stop for funky fashions in this season's color palette, from knits to leather jackets. The boutique **rose d.** (⊠ Corso Rinascimento 60, Piazza Navona ☎ 06/6867641) showcases upbeat urban fashions. (The unusual display racks can give taller customers a case of "shopper's crouch.")

The garments at **Luisa Spagnoli** (⊠ Via del Tritone 30, near Piazza di Trevi ☎ 06/69202220) are elegant but contemporary, and they go to large sizes. **Alternative** (⊠ Piazza Mattei 5, Jewish Ghetto ☎ 06/68309505) is a gorgeous addition to a beautiful piazza. Amid sparkling floor-to-ceiling crystal chandeliers, black walls, and colorful plush seating, you'll find select styles from cutting-edge designers such as Antonio Berardi, Alessandro dell-Acqua, Michael Kors, and Catherine Malandrino.

Embroidery & Linens

Frette (⊠ Piazza di Spagna 11 ☎ 06/6790673) is a Roman institution for luxurious linens. **Venier Colombo** (⊠ Via Frattina 79, near Piazza di Spagna ☎ 06/6787705) has a selection of exquisite lace goods, including lingerie and linens. **Lavori Artigianali Femminili** (⊠ Via Capo le Case

6, near Piazza di Spagna ☎ 06/6781100) sells delicately embroidered household linens, infants' and children's clothing, and blouses.

Food

There are several hundred *salumerie* (gourmet food shops specializing in fresh and cured meats and cheeses) in town, but a few stand out for a particularly ample selection and items of rare, superior quality. Foodies should head straight for **Franchi** (✉ Via Cola di Rienzo 200, near San Pietro ☎ 06/6864576) to check out the sliced meats and cheeses that you can have vacuum-packed for safe transport home. They also sell the city's best take-out treats, including salmon mousse, roast beef, and vegetable fritters. **Castroni** (✉ Via Cola di Rienzo 196, near San Pietro ☎ 06/6864383) is an excellent general food shop with lots of imported items. **Volpetti** (✉ Via Marmorata 47, Testaccio ☎ 06/5742352) has high-quality meats and aged cheeses from small producers. The men behind the counter will be happy to let you take a taste.

A bottle of liqueur, jar of marmalade, or bar of chocolate made by Cistercian monks at Italian monasteries makes an unusual and tasty treat to take home. Choose from the goodies at **Ai Monasteri** (✉ Corso Rinascimento 72, near Piazza Navona ☎ 06/68802783). Drop into **Panella** (✉ Via Merulana 54, near Santa Maria Maggiore ☎ 06/4872344), one of Rome's most spectacular bakeries, for exquisite bread sculptures and a fine selection of pastas, oils, and preserves to take home.

Housewares

The kitchen shop at **'Gusto** (✉ Piazza Augusto Imperatore 9, near Piazza di Spagna ☎ 06/3226273) has a great selection of cookbooks, including some in English. Pricey **C.u.c.i.n.a.** (✉ Via Mario de' Fiori 65, near Piazza di Spagna ☎ 06/6791275) is one of the best kitchen-supply stores in town. **D Cube** (✉ Via della Pace 38, near Piazza Navona ☎ 06/6861218) is a kitschy boutique with colorful, architectural gadgets for the home. From within a striking frescoed 17th-century palazzo, **Spazio Sette** (✉ Via dei Barbieri 7, near Campo de' Fiori ☎ 06/6869747) sells gadgets and furniture created by the biggest names in Italian and international design. **Leone Limentani** (✉ Via Portico d'Ottavia 47, Ghetto ☎ 06/68806686) is a warehouse full of discounted kitchenware, by such names as Richard Ginori, Bernardaud, Reidel, and Baccarat.

Jewelry & Silver Objects

★ **Fornari & Fornari** (✉ Via Frattina 133, Piazza di Spagna ☎ 06/6980105) has a vast selection of silver pieces, as well as fine crystal and china. What Cartier is to Paris, **Bulgari** (✉ Via Condotti 10, near Piazza di Spagna ☎ 06/6793876) is to Rome; the shop's elegant display windows hint at what's beyond the guard at the door. **Buccellati** (✉ Via Condotti 31, near Piazza di Spagna ☎ 06/6790329) is a tradition-rich Florentine jewelry house renowned for its silver work; it ranks with Bulgari for quality and reliability.

At **Liliana Michilli** (✉ Via Dei Banchi Vecchi 37, near Campo de' Fiori ☎ 06/68392154) you can buy convincing copies of Bulgari and Gucci rings for a fraction of the price. The craftswomen of **Danae** (✉ Via della Maddalena 40, near Pantheon ☎ 06/6791881) make original jewelry pieces, working with metals and chunky stones like amber, milky aquamarine, and turquoise. **Quattrocolo** (⊠ Via della Scrofa 54, near Pantheon ☎ 06/68801367) has been specializing in antique micro-mosaic jewelry and baubles from centuries past since 1938.

Shoes & Leather Accessories

It's the women's accessories—Luella bags to Marc Jacobs shoes—that bring shoppers back to the **Tad Concept Store** (⊠ Via del Babuino 155a, near Piazza di Spagna ☎ 06/32695131). Also sold are fabulous home-decorating items and *the* music you should be listening to; there's even a café. For gloves as pretty as Holly Golightly's, shop at **Sermoneta** (⊠ Piazza di Spagna 61 ☎ 06/6791960). Any color or style one might desire, from elbow-length black leather to scallop-edged lace-cut lilac suede, is available at this glove institution. For the latest, Italian-made styles in mid-range handbags, shoes, scarves, and costume jewelry, go to **Furla** (⊠ Piazza di Spagna 22 ☎ 06/69200363), which has a number of stores in the city center.

Ferragamo Uomo (⊠ Via Condotti 65, near Piazza di Spagna ☎ 06/6781130) sells classic shoes for men. **Di Cori** (⊠ Piazza di Spagna 53 ☎ 06/6784439) has gloves in every color of the spectrum. **Bruno Magli** (⊠ Via del Gambero 1, near Piazza di Spagna ☎ 06/6793802 ⊠ Via Veneto 70 ☎ 06/42011671) is known for well-made shoes and matching handbags at both moderate and high prices. **Campanile** (⊠ Via Condotti 58, near Piazza di Spagna ☎ 06/6790731) has two floors of shoes in classic styles; they also sell other leather goods. The **Tod's** (⊠ Via Foontanella di Borghese 56 a/c, near Piazza di Spagna ☎ 06/68210066) central boutique sells signature button-sole moccasins made by Italian shoe maestro Diego della Valle, as well as a line of handmade bags.

Federico Polidori (⊠ Via Pie di Marmo 7, near Pantheon ☎ 06/6797191) crafts custom-made leather bags and briefcases complete with monograms. For original, handcrafted bags and purses (some based on styles from names like YSL), **Sirni** (⊠ Via della Stelletta 33, near Pantheon ☎ 06/68805248) is worth seeking out.

For a vast selection of affordable, high-quality, Italian bags and accessories, head for **Regal** (⊠ Via Nazionale 254, near Termini ☎ 06/4884893). **Calzature Fausto Santini** (⊠ Via Santa Maria Maggiore 165, near Santa Maria Maggiore ☎ 06/6784114) is the place for colorful, offbeat Santini shoes at half price. (The flagship store is on upmarket Via Frattina.)

Silks & Fabrics

Fratelli Bassetti (⊠ Corso Vittorio Emanuele II 73, near Campo de' Fiori ☎ 06/6892326) has a vast selection of world-famous Italian silks and fashion fabrics in a rambling palazzo. **Aston** (⊠ Via Boncompagni 27, near Via Veneto ☎ 06/42871227) stocks couture-level fabrics for men and women. You can find some real bargains if there are *scampoli* (remnants).

Stationery & Gifts

Fabriano (⊠ Via del Babuino 173, near Piazza di Spagna ☎ 06/6864268) sells stylish stationery, organized by color, as well as leather albums and pens of every description. Present your gifts with Italian flair: **Daniela Rosati** (⊠ Via della Stelletta 27, Pantheon ☎ 06/68802053) has beautifully handmade gift boxes covered in colorful paper.

ROME ESSENTIALS

Transportation

BY AIR

Most international flights and all domestic flights arrive at Aeroporto Leonardo da Vinci, also known as Fiumicino, 30 km (19 mi) southwest of Rome. Some international and charter flights and most low-cost carriers land at Ciampino, a civil and military airport 15 km (9 mi) southeast of Rome. To get to the city from Fiumicino by car, follow the signs for Rome on the expressway from the airport, which links with the GRA, the beltway around Rome. The direction you take on the GRA depends on where your hotel is, so get directions from the car-rental people at the airport. A taxi from Fiumicino to the center of town costs about €50, including *supplementi* (extra charges) for airport service and luggage, and the ride takes 30–40 minutes, depending on traffic. Private limousines can be hired at booths in the arrivals hall; they charge a little more than taxis but can take more passengers. Ignore gypsy drivers who approach you inside the terminal; stick to the licensed cabs, yellow or white, that wait by the curb. A booth inside the arrivals hall provides taxi information.

You have a choice of two trains to get to downtown Rome from Fiumicino Airport. Ask at the airport (at APT or train information counters) which train takes you closer to your hotel. The nonstop Airport–Termini Leonardo Express takes you directly to Track 22 at Stazione Termini, Rome's main train station, which is well served by taxis and is the hub of metro and bus lines. The ride takes 30 minutes; departures are every half hour beginning at 6:37 AM from the airport, with a final departure at 11:37 PM. From Termini to the airport, trains leave at 21 and 51 minutes past the hour. Tickets cost €9.50 at the main ticket counters in the station, or €10.50 if purchased at the little booth beside Track 22.

FM1, the other airport train, runs from the airport to Rome and beyond, terminating in Monterotondo, a suburban town to the east. The main stops in Rome are at Trastevere, Ostiense, and Tiburtina stations; at each you can find taxis and bus and/or metro connections to other parts of Rome. This train runs from Fiumicino from 6:35 AM to 12:15 AM, with departures every 20 minutes, a little less frequently in off-hours. The ride to Tiburtina takes 40 minutes. Tickets cost €5. For either train buy your ticket at automatic vending machines. There are ticket counters at some stations (at Termini/Track 22, Trastevere, Tiburtina). Date-stamp the ticket at the gate before you board.

🛃 **Airport Information** **Aeroporto Leonardo da Vinci** (also known as Fiumicino) ☎ 06/65951, 06/65953640 English-language flight information ⊕ www.adr.it. **Ciampino** ⊠ Via Appia Nuova ☎ 06/794941.

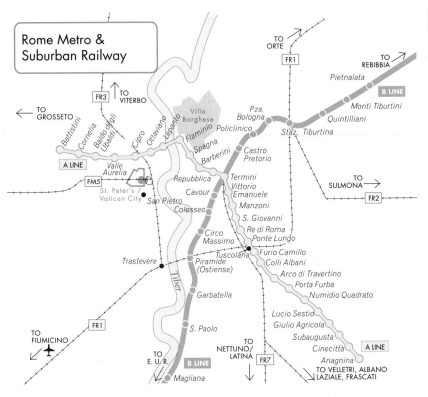

Rome Metro & Suburban Railway

BY BUS, METRO & TRAM

There's no central bus terminal in Rome. COTRAL is the suburban bus company that connects Rome with outlying areas and other cities in the Lazio region. Long-distance and suburban buses terminate either near Tiburtina Station or near outlying metro stops such as Rebbibia and Anagnina. For COTRAL bus information, call weekdays 8 AM–6 PM.

Rome's metro (subway) is somewhat limited, but it's a quick, safe, and relatively low-stress way to get around town if there's a stop where you're going. The public bus and tram system is the opposite—routes are extensive, but the city's narrow streets and chronic traffic can make street-level transport slow. Metro service begins at 5:30 AM, and the last trains leave the most distant station at 11:30 PM (on Saturday night, trains run until 12:30 AM). Buses run day and night, although some routes change after 10 PM or midnight. Stops are marked by high white signs on yellow poles listing bus numbers and upcoming stops, but for serious exploring, a bus map (available at newsstands) is invaluable. The compact electric buses of Lines 117 and 119 take routes through the center of Rome that can save lots of walking. Routes change frequently; if you know a little Italian, you can plan itineraries and download maps before you go at ATAC's Web site.

ATAC city buses and tram lines run from about 6 AM to midnight, with night buses (indicated N) on some lines. A ticket valid for 75 minutes on any combination of buses and trams and one entrance to the metro costs €1. You are expected to date-stamp your ticket when you board the first vehicle, stamping it again when boarding for the last time within 75 minutes (the important thing is to stamp it the first time). Tickets for the public transit system are sold at tobacconists, newsstands, some coffee bars, green machines positioned in metro stations and some bus stops, and at ATAC and COTRAL ticket booths (in some metro stations, on the lower concourse at Stazione Termini, and at a few main bus terminals). A BIG tourist ticket, valid for one day on all public transport, costs €4. A weekly ticket (Settimanale, also known as CIS) costs €16 and can be purchased only at ATAC booths.

🚍 **Bus & Metro Information ATAC** ☎ 800/431784 toll free ⊕ www.atac.roma.it. **CO-TRAL** ☎ 800/150008 toll-free.

BY CAR

The main access routes from the north are A1 (Autostrada del Sole) from Milan and Florence and the A12–E80 highway from Genoa. The principal route to or from points south, including Naples, is the A2. All highways connect with the Grande Raccordo Anulare (GRA), which channels traffic into the city center. As elsewhere in Italy, road signs for the center of town are marked with a bull's-eye. Signs on the GRA are confusing: take time to study the route you need.

Romans park wherever they find space, and sidewalk, double- and triple-parking is common. Parking spaces outlined in blue are paid by buying a ticket from a small gray machine, located along the street. Leave the ticket, which shows how long you've paid to park, visible on the dashboard. Spaces outlined in yellow are not parking spaces at all—stay away to avoid being towed. If you rent a car in the city, make sure the rental desk gives you specific directions for getting out of town, and invest in a detailed city map (available at most newsstands).

BY MOPED

Zipping and careening through traffic on a *motorino* (moped) in downtown Rome is an attractive way to visit the city for some, but if you're averse to risk, pass on it. If your impulses—and reflexes—are fast, you can join the craziness of Roman traffic by renting a moped and the mandatory helmet at numerous rental spots throughout the city. Be extremely careful of pedestrians when riding: Romans are casual jaywalkers and pop out frequently from between parked cars.

🛵 **Moped Rentals Enjoy Rome** ✉ Via Margbera 8A, Termini, 00185 ☎ 06/4451843 ⊕ www.enjoyrome.com. **Scoot-a-Long** ✉ Via Cavour 302, Termini ☎ 06/6780206. **St. Peter Moto** ✉ Via di Porta Castello 43, San Pietro ☎ 06/5757063. **Trevi Tourist Service** ✉ Via dei Lucchesi 2, Piazza di Spagna ☎ 06/69200799.

BY TAXI

Taxis in Rome do not cruise, but if empty (look for an illuminated TAXI sign on the roof) they will stop if you flag them down. There is a taxi shortage in the city, so your best bet—especially during peak hours—is to wait at one of the city's many taxis stands or call by phone, in which case the meter starts when the taxi receives the request for a pickup. The meter price begins at €2.33 from 7 AM to 10 PM, at €3.36 on Sunday and holidays, and at €4.91 after 10 PM. Each piece of baggage will add an extra €2.03 to your fare. There are two different fare systems, one for outside the city and one for inside, shown on the LED meter display. Make sure your cab is charging you *tariffa uno*—the cheaper one—when you're in town. Use only licensed, metered yellow or white cabs, identified by a numbered shield on the side, an illuminated taxi sign on the roof, and a plaque next to the license plate reading SERVIZIO PUBBLICO. Avoid unmarked, unauthorized, unmetered cabs (common at airports and train stations), whose renegade drivers actively solicit your trade and often demand astronomical fares. Most taxis accept credit cards, but make sure to specify when calling that you will pay that way.

🚕 Taxi Companies **Taxi** ☎ 06/5551, 06/3570, 06/4994, or 06/88177.

BY TRAIN

Stazione Termini is Rome's main train terminal; the Tiburtina and Ostiense stations serve some long-distance trains, many commuter trains, and the FM1 line to Fiumicino Airport. Some trains for Pisa and Genoa leave Rome from, or pass through, the Trastevere Station. You can find English-speaking staff at the information office at Stazione Termini, or ask for information at travel agencies. You can purchase tickets up to two months in advance at the main stations or at most travel agencies. Lines at station ticket windows may be very long: you can save time by using the electronic ticket machines, which have instructions in English, or by buying your ticket at a travel agency. You can reserve a seat up to one day in advance at a travel agency or up to an hour in advance at a train station. Tickets for train rides within a radius of 100 km (62 mi) of Rome can be purchased at tobacco shops and at some newsstands, as well as at ticket machines on the main concourse. All train tickets must be date-stamped before you board, at the machine near the track, or you may be fined.

🚆 Train Information **Trenitalia** ☎ 892021 [a small service charge applies] ⊕ www.trenitalia.it.

Contacts & Resources

EMERGENCIES

Farmacia Internazionale Apotheke, Farmacia Trinità dei Monti, and Laltrafarmacia are pharmacies that have some English-speaking staff. Most pharmacies are open 8:30–1 and 4–8; some are open all night. A schedule posted outside each pharmacy indicates the nearest pharmacy open during off-hours (afternoons, through the night, and Sunday). Dial ☎ 1100 for an automated list of three open pharmacies closest to the telephone from which you call. The hospitals listed below have English-speaking doctors. Rome American Hospital is about 30 minutes by cab from the center of town.

🚑 Emergency Services **Ambulance** ☎ 118. **Police** ☎ 112 or 113. **Red Cross** ☎ 06/5510.
🏥 Hospitals **Rome American Hospital** ✉ Via Emilio Longoni 69, Via Prenestina ☎ 06/22551 ⊕ www.rah.it. **Salvator Mundi International Hospital** ✉ Viale delle Mura Gianicolensi 67, Trastevere ☎ 06/588961 ⊕ www.smih.pcn.net.

🔳 Pharmacies **Farmacia Internazionale Apotheke** ✉ Piazza Barberini 49, near Via Veneto ☎ 06/4825456. **Farmacia Trinità dei Monti** ✉ Piazza di Spagna 30 ☎ 06/6790626. **Laltrafarmacia** ✉ Via Torino 21, near Termini ☎ 06/4881625.

TOURS

BIKE TOURS Enjoy Rome organizes all-day bike tours of Rome for small groups covering major sights and some hidden ones. Remember, Rome is famous for its seven hills; be prepared for a workout.

🔳 Fees & Schedules **Enjoy Rome** ✉ Via Marghera 8A, near Termini ☎ 06/4451843 ⊕ www.enjoyrome.com.

BUS TOURS American Express and CIT offer general orientation tours of the city, as well as specialized tours of particular areas such as the Vatican or Ancient Rome. Stop-'n'-go City Tours has English-speaking guides and the option of getting off and on at 14 key sites in the city. A day pass costs €12.

🔳 Fees & Schedules **American Express** ☎ 06/67641. **Appian Line** ☎ 06/487861. **CIT** ✉ Piazza della Repubblica 64, near Termini ☎ 06/4620311. **Stop-'n'-go City Tours** ☎ 06/47826379 ⊕ www.romecitytours.com.

WALKING TOURS All About Rome, American Express, Context: Rome, Enjoy Rome, Through Eternity, and Walks of Rome offer walking tours of the city and its sites.

🔳 Fees & Schedules **All About Rome** ☎ 06/7100823 ⊕ www.allaboutromewalks. netfirms.com. **American Express** ☎ 06/67641. **Context: Rome** ✉ Via Baccina 40, near Termini ☎ 06/4820911 or 888/4671986 ⊕ www.contextrome.com. **Enjoy Rome** ✉ Via Marghera 8A, near Termini ☎ 06/4451843 ⊕ www.enjoyrome.com. **Through Eternity** ☎ 06/7009336 ⊕ www.througheternity.com. **Walks of Rome** ✉ Via Urbana 38, Quirinale ☎ 06/484853.

VISITOR INFORMATION

🔳 Tourist Information **Tourist office** (Azienda di Promozione Turistica di Roma/APT) ✉ Via Parigi 5, near Termini ☎ 06/488991 ۞ Mon.–Sat. 9–7 ✉ Aeroporto Leonardo da Vinci ☎ 06/65956074 ۞ Daily 8:15–7.

Side Trips
from Rome

Villa Adriana, Tivoli

WORD OF MOUTH

"If you have a few extra days in Rome, northen Lazio, including Viterbo and small jewels like Tuscania, is worth checking out. If you'd like to see Etruscan tomb paintings in their original underground state, Tarquinia is the place, and you can easily drive to the airport from there and catch your flight home."

—alohatoall

WELCOME TO LAZIO

In Tuscia, the San Pellegrino district of **Viterbo** is a 13th-century time capsule, while at the gardens and palaces of nearby **Bagnaia, Caprarola,** and **Bomarzo** you can relive the Renaissance.

The ruins and tombs found along the **Etruscan Seaboard** in **Cerveteri, Tarquinia,** and **Tuscania** hold clues to the identity of the civilization that dominated central Italy prior to the Romans.

Bomarzo

Aqua Claudia

204

Bagnaia
Viterbo
Caprarola

Vetralla

1

A1

Tuscania

2

Tarquinia

3

Lago di
Bracciano

Civitavecchia

Cerveteri

1

Rome

A12

Mare Tirreno

A91

Ostia Antica
Lido di Ostia

601

Getting Oriented

All roads may indeed lead to Rome, but for thousands of years emperors, popes, and princes have been heading *fuori porta* (beyond the gates) for a change of pace from city life. To the west lies ancient Ostia Antica; as you work your way north you encounter the Etruscan seaboard and lava-rich Tuscia, with its Renaissance gardens. East of Rome is Tivoli, famed for retreats ranging from the noble—the Villa d'Este—to the imperial—Villa Adriana (Hadrian's Villa).

Ostia Antica, once ancient Rome's port, is now a parklike archaeological site.

Roman Theater, Ostia Antica   Sperlonga

Amatrice

Rieti

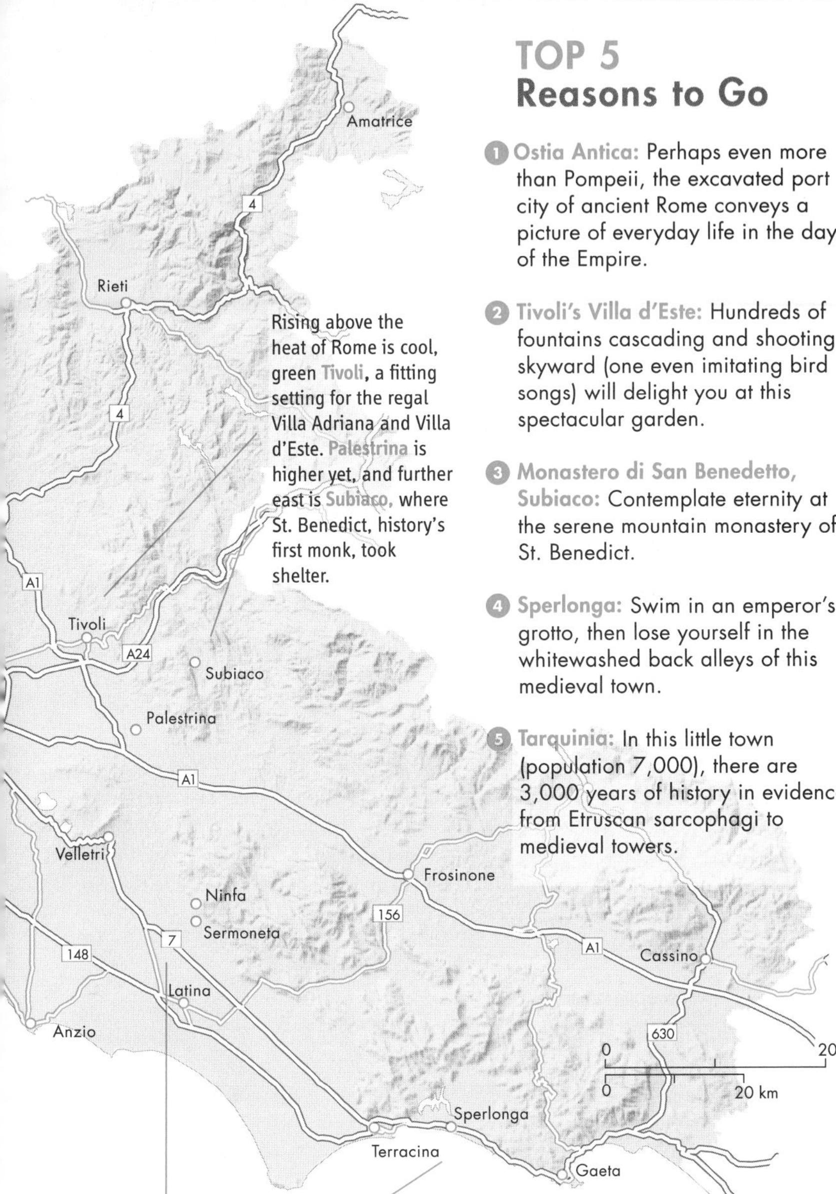

Rising above the heat of Rome is cool, green Tivoli, a fitting setting for the regal Villa Adriana and Villa d'Este. Palestrina is higher yet, and further east is Subiaco, where St. Benedict, history's first monk, took shelter.

Tivoli

A1

A24

Subiaco

Palestrina

A1

Velletri

148

Ninfa

7 Sermoneta

Latina

Anzio

Frosinone

156

A1 Cassino

630

0 _____ 20 mi

0 _____ 20 km

Sperlonga

Terracina

Gaeta

Sermoneta is famed for its Borgia castle, Ninfa for the most poetic garden in Italy, and Sperlonga— today an artists' idyll—as the original site of one of Emperor Tiberius's grandest villas.

Villa Adriana

TOP 5
Reasons to Go

① **Ostia Antica:** Perhaps even more than Pompeii, the excavated port city of ancient Rome conveys a picture of everyday life in the days of the Empire.

② **Tivoli's Villa d'Este:** Hundreds of fountains cascading and shooting skyward (one even imitating bird songs) will delight you at this spectacular garden.

③ **Monastero di San Benedetto, Subiaco:** Contemplate eternity at the serene mountain monastery of St. Benedict.

④ **Sperlonga:** Swim in an emperor's grotto, then lose yourself in the whitewashed back alleys of this medieval town.

⑤ **Tarquinia:** In this little town (population 7,000), there are 3,000 years of history in evidence, from Etruscan sarcophagi to medieval towers.

ROME SIDE TRIPS PLANNER

Making the Most of Your Time

Ostia Antica is in many ways an ideal day trip from Rome: it's a fascinating sight, not far from the city, reachable by public transit, and takes about half a day to "do." Villa d'Este and Villa Adriana in Tivoli also make for a manageable, though fuller, day trip. Other destinations in Lazio can be visited in a day, but you'll get more out of them if you stay the night. A classic two-day itinerary would have you exploring Etruscan history in Cerveteri, Tarquinia, and Tuscania on Day 1, then visiting Viterbo's medieval borgo and hot springs or the gardens of Bomarzo, Bagnaia, and Caprarola on Day 2. An overnight to Sperlonga, Ninfa, and Sermoneta, is a summer trip —Ninfa is open only then, and in warm weather you can take advantage of Sperlonga's gorgeous beach.

Lazio, the Romans' Holiday

Foreign travelers aren't the only ones making day trips into the countryside of Lazio—on weekends, many Romans escape to the country, where they indulge in long, languorous meals. The good news is there are restaurants in the region that meet their standards. The bad news is on weekends when you'll be competing with natives for a table.

Getting Around

There's reliable public transit from Rome to Ostia Antica, Tivoli, and Viterbo. For other destinations in the region, a car is a big advantage—going by train or bus can add hours to your trip, and routes and schedules often seem like puzzles created by the Italian chapter of Mensa. For more about car, bus, and train travel, see "Essentials" at the end of this chapter.

Finding a Place to Stay

With relatively few exceptions (spas, beaches, and hill resorts such as Viterbo), accommodations in Lazio cater more to commercial travelers than to tourists. Rooms tend to be short on character, but they'll do the trick for an overnight.

Dining & Lodging Price Categories

WHAT IT COSTS in Euros					
	$$$$	$$$	$$	$	¢
Restaurants	over €45	€35–€45	€25–€35	€15–€25	under €15
Hotels	over €220	€160–€220	€110–€160	€70–€110	under €70

Restaurant prices are for a first course (primo), second course (secondo), and dessert (dolce). Hotel prices are for two people in a standard double room in high season, including tax and service.

Updated by
Patricia Rucidlo

A TRIP OUT OF ROME introduces you to a different kind of Italy: people are friendlier (but speak less English), schedules are looser, and it feels as though you've stepped a few years back in time. You'll find fewer lines, lower prices, and a tourism culture not so focused on the almighty euro. The monastery of San Benedetto at Subiaco is a good example of small-town charm: the monks and nuns there will take you in as a pilgrim, just as they've done for centuries.

Ostia Antica, Ancient Rome's seaport, is one of the region's top attractions—it rivals Pompeii in the quality of its preservation, and for evocativeness and natural beauty, it easily outshines the Roman forum. The pre-Roman inhabitants of the area were wiped out in the city, but their remains—and some say, their bloodlines—persist in the rolling hills of Tuscia and the Etruscan seaboard north and northeast of Rome. So if the screeching traffic and long lines at the Colosseo start to wear on you, do as the Romans do—get out of town. There's plenty to see and do.

OSTIA ANTICA

Founded around the 4th century BC, Ostia served as Rome's port city for several centuries until the Tiber changed course, leaving the town high and dry. What has been excavated here is a remarkably intact Roman town in a pretty, parklike setting. Fair weather and good walking shoes are essential. On hot days, be here when the gates open or go late in the afternoon. A visit to the excavations takes two to three hours, including 20 minutes for the museum. Ostia Antica is 30 km (19 mi) southwest of Rome.

❶ Before exploring Ostia Antica's ruins, it's worthwhile to take a tour through the medieval *borgo* (town). The distinctive **Castello della Rovere,** easily spotted as you come off the footbridge from the train station, was built by Pope Julius II when he was the Cardinal Bishop of Ostia in 1483. Its triangular form is unusual for military architecture. Inside are (badly faded) frescoes by Baldassare Peruzzi. ✉ *Piazza della Rocca* ☎ *06/56358024* 🎟 *Free* ☉ *Wed. and Fri.–Sun. 10–noon, Tues. and Thurs. 10–noon and 3–4.*

Fodor'sChoice
★

Tidal mud and windblown sand covered the ancient port town, which lay buried until the beginning of the 20th century when it was extensively excavated. The **Scavi di Ostia Antica** (Ostia Antica excavations) continue to be well maintained today. A cosmopolitan population of rich businessmen, wily merchants, sailors, slaves, and their respective families once populated the city. The great warehouses were built in the 2nd century AD to handle huge shipments of grain from Africa; the *insulae* (forerunners of the modern apartment building) provided housing for the city's growing population. Under the combined assaults of the barbarians and the malaria-carrying mosquito, and after the Tiber changed course, the port was eventually abandoned. ✉ *Viale dei Romagnoli 717* ☎ *06/56358099* ⊕ *www.itnw.roma.it/ostia/scavi* 🎟 *€4, includes admission to Museo Ostiense* ☉ *Nov.–Feb., Tues.–Sun. 8:30–4; Mar., Tues.–Sun. 8:30–5; Apr.–Oct., Tues.–Sun. 8:30–6.*

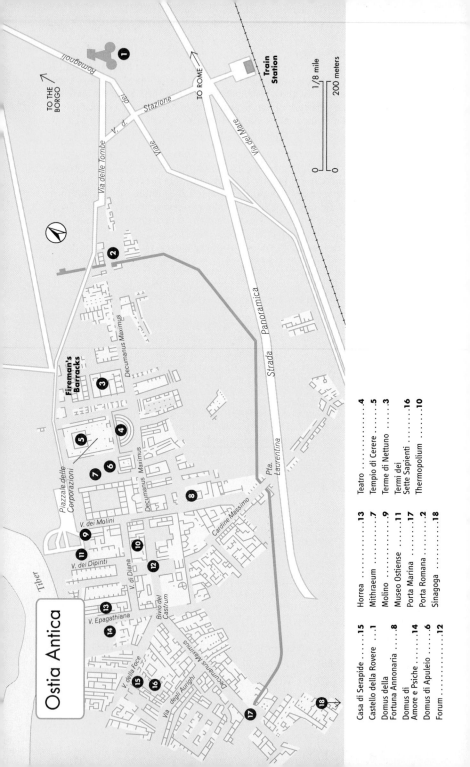

Ostia Antica

Casa di Serapide **15**

Castello della Rovere . . .**1**

Domus della
Fortuna Annonaria **8**

Domus di
Amore e Psiche **14**

Domus di Apuleio **6**

Forum **12**

Horrea **13**

Mithraeum **7**

Molino **9**

Museo Ostiense **11**

Porta Marina **17**

Porta Romana **2**

Sinagoga **18**

Teatro **4**

Tempio di Cerere **5**

Terme di Nettuno **3**

Termi dei
Sette Sapienti **16**

Thermopolium **10**

Train
Station

TO ROME

1/8 mile

200 meters

TO THE
BORGO

Fireman's
Barracks

2 The **Porta Romana,** one of the city's three gates, is where you enter the Ostia Antica excavations. It opens onto the Decumanus Maximus, the main thoroughfare crossing the city from end to end. To your right, a staircase leads up to a platform—the remains of the upper floor of the

3 **Terme di Nettuno** (Baths of Neptune)—from which you get a good view of the black-and-white mosaic pavements representing a marine scene with Neptune and the sea goddess Amphitrite. Directly behind the baths is the barracks of the fire department, which played an important role in a town with warehouses full of valuable goods and foodstuffs.

4 On the north side of the Decumanus Maximus is the beautiful **Teatro** (Theater), built by Agrippa, remodeled by Septimius Severus in the 2nd century AD, and finally restored by the Rome City Council in the 20th century. In the vast Piazzale delle Corporazioni, where trade organiza-

5 tions similar to guilds had their offices, is the **Tempio di Cerere** (Temple of Ceres), which is only appropriate for a town dealing in grain imports— Ceres, who gave her name to cereal, was the goddess of agriculture. You

6 can visit the **Domus di Apuleio** (House of Apuleius), built in Pompeian style, lower to the ground and with fewer windows than was character-

7 istic of Ostia. Next door, the **Mithraeum** has balconies and a hall deco-rated with symbols of the cult of Mithras. This male-only religion, imported from Persia, was especially popular with legionnaires.

8 On Via Semita dei Cippi, just off Via dei Molini, the **Domus della Fortuna Annonaria** (House of Fortuna Annonaria) is the richly decorated residence of a wealthy Ostian, which displays the skill of the mosaic artists of the period. One of the rooms opens onto a secluded garden.

9 On Via dei Molini you can see a **molino** (mill), where grain for the ware-houses next door was ground with stones that are still here. Along Via

10 di Diana you come upon a **thermopolium** (bar) with a marble counter and a fresco depicting the fruit and foodstuffs that were sold here. At

11 the end of Via dei Dipinti is the **Museo Ostiense** (Ostia Museum), which displays sarcophagi, massive marble columns, and statuary too large to be shown anywhere else. A beautiful statue of Mithras slaying the bull that was taken from the underground Mithraeum and placed here. (The last entry to the museum is a half hour before the Scavi closes.)

12 The **Forum,** on the south side of Decumanus Maximus, holds the mon-umental remains of the city's most important temple, dedicated to Jupiter, Juno, and Minerva. It's also the site of other ruins of baths, a basilica (which in Roman times was a secular hall of justice), and smaller temples.

13 Via Epagathiana leads toward the Tiber, where there are large **horrea** (warehouses) erected during the 2nd century AD to receive the enormous amounts of grain imported into Rome during that period, the height of the Empire.

14 West of Via Epagathiana, the **Domus di Amore e Psiche** (House of Cupid and Psyche), a residence, was named for a statue found there (now on display in the museum); you can see what remains of a large pool in an enclosed garden decorated with marble and mosaic motifs. Even in ancient times a premium was placed on water views: the house faces the shore, which would have been only about ⅓ km (⅕ mi) away. The

⑮ Casa di Serapide (House of Serapis) on Via della Foce is a 2nd-century multilevel dwelling; another apartment building stands one street over
⑯ on Via degli Aurighi. Nearby, the **Termi dei Sette Sapienti** (Baths of the Seven Wise Men) are named for a group of bawdy frescoes found there.

⑰ The **Porta Marina** leads to what used to be the seashore. About 1,000
⑱ feet to the southeast are the ruins of the **sinagoga,** one of the oldest in the Western world (from the 4th century AD).

Where to Eat

$ ✕ **Cipriani.** In the little medieval borgo near the excavations is an elegant trattoria serving Roman specialties and seafood. A businesslike mood at lunchtime contrasts with an upgrade in menu, style, and price in the evening. The wine list is exquisite. ⊠ *Via del Forno 11* ☎ *06/56359560* ▭ *AE, DC, MC, V* ☉ *Closed Wed.*

THE ETRUSCAN SEABOARD

Northwest of Rome lie Etruscan sites on coastal hills that dominate approaches from all directions. The Etruscans held sway over a vast territory mainly north of Rome from the 8th to the 4th century BC, before the Roman Republic's gradual expansion northward. According to the literary sources—mainly written by their Greek and Roman adversaries—Etruscans lived a fairly decadent life and had an unsurpassed reputation in fields as diverse as bronze-working and soothsaying. Though there are few remains of their settlements, they reserved some of their finest construction skills for assuring comfort and style in the afterlife: the Etruscan necropolis, or "city of the dead," was an agglomeration of tombs that most likely aimed to reproduce the homes and lifestyles of the living.

As you make the trip north beyond Rome's city limits, you traverse green countryside with pastures and endless fields of artichokes, a premium crop in these parts. You catch glimpses of the sea to the west, where the coast is dotted with suburban developments. Because the beaches in this area are popular with today's Romans, highways (especially the coastal Via Aurelia) and public transportation can be crowded on weekends from spring to fall. Exploring the Etruscan sites requires some agility in climbing up and down uneven stairs, and you need shoes suitable for walking on rough dirt paths.

Cerveteri is the principal Etruscan site closest to Rome and features the Necropoli della Banditaccia, a sylvan setting among mossy stones and variously shaped monuments that are memorials to revered ancestors. Tarquinia is farther north and has impressive painted tombs, as well as an excellent museum full of objects recovered from tombs throughout the region. On the way, you pass Civitavecchia, Rome's principal port. From the highway or train you can see the port installations, which include a fort designed by Michelangelo. Northeast of Tarquinia is Tuscania, a finely preserved town brimming with cultural heritage and medieval buildings.

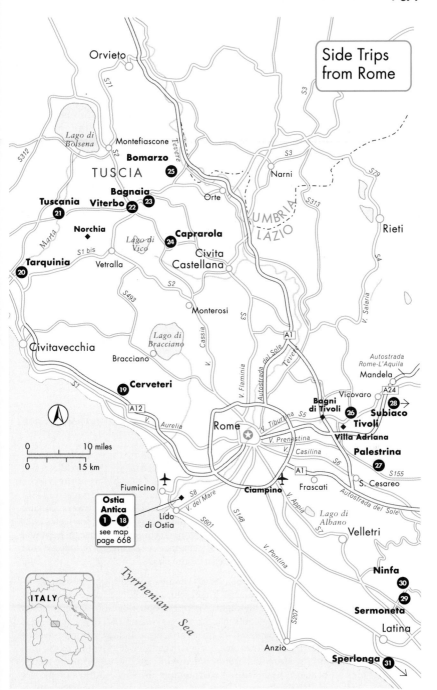

Side Trips
from Rome

Orvieto

*Lago di
Bolsena*

Montefiascone

Bomarzo
25

TUSCIA

Narni

Bagnaia
23

Tuscania **Viterbo** **22**
21

Orte

UMBRIA
LAZIO

Rieti

Norchia ◆

*Lago di
Vico*

Caprarola
24

Civita
Castellana

Tarquinia
20

Vetralla

Monterosi

*Lago di
Bracciano*

Civitavecchia

Bracciano

Cerveteri
19

A12

*Autostrada
Rome-L'Aquila*

Mandela

Vicovaro   A24

**Bagni
di Tivoli**   **Subiaco**
26   **28**

Rome ✪   **Tivoli**
Villa Adriana ◆

Palestrina
27

S. Cesareo

Fiumicino ✈

**Ostia
Antica**
1 - **18**
see map
page 668

Lido
di Ostia

Ciampino ✈   Frascati

A1

*Lago di
Albano*

Velletri

Ninfa
30
29

Sermoneta

Latina

0 ___ 10 miles
0 ___ 15 km

*Tyrrhenian
Sea*

ITALY

Anzio

Sperlonga **31**

Cerveteri

 42 km (26 mi) northwest of Rome.

The nucleus of Cerveteri, in the shadow of a medieval castle, stands on a spur of tufa rock that was the site of the Etruscan city of Caere, a thriving commercial center in the 6th century BC.

In the **Necropoli della Banditaccia** the Etruscan residents of Caere left a monumental complex of tombs constructed during more than 500 years (from the 7th to the 1st century BC). Some are laid to rest in simple graves, others in burial chambers that are replicas of Etruscan dwellings. The round tumuli are prototypes of Rome's tombs of Augustus and Hadrian (in the Mausoleo di Augusto and Castel Sant'Angelo) and the Tomb of Cecilia Metella on the Via Appia. Look for the **Tomba dei Capitelli,** with carved capitals, and the **Tomba dei Rilievi,** its walls decorated with stucco reliefs of household objects. The **Tomba Moretti** has a little vestibule with columns. The necropolis is about 2 km (1 mi) northeast of Cerveteri's main piazza, a trip you can make on foot or by taxi. ⊠ *Piazza della Necropoli* ☎ *06/9940001* ⊡ *€4* ⊙ *Tues.–Sun. 8:30–1 hr before sunset.*

Where to Eat

¢ ✕ **Tuchulcha.** Enjoy simple and satisfying home-style food at a country trattoria. Two of the specialties are handmade fettuccine and locally grown artichokes served in various ways. You can dine outside in good weather. Tuchulcha is about ½ km (⅓ mi) from the entrance to the Banditaccia Necropolis, on the road leading to the site. ⊠ *Via della Necropoli Etrusca 28* ☎ *06/9914075* ⊟ *No credit cards* ⊙ *Closed Mon.*

Tarquinia

 About 90 km (55 mi) northwest of Rome, 50 km (30 mi) northwest of Cerveteri.

Fortified Tarquinia sprawls on a hill overlooking the sea. Once a powerful Etruscan city, it was also a major center in the Middle Ages. Though it is not as well preserved as some other towns in the region, there are unexpected pleasures, including the sight of the majestic 12th-century church of Santa Maria di Castello encircled by towers. Be sure to walk to the medieval wall at the inland edge of town for views over the Etruscan countryside. To explore Tarquinia's Etruscan heritage, visit the museum in Palazzo Vitelleschi, then see the frescoed underground tombs in the necropolis just east of the city.

The **Museo Nazionale Tarquiniense** contains a wealth of Etruscan treasures and is housed in **Palazzo Vitelleschi,** a splendid 15th-century building. The undisputed highlight is a terra-cotta relief of two marvelous winged horses that gleams against the gray-stone wall of the main hall. The horses once decorated an Etruscan temple and are vibrant proof of the degree of artistry attained in the 4th century BC. The rest of the museum and its courtyard are crowded with sarcophagi from the tombs found beneath the meadows surrounding the town: figures of the deceased recline on their stone couches, mouths curved in enigmatic smiles.

Uncovering the Etruscan Past

The countryside in northern Lazio is generously dotted with Etruscan ruins and tombs. For centuries these remnants offered the only insight into the mysterious civilization that dominated the area before the rise of Rome and set the precedent for many of Rome's accomplishments. In his 1920s travelogue *Etruscan Places*, D. H. Lawrence wrote, "We know nothing about the Etruscans except what we find in their tombs." Fortunately, modern scientific techniques have since delved much further, and museums in Cerveteri, Tarquinia, and Tuscania, along with the main Etruscan museum in Rome, the Villa Giulia, regularly offer new exhibits. Still, basic questions remain unanswered, such as where exactly the Etruscans came from, what family of languages Etruscan belongs to, and why they left no proper literature to posterity. But wherever you go in northern Lazio, the Etruscans are never far away: signs point to *Riva degli Etruschi* (Shore of the Etruscans), shops and businesses use imitation Etruscan lettering, and right in the middle of Tuscania, Etruscan sarcophagi are laid out by the main square.

✉ *Piazza Cavour 1* ☎ *0766/856036* 🖃 *€4, €6.50 including necropolis* ☉ *Tues.–Sun. 8:30–7:30.*

The **Necropolis** tombs, painted with lively scenes of Etruscan life, date from the 6th to the 2nd century BC. The colors are amazingly fresh in some tombs, and the scenes show the vitality and highly civilized lifestyle of this ancient people. Apart from the wall paintings, the only evidence of the original function of the burial chambers is the stone platforms on which sarcophagi once rested. The tombs have been plundered by *tombaroli*, who dig illegally, usually at night. Of the thousands of tombs that exist throughout the territory of Etruria (there are 40,000 in the vicinity of Tarquinia alone), only a small percentage have been excavated scientifically. A thorough visit takes about 90 minutes, and good explanations in English are posted outside each tomb. The entrance is 1½ km (1 mi) southeast of the town walls, about a 20-minute walk from the main square, Piazza Matteotti. There's also infrequent bus service from Piazza Cavour. Ask at the Museo Nazionale Tarquiniense ticket counter or the tourist office for bus information. ✉ *Monterozzi, on Strada Provinciale 1/b, Tarquinia–Viterbo* ☎ *0766/856308* 🖃 *€4, €6.50 including Museo Nazionale Tarquiniense* ☉ *Nov.–Mar., Tues.–Sun. 8:30–2; Apr.–Oct., Tues.–Sun. 8:30–1 hr before sunset.*

OFF THE BEATEN PATH

NORCHIA – About 20 km (13 mi) northeast of Tarquinia on the road to Vetralla (S1bis) is the junction for the Etruscan necropolis of Norchia, which lies about 5 km (3 mi) farther to the north. From the far corner of the parking lot, a five-minute walk along a path between fields takes you to the edge of a thickly wooded gorge where Etruscan tombs are sculpted out of the cliff face. You're unlikely to see other visitors here, everything is covered in thick vegetation, *and* the site is unguarded. As you walk down to the bottom of the gorge—though it is not steep, good walking shoes and water bottles are recommended—look at the way parts of the rock face have been modeled to imitate architectural styles. To top it off, there are medieval ruins and a photogenic vantage point up the other side of the gorge (about 10 minutes away). As there is no site map on display and little by way of site information, stick to well-trodden paths.

Where to Stay & Eat

★ ¢ ✕ **Il Grappolo.** This central wine bar is the antidote to another plate of pasta—a great place for a snack, a drink, or a light meal built around wine and good company. It's cold food only, but the menu includes such fresh creations as *insalata di pera, speck, e grana* (salad with pear, cured ham, and flakes of *grana*, aged granulated cheese), perhaps accompanied by Paterno wine, a local Sangiovese thoroughbred, considered Lazio's rival to fine Tuscan reds. The vibe is modern, youthful, and welcoming. ✉ *Via Alberata Dante Alighieri 3* ☎ *0766/857321* 🗖 *AE, DC, MC, V* ⊘ *Closed Mon. and Jan. 7–31. No lunch Nov.–Mar.*

$ ✕🖾 **San Marco.** It would be impossible to find a better location for exploring the old center of Tarquinia than this ancient monastery, a huge, complex structure on the town's main square that's been operating as an inn since 1876. In the 1500s these hallowed halls housed the mysterious order of the Frati Neri (Black Monks)—an Augustinian sect whose cloisters remain intact in the hotel's courtyard. Rooms are simple, clean, and inviting; the bar hops with locals on weekend nights. The excellent restaurant ($–$$) uses recipes reconstructed from the brothers' 16th-century cookbooks (as well as pizza, for the less daring). ✉ *Piazza Cavour 18, 01016* ☎ *0766/842234* 🖨 *0766/842306* ⊕ *www.san-marco.com* ⤴ *16 rooms* ◔ *Restaurant, pizzeria, bar, wine bar, dance club, babysitting, meeting rooms; no a/c* 🗖 *AE, DC, MC, V* ⦿ *MAP.*

Tuscania

★ ㉑ *24 km (15 mi) northeast of Tarquinia, 25 km (16 mi) west of Viterbo.*

Given its small size—a population of only 7,000—Tuscania seems to overflow with sites from a number of historical periods, much more so than neighboring Tarquinia and Viterbo. The medieval city walls were tastefully restored after a devastating earthquake in 1971, and the interior abutting the walls has been pleasingly landscaped with lawns and gardens. Narrow cobblestone streets dotted with medieval towers make for great walks. Piazza Basile, in front of the Palazzo Comunale, has a parapet with the sculpted lids of nine Etruscan sarcophagi; below is the Fontana di Sette Cannelle, the restored city fountain dating from Etrusco-Roman times. North of the city walls is the Museo Archeologico Tuscanese, housed in what was the convent of the adjacent 15th-century church, Santa Maria del Riposo. The long-abandoned ancient nucleus of the town, which includes the two outstanding Romanesque churches of Santa Maria Maggiore and San Pietro, is a 20-minute walk outside the city walls to the southeast.

12

The **Museo Archeologico Tuscanese** displays the necropolis material from two main Etruscan families, the Curunas and Vipinanas, dating from the 4th to 2nd century BC. The family members are depicted on the sarcophagi in typical banqueting position, looking far from undernourished. Also displayed are the grave goods, which would have been buried with them, as well as some helpful photographs showing what the tombs looked like when first excavated. The rooms above have finds stretching back to the 8th century BC, along with some information panels in English. ⊠ *Via della Madonna di Riposo 36* ☎ *0761/436209* ⚐ *Free* ⊘ *Tues.–Sun. 8:30–7:30.*

Where to Stay & Eat

★ **$–$$** ✕ **La Torre di Lavello.** Opposite the town's medieval tower, this trattoria-cum-pizzeria combines efficient service with stylish presentation at very reasonable prices. The menu is varied and imaginative. Highly recommended is the fettuccine *al ragù bianco* (a white sauce with beans), as well as the ricotta cheese *con miele* (with honey) for dessert. To be assured of a seat, arrive early or make a reservation. ⊠ *Via Torre di Lavello 27* ☎ *0761/434258* ⊟ *DC, MC, V* ⊘ *Closed Wed.*

¢ ✕▦ **Locanda di Mirandolina.** Rooms are distinguished by door color rather
Fodor'sChoice than number at a courteously run guesthouse in Tuscania's old town.
★ Simple beds and side chairs furnish the immaculately kept spaces. The intimate restaurant ($$) is an excellent place to sample local recipes such as *pappardelle al cinghiale* (wide, flat pasta with a wild boar sauce). Book well in advance as this is a popular choice, especially with northern Europeans. Locanda di Mirandolina makes a great base for visiting ancient Etruria. ⊠ *Via del Pozzo Bianco 40/42, 01017* ☎▦ *0761/436595* ⊕ *www.mirandolina.it* ⇌ *10 rooms* ⌂ *Restaurant* ⊟ *MC, V* ▯◎ *BP* ⊘ *Closed Jan. 6–Feb. 12. Restaurant closed Tues.*

TUSCIA

The region of Tuscia (the modern name for the Etruscan domain of Etruria) is a landscape of dramatic beauty punctuated by deep, rocky gorges and thickly forested hills, with dappled light falling on wooded paths. This has long been a preferred locale for the retreats of wealthy Romans, a place where they could build grand villas and indulge their sometimes eccentric gardening tastes. The provincial capital, Viterbo, which overshadowed Rome as a center of papal power for a time during the Middle Ages, lies in the heart of Tuscia. The farmland east of Viterbo conceals small quarries of the dark, volcanic peperino stone, which shows up in the walls of many buildings here. Lake Bolsena is an extinct volcano, and the sulfur springs still bubbling up in Viterbo's spas were used by the ancient Romans. Bagnaia and Caprarola are home to palaces and gardens; the garden statuary at Bomarzo is in a league of its own—somewhere between the beautiful and the bizarre.

The ideal way to explore this region is by car. By train from Rome, you can start at Viterbo and get to Bagnaia by local bus. If you're traveling by train or bus, check schedules carefully; you may have to allow for an overnight if you want to see all four locations.

Viterbo

 25 km (16 mi) east of Tuscania, 104 km (64 mi) northwest of Rome.

Viterbo's moment of glory was in the 13th century, when it became the seat of the papal court. The medieval core of the city still sits within 12th-century walls. Its old buildings, with windows bright with geraniums, are made of dark peperino, the local stone that colors the medieval part of Viterbo a dark gray, contrasted here and there with the golden tufa rock of walls and towers. Peperino is also used in the characteristic and typically medieval exterior staircases that you see throughout the old town. More recently, Viterbo has blossomed into a regional commercial center, and much of the modern city is loud and industrial. However, Viterbo's San Pellegrino district is a place to get the feel of the Middle Ages, seeing how daily life is carried on in a setting that has remained practically unchanged over the centuries. The Palazzo Papale and the cathedral enhance the effect. The city has also remained a renowned spa center for its natural hot springs just outside of town, frequented by popes—and the laity—since medieval times.

The Gothic **Palazzo Papale** (Papal Palace) was built in the 13th century as a residence for popes looking to get away from the city. At that time Rome was a notoriously unhealthy place, ridden with malaria and plague and rampaging factions of rival barons. In 1271 the palace was the scene of a novel type of rebellion. A conclave held here to elect a new pope had dragged on for months, apparently making no progress. The people of Viterbo were exasperated by the delay, especially as custom decreed that they had to provide for the cardinals' board and lodging for the duration of the conclave. So they tore the roof off the great hall where the cardinals were meeting, and put them on bread and water. Sure enough, a new pope—Gregory X—was elected in short order. ⊠ *Piazza San Lorenzo* 🕾 *0761/341124.*

The facade and interior of Viterbo's Duomo, **Chiesa di San Lorenzo,** date from the Middle Ages. On the ancient columns inside the cathedral you can see the chips that an exploding bomb took out of the stone during World War II. There's a small adjoining **museum** with a muddle of 18th-century reliquaries, Etruscan sarcophagi, and a crucifixion painting attributed to Michelangelo. ⊠ *Piazza San Lorenzo* 🕾 *0761/ 309623* 🖂 *Church free, museum €3* ☉ *Church 8–12:30 and 3:30–7, museum Fri.–Sun. 9:30–1 and 4–6.*

The medieval district of **San Pellegrino** is one of the best-preserved of such neighborhoods in Italy. It has charming vistas of arches, vaults, towers, exterior staircases, worn wooden doors on great iron hinges, and tiny hanging gardens. You pass many antiques shops as you explore the little squares and byways. The **Fontana Grande** in the piazza of the same name is the largest and most extravagant of Viterbo's authentic Gothic fountains. ⊠ *Via San Pellegrino.*

☪ Viterbo has been a spa town for centuries, and the **Terme dei Papi** continues the tradition. This excellent spa has the usual rundown of health and beauty treatments with an Etruscan twist: try a facial with local volcanic mud, or a steam bath in an ancient cave, where scalding hot mineral water direct from the Bullicam spring splashes down a waterfall to a pool under your feet. The Terme dei Papi's main draw, however, is the *terme* (baths) themselves: a 21,000-square-foot outdoor limestone pool into the shallow end of which Viterbo's famous hot water pours at 59°C (138°F)—and intoxicates with its sulfurous odor. Floats and deck chairs are for rent, but bring your own bathrobe and towel unless you're staying at the hotel. ⊠ *Strada Bagni 12, 5 km (3 mi) west of town center* ☎ *0761/3501* ⊕ *www.termedeipapi.it* ⊠ *Weekdays €12, weekends €15* ⊙ *Pool Wed.–Mon. 9–7, spa daily 9–7.*

Where to Stay & Eat

★ **$$$** ✗ **Enoteca La Torre.** One of the best wine cellars in Italy takes center stage at the elegant Enoteca La Torre. It's also a temple to good eating: in addition to an ever-changing menu there are lists for cheeses, mineral waters, oils, and vinegars. Chestnut fritters and rabbit stew are unusual delicacies, but whatever you choose will be local, traditional, and of the highest quality. ⊠ *Via della Torre 5* ☎ *0761/226467* ⊟ *AE, DC, MC, V* ⊙ *Closed Mon. No lunch Sun.*

★ **¢–$** ✗ **Tre Re.** Viterbo's oldest restaurant—and one of the most ancient in Italy—has been operating in the *centro storico* (historic center) since 1622. The kitchen still focuses on nothing but traditional local cooking and the staff provides open, friendly service. A gregarious buzz of Viterbese businessmen and families fills the small, wood-paneled and white-walled room to overflowing at lunchtime, as diners enjoy the truest versions of specialties such as *acquacotta viterbese* (literally "cooked water") a hearty vegetable and hot-pepper soup that was the ancient sustenance of shepherds and stockmen. ⊠ *Via Macel Gattesco 3* ☎ *0761/304619* ⊟ *AE, MC, V* ⊙ *Closed Thurs.*

¢ ✗ **Cantina Palazzo dei Mercanti.** Enjoy impeccably executed classics for
Fodor'sChoice pocket change at the casual Cantina, which shares a kitchen with the
★ elegant Enoteca La Torre—it's the best lunch value in town. Try whatever is listed as the daily rotating special, such as pappardelle with a tomato-and-meat sauce. You can select a glass or bottle from the Enoteca's epic wine list, which includes a complex matrix of ratings from Italy's foremost wine reviewers. ⊠ *Via della Torre 1* ☎ *0761/226467* ⊟ *AE, DC, MC, V* ⊙ *Closed Sun.*

$$$$ 🏨 **Hotel Niccolò V.** This upscale, airy hotel is connected to Viterbo's mineral baths and spa at Terme dei Papi. The complex is a surreal mix of doctors in scrubs, bathers in bathrobes, and lost hotel guests wandering through an enormous mazelike lobby. In the guest rooms, though, marble baths and wooden floors provide a country-house elegance. Breakfast, a sumptuous buffet, is taken in a wood-beam gallery overlooking a small garden. Hotel guests have free use of the baths, as well as the option of half or full pension. ⊠ *Strada Bagni 12, 01100, 5 km (3 mi) west of center* ☎ *0761/350555* 🖷 *0761/350273* ⊕ *www. termedeipapi.it/soggiornare/hotel.html* ⇋ *20 rooms, 3 suites* ⟢ *Restaurant, in-room safes, minibars, pool, spa, bar, meeting rooms* ⊟ *AE, DC, MC, V* ⊙ *Pool closed Tues.* ⎮⊙⎮ *BP.*

Bagnaia

 5 km (3 mi) east of Viterbo.

The village of Bagnaia is the site of 16th-century cardinal Alessandro Montalto's summer retreat. The hillside garden and park that surround the two small, identical residences are the real draw, designed by virtuoso architect Giacomo Barozzi (circa 1507–73), known as Vignola, who later worked with Michelangelo on St. Peter's.

Villa Lante is a terraced extravaganza. On the lowest terrace a delightful Italian garden has a centerpiece fountain fed by water channeled down the hillside. On another terrace, a stream of water runs through a groove carved in a long stone table where the cardinal entertained his friends alfresco, chilling wine in the running water. That's only one of the most evident and of the whimsical water games that were devised for the cardinal. The symmetry of the formal gardens contrasts with the wild, untamed park adjacent to it, reflecting the paradoxes of nature and artifice that are the theme of this pleasure garden. ⊠ *Via G. Baroni 71* ☎ *0761/288008* 🖾 *Park free, gardens and residences €2* ☉ *Tues.–Sun. 8:30–1 hr before sunset.*

Caprarola

 21 km (16 mi) southeast of Bagnaia, 19 km (12 mi) southeast of Viterbo.

The wealthy and powerful Farnese family took over this sleepy village in the 1500s and had Vignola design a huge palace and gardens to rival the great residences of Rome. The architect also rearranged the little town of Caprarola, to enhance the palazzo's setting.

The massive, magnificent, 400-year-old **Palazzo Farnese,** built on an unusual pentagonal plan, has an ingenious system of ramps and terraces that leads right up to the main portal. This nicely allowed carriages and mounts to arrive directly in front of the door. Though the salons are unfurnished, the palace's grandeur is still evident. An artificial grotto decorates one wall, the ceilings are covered with frescoes glorifying the Farnese family, and an entire room is frescoed with maps of the world as it was known to 16th-century cartographers. From the windows you can glimpse the garden, which can be visited on weekdays and Saturday with a guided tour (departing every half hour at 10, 11, noon, and 3) and Sunday at 10, noon, 3, and 5. ⊠ *Piazza Farnese* ☎ *0761/646052* 🖾 *€2* ☉ *Tues.–Sun. 8:30–1 hr before sunset.*

Bomarzo

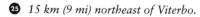 *15 km (9 mi) northeast of Viterbo.*

🕙 The eerie 16th-century **Parco dei Mostri** (Monster Park) is populated by weird and fantastic sculptures of mythical creatures and eccentric architecture. It was created by Prince Vicino Orsini for his wife, Giulia Farnese, who is said to have taken one look at the park and died of heart failure. No one really knows why the prince had the sculptures carved in outcroppings of stone in a dusky wood on his estate, but it probably has something to do with the artifices that were an artistic conceit of his time. Children love it, and there are photo ops galore. ✛ *1½ km (1 mi) west of town* ☎ *0761/924029* 🎟 *€8* ☉ *Daily 8:30–1 hr before sunset.*

TIVOLI, PALESTRINA & SUBIACO   12

East of Rome are two of Lazio's star attractions—the Villa Adriana and the Villa d'Este in Tivoli—and in the mountains beyond them, the lesser-known and wonderfully peaceful Palestrina and Subiaco. The road from Rome to Tivoli passes through uninspiring industrial areas and burgeoning suburbs that used to be lush countryside. You know you're close to Tivoli when you see vast quarries of travertine marble and smell the sulfurous vapors from the not-so-interesting Bagni di Tivoli spa.

With a car you can continue your loop through the mountains east of Rome, taking in two very different sights that are both focused on religion. The ancient pagan sanctuary at Palestrina is set on the slopes of Mt. Ginestro, from which it commands a sweeping view of the green plain and distant mountains. Subiaco, the cradle of Western monasticism, is tucked away in the mountains above Tivoli and Palestrina. Unless you start out very early and have lots of energy, plan an overnight stop along the way if you want to take in all three.

Tivoli

㉖ *36 km (22 mi) northeast of Rome.*

★ **Villa Adriana** (Hadrian's Villa) was an exclusive retreat, where the marvels of the classical world were reproduced for the ruler's pleasure. Hadrian, who succeeded Trajan as emperor in AD 117, was a man of genius and intellectual curiosity. From AD 118 to 130, architects, laborers, and artists worked on the villa below the ancient settlement of Tibur, periodically spurred on by the emperor himself when he returned from a voyage full of new design ideas. After his death in AD 138 the fortunes of his villa declined. It was sacked by barbarians and Romans alike; many of his statues and decorations ended up in the Vatican Museums, but the expansive ruins are nonetheless compelling.

It's not the single elements but the delightful effect of the whole that makes Hadrian's Villa a treat. Oleanders, pines, and cypresses growing among the ruins heighten the visual impact. To help you get your bearings, maps are issued free with the audio guides (€4). A visit here takes about two hours, more if you like to savor antiquity slowly. After sunset on Friday from June through August, a one-hour tour under spotlights is available for €8. It must, however, be booked in advance. Otherwise, in summer visit early to take advantage of cool morn-

> **WORD OF MOUTH**
>
> "Villa d'Este's gardens lived up to everything they were supposed to be, though the villa itself was nothing special and unfurnished. The fountains were spectacular, and I can only imagine how they must have been new."
>
> –Vickitty

ings. ☒ *Bivio di Villa Adriana off Via Tiburtina, 6 km (4 mi) southwest of Tivoli* ☏ *0774/530203, 0774/382733 reservations* ☒ *€6.50* ⊗ *Daily 9–1 hr before sunset.*

★ **Villa d'Este,** a late-Renaissance estate, is a playground of artistic whimsy, manifested in the 80-some fountains of all shapes and sizes that tumble down the vast, steep hillside garden. Cardinal Ippolito d'Este (1509–72), an active figure in the political intrigues of mid-16th-century Italy, set about proving his dominance over man and nature by commissioning this monument to architectural excess. His builders tore down part of a Franciscan monastery to clear the site, then diverted the Aniene River to water the garden and feed the fountains. The musical **Fontana dell'Organo** and the animated **Fontana della Civetta** have been restored to working order: the organ plays a watery tune every two hours 10:30–6:30, and the mechanical *civetta* (owl) chases warbling sparrow figures out of the bath every two hours 10–6. On the other side of the garden the more timeworn **Fontana di Roma** is a scale model representing Rome's river network and mythology as well as some of its ancient buildings. Allow an hour for this visit, and bear in mind that there are a lot of stairs to climb. ☒ *Piazza Trento 1* ☏ *0774/312070* ⊕ *www. villadestetivoli.info* ☒ *€6.50* ⊗ *Tues.–Sun. 8:30–1 hr before sunset.*

Where to Stay & Eat

$ ✕ **Del Falcone.** A central location—on Tivoli's main street leading off Largo Garibaldi—means that this restaurant is popular and often crowded. In the ample and rustic dining rooms you can try homemade *crespella* (a rolled pancake), flavored with nuts or ricotta cheese and spinach. Country-style grilled meats are excellent. ☒ *Via Del Trevio 34* ☏ *0774/312358* ▤ *AE, DC, MC, V.*

$$ ✕▣ **Adriano.** The green surroundings here, at the entrance to Hadrian's Villa, provide a restful backdrop for the Adriano's 10 rooms, which are casually elegant and immaculately kept. Some have ironwork beds and some wood. The restaurant ($$–$$$) is sophisticated Italian, as in the risotto *ai fiori di zucchine* (with zucchini flowers). You can relax and dine at outdoor tables in summer. ☒ *Via di Villa Adriana 194, 00010* ☏ *0774/382235* ☒ *0774/535122* ⊕ *www.hoteladriano.it* ☞ *7 rooms, 3 suites* ᓑ *Restaurant, in-room safes, refrigerators, cable TV, tennis court, bar, meeting room, some pets allowed (fee); no smoking* ▤ *AE, DC, MC, V* ⊗ *No dinner Sun. Nov.–Mar.* ⦿ *BP.*

Palestrina

㉗ *27 km (17 mi) southeast of Tivoli, 37 km (23 mi) east of Rome.*

Except to students of ancient history and music lovers, Palestrina is surprisingly little known outside Italy. Its most famous native son, Giovanni Pierluigi da Palestrina, born here in 1525, was the renowned composer of 105 masses, as well as madrigals, magnificats, and motets. But the town was celebrated long before the composer's lifetime.

Ancient Praeneste (modern Palestrina) flourished much earlier than Rome. It was the site of the Temple of Fortuna Primigenia, which dates from the 2nd century BC. This was one of the largest, richest, most frequented temple complexes in all antiquity—people came from far and wide to consult its famous oracle. In modern times no one had any idea of the extent of the complex until World War II bombings exposed ancient foundations occupying huge artificial terraces stretching from the upper part of the town as far downhill as its central Duomo.

Large arches and terraces scale the hillside up to the imposing **Palazzo Barberini,** built in the 17th century along the semicircular lines of the original temple. It now contains the **Museo Nazionale Archeologico di Palestrina,** with material found on the site that dates from throughout the classical period. This well-labeled collection of Etruscan bronzes, pottery, and terra-cotta statuary as well as Roman artifacts takes second place to the chief attraction, a 1st-century BC mosaic representing the Nile in flood. This delightful work—a large-scale composition in which form, color, and innumerable details captivate the eye—is alone worth the trip to Palestrina. But there's more: a model of the temple as it was in ancient times helps you appreciate the immensity of the original construction. ⊠ *Piazza della Cortina 1* ☎ *06/9538100* ✎ *€3* ⊙ *Museum daily 9–7, archaeological temple zone daily 9–1 hr before sunset.*

Where to Stay & Eat

$ ✕⌂ **Hotel Stella.** Expect a cordial welcome at the restaurant ($–$$) of the central Hotel Stella in Palestrina's public garden. The menu lists local dishes such as light and freshly made fettuccine served with a choice of sauces, as well as unusual combinations such as *pasta e fagioli con frutti di mare* (pasta and bean soup with shellfish). Decor tends toward the bright and fanciful. The guest rooms are frilly and a bit worn, but clean and comfortable. ⊠ *Piazzale Liberazione 3, 00036* ☎ *06/9538172* 🖷 *06/9573360* ⊕ *www.hotelstella.it* ✄ *30 rooms* ⌂ *Restaurant, cable TV, bar; no a/c in some rooms* ⊟ *AE, DC, MC, V* ¹⊙¹ *BP.*

Subiaco

🛎 *38 km (24 mi) northeast of Palestrina, 54 km (33 mi) northeast of Rome.*

Among wooded mountains in the deep and narrow valley of the Aniene River, Subiaco is a modern town built over World War II rubble. It is chiefly known (aside from being the birthplace of Gina Lollobrigida, whose family name is common in these parts) as the site of the cave where St. Benedict retreated into meditation and prayer and later founded the Benedictine order in the monastery that still stands today. Even earlier, the place was a refuge of Nero, who built a villa here said to have rivaled that of Hadrian at Tivoli, damming the river to create three lakes and a series of waterfalls. The road to the monastery passes the ruins of the emperor's villa.

Convento di Santa Scolastica, between Subiaco and St. Benedict's hermitage on the mountainside, is the only hermitage founded by St. Benedict to have survived the Lombard invasion of Italy in the 9th century. It has three cloisters extant; the oldest dates from the end of the 12th century. The monastery was the site of the first print shop in Italy, set up in 1464, and the library houses priceless ancient manuscripts and extensive archives.

The museum displays an interesting mix of archaeological, geological, and ethnological finds from the area in vaulted cellars beneath the monastery. ⊠ *Road to Jenne and Vallepietra, 3 km (2 mi) east of Subiaco* ☎ *0774/ 82421* 🖾 *Hermitage free, museum €2.50* ⊘ *Daily 9–12:15 and 3:30–6:30.*

The 6th-century **Monastero di San Benedetto**—still active—is a landmark of Western monasticism. It was built over the grotto where the saint lived and meditated. Clinging to the cliff on nine great arches, it has resisted assaults for almost 900 years. Over the little wooden veranda at the entrance, a Latin inscription wishes PEACE TO THOSE WHO ENTER. The upper church is covered with frescoes by Umbrian and Sienese artists of the 14th century. In front of the main altar a stairway leads to the lower church, carved out of the rock, with another stairway leading down to the grotto where Benedict lived as a hermit for three years. The frescoes here are even earlier than those above; look for the portrait of St. Francis of Assisi, painted in the early 13th century, in the **Cappella di San Gregorio** (Chapel of St. Gregory), and for the monastery's oldest fresco, painted in the Byzantine style in the 7th century, in the **Grotta dei Pastori** (Shepherds' Grotto). ⊠ *Subiaco* ☎ *0774/85039* ⊕ *www. benedettini-subiaco.it* 🖾 *Free* ⊘ *Daily 9–12:30 and 3–6:30.*

Where to Stay & Eat

¢–$$ ✕ **Frà Diavolo.** About 5 km (3 mi) outside Subiaco on the road up to Cervara—right at the junction to Monte Livata—is this cheerful restaurant-cum-pizzeria. Choose between the sunny eating area inside or the fairly makeshift outdoor terrace. Brisk but courteous servers bring local specialties such as *strozzapreti alla Frà Diavolo* (homemade pasta with tomatoes, eggplant, mozzarella, and basil) to your table. ⊠ *Contrada Colle Perino 15* ☎ *0774/83850* ☰ *AE, DC, MC, V* ⊘ *Closed Mon.*

$ 🏠 **Foresteria del Monastero.** Part of the Santa Scolastica monastery complex has been tastefully renewed to create an efficient hotel. Doubles and triples have inexpensive modern furnishings. You have the option of half board per day or full board. Well-marked trails lead from the Foresteria up to the monastery of St. Benedict. The monastery's bells start ringing at 8 AM, so late sleepers might think twice. ⊠ *Monastero Santa Scolastica, Piazzale dei Monasteri, 00028* ☎ *0774/85569* 🖶 *0774/ 822862* ⊕ *www.benedettini-subiaco.it* 🛏 *46 rooms* 🍴 *Restaurant, bar, 2 meeting rooms; no smoking* ☰ *AE, DC, MC, V* 🍽 *BP, MAP, FAP.*

SERMONETA, NINFA & SPERLONGA

This trio of romantic places south of Rome, set in a landscape defined by low mountains and a broad coastal plain, lures you into a past that seems centuries away from the city's bustle. Sermoneta is a castle town. Ninfa, nearby, is a noble family's fairy-tale garden that is open to the public only at limited times. Both are on the eastern fringe of the Pontine Plain, once a malaria-infested marshland that was ultimately reclaimed for agriculture by one of the most successful projects of Mussolini's regime. Sperlonga is a medieval fishing village perched above the sea near one of emperor Tiberius's most fabulous villas. You need a car to see them all in a day or so, and to get to Ninfa. But Sermoneta and Sperlonga are accessible by public transit.

Sermoneta

 80 km (50 mi) southeast of Rome.

In Sermoneta the town and castle are one. In medieval times concentric rings of walls protected the townspeople and provided shelter from marauders for nearby farmers. The lords—in this case the Caetani family—held a last line of defense in the tall tower, where if necessary they could cut themselves off by pulling up the drawbridge.

The **Castello Caetani** dates from the 1200s. In the 15th century, having won the castle by ruse from the Caetanis, Borgia Pope Alexander VI transformed it into a formidable fortress and handed it over to his son Cesare. The chiaroscuro of dark and light stone, the quiet of the narrow streets, and the bastions that hint at siege and battle take you back in time. Admission is by guided tour (in Italian) only; tours leave on the hour. ✉ *Via della Fortezza* ☎*0773/695404* 💲*€5* ⊘ *Apr.–Oct., Fri.–Wed. 10:30–11:30 and 3–6; Nov.–Mar., Fri.–Wed. 10:30–11:30 and 2–4.*

Ninfa

 5 km (3 mi) south of Ninfa, 75 km (47 mi) southeast of Rome.

A place of rare beauty, a dream garden of romantic ruins and rushing waters, of exotic flora and fragrant blooms: Ninfa today is a preserve of the Worldwide Fund for Nature (WWF), managed in collaboration with Caetani heirs. In the Middle Ages, this was a thriving village, part of the Caetani family's vast landholdings around Sermoneta. It was abandoned when malaria-carrying mosquitoes infested the plain, and it fell into ruin. Over the course of the 20th century, generations of the Caetani family, including English and American spouses and gardening buffs, created the garden and brought Ninfa back to life. You can visit by guided tour only; call ahead for reservations. ✉ *Via Ninfina, Doganella di Ninfa* ☎ *0773/354241, 0773/695404 APT Latina-Provincial Tourist Office* 💲*€8* ⊘ *Apr.–Oct, weekends 9:30–noon and 2:30–6.*

Sperlonga

 64 km (40 mi) southeast of Ninfa, 127 km (79 mi) southeast of Rome.

Sperlonga is a labyrinth of whitewashed alleys, arches, and little houses, like a casbah wrapped around a hilltop overlooking the sea, with broad, sandy beaches on either side. Long a favorite haunt of artists and artisans in flight from Rome's quick pace, the town has ancient origins. The medieval town gates, twisting alleys, and watchtower were vital to its defense when pirate ships came in sight. Now they simply make this former fishing town even more pictorial.

> **WORD OF MOUTH**
>
> "You can take a train from Rome's Termini to Sperlonga, then a local bus to the beach front. There are miles of unspoilt beaches, as well as the remains of Roman emperors' homes and a notable museum close by."
>
> —Huitres

Under a cliff on the shore only 1 km (½ mi) south of Sperlonga are the ruins of a grandiose villa built for Roman emperor Tiberius and known as the **Grotta di Tiberio.** The villa incorporated several natural grottoes, in one of which Tiberius dined with guests on an artificial island. The various courses were served on little boats that floated across the shallow seawater pool to the emperor's table. Showpieces of the villa were the colossal sculpture groups embellishing the grotto. The **Museo Nazionale** was built on the site especially to hold the fragments of these sculptures, discovered by chance by an amateur archaeologist. The huge statues had been smashed to pieces centuries earlier by Byzantine monks unsympathetic to pagan images. For decades the subject and appearance of the originals remained a mystery, and the museum was a work in progress as scholars there tried to put together the 7,000 pieces of this giant puzzle. Their achievement, the immense Scylla group, largest of the sculptures, is on view here. ⊠ *Via Flacca (SS213), Km 16.5, 2 km (1 mi) southwest of Sperlonga* ☎ *0771/548028* ⊠ €2 ⊗ *Daily 8:30–7:30.*

Where to Stay & Eat

$$–$$$ ✕ **Gli Archi.** On a landing of one of Sperlonga's myriad stairways, Gli Archi has a cute *piazzetta* with tables for fair-weather dining. Brick-arch interiors add a touch of refinement that puts this restaurant a cut above establishments closer to the beach. The owners take pride in serving high-quality ingredients with culinary simplicity. Seafood, including the house favorite *pennette alla seppiolina* (pasta with cuttlefish ink), predominates, but there are a few meat platters, too. ⊠ *Via Ottaviano 17* ☎ *0771/ 548300* ▭ *AE, DC, MC, V* ⊗ *Closed Wed. and Jan.*

$$$ ▣ **La Sirenella.** Rest a night at a family-run hotel occupying a prime position on Sperlonga's sandy beach, which is short walk from the old town. Rooms are bright and airy with blue-and-white striped spreads and some French doors that open to small balconies. Ask for a room on one of the upper floors in the *ala mare* (sea wing) to enjoy views of the Circeo promontory and the lapping waves. ⊠ *Via Cristoforo Colombo 25, 01100* ☎ *0771/549186* 🖶 *0771/549189* ⊕ *www.lasirenella.com* ⮢ *40 rooms* ♻ *Restaurant, cable TV, in-room data ports, beach, bar* ▭ *MC, V* ⦿ *FAP.*

ROME SIDE TRIPS ESSENTIALS

Transportation

BY BUS

COTRAL buses leave Rome for Cerveteri from the Lepanto stop of Metro A, with service every 40 minutes or so during the day. The ride takes about 70 minutes. Tuscania has a regular bus connection with Viterbo.

Buses leave Rome for Tivoli every 15 minutes from the terminal at the Ponte Mammolo stop on Metro B, but not all take the route that passes near Hadrian's Villa. Inquire which bus passes closest to the villa and tell the driver to let you off there. The ride takes about one hour. From Rome to Palestrina, take the COTRAL bus from the Anagnina stop on Metro A. From Rome to Subiaco, take the COTRAL bus from the

Ponte Mammolo stop on Metro B; buses leave every 40 minutes; the circuitous trip takes one hour and 45 minutes.

COTRAL buses for Viterbo depart from the Saxa Rubra stop of the Ferrovie COTRAL train. The *diretta* (direct) bus takes about 75 minutes. Bagnaia can be reached from Viterbo by local city bus. For Caprarola, COTRAL buses leave from the Saxa Rubra station on the Roma Nord line.

COTRAL buses for Sermoneta leave Rome from the EUR Fermi stop of Metro B. The ride takes about one hour.

🚍 Bus Information **COTRAL** ☎ 800/431784 ⊕ www.cotralspa.it.

BY CAR

To get from Rome to Ostia (a 30- to 40-minute trip), follow Via del Mare southwest, which leads directly there. If approaching from Rome's ring road, look for the Ostiense or Ostia Antica exit.

For Cerveteri, take either the A12 Rome–Civitavecchia toll highway to the Cerveteri-Ladispoli exit. There's also the Via Aurelia, a scenic coastal route, although it has stoplights and is subject to traffic. The trip takes about 40 minutes on the autostrada, twice that on the slow road. To get to Tarquinia, take the A12 Rome–Civitavecchia highway all the way to the end, where you continue on the Via Aurelia to Tarquinia. The trip takes about one hour. From that point, Tuscania is inland another half hour.

For Tivoli, take the Rome–L'Aquila autostrada (A24). To get to Palestrina directly from Rome, take the Autostrada del Sole (A2) to the San Cesareo exit and follow signs for Palestrina; this trip takes about one hour. From Rome to Subiaco, take S155 east for about 40 km (25 mi) and the S411 for 25 km (15½ mi); the trip takes about 70 minutes.

For Viterbo, Bagnaia, and Bomarzo, head out of Rome on the A1 autostrada, exiting at Attigliano. Bomarzo is only 3 km (2 mi) from the autostrada. The trip takes one hour.

The fastest route to sites south of Rome is the Via Pontina, an expressway. For Sermoneta, turn northeast at Latina. The trip takes about 50 minutes. For out-of-the-way Ninfa, proceed as for Sermoneta, but before reaching Sermoneta follow the signs for Doganella/Ninfa. The trip takes about one hour. For Sperlonga, take the Via Pontina to Latina, then the Via Appia to Terracina and Sperlonga. The trip takes about 1½ hours.

EMERGENCY SERVICES Your car-rental company should be your first resource if you have car trouble, but it's good to know that ACI, the Italian auto club, offers 24-hour roadside assistance (free to members, for a fee to nonmembers).
🚗 **ACI** ☎ 803/116.

BY TRAIN

Regular train service links the Ostia Antica station with Rome's Piramide Metro B Line station, near Porta San Paolo. Exit the Metro and go to the station called Ostia Lido adjacent to the Metro station. The ride takes about 35 minutes. Trains depart every half hour throughout the day.

For many destinations, you may need to take a combination of train and bus. From stations in Rome, FS and Metropolitana suburban trains take you to the Cerveteri-Ladispoli station, where you can get a bus for Cerveteri. The train takes 30 minutes; the bus ride then takes 15 minutes. To get to Tarquinia, take an FS train (Rome–Genoa line) from Rome or from Cerveteri to the Tarquinia station (this service is sometimes operated by bus between Civitavecchia and Tarquinia), then a local bus from the station up to the hilltop town. The trip takes about 75–90 minutes. There's a fast train service, the FM3, from Rome to Viterbo, which takes an hour and 40 minutes. Tuscania is accessible by bus from Viterbo. Trains also stop at Bagnaia, 10 minutes beyond Viterbo.

FS trains connect Rome's Termini and Tiburtina stations with Tivoli in about one hour. Villa d'Este is about a 20-minute uphill walk from the station at Tivoli. The FS train from Stazione Termini to Palestrina takes about 40 minutes; you can then board a bus from the train station to the center of town.

FS trains on the Rome–Formia–Naples line stop at Latina, where you can get a local bus to Sermoneta, though service is erratic. Traveling time is about one hour. For Sperlonga, on the same line, get off at the Itri station, from which buses leave for Sperlonga. The trip takes about 1½ hours.

▪ Train Information **FS–Trenitalia** ☎ 892021 ⊕ www.trenitalia.com.

Contacts & Resources

EMERGENCIES

Emergency numbers (listed below) are accessible from every phone, including cellular phones, all over Italy. If you have ongoing medical concerns, it's a good idea to make sure someone is on duty all night where you're staying—not a given in Lazio. As elsewhere in Italy, every pharmacy in Lazio bears a sign at the door listing area pharmacies open in off-hours, though in the countryside you may need a car to get to one.

▪ **Ambulance** ☎118. **Carabinieri** (Military Police) ☎112. **Emergencies** ☎113. **Fire** ☎115.

TOURS

CIT has half-day excursions to Villa d'Este in Tivoli. American Express has tours to Hadrian's Villa. Appian Line has excursions to Hadrian's Villa. Carrani Tours has tours that include Hadrian's Villa. For Viterbo, authorized guides are available through the APT office.

▪ Fees & Schedules **American Express** ☎ 06/67641. **Appian Line** ☎ 06/487861. **Carrani Tours** ☎06/4742501. **CIT** ☎06/478641. **Viterbo APT** ✉Piazza San Carluccio ☎0761/304795.

VISITOR INFORMATION

▪ Tourist Information **Cerveteri** ✉Piazza Aldo Moro 1 ☎06/99552637 ⊕www.comune.cerveteri.rm.it. **Palestrina** ✉ Piazza Santa Maria degli Angeli ☎ 06/9573176. **Subiaco** ✉ Via Cadorna 59 ☎ 0774/822013. **Tarquinia** ✉ Piazza Cavour 1 ☎ 0766/856384 ⊕ www.tarquinia.net. **Tivoli** ✉ Largo Garibaldi ☎ 0774/334522 ⊕ www.tivoli.it/turismo.htm. **Tuscania** ✉ Via del Comune 1 ☎ 0761/436371. **Viterbo** ✉ Piazza San Carluccio 5 ☎ 0761/304795.

Naples & Campania

Villa Cimbrone, Ravello

WORD OF MOUTH

"Pompeii was everything I expected and more. I swear I could feel the spirits of the people going about their daily tasks, visiting the bar, the bakery, the spa, whisking down the street, being mindful to stay on the sidewalk and not step in the 'gutter.'"

—artstuff

"Napoli is a lively, vibrant and chaotic town. In short, it swings."

—ira

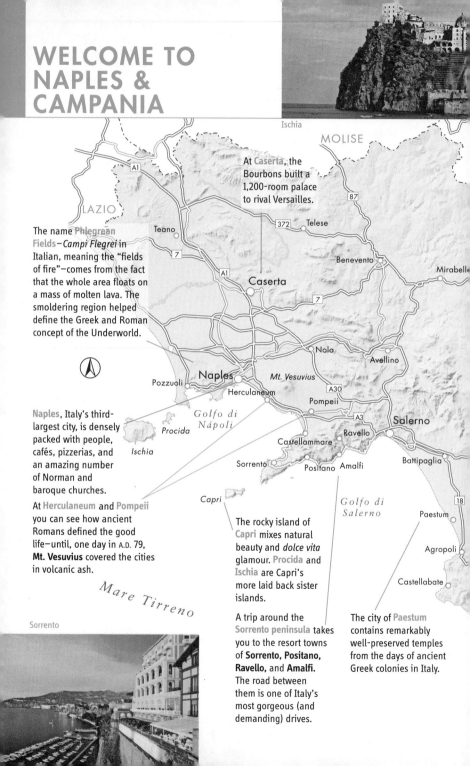

WELCOME TO NAPLES & CAMPANIA

Ischia

MOLISE

At **Caserta**, the Bourbons built a 1,200-room palace to rival Versailles.

The name **Phlegrean Fields**—*Campi Flegrei* in Italian, meaning the "fields of fire"—comes from the fact that the whole area floats on a mass of molten lava. The smoldering region helped define the Greek and Roman concept of the Underworld.

LAZIO

Teano

372 Telese

Benevento

Mirabell

Caserta

Nola

Avellino

Naples, Italy's third-largest city, is densely packed with people, cafés, pizzerias, and an amazing number of Norman and baroque churches.

Pozzuoli

Naples

Herculaneum

Mt. Vesuvius

A30

Pompeii

A3

Salerno

Golfo di Nápoli

Procida

Ischia

Ravello

Castellammare

Battipaglia

Sorrento

Positano Amalfi

At **Herculaneum** and **Pompeii** you can see how ancient Romans defined the good life—until, one day in A.D. 79, **Mt. Vesuvius** covered the cities in volcanic ash.

Capri

Golfo di Salerno

18

Paestum

Agropoli

Mare Tirreno

The rocky island of **Capri** mixes natural beauty and *dolce vita* glamour. **Procida** and **Ischia** are Capri's more laid back sister islands.

Castellabate

Sorrento

A trip around the **Sorrento peninsula** takes you to the resort towns of **Sorrento, Positano, Ravello,** and **Amalfi.** The road between them is one of Italy's most gorgeous (and demanding) drives.

The city of **Paestum** contains remarkably well-preserved temples from the days of ancient Greek colonies in Italy.

Getting Oriented

The Golfo di Napoli (Bay of Naples) holds most of Campania's attractions, including Italy's most famous resort towns, its greatest archaeological sites, and the city of Naples itself. Farther south are Greek ruins and the main draw inland is a monumental Bourbon palace.

Street, Pompeii

PUGLIA

A16

BASILICATA

Polla

Teggiano

A3

18

0   20 mi

0   20 km

TOP 5
Reasons to Go

1 **Walking the streets of Naples:** Its energy, chaos, and bursts of beauty make Naples the most operatic of Italian cities.

2 **Exploring Pompeii:** The excavated ruins of Pompeii are a unique and occasionally spooky glimpse into everyday life—and sudden death—in Roman times.

3 **Ravello:** High above the Amalfi coast, two spectacular villas compete for the title of most beautiful spot in southern Italy.

4 **The gardens of the Reggia di Caserta:** The Reggia (royal palace) in Caserta was the Bourbon monarchs' attempt to outdo Versailles. With the splendid gardens, covering 296 acres, they almost succeeded.

5 **Fresh buffalo-milk mozzarella:** One of the region's unique culinary experiences, the softball-sized white cheese is served without unnecessary garnish (other than perhaps a slice of tomato and a sprig of basil) in practically any of Campania's restaurants.

Plaster Cast, Pompeii   Royal Palace, Naples

NAPLES & CAMPANIA PLANNER

Making the Most of Your Time

In Campania, there are three primary travel experiences: Naples, with its restless exuberance; the resorts (Capri, Sorrento, the Amalfi Coast), dedicated to leisure and indulgence; and the archaeological sights (Pompeii, Herculaneum, Paestum), where the ancient world is frozen in time. Each is wonderful in its own way. If you have a week, you can get a good taste of all three, but with less time, you're better off choosing between them rather than stretching yourself thin.

Pompeii is the simplest to plan for: it's a day trip. You can easily spend the full day there, but moving at a fast clip you can see the highlights and head on to Herculaneum (if you're into archaeology) or back to your home base (if you're not). To get a feel for Naples, you should give it a couple of days at a minimum. The train station makes a harsh first impression, but the city grows on you as you take in the sights and interact with the locals.

That said, many people bypass Naples and head right for the resorts. More than anywhere else in Campania, you're rewarded here for slowing down and taking your time. These places are all about relaxing—you'll miss the point if you're in a rush. Sorrento isn't as spectacular as Positano or Capri, but it's a good base because of its central location.

Getting Around

You can get along fine without a car in Campania, and there are plenty of reasons not to have one: traffic in Naples is even worse than in Rome; you can't bring a car to Capri or Ischia (except in winter, when everything's closed); and parking in the towns of the Amalfi Coast is hard to come by.

The efficient (though slightly rundown) Circumvesuviana train travels around the bay from Naples to Sorrento, with stops at Pompeii and Herculaneum. Ferries and hydrofoils connect Naples with the islands and Sorrento, and there's ferry service between the islands, Sorrento, and the Amalfi Coast.

The SITA public bus system's Blue Line makes hourly runs along the spectacular coast road between Sorrento and Positano. It's inexpensive and efficient, and you're spared a white-knuckle driving experience. Aim for a seat on the side of the bus facing the water. For more about transportation throughout the region, see "Essentials" at the end of this chapter.

Pompeii Prep

Pompeii is impressive under any circumstances, but it comes alive if you do some preparation before your visit:

■ First, read up—there are piles of good books on the subject, including these engaging, jargon-free histories: *Pompeii: The Day a City Died* by Robert Etienne, *Pompeii: Public and Private Life* by Paul Zanker, and *The Lost World of Pompeii* by Colin Amery. For accurate historical information woven into the pages of a thriller, pick up *Pompeii: A Novel* by Robert Harris.

■ Second, be sure to visit the Museo Archeologico Nazionale in Naples. Most of the finest art from Pompeii now resides in the museum.

Safety Tips

Don't let fear of crime keep you away from Naples, but, just as in other large Italian cities, take common-sense precautions—look under "Safety" in the Smart Travel Tips section at the back of this book for pointers. The main risks in Naples are car break-ins, bag-snatching, pick-pocketing, and fraud. Give twosomes on scooters a wide berth—this is a favored method of bag-snatchers. Never make major purchases, such as digital cameras, from unlicensed dealers as goods can be artfully switched with worthless packages right under your nose. And be particularly vigilant around the central station area of Piazza Garibaldi.

Testing the Waters

Beaches here can be disappointing—most are patches of coarse sand. That doesn't mean you shouldn't pack your swim suit, but leave any Caribbean-inspired expectations behind. The area around Positano has the best beach options: Spaggia Grande (the main beach) is pleasant; a little further west, Spaggia di Fornillo gets better; and you can go by boat to the remote Spaggia di Laurito for a leisurely day of swimming and lunching on seafood. On Ischia, there's a half-mile stretch of fine sand at Ischia Ponte, and on Capri you can take a dip in the waters around the famous Faraglioni rock formation. You may not be won over by the sand, but the water itself is spectacular, with infinite varieties of blue shimmering in the sun, turning transparent in the coves.

Choosing a Place to Stay

Most parts of Campania have accommodations in all price categories, but they tend to fill up in high season, so reserve well in advance. In summer, hotels on the coast that serve meals almost always require you to take half board.

Dining & Lodging Price Categories

WHAT IT COSTS in Euros

	$$$$	$$$	$$	$	¢
Restaurants	over €45	€35–€45	€25–€35	€15–€25	under €15
Hotels	over €220	€160–€220	€110–€160	€70–€110	under €70

Restaurant prices are for a first course (primo), second course (secondo), and dessert (dolce). Hotel prices are for two people in a standard double room in high season, including tax and service.

13

How's the Weather?

Campania is not at its best in summer, when Naples swelters and Vesuvius is obscured by haze. Optimum times are May–June and September–October. Visiting in winter can be an appealing choice—the temperature remains comfortable and rain is relatively rare. Be aware, though, that while a few hotels and restaurants in Sorrento and along the Amalfi Coast are open year-round, the islands of the bay shut down from November to March.

Amalfi Coast

TOP PASSEGGIATA

Chic Neapolitans take their evening stroll on and around Piazza dei Martiri, stopping at the boutiques, bookstores, and antiques shops of the neighboring streets, particularly the stretch between Via Carlo Poerio and Via dei Mille.

Updated by
Chris Rose

CAMPANIA IS A REGION OF EVOCATIVE NAMES—Capri, Sorrento, Pompeii, Herculaneum—that conjure up visions of cliff-shaded coves, sundappled waters, and mighty ruins. The area's unique geology is responsible for its gorgeous landscape. A languid coastline stretches out along a deep blue sea, punctuated by rocky islands. Heading inland, the hills at first roll gently, then transform into mountains. Dense olive groves line the southern Cilento peninsula; vineyards flourish near Benevento and Avellino; and, spreading north toward Caserta and Rome, are the mozzarella- and tomato-producing plains.

Through the ages, the area's temperate climate, warm sea, fertile soil, and natural beauty have attracted Greek colonists, then Roman tourists—who gave the region the Campania Felix ("the happy land")—and later Saracen raiders and Spanish invaders. The result has been a rich and varied history, reflected in everything from architecture to mythology. The highlights span millennia: the near-intact Roman towns of Pompeii and Herculaneum, the amphitheaters of Pozzuoli and Capua, the Greek temples in Paestum and Cuma, the Norman and baroque churches in Naples, the white-dome fisherman's houses on the island of Procida. In the realm of myth, Cuma was home to the fortune-telling Sibyl, Herculaneum was built by Hercules, and Lake Averno was the gateway to the underworld.

Campania's complex identity is most intensely felt in its major city, Naples. It sprawls around its bay as though attempting to embrace the island of Capri, while behind it Mt. Vesuvius glowers. Naples is lush, chaotic, scary, funny, confounding, intoxicating, and very beautiful. Few who visit remain ambivalent. You needn't participate in the mad whirl of the city, however. The best pastime in Campania is simply finding a spot with a stunning view and indulging in *"la dolce far niente"* ("the sweetness of doing nothing").

NAPLES

In the period before the Italian unification of 1860, Naples rivaled Paris as a brilliant and refined cultural capital, the ultimate destination for northern European travelers on their Grand Tour. A decade of far-sighted city administration and a massive injection of European Union funds have kick-started the city back on course, though it is still a difficult place for the casual visitor to take a quick liking to: noise and air pollution levels are uncomfortably high; unemployment protest marches and industrial disputes frequently disrupt public transportation and may even result in the temporary closure of major tourist attractions. Armed with the right attitude—"be prepared for the worst but hope for the best"—you will find that Napoli does not disappoint. Among other things, it's one of Italy's top *città d'arte,* with world-class museums and a staggering number of fine churches. The most important finds from Pompeii and Herculaneum are on display at the Museo Archeologico Nazionale—a cornucopia of sculpture, frescoes, and mosaics—and seeing them will add to the pleasure of trips to the ancient ruins. And Naples has a wonderful location: thanks to the backdrop of Vesuvius and the

CAMPANIA THROUGH THE AGES

13

Ancient History. Lying on Mediterranean trade routes plied by several pre-Hellenic civilizations, Campania was settled by the ancient Greeks from approximately 800 BC onward. Here myth and legend blend with historical fact: the town of Herculaneum is said—rather improbably—to have been established by Hercules himself, and Naples in ancient times was called Parthenope, the name attributed to one of the Sirens who preyed on hapless sailors in antiquity. Thanks to archaeological research, some of the layers of myth have been stripped away to reveal a pattern of occupation and settlement well before Rome became established. Greek civilization flourished for hundreds of years all along this coastline, but there was nothing in the way of centralized government until centuries later when the Roman Republic, uniting all Italy for the first time, absorbed the Greek colonies with little opposition. Generally, the peace of Campania was undisturbed during these centuries of Roman rule.

Foreign Influences. Naples and Campania, with the rest of Italy, decayed with the Roman Empire and collapsed into the abyss of the Middle Ages. Naples itself regained some importance under the rule of the Angevins in the latter part of the 13th century and continued its progress in the 1440s under Aragonese rule. The nobles who served under the Spanish viceroys in the 16th and 17th centuries enjoyed their pleasures, even as Spain milked the area for taxes. After a short Austrian occupation, Naples became the capital of the Kingdom of the Two Sicilies, which the Bourbon kings established in 1738. Their rule was generally benevolent as far as Campania was concerned, and their support of papal authority in Rome was important in the development of the rest of Italy. Their rule was important artistically, too, contributing to the architecture of the region and attracting musicians, artists, and writers drawn by the easy life at court. Finally, Giuseppe Garibaldi launched his famous expedition, and in 1860 Naples was united with the rest of Italy.

Modern Times. Things were relatively tranquil through the years that followed—with visitors thronging to Capri, to Sorrento, to Amalfi, and, of course, to Naples—until World War II. Allied bombings did considerable damage in Naples and the bay area. At the fall of the fascist government the sorely tried Neapolitans rose up against Nazi occupation troops and in four days of street fighting drove them out of the city. A monument was raised to the *scugnizzo* (the typical Neapolitan street urchin), celebrating the youngsters who participated in the battle. The war ended. Artists, tourists, writers, and other lovers of beauty returned to the Campania region. As the years have gone by, some parts gained increased attention from knowing visitors, while others lost the cachet they once had. Though years of misgovernment have left an indelible mark, the tide appears to be turning: the region's cultural and natural heritage is finally being revalued as local authorities and inhabitants alike appreciate the importance of nurturing the area's largest industry—tourism.

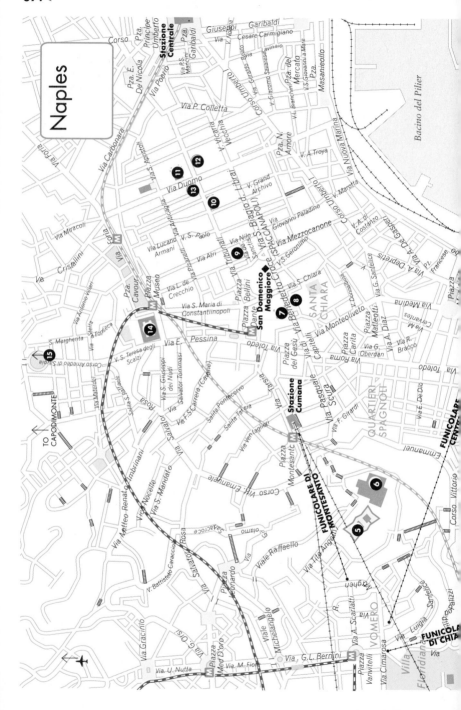

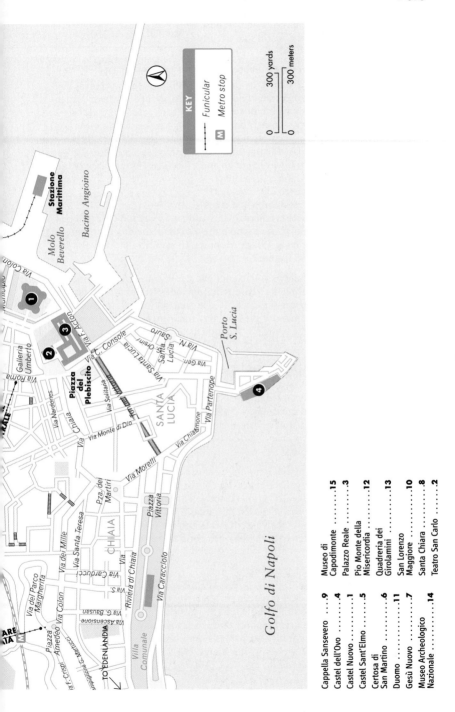

Golfo di Napoli

Cappella Sansevero **9**

Castel dell'Ovo **4**

Castel Nuovo **1**

Castel Sant'Elmo **5**

Certosa di
San Martino **6**

Duomo **11**

Gesù Nuovo **7**

Museo Archeologico
Nazionale **14**

Museo di
Capodimonte **15**

Palazzo Reale **3**

Pio Monte della
Misericordia **12**

Quadreria dei
Girolamini **13**

San Lorenzo
Maggiore **10**

Santa Chiara **8**

Teatro San Carlo **2**

KEY

┉ *Funicular*

Ⓜ *Metro stop*

0 ⊢ 300 yards

0 ⊢ 300 meters

islands in the bay, it's one of those few cities in the world that are instantly recognizable.

In Naples you need a good sense of humor and a firm grip on your pocketbook and camera. Expect to do a lot of walking (take care crossing the chaotic streets); buses are crowded, and taxis often get held up in traffic. Use the funiculars or the new metro Line 1 to get up and down the hills, and take the quick—but erratic—metro Line 2 (the city's older subway system) when crossing the city between Piazza Garibaldi and Pozzuoli. For Pompeii, Herculaneum, and Sorrento, take the Circumvesuviana train line, and the Cumana line from Piazza Montesanto goes to Pozzuoli and leads toward Baia and Cumae.

The *artecard* allows you to combine public transport and entry to major museums: a three-day card (€25) includes free entry to two museums or archaeological sites, a 50% discount on other attractions, and free transport throughout the museum area—including return trips on fast craft across the bay from Pozzuoli as far afield as Salerno. A seven-day card (€28) gives free entry to all sights covered by the program but doesn't include a travel pass. You can purchase the artecard and find out more information on the sights covered at the airport stand (outside customs), at the train station at Piazza Garibaldi, and at the Web site ⊕ www.artecard.it. The Naples and Campi Flegrei card (€13) gives access to two museums, a 50% discount on all other museums in the Flegrean area, and transport throughout the area.

Royal Naples

Naples hasn't been a capital for more than 150 years, but it still prides itself on its royal heritage. Most of the modern center of the town owes its look and feel to various members of the Bourbon family, who built their palaces and castles in this area. Allow plenty of time for museum visits, especially the Palazzo Reale and the Castel dell'Ovo. The views from the latter over the bay are good at any time, but are especially fine at sunset.

The Main Attractions

❹ **Castel dell'Ovo.** Dangling over the Porto Santa Lucia on a thin promontory, this 12th-century fortress built over the ruins of an ancient Roman villa overlooks the whole harbor—proof, if you need it, that the Romans knew a premium location when they saw one. For the same reason, some of the city's top hotels share the site. It's a peaceful spot for strolling and enjoying the views. ⊠ *Santa Lucia waterfront, Via Partenope, Santa Lucia* ☎ *081/2400055* ⌨ *Free* ☉ *Mon.–Sat. 8:30–5, Sun. 8:30–2.*

1 **Castel Nuovo.** Also known as the Maschio Angioino, this massive fortress was built by the Angevins (related to the French monarchy) in the 13th century and completely rebuilt by the Aragonese rulers (descendants of an illegitimate branch of Spain's ruling line) who succeeded them. The decorative marble triumphal arch that forms the entrance was erected during the Renaissance in honor of King Alfonso V of Aragon (1396–1458), and its rich bas-reliefs are credited to Francesco Laurana (circa 1430–1502). Set incongruously into the castle's heavy stone walls, the arch is one of the finest of its kind. Within the castle you can see sculptures and frescoes from the 14th and 15th centuries, as well as the city's **Museo Civico,** comprising mainly local artwork from the 15th to 19th century. It's hard to avoid the impression that these last were rejects from the much finer collection at the Museo di Capodimonte, though there are also regular exhibitions worth visiting. You can also visit the Palatine Chapel and the octagonal **Sala dei Baroni,** where Ferrante I disposed of a group of rebellious barons in 1485 by inviting them to a mock wedding party and then pouring boiling oil on their heads from the ceiling. The room is still regularly used for city council meetings. In the left corner of the courtyard is the **Sala dell'Armeria,** the Armory, where part of the flooring has been conveniently glassed over to reveal the remains of a Roman villa and a medieval necropolis. ✉ *Piazza Municipio* ☎ 081/7955877 ✆ €5 ☾ *Mon.–Sat. 9–7 (ticket office closes at 6); Sun. courtyard only 9–1.*

3 **Palazzo Reale.** Dominating Piazza del Plebiscito, the huge palace—best described as overblown imperial—dates from the early 1600s. It was renovated and redecorated by successive rulers, including Napoléon's sister Caroline and her ill-fated husband, Joachim Murat (1767–1815), who reigned briefly in Naples after the French emperor had sent the Bourbons packing and before they returned to reclaim their kingdom. Don't miss seeing the **royal apartments,** sumptuously furnished and full of precious paintings, tapestries, porcelains, and other objets d'art. The monumental marble staircase gives you an idea of the scale on which Neapolitan rulers lived. ✉ *Piazza del Plebiscito* ☎ 081/400547 ✆ €4 ☾ *Thurs.–Tues. 9–7.*

NEED A BREAK?
Kitty-corner to the Palazzo Reale is the most famous coffeehouse in town, the **Caffè Gambrinus** (✉ Piazza Trieste e Trento, near Piazza Plebiscito ☎ 081/417582). Founded in 1850, this 19th-century jewel functioned as a brilliant intellectual salon in its heyday but has fallen into a Sunset Boulevard–type existence, relying on past glamour, at the mercy of tourists and their pitiless cameras, and with often-indifferent service. But the inside rooms, with amazing mirrored walls and gilded ceilings, makes this an essential stop for any visitor to the city.

Piazza del Plebiscito. The vast square next to the Palazzo Reale was laid out by order of Murat, whose architect was clearly inspired by the colonnades of St. Peter's in Rome. The large church of **San Francesco di Paola** in the middle of the colonnades was added as an offering of thanks for the Bourbon restoration by Ferdinand I, whose titles reflect the somewhat garbled history of the Kingdom of the Two Sicilies, which

VOICES OF ITALY

Imma Marsella
architect, Naples

Imma Marsella is passionate about the buildings, art, landscape, and history of her native Naples. She's turned that passion into a career, overseeing restoration projects for the city architect's office. One afternoon she takes time out from work (restoring an ancient Roman tunnel) to identify what she considers the most important buildings of Naples and the region. The question sends her darting about her office, grabbing books from overburdened shelves; her reply is filled with tangents, as she recalls one fascinating building after another.

Fitting In. The best buildings, she feels, harmonize with the landscape. "A great starting point is the Castel dell'Ovo, one of the city's oldest buildings, on the Borgo Marinaro. It looks like part of the island itself, rising up out of the sea. If you walk around the various levels of terraces, at each turn there's a new and unexpected view of the city and the bay. From there you can see the Castel Sant'Elmo up on the hill. It's made from tufa stone quarried from the hill it stands on. It was originally built in the 1200s but has been modified many times, like many buildings in this city where space is such a problem." The castle is connected to the San Martino monastery, another essential stop. "From its perch on the edge of the hill you get a series of views right around the bay."

Many of the finest buildings in the area date from the 18th century. "It was one of the largest and most important cities in Europe at the time. If the Bourbon royal family wanted a new Versailles, they got it!" The "new Versailles" was the Reggia palace in Caserta. "The gardens in particular are worth seeing. They're laid along a long avenue with an infinite vanishing point."

Neapolitan buildings often have an interesting anthropological element to them. "In the San Gaudioso catacombs, for example, a cult of the dead grew up around the former cemetery. The majolica tiles in the cloister of Santa Chiara portray scenes of everyday life, so it's not just a beautiful space, but a historical record. The church of San Lorenzo encapsulates its own history—underneath it you can see the remains of a Roman street, then the church uses the Roman columns in its construction."

Minimal Modernism. Imma laments the lack of great modern architecture in the city, but says a walk up Via Parco Margherita is worth making to see its art deco, or "Liberty style," palazzi. "At the top stands a building by the eccentric Scottish architect Lamont Young. He landed in Naples at the end of the 19th century and left behind fake castles, Renaissance palaces, and Swiss chalets." For a fine example of modernism, the Mostra d'Oltremare exhibition center in Fuorigrotta is a must—"though perhaps only for real enthusiasts," Imma concedes. "Otherwise, if you visit Capri, the Villa Malaparte is a great example of how modernism fits in with the landscape, the way the building stretches across the rocks, both part of it and different. Much like the Castel dell'Ovo—exactly where we started!"

was made up of Naples (which included most of the southern Italian mainland) and Sicily. They were united in the Middle Ages, then separated, then unofficially reunited under Spanish domination during the 16th and 17th centuries. In 1816, with Napoléon out of the way on St. Helena, Ferdinand IV (1751–1825) of Naples, who also happened to be Ferdinand III of Sicily, officially merged the two kingdoms, proclaiming himself Ferdinand I of the Kingdom of Two Sicilies. His reactionary and repressive rule earned him a few more colorful titles among his rebellious subjects.

Via Toledo. Sooner or later you'll wind up at one of the busiest commercial arteries, also known as Via Roma, which has thankfully been closed to through traffic—at least along the stretch leading from the Palazzo Reale. Don't avoid dipping into this parade of shops and coffee bars where plump pastries are temptingly arranged.

Also Worth Seeing

Quartieri Spagnoli. The garrison for Spanish troops in the 17th century has become one of Naples most densely inhabited neighborhoods. A tight grid of decaying tenements lining incredibly narrow alleys, the *Quartieri* lie between Via Toledo (downhill border) and Via Pasquale Scura (western leg of Spaccanapoli). The area is hectic, sometimes dangerous, and chock-full of local color. It's a five-minute walk west of Piazza Municipio, accessible from Via Toledo.

2 **Teatro San Carlo.** This large theater was built in 1737, 40 years earlier than Milan's La Scala—though it was destroyed by fire and had to be rebuilt in 1816. You can visit the impressive interior, decorated in the white-and-gilt stucco of the neoclassical era, as part of a prearranged tour, and visitors are sometimes allowed in during morning rehearsals. ✉ *Via San Carlo between Piazza Municipio and Piazza Plebiscito, Piazza Plebiscito* ☎ *081/7972331 or 081/7972412* ⊕ *www.teatrosancarlo. it* ✉ *€5* ☉ *Tours by appointment; call 081/664545.*

NEED A BREAK?	Across from the Teatro San Carlo towers the imposing entrance to the glass-roof neoclassical **Galleria Umberto** (✉ Via San Carlo, near Piazza Plebiscito), a late-19th-century shopping arcade where you can sit at one of several cafés and watch the vivacious Neapolitans as they go about their business.

Vomero

Heart-stopping views of the Bay of Naples are framed by this gentrified neighborhood on a hill served by the Montesanto, Centrale, and Chiaia funiculars. Stops for all three are an easy walk from Piazza Vanvitelli, a good starting point for exploring this thriving district with no shortage of smart bars and trattorias.

The Main Attractions

5 **Castel Sant'Elmo.** Perched on the Vomero, this castle was built by the Angevins in the 14th century to dominate the port and the old city and remodeled by the Spanish in 1537. The stout fortifications are still in use today by the military, and occasionally there are performances, exhibitions, and fairs. ✉ *Largo San Martino, Vomero* ☎ *081/5784030* 💳 *€3* 🕐 *Thurs.–Tues. 8:30–7:30.*

★ ❻ **Certosa di San Martino.** A Carthusian monastery restored in the 17th century in exuberant Neapolitan baroque style, this structure has now been transformed into a diverse museum. The gorgeous Chiostro Grande (great cloister) and the panoramic garden terraces—strangely quiet, with a view of the city sprawling below—are among the most impressive spots in the city. Popular exhibits include the *presepi* (Christmas crèches) and an anonymous painting that depicts the Naples waterfront in the 15th century and the return of the Aragonese fleet from the Battle of Ischia. Take the funicular from Piazza Montesanto to Vomero. ✉ *Museo Nazionale di San Martino, Vomero* ☎ *081/5585942* 💳 *€6, includes admission to Castel Sant'Elmo* 🕐 *Tues.–Thurs. 8:30–7:30.*

Spaccanapoli & Capodimonte

Nowhere embodies the spirit of Naples better than the arrow-straight street informally known as Spaccanapoli (literally, "split Naples"). Gazing down it, you can sense where the name comes from—the street resembles a trench, running from the central station (where the old city walls stood) up to the San Martino hill, retracing one of the main arteries of the ancient Greek, and later Roman, settlements. At its western end, Spaccanapoli is officially named Via Benedetto Croce, in honor of the illustrious philosopher born there in 1866, in the building at No. 12. As it runs its course, the street name changes to Via San Biagio dei Librai and then Via San Gregorio Armeno. No matter the name, it's a place of vibrant street culture.

Capodimonte, to the north, was open countryside until the Bourbon kings built a hunting lodge there, after which it rapidly became part of the city proper. Between the two neighborhoods is the Museo Archeologico, Naples's finest museum. It's best to visit shortly after lunchtime, when the crowds have thinned out. Two hours will be just enough to get your bearings and cover the more important collections. The museum in Capodimonte—unlike many of the churches and the archaeological museum—is well lighted and can be viewed in fading daylight, so it's best left until last.

WALKING SPACCANAPOLI

Vibrant, chaotic Spaccanapoli is the essence of Naples. A walk along it takes you past peeling palaces, artisans' workshops, many churches and street shrines, stores of all sorts, bars, and people young and old.

Start at **Piazza Gesù Nuovo**, the area's largest square. (At this point Spaccanapoli goes by the name Via Benedetto Croce.) The forbidding exterior of the church of **Gesù Nuovo** ❼ dominates the piazza. For a complete contrast, cross the road and enter **Santa Chiara** ❽.

Originally built in the early 1300s and reconstructed after a direct hit from a bomb in 1943, the church is light, airy, and spacious. Look for the traces of Giotto frescoes behind the altar. A side door leads into its delightful vine-laden cloister decorated with hundreds of hand-painted majolica tiles, an unexpected outbreak of peace in noisy Naples.

Back out on Spaccanapoli, heading east you cross **Via San Sebastiano**, a street filled with music shops frequented by students from the nearby conservatory; it can be a veritable symphony in the morning. **Palazzo**

The Main Attractions

9 Cappella Sansevero. Off Spaccanapoli, the Cappella di Santa Maria della Pietà dei Sangro, better known as the Cappella Sansevero, holds the tombs of the noble Sangro di San Severo family. Much of it was designed in the 18th century by Giuseppe Sammartino, including the centerpiece, a striking *Veiled Christ* carved from a single block of alabaster. If you can stomach it, take a peek in the crypt, where some of the anatomical experiments conducted by Prince Raimondo, a scion of the family and noted 18th-century alchemist, are gruesomely displayed. ⊠ *Via de Sanctis 19, Spaccanapoli* ☎ *081/5518470* ⊕ *www.museosansevero.it* ⊠ €6 ⊙ *Oct.–Apr., Mon. and Wed.–Sat. 10–5:40, Sun. 10–1; May–Sept., Mon. and Wed.–Sat. 10–6:40, Sun. 10–1.*

11 Duomo. Though the Duomo was established in the 1200s, the building you see was erected a century later and has since undergone radical changes, especially during the baroque age. Inside the cathedral, 110 ancient columns salvaged from pagan buildings are set into the piers that support the 350-year-old wooden ceiling. Off the left aisle you step down into the 4th-century church of **Santa Restituta,** which was incorporated into the cathedral; though Santa Restituta was redecorated in the late 1600s in the prevalent baroque style, a few very old mosaics remain in the **Battistero** (Baptistery). The chapel also gives access to an archaeological zone, a series of Paleo-Christian rooms dating from the Roman era.

On the right aisle of the cathedral, in the **Cappella di San Gennaro,** are multicolor marbles and frescoes honoring St. Januarius, miracle-working patron saint of Naples, whose altar and relics are encased in silver. Three times a year—on September 19 (his feast day); on the Saturday preceding the first Sunday in May, which commemorates the transference of his relics to Naples; and on December 16—his dried blood, contained in two sealed vials, is believed to liquefy during rites in his honor. On these days large numbers of devout Neapolitans offer up prayers in his memory. The **Museo del tesoro di San Gennaro** houses a rich collection of treasures associated with the saint. Paintings by Solimena and Luca Giordano hang alongside statues, busts, candelabras, and tabernacles in gold, silver, and marble by Cosimo Fanzago and other 18th-century baroque masters. A guided visit is included in the ticket price. ⊠ *Via Duomo*

Filomarino, former home of philosopher Benedetto Croce and now the site of his library, is on the left as you continue. Next on your right is **Palazzo Carafa della Spina**; coachmen once used the mouths of the gargoyles at the entrance to tamp out their torches.

Continuing on, **Piazza San Domenico Maggiore** opens up to your left. The the church of San Domenico Maggiore, the Palazzo Corigliano (today part of the university), and spire contribute to one of Naples's most charming set pieces. Various cafés (including Scaturchio, a celebrated *pasticcerie*) give the square the feel of an open-air living room. Heading up the right side of the piazza, swing right onto Via Francesco de Sanctis to visit the fascinating **Cappella Sansevero 9**. Return to Spaccanapoli on Via Nilo, to the east of the chapel; where the two streets intersect you pass a statue of the Egyptian river god Nile reclining on a pedestal. (A few steps beyond, Spaccanapoli's street name changes to Via San Biagio dei Librai.) A little farther along is **Via San Gregorio Armeno,** a narrow street bridged by a tower linking two sections of a closed monastery. The street is filled with stalls selling the tiny

147, Spaccanapoli ☎ *081/449097 Duomo, 081/294764 museum* 🖃 *Duomo and Cappella di San Gennaro free, Battistero and archaeological zone €3, museum €5.50* ☉ *Duomo and Cappella di San Gennaro daily 8–12:30 and 4:30–7; Battistero and archaeological zone Mon.–Sat. 9–noon and 4:30–6:30, Sun. 9–noon; museum Tues.–Sun. 10–6.*

❼ Gesù Nuovo. The oddly faceted stone facade of the church was designed as part of a palace dating from between 1584 and 1601, but plans were changed as construction progressed, and it became the front of an elaborately decorated baroque church. Be sure not to miss the votive chapel dedicated to San Ciro (Saint Cyrus) in the far left corner of the church. Here hundreds of tiny silver ex-voto images have been hung on the walls to give thanks to the saint for his assistance in medical matters. You can buy ex-votos at any of the jewelers that line the street outside. ⊠ *Piazza Gesù Nuovo, Spaccanapoli* ☎ *081/5518613* ☉ *Mon.–Sun. 7–1 and 4–7.*

⓮ Museo Archeologico Nazionale. The

FodorśChoice
★

National Archaeological Museum's huge red building, a cavalry barracks in the 16th century, is undergoing a seemingly permanent restoration program, which means that at any given time, rooms are likely to be closed to the public with little prior warning.

> ### WORD OF MOUTH
>
> "The Naples Archaeological Museum has an incredible collection of real treasures, but the displays keep changing, and they close wings without notice or seeming reason."
>
> –mowmow

The museum holds one of the world's great collections of Greek and Roman antiquities, including such extraordinary sculptures as the *Hercules Farnese,* an exquisite Aphrodite attributed to the 4th-century BC Greek sculptor Praxiteles, and an equestrian statue of Roman emperor Nerva. Vividly colored mosaics and countless artistic and household objects from Pompeii and Herculaneum provide insight into the life and art of ancient Rome. The Gabinetto Segreto and its collection of occasionally shocking erotic art is now permanently open, after being kept under lock and key for many years. Invest in an up-to-date printed museum guide or audio guide, because exhibits tend to be poorly la-

---

presepi, figures Neapolitans use to make Nativity scenes. Take San Gregorio Armeno north; turning right at Via Tribunali brings you to **San Lorenzo Maggiore**⑩, whose 18th-century facade hides a Gothic-era nave and–surprise–one of the most interesting archaeological sites in the city, showing the streets of ancient Naples as they were 2,000 years ago. Continue along Via Tribunali, crossing Via Duomo (note the **Duomo**⑪ to the left) as far as **Pio Monte della Misericordia**⑫, which has one of the greatest 17th-century altarpieces in Europe, Caravaggio's *Seven Acts of Mercy.*

Head back west along Via Tribunali, stopping to note the curious brass skulls outside the church of **Purgatorio ad Arco** on your right–touch them to bring good luck. At the end of Via Tribunali, turn right into **Piazza Bellini** and stop for a drink at one of the leafy square's many cafés. By now, you'll have earned it.

beled. ⊠ *Piazza Museo 19, Spaccanapoli* ☎ *081/440166* ⊕ *www. archeona.arti.beniculturali.it* ▣ €9 ⊙ *Wed.–Mon. 9–7.*

Timpani e Tempura (⊠ Vico della Quercia 17, Spaccanapoli ☎ 081/5512280) is a tiny shrine to local culinary culture. There are no tables; instead, you perch yourself at the counter, but it's worth squeezing in for the *timballi di maccheroni* (baked pasta cakes) and the unique *mangiamaccheroni* (spaghetti in broth with *caciocavallo* cheese, butter, basil, and pepper). High-quality wines by the glass make this a place for a quick, delicious lunch. You can also buy cheese and salami to take home with you.

★ ⓯ **Museo di Capodimonte.** The grandiose 18th-century neoclassical Bourbon royal palace houses an impressive collection of fine and decorative art. Capodimonte's greatest treasure is the excellent collection of paintings well displayed in the **Galleria Nazionale,** on the palace's first and second floors. Besides the art collection, part of the **royal apartments** still has a complement of beautiful antique furniture, most of it on the splashy scale so dear to the Bourbons, and a staggering collection of porcelain and majolica from the various royal residences. The walls of the apartments are hung with numerous portraits, providing a close-up of the unmistakable Bourbon features, a challenge to any court painter. Most rooms have fairly comprehensive information cards in English, whereas the audio guide is overly selective and somewhat quirky. The main galleries on the first floor are devoted to work from the 13th to 18th centuries, including many pieces by Dutch and Spanish masters, as well as by the great Italians. On the second floor look out for stunning paintings by Simone Martini (circa 1284–1344), Titian (1488/90–1576), and Caravaggio (1573–1610). The palace is situated in the vast Bosco di Capodimonte (Capodimonte Park), which served as the royal hunting preserve and later as the site of the Capodimonte porcelain works. ⊠ *Via Miano 2, Porta Piccola, Via Capodimonte* ☎ *848/800288 information and bookings for special exhibitions* ▣ €7.50 ⊙ *Thurs.–Tues. 8:30–7:30 (ticket office closes 6:30).*

★ ⓬ **Pio Monte della Misericordia.** One of the defining landmarks of Spaccanapoli, this octagonal church was built around the corner from the Duomo for a charitable institution founded in 1601 by seven noblemen. The institution's aim was to carry out acts of Christian charity: feeding the hungry, clothing the poor, nursing the sick, sheltering pilgrims, visiting prisoners, ransoming Christian slaves, and burying the indigent dead—acts immortalized in the history of art by the famous altarpiece painted by Caravaggio (1571–1610) depicting the *Sette Opere della Misericordia* (*Seven Acts of Mercy*) and now the celebrated focus of the church. In this haunting work the artist has brought the Virgin, borne atop the shoulders of two angels, right down into the street—and not a rhetorical place, but a real street of Spaccanapoli (scholars have suggested a couple of plausible locations) populated by figures in whose spontaneous and passionate movements the people could see themselves. The original church was considered too small and destroyed in 1655 to make way for a new church, designed by Antonio Picchiatti and built between 1658 and 1678. Pride of place is given to the great Caravaggio above the altar, but there are other important baroque-era paintings on view here; some hang in the church while others are in the adjoining *pinacoteca* (picture gallery). ⊠ *Via Tribunali 253, Spaccanapoli* ☎ *081/446944* ⊙ *Thurs.–Tues. 9–2.*

⑬ Santa Chiara. This monastery church is a Neapolitan landmark and the subject of a famous old song. It was built in the 1300s in Provençal Gothic style, and it's best known for the quiet charm of its cloister garden, with columns and benches sheathed in 18th-century ceramic tiles painted with delicate floral motifs and vivid landscapes. An adjoining museum traces the history of the convent; the entrance is off the courtyard at the left of the church. ⊠ *Piazza Gesù Nuovo, Spaccanapoli* ☎ *081/5521597* 🎟 *Museum and cloister €4* ⊙ *Church daily 9:30–noon and 5–7; museum and cloister Mon.–Sat. 9:30–7, Sun. 9:30–1.*

NEED A BREAK? While you're exploring the old part of town, take a break at what the Neapolitans call "the best pastry shop in Italy"–**Scaturchio** (⊠ Piazza San Domenico Maggiore 19, Spaccanapoli ☎ 081/5516944). The café was founded in 1918 by two brothers, one of whom, Francesco, invented the cakes called *ministeriali* to attract Anna Fouché, a famous actress of the time. You can still buy these cakes today, along with other Neapolitan specialties such as *babà, rafioli,* and *pastiera,* which you can eat there with a coffee or have gift-wrapped.

Also Worth Seeing

Napoli Sotteranea. From two different locations, it is possible to explore the foundations of the city, some of which date back as much as 4,000 years. About 131 feet underground, guides will show you ancient aqueducts built by the Greeks and Romans, which later served as a bomb shelter during World War II. The commentary is normally in Italian, though some of the guides speak English, and a printed guide in English is available. ⊠ *Piazza San Gaetano 68, Spaccanapoli* ⊠ *Vico S. Anna di Palazzo 52, Piazza Plebiscito* ☎ *081/400256* ⊕ *www.napolisotterranea. org* 🎟 *€7* ⊙ *Tours Sat. at 10, noon, and 6; Sun. at 10, 11, noon, and 6; Thurs. at 9 PM; or call to arrange other times. Meet at Piazza Trieste e Trento, by Caffè Gambrinus.*

⑬ Quadreria dei Girolamini. Off an improbably quiet cloister enclosing a prolific forest of lemon and loquat trees, the Girolamini art museum is attached to the restored Girolamini church. Its intimate, high-quality collection of 16th- and 17th-century paintings is one of the city's best-kept secrets, well worth a half-hour visit. ⊠ *Via Duomo 142, Spaccanapoli* ☎ *081/294444* 🎟 *Free* ⊙ *Daily 9:30–12:30.*

⑩ San Lorenzo Maggiore. It's unusual to find French Gothic style in Naples, but it has survived to great effect in this church, which was built in the Middle Ages and decorated with 14th-century frescoes. Outside the 17th-century cloister is the entrance to **excavations** revealing what was once part of the Roman forum, and before that the Greek agora. You can walk among the streets, shops, and workshops of the ancient city and see a model of how the Greek Neapolis might have looked. ⊠ *Via Tribunali 316, Spac-*

Neapolitan Art in the Present Tense

For fans of contemporary art, Naples has two new exhibition spaces that are worth checking out. In keeping with the style of similar museums all over the world, they're both known by their acronyms; together they've given a dose of adrenaline to the city's art scene.

PAN (Palazzo delle Arti Napoli) is an impressively restored palazzo on Via dei Mille. It has no permanent collection, but hosts a wide range of traveling exhibitions as well as regular performances, film screenings, and presentations. ⊠ *Via dei Mille 60, Chiaia* ☎ *081/7958653* ⊕ *www.*

palazzoartinapoli.net ⊠ €5 ⊙ *Mon.-Sat. 9:30-6, Sun. 9:30-1.*

MADRE (Museo d'Arte di Donna Regina), in an 18th-century palazzo restored by the architect Alvaro Siza, has a significant collection of works by major figures in contemporary art, including Francesco Clemente, Joseph Kosuth, Anish Kapoor, and Richard Serra, as well as regularly rotating exhibitions of less-established artists. ⊠ *Via Settembrini 79, Spaccanapoli* ☎ *081/5624561* ⊕ *www.museomadre. it* ⊠ €3.50 ⊙ *Mon.-Thurs. and Sun. 10-9; Fri. and Sat. 10-midnight.*

canapoli ☎ *081/2110860* ⊕ *www.sanlorenzomaggiorenapoli.it* ⊠ *Excavations* €4 ⊙ *Mon.–Sat. 9:30–5:30, Sun. 9:30–1:30.*

Where to Eat

★ **$$$$** ✕ **Da Dora.** Despite its location up an unpromising-looking *vicolo* (alley) off the Riviera di Chiaia, this small restaurant has achieved cult status for its seafood platters. It's remarkable what owner-chef Giovanni can produce in his tiny kitchen. Start with the pasta dish *linguini alla Dora,* laden with local seafood and fresh tomatoes, and perhaps follow up with grilled *pezzogna* (blue-spotted bream). Like many restaurants on the seafront, Da Dora has its own guitarist, who is often robustly accompanied by the kitchen staff. ⊠ *Via Fernando Palasciano 30, Mergellina* ☎ *081/680519* ⌕ *Reservations essential* ⊟ *AE, DC, MC, V* ⊙ *Closed Sun. and 2 wks in Dec., 2 wks mid-Aug.*

$$$$ ✕ **La Sacrestia.** Neapolitans flock to this upscale patrician villa for the restaurant's location—on the slopes of the Posillipo hill—and high culinary standards. The specialties include tasty antipasti, linguine in *salsa di scorfano* (scorpion-fish sauce), and fettuccine with small squid, black olives, and potatoes. ⊠ *Via Orazio 116, Posillipo* ☎ *081/664186* ⌕ *Reservations essential* ⊟ *AE, DC, MC, V* ⊙ *Closed 2 wks mid-Aug.*

★ **$$$–$$$$** ✕ **La Stanza del Gusto.** The name means "The Room of Taste," and this restaurant lives up to the billing. A minute's walk from some of the city's busiest streets, up a flight of stairs opposite the Teatro Sannazzaro on Via Chiaia, it feels removed from the hectic world outside. Chef Mario Avallone mixes traditional, but often forgotten, Southern recipes with modern trends—hence the presence of the *tempura di verdura* (Japanese-style fried vegetables) alongside the *bomba savoia* (a savory cake of

CLOSE UP

Folk Songs à la Carte

IF YOU WANT TO HEAR *canzoni napoletane*—the fabled Neapolitan folk songs—performed live, you can try to catch the city's top troupes, such as the Cantori di Posillipo and I Virtuosi di San Martino, in performances at venues like the Teatro Trianon. But an easier alternative is to head for one of the city's more traditional restaurants, such as La Bersagliera or Mimì alla Ferrovia, where most every night you can expect your meal to be interrupted by a *posteggiatore*. These singers aren't employed by the restaurants, but they're encouraged to come in, swan around the tables with a battered old guitar, and belt out classics such as "Santa Lucia," "O' Surdat' Innamurate," "Torna a Surriento" (Come Back to Sorrento), and, inevitably, "Funiculì Funiculà."

These songs are the most famous of a vast repertoire that found international fame with the mass exodus of southern Italians to the United States in the early 20th century. "Funiculì Funiculà" was written by Peppino Turco and Luigi Danza in 1880 to herald Naples's new funicular railways. "O Sole Mio," by Giovanni Capurro and Eduardo di Capua, has often been mistakenly taken for the Italian national anthem. "Torna a Surriento" was composed by Ernesto di Curtis in 1903 to help remind the current Italian prime minister how wonderful he thought Sorrento was (and how many government subsidies he had promised the township).

The singers are more than happy to do requests, even inserting the name of your *innamorato* or *innamorata* into the song. When they've finished they'll stand discreetly by your table. Give them a few euros and you'll have friends for life (or at least for the night).

---

rice and potatoes). Save room for the delicious sweets. ⊠ *Vicoletto Sant'Arpino 21, Piazza Plebiscito* ☎ *081/401578* ⌕ *Reservations essential* ▭ *AE, DC, MC, V* ⊘ *Closed Sun. and Mon., and Aug. Lunch by appointment only.*

$$$ ✕ **Umberto.** Run by the Di Porzio family since 1916, Umberto is one of the city's classic restaurants. It's divided into a simple pizzeria and a more elegant restaurant, both of which offer the class of the Chiaia neighborhood and the friendliness of other parts of the city. Try the *tubettini 'do tre dita* ("three finger maccheroni" with a mixture of seafood), which bears the nickname of the original Umberto. Owner Massimo and sister Lorella (Umberto's grandchildren) are both wine experts and oversee a fantastically well-curated cellar. Umberto is also the only restaurant in the city that caters to those who have a gluten allergy. ⊠ *Via Alabardieri 30–31, Chiaia* ☎ *081/418555* ▭ *AE, DC, MC, V* ⊘ *Closed Mon.*

$$–$$$ ✕ **La Bersagliera.** You'll inevitably be drawn to eating at the Santa Lucia waterfront, in the shadow of the looming medieval Castel dell'Ovo. This spot is big and touristy but fun, with an irresistible combination of spaghetti and mandolins. The menu suggests uncomplicated, timeworn classics, such as spaghetti *alla pescatora* (with seafood sauce) and tagliatelle *alla bersagliera* (with handmade pasta, cherry tomatoes, tiny oc-

topi, and clams). ⊠ *Borgo Marinaro 10, Santa Lucia* ☎ *081/7646016* 🖃 *AE, DC, MC, V* ⊘ *Closed Tues.*

$$–$$$ ✕ **Mimì alla Ferrovia.** Near the central station, this bustling fish restaurant is as close as you get in Naples to a Parisian brasserie. It's a local institution popular with lawyers from the nearby courts and local business executives. The service is polite but not obsequious, the atmosphere relaxed but sometimes noisy. Try the range of antipasti, both fish- and vegetable-based, followed by *paccheri ai frutti di mare* (flat pasta with seafood) or the rigatoni *fiori di zucca e gamberetti* (pasta tubes with zucchini flowers and shrimp). ⊠ *Via Alfonso D'Aragona 21, Piazza Garibaldi* ☎ *081/5538525* 🖃 *AE, DC, MC, V* ⊘ *Closed Sun. and last 2 wks in Aug.*

★ **$$–$$$** ✕ **Vadinchenia.** Though it identifies itself as a cultural and gastronomic association, Vadinchenia has all the trimmings of a high-class restaurant. Husband-and-wife team Saverio and Silvana steer their guests through an innovative menu against a backdrop of refreshingly minimalist decor. Adventurous palates will enjoy such bold combinations as *paccheri alle alici e pecorino* (pasta with sardines and sheep's cheese), and meat eaters will delight in the *filletto al vino e sale grosso* (steak cooked in wine and rock salt). In winter round off the meal with the *purée di castagna* made from local chestnuts. ⊠ *Via Pontano 21, Chiaia* ☎ *081/660265* ⌖ *Reservations essential* 🖃 *AE, DC, MC, V* ⊘ *Closed Sun. and Aug. No lunch.*

$–$$ ✕ **L'Ebbrezza di Noè.** A small bar leads into a larger dining area decorated in the style of a very elegant farmhouse. Owner Luca has an enthusiasm for what he does that is quite moving—as you sip a recommended wine you can sense that he hopes you like it as much as he does. The attention paid to the quality of the wine carries over to the food—here you can taste delicate *carpaccio di chianina* (thinly sliced Tuscan steak), rare cheeses such as the Sicilian *ragusano di razza modicani,* and the local *caciocavallo podolico.* ⊠ *Vico Vetriera a Chiaia 8b/9, Chiaia* ☎ *081/400104* 🖃 *AE, DC, MC, V* ⊘ *Closed Mon. No lunch.*

$ ✕ **Osteria Castello.** The walls are covered with shelves full of wine bottles, and there are red-check tablecloths with candles on them—it looks like the quintessential Italian restaurant, and it is, with simple dishes at affordable prices and friendly service. Start at the excellent antipasto buffet, followed by the essential pasta *e patate con la provola* (with potatoes and smoked mozzarella—it sounds like carbohydrate overload, but it's actually divine) and then the grilled, flat *pleos* mushrooms. You can sip wine (preferably the local *aglianico* red) or a liqueur and sit for hours talking with friends. ⊠ *Via S. Teresa a Chiaia 38, Chiaia* ☎ *081/400486* 🖃 *AE, DC, MC, V* ⊘ *Closed Sun.*

$ ✕ **Vecchia Cantina.** The location is on a rather dark side street in the tattier section of the Spaccanapoli, but this place is well worth seeking out for its combination of old-style Neapolitan hospitality, high-quality food and wine, and excellent prices. It's a family affair, with Gianni out front and his mother, Nunzia, and wife, Maria, busy in the kitchen—much like in a typical Neapolitan household. The decorations are an accumulation of kitsch, and everyone who comes here seems to know everyone else. The pasta *e ceci* (with chickpeas) shouldn't be missed, and *baccalà fritto* (fried salt cod) is a specialty. The wine list includes selections from all over Italy. ✉ *Via S. Nicola alla Carità 13–14, Spaccanapoli* ☎ 081/5520226 ⚒ *Reservations essential* ▭ AE, DC, MC, V ⊘ *Closed Tues.*

¢–$ ✕ **Cantina della Tofa.** Located on one of the narrow alleys that lead off Via Toledo up into the Quartieri Spagnoli, this small, welcoming restaurant serves traditional Neapolitan fare that goes beyond standard pasta with seafood or tomatoes. Try the *vellutata di cicerchie*, a creamy soup made from beans that are a cross between chickpeas and fava beans. The orange-wall dining room has large wooden tables that seem more Tuscan than Campanian. The service is friendly and unhurried. ✉ *Vico Tofa 71, Piazza Municipio* ☎ 081/406840 ▭ *No credit cards* ⊘ *Closed Sun.*

¢ ✕ **Da Michele.** You have to love a place that has, for more than 130 years,
FodorśChoice offered only two types of pizza—marinara (with tomato, garlic, and
★ oregano) and margherita (with tomato, mozzarella, and basil)—and a small selection of drinks, and still manages to attract long lines. The prices have something to do with it, but the pizza itself suffers no rivals, and even those waiting in line are good-humored; the boisterous, joyous atmosphere wafts out with the smell of yeast and wood smoke onto the street. ✉ *Via Sersale 1/3* ☎ 081/5539204 ▭ *No credit cards* ⊘ *Closed Sun. and last 2 wks in Aug.*

¢ ✕ **Lombardi.** Lombardi is one of the city's most highly regarded old-style pizzerias. Simple decor and slightly cramped tables are more than compensated for by the excellent pizzas. The location is handy for a quick meal before or after a visit to the archaeological museum. ✉ *Via Foria 12, near Museo* ☎ 081/456220 ▭ AE, DC, MC, V ⊘ *Closed Mon.*

★ ¢ ✕ **Sorbillo.** Don't be put off by the lines—the locals know the wait is worth it. Take their advice and order a basic Neapolitan pizza (try the unique pizza al pesto or the stunningly simple marinara—just tomatoes and oregano). They're cooked to perfection by the third generation of pizza makers who run the place. Don't expect tablecloths: here you have the joy of eating on traditional white-marble tabletops. ✉ *Via dei Tribunali 32, Spaccanapoli* ☎ 081/446643 ▭ AE, DC, MC, V ⊘ *Closed Sun. (except Dec.) and& 2 wks in Aug.*

Where to Stay

$$$$ ⬚ **Grand Hotel Vesuvio.** You'd never guess from the somewhat dull exterior that this is the oldest of Naples's great seafront hotels—the place where Enrico Caruso died, Oscar Wilde escaped with lover Lord Alfred Douglas, and Bill Clinton charmed the waitresses. Fortunately, the spacious, soothing interior compensates for what's lacking on the outside. Guest rooms are done in luxurious, traditional style with antique accents, vibrantly colored walls, and gleaming bathrooms; many overlooking the bay. You can pamper yourself at the spa, where there are myriad special services. The famous Caruso restaurant sits atop the hotel, affording wonderful views. ✉ *Via Partenope 45, Santa Lucia, 80121* ☎ 081/7640044 🖶 081/7644483 ⊕ *www.vesuvio.it* ⇔ *163 rooms, 17 suites* ⚒ *Restaurant, in-room safes, minibars, cable TV, in-room data ports, health club, bar, babysitting, meeting room, some pets allowed* ▭ AE, DC, MC, V ⦿ BP.

$$$$ 🏨 **Palazzo Alabardieri.** One of the newest of the city's rapidly expanding list of luxury hotels, Palazzo Alabardieri welcomes guests into a small courtyard just behind the upmarket chic of the Piazza dei Martiri. A spacious marble-floor lobby makes the place feel bigger than it actually is, yet maintains a feeling of discretion and intimacy. The hotel prides itself on its marble bathrooms. ⊠ *Via Alabardieri 38, Chiaia, 80121* ☎ *081/415278* ⊕ *www.palazzoalabardieri.it* ⮌ *29 rooms* ⌂ *In-room safes, cable TV, in-room data ports, bar, parking, some pets allowed* ▤ *AE, DC, MC, V* ⎮⊙⎮ *BP.*

★ $$$$ 🏨 **Parker's.** This landmark hotel has been serving up doses of elegant, old-style atmosphere to visiting VIPs since 1870. The gilt-trimmed Empire bureaus, 19th-century paintings, shimmering chandeliers, fluted pilasters, and ornate ceilings all create a splendidly glittering environment. From the hotel's perch midway up the Vomero Hill (and convenient to funicular lines) you get fine views of the bay and Capri; if your room doesn't have one of these vistas, drink it all in from the excellent rooftop restaurant. There's also a day spa providing a full complement of health and beauty treatments. ⊠ *Corso Vittorio Emanuele 135, Chiaia, 80121* ☎ *081/7612474* ☐ *081/663527* ⊕ *www.grandhotelparkers.it* ⮌ *72 rooms, 9 suites* ⌂ *Restaurant, in-room safes, minibars, cable TV, gym, massage, sauna, spa, bar, meeting rooms, parking (fee)* ▤ *AE, DC, MC, V* ⎮⊙⎮ *BP.*

$$$–$$$$ 🏨 **San Francesco al Monte.** This high-end hotel retains hints of its former life as a Franciscan monastery: the small lobby leads to narrow corridors lined with doors that look dauntingly cell-like, until you enter and find surprisingly spacious, simply decorated rooms, many with their own hot tubs, antique furnishings, majolica-tile floors, and stunning views of the city below and the bay beyond. The hotel's restaurant is equally upscale, its French chef adding a Gallic twist to Italian fare. ⊠ *Corso Vittorio Emanuele 328, 80135* ☎ *081/4239111* ☐ *081/2512485* ⊕ *www.hotelsanfrancesco.it* ⮌ *50 rooms* ⌂ *Restaurant, in-room safes, minibars, cable TV, pool, bar, meeting rooms* ▤ *AE, DC, MC, V* ⎮⊙⎮ *BP.*

$$$ 🏨 **Caravaggio Hotel.** The old town's first luxury hotel, in a 17th-century palazzo on a tiny square behind the Duomo, takes its name from the painter of the amazing *Sette Opere della Misericordia,* which can be seen in the chapel opposite. The entrance hall is atmospherically furnished with blocks of volcanic stone, and the remains of the city's original Greek walls are visible. The guest rooms are all modern—each even has a power shower. Breakfast includes a selection of meats and cheeses from local Campanian farms. ⊠ *Via Riario Sforza 157, Spaccanapoli, 80139* ☎ *081/2110066* ☐ *081/4421578* ⊕ *www.caravaggiohotel.it* ⮌ *16 rooms* ⌂ *Cable TV, in-room data ports, bar, some pets allowed* ▤ *AE, DC, MC, V* ⎮⊙⎮ *BP.*

$$$ 🏨 **Il Convento.** In a 17th-century palazzo tucked away in the Quartieri Spagnoli, the Convent is conveniently close to Via Toledo. Rooms are small but elegant, with original architectural features such as arched or beamed ceilings. They are decorated in simple, modern Mediterranean style. Two junior suites have private roof gardens. ⊠ *Via Speranzella 137/A, Piazza Municipio, 80132* ☎ *081/403977* ☐ *081/400332* ⊕ *www.*

hotelilconvento.com ⇥ *12 rooms, 2 suites* ⌂ *Minibars, cable TV, bar, Internet point* ⊟ *AE, DC, MC, V* ᵗᏫ BP.

$$$ 🏨 **Costantinopoli 104.** An oasis of what Italians call *stile liberty* (art deco style), this calm and elegant hotel sits in the bustling centro storico near the Museo Archeologico Nazionale. Each room is individually decorated. Ask for a room with a balcony in the warmer months and enjoy your breakfast alfresco, or opt for one of the garden rooms that open out onto the small swimming pool. ⊠ *Via Costantinopli 104, Spaccanapoli, 80139* ☎ *081/5571035* 🖷 *081/5571051* ⊕ *www.costantinopoli104.com* ⇥ *8 rooms* ⌂ *Cable TV, in-room data ports, pool, bar, laundry service, parking* ⊟ *AE, DC, MC, V* ᵗᏫ BP.

$$–$$$ 🏨 **Hotel Toledo.** A centuries-old palazzo has been tastefully transformed into this boutique hotel a two-minute walk up from Via Toledo. Rooms are furnished in a pleasing rustic style, and the leafy rooftop terrace provides a quintessentially Neapolitan backdrop for your breakfast. ⊠ *Via Montecalvario 15, Quartieri Spagnoli, 80134* ☎🖷 *081/406800* ⊕ *www.hoteltoledo.com* ⇥ *18 rooms* ⌂ *Minibars, bar* ⊟ *AE, DC, MC, V* ᵗᏫ BP.

$$ 🏨 **Chiaja.** A two-minute walk from Piazza Plebiscito takes you to this hotel in a spruced-up 18th-century palazzo, part of which was once a brothel. Above the fireplace in the homely entrance hall is a portrait of the marchese Nicola Le Caldano Sasso III, original owner of the building; her granddaughter Mimi now runs the place. Rooms are small but comfortable; any sense of claustrophobia (a hazard with buildings in this old part of town) is compensated for by the opulent period furnishings. Vouchers for breakfast at the nearby Gambrinus café are available. ⊠ *Via Chiaia 216, Chiaia, 80121* ☎ *081/415555* 🖷 *081/422344* ⊕ *www.hotelchiaia.it* ⇥ *27 rooms* ⌂ *Minibars, cable TV, bar, Internet point* ⊟ *AE, DC, MC, V* ᵗᏫ EP.

$$ 🏨 **Neapolis.** Situated on a narrow alley just off the humming Via Tribunali and close to Piazza Bellini, this small hotel looks out over the 13th-century Pietrasanta bell tower. The mix of modern and traditional furnishings, the lovely terra-cotta floors, and data ports in every room make this a good base for exploring Napoli's medieval center. ⊠ *Via Francesco Del Giudice 13, Spaccanapoli, 80138* ☎ *081/4420815* 🖷 *081/4420819* ⊕ *www.hotelneapolis.com* ⇥ *19 rooms* ⌂ *Minibars, in-room data ports, bar* ⊟ *AE, DC, MC, V* ᵗᏫ BP.

$$ 🏨 **Pinto Storey.** This fascinating old pensione overflows with warmth and charm. The simple and airy guest rooms are on the fourth floor of an elegant late-19th-century building off the chic Piazza Amedeo. Rooms here are always in demand, so book early. ⊠ *Via G. Martucci 72, Chiaia, 80121* ☎ *081/681260* 🖷 *081/667536* ⊕ *www.pintostorey.it* ⇥ *16 rooms* ⌂ *Minibars, cable TV, in-room data ports* ⊟ *AE, MC, V* ᵗᏫ EP.

$ 🏨 **Soggiorno Sansevero.** In the heart of Spaccanapoli, this pensione occupies a floor in the former palace of the princes di Sangro di San Severo. Although Palazzo Sansevero overlooks the opera-set Piazza San Domenico, this tiny lodging is on a quiet inner courtyard. Rooms are simply furnished—linoleum floors, modern beds, great-grandmama's bureau—and may even come with ghosts: Renaissance composer Carlo Gesualdo murdered his wife and her lover on the palace's staircase. ⊠ *Piazza San Domenico 9,*

Spaccanapoli, 80131 ☎ *081/4201336* 🖷 *081/211698* ⊕ *www. albergosansevero.it* 🛏 *6 rooms, 4 with bath* 🖃 *AE, DC, MC, V* 🍽 *BP.*

Nightlife & the Arts

The Arts

Opera is a serious business in Naples—not in terms of the music so much as the costumes, the stage design, the players, and the politics. What's happening on stage can be secondary to the news of who's there, who they're with, and what they're wearing. Given the circumstances, it's hardly surprising that the city's famous San Carlo company doesn't offer a particularly innovative repertoire. Nonetheless, the company is usually of very high quality—and if they're not in form the audience lets them know it. Performances take place in the luxury liner of southern Italian opera houses, the historic **Teatro San Carlo** (✉ Via San Carlo, Piazza Plebiscito ☎ 081/7972331 or 081/7972412 ⊕ www.teatrosancarlo.it). The hall still gleams with its mid-19th-century gilded furnishings and thick red-velvet drapes. For the opera and ballet seasons (generally December through June), many seats are presold by subscription, but there are often some available at the box office a few days before the performance. You can also book ahead by calling **Concerteria** (✉ Via Schipa 23, Chiaia ☎ 081/7611221). For an additional fee you can order tickets on the theater Web site.

Nightlife

Bars and clubs are found in many areas around Naples. The sophisticated crowd heads to Posillipo and the Vomero, Via Partenope along the seafront, and the Chiaia area (between Piazza dei Martiri and Via Dei Mille). A more bohemian crowd makes for the centro storico and the area around Piazza Bellini. The scene is relatively relaxed—you might even be able to sit down at a proper table. Keep in mind that clubs, and their clientele, can change rapidly, so do some investigating before you hit the town.

Caffè Intramoenia (✉ Piazza Bellini 70, Spaccanapoli ☎ 081/290720) is the granddaddy of all the bars in Piazza Bellini; it was set up as a bookshop in the late 1980s and still has its own small publishing house with a variety of attractive titles. Seats in the heated veranda are at a premium in winter, though many sit outside all year round. **Bere Vino** (✉ 62 Via San Sebastiano, Spaccanapoli ☎ 081/29313) looks like a shop from the outside, but inside you'll find long wooden tables and shelves of wine from all over Italy that are consumed on the premises. Peppery *taralli* biscuits, olives, and selections of cheeses and smoked meats can be used to *apoggiare* ("prop up") whatever you're drinking. Look for recommended wines by the glass on the chalkboard or spend ages perusing the encyclopedic list. **Aret' 'a Palm** (✉ Piazza Santa Maria la Nova, Spaccanapoli) is Neapolitan for "behind the palm tree," and that's exactly where you'll find this agreeably dark bar on Piazza Santa Maria La Nova. Its long marble bar and mirrored walls suggest Paris more than Naples.

The **Enoteca Belledonne** (✉ Vico Belledonne a Chiaia 18, Chiaia ☎ 081/ 403162) is something of an institution among inhabitants of the more upscale Chiaia area. Between 8 and 9 in the evening it seems like the whole neighborhood has descended into the tiny space for an *aperitivo* (cocktail). The small tables and low stools are notably uncomfortable, but the cozy atmosphere and the pleasure of being surrounded by glass-fronted cabinets full of wine bottles with beautiful labels more than makes up for it. Excellent local wines are available by the glass at great prices. **66** (⊠ Via Bisignano 66, Chiaia ☎ 081/5720269) is a good place to meet for an aperitivo; the range of snacks on the bar (several types of olives, fresh capers, spinach-and-ricotta pies, and even small helpings of spaghetti—virtually a meal in itself) makes the crowds of young professionals and steep drink prices worth it. **Spacafé Culti** (⊠ Via Carlo Poerio 47, Chiaia ☎ 081/7644619) is the latest addition to the swish Chiaia district, an unusual combination of day spa, furniture shop, and a classy bar/restaurant. It's refreshingly quiet and beautifully designed, with long low chairs and lots of black lacquered wood.

Sports & the Outdoors

Bicycling

To rent a bike in town and for information on group excursions (including rides up Mt. Vesuvius), contact **Napoli Bike** (⊠ Riviera di Chiaia 201 ☎ 081/411934 ⊕ www.napolibike.com), conveniently close to the Villa Comunale.

Boating

Summer evening boat tours take in the Naples waterfront from the port at Mergellina to Cape Posillipo, with a view of Castel dell'Ovo on the way back. For bookings contact **Seafront Tours** (⊠ Galleria Umberto I 17, Piazza Plebiscito ☎ 081/5519188).

Shopping

Leather goods, jewelry, and cameos are some of the best items to buy in Campania. In Naples you'll generally find good deals on handbags, shoes, and clothing. If you want the real thing, make your purchases in shops, but if you don't mind imitations, rummage around at the various street-vendor *bancherelle* (stalls). Most boutiques and department stores are open Monday 4:30–8, Tuesday–Saturday 9:15–1 and 4:30–8. Food shops are open Monday morning, but most close about 2 PM on Thursday afternoon.

Shopping Districts

The immediate area around **Piazza dei Martiri,** in the center of Chiaia, has the densest concentration of luxury shopping, with perfume shops, fashion outlets, and antiques on display. **Via dei Mille** and **Via Filangieri,** which lead off Piazza dei Martiri, are home to Bulgari, Mont Blanc, and Hermes stores. The small, pedestrian-only **Via Calabritto,** which leads down from Piazza dei Martiri toward the sea, is where you'll find high-end retailers such as Prada, Gucci, Versace, Vuitton, Cacharel, Damiani, and Cartier. **Via Chiaia** and **Via Toledo** are the two busiest shopping streets for most Neapolitans; there you'll find reasonably priced clothes and shoes, with a sprinkling of cafés and food shops. The **Vomero** district yields more commercial shops, especially along Via Scarlatti and

13

Via Luca Giordano. **Via Santa Maria di Costantinopoli,** which runs from Piazza Bellini to the Archaeological Museum, is the street for antiques shops. You'll also find an antiques market on the third weekend of each month in the gardens of Villa Comunale and a flower market early every morning in the Castel Nuovo moat.

Specialty Stores

CHIAIA **Gay Odin** (✉ Via Toledo 214, Piazza Plebiscito ☎ 081/400063) produces handmade chocolates that you can find only in its Naples shops. Buy a delicious chocolate Mt. Vesuvius, or try the famous *foresta* (flaked chocolate). **Lo Stock** (✉ Via Fiorelli 7, Piazza dei Martiri ☎ 081/2405253) is a large basement in which designer-label remainders can be found at hugely reduced prices. Be prepared to rummage and hope they have your size. **Marinella** (✉ Via Riviera di Chiaia 287/a, Chiaia ☎ 081/2451182) sells old-fashioned made-to-measure ties that are favorites of the British royal family.

SPACCANAPOLI **Colonnese** (✉ Via San Pietro a Maiella 32/33, Spaccanapoli ☎ 081/459858) is an old-fashioned bookstore with antique wooden cabinets and tables laden with volumes on art, local history, and esoterica. **Melinoi** (✉ Via Benedetto Croce 34, Spaccanapoli ☎ 081/5521204) stands out from the many small boutiques in Naples for its originality; it stocks clothes and accessories by Romeo Gigli as well as a number of French designers. **Mario Raffone** (✉ Via Santa Maria di Costantinopoli 102, Spaccanapoli ☎ 081/459667) is a family printing business where they still use old presses. They sell prints of Nativity figures and Vesuvius and have a catalog of antique prints.

☺ The **Ospedale delle Bambole** (✉ Via San Biagio dei Librai 81, Spaccanapoli ☎ 081/203067), a tiny storefront operation, is a world-famous "hospital" for dolls. It's a wonderful place to take kids. **Nel Regno di Pulcinella** (✉ Vico San Domenico Maggiore 9, Spaccanapoli ☎ 081/5514171) is the workshop of Lello Esposito, renowned maker of Neapolitan puppets. The shop, a converted 16th-century stable, also has wonderful model volcanoes and the traditional good-luck symbol of the city, a red horn.

THE PHLEGREAN FIELDS

The name Campi Flegrei—the fields of fire—was once given to the entire region west of Naples, including the island of Ischia. The whole area floats freely on a mass of molten lava very close to the surface. The fires are still smoldering. Greek and Roman notions of the underworld were not drawn strictly from imagination; they were the creations of poets and writers who stood on this very ground and wrote down what they saw. Today it should take about half a day to assess it yourself.

Solfatara

🖲 *8 km (5 mi) west of Naples.*

At the sunken crater of Solfatara, a semiextinct volcano that last erupted in 1198, you can experience firsthand the volcanic nature of this otherworldly terrain. According to one legend, every crater in the Phlegrean

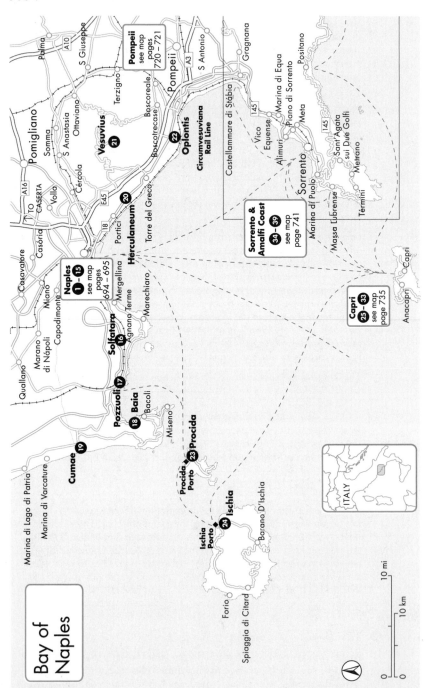

Bay of Naples

Pompeii see map pages 720–721

Naples 1–15 see map pages 694–695

Sorrento & Amalfi Coast 34–39 see map page 741

Capri 25–33 see map page 735

Pompeii

S Antonio

Gragnana

Positano

Marina di Equa

Marina di Sorrento

Piano di Sorrento

Meta

Sant'Agata sui Due Golfi

Metrano

Términi

Vico Equense

Allimuri

Sorrento

Marina di Puolo

Massa Lubrense

Capri

Anacapri

Castellammare di Stábia

Circumvesuviana Rail Line

Oplontis 22

Vesuvius 21

Terzigno

Boscoreale

Boscotrecase

Herculaneum 20

Torre del Greco

Portici

Mergellina

Marechiaro

Solfatara 16

Agnano Terme

Capodimonte

Pozzuoli 17

Baia 18

Bácoli

Miseno

Cumae 19

Marina di Lago di Patria

Marina di Varcature

Quallano

Marano di Nápoli

Casavatore

Miano

Casória

Volla

Cércola

Cásoria

S Anastasia

Somma

Ottaviano

S Giuseppe

Pálma

S Antonio

Pomigliano

Procida 23
Procida Porto

Ischia 24
Ischia Porto

Barano D'Ischia

Forio

Spiaggia di Citard

ITALY

10 mi

10 km

0

0

Fields is one of the mouths of a hundred-headed dragon named Typhon that Zeus hurled down the crater of Epomeo on the island of Ischia. Another asserts that the sulfurous springs are poisonous discharges from the wounds the Titans received in their war with Zeus. The stark, scorched area, scattered with pools of boiling mud, exerts a strange fascination. The area has good visitor facilities, is well signposted, and is safe for walking if you stick to the path. ☎ *081/5262341* ⊕ *www. solfatara.it* ✉ *€5.50* ☉ *Daily 8:30–4:30.*

Pozzuoli

13

⑰ *2 km (1 mi) west of Solfatara, 8 km (5 mi) west of Naples.*

The small fishing town of Pozzuoli once boasted of its difference from nearby Naples, and though in recent years it has become a suburb of its neighbor, it still retains enough character and sights of interest to make it worth at least a half-day trip—or longer if you want to visit one of the town's famous fish restaurants. The **Anfiteatro Flavio** is the third-largest amphitheater in Italy, after the Colosseum and Santa Maria Capua Vetere, and once held 40,000 spectators. Judging from the underground network of *carceres* (cells), which definitely merit a visit, entertainment consisted mainly of *venationes* (fights), often involving exotic animals such as lions and tigers brought from far-flung corners of the Roman Empire. The *fossa*, the large ditch in the middle of the arena, may well have contained the stage, which could be raised when necessary. If visiting between June and September, ask at the ticket office about evening concerts. ☎ *081/5266007* ✉ *€4, includes Cumae and museum and site of Baia* ☉ *Daily 9–4.*

You may want to make a short trip to Pozzuoli's **harbor** and imagine St. Paul landing here en route to Rome in AD 61, only 18 years before the eruption of Vesuvius. His own ship had been wrecked off Malta, and he was brought here on the *Castor and Pollux,* a grain ship from Alexandria.

Where to Eat

Pozzuoli is justly famed for its fish restaurants. On weekends in summer the town's narrow streets are packed with Neapolitans.

$$ ✕ **Nero di Seppia.** With its low wooden beams and fishnet-covered walls, Nero di Seppia resembles ship's cabin, which is appropriate given the fare on offer. Start by choosing from the wide range of antipasti, both seafood and vegetable, and follow up with the house speciality, spaghetti with black squid ink (*nero di seppia*). It might look strange, but it's delicious. ✉ *Corso della Repubblica 139* ☎ *081/5261840* ▤ *No credit cards* ☉ *Closed Tues.*

$ ✕ **Ristorante Don Antonio.** On weekends Neapolitans flock to this restaurant in a *vicolo* (alley) one block from the waterfront for fresh seafood and unbeatable prices. Unlike most other restaurants in the area, which happily serve well into the afternoon or late night, Don Antonio rolls down the shutters as soon as the day's catch has been consumed. ✉ *Via Magazzini 20, off Piazza San Paolo* ☎ *081/5267941* ⌦ *Reservations not accepted* ▤ *No credit cards* ☉ *Closed Mon.*

EATING WELL IN CAMPANIA

Campania's cuisine relies heavily on the bounty of the region's fertile farmland. Locally grown tomatoes are exported all over the world, but to try them here is another experience completely. Pasta is a staple, and spaghetti *al pomodoro* (with tomato sauce) and *alle vongole* (with clam sauce, either white or red) appear on most menus. Mozzarella—produced by Campania's thriving buffalo population—is used in many dishes; one of the most gratifying on a hot day is *insalata caprese* (salad with mozzarella, tomatoes, and basil). *Melanzane* (eggplant) and even zucchini are served *parmigiana* (fried and layered with tomato sauce and mozzarella).

Naples is the homeland of pizza, and you'll encounter it here in two classic forms: *alla margherita* (with tomato, mozzarella, and basil) and

marinara (with tomato, garlic, and oregano). Meat may be served *alla pizzaiola* (cooked in a tomato-and-garlic sauce). Fish and seafood in general can be expensive, though fried calamari and *totani* (cuttlefish) are usually reasonably priced. Lemons, grown locally, are widely used in cooking and for the sweet and heady limoncello (the famous lemon liqueur), especially popular around Sorrento and on the Amalfi Coast. Among the region's grape varieties, Fiano, Greco di Tufo, and Falanghina make fine whites, and the Aglianico grape produces Campania's prestigious red, Taurasi. Wine production here has an impressive pedigree: Falerno wines (red and white) are mentioned by the Latin poet Horace, and Lacryma Christi (a blend of grape varieties) is produced from grapes grown around the slopes of Vesuvius.

Baia

18 *7 km (4½ mi) south of Pozzuoli, 12 km (7 mi) west of Naples.*

Now largely under the sea, this was once the most opulent and fashionable resort area of the Roman Empire, a place where Sulla, Pompey, Cicero, Caesar, Tiberius, and Nero all built holiday villas. Petronius's *Satyricon* is a satire on the corruption, intrigue, and wonderful licentiousness of Roman life at Baia. (Petronius was hired to arrange parties and entertainments for Nero, so he was in a position to know.) It was here at Baia that Emperor Claudius built a great villa for his wife, Messalina (who spent her nights indulging herself at public brothels); here that Agrippina poisoned her husband and was, in turn, murdered by her son Nero; and here that Cleopatra was staying when Julius Caesar was murdered on the Ides of March in 44 BC. You can visit the excavations of the famous *terme* (baths). ⊠ *Via Fusaro 35* ☎ *081/8687592* ⊠ *€4, includes Cumae, the museum of Baia, and the Pozzuoli amphitheater* ⊗ *Tues.–Sun. 9–4.*

EN
ROUTE
Follow the southern loop around Lago Miseno (a volcanic crater believed by the ancients to be the Styx, across which Charon ferried the souls of the dead) and Lago del Fusaro. You'll take in some fine views of the Golfo di Pozzuoli.

A Stop on the Way to Hell

In his epic *The Aeneid*, Virgil (70–19 BC) wrote of the Trojan prince Aeneas's descent to the underworld, where he went to speak to his father. To find his way, Aeneas needed the guidance of the Cumaean Sibyl.

Virgil did not dream up the Sibyl's cave—it almost certainly stood in her chamber at Cumae. When he wrote *"Facilis descensus Averno"*—"The way to hell is easy"—it was because he knew the way. In Book VI of the *Aeneid* Virgil described how Aeneas, arriving at Cumae, sought Apollo's throne (remains of the Tempio di Apollo can still be seen) and "the deep hidden abode of the dread Sibyl / An enormous cave. . . ."

13

Cumae

⑲ *5 km (3 mi) north of Pozzuoli, 16 km (10 mi) west of Naples.*

Perhaps the oldest Greek colony in Italy, Cumae (Cuma in Italian) overshadowed the Phlegrean Fields, including Naples, in the 7th and 6th centuries BC. The **Antro della Sibilla** (Sibyl's Cave)—one of the most venerated sites in antiquity—is in Cumae. In the 6th or 5th century BC the Greeks hollowed the cave from the rock beneath the present ruins of Cumae's acropolis. You walk through a dark, massive stone tunnel that opens into a vaulted chamber where the Sibyl uttered her oracles. Standing here, the sense of mystery is overwhelming. "This is the most romantic classical site in Italy," wrote the English travel writer H. V. Morton (1892–1979). "I would rather come here than to Pompeii."

Little of ancient Cumae now stands aboveground—its Temple of Apollo has suffered woefully over the millennia—but the underground passages are virtually intact, though not all are visitable. There are detailed information panels to guide you through the site, with extra information on flora and fauna supplied by the local Worldwide Fund for Nature. As you walk through, you'll soon appreciate why this was a good location: it was surrounded by fertile land, had relatively easy access to the sea (though no natural harbor), and had an acropolis at the top providing an excellent vantage in all directions. Allow at least two hours for this visit to soak up the ambience, study the ruins, and reach the top level overlooking the Acherusia Palus—now Lago Fusaro—to the south and part of the Silva Gallinaria, the thick holm-oak ground cover to the north, once an immense forest stretching almost all the way to Rome. ✉ *Via Acropoli 39* ☎ *081/8543060* 🎫 *€4, includes Pozzuoli amphitheater and museum and site of Baia* ☉ *Daily 9–4:30.*

Regarded by the ancients as the gateway to Hades, the fabled **Lago d'Averno** (Lake Avernus) was well known by the time Virgil settled here to write *The Aeneid*. Today the scene has changed a fair amount: in summer the area pulsates to the sound of disco music, and you would be more likely to come across members of the 21st-century underworld than meet the shades of the dead that Virgil so evocatively describes. As with Lago Lucrino (the Lucrine Lake) less than 1 km (½ mi) to the south, a tarmac road skirts much of the lake. However, some of the spell is restored by the backdrop: forested hills rise on three sides and the menacing cone of Monte Nuovo looms on the fourth. The smell of sulfur sometimes hangs over the landscape, and blocked-off passages lead into long-abandoned caves into which Virgil might well have ventured. ⊠ *4 km (2½ mi) south of Cumae.*

HERCULANEUM, VESUVIUS & POMPEII

Volcanic ash and mud preserved the Roman towns of Herculaneum and Pompeii almost exactly as they were on the day Mt. Vesuvius erupted in AD 79, leaving them not just archaeological ruins but museums of daily life in the ancient world. The two cities and the volcano that buried them can be visited from either Naples or Sorrento, thanks to the Circumvesuviana, the suburban railway that provides fast, frequent, and economical service.

Herculaneum

★ ⑳ *10 km (6 mi) southeast of Naples.*

Lying more than 60 feet below the town of Ercolano, the ruins of Herculaneum are set among the acres of greenhouses that make this area one of Europe's principal flower-growing centers. About 5,000 people lived here when it was destroyed; many of them were fishermen, craftsmen, and artists. In AD 79 the gigantic eruption of Vesuvius (which also destroyed Pompeii) buried the town under a tide of volcanic mud. The semiliquid mass seeped into the crevices and niches of every building, covering household objects and enveloping textiles and wood—sealing all in a compact, airtight tomb.

Casual excavation—and haphazard looting—began in the 18th century, but systematic digs were not initiated until the 1920s. Today less than half of Herculaneum has been excavated; with present-day Ercolano and the unlovely Resina Quarter (famous among bargain hunters for its secondhand-clothing market) sitting on top of the site, progress is limited. From the ramp leading down to Herculaneum's well-preserved edifices, you get a good overall view of the site, as well as an idea of the amount of volcanic debris that had to be removed to bring it to light.

> **WORD OF MOUTH**
>
> "Herculaneum is definitely not to be missed. The buildings look as if you could move in with just a little restoration."
>
> –Juneisy

Though Herculaneum had only one-fourth the population of Pompeii and has been only partially excavated, what has been found is generally better preserved. In some cases you can even see the original wooden beams, staircases, and furniture. Much excitement is presently focused on one excavation in a corner of the site, the Villa dei Papiri, built by

Continued on page 729

ANCIENT POMPEII
TOMB OF A CIVILIZATION

The Scavi di Pompeii, petrified memorial to Vesuvius's eruption on the morning of August 23, AD 79, is the largest, most accessible, and probably most famous of excavations anywhere.

A busy commercial center with a population of 10,000–20,000, ancient Pompeii covered about 160 acres on the seaward end of the fertile Sarno Plain. Today Pompeii is choked with both the dust of 25 centuries and more than 2 million visitors every year; only by escaping the hordes and lingering along its silent streets can you truly fall under the site's spell. On a quiet backstreet, all you need is a little imagination to sense the shadows palpably filling the dark corners, to hear the ancient pipe's falsetto and the tinny clash of cymbals, to envision a rain of rose petals gently covering a Roman senator's dinner guests. Come in the late afternoon when the site is nearly deserted and you will understand that the true pleasure of Pompeii is not in the seeing but in the feeling.

A FUNNY THING HAPPENS ON THE WAY TO THE FORUM as you walk through Pompeii. Covered with dust and decay as it is, the city seems to come alive. Perhaps it's the familiar signs of life observed along the ancient streets: the beer shops with tumblers' rings still fresh in the counter, the stanchion where horses were tethered outside the taverna, the tracks of chariot wheels cut in the pavement. Coming upon a *thermopolium* (drinking bar), you imagine natives calling out, "One for the road." But a glance up at Vesuvius, still brooding over the scene like an enormous headstone, reminds you that these folks—whether imagined in your head or actu-

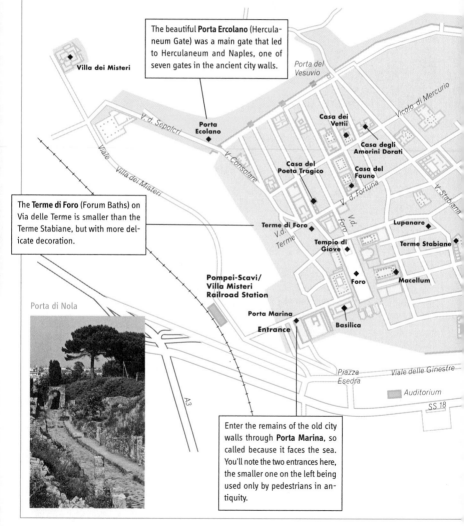

The beautiful **Porta Ercolano** (Herculaneum Gate) was a main gate that led to Herculaneum and Naples, one of seven gates in the ancient city walls.

Villa dei Misteri

Porta del Vesuvio

V. d. Sepolcri

Porta Ecolano

Viale Villa dei Misteri

V. Consolare

Vicolo di Mercurio

Casa dei Vettii

Casa degli Amorini Dorati

Casa del Poeta Tragico

Casa del Fauno

V. d. Fortuna

V. Stabiana

The **Terme di Foro** (Forum Baths) on Via delle Terme is smaller than the Terme Stabiane, but with more delicate decoration.

Terme di Foro

V. d. Foro

V. d. Terme

Tempio di Giove

Lupanare

Terme Stabiane

Porta di Nola

Pompei-Scavi/ Villa Misteri Railroad Station

Foro

Macellum

Porta Marina

Entrance

Basilica

Piazza Esedra

Viale delle Ginestre

Auditorium

A3

SS 18

Enter the remains of the old city walls through **Porta Marina**, so called because it faces the sea. You'll note the two entrances here, the smaller one on the left being used only by pedestrians in antiquity.

ally wearing a mantle of lava dust—have not taken a breath for centuries.

The town was laid out in a grid pattern, with two main intersecting streets. The wealthiest took a whole block for themselves;

Via dell'Abbondanza

those less fortunate built a house and rented out the front rooms, facing the street, as shops. There were good numbers of *tabernae* (taverns) and *thermopolia* on almost every corner, and frequent shows at the amphitheater.

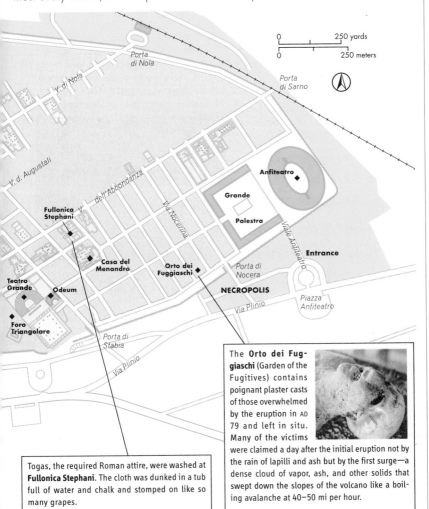

Togas, the required Roman attire, were washed at **Fullonica Stephani**. The cloth was dunked in a tub full of water and chalk and stomped on like so many grapes.

The **Orto dei Fuggiaschi** (Garden of the Fugitives) contains poignant plaster casts of those overwhelmed by the eruption in AD 79 and left in situ. Many of the victims were claimed a day after the initial eruption not by the rain of lapilli and ash but by the first surge—a dense cloud of vapor, ash, and other solids that swept down the slopes of the volcano like a boiling avalanche at 40–50 mi per hour.

PUBLIC LIFE IN ANCIENT POMPEII

Forum

THE CITY CENTER

As you enter the ruins at Porta Marina, make your way to the **Foro** (Forum), which served as Pompeii's cultural, political, and religious center. You can still see some of the two stories of colonnades that used to line the square. Like the ancient Greek *agora* in Athens, the Forum was a busy shopping area, complete with public officials to apply proper standards of weights and measures. Fronted by an elegant three-column portico on the eastern side of the forum is the **Macellum,** the covered meat and fish market dating to Augustan times; here vendors sold goods from their reserved spots in the central market. It was also in the Forum that elections were held, politicians let rhetoric fly, speeches and official announcements were made, and worshippers crowded the **Tempio di Giove** (Temple of Jupiter), at the northern end of the forum.

Basilica

On the southwestern corner is the **Basilica**, the city's law court and the economic center. These oblong buildings ending in a semicircular projection were the model for early Christian churches, which had a nave (central aisle) and two side aisles separated by rows of columns. Standing in the Basilica, you can recognize the continuity between Roman and Christian architecture.

THE GAMES

The **Anfiteatro** (Amphitheater) was the ultimate in entertainment for local Pompeians and offered a gamut of experiences, but essentially this was for gladiators rather than wild animals. By

Amphitheater

Roman standards, Pompeii's amphitheater was quite small (seating 20,000). Built in about 80 BC, it was oval and divided into three seating areas like a theater. There were two main entrances—at the north and south ends—and a narrow passage on the west called the Porta Libitinensis, through which the dead were most probably dragged out. A wall painting found in a house near the theater (now in the Naples Museum) depicts the riot in the amphitheater in AD 59 when several citizens from the nearby town of Nucera were killed. After Nucerian appeals to Nero, shows in the amphitheater were suspended for 10 years.

Fresco of Pyramus & Thisbe in the House of Loreius Tiburtinus

BATHS & BROTHELS

In its day, Pompeii was celebrated as the Côte d'Azur, the seaside Brighton, the Fire Island of the ancient Roman empire. Evidence of a Sybaritic bent is everywhere—in the town's grandest villas, in its baths, and especially in its rowdiest *lupanaria* (brothels), murals still reveal a worship of hedonism. Satyrs, bacchantes, hermaphrodites, and acrobatic couples are pictured indulging in hanky-panky.

The first buildings to the left after you've gone through the ticket turnstiles are the **Terme Suburbane** (Suburban Baths), built—by all accounts without planning permission—right up against the city walls. The baths have eyebrow-raising frescoes in the *apodyterium* (changing room) that strongly suggest that more than just bathing and massaging went on here.

On the walls of **Lupanare** (brothel) are scenes of erotic games in which clients could engage. The **Terme Stabiane** (Stabian Baths) had underground furnaces, the heat from which circulated beneath the floor, rose through flues in the walls, and escaped through chimneys. The water temperature could be set for cold, lukewarm, or hot. Bathers took a lukewarm bath to prepare themselves for the hot room. A tepid bath came next, and then a plunge into cold water to tone up the skin. A vigorous massage with oil was followed by rest, reading, horseplay, and conversation.

GRAFFITI

Thanks to those deep layers of pyroclastic deposits from Vesuvius that protected the site from natural wear and tear over the centuries, graffiti found in Pompeii provide unique insights into the sort of things that the locals found important 2,000 years ago. A good many were personal and lend a human dimension to the disaster that not even the sights can equal.

At the baths: **"What is the use of having a Venus if she's made of marble?"**

At the entrance to the front lavatory at a private house: **"May I always and everywhere be as potent with women as I was here."**

On the Viale ai Teatri: **"A copper pot went missing from my shop. Anyone who returns it to me will be given 65 bronze coins."**

In the Basilica: **"A small problem gets larger if you ignore it."**

PRIVATE LIFE IN ANCIENT POMPEII

The facades of houses in Pompeii were relatively plain and seldom hinted at the care and attention lavished on the private rooms within. When visitors arrived they passed the shops and entered an open atrium, from which the occupants received air, sunlight, and rainwater, the latter caught by the *impluvium*, a Jacuzzi-shaped receptacle under the sloped roof. In the back was a receiving room, and behind was

House of Paquius Proculus

another open area, the *peristylum*. Life revolved around this uncovered inner courtyard, with rows of columns and perhaps a garden with a fountain. Only good friends ever saw this part of the house, which was surrounded by *cubiculae* (bedrooms) and the *triclinium* (dining area). Interior floors and walls usually were covered with colorful marble tiles, mosaics, and frescoes.

Several homes were captured in various states by the eruption of Vesuvius, each representing a different slice of Pompeiian life.

The **Casa del Fauno** (House of the Faun) displayed wonderful mosaics, now at the Museo Archeologico Nazionale in Naples. The **Casa del Poeta Tragico** (House of the Tragic Poet) is a typical middle-class house. On the floor is a mosaic of a chained dog and the inscription *cave canem* ("Beware of the dog"). The **Casa degli Amorini Dorati** (House of the Gilded Cupids) is an elegant, well-preserved home with original marble decorations in the garden. Many paintings and mosaics were executed at **Casa del Menandro** (House of Menander), a patrician's villa named for a fresco of the Greek playwright. Two blocks beyond the Stabian Baths you'll notice on the left the current digs at the **Casa dei Casti Amanti** (House of the Chaste Lovers). A team of plasterers and painters were at work here when Vesuvius erupted, redecorating one of the rooms and patching up the cracks in the bread oven near the entrance—caused by earth tremors a matter of days before.

Small Garden
Triclinium
Owner's Quarters
Kitchen
Servant's Quarters
Secondary Atrium
Entrance
Main Atrium
Impluvium
Garden
Peristyle

CASA DEI VETTII

The **House of the Vettii** is the best example of a house owned by wealthy *mercatores* (merchants). It contains vivid murals—a magnificent *pinacoteca* (picture gallery) within the very heart of Pompeii. The scenes here—except for those in the two wings off the atrium—were all painted after the earthquake of AD 62. Once inside, cast an admiring glance at the delicate frieze around the wall of the *triclinium* (on the right of the peristyle garden as you enter from the atrium), depicting cupids engaged in various activities, such as selling oils and perfumes, working as goldsmiths and metalworkers, acting as wine merchants, or performing in chariot races. Another of the main attractions in the Casa dei Vettii is the small cubicle beyond the kitchen area (to the right of the atrium) with its faded erotic frescoes now protected by Perspex screens.

UNLOCKING THE VILLA DEI MISTERI

Villa dei Misteri

There is no more astounding, magnificently memorable evidence of Pompeii's devotion to the pleasures of the flesh than the frescoes on view at the **Villa dei Misteri** (Villa of the Mysteries), a palatial abode built at the far northwestern fringe of Pompeii. Unearthed in 1909, this villa had more than 60 rooms painted with frescoes; the finest are in the *triclinium*. Painted in the most glowing Pompeiian reds and oranges, the panels relate the saga of a young bride (Ariadne) and her initiation into the mysteries of the cult of Dionysus, who was a god imported to Italy from Greece and then given the Latin name of Bacchus. The god of wine and debauchery also represented the triumph of the irrational—of all those mysterious forces that no official state religion could fully suppress.

Pompeii's best frescoes, painted in glowing reds and oranges, retain an amazing vibrancy.

The Villa of the Mysteries frescoes were painted circa 50 BC, most art historians believe, and represent the peak of the Second Style of Pompeiian wall painting. The triclinium frescoes are thought to have been painted by a local artist, although the theme may well have been copied from an earlier cycle of paintings from the Hellenistic period. In all there are 10 scenes, depicting children and matrons, musicians and satyrs, phalluses and gods. There are no inscriptions (such as are found on Greek vases), and after 2,000 years historians remain puzzled by many aspects of the triclinium cycle. Scholars endlessly debate the meaning of these frescoes, but anyone can tell they are the most beautiful paintings left to us by antiquity. In several ways, the eruption of Vesuvius was a blessing in disguise, for without it, these masterworks of art would have perished long ago.

PLANNING FOR YOUR DAY IN POMPEII

GETTING THERE

The archaeological site of Pompeii has its own stop (Pompei–Villa dei Misteri) on the Circumvesuviana line to Sorrento, close to the main entrance at the Porta Marina, which is the best place from which to start a tour. If, like many potential visitors every year, you get the wrong train from Naples (stopping at the other station "Pompei"), all is not lost. There's another entrance to the excavations at the far end of the site, just a seven-minute walk to the Amphitheater.

ADMISSION

Single tickets cost €10 and are valid for one full day. The site is open Apr.–Oct., daily 8:30–7:30 (last admission at 6), and Nov.–Mar., daily 8:30–5 (last admission at 3:30). For more information, call 081/8575347 or visit www.pompeiisites.org.

WHAT TO BRING

The only restaurant inside the site is both overpriced and busy, so it makes sense to bring along water and snacks. If you come so equipped, there are some shady, underused picnic tables outside the Porta di Nola, to the northeast of the site.

MAKING THE MOST OF YOUR TIME

Visiting Pompeii does have its frustrating aspects: many buildings are blocked off by locked gates, and enormous group tours tend to clog up more popular attractions. But the site is so big that it's easy to lose yourself amid the quiet side streets. To really see the site, you'll need four or five hours.

Two buildings within Pompeii—Terme Suburbane (daily 10–2) and Casa del Menandro (weekends 2–4)—are open for restricted viewing on a first-come, first-served basis. Ask for a free coupon when you purchase your ticket and you will be assigned a visiting time.

TOURS

To get the most out of Pompeii, rent an audio guide (€6 for one, €9 for two; you'll need to leave an ID card) and opt for one of the three itineraries (2 hours, 4 hours, or 6 hours). If hiring a guide, make sure the guide is registered for an English tour and standing inside the gate; agree beforehand on the length of the tour and the price, and prepare yourself for soundbites of English mixed with dollops of hearsay.

MODERN POMPEI

Caught between the hammer and anvil of cultural and religious tourism, the modern town of Pompei (to use the modern-day Italian spelling, not the ancient Latin) is now endeavoring to polish up its act. In attempts to ease congestion and improve air quality at street level, parts of the town have been pedestrianized and parking restrictions tightened. Several hotels have filled the sizable niche in the market for excellent deals at affordable prices. As for recommendable restaurants, if you deviate from the archaeological site and make for the center of town, you will be spoiled for choice.

IF YOU LIKE POMPEII

If you intend to visit other archaeological sites nearby during your trip, you should buy the *biglietto cumulativo* pass, a combination ticket with access to five area sites (Herculaneum, Pompeii, Oplontis, Stabiae, Boscoreale). It costs €18 and is valid for three days. Unlike many archaeological sites in the Mediterranean region, those around Naples are almost all well served by public transport; ask about transportation options at the helpful Porta Marina information kiosk.

Julius Caesar's father-in-law. The building is named for the 1,800 carbonized papyrus scrolls dug up here in the 18th century, leading scholars to believe that this may have been a study center or library. Given the right funds and political support, it is hoped that the villa can be properly excavated and ultimately opened to the public.

At the entrance to the archaeological park, pick up a map showing the gridlike layout of the dig. Splurge on an audio guide (€6 for one, €9 for two) and head down the tunnel to start the tour at the old shoreline. Though many of the houses are closed and some are in dire need of restoration, a fair cross section of domestic, commercial, and civic buildings is still accessible. Decorations are especially delicate in the **Casa del Nettuno ed Anfitrite** (House of Neptune and Amphitrite), named for the subjects of a still-bright mosaic on the wall of the nymphaeum (a recessed grotto with a fountain), and in the **Terme Femminili** (Women's Baths), where several delicate black-and-white mosaics embellished the rooms. Annexed to the former house is a remarkably preserved wineshop, where amphorae still rest on carbonized wooden shelves. On the other side of the house is the **Casa del Bel Cortile** (House of the Beautiful Courtyard). In one of its inner rooms is the temporary display of a cast taken of some skeletons found in the storerooms down at the old seafront, where almost 300 inhabitants sought refuge from the eruption and were ultimately encapsulated for posterity. The sumptuously decorated **Terme Suburbane** (Suburban Baths)—open only mornings—and the **Casa dei Cervi** (House of the Stags), with an elegant garden open to the sea breezes, are all evocative relics of a lively and luxurious way of life. ⊠ *Corso Ercolano, a 5-min walk downhill from Ercolano Circumvesuviana station* ☎ *081/8575347* ⊕ *www.pompeiisites.org* ✉ *€10; €18 including Oplontis, Pompeii, and 2 other sites over 3 days* ☉ *Apr.–Oct., daily 8:30–7:30 (ticket office closes at 6); Nov.–Mar., daily 8:30–5 (ticket office closes at 3:30).*

Vesuvius

㉑ *8 km (5 mi) northeast of Herculaneum, 16 km (10 mi) east of Naples.*

As you tour the cities that it destroyed, you may be overwhelmed by the urge to explore Vesuvius. In summer especially, the prospect of rising above the sticky heat of Naples is a heady one. The view when clear is magnificent, with the curve of the coast and the tiny white houses among the orange and lemon blossoms. If the summit is lost in mist you'll be lucky to see your hand in front of your face. When you see the summit clearing—it tends to be clearer in the afternoon—head for it. If possible, see Vesuvius after you've toured the ruins of buried Herculaneum to appreciate the magnitude of the volcano's power.

Reaching the crater takes some effort. From the Ercolano stop of the Circumvesuviana, take scheduled buses (trip takes one hour; there are four or five departures a day—check for the latest schedule at the bar just outside the train station) or your own car to Quota 1000 (the parking lot and cafeteria area near the top). From here you must make the 30-minute ascent up a soft, slippery cinder track by foot. The €6 admission includes compulsory guide service, usually young geologists with a smattering of English. At the bottom you'll be offered a stout walking stick (a small tip is appreciated on return). The climb can be tiring if you're not used to steep hikes. Wear nonskid shoes (not sandals). ☎ *081/ 7775720* 🖭 *€6* ☉ *Daily 9 AM–2 hrs before sunset.*

You can visit **Osservatorio Vesuviano** (Vesuvius Observatory)—2,000 feet up—and view instruments used to study the volcano, some dating back to the mid-19th century. ☎ *081/6108483* ⊕ *www.ov.ingv.it* 🖭 *Free* ☉ *Weekends 10–2.*

Oplontis

 20 km (12 mi) southeast of Naples, 5 km (3 mi) west of Pompeii.

The spectacular archaeological site of Oplontis (surrounded by the fairly drab urban landscape of Torre Annunziata) is a villa complex that's been imaginatively ascribed—based on a mere inscription on an amphora—to Nero's second wife, Poppaea Sabina, whose family was well known among the landed gentry of neighboring Pompeii. As Roman villas go, Poppaea's Villa is truly exceptional. Excavation so far has uncovered an area of more than 325 feet by 250 feet, and because the site is bound by a road to the west and a canal to the south, it may never be possible to gauge its full extent. What's been found includes porticoes, pools, baths, and extensive gardens, as well as the standard atria, triclinia, and a warren of *cubicula* (bedrooms).

Access is easiest from the Circumvesuviana station of Torre Annunziata, about 650 feet away. Outside the station turn left and then right downhill; the site is just after the crossroads on the left. If coming by car, take the Torre Annunziata turnoff from the Naples–Salerno autostrada, turn right, and then look for signs on the left for Oplontis at the first major crossroads. The main entrance to the site is from the north— you basically go into the villa through the gardens, with the atrium on the southern side lying under about 10 feet of pumice and pyroclastic material from Vesuvius.

✉ *Via Sepolcri 1, Torre Annunziata* ☎ *081/8575347* ⊕ *www. pompeiisites.org* 🖭 *€5, including Boscoreale and Stabiae in 1 day; €18 including Herculaneum, Pompeii, and the 2 other sites over 3 days* ☉ *Apr.–Oct., daily 8:30–7:30 (ticket office closes at 6); Nov.–Mar., daily 8:30–5 (ticket office closes at 3:30).*

CASERTA & BENEVENTO

Campania's inland highlights are Caserta—the Italian answer to Versailles—and Benevento, home to an almost perfectly preserved Roman arch. Benevento was badly damaged by World War II bombings, but among the modern structures there are some medieval and even older relics still standing in the old town. If you go by car, make a brief detour to the medieval hamlet of Caserta Vecchia on the hillside, where there are one or two good restaurants and a very old cathedral.

Caserta

★ *11 km (7 mi) northeast of Herculaneum, 25 km (16 mi) northeast of Naples.*

The palace known as the **Reggia** shows how Bourbon royals lived in the mid-18th century. Architect Luigi Vanvitelli devoted 20 years to its construction under Bourbon ruler Charles III, whose son, Ferdinand IV (1751–1825), moved in when it was completed in 1774. Both king and architect were inspired by Versailles, and the rectangular palace was conceived on a massive scale, with four interconnecting courtyards, 1,200 rooms, and a vast park. Though the palace is not as well maintained as its French counterpart, the main staircase puts the one at Versailles to shame, and the **royal apartments** are sumptuous. It was here, in what Eisenhower called "a castle near Naples," that the Allied High Command had its headquarters in World War II, and here German forces in Italy surrendered in April 1945. There's a museum of items relating to the palace and the region. Most enjoyable are the gardens and parks, particularly the Cascades, adorned with sculptures of the goddess Diana and her maidens. A minibus takes you along the 5-km (3-mi) path from the palace to the end of the gardens. ⊠ *Piazza Carlo III ☎ 0823/ 448084 ⊕ www.reggiadicaserta.org ⌨ Royal apartments, Museo dell'Opera, park, and English garden €6; park only €2; minibus €1 ⊙ Royal apartments Wed.–Mon. 8:30–7:30 (ticket office closes at 7). Park Wed.–Mon.: Nov.–Feb. 8:30–2:30; Mar. 8:30–4; Apr. 8:30–5; May and Sept. 8:30–5:30; June–Aug. 8:30–6; Oct. 8:30–4:30.*

Benevento

35 km (22 mi) east of Caserta, 60 km (37 mi) northeast of Naples.

Benevento owes its importance to its establishment as the capital of the Lombards, a northern tribe that invaded and settled what is now Lombardy when they were forced to move south by Charlemagne's conquests in the 8th century. The tough and resourceful Lombards moved farther south and set up a new duchy in Benevento, later moving its seat to Salerno, where they saw the potential of the natural harbor. Under papal rule in the 13th century, Benevento built a fine cathedral and outfitted it with bronze doors that were a pinnacle of Romanesque art. The cathedral, doors, and a large part of the town were blasted by World War II bombs. The **Duomo** has been rebuilt, and the remaining panels of the original bronze doors are in the chapter library. Fortunately, the majes-

★ tic 2nd-century AD **Arco di Traiano** (Trajan's Arch) was unscathed by the bombing. Roman emperor Trajan, who sorted out Rome's finances, extended the Appian Way through Benevento to the Adriatic. The ruins of the **Teatro Romano** (⊠ Take Via Carlo from Duomo ⌨ €2.50 ⊙ Daily 9–1 hr before sunset), which had a seating capacity of 20,000, have been extensively restored and host a summer music and theater season.

ISCHIA & PROCIDA

Though Capri gets star billing among the islands that line the bay of Naples, Ischia and Procida also have their own, lower-key appeal. Ischia is a popular destination on account of its spas, beaches, and hot springs. Procida, long the poor relation of the three, and the closest to Naples, is starting to capitalize on its chief natural asset, the unspoiled isle of Vivara. The pastel colors of Procida will be familiar to anyone who has seen the widely acclaimed film *Il Postino*.

Procida

㉓ *35 mins by hydrofoil, 1 hr by car ferry from Naples.*

Lying barely 3 km (2 mi) from the mainland and 10 km (6 mi) from the nearest port of Pozzuoli, Procida is an island of enormous contrasts. It is the most densely populated island in Europe—almost 11,000 people crammed into less than 3½ square km (2 square mi)—and yet there are oases such as Marina Corricella and Vivara that seem to have been by-passed by modern civilization. It's no surprise that picturesque Procida has strong artistic traditions and is widely considered a painters' paradise.

The sleepy fishing village of **Corricella,** used as the setting for the water-front scenes in the Oscar-winning film *Il Postino,* has been relatively im-mune to life in the limelight. Apart from the opening of an extra restaurant and bar there have been few changes. This is the type of place where even those with failing grades in art class feel like reaching for a paintbrush to record the delicate pinks and yellows of the buildings. The **Graziella** bar at the far end of the seafront offers the island's famous lemons squeezed over crushed ice to make an excellent granita.

Where to Eat

$–$$ ✕ **La Gorgonia.** This restaurant sits right on the waterfront, which draws in the crowds. The specialties here are combinations of seafood and lo-cally grown vegetables, such as pasta *con fagioli e cozze* (with beans and mussels). ✉ *Marina Corricella 50* ☎ *081/8101060* 🖃 *AE, DC, MC, V* ⊗ *Closed Mon. and Nov.–Feb.*

Ischia

㉔ *45 mins by hydrofoil, 90 mins by car ferry from Naples; 60 mins by ferry from Pozzuoli.*

Whereas Capri wows you with its charm and beauty, Ischia takes time to cast its spell. In fact, an overnight stay is probably not long enough for the island to get into your blood. It does have its share of vine-grow-ing villages beneath the lush volcanic slopes of Monte Epomeo, and un-like Capri it enjoys a life of its own that survives when the tourists head home. But there are few signs of antiquity here, the architecture is un-remarkable, the traffic can be overwhelming, and hoteliers have yet to achieve a balanced mix of clientele—most are either German (off-sea-son) or Italian (in-season). But should you want to plunk down in the sun for a few days and tune out the world, this is an ideal spot; just don't expect an unspoiled, undiscovered Capri. When Augustus gave the Neapolitans Ischia for Capri, he knew what he was doing.

Ischia is volcanic in origin. From its hidden reservoir of seething molten matter come the thermal springs said to cure whatever ails you. As early as 1580 a doctor named Lasolino published a book about the mineral wells at Ischia. "If your eyebrows fall off," he wrote, "go and try the baths at Piaggia Romano. If you know anyone who is getting bald, anyone who suffers from elephantiasis, or another whose wife yearns for a child, take the three of them immediately to the Bagno di Vitara; they will bless you." Today the island is covered with thermal baths, often surrounded by tropical gardens.

A good 35-km (22-mi) road makes a circuit of the island; the ride takes most of a day if you stop along the way to enjoy the views and perhaps have lunch. You can book a boat tour around the island at the booths in various ports along the coast; there's a one-hour stop at Sant'Angelo. The information office is at the harbor. You may drive on Ischia year-round. There's also fairly good bus service, and you'll find plenty of taxis.

Ischia Porto is the largest town on the island and the usual point of debarkation. It's no workaday port, however, but a lively resort with plenty of hotels, the island's best shopping area, and low, flat-roof houses on terraced hillsides overlooking the water. Its narrow streets often become flights of steps that scale the hill, and its villas and gardens are framed by pines.

Most of the hotels are along the beach in the part of town called **Ischia Ponte,** which gets its name from the *ponte* (bridge) built by Alfonso of Aragon in 1438 to link the picturesque castle on a small islet offshore with the town and port. For a while the castle was the home of Vittoria Colonna, poetess, granddaughter of Renaissance Duke Federico da Montefeltro (1422–82), and platonic soul mate of Michelangelo, with whom she carried on a lengthy correspondence. You'll find a typical resort atmosphere: countless cafés, shops, and restaurants, and a 1-km (½-mi) stretch of fine-sand beach. **Casamicciola,** a popular beach resort, is 5 km (3 mi) west of Ischia Porto. Chic and upscale **Lacco Ameno,** next to Casamicciola, is distinguished by a mushroom-shape rock offshore and some of the island's best hotels. Here, too, you can enjoy the benefits of Ischia's therapeutic waters.

The far western and southern coasts of Ischia are more rugged and attractive. **Forio,** at the extreme west, has a waterfront church and is a good spot for lunch or dinner.

The sybaritic hot pools of the **Giardini Poseidon Terme** (Poseidon Gardens Spa) are on the Citara beach, south of Forio. You can sit like a Roman senator on a stone chair recessed in the rock and let the hot water cascade over you—all very campy, and fun.

Sant'Angelo, on the southern coast, is a charming village; the road doesn't reach all the way into town, so it's free of traffic, and it's a five-minute boat ride from the beach of Maronti, at the foot of cliffs.

The inland town of Fontana is the base for excursions to the top of **Monte Epomeo,** the long-dormant volcano that dominates the island landscape. You can reach its 2,585-foot peak in less than 1½ hours of relatively easy walking.

13

Where to Stay & Eat

★ **$$$$** ✕ **Il Melograno.** A 10-minute walk south from the center of Forio takes you to the tranquil setting of one of Campania's finest restaurants. With antipasti such as *calamaretti crudi con pera* (raw squid with pears) and many tempting pasta dishes, you could be forgiven for skipping the main course. Try the very reasonably priced local wines (both white and red) from the Pietratorcia winery up the road. Dessert, appropriately called *dulcis in fundo* (the best for last), also merits attention. ⊠ *Via G. Mazzella 110, Forio* ☎ *081/998450* ⊕ *www.ilmelogranoischia.it* ⚐ *Reservations essential* ▤ *AE, DC, MC, V* ☉ *Closed Mon. and Tues. in Nov. and Dec., closed Jan. 7–Mar. 15.*

$–$$ ✕ **Gennaro.** This small family restaurant on the seafront in Ischia Porto serves excellent fish in a convivial atmosphere. Specialties include spaghetti *alle vongole* (with clam sauce, either white or red) and linguine *all'aragosta* (with lobster). ⊠ *Via Porto 66, Ischia Porto* ☎ *081/992917* ▤ *AE, DC, MC, V* ☉ *Closed Nov.–mid-Mar.*

$$$$ 🏨 **Grand Hotel Punta Molino.** Set in its own pine forest on the island's northeastern coastline, this hotel is still within walking distance of the best shopping. This pleasingly modern establishment provides privacy, relaxation, and low-key evening entertainment. Rooms are decorated in gentle Mediterranean hues—some of the best are in the villa annex. A crescent-shape swimming pool wraps around part of the main building, and the gardens have walkways leading to shady pergolas. Rates include a buffet lunch or candlelight dinner. ⊠ *Lungomare C. Colombo 23, 80077* ☎ *081/991544* 🖷 *081/9991562* ⊕ *www.puntamolino.it* ➥ *90 rooms* ⚒ *2 restaurants, 3 pools, health club, spa, beach, piano bar, meeting rooms* ▤ *AE, DC, MC, V* ☉ *Closed Oct.–Mar.* ⊁⊜⊢ *MAP.*

$$$–$$$$ 🏨 **Hotel San Montano.** The modern San Montano is perched commandingly 300 feet up on Monte Vico. Nautical motifs are used in much of the hotel, so you'll find portholes in the lobby, brass finishings to the room furniture, and tiller-shape headboards. With the full gamut of treatments available at the spa, you could be forgiven for not venturing down to sea level. Note that half board is required in high season. ⊠ *Via Montevico 20, 80076 Lacco Ameno* ☎ *081/994033* 🖷 *081/980242* ⊕ *www.sanmontano.com* ➥ *65 rooms, 12 suites* ⚒ *Restaurant, in-room safes, minibars, cable TV, tennis court, 2 pools, spa* ▤ *AE, DC, MC, V* ☉ *Closed Nov.–Mar.* ⊁⊜⊢ *MAP.*

$$$ 🏨 **Villarosa.** A highlight at this gracious family-run hotel—a villa with bright and airy rooms—is the thermal pool in the garden. In high season, half board is required, and you must reserve well in advance. It's in the heart of Ischia Porto and only a short walk from the beach. ⊠ *Via Giacinto Gigante 5, 80077 Ischia Porto* ☎ *081/991316* 🖷 *081/992425* ⊕ *www.lavillarosa.it* ➥ *37 rooms* ⚒ *Restaurant, pool* ▤ *AE, DC, MC, V* ☉ *Closed Nov.–Mar.* ⊁⊜⊢ *MAP.*

$ 🏨 **La Pergola.** The chance to stay on a working farm is the draw at La Pergola, a whitewashed villa perched on the slopes of Monte Epomeo. Surrounded by vineyards and olive and fruit trees, the villa has sweeping views westward over Citara Beach. Its dynamic young owners also operate a thriving restaurant serving local specialties including the fabled *coniglio all'ischitana* (rabbit simmered with tomatoes). ⊠ *Via San*

Giuseppe 8, 80077 Forio ☎☎ *081/909483* ⊕ *www.agriturismolapergola.*
it ➟ *7 rooms* ⚄ *Restaurant; no a/c, no room phones, no room TVs* ⊟ *No*
credit cards ❘◯❘ *MAP.*

CAPRI

Once a pleasure dome to Roman emperors and now Italy's most glamorous seaside getaway, Capri (pronounced with an accent on the first syllable) is a craggy island at the southern end to the bay, 75 minutes by boat, 40 minutes by hydrofoil from Naples. The summer scene on Capri calls to mind the stampeding of bulls through the narrow streets of Pamplona: if you can visit in spring or fall, do so. Yet even the crowds are not enough to destroy Capri's very special charm. The town is a Moorish opera set of shiny white houses, tiny squares, and narrow medieval alleyways hung with flowers. You can take a bus or the funicular to reach the town, which rests on top of rugged limestone cliffs hundreds of feet above the sea, and on which herds of *capre* (goats) once used to roam (giving the name to the island). Unlike the other islands in the Bay of Naples, Capri is not of volcanic origin; it may be a continuation of the limestone Sorrentine peninsula.

Limestone caves on Capri have yielded rich prehistoric and Neolithic finds. The island is thought to have been settled by Greeks from Cumae in the 6th century BC and later by other Greeks from Neapolis, but it was the Romans in the early imperial period who really left their mark. Emperor Augustus vacationed here; Tiberius built a dozen villas around the island, and, in later years, he refused to return to Rome, even when he was near death. Capri was one of the strongholds of the 16th-century pirate Barbarossa, who first sacked it and then made it a fortress. In 1806 the British wanted to turn the island into another Gibraltar and were beginning to build fortifications until the French took it away from them in 1808. Over the next century, from the opening of its first hotel in 1826, Capri saw an influx of visitors that reads like a Who's Who of literature and politics, especially in the early decades of the 20th century.

Like much else about Capri, the island's rare and delicious white wine is sensuous and intoxicating. Note that most of the wine passed off as "local" on Capri comes from the much more extensive vineyards of Ischia.

On arrival at the port, pick up the excellent map of the island at the tourist office (€1). You may have to wait in line for the cog railway (€2.60 round-trip) to **Capri Town,** perched some 450 feet above the harbor. If it's not operating, there's a bus and taxi service, as well as a network of steps leading all the way up. From the upper station, walk out into Piazza Umberto I, much better known as the Piazzetta, the island's social hub. You can window-shop in expensive boutiques and browse in souvenir shops along Via Vittorio Emanuele, which leads south toward the many-domed **Certosa di San Giacomo.** You can visit the church and cloister of this much-restored monastery and also pause long enough to enjoy the breathtaking view of Punta Tragara and the Faraglioni, three towering crags, from the viewing point at the edge of the cliff. ⊠ *Via Certosa* ☎ *081/8376218* ☯ *Tues.–Sun. 9–2.*

OFF THE
BEATEN
PATH

VILLA JOVIS – From Capri Town, the 45-minute hike east to Villa Jovis, the grandest of those built by Tiberius, is strenuous but rewarding. Follow the signs for Villa Jovis, taking Via Le Botteghe from the Piazzetta, then continuing along Via Croce and Via Tiberio. At the end of a lane that climbs the steep hill, with pretty views all the way, you come to the precipice over which the emperor reputedly disposed of the victims of his perverse attentions. From a natural terrace above, near a chapel, are spectacular views of the entire Bay of Naples and, on clear days, part of the Gulf of Salerno. Below are the ruins of Tiberius's palace. Allow 45 minutes each way for the walk alone. ⊠ *Via Tiberio* ☎ *081/8370381* ⊠ *€5* ☯ *Daily 9–1 hr before sunset.*

㉗ Only when the **Grotta Azzurra** was "discovered" in 1826 by the Polish poet August Kopisch and Swiss artist Ernest Fries, did Capri become a tourist haven. The watery cave's blue beauty became a symbol of the return to nature and revolt from reason that marked the Romantic era, and it soon became a required stop on the Grand Tour. In fact, the grotto had long been a local landmark. During the Roman era—as testified by the extensive remains, primarily below sea level, and several large statues now at the Certosa di San Giacomo—it had been the elegant, mosaic-decorated nymphaeum of the adjoining villa of Gradola. Historians can't quite agree if it was simply a lovely little pavilion where rich patricians would cool themselves or truly a religious site where sacred mysteries were practiced. The water's extraordinary sapphire color is caused by a hidden opening in the rock that refracts the light. At highest illumination the very air inside seems tinted blue.

> **WORD OF MOUTH**
>
> "The Blue Grotto (Grotta Azzurra) really is worth it; the color is not to be believed. But . . . you have to sit in the little motorboat outside the grotto with all the other boats until it is your turn. Bad fumes, queasiness in everyone. . . . But I loved loved loved Capri. Not the main streets, but all the small byways."
> –humanone

The Grotta Azzurra can be reached from Marina Grande or from the small embarkation point below Anacapri on the northwest side of the island, accessible by bus from Anacapri. If you're pressed for time, however, skip this sometimes frustrating and disappointing excursion. You board one boat to get to the grotto, then transfer to another smaller boat to take you inside. If there's a backup of boats waiting to get in, you'll be given precious little time to enjoy the gorgeous color of the water and its silvery reflections. ⊠ *Marina Grande* ⊠ *About €15–€20, depending on boat company, including admission to grotto* ☯ *Apr.–Sept., daily 9:30–2 hrs before sunset; Oct.–Mar., daily 10–noon.*

㉘ From the terraces of the **Giardini di Augusto** (Gardens of Augustus), a beautifully planted public garden with excellent views, you can see the village of Marina Piccola below—restaurants, cabanas, and swimming platforms huddle among the shoals—and admire the steep and wind-

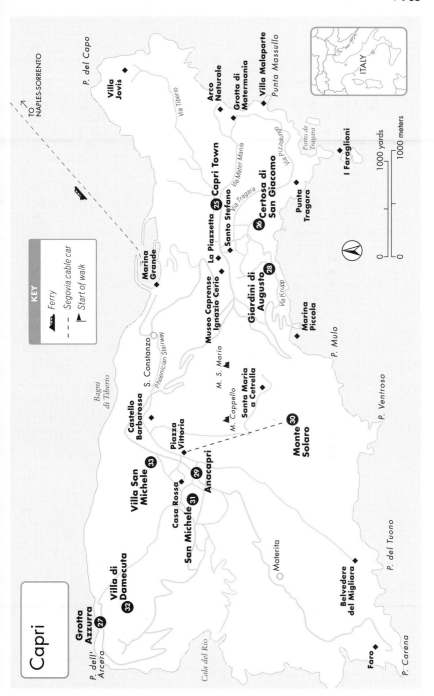

Capri

KEY

- 🚢 Ferry
- – – – Segovia cable car
- ▲ Start of walk

ITALY

TO NAPLES-SORRENTO

P. del Capo

Villa Jovis

Via Tiberio

Arco Naturale

Grotta di Matermania

Villa Malaparte
Punta Massullo

Via Mater Mania

La Piazzetta **25 Capri Town**

Santo Stefano

26 Certosa di San Giacomo

Via Tragara

Via Pizzolungo

Porto de Tragara

I Faraglioni

Punta Tragara

Marina Grande

Museo Caprense Ignazio Cerio

Giardini di Augusto **28**

Via Krupp

Marina Piccola

P. Mulo

Bagni di Tiberio

S. Constanzo

Phoenician Stairway

M. S. Maria

M. Cappello

Santa Maria a Cerella

Monte Solaro 30

Castello Barbarossa

Piazza Vittoria

Villa San Michele 33

Casa Rossa 29

San Michele 31

Anacapri

Materita

P. Ventroso

P. del Tuono

Grotta Azzurra 27

P. dell' Arcera

Villa di Damecuta 32

Cala del Rio

Belvedere del Migliara

Faro

P. Carena

0   1000 yards

0   1000 meters

ing Via Krupp, actually a staircase cut into the rock. Friedrich Krupp, the German arms manufacturer, loved Capri and became one of the island's most generous benefactors. The staircase has been closed for years, but you can reach the beach by taking a bus from the Via Roma terminus down to Marina Piccola. ⊠ *Via Matteotti beyond monastery of San Giacomo* ☉ *Daily dawn–dusk.*

㉙ A tortuous road leads up to **Anacapri,** the island's "second city," about 3 km (2 mi) from Capri Town. To get there you can take a bus either from Via Roma in Capri Town or from Marina Grande (both €1.30), or a taxi (about €15 one-way; agree on the fare before starting out). Crowds are thick down Via Capodimonte leading to Villa San Michele and around the square, Piazza Vittoria, which is the starting point of the chairlift to the top of Monte Solaro. Elsewhere, Anacapri is quietly appealing. It's a good starting point for walks, such as the 80-minute round-trip journey to the **Migliara Belvedere,** on the island's southern coast.

㉚ An impressive limestone formation and the highest point on Capri (1,932 feet), **Monte Solaro** affords gasp-inducing views toward the bays of both Naples and Salerno. A 12-minute chairlift ride will take you right to the top (refreshments available at the bar), which is a starting point for a number of scenic trails on the western side of the island. Picnickers should note that even in summer it can get windy at this height, and there are few trees to provide shade or refuge. ⊠ *Piazza Vittoria, Anacapri* ☎ *081/8371428* 🎫 *€5 one-way, €6.50 round-trip* ☉ *Daily 9:30–5:30.*

㉛ In the heart of Anacapri, the octagonal baroque church of **San Michele,** finished in 1719, is best known for its exquisite majolica pavement designed by Solimena and executed by the *mastro-riggiolaro* (master tiler) Chiaiese from Abruzzo. A walkway skirts the depiction of Adam and a duly contrite Eve being expelled from the Garden of Eden, but you can get a fine overview from the organ loft, reached by a winding staircase near the ticket booth (a privileged perch you have to pay for). Outside the church is the Via Finestrale, which leads to Anacapri's noted **Le Boffe quarter.** This section of town, centered on the Piazza Ficacciate, owes its name to the distinctive domestic architecture prevalent here, which uses vaults and sculpted groins instead of cross beams. ⊠ *Piazza Nicola, Anacapri* ☎ *081/8372396* 🎫 *€3* ☉ *Nov.–Mar., daily 9:30–5; Apr.–Oct., daily 9–7.*

㉜ One of the best excursions from Anacapri is to the ruins of the Roman **Villa di Damecuta.** Sited strategically on a ridge with views sweeping across the Bay of Naples toward Procida and Ischia, the villa would have had its main access point at the landing stage right by the Blue Grotto at Gradola. This was probably one of the villas mentioned by Tacitus in his *Annals* as having been built by Tiberius: "Here on Capreae, in twelve spacious, separately named villas, Tiberius settled." Like Villa Jovis to the east, Villa di Damecuta was extensively plundered over the centuries prior to its proper excavation in 1937. Below the medieval tower (Torre Damecuta) there are two rooms (*domus* and *cubiculum*) that are thought to have been Tiberius's secret summer refuge. Affinities with Villa Jovis may be seen in the *ambulatio* (walkway) complete with seats and a stunning backdrop. To reach Villa Damecuta, get the bus from

Anacapri to Grotta Azzurra and ask the driver to let you off at the proper stop. Alternatively, you can walk from the center of Anacapri down the bus route (about 30 minutes, but no sidewalks) or try your luck in the network of virtually traffic-free little alleyways running parallel to the main road. ⊠ *Via A. Maiuri* ⊠ *Free* ⊙ *Daily 9–1 hr before sunset.*

★ ㉝ From Anacapri's Piazza Vittoria, picturesque Via Capodimonte leads to **Villa San Michele,** the charming former home of Swedish doctor and philanthropist Axel Munthe (1857–1949) that Henry James called "the most fantastic beauty, poetry, and inutility that one had ever seen clustered together." At the ancient entranceway to Anacapri at the top of the Scala Fenicia, the villa is set around Roman-style courtyards, marble walkways, and atria. Rooms display the doctor's varied collections, which range from bric-a-brac to antiquities. Medieval choir stalls, Renaissance lecterns, and gilded statues of saints are all part of the setting, with some rooms preserving the doctor's personal memorabilia. A spectacular pergola path overlooking the entire Bay of Naples leads from the villa to the famous Sphinx Parapet, where an ancient Egyptian sphinx looks out toward Sorrento; you cannot see its face—on purpose. It is said that if you touch the sphinx's hindquarters with your left hand while making a wish, it will come true. The parapet is connected to the little Chapel of San Michele, on the grounds of one of Tiberius's villas.

Besides hosting summer concerts, the Axel Munthe Foundation has an ecomuseum that fittingly reflects Munthe's fondness for animals. There you can learn about various bird species—accompanied by their songs— found on Capri. Munthe bought up the hillside and made it a sanctuary for birds. ⊠ *Via Axel Munthe* ☎ *081/837401* ⊕ *www.sanmichele. org* ⊠ €5 ⊙ *May–Sept., daily 9–6; Mar., daily 9:30–4:30; Apr. and Oct., daily 9:30–5; Nov.–Feb., daily 10:30–3:30.*

Where to Stay & Eat

$$$–$$$$ ✕ **La Capannina.** One of Capri's finest restaurants, La Capannina is only a few steps from the busy social hub of the Piazzetta. It has a discreet covered veranda—open in summer—for dining by candlelight; most of the regulars avoid the stuffy dining rooms. The specialties are homemade ravioli and linguine *con lo scorfano* (with scorpion fish). Look for the authentic Capri wine with the house label. ⊠ *Via Le Botteghe 12bis and 14, Capri Town* ☎ *081/8370732* ⌛ *Reservations essential* ⊟ *AE, DC, MC, V* ⊙ *Closed mid-Jan.–mid-Mar. and Wed. in Mar. and Nov.*

$$$ ✕ **La Canzone del Mare.** This is the legendary spot at the Marina Piccola, erstwhile haunt of Grace Fields, Emilio Pucci, Noël Coward, and any number of '50s and '60s glitterati. The VIPs may have departed for the beach at the Bagni di Tiberio, but the setting is as magical as ever. Enjoy lunch (no dinner is served) in the thatch-roof pavilion looking out over the sea and I Faraglioni in the distance—this is Capri as picture-perfect as it comes. ⊠ *Via Marina Piccola 93, Capri Town* ☎ *081/ 8370104* ⊟ *AE, DC, MC, V* ⊙ *Closed Nov.–Mar. No dinner.*

★ $$–$$$ ✕ **Da Tonino.** It is well worth making a trip to the Arco Naturale, a rock formation east of Capri Town, to be pampered by creative chef Tonino. The emphasis here is on land-based dishes; try the *terrina di coniglio* (rabbit terrine) or ask for the pigeon with pesto, rosemary, and pine nuts, accompanied by wine from a well-stocked cellar. ✉ *Via Dentecala 34, Capri Town* ☎ *081/8376718* 💳 *AE, DC, MC, V* ⊗ *Closed Jan. 10–Mar. 15.*

$$ ✕ **Al Grottino.** At this small and friendly family-run restaurant near the Piazzetta you'll find vaulted ceilings and autographed photos of celebrity customers hanging on the walls. House specialties include gnocchi with tomato sauce and mozzarella, and linguine *ai gamberetti* (with shrimp and tomatoes). ✉ *Via Longano 27, Capri Town* ☎ *081/8370584* ✍ *Reservations essential* 💳 *AE, DC, MC, V* ⊗ *Closed Tues. and Nov. 3–Mar. 20.*

$$ ✕ **I Faraglioni.** With shade provided by a 100-year-old wisteria plant, this popular restaurant is immersed in Mediterranean greenery. Meals in the fairly stylish dining room usually kick off with *uovo alla Monachina,* an egg-shape dish stuffed with mystery ingredients. For the first course, try the *straccetti con gamberi e pomodorini* (fresh green pasta with shrimp and cherry tomatoes). ✉ *Via Camerelle 75, Capri Town* ☎ *081/8370320* ✍ *Reservations essential* 💳 *AE, DC, MC, V* ⊗ *Closed Nov.–Mar.*

$–$$ ✕ **La Giara.** A two-minute walk from Anacapri's bustling Piazza Vittoria, this casual eatery has a variety of delicious dishes served briskly and courteously. For a change from seafood, try the *pennette aum aum,* pasta pleasingly garnished with eggplant, mozzarella, cherry tomatoes, and basil. ✉ *Via Orlandi 67, Anacapri* ☎ *081/8373860* 💳 *AE, DC, MC, V* ⊗ *Closed Wed., and Dec. and Jan.*

$–$$ ✕ **Ristorante Pizzeria Aurora.** Though often frequented by celebrities—their photographs adorn the walls—this restaurant offers *simpatia* to all its patrons. Sit outside for maximum visibility or opt for extra privacy within. The cognoscenti start off by sharing a pizza *all'acqua,* a thin pizza with mozzarella and a sprinkling of *peperoncino* (dried chili peppers). If tiring of pasta, try the *sformatino alla Franco* (rice pie in a prawn sauce). Reservations are essential for dinner. ✉ *Via Fuorlovado 18–20, Capri Town* ☎ *081/8370181* 💳 *AE, DC, MC, V* ⊗ *Closed Jan. and Feb.*

$$$$ ✕🏨 **Villa Brunella.** This gem is in a garden just below the lane leading to the Faraglioni. Comfortable and tastefully furnished, the family-run hotel has spectacular views and a swimming pool overlooking the sea. The terrace restaurant ($$) also benefits from the superb panorama and is renowned for its seafood and other local dishes. ✉ *Via Tragara 24, 80073 Capri Town* ☎ *081/8370122* 📠 *081/8370430* 🌐 *www.villabrunella.it* ⇆ *20 rooms* ♨ *Restaurant, cable TV, pool, bar* 💳 *AE, DC, MC, V* ⊗ *Closed Nov.–Mar.* 🍽 *BP.*

$$$$ 🏨 **Punta Tragara.** Clinging to the Punta Tragara, this gorgeous hotel has
Fodor'sChoice ★ a hold-your-breath perch directly over the rocks of I Faraglioni. Originally a villa visited by Churchill and Eisenhower, its exterior was renovated by Le Corbusier in traditional Capri style, then opened as a hotel in the 1970s. Baronial fireplaces, gilded antiques, and travertine marble set the style in the main salons, while guest rooms—no two are alike—are sumptuous. The garden area has two beautiful saltwater pools and an arbor-covered restaurant, La Bussola, which might be the prettiest spot on the island. To top it off, the staff seems to have been sent to the finest finishing schools. ✉ *Via Tragara 57, 80073 Capri Town* ☎ *081/8370844* 📠 *081/8377790* 🌐 *www.hoteltragara.com* ⇆ *48 rooms* ♨ *Restaurant, 2 pools, bar* 💳 *AE, DC, MC, V* 🍽 *BP.*

$$$$ ▦ **Quisisana.** This grand hotel, one of the island's most luxurious, sits in the center of Capri Town. The bright and spacious rooms have some antique accents. Many have arcaded balconies with views of the sea or the charming enclosed garden surrounding a swimming pool. The Quisisana is particularly popular with Americans. ⊠ *Via Camerelle 2, 80073 Capri Town* ☎ *081/8370788* 🖷 *081/8376080* ⊕ *www.quisi.com* ⤴ *149 rooms* △ *2 restaurants, cable TV, in-room data ports, tennis court, pool, gym, sauna, bar, convention center* ▭ *AE, DC, MC, V* ☉ *Closed Nov.–mid-Mar.* ⊙⊙ *MAP.*

★ **$$$$** ▦ **Scalinatella.** The name means "little stairway," and that's how this charming but modern small hotel is built, on terraces following the slope of the hill, overlooking the gardens, pool, and sea. The Scalinatella is the more private neighbor of the nearby Quisisana, with intimate bedrooms in fresh, bright colors; the bathrooms have whirlpool baths. ⊠ *Via Tragara 8, 80073 Capri Town* ☎ *081/8370633* 🖷 *081/8378291* ⊕ *www.scalinatella.com* ⤴ *30 rooms* △ *Restaurant, tennis court, pool, bar* ▭ *AE, DC, MC, V* ☉ *Closed Nov.–mid-Mar.* ⊙⊙ *BP.*

$$–$$$ ▦ **Il Girasole.** A popular option for those on a budget, il Girasole is set in a grove of olive trees. It has small but bright rooms that look out onto a flower-filled terrace. ⊠ *Via Linciano 47, 80071 Anacapri* ☎ *081/ 8372351* ⊕ *www.ilgirasole.com* ⤴ *18 rooms* △ *No a/c* ▭ *No credit cards* ☉ *Closed Oct.–May* ⊙⊙ *BP.*

$$–$$$ ▦ **Villa Sarah.** This whitewashed Mediterranean building has a homey look and bright, simply furnished rooms. It's close enough to the Piazzetta (a 10-minute walk) to give easy access to the goings-on there, yet far enough away to ensure restful nights. There's a garden and a small bar. ⊠ *Via Tiberio 3/a, 80073 Capri Town* ☎ *081/8377817* 🖷 *081/8377215* ⊕ *www.villasarah.it* ⤴ *20 rooms* △ *Cable TV, bar, Internet point* ▭ *AE, DC, MC, V* ☉ *Closed Nov.–Mar.* ⊙⊙ *BP.*

$$ ▦ **Villa Krupp.** Occupying a quiet location near the Gardens of Augustus, this historic hostelry was once the home of Maxim Gorky, whose guests included Vladimir Lenin. Rooms are plain but spacious. ⊠ *Viale Matteotti 12, 80073 Capri Town* ☎ *081/8370362* 🖷 *081/8376489* ⤴ *12 rooms* △ *No a/c in some rooms, no room TVs* ▭ *MC, V* ☉ *Closed Nov.–Mar.* ⊙⊙ *BP.*

$ ▦ **Aida.** On a tiny lane that borders the Gardens of Augustus, the Aida offers a tranquil haven from the island's hustle and bustle. The staff is sociable, and the rooms, which look onto a small garden, are spacious, comfortably furnished, and immaculately clean. ⊠ *Via Birago, 80073 Capri Town* ☎ *081/8370366* ⤴ *4 rooms* △ *No a/c* ▭ *No credit cards* ☉ *Closed Oct.–May* ⊙⊙ *BP.*

SORRENTO & THE AMALFI COAST

As you journey down the fabled Amalfi Coast, your route takes you past rocky cliffs plunging into the sea and small boats lying in sandy coves like brightly colored fish. Erosion has contorted the rocks into shapes resembling figures from mythology and hollowed out fairy grottoes where the air is turquoise and the water an icy blue. In winter Nativity scenes of moss and stone are created in the rocks. White villages dripping with flowers nestle in coves or climb like vines up the steep, terraced hills. Lemon trees abound, loaded with blossom or fruit (and netting in winter to protect the fruit—locals joke that they look after their lemons better than their children). The road must have a thousand turns, each with a different view, on its dizzying 69-km (43-mi) journey from Sorrento to Salerno.

Sorrento

34 *50 km (31 mi) south of Naples, 50 km (31 mi) west of Salerno.*

Sorrento is across the Bay of Naples from Naples itself, on autostrada A3 and SS145. The Circumvesuviana railway, which stops at Herculaneum and Pompeii, provides another connection. The coast between Naples and Castellammare, where road and railway turn off onto the Sorrento peninsula, seems at times depressingly overbuilt and industrialized. Yet Vesuvius looms to the left, you can make out the 3,000-foot-high mass of Monte Faito ahead, and on a clear day you can see Capri off the tip of the peninsula. The scenery improves considerably as you near Sorrento, where the coastal plain is carved into russet cliffs rising perpendicularly from the sea. This is the Sorrento (north) side of the peninsula; on the other side is the more dramatically scenic Amalfi Coast. But Sorrento has at least two advantages over Amalfi: the Circumvesuviana railway terminal and a fairly flat terrain. A stroll around town is a pleasure—you'll encounter narrow alleyways and interesting churches, and the views of the Bay of Naples from the Villa Comunale and the Museo Correale are priceless.

Until the mid-20th century Sorrento was a small, genteel resort favored by central European princes, English aristocrats, and American literati. During World War I American soldiers came to recuperate at the Hotel Vittoria. Now the town has grown and spread out along the crest of its famous cliffs, and apartments stand where citrus groves once bloomed. Like most resorts, Sorrento is best off-season, in spring, autumn, or even winter, when Campania's mild climate can make a stay pleasant anywhere along the coast.

A highlight of Sorrento is **Museo Correale di Terranova,** an 18th-century villa with a lovely garden on land given to the patrician Correale family by Queen Joan of Aragon in 1428. It has an excellent private collection amassed by the count of Terranova and his brother. The building itself is fairly charmless, with few period rooms, but the garden offers an allée of palm trees, citrus groves, floral nurseries, and an esplanade with a panoramic view of the Sorrento coast. The collection itself is one of the finest devoted to Neapolitan paintings, decorative arts, and porcelains, so for connoisseurs of the *seicento* (Italian 17th century), this museum is a must. Magnificent 18th-century inlaid tables by Giuseppe Gargiulo, Capodimonte porcelains, and rococo portrait miniatures are reminders of the age when pleasure and delight were all. Also on view are regional Greek and Roman archaeological finds, medieval marble work, glasswork, old master paintings, 17th-century majolicas—even Tasso's death mask. ⊠ *Via Correale* ☎ *081/8781846* ⊕ *www.sorrento-online.com/museocorreale* ⊠ *€6* ⊙ *Wed.–Mon. 9–2.*

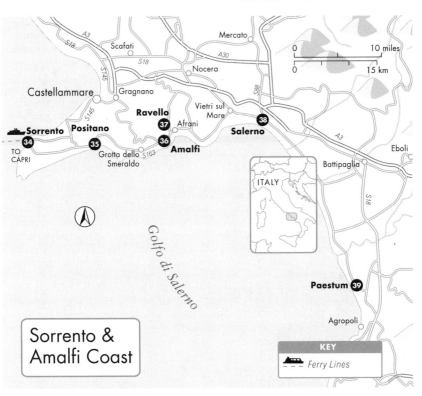

Mercato

0 ──────── 10 miles
0 ──────── 15 km

Scafati
S18
A30
Nocera
S145
Castellammare   Gragnano
S88
Ravello
Vietri sul
Mare
37 Afrani
Sorrento Positano   **38**
34   **35** Grotta dello S163 **Salerno**
TO   Smeraldo   **36** **Amalfi**
CAPRI   A3
Eboli

ITALY

Battipaglia
S18

Golfo di Salerno

Paestum **39**

Agropoli

Sorrento & Amalfi Coast

KEY
⚓ Ferry Lines

13

Worth checking out is the **Museo Bottega della Tarsialignea,** set up by local architects to ensure the continuity of the intarsia (wood inlay) tradition. It houses historical collections as well as exhibitions of modern work. Guided tours, the only way to see the displays, depart every half hour. There's a shop where you can pick up an unusual souvenir. ⊠ *Via San Nicola 28* ☏ *081/8771942* ⊕ *www.alessandrofiorentinocollection.it* 🎫 *€8* ⏱ *Apr.–Oct., Tues.–Sun. 9:30–noon and 5–7; Nov.–Mar., Tues.–Sun. 9:30–noon and 3–5. Shop Tues.–Sun. 9:30–1 and 5–8 (Nov.–Mar. 3–6).*

Via Marina Grande turns into a pedestrian lane, then a stairway leading to Sorrento's only real beach at **Marina Grande,** where fishermen pull up their boats and there are some good seafood restaurants. A frequent bus also plies this route; tickets are sold at the *tabacchi* (tobacconist).

Where to Stay & Eat

★ **$$$$** ✕ **Don Alfonso 1890.** The most heralded restaurant in Campania is the domain of Alfonso Iaccarino; *haute*-hungry pilgrims come here to feast on culinary rarities, often centuries-old recipes given a unique spin. The braciola of lamb with pine nuts and raisins is a recipe that dates back to the Renaissance, and the cannoli stuffed with foie gras pays homage to the Neapolitan Bourbon court. Nearly everything is homegrown, and the wine cellar is one of the finest in Europe. Those who want to make a night of it can stay in one of five apartments above the restaurant. ✉ *Corso Sant'Agata 13, Sant'Agata sui due Golfi, 7 km (4 mi) south of Sorrento* ☎ *081/8780026* ▤ *AE, DC, MC, V* ⊘ *Closed Mon. and Jan. 10–Mar.; closed Tues. Oct.–May.*

$$ ✕ **Antica Trattoria.** An old-fashioned dining room inside and garden tables in fair weather make this a pleasant place to enjoy the local cooking. The atmosphere is homey and the menu is voluminous; specialties include spaghetti alle vongole and *pappardelle all'antica trattoria* (fresh pasta with porcini mushrooms, prosciutto, tomatoes, and basil). You can also opt for one of four prix-fixe menus. ✉ *Via Giuliani 33* ☎ *081/8071082* ▤ *AE, DC, MC, V* ⊘ *Closed Mon. and 4 wks in Jan. and Feb.*

$$ ✕ **Antico Francischiello da Peppino.** Overlooking rows of olive trees that seem to run into the sea, this eatery is away from the throng, halfway between Sorrento and Massa Lubrense. Two huge, beamed dining rooms with brick archways, old chandeliers, antique mirrored sideboards, hundreds of mounted plates, and tangerine-hue tablecloths make for quite a sight. Specialties at this fourth-generation establishment include ravioli filled with sea bass, baked bream in a potato crust with lemon, and limoncello (lemon liqueur) ice cream. ✉ *Via Partenope 27, Massa Lubrense* ☎ *081/5339780* ▤ *AE, DC, MC, V* ⊘ *Closed Wed. in winter.*

★ $$ ✕ **La Favorita—O' Parrucchiano.** Set in a high-ceiling greenhouse, this sprawling eatery has enough tables and chairs amid enough tropical greenery to fill a Victorian conservatory. Opened in 1890 by a former priest (the name means "the priest's place" in the local dialect), La Favorita continues to serve classic Sorrentine cuisine. Though the prawns baked in lemon leaves, the long *candele* pasta with traditional meat and tomato *ragu* sauce, and the lemon tart are all excellent, it's the unique decor that sets La Favorita apart. ✉ *Corso Italia 71* ☎ *081/8781321* ▤ *MC, V* ⊘ *Closed Wed. Nov.–Mar.*

$ ✕ **Trattoria da Emilia.** You can sit outside at this trattoria on the Marina Grande and watch the life of the port go by. This simple, rustic restaurant with wooden tables has been run by Donna Emilia and her offspring since 1947 and provides typical Sorrento home cooking and a family atmosphere. Fried seafood is the specialty. Sofia Loren ate here while filming *Pane, amore . . ..* ✉ *Via Marina Grande 62* ☎ *081/8072720* ▤ *No credit cards* ⊘ *Closed Tues. Oct.–Mar. No dinner Oct.–Mar.*

$$$$ ▦ **Bellevue Syrene.** Set in a cliff-top garden close to the center of Sorrento, this exclusive hotel retains its old-fashioned comforts and sumptuous charm with Victorian nooks and alcoves, antique paintings, and exuberant frescoes. You can find interior-facing rooms at lower prices if you're willing to forgo the splendid views over the sea. Try breakfast on the sunny terrace in summer. ✉ *Piazza della Vittoria 5, 80067* ☎ *081/8781024* 🖷 *081/8783963* ⊕ *www.bellevuesyrene.it* 🛏 *73 rooms* ☕ *2 restaurants, minibars, gym, beach, dock, bar, meeting room, some pets allowed* ▤ *AE, DC, MC, V* ⊖| *BP.*

$$$$ ▦ **Cocumella.** A grand hotel in every sense, the Cocumella seems little changed since the days when Goethe and the Duke of Wellington stayed here. Overlooking the Bay of Naples, the hotel occupies a 17th-century monastery complete with frescoed ceilings and antique reliquaries. The amenities are hardly monastic: they include a spectacular pool area, a workout room, summer concerts in the hotel's baroque church, and Empire-style suites, some with fireplaces. For around €140 per person you can spend a day cruising in the hotel's 90-foot-long 19th-century yacht. Given the hotel's high standards, the restaurant is a disappointment. ⊠ *Via Cocumella 7, Sant'Agnello, 80065* ☎ *081/8782933* 📠 *081/8783712* ⊕ *www.cocumella.com* ↪ *50 rooms, 18 suites* ♿ *Restaurant, cable TV, in-room data ports, pool, gym, spa, bar, some pets allowed* ⊟ *AE, DC, MC, V* ☺ *Closed Nov.–Mar.* ⊙⊙ *BP.*

★ **$$$$** ▦ **Excelsior Vittoria.** Magnificently situated overlooking the Bay of Naples, this is a belle-epoque dream come true. Gilded salons, stunning gardens, and an impossibly romantic terrace where orchestras lull you twice a week with Neapolitan and modern music: in all, it's a truly intoxicating experience. Caruso stayed here and, more recently, Luciano Pavarotti. An outdoor swimming pool and gym add more modern comforts. ⊠ *Piazza Tasso 34, 80067* ☎ *081/8071044* 📠 *081/8771206* ⊕ *www.exvitt.it* ↪ *98 rooms, 20 suites* ♿ *Restaurant, cable TV, in-room data ports, pool, bar, meeting room, some pets allowed* ⊟ *AE, DC, MC, V* ⊙⊙ *BP.*

$$ ▦ **Settimo Cielo.** Even if your wallet won't allow a stay at one of Sorrento's grand hotels, you can still find lodgings right on the water. This hotel, an excellent choice for budget travelers, is a few steps away from the beach. The grounds have pretty gardens and a swimming pool. The rooms, which all face the sea, are simple and modern. ⊠ *Via Capo 27, 80067* ☎ *081/8781012* 📠 *081/8073290* ⊕ *www.hotelsettimocielo. com* ↪ *20 rooms* ♿ *Restaurant, pool, bar, Internet point* ⊟ *AE, DC, MC, V* ☺ *Closed Nov.–mid-Dec. and Jan.–Mar.* ⊙⊙ *BP.*

★ **$** ▦ **Lorelei et Londres.** Once favored by room-with-a-view ladies on holiday, this relic still looks like E. M. Forster's Lucy Honeychurch might pull up at any moment. In front is a beautiful terrace café, aflutter with red awnings and tablecloths. The welcoming lobby always seems to be filled with laughter, so apparently few guests mind that the linoleum-floored rooms upstairs are furnished with simple beds and creaking cupboards. Ask for sea-view rooms away from the noisy road. For luxe and modernity, go elsewhere; come here to take a trip back to the *bella* 19th century. ⊠ *Via Califano 2, 80067* ☎ *081/8073187* 📠 *081/5329001* ↪ *27 rooms* ⊟ *AE, DC, MC, V* ☺ *Closed mid-Nov.–mid-Mar.* ⊙⊙ *BP.*

$ ▦ **Mignon Meublé.** Spacious and simple yet stylish accommodations, a central location, friendly service, and bargain rates—with this winning combination, it's understandable why you should book well in advance. Breakfast is served in your room, but there's also a small sitting area where you can relax. ⊠ *Via Sersale 9, 80067* ☎ *081/8073824* 📠 *081/ 5329001* ↪ *23 rooms* ♿ *No room phones* ⊟ *AE, DC, MC, V* ⊙⊙ *BP.*

Nightlife

BAR At **Circolo dei Forestieri** (⊠ Via de Maio 35 ☎ 081/8773263) you'll get a memorable view of the Bay of Naples from the terrace. Drinks are moderately priced, and there's live music nightly in summer and every weekend the rest of the year. It's closed January and February.

Shopping

You may want to stop in one of the many shops selling limoncello, the famous lemon liqueur. Piemme and Villa Massa are recommended brands; the latter is exported to the United States.

Around **Piazza Tasso** are a number of shops selling embroidered goods and intarsia woodwork, a centuries-old tradition in Sorrento. **Fattoria Terranova** (✉ Piazza Tasso 161 ☎ 081/8781263) sells all kinds of foods ranging from cheeses to preserves, all made on a family-run farm in nearby Massa.

Along narrow **Via San Cesareo**, where the air is pungent with the perfumes of fruit and vegetable stands, there are shops selling local and Italian crafts—everything from jewelry boxes to trays and coffee tables with intarsia decoration. **Ferdinando Corcione**, in his shop on Via San Francesco, gives demonstrations of intarsia work, producing decorative plaques with classic or contemporary motifs.

Positano

★ ❸ *14 km (9 mi) east of Sorrento, 57 km (34 mi) south of Naples.*

When John Steinbeck lived here in 1953, he wrote that it was difficult to consider tourism an industry because "there are not enough *tourists*." It's safe to say that Positano, a village of white Moorish-style houses clinging to slopes around a small sheltered bay, has since been discovered. Another Steinbeck observation still applies, however: "Positano bites deep. It is a dream place that isn't quite real when you are there and becomes beckoningly real after you have gone. . . . The small curving bay of unbelievably blue and green water laps gently on a beach of small pebbles. There is only one narrow street and it does not come down to the water. Everything else is stairs, some of them as steep as ladders. You do not walk to visit a friend, you either climb or slide."

In the 10th century Positano was part of Amalfi's maritime republic, which rivaled Venice as an important mercantile power. Its heyday was in the 16th and 17th centuries, when its ships traded in the Near and Middle East carrying spices, silks, and precious woods. The coming of the steamship in the mid-19th century led to the town's decline; some three-fourths of its 8,000 citizens emigrated to America, most to New York.

What had been reduced to a forgotten fishing village is now the number one attraction on the coast. From here you can take hydrofoils to Capri in summer, escorted bus rides to Ravello, and tours of the Grotta dello Smeraldo. If you're staying in Positano, check whether your hotel has a parking area. If not, you will have to pay for space in a

> ### WORD OF MOUTH
>
> "For our honeymoon we went to Positano (and did day trips to Capri, Ravello, Sorrento, Amalfi, and Pompeii). It was the most romantic place—so beautiful. Wonderful shops and restaurants were everywhere! The drive along the cliffs was scary, but exhilarating, too!"
>
> –Gemini MBA

parking lot, which is almost impossible to find during the high season, from Easter to September. The best bet for day-trippers is to arrive by bus—there is a good, regular service—or else get to Positano early enough to find a parking space.

No matter how much time you spend in Positano, make sure you have some comfortable walking shoes (no heels) and that your back and legs are strong enough to negotiate those daunting *scalinatelle* (little stairways). Alternatively, you can ride the municipal bus, which frequently plies along the one-and-only-one-way Via Pasitea, a hairpin road running from Positano's central Piazza dei Mulini to the mountains and back, making a loop through the town every half hour. Heading down from the Sponda bus stop toward the beach, you pass Le Sirenuse, the hotel where John Steinbeck stayed in 1953. Its stepped terraces offer vistas over the town, so you might splurge on lunch or a drink here on the pool terrace, a favorite gathering place for Modigliani-sleek jet-setters. Continue to Piazza dei Mulini, and make a left turn onto Via dei Mulini.

NEED A BREAK? If you want to catch your breath after a bus ride to Positano, take a quick timeout for an espresso, a slice of Positanese (a delectable chocolate cake), or a fresh-fruit iced granita in the lemon-tree garden at **Bar-Pasticceria La Zagara** (✉ **Via Mulini 8** ☎ **089/875964**).

Past a bevy of resort boutiques, head to Via dei Mulini 23 to view the prettiest garden in Positano—the 18th-century courtyard of the **Palazzo Murat**, named for Joachim Murat, who sensibly chose the palazzo as his summer residence. This was where Murat, designated by his brother-in-law Napoléon as King of Naples in 1808, came to forget the demands of power and lead the simple life. Since Murat was one of Europe's leading style setters, it couldn't be *too* simple, and he wound up building a grand abode (now a hotel) just steps from the main beach.

Beyond the Palazzo Murat is the Chiesa Madre, or parish church of **Santa Maria Assunta**, its green-and-yellow majolica dome topped by a perky cupola visible from just about anywhere in town. Built on the site of the former Benedictine abbey of St. Vito, the 13th-century Romanesque structure was almost completely rebuilt in 1700. The last piece of the ancient mosaic floor can be seen under glass near the apse. Note the carved wooden Christ, a masterpiece of devotional religious art, with its bathetic face and bloodied knees, on view before the altar. At the altar is a Byzantine 13th-century painting on wood of Madonna with Child, known as the Black Virgin, carried to the main beach every August 15 to celebrate the Feast of the Assumption. Legend claims that the painting was once stolen by Saracen pirates, who, fleeing in a raging storm, heard from a voice on high saying, *"Posa, posa"*—"Put it down, put it down." When they placed the image on the beach near the church, the storm calmed, as did the Saracens. Positano was saved, and the town's name was established (yet again). Embedded over the doorway of the church's bell tower, set across the tiny piazza, is a medieval bas-relief of fishes, a fox, and a pistrice, the mythical half-dragon, half-dog sea monster. This is one of the sole relics of the medieval abbey of St. Vito.

✉ *Piazza Flavio Gioia above main beach* ☎ *089/875067* ⊙ *Daily 8:30–noon and 4:30–7.*

The walkway from the Piazza Flavio Gioia leads down to the **Spaggia Grande,** or main beach, bordered by an esplanade and some of Positano's best restaurants. Head over to the stone pier to the far right of the beach as you face the water. A staircase leads to the **Via Positanesi d'America,** a lovely seaside walkway. Halfway up the path you'll find the Torre Trasìta, the most distinctive of Positano's three coastline defense towers, which, in various states of repair, define the edges of Positano. The Trasìta— now a residence occasionally available for summer rental—was one of the defense towers used to warn of pirate raids. Continuing along the Via Positanesi d'America you pass tiny inlets and emerald coves until the large beach, Spaggia di Fornillo, comes into view.

If the Spaggia Grande is too orderly for you, take the small boat to the **Spaggia di Laurito.** (Look for the boat on the right side of the harbor as you approach the beach—it has a sign with a big red smiling fish on it.) You can spend an entire day in this little cove, taking the two steps up to the restaurant **Da Adolfo** when the exertion of swimming has worked up your appetite.

Where to Stay & Eat

$$–$$$ ✕ **Buca di Bacco.** After an aperitif at the town's most famous and fashionable café downstairs, you dine on a veranda overlooking the beach. The specialties include *zuppa di cozze* (mussel soup), fresh *spigola* (sea bass), and figs and oranges in caramel. ✉ *Via Rampa Teglia 8* ☎ *089/875699* ▭ *AE, DC, MC, V* ⊙ *Closed Nov.–Mar.*

$$–$$$ ✕ **Donna Rosa.** This minimalist little hideaway in one-street Montepertuso, the hamlet high over Positano, is truly original. Everybody gets into the act: Mamma does the creative cooking to order, Pappa "makes noise," and the daughters rule out front. Homemade pasta is the house specialty, along with delectable desserts, which may include walnut or strawberry mousse and *crostata all'arancio* (orange tart). A wide selection of fine wines is on hand, and live music can be anything from jazz to Australian gospel, sweetly sung by one of the daughters. Reservations are essential at dinner. ✉ *Via Montepertuso* ☎ *089/811806* ▭ *AE, DC, MC, V* ⊙ *Closed Mon.*

$$–$$$ ✕ **'O Capurale.** Even though *'o capurale* ("the corporal") himself no longer runs the place, his eponymous restaurant is still a great find in the crowded center of Positano. There's one large dining room with simple wooden tables, a marble floor, and a high coved ceiling with Fauvist-style frescoes. The space remains cool even in the height of summer when filled with diners digging into fresh pasta with mussels and pumpkin or rockfish *all'acqua pazza*, with a few tomatoes and garlic. ✉ *Via Regina Giovanna 12* ☎ *089/875374* ▭ *AE, DC, MC, V* ⊙ *Closed Nov.–mid-Feb.*

$$–$$$ ✕ **Il Ritrovo.** Stretching alongside the tiny town square of the mountain
Fodor'sChoice hamlet of Montepertuso is one of the finest restaurants in the area. Ta-
★ bles outside (heated in winter) provide a dizzying view of the coast, and inside, the wood-paneled room has the feel of a ship's cabin. The menu is a mix of sea and mountain food; try the *scialatielli ai frutti di mare*

(thick spaghetti with all manner of things from the sea), accompanied by grilled vegetables or followed by *scamorza* (a mozzarella-like cheese) baked in lemon leaves. Save room for hazelnut *semifreddo* (soft ice cream) and a homemade liqueur. The wine list is excellent. ☒ *Via Montepertuso 77* ☎ *089/812005* ⚖ *Reservations essential* ▭ *AE, DC, MC, V.*

$ ✗ **Da Adolfo.** At this completely informal spot on Spaggia di Laurito, most diners sit for hours in their swimsuits, whiling away the time reading or chatting over a jug of the light local wine (with peaches in summer) or a hefty plate of *totani con patate* (squid and potatoes with garlic and oil). The brusque but amusing waiters are part of the scene. ☒ *Spaggia di Laurito* ☎ *089/875022* ⚖ *Reservations not accepted* ▭ *No credit cards* ☉ *Closed Oct.–Apr.*

$$$$ ⊡ **Casa Albertina.** Clinging to the cliff, this little house is well loved for its Italian charm, its homey atmosphere, and its owners, the Cinque family. Rooms have high ceilings, bright fabrics, tile flooring, and sunny terraces or balconies overlooking the sea and coastline. Cars can't drive to the doorway, but porters will ferry your luggage. Note: it's 300 steps down to the main beach. Half or full board is required in summer. ☒ *Via della Tavolozza 3, 84017* ☎ *089/875143* 🖷 *089/811540* ⊕ *www.casalbertina.it* ⤏ *21 rooms* ⚘ *Restaurant, minibars, cable TV, parking (fee), some pets allowed* ▭ *AE, DC, MC, V* ⦿ *MAP.*

$$$$ ⊡ **Il San Pietro.** An oasis for its affluent international clientele, the San Pietro lies a few bends outside the town and is set amid gardens high above the sea. The hotel has sumptuous Neapolitan baroque decor and masses of flowers in the lounges, elegantly understated rooms (most with terraces), and marvelous views. There's a pool on an upper level, and an elevator whisks you down to the private beach and beach bar. The proprietors organize boating excursions and provide car and minibus service into town. There is a three-night minimum stay. ☒ *Via Laurito 2, 84017* ☎ *089/875455* 🖷 *089/811449* ⊕ *www.ilsanpietro.it* ⤏ *60 rooms* ⚘ *Restaurant, cable TV, in-room data ports, tennis court, pool, gym, beach, dock, 2 bars* ▭ *AE, DC, MC, V* ☉ *Closed mid-Nov.–mid-Mar.* ⦿ *BP.*

★ $$$$ ⊡ **Le Sirenuse.** A handsome 18th-century palazzo in the center of town has been transformed into this luxury hotel with bright tile floors, precious antiques, and tasteful furnishings. The bedrooms are spacious and comfortable; most have splendid views from balconies or terraces. The top-floor suites have huge bathrooms and whirlpool baths. One side of a large terrace has an inviting swimming pool; on the other is an excellent restaurant. ☒ *Via Cristoforo Colombo 30, 84017* ☎ *089/875066* 🖷 *089/811798* ⊕ *www.sirenuse.it* ⤏ *60 rooms* ⚘ *Restaurant, cable TV, pool, gym, sauna, bar* ▭ *AE, DC, MC, V* ⦿ *BP.*

$$$–$$$$ ⊡ **Palazzo Murat.** The location is perfect—in the heart of town, near the beachside promenade, but set inside a quiet, walled garden. The older wing is a historic palazzo with tall windows and wrought-iron balconies; the modern wing is a whitewashed Mediterranean building with arches and terraces. You can relax in antiques-accented lounges or in the charming vine-draped patio and enjoy gorgeous views from the comfortable bedrooms. ☒ *Via dei Mulini 23, 84017* ☎ *089/875177* 🖷 *089/*

13

811419 ⊕ *www.palazzomurat.it* ⋈ *31 rooms* ♿ *Restaurant, mini-bars, bar* ☰ *AE, DC, MC, V* ⊗ *Closed Nov.–Mar.* ⋄ *BP.*

$$ ⌑ **La Fenice.** This tiny, friendly, unpretentious hotel on the peaceful outskirts of town beckons with bougainvillea-laden vistas, castaway cottages, and a turquoise pool, all perched over a private beach. Guest rooms—accented with coved ceilings, whitewashed walls, and native folk art—are simple and tranquil; book the best, those closest to the sea, only if you can handle *very* steep walkways. ⊠ *Via G. Marconi 4, 84017* ☎ *089/875513* 🖷 *089/811309* ⋈ *9 rooms, 6 cottages* ♿ *Pool; no a/c, no room phones, no room TVs* ☰ *No credit cards* ⋄ *BP.*

$$ ⌑ **Villa Rosa.** Sharing almost the same views as hotels that go for twice the price, this family-run lodging has long been a favorite with independent travelers. It's centrally located but slightly set back from the road up the inevitable steps. Ask for one of the rooms on the first floor, which are quieter and have better views. Breakfast is served in your room. ⊠ *Via Cristoforo Colombo 127, 84017* ☎ *089/811955* 🖷 *089/812112* ⊕ *www.villarosapositano.it* ⋈ *18 rooms* ♿ *Laundry service* ☰ *AE, DC, MC, V* ⊗ *Closed Nov.–Feb.* ⋄ *BP.*

$ ⌑ **La Ginestra.** Set in hikers' paradise about 2,000 feet over Positano, the farming cooperative La Ginestra dominates the coastline with its converted 18th-century manor house. The peasants' quarters have been transformed into a thriving restaurant, and the guest rooms above are decorated in simple country style. Positano is reached via a network of footpaths—it's a good hour's slog up from the bottom. If arriving by train, get off the Circumvesuviana train at Vico Equense and take the local orange bus uphill to the village of Santa Maria del Castello, which is about 980 feet from the cooperative. Access by car is also easiest from Vico Equense. ⊠ *Via Tessa 2, 80069 Santa Maria Del Castello, Vico Equense* ☎🖷 *081/8023211* ⊕ *www.laginestra.org* ⋈ *7 rooms* ♿ *Restaurant; no a/c, no room phones* ☰ *MC, V* ⋄ *MAP.*

Nightlife

L'Africana (⊠ Vettica Maggiore, Praiano, 10 km [6 mi] east of Positano on coast road ☎ 089/874042) is the premier nightclub on the Amalfi Coast, built into a fantastic grotto above the sea.

Grotta dello Smeraldo

13 km (8 mi) east of Positano, 27 km (17 mi) east of Sorrento.

A peculiar green light that casts an eerie emerald glow over impressive formations of stalagmites and stalactites, many of them underwater, inspired the name of the Grotta dello Smeraldo (Emerald Grotto). You can park at the signposts for the grotto along the coast road and take an elevator down, or you can drive on to Amalfi and return to the grotto by more romantic means—via boat. Boat tours leave from the Amalfi seafront regularly, according to demand; the charge is €6 per person. Call ahead, as hours are subject to change. ☎ 089/871107 🎫 Grotto €5.50 ⊗ Apr.–Sept., daily 9–5; Oct.–Mar., daily 10–4.

Amalfi

36 *17 km (11 mi) east of Positano, 35 km (22 mi) east of Sorrento.*

"The sun—the moon—the stars—and Amalfi," Amalfitans used to say. During the Middle Ages Amalfi was an independent maritime state with a population of 50,000. The republic also brought the art of papermaking to Europe from Arabia. Before World War II there were 13 mills making paper by hand in the Valle Molini, but now only two small ones remain. The town is romantically situated at the mouth of a deep gorge and has some good-quality hotels and restaurants. It's also a convenient base for excursions to Capri and the Grotta dello Smeraldo. The parking problem here is as bad as that in Positano. The small lot in the center of town fills quickly; if you're willing to pay the steep prices, make a lunch reservation at one of the hotel restaurants and have your car parked for you.

★ Amalfi's main historical sight is its **Duomo** (also known as Cattedrale di Sant'Andrea), which shows an interesting mix of Moorish and early Gothic influences. You're channeled first into the adjoining **Chiostro del Paradiso** (Paradise Cloister), built around 1266 as a burial ground for Amalfi's elite and one of the architectural treasures of southern Italy. Its flower-and-palm-filled quadrangle has a series of exceptionally delicate intertwining arches on slender double columns in a combination of Byzantine and Arabian styles. Next stop is the 9th-century basilica, a **museum** housing sarcophagi, sculpture, Neapolitan gold artifacts, and other treasures from the cathedral complex.

Steps from the basilica lead down into the **Cripta di Sant'Andrea** (Crypt of St. Andrew). The cathedral above was built in the 13th century to house the saint's bones, which came from Constantinople and supposedly exuded a miraculous liquid believers call the "manna of St. Andrew." Following the one-way traffic up to the cathedral itself, you finally get to admire the elaborate polychrome marbles and painted, coffered ceilings from its 18th-century restoration; art historians shake their heads over this renovation, as the original decoration of the apse must have been one of the wonders of the Middle Ages. ✉ *Piazza del Duomo* ☎ *089/ 871059* 💶 *€2.50* ⊙ *Mar.–June and Oct., daily 9–7; July–Sept., daily 9–9; Nov.–Feb., daily 10–1 and 2:30–5:30.*

The **Valle dei Mulini** (Valley of the Mills), uphill from town, was for centuries Amalfi's center for papermaking, an ancient trade learned from the Arabs (who learned it from the Chinese). Beginning in the 12th century, former flour mills in the town were converted to produce paper made from cotton and linen, being among the first in Europe to do so. In 1211 Frederick II of Sicily prohibited this lighter, more readable paper for use in the preparation of official documents, favoring traditional sheepskin parchment, but by 1811 more than a dozen mills here, with more along the coast, were humming. Natural waterpower ensured that the handmade paper was cost-effective, but catastrophic flooding in 1954 closed most of the mills for good, and many of them have now been converted into private housing. The **Museo della Carta** (Museum of Paper) opened in 1971 in a 15th-century mill; paper samples, tools of the trade, old machinery, and the audiovisual presentation are all enlightening. ✉ *Via delle Cartiere 23* ☎ *089/8304561* 🌐 *www.museodellacarta.it* 🎟 *€4* ⏲ *Nov.–Mar., Tues.–Sun. 10–3:30; Apr.–Oct., daily 10–6:30.*

Where to Stay & Eat

★ $$$–$$$$ ✕ **Da Gemma.** Since 1872 cognoscenti have sung the praises of this understated landmark, which has a terrace set above the main street. The menu, printed on local handmade paper, announces such favorites as oven-baked fish with lemon peel and the *tubettoni alla masaniello* (tiny pieces of pasta with capers, mussels, and prawns). Traces of Amalfi's Arabic roots can be found in the sweets made with almonds and citrus fruits that come from the glistening kitchen. ✉ *Via Fratello Gerardo Sasso 9* ☎ *089/871345* ▭ *AE, DC, MC, V* ⏲ *Closed mid-Jan.–mid-Feb. and Wed. Sept.–June.*

$$ ✕ **A Paranza.** Located in the hamlet of Atrani, a 15-minute walk from the center of Amalfi along the road to Salerno, this seafood restaurant is worth the walk. With coved ceilings and immaculate linen tablecloths, the two dining rooms are at once homey and quite formal. Each day's menu depends on the catch; the tasting menu (antipasti ranging from marinated tuna to fried rice balls, pasta, and risotto, and a choice of dessert) is a good option. If that sounds like too much, go for the scialatielli ai frutti di mare. Finish your meal with one of the divine cakes. ✉ *Via Dragone 1/2* ☎ *089/871840* ▭ *AE, DC, MC, V* ⏲ *Closed Dec. 8–26 and Tues. Oct.–May.*

$$ ✕ **Trattoria di Maria.** At this friendly establishment presided over by the convivial Enzo (son of Maria) you can dine with the locals on delicious pizza baked in a wood oven, local fish dishes, and lemon profiteroles. Ask for a glass of the limoncello or one of the other homemade liqueurs made from bay leaves, fennel, or bilberries (similar to blueberries). ✉ *Piazza ad Amalfi* ☎ *089/871880* ▭ *AE, DC, MC, V* ⏲ *Closed Mon. and Nov.*

★ $$$$ 🏨 **Santa Caterina.** A large mansion perched above a terraced and flowered hillside just outside Amalfi proper, the Santa Caterina is one of the top hotels on the coast. The rooms are tastefully decorated; most have small terraces or balconies with spectacular views. There are lovely lounges, gardens, and terraces for relaxing, and an elevator delivers you to the seaside saltwater pool, bar, and swimming area. On grounds lush with lemon and orange groves, there are two romantic villa annexes. ✉ *Strada Amalfitana 9, 84011* ☎ *089/871012* 📠 *089/871351* 🌐 *www.hotelsantacaterina.it* 🛏 *66 rooms* 👍 *2 restaurants, cable TV, in-room data ports, saltwater pool, gym, beach, 2 bars, meeting room, free parking* ▭ *AE, DC, MC, V* 🍽 *BP.*

$$ 🏨 **Hotel dei Cavalieri.** This gleaming white Mediterranean-style hotel sits on the road outside Amalfi. Three villas across the road extend all the way to a beach below. Bright rooms are functionally furnished, with splashy majolica-tile floors. An ample buffet breakfast is served. ✉ *Via M. Comite 32, 84011* ☎ *089/831333* 📠 *089/831354* 🌐 *www.hoteldeicavalieri.it* 🛏 *54 rooms* 👍 *Restaurant, cable TV, bar* ▭ *AE, DC, MC, V* 🍽 *BP.*

$$ ⊞ **Piccolo Paradiso.** This upscale bed-and-breakfast, painted a sunny yellow with green shutters, is a special choice because of its location near the harbor. A small elevator deposits you in the cozy house, which has a casually furnished, sun-bright terrace. Guest rooms are smallish but comfortable, with wicker seating and wrought-iron headboards. Some rooms have private terraces. ⊠ *Via M. Camera 5, 84011* ☎ *089/873001* ⤳ *6 rooms* ⊟ *AE, MC, V* ⊚ *BP.*

Shopping

A must for lovers of art, vintage prints, and fine books is down by the waterfront: **Andrea de Luca** (⊠ Largo Cesareo Console 8 ☎ 089/871954), a publisher of fine books and postcards, sells desk accessories, objets d'art, and art tomes. You'll find paper creations, maps, and other souvenirs near the Duomo at **Amalfi nelle Stampe Antiche** (⊠ Piazza del Duomo 10 ☎ 089/872368).

Ravello

㊲ *5 km (3 mi) northeast of Amalfi, 40 km (25 mi) east of Sorrento.*

Fodor'sChoice ★

Perched on a ridge high above Amalfi and the neighboring town of Atrani, the enchanting village of Ravello has stupendous views, quiet lanes, two important Romanesque churches, and several irresistibly romantic gardens. Set "closer to the sky than the sea," according to André Gide, the town has been the ultimate aerie ever since it was founded as a smart suburb for the richest families of Amalfi's 12th-century maritime republic. Rediscovered by English aristocrats a century ago, the town now hosts one of Italy's most famous music festivals.

The **Duomo,** dedicated to patron saint Pantaleone, was founded in 1086 by Orso Papiro, the town's first bishop. Rebuilt in the 12th and 17th centuries, it retains traces of medieval frescoes in the transept, an original mullioned window, a marble portal, and a three-story 13th-century bell tower playfully interwoven with mullioned windows and arches. The 12th-century bronze door has 54 embossed panels depicting Christ's life, and saints, prophets, plants, and animals, all narrating biblical lore. It was crafted by Barisano da Trani, who also fashioned the doors of the cathedrals of Trani and Monreale. The

> **WORD OF MOUTH**
>
> "Ravello was absolutely the best part of our honeymoon. It had unbelievable views of the coast and sea; far better than Positano in my opinion."
>
> −sam

nave's three aisles are divided by ancient columns, and treasures include sarcophagi from Roman times and paintings by southern Renaissance artist Andrea da Salerno. Most impressive are the two medieval pulpits: the earlier one (on your left as you face the altar), used for reading the Epistles, is inset with a mosaic scene of Jonah and the whale, symbolizing death and redemption. The more famous one opposite, used for reading the Gospels, was commissioned by Nicola Rufolo in 1272 and created by Niccolò di Bartolomeo da Foggia. It seems almost Tuscan in style, with exquisite mosaic work and bas-reliefs and six twisting columns sitting on lion pedestals. An eagle grandly tops the inlaid marble lectern.

A chapel to the left of the apse is dedicated to St. Pantaleone, a physician who was beheaded in the 3rd century in Nicomedia. Every July 27 devout believers gather in hope of witnessing a miracle (similar to that of San Gennaro in Naples), in which the saint's blood, collected in a vial and set out on an inlaid marble altar, appears to liquefy and come to a boil; it hasn't happened in recent years. In the crypt is the **Museo del Duomo,** which displays treasures from about the 13th century, during the reign of Frederick II of Sicily. ⊠ *Piazza del Duomo* 🖼 *€2.50* ⊙ *Church: daily 9–1 and 3–7; museum: Apr.–Oct., daily 9:30–1 and 3–7; Nov.–Mar., weekends 9:30–1 and 3–7.*

Directly off Ravello's main piazza is the **Villa Rufolo,** which—if the master storyteller Boccaccio is to be believed—was built in the 13th century by Landolfo Rufolo, whose immense fortune stemmed from trade with Moors and Saracens. Within is a scene from the earliest days of the Crusades. Norman and Arab architecture mingle in profusion in a welter of color-filled gardens so lush that composer Richard Wagner used them as his inspiration for the home of the Flower Maidens in his opera *Parsifal.* Beyond the Arab-Sicilian cloister and the Norman tower are two flower-bedded terraces that offer a splendid vista of the Bay of Salerno; the lower "Wagner Terrace" is the site for the yearlong **Festival Musicale di Ravello** (🕾 089/858149 ⊕ www.ravelloarts.org). ⊠ *Piazza Duomo, 84010* 🖼 *€4* ⊙ *Daily 9–sunset.*

From Ravello's main piazza, head west along Via San Francesco and Via Santa Chiara to the **Villa Cimbrone,** a medieval-style fantasy that sits 1,500 feet above the sea. Created in 1905 by England's Lord Grimthorpe and made world famous when Greta Garbo stayed here in 1937, the Gothic castle is set in fragrant rose gardens that lead to the **Belvedere dell'Infinità** (Belvedere of Infinity), a grand stone parapet that overlooks the impossibly blue Gulf of Salerno and frames a panorama that former Ravello resident Gore Vidal has called "the most beautiful in the world." The villa itself is now a hotel. ⊠ *Via Santa Chiara 26* 🖼 *089/857459* 🖼 *€4.50* ⊙ *Daily 9–sunset.*

Where to Stay & Eat

★ ¢–$ ✕ **Cumpà Cosimo.** This family-run restaurant a few steps from the Piazza del Duomo offers a cordial welcome in two simple but attractive dining rooms. There's no view, but the food is excellent, most of it coming from owner Donna Netta's garden or her butcher shop next door. Among the specialties are cheese crepes, roast lamb, and a dish including seven types of homemade pasta. ⊠ *Via Roma 44* 🕾 *089/857156* 🖃 *AE, DC, MC, V* ⊙ *Closed Mon. and Jan. 10–Feb.*

¢ ✕ **Vittoria.** Down the bustling arcade of pottery shops adjacent to the Villa Rufolo, this is a good place to escape the crowds. Vittoria's thin-crust pizza with loads of fresh toppings is the star attraction, but also consider the pasta, maybe fusilli with tomatoes, zucchini, and mozzarella. The decor is extremely simple, with white walls and a few etchings of

Ravello. ✉ *Via dei Rufolo 3* ☎ *089/857947* ▭ *AE, DC, MC, V* ⊘ *Closed Tues. Nov.–Mar.*

$$$$ ⊞ **Hotel Palumbo.** Occupying a 12th-century patrician palace outfitted with antiques and modern comforts, this elegant hotel has the feel of a private home as well as its own annexed winery. It has beautiful garden terraces, breathtaking views, and a sumptuous upstairs dining room. In summer you can descend to a villa and be pampered in the hotel's seaside retreat. Half board is compulsory except in winter, when the restaurant is closed. ✉ *Palazzo Confalone, Via San Giovanni del Toro 16, 84010* ☎ *089/857244* 🖷 *089/858133* ⊕ *www.hotel-palumbo.it* ⤶ *20 rooms* ⌂ *Restaurant, cable TV, pool, beach, bar, laundry facilities, meeting room, parking* ▭ *AE, DC, MC, V* ⏐⊙⏐ *MAP.*

★ **$$$$** ⊞ **Palazzo Sasso.** One of the finest hotels in southern Italy, this 12th-century palace dazzles you with a marble atrium and lofty coastal views. No less impressive is the courteous, attentive service. The Rossellini restaurant, open to the public only in the evenings, is also highly recommended. Every room has an ocean view, with high arched ceilings and tile floors that lend a Mediterranean feel. They are furnished with antiques. The "infinite suite" has to be seen to be believed, though its price also approaches infinity. ✉ *Via San Giovanni del Toro 28, 84010* ☎ *089/818181* 🖷 *089/858900* ⊕ *www.palazzosasso.com* ⤶ *36 rooms, 8 suites* ⌂ *Restaurant, minibars, cable TV, in-room data ports, pool, outdoor hot tub, bar, library, some pets allowed* ▭ *AE, DC, MC, V* ⊘ *Closed Nov.–Mar* ⏐⊙⏐ *BP.*

★ **$$$$** ⊞ **Villa Cimbrone.** Suspended over the azure sea and set amid rose-laden gardens, this magical place was once the home of Lord Grimthorpe and the holiday hideaway of Greta Garbo. Now the Gothic-style *castello* (castle) has guest rooms ranging from palatial to cozy (opt for the Peony Room, which has its own terrace). Tapestried armchairs, framed prints, vintage art books, and other antiques that belonged to Viscountess Frost, the lord's daughter, still grace the enchantingly elegant sitting room. Best of all, guests have the villa's famous gardens all to themselves once their gates are closed at sunset. The villa is a strenuous hike from the town center, but porters will carry your luggage and the distance helps keep this the most peaceful place on the Amalfi Coast. ✉ *Via Santa Chiara 26, 84010* ☎ *089/857459* 🖷 *089/857777* ⊕ *www.villacimbrone.it* ⤶ *13 rooms* ⌂ *Minibars, cable TV, in-room data ports, hot tub, library* ▭ *AE, DC, MC, V* ⊘ *Closed Nov.–Easter* ⏐⊙⏐ *BP.*

$ ⊞ **Villa Amore.** A 10-minute walk from the Piazza Duomo, this family-run hotel has a pretty garden and an exhilarating view of the sea from most of its bedrooms. If you're looking for tranquillity, you've found it, especially at dusk, when the valley is tinged with a glorious purple light. Rooms are small, with modest modern furnishings. One of the treats is delicious homemade jam at breakfast. Full board is available, and at least half board is required from July through September. Reserve ahead, and specify time of arrival if you need help with luggage from the parking lot or bus stop; you'll pay €4 per bag. ✉ *Via del Fusco 5, 84010* ☎🖷 *089/857135* ⤶ *12 rooms* ⌂ *Restaurant, bar, some pets allowed; no a/c, no room TVs* ▭ *DC, MC, V* ⏐⊙⏐ *MAP.*

13

Salerno

❸ *6 km (4 mi) east of Vietri sul Mare, 56 km (35 mi) southeast of Naples.*

Spread out along its bay, Salerno was long a sad testimony to years of neglect and overdevelopment, but the antique port is now reevaluating its artistic heritage. It's a well-connected base for exploring the Cilento area to the south, which has such lovely sea resorts as San Marco di Castellabate and Palinuro, and inland some fine mountain walks and spectacular gorges and caves, such as Castelcivita and Pertosa.

Salerno has an imposing Romanesque **Duomo** founded in the mid-9th century and substantially rebuilt by Robert Guiscard from 1076 to 1085. The scene is set by the doorway—see the marble lions at the base—which gives way to a spacious atrium. The Cosmatesque pulpits rival Ravello's for elegance, and ornately carved marbled sarcophagi reinforce the cathedral's stately pedigree. ⊠ *Piazza Duomo* ☎ *089/231387* ☉ *Daily 10–1:30 and 3–6.*

The **Museo Archeologico Provincale,** in Salerno's medieval Benedictine abbey, has interesting displays of ancient artifacts from the region, with many of the higher-quality finds coming from the Greco-Etruscan necropolis in what is now the suburb of Fratte. Some fine Attic and Corinthian vases are on the upper floor, but the show-stealer is the 1st-century BC bronze head of Apollo fished out of the Gulf of Salerno in 1930. ⊠ *Via San Benedetto 28* ☎ *089/231135* ☜ *Free* ☉ *Mon.–Sat. 9–7, Sun. 9–1.*

Where to Stay

$ ▦ **Plaza.** You can easily walk to the harbor, shops, and transportation from this clean, no-frills lodging across from the train station. The interior is decorated in warm, mellow tones, and guest rooms are spacious. When booking, ask for a room on one of the upper floors or in the back over the courtyard, as these tend to be quieter. ⊠ *Piazza Vittorio Veneto 42, 84123* ☎ *089/224477* ▤ *089/237311* ⊕ *www.plazasalerno.it* ▚ *42 rooms* ⚬ *Minibars, cable TV, lobby lounge; no a/c in some rooms* ▤ *AE, DC, MC, V* ⏷❶ *BP.*

Paestum

★ ❹ *42 km (26 mi) southeast of Salerno, 99 km (62 mi) southeast of Naples.*

One of Italy's most majestic sights lies on the edge of a flat coastal plain: the remarkably well-preserved **Greek temples** of Paestum. SS18 from the north passes the train station (Stazione di Paestum), which is about 800 yards from the ruins through the perfectly preserved **Porta Sirena** archway. This is the site of the ancient city of Poseidonia, founded by Greek colonists probably in the 6th century BC. When the Romans took over the colony in 273 BC and the name was latinized to Paestum, they changed the layout of the settlement, adding an amphitheater and a forum. Much of the archaeological material found on the site is displayed in the well-labeled **Museo Nazionale,** and several rooms are devoted to the unique tomb paintings discovered in the area, rare examples of Greek and pre-Roman pictorial art.

At the northern end of the site opposite the ticket barrier is the **Tempio di Cerere** (Temple of Ceres). Built in about 500 BC, it's now thought to have been originally dedicated to the goddess Athena. Follow the road south past the **Foro Romano** (Roman forum) to the **Tempio di Nettuno** (Temple of Poseidon), a magnificent Doric edifice with 36 fluted columns and an extraordinarily well-preserved entablature (area above the capitals) that rivals those of the finest temples in Greece. Beyond is the so-called **Basilica,** the earliest of Paestum's standing edifices; it dates from early in the 6th century BC. The name is an 18th-century misnomer, for the structure was in fact a temple to Hera, the wife of Zeus. Try to see the temples in the late afternoon, when the light enhances the deep gold of the limestone and the temples are almost deserted. ☎ *0828/722654 ✆ Excavations €4, museum €4, excavations and museum €6.50 ⊙ Excavations July–Sept., daily 9 AM–10 PM; Oct.–June, daily 9–1 hr before sunset. Museum July–Sept., daily 9 AM–10 PM; Oct.–June, daily 9–6:30; closed 1st and 3rd Mon. of each month.*

Where to Stay & Eat

¢–$ ✕🏨 **Helios.** A few steps from the temples, the Helios has cottage-type rooms in a garden setting surrounded by olive trees. Seven rooms have their own whirlpool baths. A pleasant restaurant serves local specialties that emphasize seafood. The ricotta and mozzarella made on the premises are especially good. The hotel also organizes visits to a local mozzarella producer and excursions around the area on horseback. ⊠ *Via Nettuno 7, 84063* ☎ *0828/811451* 🖷 *0828/811600* ⇖ *27 rooms ⌂ Restaurant, pool; no a/c in some rooms, no TV in some rooms* ▭ *AE, DC, MC, V* ⭐ *MAP.*

NAPLES & CAMPANIA ESSENTIALS

Transportation

BY AIR

Aeroporto Capodichino, 8 km (5 mi) north of Naples, serves the Campania region. It handles domestic and international flights, including several daily between Naples and Rome (flight time 45 minutes). Throughout the year there is direct helicopter service with Cab Air between Aeroporto Capodichino and Capri, Ischia, or Positano. The cost is €1,400, regardless of the destination.

Taxis are available at the airport for the ride to downtown Naples (€15–€20). The transportation company ANM runs the Alibus service, which leaves the airport every 30 minutes with stops at Piazza Garibaldi and Piazza Municipio (€3). The more frequent but slightly slower Bus 3S also goes to Piazza Garibaldi and to the port (Molo Beverello) beyond. Tickets can be bought from the newsstands inside the airport (€1).

🛈 **Airport Information Aeroporto Capodichino** ☎ 081/7896259. **ANM (Azienda Napoletana Mobilità)** ☎ 081/7631111. **Cab Air** ☎ 081/2587110.

BY BOAT & FERRY

A variety of fast craft and passenger and car ferries connect the islands of Capri and Ischia with Naples and Pozzuoli year-round. In summer Capri and Ischia are serviced by boats from the Amalfi Coast. Boats and hydrofoils for these islands and for Sorrento leave from Naples's Molo Beverello. Hydrofoils also leave from Mergellina. From June to September, the Metro del Mare runs a hydrofoil service from Bacoli as far as Sapri, with various stops in between. Ticket prices depend on the journey you make, but range from €2.50 to €10.

Information on departures is published every day in the local paper, *Il Mattino*, and in local editions of national dailies *Corriere della Sera* and *La Repubblica*. Alternatively, ask at the tourist office or at the port, or contact the companies—Caremar, Navigazione Libera del Golfo, SNAV, and Alilauro—directly. Always double-check schedules in stormy weather.

🚢 Boat & Ferry Information **Alilauro** ☎ 081/7614909 ⊕ www.alilauro.it. **Caremar** ☎ 081/5513882 ⊕ www.caremar.it. **Coop Sant'Andrea** ☎ 089/873190 ⊕ www.coopsantandrea.it. **Mergellina** ✉ About 1½ km [1 mi] to west of Piazza Municipio. **Metro del Mare** ☎ 199/446644 ⊕ www.metrodelmare.com. **Molo Beverello** ✉ Southeast of Piazza Municipio. **Navigazione Libera del Golfo** (NLG) ☎ 081/5527209 ⊕ www.navlib.it. **SNAV** ☎ 081/7612348 ⊕ www.snavali.com.

BY BUS

Marozzi, a Rome-based line, runs direct air-conditioned buses from Rome to Pompeii, Salerno, Sorrento, and Amalfi. Buses leave Rome's Stazione Tiburtina weekdays at 3 PM, weekends at 7 AM. This service aside, trains are a much better option for getting in and out of the region than buses.

Within Campania, there's an extensive network of local buses. ACTP buses connect Naples with Caserta in one hour, leaving every 20 minutes from Piazza Garibaldi (every 40 minutes on Sunday). Buses to Santa Maria Capua Vetere leave Piazza Garibaldi approximately every 30–40 minutes Monday to Saturday (travel time 45 minutes). There are six buses a day Monday to Saturday from Piazza Garibaldi to Benevento. The trip takes 90 minutes. SITA buses for Salerno leave every 30 minutes Monday to Saturday and every two hours on Sunday from the SITA terminal on Via Pisanelli. SITA buses also serve the Amalfi Coast, connecting Sorrento with Salerno. Curreri operates a service (six runs daily) between Sorrento and Aeroporto Capodichino.

🚌 Bus Information **ACTP** ☎ 081/7001111. **Curreri** ☎ 081/8015420. **Marozzi** ☎ 06/4076140. **SITA** ✉ Via Pisanelli near Piazza Municipio ☎ 081/5522176 ⊕ www.sita-on-line.it.

BY CAR

Italy's main north–south route, the A2 (also known as the Autostrada del Sole), connects Rome with Naples and Campania. In good traffic the drive to Naples takes less than three hours. Autostrada A3, a continuation of the A2, runs south from Naples through Campania and into Calabria. It also connects with the autostrada A16 to Bari, which passes Avellino and is linked with Benevento by expressway.

Herculaneum (Ercolano), Pompeii (Pompei), and Oplontis all have marked exits off the A3. For Vesuvius, take the Ercolano exit. For the Sorrento peninsula and the Amalfi Coast, exit at Castellammare di

Stabia. To get to Paestum, take A3 to the Battipaglia exit and take the road to Capaccio Scalo–Paestum.

The roads on the Sorrento peninsula and Amalfi Coast are narrow and twisting, but they have outstanding views. In high season, from about April through October, only residents' cars are allowed on Ischia and Capri.

GARAGES If you come to Naples by car, park it in a garage, agree on the cost in advance, and then keep it there for the duration of your stay. (If you park on the street, you run the risk of being broken into.) Garage dei Fiori (near Villa Pignatelli), Grilli (near Stazione Centrale), and Turistico (near the port) are all centrally located and safe.

13

Garage dei Fiori ⊠ Via Colonna 21 ☎ 081/414190. **Grilli** ⊠ Via Ferraris 40 ☎ 081/264344. **Turistico** ⊠ Via de Gasperi 14 ☎ 081/5525442.

BY PUBLIC TRANSIT IN NAPLES

Naples's rather old Metropolitana (subway system), also called Linea 2, provides frequent service and can be the fastest way to get across the traffic-clogged city. The other urban subway system, Metropolitana Collinare (or Linea 1), links the hill area of the Vomero and beyond with the National Archaeological Museum and Piazza Dante. Trains on both lines run from 5 AM until 10:30 PM.

For standard public transportation, including the subways, buses, and funiculars, a Giranapoli pass costs €1 and is valid for 90 minutes within the city boundaries; €3 buys a *biglietto giornaliero,* good for the whole day. Bus service has become viable over the last few years, especially with the introduction of larger buses and the regular R1, R2, and R3 routes.

BY TRAIN

There are trains every hour between Rome and Naples. Eurostar and Intercity, the fastest types of train service, make the trip in less than two hours. Trains take either the inland route (through Cassino) or go along the coast (via Formia). Almost all trains to Naples stop at Stazione Centrale.

A network of suburban trains connects Naples with several points of interest. The line used most by visitors is the Circumvesuviana, which runs from Corso Garibaldi Station and stops at Stazione Centrale before continuing to Ercolano (Herculaneum), Pompeii, and Sorrento. Frequent local trains connect Naples with Caserta and Salerno. Travel time between Naples and Sorrento on the Circumvesuviana line is about 75 minutes. Benevento is on the main line between Naples and Foggia. The Circumflegrea runs from Piazza Montesanto Station in Naples toward the archaeological zone of Cumae, with three departures in the morning. The Ferrovia Cumana runs from Piazza Montesanto Station to Pozzuoli and Lucrino. For the archaeological zone of Baia, get the shuttle bus outside Lucrino station.

A Fascia 1 ticket (€1.50 for 100 minutes) covers trips between Naples and a radius of about 10 km (6 mi), which includes Pozzuoli and Portici; Fascia 2 (€2 for 120 minutes) takes in Ercolano (Herculaneum), Baia, and Cumae; Fascia 3 (€2.50 for 140 minutes) includes Pompeii, Boscoreale, and Castellammare; Fascia 4 (€3 for 160 minutes) will take you as far as Vico Equense; and Fascia 5 (€3.50 for 180 minutes) covers trips to Sorrento and beyond.

⚡ Train Information **Circumflegrea and Cumana** ☎ 081/5513328 ⊕ www.sepsa.it. **Circumvesuviana** ☎ 081/7722444 ⊕ www.vesuviana.it. **Stazione Centrale** ✉ Piazza Garibaldi ☎ 892021 ⊕ www.trenitalia.it.

Contacts & Resources

EMERGENCIES

⚡ Police ☎ 112. **Ambulance** ☎ 118.

⚡ Pharmacies **Farmacia Helvethia** ✉ Piazza Garibaldi 11, opposite Stazione Centrale, Naples ☎ 081/5548894.

ENGLISH-LANGUAGE MEDIA

The monthly *Qui Napoli,* free from tourist offices, has useful information in English on museums, exhibitions, and transportation.

TOURS

The Associazione di Donnaregina, run by two Neapolitan artists, organizes small group tours (six to eight people) of Naples and surroundings, offering insights into the culture, traditions, and lesser-known places of the region. Other operators include Milleviaggi, Tourcar, and STS. A welcome center for visitors to Naples's old town, the Centro di Accoglienza Turistica Museo Aperto Napoli, offers a museum-style audio guide (€6) you can to listen to as you wander the area.

⚡ Associazione di Donnaregina ✉ Via Luigi Settembrini 80, Naples ☎ 081/446799 or 338/6401301. **Centro di Accoglienza Turistica Museo Aperto Napoli** ✉ Via Pietro Colletta 89 ☎ 081/5636062 ⊕ www.museoapertonapoli.com. **Milleviaggi** ✉ Riviera di Chiaia 252, Naples ☎ 081/7642064. **STS** ✉ Via Bernini 90, Naples ☎ 081/5565164. **Tourcar** ✉ Piazza Matteotti 1, Naples ☎ 081/5521938 ⊕ www.tourcar.it.

VISITOR INFORMATION

The EPT (Ente Provinciale per il Turismo) handles information for the province (Naples, Salerno, Caserta, Benevento or Avellino), whereas information offices run by the local tourist organizations are more ubiquitous, though they cover much the same ground.

⚡ Tourist Information **EPT** ✉ Piazza dei Martiri 58, 80121 Naples ☎ 081/4107211 ✉ Stazione Centrale, 80142 Naples ☎ 081/268779 ✉ Stazione Mergellina, 80122 Naples ☎ 081/7612102.

Amalfi ✉ Corso delle Repubbliche 27, 84011 ☎ 089/871107. **Benevento** ✉ Piazza Roma 11, 82100 ☎ 0824/319938 ⊕ www.eptbenevento.it. **Capri** ✉ Marina Grande pier, 80073 ☎ 081/8370634 ✉ Piazza Umberto I, 80073 Capri Town ☎ 081/8370686 ⊕ www.capritourism.com. **Caserta** ✉ Piazza Dante 35, 81100 ☎ 0823/321137. **Ercolano** ✉ Via 4 Novembre 82, 80056 ☎ 081/7881243. **Naples** ✉ Piazza del Gesù, 80135 ☎ 081/5523328. **Pompeii** ✉ Via Sacra 1, 80045 ☎ 081/8507255. **Porto d'Ischia** ✉ Via Iasolino, Porto Salvo, 80077 ☎ 081/5074231. **Ravello** ✉ Piazza Duomo 1, 84010 ☎ 089/857096. **Salerno** ✉ Piazza Vittorio Veneto, 84100 ☎ 089/231432, 800/213289 toll-free ⊕ www.crmpa.it/ept. **Sorrento** ✉ Via de Maio 35, 80067 ☎ 081/8074033 ⊕ www.sorrentotourism.com.

The Mezzogiorno

Trulli, Alberobello

WORD OF MOUTH

"I'd expected Puglia to be quaint, charming, but a little in need of some loving care. How wrong was I! Every town we visited had elegant centers with smart shops and restaurants. Puglia hasn't yet made it into the touring crowd's itinerary, but I feel this will change very soon, so go now! It's almost like someone mixed the best of Italy and Greece together: food, medieval towns, whitewashed houses, beaches, palm trees, endless olive groves, great local wine."

–Kate

WELCOME TO
THE MEZZOGIORNO

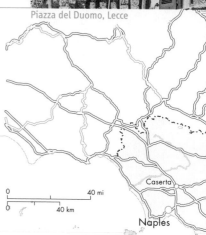

Piazza del Duomo, Lecce

TOP 5
Reasons to Go

1 A wander through Matera's sassi: A complex network of ancient cave dwellings partially hewn from rock, some of which now house chic bars and restaurants, endow this simple Basilicata town with one of the most unique landscapes in Europe.

2 A trip to peasant-food heaven: Dine on Puglia's famous purée of fava beans with chicory and spicy olive oil in a humble country restaurant, and you'll be transported back to a simpler culinary era.

3 A summer day on the beach of Puglia's Gargano Promontory: Some of Italy's most pristine coastline is still little known to foreign vacationers, so the beach culture on this peninsula remains unusually humble and relaxing.

4 Lecce and its baroque splendors: The beautiful, friendly city of Lecce might be known for its peculiar brand of fanciful baroque architecture, but it's not yet famous enough to have lost even an ounce of its Pugliese charm.

5 The trulli of Alberobello: Strange, conical homes—many of them still in use—dot the rolling countryside of Puglia, centering around Alberobello, a town still composed almost entirely of these trulli—they must be seen to be believed.

Caserta

```
0            40 mi
0        40 km
```

Naples

Getting Oriented

The *mezzogiorno* ("midday") is the informal name for Italy's languid deep south, known for its sun-drenched olive groves, fertile hills, and time-frozen towns. The area includes the regions of Calabria, the toe of Italy's boot, on the Tyrrhenian Sea; Puglia, the heel, on the Adriatic; and between them, Basilicata, the instep. Along both coasts, stretches of pristine coastline are interspersed with rough-and-tumble fishing and shipping ports.

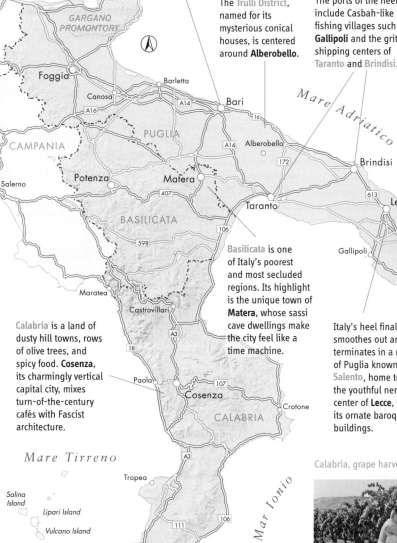

The **Gargano Promontory** juts into the Adriatic like a spur. It's full of summertime beaches, wooded campgrounds, and cliff-hanging hotels.

Bari, a lively, quirky, and sometimes seamy port city on Puglia's Adriatic Coast, is the biggest city in the mezzogiorno and home to its principal airport.

Trulli in Alberobello

The **Trulli District**, named for its mysterious conical houses, is centered around **Alberobello**.

The ports of the heel include Casbah-like fishing villages such as **Gallipoli** and the gritty shipping centers of **Taranto** and **Brindisi**.

Basilicata is one of Italy's poorest and most secluded regions. Its highlight is the unique town of **Matera**, whose sassi cave dwellings make the city feel like a time machine.

Calabria is a land of dusty hill towns, rows of olive trees, and spicy food. **Cosenza**, its charmingly vertical capital city, mixes turn-of-the-century cafés with Fascist architecture.

Italy's heel finally smoothes out and terminates in a region of Puglia known as **Salento**, home to the youthful nerve center of **Lecce**, with its ornate baroque buildings.

Map labels:
Vieste, GARGANO PROMONTORY, Foggia, Barletta, Canosa, Bari, CAMPANIA, PUGLIA, Salerno, Potenza, Matera, Alberobello, Brindisi, BASILICATA, Taranto, Lecce, Otranto, Gallipoli, Gagliano, Maratea, Castrovillari, Calabria, Paola, Cosenza, Crotone, CALABRIA, Mare Tirreno, Tropea, Salina Island, Lipari Island, Vulcano Island, Messina, Reggio di Calabria, SICILY, Mare Adriatico, Mar Ionio

Road numbers: A16, A14, 16, 172, 407, 106, 598, 613, 18, A3, 107, 111, 106

Calabria, grape harvest

THE MEZZOGIORNO PLANNER

Making the Most of Your Time

If your priority is relaxing on the beach, plan on a few days in the Gargano Promontory's seaside fishing villages-cum-resorts, such as Peschici, Rodi Garganico, and Vieste; and perhaps a further stay at one of the Calabrian coastal resorts, such as Diamante, Pizzo, Tropea, or Bagnara or Maratea in Basilicata.

Otherwise, begin your jaunt in Bari, where you should spend a day or two exploring the atmospheric old town and bustling port. Take a day trip to touristy but interesting Alberobello and its conical trulli, then head east along the Adriatic route (SS16), stopping to see Polignano a Mare and idyllic hilltop Ostuni before continuing on to Lecce, where you'll want to spend at least two to three nights exploring the city's baroque wonders and taking a day trip down the coast to Otranto.

Next, take regional roads and Via Appia (SS7) to reach Matera, whose sassi cave dwellings are a mezzogiorno highlight; allow at least two nights there. Then it's back out to the SS106, stopping at Metaponto's ruins before moving on to Calabria and picturesque, time-frozen Cosenza. Reggio di Calabria is worthwhile only if you're an archeology buff and must see its museum.

Getting Around

Trains are serviceable, but it's hard to get a good look at the countryside of Puglia and Calabria without wheels. This is particularly true if you want to hit the beaches along the coastline, or stay in agriturismi in the hill towns. Winding country roads are generally wide open and have little traffic, but allow plenty of time to get from place to place—slow trucks on two-lane roads abound. Fill up on gas whenever possible. In the towns of Bari, Brindisi, Lecce, Cosenza, and Matera, you'll want to leave your car and get around on foot.

Sasso Barisano, Matera

Speaking the Language

The dialects of Puglia, Basilicata, and Calabria, generally spoken only by town elders, are impenetrable to anyone with knowledge of only textbook Italian. A further twist is the presence of *albanesi* (Albanian-speaking locals) in upland areas, especially around Bari and the Pollino massif. Everyone speaks Italian as well; English-speakers aren't as prevalent as in points north.

On the Beach

Italians and foreign visitors alike return summer after summer to the beaches of the mezzogiorno, where the relative lack of industry has preserved mile after mile of largely unpolluted coastline.

Southern Italy's most popular vacation destinations among domestic tourists is the Gargano Promontory, where safe, sandy shores and secluded coves are nestled between whitewashed coastal towns and craggy limestone cliffs, and the well-developed Tyrrhenian coast of Calabria. The beaches are visually stunning, and they fill up quickly in summertime.

Elsewhere in the mezzogiorno, the beach scene is more laid back. You won't find impeccably manicured sand lined with regiments of sunbathers, but you can pick and choose strands at whim and spread out.

Finding a Place to Stay

Hotels in the mezzogiorno range from grand, if slightly faded, high-class resorts to family-run rural *agriturismi* (country inns, often part of farms), which compensate for a lack of amenities with their famous southern hospitality. *Fattorie* and *masserie* (small farms and grander farm estates) offering accommodation are listed at local tourist offices. Children are welcome everywhere.

In beach areas such as the Gargano Promontory, campgrounds and bungalow lodgings are ubiquitous and popular with families and young budget travelers alike. Note that many seaside hotels open up just for the summer season, when they often require several-day stays with full or half board. And do remember that in a region like this—blazingly hot in summer and chilly in winter—air-conditioning and central heating can be important.

How's the Weather?

Summers are torrid this far south, and even the otherwise perfect villages of the mezzogiorno's interior are too dazzlingly white for easy comfort from July to early September. If you seek the sand in that season, keep in mind that during *ferragosto*, the period in mid-August during which all of Italy flocks to the shores, even relatively isolated resorts can be overrun by weeklong package tourists; reserve well in advance, and be prepared to pay extra.

In April, May and June, on the other hand, the weather is clear and warm, and you'll often have the beach to yourself. Swimming temperatures last through October. Wintertime in the mezzogiorno can see heavy rain and wind, but temperatures rarely fall below freezing.

Dining & Lodging Price Categories

WHAT IT COSTS in Euros					
	$$$$	**$$$**	**$$**	**$**	**¢**
Restaurants	over €45	€35–€45	€25–€35	€15–€25	under €15
Hotels	over €220	€160–€220	€110–€160	€70–€110	under €70

Restaurant prices are for a first course (primo), second course (secondo), and dessert (dolce). Hotel prices are for two people in a standard double room in high season, including tax and service.

TOP PASSEGGIATA

The walk along the ancient walls of Bari's old town reveals a new view with every turn: the castle, the port, the harbors, and the wide-open sea.

Updated by
Robin
Goldstein

MAKING UP THE HEEL AND TOE OF ITALY'S BOOT, the Puglia, Basilicata, and Calabria regions are known informally as the *mezzogiorno*, a name that translates literally as "midday." It's a curiously telling nickname, because midday is when it's quietest here. While the blazing sun bears down, cities, fishing ports, and sleepy hillside villages turn into ghost towns, as residents retreat to their homes for four or more hours. This is Italy's deep south, where whitewashed buildings stand silently over the turquoise Mediterranean, castles guard medieval alleyways, and grandmothers dry their handmade *orecchiette*, the most Puglian of pastas, in the mid-afternoon heat. The city-states of Magna Graecia (Greek colonies) once ruled here, and ancient names, such as Lucania and Salento, are still commonly used.

At every turn, these three regions boast unspoiled scenery, a wonderful country food tradition, and—especially in Puglia and Basilicata—an openness to outsiders that's unequaled elsewhere on the boot. It's here that the Italian language is at its lilting, hand-gesturing best, and it's here that a local you've met only minutes before is most likely to whisk you away to show you the delights of the region. When locals speak among themselves, though, their conversations revert to local dialects unintelligible to the student of textbook Italian.

Some of Italy's finest beaches grace the rugged Gargano peninsula and the coastline of Calabria, and there are cultural gems everywhere, from Alberobello's fairy-tale *trulli* (curious conical structures dating from the Middle Ages) to Matera's *sassi* (a network of ancient dwellings carved out of rock) to the baroque churches in vibrant Lecce, the town that's the jewel of the south. Beyond the cities, seaside resorts, and the few major sights, there's a sparsely populated, sunbaked countryside where road signs are rare and expanses of silvery olive trees, vineyards of *primitivo* and *aglianico* grapes, and giant prickly pear cacti fight their way through the rocky soil in defiance of the relentless summer heat. Farmhouses, country trattorias, and weary low-lying factories sit among eternally half-built structures that tell a hard-luck story of economic stagnation. Organized crime, still a strong force in the region, poses no threat to tourists, but together with government neglect and archaic social patterns, it has long helped to prevent the development that other parts of the country have enjoyed—for better or for worse. Year after year, even as tourism grows in the region—especially in Salento—economic woes strangely persist. Locals will tell you it's due to the inflation that was spurred by the adoption of the euro, but clearly, the Mafia still plays a big role. In any case, the mezzogiorno still doesn't make it onto the itineraries of most visitors to Italy. This translates into an unusual opportunity to engage with a rich culture and landscape virtually untouched by mass tourism.

BARI & THE ADRIATIC COAST

The coast of Puglia has a strong flavor of the Norman presence in the south, embodied in the distinctive Puglian-Romanesque churches, the most atmospheric being in Trani. The busy commercial port of Bari offers architectural nuggets in its compact, labyrinthine Old Quarter abut-

PUGLIA, PAST & PRESENT

Puglia has long been inhabited, conquered, and visited. On sea voyages to their colonies and trading posts in the west, the ancient Greeks invariably headed for Puglia first—it was the shortest crossing—before filtering southward into Sicily and westward to the Tyrrhenian coast. In turn, the Romans—often bound in the opposite direction—were quick to recognize the strategic importance of the peninsula. Later centuries were to see a procession of other empires raiding or colonizing Puglia: Byzantines, Saracens, Normans, Swabians, Turks, and Spaniards all swept through, each group leaving its mark. Romanesque churches and the powerful castles built by 13th-century Holy Roman Emperor Frederick II (who also served as king of Sicily and Jerusalem), are among the most impressive of the buildings in the region. Frederick II, dubbed *Stupor Mundi* (Wonder of the World) for his wide-ranging interests in literature, science, mathematics, and nature, was one of the foremost personalities of the Middle Ages.

The last 50 years have brought a huge economic revival after the centuries of neglect following Puglia's golden age under the Normans and Swabians. Having benefited from EU funding, state incentive programs, and subsidies for irrigation, Puglia is now Italy's second-biggest producer of wine, with most of the rest of the land devoted to olives, citrus fruits, and vegetables. The main ports of Bari, Brindisi, and Taranto are thriving centers, though there remain serious problems of unemployment and poverty. However, the much-publicized arrival of thousands of asylum seekers from Eastern Europe and beyond has not significantly destabilized these cities, as had been feared, and the economic and political refugees have dispersed throughout Italy. Compared with neighboring Albania a mere 70 km (44 mi) away across the Straits of Otranto, Puglia oozes with prosperity.

ting the sea, while Polignano a Mare combines accessibility to the major centers with the charm of a medieval town. For a unique excursion, drive inland to the imposing Castel del Monte, an enigmatic 13th-century octagonal fortification.

Bari

❶ *260 km (162 mi) southeast of Naples, 450 km (281 mi) southeast of Rome.*

The biggest city in the mezzogiorno, Bari is a major port and a transit point for travelers catching ferries across the Adriatic to Greece, but it's also a cosmopolitan city with one of the most interesting historic centers in the region. Most of Bari is set out in a logical 19th-century grid, following the designs of Joachim Murat (1767–1815), Napoléon's brother-in-law and King of the Two Sicilies. The heart of the modern town is **Piazza della Libertà**, but just beyond it, across Corso Vittorio Emanuele, is the *città vecchia* (old town), a maze of narrow streets on the promontory that juts out between Bari's old and new ports, circumscribed by Via Venezia, offering elevated views of the Adriatic in every direction. Stop for an outdoor drink at **Greta** (⊠ Via Venezia 24) for a commanding view of the port and sea. By day, explore the old town's winding alleyways, where Bari's open-door policy offers a glimpse into the daily routine of southern Italy—matrons hand-rolling pasta with their grandchildren home from school for the midday meal, and handymen perched on rickety ladders, patching up centuries-old arches and doorways. Back in the new town, join the evening *passeggiata* (stroll) on pedestrian-only **Via Sparano**, then, when night falls, saunter among the exploding scene of outdoor bars and restaurants in Piazza Mercantile, past Piazza Ferrarese at the end of Corso Vittorio Emanuele.

In the città vecchia, overlooking the sea and just off Via Venezia, is the **Basilica di San Nicola,** built in the 11th century to house the bones of St. Nicholas, also known as St. Nick, or Santa Claus. His remains, buried in the crypt, are said to have been stolen by Bari sailors from Myra, where St. Nicholas was bishop, in what is now Turkey. The basilica, of solid and powerful construction, was the only building to survive the otherwise wholesale destruction of Bari by the Normans in 1152. ⊠ *Piazza San Nicola* ☎ *080/5737111* ☉ *Daily 9–1 and 4–7.*

Bari's 12th-century **Cattedrale** is the seat of the local bishop and was the scene of many significant political marriages between important families in the Middle Ages. The cathedral's solid architecture reflects the Romanesque style favored by the Normans of that period. ⊠ *Piazza dell'Odegitria* ☎ *080/5288215* 🎟 *Free.*

Looming over Bari's cathedral is the huge **Castello Svevo.** The current building dates from the time of Holy Roman Emperor Frederick II (1194–1250), who rebuilt an existing Norman-Byzantine castle to his own exacting specifications. Designed more for power than beauty, it looks out beyond the cathedral to the small Porto Vecchio (Old Port). Inside are a haphazard collection of medieval Puglian art and archaeological artifacts and rotating exhibits of works by local artists. At press time the castle was under restoration and could only be viewed from the outside; call, or ask at the tourist office, for the latest. ⊠ *Piazza Federico II di Svevia* ☎ *080/5286218* 🎟 *€2* ☉ *Temporarily closed for renovation.*

Where to Stay & Eat

$$$ ✕ **Ristorante al Pescatore.** This is one of Bari's best fish restaurants, in the old town opposite the castle and just around the corner from the cathedral. Summer cooking is done outside, where you can sit amid a cheerful clamor of quaffing and dining. Try a whole grilled local fish, accompanied by crisp salad and a carafe of invigorating local wine. Reservations are essential in July and August. ⊠ *Piazza Federico II di Svevia 6* ☎ *080/5237039* ▭ *AE, MC, V.*

★ **$$$$** 🏨 **Hotel Palace.** This downtown landmark is stationed steps away from Corso Vittorio Emanuele in the new city, but is also extremely convenient to the medieval center. The large, comfortable rooms are furnished lightly and tastefully. There are whimsical special pet rooms, children's rooms, and a room for music lovers, complete with stereo and classical CD collection. Other amenities include Smart Car rental service (€36

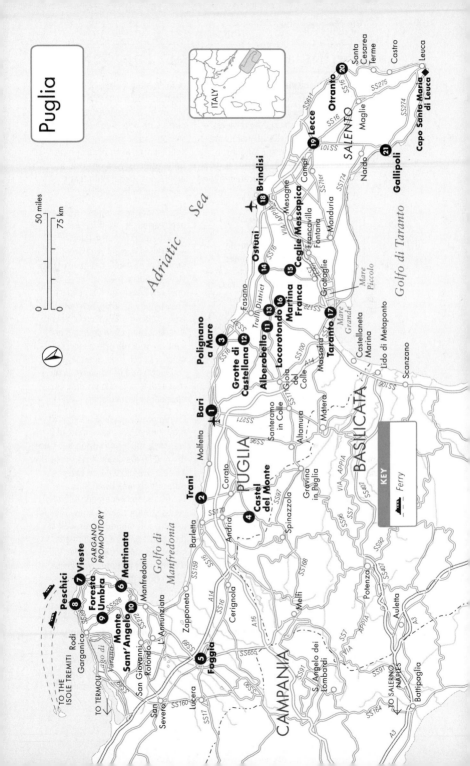

EATING WELL IN THE MEZZOGIORNO

Southern cuisine is hearty and healthful, based around homemade pastas and cheeses, fresh vegetables, seafood, and olive oil. The best—and cheapest—meals are often found at a rustic family-run trattoria (sometimes referred to as a *casalinga*), commonly located in the countryside or city outskirts. These bare-bones places usually specialize in *casareccia* pasta (doughy, handmade twists) or gnocchi, as well as homemade ricotta; they rarely offer printed menus—just flavors that rival those of any highbrow restaurant. Assent to the waiter's suggestions with a simple *va bene* (that's fine) and leave yourself in the chef's hands. Note that in many such restaurants you pay a set price for your meal, regardless of what you order.

On the coast, the star attraction is fish, served grilled (*alla griglia*), baked (*al forno*), roasted (*arrosto*), or steamed (*al umido*). Among the highlights are delicate *orata* (sea bream), *branzino* (sea bass), swordfish, and calamari.

All over the mezzogiorno you find dishes unavailable elsewhere in Italy, such as *'ncapriata*, also called *favi e fogghi* (a fava-bean puree topped with vegetables and drizzled with olive oil; mix it all together before eating). Particularly at the more humble country restaurants, look for pasta *fatto in casa* or *fatto a mano*—rolled out only hours before serving, and usually prepared with a thick tomato sauce or meat ragù. And don't miss the intensely flavorful and salty ricotta *forte*.

Each of the regions has its own specialties. In Puglia, look for focaccia *barese* (stuffed with fried onions, black olives, anchovies, and ricotta), which makes a great snack or lunch; *strascenate* (rectangles of pasta with one rough side and one smooth side); and *orecchiette* (ear-shape pasta) with *cime di rape* (bitter greens) and olive oil, a melodious preparation that's wondrous in its simplicity.

Basilicata is known for its excellent beef, various types of *funghi* (mushrooms) from the forest, antipasti of roasted vegetables soaked in olive oil, and hearty lamb stew. Calabria, meanwhile, is uniquely known for hot peppers. They pop up in *salame piccante* (spicy salami) and *salsiccia piccante* (hot sausage), often sold by street vendors on a roll with peppers, onions, french fries, and mayonnaise. You'll also find dried *peperoncini* (hot peppers) or *olio piccante* (spicy olive oil) in pasta dishes.

Puglia produces almost a fifth of Italy's wine. For years, most of it was *vino sfuso* (jug wine), but since the mid-1990s quality has risen. The ancient primitivo grape (which purportedly was brought to California and renamed zinfandel), yields strong, heady wines. Look for primitivo di Manduria, as well as the robust Salice Salentino and sweet red aleatico di Puglia. Top winemakers include Conti Zecca, Leone di Castris, Rubino, and Tormaresca. In Basilicata, producers use the aglianico grape variety to outstanding effect—try Paternoster's range of wines, and any Aglianico del Vulture. In Calabria, producers such as Librandi have worked wonders with the gaglioppo variety; their gravello is outstanding.

per day). The rooftop restaurant has great views outdoors in summer. ✉ *Via Lombardi 13, 70122* ☎ *080/5216551* 📠 *080/5211499* ⊕ *www. palacehotelbari.it* ⤳ *189 rooms* ⚲ *Restaurant, bicycles, bar, meeting room, convention center, parking (fee), some pets allowed (fee)* ▤ *AE, DC, MC, V* ¶ *MAP.*

Trani

② *43 km (27 mi) northwest of Bari.*

Smaller than the other ports along this coast, Trani has a quaint old town with polished stone streets and buildings, medieval churches, and a harbor filled with fishing boats. Trani is also justly famous for its sweet dessert wine, Moscato di Trani. The stunning, pinkish-white-hue 11th-century **Duomo** (✉ Piazza Duomo ⊙ Daily 8–noon and 3:30–7), considered one of the finest in Puglia, is built on a spit of land jutting into the sea. The boxy, well-preserved **Castle** (☎ 0883/506603 ⊙ Daily 8:30–7:30; last entrance at 7 PM) was built by Frederick II in 1233. The Jewish community flourished here in medieval times, and on **Via Sinagoga** (Synagogue Street) two of the four synagogues still exist: **Santa Maria Scolanova** and **Santa Anna,** both built in the 13th century; the latter still bears a Hebrew inscription.

Where to Stay & Eat

★ **$$** ✕▦ **La Regia.** This small hotel-restaurant occupies a 17th-century palazzo superbly positioned in front of the Duomo, on a swath of land jutting out into the sea. Don't expect grand or spacious rooms, though they are perfectly adequate. The restaurant ($$) has attractive stonework, vaulted ceilings, and a terra-cotta tiled floor. Regional specialties are presented imaginatively: try the baked crepes (similar to cannelloni) or grilled fish. Reservations are essential for Sunday lunch and for dinner on summer weekends. ✉ *Piazza Mons. Addazi 2, 70059* 📠 *0883/584444* ⤳ *10 rooms* ⚲ *Restaurant, bar* ▤ *MC, V* ⊙ *Restaurant closed Mon. Hotel and restaurant closed 15 days in Jan.* ¶ *BP.*

Polignano a Mare

③ *40 km (24 mi) southeast of Bari, 14 km (9 mi) north of Castellana.*

With a well-preserved whitewashed old town perched on limestone cliffs overlooking the Adriatic, Polignano a Mare makes an atmospheric base for exploring the surrounding area. Bari is only a half-hour train ride up the coast. The town is virtually lifeless all winter, but becomes something of a weekend hot spot for city dwellers in summer.

Where to Stay & Eat

★ **$$** ✕▦ **Grotta Palazzese.** Carved out of a cliff opening onto the Adriatic, the Grotta Palazzese inhabits a stunning group of rocks and grottoes that have wowed onlookers from time immemorial. Though all rooms but one have sea views, ask for one of the cave-apartments across the road rather than the more boxlike rooms in the main 1960s block. (Rooms 18, 25, and 139 are the most impressive.) The Grotta Palazzese's true tour de force is its summer restaurant ($$$$), serving impeccably prepared fish (try the assortment of raw Adriatic shellfish called *frutti di mare crudi*). The dramatic setting incorporates rock formations, with tables actually standing on an implausible bridge inside a jagged cave, while waves cast blue-green shadows on the grotto walls. It's one of the most romantic settings in all Italy. ☒ *Via Narciso 59, 70059* ☎ *080/ 4240677* 🖶 *080/4240767* ⊕ *www.grottapalazzese.it* ⇄ *24 rooms* & *2 restaurants, beach, bar, meeting room, parking (fee)* 🖃 *AE, DC, MC, V* ☉ *Outdoor restaurant closed Oct.–Apr.* ❅ *BP.*

Castel del Monte

★ ❹   *30 km (19 mi) south of Barletta, 56 km (35 mi) southwest of Bari.*

Built by Frederick II in the first half of the 13th century on an isolated hill, Castel del Monte is an imposing octagonal castle with eight austere towers. Very little is known about the structure, since virtually no records exist: the gift shop has many books that explore its mysterious past and posit fascinating theories based on its dimensions and Federico II's love of mathematics. It has none of the usual defense features associated with medieval castles, so it probably had little military significance. Some theories suggest it might have been built as a hunting lodge or may have served as an astronomical observatory, or even a stop for pilgrims on their quest for the Holy Grail. ☒ *On signposted minor road 18 km (11 mi) south of Andria* ☎ *0883/569997, 0340/ 5156754 Italian tour reservations, 0338/2102755 English tour reservations (ask for Angela)* ⊕ *www.castellipuglia.it* ☕ *€3* ☉ *Daily 9–6:30. Optional guided tours in English and Italian available every 1¼ hrs; call to reserve.*

Foggia

❺   *95 km (60 mi) west of Bari.*

Foggia, the chief city in Puglia's northernmost province, is not the most inspiring destination, though it makes a useful overnight stop for visitors to the Gargano. The old town is pleasant but fairly modern, having sustained significant war damage. On the main line from Rome and Naples, and easily accessible from the autostrada, Foggia has all the amenities you would expect from a major commercial center, hosting numerous fairs and conventions throughout the year. This means that, although it enjoys a decent selection of lodgings and restaurants, you'll need to reserve to ensure accommodations. This is the place to rent a car for excursions to the Gargano.

Where to Stay & Eat

★ **$$$** ✕ **La Nuova Mangiatoia.** Set in an old farmhouse, this seafood restaurant looks like a medieval tavern, with arches and wood-beam ceilings. You can also dine in a large garden, where tables made from wagon wheels surround an old well. If you're lucky, game might be roasted on a spit right in the middle of the restaurant. The location is on the main road to Bari, near the Foggia Agricultural Fairgrounds. Reservations are essential on weekends. ☒ *Via Virgilio 2* ☎ *0881/634457* 🖃 *AE, DC, MC, V* ☉ *Closed Tues.*

$–$$ ✗ **Ambasciata Orsarese.** This hidden pizzeria and restaurant near Foggia's market, also referred to as "Trilussa," is very local, very good, and very small. In the tiny dining room the few tables are surrounded by rows of bottles of the region's best wines, which accompany pizza prepared in a 16th-century oven. Local antipasti and *primi* (first courses) are also available. Try their famed *pane divino,* a tasty and healthful bread that apparently aids digestion. ⊠ *Via Tenente Iorio 50, corner of Rosati* ☎ *0881/709253* ▤ *AE, MC, V* ⊘ *Closed Wed.*

★ **$$$** ✗▥ **Cicolella.** Part of the Mercure chain, this 1920s hotel near the station, on a tree-lined road, has tasteful rooms with floor-length curtains, regal wallpaper, and restful, discreet lighting. Some have balconies. The excellent restaurant ($$) serves international cuisine, but is at its best with local dishes. Service is impeccable, and a good regional wine list complements such country classics as puree of fava beans with chicory, drizzled with Puglian olive oil infused with hot peppers. ⊠ *Viale Ventiquattro Maggio 60, 71100* ☎ *0881/566111* 🖷 *0881/778984* ⊕ *www.hotelcicolella. it* ⤢ *91 rooms, 8 suites* ♨ *Restaurant, meeting room* ▤ *AE, DC, MC, V* ⊘ *Restaurant closed weekends and Aug. 1–20* ⟦◎⟧ *BP.*

GARGANO PROMONTORY

Forming the spur of Italy's boot, the Gargano Promontory (Promontorio del Gargano) is a striking contrast to the Adriatic's generally flat, unenthralling coastline. This is a land of whitewashed coastal towns, wide sandy beaches interspersed with secluded coves, and craggy limestone cliffs topped by deep-green pine and lush Mediterranean maquis. Not surprisingly, it pulls in the crowds in July and August, including many Germans and northern Italians. Prices are higher than elsewhere in Puglia as a result of its popularity. Camping is almost always an option, as plentiful and pretty campgrounds dot the Gargano's curvy, cliff-hugging roads. For the kids, the beaches and the Foresta Umbra national park are great places to let off steam, and many towns stage puppet shows in public gardens.

Mattinata

❻ *53 km (32 mi) northeast of Foggia, 138 km (86 mi) northwest of Bari.*

Just inland from a fine sandy beach, where you'll find most of the campsites and hotels, this is a generally quiet village that comes into its own in the summer season.

Where to Stay & Eat

$$ ✗ **Trattoria dalla Nonna.** The waves lapping at the shore just inches outside the picture windows of this elegant but unpretentious coastal restaurant, a few kilometers outside Mattinata, are an indication of how fresh the fish will be. The memorable assorted raw seafood antipasto includes some shellfish you might not find anywhere else. *Cozze pelose* (an indigenous Puglian clam), hiding inside spiked-hair shells, are briny and buttery; tiny *noci* shellfish have a wonderful sweetness; and big, rich local oysters are all about texture. Try sweet grilled scampi with oil and lemon, and wash it all down with one of the great white wines on the extensive list. ✉ *Mattinata Mare* ☎ *0884/559205* ⊕ *www.dallanonna. it* ▭ *AE, DC, MC, V* ⊗ *Closed Tues. Oct.–Apr., 15 days in Nov., and 15 days in Jan.*

$$$ ⊞ **Baia delle Zagare.** This secluded, modern group of cottages overlooks an inlet and lies on the shore road around the Gargano Promontory, well north of Mattinata. An elevator built into the cliffs takes you down to a long private beach complete with limestone caves. The hotel restaurant is good enough to warrant staying on the premises all day. (You're expected to take half board in August.) Be careful when approaching on the road, as the gated entrance is easy to miss. ✉ *Località Valle dei Mergoli, 17 km (10 mi) northeast of Mattinata, 71030* ☎ *0884/550155* 🖷 *0884/550884* ⊕ *www.hotelbaiadellezagare.it* ⇌ *150 rooms* ⌂ *Restaurant, minibars, tennis court, pool, health club, beach, dance club, theater, children's programs (under 12 years)* ▭ *MC, V* ⊗ *Closed Sept. 15–May* ⏐⊙⏐ *MAP.*

Vieste

❼ *93 km (58 mi) northeast of Foggia, 179 km (111 mi) northwest of Bari.*

This large, whitewashed town jutting off the tip of the spur of Italy's boot is the Gargano's main commercial center and an attractive place to wander around. Though curvy mountain roads render it slightly less accessible from the autostrada and mainline rail stations than, say, Peschici and Mattinata, the range of accommodations (including camping) makes it a useful base for exploring Gargano. The resort attracts legions of tourists in summer, some bound for the Isole Tremiti, a tiny archipelago connected to Vieste by regular ferries. While in Vieste, make for the **castle.** Its interior has reopened to the public; check the tourist office for hours of operation. There are good views from its high position overlooking the beaches and town.

Where to Stay & Eat

★ **$$–$$$** ✕ **San Michele.** Dine on exquisite Gargano fare at this charmingly intimate eatery on the town's main street. Their legendary antipasti include grilled eggplant and marinated anchovies. The porcini mushrooms picked from the region's Foresta Umbra are worth the visit alone. ✉ *Viale XXIV Maggio 72* ☎ *0884/708143* ▭ *AE, DC, MC, V* ⊗ *Closed Mon. and Jan.–mid-Mar.*

★ **$$$–$$$$** ⊞ **Pizzomunno.** Probably the most luxurious resort on the Gargano, Pizzomunno is right on the beach and surrounded by an extensive park. It is large, white, modern, air-conditioned, and well equipped. The rooms are ample and plush, all with terraces. Here you can unwind, or try your hand at tennis or archery. One-week minimum stays are required in some parts of high season. ✉ *Spiaggia di Pizzomunno, 71019* ☎ *0884/ 708741* 🖷 *0884/707325* ⊕ *www.ventaclubhotels.com* ⇌ *190 rooms, 10 suites* ⌂ *2 restaurants, tennis court, 2 pools, health club, sauna, archery, cinema, dance club, children's programs (ages 3–12)* ▭ *AE, DC, MC, V* ⊗ *Closed mid-Oct.–early May* ⏐⊙⏐ *BP.*

¢–$$ ⊞ **Punta San Francesco.** After starting its life as an olive-oil factory, this hotel was tastefully refurbished in the mid-1990s. Thanks to its location near the waterfront in the heart of old Vieste, it is both quiet and close to the action. The owner is a warm, welcoming friend (and ardent promoter of local culture) to all who arrive, and the view from the rooftop is beautiful, especially at dawn. ✉ *Via San Francesco 2, 71019* ☎ *0884/ 701422* 🖷 *0884/701424* ⊕ *www.hotelpuntasanfrancesco.it* ⇆ *14 rooms* ⚶ *Restaurant, minibars, bar* ▬ *MC, V* ❚❘ *EP.*

Peschici

❽ *22 km (14 mi) northwest of Vieste, 199 km (124 mi) northwest of Bari.*

Peschici is a pleasant resort on Gargano's north shore, a cascade of white-washed houses and streets with a beautiful view over a sweeping cove. Some surrounding areas are particularly popular with campers from northern Europe. Development has not wreaked too much havoc on the town: the mazelike center retains its characteristic low houses topped with little Byzantine cupolas.

OFF THE BEATEN PATH

ISOLE TREMITI – A ferry service from Termoli, west of the Gargano (1¾ hours), and hydrofoil service from Vieste, Peschici, and Rodi Garganico (40 minutes to one hour) connect the mainland with these three small islands north of the Gargano. Although somewhat crowded with Italian tourists in summer, they are famed for their sea caves, pine forests, and craggy limestone formations. Interesting medieval churches and fortifications dot the islands. ☎ *199/123199 ferry reservations, 081/ 3172999 from outside Italy* ⊕ *www.adriatica.it/it/tremiti-orari.htm.*

Foresta Umbra

★ ❾ *25 km (16 mi) south of Rodi Garganico, 30 km (19 mi) southwest of Vieste.*

In the middle of the Gargano Promontory is the majestic Foresta Umbra (Shady Forest), a dense growth of beech, maple, sycamore, and oak generally found in more northerly climates, thriving here because of the altitude, 3,200 feet above sea level. Between the trees in this national park are occasional dramatic vistas opening out over the Golfo di Manfredonia. From the north coast, take harrowingly curvy S528 (midway between Peschici and Rodi Garganico) south to head through the interior of the Gargano (do it during the day), or try the gentler ascent between Mattinata and Vieste on S89.

Monte Sant'Angelo

★ ❿ *16 km (10 mi) north of Manfredonia, 60 km (19 mi) southwest of Vieste.*

Perched amid olive groves on the limestone cliffs overlooking the gulf is the town of Monte Sant'Angelo. Pilgrims have flocked here for nearly 1,500 years—among them, St. Francis of Assisi and crusaders setting off for the Holy Land from the then-flourishing port of Manfredonia. Monte Sant'Angelo is centered on the **Santuario di San Michele** (Sanctuary of San Michele) (☎ *0884/561150* ⊗ *May–Oct., daily 7:30–5; Nov.–Apr., daily 7:30–12:30*), built over the grotto where the archangel Michael is believed to have appeared before shepherds in the year 490.

14

Walk down a long series of steps to get to the grotto itself; on its walls you can see the hand tracings left by pilgrims.

The **Tomba di Rotari** (Tomb of Rotari) (☉ *Daily 9–1 and 3–dusk*), believed to have been a medieval baptistery, has some remarkable 12th-century reliefs. It's reached by steps down and to the left from the Santuario di San Michele. Steep steps lead up to the large, ruined **Castello Normano** (Norman Castle; ☎ *0884/565444* ☉ *Daily 9–7*) that dominates the town, with a view of the intricate pattern of the streets and steps winding their way up the side of the valley. Monte Sant'Angelo's medieval quarter, the **Rione Junno,** is a maze of little white houses squeezed into a corner of the narrow valley.

Where to Stay

$ ▦ **Rotary Hotel.** This simple but welcoming modern hotel is set amid olive and almond groves just outside town. Most rooms have basic decor and terraces with views of the Golfo di Manfredonia. ✉ *Via Pulsano, Km. 1, 71037* ☎ *0884/562147* 🖷 *0884/562147* ⊕ *www.rotary.it* 🛏 *24 rooms* ♿ *Restaurant, bar* ▤ *AE, MC, V* ⧊ *BP.*

THE TRULLI DISTRICT

The inland area to the southeast of Bari is one of Italy's oddest enclaves, mostly flat terrain given over to olive cultivation and interspersed with the idiosyncratic habitations that have lent their names to the district. The origins of the beehive-shape trulli go back to the 13th century and maybe further. The trulli, found nowhere else in the world, are built of local limestone, without mortar, and with a hole in the top for escaping smoke. Some are painted with mystical or religious symbols; some are isolated, and others are joined together with roofs on various levels. Legends of varying credibility surround the trulli (for example, that they were originally built so that residents could quickly take apart their homes when the tax collectors came by). The center of trulli country is Alberobello in the enchanting Valle d'Itria: it has the greatest concentration of the buildings. You will spot them all over this region, some in the middle of desolate fields, and many in disrepair, but always adding a quirky charm to the landscape.

Alberobello

⓫ *59 km (37 mi) southeast of Bari, 45 km (28 mi) north of Taranto.*

Although Alberobello is something of a tourist trap, the amalgamation of more than 1,000 trulli huddled together along steep, narrow streets is nonetheless an unusual sight (as well as a national monument and a UNESCO World Heritage Site). As one of the most popular tourist destinations in Puglia, Alberobello has spawned some excellent restaurants (and some not-so-excellent trinket shops). Alberobello's largest trullo, the **Trullo Sovrano,** is up the hill through the trulli zone (head up Corso Vittorio Emanuele past the obelisk and the basilica). Though you can go inside, where you'll find a fairly conventional domestic dwelling, the real interest is the structure itself.

The trulli in Alberobello itself are impressive, but the most beautiful concentration of trulli are along **Via Alberobello–Martina Franca.** Numerous conical homes and buildings stand along a stretch of about 15 km (9 mi) between those two towns. Amid expanses of vineyards, you'll see delightfully amusing examples of trulli put to use in every which way—as wineries, for instance.

> ### WORD OF MOUTH
>
> "We spent a week in Puglia last fall. It's very worth the visit, but a car is almost mandatory to see the countryside and small cities like Alberobello, Lecce, Martina Franca (our favorite)."
>
> –DRJ

Where to Stay & Eat

$$$
FodorsChoice ★ ✕ **Il Poeta Contadino.** Proprietor Marco Leonardo serves "creative regional cooking" in this upscale country restaurant in the heart of the attractive trulli zone. The room features ancient stone walls, candlelit tables, and a refined, understated ambience. Dishes might include *triglie vinaigrette alla menta* (red mullet with a mint vinaigrette) or *coda di rospo incrostita di patate* (monkfish in a potato crust). In season, try anything with white truffle. ⊠ *Via Indipendenza 21* ☎ *080/4321917* ⌂ *Reservations essential* ▭ *AE, DC, MC, V* ⊗ *Closed Mon. and 3 wks in Jan. No dinner Sun.*

★ **$–$$$** ✕ **Trullo d'Oro.** This welcoming rustic restaurant set in five trulli houses has dark-wood beams, whitewashed walls, and an open hearth. Local country cooking includes dishes using lamb and veal, vegetable and cheese antipasti, pasta dishes with crisp raw vegetables on the side, and almond pastries. Among the specialties are roast lamb with *lampasciuni* (a type of wild onion) and spaghetti *al trullo*, made with tomatoes, *rughetta* (arugula), and four cheeses. ⊠ *Via F. Cavallotti 27* ☎ *080/4323909* ⌂ *Reservations essential* ▭ *AE, DC, MC, V* ⊗ *Closed Mon. (except in June–Aug.) and Jan. 8–28. No dinner Sun. except in Aug.*

$$$ ▥ **Dei Trulli.** Trulli-style cottages in a pine wood near the trulli zone make this a magical place to stay. It's decorated with rustic furnishings and folk-art rugs. The modestly priced restaurant serves local specialties. You're required to take half or full board in high season. ⊠ *Via Cadore 32, 70011* ☎ *080/4323555* ▤ *080/4323560* ⊕ *www.hoteldeitrulli.it* ⇱ *28 rooms* ⌂ *Restaurant, minibars, pool* ▭ *AE, DC, MC, V* ⊚ *MAP.*

Grotte di Castellana

☾ ⑫ *20 km (12 mi) northwest of Alberobello, 63 km (52 mi) southeast of Bari.*

The Grotte di Castellana is a huge network of caves discovered in 1938. Visits are by tour only; you can take one of the hour-long guided walks through the grottoes filled with fantastically shaped stalagmites and stalactites, part of the largest network of caves on the Italian mainland. A two-hour tour takes you on an extra 2-km (1½-mi) hike to another cave, Grotta Bianca. ⊠ *Piazzale Anelli* ☎ *080/4998211* ⊕ *www.grottedicastellana.it* ▱ *€8 1-hr tour, €13 2-hr tour* ⊗ *Apr.–Oct., daily*

8:30–7, every hr; Nov.–Mar., daily 9:30–12:30, every hr. Last 2-hr tour leaves 1 hr before closing.

Locorotondo

⑬ *9 km (5½ mi) southeast of Alberobello, 40 km (25 mi) north of Taranto.*

Locorotondo is an attractive hilltop town within the trulli district in the Itria Valley (take S172 from Alberobello). The *rotondo* in the town's name refers to the circular pattern of the houses, swirling down from the top. From the top of the town, on the road to Martina Franca, a verdant public garden gives way to lookout points over the entire Valle d'Itria, a landscape dotted with olive groves and trulli. Wander around the evocative alleyways of the *centro storico* (historic center) and look for the blazing yellow cathedral in Piazza Fra Giuseppe Andria Rolleo.

Where to Eat

$–$$ ✕ **Centro Storico.** The refined ambience and cuisine of this restaurant, set apart from the tourist haunts, make it a little pricier than its neighbors, but the food and service are worth it. Try such regional dishes as *sformato di verdura* (like a vegetable mousse) and *agnello alla castellanese* (local lamb). ⊠ *Via Eroi di Dogali 6* ☎ *080/4315473* ⌖ *Reservations essential* ⊟ *AE, DC, MC, V* ☯ *Closed Wed. and 2 wks in Mar.*

Ostuni

⑭ *50 km (30 mi) west of Brindisi, 40 km (25 mi) northeast of Locorotondo.*

This sun-bleached, medieval town lies on three hills a short distance from the coast. From a distance, Ostuni is a jumble of blazingly white houses and churches spilling over a hilltop and overlooking the sea—thus earning it the nickname *la città bianca* (the White City). The **old town,** on the highest of the hills, has steep cobbled lanes, wrought-iron lanterns, some good local restaurants, and stupendous views out over the coast and the surrounding plain. **Piazza Libertà,** the city's main square, divides the new town to the west and the old town to the east.

Where to Eat

$$ ✕ **Osteria del Tempo Perso.** Buried in the side streets of the old town, this laid-back restaurant has rough-hewn stone interiors, with intriguing objects adorning the walls. It is open July–September nightly and October–June for Saturday dinner and Sunday lunch. Service is friendly and preparations focus on local cuisine such as delectable stuffed hot peppers and orecchiette with bitter greens and olive oil. ⊠ *Via G. Tanzarella Vitale 47* ☎ *0831/303320* ⊕ *www.osteriadeltempoperso.com* ⊟ *AE, DC, MC, V* ☯ *Closed Mon. and Jan. 10–31. No lunch July–Sept.; Oct.–June: no dinner Sun.–Fri.; no lunch Mon.–Sat.*

Ceglie Messapica

⑮ *11 km (7 mi) southwest of Ostuni, 18 km (11 mi) southwest of Martina Franca.*

With its 14th-century Piazza Vecchia, tattered baroque balconies, and lordly medieval castles, the little whitewashed town of Ceglie Messapica is a jewel along the lines of Ostuni and Locorotondo. The town, at the center of the triangle formed by Taranto, Brindisi, and Fasano, was once the military capital of the Messapia region, and often defended itself against invasions from the Taranto city-state, which wanted to clear a route to the Adriatic. Nowadays, more and more visitors come to Ceglie Messapica for its restaurants alone.

Where to Eat

★ **$$$$** ✕ **Al Fornello Da Ricci.** Any respectable culinary tour of Puglia must pass through this high-priced, elegant dining room run by Antonella Ricci and her husband Vinod Sookar, who hails from Mauritius. The distinguished kitchen sends out *antipasti* in a long succession, all inspired by ancient Pugliese traditions—meats, cheeses, perhaps fried zucchini flowers stuffed with fresh goat's ricotta. Then come delicate pasta dishes and ambitious meat preparations such as *controfiletto di vitello con insalata di frutta piccante* (fillet of veal with spicy fruit salad). It's an haute Pugliese experience not to be missed. ⊠ *Contrada Montevicoli* ☎ *0831/377104* ⌂ *Reservations essential* ▭ *AE, DC, MC, V* ⊘ *Closed Feb. 1–10 and Sept. 10–30. No dinner weekdays.*

$$–$$$ ✕ **Cibus.** Amid the vaulted stone archways of this humble but elegant *osteria* (tavernlike restaurant) in the centro storico sit rows of bottles and books devoted to the worship of food and wine. It's no wonder, then, that the food is so good: after an *antipasto del territorio* (sampling of local meats, cheeses, and other delights) comes lasagne *di pasta fresca con cime di rape e bottarga* (with bitter greens and cured fish roe), and then perhaps an *arrosto misto di capretto, capocollo, e salsiccia* (a mixture of roast meats including baby goat and sausage). For the more adventurous: stuffed horse meat with ragù (a slow-cooked, tomato-based meat sauce). ⊠ *Via Chianche di Scarano 7* ☎ *0831/388980* ▭ *AE, DC, MC, V* ⊘ *Closed Tues. and 1st 2 wks of July.*

Martina Franca

⑯ *6 km (4 mi) south of Locorotondo, 36 km (22 mi) north of Taranto.*

Martina Franca is a beguiling town with a dazzling mixture of medieval and baroque architecture in the light-color local stone. Ornate balconies hang above the twisting, narrow streets, with little alleys leading off into the hills. Martina Franca was developed as a military stronghold in the 14th century, when a surrounding wall with 24 towers was built, but now all that remains of the wall are the four gates that had once been the only entrances to the town. Each July and August, the town holds a music festival.

Where to Stay & Eat

$ ✕ **La Cantina del Toscano.** This restaurant has a convenient location under the *portici* (archways) of one of the city's main piazzas, but it's not a tourist joint. Locals love the pizzas, grilled meats (lamb chops and sausage are first-rate), and whole fish that are prepared with skill and love in the kitchen. The atmosphere is warm and cozy. ⊠ *Piazza Maria Immacolata* ☎ *080/4302827* ▭ *AE, DC, MC, V.*

$$ ▣ **Park Hotel San Michele.** This garden hotel makes a pleasant base in the warm months, thanks to its pool. The two categories of single rooms have a small price difference; if alone, opt for the higher-priced ones. All rooms are spacious, and include complimentary bowls of fruit, but showers are old-school, hand-held Euro-style, without wall hooks. ✉ *Viale Carella 9, 74015* ☎ *080/4807053* 🖷 *080/4808895* ⊕ *www. parkhotelsm.it* ⇆ *85 rooms* ☪ *Restaurant, pool, bar* ▤ *AE, DC, MC, V* ⵏⵎ *BP.*

SALENTO & PORTS OF THE HEEL

This far south, the mountains run out of steam and the land is uniformly flat. The monotonous landscape, besides being agriculturally important, is redeemed by some of the region's best sandy coastline and a handful of small, alluring fishing towns, such as Otranto and Gallipoli. Taranto and Brindisi don't quite fit this description: both are big ports where historical importance is obscured by unsightly heavy industry. Nonetheless, Taranto has its archaeological museum, and Brindisi, an important ferry jumping-off point, marks the end of the Via Appia (the Imperial Roman road). Farther south, Salento (the Salentine Peninsula) is the local name for the part of Puglia that forms the end of the heel. Lecce is an unexpected oasis of grace and sophistication, and its swirling architecture will melt even the most uncompromising critic of the baroque.

Taranto

🛈 *100 km (62 mi) southeast of Bari, 40 km (25 mi) south of Martina Franca.*

Taranto (the stress is on the first syllable) was an important port even in Roman times. It lies toward the back of the instep of the boot on the broad Mare Grande bay, which is connected to a small internal Mare Piccolo basin by two narrow channels, one artificial and one natural. The old town is a series of old palazzi in varying states of decay and narrow cobblestone streets on an island between the larger and smaller bodies of water, linked by causeways; the modern city stretches inward along the mainland. Circumnavigate the old town and take in a dramatic panorama to the north, revealing Italy's shipping industry at its busiest: steelworks, dockyards, a bay dotted with fishing boats, and a fish market teeming with pungent activity along the old town's western edge. Little remains of Taranto's past except the 14th-century church of **San Domenico** (✉ Via Duomo 33 ☎ 099/4713511 ☉ Daily 8:30–7) jutting into the sea at one end of the island, and its famous naval academy.

★ A compendium on the millennia of local history, Taranto's **Museo Nazionale** has a large collection of prehistoric, Greek, and Roman artifacts discovered mainly in the immediate vicinity, including Puglian tombs dating from before 1000 BC. The museum is just over the bridge from the old town, on the promontory. The collection is a testament to the importance of this ancient port, which has always taken full advantage of its unique trading position at the end of the Italian peninsula. Telephone ahead before visiting the museum, as hours can be irregular. ✉ *Corso Umberto 41* ☎ *099/4532112* 🖷 €2 ☉ *Daily 8:30–7:30.*

Where to Stay

$$$ ⊞ **Grand Hotel Delfino.** This well-equipped hotel on the waterfront caters mainly to business clients, but it's a good, central place to unwind after exploring the city. There are sea views from the large modern lounge, the attractive terrace, and the airy rooms with balconies. The restaurant features regional seafood. ⊠ *Viale Virgilio 66, 74100* ☎ *099/7323232* 🖷 *099/7304654* ⊕ *www.grandhoteldelfino.it* ⇨ *200 rooms* ♨ *Restaurant, minibars, outdoor pool, bar, meeting rooms* ▤ *AE, DC, MC, V* �101 *BP.*

Brindisi

⑱ *114 km (71 mi) southeast of Bari, 72 km (45 mi) east of Taranto.*

14

Occupying the head of a deep inlet on the eastern Adriatic coast, Brindisi (the stress is on the first syllable) has long been one of Italy's most important ports. Today most travelers think of it only as a terminus for the ferry crossing that links Italy with Greece, and the seedy area around the port seems to confirm this. However, there are some interesting 13th- and 14th-century churches in the old town.

The core of Brindisi is at the head of a deep channel, which branches into two harbors, with the city between them. Down by the water is a tall **Roman column** and the base of another one next to it. These columns were built in the 2nd century AD and marked the end of the Via Appia (Appian Way), the Imperial Roman road that led from the capital to this important southeastern seaport. ⊠ *Viale Regina Margherita.*

The **Duomo,** a short walk from Brindisi's Roman column, has a mosaic floor in its apse that is worth the stop; the floor dates from the 12th century, although much of the rest of the cathedral was rebuilt in the 18th. ⊠ *Piazza Duomo* ⊙ *Daily 7–noon and 4–8.*

Lecce

⑲ *40 km (25 mi) southeast of Brindisi, 87 km (54 mi) east of Taranto.*

Fodor'sChoice
★

Lecce is the crown jewel of the mezzogiorno. The city is affectionately referred to as "the Florence of the south," but that sobriquet doesn't do justice to Lecce's uniqueness in the Italian landscape. Though its great shopping, modern bars, and the impossibly intricate baroque architecture draw comparisons to the Renaissance masterpieces of the north, Lecce's lively streets, laid-back student cafés, magical evening passeggiata, and openness to visitors are distinctively southern. The city is a cosmopolitan oasis two steps from the idyllic Otranto–Brindisi coastline and a hop from the olive-grove countryside of Puglia. Undiscovered by tourists, Lecce exudes an optimism and youthful joie de vivre unparalleled in any other baroque showcase. There is no Lecce of the north.

Although Lecce was founded before the time of the ancient Greeks, it's often associated with the term *Lecce baroque,* the result of a citywide impulse in the 17th century to redo the town in the baroque fashion. But this was baroque with a difference. Such architecture is often heavy and monumental, but here it took on a lighter, more fanciful air. Just look at the church of **Santa Croce,** with the **Palazzo della Prefettura** abutting it. Although every column, window, pediment, and balcony is given a curling baroque touch—and then an extra one for good measure—the overall effect is light-hearted. The buildings' proportions are unintimidating, and the local stone is a glowing honey color: it couldn't look menacing if it tried. ⊠ *Via Umberto I* ☎ *0832/241957* ☾ *Daily 8–1 and 5–8.*

Lecce's ornate **Duomo,** first built in 1114 but reconstructed in baroque style from 1659 to 1670, is uncharacteristically set in a solitary lateral square off a main street, rather than at a crossroads of pedestrian traffic. To the left of the Duomo, the more austere **bell tower,** reconstructed by master baroque architect Giuseppe Zimbalo in the 17th century, takes on a surreal golden hue at dusk. The facades of the adjoining 18th-century **Palazzo Vescovile,** (Bishops' Palace) farther past the right side of the Duomo, and the **Seminario** on the piazza's right edge, complement the rich ornamentation of the Duomo to create an effect almost as splendid as that of Santa Croce. The Seminario's tranquil **cloister** is also worth a visit. ⊠ *Piazza Duomo, off Corso Vittorio Emanuele* ☎ *0832/308884* ☾ *Daily 8–1 and 5–8.*

In the middle of **Piazza Sant'Oronzo,** the city's putative center, surrounded by cafés, pastry shops, and newsstands, is a **Roman column** of the same era and style as the one in Brindisi, but imaginatively surmounted by an 18th-century statue of the city's patron saint, Orontius. Next to the column, the shallow rows of seats in the **Anfiteatro Romano** suggest Verona's arena or a small-scale Roman Colosseum.

Where to Stay & Eat

$$ ✕ **Villa G. C. della Monica.** Set in a gracious 17th-century villa complete with palm trees, courtyard, and fountain, this restaurant comes into its own with summer alfresco dining in the garden. The menu focuses almost entirely on seafood, with the traditional Puglian *antipasto misto,* a generous spread of appetizers, followed by seasonal seafood dishes such as *maccheroni con vongole veraci, cozze tarantine, e fagioli bianchi* (pasta tubes with small Adriatic clams, mussels, and white beans) and fresh grilled fish. It's particularly suitable for families with young children, as there's lots of space to run around. ⊠ *Via SS Giacomo e Filippo 40* ☎ *0832/458432* ⊟ *AE, DC, MC, V* ☾ *Closed Tues., Jan., and 2 wks in Mar.*

$ ✕ **Alle Due Corti.** Rosalba de Carlo, a local character, runs this traditional trattoria. The menu is printed in the ancient *leccese* language; the adventurous can try country dishes like *pezzetti te cavallu* (spicy horse meat in tomato sauce) or *turcineddhi* (roasted baby goat entrails)—a crisp, gamy, fully flavored delight. The white-walled decor is stark, but character comes from the red-and-white checked tablecloths and the gregarious local families and groups of friends that inevitably fill the place. ⊠ *Via Leonardo Prato 42* ☎ *0832/242223* 🖃 *AE, DC, MC, V* ☉ *Closed Sun.*

★ $ ✕ **Trattoria Casareccia.** This is an excellent place to try traditional Pugliese cooking in a warm, casual setting of white walls and loud chatter. Don't expect a menu; choose from the daily specials, which might include home-made whole-wheat pasta served with a delicate sauce of tomato and sharp, aged ricotta *forte*. The rustic *purè di fave e cicoria* (puree of fava bean with chicory) is topped with local olive oil and hot peppers; mix it to-gether before eating. Service is informal and welcoming. ⊠ *Via Costadura 19* ☎ *0832/245178* 🖃 *AE, DC, MC, V* ☉ *Closed Mon., Aug. 27–Sept. 11, 1 wk at Easter, and Dec. 23–Jan. 2. No dinner Sun.*

★ $ ✕ **Wine Bar Corte dei Pandolfini.** At this wonderfully happening local spot you can choose from a vast list of Salento's best wines and feast on an unparalleled spread of artisanal *salumi* (cured meats) and local cheeses, accompanied by delicious local honey and *mostarda* (preserved fruit). It's all small plates here rather than the traditional *primi* and *secondi*, but you can easily make a meal of them. The location is on a little pi-azza just off Via degli Ammirati, which starts on the back side of the Duomo. You can dine here until 1:30 AM. ⊠ *Piazzetta Orsini* ☎ *328/ 0993709* 🖃 *AE, V* ☉ *Closed Mon. No dinner Sun.*

★ $$$$ 🏨 **Patria Palace.** It's convenient that the best hotel in Lecce also hap-pens to be in one of the best possible locations, steps from all the ac-tion. This Starwood Luxury Collection property is impeccable, top to bottom, from the warm and elegant lobby with its recessed bar to the rooms, which are sumptuous without being over the top. For 50 well-spent euros more, you can reserve a room with a stunning private ter-race overlooking Santa Croce, the crown jewel of Lecce baroque. If not, there's a beautiful rooftop gazebo for all. ⊠ *Piazzetta Riccardi, 73100* ☎ *0832/245111* 🖷 *0832/245002* ⊕ *www.patriapalacelecce.com* ➪ *67 rooms* ⚫ *Restaurant, minibars, bar, lounge, meeting room, parking (fee)* 🖃 *AE, DC, MC, V* ¶○¶ *BP.*

$–$$ 🏨 **President.** Rub elbows with visiting dignitaries at this business hotel near Piazza Mazzini. The reception is expansive and furnishings are 1980s tasteful, with an emphasis on primary colors and modernist lamps. ⊠ *Via Salandra 6, 73100* ☎ *0832/456111* 🖷 *0832/456632* ⊕ *www. hotelpresidentlecce.it* ➪ *150 rooms, 4 suites* ⚫ *Restaurant, minibars, bar, lounge, meeting room, parking (fee)* 🖃 *AE, DC, MC, V* ¶○¶ *BP.*

$–$$ 🏨 **Risorgimento.** An old-fashioned Liberty-style hotel in an 18th-century palace, Risorgimento combines historic charm with modern comfort. For undisturbed sleep and summertime siestas during longer stays, ask for rooms overlooking the backstreets or the courtyard. The roof gar-den has great views. ⊠ *Via Augusto Imperatore 19, Piazza S. Oronzo, 73100* ☎ *0832/242125* 🖷 *0832/245571* ⊕ *www.webshop.it/ hotelrisorgimento* ➪ *57 rooms* ⚫ *Restaurant, minibars, bar, lounge, meeting room, parking (fee)* 🖃 *AE, DC, MC, V* ¶○¶ *BP.*

Shopping

The best place in town to buy gastronomical delights from the Salento region, including olive oil, ricotta forte, hot pepper sauce, and an assortment of local baked goods, is **Golosità del Salento da Valentina** (✉ Via A. Petronelli 3 ☎ 0832/300549), a few steps from the Piazza del Duomo. The friendly and helpful owner presses his own olive oil and has infinite patience with—and interest in—visitors from abroad.

Nightlife & the Arts

The most popular hangout for the university crowd is **I Merli** (✉ Via Federico D'Aragona 29 ☎ 0832/241874), a classy café where scores of locals gather each afternoon and evening for coffee, spirits, and gossip. Hours are 5:30 PM–2 AM (open earlier on weekends); closed Monday.

In July, courtyards and piazzas throughout the city are the settings for **drama productions** and, sometimes, opera. A **baroque music festival** is held in churches throughout the city in September. For details on forthcoming events call the **Tourist Information Office** (☎ 0832/248092).

Culinary Tours

In response to the gastronomical tourism craze, the Lecce area has thrown its hat into the ring with the **Hidden Apulia** (⊕ www.thehiddenapulia.com ☎ 0832/300549 ⌁ full wks €760–€890, weekends €450–€525), an outfit run by three Anglophone Leccese women. Their food-and-wine-theme excursions cover both the city and the nearby countryside. The weeklong program includes a full six days of activities, with delights such as two days of cooking classes plus market visits, olive oil and wine tastings at a *masseria* outside Lecce, traditional dance lessons, and side trips to Gallipoli, Otranto, or Ostuni.

Otranto

 36 km (22 mi) southeast of Lecce, 188 km (117 mi) southeast of Bari.

In one of the first great Gothic novels, Horace Walpole's 1764 *The Castle of Otranto,* the English writer immortalized this city and its mysterious medieval fortress. Otranto (the stress is on the first syllable) has likewise had more than its share of dark thrills. As the easternmost point in Italy—and therefore closest to the Balkan peninsula—it has often borne the brunt of foreign invasions during its checkered history. A flourishing port from ancient Greek times, Otranto (*Hydruntum* to the Romans) has a history like most of southern Italy: after the fall of the western Roman Empire, centuries of Byzantine rule interspersed with Saracen incursions, followed by the arrival of the Normans. Modern Otranto's dank cobblestone alleyways alternatively reveal dusty, forgotten doorways and modern Italian fashion chains, and the spooky castle still looms above, between city and sea. On a clear day you can see across to Albania.

The historic city center nestles within impressive city walls and bastions, dominated by the famous **Castello,** which is attributed to the Spanish of the 16th century. ✉ *Piazza Castello* ⌁ *Free* ☉ *Tues.–Sun. 9–1.*

The real jewel in Otranto is the **Cattedrale,** originally begun by the Normans and conserving an extraordinary 12th-century mosaic pavement in the nave and aisles. ✉ *Piazza Basilica* ☎ *0836/802720* ⌁ *Free* ☉ *Daily 7–noon and 3–6.*

OFF THE BEATEN PATH

COASTLINE SOUTH TO LEUCA – The coastal road between Otranto and Leuca is one of the most beautiful in southern Italy. Sandy beaches are replaced by rocky outcrops and sheer cliffs watched over by scattered castles and seaside pleasure palaces. Along the way, **Santa Cesarea Terme,** with a pleasant shoreline and famous fanciful Moorish resort, and **Castro,** with another attractive marina, are worthwhile stops; this is land that few foreign tourists traverse. At the end of the journey, **Capo Santa Maria di Leuca** has a lighthouse at the most southeastern point in Italy, the end of the Puglian Aqueduct, and the quiet, sparse basilica of **Santa Maria Finibus Terrae** (land's end). From here, you are only 70 km (44 mi) from Albania. The **Marina di Leuca,** below, is a little fishing village with excursion boats and a few summertime hotels and bars. If, after the drive, you're heading back to Lecce or points east, the inland highway is a faster route.

Gallipoli

㉑ *37 km (23 mi) south of Lecce, 190 km (118 mi) southeast of Bari.*

The fishing port of Gallipoli, on the Golfo di Taranto, is divided between a new town, on the mainland, and a beautiful fortified town, across a 17th-century bridge, crowded onto its own small island in the gulf. The Greeks called it Kallipolis, the Romans Anxa. Like the infamous Turkish town of the same name on the Dardanelles, the Italian Gallipoli occupies a strategic location and thus was repeatedly attacked through the centuries—by the Normans in 1071, the Venetians in 1484, the British in 1809. Today, life in Gallipoli revolves around its fishing trade. Bright fishing boats in primary colors breeze in and out of the bay during the day, and Gallipoli's fish market, below the bridge, throbs with activity all morning.

Gallipoli's historic quarter, a mix of narrow alleys and squares, is guarded by **Castello Aragonese,** a massive fortification that grew out of an earlier Byzantine fortress you can still see at the southeast corner. After being an operative base for the busy *Guardia di Finanza* (revenue police), it's now being renovated and adapted for future use as a public monument. Gallipoli's **Duomo** (✉ Via Antonietta de Pace ☎ 0833/261987), open daily 9–12:30 and 5–8, is a notable baroque church. The church of **La Purissima** (✉ Riviera Nazario Sauro ☎ 0833/261699) has a stuccoed interior as elaborate as a wedding cake, with an especially noteworthy tiled floor. You can visit daily 9–12:30 and 5–7:30.

Where to Stay & Eat

$$–$$$ ✕ **Marechiaro.** Unless you arrive by boat—as many do—you have to cross a little bridge to reach this simple port-side restaurant, not far from the town's historic center. It's built out onto the sea, replete with wood paneling, flowers, and terraces, with panoramic coastal views. Try the renowned *zuppa di pesce alla gallipolina* (a stew of fish, shrimp, clams, and mussels) and linguine with seafood. ✉ *Lungomare Marconi* ☎ *0833/266143* ▭ *AE, DC, MC, V.*

★ **$$$$** ▢ **Costa Brada.** The rooms all have terraces with sea views at this modern white beach hotel of classic Mediterranean design. The interiors are uncluttered and tasteful; rooms 110 through 114 are particularly spacious and overlook the beach. The hotel accepts only half- or full-board guests in summer. Room rates go down significantly at other times of year. ⊠ *Baia Verde, Litoranea Santa Maria di Leuca, 73014* ☎ *0833/ 202551* 🖷 *0833/202555* ⊕ *www.grandhotelcostabrada.it* 🛏 *90 rooms* ⚲ *2 restaurants, snack bar, 2 pools (1 indoor), gym, sauna, beach, shop* ⊟ *AE, DC, MC, V* ⦿⦿ *MAP.*

Beaches

Ample swimming, water sports, and clean, fine sand make Gallipoli's **beaches** a good choice for families. The 5-km (3-mi) expanse of sand sweeping south from town has both public and private beaches, the latter equipped with changing rooms, sun beds, and umbrellas. Water-sports equipment can be bought or rented at the waterfront shops in town.

BASILICATA

Occupying the instep of Italy's boot, Basilicata has long been one of Italy's poorest regions, memorably described by Carlo Levi (1902–75) in his *Christ Stopped at Eboli,* a book that brought home to the majority of the Italians the depths of deprivation to which this forgotten region was subject. (The tale of Levi's internment was poignantly filmed by Francesco Rosi in 1981.) Basilicata was not always so desolate, however. For the ancient Greeks, the area formed part of Magna Graecia, the loose collection of colonies founded along the coasts of southern Italy whose wealth and military prowess rivaled those of the city-states of Greece itself. The city of Matera, the region's true highlight, is built on the side of an impressive ravine that is honeycombed with sassi, some of them still occupied, forming a separate enclave that contrasts vividly with the attractive baroque town above.

Matera

㉒ *62 km (39 mi) south of Bari.*

Matera is one of southern Italy's most unusual towns. On their own, the elegant baroque churches, palazzi, and broad piazzas—filled to bursting during the evening passeggiata, when the locals turn out to stroll the streets—as well as the outstanding modern cuisine, would make Matera stand out in Basilicata's impoverished landscape. But what really sets this town apart is its sassi.

Fodor'sChoice Matera's **sassi** are rock-hewn dwellings piled chaotically atop one another, strewn across the sides of a steep ravine. They date from Paleolithic times, when they were truly cave homes. In the years that followed, the grottoes were slowly adapted as houses only slightly more modern, with their exterior walls closed off and canals regulating rainwater and sewage. Until relatively recently, these troglodytic abodes presented a Dante-esque vision of squalor and poverty, graphically described in Carlo Levi's *Christ Stopped at Eboli,* but in the 1960s most of them were emptied of their inhabitants, who were largely consigned to the ugly block structures seen on the way into town. Today, having been designated a World Heritage Site, the area has been cleaned up and is gradually being populated once again—and even gentrified,

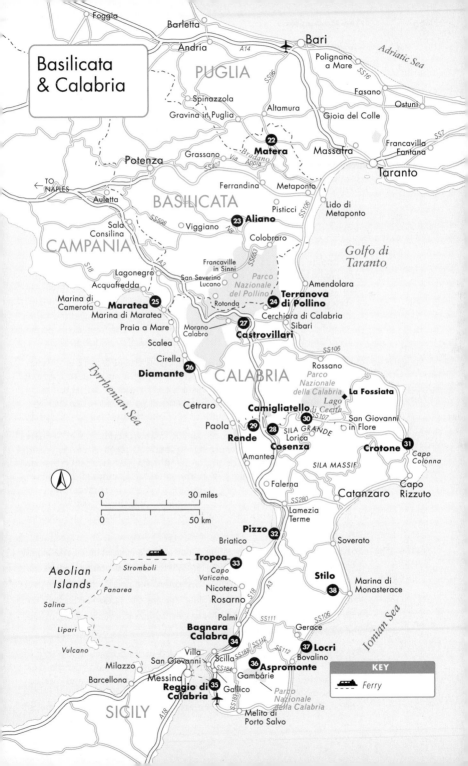

Basilicata & Calabria

PUGLIA

Foggia
Barletta
Andria
Bari
A14
Polignano a Mare
Spinazzola
SS96
Altamura
Fasano
Ostuni
Gravina in Puglia
Gioia del Colle
Francavilla Fantana
SS7
Grassano
Via Appia
Bradano
Matera **22**
Massatra
Taranto
Potenza
SS407
Ferrandina
Metaponto
TO NAPLES
Auletta
Golfo di Taranto
BASILICATA
Pisticci
Lido di Metaponto
Sala Consilina
Viggiano
Aliano **23**
SS106
Colobraro
CAMPANIA
SS508
N6
S18
SS683
Lagonegro
Francaville in Sinni
Amendolara
A3
San Severino Lucano
Parco Nazionale del Pollino
Acquafredda
Marina di Camerota
Maratea **25**
Rotonda
Terranova **24** di Pollino
Marina di Maratea
Cerchiara di Calabria
Praia a Mare
Morano Calabro
Castrovillari **27**
Sibari
Scalea
Rossano
SS106
Cirella
Diamante **26**
Tyrrhenian Sea
CALABRIA
Parco Nazionale della Calabria
La Fossiata
Lago di Cecita
Cetraro
Camigliatello **30** *SS107*
San Giovanni in Fiore
Paola
Rende **29** **28** *SILA GRANDE*
Lorica
Amantea
Cosenza
Crotone **31**
SILA MASSIF
Capo Colonna
Falerna
Catanzaro
Capo Rizzuto
SS280
Lamezia Terme
Pizzo **32**
Soverato
Briatico
30 miles
50 km
Aeolian Islands
Stromboli
Tropea **33**
Capo Vaticano
Stilo **38**
Marina di Monasterace
Panarea
Nicotera
Rosarno
S18
A3
Salina
Palmi
SS111
SS106
Gerace
Lipari
Bagnara Calabra **34**
Locri **37**
SS183
SS112
Bovalino
Vulcano
Villa
Scilla
Aspromonte **36**
Ionian Sea
Milazzo
San Giovanni
SS184
Gambàrie
Barcellona
Messina
Reggio di Calabria **35**
Gallico
Parco Nazionale della Calabria
SICILY
A18
SS183
Melito di Porto Salvo

Adriatic Sea
SS16

KEY
🚢 Ferry

as evidenced by the bars and restaurants that have moved in. (The filming here of Mel Gibson's controversial film *The Passion of the Christ* also raised the area's profile.) The wide Strada Panoramica leads you safely through this desolate region, which still retains its eerie atmosphere and panoramic views.

There are two areas of sassi, the **Sasso Caveoso** and the **Sasso Barisano,** and both can be seen from vantage points in the upper town. Follow the Strada Panoramica down into the sassi and feel free to ramble among the strange structures, which, in the words of H. V. Morton in his *A Traveller in Southern Italy,* "resemble the work of termites rather than of man." Among them you will find several *chiese rupestri,* or rock-hewn churches, some of which have medieval frescoes, notably **Santa Maria de Idris,** right on the edge of the Sasso Caveoso, near the ravine. ⊠ *Sasso Caveoso* ☎ *0835/319458* 🖃 *€2.50* ☉ *Oct.–Mar., daily 9–1 and 3:30–5:30; Apr.–Sept., daily 9–1 and 3:30–7.*

The **Duomo** in Matera was built in the late 13th century and occupies a prominent position between the two areas of sassi. It has a pungent Apulian-Romanesque flavor; inside, there's a recovered fresco, probably painted in the 14th century, showing scenes from the *Last Judgment.* On the Duomo's facade the figures of Sts. Peter and Paul stand on either side of a sculpture of Matera's patron, Madonna della Bruna. ⊠ *Via Duomo* ☎ *0835/335201* ☉ *Daily 8–12:30 and 3:30–7.*

The agency **SIC** (⊠ Via Casalnuovo 15, 75100 ☎ 0835/314244 ⊕ www. stoneincoming.it) arranges tours of the sassi area on request, charging around €10 per person for groups of four or more. Call ahead to request an English-speaking guide. Independent guides also offer their services on the spot, pricing by length of tour and the number in your party.

In town you'll find the 13th-century Romanesque church of **San Giovanni Battista,** restored to its pre-baroque simplicity in 1926. As you go in through a side door—the original end door and facade were incorporated into later buildings—note the interesting sculpted decorations in the porch. The interior still maintains its original cross vaulting, ogival arches, and curious capitals. At this writing the church was under construction; check with the tourist office for the latest on re-opening. ⊠ *Via San Biagio.*

NEED A BREAK?

The distinguished, timeworn patina of downtown's elegant little **Caffè Tripoli** (⊠ Piazza Vittorio Veneto 17 ☎ 0835/333991) only hints at the treasures that lie within: some of southern Italy's best coffee and gelato, including memorable versions of hazelnut and chocolate. They're also renowned for their unbelievably rich hot chocolate and other decadent drinks that blend coffees, creams, and gelatos. You can't go wrong.

Matera's excellent **Museo Ridola** is housed in the former monastery of Santa Chiara. Illustrating the human and geological history of the area, the museum includes an extensive selection of prehistoric and classical finds, notably Bronze Age weaponry and beautifully decorated Greek pottery. One room displays stolen art treasures recovered by a special department of the *carabinieri* (national police). ⊠ *Via Ridola 24* ☎ *0835/ 310058* ✍ *€2.50* ⊘ *Tues.–Sun. 9–8, Mon. 2–8.*

Where to Stay & Eat

$$–$$$

Fodor'sChoice

★

✕**Lucanerie.** Within the airy vaulted stone dining room of this casual restaurant you'll find some of southern Italy's most exciting food. A series of 17 or 18 small tasting plates, served at the beginning of the meal, steal the show. These creative antipasti might include bitter orange slices sprinkled with lemon zest and ground hot peppers, fried zucchini flowers, a memorable goat's ricotta with a sweet glaze of persimmon, or an herbaceous slice of rich *lardo* (lard) atop a crusty piece of bread whose texture approaches the apex of perfection. Other courses might include delectable hand-rolled pasta tubes or a fillet of local beef, though it takes a truly insatiable appetite to make it through both a primo and a secondo after such an opening spread. ⊠ *Via Santo Stefano 71* ☎ *0835/ 332133* ✍ *Reservations essential* ⊟ *AE, DC, MC, V* ⊘ *Closed Mon.*

★ $–$$

✕ **Le Botteghe.** This stylish restaurant is right in the heart of the sassi, occupying pleasingly restored vaulted premises. Carnivores will delight in the charcoal-grilled steak, which comes from the friendly owner's herd of grass-fed cows. Cooked wonderfully rare, this is one of the finest pieces of meat in the region. It's best washed down with local Aglianico del Vulture red wine. Solid renditions of local pasta dishes are also available. ⊠ *Piazza San Pietro Barisano 22* ☎ *0835/344072* ✍ *Reservations essential* ⊟ *DC, MC, V* ⊘ *Closed Feb. No dinner Sun. No lunch Tues.–Fri. Oct.–Apr.*

$–$$

Fodor'sChoice

★

▥ **Locanda di San Martino.** Combining good taste, an agreeable ambience, and value, the Locanda is a prime place to stay among Matera's sassi— and you can drive right up to it. The historic rooms—formerly cave dwellings—have been impeccably restored under the guidance of owner Antonio Panetto and American anthropologist Dorothy Zinn. Stepping out onto your terrace overlooking the old town is like being on a film set. ⊠ *Via San Martino 22, 75100* ☎ *0835/256600* ▤ *0835/256472* ⊕ *www. locandadisanmartino.it* ↴ *28 rooms, 6 suites* ⚹ *Breakfast room, minibars, bar, library, some free parking* ⊟ *AE, DC, MC, V* ▥◯▯ *BP.*

$

▥ **Hotel Sassi.** This unusual hotel lies right in the heart of the Sasso Barisano, directly across from the Duomo. It has a raw, cavelike design, with rough-hewn walls and stairs (making it inhospitable to people with limited mobility). Facilities are minimal; rooms are small and plain but clean, comfortable, and air-conditioned. Two rooms are set aside for hostel-type bunk accommodations at budget rates. Parking is a bit of a hike from the hotel, something to consider if you have heavy baggage. ⊠ *Via San Giovanni Vecchio 89, 75100* ☎ *0835/331009* ▤ *0835/333733* ⊕ *www.hotelsassi.it* ↴ *26 rooms, 2 suites* ⚹ *Breakfast room, minibars, bar* ⊟ *AE, DC, MC, V* ▥◯▯ *BP.*

Aliano

➋➌ *127 km (79 mi) southwest of Matera, 102 km (63 mi) southeast of Potenza.*

This remote village off S598 in the center of Basilicata's empty interior was the site of Carlo Levi's internment during 1936 and 1937. After the war, Levi published his account of that time in his classic *Christ Stopped at Eboli,* later filmed by Francesco Rosi. Not significantly different from any of the countless villages scattered over the featureless clay gullies and outcrops stretching out on all sides, Aliano (called Gagliano by Levi) has not altered much, and readers can identify the church, the piazza where the Fascist mayor addressed the impassive peasants, and the timeless views. The house in Aliano where Carlo Levi stayed has been preserved as the **Museo Storico Carlo Levi,** displaying some personal artifacts as well as other articles of local interest. The old post office nearby in Piazza Garibaldi—where you will find the custodians to both buildings—has been converted into an art gallery. ⊠ *Palazzo Caporale* ☎ *0835/568315* ⊠ *€3 for both museum and art gallery* ⊘ *Sept.–May, Thurs.–Tues. 10–12:30 and 4–6; June–Aug., daily 10:30–12:30 and 4–7. Closed Wed.*

Terranova di Pollino

㉔ *70 km (43 mi) south of Aliano, 125 km (78 mi) east of Matera.*

Founded in the 16th century as part of the Duchy of Noja, Terranova is a quiet village—the end of the road for local buses—lying at the foothills of Italy's largest nature preserve, the Pollino National Park. It is base camp for hikes to sleepy Albanian hill communities and to the higher reaches of the spectacular Pollino massif. Thanks to a relatively low population density, wildlife thrives within the park, its best-known inhabitants being the golden eagle and the endangered wolf—there were 34 at the latest count, making up almost 10% of the population in all of Italy.

Where to Stay & Eat

★ ¢ ✕▣ **Hotel Picchio Nero.** Situated just below the village of Terranova, this hotel combines rustic simplicity and excellent dining ($–$$). At the helm is the energetic Pino Golia, a welcoming, attentive host who has set up this first-class base for mountain hikers and dispenses copious information on local trails and history. The rooms are paneled in Alpine style and look out onto soothing woods and valleys; the grounds include the hotel's own gardens. The name *picchio nero* means "black woodpecker," one of the Pollino's conservation flagship species. ⊠ *Via Mulino 18, 85030* ☎ *0973/93170* ⊠ *0973/93170* ⊕ *www.picchionero. com* ⇋ *25 rooms, 2 family suites* ♨ *Restaurant, bar; no a/c* ⊟ *AE, DC, MC, V* ⍟ *BP.*

Maratea

㉕ *103 km (64 mi) southwest of Aliano, 217 km (135 mi) south of Naples.*

When encountering Maratea for the first time, you can be forgiven for thinking you've somehow arrived at the French Riviera. The high, twisty road resembles nothing so much as a corniche, complete with glimpses of a turquoise sea below. Divided by the craggy rocks into various separate localities—Maratea, Maratea Porto, Maratea Marina—the sequence ends above the main inland village, a tumble of cobblestone streets where the ruins of a much older settlement (Maratea Antica) can be seen. At the summit of the hill stands a dramatic, gigantic Christ, a floating white ghost in the night sky reminiscent of the one in Rio de Janeiro. There's no shortage of secluded sandy strips in between the rocky headlands, which can get crowded in August. A summer minibus service connects all the different points once or twice an hour.

Where to Stay & Eat

$$–$$$ ✕ **Taverna Rovita.** Housed in a former convent with exposed beams, this restaurant in the heart of the old town offers a menu based on traditional recipes, but the food here is in a different league from that of Maratea's other eateries. The antipasti, for a start, are varied and abundant, and the homemade pasta comes with a selection of rich sauces that changes according to the season. Choose a locally caught fish for your second course. ⊠ *Via Rovita 13* ☎ *0973/876588* ▭ *AE, MC, V* ⊗ *Closed Tues.*

$$–$$$ ✕▢ **Villa Cheta Elite.** Immersed in Mediterranean greenery, this large historic villa in the seaside village of Acquafredda is strategically close to the beach (reached by elevator). Rooms are spruce and stylish without being overfurnished, while dining out on the restaurant's garden terrace ($$) against the backdrop of Basilicata's rugged coastline is simply fabulous. ⊠ *Via Nazionale, Loc. Acquafredda Maratea, 85041* ☎ *0973/878134* 🖷 *0973/878135* ⊕ *www.villacheta.it* ↩ *23 rooms* △ *Restaurant, minibars, beach, bar* ▭ *AE, DC, MC, V* ⊗ *Closed Dec.–Mar. 15* ⍩ *MAP.*

14

CALABRIA

Italy's southernmost mainland region has seen more than its fair share of oppression, poverty, and natural disaster, but this land of Magna Graecia, mountains, and *mare* (sea) also claims more than its share of fantastic scenery and great beaches. The accent here is on the landscape, the sea, and the constantly changing dialogue between the two. Don't expect much in the way of sophistication in this least trodden of regions, but do remain open to the simple pleasures to be found—the country food, the friendliness, the disarming hospitality of the people. Aside from coast and culture, there are also some sights worth going out of your way for, from the vividly colored murals of Diamante to the ruins of Magna Graecia at Locri. Inland, the Parco Nazionale Pollino and mountainous Sila Massif, which includes a nature reserve, are draws for hikers.

The drive on the southbound A3 highway alone is a breathtaking experience, the more so as you approach Sicily, whose image grows tantalizingly nearer as the road wraps around the coastline once challenged by Odysseus. This is the road you should take to get the big picture—but don't forget to stop for a bit to get a closer view of this fascinating land.

Diamante

❷⑥ *51 km (32 mi) south of Maratea, 225 km (140 mi) south of Naples.*

One of the most fashionable of the string of small resorts lining Calabria's north Tyrrhenian coast, Diamante makes a good stop for its white-

VOICES OF ITALY

Andrea Peiser
hotelier, Cetraro, Calabria

Andrea Peiser is an accomplished marine biologist, diver, and now hotel manager. He has studied environmental science and zoology at the University of Hawaii, been a member of the Italian civil defense as a forest-fire fighter, and led an underwater search-and-rescue squad. He returned to the family business as general manager of the Grand Hotel San Michele in Cetraro, Calabria, helping his illustrious mother, Claudia Sinisalchi. Mrs. Sinisalchi once built dams in Nigeria and was a professor of hydrology in Rome, but eventually came back to Calabria to run the family hotel. Now it is Andrea's turn. He explains aspects of life in his native land.

On the concept of time: "Sometimes it's difficult to understand the way of living of some of my countrymen. They seem to have lost the concept of time. If you fix an appointment, it won't be at 10 AM sharp, but rather 'sometime in the morning or afternoon'—and which day is unknown. If you wait for someone the whole afternoon, the person might show up three days later in the morning. It's not too bad in the end; you have just to expect the unexpected."

The 'Ndrangheta: "There are a lot of small fishing boats in Calabria, and most are run or controlled by people involved with 'Ndrangheta, the Calabrian version of the Mafia. This means that the whole fishing market is a sort of 'washing machine' for the dirty money from drugs, guns, and illegal aliens. With the 'Ndrangheta, everything passes by, but nothing goes away. The organization has just changed a bit the way it makes money. Nowadays, they are more involved in the drug and gun trades, like organized crime everywhere. Still, the 'Ndrangheta isn't a threat to tourists—that's a common misconception."

Why his hotel won't serve swordfish: "Because in Calabria, they are caught with devices that are illegal, such as 'drifting nets,' which go through the water catching everything in sight. Although illegal, they're used by several boats departing from the small harbor of Cetraro and elsewhere. The coast guard organizes raids three or four times per year, confiscating boats and nets, but after a week everything is forgotten."

The pitfalls of running an old-world hotel: "A rich lady always requested breakfast in her room and ate on the balcony. The problem was that we had to evacuate the terrace below where the 'common' people ate because as she finished her breakfast she just tossed it off the balcony, bombarding our poor guests with dishes and empty teapots. We nicknamed her 'the throwing lady.'

"Another thing that happened last year: a bat took up residence under an umbrella by the pool. Early in the morning, a lady from northern Italy would go to the pool and open the umbrella housing the bat—which would cause her to scream. Why she chose that particular umbrella each time is a mystery, but bats, foxes, and even snakes are realities of life in Calabria."

14

washed maze of narrow alleys, brightly adorned with a startling variety of large-scale murals. The work of local artists, the murals—which range from cartoons to poems to serious portraits, and from tasteful to downright ugly—give a sense of wandering through a huge open-air art gallery. Flanking the broad, palm-lined seaside promenade are sparkling beaches to the north and south.

Where to Stay

$$$ 🏨 **Grand Hotel San Michele.** A survivor from a vanishing age, the San Michele, operated by the illustrious Claudia Sinisalchi and her marine biologist son Andrea, occupies a belle epoque–style, cliff-top villa near the village of Cetraro, 20 km (12 mi) south of Diamante on SS18. Mingling Mediterranean charm with old-style elegance, the hotel is set within extensive gardens, and an elevator takes you down to the private beach at the base of the cliff. As with most hotels on Calabria's coast, substantial bargains are available on room rates outside July and August. ✉ *Località Bosco 8/9, 87022 Cetraro* ☎ *0982/91012* 🖷 *0982/91430* ⊕ *www.sanmichele.it* ➳ *84 rooms, 10 suites, 40 apartments* ♿ *Restaurant, 9-hole golf course, tennis court, beach (fee), bar, convention center, car rental* ▤ *AE, DC, MC, V* ⊘ *Closed Nov.* ¶❍¶ *BP.*

Castrovillari

㉗ *68 km (43 mi) east of Diamante, 75 km (48 mi) north of Cosenza.*

Accent the first "i" when you pronounce the name of this provincial Calabrian city, notable for its Aragonese castle, Jewish synagogue, and 16th-century San Giuliano church. It's also a great jumping-off point for the Parco Nazionale Pollino. Castrovillari's world-class restaurant-inn, La Locanda di Alia, has made the city something of an out-of-the-way gastronomical destination in Calabria.

⌐ **OFF THE BEATEN PATH**

CERCHIARA DI CALABRIA – There may be no more characteristically Calabrian, time-frozen village than this community of 2,800 people, which can be reached by a winding 32-km (20-mi) climb from Castrovillari via SS105 and SS92. Like so many rural towns in southern Italy, this one is aging and shrinking: the death rate is about double the birthrate. You may get some curious stares as you ramble through the ancient sloping cobblestone streets and take in the memorable views straight across to the Ionian Sea—but the experience will transport you back a century.

Where to Eat

$–$$ ✕🏨 **La Locanda di Alia.** It's hard to say what's more surprising about this inn and gastronomical temple: its improbable location in Castrovillari, or the fact that it's been here since 1952. At the restaurant ($$$–$$$$), Chef Gaetano Alia's menu swerves from the comforting (pork liver with bay leaf and orange, with a flavorful juice to sop up with deliciously crusty bread) to the dangerously spicy (*candele*, like rigatoni without the ridges, in a tomato, pork, and hot pepper sauce). Delightful, luxurious rooms are decorated in bright colors with local art; some have separate living rooms and bedrooms. ✉ *Via Jetticelle 55* ☎ *0981/46370* ⊕ *www.alia.it* ♦ *Reservations essential* ▤ *AE, DC, MC, V.*

Cosenza

28 *75 km (48 mi) south of Diamante, 185 km (115 mi) north of Reggio di Calabria.*

Cosenza, Calabria's biggest city, has a steep, stair-laden centro storico (historic city center) that truly hails from another age. Wrought-iron balconies overlook narrow alleyways with old-fashioned storefronts and bars that have barely been touched by centuries of development. Flung haphazardly—and beautifully—across the top and side of a steep hill ringed by mountains, and watched over by a great, crumbling medieval castle, Cosenza also provides the best gateway for the Sila, whose steep walls rear up to the town's eastern side. Though Cosenza's outskirts are largely modern and ugly, culinary and photographic gems await in the rolling farmland nearby and the mountains to the east.

Crowning the Pancrazio hill above the old city, with views across to the Sila mountains, **Castello Svevo** is largely in ruins, having suffered successive earthquakes and a lightning strike that ignited gunpowder stored within. The castle takes its name from the great Swabian emperor Frederick II (1194–1250), who added two octagonal towers, though it dates back originally to the Normans, who fortified the hill against their Saracen foes. Occasional exhibitions and concerts are staged here in summer, and any time of year it's fun to check out the old ramparts and take in the views of the old and new cities—a shocking study in contrast. ⊠ *Porta Piana* 🎫 *Free* ☉ *Daily 8 AM–1 PM and 2–8.*

Cosenza's noblest square, **Piazza XV Marzo** (commonly called Piazza della Prefettura), houses government buildings as well as the elegant **Teatro Rendano**. From the square, the **Villa Comunale** (public garden) provides plenty of shaded benches for a rest.

NEED A BREAK? In the heart of the centro storico, the charming and historic **Gran Caffè Renzelli** (⊠ Corso Telesio 46 ☎ 0984/46814) makes a fine spot for a pause. At tables inside or out (there is a no-smoking room as well as an outside terrace), you can enjoy *varchiglia* (a dry almond cake) along with a host of sweet and wonderful coffee-liqueur combinations, each served with lightly whipped cream in a tall glass. Join in the *chiacchiere al caffè* (talks over coffee), echoing the discussions of the literary salon that once met here.

Cosenza's original **Duomo** was probably built in the middle of the 11th century but was destroyed by the earthquake of 1184. A new cathedral was consecrated in the presence of Emperor Frederick II in 1222. After many baroque additions, later alterations have restored some of the Provençal Gothic style. Inside, look for the lovely tomb of Isabella of Aragon, who died after falling from her horse en route to France in 1271. ⊠ *Piazza del Duomo* ☎ *0984/77864* ☉ *Daily 8–noon and 3:30–7.*

Where to Stay & Eat

$$ ✕ **Osteria dell'Arenella.** Right on the banks of the river, this grilled meat specialist caters to the local bourgeoisie with a comfortable, friendly set of rooms under old archways. The place is for carnivores only; go for the *grigliata mista* and enjoy the wonderful meatiness of local grass-fed beef—but be sure to ask for it all *al sangue* (rare). The wine list, too, is excellent. ✉ *Via Arenella 12* ☎ *0984/76573* ▭ *AE, DC, MC, V* ⊘ *Closed Mon. No lunch Tues.–Sat.*

$–$$ ✕ **Da Giocondo.** In the new part of town, but near the centro storico, you can sample simple homemade dishes in a modern yet homey setting. Go for freshly picked mushrooms from the Sila as an antipasto, followed by *rigatoni alla silana* (pasta with tomato, basil, peppers, and local caciocavallo cheese), washed down with local Cirò wine. ✉ *Via Piave 53* ☎ *0984/29810* ▭ *AE, DC, MC, V* ⊘ *Closed Aug. No dinner Sun.*

$ ✕ **Taverna L'Arco Vecchio.** This tavern-restaurant, right in the middle of the old town along the path up to the castle, appropriately under the famous Arch of Ciaccio, serves traditional Calabrian dishes in a warm, elegant vaulted room. Try the excellent *lagane e ceci* (homemade pasta with chickpeas, garlic, and oil). ✉ *Via Archi di Ciaccio 21* ☎ *0984/72564* ⊕ *www.arcovecchio.it* ▭ *AE, DC, MC, V* ⊘ *Closed Mon. and 2 wks in Aug.*

★ ¢–$$ ✕ **Wine Bar DOC.** Representing the contemporary edge of Cosenza, this postmodern feat of interior decorating oozes fusion, whimsically plopping spreads of tempting traditional Calabrian salumi and a superlative collection of wines amid a whirl of glass and exposed stone, all tucked into the cozy arches of an ancient palazzo. All the trendiest locals come out not just for the voluminous wine list, which showcases Calabria's absolute best, but also for the wonderful smoked meats, cheeses, and inventive pasta dishes. Come to eat or just to drink. ✉ *Vico San Tommaso 13, off Corso Telesio* ☎ *0984/73110* ▭ *DC, MC, V* ⊘ *Closed Mon. No lunch.*

¢–$ ▦ **Royal Hotel.** This hotel is a few blocks into the new center, away from the centro storico, but it's worth the 15-minute walk to stay in the best of Cosenza's less-than-stellar accommodation lineup. The lobby is regal, the rooms not so much; still, they're simple and clean, with sober furnishings. ✉ *Via Molinella 24/e, 87100* ☎ *0984/412165* ☎ *0984/412461* ⊕ *www.hotelroyalsas.it* ⇄ *45 rooms* ⌂ *Restaurant, bar, Internet terminal* ▭ *AE, DC, MC, V* ⏐◯⏐ *BP.*

Rende

㉙ *13 km (8 mi) northwest of Cosenza.*

Rende is a pleasing stop on the way to or from Cosenza. Leave your car in the parking lot at the base of a long and bizarre series of escalators and staircases, which will whisk you off to this pristine, cobblestoned hilltop town, whose winding streets and turrets preside over idyllic countryside views.

Where to Eat

★ $$$ ✕ **Pantagruel.** You are completely in the hands of the chef at this prix-fixe-only temple to seafood. But they are good hands indeed, which is why Pantagruel is one of the most respected restaurants in Calabria. The set menu changes daily, but you'll surely encounter something memorable: for instance, a salad of octopus so thinly sliced and delicate that it's reminiscent of carpaccio, or a tender fillet of *spigola* (Mediterranean bass) with a sweet sauce of brandy, cream of licorice, and lemon rind. It's set in an elegant old house with sweeping views of hills dotted with little towns. ⊠ *Corso Vittorio Emanuele 217* ☎ *0966/372260* ▤ *AE, DC, MC, V* ⊘ *Closed Mon. and Tues., Aug. 15–Sept. 15, and Dec. 20–Jan. 10.*

Camigliatello

③⓪ *36 km (22 mi) east of Cosenza.*

Lined with chalets, Camigliatello, between Crotone and Cosenza, is one of the Sila Massif's major resort towns. Most of the Sila is not mountainous at all; it is, rather, an extensive, sparsely populated plateau with areas of thick forest. Unfortunately, the region has been exploited by construction and fuel industries, resulting in considerable deforestation. However, since 1968, when the area was designated a national park (Parco Nazionale della Calabria), strict rules have limited the felling of timber, and forests are now regenerating. There are well-marked trails through pine and beech woods, and ample opportunities for horseback riding. Fall and winter see droves of locals hunting mushrooms and gathering chestnuts, while ski slopes near Camigliatello also draw crowds. A couple of miles east of town, Lago Cecita makes a good starting point for exploring **La Fossiata,** a lovely wooded conservation area within the park.

Where to Stay

$ 🏨 **Tasso.** On the edge of Camigliatello, less than 1 km (½ mi) from the ski slopes, this hotel is in a peaceful, picturesque location. Don't be put off by its oddly futuristic 1970s look—it's well equipped, with plenty of space for evening entertainment, including live music, and relaxation after a day of hiking or skiing. The restaurant has a terrace shaded by a walnut tree, and all rooms have balconies. There are sometimes good full-board deals for seniors in summer. ⊠ *Via degli Impianti Sportivi, Spezzano della Sila, 87058* ☎ *0984/578113* ⊕ *www.hoteltasso.it* ⏎ *82 rooms* ⚭ *Restaurant, bar, lounge, nightclub, recreation room, meeting room, free parking; no a/c* ▤ *AE, DC, MC, V* ⊘ *Closed Mar.–May and Nov.* ⧒ *BP.*

Crotone

③① *105 km (65 mi) east of Cosenza, 150 km (94 mi) northeast of Locri.*

Occupying the main bulge along Calabria's Ionian coastline, Crotone was founded by Achaeans from the Greek mainland in about 708 BC and soon became one of the great cities in Magna Graecia. Though the drab modern town has obliterated most of the ancient settlement, a remarkable gold hoard was found at the **Santuario di Hera Lacinia** on a promontory 11 km (7 mi) to the south, known as Capo Colonna for the single remaining column from the temple of Hera. The area has free access during daylight hours and is well worth a visit, especially in April and May, when it is awash with wildflowers. The **Museo Archeologico Nazionale,** close to the seafront castle in Crotone, features treasure from the Santuario di Hera Lacinia, including Hera's gold crown with intertwined fig and myrtle leaves. ⊠ *Via Risorgimento 14* ☎ *096/223082* 🎫 *€2* ⊗ *Tues.–Sun. 9–7:30.*

Pizzo

32 *148 km (92 mi) south of Diamante, 107 km (66 mi) north of Reggio di Calabria.*

Built up along the slope of a steep promontory overlooking the coast and a fishing port, Pizzo has a good selection of seafood restaurants and a small cliff-top Aragonese castle (built in 1486) near the center of town. Here the French general Joachim Murat was imprisoned, tried, and shot in October 1815, after a bungled attempt to rouse the people against the Bourbons and reclaim the throne of Naples given him by his brother-in-law Napoléon.

While in Pizzo, sample the renowned *gelato di Pizzo,* a rich, creamy delight available in many flavors at any of the outdoor bars in the central Piazza della Repubblica.

The **Chiesetta di Piedigrotta,** a little over a mile north of Pizzo's castle, at the bottom of a flight of steps leading down to the beach, is a 17th-century church implausibly hewn out of rock by shipwrecked Neapolitan sailors in thanks for their rescue. They filled it with statues of biblical and historical figures, and the collection today includes a bizarre ensemble showing Fidel Castro kneeling before Pope John XXIII (1881–1963) and President John F. Kennedy (1917–63). Call the tourist office to book ahead, as hours can vary. ⊠ *Via Prangi* ☎ *0963/531310 Pizzo tourist office* ⊕ *www.chiesettadipiedigrotta.it* ⊗ *Daily 9–12:30 and 3–7:30; call ahead since hrs irregular.*

Tropea

33 *28 km (17 mi) southwest of Pizzo, 107 km (66 mi) north of Reggio di Calabria.*

Ringed by cliffs and wonderful sandy beaches, the Tropea promontory is still undiscovered by the big tour operators. The main town, Tropea, easily wins the contest for prettiest town on Calabria's Tyrrhenian coast, its old palazzi built in simple golden stone on an elevation above the sea. On a clear day the seaward views from the waterfront promenade extend to embrace Stromboli's cone and at least four of the other Aeolians—the islands can be visited by motorboats that depart daily from Tropea in summer. Accommodations are good, and beach addicts will not be disappointed by

> **WORD OF MOUTH**
>
> "I just returned from a week in Calabria, staying in the lovely coastal town of Tropea. The area is incredibly beautiful—so green and lush with pine and chestnut forests, cleanest air and sunny beaches. . . . The local people are beyond friendly, and there are many restaurants where the fruits of the Mediterranean are deftly prepared and offered cheaply. Go!"
> –Donna

the choice of magnificent sandy bays within easy reach of here. Some of the best are south at Capo Vaticano and north at Briatico.

In Tropea's harmonious warren of lanes, seek out the old Norman **Cattedrale,** whose interior displays a couple of unexploded U.S. bombs from World War II, with a grateful prayer to the Madonna attached to each. ⊠ *Piazza Sedile* ☉ *Daily 6–noon and 4–5:30.*

From the belvedere at the bottom of the main square, Piazza Ercole, the church and Benedictine monastery of **Santa Maria della Isola** glisten on a rocky promontory above an aquamarine sea. Stroll out to visit the church on a path lined with fishermen's caves. Dating back to medieval times, the church was remodeled in the Gothic style, then given another face-lift after an earthquake in 1905. The interior has an 18th-century nativity and some fragments of medieval tombs. ⊠ *Santa Maria della Isola* ☉ *Daily 7–noon and 4–7.*

Where to Stay & Eat

$$–$$$ ✕ **Pimm's.** Since its glory days in the 1960s, this underground restaurant in Tropea's historic center has offered the town's top dining experience. Seafood is the best choice, with such specialties as pasta with sea urchins, smoked swordfish, and stuffed squid. The splendid sea views are an extra enticement. ⊠ *Corso Vittorio Emanuele 2* ☎ *0963/666105* 🖃 *AE, DC, MC, V* ☉ *Closed Mon. and Nov. 15–Dec. 15.*

$$$ 🏨 **Rocca Nettuno.** Perched on the cliffs a 10-minute walk south of Tropea's town center, this deceptively large complex has reasonably spacious rooms, almost all with balconies. Some of the best—and quietest—are immersed in greenery near the cliff top. There is an all-inclusive package in summer months that includes a dine-around option so you can enjoy meals in town, too. ⊠ *Via Annunziata* ☎ *0963/998111* 🖨 *0963/603513* ⊕ *www.roccanettuno.com* ⇥ *264 rooms* ♨ *2 restaurants, pizzeria, minibars, tennis court, massage, sauna, beach, 2 bars, theater* 🖃 *AE, DC, MC, V* ☉ *Closed Jan. 9–Mar. 25* ¶◎¶ *FAP.*

Bagnara Calabra

③④ *11 km (7 mi) south of Palmi, 36 km (22 mi) north of Reggio di Calabria.*

Fishing is in the blood of the local villagers in Bagnara Calabra, particularly when in pursuit of swordfish, for which the town has long enjoyed widespread fame. Casual trattorias make this a great lunch stop.

Where to Eat

$–$$ ✕ **Taverna Kerkira.** Centrally located on Bagnara's main street, this casual restaurant emphasizes food above all else. The chef's mother hails from Corfu, and as a result dishes represent creative Greek spins on Calabrian classics. Antipasti feature fish you'll encounter in few other places, such as delicately marinated, sashimi-like *carpaccio di alalonga* (raw Tyrrhenian tuna with olive oil and soy sauce). Farfalle pasta is prepared with Greek yogurt, lemon zest, cucumber, and a hint of mullet—a sublime creation. The chef also excels at *pesce spada* (swordfish)—try it breaded and baked with mint, vinegar, and Parmesan. ⊠ *Corso Vittorio Emanuele 217* ☎ *0966/372260* 🖃 *AE, DC, MC, V* ☉ *Closed Mon. and Tues., Aug. 1–Sept. 9, and Dec. 20–Jan. 10.*

FodorśChoice
★

Reggio di Calabria

35 *26 km (16 mi) south of Scilla, 499 km (311 mi) south of Naples.*

Reggio di Calabria, the city on Italy's toe tip, is the jumping-off point for Messina- and Sicily-bound ferries, and was laid low by the same catastrophic earthquake that struck Messina in 1908. This raw city is one of Italy's most active ports, where you'll find every category of container ship and smokestack, but there's also a pleasant lido lined with palm fronds and urban beaches.

★ Reggio has one of southern Italy's most important archaeological museums, the **Museo Nazionale della Magna Grecia.** Prize exhibits here are two statues, known as the **Bronzi di Riace,** that were discovered by an amateur deep-sea diver off Calabria's Ionian coast in 1972. Flaunting physiques that gym enthusiasts would die for, the pair are thought to date from the 5th century BC and have been attributed to both Pheidias and Polykleitos. It's possible that they were taken by the Romans as trophies from the site of Delphi and then shipwrecked on their return to Italy. Coins and votive tablets are among the numerous other treasures from Magna Graecia contained in the museum. ⊠ *Piazza de Nava, Corso Garibaldi* ☎ *0965/812255* ▤ *€4* ⊙ *Tues.–Sun. 9–7:30. Closed Mon.*

Where to Stay

$$$ ▦ **Grande Albergo Miramare.** On the seafront midway between the port and the station, Miramare has one of the best locations in Reggio. It has been restored to evoke the charm of the early 20th century, yet has modern facilities. ⊠ *Via Fata Morgana 1, 89127* ☎ *0965/812444* ▤ *0965/812450* ⊕ *www.montesanohotels.it* ⇆ *96 rooms* ♢ *Restaurant, bar, parking (fee)* ▤ *AE, DC, MC, V* |◯| *BP.*

Aspromonte

36 *Gambarie: 42 km (26 mi) northeast of Reggio di Calabria.*

Rising to the east of Reggio di Calabria, Aspromonte is the name of the sprawling massif that dominates mainland Italy's southern tip. Long the haunt of brigands, this thickly forested range reaches an elevation of nearly 6,560 feet. In summer it makes a cool respite from the heat of the coast, offering endless opportunities for hiking and shady picnicking. On a clear day you can see Mt. Etna. To get here going north from Reggio, turn inland off the autostrada or coast road at Gallico, 12 km (7 mi) north of town; driving east from Reggio on S184, turn left onto the S183 at Melito di Porto Salvo. Ask at **Reggio's tourist office** (⊠ Corso Garibaldi 329 ☎ 0965/21171) for Aspromonte walking itineraries.

┌─
│ EN
│ ROUTE   The fast S106 hugs Calabria's Ionian coast, leading south out of Reggio di Calabria and curving around Aspromonte to your left. Having rounded Capo Spartivento, the road proceeds north. If you don't want to continue farther north, turn left onto the S112dir, shortly before Bovalino and 14 km (9 mi) before reaching Locri. This winding mountain road takes you around the rugged northern slopes of Aspromonte, a highly scenic but rigorously winding route.

Locri

㊲ *100 km (62 mi) east of Reggio di Calabria.*

South of the seaside town of Locri are the excavations of **Locri Epizefiri,** where one of the most important of Magna Graecia's city-states stood. Founded around the 7th century BC, Locri became a regional power when—apparently assisted by Castor and Pollux—10,000 Locrians defeated an army of 130,000 from Kroton on the banks of the Sagra River, 25 km (16 mi) north. Founding colonies and gathering fame in the spheres of horse breeding and music, Locri was responsible for the first written code of law in the Hellenic world. The walls of the city, parts of which are still visible, measured some 8 km (5 mi) in circumference, and the ruins within are scattered over a vast area. The museum is on the main coast road (S106) and the remains of a 5th-century BC Ionic temple are settled just behind it. ☎ *0964/390023* ✉ *Museum and site €2* ☉ *Site Tues.–Sun. 9 AM–1 hr before sunset, museum Tues.–Sun. 9–7:30; museum and archaeological zone closed Mon.*

Stilo

㊳ *50 km (31 mi) north of Locri, 138 km (86 mi) northeast of Reggio di Calabria.*

Grandly positioned on the side of the rugged Monte Consolino, the village of Stilo is known for being the birthplace and home of the philosopher Tommaso Campanella (1568–1639), whose magnum opus was the socialistic *La Città del Sole* (*The City of the Sun,* 1602)—for which he spent 26 years as prisoner of the Spanish Inquisition. A more tangible reason to visit the village is the tiny 10th-century Byzantine temple **La Cattólica.** Standing on a ledge above the town, this tiled and three-turreted building is believed to be the best preserved of its kind. ✉ *Via Cattólica* ✉ *Free* ☉ *Daily 8–8.*

Where to Stay

$$ 🏨 **San Giorgio.** Tucked away off Stilo's main Via Campanella, this hotel is housed in a 17th-century cardinal's palace, Palazzo Lamberti, and decked out in the style of that period, with elegantly furnished guest rooms. There are exhilarating views seaward from the garden. Half or full board is required. The food is acceptable, and there's nowhere else in town to eat anyway. ✉ *Via Citarelli 8, 89049* ☎ *0964/629306* ⤴ *10 rooms* ⚐ *Restaurant, pool, bar; no a/c in some rooms* ▱ *AE, DC, V, MC* ☉ *Closed Oct. 20–Mar.* ❢❢ *MAP.*

EN ROUTE   From Stilo you can take the S110 inland—a long twisty road that goes through the high Serra region, covered with a thick mantle of chestnut forest. There are terrific views to be enjoyed over the Ionian coast, and you can continue across the peninsula to Calabria's Tyrrhenian littoral, emerging at Pizzo. The total road distance between Stilo and Pizzo is around 80 km (50 mi).

MEZZOGIORNO ESSENTIALS

Transportation

BY AIR

Several airlines serve the cities of Bari and Brindisi in Puglia: Alitalia flies regularly between Bari and Brindisi and Rome and Milan; VolareWeb connects Bari, Brindisi, and Lamezia Terme with Milan; Ryanair operates service to Bari and Brindisi from London's Stansted, and between Bari and Frankfurt; Air Dolomiti, a Lufthansa partner, connects Bari with Munich, Vienna, and Verona; and Air One, another Lufthansa partner, connects Bari and Brindisi with Venice and Milan. Alpi Eagles connects Brindisi with Venice and Bari with Milan, Venice, Verona, and Olbia, Sardinia. In Calabria, Aeroporto di Reggio di Calabria handles mostly Alitalia domestic flights to Rome and Milan, with one Alpi Eagles service to Venice. Twenty-seven kilometers (17 mi) north of Pizzo, you can fly out of the most convenient airport to Cosenza, Aeroporto di Lamezia, on Alitalia to Rome and Milan; on Air One to Rome, Milan, Turin, and Bologna; on Ryanair to London's Stansted; and on Alpi Eagles to Venice.

🛈Airport Information **Aeroporto di Lamezia** ☎0968/419402 ⊕www.lameziatermeairport. it. **Aeroporto di Reggio di Calabria** ☎ 0965/640517 ⊕ www.sogas.it. **Bari-Palese** ✉ Strada Provinciale Aeroporto ☎ 080/5800200 ⊕ www.seap-puglia.it. **Brindisi-Papola** ✉ Via de Simone Ruggero 1 ☎ 0831/4117208 ⊕ www.seap-puglia.it.

🛈 Airlines & Contacts **Air Dolomiti** ☎ 045/2886140 or 800/013366 ⊕ www.airdolomiti. it. **Air One** ☎ 199/207080 ⊕ www.flyairone.it. **Alitalia** ☎ 06/2222 ⊕ www.alitalia.com. **Alpi Eagles** ☎ 899/500058 ⊕ www.alpieagles.com. **Ryanair** ☎ 899/678910 ⊕ www. ryanair.com. **VolareWeb** ☎ 848/848130 or 070/4603397 ⊕ www.volareweb.com.

TRANSFERS A regular bus service connects Bari–Palese (about 10 km [7 mi] northwest of the city center) and Brindisi–Papola (8 km [5 mi] to the north) with their respective cities. Alitalia buses provide service to and from both cities. Many hotels and taxis within other outlying cities provide service directly to and from the airports, which can be much simpler than public transport—contact your hotel for details.

BY BOAT

Puglia and Calabria are major launching points for boat travel. Ferries go from Bari and Brindisi to Greece (Corfu, Igoumenitsa, Patras, and Kephalonia), Turkey, Albania, and even Egypt and Croatia. In Calabria, ferries ply the Straits of Messina to Sicily every 15 minutes or so, day and night, from Villa San Giovanni and Reggio di Calabria. Crossings take 20–40 minutes, and reservations are not needed. Villa is preferable for car ferries, with frequent service from Caronte & Tourist. Ferry entrances in Villa are well marked from the A3 autostrada. Allow extra time to sit in line waiting to get on the next boat.

🛈 Boats & Ferries from Puglia **Maritime Way** ✉ Piazza della Borsa 10, Trieste ☎ 040/ 368919 ⊕ www.maritimeway.com. **Tirrenia** to Albania and Tremiti islands; agents at A. Galli e Figlio ✉ Corso Manfredi 4, 71043 Manfredonia ☎ 892123 from within Italy, 081/ 8449297 from outside Italy ✉ Gargano Viaggi, Piazza Roma 7, 71019 Vieste ☎ 892123 from within Italy, 081/8449297 from outside Italy ⊕ www.tirrenia.it. **Superfast Ferries** ⊠ Via XXIX Settembre 2/0, 60122 Ancona ☎ 071/202033 ⊕ www.superfast.com. 🚢 Boats & Ferries from Calabria **Caronte & Tourist** ☎ 0965/793111. **FS** ☎ 0965/863545 ⊕ www.carontetourist.it. **SNAV** ☎ 0831/525492 in Brindisi ⊕ www.snav.it.

BY BUS

Compared with rail, travel times by bus into Puglia from Naples on the far side of the Apennines are substantially shorter. If traveling between Naples and Foggia, contact CLP. Miccolis runs a daily Naples–Lecce service, which takes five hours, about half as long as by train. For bus travel from Rome, contact Autolinee Marozzi, at their Rome office or in Bari.

Direct, if not always frequent, connections operate between most destinations within Puglia, Calabria, and Basilicata. SITA is the main bus company operating in the region. In many cases bus service is the backup when problems with train service arise. Matera is linked with Bari by frequent buses operated by Ferrovie Appulo-Lucane, and with Taranto by SITA buses. In Calabria various bus companies make the north–south run with stops along both coasts; Ferrovie della Calabria operates many of the local services. From Reggio di Calabria, Salzone runs to Scilla.

🚌 Bus Information **Autolinee Marozzi** ☎ 06/97749130 in Rome, 080/5562446 in Bari. **CLP** ☎ 081/5311706. **Ferrovie Appulo-Lucane** ☎ 0835/332861. **Miccolis** ☎ 081/200380. **Ferrovie della Calabria** ☎ 0961/896111 ⊕ www.ferroviedellacalabria.com. **Miccolis** ☎ 081/200380. **Salzone** ☎ 0965/751586. **SITA** ⊠ Piazza Aldo Moro 15/a, Bari ☎ 080/5213714.

BY CAR

The mezzogiorno is a fairly easy place to get around by car, and with erratic train and bus service, a car is often your best transportation option—it's the only way to see the more remote sights.

Coming from the Adriatic coast to the north, the A14 goes as far as Bari and Matera. Rome to Bari takes four or five hours by car. The A3, meanwhile, comes from Naples and Salerno on the west coast and continues all the way through Calabria to Reggio, meeting the Sicily ferries at Villa San Giovanni. As long as the construction continues (and it shows no signs of coming down), the trip from Naples to Reggio can take up to seven hours (three hours from Naples to Cosenza, and four hours from Cosenza to Reggio).

Roads are good, and major cities are linked by fast autostrade. From Puglia's Bari, take the S96 south for 44 km (28 mi) to Altamura, then the S99 south 19 km (12 mi) to Matera. The A3 Autostrada del Sole runs between Salerno and Reggio di Calabria, with exits for Crotone (the Sila Massif), Pizzo, Rosarno (for Tropea), Palmi, and Scilla; it takes an inland route as far as Falerna, then tracks the Tyrrhenian coast south (except for the bulge of the Tropea promontory). A3 is toll-free, but you get what you pay for: it's under eternal construction, so factor in time for delays. Take the S18 for coastal destinations—or for a better view—on the Tyrrhenian side, and likewise the S106 (which is uncongested and fast) for the Ionian. You can cross the Strait of Messina from Villa San Giovanni or Reggio.

Note that entering the historic centers of many towns requires a small car, folding side-view mirrors, and a bit of nerve; tentative drivers should park outside the center and venture in by foot. If you're squeamish about getting lost, don't plan on any night driving in the countryside—the roads can become confusing without the aid of landmarks or large towns. Bari, Brindisi, and Reggio di Calabria are notorious for car thefts and break-ins. If you are driving in these cities, do not leave valuables in the car or trunk, and find a guarded parking space if possible.

EMERGENCY SERVICES ACI Emergency Service offers 24-hour roadside assistance.
🚹 **ACI dispatchers** ☎ 803/116.

BY TRAIN

Bari is a transit hub for train connections with northern Italy. Rome to Bari, with frequent service, takes about four hours. On the Calabria side, the main north–south FS (Italian State Railways) line has hourly services from Reggio north to Pizzo, Diamante, and Maratea, continuing on as far as Salerno, Naples, and Rome. There are nine daily Intercity or Eurostar trains linking Reggio di Calabria with Naples (4–5 hours) and Rome (6–7 hours). All FS trains also stop at Villa San Giovanni (for connections to Sicily), a 20-minute ride from Reggio.

Within the region, FS service links Bari to Brindisi, Lecce, and Taranto, but smaller destinations can often be reached only by completing the trip on a connecting bus operated by the railroad. The private Ferrovie Sud-Est (FSE) line connects the trulli area and Martina Franca with Bari and Taranto, and the fishing port of Gallipoli with Lecce. The main FS line from Taranto stops in Metaponto, from which there are regular departures to Matera on Ferrovie Appulo-Lucane (FAL) trains. The FAL rail line links Matera to Altamura in Puglia (for connections to Bari) and to Ferrandina (for connections to Potenza). South of Metaponto, FS trains run into Calabria, either following the Ionian coast as far as Reggio di Calabria or swerving inland to Cosenza and the Tyrrhenian coast at Paola. Main FS services run along both coasts but can be crowded along the Tyrrhenian.

🚹 Train Information **FS** ☎ 892021 ⊕ www.trenitalia.com. **Ferrovie Appulo-Lucane** ☎ 0835/332861 ⊕ www.fal-srl.it. **Ferrovie Sud-Est (FSE)** ☎ 080/5462111 or 0832/668111 ⊕ www.fseonline.it.

Contacts & Resources

EMERGENCIES

For general emergencies, dial 113. Pharmacies take turns staying open late and on Sunday. A list of hours is posted on each *farmacia* (pharmacy).

In Reggio di Calabria, the pharmacies Curia and Caridi are open at night. Elsewhere, late-night pharmacies are open on a rotating basis; information on current schedules is posted on any pharmacy door.

🚹 **Ambulance, Fire, Police** ☎ 113. **Caridi** ✉ Corso Garibaldi 327 ☎ 0965/24013. **Curia** ✉ Corso Garibaldi 455 ☎ 0965/332332. **Hospital** ☎ 0965/8501 in Reggio di Calabria, 0835/253111 in Matera.

VISITOR INFORMATION

🚩 Tourist Information **Alberobello** ✉ Piazza Ferdinando IV, 70011 ☎ 080/4325171. **Bari** ✉ Piazza Moro 32/a, 70122 ☎ 080/5242361. **Brindisi** ✉ Lungomare R. Margherita, 72100 ☎ 0831/523072. **Cosenza** ✉ Via P. Rossi, 87100 ☎ 0984/578243. **Foggia** ✉ Via Perrone 17, 71100 ☎ 0881/723141. **Lecce** ✉ Corso Vittorio Emanuele 43, 73100 ☎ 0832/248092. **Maratea** ✉ Piazza del Gesù 32, 85046 ☎ 0973/876908. **Matera** ✉ Via Spine Bianche 22, 75100 ☎ 0835/331817. **Ostuni** ✉ Corso Mazzini 6, 72017 ☎ 0831/301268. **Pizzo** ✉ Piazza della Repubblica, 88026 ☎ 0963/531310. **Reggio di Calabria** ✉ Corso Garibaldi 329, 89100 ☎ 0965/21171. **San Giovanni Rotondo** ✉ Piazza Europa 104, 71013 ☎ 0882/456240. **Taranto** ✉ Corso Umberto 113, 74100 ☎ 099/4532392. **Trani** ✉ Piazza Trieste 10, 70059 ☎ 0883/588830. **Tropea** ✉ Piazza Ercole, 88038 ☎ 0963/61475. **Vieste** ✉ Piazza Kennedy, 71019 ☎ 0884/708806 ✉ Kiosk in Piazza della Repubblica (summer only) ☎ 0883/43295.

Sicily

Lipari

WORD OF MOUTH

"Palermo/Monreale was our first stop. Come here for the monuments and churches . . . an endless array. If I had to pick a favorite place, it would be the Palatine Chapel in Palazzo Reale. It managed to be dazzlingly beautiful, while retaining a remarkable sense of warmth."

–Elizabeth S

www.fodors.com/forums

WELCOME TO SICILY

Teatro Greco, Siracusa

TOP 5
Reasons to Go

1 A walk on Siracusa's Ortygia Island: Classical ruins rub elbows with faded seaside palaces and fish markets in Sicily's most beautiful port city, whose Duomo is literally built upon the columns of an ancient Greek temple.

2 The palaces, churches, and crypts of Palermo: Virtually every great European empire once ruled Sicily's strategically positioned capital, and it shows through most of all in the diverse architecture, from Roman to Byzantine to Arab-Norman.

3 The Valley of the Temples, Agrigento: This stunning set of ruins is proudly perched above the sea in a grove full of almond trees; not even in Athens will you find Greek temples this finely preserved.

4 Taormina's Teatro Greco: Watch a Greek tragedy in the very amphitheater where it was performed two millennia ago—in the shadow of smoking Mount Etna.

5 Sicilian cuisine: The quickest way to absorb Sicily's character is through a meal of pasta with sardines and raisins, a simply grilled whole fish, ricotta-stuffed cannoli, and a glass of deliciously sweet *passito*.

The Western Coast follows the island's northern edge west of Palermo, past **Monreale's** mosaics, **Segesta's** Doric temple, and the fairy-tale town of **Erice**.

Palermo, Sicily's capital and one of Italy's most hectic cities, conceals notes of extraordinary beauty amid the uncontained chaos of fish markets and impossible traffic.

To the south, Greek ruins stand sentinel in **Agrigento's Valley of the Temples**, blanketed in almond and juniper blossoms.

Cefalù

Getting Oriented

This splendid island is known as *trinacria* for its three corners. At the northeastern corner is Messina, connected by car and train ferry to the mainland. The eastern edge of Sicily is its Ionian Coast, which continues south to Catania, Siracusa, and the island's southeastern corner. Sicily's northern edge is the Tyrrhenian Coast, which includes Palermo and extends out to the island's third corner—the western one.

You may know the tranquil, wind-swept Aeolian Islands from the *Odyssey*, and some of them seem to have changed little since Homer.

The Tyrrhenian Coast is filled with summer beachgoers, but it also boasts the quaint town of **Cefalù**, with its famous cathedral.

For many, the Ionian Coast is all about touristy Taormina, spectacularly perched on a cliff near **Mount Etna**; but don't overlook lively Catania, Sicily's modern nerve center.

In hill towns such as **Enna**, the interior of Sicily reveals a slower pace of life than in the frenetic coastal cities. **Piazza Armerina** features the Villa Casale and its ancient Roman mosaics.

Seafaring Siracusa (Syracuse) was one of the great powers of the classical world. Today, full of fresh fish and remarkable ruins, it's content to be one of Italy's most charming cities.

Map labels: Stromboli, Panarea, Salina, Alicudi, Filicudi, Lipari, Vulcano, Mare Tirreno, Cefalù, Milazzo, Messina, Villa San Giovanni, A20, Capo d'Orlando, A20, 284, Taormina, Mt. Etna, A18, Mare Iónio, A19, Acireale, 89, Enna, A19, Catania, Caltanissetta, 640, 417, 194, Siracusa, Gela, 115, Ragusa, Noto

15

0   20 mi
0   20 km

SICILY PLANNER

Making the Most of Your Time

You should plan a visit to Sicily around Palermo, Taormina, Siracusa, and Agrigento, four not-to-be-missed destinations. The best way to see them all is to travel in a circle. Start your circuit in the northeast in Taormina, worth at least a night or two. If you have time, stay also in Catania, a lively, fascinating city that's often overlooked. From there, connect to the regional SS114 toward the spectacular ancient Greek port of Siracusa, which merits at least two nights.

Next, backtrack north on the SS114, and take the A19 toward Palermo. Piazza Armerina's impressive mosaics and Enna, a sleepy mountaintop city, each make worthwhile stops in the interior. Take the SS640 until you reach Agrigento, whose valley of Greek temples is one of Sicily's most photographed sights. Stay there for a night before driving west along the coastal SS115, checking out Selinunte's ruins and stopping for a meal in Marsala before reaching magical Erice, a good base for one or two nights. You're now near some of Sicily's best summertime beaches at San Vito Lo Capo. Take the A19 to Palermo, Sicily's chaotic and wonderful capital city, to wrap up your Sicilian experience.

Getting Around

There are three ways to begin a trip through Sicily: flying into Palermo, flying into Catania, or coming down from the train or car ferry from Villa San Giovanni, near Reggio di Calabria. Renting a car is easily the best way to experience Sicily. Trains are unreliable, and roads are easy and scenic throughout most parts of the island. Note that triangular yield signs function as stop signs. If you pick up a car in Catania, you might want to drop it off in Palermo, or vice versa; one-way car rentals aren't prohibitively expensive. In Palermo and Catania, park in a garage as per instructions from your hotel, and don't touch your car until you leave town.

Snacking in Sicily

Sicily is famous for its bar snacks, from the ubiquitous *arancini* (fried balls of creamy rice stuffed with meat ragu or other fillings) to the wonderful pastries, marzipan creations, and ricotta-stuffed cannoli. Some of the island's best edibles are things that you'll never find at upscale restaurants. A coffee or almond *granita* (slush), for example, which is typically served with a brioche for dipping, is one of the world's most perfect midsummer snacks. So don't plan for a big meal every lunch and dinner. Instead, leave plenty of time and stomach space for frequent, spontaneous pit stops at small bars and *pasticcerie*, and don't be afraid to point; practically every town has its own trademark bar snack.

Safety Tips

Don't be paranoid about safety in Sicily, but do be careful. You have little to worry about in the smaller towns, but in the big cities, particularly Palermo and Catania, it's not recommended to wander around unpopulated streets, especially at night, and you should never flaunt expensive watches, jewelry, and the like. Women traveling alone should keep out of deserted areas at all times. Don't leave exposed luggage in the car. Take precautions; then enjoy the company of the Sicilians. You will find them friendly and often willing to go out of their way to help you.

The Mob Mentality

Though Sicily may conjure up images of Don Corleone and his Hollywood progeny, you won't come in contact with the Mafia during your time in Sicily anywhere other than in the newspapers. The "Cosa Nostra," as the Italians sometimes refer to it (don't use the term yourself) is focused on its own business and poses virtually no risk to tourists. Wandering through sleepy interior Sicilian hill towns like Corleone (yes, it's a real place) and Prizzi, you might be subject to some curious and guarded stares by the locals and feel the haze of a silent old-boy network, but nothing more than that.

Finding a Place to Stay

The good-quality hotels tend to be limited to the major cities and resorts of Palermo, Taormina, Siracusa, and Agrigento, along with the odd beach resort, but there has also recently been an explosion in the development of *agriturismo* lodgings (rural bed-and-breakfasts), many of them quite basic, but others providing the same facilities found in hotels. These country houses also offer all-inclusive, inexpensive full-board plans that can make for some of Sicily's most memorable meals.

Dining & Lodging Price Categories

	$$$$	$$$	$$	$	¢
Restaurants	over €45	€35–€45	€25–€35	€15–€25	under €15
Hotels	over €220	€160–€220	€110–€160	€70–€110	under €70

WHAT IT COSTS in Euros

Restaurant prices are for a first course (primo), second course (secondo), and dessert (dolce). Hotel prices are for two people in a standard double room in high season, including tax and service.

How's the Weather?

Sicily comes into its own in spring, but you're not alone in knowing this. Taormina and Erice attract a flood of visitors around Easter, so avoid it or reserve early. Many sights like inland Segesta are at their best in the clear spring light. August is hot and crowded, and beaches are clogged with vacationers. Come in September or October and you'll find gentle, warm weather and acres of beach space. Reserve rooms well in advance for Easter, Christmas, Agrigento's almond festival in February, and the Carnevale in Acireale.

15

TOP PASSEGGIATA

In Palermo, the area around the Politeama and adjacent shopping streets turn into an enormous party come early evening.

Updated by
Robin S.
Goldstein

SICILY HAS BECKONED SEAFARING WANDERERS since the trials of Odysseus were first sung in Homer's *Odyssey*—perhaps the world's first travel guide. Strategically poised between Europe and Africa, this mystical land of three corners and a fiery volcano once hosted two of the most enlightened capitals of the West—one Greek, in Siracusa, and one Arab-Norman, in Palermo. The island has been a melting pot of every great civilization on the Mediterranean: Greek and Roman; then Arab and Norman; and finally French, Spanish, and Italian. Today, the ancient ports of call peacefully fuse the remains of sackings past: graceful Byzantine mosaics rubbing elbows with Greek temples, Roman amphitheaters, Romanesque cathedrals, and baroque flights of fancy.

The invaders through the ages weren't just attracted by the strategic location; they recognized a paradise in Sicily's deep blue skies and temperate climate, its lush vegetation and rich marine life—all of which prevail to this day. Factor in Sicily's unique cuisine—another harmony of elements, mingling Arab and Greek spices, Spanish and French techniques, and some of the world's finest seafood, all accompanied by big, fruity wines—and you can understand why visitors continue to be drawn here, and often find it hard to leave.

In modern times, the traditional graciousness and nobility of the Sicilian people have survived side by side with the destructive influences of the Mafia under Sicily's semiautonomous government. Alongside some of the most exquisite architecture in the world lie the shabby, half-built results of some of the worst speculation imaginable. In recent years coastal Sicily, like much of the Mediterranean coast, has experienced a surge in condominium development and tourism. The island has emerged as something of an international travel hot spot, drawing increasing numbers of visitors. Brits and Germans flock in ever-growing numbers to Agrigento and Siracusa, sometimes speculating in real estate; and in high season, Japanese tour groups seem to outnumber the locals in Taormina, where chic boutiques selling lace and linen in resort towns give no clue of the lingering poverty in which their wares are produced. And yet, in Sicily's windswept heartland, a region that tourists have barely begun to explore, vineyards, olive groves, and lovingly kept dirt roads leading to family farmhouses still tie Sicilians to the land and to tradition, forming a happy connectedness that can't be defined by economic measures.

THE IONIAN COAST

On the northern stretch of Sicily's eastern coast, Messina commands an unparalleled position across the Ionian Sea from Calabria, the mountainous tip of mainland Italy's boot. Halfway down the coast, Catania has the vivacity of Palermo, if not the artistic wealth; the city makes a good base for exploring lofty Mt. Etna, as does Taormina.

Messina

❶ *8 km (5 mi) by ferry from Villa San Giovanni, 94 km (59 mi) northeast of Catania, 237 km (149 mi) east of Palermo.*

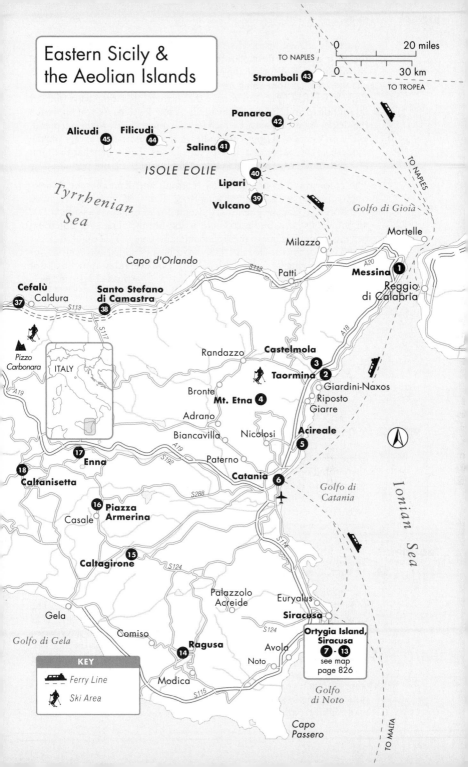

Messina's ancient history lists a series of disasters, but the city nevertheless managed to develop a fine university and a thriving cultural environment. At 5 o'clock in the morning on December 28, 1908, Messina changed from a flourishing metropolis of 120,000 to a heap of rubble, shaken to pieces by an earthquake that turned into a tidal wave and left 80,000 dead and the city almost completely leveled. As you approach the sickle-shape bay, across which ferries connect Sicily to the mainland, you won't notice any outward indication of the disaster, except for the modern countenance of a 3,000-year-old city. The somewhat flat look is a precaution of seismic planning: tall buildings are not permitted.

The reconstruction of Messina's Norman and Romanesque **Duomo**, originally built by the Norman king Roger II in 1197, has retained much of the original plan, including a handsome crown of Norman battlements, an enormous apse, and a splendid wood-beam ceiling. The adjoining **bell tower** contains one of the largest and most complex mechanical clocks in the world, constructed in 1933 with a host of gilded automatons, including a roaring lion, that spring into action every day at the stroke of noon. ⊠ *Piazza del Duomo* ☎ *090/675175* ☉ *Daily 8–12:30 and 4–7.*

Where to Stay & Eat

$$–$$$$ ✕ **Da Piero.** An institution in Messina for decades, this central restaurant (four blocks up from Piazza Cairoli) trades on its well-deserved reputation for classic Sicilian dishes, particularly seafood. Skip the smoked fish, shrimp cocktail, and risotto, but try the very good mussels *gratinate* (with cheese), the spaghetti *alle vongole* (with clams), or pleasing pasta *alla carrettiera* (with sliced tomatoes, garlic, and slightly spicy, aged pecorino cheese). Marsala sipped with one of the rich homemade desserts makes for a grand finale. ⊠ *Via Ghibellina 119* ☎ *090/718365* ▭ *AE, DC, MC, V* ☉ *Closed Sun. and Aug.*

$$$–$$$$ ▦ **Grand Hotel Liberty.** Across the piazza from the train station, this hotel—at the top end of Messina's offerings—is a cool haven from the bustle of the surrounding streets. The entrance and public rooms are sumptuously fitted out in a white-marble neoclassical style with a meticulous attention to detail, whereas bedrooms are plainer but comfortably equipped. ⊠ *Via I Settembre 15, 98123* ☎ *090/6409436* 🖷 *090/6409340* ⊕ *www.framon-hotels.com* ⬦ *51 rooms* ♨ *Restaurant, minibars, 2 bars, meeting rooms* ▭ *AE, DC, MC, V* ¶⊙ *BP.*

Taormina

❷ *43 km (27 mi) southwest of Messina.*

The medieval cliff-hanging town of Taormina is overrun with tourists and trinket shops, but its natural beauty is still hard to argue with. The view of the sea and Mt. Etna from its jagged cactus-covered cliffs is as close to perfection as a panorama can get, especially on clear days, when the snowcapped volcano's white puffs of smoke rise against the blue sky. Writers have extolled Taormina's beauty almost since its founding in the 6th century BC by Greeks from Naples; Goethe and D. H. Lawrence were among its more recent well-known enthusiasts. The town's boutique-lined main streets get old pretty quickly, but don't overlook the many hiking paths that wind through the beautiful hills surrounding

Taormina. Nor should you miss the trip up to stunning Castelmola—whether by foot or by car.

Down below the main city of Taormina, at sea level, is **Taormina Mare,** where beachgoers hang out in summer. It's accessible by a jaw-dropping *funivia* (gondola) that glides past incredible views on its way down. (✉ €1.80 ⊙ *Apr.–Oct. daily, every 15 mins 8 AM–midnight, Nov.–Mar. daily, every 15 mins 8 AM–8 PM.*)

The Greeks put a premium on finding impressive locations to stage their dramas, and the site of Taormina's hillside **Teatro Greco** is a fine one. Beyond the columns you can see the town's rooftops spilling down the hillside, the arc of the coastline, and Mt. Etna in the distance. The theater was built during the 3rd century BC and rebuilt by the Romans during the 2nd century AD. Its acoustics are exceptional: even today a stage whisper can be heard in the last rows. In summer Taormina hosts an arts festival of music and dance events and a film festival; many performances are held in the Teatro Greco. ✉ *Via Teatro Greco* ☎ *0942/23220* ✉ *€6* ⊙ *Daily 9–1 hr before sunset. Closed Mon. Oct.–Mar.*

Many of Taormina's 14th- and 15th-century palaces have been carefully preserved. Especially beautiful is the **Palazzo Corvaja,** with characteristic black-lava and white-limestone inlays. Today it houses the tourist office and the **Museo di Arte e Storia Popolare,** which has a collection of puppets and folk art, carts and cribs. ✉ *Largo Santa Caterina* ☎ *0942/610274 Palazzo* ✉ *Museum €2.50* ⊙ *Museum Tues.–Sun. 9–1 and 4–8.*

NEED A BREAK? A marzipan devotee should not leave Taormina without trying one of the gooey sweets—maybe in the guise of the ubiquitous *fico d'India* (prickly pear)—at Pasticceria Etna (✉ Corso Umberto 112 ☎ 0942/24735 🖷 0942/21279). Locals also swear by the cannoli, and a block of almond paste makes a good souvenir—you can bring it home to make an almond latte or granita.

★ Stroll down Via Bagnoli Croce from the main Corso Umberto to the **Villa Comunale** (⊙ May–Oct. daily, 9–10; Nov.–Apr. daily, 9–5). Also known as the Parco Duca di Cesarò, the lovely public gardens were designed by Florence Trevelyan Cacciola, a Scottish lady "invited" to leave England following a romantic liaison with the future Edward VII (1841–1910). Arriving in Taormina in 1889, she married a local professor and devoted herself to the gardens, filling them with Mediterranean plants, ornamental pavilions (known as the beehives), and fountains. Stop by the panoramic bar, which has stunning views.

By footpath or car you can approach the medieval **Castello Saraceno** (✉ Monte Tauro), enticingly perched on an adjoining cliff above town, but you cannot continue all the way to the castle itself.

Where to Stay & Eat

$$$$ ✕ **La Giara.** Syracuse stone columns sculpted by local master stonecutters, and an open atrium in the back overlooking the coast, enhance the elegant and classical in one of Taormina's oldest restaurants. The kitchen blends upscale modern techniques with the simple flavors of

15

EATING WELL IN SICILY

Sicilian cuisine is one of the oldest in existence, going back to Siracusan cooking competitions in 600 BC. The Sicilians even have a reasonable claim to the invention of pasta; present-day *maccheroni* (long, thin pasta tubes) may bear the closest resemblance to the original. Today's cuisine represents Sicily's unique cultural mix, imaginatively combining fish, fruits, vegetables, and nuts with Italian pastas and Arab and North African ingredients such as *cus cus* (couscous).

In Sicily, naturally, you'll enjoy some of the freshest seafood in all of Italy. Pasta *con le sarde* (an emblematic dish that goes back to the Saracen conquerors, with fresh sardines, olive oil, raisins, pine nuts, and wild fennel) is different at every restaurant. Grilled *tonno* (tuna) and *orata* (daurade) are reliable coastal staples. King, however, is *pesce spada* (swordfish), best enjoyed marinated (*marinato*), smoked (*affumicato*), or as the

traditional *involtini di pesce spada* (swordfish roulades). Delicate *ricci* (sea urchins) are a specialty, as is spaghetti *alla Norma* (with a sauce of tomato, fried eggplant, ricotta, and basil). Meanwhile, the Sicilian bitter almond (*mandorla*), the pride of Agrigento, plays into everything from risotto *alle mandorle* (almond risotto) to sweet almond liqueur to incomparable almond granita, an absolute must in summer.

Long neglected, Sicilian wines are some of the most up-and-coming in the world, but they're still the bargains of Italy. The earthy Nero d'Avola grape bolsters many of Sicily's traditionally sunny, expansive reds, but lately it's often cut with cabernet or merlot. The islands of Lipari and Pantelleria offer sweet, golden dessert wines, Malvasia and Passito. Marsala remains Sicily's most famous dessert wine. Look for anything from the world-renowned winemaker Planeta.

traditional specialties. Try scallops with *lardo di collonnata* (lard). You can extend your evening by taking an after-dinner drink at the popular piano bar. (The place is named after a giant Roman vase discovered underneath the bar.) ⊠ *Vico La Floresta 1* ☎ *0942/23360* ⊕ *www.lagiara-taormina.com* ⊟ *AE, DC, MC, V* ☉ *Closed Sun. Closed Sun.–Fri. Nov.–Mar. No lunch.*

$$–$$$ ✕ **La Dracena.** Enjoy an ideal alfresco meal in the garden near the dragon tree that is this restaurant's namesake. The *mezzelune* (half-open ravioli) with zucchini and Parmesan-like caciocavallo cheese is very good. La Dracena is just behind the castle. ⊠ *Via Michele Amari 4* ☎ *0942/23491* ⊕ *www.ladracena.it* ⊟ *AE, DC, MC, V* ☉ *Closed Mon. and Nov. 1–Mar. 1.*

$$ ✕ **La Piazzetta.** Reasonable prices bring in real Italian families to La Piazzetta. Classics such as pasta *con le sarde* (with sardines and bread crumbs) are competently prepared, the grilled fish is extremely fresh, the menu is poorly translated (always a good sign), and the service is informal and friendly. The modest room has simple white walls—you're not paying for a view. ✉ *Vico Paladino 57, off Corso Umberto* 🖼 *0942/ 626317* 🖃 *AE, DC, MC, V* ☉ *Closed Mon. and Nov. 10–Dec. 1.*

$–$$ ✕ **Taverna al Paladino.** On a little side street, you can enjoy ancient dishes at this dim haunt, which feels like an old wine bar. The traditional Sicilian *sarde a beccaficu* is a sweet-and-sour dish of sardines marinated in lemon juice, split open, and stuffed with bread crumbs, pine nuts, and sugar. Also on the menu is risotto with wild fennel. ✉ *Via Naumachia 21* 🖼 *0942/24614* 🖃 *AE, DC, MC, V* ☉ *Closed Jan.*

$–$$ ✕ **L'Arco dei Cappuccini.** Just off the radar screen of the main tourist strip lies this clean, diminutive restaurant with white tablecloths. Outdoor seating and an upstairs kitchen help make room for a few extra tables— necessary because the locals are well aware that both the price and the quality cannot be beat elsewhere in town. Indulge in *sopressa di polipo* (steamed octopus carpaccio), gnocchi *con pistacchi* (with pistachio cream sauce), or the fresh catch of the day. ✉ *Via Cappuccini 7, off Via Costanino Patricio near Porta Messina* 🖼 *0942/24893* ⌁ *Reservations essential* 🖃 *AE, DC, MC, V* ☉ *Closed Wed.*

★ ¢–$ ✕ **Vecchia Taormina.** Warm, inviting, and unassuming, Taormina's best pizzeria produces deliciously seared crusts topped with fresh, well-balanced ingredients. Try the pizza *alla Norma*, featuring the classic Sicilian combination of eggplant and ricotta—here, in the province of Messina, it's made with ricotta *al forno* (cooked ricotta), while in the province of Catania, it's made with ricotta *forte* (strong, uncooked ricotta). ✉ *Vico Ebrei 3* 🖼 *0942/625589* 🖃 *AE, DC, MC, V.*

¢ ✕ **Bella Blu.** If you fancy a meal with a view but don't want to spend much, it would be hard to do much better than to come here for the decent €13 two-course prix-fixe meal. Seafood is the specialty; try the spaghetti with fresh clams and mussels. Through giant picture windows you can watch the gondola fly up and down from the beach, with the coastline in the distance. The joint turns into a disco on weekend nights. ✉ *Via Pirandello 28* 🖼 *0942/24239* ⊕ *www.bellablu.it* 🖃 *AE, DC, MC, V.*

$$$$ 🏨 **Grand Hotel Timeo and Villa Flora.** The deluxe Timeo—on a princely
Fodor'sChoice perch overlooking the town and below the Teatro Greco—wears a
★ graceful patina that suggests the dolce vita. A splash of baroque mixes with the Mediterranean in the lobby, which has tile- and brickwork and vaulted ceilings. Wrought-iron and wicker chairs surround marble tables in the original bar from 1873 (made of gesso) and on the adjoining palatial patio. Exquisite moldings hang on butter-color walls. Fine earth-tone linens and drapes, Oriental rugs, and gilt-frame prints decorate the rooms, 31 of which are in the neighboring Villa Flora. Ask for a room with a "terrazzo"—it's worth the extra few euros to sit at a private table gazing over one of Italy's most memorable vistas. ✉ *Via Teatro Greco 59, 98039* 🖼 *0942/23801* 🖶 *0942/628501* ⊕ *www.framonhotels. com* ⇨ *84 rooms* ⌂ *Restaurant, room service, in-room safes, minibars, pool, gym, bar, convention center* 🖃 *AE, DC, MC, V* ⫶◯⫶ *MAP.*

$$$$ 🏨 **San Domenico Palace.** Sweeping views from this converted 15th-cen-
Fodor'sChoice tury Dominican monastery linger in your mind: the sensuous gardens—
★ full of red trumpet flowers, bougainvillea, and lemons—afford a dramatic vista of the castle, the sea, and Mt. Etna. Expect luxury and ease at this extraordinarily expensive hotel, which is considered by some to be

among the best in Europe. Rooms have hand-painted or hand-carved furnishings, exquisite linens, and ultramodern amenities. The San Domenico's Renaissance flavor is preserved by two exquisite cloisters, convent rooms, and the chapel, now a banquet-and-conference facility. ⊠ *Piazza San Domenico 5, 98039* ☎ *0942/613111* 📠 *0942/625506* ⊕ *www.sandomenico.thi.it* 🛏 *93 rooms, 15 suites* ♨ *2 restaurants, room service, minibars, pool, gym, bar, Internet room* 🚭 *AE, DC, MC, V* ⅋ *BP.*

$$$–$$$$ 🏨 **Romantik Villa Ducale.** The former summer residence of a local aristocrat has been converted into a luxurious villa hotel a 10- to 15-minute walk from the center of Taormina. Individually styled rooms, furnished with antiques, each have their own balconies. An intimate wood-paneled library is at once homelike and romantic, and the vast roof terrace, where a fantastic breakfast is served, takes full advantage of the wide panorama embracing Etna and the bay below. In summer a free shuttle bus connects the hotel with the area's best beaches. ⊠ *Via L. da Vinci 60, 98039* ☎ *0942/28153* 📠 *0942/28710* ⊕ *www.hotelvilladucale.it* 🛏 *10 rooms, 6 suites* ♨ *Minibars, in-room broadband, bar, health club* 🚭 *AE, DC, MC, V* ⊘ *Closed Jan. 10–Feb. 20* ⅋ *BP.*

$$$ 🏨 **Hotel Villa Paradiso.** On the edge of the old quarter, overlooking the lovely public gardens and facing the sea, this smaller hotel is not as well known as some of the blockbusters nearby, but with views of Etna from many rooms, delightful service, and a good restaurant, it's only a matter of time. Proprietor Salvatore Martorana will gladly share stories of Taormina in Goethe's day over an *aperitivo.* A regular hotel bus service runs to the beach. ⊠ *Via Roma 2, 98039* ☎ *0942/23921* 📠 *0942/625800* ⊕ *www.hotelvillaparadisotaormina.com* 🛏 *20 rooms, 17 junior suites* ♨ *Restaurant, cable TV, tennis court, beach, bar, library* 🚭 *AE, DC, MC, V* ⅋ *BP.*

$$ 🏨 **Arathena Rocks Hotel.** Here's a good choice if you want to stay near the sea. The hotel stands at one end of the bay, right on the cape where Greek settlers first landed in Sicily. There's a large pool, around which Sicilian singers and musicians entertain you every other night in summer. A twice-daily free bus service links the hotel to Taormina. The town of Giardini Naxos, 8 km (5 mi) south of Toarmina, makes a great base—in summer it's just as lively as Taormina, and the broad sandy beach is nearby. ⊠ *Via Calcide Eubea 55, 98034 Giardini Naxos* ☎ *0942/51349* 📠 *0942/51690* ⊕ *www.hotelarathena.com* 🛏 *49 rooms* ♨ *Restaurant, pool, bar, Internet room; no a/c in some rooms* 🚭 *AE, DC, MC, V* ⊘ *Closed Nov.–Easter* ⅋ *BP.*

$$ 🏨 **Villa Fiorita.** This converted private home near the Teatro Greco has excellent north-coast views from nearly every room. Rooms vary in size and furnishings, but most are bright, breezy, and colorful, with large windows and balconies (do ask). Prices are reasonable considering the views, the compact swimming pool, and the garden. You have to climb 65 steps to get to the Villa. ⊠ *Via Pirandello 39, 98039* ☎ *0942/24122* 📠 *0942/625967* ⊕ *www.villafioritahotel.com* 🛏 *24 rooms, 1 suite* ♨ *In-room safes, minibars, pool, bar* 🚭 *AE, MC, V* ⅋ *BP.*

Nightlife & The Arts

The Teatro Greco and the Palazzo dei Congressi, near the entrance to the theater, are the main venues for the summer festival dubbed **Taoarte**

(☎ 0942/21142 ⊕ www.taormina-arte.com), held each year from May to August. Performances encompass classical music, ballet, and theater. The famous **film festival** (⊕ www.taorminafilmfest.it) in June is part of the Taoarte festival.

The **Teatro dei Due Mari** (✉ Via Teatro Greco ☎ 0941/243176) stages Greek tragedy at the Teatro Greco during the month of May.

EN ROUTE The 50-km (30-mi) stretch of road between Taormina and Messina is flanked by lush vegetation and seascapes. Inlets are punctuated by gigantic, oddly shaped rocks. It was along this coast, legend says, that the giant cyclops hurled his boulders down on Ulysses and his terrified men as they fled to the sea in Homer's *Odyssey*.

Castelmola

❸ *5 km (3 mi) west of Taormina.*

You may think that Taormina has spectacular views, but tiny Castelmola, floating 1,800 feet above sea level, takes the word "scenic" to a whole new level. Along the cobblestone streets within the ancient walls, the 360-degree panoramas of mountain, sea, and sky are so ubiquitous that you almost get used to them (but not quite). Collect yourself with a sip of the sweet almond wine (best served cold) made in the local bars, or with lunch at one of the humble pizzerias or panino shops.

Fodor'sChoice ★ The best place to take in Castelmola's views is from the old **Castello Normanno** ruin, reached by a set of steep staircases rising out of the town center. In all Sicily, there may be no spot more scenic than atop the castle ruins, where you can gaze upon two coastlines, smoking Mt. Etna, and the town spilling down the mountainside.

A 10-minute drive on a winding but well paved road leads from Taormina to Castelmola; you must park in one of the public lots on the hillside below and climb a series of staircases to reach the center. On a nice day, hikers are in for a treat if they walk instead of driving. It's a serious uphill climb, but the 1½-km (¾-mi) path is extremely well maintained and not too challenging. You'll begin at Porta Catania in Taormina, with a walk along Via Apollo Arcageta past the Chiesa di San Francesco di Paolo on the left. The Strada Comunale della Chiusa then leads past Piazza Andromaco, revealing good views of the jagged promontory of Cocolanazzo di Mola to the north. Allow 45 minutes on the way up, a half hour down. There's another, slightly longer—2-km (1-mi)—path that heads up from Porta Messina past the Roman aqueduct, Convento dei Cappuccini, and the northeastern side of Monte Tauro. You could take one path up and the other down.

Where to Stay & Eat

$ ✕ **Terrazza Auteri.** Just below Castelmola's center, on the road heading down to Taormina, stands this

> **WORD OF MOUTH**
>
> "My most memorable moment in Sicily was sitting on a terrace in Castelmola above Taormina with a cappuccino and a freshly made lemon ricotta cannolo, and Mt. Etna in the background and the sea far below."   –Lina

15

three-level, multi-terraced restaurant and pizzeria. The food—seafood dishes like mixed shellfish risotto, grilled prawns or swordfish, along with pizzas from a wood-burning oven and a standard assortment of pastas—is eclipsed by the memorable views from almost every table on the terraces. ⊠ *Via Madonna della Scala 1* ☎ *0942/28603* ⊕ *www. terrazza-auteri.com* ⊟ *AE, DC, MC, V* ⊘ *Closed Mon. Oct.–Apr.*

¢ ✕ **Pizzeria Europa.** This is one of the simpler dining choices in town, and also one of the better ones. It might not boast the views you'll find at some of the competition, but a great selection of *forno a legna* (wood-fired oven) pizzas makes up for that shortcoming. Friendly staff serves the food in a pleasant little room along a side street. ⊠ *Via Pio IX 26* ☎ *0942/28481* ⊟ *No credit cards.*

$$$ ▦ **Villa Sonia.** All of the rooms at Castelmola's best hotel have terraces with (of course) spectacular views. Along with a refreshing swimming pool, public spaces include a lobby, bar, and lounge that take advantage of the vistas, plus a restaurant with a wine bar and wine store called Enoteca Divino. The relatively high room rates are a good value when you bear in mind the price-gouging at the hotels in Taormina below. ⊠ *Via Porta Mola 9, 98030* ☎ *0942/28082* 🖷 *0942/28083* ⊕ *www.hotelvillasonia. com* ⇥ *31 rooms, 3 suites* ⚖ *Restaurant, in-room safes, minibars, pool, bar, lounge, wine bar, shop, free parking* ⊟ *AE, MC, V* ⦿ *BP.*

Mt. Etna

❹ *64 km (40 mi) southwest of Taormina, 30 km (19 mi) north of Catania.*

Fodor'sChoice
★

Mt. Etna is one of the world's major active volcanoes and is the largest and highest in Europe—the cone of the crater rises to 10,902 feet above sea level. Plato sailed in just to catch a glimpse in 387 BC; in the 9th century AD, the oldest gelato of all was shaved off of its snowy slopes; and in the 21st century the volcano still claims annual headlines. Etna has erupted 11 times in the past 30 or so years, most spectacularly in 1971, 1983, 2001, and 2002, when in each case rivers of molten lava destroyed the two highest stations of the cable car that rises from the town of Sapienza. Although each eruption is predictably declared a "tragedy" by the media, owing to the economic losses, Etna almost never threatens human life. Travel in the proximity of the crater depends on Mt. Etna's temperament, but you can walk up and down the enormous lava dunes and wander over its moonlike surface of dead craters. The rings of vegetation change markedly as you rise, with vineyards and pine trees gradually giving way to growths of broom and lichen. Catania and Taormina are the departure points for excursions around—but not always to the top of—Mt. Etna. Buses leave from Catania's train station in early morning.

Instead of going up Mt. Etna, you can circle it on the **Circumetnea railroad,** which runs near the volcano's base. The private railway almost circles the volcano, running 114 km (71 mi) between Catania and Riposto—the towns are 30 km (19 mi) apart by the coast road. The line is small, slow, and only single-track, but has some dramatic vistas of the volcano and goes through lava fields. The round-trip takes about five hours, there are about 10 departures a day. ⊠ *Via Caronda 352, Catania* ☎ *095/541243* ⊕ *www.circumetnea.it* 🎟 *€6 round-trip* ⊘ *Mon.–Sat. 6 AM–9 PM.*

If you're a beginning climber, call the **Gruppo Guide Etna Nord** to arrange for a guide. Their service is a little more personalized—and expensive—than others. Reserve ahead. ✉ *Via Roma 93, Linguaglossa* ☎ *095/7774502* ⊕ *www.guidetnanord.com.*

Club Alpino Italiano in Catania is a great resource for Mt. Etna climbing and hiking guides. If you have some experience and don't like a lot of hand-holding, these are the guides for you. ✉ *Piazza Scammacca* ☎ *095/7153515* ⊕ *www.cai.it.*

Etna Sci (⊕ *www.etnasci.it.*) handles skiing operations on Mt. Etna. Destroyed by 2002 eruptions, the southern funivia at the village of Nicolosi reopened in November of 2005. Weather allowing, you can once again ski Etna from that area. Its bottom station is accessible by car. Work continues on the northern ski-lift station, Linguaglossa, which at this writing was not yet open.

For a bird's-eye view of Mt. Etna, you can try paragliding or hang gliding; contact **No Limits Etna Center** (✉ Via Milano 6/a, Catania ☎ 095/7213682 ⊜ 095/387313 ⊕ www.etnacenter.net). The company also organizes climbing, caving, and diving expeditions.

15

Where to Stay

$$$$ 🏨 **Hotel Villa Paradiso Dell'Etna.** This 1920s hotel 10 km (6 mi) northeast of Catania was a haunt for artists before General Rommel took over during World War II. When the tide turned in the war, it became a military hospital. Today, after a painstaking renovation, Paradiso Dell'Etna resembles an elegant private villa housing mementos of a memorable past, the hotel has four exceptional suites and 30 sumptuous rooms, each filled with tasteful 19th-century Sicilian antiques and all the modern accessories befitting a four-star hotel—the pool is even heated. ✉ *Via per Viagrande 37, exit A18 toward San Gregario, 95036 S. G. La Punta* ☎ *095/7512409* ⊜ *095/7413861* ⊕ *www.paradisoetna.it* ⃔ *30 rooms, 4 suites* ⬧ *Restaurant, room service, in-room safes, minibars, cable TV, tennis court, pool, gym, massage, sauna, bar, dance club, Internet room, meeting room* ▭ *AE, DC, MC, V* ⦿ *BP.*

Acireale

➎ *40 km (25 mi) south of Taormina, 16 km (10 mi) north of Catania.*

Acireale sits amid a clutter of rocky pinnacles and lush lemon groves. The craggy coast is known as the Riviera dei Ciclopi, after the legend narrated in the *Odyssey* in which the blinded cyclops Polyphemus hurled boulders at the retreating Ulysses, thus creating spires of rock, or *faraglioni* (pillars of rock rising dramatically out of the sea). Tourism has barely taken off here, so it's a good destination if you feel the need to put some distance between yourself and the busloads of tourists in Taormina. And, though the beaches are rocky, there's good swimming here, too.

During Carnival celebrations (in the two weeks before Lent), considered the best in Sicily, streets are jammed with thousands of fancy-dressed revelers and floats dripping with flowers and gaudy papier-mâché models. Acireale is an easy day trip from Catania.

Sweet Sicily

SICILY IS FAMOUS for its desserts, none more than the wonderful cannoli (*cannolo* is the singular), whose delicate pastry shell and just-sweet-enough ricotta barely resemble their foreign impostors. They come in all sizes, from pinkie-size bites to holiday cannoli the size of a coffee table. Even your everyday bar will display a window piled high with dozens of varieties of ricotta-based desserts, including delicious fried balls of dough. The traditional cake of Sicily is the *cassata siciliana*, a rich chilled sponge cake with sheep's ricotta and candied fruit. It's the most popular dessert at many Sicilian restaurants, and you shouldn't miss it.

From behind bakery windows and glass cases beam tiny marzipan sweets fashioned into brightly colored apples, cherries, and even hamburgers and prosciutto.

Do as the locals do and dip your summer morning brioche—the best in Italy—into a cup of brilliantly refreshing coffee or almond granita. The world's first ice cream is said to have been made by the Romans from the snow on the slopes of Mt. Etna, and the practice of producing top-quality gelato, and eating it in great quantities, is still prevalent throughout the island.

Begin your visit to Acireale with a stroll down to the public gardens, **Villa Belvedere**, at the end of the main Corso Umberto, for superb coastal views.

With its cupola and twin turrets, Acireale's **Duomo** is an extravagant baroque construction dating back to the 17th century. In the chapel to the right of the altar, look for the 17th-century silver statue of Santa Venera, patron saint of Acireale, made by Mario D'Angelo, and the early-18th-century frescoes by Antonio Filocamo. ⊠ *Piazza Duomo* ☎ *095/601797* ☉ *Daily 8–noon and 4–7.*

NEED A BREAK?   **El Dorado (⊠ Corso Umberto 5 ☎ 095/601464) serves delicious ice creams, and the granita *di mandorla* (almond granita), available in summer, invites a firsthand acquaintance.**

The sulfur-rich volcanic waters from Mt. Etna found at **Terme di Acireale** were first enjoyed by the Greeks. In the 2nd century AD Acireale's patron saint, Venera, was martyred, after which the waters were accorded miraculous powers. After 1873, when the Santa Venera bathing establishment with its park was created, the baths attracted a stream of celebrated visitors, including Wagner. Book in advance to use the baths and have mud treatments and massages (multiday treatment packages are available). Nonpatrons can wander the gardens for free. ⊠ *Via delle Terme 47* ☎ *095/601508* ⊕ *www.terme-acireale.com* ⊡ *Baths €13 and up, gardens free* ☉ *Treatments by appointment daily 7–2; gardens daily 9–8.*

Lord Byron (1788–1824) visited the **Belvedere di Santa Caterina** to look out over the Ionian sea during his Italian wanderings. The Santa Caterina viewing point is south of the old town, near the Terme di Acireale, off SS114.

Where to Eat

$ ✕ **La Grotta.** A conventional-looking trattoria entry fronts a dining room within a cave, part of whose wall is exposed. Try the *insalata di mare,* a selection of delicately steamed fish served with lemon and olive oil, or fish grilled over charcoal. Chef-proprietor Carmelo Strano's menu is small, but there isn't a dud among the selections. ⌖ *Via Scalo Grande 46* ☎ *095/7648153* ⌖ *Reservations essential* ▤ *AE, DC, MC, V* ⊘ *Closed Tues. and Oct. 15–Nov. 5.*

Nightlife & the Arts

Sicily's puppet theater tradition carries on in Acireale, although it has all but died out in other parts of the island (with the exception of Palermo). The **Teatro dell'Opera dei Pupi** (⌖ Via Alessi 11 ☎ 095/606272 ⊕ www.teatropupimacri.it) has puppet shows and a puppet exhibit.

Shopping

Acireale is renowned in Sicily for its marzipan, made into fruit shapes and delicious biscuits available at many *pasticcerie* (pastry shops) around town. **Castorina** (⌖ Piazza del Duomo 20 ☎ 095/601546) sells marzipan candies (and cute gift boxes for them). A unique creation at **Belvedere** (⌖ Corso Umberto 230 ☎ 095/894164) is the *nucatole,* a large cookie made with heaping quantities of chocolate, Nutella, nuts, and other wholesome ingredients.

OFF THE BEATEN PATH

ACI CASTELLO AND ACI TREZZA – These two gems of the coastline between Acireale and Catania—the "Riviera Jonica" (Ionian Riviera)—fill with city dwellers in the summer months, but even in colder weather their beauty is hard to fault. Heading south from Acireale on the coast-hugging *litoranea* road, you'll first reach Aci Trezza, said to be the land of the blind Cyclops in Homer's *Odyssey.* Legend has it that when the Cyclops threw boulders at Odysseus they became the faraglioni offshore. Aci Trezza is also famous as the setting for *I Malavoglia,* the 1881 novel by Giovanni Verga. It should be easy to satisfy your literal rather than literary hunger at **Da Federico** (⌖ Via Magrì 4, Aci Trezza ☎ 095/276364 ⊘ Closed Mon.), which lays out a sprawling antipasto buffet featuring delectable marinated anchovies and eggplant parmigiana, along with excellent grilled whole fish and sweet *scampi* (thin, delicate crustaceans). Less developed than Aci Trezza, Aci Castello has its own fish houses plus the imposing Castello Normanno (Norman Castle), which sits right on the water. The castle was built in the 11th century with volcanic rock from Mt. Etna—the same rock that forms the coastal cliffs.

Catania

❻ *16 km (10 mi) south of Acireale, 94 km (59 mi) south of Messina, 60 km (37 mi) north of Siracusa.*

The chief wonder of Catania, Sicily's second city, is that it is there at all. Its successive populations were deported by one Greek tyrant, sold into slavery by another, and driven out by the Carthaginians. Every time

VOICES OF ITALY

Francesco Pensovecchio
wine critic, Palermo

Francesco Pensovecchio is one of the elite tasters who contribute to *Vini d'Italia*, Italy's definitive wine guide, published by the food and wine organization Gambero Rosso. Its Tre Bicchieri (three glasses) designation is the ultimate honor for Italian wines.

On Sicilian wine: "Sicily, between the 35th and 45th northern parallels, is quite simply one of the best places in the world for producing wine. Sicily also has diverse and interesting microclimates: volcanic soil that's moistened and chilled by Etna; the sun-soaked red sands of the Ragusa region; the salty marine microclimates of the Aeolian Islands and Pantelleria; and the strong, scorched clay of the interior.

"Right now, Sicily produces just under 20% of the wine in all of Italy. In the past few years, Sicily has been as successful with so-called 'international' varietals (e.g., chardonnay) as with the great native grape, Nero d'Avola, which has long been grown all over Sicily.

"Important Italian producers have begun to notice Sicily's abundance of cheap, high-quality land. Mainland producers like Mezzocorona, Zonin, Marzotto, and Illva have bought big—500 or 600 hectares. What they plan to do with all this wine is still unclear: blend it with the wines of the north? Make new lines of wine for sale abroad? Maybe both. If you know the story of Sicily, you know that colonization by foreign investors is nothing new."

On Planeta, Sicily's biggest success story: "People say that Planeta was born in 1995. This is partially true, but the other part of the truth is that the Planeta family has been working in agriculture in Sicily since the 1600s. In 1985 a fire in the vineyards around Lake Arancio, in western Sicily, presented the possibility of starting something new in the region. An institute whose president was Diego Planeta began to plant chardonnay, and the results were extraordinary.

"In 1995 the winery completed its first vintage. The Tre Bicchieri awards quickly followed, and in 1999 Planeta was selected Winery of the Year by Gambero Rosso. As it has grown, Planeta has begun producing Cerasuolo di Vittoria (a traditional southeastern wine) and expanded to Noto, a return to the origins of Nero d'Avola. The winery now produces more than 2 million bottles per year."

On how to choose Sicilian wines: "The most important thing is to get a sense of the many styles. Among the wines of western Sicily, try Planeta's Chardonnay, Ceuso's Custera, Furat's Ajello, Duca di Salaparuta's Duca Enrico, Morgante's Nero d'Avola, and Donnafugata's Mille e Una Notte. Among the wines of the east, try Planeta's Santa Cecilia (a Nero d'Avola from Noto) and Gulfi's Nerojbleo (another Nero d'Avola). And be sure to try any Cerasuolo di Vittoria, the most characteristic wine from Iblea, bolstered by the fruity Frappato grapes. Great versions come from Planeta, Valle dell'Acate, and Avide."

the city got back on its feet it was struck by a new calamity: plague decimated the population in the Middle Ages, a mile-wide stream of lava from Mt. Etna swallowed most of the city in 1669, and 25 years later a disastrous earthquake forced the Catanese to begin again.

Today Catania is completing yet another resurrection—this time from crime, filth, and urban decay. Although the city remains loud and full of traffic, signs of gentrification are everywhere. The elimination of vehicles from the Piazza del Duomo and scrubbing of a lot of the historic buildings has added to Catania's newfound charm. Home to what is arguably Sicily's best university, Catania is full of exuberant youth, and it shows in the chic *osterie* (taverns) that serve wine, designer bistros, and trendy ethnic boutiques that have popped up all over town. Even more impressive is the vibrant nightlife—theater, dance, and live music—to which the town now sways. Every year Catania becomes more and more worthwhile as a stop on a tour of Sicily—especially in summer, when the nearby beach and fishing towns become hot spots.

Catania's greatest native son was the composer Vincenzo Bellini (1801–35), whose operas have thrilled audiences since their premieres in the first half of the 19th century. Many of the town's buildings are constructed from three-century-old lava; the black lava-stone buildings combine with baroque architecture to give the city a singular appearance. Nowhere is this clearer than in the *centro storico* (historic center). Don't miss the stunning **Piazza Universitaria,** a nerve center made interesting by the facade of a majestic old university building, and the nearby Castello Ursino. The tourist board gives free **city tours** (☎ 095/7306222 ⊕ www.apt.catania.it) in English, Italian, and French, departing each morning from the tourist office at Via Cimarosa 12. There's a different tour theme each day; on Friday evenings you can take a reservations-only tour of the city's baroque buildings when they're lighted up at night.

At the heart of **Piazza del Duomo,** which is closed to traffic, stands an elephant carved out of lava, balancing an Egyptian obelisk—the city's informal mascot. The piazza shines from a 21st-century renovation. From here you can look way down the long, straight Via Garibaldi to see a black-and-white-striped fortress and entrance to the city, the Porta Garibaldi.

The Giovanni Vaccarini–designed facade of the **Cattedrale di Sant'Agata (Duomo)** dominates the Piazza del Duomo. Inside the church, composer Vincenzo Bellini is buried. Also of note are the three apses of lava that survive from the original Norman structure and a fresco from 1675 in the sacristy that portrays Catania's submission to Etna's attack. ⊠ *Piazza del Duomo, bottom end of Via Etnea* ☎ *095/320044* ☉ *Mon.–Sat. 8–noon and 4–7, Sun. 4–7.*

Evenings **Via Etnea** is host to one of Sicily's most enthusiastic *passeggiate* (predinner stroll), in which Catanese of all ages take part. Closed to automobile traffic until 10:30 PM, the street is lined with cafés and clothing, jewelry, and shoe stores.

15

NEED A BREAK?

The lively **Savia** (✉ Via Etnea and Via Umberto near Villa Bellini) makes superlative *arancini* (fried risotto balls) with *ragù* (a slow-cooked, tomato-based meat or seafood sauce). Or you could choose cannoli or other snacks to munch on while you rest.

An underground river, the Amenano, flows through much of Catania. You can glimpse it at the Fontana dell'Amenano, but the best place to experience the river is at the wine bar of the **Agorà Youth Hostel**. Here you can sit at a table near a grotto as swirls of water rush by. ✉ *Piazza Currò 6* ☎ *095/7233010* ☉ *Bar daily 12:30 PM–2 AM; other times, ask at the reception to see the grotto.*

Where to Stay & Eat

★ **$$$$** ✕ **La Siciliana.** Salvo La Rosa and sons serve memorable seafood and meat dishes, exquisite homemade desserts, and a choice of more than 220 wines. The restaurant specializes in the ancient dish *ripiddu nivicatu* ("black" risotto with cuttlefish ink and fresh ricotta cheese), as well as *le sarde a beccafico* (stuffed sardines) and calamari *ripieni alla griglia* (stuffed and grilled). A meal at this fine eatery more than justifies the short taxi ride 3 km (2 mi) north of the city center. ✉ *Viale Marco Polo 52* ☎ *095/376400* ⊕ *www.lasiciliana.it* ▭ *AE, DC, MC, V* ☉ *Closed Mon. No dinner Sun.*

$$–$$$$ ✕ **Costa Azzurra.** Reserve in advance for a table on the veranda, where you sit by the edge of the sea with good views of the harbor in the Ognina district. The *fritto misto* (assorted fried appetizers) can be ordered as an antipasto or a main course, and the *pesce spada* (swordfish) steak is a classic, served grilled with a large slice of lemon. ✉ *Via De Cristofaro 4, north of old town center on way to Taormina* ☎ *095/497889* ▭ *AE, DC, MC, V* ☉ *Closed Mon. and last 2 wks in Aug.*

$–$$$ ✕ **Ambasciata del Mare.** When a seafood restaurant sits next door to the fish market, it bodes well for the food's freshness. Choose swordfish or *gamberoni* (large shrimp) from a display case in the front of the restaurant, for instance, and then enjoy it simply grilled with oil and lemon. This simple, bright, and cozy place could not be friendlier or more easily accessed—it's right on the corner of Piazza Duomo by the fountain. ✉ *Viale Marco Polo 52* ☎ *095/341003* ⊕ *www.ambasciatadelmare.it* ▭ *AE, DC, MC, V* ☉ *Closed Mon. No dinner Sun.*

★ **¢–$** ✕ **Pizzeria Vico Santa Filomena.** This typical *forno a legna* (wood-burning oven) pizzeria, on a narrow side street off Via Umberto, is one of the most respected in the city for its outstanding "apizza," as the locals call it. Enjoy it as Catanians do: only at night, and with a beer (or soda)—never wine. The antipasti spreads are also delicious, and there's an outdoor garden. Expect a long wait with the hungry local youth on weekend evenings. ✉ *Vico Santa Filomena 35* ☎ *095/316761* ▭ *No credit cards.*

$$$$ ⊞ **Excelsior Grand Hotel.** Ask for a room facing Piazza Verga, a neat tree-lined square in a quiet but central district of Catania. Sound-insulated windows add to the peace. Impeccably designed rooms have a careful balance of neoclassical and new furnishings. The American Bar should provide solace if you're craving a Manhattan. ✉ *Piazza Verga 39, 95129* ☎ *095/7476111* 🖷 *095/537015* ⊕ *www.excelsiorcatania.thi.it*

🛏 *158 rooms, 13 suites, 5 junior suites* ♦ *Restaurant, gym, steam room, bar* ▭ *AE, DC, MC, V* ⏀ *BP.*

$$–$$$ 🏨 **Residence Angiolucci.** This freshly renovated 19th-century *palazzo* is
Fodor's Choice stunning not just for the impressive detail of the restoration work, but
★ even more for the elegant modernity of the mini-apartments that have
been built inside. The gleaming units, unique in eastern Sicily, each
have two floors (even the single rooms) and a full kitchen. Some also
have large living rooms and windows overlooking one of Catania's
main streets. The location is ideal and there are discounts for weeklong
stays. ✉ *Via E. Pantano 1, 95129* ☏ *095/3529420* 📠 *0931/464611*
⊕ *www.agniolucc150residence.com* 🛏 *30 apartments* ♦ *In-room safes,
kitchens, minibars, in-room broadband* ▭ *AE, DC, MC, V* ⏀ *EP.*

Shopping

Catania is justly famous for its sweets and bar snacks. Of the numerous pastry shops along Via Etnea, **Al Caprice** (✉ Via Etnea 32, near Piazza Universitaria ☏ 095/320840) has the largest variety of homemade goodies and edible gifts, plus hot and cold snacks. The selection of almond-based delights from **I Dolci di Nonna Vincenza** (✉ Palazzo Biscari, Piazza San Placido 7 ☏ 095/7151844 ⊕ www.dolcinonnavincenza.it ✉ Aeroporto Fontanarossa ☏ 095/7234522) may be small, but everything is fresh and phenomenally good. Nonna Vincenza ships abroad and even has an outlet in the Catania airport.

The **outdoor fish and food market,** which begins on Via Zappala Gemelli and emanates in every direction from Piazza di Benedetto, is one of Italy's most memorable. It's a feast for the senses: thousands of impeccably fresh fish, some still wriggling, plus endless varieties of meats, ricotta, and fresh produce, and a symphony of vendor shouts to fill the ears. Open Monday–Saturday, the market is at its best in the morning.

SIRACUSA

Siracusa (known to English-speakers as Syracuse), old and new, is a wonder to behold. One of the great ancient capitals of Western civilization, the city was founded in 734 BC by Greek colonists from Corinth and soon grew to rival, and even surpass, Athens in splendor and power; Siracusa became the largest, wealthiest city-state in the West and a bulwark of Greek civilization. Although the city lived under tyranny, rulers such as Dionysus filled their courts with Greeks of the highest artistic stature—among them Pindar, Aeschylus, and Archimedes. The Athenians did not welcome the rise of Siracusa and set out to conquer Sicily, but the natives outsmarted them in what was one of the greatest naval battles of ancient history (413 BC). Siracusa continued to prosper until it was conquered two centuries later by the Romans.

Siracusa still has some of the finest examples of baroque art and architecture; dramatic Greek and Roman ruins; and a Duomo that is the stuff of legend, a microcosm of the city's entire history in one building. The modern city also has a wonderful lively baroque old town worthy of extensive exploration, pleasant piazzas, outdoor cafés and bars, and a wide assortment of excellent seafood. There are essentially two areas

15

to explore in Siracusa: the Parco Archeologico, on the mainland; and the island of Ortygia, the ancient city first inhabited by the Greeks, which juts out into the Ionian sea and is connected to the mainland by two small bridges.

Siracusa's old nucleus of Ortygia is a compact area, a pleasure to amble around without getting unduly tired. In contrast, mainland Siracusa is a grid of wider avenues. At the northern end of Corso Gelone, above Viale Paolo Orsi, the orderly grid gives way to the ancient quarter of Neapolis, where the sprawling Parco Archeologico is accessible from Viale Teracati (an extension of Corso Gelone). East of Viale Teracati, about a 10-minute walk from the Parco Archeologico, the district of Tyche holds the archaeological museum and the church and catacombs of San Giovanni, both off Viale Teocrito (drive or take a taxi or city bus from Ortygia). Coming from the train station, it's a 15-minute trudge to Ortygia along Via Francesco Crispi and Corso Umberto.

Archaeological Zone

The Main Attractions

Parco Archeologico. Siracusa is most famous for its dramatic set of Greek and Roman ruins. Though the various ruins can be visited separately, see them all, along with the Museo Archeologico. If the park is closed, go up Viale G. Rizzo from Viale Teracati to the belvedere overlooking the ruins, which are floodlighted at night. The last tickets are sold one hour before closing.

Before the park's ticket booth is the gigantic **Ara di Ierone** (Altar of Hieron), which was once used by the Greeks for spectacular sacrifices involving hundreds of animals. The first attraction in the park is the **Latomia del Paradiso** (Quarry of Paradise), a lush tropical garden full of palm and citrus trees. This series of quarries served as prisons for the defeated Athenians, who were enslaved; the quarries once rang with the sound of their chisels and hammers. At one end is the famous **Orecchio di Dionisio** (Ear of Dionysus), with an ear-shape entrance and unusual acoustics inside, as you can hear if you clap your hands. The legend is that Dionysus used to listen in at the top of the quarry to hear what the slaves were plotting below.

★ The **Teatro Greco** (Greek Theater) is the chief monument in the Archaeological Park—and indeed one of Sicily's greatest classical sites and the most complete Greek theater surviving from antiquity. Climb to the top of the seating area (which could accommodate 15,000) for a fine view: all the seats converge upon a single point—the stage—which has the natural scenery and the sky as its background. Hewn out of the hillside rock in the 5th century BC, the theater saw the premieres of the plays of Aeschylus. Greek tragedies are still performed here every year in May and June. Above and behind the theater runs the Via dei Sepulcri, in which streams of running water flow through a series of Greek sepulchres.

The well-preserved and striking **Anfiteatro Romano** (Roman Amphitheater) reveals much about the differences between the Greek and Roman personalities. Where drama in the Greek theater was a kind of religious ritual, the Roman amphitheater emphasized the spectacle of combative sports and the circus. This arena is one of the largest of its kind and was built around the 2nd century AD. The corridor where gladiators and beasts entered the ring is still intact, and the seats, some of which still bear the occupants' names, were hauled in and constructed on the site from huge slabs of limestone. ⊠ *Viale Teocrito, Archaeological Zone* ☎ *0931/ 65068* ⊑ *€6* ◷ *Apr.–Sept., daily 9–7; Oct., daily 9–5; Nov.–Feb., daily 9–4; Mar., daily 9–6.*

| NEED A BREAK? | For some great Sicilian cakes and ice cream on your way to the Archaeological Park, visit **Leonardi** (⊠ Viale Teocrito 123, Archaeological Zone ☎ 0931/ 61411), a bar-cum-pasticceria. It's popular with the locals, so you may have to line up for your cakes in holiday times. It's closed Wednesday. |

Also Worth Seeing

Catacombe di San Giovanni. Not far from the Archaeological Park, off Viale Teocrito, the catacombs below the church of San Giovanni are one of the earliest-known Christian sites in the city. Inside the crypt of San Marciano is an altar where St. Paul preached on his way through Sicily to Rome. The frescoes in this small chapel are mostly bright and fresh, though some dating from the 4th century AD show their age. Open hours may be extended in summer. ⊠ *Piazza San Giovanni, Archaeological Zone* ☎ *0931/64694* ⊑ *€4* ◷ *Daily 9:30–12:30 and 2:30–6.*

Museo Archeologico. The impressive collection of Siracusa's splendid archaeological museum is organized by region around a central atrium and ranges from Neolithic pottery to fine Greek statues and vases. Compare the *Landolina Venus*—a headless, stout goddess of love who rises out of the sea in measured modesty (a 1st-century AD Roman copy of the Greek original)—with the much earlier (300 BC) elegant Greek statue of Hercules in Section C. Of a completely different style is a marvelous fanged Gorgon, its tongue sticking out, that once adorned the cornice of the Temple of Athena to ward off evildoers. The last tickets are sold an hour before closing. ⊠ *Viale Teocrito, Archaeological Zone* ☎ *0931/464022* ⊑ *€6* ◷ *Tues.–Sat. 9–7, Sun. 9–1.*

Museo del Papiro. Close to Siracusa's Museo Archeologico, the Papyrus Museum demonstrates how papyri are prepared from reeds and then painted—an ancient tradition in the city. Siracusa, it seems, has the only climate outside the Nile Valley in which the papyrus plant—from which the word "paper" comes—thrives. ⊠ *Viale Teocrito 66, Archaeological Zone* ☎ *0931/61616* ⊑ *Free* ◷ *Tues.–Sun. 9–1:30.*

Ortygia Island

The Main Attractions

❿ Duomo. Siracusa's Duomo is an archive of island history: the bottommost excavations have unearthed remnants of Sicily's distant past, when the Siculi inhabitants worshipped their deities here. During the 5th century BC (the same time as Agrigento's Temple of Concord was built), the Greeks built a temple to Athena over it, and in the 7th century Siracusa's first Christian cathedral was built on top of the Greek structure.

FodorsChoice
★

15

Castello
Maniace **13**

Duomo **10**

Fonte
Aretusa **12**

Palazzo
Beneventano
del Bosco **11**

Piazza
Archimede **8**

Piazza del
Duomo **9**

Tempio di
Apollo **7**

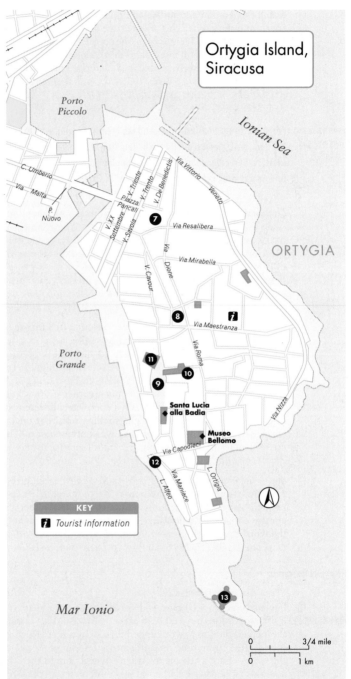

Ortygia Island,
Siracusa

The massive columns of the original Greek temple were incorporated into the present structure and are clearly visible, embedded in the exterior wall along Via Minerva. The Greek columns were also used to dramatic advantage inside, where on one side they form chapels connected by elegant wrought-iron gates. The baroque facade, added in 1700, displays a harmonious rhythm of concaves and convexes. In front, the piazza is encircled by pink and white oleanders and elegant buildings ornamented with filigree grillwork. ⊠ *Piazza del Duomo, Ortygia* ☎ *0931/65328* ⊙ *Daily 7:30 AM–7:30 PM.*

🔢 **Fonte Aretusa.** A freshwater spring, the Fountain of Arethus, sits next to the sea, studded with Egyptian papyrus that is reportedly natural. This anomaly is explained by a Greek legend that tells how the nymph Arethusa was changed into a fountain by the goddess Artemis (Diana) when she tried to escape the advances of the river god Alpheus. She fled from Greece, into the sea, with Alpheus in close pursuit, and emerged in Sicily at this spring. It's said if you throw a cup into the Alpheus River in Greece it will emerge here at this fountain, which is home to a few tired ducks and some dull-color carp—but no cups. If you want to stand right by the fountain, you need to gain admission through the aquarium; otherwise look down on it from Largo Aretusa. ⊠ *Off promenade along harbor, Ortygia.*

🔢 **Piazza Archimede.** The center of this piazza has a baroque fountain, the *Fontana di Diana,* festooned with fainting sea nymphs and dancing jets of water. Look for the Chiaramonte-style **Palazzo Montalto,** an arched-window gem just off the piazza on Via Montalto.

🔢 **Piazza del Duomo.** In the heart of Ortygia, this ranks as one of Italy's most beautiful piazzas, its elongated space lined with Sicilian baroque treasures and outdoor cafés.

🔢 **Tempio di Apollo.** Scattered through the piazza just across the bridge to Ortygia are the ruins of a temple dedicated to Apollo, a model of which is in the Museo Archeologico. In fact, little of this noble Doric temple still remains except for some crumbled walls and shattered columns; the window in the south wall belongs to a Norman church that was built much later on the same spot. ⊠ *Piazza Pancali, Ortygia.*

Also Worth Seeing

🔢 **Castello Maniace.** The southern tip of Ortygia island is occupied by a castle built by Frederick II (1194–1250), now an army barracks, from which there are fine views of the sea.

🔢 **Palazzo Beneventano del Bosco.** On a corner of the Piazza del Duomo, this elegant palazzo is a private residence, but you can take a peek at the impressive interior courtyard, ending in a grand winding staircase. ⊠ *Piazza del Duomo, Ortygia.*

Where to Stay & Eat

$$$–$$$$
FodorsChoice
★
✕ **Don Camillo.** A gracious series of delicately arched rooms, lined with wine bottles and sepia-tone images of Old Siracusa, overflows with locals in the know. Preparations bring together fresh seafood and inspired

15

creativity: taste, for instance, the sublime spaghetti *delle Sirene* (with delicate *ricci* [sea urchin] and shrimp in butter) a delicate *zuppa di mucca* (tiny fish floating in a scampi broth with cherry tomatoes, olive oil, and egg); or *gamberoni* (sweet, large prawns) prepared, unexpectedly (and wonderfully), in pork fat. The wine list is, in a word, extraordinary. ✉ *Via Maestranza 96, Ortygia* ☎ *0931/67133* ▭ *AE, DC, MC, V* ⊘ *Closed Sun., 1st 15 days in Nov., and 1st 15 days in July.*

$$–$$$$ ✕ **Oinos.** This wine bar and restaurant's ambitious food represents the most modern face of Siracusa. The rooms are stark but inviting, carefully balancing style consciousness with restrained refinement. Surrender to the sensational antipasto *sformatino di verdure e ricotta profumato al Ragusano,* a molded cheese-and-vegetable tart with ricotta and Ragusano DOP (*denominazioni di origine protette,* meaning only certified producers may use the name Ragusano on their goods) cheese, a melting delight. In season, special dishes spotlight white truffle from Alba priced by the gram (as is customary) and worth every penny. ✉ *Via della Giudecca 71, at Via Minniti, Ortygia* ☎ *No phone* ▭ *AE, DC, MC, V.*

★ $–$$$ ✕ **Vite e Vitello.** Sooner or later, you'll need a break from the nonstop seafood of the Sicilian coast, and you'll find just that in a couple of simple white rooms with an open kitchen. A menu of some of the best beef and veal in Sicily includes an antipasto sampler with cubes of veal gelatin and homemade ricotta. Your primi might be *cavatelli* (small pasta twists) with *guanciale* (pig's jowl bacon) and delicious pistachios, and your secondi an incredible Angus steak shipped in from Ireland. For dessert, try the *cannollata,* a cake that resembles a deconstructed *cannolo* (singular of cannoli). ✉ *Piazza Francesco Corpaci 1, Ortygia* ☎ *0931/464269* ▭ *AE, DC, MC, V.*

$–$$ ✕ **Ionico.** Enjoy seaside dining in the coastal Santa Lucia district. The Ionico has a terrace and veranda for alfresco meals, and the interior is plastered with diverse historical relics and has a cheerful open hearth for winter. Chef-proprietor Roberto Giudice cooks meals to order or will suggest a specialty from a selection of market-fresh ingredients. Try the pasta *con acciughe e il pan grattato* (in an anchovy sauce). ✉ *Riviera Dionisio il Grande 194, Santa Lucia* ☎ *0931/65540* ▭ *AE, DC, MC, V* ⊘ *Closed Tues.*

$–$$ ✕ **La Siciliana.** More than 54 varieties of inexpensive pizza top the menu here. The traditional *siciliana,* a crusty and flavorful fried calzone stuffed with *tuma* (fresh unsalted cheese) and anchovies, is served only in the evening. Other choices on the menu include pasta and fish. It's a good place to enjoy a cold beer or a white wine. ✉ *Via Savoia 17, Ortygia* ☎ *0931/68944* ▭ *DC, MC, V* ⊘ *Closed Mon.*

¢–$ ✕ **Fermento.** This hip wine bar–restaurant–Internet café is graced with warm lighting, dark vaulted stone, candles everywhere, a dim buzz, and Sicilian wines served in huge, beautiful tasting glasses. The menu really revolves around wine, with a decent (if pricey) selection of local classics. Stick to the pasta dishes and creative salads rather than the meats, or come just for the wine. ✉ *Via Crocifisso 44/46, Ortygia* ☎ *0931/ 60762* ▭ *AE, DC, MC, V* ⊘ *Closed Tues.*

$$$$ ▦ **Grand Hotel Ortigia.** An elegant, fantasy-inspired design prevails at this venerable institution, which has enjoyed a prime position the Porto

Grande, at the base of Ortygia, since 1898. A surreal seascape painting and a whimsical chandelier set a dreamy tone in the lobby. Guest rooms have fine wood floors, inlaid wood furniture, and stained-glass windows. Spacious bi-level suites with staircases cost about €60 extra. Look out from roof-garden restaurant at superb views over the harbor and seafront, while you indulge in excellent food. A shuttle service is provided to the hotel's private beach nearby. ⊠ *Viale Mazzini 12, Ortygia, 96100* ☎ *0931/464600* ⓐ *0931/464611* ⊕ *www.grandhotelsr.it* ⌂ *39 rooms, 19 suites* ⚬ *Restaurant, in-room safes, minibars, cable TV, beach, bar, meeting room, free parking* ⊟ *AE, DC, MC, V* ⫶⏶⫶ *BP.*

★ **$$$$** ⬚ **Hotel des Étrangers et Miramare.** After a revamp of the old Miramare, which took the better part of a decade, this imposing hotel opened in 2004 and quickly became the city's top address for visiting dignitaries and luxury tourists. Rooms are refreshingly simple for a hotel of this caliber, but at the same time elegant, and some have balconies overlooking the sea. The hotel, which stands beside the Fonte Aretusa in Ortygia, has a rooftop restaurant with nice views of the city—a great place to meet for a cocktail. ⊠ *Passeggio Adorno 10/12, Ortygia 96100* ☎ *0931/62671* ⓐ *0931/65124* ⊕ *www.medeahotels.com* ⌂ *67 rooms, 13 suites* ⚬ *Restaurant, in-room safes, minibars, pool, 2 bars, Internet room, meeting rooms, free parking* ⊟ *AE, DC, MC, V* ⫶⏶⫶ *BP.*

$$ ⬚ **Domus Mariae.** You can see the sea at the end of the corridor as you enter this hotel on Ortygia's eastern shore. In an unusual twist, it's run by nuns of the Ursuline order, who help to make the mood placid and peaceful—and couldn't possibly be nicer hosts. Don't expect monastic conditions, however: refined furnishings distinguish the public rooms. Guest rooms—six with sea views (an extra €15) and others with great Ortygia street balconies—are bright, modern, and comfortable. ⊠ *Via Vittorio Veneto 76, Ortygia, 96100* ☎ *0931/24854 or 0931/24858* ⊕ *www.sistemia.it/domusmariae* ⌂ *12 rooms* ⚬ *Bar, free parking* ⊟ *AE, DC, MC, V* ⫶⏶⫶ *BP.*

¢–$ ⬚ **Airone.** In a pretty old palazzo in the heart of Ortygia, this bed-and-breakfast (liberally interpreted—breakfast at a nearby bar is included) caters mostly to backpackers and those who have the stamina to brave the four-story climb. Service is friendly and hassle-free (you get your own keys to the building), and the price and location can't be beat. Rooms are aging but spotless and spacious, some overlooking the coastline. Some rooms share baths. ⊠ *Via Maestranza 111, Ortygia 96100* ☎ *0931/ 69005* ⓐ *178/2280482* ⊕ *www.bedandbreakfastsicily.com* ⌂ *16 rooms, 10 with bath* ⚬ *Breakfast room, lounge, parking (fee)* ⊟ *No credit cards* ⫶⏶⫶ *BP.*

Nightlife & the Arts

Every May and June, Siracusa's **Teatro Greco** (⊠ Parco Archeologico, Archaeological Zone ☎ 0931/465831 ⊕ www.indafondazione.org) stages performances of classical drama and comedy.

★ One of Sicily's best wine bars, **Peter Pan** (⊠ Via Castello Maniace, Ortygia ☎ 0931/468937) remarkably serves absolutely any wine on its voluminous list by the glass. The place doubles as a haunt of the city's far-left youth. Popular and filled with locals, **Il Bagatto** (⊠ Piazza S. Giuseppe 1, Ortygia ☎ 0931/464076) is a bar in the heart of Ortygia.

Shopping

Siracusa's specialty is papyrus paper. But beware—most of what you buy is commercially produced, hard, and of inferior quality to the hand-made paper, which feels like fabric. One of the best of the few places to buy the genuine article is **Galleria Bellomo** (⊠ Via Capodieci 15, Ortygia ☎ 0931/61340 ⊙ Closed Sun.), opposite the currently closed Museo Bellomo. It's run by an artist who sells cards and paintings and may also give a demonstration of how to make the paper.

THE INTERIOR

Sicily's interior is for the most part underpopulated and untrammeled, though the Imperial Roman Villa at Casale, outside Piazza Armerina, gives precious evidence from an epoch gone by. Don't miss windy mountaintop Enna, called the Navel of Sicily, or Caltagirone, a ceramics center of renown.

Ragusa

⓮ *90 km (56 mi) southwest of Siracusa.*

Ragusa and Modica are the two chief cities in Sicily's smallest and sleepiest province, and the centers of a region known as Iblea. The dry, rocky, gentle countryside filled with canyons and grassy knolls is a unique landscape in Sicily. Iblea's trademark squat stone walls divide swaths of land in a manner reminiscent of the high English countryside—but summers are decidedly Sicilian, with dry heat so intense that life grinds to a standstill for several hours each day. This remote province hums along to its own tune, clinging to local customs, cuisines, and traditions in aloof disregard even for the rest of Sicily.

Ragusa is known for some great local red wines and its wonderful cheese, Ragusano DOP, a creamy, doughy, flavorful version of caciocavallo, made by hand every step of the way. It's a modern city ★ with a beautiful old town called **Ibla**, which was completely rebuilt after the devastating earthquake of 1693. A tumble of buildings perched on a hilltop and suspended between a deep ravine and a sloping valley, Ibla's tiny squares and narrow lanes make for pleasant meandering. The **Basilica di San Giorgio**, designed by Rosario Gagliardi in 1738, is a fine example of Sicilian baroque.

> **WORD OF MOUTH**
>
> "Ragusa was probably the biggest surprise of any place in Sicily for me. The first view of the town built on what seem to be practically vertical walls is stunning. Then climbing up through the town's twisty stairways and alleys and through arches and narrow passageways . . . you feel transported clear out of the 21st century."   −RAR

Caltagirone

⑮ *66 km (41 mi) northwest of Ragusa.*

Built over three hills, this charming baroque town is a center of Sicily's ceramics industry. Here you can find majolica balustrades, tile-decorated windowsills, and a monumental tile staircase of 142 steps—each decorated with a different pattern—leading up to the neglected **Santa Maria del Monte.** On the feast of San Giacomo (July 24), the staircase is illuminated with candles that form a tapestry design over the steps. It's the result of months of work preparing the 4,000 *coppi*, or cylinders of colored paper that hold oil lamps. At 9:30 PM on the nights of July 24, July 25, August 14, and August 15 a squad of hundreds of boys springs into action to light the lamps, so that the staircase flares up all at once. ☺ *Daily 7–noon and 4–7.*

Shopping

Of the numerous ceramic shops in Caltagirone's old center, **Branciforti** (✉ Scala Santa Maria del Monte 3 ☎ 0933/24427 ⊕ www.ceramichebranciforti.it), right on Caltagirone's fabled ceramic steps, is one of the best, selling eye-catching work with deep shades of blue and swirling arabesques.

Piazza Armerina

⑯ *30 km (18 mi) northwest of Caltagirone.*

A quick look around the fanciful town of Piazza Armerina is rewarding—it has a provincial warmth, and the crumbling yellow stone architecture with Sicily's trademark bulbous balconies creates quite an effect. The greatest draw, however, lies just down the road. The exceptionally

FodorsChoice well-preserved **Imperial Roman Villa,** 4 km (2½ mi) southwest of Piazza
★ Armerina, is thought to have been a hunting lodge of the emperor Maximianus Heraclius (4th century AD). The excavations were not begun until 1950, and the wall decorations and vaulting have been lost. However, some of the best mosaics of the Roman world cover more than 12,000 square feet under a shelter that hints at the layout of the original buildings. The mosaics were probably made by North African artisans; they are similar to those in the Tunis Bardo Museum. The entrance was through a triumphal arch that led into an atrium surrounded by a portico of columns, after which the *thermae,* or bathhouse, is reached. It's colorfully decorated with mosaic nymphs, a Neptune, and slaves massaging bathers. The peristyle leads to the main villa, where in the Salone del Circo you look down on mosaics illustrating Roman circus sports. Room 38 even reveals a touch of eroticism—surely only scratching the surface of the bacchanalian festivities that Maximianus conjured up. ✉ SP15, Casale ☎ 0935/680036 ☐ €6 ☺ *Mar.–Sept., daily 8–5; Oct.–Feb., daily 8–4.*

Where to Eat

$$–$$$ ✕ **Al Fogher.** A beacon of culinary light shines in Sicily's interior, a region generally filled with good, but simple, places to eat. Ambitious—and successful—dishes include tuna tartare with potato puree and a fillet

15

of baby pig crusted with black pepper and pistachio that's served with a sauce made from *bottarga* (cured tuna roe) and asparagus. Decor is simple and elegant. ✉ *Contrada Bellia near SS117bis exit* ☎ *0935/684123* ▤ *AE, DC, MC, V* ⊗ *Closed Mon. and 2 wks in Aug.*

Enna

⑰ *33 km (20 mi) northwest of Piazza Armerina, 136 km (85 mi) southeast of Palermo.*

Deep in Sicily's interior, the fortress city of Enna (altitude 2,844 feet) commands exceptional views of the surrounding rolling plains, and, in the distance, Mt. Etna. It is the highest provincial capital in Italy and, thanks to its central location, it is known as the Navel of Sicily. Virtually unknown by tourists and relatively untouched by industrialization, this sleepy town charms and prospers in a distinctly old-fashioned, provincial, and Sicilian way. Enna makes a good stopover for the night or just for lunch, as it's right along the autostrada between Palermo and Catania (and thus Siracusa).

The narrow, winding streets are dominated at one end by the impressive cliff-hanging **Castello di Lombardia,** built by Frederick II, easily visible as you approach town. Inside the castle, you can climb up the tower for great views from the dead center of the island; on a very clear day, you can see to all three coasts. ▤ *Free* ⊗ *Daily 8–8.*

★ The Greek cult of Demeter, goddess of the harvest, was said to have centered around Enna. It's not hard to see why its adherents would have worshipped at the **Rocca di Cerere** (rock of Demeter), protruding out on one end of town next to the Castello di Lombardia. The spot enjoys spectacular views of the expansive countryside and windswept Sicilian interior.

In town, head straight for Via Roma, which leads to **Piazza Vittorio Emanuele,** the center of Enna's shopping scene and evening passeggiata. The attached **Piazza Crispi,** dominated by the shell of the grand old Hotel Belvedere, affords breathtaking panoramas of the hillside and smoking Etna looming in the distance. The bronze fountain at the center of the piazza is a reproduction of Gian Lorenzo Bernini's famous 17th-century sculpture *The Rape of Persephone,* a depiction of Hades (Plutone) abducting Persephone (Proserpina) to take her to the underworld. According to several versions of the myth, including Aristotle's, the abduction occurred around Lake Pergusa, near Enna.

The mysterious **Torre di Federico II** stands above the lower part of town. This octagonal tower, of unknown purpose, has been celebrated for millennia as marking the exact geometric center of the island—thus the tower's, and city's, nickname, Umbilicus Siciliae (Navel of Sicily). The inside of the tower is not open to the public, but the surrounding park is, and you can admire the tower up close from the outside.

Where to Stay & Eat

$–$$ ✕ **Centrale.** This casual place has served meals since 1889. The bright walls of an old palazzo are adorned with Sicilian pottery, and an outdoor terrace soothes diners in summer. The varied menu includes local preparations such as *coppole di cacchio* (peppers stuffed with spaghetti, potato, and basil) and grilled pork chops. Choose from a decent selection of Sicilian wines to accompany your meal. ⊠ *Piazza VI Dicembre 9* ☎ *0935/500963* ☐ *AE, DC, MC, V* ⊗ *No lunch Sat. Oct.–Mar.*

$ ✕ **La Botte.** At this glass-enclosed restaurant along an old street, the menu pays homage to tradition—the *orrecchiette* (small, ear-shape pasta) served *alla Norma* is a Sicilian classic—and has tasty dishes like the *pappardelle alla botte,* wide noodles with a meat sauce. Order off the wine list or let the friendly staff fill your carafe with the good local table wine from *la botte* (the barrel). There's a fixed lunch menu on Monday and Wednesday. ⊠ *Via Roma 488* ☎ *0935/502331* ☐ *AE, DC, MC, V* ⊗ *Closed Tues.*

$–$$ ▥ **Hotel Sicilia.** Sicily's interior has few decent accommodations, so if overnighting you have little choice but to stay at the central Hotel Sicilia. The place is institutional feeling and monopoly priced, but its bright rooms (some with excellent views) are reliably clean and adequate. Reserve ahead for one with a bathtub (Room 10), air-conditioning, or a view over the town and hillside rather than onto the piazza. Low-season or Internet discounts can be as much as 50%. ⊠ *Piazza Napoleone Colajanni 7, 94100* ☎ *0935/500850* ☐ *0935/500488* ⊕ *www.hotelsiciliaenna.it* ⇄ *65 rooms* ⌂ *Minibars, bar; no a/c in some rooms* ☐ *AE, DC, MC, V* ⦿ *BP.*

Caltanisetta

⑱ *35 km (21 mi) southwest of Enna.*

Caltanisetta, completely off the tourist track, is about as characteristic an interior Sicilian city as you'll find. The truest pleasure here is simply walking around and absorbing the mysterious vibe of a place whose residents seem almost shell-shocked by the creeping arrival of modernity. Notable in the historic center are the colors of the churches, domes, and palazzi—bright, primary colors that give the city an uncommon glow.

Where to Eat

★ **¢–$** ✕ **Boccondivino.** This wonderful restaurant in the city center alone justifies a trip to Caltanisetta. The theme here is local *piatti della tradizione* (plates of tradition), from an antipasto of the typical cheeses and *salumi* (cured meats) of Sicily, to *casarecce* (hand-rolled pasta tubes) with broccoli, tomatoes, and anchovies, to a mind-blowing sampler of three different juicy grilled sausages: *lepre* (hare), *cinghiale* (wild boar), and *al limone* (lemon-infused). The yellow walls, painted with Goethe's words of praise for Sicily, give a warmth to the space. The price is right, too. ⊠ *Corso Umberto I 146* ☎ *0934/582764* ☐ *AE, DC, MC, V.*

AGRIGENTO & WESTERN SICILY

The crowning glory of western Sicily is the concentration of Greek temples at Agrigento, on a height between the modern city and the sea. The mark of ancient Greek culture also lingers in the cluster of ruined cliff-side temples at Selinunte and at the splendidly isolated site of Segesta. Traces of the North African culture that for centuries exerted a strong influence on this end of the island are most tangible in the coastal towns of Trapani and Marsala, and on the outlying island of Pantelleria, nearer to the Tunisian coast than the Sicilian. In contrast, the cobbled streets of hilltop Erice, outside Trapani, retain a strong medieval complexion, giving the town the air of a last outpost on the edge of the Mediterranean. On the northern coast, not far outside Palermo, Monreale's cathedral glitters with mosaics that are among the finest in Italy.

Agrigento

⑲ *60 km (37 mi) southwest of Caltanisetta*

Agrigento owes its fame almost exclusively to its ancient Greek temples—though it was also the birthplace of playwright Luigi Pirandello (1867–1936). Among the reasons to go up the hill from Valle dei Templi to the modern city is the opportunity to eat a more-local, less-over-priced meal or to stay at an inexpensive hotel; another is to ring the doorbell at the **Convento di Santo Spirito** and try the *kus-kus* (sweet cake), made of pistachio nuts and chocolate, that the nuns prepare. ⌧ *Salita di Santo Spirito off Via Porcello* ☏ *No phone.*

Valle dei Templi   See Page 836

Where to Stay & Eat

$–$$ ✕ **Kokalos.** On a hillside opposite the temple ridge, 6 km (4 mi) to the southeast, this large restaurant in an old village house has beautiful views over the temples. As well as serving local specialties, Kokalos has a pizzeria and enoteca—it hops on weekend nights. ⌧ *Via Cavaleri Magazzeni 3, Villagio Mosè* ☏ *0922/606427* ▭ *AE, MC, V.*

$–$$ ✕ **Trattoria dei Templi.** Along a road on the way up to Agrigento proper from the temple area, this simple vaulted restaurant can get very busy after it becomes too dark for temple exploring. The menu has all the classic Sicilian dishes, including satisfying homemade *maccheroni* (tubular pasta) and plenty of grilled fish. The antipasti, such as the carpaccio of *cernia* (grouper), are exceptional. ⌧ *Via Panoramica dei Templi 15* ☏ *0922/403110* ▭ *AE, DC, MC, V* ⊙ *Closed July 1–15 and Sun. July and Aug.*

$$$$ ✕⌂ **Foresteria Baglio della Luna.** Fiery sunsets and moonlight cast a glow over a tower dating from the 8th century, which is central to the farmhouse-hotel complex. Stone buildings surround around a peaceful geranium- and ivy-filled courtyard and a garden beyond. Standard rooms, some with views of the temples, are nothing fancy, with mellow walls and wooden furniture. The intimate, rustic restaurant, Il Dehors ($$$$), serves extremely expensive foodie fare that is ambitious and impressive. *Spigola* (Mediterranean bass) comes in a delicate potato crust with baby broccoli and asparagus. The hotel is in the valley below the temples: note that the dirt road up to the hotel is unmarked. Prices are very high for what you get, and there have been complaints about the service, but such is the touristy temple area. ⊠ *Contrada Maddalusa, Valle dei Templi, 3 km (2 mi) southeast of old town, 92100* ☎ *0922/ 511061* 🖷 *0922/598802* ⊕ *www.bagliodellaluna.com* ⇨ *23 rooms, 4 suites* ♨ *Restaurant, minibars, bar* ▤ *AE, DC, MC, V* ⏐◎⏐ *BP.*

$$$–$$$$ ⊞ **Villa Athena.** The price here reflects the privileged position of the 18th-century Villa Athena, with a view over the Temple of Concordia. The lodging itself, although pleasant, is not outstanding. Many rooms have terraces overlooking the large gardens and the swimming pool. The temples are an easy walk away, and there's a convivial bar, where a multi-national crowd swaps stories. The only hotel right in the midst of the archaeological zone is in much demand, so make reservations as early as possible. ⊠ *Via Passeggiata Archeologica 33, 92100* ☎ *0922/596288* 🖷 *0922/402180* ⊕ *www.athenahotels.com* ⇨ *40 rooms* ♨ *Restaurant, minibars, pool, bar, Internet room* ▤ *AE, DC, MC, V* ⏐◎⏐ *BP.*

$$ ⊞ **Tre Torri.** Stay here if you are sports-minded and bent on exploring the countryside around Agrigento. Bicycle tours, bicycle rental, and na-ture walks can be arranged or a boat booked for fishing trips and water sports. The heated pool is pleasant, the public areas spacious, and the modern rooms furnished with some panache. The hotel's location, Vil-lagio Mosè, 5 km (3 mi) southeast of town, is on a regular bus route. ⊠ *Villagio Mosè, 92100* ☎ *0922/606733* 🖷 *0922/607839* ⊕ *www. htretorri.com* ⇨ *118 rooms* ♨ *Restaurant, indoor pool, gym, sauna, bicycles, bar, meeting room* ▤ *AE, DC, MC, V* ⏐◎⏐ *BP.*

Selinunte

⓴ *100 km (60 mi) northwest of Agrigento, 114 km (71 mi) south of Palermo.*

★ Near the town of Castelvetrano, numerous **Greek temple ruins** perch on a plateau overlooking an expanse of the Mediterranean at Selinunte (or Selinus). The city was one of the most superb colonies of ancient Greece. Founded in the 7th century BC, Selinunte became the rich and prosper-ous rival of Segesta, which in 409 BC turned to the Carthaginians for help. The Carthaginians sent an army commanded by Hannibal to de-stroy the city. The temples were demolished, the city was razed, and 16,000 of Selinunte's inhabitants were slaughtered. The remains of Selinunte are in many ways unchanged from the day of its sacking—burn marks still scar the Greek columns, and much of the site still lies in rubble at its exact position of collapse at the hands of the Carthaginian attack. The original complex held seven temples scattered over two sites sepa-rated by a harbor. Of the seven, only one—reconstructed in 1958—is whole. Selinunte is named after a local variety of wild parsley (*Apium graveolens* or *petroselinum*) that in spring grows in profusion among the ruined columns and overturned capitals. Although there aren't many places to stay right around Selinunte, it's an easy stop along the road to or from Agrigento and it only takes an hour or two to see—a richly rewarding stopover. ⊠ *SS115* ☎ *0924/46277* 🎫 *€6* ☉ *Apr.–Oct., Mon.–Sat. 9–4; Nov.–Mar., daily 9–4.*

VALLE DEI TEMPLI

Built on a broad open field that slopes gently to the sun-simmered Mediterranean, Akragas (ancient Agrigento's Greek name) was a showpiece of temples erected to flaunt a victory over Carthage. Despite a later sack by the Carthaginians, mishandling by the Romans, and neglect by the Christians and Muslims, the eight or so monuments in the Valle dei Templi are considered to be, along with the Acropolis in Athens, the finest Greek ruins in all the world.

 TIMING TIP

The temples are at their very best in February, when the valley is awash in the fragrant blossoms of thousands of almond trees.

Whether you first come upon the Valle dei Templi in the early morning light, or bathed by golden floodlights at night, it's easy to see why Akragas was celebrated by the Greek poet Pindar as "the most beautiful city built by mortal men."

MAKING THE MOST OF YOUR VISIT

GETTING AROUND

Though getting to, from, and around the dusty ruins of the Valle dei Templi is no great hassle, this important archaeological zone deserves several hours. The site, which opens at 8:30 AM, is divided into western and eastern sections. For instant aesthetic gratification, walk through the eastern zone; for a more comprehensive tour, start way out at the western end and work your way back uphill.

The temples are a bit spread out, but the valley is all completely walkable and generally toured on foot. However, note that there is only one hotel (Villa Athena) that is close enough to walk to the ruins, so you will most likely have to drive to reach the site; parking is at the entrance to the temple area.

WHAT TO BRING

It's a good idea to pack your own snacks and drinks, as there are hardly any restaurants in the temple area, and the handful of high-priced bars around the site cater mostly to tourists.

In summer the site can get extremely hot, so wear light clothing, a hat, and sun protection if possible.

15

VALLE DEI TEMPLI

A BRIEF HISTORY OF AGRIGENTO

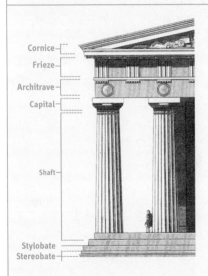

Cornice
Frieze
Architrave
Capital
Shaft
Stylobate
Stereobate

KEY DATES	
750 BC	Greek city-states begin to colonize Sicily and southern Italy.
734 BC	Neighboring Siracusa founded.
582 BC	Akragas settled. The city grows wealthy through trade with Carthage, just across the Mediterranean.
ca. 450 BC– 350 BC	Temples at Akragas erected over a period of about 100 years to celebrate the city's propserity.
413 BC	Battle of Siracusa vs. Athens.
406 BC	Fire from Carthaginian attack destroys much of Akragas. Despite this and future attacks, the city and its temples survive through the Roman era, the Middle Ages, and into the modern age.

The natural defenses of ancient Akragas depended on its secure and quite lovely position between two rivers on a floodplain a short distance from the sea. In Agrigento you will be treated to what many experts consider the world's best-preserved remains of classical Greece. All of the temples in the Valle dei Templi are examples of Doric architecture, the earliest and simplest of the Greek architectural orders (the others are Ionic and Corinthian). Some retain capitals in addition to their columns, while others are reduced to nothing more than fragments of stylobate.

THE TEMPLES

TEMPIO DI ERCOLE

The eight pillars of the **Temple of Hercules**, down the hill from the Temple of Concord, make up Agrigento's oldest temple complex (dating from the 6th century BC), dedicated to the favorite god of the often-warring citizens of Akragas. Partially reconstructed in 1922, it reveals the remains of a large Doric temple that originally had 38 columns. Like all the area temples, it faces east. The nearby Museo Archeologico Regionale contains some of the marble warrior figures that once decorated the temple's pediment.

Tempio di Ercole

TEMPIO DELLA CONCORDIA

The beautiful **Temple of Concord** is perhaps *the* best-preserved Greek temple in existence. The structure dates from about 430 BC, and owes its exceptional state of preservation to the fact that it was converted into a Christian church in the 6th century and was extensively restored in the 18th century. Thirty-two Doric columns surround its large interior, and everything but the roof and treasury are still standing. For preservation, this temple is blocked off to the public, but you can still get close enough to appreciate how well it's withstood the past 2,400 years.

TEMPIO DI GIUNONE

The **Temple of Juno,** east on the Via Sacra from the Temple of Concord, commands an exquisite view of the valley, especially at sunset. It's similar to but smaller than the Concordia and dates from about 450 BC. Traces of a fire that probably occurred during the Carthaginian attack in 406 BC,

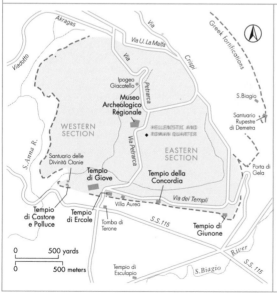

Valle dei Templi
Phone: 0922/621611
Web site:
www.valledeitempli.net
Admission: Site €6, with museum €10. One ticket covers all temples.
Open daily 8:30–7.

Museo Archeologico Regionale
Contrada San Nicola, 12
Phone: 0922/401565
Admission: €6, with temples site €10
Open Tues.-Sat. 9-7:30, Sun.-Mon. 9-1:30

Agrigento tourist information
Via Cesare Battisti 15, 92100
Phone: 0922/20454

which destroyed the ancient town, can be seen on the walls of the cellar. Thirty of the original 34 columns still stand, of which 16 have retained their capitals.

TEMPIO DI GIOVE

Though never completed, the **Temple of Jupiter** was considered the eighth wonder of the world. With a length of more than 330 feet, it was once the biggest of the Akragas temples and one of the largest temples in the Greek world. The temple was probably built in gratitude for victory over Carthage and was constructed by prisoners captured in that war. Basically Doric in style, it did not have the usual colonnade of freestanding columns but rather a series of half columns attached to a solid wall. This design is unique among known Doric temples—alas, only the stereobate was left behind. Inside the excavation you can see a cast (not the original) of one of the 38 colossal Atlas-like figures, or telamones, that supported the temple's massive roof.

Tempio di Giove

TEMPIO DI CASTORE E POLLUCE

The **Temple of Castor and Pollux** is a troublesome reconstruction of a 5th-century BC temple. It was pieced together by some enthusiastic if misguided 19th-century romantics who, in 1836, haphazardly put together elements from diverse buildings. Ironically, the four gently crumbling columns supporting part of an entablature of the temple have become emblematic of Agrigento.

OTHER SITES OF INTEREST

To the left of the Temple of Concord is a Paleochristian **necropolis**. Early Christian tombs were both cut into the rock and dug into underground catacombs.

Right opposite the Temple of Castor and Pollux, facing north, the **Santuario delle Divinità Ctonie** (Sanctuary of the Chthonic Divinities) has cultic altars and eight small temples dedicated to Demeter, Persephone, and other Underworld deities. In the vicinity are two columns of a temple dedicated to Hephaestus (Vulcan).

At the end of Via dei Templi, where it turns left and becomes Via Petrarca, stands the **Museo Archeologico Regionale**. An impressive collection of antiquities from the site includes vases, votives, everyday objects, weapons,

statues (including one of the surviving original telamones from the Temple of Jupiter), and models of the temples.

The **Hellenistic and Roman Quarter**, across the road from the archaeological museum, consists of four parallel streets, running north-south, that have been uncovered, along with the foundations of some houses from the Roman settlement (2nd century BC). Some of these streets still have their original mosaic pavements, and the complex system of sidewalks and gutters is easy to make out—reminding you that the ancient world wasn't all temples and togas.

15

VALLE DEI TEMPLI

Marsala

 88 km (55 mi) northwest of Selinunte.

The quiet seaside town of Marsala was once the main Carthaginian base in Sicily, from which Carthage fought for supremacy over the island against Greece and Rome. Nowadays it's more readily associated with the world-famous, richly colored sweet wine named after the town. In 1773 a British merchant named John Woodhouse happened upon Marsala and discovered that the wine here was as good as the port the British had long imported from Portugal. Two other wine merchants, Whitaker and Ingram, rushed in, and by 1800 Marsala was exporting its wine all over the British Empire.

A sense of Marsala's past as a Carthaginian stronghold is captured by the well-preserved Punic warship displayed in the town's **Museo Archeologico Baglio Anselmi,** along with some of the amphoras and other artifacts recovered from the wreck. The vessel, which was probably sunk during the great sea battle that ended the First Punic War in 241 BC, was dredged up from the mud near the Egadi Islands in the 1970s and is now installed under a climate-controlled plastic tent. ⊠ *Lungomare Boéo 2* ☏ *0923/952535* 🖾 *€3* ☉ *Tues.–Sat. 9–6, Sun. 9–1.*

One of Sicily's foremost wine producers, the 150-year-old **Donnafugata Winery** is open for tours of their Cantina (reservations required) right in downtown Marsala. It's an interesting look at the wine-making process in Sicily, and it ends with a tasting of several whites and reds and a chance to buy; don't miss the delicious, full-bodied red Mille e Una Notte, and the famous Ben Ryè Passito di Pantelleria, a sweet dessert wine made from dried grapes. ⊠ *Via Lipari 18* ☏ *0923/724200* ⊕ *www.donnafugata.it* 🖾 *Free* ☉ *Weekdays 8:30–1 and 2:30–5:30, by appointment only; other times sometimes possible.*

Trapani

 30 km (18 mi) north of Marsala.

The modern town of Trapani is the departure point for ferries to Sardinia and to the island of Pantelleria, near the African coast. Many spaghetti Westerns were filmed on this rugged western end of Sicily.

The historic center is a well-kept secret. The lanes near Corso Italia hold a handful of churches worth wandering into. **Santa Maria di Gesù** (⊠ Via San Pietro ☏ 090/323362) has Gothic and Renaissance doors and a Madonna by Andrea della Robbia (1435–1525). **Sant'Agostino** (⊠ Piazzetta Saturno), behind the town hall, has a 14th-century rose window.

Where to Stay & Eat

$ ✕🖾 **Ai Lumi.** If you're still hungry after the abundance of the antipasto buffet, try the restaurant's ($$) hearty traditional soups and variety of tasty fish and meat dishes. Salami hangs from the ceiling in this appealing and attentive *tavernetta* (cozy tavern) with a medieval door. The bed-and-breakfast upstairs offers simple rooms with local Trapani ironwork beds, and inexpensive mini-apartments with kitchens. The facilities are comfortable and the location couldn't be any more central. ⊠ *Corso Vittoria Emanuele*

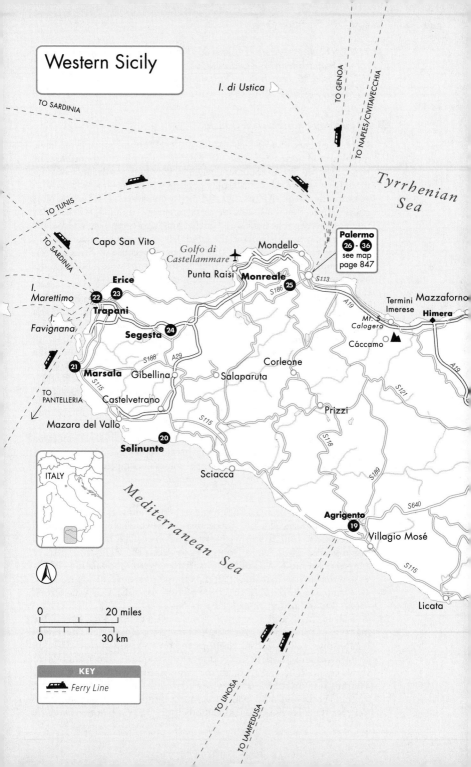

71/75, 91100 ☎ 0923/872418 or 0347/8566570 ⊕ www.ailumi.it ⇴ 5 rooms, 9 apartments ♿ Restaurant, some kitchens, bar ⊟ AE, DC, MC, V ⊘ Closed 20 days in June. Restaurant closed Sun. No lunch ⍟ BP.

Erice

㉓ *15 km (9 mi) northeast of Trapani.*

Erice is perched 2,450 feet above sea level, an enchanting medieval mountaintop aerie of castles and palaces, fountains, and cobblestone streets. Shaped like an equilateral triangle, the town was the ancient landmark Eryx, dedicated to the fertility goddess whom the Phoenicians called Astarte, the Greeks Aphrodite, and the Romans Venus. When the Normans arrived they built a castle on Monte San Giuliano, where today there's a lovely public park with benches and belvederes from which there are striking views of Trapani, the Egadi Islands offshore, and, on a *very* clear day, Cape Bon and the Tunisian coast. Because of Erice's elevation, clouds conceal much of the view for most of the winter. Sturdy shoes and something warm to wear are recommended.

Fans of Sicilian sweets make a beeline for **Pasticceria Grammatico** (✉ Via Vittorio Emanuele 14 ☎ 0923/869390). The place is run by Maria Grammatico, a former nun who gained international fame with *Bitter Almonds,* her life story cowritten with Mary Taylor Simeti. Her almond-paste creations are works of art, molded into striking shapes, including dolls and animals. The balcony from the tearoom upstairs has wonderful views. At **Pasticceria del Convento** (✉ Via Guarnotta 1 ☎ 0923/ 869777), Maria Grammatico's sister sells similar delectable treats.

Capo San Vito, 40 km (25 mi) from Erice, is a cape with a long sandy beach on a promontory overlooking a bay in the Gulf of Castellammare. The town there, San Vito Lo Capo, is famous for its North African couscous, made with fish instead of meat. In late September it hosts the five-day **Cus Cus Fest,** a serious international couscous competition and festival with live music and plenty of free tastings.

Where to Stay & Eat

$ ✕ **Monte San Giuliano.** Sit out on the tree-lined stone patio and sample spicy Arab-influenced seafood couscous—served with a bowl of fish broth on the side to add as you wish—or delicious grilled tuna. Wash it all down with a good white Donnafugata, from the Rallo vineyards at Marsala. Monte San Giuliano is satisfyingly traditional. It's hidden within the labyrinth of lanes that makes up Erice, near the main piazza. ✉ *Vicolo San Rocco 7* ☎ *0923/869595* ⊟ *AE, DC, MC, V* ⊘ *Closed Mon., 2 wks mid-Jan., and 1st 2 wks Nov.*

$$ ✕⌂ **Elimo.** Because it's on one of Erice's main cobblestone streets, the majority of the spacious rooms at this hotel have superb views overlooking the town's characteristic rooftops and the vast valley below. The mix of antiques and plasticky room doors adds a quirky dimension. Great views can also be had through the large picture window in Carmelo Tilotta's restaurant ($$–$$$), where fresh local ingredients take center stage. (Tilotta and marzipan guru Maria Grammatico have appeared together at the James Beard Foundation House.) ✉ *Via Vittorio Emanuele*

75, 91016 ☎ *0923/869377* 🖷 *0923/869252* ⇱ *21 rooms* ⚒ *Restaurant, minibars, bar, lounge, library* ⊟ *AE, DC, MC, V* ⍾ *BP.*

$-$$ ✕⊞ **Moderno.** This modern, delightful hotel is decorated with local crafts and has a lovely terrace and a well-known restaurant ($$) serving seafood pasta and homemade desserts. In winter the lobby fireplace is always blazing. Some rooms, along with a large lounge and bar, are directly across the street from the main hotel. ⊠ *Via Vittorio Emanuele 67, 91016* ☎ *0923/869300* 🖷 *0923/869139* ⊕ *www.hotelmodernoerice. it* ⇱ *40 rooms* ⚒ *Restaurant, minibars, bar* ⊟ *AE, DC, MC, V* ⊘ *Restaurant closed Mon. Apr.–Oct. No dinner Sun. Apr.–Oct.* ⍾ *BP.*

Segesta

㉔ *35 km (22 mi) east of Erice, 85 km (53 mi) southwest of Palermo.*

★ Segesta is the site of a **tempio Dorico** (Doric temple), one of Sicily's most impressive, constructed on the side of a windswept barren hill overlooking a valley of wild fennel. Virtually intact today, the temple is considered by some to be finer in its proportions and setting than any other Doric temple left standing. The temple was actually started in the 5th century BC by the Elymian people, who some believe were refugees from Troy. At the very least, evidence indicates that they were non-Greeks; for example, they often sided with the Carthaginians. However, the style is in many ways Greek. The temple was never finished; the walls and roof never materialized, and the columns were never fluted. A little more than 1 km (½ mi) away, near the top of the hill, are the remains of a fine **amphitheater,** with impressive views, especially at sunset, of nearby Monte Erice and the sea. ☎ *0924/952356* ⌧ €6 ⊘ *Oct.–Apr., Mon.–Sat. 9–4, Sun. 9–2; May–Sept., Mon.–Sat. 9–6, Sun. 9–2.*

Monreale

㉕ *59 km (37 mi) northeast of Segesta, 10 km (6 mi) southwest of Palermo.*

★ Monreale's splendid **Duomo** is lavishly executed with mosaics depicting events from the Old and New Testaments. After the Norman conquest of Sicily the new princes showcased their ambitions through monumental building projects. William II (1154–89) built the church complex with a cloister and palace between 1174 and 1185, employing Byzantine craftsmen. The result was a glorious fusion of Eastern and Western influences, widely regarded as the finest example of Norman architecture in Sicily.

> ## WORD OF MOUTH
>
> "The Cathedral of Monreale dwarfs everything in Palermo, and I mean everything. It's the grandest and most spectacular church in all of southern Italy." —GAC

The major attraction is the 68,220 square feet of glittering gold mosaics decorating the cathedral interior. *Christ Pantocrator* dominates the apse area; the nave contains narratives of the Creation; and scenes from the life of Christ adorn the walls of the aisles and the transept. The painted wooden ceiling dates from 1816–37. A small pair of binoculars will make

Prizzi's Honor

BURIED IN THE HEART of Mafia country (22 km [14 mi] west of Lercara Friddi, which gave the world the mobster Lucky Luciano), Prizzi, population 6,000, is a fairy-tale aerie, a floating apparition of twisting stone alleyways and brown rooftops gently dusting the peak of a 3,267-foot mountain. Its medieval layout and architecture—surreally frozen in another age—and dreamy views of the surrounding countryside, perhaps best seen at sunset, make it well worth a stop along the way between Palermo and Agrigento. Prizzi was founded by the Greeks in about 480 BC, and was alternately conquered by the Byzantines (8th century AD) and Saracens (9th century AD), the latter of whom built three lofty castles and created a "cult of water" with an elaborate network of drinking troughs. Christian conquest came in the 11th century.

The name "Prizzi" became known to the outside world through 1985's wryly comic mobster movie *Prizzi's Honor,* but the town feels as far removed as imaginable from Hollywood glamour and glitz. There's little in the way of significant art or monuments, and the secrets of the Mafia presence lie out of reach to visitors, buried in inaccessible crevices of local culture. But you can spend hours wandering in and out of the maze of steeply sloped alleyways, with tiny, still-inhabited houses built into the rock, eventually giving way to the remains of the three castles and the mountain's dazzling peak, from which, on a clear day, you can view the sea of Sciacca to one side and the cone of Mt. Etna to the other.

Coming from Palermo, follow the signs to Sciacca; both Prizzi and Corleone—another name familiar to moviegoers—are on the way.

---

it easier to read the Latin inscriptions. The roof commands a great view (a reward for climbing 172 stairs).

Bonnano Pisano's **bronze doors,** completed in 1186, depict 42 biblical scenes and are considered among the most important of medieval artifacts. Barisano da Trani's 42 panels on the north door, dating from 1179, present saints and evangelists. ⊠ *Piazza del Duomo* ☎ *091/6404413* ⊙ *May–Sept., daily 8–6; Oct.–Apr., daily 8–12:30 and 3:30–6.*

The lovely **cloister** of the abbey adjacent to the Duomo was built at the same time as the church but enlarged in the 14th century. The beautiful enclosure is surrounded by 216 double columns, every other one decorated in a unique glass mosaic pattern. Note the intricate carvings on the bases and the capitals. Afterward, don't forget to walk behind the cloister to the **belvedere,** with stunning panoramic views over the Conca d'Oro (Golden Conch) valley toward Palermo. The last tickets are sold a half hour before closing. ⊠ *Piazza del Duomo* ☎ *091/6404403* ▨ *€4.50* ⊙ *Mon.–Sat. 9–6:30, Sun. 9–1:30.*

Where to Eat

¢ ✕ **La Botte 1962.** It's worth the short drive or inexpensive taxi fare from Monreale to reach this restaurant, a good value for well-prepared local specialties. Dine alfresco on seafood-centered dishes such as *bavette don Carmelo,* a narrow version of tagliatelle with a swordfish ragù, squid, shrimp, and pine nuts. Other regular favorites include *involtini alla siciliana,* meat roulades stuffed with salami and cheese. Local wines are a good accompaniment. ☒ *Contrada Lenzitti 20, S186* ☎ *091/414051* ⊕ *www.mauriziocascino.it* ▤ *AE, DC, MC, V* ☉ *Closed Mon. and Aug. No dinner Sun.*

PALERMO

Once the intellectual capital of southern Europe, Palermo has always been at the crossroads of civilization. Favorably situated on a crescent-shape bay at the foot of Monte Pellegrino, it has attracted almost every culture touching the Mediterranean world. To Palermo's credit, it has absorbed these diverse cultures into a unique personality that is at once Arab and Christian, Byzantine and Roman, Norman and Italian. The city's heritage encompasses all of Sicily's varied ages, but its distinctive aspect is its Arab-Norman identity, an improbable marriage that, mixed in with Byzantine and Jewish elements, created some resplendent works of art. These are most notable in the churches, from small jewels such as San Giovanni degli Eremiti to larger-scale works such as the cathedral. No less noteworthy than the architecture is Palermo's chaotic vitality, on display at some of Italy's most vibrant outdoor markets, public squares, street bazaars, and food vendors, and above all in its grand, discordant symphony of motorists, motor bikers, and pedestrians that triumphantly climaxes in the new town center each evening with Italy's most spectacular passeggiata (the leisurely social stroll along the principal thoroughfare).

Exploring Palermo

Sicily's capital is a multilayered, vigorous metropolis; approach with an open mind when exploring the enriching city with a strong historical profile. You're likely to encounter some frustrating instances of inefficiency and, depending on the season, stifling heat. If you have a car, park it in a garage as soon as you can, and don't take it out until you are ready to depart.

Palermo is easily explored on foot, though you may choose to spend a morning taking a bus tour to help you get oriented. The Quattro Canti, or Four Corners, is the hub that separates the four sections of the old city: La Kalsa (the old Arab section) to the southeast, Albergheria to the southwest, Capo to the northwest, and Vucciria to the northeast. Each of these is a tumult of activity during the day, though at night the narrow alleys empty out and are best avoided altogether in favor of the more animated avenues of the new city north of Teatro Massimo. Sights to see by day are scattered along three major streets: Corso Vittorio Emanuele, Via Maqueda, and Via Roma. The tourist information office in Piazza Castelnuovo will give you a map and a valuable handout that lists opening and closing times, which sometimes change with the seasons.

PALERMO'S MULTICULTURAL PEDIGREE

Palermo was first colonized by Phoenician traders in the 6th century BC, but it was their descendants, the Carthaginians, who built the important fortress here that caught the covetous eye of the Romans. After the First Punic War the Romans took control of the city in the 3rd century BC. Following several invasions by the Vandals, Sicily was settled by Arabs, who made the country an emirate and established Palermo as a showpiece capital that rivaled both Cordoba and Cairo in the splendor of its architecture. Nestled in the fertile Conca d'Oro (Golden Conch) plain, full of orange, lemon, and carob groves and enclosed by limestone hills, Palermo became a magical world of palaces and mosques, minarets and palm trees.

It was so attractive and sophisticated a city that the Norman ruler Roger de Hauteville (1031–1101) decided to conquer it and make it his capital (1072). The Norman occupation of Sicily resulted in Palermo's golden age (1072–1194), a remarkable period of enlightenment and learning in which the arts flourished. The city of Palermo, which in the 11th century counted more than 300,000 inhabitants, became the European center for the Norman court and one of the most important ports for trade between East and West. Eventually the Normans were replaced by the Swabian ruler Frederick II (1194–1250), the Holy Roman Emperor, and incorporated into the Kingdom of the Two Sicilies. You will also see plenty of evidence in Palermo of the baroque art and architecture of the long Spanish rule. The Aragonese viceroys also brought the Spanish Inquisition to Palermo, which some historians believe helped foster the protective secret societies that evolved into today's Mafia.

The Main Attractions

★ ㉘ **Cattedrale.** This church is a lesson in Palermitan eclecticism—originally Norman (1182), then Catalan Gothic (14th–15th century), then fitted out with a baroque and neoclassical interior (18th century). Its turrets, towers, dome, and arches come together in the kind of meeting of diverse elements that King Roger II (1095–1154), whose tomb is inside along with that of Frederick II, fostered during his reign. The back of the apse is gracefully decorated with interlacing Arab arches inlaid with limestone and black volcanic tufa. ✉ *Corso Vittorio Emanuele, Capo* ☎ *091/ 334373* ⊕ *www.cattedrale.palermo.it* 🎫 *Church free, crypt €2* ◷ *Mon.–Sat. 8:30–1 and 4–5:30, Sun. 7:30–1:30 and 4–7.*

㊱ **Convento dei Cappuccini.** The spookiest sight in all of Sicily, this 16th-century catacomb houses more than 8,000 corpses of men, women, and young children, some in tombs but many mummified and preserved, hanging in rows on the walls. Many of the fully clothed corpses wear priests' smocks (most of the dead were Capuchin monks). The Capuchins were

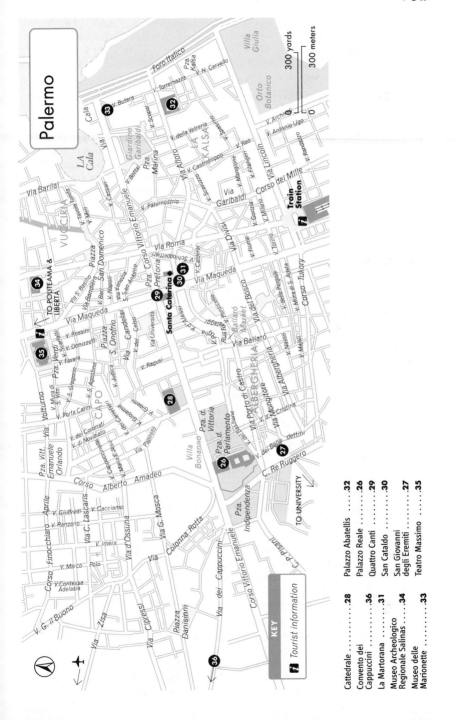

Palermo

KEY

i *Tourist information*

Cattedrale **28**

Convento dei
Cappuccini **36**

La Martorana **31**

Museo Archeologico
Regionale Salinas **34**

Museo delle
Marionette **33**

Palazzo Abatellis **32**

Palazzo Reale **26**

Quattro Canti **29**

San Cataldo **30**

San Giovanni
degli Eremiti **27**

Teatro Massimo **35**

300 yards

300 meters

founders and proprietors of the bizarre establishment from 1559 to 1880. It's memorable and not for the faint of heart; children might be frightened or disturbed. ⊠ *Piazza Cappuccini off Via Cappuccini, near Palazzo Reale* ☎ *091/212117* 🏛 *€1.50* ☉ *Thurs.–Sat., Mon., and Tues. 9–noon and 3–5; Sun. 3–5.*

③① La Martorana. Distinguished by an elegant Norman campanile, this church was erected in 1143 but had its interior altered considerably during the baroque period. High along the western wall, however, is some of the oldest and best-preserved mosaic artwork of the Norman period. Near the entrance is an interesting mosaic of King Roger II being crowned by Christ. In it Roger is dressed in a bejeweled Byzantine stole, reflecting the Norman court's penchant for all things Byzantine. Archangels along the ceiling wear the same stole wrapped around their shoulders and arms. The striking San Cataldo is adjacent; plan on visiting both churches in one outing. ⊠ *Piazza Bellini 3, Kalsa* ☎ *091/ 6161692* ☉ *Apr.–Oct., Mon.–Sat. 8–1 and 3:30–5:30, Sun. 3:30–7; Nov.–Mar., Mon.–Sat. 8–1 and 3:30–5:30.*

②⑥ Palazzo Reale (Royal Palace). This historic palace, also called Palazzo dei Normanni (Norman Palace), was for centuries the seat of Sicily's semiautonomous rulers. The building is an interesting mesh of abutting 10th-century Norman and 17th-century Spanish structures. Because it now houses the Sicilian Parliament, little is accessible to the public. The **Cappella Palatina** (Palatine Chapel) remains open. Built by Roger II in 1132, it's a dazzling example of the harmony of artistic elements produced under the Normans. Here the skill of French and Sicilian masons was brought to bear on the decorative purity of Arab ornamentation and the splendor of 11th-century Greek Byzantine mosaics. The interior is covered with glittering mosaics and capped by a splendid 10th-century Arab honeycomb stalactite wooden ceiling. Biblical stories blend happily with scenes of Arab life—look for one showing a picnic in a harem—and Norman court pageantry.

Upstairs are the royal apartments, including the **Sala di Re Ruggero** (King Roger's Hall), decorated with medieval murals of hunting scenes—an earlier (1120) secular counterpoint to the religious themes seen elsewhere. To see this area of the palace, ask one of the tour guides (free) to escort you around the halls once used by one of the most splendid courts in Europe (call in advance if you want to be sure a guide is available). French, Latin, and Arabic were spoken here, and Arab astronomers and poets exchanged ideas with Latin and Greek scholars in one of the most interesting marriages of culture in the Western world. ⊠ *Piazza Indipendenza, Albergheria* ☎ *091/7056001* 🏛 *Free* ☉ *Mon.–Sat. 8:30–noon and 2–5.*

★ ③⓪ San Cataldo. Three striking Saracenic scarlet domes mark this church, built in 1154 during the Norman occupation of Palermo. The church now belongs to the Knights of the Holy Sepulchre, and the spare but intense stone interior is rarely open to the public. Call ahead to arrange the requisite guided tour, or ask next door at La Martorana church. ⊠ *Piazza Bellini 3, Kalsa* ☎ *091/6375622* ☉ *By tour Sept.–May, Mon.–Sat. 9–1:30; June–Aug., Mon.–Sat. 9–12:30 and 4–7, Sun. by appointment only.*

27 **San Giovanni degli Eremiti.** Distinguished by its five reddish-orange domes and stripped-clean interior, this 12th-century church was built by the Normans on the site of an earlier mosque—one of 200 that once stood in Palermo. The emirs ruled Palermo for nearly two centuries and brought to it their passion for lush gardens and fountains. One is reminded of this while sitting in San Giovanni's delightful cloister of twin half columns, surrounded by palm trees, jasmine, oleander, and citrus trees. The last tickets are sold a half hour before closing. ⊠ *Via dei Benedettini, Albergheria* ☎ *091/6515019* ⊠ *€6* ⊗ *Mon.–Sat. 9–7, Sun. 9–1:30.*

35 **Teatro Massimo.** Construction of this formidable neoclassical theater was started in 1875 by Giovanni Battista Basile and completed by his son Ernesto in 1897. A fire in 1974 rendered the theater inoperable but it reopened with great fanfare in 1997, its interior as glorious as ever. *The Godfather Part III* ended with a famous shooting scene on the theater's steps. Visits are by 25-minute guided tour only; English-speaking guides are available 10–2 and 3–4. ⊠ *Piazza Verdi 9, at top of Via Maqueda, Olivella* ☎ *091/6090831, 0800/907080 ticket office* ⊕ *www. teatromassimo.it* ⊠ *€3* ⊗ *Tues.–Sun. 10–3:30, except during rehearsals; ticket office daily 10–5.*

Also Worth Seeing

34 **Museo Archeologico Regionale Salinas** (Salinas Regional Museum of Archaeology). Especially interesting pieces in this small but excellent collection are the examples of prehistoric cave drawings and a marvelously reconstructed Doric frieze from the Greek temple at Selinunte. The frieze reveals the high level of artistic culture attained by the Greek colonists in Sicily some 2,500 years ago. ⊠ *Piazza Olivella 24, Via Roma, Olivella* ☎ *091/6116805* ⊠ *€6* ⊗ *Tues.–Sat. 8:30–1:45 and 2:30–6:30, Sun. and Mon. 8:30–1:45.*

33 **Museo delle Marionette.** The traditional Sicilian *pupi* (puppets), with their glittering armor and fierce expressions, have become a symbol of Norman Sicily. Plots of the weekly performances center on the chivalric legends of the troubadours, who, before the puppet theater, kept alive tales of Norman heroes in Sicily such as Orlando Furioso and William the Bad (1120–66). ⊠ *Piazzetta Niscemi 1, at Via Butera, Kalsa* ☎ *091/ 328060* ⊕ *www.museomarionettepalermo.it* ⊠ *€5* ⊗ *Weekdays 10–1 and 3:30–6:30. Closed 2 wks in Aug.*

32 **Palazzo Abatellis.** Housed in this late-15th-century Catalan Gothic palace with Renaissance elements is the **Galleria Regionale**. Among its treasures are an *Annunciation* (1474) by Sicily's prominent Renaissance master Antonello da Messina (1430–79) and an arresting fresco by an unknown painter, titled *The Triumph of Death,* a macabre depiction of the plague years. ⊠ *Via Alloro 4, Kalsa* ☎ *091/6230011* ⊕ *www.regione.sicilia.it/ beniculturali/dirbenicult/palazzoabatellis/index.htm* ⊠ *€4.50, additional €3.50 for guided tour* ⊗ *Mon.–Sat. 9–1 and 2:30–7, Sun. 9–1.*

Piazza Pretoria. The square's centerpiece, a lavishly decorated fountain with 500 separate pieces of sculpture and an abundance of nude figures, so shocked some Palermitans when it was unveiled in 1575 that it got

15

the nickname "Fountain of Shame." It's even more of a sight when illuminated at night.

㉙ Quattro Canti. The Four Corners is the intersection of Corso Vittorio Emanuele and Via Maqueda. Four rather exhaust-blackened baroque palaces from Spanish rule meet at concave corners, each with its own fountain and representations of a Spanish ruler, patron saint, and one of the four seasons.

Where to Stay & Eat

$$$$ ✕ **Il Ristorantino.** Pippo Anastasio, one of the true personalities of Sicilian cooking, has created one of the most modern restaurants on the island. Here pesce spada reaches its loftiest heights, served simply marinated with olive oil, lemon, herb butter, and toast; meanwhile, Pippo's flights of fancy include *astice* (lobster) tortellini with cherry tomatoes, *bottarga* (cured tuna roe), and hot pepper. Dark wood contrasts with recessed lighting and stylized wall panels to create a design fusion that echoes the creativity of the menu. The suburban restaurant is an easy taxi ride from the center. ⊠ *Piazzale Alcide De Gasperi 19, Resuttana* ☎ *091/ 512861* ▤ *AE, DC, MC, V* ☿ *Closed Mon. and 2 wks in Aug.*

$$$ ✕ **Strascinu.** The region's ubiquitous Arab-Sicilian dish, pasta *con sarde* (with sardines and *mollica tostata*, the trademark toasted bread crumbs), takes center stage at this informal and busy restaurant on the city outskirts. Amphoras, Sicilian ceramics, and even a miniature, electrically operated puppet theater enliven the rustic decor, and there's a large garden with gazebos. ⊠ *Viale Regione Siciliana 2286, Circunvallazione* ☎ *091/401292* ▤ *AE, DC, MC, V* ☿ *Closed Aug. 14–28.*

★ $$$ ✕ **Osteria dei Vespri.** A foodie paradise occupies a cozy-but-elegant space on an unheralded piazza in the historic city center. Try the superb antipasto *sei variazioni di crudo dal mare* (six variations of raw delicacies from the sea). Sheep's cheese ravioli with basil, fresh tomato, eggplant, and crispy onions adds creative depth to traditional preparation. Local fish is presented in dishes like a *tagliata di tonno al pepe nero e semi di papavero* (cut of tuna with black pepper and poppy seeds), which is served with herb-infused oil, sweet and sour Tropea onions, and steamed spinach. The wine list is one of the best in Palermo. ⊠ *Piazza Croce dei Vespri 6, Kalsa* ☎ *091/6171631* ⊕ *www.osteriadeivespri.it* ▤ *AE, DC, MC, V* ☿ *Closed Sun. and 1 wk in Aug.*

$$$ ✕ **Ristorante Graziano.** Palermitans drive the 45 minutes to savor modern and startling combinations in chef Nino Graziano's traditional country house—probably Sicily's best restaurant. *Macco* (fava-bean puree), a staple of the rural poor, is playfully paired with scampi and finished with ricotta, *speck* (cured ham), peppercorns, and fried basil. Pistachios encrust a delicate pork fillet served with chocolate sauce, rice fritters, cinnamon applesauce, and swirls of raspberry. The wine list is excellent, and prices are reasonable—even for the spectacular tasting menu. Look for Ristorante Graziano (formerly called Il Mulinazzo) on the right side of SS121, after a car dealership; the tiny sign is easy to miss. ⊠ *SS121, Località Bolognetta Nord, 17 km (11 mi) southeast of Palermo, Villafrati* ☎ *091/8724870* ⊕ *www.ristorantegraziano.it* ▤ *AE, DC, MC, V* ☿ *Closed Mon., Jan., and July. No dinner Sun.*

FodorsChoice ★

$$ ✕ **Casa del Brodo.** On the edge of the Vucciria is a restaurant that dates to 1890, one of Palermo's oldest. In winter, tortellini *in brodo* (in beef broth), the restaurant's namesake, is the specialty of the house. Year-round you can't go wrong with *carni bollite* (boiled meats) or the *fritella di fave, piselli, carciofi, e ricotta* (fried fava beans, peas, artichokes, and ricotta). A mix of tourists and locals crowd the two small rooms. ⊠ *Corso Vittorio Emanuele 175, Vucciria* ☎ *091/321655* ⊕ *www.casadelbrodo.it* ⊟ *AE, DC, MC, V* ⊘ *Closed Tues. Nov.–Apr., Sun. May–Oct.*

$$ ✕ **Capricci di Sicilia.** Rumor has it that Capricci di Sicilia, in the heart of Palermo next to the Teatro Politeama, is the best place in town for *cassata siciliana* (sponge cake with sheep's-milk ricotta and candied fruit). Only typical Sicilian specialties are served here, such as tuna with garlic and mint, sardine *polpette* (minced sardine balls) in summer, and spaghetti with sausage and fresh ricotta. The place is a bit impersonal. ⊠ *Via Pignatelli 6, Piazza Luigi Sturzo, Vucciria* ☎ *091/327777* ⊟ *AE, DC, MC, V* ⊘ *Closed Mon.*

★ **$** ✕ **Osteria Altri Tempi.** The "olden days" restaurant is a favorite among locals searching for the true rustic cooking of their Sicilian ancestors. Knickknacks fill the walls of the small friendly space. A meal begins with a carafe of the house red set down without asking and a superb spread of traditional antipasti. Dishes have old Palermitan names: *fave a cunigghiu* is fava beans prepared with olive oil, garlic, and remarkably flavorful oregano; and *vampaciucia c'anciova* is a lasagna-like pasta dish with a concentrated sauce of tomatoes, anchovies, and grapes. The meal ends well, too, with free house-made herb or fruit liquors and excellent cannoli. ⊠ *Via Sammartino 65/67, Libertà* ☎ *091/323480* ⊟ *MC, V* ⊘ *Closed Aug. 15–Sept. 15. No dinner Sun.*

★ **¢** ✕ **Antica Focacceria San Francesco.** Turn-of-the-20th-century wooden cabinets, marble-top tables, and cast-iron ovens characterize this neighborhood bakery. Come here for the snacks that locals love—and from which you can make an inexpensive meal. The big pot on the counter holds the delicious regional specialty *pani ca meusa* (boiled, sliced calf's spleen with caciocavallo cheese and salt). The squeamish can opt for the *panelle* (chickpea flour fritters), the fantastic fritto misto, or an enormous *arancino* (breaded, deep-fried ball of rice) with tomato and meat or vegetable filling. ⊠ *Via Paternostro 58, Kalsa* ☎ *091/320264* ⊟ *AE, DC, MC, V* ⊘ *Closed Tues. Nov.–May and Jan. 9–24.*

¢ ✕ **Pani Ca Meusa.** This supremely local institution facing Palermo's old fishing port has had only one item on the menu—and one legendary manager–cum–sandwich maker—for more than 50 years. Calf's spleen sandwich, the joint's namesake, is sprinkled with a bit of salt and some lemon and served with or without cheese to a buzzing crowd of Palermo's battle-wearied elders. In our book, their sandwich beats the Antica Focacceria San Francesco's for the title of best in town. There's no seating, though—only counters—and the overall menu is better at San Francesco. ⊠ *Porta Carbone, Via Cala 62, Kalsa* ☎ *No phone* ⚓ *Reservations not accepted* ⊟ *No credit cards* ⊘ *Closed Sun. and Mon., and unpredictable other days.*

★ **$$$–$$$$** ▦ **Centrale Palace Hotel.** A stone's throw from Palermo's main historic sites, the Centrale is the only hotel in the heart of the centro storico that

15

was once a stately private palace. Built in 1717, the hotel weaves old-world charm with modern comfort like few establishments on the island. Salons are ornately furnished and "classic" rooms have antiques and reproductions. Forty "neoclassic" rooms (which are slightly pricier and done in a more modern elegance) were part of a 2003 expansion as were six spacious junior suites. The young, welcoming staff provides professional service. The rooftop restaurant serves creative Sicilian cuisine. ☒ *Corso Vittorio Emanuele 327, Vucciria, 90134* ☎ *091/336666* 🖷 *091/334881* ⊕ *www.centralepalacehotel.it* ⤺ *104 rooms* ⚉ *Restaurant, some in-room safes, some in-room hot tubs, minibars, cable TV, in-room broadband, bar, free parking* ⊟ *AE, DC, MC, V* ⓧ *BP.*

$$$$ 🏨 **Villa Igiea.** Take a short taxi ride (through some rough-looking districts of Palermo) to an oasis of luxury and comfort in a private tropical garden at the edge of the bay. A meander through the grounds reveals such relics as an ancient Greek temple at the water's edge. Large rooms are furnished individually, the nicest with an Italian art nouveau flavor. Spacious lobbies and public rooms unfold onto a terrace and restaurant. There's infrequent shuttle service to the city center; a €12 taxi ride is more convenient. ☒ *Salita Belmonte 43, 90142 Acquasanta, 3 km (2 mi) north of Palermo* ☎ *091/6312111* 🖷 *091/547654* ⊕ *www.villaigieapalermo.it* ⤺ *110 rooms, 6 suites* ⚉ *Restaurant, minibars, tennis court, pool, gym, bar, free parking* ⊟ *AE, DC, MC, V* ⓧ *BP.*

$$$ 🏨 **Hotel Principe di Villafranca.** Fine Sicilian antiques, imperial striped silks, creamy marble floors, and vaulted ceilings evoke a luxurious private home not far from Palermo's glitzy shopping district. It's easy to get comfortable in the understated surroundings: relax in the library with an aperitif or savor an authentic meal in the rustic adjoining Ristorante Firriato, which drizzles its dishes with a sublime, homemade balsamic vinegar. Rooms are elegant, with fine linens and more antiques. Ask for a room on the street side; back rooms can actually be noisier. ☒ *Via G. Turrisi Colonna 4, Libertà, 90141* ☎ *091/6118523* 🖷 *091/588705* ⊕ *www.principedivillafranca.it* ⤺ *32 rooms, 2 suites* ⚉ *Restaurant, café, Wi-Fi, gym, library, meeting room, free parking* ⊟ *AE, DC, MC, V* ⓧ *BP.*

$$$ 🏨 **Massimo Plaza Hotel.** This hotel has one of Palermo's best locations—opposite the renovated Teatro Massimo. It is small and select; the few rooms are spacious, comfortably furnished, and well insulated from the noise on Via Maqueda. Service is personal and polite, with continental breakfast served in your room with the newspaper of your choice. Book in advance for one of the seven rooms that have theater views. ☒ *Via Maqueda 437, Vucciria, 90133* ☎ *091/325657* 🖷 *091/325711* ⊕ *www.massimoplazahotel.com* ⤺ *15 rooms* ⚉ *Minibars, cable TV, bar, Internet room, parking (fee)* ⊟ *AE, DC, MC, V* ⓧ *BP.*

$$$ 🏨 **Mondello Palace.** In summer, Mondello Palace, the leading hotel at the Mondello resort, is indisputably the place to be. Making the best use of its private beach location just north of Palermo, there are cabins and changing rooms for the use of hotel patrons. The rooms are large, with luxury baths, and most have balconies. ☒ *Viale Principe di Scalea, 90139 Mondello Lido* ☎ *091/450001* 🖷 *091/450657* ⊕ *www.mondellopalace.it* ⤺ *83 rooms, 9 suites* ⚉ *Restaurant, minibars, pool, beach, bar, free parking, some pets allowed* ⊟ *AE, DC, MC, V* ⓧ *BP.*

$ 🏨 **Hotel Moderno.** Right down to the 1930s technology at the reception desk, this third-floor hotel is a slice of slow old Palermo—perhaps the name is meant to be ironic. But the location and rates couldn't be better. (Singles are a particularly good deal, at not much more than half the double room rate.) A slightly shabby, mirrored reception area and bar give way to simple but clean and comfortable rooms, some with balconies overlooking Via Roma. ⊠ *Via Roma 276, corner of Via Napoli, Vucciria, 90139* ☎*091/588683* 🖷*091/588260* ⊕*www.hotelmodernopa. com* ⇄ *38 rooms* ⚐ *Bar, parking (fee)* ▭ *AE, DC, MC, V* ⦿ *BP.*

Nightlife & the Arts

The Arts

CONCERTS & **Teatro Massimo** (⊠ Piazza Verdi at the top of Via Maqueda, Capo ☎ 091/
OPERA 6053111 ⊕ www.teatromassimo.it), modeled after the Pantheon in Rome, is truly larger than life—it's the biggest theater in Italy. Concerts and operas are presented throughout the year. Live out your *Godfather* fantasies; an opera at the Massimo is an unforgettable Sicilian experience. The shamelessly grandiose neoclassical **Teatro Politeama Garibaldi** (⊠ Piazza Ruggero Settimo, Libertà ☎ 091/6053315) stages a season of opera and orchestral works from November through May.

FESTIVALS The **Festa di Santa Rosalia** street fair is held July 10–15 in honor of the city's patron saint. Fireworks light up the evenings. **Epiphany** (January 6) is celebrated with Byzantine rites and a procession of townspeople in local costume through the streets of Piana degli Albanesi, 24 km (15 mi) south of Palermo. The village is named for the Albanian immigrants who first settled there, bringing with them the Byzantine Catholic rite.

PUPPET SHOWS Palermo's tradition of puppet theater holds an appeal for children and adults alike. Street artists often perform outside the Teatro Massimo in summer. The **Figli d'Arte Cuticchio Association** (⊠ Via Bara all'Olivella 95, Kalsa ☎ 091/323400 ⊕ www.figlidartecuticchio.com ⧉ €6) hosts performances September–May on most Saturdays and Sundays at 6:30, with the occasional morning performance scheduled as well.

Nightlife

Each night between 6 and 9 PM, Palermo's youth gather to shop, socialize, flirt, and plan the evening's affairs in an epic passeggiata along Via Ruggero Settimo (a northern extension of Via Maqueda) and filling Piazza Ruggero Settimo in front of Teatro Politeama. Some trendy bars also line Via Principe del Belmonte, intersecting with Via Roma and Via Ruggero Settimo.

BARS & CAFÉS **Kursaal Kalhesa** (⊠ Foro Umberto I 21, Kalsa ☎ 091/6162111 ⊕ www. kursaalkalhesa.it) is one of the most fascinating places to drink or socialize down by the port and the Porta Felice. An energetic, eclectic crowd of Palermitan youth takes in lively jazz, coffee, and drinks inside an ancient city wall with spectacular 100-foot ceilings and an idyllic courtyard—it's truly representative of the New Palermo. There's live music (primarily jazz) Thursday night. Excellent, if pricey, Sicilian food with an Arab touch is served in the adjacent restaurant. Kursaal Kalhesa is closed Sunday night and Monday.

15

Parco Letterario Giuseppe Tomasi di Lampedusa (✉ Vicolo della Neve al-l'Alloro 25, near Piazza Marina, Kalsa ☎ 091/6160796 ⊕ www.parcotomasi.it) is a cultural center, wine bar, café, language school, and historic-tour operator. The center, open Tuesday–Sunday 9 AM–1 AM, runs courses in Italian for foreigners, has excellent local wines and a student social scene, and hosts art shows. The little library (and just about everything else) focuses not just on Palermitan history but on the life and times of the center's namesake, Lampedusa, author of the canonical *Il Gattopardo (The Leopard)*. ˙

NIGHTCLUBS   Most nightclubs and discotheques are scattered around the northern, newer end of town. In summer the nightlife scene shifts to Mondello, Palermo's seaside satellite town on the other side of Monte Pellegrino. **Bar Costa** (✉ Via G. D'Annunzio 15, Libertà ☎ 091/334835) overflows with Italian bar-style treats, coffee, and so on; they also ship their famous delicacies abroad. **Mikalsa** (✉ Via Torremuzza 27, Kalsa ☎ 339/3146466) is a hip, coolly lighted nightspot with Sicily's best selection of Belgian beers. Try the interesting, unpasteurized Wild Spirit beer, a painstaking product of one of Sicily's first microbreweries (also available elsewhere around town). **Tonnara Florio** (✉ Discesa Tonnara 4, Arenella suburbs ☎ 091/6375611) is a striking disco-bar-restaurant in a former tuna-packing plant.

Shopping

North of Piazza Castelnuovo, Via della Libertà and the streets around it represent the luxury end of the shopping scale, with some of Palermo's best-known stores. A second nerve center for shoppers is the pair of parallel streets connecting modern Palermo with the train station, Via Roma, and Via Maqueda, where boutiques and shoe shops become increasingly upmarket as you move from the Quattro Canti past Teatro Massimo to Via Ruggero Settimo.

Most shops are open 9–1 and 4 or 4:30–7:30 or 8 and closed Sunday; in addition, most food shops close Wednesday afternoon, and other shops normally close Monday morning.

A GOOD WALK: PALERMO PASSEGGIATA

It is surely one of Sicily's—and Italy's—greatest pleasures to take one's place in the procession of the evening's passeggiata. The passeggiata may be roughly translated as "a walk around," but it is more than that. The Sicilian passeggiata is a graceful dance of Italian pedestrians flirting with shop windows, with ice cream, and with each other, a nightly voyage whose provenance is also its only destination: the city street.

Generally speaking, in Palermo, as elsewhere, the passeggiata begins somewhere around 7 PM on most nights, and continues until 9 PM or so. On Friday and Saturday, the pedestrians stay out later—until at least 10 PM, which is when many Italians go out for pizza on weekend evenings—and even past that hour, there is no letup in the amount of foot traffic as the evening wears on, just a gradual replacement of the older crowd with younger carousers.

Clothing & Fabric

The classy **Carieri & Carieri** (✉ Via E. Parisi 4, Libertà ☎ 091/321846) has an extensive selection of men's suits and shirts. For men's shirts and suits near the Quattro Canti, try the elegant but friendly **Barbisio** (✉ Corso Vittorio Emanuele 284–298, Quattro Canti ☎ 091/329992).

Seekers of fringes, tassels, and heavy fabrics stop at **Giuseppe Gramuglia** (✉ Via Roma 412–414, at Via Principe di Belmonte, Vucciria ☎ 091/583262).

Food & Wine

Enoteca Picone (✉ Via Marconi 36, Libertà ☎ 091/331300 ⊕ www.enotecapicone.it) is the best wine shop in town, with a fantastic selection of Sicilian and national wines. You can taste a selection of wines by the glass in the front of the store; sometimes there's also table service in the back, where meats and cheeses are also served. **Pasticceria Alba** (✉ Piazza Don Bosco 7/c, off Via della Libertà near La Favorita Park, Libertà ☎ 091/309016 ⊕ www.albasrl.it) is the place to find all the favorite Sicilian pastries such as cannoli and cassata siciliana.

The charming **I Peccatucci di Mamma Andrea** (Mamma Andrea's Small Sins; ✉ Via Principe di Scordia 67, near Piazza Florio, Vucciria ☎ 091/334835) sells a plethora of mouthwatering original creations, including jams, preserves, candies, liqueurs, honey, and Sicilian treats like superb *frutta di Martorana,* fruits, and other shapes made out of marzipan.

Markets

If you're interested in truly connecting with local life while searching for souvenirs, a visit to one of Palermo's many bustling markets is essential. Between Via Roma and Via Maqueda the many **bancherelle** (market stalls) on Via Bandiera sell everything from socks to imitation designer handbags.

★ It's easy to see how the **Vucciria Market** got its name, which translates in dialect as "voices" or "hubbub." Palermo's most established outdoor market in the heart of the centro storico is a maze of side streets around Piazza San Domenico, where hawkers deliver incessant chants from behind stands brimming with mounds of olives, blood oranges, wild fennel, and

Palermo has one of Sicily's—and all of Italy's—most vibrant evening passeggiate, and it's centered around Piazza Ruggero Settimo in front of the **Teatro Politeama.** Pedestrians stream in two different directions from the Politeama; to join in the passeggiata, you can take either route (or both). One streams up **Viale della Libertà,** where the most elegant boutiques lie; the other heads down **Via Ruggero Settimo** at least as far as the impressive **Teatro Massimo** ㉟, which will be on your right coming from the Politeama. There, you can stop for a moment to reenact the last scene of *The Godfather 3.* On either of those wide avenues you'll doubtless find yourself window-shopping at the boutiques that deck out Palermo's most modern quarter, as the Italians do—it's perhaps the most characteristic aspect of the passeggiata.

Drinking a coffee, eating gelato, or taking an *aperitivo*—a short, lightly alcoholic drink such as Campari or Aperol that whets the appetite for dinner—is also an essential part of the passeggiata. However, in stark contrast to the café cultures in other parts of Europe such as France and Spain, don't expect to see many

long-stem artichokes. One hawker will be going at the trunk of a sword-fish with a cleaver while across the way another holds up a giant squid or dangles an octopus. Morning is the best time to see the market in full swing.

Wind your way through the Albergheria district and the historic **Ballarò Market,** where the Saracens did their shopping in the 11th century—joined by the Normans in the 12th. The market remains faithful to seasonal change as well as the original Arab commerce of fruit, vegetables, and grain. Go early; the action dies out by 4 PM most days.

> **WORD OF MOUTH**
>
> "The Vucciria market: what a sight! Every kind of fresh meat (by fresh I mean the whole animal hanging by rope), fish, vegetables, etc. We bought several vacuum-packed packages of olives and sun-dried tomatoes to bring back as gifts."
> —AP6380

THE TYRRHENIAN COAST

Sicily's northern shore, the Tyrrhenian coast, is mostly a succession of small holiday towns interspersed with stretches of sand. It's often difficult to find a calm spot among the thousands of tourists and locals in high summer, though the scene quiets down considerably after August. The biggest attraction is the old town of Cefalù, with one of Sicily's most remarkable medieval cathedrals, encrusted with mosaics. The coast on either side is dotted with ancient archaeological remains and Arab-Norman buildings. A couple of miles south of Cefalù, Pizzo Carbonara (6,500 feet) is the highest peak in Sicily after Mt. Etna. Piano della Battaglia has a fully equipped ski resort with lifts. The area has a very un-Sicilian aspect, with Swiss-type chalets, hiking paths, and even alpine churches.

Cefalù

★ *70 km (42 mi) east of Palermo, 161 km (80 mi) west of Messina.*

Cefalù is a classically appealing Sicilian old town built on a spur jutting out into the sea. It's dominated by a massive rock—*la rocca*—and a 12th-century Romanesque **Duomo,** one of the finest Norman cathedrals in Italy.

folks relaxing at tables and chairs with their libations, watching the world go by. This is a standing culture, not a sitting one, and if you want to do as the Italians do, you'll down your diminutive cup of coffee or little glass of bright red bitter liqueur in a few seconds, or get your ice cream to go, and continue on your way. There are scores of coffeeshops and ice-cream joints all along Viale Libertà and Via Ruggero Settimo, as well as around the Politeama; most are essentially similar, so you shouldn't worry too much about trying to find the best or most famous place for a refreshment. After all, the real experience is to be had outside.

Ruggero II began the church in 1131 as an offering of thanks for having been saved here from a shipwreck. Its mosaics rival those of Monreale; whereas Monreale's Byzantine Pantocratic Christ figure is an austere and powerful image, emphasizing Christ's divinity, the Cefalù Christ is softer, more compassionate, and more human. The traffic going in and out of Cefalù town can be heavy in summer; you may want to take the 50-minute train ride from Palermo instead of driving. At the Duomo you must be suitably attired—no shorts or beachwear are permitted. ⊠ *Piazza Duomo* ☎ *0921/922021* ⊘ *Daily 8–6.*:

Where to Stay & Eat

$–$$$ ✕ **Al Gabbiano.** Its name, which translates "seagull," is an appropriate name for a beachside seafood restaurant with a nautical theme. House specialties are *involtini di pesce spada* (swordfish roulades) and spaghetti marinara. ⊠ *Via Lungomare Giardina 17* ☎ *0921/421495* ▭ *AE, DC, MC, V* ⊘ *Closed Wed. and Nov.–Jan.*

$$ ✕ **Al Porticciolo.** Nicola Mendolia's restaurant is comfortable, casual, and faithfully focused on the food. You might start with the *calamaretti piccoli fritti* (fried baby squid and octopus) and then follow with one of the chef's specials, which change weekly. Regardless, a refreshing *sgroppino* (whipped lemon sorbet with spumante) should end the meal. Dark, heavy, wooden tables create a comfortable environment filled with a mix of jovial locals and businesspeople. ⊠ *Via C. Ortolani di Bordonaro 66* ☎ *0921/921981* ▭ *AE, DC, MC, V* ⊘ *Closed Wed. Nov.–Apr. and Dec.*

$$ ▦ **Kalura.** Caldura, 2 km (1 mi) east along the coast, is the site of this modern hotel on a small promontory that's hard to reach without a car; it's only a few minutes by taxi from Cefalù, however. Sports facilities keep you from getting too sedentary, and the private beach is ideal for swimming. Rooms are bright and cheerful. Half board is required in July and August. ⊠ *Via V. Cavallaro 13, 90015 Località Caldura* ☎ *0921/421354* ▭ *0921/423122* ⊕ *www.hotelkalura.com* ⇨ *65 rooms* ⊘ *Restaurant, tennis court, pool, beach, bar, Internet room* ▭ *AE, DC, MC, V* ℺ *MAP.*

Santo Stefano di Camastra

38 *33 km (20 mi) east of Cefalù, 128 km (80 mi) west of Messina.*

When the original village of Santo Stefano di Camastra was destroyed in a landslide in 1682, the local duke, Giuseppe Lanza, rebuilt it on the coast according to strict military principles—a geometric street grid and artery roads connecting the center with the periphery. Today Santo Stefano is filled with the vividly colored pottery for which the town has an international reputation. For a comprehensive pottery education, drop in on the **Museo della Ceramica** in the center of town. ⊠ *Via Palazzo* ☎ *0921/331110* ▱ *Free* ⊘ *June–Sept., weekdays 9–1 and 4–8; Oct.–May, weekdays 9–1 and 3:30–7:30.*

Shopping

The Franco family has a long tradition of creating ceramic objets d'art by borrowing styles from past eras. Thus, Renaissance Madonnas rub

15

shoulders with florid baroque vases, all richly colored and skillfully finished. Call ahead to visit their ceramic laboratory or the two outlets of **Ceramiche Franco** (✉ Via Nazionale 8 ☎ 0921/337222, 347/6004506 for reservations ✉ Via Vittoria 4 ☎ 0921/339925), as the stores don't have set hours.

THE AEOLIAN ISLANDS

Off Sicily's northeast coast lies an archipelago of seven spectacular islands of volcanic origin. The Isole Eolie (Aeolian Islands), also known as the Isole Lipari (Lipari Islands), were named after Aeolus, the Greek god of the winds, who is said to keep all the Earth's winds stuffed in a bag in his cave here. The Aeolians are a world of grottoes and clear-water caves carved by waves through the centuries. Superb snorkeling and scuba diving abound in the clearest and cleanest of Italy's waters. The beautiful people of high society discovered the archipelago years ago—here Roberto Rossellini courted his future wife, the star Ingrid Bergman, in 1950—and you should not expect complete isolation, at least on the main islands. August, in particular, can get unpleasantly overcrowded, and lodging and travel should always be booked as early as possible.

Lipari provides the widest range of accommodations and is a good jumping-off point for day trips to the other islands. Most exclusive are Vulcano and Panarea, the former noted for its black sands and stupendous sunsets (and prices), as well as the acrid smell of its sulfur emissions, whereas the latter is, according to some, the prettiest. Most remarkable is Stromboli (pronounced with the accent on the first syllable) with its constant eruptions, and remotest are Filicudi and Alicudi, where electricity was introduced only in the 1980s. Access to the islands is via ferry and hydrofoil from Milazzo (on Sicily) or from Naples. The bars in the Aeolian Islands, and especially those on Lipari, are known for their granitas of fresh strawberries, melon, peaches, and other fruits. Many Sicilians on the Aeolians (and in Messina, Taormina, and Catania) begin the hot summer days with a granita *di caffè* (a coffee ice topped with whipped cream), into which they dunk their breakfast rolls. You can get one any time of day.

Vulcano

❸❾ *18 km (11 mi) south of Lipari, 25 mins by ferry, 10 mins by hydrofoil; 55 km (34 mi) northwest of Milazzo, 90 minutes by ferry.*

True to its name—and the origin of the term—Vulcano has a profusion of fumaroles sending up jets of hot vapor, but the volcano here has long been dormant. Many come to soak in the strong-smelling sulfur springs: when the wind is right, the odors greet you long before you disembark. The island has some of the archipelago's best beaches, though the volcanic black sand can be off-putting at first. You can ascend to the crater (1,266 feet above sea level) on muleback for a wonderful view or take boat rides into the grottoes around the base. From Capo Grillo there is a view of all the Aeolians.

Where to Stay

★ **$$$–$$$$** ⊞ **Les Sables Noires.** Named for the black sands of the private beach in front, this luxury hotel is superbly sited on the beautiful Porto di Ponente. The cool modern furnishings and inviting pool induce a sybaritic mood, and the white-wall guest rooms are tasteful and spacious. The restaurant, naturally, looks out over the bay: sunsets are framed by the towering faraglioni. Weeklong stays are required in high season. ⊠ *Porto di Ponente, 98050* ☎ *090/9850* 🖶 *090/9852454* ⊕ *www.framonhotels.com* ⤴ *48 rooms* ♨ *Restaurant, pool, beach, bar* ▭ *AE, DC, MC, V* ⊘ *Closed mid-Oct.–mid-Apr.* �‖ *BP.*

Lipari

❹⓿ *37 km (23 mi) north of Milazzo, 2 hrs, 10 mins by ferry, 1 hr by hydrofoil; Milazzo: 41 km (25 mi) west of Messina.*

The largest and most developed of the Aeolians, Lipari welcomes you with distinctive pastel-color houses. Fields of spiky agaves dot the northernmost tip of the island, Acquacalda, indented with pumice and obsidian quarries. In the west is San Calogero, where you can explore hot springs and mud baths. From the red-lava base of the island rises a plateau crowned with a 16th-century castle and a 17th-century cathedral.

★ The vast, multibuilding **Museo Eoliano** is a terrific archaeological museum, with an intelligently arranged collection of prehistoric finds—some dating as far back as 4000 BC—from various sites in the archipelago. ⊠ *Via Castello* ☎ *090/9880174* 🎟 *€6* ⊘ *Daily 9–1:30 and 3–7; ticket booth closes at 1 PM for morning visits and 6 PM for afternoon visits.*

Where to Stay & Eat

$$$ ⊞ **Gattopardo Park Hotel.** Bright bougainvillea and fiery hibiscus set the tone at this grand villa, and its restaurant has sweeping views of the sea. Guest quarters are in the 19th-century main villa or in whitewashed bungalows in the surrounding tranquil parkland. Public rooms have wood-beam ceilings and rustic-style furnishings. A minibus shuttles between the hotel and Spiagge Bianche, one of Lipari's better beaches. There are also trips around the island, boat excursions to Vulcano and Stromboli, and folklore evenings. Weekly discounts are available. ⊠ *Via Diana, 98055* ☎ *090/9811035* 🖶 *090/9880207* ⊕ *www.gattopardoparkhotel.it* ⤴ *53 rooms* ♨ *Restaurant, bar, pool* ▭ *MC, V* ⊘ *Closed Nov.–Mar.* �‖ *MAP.*

★ **$$$** ✕⊞ **Il Filippino.** The views from the flower-strewn outdoor terrace of this restaurant in the upper town are a fitting complement to the superb fare. Founded in 1910, the restaurant ($$–$$$) is rightly rated one of the archipelago's best. Top choice is seafood: the *zuppa di pesce* (fish soup) and the antipasto platter of smoked and marinated fish are absolute musts. Leave some room for the local version of cassata siciliana, accompanied by sweet Malvasia wine from Salina. The restaurant also runs Residence Mendolita, a comfortable B&B 300 yards away. The basic rooms are furnished in a style a bit reminiscent of a kids' rec room. ⊠ *Piazza Municipio* ☎ *090/9811002, 090/9812374 Mendolita* 🖶 *090/9812878* ⊕ *www.bernardigroup.it* ⤴ *18 rooms, 1 suite* ♨ *In-room safes, minibars, in-room data ports* ▭ *DC, MC, V* �‖ *BP.*

15

Salina

❹❶ *15 km (9 mi) north of Lipari, 50 mins by ferry, 20 mins by hydrofoil; 52 km (38 mi) northwest of Milazzo.*

The second largest of the Aeolian Islands, Salina is also the most fertile—which accounts for its excellent Malvasia dessert wine, unlike that found on other islands. Salina is also the highest of the islands, Mt. Fossa delle Felci rises to more than 3,000 feet, and the vineyards and fishing villages along its slopes add to its allure. Accommodations and restaurants are reasonable, and there are smaller crowds than on Lipari.

Where to Stay

$$$ 🏨 **Bellavista.** This is a quiet hotel in a quiet location, even though it's right next to the port. Rooms are simply furnished and cheerfully decorated with bright materials and ceramic tiles. Almost all have sea views, which can be enjoyed from the balconies. The management provides a list of things to do while on Salina and can organize boat excursions and transport around the island, though you may well opt for the *dolce far niente* (idle life). ⊠ *Via Risorgimento, Santa Marina Salina, 98050* 🖂📠 *090/9843009, 090/9281558 in winter* 🛏 *13 rooms* ☖ *Bar* 🖃 *No credit cards* ⊘ *Closed Oct.–Mar.* �“⊙| *BP.*

Panarea

❹❷ *18 km (11 mi) north of Lipari, 2 hrs by ferry, 25–50 mins by hydrofoil; 55 km (33 mi) north of Milazzo.*

Panarea has some of the most dramatic scenery of the islands: wild caves carved out of the rock and dazzling flora. The exceptionally clear water and the richness of life on the sea floor make Panarea especially suitable for underwater exploration, though there is little in the way of beaches. The outlying rocks and islets make a gorgeous sight, and you can enjoy the panorama on an easy excursion to the small Bronze Age village at Capo Milazzese.

Where to Stay

$$$$ 🏨 **La Raya.** This discreet, expensive hotel is perfectly in keeping with the elite style of Panarea, most exclusive of the Aeolian islands. Public rooms, including bars, a broad terrace, and an open-air restaurant, are built into a hillside right on the port; the residential area is a 10-minute walk inland, though the rooms still enjoy the serene prospect of the sea and Stromboli from their balconies. The decor is elegant and understated, with Moorish-type hangings and low divans helping to create a tone of serene luxury. Families with young children are asked to book elsewhere. ⊠ *San Pietro, 98050* 🖂📠 *090/983103* ⊕ *www.hotelraya.it* 🛏 *30 rooms* ☖ *Restaurant, minibars, bar, nightclub* 🖃 *AE, DC, MC, V* ⊘ *Closed Oct. 17–Mar. 25* �“⊙| *BP.*

Stromboli

❹❸ *40 km (25 mi) north of Lipari, 3 hrs, 45 mins by ferry, 65–90 mins by hydrofoil; 63 km (40 mi) north of Milazzo.*

This northernmost of the Aeolians (also accessible from Naples) consists entirely of the cone of an active volcano. The view from the sea—especially at night, as an endless stream of glowing red-hot lava flows into the water—is unforgettable. Stromboli is in a constant state of mild dissatisfaction, and every now and then its anger flares up, so authorities insist that you climb to the top (about 3,031 feet above sea level) only with a guide. The round-trip—climb, pause, and descent—usually starting around 6 PM, takes about four hours; the lava is much more impressive after dark. Some choose to camp overnight atop the volcano—again, a guide is essential. The main town has a small selection of reasonably priced hotels and restaurants and a choice of lively clubs and cafés for the younger set. In addition to the island tour, excursions might include boat trips around the naturally battlemented isle of Strombolicchio.

Numerous tour operators have guides that can lead you up Stromboli, among them **Società Navigazione Pippo** (☎ 090/986135 or 0338/9857883). Rates are around €20 per person for four hours.

15

Filicudi

④④ *30 km (16 mi) west of Salina, 30–60 mins by hydrofoil; 82 km (54 mi) northwest of Milazzo.*

Just a dot in the sea, Filicudi is famous for its unusual volcanic rock formations and the enchanting *Grotta del Bue Marino* (Grotto of the Sea Ox). The crumbled remains of a prehistoric village are at Capo Graziano. The island, which is spectacular for walking and hiking and is still a truly undiscovered, restful haven, has a handful of hotels and pensions, and some families put up guests. Car ferries are available only in summer.

Where to Stay

★ $$$ 🏨 **La Canna.** Set on a height above the tiny port, this hotel commands fabulous views of sky and sea from its flower-filled terrace. It's wonderful to wake up to the utter tranquillity that characterizes any stay on this island. Rooms are small but adequate, kept clean and tidy by the friendly family staff. The cooking is quite good, usually centered around the day's catch (half or full board required in peak season). Arrange ahead of time to be collected at the port. ⊠ *Via Rosa 43, 98050* ☎ *090/9889956* 🖷 *090/9889966* ⊕ *www.lacannahotel.it* ⇆ *14 rooms* ⚘ *Restaurant, in-room safes, bar, pool* ⊟ *DC, MC, V* ⊙❘ *MAP.*

Alicudi

④⑤ *65 km (40 mi) west of Lipari, 3 hrs, 25 mins–3 hrs, 50 mins by ferry, 60–95 mins by hydrofoil; 102 km (68 mi) northwest of Milazzo.*

The farthest outpost of the Aeolians remains sparsely inhabited, wild, and at peace. Here and on Filicudi there is a tiny selection of accommodations, but you can rent rooms cheaply. Only the coming and going of hydrofoils (which run only occasionally, especially October–April) disturbs the rhythm of life here, and the only noise is the occasional braying of donkeys.

SICILY ESSENTIALS

Transportation

BY AIR

Sicily can be reached from all major international cities on flights connecting through Rome, Milan, or Naples on Alitalia. Meridiana, Air One, and Volare also connect Catania and Palermo to other cities all over Italy, and Alitalia operates periodic connections to Cagliari in Sardinia. There are also direct flights to Sicily from London on Meridiana and from Munich on Lufthansa. Note that domestic flights to and from Sicily, especially one-way flights, are much cheaper when purchased from travel agencies in Italy than internationally or through Web sites.

Planes to Palermo land at Aeroporto Falcone-Borsellino (named in memory of two anti-Mafia judges famously assassinated in 1992) in Punta Raisi, 32 km (19 mi) west of town. Catania's Aeroporto Fontanarossa, 5 km (3 mi) south of the city center, is the main airport on Sicily's eastern side.

Airport Information **Aeroporto Falcone-Borsellino** ☎ 091/7020127 ⊕ www.gesap. it. **Aeroporto Fontanarossa** ☎ 095/340505 ⊕ www.aeroporto.catania.it.

TRANSFERS Prestia & Comandè buses run every half hour between Palermo's Punta Raisi airport and the city center (Piazza Castelnuovo and the central station); tickets cost €4.80. Taxis charge around €35 for the same 45-minute trip. To get directly to the train station, take the hourly train leaving from the airport, Trinacria Express, which takes 40 minutes and costs €4.50. There are also less-frequent bus connections directly to and from Agrigento and Trapani on Sal and Segesta lines, respectively. Catania's Fontanarossa airport is served by Alibus, which leaves about every 20 minutes from the airport and the central train station, with stops at Piazza Stesicoro, on Via Etnea, at the Duomo, and so on. The journey takes around 25 minutes; tickets cost €1. Taxis cost around €20.

Taxis & Shuttles **Alibus** ☎ 095/7360450. **Prestia & Comandè** ☎ 091/580457 or 091/586351. **Sal Lines** ☎ 0922/401360. **Segesta Lines** ☎ 091/6167919

BY BOAT & FERRY

Frequent car ferries, run by Caronte & Tourist, cross the strait between Villa San Giovanni in Calabria and Messina on the island, costing €23 per car. The crossing usually takes about a half hour, and ferries leave about every 15 minutes, but during the summer months there can be considerable delays. Overnight car ferries operated by Tirrenia run all year between Naples and Palermo. Tirrenia also runs regular service between Palermo and Cagliari, Sardinia. SNAV has faster service between Palermo and Naples during the day, as well as a route between Palermo and Civitavecchia (near Rome). Passenger-only hydrofoils also cross the strait from Reggio di Calabria to Messina in about 15 minutes. Grimaldi Lines' Grandi Navi Veloci run beautiful cruise-ship-like ferries to Genoa (a 20-hour trip) year-round. Milazzo is the main port of departure for the Aeolian Islands, with Navigazione Generale Italiana (NGI) the main operator of those ferries, as well as of boats between the various islands. Medmar and SNAV also have service between Naples and the Aeolians.

🚢 Boat & Ferry Information **Caronte & Tourist** ☎ 0965/793111 ⊕ www.carontetourist.
it. **Grandi Navi Veloci** ☎ 091/587404 in Palermo ⊕ www.gnv.it. **Medmar** ☎ 081/
3334411 in Naples ⊕ www.medmargroup.it. **NGI** ☎ 090/9284091 in Milazzo ⊕ www.
ngi-spa.it. **SNAV** ☎ 091/6317900 in Palermo, 081/4285555 in Naples ⊕ www.snav.it.
Tirrenia ☎ 892123 ⊕ www.tirrenia.it.

BY BUS

Air-conditioned coaches connect major and minor cities and are often
faster and more convenient than local trains but slightly more expensive. Various companies serve the different routes. SAIS runs frequently
between Palermo and Catania, Messina, and Siracusa, in each case arriving at and departing from near the train stations. Cuffaro runs between Palermo and Agrigento. On the south and east coasts and in the
interior, SAIS connects the main centers, including Catania, Agrigento,
Enna, Taormina, and Siracusa. Etna Trasporti operates between Catania, Caltagirone, Piazza Armerina, and Taormina. Interbus serves the
routes between Messina, Taormina, Catania, and Siracusa.

🚌 Bus Information **Cuffaro** ☎ 0922/403157 ⊕ www.cuffaro.it. **Etna Trasporti** ☎ 0935/
530396 ⊕ www.etnatrasporti.it. **Interbus** ☎ 0935/565111 ⊕ www.interbus.it. **SAIS**
☎ 091/6166028 Palermo, 095/536168 Catania ⊕ www.saistrasporti.it.

BY CAR

This is the ideal way to explore Sicily. Modern highways circle and bi-
sect the island, making all main cities easily reachable. A20 (supplemented
by S113 at points) connects Messina and Palermo; Messina and Catania are linked by A18; running through the interior, from Catania to
west of Cefalù, is A19; threading west from Palermo, A29 runs to Trapani and the airport, with a leg stretching down to Mazara del Vallo.
The *superstrada* (highway) SS115 runs along the southern coast, and
connecting superstrade lace the island.

You will likely hear stories about the dangers of driving in Sicily. Some
are true, and others less so. In the big cities—especially Palermo, Catania, and Messina—streets are a honking mess, with lane markings and
traffic lights taken as mere suggestions; you can avoid the chaos by leaving your car in a garage. However, once outside the urban areas, the
highways and regional state roads are a driving enthusiast's dream—
they're winding, sparsely populated, and well maintained, and around
most bends there's a striking new view.

BY TRAIN

There are direct express trains from Milan and Rome to Palermo, Catania, and Siracusa. The Rome–Palermo and Rome–Siracusa trips take at
least 10 hours. After Naples, the run is mostly along the coast, so try
to book a window seat on the right if you're not on an overnight train.
At Villa San Giovanni, in Calabria, the train is separated and loaded
onto a ferryboat to cross the strait to Messina.

With Sicily, main lines connect Messina, Taormina, Siracusa, and
Palermo. Secondary lines are generally very slow and unreliable. The
Messina–Palermo run, along the northern coast, is especially scenic.

🚆 Train Information **FS** (Italian State Railways) ☎ 892021 ⊕ www.trenitalia.com.

Contacts & Resources

EMERGENCIES

🔲 **Ambulance, Police, Fire** ☎ 113. **Hospital** ☎ 091/288141 in Palermo, 095/7591111 in Catania.

VISITOR INFORMATION

🔲 Tourist Information **Acireale** ✉ Via Oreste Scionti 15, 95024 ☎ 095/892129 ⊕ www.acirealeturismo.it. **Agrigento** ✉ Viale della Vittoria 225, 92100 ☎ 0922/401352 ✉ Via Cesare Battisti 15, 92100 ☎ 0922/20454. **Caltagirone** ✉ Via Duomo 7, 95041 ☎ 0933/34191 ⊕ www.comune.caltagirone.ct.it/turismo2.htm. **Caltanisetta** ✉ Corso Vittorio Emanuele 109, 93100 ☎ 0934/530411 ⊕ www.aapit.cl.it. **Catania** ✉ Via Cimarosa 10, 95124 ☎ 095/7306211 ⊕ www.apt.catania.it ✉ Stazione Centrale, 95129 ☎ 095/7306255 ✉ Aeroporto Fontanarossa, 95100 ☎ 095/7306266. **Cefalù** ✉ Corso Ruggero 77, 90015 ☎ 0921/421050. **Enna** ✉ Via Roma 411, 94100 ☎ 0935/528288 ⊕ www.apt-enna.com. **Erice** ✉ Via Conte Pepoli 56, 91016 ☎ 0923/869388. **Lipari** ✉ Corso Vittorio Emanuele 202, 98055 ☎ 090/9880095. **Marsala** ✉ Via XI Maggio 100, 91025 ☎ 0923/714097. **Messina** ✉ Piazza della Repubblica, 98122 ☎ 090/672944 ✉ Via Calabria 301bis, 98123 ☎ 090/674236 ⊕ www.azienturismomessina.it. **Monreale** ✉ Piazza Duomo, 90046 ☎ 091/540122. **Palermo** ✉ Piazza Castelnuovo 34, 90141 ☎ 091/586338 ⊕ www.palermotourism.com ✉ Stazione Centrale, Piazza Giulio Cesare, 90100 ☎ 091/6165914 ✉ Aeroporto Falcone-Borsellino, 90045 ☎ 091/591698. **Piazza Armerina** ✉ Via Cavour 15, 94015 ☎ 0935/680201. **Siracusa** ✉ Via San Sebastiano 43, 96100 ☎ 0931/481200 ⊕ www.apt-siracusa.it ✉ Via Maestranza 33, 96100 ☎ 0931/464255. **Taormina** ✉ Palazzo Corvaja, Largo Santa Caterina, 98039 ☎ 0942/23243 ⊕ www.gate2taormina.com. **Trapani** ✉ Piazza Saturno, 91100 ☎ 0923/29000 ⊕ www.apt.trapani.it.

Sardinia

Oristano

WORD OF MOUTH

"All in all I loved Sardinia. It's a totally different experience from other areas I've been to in Italy. The itinerary wasn't so driven by historical sites as it was by beaches, towns, and just plain gorgeous scenery."

—AP6380

WELCOME TO SARDINIA

Alghero

TOP 5
Reasons to Go

1 Su Nuraxi: This UNESCO World Heritage Site is the most impressive of Sardinia's enigmatic *nuraghi* (bronze-age stone fortresses).

2 Grotta di Nettuno: Near Alghero, a wonderland of sea-soaked stalactites and stalagmites awaits visitors arriving by water or down an infamously steep stairway along the limestone cliffs.

3 Cagliari's Museo Archeologico: The artifacts here from the island's nuraghi are the only clues to the mysterious prehistoric people who built them.

4 Nora: These partially submerged (but otherwise well-preserved) ruins near Pula were first settled as a Phoenician port and later built up by the Carthaginians and Romans.

5 Porto Cervo: Even if you can't bring your own 100-foot yacht, you still may be able to splurge on one of the exclusive hotels here and sunbathe on some of Europe's most expensive sand.

Getting Oriented

Sardinia is a world apart from the rest of Italy. It's the second largest island in the Mediterranean—just smaller than Sicily—and its landscape closely resembles that of Corsica, 16 km (10 mi) to the north, with miles of untamed beaches and a rugged, mountainous inland. There's little sophistication in Sardinia, aside from the opulence of the Costa Smeralda, the island's outpost for the rich and famous.

Su Nuraxi   Cathedral, Cagliari   Ruins at Nora

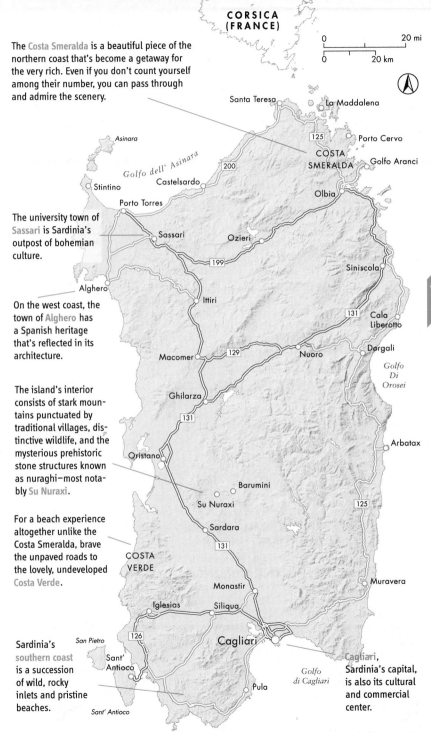

CORSICA
(FRANCE)

0 ——————— 20 mi
0 ——————— 20 km

The Costa Smeralda is a beautiful piece of the
northern coast that's become a getaway for
the very rich. Even if you don't count yourself
among their number, you can pass through
and admire the scenery.

Santa Teresa

La Maddalena

Asinara

125

Porto Cervo

COSTA
SMERALDA

Golfo Aranci

Golfo dell' Asinara

200

Stintino

Castelsardo

Olbia

Porto Torres

The university town of
Sassari is Sardinia's
outpost of bohemian
culture.

Sassari

Ozieri

Siniscola

199

16

Alghero

Ittiri

131

Cala
Liberotto

On the west coast, the
town of Alghero has
a Spanish heritage
that's reflected in its
architecture.

Macomer

129

Nuoro

Dorgali

Golfo
Di
Orosei

The island's interior
consists of stark moun-
tains punctuated by
traditional villages, distinctive wildlife, and the
mysterious prehistoric
stone structures known
as nuraghi—most nota-
bly Su Nuraxi.

Ghilarza

131

Oristano

Barumini

Su Nuraxi

Arbatax

For a beach experience
altogether unlike the
Costa Smeralda, brave
the unpaved roads to
the lovely, undeveloped
Costa Verde.

COSTA
VERDE

Sardara

131

125

Monastir

Muravera

Iglesias

Siliqua

San Pietro

126

Cagliari

Sardinia's
southern coast
is a succession
of wild, rocky
inlets and pristine
beaches.

Sant'
Antioco

Golfo
di Cagliari

Cagliari,
Sardinia's capital,
is also its cultural
and commercial
center.

Pula

Sant' Antioco

SARDINIA PLANNER

Making the Most of Your Time

Cagliari is a popular point of entry for visitors to Sardinia and makes an excellent base for a general island tour. Its archaeological museum has the island's best antiquities collection, and both the ruins at Nora and the wild, deserted Costa Verde are nearby. Oristano is a good base for exploring the interior region's villages, wildlife, and ruins; the fortress at Su Nuraxi is an easy trip from either Cagliari or Oristano.

Though crowded in summer, the coastal beach and resort towns are ideal retreats in spring and fall; relax in luxury in Porto Cervo, or head to the southern coast for a less pricey alternative. On the western shoreline, near Alghero, the Grotto di Nettuno sits below the dramatic headlands of Capo Caccia, waiting to be explored.

Finding a Place to Stay

The Costa Smeralda has the most posh and costly hotels in all of Italy. Other resort areas are more affordable. Most lodgings on the coast shut down from October through April. Small-town hotels are basic, with restrained but genuine hospitality and low rates. Hotels of any vintage are hard to find inland.

Dining & Lodging Price Categories

WHAT IT COSTS in Euros					
	$$$$	$$$	$$	$	¢
Restaurants	over €45	€35–€45	€25–€35	€15–€25	under €15
Hotels	over €220	€160–€220	€110–€160	€70–€110	under €70

Restaurant prices are for a first course (primo), second course (secondo), and dessert (dolce). Hotel prices are for two people in a standard double room in high season, including tax and service.

Getting Around

You need a car if you want to explore the island. Smaller roads often provide better views and give you a better sense of place. Cagliari is the public transit hub, with bus or train service to most larger towns. For details about transportation, see "Essentials" at the end of this chapter.

Speaking the Language

The Sard language is incomprehensible to mainland Italians, let alone to foreigners, but most locals can switch from Sardinian to perfect Italian with ease. In the main tourist areas, most people you deal with will speak some English, though often less than elsewhere in Italy.

TOP PASSEGGIATA

Just off the western coast, the appealing town of Oristano has a vibrant predinner stroll with a family-friendly spirit.

How's the Weather?

Try to avoid the coastal resorts in steamy August, when they're swamped not only with tourists but also with locals on their annual break. May and September are much quieter and still temperate; the sea remains warm enough for swimming well into October. The mild spring and fall weather is also ideal for inland travel; from November through February the maestrale (winter winds) are fierce, and it snows most years in the Barbagia region. Quiet towns like Oristano and Sassari are pleasant stops any time of year.

Updated by
Peter Blackman

AN UNCUT JEWEL OF AN ISLAND, Sardinia remains unique and enigmatic. Would-be conquerors from all directions—Phoenicians, Carthaginians, Romans, Catalans, Pisans, Piemontese—have left their marks, but no single outside culture has had a dominant impact. Pockets of foreign influence persist along the coasts (for example, the walled Catalan city of Alghero), but inland, a proud Sard culture and language flourish.

Sardinia's identity as a travel destination is split: the island has some of Europe's most expensive resorts, but it's also home to areas as rugged and undeveloped as anywhere on the continent. Fine sand, clean waters, and relative lack of crowds draw summer sun-seekers to beaches that are unquestionably among the best in the Mediterranean. Best known are those along the Costa Smeralda (Emerald Coast), where the super-rich have anchored their yachts since the 1960s. Less exclusive beach holidays can be found elsewhere on the island at La Maddalena, Villasimius, and Pula. There are also wonderfully undertouristed medieval towns—Cagliari, Oristano, Sassari—on or near the water.

But most of the coast is unsettled, a jagged series of wildly beautiful inlets accessible only by sea. And inland, Sardinia remains shepherd's country, silent and stark. Spaghetti Westerns were once filmed here, and it's not hard to imagine why: the desolate mountainous terrain seems the perfect frontier set, and the towns, such as Nuoro, have an air of deliberate provinciality. Against this landscape are the striking and mysterious stone *nuraghi* (ancient defensive structures), which provide clues to the lifestyles of the island's prehistoric peoples.

16

CAGLIARI & THE SOUTHERN COAST

Cagliari (pronounced *Cahl*-yah-ree) is Sardinia's capital and largest city; it contains the island's principal art and archaeology museums as well as an old cathedral and medieval towers that have lofty views of the surrounding sea, lagoons, and mountains. East of Cagliari the coast is no less scenic, but it's more built up; though blissfully uncommercialized for the most part, the coast does have pockets of development that have sprouted as tourism has found a niche. To the southwest, Pula is an inland town within easy reach of both good beaches and the excavated ruins at Nora. Swaths of eucalyptus and lush pine groves artfully conceal hotels at Santa Margherita di Pula, one of Sardinia's most luxurious holiday enclaves. South and west of Santa Margherita, the protected coast contains few beaches but does have jaw-dropping vistas unspoiled by construction.

Cagliari

❶ *268 km (166 mi) south of Olbia.*

The island's capital has steep streets and impressive Italianate architecture and churches in differing styles. Cagliari is characterized by its busy commercial center and waterfront with broad avenues, as well as by the typically narrow streets of the old hilltop citadel (called, simply, *Castello*). An ongoing revitalization effort has restored the nobility of several me-

SARDINIA, PAST & PRESENT

A Phoenician stronghold in ancient times and later a Spanish dominion, Sardinia doesn't seem typically Italian in its color and flavor. It was a bit too far from imperial and papal Rome and from the palaces of the Savoy dynasty to have been transformed by the events that forged the national character of the mainland. Yet Giuseppe Garibaldi, the charismatic national hero who led his troops in fervid campaigns to unify Italy in the mid-19th century, chose to spend his last years in relative isolation on the small island of Caprera, just off the coast of Sardinia. Later political leaders such as Antonio Gramsci and Francesco Cossiga, and such radical parties as the still-strong Partito Sardo d'Azione, have advocated Sardinian independence. It is one of the few regions that retains semi-autonomous political status.

Sardinians are courteous but remote, often favoring their forbidding regional language over Italian. In hamlets, women swathed in black shawls and long, full skirts look with suspicion upon strangers passing through. Like mainland Italians, the Sardinians are of varied origin. On the northwest coast, fine traceries of ironwork around balconies underscore the Spanish influence. In the northeast, the inhabitants have Genoese or Pisan ancestry, and the headlands display the ruined fortresses of the ancient Pisan duchy of Malaspina. As you explore the southern coast, you come upon the features, customs, dialects, place names, and holy buildings of the Turks, Moors, Phoenicians, Austrians, and mainland Italians. If there are any pure Sardinians—or Sards—left, perhaps they can be found in the mountains south of Nuoro, under the 6,000-foot crests of the Gennargentu Massif, in the rugged country still called, ironically, Barbagia, "Land of Strangers."

dieval landmarks, but has done little to alter the appealingly dilapidated feel of the old town. Medieval Spanish conquerors from Aragon as well as Pisans and Piemontese all left their marks, and grand, decaying castles, floodlighted by night, overlook the old center's winding streets and bustling port from far above.

Begin your visit at the **Museo Archeologico,** within the walls of a castle erected by Pisans in the early 1300s to ward off the Aragonese and Catalans (attacking from what is now Spain). Among the intriguing artifacts are bronze statuettes from the tombs and dwellings of Sardinia's earliest inhabitants, who remain a prehistoric enigma. Ancient writers called them the nuraghic people, from the name of their curious stone dwellings, the nuraghi, which are unique to Sardinia. Archaeologists date most of the nuraghi to about 1300–1200 BC, the same time the ancient Israelites were establishing themselves in Canaan. ✉ *Cittadella dei Musei, Piazza Arsenale* ☎ *070/684000* 🖭 *€4* 🕐 *Tues.–Sun. 9–7:15.*

The 1305 **Torre di San Pancrazio,** part of the imposing medieval Pisan defenses, is just outside Cagliari's archaeological museum, and it marks the edge of the Castello district. You can climb up the tower for a fabulous panorama of the city and its surroundings. Curiously enough, the tower's back wall is missing, which allows you to see the series of wooden stairs and landings inside without climbing a step. ⊠ *Piazza Indipendenza* ☎ *070/41108* 🎟 *€2* ⊗ *Tues.–Sun. 9–1 and 3:30–7:30.*

Torre dell'Elefante, twin to the tower of San Pancrazio, stands at the seaward end of Cagliari's bastions. Built in 1307, it was used as a prison in the 1800s. ⊠ *Via Università* ☎ *070/659674* 🎟 *€2* ⊗ *Apr.–Sept., Tues.–Sun. 9–1 and 3:30–7:30; Oct.–Mar., Tues.–Sun. 9–4:30.*

Cattedrale di Santa Maria, also known as the **Duomo,** was originally constructed in the 17th century, but the look was changed during construction in the mid-1930s. The tiers of columns on the facade resemble those of medieval Romanesque Pisan churches, but only the central portal is an authentic relic of that era. ⊠ *Piazza Palazzo off Via Martini* ☎ *070/663837* ⊗ *Daily 8–noon and 4–8.*

On the narrow streets of the **Castello,** the quarter below the Duomo, humble dwellings still open directly onto the sidewalk and the wash is hung out to dry on elaborate wrought-iron balconies.

The **Terrazza Umberto I** is a monumental neoclassical staircase and arcade added in the 19th century to the Bastion of St. Remy (built by the Spaniards 400 years earlier). It has long been covered by graffiti, but a massive restoration is under way. ⊠ *Piazza Costituzione.*

The **Anfiteatro Romano** dates from the 2nd century AD. The well-preserved amphitheater arena—complete with underground passages and a beasts' pit—is evidence of the importance of this Roman outpost. ⊠ *Viale Fra' Ignazio* ☎ *070/652956* 🎟 *€3.30* ⊗ *Apr.–Oct., Mon.–Sat. 9:30–1:30, Sun. 10–1 and 3–6; Nov.–Mar., Mon.–Sat. 9:30–1:30, Sun. 10–4.*

OFF THE BEATEN PATH

SAN SPERATE – Walls throughout this small town 20 km (12 mi) north of Cagliari have been brightened with *murales* (murals) by local artists and some well-known Italian painters. The murals were begun in 1968 and continue to be expanded upon today, transforming the entire town into an open-air art gallery.

Where to Stay & Eat

$$$$ ✕ **Dal Corsaro.** This formal restaurant near the port is one of the island's most recommended, so make reservations. The interior is refined, the welcome cordial. The menu includes fish and meat, with such dishes as seafood antipasto and *porcheddu* (roast suckling pig). At various unpredictable times each year—always including August—the restaurant opens a branch at the seaside. ⊠ *Viale Regina Margherita 28* ☎ *070/664318* ⊠ *Marina Piccola* ☎ *070/370295* ⌂ *Reservations essential* ▤ *AE, DC, MC, V* ⊗ *Closed Sun. and 2 wks in Jan.*

$$$–$$$$ ✕ **S'Apposentu.** Informed by his studies in Corsica and mainland France,
Fodor'sChoice young chef Roberto Petza has quietly created a new model of Sardinian cuisine, one deeply entrenched in the ingredients of his native island.
★ Petza's otherworldly creations might include a stunning plate of *lasagnette* (thin, flat noodles) with San Gavino saffron, sausage, and local ri-

16

cotta; spectacular Sardinian *agnellino* (baby lamb); or roast pigeon with a sauce made from white vernaccia wine and *mirto*, a local digestive. The stage is a soaring, ultramodern space—even the place settings are cutting-edge—that's set in Cagliari's opera house, the Teatro Lirico. ⊠ *Teatro Lirico di Cagliari, Via Sant'Alenixedda* ☎ *070/4082315* ⊕ *www.sapposentu.it* ⌕ *Reservations essential* ⊟ *AE, DC, MC, V* ⊘ *Closed Sun. and Mon.*

$ ✕ **Antico Caffè.** The gilded Antico Caffè has anchored the base of Terrazza Umberto I since 1855, serving as a social center from breakfast until well after midnight. A daily set menu (€12) lists local specialties like *burrida* (marinated dogfish) and the pastas and salads are reliable à la carte choices. Desserts are the real attraction here: try the flavorful *crema catalana* (crème caramel) or one of the elaborate ice cream concoctions. ⊠ *Piazza Costituzione 10* ☎ *070/658206* ⊟ *AE, DC, MC, V.*

$$ ▦ **Panorama.** The exterior is nondescript, but this hotel just outside downtown Cagliari is geared to the business class—with high-speed Internet connections in the rooms and modern, functional furnishings. Rooms are spacious; try to reserve one on a high floor to enjoy the view over the harbor and bay. There's also a bar with—appropriately enough—a panoramic view on the top floor. ⊠ *Viale Armando Diaz 231, 09126* ☎ *070/307691* ⊟ *070/305413* ⊕ *www.hotelpanorama.it* ⇗ *80 rooms, 20 suites* ⌕ *Restaurant, café, minibars, cable TV, pool, gym, Turkish bath, bar, meeting rooms* ⊟ *AE, DC, MC, V* ▯◊ *BP.*

$ ▦ **AeR Bundes Jack.** Courtyard-facing rooms and simple furnishings make this central *secondo piano* (third-floor) pension cozy. Expect polite, friendly service. And yes, there's an elevator. The port is directly opposite the nondescript entrance under the arcades of Via Roma and the street itself presents an entertaining parade of shops and sit-down bars. The bus and train stations are steps away. ⊠ *Via Roma 75, 09100* ☎☎ *070/657970* ✍ *hotel.aerbundesjack@libero.it* ⇗ *28 rooms, 16 with bath* ⌕ *Bar* ⊟ *No credit cards* ▯◊ *BP.*

Nightlife & the Arts

Cagliari's university stages concerts throughout the academic year; contact the tourist office for information.

Fodor's Choice
★

Thousands of costumed villagers, many of them on horseback, parade through town during Sardinia's greatest annual festival, the **Festa di Sant'Efisio** (May 1–4). It's part of a four-day procession from Cagliari to Nora and back again, and it's a good chance to take part in a centuries-old event.

CAFÉS The **Libarium Nostrum** (⊠ Bastioni di Santa Croce ☎ 070/650943) might well be the coolest café-bar in Sardinia: it's a dim, bohemian haunt full of nooks, crannies, wood beams, and castle walls. Contemporary art, electronic music, and a kitchen open until midnight attract university students to **Ritual's Cafe** (⊠ Via Università 33 ☎ 070/652071). The central **Caffè dell'Elfo** (⊠ Salita Santa Chiara 4/6 ☎ 070/682399) is favored by local professionals who linger over wine and conversation. The terrace of **Caffè de Candia** (⊠ Via Maria de Candia ☎ 070/655884), built directly into the castle walls near Terrazzo Umberto I, catches the afternoon sun—it's a great place to enjoy wine or coffee after exploring the Castello quarter.

Shopping

Cagliari's two best shopping streets, full of boutiques, clothing stores, and such, are Via Manno and Via Garibaldi, just up from the port. **ISOLA** (✉ Via Bacaredda 176 ☎ 070/492756 ✉ Via Santa Croce 34 ☎ 070/651488) is a government-sponsored exhibition of artisan crafts; most of the work is for sale.

Sports

The **Lega Navale Italiana** (✉ Marina Piccola ☎ 070/370380 ⊕ www.leganavale.it) has information on the island's sailing facilities. Sardinia has some of the best windsurfing spots in Europe; the **Windsurfing Club Cagliari** (✉ Marina Piccola ☎ 070/380918 ⊕ www.windsurfingclubcagliari.it) can provide advice to beginners and experts alike.

EN ROUTE Driving east from Cagliari takes you through some dismal industrial suburbs on the road that leads to the scenic coast and beaches of Capo Boi and Capo Carbonara. **Villasimius,** 50 km (31 mi) east of Cagliari, is the chief resort here; the beautiful beaches lie a couple of miles north of the town center, on the golden sands of the Costa Rei.

16

Pula

➋ *29 km (18 mi) southwest of Cagliari, 314 km (195 mi) southwest of Olbia.*

Resort villages sprawl along the coast southwest of the capital, which has its share of fine scenery and good beaches. On the marshy shoreline between Cagliari's Aeroporto di Elmas and Pula, huge flocks of flamingos are a common sight. From Cagliari, first follow the S195 toward Teulada, then take the turnoff for Pula at Km 27. Nora is the headland south of Pula that has a rich Roman archaeological site.

Beaches and lodging catering to summer crowds are concentrated 4 km (2½ mi) south of Pula, a little more than 1½ km (1 mi) south of Nora, in a conglomeration that makes up the town of Santa Margherita di Pula.

The small **Museo Archeologico Comunale** has archaeological finds from excavations of a site at Nora, including amphoras, anchors, and inscribed stones, mostly dredged up from the sea. ✉ *Corso Vittorio Emanuele 67* ☎ *070/9209610* 🎟 *€2.50, €5.50 including archaeological site at Nora* ☉ *Daily 9–8.*

★ The narrow promontory outside Pula, **Nora,** was the site of a Phoenician, then Carthaginian, and later a Roman settlement. An old Roman road passes the moss-covered ruins of temples, an amphitheater, and a small Roman theater. Nora was a prime location—the Phoenicians scouted for good harbors, cliffs to shelter their craft from the wind, and an elevation from which they could defend themselves against attack. Extensive excavations have shed light on life in this ancient city from the 8th century BC onward. You can make out the channels through which hot air rose to warm the Roman baths; note the difference between the Carthaginians' simple mosaic pavements and the Romans more elabo-

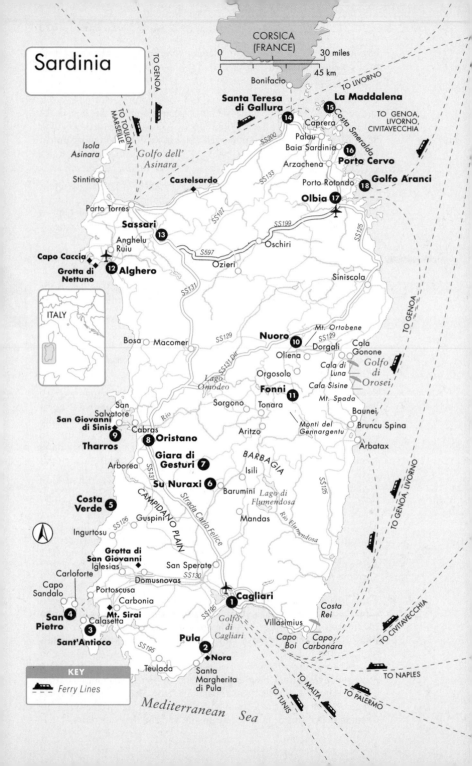

rate designs. If the sea is calm, look under the clear waters along the shore for more ruins of the ancient city, submerged by earthquakes, rough seas, and erosion. Guided tours begin on the hour. ⊕ *3 km (2 mi) south of Pula* ☎ *070/9209138* ✉ *€5.50, including Museo Archeologico Comunale* ⊙ *Daily 9–dusk; last entrance ½ hr before closing.*

Sant'Efisio, the little Romanesque church at the base of the Nora promontory, plays a part in one of the island's most colorful annual events. A four-day procession during the Festa di Sant'Efisio accompanies a statue of the saint all the way from Cagliari and back again, culminating in a huge parade down Cagliari's main avenue. If you're in Sardinia from May 1 to May 4, don't miss it. ⊕ *3 km (2 mi) south of Pula* ☎ *070/ 9208473* ⊙ *Apr.–Sept., Sat. 3–6, Sun. 9:30–1 and 3–7:30; Oct.–Mar., Sun. 9:30–noon and 3–5.*

Where to Stay

$$$$ ▨ **Flamingo.** Eucalyptus trees surround the main building and the six, two-story cottages of this shady beachside resort hotel. Balconied rooms are light and airy, overlooking park or sea. Sports facilities abound, and the outdoor pool is open late into the night—a welcome treat in the balmy summer. ✉ *4 km (2½ mi) south of Pula, 09010 Santa Margherita di Pula* ☎ *070/9208361* 🖷 *070/9208359* ⊕ *www.hotelflamingo.it* 🛏 *188 rooms* ♿ *Restaurant, minibars, miniature golf, tennis court, pool, gym, sauna, Turkish bath, beach, dive shop, windsurfing, piano bar, dance club* 🚭 *AE, DC, MC, V* ⊙ *Closed Nov.–Apr. 15* 🍽 *BP.*

Sports

The 18-hole **Is Molas** (✉ Santa Margherita di Pula ☎ 070/9241014 ⊕ www. ismolas.it) has won tributes from Tom Watson and Jack Nicklaus.

Sant'Antioco

❸ *75 km (47 mi) west of Pula, 100 km (62 mi) west of Cagliari.*

Off Sardinia's southwest coast is the sleepy island of Sant'Antioco—the most hectic activity seems to be the silent repairing of nets by local fishermen who have already pulled in their daily catch. It has become a popular holiday spot because of its good beaches. The island has been connected to the mainland since Roman times by a still-standing causeway (the modern causeway that you traverse runs parallel).

Before leaving the main town, also called Sant'Antioco, take time to visit the **Zona Archeologica** at the top of the old section, which has terrific views of the Sardinian mainland. Here you can see a Punic necropolis and a burial site scattered with urns that contained the cremated remains of stillborn children. Admission includes a guided tour and entry to the on-site ethnographic and archaeological museums. ✉ *Sant'Antioco* ☎ *078/183590* ✉ *€5* ⊙ *Apr.–Sept., daily 9–1 and 3:30–7; Oct.–Mar., daily 9–1 and 3:30–6.*

Also of note on the island is the tiny fishing village of **Calasetta.** Its name literally means "silk cove," and it was from a villa outside this town that generations of an Armenian silk-trading family once supported much of the island's economy. ⊕ *10 km (6 mi) northeast of Sant'Antioco town.*

16

EATING WELL IN SARDINIA

Sardinian cuisine is sharply divided between hearty, meat-based dishes from the interior and Mediterranean seafood fare with Catalan and North African influences along the coast. Meat dishes are most commonly veal, roast *agnello* (lamb) and *agnellino* (baby lamb), or *porcheddu* (roast suckling pig, most often available at Easter). *Cavallo,* or *carne equino* (horse meat), is also a common specialty of Sardinia; it's generally served in the form of a *bistecca* (thin steak), which can be a bit chewy, but when properly grilled, also intensely flavored and delicious. Homemade pastas might be topped with a wild boar sauce. Finally, Italy's original and best, pecorino cheese, made from sheep's milk, comes from the rugged slopes of the interior.

Langouste or *aragosta* (lobster) is a seafood specialty of the northern coast that can get pricey. Looking for the unusual? Try the *ricci* (sea urchins), which, unlike the Japanese

uni, are served atop pasta. *Bottarga,* another prized Sardinian product, is a dried, cured tuna roe that's best when shaved off a block directly onto spaghetti or with butter on *crostini* (thin slices of toasted bread). Foreign conquerors left their legacies of bouillabaisse (known here as *zimino*), paella, and *cuscus* (couscous), also called *cashkà.*

Native pastas include *malloreddus* (small shells of bran pasta sometimes flavored with saffron), *culurgiones* (the Sardinian version of ravioli), and *maccarones de busa* (thick pasta twists). And crispy bread called *pane carasau* (*carta di musica* in Italian) is typical island fare. Prized around Italy and around the world is Sardinia's *amaro di corbezzolo,* a honey with a bouquet and taste primordially foresty, slightly bitter, and dazzlingly complex. It's made by bees that suck nectar from a plant known as *arbutus,* the tree strawberry.

San Pietro

4 *5 km (3 mi) northwest of Sant'Antioco.*

A ferry at the small northern port of Calasetta connects Sant'Antioco with Carloforte, the main town on the smaller island of San Pietro. This classic little Italian port village and its surrounding coastline are a favorite of wealthy Cagliarians, many of whom have built weekend cottages here. The best views are from Capo Sandalo, on San Pietro's rugged western coast, but head to the island's southern tip for the beaches. During daylight hours the ferry departs every 20 minutes in summer and every 30 in winter—the trip takes 20 minutes.

Where to Stay

$ ☐ **Hieracon.** An art nouveau building with modern whitewashed rooms sits on the harbor in Carloforte. A few palm trees grow in the small courtyard garden near the bungalow-style apartments. Try to get a front-facing room for a harbor view, though there may be some traffic noise. Avoid rooms at the top, which have low ceilings and no view. The central location means that you're a short walk from some good restaurants. ⊠ *Via Cavour 63, 09014 Carloforte* ☎*0781/854028* 📠*0781/854893* ⬧*hotel-hieracon@tiscali.it* 🛏 *17 rooms, 7 apartments* ⚓ *Restaurant, some kitchenettes, minibars, bar* ⊟ *AE, MC, V* ⦿ *BP.*

Costa Verde

⑤ *35 km (22 mi) northwest of San Pietro, 80 km (50 mi) northwest of Cagliari.*

If you've come to Sardinia in search of untrammeled wilderness and sweeping sands as far as the eye can see, then this deserted coast is the place to find them. Hidden away in the forgotten southwest corner of Cagliari province, the Costa Verde is accessible only by a bumpy, unpaved track. The effort is worth it. The dune-backed sands shelter rare grasses and birdlife, as well as provide magnificent swimming.

You can approach the coast either from the town of Guspini, on the straggling S126, or from a turnoff a couple of miles farther south, which leads through the abandoned mining town of **Ingurtosu.** It's a strange, ghostly cluster of chimneys and workers' dwellings, forlorn amid the encroaching scrubland. Drive down the dirt track another 10 km (6 mi) or so, through woods of juniper, to reach the sea.

> ### WORD OF MOUTH
>
> "Unfortunately, too many travelers make the mistake of focusing on the Costa Smeralda area, which is *least* representative of Sardinia. By contrast, there are numerous interesting towns in the hinterland which are worth visiting, lovely medieval basilicas scattered about the lonely countryside, as well as beautiful Roman ruins along the coasts."
>
> –gac

Where to Stay

★ **$$$$** 🏨 **Hotel Le Dune.** A remote oasis on the beach, this hotel was formerly a depot for the minerals dug out from the surrounding hills; you can still see the remains of wagons, rails, and other mining bric-a-brac scattered about, which adds to the desolate allure. Bamboo furnishings give simple guest rooms a light, spacious feel. Eleven of the rooms have their own sitting areas. There's a good cocktail bar, where you can contemplate the limitless sands stretching out on either side. For exploring, guided tours are available on request. Half board is required year-round; rates drop to €180 for a double September–July. ⊠ *Via Bau 1, 09031 Ingurtosu* ☎ *070/977130* 📠 *070/977230* ⊕ *www.leduneingurtosu.it* 🛏 *27 rooms* ⚓ *Restaurant, in-room safes, minibars, pool, bar, meeting room, travel services; no room TVs* ⊟ *AE, DC, MC, V* ⦿ *MAP.*

SU NURAXI TO THE COSTA SMERALDA

A more traditional—and wild—Sardinia awaits the traveler who ventures into the island's mountainous interior. The Taviani brothers, noted Italian filmmakers, made the hinterland of the Barbagia region, where

16

traditional Sardinian customs are maintained in remote hilltop villages, the subject of the extraordinary film *Padre Padrone* (1977). Inland Sardinians are hardy souls, used to living in a climate that is as unforgiving in winter as it is intolerable in summer. Old traditions, including the vendetta, are firmly rooted in the social fabric of this mountainous land, which is barren and beautiful. Here, rare species of wildlife share the rocky uplands with sturdy medieval churches and the mysterious *nuraghi* (ancient stone defensive structures) left by prehistoric people. The nuraghi were built beginning in the 16th century BC, and they vary from single defensive towers to multitower complexes sheltering whole communities—prehistoric versions of medieval walled towns. You may want to make your base Oristano, on the west coast and the medieval center of Sardinian nationalism.

As you move northward, the timeless beauty of the landscape begins to show greater signs of 20th-century development. The sunny resort of Alghero, the Spanish-influenced port on the west coast, is one of the island's premier holiday spots. Costa Smeralda, the luxury resort complex on the northeast corner of Sardinia, is as prestigious a summer getaway as any in Italy.

Su Nuraxi

❻ *64 km (40 mi) northeast of Ingurtosu on the Costa Verde, 60 km (37 mi) north of Cagliari.*

Fodor'sChoice
★

It's definitely worth a detour to see the extraordinary stone fortress-village of Su Nuraxi, near the quiet town of Barumini. The most extensive of the island's 7,000 discovered nuraghi, Su Nuraxi's significance merits its inclusion on the UNESCO World Heritage List. Concentric rings of thick stone walls conceal dark chambers and narrow passages in a central, beehive-shape tower. The excellent guided tour (available in English) allows you to explore the interior. In the ruins of the surrounding village there are benches, ovens, wells, and other remnants of middle bronze–age society.

The specific functions of individual nuraghi remain a mystery, largely because their construction predates written or pictorial history. Though this particular type of construction is unique to Sardinia in Italy, similar buildings dating from the same era are found in other parts of the Mediterranean, such as Cyprus and the Balearic islands off Spain. If driving from SS131, don't be misled by other, lesser nuraghi—follow signs all the way to Barumini. ⊠ *SP Barumini-Tuilli, 1 km (½ mi) west of Barumini* ☎ *070/9368128* 🖅 *€5* ☉ *Daily 9–2 hrs before dusk.*

Giara di Gesturi

❼ *8 km (5 mi) north of Barumini, 68 km (42 mi) northwest of Cagliari.*

On the 45-square-km (28-square-mi) basalt plateau of Giara di Gesturi roams some of the island's more exotic wildlife, including a species of wild dwarf horse. Another rare species in the Giara is the mouflon, a wild sheep distinguishable from its domesticated counterpart by its lengthy, curving horns and skittishness. Long hunted for their horns, the mouflon are now an endangered species, with only a few surviving on Sardinia and Corsica. ⊠ *Off S197, north of Gesturi.*

Oristano

❽ *25 km (16 mi) north of Giara di Gesturi, 93 km (58 mi) northwest of Cagliari.*

The beautiful small colonial center exudes a distinct serenity. Oristano's evening *passeggiata* (predinner stroll) teems with vivacious young children and has a relaxed friendliness about it. The city's star shone most brightly in the Middle Ages, when it was capital of an independent duchy led by Sardinia's own Joan of Arc–type heroine, Eleanora di Arborea (circa 1340–1402). Oristano is now the scene of livestock fairs and a rousing series of horseback competitions, called Sa Sartiglia, marking the end of February's Carnival.

Where to Stay & Eat

$$ ✕ **Trattoria Gino.** The same family has run Trattoria Gino, under different names, for nearly a century. Authentic local seafood dishes include the *antipasto mare* (mixed seafood appetizer) and the delicious spaghetti *ai ricci* (with sea urchin). The lobster is a memorable splurge. Light walls lined with bottles of wine and simple rows of tables deck out the single room, and service is friendly and attentive. It's a popular spot for locals and an ideal lunch stop. ⊠ *Via Tirso 13* ☎ *0783/71428* ▤ *MC, V* ☉ *Closed Sun., 1 wk in Jan., and 3 wks in Aug.*

$ ▦ **I.S.A. Hotel.** This central downtown hotel has a clean and elegant (if a bit dated) lobby with chandeliers. Rooms, too, are well kept and comfortable, with simple white walls and wood furnishings, and excellent bathrooms. Nothing at the I.S.A. blows you away, but Oristano does everything in moderation, and the town's hotels are no exception. ⊠ *Piazza Mariano 50, 09170* ☎ *0783/360101* ⤽ *49 rooms* ⚲ *Restaurant, minibars, bar, meeting room* ▤ *AE, DC, MC, V* ⑩ *BP.*

Nightlife & the Arts

☾ The **Sa Sartiglia** festival, on the last Sunday of February's Carnival season, includes rich costumes and ritual joustlike competitions on horseback. Each summer the town holds an **arts and crafts exhibition** (Tourist office ⊠ Via Cagliari 278 ☎ 0783/74191), with local foods and wines given prominence.

Tharros

❾ *20 km (12 mi) west of Oristano, 113 km (70 mi) northwest of Cagliari.*

The site of the Carthaginian and Roman city of Tharros (Cabras in Italian), like Nora to the south, was chosen because it commanded the best views of the harbor and could provide an easy escape route if inland tribes threatened. Today the roadside ruins afford a scenic view over the Sinis Peninsula. Four Corinthian columns still stand, and there are baths and fragments of mosaics from the Roman city. As at Nora, there is much more submerged under water. ⊠ *San Giovanni in Sinis* ☎ *0783/370019* ⊕ *www.penisoladelsinis.it* ▦ *€4 includes the Museo Civico di Cabras* ☉ *Daily 9–1 hr before sunset.*

16

At the **Museo Civico di Cabras** you can view many of the better-preserved urns and other artifacts that have been recovered from the ruins at Tharros. ⊠ *Via Tharros* ☏ *0783/290636* ⊕ *www.penisoladelsinis.it* ⌨ *Museum €2; museum and archaeological site at Tharros €4* ⊗ *June–Aug., daily 9–1 and 4–8; Sept.–May, daily 9–1 and 3–7.*

EN ROUTE On the way to Tharros you pass the ghost town of **San Salvatore**, revived briefly in the 1960s as a locale for spaghetti Westerns and since abandoned. The saloon from the movie set still stands. Among the dunes past San Salvatore are large rush huts formerly used by fishermen and now much in demand as back-to-nature vacation homes. The 5th-century church of **San Giovanni di Sinis,** on the Sinis Peninsula, is the oldest Christian church in Sardinia.

Nuoro

⑩ *107 km (67 mi) northeast of Tharros, 181 km (113 mi) north of Cagliari.*

The somewhat shabby provincial capital of Nuoro is on the edge of a gorge in the harsh mountainous area that culminates in Gennargentu, the island's highest massif (6,000 feet). Not much happens here; you can do some (relatively inexpensive) shopping amid strolling locals, or try the local Barbagia sausage, a sweet, fatty delight. The most interesting things in Nuoro are the views from the park on Sant'Onofrio Hill and the **Museo della Vita e delle Tradizioni Popolari Sarde** (Museum of Sardinian Life and Folklore), where you can see some domestic and agricultural implements, traditional jewelry, and local costumes worn by mannequins. ⊠ *Via Mereu 56* ☏ *0784/257035* ⌨ *€5* ⊗ *May–Oct., daily 9–8; Nov.–Apr., daily 9–1 and 3–7.*

Make an excursion about 3 km (2 mi) east of Nuoro to **Monte Ortobene** (2,900 feet) for lofty views over the gulch below. Here you can also see up close the imposing statue of Christ the Redeemer overlooking the city. Picnic tables make this a handy spot for an alfresco lunch.

Where to Stay & Eat

$$$$
Fodor'sChoice
★

✕⊞ **Su Gologone.** Rooms here are impeccable retreats, decked out with traditional Sardinian fabrics, wood chests, paintings, and wood beam ceilings. Staff members organize jeep and hiking expeditions. Stop in the rustic restaurant for an authentic Sardinian meal. Specialties include *maccarones de busa* (thick homemade pasta twists) and *culurgiones* (ravioli), *sebadas* (pockets of fried dough stuffed with cheese and lemon peel), and roast suckling pig. Much of the local Cannonau, a heady red wine, is made from grapes grown in the countryside around the inn. Su Gologone attracts droves, but for good reason. ⊠ *Località Su Gologone, 08025 Oliena, 17 km (11 mi) southeast of Nuoro* ☏ *0784/287512* 🖷 *0784/287668* ⊕ *www.sugologone.it* ⇙ *60 rooms, 8 suites* ⌂ *Restaurant, miniature golf, 2 tennis courts, pool, gym, massage, bicycles, bar, meeting rooms, some pets allowed* ▤ *AE, DC, MC, V* ⊗ *Closed Nov.–mid.-Mar.* ⍔⏐ *MAP.*

★ **$** ⊞ **Barbagia.** Rooms at this very simple, modern block-style hotel—more or less standard for provincial Nuoro—are quite comfortable, and those on the upper floor rooms have nice views out over the hills. Barbagia is out by the stadium on the fringes of downtown. ⊠ *Via Aosta 44, 08100* ☎*0784/35585* 📠*0784/232782* ⇋*42 rooms* ᐦ*Restaurant, mini-bars, bar, lounge* 🖃 *AE, DC, MC, V* 🍽 *BP.*

Nightlife & the Arts

Nuoro's **Festa del Redentore** (Feast of the Redeemer) is held on the next-to-last Sunday in August. It's the best time to view the various traditional costumes of Sardinia's interior all in one place.

Shopping

Crafted for local festivals, wooden masks make unusual and festive souvenirs. The local shop of **ISOLA** (⊠ Via Monsignor Bua 10 ☎ 0784/31507) is in the middle of the old town.

EN ROUTE
Orgosolo, the old center of banditry halfway between Nuoro and Fonni, is still a poor and undeveloped village, but the houses have been painted with murals vividly depicting political and cultural issues. The effect is startling and lively. The forest and grassy plain above the village make fine walking country. ⊕ *15 km (9 mi) south of Nuoro.*

Fonni

16

⓫ *30 km (19 mi) south of Nuoro, 137 km (85 mi) south of Olbia.*

In the heart of the Barbagia region, Fonni, with walls covered in murals, is the highest town on the island. This mountainous district, including Monte Spada and the Bruncu Spina refuge on the Gennargentu Massif, is Sardinia's most primitive. Life in some villages seems not to have changed much since the Middle Ages. Here a rigidly patriarchal society perpetuates the unrelenting practice of vendetta. Although as a tourist you may be looked at with curiosity, a smile goes a long way. High mountain roads wind and loop through the landscape; towns are small and undistinguished, their social fabric formed in complete isolation. On feast days elaborate regional costumes are taken out of mothballs and worn as an explicit statement of community identity.

Where to Eat

$ ✕ **Barbagia.** The best place downtown for a midday meal is also one of the most friendly to foreigners—a prize in this aloof village. The cheerful owners usher you into a rustic room full of nicely made-up tables, the obligatory TV in the corner, and not much else. Try the assortment of local *salumi* (cured meats), the maccarones de busa, and the typical grilled *bistecca di cavallo* (horse-meat steak), which is excellent. ⊠ *Via Umberto 106* ☎ *0784/58329* 🖃 *No credit cards* ⊘ *Closed Mon.*

Nightlife & the Arts

You can see one of the most characteristic of the Barbagia's celebrations in local costume during the **Festa di San Giovanni,** held June 24.

Shopping

Special candies are made from honey and nougat and sold in hilltop **Tonara,** 15 km (9 mi) southwest of Fonni. In the mountain village of **Aritzo,** about 45 km (28 mi) south of Fonni, high up in the Barbagia, you can find handcrafted wooden utensils and furniture.

CLOSE UP

Sardinia by Rail

If you can stand a little agitation, consider taking a trip on the rickety old single-gauge railroad that runs between Cagliari and Arbatax, midway up the east coast (with a change at Mandas). The line has been operating since 1893; it takes about seven hours to cover the approximately 250 km (155 mi) of track. The train rattles up into the Barbagia district through some breathtaking mountain scenery, then eases down into desert inland landscape before arriving at Arbatax, where the trip ends on the dock next to the fishing boats. The daily (early-morning) departures are run by the **Trenino Verde della Sardegna** (☎ 070/342341 or 800/460220 ⊕ www.treninoverde.com ⊘ June–mid-Sept.). In Tortoli, just outside Arbatax, **Dolce Casa** (✉ Via Sarcidano 3 ☎🖨 0782/623484) is a modest hotel run by an English-speaking couple. It's the best lodging option in the area, but it's open only from June through September.

EN ROUTE — Head back to Nuoro, and from there take the S129 west about 65 km (40 mi) to coastal **Bosa**, where you turn north into hilly and arid scrub country, with an abundance of cactus and juniper. Pines and olive trees shelter low buildings from the steady winds that make these parts ideal for sailing. About the only cash crop here is cork from the cork trees dotting the landscape. Yet in the low valleys and along the riverbeds, masses of oleanders bloom in June and July, creating avenues of color.

Alghero

 135 km (84 mi) northwest of Fonni, 137 km (85 mi) southwest of Olbia.

A tourist-friendly town with a distinctly Spanish flavor, Alghero is also known as Barcelonetta (little Barcelona). Rich wrought-iron scrollwork decorates balconies and screened windows; a Spanish motif appears in stone portals and in bell towers. The town was built and inhabited in the 14th century by the Aragonese and Catalans, who constructed seaside ramparts and sturdy towers encompassing an inviting nucleus of narrow, winding streets with whitewashed palazzi. The native language spoken here is a version of Catalan, not Italian, although you probably have to attend one of the masses conducted in Algherese (or listen in on stories swapped by older fishermen) to hear it.

The **Museo Diocesano d'Arte Sacra** (Diocesan Museum of Sacred Art) is housed in a 13th-century church. The usual assortment of religious treasures—paintings, wooden sculptures, and bronzes—is on display; look for the masterful 16th-century Catalan silverware. ✉ *Via Maiorca 1* ☎ *079/9733041* 🎫 *€2.50* ⊘ *Jan.–Mar., Thurs.–Tues. by appointment; Apr., May, and Oct., Thurs.–Tues. 10–1 and 5–8; June and Sept., Thurs.–Tues. 10–1 and 5–9; July and Aug., Thurs.–Tues. 10–1 and 6–11; Dec., Thurs.–Tues. 10–1 by appointment and 4–7; the museum is closed Nov.*

West of Alghero are broad sandy beaches and the spectacular heights of **Capo Caccia**, an imposing limestone headland. At the base of a sheer cliff the pounding sea has carved an entrance to the vast **Grotta di Nettuno** (Neptune's Caves), a fantastic cavern filled with water pools, stalactites, and stalagmites. You must visit with a guide; tours start on the hour. ✛ *13 km (8 mi) west of Alghero* ☎ *079/946540* 🎫 *€10* ☉ *Apr.–Sept., daily 9–7; Oct., daily 9–5; Nov.–Mar., daily 9–4.*

By land you can reach the entrance to the Grotta di Nettuno by descending the 654 dizzying steps of the aptly named *escala del cabirol* (mountain goat's stairway). The trip to the top of the stairway takes about 50 minutes by **public bus**. ✉ *Via Catalogna* ☎ *079/950179* 🎫 *€4 round-trip* ☉ *From Alghero 9:15 year-round and 3:10 and 5:10 June–Sept. From Capo Caccia noon year-round and 4:05 and 6:05 June–Sept.*

Taking a **boat tour** from Alghero to see Neptune's caves takes 2½ hours and is much less exhausting than approaching on foot, but is not possible November–March and when seas are rough. The boat departs from docks near Bastione della Maddalena, on the northeast edge of the old town. ✉ *Navisarda* ☎ *079/950603* 🎫 *€12, plus cave admission* ☉ *Apr., May, and Oct., daily 9, 10, and 3; June–Sept., daily 9–5 on the hr.*

Where to Stay & Eat

★ **$$$$** ✗ **Andreini.** Traverse the loftiest heights of Sardinian elegance at an expensive, opulent, ambitious—yet somehow cozy—restaurant. The place is set to the nines: candles, tablecloths, and waiters abound; the service and wine list are just so. The food is equally romantic; a great tasting menu highlights the Andreini brothers' artful use of local ingredients like pecorino cheese and wild fennel. Creations might include homemade cuttlefish-ink tagliatelle with asparagus or wild boar with Cannonau wine sauce. The weekday three-course "business lunch" is a good value. ✉ *Via Arduino 45* ☎ *079/982098* ⚓ *Reservations essential* ▭ *AE, DC, MC, V* ☉ *Closed Mon. Sept.–May.*

$ ✗ **Da Pietro.** A menu that includes *bucatini all'algherese* (hollow, spaghetti-like pasta with a sauce of clams, capers, tomatoes, and olives) and baked fish with a white-wine sauce keeps this seafood restaurant bustling below its vaulted ceilings. Look for Da Pietro in the old town near Largo San Francesco. ✉ *Via Ambrogio Machin 20* ☎ *079/979645* ▭ *AE, MC, V* ☉ *Closed Wed. and Dec. 15–27.*

$$$$ 🏨 **Carlos V.** On the shore boulevard opposite the Villa Las Tronas, this modern hotel (pronounced Carlos Quinto) has an array of gardens and terraces, and a big pool overlooking the sea. Don't settle for a slightly cheaper room facing the back; the pleasure here is all in the magnificent view from your balcony. Low-season rates are a bargain. ✉ *Lungomare Valencia 24, 07041* ☎ *079/9720600* 🖨 *079/980298* ⊕ *www.hotelcarlosv.it* ⇒ *110 rooms* ⚬ *Restaurant, minibars, cable TV, miniature golf, 2 tennis courts, 2 saltwater pools, 2 bars, playground, business services, meeting rooms* ▭ *AE, DC, MC, V* 🍽 *BP.*

★ **$$$$** 🏨 **Villa Las Tronas.** Gardens surround a narrow drive that separates this hotel's little island from the road, imparting a regal sense of seclusion

16

to what was once a royal mansion. Belle epoque interiors have ornate gilt chairs or canopy-draped beds. The Villa is on a rocky promontory—above the sea but still near the center—and there are great views from most rooms. Service is elegant and impeccable, from reception to the restaurant. It's open year-round, a rarity in these parts. ⊠ *Lungomare Valencia 1, 07041* ☎ *079/981818* 🖷 *079/981044* ⊕ *www.hvlt.com* 🛏 *22 rooms, 3 suites* ᝕ *Restaurant, minibars, Wi-Fi, saltwater pool, gym, beach, bicycles, billiards, Internet room, meeting room, some pets allowed* ☰ *AE, DC, MC, V* ❢❍❘ *MAP.*

$ 🏨 **San Francesco.** The convent that was once attached to the church of San Francesco has been reinvented as a hotel. The rooms are grouped around the 14th-century cloister and, though somewhat cramped, are modern and quiet. It's quite central, in Alghero's Spanish quarter. ⊠ *Via Machin 2, 07041* ☎ *079/980330* ⊕ *www.sanfrancescohotel. com* 🛏 *21 rooms* ᝕ *Bar, meeting room* ☰ *MC, V* ⊗ *Closed Nov.–mid-Dec.* ❢❍❘ *BP.*

Nightlife

The **Caffè Costantino** (⊠ Piazza Civica 30 ☎ 079/976154) is sumptuous and elegant, with yellow flowered walls, chandeliers, classical music, and a warm crowd of distinguished, well-dressed Algherese. Stop in for a glass of local wine or just a coffee; it's open until midnight.

Baraonda (⊠ Principe Umberto 75 ☎ 079/975922), a marvelous local wine bar, also carries specialty liqueurs and grappas from all over Sardinia.

The hip **Il Tunnel** (⊠ Via G. Ferret 37 ☎ 340/2476190) bar, inside an ancient tunnel, is striking and open late into the night.

Shopping

Jewelry purveyors dot Alghero's old quarter; Via Carlo Alberto is especially good for handmade coral products. A great place to buy wine is **Bacco e Tabacco** (⊠ Via Roma 91 ☎ 079/9735030 ⊕ www. baccoetabacco.it), which ships all over the world.

Sassari

⓭ *34 km (21 mi) northeast of Alghero, 212 km (132 mi) north of Cagliari.*

Inland Sassari is an important university town and administrative center, notable for its history of intellectualism and bohemian student culture, an ornate old cathedral, and a good archaeological museum. Look for downtown vendors of *fainè,* a pizzalike chickpea-flour pancake glistening with olive oil, which is a Genovese and Sassarese specialty. Sassari is the hub of several highways and secondary roads leading to various coastal resorts, among them Stintino and Castelsardo.

Sassari's excellent **Museo Sanna** has the best archaeological collection outside Cagliari, spanning nuraghic, Carthaginian, and Roman histories, including well-preserved bronze statues and household objects from the second millennium BC. Summer hours vary from one year to the next. ⊠ *Via Roma 64* ☎ *079/272203* 💷 *€2* ⊗ *Tues.–Sun. 9–8.*

Where to Eat

¢ ✕ **L'Assassino.** Get a true taste of great local Sassarese cooking—and many of the other obscure Sardinian specialties you might have been looking for but not yet found. Horse, donkey, and roast pig figure prominently on the menu; best of all is a *cena sarda*, a 10-dish tasting menu with *porcetto* (roast suckling pig), also spelled *porcheddu*. The service is friendly, and the room is warm and cozy. Food is, unusually, served all afternoon long. ✉ *Vicolo Ospizio Cappuccini 1, near Via Rosello* ☎ *079/235041* ⊟ *AE, DC, MC, V* ☺ *Closed Sun.*

Shopping

Sassari has Sardinia's main **ISOLA** (✉ Giardini Pubblici ☎ 079/230101), a craft exhibition center in the public gardens next to Viale Mancini built specifically as a showcase for gifts and souvenirs.

On the way to Santa Teresa di Gallura, the walled seaside citadel of **Castelsardo,** 32 km (20 mi) northeast of Sassari, is a delight for basket lovers. Roadside stands and shops in the old town sell woven baskets, as well as rugs and wrought iron. The appropriately shaped **Roccia dell'Elefante** (Elephant Rock) on the road into Castelsardo was hollowed out by primitive man to become a *domus de janas* (literally, "fairy house," in fact a Neolithic burial chamber).

16

Santa Teresa di Gallura

⑭ *100 km (62 mi) northeast of Sassari, 65 km (41 mi) northwest of Olbia.*

At the northern tip of Sardinia, Santa Teresa di Gallura retains the relaxed, carefree air of a former fishing village. Nearby beaches rival those farther down the coast but manage not to seem overtouristed.

Where to Stay & Eat

¢ ✕🖼 **Canne al Vento.** Step into a family-run hotel and restaurant that is a quiet, cheerful haven in town. Despite a bland exterior, the place has a defiantly rustic feel, with a bamboo-roof restaurant and the odd ornamental wagon wheel. Rooms are sparsely furnished but cool and comfortable. The restaurant ($$$) specializes in authentic island cuisine, for example *zuppa cuata* (bread, cheese, and tomato soup), porcheddu, and seafood. ✉ *Via Nazionale 23, 07028* ☎ *0789/754219* 🖨 *0789/754948* ↩ *22 rooms* ⚭ *Restaurant, minibars* ⊟ *AE, DC, MC, V* ☺ *Closed Oct.–Mar. Restaurant closed Mon.* ⏐◉⏐ *BP.*

$$$$ 🖼 **Grand Hotel Corallaro.** This hotel has luxury accommodations in a panoramic spot right by the beach, a brief walk from the town center. Rooms are functional and some have balconies. Public rooms are much grander, furnished with wicker chairs, and there are terraces and lawns on which to sip drinks. Half board and a seven-day minimum stay are required in August; the rest of the year, the minimum stay is three days (sizeable discounts are available). ✉ *Località Rena Bianca, 07028* ☎ *0789/755475* 🖨 *0789/755431* ⊕ *www.hotelcorallaro.it* ↩ *85 rooms* ⚭ *Restaurant, indoor pool, gym, Turkish baths, beach* ⊟ *AE, DC, MC, V* ☺ *Closed mid-Oct.–Easter* ⏐◉⏐ *MAP.*

La Maddalena

⑮ *30 km (19 mi) east of Santa Teresa di Gallura, 45 km (20 mi) northwest of Olbia.*

From the port of Palau you can visit the archipelago of La Maddalena, seven granite islands embellished with lush green scrub and wind-bent pines. Car ferries make the 3-km (2-mi) trip about every half hour.

Pilgrims pay homage to national hero **Giuseppe Garibaldi's tomb** (1807–82) on the grounds of his hideaway. Take the ferry to Isola Maddalena and then the bridge to Isola Caprera. ⚓ *7 km (4½ mi) east of Isola Maddalena* ☎ *0789/727162* 🖃 *€2* ☉ *Oct.–Apr., Tues.–Sun. 9–1:30; May–Sept., Tues.–Sun. 9–6:30.*

Porto Cervo

★ **⑯** *35 km (22 mi) southeast of La Maddalena, 30 km (19 mi) north of Olbia.*

Sardinia's northeastern coast is fringed with low cliffs, inlets, and small bays. This has become an upscale vacationland, with glossy resorts such as Baia Sardinia and Porto Rotondo just outside the confines of the famed Costa Smeralda, developed by the Aga Khan (born 1936), who in 1965 accidentally discovered the coast's charms—and potential—when his yacht took shelter here from a storm. In the late '60s and '70s, the Costa Smeralda, with its heart in Porto Cervo, was *the* place to summer. The attractions remain geared to those who can measure themselves by the yardstick of Khan's fabled riches. Italy's most expensive hotels are here, and the world's most magnificent yachts anchor in the waters of Porto Cervo.

All along the coast, carefully tended lush vegetation surrounds vacation villages and discreet villas that have sprung up over the past decade in spurious architectural styles best described as bogus Mediterranean. The trend has been to keep this an enclave of the very rich. Outside the peak season, however, prices plunge and the majesty of the natural surroundings shines through, justifying all the hype and the Emerald Coast's fame as one of the truly romantic corners of the Mediterranean.

Where to Stay

$$$$ 🏨 **Cala di Volpe.** Long a magnet for the beautiful people, this hyper-glamorous establishment, now part of the Starwood Luxury Collection, was built to resemble an ancient Sardinian village, albeit one with high-speed Internet access. The rustic-elegant interior has wood-beam ceilings, terra-cotta floors, Sardinian arts-and-crafts decorations, and porticoes overlooking the sea. The Presidential Suite, in the highest tower, has a private pool. Summer prices, including the requisite half board, are so high (€2,000 and up) that you may think you've got the exchange rate wrong by a factor of 10—this is one of the most expensive hotels in the world (rates outside of July and August drop to just €1,000 and up).

✉ *Cala di Volpe, 07020* ☎ *0789/976111* 🖷 *0789/976617* 🌐 *www.luxurycollection.com* ➷ *122 rooms, 3 suites* ⚴ *2 restaurants, room service, in-room safes, cable TV with movies, in-room VCRs, in-room data ports, putting green, 3 tennis courts, saltwater pool, wading pool, spa, beach, boating, waterskiing, 3 bars, shops, babysitting, laundry service, concierge, business services, convention center, airport shuttle, car rental* 🖃 *AE, DC, MC, V* ⊗ *Closed mid-Oct.–mid-Apr.* ❢❶ *MAP.*

$$$$ 🏨 **Cervo Hotel.** Low Mediterranean buildings surround a large pool and garden in the heart of the Costa Smeralda's Porto Cervo. Colorful painted wood furniture and slip-covered pieces fill up the large rooms; most have a terrace. The five tennis courts are well-lighted at night. High-season prices (half board required) are through the roof, but in winter, prices fall to as low as one-tenth the summer rate. This Starwood Sheraton hotel complex is next to the marina and *piazzetta* (small piazza)—a popular spot to see and be seen. ✉ *Waterfront, 07020* ☎ *0789/931111* 🖷 *0789/931613* 🌐 *www.sheraton.com/cervo* ➷ *86 rooms, 6 suites* ⚴ *5 restaurants, room service, minibars, cable TV with movies, in-room data ports, 5 tennis courts, 3 pools (1 indoor), gym, beach, boating, waterskiing, squash, 4 bars, piano bar, babysitting, concierge, business services, convention center, travel services, no-smoking rooms* 🖃 *AE, DC, MC, V* ❢❶ *MAP.*

$$$$ 🏨 **Nibaru.** Pinkish-red brick buildings with tiled roofs stand on a secluded inlet amid lush gardens. Nibaru has all the best features of the Costa Smeralda at comparatively low rates: guest rooms are just a few yards from some superb ocean swimming spots, as well as from Nibaru's lagoonlike pool. From here you have easy access of the Pevero Golf Club and the tennis courts of Porto Cervo. ✉ *Località Cala di Volpe, 07020* ☎ *0789/96038* 🖷 *0789/96474* 🌐 *www.hotelnibaru.it* ➷ *50 rooms, 2 suites* ⚴ *Minibars, pool, bar* 🖃 *AE, DC, MC, V* ⊗ *Closed mid-Oct.–mid-Apr.* ❢❶ *BP.*

Sports & the Outdoors

The world-class, 18-hole **Pevero Golf Course** (✉ Bay of Pevero ☎ 0789/96210) was designed by Robert Trent Jones.

The **Yacht Club Costa Smeralda** (✉ Via della Marina ☎ 0789/902200 🌐 www.yccs.it) provides use of its pool, restaurant, bar, and guest rooms to those with memberships at other yacht clubs.

Olbia

⑰ *30 km (19 mi) south of Porto Cervo, 106 km (66 mi) north of Nuoro.*

Set amid the resorts of Sardinia's northeastern coast, Olbia is a lively little seaport and port of call for mainland ferries at the head of a long, wide bay. The little basilica of **San Simplicio**, a short walk behind the main Corso Umberto, is worth searching out if you have any spare time in Olbia. The simple granite structure dates from the 11th century, part of the great Pisan church-building program, using pillars and columns recycled from Roman buildings. ⊠ *Via San Simplicio* ☎ *0789/23358* ⊙ *Daily 6:30–12:30 and 4–7.*

Where to Stay & Eat

$$ ✕ **Barbagia.** Traditional dishes from Sardinia's wild interior fuse with local ingredients here. Antipasti might be a refreshing salad of sliced tomato and fresh cheese (called *sa t'amata chi sa frughe*). Then try maccarones de busa with a wild boar sauce; you might also find roast lamb and suckling pig in season. A good selection of pizza is served for dinner only. This is a classic downtown gathering place with a simple, bright array of tables. ⊠ *Via Galvani 94* ☎ *0789/51640* ▤ *AE, DC, MC, V* ⊙ *Closed Wed. Oct.–June.*

$$ ▥ **Martini.** Plush, modern, and businesslike, Martini occupies an eye-catching site on the shore of a lagoon north of town. The hotel has lounge chairs on the roof with views of the port. Most of the classic bedrooms also benefit from the excellent vista. It's a 20-minute walk or easy taxi ride from the port and center, and is thankfully detached from the early-morning and late-night comings and goings of ferries. ⊠ *Via G. D'An-nunzio 21, 07026* ☎ *0789/26066* ▧ *0789/26418* ⊕ *www.hotelmartiniolbia.com* ⤺ *70 rooms* ⚭ *Restaurant, in-room safes, mini-bars, bar, meeting room* ▤ *AE, DC, MC, V* ▥◯ *BP.*

Golfo Aranci

⓲ *19 km (12 mi) northeast of Olbia.*

At the mouth of the Gulf of Olbia, Golfo Aranci is a small-scale resort and major arrival point for ferries from the mainland. The craggy headland west of town has been left undeveloped as a nature reserve, and there are some inviting beaches within an easy drive.

SARDINIA ESSENTIALS

Transportation

BY AIR

Flying is by far the fastest and easiest way to get to the island. Sardinia's major airport is in Cagliari, with smaller ones at Alghero and Olbia, the latter serving the Costa Smeralda. Cagliari's Aeroporto di Elmas is about 6 km (4 mi) west of town center, and there is regular bus service from the airport to Piazza Matteotti, in front of the train station. Alghero's Aeroporto Fertilia is 13 km (8 mi) from the city. A bus links the airport with the bus station in the center of town. Aeroporto Costa Smeralda is 4 km (2½ mi) southeast of Olbia, linked by local bus to Olbia.

Alitalia offers frequent direct flights between Cagliari and Rome's Fiumicino Airport; the trip takes about 40 minutes. Meridiana provides service between Cagliari and Bologna, Naples, Paris, Turin, and London's Gatwick; between Olbia and Bologna, Florence, Milan, and Rome; and between Cagliari and Olbia. Air One connects Cagliari with Milan, Pisa, and Turin; and Alghero with Milan and Rome. RyanAir has direct flights between Alghero and secondary airports of major Euopean cities: London's Stansted, Frankfurt's Hahn, Barcelona's Girona, and Rome's Ciampino. EasyJet provides service between Olbia and London's Gatwick and Berlin's Schönefeld, and between Cagliari and London's Luton.

🔢 Airport Information **Aeroporto Alghero-Fertilia (AHO)** ☎ 079/935282 ⊕ www. aeroportodialghero.it. **Aeroporto Cagliari-Elmas (CAG)** ☎ 070/211211 ⊕ www.sogaer. it. **Aeroporto Oblia Costa Smeralda (OLB)** ☎ 0789/563444 ⊕ www.geasar.com.

🔢 Airlines & Contacts **Air One** ☎ 199/207080 toll-free, 06/48880069 from outside Italy) ⊕ www.flyairone.it. **Alitalia** ☎ 800/223-5730 in U.S., 020/7602-7111 in London, 0990/ 448-259 in U.K., 06/65641 in Rome, 848/865641 elsewhere in Italy ⊕ www.alitalia.it. **EasyJet** ⊕ www.easyjet.com. **Meridiana** ☎ 199/111333 toll-free, 0789/52682 from outside Italy ⊕ www.meridiana.it. **RyanAir** ☎ 0870/1-569-569 in U.K., 899/678910 in Italy, 353/12497700 from elsewhere to headquarters in Ireland ⊕ www.ryanair.com.

BY BOAT & FERRY

Large modern ferries run by Tirrenia Lines and Moby Lines, and Corsica Ferries connect Sardinian ports at Porto Torres, Olbia, Arbatax, and Cagliari with the mainland. These ferries are a popular mode of transport. Tirrenia connects Naples with Cagliari; Genoa with Porto Torres, Olbia, and Arbatax; Civitavecchia (near Rome) with Olbia, Arbatax, and Cagliari; Fiumicino (near Rome) with Golfo Aranci and Arbatax; and Cagliari with Palermo and Trapani. Vehicles can generally be transported on Tirrenia ferries. Moby Lines carries passengers and cars between Olbia and Civitavecchia, Genoa, and Livorno. Corsica Ferries, for passengers and cars, sail from Civitavecchia to Golfo Aranci, near Olbia. Grandi Navi Veloci run comfortable ferries that resemble cruise ships between Genoa and Porto Torres (year-round) and Genoa and Olbia (June–September). French SNCM ferries transport passengers to and from Marseille, France.

FARES & SCHEDULES The ferry ride on Tirrenia from Naples to Cagliari takes about 17 hours and costs approximately €75 for first-class passage in mid- or high season with a berth (and €100 for automobile transport). The Civitavecchia–Olbia/Golfo Aranci run (€50) takes about eight hours, and there are overnight trips; or you can choose a high-speed ferry (summer only), which takes just four to six hours but costs more and gets booked up weeks ahead during the peak of the season in mid-August. Normal ferry service is scheduled two or three times a week, and high-speed ferries depart one to four times daily.

🔢 Boat & Ferry Information **Corsica Ferries** ☎ 199/400500 ⊕ www.corsicaferries. it. **Grandi Navi Veloci** ☎ 02/89012281 ⊕ www.gnv.it. **Moby Lines** ☎ 06/42011455 or 0586/826824 ⊕ www.mobylines.it. **SNCM** ☎ 33/0825888088 to France ⊕ www.sncm. fr. **Tirrenia** ☎ 199/123199, 081/3172999 from cellular phones and outside Italy ⊕ www. tirrenia.it.

BY BUS

Cagliari is linked with the other towns of Sardinia by a network of buses. Local destinations are served by ARST. Major cities, excluding Olbia, are served by PANI. The heart of the Sardinian bus system is the Stazione

16

Autolinee, across the square from the main tourist office in Cagliari. City buses in Cagliari and Sassari operate on the same system as those on the mainland: buy your ticket first, at a tobacco shop or machine, and punch it in the machine on the bus. Fares are €1 per ride.

Bus Information **ARST** ☎ 070/40981 ⊕ www.arst.sardegna.it. **PANI** ☎ 070/652326. **Stazione Autolinee** ✉ Piazza Matteotti, Cagliari ☎ 070/4098324.

BY CAR

Sardinia is about 260 km (162 mi) long from north to south and takes three to four hours to drive on the main roads; it's roughly 120 km (75 mi) across. Cars may be taken on board most of the ferry lines connecting Sardinia with the mainland.

The main highway linking Cagliari with Sassari was begun in 1820 by the Savoy ruler Carlo Felice; designated S131, but still referred to as the Strada Carlo Felice by the islanders, it runs through the fertile Campidano Plain, bordered by rhododendrons for virtually all of the 216 km (134 mi) between the two cities. The S131dir (not to be confused with the S131) and S129 connect the Strada Carlo Felice with Nuoro and the Barbagia. The S597 connects Sassari and Olbia.

Roads are generally in good condition, but bear in mind that roadside facilities are infrequent, especially in the east. Try to avoid driving at night, when mountain roads are particularly hazardous and slow. Fog is an issue in winter.

BY TRAIN

The Stazione Centrale in Cagliari is next to the bus station on Piazza Matteotti. There are fairly good connections between Olbia, Cagliari, Sassari, and Oristano. You can reach Nuoro via Macomer; Alghero is reached via Sassari. Service on the few other local lines is infrequent and slow. The fastest train between Olbia and Cagliari takes more than four hours. Local trains connect Golfo Aranci, the Ferrovie dello Stato (Italian State Railways, or Trenitalia) port for the train ferry, with Olbia (20 minutes) and Sassari with Alghero (35 minutes).

Train Information **Ferrovie dello Stato** ☎ 892021 ⊕ www.trenitalia.com.

Contacts & Resources

EMERGENCIES

Late-night pharmacies are open on a rotating basis; information on current schedules is pinned up on any pharmacy door or can be obtained by calling 192.

ACI provides 24-hour roadside assistance for emergencies.

ACI ☎ 803/116. **Ambulance** ✉ Cagliari ☎ 070/4092901. **Hospital** Ospedale Civile San Michele ✉ Via Peretti, Cagliari ☎ 070/543266. **Police** ☎ 112 or 113.

TOURS

Cagliari travel agency conducts tours of Sardinia. The Associazione Nazionale di Turismo Equestre can provide information on horseback riding tours both along the coast and inland. The Centro Vacanze Ala Birdi organizes riding vacations.

▣ Horseback Riding Tours **Associazione Nazionale di Turismo Equestre** ⊠ Via Carso 35/a, Sassari ☎ 079/299889. **Cagliari** Viaggi Orrù ⊠ Via Roma 95, Cagliari ☎ 070/659858 ⊕ www.viaggiorru.it. **Centro Vacanze Ala Birdi** ⊠ Strada a Mare 24/27, 09092 Arborea, near Oristano ☎ 0783/80500 ⊕ www.hotelalabirdi.it.

VISITOR INFORMATION

The official Sardinia Web site has information for many island towns. ▣ Tourist Information **Sardinia** ⊠ Viale Trieste 105 ☎ 070/606280 ⊕ www.regione.sardegna.it. **Alghero** ⊠ Piazza Porta Terra 9, 07041 ☎ 079/979054. **Cagliari** ⊠ Piazza Matteotti 9, 09100 ☎ 070/669255 ⊠ Aeroporto di Elmas ☎ 070/240200. **Golfo Aranci** ⊠ City Hall, 07026 ☎ 0789/21672 June–Aug. **Nuoro** ⊠ Piazza Italia 19, 08100 ☎ 0784/30083. **Olbia** ⊠ Via Castello Piro 1, 07026 ☎ 0789/21453 ⊠ Aeroporto Costa Smeralda ☎ 0789/52634. **Oristano** ⊠ Piazza Eleonora 19, 09170 ☎ 0783/36831. **Sassari** ⊠ Via Roma 62, 07100 ☎ 079/231777.

16

ITALIAN VOCABULARY

English	Italian	Pronunciation

Basics

Yes/no	Sí/No	see/no
Please	Per favore	pear fa-**vo**-ray
Yes, please	Sí grazie	see **grah**-tsee-ay
Thank you	Grazie	**grah**-tsee-ay
You're welcome	Prego	**pray**-go
Excuse me, sorry	Scusi	**skoo**-zee
Sorry!	Mi dispiace!	mee dis-spee-**ah**-chay
Good morning/ afternoon	Buongiorno	bwohn-**jor**-no
Good evening	Buona sera	**bwoh**-na **say**-ra
Good-bye	Arrivederci	a-ree-vah-**dare**-chee
Mr. (Sir)	Signore	see-**nyo**-ray
Mrs. (Ma'am)	Signora	see-**nyo**-ra
Miss	Signorina	see-nyo-**ree**-na
Pleased to meet you	Piacere	pee-ah-**chair**-ray
How are you?	Come sta?	**ko**-may **stah**
Very well, thanks	Bene, grazie	**ben**-ay **grah**-tsee-ay
And you?	E lei?	ay **lay**-ee
Hello (phone)	Pronto?	**proan**-to

Numbers

one	uno	**oo**-no
two	due	**doo**-ay
three	tre	tray
four	quattro	**kwah**-tro
five	cinque	**cheen**-kway
six	sei	say
seven	sette	**set**-ay
eight	otto	**oh**-to
nine	nove	**no**-vay
ten	dieci	dee-**eh**-chee
eleven	undici	**oon**-dee-chee
twelve	dodici	**doe**-dee-chee
thirteen	tredici	**tray**-dee-chee

fourteen	quattordici	kwa-**tore**-dee-chee
fifteen	quindici	**kwin**-dee-chee
sixteen	sedici	**say**-dee-chee
seventeen	diciassette	dee-cha-**set**-ay
eighteen	diciotto	dee-**cho**-to
nineteen	diciannove	dee-cha-**no**-vay
twenty	venti	**vain**-tee
twenty-one	ventuno	vain-**too**-no
twenty-two	ventidue	vain-tee-**doo**-ay
thirty	trenta	**train**-ta
forty	quaranta	kwa-**rahn**-ta
fifty	cinquanta	cheen-**kwahn**-ta
sixty	sessanta	seh-**sahn**-ta
seventy	settanta	seh-**tahn**-ta
eighty	ottanta	o-**tahn**-ta
ninety	novanta	no-**vahn**-ta
one hundred	cento	**chen**-to
one thousand	mille	**mee**-lay
ten thousand	diecimila	dee-eh-chee-**mee**-la

Useful Phrases

Do you speak English?	Parla inglese?	**par**-la een-**glay**-zay
I don't speak Italian	Non parlo italiano	non **par**-lo ee-tal-**yah**-no
I don't understand	Non capisco	non ka-**peess**-ko
Can you please repeat?	Può ripetere?	pwo ree-**pet**-ay-ray
Slowly!	Lentamente!	**len**-ta-men-tay
I don't know	Non lo so	non lo **so**
I'm American/ British	Sono americano(a) Sono inglese	**so**-no a-may-ree-**kah**-no(a) **so**-no een-**glay**-zay
What's your name?	Come si chiama?	**ko**-may see kee-**ah**-ma
My name is . . .	Mi chiamo . . .	mee kee-**ah**-mo
What time is it?	Che ore sono?	kay **o**-ray **so**-no
How?	Come?	**ko**-may
When?	Quando?	**kwan**-doe
Yesterday/today/ tomorrow	Ieri/oggi/domani	**yer**-ee/**o**-jee/ do-**mah**-nee

This morning/ afternoon	Stamattina/Oggi pomeriggio	sta-ma-**tee**-na/**o**-jee po-mer-**ee**-jo
Tonight	Stasera	sta-**ser**-a
What?	Che cosa?	kay **ko**-za
What is it?	Che cos'è?	kay ko-**zay**
Why?	Perché?	pear-**kay**
Who?	Chi?	kee
Where is . . .	Dov'è . . .	doe-**veh**
the bus stop?	la fermata dell'autobus?	la fer-**mah**-ta del ow-toe-**booss**
the train station?	la stazione?	la sta-tsee-**oh**-nay
the subway station?	la metropolitana?	la may-tro-po-lee-**tah**-na
the terminal?	il terminale?	eel ter-mee-**nah**-lay
the post office?	l'ufficio postale?	loo-**fee**-cho po-**stah**-lay
the bank?	la banca?	la **bahn**-ka
the . . . hotel?	l'hotel . . .?	lo-**tel**
the store?	il negozio?	eel nay-**go**-tsee-o
the cashier?	la cassa?	la **kah**-sa
the . . . museum?	il museo . . .?	eel moo-**zay**-o
the hospital?	l'ospedale?	lo-spay-**dah**-lay
the first-aid station?	il pronto soccorso?	eel **pron**-to so-**kor**-so
the elevator?	l'ascensore?	la-shen-**so**-ray
a telephone?	un telefono?	oon tay-**lay**-fo-no
Where are the restrooms?	Dov'è il bagno?	do-**vay** eel **bahn**-yo
Here/there	Qui/là	kwee/la
Left/right	A sinistra/a destra	a see-**neess**-tra/ a **des**-tra
Straight ahead	Avanti dritto	a-**vahn**-tee **dree**-to
Is it near/far?	È vicino/lontano?	ay vee-**chee**-no/ lon-**tah**-no
I'd like . . .	Vorrei . . .	vo-**ray**
a room	una camera	**oo**-na **kah**-may-ra
the key	la chiave	la kee-**ah**-vay
a newspaper	un giornale	oon jor-**nah**-lay
a stamp	un francobollo	oon frahn-ko-**bo**-lo
I'd like to buy . . .	Vorrei comprare . . .	vo-**ray** kom-**prah**-ray
a cigar	un sigaro	oon see-**gah**-ro
cigarettes	delle sigarette	**day**-lay see-ga-**ret**-ay
some matches	dei fiammiferi	**day**-ee **fee**-ah-**mee**-fer-ee
some soap	una saponetta	**oo**-na sa-po-**net**-a
a city plan	una pianta della città	**oo**-na **pyahn**-ta day-la chee-**tah**

a road map of . . .	una carta stradale di . . .	**oo**-na **cart**-a stra-**dah**-lay dee
a country map	una carta geografica	**oo**-na **cart**-a jay-o-**grah**-fee-ka
a magazine	una rivista	**oo**-na ree-**veess**-ta
envelopes	delle buste	**day**-lay **booss**-tay
writing paper	della carta da lettere	**day**-la **cart**-a da **let**-air-ay
a postcard	una cartolina	**oo**-na car-toe-**lee**-na
a guidebook	una guida turistica	**oo**-na **gwee**-da too-**reess**-tee-ka
How much is it?	Quanto costa?	**kwahn**-toe **coast**-a
It's expensive/cheap	È caro/economico	ay **car**-o/ay-ko-no-**mee**-ko
A little/a lot	Poco/tanto	**po**-ko/**tahn**-to
More/less	Più/meno	pee-**oo**/**may**-no
Enough/too (much)	Abbastanza/troppo	a-bas-**tahn**-sa/**tro**-po
I am sick	Sto male	sto **mah**-lay
Call a doctor	Chiama un dottore	kee-**ah**-mah oon doe-**toe**-ray
Help!	Aiuto!	a-**yoo**-toe
Stop!	Alt!	ahlt
Fire!	Al fuoco!	ahl **fwo**-ko
Caution/Look out!	Attenzione!	a-ten-**syon**-ay

Dining Out

A bottle of . . .	Una bottiglia di . . .	**oo**-na bo-**tee**-lee-ah dee
A cup of . . .	Una tazza di . . .	**oo**-na **tah**-tsa dee
A glass of . . .	Un bicchiere di . . .	oon bee-key-**air**-ay dee
Bill/check	Il conto	eel **cone**-toe
Bread	Il pane	eel **pah**-nay
Breakfast	La prima colazione	la **pree**-ma ko-la-**tsee**-oh-nay
Cocktail/aperitif	L'aperitivo	la-pay-ree-**tee**-vo
Dinner	La cena	la **chen**-a
Fixed-price menu	Menù a prezzo fisso	may-**noo** a **pret**-so **fee**-so
Fork	La forchetta	la for-**ket**-a
I am diabetic	Ho il diabete	o eel dee-a-**bay**-tay
I am vegetarian	Sono vegetariano/a	**so**-no vay-jay-ta-ree-**ah**-no/a
I'd like . . .	Vorrei . . .	vo-**ray**

I'd like to order	Vorrei ordinare	vo-**ray** or-dee-**nah**-ray
Is service included?	Il servizio è incluso?	eel ser-**vee**-tzee-o ay een-**kloo**-zo
It's good/bad	È buono/cattivo	ay **bwo**-no/ka-**tee**-vo
It's hot/cold	È caldo/freddo	ay **kahl**-doe/**fred**-o
Knife	Il coltello	eel kol-**tel**-o
Lunch	Il pranzo	eel **prahnt**-so
Menu	Il menù	eel may-**noo**
Napkin	Il tovagliolo	eel toe-va-lee-**oh**-lo
Please give me . . .	Mi dia . . .	mee **dee**-a
Salt	Il sale	eel **sah**-lay
Spoon	Il cucchiaio	eel koo-kee-**ah**-yo
Sugar	Lo zucchero	lo **tsoo**-ker-o
Waiter/Waitress	Cameriere/ cameriera	ka-mare-**yer**-ay/ ka-mare-**yer**-a
Wine list	La lista dei vini	la **lee**-sta **day**-ee **vee**-nee

MENU GUIDE

English	Italian
Set menu	Menù a prezzo fisso
Dish of the day	Piatto del giorno
Specialty of the house	Specialità della casa
Local specialties	Specialità locali
Extra charge	Extra . . .
In season	Di stagione
Cover charge/Service charge	Coperto/Servizio

Breakfast

Butter	Burro
Croissant	Cornetto
Eggs	Uova
Honey	Miele
Jam/Marmalade	Marmellata
Roll	Panino
Toast	Pane tostato

Starters

Assorted cold cuts	Affettati misti
Assorted seafood	Antipasto di pesce
Assorted appetizers	Antipasto misto
Toasted rounds of bread, fried or toasted in oil	Crostini/Crostoni
Diced-potato and vegetable salad with mayonnaise	Insalata russa
Eggplant parmigiana	Melanzane alla parmigiana
Fried mozzarella sandwich	Mozzarella in carrozza
Ham and melon	Prosciutto e melone
Cooked sausages and cured meats	Salumi cotti
Filled pastry shells	Vol-au-vents

Soups

"Angel hair," thin noodle soup	Capelli d'angelo
Cream of . . .	Crema di . . .
Pasta-and-bean soup	Pasta e fagioli
Egg-drop and Parmesan cheese soup	Stracciatella

Pasta, Rice, and Pizza

Filled pasta	Agnolotti/ravioli/tortellini
Potato dumplings	Gnocchi

Semolina dumplings	Gnocchi alla romana
Pasta	Pasta
with four cheeses	*al quattro formaggi*
with basil/cheese/pine nuts/ garlic sauce	*al pesto*
with tomato-based meat sauce	*al ragù*
with tomato sauce	*al sugo* or *al pomodoro*
with butter	*in bianco* or *al burro*
with egg, Parmesan cheese, and pepper	*alla carbonara*
green (spinach-based) pasta	*verde*
Rice	Riso
Rice dish	Risotto
with mushrooms	*ai funghi*
with saffron	*alla milanese*
Noodles	Tagliatelle
Pizza	Pizza
Pizza with seafood, cheese, artichokes, and ham in four different sections	Pizza quattro stagioni
Pizza with tomato and mozzarella	Pizza margherita
Pizza with oil, garlic, and oregano	Pizza marinara

Fish and Seafood

Anchovies	Acciughe
Bass	Persico
Carp	Carpa
Clams	Vongole
Cod	Merluzzo
Crab	Granchio
Eel	Anguilla
Lobster	Aragosta
Mackerel	Sgombro
Mullet	Triglia
Mussels	Cozze
Octopus	Polpo
Oysters	Ostriche
Pike	Luccio
Prawns	Gamberoni
Salmon	Salmone
Shrimp	Scampi
Shrimps	Gamberetti
Sole	Sogliola
Squid	Calamari
Swordfish	Pescespada

Trout	Trota
Tuna	Tonno

Methods of Preparation

Baked	Al forno
Cold, with vinegar sauce	In carpione
Fish stew	Zuppa di pesce
Fried	Fritto
Grilled (usually charcoal)	Alla griglia
Seafood salad	In insalata
Smoked	Affumicato
Stuffed	Ripieno

Meat

Boar	Cinghiale
Brain	Cervella
Braised meat with wine	Brasato
Chop	Costoletta
Duck	Anatra
Lamb	Agnello
Baby lamb	Abbacchio
Liver	Fegato
Pheasant	Fagiano
Pork roast	Arista
Rabbit	Coniglio
Steak	Bistecca
Sliced raw steak with sauce	Carpaccio
Mixed boiled meat	Bollito misto

Methods of Preparation

Battered with eggs and crumbs and fried	. . . alla milanese
Grilled	. . . ai ferri
Grilled (usually charcoal)	. . . alla griglia
Raw, with lemon/egg sauce	. . . alla tartara
Roasted	. . . arrosto
Very rare	. . . al sangue
Well done	. . . ben cotta
With ham and cheese	. . . alla valdostana
With Parmesan cheese and tomatoes	. . . alla parmigiana

Vegetables

Artichokes	Carciofi
Asparagus	Asparagi
Beans	Fagioli

Brussels sprouts	Cavolini di Bruxelles
Cabbage	Cavolo
Carrots	Carote
Cauliflower	Cavolfiore
Cucumber	Cetriolo
Eggplants	Melanzane
Green beans	Fagiolini
Leeks	Porri
Lentils	Lenticchie
Lettuce	Lattuga
Mushrooms	Funghi
Onions	Cipolle
Peas	Piselli
Peppers	Peperoni
Potatoes	Patate
Roasted potatoes	*Patate arroste*
Boiled potatoes	*Patate bollite*
Fried potatoes	*Patate fritte*
Small, roasted potatoes	*Patatine novelle*
Mashed potatoes	*Purè di patate*
Radishes	Rapanelli
Salad	Insalata
vegetable	*mista*
green	*verde*
Spinach	Spinaci
Tomatoes	Pomodori
Zucchini	Zucchini

Sauces, Herbs, and Spices

Basil	Basilico
Bay leaf	Lauro
Chervil	Cerfoglio
Dill	Aneto
Garlic	Aglio
Hot dip with anchovies (for vegetables)	Bagna cauda
Marjoram	Maggiorana
Mayonnaise	Maionese
Mustard	Mostarda *or* senape
Oil	Olio
Parsley-based sauce	Salsa verde
Pepper	Pepe
Rosemary	Rosmarino
Tartar sauce	Salsa tartara
Vinegar	Aceto
White sauce	Besciamella

Cheeses

Fresh:	Caprino fresco
	Mascarpone
	Mozzarella
	Ricotta
Mild:	Caciotta
	Caprino
	Fontina
	Grana
	Provola
	Provolone dolce
	Robiola
	Scamorza
Sharp:	Asiago
	Gorgonzola
	Groviera
	Pecorino
	Provolone piccante
	Taleggio
	Toma

Fruits and Nuts

Almonds	Mandorle
Apple	Mela
Apricot	Albicocca
Blackberries	More
Black currant	Ribes nero
Blueberries	Mirtilli
Cherries	Ciliege
Chestnuts	Castagne
Coconut	Noce di cocco
Dates	Datteri
Figs	Fichi
Green grapes	Uva bianca
Black grapes	Uva nera
Grapefruit	Pompelmo
Hazelnuts	Nocciole
Lemon	Limone
Melon	Melone
Nectarine	Nocepesca
Orange	Arancia
Pear	Pera
Peach	Pesca
Pineapple	Ananas
Plum	Prugna/Susina
Prune	Prugna secca

Raisins	Uva passa
Raspberries	Lamponi
Red currant	Ribes
Strawberries	Fragole
Tangerine	Mandarino
Walnuts	Noci
Watermelon	Anguria/Cocomero
Dried fruit	Frutta secca
Fresh fruit	Frutta fresca
Fruit salad	Macedonia di frutta

Desserts

Custard filed pastry, with candied fruit	Cannoli
Ricotta filled pastry shells with sugar glaze	Cannoli alla siciliana
Ice cream with candied fruit	Cassata
Ricotta filed cake with sugar glaze	Cassata siciliana
Chocolate	Cioccolato
Cup of ice cream	Coppa gelato
Caramel custard	Crème caramel
Pie	Crostata
Fruit pie	Crostata di frutta
Ice cream	Gelato
Flaked pastry	Millefoglie
Chestnuts and whipped-cream cake	Montebianco
Whipped cream	Panna montata
Pastries	Paste
Sherbet	Sorbetto
Chocolate-coated ice cream	Tartufo
Fruit tart	Torta di frutta
Apple tart	Torta di mele
Ice-cream cake	Torta gelata
Vanilla	Vaniglia
Egg-based cream with sugar and Marsala wine	Zabaione
Ice-cream filled cake	Zuccotto

Alcoholic Drinks

On the rocks	Con ghiaccio
Straight	Liscio
With soda	Con seltz
Beer	Birra
light/dark	*chiara/scura*

Bitter cordial	Amaro
Brandy	Cognac
Cordial	Liquore
Aniseed cordial	Sambuca
Martini	Cocktail Martini
Port	Porto
Vermouth	Vermut/Martini
Wine	Vino
blush	*rosé*
dry	*secco*
full-bodied	*corposo*
light	*leggero*
red	*rosso*
sparkling	*spumante*
sweet	*dolce*
very dry	*brut*
white	*bianco*
Light wine	Vinello
Bottle	Bottiglia
Carafe	Caraffa
Flask	Fiasco

Nonalcoholic Drinks

Mineral water	Acqua minerale
carbonated	*gassata*
still	*non gassata*
Tap water	Acqua naturale
Tonic water	Acqua tonica
Coffee with steamed milk	Cappuccino
Espresso	Caffè espresso
with milk	*macchiato*
decaffeinated	*decaffeinato*
lighter espresso	*lungo*
with cordial	*corretto*
Fruit juice	Succo di frutta
Lemonade	Limonata
Milk	Latte
Orangeade	Aranciata
Tea	Tè
with milk/lemon	*col latte/col limone*
iced	*freddo*

SMART TRAVEL TIPS

Air Travel
Airports
Beaches
Bike Travel
Bus Travel
Business Hours
Car Rental
Car Travel
Computers on the Road
Consumer Protection
Customs & Duties
Eating & Drinking
Electricity
Embassies
Emergencies
English-Language Media
Etiquette & Behavior
Hiking & Walking
Holidays
Insurance
Language
Lodging
Mail & Shipping
Money Matters
Packing
Passports & Visas
Restrooms
Safety
Shopping
Sightseeing Guides
Smoking
Taxes
Telephones
Time
Tipping
Tours & Packages
Train Travel
Travel Agencies
Visitor Information
Web Sites

There are planners and there are those who, excuse the pun, fly by the seat of their pants. We happily place ourselves among the planners. Our writers and editors try to anticipate all the issues you may face before and during any journey, and then they do their research. This section is the product of their efforts. Use it to get excited about your trip to Italy, to inform your travel planning, or to guide you on the road should the seat of your pants start to feel threadbare.

AIR TRAVEL

The price of flying within Italy is often comparable to the cost of train travel, but be sure to factor in the expense of getting to and from the airport. When flying out of Italian airports, always check with the airport or tourist agency about upcoming strikes, which are frequent in Italy and often affect air travel.

BOOKING

When you book, look for nonstop flights and remember that "direct" flights stop at least once. If it's feasible, avoid connecting flights, which require a change of plane—though for many Italian cities, a connection is your only option when coming from overseas. Two airlines may operate a connecting flight jointly, so ask whether your airline operates every segment of the trip; you may find that the carrier you prefer flies you only part of the way. To find more booking tips and to check prices and make online flight reservations, log on to www.fodors.com.

CARRIERS

When flying internationally, you must usually choose between a domestic carrier, the national flag carrier of the country you are visiting (Alitalia for Italy), and a foreign carrier from a third country. National flag carriers have the greatest number of nonstops. Domestic carriers may have better connections to your hometown and serve a greater number of gateway cities. Third-party carriers may have a price advantage.

On flights from the United States, Alitalia and Delta Air Lines serve Rome, Milan, and Venice. The major international hubs in Italy, Milan and Rome, are also served by Continental Airlines and American Airlines, and US Airways serves Rome. From April through October, the Italy-based EuroFly has nonstop flights from New York to Rome, Naples, Bologna, and Palermo.

Alitalia and British Airways have direct flights from London to Milan, Venice, Rome, and 10 other locations in Italy. Smaller, no-frills airlines also provide service between Great Britain and Italy. EasyJet connects Gatwick with Milan, Venice, Rome, and Bologna. British Midland connects Heathrow and Milan (Linate), Naples, and Venice. Ryanair, departing from London's Stansted Airport, flies to Milan, Rome, Pisa, and Venice. Meridiana has flights between Gatwick and Olbia on Sardinia in summer, and flights to Rome and Florence throughout the year.

Tickets for flights within Italy, on Alitalia and small carriers such as EuroFly, Meridiana, and Air One, cost less when purchased from agents within Italy. Tickets are frequently sold at discounted prices, so check the cost of flights, even one-way, as an alternative to train travel.

⊞ International Carriers **Air Canada** ☎ 888/247-2262 in U.S. and Canada, 0870/524-7226 in U.K., 800/919091 in Italy ⊕ www.aircanada.com. **Alitalia** ☎ 800/223-5730 in U.S., 0870/544 in U.K., 06/65641 in Rome, 848/865641 elsewhere in Italy ⊕ www.alitalia.it. **American Airlines** ☎ 800/433-7300 in U.S., 02/69682464 in Milan ⊕ www.aa.com. **British Airways** ☎ 800/403-0882 in U.S. and Canada, 0870/850-9850 in U.K., 06/52492800 in Italy ⊕ www.britishairways.com. **British Midland** ⊕ www.flybmi.com **Continental** ☎ 800/231-0856 in U.S., 02/69633256 in Milan, 800/296230 elsewhere in Italy ⊕ www.flycontinental.com. **Delta** ☎ 800/241-4141 in U.S., 06/65954406 in Italy ⊕ www.deltaairlines.com. **EasyJet** ☎ 0870/607-6543 in U.K., 848/887766 in Italy ⊕ www.easyjet.com. **EuroFly** ☎ 800/459-0581 in U.S., 199/509960 in Italy ⊕ www.euroflyusa.com, www.eurofly.it. **Ryanair** ☎ 08701/569569 in U.K., 199/114114 in Italy ⊕ www.ryanair.com. **US Airways** ☎ 800/428-4322 in U.S., 848/813177 in Italy ⊕ www.usairways.com. ⊞ National Carriers **Air One** ☎ 06/488800 in Rome, 800/900966 elsewhere in Italy ⊕ www.flyairone.it. **Meridiana** ☎ 199/111333 in Italy ⊕ www.meridiana.it.

CHECK-IN & BOARDING

Always **find out your carrier's check-in policy.** Plan to arrive at the airport about 2 hours before your scheduled departure time for domestic flights and 2½–3 hours before international flights. You may need to arrive earlier if you're flying from one of the busier airports or during peak air-traffic times. To avoid delays at airport-security checkpoints, try not to wear any metal. Jewelry, belt and other buckles, steel-toe shoes, barrettes, and underwire bras are among the items that can set off detectors.

Assuming that not everyone with a ticket will show up, airlines routinely overbook planes. When everyone does, airlines ask for volunteers to give up their seats. In return, these volunteers usually get a several-hundred-dollar flight voucher, which can be used toward the purchase of another ticket, and are rebooked on the next available flight out. If there are not enough volunteers, the airline must choose who will be denied boarding. The first to get bumped are passengers who checked in late and those flying on discounted tickets, so get to the gate and check in as early as possible, especially during peak periods.

Always **bring a government-issued photo ID** to the airport; even when it's not required, a passport is best.

CUTTING COSTS

The least expensive airfares to Italy are often priced for round-trip travel and must usually be purchased in advance. Airlines generally allow you to change your return date for a fee; most low-fare tickets, however, are nonrefundable. It's smart to call a number of airlines and check the Internet; when you are quoted a good price, book it on the spot—the same fare may not be available the next day, or even the next hour. Always check different routings and look into using alternate airports. Also, price off-peak and red-eye flights, which may be significantly less expensive than others. Travel agents, especially low-fare specialists (⇨ Discounts & Deals), are helpful.

Consolidators are another good source. They buy tickets for scheduled flights at reduced rates from the airlines, then sell them at prices that beat the best fare available directly from the airlines. (Many also offer reduced car-rental and hotel rates.) Sometimes you can even get your money back if you need to return the ticket. Carefully read the fine print detailing penalties for changes and cancellations, purchase the ticket with a credit card, and confirm your consolidator reservation with the airline.

When you fly as a courier, you trade your checked-luggage space for a ticket deeply subsidized by a courier service. There are restrictions on when you can book and how long you can stay. Some courier companies list with membership organizations, such as the Air Courier Association and the International Association of Air Travel Couriers; these require you to become a member before you can book a flight.

Many airlines, singly or in collaboration, offer discount air passes that allow foreigners to travel economically in a particular country or region. These visitor passes usually must be reserved and purchased before you leave home. Information about passes often can be found on most airlines' international Web pages, which tend to be aimed at travelers from outside the carrier's home country. Also, try typing the name of the pass into a search engine, or search for "pass" within the carrier's Web site.

🛂 Consolidators **AirlineConsolidator.com** ☎ 888/468-5385 ⊕ www.airlineconsolidator.com, for international tickets. **Best Fares** ☎ 800/880-1234 ⊕ www.bestfares.com; $59.90 annual membership. **Cheap Tickets** ☎ 800/377-1000 or 800/652-4327 ⊕ www.cheaptickets.com. **Expedia** ☎ 800/397-3342 or 404/728-8787 ⊕ www.expedia.com. **Hotwire** ☎ 866/468-9473 or 920/330-9418 ⊕ www.hotwire.com. **Now Voyager Travel** ✉ 1717 Ave. M, Brooklyn, NY 11230 ☎ 212/459-1616 🖷 718/504-4762 ⊕ www.nowvoyagertravel.com. **One-travel.com** ☎ 888/656-4546 ⊕ www.onetravel.com. **Orbitz** ☎ 888/656-4546 ⊕ www.orbitz.com. **Priceline.com** ⊕ www.priceline.com. **Travelocity** ☎ 888/709-5983, 877/282-2925 in Canada, 0870/111-7061 in U.K. ⊕ www.travelocity.com.

🛂 Courier Resources **Air Courier Association/Cheaptrips.com** ☎ 800/211-5119 ⊕ www.aircourier.org or www.cheaptrips.com; $20 annual membership. **Courier Travel** ☎ 303/570-7586 🖷 313/625-

6106 ⊕ www.couriertravel.org; $50 annual membership. **International Association of Air Travel Couriers** ☎ 308/632-3273 🖷 308/632-8267 ⊕ www.courier.org; $45 annual membership.

ENJOYING THE FLIGHT

State your seat preference when purchasing your ticket, and then repeat it when you confirm and when you check in. For more legroom, you can request one of the few emergency-aisle seats at check-in, if you're capable of moving obstacles comparable in weight to an airplane exit door (usually between 35 pounds and 60 pounds)—a Federal Aviation Administration requirement of passengers in these seats. Seats behind a bulkhead also offer more legroom, but they don't have underseat storage. Don't sit in the row in front of the emergency aisle or in front of a bulkhead, where seats may not recline. SeatGuru.com has more information about specific seat configurations, which vary by aircraft.

Ask the airline whether a snack or meal is served on the flight. If you have dietary concerns, request special meals when booking. These can be vegetarian, low-cholesterol, or kosher, for example. It's a good idea to pack some healthful snacks and a small (plastic) bottle of water in your carry-on bag. On long flights, try to maintain a normal routine, to help fight jet lag. At night, get some sleep. By day, eat light meals, drink water (not alcohol), and **move around the cabin** to stretch your legs. For additional jet-lag tips consult *Fodor's FYI: Travel Fit & Healthy* (available at bookstores everywhere).

FLYING TIMES

Flying time to Milan or Rome is approximately 2½ hours from London, 8–8½ hours from New York, 10–11 hours from Chicago, 11½ hours from Los Angeles, and 23½ hours from Sydney.

HOW TO COMPLAIN

If your baggage goes astray or your flight goes awry, complain right away. Most carriers require that you **file a claim immediately.** The Aviation Consumer Protection Division of the Department of Transportation publishes *Fly-Rights*, which discusses airlines and consumer issues and is available online. You can also find articles and information on mytravelrights.com, the Web site of the nonprofit Consumer Travel Rights Center.

🔁 Airline Complaints **Aviation Consumer Protection Division** ✉ U.S. Department of Transportation, Office of Aviation Enforcement and Proceedings, C-75, 400 7th St. SW, Room 4107, Washington, DC 20590 ☎ 202/366-2220 ⊕ airconsumer.ost.dot.gov. **Federal Aviation Administration Consumer Hotline** ✉ For inquiries: FAA, 800 Independence Ave. SW, Washington, DC 20591 ☎ 800/322-7873 ⊕ www.faa.gov.

RECONFIRMING

Check the status of your flight before you leave for the airport. You can do this on your carrier's Web site, by linking to a flight-status checker (many Web-booking services offer these), or by calling your carrier or travel agent. Always confirm international flights at least 72 hours ahead of the scheduled departure time. Confirm flights within Italy the day before travel. Labor strikes are frequent in Italy and can affect air and train travel. Your airline will have information about strikes directly affecting its flight schedule. If you are taking a train to get to the airport, check with the local tourist agency or rail station about upcoming strikes.

AIRPORTS

The major gateways to Italy are Rome's **Aeroporto Leonardo da Vinci,** better known as **Fiumicino** (FCO), and Milan's **Aeroporto Malpensa 2000** (MXP). There are direct connections from both airports to Florence and Venice. For information about regional airports, *see* the Essentials sections at the end of each chapter.

🔁 Airport Information **Aeroporto Leonardo da Vinci** ✉ 35 km (20 mi) southeast of Rome ☎ 06/5951 ⊕ www.adr.it. **Aeroporto Malpensa** ✉ 45 km (28 mi) north of Milan ☎ 02/74852200 ⊕ www.sea-aeroportimilano.it.

BEACHES

With 7,420 km (4,610 mi) of coastline facing three seas—the Adriatic to the northeast, the Ionian to the southeast, and the Tyrrhenian to the west—Italy offers every type of seaside scene. Italy has several world-famous beaches, like those along the Costa Smeralda in Sardinia, and great stretches of deserted and untouched coastline, many found in eastern Calabria, Sardinia, and the islands around Sicily. In Emilia-Romagna, Riccione and Rimini beaches are famous for their nightlife and seaside fitness programs (Spinning to weight lifting, water gymnastics to dance). The Tremiti Islands (off the Adriatic Coast, between Molise and Puglia), the Gargano Peninsula (in Puglia), Tropea (in Calabria), Taormina (in Sicily), the islands of Capri and Ischia (in the Gulf of Naples), the Amalfi Coast (in Campania), Ponza (off the coast of Lazio), and the island of Elba (off the coast of Livorno in Tuscany) bring together a natural beauty with a low-key worldliness.

Public beaches are free, but offer no services. On the most popular ones it's sometimes possible to buy sandwiches and soft drinks, but don't depend on it. They also often lack telephones, toilets, and showers. Private beaches charge admission and range from downright spartan (cold showers and portable toilets) to luxurious (with gardens, stylish bars, fish restaurants, and private guest huts). Admission policies and prices vary accordingly. Most establishments offer a chaise longue, chair, and umbrella for between €20 and €50 a day. Some of the most exclusive places cater only to patrons who pay by the week or month. Inquire at local tourist offices.

Don't underestimate the scorching power of the Italian sun. The "tanning season" begins in early May, and beach life starts in earnest in early June, with the opening of beach concessionaires, called *stabilimenti balneari* or *bagni*. During weekends and holidays and in August, most sea resorts and beaches tend to be very crowded, some posting "no vacancy" (*completo*) signs by 10 AM, so an early start is essential. In northern and central Italy, it's common to see topless sunbathing; in the south it could lead to undesired attention from local men. Wearing beach attire (bare chests and thighs) in town is frowned upon. The summer season ends in early September.

BIKE TRAVEL

Biking is a terrific way to see Italy, particularly in places such as Tuscany, where two-lane roads wind through startlingly beautiful countryside. The best times to bike are in spring and fall; July and August are unbearably hot in most places. Rentals are easily obtained in most cities. Given the generally hilly terrain, it's essential to have a good map with elevations, distances, and the various types of roads clearly marked. An excellent map choice is the green regional series issued by the Italian Touring Club, available at major bookstores. Topographical maps by Kompass Wanderkarten, distributed by Omni Resources, show both hiking and biking routes and are available in large bookstores and map shops. The *Federazione Italiana Amici della Bicicletta* (Italian Federation of Friends of the Bicycle) has a useful Web site (in English as well as Italian) with information about bicycle routes, events, and services.

Road conditions are generally good throughout Italy, but, as you move along it's always a good idea to ask local tourist information offices about bike-friendly routes. Especially in smaller towns and villages cyclists do not go unnoticed, and if you speak a little Italian you'll be likely to meet sympathetic native cyclists eager to give valuable tips about the region. If you're not familiar with the countryside, joining an organized tour is a great idea. To be on the safe side, always lock your bike inside your hotel for the night.

🚲 Bike Maps **Omni Resources** ⊠ 1004 S. Mebane St., Burlington, NC 27216-2096 ☎ 336/227-8300 📠 336/227-3748 ⊕ www.omnimap.com.
🚲 Bike Organization *Federazione Italiana Amici della Bicicletta* ⊠ Viale Col Moschin 1, 30171 Mestre, Veneto 📠☎ 041/921515 ⊕ www.fiab-onlus.it.
🚲 Bike Tours **Backroads** ⊠ 801 Cedar St., Berkeley, CA 94710 ☎ 800/462-2848 or 510/527-1555 ⊕ www.backroads.com. **Bike Riders** ⌂ Box 130254, Boston, MA 02113 ☎ 800/473-7040 or 617/723-2354 ⊕ www.bikeriderstours.com. **Butterfield & Robinson** ⊠ 70 Bond St., Suite 300, Toronto, Ontario M5B 1X3 Canada ☎ 800/678-1147 or 416/864-1354 ⊕ www.butterfield.com. **Ciclismo Classico** ⊠ 30 Marathon St., Arlington, MA 02474 ☎ 800/866-7314 or 781/646-3377 ⊕ www.ciclismoclassico.

com. **EEI Travel** ⊠ 19021 120th Ave., Suite 102, Bothell, WA 98011 ☎ 800/927-3876 or 425/487-6711 ⊕ www.europeexpress.com). **Euro-Bike Tours** ⌂ Box 990, De Kalb, IL 60115 ☎ 800/321-6060 ⊕ www.eurobike.com. **Europeds** ⊠ 761 Lighthouse Ave., Monterey, CA 93940 ☎ 831/646-4920 ⊕ www.europeds.com. **I Bike Italy** ☎ 772/388-0783 in U.S., 055/2342371 in Italy ⊕ www.ibikeitaly.com. **Naturequest** ⊠ 30872 S. Coast Hwy., Suite 185, Laguna Beach, CA 92651 ☎ 800/369-3033 or 949/499-9561 ⊕ www.naturequesttours.com.
🚲 Rentals **Alinari** ⊠ Via Guelfa 85/r, Florence ☎ 005/271871. **Florence By Bike** ⊠ Via San Zanobi 90/r-120/r, Florence ☎ 005/488992 ⊕ www.florencebybike.it. **Happy Rent** ⊠ Via Farini 3, Rome ☎ 06/4818185. **Scooter Hire** ⊠ Via Cavor 80, Rome ☎ 06/4815669 ⊕ www.scooterhire.it.

BIKES IN FLIGHT

Most airlines accommodate bikes as luggage, provided they are dismantled and boxed; check with individual airlines about packing requirements. Some airlines sell bike boxes, which are often free at bike shops, for about $20 (bike bags can be considerably more expensive). International travelers often can substitute a bike for a piece of checked luggage at no charge; otherwise, the cost is about $100. Most U.S. and Canadian airlines charge $40–$80 each way.

BUS TRAVEL

Italy's bus network is extensive, although buses are not as attractive an option as in other European countries, partly because of cheap, convenient train travel. In some areas buses are faster, so **compare bus and train schedules.** To reach some smaller towns, a bus may be your only option.

If you're traveling by bus from the United Kingdom, **have some euros on hand** to spend along the way. Eurolines runs bus service to Rome once a week from London, three times a week June–September.

CUTTING COSTS

Bus service is provided by regional companies, some of which run day trips from their base of operations. Children under two usually ride for free, and children under eight travel at half price. If you need a car seat for your child, it's best to bring your own.

FARES & SCHEDULES

Unlike city buses, for which you must buy your ticket from a machine, newsstand, or tobacco shop and stamp it after you board, private bus lines usually have a ticket office in town or allow you to pay when you board.

🚌 **Bus Information Eurolines** ✉ 52 Grosvenor Gardens, London SW1W OAU ☎ 020/7730-8235 or 020/7730-3499 ⊕ www.eurolines.com.

BUSINESS HOURS

Religious and civic holidays are frequent in Italy. Depending on the holiday's local importance, businesses may close for the day. Businesses do not close on a Friday or Monday when the holiday falls on the weekend.

BANKS & POST OFFICES

Banks are open weekdays 8:30–1:30 and for an hour in the afternoon, depending on the bank. Most post offices are open Monday–Saturday 9–12:30; central post offices are open 9–6:30 PM weekdays, 9–12:30 on Saturday. On the last day of the month all post offices close at midday.

MUSEUMS & SIGHTS

Most churches are open from early morning until noon or 12:30, when they close for three hours or more; they open again in the afternoon, closing at about 6 PM. A few major churches, such as St. Peter's in Rome and San Marco in Venice, remain open all day. Walking around during services is discouraged. Many museums are closed one day a week, often Monday. During low season, museums often close early; during high season, many stay open until late at night.

PHARMACIES

Pharmacies are generally open weekdays 8:30–1 and 4–8, and Saturday 9–1. Local pharmacies cover the off-hours in shifts: on the door of every pharmacy is a list of which pharmacies in the vicinity will be open late.

SHOPS

Most shops are open Monday–Saturday 9–1 and 3:30 or 4–7:30. Clothing shops are generally closed Monday mornings. Barbers and hairdressers, with some exceptions, are closed Sunday and Monday. Some bookstores and fashion and tourist-oriented shops in places such as Rome and Venice are open all day, as well as Sunday. Large chain supermarkets such as Standa, COOP, and Eselunga do not close for lunch and are usually open Sunday; smaller *alimentari* (delicatessens) and other food shops are usually closed one evening during the week (it varies according to the town) and are almost always closed Sunday.

CAR RENTAL

Renting a car in Italy is essential for exploring the countryside, but not if you plan to stick to the cities. Signage on country roads is usually good, but be prepared for fast and impatient fellow drivers.

Hiring a car with a driver can come in handy, particularly if you plan to do some wine tasting or drive along the Amalfi Coast. Ask at your hotel for recommended drivers, or inquire at the local tourist office. Drivers are paid by the day, and are usually rewarded with a tip of about 15% upon completion of the journey.

Fiats and Fords in a variety of sizes are the most typical rental cars. Remember that most Italian cars have standard transmissions. **If you want to rent an automatic, be specific when you reserve the car.** Higher rates will apply.

🚗 **Major Agencies Alamo** ☎ 800/522-9696 ⊕ www.alamo.com. **Avis** ☎ 800/331-1084, 800/879-2847 in Canada, 0870/606-0100 in U.K., 02/9353-9000 in Australia, 09/526-2847 in New Zealand ⊕ www.avis.com. **Budget** ☎ 800/527-0700 ⊕ www.budget.com. **Dollar** ☎ 800/800-6000, 0800/085-4578 in U.K. ⊕ www.dollar.com. **Hertz** ☎ 800/654-3001, 800/263-0600 in Canada, 0870/844-8844 in U.K., 02/9669-2444 in Australia, 09/256-8690 in New Zealand ⊕ www.hertz.com. **National Car Rental** ☎ 800/227-7368 ⊕ www.nationalcar.com.

CUTTING COSTS

Most American chains have affiliates in Italy, but the rates are usually lower if you book a car before you leave home. A company's rates are the same throughout the country: you will not save money, for example, if you pick up a vehicle in a city rather than at an airport. For a good deal, book through a travel agent who will shop around.

Do look into wholesalers, companies that do not own fleets but rent in bulk from those that do and often offer better rates than traditional car-rental operations. Prices are best during off-peak periods. Rentals booked through wholesalers often must be paid for before you leave home.
📶 **Wholesalers Auto Europe** ☎ 800/223-5555 or 207/842-2000 🖷 207/842-2222 ⊕ www. autoeurope.com. **Destination Europe Resources** (DER) ⊠ 9501 W. Devon Ave., Rosemont, IL 60018 ☎ 800/782-2424 🖷 800/282-7474. **Europe by Car** ☎ 800/223-1516 or 212/581-3040 🖷 212/246-1458 ⊕ www.europebycar.com. **Kemwel** ☎ 877/820-0668 or 800/678-0678 🖷 207/842-2124 or 866/726-6726 ⊕ www.kemwel.com.

INSURANCE

When driving a rented car you are generally responsible for any damage to or loss of the vehicle. Collision policies that car-rental companies sell for European rentals typically don't cover stolen vehicles. Indeed, all car-rental agencies operating in Italy require that you buy a theft-protection policy. Before you rent—and purchase collision coverage—see what coverage you already have under the terms of your personal auto-insurance policy and credit cards.

REQUIREMENTS & RESTRICTIONS

In Italy your driver's license is acceptable. However, a universally recognized International Driver's Permit may save you a problem with the local authorities. They are available from the American or Canadian Automobile Association and, in the United Kingdom, from the Automobile Association or Royal Automobile Club. In Italy you must be 21 to rent a car, and most companies require those under 23 to pay by credit card.

In Sicily there are some roads for which rental agencies deny coverage; ask in advance if you plan to travel in remote regions.

Children under three are required to ride in a car seat, which must be booked in advance. The cost ranges from €26 to €40 for the duration of the rental.

SURCHARGES

Before you pick up a car in one city and leave it in another, ask about drop-off charges or one-way service fees, which can be substantial. Also inquire about early-return policies; some rental agencies charge extra if you return the car before the time specified in your contract while others give you a refund for the days not used. Most agencies note the tank's fuel level on your contract; to avoid a hefty refueling fee, return the car with the same tank level. If the tank was full, refill it just before you turn in the car, but be aware that gas stations near the rental outlet may overcharge. It's almost never a deal to buy a tank of gas with the car when you rent it; the understanding is that you'll return it empty, but some fuel usually remains. The cost for an additional driver is about €5 per day.

CAR TRAVEL

Italy has an extensive network of *autostrade* (toll highways), complemented by equally well-maintained but free *superstrade* (expressways). Save the ticket you are issued at an autostrada entrance, as you need it to exit; on some shorter autostrade, you pay the toll when you enter. Viacards, on sale for €25 at many autostrada locations, allow you to pay for tolls in advance. At special lanes you simply slip the card into a designated slot.

An *uscita* is an "exit." A *raccordo* is a ring road surrounding a city. *Strade regionale* and *strade provinciale* (regional and provincial highways, denoted by S, SS, SR, or SP numbers) may be two-lane roads, as are all secondary roads; directions and turnoffs aren't always clearly marked.

EMERGENCY SERVICES

Automobile Club Italiano offers 24-hour road service. English-speaking operators are available. Your rental-car company may also have an emergency tow service with a toll-free call. Be prepared to tell the operator which road you're on, the *verso* (direction) you're headed, and your *targa* (license plate number).

When you're on the road, always carry a good road map, a flashlight, and, if possible, a cellular phone for emergencies. On the autostrade and superstrade, emergency phones are available. To find the nearest one, look on the pavement for painted arrows and the term "SOS."

⚐ Automobile Club Italiano ☎ 803/116.

GASOLINE

Gas stations are located along the main highways. Those on autostrade are open 24 hours. Otherwise, gas stations generally are open Monday–Saturday 7–7, with a break at lunchtime. At self-service gas stations the pumps are operated by a central machine for payment, which don't take credit cards; accept only bills in denominations of 5, 10, 20, and 50 euros; and do not give change. Those with attendants accept cash and credit cards. It's not customary to tip the attendant.

Gasoline (*benzina*) costs about €1.20 per liter and is available in unleaded (*verde*) and super-unleaded (*super*). **Many rental cars in Italy use diesel** (*gasolio*), which costs about €1 per liter.

PARKING

Parking is at a premium in most towns, especially in the *centri storici* (historic centers). Fines for parking violations are high, and towing is common. Don't think about tearing up a ticket, as car-rental companies may use your credit card to be reimbursed for any fines you incur. It's a good idea to park in a designated (and preferably attended) lot. And **don't leave valuables in your car,** as thieves often target rental cars.

In congested cities like Rome and Florence, indoor parking costs €23–€30 for 12–24 hours; outdoor parking costs about €10–€20. Parking in an area signposted ZONA DISCO (disk zone) is allowed for short periods (from 30 minutes to two hours or more—the time is posted); if you don't have a cardboard disk (get one at the tourist office or car-rental company) to show what time you parked, you can use a piece of paper. The *parcometro,* a central parking meter that, after coins are inserted, prints a ticket that you leave on your dashboard, has been introduced in most metropolitan areas.

ROAD CONDITIONS

Autostrade are generally well maintained, well marked, and easy to navigate, as are most regional roads. The condition of smaller roads varies, but road maintenance is generally good in Italy.

ROAD MAPS

Street signs are often challenging—a good map and lots of patience are essential. Local maps are available at rental agencies. Most bookstores sell them, as do most gas stations. The best road maps are those produced by Michelin. Before taking a journey through the Italian countryside by car, it is a good idea to go online at viamichelin.com to print out route instructions and maps.

RULES OF THE ROAD

Driving is on the right. Regulations are largely the same as in Britain and the United States, except that the police have the power to levy on-the-spot fines. Using handheld mobile phones while driving is illegal; fines can exceed €100. In most Italian towns the use of the horn is forbidden in many areas; a large sign, ZONA DI SILENZIO, indicates a no-honking zone. Speed limits are 130 kph (80 mph) on autostrade and 110 kph (70 mph) on state and provincial roads, unless otherwise marked.

The blood-alcohol content limit for driving is 0.5 gr (stricter than U.S. limits) with fines up to €5,000 for surpassing the limit and the possibility of six months' imprisonment. Although enforcement of laws varies depending on region, fines for speeding are uniformly stiff: 10 kph over the speed limit can warrant a fine of up to €500; greater than 10 kph, and your license could be taken away from you.

Nonetheless, Italians drive fast and are impatient with those who don't. Tailgating is the norm here—the only way to avoid it is to get out of the way. Right turns on red lights are forbidden. Headlights are not compulsory in cities when it rains or snows, but it's a good idea to turn them on. However, you must **turn on your headlights** outside city limits at all hours. You must **wear seat belts** and **strap young children into car seats** at all times.

COMPUTERS ON THE ROAD

Getting online in Italian cities isn't difficult. Internet cafés, some open 24 hours a day, are common. Prices differ, so **shop for the best deal.** Some hotels have in-room modems, but using the hotel's line is usually expensive. Always check the rates before plugging in. You may need an adapter for your computer for the European-style plugs. As always, if you are traveling with a laptop, carry a spare battery and an adapter. Wireless Internet is available in high-end hotels, airports, train stations, and shopping centers.

CONSUMER PROTECTION

Most stores in Italy do not allow customers to return or exchange merchandise, even if there is a minor flaw in the product. Clothing stores are particularly inflexible.

Whether you're shopping for gifts or purchasing travel services, **pay with a major credit card** whenever possible, so you can cancel payment or get reimbursed if there's a problem (and you can provide documentation). If you're doing business with a particular company for the first time, contact your local Better Business Bureau and the attorney general's offices in your state and (for U.S. businesses) the company's home state as well. Have any complaints been filed? Finally, if you're buying a package or tour, always consider travel insurance that includes default coverage (⇨ Insurance).

🖪 BBBs **Council of Better Business Bureaus** ✉ 4200 Wilson Blvd., Suite 800, Arlington, VA 22203 ☏ 703/276-0100 🖷 703/525-8277 ⊕ www.bbb.org.

CUSTOMS & DUTIES

You're always allowed to bring goods of a certain value back home without having to pay any duty or import tax. There's also a limit on the amount of tobacco and liquor you can bring back duty-free, and some countries have separate limits for perfumes; for exact figures, check with your customs department. The values of so-called "duty-free" goods are included in these amounts. When you shop abroad, save all your receipts as customs inspectors may ask to see them as well as the items you purchased. If the total value of your goods is more than the duty-free limit, then you'll have to pay a tax (most often a

flat percentage) on the value of everything beyond that limit.

🖪 **U.S. Customs and Border Protection** ✉ For inquiries and complaints, 1300 Pennsylvania Ave. NW, Washington, DC 20229 ⊕ www.cbp.gov ☏ 877/227-5551 or 202/354-1000.

EATING & DRINKING

The restaurants we list are the cream of the crop in each price category. Properties indicated by a ✕🖾 are lodging establishments whose restaurant warrants a special trip.

CATEGORY	COST
$$$$	over €45
$$$	€35–€45
$$	€25–€35
$	€15–€25
¢	under €15

Prices are for a first course (primo), *second course* (secondo), *and dessert* (dolce) *and are given in euros.*

A few pointers on Italian dining etiquette: menus are posted outside most restaurants (in English in tourist areas); if not, you might step inside and ask to take a look at the menu, but don't ask for a table unless you intend to stay. Italians take their food as it is listed on the menu, seldom making special requests such as "dressing on the side" or "hold the olive oil." If you have special dietary needs, though, make them known, and they can usually be accommodated. Although mineral water makes its way to almost every table, you can always order a carafe of tap water (acqua di rubinetto or acqua semplice). Doing this, however, will mark you as a tourist.

Spaghetti should be eaten with a fork rolled against the side of the dish, although a little help from a spoon will not horrify the locals the way cutting spaghetti into little pieces might. Wiping your bowl clean with a (small) piece of bread is fine in less-formal eateries. Order your espresso (Italians almost never drink a cappuccino after breakfast) after dessert, not with it. You usually have to ask for il conto (the bill). Unless it's well past closing time, no waiter will put a bill on your table until you request him to do so. Don't ask for a doggy bag.

MEALS & SPECIALTIES

What's the difference between a ristorante and a trattoria? Can you order food at an enoteca? Can you go to a restaurant just for a snack, or order just a salad at a pizzeria? The following definitions should help.

Not too long ago, restaurants tended to be more elegant and expensive than trattorias and osterie, which served more traditional, home-style fare in an atmosphere to match. But the distinction has blurred considerably, and an osteria in the center of town might be far fancier (and pricier) than a ristorante across the street. In all these types of places you are generally expected to order at least a two-course meal, such as: a *primo* (first course) and a *secondo* (main course) or a *contorno* (vegetable side dish); an antipasto (starter) followed by either primo or secondo; or a secondo and a *dolce* (dessert).

In an *enoteca* (wine bar) or pizzeria it's common to order just one dish. An enoteca menu is often limited to a selection of cheese, cured meats, salads, and desserts, but if there's a kitchen you'll also find soups, pastas, and main courses. The typical pizzeria fare includes *affettati misti* (a selection of cured pork), simple salads, various kinds of bruschetta, crostini (similar to bruschetta, sometimes topped with cheese and broiled) and, in Rome, *fritti* (deep-fried finger food) such as *olive ascolane* (green olives with a meat stuffing) and *supplì* (rice balls stuffed with mozzarella). All pizzerias serve fresh fruit, ice cream, and simple desserts.

Throughout the country the handiest and least expensive places for a quick snack between sights are probably bars, cafés, and pizza *al taglio* (by the slice) spots. Bars in Italy are primarily places to get a coffee and a bite to eat rather than drinking establishments. Most have a selection of *panini* (sandwiches) warmed up on the griddle (*piastra*) and *tramezzini* (sandwiches made of untoasted white bread triangles). In larger cities, bars also serve vegetable and fruit salads, cold pasta dishes, and yogurt around lunchtime. Most bars offer beer and a variety of alcohol as well as wines by the glass (sometimes good but more often mediocre). A café (*caffè* in Italian) is like a bar but usually with more tables. Pizza at a café should be avoided—it's usually heated in a microwave. If you place your order at the counter, ask if you can sit down: some places charge for table service, others do not. In self-service bars and cafés it's good manners to clean your table before you leave. Note that in some places you have to pay a cashier, then place your order and show your *scontrino* (receipt) at the counter. Pizza al taglio shops sell pizza by weight: just point out which kind you want and how much. Very few pizza al taglio shops have seating.

Italian cuisine is still largely regional. Ask what the local specialties are: by all means, have spaghetti *alla carbonara* (with bacon and egg) in Rome, pizza in Rome or Naples, *bistecca alla fiorentina* (steak) in Florence, *chingale* (wild boar) in Tuscany, truffles in the Piedmont, and risotto *alla milanese* in Milan.

MEAL TIMES

Breakfast (*la colazione*) is usually served from 7 to 10:30, lunch (*il pranzo*) from 12:30 to 2:30, dinner (*la cena*) from 7:30 to 10. Peak times are usually 1:30 for lunch and 9 for dinner. Enoteche and *bacari* (wine bars) are open also in the morning and late afternoon for a snack at the counter. Most pizzerias open at 8 PM and close around midnight—later in summer and on weekends. Most bars and cafés are open from 7 AM until 8 or 9 PM; a few stay open until midnight. Unless otherwise noted, the restaurants listed in this guide are open daily for lunch and dinner.

PAYING

Most restaurants charge a "cover" charge per person, usually listed at the top of the check as *"coperto"* or *"pane e coperto."* It should be a modest charge (€1–€2.50 per person) except at the most expensive restaurants. Whenever in doubt, ask before you order to avoid unpleasant discussions later. It is customary to leave a small tip (around 10%) in appreciation of good service. If *servizio* is included at the bottom of the check, no tip is necessary. Tips are always given in cash.

The price of fish dishes is often given by weight (before cooking), so the price you see on the menu is for 100 grams of fish, not for the whole dish. An average fish portion is about 350 grams. In Tuscany, *bistecca alla fiorentina* (florentine steak) is also often priced by weight.

Major credit cards are widely accepted in Italy, though cash is usually preferred. More restaurants take Visa and Master-Card than American Express.

RESERVATIONS & DRESS

Reservations are always a good idea; we mention them only when they're essential or not accepted. Book as far ahead as you can, and reconfirm as soon as you arrive. (Large parties should always call ahead to check the reservations policy.) Pizzerias and enoteche usually accept reservations only for large groups.

We mention dress only when men are required to wear a jacket or a jacket and tie. But unless they're dining outside or at an oceanfront resort, Italian men never wear shorts or running shoes in a restaurant. The same applies to women: no casual shorts, running shoes, or plastic sandals when going out to dinner. Shorts are acceptable in pizzerias and cafés.

WINE, BEER & SPIRITS

If you're in a restaurant or trattoria, ask your waiter about the house wine; sometimes it's very good indeed, sometimes it isn't. Wine in Italy is considerably less expensive than almost anywhere else. Beer can be more expensive than a glass of wine, and though Italy does produce beer it's not nearly as notable as its wine.

Beer, wine, and spirits can be purchased in any bar, grocery store, or enoteca, any day of the week. There's no minimum drinking age in Italy. Italian children begin drinking wine mixed with water at mealtimes when they're teenagers or even younger.

Many bars have their own *aperitivo della casa* (house aperitif). Italians are most imaginative with their mixed drinks—usually shaken, rarely blended.

ELECTRICITY

To use electric-powered equipment purchased in the United States or Canada, **bring a converter and an adapter.** The electrical current in Italy is 220 volts, 50 cycles alternating current (AC); wall outlets take Continental-type plugs, with two or three round prongs.

If your appliances are dual-voltage, you'll need only an adapter. Don't use 110-volt outlets marked FOR SHAVERS ONLY for high-wattage appliances such as blow-dryers. Most laptops operate equally well on 110 and 220 volts and so require only an adapter.

EMBASSIES

🚩 Australia **Australian Embassy** ✉ Via Alessandria 215, 00198 Rome ☎ 06/852721 ⊕ www.australian-embassy.it.

🚩 Canada **Canadian Embassy** ✉ Via G. B. de Rossi 27, 00161 Rome ☎ 06/445981 ⊕ www.dfait-maeci.gc.ca/canadaeuropa/italy.

🚩 New Zealand **New Zealand Embassy** ✉ Via Zara 28, 00198 Rome ☎ 06/4417171.

🚩 U.K. **British Embassy** ✉ Via XX Settembre 80A, 00187 Rome ☎ 06/42200001 ⊕ www.britain.it.

🚩 U.S. **U.S. Embassy** ✉ Via Veneto 121, 00187 Rome ☎ 06/46741 ⊕ www.usembassy.it.

EMERGENCIES

No matter where you are in Italy, you can **dial 113 in case of emergency.** Not all 113 operators speak English, so you may want to ask a local person to place the call. Asking the operator for *"pronto soccorso"* (first aid) should get you an *ambulanza* (ambulance). If you just need a doctor, ask for *"un medico."*

Italy has the *carabinieri* (national police force) as well as the *polizia* (local police force). Both are armed and have the power to arrest and investigate crimes. Always **report the loss of your passport** to the police as well as to your embassy. When reporting a crime, you'll be asked to fill out an *una denuncia* (official report); keep a copy for your insurance company.

Local traffic officers, known as *vigili,* are responsible for, among other things, giving out parking tickets. They wear white (in summer) or black uniforms. Should you find yourself involved in a minor car accident, contact the vigili.

▣ Emergencies ☎ 113. **National police** ☎ 112.

ENGLISH-LANGUAGE MEDIA

BOOKS

Most major cities have bookstores that cater to English speakers. The nationwide chain Feltrinelli International, for example, has a large English-language section (expensive, since they are all imported). Rome has several independent English-language bookstores, as do several other cities, including Florence.

NEWSPAPERS & MAGAZINES

The best source for news in English is the *International Herald Tribune,* sold at newsstands in major cities. *USA Today* and most of the London newspapers are also available. You can sometimes find a week-old Sunday *New York Times,* but be prepared to pay €12. Various national versions of *Vogue* are available, as are English-language versions of *Time, Newsweek, The Economist, The New Yorker, Vanity Fair, In Style,* and *People,* among others. But they don't come cheap: *Vanity Fair,* for example, costs about €8.

RADIO & TELEVISION

Unless your hotel gets CNN, BBC, or SkyNews, every television program you see will be in Italian. (MTV is sometimes broadcast in English with Italian subtitles—but that's the exception, not the rule.) Aside from Vatican Radio, which broadcasts world news in English three times a day, radio broadcasts are all in Italian.

ETIQUETTE & BEHAVIOR

Be sure to **dress appropriately** when visiting a church in Italy. Shorts, tank tops, and sleeveless garments are taboo in most churches throughout the country. In summer carry a sweater or other item of clothing to wrap around your bare shoulders before entering a church. You should **never bring food into a church,** and do not sip from your water bottle while inside. And **never enter a church when a service is in progress,** especially if it is a private affair such as a wedding or baptism.

Italians who are friends greet each other with a kiss, usually first on the right cheek, then on the left. When you meet a new person, shake hands.

HIKING & WALKING

Italy has many good places to hike and an extensive network of long trails. The Sentiero Italia is a national trail running from Reggio Calabria on the toe of Italy's boot to the central section of the Apennine mountains. There are plans to lengthen it farther north and to the western Alps, and from there to the Dolomites and Udine in the Friuli region. For detailed information on the Sentiero Italia contact the Club Alpino Italiano headquarters or one of the local offices. Local tourist information offices can also be helpful.

▣ Hiking Organization Club Alpino Italiano ✉ Via Petrella 19, 20124 Milan ☎ 02/2057231 🖷 02/205723201 ⊕ www.cai.it.

▣ Hiking & Walking Tours Above the Clouds Trekking 🖅 Box 388, Hinesburg, VT 05461 ☎ 800/233-4499 or 802/482-4848 🖷 802/482-5011 ⊕ www.abovecclouds.com. **Backroads** (⇨ Bike Travel). **Butterfield & Robinson** (⇨ Bike Travel). **Ciclismo Classico** (⇨ Bike Travel). **Country Walkers** 🖅 Box 180, Waterbury, VT 05676-0180 ☎ 800/464-9255 or 802/464-9255 ⊕ www.countrywalkers.com. **EEI Travel** (⇨ Bike Travel). **Italian Connection, Walking & Culinary Tours** ✉ 11 Fairway Dr., Suite 210, Edmonton, Alberta T6J 2W4 Canada ☎ 800/462-7911 ⊕ www.italian-connection.com. **Mountain Travel-Sobek** ✉ 6420 Fairmount Ave., El Cerrito, CA 94530 ☎ 510/527-8100 or 888/687-6235 🖷 510/525-7710 ⊕ www.mtsobek.com. **Wilderness Travel** ✉ 1102 9th St., Berkeley, CA 94710 ☎ 800/368-2794 or 510/558-2488 🖷 510/558-2489 ⊕ www.wildernesstravel.com.

HOLIDAYS

If you can avoid it, don't travel through Italy in August, when much of the population is on vacation. Most cities are deserted (except for foreign tourists) and many restaurants and shops are closed.

National holidays in 2007 include January 1 (New Year's Day); January 6 (Epiphany); April 8 and April 9 (Easter Sunday and Monday); April 25 (Liberation Day); May 1 (Labor Day or May Day); June 2 (Festival of the Republic);

August 15 (Ferragosto); November 1 (All Saints' Day); December 8 (Immaculate Conception); December 25 and 26 (Christmas Day and the feast of St. Stephen).

Feast days of patron saints are observed locally. Many businesses and shops may be closed in Florence, Genoa, and Turin on June 24 (St. John the Baptist); in Rome on June 29 (Sts. Peter and Paul); in Palermo on July 15 (St. Rosalia); in Naples on September 19 (San Gennaro); in Bologna on October 4 (San Petronio); in Trieste on November 3 (San Giusto); and in Milan on December 7 (St. Ambrose). Venice's feast of St. Mark is April 25, the same as Liberation Day, so the Madonna della Salute on November 21 makes up for the lost holiday.

INSURANCE

The most useful travel-insurance plan is a comprehensive policy that includes coverage for trip cancellation and interruption, default, trip delay, and medical expenses (with a waiver for preexisting conditions).

Without insurance you'll lose all or most of your money if you cancel your trip, regardless of the reason. Default insurance covers you if your tour operator, airline, or cruise line goes out of business—the chances of which have been increasing. Trip-delay covers expenses that arise because of bad weather or mechanical delays. Study the fine print when comparing policies.

If you're traveling internationally, a key component of travel insurance is coverage for medical bills incurred if you get sick on the road. Such expenses aren't generally covered by Medicare or private policies. U.K. residents can buy a travel-insurance policy valid for most vacations taken during the year in which it's purchased (but check preexisting-condition coverage). British and Australian citizens need extra medical coverage when traveling overseas.

Always **buy travel policies directly from the insurance company**; if you buy them from a cruise line, airline, or tour operator that goes out of business you probably won't be covered for the agency or operator's default, a major risk. Before making

any purchase, review your existing health and home-owner's policies to find what they cover away from home.

◪ Travel Insurers In the United States: **Access America** ✉ 2805 N. Parham Rd., Richmond, VA 23294 ☎ 800/284-8300 🖷 800/346-9265 or 804/673-1469 ⊕ www.accessamerica.com. **Travel Guard International** ✉ 1145 Clark St., Stevens Point, WI 54481 ☎ 800/826-1300 or 715/345-1041 🖷 800/955-8785 or 715/345-1990 ⊕ www.travelguard.com.
◪ In the United Kingdom: **Association of British Insurers** ✉ 51 Gresham St., London EC2V 7HQ ☎ 020/7600-3333 🖷 020/7696-8999 ⊕ www.abi.org.uk. In Canada: **RBC Insurance** ✉ 6880 Financial Dr., Mississauga, Ontario L5N 7Y5 Canada ☎ 800/387-4357 or 905/816-2559 🖷 888/298-6458 ⊕ www.rbcinsurance.com. In Australia: **Insurance Council of Australia** ✉ Level 3, 56 Pitt St., Sydney, NSW 2000 ☎ 02/9253-5100 🖷 02/9253-5111 ⊕ www.ica.com.au. In New Zealand: **Insurance Council of New Zealand** ✉ Level 7, 111-115 Customhouse Quay, Box 474, Wellington ☎ 04/472-5230 🖷 04/473-3011 ⊕ www.icnz.org.nz.

LANGUAGE

In larger cities such as Venice, Rome, and Florence, language is not a big problem. Most hotels have English speakers at their reception desks, and if not, they can always find someone who speaks at least a little English. You may have trouble communicating in the countryside, but a phrase book and expressive gestures will go a long way. Try to **master a few phrases for daily use** and familiarize yourself with the words you'll need for deciphering signs and menus. A phrase book and language-tape set can help get you started. *Fodor's Italian for Travelers* is available at bookstores everywhere.

LODGING

The lodgings we list are the cream of the crop in each price category. We always list the facilities that are available, but we don't specify whether they cost extra; when pricing accommodations, always ask what's included and what costs extra. Properties are assigned price categories based on the range between their least and most expensive standard double room at high season (excluding holidays). Properties marked ✕▦ are lodging establishments whose restaurants warrant a special trip. Hotels with the designation **BP** (for Breakfast Plan) at the end of their listing include breakfast in their rate; offerings can vary from coffee and a roll to an elaborate buffet. Those designated **EP** (European Plan) have no meals included; **MAP** (Modified American Plan) means you get breakfast and dinner; **FAP** (Full American Plan) includes all meals.

CATEGORY	MAIN CITIES	ELSEWHERE
$$$$	over €290	over €220
$$$	€210–€290	€160–€220
$$	€140–€210	€110–€160
$	€80–€140	€70–€110
¢	under €80	under €70

Prices are for two people in a standard double room in high season, including tax and service, and are given in euros. "Main cities" are Florence, Milan, Rome, and Venice.

APARTMENT & VILLA RENTALS

If you want a home base that's roomy enough for a family and comes with cooking facilities, consider a furnished rental. These can save you money, especially if you're traveling with a group. Home-exchange directories sometimes list rentals as well as exchanges.

In the capital, *Wanted in Rome* is a bimonthly magazine with extensive listings for short-term rentals all over the country. Another good source for rentals is *EYP*, available at English-language bookstores.

⛫ International Agents At Home Abroad ⌕ 163 3rd Ave., No. 319, New York, NY 10003 ☎ 212/421-9165 🖷 212/533-0095 ⊕ www.athomeabroadinc.com. **Drawbridge to Europe** ✉ 98 Granite St., Ashland, OR 97520 ☎ 541/482-7778 or 888/268-1148 🖷 541/482-7779 ⊕ www.drawbridgetoeurope.com. **Hideaways International** ✉ 767 Islington St., Portsmouth, NH 03801 ☎ 800/843-4433 or 603/430-4433 🖷 603/430-4444 ⊕ www.hideaways.com; annual membership $185. **Hometours International** ✉ 1108 Scottie La., Knoxville, TN 37919 ☎ 865/690-8484 or 866/367-4668 ✎ hometours@aol.com ⊕ thor.he.net/~hometour/. **Interhome** ✉ 1990 N.E. 163rd St., Suite 110, North Miami Beach, FL 33162 ☎ 800/882-6864 or 305/940-2299 🖷 305/940-2911 ⊕ www.interhome.us. **Solemar** ✉ 1990 N.E. 163rd St., Suite 110, North Miami Beach, FL 33162 ☎ 800/882-6864 or 305/940-2299 🖷 305/940-2911 ⊕ www.solemar.us. **Vacation**

Home Rentals Worldwide ✉ 235 Kensington Ave., Norwood, NJ 07648 ☎ 800/633-3284 or 201/767-9393 🖷 201/767-5510 ⊕ www.vhrww.com. **Villanet** ✉ 1251 N.W. 116th St., Seattle, WA 98177 ☎ 800/964-1891 or 206/417-3444 🖷 206/417-1832 ⊕ www.rentavilla.com. **Villas and Apartments Abroad** ✉ 183 Madison Ave., Suite 201, New York, NY 10016 ☎ 800/433-3020 or 212/213-6435 🖷 212/213-8252 ⊕ www.vaanyc.com. **Villas International** ✉ 4340 Redwood Hwy., Suite D309, San Rafael, CA 94903 ☎ 800/221-2260 or 415/499-9490 🖷 415/499-9491 ⊕ www.villasintl.com.

⛫ Local Agents Homes International ✉ Via Bissolati 20, 00187 Rome ☎ 06/4881800 🖷 06/4881808 ⊕ www.homeinternational.it. **Property International** ✉ Viale Aventino 79, 00153 Rome ☎ 06/5743170 🖷 06/5743182 ⊕ www.propertyint.net.

⛫ Roman Publications *EYP* ⊕ www.intoitaly.it. *Wanted in Rome* ✉ Via dei Delfini 17, 00186 Rome, Italy ☎ 06/6790190 🖷 06/6783798 ⊕ www.wantedinrome.com.

FARM HOLIDAYS & AGRITOURISM

Staying on working farms or vineyards, often in old stone farmhouses that accommodate a number of guests, has become more and more popular. Contact local tourist offices or consult *Agriturism* (www.agriturismo.com) for more than 1,600 farms in Italy. Although it's in Italian, the publication has photos and descriptions that make it a useful resource.

⛫ Agency Italy Farm Holidays ✉ 547 Martling Ave., Tarrytown, NY 10591 ☎ 914/631-7880 🖷 914/631-8831 ⊕ www.italyfarmholidays.com.

HOME EXCHANGES

If you would like to exchange your home for someone else's, join a home-exchange organization, which will send you its updated listings of available exchanges for a year and will include your own listing in at least one of them. It's up to you to make specific arrangements.

⛫ Exchange Clubs HomeLink USA ✉ 2937 N.W. 9th Terr., Wilton Manors, FL 33311 ☎ 800/638-3841 or 954/566-2687 🖷 954/566-2783 ⊕ www.homelink.org; $75 yearly for a listing and online access; $45 additional to receive directories. **Intervac U.S.** ✉ 30 Corte San Fernando, Tiburon, CA 94920 ☎ 800/756-4663 🖷 415/435-7440 ⊕ www.intervacus.com; $128 yearly for a listing, online access, and a catalog; $68 without catalog.

HOSTELS

Hostels offer barebones lodging at low, low prices—often in shared dorm rooms with shared baths—to people of all ages, though the primary market is young travelers, especially students. Most hostels serve breakfast; dinner and/or shared cooking facilities may also be available. In some hostels, you aren't allowed to be in your room during the day, and there may be a curfew at night. Nevertheless, hostels provide a sense of community, with public rooms where travelers often gather to share stories. Many hostels are affiliated with Hostelling International (HI), an umbrella group of hostel associations with some 4,500 member properties in more than 70 countries. Other hostels are completely independent and may be nothing more than a really cheap hotel.

Membership in any HI association, open to travelers of all ages, allows you to stay in HI-affiliated hostels at member rates. One-year membership is about $28 for adults; hostels charge about $10–$30 per night. Members have priority if the hostel is full; they're also eligible for discounts around the world, even on rail and bus travel in some countries.

🎫 Organizations **Hostelling International–USA** ✉ 8401 Colesville Rd., Suite 600, Silver Spring, MD 20910 ☎ 301/495-1240 📠 301/495-6697 ⊕ www. hiusa.org. **Hostelling International–Canada** ✉ 205 Catherine St., Suite 400, Ottawa, Ontario K2P 1C3 ☎ 800/663-5777 or 613/237-7884 📠 613/ 237-7868 ⊕ www.hihostels.ca. **YHA England and Wales** ✉ Trevelyan House, Dimple Rd., Matlock, Derbyshire, DE4 3YH U.K. ☎ 0870/870-8808, 0870/ 770-8868, or 0162/959-2600 📠 0870/770-6127 ⊕ www.yha.org.uk. **YHA Australia** ✉ 422 Kent St., Sydney, NSW 2001 ☎ 02/9261-1111 📠 02/9261-1969 ⊕ www.yha.com.au. **YHA New Zealand** ✉ Level 1, Moorhouse City, 166 Moorhouse Ave., Box 436, Christchurch ☎ 0800/278-299 or 03/379-9970 📠 03/365-4476 ⊕ www.yha.org.nz.

HOTELS

All Italian hotels are graded on a star scale, from five stars for the most deluxe hotels to one star for the most modest. This system can be misleading, as it reflects a hotel's facilities, not how well it is maintained. Some four- or five-star accommodations are past their prime, and some two- and three-star places might be sparkling. Except in the most expensive hotels, rooms may be very small by U.S. standards.

The quality of rooms in older hotels may be very uneven; if you don't like the room you're given, request another. A front room may be larger or have a view, but it also may have a lot of street noise. If you're a light sleeper, **request a quiet room** when making a reservation. Rooms in lodgings listed in this guide have a shower and/or tub unless noted otherwise. (Hotels with three or more stars always have private bathrooms). Remember to **specify whether you prefer to have a bathtub or shower.**

In all hotels there will be a card inside the door of your room stating the basic rate (which often varies according to the location and size of the room). Any discrepancy between the posted rate and what you are charged is cause for complaint to the manager and to the police. By law, breakfast is supposed to be optional, but most hotels quote room rates including breakfast. When you book a room, **ask whether the rate includes breakfast.** You are under no obligation to take *colazione* (breakfast) at your hotel, and can have the charge removed from your bill if you decide to eat elsewhere.

You'll find some familiar chains, such as Best Western and Sheraton. Other chains include Atahotels, with mostly four- and five-star hotels; Agip, which has four-star motels along main highways; Jolly, which has four-star hotels; Space Hotels, which has 80 independently owned four- and three-star hotels; and Starhotels, which has mainly four-star lodgings.

RESERVING A ROOM

High season in Italy generally runs from Easter through the beginning of November, and then for two weeks at Christmas. During low season, many hotels reduce their prices. Always **inquire about special rates.** It's always a good idea to **confirm your reservation** by e-mail or fax. If you need to cancel your reservation, do so by e-mail or fax and keep a record of the transmission. If you don't have a reservation, most cities have reservation booths in train stations.

Useful terms to know when booking a room are *aria condizionata* (air-conditioning), *bagno in stanza* (private bath), *letto matrimoniale* (double bed), *letti singoli* (twin beds), and *letti singoli uniti* (twin beds pushed together). Italy does not really have queen- or king-size beds, but larger beds are sometimes available in four- and five-star accommodations.

Other useful phrases include: *una camera su un piano alto e con vista* (a room on a high floor with a view), *una camera a un piano basso* (a room on a low floor), and *una camera silenziosa* (a quiet room).

MAIL & SHIPPING

The Italian mail system is notoriously slow. Allow up to 15 days for mail to get to the United States, Canada, Australia, and New Zealand. It takes about a week to the United Kingdom and within Italy. Posta Prioritaria (for Italy only) and Postacelere (for Italy and abroad) are special-delivery services from the post office that guarantee delivery within 24 hours in Italy and within three to five days abroad.

Most post offices are open Monday–Saturday 9–12:30; central post offices are open weekdays 9–6:30, Saturday 9–12:30. On the last day of the month, post offices close at midday. You can buy stamps at tobacco shops as well as post offices.

OVERNIGHT SERVICES

Overnight mail is generally available during the week in all major cities and at popular resorts. Service is reliable; a Federal Express letter to the United States costs about €30, to the United Kingdom, €51, and to Australia and New Zealand, €33. Overnight delivery usually means 24–36 hours.

If your hotel can't assist you, try an Internet café, many of which also offer overnight mail services using major carriers at reasonable rates.

🖼 Major Services **DHL** ☎ 199–199–345 ⊕ www. dhl.it. **Federal Express** ☎ 800/123800 ⊕ www. fedex.com. **SDA** ☎ 800/016027 ⊕ www.sda.it.

POSTAL RATES

Airmail letters and postcards sent *ordinaria* to the United States and Canada cost €0.65 for up to 20 grams, €1 for 21–50 grams,

and €1.30 for 51–100 grams. Always stick the blue airmail tag on your mail, or write AIRMAIL in big, clear letters beside the address. Mail sent *ordinaria* to Italy, the United Kingdom, and other EU countries costs €0.45 for the first 20 grams.

For faster service, use priority delivery *Posta Prioritaria* (for small letters and packages), which guarantees delivery within Italy in three to five business days and abroad in five to six working days. The more-expensive express delivery, *Postacelere* (for larger letters and packages), guarantees one-day delivery to most places in Italy and three- to five-day delivery abroad.

Mail sent as Posta Prioritaria to the United States and Canada costs €0.80 for up to 20 grams, €1.50 for 21–50 grams, and €1.80 for 51–100 grams; to Italy, the United Kingdom, and other EU countries it costs €0.62. Mail sent as Postacelere to the United States and Canada costs €35.05 for up to 500 grams. If you're shipping to the United Kingdom or elsewhere in Europe, the cost is €28.15.

Other package services to check are Quick Pack Europe, for delivery within Europe; and EMS ExpressMail Service, a global three- to five-day service for letters and packages that can be less expensive than Postacelere.

RECEIVING MAIL

Correspondence can be addressed to you in care of any Italian post office. Letters should be addressed to your name, "c/o Ufficio Postale Centrale," followed by "Fermo Posta" on the next line, and the name of the city (preceded by its postal code) on the next. You can **collect it at the central post office** by showing your passport or photo-bearing ID and paying a small fee. American Express also has a general-delivery service. There's no charge for cardholders, holders of American Express traveler's checks, or anyone who booked a vacation with American Express.

SHIPPING PARCELS

You can ship parcels via air or surface. Air takes about two weeks, and surface anywhere up to three months to most countries. If you have purchased antiques, ceramics, or other objects, **ask if the vendor will do the shipping** for you; in most cases, this is a possibility. If so, ask if the article will be insured against breakage.

MONEY MATTERS

Prices vary from region to region and are substantially lower in the country than in the cities. Of Italy's major cities, Venice and Milan are by far the most expensive. Resorts such as the Costa Smeralda, Portofino, and Cortina d'Ampezzo cater to wealthy people and charge top prices. Good values can be had in the scenic Trentino–Alto Adige region and the Dolomites and in Umbria and the Marches. With a few exceptions, southern Italy, Sicily, and Sardinia also offer good values.

Prices throughout this guide are given for adults. Substantially reduced fees are almost always available for children, students, and senior citizens from the EU; citizens of non-EU countries rarely get discounts. For information on taxes, *see* Taxes.

ATMS

An ATM (*bancomat* in Italian) is the easiest way to get euros in Italy. There are numerous ATMs in large cities and small towns, as well as in airports and train stations. They are not common in places such as grocery stores. Be sure to **memorize your PIN number,** as ATM keypads in Italy don't always display letters.

CREDIT CARDS

MasterCard and Visa are preferred by Italian merchants, but American Express is usually accepted in tourist spots. Credit cards aren't accepted everywhere; if you want to pay with a credit card in a small shop, hotel, or restaurant, it's a good idea to make your intentions known early on. Throughout this guide, the following abbreviations are used: **AE,** American Express; **DC,** Diners Club; **MC,** MasterCard; and **V,** Visa.

🔢 Reporting Lost Cards **American Express** 🖷 800/874333 international collect. **Diners Club** 🖷 702/797–5532 collect. **MasterCard** 🖷 800/

870866 toll free in Italy. **Visa** 🖷 800/877232 toll free in Italy.

CURRENCY

The euro is the main unit of currency in Italy, as well as in 11 other European countries. Under the euro system there are 100 *centesimi* (cents) to the euro. There are coins valued at 1, 2, 5, 10, 20, and 50 cents, as well as 1 and 2 euros. There are seven notes: 5, 10, 20, 50, 100, 200, and 500 euros.

CURRENCY EXCHANGE

At this writing, the exchange rate was about 0.76 euros to the U.S. dollar; 0.70 euros to the Canadian dollar; 1.47 euros to the pound sterling; 0.60 euros to the Australian dollar; and 0.49 euros to the New Zealand dollar.

For the most favorable rates, **change money through banks.** Although ATM transaction fees may be higher abroad than at home, ATM rates are excellent because they're based on wholesale rates offered only by major banks. You won't do as well at exchange booths in airports or rail and bus stations, in hotels, in restaurants, or in stores. To avoid lines at airport exchange booths, get a bit of local currency before you leave home. Post offices also exchange currency at good rates.

🔢 Exchange Services **International Currency Express** ✉ 427 N. Camden Dr., Suite F, Beverly Hills, CA 90210 🖷 888/278–6628 orders 🖷 310/278–6410 ⊕ www.foreignmoney.com. **Travel Ex Currency Services** 🖷 800/287–7362 orders and retail locations ⊕ www.travelex.com.

TRAVELER'S CHECKS & CARDS

Some consider traveler's checks the currency of the cave man, and it's true that fewer establishments accept them these days. Nevertheless, they're a cheap and secure way to carry extra money, particularly on trips to urban areas. Both Citibank (under the Visa brand) and American Express issue traveler's checks in the United States, but Amex is better known and more widely accepted; you can also avoid hefty surcharges by cashing Amex checks at at Amex offices. Whatever you do, keep track of all the serial numbers in case the checks are lost or stolen.

American Express now offers a stored-value card called a Travelers Cheque Card, which you can use wherever American Express credit cards are accepted, including ATMs. The card can carry a minimum of $300 and a maximum of $2,700, and it's a very safe way to carry your funds. Although you can get replacement funds in 24 hours if your card is lost or stolen, it doesn't really strike us as a very good deal. In addition to a high initial cost ($14.95 to set up the card, plus $5 each time you "reload"), you still have to pay a 2% fee for each purchase in a foreign currency (similar to that of any credit card). Further, each time you use the card in an ATM you pay a transaction fee of $2.50 on top of the 2% transaction fee for the conversion—add it all up and it can be considerably more than you would pay for simply using your own ATM card. Regular traveler's checks are just as secure and cost less.

🇮🇹 **American Express** ☎ 888/412–6945 in the U.S., 801/945–9450 collect outside of the U.S. to add value or speak to customer service ⊕ www. americanexpress.com.

PACKING

The weather is considerably milder, in winter at least, in Italy than in the north and central United States or Great Britain. At the height of summer stick with very light clothing, as it can get steamy. But even during summer months a sweater may be necessary for cool evenings, especially in the mountains and on the islands. Sunglasses, a hat, and sunblock are essential. Brief summer afternoon thunderstorms are common in Rome and inland cities, so a small umbrella will come in handy. In winter bring a medium-weight coat and a raincoat for Rome and farther south. Northern Italy calls for heavier coats, gloves, hats, scarves, and boots. Bring sturdy shoes for winter and comfortable walking shoes in any season.

Living up to their reputation, Italians dress exceptionally well. Men aren't required to wear ties or jackets to dinner, except in some of the grander hotel dining rooms and top-level restaurants, but are expected to look reasonably sharp—and they do.

For sightseeing **pack a pair of binoculars**; they will help you get a good look at painted ceilings and domes. If you stay in budget hotels **take your own soap and towel.** Many such hotels either do not provide soap or give guests only one tiny bar per room, and towels are often small and thin.

In your carry-on luggage, pack an extra pair of eyeglasses or contact lenses and enough of any medication you take to last a few days longer than the entire trip. You may also ask your doctor to write a spare prescription using the drug's generic name, as brand names may vary from country to country. In luggage to be checked, **never pack prescription drugs, valuables, or undeveloped film.** And don't forget to carry with you the addresses of offices that handle refunds of lost traveler's checks. Check *Fodor's How to Pack* (available at online retailers and bookstores everywhere) for more tips.

To avoid customs and security delays, carry medications in their original packaging. Don't pack any sharp objects in your carry-on luggage, including knives of any size or material, scissors, nail clippers, corkscrews, or anything else that might arouse suspicion.

To avoid having your checked luggage chosen for hand inspection, don't cram bags full. The U.S. Transportation Security Administration suggests packing shoes on top and placing personal items you don't want touched in clear plastic bags.

CHECKING LUGGAGE

You're allowed to carry aboard one bag and one personal article, such as a purse or a laptop computer. Make sure what you carry on fits under your seat or in the overhead bin. Get to the gate early, so you can board as soon as possible, before the overhead bins fill up.

Baggage allowances vary by carrier, destination, and ticket class. On international flights, you're usually allowed to check two bags weighing up to 70 pounds (32 kilograms) each, although a few airlines allow checked bags of up to 88 pounds (40 kilograms) in first class. Some international carriers don't allow more than 66 pounds (30 kilograms) per bag in business class and 44 pounds (20 kilograms) in economy. If you're flying to or through the United Kingdom, your luggage cannot exceed 70 pounds (32 kilograms) per bag. On domestic flights, the limit is usually 50 to 70 pounds (23 to 32 kilograms) per bag. In general, carry-on bags shouldn't exceed 40 pounds (18 kilograms). Most airlines won't accept bags that weigh more than 100 pounds (45 kilograms) on domestic or international flights. Expect to pay a fee for baggage that exceeds weight limits. Check baggage restrictions with your carrier before you pack.

Airline liability for baggage is limited to $2,500 per person on flights within the United States. On international flights it amounts to $9.07 per pound or $20 per kilogram for checked baggage (roughly $640 per 70-pound bag), with a maximum of $634.90 per piece, and $400 per passenger for unchecked baggage. You can buy additional coverage at check-in for about $10 per $1,000 of coverage, but it often excludes a rather extensive list of items, shown on your airline ticket.

Before departure, itemize your bags' contents and their worth, and label the bags with your name, address, and phone number. (If you use your home address, cover it so potential thieves can't see it readily.) Include a label inside each bag and **pack a copy of your itinerary.** At check-in, make sure each bag is correctly tagged with the destination airport's three-letter code. Because some checked bags will be opened for hand inspection, the U.S. Transportation Security Administration recommends that you leave luggage unlocked or use the plastic locks offered at check-in. TSA screeners place an inspection notice inside searched bags, which are resealed with a special lock.

If your bag has been searched and contents are missing or damaged, file a claim with the TSA Contact Center as soon as possible. If your bags arrive damaged or fail to arrive at all, file a written report with the airline before leaving the airport.

🛄 Complaints **U.S. Transportation Security Administration Contact Center** 📞 866/289-9673 🌐 www.tsa.gov.

PASSPORTS & VISAS
When traveling internationally, carry your passport even if you don't need one (it's always the best form of ID) and **make two photocopies of the data page** (one for someone at home and another for you, carried separately from your passport). If you lose your passport, promptly call the nearest embassy or consulate and the local police.

U.S. passport applications for children under age 14 require consent from both parents or legal guardians; both parents must appear together to sign the application. If only one parent appears, he or she must submit a written statement from the other parent authorizing passport issuance for the child. A parent with sole authority must present evidence of it when applying; acceptable documentation includes the child's certified birth certificate listing only the applying parent, a court order specifically permitting this parent's travel with the child, or a death certificate for the nonapplying parent. Application forms and instructions are available on the Web site of the U.S. State Department's Bureau of Consular Affairs (🌐 travel.state.gov).

ENTERING ITALY
Citizens of Australia, Canada, New Zealand, and the United States need only a valid passport to enter Italy for stays of up to 90 days. Citizens of the United Kingdom need only a valid passport to enter Italy for an unlimited stay.

PASSPORT OFFICES
The best time to apply for a passport or to renew is in fall and winter. Before any trip, check your passport's expiration date, and, if necessary, renew it as soon as possible.

🛄 Canadian Citizens **Passport Office** ✉ To mail in applications: 70 Cremazie St., Gatineau, Québec J8Y 3P2 📞 800/567-6868 or 819/994-3500 🌐 www. ppt.gc.ca.
🛄 U.K. Citizens **U.K. Passport Service** 📞 0870/ 521-0410 🌐 www.passport.gov.uk.
🛄 U.S. Citizens **National Passport Information**

Center ☎ 877/487-2778, 888/874-7793 TDD/TTY ⊕ travel.state.gov.

RESTROOMS

Public restrooms are rather rare in Italy. Pay toilets are the exception, not the rule. In Rome, Florence, and Venice, a few public pay toilets costing €0.50 are strategically located in the city centers. Although private businesses can refuse to make their toilets available to the passing public, some bars will allow you to use the restroom if you ask politely. Alternatively, it is not uncommon to pay for a little something—a mineral water or coffee, for example—to get access to the facilities. Standards of cleanliness and comfort vary greatly. In cities, restaurants, hotel lobbies, and high-end department stores such as La Rinascente and Coin tend to have the cleanest restrooms. Pubs and bars rank among the worst. In general, it's in your interest to carry some toilet paper with you. There are bathrooms in museums and in airports and train stations (in major train stations you'll also find well-kept pay toilets for €0.50–€1). There are also bathrooms at highway rest stops and gas stations: a small tip (€0.25–€0.50) to the attendant is always appreciated. There are no bathrooms at churches, post offices, subway stations, or public beaches.

SAFETY

The best way to protect yourself against purse snatchers and pickpockets is to wear a concealed money belt or a pouch on a string around your neck. Be on your guard when in buses and subways, when making your way through crowded trains, and in busy piazzas and other tourist spots. Don't wear a waist pack, which pegs you as a tourist. Distribute your cash and any valuables (including your credit cards and passport) between a deep front pocket, an inside jacket or vest pocket, and a hidden money pouch. Do not reach for the money pouch once you're in public.

LOCAL SCAMS

In larger cities, some children have been trained to be adept pickpockets. One tactic is to proffer a piece of cardboard with writing on it. While you attempt to read the message *on* it, the children's hands are busy *under* it, trying to make off with purses or valuables. If you see such a group, avoid them—they are quick and know more tricks than you do. If traveling in a rental car, have someone remain near the car when you stop at rest areas. Thieves often target rental cars.

WOMEN IN ITALY

Purse-snatching is not uncommon, and thieves operate on foot as well as on *motorini* (mopeds). If you carry a purse, choose one with a zipper and a thick strap that you can drape across your body; adjust the length so that the purse sits in front of you at or above hip level. (Don't wear a waist pack.) Store only enough money in the purse to cover casual spending. Distribute the rest of your cash and any valuables between deep front pockets, inside jacket or vest pockets, and a concealed money pouch.

The difficulties encountered by women traveling alone in Italy are often overstated. Younger women have to put up with much male attention, but it is rarely dangerous or hostile. Ignoring whistling and questions is the best response; a firm *no, vai via* ("no, go away") usually works, too.

SENIOR-CITIZEN TRAVEL

To qualify for age-related discounts, mention your senior-citizen status up front when booking hotel reservations (not when checking out) and before you're seated in restaurants (not when paying the bill). Be sure to have identification on hand. When renting a car, ask about promotional car-rental discounts, which can be cheaper than senior-citizen rates.

🄵 Educational Programs **Elderhostel** ✉ 11 Ave. de Lafayette, Boston, MA 02111 ☎ 877/426-8056, 978/323-4141 international callers, 877/426-2167 TTY 🖷 877/426-2166 ⊕ www.elderhostel.org. **Interhostel** ✉ University of New Hampshire, 6 Garrison Ave., Durham, NH 03824 ☎ 800/733-9753 or 603/862-1147 🖷 603/862-1113 ⊕ www.learn.unh.edu.

SHOPPING

Italy produces fine wines, beautiful clothes, and exquisite jewelry, among other things. The notice PREZZI FISSI (fixed prices) means just that—it's a waste of time to bargain unless you're buying a sizable quantity of goods or a particularly costly object. You can bargain, however, at outdoor markets and when buying from street vendors.

WATCH OUT

Be careful about purchasing art: any painting, sculpture, or other work of art more than 50 years old must receive clearance from the Italian government to leave the country.

If you're purchasing an antique, have the dealer provide you with a certificate attesting to the integrity of the piece and the price paid. Some dealers will ship the object for you; others leave it to you to arrange shipping.

SIGHTSEEING GUIDES

Every province in Italy has tour guides licensed by the government. Some are eminently qualified in relevant fields such as architecture and art history; others have simply managed to pass the test. Tourist offices can provide the names of knowledgeable guides and the rates for certain services. Before you hire a guide, ask about their background and qualifications and make sure you can understand each other. Tipping is appreciated but not obligatory.

SMOKING

In 2005, smoking was banned in many public places, including bars and restaurants. Although Italians are for the most part unrepentant smokers, they are begrudgingly obeying the law. Always check to see if there's a VIETATO FUMARE (no smoking) sign before lighting up. All Italian trains are smoke-free.

LOCAL RESOURCES

The Centro Turistico Studentesco (CTS) is a student and youth travel agency with offices in major Italian cities. CTS helps its clients find low-cost accommodations and bargain fares for travel in Italy and elsewhere. CTS is also the Rome representative for EuroTrain International.

TAXES
HOTELS

A 9% V.A.T. (value-added tax) is included in the rate at all hotels except those at the upper end of the range. At luxury hotels a 12% tax is added to the bill.

RESTAURANTS

No tax is added to the bill in restaurants. A service charge of approximately 10%–15% is often added to your check; in some cases a service charge is included in the prices.

VALUE-ADDED TAX

The V.A.T. is 20% on clothing, wine, and luxury goods. On consumer goods it's already included in the amount shown on the price tag, whereas on services it may not be. If your purchases total more than €155 you may be entitled to a refund of the V.A.T.

When making a purchase, **ask for a V.A.T. refund form** and find out whether the merchant gives refunds—not all stores do, nor are they required to. Have the form stamped like any customs form by customs officials when you leave the country or, if you're visiting several European Union countries, when you leave the EU. Be ready to show customs officials what you've bought (pack purchases together, in your carry-on luggage); budget extra time for this. After you're through passport control, take the form to a refund-service counter for an on-the-spot refund (which is usually the quickest and easiest option), or mail it to the address on the form (or the envelope with it) after you arrive home.

A service processes refunds for most shops. You receive the total refund stated on the form. Global Refund is a Europe-wide service with 210,000 affiliated stores and more than 700 refund counters—located at major airports and border crossings. Its refund form is called a Tax Free Check. The service issues refunds in the form of cash, check, or credit-card adjustment. If you don't have time to wait at the refund counter, you can mail in the form to an office in Europe or Canada instead.

🚩 **V.A.T. Refunds Global Refund Canada** 🗐 Box 2020, Station Main, Brampton, Ontario L6T 3S3 ☎ 800/993-4313 🖷 905/791-9078 ⊕ www. globalrefund.com.

TELEPHONES

Italy's telephone system is quite reliable. Remember that telephone numbers do not have a standard number of digits (they can range anywhere from four to seven) and that the entire area code must be included even when calling a number in the same city.

Cell phones are widely used by Italians, so there are fewer public pay phones. If you need to make a lot of calls, consider renting or even buying a cell phone. Renting one costs about €20 per week plus the cost of a calling card. There is no charge for the phone, but a €100 deposit is normal. Buying a basic phone runs between €80 and €125.

Public pay phones may take coins, but usually require a *carta telefonica* (phone card) purchased at newsstands and tobacco shops. There are national cards and international cards, so make sure to specify which you want.

AREA & COUNTRY CODES

The country code for Italy is 39. Here are the area codes for major cities: Bologna 051; Brindisi 0831; Florence 055; Genoa 010; Milan 02; Naples 081; Palermo 091; Perugia 075; Pisa 050; Rome 06; Siena 0577; Turin 011; Venice 041; Verona 045. A call from the United States to Rome would be dialed as 011 + 39 + 06 + phone number.

The country code is 1 for the United States and Canada, 61 for Australia, 64 for New Zealand, and 44 for the United Kingdom.

DIRECTORY & OPERATOR ASSISTANCE

For general information in English, dial 4176. To place international calls through an operator, dial 170.

INTERNATIONAL CALLS

Since hotels charge exorbitant rates for long-distance and international calls, it's best to call from public phones using telephone cards. You can **make collect calls from any phone by dialing 170,** which will get you an English-speaking operator. Rates to the United States are lowest all day Sunday and 10 PM–8 AM the rest of the week.

LOCAL & LONG-DISTANCE CALLS

For all calls within Italy, whether local or long-distance, dial the area code followed by the number. Rates for long-distance calls vary according to the time of day; it's cheaper to call before 9 AM and after 7 or 8 PM.

LONG-DISTANCE SERVICES

AT&T, MCI, and Sprint access codes make calling long-distance relatively convenient, but you may find the local access number blocked in many hotel rooms. First ask the hotel operator to connect you. If the hotel operator balks, ask for an international operator, or dial the international operator yourself. One way to improve your odds of getting connected to your long-distance carrier is to travel with more than one company's calling card (a hotel may block Sprint, for example, but not MCI). If all else fails, call from a pay phone. If you are traveling for a longer period of time, consider renting a cell phone from a local company.

🚩 **Access Codes AT&T Direct** ☎ 800/172-444. **MCI WorldPhone** ☎ 800/172-401 or 800/172-404. **Sprint International Access** ☎ 800/172-405.

PHONE CARDS

Prepaid *carte telefoniche* (phone cards) are available throughout Italy. Cards in different denominations are sold at post offices, newsstands, tobacco shops, and bars. For local or national cards, tear off the corner of the card and insert it in the slot. When you dial, its value appears in the window. After you hang up, the card is returned. International calling cards are different; you must call a toll-free number and dial a code number on the back of the card. The best card to use when calling North America or Europe is the €5 or €10 Europa card, which gives you a local number to dial and 180 minutes and 360 minutes of calling time.

PUBLIC PHONES

Public pay phones are scarce, although they can be found at train and subway stations, post offices, in hotel lobbies, and in some bars. In rural areas, town squares usually have a pay phone. Some accept coins, but most use only prepaid phone cards.

TIME

Italy is 6 hours ahead of Eastern Standard Time, 1 hour ahead of Great Britain, 10 hours behind Sydney, and 12 hours behind Auckland. Like the rest of Europe, Italy uses the 24-hour (or "military") clock, which means that after noon you continue counting forward: 13:00 is 1 PM, 23:30 is 11:30 PM.

TIPPING

In restaurants a service charge of 10% to 15% may appear on your check. If so, it's not necessary to leave an additional tip. If service is not included, leave a tip of up to 10%. Tip checkroom attendants €1 per person and restroom attendants €0.50 (more in expensive hotels and restaurants). In major cities tip €0.05 for whatever you drink standing up at a coffee bar, €0.50 or more for table service in cafés. At a hotel bar tip €1 and up for a round or two of drinks.

Italians rarely tip taxi drivers, which is not to say that you shouldn't do it. A euro or two, depending on the length of the journey, is appreciated, particularly if the driver helps with luggage. Service-station attendants are tipped only for special services; give them €1 for checking your tires. Railway and airport porters charge a fixed rate per bag. Tip an additional €0.25 per person, more if the porter is helpful. Give a barber €1–€1.50 and a hairdresser's assistant €1.50–€4 for a shampoo or cut, depending on the type of establishment.

On sightseeing tours, tip guides about €1.50 per person for a half-day group tour, more if they are especially knowledgeable. In monasteries and other sights where admission is free, a contribution (€0.50–€1) is expected.

In hotels give the *portiere* (concierge) about 10% of his bill for services, or €2.50–€5 for help with dinner reservations and such. For two people in a double room leave the chambermaid about €0.75 per day, or about €4.50–€5 a week in a moderately priced hotel; tip a minimum of €1 for valet or room service. Double these amounts in an expensive hotel. In expensive hotels tip doormen €0.50 for calling a cab and €1.50 for carrying bags to the check-in desk, bellhops €1.50–€2.50 for carrying your bags to the room, and €2–€2.50 for room service.

TOURS & PACKAGES

Packages *are not* guided tours. Packages combine airfare, accommodations, and perhaps a rental car or other extras (theater tickets, guided excursions, boat trips, reserved entry to popular museums, transit passes), but they let you do your own thing. During busy periods, packages may be your only option because flights and rooms may be otherwise sold out. Packages will definitely save you time. They can also save you money, particularly in peak seasons, but—and this is a really big "but"—you should price each part of the package separately to be sure. And be aware that prices advertised on Web sites and in newspapers rarely include service charges or taxes, which can up your costs by hundreds of dollars.

Note that local tourism boards can provide information about lesser-known and small-niche operators that sell packages to just a few destinations. And don't always assume that you can get the best deal by booking everything yourself. Some packages and cruises are sold only through travel agents.

Each year consumers are stranded or lose their money when packagers—even large ones with excellent reputations—go out of business. How can you protect yourself? First, always pay with a credit card; if you have a problem, your credit-card company may help you resolve it. Second, buy trip insurance that covers default. Third, choose a company that belongs to the United States Tour Operators Association, whose members must set aside funds ($1 million) to cover defaults. Finally choose a company that also participates in the Tour

Operator Program of the American Society of Travel Agents (ASTA), which will act as mediator in any disputes. You can also check on the tour operator's reputation among travelers by posting an inquiry on one of the Fodors.com forums.

⚡ Organizations American Society of Travel Agents (ASTA) ☎ 703/739–2782 or 800/965–2782 24-hr hotline ⊕ www.astanet.com. **United States Tour Operators Association (USTOA)** ☎ 212/599–6599 ⊕ www.ustoa.com.

TRAIN TRAVEL

In Italy traveling by train is simple and efficient. Service between major cities is frequent, and trains usually arrive on schedule. You can either purchase your tickets in advance (all major credit cards are accepted online at ⊕ www.raileurope.com) or after you arrive at any train station or travel agency. If you are considering using a Eurailpass or any of its variations you must **buy the pass before leaving your home country,** as they are not sold in Italy.

You must **validate your ticket before boarding** the train by punching it at a yellow box located in the waiting area of smaller train stations or at the end of the track in larger stations. Always **purchase tickets before boarding the train,** as you can no longer purchase one from a conductor. Fines are steep for passengers without tickets.

The fastest trains on the *Trenitalia,* the Italian State Railways, are the Eurostar trains that run between major cities. You will be assigned a specific seat in a specific coach. To avoid having to squeeze through narrow aisles, board only at your designated coach (the number on your ticket matches the one on near the door of each coach). The next-fastest trains are the *Intercity* (IC) trains. Reservations, required for some IC trains, are always advisable. *Diretto* and *Interregionale* trains make more stops and are a little slower. *Regionale* and *locale* trains are the slowest; many serve commuters. There are refreshments on all long-distance trains, purchased from a mobile cart or a dining car.

Traveling by night is a good deal, as you do not pay extra for a bed. More comfortable trains run on the longer routes (Sicily–Rome, Sicily–Milan, Sicily–Venice, Rome–Turin, Lecce–Milan); ask for the good-value T3, Intercity Notte, and Carrozza Comfort. The Vagone Letto Excelsior has private bathrooms, coffee machines, microwave ovens, refrigerators, and a suite with a double bed and TV.

Some cities—Milan, Turin, Genoa, Naples, Florence, and Rome included—have more than one train station, so be sure you get off at the right place. When buying train tickets be particularly aware that in Rome and Florence some trains do not stop at all of the cities' train stations and may not stop at the main central station. This is a common occurrence with regional and some intercity trains. When scheduling train travel on the Internet or through a travel agent, be sure to request a train that goes to the train station closest to you destination in Rome and Florence.

Except for Pisa and Rome, none of the major cities have trains that go directly to the airports, but there are commuter bus lines connecting train stations and airports.

Train strikes of various kinds are also common, so it's a good idea to make sure your train is running.

⚡ Train Information Trenitalia ☎ 892021 in Italy ⊕ www.trenitalia.com.

CLASSES

Most Italian trains have first and second classes. On local trains a first-class fare gets you little more than a clean doily on your headrest, but on long-distance trains you get wider seats, more legroom, and better ventilation and lighting. At peak travel times, a first-class fare is worth the price as the coaches are less crowded. In Italian, *prima classe* is first class; second is *seconda classe.*

CUTTING COSTS

To save money, **look into rail passes.** But be aware that if you don't plan to cover many miles, you may come out ahead by buying individual tickets. If Italy is your only destination, consider an Italian Flexi Rail Card Saver. Over the course of a month you can travel on 4 days ($239 first class, $191 second class), 8 days ($334 first class, $268 second class), or 12 days ($429 first class, $343 second class). These tickets are sold only outside Italy.

The *Carta d'Argento* (Silver Card), for seniors, *Cartaverde* (Green Card), for those under 26, and *Comitive Ordinarie,* for groups, have been discontinued. They have been replaced with the *Railplus* card which is used for the purchase of international tickets (25% reduction on international tickets from Italy to Austria, Germany, and France and 25% on internal ticket prices when combined with an international ticket). The *Railplus* card is purchased upon arrival in Italy and costs €45 for adults and €20 for seniors over 60 and youths under 26.

Italy is one of 17 countries that accept Eurailpass, which allows unlimited first-class travel. If you plan to rack up the miles, get a standard pass. Passes are available for 15 days ($605), 21 days ($785), one month ($975), two months ($1,378), and three months ($1,703). You also get free or discounted fares on some ferry lines. The Eurail Selectpass allows for travel in three to five contiguous countries. Five days of first-class travel in three countries is $383, four countries $428, five countries $473.

In addition to standard Eurailpasses, **ask about special plans.** Among these are the Eurail Youthpass (for those under 26), the Eurail Flexipass (which allows a certain number of travel days within a set period), the Eurail Saver Flexipass (which give a discount for two or more people traveling together), and the EurailDrive Pass (which combines travel by train and rental car). All Eurailpasses must be purchased before you leave home. Order them on the Rail Europe Web site.

Remember that you need to reserve seats even if you are using a rail pass.

⏷ Information & Passes CIT Rail ✉ 15 W. 44th St., New York, NY 10036 ☏ 800/248-7245. **DER Tours** ☏ 800/782-2424 🖷 800/282-7474. **Rail Europe** ✉ 44 S. Broadway, White Plains, NY 10601 ☏ 800/438-7245 or 877/257-2887 ⊕ www. raileurope.com.

PAYING

You can pay for your train tickets in cash or with a major credit card such as American Express, Diners Club, MasterCard, and Visa.

RESERVATIONS

Trains can be very crowded, so it's always a good idea to make a reservation. You can reserve seat up to two months in advance at the train station or at a travel agent. Simply holding a train ticket does not guarantee a seat. In summer it's fairly common to see people standing for part of the journey.

TRAVEL AGENCIES

A good travel agent puts your needs first. Look for an agency that has been in business at least five years, emphasizes customer service, and has someone on staff who specializes in your destination. In addition, **make sure the agency belongs to a professional trade organization.** The American Society of Travel Agents (ASTA) has more than 10,000 members in some 140 countries, enforces a strict code of ethics, and will step in to mediate agent-client disputes involving ASTA members. ASTA also maintains a directory of agents on its Web site; ASTA's TravelSense.org, a trip-planning and travel-advice site, can also help to locate a travel agent who caters to your needs. (If a travel agency is also acting as your tour operator, *see* Buyer Beware *in* Tours & Packages.)

⏷ Local Agent Referrals American Society of Travel Agents (ASTA) ✉ 1101 King St., Suite 200, Alexandria, VA 22314 ☏ 800/965-7782 24-hr hotline, 703/739-2782 🖷 703/684-8319 ⊕ www. astanet.com or www.travelsense.org. **Association of British Travel Agents** ✉ 68–71 Newman St., London W1T 3AH ☏ 020/7637-2444 🖷 020/7637-0713 ⊕ www.abta.com. **Association of Canadian Travel Agencies** ✉ 130 Albert St., Suite 1705, Ottawa, Ontario K1P 5G4 ☏ 613/237-3657 🖷 613/237-7052 ⊕ www.acta.ca. **Australian Federation of Travel Agents** ✉ Level 3, 309 Pitt St., Sydney, NSW 2000 ☏ 02/9264-3299 or 1300/363-416 🖷 02/9264-1085 ⊕ www.afta.com.au. **Travel Agents' Association of New Zealand** ✉ Level 5, Tourism and Travel House, 79 Boulcott St., Box 1888, Wellington 6001 ☏ 04/499-0104 🖷 04/499-0786 ⊕ www.taanz.org.nz.

VISITOR INFORMATION

Learn more about foreign destinations by checking government-issued travel advisories and country information. For a broader picture, consider information from more than one country.

Tourist Information **Italian Government Tourist Board** ✉ 630 5th Ave., Suite 1565, New York, NY 10111 ☎ 212/245-4822 🖷 212/586-9249 ✉ 500 N. Michigan Ave., Chicago, IL 60611 ☎ 312/644-0996 🖷 312/644-3019 ✉ 12400 Wilshire Blvd., Suite 550, Los Angeles, CA 90025 ☎ 310/820-1898 🖷 310/820-6357 ✉ 175 Bloor St. E, Suite 907, South Tower, Toronto, Ontario M4W 3R8 ☎ 416/925-4882 🖷 416/925-4799 ✉ 1 Princes St., London W1B 2.8AY ☎ 020/7408-1254 🖷 020/73993567 ⊕ www.italiantourism.com.

Regional Offices **Florence** ✉ Via Cavour 1/r, next to Palazzo Medici-Riccardi, 50129 ☎ 055/290832 ⊕ www.comune.firenze.it. **Milan** ✉ Stazione Centrale, 20121 ☎ 02/72524370 ⊕ www.milaninfotourist.com. **Naples** ✉ Piazza del Gesù, 80135 ☎ 081/5523328 ⊕ www.inaples.it. **Palermo** ✉ Piazza Castelnuovo 35, 90141 ☎ 091/583847 ⊕ www.palermoturismo.com. **Rome** ✉ Via Parigi 5, 00185 ☎ 06/36004399 ⊕ www.romaturismo.it. **Venice** ✉ Stazione Ferroviaria Santa Lucia ☎ 041/5298727 ⊕ www.turismovenezia.it.

Government Advisories **U.S. Department of State** ✉ Bureau of Consular Affairs, Overseas Citizens Services Office, 2201 C St. NW, Washington, DC 20520 ☎ 202/647-5225, 888/407-4747 or 317/472-2328 for interactive hotline ⊕ www.travel.state.gov. **Consular Affairs Bureau of Canada** ☎ 800/267-6788 or 613/944-6788 ⊕ www.voyage.gc.ca. **U.K. Foreign and Commonwealth Office** ✉ Travel Advice Unit, Consular Directorate, Old Admiralty Bldg., London SW1A 2PA ☎ 0870/606-0290 or 020/7008-1500 ⊕ www.fco.gov.uk/travel. **Australian Department of Foreign Affairs and Trade** ☎ 300/139-281 travel advisories, 02/6261-1299 Consular Travel Advice ⊕ www.smartraveller.gov.au or www.dfat.gov.au. **New Zealand Ministry of Foreign Affairs and Trade** ☎ 04/439-8000 ⊕ www.mft.govt.nz.

WEB SITES

Do check out the World Wide Web when planning your trip. You'll find everything from weather forecasts to virtual tours of famous cities. Be sure to visit Fodors.com (⊕ www.fodors.com), a complete travel-planning site. You can research prices and book plane tickets, hotel rooms, rental cars, vacation packages, and more. In addition, you can post your pressing questions in the Travel Talk section. Other planning tools include a currency converter and weather reports, and there are loads of links to travel resources.

INDEX

A

Abbazia di Monte Oliveto
Maggiore, *517*
Abbazia di Novacella, *185*
Abbazia di San Fruttuoso, *327*
Abbazia di San Galgano, *523*
Abbazia di Sant'Antimo, *522*
Abbazia di Sant'Antonio di
Ranverso, *283*
Accademia ☉, *167*
Accademia Carrara, *244*
Accademia delle Belle Arti,
338–339
Aci Castello, *819*
Aci Treza, *819*
Acireale, *817–819*
Acqua Alta, *58*
Acquario (Camogli), *329*
Acquario di Genova, *337*
Adler ☉, *192*
Aeolian Islands, *858–861*
Agata e Romeo ✕, *626*
Agrigento, *834–835*
Air travel, *905–907*
Airports, *907*
Al Bagatto ✕, *152–153*
Al Bersagliere ✕, *235*
Al Donizetti ✕, *245*
Al Fornello Da Ricci ✕, *777*
Al Garamond ✕, *275*
Al Sole ☉, *141–142*
Al Sole da Tiziano ✕, *139*
Alba, *292*
Albenga, *347*
Alberobello, *774–775*
Albisola Marina, *344–345*
Aleph ☉, *643*
Alghero, *882–884*
Aliano, *787–788*
Alicudi, *861*
Alla Vedova ✕, *80*
Alle Fratte ✕, *629*
Alle Testiere ✕, *81*
Alle Logge, *522*
Alle Ore, *140–141*
Allegrini (winery), *134*
Alpenhotel Ratsberg ☉,
186–187
Alto Adige & Cortina, *179–189*
Amalfi, *749–751*
Amalfi Coast, *739–755*
Amarone, *134–135*
Ambasciata ✕, *235*
Anacapri, *736*
Ancient Rome, *585–593*
Ancona, *564–567*
Andreini ✕, *883*
Anfiteatro Flavio, *715*

Anfiteatro Romano (Cagliari),
871
Anfiteatro Romano (Fiesole),
467
Anfiteatro Romano (Lecce),
780
Anfiteatro Romano (Siracusa),
824–825
Antica Focacceria San
Francesco ✕, *851*
Antica Locanda dei Mercanti
☉, *219*
Antica Osteria al Cavallino
✕, *144*
Antica Osteria al Duomo ✕,
135
Antica Osteria del Ponte ✕,
214
Antica Osteria del Teatro ✕,
365
Antico Noe ✕, *449*
Antipastoteca di Mare ✕, *153*
Antro della Sibilla, *717*
Aosta, *297–299*
Aquariums, *329, 337*
Ara Pacis Augustae, *609*
Archeological Zone, *824–825*
Arco d'Augusto (Rimini), *398*
Arco di Augusto (Aosta), *297*
Arco di Druso, *552–553*
Arco di Traiano (Ancona), *566*
Arco di Traiano (Benevento),
729
Arena di Verona (opera),
132, 136–137
Arezzo, *513, 515–516*
Arsenale, (Venice), *67–68*
Art Hotel Novecento ☉, *385*
Ascoli Piceno, *568*
Asolo, *140–142, 143*
Asplenia ☉, *286*
Aspromonte, *797*
Assisi, *538, 540, 545–546*
Asti, *287–288, 292*
ATMs, *920*
Auditorium-Parco della
Musica, *647*
Avogaria ✕, *84*

B

Badia Fiorentina, *420*
Bagnaia, *678*
Bagnara Calabra, *796*
Bagno di Romagna, *397–398*
Baia, *716*
Balzi Rossi (caves), *352*
Bancogiro ✕, *87*
Barbagia ☉, *880–879*
Bard, *293–294*

Bardineto, *347*
Bardolino, *236*
Bardonecchia, *286*
Bargello, *412, 414*
Bari, *765–766, 769*
Basilica di San Francesco
Arezzo, *513*
Assisi, *541–543*
Basilica di San Giorgi, *830*
Basilicas
Assisi, *541–543*
Loreto, *567*
Paestum, *755*
Ragusa, *830*
San Giulio, *252*
San Luca, *382*
San Marco, *52–54*
San Nicola, *766*
San Petronio, *379–380*
San Pietro, *577, 579*
San Simplicio, *887–888*
San Vitale, *401*
Sant'Ambrogio, *212*
Sant'Andrea, *234*
Sant'Antonio, *115–116*
Sant'Ubaldo, *548*
Santa Maria Finibus Terrae, *783*
Santa Maria Maggiore, *551*
Santi Maria e Donato, *77*
Santo Stefano, *380*
Superga, *274–275*
Basilicata, *784, 786–789*
Bassano del Grappa, *138–140*
Battistero
Bergamo, *244*
Florence, *414–415*
Naples, *701*
Parma, *368–369*
Pisa, *487–488*
Siena, *505*
Battistero del Duomo, *117–118*
Battistero Neoniano, *401*
Battistero Paleocristiano, *210*
Batzenhausl ✕, *177*
Beacci Tornabuoni ☉, *455*
Beaches, *99, 784, 907*
Beehive, The ☉, *642–643*
Bellagio, *245–247*
Belvedere di Santa Caterina,
818–819
Belvedere di Sardagna, *164*
Benevento, *729*
Bergamo, *243–245*
Biblioteca Medicea
Laurenziana, *431–432*
Bike travel, *908*
Boccondivino ✕, *833*
Bologna, *378–389*
Bolzano, *174–179*

Bomarzo, *678–679*
Bordighera, *350–351*
Borgo Medioevale, *273*
Bormio, *172–173*
Bosa, *881*
Bressanone, *184–185*
Breuil-Cervinia, *294–296*
Brindisi, *779*
Bristol Palace ⊞ , *341–342*
Britannia ⊞ , *641*
Brunico, *185–186*
Bucadisantantonio ✕ , *484*
Burano, *76*
Bus travel, *908–909*
Business hours, *909*
Bussana Vecchia, *349*
Busseto, *367*

C

Ca' de Ven ✕ , *404*
Ca' d'Oro, *68–69*
Ca' Gottardi ⊞ , *88–89*
Ca' Maria Adele ⊞ , *91*
Ca' Pesaro, *66*
Ca' Rezzonico (mansion), *60*
Cadran Solaire ✕ , *300*
Cafès, *451, 630–631*
Caffè culture (Trieste), *151*
Cagliari, *869–873*
Calabria, *789, 791–798*
Calasetta, *875*
Calcione Country and Castle
⊞ , *515*
Caldaro, *193–194*
Caltagirone, *831*
Caltanisetta, *833*
Camera di San Paolo, *369*
Camigliatello, *794*
Camogli, *328–329*
Campania, *692, 693.* ⇨ *Also*
Naples
Campanile
Florence, 415
Venice, 57
Campo Carlo Magno, *171*
Campo de' Fiori, *594,*
619–620, 632–633
Campo San Polo, *66*
Campo Santo Stefano, *62*
Camposanto, *489*
Canazei, *189, 192*
Candidollo ✕ , *348*
Caniparoli (shop), *487*
Cannara, *540*
Cannaregio, *67–74, 79–80,*
88–89
Canova, *334–335*
Cantina Palazzo dei Mercanti
✕ , *677*
Cantine Lungarotti, *549*
Capo Caccia, *883*

Capo San Vito, *842*
Capo Santa Maria di Leuca,
783
Capodimonte, *700–705*
Cappella Colleoni, *244*
Cappella degli Scrovegni,
116–117
Cappella del Crocifisso, *163*
Cappella del Transito, *540*
Cappella Sansevero, *701*
Cappelle Medicee, *422, 429*
Caprarola, *678*
Capri, *733–734, 736–739*
Capri Town, *733–734*
Car racing, *222*
Car rentals, *909–910*
Car travel, *910–911*
Casa Buonarroti, *441–442*
Casa del Conte Verde, *281*
Casa di Andrea Mantegna, *234*
Casa di Giorgio Vasari, *515*
Casa di Giulietta, *134*
Casa di Serapide, *670*
Casa Natale di Raffaello,
564–565
Casa Romana, *553*
Casa Romei, *391*
Casale Monferrato, *287*
Casamicciola, *731*
Cascata delle Marmore, *562*
Cascate del Gorello, *523*
Cascina Zeledria ✕ , *171*
Caserta, *729*
Casinò de la Vallée, *294*
Casinos
Italian Riviera, 349
Valle d'Aosta, 294
Venice, 98
Castel del Monte, *770*
Castel dell'Ovo, *696*
Castel Gavone, *346*
Castel Juval, *180*
Castel Mareccio, *176*
Castel Nuovo, *697*
Castel Roncolo, *176*
Castel San Giorgio, *312*
Castel Sant'Angelo, *579–580*
Castel Sant'Elmo, *699–700*
Castel Trauttmansdorff, *182*
Castelletto (Genoa), *334*
Castellina in Chianti, *497*
Castello
Asolo, 141
Cagliari, 871
Otranto, 782
Prato, 477
Udine, 146
Castello (town), *67–74, 81,*
89–91
Castello Aragonese, *783*
Castello Caetani, *683*

Castello del Buonconsiglio,
164–165
Castello della Castelluccia ⊞ ,
644
Castello della Rovere, *667*
Castello di Lerici, *310*
Castello di Lombardia, *832*
Castello di Manta, *284*
Castello di Miramare, *154*
Castello di Petrata ⊞ , *545*
Castello di San Giorgio, *326*
Castello di San Giusto, *152*
Castello di Volpaia, *495*
Castello Estense, *389–390*
Castello Fénis, *296–297*
Castello Formentini ⊞ , *150*
Castello Maniace, *827*
Castello Normano, *774*
Castello Normanno, *815*
Castello Saraceno, *811*
Castello Scaligero, *237, 241*
Castello Sforzesco, *206*
Castello Svevo
Bari, 766
Cosenza, 792
Castello Visconteo, *229*
Castelmola, *815–816*
Castelsardo, *885*
Castelvecchio, *132*
Castle (Trani), *769*
Castro, *783*
Castrovillari, *791*
Catacombe di San Giovanni,
825
Catacombs
Rome, 617
Sicily, 825, 846, 848
Catania, *819, 821–823*
Cathedrals
Acireale, 818
Amalfi, 749
Ancona, 566
Aosta, 298
Arezzo, 513, 515
Asolo, 140
Asti, 287–288, 292
Bari, 766
Benevento, 729
Bergamo, 244
Bolzano, 175
Bressanone, 184
Brindisi, 779
Cagliari, 871
Catania, 821
Cefalù, 856–857
Cividale del Friuli, 147
Como, 250
Cosenza, 792
Cremona, 232
Ferrara, 390
Fiesole, 467

Florence, 415, 418
Gallipoli, 783
Genoa, 338
Gubbio, 547
Lecce, 780
Lucca, 481, 483
Matera, 786
Merano, 181
Messina, 810
Milan, 206–207
Modena, 371
Monreale, 843–844
Naples, 701–702
Orvieto, 559
Otranto, 782
Padua, 117
Palermo, 845–846
Parma, 368
Perugia, 535
Piacenza, 364
Pienza, 520–521
Pisa, 488
Pistoia, 478
Prato, 476
Rapallo, 323
Ravello, 751–752
Rome, 605
Salerno, 754
Siena, 504–505
Siracusa, 825, 827
Spoleto, 552
Todi, 557
Trani, 769
Trento, 163
Treviso, 144
Trieste, 152
Tropea, 796
Turin, 266–267, 269
Venice, 52–55
Ventimiglia, 351
Verona, 132
Viterbo, 676
Volterra, 498
Cattedrale di San Giusto, 152
Cattedrale di San Zeno, 478
Cattedrale di Sant'Agata, 821
Cavaliere Palace Hotel ⌂, 555
Caverns, 312, 352, 734, 748, 775–776, 883
Cavour 313 ✕, 627–628
Cefalù, 856–857
Ceglie Messapica, 776–777
Cemeteries. ⇨ Also Catacombs
Genoa, 331
Rome, 594
Tuscany, 489
Umbria & the Marches, 554–555
Venice, 70, 78

Cenobio dei Dogi ⌂, 329
Centrale ✕, 233
Centrale Palace Hotel ⌂, 851–852
Centro Storico, 412, 414–415, 418–422, 452–453
Ceramics museums, 396–397, 550, 857
Cerchiara di Calabria, 791
Cernobbio, 249
Certosa (Pavia), 229, 231
Certosa di San Giacomo, 733
Certosa di San Martino, 700
Cerveteri, 672
Cervo, 347
Cesàri ⌂, 639
Chianti, 491–493, 495–497
Chiavari, 322
Chiesa dei Domenicani, 174–175
Chiesa di San Lorenzo, 676
Chiesa di Santa Croce, 491
Chiesetta di Piedigrotta, 795
Chiusa, 184
Chorus churches, 44
Christkindlmarkt, 185
Cibrèo ✕, 448
Cicolella ✕⌂, 771
Cimitero Monumentale di Staglieno, 331
Cinque Terre, 313–321
Circo di Massenzio, 619
Circumetnea railroad, 816
Civico Museo di Storia ed Arte, 152
Civico Museo Revoltella e Galleria d'Arte Moderna, 152
Cividale del Friuli, 147–148
Cogne, 301–302
Col Rodella, 189
Colle Aventino, 617
Colle Val d'Elsa, 502
Collegiata (San Gimignano), 500
Collegiata di Sant'Orso, 297
Collegio del Cambio, 532–533
Colline & Savoy Palaces, 281, 283–284, 286
Colonna di Marco Aurelio, 603
Colosseo, 633, 636
Columbus, Christopher, childhood home of, 339
Como, 250–251
Computers, traveling with, 911–912
Conegliano, 144
Consorzio Produttori Aceto Balsamico Tradizionale di Modena, 372
Consumer protection, 912

Convento dei Cappucccini, 846, 848
Convento di Santa Scolastica, 681–682
Convento di Santo Spirito, 834
Convento e Chiesa di San Francesco, 480
Cormòns, 148, 150
Corona d'Oro 1890 ⌂, 384–385
Corricella, 730
Corsa dei Ceri, 549
Corso Vannucci, 533
Corte Sconta ✕, 81
Cortina d'Ampezzo, 187–189
Cortona, 516–517
Cosenza, 792–793
Costa Brada ⌂, 783–784
Costa Verde, 877
Courmayeur, 299–301
Covered bridge (Bassano del Grappa), 138
Cracco-Peck ✕, 214
Credit cards, 9, 920
Cremona, 231–233
Cresta del Furggen, 295
Creto, 335
Cristo Salvatore, Santa Caterina d'Alessandria, e San Serafino di Sarov, 349
Crotone, 794–795
Crypta Balbi, 597–598
Cul de Sac ✕, 625
Cumae, 717
Cumpà Cosimo ✕, 752
Cura dell'Uva, 236
Customs and duties, 912

D

Da Abele ✕, 217
Da Delfina ✕, 478
Da Dora ✕, 705
Da Gemma ✕, 750
Da Michele ✕, 708
Da Tonino ✕, 737–738
Dal Mi' Cocco ✕, 535
Dar Poeta ✕, 629
De la Poste ✕⌂, 187–188
Deruta, 550
Diamante, 789, 791
Dining, 912–914. ⇨ Also Restaurants under specific areas
price categories, 79, 113, 161, 201, 265, 309, 361, 442, 475, 531, 619, 666, 691, 763, 807, 868
Dobbiaco, 186–187
Dolomites: Trentino-Alto Adige, 157–196

Domus dei Tappeti di Pietra, 402–403
Domus della Fortuna Annonaria, 669
Domus di Amore e Psiche, 669
Domus di Apuleio, 669
Don Alfonso 1890 ✕, 741–742
Don Camillo ✕, 827–828
Don Carlos ✕, 214–215
Donnafugata Winery, 840
Dorsoduro (Venice), 58, 60–63, 81, 84, 91–92
Dozza, 395–396
Drogheria della Rosa ✕, 383
Duchi d'Aosta 🏨, 153
Due Mori 🏨, 137
Duomo. ⇨ *See* Cathedrals
Duomo Cripta, 505
Duomo di San Ciriaco, 566
Duomo di San Giovanni, 266–267, 269

E

Eden 🏨, 643
Electricity, 914
Elephant 🏨, 185
Embasssies, 914
Emergencies, 914–915
Dolomites, 195
Emilia-Romagna, 406
Florence, 470
Italian Riviera, 355
Mezzogiorno, 801
Milan, Lombardy & the Lakes, 258–259
Naples and Campania, 758
Piedmont & Valle d'Aosta, 303
Rome, 661–662, 686
Sardinia, 890
Sicily, 864
Tuscany, 525
Umbria & the Marches, 570
Venetian Arc, 156
Venice, 105
Emilia-Romagna, 357–406
English-language media, 915
Enna, 832–833
Enoteca Antica Osteria Fontana ✕, 370
Enoteca di Corso (shop), 168
Enoteca Fuoripiazza ✕, 493
Enoteca Gustavo ✕, 501
Enoteca La Torre ✕, 677
Enoteca Regionale, 396
Eremo delle Carceri, 538
Erice, 842–843
Etiquette and behavior, 915
Excelsior Vittoria 🏨, 743
Exedra 🏨, 641

Explora Il Museo dei Bambini di Roma, 611

F

Faenza, 396–397
Feast of Corpus Christi, 551
Ferrara, 389–394
Ferrovia Genova-Casella, 334–335
Ferry service, 102–104, 256–257, 353, 756, 862–863, 889
Festa di Sant'Efisio, 872
Festi di San Giuseppe, 287
Fiesole, 467–468
Filicudi, 861
Finale Ligure, 346–347
Florence, 407–470
children, attractions for, 418, 420–421, 436, 444, 449–450, 461, 463
essential information, 468–470
exploring, 412–415, 418–422, 429–442
hotels, 452–458
nightlife & the arts, 458–460
price categories, 442, 452
restaurants, 442–445, 448–452
shopping, 460–465
side trips, 465–468
Foggia, 770–771
Fonni, 881
Fontana del Nettuno
Bologna, 380
Trento, 163
Fontana del Tritone, 606
Fontana delle Tartarughe, 612
Fontana di Trevi, 600
Fonte Aretusa, 827
Fonte de' Medici 🏨, 493
Foresta Umbra, 773
Forlì, 397
Forio, 731
Foro Romano, 755
Forst Brewery ✕, 180
Forte di Bard, 293–294
Fortezza, 560
Forum, 669
Friuli–Venezia Giulia, 145–148, 150–154
Fuori Porta ✕, 445

G

Galata Museo del Mare, 337
Galleria Borghese, 609
Galleria Civica d'Arte Moderna e Contemporanea (GAM), 272
Galleria d'Arte Antica, 146
Galleria d'Arte Moderna Ricci Oddi, 365

Galleria degli Uffizi, 418–419
Galleria dell'Accademia, 429–430
Galleria Nazionale
Genoa, 331
Naples, 703
Parma, 369
Galleria Nazionale dell'Umbria, 533–534
Galleria Sabouda, 269
Galleria Umberto, 699
Galleria Vittorio Emanuele, 207–208
Gallerie dell'Accademia, 60–61
Gallipoli, 783–784
Gardaland Amusement Park, 242
Gardone Riviera, 239–241
Gargnano, 238–239
Gargnano promintory, 771–774
Garibaldi, Giuseppe (tomb of), 886
Gelaterie & pasticcerie, 451, 631, 842
Gener Neuv ✕, 288
Genoa, 330–331, 334–343
Gesù Nuovo, 702
Gesuati, 62
Gesuiti, 71
Ghetto, 69–70, 390, 612, 628–629
Giara di Gesturi, 878–879
Giardini Botanici Hanbury, 352
Giardini di Augusto, 734, 736
Giardini Poseidon Terme, 731
Giardini Vaticani, 583
Giardino Botanico Hruska, 239
Giardino di Boboli, 436
Giardino Giusti, 134
Giardino Zoologico, 479
Giostra della Quintana, 568
Giudecca, 74–75, 93
Glass museums, 76–77
Golfo Aranci, 888
Gondola rides
Gubbio, 548
Taormina, 811
Venice, 102–103
Gran Hotel Gardone 🏨, 240
Gran Madre di Dio, 274
Granarolo funicular, 335
Grand Canal, 45–51
Grand Hotel 🏨, 398, 400
Grand Hotel Baglioni 🏨, 385
Grand Hotel Gianicolo 🏨, 638
Grand Hotel Miramare 🏨, 325
Grand Hotel Palace 🏨, 183

Grand Hotel Timeo and Villa Flora ☑, 813
Grand Hotel Villa Serbelloni ☑, 246
Gray, The ☑, 219
Greek temples
Paestum, 754–755
Selinunte (ruins), 839
Greve in Chianti, 491–493
Grotta Azzurra, 734
Grotta degli Animali, 465
Grotta dello Smeraldo, 748
Grotta di Nettuno, 883
Grotta di Tiberio, 684
Grotta Palazzese ☑☑, 769–770
Grotte di Castellana, 775–776
Grotte di Catullo, 241
Grotto Arpaia, 312
Gubbio, 546–549

H

Harbors
Genoa, 337
Pozzuoli, 715
Hassler ☑, 636
Heart of the Dolomites, 189, 192–194
Herculaneum, 718–719
Hermitage ☑, 295
Hiking and walking, 190–191, 382, 563, 915
Holidays, 915–916
Hostels, 918
Hotel Antico Doge ☑, 88
Hotel Belvedere ☑, 247
Hotel Clocchiatti ☑, 147
Hotel des Étrangers et Miramare ☑, 829
Hotel Farnese ☑, 640
Hotel Fortuna ☑, 537
Hotel Greif ☑, 178
Hotel Helvetia & Bristol ☑, 452–453
Hotel La Badia ☑, 560–561
Hotel Le Dune ☑, 877
Hotel Palace ☑, 766, 769
Hotel Piccho Nero ☑☑, 788
Hotel Ripagrande ☑, 393
Hotel San Luca ☑, 555–556

I

Ibla, 830
Il Bigo, 339
Il Conivivio ✕, 621
Il Desco ✕, 135
Il Don Giovanni ✕, 391–392
Il Falconiere ✕☑, 516–517
Il Filippino ✕☑, 859
Il Focolare ☑, 145
Il Gesù, 598

Il Grappolo ✕, 674
Il Melograno ✕, 732
Il Poeta Contadino ✕, 775
Il Quirinale, 606
Il Ritrovo ✕, 746–747
Il Sole di Ranco ✕☑, 255
Il Torchio (shop), 459
Il Vittoriale, 239
Imola, 394–395
Imperia, 348
Imperial Roman Villa, 831
Ingurtosu, 877
Insurance, 916
Ionian Coast, 808, 810–819, 821–823
Ischia, 730–733
Ischia Ponte, 731
Ischia Porto, 731
Islands of the Lagoon, 75–78, 93
Isola Bella, 254
Isola dei Pescatori, 254
Isola Madre, 254
Isola Tiberina, 612
Isole Borromee, 254
Isole Tremiti, 773
Istituto e Museo di Storia della Scienza, 420
Italian Riviera, 305–356

J

Jewish Ghetto
Ferrara, 390
Rome, 612, 628–629
Venice, 69–70
JK Place ☑, 455

K

Keats-Shelley Memorial House, 603
Knights of Malta, garden of, 617

L

La Bastiglia ✕, 551
La Bitta ✕, 84
La Cacciatore de la Subida ✕, 148
La Calcina ☑, 92
La Canna ☑, 861
La Castiglia, 284
La Cattólica, 798
La Favorita—O' Parrucchiano ✕, 742
La Foce ☑, 521–522
La Fortezza, 522
La Fossiata, 794
La Frasca ✕, 397
La Giostra ✕, 448–449
La Grotta ✕, 519

La Locanda di San Martino ✕, 398
La Maddalena, 886
La Martorana, 848
La Nuova Mangiatoia ✕, 770
La Pallotta ✕☑, 545
La Pergola ✕, 625
La Pigna, 349
La Siciliana ✕, 822
La Purissima (church), 783
La Regia ✕☑, 769
La Riserva ☑, 351–352
La Rocca, 553
La Spezia, 312
La Stanza del Gusto ✕, 705–706
La Suvera ☑, 502
La Torre di Lavello ✕, 675
Lacco Ameno, 731
Lace museum, 76
Lago d'Averno, 717
Lago di Carezza, 193
Lake Como, 242–251
Lake Garda, 236–242
Lake Maggiore, 252–255
Lake Orta, 252–255
L'Anfora ✕, 120
Language, 919
Largo di Torre Argentina, 594, 596
Le Botteghe ✕, 787
Le Due Spade ✕, 165
Le Due Torri, 380
Le Sirenuse ☑, 747
Leaning Tower, 488–489
Lecce, 779–782
Lerici, 310–312
Les Neiges d'Antan ✕☑, 295
Les Sables Noires ☑, 859
Levico Terme, 165
Libraries
Emilia-Romagna, 371–372, 381
Florence, 431–432
Rome, 582
Tuscany, 595
Lipari, 859
Locanda del Melarancio ✕, 403–404
Locanda dell'Amorosa ✕☑, 519
Locanda di Mirandolina ✕☑, 675
Locanda di San Martino ☑, 787
Locarno ☑, 637
Locorotondo, 776
Locri, 798
Locri Epizefiri, 798
Lodging, 916–919. ⇨ Also Hotels under specific areas

price categories, 88, 113, 161, 201, 265, 309, 361, 452, 475, 531, 632, 666, 691, 763, 807, 868
Loggia dei Mercanti (Ancona), 566
Loggia dei Mercanti (Genoa), 335
Loggia del Consiglio, 132
Lombardy, *197–259*
London ⊡, 220
Lorelei et Londres ⊡, 743
Loreto, 567
Lucanerie ✕, 787
Lucca, 481, 483–487
Lungomare Argentina, 350
Lungomare degli Artisti, 344

M

Madonna di Campiglio, *170–172*
MADRE (Museo d'Arte di Donna Regina), 705
Maggio Musicale Fiorentino, *458–459*
Mail and shipping, *919–920*
Maison de Filippo ✕, 300
Majestic Toscanelli ⊡, 121
Malcesine, 237
Mantua, *233–236*
Maratea, *788–789*
Marina di Leuca, 783
Marina Grande, 741
Mario ✕, 443
Marostica, 137
Marsala, 840
Martina Franca, *777–778*
Matera, 784, 786–787
Matterhorn, *294–296*
Mattinata, *771–772*
Mausoleo di Galla Placidia, *401–402*
Max ✕, 392
Meal plans, 917
Merano, *180–184*
Mercato Nuovo, *420–421*
Messina, 808, 810
Mezzogiorno, *759–802*
Michelangelo, 422, 429–433
Miki ✕, 321
Milan, 202, 204, 206–208, 210–225
Milan, Lombardy, and the Lakes. ⇨ *See* Lombardy
Milleluci ⊡, 298
Mithraeum, 669
Modena, *371–372*
Mole Antonelliana, 269
Monasteries
Capri, 734
Dolomites, 184

Naples, 704
Pavia, 229, 231
Tuscany, 517, 522
Subiaco, 681–682
Tropea, 796
Monastero di San Benedetto, 682
Moneglia, 322
Money matters, *920–921*
Monferrato & the Langhe, *286–288,* 292
Monna Lisa ⊡, 455
Monreale, 843–844
Montalcino, 522
Monte Baldo, 237
Monte Bianco (Mont Blanc), *299–301*
Monte Epomeo, 731
Monte Ortobene, 880
Monte Sant'Angelo, *773–774*
Monte Solaro, 736
Montefioralle, 491
Montello, 143
Montepulciano, 517, *519–520*
Monumento a Vittorio Emanuele II, *600–601*
Morandi alla Crocetta ⊡, 453
Mount Etna, *816–817*
Murano, *76–77*
Musei Civici, 44, 52
Musei Civici degli Eremitani, 118
Musei Vaticani, *580–582*
Museo Agricolo di Brunnenburg, 182
Museo Archeologico
Cagliari, 870
Chiavari, 322
Ferrara, 391
Fiesole, 467
Florence, 432
Pegli, 344
Siracusa, 825
Spoleto, 554
Verona, 134
Museo Archeologico Baglio Anselmi, 840
Museo Archeologico Comunale, 873
Museo Archeologico dell'Alto Adige, *175–176*
Museo Archeologico Nazionale
Crotone, 794–795
Naples, 702–703
Perugia, 535
Museo Archeologico Provincale, 754
Museo Archeologico Regionale Salinas, 849
Museo Archeologico Tuscanese, 675

Museo Bottega della Tarsialignea, 741
Museo Civico
Asolo, 140
Bolzano, 176
Naples, 697
Pavia, 229
Piacenza, 364
Pistoia, 479
San Gimignano, 500
Vicenza, 123
Museo Civico Archeologico, 213
Museo Civico di Cabras, 880
Museo Claudio Faina, 559
Museo Correale di Terranova, 740
Museo Correr, *57–58*
Museo d'Arte e Ammobiliamento, 281
Museo d'Arte Contemporaneo, 281
Museo d'Arte Moderna e Contemporanea, 169
Museo d'Arte Moderna e Contemporanea di Trento, 165
Museo d'Arte Orientale Chiossone, 335
Museo del Mare (Trieste), 152
Museo del Papiro, 825
Museo del Patrimonio Industriale, *382–383*
Museo del Vino, 549
Museo dell'Automobile, 273
Museo dell'Olivo, 348
Museo dell'Opera del Duomo
Florence, 421
Pisa, 489
Prato, 476–477
Museo dell'Opera Metropolitana, 505
Museo dell'Opificio delle Pietre Dure, 432
Museo della Carta, *749–750*
Museo della Ceramica, 857
Museo della Marionette, 849
Museo della Val Gardena, 192
Museo della Vita e delle Tradizioni Popolari Sarde, 880
Museo delle Ceramiche, *396–397*
Museo di Capodimonte, 703
Museo di Castelvecchio, 132
Museo di Criminologia Medievale, *500–501*
Museo di Pittura Murale, 477
Museo di San Marco, 430
Museo Didattico della Seta (Silk Museum), 250

Museo Diocesano
Bressanone, 184–185
Cortona, 516
San Miniato, 480
Museo Diocesano d'Arte Sacra, *882*
Museo Diocesano Tridentino, *164*
Museo Ebraico
Ferrara, 390
Florence, 441
Rome, 613
Venice, 70
Museo Egizio, *269–270*
Museo Eoliano, *859*
Museo Etnografico dell'Alto Adige, *186*
Museo Etrusco Guarnacci, *498*
Museo Internazionale della Musica, *381*
Museo Israelitico, *287*
Museo Marino Marini, *435*
Museo Nazionale
Florence, 412
Paestum, 754–755
Ravenna, 403
Taranto, 778
Museo Nazionale Archeologico di Palestrina, *681*
Museo Nazionale del Cinema, *269*
Museo Nazionale della Magna Grecia, *797*
Museo Nazionale della Scienza e Tecnica, *213–214*
Museo Nazionale di San Matteo, *489*
Museo Nazionale di Villa Guinigi, *483–484*
Museo Nazionale Etrusco di Villa Giulia, *611*
Museo Nazionale Romano, *596*
Museo Nazionale Tarquiniense, *672–673*
Museo Ostiense, *669*
Museo Poldi-Pezzoli, *208*
Museo Provinciale d'Arte, *165*
Museo Provinciale del Vino, *194*
Museo Regionale della Ceramica, *550*
Museo Ridola, *786–787*
Museo Sanna, *884*
Museo Storico Carlo Levi, *788*
Museo Storico in Trento, *165*
Museo Storico Italiano della Guerra, *169*
Museo Storico Navale, *71–72*
Museo Stradivariano, *232*
Museo Teatrale alla Scala, *210*

Museums. ⇨ *See* Ceramics museums; Glass museums; Lace museums; Vatican Museums; Wine museums *and specific museum names*
Myosotis ✕, *621*

N

Naples & Campania, *687–758*
Napoli Salteranea, *704*
Nardini (shop), *138–139*
Narni, *561–562*
Naturno, *180*
Naval museum (Pegli), *344*
Navigli district (Milan), *214*
Necropoli della Banditaccia, *672*
Necropolis, *673*
Nervi, *343–344*
Ninfa, *683*
Noli, *347*
Nonino, *146–147*
Nora, *873, 875*
Norchia, *673–674*
Norcia, *563*
Nuoro, *880–881*
Nuovo Batezar—da Renato ✕, *294*
Nuovo Piccolo Mondo ✕, *350*

O

Oca Bianca ✕, *324*
Olbia, *887–888*
Oltrarno, *435–439, 445, 448, 456–457*
Oplontis, *728*
Orgosolo, *881*
Oristano, *879*
Orsanmichele, *421*
Orta San Giulio, *252–253*
Ortisei, *192–193*
Orto Botanico
Padua, 118
Siena, 510
Ortygia Island, *825, 827–829*
Orvieto, *558–561*
Orvieto Underground, *559–560*
Ospedaletto, *72*
Osservatorio Vesuviano, *720*
Osteria Al Brindisi ✕, *392–393*
Osteria al Duca ✕, *135–136*
Osteria Al Vecchio Stallo ✕, *147*
Osteria Altri Tempi ✕, *851*
Osteria da Fiore ✕, *86*
Osteria de'Benci ✕, *449*
Osteria dei Vespri ✕, *850*
Osteria del Coro ✕, *511*

Osteria del Museo, *550*
Osteria del Pesce ✕, *619*
Osteria della Frezza ✕, *621*
Osteria di Passignano ✕, *492*
Osteria Piazzetta dell'Erba ✕, *545*
Osteria Ponte Dante ✕, *144*
Ostia Antica, *667, 669–670*
Ostuni, *776*
Otranto, *782*

P

Packing, *921–922*
Padua, *114–121*
Paestum, *754–755*
Palazzina di Caccia, *281*
Palazzina di Marfisa d'Este, *391*
Palazzo Abatellis, *849*
Palazzo Alexander ▣, *486*
Palazzo Altemps, *596*
Palazzo Barberini
Palestrina, 681
Rome, 608
Palazzo Beneventano del Bosco, *827*
Palazzo Bianco, *331*
Palazzo Cambiaso, *334*
Palazzo Campanella, *336–337*
Palazzo Carignano, *271*
Palazzo Carrega Cataldi, *335*
Palazzo Cattaneo Adorno, *336*
Palazzo Chiericati, *123*
Palazzo Colonna, *601*
Palazzo Comunale
Bologna, 381
Trieste, 151
Palazzo Corsini, *614*
Palazzo Corvaja, *811*
Palazzo degli Anziani, *346*
Palazzo degli Scaligeri, *132*
Palazzo dei Consoli, *546–547*
Palazzo dei Diamanti, *390–391*
Palazzo dei Musei, *371–372*
Palazzo dei Priori, *534*
Palazzo del Bo', *118*
Palazzo del Capitanio, *117*
Palazzo del Comune
Piacenza, 364
Pistoia, 479
Palazzo del Podestà
Bologna, 381
Radda in Chianti, 495
Palazzo del Popolo, *500*
Palazzo della Ragione
Padua, 117
Verona, 132–133
Palazzo della Rovere, *345–346*

Palazzo dell'Accademia delle Scienze, 269
Palazzo delle Torrette, 337
Palazzo dell'Università, 335
Palazzo di Ludovico il Moro, 391
Palazzo Doria Pamphilj, 603
Palazzo Doria Tursi, 336
Palazzo Ducale
Genoa, 337–338
Gubbio, 547–548
Mantua, 234
Urbino, 564
Venice, 55, 57
Palazzo Farnese
Caprarola, 678
Piacenza, 364
Rome, 598–599
Palazzo Gambaro, 334
Palazzo Labia, 72
Palazzo Leoni Montanari, 123
Palazzo Lercari Parodi, 334–345
Palazzo Madama, 270
Palazzo Massimo alle Terme, 606
Palazzo Medici-Riccardi, 432
Palazzo Montalto, 827
Palazzo Murat, 745
Palazzo Papale, 676
Palazzo Piccolomini, 520
Palazzo Pitti, 436–437
Palazzo Podestà, 336
Palazzo Pretorio, 164
Palazzo Ravizza ⊡ , 511
Palazzo Re Enzo, 381
Palazzo Reale
Italian Riviera, 331, 334
Naples, 697
Sicily, 848
Turin, 271–272
Palazzo Rosso, 334
Palazzo Rucellai, 435
Palazzo Sasso ⊡ , 753
Palazzo Schifanoia, 391
Palazzo Spada, 599
Palazzo Spinola, 331
Palazzo Strozzi, 433
Palazzo Te, 234–235
Palazzo Troya, 287
Palazzo Vecchio, 421–422
Palazzo Vendramin-Calergi, 72
Palazzo Venezia, 603
Palermo, 845–846, 848–856
Palestrina, 680–681
Palladio, 125–129
PAN (Palazzo delle Arti Napoli), 705
Panarea, 860
Pantagruel ✕ , 793–794
Pantheon, 596

Panzano, 495
Paolo Teverini ✕ , 397
Papá Baccus ✕ , 630
Paraggi, 327
Parco Archeologico, 824
Parco dei Mostri, 678–679
Parco del Valentino, 273
Parco Naturale Collina Torinese, 274
Parco Nazionale del Gran Paradiso, 301–302
Parco Nazionale dello Stelvio, 173
Parco Villa Grimaldi, 343
Park Hotel Laurin ✕⊡ , 177–178
Parker's ⊡ , 709
Parma, 367–371
Parma Rotta ✕ , 370
Passeggiata Anita Garibaldi, 343
Passeggiata d'Estate, 182
Passeggiate d'Inverno, 182
Passeggiata del Guncina, 176
Passeggiata delle Mura, 483
Passeggiata Tappeiner, 182
Passo dello Stelvio, 174
Passo di Sella, 192
Passports and visas, 922–923
Pasticceria del Convento, 842
Pasticceria Grammatico, 842
Patria Palace ⊡ , 781
Pavia, 229, 231
Peggy Guggenheim Collection, 61
Pegli, 344
Pensione Accademia Villa Maravege ⊡ , 92
Perugia, 532–537
Peschici, 773
Peter Pan (wine bar), 829–830
Peyrano (shop), 280
Phlegrean Fields (Campania), 713, 715–717
Piacenza, 364–365
Piano Grande, 563
Piave River, 143
Piazza Archimede, 827
Piazza Armerina, 831–832
Piazza Bocca della Vertità, 614, 616
Piazza Castello, 272
Piazza dei Cavalli, 364
Piazza dei Signori
Padua, 117
Treviso, 142, 144
Verona, 133
Vicenza, 123
Piazza del Anfiteatro Romano, 483

Piazza del Campo (Siena), 506–509
Piazza del Comune, 232
Piazza del Duomo
Catania, 821
Parma, 368
San Gimignano, 500
Siracusa, 827
Piazza del Plebiscito, 697, 699
Piazza del Popolo
Ascoli Piceno, 568
Faenza, 396
Rome, 610
Todi, 556
Piazza dell'Unità d'Italia, 151
Piazza della Borsa, 151
Piazza della Libertà
Bari, 765–766
Udine, 145–146
Piazza della Repubblica
Florence, 422
Rome, 608
Piazza della Signoria, 419–420
Piazza delle Erbe
Bolzano, 176
Verona, 133
Piazza di Santa Maria in Trastevere, 612–613
Piazza di Spagna, 601, 620–621, 636–638, 652
Piazza XV Marzo, 792
Piazza Garibaldi (Narni), 561
Piazza Garibaldi (Parma), 368
Piazza Grande (Arezzo), 513
Piazza Grande (Montepulciano), 519
Piazza Libertà, 776
Piazza Maggiore, 140
Piazza Matteotti
Greve in Chianti, 491
Udine, 146
Piazza Navona, 596–597, 621, 625, 638–639
Piazza Pretoria, 849–850
Piazza Roma, 232
Piazza San Carlo, 270
Piazza San Marco (Venice), 52–55, 57–58, 84, 86, 93–95
Piazza San Pietro, 583
Piazza Sant'Oronzo, 780
Piazza 3 Novembre, 237
Piazza Universitaria, 821
Piazza Vittoria Emanuele, 832
Piazza Walther, 176
Piazzale Michelangelo, 437
Piccola Osteria del Borgo ✕ , 396
Piccola Slam (shop), 463

Piedmont & Valle d'Aosta, *261–304*
Pienza, *520–522*
Pieve di Santa Maria, *513*
Pinacoteca Ambrosiana, *212*
Pinacoteca di Brera, *208*
Pinacoteca e Museo Civico, *498*
Pinacoteca Giovanni e Marella Agnelli, *273–274*
Pinacoteca Nazionale
Bologna, 382
Siena, 505, 510
Pinacoteca Nazionale di Palazzo Mansi, *484*
Pincio, *611*
Pio Monte della Misericordia, *703–704*
Pisa, *487–491*
Pista Olimpica di Bob, *187*
Pistoia, *478–479*
Pizza, *628*
Pizzeria Vico Santa Filomena ✕, *822*
Pizzo, *795*
Pizzomunno ⌂ , *772*
Plateau Rosa, *295*
Po River, *272–274*
Poli Grappa Museum, *139*
Polignano a Mare, *769–770*
Pompeii, *719–726*
Ponte degli Alpini, *138*
Ponte delle Bele ✕ , *124*
Ponte delle Torri, *552*
Ponte di Rialto, *63*
Ponte Santa Trinita, *434–435*
Ponte Vecchio, *420*
Porta all'Arco, *498*
Porta dello Zodiaco, *283*
Porta Marina, *670*
Porta Romana, *669*
Porta Soprana, *339*
Porto Cervo, *886–887*
Portofino, *326–328*
Portovenere, *312*
Porziuncola, *540*
Positano, *744–748*
Pozzo di San Patrizio, *560*
Pozzuoli, *715*
Prato, *476–478*
Price categories, *912, 917*
dining, 79, 113, 161, 201, 265, 309, 361, 442, 531, 619, 666, 691, 763, 807, 868
lodging, 88, 113, 161, 201, 265, 309, 361, 452, 531, 632, 666, 691, 763, 807, 868
Principe di Savoia ⌂ , *219*
Procida, *729*
Prosecco, *143*
Pula, *873, 875*

Punta Chiappa, *329*
Punta di San Vigilio, *236*
Punta Portofino, *326–327*
Punta Tragara ⌂ , *738*

Q

Quadreria dei Girolamini, *704*
Quartieri Spagnoli, *699*
Quattro Canti, *850*
Querini-Stampalia, *72*

R

Radda in Chianti, *495–496*
Ragusa, *830*
Rapallo, *322–323*
Ravello, *751–753*
Ravenna, *400–405*
Reggia (palace), *720, 729*
Reggio di Calabria, *797*
Relais Fattoria Vignale ✕⌂ , *496*
Renaissance notables, *423–428*
Rende, *793*
Renon Plateau, *177*
Residence Angiolucci ⌂ , *823*
Residenza Farnese ⌂ , *632–633*
Residenza Johanna I ⌂ , *454*
Restrooms, *923*
Rimini, *398, 400*
Rione Junno, *774*
Ristorante Arnolfo ✕ , *502*
Ristorante Graziano ✕ , *850*
Ristorante Tornasacco ✕ , *568*
Ristoro di Lamole ✕ , *492*
Riva del Garda, *237–238*
Riviera di Levante, *310–312, 322–329*
Riviera di Ponente, *344–352*
Rivoli, *281*
Rocca, *141*
Rocca di Cerere, *832*
Rocca Sforzesca di Dozza, *396*
Roccia dell'Elefante, *885*
Romagna. ⇨ *See* Emilia-Romagna
Roman aqueduct, *562*
Roman column, *779, 780*
Roman Porta Pretoria, *297*
Roman theaters, *151–152, 297, 498, 554, 729*
Romantik Hotel Villa Pagoda ⌂ , *343–344*
Rome, *571–662*
children, attractions for, 596–597, 607, 611, 616
essential information, 658–662
exploring, 576–577, 579–583, 594, 596–601, 603–614, 616–619

hotels, 632–633, 636–644
nightlife & the arts, 644–650
price categories, 619, 632
restaurants, 582, 594, 611, 619–621, 625–631
shopping, 651–658
sports & the outdoors, 651
Rovereto, *168–169*
Royal Sporting ⌂ , *312*
Ruta, *329*

S

Sacra di San Michele, *283*
Sacro Monte, *252*
Safety, *923*
Sagra del Pesce, *329*
St. Francis, *541–544*
St. Vincent, *294*
Salento, *778–784*
Salerno, *754*
Salina, *860*
Salò Market, *240*
Salumerie, *452*
Saluzzo, *283–284*
San Biagio (church)
Italian Riviera, 346
Tuscany, 519
San Callisto, *617*
San Carlino alle Quattro Fontane, *608*
San Carlo, *272*
San Cataldo, *772*
San Clemente, *604*
San Domenico ✕ , *395*
San Domenico (church)
Bologna, 382
Fiesole, 467–468
Italian Riviera, 348
Narni, 562
Mezzogiorno, 778
Siena, 510
San Domenico Palace ⌂ , *813–814*
San Donato, *339*
San Fedele, *250*
San Fermo Maggiore, *133*
San Francesco a Ripa, *616*
San Francesco della Vigna, *72–73*
San Francesco di Paola, *697, 699*
San Frediano, *483*
San Giacomo dell'Orio, *66–67*
San Gimignano, *499–501*
San Giorgio, *326*
San Giorgio Maggiore, *74–75*
San Giovanni Battista, *786*
San Giovanni degli Eremiti, *849*
San Giovanni di Sinis, *880*
San Giovanni Elemosinario, *67*

San Giovanni Evangelista, *369*
San Giovanni Fuorcivitas, *479*
San Giovanni in Laterano, *605*
San Giulio, *252–253*
San Lorenzo
*Florence, 430–431, 446,
453–454*
Genoa, 338
Rome, 626–628
Turin, 271
San Lorenzo Maggiore
Milan, 212
Naples, 704–705
San Luigi dei Francesi, *597*
San Marco, *84, 86, 93–95*
San Marino, *399*
San Matteo, *339*
San Michele
Capri, 736
Venice, 78
San Michele ✕ , *772*
San Michele in Foro, *483*
San Miniato, *479–481*
San Miniato al Monte, *438*
San Nicolò (church), *144*
San Nicolò (town), *329*
San Pellegrino, *676*
San Pietro
Rome, 625–626, 639–641
Sardinia, 876–877
San Pietro church
(Portovenere), *312*
San Pietro di Castello, *73*
San Pietro in Ciel d'Oro, *229*
San Pietro in Montorio, *616*
San Pietro in Valle, *563*
San Polo, *63–67, 86, 95*
San Procolo, *180*
San Remo, *348–350*
San Remo Casinò, *349*
San Rocco, *329*
San Rufino, *540*
San Salvatore (church),
554–555
San Salvatore (ghost town),
880
San Satiro, *212*
San Sebastiano (Rome), *617*
San Sebastiano (Venice), *62*
San Secondo, *288*
San Simplicio, *887–888*
San Siro, *336*
San Sperate, *871*
San Stae, *67*
San Zeno Maggiore, *133*
San Zulian 🏨 , *94*
Sant'Abbondio, *250*
Sant'Agostino
Genoa, 338
San Gimignano, 501
Trapani, 842

Sant'Agostino in Campo
Marzio, *597*
Sant'Anastasia, *133–134*
Sant'Andrea
Mantua, 234
Pistoia, 479
Sant'Andrea al Quirinale,
608–609
Sant'Andrea della Valle, *599*
Sant'Angelo, *731*
Sant'Antioco, *875*
Sant'Apollinare in Classe, *403*
Sant'Apollinare Nuovo, *402*
Sant'Efisio, *875*
Sant'Eufemia, *554*
Sant'Ignazio, *601*
Sant'Ivo alla Sapienza,
599–600
Sant'Olcese Tullo, *335*
Sant'Ubaldo, *548*
Santa Anna, *769*
Santa Caterina (church)
Asti, 287
Finale Ligure, 346
Santa Caterina 🏨 , *750*
Santa Caterina del Sasso
Ballaro, *255*
Santa Cecilia in Trastevere,
616
Santa Cesarea Terme, *783*
Santa Chiara (church)
Assisi, 538
Naples, 704
Santa Chiara 🏨 , *639*
Santa Cristina, *272*
Santa Croce
*Florence, 439–442, 448–450,
457–458*
Lecce, 780
Venice, 63–67, 86–87
Santa Felicita, *438*
Santa Margherita Ligure,
323–326
Santa Maria Assunta
Panzano, 495
Positano, 745–746
Venice, 77–78
Santa Maria de Idris, *786*
Santa Maria degli Angeli
Assisi, 540
Rome, 608
Santa Maria dei Miracoli,
70–71
Santa Maria del Carmine, *437*
Santa Maria del Monte
Caltagirone, 831
Turin, 274
Santa Maria del Popolo, *610*
Santa Maria della Concezione,
607

Santa Maria della
Consolazione, *557*
Santa Maria della Isola, *796*
Santa Maria della Piazza, *566*
Santa Maria della Salute,
61–62
Santa Maria della Steccata,
368
Santa Maria della Vittoria, *607*
Santa Maria delle Carceri, *477*
Santa Maria delle Grazie,
212–214
Santa Maria di Castello, *338*
Santa Maria di Gesù, *840*
Santa Maria Finibus Terrae,
783
Santa Maria Formosa, *73–74*
Santa Maria Gloriosa dei
Frari, *63–64*
Santa Maria Impensole, *561*
Santa Maria Maddalena dei
Pazzi, *432*
Santa Maria Maggiore
Rome, 604
Spello, 551
Trento, 164
Santa Maria Novella, *434,
444, 455–456*
Santa Maria Scolanova, *769*
Santa Maria sopra Minerva,
599
Santa Sabina, *617*
Santa Teresa di Gallura,
885–846
Santa Trinita, *435*
Santi Gervasio e Protasio, *323*
Santi Giovanni e Paolo, *71*
Santi Quattro Coronati, *604*
Santissima Annunziata
Florence, 432–433
Genoa, 336
Santo Spirito, *438–439*
Santo Stefano, *380*
Santo Stefano di Camastra,
857–858
Santuario della Santa Casa,
567
Santuario della Vittoria, *335*
Santuario di Hera Lacinia, *794*
Santuario di San Michele, *773*
S'Apposentu ✕ , *871–872*
Sardinia, *865–891*
Sassari, *884–885*
Sassi, *784, 786*
Sassi-Superga Cog Train, *274*
Saturnia, *523–524*
Saviona, *184*
Savoia ✕ , *275*
Savoia Palace 🏨 , *171*
Savona, *345–346*
Sbigoli Terrecotte (shop), *461*

Scala Santa, *606*
Scalinatella ⌂ , *739*
Scavi di Ostia Antica, *667*
Schloss Korb ⌂ , *178*
Scuola di San Giorgio degli Schiavoni, *74*
Scuola Grande di San Rocco, *65*
Scuola Grande dei Carmini, *62–63*
Segesta, *843*
Selinunte, *835*
Senior-citizen travel, *923*
Sentiero Botanico di Ciaé, *335*
Serègo Alighieri (winery), *134–135*
Sermoneta, *683*
Sestriere, *284, 286*
Shopping, *923–924.* ⇨ *Also* under specific areas
Siciliainbocca ✕ , *626*
Sicily, *803–864*
Siena, *503–505, 510–512*
Sightseeing guides, *924*
Sinagoga, *440–441, 613, 670*
Siracusa, *823–825, 827–830*
Sirmione, *241–242*
Sissi ✕ , *182–183*
Smoking, *924*
Soccer, *222–224, 280, 651*
Solfatara, *713, 715*
Sorbillo ✕ , *708*
Sorrento, *740–744*
Spaccanapoli, *700–705*
Spaggia di Laurito, *746*
Spaggia Grande, *746*
Spanish Steps (Piazza di Spagna), *601*
Spas
Dolomites, 165, 172–173, 182
Emilio-Romagna, 397
Naples and Campania, 731
Sicily, 818
Tuscany, 523
Viterbo, 676–677
Spedale del Ceppo, *479*
Spedale degli Innocenti, *433*
Spedale di Santa Maria della Scala, *510*
Spello, *550–551*
Sperlonga, *683–684*
Spezieria di San Giovanni, *369*
Spoleto, *552–556*
Stilo, *798*
Stradivari, Antonio, *232*
Stresa, *253–255*
Stromboli, *860–861*
Stupinigi, *281*
Su Gologone ✕⌂ , *880*
Su Nuraxi, *878*
Subiaco, *681–682*

Symbols, *9*
Synagogues
Casale Monferrato, 287
Florence, 441
Rome and environs, 613, 670
Trani, 769

T

Taggia, *348*
Taormina, *810–815*
Taormina Mare, *811*
Taranto, *778–779*
Tarquinia, *672–674*
Taverna Colleoni dell'Angelo ✕ , *244*
Taverna del Bronzino ✕ , *443*
Taverna Kerkira ✕ , *796*
Taxes, *924–925*
Teatro (Ostia Antica), *669*
Teatro alla Scala, *210*
Teatro Carlo Felice, *339*
Teatro di verdura, *484*
Teatro di Marcello, *613–614*
Teatro Farnese, *369*
Teatro Greco (Siracusa), *824*
Teatro Greco (Taormina), *811*
Teatro Massimo, *849*
Teatro Olimpico
Vicenza, 122–123
Teatro Regio, *368*
Teatro Rendano, *792*
Teatro Romano
Aosta, 297
Benevento, 729
Spoleto, 554
Trieste, 151–152
Volterra, 498
Teatro San Carlo, *699*
Teatro Verdi, *367*
Telephones, *925–926*
Tempietto Longobardo, *148*
Tempio della Fortuna Virilis, *616*
Tempio di Apollo
Cumae, 717
Siracusa, 827
Tempio di Cerere
Ostia Antica, 669
Paestum, 755
Tempio di Minerva, *538, 540*
Tempio di Nettuno, *755*
Tempio di Vesta, *616*
Tempio Dorico, *843*
Tenuta di Canonica ⌂ , *557–558*
Terme dei Papi, *676–677*
Terme di Acireale, *818*
Terme di Merano, *182*
Terme di Nettuno, *669*
Terme di Saturnia, *523*
Termi dei Sette Sapienti, *670*

Termini, *626–628, 641–643*
Terminus ✕⌂ , *251*
Terranova di Pollino, *788*
Terrazza Umberto I, *871*
Testaccio, *628–629*
Tharros, *879–880*
Time, *926*
Tipping, *926*
Tivoli, *679–680*
Todi, *556–558*
Tomba di Cecilia Metella, *617*
Tomba di Dante, *403*
Tomba di Rotari, *774*
Tomba Raggio, *331*
Torcello, *77–78*
Torgiano, *549–550*
Torrazzo, *232*
Torre Apponale, *237*
Torre Civica
Bergamo, 244
Casale Monferrato, 287
Torre Comentina, *287*
Torre del Brandale, *346*
Torre dell'Aquila, *165*
Torre dell'Elefante, *871*
Torre dell'Orologio
Padua, 117
Venice, 58
Torre di Frederico II, *832*
Torre di San Pancrazio, *870–871*
Torre Grossa, *500*
Torre Guinigi, *483*
Torre Romana, *287*
Torre Troyana, *287*
Torre Vanga, *164*
Torre Verde, *165*
Tours and packages, *926–927*
Train travel, *927–928*
Trani, *769*
Trapani, *840, 842*
Trastevere, *614, 628–629, 638, 646–648*
Trattoria Casareccia ✕ , *781*
Trattoria da Giovanni ✕ , *153*
Trattoria Montina ✕ , *216–217*
Travel agencies, *928–929*
Tre Re ✕ , *677*
Tremezzo, *247–248*
Trentino, *162–174*
Trento, *162–168*
Treviso, *142, 144–145*
Trieste, *150–154*
Tripe carts, *450*
Tropea, *795–796*
Truffles, *554*
Trulli District (Mezzogiorno), *774–778*
Trullo d'Oro ✕ , *775*
Trullo Sovrano, *774*
Turin, *266–267, 269–281*

Tuscania, *674–675*
Tuscany, *471–526*
Tuscia, *675–679*
Tyrrhenian Coast, *856–858*

U

U' Giancu ✕ , *323*
Udine, *145–147*
Umbria & the Marches, *527–570*
Umbria Jazz Festival, *537*
Università di Bologna, *380*
Uno e Bino ✕ , *627*
Urbino, *564–566*

V

Vadinchenia ✕ , *707*
Valle d'Aosta, *292–302.* ⇨ *Also* Piedmont & Valle d'Aosta
Valle dei Mulini, *749–750*
Valle dei Templi, *835–838*
Valnerina, *562–563*
Valpolicella, *134–135*
Varenna, *247*
Vatican, *576–577, 579–583, 594*
Vatican Museums, *580–582*
Vatican Necropolis, *583*
Vecchia Parrocchiale, *176*
Vecchia Taormina ✕ , *813*
Venetian Arc, *109–156*
Venice, *39–107*
children, attractions for, 57, 61, 67–68, 71–72, 76–77
essential information, 102–108
history, 56
hotels, 87–95
nightlife & the arts, 95–99
price categories, 79, 88
restaurants, 57, 58, 61, 62, 65–66, 71, 78–81, 84, 86–87
shopping, 99–102
sports, 99
Ventimiglia, *351–352*
Venus Ristorante ✕ , *253*
Verbania, *255*
Verona, *130, 132–137*
Vesuvius, *727–728*
Via Alberobello–Martina Franca, *775*
Via Appia Antica, *618*

Via Belenzani, *164*
Via del Portico d'Ottavia, *614*
Via delle Volte, *391*
Via Destra del Porto, *398*
Via Etnea, *821*
Via Garibaldi, *334*
Via Giulia, *600*
Via Nazionale, *641–643*
Via Positanesi d'America, *746*
Via Sinagoga, *769*
Via Sinistra del Porto, *398*
Via Sparano, *766*
Via Toledo, *699*
Via Veneto, *629–630, 643–644*
Vicenza, *121–124, 130*
Victoria ▦ , *277*
Vieste, *772–773*
Villa Adriana, *679–680*
Villa Balbianello, *248*
Villa Belgioioso Bonaparte-Museo dell'Ottocento, *210–211*
Villa Belvedere, *818*
Villa Bordoni ▦ , *493*
Villa Carlotta, *247–248*
Villa Cipriani ▦ , *141*
Villa Cimbrone ▦ , *752, 753*
Villa Comunale, *811*
Villa Cortine ▦ , *242*
Villa Crespi ▦ , *253*
Villa d'Este (estate), *680*
Villa d'Este ▦ , *249*
Villa del Quar ✕▦ , *136*
Villa del Sogno ▦ , *240*
Villa di Castello, *465–466*
Villa di Damecuta, *736–737*
Villa Doria, *344*
Villa Durazzo Pallavicini, *344*
Villa Faraggiana, *345*
Villa Farnesina, *614*
Villa Fiordaliso ✕▦ , *240*
Villa Gamberaia, *466–467*
Villa Jovis, *734*
Villa Lante, *678*
Villa La Petraia, *466*
Villa Las Tronas ▦ , *883–884*
Villa Medicea, *477–478*
Villa Melzi, *246*
Villa Monastero, *247*
Villa Novecento ▦ , *301*
Villa Pallavicino

Busseto, *367*
Stresa, *253*
Villa Pasini, *141*
Villa Pisani, *117*
Villa Pisani ▦ , *120–121*
Villa Poggio San Felice ▦ , *458*
Villa Reale, *484*
Villa Rufolo, *752*
Villa San Michele, *737*
Villa Sant'Agata, *367*
Villa Serbelloni, *246*
Villa Taranto, *255*
Villa Valmarana ai Nani, *123*
Villasimius, *873*
Vini da Gigio ✕ , *79*
Vintage 1997 ✕ , *275*
Vite e Vitello ✕ , *828*
Vitello d'Oro ✕ , *147*
Viterbo, *676–677*
Vocabulary, *892–896*
Volpaia, *495*
Volterra, *498–499*
Vomero, *699–700*
Vucciria Market, *855–856*
Vulcano, *858–859*

W

Weather, *17*
Web sites, 929
Wine, *121, 134–135, 137, 138–139, 143, 144, 146–147, 149, 179, 185, 236, 289–292, 366, 387–389, 396, 491, 518, 522, 549, 550, 820, 840, 855*
Wine Bar Corte dei Pandolfini, *781*
Wine Bar DOC ✕ , *793*
Wine museums
Bassano del Grappa, 139
Caldaro, 194
Torgiano, 549
Wines of Langhe, *289–291*

Z

Zecca-Righi funicular, *334*
Zona Archeologica, *875*
Zoos, *253, 479*
Zür Kaiserkron ✕ , *177*

PHOTO CREDITS

Morandi/age fotostock. 22, *Stefano Cellai/age fotostock.* 23 (left), *Atlantide S.N.C./age fotostock.* 23 (right), *Doug Scott/age fotostock.* 24, *Wojtek Buss/age fotostock.* 25 (left), *Walter Bibikow/age fotostock.* 25 (right), *Bruno Morandi/age fotostock.* 38, *Bruno Morandi/age fotostock.* **Chapter 1: Venice:** 39, *Javier Larrea/age fotostock.* 40, *Kevin Galvin/age fotostock.* 41 (top left), *Willy Matheisl/age fotostock.* 41 (top right), *Ken Ross/viestiphoto.com.* 41 (bottom), *Norma Brown Hill//viestiphoto.com.* 43, *Javier Larrea/age fotostock.* 45, *Walter Bibikow/viestiphoto.com.* 46, *Jennifer Edwards.* 47 (left), *M. Spancer/viestiphoto.com.* 47 (right), *Jennifer Edwards.* 48, *Javier Larrea/age fotostock.* 49 (left), *Steve Allen/Brand X Pictures.* 49 (right), *Doug Scott/age fotostock.* 50, *Bruno Morandi/age fotostock.* 51 (left), *Corbis.* 51 (right), *Sergio Pitamitz/age fotostock.* **Chapter 2: Venetian Arc:** 109, *Wojtek Buss/age fotostock.* 110 (top), *Wojtek Buss/age fotostock.* 110 (bottom left), *Vito Arcomano/Fototeca ENIT.* 110 (bottom right), *Vito Arcomano/Fototeca ENIT.* 111 (top), *Javier Larrea/age fotostock.* 111 (bottom), *Targa/age fotostock.* 113, *Wojtek Buss/age fotostock.* 125 and 126 (top), *from Quattro Libri by Andrea Palladio.* 126 (bottom), *Classic Vision/age fotostock.* 127, *Erich Lessing/Art Resource.* 128 (left), *Vito Arcomano/Fototeca ENIT.* 128 (right), *Wojtek Buss/age fotostock.* 129, *Wojtek Buss/age fotostock.* **Chapter 3: The Dolomites: Trentino-Alto Adige:** 157, *Angelani/fototeca Trentino S.p.A.* 158 (top), *Stefano Cellai/age fotostock.* 118 (bottom), *Angelani/ fototeca Trentino S.p.A.* 159 (top), *Kevin Galvin/age fotostock.* 159 (bottom left), *Vito Arcomano/Fototeca ENIT.* 159 (bottom right), *Vito Arcomano/Fototeca ENIT.* 161, *Stefano Cellai/age fotostock.* 190, *APT Dolomiti di Brenta-Altopiano della Paganella.* 191, *Südtirol Marketing.* **Chapter 4: Milan, Lombardy & the Lakes:** 197, *Worldscapes/age fotostock.* 198 (top), *Corbis.* 198 (bottom), *Joe Viesti/viestiphoto.com.* 199 (top), *APT del Comasco.* 199 (bottom left), *P. Narayan/age fotostock.* 199 (bottom right), *Julius Honnor.* 201, *Wojtek Buss/age fotostock.* 204-206, *Antonio Dalle Rive.* 227 (top), *Alan Copson/age fotostock.* 227 (bottom left), *Antonio Dalle Rive/Anyway Group.* 227 (bottom right), *Javier Larrea/age fotostock.* **Chapter 5: Piedmont & Valle d'Aosta:** 261, *Paroli Galperti/viestiphoto.com.* 262 (top), *Claudio Penna/ viestiphoto.com.* 262 (bottom left), *Vito Arcomano/Fototeca ENIT.* 262 (bottom right), *Roberto Borgo/ Turismo Torino.* 263 (top), *Giuseppe Bressi/Turismo Torino.* 263 (bottom), *Angelo Tondini/viestiphoto.com.* 265, *Alan Copson/Agency Jon Arnold Images/age fotostock.* 270, *Alan Copson/age fotostock.* 289 (top), *Targa/age fotostock.* 289 (bottom), *R&D Valterza/viestiphoto.com.* 290, *Michele Bella/viestiphoto.com.* 291 (top), *Targa/age fotostock.* 291 (bottom), *Targa/age fotostock.* **Chapter 6: The Italian Riviera:** 305, *José Fuste Raga/age fotostock.* 306 (top), *Sandro Vannini/age fotostock.* 306 (bottom), *Marco Simoni/age fotostock.* 307 (top), *Angelo Cavalli/age fotostock.* 307 (bottom left), *Adriano Bacchella/viestiphoto.com.* 307 (bottom center), *Ken Welsh/age fotostock.* 307 (bottom right), *Photosphere.* 308, *Kevin Galvin/age fotostock.* 313, *Walter Bibikow/viestiphoto.com.* 314 (top left), *Peter Phipp/age fotostock.* 314 (top center), *Walter Bibikow/viestiphoto.com.* 314 (top right), *Loren Irving/age fotostock.* 314 (bottom), *Carson Ganci/age fotostock.* 315 (left), *Angelo Cavalli/age fotostock.* 315 (center), *Cornelia Doerr/age fotostock.* 315 (right), *Bruno Morandi/age fotostock.* 317 (top), *Adriano Bacchella/viestiphoto.com.* 317 (bottom), *Walter Bibikow/viestiphoto.com.* 318 (top), *José Fuste Raga/age fotostock.* 318 (center), *Walter Bibikow/ viestiphoto.com.* 318 (bottom), *Vito Arcomano/Fototeca ENIT.* 319 (top), *Angelo Cavalli/age fotostock.* 319 (bottom), *Angelo Cavalli/age fotostock.* 320, *Atlantide S.N.C./age fotostock.* **Chapter 7: Emilia-Romagna:** 357, *Atlantide S.N.C./age fotostock.* 358 (top), *Atlantide S.N.C./age fotostock.* 358 (bottom), *P. Narayan/age fotostock.* 359 (top), *Javier Larrea/age fotostock.* 359 (bottom), *FSG/age fotostock.* 360, *Vito Arcomano/Fototeca ENIT.* 361, *Angelo Tondini/viestiphoto.com.* 373, *John A. Rizzo/age fotostock.* 374 (top), *Federico Meneghetti/viestiphoto.com.* 374 (second from top), *Federico Meneghetti/viestiphoto.com.* 374 (third from top), *Consorzio del Prosciutto di Parma.* 374 (fourth from top), *Federico Meneghetti/ viestiphoto.com.* 374 (bottom), *Angelo Tondini/viestiphoto.com.* 375 (top), *Consorzio del Formaggio Parmigiano-Reggiano.* 375 (second from top), *Consorzio del Formaggio Parmigiano-Reggiano.* 375 (third from top), *Federico Meneghetti/viestiphoto.com.* 375 (fourth from top), *Federico Meneghetti/viestiphoto.com.* 375 (bottom), *Vito Arcomano/Fototeca ENIT.* 376 (top), *Adriano Bacchella/viestiphoto.com.* 376 (bottom), *Federico Meneghetti/viestiphoto.com.* 377 (top), *John A. Rizzo/age fotostock.* 377 (second from top), *John A. Rizzo/age fotostock.* 377 (third from top), *Atlantide S.N.C./age fotostock.* 377 (fourth from top), *Archivio Fotografico Di Bologna Turismo.* 378 (bottom), *Artemisia/viestiphoto.com.* **Chapter 8: Florence:** 407, *Jesus Ochoa/age fotostock.* 408, *Walter Bibikow/viestiphoto.com.* 409 (top), *Photodisc.* 409 (bottom left), *Walter Bibikow/viestiphoto.com.* 409 (bottom right), *Sergio Pitamitz/age fotostock.* 410, *Planet Art.* 410, *Joe Viesti/viestiphoto.com.* 423 (left), *SuperStock/age fotostock.* 423 (center), *Classic Vision/age fotostock.* 423 (right), *Classic Vision/age fotostock.* 424 (left), *Chie Ushio.* 424 (center), *Planet Art.* 424 (right), *Paola Ghirotti/Fototeca ENIT.* 425 (top), *Classic Vision/age fotostock.* 425 (center), *Super-Stock/age fotostock.* 425 (bottom), *Corbis.* 426 (left), *Fototeca ENIT.* 426 (center), *SuperStock/age fotostock.* 426 (right), *Bruno Morandi/age fotostock.* 427 (left), *SuperStock/age fotostock.* 427 (center), *Sandro Vannini/viestiphoto.com.* 427 (right), *PTE/age fotostock.* 385 (left), *Planet Art.* 428 (center), *Planet Art.* 428 (right), *Planet Art.* **Chapter 9: Tuscany:** 471, *Stefano Cellai/age fotostock.* 472 (top), *Agen-*

zia Turismo Chianciano Terme – Valdichiana. 472 (center), *Chie Ushio*. 472 (bottom left), *Julius Honnor*. 472 (bottom right), *Photodisc*. 473 (top), *Stefano Cellai/age fotostock*. 473 (center), *Atlantide S.N.C./age fotostock*. 473 (bottom), *Javier Larrea/age fotostock*. 506, *Javier Larrea/age fotostock*. 506 (inset), *Photodisc*. 508 (top), *Vittorio Sciosia/viestiphoto.com*. 508 (center), *Vittorio Sciosia/viestiphoto.com*. 508 (bottom), *Bruno Morandi/age fotostock*. **Chapter 10: Umbria & the Marches:** 527, *Atlantide S.N.C./age fotostock*. 528 (top), *Stefano Cellai/age fotostock*. 528 (bottom left), *Stefano Cellai/age fotostock*. 528 (bottom right), *Atlantide S.N.C./age fotostock*. 529 (left), *Joe Viesti/viestiphoto.com*. 529 (right), *Atlantide S.N.C./age fotostock*. 530, *Vito Arcomano/Fototeca ENIT*. 531, *Vito Arcomano/Fototeca ENIT*. 531, *Atlantide S.N.C./age fotostock*. 542, *Picture Finders/age fotostock*. 543 (all), *Fototeca ENIT*. 544, *Atlantide S.N.C./age fotostock*. **Chapter 11: Rome:** 571, *Walter Bibikow/viestiphoto.com*. 572, *Vito Arcomano/Fototeca ENIT*. 573 (top), *Vito Arcomano/Fototeca ENIT*. 573 (bottom), *Caroline Commins/age fotostock*. 575 (left), *Corbis*. 575 (right), *Dave Drapak*. 585 (left), *Justin D. Paola*. 585 (right), *Edis Jurcys/age fotostock*. 586 (bottom), *Justin D. Paola*. 587 (top left), *Joe Viesti/viestiphoto.com*. 587 (top right), *Joe Viesti/viestiphoto.com*. 587 (bottom), *Justin D. Paola*. 588 (bottom), *Justin D. Paola*. 589 (top left), *Rome Tourist Board*. 589 (top right), *Atlantide S.N.C./age fotostock*. 589 (bottom), *Justin D. Paola*. 591 (left), *Chie Ushio*. 591 (right), *Joe Viesti/viestiphoto.com*. 593 (left), *Chie Ushio*. 593 (right), *Corbis*. **Chapter 12: Side Trips from Rome:** 663, *Joe Viesti/viestiphoto.com*. 664 (top), *Rome Tourist Board*. 664 (bottom left), *Vito Arcomano/Fototeca ENIT*. 664 (bottom right), *Atlantide S.N.C./age fotostock*. 665, *Joe Viesti/viestiphoto.com*. 666, *Stefano Cellai/age fotostock*. **Chapter 13: Naples & Campania:** 687, *Richard T. Nowitz/age fotostock*. 688 (top), *Paola Ghirotti/Fototeca ENIT*. 688 (bottom), *Demetrio Carrasco/Agency Jon Arnold Images/age fotostock*. 689 (top), *Doug Scott/age fotostock*. 689 (bottom left), *Peter Phipp/age fotostock*. 689 (bottom right), *Katie Hamlin*. 691, *Peter Phipp/age fotostock*. 719 (top), *Vincent Leblic/Photononstop*. 719 (bottom), *Robert Frerck/Odyssey Productions, Inc.* 720, *Joe Viesti/viestiphoto.com*. 721 (top), *Demetrio Carrasco/Agency Jon Arnold Images/age fotostock*. 721 (bottom), *Peter Phipp/age fotostock*. 722 (top), *Demetrio Carrasco/Agency Jon Arnold Images/age fotostock*. 722 (center), *Vito Arcomano/Fototeca ENIT*. 722 (bottom), *Joe Malone/Agency Jon Arnold Images/age fotostock*. 723, *Doug Scott/age fotostock*. 724, *Katie Hamlin*. 725, *Demetrio Carrasco/Agency Jon Arnold Images/age fotostock*. **Chapter 14: The Mezzogiorno:** 766, *José Fuste Raga/age fotostock*. 760, *Joe Viesti/viestiphoto.com*. 761 (top), *Tommaso di Girolamo/age fotostock*. 761 (bottom), *Vito Arcomano/Fototeca ENIT*. 762, *Vito Arcomano/Fototeca ENIT*. **Chapter 15: Sicily:** 803, *Charles Bowman/age fotostock*. 804 (top), *Vito Arcomano/Fototeca ENIT*. 804 (bottom left), *Andre Maslennikov/age fotostock*. 804 (bottom right), *Richard T. Nowitz/age fotostock*. 805, *Corbis*. 806, *Vito Arcomano/Fototeca ENIT*. 807, *Alvaro Leiva/age fotostock*. 836, *Alvaro Leiva/age fotostock*. 838, *Corbis*. 839, *Joe Viesti/viestiphoto.com*. 854, *Doug Scott/age fotostock*. **Chapter 16: Sardinia:** 865, *Bruno Morandi/age fotostock*. 866 (top), *Jon Arnold/Agency Jon Arnold Images/age fotostock*. 866 (bottom), *Bruno Morandi/age fotostock*. 866 (top), *Bruno Morandi/age fotostock*. 866 (bottom left), *Vito Arcomano/Fototeca ENIT*. 866 (bottom right), *Santiago Fernandez/age fotostock*. **Color Section:** The view from Ravello, high above the Amalfi Coast: *Demetrio Carrasco/Agency Jon Arnold Images/age fotostock*. Young priests stroll along Venice's Grand Canal: *Doug Scott/age fotostock*. The Regata Storica, a race of traditional Venetian boats held the first weekend in September: *Glen Allison/age fotostock*. Fashion is a passion in Milan (left): *Federico Malagoli/viestiphoto.com*. Fashion is a passion in Milan (right): *Enzo Signorelli/viestiphoto.com*. The Piazza del Duomo, in the heart of Florence: *Walter Bibikow/viestiphoto.com*. The peaks of the Dolomites: *Peter Adams/Agency Jon Arnold Images/age fotostock*. Riomaggiore, one of five towns that make up the Italian Riviera's Cinque Terre: *Angelo Cavalli/age fotostock*. Assisi, one of Umbria's definitive hill towns: *Javier Larrea/age fotostock*. The café scene outside the Arena di Verona: *Alan Copson/Agency Jon Arnold Images/age fotostock*. Rome's Bocca della Verità: *Joe Malone/Agency Jon Arnold Images/age fotostock*. Italy's national game, played in front of the Palazzo Reale in Naples: *Doug Scott/age fotostock*. The Colosseum, Rome: *John A. Rizzo/Photodisc*. Beachgoers on the Golfo di Orosei, Sardinia: *Bruno Morandi/age fotostock*. Rome's Vatican Museums: *Walter Bibikow/age fotostock*. Greek ruins at Selinunte, Sicily: *Richard T. Nowitz/age fotostock*.

ABOUT OUR WRITERS

After completing his master's degree in art history, Peter Blackman settled permanently in Italy in 1986. Since then he's worked as a biking and walking tour guide, managing to see more of Italy than most of his Italian friends. When he's not leading a trip, you'll find Peter at home in Chianti, listening to opera and planning his next journey.

While doing physics research in the same tower where Galileo once worked, Jeff Booth felt the gravitational pull of Venice. After two years of learning to row gondolas and raise a Venetian daughter, he hasn't fallen into the Grand Canal, yet. Jeff writes for *National Geographic Traveler* and *New York* magazine, among other publications.

Disinclined to stray far from superb wine and spectacular skiing, travel writer Ryan Bradley divides his days between northern Italy and northern California. Though the Dolomites are his part-time home, he's never quite prepared for the existential challenge of a face-to-face encounter with Bolzano's iceman.

Although Robin S. Goldstein is trained in philosophy at Harvard and law at Yale, his heart has always been in his travel writing. His credits include not only his home base of Italy but also Spain, Mexico, Ecuador, and the Galapagos Islands. Once a resident of Genoa, he now spends most of his time in the *mezzogiorno* and along the Sicilian coast.

Cristina Gregorin has worked as a guide in Venice since 1991. She's the author of *Venice Master Artisans,* a study of the city's traditional arts and crafts.

After many years of practicing law, Denise Hummel took up a career in journalism and now freelances for many U.S. based newspapers and magazines. She lives in Varese, between Lake Como and Lake Maggiore, where she runs a public relations and communications firm.

Madeleine Johnson is an unrepentant Midwesterner who has lived in Italy—with a two-year break in Paris—since 1988. She has degrees in art history from Wellesley College and U.C. Berkeley, and her writing has appeared in *Connoisseur, The Journal of Art,* and *The American*—where she has a monthly column about life in Milan.

Dana Klitzberg studied at the Institute of Culinary Education and worked as a chef at the renowned Manhattan restaurant San Domenico. After a stint cooking in a restaurant in Rome, she decided to make the Eternal City home. Now she runs her own company, through which she caters, gives cooking classes, and conducts culinary tours of the city.

Chris Rose arrived in Naples from Manchester, England, planning to stay for three months. Thirteen years later, he's still there, writing guidebooks, teaching English, and organizing events with writers and artists visiting from Britain. You can read his short story "The Shoemaker General of Naples" in *New Writing 10,* published by Picador.

Florence resident Patricia Rucidlo holds master's degrees in Italian Renaissance history and art history. When she's not extolling the virtues of a Pontormo masterpiece or angrily defending the Medici, she's leading wine tours in Chianti and catering private dinner parties.

California native Pamela Santini came to study art history 15 years ago at Venice's Ca' Foscari University, where she currently teaches. She's also a writer and translator, and enjoys traveling with her husband and son.

Megan K. Williams is a Rome-based writer and correspondent, covering Italy and Africa in print for many newspapers and magazines, as well as on the radio for the CBC, Marketplace, NPR, and Deutsche Welle. Her collection of short stories about life in in her adopted hometown, *Saving Rome,* was published in 2006 to rave reviews.